S0-AHV-954

Past and Present Publications

Society, Politics and Culture

Past and Present Publications

General Editor: PAUL SLACK, *Exeter College, Oxford*

Past and Present Publications comprise books similar in character to the articles in the journal *Past and Present*. Whether the volumes in the series are collections of essays – some previously published, others new studies – or monographs, they encompass a wide variety of scholarly and original works primarily concerned with social, economic and cultural changes, and their causes and consequences. They will appeal to both specialists and non-specialists and will endeavour to communicate the results of historical and allied research in readable and lively form.

For a list of titles in Past and Present Publications, see end of book.

Society, Politics and Culture

Studies in early modern England

MERVYN JAMES

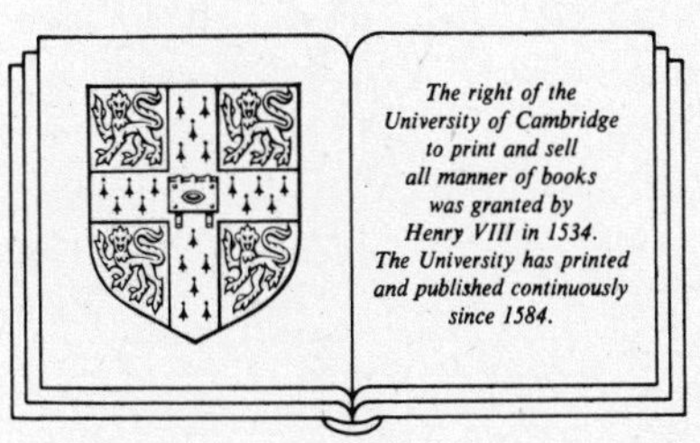

CAMBRIDGE UNIVERSITY PRESS

Cambridge
London New York New Rochelle
Melbourne Sydney

Published by the Press Syndicate of the University of Cambridge
The Pitt Building, Trumpington Street, Cambridge CB2 1RP
32 East 57th Street, New York, NY 10022, USA
10 Stamford Road, Oakleigh, Melbourne 3166, Australia

First published 1986

Printed in Great Britain at the University Press, Cambridge

British Library cataloguing in publication data

James, Mervyn
Society, politics and culture: studies in early
modern England. – (Past and present publications)
1. Great Britain – History – Tudors, 1485–1603
I. Title II. Series
942.05 DA315

Library of Congress cataloguing in publication data

James, Mervyn (Mervyn Evans)
Society, politics, and culture.
(Past and present publications)
Includes index.
1. England – Civilization – 16th century. 2. England –
Social conditions. 3. Great Britain – Politics and
government – 1485–1603. I. Title.
DA320.J36 1986 942.05 85–21277

ISBN 0 521 25718 2

WD

Contents

Preface

Of the studies included in this book, three originally appeared, under the same titles, in *Past and Present*: Chapter 1 in xcviii (February, 1983), pp. 3–29; Chapter 6 in xlviii (August, 1970), pp. 3–78; and Chapter 7 in lx (August, 1973), pp. 49–83. Chapter 8 was (again under the same title) *Past and Present* Supplement no. 3 (1978). Of the other chapters, 2 and 3 first saw light as xxx (1966) and xxvii (1965) of the Borthwick Papers published by the University of York, Borthwick Institute of Historical Research. I am grateful to Dr W. J. Sheils, the General Editor, for permission to reproduce them. Chapter 4 was first printed in *Northern History*, i (1966), pp. 43–69, and my thanks are due to the Editor, Mr G. C. F. Forster, for permission to include it here. Chapter 5 originally appeared in the *Transactions of the Cumberland and Westmorland Antiquarian and Archaeological Society*, new series, lxvi (1966), pp. 165–78. Again my grateful thanks are due to the Joint Editors, Messrs J. Hughes and B. C. Jones, for leave to republish.

I am also grateful to Mr R. C. Norris of Durham University Library for help given, during a particularly difficult period, in securing access to essential works of reference.

Stonesfield, Oxon. MERVYN JAMES

Preface

Of the studies included in this book, three originally appeared, under the same titles, in *Past and Present*: Chapter 1 in xcviii (February, 1983), pp. 3–29; Chapter 6 in xlviii (August, 1970), pp. 3–78; and Chapter 7 in lx (August, 1973), pp. 49–83. Chapter 8 was (again under the same title) *Past and Present* Supplement no. 3 (1978). Of the other chapters, 2 and 3 first saw light as xxx (1966) and xxvii (1965) of the Borthwick Papers published by the University of York, Borthwick Institute of Historical Research. I am grateful to Dr W. J. Sheils, the General Editor, for permission to reproduce them. Chapter 4 was first printed in *Northern History*, i (1966), pp. 43–69, and my thanks are due to the Editor, Mr G. C. F. Forster, for permission to include it here. Chapter 5 originally appeared in the *Transactions of the Cumberland and Westmorland Antiquarian and Archaeological Society*, new series, lxvi (1966), pp. 165–78. Again my grateful thanks are due to the Joint Editors, Messrs J. Hughes and B. C. Jones, for leave to republish.

I am also grateful to Mr R. C. Norris of Durham University Library for help given, during a particularly difficult period, in securing access to essential works of reference.

Stonesfield, Oxon. MERVYN JAMES

Introduction

There are two reasons which could be given for putting together a collection of this sort. The first is that some of these studies, while still in demand, are out of print or not easily accessible; the second, that there may be some interest in placing an author's writings side by side, so that the connections between them, and the way in which his views have developed, may be more easily traced. The first requires no further explanation. But, in the case of the second, some guidance to the various themes discussed, with some comment on their development, and to the cross-references between them from one chapter to another may be helpful; the more so because the items included in the collection are printed in their historical sequence, and not in the order of composition. If the latter were adopted, Chapter 1 would take the place of Chapter 8 as the penultimate in the book; and Chapters 2 and 3 would be transposed. The Introduction aims therefore to provide a preliminary guiding commentary, easily dispensed with by anyone who does not find such a thing at all necessary. With the exception of Chapter 9, which has not been previously published, the various items are printed here more or less as they first appeared, with no attempt at significant revision.

The studies in the Tudor north in Chapters 2, 3, 4 and 5 come first in the order of composition. These were based to a significant extent on local archive collections; and, like many of his protagonists, the author tended to see events from a localized vantage-point: through the eyes of a regional society (or several such societies) for whom the distant authority in London was something which, while legitimate, was also liable to be regarded as intrusive and largely alien. This approach tended to concentrate attention on the regional society: the institutions which articulated political and social power within it, and the attitudes in terms of which it saw itself. As a result, an emphasis emerged on the role of the households of the northern nobility as centres of patronage, sources of office and profit in terms of which clienteles formed themselves amongst the gentry of the northern communities; and which might also give access to office under the crown. At the same time, the many mesne tenures by knight service which survived on such great aristocratic estates as those of the Cliffords and Percies[1] meant that the ties of patronage were reinforced by those of feudal service based on the exaction of homage, with knights' courts at such centres as Alnwick and Skipton, which in their hey-day early in the sixteenth century still helped to express and sustain the solidarity of a clientele.[2]

At the same time a characteristic ethos tended to maintain itself in connection with these organizational forms. In northern society the stress on ties of kinship, blood and lineage found their most tenacious and binding forms amongst the Border clans, with their gavelkind tenures and extended family organization;[3] but also generally permeated the society, particularly at its upper levels. Aristocratic clienteles were frequently characterized by ties of hereditary dependence on great aristocratic houses, although admittedly from the early sixteenth century these were increasingly subject to stresses and strains which often weakened their importance. What I called an "ethos of 'service' " stressed the qualities implicit in "good lordship" as the ideal conjunctive and solidarity-promoting influences in the society; these both evoked, and were evoked by, loyalties which had an ancestral, accustomed, and "natural" resonance, sanctioned by time, and unconditional.[4] Thus a pattern of social relationships and attitudes emerged, which will be found visually projected in the colourful and characteristic funerary ritual used at the burial of William, Lord Dacre, as described in Chapter 5. In order to characterize the ethos of service, I made use of Percy estate correspondence of the late sixteenth and early seventeenth century, and the terminology used at least partly reflects the sixteenth-century cultural developments described in Chapters 7 and 8. However, the stress on good lordship and faithfulness, and on kinship, lineage, and ancestral connection marks these northern aristocratic dependencies as essentially "communities of honour" of the sort described in Chapter 8.[5]

It will be seen that by and large I took a positive view of the role

[1] See below, pp. 68 ff., 153 ff., 295 ff., 330 ff.
[2] *Ibid.* [3] Pp. 95 ff. [4] Pp. 52 ff. [5] Pp. 327 ff.

of Thomas Lord Wharton as an agent of "the Tudor revolution in the north",[6] so conforming to a dominant historical convention with regard to the Tudor achievement which had been developed and deepened by G. R. Elton and A. G. Dickens. Both these authorities on the Tudor age placed the development of the Tudor state and its successful deployment in the struggle against "overmighty subjects", feudal liberties, and the abuses of retainers, affinity, and maintenance as a prime Tudor contribution to the advancement of civilizing frontiers; to be set in this respect side by side with the achievement of the Reformation.[7] But, while accepting this approach, I also felt dissatisfied with it, was inclined to question the idea, or at least to look for some sort of reformulation. Doing this kind of history, I could not but be aware that the old order in the north had its good qualities as well as bad. The violence and competitiveness endemic in the northern communities of honour were in a measure offset by the protective and integrative influence of kinship and family loyalties; and also by the areas of relative stability and order which centred on the aristocratic connections and great households – the latter focal points not only of orderliness, but of a culture which, although not always accordant with the tendencies approved at the court and in London, nevertheless had its own validity.[8] In addition, there was an awareness of the negative, disruptive effects of Tudor policies north of the Trent. These often had the effect of destabilizing the accepted local balance of interest and power, producing reactions of violence and revolt. At the same time the agents of the government frequently showed a greed and aggressivity offensive to the northern communities which were supposedly the beneficiaries of Tudor order.[9]

The material studied tended to project, often with great vividness, the kind of conflict generated by the competing claims of local loyalties and those claimed by the crown. There was, for example, the case of the unfortunate sixth earl of Northumberland's decision, taken after much hesitation and pressure from London, to execute the family ally and former Percy officer, Sir William Lisle of

[6] P. 102.

[7] See for example G. R. Elton, *The Tudor Constitution* (1st edn, Cambridge, 1960, p. 195 ff.; A. G. Dickens, *Thomas Cromwell and the English Reformation* (London, 1959), pp. 97 ff., and *The English Reformation* (London, 1964), pp. 112 ff.

[8] See pp. 49 ff., 274 ff.

[9] See for example pp. 282, 292.

Felton, then an outlaw.[10] In the eyes of the regional society in which the Percies had traditionally played a leading role, what would be seen in London as a proper and loyal enforcement of the law would be construed as the dishonourable betrayal of a dependant. I had also already encountered, although not yet written about, the same conflict as resolved by Lord Darcy during the Pilgrimage of Grace, who opted for the connectional and local loyalty, at the expense of his loyalties to Henry VIII.[11] But at this stage I was only peripherally aware of the concept of honour, and how this might be used to arrange the components of the picture in a more satisfying pattern. My earlier inclination was to wonder whether Henry VIII might not have crossed the margin separating tyranny from what was proper to a royal leadership of the nobility; and to stress that, at least in the north, the power of the great aristocratic houses, properly exercised, complemented rather than contradicted that of the crown.[12] In the background there was the ineluctability of dissent in any political society, and the problem of the appropriate mode for its expression.

In a study of the Lincolnshire rebellion (Chapter 6), I attempted to restate the problem. It seemed that this particular regional dissident movement did not conform to the model of the "neo-feudal" revolt, led by a regionally orientated nobility and aiming, through the mobilization of aristocratic connectional power, at a change effected by force in the existing distribution of political power at court, so initiating armed rebellion or civil war. A better precedent was to be found in such broadly based popular protests against misgovernment of the late fourteenth or fifteenth century as the Peasants' Revolt or Cade's Rebellion. These had aimed to bring home to government that the very ideology of "obedience" on which its authority rested could be brought into question by policies which threatened the material and moral disruption of the regional societies over which it presided.[13] The methods used involved the weapons of riot, armed mobilization, the occupation of local centres and regional capitals, together with the promulgation of programmes of political and socio-economic demands. But at the same time the movement sought (not necessarily with success) to contain itself within a context of "obedience". The actual resort to violence, as distinct from demonstrative gesture and threat, was minimal, and

[10] Pp. 56 ff. [11] Pp. 339 ff. [12] P. 50. [13] Pp. 260 ff.

casualties were few. The "rebels" did not question the authority of the crown, but rather the abuses of its agents; and the intention was one of peaceful petition to the king's person. Upon confrontation with the royal forces, a negotiated settlement was sought, and the option of surrender more often taken than that of battle. I suggested that these modes of political mobilization and action, assuming the ostensible form of political pressure exercised from below upwards (so reversing the accepted and proper direction of political initiative), were rooted in the stock of conventional political wisdom which was presented in such widely circulated collections as Lydgate's *Fall of Princes*;[14] and which was reinforced by the deeper penetration of the language and thought-forms of the common law into lower levels of the social structure, with an attendant awareness of the boundary separating "treason" from other forms of quasi-violent disorder, such as riot, and of the limits of toleration this might encounter.[15]

By and large, I still hold to this model for a dissident movement, and think it can be quite widely applied to the Pilgrimage of Grace, and to other revolts and rebellions of the Tudor period; and it is interesting to see that a similar approach can be applied, *mutatis mutandis*, to such related forms of disorder as grain riots during the seventeenth century.[16] However it gave rise to two criticisms: firstly, that, as applied to the Lincolnshire revolt, the model excluded a truly popular initiative, the real leadership being that of the nobility and gentry exercised under a cloak of popular coercion; secondly, that this implied a "conspiracy" theory of the movement, leaving no room for any ideological motivation, in the sense of the unfavourable popular reaction to the religious changes implied by the Ten Articles and royal Injunction of 1536.[17]

14 Pp. 260 ff.

15 See also Chapters 7, pp. 283 ff., and 8, pp. 32 ff.

16 See J. Walter and K. Wrightson, "Dearth and the Social Order in Early Modern England", *Past and Present*, lxxi (May 1976), pp. 22 ff.; J. Walter, "Grain Riots and Popular Attitudes to the Law: Maldon and the Crisis of 1629", in *An Ungovernable People: The English and their Law in the Seventeenth and Eighteenth Centuries*, ed. J. Brewer and J. Styles (London, 1980), pp. 47 ff.; K. Wrightson, *English Society, 1580–1680* (London, 1982), pp. 173 ff.

17 See C. S. L. Davies, "Popular Religion and the Pilgrimage of Grace", shortly to appear in *Order and Disorder in Early Modern England*, ed. A. Fletcher and J. Stevenson (Cambridge). In the same place Dr Davies also discusses Prof. G. R. Elton's article, "Politics and the Pilgrimage of Grace", in which the interpretation of the politics of the Lincolnshire revolt advanced in Chapter 6 is taken up

As far as the notion of conspiracy is concerned, the disaffection of such leading Lincolnshire families as the Husseys, Willoughbies, Dymokes, and others, together with the likely affiliation of the Dymokes and Husseys with oppositional elements at court, make it difficult to believe that some of these did not have a hand in the disorders from the start.[18] But the part played by the shire magnates was conveniently obscured by the far more obvious and visible role of a network of insurrectionary activists, "promoters" and "stirrers" of the rising, who came from a lower social level: of local lawyers, petty officials, "new" or marginal gentry, and yeomen.[19] "Hard facts" are unlikely to be found establishing the involvement of these men with others of their like in Yorkshire and elsewhere in some kind of organization and prior planning connected with the outbreak of the Pilgrimage of Grace; for all trace of such an organization would have been carefully concealed, and transmitted by credence and word of mouth rather than by written communication. Nevertheless, the meeting between their leader in Lincolnshire, Thomas Moigne, and Robert Aske, soon to emerge as captain-general of the Pilgrimage, is significant; and the existence of prior planning and organization a reasonable hypothesis.[20] However, such an organization, working through popular leaders, and exploiting popular discontents, could scarcely have been enough in itself to indicate a viable dissident movement with a clear prospect of success. The activists could not hope, out of their own resources, and without contacts with great men at court within the royal circle, to achieve much more than a series of local riots, whose fate sooner or later could not but be repression. Discontented magnates with court affiliations and popular leaders could therefore be expected to come together sooner or later; and sooner rather than later, since the need each had of the other was so obvious. Again, prior understandings and consultations were to be expected, extending to the encouragement or contrivance of initial disturbances which pre-

and more widely applied, and which Davies thinks open to much the same criticisms as my own. For Elton's article, see *After the Reformation: Essays in Honor of J. H. Hexter*, ed. Barbara Malament (Pennsylvania, 1980), pp. 25 ff.; reprinted in G. R. Elton, *Studies in Tudor and Stuart Politics and Government*, iii (Cambridge, 1983), pp. 183 ff.

18 See below, pp. 226 ff., 221 ff.

19 Pp. 209 ff.

20 On the traces of organization and planning in Lincolnshire, see pp. 206 ff.

sented the possibility of exploitation with a view to the broadening of the movement.

To that extent, therefore, a "conspiracy" involving the harnessing of popular discontents to the designs of the great, and plans to exploit the latter by an active "stirring" of the people, was certainly very much a part of such a movement as the Lincolnshire revolt. But on the other hand, while magnates and activists certainly needed each other, their roles in the movement being complementary, a continuing tension between them was also inherent in the situation. For the popular leaders were more exposed than the great men, who, because of the ostensible popular initiative with which the rising had originated, could present themselves as the victims of the popular hatred of authority. As a result, fear of compromises and surrender settlements entered into at their expense made the popular leaders prone to extremist policies. As a result, at critical points the movement was liable to disintegrate into moderates and extremists, with "the people" turning against "the gentry", charging them with a betrayal of the cause.[21] In addition, the factors of distance, slow communications, and the need for secrecy multiplied misunderstandings, misinformation, hesitations, and changes in attitude. Such contingencies limited what any conspiratorial prearrangements could achieve, and made a revolt what it was generally recognized to be: a gamble with Fortune of a particularly hazardous and uncertain kind. Many found that their nerve and courage failed them when the decisive moment came. Conspiracy could play its part in the initiation of such a movement; but thereafter the outcome depended both on the skilful manipulation of local discontents and of successive changing situations as they arose.[22]

As far as religion is concerned, no one can doubt that the Reformation, with its defacement of powerfully protective and socially integrative religious symbols, caused a painful lesion in the popular consciousness. A sense of religious shock and outrage may well have been a major factor enhancing support for the Lincolnshire

[21] Pp. 256 ff.

[22] The margin of difference (which is not a wide one) between my own view, as here expressed, and that of Dr Davies emerges in the conclusion to the Appendix of his article: " 'Conspiracy' undoubtedly shaped the form the Pilgrimage took; it is far from providing a complete examination of how it broke out, let alone its subsequent extent and force."

rising, and later for the Pilgrimage of Grace. Yet the evidence for the nature and direction of popular religious preferences, as far as Lincolnshire is concerned, tends to be sparse. We know little beyond that the common people "grudged" at the new opinions concerning Our Lady and Purgatory, two themes towards which much popular piety was certainly directed. I probably placed too much emphasis, to the exclusion of religious commitment, on the popular outcry at the prospect of the plunder of the parish treasures of Louth church by the royal commissioners, with the implication that the cause was rooted in material interest, not religious sentiment.[23] I would certainly accept C. S. L. Davies's more sensitive and balanced view that, in this case as in others, "the sense of communal proprietorship strengthened the natural conservative commitment to familiar [religious] forms, and was in fact an integral part of it".[24]

I may also have been unfair to the religious point of view of the Lincolnshire parish priests, whose political importance (with that of the monastic clergy) as "stirrers" and leaders of their parishes into the revolt I emphasized, but whose reaction to the religious changes I described as "that of a conservative professional group which wished to pursue undisturbed its established habits and bucolic routines".[25] Yet, as Mrs Bowker has pointed out, the material available from which to judge the religious opinions of the priesthood is limited. We know that some feared for the mass, as well as for the traditional teaching concerning Purgatory and Our Lady; and some "saw the source of the trouble in the change in the precise location of authority in the Church". Nevertheless, "For the rest the protest was against religious legislation which had far-reaching economic consequences", and "against a prince who saw the Church as a milch cow".[26] It required a mind trained in theological subtleties to detect that a fundamental threat to traditional religion was already implicit in the king's doings, and only Thomas Kendall, vicar of Louth, the university theologian, was equal to the task.[27] There was also the disquieting development that, whereas traditional belief had always

[23] See pp. 202–3.
[24] Davies, "Popular Religion". [25] See below, p. 202.
[26] Margaret Bowker, "Lincolnshire 1536: Heresy, Schism, or Religious Discontent", in *Studies in Church History*, ix: *Schism, Heresy, and Religious Protest*, ed. Derek Baker (Cambridge, 1972), pp. 195 ff., 200, 207, 210–11, 212.
[27] *Ibid.*, p. 209. Cf. below, p. 202.

rested on its unquestioned legitimization by both ecclesiastical and secular authority, now the role of authority in relation to religion as commonly understood had assumed an ambiguous, even hostile, character. Priests and people could grasp the danger of a raid on parish treasures by a greedy king, but could not yet clearly conceive of an alliance between the crown and heresy. Yet the sense of this unbelievable possibility had at least begun to dawn, and would eventually compel a revaluation of the implications of heresy itself, which would gradually establish itself as an orthodoxy. Thus the religious motif, while present, was liable to be muted and confused by comparison with the less complex material issues; and this in spite of the probable informed conservative commitment of such leaders as the Dymokes and Lord Hussey.

In a book called *Family, Lineage and Civil Society*[28] I had aimed to analyse the evolution of the Durham region between 1500 and 1640 in terms of a development from a "lineage society" to a "civil society". The former was bonded by kinship and the ties of the extended family, its socio-political pattern determined by loyalties which centred on the aristocratic great household. In the latter, the family had become more privatized, and loyalties centred more on the state, with the local society conforming to the generalized pattern of the body of the realm, bonded by law, humanistic wisdom, and Protestant religion. In Chapter 7 this pattern will be found applied to a similar evolution in Northumberland, during the generation before the Northern Rising of 1569. This chapter develops the theme of the penetration of the Percy estate community and its organization (itself an instance of a typical northern "lineage" socio-political grouping) by concepts of legality and rationality, with accompanying changes in socio-political attitudes and political practice. This development, and others associated with it, both accompanied and furthered a decline in the effectiveness of the aristocratic leadership of the region traditionally exercised by the Percy earls of Northumberland, whose weakness showed itself during the rising, the outcome of which in effect ended their power in its traditional form. In this study, the culture of the lineage society is characterized as centred on lineage and lordship, faithfulness and service, its standards of acceptable behaviour on the code of honour; its thinking pre-conceptualized and particularized, typi-

[28] Oxford, 1974.

cally taking the form of the exemplary myth and tale, rather than more discursive, generalizing modes of expression.

This approach is given a wider scope in Chapter 8, which applies these ideas to the general development of political attitudes and practice during the Tudor and earlier Stuart period, with particular reference to the problem of order, and its antithesis: the politics of violence whose typical expression consisted in armed revolt or rebellion. An interest in the concept of honour arose partly out of the concern with the typical structure of Tudor revolt, and with the motivation of Tudor dissidence, which finds expression in Chapter 6. But, in addition, involvement with the history of the decline of the Percy power in the north under the Tudors had raised the issue of the changes in aristocratic mentality, and particularly in the aristocratic attitude to the crown and political dissidence, of which the cases of the fifth and sixth earls of Northumberland, and the first earl of Cumberland, discussed in Chapters 2, 3 and 4, illustrate. What seemed to be happening was characterized by the late K. B. McFarlane as the emergence, with the Tudor advent, of a "chastened, indeed craven, mood" amongst the old nobility, who had become "more self-effacing, less sure of their mission to coerce high-handed rulers, congenitally wary, convinced of the benefits of passive obedience",[29] states of mind whose operation may be seen in the weak and uncertain reaction of the northern lords to the Pilgrimage of Grace.[30] Macfarlane qualifies his characterization by pointing out that the aristocracy had, in all probability, already learnt the lesson of obedience by 1450;[31] and it is indeed the case that the processes which broke the will of aristocratic dissidence, and changed the character of aristocratic influence, have their roots far back in the fifteenth century, and beyond.

Nevertheless, these were decisively reinforced and carried to their conclusion by the developments of the Tudor period. In the first place, there was the political practice of the first two Tudor kings. This aimed at disciplining the great nobility, while at the same time encouraging the re-emergence of local articulations of royal

[29] K. B. McFarlane, "The Wars of the Roses", *Proceedings of the British Academy*, 1 (1964), pp. 87–119; reprinted in K. B. McFarlane, *England in the Fifteenth Century: Collected Essays*, intro. by G. L. Harriss (London, 1981), from which it is here cited.

[30] See below, p. 353 ff.

[31] *England in the Fifteenth Century*, p. 260.

influence and power, based on the gentry, able where necessary to counter-poise that of the aristocratic connections.[32] The result might have been ephemeral, and an aristocratic reaction can in fact be seen under way in the reigns of Edward VI and Queen Mary. But Henrician policies tended to be underwritten by long-term structural changes: the extinction of noble families, and the break-up of their estates; an altered relationship between lords and tenants; and changes in the social composition and size of gentry communities which tended to disrupt the traditional aristocratic dependencies amongst them. The cultural landslide of the Reformation ushered in providentialist religion, consolidated and extended humanistic education, and was accompanied by a deeper penetration into society of common-law concepts; all tendencies which encouraged related political attitudes, with the stress on order and obedience.[33] In Chapter 8 the influences are traced which changed the emphasis of honour. From a code of "faithfulness" to lords and "friends", in terms of which nobles might confront unworthy kings, it becomes the mark and reward of service to the monarchical state. This process, it is suggested, involved the incorporation of honour as one component in a cultural synthesis which also included religion, humanism, and law, and whose dominant motifs harmonized with the needs and disciplines of a civil society. The cultural pattern which resulted received its most complete and influential expression in the literary products of the Sidney circle, and particularly in Sir Philip Sidney's own *Arcadia*. It is suggested, however, that during the early seventeenth century the pattern ceased either to convince

[32] Possibly the main area of disagreement between Dr M. L. Bush and myself (see M. L. Bush, "The Problem of the Far North . . . ", in *Northern History*, vi, 1971, pp. 40 ff.) relates to this point. I would not dispute Dr Bush's view that neither Henry VII nor Henry VIII showed an "unwillingness" to employ magnates in Border offices where they could "adequately fulfil" those entrusted to them. It does seem to me however that the crown was concerned, particularly during the ministries of Wolsey and Cromwell, to encourage and support the gentry of the Marches to form local concentrations of influence and power, based on kinship and affinity, which were detached from the traditional aristocratic connections. These provided the crown, on occasion, with an alternative source of recruitment to office, while also consolidating a local balance of power which facilitated an assured crown control of the great lords. But the policy also had the effect of dividing the Border communities, and of disrupting established loyalties, while also inviting a defensive aristocratic reaction, so that, at least in the shorter term, the problem of maintaining order was exacerbated. As Dr Bush points out, it did not always increase the efficiency of Border administration, either.

[33] Below, pp. 302 ff., 357 ff., 370 ff.

or to motivate a significant sector of the governing class, under the stress of disillusionment with the Stuart political system, religion, and policies. As a result the way was opened for the emergence of attitudes which could once more impart to political conflict the edge of violent intransigence: those of Puritan millenarianism, and of honour "cut loose from its moorings in religion and wisdom".[34]

The curve of development therefore involved a change in the emphasis of honour, which from a motive for dissidence becomes the mark of obedience; and its union with religion, wisdom and law into a unified pattern which subsequently showed signs of disintegration under stress. The process cannot be understood, however, except in relation to deep-seated cultural changes, reaching back at least as far as the late fourteenth century. The most important of these, so this chapter maintains, is the extension of literacy, and the rise of a larger and socially more varied reading public. A wider access to popularized versions of the learned culture brought with it "the urge to understand one's place in space and time"; and the hope that, by right understanding and right action, the area of instability and recurrent disaster resulting from the rule of Fortune over events and history might be reduced. The need was met by the wider dissemination of a particular religious emphasis, originally a mark of the religious and political culture of urban communities, and particularly of urban élites: that of providentialist religion. This, given a more sophisticated theological framework by the Reformation, would in due course emerge, universalized, as the religion of the state.[35]

Protestantism was then the developed form. But in the more primitive version providentialism had done no more than express the conviction of urban communities that prosperity and well-being arose out of the continuing favour of Providence, which itself depended on the moral quality of social and political life: its inner orderliness, its obedience to law, human and divine. Hence the concern, in the city, with religious and personal purity and conformity, seen as the means of containing the unpredictable pressures of Fate and Fortune. The nature of the complex of attitudes involved is indicated in Chapter 1, where the religious frame of mind favoured amongst some of the London élite in the early fifteenth century is discussed. This was characterized by a didactic approach to the content of religion, with a stress on the sermon rather than the sacra-

[34] See p. 309. [35] Pp. 358 ff.

ments, and on moral rather than ritualistic observance. This religious emphasis, gradually built into the London chronicle tradition as the fifteenth century proceeds, produces a moralized and providentialist history which in due course surfaces in Fabyan, and shapes the Tudor historiography of Hall and his successors; while also contributing to the popularity of the poet Lydgate's *Fall of Princes*, which adapted for English use the historical and moral attitudes of Florentine civic humanism, as codified by Boccaccio.[36]

Universalized therefore by the Reformation, and so applied to the whole of society, providentialism became the mark of the Protestant religion of the state. Protestantism provided the terms in which the English polity, structured as the body of the realm, its religious and secular aspects unified under its monarchical Head, its inner life articulated by religion and law, could be seen as historically unfolding in time under divine protection: its security and prosperity conditional on its conformity to the divinely appointed mission entrusted to it, consisting in the maintenance and furtherance of the providential Protestant order. For the individual, divine protection against the inroads of Fate and Fortune required, in this context, conformity to this order, and obedience to the Protestant state and its monarchical Head. The honourable man, in the Protestant civil society, earned repute and esteem by his deliberate obedience to, and service of, a providentially favoured political order. As a result, the political style requires a different tone from that appropriate to the man of honour in the lineage society. For the man of honour, events, being ruled by Fortune and not providentially ordered, are intractable except in so far as order can be imposed on them by the force of the political will. He has no "remedy against Fortune", beyond his confidence in his own inner resources and worth, which would either triumph over circumstances, or bring the reward of a worthy death and heroic fame: a triumph of another kind.[37] In the civil society these tendencies were qualified by a required submission, in obedience, to a religious and moral order identified with the Protestant state. At pp. 319–22 I propose reasons why the discipline thus imposed may have been, in intention, closer and less qualified under the Protestant than it had been under the Catholic order, and therefore more far-reaching in effect.

At the conclusion of Chapter 1 it is suggested that "the desire and

[36] *Ibid.*, and pp. 38 ff., 261 ff.

[37] See pp. 314 ff.

pursuit of the whole"[38] (in the sense that the "good society" involved the harmonious incorporation of the members, each in his own appropriate way, into the wholeness of the body of the realm) presents itself as a dominant theme of Tudor and early Stuart socio-political aspiration. In Chapter 1 some of the religious aspects of social wholeness, as manifested in an urban setting under the ritual forms of the Corpus Christi cult, are discussed; and reasons are put forward for the emerging dissatisfaction with, and critique of, these forms and of their appropriateness and effectiveness in the urban milieu in which they had been most widely used.[39] At the end of the book, I argue that the established religious order was rejected at the Reformation, not only because of its supposed inadequacy as a means of personal salvation; but also because of the socially divisive aspects attributed to the Catholic order by Protestant polemic, and manifested both in the separation of secular from ecclesiastical authority, and of priesthood from laity through the former's monopoly of the "sacrifice of the mass", which had thus become the sacrament not of unity but of separation.[40] Thus a deeply rooted concern with the promotion of social wholeness and unity accompanied the Reformation, placing the religious movement in harmony with, and in a supportive relationship to, the secular stress on the body of the realm, with its religious and secular aspects unified under the crown, and in which both religion and governance aimed to evoke the same response of obedience and service. Against this strongly unitive background, the eclipse of aristocratic dissidence, the tendency for even "rebels" to opt for non-violent modes for the expression of dissent, together with the strong resistances to the emergence of Parliament as a platform for political conflict, become more comprehensible.

Nevertheless, the unity thus adumbrated as aspiration could never be wholly translated into fact. In practice the Reformation, while projecting unity, also promoted divisiveness, not only through the break with Rome, but also because of the tendencies within itself promoting sectarian fissiparity. Moreover, by the end of the sixteenth century, further tensions had been introduced into the unitive order of the providentialist state by the emergence of an

[38] A phrase appropriated from the title of a novel by Frederick Corvo.
[39] See pp. 38 ff.
[40] See pp. 459 ff.

increasingly many-sided secular multi-culturality, expressed in ways of thinking and forms of affectivity rooted in humanism and pyrrhonism, which were autonomous in relation to religion, and sometimes sceptical of its claims. In Chapter 9 the theme of fissiparity is developed as seen in the context of the circle of the second earl of Essex; and the various influences circulating amongst the group, forming its outlook and patterning its action, are discussed. The mentality of the Essex circle reveals a spectrum of attitudes, ranging from the Catholic to the Puritan, with a strong Tacitean and "politic" tone, and a concern with the traditional preoccupations of honour. But in the end, when it came to revolt, it was the latter which provided the only language of dissent which all could share. Thus the idiom of the Essex revolt, in spite of its occasional resort to Tacitean modes of expression, in fact reverts to medieval models, with men of blood and lineage bound together by honour, and led by an earl marshal, confronting "base-born and unworthy" ministerial favourites with a view to their forcible removal from office and "the reform of the commonwealth". But at the same time the revolt underlines the inadequacy of the honour motivation, which emerges in the uncertainties, divided minds, hesitations, and split loyalties which characterized the leadership, so contributing to the final material failure and moral collapse. The Essex revolt proved to be, in England, the last of the honour rebellions. Yet the Essex circle, reincorporated by the repentance and exemplary death of their leader in the body of the realm, survived to make a significant contribution to the changed forms in which dissidence would receive expression during the seventeenth century.

Almost inevitably, a collection of this sort leaves an impression of incompleteness. Many gaps have been left unfilled, and themes touched upon have not been carried to a conclusion; for the work is still in progress. The influences it shows are fairly diverse. In some chapters the leaven of social anthropology is strongly present; others follow more traditional modes of exposition. It is to be hoped nevertheless that the studies, taken altogether, will reveal, if not a continuity, at least a connection and correspondence of theme. If so, the collection will have its uses, whatever its omissions, and whatever misunderstandings and errors it no doubt contains.

1. *Ritual, drama and social body in the late medieval English town**

This article aims to discuss a specific late medieval cult as practised in a specific context: that of the late medieval town. The kind of town to be considered falls typically into the category of "provincial capital", or at least of "county town", in terms of a recently suggested classification.[1] The cult in question is the cult of Corpus Christi. Corpus Christi was celebrated annually on a day which fell sometime between the end of May and the end of June.[2] What I propose to discuss are the various rites which were celebrated on Corpus Christi Day, the various dramatic, theatrical manifestations which took place in connection with the occasion, and the mythology associated with both. By and large, Corpus Christi has received more attention from literary scholars than from historians. This is because the famous Corpus Christi play cycles developed in connection with the Corpus Christi cult. The mythology of Corpus Christi has been very interestingly discussed by, for example, V. A. Kolve and Jerome Taylor.[3] Much has been written about the ways the plays were presented and produced, some of this by scholars with a strong historical sense, as more recently Alan Nelson and

* This paper was put together while I was a member of the Institute of Advanced Study, Princeton, New Jersey, during the session 1976–7. I owe a debt of gratitude to that distinguished institution, and in particular to its School of Historical Studies, whose Chairman, John Elliott, and fellow-members provided so much by way of hospitality, stimulating discussion and conversation. I am also grateful to Michael Hunter and Bob Scribner, who organized the London University seminar on "Ritual, Myth and Magic in Early Modern Europe" to which it was delivered in November 1979.

1 See P. Clark and P. Slack, *English Towns in Transition, 1500–1700: Essays in Urban History* (London, 1976), pp. 8 ff.

2 The date of Corpus Christi Day was determined by that of Easter Sunday and showed the same variation from year to year.

3 V. A. Kolve, *The Play Called Corpus Christi* (London, 1966); Jerome Taylor, "The Dramatic Structure of the Corpus Christi Play", in Jerome Taylor and Alan H. Nelson (eds.), *Medieval English Drama: Essays Critical and Contextual* (Chicago, 1972), pp. 148 ff.

Margaret Dorrell.[4] Nevertheless, there does seem to be lacking amongst most of these writers anything more than a very generalized idea[5] of the late medieval social background against which the cult was practised and the plays performed; and very little sense of the specific social needs and pressures to which both responded. What I aim to do here therefore is to fill in the social dimension. Briefly, I propose to argue that the theme of Corpus Christi is society seen in terms of body; and that the concept of body provided urban societies with a mythology and ritual in terms of which the opposites of social wholeness and social differentiation could be both affirmed and also brought into a creative tension, one with the other.[6] The final intention of the cult was, then, to express the social bond and to contribute to social integration. From this point of view, Corpus Christi expresses the creative role of religious rite and ideology in urban societies, in which the alternative symbols and ties

[4] Alan H. Nelson, *The Medieval English Stage: Corpus Christi Pageants and Plays* (Chicago, 1974); Margaret Dorrell, "The Mayor of York and the Coronation Pageant", *Leeds Studies in English*, new ser., v (1971), pp. 34–45; Margaret Dorrell and Alexandra F. Johnston, "The Domesday Pageant of the York Mercers", *Leeds Studies in English*, new ser., v (1971), pp. 29–34.

[5] As expressed for example by Taylor, "Dramatic Structure of the Corpus Christi Play", pp. 152–3.

[6] The general approach owes much to Mary Douglas, *Natural Symbols: Explorations in Cosmology* (London, 1970); Mary Douglas, *Purity and Danger: An Analysis of Concepts of Pollution and Taboo* (London, 1966). For the background of ideas, see Leonard Barkan, *Nature's Work of Art: The Human Body as Image of the World* (New Haven, Conn., 1975); S. B. Chrimes, *English Constitutional Ideas in the Fifteenth Century* (London, 1936); D. G. Hale, *The Body Politic: A Political Metaphor in Renaissance English Literature* (The Hague, 1971); E. H. Kantorowicz, *The King's Two Bodies: A Study in Medieval Political Theology* (Princeton, 1957); F. W. Maitland, "The Body Politic", in his *Selected Essays*, ed. H. D. Hazeltine (Cambridge, 1936), pp. 240 ff. The concept of body was of course by no means solely applied to urban societies; it provided a symbolism in terms of which all kinds of human social organization, including the unity of mankind itself and its relationship to the cosmos, could be expressed. See Barkan, *Nature's Work of Art, passim*; Otto Gierke, *Political Theories of the Middle Age*, trans. F. W. Maitland (Cambridge, 1922), p. 10.

It is likely that the role attributed in this paper to the Corpus Christi celebrations in English urban society was at least similar to that of the feast and its cultus in the larger towns of western Europe in general. For the European dimension, see for example Natalie Zemon Davis, "The Sacred and the Body Social in Sixteenth Century Lyon", *Past and Present*, xc (Feb. 1981), pp. 40 ff.; Neil C. Brooks, "Processional Drama and Dramatic Procession in Germany in the Late Middle Ages", *Jl English and Germanic Philology*, xxxii (1933), pp. 141 ff.; Edwin Muir, *Civic Ritual in Renaissance Venice* (Princeton, 1981), pp. 223 ff.; F. G. Very, *The Spanish Corpus Christi Procession: A Literary and Folkloric Study* (Valencia, 1962), *passim*.

of lordship, lineage and faithfulness, available in countrysides, were lacking.

The feast of Corpus Christi, authorized by a papal bull of 1264 which was published in 1317,[7] first receives specific mention in England when it was celebrated at Ipswich in 1325.[8] In the course of the following century, its observation spread widely; and, although never exclusively an urban feast, it soon came to occupy a particularly prominent place in the townsman's liturgical calendar. And it was in towns that the Corpus Christi celebrations assumed their most elaborate and developed form.[9] What happened on Corpus Christi Day was that first of all a mass took place, after which the congregation formed a procession in which the Corpus Christi, the Body of Christ, in the form of the host consecrated at the mass, was ceremonially carried through the principal thoroughfare of the place where the feast was being celebrated. It was attended by clergy and layfolk, and in the larger towns the mayor, aldermen, councillors and other municipal officials took a prominent part in the proceedings. The gilds were also required to attend, dressed in their gild uniform, or livery; and these processed in accordance with a carefully defined order of precedence, the humbler crafts going first, the wealthier and more important, in ascending order, coming behind them. Last of all came the aldermen, councillors, sheriffs: the town magistracy, in fact; and last of all, marching next to the host with its attendant clergy, came the mayor. The procession made its way to some other church at the other end of the processional route, where the host was deposited, and the religious side of the celebrations were there completed. Feasting and other kinds of more secular celebration then followed.[10] The feature to note

[7] For the foundation of the cult of Corpus Christi, and the circumstances of the bull, see P. Browe, *Die Verehrung der Eucharistie im Mittelalter* (Munich, 1933), pp. 70 ff.; *Acta sanctorum*, x *Aprilis*, i, (Paris, 1866), pp. 457–64; for the bull *Transiturus*, see *Magnum bullarium Romanum*, iii (Turin, 1858), pp. 705–8.

[8] According to M. L. Spencer, *Corpus Christi Pageants in England* (New York, 1911), p. 11; cf. E. K. Chambers, *The Medieval Stage*, 2 vols. (Oxford, 1903), ii, p. 371. But the feast may already have been widely observed by 1318. See Glynne Wickham, *Early English Stages, 1300 to 1600*, 2 vols. in 3 (London, 1959–72), i, *1300 to 1576*, 2nd edn (London, 1980), p. 130.

[9] For reasons succinctly outlined by Glynne Wickham, *The Medieval Theatre* (London, 1974), pp. 59 ff., and by Nelson, *Medieval English Stage*, pp. 10 ff.

[10] William Tydeman, *The Theatre in the Middle Ages: Western European Stage Conditions, c. 800–1576* (Cambridge, 1978), pp. 96 ff.; Spencer, *Corpus Christi Pageants*, pp. 61 ff.

however is the procession, in which the Corpus Christi becomes the point of reference in relation to which the structure of precedence and authority in the town is made visually present on Corpus Christi Day.

In addition, in many towns the gild contingents in the procession were accompanied by "pageants" – moving waggon platforms. On these, theatrical properties and actors were assembled into depictions of Scriptural scenes and incidents, each one being the responsibility either of one, or collectively of several, of the gilds marching in the procession. The pageants might take the form of mute shows. But in some towns they stopped at predetermined stations to present brief speeches accompanied by dramatic actions. In others, full-length plays might be acted at some stage in the proceedings.[11] The assembled texts of the latter constitute the well-known Corpus Christi cycles, of which more or less complete examples survive from Coventry, York, Wakefield, Chester and from another town which was probably Lincoln.[12] Some of these play cycles were so elaborate – involving in York, for example, the presentation of over fifty plays – that the dramatic aspects of the feast were liable to conflict with the processional and liturgical aspects. Where this happened, the two became separated. In some towns the procession took up the morning of the feast-day, the plays the afternoon. In Chester the plays were shifted to Whitsun week; in York the plays continued to be presented on Corpus Christi Day, but the procession and mass took place the morning after.[13] As a result of this separation two aspects of the celebration emerged – the procession and the plays – each with a different significance and function which I will later discuss.

What is the meaning of all this? One thing that seems to be clear

[11] Most of the extensive material relating to the nature of the "pageants" and the manner in which the plays were presented is summarized with bibliographies, but with polemical intent, in Nelson, *Medieval English Stage*, *passim*.

[12] See *Two Coventry Corpus Christi Plays*, ed. Hardin Craig, 2nd edn (Early English Text Soc., extra ser., lxxxvii, London, 1957); *York Plays*, ed. L. Toulmin Smith (Oxford, 1885); *The Towneley Plays*, ed. George England and A. W. Pollard (Early English Text Soc., extra ser., lxxi, London, 1897); *The Wakefield Pageants in the Towneley Cycle*, ed. A. C. Cawley (Manchester, 1958); *The Chester Plays*, ed. H. Deimling (Early English Text Soc., extra ser., lxii, London, 1892; re-ed. J. Matthews, Early English Text Soc., extra ser., cxv, London, 1916); *Ludus Coventriae: or, The Plaie Called Corpus Christi*, ed. K. S. Block (Early English Text Soc., extra ser., cxx, London, 1920).

[13] Spencer, *Corpus Christi Pageants in England*, pp. 96 ff.

is that in some kind of way the feast and its season is about body – a special kind of body admittedly: the Corpus Christi; but body nevertheless, and as such related to and modelled on the human psychosomatic self, and to the way in which this is experienced. So my starting point is going to be from the idea – developed by Mary Douglas for example in *Natural Symbols*[14] – that the human experience of body tends to sustain a particular view of society, the latter in turn constraining the way in which the body itself is regarded. Of course, the body of Christ was an essentially religious conception, involving a relationship between the self and a supernatural order. But the idea also had a secular and social relevance. "Body" was the pre-eminent symbol in terms of which society was conceived.[15] Other images were available – the social order might be seen as a tree, or as a ship, as a vineyard with its graduated hierarchy of labourers, or as a church building with its component parts.[16] All had the advantage of suggesting structure – separate parts related to each other within a larger whole. But it was the idea of the social order as body which had the widest connotation, and which was most obsessive and fruitful. It suggested in the first place the intimacy and naturalness of the social bond, since it was presented as a kind of extension of the psychosomatic self.[17] Natural body and

[14] Douglas, *Natural Symbols*, pp. 65, 70.

[15] By and large this paper inclines to the kind of "structuralist" approach developed in relation to systems of religious ritual and belief by Claude Lévi-Strauss in his *Le totémisme aujourd'hui* (Paris, 1962), and in his *La pensée sauvage* (Paris, 1962). The view developed is that, through the medium of eucharistic beliefs, a language of ritual and symbol is set up, in terms of which an "ideal" order is projected which stands in a dialectical (or "binary") relationship to the actual order, generating a pressure towards a conformity of the latter to the former.

[16] Edmund Dudley, *The Tree of Commonwealth*, ed. D. M. Brodie (Cambridge, 1948); G. R. Owst, *Literature and Pulpit in Medieval England*, 2nd edn (Oxford, 1966), pp. 72, 549.

[17] The idea of a close analogy between the body politic and the body natural originates in the pre-Socratic idea that the world of nature is saturated with mind, and that therefore all bodies within it were constructed in accordance with similar principles, and displayed a similar structure, being those perceived in mind. For Plato, in accordance with his doctrine of "ideas", all living creatures similarly conformed to an "ideal" primordial model. Aristotle clearly enunciated the structural similarity of social and psychosomatic bodies, laying down the principle that "the constitution of an animal must be regarded as resembling that of a well-governed city state"; Aristotle, *On the Movement of Animals*, trans. E. S. Forster (Cambridge, Mass., and London, 1937), p. 475. The concept received much emphasis in the writings of the Roman Stoics, as in Seneca: "We are all parts of one great body. Nature produced us related to one another, since she created us for the same end": Seneca, *Ad Lucilium epistolae morales*, trans.

social body indeed reacted on each other with a closeness which approaches identity. Thus actions which affected the social body reacted back on the physical body – physical ailments, for example, being seen as the result of sins, lapses or crimes which had inflicted harm on the social body.[18] And, just as in the natural body the physiological danger points were at the joints, where member met member, or at the openings where the body could be invaded by harmful influences from without, so in the social body tensions arose at the jointures which linked group to group, class to class; and

R. M. Gummere, 3 vols. (Cambridge, Mass., and London, 1917–43), iii, p. 91. The idea passed into the Christian tradition by way of St Paul's First Epistle to the Corinthians xii. 12, 14–23, 25–6. For these and other authorities, see Hale, *Body Politic*, pp. 18 ff.; Barkan, *Nature's Work of Art*, pp. 8 ff., 64 ff., and references there given.

18 The concept of body meant that social dysfunction was presented in terms of disease, as in Cicero, *De officiis*, iii. 5. 22, quoted in Hale, *Body Politic*, p. 25: "As, supposing each member of the body were so disposed as to think it could be well if it should draw to itself the health of the adjacent member, it is inevitable that the whole body would be debilitated and would perish." The interest in medicine among the early Tudor humanists, particularly in Cardinal Pole's household at Padua, led to one of the most elaborate surviving expositions of social ills in terms of disease. This was Thomas Starkey's *Dialogue between Cardinal Pole and Thomas Lupset*, ed. J. M. Cowper (Early English Text Soc., extra ser., xii, London, 1871). Starkey sees the English body politic as afflicted by consumption (loss of population); dropsy (idleness); palsy (luxury); and pestilence (social conflict). By the same principle, applied in reverse, an explanation for the misfortunes and ills which afflicted the psychosomatic body of the individual person was sought in the latter's moral lapses and sins, which in turn caused disorders in the social body. See K. V. Thomas, *Religion and the Decline of Magic: Studies in Popular Beliefs in Sixteenth and Seventeenth Century England* (London, 1971), pp. 106–7. Hence the importance given, particularly in urban societies, to the moral purity of office-bearers, and the enforcement by urban magistracies of moral policies on whose effectiveness the well-being of the town and its inhabitants was thought to depend: Bernd Moeller, *Imperial Cities and the Reformation: Three Essays*, ed. and trans. H. C. E. Midelfort and M. U. Edwards Jr (Philadelphia, 1972), pp. 45–6. In the larger English towns, magistrates were commonly disqualified from office by immorality, and urban governments enforced a sexual code which involved punishing or penalizing adultery, fornication and prostitution; before the Reformation, as after it, Sabbatarianism was an issue, leading to spasmodic Sabbatarian legislation. For the attitudes involved, see for example John Stow, *A Survey of London*, ed. C. L. Kingsford, 2 vols. (Oxford, 1908), i, pp. 189–90, where he reports that in 1383 the citizens of London, "taking upon them the rights which belonged to their bishops", proceeded to punish on their own initiative the prostitutes and procurers in the city, "saying, they abhorred . . . the negligence of their prelates . . . wherefore they would themselves, they said, purge their Citie from such filthiness, least through God's vengeance, either the pestilence or sworde should happen to them, or that the earth should swallow them".

in the social body too there were the openings through which might pour invasion from without.[19]

The language of body also provided an instrument by means of which social wholeness and social differentiation could be conceived and experienced at many different levels. Social differentiation could be apprehended in terms of the various limbs and organs, all arranged in a hierarchical structure of different roles and functions under the overall direction of the head: the magistracy. Wholeness was seen in terms of the necessary interdependence of the constituting limbs and organs. None could subsist of themselves; their survival depended on an effective incorporation into the wholeness of the social body, and in subordination to its head.[20] But of course these attitudes, which conceived of society as a body in which differentiation was taken up into social wholeness, were in historical fact projected by societies which were deeply divided –

[19] The supposition that disease invaded the body through its openings, particularly the mouth, but also the pores and even the eyes, was strengthened by the theories, increasingly popular after the fourteenth century, of the infectious and contagious spread of such illnesses as bubonic plague, erysipelas, smallpox, influenza, diphtheria, typhoid fever and later syphilis. These theories explained the spread of these diseases by the infectious or contagious dissemination of the "seeds" of the fever (a term which had the authority of Galen behind it) which, entering the body, upset the balance of the humours on which health depended. See A. C. Crombie, *Augustine to Galileo: Science in the Middle Ages*, 2nd edn, 2 vols. (London, 1964), i, *Fifth to Thirteenth Centuries*, pp. 228 ff., and ii, *Thirteenth to Seventeenth Centuries*, pp. 284 ff. For examples of how infection, taken into the body through the mouth in "corrupted" water or air, undermined the whole body, see Lynn Thorndike, *A History of Magic and Experimental Science*, 8 vols. (New York, 1923–58), iii, pp. 244–5, and iv, pp. 254–5.

For Galen, the dominant authority on which medieval medicine was based, the form of the bodily structure was determined by the bones: " . . . as poles to tents, and walls to houses, so are bones to all living creatures, for other features naturally take form and change from them": Galen, *On Anatomical Procedures*, ed. Charles Singer (London, 1959), p. 4. Hence, according to Sir John Cheke, a body politic, as well as a body natural, "cannot bee without much griefe of inflammacon, where any least parte is out of joynt, or not duely set in his owne natural place": John Cheke, *The Hurt of Sedicion Howe Grevous it is to a Communewelth* (London, 1549; A. W. Pollard and G. R. Redgrave, *A Short Title Catalogue of Books Printed in England and Ireland 1475–1640*, 2 vols., London, 1926 (henceforth cited as S.T.C.), 5109), quoted in Hale, *Body Politic*, p. 58.

[20] The medical theory that health depended on a balance of the four "humours" within the body natural, which therefore needed to maintain a proper hierarchical relationship to each other, corresponding to that of the four elements, was also invoked to explain "sickness" in the social body. For the hierarchical classification of the bodily parts, and their correspondence to the social hierarchy, see Hale, *Body Politic*, p. 15, and *passim*.

riven by an intense competitiveness: by the struggle for honour and worship, status and precedence, power and wealth. Conflict was the dark side of the moon of unity. However, without conflict, no social wholeness either. Conflict strengthened the need for participation and support which wholeness implied. Participation was to be found in family, neighbourhood, craft and gild fraternity, and in citizenship. But the persisting tension between whole and differentiation meant that the process of incorporation into the social body needed to be continually reaffirmed, and the body itself continually recreated. Ritual, in an affective and visual way, projected the tensions and aspirations, and the resolution of these, which this process involved. From this point of view the archetypal symbol was the mass, which both affirmed and created the symbol of social body, which was the Body of Christ. The Corpus Christi procession involved the application of this theme to a specific community and place, presenting in visual form the structure of social differentiation taken up into the social wholeness which was the town itself.[21]

Thus Corpus Christi resolves into what could be seen as the binary terms of a typical Lévi-Straussian mythological contradiction: social wholeness versus social differentiation.[22] Certainly it is this contradiction and its resolution which is the message spelt out in the liturgical texts of the feast, and which is conveyed through the ritual forms. Thus, according to the Sequence for the Mass of Corpus Christi Day, just as social particularity involves social participation, so each fragment of the consecrated host shares in the wholeness of the Body of Christ, "Not a single doubt remain", the Sequence says, "When they break the host in twain,/ But that in each part remain/ What was in the whole before." Similarly:

[21] For the role of the church as a peace-making and conflict-resolving institution, and for some of the ways in which this role was related to the mass (while later also receiving expression in the Protestant communion rite), see John Bossy, "Blood and Baptism: Kinship, Community and Christianity in Western Europe from the Fourteenth to the Seventeenth Centuries", in D. Baker (ed.), *Sanctity and Secularity: The Church and the World* (Studies in Church Hist., x, London, 1973), pp. 138 ff. For the consecrated host as a peace-making symbol, used to separate the participants in a violent riot in London, see *Bales' Chronicle*, printed in *Six Town Chronicles*, ed. Ralph Flenley (Oxford, 1911), p. 146, under the year 1458–9. For a similar use of the host to quell urban riots in Spain, see Henry Kamen, *Spain in the Later Seventeenth Century* (London, 1980), p. 180.

[22] See the exposition by Robert C. Poole, in Claude Lévi-Strauss, *Totemism*, trans. Rodney Needham (Harmondsworth, 1969), Introduction, pp. 9 ff.

"Whether one or thousands eat/ All receive the self-same meat."[23] The social reference emerges in a less encoded and abstract kind of way in the sermon of St John Chrysostom read at matins during the Corpus Christi season: "Christ hath mingled himself with us, and infused his Body into our bodies, that we may be one together, as limbs of one body."[24] Another lesson also read at matins during the season affirmed: "Let him come near, let him enter that Body, that he may be quickened. Let him not sever himself from the fit joining together of all the members . . . let him be goodly, and useful, and healthy."[25] Finally, the nature of the Body of Christ as social body is made clear by the offertory prayer of the mass, which asserted that the Body of Christ signified "the peace and unity" of the church, the sacral society which *was* Christ's mystical Body.[26]

Of course, in these ritual formulas the concepts are stated in an extremely compressed and coded form. However, just as the Corpus Christi mass extended itself into the secular ritual of the Corpus Christi procession, so the liturgical formulas projected themselves into secular usage, in which their themes are given an explicitly social reference. For example, the "peace and unity" of the offertory echoes in the reiterated phrases used in urban documents to designate the social bond. The leet of Coventry in 1494 spoke of "unity, concord, and amity" as what was aimed at in the governance of cities.[27] Similarly, John Hooker, town clerk of Exeter

23 For the Latin text, see *Missale ad usum . . . ecclesiae Sarum*, ed. F. H. Dickinson (Oxford and London, 1861–83), pp. 457–8.

24 *The Roman Breviary*, trans. John, Marquess of Bute, 2 vols. (London, 1879), ii, p. 575. Cf. the Sarum Breviary, Response to the Third Nocturn of the Feast of Corpus Christi: "We are one bread and one body. All of us share in one bread and one cup"; and also a Lesson in the same Nocturn: "Our Lord Jesus Christ entrusted his Body and Blood to things which constitute themselves into a whole. For one loaf is made of many grains, and wine flows out of many grapes": *Breviarium ad usum . . . ecclesiae Sarum*, ed. F. Proctor and C. Wordsworth, 3 vols. (Cambridge, 1879–86), i, col. 1070.

25 *Roman Breviary*, ii, p. 582. Cf. *Breviarium ad usum . . . ecclesiae Sarum*, ed. Proctor and Wordsworth, i, col. 1084: "For this [that is, the Body and Blood of Christ] is the sacrament of duty towards others, the sign of unity, the bond of charity" (First Lesson for Sunday within the Octave of Corpus Christi).

26 *Missale ad usum . . . ecclesiae Sarum*, ed. Dickinson, p. 459. Cf. *Breviarium ad usum . . . ecclesiae Sarum*, ed. Proctor and Wordsworth, i, col. 1101: "Who has received the mystery of unity, and does not hold to the bond of peace, does not receive the mystery for himself, but as a testimony against himself" (Fourth Lesson at Matins within the Octave of Corpus Christi).

27 *The Coventry Leet Book*, ed. M. D. Harris, 4 vols. (Early English Text Soc., original ser., cxxxiv, cxxxv, cxxxviii, cxlvi, London, 1907–13), p. 555.

in the mid-sixteenth century: "Wheresoever love, concord, and unity are not, there is disorder and confusion . . . for where every singular member . . . will . . . swerve from that unity we are all conjoined in, let him surely await for destruction."[28] At Newcastle upon Tyne, Corpus Christi was associated with the "good unity, concord, and charity", which ought to subsist among the crafts and occupations, which received expression on the feast-day, when the gild brothers "amicably and lovingly . . . in their best apparel and array . . . go in the procession".[29] In York the Corpus Christi fraternity saw itself as characterized by a "unity and concord" rooted in charity and in the veneration of the Body of Christ.[30] At Beverley the worshipful men of the town contributed to the Corpus Christi procession "For the praise and honour of God and the Body of Christ, and for the peaceful union of the worthier and lesser commons of the town".[31]

The cultic terminology, then, with its overflow into secular usage, provides an apt commentary on the aspect of the feast in which social wholeness was the central emphasis. This aspect received proper visual expression in the nature of the procession, which was itself the wholeness of the urban social body, gathered in unity and concord to venerate the Corpus Christi, itself a central symbol of social wholeness, and joined in this by the massed crowds through which it moved. From this point of view, the occasion was one in which specialized roles and differences of function and status were dissolved into a simple membership of the social body, and the undifferentiated togetherness which this implied. The stage is thus

[28] John Hooker's Oration to the Commons, 25 Jan. 1559, in W. Cotton, *An Elizabethan Guild* (Exeter, 1873), pp. 99 ff.

[29] Ordinance of the Company of Tailors of Newcastle upon Tyne, 8 Oct. 1536, printed in R. Welford, *History of Newcastle and Gateshead*, 3 vols. (London, 1884–7), ii, p. 154.

[30] *The Register of the Guild of Corpus Christi in the City of York*, ed. R. H. Skaife (Surtees Soc., lvii, Durham and London, 1871), p. 4. At York, as elsewhere, "unity and concord" implied the process of negotiation, compromise and agreement which enabled decisions to be made with a show of unity. Thus disputed aldermanic elections 1516–17 led to riots, and a breakdown in civic peace and order. The mayor and aldermen, summoned before Wolsey, promised henceworth to be "in oon unity and concord without any part taking in any": D. M. Palliser, *Tudor York* (Oxford, 1979), p. 67; *York Civic Records*, ed. A. Raine, 8 vols. (London and York, 1939–52), iii, pp. 57 ff. The beliefs associated with Corpus Christi tended to promote the ethic of unity and social peace.

[31] *Beverley Town Documents*, ed. A. F. Leach (Selden Soc., xiv, London, 1900), p. 34.

set for the kind of social experience which Victor Turner in *The Ritual Process*[32] calls "communitas", in which, as he puts it, the structural aspects of society are reversed in order to give expression "to an essential and generic human bond without which there would be *no* society".[33] Yet the opposite emphasis, that of social differentiation, with its stress on the segmented occupational roles in the urban community, and its vertical structure of status and authority, is if anything even more emphatically spelt out, as the gilds file past in the due order and precedence laid down by authority, the procession culminating in the representatives of the magistracy and their head, the mayor, whose place is next to the Corpus Christi. This aspect of the proceedings is paralleled by the liturgical texts of the season which celebrate the sovereignty of God, and the rule of Christ, as head, over his members in the body of the church.[34] Several urban texts of the fourteenth to fifteenth century use this imagery of head and members to define the relationship which ought to subsist between the mayoral office and the citizenry. For the fourteenth-century London alderman Andrew Horn, for example, the mayor required reverence from his burghers and subjects because his authority rested on divine, as well as human, election: he was the head, and they the members.[35] Moreover, the idea persisted that, just as the person of Christ as its head constituted the corporate identity of the church, so it was the person of the mayor as head which gave a town the corporate identity which, for example, enabled it to plead or be pleaded at law.[36] Thus the

[32] Victor W. Turner, *The Ritual Process: Structure and Anti-Structure* (Harmondsworth, 1969), pp. 82 ff.

[33] *Ibid.*, p. 83.

[34] Jerome Taylor, "Dramatic Structure of the Corpus Christi Play", pp. 151 ff., and the references there given.

[35] *Munimenta Gildhallae Londoniensis*, ed. H. T. Riley, 3 vols. in 4 (Rolls Series, London, 1849–62), ii, *Liber custumarum*, pt. 2, p. 517. On Andrew Horn, see Jeremy Catto, "Andrew Horn: Law and History in Fourteenth-Century England" in R. H. C. Davis and J. M. Wallace-Hadrill (eds.), *The Writings of History in the Middle Ages: Essays Presented to Richard William Southern* (Oxford, 1981), pp. 367 ff.

[36] As late as 21 Edward IV a judge could declare: "The political body is made up of men like us. If the man's head is decapitated, he himself is dead. In the same way, if the mayor who is the head of the 'corps politike' die, the writ abates. And if the community without the mayor wish to enforce such an act, it cannot be done, because the mayor did not give his assent . . . " Similarly Chief Justice Brian: "And as to that which is said, that such a body politic cannot be severed, it is not so, for if the mayor dies, they are severed, and when a new mayor is appointed

Corpus Christi could function as the symbol of the principle of magisterial authority, on which depended the whole structure of social differentiation and social status in the urban community. The procession therefore spelt out the nature of this authority as imparting to the wholeness of the social body an ordered structure which it would otherwise lack.

But where do the Corpus Christi plays come into all this? How do they contribute to the expression of that tension between social wholeness and social differentiation which I have characterized as the essence of the celebration of Corpus Christi? Certainly the plays gave a wider range of resonance to the celebration of the feast. They did so, in the first place, because the Corpus Christi play cycle, in such great towns as Coventry, Chester, York, where it assumed the form of a grandiose celebration of the total content of Christian mythology, from the Creation to the Last Judgement,[37] helped to make Corpus Christi an occasion on which the urban community could effectively present and define itself in relation to the outside world. One respect in which the plays did this was that they attracted a numerous extramural audience: firstly, of gentry and common people from the surrounding countryside; but they also provided the occasion for visits by monarchs, members of the royal family, great nobles, and prominent merchants from other towns.[38] A routine of entertainment and conviviality therefore established

they are as before . . . " H. Ke Chin Wang, "The Corporate Entity Concept (or Fiction Theory) in the Year Book Period", in *Law Quart. Rev.*, lix (1943), p. 79.

37 Such a celebration seems to have been the intention, although the cycles themselves only approximate to the ideal prototype based on the Seven Ages of the World, and figural representations of each, postulated by Kolve, *Play Called Corpus Christi*, pp. 57 ff.

38 Kolve, *Play Called Corpus Christi*, pp. 6–7. The York Corpus Christi plays were seen by Richard II in 1397: Robert Davies, *Extracts from the Municipal Records of the City of York* (London, 1843), pp. 230–1; and by Henry VII in 1487: *York Civic Records*, ed. Raine, ii, p. 25. On more ordinary occasions the plays were presented before an audience of "knights, ladies, gentlemen and noblemen then within the city": Davies, *Extracts from the Municipal Records of the City of York*, pp. 74–7. The Coventry Corpus Christi plays were seen by Queen Margaret in 1457, by Richard III, and Henry VII: Chambers, *Medieval Stage*, ii, pp. 357–8. At Chester, plays from the cycle were presented before Lord Strange in 1488, Prince Arthur in 1497 and the earl of Derby in 1578: R. H. Morris, *Chester in the Plantagenet and Tudor Reigns* (Chester, n.d.), pp. 322, 353; *Digby Plays*, ed. F. J. Furnivall (Early English Text Soc., extra ser., lxx, London, 1897), p. xxvi. At Beverley in 1423 the earl of Northumberland was the principal guest for the plays and Corpus Christi celebrations: *Report on the Manuscripts of the Corporation of Beverley* (Hist. MSS. Comm., London, 1900), p. 160.

itself in connection with the presentation of the cycles which helped to extend and confirm the network of contacts with those whose wealth and power made them significant in the external relationships of the community. The influx of strangers also brought a brief flurry of enhanced commercial activity to the urban markets.[39] More important than the latter, however, is the fact that a famous dramatic cycle promoted the prestige of the community with which it was associated, and so enhanced the latter's "honour".[40] It did this by witnessing to the communal piety of the community, and to the resources of ingenuity and surplus wealth at its disposal, which were potent enough to draw the outer world into its streets and markets, attracting the admiring attention of great nobles and even of kings. "Honour" in this sense received expression in the wealth of human and material resources deployed in the plays, and also in the elaborateness of the Corpus Christi procession, affording as this did an occasion for the display of costly artefacts and costumes. So that *sumptuosus*, a word with implications of lavishness and luxury, was the typical adjective applied to the great play cycles.[41] "Honour"

[39] Such at any rate seems to have been the case at Warwick, according to Sir William Dugdale: Spencer, *Corpus Christi Pageants*, p. 17. At Chester in 1575 dominant opinion was of the view that the plays advanced the "comen welthe, and benefit, and profite" of the city: Morris, *Chester in the Plantagenet and Tudor Reigns*, p. 321.

[40] At Beverley, by an ordinance of 1411, the Corpus Christi play was to be presented "for ever", "ut honor dei et honestas ville . . . exaltentur" ("in order that the honour of God and the repute of the town . . . may be enhanced"): *Beverley Town Documents*, ed. Leach, p. 34. At Coventry, in 1494, the Corpus Christi pageants were "for the welth and worship of the whole city", and contributions were to be paid to maintain them to "please God and contynewe the goode name and fame that this citie hath had": *Coventry Leet Book*, ed. Harris, p. 558. At Chester, a typical usage was "to the pleasure of God, worship of Master Maire, and the city" (1523): Morris, *Chester in the Plantagenet and Tudor Reigns*, p. 316. At York the formula was "for the honour of God, and worship of the Cite": *York Civic Records*, ed. Raine, i, p. 56, and iv, p. 109.

[41] Used, for example, of the great London cycle, now lost, described by the chronicler Malvern in 1384 as "quendam ludum sumptuosum duravit quinque diebus" ("A certain very sumptuous play that lasted five days"): Chambers, *Medieval Stage*, ii, p. 380. Cf. *York Memorandum Book*, ed. Maud Sellars (Surtees Soc., cxxv, Durham, 1915), p. 156: " . . . universari artifices civitatis Ebor' annis singulis suis sumptibus fecerent quendam ludum sumptuosum, in diversis paginis compilatum" (" . . . all the craftsmen of the city of York each year at their own expense presented a certain sumptuous play, composed of diverse pageants") (1425). The "sumptuousness" of the play procession arose partly from the richness of the costumes of the actors (these were sometimes vestments borrowed from the churches: Morris, *Chester in the Plantagenet and Tudor Reigns*, p. 311 n.); at Lincoln, costumes were borrowed from the local gentry and

therefore was a factor which impelled urban ruling groups to develop the scale and complicate the nature of the Corpus Christi festivities, in particular by the promotion of the play cycles.

It is likely that it was these external aspects of the Corpus Christi plays, as an enhancement of urban honour in the world at large, which most appealed to the urban magistracies, or many of them.[42] This seems to have been the case at Beverley, for example, where there is little evidence, in the production of the play cycle, for the kind of middle-class dramatic initiative, exercised through the gild organizations, which is encountered elsewhere.[43] A lack of interest in the borough plays on the part of the crafts is suggested by the fact that, for nearly every year that information survives, records of fines also exist, levied on the gilds for careless playing or other misconduct in connection with their play assignments.[44] The Beverley plays abruptly ceased in 1520, when the ruling group became aware that literary fashion was changing, that the cycle form no longer inspired admiration, or attracted prestige.[45] As a result, abandoned

their ladies: see *The Manuscripts of the Corporation of Lincoln* (Hist. MSS. Comm., 14th Rept, Appendix, pt. 8, London, 1895), pp. 25, 29; and partly from the effect created by the gilded and brightly coloured pageant waggons. Corpus Christi processions were also characterized by a display of valuable gold and silver artifacts, like those belonging to the York Corpus Christi Gild: see *Register of the Guild of Corpus Christi*, ed. Skaife, pp. 296–7.

42 The "honour" motivation did not of course conflict with an occasionally asserted didactic purpose of the cycles, as in the 1544 proclamation of the Chester plays: "To exort the mynds of the common people to good devosion and holsome doctryne . . . ": Morris, *Chester in the Plantagenet and Tudor Reigns*, p. 349.

43 Nelson, *Medieval English Stage*, p. 92, comments: " . . . the Beverley corporation remained more closely identified with the actual production of the pageants than the governments of most other English cities", and cites the case of the Hairers' gild in 1391, when it was the town corporation and not the gild itself (as in other towns) which provided the pageant waggon and at least some of the costumes and properties required for the gild play: *Beverley Town Documents*, ed. Leach, p. 37.

44 Nelson, *Medieval English Stage*, p. 94, and references there given. The concern with town "honour", "worship" and "repute" in relation to the outside world, which motivated the penalization of gilds which neglected their obligations towards the play, emerges from the case of the aldermen of the Painters' gild, fined in 1519 because the gild play, *The Three Kings of Cologne*, was badly and disorderly played, "in contempt of the whole community, in the presence of many strangers": *Report on the Manuscripts of the Corporation of Beverley*, p. 172.

45 Such seems to be the implication of the attempt made in 1520 to "transpose" and "alter" the play, William Peeris, chaplain to the earl of Northumberland, being called in for this purpose, the title of *poeta* attributed to him suggesting a possible "humanist" orientation. See Nelson, *Medieval English Stage*, p. 99, and *Report*

by the magistracy, and having no deep roots in the gilds, the plays simply disappeared; not even their text has survived. But there is a contrast between the fate of the Beverley cycle and the tenacity with which, for example, those of York and Chester fought for survival in the face of changing fashion and, after the Reformation, also of governmental and ecclesiastical disapproval. In such towns the plays enjoyed a wider support, and met a deeper need, felt by a wider spectrum of the urban community than at Beverley.[46]

What was the nature of this need? I would suggest that, in towns like York and Chester, characterized by numerous crafts and gild organizations which preserved their vitality far into the sixteenth and even the seventeenth centuries, the play cycles provided a mechanism, which I shall later describe, by which the tensions implicit in the diachronic rise and fall of occupational communities could be confronted and worked out. In addition, they made available a means by which visual and public recognition could be given to changes in the relationships of superiority, dependence or co-operation which existed between occupations. And from this point of view the play cycles constitute the natural complement of the Corpus Christi procession. For the procession, as we have seen, assumed the essentially synchronic form of a static hierarchical structure, defined by the magistracy, in which change therefore could take place only by publicly dramatized conflict, resolved by arbitration or judicial decision. But the play cycles worked by means which were essentially informal, by which nevertheless the implications of change could be given recognition and incorporated

on the Manuscripts of the Corporation of Beverley, p. 171. For Peeris's connection with the earl of Northumberland, see below, p. 86.

46 At both Chester and York there was strong popular support for the continuation of the plays. Sir John Savage, mayor of Chester, summoned before the Privy Council for permitting the last presentation of the Chester cycle (in 1574) in spite of an inhibition from the Council in the North and the archbishop of York, based his defence on "the assente, consente, and agreement of his saide then brethrene the aldermen of the saide citie and of the comen counsell of the same": Morris, *Chester*, p. 321. See also H. C. Gardiner, *Mysteries' End: An Investigation of the Last Days of the Medieval Religious Stage* (New Haven, Conn., 1946), pp. 72 ff. At York, the last we hear of the Corpus Christi cycle is when in 1580 the York commons "did earnestly request my L. Maiour . . . that Corpus Christi play might be played this yere", but to no effect. The play-book had been impounded by Archbishop Sandys and Dean Hutton for revision, and was never returned: *York Civic Records*, ed. Raine, iii, pp. 7, 26; see also Palliser, *Tudor York*, pp. 246–7; A. G. Dickens, "Tudor York", in *Victoria County History, Yorkshire: The City of York* (London, 1961), p. 152.

with a minimum of friction in the structure of the social body. The plays were in fact, both by their symbolism and the way in which they were organized and built up, well suited to function in this way. Indeed, the social pressures which contributed to their development have been probably too little appreciated.

As a symbolic system, the Corpus Christi play cycle, like the Corpus Christi procession, expressed wholeness. As I have said, the typical cycle aimed to present, through a series of connected play-episodes, the whole spectrum of sacred history, from the Creation to Domesday.[47] Thus a connected mythological world-view emerged, but one which was built up out of a series of linked but autonomous play-units, each one complete, and with its own specific dramatic character. This structure projected the nature of the society whose world-view it expressed. For, in the presentation of a cycle, each play-unit was associated, at least in part, with a movable wheeled platform, equipped with the appropriate theatrical properties, from which the play-unit was wholly or partly performed. Each of these "pageants" and its associated play was, by command of the magistracy, made the responsibility of a specific occupational gild. This was charged with the task of mobilizing the human and material resources required for its proper performance.

[47] See p. 27 and n. 37 above, this chapter; Kolve, *Play Called Corpus Christi*, pp. 48 ff.; Taylor, "Dramatic Structure of the Corpus Christi Play", pp. 148 ff.; O. B. Hardison, *Christian Rite and Christian Drama in the Middle Ages* (Baltimore, 1965), pp. 286–7; Hardin Craig, *English Religious Drama of the Middle Ages* (Oxford, 1955), p. 133; Wickham, *Medieval Theatre*, pp. 59 ff.; Wickham, *Early English Stages*, i, pp. 130 ff. These authors argue for or support the idea that a close connection existed between this synoptic character of the cycles, and the nature and doctrinal content of the Corpus Christi feast, which was both the end and culmination of the liturgical year, and therefore an appropriate time for presenting, in summarized form, its total content. In addition, the cycles projected a representational unfolding, in space and time, of the compressed, timeless content of the central symbol of the feast, that is the Corpus Christi itself. There are some variations on this theme. Alan H. Nelson thinks that the cycles were based on festival processions which pre-dated the Corpus Christi feast, and that any connection with its doctrinal content was incidental; more important were the pressures on town authorities, who had to accommodate perhaps a score or two of gilds, each of them eager to put on a pageant, while at the same time the whole procession had to be given a connected theme, and "clear, sequential, and familiar iconography": Nelson, *Medieval English Stage*, pp. 10 ff. Glynne Wickham also holds that in some form processions and plays pre-dated the feast: Wickham, *Early English Stages*, i, pp. 127 ff. For Rosemary Woolf, *The English Mystery Plays* (London, 1972), the cycles became linked to the feast for didactic and propagandist, rather than doctrinal reasons. None of these views are incompatible with the argument developed here – or, for that matter, with each other.

As a result, therefore, the Corpus Christi cycle, by the nature of its structure, gathered together the different occupational gild groupings into a visibly presented unity.[48] Here then, once again, was presented, as in the Corpus Christi procession, the wholeness of the social body and of its mythological world-outlook, into which each occupation was incorporated.

For the full expression of its place in the social body, an occupation and its ruling gild needed its place in the Corpus Christi play cycle, as well as its place in the procession. This was true in a very concrete and practical, as well as symbolic kind of way. In the first place, the identity and inner cohesion of an occupation was closely linked to the co-operative enterprise in which its Corpus Christi play-unit involved the membership. Indeed, it was often the case in those towns where elaborate Corpus Christi cycles grew up, that membership of a specific occupation was most readily established by the payment of the dues called "pageant-money", which were levied for the support of the gild play-unit. And the requirement, laid down in gild regulations, that all members should attend the performance of the gild play, attired in their liveries, made it an occasion on which the gild defined itself, and assumed a publicly visible form.[49] Thus the need of the play for financial and moral support also defined the boundaries of an occupational jurisdiction, marking it off from others of the same sort. Indeed, gilds which gave no play, and collected no pageant-money, commonly represented occupations which, being unskilled, were loose in their organization; or else crippled by poverty and dwindling numbers. And with such, of course, the plays were bound to be unpopular; and it was from them, by and large, that complaints about the financial burden they involved were most likely to arise.[50]

[48] Spencer, *Corpus Christi Pageants*, pp. 19 ff.; Tydeman, *Theatre in the Middle Ages*, pp. 95 ff.; Wickham, *Early English Stages*, i, pp. 130 ff.

[49] Wickham, *Early English Stages*, i, pp. 294 ff.; Spencer, *Corpus Christi Pageants*, pp. 20 ff.; M. Rogerson, "The York Corpus Christi Play: Some Practical Details", *Leeds Studies in English*, new ser., x (1978), pp. 97 ff.; Toulmin Smith, *York Plays*, p. xxxviii; *York Civic Records*, ed. Raine, iii, p. 178; Thomas Sharp, *Dissertation on the Pageants or Dramatic Mysteries Anciently Performed at Coventry* (Coventry, 1825), pp. 22, 78–9, 164; *Coventry Leet Book*, ed. Harris, pp. 205–6, 417; *Two Coventry Corpus Christi Plays*, ed. Craig, p. 80; *Report on the Manuscripts of the Corporation of Beverley*, pp. 96–7, 100–1; Welford, *History of Newcastle and Gateshead*, ii, pp. 133, 151, 238, 364.

[50] For a generalized complaint about the burden of pageant charges, due to gild poverty and dwindling numbers, see *Coventry Leet Book*, ed. Harris, p. 556; for

But again, a question of honour was involved. That is, just as the cycle as a whole defined the identity and projected the honour of the town community in relation to the world outside it, so the play-unit defined the identity and projected the honour of the particular occupational community in relation to the social body in which it was involved. The honour of a gild became visible in its painted and gaily decorated pageant waggon,[51] as well as in the wealth of costume, accessories and histrionic skills which the latter involved – all giving visible proof of its vitality, and of the surplus resources among its members which could be put to this communal use. By contributing its pageant to the cycle which was performed to "the honour of God, and the honour and profit of this city", an occupation enhanced its own honour,[52] and established its status as an active and valued member of the urban body, able to make a defined contribution to the latter's standing and well-being. By so doing it acquired a claim to reciprocal support from the urban authorities when its own interests were endangered – as in the case, for example, of the Chester gild of Cappers, who threatened in 1523 to withdraw their play if the magistrate failed to remedy the encroachments made on their occupation by the Mercers.[53] The York Armourers in 1475 had similarly threatened a withdrawal of their play if the magistracy failed to approve the reforms they desired in their ordinances.[54] Thus from the point of view of a gild, or at least of its ruling circle, the play was a desirable status symbol; and as such eagerly sought after, particularly by newly rich occupations which had recently acquired gild status. Indeed, one of the advantages of the cycle form was that new play-units could be inserted into

a particular instance, *ibid.*, p. 708. See also *York Civic Records*, ed. Raine, iii, pp. 14, 176, and vi, pp. 11 ff.

51 See Dorrell and Johnston, "Domesday Pageant of the York Mercers", pp. 11 ff.

52 Thus in 1476 the York magistracy ordered that the "iiij of the most conyng, discrete and able players within this Citie" were to "examine all the players and plaies and pagents throughout all the artificiers belonging to the Corpus Christie plaie", to ensure that they were "sufficient . . . to the honour of the Citie and worship of the saide Craftes . . . ": *York Civic Records*, ed. Raine, i, p. 5. Similarly, at Coventry the rules of the Smiths' Company required the company's journeymen "to waite upon the maysters and attend upon the pageant to the worshipe of this citie and the crafte": *Two Coventry Corpus Christi Plays*, ed. Craig, p. 85. See also the remarks of Charles Phythian-Adams, in his *Desolation of a City: Coventry and the Urban Crisis of the Late Middle Ages* (Past and Present Pubns., Cambridge, 1979), pp. 111, 130.

53 Morris, *Chester in the Plantagenet and Tudor Reigns*, p. 316 and n. 4.

54 *York Civic Records*, ed. Raine, iii, pp. 176–7.

it, or old ones divided, to accommodate newcomers. Similarly, a play which had become too much of a burden for a declining gild might be sold, with its pageant-waggon and appurtenances, to a more vigorous and rising occupational body; or else it might be amalgamated with the play of a more prosperous occupation.[55] In the process, the play cycle also came to express the diachronic changes in the social body to which I earlier referred, which were the result of shifts in the status and economic well-being of its constituent gilds. Gilds which lost their play lost their cohesion and identity, drifting to the bottom of the gild hierarchy, losing their place in the Corpus Christi procession or perhaps disappearing altogether. Others, whose plays were amalgamated with those of stronger occupational bodies, tended to assume a position of subordination to the latter, or might be absorbed into them. The point about the Corpus Christi play cycle then is that it projected a symbolism of temporal mutation within the urban body, while also providing in this respect a necessary complement to the Corpus Christi procession, which defined the static order prevailing in the urban world.

However, the Corpus Christi play did more than merely register change; it also provided a mechanism by means of which status, and

[55] Thus the rising occupation of the Cappers at Coventry, whose mastership trebled between 1496 and 1550, and whose ordinances were first admitted by the Leet only at the former date, in 1529 took over the pageant of the declining Weavers (*Coventry Leet Book*, ed. Harris, p. 697), and then in 1531 that of the declining Cardmakers and Saddlers (*ibid.*, pp. 707–8) with their gild chapel. At York similarly gilds without pageants tended to acquire one as soon as their standing and prosperity became sufficient to enable them to do so. Thus in 1476 the Linen Weavers petitioned to be discharged from their dependent status as mere contributors to the Tapiters' pageant, and to be allowed to put on their own play, *Fergus*: *York Civic Records*, ed. Raine, i, p. 6; in 1477 the Masons took over the pageant and play formerly of St Leonard's Hospital, in whose possession they were joined in 1493 by the newly incorporated Hatmakers: *York Plays*, ed. Toulmin Smith, p. xxi, n. 4; in 1561 the newly incorporated Minstrels, at "their humble sute and prayers", received the pageant of *Herod*, formerly of the Masons: *York Civic Records*, ed. Raine, vi, pp. 30–1; *York Plays*, ed. Toulmin Smith, p. 125, n. 1. At Chester, prospering occupations like those of the Painters, the Tanners and the Vintners were accommodated with plays in the cycle between 1470 and 1540; F. M. Salter, "The Banns of the Chester Plays", *Rev. Eng. Studies*, xv (1939), pp. 452, 456, and xvi (1940), p. 1. At Norwich, the rising Worsted Weavers were first allocated a pageant in 1530, and in due course usurped the place of the declining Painters of the Gild of St Luke: J. Dutka, "Mystery Plays at Norwich: Their Formation and Development", *Leeds Studies in English*, new ser., x (1978), p. 110.

the honour which went with status, could be distributed and redistributed with a minimum of conflict resulting. It seems paradoxical that Corpus Christi, the feast of concord and unity, should occasion conflict. But this was in fact often the case. In towns like York and Chester, for example, the Corpus Christi procession was accompanied again and again by lawsuits, riots and even bloodshed between gilds competing for the symbols of precedence and esteem which the procession conferred.[56] The fact is that urban societies, no less than landed, aristocratic societies, constituted communities of honour, and were therefore intensely competitive in their internal structure.[57] The difference lay simply in the fact that, whereas in aristocratic societies the honour to be asserted and enhanced derived from blood and lineage, in urban societies honour had a corporative character. Individuals in the urban world derived their sense of worth not from their descent, but from the corporate status of their gild or town; the latter being derived ultimately from a religious source – the honour of God himself.[58] The fact, then, that

[56] *York Civic Records*, ed. Raine, ii, pp. 56, 59, 71, 96; Palliser, *Tudor York*, p. 106; D. Jones, *The Church in Chester, 1300–1540* (Chetham Soc., 3rd ser., vii, Manchester, 1957), p. 117; Morris, *Chester in the Plantagenet and Tudor Reigns*, pp. 50, 405, 572; Nelson, *Medieval English Stage*, p. 13.

[57] See Chapter 8 below.

[58] On the place of honour in a late medieval urban society, see Phythian-Adams, *Desolation of a City*, p. 130. A long-established urban aristocracy, adopting the symbols and styles of the lineage and honour culture of the gentry and nobility, did not develop in late medieval English towns, in spite of the presence of many individuals of gentry descent amongst the merchant class. Those who made large enough fortunes tended to quit the town for the countryside, there to found county families. Specifically urban nobility, and the armorial bearings which went with it, arose out of urban office, and were only incidentally related to lineage; as for example in the case of the London aldermen: S. L. Thrupp, *The Merchant Class of Medieval London* (Michigan, 1948), pp. 249–50. Cf. Caxton's remarks on London merchant families: "I have sene and knowen in other landes in dyverse cities that of one name and lygnage successyvely have endured prosperously many heyres ye a v or vi hondred yere and somme a thousand, and in this noble cytie of London it can unnethe contynue unto the thyrd heyre or scarcely the second . . . ": *The Prologues and Epilogues of William Caxton*, ed. W. J. B. Crotch (Early English Text Soc., original ser., clxxvi, London, 1927), pp. 77–8. The corporate quality of urban life, permeating social life at every level, promoted the stress on solidarity characteristic of urban élites, self-assertiveness and competition being deprecated where it occurred: see Frank F. Foster, *The Politics of Stability: A Portrait of the Rulers in Elizabethan London* (London, 1977), pp. 152 ff. Characteristically, armorial bearings of urban origin often displayed a peaceful commercial symbolism, or religious signs (cups, fishes, buckles or cloves; crosses, scallop shells, the lamb-and-flag), instead of the predatory

one's place in the Corpus Christi procession involved honour means that violence could result if conflict arose about this.

From this point of view, therefore, it was important that the setting for the symbolism of temporal mutation provided by the Corpus Christi cycle should have been one in which the emphasis was placed not on the structural aspects of urban society, but instead (to quote Victor Turner again) on the "essential and generic human bond".[59] The stress, in the first place, is on the creation of wholeness: the wholeness, that is, of the total dramatic enterprise of the cycle, emerging by the co-operative action of the whole community of different gilds and occupations out of the particularity of the separate play-units. Secondly, the play enterprise is seen as projected by a community of equals, the gilds and occupations taking part sharing a status which is the same for all. This egalitarianism receives expression through the mode adopted for the assignment by the magistracy of the various play-units in the cycle to the various gilds taking part. We might expect this to follow the hierarchical sequence stressed in the Corpus Christi procession, with the more prestigious and impressive play-units going to the gilds which enjoyed most social status. However, this was not the case; and plays were in fact assigned by criteria which emphasized the random and symbolic, rather than status.[60] When the play-sequences were

symbols (birds and beasts of prey) tending to predominate in the heraldry of the gentry and nobility.

God conferred "honour" on a town by the divine favour which permitted its foundation and continued prosperity. In return the town "honoured" God by its cult (as in the Corpus Christi procession), or by such a "work" as the play cycles, which were presented "to the honour of God", as well as of the town.

[59] Turner, *Ritual Process*, p. 83.

[60] True, there was a tendency for the richest and most spectacular pageants to come into the hands of the richest and socially superior gilds, usually the Mercers. Thus at Coventry the cycle concluded with the pageant of the *Assumption and Domesday*, presented respectively by the Mercers and Drapers, the two leading gilds; similarly at York, the last pageant was the Mercers' *Domesday*: *Two Coventry Corpus Christi Plays*, ed. Craig, pp. xv–xviii; *York Plays*, ed. Toulmin Smith, p. xxvii. At Norwich, the Mercers had the first pageant, the *Creation of the World*: Dutka, "Mystery Plays at Norwich", p. 110. But at Chester, the leading gilds, the Mercers, Vintners and Goldsmiths, collaborated in presenting pageants of *The Adoration of the Magi*, acquired as a result of the fortuitous symbolic affinity between the gold offered by the Magi at the nativity, and the Goldsmiths' occupation. These pageants did not confer a leading or important place in the cycle. At Chester, the prestigious *Domesday* pageant was presented by the Weavers, a large and ancient, but not rich or influential gild.

first devised, the play-unit given a gild might simply be determined by the cultus of its associated religious fraternity. Thus the York Carpenters, who maintained a Fraternity of the Resurrection, presented the Resurrection play in the York cycle; and the Coventry Fullers, who had originated as a gild of the Nativity, presented the Nativity play in the Coventry cycle.[61] Or else plays were allocated on the basis of a symbolic affinity between the occupation and the Scriptural episode which the play represented. So that Bakers, connected with bread, were commonly given the Last Supper play; Watermen and Shipwrights almost always furnished the plays of the Flood and Noah's Ark; and so on.[62]

However, this primitive assignment of plays, on whatever criteria originally established, was soon disrupted by the course of time, for reasons already indicated. Some gilds declined or ceased to exist; their plays had to be handed over to others. Room had to be made in the cycles for new occupations.[63] Some gilds would coalesce, and their plays merge; others drifted into dependence on stronger gilds to whose plays they contributed.[64] The community of the play enterprise was therefore a community of equals, but one in which social mobility prevailed, registering the rise and fall of occupations. But at the same time these relationships emerged as a consequence of the play of impersonal pressures, economic and other; they were the result of something like the "invisible hand" of a later age, and more acceptable for that reason. Thus, in the setting of the play community, changes in the relative status of gilds could be brought about and registered in a setting which reduced the likelihood of conflict resulting. Eventually these changes worked through into the order of the Corpus Christi procession, there receiving the

[61] *York Memorandum Book*, ed. Sellars, ii, p. xxxix; *Coventry Leet Book*, ed. Harris, p. xxxiii.

[62] Spencer, *Corpus Christi Pageants*, pp. 34–6.

[63] For the influence of the rise and decline of gilds on the evolution of a cycle, see for example Salter, "Banns of the Chester Plays", *passim*; F. M. Salter, *Medieval Drama in Chester* (New York, 1968), pp. 65 ff.; cf. the case of Norwich, as described by Dutka, "Mystery Plays at Norwich", *passim*.

[64] Spencer, *Corpus Christi Pageants*, pp. 23 ff.; S. Kramer, *The English Craft Gilds* (New York, 1927), pp. 57 ff.; Phythian-Adams, *Desolation of a City*, pp. 101, 111–12, 263–4; *Two Coventry Corpus Christi Plays*, ed. Craig, pp. xii–xiii; *York Memorandum Book*, ed. Sellars, ii, pp. 172 ff., 176 ff., 277 ff.; *York Civic Records*, ed. Raine, iii, pp. 65, 176 ff.; *York Plays*, ed. Toulmin Smith, pp. xxxviii ff.

formal sanction of the magistracy.[65] The play cycle therefore, with its stress on equality, change and social mobility, provided the appropriate counterbalance to the procession, with its stress on status, hierarchy and the role of authority. Both, play cycles and procession, were needed to mediate the full meaning of Corpus Christi.

By way of conclusion I would like to raise some points about the abandonment of the observance of Corpus Christi,[66] of the mythology associated with the feast, and of the cycle plays. This of course arose from the Protestant critique of Corpus Christi, in due course implemented by the Protestant church, with the support of the Protestant state.[67] But this critique, I would suggest, has deep roots in English urban culture – roots which reach back at least to the turn of the fourteenth and fifteenth centuries. The critique arises from the increasingly moralistic and anti-ritualistic bent which characterizes a significant sector of urban opinion as the fifteenth century proceeds.[68] This is connected with the rise of a literate and cultured

[65] For examples of revised Corpus Christi processional order lists, see *The Records of the City of Norwich*, ed. William Hudson and J. C.Tingey, 2 vols. (Norwich and London, 1906–10), ii, pp. lii, 297–8, 312; Dutka, "Mystery Plays at Norwich", p. 110, the later list showing changes in gild precedence first finding expression in the pageant-order.

[66] As expressed, for example, in Article xxviii of the Anglican Thirty-Nine Articles of 1563: "The Sacrament of the Lord's Supper was not by Christ's Ordinance reserved, carried about, lifted up, or worshipped . . . ", and by the excision of the feast of Corpus Christi from the Calendar of the Elizabethan Book of Common Prayer.

[67] Gardiner, *Mysteries' End*, pp. 65 ff.

[68] An aspect of this climate of opinion is the increasing stress on moral conformity in urban life, and on the religious and moral status of urban office, the latter seen for example in the insistence on the role of the Holy Ghost in mayoral elections which emerges in London after 1406: C. L. Kingsford, *Prejudice and Promise in 15th Century England* (Oxford, 1925), p. 108; and which is also apparent in Bristol rather later in the century: *The Maire of Bristowe is Kalendar, by Robert Ricart, Towns Clerk of Bristol*, ed. L. Toulmin Smith (Camden Soc., new ser., v, London, 1872), p. 414. The late fifteenth century sees a stronger stress on moral conformity to the sexual code at Coventry, senior civic officials being specifically debarred in 1492 from adultery and usury, as well as fornication: Charles Phythian-Adams, "Ceremony and the Citizen: The Communal Year at Coventry, 1450–1550", in P. Clark and P. Slack (eds.), *Crisis and Order in English Towns, 1500–1700* (London, 1972), p. 61. Cf. n. 18 above. Sabbatarianism was increasingly a feature of many fifteenth- and early sixteenth-century gild ordinances, and can be traced at Norwich in 1448: F. Blomefield, *An Essay towards a Topographical History of the County of Norfolk*, 11 vols. (London, 1805–10 edn), iii (1), p. 157; Coventry in 1493, 1514, 1539 and 1555: *Coventry Leet Book*, ed. Harris, pp. 547, 640, 739, 812; and at York in 1418 and

laity, and its influence spreads out from London.[69] A typical manifestation of the trend is provided by the case of Bishop Reginald Pecock, condemned for heresy in 1457 for promulgating opinions which, significantly, in many respects anticipate those of Protestantism.[70] The formative years of Pecock's career however had been spent in London, as one of a circle of learned city clergy and laymen, the latter including the cultured town clerk John Carpenter, author of a famous compilation of London lore and custom, the *Liber albus*.[71] Pecock declared his aim to be the adaptation

1490: *York Memorandum Book*, ed. Sellars, i, pp. 197, 201, 279; and elsewhere. In the case of gild fraternities, ritual requirements and moral claims (in the sense of the charitable obligations of the fraternity towards its members) could conflict. Thus the Cambridge gild of the Holy Trinity bound itself to maintain a chaplain and a candlebearer, and to burn three candles before a carving of the Holy Trinity on Sundays and feast days; but only "if the means of the Gild enable it", and the needs of the poor were to come first. Priests were excluded from all gild offices on the grounds that "it is not seemly or lawful that a parson should . . . mix himself up with secular business". Other Cambridge gilds made similar provisions, as did the Coventry Gild Merchant in 1388: *Ordinances of English Gilds*, ed. L. Toulmin Smith (Early English Text Soc., original ser., xl, London, 1870), pp. 228, 263 ff.

69 The culture of the London élite in the fifteenth century was marked by an interest in books and education, in preaching, and in an educated clergy: Thrupp, *Merchant Class of Medieval London*, pp. 155 ff., 181; Nicholas Orme, *English Schools in the Middle Ages* (London, 1973), pp. 43 ff.; and in a moralized and providentialist history which found expression in the London chronicle tradition, culminating in the work of Fabyan and Hall. Biblical and historical material figures prominently among the twenty books found by Thrupp among sixteen London bequests made between 1403 and 1483; three bibles, a book of Job, a book of the Gospels, with a Brut, and two copies of a polychronicon: Thrupp, *Merchant Class of Medieval London*, pp. 162–3. The parish library of St James Garlickhithe included a French translation of Scripture: *ibid.* The interest in the Bible in the city is also suggested by the fact that Caxton, a shrewd business man, found it worth his while to append a number of "storyes of the Byble" to his 1483 printing of the *Golden Legend*, although it was an innovation to add such stories to a compendium of the lives of the saints, the more so in that the Scriptural text was followed with considerable accuracy. See Helen C. White, *Tudor Books of Saints and Martyrs* (Madison, Wisc., 1962), p. 33. One motive for seeking education was to secure direct access to the Scriptures. Caxton's "Repressor of Overmuch Blaming of the Clergy" put into English ancient commonplaces which required every Christian to cause his friends and children to read the Scriptures; otherwise they would suffer God's vengeance: *Caxton's Dialogues, English and French*, ed. H. Bradley (Early English Text Soc., extra ser., lxxix, London, 1900), pp. 9, 37.

70 See Joseph F. Petrouch, *Reginald Pecock* (New York, 1970); V. H. H. Green, *Bishop Reginald Pecock* (Cambridge, 1945).

71 See Thomas Brewer, *Memoir of the Life and Times of John Carpenter* (London, 1856). Pecock was left a legacy in Carpenter's will, and given discretionary power to dispose of his books: *ibid.*, pp. 64–5. For the circle of Carpenter's friends, see

of the teaching of the church to the needs of precisely the kind of intelligent, literate and book-loving laity which was to be found in his own circle.[72] His writings cry up the study of Scripture and practice of good works, and denigrate rites, ceremonies and sacraments. His stress is on the written and spoken word, his approach didactic; and he shows a consistent distrust of the kind of learning through visual experience and bodily involvement which was characteristic of ritual.[73]

Pecock's views provide a religious counterpart to the lay approach in this milieu to the social and political order. For John Carpenter, similarly, the ritual of the cult of Corpus Christi could have no place in the affirmation of the unity and wholeness of the social body. This he seems to have conceived as simply secular: the *universitas civium*, grounded in law and constituted by conformity to the legal disciplines imposed by the magistracy. Indeed, it was to the latter alone, in the person of the mayor and his officers, that Carpenter in the *Liber albus* applied the conventional body imagery.[74] These are attitudes which harmonize too with the moralized and providentialist history which is gradually built into

ibid., pp. 61 ff. See also Green, *Bishop Reginald Pecock*, pp. 20–1, 26. For the *Liber albus*, see *Munimenta Guildhallae, Londoniensis*, ed. Riley, i, iii.

[72] See Petrouch, *Reginald Pecock*, pp. 123 ff. In Reginald Pecock, *The Reule of Crysten Religion*, ed. W. C. Greet (Early English Text Soc., original ser., clxxi, London, 1927), the author aims to show the laity how to pursue the good life, and provides the knowledge needed for this purpose. He wrote in the vernacular in order to appeal to a lay audience.

[73] Thus in his popularizing work, *The Donet*, ed. E. V. Hitchcock (Early English Text Soc., original ser., clvi, London, 1918), Pecock devoted 64 pages to God's "law and service", and only 18 to the dogmatic aspects of his exposition of Christianity. In his *Reule of Crysten Religion* (of which *The Donet* was intended to be a simplified summary), p. 244, he asserted that "God's holy wordes" were more profitable in stirring up good will towards God and his service than were "the other signs" (that is, rites and sacraments); and he insisted that the sacrament of the altar signified not only Christ's Body and Blood, but also the "charite whiche should be betwine us and all oure neighbours". Good works offered to God availed more in prayer than mere petitions, and more truly honoured God than mere praise: *ibid.*, p. 412.

[74] Significantly enough, however, Carpenter did have an interest in the kind of secular urban ceremonial which would survive the Reformation. Thus it was he who collaborated with John Lydgate in devising and directing the pageants which greeted Henry VI's entry into London after his coronation: Derek Pearsall, *John Lydgate* (London, 1970), p. 171. The *Liber albus* shows little sense of the concept of body; but this is present implicitly in the description of the sheriffs as the "eyes" of the mayor as head, the other officers being his "limbs": *Liber albus*, in *Munimenta Gildhallae Londoniensis*, ed. Riley, i, p. 42.

the London chronicles as the century proceeds, and eventually emerges in Fabyan and Hall, while also preparing the way for the civic humanism of the Colet circle and the Erasmians. Finally, under Protestantism, the Corpus Christi becomes the Body of the Realm; and urban rituals, like religious rituals, tend to become progressively secularized, privatized and monopolized by the magistracy.[75]

It is probably significant that the attitudes just discussed arise in a great city – London – governed by a magistracy which had already, in the late fourteenth century, triumphed over the crafts, and in which the rule of the oligarchy was not seriously qualified by the need to come to terms with the oppositionist elements, political and social. London was a town in which there was no serious challenge to the dominance of a self-co-opting élite.[76] There were others of the same sort: Exeter, for example.[77] Significantly, in such towns the celebration of Corpus Christi never acquired a public and civic status, and play cycles of the Corpus Christi type never developed.[78]

[75] For the London chronicle tradition, see C. L. Kingsford, *English Historical Literature in the Fifteenth Century* (Oxford, 1913), pp. 70 ff.; Flenley, *Six Town Chronicles*, pp. 7 ff. For the privatization of urban ritual, see Phythian-Adams, "Ceremony and the Citizen", pp. 79–80.

[76] Thrupp, *Merchant Class of Medieval London*, p. 81: "Although isolated groups of journeymen periodically . . . agitated for better wages and working conditions . . . the 'small people' . . . lacked leadership and lost their political ambition. Throughout the fifteenth century, London appears to have been stolidly content with merchant government." *Ibid.*, p. 85: "In terror at the revival of intercraft faction . . . the small free masters were probably quite content to efface themselves, and accept a subordinate role." This situation persisted throughout the sixteenth century and later. See Foster, *Politics of Stability . . . in Elizabethan London*, p. 4.

[77] See W. T. MacCaffrey, *Exeter, 1540–1640* (Cambridge, Mass., 1958), p. 18. Exeter had an uneventful history, in the course of which the rule of the élite was only questioned once (in the middle of the fifteenth century) by the then rising and prosperous Tailors' gild, which was however soon defeated by the corporation in the courts, and sank into obscurity: M. A. E. W. Green, *Town Life in the Fifteenth Century*, 2 vols. (London, 1894), ii, pp. 172–81. Troubles arising in the mayoral election of 1496 led to the reconstitution of the ruling Council of Twenty-Four as a wholly self-co-opting body: B. Wilkinson and R. L. E. Easterling, *The Medieval Council of Exeter* (Exeter, 1931), pp. 25 ff. The rulers of Exeter were chosen from a very select circle, the gilds were kept in strict subordination to the city chamber, and the commons had no part in civic government.

[78] Thus at Exeter Corpus Christi had no civic relevance, but was a merely ecclesiastical occasion, the procession being the concern of the Grey and Black Friars. In the fifteenth century however the Skinners' Company did it seems present some kind of play on Corpus Christi: A. G. Little and R. C. Easterling, *The Franciscans and Dominicans at Exeter* (Exeter, 1927), p. 26.

London had its great cycle plays; but the London cycle was performed by professional actors, and had no connection either with Corpus Christi or the city gilds, being probably the responsibility solely of the rich merchants of the Skinners' Company.[79] The public and civic celebration of Corpus Christi, and the creation of the Corpus Christi drama, does seem to have the background of a specific kind of community – one in which there existed a certain tension and free play of political and social forces, and in which order and unity needed therefore to be continually affirmed in terms of shared rite and shared ritual. Such were towns like Lincoln,[80] York, Newcastle, Coventry,[81] Chester and Norwich,[82] in

[79] The London cycle plays performed at Skinners Well and Clerkenwell in the late fourteenth and the fifteenth century contained "Some large hystorie of holy Scripture", and "matter from the creation of the world": Stow, *Survey of London*, i, pp. 15–16. Their content therefore may have been synoptic and historical, and so not unlike that of the typical Corpus Christi cycle. But they had no relevance to the internal relationships of the city community. Rather their purpose was to impress by their great length and "sumptuousness", and thus to project the honour and "worship" of the city. Thus they were directed primarily at an external audience, which frequently included the nobility and members of the royal family. In 1409, for example, they were played before the king, the Prince of Wales, and "nobles and gentles": Chambers, *Medieval Stage*, ii, p. 380. Stow, *Survey of London*, i, pp. 15–16, affirmed that the play at Skinners' Well was the responsibility of the Skinners' Company.

[80] Lincoln affords an interesting example of the interplay of intra-urban faction and conflict with the development of processional and dramatic rituals so as to express urban solidarities. The late fourteenth and the fifteenth century saw recurring tensions and constitutional conflicts at Lincoln, involving an office-holding élite of "more worthy" citizens, and a larger group of *minores*, whose role was at best merely consultative. By 1530 the conflict had been resolved in favour of the élite. See J. W. F. Hill, *Medieval Lincoln* (Cambridge, 1948), pp. 260–1, 275–6, 277–8, 301–2. In addition, cross-currents of conflict over the rival jurisdictions exercised over the cathedral close by the city and the dean and chapter set corporation and cathedral at loggerheads. The divided state of Lincoln in the fourteenth century found expression in the foundation of a Corpus Christi gild, in 1350, as a fraternity of "folks of common and middling rank", from which office-holders were excluded, unless approved of as "humble" and "of good conversation". The fraternity of the élite, on the other hand, was the St Anne's gild: Hill, *Medieval Lincoln*, p. 298; J. W. F. Hill, *Tudor and Stuart Lincoln* (Cambridge, 1956), pp. 3 ff. Both bodies mounted processions, with pageants, on their respective days, to each of which the crafts contributed; and each developed (if we accept the thesis summarized by Hardin Craig in his *English Religious Drama*, Oxford, 1955, p. 260 ff.) a play cycle. One of the latter was a typical Corpus Christi sequence; the other, the St Anne's play, was characterized by an appropriately strong Marian emphasis. In 1493 the latter was extended by the addition of an Assumption play, previously the possession of the cathedral, a development which probably reflects an adjustment of interests, and so better relations, between the dean and chapter and the corporation: Virginia Shull, "Clerical Drama in Lincoln Cathedral", *Pubns Mod. Language Assoc. America*, lii (1937), p. 958. After 1530, with the final adjustment of the tensions which had

divided the two gilds, the differences between them faded. The Corpus Christi gild was opened to all citizens, who were required to contribute to its pageants, as also to those of the St Anne gild: *Manuscripts of the Corporation of Lincoln*, p. 32. The so-called *Ludus Coventriae* cycle is thought to represent a conflated version of the originally independent cycles evolved by each of the two gilds: Hardin Craig, *English Religious Drama*, p. 260 ff.; K. Cameron and S. J. Kahrl, "The N-Town Plays at Lincoln", *Theatre Notebook*, xx (1965–6), pp. 61 ff.; A. S. Loomis, "Lincoln as a Dramatic Centre", in *Mélanges d'histoire du théâtre . . . offerts à Gustave Cohen* (Paris, 1950), pp. 246 ff. Be it said, however, that more recently a lone voice, that of Mark Eccles, "*Ludus Coventriae*: Lincoln or Norfolk?", *Medium aevum*, xl (1971), pp. 135–41, has questioned the otherwise generally accepted Lincoln provenance of the N-Town plays.

81 York, Newcastle and Coventry were towns in which the gild occupational fellowships played a significant part in a "continuous process whereby the life-cycle of the citizen was related to the working of the urban system as a whole": Phythian-Adams, *Desolation of a City*, p. 117. They were "transforming agencies" whereby gild masters were introduced into the office-holding system, and from which they might begin their ascent of the urban hierarchy. In all these towns, gilds played a significant role in the constitutional structure. In York the Common Council, both before and after the constitutional changes of 1516–17, was chosen by the gilds, and consisted of gild officials, its members playing a part in the choice of mayor, sheriffs and aldermen: Palliser, *Tudor York*, pp. 67 ff. In Newcastle similarly, twelve "mysteries" had a part in the constitution of the Council of Twenty-Four which chose mayor, aldermen and sheriffs: J. F. Gibson, *The Newcastle-upon-Tyne Improvement Acts and Bye-Laws 1837 to 1877, with an Introductory Historical Sketch* (Newcastle upon Tyne, 1881), pp. xi–lx; R. Howell, *Newcastle upon Tyne and the Puritan Revolution* (Oxford, 1967), pp. 35 ff. In Coventry, the office-holding élite of the craft fellowships were recruited into the two civic gilds of Corpus Christi and the Holy Trinity, from which the ascent of the hierarchy of civic offices could be commenced: Phythian-Adams, *Desolation of a City*, pp. 118 ff.

Although in these towns there was no necessary or inevitable conflict between the crafts and the ruling élites, friction could arise between aspirants to civic office, arising within and supported by one or other occupational fellowship, and the established ruling group, as a result of the veto which might be exercised by the latter over particular aspirants to office. Those thus excluded were liable to mobilize their following in the craft, and among rank-and-file citizens and the poor, to contest elections, and raise disorders in connection with issues in which popular passions became involved, such as the disposal of town common pastures. Thus there were electoral quarrels and disorders at York in 1471, 1475, 1482, 1494, 1504 and 1516–17, with recurring friction over enclosures of commons: *V.C.H., Yorkshire: The City of York* (London, 1961), pp. 82–4; Palliser, *Tudor York*, pp. 68–9, 84. In Coventry, the second half of the fifteenth century saw the long quarrel between the corporation, and the then rising and prosperous Dyers' gild, led by Laurence Saunders, which was accompanied by riots over the enclosure of the commons: M. D. Harris, *The Story of Coventry* (London, 1911), pp. 181 ff., 220. Dissensions at Newcastle led in 1518 to a Star Chamber revision of the constitution, restricting the electoral role of the gilds: Gibson, *Newcastle-upon-Tyne Improvement Acts*, pp. xlii ff. All three towns provided a setting in which gild fellowships needed to affirm their identity and "honour" in a clearly defined, spectacular, processional and dramatic form; but these were also communities in which, because of the ever-present possibility of conflict, the ethic of "unity and concord" needed to be continually reaffirmed.

82 The place of the gild fellowships in the government of Chester and Norwich

all of which Corpus Christi played precisely such an affirmative role. But of course during the sixteenth century, this kind of social and political balance is progressively upset. The decline and impoverishment of gild organizations, the pauperization of town populations, the changing character and role of town societies, and the increasing government support of urban oligarchies were all factors tending towards urban authoritarianism. As a result urban ritual and urban drama no longer served a useful purpose; and were indeed increasingly seen as potentially disruptive of the kind of civil order which the magistracy existed to impose.[83]

The Corpus Christi drama was undermined in part by the rise of the new humanistic dramatic style finding expression in the interlude and Biblical stage play.[84] The new dramatic fashion made it impossible for the traditional drama, now seen as primitive, ridiculous and naive, to project any longer the honour of a town.[85] But

seems at present not precisely ascertainable, but was probably similar to that of the York gilds. Norwich during the fifteenth century was a deeply divided city, with rival civic factions respectively supporting and opposing the prior of the cathedral abbey in his feud with the corporation, the quarrel eventually leading to royal intervention, and suspension of the city's liberties. On Chester, see Morris, *Chester in the Plantagenet and Tudor Reigns*, *passim*; on Norwich, see Blomefield, *Essay Towards a Topographical History of the County of Norfolk*, iii, pt. 1, pp. 120 ff.

83 C. Phythian-Adams, "Urban Decay in Late Medieval England", in P. Abrams and E. A. Wrigley (eds.), *Towns and Societies: Essays in Economic History and Historical Sociology* (Past and Present Pubns, Cambridge, 1978), pp. 159 ff.; Phythian-Adams, "Ceremony and the Citizen", pp. 79 ff.; Clark and Slack (eds.), *Crisis and Order in English Towns*, Introduction, pp. 1–51.

84 Woolf, *English Mystery Plays*, pp. 312 ff.; L. B. Campbell, *Divine Poetry and Drama in Sixteenth Century England* (Cambridge and Los Angeles, 1959); M. Rostan, *Biblical Drama in England* (London, 1968); Wickham, *Early English Stages*, i, pp. 234 ff.; Chambers, *Medieval Stage*, ii, pp. 179 ff.

85 This insight was however confined to the urban élites. As seen above, the likelihood is that the cycles remained popular until the end among the "middling" groups and occupations. However, Chester, when honoured in 1577 by a visit of the earl of Derby, entertained him with a "comedy" presented by "the scollers of the frescole": Chambers, *Medieval Stage*, ii, p. 168; whereas in 1488 it had been the cycle play of the Assumption which had been played before Lord Strange, as before Prince Arthur in 1497: Morris, *Chester in the Plantagenet and Tudor Reigns*, pp. 322–3. In other cycle towns attempts were made, usually with the help of the local schoolmaster, to replace the cycle with an interlude or biblical play. At York in 1585 Thomas Grafton, schoolmaster, was authorized to proceed with an interlude: Nelson, *Medieval English Stage*, pp. 69–70. In 1564–6 Lincoln adopted a biblical play, *Tobias*: *ibid.*, p. 118; Chambers, *Medieval Stage*, ii, p. 379. At Norwich in 1541/2, and again in 1543/4, the authorities paid for making

those who viewed the Corpus Christi plays as increasingly superfluous and potentially disruptive were also able to fasten on the tension which had always existed within the cycles between their quality as "ritual", arising from their nature as a "work" done for "the honour of God and the city"; and their quality as *ludus*, that is a kind of "play" in the literal sense: a game.[86] As *ludus*, as game, the plays were carried into the region of popular culture:[87] the world of mime, mumming, carnival and the rituals of reversal.[88] This side of things surfaces in the ridiculing of authority we find in some of the plays: in the presentation of such figures as Herod, Pilate, Annas and Caiaphas; and in the near-blasphemous treatment of the Virgin Birth found in the plays of "Joseph's Doubts".[89] True, the sting is taken out of such presentations by the fact that they are firmly contained within the general structure of the cycle, with its dominantly

a stage from which to present an interlude: Nelson, *Medieval English Stage*, pp. 136–7, the first of several such performances. Coventry in 1584 replaced its Corpus Christi play with a "tragedy", *The Destruction of Jerusalem*: Chambers, *Medieval Stage*, ii, p. 361.

86 See Woolf, *English Mystery Plays*, pp. 33–5; Kolve, *Play Called Corpus Christi*, pp. 12 ff.

87 The use of the word *ludus* to describe late medieval street plays, like the Corpus Christi cycles, involved a degree of demotion of the sacred play from the status it had held when presented in church, and within the context of the liturgy, when the descriptive word used had been *ordo*, *processio* or *officium*. For Geroh of Reichersberg, in the twelfth century, *ludus* implied all that was most undesirable in religious plays. The word was used for popular revelling, involving the grotesque, farcical acting styles, and deceptive, illusion-creating tricks characteristic of the *mimi*, or popular entertainers. See Karl Young, *The Drama of the Medieval Church*, 2 vols. (Oxford, 1933), ii, pp. 407–-10. Cf. Wickham, *Early English Stages*, i, p. 319.

88 The use of the word *scena* (that is, theatrical representation, stage show) as implying both "play", absurd illusion, and a disquieting sense of social reversal is well brought out in a late fifteenth-century Latin–German dictionary, Johannes Melber's *Vocabularius praedicantium* (Reuchlingen [*c*. 1479–82]): "*Scena* is the kind of game in which a peasant is made a king or knight, and once it is over becomes once more a peasant": see Mary H. Marshall, "*Theatre* in the Middle Ages: Evidence from Dictionaries and Glosses", *Symposium: A Journal Devoted to Modern Languages and Literatures* [New York], iv (1950), pp. 380 ff.; Kolve, *Play Called Corpus Christi*, p. 19. Cf. Calvin's dictum that the Biblical prohibition of exchanges of apparel between the sexes (Deuteronomy xxii. 5) had a special relevance to dramatic performances. For the links between carnival and stage representations, see Peter Burke, *Popular Culture in Early Modern Europe* (London, 1978), p. 182.

89 On the satirical aspects of "Joseph's Doubts", and on the satirical treatment of Herod, Pilate and the rest, see Woolf, *English Mystery Plays*, pp. 170 ff., 247 ff., 250 ff.; Kolve, *Play Called Corpus Christi*, pp. 223 ff., 232 ff., 247 ff.

orthodox tone.[90] Nevertheless, the element of unrestrained and coarse humour, or satire and social criticism which they contained, fed the sense, deeply rooted in late medieval culture, of all forms of mimetic activity as inherently improper; and as carrying implications disturbing to the established structure of deference and order. All this is well brought out in an early fifteenth-century Wyclifite critique of the Corpus Christi drama, which both foreshadows the later Protestant criticisms and provides a dimension of depth which the latter lack.[91] The Wyclifite preacher presents the plays as essentially rites of reversal.[92] In them, the truths of religion are turned into stage illusions; and in the audience restraint and gravity are dissolved into emotional self-indulgence and enjoyment;[93] men turn from reality to a game, and so become transformed from grown-ups into children.[94] The result is a relaxation of discipline and self-control on the part of the play audiences – the more dangerous, says the Wyclifite critic, because this takes place in the context of large public assemblies. The last point probably touches the nub of the matter, and one to which the response of urban magistrates was likely to be immediate. John Carpenter says in the *Liber albus* that all public assemblies are dangerous: a threat to the unity of the city and to magisterial authority; the fewer of

[90] See, for example, Kolve's discussion of Joseph and his doubts: Kolve, *Play Called Corpus Christi*, pp. 247 ff.

[91] "A Sermon against Miracle-Plays", ed. Deuard Mätzner, in his *Altenglische Sprachproben nebst einem Wörterbuche*, i (2) (Berlin, 1869), pp. 222–41.

[92] "No man shulde usen in bourde [joke] and pleye the myraclis and werkes that Crist . . . wroughte to oure helthe; for whoever so doth, he errith in the byleve, reversith Crist, and scornyth God . . . A! Lord! Sythen an ertheley servaunt dar not taken in pleye and bourde that his erthely lord takith in ernest, myche more we shulden not maken our pleye and bourde of the myraclis and werkis that God so ernestfully wrought to us; for sothely whan we so done, drede to synne is taken away, as a servaunt when he bourdith with his mayster, leesith his derde to offendym him . . . ": *ibid.*, pp. 225–6.

[93] " . . . sythen myraclis pleyinge is of the lustis of the fleyssh and myrthe of the body . . . so myraclis pleyinge reversith discipline . . . also sithen it makith to se vayne sightis of degyse, aray of men and symmen by yvil continaunse, eyther stirynge othere to lecherie and debatis, as aftir most bodily myrthe comen moste debatis, as siche myrthe more undisposith a man to paciencie and ablith to glotonye and to othere vicis . . . ": *ibid.*, p. 228.

[94] " . . . dere frend, beholdith how kynde tellith that the more eldre a man waxith the more it is agen kynde hym for to pleyn, and therfor seith the booc, 'Cursid be the childe of han hundred yere' . . . therefore agen kynde of all creaturis it is now myraclis pleyinge": *ibid.*, p. 241.

them the better.[95] Certainly the Corpus Christi celebrations could raise difficult problems of public order for those towns in which they took place.[96] And plays could undoubtedly be unsettling, even when they contained no potentially subversive content, simply because of their tendency to loosen social constraints and inner controls.[97] A case in point is that of the York *Fergus* play: a straightforward cycle play on the theme of the funeral of the Virgin Mary, but which included some particularly hilarious slapstick comedy effects. According to its sponsors, the Masons' gild, however, it not only caused irreverent noise and laughter, but also quarrels, fights and lawsuits among the onlookers.[98] There is no doubt that assemblies for play and game, whether these were of the dramatic sort, or had the character of folk festival, could lead to sedition. A Lent carnival at Norwich in 1443 precipitated a revolt.[99] Sometime in the 1550s the staging of one of the cycle plays at York – the play of Thomas the Apostle – provided the occasion for a papist disturbance. The Kett revolt was sparked off by a play at Wymondham.[100] All this is a large part of the explanation why folk festivals, like the Hox play at Coventry or the Yule Riding at York, aroused the same sort of disapproval in Puritan circles as did the cycle plays, and were done away with more or less at the same time. The sixteenth-century privatization of the drama by the development of the stage play, the theatre and the professional actor parallels the privatization of religious and civic ritual, and arose from much the same causes. In this setting, then, the public ritual and public drama of the Corpus Christi feast no longer had any place.

[95] *Liber albus*, in *Munimenta Gildhallae Londoniensis*, ed. Riley, i, pp. 18–19.

[96] As at Chester in 1358, when the Corpus Christi procession was made the occasion for an attack by the Master Weavers on their journeymen. Morris, *Chester in the Plantagenet and Tudor Reigns*, pp. 405–8. Public holidays, and the "multitude" of people then loosed on to city streets, often raised problems of public order. Thus at Coventry the civic ridings on Midsummer Eve and St Peter's Night occasioned "great debate and manslaughter": Sharp, *Dissertation on the Pageants*, p. 180; and on Corpus Christi Eve in 1458 there was a fray in which one person was killed and others were wounded: *ibid.*, p. 169.

[97] Cf. n. 93 above, this chapter.

[98] *York Memorandum Book*, ed. Sellars, ii, p. 124.

[99] Blomefield, *Essay Towards a Topographical History of the County of Norfolk*, iii pt. 1, pp. 149–50.

[100] Gardiner, *Mysteries' End*, p. 49; F. W. Russell, *Kett's Rebellion in Norfolk* (London, 1859), p. 25.

2. *A Tudor magnate and the Tudor state: Henry fifth earl of Northumberland*

I

Perhaps the most remarkable fact about the fifth earl of Northumberland[1] is that he successfully imposed his will on King Henry VIII, an achievement which can be put to the credit of very few. For although most of the life of this great lord was spent in disfavour, and in exclusion from the great offices (particularly the northern lieutenancies and Border wardenries) which had been held by his ancestors, he was nevertheless able to create conditions which eventually compelled the crown (but only after his own death) to confer these same offices on his heir, and so restore the traditional Percy ascendancy in the north. The earl therefore succeeded in reversing the political eclipse which had overshadowed his family in his own lifetime, and seemed to have ensured its future. The following pages attempt to explain how he did so, and also seek to throw light on the tactics by which the Tudors sought to undermine the influence of subjects thought to be "overmighty", as well as the defensive reactions to which these gave rise on the latter's part. In this way it is hoped to clothe with flesh and blood some aspects of the successful struggle of the Tudor crown with those "rival powers" and "overmighty subjects" which established historical convention has seen as a prime Tudor contribution to the emergence of a more modern state. Some attempt has also been made to evoke the kind

[1] For the fifth earl, treated as an instance of the economic and political "decline" of the upper nobility, see J. D. Mackie, *The Early Tudors* (Oxford, 1952), p. 16. For his estates and finances see J. M. W. Bean, *The Estates of the Percy Family 1416–1537*, (Oxford, 1958). The fullest account of the earl's life is in E. B. Barrington de Fonblanque, *Annals of the House of Percy*, 2 vols. (London, 1887), i, pp. 310 ff., which however contains inaccuracies, and should be treated with caution. The earl's *Household Book* was edited by Thomas Percy (*The Northumberland Household Book*, London, 1777 and 1827) and reprinted in Grose's *Antiquarian Repertory* (London, 1809), iv.

of literary influences to which this great lord responded, to explain the attraction which he seems to have felt for certain literary themes, and to relate these to the political tensions and dilemmas which confronted him during his lifetime.

One point which may be noted, as the contest between Tudor and Percy unfolds, is that both parties sought to prevail by means which were basically similar. It is not easy to see the crown, in its relations with the fifth earl, straightforwardly as the upholder of the "rule of law" and equal justice against the "unruliness" and "feudal anarchy" of a great lord. There can be no doubt, as will be seen, that the earl patronized and supported violent elements amongst the gentry, whose activities threatened the authority of the crown, particularly in the Marches. But it is also true that the crown sought to advance its power by drawing into its service men of exactly the same sort, on whom it relied for support, and whose interests it sought to protect and advance. From this point of view the "law of Star Chamber" implies less an equal justice than a means by which the crown could give effective protection to the factions it supported.[2] Nor can we be sure that the dominance of these latter would have ensured greater tranquillity and good governance in the north. There was little to choose, for violence and tyranny, between men like Sir Robert Constable[3] or Sir John Hotham, who served the crown, and such Percy followers as Sir William Lisle and Sir John Heron. And there is at least a case for the view that "good rule" in

2 It is not likely, for example, that it was the earl who initiated the quarrel with Sir John Hotham in Scorborough which brought him before Star Chamber in 1506. It is not easy to be certain about the rights and wrongs of this matter, which seems to have been a dispute about boundaries in a district where both held property. But a man of such vast landed wealth as the earl would scarcely have deliberately embarked on a fray with a royal knight of the body (which Hotham was) for the sake of the few "meyres and pastures" which were in dispute. Hotham, on the other hand, strengthened by the support of his friends and fellow king's servants Sir Robert Constable and the Archbishop of York could expect a large enhancement of standing if he successfully bearded his powerful neighbour. And in Star Chamber, "Your highness . . . true servant and liegeman John Hotham Knyght of your bodye" could expect the "good lordship" of the crown. With that backing he could afford to make trouble. See below, p. 000 and n. 66.

3 See below, pp. 66–7. Constable (eventually executed as a rebel for his part in the Pilgrimage of Grace) was particularly notorious for his violent and "dangerous" temperament. See Lord Darcy's view of him in *Letters and Papers, Henry VIII* (hereafter cited as *L.P.*), iii (i), 1236; an anonymous memorandum of 1534 to Cromwell recommended his removal from the commission of the peace for the East Riding, since this would "quiet the shire and further justice".

the north would have been better ensured if the crown had not been so determined to challenge the Percy predominance. The influence of a great lord, exercised through his council,[4] and through such instruments as his knights' courts,[5] could stabilize a country, and hold the gentry together. But the crown's policies, since they brought the authority of the Percy into question, encouraged faction and created tensions which eventually contributed to the Pilgrimage of Grace. This was the price the first two Tudors paid for their unwillingness to place their confidence in the earls of Northumberland; and perhaps on occasion their distrust of the Percies led both to cross the margin separating tyranny from that necessary dominance and leadership of the nobility which was of the essence of kingship.

It may be thought surprising that the fifth earl (as will be seen) could command such a powerful following, and could dominate a countryside with such effect, after the strong rule of Henry VII and the enforcement of the laws against livery and maintenance by this king and then Wolsey. It is increasingly recognized, however, that the liveried retinues against which these laws were directed in fact persisted throughout most of the Tudor period. This can be explained in part by the willingness of the crown to license retainder for service in war, and even in time of peace in the case of its followers and those lords whom it trusted; and by the assumption that in practice there was extensive evasion of the law's requirements in this matter.[6] But perhaps insufficient attention has been given to the

[4] The role of the Percy council in Northumberland was still remembered in the 1590s, when a Percy officer recommended its revival to the earl: "For these and lyke controversies yt wer good yf yt might so stand with his Lordships pleasur, that he wold nominate and appoynt certeyn gentlemen of the country of the worship, and wysest, and such as wer his Lps: frends, to be as it wer a counsell for ayding and assisting to his officers here, as his Lps: uncle and father and others his auncestors before him have had, and allwayes all or some of them to sytt in Courte and heare and determine premisses" (Syon House MS. Q 2 (4), Notes and Remembrance from Robert Helme 1592).

[5] See below, p. 69 and n. 74.

[6] For the traditional view of the Tudor policy with regard to retainder, livery and maintenance, see J. R. Tanner, *Tudor Constitutional Documents* (Cambridge, 1948), p. 7; Tanner's views are restated and modified by G. R. Elton in *The Tudor Constitution* (Cambridge, 1960), p. 30. For the survival of retinues in Tudor England and the whole question of retainder, see W. H. Dunham, *Lord Hastings' Indentured Retainers* (Trans. Connecticut Academy of Arts and Sciences, xxxix, New Haven, Sept. 1955), ch. 5, and L. Stone, *The Crisis of the Aristocracy 1558–1641* (Oxford, 1965), ch. 5.

implications of the fact that even the Statute of Liveries of 1504[7] exempted from any penalties those who retained persons as their servants, household or manual, or as estate officers or counsel learned. This was a loophole big enough to ensure that any magnate with large estates at his disposal, and presiding over a great household (such as that described in the fifth earl's *Household Book*), could, whether in peace or war, command a sufficient retinue. His estates enabled him to dispense a large fund of patronage in the way of constabularies, bailiwicks, stewardships, and receiverships; and the fees and other perquisites (such as profitable leaseholds) attached to these offices were sufficient to attract the service of the gentry. The same is true of the emoluments and honour which went with office and place in the household of a great lord. There is no hint that the fifth earl retained or gave his livery illegally. His power was based on the men he appointed as constables of his castles, receivers of his lands and bailiffs and stewards of his lordships, and who also served in his household.[8] This last was no mere domestic

[7] 19 Henry VII, c. 14; for this famous act see Tanner, and Elton, *loc. cit.*; Dunham, *op. cit.*, p. 95. It was the most vigorous of all the acts against livery and maintenance (although exemption could be obtained from its operation by royal licence), and did away with the permissive clause in the act of 1468 (8 Edw. IV, c. 2), which allowed private persons, as well as the crown, to give fees to others than counsel, officers, and household servants "for lawful service done". The act of 1504 lapsed on the death of Henry VII. Policy in Henry VIII's reign seems to have been based on the royal proclamation of 3 July 1511 (*Tudor Royal Proclamations*, ed. P. L. Hughes and J. F. Larkin, i, New Haven, 1964, p. 84) and of 12 Oct. 1514 (*ibid.*, p. 124; see Dunham, *op. cit.*, p. 100) which firmly prohibited all retainders contrary to the form of existing statutes. These, however, amply safeguarded the rights of private persons to give their fee to officers, household servants, and counsel learned.

[8] The following of a great lord could be enlarged by multiplying estate offices. Thus the sixth earl of Northumberland appointed no less than six stewards to rule his lands in Yorkshire, whereas his father had been able to make do with two. The multiplication of offices enabled him to give his fee and livery to such men as Sir Thomas Wharton, Sir Stephen Hamerton, William Babthorpe and Robert Lascelles, all men of standing in their countries. The appointments are recorded in the earl's Book of Grants (Alnwick Castle MS., Letters and Papers, ii). The purpose of such appointments is made clear in the deposition of Robert Gilbert, chancellor to the last Stafford duke of Buckingham, at his master's trial for treason in 1521: "Also he saith that the said Duke . . . hath much studied to make many particular offices in his lands, to the intent that he might retain as many men by the said offices as he could" (*L.P.*, iii (1), p. cxxx).

establishment, but rather the organizing centre and ceremonial expression of a magnate connection.[9]

Thus it would be misleading to assume that the men to whom the fifth earl (with complete legality) gave his livery and fee were no more than a body of estate agents and domestic servants, bound to their master by a mere cash-nexus. Throughout the Tudor period, and indeed far into the seventeenth century, the relationship between a lord and his fee'd man was based on the traditional ethos of "service" on the one hand, in return for which support, protection and reward – everything implied in "good lordship" – were made available. Some of the content of the attitudes which these terms imply may be illustrated from statements and comments made by Percy servants of the sixteenth and earlier seventeenth century. "Service", for example, implied something both "honourable" and "natural", in the same sense as "It is most naturall, and no less honourable that his Lordship [the earl of Northumberland] should have the government and ruell under the Prince here in this countrie of Northumberland."[10] Service was honourable, since it involved participation in the earl's authority, and the grant of "his especiall trust and confidence";[11] natural, because that authority was the keystone of a regional structure of order and governance which also had its place in the body of the kingdom as a whole, being "under the Prince". But the sanction of nature was time; the mark of the natural was long continuance, receiving expression in custom. Servants received "accustomed" fees, and performed "accustomed" duties;[12] and it was "natural" then that a man whose ancestors had served the earls of Northumberland should do so himself. Descent,

9 The provision made in the fifth earl's *Household Book* (London, 1827 edn, pp. 53–4) that the earl should be waited on in household by the officers of his Yorkshire lands from Michaelmas to Lady Day, of his Cumberland estates from Lady Day to Midsummer, and the Northumberland estates from Midsummer to Michaelmas, brought these into regular contact with their master, and underlined the role of the household as the unifying centre of the Percy following.

10 This remark is made by George Clarkson in his survey of the seventh earl of Northumberland's parks at Alnwick in the 1560s (Syon House MS. A I 1b).

11 Letters patent making grants of offices always began by reciting the "especiall trust and confidence" which the earl had in the grantee.

12 Letters patent authorized the officer "to execute perform and do all such lawful act and acts in the execution of the said office as have been hitherto accustomed to be performed and done" and "to take and receive such several fees and allowances as have been heretofore . . . accustomed to be taken". Many examples of such grants by letters patent survive amongst the Syon House MSS.

therefore, was a prime qualification for service, and offices were claimed because such-and-such "have been bailiffs to your lordshippe and your right noble progenitors earles of Northumberland these many hundreth years".[13] This sense of "service" as something which was both "honourable" and binding on successive generations could emerge as late as the reign of James I even in a great man like Sir Henry Curwen, sheriff and knight of the shire, of Workington in Cumberland, who wrote to the ninth earl of Northumberland in 1619: "My ancestors alwayes have been imployed in service in that noble house of Northumberland, and although I acknowledge myself inferior to the meanest of them, yet none of them have ever borne a more faithful affection to that famous house. My humble suit now is that your lo : wilbe pleased to take notice that I doe hereby humbly tender my service to your lo : in that place wherein many of my ancestors have been servants . . . "[14] There was nothing ephemeral or unstable about such relationships, based though they were on fees not fiefs, and on money instead of land.

The "faithfull affection" of which Curwen spoke (or more simply "faithfulness") was the mark of the good servant. Thus a servant could say, in the early seventeenth century, "my care shall be only to deal faithfully with your lordship, as I may answere before God as a true Christiane, and before the world as a faithful steward and true servant".[15] "Faithfulness", moreover, so far from being linked to any cash-nexus, was thought of as unconditional; it sought no reward, and reflected an absolute dependence on the lord. "When war you to take from me my office, may not discontent me, for he that gives all may take all"[16] wrote another Percy servant in James I's reign. For some service could mean a total commitment, extending to life itself, and charged with strong emotive overtones. Thus: "I wish you may be long from occasion; yet it is not unnecessary your lordship should know you have a man ever redy to lay down

[13] Syon House MS. R V 1, Petition of Roland Green, formerly bailiff of Rothbury lordship, to the ninth earl of Northumberland, 1601.
[14] *Ibid.*, X II 3.
[15] George Whitehead, receiver and deputy-captain of Tynemouth, to the ninth earl, Feb. 1612 (Syon House MS. Q I 39).
[16] *Ibid.*, Q I 12, Thomas Percy, constable of Alnwick castle, to the ninth earl, Feb. 1602.

his life at your command."[17] "Faithfulness" implied too that the total loyalty owed by a servant to his master should not be attenuated by ties entered into with other men. The faithful servant could say "Frendes my goode lorde I have none above you . . . but stand only upon your lordships goode selfe . . . "[18]

But if the servant was expected to be faithful, the reciprocal character of the relationship is indicated by the "good lordship" his master was required to show in return. "Good lordship" was not an institution which died with the advent of "the Tudor peace". As late as 1595 a servant could say "I praye yow Sir move my lord to stand my good lord, and I shall showe my selfe as thankfull and as serviceable as any appertains his honour."[19] In fact this servant, by openly making his service appear to be conditional on good lordship, transgressed the unwritten code of service, and so found himself in trouble; good lordship was something to which a servant could appeal, and for which he could beg, but it could not be insisted on as a matter of right. "Good lordship" consisted above all of the "favours" which the master conferred on his "faithful" servants; one went with the other, so that a servant could tell his master: "I stand fully resolved you are my good lord, so that I may bouldly build upon your . . . continewance of good favors."[20] "Favours" like "faithfulness" were unconditioned by any contractual obligations or legal framework; they were free gifts beyond what a servant could claim by his letters patent or indenture as his fee or annuity. Most commonly they took the form of the leaseholds, or even outright

[17] *Ibid.*, P II 2 (1), the same to the same, 31 Aug. 1602. "Faithfulness" required from servants (however humble) a willingness both to undergo and inflict violence in their lord's quarrels. Thus on 4 May 1569, "William Harrison, Odinell Selbye, Christopher Armourer, John Urpeth and John Harrison being your lordship's servants [they were parkers and agisters to the seventh earl at Alnwick] with others did drive Sir John Fosters cattell forth of your Lops: parke of Hulne and remained at Hynden gaitte to se if the said Cattell should by any person be put agayne in the said parke. In whiche tyme xvi of the same Sir John Fosters servantes weapynned with speares bylles and lances ryotously and with greate force dyd expulse y^r Lops: said servantes from the said gayte of the said parke and Thomas Sallgheld dyd smyte Odinell Selbye on the face with his hand, the others mayntening the same with ther weapynges bent for that purpose and y^r Lops: said servantes thereby compelled to give plaice" (Syon House MS. Q XI 1, Robert Collingwood and George Clarkson to the seventh earl, 8 May 1569).

[18] Syon House MS. X II 8, Christopher Vavasour, steward in Yorkshire, to the ninth earl, 16 May 1596.

[19] *Ibid.*, X II 8, Richard Green to the ninth earl, 31 Oct. 1595.

[20] *Ibid.*, X II 6 (11), Christopher Vavasour to the ninth earl, 26 April 1596.

grants of land, with which a good lord enriched his servants.[21] Good lordship however involved more than the conferment of benefits of this kind. A "good lord" might, for example, overlook his servant's lapses, and forgive inefficiencies or debts, or even downright dishonesty;[22] he would provide support against rivals and enemies, and succour if the servant's duties brought him into difficulties or danger. These then were the marks of magnanimity which made a nobleman an "honourable personage", worthy of faithfulness. By these means he gained eternal remembrance and the gratitude of posterity. "It hath been an ancient use", wrote a servant to his master in 1609, " as is dailie scene and knowne not onely amongst princes, but great noble personages . . . to purchase to themselves a name of perpetuall memorye unto all posterities: and this soe laudable use hath bene much observed, not to be unregarded by your honors selfe: and being speciallie manifested in your lordshipes singular bountie and liberalitie to dyverse and manie your servants and followers . . . "[23] Here humanist influences have left their mark on the terms used.

Enough has been said to show the kind of loyalties on which a great nobleman could draw to sustain his influence and power, and the kind of obligations he incurred towards those who followed him. A moral content is implied in these relationships[24] which does not make it easy to dismiss a great lord who incurred the disfavour of the

[21] Thus Sir Henry Curwen, *loc. cit.*, n. 14 above, at the same time as he proffered his service, begged for a lease to make a dam over the Eden, and for a warrant for a stag and a hind every year, "that in this I might glory in your lordship's favours".

[22] Thus one of the ninth earl's receivers in Cumberland, Henry Patrickson, called to account in respect of arrears of rents in his receipt which he had pocketed, wrote on 18 May 1597, "I promise to shewe matter to excuse the nott present payment . . . and to submitt myself to his Lordship's owne order: so as I trust his honor upon the perusing of my letter will stand my good lord and maister as for to staye suite untill the beginning of Michaelmas terme" (Syon House MS. X II 3). The suit was, in fact, dropped, and an amicable arrangement reached between Patrickson and his master.

[23] Syon House MS. X II 6 (18), William Stockdale to the ninth earl, 1609.

[24] Something of the quality of the bond between lord and servant is suggested by a provision made in the will of Odinell Selby, parker of Hulne park at Alnwick (see n. 17 above; his office involved him in the fray between the seventh earl's men and Sir John Forster's in May 1569); he gave "my sonne Raphe Selby unto the right honourable Earle of Northumberland, my good lorde and master, as frely as God gave him to me, yf it shall please his honor to taik hym to his service, to serve hym in my place, as I have done his lordships father, and the Earle his late brother, these sex and thirtye years" (Surtees Soc., xxviii, Durham and London, 1860, p. 135).

crown merely as a patron of violence and anarchy presiding over illegally recruited bands of hired thugs. There were bad lords and unfaithful servants; tyranny and dishonesty were as endemic in this sphere as in any other of Tudor society. But we cannot doubt that the relationship between lord and servant contained sufficient that was positive to make it one of the prime cohesive forces of that society. The regional communities which made up the totality of Tudor England regarded it as "natural" that the local great household (if such there was) should "rule, under the Prince". From this point of view the great nobility were less the "rivals" of the Tudor crown than a necessary complement to its authority.

Perhaps the character of the fifth earl's policies, and the nature of his political achievement may be most vividly seen by considering events which took place in Northumberland less than a year after his death. These will first be related, by way of prologue, in the pages that follow. The principal actors involved were the fifth earl's heir and political legatee, Henry sixth earl of Northumberland, and Sir William Lisle, whom the fifth earl had made his constable of Alnwick castle.

II

On a Sunday late in January 1528, as the young sixth earl of Northumberland, only lately appointed warden of the East and Middle Marches, made his way from mass along the Canongate at Alnwick to the great fourteenth-century gatehouse of the castle, he was encountered by a melancholy little group of suppliants, lightly clad, and shivering in the cold wind. They wore only white shirts, and there were halters about their necks, symbols of abasement and repentance. Kneeling in the mud, all fifteen of them made unconditional submission to the king's authority, and were immediately committed to the castle prison.[25] Amongst them there were gentlemen of worship in Northumberland, particularly Sir William Lisle, lord of Felton near Alnwick, and Humphrey his young heir; but also John Ogle, William Shaftoe, and Thomas Fenwick.[26] All were

[25] The earl described the scene in a letter of 28 January 1528 to the king. See *L.P.*, iv (2), 3820. Most of the text of the letter is reproduced in Fonblanque, *Annals of the House of Percy*, i, pp. 388–9.

[26] *L.P.*, iv (2), 4133.

bandits, who since the previous summer, when Lisle had escaped from imprisonment at Newcastle, had kept the Marches in an uproar, helped by a band of "broken men" from Tynedale and Redesdale, and from over the Border. They had sought the life of the sheriff of Northumberland, Sir William Ellerker, at Widdrington, burning his tenements and carrying away his stock. Roger Heron's lordship of Eshott had been raided, and his house burnt down, together with Ellerker's town of Humshaugh.[27] Not even the all-powerful but remote cardinal had been spared Lisle's attentions. His regality of Hexham had been raided, and twenty-four of the tenants taken prisoner.[28] By December 1527 Lisle was even known abroad, and the French ambassador informed Paris that the earl of Northumberland had been sent against him.[29]

It was a commonplace that there were few of the Northumbrian gentry who were not involved in banditry, and "who have no thieves belonging to them".[30] This was a society where the strong lived on the weak, and where "reiving", with its attendant arts of blackmail and murder, were not thought of as crime, but as the expression of a way of life. Violence was stimulated by the proximity of the Border, and by a mounting population pressure on the available agrarian resources. The Lisles may have been outstanding for their courage and ferocity, but theirs was no more than a typical example of the local mores. Apart from their lordship of Felton, the family held the manor of Woodburn and other lands in Redesdale, the latter the stronghold of the Hedleys, Halls, and other warlike border clans which "doe inhabite in some places three or fower houshold, soe that they cannot uppon soe small fermes without any other craftes live truely but either be stealing in England or Scotland."[31] The Lisles were well regarded in Redesdale as gentlemen of worship, patrons and protectors who might help in time of trouble, and who were to be reciprocally supported in their own enterprises and trials. But their relations with the Tudor monarchy were uneasy. Sir

[27] *Ibid.*, iv (2), 3344, 3370, 3383, 4336.

[28] *Ibid.*, 3552.

[29] *Ibid.*, 3691.

[30] *Ibid.*, iv (1), 1482; iii (2), 3240.

[31] Sir Robert Bowes, "A Book on the State of the Frontiers and Marches", printed in J. Hodgson, *History of Northumberland*, iii (2) (Newcastle upon Tyne, 1828), p. 243. For the history of the Lisles, see *Northumberland County History*, vii (Newcastle upon Tyne, 1904), pp. 244 ff.

William's father, Sir Humphrey Lisle, had been exempted from the general pardon of 1509,[32] and was for a time imprisoned in London. In 1512 he was in trouble again for a debt to the crown.[33] Perhaps these difficulties arose because of Sir Humphrey's feud over tithes with the canons of Brinkburn.[34] This led to an attack on Brinkburn priory, and eventually (in 1521) to the murder of one of the canons by Sir Humphrey's grandson.[35] Perhaps it was this incident which first brought the Lisles to Wolsey's attention.

Sir William Lisle's troubles had begun when a squabble of a kind common enough in Northumberland had flared up between him and his neighbour, Roger Heron of Eshott, probably over disputed boundaries.[36] Lisle had impounded some of Heron's cattle, found no doubt grazing on land he claimed as part of the lordship of Felton. Heron appealed to the sheriff, Sir William Ellerker, who awarded him a replevin of his property, and this was apparently executed. At any rate, Lisle retaliated against Ellerker, raiding his lands with a hundred men, and carrying off forty cattle. Perhaps even these violent proceedings might eventually have been overlooked in the harsh world of the Marches but for the words which Lisle used in confrontations with his enemies. The most expressive exchange was with the sheriff, himself of a family notable for its loyalty to the Tudor monarchy, and who had spent much of his life in the service of the crown. "Sir William Lisle", Ellerker remarked, "have we not a God and a King to live under?" The words evoke the sense of an order reaching down from supernature to nature, and of which the authority of the crown was the earthly keystone, which was one of the commonplaces of the political theory of the age. They would have met a ready echo amongst the intellectuals and civil servants of the Tudor court, particularly in those quarters where humanist influences had already made themselves felt, and where there was a quickened sense of the significance of the "Christian Prince". But such attitudes were remote from the rude, archaic world of the border where men of worship were more

[32] *L.P.*, i (1), 11 (10).
[33] *Ibid.*, i (1), 289 (35), 1493 (3).
[34] See Lord Dacre's undated letter to the Council printed in *Northumberland County History*, vii, p. 245.
[35] *L.P.*, iii (2), 1920.
[36] For an account of the course of the feud and Lisle's words to Ellerker and Heron, see *L.P.*, iv (2), 2370, 2402.

inclined to emphasize their liberties, after the fashion of an earlier age, than the authority of the crown. Lisle's reply expresses much of what Wolsey and his like were determined to put down. "By God's blood", he said, "there is nother king nor his officers that shall take any distress on my ground, or have ado within the liberties of Felton, but I shall take another for it, if I be as strong as he, and able to make my party good." A more direct challenge to the cardinal himself was implied in the words Lisle exchanged with Heron: "What! Meanest thou to strive with me? Wilt thou win anything at my hands? I have ruffled with the Warden, and also with the Cardinal, and trust to pluck him by the nose." Lisle's quarrels with the late warden of the Marches towards Scotland, Lord Dacre, were notorious; and his son had given practical expression to the family dislike of the cardinal by clapping in the stocks an agent of the legate's commissary who attempted to serve a citation at Felton. No doubt Lisle's words were in part due to the heat of the moment, but they also reflect an environment in which there was a rooted hatred of Wolsey and his policies, and, at a deeper level, a kind of anarchic repugnance to order and law in any form.

Lisle's rashness, however, laid him open to his enemies, and retribution followed. A complaint was laid against him in Star Chamber, and, after examination at York, he was committed to imprisonment at Newcastle.[37] There he remained for a year until, in August 1527, with characteristic impetuosity (his release was then under consideration) he broke gaol and began his career as a border terrorist. By so doing he laid himself open to the penalties of attainder, with the loss of his lands and goods, as well as his life, and events moved inexorably towards the scene at Alnwick in January 1528. But his lawless exploits had a political significance of importance. It was the case of Sir William Lisle which proved that the Marches could not be ruled without the earl of Northumberland. The paralysis of government emerges most clearly in the ineffectiveness of Sir William Eure, the king's lieutenant of the Middle March, whose duty it was to lay Lisle by the heels. He refused to emerge from Harbottle castle, and confessed he could no longer rule the country against Lisle and his adherents, since none of the gentry would do anything for him, and he could not trust them.[38] It was, in fact, Eure's confessions of failure which led the duke of Richmond's

[37] *L.P.*, iv (2), 2450, 3230.

[38] *Ibid.*, iv (2), 3552.

council to recommend to Wolsey, on 3 November 1527, that Lisle could not be apprehended "except by the power of some nobleman continually lying in Northumberland",[39] particularly since Lisle was given refuge by the Scots. It is unlikely that the council had any other than the head of the house of Percy in mind, and it was Wolsey himself who secured the appointment of the sixth earl of Northumberland to the East and Middle Marches a month later.

Thus the sixth earl owed Sir William Lisle a considerable debt of gratitude. Lisle's lawlessness had secured for him offices which so many of his predecessors had enjoyed but from which his father had been excluded throughout his lifetime. The Percy influence, which had been in eclipse in the Marches since the assassination of the fourth earl in 1489, now found itself once more in the ascendant. Moreover, the obligation under which the earl lay to his prisoner was deepened by the ties of "good lordship" and service which bound the two men together, and which were so potent in the Border society. For Sir William Lisle, the violent brigand and outlaw, was also none less than constable of Alnwick castle, to which office he had been appointed on 25 March 1525 by the earl's late father.[40] As custodian of the principal Percy stronghold in the Eastern Marches Lisle acquired a status in Northumberland far beyond that justified by his own resources. As constable he led the Percy tenants on service against the Scots, a force of nearly nine hundred horse and over a thousand foot;[41] "in time of service wher was ther", wrote nostalgically a Percy officer of a later age, "in all the countrie one gentleman of honnoure or worshipe that had such a company of gentlemen and good servitours as the cheife constable's of the said castle and barony of Alnwyck?"[42] As constable, Lisle would have been the natural link between the gentry communities of the East

[39] *Ibid.*

[40] See Syon House MS. C III 5 c, Account of Geo. Swinburne, Receiver in Northumberland.

[41] Syon House MS. A I 2, Abstract of the Survey of the lands purchased by the King's Highness of Henry earl of Northumberland, n.d., but of the 1530s: "Also there be of Tennants and Hablemen Resyiante and Inhabytinge with the said Lordshippes and manors [in Northumberland] redy to serve the Kyng having Jacks cote of fens and harnys with long speres bowes and other weapons in a redyness whensoever they shall be called upon to the nombre of mdccccIxvij whereof horsemen dccccxlix fotemen mcxviii."

[42] Syon House MS. A II 2, The Red Book of Alnwick, p. 55. "Opinio Scriptoris". This is in the handwriting of George Clarkson, surveyor to the seventh earl in the 1560s.

and Middle Marches which followed the house of Percy and the earl himself. His office explains the difficult position of the new warden confronted by this embarrassing outlaw, and the devious manoeuvres to which the earl had to resort to extricate himself.

For it is likely that Lisle's surrender had, in fact, been voluntary. The duke of Richmond's council had been baffled by the succour he received in Scotland, and confessed they could not see how he could be apprehended as long as this persisted.[43] And in spite of reassuring replies sent to Henry VIII, and Wolsey's letters to James V and to the earl of Angus, the Scottish warden of the Marches, it seems that Lisle could rely on the help of the Scottish Border magnates right to the end, and that his surrender took place against their advice.[44] It is clear that Lisle submitted to the earl of Northumberland because the latter's appointment as warden presaged a new régime in the Eastern Marches. Sir William had already disseminated a wholly erroneous report that the king had not been privy to his imprisonment, which had been procured by Wolsey and his other enemies.[45] But now surely the outlawed knight could expect succour and good lordship from his own master's son, whose power in the country he had done so much to restore. He came to Alnwick in the garb of a penitent, but also full of hopes for the future, and he must have known that the earl would disappoint these at his own peril. Because, if the latter disowned and condemned one of his own chief servants and followers, he would make himself an object of contempt in the March society, and his authority would crumble. As the earl himself explained to Wolsey, "William Lysle is kyned and allied of the borders amongst them that I must need put my lyfe in trust with many times, if I serve the King's grace in this office."[46] Already, in fact, the gentry community stood ominously aloof from the new warden, who could rely only on the king's servants and his own, together with one or two relatives, to apprehend malefactors.[47] Thus the earl, in spite of the letters he had received both from king and cardinal to proceed at once to the attainder of the two

43 *L.P.*, iv (2), 3552.
44 The sixth earl of Northumberland was told by Nicholas Lisle that Sir William and his adherents were supported by Lord Maxwell and the earls of Angus and Bothwell, who were opposed to any policy of submission. See *L.P.*, iv (2), 3914.
45 *L.P.*, iv (2), 3383.
46 *Ibid.*, iv (2), 4093; Fonblanque, *Annals of the House of Percy*, i, pp. 391–2.
47 Fonblanque, *op. cit.*, p. 389.

Lisles, father and son,[48] was bound to seek some mitigation of the penalties they had incurred. He manoeuvred first for time, in order that he could bring his influence at court to bear, writing to request that the justices of assize at York should be joined with him in the commission to impose sentence, since he was inexperienced in the procedures of attainder.[49] And in the meanwhile letters were sent to Sir Brian Tuke, treasurer of the chamber, and to Tunstall, bishop of London, requesting their intervention on behalf of the prisoners.[50] Wolsey was willing that the life of the heir, young Humphrey Lisle, should be spared. But it is clear that the earl was not satisfied with this, and that he still hoped to save the chief offender, Sir William himself. The result was an angry letter from Wolsey on 28 March 1529,[51] denouncing the earl's delays as a pretence. "You should not use", the cardinal wrote, "such cautelous and colorable dealing with one [Wolsey] that thus both tenderly . . . set you forward, and by whose only means the King hath put you in such authority. I know the whole discourse of your privy suits and dealing . . . " Humphrey Lisle's life was to be spared, and he was to be sent up to London; but sentence was immediately to be executed against his father. The earl could do no more, and within a few days Sir William Lisle had been hanged, drawn and quartered.[52] But it may well be that one result of the incident was to drive a wedge between the earl and some of his followers in the easternmost Marches, who would turn increasingly to the more romantic rash and impulsive leadership of his brother, Sir Thomas Percy.

III

The case of Sir William Lisle, then, reveals the two Percies, father and son, as maintainers of Border violence and lawlessness. Both were involved in courses of action which helped to disrupt good rule in the Marches, and to weaken the Border. As a result the Percy interest became inevitably entangled in an underground struggle with the crown, whose ultimate outcome was the collapse of the

48 *L.P.*, iv (2), 3967.
49 *Ibid.*
50 The letters have not survived, but the earl refers to them when writing to Wolsey on 24 March 1528 (*L.P.*, iv (2), 4093; Fonblanque, *op. cit.*, i, pp. 391–2).
51 *L.P.*, iv (2), 4082; Fonblanque, *op. cit.*, pp. 390–1.
52 *Ibid.*, iv (2), 4133.

power of the family when its lands came into the king's possession on the death of the sixth earl in 1537. There is something tragic about this result, leading as it did to the latter's death in poverty and disgrace; and there is an implacable quality about Henry VIII's pursuit both of him and his father. For the fifth earl, too, had died under the shadow of the royal displeasure, the government exploiting a shortage of cash in his household to curtail his funeral and to heap humiliations on his family.[53] Yet the policies of the Percies had more affinities with those of families like the Howards and the Talbots, who sought advancement by service to the Tudor state, than with those of the legatees of the White Rose and their allies, who could hope for benefits from a change of régime. The fourth earl of Northumberland had, after all, held high office under Henry VII, and had met his death (in 1489) while seeking to quell a riot occasioned by the king's tax demands. His grandson, the sixth earl, although successively bullied and humiliated by Wolsey and Henry VIII, nevertheless served the crown as a conscientious warden of the Marches. And, although the fifth earl had fewer claims on the gratitude of the Tudor rulers, who failed to employ him in the office he thought befitted his rank, we can scarcely doubt his desire to serve. This was, in fact, given graphic expression, sometime between 1516 and 1523, in one of the earliest English emblem drawings,[54] executed by some artist in his household, depicting Henry VIII, holding the sun, in the centre of a Tudor rose emitting fire and drops of liquid falling on to an eye let within a silver crescent (one of the Percy badges); below the crecent is a scroll, and at the bottom of the drawing the drops fall on to the letters COR. On the scroll are the verses:

I receyve noo lighte but from thy bearmes bright,
The leight benevolent causith cor to relent,
For remembryng thy goodness contenuall, which remanith
perpetuall,

[53] Wolsey interfered incessantly in the affairs of the dead earl, arranging for plate to be pledged to pay for his burial, and fixing a limit for what was to be spent on the burial; the dowager countess even had to petition to be allowed to remain in her home at Wressle castle, promising that she would "live poorly" and be at pains to please the cardinal. See *L.P.*, iv (2), 3134, 3184.

[54] See A. G. Dickens, "A Tudor Percy Emblem in Royal MS. 18 D ii", in *Archaeol. Jl*, cxii (1955), p. 95.

Cor cannot but of dutie he muste distill;
Yet he saith dutie cannot recompense a cordinge to his goode will.

But in spite of these unexceptionable sentiments, Henry VIII's distrust of his powerful subject persisted. For behind it there was an awareness that the earl was not above the temptation to seek to compel his master's favour. It was this which confirmed the king in the settled Tudor hostility to the house of Percy.

But what magnate was exempt from such temptation? The immense prestige of monarchy, combined with the inadequate resources of even the greatest lords compared with those of the crown, ensured that none could aspire to sovereign principalities. The days were past when an earl of Northumberland could scheme, like the first of the line, to partition England with his allies; the sixteenth-century Percies were well aware (in spite of Hunsdon's much quoted phrase)[55] that the north did not know them as princes. The magnates of Tudor England, conscious that rebellion against a united and effective government was a desperate expedient, in fact sought the favour of the crown, rather than to tear themselves away from it. Thus the Percy ambition was no more than to exercise the king's authority in the north as lieutenants and wardens of the Marches. But the rub arose if favour and office commensurate with dignity were withheld. For no great lord lacked the means to bring pressure on the government. Local influence, based on great estates and a large following, could be mobilized to promote disorder, and so demonstrate (as Lisle so effectively succeeded in doing) the indispensability of the local magnate. In court circles however there was an awareness that such tactics tended to make government the plaything of local pressures, and to remove governmental initiative from London to the provinces; and it was Edmund Dudley who, at the beginning of Henry VIII's reign, formulated the Tudor rule with regard to magnate aspirations to office. "Though it be . . . tollerable for them to desier yt [office] when they are mete therefore", Dudley had written, "yet it is more lawdable to have it of the fre disposicion of ther sovereigne: but in all cases lett them not presume to take it of ther owne auctoritie, for then it will suerly choke them."[56] Thus

[55] Made at the time of the Rebellion of the Earls, on 31 Dec. 1569. See *Cal. State Papers, Foreign, Eliz. 1569–71*, 568.

[56] Edmund Dudley, *The Tree of Commonwealth*, ed. D. M. Brodie (Cambridge, 1948), p. 57.

declarations of loyalty and even willing service could not exempt a great lord from the unremitting suspicion of the king, quick to detect the slightest hint of disobedience behind outward conformity. So that the Howards, for example, raised to heights never attained by the Percies, also trod an even narrower knife-edge between greatness and ruin.

But there were few lords better placed than the earl of Northumberland (if he were so inclined) to play the game of magnate politics with London. His connection and lands, based on half-a-dozen of the most formidable strongholds in the north, ramified through the Border counties, and down into Yorkshire, with outliers in Lincolnshire, Sussex, Kent and the Southwest. Since the fall of the Nevilles, none of the surviving northern magnates could rival his wealth and power; and if the still precarious unity founded on Tudor rule were to break, the earl was the man who could lead north against south. He was a factor of importance, too, in the increasingly delicate pattern of Anglo-Scottish relations. Thus the Percy was the type of the "over-mighty subject", too indispensable to be tolerated by kings of the kind of Henry VII or Henry VIII. The earls of Northumberland were all too liable to conceive the governmental process as a dialogue between the kind of regional influence they exercised, and the power of the crown. The Tudors, on the other hand, were merely concerned to be obeyed, and that without second thoughts or reservations. And so the politics of the fifth earl, which entangled him with other discontented magnates, and made him the patron, not only of Sir William Lisle, but also (as will be seen below) of other dissident elements in the north, was bound to lead to implacable conflict with the crown, and so ultimately to the downfall of his house.

The power of the Percies, then, made it almost inevitable that first Henry VII, then Henry VIII should seek to prune the excessive influence of the family. Something was done from this point of view even during the lifetime of the fourth earl of Northumberland, who, although he remained a vice-regal figure in the north, holding the great offices of king's lieutenant and warden of the East and Middle Marches, was nevertheless removed by Henry VII from the rule of the West March and Berwick. Henry was less ready than his predecessors to rule the north through the agency of the great houses, and by balancing one magnate against another. His object was rather to make the royal presence directly felt. Partly this could be achieved by the increasingly vigorous and powerful action of royal agents sent into the north on commission, partly by the effective use of the king's summary jurisdiction in Star Chamber. But policies of this sort could only succeed (since the crown had no sufficient standing reserve of force at its disposal) to the extent that the king could rely on local support, and this meant the intrusion of the royal power into the web of alliance and dependence which bound the northern gentry to the great houses. An opportunity to bring this about, as far as the Percy influence was concerned, was afforded as a result of the assassination of the fourth earl near Thirsk in 1489. This event involved the succession of a minor, and so placed the Percy estates for a decade in the hands of the crown.

One consequence of this was a crumbling of the Percy influence which set in during the fifth earl's minority, when a movement began of prominent northern families from the Percy service into that of the crown. The Radcliffes of Dilston[57] in Northumberland, for example, the Curwens[58] and Penningtons[59] in Cumberland, were all families which had served the fourth earl of Northumberland, but opted for office in the royal household in the next generation. In Yorkshire there was Sir Robert Plumpton, the fourth earl's forester and steward of the lordship of Spofforth, whom Henry VII made a knight of the body after his master's death;[60] or the first lord Eure, ennobled for his services to Henry VIII, but also of a family which had taken the fourth earl's fee.[61] So was Sir Robert Constable of Flamborough, another of Henry VII's knights of the body, but whose grandfather had been close to the fourth earl, and had been

57 Thomas Radcliffe of Derwentwater, a Percy fee'd man mentioned in the fourth earl's will (Surtees Soc., xlv, Durham and London, 1865, p. 308), was father to Sir Edward Radcliffe, appointed one of the king's esquires of the body sometime before 1516; he acquired Dilston and other lands in Northumberland in the right of his wife (*L.P.*, ii (i), 2735).

58 The Curwens had a long tradition of Percy service (see above, p. 53) which seems to have survived the fifth earl's minority, since Sir Thomas Curwen acted as his Receiver in Cumberland (Syon House MS. C. III 2a); but the rot set in with Curwen's grandson of the same name, who was a courtier, an esquire of the body, and the king's steward of Galtres forest and of Sheriff Hutton lordship in Yorkshire.

59 Sir John Pennington (d. 1518) was made a knight banneret by the fourth earl, and held several offices under him in Cumberland (Hist. MSS. Comm., 10th Rept, App. IV, p. 228); but his heir John Pennington was already of the king's household in 1495–6 (J. Foster, *Penningtoniana*, London, 1878, pp. vi–viii).

60 *Plumpton Correspondence* (Camden Soc., 1st series, iv, 1839, pp. xcix, cxii).

61 *Testamenta Eboracensia*, ed. by J. Raine, iii (Surtees Soc., xlv, Durham and London, 1865), p. 307.

remembered in the latter's will.[62] Doubtless no hard and fast shift of loyalty was necessarily involved in the readiness of many of the gentry to seize on the openings offered by the service of the crown. Sir Edward Radcliffe, for example, took the fee of the fifth earl as well as that of the king, although he could hardly be said to have served the former loyally.[63] Constable's heir served the sixth earl;[64] and Sir John Hotham of Scorborough, although a knight of the body and at one time an enemy of the Percies, was also one of Northumberland's captains in the French campaign of 1513, and the Scottish campaign of 1523.[65] All the same, it can hardly be a coincidence that the fifth earl was early made aware of the intrusive presence of the crown's influence in the heart of his own country in the East Riding as a result of a combination of two knights of the body, Hotham and Constable, with the courtier and civil servant Thomas Savage, archbishop of York. Hotham trespassed on lands claimed by the earl at Scorborough; Constable had his feud with the earl's brother, Sir William Percy, and supported the archbishop in his attempt to break the earl's predominant influence in the archiepiscopal town of Beverley. As a result there were frays with the earl's servants and followers, which gave Hotham and Savage the opportunity to cite him before Star Chamber, because (as Hotham put it) "Your saide besecher is not able nor of poure to sue against the saide Erle, beyng a greate lorde aod of greate poure and myght in that countrie."[66] The earl seems to have emerged unscathed from these troubles, but only at the price of a letter to Sir Reginald Bray begging for his support against the archbishop, and of £100 paid to the king (early in

[62] Sir Robert Constable the elder was one of the fee'd men who accompanied the fourth earl to meet Henry VII at York in the first year of the reign (*Plumpton Corres.*, p. xcvi); for the earl's will see Surtees Soc., xlv, p. 308. Sir Robert Constable the younger is mentioned as a knight of the body *c.* 1505–6: *Yorkshire Star Chamber Proceedings* (Yorkshire Archaeological Society, Record Series, 4 vols., London and York, 1909–27), iii, p. 96.

[63] He was steward in Northumberland and counsellor-at-law to the fifth earl (Syon House MS. C. III 5a); for his loyalty see n. 92 below.

[64] The sixth earl appointed Sir Marmaduke Constable his bailiff of Hundmanby in 1532 (Alnwick Castle MS., Letters and Papers, ii, Book of Grants, p. 74).

[65] Grose's *Antiquarian Repertory* (1809), iv, pp. 346 and 351; Public Record Office, E101/531/34, "The erle of Northumberlands Retynewe at Newcastell the xxj daie of October Ao XV Regis Henrici viii".

[66] For Hotham's quarrel with the earl see *Yorkshire Star Chamber Proceedings*, ii, p. 134; for Constable's quarrels with Sir William Percy and the earl, see *ibid.*, iii, pp. 18, 96; for Archbishop Savage's complaints about the earl's proceedings in Beverley and elsewhere, see *ibid.*, p. 18.

1507) for his favour "in the matter of Sir John Hotham".[67] Such shifts would alone have been enough to show that his power was no longer certain and assured as it had been in his father's time.

But there were other ways in which this realization was being brought home in the countries where the earl had rule. For example there were the pressures arising from the new concern to establish and enforce the king's feudal prerogatives by means of the commissions which Henry VII sent out to enquire into royal wardships and concealed lands.[68] These touched on the sensitive nerve of a society in which the family, whose life was sustained and transmitted on a basis of landed property, was the primary grouping. A new awareness therefore was created of the power of the crown as an active presence in the midst of the northern gentry communities; a presence moreover from which very concrete benefits could accrue, and which it would be perilous to ignore. For the dominant gentry groups now discovered that questions relating to the disposal of landed estates (particularly the marriage of heiresses) could no longer be decided merely by private agreement amongst themselves, or by force. Sir Robert Plumpton, for example, pursued by Empson through the Westminster courts over the disposal of the Babthorpe inheritance (Plumpton's son had married the Babthorpe heiress) was compelled to seek the protection he hoped the royal service would confer.[69] Even this, however, could prove a broken reed, as Sir Robert Constable discovered in 1523, when, having abducted an heiress claimed as a ward of the crown, and contracted her to his son, he was summoned before the Council and compelled to submit, in spite of his claims on the king's "good lordship" for his past services.[70]

Feudal tenures, however, were a source of fiscal profit and social influence not only to the crown, but also to the northern lords. Scores of knights' fees were held of the Percy honour of Cockermouth and barony of Alnwick, of the Clifford honour of Skipton and barony of Westmorland, of the Dacre barony of Greystoke, and

[67] Fonblanque, *Annals of the House of Percy*, i, p. 319.

[68] See W. C. Richardson, "The Surveyor of the King's Prerogative", in *Eng. Hist. Rev.*, lvi (1941), p. 52.

[69] *Plumpton Correspondence*, pp. cxi–cxii.

[70] *L.P.*, iv (1), 1115, 1136. This was one of a number of incidents which in time made Constable too disreputable to remain in the crown's service.

of other great northern estates.[71] Knight-service tenures could bring appreciable financial windfalls into the coffers of the northern magnates, particularly by way of wardships.[72] But probably more significant than the financial gains were the relationships of affinity and service which supplemented the tenurial connections linking so many of the northern squires to the great families. Military tenure created a bond, transmitted from generation to generation, between a lord and his mesne dependants which found natural expression in the latter's service as their lord's fee'd men and officers;[73] and in the greater liberties the knights' court to which mesne tenants made their suit was also a tribunal where disputes arising within the following of a great lord were resolved; so that the knight court of the barony of Alnwick, for example, was a material factor in the assertion of the Percy influence in Northumberland, and in the maintenance of good order there.[74] And so, amongst the

71 Material amongst the Syon House MSS. suggests that some thirty families held land by knight service of the Percies in Northumberland. Most of these were small squires, but there were some houses of importance, like the Greys of Chillingham, the Horsleys of Scrainwood, and the Shaftoes of Great Bavington. A score of tenants did suit to the knights' court of the honour of Skipton in 1522 (Bodleian Library, Dodsworth MS. 83, fo. 114 b). A survey of 1526, Carlisle County Record Office, shows that there were over forty knights' fees in the barony of Westmorland.

72 The tenth Lord Clifford, for example, sold the wardship of Thomas Wharton (later the first Lord Wharton), who held Nateby of him by knight service, for 200 marks, and that of John Warcop of Smardale for £40.

73 The Whartons and Tempests, for example, both knight-service tenants for lands in the barony of Westmorland and the honour of Skipton respectively, provided the Cliffords with many officers. In Cumberland the Curwens, with their tradition of service to the Percies, held their lordship of Workington of Percy honour of Cockermouth. The Horsleys of Scrainwood, a fee held by knight service of Alnwick, were servants of the fifth and sixth earls of Northumberland. But relations between the northern magnates and their mesne tenants were not always amicable. Disputes over reliefs and suits of court exacerbated bitterness between the Percies and the Greys of Chillingham in Northumberland (Syon House MSS., *passim*).

74 For the importance of the knights' court of the barony of Alnwick as a means whereby disputes were resolved and the outbreak of feuds prevented, see the remarks of the Elizabethan surveyor quoted at n. 18 above: "At wch court by the said good appearance of the freeholders, yf ether they had travers or controversies for any parcell of inherytannce amongst or betwyxte any of them . . . xii of the saide freeholders was Impannallyd who by ther othes the same controversye did mittigait and did ther in give order . . . Itm the goode order above mentioned maid and caused suche ferme and steadfast love amongst the inhabitants and gentlemen of the same baronye That upon any grudge stirred or moved among any of them it was straightway appeased and the commonaltie of

troubles which the fifth earl encountered over the years 1505–7, not the least was the appearance in Northumberland (in 1505) of a royal commission of concealments, which found that over twenty of his mesne tenancies there were in fact held of the crown.[75] One result of this was that some dozen Northumbrian squires, all of them Percy knight-service tenants, were compelled into the trouble and expense of traversing the commission's findings in the court of King's Bench.[76] And, although most of the traverses were upheld, once again in a disquieting kind of way the royal power had made itself felt within a network of traditional ties of dependence, even in the remote backwoods of Northumberland.[77]

the said baronye to leve so quietlie that they feared neyther the evyll and ungodly persones either of England or Scotland . . . Nor yet the malice or evill will of others . . . for yf they or any of them were oppressed the said cheife constable [of Alnwick castle] and other the lords officers did find forthwith present remedie therein. And then the tennants and farmours was not only both able in bodie and goods to serve the lorde, but also thereunto was encouraged" (Syon House MS. A II 2, The Red Book of Alnwick, p. 54 ff.).

75 See *Calendar of the Inquisitions Post Mortem, Henry VII*, iii, nos. 6 and 7. There was a commission at the same time to enquire into encroachments made by the earl and others in Cumberland. See *ibid.*, p. 597.

76 These were Robert Hoppen for the manors of Hoppen and Lucker (Public Record Office, KB 27/988/ixd); Sir Robert Tailbois for Chirmondesden, Netherton and Alwinton (KB 27/988/Rex Vd e 992/Rex iv); Robert Raymes for Witton North (KB 27/988/xi d); Ralph Hebburn for Hebburn (KB 27/988/xiii and 992/6); John Swinhoe for Swinhoe (KB 27/988/ix); Robert Aynsley for Shaftoe (KB 27/988/xi); Thomas Horsley for Screnwood and Horsley (KB 27/988/xvii); William Lawson for Cramlington (KB 27/988/xix); James Lilburne and John Burgh for Leversheels (KB 27/988/v); Robert Bellingham for half Howick and Abberwick (KB 27/988/ii d); Robert Loraine for Kirkharle (KB 27/988/xi d); Sir Ralph Bowes for Spindleston and Budle (KB 27/877/xv). The priors of Tynemouth and Carlisle and the abbot of Newminster also had to make traverses. I owe these references (taken from the Rex Roll of the term) to Mr J. P. Cooper.

77 Some kind of assault on the earl's mesne tenures, this time in Sussex, where his honour of Petworth lay, seems to be behind the complaints made against him in Star Chamber by one John Goring, probably in 1500. The earl claimed that Goring's grandfather (whose heir the latter was) had held his lands of the Percies by knight service, and detailed Goring himself as his ward at his house. Goring denied that his lands had been so held, and demanded his release on surety. Probably he had been encouraged to defy the earl by his relative the court magnate Sir Reginald Bray, one of the leading councillors of Henry VII, to whom the two justices appointed to adjudicate the dispute were to report. It was only after the earl's counsel sought to delay the matter until Bray had left London that Goring took his cause into Star Chamber, evidently unsure that the justices would uphold it without prompting from his powerful relative. John Goring the grandfather, whether or not a Percy tenant, certainly had close Percy affiliations, and was one of the fifth earl's mother's trustees. Characteristically, however, John Goring the grandson's heir, Sir William Goring, passed into the orbit of the court, and died

If developments of this kind were bound to shake the confidence of those accustomed to put their trust in the power of the Percy, we may assume that this trust was further and drastically undermined in 1506 as a result of the case of Elizabeth Hastings, so often quoted in the text books as an instance of Henry VII's stern treatment of the great lords. Damages of £10,000 were found against Northumberland for the ravishment of this lady, the daughter of Sir John Hastings of Fenwick in the West Riding, and one of the king's wards.[78] Precisely what lay behind the incident cannot now be said. No indication has survived that the earl himself had a claim to the wardship of Elizabeth Hastings, as the heiress of one of his mesne tenants, although it is tempting to assume that this was the case; nor can we know how or why he became involved in her abduction. But the enormous fine imposed on him must have been a severe blow to his prestige. Eventually he was allowed to clear himself by the payment of £5,000 in annual instalments of 1,000 marks; the price of this arrangement to be the transfer of a large number of Percy manors in Yorkshire to feoffees (these included Empson and Dudley) to the king's use, to guarantee the payments.[79] And so a beginning was made of that royal intrusion into the Percy properties which was to be carried so much further in the next reign. We may doubt whether the pardon and remission which the earl received at the beginning of Henry VIII's reign[80] wholly healed the wounds caused by this incident.

But it is likely that the earl was most embittered by his complete exclusion from the great offices which his father had held. He was sworn to the council on reaching his majority, and placed on the commission of the peace for the counties where his estates lay; he served on commissions of sewers, and of oyer and terminer; and he was made steward and constable of Knaresborough lordship and castle. But, apart from two unsupported assertions made in Hall's chronicle,[81] there is no evidence that he ever held for any significant

a gentleman of the Privy Chamber to Edward VI. See *Select Cases in the Star Chamber*, ed. J. S. Leadam, (Selden Soc., xvi, London, 1903), pp. cxiv–cxx; 95–105.

78 See W. C. Richardson, *Tudor Chamber Administration, 1485–1547* (Baton Rouge, 1952), p. 150.

79 Bean, *The Estates of the Percy Family*, p. 143.

80 *L.P.*, i (1), 414 (58).

81 Hall's chronicle says that the earl was made warden of the Marches *ad hoc* when in 1503 he accompanied Princess Margaret on her marriage journey to Scotland

period of time either the royal lieutenancy through which the fourth earl had ruled Yorkshire, or any of the March wardenries which had come to be regarded as almost a patrimonial dignity of the house of Percy. Henry VII seems to have hoped to turn the young nobleman into a courtier, and to have cast him for the role of a satellite obediently circling around the Tudors and their affairs. The marriage which the king arranged for his ward was significant, because this made him a relative of the royal house. The new countess of Northumberland, Catherine Spencer, daughter of Sir Robert Spencer of Spencercombe in Devon, was, like the king's mother (who was her great-aunt), of the house of Beaufort, and great-great-granddaughter of John of Gaunt.[82] And then there were the many ceremonial duties which the earl was called upon to perform particularly on Tudor family occasions, but also on occasions of state. He bore a rod of gold, for example, at the creation of Prince Henry as duke of York in 1494,[83] and in 1503 accompanied Princess Margaret on her marriage journey to Scotland.[84] In 1507 and 1508 he was sent on the embassy to negotiate a marriage between Princess Mary and the Archduke Charles,[85] and as late as 1525 he was inexorably called into service to carry a duke's robe of estate at the creation of the duke of Richmond.[86] In addition, he attended Henry VII at his meeting with the Archduke Philip in 1500,[87] and in 1520 was present at the Field of the Cloth of Gold, where he was a judge of the lists.[88]

All these duties no doubt constituted marks of the king's favour towards the earl, and were routine in the life of a great nobleman; but they also gave symbolic expression to the kind of unconditional obedience and subordination which the Tudor rulers expected from

(Edward Hall, *The Union of . . . York and Lancaster . . .* , ed. H. Ellis (London, 1809), p. 498); he also states that Northumberland was made warden of "the whole marches" in 14 Henry VIII (1522/3) but that he made suit to be discharged of the office, and the earl of Surrey was appointed in his place (*ibid.*, pp. 651–2). Although these appointments are not confirmed by any other source, there is nothing unlikely about either. See below, p. 81.

82 G.E.C. *et al.*,*Complete Peerage*, ix, p. 720.

83 *Letters and Papers . . . of the Reigns of Richard III and Henry VII*, ed. J. Gairdner, 2 vols. (Rolls Series, 1861–3), i, p. 392.

84 Hall, *loc. cit.*

85 T. Rymer, *Foedera*, 20 vols. (London, 1704–35), xiii, pp. 177, 238.

86 *L.P.*, iv (1), 1431 (8).

87 *Chronicle of Calais*, ed. J. G. Nichols (Camden Soc., London, xxxv, 1846).

88 *L.P.*, iii, pp. 313, 326.

the great lords. At the same time, however, there must have been something infuriating about them to a man who was refused the power and dignity his family had in the past enjoyed under the crown. And a note of exasperation is struck in Northumberland's letter in May 1517 to the earl of Shrewsbury, seeking mitigation of the duty which had been placed on him to conduct the queen dowager of Scotland from York to Newburgh. "My lord", wrote the earl, "methinks I nede not be put to this business if they would have pondered the charge that they have of late put upon me, and the payments I have made of late."[89] Perhaps King Henry VII, and his heir after him, may have hoped that the Percy energies could find sufficient outlet in conspicuous expenditure, and in the life of a rich and cultured nobleman. The earl's "magnificence", at any rate, dazzled amongst others the chronicler Hall, and he can also claim some credit as a patron of learning and the arts.[90] All this however would be unlikely to sweeten the bitter flavour of disrepute which clung to the unemployed magnate. Hall's words about the reaction of Northumberland's own country to the earl's supposed refusal of the warden-generalship of the Marches in 1523 would also describe the effect on his following of tame acquiescence in exclusion from the dignities due to his name. "For refusing this office", Hall wrote, "the earl of Northumberland was not regarded of his owne tenaunts, which disdained him and his blode, and much lamented

[89] *Ibid.*, ii (2), 3278, printed in Edmund Lodge's *Illustrations of British History*, 3 vols. (London, 1838), i, p. 25. The "charge" and "payments" to which the earl refers arose probably from his examination before the Council, and his committal to the Fleet in the previous year.

[90] But the title of "magnificent" so often applied to the earl goes no further back than Brydges edition of Collins's *Peerage* (Arthur Collins, *Peerage of England*, ed. Sir S. E. Brydges, London, 1812), and seems to have arisen from the impression made by his *Household Book*, and the comments on this made by Bishop Percy in his edition of 1777. A reference in Hall (*op. cit.*, p. 498), a Dodsworth MS. ("Equipage of the . . . Earl of Northumberland at the siege of Turwen in France", printed in Grose's *Antiquarian Repertory*, iv, p. 346), and the herald John Younge's account of "The Fyancells of Margaret eldest daughter of King Henry VII to James King of Scotland" (John Leland, *De rebus Britannicus collectanea*, ed. Thomas Hearne, 6 vols., Oxford, 1815, iv, p. 271) are also often quoted to illustrate the "magnificence" of his dress and accoutrements and those of his followers. It is unlikely however that Northumberland was exceptional in his expenditure on personal display or on his household as compared with other noblemen of similar wealth and status, like the duke of Buckingham, and there is no evidence to confirm the common opinion that the earl impoverished himself by his extravagance (Bean, *Estates of the Percy Family*, pp. 135–43). For the earl's cultural interests see below, pp. 83 ff.

his chivalrie."[91] The situation was one which it was not possible for a nobleman of Northumberland's standing and background to tolerate indefinitely.

IV

In these circumstances the earl was drawn into two courses of action, one of which was unsuccessful, and indeed almost, if not quite, disastrous; while the other brought a persistent and steady pressure to bear on the crown, which eventually resulted (but only after his death) in a surrender to the Percy claims. The first course consisted of an alliance with his brother-in-law, the duke of Buckingham, and other discontented magnates to bring pressure on the government, and to exploit the relaxed political climate which followed the death of Henry VII. The earl's objectives at this time are probably accurately outlined in some indiscreet statements made by his servants towards the end of 1509, which Lord Darcy reported to the government.[92] One of these was "that if their lord [Northumberland] had not room in the north as his father had before him, it should not long be well"; the other that "my lord of Buckingham should be protector of England, and that their master should rule all from Trent north, and have Berwick and the Marches". And a reference to Rhys ap Thomas in the same report suggests the same kind of alignment between Wales, the Welsh Marches (where so much of Buckingham's power lay), and the north as had threatened the rule of of Henry IV a century before.

But it is unlikely that all this amounted to much more than talk. Buckingham lacked the resolution, the resources, and a wide enough basis of support to be a serious threat to the government. As he himself is reported to have said, "It would do well enough if the noblemen durst break their minds together, but some of them mistrusteth, and feareth to break their minds to other, and that marreth all."[93] Nor could Northumberland rely on the united support of the north, where the Neville interest presided over by Lord Darcy resisted Percy leadership, and where Lord Dacre was allied to the

91 Hall, *Union of . . . York and Lancaster* (1809 edition), pp. 651–2.
92 *L.P.*, i (1), 157. Darcy's informant was Sir Edward Radcliffe, who as the earl's steward in Northumberland must have had many opportunities to spy on the Percy household.
93 *Ibid.*, iii (1), p. cxxx.

crown. Probably, in fact, the most important result of the earl's association with the duke was that by it he incurred the distrust and therefore disfavour of Henry VIII. This finds expression, for example, in an undated letter to Wolsey, in which the king instructed the cardinal, "I wolde you shoulde make good watche on the duke of Suffolke, on the duke of Buckingham, on my lorde of Northe Omberland, on my lord of Darby, on my lord of Wylshere, and others which you think suspect . . . "[94] Polydore Vergil says that Wolsey deliberately incensed Henry against Northumberland because he saw the earl as Buckingham's principal supporter, who needed to be neutralized before Buckingham himself could safely be struck down; and he adds that the cardinal stirred up another quarrel between earl and crown over an abducted ward to bring the former into deeper discredit.[95] Probably it was in connection with this matter that in 1516 Northumberland was examined before Star Chamber, and committed to a brief imprisonment in the Fleet.[96]

But it is likely that the confrontation which took place in 1516 between the king and Northumberland[97] in due course brought about a change of heart in the latter which finds expression in the symbol and verses referred to above,[98] which were drawn and written sometime between 1516 and 1523. Perhaps Henry, at the interview he had with the earl in May 1516, upon his release from the Fleet, may have brought to bear the charm and graciousness at which he was so expert when occasion demanded, so that his "leight benevolent" caused Northumberland's "cor to relent". At any rate, when Buckingham was attainted and went to his death in 1521, Wolsey himself absolved the earl of any suspicion of collusion with the fallen magnate.[99] Thereafter, outwardly at any rate, his demeanour was that of the model Henrician courtier, submissive and deferential in his approaches to both king and cardinal. The speech which Cavendish[100] put into his mouth when he reproved his

94 *Ibid.*, iii (1), 1. The letter is calendared under 1519.

95 *Anglica Historia*, ed. D. Hay (Camden Soc., lxxiv, London, 1950, p. 264).

96 *L.P.*, ii (1), 1836, 1861, 1870.

97 *Ibid.*, 1861, 1893.

98 Pp. 63–4.

99 *L.P.*, iii (1), 1293. Holinshed's statement that the earl was in fact imprisoned at the same time as Buckingham must therefore be regarded as extremely dubious (*Chronicle*, London, 1585, iii, p. 855).

100 George Cavendish, *The Life and Death of Cardinal Wolsey*, ed. R. S. Sylvester (Early English Text Soc., original ser., ccxliii, 1959, pp. 32–4). The following extract from the earl's speech, for example, suggests the practised Henrician courtier: "Therefore what Ioy, what Comfort, what pleasure or solace shold I

heir for his indiscreet attachment to Anne Boleyn, with its emphasis on the self-effacement, devotion and gratitude to the king, may well reflect an actual mastery of the Henrician court idiom which the earl had achieved by the end of his life.

Northumberland, then, gained little from his association with Buckingham, and if we are to assess his quality as a politician we must look elsewhere, at the earl's own country, rather than at the court. For it was the earl's chief preoccupation throughout his life to conserve and strengthen the Percy influence there, and to prove that the north, and particularly the Marches, could not be ruled without its support. Because, although the policies of Henry VII, and of Wolsey after him, had made the crown a factor to be reckoned with even in the remote societies of Yorkshire and the Marches, here the tension between king and Percy had not yet been conclusively resolved in favour of the former, and the earl still had large reserves of strength on which he could draw. There was the obvious fact of his great estates, whose resources enabled him to command a patronage second only to that of the king himself. Few of the gentry of Yorkshire, Northumberland, and Cumberland could afford to despise the lucrative leases and offices, and the place and power, which could come their way through the Percy service. Then there was the military importance which those same estates commanded. The Percy tenants, mustered under their officers, were, as has been seen above,[101] an essential component of the defence of the Marches, and also constituted an important reservoir from which the king could recruit a sufficient force of the tough northern light horse for his campaigns abroad. Henry VIII's wars, both on the Border and in France, must have tended to underline the earl's role as one of the leading northern warlords, and the military patronage which they put at his disposal must have helped to

conceyve in the that thus w[t]out discession or advisement hast mysused thy self havying no maner of regard to me thy naturall father, ne inespecyall vnto thy soverayn lord to whome all honest and loyall subiectes berythe faythfull and humble obedyence, ne yet to the welthe of thyn owen estate but hath so onadvysedly ensured thy selfe to hir [Anne Boleyn] for whome thou hast purchased the kynges displeasure intollerable for any sibjecte to susteyn but that his grace of his mere wisdome dothe consider the lightnes of thy hed and wilfull qualities of thy person his displeasure and Indignacon were sufficient to cast me and all my posterytie in to utter subvercion and dyssolucion . . . " Cavendish says that these words were spoken in his hearing.

101 Page 60. The earl's Yorkshire lands could muster 2,280 horse and 3,953 foot; the Cumberland lands 1,030 horse and 2,011 foot (SYon House MS. A I 1a).

strengthen the ties which bound his clientele to him. So that both in the French campaign of 1513, and in the Scottish of 1523, the names of the earl's captains read almost like a roll-call of the Percy following.[102] Again, too much emphasis cannot be placed on the earl's continuous residence in his country, and the splendid household he maintained at Leconfield and Wressle. There, dining in public in the great chamber, waited on by ushers and sewers, carvers and cupbearers who were also the officers presiding over his honours, castles, and baronies,[103] the earl gave visible and ceremonial expression to the great *familia* over which he presided.

Into all this, however, as has been seen, the power of the crown had made inroads, and there had been significant defections from the Percy service to that of the king. But it was rarely possible for the crown to scatter the bounties which its patronage brought either widely enough or evenhandedly enough amongst the touchy and jealous factions into which the northern gentry were divided. Inevitably there were those who were hostile, disappointed or disillusioned, and it was these who turned hopefully to the Percy for protection and advancement. Many opportunities of this sort were put in the earl's way, for example, by the alliance which Henry VII made between the crown and Thomas Lord Dacre of Gilsland, which lasted, in spite of many stresses and strains, until the latter's death in 1525. Appointed warden of the West March in 1486, Dacre was given the wardenries of the East and Middle Marches (where he

[102] The captains of the earl's companies of demi-lances of Northumberland, Cumberland and Yorkshire in the French campaign of 1513 included Sir John Normanville and Sir John Notham of Scorborough in Yorkshire; John Lamplugh, lieutenant of the Percy honour of Cockermouth in Cumberland, and Cuthbert Musgrave, the earl's feodary in the same county; Roger Lascelles of Brakenborough, deputy-steward of the earl's lordship of Topcliffe in Yorkshire; John Heron of Chipchase, constable of Warkworth castle; George Swinburne, constable of Alnwick castle; and Thomas Errington, constable of Langley castle in Northumberland. When the earl mustered his Yorkshire tenants in 1523 in readiness for service against Scotland the following Yorkshire gentry brought retinues to serve under him: Sir John Hotham of Scorborough; Sir Ralph Salvin of Newbiggin; William Thwaites "from Lande of the Wolde"; Stephen Hamerton of Giggleswick; Nicholas Palmes of Naburn. On this occasion the earl's Yorkshire companies totalled 762 men, under seven captains. Of these, 170 were contributed by the monastic or crown stewardships of Holderness, Kirkbyshire, and Whitby Strand which the earl held. See Grose's *Antiquarian Repertory*, iv, pp. 346 and 351; Public Record Office, E101/531/34, "The erle of Northumberlands Retynewe at Newcastell the xxj daie of October Ao XV Regis Henrici viii".

[103] *Household Book*, pp. 53–4.

had served for some years previously as Surrey's and Lord Darcy's deputy) in 1515.[104] It was in the latter two offices, into which Northumberland was divided, that Dacre (whether as warden, lieutenant or deputy) could never make himself at home. He had some following amongst the thieves and small squires of the north Tyne, and the barony of Morpeth which he had acquired by his Greystoke marriage gave him a territorial base in the Middle March. But he was disliked and distrusted by the Northumberland gentry, who saw him as the outsider and upstart who had stepped into the Percy's shoes.[105]

In particular, almost from the start of his attempt to rule the easternmost Marches, Dacre ran into trouble with the powerful Heron clan, whose head, Sir William Heron, from his castle at Ford, commanded a large influence and wide estates close to the Border.[106] Most of this arose from the simple fact that the Herons, like the Percies, were excluded from the March offices which they conceived theirs by right. Sir Roger Heron, William's father, had been lieutenant of the East and Middle Marches during the wardenry of the fourth earl of Northumberland, whose fee'd man he was.[107] John Heron, Sir William's elder brother, had been appointed to the same office in 1494,[108] and Sir William himself had held the lieutenancy of the Middle March in 1500.[109] Probably the Percy connection is a sufficient explanation for the unwillingness of the government subsequently to entrust Herons with the rule of the Marches, and they were passed over in favour of Fenwicks, Widdringtons, and Radcliffes, or even of outsiders like Sir William Eure or Sir William Bulmer. It was not until 1523 that Sir William Heron was appointed even to the subordinate office of keeper of Redesdale.[110] The result was to breed in the Herons an intense

104 Public Record Office, E10/72/1062; *L.P.*, iv (2), 3119.

105 See below, pp. 97 ff., 142 ff.

106 For the Herons of Ford, see *Northumberland County History*, xi (Newcastle upon Tyne, 1922), pp. 369 ff.

107 *L.P.*, iv (1), 1460; in his will (Surtees Soc., xlv, Durham and London, 1865, p. 304), the fourth earl provided that John Heron, son and heir of Sir Roger Heron of Ford, should receive his father's fee and annuity.

108 *Calendar of Documents Relating to Scotland . . . 1547–1603*, ed. Joseph Bain, 9 vols. (Edinburgh, 1898–1915), iv, p. 418.

109 *Ibid.*, p. 333.

110 Heron had been appointed to this office by October 1523, when he led the men of Redesdale on one of Surrey's raids into Scotland (*L.P.*, iii (2), 3381). It must

hatred of government and its agents, which had the same anarchic violence of tone as Sir William Lisle's. When in 1525 royal commissioners were sent into the north to recruit retinues for service with the king in France, these were scandalized by Sir William Heron's behaviour. He attended them in Newcastle "in a froward manner, rather like a quarrel then otherwise", and "said openly 'the lieutenants undoys the countrie', with divers other froward wordes, and if his power [i.e. his retinue] had been better than ours, further trouble had been like to have growen emongs us".[111] But such trouble-makers were all grist to the Percy mill, and long before Sir William Lisle had held that office, the fifth earl by 1514 had made Heron his constable of Alnwick castle,[112] so greatly increasing his capacity to disrupt the organization of the Marches.

Sir William's distant relative Sir John Heron of Chipchase in Tynedale[113] was another important Percy ally. From Chipchase, Heron exercised a wide influence amongst the reivers and thieves of the north Tyne. Like Sir William Lisle in Redesdale, he was the obvious person to mediate between the lawless Tyne upland and the larger and more settled world of the lowland. Yet for many years he was excluded from the keepership of Tynedale, which he regarded as his by right; and, since Lord Dacre competed with him for the trust and favours of the Tynedale clans, this gave a sharper edge to Heron's hatred of him. But his relations with the Percies were good. The earl made him constable of Warkworth castle, and he in due course succeeded Sir William Heron as constable of Alnwick.[114] Heron was a character of the same cut as Sir William Lisle, although to the latter's boldness and violence he could add cunning and treachery; and his rule at Warkworth was mainly remarkable for the oppressions and murders he and his sons committed against the

have been galling for him to serve under the "foreigner" Sir William Eure, who had been appointed lieutenant of the Middle March in the same year.

111 *L.P.*, iv (1), 1289; *Northumberland County History*, xi (Newcastle upon Tyne, 1922), pp. 385–6.

112 Syon House MS. C III 5a, Account of George Swinburne, Receiver in Northumberland, 1519, specifies Sir William Heron as constable of Alnwick castle, 6 Henry VIII.

113 For the Herons of Chipchase see *Northumberland County History*, iv (2) (Newcastle upon Tyne, 1897), p. 340.

114 Sir John Heron was constable of Alnwick castle in 1519, and probably graduated to the office in that year from Warkworth: Syon House MS. C III 5a; *Northumberland County History*, v (Newcastle upon Tyne, 1899), p. 54.

unfortunate tenants.[115] Still, he was well qualified to make trouble, and to bring home to the government that the Marches could not be ruled without the earl of Northumberland.

There were other Percy allies, like the Swinburnes of Capheaton, whose head William Swinburne was the earl's bailiff of Corbridge;[116] his relative George Swinburne of Edlingham was the Percy receiver in Northumberland,[117] whose daughter was married to one of Sir John Heron's sons. Thus the earl had given his countenance to this powerful kinship grouping whose hostility to Dacre made them more than ready to disrupt his rule and to open the way to a Percy restoration. This was a state of affairs which had particularly dangerous implications in time of war, when the warden could never be sure of the support of the Percy power and the Percy allies either for the defence of the frontier or for his "rodes" into Scotland. As early as 1513 Dacre complained that the gentry were "backward" in joining the foray into Scotland he had made at the beginning of the winter, and cited the constable of Alnwick (with Lord Ogle) as particularly remiss in this respect.[118] In the next year he reported that Sir William Heron, now that he had entered the Percy service, refused to serve under him.[119] There was more trouble in the Scottish campaigns of 1523 and 1524, when the Herons and Swinburnes again refused to join the warden's "rodes";[120] and there was friction between Sir William Percy, the earl's brother, and Dacre, Percy complaining of the disproportionate burdens placed on the earl's tenants, and even making charges of betrayal to the Scots during Dacre's raid on Kelso.[121] In peacetime matters were not much better, since the Percy faction sabotaged Dacre's intermittent attempts to enforce March law and suppress banditry, besides exploiting the warden's contacts with the border reivers to discredit him with the government. Thus there

[115] *L.P.*, iii (2), 1920.

[116] William Swinburne was one of the earl's servants in 1509, and was bailiff of Corbridge in 1523 (Syon House MSS. C III 2a; C III 5b).

[117] Three of his accounts survive amongst the Syon House MSS., C III 2a; C III 5a; and C III 5b. For his pedigree see *Northumberland County History*, vii (Newcastle upon Tyne, 1904), p. 132.

[118] *L.P.*, i (2), 2443; the constable was then John Swinhoe, Sir William Heron's predecessor.

[119] J. Raine, *The History and Antiquities of North Durham* (London, 1812), p. vii.

[120] *L.P.*, iv (1), 278.

[121] *Ibid.*, iii (2), 2402, 3100, 3110, 3603.

were complaints from the Northumberland gentry in 1518, and again in 1524,[122] that Dacre was hand-in-glove with thieves, and on the latter occasion the warden, involved in an acrimonious correspondence with Wolsey, was called up to London to explain himself. And so, while these factions prevailed in the easternmost Marches, their defence was precarious, and even a semblance of law and order could scracely be maintained within them. Men's minds turned increasingly as a result to the Percy as alone able to keep the East and Middle Marches.

In fact, it was a group of gentry associated with the service of the crown which first proposed (in 1523) that Dacre should be displaced, and "some great and discreet nobleman" should be made warden of the East and Middle Marches, "to live in the country, and keep all men to their duty".[123] We cannot be certain that the "nobleman" was the earl of Northumberland, but it is unlikely that these experienced borderers would have considered a magnate without lands and following in the Marches as capable of ruling them, and the circumstances make it improbable that they could have had any other in mind.[124] Perhaps Northumberland (if we are to believe Hall) was in fact offered, but refused, the warden-generalship of "the whole Marches" at this time, having already in 1522 been appointed a member of Shrewsbury's council as lieutenant of the north.[125] It may be that the earl now felt that he was strong enough to bargain with the king, and was dissatisfied with the terms on which he had been offered office. From this point of view Sir William Lisle's appointment as constable of Alnwick a little later was significant.[126] In this tempestuous Borderer the Percy interest acquired a new and powerful ally, and a most effective means of bringing further pressure on the government. Such policies explain the disfavour into which the earl again fell towards the end of his

[122] *Ibid.*, ii (2), 4452; iv (1), 682. See below, pp. 98, 143.

[123] *L.P.*, iii (2), 3286. The gentry were Sir William Eure, Sir John Widdrington, Cuthbert Radcliffe, John Horsley, and Lionel Grey.

[124] Noblemen without lands and following on the Borders tended to be failures as wardens, at any rate in time of peace, when there was no royal army on hand to support their authority. The earl of Cumberland in the West March, as well as the earl of Westmorland in the East and Middle, both appointed on the death of Thomas Lord Dacre in 1525, were unsuccessful deputy wardens for this reason.

[125] Hall's *Chronicle* (ed. Ellis, 1809 edn), pp. 651–2; *L.P.*, iii (2), 2412.

[126] See above, p. 60.

life,[127] and make the circumstances of his death more comprehensible.[128] He and his followers had, in fact, sabotaged the Tudor policy of excluding the house of Percy from the rule of the Marches. The success of the earl's proceedings became patent after Dacre's death in 1525, when the slow crumbling of good order which characterized his rule broke into chaos as Sir William Lisle rampaged across Northumberland on his missions of violence and vengeance. The earl of Westmorland, appointed as vice-warden,[129] was no more able to control the situation than his lieutenants Eure and Bulmer, and, although there was still no hint that the head of the house of Percy should be given office on the Border, the appointment of his heir as warden of the East and Middle Marches, first mooted in 1523,[130] now became increasingly inevitable, and indeed (as has been seen) transpired towards the end of 1527.[131] The fifth earl died in disfavour and without having achieved the offices he regarded as his right; but he must also have been aware that he had opened the way for the restoration of the greatness of his family in the person of his son.

[127] Suggested, for example, by Henry VIII's quick suspicion on hearing a report that the earl and his retinue had worn the device of "the cross keys" on the Border in 1523. The cross keys were the arms of the see of York, and the king seems to have feared that Northumberland had taken Wolsey's livery as archbishop. Wolsey hastily wrote to say that the earl had not in fact borne the device (*L.P.*, iii (2), 3563). Towards the end of 1526 the earl was in trouble with the duke of Richmond's council, which proposed to examine witnesses relative to his indictment as accessory (with one James Dryland as principal) as soon as Wolsey set down the writ of *certiorari* (*L.P.*, iv (2), 2729). What the matter was cannot now be ascertained, beyond that Dryland was a member of a family which had claims on the lands of Sir Edward Poynings (see *Cal. Inq. Post Mortem, Henry VII*, iii, no. 131) a large part of which had reverted to the earl in 1521 (Bean, *The Estates of the Percy Family*, p. 126). Perhaps therefore some dispute over property was involved. What is interesting is Wolsey's quick interest in the earl's affairs; he wrote to the Council on 29 Nov. 1526 directing them "how to treat the earl of Northumberland and his causes".

[128] See above, pp. 57 ff.

[129] He is referred to as such in January 1527; by then he had probably held the office for a year (*L.P.*, iv (2), 2801).

[130] There are references in Surrey's letters to Wolsey in Sept. 1523 to a decision taken to make Lord Percy warden (*L.P.*, iii (2), 3321, 3365), perhaps with Lord Dacre as his deputy. The decision was never implemented, but was perhaps motivated by Northumberland's refusal to become warden himself; no doubt too, it was reasonable to suppose that the heir, brought up in Wolsey's household, would be more submissive than his father.

[131] Above, pp. 59–60.

V

The fifth earl owes most of his reputation as a cultivated nobleman to Bishop Percy, who in his preface to the *Household Book* asserted that "He appears to have had a great passion for literature, and was a liberal patron of such genius as that age produced."[132] Percy's evidence for the earl's literary enthusiasms came principally from the splendid manuscript preserved in the British Library (Roy. MS. 18 D ii) to which reference has already been made, and which is the most impressive of the two known survivals from his library.[133] The bishop also referred with approval to the "remarkable provision" made in the *Household Book* that the earl's almoner should be "a maker of Interludys".[134] Warton, following in Percy's footsteps, maintained that the earl "loved literature", and "was the general patron of such genius as his age produced. He encouraged Skelton, almost the only professed poet of the reign of Henry VII, to write an elegy on the death of his father, which is still extant."[135] Thus the way was opened for a later panegyrist of the earl's literary good taste to state that he had also been Lydgate's patron, in spite of the fact that this poet had died long before the earl was born.[136] Warton also noted (from information supplied to him by Percy) that the earl had endowed a teacher of grammar and philosophy at Alnwick abbey, and added "His cultivation of the arts of external elegance appears from the stately sepulchral monuments which he erected in the minster . . . of Beverley in Yorkshire, to the memory of his father and mother; which are executed in the richest style of the florid Gothic architecture, and remain to this day, the conspicuous and striking evidence of his taste and magnificence."[137]

Probably, however, the earl's enthusiasm for the arts, just like his

132 1827 edn, p. xxi.

133 The other is Bodleian Library MS. 3356 which consists principally of Hardyng's "Chronicle of England", in a hand of *c.* 1464, to which "The Proverbes of Lydgate upon the fall of prynces" (in a hand of *c.* 1520) has been bound. The "Chronicle" is followed by a depiction of the fifth earl's arms added sometime after 1495. The earl's addition of "The Proverbes" to this MS. suggests again his concern with the theme of "mutabilitie" discussed below.

134 *Household Book*, p. xxii.

135 Thomas Warton, *History of English Poetry*, 4 vols. (London, 1824 edn), ii, p. 164.

136 Fonblanque, *Annals of the House of Percy*, i, p. 322.

137 Warton, *loc. cit.*, pp. 165–6.

"magnificence", has been exaggerated. There is no evidence, for example, that he patronized Skelton. This poet did, it is true, write an elegy, prefaced by Latin couplets in which he offered the young earl his service, on the "dolorous dethe" of his murdered father. But it is unlikely that the earl should have "encouraged" him to do this, since he was then a boy of only twelve years of age. If there was any encouragement, it is more likely to have come from Dr William Rukshaw, vicar of Topcliffe, and one of the earl's trustees. A man of considerable learning, he must have known the fourth earl well, and been aware of the circumstances of his death; it was to him that Skelton dedicated his verses.[138] Subsequently the name of the earl of Northumberland appears only once, and then not in a particularly flattering context, in the whole corpus of Skelton's writings.[139] Nor are there any facts which suggest that the earl patronized other prominent literary figures of his day. His name can be linked only with his secreatry William Peeris,[140] who wrote the verse Percy-family chronicle bound into Roy. MS. 18 D ii, and with the musician and poet William Cornyshe, one of whose works is included in the same manuscript.[141] Thus the earl's record as a patron of the arts is meagre, and cannot be compared with the princely patronage exercised, for example, by the Howard household, which had a long connection not only with Skelton but also with Barclay and William Roy.[142] It is probably not coincidental, however, that the earl's literary contacts, such as they were, brought him into touch with men of

[138] For the text of Skelton's elegy, see his *Works*, ed. A. Dyce, 2 vols. (London, 1843), i, p. 6. For William Rukshaw, see T. A. Walker, *Biographical Index of Peterhouse Men* (Cambridge, 1912), pt. 1, pp. 56–7; A. B. Emden, *Biographical Register of the University of Cambridge to 1500* (Cambridge, 1963), p. 493.

[139] The mention occurs in Skelton's vituperative attack on Wolsey, *Why come ye not to Courte*, written in 1522:

> The Erle of Northumberland
> Dare take nothynge on hande:
> Our barons be so bolde,
> Into a mouse hole they wolde
> Rynne away and crepe
> Like a mayny of shepe . . .

See *Works*, ii, p. 36.

[140] Nothing is certainly known about Peeris, except that he was a priest, and the earl's secretary.

[141] This is "A parable betwene enformacon and musike", bound into the MS. between *The Siege of Thebes* and Skelton's elegy.

[142] See Skelton's *Magnyficence*, ed. Robert Lee Ramsay (Early English Text Soc., extra ser., xcviii, London, 1906), intro., pp. cxxvi–cxxviii.

the literary opposition. Skelton was the "laureate of the nobles",[143] and his bitter political satires directed against Wolsey's régime are well known. Cornyshe, too, had his quarrel with Wolsey, and, if tradition is to be believed, was imprisoned for a satire against Sir Richard Empson.[144] Similarly, the local and family orientation of so much of the earl's expenditure on the arts suggests again the concern for prestige and power in his own "country" which also marked his political approach. The stately chantry at Beverley, the endowment of grammar and rhetoric at Alnwick abbey, the maker of interludes to amuse the assembled household, and Peeris's verse chronicle all attest the setting in which the earl particularly wished his family and himself to be associated with splendour, learning, revelry and antiquity.

But even if the earl was not outstanding as a patron of literature, there can be no doubt that he had definite literary tastes and preferences. These find expression in the verse and prose items bound together in the British Library Percy manuscript,[145] some of which come close to the earl as a man, and to his personal preoccupations. The core of the manuscript consists of Lydgate's *Siege of Thebes* and *Troy Book*, which had belonged to the first Herbert earl of Pembroke, and which had come to Northumberland from his Herbert mother. Evidently the earl enjoyed Lydgate's epic romances, since he took the trouble to fill in the blank miniature spaces which remained in the unfinished manuscript which he inherited, employing a good artist of the Flemish School for this purpose. Apart from the skill and liveliness of Skelton's narrative, he may well have particularly relished the poet's strictures on the "faithless" king whose unwillingness to keep his word brought such disasters on Thebes, as well as his condemnation of tyrannical rule. And at a deeper level the theme of Fortune's mutability to which Lydgate gave expression in the *Troy Book* seems to have been one which the earl found particularly appealing, as will appear below.

143 *Ibid.*, p. cxxv.

144 See *Dict. Nat. Biog.* and Sir G. Grove, *Dictionary of Music and Musicians*, ed. E. Blom, 5th edn, 9 vols., 11 (1954), p. 452. For his satire or ballad against Empson, see *The Great Chronicle of London*, ed. A. H. Thomas and I. D. Thornley (London, 1938), pp. 344–7, and p. 454. "A parable betwene enformacon and musike" was, as its heading states, composed by Cornyshe in the Fleet prison.

145 The contents of Roy. MS. 18 D ii are fully described in Sir G. F. Warner and J. P. Gilson, *Catalogue of Western MSS. in the Old Royal and King's Collections*, 4 vols. (London, 1921), ii, p. 309.

To these works the earl had bound two other Lydgate poems, the *Testament* and *The Assembly of Gods*. The emotive Christo-centric piety of the former suggests the process whereby devotions originally devised for the cloister were infiltrating into the lives of the literate laity; the latter, on the other hand, is more mundane and matter-of-fact in tone, and aims at conveying a corpus of doctrine and divinity through the medium of allegory and narrative.

We come closer, however, to the events of the earl's own lifetime when we turn from the histories of Thebes and Troy to that of his own family, written sometime between 1516 and 1523, in lumbering broken-backed verse by William Peeris, the earl's secretary, who presented it to his master as a New Year's gift.[146] The Percy history, however, is set in context by the two items which precede it in the manuscript. First of all the background of Christendom is suggested by a book of "The armes of certeyne kyngis cristanyde, blasyde and translatyde oute of latyn to inglyshe as hereaftere folowethe."[147] The first "blasyorre" was of the city of Jerusalem, with its "sylver a crosse potonce between iiij crosslettis golde", and the Christian potentates included the Three Kings of Cologne, Prester John, and "the Emperor of Constantobyll". Here the earl was drawn into a romantic view of a past, crusading and chivalric, in which the house of Percy-Louvain, descended from Louis IV of France, could feel thoroughly at home. Next to "The armes", however, Lydgate's "The reignes of the kingis of Englande",[148] brought down to the reign of Henry VIII by an anonymous writer, must have reminded the earl of the more uncomfortable realities of his own day. The concluding lines, addressed to Henry VIII, "God graunt to hym grace of his mercyfull benygnitie / Longe to enjoy his septure with honoure and felicitie", take up the theme of loyalty which is resumed in the emblem and verses discussed above,[149] which is the last item bound into the manuscript.

All the same, the difficulties and tensions which bedevilled relations between the Percies and the house of Tudor have left their mark on Peeris's chronicle. For example, it is plain that Henry VII's removal of the fourth earl of Northumberland in 1489

[146] Roy. MS., fos. 186–99. Peeris's Percy Chronicle has been edited, with some omissions, by John Besley (Newcastle upon Tyne, 1845).
[147] *Ibid.*, fos. 183–5.
[148] *Ibid.*, fos. 181–3.
[149] *Ibid.*, fo. 200; see above, p. 60

from the captaincy of Berwick (conferred again on a Percy only for a brief period in Mary's reign) was still remembered as a grievance by the family. Peeris put the Percy case against the encroachments of the crown when he claimed in his chronicle that Berwick castle had originally been a part of the Percy inheritance, and that it had come into the hands of the king only because the first earl of Northumberland had made a gift of it to Edward III. Therefore "the heires of the Pearcies by lineall descent" ought "of right title and Justice evident" to be constables of the great stronghold which was the key to the eastern Borders.[150] A sense of injustice at the earl's exclusion from the offices his ancestors had held here peers through the lumbering verses. Another sensitive and still topical theme was the assassination of the fifth earl's father in 1489 by the commons at Thirsk, which is recounted at length not only in Peeris's chronicle, but in Skelton's *Elegy* as well, the only surviving manuscript of which is also bound into Roy. MS. 18 D ii.[151] The incident had many sinister overtones.[152] Henry VII had much to gain from the death of the fourth earl, which left his heir a ward in the hands of the crown, and it is a remarkable fact that the assassination was committed by a royal officer, one of the foresters of Galtres forest. And not only was the murdered man abandoned by his retinue, but also one of his relatives, Sir John Egremont, was involved in the disturbances which followed the earl's death. Nevertheless he appears to have been subsequently pardoned (in spite of his supposed Yorkist affiliations) and even received grants of Percy lands. if the young fifth earl was aware of these circumstances (and it will be seen that he was warned), the years of his youth could scarcely have been happy or secure, or calculated to reconcile Percy and Tudor; and, since these were followed by a lifetime of disfavour, it is not surprising that his approach to men and affairs should have been sceptical and pessimistic. And so he became particularly drawn to the themes of "mutabilitie" and of Fortune's fickleness. These, it will be seen, are well represented amongst the items in his book.

This then was the sinister happening which stirred Peeris into something like eloquence. Apart from his horror at the "detestable"

[150] *Ibid.*, fo. 192.

[151] For Peeris's account see *ibid.*, fo. 194.

[152] For a discussion of the circumstances of the earl's assassination, see M. E. James, "The Murder at Cocklodge, 28th April, 1489" (*Durham University Jl*, March 1965), pp. 80 ff.

crime of the commons against their "naturall Lorde", his main emphasis is on the abandonment of the fourth earl by his retinue, "those to whom he gave fees, and was right speciall lord", who fled, leaving their master to the mercy of his enemies. He concludes, "There was some privie treason, the truth to record".[153] Peeris drives home the point that treachery had been behind the assassination. Skelton does the same, although with a greater degree of literary elegance and sophistication than Peeris could achieve. Like Peeris he denounced the earl's servants and retinue for their abandonment of their master, and raised again the accusation of treachery in the dead earl's household. He explained the commons' crime against their natural lord by the use of the dichotomy of "will" versus "wit", the revolt of arrogant impulse against the restraints of reason, which he employed elsewhere in his political satires. But he also put the earl's death at Fortune's door. The earl had prospered till "fykkel Fortune began on hym to frowne" and "Tyll the chaunce ran agayne hym of Fortunes duble dyse".[154] And the theme of Fortune recurs in the Latin elegiac couplets addressed to the murdered nobleman's heir, with which Skelton prefaced his poem. It was in these that the poet warned the young earl, the "lion" to whom he sent his verses, of the perils which now surrounded him.

> Ast ubi perlegit, dubiam sub mente volutet
> Fortunam, cuncta quae malefida rotat
> Qui leo sit felix, et Nestoris occupet annos;
> Ad libitum cujus ipse paratus ero.[155]

"But when he has read them [Skelton's verses] let him consider in his mind his own uncertain fortune, surrounded as it is by treachery in all its forms. May the Lion be lucky, and may he attain Nestor's years . . . " And the poet concludes with the offer of his service. From his boyhood, then, the fifth earl learnt of the uncertainties of Fortune, as well as of the perils which confronted him as head of the house of Percy. Skelton has driven home the lesson in another couplet which he placed at the end of his elegy.

> Non sapit, humanis qui certam ponere rebus
> Spem cupit; est hominum raraque ficta fides.[156]

[153] Roy. MS. 18 D ii, fo. 194.
[154] *Ibid.*, fo. 166; *Works*, i, p. 11.
[155] *Ibid.*, fo. 165; *Works*, i, p. 6.
[156] *Ibid.*, fo. 166; *Works*, i, p. 14.

The lines were a play on the Percy motto, *esperaunce ma comforte*, in which the earl was warned not to place his hope in men; it was only rarely that they kept faith, and their loyalty could not be relied upon.

But Skelton's concern with Fortune's fickleness and men's unreliability is also echoed in those "Proverbis" painted on the walls and ceilings of the earl's houses at Leconfield and Wressle whose text was bound into his manuscript next to Peeris's chronicle.[157] Perhaps the most significant of these are "The proverbis in the rooffe of the hyest chawmbre in the gardynge at Lekingfelde" which, like Skelton's couplet, treat of hope, and use the Percy motto as a refrain, but with a significant difference. The fifth earl changed his father's *esperaunce ma comforte* into *esperaunce en dieu*,[158] and around this device a poem was constructed which sought a religious resolution of the tension between hope and fortune, faith and fickleness, which had been Skelton's theme. The first dozen lines catch the essence of the work:[159]

Esperaunce en dyeu
Trust hym he is moste trewe.

En dieu esperaunce.
In hym put thyne affiaunce.

Esperaunce in the worlde nay.
The worlde variethe every day.

Esperaunce in riches nay not so.
Riches slidethe and sone will go.

Esperaunce in exaltation of honoure.
Nay it widderethe away lyke a floure.

[157] Fos. 201–5. The text of the "proverbis" (their authorship is unknown) has been printed in Grose's *Antiquarian Repertory* (1809 edn), iv, pp. 338–40 and 393–421; and in *Anglia*, xiv (1891), pp. 471–97, ed. E. Flügel.

[158] This was the motto the fourth earl had carved above the doorway of the Barbican at Alnwick castle (*Household Book*, p. 461; G. R. Batho in *Archaeologia Aeliana*, 4th ser., xxxvi (1958), p. 132). The motto *esperaunce en dieu* appears in the fifth earl's arms as depicted in Bodleian Library MS. 3356. Both he and his heir however also used the shorter form *esperaunce*, at any rate on seals. See Bodleian Library Dodsworth MS. 83, fo. 36, and *Complete Peerage*, ix, p. 722, n. 6.

[159] *Antiquarian Repertory*, iv, pp. 338–9; Flügel, *op. cit.*, pp. 480–1; Roy. MS. 18 D ii, fo. 201.

Esperaunce en dieu in him is all
Which is above fortunes fall.

These are sentiments echoed so frequently in the other "proverbis" with which the earl adorned his houses, and they have such a poignant relevance to his own experience that it is difficult not to feel that here the unknown poet hit on something bound to elicit a deep response from his patron; for his poem pointed to a stability beyond the shifting political contours of the time, and the perils which confronted the earl and his family as a result of the challenging power of the Tudor state. No doubt, within a generation or so, when fashions had changed, the earl could have been equally comforted by the Stoic eudaimonia of the humanists. It was in this that his great-grandson found consolation during his long imprisonment in the Tower a century later. "A well-fashioned mind I call it", wrote the ninth earl of Northumberland in James I's reign, "when it is free from perturbations and unseemly affections . . . for the very means to quit ourselves of these ugly perturbations are to esteem nothing of the world at an over-value, for so shall we sorrow ever . . . "[160] This aristocratic detachment went well with great possessions and high rank which could survive even the displeasure of kings. But a gulf separated it from the Puritan influences which would soon be popular with many of the Tudor "new men". These rejoiced in the service of a God who was more than a refuge from, and appeal against, the course of history; and whose commands, exhortations and judgements could be seen at work in the policies and events in which they themselves were engaged. They were too involved in their tasks to sympathize with the sceptical, withdrawn attitudes which the two Percies, great-grandfather and great-grandson, each in his own way found congenial.

[160] *Advice to His Son by Henry Percy Ninth Earl of Northumberland*, ed. G. B. Harrison (London, 1930), pp. 71–2.

3. *Change and continuity in the Tudor north: Thomas first Lord Wharton*

I

Frontiers are synonymous with violence, and the barmkin, peel-tower and beacon of an earlier age have only given place to the look-out post, barbed wire and strong-point of our own day. But in the pre-industrial era, when techniques of defence and control were crude and unsophisticated, the frontier was less a line than a region, with its distinctive way of life, largely determined by the latent or open violence implied in the boundary which traversed it, where unrestrained sovereignties met. And so still, during the Tudor period, the typical frontier was a March, with its own specific characteristics marking it off from territories lying away from the exposed periphery. Such was the English Border towards Scotland.[1] It was a chain of marchlands spanning the country from sea to sea; the West March grouping together Cumberland and Westmorland, Northumberland comprised in the East and Middle Marches. North of the frontier line the Scottish East, Middle and West Marches sprawled across Berwickshire, Roxburgh, Selkirk, Peebles and Dumfries, carrying the Border region fifty miles or more into the territory of the opposite kingdom.[2]

In spite of the proximity of the frontier, the machinery of law and good rule was available in the English Marches as elsewhere in the country. Each of the Border shires had its sheriff, there were

[1] There is no general account of the Border in the early Tudor period; but much of the matter in D. L. W. Tough, *The Last Years of a Frontier: A History of the Borders during the Reign of Elizabeth* (Oxford, 1928) is relevant. See also C. M. L. Bough and G. P. Jones, *The Lake Counties 1500–1830* (Manchester, 1961) and G. M. Trevelyan, "The Middle Marches", in *Clio, A Muse and Other Essays* (London, 1930).

[2] See T. I. Rae, "Some Aspects of Border Administration in the Sixteenth Century", in *Hawick Archaeological Society Transactions* (1958).

The Marches towards Scotland in the Tudor period

justices of the peace, and assizes at Carlisle and Newcastle. But the weight of authority in each March lay with the man appointed as its warden and "governour" by the crown.[3] The warden was required to "indevor himself aswell in tyme of warre as in tyme of peas for the sure keping savegard and defence of the . . . marche and subiects of oure saide sovran lordes inhabited within the same from al maner

[3] For the warden's office see W. Nicolson, *Leges Marcharum* (London, 1747), and J. Nicolson and R. Burn, *History and Antiquities of the Counties of Westmorland and Cumberland*, 2 vols. (London, 1777), i, chs. 1, 2 and 3.

invasione roodes excursiones roberyes hereships burnynges murdours and all other violences and unlawfull attemptates of the Scottes . . . ".[4] The officers of all the lordships of the March were at the warden's command, and were required to muster the tenants at his orders to resist invasion or raidings, and to maintain a watch day and night on the frontier. In time of peace he punished breaches of March law and custom in his own court, and at the periodic "days of truce" he conferred with the warden of the opposing Scottish March, and negotiated redress for those within his jurisdiction, claiming damage at the hands of the Scots. Much of his business related to the affairs of the Border clans, those chronically violent societies inhabiting the upland dales scoring the slopes of both sides of the watershed along which the frontier ran, and which so largely lived by raiding and robbery. From one point of view the warden, as the embodiment of the king's authority, was the enemy of this whole way of life. But in practice he often had to set thieves to catch thieves, and so was often the protector of some of the "reiving" clans, at the same time as he was hunting down and punishing others accused of breaches of March law; and the tough light horse so readily available in these upland dales, which was so willing to burn and terrorize, could be a valuable reinforcement for the warden's own influence and power.

Like marches everywhere, those of England and Scotland had their Border barons, each presiding over a warlike clientele, bound together by ties of kinship and patronage. Scotland had its Lord Home, its earl of Angus, and its lairds of Cessford and Ferniehurst in the East and Middle Marches; in the West there were Johnstone and Lord Maxwell. The English magnates were fewer and more formidable. The Percy interest, headed by the earl of Northumberland, ramified through the whole length of the Border, based on great estates in Cumberland and Northumberland, centring on the castles at Cockermouth and Alnwick, and supported by vast landed wealth outside the Marches in Yorkshire and elsewhere.[5] A long roll of the leading gentry of the north were to be found serving in the Percy household; and the influence of the family had been succinctly described by a chronicler of Edward IV's reign: "The

[4] William Lord Dacre's indenture for the wardenry of the West March, 1 December, 19 Henry VIII (Public Record Office, E101/72/7).

[5] See J. M. W. Bean, *The Estates of the Percy Family, 1416–1537* (Oxford, 1958).

noble men and commons in those parties", he wrote, "were towardes th'erle of Northumberlande, and would not stir with any lord or nobleman other than the sayd earl . . . "[6] Tudor rule had eroded the earl's authority, but in Henry VIII's reign this was still unrivalled by any other of the northern magnates. The fall of the Nevilles and the annexation of so many of their estates to the crown had left the house of Percy on a lonely eminence. But the Cliffords, with extensive lands in Westmorland and Yorkshire, castles at Brough, Appleby and Brougham, and with their great stronghold at Skipton in the background, were a power in the West March.[7] And here too were the Dacres, hereditary rivals of the Cliffords, made immeasurably more formidable by the marriage of Thomas, third Lord Dacre, to the heiress of the last Lord Greystoke. This alliance had doubled the Dacre estates in Cumberland, and founded a Dacre influence in Northumberland, through the acquisition there of the barony of Morpeth.[8]

The wardens were recruited from the heads of these great families, and the Marches, if not ruled by members of the royal family, had been entrusted to Percies or Nevilles, Cliffords or Dacres as far as the memory of man could reach.[9] The wardenries had been valued partly because of the prestige and influence they conferred, and partly, until the advent of the Tudors, for the generous wages paid by the crown, and for the profits which could be made from leases of crown lordships. And, as far as the crown was concerned, since no strong and independent royal interest existed in the Marches which could confront the clienteles of the great lords, there was no alternative to the indirect rule of the latter. Not even

[6] "Historie of the Arrivall of Edward IV in Englande . . . . " (Camden Soc., xxxix, London, 1847), pp. 6–7.

[7] For the Cliffords see *Clifford Letters of the Sixteenth Century*, ed. A. G. Dickens (Surtees Soc., clxxii, Durham and London, 1962); T. D. Whitaker, *History and Antiquities of the Deanery of Craven*, 1st edn (London, 1805), p. 223; J. W. Clay, "The Clifford Family", in *Yorkshire Archaeological Jl*, ed. A. G. Dickens, xviii (1905), p. 355; R. T. Spence, *The Cliffords, Earls of Cumberland, 1576–1646* (London, Ph.D. thesis, 1959); *Complete Peerage*, iii, pp. 290 ff., 566 ff.; *Dict. Nat. Biog.*, iv, *passim*.

[8] For the third Lord Dacre see *Dict. Nat. Biog.* and *Complete Peerage*, iv, pp. 20 ff.; for the Dacre lands in the West March see Nicolson and Burn, *op. cit.*, ii, p. 351. Some account of the Greystoke family and of their lands in Northumberland is given by J. Hodgson, *History of Northumberland*, ii (2) (Newcastle upon Tyne, 1832), p. 373.

[9] See R. L. Storey in *Eng. Hist. Rev.*, lxxii, p. 593.

Henry VII was able to change this state of affairs in any basic kind of way, although there were significant developments in his reign. For example, like Richard III he kept the wardenry of the West March in his own hands, ruling it through Thomas Lord Dacre as his lieutenant. This appointment founded the alliance between this lord and the new dynasty which lasted till Dacre's death, and which helped to offset the dominant Percy influence.[10] The latter was further weakened when the king removed the fourth earl of Northumberland from the captaincy of Berwick, which he conferred on a courtier, Sir William Tyler.[11] In this respect Henry began a policy from which no Tudor subsequently deviated, which made sure that this great fortress, the gateway into England, would be in obedient and loyal hands. Other changes were made possible by the assassination of Northumberland in 1489, leaving his heir a ward in the king's hands.[12] This event broke the Percy grip on the two eastern wardenries, and for a generation enabled Henry to rule them through lieutenants, or through such a man as the newly ennobled Lord Darcy, who was both a courtier and (through his second marriage to the earl of Westmorland's mother) legatee of the Neville interest. Then in 1515 Lord Dacre was appointed warden of the West, East and Middle Marches,[13] and thereafter controlled the whole Border until his death in 1525. But Dacre did not find it easy to rule in Northumberland against the opposition of the Percy interest, and it is an index of how little had been changed that in 1527 the sixth earl of Northumberland had to be given the East and Middle wardenries because it had become clear that nobody else could govern them.[14]

The rule of law and loyalty to such a remote authority as the crown had no deep roots in the March society. What counted was blood and kin, and in the archaic communities of Redesdale, Tynedale and Coquetdale in the upland of the East and Middle Marches, and in Bewcastle and Eskdale in the West, the joint family seems to have survived until well into the Tudor period, centring on the "stronge houses" built of "great sware oke trees strongly bounde

[10] Storey, *ibid.*, pp. 608, 615.

[11] A. Conway, *Henry VII's Relations with Scotland and Ireland* (Cambridge, 1932), p. 34; *Letters of Richard Fox*, ed. P. S. and H. M. Allen (Oxford, 1929), p. 137.

[12] See R. R. Reid, *The King's Council in the North* (London, 1921), pp. 75–7.

[13] *L.P.*, ii (1), 514.

[14] *L.P.*, iv (2), 3628.

and joined together with great tenors of the same" occupied by the headsmen of the "graynes" or clans.[15] The "deadly feude" whereby the violence done to any member of the clan was implacably avenged by the kin was the natural outcome of the close identification of individual and family. But violence also had an economic function. Tynedale, for example, was "overcharged with so greatt a number of people mo then suche profyttes as may be gotten . . . out of the grounde", and this overpopulation drove "the yonge and actyve people for lack of lyvynge . . . to steal or spoyle contynually either in England or Scotland . . . ".[16] In many respects these upland clans, in which violence had come to be accepted as a normal part of the pattern of living, were best equipped to survive and increase in a world where lawlessness ruled, and they prospered by battening on the lowland. There was a delight too in the epic quality of the Border way of life, which so often stretched courage and physical endurance to the utmost limits.[17] Theft, robbery, and murder did not meet with the disapproval such crimes incurred in more settled societies. On the contrary, the Borderers "most prayses and cheryshes suche as begynne sonest in youthe to practise themselves in theftes and robberies contrary to the kinges graces lawes . . . ".[18] The ballad of Kinmont Willie's celebrated escape from Carlisle vividly celebrates one such feat of energy and daring on which the Border community set its stamp of approval,[19] just as *The Death of Percy Reed*[20] recreates the senseless atrocities which were the other side of the picture:

> They fell upon him all at once,
> They mangled him most cruellie;
> The slightest wound might caused his deid,
> And they hae gi'en him thirty-three;
> They backit off his hands and feet,
> And left him lying on the lee.

[15] Bowes and Ellerker's "Survey of the Borders 1542", printed in Hodgson, *op. cit.*, iii (2) (1828), p. 232.

[16] *Ibid.*, p. 233.

[17] See M. J. C. Hodgart, *The Ballads* (London, 1950), ch. 7, "Some Ballad Communities".

[18] Bowes and Ellerker, *op. cit.*, p. 234.

[19] See F. J. Child, *The English and Scottish Popular Ballads* (Boston, 1882–98), iii, p. 469.

[20] *Ibid.*, iv, p. 24.

Such was the fate of one of the royal keepers of Redesdale in Elizabeth's reign, who was set upon by the Croziers, with whom he was at deadly feud.

Little love was lost between the upland and the lowland, the Border clans, and the more settled March communities of the coastal plains of Cumberland and Northumberland. The common people, so it was observed in 1542, were exhausted and out of heart "by the greatt and manyfolde losses, hurtes and overthrowes" sustained as a result of raids from Tynedale, Redesdale, and Liddesdale, so that there was a danger that the "waste and desolate cuntries be lyke to encrease and waxe greater".[21] A real possibility existed that the lawless Border way of life would overwhelm all civil order. Many of the gentry of the lowland conformed to the violent ways of the upland, and the attitude of Sir William Lisle of Felton in Northumberland, who remarked "By God's blood, there is nother King nor his officers that shall take any distress of my ground, or have ado within the liberties of Felton, but I shall take another for it, if I be as strong as he, and able to make my party good",[22] expresses an approach to authority which was common in the March gentry communities.

The endemic violence, and the introverted regional loyalties, so fiercely resistant to interference from without, fed the power of the great lords. For the gentry of the Marchland the crown was alien and remote, but the great households at Naworth castle where Lord Dacre ruled, or at Alnwick or Brougham when the earl of Northumberland or the earl of Cumberland were in residence, represented the acme of power and magnificence, and were the sources from which favours and patronage flowed. The Percy household, with the elaborate organization and almost liturgical solemnity which still meets us in the pages of the *Northumberland Household Book*,[23] was a true regional court with which most of the leading northern gentry stocks had some contact. The Dacre influence was more localized, and centred mainly on Cumberland and the North Tyne, but here it was uncontested. "The cuntrey", said one observer in 1534, "has been so overlayd with the lord Dacres they thowght there was non other Kyng".[24] There were Dacre followers, too, in West-

[21] Bowes and Ellerker, *op. cit.*, p. 229.
[22] *L.P.*, iv (2), 2370.
[23] Ed. Thomas Percy (London, 1770, 1827).
[24] See below, p. 110. For the Dacre connection, see Appendix I, p. 142 ff.

morland, but here the majority of the gentry followed the Cliffords, whose influence extended over into the West Riding. The great households presented an orderly and decorous front, and there was a sense of responsibility to dependants and inferiors which was rare elsewhere. "See that ye keep a noble house for beef and beer, that thereof may be praise given to God and your honour . . . Have no dice, but pastimes of hunting and hawking . . . Ride always with a noble company of servants, and orderly apparelled . . . Bid your tenants come to you if wronged by your officers . . . "[25] was the advice given in Elizabeth's reign to the last of the Dacres to reside at Naworth. But behind the decorous façade all too often the great lords were bound in a close mafia with the upland thieves, and patronized and protected Border lawlessness. The Dacres were most at home in this world, to which their lordships of Burgh and Gilsland were so close. Thomas Lord Dacre, for example, owed much of his power to rule and terrorize along the whole length of the Border to his alliance with the Armstrongs of Bewcastle and Liddesdale, Scots as well as English, and to his contacts with Tynedale and Redesdale through the Charletons, Ridleys, and other families.[26] But the Percies, too, particularly the dissident fifth earl of Northumberland, who was excluded all his life from office in the Marches, had their allies in Tynedale and Redesdale.[27] No great lord could afford to ignore communities where forces of light horse were available with a readiness which contrasted with the reluctance of the less warlike lowland tenantry to muster under their officers. The Cliffords were weakened by their lack of contact with

[25] "Advice given by Richard Atkinson to Leonard Dacre", *c.* February 1570 (*Cal. State Papers, Domestic, Addenda, 1566–79*, p. 255). This document relates to a great household under stress, since the rebel Leonard Dacre would soon be attacked by Lord Hunsdon's government troops. But the advice given would be equally applicable to earlier and more secure times. In case it should be thought that the great northern lords were particularly benevolent and "uneconomic" in their approach to their tenants, the last sentence of this quotation needs to be completed: " . . . and they will not think much of their rent doubling". In normal times Dacre would not have been advised to squeeze his tenants as hard as this; but money must have been desperately needed to finance rebellion.

[26] Appendix I, below, pp. 142 ff.

[27] The Percies had contacts with Tynedale through John Heron of Chipchase, and with Redesdale through Sir William Lisle of Felton; the latter was employed by the fifth earl of Northumberland as constable of Alnwick castle (Syon House MS. C III 5b); the former by the sixth earl as constable of Warkworth castle (Alnwick Castle MS., Letters and Papers, ii, Book of Grants).

the Border dales, and it is probably for this reason that the first earl of Cumberland was a failure in the wardenry of the West March to which he was appointed on the third Lord Dacre's death in 1525.[28] His own power was not sufficient to rule against the enmity of the Dacres, who stirred up the Border thieves and harassed the earl's officers.[29] At last, in 1527, Cumberland had to be dismissed and William fourth Lord Dacre put in his place.[30]

But in London the proceedings of the Border lords were watched with mounting disapproval and distrust. Henry VII had been aware how often, under his predecessors, northern violence had been unleashed to "the subversion of the politeque weal . . . and to robbe, dispoyle and destroye all the southe partes of this . . . realme".[31] With the accession of Henry VIII deteriorating relations with Scotland made it more urgent that the Marches should be ruled by wardens whom the crown could trust and control, and that the Border should not be weakened by the incessant quarrels between Dacres and Cliffords, and Dacres and Percies. And Wolsey, with his new law of Star Chamber, was not disposed to tolerate patronage of Border lawlessness by the king's wardens. Thomas Lord Dacre, for example, whose rule in the Marches had been unquestioned for so long, found that his contacts with the upland clans, reported to London by his enemies in Northumberland, exposed him to Wolsey's distrust and anger.[32] There were acrimonious exchanges between the two men in the spring of 1524, and when Dacre asked to be discharged of the rule of the East and Middle Marches he was told to stay at his post till he had repressed the disorders with which he was charged.[33] Eventually, he went up to London to answer the accusations which were being made against him, and perhaps only his death in October 1525 spared him further troubles.[34] His heir, at any rate, was not appointed to succeed his father in the East and Middle Marches, and the abortive attempt mentioned above to exclude him even from the western wardenry suggests the disfavour into which the family had fallen.

28 *L.P.*, iv (1), 1727.
29 *Ibid.*, iv (2), 4421.
30 Dacre was appointed on 1 December 1527 (Public Record Office, E101/72/7).
31 Henry VII's proclamation against the northern rebels, 10 May 1489, W. Campbell, *Materials for a History of the Reign of Henry VII*, 2 vols. (Rolls Series, 1873), ii, p. 447.
32 Hodgson, *op. cit.*, pt. 3, i, p. 31.
33 *L.P.*, iv (1), 133, 220, 279.
34 *Ibid.*, iv (1), 1727.

In the background of these events, however, there were broad tendencies at work of significance for the future. In particular, direct contact became more frequent between leading gentry houses of the Marches and the court, so that a crown interest began to shape itself in these remote countries where the power of the great lords had been unchallenged for so long. Instances of this were numerous in the West March, where for example both the brother and eldest son of Sir John Pennington of Muncaster, a Percy officer and follower, were serving in the royal household as early as 1495–6.[35] Then there was the case of Sir William Musgrave, whose father Sir Edward was allied to the Dacres.[36] But Sir William became one of the royal knights of the body, and had been made treasurer of Berwick in 1529.[37] His appointment over Lord Dacre's head in 1531 as constable of Bewcastle,[38] the isolated crown outpost on the western Border, an office which had been promised to Dacre, was one of the causes of the bitter feud between the two men which was soon to raise an uproar in Cumberland. Sir Thomas Curwen of Workington was another who gave up the traditional allegiance of his family to the Percies,[39] and opted for the service of the crown, carrying many of his influential relatives with him. Two of his uncles, for example, Sir John Lamplugh[40] (another Percy

[35] For the Penningtons and their Percy and crown affiliations, see J. Foster, *Penningtoniana* (London, 1878) and Hist. Mss. Comm., 10th rept, App. pt. 4, *Muncaster MSS.*, p. 228, no. 36; 70, A3.

[36] There is a convenient pedigree of the Musgraves of Hartley castle and Edenhall in *Transactions of the Cumberland and Westmorland Antiquarian and Archaeological Society* (Kendal, 1874 ff.) (cited hereafter as *Trans. C. & W. A. & A. Soc.*), new series, xi (1911), facing p. 54. One of Thomas Lord Dacre's daughters had married a Musgrave, and Sir Edward Musgrave seems to have been involved in plans to draw the two families closer together by a match between his grandson (Sir William's heir) and one of the Dacres. Sir William was opposed to the Dacre alliance, and the quarrel between the two generations, father and son, emerges in *L.P.*, vii, 1647, a document which seems to belong to 1534 or 1535.

[37] *L.P.*, iv (3), 6135 (20).

[38] *Ibid.*, v, 220 (b14).

[39] The Curwens held Workington by knight service of the Percy barony of Egremont (Petworth House MS., Survey 1577; Egremont). Sir Thomas Curwen's grandfather had been receiver of the Percy lands in Cumberland (Alnwick Castle MS. C III 2a). For the family see J. F. Curwen, *The Curwens of Workington* (Kendal, 1928); W. Jackson, *Papers and Pedigrees*, 2 vols. (London, 1892), i, p. 288; Surtees Soc., xli (Durham and London, 1848), p. 100.

[40] For the Lamplughs, see *Trans. C. & W. A. & A. Soc.*, new ser., xxxviii (1938), p. 71. Sir John Lamplugh was another ex-Percy servant, who had been lieutenant

officer) and Sir John Lowther,[41] acted for the crown in riots which broke out in Cumberland in 1531 and 1532;[42] and a third, Sir James Leyburn,[43] steward of Kendal (an office he shared with the Stricklands of Sizergh, also allied to the Curwens),[44] became one of Thomas Cromwell's intelligencers, sending up news of Lord Dacre's doings.[45] Curwen himself had been an esquire of the body.[46] He became forester of Galtres forest near York in 1523, and in 1531 displaced Sir Robert Constable, soon to be a leading Pilgrim, as steward of the nearby royal lordship of Sheriff Hutton.[47] Sir William Musgrave was his brother-in-law.

There were other instances of the same kind in the East and Middle Marches, where for example the Radcliffes of Dilston and the Forsters of Adderstone, again both Percy families, came to serve the king.[48] Probably the long minority of the fifth earl of Northumberland, when he was the king's ward, was the occasion of some of these defections from the Percy service to that of the crown. But there was also the policy of securing the Percy lands to strengthen the crown's authority in the north, which was almost certainly conceived by Wolsey,[49] but which did not begin to be implemented until after Cromwell's appointment to the Council. This coincided with the negotiations between the sixth earl of Northumberland and the king, which led on 7 July 1531 to the transfer of all the Percy lands in Cumberland to the crown, in whose hands they remained until February 1535.[50] The new crown landed

of the honour of Cockermouth from 1527 to 1530 (Alnwick Castle MS., Letters and Papers, ii, Book of Grants). He married Isabella Curwen, Sir Thomas's great-aunt.

41 He married Lucy Curwen. See J. Foster (ed.), *Visitations of Cumberland and Westmorland* (Carlisle, 1891), p. 84.

42 *L.P.*, v, 477, 1433.

43 He married Helen Curwen, and his mother was a Pennington (Surtees Soc., xli, 1848), p. 95.

44 See H. Hornyold-Strickland, *The Stricklands of Sizergh* (Kendal, 1928).

45 *L.P.*, v, 1224.

46 *Ibid.*, iv (3), 6248 (11).

47 *Ibid.*, iv (2), 5243 (21); v, 506 (10).

48 Sir Edward Radcliffe was Percy steward in Northumberland under the fifth earl, but also a knight of the body, and held various offices under the crown. Sir Thomas Forster (d. 1526) was the king's marshal of Berwick; but his father of the same name had been one of the Percy bailiffs (Alnwick Castle MS. C III 4a).

49 For Wolsey's intrusive meddling with the Percy properties, which eventually led to the sixth earl of Northumberland's indignant protest that "he would be no ward", see *L.P.*, iv (2), 3119, 4603, 4698.

50 Bean, *The Estates of the Percy Family*, p. 151.

endowment must have opened out attractive prospects of grants, offices and leases. Appetites were whetted, and the standing of the crown interest in the West March enhanced. It is not surprising therefore, at this point, that the circle of Curwen kin should receive a new recruit closely connected with the Percy estate administration. This was the man whose career will be traced in this essay, Sir Thomas Wharton, lieutenant (as he then was) of the honour of Cockermouth, and principal officer therefore of the Percy lands which passed to the crown in 1531. Wharton's friendship with Curwen went back at least to 1533,[51] but it was cemented in October of the following year by the marriage of his daughter Agnes to Curwen's heir.[52] Later Sir Thomas Curwen married Wharton's widowed sister, and an intimacy and trust grew up between the two men which was broken only by death.[53]

Probably nobody could have foreseen in 1534 that only ten years later Wharton would be raised to a barony and to the great office of warden of the West March, at the same time as Sir William Eure was ennobled and appointed to the east wardenry.[54] Both men were the first to break the long monopoly of these offices enjoyed by the great lords, and their appointment was a step in the long and gradual Tudor revolution in the north, which, after many set-backs, changes of policy, and tactical retreats, had within a generation broken the power of the northern magnates. Their rise to greatness also suggests a shift in the political balance within the landed class. The gentry were acting with greater initiative and independence, and new leaders were emerging from their ranks. The great houses did not enjoy unquestioned deference as in the past. But even in 1534 it must already have been clear that the Dacre interest in the West

51 *L.P.*, vi, 907.

52 The marriage of Henry Curwen and Agnes Wharton did not lead to a permanent union, and is not mentioned in Curwen or in some Wharton pedigrees. But evidence that it took place was given before a commission of the archbishop of Canterbury on 16 July 1566 (*Cal. of Patent Rolls, 1563–6*); I owe this reference to Mr C. R. Hudleston.

53 Curwen died in 1543 (*L.P.*, xviii (2), 332). Wharton was present at his death-bed and an executor of his will. Six years before, the duke of Norfolk, when lieutenant in the north, had noted that Curwen was the man Wharton trusted most (*ibid.*, xii (2), 248, July 1537).

54 For a description of the presentation of their letters patent to Wharton and Eure by the earl of Hertford, lieutenant in the north, at Newcastle upon Tyne on 20 March 1544, see *The Hamilton Papers*, ed. J. Bain (Edinburgh, 1890–2), ii, p. 303.

March was confronted by a powerful group of interrelated families based on the former Percy lands and influence, and supported by the crown. In the background there was the hostility of the earl of Cumberland, and of his brother-in-law the sixth earl of Northumberland. These were formidable opponents if it came to a fight, and it was not long before Lord Dacre fell before them.

II

But before the downfall of Lord Dacre is related, some attention must be given to Sir Thomas Wharton's background and early career. The Whartons, of Wharton, near Kirkby Stephen, belonged to the minor gentry. They may have been seated at Wharton as far back as the reign of Edward I. But it is possible that their gentry status was of comparatively recent origin; for, when the future first lord submitted his pedigree to the herald Tonge at the visitation of 1530, this began only with his great-grandfather, who had been M.P. for Appleby in 1435–7;[55] and the Wharton armorial bearings, with their maunch and bull's head crest, may have been brought into the family by the first lord's grandmother, a Conyers of Hornby, whose coat this was.[56] The Whartons, however, had long been dependants of the Cliffords, from whom they held the ancestral manors of Wharton and Nateby, and Wharton's father, also named Thomas, had been an officer of the tenth Lord Clifford.[57] But he had also served the crown in 1513 as clerk of the wars in Surrey's army in the north, and the following year he was appointed escheator in Cumberland and Westmorland.[58] We may perhaps therefore visualize a stock whose modest landed endowment needed to be supplemented by the profits of a profession, and who had been accustomed to serve the local great family as estate administrators and men of business. If this was so, the first lord was in line with the family tradition when he embarked on a career in the service of the house of Percy, who had close and friendly links with the Cliffords. Perhaps too it was through his father that he formed

55 Surtees Soc., xli (Durham and London, 1848), p. 99.

56 *Complete Peerage*, xii (2), p. 594; Nicolson and Burn, *History of Westmorland*, ii, p. 433; *The Genealogist*, new ser., viii (1891), pp. 7, 127.

57 *Clifford Letters*, p. 30.

58 *L.P.*, i, 1450, 3499 (68).

his first connections with Tudor administration and the Tudor court.

The first Lord Wharton came then of a respectable stock whose resources were not large enough to make sloth a temptation. Industry, professional competence, and the pursuit of a career were the marks of the family tradition. But the corollary of this modest status was that Wharton could expect little from family alliance and affinity to secure his own advancement. In fact, until his connection with Curwen was formed he was poor in kin and friends, and had few links with the leading houses of the West March. Through his mother's family, the Warcops of Smardale, again of modest gentry stock, Wharton was related to the Sandfords of Askham, and to a Northumbrian squire, Cuthbert Carnaby of Halton, who had married Wharton's aunt, Mabel Warcop.[59] Their son, Sir Reynold Carnaby, was probably brought into the Percy service by Wharton himself, and later became a prominent figure in the politics of the East and Middle Marches. In addition the Wharton kin included the cadet Whartons of Kirkby Thore,[60] whose head Gilbert Wharton the first lord subsequently employed. Probably, however, the latter's career was materially advanced by his marriage in July 1518 to Eleanor Stapleton, third daughter of Sir Brian Stapleton of Wighill in the West Riding. The Stapletons[61] were Percy followers, and Sir Brian's brother William[62] became attorney to the sixth earl of Northumberland. The connection may have given Wharton his entry into the Percy service, but when or how this took place cannot be ascertained. Apart from the fact that he was placed on the commission of the peace for Westmorland in February 1524, all that can be known of his career in the early 1520s is that in April 1522 he

[59] For the Sandfords see *Trans. C. & W. A. & A. Soc.*, new ser., xxi (1921), p. 174. For the Carnabies, *Northumberland County History*, x (Newcastle upon Tyne, 1914), opp. p. 408. There is a pedigree of the Warcops in Foster (ed.), *Visitations of Cumberland and Westmorland*, p. 138, and in *Heraldic Visitation of the Northern Counties Made in 1530 by Thomas Tonge*, ed. W. H. D. Longstaffe (Surtees Soc., xli, Durham and London, 1848), p. 100.

[60] The Whartons of Kirkby Thore were descended from a younger brother of the Thomas Wharton who heads the family pedigree in Tonge's *Visitation* (*Visitation of Yorkshire 1612*, ed. J. Foster, London, 1875, p. 589).

[61] The fullest pedigree of the Stapletons is in J. Foster, *Yorkshire Pedigrees*, 3 vols. (London, 1874), ii, West Riding. See also Tonge's *Visitation*, p. 16.

[62] He was appointed attorney, at a fee of £10, on 10 June 1533; later in the same year he became the earl's feodary in Yorkshire and was granted an annuity (Alnwick Castle MS., Letters and Papers, ii, Book of Grants).

served under Sir Anthony Ughtred, captain of Berwick, on a raid into Scotland.[63] Amongst his companions were two sons of the fifth earl of Northumberland, Sir Thomas and Sir Ingram Percy. The pattern thus suggested of a connection both with the service of the crown and with the Percy family would persist in Wharton's career till the death of the sixth earl in 1537 and the transfer of the Percy estates into the hands of the king.

If more were known of Wharton's activities during these obscure years perhaps his swift advancement in the Percy service in 1528 and 1530 would seem less mysterious. Because in May of the former year the sixth earl of Northumberland appointed him comptroller of his household and steward of the Percy lordships of Tadcaster and Healaugh in the West Riding, all of which offices he was to hold for life. And on 18 October 1530 he became steward of the earl's lordships of Eskdale and Wasdale, constable of Egremont castle, and lieutenant of Cockermouth.[64] The last two posts were of particular importance since they carried with them the command of the earl's tenants in the West March on Border service. But what was remarkable about the grants of 1530 was that the earl alienated these offices not only to Wharton for his lifetime, but also to his heirs, so divesting himself and his successors in the earldom of much of the traditional Percy authority in Cumberland. Even more remarkable was the large landed endowment which the earl conferred on Wharton at the same time. This consisted of the Percy manors of Great Broughton and Little Broughton, Dean, Whinfell, Birkby, and Caldbeck Underfell, together with Cockermouth mill and the herbage of Cockermouth park, and a number of smaller items which included the tolls and customs of the honour of Cockermouth.[65] These were all granted to Wharton and his heirs against reserved rents, which were however to be paid out of an annuity of 100 marks which the earl made over simultaneously and on the same terms. A few years later, probably in 1536, Wharton further received from his master the manors of Healaugh and Catterton in Yorkshire.[66] All

[63] *L.P.*, iii (2), 2186; *ibid.*, iv (1), 137 (10).

[64] Wharton's appointments are specified in the sixth earl of Northumberland's Book of Grants at Alnwick castle (Alnwick Castle MS., Letters and Papers, ii).

[65] There is a copy of the grant in the Bodleian Library, Carte MA., 117.

[66] These manors are reserved to Wharton in the Act of 1536 assuring the Percy lands to the king and his heirs (*Statutes of the Realm*, ed. A. Luders *et al.*, 11 vols., London, 1810–28, iii, p. 611).

this amounted to a considerable landed estate, whose rental alone was over £150,[67] and its acquisition must have greatly enhanced Wharton's status in the West March. There, as lieutenant of Cockermouth and a considerable landowner, he must after 1530 have been a person to reckon with.

Estate administration in the sixteenth century could lay the foundation of considerable fortunes. But Wharton's gains are on an extraordinary scale, matched in fact only by those made by his relative Sir Reynold Carnaby in Northumberland, also at the expense of the Percy inheritance. Not surprisingly therefore the earl's motives have aroused speculation, and have sometimes been ascribed to plain folly which led him to indulge favourites among his servants to the detriment of his heirs.[68] But it is significant that less than a year after the grants to Wharton the sixth earl (as we have seen) made over his lands in Cumberland to the king, on whom therefore fell the charge of the earl's generosity. Similarly it is likely that Wharton's manors of Healaugh and Catterton were granted him after the earl had decided, in January 1536, to make the crown his heir. He may have reasoned that the grants would bind to him, by ties of regard and gratitude, a man of growing importance and power in the West March, and that by this means a Percy influence would persist there, even if the Percy lands had passed to the crown. if this was the earl's assumption, it was confirmed by events. A close relationship, which seems to have been one of trust and regard, persisted between Wharton and his master until the latter's death. Sir George Lawson, for example, noted in 1533 how influential Wharton was in the earl's counsels, an observation which is confirmed by the earl's description of him, in 1534, as "mine one hand".[69] And it is Wharton whom the earl entrusted, in January 1536, with an important role in the transactions to give effect to his decision to bequeath his lands to the king.[70] Wharton, on his side, repaid his master's trust with loyalty, in spite of his many and close connections with the court. A letter to Cromwell, which seems to date from 1531, in which the latter was thanked for his continual kindness, and promised reports hereafter, might arouse our suspicions in this respect but for its con-

[67] Wharton's Cumberland grants had an annual clear value of £102: Healaugh and Catterton brought in £51 a year clear value. See Appendix III, below.

[68] See Bean, *op. cit.*, pp. 144–57, for the most cogent statement of this view.

[69] *L.P.*, vi, 16; vii, 896.

[70] *Ibid.*, viii, 166.

clusion, in which Wharton added that his acts were always not only to the satisfaction of the king, but also to the honour of his master; and in January 1533 he evaded Cromwell's request for news by pointing out that full reports were always forwarded by the earl and his council.[71]

But, if Wharton remained the confidant and favourite of his master, there can be no doubt that during these years he was also increasingly trusted and approved by the government. He received marks of favour, and was increasingly employed. In 1529, for example, he was pricked sheriff of Cumberland, although he then had no lands in the county; and in that same year he sat in Parliament for Appleby, a Clifford borough.[72] Soon after he received the honour of knighthood. In 1531 he was a commissioner of redress of injuries in the West March, and in this capacity negotiated with James V.[73] In the next year his appearance on the commission of the peace for Northumberland and the East Riding, as well as Cumberland and Westmorland, showed that he was already a figure of more than merely local importance.[74] And in 1533 he was a commissioner for the truce with Scotland.[75] All these activities inevitably brought him into closer contact with the court. On many occasions the earl of Northumberland sent him up with missives and credences to Wolsey, the king, and Cromwell.[76] He received letters as we have seen, from the last, and began to correspond with Henry VIII.[77] Wharton, in fact, now came to be known in a wider world than that of the Marches. Sir George Lawson, for example, commented to Cromwell on the good service he did the king by his wise counsel and experience, and urged that he should be sent a letter of thanks.[78] There can be little doubt therefore that he was regarded with increasing favour in London, and that the king trusted the man who had been so opportunely placed in the lieutenancy of Cockermouth only a few months before the Percy lands in Cumberland passed into the hands of the crown. His alliance with Sir Thomas Curwen and his friends could only have enhanced the confidence in which he was held.

[71] *Ibid.*, v, 412; vi, 17. [72] *Ibid.*, iv (3), 6072. [73] *Ibid.*, v, 434.
[74] *Ibid.*, v, 838 (30), 909 (23), 1694.
[75] *Ibid.*, vi, 745.
[76] See e.g. *ibid.*, v, 609; vi, 1019; vii, 886, 896.
[77] Wharton began to correspond directly with the king in July 1533; *ibid.*, vi, 892.
[78] *Ibid.*, vi, 16.

III

In July 1534 William Lord Dacre was arraigned before his peers on charges of treason arising out of his supposed collusion with the Scots, in time of war, to harm the king's lieges in the Marches.[79] To the surprise of his contemporaries he was acquitted by the house of lords, but although this saved his life and lands it could not protect him from all the dire consequences of the king's displeasure. He had been unwise enough to conceal letters, probably innocent enough in themselves, written by his uncle, Sir Philip Dacre, and himself to Robert Charteris of Hempsfield, one of James V's agents, and so he was not only dismissed from his wardenry but also fined £10,000.[80] These events showed that not even the most formidable of Border barons could be certain of eluding the long arm which stretched from London. And it is significant that a leading role in the drama was played by Sir William Musgrave, acting with the collusion of the government, and the support of his Curwen relatives and of Wharton in the West March. Lord Dacre's troubles certainly arose out of his enmity with Musgrave, embittered as this had been by the latter's appointment over the warden's head as constable of Bewcastle. In October 1531 there had been a fray at Bewcastle between the Musgraves and the Forsters, in the course of which a Forster had been killed. The feud which arose out of this incident opened the way for Dacre to unleash some of the Border clans against his enemies. And so on 8 November 1532 his uncle Sir Christopher Dacre had made an agreement with Thomas Armstrong, the Elwoods, and other Scots of Liddesdale, under which these were promised indemnity and freedom from reprisals in respect of all attacks made on Sir William Musgrave and his tenants. As a result Bewcastle was raided on 1 July 1533, one of Musgrave's men was slain, and many other robberies and murders committed, for which no redress could be obtained. So at any rate the indictment stated which was found against Dacre at Carlisle in July 1534, and there is an inherent probability in the charge.[81] The Dacres were only too ready to use the Border clans both English and Scottish to terrorize their enemies and bolster up their own power.

79 See *A Complete Collection of State Trials*, ed. W. Cobbett *et al.*, 42 vols. (London, 1816–98; hereafter cited as *State Trials*), i, p. 407; *L.P.*, vii, 1013.

80 *L.P.*, vii, 1270.

81 *Ibid.*, vii, 962.

Other and graver charges were brought against the warden at the same time. He had, for example, "sought the destruction" of the earl of Northumberland by an agreement made with William Scott of Buccleuch, whom Dacre promised not to molest if he invaded the East March. There had been an arrangement too with Lord Maxwell, under which the latter was to invade the West March and spoil the king's lieges, especially the Musgraves, while sparing the Dacre lands. Maxwell had visited Dacre secretly in time of war, and he too had been encouraged to attack the earl of Northumberland.[82] But these charges suggest plotting on a fantastic and implausible scale which is remote from Dacre's hard-headed and experienced approach to Border politics. Intrigue with petty Border chiefs to terrorize his enemies was one thing; but treason at this level involved too many risks and too doubtful a return. Nor could the charges be substantiated, as the lords' verdict showed. The indications in fact are that in the spring of 1534 there was a deliberate determination to ruin Dacre, and an awareness that circumstances had placed him in the hands of his enemies. Since March he was in London,[83] and therefore could easily be arrested; and forces were available which could be mobilized against him in the north. There was, for example, Sir William Musgrave, more than willing, given support from London, to prefer his damaging charges. Thomas Cromwell, recently appointed secretary of state, sent encouragement and instructions, warning Musgrave to be precise and circumstantial in his accusations. The latter replied with an agitated missive written on 12 June 1534,[84] just as the commissioners to investigate Dacre's treasons approached Carlisle. The day and time of every indictment, he said, would be perfectly stated "so that as concernyng my buke there shall be nothing reprovable against me", and he was convinced that his allegations were so substantially set out that none of them could be denied. The whole affair, he added, was from his point of view a service to the king, and a chargeable one at that, "for, Sir, in thys mater yor worship and I spesally beryth all the blame". Dacre had many followers, for "dyvers of this country . . . will in nowise trust that he will have any overthrow but . . . is of his partye". As soon as they see "he shall goe dowyn they

[82] *Ibid.*
[83] Dacre had gone up for the spring session of Parliament (*ibid.*, vii, 391).
[84] Public Record Office, SP1/84, p. 199.

will say *Crucifige*. The cuntrey has been so overlayd with the lord Dacres they thowght there was non other Kyng." Success depended on unwavering support from London. "Therefore Sir", urged Musgrave, "I pray you stand styffly in thys mater and that I may have your gentyll ayd." In the tense, fear-laden phrases we touch the quick of the struggle between the Tudors and the great lords in the Marches.

Musgrave, however, could rely on powerful support. The commission,[85] for example, appointed to sit at Carlisle to investigate the charges against Dacre could be relied on not to find him innocent. Only one of the members, the earl of Westmorland, had no axe to grind in the case. Otherwise there were the earls of Northumberland and Cumberland, Dacre's two greatest enemies, who were supported by Cumberland's brother, Sir Thomas Clifford, and by Wharton himself. The remaining two members were servants of the crown, the lawyers Robert Challoner and Thomas Fairfax. Dacre could not hope for mercy from such judges. Nor would the two juries[86] who tried him be likely to find anything other than a true bill. Both were well packed with Wharton and Curwen kin, and with Percy and Clifford followers. The first group, for example, included Sir John Lowther, supported by two other Lowthers, and by three Wharton relatives.[87] There were also Richard Barwise,[88] a Percy officer and the king's feodary in Cumberland, together with his father-in-law Robert Briscoe, and Thomas Dalston, a Clifford servant.[89] Sir Edward Musgrave may have favoured Dacre, but at least nine of the fifteen jurors could be relied on to find against him. The second jury was made up for the most part of small and obscure squires who could be expected to find as directed by the two great men, Sir Cuthbert Radcliffe (head of a family notable for its connec-

[85] *L.P.*, vii, 962.

[86] Both are listed, and the indictment found given, in *ibid.*, vii, 962.

[87] The three were Gilbert Wharton of Kirkby Thore, Robert Warcop, and Guy Machell.

[88] Richard Barwise of Ilekirk was the Percy feodary in Cumberland in 1530 (Account of John Wodehall, Receiver in Cumberland, 1530, Alnwick Castle MS., X II 3), and was appointed learned steward there by the sixth earl in 1533 (Book of Grants, Alnwick Castle MS., Letters and Papers, ii). For his career and connections see *Trans. C. & W. A. & A. Soc.*, new ser., xxxvii (1937), p. 106.

[89] Dalston had been made deputy steward of Holme Cultram abbey by the earl of Cumberland (*L.P.*, iv (2), 4421).

tions with the Percies and the court[90]), and Sir Thomas Curwen himself, who headed the jury list. All should have gone well, but for the fact that the elaborate arrangements made to trap Dacre suggested a frame-up all too obviously, even to the hand-picked group of peers appointed to try him. Dacre, according to Hall, "improved the sayd indictment as false and maliciously devised against hym, and answered every point and matter therein contained . . . and directly confuted his accusors".[91] And the evidence of the "mean and provoked Scottish men" brought by Musgrave against him was rejected by the peers as malicious and "suborned".[92] But, if Dacre was acquitted, his political ascendancy in the West March now went into eclipse. The earl of Cumberland took his place as warden, and the crisis was over. But its course had revealed how cohesively and powerfully the substantial squirearchy of the March, given government backing, could act against its enemies. Wharton and Curwen, Lowther, Musgrave and their like, now confronted the traditional dominance of Dacre, Clifford and Percy. And there was a widespread appreciation too that the fall of ancient landed interests could bring substantial rewards to those who were on the right side of the political fence. Edward Aglionby, one of the officers of the Carlisle garrison, wrote hastily to Cromwell on 28 June, begging to be remembered if Lord Dacre's lands, as well as his goods, were forfeited.[93] Soon the dissolution of the monasteries would open out unprecedented prospects of gain for those who enjoyed the favour and trust of the court.

Over this lowering scene a little more than two years later there broke the thunderclap of the Pilgrimage of Grace, in which Sir Thomas Wharton played an important, if equivocal role. The part which he and his friends had taken in Dacre's downfall had emphasized that he must now be regarded as a leading personage in the West March, and there are indications that his prestige and influence grew in the months which intervened before the outbreak

[90] See n. 48 above.

[91] Edward Hall, *The Union of . . . York and Lancaster* (London, 1550 edn; S.T.C. 12723), fo. ccxxv. Perhaps Dacre owed something to the fact that the duke of Norfolk presided over the lord steward's court which tried him.

[92] Edward Lord Herbert of Cherbury, *The Life and Raigne of Henry VIII* (1683 edn), p. 407. Herbert couples Sir Ralph Fenwick with Musgrave as Dacre's principal accusers. Fenwick was one of the deputies of the Middle March under the sixth earl of Northumberland (*L.P.*, iv (2), 5085).

[93] *L.P.*, vii, 895.

of the rebellion. He was not without his troubles at this time, but he emerged from them on the whole triumphantly. For example, there was the feud with Sir Edward Musgrave, which took up the summer months of 1535. Musgrave became, as has been seen, a supporter of the Dacre interest. He disapproved of his courtier heir, Sir William, and disliked the latter's friendship with Wharton. The mutual hatred exploded into hunting disputes and frays in Westmorland, where one of the Musgrave houses, Hartley castle, stood within a few miles of Wharton Hall. Christopher Wharton, Sir Thomas's brother, slew a Musgrave servant; significantly, Dacre tenants joined in the disorders on the Musgrave side. Agrarian grievances became entangled in the dynastic quarrels, so that Lancelot Lancaster, one of Dacre's officers in Westmorland, assembled his master's tenants, and led them to throw down certain enclosures which had been made by John Warcop, Wharton's brother-in-law. Eventually the earl of Westmorland and then Lord Monteagle were sent to the scene to restore peace. The murderer Christopher Wharton escaped lightly. He was merely bound over to keep the peace, together with the aggrieved Sir Edward Musgrave. But Lancelot Lancaster was imprisoned at Appleby castle.[94] Wharton could feel that his interests had been given a just measure of support, particularly since other marks of favour also came his way at this time. The abbot of St Mary's, York, for example, had hastened to grant him the presentation to Kirkby Stephen vicarage,[95] and in 1535 he had once more been appointed sheriff of Cumberland.[96] In 1536 he was taking an active part in the March administration, and above all he still held Cromwell's ear, sending him commendations of those gentlemen who had done good service, and who could therefore expect thanks and rewards.[97] Thus hopes and expectations must have fastened increasingly on the man who could mediate between London and the West March, besides being the principal Percy officer in Cumberland. So that inevitably Wharton grew in political stature and importance.

This was why he came to figure so prominently in the plans of the leaders of the Pilgrimage of Grace. For obvious reasons the Pilgrims needed to control the Marches, since the power to open the frontier to the Scots enemy (or to keep it closed) would have been an invalu-

94 *Ibid.*, viii, 1030, 1046.

95 *Ibid.*, viii, 167.

96 *Ibid.*, ix, 914 (22).

97 *Ibid.*, xi, 666.

able bargaining counter in any negotiations with the government. As far as the East and Middle Marches were concerned, powerful forces were working in their favour. There much could be expected from the discontents and hatreds of Sir Thomas and Sir Ingram Percy. But where were the rebel leaders to come from in the West March? There was of course Lord Dacre. But his contacts with Lord Darcy and his friends, and with the representatives of the Percy interest which figured so prominently in the rebel leadership, were few and, as often as not, hostile. Dacre too had been chastened by his late troubles, and was probably already under the duke of Norfolk's influence, which was always exercised in favour of cautious and loyal policies. At any rate, Dacre did not commit himself to the Pilgrims. Instead he sent his uncle, Sir Christopher Dacre, to restrain the commons from besieging Carlisle, and even offered his help to Lord Clifford, heir to the hated earl of Cumberland, who had taken refuge there.[98] Finally, early in November 1536, he decided to make assurance doubly sure and took himself off to London, where he remained till the commotions in Cumberland and Westmorland were over.[99] It is true that his absence did not prevent his tenants from mustering and taking the Pilgrims' oath under the captaincy of one of his servants, Richard Dacre. But it is plain that this was with the strictly limited object of wreaking revenge on Sir William Musgrave, who early in December came within an inch of assassination by Richard Dacre and his henchmen as he emerged from church in Carlisle.[100] Thereafter any Dacre interest in the rebellion lapsed, and during the second rising in the West March in February 1537 Sir Christopher Dacre was able to prove the loyalty of his house by scattering the besiegers of Carlisle with a force of five hundred Border spearmen, so ending the rebellion and earning the thanks of the king himself.[101] The Dacres in fact played their own game circumspectly and skilfully, and emerged from the rebellion with their interests intact and their credit enhanced.

Still less could the Pilgrims expect any aid from the Cliffords. The harsh, angular personality of the earl of Cumberland, and his repu-

[98] *Ibid.*, xi, 1331.

[99] *Ibid.*

[100] *Ibid.*

[101] *Ibid.*, xii, 448, 479; M. H. and R. Dodds, *The Pilgrimage of Grace 1536–7, and the Exeter Conspiracy, 1538*, 2 vols. (Cambridge, 1915), ii, pp. 116–17.

tation as an unreasonable and grasping landlord made him hated in his own country.[102] He could only hope to stand with help from outside, from London, and from the start his policy was one of consistent and unwavering loyalty. The earl himself held Skipton against the rebels, while his eldest son and brother ensured the safety of Carlisle,[103] so that only one interest remained to which the Pilgrims could hope to appeal. And this was that powerful widely ramified kinship which centred on Sir Thomas Curwen and Wharton, in which the latter had emerged as the most significant political figure, and whose members had so many contacts with the Percy service. This was a material point when we recall the close involvement of the Percy interest in the leadership of the Pilgrimage, and the fact that Wharton himself was one of the chief officers of the earl of Northumberland. Because, given the corporate sense of a great household, the Pilgrims must have reasoned that Wharton would not find it easy to hold aloof from a movement in which so many of his fellow-officers were involved. The siege of Hull, after all, had been presided over by Wharton's own brother-in-law, William Stapleton, attorney to the earl of Northumberland;[104] the siege of Skipton by John Norton, treasurer of the household of which Wharton was comptroller.[105] Sir Stephen Hamerton, steward of the Percy manor of Preston in Craven, soon to die a traitor's death, was captain of the rebel host of Ribblesdale, and had lately married his heir to Joan Stapleton, Lady Wharton's niece.[106] Other Percy officers, like Sir Roger Lassells,[107] the earl's steward of house-

[102] See A. G. Dickens in Surtees Soc., clxxii, Durham and London, 1957, pp. 24–5, and below, pp. 162, 168–9.

[103] Dodds, *op. cit.*, i, pp. 207 ff. and p. 223.

[104] See above, nn. 61 and 62.

[105] Foster, *Yorkshire Pedigrees* contains the fullest family tree of the Nortons. For John Norton's feud with the earl of Cumberland and his siege of Skipton, see Dodds, *op. cit.*, i, pp. 52, 209. He was probably appointed treasurer in household by the fifth earl of Northumberland, and is referred to under this title in 1528 in the sixth earl's Book of Grants (Alnwick Castle MS., Letters and Papers, ii).

[106] The marriage covenant is dated 8 May 1535 (*Yorkshire Pedigrees*, i, West Riding). Sir Stephen Hamerton had been appointed steward of Preston in Craven by the sixth earl in 1528 (Alnwick Castle MS., Book of Grants). For his role in the Pilgrimage see Dodds, *op. cit.*, *passim*.

[107] The sixth earl appointed Lassells his steward in household a few months after his accession in 1527 (Book of grants). With John Norton (his father-in-law), and Sir Robert Constable, he had been denounced to Cromwell in an undated letter (perhaps of 1534) by an unknown informer as one of the leading trouble-makers in the North and East Ridings (*L.P.*, vii, 1669). The family was of Brecken-

hold, and his constable of Wressle castle, William Babthorpe,[108] were prominent in the rebels' counsels. Wharton's master himself, the earl of Northumberland, had shown favour to Robert Aske, once a Percy servant, but now grand captain of the Pilgrimage, and had given him the use of Wressle castle as his headquarters.[109] In fact, many and powerful ties both of loyalty and kin must have drawn Wharton towards the vortex of rebellion. Every effort was made by the Pilgrims themselves to attract him into their ranks. Robert Aske himself, hearing that a bill had been set up in Workington threatening Wharton with death "for old displeasures between him and lord Dacres", sent letters to rescue him from the irate commons of Westmorland.[110] William Stapleton similarly sent a safe conduct for him to come into Yorkshire.[111] And it is significant that the disorders in the West March first broke out in Kirkby Stephen, Wharton's own parish, where the insurgents immediately came to Wharton Hall in search of him. Failing to find him there they seized his eldest son as a hostage, and went to look for him next day (but with no more success) at the Warcop house at Lammerside.[112] But thereafter, during the crucial weeks when the Pilgrimage was at its height, Wharton disappears from the scene. For nearly two months nothing is known of his whereabouts or activities. Probably he was unaware that he and Sir William Musgrave had been

brough, near Topcliffe, one of the Percy lordships (see J. Foster, *Glover's Visitation of Yorkshire* (London, 1875), p. 61). When the Pilgrimage broke out Lassells joined Lord Darcy at Pontefract castle, where he was one of those "called aside" into a "deep window" to consult with Aske and Darcy (*L.P.*, xii (1), 393). He marshalled a company of rebels at the first appointment with Norfolk at Doncaster (*ibid.*, xii (1), 29) and was present at the rebel council at Pontefract early in December 1536, where he was appointed with others (who included John Norton and William Babthorpe) to lay the rebel articles before Norfolk (*ibid.*, xi, 1243 (2)).

108 Babthorpe had been appointed one of the sixth earl's counsellors learned in 1533; he became constable of Wressle castle, steward of Wressle and Neasham, and master forester of Wressle in November 1535, with the reversion of these offices to his son. He joined Darcy at Pontefract, and was present with Lassells at the consultation there mentioned in n. 107 above. He also went to the rebel councils at York and Pontefract, and was one of those appointed to lay the rebel articles before Norfolk (see the references cited in n. 107 above).

109 For Aske's service with the sixth earl of Northumberland, see *Notes and Queries*, 11th ser., iv (1911), p. 441. For the earl's surrender of Wressle see *L.P.*, xii (1), 849, p. 382.

110 *L.P.*, xi, 1046 (3).

111 *Ibid.*, xii (1), 392, p. 193.

112 *Ibid.*, 687 (2).

nominated as the two representatives of Westmorland at the rebels' council at York in November 1536.[113]

Many northern notables, of course, sought to avoid the consequences of involvement in the Pilgrimage by flight and concealment. The cases of Lord Scrope and Sir Francis Bigod came to mind in Yorkshire, and of the Lumleys and Sir Thomas Hilton in the Bishopric. The behaviour of such men however was not that of firm and consistent loyalists. Sooner or later they were in fact drawn into the leadership of the Pilgrimage, and the suspicion is often present that their flight was a tactic which would enable them to plead that they had been coerced into rebellion. The committed royalists followed a different pattern of behaviour. They resisted the rebellion arms in hand. The Cliffords, as has been seen, held out in Skipton and Carlisle, the Eures at Scarborough, the Carnabies and Greys at Chillingham in Northumberland, Sir Thomas Clifford at Berwick. Sir William Musgrave made his way to Carlisle and joined the Cliffords there. Perhaps Wharton's much more passive role can be explained by the chance that the rebellion broke on him near Kirkby Stephen, where he was separated by many miles of wild and hostile country from the nearest loyalist stronghold at Skipton castle. But it may also be that he was paralysed by the contradictory loyalties in which his own career had involved him. Bound as he was by ties of obligation, loyalty and kin to the Percy interest, to which he owed so much of his rise in the world, he was also trusted and well regarded by the court. It is possible, then, that he took advantage of his isolation in hostile country to stand aside from the whole conflict. Whether by chance or deliberation, in fact, he played a waiting game, until he could emerge on the winning side. Where and how Wharton remained concealed from 17 October 1536, when the Kirkby Stephen insurgents came in search of him, until 12 January 1537, when he re-appears (together with Sir Thomas Curwen and Sir William Musgrave) at Skipton castle,[114] we do not know. At any rate by the end of this period the government was in touch with him through the duke of Norfolk. But on 18 December he had refused to attempt the journey to court, in spite of the command to do so received from the duke.[115] By January, however, the truce had been declared, and the Pilgrimage had lost its impetus. The presence of the king's lieutenant compelled Wharton to emerge and declare

[113] *Ibid.*, xi, 1155.
[114] *Ibid.*, xii (1), 71.
[115] *Ibid.*, xi, 1339.

himself, and to do so with the expectation that he had committed himself to the victorious party.

An aggrieved gentleman (John Leigh of Isel), who had been the subject of complaints about his passive demeanour in the time of the insurrection in the West March, justified himself by pointing out that the sheriff and those in authority under the crown had failed to provide the leadership which loyalists expected of them, and had not called for the attendance of the gentry to subdue the king's enemies.[116] This was a charge which must have struck home, not only at Wharton, who had been sheriff of Cumberland at the outbreak of the Pilgrimage, but also at Sir Thomas Curwen, who succeeded him in the office on 11 November 1536.[117] Neither of the sheriffs could claim the credit for any energetic resistance to rebellion, and in January 1537 Curwen had actually deserted his post and fled to Sheriff Hutton to be away from the commotions in the West March.[118] Leigh's strictures also touched two Curwen uncles and two Wharton kin, all of them justices of the peace, who had also done nothing to restrain the rebellion. Wharton's servant and kinsman Gilbert Wharton, and his brother-in-law John Warcop, both of them justices,[119] may have gone into hiding as he did himself. So perhaps did Sir John Lamplugh, also a justice, for all we know of his activities while the rebels were mustering in the March. Sir John Lowther, another J.P., even joined the muster at Cartlogan Thorns in Cumberland.[120] Other Curwen kin, who were not trammelled by office under the crown, had an even more dubious record. Sir Robert Bellingham and Sir James Leyburn joined the rebel host at Kendal, although under duress.[121] Walter Strickland of Sizergh was also involved in the Kendal disturbances, influenced perhaps by his prospective father-in-law Sir Stephen Hamerton.[122] In fact, out of all the government's previous sup-

[116] *Ibid.*, xii (1), 904. Leigh hints that the sheriff of Cumberland "was the first that was sworn in Westmorland". He seems to refer here to Wharton, but none of the other evidence suggests that the latter was ever in fact sworn to the rebels. The possibility cannot however be excluded.

[117] *Ibid.*, xi, 1217 (23).

[118] *Ibid.*, xii (1), 185.

[119] *Ibid.*, viii, 149 (82). Thomas Sandford is another Wharton relative and a J.P. for Westmorland who seems to have done nothing to check the outbreaks in the county.

[120] *Ibid.*, xii (1), 687.

[121] *Ibid.*, xii (1), 914.

[122] *Ibid.*

porters in the West March, only Sir William Musgrave and the Cliffords were exceptions to the passive or non-committal stance taken up by the rest. From the point of view of the government, therefore, the whole group proved to be a broken reed when the test came.

This may in part be explained by the bitter flavour of social conflict which crept into the Pilgrimage in the West March. "Never were people so set against the nobles as in these parts", commented the duke of Norfolk on 4 February 1537.[123] This was natural, since the inherent sparseness and instability of the economy of the West March left only a small surplus product to be divided between tenant and landlord; and in the inland districts away from the Border this could not be enlarged by raiding and robbery. Cornland was scarce, and the frequent wet summers had their sequel of famine and plague. A mounting population pressed against the supply of available land, and the typical tenant was a small-holder whose livelihood depended on the extensive grazing rights in the fells which went with his farm.[124] This was why enclosure roused such passionate opposition. Landlords eager to increase the profitability of their estates made intakes from the wastes and let them to their more prosperous tenants, so swelling their rent-rolls. The earl of Cumberland was particularly notorious in this respect, and his enclosures were thrown down in the second rising in Westmorland and in February 1537.[125] Curwen and Wharton had both been involved in April 1536 in a riot of the tenants of Galtres forest, near York, which probably had to do with intakes.[126] John Warcop, as we have seen, had his enclosures thrown down in the summer of 1535. Wharton had a reputation as a harsh landlord which survived for generations in his native Westmorland, and was particularly notorious for the greatly enhanced entrance fines he exacted from his tenants.[127] There is reason to believe that the Percy tenants in

123 *Ibid.*, xii (1), 336.

124 For some evidence of high population in the Westmorland dales in the later sixteenth century, see Joan Thirsk in *Essays in the Economic and Social History of Tudor and Stuart England, in Honour of R. H. Tawney*, ed. F. J. Fisher (London, 1961), p. 81.

125 *L.P.*, xii (1), 319.

126 *Ibid.*, x, 733.

127 *Ibid.*, xii (2), 548; E. R. Wharton, *The Whartons of Wharton Hall* (Oxford, 1898), p. 25. Later in his career Wharton, it seems, became notorious as the encloser of Ravenstonedale Park (*Trans. C. & W. A. & A. Soc.*, new ser., ii (1902), p. 400).

Cumberland had also been immoderately squeezed in the matter of fines,[128] and there was much resentment at the exaction of ancient rents like "neat geld" and "serjeant corn", probably mainly on the great estates owned by the Cliffords.[129] It is not surprising, then, that agrarian grievances should figure so largely in the rebel demands in the West March, or that the captains of the commons of Westmorland should tell Darcy that they had no gentry of their counsel, because they were afraid of them "as yet".[130]

But the "as yet" of the Westmorland commons shows that they too hoped that in time allies from amongst their landlords would join their cause. And we may doubt whether fear of their tenants was the only or even the main reason for the inactivity of so many of the gentry. Norfolk was convinced that they could keep order, as long as they resided and asserted their authority.[131] Ralph Sadler had been given the same opinion with regard to the Yorkshire outbreaks by the inhabitants of Tadcaster, who told him "Yee yee an the gentlemen had been as they should be, they might have stayed them well enough at the first . . . "[132] It seems in fact as though Wharton's friends may have been paralysed and thrown into disarray by the same contradictory loyalties as had been brought to bear in Wharton's own case, and that they too may have felt the powerful attraction of the Percy interest. At any rate, it was not until February 1537 that these men recovered something of their strength and cohesiveness. The arrival of the duke of Norfolk on the scene as the king's lieutenant, and probably too Wharton's re-emergence, had much to do with this. The first sign of a positive and committed loyalty came on 10 February when the fugitive Sir Francis Bigod was arrested in Cumberland by Sir John Lamplugh on information provided by Sir Thomas Curwen.[133] Then on 16 February, after the news of the disorders at Kirkby Stephen, and the spread of a new rebellion, Wharton and Curwen were sent into Westmorland to steady the country and raise men.[134] Both were commended to the king after the collapse of the revolt (together with Lamplugh and Sir Christopher Dacre) as Norfolk's chief helpers in the work of sup-

[128] Bean, *The Estates of the Percy Family*, p. 65.
[129] *L.P.*, xi, 1080; xii (1), 687, p. 304; Dodds, *op. cit.*, i, pp. 370–1.
[130] *L.P.*, xi, 1080.
[131] *Ibid.*, xii (1), 336.
[132] *Ibid.*, 200.
[133] *Ibid.*, 301.
[134] *Ibid.*, 439.

pression.[135] Even Sir John Lowther was able to retrieve his reputation by taking part in the defence of Carlisle.[136] There was trouble again in May when the bodies of the rebels whom Norfolk had executed by martial law were secretly taken down and buried, a proceeding to which Cromwell insinuated the duke had consented.[137] Norfolk hastily tried to fasten the blame on Wharton, Curwen and Lowther, but the two former soon cleared themselves by prompt action in searching out and examining the unfortunate women who had been responsible.[138] And by the end of the month both were acquiring further merit by searching out evidence of the treasons of the abbot of Holme Cultram.[139] Passivity in the first revolt was in fact atoned for by a prompt and energetic reaction to the second.

IV

One of the most remarkable sequels of the Pilgrimage of Grace was the shabby way in which the earl of Cumberland was treated. The earl and his family, as has been seen, had been devoted and consistent supporters of the crown throughout the rebellion. Nevertheless on 8 February 1537 Cumberland was told by the king to quit his wardenry and he hastened to obey.[140] Henry, however, does not seem to have been actuated by any personal dislike or distrust of the earl, in spite of the latter's close relationship with the fallen earl of Northumberland, and in fact (as he subsequently made clear to the duke of Norfolk) was appreciative of the Cliffords' services during the rebellion. So that sometime early in the next month the king relented, and Cumberland was told (perhaps on 9 March) that there had been a change of policy, and that he was after all to remain warden.[141] In April the earl was made a knight of the Garter and in the summer his heir entered the circle of the royal family through his marriage to Elizabeth Brandon, the king's niece.[142] But we may doubt whether these honours compensated for the hard fact of the collapse of the Clifford ascendancy in the West March which took place in that same summer of 1537. Because on 28 June Sir Thomas

[135] *Ibid.*, 498.
[136] *Ibid.*, 427. [137] *Ibid.*, 1156.
[138] *Ibid.*, 1156, 1214, 1246, 1258.
[139] *Ibid.*, 1259.
[140] *Ibid.*, xii (1), 372. [141] *Ibid.*, 614.
[142] *Ibid.*, 1008; *Complete Peerage*, iii, p. 567.

Wharton received letters patent making him deputy warden of the West March.[143] The appointment might not in itself have caused the earl any misgivings; but it soon became apparent that the new deputy warden was to have the substance of power in the March, while Cumberland would retain only an empty title. Wharton, for example, was given the stewardships of the bishopric and priory of Carlisle, and of Holme Cultram abbey and Wetherall priory, together with the profits of certain crown lands in Cumberland, "in order to have the men of the country under command".[144] But just for this reason these were normally the warden's perquisites, and as such had been enjoyed by the earl of Cumberland. Now he had to surrender his patents. Then it was noted that when some thirty gentry of the West March were fee'd to serve the crown on the Border, these consisted preponderantly of Wharton allies and kin, balanced by a few Dacre followers: but the Clifford connection was scarcely represented at all.[145] Even more devastating was the fact that the fee'd gentry were not to serve under the warden, but under the new deputy warden.[146] Thus, although the earl retained his office until his death in 1542, in practice he had played no part in the administration of the West March since the appointment of his intrusive deputy five years before. In fact, when Wharton was raised from his deputyship to the wardenry in 1544, he merely acquired the title of an office whose substance he had long enjoyed.

But Wharton's rule, it has been seen, involved a break with the tradition whereby the Marches had been entrusted to great lords, and its novelty inevitably gave rise to controversy. What after all qualified a man to serve the crown in high office? Was it noble blood and the high status which nobility conferred? Or was the mere appointment of the crown enough to invest any person whom the king trusted with something of the majesty of royalty. Norfolk was insistent that only noblemen could maintain the king's authority in the Marches. As early as 7 March he had written to urge that the western wardenry should not be conferred on a "mean person", and that "men of estimation and nobility" were also required to rule the eastern Border.[147] But the only result was to produce a weighty rebuke from the Council. "If it shall please his Majesty", Norfolk

143 *L.P.*, xii (2), 154.
144 *Ibid.*, Add. i (1), 1229.
145 *Ibid.*, xii (2), 249. See below, p. 133.
146 *Ibid.*
147 *Ibid.*, xii (1), 594.

was told, "to appoynt the meanest man to rule and govern in that place, is not his Graces authoritie sufficient to cause al men to serve his Grace under him without respect of the verie estate of the personage?"[148] To this the king himself added, "For surely we woll not be bound of a necessitie to be served with lordes. But we woll be served with such men what degree soever as we shall appointe to the same."[149] There seems to be an echo here (although with a characteristic Henrician emphasis on the force of the royal appointment) of the arguments for merit and capacity to serve, as opposed to mere inherited rank, which had been put forward during the Pilgrimage by humanist propagandists of Cromwell's entourage like Richard Morison.[150] And in fact it seems likely that Cromwell's was the most important influence at work at this time to secure the rejection of Norfolk's insistence on the appointment of great nobles to the Marches. He and Wharton were closely in touch during the spring and summer months of 1537,[151] and Wharton thought he owed his deputy wardenry to the lord privy seal, to whom he wrote on 13 July, in one breath acknowledging his advancement and expressing his "devotion".[152] Wharton's own approach to the work of his office expressed an impatience with the rule of the great lords which followed naturally from the circumstances of his appointment. "In the late lord Dacre's time", he told Cromwell on 4 September 1537, "there was a cry 'A Dacre, a Dacre' and afterwards 'A Clifford, a Clifford' and even then 'A Dacre, a Dacre'. Now only 'A King, a King'."[153] What could express better the start of the slow Tudor revolution in the north (not to be completed however for another generation) of which Wharton had become a prime agent? His old master the earl of Northumberland had died within a few days of his appointment. Released from the service of the house of Percy, he could now devote himself wholeheartedly to that of the crown.

The Pilgrimage of Grace, then, provided the government with the opportunity to end Clifford rule in the West March, just as the

[148] *Ibid.*, 636.
[149] *Ibid.*, 1118.
[150] See W. G. Zeeveld, *Foundations of Tudor Policy* (Cambridge, Mass., 1948), ch. 8.
[151] For example on 14 April Wharton sent up his brother with "news" of the West March (*L.P.*, xii (1), 935).
[152] *L.P.*, xii (2), 254.
[153] *Ibid.*, xii (2), 642.

Dacre dominance had been broken a few years before. A "new man" was instead to be set over the March. This was a policy dictated as much by administrative convenience as by mistrust of the great lords, for the March would always be weak and disorderly as long as the warden, whether Clifford or Dacre, exploited his office to pursue family feuds and rivalries.[154] But Wharton also owed his office to the suspicion aroused by the ambitions of the king's lieutenant in the north, the duke of Norfolk. Norfolk's opposition to the rule of "mean men" in the Marches had originally been motivated by the hope that he might be appointed warden-general of all three Marches.[155] With this office, combined with his lieutenancy, he would exercise wide powers over the north, and control an extensive patronage. But when hints of his willingness to serve in these capacities got no response from the king, Norfolk turned to the tactic of pushing the claims of the great northern lords to the March offices. He urged the appointment of either the earl of Rutland or the earl of Westmorland to the East and Middle Marches (where two "mean men", Sir William Eure and Sir John Widdrington, had been appointed as deputies) even after both had refused to serve.[156] In the West he was insistent on Dacre as warden, and, although here he at last resigned himself to the continuance of Cumberland's rule, his opposition to Wharton's advancement ("I think", he said, "Sir Thomas Wharton will never serve the King well as warden") persisted to the end.[157] In the background, too, there were hints of other ambitions. Norfolk saw himself as the heir of the crumbling Percy influence in the north, undermined by the Pilgrimage and the disgrace of the earl of Northumberland. Were it not to serve the king, the duke wrote, he would not have tarried in the north for all the earl of Northumberland's lands; and Cromwell, the duke added, would wonder if he knew how much Norfolk had been urged to ask for Percy lands, and so remain inhabited in the north.[158] It was said too that the duke had called his son to him in order that he might learn what was necessary to succeed in his room.[159] Norfolk seems in fact to have envisaged a new Howard territorial power in the north which, buttressed by office under the crown,

[154] *Ibid.*, xii (1), 636, 667.

[155] *Ibid.*, 595. There can be little doubt that Norfolk was the "nobleman" who, under this remembrance, would be made lieutenant of the north and warden-general.

[156] *Ibid.*, 667, 919.

[157] *Ibid.*

[158] *Ibid.*, 1157; xii (2), 291.

[159] *Ibid.*, xii (1), 1162.

would lead the northern magnates, and mediate between London and the remote communities of the Marches and Yorkshire. In short, the duke showed too many of the makings of an over-mighty subject to be trusted. No doubt his ambitions were too broadly and unskilfully pressed to have any hope of success. But all the same it would have been the height of folly to strengthen his following and reputation by appointing the men whom he backed for high office in the Marches. And so the very fact of Norfolk's patronage of the great lords compelled the government to turn to "mean men" to occupy the wardenries. In the West March, as has been seen, the way had been prepared for an alternative to the see-saw of Clifford and Dacre rule, as the crown's grip on the Percy lands and following in Cumberland had tightened. This was a process which was completed by the disgrace of the earl of Northumberland after the Pilgrimage. He was in London by February 1537, ill and destitute, with his suits on behalf of his servants and his requests for money all ignored.[160] Norfolk even prevented him from meeting his needs by selling timber from his own estates.[161] And in the background there was the shadow of treason and the need to explain the surrender of Wressle castle to Robert Aske.[162] It is not surprising that early in May the earl should have agreed to make over his lands forthwith and unconditionally to the crown, begging Cromwell for such recompense and maintenance as the king might determine.[163] By 2 July he was dead, and the king succeeded to the vast Percy interests in the north. This very fact made Wharton, the man who, as lieutenant of Cockermouth, commanded the Percy tenants in Cumberland, an obvious choice to rule the March. But in addition of course there was his kinship with Curwen; this had brought him into the circle of the court-orientated families in the March, which gave him a powerful following, while his Percy grants had made him a substantial landowner there in his own right. Above all his service with the earl of Northumberland had given him experience both of the Border administration and of the court.

Still, all these things might not have been decisive but for Wharton's own character and temperament which made him better fitted than the other men available in his own circle for the tasks which would now have to be faced. Both Sir William Musgrave and

[160] *Ibid.*, xii (1), 328, 774, 1211.
[161] *Ibid.*, 1173.
[162] *Ibid.*, 849 (p. 382), 1062.
[163] *Ibid.*, 1121, 1304.

Sir Reynold Carnaby,[164] for example, were given opportunities not unlike those afforded Wharton, but shied away from the harsh duties which rule in the Marches involved. In Wharton however there was a combination of toughness, unselfconscious bravery, and even delight in violence, which made him at home in this world. He was, in the jargon of the time, a "good Borderer". His feuds, for example, were pursued with an implacability which made him hated, but also feared, and which more than matched the Border chiefs and lords at their own game.[165] His toughness, bravery, and steady nerve emerge in the famous victory at Solway Moss where on 24 November 1542 he coolly confronted and then put to rout a Scots army many times the size of his own.[166] And the steadily deteriorating relations between James V and Henry VIII after 1537, due largely to the latter's violent and provocative policy towards Scotland, threw many opportunities in his way to prove his skill in Border raid, counter-raid, and espionage. But in addition to Wharton the Borderer there was also the Wharton who had known the ordered dignified world of the great households, whose forebears had served the Cliffords, and who had himself been a Percy officer. There he had learnt the sense of system and order, of deference and degree which made the former Percy comptroller an equally faithful and able servant of the crown. It is well to bear in mind that Wharton's peerage was not simply the result of the sen-

[164] Carnaby was a failure as keeper of Redesdale, an office to which he was appointed soon after the Pilgrimage, and eventually had to be superseded by his enemy Sir John Heron. Sir William Musgrave was discredited by his debts, and his failure to reside at Bewcastle, where effective rule was exercised by his deputy, John Musgrave.

[165] Wharton's self-assertive quarrelsomeness helped him to challenge the dominance of the great lords in the March society. But his incessant feuds, particularly with his fellow officers in the March administration, had their embarrassing side. For the consequences of his enmity with Lord Grey of Wilton, warden of the East March in Edward VI's reign, see below, p. 135; and his execution of the Maxwell hostages in 1548 (after betrayal by the Maxwells had led to the failure of Wharton's raid on Dumfries early in the year) was an impulsive and impolitic move which generated a feud of such violence that it was one of the factors which led to Wharton's removal from the rule of the West March. There were also quarrels with Sir Thomas Wentworth, whom Wharton eventually displaced as Captain of Carlisle, with Lord Eure, deputy warden of the Middle March, and with Sir William Vavasour over the captaincy of Berwick. Wharton, with his Borderer's passion and violence, was never wholly at home in the ordered world of Tudor administration.

[166] See e.g. Sir William Musgrave's account of the battle, in *Hamilton Papers*, ed. J. Bain, 2 vols. (Edinburgh, 1890–2), i, p. 307.

sational stroke of luck which made him the victor of Solway Moss, since Sir William Eure, who had no such feat of arms to his credit, was ennobled at the same time. Rather these titles were intended to signalize the success of the Tudor policy of ruling the Marches through the "new men" whose service to the crown had now raised them to a place in the peerage side by side with the great lords they had displaced.

V

Wharton probably inherited an income of about £100 a year from his ancestral estate, and a status therefore of modest prosperity rather than great wealth.[167] Office however made him a rich man. Already in 1537, as deputy warden of the West March, he received a fee of 200 marks a year, which rose to 300 when in October 1541 he also became captain of Carlisle.[168] His appointment as warden of the March in 1544 doubled his salary,[169] which soared again to 1,000 marks when in July 1552 he became deputy warden-general of all three marches under John Dudley duke of Northumberland.[170] This was an income which few but the great lords of the north or the richest of the squirearchy could have equalled, but Wharton enjoyed it for only two years. The Marian régime relegated him to the Middle March, with a salary of only 500 marks.[171] But his

167 This estimate is based on the inquisition post mortem of Philip third Lord Wharton of 1625 (see below, pp. 000–00 and Appendix III), in which the rental of the first lord's inheritance is specified as follows:

	£	*s.*	*d.*
Wharton	23	6	8
Lammerside	10	0	0
Nateby	27	12	6
Tebay and Roundthwaite	38	10	3
	£99	9	5

It may reasonably be assumed that this rental approximates to that received at the time of the first lord's death in 1569.

168 *L.P.*, xii (2), 249 (6); xvi, 1282.

169 Wharton's fee as warden was 500 marks: *Calendar of Patent Rolls, Edward VI*, ed. R. H. Brodie, 5 vols. (London, 1924–9; hereafter cited as *C.P.R., Edw. VI*), ii, p. 401; he also retained the captaincy of Carlisle, with its 100 mark fee.

170 *C.P.R., Edw. VI*, iv, pp. 195, 258; *Literary Remains of Edward VI*, ed. J. G. Nichols (London, 1857), pp. 439–40; *Acts of the Privy Council*, by J. R. Dasent, 32 vols. (London, 1890–1907; hereafter cited as *A.P.C.*), 1552–4, p. 137.

171 *Calendar of Patent Rolls, Philip and Mary*, 4 vols. (London, 1936–9; hereafter cited as *C.P.R., Ph. & M.*), iii, p. 27.

fortunes began to soar again in December 1555, when he was made warden of the East and Middle Marches, with fees totalling 700 marks.[172] Office also brought him other perquisites. He enjoyed a long list of stewardships of monastic, church and crown lands, all with fees annexed to them.[173] From 1553 he was master of the queen's henchmen, with a wage of £100 a year, and doubtless other perquisites as well.[174] Windfalls came his way like the wardship of Sir William Musgrave's heir, and then of Sir Reynold Carnaby's.[175] All in all, at the height of his prosperity, his income from office, by way of fees and wages alone, must have been in the region of £600–£700 a year. We can understand, therefore, his reluctance to quit the East March in the summer of 1557, when the earl of Northumberland was associated with him in the wardenry, finally supplanting him in January 1559. Thereafter Wharton withdrew into the semi-retirement which lasted until his death in 1569.[176] Wharton's official revenues almost equalled, and may have exceeded, his income from land, even after he had built up the great estate which he left to his heir; and retirement, if made inevitable by advancing years, must nevertheless have involved a drastic reduction in his resources, as well as a blow at his self-esteem. Perhaps, as long as Queen Mary was alive, he could draw solace from the favour with which his eldest son, Sir Thomas Wharton, a member of the Queen's Council, was regarded by the Marian régime. The Whartons, in fact, were already establishing themselves as one of the great political dynasties. Both interest and inclination, and later religion as well, drew them towards politics. The first lord had set his family on the course, as exhilarating as it was perilous, which would end a century

172 He was also captain of Berwick (*ibid.*, pp. 182–3).

173 While he was warden of the West March Wharton also held the stewardships of the lands of Holme Cultram abbey, of Carlisle and Wetherall priories, and of Penrith (*L.P.*, *Add.* i (1), 1229). He was appointed steward, bailiff and receiver of the liberty of Hexhamshire, constable of Alnwick castle and forester of all forests and chases appertaining thereto, at the same time as he became warden of the Middle March. He combined the stewardship of Rothbury lordship with the wardenry of the East March. He was also steward of Furness Abbey (Sir R. Somerville, *History of the Duchy of Lancaster*, 2 vols., London, 1953 and 1979, i, p. 510).

174 *C.P.R., Ph. & M.*, ii, p. 277.

175 *L.P.*, xxi (1), 1166 (33); *C.P.R., Edw. VI*, iv, p. 36.

176 *A.P.C.*, vi, 1556–8, pp. 137–8; *Calendar of Patent Rolls, Elizabeth I* (London, 1939–), hereafter cited as *C.P.R., Eliz.*, i, pp. 56, 58; see below, p. 135.

and a half later with the shipwreck of its fortunes, and the impecunious exile of the Jacobite duke of Wharton, the last of his line.

But in addition to the offices there were the lands, for Wharton's career made him a great landowner as well as a great official. Characteristically, his estate was built up mostly at the expense of those powers and interests in the north which had declined before the rising sun of Tudor supremacy. There were, for example, the early grants of Percy lands in Cumberland and Yorkshire, made over to Wharton by the unfortunate sixth earl of Northumberland.[177] The later acquisitions were mostly made out of monastic lands, but there were also significant gains from the escheated estates of Sir Francis Bigod, the traitor and eccentric Pilgrim,[178] another of the defeated. The outcome was not a consolidated estate, although there was a tendency for the main weight of the properties to lie in Westmorland and north-west Yorkshire around the ancient Wharton inheritance there, with Wharton Hall, enlarged and beautified, as its centre. But there was also the Cumberland complex, and another near Tadcaster, on the borders of the West and East Ridings. These made Wharton a considerable member of two other gentry communities in addition to that of his native Westmorland. And his acquisition of Healaugh priory in the West Riding, together with his lease of Holme Cultıram abbey in Cumberland, enabled him to reside and therefore to make his influence felt in both. The distribution of his estates helped to make him known and respected throughout the north, and so increased his political stature.

No doubt family pride was a motive behind Wharton's extensive acquisitions of lands in Westmorland and the North Riding, which provided such tangible evidence of the new status he had conferred on his house. Doubtless too it was satisfying for a descendant of Clifford servants to confront the earl of Cumberland in an area where the Clifford predominance had previously been unquestioned. At any rate the estate as Wharton built it up dominated the uplands west of the vale of Eden, looking down towards Appleby with its Clifford castle, besides straddling the Pennines from Kirkby Stephen (only a few miles from another Clifford castle at Brough)

[177] See above, pp. 105–6.

[178] On Bigod see A. G. Dickens, *Lollards and Protestants in the Diocese of York* (Oxford, 1959), ch. 3.

down into Swaledale. It was gradually acquired in stages, beginning in August 1544, when Wharton received an extensive block grant of monastic property.[179] This included the lands of Shap abbey (or most of them) in the central uplands of Westmorland, and these were joined to the ancestral Wharton inheritance (Wharton, Nateby and Tebay) by the grant in 1545 and 1546 of two other Westmorland manors, Bretherdale (late of Byland abbey) and Ravenstonedale, which had belonged to Watton priory.[180] The acquisition at the same time of Muker and Keld, two manors which had been part of the Rievaulx abbey lands, carried the estate over into upper Swaledale.[181] It was in 1546 too that the manor of Kirkby Stephen, late of St Mary's abbey, York, came into Wharton's hands.[182] Perhaps it was to overawe this tumultuous community which had driven him into exile ten years before that he left in the parish church a memorial of his greatness in the cenotaph on which he lies in effigy between Dorothy Stapleton and Lady Anne Bray, the latter a daughter of the earl of Shrewsbury, and the wife of his old age.[183] Here too he founded his Free School, bringing the Erasmian ideals of the Tudor governing class to this remote revion where so recently the monastic culture had held unchallenged sway.

There were more additions to the lands in the North Riding and Westmorland during Edward's and Mary's reigns. The most important was the manor of Healaugh in Swaledale, late Sir Francis Bigod's, in May 1556, which brought the Wharton lands down into lower Swaledale.[184] But there had also been the Westmorland manor of Thrimby, acquired in May 1547 by an exchange with the archbishop of York;[185] and another Westmorland manor, Marton, late of the duchy of Richmond, came into Wharton's possession in 1558.[186] Meanwhile the complex of lands near Tadcaster had also been enlarged. The nucleus here were the two Percy manors of Healaugh (not to be confused with Healaugh in Swaledale) and Catterton, both grants of the earl of Northumberland. To these had

179 Public Record Office, E318/1203.
180 Public Record Office, E318/1203 and 1205.
181 *Ibid.*, E318/1203.
182 *Ibid.*, E318/204.
183 For a description of the cenotaph at Kirkby Stephen, see *Trans. C. & W. A. & A. Soc.*, iv (1878–9), p. 206.
184 *C.P.R., Ph. & M.*, iii, p. 203.
185 *C.P.R., Edw. VI.*, i, p. 50.
186 *C.P.R., Ph. & M.*, iii, p. 409.

been added in 1538 the buildings and demesnes of Healaugh priory, where Wharton lived in his later years, and where he lies buried in the nearby parish church.[187] Perhaps the attraction was the close vicinity of his wife's family, at Wighill. The acquisition of the lands of Sinningthwaite priory by exchange in 1558 gave him a sizeable estate in this district.[188] No additions were subsequently made to the Percy grants in Cumberland, beyond the lease of Holme Cultram abbey, which expired in 1560.[189] But two outlying manors were acquired in north Yorkshire, Thormanby and Kipling Grange, the former a Gisburn estate, the latter of Easby abbey; and there was the manor of Trimdon in the Bishopric, also Gisburn abbey property.[190]

What the annual rental of these lands may have been we can only guess. Wharton's inquisition post mortem of 1569 has survived, but is an even more misleading guide to rental values than most documents of this class, since the Cumberland and Westmorland estates are not included. The annual value of the Yorkshire lands are given as £114, obviously an underestimate. The figures given in the grants and particulars of sale suggest a rental of over £230 a year, without fines and other casual profits. The Cumberland estates would bring in another £100 a year, again without casual profits. Those in Westmorland, absent from the first lord's inquisition, are detailed in that of the third lord, taken in 1625, and in spite the lapse of over half a century the annual values specified in this seventeenth-century inquisition, where they can be compared, are identical with those of 1569. From these figures, together with those contained in the grants and particulars of sale, we may conclude that the rental of £364 given for the fourth lord's Westmorland estates also represents, more or less, the value of these lands at the time of the first lord's death. To this the Durham lands added another £65. Wharton therefore came to enjoy an income from land which (if casual profits are also taken into account) must have been over £750 a year. He had almost increased eightfold the rental he had inherited from his father.[191]

187 *L.P.*, xiii (1), 1520, p. 578. Public Record Office, E318/1201.

188 *C.P.R., Ph. & M.*, iii, p. 409.

189 *C.P.R., Eliz.*, ii, pp. 108–9.

190 Trimdon and Thormanby were included in the grant of 1544 (see n. 179 above); Kipling Grange is listed in Wharton's i.p.m. as late of Easby abbey.

191 For an approximate rental of Wharton's properties see Appendix III, below, p. 146.

The rise of the Wharton family to the status of great landowners must have seemed something of a portent in the conservative society of the north. It was remarkable, for example, that a single lifetime had sufficed for the accumulation of such a large mass of landed property. The great northern estates were ordinarily the result of generations of slow accumulation and careful marriage alliances, and newcomers were rare in the circle of the greater landed families. The *arriviste* Wharton was therefore a novel phenomenon. Perhaps even more novel was the fact that this was an *arriviste* who had been enriched, on an unexampled scale, by the service of the crown. Because, although Wharton did expend over £2,000 on the purchase of land,[192] the overwhelming bulk of his landed acquisitions came to him by way of gift from the crown, and as a reward for service done. Probably few or none of Wharton's contemporaries could remember the case of the first Lord Ogle,[193] in the reign of Edward IV, who also owed the extensive, if largely ephemeral, estate he built up in Northumberland to politics and office. But with the ending of the Wars of the Roses opportunities for those in the lower reaches of the landed class to better themselves by such methods had become increasingly rare. New openings however presented themselves when the mounting tension between Henry VIII and the northern magnates once more raised hopes of confiscatory measures from which faithful servants of the crown might profit. Lord Dacre's troubles in 1534, for example, had aroused expectations (doomed to disappointment) of lucrative grants and leases of escheated Dacre estates.[194] And the annexation of the Percy lands to the crown (from which many more than Wharton profited) must have drawn the ambitious and land-hungry amongst the gentry towards the king's service, since "worthy service" came to be the condition on which "preferment" to those lands could be obtained.[195] But above all of course the dissolution of the monasteries made possible extensive changes in the distribution of landed property, and the rise to affluence of families previously often of modest status. In fact a measure of reconstruction of the

[192] Wharton purchased the demesnes of Healaugh priory, and the manors of Brotherdale, Kirkby Stephen, Ravenstonedale and Marton (Public Record Office, E318/1202, 1204, 1205; *C.P.R., Ph. & M.*, iv, p. 409).
[193] See *Dict. nat. Biog.*; Hodgson, *History of Northumberland*, pt. 2, p. 384.
[194] See above, p. 111.
[195] *A.P.C., 1542–7*, p. 383.

landed class became possible, and this was done in such a way as to enhance the power of the crown by rewarding those who served it faithfully, and by making available career prospects beyond those which any magnate could offer.[196]

Wharton of course was a leading beneficiary of this process in the north, but not the only one. The affluence which came his way was shared with the relatives, friends, and political associates on whom he had come to rely for backing and support. The party, in fact, and not just an individual was refreshed by the shower of royal bounty. Some made gains comparable to Wharton's own. His nephew, Sir Reynold Carnaby, for instance, was able to build up a great estate in Northumberland, mostly from monastic properties, particularly those of Hexham abbey.[197] So was his brother-in-law Sir John Forster, who married his daughter to the heir of an earldom.[198] Of Wharton's old associates in the West March Sir Thomas Curwen acquired a lease of Furness abbey lands which subsequently became legendary;[199] Sir John Lamplugh profited at the expense of St Bees and other monastic houses.[200] Thomas Dacre, who abandoned his own family to serve Wharton, was rewarded with Lanercost priory and its lands, where his descendants were to remain for five generations;[201] and Thomas Sandford, as well as Christopher Crakenthorpe, could probably both thank their kinsman Lord Wharton for the Shap abbey and Byland estates which rounded off their ancestral possessions.[202] There seems to be a pattern here which was initiated, according to a contemporary observer, by Thomas Cromwell, who caused the King to prefer "many sufficient persons to the kingis servis who were some raised to nobilitie and to worshipe and good calling, and all indewed with maintenance out of the

196 See e.g. *ibid.* for the use made of Holme Cultram abbey lands and chantry lands to reward good service in the West March upon recommendation by Wharton.

197 See *Northumberland County History*, x (Newcastle upon Tyne, 1914), p. 408.

198 *Ibid.*, i (1893), pp. 154–60. Forster's grandson was the third Russell earl of Bedford.

199 *Victoria County History, Lancashire*, 8 vols. (London, 1906–14), viii, p. 311 n. Curwen preceded Wharton as steward of the Furness abbey lands. For the legend, and a tradition of his intimacy with Henry VIII, see Edmond Sandford, *Relation of all the Antiquities and Familyes in Cumberland* (Kendal, 1675), p. 20.

200 *Trans. C. & W. A. & A. Soc.*, new ser., xxxviii (1938), p. 89.

201 *Victoria County History, Cumberland* (London, 1901–), ii (1905), p. 160.

202 *L.P.*, xix (1), 1035 (159); *Hist. MSS. Comm.*, 9th Rept (1883), App. II, p. 195.

revenewes of the abbyes".[203] Cromwell however can hardly claim the credit for the policy of taking the leading gentry into the fee of the crown in return for their "assistance" to the warden (or deputy warden) and service under him when summoned. Although fees were first paid in the West March in 1537, at the same time as Wharton's appointment to the deputy wardenry, Wolsey had made use of this device in the East March as early as 1525.[204] It was an obvious complement to the policy of appointing "mean men" to rule the Marches, since these, unlike the great lords, were without the resources to fee the gentry themselves, or reward with grants, leases, and estate offices, as a Dacre, Clifford, or Percy could. But the fees were also of course a means of sharing out amongst a broad cross-section of the gentry those profits of office from which Wharton had benefited, although on a very much larger scale. And so, more or less at the same time as Wharton's appointment to the deputy wardenry, thirty-four of the gentryof the West March were fee'd at a total cost of £273 a year.[205] Amongst these Wharton's friends were largely represented, and in fact of the thirteen leading gentry of the March who received the larger fees of £10 or more, nine were Wharton or Curwen kin. These included Curwen himself, Lamplugh, Lowther, Sir William Musgrave, and Walter Strickland of Sizergh, as well as Sir James Leyburn and Sir Robert Bellingham. The lesser gentry, with fees of £6 13*s* 4*d*, included another four Wharton relatives,[206] but a significant feature of this grouping was that in it were at least five Dacre followers.[207] In fact the Dacre influence, thanks largely to the support of the duke of Norfolk, remained strong and lively, and could not be denied recognition. It continued to exist as the opposition party confronting the dominant Wharton connection, never losing hope of a reversal of fortunes. The Cliffords, as has been seen, limped behind as a poor third. Only Thomas Clifford and Thomas Dalston,[208] one of the earl of Cumberland's stewards, received fees in the West March.

[203] *Letters Relating to the Suppression of the Monasteries*, ed. T. Wright, Camden Soc., xxvi (London, 1843), p. 112.

[204] *L.P.*, iv (2), 5085.

[205] *Ibid.*, xii (2), 249, 250.

[206] These were Christopher Crackenthorpe, John Warcop, Gilbert Wharton, and Hugh Machel.

[207] I.e. John Leigh, Cuthbert Hutton, Thomas Blennerhasset, Alexander Appleby, and Lancelot Lancaster.

[208] But Dalston was a notable grantee both of monastic and Percy properties. He purchased two Percy manors in Cumberland, and many of the lands of Holme Cultram abbey (Hist. Mss. Comm., *9th Rept*, p. 197).

VI

It is significant that Wharton was regarded not merely with hatred by the great houses he had supplanted, but also with contempt. He himself commented, in a letter of September 1538 to Cromwell, on the "disdain" with which his friends were regarded, and remarked that no love was lost between him and the earl of Cumberland and Lord Dacre.[209] Robert Holgate, early in 1539, also used the word "disdain" to describe his neighbours' bearing towards the new deputy warden.[210] Wharton in fact was treated as a parvenu. He was the radical who had successfully challenged an entrenched establishment, the upstart who, in the name of the king's authority, had violated traditional loyalties and due order and degree. The Cliffords seem to have resented his ascendancy with a particular bitterness, which is understandable when we recall that they had been outstripped by one of their own tenants whose father had been a Clifford servant. And the second earl of Cumberland found it difficult to forget and forgive the slights offered to his father, particularly since in 1543 he himself was passed over for the western wardenry, and Wharton appointed in his place.[211] Then there was Wharton's new estate in Westmorland, all too close to the traditional Clifford centres of power at Appleby and Brough. Bitter disputes arose over boundaries and rights, like the Cliffords' claim to hold a market at Kirkby Stephen, one of Wharton's new acquisitions.[212] And so there were the inevitable rufflings and riots between servants and tenants, culminating in the intervention of the Council, who summoned both Cumberland and Wharton before them (together with Lord Dacre) and forced a public reconciliation.[213] Cumberland and Dacre seem to have been ready to mitigate the ancient enmity of their houses. But the feud between the earl and Wharton was less easy to resolve, and was still smouldering as late as 1558.[214]

Lord Dacre was a more formidable antagonist than Cumber-

[209] *L.P.*, xiii (2), 115, 309.
[210] *Ibid.*, xiv (1), 50.
[211] Cumberland was also passed over for the wardenry of the East March (*ibid.*, xvii, 1048).
[212] *A.P.C., 1547–50*, p. 553; *ibid., 1552–4*, p. 271; *ibid., 1554–6*, p. 43.
[213] *Ibid., 1554–6*, p. 86.
[214] *Ibid., 1558–70*, p. 10.

land. It is a remarkable fact that only six years after Wharton's appointment as warden Dacre succeeded in breaking his ascendancy, and on 17 April 1549[215] took his place in the wardenry, which he held thereafter till his death in 1562. Wharton himself was partly responsible for his own downfall. His quarrelsomeness and ferocity had made him many enemies, including Lord Grey of Wilton, who had been appointed warden of the East March in 1547. The enmity between the two men[216] was one cause of the disastrous failure of their joint invasion of Scotland early in 1548, which weakened and discredited Wharton. But the political conditions which prevailed during the reign of Edward VI[217] were an equally important factor at work. Dacre had remained cautious and quiescent as long as Henry VIII's strong rule prevailed. But the party conflict between Somerset and John Dudley, soon to become duke of Northumberland, raised the hopes of every interest which had been excluded from favour in the previous reign. Dacre, like most of the northern magnates from the earl of Shrewsbury downwards, supported Somerset. But Wharton's dismissal made him one of the chief props of Northumberland's party in the north. In due course Dudley's gratitude for his services brought him back into the administration of the Border in the high office of deputy warden-general of all three marches.[218] And even under the conservative Marian régime he continued to rule the East and Middle Marches until August 1557, when (as has been seen) he had to share his office with the seventh earl of Northumberland, heir of the condemned traitor Sir Thomas Percy, who finally replaced him in January 1559.[219] This appointment is significant, because it suggests a complete reversal of the Henrician and Cromwellian revolution in the Marches. With Wharton in retirement, Percy rule in the East and Middle Marches, and Dacre rule in the West, the clock had been put back a generation. But in fact the reaction depended on the fragile life of Queen Mary, and when this ended Elizabeth's government

215 *C.P.R., Edw. VI*, ii, p. 401.

216 It emerges in Somerset's letter of 6 Oct. 1549 to Grey, forbidding him to fight a duel with Sir Henry Wharton (*Cal. State Papers, Domestic, Addenda, 1547–65*, p. 401).

217 Some account of the relevance of these to the situation in the Marches is given in R. R. Reid, "The Political Influence of the North Parts under the later Tudors", in *Tudor Studies*, ed. R. W. Seton-Watson (London, 1924), pp. 208 ff.

218 See n. 170 above.

219 See above, p. 127.

(after a brief initial period of hesitation) resumed the Henrician policies Mary had abandoned. The Dacre influence died for good on 15 February 1570 with the gallant but ineffectual charge of Leonard Dacre's Gilsland spearmen against the shot of Lord Hunsdon's government forces.[220] The last Percy warden disappeared from the scene a little later with the execution of the rebel earl of Northumberland at York in August 1572, a dozen years after his dismissal from the East and Middle Marches. Thereafter the bureaucrats Hunsdon, Scrope, and Sir John Forster ruled, men whose authority had its root not in the soil of the Marches themselves, but in London. The course of events had, after all, vindicated Wharton and his kind. The future lay with the "new men".

We cannot be wholly sure that Wharton himself would have rejoiced at this. It may be useful to characterize him as a Tudor radical, but with the qualification that he was a curious one by our standards. Even politically his background was the world of the great households from which he came, and he always remembered his first master, the dead and disgraced sixth earl of Northumberland (a proper subject for contempt in most quarters), with due regard and reverence. His personal tastes looked back to that dying world, and remained obstinately medieval,[221] so that the luxury displayed in his house at Healaugh when he died was essentially the luxury of the middle ages, made up of tapestries, hangings, cushions and plate which, bundled into the baggage waggons, could accompany the household on the slow progress over the Pennines to the recently enlarged house at Wharton, and then back to Healaugh. Such equipment was a necessary part of peripatetic existence liked by the great lords of the old school, constantly on progress from estate to estate and castle to castle. Wharton had purchased none of the new-fangled glass vessels, and his furniture was solid, unadorned, and of the plainest sort. His buildings at Wharton – the new spacious hall, kitchen, and gatehouse – were solid and handsome, and properly expressive of the new dignity and eminence of the family. But the style again struck a conservative

[220] Hunsdon's description of the action is printed in Sir C. Sharp, *Memorials of the Rebellion of 1569* (London, 1840), p. 219.

[221] See Joan Evans, "An Inventory of Thomas Lord Wharton 1568", in *Archaeol. Jl*, cii (1945), pp. 134 ff.

note, and there was no trace of the newer Italianate influences.[222] Nor did Wharton show any enthusiasm for the novel religious tendencies of his time. Like a good Henrician he conformed to the church by law established, and the Elizabethan régime appointed him a commissioner to enquire into offences against the Acts of Supremacy and Uniformity.[223] But in Edward's reign, although characteristically he acted as a commissioner for the dissolution of the chantries,[224] he had nevertheless voted against the Acts of 1549 authorizing priests to marry and the destruction of old service books, and had opposed the Act of Uniformity of 1552.[225] In his will,[226] made in 1568, he desired "the Blessed Virgin Marie and all the hollie Companye in heaven and earth to praye for me", a request whose theology was ambiguous, but which would scarcely have been made by any ardent Protestant. And the terms of the schoolmaster's oath which he included in the statutes of his school at Kirkby Stephen (which must have been suggested to him by the Marian reactionary Dr John Dakyn) also hints at a nostalgia for the old faith. "I shall not read", so the oath ran, "to them [i.e. to the pupils] any corrupt or reprobate books set forth at any time contrary to the determination of the universal catholique church, whereby they may be infected in their youth in any kind of heresie or corrupt doctrine, or else be induced to an insolent manner of living."[227] This sense of the unity of Christendom, set against "heresy" and an "insolent manner of living", suggests the old lord's distaste for the new religious attitudes which challenged authority and disrupted an established order. Wharton would hardly have disagreed with that

[222] For a description of Wharton Hall see M. W. Taylor, *Manorial Halls of Westmorland and Cumberland* (Kendal, 1892), p. 165; Royal Commission on Historical Monuments, *An Inventory of the Historical Monuments in Westmorland* (London, 1936), p. 240.

[223] *C.P.R., Eliz.*, ii, p. 170.

[224] See A. F. Leach, *English Schools at the Reformation, 1546–8* (Westminster, 1896), pt. 2, p. 44.

[225] *Dict. Nat. Biog.*

[226] See *Trans. C. & W. A. & A. Soc.*, iv (1878–9), p. 240.

[227] See Bishop William Nicolson, *Miscellany Accounts of the Diocese of Carlisle*, ed. R. S. Ferguson (Carlisle, 1877), pp. 226–7; N. Carlisle, *Endowed Grammar Schools*, 2 vols. (London, 1818), ii, p. 715. The terms of the oath reproduces that devised by Dr John Dakyn, one of the judges in the York Court of Audience in Mary's reign, for the school he founded at Kirkby Ravensworth in 1556. See A. G. Dickens, *The Marian Reaction in the Diocese of York*, St Anthony's Hall Publications, no. 11 (York and London, 1957), i, p. 8.

arch-conservative the rebel seventh earl of Northumberland, who late in the summer of 1572 drew the attention of his captors to the "dangerous sects" and "great dissentyon contynually growying" amongst Protestants, which he contrasted with "the amytie which ever hath beyn, throughout Crystendom, among those called Papysts".[228] Both the defeated great nobleman of ancient blood and the newly risen Tudor peer shared a dislike of that fragmentation of authoritative order and accepted hierarchy which Protestantism so often brought in its wake.

This of course is only to say that Wharton and his friends, no less than the Dacres, Cliffords, Percies and their kind, belonged, below the level of their disagreements, to the same landed and gentle society, whose members shared a basic ethos and outlook. None would wish to quarrel with the traditional ideals of order, degree and due subordination, service and obedience, even if some were disposed to ignore them in practice. Wharton's career in fact merely reflects a shift in power and influence within the traditional governing class, and the emergence of new elements within that class, which was such a widespread Tudor phenomenon. It was the result (as Wharton's case suggests) more often of political than economic enterprise, and there was little about it of that "rise of the middle class" of out-dated historical convention. But changes in religion, culture, and the climate of opinion nevertheless often became entangled (more by accident than set design) in the hatreds, ambitions and appetites of such men, compelling them to come to terms with ideas and movements for which in themselves they had little sympathy. The conservative Wharton is a case in point, for in his will he made provision for the foundation of that Free Grammar School at Kirkby Stephen mentioned above. Latin was to be taught there, but also "other humane doctrine"[229] was to be inculcated. Here Wharton conformed to the tendencies which were changing the shape of the world in which he lived, because his school (apart from Henry VIII's foundation at Carlisle) was the first of its kind in the West March. Educational opportunities there had been few,

228 Sharp, *Memorials*, p. 213.

229 This is the phrase used in Bishop Nicolson's version of the School Statutes, *loc. cit.* n. 227 above. Carlisle has "I will that the said Schoolmaster . . . shall interpret and reade those authors which may lead them [the Scholars] to vertue, to godliness, and to honest Behaviour, and to the knowledge of humanity" (*loc. cit.*, p. 717).

and such schools as were available had been designed exclusively to meet the needs of the church and monasteries, like the abbot of Shap's school at Brough, or the chantry schools at Penrith and Kendal,[230] where the stock subjects had been church music and liturgical Latin. Wharton's foundation aimed at more than this. The emphasis on "humanity" and the character of the syllabus taught (although it seems Greek was absent) suggests Erasmian influences[231] and a bent towards the new-fangled humanist rhetoric, and therefore towards that great world of courtiers, administrators, and upper clergy where the humanist culture ruled. Moreover the bursaries which Wharton endowed to take two of his scholars to the Universities underlines the wider scope of the school at Kirkby Stephen as compared with the traditional chantry foundations which had no university connections. Here once again, then, consciously or unconsciously, Wharton sheds his conservative guise. Instead he appears as the ally of the kind of Tudor radicalism which was eager to afford more opportunity for exceptional merit to leap the barriers to advancement which hedged the traditional society. And his school also provides an early instance of that new and powerful charitable impulse, lay in origin, and therefore orientated towards the needs of the laity, which was such a striking feature of the later Tudor and early Stuart social scene. In the north particularly a contrast can be seen here with the charity of the older generation, which had been so largely confined to the pious benefactions which the great northern families liked to make particularly to the monasteries.[232] But the emerging *esprit laïque* of the Protestant north preferred to endow education, so that Wharton's

[230] Carlisle, *op. cit.*, i, p. 191; ii, pp. 706, 711; Leach, *op. cit.*, pp. 251–3.

[231] Nicholson's version of Wharton's statutes specifies the following authors to be read in the school: Cato (Disticha); Tully (Offices, *De amicitia* and *De senectute*); Sallust; Vergil; Terence, "and such others". This list is almost identical with that given by Erasmus in his *De ratione studii* as a suitable basis for a training in humanist rhetoric. The curriculum of the new humanist schools at St Paul's and Ipswich was based on these same authors. See T. W. Baldwin, *William Shakspere's Small Latine and Lesse Greeke* (Urbana, 1944), i, ch. 5.

[232] See e.g. A. G. Dickens in Surtees Soc., clxxii (Durham and London, 1957), p. 28, on the Cliffords' patronage of Mountgrace priory. The fifth earl of Northumberland made considerable subventions to Alnwick abbey, and paid the salary of a master to teach philosophy and grammar there; he also paid an annuity to the monks of Holy island, and to the hermit at Warkworth, besides maintaining a light at St Cuthbert's tomb at Durham (Alnwick Castle MS., Receiver's Account, Northumberland, 1523).

foundation proved to be the first of nearly a dozen new grammar schools set up in Cumberland and Westmorland before 1640, all but three founded by laymen.[233]

Like many other benefactors, before and since, Wharton wished to be remembered. Perhaps he would have liked a chantry and masses for his soul had this been practicable. As it was he provided in the statutes of his school

> that every morning and evening at six of the clock . . . the Schollers by two and two, and the Schoolmaster, shall goe from the School-house into the Parish Church, and there devoutly upon their knees before they doe entre the quire say some devout prayer, and after the same they shall repaire together into the Chappell or quire, where I have made and sett up a tomb, and there sing together one of these psalms hereafter instituted, such as the Schoolmaster shall appoint . . . [234]

The psalms follow no particular liturgical pattern. They were, we may assume, the personal choice of the old lord himself, and as such they are of interest as illustrating the kind of religious attitudes within whose framework he sought to give significance to the events of his own life, and from which he drew consolation. The note of penitence, for example, is sounded by the inclusion of the *Miserere mei deus*;[235] and with this there went an emphasis on the terror of divine judgements which awaited the ungodly: "For we consume away in thy displeasure", Wharton's scholars sang in the *Domine, refugium*,[236] " . . . thou hast set our misdeeds before thee; and our secret sins in the light of thy countenance. For when thou art angry all our days are gone." But there were also the divine favours which awaited those who, having clean hands and a pure heart, could hope to ascend the hill of the lord; and these, as described by the Psalmist, so often assumed that thoroughly temporal and concrete character which Wharton could so easily comprehend. There must have been a satisfaction for the successful, thrusting old man in the thought that his scholars would sing from the Thirtieth Psalm "I will magnify

[233] These were the schools at Appleby, Bampton, Haversham, Kirkby Lonsdale, and Lowther in Westmorland, and at St Bees, Great Blencow, Bromfield, Crosthwaite, Dean, and Maughanby in Cumberland. Brampton grammar school, Maughanby grammar school, and St Bees were founded by clergy. See Carlisle, *op. cit*, *passim*.

[234] Nicolson, *op. cit.*, pp. 227–8.

[235] Ps. 51.

[236] Ps. 90.

thee, O Lord, for thou hast set me up, and not made my foes to triumph over me . . . And in my prosperity I said, I shall never be removed; thou, Lord, of thy goodness hast made my hill so strong." And what could Wharton have seen in the Forty-Fifth Psalm but a vivid delineation of his own ferocity and energy, his devotion to the service of the crown, and the fame and honour his career had brought him. "Gird thee with thy sword upon thy thigh, O thou most mighty," the Hebrew poet wrote, "according to thy worship and renown. Good luck have thou with thine honour: ride on . . . and thy right hand shall teach thee terrible things. Thy arrows are very sharp, and the people shall be subdued unto thee: even in the midst among the King's enemies . . . Thou hast loved righteousness, and hated iniquity: wherefore God, even thy God, hath anointed thee with oil of gladness above thy fellows." For Wharton, then, the psalms had come to express not merely the dramas of the soul, but the temporal drama of his own career. He seems to have had a strong sense of a providence at work in the events of his own lifetime, of which he himself had been a special instrument. Lamenting his sins, continually seeking to fear the divine judgement, obeying the law of the lord, he had earned the divine favour which had brought him to such high places. Now his gaze turned to the heavenly reward which still awaited him. "My soul hath a desire and longing to enter into the courts of the lord", his scholars were to sing, " . . . For one day in thy courts is better than a thousand."[237] But what were these but Puritan attitudes? Wharton, as much as any Calvinist, had come to see himself as a chosen vessel, called in a remote part of England to advance the coming of the sanctified society which lay within the divine purpose. Almost insensibly, it seems, his inner life had responded to the changing religious pattern of the time, in spite of his distrust of heresy, his sense of a universal catholic order, and his devotion to the Blessed Virgin and the angels. Wharton, in fact, like his less fortunate contemporary Sir Francis Bigod, stood at one of the cross-roads of his time, and in religion, as in so many other matters, he faced now towards the past, now towards the future.

[237] Ps. 84.

Appendix I

THE DACRE CONNECTION

The Dacre following is of interest as illustrating the kind of support on which the power of the great Border lords was founded. It included a number of Cumberland families, mainly of the middle or lower range of the squirearchy. Amongst these were the Threlkelds of Melmerby, whose head, William Threlkeld, was one of those nominated by Lord Dacre to the king in 1516 for appointment as sheriff of Northumberland (*L.P.*, ii (1), 2460). William's son Richard was a Dacre servant (*ibid.*, iii (2), 3671) and another, Roland, rector of Kirkoswald, was receiver-general to the fourth lord (*ibid.*, vii, 676). The Dentons of Warnell were another Dacre house. John Denton of Warnell was a natural son of Humphrey Lord Dacre, and in 1509 exchanged his ancestral manor of Denton for Warnell with his cousin, the third lord (*Trans. C. & W. A. & A. Soc.*, new series, xvi, 1915–16, p. 40). He (or his heir) was still a Dacre officer in 1534 (*L.P.*, vii, 676). Thomas Sandford of Askham and his father also served the third lord (*ibid.*, iii (2), 3427), but not surprisingly the former in due course transferred his allegiance to Wharton, who was his cousin. Thomas Salkeld of Corby was a servant of the fourth lord (*ibid.*, v, 1394), as was John Leigh of Isel, who had married a Threlkeld, and whom his master made a deputy of the West March in 1533 (*ibid.*, vi, 1167). The Blennerhassets of Carlisle were another family which followed the Dacres, and there are numerous references in *Letters and Papers, Henry VIII* to Thomas Blennerhasset, land serjeant of the Dacre lordship of Gilsland; so in all probability were the Dudleys of Yanwath, who held their lands of the barony of Greystoke, and who had married one of the co-heiresses of the senior line of the Threlkelds. There was also support from smaller men – Applebies, Porters, Huttons, and others.

Like other groupings of the same sort, the Dacre connection was strongly regional in character (its main weight was in northern Cumberland, and most of these families were seated near the Dacre houses and lands) and was based on ties of tenure and kin. The dominant impression is one of weakness, since none of these families (perhaps with the exception of the Leighs) belonged to the leadership of the county. Even after the Dacres had secured the Greystoke inheritance, they could still not challenge effectively the weight of Percy influence and landed wealth in Cumberland. The wealthy squires might seek the leadership of the earl of Northumberland or the crown, but not that of Lord Dacre. The latter's following was even weaker in Westmorland, where there was only the Dacre steward, Lancelot Lancaster of Sockbridge, who however could be relied on, when required, to push his master's quarrels with the dominant local Clifford interest to the point of violence (*ibid.*, iv (2), 4421). And in Northumberland Dacre found he could make little headway against the ubiquitous Percy influence at Alnwick, and the crown interest centred on Berwick, Dunstanburgh, and Bamburgh. In the West March, he lamented to Wolsey in April 1524, he had trusty tenants and friends; but in Northumberland only few (*ibid.*, iv (1), 220).

The political resources of the third Lord Dacre must therefore have been stretched, particularly when from 1515–25 he was ruling all three Marches. And, since he received insufficient support from the solid well-established families, he had to seek more dubious friends. In Northumberland these included Sir Nicholas Ridley of Willimoteswick, whose lawless relatives Dacre proved so reluctant to lay by the heels (*ibid.*, iv (1), 405). There was also Ridley's neighbour, Alexander Fetherstonehaugh, a ward of the third lord, who probably also followed his son. Friends of this kind brought Dacre close to the lawless and violent world of the North Tyne and of the Border clans. But here he also had more direct allies. The gentry of Northumberland were convinced that Dacre was in league with the Armstrongs of Bewcastle and Liddesdale, who could put three hundred horse at his disposal, and that he was "dayle conversaunte" with Hector Charleton of Bellingham, "oon of the grettest theves" of Tynedale (Hodgson, *History of Northumberland*, iii (1), pp. 34, 38). And when some of the Northumberland gentry proceeded sternly against the thieves of Redesdale, at the command of the duke of Norfolk, the king's lieutenant, Dacre told them "I pray god that I may leve and juge you . . . as soore as you now juge my friendes . . . " (*ibid.*, p. 40). Dacre was ready with his denials, but there can be little doubt of his alliances with the Border clans, or that these were his principal asset, "done upon sinister policy to make the King think the country cannot be quieted without the help of Dacre and his adherents . . . " (*L.P.*, iv (1), 1223). Dacre's financial resources, as well as his political resources, may have been stretched to pay for his greatness. In 1523, for example, he was defending the West March at his own charges (*ibid.*, iii (2), 3106), and his castle-building activities (see *Trans. C. & W. A. & A. Soc.*, new series, xi, 1911, p. 242) must have involved considerable expenditure, which could scarcely have been wholly met out of his fee. He may have been glad therefore to share in the profits of robbery and blackmail with his reiving friends. William Lord Dacre's use of the Armstrongs against Sir William Musgrave and his allies at Bewcastle shows that the alliances made by the third lord did not lapse after his death. One of the results of this state of affairs, however, was to give the Dacres a vested interest in Border violence, and to expose them as a result to the dislike and distrust of the sober officials in London who were determined to suppress it.

Appendix II

CURWEN AND WHARTON GENEALOGIES

The Curwens

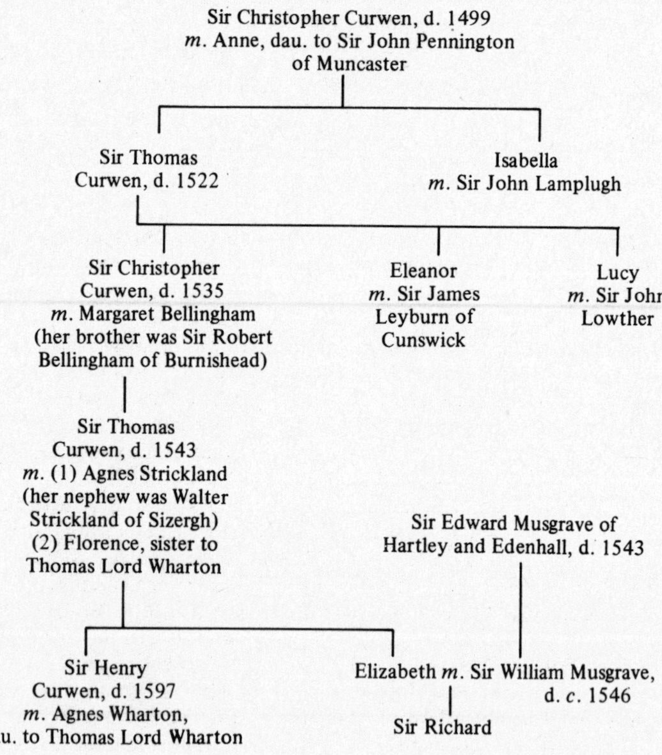

Sir Christopher Curwen, d. 1499
m. Anne, dau. to Sir John Pennington
of Muncaster
Sir Thomas
Curwen, d. 1522
Isabella
m. Sir John Lamplugh
Sir Christopher
Curwen, d. 1535
m. Margaret Bellingham
(her brother was Sir Robert
Bellingham of Burnishead)
Eleanor
m. Sir James
Leyburn of
Cunswick
Lucy
m. Sir John
Lowther
Sir Thomas
Curwen, d. 1543
m. (1) Agnes Strickland
(her nephew was Walter
Strickland of Sizergh)
(2) Florence, sister to
Thomas Lord Wharton
Sir Edward Musgrave of
Hartley and Edenhall, d. 1543
Sir Henry
Curwen, d. 1597
m. Agnes Wharton,
dau. to Thomas Lord Wharton
Elizabeth m. Sir William Musgrave,
d. c. 1546
Sir Richard

The Whartons

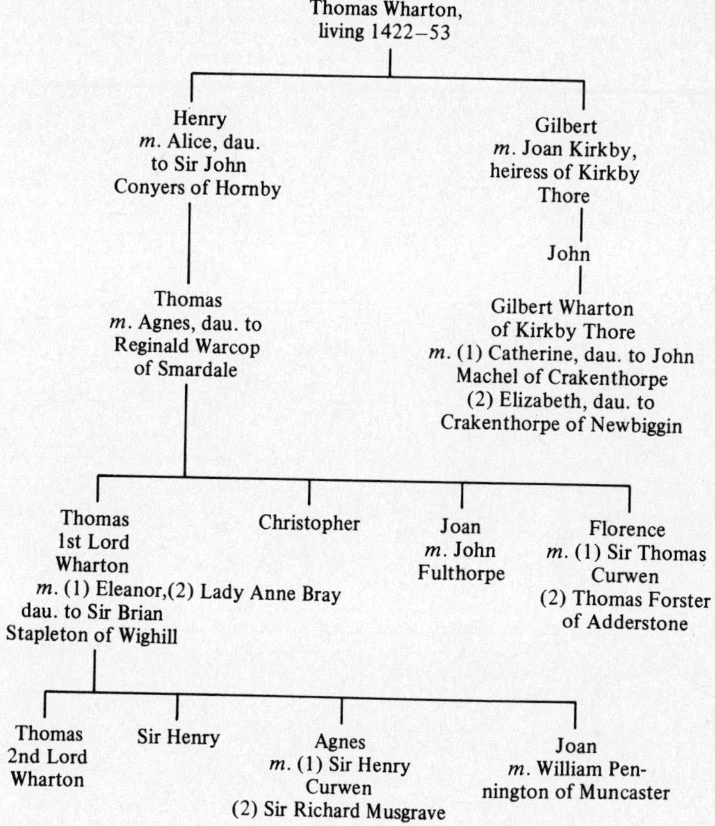
Thomas Wharton,
living 1422–53
Henry
m. Alice, dau.
to Sir John
Conyers of Hornby
Gilbert
m. Joan Kirkby,
heiress of Kirkby
Thore
John
Thomas
m. Agnes, dau. to
Reginald Warcop
of Smardale
Gilbert Wharton
of Kirkby Thore
m. (1) Catherine, dau. to John
Machel of Crakenthorpe
(2) Elizabeth, dau. to
Crakenthorpe of Newbiggin
Thomas
1st Lord
Wharton
m. (1) Eleanor,(2) Lady Anne Bray
dau. to Sir Brian
Stapleton of Wighill
Christopher
Joan
m. John
Fulthorpe
Florence
m. (1) Sir Thomas
Curwen
(2) Thomas Forster
of Adderstone
Thomas
2nd Lord
Wharton
Sir Henry
Agnes
m. (1) Sir Henry
Curwen
(2) Sir Richard Musgrave
Joan
m. William Pen-
nington of Muncaster

Appendix III

Annual values of Lord Wharton's estates

An approximate rental of Wharton's properties may be constructed as follows:

Yorkshire lands		*£*	*s*	*d*
Sinningthwaite	*C.P.R. Ph. & M.*, 1557–8, p. 409	13	6	8
Muker and Keld	Public Record Office, E318/1203	46	16	8
Healaugh (Swaledale)				
Manor	*C.P.R. Ph. & M.*, 1555–7, p. 203	53	6	7
Free rents		49	1	7½
Healaugh (W. Riding)	Alnwick Castle MS. X II 6(28)	48	15	5
Catterton	Alnwick Castle MS. X. II 6(28)	23	10	2
Thormanby	Public Record Office, E318/1203	20	9	11
		£255	7	0½
Less reserved rents	*£ s d*			
of Catterton	10 15 0½			
Healaugh	10 10 4	21	5	4½
	Clear annual value	£234	1	8

Durham lands				
Trimdon manor and rectory, and Castleton	Public Record Office, E318/1203	£65	2	0

Cumberland lands				
Great Broughton	Alnwick Castle MS. X II 3	£23	16	4
Little Broughton	Alnwick Castle MS. X II 3	3	14	8
Caldbeck underfell	Alnwick Castle MS. X II 3	21	7	8
Birkby	Alnwick Castle MS. X II 3	6	5	4
Dean	Alnwick Castle MS. X II 3	13	18	5
Whinfell	Alnwick Castle MS. X II 3	7	10	4
Cockermouth park etc.	Alnwick Castle MS. X II 3	34	8	10
Wharton's annuity	Alnwick Castle MS. X II 3	66	13	4
		£177	14	11
Less reserved rents of £75 0*s* 11*d*	Bodleian Library, Carte MSS	75	0	11
	Clear annual value	£102	14	0

Lands in Westmorland				
Wharton	i.p.m. 1625	£23	6	8
Lammerside	i.p.m. 1625	10	0	0
Kirkby Stephen rectory and vicarage	i.p.m. 1625	27	13	4
Nateby	i.p.m. 1625	27	12	6
Tebay and Roundthwaite	i.p.m. 1625	38	10	3
Kirkby Stephen manor	Public Record Office, E318/204	11	2	8½
Brotherdale	Public Record Office, E318/1202	13	13	4
Shap and Sleagill	Public Record Office, E318/1203	96	8	2½
Marton	i.p.m. 1625	14	6	8
Thrimby	i.p.m. 1625	1	13	1
Ravenstonedale	Public Record Office, E318/1205	100	2	8
		£364	9	5

Both the first lord's inquisition post mortem of 1569 and the third lord's of 1625 (above, p. 130) are transcribed amongst the Wharton MSS (Bodleian Library), i, pp. 28 and 57.

4. *The first earl of Cumberland (1493–1542) and the decline of northern feudalism*

I

However much Henry VIII might insist that "we woll not be bound of a necessitie to be served with lordes. But we woll be served with such men what degree soever as we shall appointe to the same",[1] the crown during his reign, as before it, could not dispense with the services of the nobility if the realm were to be maintained in ordered governance. Out of "the unstable and waverynge rennynge water" of the people "the noble persons of the worlde" were the indispensable islands of "ferme grounde" without which there could be no good rule.[2] In this respect the advent of the Tudors had changed little in the essentials of the situation, and Thomas Starkey in the 1530s saw it in much the same way as Bishop Russell at the end of the reign of Edward IV. The "office and duty" of the "nobylytie and gentylmen of every schyre", he wrote, "ys chefely to see justyce among theyr servanntys and subiectys and to kepe them in unytie and concorde".[3] From this point of view those great lords in the upper levels of the peerage, whose possessions and following were wide enough to enable them to lead and rule whole "countries", had a special importance. Henry VIII and his father might be wary of the type as potential "over-mighty subjects"; nevertheless these were the first to be sent the royal commands and missives if a riot was to be checked, a rebellion suppressed, or an army raised and led to

[1] *L.P.*, xii (1), 1118; W. G. Zeeveld, *Foundations of Tudor Policy* (Cambridge, Mass., 1948), pp. 201–2.

[2] The quotations are from Bishop Russell's draft sermon, prepared for the intended Parliament of Edward V, printed in S. B. Chrimes, *English Constitutional Ideas in the Fifteenth Century* (Cambridge, 1936), p. 169.

[3] Thomas Starkey, *A Dialogue between Cardinal Pole and Thomas Lupset*, ed. J. W. Cowper, Early English Text Soc., extra ser., xxxii (1878), p. 190.

war.[4] And in the governance of the north particularly the great aristocratic houses had a special place; without them order in the northern shires could crumble into rebellion as late as 1569. Good rule could not be guaranteed in Northumberland and the East Riding without the Percies; in Westmorland and the western dales without the Cliffords; in Cumberland and Lancashire without the Dacres and Stanleys. It was to the world of these great lords that the earl of Cumberland belonged, and he was distinguished from other members of his class only by the special relationship he enjoyed with Henry VIII. But during the latter's reign, as became evident during the crisis of the Pilgrimage of Grace, his power to rule in his country had become weakened to the point at which it could no longer function effectively, so raising the question of what was to take its place. The following deals with the nature and basis of the earl's authority, and the causes of its decline.

Henry first earl of Cumberland was head of the house of Clifford.[5] From his Bromeflete grandmother he had inherited extensive estates in the East Riding.[6] But the power of his family rested on lands which had been in its possession for a much longer period. These comprised the honour of Skipton in Craven in the West Riding, with its great castle; and the barony of Westmorland, where the Cliffords were hereditary sheriffs, and had the three castles of Brough, Appleby and Brougham.[7] Thus their power was preponderant in the upland communities of west Yorkshire and

[4] For the continued importance of the peerage from these points of view during the Tudor period, see W. H. Dunham, *Lord Hastings' Indentured Retainers* (Trans. Connecticut Academy of Arts and Sciences, xxxix, New Haven, Sept. 1955), ch. 5; L. Stone, *The Crisis of the Aristocracy 1558–1641* (Oxford, 1965), ch. 5.

[5] For the Cliffords in the early Tudor period see particularly *Clifford Letters of the Sixteenth Century*, ed. A. G. Dickens (Surtees Soc., clxxii, Durham and London, 1962). Also *Complete Peerage*, iii; J. W. Clay, "The Clifford Family", in *Yorkshire Archaeological Jl*, xviii (1905), p. 355; R. T. Spence, *The Cliffords, Earls of Cumberland, 1576–1646* (London Ph.D. thesis, 1959); T. D. Whitaker, *History and Antiquities of the Deanery of Craven*, 1st edn (London, 1805), p. 223; *Lives of Lady Anne Clifford*, ed. J. P. Gilson (Roxburghe Club, 1916).

[6] These were the Vesci manors of Londesborough, Weighton, Brompton, Whyrethorpe, Welham and Barlby.

[7] The greatness of the Cliffords had been founded on a Vipont marriage. Robert first Lord Clifford inherited a moiety of the Vipont possessions in Westmorland from his mother Isabella in 1299. To this he added the honour and castle of Skipton (with the manors of Silsden, Skibeden, Holme, Sturton, Thorsby, Crookrise, and Barden forest) granted him by Edward II in 1310 against the exchange of Clifford lands in Monmouthshire and Scotland. The third lord

Westmorland, but also spilled over into Cumberland, where, however, the rivalry of the Lords Dacre was to be encountered. The importance of the family in the political pattern of the north, although not equal to that of the Nevilles and Percies, was nevertheless large enough to bring them into close contact with the crown. The Clifford tradition was Lancastrian, and from the start the Tudors saw them as allies. The first earl's father, the tenth Lord Clifford, had been brought by Henry VII into the circle of the royal family by his marriage to Anne St John, the king's cousin german.[8] And, although this lord, in spite of his creditable service at Flodden and his conscientious performance of the routine chores and duties which came his way, may have incurred governmental disfavour,[9] this did not prevent his heir from being bred up with Henry VIII, whom he therefore knew intimately from childhood.[10]

There is no reason to doubt Lady Anne Clifford's view that this common upbringing "ingrafted such a love in the said Prince towards him, that it continued to the very end",[11] since this found expression in the many favours which came Cumberland's way. Perhaps the most obvious of these was the earldom Henry conferred on him in 1525, which at last raised the Cliffords from their barony to an equal status with the great Neville, Stanley and Percy dynasties of the north.[12] Cumberland was also generously endowed with lands and office. He was given the royal manor of Bawtry in Nottinghamshire and of Kimberworth in Yorkshire,[13] and towards the end of 1525 he was made warden of the West March.[14] Displaced in this office by his enemy William Lord Dacre,[15] he was restored to it in 1534,[16] after Dacre's disgrace and trial for treason. Thereafter (although the question of his replacement was again raised in 1537) he remained warden until his death, but was overshadowed during these later years by the intrusive deputy, Sir Thomas Wharton, whom the king had put in to do most of the work involved in the

(d. 1344) succeeded to the other moiety of the Vipont lands on the death of his great-aunt Idonea Vipont. Thus the Cliffords became lords and hereditary sheriffs of Westmorland. See Clay, *op. cit.*

8 *Complete Peerage*, iii, p. 254.

9 See below, pp. 157–8.

10 *Clifford Letters*, p. 140.

11 *Ibid.*

12 *L.P.*, iv, 1431, 1433.

13 *Ibid.*, 1043; ii, 1695; x, 777.

14 *Ibid.*, iv, 1727, 2402.

15 Dacre's indenture of appointment (Public Record Office, E101/72/7) is dated 1 Dec. 1527.

16 *L.P.*, vii, 1217.

office.[17] In 1535 there had been the great match between Cumberland's heir, and Lady Eleanor Brandon, "daughter of the ryght high and gratious Princess Mary late the French quene" and niece to Henry VIII.[18] Two years later there was the order of the Garter and preferment to the Council in the north, rewards for the earl's loyalty during the Pilgrimage of Grace.[19] Through his marriage into the Percy family Cumberland was also able to round off the Clifford possessions in Craven by securing the Percy lands there for his heir, to whom his brother-in-law the sixth earl of Northumberland bequeathed them.[20] And he made further important addition to the family estates by buying up the lease of the lands of Bolton abbey.[21]

By and large, then, a conventional Tudor success story. But Cumberland's failures are more interesting than his successes. He seems, for example, to have had little taste for business, and partly for this reason to have been an indifferent warden. Few letters have survived from his hand about the affairs of the West March,[22] which he tried to rule from Skipton, a castle which was too remote from the frontier. Most of the work was done by Sir John Lowther, whom Cumberland made his deputy;[23] and his own interest in the office seems to have been confined to the opportunities it gave to pursue his feud with Lord Dacre.[24] The earl's ineffectiveness as warden was in fact the cause of the humiliation he suffered when, after 1537, the king made Sir Thomas Wharton deputy warden, fee'd some thirty of the March gentry to serve under him, instead of under the warden, and transferred to him the royal lands and offices normally attached to the warden's office. Cumberland retained only an empty title, and the substance of power in the March, previously monopolized

[17] Cf., above pp. 120 ff.

[18] The indenture between Cumberland and Lady Eleanor's father, the duke of Suffolk, was signed on 9 May 1535; the marriage was to take place before 1 July in the same year. See *Statutes of the Realm*, iii (1817), p. 587.

[19] *L.P.*, xii (1), 1008.

[20] See below, pp. 169 ff.

[21] *L.P.*, xvi, p. 721.

[22] Only one letter written by the earl on March business exists for his first period as warden, from 1525–7 (*L.P.*, iv, 4211); for his second period of office, there are two for 1534 (*L.P.*, vii, 1312, 1588); none for 1535; two for 1536 (*ibid.*, x, 160, 161) and three for 1537 (*ibid.*, xii, 882, 883, 993). Thereafter the business of the March was conducted by Sir Thomas Wharton as deputy warden. By then, mountainous arrears of business had accumulated (*L.P.*, xii (2), 537).

[23] *L.P.*, xii (1), 843, 882, 1026, 1038.

[24] The quarrels between Dacre and Cumberland are amply documented. See *L.P.*, iv, 1762, 1763, 2052, 2110, 2483, 4132, 4421, 4495, 4531, 4790, 4828, 4855; vii, 1365, 1549, 1589; viii, 310, 1041; xi, 477.

by the great families, now passed to a man of modest gentry stock who was one of the earl's freeholders and the descendant of a line of Clifford servants. Cumberland's inadequacies as warden had helped forward the emergence of a new-style leadership of the March community as an alternative to that of the great lords.[25] The king seems to have sensed that Cumberland would be content to exchange the reality of regional power for lands, empty titles, and status symbols. In his case the role of feudal magnate had been overshadowed by that of courtier and landowner.

Perhaps more significant, however, was the failure of Cumberland's ability to lead and command in the countries of Craven and Westmorland, and in the west-Yorkshire dales, where his family had traditionally held dominance and rule. This became apparent during the two critical years of 1535 and 1536. During the former there was an insurrection on his own doorstep, in Craven, directed against the earl and his steward John Lambert, and which was the result of enclosures, evictions of tenants, and enhancements of rents and fines. Order was restored not by the earl or his officers but by a session of J.P.s led by Sir Richard Tempest, one of the king's servants, appointed by the earl of Northumberland, the king's lieutenant in Yorkshire.[26] Even more striking was the collapse of the earl's authority in the following year, during the Pilgrimage of Grace. The men to whom Cumberland wrote, towards the end of the first week of October 1536, to "stay" the countries of Dent, Sedbergh, and Wensleydale, where unrest had been reported, all disobeyed him;[27] and his son-in-law Lord Scrope abandoned his castle at Bolton, the strongest house in Wensleydale, at the approach of the rebels, and eventually became sworn to them. The earl himself was deserted at Skipton by the gentry of his retinue, who scattered (so they said) to see to the safety of their houses, leaving him to defend the castle with his household servants and a force hastily recruited by his man of business, Christopher Aske.[28] Thereafter Skipton was besieged by the Craven commons, led by the mysterious "Merlioune", reinforced by a group of dissident gentry from Richmondshire and

[25] See above, Chapter 3.

[26] *L.P.*, vii, 893, 970, 974, 992–3.

[27] *Ibid.*, xi, 604. Cumberland wrote to Sir James Metcalf, Sir Geoffrey Middleton, "and others", presumably including Lord Scrope. For Scrope, see *Clifford Letters*, pp. 49–51.

[28] *L.P.*, xii (1), 1186.

Mashamshire, which included the earl's old enemy and disloyal vassal, John Norton of Norton Conyers. Cumberland was safe in his strong castle, which the rebels had no artillery to batter down, and probably the siege lasted less than a fortnight.[29] But the countryside remained uneasy, and it was not until the new year, with the collapse of the Pilgrimage and of the subsequent insurrections in the West March, followed by the advent of the king's lieutenant, the duke of Norfolk, that normality was restored. Thus, while Cumberland had ensured his own safety, he had failed to prevent the outbreak and progress of rebellion, and had to be rescued from the consequences of his failure by the king.

Some of the causes of the erosion of the earl's authority may now be considered. And here one of the first points to be borne in mind is that the power of the head of the house of Clifford to lead and command in his country was still related, during the early Tudor period, to those tenurial bonds between lord and mesne tenant on which great honours like the Skipton Fee and the barony of Westmorland[30] had originally been founded. In so far as these bonds had become eroded, Cumberland's rule had been correspondingly weakened; in so far as they survived, the Clifford dominance remained a reality. For the following which the family could command amongst the gentry community consisted mostly of those freeholders who held fees by knight service, and did suit to the military court at Skipton, or to the similar court at Westmorland.[31] The continued vitality of the feudal bond is suggested by the persistence of the ceremony of homage, which the earl's father, the tenth Lord Clifford (who died in 1523), still performed in person, so giving

[29] Skipton was under siege by the commons of Craven by 18 Oct., the day on which Sir Stephen Hamerton was seized by the insurgents and sent to the castle to negotiate with the earl (*L.P.*, xii (1), 1034). On 21 Oct. John Norton, Sir Christopher Danby, Sir William Mallory and others from Mashamshire and Richmondshire set out for Craven to join the besiegers (*ibid.*, 392). They continued there until Norton was summoned to Doncaster on 26 Oct. (*ibid.*, 6). The proclamation of the truce on 28 Oct. must have ended overt hostilities against Skipton.

[30] For the barony of Westmorland, see J. Nicolson and R. Burn, *History and Antiquities of Westmorland and Cumberland* (London, 1777), i, p. 265; for the honour of Skipton, see Whitaker, *History and Antiquities of . . . Craven*, p. 209.

[31] The military court of the honour of Skipton continued to be held until 1650. The court rolls from the reign of Henry VI to that of Elizabeth, and for the years 1619 to 1650 are preserved amongst the Skipton Castle MSS. in the library of the Yorkshire Archaeological Society, Leeds.

direct and visible expression to the tie between lord and vassal.[32] Moreover, since most of the Clifford military fees were within striking distance of Skipton castle, or of Appleby, Brougham or Brough, the tenurial link could be strengthened by personal contact resulting from the service of mesne tenants in the household and estate administration. Thus, out of the ten servants who accompanied Cumberland to London for his creation in 1525, all but three belonged to families which were Clifford mesne tenants.[33] Stewards of lordships were normally recruited from these families; and so were most of the constables of the Clifford castles.[34]

Mesne feudalism then continued to survive within a context of service, with all that this implied of "good lordship" as one side of the relationship, and "faithfulness" on the part of the tenant.[35] Moreover the tenurial link, spanning the generations, had its importance as implying a relationship which was larger than the life of any single individual, and as long-lasting as the family itself. Mesne tenants were likely to be involved in a more stable tradition of dependence on and service to the Cliffords than those who were merely employed by them. Nor ought we to assume that the military service on which knightly tenures were based had ceased to have any reality by the Tudor period. Cumberland, like his ancestors, was one of the great northern war-lords, whose tenants served under him and his officers for the defence of the Border against the Scots, as they had done for example during his father's lifetime, at

[32] For example on 27 Oct. 1515 Lord Clifford received "att my lodge at Barden" the homage and relief of Henry Marton "for all suche landes as he holdeth of me by knyght service in Essleton, Kyghley, Utterlay, and Halton on the Hyll, as of my castle of Skipton" (Bodleian Library, Dodsworth MS. 83, fo. 11).

[33] Of the earl's servants at board wages who went to London, Lionel Marton, Lancelot Marton, Stephen Tempest, George Blenkinsop, Christopher Wharton, Anthony Hoton, and Thomas Blenkinsop were of families which were Clifford military tenants. The remaining three servants (Laurence Hamerton, Robert Bellingham, and Roland Thompson) were not of such families. Whitaker, *op. cit.*, p. 234.

[34] Sir Thomas Tempest, steward of Skipton in 1499, Roger Tempest, steward in 1514, and John Lambert, steward in 1522, were all knight-service tenants (Dodsworth MS. 83, fos. 116, 113b, 114b). The first earl's steward of Appleby, Thomas Sandford, and John Blenkinsop, his constable of Brough castle, both came of families which were military tenants of the barony of Westmorland. An exception was Thomas Fallowfield, constable of Brougham castle, who was not one of the earl's tenants (Appleby Castle MS., Carlisle County Record Office).

[35] For some of the implications of these terms see above, Chapter 2.

Flodden.[36] Indeed the prestige which the head of the house of Clifford enjoyed as a military leader entitled to demand devoted service (in return for which he was expected to extend the benefits of "good lordship" to his dependants) coloured the relationship between him and his tenants at all levels.[37]

By and large the Clifford mesne tenants belonged to the middle or lower ranges of the gentry. Nevertheless tenure and service, continued over generations, could also hold families of substance and power within the Clifford orbit. Under the tenth Lord Clifford, for example, Sir Thomas Tempest of Bracewell, head of a family with extensive lands in Yorkshire and Lincolnshire, but with a long Clifford connection based on the tenure of Thorpe, Burnsall, and other Clifford knights' fees in Craven, had served as steward of Skipton. So had Roger Tempest of Broughton, another Skipton knights' fee, head of a junior branch of the same family.[38] The Lowthers of Westmorland, whose ancestral manors of Lowther William and Lowther John were both Clifford fees,[39] were another prominent family of Clifford followers. Sir John Lowther served the first earl both as under-sheriff of Westmorland and as one of his deputies as warden of the West March.[40] So did Thomas Blenkinsop of Helbeck, another military tenant of the barony of Westmorland.[41] Sometimes the Clifford connection with families of this degree of importance was strengthened by marriage alliances.

[36] At Flodden Lord Clifford commanded a company in the vaward: Hall's *Chronicle* (London, 1809), p. 557. The first earl was thought to be able to raise about 1,000 "footmen" in Craven and Westmorland for service on the Border (*L.P.*, xii (1), 1092).

[37] Nostalgic recollections of the "service" relationship between the Cliffords and their tenants persisted far into Elizabeth's reign, to be contrasted with the more "economic" relationships which increasingly prevailed. Thus, when the inhabitants of Great Stainforth in Craven were being oppressed by their landlord, they turned for help to the third earl of Cumberland. Recalling that "we and our ancestors have at all tymes heretofore bene under the rule of your honours ancestors in tyme of service" they begged the earl "to buy and purchase us, that we might be wholly under your honours rule". Characteristically, the third earl rejected the offer, and the tenants enfranchised themselves (Whitaker, *op. cit.*, p. 125).

[38] n. 34.

[39] Appleby Castle MS., County Record Office, Carlisle: Survey of the Earl of Cumberland's Knights' Fees, 1526.

[40] Cumberland made Lowther his under-sheriff in 1530 (Dodsworth MS., 83, fo. 55). He is mentioned as one of the earl's deputies in the West March in *L.P.*, xii (1), 121.

[41] Nicolson and Burn, *op. cit.*, i, p. 500.

Thus, when the Musgraves of Hartley castle, tenants of the barony of Westmorland, acquired large estates in Cumberland through an alliance with the heiress of the Stapletons of Edenhall, Sir Richard Musgrave was brought into the Clifford family circle by a marriage to a daughter of the tenth lord.[42] And Sir Christopher Metcalf of Nappa in Wensleydale, who had inherited half a dozen Clifford fees in Craven from his grandmother, became one of Cumberland's sons-in-law.[43]

Such ties then were surprisingly persistent in their capacity to evoke loyalty and service. Nevertheless a system of service which rested on grants of land which were also heritable patrimonies had about it an inherent element of instability; and this was one reason why Cumberland's authority faltered when the moment of crisis came. Thus marriage and inheritance, and the extinction of male heirs, had carried five of the Clifford fees in Westmorland into the hands of his enemy, Lord Dacre.[44] Similar processes in Craven had led to the succession of John Norton of Norton Conyers to the Skipton knights' fee of Rylstone, previously held by a family of Clifford servants, the Radcliffes.[45] As a result the earl acquired a new and obstreperous vassal with whom he was soon involved in a dangerous feud. And the manor of Gargrave, held of Skipton, ceased to reinforce the authority of the Cliffords when it passed to the Danbies of Mashamshire, who were Neville not Clifford followers.[46] Moreover, even when fees remained in the hands of

[42] The Musgraves held Hartley, Langton, Musgrave, Marton, and Soulby of the barony of Westmorland. The family intermarried with the co-heiresses of the Stapletons of Edenhall in the reign of Edward IV. Sir Richard Musgrave, living in 1492, married Joan, daughter of Thomas Lord Clifford. See Nicolson and Burn, *op. cit.*, i, p. 580, and *Trans. C. & W. A. & W. Soc.*, new ser., xi (1911), p. 54, Pedigree E.

[43] Metcalf's grandmother was Elizabeth Hartlington, heiress of an ancient family of Clifford tenants who had been bailiffs of Kettlewelldale. She married Thomas Metcalf, builder of Nappa Hall, who rose to be chancellor of the duchy of Lancaster and a privy councillor of Richard III. See Whitaker, *op. cit.* (3rd edn, London, 1878), p. 514.

[44] In the 1526 survey Dacre held Dufton, Yanwath, Bolton, Brampton, and a moiety of Overton of the barony of Westmorland.

[45] Whitaker, *op. cit.* (1st edn, 1805), p. 379.

[46] *Ibid.*, p. 168. Dodsworth MS. 83, fo. 116, shows that the Danbies held Gargrave as early as 1499. For the family, see Harleian Soc., xvi (1881), p. 88. Sir Christopher Danby, who came with his fellow Clifford vassal John Norton to besiege Skipton castle in 1536, was married to a daughter of Richard Neville, Lord Latimer.

families with a traditional Clifford connection, these could nevertheless be carried out of the Clifford orbit by marriage to heiresses outside the Clifford countries, bringing with them new lands, new interests, and new masters. And so the Musgraves, for example, with the new Cumberland estate, were closer to the Dacres than the Cliffords during the first earl's lifetime, in spite of Sir Richard's Clifford marriage in the previous generation; and the heir, Sir William, was a courtier.[47] The Tempests of Bracewell were another case in point, with their new lands around Bradford and in Lincolnshire. Sir Richard Tempest was not content, like his father, to serve the Cliffords. He hoped for greater things from the service of the crown, and from his relative the court magnate Lord Darcy.[48] It was becoming increasingly difficult therefore to keep alive a connection with the bigger men of the Clifford following; and even amongst the smaller squires orientated towards Skipton or Appleby the traditional loyalties were increasingly insecure.

To this outcome the policies of Henry VII made their contribution. For (like many other of his kind) the tenth Lord Clifford was subjected to those commissions to enquire into wardships and concealed lands by means of which the king sought both to enforce his feudal prerogatives and also to bring pressure to bear on recalcitrant magnates. The tenth lord, in spite of his marriage to Henry's cousin, was not favoured by the Tudor régime (he may have countenanced some movement to resist the payment of taxes[49]) as the findings of an inquisition of 8 May 1504[50] must have made clear to the countries he ruled. These asserted that Lord Clifford had "unjustly", "by usurpation upon the title of the king", profited from the wardship marriage and relief of Thomas Blenkinsop of Helbeck; at the same time his right to the hereditary sheriffwick of Westmorland was brought into question, and fifteen Clifford fees there were claimed

[47] Sir Richard's heir, Sir Edward Musgrave, planned to marry his grandson into the Dacre family (*L.P.*, vii, 1647); his eldest son Sir William was one of the king's knights of the body. See above, pp. 100, 68 ff.

[48] For the Tempests see *Yorkshire Archaeological Jl*, xi (1890), p. 246. Like Sir William Musgrave, Sir Richard Tempest became a royal knight of the body (*L.P.*, ii (1), 2735). He was also a servant of the duke of Richmond (*ibid.*, iv (1), 3551) and steward of the crown lordship of Wakefield (*ibid.*, vi, 1595). For his relationship to Lord Darcy, with whom he was associated in many commissions and business matters, see *L.P.*, iv, 378, and *L.P.*, xi, 741.

[49] According to Lady Anne Clifford (*Clifford Letters*, pp. 130, 135).

[50] *Cal. Inq., Henry VII*, ii (1915), pp. 810–22.

for the crown. Eventually Clifford was able to traverse the findings of the inquisition, and his tenures and office were confirmed.[51] But, although he received a general pardon in 1506,[52] his fine of 1,300 marks was not remitted. The whole incident must have made the Clifford countries aware of a new immediacy of the power of the crown. And this impression must have been strengthened, during Cumberland's lifetime, by his failure in 1532 to enforce (through his under-sheriff Sir John Lowther) the jurisdiction of his sheriff's tourn within the barony of Kendal, which had been set up as a liberty for the duke of Richmond,[53] an incident which involved him in a quarrel with the crown. Although Cumberland was pardoned, his standing in his country and his power to maintain his followers must have been brought into question, particularly as far as the Lowthers were concerned. Such factors help to explain the tendency for families which had been orientated towards Clifford service, to turn increasingly towards that of the king during Cumberland's lifetime. The case of Sir Richard Tempest has been cited; he became a knight of the body and steward of the royal lordships of Halifax and Wakefield.[54] So has that of Sir Thomas Wharton, whose service to the crown brought him a peerage and great estate which eventually enabled him to challenge the Clifford influence in Westmorland itself.[55] In his wake a number of other Westmorland families, which were Clifford mesne tenants and followers, like the Warcops, Sandfords, and Lowthers, passed in the years immediately following the Pilgrimage of Grace into the crown service.

Just as the two-fold character of a fief as a piece of property and as the basis of a system of service contained contradictions not easily reconciled, so there was a latent tension between the "good lordship" which the head of a great estate was expected to dispense and his role as a landlord. Cumberland in fact seriously damaged his image in his country by unpopular estate policies aiming at maximum economic gain, which gave him the reputation of a harsh landlord. Fines of seven or eight years' rent were taken from tenants

[51] A copy of the confirmation is amongst the Appleby Castle MSS. in the Carlisle County Record Office.

[52] *Calendar of Patent Rolls, Henry VII*, 2 vols. (London, Public Record Office, 1914–16; hereafter *C.P.R., Henry VII*), ii (1494–1509), p. 466.

[53] See *L.P.*, v, 951, 966; vi, 299, 306, 1620; vii, 55, 257.

[54] See above, n. 48.

[55] See above, p. 151 and n. 25.

entering on intakes made in the earl's forests of Stainmore and Mallerstang, and five years' fine from tenants in townships.[56] In Craven his officers had been at work making enclosures,[57] enhancing rents, and ill-treating the tenants of the lordship of Winterburn (Cumberland claimed a lease of this from Furness abbey), some of whom were evicted and others imprisoned in Skipton castle.[58] If, as there is evidence to suggest, competition amongst a rising population for the available land enhanced the hazards of frequent wet summers and scarce cornland, the balance of the peasant economy was precarious.[59] Cumberland's policies, if persisted with in time of dearth (such as the years 1535–6), could drive peasant communities to desperation. Moreover, so many such communities conceived themselves endangered partly because of the extent of Cumberland's estates and partly because his example[60] encouraged the

56 A note added to a copy of the 1526 survey of Clifford knights' fees in Westmorland (Carlisle County Record Office) sometime between 1526 and 1542 states "the forrests of Stanesmore and Mallerstang: The new tenants that never take nor paid gressom to be rated after vii or viii penny gressom . . . The townes in the countrie: The new tenants that never toke nor paid gressom to be rated after v penny gressom". Old tenants that had already paid gressum "once or twice" were to be rated at four penny gressum in the forests and at three penny gressum in the towns.

57 These were thrown down in the Craven riot of 1535 (*L.P.*, viii, 991). The earl's enclosures in Westmorland were similarly treated in the rising there in Jan. 1536 (*L.P.*, xii (1), 319).

58 *Yorks. Star Chamber Proc.*, iv, Yorkshire Archaeological Soc. Record Series, lxx (1927), pp. 52, 136.

59 The increase in population seems to have been most marked after the middle years of the century: see e.g. Joan Thirsk, "Industries in the Countryside", in *Essays in the Economic and Social History of Tudor and Stuart England in Honour of R. H. Tawney*, ed. F. J. Fisher (Cambridge, 1961); G. H. Tupling, *The Economic History of Rossendale* (Chetham Soc., 1927), ch. 2; G. Elliott in *Trans. C. & W. A. & A. Soc.*, new ser., lix (1959), p. 85. In Craven, population pressure is suggested by the settlement of the forests, which was far advanced by Henry VIII's reign. The forest of Langstrothdale was tenement land rented at £139 in 1518 (Syon House MS. A I 1a); the forest of Ribblesdale had a rental of £86 at the same date. By 1537 only 60 deer survived in Ribblesdale, and "little timber or other wood, but only enough for the tennants there".

60 The example set by great lords or by others in positions of authority, particularly the king's officers, who treated tenants oppressively, had an unsettling effect wider than the lands and persons immediately affected. It is likely, for example, that the unrest which came to the surface amongst the tenantry at Sedbergh, Dent, and Mashamshire, as well as Richmondshire, during the Pilgrimage of Grace was related to the conduct of William Lord Conyers, who in the 1520s, as the king's steward of Richmond, had ill-treated the tenants of Arkengarthdale, and violated their customs (*Yorks. Star Chamber Proc.*, ii, Yorkshire Archaeological Soc., Record Series, xlv (1911), p. 178). Similarly, Sir James

gentry to follow similar courses. Nobody, whether amongst the plebeians or their betters, would have disputed that "It is most naturall . . . that his lordship should have government and ruell under the Prince here in this countrie . . . "[61] but this kind of rule implied that "the poor people be not oppressed but that they may live after their sorts and qualities".[62] Ultimately the outcome was to be "the earl of Cumberland is in great danger of his life, for no man is worse beloved".[63]

It was unwise to increase the burdens of the peasantry beyond what could be endured; but Cumberland was also foolish enough to irritate and alienate the gentry by the enhanced rents and dues he tried to squeeze out of his mesne tenants. Thus the rents paid for the knights' fees of the barony of Westmorland, which totalled £27 9*s* 8*d* in 1526, were raised to £42 4*s* 7*d* in the years immediately following. Some of the military tenants were particularly hard hit. Gilbert Wharton, for example, had his rent for the manor of Kirkby Thore raised from 19*s* 10*d* to £4 3*s* 0*d*. The Crakenthorpes had to pay 26*s* instead of 1*s* 8*d* for Newbiggin, and £5 5*s* 8*d* instead of 21*s* 8*d* for Milburne. An attempt was to be made to extract £3 11*s* 6*d* instead of 25*s* 6*d* from Lord Dacre for the Westmorland fiefs he had inherited from the Greystokes.[64] These were considerable sums, involving a very real burden, particularly for the smaller squires. There are hints too that the earl's men of business were not satisfied with the profits made from wardships, and there may have been

Leyburn, steward of the barony of Kendal (another crown lordship), by enhancing fines on his own estate, gave rise to fears that, to profit the king, he might break the Kendal customs, and that his example would encourage other freeholders of the barony to squeeze their tenants in the same way. As a result Kendal was drawn into the Pilgrimage. The fact that fines had been so frequently exacted and perhaps enhanced on the Percy lands in Cumberland (J. M. W. Bean, *The Estates of the Percy Family, 1416–1537* (Oxford, 1958), pp. 65–6) as well as on the Clifford estates accentuated peasant unrest. The impression must have been present, during the decade before the Pilgrimage, of a general offensive against custom on the part of the great lords and the king's officers. This made it easy for the tenantry in the West March, and in the north Pennine dales, to be drawn into rebellion.

61 A remark made in a Percy survey of the 1560s (Syon House MS.).

62 Instructions to the Council in the North, 1538; see R. R. Reid, *The King's Council in the North* (London, 1921), p. 15.

63 *L.P.*, viii, 991.

64 The enhanced rents are entered in the copy of the 1526 survey of knights' fees in Westmorland made sometime between 1526 and 1542, cited at n. 56 above, this chapter.

attempts to squeeze more out of these, as well as raise rents.[65] Nor is it likely that the military tenants of Skipton would have been exempt from the pressures brought to bear on those of Westmorland. It is clear, at any rate, that suit of court by military tenants was more strictly enforced there after 1522, and this of course was an essential pre-condition for the financial exploitation of military tenures.[66] But, however this may be, the outcome of policies of this kind cannot be doubted. Cumberland may have been unaware of the case of the third duke of Buckingham, whose exploitation of feudal revenues in his Marcher lordships made him so unpopular that it became unsafe for him to visit them without a large armed escort, and whose financial exactions so alienated the support of his tenants that it was easy for Henry VIII to destroy him in 1521.[67] Cumberland's isolation became apparent during the Pilgrimage of Grace, and the duke of Norfolk went to the heart of the matter when he told Cromwell in April 1537 that if the earl were to serve the king in the marches "he must be brought to change his conditions, and not be so greedy to get money of his tenants".[68]

Thus one feature of the Pilgrimage, as it affected Cumberland's country, was that many of his vassals joined the rebels. These came mostly from families like the Musgraves and Tempests with inherited lands and interests which had carried them out of the Clifford orbit, or who had inherited Clifford fiefs but had no tradition of Clifford service. Amongst these were Sir Richard Tempest of Bracewell, who had offered to take Lord Darcy's part against "any lord in England", and whose brother Nicholas was one of the captains of the rebel host of Craven and Ribblesdale;[69] Sir Edward Musgrave of Hartley, who was sworn to the Cumberland commons;[70] and Sir Christopher Danby and John Norton, who were

[65] A note in the same copy of the 1526 survey states that the wardship of John Warcop of Smardale had been sold by the tenth Lord Clifford for £40 to William Tunstall, who was able to dispose of it to a third party for £120. The object seems to have been to warn the lord against the disposal of wardships at under-rates, to the profit of others.

[66] Thus at the military court held at Skipton in 1499, only 13 military tenants out of a total of 22 did suit as required by their tenures (Bodleian Lib., Dodsworth MS. 83, fo. 116), and in 1522 only 12 tenants did suit (*ibid.*, fo. 114b). By 1552, on the other hand, 19 tenants are named as doing suit.

[67] See *The Marcher Lordships of South Wales, 1415–1536: Select Documents*, ed. T. B. Pugh (Cardiff, 1963), intro., pp. 260, 523.

[68] *L.P.*, xii (1), 919.

[69] *L.P.*, xi, 741; xii (1), 1034.

[70] *Ibid.*, xii (1), 687 (2).

with the besiegers of Skipton castle.[71] The case of John Norton, who was the bitterest of Cumberland's enemies, deserves special mention, and will be further considered below in connection with the earl's relations with his brother-in-law, the earl of Northumberland. Norton had quarrelled with Cumberland in 1531 over the lordship of Kirkby Malzeard and Netherdale, belonging to Anne countess of Derby, both men seeking "rule and governance" of the tenants, and claiming rival grants of the stewardship. There had been frays at Kirkby between the earl's followers and Norton's, and quarrels at Rylstone over the earl's hunting rights and his enclosure of a common there, which led to litigation in Star Chamber.[72] From Norton's point of view the Pilgrimage provided the opportunity to secure the support of the gentry of Mashamshire and Richmondshire of the Neville and Darcy affiliation to settle scores with his old enemy.[73] But, even in the case of those mesne tenants who did not actually join the rebellion, there could have been little desire to endanger themselves in the service of a lord who was eager to enhance their rents. There must have been many such amongst the gentry who deserted Cumberland at Skipton when the siege became imminent.

The earl's reputation as an oppressive landlord had already led in 1535 to the Craven revolt against his enclosures; in 1536 his estate policies were a principal cause of the mass support which the Pilgrimage secured amongst the peasantry of Westmorland. It is significant that the rebellion there should have flared up on 17 October 1536 at Kirkby Stephen, at the centre of those Clifford lands and forests of Stainmore and Mallerstang where the earl had been

[71] *L.P.*, vii (1), 392.

[72] See *Yorks. Star Chamber Proc.*, iii, Yorkshire Archaeological Soc. Record Series, li, (1914), pp. 200, 202; *ibid.*, ii, Yorkshire Archaeological Soc. Record Series, xlv (1911), p. 48.

[73] When in 1531 John Norton had contested Cumberland's exercise of the stewardship of Kirkby Malzeard, his principal supporters "of worship", with the help of whose armed followers he had confronted the earl's heir and officers, had been Sir Christopher Lascelles, Sir William Mallory of Studley, and Christopher Wandsforth of Kirtlington: Public Record Office, Star Chamber 2/18/164. These men, who had been cited by Cumberland before Star Chamber for their part in the riot at Kirkby Malzeard, also (Lascelles excepted) accompanied Norton to the siege of Skipton castle in Oct. 1536. But they were now reinforced by Sir Christopher Danby, the Inglebies and Markenfields, Ralph Gower of Richmond, and others of the gentry of Mashamshire and Richmondshire. In Mashamshire the principal influence, exercised from Snape castle, was that of Lord Latimer, head of a junior branch of the Nevilles. The chief of the Neville clan was the earl of Westmorland, stepson to Lord Darcy, who had been steward of his estates.

forcing up fines, and probably too making the enclosures which were thrown down in the second Westmorland rising of February 1537.[74] Thus it was to be expected that the programme of the Westmorland commons, as set out in their petition of 15 November 1536, should include the demand that gressums should not exceed one year's rent, and that "all intaykes that [are] noysom for power men to be layd downe".[75] What is more surprising is that the petition of the peasantry touched on grievances felt by many of the gentry as well as the commons. For this envisaged the abolition of "neat geld", or cornage, as well as "sergeant food".[76] These were rents payable not only collectively by the Westmorland townships, and therefore a "greate welthe for all the power men to bee layd downe", but also by the mesne tenants of the barony of Westmorland;[77] and those free rents which Cumberland aimed to enhance were in fact cornage rents. It was not then without reason that the captains of the Westmorland commons registered their expectation that allies from amongst the gentry might in due course join them, when they told Darcy in the early days of the revolt that they had none such of their counsel "as yet".[78] Cumberland's desertion by the gentry of his retinue, and the lack of resistance to the rebellion in Westmorland, suggests that such an expectation was not unfounded. It is possible too that these features of the rebellion left their impression on the Cliffords themselves; for the second earl of Cumberland did not persist in his father's policy of squeezing the mesne tenants and enhancing free rents: he restored them to what they had been in the reign of Henry VI.[79]

74 *L.P.*, xii (1), 319, 687 (2).
75 *Ibid.*, xi, 1080.
76 *Ibid.* On cornage, see Nicolson and Burn, *History and Antiquities*, i, pp. 292–4.
77 Thus a Clifford survey of Westmorland knights' fees of 1 & 2 Ph. and M. is headed "The Cornage of Westmorland", and begins: "Of the farmes Services and Rents of all the Free Tenants within the county of Westmorlande which they hould free . . . by cornage, that is to say by knights service" (Carlisle County Record Office).
78 *L.P.*, xi, 1080.
79 This is clear from the Marian survey cited at n. 77 above, made during the lifetime of the second earl. In this the enhanced cornage rents which appear in the amended survey of 1526 have all been dropped.

II

Although the Pilgrimage of Grace in Westmorland and Cumberland (where the plebeian element in the movement was most pronounced) has been presented as "essentially a rising of the poor against the rich",[80] the concept of class conflict has its limits as a useful descriptive term. The governing class (which was also the landlord class) certainly feared the destruction and dislocation which resulted from such movements, and, unless they could be exploited for political ends, sought to repress them. But they were not regarded as a threat to the existing social order; and if some landlords felt themselves endangered in 1536–7, this was because of political enmities they had incurred, and not merely because they had oppressed their tenants.[81] Some of the gentry (including two of the most prominent) in fact showed themselves tolerant to the commons, or actually joined them, accompanied by their tenants.[82] The commons in their turn, although the disorders tended to be initiated by leaders from their own ranks, were eager for the countenance and help of those in authority.[83] There was little of the class-consciousness needed to make a real peasant war, although the plebeian leaders were uneasily aware that, if things went wrong, they would be the first to be sacrificed by their betters to the king's

[80] M. H. and R. Dodds, *The Pilgrimage of Grace 1536–7, and the Exeter Conspiracy, 1538*, 2 vols. (Cambridge, 1915), i, p. 225.

[81] Sir Thomas Curwen of Workington seems to have been the gentleman who was most frightened of the commons. To escape being taken by them in Jan. 1537, he fled to Sheriff Hutton in Yorkshire, in which lordship he was the king's steward. There is no evidence that he was an oppressive landlord. He had had his disputes with the tenants of Sheriff Hutton, but by Jan. 1537 relations were good enough for him to be convinced they would defend him. But with Sir William Musgrave he was the principal loyalist in Cumberland, being a knight of the body and sheriff; and he had been abandoned by his fellow gentry, who had gone up to London to make their peace with the king. In 1531 he had displaced the rebel leader Sir Robert Constable as steward of Sheriff Hutton. It was for political, not social, reasons that he feared the commons. See *L.P.*, v, 506 (10); xii (1), 195.

[82] In Oct. 1536 Sir Edward Musgrave took the commons' oath, together with his tenants of Edenhall (*L.P.*, xii (1), 687). Sir John Lowther attended the muster of the commons at Cartlogan Thorns in Cumberland. "He does not seem to have been brought in by force, and the commons looked upon him as their friend" (Dodds, *op. cit.*, i, p. 222).

[83] In the West March, as elsewhere, the first objective of the commons was to compel the gentry to take their oath and assume the leadership of the risings. Where the initiative was taken by leaders who were not gentlemen, these were often on the fringes of the landed establishment, being either estate officers or clergy.

anger.[84] The commons thought of themselves in religious terms, as "brethren in Christ"[85] under the leadership of Poverty, Pity, Charity and Faith.[86] Their appeal was not against the existing order, to which they had no alternative to put forward, but to the compassion and conscience of the great and powerful, whose oppression had made intolerable the peasant's harsh life, weighed down as it was by recurrent dearth and natural calamities. The commons' actions reminded those in authority that the stability of their world too required that "the poor people be not oppressed but that they may live after their sorts and qualities".[87]

The commons then sought less the overthrow of their betters than their countenance and support; and this in a measure they obtained. But the gentry, in their turn, were no more ready than the poor to make a rebellion from below; they too needed the countenance of the great. Thus the failure of Cumberland's rule cannot be wholly explained by the breakdown of tenurial bonds, oppressive estate policies, and the resentment of vassals and tenants. The latter were

[84] The fear of the commons that they would be made the scapegoats of rebellion was the cause of the second insurrection in Cumberland and Westmorland of Jan. 1537, in which no gentlemen or clergy took part. The rising began in Westmorland when the gentry had all gone up to court to make their peace with the king, and when the commons' leaders had become convinced that nothing but enmity could henceforth be expected from them (*L.P.*, xii (1), 411). Even at this stage, however, the commons' leaders hoped that they might be countenanced by one of the Percies (*L.P.*, xii (1), 520), and the duke of Norfolk was convinced the disorders could be contained if the gentry had remained in residence and given firm leadership (*ibid.*, 336). There was little social content in the rising, which was one of desperation led by a plebeian political élite which, having been encouraged by its betters to use peasant grievances to raise disorders, had then been abandoned by the latter to the king's anger. A similar situation had developed in the Lincolnshire rising of Oct. 1536, when the commons, suspecting correctly that the gentry intended to submit, planned to kill them (*L.P.*, xi, 971).

[85] This was the form of address used by the commons of Richmondshire to those of Westmorland: *L.P.*, xii (1), 687 (1).

[86] These were the titles takien by the four captains of the commons in Westmorland and Cumberland at their assembly near Penrith: *L.P.*, xii (1), 687 (1). The religious idiom in which the peasantry voiced their protest has all the marks of "the Piers Plowman tradition" (see Helen C. White, *Social Criticism in Popular Religious Literature of the Sixteenth Century*, New York, 1944, ch. 1), mediated presumably through the strong clerical element amongst the leadership. The tradition imparted a charismatic significance to poverty, as the state of life in which Christ could be most truly followed; there was no encouragement of revolt against the rich, although their failings were denounced; and patience was enjoined on those who suffered. See White, *op. cit.*, pp. 9–10.

[87] See n. 62.

unlikely to challenge a great lord like Cumberland, "a man of great poure and mighte in those parties",[88] without the encouragement of another as great. There was only one person who could have fulfilled this role in Cumberland's countries, and that was his brother-in-law the sixth earl of Northumberland. The latter, as lord of Percy Fee, which included the manors of Preston-in-Craven and Gisburn, as well as Langstrothdale and Ribblesdale, ruled north Craven, as Cumberland ruled the south from Skipton.[89] Not far away there were the great Percy estates in Cumberland, based on Cockermouth castle; and the sixth earl, through Sir Thomas Wharton, who was comptroller of his household, had a useful contact with the gentry of Westmorland.[90] It is to the relations between the two earls that we must now turn.

Although Northumberland was fond of his sister the countess of Cumberland, it is difficult to resist the impression that he nevertheless aimed at undermining her husband's authority, and at ensuring that this should not be secure, even in his own country, in spite of the king's favour. The earl's hand can be traced, for example, in Cumberland's damaging feud, already mentioned, with John Norton. Norton was a Percy follower, holding the office of treasurer of the Percy household,[91] which must have brought him into the circle of the earl's intimates. Norton's fortunes had risen with those of the Percies, and after Northumberland's appointment to the East and Middle Marches he had become a member of the new warden's council, and a J.P. for Northumberland as well as for the North and West Ridings.[92] A mounting sense of his own importance must have contributed to his quarrel with Cumberland over Kirkby Malzeard. But he would hardly have ventured to challenge a man so much his superior in wealth and status without the knowledge and backing of his master. And it emerges from the terms of his petition to Star Chamber, made after the fray with Cumberland's men at Kirkby, that he was convinced the latter would be available. For in this he stated that Anne countess of Derby had made over to him the farm and stewardship of Kirkby Malzeard "at the especiall instans

[88] *Yorks. Star Chamber Proc.*, iv (1927), p. 136.

[89] Other places within the Fee were Settle, Giggleswick, Buckden, and Starbotton.

[90] Wharton's ancestral estates were around Wharton and Nateby in Westmorland. He was related to the Sandfords, Warcops, and other Westmorland houses.

[91] Alnwick Castle MS., Letters and Papers, ii, Book of Grants.

[92] *L.P.*, iv (1), 3629, 5083, 6803; v, 1694, 119 (53).

request and desyre of the right honorabyll Harry erle of Northumberland".[93] Northumberland had an interest in the premises since the stewardship of Kirkby had been granted first to his father, then to himself, by the countess.[94] But the deviousness of Northumberland's conduct becomes apparent from the fact that, only a few months before the grant to Norton, he had assigned his offices in Kirkby for life to the earl of Cumberland "for the tender zele and love" he bore to his brother-in-law.[95] Thus Northumberland, by making one grant but also requesting and consenting to another which contradicted it, must be seen as ultimately responsible for the feud between Norton and Cumberland, which culminated in the siege of Skipton castle.

There are features too of the Craven insurrection of 1535 which suggest that Northumberland was no friend of his brother-in-law. For example, although it was Cumberland's enclosures which were thrown down, the disorders centred on Giggleswick, which was a Percy, not a Clifford estate; and, of the four score tenants indicted for taking part in them (out of 400 who participated), only half were Cumberland's or John Lambert's, the rest being the earl of Northumberland's.[96] Then there is Northumberland's reluctance to participate in person in the work of repression. As the king's lieutenant in Yorkshire he appointed a commission of J.P.'s to enquire into the rising, but neither he nor the earl of Westmorland attended its sessions, although instructed by the king to do so. Instead Sir Marmaduke Constable from the East Riding, who would not have been readily identifiable as one of Northumberland's men in Craven, was sent to represent the Percy interest.[97] And the principal Percy officer on the spot, Sir Stephen Hamerton, steward of Percy Fee, did nothing to assist the justices, having been

[93] Public Record Office, Star Chamber, Henry VIII, 27/135. The sentence has been excluded from the transcript in *Yorks. Star Chamber Proc.*, iii (1914), p. 200.

[94] Bodleian Library, Dodsworth MS. 83, fos. 36 and 68.

[95] *Ibid.*, fo. 36.

[96] *L.P.*, viii, 991.

[97] Northumberland used two excuses to explain his non-attendance. One (*L.P.*, viii, 991) was that the letters from Cromwell and others commanding his presence at the commission's proceedings reached him too late. The other, reported by Sir Richard Tempest (*L.P.*, viii, 993), was that he was too sick to act. Neither excuse satisfied the king, with whom by Sept. 1535 Northumberland was in trouble (*L.P.*, ix, 371); a royal rebuke had been administered because his response to the Craven riots had been insufficiently vigorous.

merely instructed by his master to "put himself in readiness" to do so.[98] Nor did Northumberland commit any of the rioters, as he had been ordered by the king, to his castle at Wressle; and his officers even took the prisoners who had been sent to York castle by Sir Richard Tempest (the justice who had done most to restore order) out of the hands of the latter's servants.[99] The sixth earl (as one piece of evidence suggests) may well also have been encouraging the tenants of Winterburn to resist Cumberland's oppressions.[100] He was certainly eager to dissociate himself from his unpopular brother-in-law, even at the price of disobedience to the king.

Percy influences are even more obviously present in the course taken in Craven by the Pilgrimage of Grace in the following year. The rising of the Craven commons, in 1536 as in 1535, began on Percy ground at Giggleswick. It was there that Sir Stephen Hamerton first learnt of it from a bill set on the church door summoning all the inhabitants to a muster; it was there that he was seized by a band of armed Percy tenants and forced (so he said) to take the commons' oath.[101] But subsequently this Percy officer was a leader of the revolt, first going to Skipton to negotiate the surrender of the castle with Cumberland, and then marching with Nicholas Tempest and the host of Ribblesdale against the earl of Derby.[102] Early in 1537 he joined Tempest in the "rising" which led to their execution for treason.[103] There is no need to emphasize any further the Percy affiliations of John Norton, who arrived in Craven on 21 October to join the commons in the siege of Skipton. His friends and relatives were reinforced however on this occasion by Sir

98 *L.P.*, viii, 991, 995.

99 In his letter of 5 June 1535 to the king (*L.P.*, viii, 991), Northumberland stated that the rioters had been committed to Wressle, as well as to Skipton and Sandall castles; but on 15 Sept. he told Henry there had been no time to commit the prisoners either to Wressle or Skipton. For the incident at York, see *L.P.*, viii, 946.

100 Why else should one of Northumberland's chaplains, Robert Suthayke, have incurred the earl's disfavour because he became involved in a quarrel with the Proctors, the family which was most obstinate in resisting Cumberland at Winterburn? Suthayke, having been attacked by the Proctors, could get no remedy from his master, who was told that the chaplain "hath not done him trow suit, and syth that tyme the said herlle [earl] hath not byn good lord to hys chaplin" (Public Record Office, Star Chamber, 2/32/34). He therefore initiated a suit in Star Chamber against the Proctors.

101 *L.P.*, xii (1), 1034.

102 *Ibid.*

103 Dodds, *The Pilgrimage of Grace*, ii, pp. 83–5.

Christopher Danby and other followers of the Neville interest in Richmondshire and Mashamshire, which also (like the Tempests) had its affiliations with Lord Darcy.[104] The events in Craven in fact suggest an alliance of the Percy interest with Darcy and the Nevilles behind the Pilgrimage. And, although we might be tempted to absolve Northumberland himself, away in London in the early stages of the revolt and then on his sick-bed at distant Wressle, from any personal responsibility, there is one hint that his officers and agents did not act without first securing his approval. Towards the end of 1536 Hamerton was summoned by Cumberland to Skipton castle, probably to discuss the release of his son (or grandson) who was being held as a hostage there. Nevertheless Hamerton would not go until he had first sent a servant to his master "to know his pleasure". Northumberland vetoed the interview. In the brief phrase (according to one of Darcy's agents) "we do not know my lord" he set the seal on his estrangement from his brother-in-law.[105]

Why then had Northumberland become so ill-disposed to a man who had married the sister he held in such affection? The lands of Percy Fee may have been a factor in the situation. Lady Anne Clifford says that when the marriage took place (on 2 February 1513) between Lady Margaret Percy, daughter of the fifth earl of Northumberland, and Sir Henry Clifford (as Cumberland was then called), Lady Margaret "had given her dowry by her father, and afterwards confirmed by her brother, all those lands in Craven called Percy Fee . . . ".[106] The fifth earl, however, did not "give" his daughter the lands of Percy Fee, but merely the income from them for life, against a dowry of approximately the same rental out of the Clifford estates.[107] This was no more than normal endowment for a marriage which was, after all, a great match, since Clifford was heir to a barony and favoured at court. The fee simple, however, passed to the sixth earl, who on 5 February 1528 apointed Sir Stephen Hamerton his steward in Craven.[108] It was this earl who converted his father's proper provision for Lady Margaret's marriage into an act of extravagant generosity towards the Cliffords. For in August

104 See above, n. 73.
105 *L.P.*, xii (1), 7.
106 *Clifford Letters*, p. 138.
107 Bodleian Lib., Dodsworth MS. 70, fo. 49. Lady Margaret's jointure was to consist of Clifford lands of an annual rental of £120.
108 Alnwick Castle MSS., Letters and Papers, ii, Book of Grants, p. 135.

1532 he entered into an indenture[109] whereby the fee simple of Percy Fee was vested in trustees to his own use and that of the issue male of his body, but with the provision that if the latter were not forthcoming, the heir was to be Henry Lord Clifford, eldest son of the earl of Cumberland.

The date of this transaction however ought to be noted, because only a month before the indenture was made Northumberland had been involved in a dangerous crisis whose outcome could have been his ruin. In July 1532 he had been examined before the Council because he had stated to his wife that, many years before, he had been betrothed to Anne Boleyn, and that in view of this pre-contract any marriage he had subsequently entered into was invalid.[110] The countess had revealed this statement to her father, the earl of Shrewsbury (from whom it was eventually transmitted to the king), in the hope that it might end her own unhappy marriage and that the supposed pre-contract might prevent any marriage between the king and Anne. But the result was to expose Northumberland to great peril for having concealed a matter which affected the king so closely. He was able to extricate himself only by the most solemn denials before the Council and before the archbishops of Canterbury and York, and by an oath on the sacrament. Thus his position in the summer of 1532 was weak. He was not well placed to resist any pressures that might be brought to bear, and he needed friendship, particularly from those who enjoyed the king's favour. There was more than simply family affection in his words on 12 July 1532 (they must have been written just before his departure to London for his examination) to Cumberland and his wife: ". . . the King excepted, ye be the persons in the wordell [world] I would faynest see, and that my comforth doth rest in". The Cliffords then may have owed the Percy Fee to Northumberland's troubles in London. If so, on the latter's side there may have been resentment and a sense of victimization.

But the two earls were also divided by differences of political attitude which both pre-dated and went deeper than the affair of Percy Fee. The sixth earl of Northumberland, warden of the East

[109] There is a copy amongst the Syon House MSS. X II 3 (at Alnwick), "Therle of Cumberlands indenture for lands in Langstroth".

[110] *Clifford Letters*, p. 110; P. Friedmann, *Anne Boleyn*, 2 vols. (London, 1884), i, pp. 159–61; *L.P.*, x, 864.

and Middle Marches since 1527,[111] sheriff of Northumberland for life, lieutenant in Yorkshire, and after 1533 the leading member of the Council in the North,[112] had raised his family to a power such as it had not enjoyed since the previous century. But the earl's eminence was precarious. The Percies were not trusted by Henry VIII,[113] and the future of the family was in doubt. The earl was estranged from his wife, and had no children; the heir male, his brother Sir Thomas Percy, had received no marks of royal favour. The earl himself was in peril, as has been seen, because of his supposed pre-contract to Anne Boleyn, which was used against him in 1532, and again in 1536.[114] His conviction for treason would have transferred the Percy estates into the king's hands, and so would have achieved at one stroke what it had long been the policy of the crown to bring about. It is not surprising then that the earl should have sought to fortify his position in the north by a multiplication of offices and fees,[115] in order to extend his following amongst the northern gentry; or that he should have rewarded the more able and influential of his servants in an exceptionally generous way.[116] Nor is it unlikely that he came to see the desperate expedient of rebellion as the one means by which his own standing and the future of his house might be assured. By January 1535 he had already made the disloyal gesture of an approach to Chapuys to sound the possibility of the emperor's help for a revolt,[117] and he was probably already in touch with Lord Darcy.[118] And it is difficult to conclude from his actions during the rebellion, as distinct from his public posture and statements, that he opposed the Pilgrimage of Grace.[119]

[111] *L.P.*, iv (2), 3628.

[112] *L.P.*, vi, 15; vii, 262 (22); Reid, *The King's Council*, pp. 115–16, 487.

[113] See above, Chapter 2.

[114] *L.P.*, x, 164.

[115] Bean, *The Estates of the Percy Family*, pp. 145–7.

[116] *Ibid.*, n. 25, p. 11.

[117] *L.P.*, vii, 1; *Cal. State Papers, Spanish, 1534–5*, p. 354.

[118] Darcy at any rate knew about Northumberland's approaches to Chapuys (*L.P.*, viii, 121).

[119] Thus, immediately on his return from London to the north on 10 Oct., the earl offered to surrender himself to one of the rebel leaders, Thomas Maunsell, vicar of Braynton, one of Darcy's agents; but the latter allowed him to proceed on his way to Topcliffe, in view of his illness. Subsequently the earl dismissed the royalist Lord Ogle, who had been his vice-warden, and appointed his insurgent brother Sir Ingram Percy to this post, and to the sheriffwick of Northumberland and lieutenancy of the East March (E. B. Barrington de Fonblanque, *Annals of the House of Percy*, 2 vols. (London, 1887), i, Appendix lii, p. 565). The earl may

This then is the background against which Northumberland's sensational gesture whereby, early in 1536, he made the king heir to the Percy lands[120] in place of his brother, ought to be seen. No doubt his childlessness and differences with his brothers, particularly with Sir Thomas Percy, together with his expectation (because of his ill-health and the political perils to which he was exposed) of a short life, were all factors which played their part in the earl's decision.[121] Sir Thomas Percy, who was not faced with the problem of relations with an all-powerful and suspicious master, and who knew little of the ways of the court, found it hard to appreciate the earl's manoeuvres, which were often damaging to his own interests.[122] Yet the two brothers must also have been held together, in spite of their differences and conflicts, by a common concern for the future of the family; in this Sir Thomas Percy had a special interest since, in view of the earl's childlessness, it lay with his eldest son Thomas, born in 1528. And it is likely that it was precisely to ensure that future, and to protect the long-term interests of his house, that the earl disinherited his brother.[123] For by making the king his heir he elimin-

have been misinformed about the position in Northumberland; he subsequently withdrew Sir Ingram's offices and restored Ogle to the vice-wardenship. Nevertheless his earlier actions must have strengthened the dominance of his two insurgent brothers there, and made it easier for Sir Thomas Percy to claim (as he did do) that the earl had appointed him lieutenant of the Middle March. Northumberland, here as elsewhere, in practice advanced the cause of rebellion, although he always had plausible excuses ready and lines of retreat available. He also surrendered Wressle castle to Robert Aske, the chief captain of the Pilgrimage, and recognized him as "captain of the baronage" (*L.P.*, xii (1), 1062 and p. 352).

120 Fonblanque, *op. cit.*, i, pp. 469–71; *Archaeologia*, xxxiii (1849), p. 4.

121 Bean, *op. cit.*, p. 157.

122 Only one letter (*L.P.*, viii, 1143) has survived from Thomas Percy to a prominent court personality. Sir Thomas's strength lay in his local influence in Northumberland, which rested on friendships with the Tynedale clans (the Robsons and Charltons) and with such gentry as Sir John Heron of Chipchase and Sir Humphrey Lisle of Felton, whose lawlessness made them suspect in London. For Sir Thomas's grievances against Northumberland, see *L.P.*, viii, 1143 (4).

123 There is no evidence that, during the Pilgrimage, Sir Thomas Percy ever contested Northumberland's decision to make the king his heir. When the commons at York and Pontefract called him "Lord Percy" (the title borne by the Percy heir) he "lighted off his horse, and took off his cap, and desired they would not so say" (*L.P.*, xii (1), 393). It was Sir Ingram, not Sir Thomas, who said he would be revenged on Sir Reynold Carnaby, for being "the destruction of our house, for by his means the King shall be my lord's heir". Sir Thomas's silence on his brother's disinheritance of him does not of course mean that he was not willing to further rebellion. A successful revolution might have created a far more favourable

ated one of the principal motives which might have induced the crown to seize the Percy lands. And by a gesture of unparalleled generosity, he made a claim on the gratitude of the Tudor dynasty from which a later generation of his house might benefit,[124] particularly should the Lady Mary (with whose cause Northumberland, by his approach to Chapuys, had sufficiently identified himself) occupy the throne. The earl was unable to foresee the outcome of the Pilgrimage of Grace, which resulted in the attainder of Sir Thomas Percy, and his own death in disgrace, followed by the inevitable inheritance of the Percy lands by the crown. Nevertheless he had opened the way for the restoration of the Percy titles and properties in the person of his nephew, the seventh earl, Sir Thomas' heir, in

political context in which his own future and that of his family might have been guaranteed. But the earl, by bequeathing the Percy estates to the crown, also made provision for the contingency of an unsuccessful rebellion.

124 Northumberland, in the letters to the king and Cromwell in which he announced his intention to make the former his heir, was careful to stress that his action was not merely one of expediency, but of love and devotion to the king's person. Thus he told the king, "Sir the debility of my blood . . . is not the only occasion that forceth me thus to do, but assuredly the inward heart and love I bear, as ever I have borne, to your majesty as a true and most bounden subject, and one of the poorest of your blood . . . " Such phrases touched on deep chords in the life of the time. The earl's "devotion", carried to the extreme point of willingness to sacrifice his own family to his master, involved "good lordship" on the latter's part as the only appropriate response. The theme of "kinship" which the earl also raised invited a generous response on the part of the royal house to the extraordinary fidelity of a servant who was also a "poor" relative (Fonblanque, *op. cit.*, i, pp. 469–71). Northumberland deepened the note of utter submission to his master early in June 1537, after the attainder of Sir Thomas Percy, when he made over his inheritance to the crown wholly unconditionally, resigning even his own maintenance to the king's generosity.

The closest parallel to Northumberland's action is provided by the case of William Marquess Berkeley, who in 1487–8 bequeathed to Henry VII the extensive possessions of his family in England, Wales, Ireland and Calais, so disinheriting his brother (John Smyth, *Lives of the Berkeleys* in *The Berkeley MSS.*, ed. Sir J. Maclean, 3 vols. (Gloucester, 1883–5), ii, pp. 126 ff.). Berkeley's gift to the king, however, had none of the absolute and unconditional character of Northumberland's. It was in fact the result of a bargain, whereby the king undertook to gratify Berkeley's appetite for titles and offices of honour by creating him a marquess and earl marshal of England. Moreover Berkeley limited his grant to the king in tail male, so ensuring the return of the Berkeley lands to his own heirs, should the king's male issue become extinct, as happened with the death of Edward VI. By contrast, Northumberland left the Percy inheritance " . . . to the Kyng oure Sovereign Lorde and to his heyres and successors for ever" (*Statutes of the Realm*, iii, p. 611). His motive was simply to provide "for the augmentacon and increase of his [majesty's] Imperiall Crowne".

the Marian period.[125] His act of faith whereby he appealed to the future against the darkly tinted present was vindicated.

The earl of Cumberland, on the other hand, was never faced with the perils or involved in the dilemmas which confronted his brother-in-law. However inefficient he may have been in office, and however unattractive his oppression of his tenants may appear, in one respect he was completely consistent, and that was in his loyalty to Henry VIII. Although he was dismissed from the wardenship of the West March in 1528, and threatened with the loss of the same office in 1537, in spite of his services to the king during the Pilgrimage, his obedience was absolute. This received characteristic expression in phrases which echo again and again in his letters. He would "obey with all his heart"[126] and "be agreeable to the King's pleasure with his whole heart and mind"[127] when discharged from his wardenship; he "would always he ready to follow his highnesses pleasure".[128] And his reply to the emissaries of the rebel host besieging his castle during the Pilgrimage is a model of straightforwardness compared

[125] Thomas Percy, who had been restored in blood and to his father's lands in the reign of Edward VI, was created earl of Northumberland on 1 May 1557. On 16 Aug. he was restored to all the lands his uncle, the sixth earl, had made over to Henry VIII, a few Yorkshire manors which had been granted to Matthew duke of Lennox alone excepted (*C.P.T.*, Ph. & M., iv, p. 179). Percy even received back some of the lands his uncle had sold (those in Somerset purchased by the marquess of Exeter which had come into the crown's hands following his attainder). He was also compensated for Percy Fee in Craven, since, although this remained in fee tail in the hands of the earl of Cumberland, Percy was granted the rents due out of it to the crown. There was also the remarkable provision whereby the title and inheritance were granted with remainder in tail male to the earl's brother, Sir Henry Percy, which enabled both to survive a second Percy catastrophe, the rising of 1569.

With the exception of Edward Courtenay earl of Devon (whose royal blood placed him in a special category) and the duke of Norfolk (against whom the sentence of attainder had never been carried out), no aristocratic victims of the Henrician attainders were restored as completely as the Percies. Thus the Staffords received back Thornbury and Stafford, but not their great Marcher lordships and Yorkshire lands. George Lord Darcy of Aston was restored in blood and title, but only to the reversion of the family estate, after the extinction of the heirs of the grantees. Gregory Lord Cromwell received one of his father's titles and his lands of Launde abbey, and the lordships of Oakham and North Elmham. But the lands of St Osyth's abbey in Essex, of Grey Friars, Yarmouth, and the extensive estates of Lewes priory, which had belonged to Thomas Cromwell earl of Essex, remained with the crown. The Boleyns were lucky in that, although Viscount Rochford, heir to Thomas Boleyn earl of Wiltshire, was attainted, one of the co-heiresses, the Princess Elizabeth, eventually ascended the throne. The estates of Lord Hussey and of the Poles were never restored.

[126] *L.P.*, xii (1), 372.

[127] *Ibid.*, 614.

[128] *Ibid.*, 373.

with the evasiveness of so many of the northern gentry and nobility, who were content to flee or become sworn to the commons. "I defy you", Cumberland told the messengers who came to him at Skipton, "and do your worse, for I will not meddle with you."[129]

By this forthright statement Cumberland, although he had failed to prevent the rebellion or check its spread, in fact did the king a great service, because his refusal to have any dealings with the Pilgrimage showed that the north was not united in its resistance to the king's policies; and that the great lords, the natural leaders of northern society, were divided on this issue. Skipton became the centre towards which those who were opposed to, or uncertain about, the rebellion could look; and Lancashire, Cheshire and Derbyshire would not rise till all the country from Trent northwards was made sure.[130] Moreover the earl's heir, Lord Clifford, had ensured the loyalty of Carlisle, and his half-brother Sir Thomas Clifford had held Berwick, so that the Pilgrims were denied the keys of the frontier. Cumberland's stand, then, checked the impetus of the rising. The peace party amongst the leadership (Bowes, Babthorpe, Sir Thomas Tempest of the Bishopric) was able to assert itself against the irreconcilables like Sir Robert Constable, and impose a policy of negotiation without any consolidation of the ground the revolt had conquered. And so the psychological moment passed as week followed week with the messages circulating between Whitehall and the north; the musters disintegrated, and the king's authority grew. The earl of Northumberland could hardly have foreseen these consequences of his brother-in-law's loyalty; but he must have been aware that no other northern house owed more to, and could expect more from, the crown. The Cliffords, dedicated by Cumberland's motto *Desormais* to a great destiny, could hope for advancement into the top flight of the great families only by an absolute dependence on the crown. Unlike the Percies they were not gorged with office and status, nor did they possess the latter's vast resources and influence which made it possible to bargain and manoeuvre. Thus the family was a stumbling block in the way of that secure leadership of the north which was the surest guarantee of Northumberland's greatness, and even of his survival. Marriage alliances failed to reconcile two such opposed postures; when it came to the point there could only be hostility between the two earls.

129 *Ibid.*, 1034.

130 *Ibid.*, 392 (p. 194), 466.

5. *Two Tudor funerals*

However much we may deplore the expense and lavish display involved in the funerals of Tudor peers as manifestations of conspicuous extravagance on the part of a status-ridden aristocracy,[1] it is doubtful whether those who lived in the Tudor age would have regarded them in quite this kind of way, at least until Puritan attitudes began to gain a wide acceptance. For at all times, particularly at those crises of transition when human list passes from one state to another (birth, initiation, marriage, death) men have felt the need of rituals which, by projecting ideal images of the human condition and making these available for social participation, made it easier to surmount the stresses of change. The Tudor funeral was one of these *rites de passage*. But the death of a peer was more than just a crisis in the life of an individual. At least as far as the more conservative area of Tudor society was concerned, the death of a lord of great possessions, presiding over a great household and a large following, was also a crisis in the life of the community over which he presided. Would the heir, for example, favour and cherish those who had given faithful service to his predecessor? The accepted canons of behaviour appropriate to a great lord required that he should do so; but in practice, conflicts between the generations could lead to instances of maltreatment of his father's servants by the heir.[2] Death and a new succession also could lead to shifts in the

[1] See Lawrence Stone, "The Anatomy of the Elizabethan Aristocracy", in *Econ. Hist. Rev.*, xviii (1948), p. 12; the fullest account of the Tudor aristocratic funeral is in the same author's *The Crisis of the Aristocracy 1558–1641* (Oxford, 1965), p. 572.

[2] The eleventh Lord Clifford, for example, having quarrelled with his father, maltreated the latter's servants (T. D. Whitaker, *History and Antiquities of the Deanery of Craven*, London, 1805, p. 255). The ninth earl of Northumberland had his differences with his father's officers, particularly with Francis Fitton who had opted to serve his mother (E. B. Barrington de Fonblanque, *Annals of the House of Percy*, 2 vols., London, 1887, ii, pp. 189 ff.; *Advice to his Son by Henry Percy Ninth Earl of Northumberland*, ed. G. B. Harrison, London, 1930, p. 78).

centres of power within an aristocratic household. This was the more likely to happen if the title and lands passed not to a son, but to a distant relative; and a failure of heirs male, bringing the estates into the hands of one or more female heirs who would carry them by marriage into other lines, involved the most extreme forms of upheaval, perhaps leading to a dissolution of the household and the break-up of the inheritance.[3] For tenants, too, as well as for officers and servants, the death of a great lord brought uneasiness. Would fines be enhanced and rents raised under the heir, or would the old ways be held to?[4]

It is not surprising, then, that in the face of impending change one of the notes struck in funeral ceremonies should be that of continuity. The display of heraldic family symbols in particular tended to stress the persistence of the line, as against the transience of its individual head. This having been said, however, there can be no doubt that the principal emphasis in the funerary ritual was on the greatness of the dead man. This was emphasized by the expensive stateliness of the ceremonial, the sombre and impressive procession of mourners, officers, and followers, with the chariot and hearse draped in black velvet, all contrasting with the colourful brilliance of heraldic banners and escutcheons.[5] But again, it ought to be remembered that more than just the vanity of a powerful and wealthy individual was involved in the display. A whole community of dependants participated in these prestigious symbols; all the brilliance and pageantry was, in due measure, theirs as well as the dead man's.

The funeral of a peer followed a set form laid down by the

[3] This disaster struck the Dacres in 1569, when George Lord Dacre died leaving no heir male, and commissioners appointed by the earl marshal adjudicated that the barony of Dacre was a barony by writ, and therefore in abeyance between the last lord's three sisters, his co-heiresses. The Dacre lands were divided between the co-heiresses. By an arbitrament of Edward IV in 1473, however, both barony and lands had been entailed on the heirs male of Thomas Lord Dacre (d. 1485), and should therefore have passed to Leonard Dacre, uncle to the last lord. The adjudication of the commissioners (which ignored the 1473 arbitrament) was probably influenced by political considerations and the interest of the duke of Norfolk, who was earl marshal, and whose three sons were married to the three co-heiresses. See *Complete Peerage*, iv, pp. 19, 23, and below, p. 187.

[4] Thus, once the Dacre lands had come into the possession of the Howards, assaults on tenant right in due course followed. See *Household Books of Lord William Howard*, ed. G. Ornsby (Surtees Soc., lxviii, Durham and London, 1878, pp. 413, 425).

[5] See Stone, *ibid.*

heralds, who played the principal role in the ceremonies, and provision was made for varying degrees of pomp and ceremonial elaboration according to the rank of the dead lord.[6] That of William Lord Dacre, which wound its way through the streets of Carlisle from St Cuthbert's church to the cathedral on 15 December 1563[7] in general followed the set form, although there were some unusual features which will be noticed below. First came two of the late lord's porters (probably one from Kirkoswald castle, the other from Naworth) with black staves to conduct the procession. These were followed by a troop of twenty-three poor men, beneficiaries of the dead man's charity, who walked two by two in black gowns. On their heels came the cathedral singing-men and priests in their surplices followed by the dean. Thereafter the procession (although Dacre's chaplains and the bishop, who was probably to preach the sermon at the funeral service, were still to come) struck a note which was predominantly secular and chivalric rather than religious. Next to the dean came the Dacre standard, the battle flag that is, behind which the Dacre tenantry went to war. This was followed by the late lord's gentlemen, in black gowns and hoods, and by the chaplains and bishop. Then came the great banner, carried by Richard Dacre, which displayed the family escutcheon in full with all its quarterings, the symbol therefore of the family greatness and continuity (not, like the standard, of its solidarity in war) on which the initiated could see portrayed the Dacre alliances and descent.

The heralds in their armorial tabards contributed a further element of colour and brilliance to offset the dominant sombreness

6 For these forms as prescribed for each rank of the peerage, see Bodleian Library, Ashmole MSS. 763/178; 178b; 179b; 836/39–42.

7 Ashmole MS. 836/181: "Hereafter foloweth the ordre of the procedinge to the buryall with the bodye of the Ryght honorable Wylliam lorde Dacres from the church of saynte Cuthbertes in Carlell to the cathedrall churche of Sainct Maryes there the xiith daye of Decembre, ano 1563." I owe the following account of Lord Dacre's death, taken from a Chancery deposition (Public Record Office, C3/50/117), to Mr C. R. Hudleston: "Leonard and Edward Dacre say that on Sunday Nov. 14th 1563, their father being ready to dinner at Kirkoswald castle, it pleased Almighty God to visit and strike with deadly sickness the said late lord Dacre who then said to the complainant [Thomas, Lord Dacre's eldest son]: Thomas, take my place, for I am sick: and thereupon the late lord Dacre did go to his chamber called the Great Chamber and shortly after to his bedchamber and there continued in sickness until Thursday then next following . . . early in the morning about four or five of the clock it pleased Almighty God to call the said lord Dacre to his mercy." The funeral cost £300.

of a funeral procession. Dacre's coffin was preceded by Chester herald who carried (or perhaps wore emblazoned on his tabard) the dead peer's coat of arms, and by Norroy king at arms. Lord Dacre's sword, target and helm ought to have been carried at this central point in the procession; surprisingly, however, no mention is made of these in the funeral arrangements, and this traditional feature was apparently omitted. The coffin was borne by six bearers, with four "assistants". At each of its four corners a servant carried a "banner rolle" which, like the great banner, depicted heraldically the family alliances and descent. Behind the coffin came the mourners, all but two of them the dead man's sons. The rear was brought up by the mayor and corporation of Carlisle, the remaining Dacre servants in black coats, and the gentlemen of the country who had attended the funeral.

As has been said, the most surprising feature of Lord Dacre's funeral is that the dead peer's helm, target and sword, the emblems of chivalry and of his knightly status, were not given any place in the procession. The common form of a baron's funeral required the attendance of three heralds and a king at arms, the former to carry the deceased's helm, sword and target, the latter his coat of arms.[8] Only two heralds, however, took part in the Dacre procession, and only his coat of arms was displayed. But arrangements were made that helm, sword and target were to be produced in the cathedral, where they were to be "offered" by the chief mourners, although at what precise point in the funeral service is not made clear.[9] Whatever the significance of these omissions (this will be discussed below), we also find them made in the second funeral procession here considered, that of Thomas Lord Wharton, which took place five years after Dacre's on 22 September 1568, at Healaugh parish church near York.[10] By and large, in Wharton's burial as in Dacre's,

[8] Ashmole MS. 736/179b.

[9] Ashmole MS. 836/181: "The ordre of the proceedinge to the offeringe. Fyrst my lorde Dacres chefe morner . . . wente upe alone and offered for hymselfe and before hym norrey kinge of armes . . . then my lord Scrope and Leonard Dacres dyd offer the cote of his armes then Edward Dacres and Mr Francys Dacres dyd offer the sworde and Mr Edward Scrope and parson Dacres dyd offer the target and Mr Leonard Dacres dyd offre hys helme and creste and at every tyme wente before them Chester herauld and norrey kinge of armes . . . "

[10] Ashmole MS. 836/189: "The order of the procedinge to the churche att the funerall of the righte honorable Thomas lord Wharton from his manor house of Heley unto the parishe churche of the same beinge in distance one myle the xxii daye of September Ano dni 1568." Ashmole MS. 836/101 gives a fuller "order"

the traditional forms were observed. There were the yeomen conductors with their black staves, the poor men, the standard, the surpliced clergy, the late lord's gentlemen, the great banner, the coffin surrounded by bannerols, followed by the mourners, and the late lord's yeomen. But only one herald was present, and it is not certain whether even Wharton's coat of arms, let alone the other emblems of chivalry, were displayed. And the ritual had been further simplified in that no provision was made for any "offering" during the funeral service, as in Dacre's case.[11]

The offering of the dead peer's helm, sword, target and coat had fitted naturally into the structure of the requiem mass of the old religious régime. Presented at the altar at the same time as the priest's offertory of the elements, they were a means whereby the deceased was associated symbolically with the sacrifice of the mass, which made available to him benefits which might shorten the pains of purgatory. That some thought had been given to the theological aspects of the matter is suggested by the distinction made in funerary rites between the personal emblems of the dead man (his sword, helm and target) and the standard, banner and bannerols carried in the funeral procession, which were family emblems, and could have no religious significance. It was only after "the masse fynished, at verbum caro factum"[12] that those were to be offered to the priest. But in the climate of the first decade of Elizabeth's reign it was not easy to reconcile such ceremonies with the Prayer Book funeral service which had been brought in once more. The Dacres, conservative in religion as in other respects, had insisted on as much as possible of the old ceremonial. Perhaps the late Lord Dacre's arms, sword, helm and target had been simply placed on the communion table in Carlisle cathedral during the funeral service. Or the bishop may have allowed the communion to be said and the offering to

of the funeral which includes the names of those present. The transcript in *Trans. C. & W. A. & A. Soc.*, old ser., iv (1878–9), p. 243, is misleading in some respects since it conflates both these MSS. into a single document.

11 Ashmole MS. 836/189 provided that Norroy king at arms should walk in Wharton's funeral procession "bearing the cote of his armes". But Ashmole MS. 836/191, which sets out the detailed arrangements for the funeral, omits the latter phrase. Neither document mentions any "offering".

12 Ashmole MS. 818/12: Sir Anthony Browne's funeral (1548). In the Dacre funeral this practice was still followed: "And as service was done his greate banner was offered and then went awaye with the chefe mourners and then Chester herauld procedet to the buriall with the body" (Ashmole MS. 836/181).

have been made with that of the alms. But this would have been dangerously near, at that time and place, to the prohibited "communion for the dead".[13] The Whartons, new men with no tradition of great family funerals to keep up, and closer to the Tudor establishment, preferred to abandon such ceremonies. It was not until later in the reign, with the growth of the self-confidence of the Elizabethan régime, that they came generally into use once more.[14] But their meaninglessness in a Protestant context underlined their essentially secular character as chivalric or heroic rather than Christian rites, and so exposed them to Puritan disapproval. "As if Duke Hector or Ajax, or Sir Lancelot were buried", wrote one critic.[15]

Most can be learnt, however, about the shifts and changes, social and political, of the Tudor age by considering the kind of people who attended these two funerals. Each of the latter from this point of view had its own sharply defined character. The late William Lord Dacre was a Border magnate of the old school, expert in Border laws and know-how, knowledgeable in the alliances, feuds and ambitions of the Border clans, English and Scottish. Uniting in his person the great inheritance of Greystoke with that of Dacre of the north, he and his father (with relatively brief intervals of disfavour) had ruled the West March almost from the beginning of the Tudor period. Dacre's power had depended on the faithfulness of his tenants, and on that of gentry stocks bound to his family by ties of tenure, kin and service often extending over several generations.[16] Thus a network of loyalties, feudal and patriarchal, centred on the Dacre castles and households at Kirkoswald and Naworth; a world to which London, the court at York and the queen's justice was remote, and in which quarrels were decided by violence, or else by recourse to Lord Dacre and his officers. It was men who found it natural to move within this orbit who assembled to follow the late lord's body from Kirkoswald, where he had died nearly a month before, to Carlisle.

13 See *Tudor Parish Documents of the Diocese of York*, ed. J. S. Purvis (Cambridge, 1948), pp. 14, 23, 30, 33.

14 See for example Ashmole MS. 818/21, Lord Grey of Wilton's Funeral 1593, when crest, sword, coat and target were carried in the funeral procession, and offered at the communion table in the course of the service.

15 *The Writings of Henry Barrow*, ed. L. H. Carlton (London, 1962), p. 459.

16 For William Lord Dacre and his father see above, p. 000.

Thus the Dacre standard was carried by Richard Salkeld of Corby, whose father was (like himself) one of the late Lord Dacre's gentlemen, and a bearer of his coffin.[17] Richard Dacre, who bore the great banner, was the Tybalt of the family, a killer who in the time of the Pilgrimage of Grace had been sent with a company of tenants into Carlisle to murder Sir William Musgrave, the king's captain of Bewcastle, Lord Dacre's enemy.[18] Leonard Musgrave, another of the bearers, had served both the dead lord and his father, and under the former had become deputy captain of Bewcastle, receiving a lease of the Dacre lands at Cumcatch for his services.[19] He was a member of a junior branch of the Musgrave family, whose loyalty to the Dacres had been assured by a match with a daughter of the third lord.[20] There was also a Denton, descended from a natural son of Humphrey Lord Dacre;[21] a Leigh of Isel, of a family whose head Lord Dacre had made his deputy in the West March;[22] a Pickering and a Hutton, both knight-service tenants of the barony of Greystoke;[23] Thomas Bates, an officer of the Dacre lordship of Morpeth;[24] and two Middletons, Thomas and his brother John, the former another Greystoke tenant.[25]

The dominant impression, therefore, is of a tightly regional connection, bound together by bonds of tenure, kinship, and service.

[17] For the Salkelds see *Trans. C. & W. A. & A. Soc.*, new ser., xiv (1949), p. 253.

[18] *L.P.*, xi, 1331. See above, p. 113.

[19] *Cal. State Papers, Domestic, Addenda, 1566–79*, p. 35.

[20] *Trans. C. & W. A. & W. Soc.*, xi (1911), opp. p. 254, Pedigree E.

[21] *Ibid.*, xvi, p. 40.

[22] *L.P.*, vi, 1167.

[23] J. Nicolson and R. Burn, *History and Antiquities of the Counties of Westmorland and Cumberland*, 2 vols. (London, 1777), i, p. 498; ii, p. 365.

[24] He was tenant of Morpeth mills, and probably receiver there, since a letter has survived from William Lord Dacre authorizing him to make out-payments on the latter's behalf. He had been M.P. for Morpeth, and distinguished himself by his services on the Border, for which he received a letter of thanks from Queen Mary. He subsequently entered the Percy service, becoming steward of Alnwick, and played an important role in the events leading to the Rising of the North, acting as interpreter between the seventh earl of Northumberland and the Spanish ambassador, and as intermediary between the former and Leonard Dacre. Arraigned of treason, he was subsequently pardoned. See *Northumberland County History*, ix (Newcastle upon Tyne, 1909), pp. 84–6; Sir C. Sharp, *Memorials of the Rebellion of 1569* (London, 1840), pp. 360–3.

[25] The Middletons, I am informed by Mr C. R. Hudleston, appear as tenants of Greystoke in an Elizabethan survey of the barony in the Prior's Kitchen, Durham.

The impression would have been strengthened if the herald had found it necessary to include in his schedule of funeral arrangements the names of those other servants who followed behind the mourners in the procession. These must have included Christopher Elwood of Denton Hall, keeper of Naworth park under the late lord, and son of his chief of ordnance, who had served under him at the battle of Musselburgh;[26] Thomas Farlam, tenant and bailiff of Askerton under Lord Dacre and his father, who for twenty years had carried the banner of the barony of Gilsland on Border raids;[27] and Christopher Blackborne, tenant of the barony of Greystoke, who had been Dacre's standard-bearer at Musselburgh field.[28] Such names and callings strike the epic Border note, violent and warlike. On the other hand representatives of the government were almost entirely lacking. There was only Lord Scrope, who had succeeded Dacre as warden of the West March in the previous year. He took his place in the procession with the late lord's sons, Thomas fifth Lord Dacre, Leonard, Edward and Francis, the last three men who would live to see the fall of their house. These were the chief mourners.

Although both Dacre and Wharton were peers, there were differences in their background and in the context in which each had spent his life. Lord Wharton, the first baron,[29] came not of any great feudal family, but of modest gentry stock settled at Wharton in Westmorland, where his ancestors had been tenants and followers of the Cliffords. Beginning his career in the service of the earl of Northumberland, Wharton had subsequently risen by that of the crown to a peerage and extensive estates. He had been the first to break the hold of the Border magnates on the great March offices. In 1542 he had succeeded the earl of Cumberland as warden of the West March. In the reign of Edward VI he had been deputy warden-general of all three Marches under the duke of Northumberland, and later still he ruled the East and Middle Marches. Lord Dacre had been one of his principal political rivals, and little love had been lost between the two men. Wharton, a member of the new Tudor political establishment, could depend to a much lesser extent than Dacre could on the support of a regional influence based on the loyalties of tenants and followers, and the prestige of a great name.

[26] *Cal. State Papers, Domestic Addenda, 1566–79*, p. 35.
[27] *Ibid.*, p. 36.
[28] *Ibid.*, p. 37.
[29] See above, p. 103 ff.

The Wharton lands, while extensive, were spread over three counties, and most of them had recently belonged either to monasteries or to the house of Percy. There were no gentry houses with a tradition of service to the Whartons, as so many had to the Dacres, Nevilles or Percies; and Wharton had ruled the Marches by means of those gentlemen who had been fee'd by the crown to serve under him. His power had depended on the great offices he held, and on the support of such of the northern gentry as identified themselves not with any of the great aristocratic households but with the crown. These were men to most of whom the Border world familiar to lord Dacre was alien, but who were closely involved in the work of the commissions of the peace and of "the court at York". Some of them were also members of the house of commons, and learned in, indeed often professionally involved with, those processes of common law whereby they and the properties they had inherited were integrated into a stable regulated order whose keystone was the crown. In such circles there was a distaste for the rambling strongholds of the great families ("A marvellous huge house", wrote one of them of the Neville castle at Raby, " . . . and yet is there no ordre or proporcion in the buyldinge thereof . . . but lyke a monstrous old abbey and will soone decay yf yt be not contynually repayred")[30] with their gregarious social routines, swollen retinues and touchy loyalties. Wharton, although he rebuilt Wharton Hall to be the traditional kind of setting for a great household, nevertheless preferred to live at his relatively modest manor-house at Healaugh, lately a small monastery, in a part of the country where his family had no roots, and away from the main body of his estates. But here he was close to his Stapleton relatives by marriage, and to York, the administrative capital of the north, where so many of his friends and acquaintances of the Tudor governmental élite were to be encountered. And it was at Healaugh that Wharton directed he should be buried, not at Kirkby Stephen in the heart of the Wharton country, where stood the parish church of his ancestors.[31]

Thus his funeral would be unlikely to give collective expression to a tight, regional and feudal connection, as Dacre's had done. It was in the first place much more a restricted and exclusively family

[30] Public Record Office, E164/37: Hall and Humblestone's Survey of Raby.

[31] See his will, printed in *Trans. C. & W. A. & C. Soc.*, old ser., i (1878–9), p. 240. A cenotaph was erected to his memory in Kirkby Stephen church.

affair. Wharton recruited the majority of his gentlemen and servants from amongst his relatives, probably most of them from the Kirkby Thore branch of his house, and these were well represented in his funeral procession. Richard Wharton carried the standard, and Anthony Wharton the great banner. John Wharton, one of the late lord's commissioners, and Charles Wharton carried two of the bannerols. Michael Wharton was one of the bearers. These were not supported, as in Dacre's case, by any great concourse of client gentry and tenants. Of Wharton's gentlemen present who were not of his family, Avery Copley of Batley in the West Riding was his nephew by marriage;[32] Richard Cliburn, of the Westmorland family of that name, had probably entered the Wharton service when the first lord had been warden of the West Marches;[33] John Herbert was a member of the great family whose head, the earl of Pembroke, was one of Wharton's executors.

This miscellaneous grouping suggests the narrowness of Wharton's following, outside his own kin. A few of the local gentry were also present, like Sir Oswald Wilstropp of Wilstropp, and John Thwaites of Marston in the Ainsty. These again, however, were neighbours and personal friends, not Wharton followers. But one of the most remarkable features of the funeral procession is the absence from it of all of Wharton's sons, including the second lord, who should have been chief mourner. Whatever the reason may have been, this cannot be explained by lack of time, since a month elapsed between the first lord's death and his burial. Perhaps the second generation of Whartons, whose interests were increasingly orientated towards London and the south, were little concerned with a remote ceremony in a part of the country distant even from the main family seat.[34] And the Whartons had no tradition of great family funerals to be upheld. Nor did the three great lords, the earls of Shrewsbury, Sussex and Pembroke (the first two of them relatives by marriage), whom the first lord had appointed his executors, feel it incumbent upon them to attend the burial of a newly risen

32 *Heraldic Visitation of the Northern Counties Made in 1530 by Thomas Tonge*, ed. W. H. D. Longstaffe (Surtees Soc., xli, Durham and London, 1848), p. 81.

33 *Trans. C. & W. A. & A. Soc.*, new ser., xxviii (1928), pp. 207 ff.

34 The second Lord Wharton, for example, although he occasionally resided at Wharton, was more often to be found at New Hall, Boreham, Essex, of which honour and manor he was chief steward and keeper of the capital mansion under the crown.

provincial peer who, whatever his prestige in the Marches, had lately counted for little at court.

Nevertheless, Wharton's funeral was an impressive occasion. What made it so was no assembly of client gentry and tenants but rather the powerful representation of the Tudor administrative élite which attended. Thus Wharton's chief mourners included Sir Thomas Gargrave, one of the common-law members of the Council in the North (a judge, therefore, of "the court at York") as well as queen's receiver in Yorkshire, and deputy constable of the royal castle of Pontefract.[35] There was Sir Henry Saville of Lupset, like Gargrave a judge of the court at York and surveyor of crown lands beyond Trent.[36] Present also were two other members of the Council in the North: Sir George Bowes, steward of the royal lordship of Barnard castle, and John Vaughan, steward of crown lands in Cumberland and Westmorland.[37] Sir Richard Lowther, sheriff of Cumberland, was another mourner, and in the procession was Robert Bowes, younger brother of Sir George, soon to be treasurer of Carlisle and ambassador to Scotland.[38] Here we have the public-spirited active gentry, administratively inclined, and obedient to authority. This was the community to which Wharton had come to belong. And the emphasis on the ordered disposal of property by due process of law which had such an appeal in this ambience was underlined by the men who walked before Wharton's great banner. These were no family retainers or veteran Border warriors, but three lawyers: Mr Monson, the late lord's counsel,[39] Mr Swyft (probably of the Rotherham family whose head had lately been steward to the earl of Shrewsbury),[40] and Mr Rodes, serjeant-at-law, soon to be a justice of the common pleas, and a member of the Council in the North.[41] They were there "in place of executors".

[35] R. R. Reid, *The King's Council in the North* (London, 1921), App. II, p. 492.
[36] *Ibid.*, p. 493.
[37] *Ibid.*, pp. 493–4. For Sir George Bowes see Sharp, *op. cit.*, App., p. 366, and *Dict. Nat. Biog.*, ii, p. 964.
[38] It was Lowther who, as sheriff, removed Mary Queen of Scots from the custody of the earl of Northumberland's officers, after she had landed at Workington, and conveyed her to Carlisle castle. See *Cal. State Papers, Scotland*, ii, pp. 410–13. For Robert Bowes, see *Dict. Nat. Biog.*
[39] See Wharton's will, which made him a legacy.
[40] J. Hunter, *South Yorkshire*, 2 vols. (London, 1828–31), i, p. 204; *Dict. Nat. Biog.*, xix, p. 227.
[41] Reid, *op. cit.*, p. 495.

Thus in these two funeral processions we find presented in miniature the picture of two contrasting societies. The one, with its roots far in the past, had its points of contact with the world of the *comitatus*, the war-band mourning its dead chieftain. The other attended the burial of the founder of a family whose fortunes would culminate in the career of a Whig marquess and party manager[42] of the reign of Queen Anne. It was the emerging polity of that England therefore which followed Wharton to his tomb. For the Dacres there was no such future in prospect. The early death of Thomas the fifth lord in 1566, followed by that of his heir three years later while still a ward of the duke of Norfolk, brought disaster to the family. The estate, divided amongst heiresses, passed by marriage to the Howards, and the title became extinct. The attempt of Leonard Dacre, the fifth lord's brother, to assert his claims as heir male[43] by force, and his consequent involvement in the Rising of the North, gave the government the opportunity to uproot the Dacre influence. So that, of the family mourners who followed the fourth lord's heir, Leonard Dacre died in Brussels ten years later, attainted and in poverty; Edward Dacre, also attainted, ended his days in the Spanish service, which provided a refuge too for the youngest brother, Francis, attainted in 1591 after his abortive attempt to claim the family title and estates. He and his son survived into the reign of Charles I, intermittently pensioned by the Stuart monarchy.[44] After that only the Dacre estates remained, and these became the endowment of another great Whig interest, that of the Howard earls of Carlisle.

[42] The fifth lord and first marquess of Wharton. It was his heir Philip, first and only duke of Wharton, who ruined the family by his extravagance and Jacobite politics.

[43] See n. 3, above.

[44] See *Complete Peerage*, iv, pp. 25–6.

6. *Obedience and dissent in Henrician England: the Lincolnshire rebellion, 1536*

I

Any approach to the subject of this essay must begin from the massive and well-known work of the Misses Dodds, *The Pilgrimage of Grace 1536–7, and the Exeter Conspiracy, 1538.*[1] We still owe to these two historians most of what can be said about the supreme crisis of the reign of Henry VIII, indeed perhaps of the Tudor dynasty. And the merits of their account have lately been recalled by another authority in the same field, Professor A. G. Dickens.[2] There will be widespread agreement that as a work of narrative history their book is unlikely to call for major revision. It is when it comes to the matter of interpretation however that one senses a feeling of persistent uneasiness, which comes through particularly strongly perhaps less in connection with the Pilgrimage of Grace than in the case of its prelude the Lincolnshire movement. Whatever explanations may be offered for the Pilgrimage (and it may be doubted whether here too we are anywhere near finality),[3] events in Lincolnshire baffle by their paradoxical character and the obscurity of their motivation.

Some of the bafflement emerges in *The Pilgrimage of Grace*. Thus "It was a most curious movement, both in its sudden outbreak and its still more sudden collapse."[4] Professor Dickens speaks of the events in Lincolnshire as "confused", and characterized by mob law

[1] By M. H. and R. Dodds, i and ii (Cambridge, 1915).
[2] In "Religious and Secular Motivation in the Pilgrimage of Grace", *Studies in Church Hist.*, iv, ed. G. J. Cuming (Leiden, 1968), pp. 39–54.
[3] For a stimulating recent discussion of the pilgrimage, see C. S. L. Davies, "The Pilgrimage of Grace Reconsidered", *Past and Present*, xli (Dec. 1968), pp. 54–76.
[4] Dodds, *op. cit.*, i, p. 138.

and meaningless violence,[5] an impression which is shared by Professor Dom David Knowles, who contrasts "the riotous violent character" of the Lincolnshire men with the more creditable behaviour of Yorkshire.[6] Explanations for the apparent meaninglessness and chaotic violence of the Lincolnshire movement have been sought in the isolation of the region, and the brutal and backward character of the society. Thus Henry VIII's characterization of the shire as "one of the most brute and beastly of the whole realm", and John Williams's description of the Lincolnshire gentry as "such a sight of asses, so unlike gentlemen as the most part of them be" are quoted to this effect.[7] Yet the rebellion received more support from the docile landlord-dominated Lincolnshire Vale[8] and from the thriving marshland and wolds,[9] regions of rich squires and a prosperous rural middle class, than from the traditionally turbulent and poor fens. Nor were the Lincolnshire gentry a rustic or backwoods group. The leading families, including those involved in the rebellion, knew London and the court, and not just their own backyards. There were many contacts with the royal household and with office under the crown.[10] Of the brutal murder

[5] *Loc. cit.*, pp. 51–2; and A. G. Dickens, *The English Reformation* (London, 1964), p. 125.

[6] David Knowles, *The Religious Orders in England*, iii (Cambridge, 1961), p. 322. Cf. P. Hughes, *The Reformation in England*, 5th edn (London, 1963), i, pp. 296–302, who sees the Lincolnshire movement as "unplanned", "confused and incoherent".

[7] Dodds, *op. cit.*, i, p. 89; Knowles, *loc. cit.*; Dickens, "Religious and Secular Motivation", p. 52.

[8] I.e. the clayland between the wolds and the limestone cliff. For conditions here see Joan Thirsk, *English Peasant Farming: The Agrarian History of Lincolnshire from Tudor to Recent Times* (London, 1957), ch. 4. The peasantry here was, on the average, poorer than that of the fenland, but land tended to be held in a strong manorial framework, and in one-manor villages the squire and his steward enjoyed undivided authority over the community. See also Joan Thirsk, "The Farming Regions of England", *The Agrarian History of England and Wales*, iv, ed. Joan Thirsk (Cambridge, 1967), pp. 32–3.

[9] For the marshland and wolds, see Thirsk, *English Peasant Farming*, chs. 2 and 3.

[10] Of the gentlemen involved in or close to the rebellion, both Sir Robert Dymoke and Sir Christopher Willoughby had been knights of the body, and Dymoke had been treasurer of Tournai and chancellor to Queen Catherine of Aragon. Sir William Ayscough had served in the French war of 1512–13, attended Henry VIII at the Field of the Cloth of Gold, and been a knight attendant (with Sir William Skipwith) at the coronation of Anne Boleyn. Both his sons were of the king's household. John Heneage was brother to Sir Thomas Heneage of Hainton, keeper of the king's privy purse. Sir William Skipwith and Sir Robert Tyrwhitt had represented the shire in Parliament, and the latter's son of the same name

of Thomas Wolsey and Dr Raynes there can be no doubt, but reasons are adduced below[11] to suggest that these killings were not pointless cruelties, but meaningful in the political sense: a state of affairs which does not of course make them any less repugnant from a moral point of view.

Some of the sense of bafflement and meaninglessness may perhaps be dissipated by a more careful look at the socio-political scene in Lincolnshire. In particular the gentlemen and magnates of the shire need to be seen less as cardboard figures, and their background, past and even future, filled out. On this basis alone a picture then emerges of a community which in 1536 was disgruntled in important respects, and could be expected to seize opportunities to vent its discontents. And, even if religion cannot be seen at work in the rebellion as an effective mass force, the presence of religious fervour in restricted but nevertheless decisive circles connected with the movement needs to be stressed. Again the tensions generated by what seemed to be a threat to the traditional role of an all-important professional group, the clergy, could usefully be re-emphasized. More attention also needs to be given to the actual structure of the mobs which initiated the disturbances, and to the character of the plebeian élite whose activities in the leadership of "the commons" has left such a mark on the movement that its democratic origins are still stressed.[12] In this connection the whole idea of "class conflict" as the key to the collapse of the rebellion may be usefully reconsidered. The Misses Dodds thought that the gentlemen "feared their allies [the commons] quite as much as the troops which opposed them: and recollections of the German Peasant Revolt of 1525 would increase their alarm".[13] Hence they deserted the commons, and submitted to the king. It is contended below however that a *jacquerie* in Lincolnshire in 1536 was a remote prospect; and that the plebeians with whom the gentlemen quarrelled were not the leaders of a peasant mass movement, but represented mainly themselves, most of "the commons" being content to submit to the leadership of their betters. Again the verdict that the movement's

was an esquire of the body and chamberlain of Berwick. Sir Edward Madison was M.P. for Hull, and Vincent Grantham for the city of Lincoln. This was no group of backwoods gentry.

[11] See below, p. 219.

[12] For example, by Dickens, "Religious and Secular Motivation", p. 51.

[13] Dodds, *The Pilgrimage of Grace*, i, p. 126.

"most obvious weakness was that it had no leader" and lacked "the inspiration of a great leader and a great cause"[14] may be questioned. For it prejudges the whole character of the rebellion, seeing it as a failed religious war. If in fact it was something more limited and less spectacular, Lord Hussey's leadership is less to be despised. Part then of the intention in the pages that follow is to fill in some of the gaps and suggest the revisions indicated above, in the hope that the area of comprehension may be extended.

A more difficult task, however, remains which could well take its start from a comment of Professor G. R. Elton: "All through they [the Lincolnshire rebels] declared themselves to be loyal to the crown; and perhaps the most remarkable thing about the whole rising was the confidence of these deluded men that the king was on their side, and they on his."[15] What was the meaning then of a "rebellion" whose participants took up such a curious stance? It is equally present in the Pilgrimage of Grace, and in other Tudor and pre-Tudor (and continental) dissentient movements, just as we encounter other paradoxes in these same rebellions, like the "coercion" of gentlemen "compelled" to take part in risings which they subsequently led.[16] Was the loyalty of the Lincolnshire men merely delusion or deceit? Did the gentlemen rise only because "coerced" by rebel plebeians? By and large both questions tend to be answered in the affirmative by current historical writing, which has a short and sharp way with Tudor dissentients, seeing behind them (particularly in the Pilgrimage of Grace) neo-feudal instigators of civil conflict, conniving at the renewal of the Wars of the Roses and seeking to plunge the country into prolonged anarchy and bloodshed.[17] The approach shows a fascination with Tudor

[14] *Ibid.*, pp. 138, 139.

[15] G. R. Elton, *England under the Tudors* (London, 1955), p. 146.

[16] Professor A. G. Dickens, in his valuable essay on Sir Francis Bigod in *Lollards and Protestants in the Diocese of York* (Oxford, 1959), ch. 3, pp. 90–1, notes how strangely this behaviour appears to modern eyes, when encountered in the Pilgrimage of Grace. He suggests, as a possible explanation of the phenomenon, a psychology arising from the interplay of neo-feudal habits of mind with the economic tensions which divided gentry and commons, so that the latter's behaviour vacillated between the coercion of their letters and submission to them (*ibid.*, p. 91). Another approach to the problem is attempted below.

[17] Dickens is perhaps the most forthright in his condemnation of the Pilgrimage and its leaders from this point of view: see e.g. his *Thomas Cromwell and the English Reformation* (London, 1959), pp. 94–5, 102; *The English Reformation* (London, 1964), p. 125; *Lollards and Protestants*, pp. 112–13. On the other hand he also

"order",[18] that correspondence of cosmic and political harmony which was the ideal image of Tudor rule, celebrated in the stately sentences of the *Homily on Obedience*, and by so many Tudor writers and intellectuals, including William Shakespeare. Inevitably, then, "rebels" get a bad press. Yet this is to by-pass the problem of how dissidence was to express itself in a society like that of Tudor England, which was surely remote from any Byzantine immobility, and in which there were tensions in plenty to feed dissent. Moreover, even by the end of the period we may doubt whether Parliament had so developed itsconventions and rules of non-violent political warfare as to function as the effective conflict-resolving mechanism of the society.

An attempt is made below to present a different point of view, using the Lincolnshire rebellion as a useful model. The latter is here approached not in the terms of a neo-feudal conspiracy aiming at levying war against the king, but as a means whereby a profound sense of disagreement with the king's policies, and of injustice at supposed injuries inflicted by his agents on individuals, could receive expression. The methods used ranged from riots in market towns to mass popular demonstrations involving the armed occupation of the shire capital and the drafting of programmes of political demands: manifestations in fact which the government could not possibly ignore. At the same time, however, the contention is that these were constrained within a framework of form and convention which aimed at limiting the disruptive effects of the movement and the amount of damage which might result, particularly to the landed governing class whose members (unlike "the commons" or even the clergy) constituted the essence of "polity" within the commonwealth over which the king presided. Thus while the rebellion assumed the initial form of popular commotions, which were

notes that "paradoxically", and "by reaction" the movement had its positive side, since it opened the way to the more effective government of the north: *Thomas Cromwell*, p. 102; *The English Reformation*, p. 127. For Elton the Pilgrimage was a movement of the "backward and barbarous north", which was "futile, misdirected and ill-considered" (*England under the Tudors*, pp. 147–8).

[18] Elton, for example, thought that the movement was bound to fail, for "Loyalty and obedience to the King, the guardian of peace and order, and the symbol of the state, dominated everything. Even the rebels used the language of loyalty" (*loc. cit.*). Professor J. D. Mackie, *The Earlier Tudors* (Oxford, 1952), considered that Henry VIII could calculate that "the prestige of the Crown, which stood for good order, would defeat the assaults of rebellious subjects" (p. 394).

accompanied by some, if restricted, popular violence, the leadership of "the commons" soon gave way to that of J.P.s and gentlemen, although supposedly "coerced" into this position. Respect for established authority, including that of the king, was maintained throughout; and when, as the movement began to disintegrate, some of the popular leaders sought to assert themselves against their betters, the majority of the commons supported the latter. Moreover, when the prospect confronted them, the leadership shied violently away from civil war, preferring submission, although if it had come to a battle the military odds were not unduly weighted against the insurgents. The government, on its side, acted with studied moderation. The blame for the commotions in Lincolnshire was fastened on the commons and the clergy, and only two of the landed establishment involved had to suffer the penalties of treason. The movement was not an unredeemed failure. Some, if not all, of the grievances which had caused it were subsequently remedied.

Looked at this way, the Lincolnshire rebellion points back less to the medieval baronial revolts against tyrannical kings, or civil wars between rival claimants to the throne, than to the fourteenth- and fifteenth-century protests against misgovernment, particularly the Peasants' Revolt and Cade's Rebellion (with the difference that in these movements popular violence was less effectively controlled, and some of the upper classes more roughly handled); and the closest Tudor precedent is probably that of the disorders of 1525 directed against Wolsey. Disturbances of this kind, however, may also be usefully considered in connection with a framework of political commonplace and moralizings from historical *exempla*, which received literary expression in the immensely popular tragic tales of the downfall of princes and great men included in Lydgate's *Fall of Princes* and its continuation, the Tudor *Mirror for Magistrates*. This literature, which is considered in more detail below, while insistent on "obedience" as the prime political and social virtue, and never condoning rebellion, nevertheless threw the responsibility for dissident insurgency on the prince himself, for the true cause of such disorders was misgovernment. The function of rebellion, then, was positive in so far as it called the prince to self-examination and the correction of misrule, and not to mere repression, necessary though this might be. From this point of view it played a positive role in the polity, for, by releasing tensions, compelling readjustments and correcting injustices, it conduced to the prince's own preservation, and so to stability.

Of course the expression of dissidence in this way did not necessarily conform to the ideal pattern. Things could go wrong, and damaging social and political conflict result. Dissident nobles and gentlemen could become convinced that their own lives and the future of their families had become so endangered through their involvement in a dissident movement as to leave no alternative but to attempt the arbitrament of a civil war. Or dissidence could assume an exclusively plebeian character, divorced from the ruling classes, and collapse into fantasy, violence and the pursuit of plunder. But this is only to say that "rebellion" raised more political than military problems. Both on the king's part, and on that of the insurgents, moderation and willingness to compromise had to be combined with boldness and the firm assertion of authority. As will be seen, these qualities were not absent on either side in the Lincolnshire rising; and amongst the rebels there were those who, like Hussey, preferred to risk the penalties of treason rather than encourage the Lincolnshire men to carry their protest out of the context of obedience into that of civil war.

II

"How presumptuous therefore are ye, the rude commons of one shire", Henry VIII told the Lincolnshire rebels, "and one of the most brute and beastly of the whole realm . . . to take upon you, contrary to God's law, and man's law, to rule your prince, whom ye are bound by all laws to obey and serve."[19] There was no need for the king to tone down the insulting phrases, for the Lincolnshire rebellion had already collapsed, and soon the hangman and the axe would take their toll of the leadership. The importance of the royal missive, however, was that it expressed the official view of the Lincolnshire disturbances which would be disseminated by authority. These had been the result of an elemental rising of the "rude and ignorant common people",[20] incited by a few erring monks and clergy. These latter had plotted with plebeian leaders as obscure and anonymous as the multitude they had led astray, hoping "to rule

19 *L.P.*, xi, 780 (2); *State Papers, Henry VIII*, i, p. 463.
20 *Ibid.*

and govern the King against his will, and deprive him of his royal liberty and power".[21] By contrast the same official version of events absolved the governing establishment of landed families, with two exceptions, from blame. The great men of the shire, it was emphasized, had been the first victims of rebel violence. Their authority had been flouted, and they had been compelled to flee or else had been coerced into joining the insurrection.[22] Thus it was appropriate that, when order was restored, almost all those who suffered the penalties of treason should be of "the commons". The presence of the before-mentioned two exceptions among the victims might seem to render implausible this version of events, since one of them was a shire magnate, Lord Hussey of Sleaford, and the other the recorder of Lincoln, Thomas Moigne. But both of these in fact accepted it. Hussey protested his loyalty to the end, asserting that only the hostility of his tenants, who sided with the commons, and lack of men, had prevented him from taking active measures against the rebels.[23] Moigne maintained that he had been compelled by the commons to take their oath, and submitted because he feared for the safety of his sick wife and house.[24] The most prominent clergyman among the rebels, the abbot of Barlings, made much the same defence.[25] He too had been coerced into aiding the rebels.

And so the view established itself that the Lincolnshire insurrection was a spontaneous explosion of popular anger due to those "rumours" of impending confiscations of property and church goods and the destruction of parish churches which had aroused the fears of the multitude. The gentry and upper clergy were dragged behind the popular movement, and in due course the inevitable tensions asserted themselves between the commons and their betters which was one of the causes of the failure of the rebellion. Such then was the official version. But an element of paradox is brought into the situation by the fact that behind the scenes this same version was received with scepticism, and indeed incredulity, in those same governmental circles which disseminated it. For it was a view of events which had originated as the defence of those of the gentry who had been involved in the rebellion and had indeed emerged as its leaders, although (so they said) under duress. Those in the know found it hard to absolve the gentlemen, and in private said so. The

[21] *L.P.*, xii (1), 734 (3).
[22] *Ibid.*
[23] *L.P.*, xi, 852; xii (1), 599.
[24] *L.P.*, xi, 971.
[25] *Ibid.*, 805.

king himself was one of the sceptics. Thus he urged the duke of Suffolk, his lieutenant in Lincolnshire whose task it was to ascertain the causes of the rising, to put to those he examined "if it be likely that so few villains and labourers could have stirred or raised, in despite of so many gentlemen, their own tenants against themselves or us".[26] And he warned Suffolk that "perceiving by the examination of divers traitors of the faction taken . . . that many of the gentlemen be not as whole as they pretend, we advise you to trust them no further than you must".[27] Distrust had been Henry's reaction, at an early stage of the rising, to the news that some of the commissioners of the subsidy had been taken prisoner by the rebellious commons of Caistor and Louth. The king had written words of small consolation to the captives, expressing his astonishment "that you, being our sworn servants, should place yourselves in their hands, instead of assembling for the surety of your persons, and for their suppression".[28] The same point of view was subsequently put in one of the interrogatories to the vicar of Louth: "How was it so many gentlemen and others were taken . . . and none sore stricken?"[29] Thus amongst the king's servants the notion that the rising was a mere plebeian revolt received scant credence. But were there any grounds for such suspicions? And if so why was the fiction persisted in which placed the responsibility on "the rude commons"?

III

The action of the common people in precipitating the Lincolnshire rebellion can be seen at its most dramatic in the succession of riots in market towns which initiated the movement. These began at Louth, and then spread to Caistor and Horncastle. If the disturbances were the result of deliberate contrivance, there were good reasons why these three places should have been chosen by the instigators. Louth was not only an important market and route centre, and the chief town of a wapentake and rural deanery, but also next to Boston and Lincoln itself, the largest urban community in the shire.[30] To the west it faced towards the wold country, which

[26] *Ibid.*, 843. [27] *Ibid.*, 883. [28] *Ibid.*, 569. [29] *L.P.*, xii, 69.

[30] According to the archdeacon's return of 1563 (British Lib., Harleian MS. 618) Louth had a population of about 400 families; Boston had 471, and the ten parishes of Lincoln included in the return had 459. Stamford came next with 213.

in the sixteenth century was a fertile field for the development of large-scale capitalist farming;[31] and to the east there was the marshland, where there were many wealthy yeomen, as well as rich squires.[32] Such prosperous middle-class farmers provided a good many of the leaders of the rebellion. Horncastle, although less than half the size of Louth,[33] was also a route and market centre, and the capital of a soke and rural deanery. It drew too on a social environment much the same as that of Louth, although Horncastle was closer to the world of the fens, where gentlemen were few. In this respect there was a contrast with the third centre, Caistor, eighteen miles north-west of Louth. Although a market town of the hundred of Yarborough, Caistor was much smaller even than Horncastle. But its importance arose from the many great estates and houses of great families which surrounded it.[34] As a result it was the centre where many of the leading gentlemen of the shire assembled to carry out their duties as justices, commissioners and such-like. One such gathering in fact was in progress on 2 October 1536, when a meeting of the king's commissioners for the subsidy, comprising seven of the leading gentry of the shire and a peer,[35] was being held at Caistor Hill outside the town. Inside it at the same time was an assembly of substantial men of four wapentakes, come to negotiate the incidence of the subsidy with the commissioners, and 160 clergy summoned to undergo the visitation of which more will be said below.[36] Thus in these early days of October Caistor acquired an importance as a political and social nerve-centre quite out of proportion to its size. But Louth and Horncastle too, on 2 and 3 October, had their gatherings of clergy awaiting visitation, whose

[31] As also were the Yorkshire wolds: see Thirsk, "The Farming Regions of England", p. 34.

[32] *Ibid.*, p. 36; Thirsk, *English Peasant Farming*, p. 54.

[33] With 164 families in 1563.

[34] Near Caistor (which had a population of 53 families in 1563) or within striking distance were the houses of Sir William Ayscough at Stallingborough, Sir Edward Madison at Fonaby, Sir William Skipwith at South Ormsby, Sir Robert Tyrwhitt at Kettleby, Thomas Moigne at North Willingham, Henry Booth at Killingholme, Sir Thomas Heneage at Hainton and Sir Thomas Mussenden at Healing.

[35] The gentlemen were Sir Thomas Mussenden, Thomas Moigne, Sir William Ayscough, Sir Edward Madison, Henry Booth, Sir Robert Tyrwhitt and Thomas Portington; the peer was Lord Burgh.

[36] *L.P.*, xi, 853. Apparently the clergy included those of the deanery of Grimsby and Rasen, as well as of Yarborough, which accounts for the large number present at Caistor.

presence imparted an air of excitement also to these towns.[37] And in all three centres these parish priests would subsequently play an important role in ensuring the participation of the countryside in the agitation which had begun in the market towns.

No clear evidence exists that the disturbances were the result of economic stress or social conflict. There is no hint, for example, that the common people in town or country rose because of the dearness of corn, although the majority of those involved in the riots at Louth were wage-labourers and craftsmen, and in those at Horncastle "poor men", groups vulnerable to dearth. But the harvest year 1536–7 was it seems one of relative abundance, at least as compared with the dearth of 1535–6.[38] Even so it is clear that there were many in this society willing to riot if they were paid for it. William Leech, for example, began the disturbances at Horncastle with the help of some forty "poor men" to whom he gave a shilling each; and Nicholas Melton at Louth stirred up that town with the support of a similar band whose members received disbursements from the funds of the parish church.[39] Both sides in fact were conscious of the importance of money in raising the people, the earl of Shrewsbury telling the king that "money is the thing that every poor man will call for",[40] while the Horncastle clergy urged their parishioners "to proceed on this journey" because "they would lack neither gold nor silver".[41] Since however none of the disturbances assumed the form of corn-riots, nor was the price of corn mentioned in any rebel pro-

[37] See below, p. 200.

[38] See W. G. Hoskins, "Harvest Fluctuations and English Economic History 1480–1619", in *Agricultural Hist. Rev.*, xii (1964), p. 28. With wheat at an average price of 12.67 a quarter for 1535–6, and deviating by + 35.7 from the 31-year moving average which he took as its norm, Hoskins classified the harvest of this year as "Bad". By contrast for 1536–7 the average fell to 9.17 a quarter, deviating by − 4.61 from the norm, and the harvest for this year was therefore classified as "Average". On Thorold Rogers's evidence, too, 1535–6 was a bad year, with a general average of 10*s* 3½*d* a quarter for wheat in 1535, and 10*s* 7½*d* in 1536, the highest price since 1527 (12*s* 11*d*). The high prices maintained themselves in 1536 until September, when it became obvious that an abundant harvest was in hand, and a fall began to the old level of 1534 (7*s*): *History of Agriculture and Prices in England*, 7 vols. (Oxford, 1866–1900), iv, pp. 258–9, 288. The list of corn prices returned by leet juries at Lincoln for the years 1513–1712, printed in J. W. F. Hill, *Tudor and Stuart Lincoln* (Cambridge, 1956), Appendix iii, does not unfortunately include any returns for the years 1534–8. See also the remarks of C. S. L. Davies, "The Pilgrimage of Grace Reconsidered", pp. 57–8.

[39] *L.P.*, xi, 967 (iii) and (v); 828 (i) (1).

[40] *L.P.*, xi, 5 and 7.

[41] *L.P.*, xii, 70 (ix).

gramme, it seems unlikely that the poor, in spite of their appetite for pay, confronted conditions of exceptional hardship in October 1536.

Nor did the commons give any hint that they felt strongly about such agrarian grievances as enclosures or the level of rents and fines. In spite of the trivial scale of depopulating enclosure in Lincolnshire revealed by the surviving returns of the Inquisition of 1517,[42] there were instances of bitter conflict between the big sheep- and cattle-farmers who overstocked commons or turned them into private pastures and the lesser men who were the losers.[43] But these do not seem to have been wide enough in their effect to have permeated the popular consciousness sufficiently to produce a mood of mass insurgency, any more than quarrels between landlords and tenants over rents and fines. Thus in the Lincolnshire movement there is no hint of the peasant agitation against oppressive lords characteristic of the Pilgrimage of Grace in the Pennine dales and West March. We might be tempted to see a trace of class conflict between rich and poor at Louth in the rough treatment (but it did not go beyond words) meted out to "the heads of the town" and "the rich men" by the mob, the former being summoned "by the name of churls" to take the oath and join the insurgents, and the latter threatened with hanging at their own doors.[44] But in fact at least some town notables, including the bailiff William King, helped to raise and sustain these disturbances.[45]

[42] Which relate only to the sokes of Bolingbroke and Horncastle, and the wapentake of Candleshoe. See *The Domesday of Inclosures*, ed. I. S. Leadman (London, 1897), i, pp. 243–66. Cases heard in the court of exchequer as a result of the Act of 1533 forbidding flocks of more than 2,400 sheep resulted however in only two suits affecting Lincolnshire; and only four of the 583 prosecutions in the same court relating to enclosures between 1518 and 1568 arose in the county. See Thirsk, *English Peasant Farming*, pp. 159–60, and M. Beresford, *The Lost Villages of England* (London, 1954), pp. 396–8.

[43] Vincent Grantham, for example, who will be encountered below as one of the leaders of the rebellion, had his enclosures at Langton thrown down in 1531 in a riot which led to a suit in Star Chamber: Public Record Office, Star Chamber 2/16/206. In 1539 Grantham was involved in another Star Chamber suit arising from his overcharging the common of Bracebridge with his sheep (Star Chamber 2/3/41), and an assault which he and his servants made on Thomas Bagger, a husbandman, whose sheep had been driven from the common.

[44] *L.P.*, xi, 854, 970.

[45] For King's involvement, see *L.P.*, xi, 828 (i) (1), 843. A Louth magnate, John Chapman of Thorpe Hall, and a gentleman who was probably John Elton of Frisby brought pressure on the vicar of Louth to make church money available to

It seems then that the Lincolnshire movement originated less in tensions within the society than in its fears of invasion from without, which it will be seen were present at all its levels, high as well as low. But probably it was to the clergy that the unrest communicated itself most strongly and directly. For in June 1536 the promulgation of the Ten Articles had brought the first clear indication that the new Supreme Headship of the church would involve changes in the traditional religious practices and forms. The Ten Articles were underlined by the royal Injunctions of August 1536, which provided for the enforcement of the Articles at the parochial level by means of a visitation to be made in the king's name by Thomas Cromwell, as viceregent in spirituals, who was authorized to appoint commissaries for this purpose.[46] It was this visitation which was under way in Lincolnshire as early as September 1536, with Dr John Raynes, already the bishop's commissary, acting as one of Cromwell's for this purpose.[47] In the deanery of Louth and Louthesk the visitation proceedings were due to begin on Monday 2 October, with Dr Frankish, the diocesan registrar, acting as commissary there and in the deanery of Yarborough, whose clergy had been assembled at Caistor.[48] Raynes was to act in the deanery of Horncastle and Hill, whose clergy had also been assembled.[49]

The anxieties aroused by the visitation centred on the changed role which the new religious trends required of the priesthood. There was for example the emphasis on "exhortation" and the sermon in the visitation articles. The clergy were required to preach up the Supremacy and Articles, urge their flocks into works of charity and the keeping of God's commandments, and to the reading of the Bible, which was to be set up in each church, but without contention.[50] Such duties contrasted with the traditional function of the priest, which the parishioners had tended to see as ritualistic rather than didactic in character. For the good priest was not required to be assiduous in preaching, but rather punctual at the altar, in burying

pay "the poor men" who started the riots. Both were subsequently captains in the host of Louth and Louthesk. See *L.P.*, xi, 968.

46 See Burnet's *History of the Reformation*, ed. N. Pocock (Oxford, 1865), iv, p. 308, where the Injunctions are printed.

47 See *Visitations of the Diocese of Lincoln, 1517–31*, ed. A. Hamilton Thompson (Linc. Rec. Soc., xxxiii, xxxv, xxxvii), ii (1944), pp. 219–20.

48 *L.P.*, xii (1), 380; xi, 853.

49 *Visitations, loc. cit.*

50 Burnet, *loc. cit.*

and marrying, in visiting the sick, and in confession.[51] And of course the emphasis on the sermon was bound to raise the question of the "learning" of the clergy, that is their capacity to preach, which it seems was often doubtful. Anxieties on this score had at any rate been stimulated by an overzealous clerk of Raynes's, who had told the clergy assembled at Bolingbroke to "look to their books" or "it would be worse for them".[52] It seems no longer possible to establish the exact provenance of the wild rumours which excited the priests, and which they disseminated. It is understandable, however, that these should have been readily listened to and passed on. For the attack on the monasteries and the devaluation of important aspects of traditional religion apparent in the Articles and visitation Injunctions must have made anything seem possible in the eyes of a conservative priesthood. It was natural to assume, for example, that if only preachers were required, non-preaching incumbents would be dispensed with,[53] and no doubt their parish churches with them. And, if the king had not hesitated to plunder the goods and treasures of the monasteries, it seemed unlikely that he would spare those of the parishes. Hence the rumours about the proposed suppression of parish churches and the seizure of their plate. And the fears of the clergy, which were shared by the laity, that they would be taxed to the bone by the Supreme Head,[54] could not have been assuaged by the requirement of the Visitation Articles that they

51 *Visitations*, i (1940), p. xxxix. In her recent *The Secular Clergy in the Diocese of Lincoln, 1495–1520* (Cambridge, 1968), however, Mrs M. Bowker concludes: "A modicum of preaching also appears to have been expected. Some slight evidence survives to suggest that the clergy were preaching and that those reported for not doing so were the exception not the rule" (p. 112).

52 *L.P.*, xii (1), 481.

53 According to William Morland, there were priests who expected this fate, and spread the rumours "to persuade the common people that they also should be as ill handled" (*ibid.*).

54 Some priests thought the object of the visitation was to deprive as many clergy as possible in order that first-fruits could be levied on their benefices: *L.P.*, xii (1), 481. The eagerness of the insurgents at Louth to secure Frankish's "book of reckonings" may have been connected with such preoccupations: *L.P.*, xii (1), 380. Raynes, it seems, had been engaged at Bolingbroke on the valuation of benefices, which according to one report, determined a group of priests "to strike him down": *L.P.*, xi, p. 401. For the great increase in clerical taxation initiated in 1635, see Davies, "The Pilgrimage of Grace Reconsidered", pp. 63–4, and J. J. Scarisbrick, "Clerical taxation in England, 1485–1547", in *Jl of Eccles. Hist.*, xi (1960), pp. 41–54.

should bestow specified proportions of their stipends on the poor, the repair of church buildings, and on exhibitions to scholars.[55]

It is difficult to see much religious fervour in these doubts and fears, at least as expressed by the activists and "stirrers" among this rural priesthood confronted by the prospect of religious change. In fact the latter was regarded primarily as a threat to the way of life of a conservative professional group which wished to pursue undisturbed its established habits and bucolic routines,[56] and was doubtful of its capacity to measure up to the new demands made on it and fearful of the new fiscal burdens. There is evidence of only one case of a Lincolnshire clergyman who, in the course of the rebellion, displayed a strong religious commitment. This was the vicar of Louth, Thomas Kendal, who was deeply concerned about the doctrinal matters at issue, counselling the rebels to make the repression of heresy and the maintenance of the faith their first objective.[57] He may have been right in his conviction that the common people "grudged" at the "new opinions" concerning Our Lady and Purgatory, two themes towards which it is certainly true that much popular piety was directed, as well as at the Royal Supremacy and abrogation of holy days.[58] But it is significant that in his sermon of Sunday 1 October which sparked off the disturbances at Louth, the vicar's emphasis was less on such matters than on "such things as would be required of them in the said visitation" whose safety he urged his parishioners to "go together" to protect, that is the jewels of Louth church.[59] The people, it seems, were more easily roused by the prospect of the plunder of the parochial treasures by the king's

[55] The Articles required all parsons to bestow ⅕ of their benefice on repairs, 1/40 of benefices of £20 a year or more on the poor, and an exhibition for each £100 received from a benefice. What had previously been generalized obligations were now to be precisely quantified.

[56] For these, see *Visitations*, i, intro. pt. 3, p. xxxix.

[57] *L.P.*, xii (1), 70.

[58] *L.P.*, xi, 90 (i); xii (1), 70. The vicar's opinion as to the religious preoccupations of the common people, and their dislike of religious innovation, may appear to be confirmed by the action of the rioters at Louth, who burned "all English books of the New Testament, and other new books they could get by proclamation" including a copy of "Frythe his booke". But the burning was the work of Melton and his company, i.e. the band of "poor men" who initiated the disturbances, and who had been paid out of the funds of Louth church. The cobbler Nicholas Melton was much under the vicar's influence, who "encouraged him to proceed in this business", and subsequently "comforted" him. See *L.P.*, xi, 828 (i); iii, 968.

[59] *L.P.*, xii (1), 481.

agents than by that of invasion by an alien religion. And such a concern was easily joined in the minds of the commons, particularly at Caistor where the work of assessing the subsidy was about to begin, with the fear that they too, as well as the clergy, would suffer from the apparently limitless royal fiscal demands which already threatened the church.[60] This fear received expression in the rumour that all unmarked cattle would be seized to the king's use.[61] Such matters were a common denominator bringing clergy and commons together.

The clergy were subsequently to claim, like the gentlemen, that they joined the rebellion only because they were coerced into doing so by the commons. But it could not have been easy for the mobs to coerce the large assemblies of priests at Louth, Horncastle and Caistor, many among which were just as capable of violence as the laity. The riot at Louth, for example, was the work of a crowd about a hundred strong,[62] out of which the activists probably numbered barely twenty.[63] This was a considerable number in a town of four hundred families or thereabouts; but the clergy assembled at Louth numbered sixty,[64] and they could undoubtedly have put up a forceful resistance had they been disposed to do so. The number of clergy at Caistor was about a hundred and sixty,[65] and there could scarcely have been less than fifty at Horncastle.[66] On the other hand, in both

[60] The commons at Caistor, while willing that the king should be Supreme Head, and have first-fruits and tenths, together with the subsidy, demanded that he should ask no more money of the commons during his lifetime, and suppress no more abbeys (*L.P.*, xi, 853). The main preoccupation was to restrain further royal inroads on property, clerical and lay. The "religious" implications of the Supreme Headship, on the other hand, were ignored. See also Davies, "The Pilgrimage of Grace Reconsidered", pp. 69–71.

[61] This rumour, together with that relating to the confiscation of "church jewels", was circulating at Sleaford on Michaelmas Day (*L.P.*, xi, 828 (vi)).

[62] *L.P.*, xi, 828 (i) (1).

[63] *Ibid.* The names of seventeen activists are given who worked up the crowd to the point of ringing the common bell and raising the town. Undoubtedly once the bell had been rung the original crowd of about a hundred would have increased in number, and it is possible that William Morland's estimate (*L.P.*, xii (1), 380) that, later in the day, he was surrounded by a mob of three to four hundred may be near the truth, for "meanwhile the country had resorted to them" (*L.P.*, xi, 828). The clergy, however, had submitted at an early stage in the disturbances, before the arrival of Heneage and Frankish, some of them accompanying the commons to meet and seize the latter.

[64] *L.P.*, xii, 70 (i).

[65] *L.P.*, xi, 853.

[66] There were forty-six benefices in the deaneries of Horncastle, Hill and Gartre, and there were many clergy from other deaneries, particularly Bolingbroke, in the town at the time of the disturbances.

these smaller places the mobs are not likely to have been more numerous than at Louth.[67] It is difficult then to believe that the clergy took the commons' oath other than willingly.[68] This supposition is confirmed by their subsequent behaviour. At Louth they promised to raise their parishes, and did so by ringing their church bells.[69] Probably the same undertaking was given at Horncastle and Caistor, for in all three deaneries clergy were subsequently named who were active in raising the peasantry. Thus the priests played a role of great importance, since they initiated the mobilization of the countryside which was to transform what had begun as an urban riot into a regional mass movement.

Again it is sometimes taken for granted that the monastic clergy were too apathetic and cowed to take part in any dissentient movement, and that those who did so were coerced.[70] Three houses became involved in the rebellion: Bardney (Benedictine), Kirkstead (Cistercian) and Barlings (Premonstratensian); and in these, if Barlings was typical, an atmosphere of unsettlement and near-desperation prevailed in the months immediately before Lincolnshire rose. This mood was the result of the conviction that the larger monasteries would not long survive the dissolution of the lesser, and the monks feared for their future.[71] It is not surprising then that they should have rallied to the support of a movement which had already stopped the dissolution of one house (Legbourne

[67] On the first day of the disturbances at Horncastle the insurgents numbered about a hundred (*L.P.*, xii (1), 70 (viii) and (x)). At Caistor there were large numbers of commons in the town, although George Hudswell's figure of two thousand seems exaggerated (*L.P.*, xi, 853). William Morland's one thousand (*L.P.*, xii (1), 380) may be more accurate, but these were unarmed and constituted an audience of, rather than participants in, the events of the day. The only figure available for the activists is that of a hundred given by Thomas Moigne (*L.P.*, xi, 971) as the number of commons who came to confront the subsidy commissioners at Caistor Hill. The recurrence of the figure of a hundred at Louth, Horncastle, and Caistor is suspicious, but may nevertheless be a rough approximation to the actual number of those prepared to lead and actively participate in disorders in all three places.

[68] At Caistor the clergy straightforwardly joined the commons, led by the deans of Grimsby and Rasen, without any show of resistance (*L.P.*, xi, 853).

[69] *L.P.*,. xii, 70 (1).

[70] Dodds, *The Pilgrimage of Grace*, ii, p. 156; Knowles, *The Religious Orders*, iii, p. 323; Dickens, *The English Reformation*, p. 126.

[71] The abbot of Barlings expected the dissolution of the greater monasteries would begin soon after Michaelmas. He had called his monks together and advised the sale of the plate and vestments of the house to provide for themselves, in view of the inadequacy of the government pension for monks. See *L.P.*, xii (1), 702.

nunnery), and whose programme was to oppose any resumption of the dissolution policy. Thus all the monks of Kirkstead, with the exception of the abbot, joined the rebel host horsed and armed, as did six monks from Barlings, and at least four from Bardney. All said they had acted out of fear, because of threats by the commons to burn their houses and the murder of Dr Raynes at Horncastle on Wednesday 4 October.[72] But the case of Dr Matthew Mackerell, bishop of Chalcedon, suffragan bishop of Lincoln and abbot of Barlings, suggests that such excuses were not sincere. Mackerell has left a particularly vivid description, frequently quoted, of his fear when a band of commons occupied Barlings.[73] Yet not only did he join the insurgents at the head of his monks in harness,[74] but he soon also became deeply involved in the movement. He supplied the host with food,[75] and urged the commons to "go forward" and "stick to this matter";[76] these "comfortable words" of his, and his "great gift" of provisions were shortly to be remembered by a witness who reported them to the Beverley insurgents.[77] The hollowness of Mackerell's excuse of fear of the commons is suggested by the fact that, although given a passport to leave the host to gather provisions from the abbey manors, he made no attempt to escape.[78] As the government which executed him saw, he was in fact wholly committed to the rebel cause.[79]

Sir William Fairfax, in a letter to Cromwell,[80] ascribed both the Lincolnshire rebellion and the Pilgrimage of Grace to the power of the church, pointing out that the people had been most ready to rise where archbishops, bishops and abbots had rule and appointed

[72] *L.P.*, xi, 828 (viii), 828 (v), 828 (vii.

[73] *L.P.*, xi, 805.

[74] *L.P.*, xi, 828 (v).

[75] *L.P.*, xi, 805; xii, 70 (viii). The abbot admitted to supplying the host with six bullocks, beer, bread and cheese; another witness maintained he also sent eighty wethers, which the abbot denied.

[76] *L.P.*, xii, 70 (viii). The abbot denied using these words.

[77] The Yorkshire men were so impressed by the abbot's demeanour that "any man counted themselves ashamed to be so far behind them [of Lincolnshire] and then longer stay could not be taken . . . " (*L.P.*ı, xii (1), p. 185).

[78] Mackerell's cellarer, Henry Thornbeck, reported that the abbot, although given a passport to leave the host and go to his lordship of Sweton, in fact never used it (*L.P.*, xi, 828 (vi)). Mackerell said he was stayed by hearing other counties had risen (*ibid.*, 805).

[79] One of the surveyors of monastic properties claimed that Mackerell had planned to kill him, and procured the plunder of his house by the commons (*L.P.*, xi, 725).

[80] *L.P.*, xii (1), 192.

officers. As examples he instanced Louth, a lordship of the bishop of Lincoln; Hedon, belonging to the bishop of Durham; and Beverley, a town of the archbishop of York. He might have added Horncastle, a manor of the bishop of Carlisle, to his list. Undoubtedly the church played a part of first importance in the Lincolnshire movement, even if monks and clergy did little to infuse religious fervour into the rebellion. The paradox of the position of John Longland, bishop of Lincoln, tends to conceal this fact. For, though a conservative in religion, he was compromised (as will be seen) by his involvement in Queen Catherine's divorce, which led to his inclusion in the list of "heretic bishops" whom the rebels demanded should be punished. He had no choice but to keep out of the way and remain "loyal". But the adhesion of his suffragan Mackerell, perhaps a more familiar representative of authority than the absentee bishop, must have gone a long way to convince the clergy that their doings were countenanced from above. Moreover the whole orientation of the rebel demands confirms the sense of a powerful clerical initiative at work. The disturbances at Louth were begun by a mob roused by the vicar, paid out of church funds, and determined to defend the rights of parish churches. The commons stopped the dissolution of Legbourne nunnery, and arrested the dissolution commissioners. The agents of the hated viceregent's visitation were ill-treated, Frankish being threatened with hanging at Louth, and Raynes murdered at Horncastle. The latter place rose too in defence of the parish churches, and, although at Caistor the fiscal grievances of the laity bulked largest, there also the cause of the monasteries was taken up. It was only as the movement broadened and the gentry began to participate that a political programme shaped itself side by side with the demands of the conservative clergy.

IV

But, apart from the mass response to fears stimulated by rumour and magnified by ignorance, did conscious planning have any role in causing the disturbances? Something of this was certainly present from the start. At Louth, for example, it is clear that the insurrection was begun and directed by a small band of activists, less than a score strong, led by Nicholas Melton the cobbler and these (as has been seen) were paid to do their work.[81] The composition of the group is interesting, and the core plainly consisted of Melton's workmates, since out of the seventeen involved five were cobblers or shoemakers. Among the rest there were two weavers, two sawyers, a singing-man, a smith, and three labourers. Thomas Manby, one of the most active after Melton himself, is variously described as a "labourer" and "victualler"; he may have been a bankrupt shopkeeper.[82] It was this group (whose members were, it seems, armed[83]) which, led by Melton, on Sunday evening after Kendal's inflammatory sermon, seized the keys of the church from the churchwardens, and locked it to ensure that none of the treasures were removed. The keys were then handed over to Melton's custody.[84] On Monday morning a crowd gathered at the church door, and were there addressed by Melton's men, and it was agreed to ring the common bell, so alerting the town against the arrival of John Heneage, the bishop's steward, who was due that day at Louth to select new officers for the town, and of Frankish, expected for the visitation.[85] Upon their arrival both were seized, but Heneage was less roughly treated than the commissary, being merely forced to take the commons' oath with the rest of the town and shut in the church.[86] Thus a first contact was made with the gentry, and there was a second when Sir William Skipwith, the head of a local great family, encountered by some of the crowd near the town, took the oath. He did so willingly according to some, under coercion according to others.[87] The capture at Legbourne of the commissioners, engaged on the dissolution of the nunnery there, the swearing of the clergy, and the baiting of Frankish completed the events of the first day of the disturbances at Louth.[88] Thereafter as the movement broadened Melton and his friends play a much less prominent role, and the gentry move into the foreground.

The pattern whereby a group of activists stirred up the crowd and initiated disturbances was repeated both at Horncastle and Caistor. At Horncastle the leader was William Leech, a much more substantial and impressive figure than Melton, who was helped by his brothers Nicholas (parson of nearly Belchford) and Robert, all

[81] Above, pp. 198–9.
[82] Public Record Office, SP 1, 109/1.
[83] *L.P.*, xi, 854.
[84] *L.P.*, xi, 828 (i).
[85] *Ibid.*
[86] *L.P.*, xii (1), 380.
[87] *L.P.*, xi, 828 (i), 854.
[88] *L.P.*, xii (1), 380.

three being members of a prosperous local yeoman family.[89] Like Melton, however, Leech was the leader of an activist group some forty strong, consisting as has been seen of "poor men" who were paid for their services.[90] There is evidence of prior planning, since these were under orders to be at Horncastle on Tuesday morning.[91] Like the men at Louth, and for the same reasons, they seized control of the church from the churchwardens, and then roused the town by ringing the common bell. As a result a crowd gathered.[92] Apart from his two brothers, Leech seems to have had other lieutenants, more substantial men than the rank and file, who were entrusted with specific tasks, particularly the capture of prominent personages. Thus, while Leech himself went towards Scrivelsby to bring in the Dymokes, the local great family, one Philip Trotter, a mercer, was sent ahead with half-a-dozen men to confront Sir Robert Dymoke and his sons at the house; and he seems subsequently to have played a similar role at Bolingbroke, at the capture of Raynes, Cromwell's commissary.[93] William Longbottom, a barber, was sent to swear two gentlemen, Thomas Littlebury and Sir John Copledike, and to fetch the Dymoke banner from Horncastle church.[94] Robert Nele, a tanner, was sent to gather money from various persons in Horncastle, and Ralph Green of Pertney, a yeoman and an old associate of Leech's, was prominent in haranguing the crowd.[95] Just as at Louth, however, the role of the popular leaders and their bands fall into the background after the first day of the disturbances. On Wednesday, as will be seen, the leadership was assumed by the gentry.

Fewer details have survived of the rising at Caistor, where it seems substantial men of the wapentakes of Yarborough, Walshcroft, Bradley and Haverstoe were assembled to confer with the commissioners of the subsidy, who were meeting near at hand at Caistor Hill. Their numbers were swollen by a crowd of "the commons", and the fact that these had assembled suggests that something out of the ordinary was expected.[96] These latter were addressed, as at Louth, by a number of activists, of whom however

89 See below, pp. 211–12.

90 Above, p. 198. *L.P.*, xi, 967.

91 *L.P.*, xi, 967 (v).

92 *L.P.*, xi, 828 (i) and (2); 967.

93 *L.P.*, xi, 828 (i) and (2). Trotter was also subsequently sent with a message to the gentlemen at Louth.

94 Accompanied by Trotter. See *L.P.*, xi, 828 (ii).

95 *L.P.*, xi, 967; xii (1), 70 (xii).

96 *L.P.*, xi, 853, 971.

the names of only two (who subsequently disappear from the scene)[97] have survived. They roused their audience by asserting that the justices had been commanded to disarm the common people, obviously a measure which would facilitate those oppressive taxes which popular rumour anticipated.[98] At Caistor therefore the emphasis was more on the laity's fears of fiscal exploitation than on the danger to the parish churches. As a result of the harangues, the commons banded themselves together under the leadership of one George Hudswell who was elected their captain. The clergy gathered for the visitation then threw in their lot with the commons, and the latter were joined by a contingent of the commons at Louth, a move which had been plainly pre-arranged. Both contingents then went in pursuit of the subsidy commissioners, just as at Horncastle Leech and his men had sought out the Dymokes and other local gentry.[99] As a result two of the leading gentlemen of the shire, Sir William Ayscough and Sir Robert Tyrwhitt, were captured, together with Sir Edward Madison, Henry Booth and Thomas Portington. Lord Burgh, Sir Thomas Mussenden and Thomas Moigne escaped, but the latter nevertheless joined the commons that same evening.[100] Once again with the appearance of the gentlemen on the scene, much less is heard of the popular leaders responsible for the first initiative.

Inevitably, however, the element of planning and initiative which had been present in the raising of the initial disturbances assumed greater importance as the rebellion shaped itself into a coherent political movement. As this happened so the payment and victualling of the rebel host had to be organized. Contact had to be made with the established centres of power represented by the shire magnates, and a political programme had to be drawn up. And the Lincolnshire movement needed to be co-ordinated with that in Yorkshire once this got under way. It is in connection with functions of this sort that we become aware of an organizing élite at work which included some, but not all, of the popular leaders and mob-raisers so far encountered. We can see two of these men, for example, active in the disturbances at Louth and Caistor, seeking to effect a conjunction between the rioting commons and the gentry,

[97] Anthony Williamson and Harry Pennell of Saxby.
[98] *L.P.*, xi, 853.
[99] *Ibid.*
[100] *Ibid.*, 971; xii (1), 380.

and to bring the latter into the leadership of the movement. One was an ex-monk William Morland, of the dissolved abbey of Louth Park, the other his friend Guy Kyme. Morland made the first contact both with Heneage and Frankish at Louth, and with the captured subsidy commissioners at Caistor.[101] In both places he acted to check popular violence, and to reassure those who had fallen into the rebels' hands. Kyme placed his house at Louth at the disposal of the commissioners, and it was from there that the latter despatched their letter to the king asking for a general pardon, so making the first contact between the government and the insurgents. Subsequently Kyme went to Beverley to act as the link between the Lincolnshire and Yorkshire movements.[102] Another such contacts-man was Anthony Curtis, who with his family had been prominent in ensuring the adherence of Grimsby to the rebellion, but who also accompanied Kyme on his mission to Beverley.[103]

Apart from the contacts-men, however, there were also the opinion-makers and policy-drafters. George Stones of Haltham is a good example of the type. Of yeoman or small gentry stock,[104] he makes his first appearance as one of the leaders of the commons at Louth.[105] Subsequently he devised the "articles" setting out the rebel programme, which he drew up so skilfully that his version superseded that of a gentleman, Robert Dighton.[106] Stones showed great energy in forming and mobilizing opinion among the rank and file of the movement. He rode from wapentake to wapentake to ensure that his programme was known and approved by the commons, and subsequently read out his articles for acceptance by the acclamation of the assembled rebel host at its muster near Lincoln.[107] He was then sent up with the articles to London, but was captured *en route* by Richard Cromwell and placed in Suffolk's

[101] See his confession, *L.P.*, xii (1), 380.
[102] *L.P.*, xi, 828 (xii).
[103] *L.P.*, xii (1), 70 (viii), 392, p. 185, xi, 593.
[104] Thomas Stones of Haltham was one of those returned as having made enclosures in the township of Low Toynton by the inquisition of 1517. See Leadam, *Domesday*, i, p. 258.
[105] If he was the "Stones" specified as such by Sir Edward Madison, *L.P.*, xi, 568. He seems to have been mainly active however in the Horncastle region, which was only four or five miles from Haltham.
[106] *L.P.*, xii, 70 (iii) and (iv).
[107] *L.P.*, xi, 828 (v).

custody.[108] Another such policy-drafter was John Porman, also of the Caistor commons, who expounded an early version of the rebel articles to the captured subsidy commissioners;[109] and a third perhaps was Richard Curson of Louth, who wrote the commissioners' letter to the king.[110] Finally there were the men who saw to the financial and provisioning side of the movement, like William King, the bailiff of Louth, who collected money and paid the host during the whole course of the advance on Lincoln.

One characteristic which these men shared, whether they were popular leaders or belonged to the organizing group, is that they were all outside the shire establishment. With the exception of Kyme,[111] none of these names suggest any connection with a county family, and most seem to have come from one or other level of that rural middle class which made up the "yeomanry" and "parish gentry". William Leech and his family are typical of the kind of background. William Leech the elder of Fulletby, whose will dated 1532 has survived,[112] and who was perhaps the uncle of William Leech the rebel leader, owned land of his own as well as occupying a rented tenement; his son Robert, a priest, was rich enough to rent Belchford grange from St Katherine's priory, Lincoln;[113] and William the rebel, only a year before the rebellion, had bought the title to a messuage and eighty acres of land in Withcall.[114] The family still had its roots in the common people, William Leech the elder being content to describe himself as "husbandman" and to marry his daughter to a farm labourer.[115] But a certain rise in the social scale may be suggested by the many clerical connections of the family (Nicholas Leech, parson of Belchford, seems to have been its most

108 *L.P.*, xi, no. 658. With Thomas Stones however he reappears as one of those sworn before the king's commissioners on 19 and 20 October (*ibid.*, 842 (3)).
109 *L.P.*, xi, 853.
110 *L.P.*, xi, 568, 828 (iii). He was one of the "chief captains" at Louth (*ibid.*, 853).
111 Who may have been one of the Kymes of Friskney.
112 *Lincoln Wills*, ed. C. W. Fosıter, iii (Linc. Rec. Soc., xxiv, 1930), p. 208.
113 Public Record Office, Star Chamber 2/29/40. The lease in 1515 was held jointly with John Denys of Belchford, husbandman. The grange comprised 100 acres land, 3 acres meadow, and 20 acres pasture. A rival claim to the lease by one Richard Backworth, supported by Sir Christopher Willoughby, led Leech to cite the latter before Star Chamber.
114 *Ibid.*, 2/13/239. The title had been bought from John Yarburgh, probably cheaply, since it was a doubtful one, and led to a Star Chamber case.
115 *Lincoln Wills*, *loc. cit.*

prominent clerical member[116]); and William Leech the rebel had, it seems, entered the social circle of a great family, the Dymokes of Scrivelsby.[117] Others of the group, however, belonged in a more pronounced kind of way to those upper levels of the yeomanry which already claimed gentility. Thus two popular leaders, George Hudswell and Porman,[118] used the title gentleman, and George Stones together with his relative (perhaps his father) Thomas also had this designation.[119] Perhaps Anthony Curtis, with his Gray's Inn education and kinship to the Askes of Aughton, was most securely one of the gentry, in spite of the fact that he had no more than forty marks a year of land.[120]

But in addition many of these men were characterized by a professional background of a minor administrative and legal kind, implying that if few of them (like Curtis) had attended the Inns of Court, most must at least have been literate. Guy Kyme, for example, was some kind of official (perhaps clerk) of the commission of the peace.[121] William King was a bailiff, as were some of the leaders of the commons.[122] Stones had been "sometime clerk to the king's late attorney", that is to John Roper, a connection which gave him a contact with the More circle.[123] Richard Curson too seems to have been a clerk of some kind, and Anthony Curtis was a

116 Although not given the clerical title "Sir", he is presumably the Nicholas Leech mentioned, with his two brothers the rebel leaders William and Robert, in William Leech the elder's will. The many clerical connections of the family are suggested too by the legacies left to Robert, Nicholas and William Leech by the parson of Fulletby, in his will of 1520: *Lincoln Wills*, ii (Linc. Rec. Soc., x), p. 211. William Leech the elder of Fulletby left a house and intake to his daughter but for four years only. At the end of this term his executors were to dispose of it "for my soule and my frendys soules and all crysten soules", rather generous provision for this purpose. This and the many other religious bequests in Leech's will suggest a preoccupation with traditional forms of piety, as well as with clerical careers, in the family. William Leech the rebel had originally been intended to enter the church, the will of a Belchford neighbour (dated 1531/2) leaving him a bequest to sing a trental for the souls of the testator's father, mother, and friends "yff he be preste" (*Lincoln Wills*, iii, p. 212).

117 *L.P.*, xii, 70 (xiii).

118 *L.P.*, xii (1), 743 (3); xi, 853.

119 *L.P.*, xi, 842 (3).

120 *L.P.*, xi, 1104, 1120; xii (1), p. 185.

121 *L.P.*, xi, 828 (12).

122 *L.P.*, xi, 568. One of the leaders at Horncastle, Andrewson, was a schoolmaster (*ibid.*).

123 *L.P.*, xi, 658.

collector of the subsidy as well as being a lawyer.[124] Such callings underline the fact that these men, in their professional life as in their social background, tended to form a "fringe" group, within hailing distance if yet firmly outside the administrative and judicial, as well as the landed, establishment. At the same time, however, many of them were bold and thrusting, and possessed gifts of leadership as well as organizing powers. Only a year before the rebellion William Leech, in association with Ralph Green, had dared to assert his title to his land in Withcall against the customer of Boston, Robert Pulvertoft, who was supported by a powerful group of gentlemen. As a result both he and Green had been cited before Star Chamber.[125] Anthony Curtis had also appeared in Star Chamber in connection with a dispute over a legacy which had led to violence, and had been involved in much litigation in Chancery.[126] Robert Leech the priest had been involved in a quarrel with Sir Christopher Willoughby which led to a Star Chamber case.[127] These incidents suggest a determined appetite for property and the wealth and status it conferred, together with a willingness to risk litigation,[128] violence and even the hostility of the great families. Robert Carr of Sleaford is a good example of the type.[129] The son of a successful merchant, and connected with the administration of monastic estates, he became a captain of the commons in 1536. A persistent tradition, reported in the seventeenth century, affirmed however he was also one of Lord Hussey's officers.[130] In the outcome he saved

[124] Public Record Office, Star Chamber 2/2/101 (1535), in which Curtis is referred to as "collector appoynted by the commyssioners of the subsidie in the partes of Lyndesey".

[125] *Ibid.*, 2/13/239; *ibid.*, 2/13/237–8. Pulvertoft was supported by Sir Robert Dymoke and Sir Christopher and Sir Thomas Willoughby.

[126] *Ibid.*, 2/2/101; C1/611/23; C1/733/53.

[127] *Ibid.*, 2/29/40.

[128] Litigation, as a means of defending property and prestige, and often involving a judicious combination of violence and resort to law, was of course very much a part of the way of life of the upper gentry; for those outside the landed establishment, however, the ways of the law were liable to be uncertain, expensive, and hazardous, to be trodden only by the bold and determined.

[129] See *Lincolnshire Pedigrees* (Harleian Soc., l–lii, London, 1902–4, and lv, London, 1906), i, p. 228; *The Genealogist*, 1st ser., ed. G. W. Marshall, 7 vols. (London, 1877–83), iii (1879), p. 193.

[130] Recorded in Sir Joseph Williamson's notes on the Lincolnshire gentry, of 1667. He described Robert Carr as "a kind of auditor at the dissolution of the monasteries, and on that fall made advantage; and by consequence most of their [the Carrs'] estates in church land, save part of which he got from Lord Hussey's

his skin and acquired favour by changing sides, for he provided damaging evidence against his late master,[131] and so was discharged on Cromwell's own orders.[132] His role in this respect may well have opened the way to the many purchases of monastic lands he was subsequently able to make,[133] and he was also thought to have profited by Hussey's downfall. The great estate he built up, and his second marriage, to Sir Edward Dymoke's widow, brought his family into the circle of the shire establishment.[134] Such a success story suggests the type of person, dexterous, bold and ambitious, whom rebellion was liable to attract, in spite of its perils. For when dissent came to the surface and "confusion" rules there were opportunities to be seized not normally present in that slow-moving and status-ridden society.

But such men had to be willing to take risks and occupy the exposed positions which were avoided by the leading gentry who had so much more to lose. It is not surprising then that by and large they dispensed with those rituals of capture and forced oath-takings which protected the latter. Moreover it follows from that very exposure that it is among these same men that we find the clearly militant attitudes, and a willingness to wage war on the king, expressed with a frankness which the gentry avoided. Thus Nicholas Melton said that the rebel purpose was to fight the king if he would not grant what they asked.[135] Philip Trotter (William Leech's lieutenant) stated that the purpose was to kill Cromwell and four or five bishops.[136] Guy Kyme told the Beverley insurgents that the army of the Lincolnshire men was eager to go forward, and "able to give battle to any king christened".[137] And it is in these quarters too

estate, to whom he was a kind of servant" (*Herald and Genealogist*, ii (1865), p. 120).

131 *L.P.*, xi, 969.

132 *L.P.*, xii (1), 591.

133 Beginning with the grant of the house and site of Catley priory with three monastic granges and a manor in 1539. See *L.P.*, xiv (2), 780 (38).

134 His plebeian origins were nevertheless remembered, and noted by Leland (*Itinerary*, ed. Lucy Toulmin Smith (London, 1906), i, p. 26): "About a mile from Hayder I saw the ruines of Cateley priory, now longyng to one Car of Sleford, a proper gentleman, whose father was a riche merchaunt of the staple." Carr's father left him lands in Kirkby, Lathorpe, Evedon, and Holdingham, but his first marriage, to a bailiff's daughter, one of the Cawdrons of Heckington, suggests a social position then still on the fringe of the gentry.

135 *L.P.*, xi 828 (i) (1).

136 *L.P.*, xii, 70 (x).

137 *L.P.*, xii (1), p. 185.

that we find the few traces of lay religious fervour that have survived, as well as such gropings as there were towards the idiom of a religious war. Guy Kyme described the supposed growth of the rebel army from a mere six persons in Louth to sixteen thousand in one day, and to twenty thousand in another, as "like to come of the Holy Ghost".[138] And it was Philip Trotter who, having first of all carried a feudal banner, the standard of the Dymoke family, later took home to Horncastle another whose iconography suggests a peasant Catholicism, for on it was painted a horn and a plough, as well as the Five Wounds and a chalice and host.[139] William Leech, recalling the rebellion in a confession made six years after its occurrence, described it as "one general commotion for maintaining Christ's Faith, Holy Church, honor of our native crown, realm, and nobility and commonwealth", giving the religious issue a priority less trenchantly apparent in other rebel programmes.[140] Finally it is among these men that we find a kind of euphoria which contrasts markedly with the doubts and caution of the gentry as they approached the rubicon of rebellion. Thus the yeoman Ralph Green, when the commons of Horncastle wavered and hesitated to "go forward" to the rendezvous at Lincoln, could cry "God's blood sirs, what will ye now do? Shall we go home and keep sheep?"[141] Perhaps such a mood may be connected with the exhilaration generated as the rigid social structure seemed to dissolve, and the landmarks of authority which hedged in the routines of everyday disappeared with the increasing momentum of rebellion. Then for a brief period a field of political activity and opportunities to exercise leadership were opened which were not normally available to those outside the ruling group.[142] But such a frame of mind, not nourished

[138] *Ibid.*

[139] *L.P.*, xi, 828 (i) (2); xii (1), 70 (xiii).

[140] *L.P.*, xviii (1), 26 (6).

[141] *L.P.*, xii, 70 (xii).

[142] Euphoric fantasy associated with a sense of the reversal of established structures of authority seems to have been part of the atmosphere of rebellions. Inevitably this was most pronounced where the stimulus of appropriate mythologies was present (such as may have been provided by the preaching of John Ball in 1381, or by Anabaptism in the Münster disturbances of 1533–5) and where class and social tension was strongly felt. The latter did not have to be present however. In the Pilgrimage of Grace the same atmosphere can be sensed in the herald Thomas Miller's shocked description of Robert Aske lording it over peers and an archbishop in the hall of Pontefract castle, "standing up in the highest place, taking the high estate upon him", and "keeping his port and countenance as though he had been a great prince, with rigour like a tyrant" (Dodds, *The Pilgrimage of Grace*, i, pp. 228–9). Michael Joseph, the blacksmith who led the

by any deeply felt ideology, soon collapsed with the circumstances which had stimulated it. It was Ralph Green who, a few weeks later, sought to save his skin by abjectly denouncing his old associates the Leeches.[143] And William, the sole survivor of the three Leech brothers (who managed for a while to escape the king's vengeance), disappeared into the Edinburgh underworld of spies and assassins, finding an outlet for his personal hatreds and bitter memories in the murder of an English herald.[144] One of the weaknesses of these popular leaders was the lack of a firm "inner direction",[145] so that their sense of purpose tended to collapse once the approval of their followers and betters was withdrawn. To this state of affairs, as will be seen, the dominant ideology of "obedience", which had no place for any sustained protest or initiative from below, made its contribution.

V

But what about the king's suspicions of the gentlemen? Were the subsidy commissioners taken at Caistor the unwilling victims, as they claimed, of the rebellious commons of Louth, and the Dymokes and their associates those of the commons of Horncastle? Certainly the hand of no gentleman can be detected in the initial disturbances, or directly in the payments made to Nicholas Melton and his men at Louth, or to William Leech and his followers at Horncastle. We can only guess from whom Leech got his money, and the source of Melton's was clerical.[146] On the other hand there is the cir-

Cornish revolt of 1497, continued to be sustained, even after his defeat and capture, by an exalted mood, so that he behaved in a way which contemporaries regarded as extraordinary for one of his station. He "held as good countenance and spak as boldly to the people as he had been at his luberte" (*Great Chronicle of London*, ed. A. D. Thomas and I. D. Thornley (London, 1938), p. 277); and while being drawn to Tyburn he boasted that "for this myschevous and facinerous acte, he should have a name perpetual and fame permanent and immortal" (Edward Hall, *The Union of . . . York and Lancaster*, ed. H. Ellis (London, 1809), p. 479). The smith's behaviour suggested to Hall that "as well poore and meane persounes as ye harte of great lords and puissant princes" could be inflamed with "that desire and ambittious cupiditie of vaine glorie and fame" (*ibid.*).

143 *L.P.*, xi, 975.
144 *L.P.*, xviii (1), 26.
145 In the sense of D. Riesman, in *The Lonely Crowd*, 2nd edn (Yale, 1961).
146 See above, p. 198.

cumstance that, at Horncastle, Leech was the intimate of the Dymokes,[147] and that the latter certainly made subventions to the insurgents once the movement got under way.[148] And two important organizers and contact-men, Guy Kyme and Anthony Curtis, who were subsequently executed for the part they had played in the rebellion, must have been well known to the justices and subsidy commissioners taken at Caistor, since Kyme was some kind of official or agent of the commission of the peace, and Curtis had acted as a collector of the subsidy.[149] The monk Morland too was suspiciously intimate with Sir William Skipwith, one of the Louth gentlemen.[150] And he seems to have known Sir Robert Constable, the Yorkshire rebel captain, whose service he entered after the collapse of the Lincolnshire movement.[151] Constable was cousin to Sir Robert Tyrwhitt, one of the captured subsidy commissioners.

But it is the pattern of behaviour of these shire magnates, both when first confronted by the rebel commons, and when in the latter's hands, which raises the most lively suspicions. For we have to account not only for their failure to resist the coercion to which they were apparently subjected, but also their subsequent silence and passivity. The king could rightly expect these great men who had been entrusted with the commission of the peace and one of whom was a sheriff, to react strongly when confronted with lawlessness, even at risk to themselves. Thus it is not surprising that Henry should "marvel" at the conduct of his subsidy commissioners at Caistor, who either evaded the issue by flight, or else tamely submitted to "villains and labourers" without resistance, none being "sore stricken".[152] No doubt there were mitigating circumstances, if we are to credit the testimony of William Morland. The latter said that the gentlemen's retinue was small,[153] and that the commons so maltreated a servant of Lord Burgh's that he subsequently died, so

147 See above, p. 212.
148 *L.P.*, xii (1), 70 (vii) and (ix).
149 Above, pp. 212–13.
150 Skipworth provided Morland with horse and armour, and seems to have used him as a contact-man, sending him to discover Lord Burgh's intentions, and with the party sent to bring in Lord Hussey (*L.P.*, xii (1), pp. 176–7).
151 *Ibid.*, p. 178.
152 Above, pp. 195–6.
153 *L.P.*, xii (1), p. 176. Morland says the commissioners' retinue was less than twenty strong. On the other hand the mounted band, led by Morland, which pursued and captured them, consisted of no more than eighteen or twenty men (*ibid.*, p. 175). The odds were not weighted against the commissioners.

showing their dangerous mood.[154] Whether they would have dared to treat J.P.s and shire magnates in this fashion is, however, another matter. For it is significant that not even that other group of commissioners whom the Louth insurgents captured, those engaged on the dissolution of Legbourne nunnery, found their lives put in question, although they were the direct agents of the hated Cromwell. In spite of the story which circulated that one of them had been blinded, wrapped in a raw cowhide and baited to death by dogs, they suffered no more than threats and a fortnight's imprisonment at Louth, two of them being clapped in the stocks for a while.[155] Nothing approaching even this degree of maltreatment was offered the Caistor gentlemen, who nevertheless submitted "for fear of their lives",[156] and then tamely accompanied their captors to Louth, there to sign the first rebel manifesto in the form of a letter to the king.

The accounts of the capture of the gentlemen at Horncastle vary in tone and emphasis, but that which was given official credence ascribed to them the same stance as that of the commissioners at Caistor, and for the same reasons. When on Thursday 3 October William Leech and his men marched on Scrivelsby, seat of the Dymoke family, several of the great men of the shire were assembled there. These included Sir Robert Dymoke, the head of the family, his heir Edward, who was sheriff, a younger son Arthur, and Thomas Dymoke of Carlton, a distant relative. Also at Scrivelsby were Robert Dighton of Great Sturton, Nicholas Saunderson of Reasby, and the latter's father-in-law Sir William Sandon. With the exception of the latter, all submitted and took the rebel oath tendered them by Leech, "on pain of death". Sandon, however, is unique in that he put up a show of resistance, telling the commons "they would be hanged for their pains". The degree of maltreatment to which he was consequently subjected, however, was not such as to confirm the view that the other gentlemen failed to follow his example because their lives were in danger. For Sandon was merely "haryed forth by the arms to Horncastle, till he was for heat and weariness almost overcome" and there put in the courthouse.[157] But he soon emerged (perhaps satisfied that he had put up enough of a show of resistance) to join the band of commons

[154] *Ibid.*, p. 176.
[155] *L.P.*, xi, 854.
[156] *L.P.*, xii (1), p. 177.
[157] *L.P.*, xi, 967.

which went to bring in John Copledike of Harrington and Thomas Littlebury of Stainsby.[158] Subsequently he accompanied the rebel host to Lincoln with the other gentlemen.

By comparison with this scene of forced acquiescence and the maltreatment of Sandon, we may contrast another picture of the behaviour of the Horncastle gentlemen which emerges from some of the depositions of the popular leaders. These may have been actuated by ill-will, since the latter may have thought themselves abandoned to the king's vengeance by their betters, or they may have hoped to save their necks by implicating the gentlemen. Nevertheless much of this testimony is difficult to dismiss. For example, while the gentlemen may have been defenceless at Scrivelsby on Tuesday, and so easily coerced, it is difficult to believe that this was still the case on Wednesday when they appeared at the rebel rally at Horncastle "being well harnessed with their tenants".[159] Thus armed and supported by their retinues they were well placed to restore order. Yet, so far from attempting to do so, by their acquiescence and presence they condoned some of the most repellent acts of violence which marked the whole course of the rebellion, which took place at this gathering. First of all there was the hanging of a certain Thomas (or George) Wolsey, thought to be a government spy, who was handed over by the gentlemen to his executioners.[160] Then there was the murder of Cromwell's commissary, Dr Raynes, captured at Bolingbroke the previous day. He was beaten to death while Edward Dymoke and John Copledike stood by, the sheriff actually distributing the dead man's clothes and money among his murderers.[161] The incident, related by one of the latter, has an air of verisimilitude, for the further development of the movement depended on some public demonstration on the part of the gentlemen of their willingness to commit themselves to the course which the commons had initiated. The sheriff's action served this purpose, since it showed that he was prepared to tolerate popular lawlessness to the point of bloodshed. As a result, "After this every parson in the field counselled their parishioners to proceed on this journey . . . ", and there was also the eager anticipation that now "they should lack neither gold nor silver", which presumably the gentlemen could be relied on to provide. Such expectations were

[158] *L.P.*, xi, 828 (i) (2).

[159] *L.P.*, xii (1), 70 (vii).

[160] *L.P.*, xii (1), p. 176.

[161] *L.P.*, xii (1), 70 (ix).

not disappointed, for the Dymokes, in particular, sent provisions and money "for the poor men in the field".[162]

These events make it harder to dismiss an alternative account of the happenings at Scrivelsby (given by Philip Trotter),[163] which depicts an open collusion between the gentlemen and commons very different from the accepted official version of what occurred. According to Trotter, the gentlemen, led by the sheriff, came to meet Leech and his band a quarter of a mile from the house. The sheriff greeted them with the words "Masters ye be welcome", and when he was told that he and his companions must be sworn, replied "With a good will". Dymoke (as sheriff) then authorized the ringing of the bells of the churches, to raise the country.[164] Whether or not all the details of this narrative actually happened, Trotter's account underlines what was to dominate the course of the rebellion from this moment: the confident assumption of leadership by the gentlemen. As a result the movement ceased to have the character of a plebeian riot, and acquired an air of legitimacy, so that most of those participating were convinced, when they mustered and marched on Lincoln, that this was in the king's service.[165] Dymoke's role as sheriff was particularly important from this point of view. Thus he was obeyed without demur at Boston when he summoned the town to rise, warning them to be ready "to serve the king".[166]

At Louth the captured subsidy commissioners played the same role. On Tuesday they were prisoners, although by the evening we find them at Guy Kyme's house, where they drew up their letter to the king informing him of the commons' grievances and asking for a general pardon.[167] It was on Wednesday, however, that the Caistor gentlemen (now reinforced by the return of Thomas Moigne and by the arrival of Sir Andrew Bilsby and Edward Forsett with the men of Alford)[168] definitely took the leadership of the commons. They sent for their armour, and each assumed the captaincy of the wapentake in which he resided.[169] At the same time the machinery of the musters was activated to mobilize the countryside. Petty captains were appointed for the townships, and these received instructions from the head constable of the hundred where and

162 *Ibid.*
163 *L.P.*, xii (1), 70 (x).
164 *Ibid.*, and (xii).
165 *Ibid.*, xi.
166 *L.P.*, xi, 973.
167 *L.P.*, xi, 568; Dodds, *The Pilgrimage of Grace*, i, pp. 98–9.
168 *L.P.*, xi, p. 395.
169 *Ibid.*, and *L.P.*, xi, 854.

when they were to rendezvous with their men.[170] Once again, for most of those involved there was no question of rebellion, but rather of obeying the commands of men who were justices and the king's representatives.[171] Thus at Louth, as at Horncastle, not one of the gentlemen "persuaded the people to desist, or showed them it was high treason". Otherwise, this deponent thought, "they would not have gone forward, for all the people . . . thought they had not offended the king, as the gentlemen caused proclamations to be made in his name".[172] By their silence and acquiescence therefore, and by their actions, the gentlemen advanced the rebellion.[173] And some of those involved were emphatic that they did not do so passively and under constraint. George Hudswell asserted that the gentlemen furthered the insurrection "to the utmost of their power";[174] Roger New thought they were among the rebels willingly; Brian Stones that "the poor men were content to be ordered by the gentlemen"; Philip Trotter that they were "the chief setters forward of the commons, who were obedient to them in all their proceedings".[175]

In the exercise of their leadership, however, a distinction emerges between those gentlemen who, like the sheriff and the subsidy commissioners, occupied positions which fell to them because of their prestige and the offices they held, and those who were subsequently identified as active "stirrers" of the people and "promoters" of the insurrection: in fact organizers, like those already encountered in the ranks of the commons. Foremost among these was Thomas Moigne, whose meeting with Robert Aske (soon to be grand cap-

[170] The Wapentake of Yarborough, for example, mustered on the orders of its head constable at Yarborough hill, with Philip Tyrwhitt as captain, and John Rud, Robert Hopkinson, and probably George Hudswell as petty captains (*L.P.*, xi, 853). At a further muster of Hambleton Hill, Sir Robert Tyrwhitt took command and chose captains.

[171] George Hudswell (*ibid.*) emphasized that Sir Robert Tyrwhitt was "chief ruler of the hundred of Yarborough", i.e. the local justice and representative of authority, whom it would be difficult for simple people to see as a rebel.

[172] *L.P.*, xii (1), 70 (xi).

[173] In the only deposition made by any of the Louth gentlemen Thomas Moigne (*L.P.*, xi, 971) denied this, claiming that gentlemen, having armed themselves and assumed the captaincies of the wapentakes, nevertheless then tried to dissuade the mustered commons from going forward to Lincoln. It was Moigne himself however who was identified by George Hudswell as in face a "great promoter" of the insurrection (*L.P.*, xi, 853).

[174] *Ibid.*

[175] *L.P.*, xii, 70 (vii), (ix), and (x).

tain of the Pilgrimage of Grace) seems to be the first identifiable contact between the Lincolnshire leaders and those in Yorkshire.[176] Later it was on Moigne's advice that, at Lincoln, the gentlemen decided on a policy of submission to the king.[177] But there were also Robert Dighton, author of one of the rebel programmes, Nicholas Saunderson, who provided the host with a banner in the form of a picture of the Trinity, so identifying the movement with the cause of religion; Vincent Grantham, and Thomas Dymoke of Carlton.[178] With the exception of Saunderson, those men belonged to a group of families associated with the city of Lincoln, whose background will be considered below.[179]

Here, however, it will be useful to note the characteristics which such "promoters" shared with the plebeian élite of leaders and organizers to which attention was drawn above. Like the latter they were something of a fringe group, for although gentlemen they were outside the circle of great families, and with the exception of Moigne their gentility was recent, most of them being of mercantile background. Again one notices the same thrusting and aggressive quality, combined with those acquisitive and litigious propensities (the latter shared too with the great families) also characteristic of the plebeian élite. Moigne, for example, was heir male of an ancient family who had been disinherited by the passage of the family estates to heirs general. But he had been able to gain possession of at least part of them, including the family seat at North Willingham, by a skilful combination of force and litigation which had involved an appearance in Star Chamber.[180] Dighton and Grantham had also appeared before this court.[181] The former, already a lessee of monastic properties, would soon emerge as a notable speculator in monastic lands;[182] and Grantham was a notorious encloser and the founder of a family of prosperous gentlemen farmers, also on

[176] *L.P.*, xi, 853 (ii); xii (1), p. 3.
[177] See below, pp. 257–9.
[178] *L.P.*, xii, 70 (ii) and (xii); xi, 853 (ii).
[179] See pp. 236 ff.
[180] Public Record Office, Star Chamber 2/20/297.
[181] *Ibid.*, 2/10/127; 2/3/41.
[182] He had leased the manor of Barlings from Mackerell's predecessor as abbot: Public Record Office C1/384/27. For his post-dissolution dealings in monastic lands, see G. A. J. Hodgett, "The Dissolution of the Religious Houses in Lincolnshire and the Changing Structure of Society", *Lincolnshire Architectural and Archaeological Soc.: Reports and Papers*, iv (1) (1948–51), p. 92.

monastic lands.[183] Saunderson, a newcomer to the shire and feodary of the Lincolnshire duchy of Lancaster lands, established a landed family on the grange at Reasby he had leased from the abbot of Barlings.[184] Such men, again like their plebeian counterparts, were willing to take risks. All subsequently pleaded coercion, but Grantham, Thomas Dymoke, Dighton and Moigne were identified in one deposition as having joined the rebellion freely and without compulsion.[185] In these quarters, however, there was none of the extremism and euphoria characteristic of the commons' leaders. Men like Moigne, who was recorder of Lincoln, and Grantham, an M.P., had at least some acquaintance with the political world and the court, and knew the limits of what a dissident movement could achieve. When those limits had been reached, as will be seen, they hastened to submit. Unlike so many of the leaders of the commons, too, most of these men survived the rebellion and prospered after it. Only Thomas Moigne was sacrificed to the king's vengeance and suffered the penalties of treason.

Inevitably the gentlemen, once they had assumed the leadership, played a decisive role in forming the character of the movement's political programme which under their influence gradually assumed a more sophisticated form. The crudest platform of rebel policy is probably that contained in the commissioners' letter[186] to the king from Louth, which merely reports the fears of the commons that "all the Jewells and goods of the churches would be taken from them", and that the people "shulde be put to enhaunsements and importunate charges, which they were not able to bear, by reason of extreme poverty". A general pardon was the sole request made. The earliest list of coherent demands, however, had been that put to the commissioners by Porman the day before, at the time of their capture at Caistor.[187] These raised no objection to the Supreme Headship (to have attacked this would have exposed Porman to the penalties of treason)[188] or to the levying of tenths and first-fruits on the clergy. But no more abbeys were to be suppressed, Cromwell

[183] See above, note 43, this chapter, and Thirsk, *English Peasant Farming*, p. 90.
[184] *L.P.*, xii, 70 (ii). R. Somerville, *History of the Duchy of Lancaster, i, 1265–1603* (London, 1953), p. 582.
[185] *L.P.*, xi, 853 (ii).
[186] Printed in Dodds, *The Pilgrimage of Grace*, pp. 98–9.
[187] *L.P.*, xi, 853 (i).
[188] Under 26 Henry VIII, c. 13.

and "the heretic bishops" were to be surrendered to the commons, and the king was to levy no more taxes during his lifetime. Out of such relatively crude material the leadership sought to shape terms which would give the impression of moderation, which had something to offer gentlemen, clergy and commons and so hold the front of all three together, but which may also have been visualized as a parliamentary programme and therefore needed to embody an appeal to a wider audience. In order to do this the gentlemen deliberated some distance away from the main body of the commons, in association with organizers like George Stones, and one or two popular leaders like William Leech.[189] The articles they drew up were then presented to the commons, and assented to by acclamation.[190]

One demand common to all the rebel programmes was that no more abbeys should be suppressed. On this point it seems that the monastic clergy, the lessees of monastic land, and those concerned with the religious issue, were all agreed. All the programmes were at one too in making no criticism of the Supreme Headship, since this would have been treason. But both the articles of the commons of Boston,[191] and also it seems those submitted to the muster of the rebel host at Lincoln,[192] demanded the restoration of the liberties and privileges of the church, and that the clergy should be spared first-fruits and tenths. There was agreement too from first to last that Cromwell and "the heretic bishops" must be delivered up to the vengeance of the commons.[193] But both the Boston and the Lincoln articles sound a note of greater political reality by the proviso that they could otherwise be banished or merely removed. And the Lincoln programme took another step in the same direction by the positive demand that the king should not merely proscribe the hated ministers, but also take noblemen for councillors.[194] Here plainly the need had been seen for something to appeal to the dissident great lords of the north, as well as to court peers like Norfolk, Shrewsbury and even Suffolk, who hated Cromwell. In this matter

189 *L.P.*, xi, p. 342; xii, 70 (xi).
190 *L.P.*, xii, 70 (iii) and (xi); xi, 828 (v).
191 *L.P.*, xi, 585.
192 Dodds, *op. cit.*, p. 114.
193 This demand was raised by Porman at Caistor, and by the sheriff, gentlemen, and William Leech at Horncastle: *L.P.*, xii, 70 (x).
194 *L.P.*, xi, 828 (v).

of the proscription of political and religious opponents, however, the behaviour of the Horncastle commons suggests how completely dependent the commons were on the gentlemen to identify the enemy. For when George Stones and William Leech submitted the Horncastle articles to the people they asked them "whether they would have the Lord Cromwell and others before named, saying to them the Lord Cromwell was a false traitor, and that he and the same bishops . . . were the devisers of all the false laws". Whereupon the commons asked the gentlemen "Masters, if he had them, would that mend the matter? And the gentlemen said, Yea, for these be the doers of all mischief."[195]

Similarly it was the initiative of the gentlemen which raised the issue of the repeal of the Statute of Uses, a demand which must have been remote from most yeomen and tenants. In fact at Horncastle the sheriff had to explain to the commons what the Act meant, for before they had never heard of it.[196] But they agreed to its repeal, and this point subsequently appeared both in the Boston and Lincoln articles. The latter also showed greater sophistication in their approach to the problem of taxation. Earlier demands had simply emphasized the poverty of the commons, or had insisted that the king should levy no more taxes during his lifetime, or that the subsidy be remitted. The Lincoln and Boston programmes went beyond this in their article that the king should levy no taxes except in time of war, so raising the constitutional notion that the king ought to live of his own except when (as Fortescue had put it) "a case exorbitant" arose for the defence of the realm or the suppression of rebellion.[197] In these matters the impression again emerges that such political initiative as the commons could muster was limited and feeble, and soon died away into a dependence on the leadership of their betters in a way that gives verisimilitude to the testimony already quoted that the gentlemen "were the chief setters forward" of the commons, who "were obedient to them in all their doings".[198]

195 *L.P.*, xii, 70 (x).
196 *L.P.*, 70 (xi). See also below, pp. 238–9.
197 Sir John Fortescue, *Works* (London, 1869), i, p. 457.
198 *L.P.*, xii, 70 (x).

VI

But, although rebellion offered tempting opportunities for ambitious plebeians and "fringe" gentry eager to rise in the world, the problem still remains of what could have induced gentlemen of the status of, for example, Edward Dymoke, Sir Robert Tyrwhitt, Sir William Ayscough or Sir William Skipwith to take the plunge into collusion with popular insurrection. For these represented the shire establishment of ancient landed families. Yet they were deeply involved in the movement, which gathered momentum around their leadership. The rule of such men was uncontested, and exercised through the commissions, above all of the peace, on which they all sat, whose sessions made them aware of each other as members of a distinctive political society, with its specific needs, resentments and grievances. Here a solidarity which could be compactly resistant to pressure from without was built up, as well as a sense of what was appropriate in the affairs of the shire; and a prickly dislike of the meddling of outsiders. At a deeper level such political and social ties were reinforced by the bonds of marriage and kin[199] which gave the community its nervous system through which private grievances ran, just as at the justices' sessions political rumour and news circulated. And here the many family ties with Yorkshire houses subsequently involved in the Pilgrimage of Grace are significant.[200] The rebellion in fact expressed the alienation of a whole gentry community (including even families of peerage status like the Husseys, Tailboys and Willoughbies) from the court. How had this come about?

Regional grievances played their part, and may first be considered. These arose largely out of a factor more the result of chance and accident than political intention. This was the decline of the families of baronial rank which had traditionally provided the gentry with their leadership, whose households had dispensed fees, offices and hospitality, and which had been a channel of communication with the court. The death of the last Viscount Beaumont in 1507 without heirs meant the end of the family which had ruled from

[199] These may be abundantly traced in the four volumes of *Lincolnshire Pedigrees* (Harleian Soc., li–liii, London, 1902–4, and lv, London, 1906).

[200] Particularly the alliances of the Husseys and Tyrwhitts with the Constables of Flamborough, the Tailboys with the Gascoignes of Gawthorpe, and the Portingtons with the Askes. See *Lincolnshire Pedigrees*, under these families.

Folkingham castle, and brought the great Bardolf–Beaumont inheritance into the hands of the crown.[201] A few years previously the last Viscount Welles had died without heirs male, and other extensive properties had consequently escheated to the king.[202] A generation before the line of the Cromwells had failed, and the great castle at Tattershall was unoccupied, with the lands annexed to the earldom of Richmond.[203] Then there was the single political casualty amongst these great houses, the de la Poles, who had fallen with the attainder of the earl of Lincoln in the reign of Henry VII.[204] Of the surviving or newly created baronial houses, the resources of Lord Burgh of Gainsborough were small, and the family influence had been weakened by the lunacy of the second lord.[205] Lunacy, as will be seen below, had also weakened and divided the Tailboys family, lords of Kyme, and lords marcher of Redesdale on the Scottish border.[206] And with the death of the tenth Lord Willoughby in 1526, the direct male line of this family had ended in an heiress.[207] Of the two new Lincolnshire peers created by Henry VIII, Lord Hussey (made a baron in 1529)[208] enjoyed immense prestige as a court magnate, but his resources were not large enough to dominate the local scene, where his influence was contested by the Willoughbies;[209] and Gilbert Tailboys, also raised to the peerage in 1529 as Lord Tailboys, died a year later.[210]

One result of the extinction of great families, and the lapse of great inheritances to the crown was that a mass of lands and offices came into the latter's disposal. Who was to benefit? The question stimulated ambitions and generated tensions. Another consequence however was the emergence of a gentry polity in which no single house could claim unquestioned deference. Lincolnshire was

[201] See *Complete Peerage*, ii, p. 62.
[202] *Ibid.*, xii (2), p. 448. [203] *Ibid.*, iii, pp. 551–4.
[204] *Ibid.*, vii, pp. 688–90.
[205] *Ibid.*, ii, pp. 422–4. The main weight of the Burgh estates were in Northumberland, where the family held the barony of Mitford.
[206] *Ibid.*, vii, pp. 358–63, and xii (1) (London, 1953), p. 602.
[207] *Ibid.*, xii (2), pp. 670–3.
[208] *Ibid.*, vii, p. 15.
[209] As emerges, e.g. in a Star Chamber case, in which in his answer to the bill of complaint Sir Christopher Willoughby asserted: "The said bill . . . is false untrewe and fayned agaynst hym by the procurement and abettyng of Syr John Hussey . . . of his malyce propensyd toward the sd Syr Chrystopher to thintent to put hym to sclaundre before the Kinges grace . . . like as he hath divers tymes done heretofore . . . " (Public Record Office, Star Chamber 2/29/40).
[210] *Complete Peerage*, xii (1), p. 602.

not one of those regions where a great family dominated the scene, like the Percies in Northumberland or the Cliffords in Westmorland. And, although the Willoughbies, in the person of Sir Christopher Willoughby the tenth lord's brother (and till 1519 his heir apparent), seem to have had the predominant place, this rested less on a great household and following of client gentry than on the deference he commanded as a justice, and the regard in which he was held by his fellow J.P.s.[211] Moreover, as the great inheritances lapsed into the hands of the crown, it was the gentry community and its leaders from the lesser baronial houses which benefited. The stewardships of the Beaumont lands were conferred on the Willoughbies and Husseys.[212] Gilbert Tailboys became bailiff of the Cromwell lands, and occupied Tattershall castle.[213] Dymokes, Tyrwhitts and Thimblebies were entrenched in the administration of the Duchy lands of the honour of Bolingbroke.[214] The same families dominated the commission of lunacy appointed to administer the Tailboys estates.[215] And the intermarriage of leading gentry houses with dwindling stocks like the Willoughbies and Tailboys opened prospects of a share of these inheritances if the male line were to fail.[216]

From the point of view of the crown, however, it is likely that this situation was not wholly satisfactory. For, although the Tudors have been credited with a predilection for the gentry rather than aristocratic "over-mighty subjects", in practice their rule tended to favour the dominance of regional societies by magnates whose influence rested on a local territorial basis, and who were entrusted with the

[211] Robert Leech, the petitioner in the Star Chamber case cited at n. 209 above, prayed for letters of Privy Seal against Willoughby on the grounds that Willoughby "bears such rule in the countrie, for he is one of your justices of the peace, and divers other of the justices of the peace ther of his assuryance and do his commandment". Although the ninth Lord Willoughby inherited a great estate of more than baronial extent in Lincolnshire, Suffolk, and elsewhere, his style of life seems to have been closer to that of the upper gentry than to that of the great lords, his principal house at Grimesthorpe being "no great place afore the building of the second court" (by the duke of Suffolk), although it was built of stone, "and the gate house was fair and strong" (Leland, *Itinerary*, i, p. 23).

[212] *L.P.*, i, 158 (14) and (17); *Complete Peerage*, xii (2), p. 670.

[213] *L.P.*, iv, 1298, 1533.

[214] See the list of officers in Somerville, *History of the Duchy of Lancaster*, pp. 575 ff.

[215] *L.P.*, ii, 2979.

[216] Willoughbies, Tailboys, Tyrwhitts, and Dymokes were much intermarried.

royal lieutenancy.[217] Always, however, with the proviso that these were well regarded by the court, a condition which Lord Hussey, for example, found it increasingly difficult to meet once the divorce crisis and religious changes got under way, as will be seen.[218] And as the 1520s proceeded indications multiplied that there were great men in the king's immediate circle who could descry new lands to conquer in Lincolnshire, who were eager to occupy the place vacated by the great families, and who could hope for the support of the crown to advance their ambitions. The first on the scene was Charles Brandon duke of Suffolk, Henry VIII's boon companion and brother-in-law.[219] As early as 1513, at the time of his creation as duke, he had been endowed with the de la Pole inheritance, part of which was in Lincolnshire.[220] The first real sign, however, of an active interest in the affairs of the shire came in 1525, when Suffolk secured the title of earl of Lincoln for his heir.[221] He may already at this time have had in mind the possibility of endowing his line with the Willoughby inheritance, which on the death of the ninth lord Willoughby (which took place a year later) would fall to an heiress. The Willoughby estates were large.[222] There were thirty manors in Lincolnshire, and another score in Norfolk and Suffolk. If the earl of Lincoln were to marry the heiress, these lands, added to the existing Brandon properties,[223] would go a long way towards giving the family a clear preponderance in the shire. But whether this development would be welcomed by the Lincolnshire landed establishment was another matter.

In fact profound resentments were to be roused by the duke's ambitions, and by the problem of the disposal of the Willoughby inheritance. For on the death of the last Lord Willoughby of the male line in 1526, the rival claims of heir male and heir general to the estates led to bitter quarrels within the family, which, like other

217 See Gladys Scott Thompson, *Lords Lieutenant in the Sixteenth Century* (London, 1923).
218 Below, pp. 241 ff.
219 See *Dict. Nat. Biog.*
220 *Complete Peerage*, xii (1), p. 455, n. 1; *L.P.*, ii (1), 94.
221 *Complete Peerage*, xii (1), pp. 460–1.
222 See the list of the Willoughby manors in Collins's *Peerage*, ed. S. E. Brydges (London, 1812), vi, p. 616.
223 The main weight of the de la Pole properties had been in East Anglia and the midlands. Those in Lincolnshire included the lordships of Harpswell and Beyborough. See *Complete Peerage*, xii (1), p. 441, n. 1.

such feuds in the previous century,[224] eventually threatened the peace of the shire. Lord Willoughby's first marriage, to Lord Hussey's sister, had been childless, and as a result the heir male, his brother Sir Christopher Willoughby, for many years occupied a special place in the succession, for on him depended the continuance of the family line. But there was little love lost between the two brothers, and each seems to have been willing to cheat the other for land or money. The main settlement of the family estates concluded between them had been made in 1512,[225] at the time of Sir Christopher's marriage to Elizabeth Tailboys, and of Lord Willoughby's departure on Dorset's expedition to Guyenne. In return for the payment of 1,000 marks by the bride's father, Sir George Tailboys, Lord Willoughby made over lands of 300 marks value in Lincolnshire to Sir Christopher and his wife and their heirs; lands in Suffolk of the same value were also made over, and if Lord Willoughby were to die without issue he was to will the barony of Eresby and its members in Lincolnshire, worth 400 marks a year, to his brother. Under these arrangements Sir Christopher Willoughby acquired prospects of succeeding to about half of the family estates.

But Lord Willoughby, having pocketed the 1,000 marks (possibly used to finance his "voyage into Spayne"), seems subsequently to have obstructed the making of the conveyances which would have assured his brother's title, perhaps because of the latter's sharp practice in securing lands in Suffolk intended for Lord Willoughby during his lifetime.[226] Certainly too the ninth lord's exotic second marriage in 1516 to a shrewd and determined Castilian noblewoman, Lady Maria Salinas, maid of honour to Queen Catherine, and with a keen eye for property, led to further bad blood between the two. For Lord Willoughby at the time of his marriage received £800 from the queen in return for the settlement of a jointure on Lady Maria which included many of the manors already covenanted to Sir Christopher;[227] the latter had to be content with a doubtful entail of the Suffolk lands, which were to go to himself and his heirs only if there were no heirs male of Lord Willoughby's marriage, and

[224] See K. B. McFarlane, "The Wars of the Roses", *Pro. British Academy*, 1 (1964), p. 105.
[225] Linc. Rec. Off., Ancaster MS. 5/B/4d.
[226] *Ibid.*, 5/B/1c.
[227] *Ibid.*, 5/B/1q.

presumably also after the expiry of Lady Maria's interest.[228] Finally the whole tangle of claims and counter-claims was further complicated and resentments embittered by the birth of a daughter, Catherine Willoughby, to Lady Maria in 1519.[229] In his will Lord Willoughby left all his properties to the heiress, reserving only his wife's interest, and passing over his brother's claims.[230]

The latter then would have to be fought in the courts. But resort to the law also involved a judicious use of force to establish positions to defend. In Lincolnshire Sir Christopher Willoughby with a band of armed servants occupied the Eresby lands soon after his brother's death. In the manor-house he seized the family muniments, said to be prejudicial to the claims of Catherine Willoughby, and there he prepared to keep household.[231] Apart from the muniments, he may have been particularly concerned to establish his rights to lands from which his brother's baronial title derived, for he may have hoped to succeed to this himself. Inevitably Lady Maria retaliated in kind, occupying the family house at Parham in Suffolk, and carrying away goods which Sir Christopher said had been bequeathed him by his brother.[232] Suits were set on foot in Chancery, and complaints and counter-complaints entered in Star Chamber.[233] Probably, if the ordinary course of law had been followed, Willoughly would have had a strong case in equity, whatever the defects in his titles. But he lacked the powerful friends Lady Maria could command at court. Sir Christopher was not likely to prevail against the duke of Suffolk.

For it was the duke who, on 12 February 1529, had been granted the wardship of Catherine Willoughby,[234] his intention being to marry her to the earl of Lincoln. But the latter had died at the beginning of 1534, so that Suffolk had had to step into the breach himself, and in the previous September the Willoughby heiress had become his wife.[235] The duke must have hoped (since Lincoln had been his

228 *Ibid.*, 5/B/1j. The entail was doubtful because it was made after Lord Willoughby's covenant with the queen for the assurance of these manors to Lady Maria, and after they had been recovered to the latter's use. So at any rate Lady Maria claimed.
229 *Complete Peerage*, xii (2), p. 673.
230 Linc. Rec. Off., Anc. MS., 5/B/10.
231 *L.P.*, iv, 3997, 4184.
232 *Ibid.*, 3474.
233 Public Record Office, Star Chamber 2/17/399; 2/21/30; 2/19/241; C1/689/32; C1/691/26; C1/665/40.
234 *L.P.*, iv, 5336 (12).
235 *L.P.*, vi, 1069.

only child) that the match would ensure the continuance of his line, as well as establish its territorial predominance in Lincolnshire. The first objective was achieved by the birth of two sons of the marriage.[236] But the second required the defeat of Sir Christopher Willoughby. Not only was Suffolk reluctant to part with the lands which Willoughby claimed, but his own standing as a magnate in Suffolk, as well as in Lincolnshire, required that he should not be successfully confronted in these counties by a man whose status was modest in comparison with his own. And so the duke had recourse to the king's mediation and an Act of Parliament.[237] The Act, of February 1536, ejected Willoughby from two manors in which his title had been established by Chancery decree of 1531,[238] but confirmed his right to eight others in satisfaction for his 300 marks rent, provided he abandoned all further claim to any lands in the shire.[239] His title to any of the Willoughby estates in Suffolk and Norfolk, on the other hand, was completely ignored, not even the manors of Parham and Bradfield in Suffolk, and Roughton in Norfolk, in whose possession he had also been confirmed by Chancery decree,[240] being mentioned.

Whatever the rights and wrongs of the settlement, in the view of the Willoughby male line it was unjust, because Suffolk and his wife, in the interests of their family, had been able to by-pass the processes of law by resorting to political pressures exercised through Parliament. Of Suffolk's determination to establish the Brandons in Lincolnshire there can certainly be no doubt. For a second Act of Parliament, of February 1536, also made over to the duke the Percy lands in the shire, lately alienated by the earl of Northumberland to the king, the latter receiving in exchange Suffolk's lands in Oxfordshire and Berkshire.[241] Later too, after the rebellion, large acqui-

236 *Complete Peerage*, xii (1), p. 461.

237 27 Henry VIII, c. 40 (*Statutes of the Realm*, iii, p. 596).

238 Public Record Office SP 1/68/68–9. The two manors were Fulstow Beck and Fulstow Arseck.

239 The eight manors were Orby, Burgh, Somercotes, Hogsthorpe, Belchford, Ingoldmells, Fulletby and Cockrington. Under the Act, Willoughby abandoned his claims in Lincolnshire to Willoughby, Eresby, Spilsby, Upper and Lower Toynton, Steeping, and Pinchbeck.

240 Linc. Rec. Off., Anc. MS., 5/B/1d(i). Under the settlement of 1512 Willoughby had claims in Norfolk and Suffolk to Parham, Bradfield, Roughton, Ufford, Wicks Ufford, Orford, Combes, Edgefield, and Bawdsey.

241 27 Henry VIII, c. 38 (*Statutes of the Realm*, iii, p. 591).

sitions of monastic properties further extended the Brandon estates.[242] How seriously Suffolk took his role as a Lincolnshire magnate is suggested by his building operations at Grimesthorpe, which aimed at converting the modest Willoughby manor-house into an early example of the Tudor-style courtier great house.[243] Subsequently however, in 1537, he acquired Tattershall castle as the principal family seat.[244] Here he would be able to "keep household" in his "country", an indispensable condition for the maintenance of a great regional connection. Only the death of the duke's two sons in the sweating sickness of 1552 in fact prevented the permanent establishment of the Brandons as the leading great family in Lincolnshire.[245]

But there was little satisfaction in the shire at this intrusion of an alien court dynasty, for the substantial squires had ruled the roost for a generation and had lost the habit of deference to great lords. Among the upper gentry too there would have been sympathy for the misfortunes of Sir Christopher Willoughby, whose "assurance and commandment" was sought by so many of his fellow justices of the peace. This showed itself for example in the rough treatment John Copledike received at the Quarter Sessions at Caistor in September 1529, which was probably connected with the latter's role as Suffolk's agent, keeping the duke informed of Willoughby's doings.[246] The bad blood roused by the quarrel with the Brandons had not died down by the autumn of 1536, in spite of the royal mediation, and in April Willoughby and the duke were still squabbling in the king's presence.[247] Thus it is not surprising that the Willoughbies should have played a prominent part in the rebellion when it got under way. This went beyond the unrest which inevitably manifested itself amongst the tenantry of the Willoughby estates, which significantly included Belchford and Fulletby, home of the Leeches. For it is one "Mr Willoughby" who is named in the abbot of Barlings's confession as "grand captain of the whole host of

242 Hodgett, *op. cit.*, pp. 86, 96.
243 H. A.Tipping, *English Homes* (London, 1928), iv (2), p. 307.
244 *L.P.*, xii (1), 1103 (5).
245 *Complete Peerage*, xii (2), p. 461.
246 See Copledike's letter to Suffolk of 28 Feb. 1528, wrongly calendared under 1534 in *L.P.*, vii, 233; also *L.P.*, iv, 3997, and Public Record Office, Star Chamber, 2/2/279.
247 *L.P.*, x, 635.

Lincolnshire", and his christian name, William, given in another confession, establishes his identity as Sir Christopher Willoughby's eldest son,[248] a rebel who in a characteristically paradoxical kind of way would subsequently become the first Lord Willoughby of Parham and a devoted servant of Queen Elizabeth. Thus from one point of view the rebellion was an extension of the quarrel of the Willoughbies and their friends with the intrusive Brandons. And the role of regional magnate to which Suffolk aspired in Lincolnshire required similarly that it should be he who must assert himself to restore order. So it was the duke who, appointed the king's lieutenant, had to play the leading part in the repression of the Lincolnshire movement.

The theme of the intrusion of the alien and predatory courtier into the Lincolnshire scene cannot be left without a glance at the troubles of a second great family. The Tailboys of Kyme[249] could point (like the Willoughbies) to an impeccable record of Lancastrian affiliation. Nevertheless relations with the Tudors had been uneasy. Sir George Tailboys had been deprived of his castle of Harbottle in Redesdale by Henry VIII to strengthen the defences of the frontier.[250] Subsequently the family played no further role in the affairs of the Marches, and the wide franchises it had enjoyed in Redesdale (which included the appointment of all justices and the return of all writs)[251] in practice fell into the hands of the king. Then in 1517 came the calamity of Sir George Tailboys's lunacy, which gave the crown a say in the disposal of the family's lands.[252] In Lincolnshire the latter were put in the custody of a commission of local gentry (Dymokes, Tyrwhitts, Heneages and Fulnetbies). But these were presided over by Wolsey as chancellor, and the opportunity was seized in 1519 to marry the heir, Gilbert Tailboys, outside the circle of local Yorkshire and Northumbrian alliances which had been characteristic of the family, to Henry VIII's discarded mistress, Elizabeth Blount.[253]

One result of this match was to generate tension between the older and younger generation of the Tailboys. Gilbert Tailboys was

[248] *L.P.*, xi, 805, 828 (vii).
[249] See above, p. 227 and n. 206.
[250] *L.P.*, i, 131.
[251] See *Calendar of Inquisitions, Henry VIII*, i, p. 414.
[252] *L.P.*, ii, 2979.
[253] *Complete Peerage*, xii (1), p. 602.

a courtier, and "of the king's chamber".[254] As a result of his marriage, he was amply endowed with royal offices, lands, and wardships;[255] "great sums of money and other benefits" were conferred on him,[256] and in due course he was made a peer.[257] The price which had to be paid, however, was the generous portion comprising eight Tailboys manors, settled on Elizabeth Blount for life in 1523 by Act of Parliament.[258] As a result of the settlement bitter disputes arose between Gilbert Tailboys and his mother, the latter holding back many of the lands made over to her daughter-in-law, claiming that without them no provision could be made for the maintenance of her other children, and particularly for the marriage money of her daughter Anne; if her son and his wife had their way she would be forced to "break" her household and disperse her servants.[259] The dispute reached its peak in the years 1528–9, at the same time as the Willoughby–Suffolk quarrel got under way. And like Suffolk it was the intrusive courtier Elizabeth Blount and her unfilial husband who had the support of the government. Cardinal Wolsey himself, according to the elder Lady Tailboys, had sent for her son "and said he should go home to see order kept, and he should have the custody of his father and his lands". This, she added, "causes me great disquiet, and makes my friends here and in the north wonder".[260]

Those friends would certainly have included Sir Christopher Willoughby, who was married to Lady Tailboys's daughter Elizabeth. No doubt his own troubles with the court would have made his sympathy more heartfelt. Another would have been Edward Dymoke, who was to play such a prominent role in the events of October 1536. For Anne Tailboys, whose marriage money was endangered by the importunities of Elizabeth Blount and her husband, was Dymoke's wife.[261] Whether or not a settlement of this issue was eventually reached cannot be known, but the exclusion of the Dymokes from the new commission made out in February 1531

[254] *L.P.*, iv, 2972.

[255] He was granted the manor of Rokeby, Warwickshire, made bailiff of Tattershall, and keeper of the castle, and given a lease of the park, with the wardship of William Ingleby. See *L.P.*, iii, 2356 (18); iv, 1298, 1533 (6), 5336 (27).

[256] 14 and 15 Henry VIII, c. 34 (*Statutes of the Realm*, iii, p. 280).

[257] *Complete Peerage*, xii (1), p. 602.

[258] 14 and 15 Henry VIII, c. 34.

[259] *L.P.*, iv, 4357.

[260] *Ibid.*, 5408.

[261] *Lincolnshire Pedigrees*, iv, p. 1205.

for the custody of Sir George Tailboys suggests that the role of the family in this affair was not regarded with favour by the court.[262] Thus the Dymokes had their private grievances, as well as a concern with more public causes which will be considered below. Moreover the sense of malaise at the intrusion of courtiers into the great matches and inheritances of the shire could hardly have been dissipated by Elizabeth Blount's second marriage in the early 1530s (Gilbert Tailboys had died in 1530) to Lord Clinton.[263] As a result yet another courtier was brought into Lincolnshire, who would build up a great estate there and who, in Elizabeth's reign as earl of Lincoln, would play the role of local magnate left vacant by the Brandons, ruling like them from Tattershall castle.[264] It can be no cause of surprise therefore that, when a band of well-horsed insurgents called at Barlings abbey in October 1536 to recruit the abbot for the rebellion, one of the leaders should have been "my old Lady Taillbois chaplain, called Sir Edmond".[265] The band probably consisted of Tailboys servants and tenants.

These then were the substantial and ancient gentry, a coherent group whose members shared an equality of wealth and social status, and the administrative duties involved in the rule of the shire. As the leaders of their class they were close in sentiments and standing to the families of peerage status like the Willoughbies and Tailboys. In addition, however, there was another gentry grouping which became associated with the rebellion, and from which in fact most of the "promoters" and "stirrers" referred to above were recruited. As has been seen, compared with the Dymokes, Skipwiths and their like, these were relative newcomers to the landed class, most of them being descended from fathers or grandfathers who had been merchants. What needs to be noted here, however, is their common connection with the city of Lincoln. Robert Dighton, for example, was the son of a mayor of Lincoln who had founded a landed family at Great Sturton.[266] Vincent Grantham was an alderman and ex-mayor of the city, and one of its M.P.s, and the mayor at the time of the rebellion was his brother-in-law Robert Sutton,

262 *L.P.*, v, 119 (67).
263 *Complete Peerage*, vii, p. 691.
264 Arthur Collins, *Peerage of England*, ed. Sir S. E. Brydges (London, 1812), ii, pp. 197–8.
265 *L.P.*, xi, 805.
266 *Lincolnshire Pedigrees*, ii, p. 298.

another member of the group who had an important role to play in the movement, and who was connected with Lord Hussey through his son's marriage to the latter's niece.[267] He came of another Lincoln merchant family now settled at Burton-by-Lincoln. Finally there was Thomas Dymoke of North Carlton and Fiskney who, although descended from the ancient Scrivelsby family, was also a freeman of Lincoln;[268] and the clever lawyer Thomas Moigne was not only squire of Willingham but also recorder of Lincoln, a post to which he had been appointed in 1532.[269]

Although the Lincoln gentlemen belonged to relatively "new" families, they were part of an ancient interest, the city of Lincoln, which was involved in an economic crisis, and which, like the Willoughbies and Tailboys, had its difficulties with the court. At Lincoln the great days of the wool trade were over, and the civic dynasties whose wealth had been derived from it, like the Suttons and their kind, had moved their capital into land. The city gilds were dwindling, population was falling, churches and houses were in decay, and an attempt to revive trade by reopening the silted-up Fossdyke, giving access to the Trent, had failed through lack of funds.[270] On this depressed and dwindling community the crown fee-farm rent of £100 a year, which had been inherited in 1524 by the newly created courtier earl of Rutland from the last Lord Ros, was a heavy burden.[271] The house of York had shown more favour to Lincoln than the Tudors, for Edward IV, in view of the impoverishment of the city, had released the fee-farm to the mayor and citizens;[272] and it was Henry VII who had restored it to Lord Ros, whose lunacy had however carried the custody of his estates to his brother-in-law Sir Thomas Lovell. Lovell was sensible enough not to exact the full amount, and until Rutland's accession to the Ros inheritance only twenty marks a year had to be paid. But thereafter the earl demanded the whole rent.[273] On its side the corporation resolved not to pay, and so began a wrangle which was not settled by

[267] *Ibid.*, ii, p. 421; iii, p. 938; *L.P.*, xi, 531.
[268] *Lincolnshire Pedigrees*, iv, p. 1203.
[269] *Ibid.*, ii, p. 679.
[270] On conditions in Lincoln in the early Tudor period, see Hill, *Tudor and Stuart Lincoln*, ch. 2.
[271] J. W. F. Hill, *Medieval Lincoln* (Cambridge, 1948), pp. 285–6.
[272] *Ibid.*, p. 281.
[273] Hill, *Tudor and Stuart Lincoln*, pp. 25–9.

the mediation of Sir William Ayscough in 1534[274] and which was still in progress in 1536.

No doubt this was one factor which predisposed the Lincoln community to dissident politics, nourished by hopes of a change of régime which might ward off the threat of Rutland's claims. Another, however, was the ambition of the Lincoln oligarchy, now composed not of cautious merchants and gildsmen but of the civic gentry (like Grantham and his friends) and of lawyers and episcopal officials who aspired to a wider role. The city, in spite of its decline, gave these men a useful political base, conferring status on them as mayors, aldermen and magistrates; and its parliamentary representation gave access to London and to wider political horizons than were open to most of the gentry. Profits too could be made from the corporation's lands and properties. Thus they had an interest in maintaining the shell of civic dignity and privilege which enclosed the shrunken economy of Lincoln; and it was appropriate that it should be Vincent Grantham, one of the most active and thrusting of the group, who in 1534 had taken steps in London to renew the decayed symbols of the city's greatness, sending down a new cap of maintenance for the corporation, and a scabbard for the city sword.[275] Grantham probably found his parliamentary role[276] profitable as well as stimulating. In the summer of 1536, for example, he was busy in London with Thomas Moigne trying to secure the lands of the cell in Lincoln of St Mary's abbey, York, for the city. He claimed £60 for his services, and was to have the demesnes of the cell on lease.[277] Whether it was Grantham who transmitted to his friends at Lincoln the tensions and excitements of the great world of London cannot be said. What is certain, however, is that the guiding star of the Lincoln group would be the great man whose niece had married Henry Sutton, himself Grantham's nephew. This was Lord Hussey. Thus ambition, capacity for leadership and a sense of opportunities to be seized impelled the group into the significant role they were to play in the rebellion.

Finally it is unlikely that any of these gentlemen, whether of the ancient families or of the Lincoln civic dynasties, were unaware of

[274] *Lincoln Corporation MSS.*: Hist. MSS. Comm., 14th Report, pt viii, p. 32.
[275] *Ibid.*, p. 33.
[276] He was elected, with alderman Sammes, in 1533 (*ibid.*, p. 32).
[277] *Ibid.*, pp. 34–5.

the implications of the Statute of Uses recently passed, sorely against its will, by Parliament. Possibly the Dymokes were particularly perceptive with regard to the implications of the Statute and its political relevance, since the demand for its repeal first appears in the Horncastle and Boston articles, two places where the influence of the family was strong; and it has been seen that at Horncastle Edward Dymoke himself made a point of explaining the new law to the assembled commons.[278] But lawyers like Moigne or M.P.s like Grantham would have been equally sensitive to this issue. For at one stroke the Act had deprived the landed class of the right to devise its estates by will, and of the protection which the device of the use gave tenants-in-chief against the claims by the crown as feudal overlord. In Lincolnshire the prospect of a strengthening of the king's feudal prerogatives could not have been made more palatable to local opinion by the way in which these had been used in the cases of the minority of Catherine Willoughby and the lunacy of Sir George Tailboys. Moreover Henry's browbeating of Parliament over the issue of the Statute, his suborning of the judges to undermine the existing law, and the vindictiveness with which, in 1535–6, he imposed a settlement overwhelmingly advantageous to the crown, had shown that the king could tyrannize over the laity as well as the clergy, and that he could not be restrained by any merely parliamentary opposition.[279]

Thus the Statute of Uses linked the private grievances and fears of the Lincolnshire landowners to those of the landed class as a whole, whose representatives had tenaciously resisted in Parliament the royal attempt to change the existing law. In this way the Lincolnshire leaders invited support from outside the shire, and their articles implied a parliamentary programme which touched on weighty secular as well as religious issues; and one too which could be expected to revive the self-respect and initiative of Parliament after its humiliating defeat at the king's hands over the issue of the Statute in 1535–6. No doubt too the article on taxation mentioned above, also included in the Lincoln and Boston programmes, with its implication of a hardening resistance to the royal fiscal demands and a tightening of parliamentary purse-strings, had its part to play from this point of view.

[278] See above, p. 225.
[279] See E. W. Ives, "The Genesis of the Statute of Uses", in *Eng. Hist. Rev.*, lxxxii (1967), p. 673.

VII

Regional and class ambitions and grievances of the kind discussed above were all very well to make discontented gentlemen ready to involve themselves in a regional riot. Few of these, however (and here there was a difference of approach as between gentlemen and commons), would be ready to be carried into waging war against the king, and doing battle with his forces. When this prospect faced them they surrendered. For the model for "rebellion" in 1536 is not likely to have been the Wars of the Roses, but the much more recent experience of the risings of 1525 against the Amicable Grant. These had been directed against an unpopular minister (Wolsey), whose power they had shaken if not overthrown; and the withdrawal of the unpopular tax which had been their cause was secured. But this had been the outcome because the rebellious commons had been cautiously "countenanced" by the anti-Wolsey party at court, and used by the dukes of Norfolk and Suffolk to discredit the cardinal.[280]

[280] There are many echoes of the Lincolnshire rebellion in the events of the spring of 1525. Wolsey was the scapegoat in 1525, and aroused the same hatred, as Cromwell in 1536. Just as Philip Trotter in Lincolnshire was told that "there was no remedy for these things . . . but only by insurrection and to beat down to the ground them that would attempt such things" (*L.P.*, xii, 69 (x)), so the commons of Kent asserted in 1525 "they will never have rest . . . as long as some liveth", by which it seems Wolsey was meant (*L.P.*, iv, 1243). According to one account (*L.P.*, iv, 1318), the dukes of Norfolk and Suffolk informed the cardinal that the commons laid the blame for their discontents on him, and that in any insurrection "the quarrel shall only be against him". Wolsey countered "that he was not alone herein", and that he was blamed because the people "dared not use their tongue against their sovereign". The king, however, was alarmed by the rising, and extricated himself by denying knowledge of the Amicable Grant, so that Wolsey had to bear the sole responsibility, asserting "I am content to take it on me, and to endure the fame and noyes of the people for my good will towards the kyng". Henry revoked the commissions to collect the grant, and sent pardons down to the shires (Hall, *The Union of . . . York and Lancaster*, pp. 700–1).

The dukes of Suffolk and Norfolk were sent down to restore order in East Anglia, but both urged moderation on the king (*L.P.*, iv, 1319), their attitude in this respect contrasting with Wolsey's insistence on severity (*ibid.*, 1324), and both asked that a Council be called to consider what should be done (*ibid.*, 1329). Relations between them and the insurgents were good, the latter telling Suffolk "that they would defende hym from all perilles if he hurt not their neighbours, but against their neighbours they would not fight" (Hall, *op. cit.*, pp. 699–700). Cf. Hussey's report of the Lincolnshire men, "they will be glad to defend me, but I shall not trust them to fight against the rebels" (*L.P.*, xi, 547). Norfolk, according to Hall (p. 700), told the rebels of his own county "he was sorry to hear their complaint, and well he knew it was true . . . on my honour I will send to the kyng, and

Similarly, then, the success of the Lincolnshire movement depended less on the military strength it could mobilize than on the patronage of the great men at court who were just as opposed as the Lincolnshire gentlemen to everything associated with "Cromwell" and "the heretic bishops". Only they could transform "rebellion" into a "loyal" demonstration against unworthy councillors, and precipitate a change of régime at the centre. And without this possibility it is unlikely that the gentlemen could have seen much future in a movement whose outcome could then only be a doubtful civil war against Henry VIII. The decisive leadership must therefore come not from discontented feudal houses and backwoods gentry, but from discontented courtiers: that is from within the Tudor establishment itself. There were two such in Lincolnshire, Lord Hussey and Sir Robert Dymoke. The former particularly was the central figure around whom the Lincolnshire movement both gathered momentum and eventually collapsed.

Hussey's importance lay in his long experience of the court, his friendships with the great, and his intimacy with Lord Darcy and the earl of Shrewsbury.[281] Nobody else within the horizon of the Lincolnshire insurgents was better placed to turn a regional demonstration into a serious political manoeuvre aiming at changes in the government. As a result all looked to him for leadership, and followed it when given. At first sight it is surprising to find Hussey in this role, in view of his long service to the two Tudors, father and son, which had brought him the great honorific office of chief butler of England, and in 1529 a peerage.[282] But there were signs in the years immediately preceding 1536 that he no longer enjoyed the king's favour. In September 1535, for example, the reversion of his office of chief butler had been granted to Sir Francis Bryan; and in March that of his master forestership of Waybridge and Sapley, was transferred to Richard Cromwell.[283] Throughout 1534 and 1535 pressure was being brought to bear for the repayment of his debts to the crown, although these had been incurred (so Hussey said) in the

make humble intercession for your pardon, which I trust to obtein, so you depart, then al they answered they would, and so they departed home". It was no doubt this kind of role that Hussey had in mind in Lincolnshire.

281 See *Dict. Nat. Biog.*; *Complete Peerage*, vii, p. 15.

282 *Ibid.*

283 *L.P.*, viii, 481 (32); ix, 729 (15); vii, 923 (5).

king's service.[284] And in August 1536 his wife had been imprisoned in the Tower because she had called the Lady Mary by the forbidden title of princess.[285]

Hussey's decline and fall has often been ascribed to Anne Hussey, with her sympathy for and unwise friendship with Mary. And it is probably the case that he was influenced by the ambience into which he had been brought by this second marriage of his to a daughter of George Grey second earl of Kent, and his sister's to Richard the third earl. These alliances brought the parvenu Husseys into the inner circle of the ancient and prestigious noble families, but also allied them to a house whose fortunes had been made by the Yorkist dynasty, and which had declined into increasing obscurity and poverty since the death of Edward IV.[286] Richard earl of Kent however who, through his grandmother, had affiliations with the Franco-Burgundian aristocracy, is distinguished by the consistency with which he participated in the banquets and ceremonial occasions which brought together the Tudors and members of the Habsburg family, from Philip of Burgundy's visit in 1506 to Charles V's in 1522.[287] Perhaps contacts were then made which

[284] *L.P.*, vii, 1259, 1566.

[285] *L.P.*, vii, 1035, 1036; xi, 222.

[286] For the Greys, Lords Grey of Ruthin and earls of Kent, see *Complete Peerage*, vi, p. 152, and vii, p. 164; Collins's *Peerage* (1812 edn), iii, p. 343. Edward IV had made the fourth Lord Grey of Ruthin lord treasurer of England and earl of Kent. His eldest son (who predeceased him) and George second earl of Kent married daughters of Richard Widevile, first Earl Rivers, and so became brothers-in-law of Edward IV, whose queen consort was Elizabeth Widevile. The sıecond earl's subsequent marriage to Catherine Herbert, daughter of William earl of Pembroke, was less brilliant, but no doubt was intended to bring him into the inner circle of the new Tudor establishment. The marriages of Richard third earl of Kent, first to Elizabeth Hussey, daughter of a chief justice of the common pleas, and then to Margaret Dawes, widow of a London alderman, are surprising for a nobleman of his status, and were probably motivated by financial considerations. The third earl's money troubles were already apparent during his lifetime, and led him to sell land. They are usually ascribed to extravagance and gambling. As a result his heir, Sir Henry Grey, never assumed the title "by reason of his slender estate".

[287] The earl was present at the meeting of Henry VII and Philip king of Castile near Windsor in January 1506; at the ratification of the treaty between Henry VIII, the Emperor Maximilian, and Charles of Burgundy at Greenwich on 5 July 1517, and on 7 July at the royal banquet there; at Henry VIII's meeting with Charles V at Gravelines, August 1520; at the reception of Charles V on his visit to England in May 1522. He was a witness to the Treaty of Windsor on 19 June 1522, and died in the following year. Perhaps these many Habsburg contacts had to do with the

opened the way to Lady Hussey's friendship with Mary, the emperor's cousin, her husband's appointment as the latter's chamberlain in 1533,[288] and even to Hussey's approach to Chapuys, the emperor's ambassador in September 1534.[289] And the relationship with the princess may have reminded Anne Hussey of the intimacy the Greys had enjoyed with the royal family in the days of Edward IV. If Mary were to succeed to the throne, the restoration of their fortunes, as well as the enhancement of those of the Husseys, could follow.

But whatever significance may be attached to these memories of the past and hopes for the future, religion must now enter the picture if we are to explain Hussey's discontents. For the latter was in contact with the intense and emotive world of reformed Catholic piety, with its mystical overtones, through his connection with the Brigettine nunnery of Syon, near Brentford, and its associated group of cultivated priests and chaplains. Syon was both a centre of the *devotio moderna* and in due course of opposition to the Royal Supremacy.[290] As early as 1512 Hussey had given lands to Pembroke College, Cambridge, a body which had close relations with Syon.[291] And it was a former fellow of Pembroke and confessor-general of Syon, John Fewterer, who dedicated to him *The Mirrour or glasse of Christes passion*, a characteristic product of Syon, published in 1534.[292] Like other members of the Syon circle too, Hussey was "shown" the "revelations" of the Nun of Kent, which condemned Henry VIII's divorce, and prophesied he "shall not be a king a month" if he married Anne Boleyn.[293] Against this background Hussey's dislike of heresy falls into place. He himself

earl's affiliations with the Franco-Burgundian aristocracy, his grandmother being Jacqueline, daughter of Pierre de Luxembourg, count of Saint-Pol, Conversano, and Brienne, who had married the first Earl Rivers.

288 *L.P.*, vi, 1199. As Mary's chamberlain Hussey was required to be the instrument of the king's displeasure towards his daughter, being required to withdraw her jewels and plate, and her title and status of princess. See *L.P.*, vi, 849, 1009, 1041, 1139, 1186, 1382. Hussey had little relish for this role, and by January 1534 (*L.P.*, vii, 38) Mary's household had been dissolved, and the office of chamberlain abolished.

289 *L.P.*, vii, 1206.

290 See Knowles, *The Religious Orders*, iii, pp. 212–21; J. K. McConica, *English Humanists and Reformation Politics* (Oxford, 1965), pp. 56–7, 131–3.

291 *L.P.*, i, 1732 (26).

292 McConica, *op. cit.*, p. 132. Fewterer translated this book at Hussey's request.

293 *L.P.*, vi, 1468.

admitted that in 1534 he and two significant companions, Lord Darcy and Sir Robert Constable, had affirmed "we could not be heretics, but die Christian men". There is also the testimony of Chapuys that he wished Charles V to "remedy" affairs in England not only because the interests of Catherine and Mary were involved, but also because "it was God's cause, which you [the emperor] as a Catholic prince, and chief of all other princes, were bound to uphold".[294] And there is an uncorroborated piece of testimony to the effect that in 1535 he told a Yorkshire gentleman concerned about the spread of heresy "it will never mend but we fight" for holy church.[295] In practice however, as will be seen, Hussey's militancy, even in the cause of religion, had its limits. Like his friend John Fewterer, who first stood out against, but eventually accepted the Royal Supremacy, Hussey would find that while he could not be "against" the Lincolnshire rebels, neither could he be "false to his Prince". Obedience had the last word.[296]

Unlike Hussey, Sir Robert Dymoke came from an ancient Lincolnshire family, which from Scrivelsby, near Horncastle, had long exercised an influence in the shire comparable to that of the Tailboys and Willoughbies, although no Dymoke had ever been made a peer.[297] It was Sir Robert's father, Sir Thomas Dymoke, who had been the principal ally of Lord Willoughby and Welles, who in 1470 had raised Lincolnshire against Edward IV;[298] so the family had an impeccable Lancastrian tradition which gave them a claim on the favour of the Tudors. Probably Sir Robert had first entered the king's service in the reign of Henry VII, but office did not come his way until 1513 when he was made treasurer of the king's army against France, and then treasurer of Tournai, a post he held until 1516.[299] Here he was engaged in the transmission of subsidies to the Emperor Maximilian, and in negotiations with the regent of the Netherlands, Margaret of Savoy;[300] and these contacts with the Habsburg court (like those of Lady Hussey's family) may be relevant to his subsequent appearance in the service of Queen

[294] *L.P.*, vii, 1206.
[295] *L.P.*, xii (1), 576.
[296] Knowles, *op. cit.*, p. 218; *L.P.*, xii (1), 70 (iii).
[297] *Lincolnshire Pedigrees*, iv, p. 1202.
[298] "Chronicle of the Rebellion in Lincolnshire, 1470", ed. J. G. Nichols, *Camden Miscellany*, i (Camden Soc., 1847).
[299] *L.P.*, i (2), p. 928; 2414, 3114.
[300] *Ibid.*, 2528, 2992.

Catherine. It was not until 1527, however, the year in which Henry VIII instigated divorce proceedings against Catherine, that Dymoke appears as chancellor of the queen's household, ranking next to the chamberlain, Lord Mountjoy, and the vice-chamberlain, Sir Edward Darell.[301] Subsequently he remained one of Catherine's principal household officers until 1533, when her household was dissolved;[302] and it seems (according to his sister-in-law) that he had also been made one of the king's council.[303] In 1534 he is found living in retirement at Scrivelsby (his age would be a sufficient reason for his withdrawal) and he held no further office.

In the previous year Dymoke had been present at a bitter scene at Buckden, the house of the bishop of Lincoln which was then Catherine's residence. On 18 December the duke of Suffolk had been sent down from the king to compel Catherine's servants to take a new oath to her under the title of "Princess Dowager" instead of queen, and to imprison those who refused; he had also attempted (but without success) to remove Catherine herself to a remoter confinement at Somersham in the Isle of Ely.[304] Chapuys maintained that the object of the operation was to separate Katherine from her officers, and he mentioned her "almoner" (one of Sir Robert Dymoke's titles while in the queen's service) as one of these.[305] Dymoke left no hint on this occasion as on others that he sided with his mistress against the king, and, although there is no mention of his taking the new oath himself, there is no suggestion either that he resisted it. It would be strange, however, if he were not drawn into the nexus of loyalties which bound the officers of a great household to its head. And, if Dymoke had already come to dislike Suffolk because of his quarrel with Sir Christopher Willoughby, he would have additional reason to resent his treatment of Catherine on this occasion. The Dymoke connection with Catherine moreover makes it unlikely that the family would support any other than her daughter Mary as next in the succession to the crown. But Mary's prospects, after some improvement following the fall of Anne Boleyn, were once more clouded over by the autumn of 1536. She had been given no place in the new Act of Succession, and was forced into a humiliating acknowledgement of the invalidity of her mother's marriage, and so of her own claims.[306] Loyalty to Mary

301 *L.P.*, iv (2), p. 1332.
302 *L.P.*, vi, 760, 1541.
303 *L.P.*, vii, 1634.
304 *L.P.*, vi, 1541.
305 *Ibid.*, 1510.
306 *L.P.*, x, 1137.

gave the Dymokes a point of contact with Hussey, who as has been seen, was Mary's chamberlain.

Apart from this involvement with the cause of Queen Catherine, however, it is also likely that the Dymokes had little sympathy with the king's proceedings in religion. For through the Dominican priory of Dartford in Kent, where Sir Robert Dymoke was steward and his sister-in-law Elizabeth Cressener prioress,[307] like Hussey at Syon the Dymokes were in contact with much that was best in the established religion and English monasticism. For, although Dartford had a close connection with the court and royal family, like Syon (or Sheen) it fostered a strong religious life based on the *devotio moderna* and an austere discipline.[308] There were connections too with the More circle, William Roper's sister being one of the nuns; another was Elizabeth White, half-sister to Bishop John Fisher, to whom the latter dedicated his *Spiritual Consolation* of 1534.[309] There was little support for the religious changes at Dartford. The Royal Supremacy was acknowledged on 14 May 1534 before the commissioners appointed to take the oath, John Hilsey and George Browne, two Domincans whom Cromwell had appointed as provincials to visit the houses of the Order. But, although the monastic seal was fixed to the instruments, none of the nuns had to sign it. The Dymokes, however, could scarcely have relished the pressure it brought to bear on Elizabeth Cressener to part with Dartford lands to men like Hilsey, or the proposed appointment of a servant of Cromwell to succeed Sir Robert Dymoke as steward.[310]

In fact both family sentiment and religious inclination probably turned the Dymokes against the dissolution. And the Dartford connection accounts for the inclusion by name both of Hilsey (then bishop of Rochester) and Browne (as archbishop of Dublin) in the list of "heretic bishops" whom the Lincolnshire commons demanded should be punished.[311] In the case of Hilsey, however, the theme of the divorce emerges again, for at Catherine's funeral

[307] *L.P.*, vii, 1634; Harleian Soc., xiv (London, 1879), p. 721.
[308] C. F. R. Palmer, "History of the Priory of Dartford in Kent", in *Archaeol. Jl*, xxxvi, p. 241.
[309] *Complete Works of St Thomas More*, ii, ed. R. S. Sylvester (Yale edn, New Haven, 1963), pp. 158–9.
[310] Palmer, *loc. cit.*; *L.P.*, vii, 665 (3), 666, 1634; ix, 704.
[311] *L.P.*, xi, 853, 585.

he had untruthfully preached that on her deathbed she had confessed that she had not been rightfully queen of England.[312] The same issue accounts for the inclusion of Longland bishop of Lincoln (a religious conservative) in the list, since he was credited with having originally suggested the divorce to Henry VIII, and had played a prominent part in advancing it.[313] For the Dymokes then dissidence had its deepest roots in religion, and in loyalty to Sir Robert Dymoke's late mistress. But inevitably when the time for action came it was the heir Edward Dymoke, lately appointed sheriff,[314] and not the aged head of the family, who figured most prominently in the leadership.

VIII

Safe at Sleaford, thirty miles away from the disorders at Horncastle and Louth, Hussey had no contact with the events which had sparked off the rising, and so had avoided any contamination by rebellion. This was fortunate given the role he adopted as events developed, which was to mediate between the Lincolnshire dissidents and the court. For this it was essential that he should remain firmly within the context of "obedience", at any rate as far as outward appearances went. It was from this point of view that Hussey set about the task of exploring what political capital could be made out of the movement. The first of his letters with this object in mind was written to Robert Sutton as mayor of Lincoln and to Vincent Grantham on 3 October.[315] Its tone was impeccably loyal. The rebels were described as "evil disposed rebellious persons", and Sutton and Grantham were commanded to keep the city against them; they were to be ready to raise men to suppress the rising, gathering arms for this purpose. Thus the posture recommended was essentially defensive and passive, inevitably leaving the initiative to the insurgents. Moreover in the last sentence of the letter Sutton and Grantham were instructed to make no public gesture of loyalty, but to handle the whole matter secretly; and so far from placing the main emphasis on resistance to the rebels, Hussey revealed that he already visualized the possibility that the

312 *L.P.*, x, 284.
313 *L.P.*, iv, 6308; v, 45, 171, 287; vii, 14.
314 *L.P.*, ix, 914 (22).
315 *L.P.*, xi, 531.

Lincoln authorities might not find this feasible. In that case, he told Sutton and Grantham, they should send him word, and he would come to their aid. Thus the way was being prepared for an encounter between Hussey and the main body of the rebels at Lincoln. The rebel leaders, as will be seen, were eager for this to take place, and none of them anticipated that it would assume a warlike character. It was a rendezvous with the principal magnate of the shire, which they had in mind, and it is unlikely that Sutton and Grantham thought differently, or failed to grasp the finer points of the letter they had received. For as has been seen, both were actively involved in the advancement of the rebellion, Grantham being subsequently identified as one of those who openly joined the insurgents of his own free will, without the usual show of coercion being necessary. And it was the mayor who armed the commons of Lincoln, so enabling them to seize power in the city and open the gates to the rebel host.[316]

At the same time Hussey also wrote to Sir Robert Tyrwhitt (Sutton's cousin), who it will be remembered was one of the commissioners taken at Caistor. The latter set before Tyrwhitt and his associates the same prospect as had been put to Sutton and Grantham. There was to be a rendezvous at Lincoln, to which Tyrwhitt was to hasten, inevitably in the company of the Caistor and Louth insurgents, whose captive he was as Hussey was aware.[317] For in the meanwhile he had received a communication from Thomas Moigne. This has not survived, but presumably it gave an account of the events at Louth, and Hussey hastened to answer it, on the same day as he wrote to Sutton, Grantham and Tyrwhitt. His reply[318] gives some further indication of the way he was thinking. Firstly Moigne was reproved for having sent his letter "without getting the worshipful men there to set their hand to it". That is, Hussey required the gentlemen to commit themselves in writing to the events in which they were involved. The point was taken, for on the next day Tyrwhitt, Skipwith, Ayscough and their other associates wrote (each now signing their name to the letter) to know whether

[316] *Ibid.*, 879 (2). According to one deponent, Sutton asserted he had been with Lord Hussey, who could see no remedy but to do as the commons did.

[317] The letter fell into the hands of the commons, and has not survived. For its content see *L.P.*, xi, 973.

[318] *L.P.*, xi, 532.

Hussey "would come and aid the commonalty in their service to God, the king, and the commonwealth of this realm", else "the commonalty will in all haste seek you out as their utter enemy".[319] In addition, however, Hussey was concerned to ascertain from Moigne whether the insurrection was gathering momentum or not, and whether the gentlemen, and particularly his fellow-peer Lord Burgh, would appoint a meeting with him, to take place at Lincoln. Once again therefore Hussey urged the movement towards a convergence on the shire capital, where he told Moigne he would himself arrive on Wednesday night or Thursday morning.

As has been said, one of Hussey's advantages in these first two days of the rebellion was that, at Sleaford, he was safely remote from the popular insurrections at Louth and elsewhere. Thus he could view events with detachment and seek to guide and control them, and he was free from the danger of being swept away by the tide of rebellion. He probably hoped to make his own way to Lincoln, arriving there still untainted by any public involvement with the insurgents. But on Wednesday 4 October the rebellion reached Sleaford, and these plans were thrown out of gear. For it seems that on that day Hussey lost control of events on his own doorstep, and had to send a servant to seek the advice of Robert Carr,[320] the most important personage in the town after Hussey himself.[321] From that moment, however, pressure was brought to bear to compel Hussey to declare himself, and to abandon his careful posture of non-commitment. And it soon became clear that he would not be allowed to leave for Lincoln except at the head of a band of the commons of Sleaford. For the latter now rose and, led by Carr, surrounded Hussey's house, saying that they wished his aid and would "live and die with him".[322] Hussey may have regarded the agitation as worked up by Carr to compromise him, either as having declared for the rebellion or as having failed to raise his country to suppress it; and in fact it was Carr's evidence which subsequently did most to bring him to the block. In the meanwhile, however, he continued to refuse to declare himself, asserting "I would come and go as I list". But his house was now besieged, and he could not leave for Lincoln as he had planned.[323]

From one point of view, however, the rising at Sleaford had its

319 *Ibid.*, 539.
320 See above, pp. 213–14.
321 *L.P.*, xi, 969.
322 *Ibid.*
323 *Ibid.*, 852.

advantages as far as Hussey was concerned. For the most obvious weakness of his position, if he was to guard against charges of disloyalty, was his continued inactivity.[324] He had received news of the rebellion from Lord Clinton as long ago as Monday 2 October;[325] yet day followed day (as hostile witnesses were subsequently to point out) and beyond writing letters he had done nothing. Yet it was his plain duty, as the king's greatest subject in the disaffected district, to muster his tenants and followers and restore obedience. Now, however, Hussey could explain his passivity by the disloyalty of his "countrymen" who, as he told Cromwell in a letter written on Thursday 5 October, would defend him but could not be trusted to fight against the rebels.[326] And his incarceration at Sleaford could be used to account for his failure to join the earl of Shrewsbury, who was mustering the king's forces at Nottingham. "I would come to your lordship", Hussey told the earl on Friday the 6th, "but am so environed that I dare not leave my house . . . I will be with you as soon as I may."[327] Such explanations were the more necessary because emissaries from the government (Sir Marmaduke Constable, Robert Tyrwhitt and John Heneage) had reached Sleaford on Thursday with letters from the king to Hussey and the gentlemen "now in the hands of the commons".[328] That to the commissioners at Louth has survived, and expressed the king's astonishment that they should have put themselves in the hands of the rebels, instead of assembling to defend themselves, and suppress the insurrection.[329] No doubt that to Hussey had commented with equal disapproval on his failure to react energetically to the fact of rebellion.

But in the meanwhile Hussey's manoeuvres and hesitations were giving rise to mounting doubts and fears among the insurgents, and particularly among the gentlemen. For without Hussey and the support it was supposed he could command with the great, the latter could see little future for the rebellion; only with his guidance could it become effective as a lever to change the balance of power at court. On Wednesday, it is true, Hussey had sent two servants to the

[324] Cf. Robert Carr's view: "If my lord had gathered men for the King as he had done for his own pomp to ride to sessions or assize, he might have driven the rebels back" (*L.P.*, xi, 969).

[325] *Ibid.*

[326] *L.P.*, xi, 547.

[327] *Ibid.*, 561.

[328] *Ibid.*, 553, 578.

[329] *Ibid.*, 569.

Horncastle insurgents, and one of these had given an assurance that he would not raise the country against them.[330] But in reply to emissaries sent to Sleaford by Edward Dymoke he had used the formula already quoted, that "he would not be false to his Prince, nor would he be against them".[331] Probably it was this message which caused so much discontent amongst the leaders when the messengers returned with it on Saturday.[332] And this does not seem to have been much assuaged by a statement by Hussey's servant Cutler, who had reached the host the previous day, that his master and his house were at the commons' command, or by the letters he brought with him[333] although Cutler thought that in these Hussey promised to surrender to the insurgents.[334] By Saturday the rebel host had occupied Lincoln, and the rebellion had reached its climax, having attained the objective set it by Hussey himself. Its further development now depended on his leadership and advice, and the general opinion was that "if he were set like a nobleman he would come" to Lincoln.[335] It was decided, therefore, to send a body of horse under Sir Christopher Ayscough to fetch him. But these returned on Sunday empty-handed.[336] Hussey had escaped from Sleaford and fled to Nottingham to the loyalist earl of Shrewsbury. Not even Lady Hussey's persuasions could bring him back.[337] The rising survived this news barely more than two days. On Tuesday the gentlemen hastened to submit, leaving their plebeian followers in the lurch.

Why had Hussey defected? The reason lay in the attitude taken up by the earl of Shrewsbury, who had been appointed a king's lieutenant for the suppression of the rebellion.[338] This great nobleman, who had been prominently involved in so many of the campaigns and diplomatic transactions of both Tudor reigns, was a friend of Hussey and of Lord Darcy.[339] His attitude could be expected to influence that of his co-lieutenants, the dukes of Norfolk and Suffolk, who both disliked Cromwell, and of his fellow

[330] *Ibid.*, 620.
[331] *L.P.*, xii (1), 70 (iii).
[332] *L.P.*, xi, 968.
[333] *Ibid.*, p. 342.
[334] *Ibid.*, 587 (2).
[335] *Ibid.*, 968.
[336] *Ibid.*, 853, 854, 968.
[337] *Ibid.*, 852.
[338] *Ibid.*, 537. Shrewsbury first mustered men on a basis of letters missive from the king, under the Privy Seal. His commission as lieutenant was not sent him till 15 October (*L.P.*, xi, 715, 716).
[339] *Dict. Nat. Biog.*; *Complete Peerage*, xi, p. 706.

northern magnates the earl of Cumberland, Lord Dacre and the earl of Northumberland, who were (or had been) his sons-in-law, as well as the earl of Derby and perhaps the lords of the White Rose party. Shrewsbury had been involved in the aristocratic reaction against Wolsey's rule,[340] and he had reason to dislike Cromwell's régime. There had been no overt quarrel between the two, but bickerings had recurred over the disposal of monastic offices in houses where Shrewsbury was steward, and over the lands of another founded by one of his ancestors.[341] A more serious matter was the earl's aversion to the divorce[342] (although he eventually supported it), and his failure to officiate as lord steward at Anne Boleyn's coronation, the duke of Suffolk being appointed for the day to act in his place.[343] Perhaps it was this incident which occasioned the pressure brought to bear in 1534 to secure the repayment of Shrewsbury's debts to the crown (whose amount the earl said had been exaggerated), and the rumour spread by Cromwell that the king favoured the succession of the earl of Sussex as lord steward.[344] Then in May 1536 the earl had been hit in his pocket when his Irish lands were confiscated and transferred by an act of the Irish parliament to the king, to sustain his charges there.[345] Cromwell held out hopes of compensation, but nothing would come of these until late in 1537.[346]

Hussey therefore had reason to believe that the earl had his discontents, and might be inclined to benevolence towards a dissident movement. And like Hussey and the Dymokes, Shrewsbury was a conservative in religion, being a friend of Sir Thomas More and

[340] *L.P.*, iv, 6075.
[341] *L.P.*, v, 1234; vii, 818; xi, 177, 247, 459.
[342] *L.P.*, v, 120, 171, 287.
[343] *L.P.*, vi, 601.
[344] *L.P.*, vii, 991, 1407, 1442. In October 1535 Shrewsbury granted his manors of Sheffield, Hansworth, Bradfield, Southey, Ecclesfield, Treeton, Whiston, and Bolderstone to trustees to secure the payment of 220 marks a year to the king in respect of his debts: Sheffield City Library, Arundel Castle MS. SD 112. Shrewsbury claimed that the king had already recovered lands worth 500 marks in respect of these same debts.
[345] Shrewsbury's possessions in Ireland were forfeited by the Act of Absentees passed after the Geraldine rebellion, 1 May 1536 (*Statutes at Large, Ireland* (20 vols., Dublin, 1786–1802), p. 84.
[346] *L.P.*, x, 1198. On 6 October 1537 Shrewsbury was granted the site of Rufford abbey, Notts., and other lands to the value of £246 a year. See *L.P.*, xii (2), 1008 (9).

allergic to heretics.[347] In that first week of October 1536, with his headquarters at Nottingham and assisted by the earls of Rutland and Huntingdon, he was engaged in gathering forces to deal with the rebellion. But persistent rumours circulated that he favoured the commons, and these probably contributed to the story related many years later by Holinshed, that when he began to muster men the latter expected to be led to join the rebels, not against them.[348] This was the man then whose support could have taken the rebellion a long way towards its transformation into a broad movement of political opposition which the king himself could scarcely have resisted. Hussey must have felt that he had good grounds for a gamble that Shrewsbury would take this road. But Shrewsbury already owed much to Henry VIII.[349] If he suppressed a rebellion, further rewards and favours would come his way, whereas the opposite course involved incalculable uncertainties. At any rate in the outcome the earl held to the policy he had persisted in throughout his career: that of absolute loyalty.[350] And Hussey's letter to him of Friday 6 October,[351] intended to sound his intentions, contained a sentence on which Shrewsbury could seize to make his attitude absolutely clear.

Hussey had written in his letter that the emissaries which had reached him the previous day with the royal missives "showed me that dyverse things were in your lordshippes letter [from the king] which your lordship wold advertise me of". Why, Hussey must have reasoned, could the king not have put the "things" of which he was to be "advertised" in the letter which had just been delivered to him

347 For an example of Shrewsbury's short way with heretics, see Dickens, *Lollards and Protestants*, pp. 37–9.

348 Hall, *The Union of . . . York and Lancaster* (1586 edn), iii, p. 942. See also Dickens, *op. cit.*, p. 39 for an opinion circulating in clerical circles at the time of the Lincolnshire rebellion that Shrewsbury favoured the commons.

349 As for example his power in the Welsh Marches, based on crown offices. He was steward of the royal lordships of Radnor, Maelienydd, Rhayader, Cwmmwd Deuddwr, Presteign, Norton, Gatley and Knighton, granted to him and his son and heir Francis in survivorship in 1525. See R. Robinson in *Bull. of the Board of Celtic Studies*, xxi (1964–6), p. 336.

350 Even his family marriages were subject to the king's approval, which was probably withheld in the case of Buckingham's proposal for a cross match between the Staffords and Talbots, so leading Shrewsbury to reject the duke's handsome offer, Buckingham remarking to Wolsey "Nay nay my lord, I know my lord Steward's mind, that he will never marry his son without the advice of the King's grace, and there as shall be his pleasure" (*L.P.*, ii (1), 1893).

351 Public Record Office SP1/106, fo. 283; *L.P.*, xi, 561.

from the king himself? A likely explanation was that some conciliatory move had been decided on. For, if this were the case, it would certainly not be communicated directly by the king to a man whose loyalty was already suspect. If there were to be negotiations, these would be entrusted rather to the king's lieutenant who could, if necessary, be repudiated. Moreover, if the king were wavering, Shrewsbury might be more inclined to let his supposed sympathy towards the insurgents come into the open. Hussey's words then in effect were an invitation to the lieutenant to open a dialogue in which the political situation could be reviewed and its possibilities explored. Shrewsbury immediately saw the importance of the letter, and that his own reputation as the king's loyal servant depended on the kind of reply he sent, and of this he carefully preserved a copy.[352] It cut through Hussey's devious approaches by presenting him with a plain statement of his duty. "My lord and I have no oder thing in my letter", Shrewsbury wrote, "but onely comandement to represse the Kyngs Rebellyous, whiche I dowt not but ye woll put your helpying hande to." The next sentence made it clear that the earl had no underhand motives of his own, or instructions transmitted to him by the king which might be exploited, for he now stated: "My verie good lord, for the old acquaintance and familyaritie betwyxt your good lordship and me as unto hym that I entirely love, I wold wryte the playnes of my mynd to your lordship." "Ye have allwayes bene an honorable and true gentylman", Shrewsbury went on, " . . . and I dowt not but will now so prove your selff accordying to your bounded duty." Nobody, Shrewsbury thought, could do the king truer service than Hussey in those parts by "practising" to "stay" the rebels, and particularly by finding means to separate the gentlemen from the plebeian rank and file. For then the latter "could do small hurt". Finally the implications of disobedience were lightly touched upon. The king's subjects of Derby, Stafford and Shropshire, of Worcester, Leicester and Northampton, to the number of 40,000, would be with the earl at Nottingham by Saturday night, "and I trust undowtedly to have your good lordship to kepe us company . . . ".

And so Hussey the courtier, whose whole career had been spent in the service of the crown, and in a context of ordered obedience to the king, whose family had risen by that same service, was now con-

[352] Public Record Office, SP1/107, fo. 71; *L.P.*, xi, 589.

fronted unequivocally with the choice of obeying the king's lieutenant, or assuming the leadership of a regional rebellion and revealing himself as a traitor. The latter stance, however, was morally repugnant; and Hussey knew the rising had no political future now that the king had withheld any gesture of conciliation and Shrewsbury had refused to have any truck with him. Thomas Cromwell must have seen the earl's reply to Hussey, for Shrewsbury had sent up a copy with his other letters to the king, whose receipt Cromwell acknowledged on 9 October. The latter's reaction was effusive, and he wrote praising the earl "as the man and most worthy earl that ever served a Prince, and such a chieftain as is worthy of eternal glory", and assured him of the king's appreciation of his services.[353] Hussey in the meanwhile had made his decision, and set out for Nottingham on Saturday night. Subsequently, in his confession before the council, he stated that he had told Shrewsbury in his letter of Friday 6 October that he would join him on Saturday. But this was untrue. What he had said was "I will be with you as shortly as I may". It was Shrewsbury's reply a day later which had barred all ways out except that of immediate submission. There was no alternative for one who, if he would not be "against" the Lincolnshire dissidents, also "would not be fals to his Prince", and who asserted, in the letter he wrote just before his execution, that he would not include treason amongst his sins, "for that I will ask no pardon, for I have not offended his grace in treason".[354]

If the gentlemen assembled with the commons at Lincoln on that same Sunday that Sir Christopher Ayscough returned from Sleaford with the news of Hussey's defection had been intent on civil war, the military factors in the situation were not particularly weighted against them. For the king's forces were still divided and weak. Shrewsbury was at Nottingham, but the news of the risings at Halifax and Beverley, which had just reached Lincoln,[355] suggested he would be kept too busy further north to be able to deal with Lincolnshire. Thirty-six miles from Lincoln, at Stamford, Sir John Russell and Sir William Parr with a small force barred the Great North Road.[356] But on Monday they doubted whether they would

353 *L.P.*, xi, 612; E. Lodge (ed.), *Illustrations of British History* . . . , 3 vols. (London, 1838), i, p. 40.
354 *L.P.*, xii (2), 2.
355 *L.P.*, xi, 971.
356 *L.P.*, xi, 615. Parr and Russell had 900 men (*L.P.*, xi, 808).

be able to hold the town.[357] Suffolk, far to the south at Huntingdon, was pessimistic about the outcome of a battle, and uncertain whether the rebels could be held anywhere further north.[358] It was not until Wednesday that the king's forces at last concentrated at Stamford, Parr and Russell being joined there by the retinues of Suffolk, the Lord Admiral Fitzwilliam and Sir Francis Bryan.[359] And with the arrival of the artillery on Friday an advance on Lincoln became feasible.[360] But the result was a force of no more than 3,000 men,[361] probably a strength not much greater than the retinues of the Lincolnshire gentlemen together with the armed commons.[362] The host at Lincoln was not, therefore, confronted by any overwhelming odds. Nevertheless as early as Tuesday the gentlemen had decided on submission, and on that same Friday they informed Suffolk to this effect and offered to come unconditionally to Stamford on the following day.[363]

The readiness of the gentlemen to submit, and their unwillingness to respond both to the desire of the commons to "go forward", and to the offers of help of the Yorkshire rebels, has laid them open to the charge of folly and pusillanimity.[364] But the fact was that without

[357] *Ibid.*, 621.

[358] *Ibid.*, 971.

[359] *Ibid.*, 658.

[360] *Ibid.*, 661.

[361] Suffolk discharged 2,000 men who were unarmed and unhorsed, out of a total of 5,000 (*L.P.*, xi, 808).

[362] The military strength of the regions most involved in the rebellion is suggested by the 1539 musters of the Lindsey wapentakes of Hill, Candleshoe, Calceworth, Yarborough, Haverstoe, Gartree, Wraggoe, Aslacoe, Lawress, Well and Walschcroft, and the sokes of Bolingbroke and Horncastle (*L.P.*, xiv (1), p. 276). The total strength was 3,855 "able" men, of which 847 were archers, and 2,749 billmen. 827 "harnesses" were available (in the hands of the gentlemen) for mounted men, but it appears that only 159 of the latter mustered, being the household servants of the gentlemen. Louthesk wapentake, as mustered in 1542, provided a further 634 "harnesses" and men (*L.P.*, xvii, p. 503). It is reasonable to assume that in time of rebellion the gentlemen would have made more of an effort to raise armed and mounted retinues amongst their followers and tenants. Thomas Moigne, for example, brought 200 men in harness to the muster at Hamelton Hill (*L.P.*, xi, 853). The host at Lincoln was equipped with artillery, supposedly brought from Grimsby (*L.P.*, xi, p. 322). Such figures seem closer to reality than the inflated estimates of a host 30 or 40,000 strong which circulated at the time of the rebellion.

[363] *L.P.*, xi, 971, 690, 691.

[364] Dodds, *The Pilgrimage of Grace*, i: "It was a wonder the gentlemen themselves were not carried away by the surging enthusiasm of the commons. When they had already risked so much they might . . . have brought themselves to stake all" p. 115); "The commons of Lincolnshire were clamouring to be led to battle . . . But the gentlemen were afraid" (p. 128). The Misses Dodds were aware of

Hussey to mediate between themselves and the great men about the king they were demoralized and at sea. For, lacking its natural leader, it was difficult to see how the movement could be legitimized, or where it would lead, even if an advance were made towards London. It seems too that the gentlemen were finding it increasingly difficult to control the commons, and that tension was growing between them and the popular leaders. There is no need to assume that they feared a "peasant war",[365] but there can be no doubt that men like Hudswell, the Leeches, Trotter, Melton and their like were aware how exposed they were if a policy of submission were adopted. The best insurance against this, from their point of view, was to press the gentlemen to "go forward" and commit themselves to the idiom of overt resistance and rebellion which, so far, by means of the rituals of forced oath-taking and coercion they had avoided. The gentlemen, on the other hand, could have seen little more than fantasy in this kind of political initiative from below. To "go forward" as leaders of "the commons" could, in the commonplace of the day, only result in "confusion", leading perhaps even to the rise of "tyrants" out of the ranks of the people, and to the subversion of the established structure of authority, which had so far been successfully upheld.[366]

These were the factors involved then in the confrontation which, according to Thomas Moigne, took place on Tuesday in the chapter house of Lincoln cathedral between the gentlemen and a band of commons two or three hundred strong, which was occasioned by the arrival of a letter from the king, whose content the commons

another approach to the situation however: "There would have been no difficulty in making a sudden dash up to London . . . but even if they reached London, as Wat Tyler and Jack Cade did . . . it was difficult to do anything effective there" (*ibid.*, p. 125).

365 *Ibid.*, p. 126.

366 See below, pp. 264–5. The tragedy of "The Blacksmith" in *A Mirror for Magistrates*, ed. Lily B. Campbell (Cambridge, 1938), would illustrate from the fate of Lord Audley, who in the Cornish rebellion of 1497, although a peer, had submitted to the rule of "Flamoke the Smith", the fearful consequences for the rebel who "went forward" with plebeians:

> For if he once be entered to the breares
> He hath a raging wolfe fast by the eares.
> And when he is once entred to rule the beastly route
> Although he would he can no way get out:
> He may be sure none wyl to him resorte,
> But such as are the vile and rascall sorte.

insisted on knowing, and another from Suffolk.[367] These communications inclined the gentlemen, led by Moigne, to submit, but aroused the fears and suspicions of the plebeians. Probably the seriousness of the conflict has been exaggerated in Moigne's account. He claimed that the commons had planned to kill the gentlemen because of their desire to surrender, a version of events which obviously served the purpose of completing the picture already built up of the gentlemen as the victims of the popular frenzy. But trouble there certainly was, which went to the point of one of the commons crying out (as we know from testimony independent of Moigne's) that "if any were hanged for this, they would not leave one gentleman alive in Lincolnshire".[368] And it may be possible that Moigne himself, as he claimed, had been "like to be slain" for omitting a sentence from the king's letter when he read it out. The commons, for whom the terms of submission were a matter of life and death, were plainly in a violent mood. These events, however, were remote from any impending *jacquerie*. For only a minority of intransigents and activists were involved, probably led by the Leech family.[369] The "honest men" among the commons supported the gentlemen, and helped them to maintain their authority.[370] The latter had no difficulty in restoring order next day when, armed and supported by their retinues, they announced to the assembled host their intention of abandoning the rebellion;[371] and on Thursday, upon the arrival of Lancaster herald with the king's command to disperse, the host began to break up.[372] Thus the popular initiative soon died away, and Shrewsbury's dictum that the plebeians, once separated from the gentlemen, "could doe small hurt" was confirmed. But the incident also helped the gentlemen to

367 *L.P.*, xi, 971. For the king's letter see *ibid.*, 569, and Suffolk's *ibid.*, 616.

368 *Ibid.*, 975, fo. 3.

369 It was, however, Thomas Ratford vicar of Snelland who unleashed the violent scene in the chapter house by crying out that Moigne had "falsely read" the king's letter. When however the host assembled on Thursday 12 October to hear Lancaster herald's proclamation for them to disperse, it was Robert Leech who seized the gentlemen's submission and opened and read it, saying "he would see what their answer was ere it should depart" (*L.P.*, xi, 843). His brother William Leech, who escaped capture, was attempting to organize a new rising in Lincolnshire in January 1537 (*L.P.*, xii (1), 491). The Leeches seem to be the most persistently intransigent of the commons leaders, persisting in this attitude right through the rebellion, and, in the case of William Leech, beyond it.

370 *L.P.*, xi, 971.

371 *Ibid.*

372 *Ibid.*, 694.

wind up the rebellion, and gave verisimilitude to their claim that the responsibility for it ought to be placed on the people. In the event, as has been seen, this was the version of events which was accepted, with the consequence that, although many of the commons were hanged, among the gentlemen the activist Thomas Moigne was the sole casualty.

IX

In 1536 there was little of the directness of approach and fixity of purpose to be found, for example, in the Lincolnshire rebellion of 1470 against Edward IV. Then the Willoughbies and Dymokes had summoned the Lincolnshire commons to muster at Ranby Hawe "to resist the Kyng in comyng down into the said shire, sayyng that his comyng there was to destroie the comons of the said shire . . . ".[373] Reginald Pole's attempt to posit a theory of limited obedience by reminding the English that in the past they had deposed tyrannical kings, and by pointing to Henry VIII's trust in evil councillors, his oppression of the nobility and people, and his disruption of Christendom as justifying resistance,[374] found only a few meagre echoes among the activists and popular leaders, and probably the very existence of the *Pro ecclesiasticae unitatis defensione* was unknown in Lincolnshire. As far as the gentlemen and shire magnates were concerned, there was on the contrary a shrinking away from the fact of dissidence, and a reluctance to admit that rebellion might be a legitimate expression for it. Hence the paradox of Hussey's position when he asserted that, while he would not be "against" the insurgents, neither would he be false to his prince; and the odd pattern of behaviour whereby the Lincolnshire gentlemen assumed the leadership of rebellion, but insisted they were not rebels since they were acting under coercion. Even in the ranks of the commons only a few were aware of themselves as rebels. Most thought they were the king's "trewe and faithfull subjects", their cause was "Gods and the Kings", and all the people "thought they had not offended the king".[375]

373 "Chronicle of the Rebellion in Lincolnshire" (cited above n. 298, this chapter), p. 6.

374 *Pro ecclesiasticae unitatis defensione*, 1555 edn, fo. 71 v. See W. G. Zeeveld, *Foundations of Tudor Policy* (Cambridge, Mass., 1948), pp. 105–8.

375 *L.P.*, xi, 534, 853; xii (1), 70 (xi).

For, whereas in 1470 the king's tenure of the throne had been uncertain, and a prince of the blood, Clarence, had been involved in the rebellion, no such state of affairs existed in 1536. Henry VIII's title was undisputed, and Pole's voice was drowned in the chorus of writings which extolled the obedience subjects owed their rightful king, as the only insurance against the horrors of "confusion" and civil war. Richard Morison struck the prevailing note in the expressive title of his pamphlet against the Lincolnshire rebels: *A Lamentacon in whiche is showed what Ruyne and destruction cometh of seditious rebellyon* as in its complement: *A remedye for sedition: wherein are conteyned many thinges concerninge the true and loyall obeisance that comens owe unto their prince and soveraygne lorde the Kynge*.[376] These were themes which had been, or soon would be, explored and driven home by authors as diverse as Dudley and Tyndale, Fox and Gardiner, Sampson, Elyot and Hall. The resulting climate of opinion both contributed to and resulted from what has been called "the chastened, indeed craven mood" of the governing class which had set in since Bosworth.[377] Nothing could be more remote, in such conditions, than resort to any neo-feudal form of protest, so that none even of the northern lords caught up in the Pilgrimage of Grace showed any sign of resorting to the *diffidatio* which the Percies had launched against Henry IV in 1403.[378] And in Lincolnshire Hussey was quick to repudiate any such attitudes when appeal was made to them; so that when one of the Sleaford insurgents expressed his desire "In faith my lord to take your part, and to live and die with you", Hussey called him "a naughty busy knave", and sent him away "amazed".[379]

In fact the problem which arose under the strong Tudor kingship with particular urgency was how dissidence might be expressed within a context of obedience, Parliament having still not established itself as an effective and sufficient vehicle for the expression of opposition and for the resolution of political conflict. The problem was not a wholly new one. The relevant precedents and parallels are, however, best looked for not in aristocratic movements like those of 1297 and 1311, but in the great popular protests

[376] Zeeveld, *op. cit.*, pp. 174–5.
[377] McFarlane, "The Wars of the Roses", *loc. cit.*, p. 119.
[378] According to Hardyng's *Chronicle*, ed. H. Ellis (London, 1812), pp. 352–3.
[379] *L.P.*, xi, 969.

against misgovernment of the late fourteenth and fifteenth centuries. The Peasants' Revolt and Cade's Rebellion particularly show many resemblances to the Lincolnshire movement and to the Pilgrimage of Grace. Thus both the peasants in 1381 and Cade's followers in 1450 protested their loyalty to the king, whose authority was not brought into question, but merely that of "evil councillors". Again in both revolts there are instances of gentlemen playing a role of leadership, some of them coerced into taking a forced oath; and in Cade's revolt the machinery of the musters was used to mobilize the popular forces, as in Lincolnshire in 1536. In both, too, there are traces of a collusion between discontented elements among the governing classes and the commons to overthrow an unpopular government, the "people" however being abandoned by their betters once this objective had been achieved and once the popular movement showed signs of getting out of hand. When this happened nobles, gentlemen and rich merchants rallied to the crown, and showed their loyalty by joining in the work of repression, with the plebeian leaders and their followers providing most of the victims of royal justice. And, as with the Lincolnshire rebellion, an official version of events developed which emphasized the character of both movements as spontaneous risings of "the brutish and ignorant commons" which their betters had joined only under compulsion.[380] But at the same time dissidence (that of the governing class as well as of their inferiors) had received expression, unpopular ministers had been removed by death or exile, and the complaints of subjects forced on the king's attention. Yet, because rebellious actions were wrapped up in mythicized interpretations or given special ritual forms (like the forced oath-takings), "obedience" was not in principle challenged and still provided a basis on which there could be a return to political and social normality.

In a society in which legitimacy, deference and continuity were as much stressed as in Tudor England, and in which change had the

[380] A. Réville and C. Petit-Dutaillis, *Le Soulèvement des Travailleurs d'Angleterre en 1381* (Paris, 1898); E. Powell, *The Rising in East Anglia, 1381* (Cambridge, 1896); B. Wilkinson, "The Peasants' Revolt of 1381", *Speculum*, xv (1940); Helen M. Lyle, *The Rebellion of Jack Cade* (Historical Assoc., 1950). For instances of coercion and forced oath-taking in the Peasants' Revolt see Réville, p. 102; in Cade's rebellion, see William Gregory's "Chronicle of London" in *Collections of a Citizen of London*, ed. J. Gairdner (Camden Soc., 1876), p. 190. For the use of the machinery of array in Cade's rebellion, see Michael Powicke, *Military Obligation in Medieval England* (Oxford, 1962), p. 219.

connotations of "decay", such myths and rituals played an important role in absorbing the harsh facts of political change and conflict into the society with a minimum of damage. Thomas More saw as much when, in his *Richard III*, he described how Buckingham, at Baynard's castle sometime in June 1484, entreated Richard to assume the throne, the latter putting up an elaborate show of reluctance. More noted that both parties behaved as though "neither had ever communed with other before", although in fact all knew that the scene had been prearranged. Yet this was to be excused because "all must be done in good order" and the fictions involved accepted in good faith, just as the spectators of a play must not challenge the conventions of the drama even though they all know that "he that playeth the sowdayne is percase a sowter". "And so . . . ", More concluded, "these matters be Kynges games, as it were stage playes, and for the moste parte played upon scaffoldes."[381] The passage is relevant to the appeal of the historical tragedies and chronicles of Shakespeare and his contemporaries. Moreover it was Henry VIII himself who called that sequel to the Lincolnshire rebellion, the Pilgrimage of Grace, "this tragedy",[382] a term which implied not, it is true, a stage play but a tale of how great men had fallen from high estate partly through the hostility of Fortune and partly because of their own corrupted wills. "Tragedy" in this sense brings us close to the commonplace in which men thought about rebellion and to the ways in which dissidence expressed itself.

In early Tudor England the most widely read collection of tragedies was *The Fall of Princes*[383] of the poet John Lydgate, a monk of Bury St Edmunds who had died about 1450.[384] He derived his *Fall* from Boccaccio's *De casibus virorum illustrium* which he had put into English verse from a French version,[385] but with additions and omissions of his own which to some extent altered the emphases of Boccaccio's work.[386] Although Lydgate's writings belong to the reigns of Henry V and Henry VI, *The Fall of Princes*

381 St Thomas More, *Works*, ii, ed. Sylvester, pp. 80–1.
382 *L.P.*, xii (2), 77.
383 Ed. H. Bergen, 4 vols. (Early English Text Soc., extra ser., cxxi–cxxiv, 1924–7).
384 See Walter F. Schirmer, *John Lydgate: A Study in the Culture of the Fifteenth Century*, trans by A. E. Keep (London, 1961), and A. Renoir, *The Poetry of John Lydgate* (London, 1967).
385 Of Laurence de Premierfait.
386 Bergen, *op. cit.*, pt i, intro.; Schirmer, *op. cit.*, ch. 21.

retained its popularity far into the Tudor period and beyond, being printed in 1494 and 1527 and again in 1554.[387] Nor did the monkish background of its author inhibit its repute amongst Protestants. On the contrary, *The Mirror for Magistrates*,[388] first published in 1559, in spite of its Calvinist tone (it was the work of a group of Puritan intellectuals), was in fact a continuation of *The Fall*, and aimed to bring it up to date by moralizing, in Lydgate's fashion, on a series of *exempla* taken from more recent history.[389]

The theme of the tragedies included in *The Fall* was the problem of political instability, as a result of which princes and great men were cast down from their high estate. How did this come about, and how could it be prevented? As much as any Tudor publicist Lydgate insisted that the foundation of stability was obedience: "virtue of virtue" as he calls it, without which "destroied were al worldlie policie".[390] Boccaccio, however, had maintained that, sooner or later, the failure of "worldly policie" became inevitable. For in the post-lapsarian world beneath the moon the corruption of men's nature exposed his polity to the vagaries of Fortune, the instrument of God's judgements. So, inevitably, Fortune's wheel cast down the pride of princes and raised the lowly.[391] Lydgate, however, would not consistently subscribe to Boccaccio's determinism.[392] For him the issue depended on the prince's own will. In so far as this conformed to virtue and God's law the latter could not

387 Bergen, *op. cit.*, pt iv, pp. 106–24.

388 Ed. Lily B. Campbell (Cambridge, 1938 and 1946).

389 *Ibid.*, intro.

390 *The Fall*, Bk. II, l. 533: "The comendacon of Bochas upon the vertu of obedience". Lydgate however greatly extended Boccaccio's "Obedientiae commendatio".

391 For Boccaccio's views in this respect see Willard Farnham, *The Medieval Heritage of Elizabethan Tragedy* (Berkeley, 1936), ch. 3.

392 Lydgate's retention of the figure of Fortune involved him in inconsistencies. See Schirmer, *op. cit.*, pp. 212–13: "In the prologue [to *The Fall*] we are told that it is not Fortune that brings about the fall of princes but 'vicious lyvyng', and that Fortune exercises no influence over virtuous princes. This shows the intellectual dilemma in which Lydgate found himself. It was expressed still more clearly in the detailed dispute between Fortune and Cheerful Poverty in Book III: on the one hand the entire world is portrayed as a fatalistic drama of the fickleness of Fortune and the transitoriness of earthly glory: on the other hand history is seen as a manifestation in this world of divine justice. Lydgate fails to extricate himself from the toils of this contradiction." Nevertheless "no medieval narrator of tragedy did so much as Lydgate to make tragedy show retribution for sin" (Farnham, *op. cit.*, p. 170).

be subjected to Fortune's rule. Thus the great of this world were reminded that virtue must belong to dignity and was the sole guarantor of the ruler's "worldlie prosperitie".[393] It was in fact princes who neglected virtue who exposed themselves to the fickleness of Fortune,[394] and this expressed itself in the irruption of turmoil into the state. That very turmoil, however, called for more than merely repressive action, necessary though this was, on the part of the wise prince. For such stirrings were in reality symptoms of his own failings, summoning him to correct the manner of his ruling.[395] From this point of view, however, dissent, even carried to the point of rebellion (abhorrent though this was), could, in a paradoxical way, result in something positive, conducing in fact to the prince's own preservation. As such, dissidence had its place in the very structure of "order". Or, as one of the authors of the *Mirror for Magistrates* was to put it:

> Yet this I note concernynge rebelles and rebellyouns, although the deuyll raise them, yet God alwıays useth them to his glory, as a parte of his Justice. For whan Kyngs . . . suffer theyr under officers to mysuse theyr subiectes, and will not heare nor remedy theyr peoples wrongs whan they complayne, than suffereth God the Rebell to rage, and to execute that parte of his Iustice that the parcyall prince would not.[396]

Thus the complaints of the Lincolnshire men against the misgovernment of the king's unworthy councillors were an appeal to Henry VIII to mend his ways, and one which he could neglect only at his peril.

Lydgate's book provided a lively and varied catalogue of the specific failings which had occasioned the fall of princes. Lechery, insobriety, sloth, cruelty, robbery and false counsel are only a small

[393] *The Fall*, Bk IX, ll. 3541–8.
[394] *Ibid.*, ll. 3520–40.
[395] Lydgate insisted that the prince's subjects would treat him as he treated them, as e.g. in Bk I, ll. 995–1001:

> And noble Pryncis, which han the sovereyntie
> To govern the people in rihtwisnesse,
> Lik as ye cherisshe hem in pes and unyte
> Or Frowardli destroie hem or oppresse,
> So ageynward ther corages thei will dresse
> Lowli tobeie to your magnyficence,
> Or disobeie by disobedience.

[396] *A Mirror for Magistrates*, ed. Campbell, p. 178.

selection from the list. The theme of "oppression" and "tyranny", however, was one in which he took a lively interest, and it recurs again and again in *The Fall*.[397] The poet never condones rebellion, even against a tyrant; his point is rather that princes who oppressed invited the spontaneous and unthinking reaction of resistance on the part of "the people" or (as he otherwise calls them) "the poraile", that is the poor.[398] Lydgate, however, depicts the people not only as the collective victims of princely oppression, but also as an essentially blind and irrational social force, whose action when it irrupted into the political field was as fickle and incomprehensible as that of Fortune herself. For the poet, "the people" was an elemental power and alien to all "polity". For the essence of polity was reason, whereas the people followed, not truth, but "opynioun", and so could pursue no consistent political course, but were turned upside-down by every wind.[399] Their alienation from reason and so from ordered political life manifested itself clearly, Lydgate thought, when through princely misgovernment plebeians rose to exercise governance. For such were invariably tyrants, and there was "nothyng more cruel, not nothyng more vengable / Than when a beggar hath dominacioun". "Boors" were always cruel, following their churlish natures.[400] It followed, however, that when the people rose in their blind violence, although "order" required that they be beaten into obedience and their leaders punished, yet the responsibility did not lie on them since they were incapable of political choice; still less did it fall on their betters whom they compelled to join them. Once again plebeian disorders pointed to the failings of the prince, whose misrule had raised a plebeian underworld to overwhelm polity.[401]

Is it not likely then that such concepts, widely disseminated among the governing class[402] by Lydgate's vivid narratives, should

[397] E.g. Bk I, ll. 995–1001; Bk II, ll. 904–10, 1422–8; Bk IV, ll. 757–63; Bk VII, ll. 270–7; Bk IX, ll. 2041–8.

[398] *Ibid.*

[399] Bk III, ll. 4229–35; Bk IV, ll. 624–30.

[400] Bk IV, ll. 2654–60, 2955–61; Bk V, ll. 2369–75.

[401] Bk II, ll. 1457–63.

[402] That *The Fall of Princes* was not unknown in Lincolnshire appears from one of the MSS. (Corpus Christi College, Oxford MS. 242) bearing the names of two members of two Lincolnshire families, the Crathornes of Saltfleetby and the Lovedays of Bardney, with the inscription "Edwarde dymmoke yer a starke knave", but whether the "knave" was the rebellious sheriff of 1536 cannot be said. The past ownership of surviving MSS. suggests that the work circulated

form the framework of ideas on which dissident movements tended to model themselves? For if rebellions assumed the form of risings of the people, with their betters remaining within the context of obedience and taking part only under compulsion, then the fiction could establish itself that the element of willed intention in these outbreaks had been minimal. As a result the area of reprisals which could be taken against the governing class became restricted, and the damage which could result from the expression of dissidence was kept within limits, being mainly inflicted on the plebeians. Hussey at any rate seems to have thought along these lines, if we are to credit his conversation in September 1534 with Chapuys the emperor's ambassador,[403] in which (according to Chapuys) he sought imperial support for a movement against Henry VIII. This was to be popular, and was to arise out of "the indignation of the people", who would "then" be joined by the nobility and clergy. Hussey's friend Lord Darcy placed a similar emphasis, in his own communications with Chapuys, on "the poor oppressed people" who would be comforted by the emperor's intervention, and asserted his intention to "animate the people" against the religious innovations.[404] Thus the initiative would be made to arise outside the political community of lords, gentry and upper clergy, and would manifest itself as a spontaneous plebeian reaction to royal misrule. It was to this model, as has been seen, that the Lincolnshire movement, with the coercion to which the gentlemen were subjected, in general conformed.

One consequence however of expressing dissidence, but within a context of obedience, was that everything depended on "countenance" from above, and any initiative from below was at a discount. Hussey gave in when no word came from the king, and when his

widely particularly amongst the northern aristocracy, and was known in the early sixteenth century in the circles of the earls of Rutland, Cumberland, Westmorland, and Northumberland, and the Lords Lumley, as well as of the Lords Dacre of the South and Dudley (Ed. Bergen, pt. v, "Descriptions of the Manuscripts"). Dr A. I. Doyle of Durham University Library informs me that copies were also owned by Lord Monteagle at Hornby castle in 1532, by Gerald ninth earl of Kildare, and by Lady Margaret Beaufort. An instance of the way in which *The Fall* could be given a contemporary political application is provided by an inscription in MS. Harley 4197, opposite Bk I, ll. 4019–60 (Envoy on the Vice of Tyranny): "Kardinall Wolsey yoused this theame to the Duke of Suffolk when he was in the kinges displeasure' (Ed. Burgen, pt. 4, p. 55).

403 *L.P.*, vii, 1206. 404 *Ibid.*

overtures to Shrewsbury failed. The gentlemen surrendered when they were abandoned by Hussey, and despaired of royal favour. The organizers and popular leaders had no choice but to submit to punishment once the support of their betters was withdrawn. Groups and individuals were confined in a straight-jacket whose nature is suggested by the ideas discussed above. Perhaps dissident religion, whether the radical Catholicism or the militant Puritanism of a later age, was the only force which might have broken the framework, but with the probable consequence of unleashing civil war. Even so, however, it would be unwise to write off this mode of expressing dissidence, for the Lincolnshire rebellion and its sequel the Pilgrimage of Grace were not the total failures they are sometimes represented to be. Some of the larger objectives were certainly not attained, since the old religion and the monasteries were not saved; and with the commons it was the clergy who suffered most for the part they had played in it. But Cromwell survived only for another four years, and the image of the plebeian tyrant which Lincolnshire rebels and the Pilgrimage of Grace had projected on to the minister in 1536 stuck, preparing the way for the king's sacrifice of him in 1540. In that same year too the king abandoned the Statute of Uses, much of which was repealed in 1540 by the Statute of Wills.[405] And in 1543 Mary was restored by Act of Parliament to a place in the succession to the throne after Edward and his issue.[406]

Nor was nothing done to remedy the private grievances which had incensed the Lincolnshire landed establishment against the government. The Willoughbies could scarcely complain when, within a decade of the rebellion, Sir Christopher's heir William Willoughby, late captain-general of the commons, had been raised to the peerage as Lord Willoughby of Parham.[407] And within the same period Edward Dymoke, the sheriff who had presided at the murder of Dr Raynes, was granted the office of treasurer of Boulogne which his father had held.[408] Both families too were reconciled to the intrusive Elizabeth Blount. The latter inevitably retained the Tailboys manors granted her for life, but one of her daughters (by the first Clinton earl of Lincoln) married Edward Dymoke's heir,

[405] Cf. "The Genesis of the Statute of Uses", pp. 696–7.
[406] Succession Act, 1543 (35 Henry VIII, c. i; *Statutes of the Realm*, iii, p. 955).
[407] *Complete Peerage*, xii (2), p. 701.
[408] *L.P.*, xii (2), 22.

and another (by the same marriage) became the wife of the second Lord Willoughby of Parham.[409] The duchess of Suffolk's quarrel with her Willoughby relatives persisted longer, but here too a settlement was reached soon after Elizabeth's accession.[410]

Otherwise the Lincolnshire gentlemen must have been gratified at their relative immunity from reprisals. The king insisted on his victims, but only two prominent laymen, Moigne and Hussey, suffered. So, apart from the disappearance of the monasteries, few of the Lincolnshire continuities were broken by the events of 1536. Of the other active "stirrers" of rebellion, Robert Dighton soon became notable for his dealings in monastic lands, as did Robert Carr of Sleaford.[411] Thomas Dymoke became sheriff in 1542,[412] and, while Vincent Grantham turned increasingly to his acquisitive farming and land-grabbing, his son Thomas succeeded him as M.P. for Lincoln and mayor.[413] Of the older families, the Skipwiths and Tyrwhitts also profited from the dissolution, although no doubt there must have been envy in such quarters of the much vaster accumulations of monastic estates acquired by the Lincolnshire courtier dynasties, the Brandons and Clintons.[414] The rebellion made no difference in the standing of these families with the king. Sir William Skipwith's heir served Henry VIII with distinction in the Scottish wars, as well as representing Lincolnshire in Parliament,[415] and Sir Robert Tyrwhitt the younger made a career as a knight of the body and courtier.[416] One of Sir William Ayscough's sons became a member of Cranmer's household and a zealous Protestant and one of his daughters a Protestant martyr.[417] Even the Moignes and Husseys were able to save something from the catastrophe which had overwhelmed them;[418] and, more remarkably, the

409 *Lincolnshire Pedigrees*, iii, p. 1008; iv, p. 1206; *Complete Peerage*, xii (2), p. 703.

410 In June, 1561. Linc. Rec. Off., Anc. MS., 4 n. and o., being the articles of an award made after arbitration between the two parties.

411 See above, pp. 213–14, 222.

412 *Lincolnshire Pedigrees*, iv, p. 1203.

413 *Ibid.*, ii, p. 422.

414 Hodgett, "Dissolution of the Religious Houses".

415 *Lincolnshire Pedigrees*, iii, p. 895.

416 In 1542, as "the king's servant", he received a large grant of monastic lands: *L.P.*, xvii, 714 (15).

417 *Lincolnshire Pedigrees*, i, p. 61. His heir Sir Francis duly succeeded him at Stallingborough and was three times sheriff.

418 Moigne's brother Simon was made bailiff of the family estate at North Willingham forfeited by Thomas. The Moignes survived as small gentry, and pro-

plebeian Leeches survived as substantial yeomen in Belchford and Fulletby in spite of the execution of the three brothers Nicholas, Robert and William.[419] Soon, among the gentry, the very memory of the rebellion was buried. In more plebeian quarters as late as 1542 it was recalled how Lincolnshire had risen in "one general commotion for maintaining of Christs Faith, Holy Church, honor of our native crown, realm, nobility and commonwealth", and the consequence "our brethren and friends crewelly distrowed and disherced".[420] But such voices invited the attention only of the gaoler and hangman and soon they too were silent.

duced a bishop of Kilmore in the early seventeenth century (*Lincolnshire Pedigrees*, ii, p. 679). Lord Hussey's son by his first marriage, Sir William, founded a landed family at Beauvall, Notts.; Sir Giles, his eldest son by his second marriage, did the same at Caythorpe, Lincs. His two elder daughters made great matches, Elizabeth to Lord Hungerford, and Bridget first to the earl of Rutland, and then to the earl of Bedford. See *Lincolnshire Pedigrees*, ii, p. 527.

419 *Lincolnshire Pedigrees*, ii, p. 593.

420 *L.P.*, xvii (1), 26 (5). Of the leaders of the rebellion, twelve were executed at London on 27 March 1537, and of these five were priests, including the abbot of Barlings and the vicar of Louth (Camden Soc., new ser., London, 1875, xi, *Wriothesley's Chronicle*, i, p. 62; *L.P.*, xii (2), 181). Thomas Moigne, the solitary victim from the ranks of the gentry, was executed at Lincoln on 7 March, together with Guy Kyme and the abbot of Kirkstead (*L.P.*, xii (1), 590). On 8 and 9 March thirty-one condemned rebels were executed at Louth and Horncastle, of whom fourteen were monks, six parish priests and the rest commons (*L.P.*, *ibid.*, and 581; Hughes, *The Reformation in England*, i, p. 318, n. 3). Hussey was executed at Lincoln sometime in July (*Wriothesley's Chronicle*, i, p. 63). Thus there were fifty-seven victims in all, the overwhelming majority commons and clergy.

7. *The concept of order and the Northern Rising, 1569*

I

"The whole world", wrote Hooker, "consisting of parts so many, so different, is by this only thing upheld; he which framed them hath set them in order."[1] Thomas Starkey was one of the many theorists who translated the implications of an ordered creation into terms of policy and governance. More than a generation before Hooker he had pointed to "the good order and policy by good laws stablished and kept, and by heads and rulers put in effect; by which the whole body, as by reason, is governed and ruled . . . ".[2] The concept of order is often taken for granted as Tudor commonplace, written into the basic attitudes of the age.[3] Yet it was not until relatively late in the sixteenth century, when the gentry sought access in increasing numbers to the new humanist education disseminated by the grammar-school foundations and in the universities, that a style of thinking previously restricted to metropolitan and university circles of clerical and lawyer intellectuals became increasingly the common possession of the whole governing class.[4] Implicit in the concept of order was the tradition, primarily of Aristotelian rationalism, in

[1] *Of the Laws of Ecclesiastical Polity*, VIII. ii. 2.

[2] Thomas Starkey, *A Dialogue between Cardinal Pole and Thomas Lupset*, ed. J. W. Cowper (Early English Text Soc., extra ser., xxxii, 1878), p. 50.

[3] E. M. W. Tillyard, *The Elizabethan World Picture* (London, 1943), *passim*; W. H. Greenleaf, *Order, Empiricism and Politics 1500–1700* (Oxford, 1964), pp. 14 ff.; Christopher Morris, *Political Thought in England, Tyndale to Hooker* (London, 1965), pp. 68 ff.; E. W. Talbert, *The Problem of Order* (Chapel Hill, 1962), pp. 1–117.

[4] Joan Simon, *Education and Society in Tudor England* (Cambridge, 1966), pp. 291 ff.; J. H. Hexter, "The Education of the Aristocracy in the Renaissance", *Jl Mod. Hist.*, xxii (1950), pp. 1–20; M. H. Curtis, *Oxford and Cambridge in Transition, 1558–1642* (Oxford, 1959), pp. 54 ff.; Lawrence Stone, "The Educational Revolution in England, 1560–1640", *Past and Present*, xxviii (July 1964), pp. 41–80.

terms of which generalized propositions could be stated, and a discourse sustained which could claim universal validity. Thus the idea of a natural, social and political "order" became possible, with a single integrated structure and common texture throughout, in which the part found its point and purpose in a relationship to the whole.[5]

But before the political and social order had been widely thus conceived, a different kind of language had been current, in terms of which the gentry had been accustomed to articulate their sense of justice, duty, right and honour. This owed less to the systemized literary culture of school and university than to attitudes and concepts prevalent in the households of the greater landlords. Here, in the setting of the castles and greater manor houses of aristocratic and magnate lineages, communities of servants and dependent gentry gathered; petty "courts" unified by their common allegiance to the great family which dispensed the benefits of "good lordship" in return for proffered fidelity and obedience.[6] From one point of view the household mobilized and gave visible expression to the social influence and political power of its head; but from another, just as much as school and university, it was an educational institution.[7] Service in household initiated the sons of the gentry into the arts of war and chase, of manners and ceremony, which were the *raison d'être* of this way of life. The style of education provided is aptly summarized in the mid-fourteenth-century metrical romance *Ipomydon*, where the instructions of King Ermones for the upbringing of the young hero Ipomedon in his household are as follows:[8]

> Tholomew a clerk he toke
> That taught the chyld uppon the boke,
> Both to synge and to rede;

[5] R. Hoopes, *Right Reason and the English Renaissance* (Harvard, 1962), pp. 7–32, 73–85, 123 ff.

[6] See P. Van Brunt Jones, *The Household of a Tudor Nobleman* (Cedar Rapids, Iowa, 1918). For the Percy household under the fifth earl of Northumberland (1498–1527) see the *Northumberland Household Book*, ed. Thomas Percy (London, 1770, 1827). On "good lordship" and "faithfulness", see for these attitudes in a context of retaining, W. H. Dunham, *Lord Hastings' Indentured Retainers* (Trans. Connecticut Academy of Arts and Sciences, xxxix, New Haven, Sept. 1955, pp. 1–175), pp. 11–14, 18–20, 41–6, 50–5; and above, pp. 52 ff.

[7] For the household style of education, see F. J. Furnivall, *Education in Early England* (Early English Text Soc., ordinary ser., xxxii, 1868), pp. 6 ff.

[8] *Metrical Romances*, ed. H. Weber (Edinburgh, 1810), ll. 55 ff.

And after he taught him other dede:
Aftirward to serve in hall,
Bothe to grete and to smalle;
Before the kyng mete to kerve,
Hye and lowe feyre to serve;
Bothe of houndis and haukis game
After he taught hym, all and same,
In se, in field, and eke in ryvuere,
In wodde to chase the wild dere,
And in the feld to ryde a stede,
That all men had joy of his dede.

In *King Horn*, on the other hand, the musical aspects of the instruction given are more clearly indicated in the provision for the hero to learn "of harpe and songe".[9]

By the practice of these arts the values of the lineage culture received expression. But they were also transmitted through the literary genres of the tragic tale, romance and history. Thus, in the sophisticated setting of the royal household of Edward IV, the squires spent their time "talkynge of cronycles of Kings and other Polycyes", as well as in the practice of "actes martialles"; while the children of the household were taught languages as well as "curtesy", to ride, wear harness, to harp, pipe and sing.[10] In their literary manifestations, and above all in the romance and tragic history, the values of the lineage culture assumed a chivalric, and even a Christianized form. The royal court or baronial household was seen, as in Malory's *The Morte Darthur*, as a "fellowship" united in a dedicated communal quest of "worship" or honour, and in obedience and faithfulness to a lord.[11] Chivalric values, however, were liable to break down in the event of a conflict with the claims of lineage; for a man's honour was inseparable from that of his kin, with whom he shared the "blood" which conferred honourable

[9] In *The Middle English Metrical Romances*, ed. W. H. French and C. B. Hale (London, 1964), i, ll. 227 ff.

[10] *A Collection of Ordinances and Regulations for the Government of the Royal Household* (London, Society of Antiquaries, 1790), p. 45.

[11] See Sir Thomas Malory, *The Morte Darthur, Parts Seven and Eight*, ed. D. S. Brewer (York Medieval Texts, London, 1968), intro., pp. 25 ff. Cf. Elizabeth T. Pochoda, *Arthurian Propaganda: Le Morte Darthur as an Historical Ideal of Life* (Chapel Hill, 1971), particularly ch. 4.

status.[12] Malory made this conflict a prime theme of his great work, for the breach of chivalric fellowship between Gawain and Lancelot which opened the way to the fall of King Arthur and the Round Table, arose because Lancelot had slain, although only accidentally, Gawain's brother, so violating the blood of the latter's kin.[13] Chivalry may perhaps best be seen as the idealized image of itself which the lineage society projected, but which co-existed uneasily with its persistent competitiveness and assertiveness. It is probably its status as aspiration and ideal, rather than the rise of more "modern" attitudes, that accounts for the recurring laments about the decay of chivalric values, like those of Caxton at the beginning of the reign of Henry VII.[14]

The literary manifestations of lineage values, and the cult of chivalry, show that the lineage culture had its own kind of sophistication.[15] Nevertheless the contrast with the professionally intellectual and university setting in which the concept of order flourished, remains. In the lineage society the approach was personal and particularized; the validity of the modes of acceptable behaviour, based on the code of honour, being taken for granted within the restricted world to which alone they had relevance: that of the specific household community and its related clientele. The thinking of this society, unlike that of the dominant scholastic culture, was less philosophical and discursive than mythological, expressed in terms of exemplary myth and tale. Thus in *The Boke of St Albans* (1486),[16] the existence of a society of superiors and dependants is explained simply in terms of the story of the subordination of the descendants

[12] For the English traditional usage whereby "blood" is seen not only as the vital fluid and supposed seat of the emotions, but also as the shared identical inheritance of members of the same family and race, distinguishing them from other such families and races, see *The New English Dictionary on Historical Principles*, ed. J. A. H. Murray *et al.* (Oxford, 1888–1933). See also the article "Honor", by Julian Pitt-Rivers in *The International Encyclopaedia of the Social Sciences* (New York, 1968), vi, pp. 503–11, particularly pp. 505, 506.

[13] Malory, Book XX, ed. Brewer, pp. 113 ff.; cf. Brewer, *op. cit.*, intro., p. 20: in his attitude to Lancelot, Gawain is depicted "as angry and vengeful, inspired not only by love of Gareth, but by the spirit of ancient family feud".

[14] Arthur B. Ferguson, *The Indian Summer of English Chivalry* (Durham, N.C., 1960), pp. 34 ff.

[15] Particularly apparent in the intellectualized form given chivalric values in such works as Hay's (1456) and Caxton's (1486) translations of Ramón Lull under the title of *The Ordre of Chivalry*, or Stephen Hawes's *The Pastime of Pleasure* (1509; S.T.C. 12948).

[16] Ed. W. Blades (London, 1881).

of Cain to those of Seth, and by Noah's curse on his son Ham, who with his line was thus deprived of his inherited gentle status. There is little sense of any generalized order, beyond the common texture assumed by the relationships of dependence, alliance, or competitiveness in which the lineage was involved with others of its own kind, articulated in terms of the code of honour. With this there went an awareness of an overriding divine Fatum or Fortuna, Christianized in terms of a God whose judgements overthrew the wicked, but preserved the good.[17] In addition to honour and shame, the whole outlook crystallized around such terms as blood and lordship, faithfulness and service.[18] In this setting polity was lordship. "With divers stones and one cement building is raised", wrote Lord Berners in the reign of Henry VIII " . . . and of divers men and one lord is composed a common wealth."[19]

In the earlier sixteenth century, conditions in northern England provided particularly favourable soil for a flourishing lineage culture. Here many countrysides were overlain by great honorial estates,[20] ruled by Percies, Nevilles, Cliffords or Dacres, great families admired for their "ancient blood", and tough enduring persistency. Even the influence of the crown was often encountered primarily as that of a great landlord, as duke of York or duke of Lancaster.[21] The many mesne tenancies by knight service characteristic of such estates were one factor which, by creating bonds of service and office between the gentry families and the great houses, made the leadership of the latter natural and unquestioned. In this context personalized ties were decisive in the relationship between lord and client or tenant.[22] Dependants proffered their "faithful" service; while lordship was or should be "good lordship", involving restraint in the claims made on inferiors, and the provision of

[17] For the cult of Fortune in the circle of the fifth earl of Northumberland, see above, pp. 83 ff.; for some of its wider social and political implications, see above, pp. 261 ff.

[18] For these terms and the interconnection between them, see Julian Pitt-Rivers, *op. cit.* and the references there given. Cf. the same writer's "Honour and Social Status", in J. G. Peristiany (ed.), *Honour and Shame: The Values of Mediterranean Society* (London, 1965), pp. 21–39.

[19] *The Golden Boke of Marcus Aurelius*, trans. by Lord Berners (London, 1535; S.T.C. 12436), p. 28^{v}.

[20] For the role of these in the society of the West Riding, see R. B. Smith, *Land and Politics in the Reign of Henry VIII: The West Riding of Yorkshire, 1530–46* (Oxford, 1970), pp. 43–6, 133–44, 257.

[21] *Ibid.*, pp. 139, 257.

[22] See above, pp. 148 ff.

"favours" and maintenance in return for service.[23] Defined contractual relationships based on law played by comparison a secondary role. In the case of the humbler tenants they were often lacking, for until well into the sixteenth century a common tenure on northern estates was the tenancy at will.[24] Otherwise, in practice, contracts between lord and tenant were only enforceable within the context of the code of good lordship. For seigneurial courts paid heed to the latter as well as to the legal aspects of the situation; and the plaintiff who had lost the favour of his lord knew his cause was lost, unless he was bold and wealthy enough to appeal to the courts at York and London.[25] It was the sense of absolute dependence involved in "faithfulness" which was the approved and dominant attitude on the part of inferiors in these estate communities, however qualified this might be in practice by "good lordship· "He that gives all may take all", wrote an officer of the earl of Northumberland to his master as late as the reign of James I.[26]

The values of lineage, good lordship and fidelity, with the contrast between them and those involved in the concept of order, emerge clearly enough from the unsophisticated writings of Richard Atkinson, a follower of the Border baronial family of Dacre; and particularly from the "Advice" which he tendered in 1569 to Leonard Dacre, heir male to the family title and estates.[27] This was occasioned by the family quarrel arising in that year as a result of the death of George, Lord Dacre.[28] For now the claims of the latter's three sisters, as heirs general, to the family inheritance were confronted by those of the heir male. But the Dacre sisters were the daughters-in-law of the court magnate and oppositionist politician Thomas Howard, duke of Norfolk, whose ward Lord Dacre had been. Thus the quarrel became one between the duke and Leonard

[23] See n. 6 above, this chapter.

[24] See below, pp. 285 ff. Cf. E. Kerridge, *Agrarian Problems in the Sixteenth Century and After* (London, 1969), pp. 45–6, 58–9, 97.

[25] R. R. Reid, *The King's Council in the North* (London, 1921), pp. 7 ff.; see also above, pp. 48 ff. and pp. 153 ff. Cf. below, pp. 295 ff. Cf. R. L. Storey, *The Earl of the House of Lancaster* (London, 1966), p. 118.

[26] Syon House MS. Q I 12.

[27] Public Record Office, SP15/18, fo. 37; *Cal. State Papers, Domestic, Addenda, 1566–79*, p. 255.

[28] See N. Williams, *Thomas Howard Fourth Duke of Norfolk* (London, 1964), pp. 116 ff.; *Complete Peerage*, revised edn, ed. Vicary Gibbs *et al.* (London, 1910–59), iv, pp. 23 ff.

Dacre, the issue being whether the inheritance was to remain in the Dacre "name" and "blood", or pass to heiresses who would carry it to the descendants of their Howard husbands. The setting therefore was one of tension and crisis, accentuated by the outbreak in November of the Northern Rising, which Dacre was expected to join.[29] This probably contributed to the frankness, cogency and sharpness with which Atkinson stated the values of lineage, still powerfully present in the remote Border community to which he belonged. These appear in clear focus from the assumptions and arguments used to support the courses of action he urged on the man whom he regarded as the head of the house of Dacre.

The lineage society gave primacy to the sense of "blood" as the vehicle of the collective family genius and virtue, bringing these out of the past and carrying them into the future; its representative being the heir male, to whom the whole family owed loyalty as its head.[30] The wider significance of the persistence of the "blood" (usually coupled with the "name"), however, lay in its role as guarantee of the stability of the estate community; for it was thought that this would be threatened by the unjust disinheritance of the "true blood", and the intrusion of alien landlords. "The poor people", wrote Atkinson, " . . . favour you and your house, and cry and call for you and your blood to rule them."[31] There was little sense of any loyalties which overrode those imposed by the intense and particularized world of the lineage. The preservation of the line, on which this whole world rested, had an absolute priority, to be defended even at the cost of life itself. Inevitably loyalty to the crown, in spite of the deference with which the royal authority was approached, went by the board in the event of a conflict with the

[29] Sir C. Sharp, *Memorials of the Rebellion of 1569* (London, 1840), p. 211.

[30] Cf. Pitt-Rivers, "Honor", p. 505: "Since honor is felt as well as demonstrated, it is allied to the conception of the self in the most intimate ways . . . Honor is inherited through the 'blood', and the shedding of blood has a specifically honorific value in transactions of honor . . ." For the persistence of the idea in a modern Greek pastoral community, the Sarakatsani, see J. K. Campbell, *Honour, Family and Patronage* (Oxford, 1964), p. 185: "The solidarity of the corporate family is symbolized by the idea of blood . . . Relationships in the family are a participation in this common blood." The concept has a long history: see R. B. Onians, *Origins of European Thought* (London, 1951 edn), pp. 48, 121.

[31] Public Record Office, SP15/18 fo. 41; *Cal. State Papers, Domestic, Addenda, 1566–79*, p. 257. Cf. above, pp. 176–7.

interests of the lineage.[32] If the latter were brought into question there was no alternative to resistance even to the queen, to be sustained if necessary to the point of death. Dacre's brother Edward, so Richard Atkinson asserted, was willing "to suffre deathe paycently . . . so that . . . you and your blode in name might contenewe with your ancestors' levyinge".[33] It was Edward Dacre who had urged the head of the family, in January 1570, "In noo cayse be persuadyd by the fayre words of the Quene your mystresse, to yeeld to hyr desyres", and to "Gyt by every meane possible of money as you can . . . and furnysh the house with artillery, and sure men to keep the same in saffety."[34] Atkinson preferred deception to force, and advised Dacre to promise to take and send up the rebel Edward, "This shall plese the Quene . . . and never come to pass . . . it is but words spokyn." But for him, too, in the last resort the lineage world was to be defended to the death. The advice he tendered was "fly never but for advantage; better dye in honour than leve with shame". The words were unlikely to have been meant to apply solely to "the service of your Prynce", although circumstances made this careful qualification advisable.[35]

Other characteristic comments emerge from Atkinson's observations. The fortune of lineages was subject to an overriding divine providence; hence it was wise to "see that ye never miss to serve God at all times".[36] Greed for the wealth of the Dacres had made the duke of Norfolk forget God, and so brought about his downfall. For the same reason, although there would be no harm in doubling Dacre rents and fines, which were behind those of other landlords, tenants should not be oppressed, lest God be offended. Hence com-

[32] On the conflicts liable to arise between personal honour and legally constituted authority, see Pitt-Rivers, "Honor", p. 509; but personal honour was inseparable from the maintenance of the line, for "The family is the repository of personal honor, not merely in its aspect of social status, but also with regard to the moral qualities which attach to it" (*ibid.*, p. 506).

[33] Public Record Office, SP15/18, fo. 39ᵛ; *Cal. State Papers, Domestic, Addenda, 1566–79*, p. 256.

[34] Public Record Office, SP15/18, fo. 34ᵛ; *Cal. State Papers, Domestic, Addenda, 1566–79*, p. 254.

[35] *Ibid.*, fos. 38, 43; *ibid.*, p. 255.

[36] *Ibid.*, fo. 37; *ibid.*, p. 255. Cf. "Warnings and Counsels for Noblemen" (1577) in Early English Text Soc., extra ser., viii (1869), ed. F. J. Furnivall *et al.*, p. 74: "Do good whiles yow have power thereunto, and do hurte yow maie; for the teares of the offended, and the complaints of the greved, maye on day have place in the sight of God, to move him to chastise yow . . . "

plaints against unjust officers should be encouraged. The way of life of the great household, and the hospitality which was its bond, was extolled; for it was by his generous housekeeping that the fourth Lord Dacre had won praise and a following. Dacre, as head of his house, must always ride with a retinue of liveried retainers, but these should be "orderly", disciplined by the arts of hawking and the chase. Gambling was to be discouraged, as making for quarrelsomeness and disunity.[37]

It cannot be doubted that these values and the way of life based on them had their own validity in the Dacre context. But they were remote from those of the professional intelligentsia, clerical and lay. We know what would have been the comment of the humanist Starkey on the ordered stateliness of the Dacre household, so appropriate to the great lineage it served: " . . . look what an idle rout our nobles keep and nourish in their houses, which do nothing else but carry dishes to the table, and eat them when they have done; and after give themselves to hunting, hawking, dicing, carding, and all other idle pastimes and vain".[38] Similarly the Puritan Laurence Humphrey: "Nor place I the honour of Nobilytie in . . . hawkynge, huntynge, pastimes . . . traynes of horses and servauntes . . . or great lyne." For Puritan, as for humanist, true nobility was not that of lineage, but had "virtue" as its "surest sign and token". "Renown and fame of auncestry" was valid only when coupled with "Chrystian and farre spred vertue".[39]

II

The ambience in which we encounter George Clarkson is very similar to that of Richard Atkinson; Clarkson too belonged to the following of a powerful northern lineage, being an officer of the Percy estates in Northumberland. A deputy steward to the seventh earl of Northumberland, he lived to see his master executed at York, an attainted rebel who had been one of the leaders of the ill-fated Northern Rising of 1569.[40] His writings now to be considered

[37] Public Record Office, SP15/18, fos. 37, 37ᵛ, 38; *Cal. State Papers, Domestic, Addenda, 1566–79*, p. 255.

[38] Starkey, *Dialogue*, p. 77.

[39] Laurence Humphrey, *The Nobles, or of Nobilitye* (1563; S.T.C. 13964) sig. a. ivᵛ.

[40] While nothing is known of the background of Richard Atkinson, that of Clarkson is clear enough. He was a burgess of the Percy mesne borough of Alnwick, the son

were a draft survey of the manors he administered,[41] which, though in form different from those of Atkinson, resemble them in purpose. For the notes and remarks which Clarkson appended to his survey have the character of exhortation and advice addressed to the earl of Northumberland, just as those of Atkinson were directed to Leonard Dacre. Both men wrote more or less at the same time, the greater part of Clarkson's survey being in progress in 1567.[42] From its pages a picture emerges, presented with greater detail than Atkinson was concerned to provide, of an estate community which was shortly to traverse the crisis of a great rebellion; of Clarkson's own attitudes to the political issues of his day, his views on the nature of the estate community to which he belonged, on landlord–tenant relations, and on the nature and role of seigneurial authority. All this against the background of the impressive Percy inheritance which he served: the half-dozen baronies and lordships comprising nearly forty townships, the great castles at Alnwick and Warkworth, the £1,100 rental levied on a tenantry nearly two thousand strong. The earl of Northumberland was the head of the most powerful lineage in the north, and the great estate in Northumberland formed only a part of the family possessions. There were equally extensive lands in Yorkshire, Cumberland and Sussex.[43]

What is interesting about Clarkson's writings is that in them we find an attempt to articulate the social world to which he belonged,

of a merchant of that place of the same name, who had been a lessee of land and tithes from Alnwick abbey, and of a small coal mine from the earl of Northumberland (Alnwick Castle MS. A. I 1d, Clarkson's Survey, Survey of Bilton; G. Tate, *History of Alnwick* (Alnwick, 1868–9), ii, p. 26). The surveyor, with Richard Clarkson, probably his brother, held several tenements in Alnwick lately belonging to Alnwick abbey (Alnwick Castle MS. A I 1a, Survey of Alnwick) and the latter in 1562 leased from the earl the manor of Alnmouth (*Estate Accounts of the Earls of Northumberland*, ed. M. E. James, Surtees Soc., clxiii, Durham and London, 1955, p. 49). In 1562 the surveyor was steward of Alnwick, Warkworth and Rothbury lordships, and one of the earl's commissioners of survey (*ibid.*, pp. 42, 50). The family had Newcastle connections, Richard Clarkson, son of George, being admitted to the Merchant Adventurers' Company there in 1546: *Extracts from the Records of the Merchant Adventurers of Newcastle-upon-Tyne*, ii, ed. F. W. Dendy (Surtees Soc., ci, 1899), p. 199.

41 Alnwick Castle MS. A I 1a–r.

42 *Ibid.*, A I 1c.

43 For a list of Percy possessions see *Estate Accounts of the Earls of Northumberland*, pp. xi–xii; the rental of the lands in Northumberland in 1582 was £1,148 (Syon House MS. A I 8); in the 1530s the tenants and their families amounted to 1,967 "able" men, i.e. equipped for Border service.

not in the personalized categories of good lordship, faithfulness and service characteristic of a lineage society; but rather in generalized, legalistic and philosophic terms, which also had moral and contractual implications by which even authority, including that of lordship, was bound. Clarkson presents himself in fact as in the succession of the Tudor theorists of order, returning again and again to the theme of "the olde auncyente order" to which the Percy estate community ought to be conformed: the "good rule and order" in accordance with which authority ought to comport itself, and the "good order" which court procedures should reflect. The "order" he had in mind owed much to the common law, and something also to the Aristotelian and neo-Platonic tradition, lately restated in Christian terms and refurbished by such humanist writers as Elyot and Starkey. The point of view is well expressed, in terms which Clarkson would have recognized, by the quotation from Starkey's *Dialogue* given above, with its continuation stating that the end of reason and order is "to the intent this . . . whole commonalty . . . may worship God . . . every one doing his duty to other with brotherly love . . . as members and parts of one body";[44] phrases which closely echo Clarkson's own. A favourite term used by the latter however is the word "frame", used to imply (in the same way as "the frame of things" or "nature's frame" could be spoken of[45]) that society had the quality of structure. As such the social framework formed an integral part of the total natural order, the "authority" which gave the former shape and form being consequently also "natural". Therefore, "it is most naturall and no lesse honorable that his Lordshipe [i.e. the earl of Northumberland] should have the government and rule under the Prince here in this countrie of Northumberland".[46] The qualification "under the Prince" related the estate community to the larger polity of the kingdom.

There is, of course, nothing original about such ideas, which had long been a part of the university and clerical culture, as of its secular common-law counterpart. What is new is that they should be found in this remote context, and that an official of modest social

44 *Loc. cit.* n. 2 above, this chapter.

45 Cf. Shakespeare, *Much Ado*, IV.i.130: "Griev'd I, I had but one? / Chid I, for that at frugal Natures frame?"; *Macbeth*, III.ii.16: "But let the frame of things dis-ioynt / Both the worlds suffer."

46 Alnwick Castle MS. A I 1b.

status and restricted background, in the rough and warlike environment of the Marches towards Scotland, should have been able to use them to give his experience a new dimension of expressiveness. Moreover, while Clarkson was aware of the importance of education (he took a prominent part in a petition of the burgesses of Alnwick to the earl of Northumberland for the foundation of a grammar school in their town[47]), all the indications are that he had no formal schooling himself. There is no evidence that he attended either the Inns of Court or one of the universities. He could in fact have picked up the characteristic concepts used in his survey from Christopher St German's popular legal textbook *Dialogues between a Doctor of Divinity and a Student of the Lawes of England*.[48] Some acquaintance with the law must at any rate have been required in the post which Clarkson held in 1562, when he was acting as steward of the Percy lordships of Alnwick, Warkworth and Rothbury, and as a commissioner of survey.[49] By then he was already one of the leading Percy men of business in Northumberland.

The few other facts available about Clarkson's life suggest his prominent role in the defence of Percy interests in Northumberland in the 1560s, when the earl was out of favour, and his tenants and officers subjected to a good deal of pressure and provocation on the part of the agents of the Elizabethan régime in the East and Middle Marches. Thus in 1562 Clarkson was imprisoned at Berwick by Lord Grey of Wilton,[50] the earl's enemy and his successor as warden of the East March; and a vivid letter has survived from his hand of May 1569, describing a fray in which he had been involved with the bitterest of all his master's enemies, Sir John Forster.[51] His role in the rebellion of 1569 is unknown, and he may have kept clear of it; but, when last mentioned, he held the subordinate office of clerk of courts, and this may imply that, with the Percy estates now in the

47 *Ibid.*; the "free school" was to be set up by royal charter, to be obtained by the earl's mediation, and was to be endowed with former chantry lands in Alnwick.

48 1543: S.T.C. 21570; originally published in two parts in 1530–1.

49 Above, n. 33, this chapter. For the importance of the class of provincial lawyer–estate administrators to which Clarkson belonged, see E. W. Ives, "The Common Lawyers in Pre-Reformation England", *Trans. Roy. Hist. Soc.*, 5th ser., xviii (1968), pp. 145 ff.

50 *Estate Accounts of the Earls of Northumberland*, pp. 46–7.

51 Robert Collingwood and George Clarkson to the seventh earl of Northumberland, 8 May 1569: Syon House MS. Q XI 1.

hands of the crown, he had fallen into disfavour.[52] Undoubtedly the pressure of politics sharpened Clarkson's sense of "order", which stood out in clear-cut relief by contrast with the same hostile forces which he had himself confronted on his master's behalf. The peril came from those who "sought their owne private gain and comodetye", who "would exalte and extolle their owne name and fame unto honour",[53] and whose ambition threatened therefore that "natural" authority which Clarkson's master the earl ought to exercise in his country.

It was in such terms that Clarkson forebodingly characterized the activities of the faction of Northumberland gentry which followed the lead of Sir John Forster, who since his appointment in 1560 as warden of the Middle March had been the principal agent of the government in the shire.[54] Forster, of a family which had originally been one of Percy tenants and dependants, had risen in the wake of his relative, the Henrician royal officer Thomas first Lord Wharton. The latter, in the course of his long and successful career as a Borderer, had at one time or other ruled all three of the northern Marches; Forster had served under him as a deputy.[55] Between Forster and his kin and the Percies there was a feud which went back to the days of the Pilgrimage of Grace,[56] with the two factions subsequently competing for control of the March offices. The Percies had their day during the years of the Marian régime, when the family earldom and estates were restored, and the seventh earl was made warden of the East and Middle Marches. Wharton was forced into retirement, followed by Forster and his friends.[57] But then followed the Elizabethan reversal when Forster himself took over the Middle March from his old enemy, and Northumberland was replaced in the East March first by Lord Grey of Wilton, then by the

[52] Public Record Office, E164/37, Hall and Humberstone's Survey: Survey of Alnwick.
[53] Alnwick Castle MS. A I 1b.
[54] *C.P.R., Eliz.*, i, p. 411.
[55] For a pedigree of the Forster family, see *The Northumberland County History*, i, by E. Bateson (Newcastle upon Tyne, 1893), p. 228.
[56] The events of the Pilgrimage of Grace in Northumberland had involved confrontations between the following of Sir Reynold Carnaby, Wharton's nephew and Forster's brother-in-law, and that of Sir Thomas Percy, father of the seventh earl of Northumberland. See *L.P.*, xii (1), 1090.
[57] See pp. 134 ff. above; and *Illustrations of British History*, ed. Edmund Lodge (London, 1838), p. 277.

earl of Bedford, both trusted agents of the Elizabethan régime.[58] Thus the earl, forced in his turn into the background, and surrounded by an aura of disfavour, drifted into dissident politics and religion. He intrigued with the Lennox faction, with Mary Queen of Scots, with the duke of Norfolk, and formed links with the Spanish embassy.[59] Forster on the other hand, based on Harbottle castle, and supported by troops of the Berwick garrison,[60] was well placed to weaken and undermine the Percy interest. In the background there was the explosive religious issue, Forster being an aggressive Protestant. Northumberland on the other hand favoured the old religion, and in 1567 was reconciled to the Roman church.[61] For Clarkson this situation partly accounted for the "decay" of what he called "comon welthe". But the process was not solely the outcome of these extraneous pressures. Also at work were tensions within the estate community itself.

III

For Clarkson the connotation of "common wealth"[62] (or "common weal") is different from that of "order", the emphasis being less on the social structure and its place in the universal "frame" than on the benefits (involving duties and rights) arising from the social bond. The term could have subversive undertones, as when the Kentish insurgents of 1450 "wente, as they sayde, for the comyn weale of the realme of Ingelonde";[63] and it had been used in a similar context

[58] See pp. 135–6 above; *Estate Accounts of the Earls of Northumberland*, p. xix; Rymer, *Feodera* (London, 1704–35), xv, pp. 461–2; *C.P.R., Ph. & M.*, iv, p. 179; Rymer, *loc. cit.*, pp. 458, 475. *C.P.R., Eliz.*, iii, nos. 367, 379; *ibid.*, i, pp. 327, 348.

[59] *Cal. State Papers, Scotland*, ii, pp. 165, 410–13, 421; *Cal. State Papers, Spanish*, ii, pp. 95–6, 147, 195, 201.

[60] *Cal. State Papers, Foreign, Elizabeth, 1566–8*, no. 1003.

[61] James Melville gives an account of a meeting with Forster in 1585, at which the latter "began bathe to glorifie God . . . and to prophesie . . . that we arw estonished to heir the mouthe of a worldlie civill man sa opened to speak out the wounderfull warkes and prases of God wrought for us": James Melville, *Diary 1556–1601*, ed. R. Pitcairn (Wodrow Soc., iii, Edinburgh, 1842), p. 227. Sharp, *Memorials*, p. 204.

[62] See W. R. D. Jones, *The Tudor Commonwealth* (London, 1970), chs. 1 and 2.

[63] William Gregory's "Chronicle of London", in *Collections of a Citizen of London*, ed. J. Gairdner (Camden Soc., new ser., xvii, London, 1876), p. 191.

during both the Pilgrimage of Grace and Kett's rebellion.[64] Sir Thomas Elyot had shied away from such implications of common wealth, and suggested "public weal" as an alternative, remarking that "there maye appere lyke diversitie to be in englissche betwene a publike weale and a commune weale as shulde be in latin betwene *Res publica* and *Res plebeia*."[65] Berners, as has been seen, had made lordship the essence of common wealth. Clarkson, however, subscribed neither to *Res plebeia*, nor at the other extreme, to Berners's view. Instead, for him community rested on custom sanctioned by long continuance; it was this which regulated the interplay of duties, rights and benefits which was the public weal. Common wealth implied "the good and auncyent rule and government" without which "the common wealthe . . . much ys damnyfied . . . "; it was "thauncyent rites customes and orders" which were neglected only "to the utter undoing of so many good common people".[66] Once again the approach involves something different from the values of good lordship, faithfulness and service. Common wealth was rooted in a customary order handed down from the past which had the nature of law, defining the extent and limits even of the lord's authority, as well as the rights and duties of the tenant. In the context of common wealth, while authority remained basic to order, the possibility was nevertheless present that masters and their inferiors might confront each other as equals at least in their legal personalities, instead of in the relationship of responsible dominance and unqualified submission which good lordship implied. Once again, of course, Clarkson's debt to the common law becomes apparent. As Christopher St German put it, "the lawe of Englande standith upon divers generall customes of olde time used . . . And because the saide customes . . . have been alwayes taken to be good and necessarye for the common wealth . . . Therefore they have

[64] During the Pilgrimage, for example, the commons of Howdenshire and Marshland were summoned to rise "for the comen welthe", and "every man to be trewe to the kyngs issue, the noble blood . . . and to the comens and ther welthis": Dodds, *The Pilgrimage of Grace* (London, 1915), i, p. 148. Cf. the leaders of the Kett rebellion who issued warrants commanding all persons "as they tender the King's honor and roiall majestie, and the reliefe of the common welthe, to be obedient to us the Governors": F. W. Russell, *Kett's Rebellion in Norfolk* (London, 1859), p. 97.

[65] Sir Thomas Elyot, *The Boke named The Governour*, ed. from the first edition of 1531 by H. H. S. Croft, 2 vols. (London, 1880), i, p. 1.

[66] Alnwick Castle MS. A I 1m: printed in *Northumberland County History*, ii, by E. Bateson (Newcastle upon Tyne, 1895), pp. 475–6; *ibid.*, A I 1a.

obtained the strength of a law."[67] The rule of custom and common wealth involved the penetration of the common-law way of thinking into remote northern countrysides, and the conferment as a result of rights on those whose posture had previously been solely one of submission.

This can be seen in the emphasis, suggesting a significant change in the prevailing attitudes to authority, which Clarkson placed on the restraints which order and custom imposed on the exercise of lordship. These differed from the personalized code of good lordship. For they arose partly from the purpose which seigneurial rule existed to serve, which for Clarkson was the "maintenaunce of the common welthe";[68] and partly from the objective legalized norm provided by the rules of custom. The latter were known collectively as "the custom of Cockermouth", and by the 1560s the majority of the Percy tenancies in Northumberland were held "according to" this custom. The custom of Cockermouth defined the extent of the rents and the services (which included military service on the Border) attaching to the tenancy; it also conferred on the tenant an estate to himself and his assigns for the term of his life and that of the lord. When the estate terminated, whether by the death of the tenant or lord, a fine was levied on the former, this being arbitrable not by custom but "at the will of the lord".[69] It was in terms of this custom that Clarkson could assert that, while the lord was to be "fully answered of his accustomed servyce" and "auncyent rent", to exact more would be to violate order and go against "conscience".[70] The custom of Cockermouth, as used in Northumberland, was not a particularly generous one. It certainly did not amount to the copyhold of inheritance which the tenants unsuccessfully claimed in the

[67] *Dialogues between a Doctor of Divinity and a Student in the Lawes of Englande* . . . (London, 1554 edn) (S.T.C. 21571), fo. 11.

[68] E.g. Alnwick Castle MS. A. I 1a, Survey of Alnwick, in which Clarkson affirms the duty of the lord to advance the "maintenaunce of the comon welthe" of the burgesses. Cf. *ibid.*, A I 1g, on the role of the lord's officer, which was "to manetane his Lordships inheritance, and seike to provyde for the Comon Welthe of those he hath charge of . . . ".

[69] Public Record Office, E164/37, Hall and Humberstone's Survey, 1570, Survey of Alnwick: " . . . the custom of the honor of Cockermouth, which ys to make fyne at the lordes wyll and pleaser, after the death or alienacon or exchaunge of the lord or tenaunt". The estate granted is specified, in the copies which Clarkson entered in his survey, as "to have to him and his assigns (habendum sibi et assignatis suis)".

[70] Alnwick Castle MS. A I 1l, Survey of Guyzance.

course of their tenurial disputes of the early seventeenth century with the ninth earl of Northumberland.[71] But the indications are that, some half a century before Clarkson wrote his survey, the majority of these same tenants could claim no status at all beyond that of simple tenant at will. Possibly, it has been suggested, the customary régime was introduced into Northumberland in the early 1520s, at the same time as it was adopted in Yorkshire from the Cumberland Percy honour of Cockermouth. There it must already have established itself.[72]

Clarkson's appeal to "antiquity" and to the supposed immemorial origin of custom cannot therefore be taken too seriously. Customary tenure (as a status which conferred a degree of protection in the courts of common law) was in fact a relatively recent development, as far as the Percy tenants in Northumberland were concerned; the result of a bargaining process between lord and tenant whereby an enhanced status involving improved security of tenure was bartered against larger fines.[73] No doubt the tenants had previously enjoyed a *de facto* customary régime, in the sense that over the generations the same families had occupied the same tenancies. For the shortage of agricultural labour, whose effects in the fifteenth century can be seen in the persistence of decayed rents and unoccupied holdings,[74] as well as the code of "good lordship" made for stability. Nevertheless the rise of customary tenure involved a changed attitude to lord–tenant relations which is reflected in Clarkson's writings. The responsible dominance and unconditional submission characteristic of the tenancy at will no longer predominated. Instead a relationship arose which could be related to the total system of the common law, conferring rights and a legal personality on the tenant. It was this which expressed itself in Clarkson's sense of order and polity. The trend was strengthened moreover by the abortive rising of 1569. For the royal surveyors, no doubt concerned to weaken the hold of lords over tenants, asserted that the Percy lands in Northum-

[71] See G. R. Batho, "The Finances of an Elizabethan Nobleman: Henry Percy, Ninth Earl of Northumberland (1564–1632)", *Econ. Hist. Rev.*, 2nd ser., ix (1956–7), pp. 433–50.

[72] J. M. W. Bean, *The Estates of the Percy Family, 1416–1537* (Oxford, 1958), pp. 56–7, 62–4.

[73] *Ibid.*, pp. 51 ff.

[74] *Ibid.*, pp. 29 ff.

berland were copyholds of inheritance "according to the custom of Cockermouth".[75]

Clarkson was emphatic however that "good order" and "common wealth" involved more than merely legal and contractual obligations imposed on lord and tenant by the régime of custom and order. Underlying this was a system of moral values with a religious sanction. This not only required the lord to refrain from oppressing his tenants and dependants; but also placed on him the duty to provide in a positive kind of way for their well-being. When pursuing this line of thought, Clarkson sometimes appealed to the traditional code of "good lordship", or to the "honour" which was the mark of true nobility, whose very nature involved generosity to dependants.[76] In this connection, however, the surveyor also raised the sanction of "conscience". Thus, where tenants in the same township were unequally endowed with land, "conscyence wold there should be the lyke respects [i.e. a similar disproportion] in doinge ther service . . . which wer good for them which are the poorest amongest the said tennants".[77] Similarly the "disorder" in the township of Rennington needed to be "straitly looked upon" by the lord and his officers "as well for consciens sake as my lordes honour and welthe of the said tenants".[78] Clarkson could have learnt from Christopher St German that conscience is "an habit of mind discerninge betwixte good and evill" and that this was rooted in "Synderesis . . . a naturall power of the soule sett in the highest parte thereof moving and stirring it to good and abhorring evill . . . ". But the concept involved religion just as much as philosophy, for "this Synderesis our Lord put in man to the intent that order of things should be observed".[79] "Honour and conscience", therefore, required the lord to provide for the moral and religious, as well as material, well-being of his dependants. He ought for example to provide churches for his

[75] Public Record Office, E164/37, Hall and Humberstone's Survey of Cockermouth: " . . . all the most of the customarye tenants of therles [of Northumberland and Westmorland] in all the countyes of Cumberland and Northumberland York and the Busshopryk of Duresme have in all their ancient grants and copies, to hold to them and theyr heyres according to the custom of the honor of Cockermouth".

[76] E.g. Alnwick Castle MS. A I 1a, Survey of Alnwick: "To his lordship it were honor . . . to be gracious lorde unto the said burgesses and aswel graunt them suche thinges as wilbe for the setting forth of ther comon welthe."

[77] *Ibid.*, A I 1c, Survey of Denwick.

[78] *Ibid.*, A I 1p, Survey of Rennington.

[79] *Dialogues between a Doctor*, fos. 23, 25.

tenants where these were lacking, and help his burgesses of Alnwick to found a free grammar school in their town.[80]

Thus the emphasis in Clarkson's concept of honour has shifted as compared with Richard Atkinson's. Instead of expressing the competitive self-assertion of the noble person or lineage, reputation now submits to the determination of a religious and moral system external to itself. To be "honourable" becomes simply to implement, according to conscience, the obligations implicit in the status of lordship. Here Clarkson's thinking merges with the humanist–Puritan ideal which would establish itself as the Elizabethan paradigm of nobility. In terms of this "the hawtiest . . . nobilitye is that which, with renoume and fame of auncestrye, hath coupled excellent, Chrystian and farre spred vertue", by contrast with that other face of nobility as mere private repute, where "envy glorieth with bloodye looke", and "Stout stomaches cannot beare pryvate grudges . . . Hence cometh it that Nobilitye can beare no peere, and all ambition is impacient of mete", for the Christian nobleman "Justice . . . is fittest and necessariest . . . The neybour virtue to this is equitye. Not to racke all things by extreme right, to yield somewhat, and thinke nothinge more beloved than mercye and curtesye." In the Puritan ideal of nobility the more aggressive aspects of honour are played down, and its identity with conscience emphasized.[81]

Conscience bound the tenant as much as the lord, and for the former it translated itself into "duety", this being directed towards God, his neighbour, and "his lordshipe". Duty towards "God and neighbour", and involvement in "neighbourhood" implied a more voluntary and spontaneous kind of association than the primarily legalistic and contractual community of "common welthe"; nevertheless the former was seen as the necessary basis of the latter. In the widest sense "neighbourhood" required the conservation and proper management of the communal inheritance, so that "we, consideringe our duty to God and neighbour, may be ashamed not to go thorowe and accomplishe those thingis founde out for our welth by such as before us hathe bene . . . ".[82] It also implied a moral soli-

[80] Alnwick Castle MS. A I 1a, Survey of Alnwick; *ibid.*, A I 1l, Survey of Guyzance.

[81] Humphrey, *Of Nobilitye*, sig. a. iv^v; n. viii; i.i; q. vi^v. Cf. J. Pitt-Rivers, "Honor", p. 507.

[82] Alnwick Castle MS. A I 1m, Survey of Warkworth.

darity which was broken when, for example, necessary communal tasks beyond the resources of the single tenant family, like the building and repair of houses, were neglected. If carried far enough, decay of neighbourhood could disintegrate a peasant community to the point where it could no longer even defend itself against outside attack. Thus in one township the tenants "be also unquiet amongst themselves having undecent talk nor yet useth any good and neighbourly wayes for the common welthe", and in this same township "in suche tyme as any attemptate is made upon them by the enemy they do not come together to resist the same . . . ".[83] Where neighbourhood decayed, therefore, "comon welthe" also suffered, and so also did "duety" to the lord, as expressed above all in "service", that is with horse and armour under the lord's officer against the Scots. It was good neighbours, so Clarkson clearly thought, who were most likely to internalize demands made upon them from outside the neighbourhood community, and so also be good tenants. Thus in another township we encounter a model group of the latter who "be verie well horsed and dewtiful towards his lordshipe in service [i.e. military service]: there be many good orders amongst them for keeping ther order in neighbourhood".[84] Neighbourhood, order, and duty to the lord went together. But the juxtaposition required the seigneurial authority to be exercised according to conscience, and in ways responsive to the values of "neighbourhood". So that the officer worthy of his charge ought not only to refrain from extortion and oppression of the tenants, but also to "seike the favor of thinhabytors thereby his neighbours . . . and seike to provyde for the Comon welthe of those he hath charge of . . . ".[85]

These attitudes involved estate policies in which priority was never consistently or primarily given to what was to the lord's "best profit", a phrase which by the seventeenth century had become the touchstone in such matters. For Clarkson the economic motive was not as important as policies making for stability and the persistence

[83] *Ibid.*, A I 1b, Survey of Rennington.
[84] *Ibid.*, A I 1f, Survey of Swinhoe.
[85] *Ibid.*, A I 1g, Survey of Chatton. Cf. Laurence Humphrey's description of the ideal seigneurial common wealth: "Be this therefore the sum of all. That the commens win the nobles with service, the nobles the commens with benevolence. They obey lowly, thother rule favourably. They strive to excell in justice, they in obedience": *Of Nobilitye*, sig. d. iii, ff.

of the community of small to medium-sized family farmers which constituted the majority of the Percy tenantry; each with a holding substantial enough to contribute an armed horseman or footman to the levy of tenants under the lord's officers. This was therefore a "service" community, that is one whose *raison d'être* was military. But all this implies is that the other values bound up with its way of life, like neighbourhood, duty, common wealth and order were only viable, in the context of a March society, as long as effective defence guaranteed survival. For the Percy tenantry warfare was not a primary activity, as it was to some Border communities whose survival was largely dependent on the profits of raiding.[86] Preoccupations of this kind, however, made some of Clarkson's proposed courses of action in matters of estate administration appear strange to a later generation of Percy officers, one of whom annotated his Survey with the disapproving comment: "This is against his Lordshipe's profite."[87]

For example, there was his insistence that the lord must not only be content with his "accustomed" rents, but also resist the temptation to let highly rented farms of demesnes and parks to big leaseholders. For where such grounds were needed as pasture by "the poor tenants", to them, Clarkson asserted, they ought to be let at "some reasonable certain price". And, where commons were improved, these ought to be added to the existing tenement land, not retained in the lord's possession.[88] The same concern for the vigour of the service community of middling tenants emerges also from Clarkson's insistence on the need for equality of holdings, and his resistance to the emergence of any peasant élite of prosperous farmers, eager to engross tenancies to "ther owne private gain and comodety, to the utter undoinge of so many good common people . . . ".[89] In the past the lord and his officers had not permitted any tenant to occupy more than one tenement; his authority should now be used to enforce this rule where it had been broken, "to the

[86] As, for example, in Tynedale, where over-population drove "the yonge and actyve people for lack of lvynge . . . to steal or spoyle contynually ether in England or Scotland": Bowes and Ellerker's "Survey of the Borders, 1542", in J. Hodgson, *History of Northumberland*, ii (2) (Newcastle upon Tyne, 1828), p. 233.

[87] Alnwick Castle MS. A I 1a, Survey of Alnwick.

[88] *Ibid.*, A I 1p, Survey of Birling; *ibid.*, A I 1p, Survey of Acklington.

[89] *Ibid.*, A I 1a, Survey of Alnwick.

great impoverishement of all the reste of the saide tennants . . . and also no little hurt and hindrance of service to his lordshipe then prejudice to the common welthe".[90] For the same reason Clarkson, although well aware of the inadequacies of the field systems prevalent on the Percy manors, often found himself unable to recommend such improvements as the division of townships or enclosure;[91] for in his eyes the strength of the *status quo* was that it best ensured to each tenant his due share of good and bad land, and so conduced to equality.[92] "Private gain and comodety" then must be restrained and equality preserved;[93] the enhancement of the rent-roll of the estate took second place to such objectives.

IV

Thus in the context of order and common wealth, duty, service and neighbourhood, Clarkson projected the image of the lord who respected custom, was moved by conscience, and cherished his tenants. There was nothing specifically "northern" or "neo-feudal" about such an ideal, which was shared by the whole Tudor governing class, and instances of the type may be encountered as much in the midlands and south as in the northern and western "highland zones" and "peripheral areas".[94] Against the background of the rising of 1569, however, this kind of lordship has a relevance to that "devotion" of tenants to their lords which has been seen as a special feature of northern society during the Tudor period, contributing to the political instability which exploded into recurring rebellions against the dominant court cliques. Much of the evidence for this view as applied to the events of 1569 comes from Northumberland. In particular there is Lord Hunsdon's dictum, so often quoted, that

[90] *Ibid.*, A I 1c, Survey of Denwick.

[91] For example, Alnwick Castle MSS. A I 1c, Denwick; A I 1p, Acklington; A I 1d, Lesbury; A I 1f, Swinhoe.

[92] Cf. the case of Denwick: "Yt ys not convenyent that this towne shold be devided, neyther the airable landes, nor yet the common pasture . . . speciallie for that there be suche diversitie and unequalitie of the goodnes of the said groundes . . . nowe lyinge by rigge and rigge amonge the tenants . . . Yt ys the most equall partition that can be made in this towne" (*ibid.*, A I 1c).

[93] E.g. at Chatton the constable of Alnwick castle "provyded always that ther were no tenements compact together more then one, for that ys the decaye of servyce and also weakening of his strength and ayde" (*ibid.*, A I 1g).

[94] See Lawrence Stone, *The Crisis of the Aristocracy* (Oxford, 1965), pp. 303 ff.

Northumberland "knew no Prince but a Percy"; and it was Hunsdon who also informed the government that the Percy tenants there "loved" their earl "better than they do the Queen".[95] Sir John Forster testified to the same effect. He reported to the Council his own fear, surrounded as he was by the Pericy lands with their many tenants. The latter had already received warning to rise at an hour's notice, and the Percy castles at Alnwick and Warkworth had been garrisoned. He pointed to his own peril and isolation, and the need for reinforcements.[96]

Evidence of this sort needs to be cautiously handled. Neither Hunsdon nor Forster were disinterested when they transmitted such alarmist reports to their superiors. Both were concerned to magnify the difficulty of suppressing the rebellion, so as to secure reinforcements, and keep their own forces under their own control and in their own "country". They needed to ensure against failure, as well as enhance their achievement in the event of success. Thus it would not be surprising that they should exaggerate the power of the earl of Northumberland in the shire, and the devotion of his tenants. Undoubtedly, however, there were good reasons why those same tenants should have seen their own interests as bound up with those of their lord, and why they, no less than their counterparts in Sir George Bowes's "country", should have conceived that "old good wyll . . . deepe graftyd in their harts, to their nobles"[97] to which reference is so often made in accounts of the Tudor north. Few Percy tenants could have rejoiced at the results of the three decades from 1537 to 1557 when the Percy influence had been in eclipse, and the Percy estates in the hands of the crown. For during this period leases of the demesnes and manors had been made mostly to supporters of the Forster faction in Northumberland who had enclosed or encroached on commons and pastures, and impoverished the tenants.[98] Gentlemen farmers of this kind, intent on large and quick profits, were detected by Clarkson as principal

[95] *Cal. State Papers, Foreign, 1569–71*, p. 159; *Cal. State Papers, Domestic, Addenda, 1566–79*, p. 195.

[96] *Cal. State Papers, Domestic, Addenda, 1566–79*, pp. 117–19.

[97] Sharp, *Memorials*, p. x.

[98] For the effects of the rule of the Forsters and their Bradford relatives in the Percy manors of Tuggal, Lucker, and Newham, leased to them by the crown, see Alnwick Castle MS. A I 1f, and *Northumberland County History*, i, pp. 240, 350 ff., 374.

enemies of order and common wealth, as well as of the Percy ascendancy in the shire.[99] And the decline of that ascendancy, accompanied as it was by the decay of the authority of the Percy officers and courts, had as one consequence extensive encroachments by gentry or tenants of neighbouring townships (often encouraged by their landlords) on Percy commons and wastes, inevitably to the impoverishment of the earl's tenants.[100] In fact, at a time when the supply of common pasture and waste was less than in the past, and competition for it intensified, peasant communities with powerful landlords able to protect their interests were likely to come off best. Order and common wealth then had political implications; tenants were liable to suffer as the earl's authority in his country crumbled.

Yet in the outcome the Northern Rising received meagre support from the Percy tenantry in Northumberland. As Sir John Forster had reported, bodies of servants and tenants had garrisoned Alnwick and Warkworth castles. But in the event these surrendered after only a token resistance.[101] Of the rebel forces, which at the height of their strength amounted to about four thousand foot and some seventeen hundred light horse, only eighty to a hundred are reported as coming out of Northumberland, these being mostly from the upland lordship of Langley, on the south Tyne.[102] Thus, when it came to the point, "neo-feudal" loyalties were not enough to draw tenants into rebellion in support of their lord. The extent of the collapse in 1569 of the strength of the Percy levy of tenants is suggested by an estimate of that strength made in the 1530s, when there were in Northumberland "of [Percy] tennants and hablemen . . . redy to serve . . . having jacks cote of fens and harnys with long speres bowes and other weapons in a redines to be called upon to the

[99] Clarkson described them as "suche as wold exalte and extolle their owne name and fame unto honor, whiche at this present may easelye be perceyved, not onely by the . . . knyttinge together of frendeshipe in maiking of mariages, obteyninge the wardshipe of suche as be in their minoritye, and also getting the rule of lordshipes and manours . . . as well of the prince as of others, obteyninge leases of all parsonages and monasteries in the countrie . . . And anythinge of his Lordhipes landes joyninge nighe unto them, tayke it to be ther owne . . . ": Alnwick Castle MS. A I 1b, Survey of Alnwick Parks and Aydon Forest.

[100] E.g. at Wooden (*ibid.*, A I 1d), Newham and Ellingham (*ibid.*, A I 1f), Guyzance (*ibid.*, A I 1l), Chatton (*ibid.*, A I 1g).

[101] See above, n. 89 this chapter.

[102] Sharp, *Memorials*, p. 185; *Cal. Border Papers*, ii, p. 22.

number of" 849 horsemen and 1,118 foot. These figures are close to the actual number of Percy horse and foot which, under the command of the constable of Alnwick, mustered in 1539.[103] "Neo-feudal" loyalties were not compelling enough to draw more than a small minority of tenants into rebellion behind their lord.

Perhaps the poor response of the Percy tenantry in November 1569 owed something to the special circumstances in which the rebellion broke out in Northumberland, which was relatively remote from the main centres of disaffection in Durham, the North and West Ridings. The earl of Northumberland himself, with his associates, never entered the country to mobilize support; and the latter was certainly greatest in those districts where the rebel earls made a personal appearance, and were able to make the offers of pay which were essential to hold the majority of their recruits, which did not in fact consist of tenants.[104] The presence of the lord was not essential, however, for the effective mobilization of the tenantry where the machinery of seigneurial authority was in good order and energetically used. For, in the case of the Neville lordships of Bywell in Northumberland and Kirkby Moorside in Cleveland (both districts also away from the main centres of the rebellion), the stewards had raised large and virtually complete levies of tenants without the need for the presence of the earl of Westmorland.[105] Probably, however, the leadership of the Percy tenantry was less determined and energetic than that provided by these two Neville officers. For the principal Percy supporter in Northumberland, Sir

[103] Syon House MS. 1 I 2. *L.P.*, xiv, 102.

[104] The majority of the rebel forces, just under 4,000 out of a total of 5,700 or 5,800, were footmen, the "most part unarmed, arising onelie of artificers, and the meanest sort of husbandmen". It was the horsemen, 1,700 or 1,800 strong, which consisted of the gentry with their tenants and servants (including the eighty Percy tenants from Northumberland, and sixty Neville tenants from the lordship of Bywell): Sharp, *op. cit.*, pp. 184–5. On the importance of pay to recruit and retain the former, see Christopher Norton's confession: "The next day we came to Northallerton, where all the footmen of the Bishopric (of Durham) were commanded to be, and promised money". The two rebel earls had only £20 available to distribute among the one thousand men who mustered, with the result that only four hundred men could be paid, and "those who received nothing were dissatisfied, and returned home" (*Cal. State Papers, Domestic, Addenda, 1566–79*, p. 276).

[105] The high recruitment rate of 80 horse out of a total of 110 Neville tenants at Bywell was probably due to the able and energetic steward, John Swinburn; according to the earl of Sussex (*Cal. State Papers, Domestic, Addenda, 1566–79*, p. 110) Christopher Neville "raised all the earl [of Westmorland's] tenants of Kirkby Moorside": he was probably the deputy steward.

Cuthbert Collingwood of Eslington, speedily surrendered Alnwick castle, and, although some of his relatives were attainted, himself escaped all the penalties of rebellion. He may have been a follower of the rebel earl's brother Sir Henry Percy, a cautious "loyalist" and later eighth earl of Northumberland, rather than of the earl himself.[106] It would not be surprising if Collingwood's leadership contributed something to the failure of all but a small minority of the tenants to rise.[107]

Whatever weight is given to such factors, however, there are strong reasons to believe that by 1569 the military effectiveness of the tenant levy had been undermined by more long-term and fundamental weaknesses in the structure of seigneurial authority and of the service community which could not have been offset by any leadership, however determined and energetic. For Clarkson at any rate the decline of "service" was a deep-rooted and long-term tendency, a concomitant of the more fundamental process which he called "decay". This he saw as a falling away from the primeval, pristine pattern "founde oute for our welth by such as before us hath bene",[108] that is the customary foundation of order and common wealth. "Decay" was to be seen at its most catastrophic in the decline of the knights' court of the barony of Alnwick,[109] both the

106 Sir Cuthbert Collingwood, lately sheriff of Northumberland, was identified by Lord Hunsdon as "Northumberland's man", and was rumoured to have recruited 600 horse for the rebels among the Border clans (*Cal. State Papers, Domestic, Addenda, 1566–79*, p. 114); Hunsdon subsequently asserted that Collingwood had been the earl's constable of Alnwick castle during the rebellion (*Cal. Border Papers*, i, p. 557). Collingwood later held various estate offices under Sir Henry Percy when the latter succeeded his attainted brother (the earldom being entailed) as eighth earl of Northumberland: see *Estate Accounts of the Earls of Northumberland*, pp. 65, 69, 74, 76, 80, 85.

107 By contrast the strong levy of tenants which joined the rebellion from the barony of Langley was probably the result of the leadership of John Carnaby, the earl's farmer and officer there, who was subsequently attainted.

108 Alnwick Castle MS. A I 1n.

109 Clarkson's remarks about the knight's court are contained in a few leaves entitled "Opinio Scriptoris" bound into Syon House MS. A II 2 (known as the Red Book of Alnwick) beginning at fo. 54. The book also includes a rental of the reign of Edward IV, and one of Richard III, so that its contents have sometimes been attributed to the later fifteenth century. But the rentals have been transcribed in a sixteenth-century hand, and in the case of that of Edward IV for comparative purposes on the same page as one of 23 Henry VIII. At fo. 38 begins another "Opinio Scriptoris" including references to Sir John Forster which place it in the time of the seventh earl of Northumberland, probably in the early years of the reign of Queen Elizabeth. Both fos. 38 ff. and fos. 54 ff. are in Clarkson's hand.

symbol and organizing centre of seigneurial authority in the townships of the central Northumbrian coastal plain and upland which constituted the Percy heartland, as well as the means whereby the lord's will was declared and executed. In the past probably the most important function of the court had been to promote and maintain the cohesion of the Percy following in Northumberland, the core of this consisting of the tenants by knight service, who owed suit to the knight's court. It was in this court, Clarkson explained, that "good order" was kept among the gentlemen of the barony, for "upon any grudge stirred or moved among any of them, it was straitlie appeased", and so "firme and steadfast love" among them maintained.[110] It was the knight's court, too, which enforced the obligations of service, particularly important as far as the freeholders were concerned, who could supplement the levy of the tenants at will with their own retinues. Thus, as long as it functioned effectively, "in tyme of service wher was ther in all the countrie one gentleman of honnoure or worshipe that had such a company of gentlemen and good servitours as the cheife constable's . . . of Alnwyck".[111] In addition the court exercised the jurisdiction of a leet, and its authority was brought home to the tenants at will by the presentments made before it by the reeves and swornmen of each township.[112]

But the court was now, so Clarkson reported, only rarely held, and the suitors who appeared, whether freeholders or others, were few and sometimes none; nor were any amercements levied on those who failed to do suit. Thus the court which was the "keye of justice" in the barony was "brought to nothyng", and "the lorde himselfe in his owne countrie not regarded". Similar abuses were present in the manorial courts, with comparable results.[113] Manorial monopolies, like brewing and baking, could not be maintained, engrossment of tenements was not corrected, and in the pursuit of "comodety and profit" neighbourhood was neglected. Moreover, reformation was difficult because forces deeply hostile to "order" had penetrated the administrative structure of seigneurial authority. For the earl's enemies "procurethe the frienshipe companye and helpe of such as be his Lordshipes owne servants . . . so that

[110] Syon House MS. A II 2, fo. 55.
[111] *Ibid.*
[112] *Ibid.*, fo. 56.
[113] *Ibid.*, fo. 57.

nothing can be spoken or done for his Lordeshipe but shall be knowen by them and prevented".[114]

In Clarkson's view developments of this kind were partly the result of significant changes in tenant attitudes to authority, connected with the decline of tenancies at will, and the enhanced security of tenure they had come to enjoy. Tenants, he noted, now "for the moste parte do accounte themselves for ther rente payinge to be lordes of ther tenementes".[115] But there was also the effect of the hold which the Forster faction had been able to establish over the structure of the estate, as over its administration. For, during the twenty years when the Percy estates had been in the hands of the crown, many Forster relatives and friends had been granted leases of Percy manors and demesnes. In these places their authority now prevailed over that of the earl. Again and again Clarkson observed that the tenants were more willing to displease "his lordeshipe" than the "gentlemen ther neighbours there", or that "the tenants . . . stand not so much in feare of his lordshipe and his officers as of other gentlemen ther neighbours",[116] these being mostly Forster relatives. At Alnwick Sir John Forster himself took the lead in harassing the earl's authority from his house at Alnwick Abbey, whose tithes and lands he leased from the crown. These, being intermixed with the Percy properties, provided many occasions for making trouble. One of Forster's more provocative gestures, for example, was to induce the Alnwick burghers to grind their corn at his mill, instead of at the earl's, to which they owed service, thus "dishonouring" the earl and his officers in a way which, Clarkson thought, would have been inconceivable "in former times when the state of the lords of Alnwick flourished".[117] By 1569 therefore the whole structure of seigneurial administration was weakened and crumbling, and the earl's authority questioned and flouted.[118]

114 Alnwick Castle MS. A I 1b, Survey of Alnwick Parks and Aydon Forest.

115 *Ibid.*, A I 1g, Survey of Chatton.

116 *Ibid.*, A I 1f, Survey of Lucker.

117 *Ibid.*, A I 1a, Survey of Alnwick; for Forster's lease of Alnwick abbey, see Tate, *Alnwick*, ii, p. 21.

118 Cf. the graphic description in "Opinio Scriptoris", fo. 57: " . . . my lordes lands be at every place for the most part encroched, divers of his lordships freeholders using and having a great part of my lordes royallties . . . also his tennands dwelling amongst or neare to any gentlemen is so coacted with feare . . . they do both neglect . . . there dewtie to his lordship, and almost useth and honoreth the said gentlemen or other officer as the naturall lord. Notwithstanding overrun upon everie part aswell by the neighbours as also by evill dysposed persons . . . And ther ground taken . . . and have no helpe to call or redress."

Inevitably "service" and the military levy of tenants decayed as well, if only because so often the earl's officers could not enforce them, and frequently lacked the will and desire to do so. In addition, the tenants were increasingly unwilling or unable to maintain the horses, armour and weapons which made up their military equipment. Sometimes Clarkson ascribed this to neglect by tenants of any service "beyond their rent paying"; sometimes to the poverty which resulted from oppression by gentlemen, the engrossment of holdings, and raids by Scots and Border thieves, against which the military unpreparedness of many townships made them defenceless. Thus in one town the tenants "havyng neither horse nor armour can do no service"; in another "the tenants are . . . not able to keipe themselves in horse and gear"; in a third they "be neither well horsed nor yet haithe good armour"; in a fourth and for the same reason, "the lord loseth much service".[119] Disabilities of this kind, and Clarkson's laments on their score, recur in nearly half of the thirty townships he surveyed, with the result that many were plagued by "the great thefts that ys continuallie" and "manie tymes overcome and spoyled by the Scots and also by others, evill disposed persons, Englishmen".[120] A tenant community lacking the will and weapons to defend itself against border raiding was scarcely the stuff out of which effective "neo-feudal" rebellion could be raised.

V

In the drama of the estate community assailed by inward decay and outward enemies as depicted by Clarkson, perhaps the most notable absent character was the earl of Northumberland, whose "natural rule" over his tenants was now so much brought into question. The castle at Alnwick stood intact and in good repair, with "a faire hall, a greate chamber, lodgeinge and all howses of offices for the lorde and his traine",[121] providing the complete setting required for the great retinue and elaborate *familia* which had accompanied the earls in the days of their greatness from house to house and estate to estate. But the castle was empty and probably unfurnished. Work

[119] Alnwick Castle MS. A I 1g, Chatton; A I 1f, Tuggal; A I 1p, Rennington; A I 1f, Ellingham.
[120] *Ibid.*, A I 1h, Survey of Rugley.
[121] *Ibid.*, A I 1a, Survey of Alnwick.

had been begun to provide stabling and garners for 120 geldings, but this had been abandoned.[122] Without stabling on this scale a great household could not be accommodated. Moreover Sir John Forster had so plundered the woods in the parks that supplies of firewood for heating and of timber for repairs were in doubt. Clarkson hinted too that the earl's "contenuall lyeinge in this countrie" might not be wholly welcome to the tenants. For previous earls had levied hay and grain on the latter for the upkeep of the household, which had been "not so profytable for his Lordeshipe as then yt was thought, but raythe more dishonor and the undoinge of his Lordeshipes tenants". Such supplies were better paid for, and the grain imported from Lincolnshire or Holderness.[123] At the same time, in his absence it was easier for such as Clarkson to conceive his master's role as that of an abstract embodiment of authority and legal right, rather than that of the personalized "good lord". He was a figure to be invoked from afar, not a presence to be reckoned with from day to day. Of necessity he must "cleave to" and "maike accompte" of his officers,[124] and take their advice. "His Lordship and his officers" was a phrase Clarkson often used; in his eyes the Percy interest had come to assume a quasi-corporative character.

An estate régime which required, in an age of rising prices, that rents should remain "ancient" and fines "reasonable", while limiting the lord's authority by custom and conscience, tended to strengthen the prerogatives of the estate officer. From the tenant's point of view it was the latter, with his local knowledge and presence, who counted; and the widening margin between economic rent and customary rent could become a source of official gain. Fines supposedly at the lord's will, for example, were not infrequently in practice at the will of the officer who assessed and levied them, whose "goodwill" the tenant might find it worth while to buy, if the price asked were not unreasonable.[125] Cash balances in the hands of receivers of rents were valuable assets where a

122 *Ibid.*

123 *Ibid.*

124 *Ibid.*, A I 1b, Survey of Alnwick Parks.

125 Thomas Percy, the gunpowder plotter, whom the ninth earl of Northumberland made his receiver-general in the north, was particularly notorious for his exploitation of under-rented tenements. He was alleged to have taken in 1602 payments of over £200 above fines in return for his goodwill in the matter of admissions to tenements. See Syon House MS. Q I 12.

scarcity of loans and credit prevailed.[126] There were also the more straightforwardly dishonest ways in which official pockets could be lined. A discreet proportion of the money received for wardships, for forfeitures of felons' goods, for sales of timber, and for amercements might be retained in official possession.[127] Or access to woods, parks and demesnes could be sold to tenants.[128] Under the surface an informal network of ties and dependencies developed between officers and tenants, involving the transfer of a proportion of the profits of the estate into official hands.[129] Not even such a determined and energetic landlord as the ninth earl of Northumberland could wholly eliminate such practices,[130] and by and large, provided no scandalous oppression or blatant dishonesty came to light, they were tolerated. Thus officers had an interest in the maintenance of a customary régime, of which they were themselves often also the direct beneficiaries, through the under-rented leaseholds and copyholds with which they were rewarded;[131] and sometimes

126 *Estate Accounts of the Earls of Northumberland*, p. xxxvi.

127 Sir Wilfred Lawson, the ninth earl's principal officer in Cumberland, was charged in 1595 with having sold mesne wardships belonging to his master, receiving nearly £50 for them (Syon House MS. X II 3, "Mr Henry Patrikson . . . in dyverse complaints to his lo."); Thomas Percy similarly sold one of his master's wardships for £20 (*ibid.*, Q I 12). Percy's servant confessed that he had received ten times as much for forfeitures as he had paid in (*ibid.*). Both Lawson and Percy pocketed amercements. Ralph Stubbes, under-bailiff of the Yorkshire Percy lordship of Topcliffe, was thought to have taken £300 out of the proceeds of timber sales over a ten-year period in the 1590s (Information of William Percivall, 1602, *ibid.*, X II 6/2).

128 Clarkson reported that the keeper of Cawledge Park allowed the tenants of Rugley to pasture their cattle in the park in return for hay and corn harvest services (Alnwick Castle MS. A I 1h, Survey of Rugley). In 1602 the bailiff of the Yorkshire lordship of Kildale in Cleveland was informed against for allowing the tenants of neighbouring townships to cut turves on Kildalemoor (Informations against the bailiff of Kildale, Syon House MS. X II 6).

129 Even such an upright officer as Clarkson had a special relationship with the burgess community of Alnwick, to which he and his family belonged, and used his survey to plead for favours both for Alnwick, and for the little port of Alnmouth, where he and his family had property: Alnwick Castle MS. A. I 1a and 1m.

130 His advice to his son with regard to such official gains on the side was "You must not strive too much to set all these things right, for it will not be in your power to help; only this I require, that you should understand what they do . . . ": *Advice to his Son by Henry Percy Ninth Earl of Northumberland*, ed. G. B. Harrison (London, 1930), p. 119.

131 A good Northumbrian example of an under-rented official lease is that granted to Sir Cuthbert Collingwood, the eighth earl's receiver, of the manors of Fawdon and Clinche, held in 1586 at a rent well below their value at the beginning of the century: Syon House MS. A II 8, Survey of Northumberland, 1586. Cf. the case of Francis Lucas, a former Percy receiver in Yorkshire, who leased the mills of

they even made common cause with the tenants in defence of custom. In a sense the officer's authority was Janus-headed, facing both towards the lord from which it was derived, and towards the tenant community in which it was exercised. This double aspect was, of course, also characteristic of Clarkson's way of thinking. On the one hand the frame of order, as he visualized it, received its structure from the rule of the lord, by which it was governed and maintained. But on the other hand there was the sense of common wealth, rooted in custom and neighbourhood, which limited even what the lord could do.

What is perhaps most striking about Clarkson's view of things, however, is the consistently law-abiding emphasis which permeates all his attitudes. For him "honour" and "conscience" implied above all conformity to law, and the law-abiding society provided the framework within which "the state of the earls of Northumberland" could be effectively restored and maintained. In this context any right of resistance, whether by tenants or against lords, or by the latter against the crown was bound to be excluded as synonymous with "disorder". Consequently, in spite of the support extended by the government to the Forster faction, whose activities were so destructive of order and common wealth in the earl's country, nevertheless Clarkson insisted that the latter should rule only "under the Prince", and defend his causes only by their pursuit at law. He recommended therefore that the earl's rights be established by careful surveys; that his courts be regularly held in orderly fashion by officers who could be trusted; that where disputes arose the best legal counsel should be sought; and that causes once initiated in the courts be persistently pursued.[132]

In defence of his faith in law, Clarkson cited an instance where this had paid dividends.[133] In 1565 a ship from Flanders was wrecked at Boulmer within the lord's liberties, while carrying to Mary Queen of Scots "a greate masse of golde whiche was founde in one chest casten upon the rocks". The earl claimed admiralty jurisdiction, but

Wigton in Cumberland in 1603 at a rent of 20*s*, although the lease was worth £4 a year. Clarkson himself was given a grant of demesnes in Easter Seaton by copy at a rent of 68*s*. (*ibid.*, A I 1m). Such instances could be multiplied. By the turn of the sixteenth and seventeenth centuries, however, officers were increasingly under pressive to "give as much as any other man" for their leases.

132 Alnwick Castle, MS. A I 1b, Survey of Alnwick Parks.

133 *Ibid.*, A I 1e, Survey of Long Houghton.

this was contested by the earl of Bedford, as the queen's deputy admiral. But the earl's jurisdiction was upheld before the Council[134] "whereof his Lordeshipe did receave two thowsand pounds and above". Such an approach did not always lead to such a happy outcome, as the earl found when the Exchequer, in a frequently cited judgement, upheld against him the queen's right to mine copper on his lands in Cumberland.[135] The Boulmer case suggests, however, that what was lost on the swings may well have been regained on the roundabouts; and that the seventh earl had no particular reason to make a grievance of his treatment by the law. He seems in fact to have kept consistently to the law-abiding course Clarkson recommended until the sudden and tragic flurry of rebellion in 1569.

VI

Clarkson's insight that the integrating factor in his society had come to be law and custom, to which conscience and honour required lordship to conform, reflects the significant changes in outlook and social relationships in progress, by Elizabeth's reign, underneath the "feudal" integument which the great landed inheritances spread over the northern countrysides. In the Dacre setting lineage values were still powerful, sustained by family divisions, the proximity of the Border, and the military and moral support afforded by the Scottish Border lairds. Through his incorporation into this Border world Leonard Dacre, with the backing of his Scots allies, would be able in February 1570 to confront Lord Hunsdon and the government forces with a formidable levy of three thousand men, in the one brief but ferocious military encounter in the whole course of the Northern Rising. More than two hundred dead and a hundred prisoners testified to the continued force of faithfulness to "blood" and lordship.[136] But in Northumberland, for reasons which

134 This seems to have been the tribunal before which the matter was debated and decided, but the MS. is defaced at this point, and tells us only that the matter was "debated before the Quene's Majestie and hir Honorable . . . at the demand of the Queen of Scotland". Cf. *Cal. State Papers, Scotland*, ii, p. 272.

135 For an account of this dispute, see R. R. Reid in *Trans. Roy. Hist. Soc.*, new ser., xx (1906), pp. 201 ff., where, however, the date of the discovery of the copper mine is wrongly given as July 1569, instead of July 1566. For the pleadings in the case, see E. Plowden, *Commentaries* (London, 1761), pp. 310–40.

136 But Leonard Dacre's "rising" was more like a Scots Border incursion than a rebellion, and his tenants could have formed only a small proportion of the array

Clarkson made sufficiently clear, these loyalties were no longer powerful enough to be given effective military and political expression. The ordered world of Clarkson's outlook is already closer to the seventeenth-century civil society, structured by law and contract, than to the archaic heroic setting in which Atkinson's lineage loyalties were grounded. Much of Clarkson's thinking was oriented towards the future, not the past. The northern society he knew, although still plagued by poverty and Border violence, was not without its transformative aspects. For poverty itself and the pressure of population on the land stimulated the exploitation of new resources: the lead of the upland valleys, the coal and the free-stone quarrying of Durham and Northumberland, involving the rise of novel productive forms, and new styles of social organization.

Clarkson was among those keenly aware of the new opportunities. He saw that coal-mining might alleviate the poverty of the Percy tenants, and he was eager to develop Warkworth as a port, for "within this lordship . . . is diverse things to be had for the commodity of such persons as used ther traffique or trade of getting their livinge by sea, as coal mynes, grynde stone quarrels, with diverse others . . . ".[137] His many laments about "decay", and his reference to "that which hath been wrought on our behalf by those which before us hath been"[138] as the standard from which the present had sadly fallen away, should not tempt us to typify him as a backward-looking conservative obsessed with the glories of the feudal past; still less as an adherent of those theories of cosmic senescence which would become increasingly popular in the next reign. Clarkson's appeal to a mythical primal order owed more to the common-law way of thinking than to any theories of cosmic senescence; and it was in fact by the enforcement of law that decay was to be arrested and order recovered. For Clarkson, like Starkey's Thomas Lupset, "decay" was not a cosmic fate, but "The faute thereof . . . ys in the malyce of men. Therefore . . . me semyth, hyt shold be best for you to apply your mind . . . to restore this cyvile order."[139] "Civil order"

of 3,000 men which confronted Lord Hunsdon's government forces near Naworth. The great majority were Scots sent to Dacre's aid by the Border lords Hume, Cessford, Ferniehurst, Buccleuch and others. See *Cal. State Papers, Domestic, Addenda, 1566–79*, pp. 237 (XVII/97), 240 (XVII/103), 241 (XVII/107), 253 (XVIII/11, ii, 1); *Cal. State Papers, Foreign, 1569–71*, p. 157.

137 Alnwick Castle MS A I 1n, Survey of Warkworth.

138 *Ibid.*

139 Starkey, *Dialogue*, p. 10.

founded on law was just as much Clarkson's ideal as that of the sophisticated court humanist Thomas Starkey.

Clarkson's outlook, the community he described, and its behaviour during the rising of 1569 at least bring into question the accepted convention that northern society was structurally disposed, as "neo-feudal" and archaic, to rebellion and violent forms of political dissidence. From this point of view it is of interest that the mentality of the seventh earl of Northumberland had much in common with that of his surveyor. Whether Clarkson did influence his master cannot be certainly known, although it is clear that his writings, like those of Richard Atkinson in the Dacre setting, were intended for the latter's perusal, and that their content would have been in general conformity with the prevailing consensus of opinion in the earl's circle. From this point of view Clarkson's sense that it was "naturall" for the earl to have "government and ruell under the Prince"[140] in his country fell easily into step with Northumberland's own conviction that the nobility, particularly that of "the ancient blood", had a special place in the community of the realm, and represented a body of opinion and influence bound in the last resort to be decisive in the determination of policy. Indeed his faith in the two causes he had most at heart, the restoration of Catholicism, and "the preservation of the second person, the Queen of Scotts, whom we accompted by Gods law and mans lawe to be right heire, if want should be of issue of the Queens Majestys body", arose from his conviction that both policies were "greatly favoured by most part of noblemen within this realm", so that he could look "for mantenance and aide by moste of the nobilytie".[141]

There is evidence too that the seventh earl would have sympathized with Clarkson's image of the lord who respected custom, was moved by conscience, and cherished his tenants, providing particularly for their moral and religious well-being. An instance is

[140] Alnwick Castle MS. A I 1b, Survey of Alnwick Parks.

[141] Cf. the duke of Norfolk's conviction that the queen would be bound to accept his proposed marriage to the Queen of Scots, not only because he thought most of her council favoured it, but also "that the whole nobilitie abroad lyked well of it . . . for he had assayed all there minds". Similarly the queen would never be able to bring him back by force from his country, if he were to withdraw there, for "there wold no nobleman in England accept that charge at her command, for he knew there whole myndis". Sharp, *Memorials*, pp. 202, 203; William Murdin (ed.), *A Collection of State Papers Relating to Affairs in the Reign of Queen Elizabeth, from the Year 1571 to 1596* (London, 1759), p. 44.

recorded of his personal correction of an injustice done to a tenant, "being moved in his conscience".[142] He also defended the customary claims of the crown tenants of Richmondshire, where he was the queen's steward, even against the queen herself.[143] And he showed his concern for the religious welfare of his tenants by repairing and even building churches for their use.[144] Clarkson's categories of "order" and "common wealth" under assault from the forces of "decay" would also have been sympathetic, for Northumberland saw his world in much the same way, but the terms he used to describe it were those of religion. For, although a convert to Catholicism, he was aware of Protestantism less in its religious essence than for its social implications, seeing it as a disintegrative force, making for "disagreement and great discentyon contynually growing", producing "dangerous sects now sparkled abrode", and contrasting with the Catholic cohesiveness and "unytie".[145] The activities of the disreputable clique of Protestant gentry led by Sir John Forster, whose activities Clarkson discussed, may have contributed to this view of Protestantism as an essentially destructive influence.

Northumberland's views, particularly his Catholicism and emphasis on the role of the aristocracy in the English polity may seem conservative to the point of incompatibility with the Elizabethan régime. In fact during the 1560s the sense of a nobility whose inherited position conferred on it a special and privileged function was not confined to dissidents, being rather one of the unifying political commonplaces acceptable, with varying emphases, over the whole range of opinion. Thus the queen herself, addressing her Council at the beginning of the reign, spoke first to those of them who were "of the antient nobility, having your beginnings and estates of my progenitours Kings of this Realm", and who therefore ought to have "the more naturall care for maintaining of

[142] Clarkson records that the earl evicted Thomas Steile from his father's tenancy in Alnwick demesnes in favour of William Johnstone, who had paid a fine of 40*s*, "but upon sight of widow Steile, then living, very feeble and of full years, moved in conscience, he directed that the said Thomas Steile shall have the said tenancy": Alnwick Castle MS. A I 1a, Survey of Alnwick.

[143] *Cal. State Papers, Domestic, Addenda, 1547–65*, p. 551.

[144] It was the seventh earl, for example, who built the New Kirk of Westward in Cumberland, for the use of the growing population of the forest of Westward. Petworth MS., Survey of Westward Forest, 1577.

[145] Sharp, *Memorials*, p. 213.

my Estate, and this commonwealth". And when in 1568 the question arose of the guilt of the Scots queen, and so of the involvement of a person of royal status in the crimes of murder and adultery, the matter was thought to be so weighty that not only the Privy Council but also "the earls should be called to give their advice to the same"[146] Thus for Northumberland the fact that his policies of "religion" and the preservation of the second person, were "greatly favoured by the most part of noblemen within this realm" implied the conviction that, in the political nature of things, these would sooner or later assert themselves against the dominant régime at court. Catholicism was so much the "natural" religion that to adhere to it involved no Tridentine fervour or Jesuitical subversiveness, but simply "To discern cheese from chalk in matters of religion". Sooner or later Cecil and Leicester themselves, so the earl thought, would bring "her Majesty to the truwthe therein".[147]

Northumberland may well have felt "great grief . . . for that they all lived out of the lawe of the Catholic Church", and have been willing to "spend his life" for its restitution.[148] But he was better aware than some of his gentry followers and their clerical mentors, that this could be brought about only given the pre-condition of a broad spectrum of support in the politically decisive level of the upper class, and by processes of royal marriage and succession. In the tense autumn months of 1569, Norfolk's surrender to the queen, the lack of any support from Spain, and the Scots queen's own veto proved that any "stir" could achieve nothing. The earl therefore, in spite of pressure from his supporters, "uppon the Duke's repayre to court . . . sought to forebere to rise, or sturre". But eventually, in the condition of panic and despair occasioned by his summons to London, "was drawn into it perforce".[149] Both the rebel earls, Westmorland as well as Northumberland, according to the earl of Sussex, had originally been involved only in oppositional politics, dealing with matters which, while bringing them into disfavour with the queen, were "not perilous to them". But they were subsequently drawn into a treasonable revolt because "they have been put into greater fear than their case required", and so gave their "wicked

146 Public Record Office, SP12/1/8, fo. 13; C. Read, *Mr Secretary Cecil and Queen Elizabeth* (London, 1955), p. 411.
147 Sharp, *Memorials*, p. 203.
148 According to Francis Norton: Sharp, *Memorials*, p. 281.
149 *Ibid.*, pp. 201–2.

counsellors" a free hand.[150] Political errors and miscalculations rather than any settled attitude of violent dissidence, or a social context attuned to armed revolt, made the earl of Northumberland a rebel. There was no state of affairs in which tenants still proffered their landlord unquestioning "faithfulness", or knew "no Prince but a Percy".

[150] *Cal. State Papers, Domestic, Addenda, 1566–79*, pp. 107–8 (XV/25).

8. *English politics and the concept of honour, 1485–1642*★

INTRODUCTION

The problem of violence, particularly in relation to politics, is a perennial theme of Tudor historiography, discussion of which has recently been renewed in G. R. Elton's Ford Lectures.[1] These begin with an evocation of the pervasive violence of the Tudor social world. People carried weapons; there was a latent irascibility in the air. Men were prone to brawl and take offence. Silly quarrels escalated into battles in the streets.[2] Conflicts were rapidly translated into the language of the sword. This was particularly so when large issues of politics or religion were at stake. Dissidence could be conceived only in terms of a violent, disruptive stance. It was revolt, "rebellion", the waging of war against the king.[3] Symbols and scenes of violence figured prominently in manifestations of dissent. There were assemblies of armed men, and banners might be raised. Martial postures and attitudes were assumed. There were sieges and, now and then, battles. But what motivated the pervasive violence? Did it have any method, rhyme or reason? How was the language of the sword translated into politics? It will be suggested below that the root of the matter lies in the mentality defined by the concept of honour. This, emerging out of a long-established military

* This essay originated in a paper read to the Anglo-American Conference of Historians, Senate House, University of London, on 7 July 1974, entitled "Tudor Revolt: Honour Violence versus Moralized Politics". Earlier drafts were read by Professor John Elliott, Dr J. E. C. Hill and the late Mr J. P. Cooper. I owe much to their comments and criticisms.

1 G. R. Elton, *Policy and Police: The Enforcement of the Reformation in the Age of Thomas Cromwell* (Cambridge, 1972).

2 *Ibid.*, pp. 4 ff.

3 J. G. Bellamy, *The Law of Treason in England in the Later Middle Ages* (Cambridge Studies in English Legal History, Cambridge, 1970), ch. 8; Elton, *op. cit.*, ch. 6.

and chivalric tradition, is characterized above all by a stress on competitive assertiveness; it assumes a state of affairs in which resort to violence is natural and justifiable; the recurrence of personal and political situations in which conflict cannot be otherwise resolved than violently. Honour could both legitimize and provide moral reinforcement for a politics of violence.

But it will also be argued that the sense of what honour implied underwent a change of emphasis, apparent by the early seventeenth century. From this a different attitude to politically motivated violence gradually formed itself. This involved the emergence of a "civil" society in which the monopoly both of honour and violence by the state was asserted. Equally important in bringing the change about is the more or less coterminous process which I shall call "the moralization of politics". Out of these developments a shift in political culture and climate of opinion can be discerned, relevant for example to some of the peculiarities of the revolts against Tudor rule, and particularly to the fact that some of these were less violent than we might expect revolts to be. Obviously this was not the only factor at work. No doubt the Tudors did succeed, by and large, in making revolt a more dangerous and difficult proceeding. But Tudor order would not have been feasible without the collaboration of the majority of the governing class, who controlled the principal order-keeping forces available. Tudor order needed therefore to be freely accepted, assimilated, and given compelling moral force. The process whereby a system of social controls and moral sanctions was effectively internalized emerges out of the changes in attitude and mentality to which I have referred. These, it will be suggested, received comprehensive expression in the synthesis of honour, humanistic "wisdom" and Protestant religion achieved in the literary products of the Sidney circle at the Elizabethan court. It will be argued however (by way of conclusion) that this composite Tudor court culture, which aspired to be honourable, religious and wise, disintegrated under the stresses to which it became subject under the rule of the first two Stuarts. These were the result of political frustration, and of disillusionment with the Stuart political system and policies. As a result attitudes could develop which sharpened the edge of political conflict, providing the terms in which a resort to violence could once more be envisaged: either those of Puritan millenarianism; or of an honour cut loose from its moorings to religion and wisdom.

ASPECTS OF HONOUR

Honour and violence

The expositors of honour whose writings circulated in England and Scotland at the turn of the fifteenth and sixteenth centuries were unanimous that blood and lineage predisposed to honourable behaviour. Caxton, translating a French version of Raymond Lull's *The Book of the Ordre of Chyvalry* (printed sometime between 1483 and 1485), actually tightened his author's references to lineage as of the essence of knighthood, excluding the latter's occasional brief references to meritocratic criteria as also relevant to chivalric status.[4] Similarly the immensely popular *Boke of Saint Albans*, reprinted again and again between 1486 and 1610, followed the tradition which divided mankind into the descendants of Japheth, ennobled by the paternal blessing conferred on their ancestor Noah; and the descendants of Ham, rendered ignoble by Noah's curse.[5] But the Bartolan view,[6] which circulated particularly among the meritocratic nobilities of the robe of western Europe, was also reflected in the insular treatises. This emphasized the nature of honour as the reward of "virtue". Both Lull and the St Albans author, in their insistence that the nobility which lineage conferred needed to be supplemented by virtue (conceived as an unswerving exercise of will), stood within the Bartolan tradition. It was virtue which made the potential honourable quality of a man actual. *The Boke of Saint Albans* listed the virtues which gentlefolk should cultivate: fortitude, prudence, wisdom, hope, steadfastness, all related

[4] *The Book of the Ordre of Chyvalry, translated and printed by William Caxton from a French Version of Ramón Lull'a "Le libre del orde de cauayleria"*, ed. A. T. P. Byles (Early English Text Soc., clxviii, London, 1926), pp. xxxviii–xxxix.

[5] Dame Juliana Berners, *The Boke of Saint Albans . . . Containing Treatises on Hawking, Hunting and Cote Armour. Printed at Saint Albans . . . in 1486*, reproduced in facsimile with an introduction by William Blades (London, 1881), fos. A.i^{r}, A.ii.

[6] Expressed in the *Tractatus de insigniis et armis* printed in 1475, and the commentary *Ad librum duodecim Codicis. De dignitatibus*, both of the fourteenth-century civilian Bartolus de Saxoferrato; see his *Opera*, ed. P. C. Brederodius, 5 vols. (Basle, 1588–9), iv (3), pp. 114–23. See also J. P. Cooper, "General Introduction" to the *New Cambridge Modern History*, iv, *The Decline of Spain and the Thirty Years War, 1609–58–59*, ed. J. P. Cooper (Cambridge, 1970), pp. 1–66, at p. 16.

to conduct in war and battle. Peace required only courtliness and justice.[7] In Lull too, virtue was essentially "prouesse" and the "nobility of his courage" by which the knight proved his noble origin.[8]

The warlike emphasis is significant. There is no reference in these early expositions of honour to the sense, prominent in the Bartolan tradition, of learning as a qualification for nobility: that honour might be attained by the pen, as well as the sword.[9] Caxton's Raymond Lull accepted, as one of the ineluctable facts of life, that knights were not learned, and so (although otherwise excellently suited) might not be, for example, judges.[10] Alexander Barclay differentiated the man of honour from the man of the robe or the ecclesiastic by insisting that the former was the man of deeds, not of the book: "A straw for thy study, thy reason is but blind,/ To waste time in words, and on no deed to muse,/ . . . Therefore reader refuse/ Superfluous study and care superfluous,/ And turne thy chief study to deeds vertuous."[11] A more sophisticated expositor of honour like the Scots humanist Gavin Douglas could attempt in his allegorical anatomy of honour, *The Palice of Honour*[12] of 1501, to relate other value systems to those of the men of deeds. Saints and philosophers, and even poets and courtly lovers, were to be encountered on the road to, and even in the outskirts of, the allegorical Palace.[13] But they were seen only as remote and humble suppliants for the favour of its monarch, Honour himself. Such were not to be found in the presence chamber where Honour held court with his intimates. Here he sits armed, surrounded by princes in

[7] Berners, *Boke of Saint Albans*, ed. Blades, sig. a.iv[v], a.[r].
[8] *Book of the Ordre of Chyvalry*, ed. Byles, pp. 16–17.
[9] Cooper, *op. cit.*, p. 22. For the roots of the concept of a nobility of learning, as well as of arms, in the rhetorical topos *sapientia et fortitudo*, see E. R. Curtius, *Europäische Literatur und lateinisches Mittelalter* (Berne, 1948), pp. 185 ff.
[10] *Book of the Ordre of Chyvalry*, ed. Byles, p. 30.
[11] Alexander Barclay, *The Mirrour of Good Maners*, repr. from the edition of 1570 (Spenser Soc., xxxviii, Manchester, 1885), p. 18.
[12] See Gavin Douglas, *The Palice of Honour*, in *The Shorter Poems of Gavin Douglas*, ed. Priscilla J. Bawcutt (Scottish Text Soc., 4th ser., iii, Edinburgh and London, 1967), pp. 1–133.
[13] Douglas represents the different ways leading to Honour's Palace by various processions or "courts" in progress, which he encounters and describes, viz. (1) the court of Sapience, the way of wisdom, practical or contemplative; (2) the court of Diane, the way of chastity; (3) the court of Venus, the way of love; (4) the court of Rhetoric, to which the poet attaches himself. See *ibid.*, pp. xxxviii ff., and C. S. Lewis, *English Literature in the Sixteenth Century* (Oxford, 1954), pp. 76 ff.

gold armour. The antechamber is filled with "most valiant folk", slain in just battle.[14] Again it is a warlike society which is found at the heart of the whole structure, from which all value radiates: for Honour is identified with God himself.

A martial and warlike emphasis is to be found unaltered and unqualified in some of the earlier Elizabethan writers on honour. For Gerard Legh in 1562 the "virtue" which conferred honour is (as for Lull) a "glory got by courage of manhood", and "martial prowess" is "the chief advancer of gentry".[15] The martial reference, with its framework of heroic values and chivalry, thus imparted a flavour of violence to the "deeds" by which honour was earned. But the man of honour did not need to be a soldier, nor did honour necessarily require a setting of battle. In peacetime honour could become self-assertiveness: the capture of the attention of "the world", and of public esteem. For without the confirmation which the latter provided, honour remained subjective, and to indistinguishable from vanity.[16] The principle is clearly stated by Cleland early in the reign of James I: "Honour is not in his hand who is honoured, but in the hearts and opinions of other men."[17] But the same position had been that of Malory in the reign of Edward IV, for whom honour was similarly repute. Dishonour occurred, so Sir Bors told Sir Lancelot, when "the world would speak of you shame to the world's end".[18] The thirst for esteem could be slaked by a socially accorded "pre-eminence" involving the exercise of governance, which like battle had its coercive implications. For Lull the knight was entrusted with the sword to rule, as well as to slay his lord's enemies: "So much noble is chivalry that every knight ought to be governor of a great country or land . . . " The common people are defended by the knight, but it is because of their fear of him that they toil and cultivate the earth; it is his task to punish the wicked.[19] Even in peace the way of honour was the way of the sword, whose

[14] Douglas, *The Palice of Honour*, ll. 1,965–71 (ed. Bawcutt, pp. xliv–xlv, 122–3).
[15] Gerard Legh, *The Accedens of Armory* (London, 1562, S.T.C. 15388), pp. 22 ff., and (London, 1597 edn, S.T.C. 15392), fo. a.iv^{v}.
[16] Cf. J. Pitt-Rivers, "Honour and Social Status", in J. G. Peristiany (ed.), *Honour and Shame: The Values of Mediterranean Society* (London, 1965), pp. 19–77.
[17] James Cleland, *Propaideia, or the Institution of a Young Noble Man* (Oxford, 1607, S.T.C. 5393), bk. v, ch. 6.
[18] Sir Thomas Malory, *The Morte Darthur, Parts Seven and Eight*, ed. D. S. Brewer (York Medieval Texts, London, 1968), p. 108.
[19] *Book of the Ordre of Chyvalry*, ed. Byles, pp. 27, 32, 41–2.

prestige was such that those who rose by other callings were often more than ready, given the opportunity, to take it. In an honour society, violence, or the ever-present possibility of violence, was a way of life.

> Take the instant way;
> For honour travels in a strait so narrow
> Where one but goes abreast. Keep then the path,
> For emulation hath a thousand sons
> That one by one pursue. If you give way,
> Or hedge aside from the direct forthright,
> Like to an ent'red tide, they all rush by,
> And leave you hindmost . . .[20]

The competitiveness did not invariably receive violent expression. But aggressivity was always latent in the relationships of men of honour, although subject to the restraints imposed by the solidarities of honour: that is, by lordship, kinship, friendship, and the code implicit in honour itself. Where these were absent, in the company of his equals the man of honour was expected to assert his "pre-eminence", a requirement which imparted a note of tension even to ordinary social intercourse and daily conversation. So much so that Guazzo advised the gentleman to seek relaxation in the company of his inferiors. For with them "he shalbe the chiefe man . . . and rule the company as his list; neither shall he be forced to favor or do anything contrary to his mind: which libertie is seldom allowed him amongst his equals"; for they "will looke for as much prehemminence every way as himselfe".[21]

The competitiveness of honour was veiled by the routines of good manners and courtesy, which helped to contain the latent violence within acceptable limits. But even courtesy did no more than demarcate the battlefield, drawing a line between winners and losers. For it could be dispensed with and replaced by familiarity in the case of those who, for the man of honour, "be such, as he is not like any way, either to be in danger of their hurt, or in need of their help".[22] But the persistent tension means that violence was always

[20] Shakespeare, *Troilus and Cressida*, III. iii. 53–60.

[21] *The Civile Conversation of M. Steeven Guazzo*, trans. George Pettie (London, 1581, S.T.C. 12422), bk. ii, fo. 44b.

[22] Simon Robson, *The Court of Civill Courtesie* (London, 1591, S.T.C. 21136), ch. 1.

liable to escalate from its latent to an actual state, when its expression was the armed conflict of the duel. This was given an extended popularity, from the middle years of the sixteenth century, by the new art of fence of the Italiante style, using the rapier.[23] But in some form it was a feature of all honour societies. Long before the Italian fencing-masters and the touchy etiquette of the point of honour appeared on the scene, the duel had been commended by Nicholas Upton early in the reign of Henry VI, as a manner of fighting which, if authorized by authority, "is for honour", and which "is done principally to prove one his strength and manhood".[24] Conflict was least likely to arise where honour positions were clearly defined in terms of those entitled to deference, and those required to accord it. Such visible symbols as graded styles of dress, distinctive manners, and the enforcement of a table of precedence on public occasions, went some way towards ensuring this. However, the competitiveness and self-assertiveness whose ultimate sanction was violence points to the importance of will and the emphasis on moral autonomy in the structure of honour. From this arose the uneasiness of the man of honour in relation to authority, seen as liable to cabin, crib and confine this same autonomy.[25] Hence the need, so Lull tells us, that "the honour of a King or a prince . . . be according in [that is, should accord with] the honour of a knight".[26] If the accordance broke down, so did the harmonious relationship between authority and the man of honour; the latter then became the potential rebel.

Honour and fatefulness

The role of honour in revolts and rebellions cannot be explained without a consideration of its social dimension. The man of honour

[23] Lawrence Stone, *The Crisis of the Aristocracy, 1558–1641* (Oxford, 1965), pp. 242–50; Ruth Kelso, *The Doctrine of the English Gentleman in the Sixteenth Century* (Univ. of Illinois Studies in Language and Literature, xiv nos. 1–2, Urbana, Ill., 1929; repr. Gloucester, Mass., 1964), pp. 151 ff.; J. D. Aylward, *The English Master of Arms from the Twelfth to the Twentieth Century* (London, 1956).

[24] *The Essential Portions of Nicholas Upton's "De studio militari" . . . Translated by John Blount, Fellow of All Souls, c. 1500*, ed. F. P. Barnard (Oxford, 1931), p. 16.

[25] See J. Pitt-Rivers's suggestive development of this theme in the article "Honor", in *The International Encyclopaedia of the Social Sciences*, ed. D. L. Sills, 17 vols. (New York, 1968), vi, esp. pp. 505–6.

[26] *Book of the Ordre of Chyvalry*, ed. Byles, p. 116.

was not merely violent and self-assertive, he was also involved in strong solidarities, incorporated in a society with its own distinctive organization, legality and culture. As far as the latter is concerned, perhaps the most fundamental tenet of honour belief is that Fate, irrational, incomprehensible and uncontrollable, rules over human history. Events were inevitable and their causes obscure; no explanation was possible why this rather than that should have come to pass. A number of symbols, concepts and personifications has been used to express this point of view, from the *Wyrd* of Anglo-Saxon epic to the Goddess Fortuna inherited from late antiquity, and the Christian God to whom the inexorable aspect of Fate could easily be ascribed. Thus for Fabyan, in his *Chronicle* of 1516, the Norman Conquest is an event essentially unintelligible, although ascribed to God, who "of his unknown judgements to men, and by his high and hid counsel would suffer this duke [William] to conquer so noble a land".[27] Similarly, and according to decrees whose justice only the next world would reveal (so the author of the late alliterative epic *Scottish Ffeilde* tells us), had his heavenly Lord dealt with Richard III, "that rich lord in his bright armour" on the field of Bosworth.[28] The chivalric honour community of Malory's *Morte Darthur*, Christianized though it was, nevertheless projects the deterministic and fateful image of Fortune's wheel, which carries the great king upwards to the height of glory and empire but then inexorably down to defeat and death.[29]

In contrast to the moralized view of history discussed below, for the man of honour events were therefore hag-ridden by Fate. For this reason, although the quality of the assertive will was displayed in the encounter with Fate, honour was not authenticated at the bar of success, or diminished by failure. A typical exponent of the honour code such as the author of *Scottish Ffeilde* does not consider (although no Yorkist) that he has to disparage Richard because of his defeat and fall; nor does he see Bosworth as a punishment for the latter's sins. Even in his defeat Richard vindicated his honour, showing himself "no coward, for he was a king noble", who "fought full freshlie his foemen among".[30] Similarly, for Raymond Lull

[27] Lewis, *English Literature in the Sixteenth Century*, p. 148.
[28] *Scottish Ffeilde*, ed. J. P. Oakden (Chetham Miscellanies, vi; Chetham Soc., new ser., xciv, Manchester, 1935), pp. 1–2, ll. 27–35.
[29] Malory, *Morte Darthur*, ed. Brewer, pp. 8, 142.
[30] *Scottish Ffeilde*, ed. Oakden, pp. 1–2.

defeat carried no disgrace, for only the power of God could stand eternally. It was the knight who refused to die with his stricken lord who merited condemnation.[31] Honour was established, not primarily by the skill with which events and situations were manipulated with a view to a successful outcome, important though this might be to confirm and enhance standing and status, but by the determined "steadfastness" with which they were confronted.[32] Consistency in standing by a position once taken up was basic to the honour code. But, since the latter was a public one, that of a society of honourable men, there was the need to define the position to which honour was committed by a public gesture. This took the form of promise and oath, the giving of one's word, the "word of honour". Once this had been done, the man of honour could withdraw only at the expense of the diminishment involved in dishonour.[33]

Honour and religion

In some important, indeed fundamental, respects honour involved a tension with religious values which was not easily resolved. There was the problem of how a code which glorified self-esteem, and the self-assertive will in the conflict with Fate, could be reconciled with the very different emphasis of Christianity. Thus, among the theologians, for St Thomas Aquinas the way of honour, whose rewards derived from human opinion, in its nature ephemeral, could confer no more than a transient "repute". It was not therefore to be compared with the eternal beatitude which awaited those who trod the narrow and thorny path of religion.[34] But in pre-Reformation religion the tension tended to be slackened by the lines of demar-

[31] *Book of the Ordre of Chyvalry*, ed. Byles, pp. 32–3.

[32] Almost any reference to any honour culture encounters this attitude. Cf., for example, the early medieval Russian epic *Igor's Tale*, with its glorification of honour, and the comment of G. P. Fedotov: "Glory is not given by sucesss or political might, but by intrepid conduct. That is why the poem ends with a 'glory song' to Igor and his kinsmen, although from a political point of view their campaign was a failure and defeat." G. P. Fedotov, *The Russian Religious Mind. Kieven Christianity: The Tenth to the Thirteenth Centuries* (New York, 1960), p. 329.

[33] See Pitt-Rivers, "Honor", pp. 505–6, and Pitt-Rivers, "Honour and Social Status", pp. 32–4.

[34] St Thomas Aquinas, *Summa contra gentiles*, III. i. 63, and III. i. 29; St Thomas Aquinas, *Summa theologica*, I. ii. 69. See C. B. Watson, *Shakespeare and the Renaissance Concept of Honor* (Princeton, 1960), pp. 102 ff.

cation which compartmentalized the religious culture. Sacred was marked off from secular, nature from supernature, religion from "the world". Moral and religious problems were liable to be stated and resolved in legal terms rather than in those of direct personal involvement and decision. One respect in which the sense of tension between honour and religion emerged was in the distinction made, in matters of honour, between the clergy and the laity. The former, at least as far as their sacerdotal office was concerned, were outside the community of honour. In theory they had no part in honour loyalties and attachments, and were denied the coercive and militant role to which the man of honour aspired.[35] The apartness of the clergy strengthened the sense of the boundary which separated "this world" from "the world to come", religion being essentially concerned with the latter. There the destiny of the soul would be affected by the ritualistic and charitable works, particularly the administration of the sacraments, which the clergy performed. The aggressivity of honour, its wars and violence, could be subjected to trenchant criticism in terms of the evangelical precepts.[36] But in the dominant opinion it was understood in terms of the law of nature. This, since the Fall, was permeated with violence. The beasts, and even the elements, were at war with each other.[37]

Two approaches were tried which would confer on honour and its associated way of life an acceptable role within the purview of a Christian culture. The first is to be found in John of Salisbury's *Policraticus*, a mid-twelfth-century production which foreshadows many features which would later characterize the Bartolan tra-

[35] For the attitude of the church to the duel and related forms of honour violence, see Frank R. Bryson, *The Sixteenth-Century Italian Duel: A Study in Renaissance Social History* (Chicago, 1938), pp. 114 ff. For Malory, clerical status or entry into religion implied a separation from honour loyalties and attachments. When Guinevere became a nun and Lancelot a priest, both repudiated their way of life in the former Arthurian community. The "hermit" in the story of "The Fair Maid of Astolat" was once a knight, and a member of the Round Table; but, being vowed to God, he had abandoned his chivalric and Arthurian loyalties. See Malory, *Morte Darthur*, ed. Brewer, p. 33.

[36] See, for example, the self-analysis and self-criticism of a famous knight, Henry of Grosmont, duke of Lancaster, in his *Livre de seyntz medicines*, discussed by John Barnie in his *War in Medieval Society: Social Values and the Hundred Years War, 1337–99* (London, 1974), pp. 58 ff. Cf. the critique of honour values and "worship" by the "Loller" knight Sir John Clanvowe in his "The Two Ways", in *The Works of Sir John Clanvowe*, ed. V. J. Scattergood (Cambridge, 1975), p. 69.

[37] M. H. Keen, *The Laws of War in the Late Middle Ages* (London, 1965), pp. 8–9.

dition.[38] According to this work, the violence of the warrior was the vehicle of God's judgements on man's sins. The knighthood wielded the sword, not to obtain riches and glory, but "to execute the judgement that is committed to them to execute; wherein each follows not his own will, but the deliberate decision of God, the angels, and men, in accordance with equity and public utility".[39] John had little interest in the code of honour, in chivalry as such, or even in lineage and noble blood (although he thought this might be useful as conducive to courage). His concern was with the knight as the executant of divine judgement, and as the upholder of "equity and public utility". As such, he wielded the sword as the agent of constituted authority, either that of the church or of the state. His approach in this respect paralleled that of such fourteenth-century civil lawyers as Bartolus, John of Legnano and Honoré Bonet, for whom the knighthood were the instruments of "the just war", authorized by public authority (emperor, king or prince). In such a war, violence could be put to a proper constructive use in the defence of "justice" Excess would be curbed by the legal controls of the *ius gentium* and of "the law of arms". In the just war, honour, conferred by the prince in whose name the war had first been declared, could be legitimately sought.[40]

As against John of Salisbury's approach, with its affinities to the civil law and the Bartolan tradition, there was that of Raymond Lull. While the ideas of *Policraticus* found a sympathetic echo among the lawyer bureaucracies of late medieval Europe, it was Lull's book which established itself among the nobilities of the sword as the textbook of honour and chivalry. As Caxton's *Book of the Ordre of Chyvalry* it was to make a powerful contribution to Tudor concepts of gentility. Unlike John of Salisbury, Lull extolled noble blood. It has been seen above that he glorified the martial virtues and the way of honour; he approved the cult of lineage, arms and the chase.[41] Like John, he saw the knighthood as an order, or "Christian profession", parallel to that of the clergy. By the sword it imposed order and rule, defending its lord and the church in the

38 See Sidney Painter, *French Chivalry: Chivalric Ideas and Practices in Medieval France* (Baltimore, 1940), pp. 68 ff.
39 *Ibid.*, p. 70.
40 For the theory of the just war, see Keen, *op. cit.*, pp. 63 ff.
41 See above, pp. 310–11. See also Painter, *op. cit.*, pp. 76 ff.

"just war". But the emphasis in Lull is less on the role of "the prince" as the fount of honour and honourable enterprise. Instead it is the corporate authority of the code of honour and of the order of chivalry itself which is invoked. Emperors, kings and princes themselves belonged to that order, and were as much bound by it as their knights.[42] The code required not only faithfulness on the part of a knight to his lord, but also that the latter should uphold his knight's "franchise" (freedom) and honour, respecting it as much as his own.[43]

The operation of the laws of war in the later middle ages suggests that such views conformed to significant realities in what Malory called the "worshipful" way of honour. There was a strong sense of the corporate chivalric code, to which princes as well as knights were subject, and which claimed a jurisdiction as wide as Christendom itself. In the context of the code, treason could take place not only against the prince, but against the order of knighthood itself. Henry V in 1418 sentenced a French knight to death in a military court, not for treason against himself but against his enemy the king of France. He did so because the knight, by surrendering a town, had betrayed his lord. The code of honour, which all kings, themselves knights, were equally required to uphold, had thus been contravened.[44] A knight might appeal to the corporate authority of honour against the king. The seigneur de Barbason did so when condemned to death by Henry V for implication in the murder of John the Fearless. A point of honour was involved, for Barbason had fought with the king man to man; he was thus his "brother-in-arms". Chivalry required that one brother-in-arms should not put another to death. Thus Barbason was able to appeal from the king's jurisdiction to that of the heralds. As a result his life was spared.[45]

The code of honour constituted a body of custom relating to the way of life, and particularly to the warlike activities, of the western nobilities of the sword. Its authorities were experienced knights and squires, *chivalers et esquiers de valu*; the heralds, its recorders and judges. But as "the law of arms" it stood in relation to the canon and

[42] *Book of the Ordre of Chyvalry*, ed. Byles, p. 115: "yf to a kyng ne to a prynce were not noblesse of Chyvalry incorporate . . . & that they hadde not in them the vertues ne thonour that apperteyneth to thordre of chyvalry, They shold not be worthy to be kynges ne Prynces ne lordes of Countrees".

[43] See above, p. 314 and note 25.

[44] Keen, *op. cit.*, pp. 46, 53.

[45] *Ibid.*, p. 53.

civil laws, both grounded in the divine law which was binding on all Christian men.[46] Most knights, although there were notable exceptions, would no doubt not be likely to take very seriously Lull's exhortation to follow the Christian virtues, as well as those of chivalry. The former were the primary concern of monks, not knights; or could be left to old age, when the man of honour, now too enfeebled for deeds of arms, should devote himself to "ghostly chivalry and deeds of arms spiritual".[47] The horizontally demarcated lines marking off one Christian profession from another, with the vertical gradations of the hierarchy leading up from nature to supernature, from the "law of arms" to *ius divinum* and Christian perfection, all helped to clear a space for honour. As a result the warrior values of ancient Germanic society continued to flourish as a corporate way of life in a setting whose dominant tone was Christian.

In the sixteenth century however it became less easy to keep this space open. A reaction developed, particularly operative in the English social scene, against the sense of honour as a corporate code, in Lull's sense, binding on princes and subjects alike, with an independent authority of its own. In particular, honour was increasingly required to adapt itself to the demands of religion, and to those of the state. The religious pressures seem to have been as much at work in the Europe of the Counter-Reformation as in that of the Protestants. But in Tudor England it was the influence of the Reformation which was felt. This expressed itself in the demand of the Protestant expositors of honour for a total Christianization of the code. In part this involved simply a stronger emphasis on aspects of the Bartolan tradition. Protestant writers, with the Erasmians as their direct precursors, cried up the nobility of virtue, the road to which was opened by the new humanist educational programmes.[48] There was a denigration of the honour cult of lineage, ceremony and

[46] *Ibid.*, pp. 34–5, 19–20, 239 ff.

[47] As recommended to Sir John Fastolf by Stephen Scrope in the dedication of his translation of Christine de Pisan, *The Epistle of Othea to Hector: or, The Boke of Knyghthode*, ed. G. F. Warner (Roxburghe Club, London, 1904). See Arthur B. Ferguson, *The Indian Summer of English Chivalry* (Durham, N.C., 1960), p. 56.

[48] For an early instance of this approach, with a strong emphasis on learning as the root of nobility, see *The Institucion of a Gentleman* (London, 1568 edn, S.T.C. 14105).

magnificence, and of such honour symbols as coats of arms.[49] The "franchise" and autonomy which Lull had been willing to attribute to the man of honour had no place in the Protestant interpretation of the code, in which the role of authority is stressed as the fount of honour, and as the sole legitimizer of honour violence. The content of Protestant education aimed at a training in obedience as one of its primary objectives. The children of the gentry, so one of the earlier Protestant expositors of honour wrote, were to be taught to fear God, honour their parents, and to "know their obedience and duty towards the king his Majesty, his councillors, officers, and administrators, both high and low".[50]

Moreover the "king's majesty" thus conceived was more than the colourless "public authority" of Bartolus and the civilians. Instead kingship was internalized as the powerful image of the "godly prince", to be encountered in the pages of Scripture as the agent of a law which was not merely natural and human, but divine. The service of that law moreover required a total religious commitment. Protestant man, justified by faith, could not delegate this to specialized religious groups like the monastic orders, or defer it to the later years of life. It confronted him directly, at all times. John Norden therefore, writing for the swordsmen of the second earl of Essex's entourage, abandoned the traditional self-reliance and moral autonomy of the man of honour in favour of a direct religious motivation: "In vain doth he hope that feareth not God, and in vain he fighteth that fighteth without God's assistance . . . no man can be honourable without divine inspiration and inward motion." It was faith, not conformity to the code of honour, which enabled a general "to shake off the clogs of cowardice and a covetous desire, which hinder much the success of war". Hence the queen, as became a godly prince, did well when appointing a commander to consider

[49] See Erasmus, *Enchiridion militis christiani, or The Manual of the Christian Knight* (London, 1544, S.T.C. 10483), reprinted as *A Book Called in Latin 'Enchridion militis christiani'* (London, 1905), pp. 193, 222; St Thomas More, *Utopia*, ed. Edward Surtz and J. H. Hexter, in *The Complete Works of St Thomas More*, iv (Yale edn, New Haven, 1965), pp. 63, 169, 244; Thomas Starkey, *A Dialogue between Cardinal Pole and Thomas Lupset* (Early English Text Soc., extra ser., xxiv, London, 1878), pp. 77, 129, 160, 188; Laurence Humphrey, *The Nobles, or Of Nobilitye* (London, 1563, S.T.C. 13964), sig. a.iv^{r}, and a.ii^{r}.

[50] *The Institucion of a Gentleman*, sig. a.iii^{r}.

especially "his wisdom and fear of God".[51] These were attitudes closely connected with the moralization of politics.

It was over the question of honour violence in one of its most characteristic expressions, the duel, that the keenest tension developed between Christianity and honour. Duelling was forbidden by canon law in Catholic countries; Protestants pointed to the biblical commandment "Thou shalt not Kill" as proof of its absolute prohibition.[52] Duels were occasionally permitted by the states of western Europe but only under conditions of legal safeguard, and with the consent of public authority which was increasingly rarely given.[53] But the belief persisted that every gentleman had the right to defend his honour by the sword, which alone could decide disputes in which it was brought into question.[54] Thus in practice the "private" duel which had not been publicly authorized remained widespread, and its incidence probably increased in the later sixteenth century.[55] The herald William Segar, writing in 1602, admitted that duels were prohibited by church and state, but condoned those which took place in private. He gave details of the rules which ought to govern such encounters, for it was reasonable that "a martial man, justly challenged, should without offence appear in the field to defend his honour", provided the matter was settled outside

[51] John Norden, *The Mirror of Honor* (London, 1597, S.T.C. 18614), pp. 15–16.

[52] See Bryson, *Sixteenth-Century Italian Duel*, pp. 114 ff. For a statement of a Protestant approach, see *The Charge of Sir Francis Bacon . . . Touching Duells* (London, 1614, S.T.C. 1125; facsimile reprint, Amsterdam and New York, 1968).

[53] For a brief account, see John Selden, *The Duello, or Single Combat* (London, 1610, S.T.C. 22171).

[54] See Bryson, *op. cit.*, *passim*. The idea of a sovereign prince, who alone authorized war and personal combat, involved a conflict with the older view whereby it was taken for granted that any person of noble status was entitled to wage war. *Les coutumes de Beauvaisis*, as expounded by Beaumanoir, assumed the privilege of all gentlemen to settle their disputes by arms if they so wished. In England levying war, even against the king, was seldom regarded as high treason before the reign of Edward I. See Keen, *Laws of War*, pp. 72–3. Such attitudes survived and were widely tolerated into the sixteenth century and later. For Bodin "the Prince can dispose of a subject's life and goods, but not of his honour"; he maintained that, in spite of many royal edicts against duelling, the principle once enunciated by Francis I, who in council denied "that man to be worthy who, given the lie, would not spurn it with arms (*virum bonum esse qui mendacium oblatum armis non reiiceret*)" was the rule among the French nobility. See Cooper, "General Introduction" to *New Cambridge Modern History*, iv, p. 24, and Selden, *op. cit.*, p. 15.

[55] Cf. above, p. 314 and note 23.

the prince's territorial jurisdiction.[56] Nicholas Upton, early in the fifteenth century, could defend the duellist as incurring no blame as long as his intention was not malicious, but merely to display strength or gain honour.[57] But a civilian lawyer like Feretti, in the sixteenth century, regarded hatred as inherent in the nature of the duel, the result of the universal enmity which was apparent in the law of nature.[58]

Implicit in such positions was a strain of latent indifference to religion, combined with anti-clericalism, and a kind of secularism. There were Italian theorists of the point of honour who asserted (a characteristically Italian position) that the man of honour could not be subject to rules made for monks. Possevino, in the middle of the sixteenth century, even asserted that knights did not wish to be Christians;[59] Maffei, at the beginning of the eighteenth, could remark that a man who sought to avoid a duel on the grounds that he was a Christian would be banished from the profession of knighthood and honour.[60] Similar opinions circulated in the England of James I and may be found reproduced in Northampton's anti-duelling pamphlet "Duello Foiled":[61]

> *Vim vi repellere* is *juris naturae*, whether that violence be offered to a man's person or fame . . . he that wrongs me in my honour shall without peradventure know that I carry not a sword of lath but of bright metal, and revenge is necessary to keep the world in good order . . . [62]

Or there was the position of Robert, Lord Sanquhar, brought to trial by King James for an honour killing: "I considered not my

56 William Segar, *Honor Military, and Civill* (London, 1602, S.T.C. 22164), pp. 116, 125 ff.

57 *Essential Portions of Nicholas Upton's "De studio militari"*, ed. Barnard, p. 15.

58 Bryson, *op. cit.*, p. xxiii.

59 Quoted in *ibid.*, p. 120.

60 *Ibid.*

61 "Duello Foiled, or The Whole Proceedings in the Orderly Disposing of a Design for Single Fight between Two Valiant Gentlemen", in Thomas Hearne (ed.), *A Collection of Curious Discourses* . . . , 2 vols. (London, 1771 edn), ii, pp. 223–42, where it is attributed to Sir Edward Coke. The authorship of Henry Howard, earl of Northampton, seems now to be established by a manuscript of the text in Bodleian Lib., Ashmole MS. 856. This states that the work was written by Howard. I owe this information to the kindness of Miss E. M. Rainey of Durham University Library. See also F. T. Bowers, "Henry Howard, Earl of Northampton and the Jacobean Duel", *Englische Studien*, lxx (1937), pp. 350–5.

62 "Duello Foiled", pp. 228, 230.

wrongs upon terms of Christianity . . . but being trained up in the courts of princes and in arms, I stood upon the terms of honour."[63]

In a sense the true religion of the man of honour lay in the immortality which honourable deeds conferred, their memory being preserved and celebrated in the community to which he belonged. The typical vehicle for this memory was the epic poem, declaimed by a minstrel in hall before the lord and his followers. The persisting attraction of the epic for communities of honour even into the Tudor period is shown by the above-named alliterative instance of the genre, *Scottish Ffeilde*, composed shortly after Flodden, in the circle of the Stanley earls of Derby.[64] At court, during Elizabeth's reign, a minstrel was still retained on the royal cheque-roll who "commodiously sang to the harp in places of assembly, where the company shall be desirous to hear of old adventures and valiaunces of knights in times past".[65] Gavin Douglas was one of those who sought to use the resources of humanism for the needs of the community of honour, adapting classical epic by translating Virgil's *Aeneid* for this purpose.[66] In his translation he used what he called a "noble" or "knight-like" style, meaning by this literally (and not just in the rhetorical sense) a style intended not for scholars but for nobles and knights, to move them to courage and deeds of honour.[67] These were the readers Douglas sought and the critics whose good opinion he valued. "Churls" were to be snubbed if they dared question his Virgilian renderings. But nobles were to be invited to do so.[68] For Douglas men of honour were in fact endowed with a kind

[63] *State Trials*, ii, col. 747.

[64] *Scottish Ffeilde*, ed. Oakden, pp. viii–x.

[65] John Stevens, *Music and Poetry in the Early Tudor Court* (London, 1961), pp. 281–2. Significantly, minstrelsy and heraldry were originally closely connected, the herald's office evolving out of the minstrel's; see N. Denholm-Young, *History and Heraldry, 1254 to 1310: A Study of the Historical Value of the Roll of Arms* (Oxford, 1965), pp. 54 ff.

[66] *Virgil's "Aeneid" Translated into Scottish Verse by Gavin Douglas*, ed. D. F. C. Coldwell, 4 vols. (Scottish Text Soc., xxv, xxvii, xxviii and xxx, Edinburgh and London, 1957–64). Cf. Sir John Clanvowe's strictures on the "worshipful" of whom "men maken bookes and songes and reeden and syngen of them for to holde the mynde of here deedes the lengere heere upon eerth": *Works of Sir John Clanvowe*, ed. Scattergood, p. 69.

[67] See "The Proloug of the Nynth Buke", in *Virgil's "Aeneid" Translated . . . by Gavin Douglas*, ed. Coldwell, iii, pp. 169–71; Lewis, *English Literature in the Sixteenth Century*, p. 85.

[68] "Ane Exclamatioun Aganyst Detractouris and Oncurtass Redaris" (appended to "The Threttene Buke of Eneados"), ll. 37–40, in *Virgil's "Aeneid" Translated . . . by Gavin Douglas*, ed. Coldwell, iv, p. 193.

of innate insight into what an epic ought to be, and how it should be presented. For the epic immortalized what should be its own way of life.

Honour and lineage

The "steadfastness" of the man of honour, manifesting itself in a "faithfulness" to his freely given word, was of the essence of the social dimension of honour. Only one obligation went deeper than this: that to the lineage, the family and kinship group. For this, being inherited with the "blood", did not depend on promise or oath. It could neither be contracted into, nor could the bond be broken. For a man's very being as honourable had been transmitted to him with the blood of his ancestors, themselves honourable men. Honour therefore was not merely an individual possession, but that of the collectivity, the lineage. Faithfulness to the kinship group arose out of this intimate involvement of personal and collective honour, which meant that both increased or diminished together. Consequently, in critical honour situations where an extremity of conflict arose, or in which dissident positions were taken up involving revolt, treason and rebellion, the ties of blood were liable to assert themselves with a particular power. Malory, meditating the internal inconsistencies liable to disrupt honour societies, made the stronger compulsion of the claims of blood over those of chivalric fellowship a prime theme of his greatest work.[69]

Thus the man of honour would be likely to hold, even after faithfulness to king or lord had been broken, to the bond between the lineage and himself. The earl of Westmorland, in 1569, at first recoiled from treason because of the dishonour which this would bring to the lineage: "I will never blot my house, which hath been thus long preserved without staining."[70] But once the decision to rise had been taken, the house of Neville, in all its branches, rose with him. The Nortons, Markenfields and Dacres were similarly involved on the same occasion, as lineages, in collective disaster. Other loyalties were liable to be jettisoned if these brought into question the claims of "blood". Leonard Dacre found it impossible to maintain a conformity to the queen's law once this had dis-

[69] See above, pp. 272–3 and the references there given.
[70] Sir C. Sharp, *Memorials of the Rebellion of 1569* (London, 1840), p. 196.

inherited him, carrying the lands and dignities of his lineage into the hands of strangers.[71] For the man of honour personal advancement was not easily separable from that of the lineage. Gavin Douglas, recruited to be the agent of Henry VIII in the Scotland of the infant James V, was promised not merely his own advancement, but also that "your blood will be made for ever".[72] The greatest gain was to be the family's. Of course, as a result of the new pressures which made themselves felt in the course of the sixteenth century, particularly those of religion (so alien to the sense of lineage),[73] families did become divided. Religious commitment assailed the sense of lineage, as well as the honour emphasis on self-reliance and the will. For Richard Brathwait, for example, "he who prefers the care of his family before the advancement of God's glory, may seeme to be of the Cardinell Bourbon's minde, who would not lose his part in Paris, for his part in Paradise".[74] But often apparently opposed religious and political positions on the part of leading members of the same lineage simply served to ensure the preservation and continuity of the "blood".[75] The earl of Northumberland, head of the

[71] See above, pp. 275–8.

[72] Adam Williamson to Gavin Douglas, n.d. (*circa* 1515/16); printed in *The Poetical Works of Gavin Douglas*, ed. John Small, 4 vols. (Edinburgh, 1874), i, p. xxii.

[73] The disruptive pressure which religious conviction could assert in a setting of lineage loyalties is well illustrated by a letter of Sir Francis Hastings, the fervently Puritan brother of the third earl of Huntingdon, to an otherwise unknown cousin Anne, a Protestant convert in a Catholic household: "I know they will say to you, your father, your mother, all your friends and kindred are good Catholics, and in professing this religion you must needs condemn them and all your forefathers which were wise and learned, therefore beware what you do. But to this you may easily answer, 'Each one is to be saved by his own faith, and not by the faith of any other', and with Cyprian you may say, 'We are not to take what they did which were before us, but what Christ did which was before all, and follow that.'" See Claire Cross, *The Puritan Earl: The Life of Henry Hastings, Third Earl of Huntingdon, 1536–1595* (London, 1966), p. 37.

[74] Richard Brathwait, *The English Gentleman* (London, 1630, S.T.C. 3563).

[75] Even the Hastings family, fervently Protestant after the accession of the third earl in its dominant tone, nevertheless consistently retained footholds in both religious camps. The politique conformism of the second earl of Huntingdon, the fervent Catholicism of his brother Lord Hastings or Loughborough, played their part with the equally fervent Protestant convictions of the third earl in ensuring the survival of the lineage during a period of rapid religious change. Even during the third earl's lengthy tenure of the title Catholic connections persisted without any serious disruption of family unity. The third earl's brother and heir retained Catholic sympathies, and was regarded by Catholics as the true heir to the Hastings claim to the throne; so did another younger brother, Walter Hastings. The religious unity of the family became consolidated only in the reign of

house of Percy, rebelled in 1569; but his brother and heir,[76] on whom the family title and estates were entailed, took up a "loyal" position, so ensuring their preservation in the Percy line. Under the Tudors it was common for the head of the lineage to stand aloof from civil commotions. His sympathies could be sufficiently, and less dangerously, indicated by the participation of a younger son, or the head of a cadet branch. But the widely diffused sense of blood and lineage meant that the government was rarely deceived by such devices. The non-participation of the head of the family rarely preserved him from some form of reprisal, including prosecution if a case at law could be established. Sir Thomas Arundell, head of the house of Lanherne, was brought to the block as a result of the Western Prayer Book Rebellion of 1549, in spite of the fact that it was his cousin, and not himself, who had been the leading activist of that movement.[77]

Honour and lordship

The political culture of the world of honour was essentially pluralist. There was little room for the concepts of sovereignty, or of unconditional obedience, and such other *étatiste* notions whose acceptability rose and then declined in the course of the century before 1640. Both Caxton and Sir Gilbert Hay, in their versions of Lull, stated the duty of the knight to be not necessarily to the king but to his "erthely lord and naturel countrey"; or to "his naturale lord" and to "the peple in thair richtis".[78] Honour societies revered kingship, but the place which will and autonomy occupied in the honour code implied the possibility of changing one's master, if he could no longer be freely and honourably served.[79] Seen in terms of honour, that is in terms of an informal complex of attitudes and modes of behaviour, not to be confused with those of the law, kingship constituted one authority (admittedly the dominant one, whose claim to

James I when the immediate relevance of Catholicism to the interest of a great house faded away. See Cross, *The Puritan Earl*, chs. 1–2.

76 For the career of Sir Henry Percy, brother to the seventh earl of Northumberland, and subsequently eighth earl, see *Dict. Nat. Biog.*, xv, pp. 854–6; Sharp, *Memorials*, pp. 351 ff., and E. B. Barrington de Fonblanque, *Annals of the House of Percy*, 2 vols. (London, 1887), ii, pp. 126 ff.

77 F. Rose-Troup, *The Western Rebellion of 1549* (London, 1913), pp. 351 ff.

78 *Book of the Ordre of Chyvalry*, ed. Byles, p. xxvi.

79 See above, p. 314 and note 26.

"faithfulness" was the widest and most inclusive) among a number. What such authorities had in common was the institution of lordship, the king being the greatest of lords and his court the exemplar, as well as the largest, richest and most brilliant of all honour communities. Typically therefore John, Lord Berners, high priest of honour at the court of Henry VIII, conceived a commonwealth as composed "of divers men and one lord".[80]

It was only gradually, and during the Tudor period, that the realm and the community of honour came to be identical, presided over by a crown whose sovereign authority constituted the only kind of "lordship" which effectively survived. This was the result of a "nationalization" of the honour system for which Henry VIII was most, if not wholly, responsible. It was during his reign that the kingship launched a powerful initiative to establish itself as "the fount of honour", the source not only of "dignity" and office within the crown's gift, but also of gentility itself. At the same time the requirement began to establish itself whereby honourable status needed to be granted or confirmed by state-authenticated and state-supported heraldic visitations. This contrasts with the more informal arrangements which had once applied, and with the largely self-authenticating character which the honour community had previously possessed. For Chaucer, honour was conferred not by royal authority but by public recognition; for Malory, the bearer of kingship was not the fount of honour, but (if the man was equal to the office) the exemplar of all honourable men.[81]

Before the sixteenth century no disciplined organization of the heraldic office under any royal minister existed; and before the Tudor advent the evidence for any effective system of provincial heraldic jurisdiction and visitation is scanty. The doubtful authenticity of the "Ordinances" ascribed to Thomas, duke of Clarence, formerly thought to be drawn up between 1417 and 1421, removes the evidence for any such system in the reign of Henry V.[82] Royal

[80] Antonio de Guevara, *The Golden Boke of Marcus Aurelius* (London, 1535, S.T.C. 12436), p. 28v.

[81] See D. S. Brewer, "Honour in Chaucer", *Essays and Studies* [English Association], new ser., xxvi (1973), pp. 1–19, at pp. 4–5; and Malory, *Morte Darthur*, ed. Brewer, p. 30 and note 24.

[82] See A. R. Wagner, *Heralds and Heraldry in the Middle Ages: An Inquiry into the Growth of the Armorial Functions of Heralds*, 2nd edn (London, 1956), pp. 59–64; Sir Anthony Wagner, *Heralds of England: A History of the Office and College of Arms* (London, 1967), pp. 66–8, and p. 68 note 3.

heralds, and perhaps an organization of two heraldic provinces, one north and one south of Trent, each under a "king of arms", may have existed as early as the reign of Edward I.[83] By the time of the heraldic chapter held at Rouen in 1420, a precedence of royal "kings in arms" over other heralds has clearly established itself;[84] while the earliest surviving trace of a heraldic visitation seems datable to the reign of Edward IV. Richard III's incorporation of the heralds into a college in 1484 further suggests an increasingly powerful royal initiative in matters of honour.[85] But noblemen, as well as kings, had their heralds and made grants of arms. Even for royal heralds the test of honour was "common opinion, but also by the report and witness of other noble men worthy of belief", just as matters in dispute under the law of arms were referred to the arbitrament of *chivalers et esquiers de valu*.[86] Although direct evidence is lacking, the knights' courts of the greater honours, like those of the castles of Carisbrooke, Skipton and Alnwick, may have adjudged matters of honour.[87] It was not until the advent of the Tudors, when so many great aristocratic interests became merged with the crown, that there was a drastic decline in the number of seigneurial officers of arms. Even so heralds survived until the 1530s in the household of such magnates as the dukes of Suffolk and Norfolk, and the earl of Northumberland.[88]

83 Denholm-Young, *History and Heraldry, 1254 to 1310*, pp. 60–1.
84 Wagner, *Heralds of England*, pp. 68–70.
85 *Ibid.*, pp. 123 ff.
86 "par commune renommee mez aussi par le rapport et tesmoignage d'autres nobles hommes dignes de foi", from the patent of arms granted by John Smert, Garter, to Edmond Mylle, 1450; see Wagner, *Heralds and Heraldry in the Middle Ages*, Appendix A (23), pp. 125–6, and p. 77. Cf. the procedure under the law of arms, pp. 319–20 above. For private heralds, see H. S. London and A. R. Wagner, "Heralds of the Nobility", in *Complete Peerage*, xi, Appendix C, pp. 93 ff. For instances of grants of arms by private heralds, see *ibid.*, p. 146; for instances of similar grants by nobles, see Wagner, *Heralds of England*, p. 28. In the course of the fifteenth century it became the established convention that only peers of the rank of earl and above could create heralds (as distinct from pursuivants) and that such creations required royal confirmation. Sir William Bruges, on his creation as Garter King of Arms in 1417, petitioned Henry V that no herald should be created without royal licence; and some such system of control exercised by the crown may have subsequently established itself. But the only two surviving instances of a royal creation of a private herald date from the reigns of Henry VII and Henry VIII. See London and Wagner, *op. cit.*, p. 142.
87 Denholm-Young, *op. cit.*, p. 124. For the continued significance into the sixteenth century of the Alnwick knights' court, see above, pp. 295–7.
88 See London and Wagner, *op. cit.*, pp. 47–8.

Lordship emphasized the hierarchical, stratified character of honour, involving as it did a relationship between superiors and inferiors. For the man of honour it implied a relationship of "faithfulness" to his master, which was owing as long as the latter showed himself a "good" lord – that is, while he protected, was just, rewarded, and took counsel.[89] The setting in which lordship deployed itself was the household of a landed magnate (or of the king) with its inner circle of officers and servants, and its outer circle of client gentry of the "affinity", calling themselves "followers" or "friends". The code of honour required faithfulness to friends as well as to one's lord. The notion of friendship commonly indicated a relationship between equals, and often arose out of "chamber companionship", that is, the sharing of lodgings by young men serving at court or in a great household. The devotion of friends to each other in this sense was an admired feature of the world of honour idealism, celebrated in romance and story.[90] But friendship might also imply a relationship to a benefactor and patron, and as such entered into the implications of lordship.[91] A lord's friendship showed itself in the special trust, good will and "favour" extended to a dependant, requiring a response of fidelity and gratitude on the latter's part.[92]

It is possible that, after the Tudor advent, friendship was increasingly emphasized in the relationship between lordship and affinity.

[89] On "good lordship", see W. H. Dunham, *Lord Hastings' Indentured Retainers* (Trans. of the Connecticut Academy of Arts and Sciences, xxxix, New Haven, Sept. 1955), p. 13, and ch. 2. Cf. above, pp. 52–5.

[90] As, for example, in the late fifteenth-century anonymous *History of Sir Eger, Sir Gryme, and Sir Gray-Steel*, printed in *Early Popular Poetry of Scotland and the Northern Border*, ed. David Laing, and revised by W. C. Hazlitt, 2 vols. (London, 1895), ii, pp. 131–210.

[91] See *Middle English Dictionary*, ed. Hans Kurath and Sherman M. Kuhn, iii (Ann Arbor, Mich., [1952]), pp. 884–5, under the heading "Frend", for uses of the word in the senses of benefactor and patron.

[92] Friendship, trust and fidelity were closely linked. Where the character of a dependant was assumed to be of such integrity that his "faithfulness" could never be called in question, the natural response of a lord was "friendship". The most obvious expression of this would be the grant of office and favours. The common formula for grants of office included a reference to "the especial trust and confidence" placed by the lord in the grantee. The response of the latter was (or ought to be) "faithful affection", that is, a strongly emotive relationship which went beyond the more contractual implications of faithfulness. Aristotle, but above all Cicero's *De amicitia*, provided popularizing moralists like Sir Thomas Elyot with their model for faithfulness and friendship. See Watson, *Shakespeare and the Renaissance Concept of Honour*, pp. 260 ff.

This would be a natural development as the contractual bonds of mesne tenancy or retainder, which had bound lord and following, disintegrated or fell under the ban of the law. For the fourth duke of Norfolk the gentry of the Howard following in East Anglia were the "friends" on whom he could rely in his country, and whose advice was to be taken should the queen veto his proposed match to the queen of Scots.[93] The earl of Northumberland similarly spoke of the "friends" with whom there were so many consultations in the months before the Northern Rising was decided on.[94] The network of mesne tenancies by knight service which had formerly bound so many of the gentry of north Yorkshire, Northumberland and Cumberland to his family had long been undermined by the intrusions of royal authority and the decline of feudal ties. The more informal relationship of friendship was all that remained.[95] Towards the end of the century there was the following of the earl of Essex,

[93] Thus the seventh earl of Northumberland reported the receipt of a letter from the duke on the eve of the Northern Rising, "the effect whereof was, for so much as he had bene moovid by soondry noble men and his frends, he thought it appartaynid him not to enter into yt [the Rising] without the advice and consent of his deare frends": Sharp, *Memorials*, p. 195. Similarly the earl of Westmorland heard of Norfolk that "his friends and chief gentlemen in his Countrie seemed to refuse him". The duke himself told the bishop of Ross on 3 November "that he would depart to his country . . . and there would take purpose by the advice of his countrymen and friends": *A Collection of State Papers Relating to Affairs in the Reign of Queen Elizabeth, from the Year 1571 to 1596*, ed. William Murdin (London, 1759), p. 44.

[94] The news that the duke of Norfolk had gone home to his country, so Northumberland asserted, "moved me most especially . . . to assemble my friends, and to advise with them, and know their inclinations": Sharp, *op. cit.*, p. 201. Later, visiting the earl of Westmorland, he found the said earl "so furnished with his men and friends as ready to enter forthwith [into a rising]": *ibid.*, p. 109.

[95] See above, pp. 68 ff. The Percy leadership of their mesne tenants by knight service in Northumberland (of whom there were over thirty, including some leading families like the Greys, Forsters, Herons, Haggerstons and Swinburnes) had collapsed by the middle years of the sixteenth century, and the knights' court at Alnwick had ceased to meet. Those who still followed the earl were political and religious allies like the Carrs, the Swinburnes and (until the reign of Queen Mary) the Herons of Chipchase; or else recipients of favours and offices, like the Bates family, the Horsleys and the Hoppens. They were, that is, "friends". The rents and services due from the many Yorkshire mesne tenancies, also held in many cases by prominent families, were not levied after the Percy estates came into the hands of the crown in 1537. The ninth earl, in the 1590s, was attempting to revive them: Syon House MS., X. II. 8. Thus in Yorkshire too the sixteenth century saw the collapse of feudal ties, with "friendship" surviving as the cement of political and religious interest. Cf. for the same process west of the Pennines, above, pp. 148 ff.

whose relationship to the lands and traditional connections inherited by the Devereux family was, outside Wales, tenuous. Essex House, in the final stage before its disintegration, sheltered a community of honour whose bond was friendship, conceived in the powerful and passionate sense of Cicero's *De amicitia*, revived by humanism. But essentially also a "court of King Arthur", dedicated to swordsmanship and the heroic style for which there was no place in the dominant *regnum Cecilanum*.[96] Thus friendship established itself as a term denoting political association, so that it became possible to carry over an item from the vocabulary of honour into the parliamentary jargon and parlance of another age.

HONOUR AND THE STATE

The State and the community of honour

The widest social dimension of honour, embracing both lineage and lordship, was the community of honour itself. To this society all men of honour, from princes and lords down to the mere gentleman, belonged. The test for entrance was honourable descent, for "noblenes . . . is a dignity and excellencie of birth and lineage" as Gerard Legh (in common with all other expositors of honour) pointed out in 1562.[97] But the status of being honourable implied a tension between inherited status and personal quality, between "blood" and "virtue". The man of honour was required to establish the innate quality of his honourable blood by his virtuous deeds, for "as the soul is more precious than the body; so much is nobleness of virtue more precious than nobleness of lineage".[98] The stress on virtue emphasized the anomaly of those who displayed "virtue", but without possessing the qualification of lineage. From one point of view they qualified for the status of honourable men, and sometimes they were admitted to the community of honour. Edmond Mylle, in the case already quoted,[99] was ennobled by Garter Smert in 1450 because he was reported to have pursued deeds of arms, and

[96] For a picture of the circle of the second earl of Essex, its interests and outlook, see David Mathew, *The Celtic Peoples and Renaissance Europe* (London, 1933), pp. 386 ff.

[97] Legh, *The Accedens of Armory*, fo. 22.

[98] *Ibid.*

[99] See note 86 above.

to have comported himself honourably. But the herald, as seen above (and the grant is only one instance of a class of similar patents), also claimed to have taken "common opinion", and consulted "noble men worthy of belief", thus showing his sense of the pressure on his office of the community of honourable men. For honour could not be imposed by a mere exercise of royal authority; it involved admission to a group which was self-selective and self-authenticating.

This was a conviction which was weakened by, but survived, the increasingly state-controlled system of honour whose emergence was consolidated during the sixteenth century, and which subsequently lasted almost as long as the Stuart monarchy. In the reign of James I, Cowell still ascribed gentility simply to those "whom their blood and race doth make noble and known", while attributing all degrees of "nobility" (in the sense of title) and peerage to royal grant.[100] The mark of the former status was the possession of a coat of arms. But as the authenticity of this came increasingly to be founded on heraldic confirmation or grant, the heraldic order came to play an increasingly significant role in the evolution of the community of honour, particularly in the matter of the admission of newcomers to honourable status. It was by means of the herald's office that the crown sought to establish itself as the sole fount of honour.

As seen above, the activity of royal heralds in the leadership and organization of the office of arms becomes increasingly apparent as the fifteenth century proceeds. During the same century the number of grants of arms made by royal kings of arms reaches an appreciable total, sixty having survived for the period before 1484. Only after the Tudor advent did the trickle gradually swell into a flood. The heraldic prerogative of "visitation", attributed to Clarenceux king of arms south of Trent and Norroy north of it, established itself at the same time. It involved a heraldic circuit of the shires to record the arms and descents of the gentry, and to expose those falsely claiming gentle status. The first record of such a procedure belongs to the reign of Edward IV.[101] What is interesting

[100] John Cowell, *The Interpreter of Words and Terms . . . First Publish'd by . . . Dr Cowel . . . and Continu'd by Tho. Manley . . . Now Further Augmented and Improv'd* (London, 1701), under the heading "Gentleman".

[101] See Wagner, *Heralds and Heraldry in the Middle Ages*, pp. 107–9.

about the performance of these heraldic functions is that they were conceived as done *virtute officii*, under an authority which derived from the nature of the heraldic office, rather than from any direct and specific royal grant. Already, as has been seen, by the mid-fifteenth century the herald had established himself as the judge of conformity to a recognizably "honourable" style of life which justified a grant of arms to those without. The most typical formula by which he did so was "by the power and auctoritie to mine office in this partie annexed and attributed", without reference to any royal authorization.[102] Visitation was similarly regarded as a prerogative inherent in the heraldic office. Both it and the grant of arms might be regarded as duties implied by the oath which a king of arms took at his creation. This required him to have knowledge of all gentlemen within his jurisdiction, and to record their arms. He adjudged such matters with the help of the "common opinion" of local communities. He might be given the support of royal "placards" or patents which enlisted the aid of local royal officers. These of course facilitated a visitation, and would be likely to make it more effective. But visitation as such did not originally need to be authorized by a special instrument.[103]

Thus significant aspects of the heraldic office were rather loosely tied to the royal prerogative, and there was a sense in which the herald was the servant, not merely of the crown, but also of honour itself; in much the same way as a judge served the law and the realm, as well as the king.[104] Indeed it could be said that the heraldic office constituted the informal judiciary of the community of honour, and the organizing agency of its transactions. Apart from adjudging coats of arms and pedigrees, heralds regulated such honour

[102] *Ibid.*, pp. 74–5. Even in the fifteenth century instances occur of grants of arms made by provincial kings of arms which are specifically based on the royal authority; for example, the grant of William Hawkslowe, Clarenceux (*ibid.*, p. 77) made by "the power and auctoritie by the kinges goode grace to me in that behaulfe comitted". Garter, with no specific province allotted to him and with his power to grant and visit contested by the kings of arms, may have been the most concerned to rely on the inherent nature of his office rather than on royal authorization. But provincial kings of arms also did so, and by no means invariably invoked royal authority. The formula here quoted in fact occurs in a grant made not by Garter but by Clarenceux Thomas Holme in 1482. The sense of a jurisdiction inherent in the office of arms plainly survived generally even among the royal heralds.

[103] *Ibid.*, pp. 58–9, 92.

[104] Cf. Keen, *Laws of War*, pp. 194–5.

occasions as tournaments and duels, funerary ceremonies, and those of orders of knighthood; they were emissaries and go-betweens, carrying challenges, news of tournaments, and declarations of war and peace. They recorded honourable deeds, and interpreted the inherited lore and traditions of honour. The herald's oath attests the aspects of the office which related to the service of the honour community. This, as recorded by Nicholas Upton in the 1430s, required him to be faithful not only to his lord and to the king, "but also to any other noble man, though he be enemy; and thou shalt faithfully execute the business of all noble men what so ever they be, though they were enemy".[105] The form of the oath used in England preserves a similar content. The herald swore loyalty to his lord and the king, but was also required to "promise and swear that you shall be conversant and serviceable to all gentlemen, to do their commands to their worship and knighthood by your good counsel . . . and ever ready to offer your service unto them".[106]

The well-known controversy of 1530,[107] which originated in a conflict of jurisdiction between Thomas Wriothesley, Garter king of arms, and Thomas Benolt, Clarenceux, does seem to constitute a dividing line in the history of the office of arms, even if only in the sense that it dramatized and brought to a head developments which had been in progress for more than a century. After 1530 the outlines of a more definitively state-controlled system of honour can be traced in the different emphasis given the herald's role; and in the more precise way in which heraldic jurisdiction was referred to the crown as its source. One of the most interesting features of the quarrel was the occasion it provided for an interview with the king, at which both Benolt and Wriothesley (with the other kings of arms) were present. In the course of the audience Henry VIII reproached the heralds (the blame, it seems, was proved to fall on Wriothesley) for misusing their prerogatives; in particular, by giving arms to "bond men" and "vile persons unable to uphold the honour of nobles", which was "against the honour of noble men and of all gentlemen of name and arms". The king, it emerged, would have no truck with any heraldic claim to ennoble *virtute officii*. "All such authorities and privileges", he asserted, "that is to say in the giving

105 *Essential Portions of Nicholas Upton's "De studio militari"*, ed. Barnard, pp. 1–2.
106 See *The Antiquarian Repertory*, 4 vols. (London, 1807–9), i, pp. 159–61.
107 Wagner, *Heralds and Heraldry in the Middle Ages*, pp. 83 ff.

of arms and cognizances of arms to ennoble any person . . . belongeth to his prerogative";[108] they had never been granted out, and could not be proved from any herald's letters patent of appointment. The king therefore resumed into his own hands the authority to ennoble and grant arms, thus doing away with a jurisdiction which was not securely anchored in a specific royal instrument. The incident could well have led to such a collapse of heraldic jurisdiction as took place in France during the sixteenth century. There in 1615 the heralds were finally ousted by a royal *juge d'armes*. Benolt claimed the credit for the different course taken by events in England. He petitioned the king that his traditional "authorities, privileges and liberties" as a king of arms should be renewed and strengthened by a grant under royal letters patent, so giving them a secure foundation in the prerogative.[109] Probably the grant included the clause conferring the right to give arms and cognizances, and to ennoble, which appears in the surviving patent of creation of Thomas Hawley, Clarenceux, dated May 1536. That of William Fellows as Norroy, dated a few months later, went further and was more specific: it included the right to visit, and to correct arms, as well as grant them.[110] Towards the end of 1530 Benolt embarked on a visitation of his province, but one authorized by royal commission, the first of a long series which would last until 1688.[111]

In the background there was the collapse of the seigneurial heraldic jurisdictions, or their annexation to the crown with the aristocratic interests which had sustained them. After the reincorporation of the heralds under the charter of 1555, they were subordinated to a royal official, the earl marshal.[112] Moreover, Henry VIII, in the Commission of 1530, had gone a long way towards laying down tests of gentility, underwritten by the state, which the heralds

[108] *Ibid.*, p. 97. According to Benolt the idea of an autonomous heraldic jurisdiction had already been brought into question (at least as exercised by Garter) early in the reign of Henry VII. In 1492 John Writhe, then Garter, was in trouble for having granted arms by his own letters patent to unworthy persons. Some "knights and noblemen" had asserted that "it was too high a thing for Garter to ennoble any person, except the person had the king's high grant upon the same". Henry VII made no declaration on the point of principle involved. But he confirmed by a supplementary royal grant the specific Writhe ennoblement which had led to the raising of the issue. See Wagner, *Heralds of England*, pp. 136–7.

[109] Wagner, *Heralds and Heraldry in the Middle Ages*, pp. 97–8.

[110] *Ibid.*, p. 98.

[111] *Ibid.*, pp. 9 ff.

[112] Wagner, *Heralds of England*, pp. 180 ff.

were to enforce. Those of "vile blood" (that is, of unfree descent) together with rebels and heretics were excluded. As far as the laity was concerned, the test was to be "service done to us or to another", which had resulted in "possessions and riches able to maintain the same". In the case of the clergy, arms were to be given to those advanced "by grace, virtue or cunning to rooms and degrees of honour and worship".[113] Bishoprics, abbacies, deaneries and priories seem to have been the preferments meant. Thus honour became the servant of a "social policy", which involved for example the intrusion of increasing numbers of the clergy into the honour system, from which the traditional code excluded them. True, the tests for gentility subsequently became more informal. But the intention of closer state direction was implicit in the Orders which the duke of Norfolk, as earl marshal, imposed on the heralds in 1565 and 1568. Under these, no new arms were to be granted without the earl marshal's consent.[114] Only the execution of the duke in 1572, the ineffectiveness of his successors in the earl marshal's office, and the consequent squabbles, inefficiency and disorganization which prevailed in the college of heralds prevented any effective implementation of the procedure which Norfolk's orders had defined.

The reception given the visitations varied from shire to shire, and with the circumstances of each one. Certainly heralds tended to be unpopular with significant sections of the gentry. Heraldic attempts to secure parliamentary confirmation of their authority consistently failed; and the heralds (with the earl marshal's court of chivalry) were the object of attack by the parliamentary opposition of 1623 and again in 1640.[115] In the early visitations there was the fear that local opinion in matters of gentility would be overridden by heraldic authority – a feeling perhaps strongest in the more traditionalist parts of the country. Thus when William Fellows went on visitation in Lancashire and Cheshire in 1533[116] he received a cool welcome from a good many of the gentry, and sometimes encountered downright hostility. Several were not at home; others refused "to have

[113] Wagner, *Heralds and Heraldry in the Middle Ages*, pp. 9–10.

[114] Or, in his absence, that of Sir William Cecil or the earl of Leicester: Wagner, *Heralds of England*, pp. 197, 187.

[115] *Ibid.*, pp. 209, 235, 252.

[116] *The Visitation of Lancashire and a Part of Cheshire . . . A.D. 1533*, ed. W. Langton, 2 vols. (Chetham Soc., xcviii, cx, Manchester, 1876–82).

any note taken" of their arms and pedigrees. Sir Richard Houghton gave the herald "proud words" and "no good cheer". There was a chilly reception and poor reward from Sir John Townley, whom the herald had "sought . . . all day, riding in the wild country". Townley replied to his inquiries with the assertion that there was none "more gentleman" than himself in Lancashire, the two local peers, the earl of Derby and his relative Lord Mounteagle alone excepted.[117] For him and his like, gentility was a matter of traditional standing and local opinion, which needed no prying inquiry on the part of a king's herald. The Lancashire knight Sir Piers Leigh of Bradley had no qualms about submitting his armorial coat to the arbitration of the high constable of England in a well-known case of 1496, precisely because that office was then held by his own "dear lord" the earl of Derby.[118] As in many other matters, there was a preference in the regional communities for the arbitration of the local magnate if doubtful points arose in connection with pedigree and coat armour.[119]

The visitations, and the state-centred honour system which they implied, point to a trend, also apparent in other fields during the 1530s, whereby the loyalties of the community of honour are related solely to a single centre, the crown. More or less at the same time as Benolt and Fellows were perambulating the shires, Sir Thomas Elyot had embarked, with remarkable effectiveness, on the task of restating the honour code in terms of the popularized humanism of the age. In *The Boke named The Governour*,[120] directed to a noble not a learned audience, he attempted to do for honour what the church had once attempted for chivalry: to incorporate its values in a universalized moral system, and to relate it to religion. The members of the community of honour were to be transmuted into a liter-

117 *Ibid.*, i, pp. 43, 48.

118 *Ibid.*, ii, pp. 160–1.

119 The persisting strength of this sentiment emerges in the armorial case of Thomas Leigh *v*. Richard Leigh of 1582. This was tried by George, earl of Shrewsbury, then earl marshal, but also the local magnate in the "country" of the parties concerned. Shrewsbury investigated the case locally in the presence of sundry "Knights, esquires, and gentlemen" of the "blood, surname, and alliance" of the parties. But he gave no verdict and it was two years before he declared for the plaintiff by a warrant which the heralds were required to register. See G. D. Squibb, *The High Court of Chivalry: A Study of the Civil Law in England* (Oxford, 1959), pp. 32–3.

120 Sir Thomas Elyot, *The Boke named The Governour*, ed. from the first edition of 1531 by H. H. S. Croft, 2 vols. (London, 1880).

ate magistracy, wielding the sword of justice in their local communities. Significantly for Elyot the meaning of faithfulness, if not the loyalty of a servant to a master, could only be that due from a subject to his sovereign.[121] But as against this concept, soon to be reinforced by Protestantism and universalized by the new-style grammar-school education, the traditional dissidence of honour, with its turbulent emphasis on autonomy and will, persisted with much of its old force, particularly perhaps in the north and west. Here it was rooted in a pluralistic network of honour-infused bonds and dependencies still able to enforce a loyalty to friends, dependants and lords, which the king could not always overrule. Some of the events of the Pilgrimage of Grace aptly dramatize the political relevance of honour obligations, and of the different ways in which these were interpreted and understood. An honour transaction in which the rebel leader Thomas, Lord Darcy, and the king's lieutenant Thomas, duke of Norfolk, were both involved is of interest from this point of view.

"Promise" and the dissidence of honour

In November 1536 Darcy and Norfolk were required to state whether they conceived themselves bound by a "promise" given: that is by honour as publicly committed through their freely given word. The significance of such a situation arises out of the nature of honour as a public code, this public status distinguishing it from a private morality.[122] Men of honour could (and did) lie, cheat, deceive, plot, treason, seduce, and commit adultery, without incurring dishonour.[123] Such activities were of course immoral, and might compromise the perpetrator's religious status, bringing his eternal salvation into question. But as long as they were not attributed to

[121] *Ibid.*, i, pp. 226–7.

[122] See above, p. 316 and note 33.

[123] Thus machiavellism does not represent a "modern" rationalized attitude, to be contrasted with the "medieval" chivalric idealism of honour. Honour and *realpolitik* were totally compatible. Even King Arthur did not hesitate to "set a spy" on Lancelot when it appeared that the latter might have brought the royal honour into question. See also Paula S. Fichtner, "The Politics of Honor: Renaissance Chivalry and Habsburg Dynasticism", *Bibliothèque d'humanisme et renaissance*, xxix (1967), pp. 567 ff.

him in a public way, honour was not brought into question.[124] The importance of "promise" was that this gave the essence of honour, will and intention, the public status which enabled both to be brought into question. By the symbolic rite of "giving one's word" – the word of honour – promise bound honour itself to a specified position or course of action.[125] Once so bound, withdrawal was possible only at the price of public diminishment. For "steadfastness" required adherence to an honour commitment once taken up. Any other course suggested that the will had been overruled, and the autonomy of honour cancelled. Submission implied in fact cowardice, the extremity of dishonour.

The relevance of honour to aristocratic forms of dissidence emerges from the insistence of Thomas, Lord Darcy, that honour, thus bound by promise, had priority over obedience to the king. Captain of the royal castle of Pontefract, he was besieged there by the rebel host of the Pilgrimage of Grace. But after a brief resistance he surrendered, justifying his action by the weakness of the garrison and lack of supplies. He then emerged as a prominent figure in the counsels of the rebels, side by side with the lawyer Robert Aske.[126] It is November 1536, and he is engaged in a dialogue with a herald, Thomas Trehayron, sent by the government to sound out his intentions. The dialogue[127] presents the choice between honour, as Darcy conceives it, and his duty to the king. "My lord", the herald begins, " . . . in times past . . . I have heard you speak of so much honour, truth, and faithfulness, and that if you were faulty in any of them you were worthy before all other to suffer for it."[128] Then, says the herald, supposing it were put to you to seize your captain Robert

[124] In honour societies goodness tends to be fenced off from honour (cf. Pitt-Rivers, "Honour and Social Status", p. 17 note 4) in much the same way as religion (see above, pp. 316–17, 320). Nevertheless a tension persists between them, and there is a tendency to blur the distinction in much the same way as that between "virtue" and "lineage". This tension is one of the most powerful underlying themes of Malory's *The Morte Darthur*. See Malory, *Morte Darthur*, ed. Brewer, pp. 26 ff.

[125] "Giving one's word" was not the only rite which committed honour. Another was the public display of one's banner or pennon, both being personal symbols of honour. To do so committed the person concerned, on his honour and by the law of arms, to battle. See Keen, *Laws of War*, p. 107.

[126] See M. H. and R. Dodds, *The Pilgrimage of Grace, 1536–7, and the Exeter Conspiracy, 1538*, 2 vols. (Cambridge, 1915), i, ch. 8.

[127] Printed in *ibid.*, i, pp. 300–6; *L.P.*, xi, 1086, pp. 435–8.

[128] Dodds, *op. cit.*, p. 303.

Aske, and kill him or send him up to the king, would this be lawful, for Aske is said to be a rebel? For you it would be lawful, replies Darcy, but "not for me, for he that promiseth to be true to one, and deceiveth him, may be called a traitor, for what is a man but his promise?".[129] Thus for Darcy, to be a traitor is to renege on a commitment by which honour is bound. The fact that his promise is to the "traitor" Aske, and even that the fealty due to the king required his obedience, is irrelevant. For only the man of honour himself, out of his own moral autonomy, can decide where honour has been committed.[130] This being so, Darcy will not break his word to Aske, traitor or no, for by this his very self is bound. For what is a man but his promise?

When Darcy thus identified his very self with his honour, we can see that for such a man, once honour is evoked as a motive for dissidence, the latter acquires an ultimate character. Once honour is in question life itself has to be staked on it.[131] This proved to be so for Darcy. For by revealing and then standing by his promise to Aske, he provided evidence which would subsequently bring him to the block.[132] Honour could articulate a compelling network of obligation which was outside what the state, law, and even religion enforced. For this reason Thomas, duke of Norfolk, riding northward at the end of October 1536 to put down the Pilgrimage of Grace, saw that Henry VIII himself needed to be reassured against the unpredictability imparted by honour transactions even to the relations between the king and his servants. "I beseech you take in good part", he wrote to his master, "what so ever promise I shall make unto the rebels . . . for surely I shall observe no part thereof for any respect of that what other might call honour distained"; "thinking and reputing", he added, "that none oath nor promise

[129] *Ibid.*, p. 304. Cf. p. 291.

[130] This kind of situation receives recognition under the law of arms. The command of the prince did not annul the obligations of honour. Thus a knight could not "justly" wage war against a person or persons to whom he was otherwise obligated (for example, by a blood relationship, or by a solemn oath sworn between them) merely because royal authority required him to do so. See Keen, *op. cit.*, pp. 84 ff.

[131] As in the duelling code. Once honour was brought into question by an affront, life was staked on it. See Pitt-Rivers, "Honour", p. 508.

[132] Trehayron's minute of his discussion with Darcy was among the evidence prepared for use against the latter at his trial. He was interrogated on the words "for he that promiseth to be true to one and deceiveth him, may be called a traitor": *L.P.*, xii (1), 944, p. 427.

made for policy to serve you mine only master and sovereign can distain me".[133] Thus in this case honour is the crown's, to which that of its servant has been assimilated. For Norfolk's fidelity was due in a total sense to the master and sovereign who, according to Benolt, claimed honour as belonging to his prerogative, from which it derived. Appropriately, it was the house of Howard, in the person of Norfolk's grandson the fourth duke as earl marshal, which was to preside, in the 1560s, over the further development of the increasingly crown-centred system of honour which Henry VIII had set on foot. It was he who (as seen above) completed, at least in intention, the subordination of the heralds to the state, requiring all grants of arms to be confirmed by him as earl marshal, or in his absence by some other minister, like the principal secretary of state or the earl of Leicester.

Not surprisingly honour also emerges in other revolts as the ultimate motivation for an appeal to violence; and so for the commitment of life itself to a dissident cause. The northern earls in 1569 were subjected to powerful pressure to rebel, a course which flew in the face of reason and common sense, because honour had been irrevocably committed. "It would be a marvellous blot", they were told by their followers, "and discredit most to you noblemen, and something to us; . . . to depart and leave of this godly enterprise, that is so expected and looked for at our hands, and throughout the body of the realm."[134] Blot, discredit, shame – these are all keywords in the vocabulary of honour. There were similar pressures on another northern rebel – Leonard Dacre. "Better die in honour than live with shame",[135] he was told by one of his own servants. It was the communities of honour which still centred on these great northern houses asserting the code against the cautious prudentialism of the leadership. By contrast, there was the case of Lord Hussey, who abandoned his associates in the Lincolnshire rebellion of 1536 and fled to the royal forces. The commment of the rebel leaders at Lincoln was that he had failed to be "set like a nobleman".[136] That is, he had not maintained the attitude of steadfastness

[133] *L.P.*, xi, 864, p. 347; printed in Dodds, *op. cit.*, i, pp. 259–60.
[134] Sharp, *Memorials*, p. 196.
[135] Public Record Office, SP5/18, fo. 43; *Cal. State Papers, Domestic, Addenda, 1566–79*, p. 255.
[136] *L.P.*, ix, 968, p. 390; and above, p. 251.

appropriate to the man of honour (still more to a nobleman) once his word was given.

Honour therefore implied for those who professed it, a pressure towards the consistency of public (and therefore political) attitude which "faithfulness" to lords and friends involved. As such it had a natural role in the kind of political conflict in which lords confronted unworthy or tyrannical rulers, and if necessary removed them, with the violence of "war and battle" as the final sanction by means of which the conflict was resolved. The honour emphasis on will and moral autonomy precluded any sense of unconditional obedience, and provided a motive for resistance when authority, even in the person of the king himself, was felt to have failed the governing class it was expected to lead. But once such a stance of resistance had been publicly taken up, everything depended on the will of servants, retainers, friends, to stand by their lord, even to death, in the total commitment which faithfulness implied. Thus honour was the necessary body of sentiment and principle which bound together leaders and followers in a kind of politics in which conflict was liable to assume violent forms. It was the code of political activists in such movements as those which removed Edward II and Richard II; or of those who stood, with a sufficient measure of consistency, behind their leaders in the conflicts of the Wars of the Roses. Edward of York had reason to be grateful when in 1471, as his army advanced from Ravenspur into the midlands, he was met at Leicester by "a fellowship of folks" whom the chronicler singled out as being "such as were to be trusted". Mobilized by Lord Hastings, Edward's faithful servant and chamberlain, they had been "stirred" by his messages to them, and raised by his "friends and lovers".[137] Honour provided a code in terms of which this kind of response found its motivation, often more to be relied upon in the test of battle than the material inducements made available by indentures, fees and grants; or even than the loyalties claimed by a *de facto* monarch. At Bosworth, Richard of Gloucester found the dignity that hedged a king as ineffective a sanction to ensure obedience as had his namesake Richard of Bordeaux at Flint in 1399. Richard III, king of

[137] *Historie of the Arrivall of Edward IV in England and the Final Recouerye of His Kingdomes from Henry VI*, ed. John Bruce (Camden Soc., old ser., i, London, 1838), pp. 8–9. See K. B. McFarlane, "The Wars of the Roses", *Proc. British Academy*, l (1954), pp. 87–119, at p. 107.

England, was betrayed or abandoned on the battlefield by his subjects Lord Stanley and the earl of Northumberland. But the ties of lordship and honour held. Richard's following of household men and friends fought with him to the death against Henry Tudor's similar bodyguard force.[138] The competitive violence of honour culminated in the barbaric symbolism of the scene which followed the battle, intended not only to publicize Richard's death, but also to mark the fallen king with an ultimate infamy. His naked corpse had to be carried by his own herald, Blanch Sanglier, trussed to the back of a horse "as an hog or other vile beast" to a dishonourable burial in Leicester abbey.[139] Few of those who had fought at Richard's side during the battle were allowed to make their peace with the new régime; and Blanch Sanglier's office, with that of the late king's other personal king of arms, Gloucester, lapsed.[140] The community of honour which had centred on Richard of Gloucester was eliminated. Bosworth dramatized the solidarities of honour, and also gave free vent to honour violence.

Tudor revolt

Against this background of a politics of violent conflict, related to the self-assertiveness and competitive emphasis of the honour code, Tudor revolts present a number of puzzling features. In the first place, there is the relative lack of violence which characterized many of them. The most obviously destructive revolts were those of the reign of Henry VII which culminated in pitched battles. Bosworth was followed by the hard-fought fight at Stoke, in which free vent was once more given to the rival honour-claims of York and Tudor-Lancaster. Blackheath, with its many casualties, is also at least in part to be attributed to the violence of dynastic conflict. For it is unlikely that Yorkist influences were at work once the

[138] The standard account of the battle is still James Gairdner, "The Battle of Bosworth", *Archaeologia*, 2nd ser., v (1896), pp. 159–78. For a recent attempt at reconstruction which brings out the role of Richard's household men and friends, see P. M. kendall, *Richard the Third* (London, 1955; repr. London, 1972), pp. 46 ff. Cf. S. B. Chrimes, *Henry VII* (London, 1972), pp. 47 ff., and p. 46 note 2.

[139] *The Great Chronicle of London*, ed. A. H. Thomas and I. D. Thornley (London, 1938), p. 238; cf. *Ingulph's Chronicle of the Abbey of Croyland, with the Continuations* . . . , trans. H. T. Riley (London, 1854), p. 504.

[140] Wagner, *Heralds of England*, pp. 134–5.

leadership of the Cornishmen had been assumed by Lord Audley.[141] By contrast, admittedly with the two exceptions of the Kett movement in Norfolk, and the West Country rebellion of 1549, subsequent revolts are marked by a relative bloodlessness. Many of the symbols and conventions of violent conflict are still used: armed forces are raised, and there are confrontations with those of the crown; castles and towns are besieged; representatives of authority taken prisoner; provincial capitals occupied. But these operations result in few or no casualties, armed clashes tend to be small-scale, and there is no resolute appeal to the arbitrament of battle. The violence inflicted on political opponents is minimal.

Thus the Pilgrimage of Grace seems to have resulted in no more than a single casualty, and the Lincolnshire rebellion in two.[142] The small loss of life in both these movements contrasts with the many executions, whether by martial law, treason trials or attainders, which followed their suppression. As a result of these, 178 lives were lost.[143] Even in the desperate Northern Rising of 1569, if we exclude the clash between the Berwick garrison and the Scots raiders who were Leonard Dacre's allies, only six persons were killed.[144] Again, it is the number of subsequent executions which impresses. There could hardly have been less than two or three hundred of them.[145] By contrast the Edwardian and Marian revolts resulted in much loss of life due to rebel as well as government

[141] His father, who died in 1491, had been a trusted councillor of Richard III and the latter's lord treasurer: *Complete Peerage*, i, pp. 341–2, and *Dict. Nat. Biog.*, xix, pp. 1003–4, under "Touchet, James, Seventh Baron Audley (1465?–1497)".

[142] In the course of the Pilgrimage one of the Pilgrim host was accidentally killed near Doncaster during the confrontation with Norfolk's forces at the end of October 1536. This, according to Aske, "was all the men that was slain or hurt of either party during all the time of business": *L.P.*, xii (1), 901 (73), p. 412. In the subsequent Bigod rising, three persons were wounded in the course of Hallam's attempt on Hull, including Hallam himself, but no lives were lost. The two casualties of the Lincolnshire rebellion were Thomas (or George) Wolsey, hanged at Horncastle as a government spy; and Dr Raynes, murdered by the mob at Horncastle. See above, p. 219.

[143] Elton, *Policy and Police*, p. 389.

[144] Five of the casualties took place in the course of the siege of Barnard Castle. See Sir George Bowes's report on the rising, printed in Sharp, *Memorials*, pp. 184 ff.

[145] The number of persons set aside for execution in Durham alone has been estimated at three hundred and twenty; but it is likely that only a proportion of these, perhaps less than a half, were actually executed. Bowes estimated the total number appointed to be executed at seven hundred: Sharp, *op. cit.*, p. 184. See H. B. McCall, "The Rising in the North", *Yorkshire Archaeol. Jl*, xviii (1904–5), pp. 74–87.

action. They were badly handled both by their leaders and those in authority. The latter were divided and indecisive; the former were therefore tempted to hold out in the hope of greater concessions. Both sides consequently blundered into destructive military clashes with much bloodshed resulting. Hundreds of lives must have been lost in the battles which concluded Kett's revolt and the West Country rising.[146] Wyatt's revolt produced sixty or seventy battle casualties and there was about the same number of executions.[147] In these relatively violent revolts, particularly Kett's and that in the West Country, which were mass movements with an anti-gentry emphasis, we might expect the rebels to treat their enemies roughly. But there is little concrete evidence of this. Sotherton[148] did his best to build up Kett into a plebeian incendiary, intent on harrying his betters.[149] But a less biased tradition remembered that he had punished plunderers under his Oak of Reformation, and that "the mayor [of Norwich]" and "other of the gentry" were admitted to the counsels of the rebels.[150] The Cornishmen in 1549 besieged and imprisoned the pro-government gentry; but none of these was killed or complained of ill-treatment.[151] Just as in the Pilgrimage of Grace and the Lincolnshire rebellion,[152] in which popular risings also took

[146] See Rose-Troup, *Western Rebellion of 1549*, and F. W. Russell, *Kett's Rebellion in Norfolk* (London, 1859).

[147] D. M. Loades, *Two Tudor Conspiracies* (Cambridge, 1965), pp. 73, 113–14.

[148] Nicholas Sotherton was the author of "The Comocyon in Norfolk, 1549", a chronicle of the rising which was the closest to the events themselves: British Lib., Harleian MS. 1576, fos. 251 ff.

[149] Sotherton, himself a member of the Norwich patriciate and a close relative by marriage of alderman Augustine Steward (who collaborated with Kett), was concerned to whitewash the Norwich men, who had been very much implicated in the rising; indeed it was one Leonard Sotherton who had appeared before the council in London to beg a pardon for the rebels. The chronicler makes it clear that members of the gentry did supply the rebel host with money and food; he is much concerned to emphasize that in so doing they were the victims of plebeian violence. He asserts that gentry (he gives no names) were tried and threatened with death at Kett's Oak of Reformation. But none was in fact killed. Sotherton describes only two concrete cases of ill-treatment, whose effect he seeks to exaggerate, implying (in contradiction of his own account) that one of the victims was "slain". See Sotherton, *op. cit.*, fo. 253; Russell, *op. cit.*, p. 72. For the Sotherton family, see *The Visitations of Norfolk, 1563, 1589 and 1613*, ed. Walter Rye (Harleian Soc., xxxii, London, 1891), pp. 268–70.

[150] Francis Blomefield and Charles Parkin, *An Essay Towards a Topographical History of the County of Norfolk*, 11 vols. (London, 1905–10 edn), iii, p. 228.

[151] Rose-Troup, *Western Rebellion of 1549*, chs. 5, 8.

[152] See above, pp. 218 ff.

place, some of the gentry were harassed, others suffered inconvenience, but none had serious violence inflicted on them. Apart from the Devon yeoman William Hellyons, only one or two figures on which regional hatreds and fears had become focused, were subjected to the ultimate violence of death.[153] But significantly these tended to be intruders into regional societies who were regarded as the agents of unpopular London régimes. Such was Dr John Raynes, murdered at Horncastle during the Lincolnshire rebellion while acting as one of Thomas Cromwell's commissaries as vicegerent in spirituals; or William Body, archdeacon of Cornwall, whose murder at Helston in 1548 was the prelude to the rising of the West Country.[154] These were the sole victims of the anger of the commons.

Equally striking is a change in the attitude to authority, and in the language used to express this, on the part of the rebels. There is a growing reluctance, not only to appeal to violence, but also to make any public challenge to the royal authority. Unpopular ministers were attacked again and again in rebel manifestos; but never the crown or the person of the monarch. Rebels, paradoxically, thus became increasingly insistent on the maintenance of a convention of obedience. Hence the leaders of the Lincolnshire rebellion asserted that they were the king's "true and faithful subjects", and that their cause was "God and the king's".[155] The leaders of the Pilgrimage of Grace made similar protestations. Even more remarkably, they gave substance to them by winding up their formidable movement, which could have presented a powerful challenge to the royal forces, with a submissive petition to Henry VIII for a pardon. Redress of the grievances which had caused the revolt was to be left to the king, and the Parliament he was able to convoke at his will and pleasure.[156] Even Wyatt asserted "before the Judge of all Judges, I never meant hurt against her highness person".[157] The northern rebels in 1569 issued proclamations to the same effect.[158] The language of the West Country rising was probably the least

[153] Rose-Troup, *op. cit.*, pp. 122 ff.
[154] See Dodds, *Pilgrimages of Grace*, i, pp. 101–2; Rose-Troup, *op. cit.*, pp. 70 ff.
[155] See above, p. 259.
[156] Dodds, *op. cit.*, ii, pp. 13–23.
[157] *State Trials*, i, col. 862.
[158] John Strype, *Annals of the Reformation*, 4 vols. in 7 (Oxford, 1824 edn), i, pt. 2, pp. 313 ff.

respectful of authority, with the peremptory "We will have . . . " which prefaced each of the rebel articles. But the West Countrymen too maintained the distinction between the king and his "governors"; the leaders were probably of the opinion that, while Edward VI remained in his minority, Somerset and his associates had no authority to make changes in religion. It was the latter, and not Edward, that the articles addressed.[159]

Of course, attacks on ministers accompanied by disclaimers of any designs against the royal authority and person are to be encountered as a feature of dissident politics long before the Tudor advent. The manifestos of the Ordainers in the reign of Edward II, of the Appellants in that of Richard II, the Yorkist manifesto of 1460, and that of Clarence and his associates in 1469, all contained such disclaimers. But in such cases the respect thus shown for royal authority proved little more than a tactical device of great lords in no doubt that "honour and worship" required from them a confrontation, in the name of the *respublica* of the realm, with an ineffective and unpopular king; this to be carried if necessary to the point of resort to force. In the immediate aftermath of the Lancastrian usurpation, and in the course of the party struggle of York and Lancaster-Tudor even the show of respect for authority tended to be abandoned, and an open violence of intention received its appropriate language. The Percies in 1403 had no qualms about sending their "mortal *diffidatio*" to Henry IV, offering to prove it "with our own hand".[160] The leaders of the Lincolnshire rebellion against King Edward in 1470 summoned the commons to rise "to resist the king coming down to the said shire, saying that his coming there was to destroy the commons of the said shire".[161] The Cornishmen in 1497 were similarly as ready to come to blows with Henry VII as he had been with Richard III. Polydore Vergil tells us how they prepared, at Blackheath, "to fight with the king . . . For they thought verily that the king was afraid of their puissance".[162]

[159] Rose-Troup, *op. cit.*, pp. 213 ff. The articles concluded with: "Item, we pray God save king Edward, for we be his, both body and soul."

[160] *The Chronicle of John Hardyng*, ed. H. Ellis (London, 1812), pp. 352–3.

[161] "Chronicle of the Rebellion in Lincolnshire, 1470", ed. J. G. Nichols, in *Camden Miscellany*, i (Camden Soc., old ser., xxxix, London, 1847), pp. 1–28, at p. 6.

[162] Edward Hall, *The Union of . . . York and Lancaster*, ed. H. Ellis (London, 1809), p. 479. See also *The "Anglica historia" of Polydore Vergil, A.D. 1485–1537*, ed. with a translation by Denys Hay (Camden Soc., 3rd ser., lxxiv, London, 1950), p. 96.

Yet what already distinguish the Cornish rebellion[163] are the marks of hesitation and a divided mind which become apparent among the leadership once an appeal to force against the king presented itself as an immediate issue. From the start, division arose between the rival policies of the blacksmith Michael Joseph, supported in due course by Lord Audley, and those of the gentleman-lawyer Flamank. While the former led a war party ready to attempt the arbitrament of battle with the king,[164] Flamank asserted that the rebels had no quarrel with Henry VII, but only with his ministers Bray and Morton. It was they who had illegally imposed a subsidy on the Cornishmen. According to Bacon, Flamank talked "as if he would tell how to make a rebellion, and never break the peace".[165] Thus it seems that elements among the leadership (significantly associated with a lawyer) aimed to formulate some kind of alternative to the violent idiom of protest. On the eve of the battle of Blackheath a peace party emerged which sent a message to Lord Daubeny, the royal commander, suing for a general pardon, and offering to surrender their captains. There were many desertions from the rebel forces. Morale was plainly low and irresolution rife. But the men of violence nevertheless remained in control.[166] At Blackheath, Audley took his Cornish following with him into disastrous defeat at Daubeny's hands. Then he went to his death on the scaffold with the unrepentant stoicism of the man of honour.[167]

[163] See A. L. Rowse, *Tudor Cornwall* (London, 1941), pp. 114 ff.

[164] It was "the Smith and his affinitie" who, on the eve of the battle of Blackheath, prevailed against those among the rebels who "were of the mind to have yielded them unto the king's grace": *Great Chronicle of London*, ed. Thomas and Thornley, p. 276.

[165] Francis Bacon, *The History of the Reign of King Henry the Seventh* (London, 1676 edn), p. 92. Bacon's principal source was Vergil whom, however, he supplemented from the resources of the London chronicles and the manuscripts of his friend Cotton. Both Vergil and the *Great Chronicle* mentioned the rebels' animus against Morton and Bray, on whom the responsibility was placed for the heavy taxation under which the Cornishmen suffered, the king being guiltless in this respect. But Bacon alone makes Flamank the originator of this attitude, and mentions his advice that the rebels should take up arms "yet to do no creature hurt, but go and deliver the king a strong petition, for the laying down of these grievous payments . . . ": Bacon, *op. cit.*, p. 92. For Bacon's sources, and those for the Cornish rising, see W. Busch, *England under the Tudors*, i, *King Henry VII* (London, 1895), pp. 345, 416 ff.

[166] *Great Chronicle of London*, p. 276.

[167] He was convicted by a Court of Chivalry, and led to his death with "a coat armour of paper on him all torn": *Chronicles of London*, ed. C. L. Kingsford (Oxford, 1905), p. 216.

But in the Pilgrimage of Grace, as in the Lincolnshire rebellion which immediately preceded it, it was the militant exponents of "war and battle" who were defeated. A powerful non-violent impulse was apparent in the movement from the start. In this, lawyers were once more prominent. From their ranks came such able and articulate activists as Robert Aske, the captain general of the Pilgrimage, and Robert Bowes, Babthorpe, Challenor and Sir Thomas Tempest.[168] These, with the courtier Lord Darcy, were the policy-makers who handled the delicate and dangerous negotiations at Doncaster with the duke of Norfolk as the king's lieutenant, and with Henry VIII. Aske, obviously a political leader of remarkable skill and subtlety, showed himself able to forge and unify a powerful political demonstration, representative of a wide spectrum of northern society, out of disparate interests and frequently opposed political and social tendencies. There was a powerful party of violence, represented above all by "the lords of the Bishopric [of Durham]", including Lord Lumley, Lord Latimer and the Nevilles, Sir Thomas Hilton and others. Later joined by Sir Robert Constable, this was the group most ready to carry the issue to "war and battle" with the king, adopting as their badge the device of the five wounds, a protective talisman associated with the crusade and carrying implications of religious war.[169] The images and language of the crusade had been fostered in the circle of Catherine of Aragon, Fisher and More, as well as systematized by Reginald Pole in his *De unitate*.[170] Thus a potentially highly disruptive motivation was made available for resisting Henry VIII on the grounds that he had become a heretic and schismatic.[171] But the touchy self-assertiveness of

[168] Bowes, Babthorpe, Challenor and Tempest were all of the king's fee'd counsel in the north. Tempest was a sergeant-at-law, Bowes a master of requests, Aske was of Gray's Inn.

[169] The militants were predominant in the vanguard of the Pilgrim levies, this consisting of the men of the bishopric, Richmondshire and Cleveland, led by Lords Neville, Latimer and Lumley, and by Sir Thomas Hilton and Sir Thomas Percy: *L.P.*, xii (1), 6, p. 5; it was the Durham men who first adopted the badge of the five wounds: *L.P.*, xii (1), 901 (73), p. 412.

[170] Reginald Pole, *Pro ecclesiasticae unitatis defensione* (Rome, 1538).

[171] Queen Katherine herself told her nephew Charles V that she could see no difference between the Infidel and "what these people are attempting here"; she looked forward to "the defeat and death by the Pope's hand of this second Turk": *Cal. of State Papers, Spanish, Henry VIII*, iv (2) (i), 994, p. 510; *ibid.*, iv (2) (ii), 1145, p. 843. Chapuys reported at the same time (1633) Fisher's words to the emperor: "It is incumbent upon Your Majesty to interfere in this affair [the 'divorce'] and undertake a work which must be as pleasing in the eyes of God as

honour also drove the group towards violent courses. "The lords" were eager, as honour required, to take up Norfolk's challenge to battle, sent by Lancaster herald, instead of accepting his offer of a negotiation. It was Aske, supported by Darcy, who calmed the militancy of the northern honour communities. He persuaded the Durham lords that there was no "shame" involved in discussing the Pilgrims' petition with the king's lieutenant; and that indeed the Pilgrimage had been assembled for the very purpose of laying the grievances of the north before the king.[172]

Aske's approach affords a sharp contrast to the aggressiveness of the men of honour. He recoiled from the prospect of civil war. Even when, in October 1536, the opportunity offered itself to overwhelm the much weaker royal forces of Norfolk and Shrewsbury, he opposed resort to battle, pointing out that, if the day were lost, the outcome would be all the gentlemen in those parts "attainted, slain, and undone and the country made a waste for the Scots"; if won, loss to the realm and displeasure to the king.[173] The image of a "Pilgrimage" which Aske himself seems to have chosen to express the nature of the movement he led, itself suggests a search for non-violent political forms. The concept of a Pilgrimage implied an essentially peaceful kind of demonstration, set against a background of religion, not honour. The traditional objective of the dissident aristocracy, to assert the claims of the *respublica*, the realm or common weal against an unworthy king and his councillors, while present, was muted in the Pilgrim proclamations. The first sentence of the Pilgrim's oath required indeed a repudiation of any such policy: "ye shall not enter this Pilgrimage of Grace for the Commonwealth"; but rather "only for the love that ye do bear to Almighty God, his faith, and Holy Church militant" in order "to make petition to the king's highness for the reformation of that which is amiss within this his realm". The oath, and Aske's proclamation before York, may be seen as an attempt to establish a religious motivation for rebellion.[174] But, in spite of pressure from the militants, the clergy consistently refused to define any clear

war against the Turk": *ibid.*, iv (2) (ii), 1130, p. 813. Mary had written in October 1535 that a "work" in England would be as acceptable to God, and redound as much to the emperor's glory as the conquest of Tunis: *ibid.*, v (1), 218, 560.

172 *L.P.*, xii (1), 6, p. 5.

173 *Ibid.*, 1175 (2), p. 540.

174 Dodds, *Pilgrimage of Grace*, i, pp. 175–6, 182.

grounds on which "we may endanger battle".[175] Archbishop Lee indeed took up a clearly non-resistant attitude. The sword was given to none but the prince.[176] Thus the Pilgrimage never committed itself to any formula in terms of which a civil war might have been fought.

It is not easy to dismiss as mere subterfuge Aske's statement that "he ever thought that by no just law no man might rebel against their lord and king"[177] against the background of the policies he actually pursued as leader of the Pilgrimage. These, seconded by Darcy, aimed at a politics of negotiation and political manoeuvre, not of violent confrontation. The object was not a solution by "war and battle" (although this remained the last resort) but by means of the political pressures which it was hoped the duke of Norfolk and his "friends" would bring to bear at court.[178] Norfolk was loved and trusted in the north, and there seems little doubt that, in the course of the first Doncaster meeting, he was able to persuade the northern leaders that he sympathized with their cause. Norfolk was seen as the agent of a reconciliation between the king and the northern dissidents. Of course, as already seen above, both Aske and Darcy were betrayed by the man they regarded as a trusted friend. Norfolk had already assured the king that he did not regard himself as bound in honour by any promises made to rebels.[179] By exploiting the instinctive recoil from violence on the part of the leaders, and the

175 *L.P.*, xii (1), 1022, p. 466.

176 In spite of pressure from the militants (particularly Lord Latimer and Sir Robert Constable) Lee preached to this effect before the Pilgrim council at Pontefract: *ibid.*

177 *Ibid.*, 901, p. 412.

178 Norfolk's dislike of Cromwell and his alignment with the "aristocratic" party at court made him a sympathetic figure in the eyes of the northern conservatives and a likely supporter of the Pilgrim demand that "villein blood" be removed from the council. His association, as lieutenant, with the earl of Shrewsbury, a friend of Darcy and Hussey, increased the favour in which he was held. For the role of Shrewsbury in relation to Lord Hussey in the Lincolnshire rebellion, see above, pp. 251 ff.

179 See above, pp. 341–2 and note 133 above. Norfolk's false "promises" are probably referred to by Lord Herbert of Cherbury in his *The Life and Reigne of King Henry the Eighth* (London, 1649), p. 428: " . . . the Lord Darcy during his imprisonment had accused him [Norfolk] as favouring the rebels' articles when they first met at Doncaster". No contemporary confirmation of Herbert's statement has survived. But such an attitude on the duke's part would help to explain the Pilgrim decision to abandon their regional rising in order to enhance Norfolk's standing with the king, and facilitate his advancement of their policies and interests at court. See Dodds, *op. cit.*, pp. 267–8.

anxiety with which they sought a political solution, he was able to bring about their submission and the disintegration of the Pilgrimage as an organized mass movement. As a result the militant party was politically defeated and isolated. Bigod aimed to exploit the militants' distrust of the king's promises, and their fear of royal vengeance. But his hasty and badly organized revolt simply provided the government with grounds to repudiate the policy of moderation and mercy. Aske and Darcy, in the outcome, were drawn with Bigod into the common disaster which marked the collapse of the Pilgrimage.[180]

The Pilgrimage presents then the picture of a constructive search for non-violent political forms through which an opposition could express itself. But the movement also signalizes the crumbling away of the traditional oppositionist role of the great lords. In 1536 the northern magnates already confronted authority in a mood of uncertainty and moral ambivalence, characterized by a shifty evasiveness, and an unwillingness to assume any open oppositionist stance. The case of the earl of Northumberland is typical of his class.[181] The greatest landowner in the north, warden of the East and Middle Marches, lieutenant in Yorkshire, he headed a clientele whose ramifications spread widely through the northern counties. Many of his followers, and his brother Sir Thomas Percy, were involved with the militant party. But the earl's own attitude

[180] As seen above (pp. 350–1) the militants were overruled at the first encounter with Norfolk at Doncaster, Aske and Darcy insisting on a policy of peaceful negotiation instead of a battle. They were defeated again at the Pilgrim council at York, where Sir Robert Constable emerged as their most articulate representative. He wished to consolidate the Pilgrim control of the north and extend the movement into Lancashire, Cheshire and Derbyshire before negotiating with the king: *L.P.*, xii (1), 466, pp. 222–3; *ibid.*, 392, p. 194. Again the leaders of the peace party were Darcy (who had advocated immediate negotiation at a previous council meeting at Templehurst) and Aske, supported by the lawyer Babthorpe. Constable used "cruel words" against Archbishop Lee when at the council at Pontefract he committed himself in his sermon to a policy of non-resistance: *L.P.*, xi, 1300, p. 527.

On Bigod, see A. G. Dickens, *Lollards and Protestants in the Diocese of York, 1509–1558* (London, 1959), pp. 53 ff. His orientation towards the militants is shown by the regions from which he hoped for support: Cleveland (Sir Thomas Percy); Richmondshire (Latimer); Durham (Neville and Lumley); Craven (Percy). With the exception of the Lumleys (Lord Lumley's heir, George, joined Bigod) none of these general interests (with the possible exception of Sir Thomas Percy) was willing to commit itself to a new rising.

[181] See above, pp. 114–15 and 168–9.

remained doubtful. Some of his actions suggest support for the Pilgrimage. But he refused to commit himself publicly to it, and dismissed his younger brother, Sir Ingram, from his March offices when he spoke disrespectfully of Cromwell in his presence.[182] At least Northumberland was a sick man. Illness may partly account for his shifty tactics. The earl of Westmorland had no such excuse. As a result of the indiscretion of a servant[183] we know that secretly he supported the Pilgrimage. But he avoided any open commitment, although his heir, Lord Neville, led the Durham contingent of the Pilgrims. A similar attitude characterized the Border magnate, Lord Dacre. Outward loyalty went with underhand support for the local dissidents, until it became clear that the Pilgrimage had no future. Dacre then helped to suppress it.[184] The earl of Derby and the earl of Cumberland remained loyal.[185] Such attitudes were characteristic of the nobility, among whom the militants were only a small minority: Lumley, Latimer and the Nevilles, with their allies Hilton, Constable and later Bigod from the upper gentry. Among the upper class a mood of dissent carried to the point of revolt could no longer sustain itself. It was the moral force of the concept of obedience which triumphed. The Pilgrims, troubled by the conflict between their oath and the allegiance which bound them to the king, found no comfort from the clergy they had risen to defend.[186] As seen above, Archbishop Lee told them that the sword was given to none but the prince; none might draw it but in the prince's name. Lee's sermon completed the isolation of the militants, defining the mood of fear and doubt which was the context of the Bigod revolt.

The Northern Rising of 1569 affords other instances of a failure of nerve on the part of the high nobility (particularly the "high and mighty prince" Thomas, fourth duke of Norfolk) when it came to a confrontation with the crown. Like Bigod's, the context of this

182 *L.P.*, xii (1), 1090, pp. 504–8.

183 M. E. James, *Family, Lineage, and Civil Society: A Study of Society, Politics, and Mentality in the Durham Region, 1500–1640* (Oxford, 1974), p. 46.

184 See above, p. 113.

185 Christopher Haigh, *The Last Days of the Lancashire Monasteries and the Pilgrimage of Grace* (Chetham Soc., 3rd ser., xvii, Manchester, 1969), pp. 61 ff.; see also above, pp. 174 ff.

186 Among the points to be submitted to the clergy at the Pilgrim council at Pontefract was the item: "if one oath be made, and after one other oath to the contrary, and by the latter oath the party is sworn to repute and take the first oath void, whether it may be so by . . . [spiritual] . . . law or not" (*L.P.*, xi, 1182, p. 477). The clergy gave no ruling on this, and it seems that it was not even discussed.

revolt was the fear and despair of a group of militants who had been abandoned to their own devices by powerful allies who had come to terms with the government. The rebel earls of Westmorland and Northumberland were the rump of what had been a wider and more moderate movement which had the sympathies of most of the northern nobility.[187] This had acquired political plausibility from its affiliation to a powerful aristocratic pressure group at court, led by Norfolk, which was prepared to support the proposed Norfolk marriage to Mary, queen of Scots, and aimed at the overthrow of the Cecil régime.[188] But the link between the northerners and the court was broken, and the northern movement split, by the duke's defection. His decision to obey Elizabeth's summons to her presence meant the abandonment of his friends in the north.[189] Their sense of fear and isolation drove them into a disastrous revolt, with the religious extremists taking the upper hand with their policy of religious war. In the meanwhile the noble opportunists – Derby, Arundel, Lumley and Pembroke, as well as Norfolk – made their peace with the government.[190] It was the end of any significant

[187] The rising was a minority movement in the sense that those who took part consisted only of the two earls and a few gentry families closely connected with them. Among the Percy following, support was strongest in Richmondshire and north Yorkshire where the Nortons and Markenfields rose, but non-existent in Cumberland and weak in Northumberland: see above, pp. 293 ff. The Nevilles were more successful in raising Durham, but even here only three leading houses were involved – the Salvins, Claxtons and Tempests: James, *Family, Lineage, and Civil Society*, p. 51; most of the support came from minor or newly risen families not in the leadership of the Palatinate.

[188] Among the court peers Arundel, Lumley and Pembroke were Norfolk's most consistent supporters. In the north his brother-in-law Lord Scrope was warden of the West March; his cousin Sussex was lord president; his brother-in-law the earl of Westmorland actively supported his interest. The earls of Derby and Cumberland, with Lord Wharton, were sympathizers. The earl of Northumberland represented an ultra-Catholic policy not always favourable to the duke's aspirations; and Norfolk had divided the border Dacre interest by disinheriting the Dacre male heir, Leonard Dacre, and securing the succession to the Dacre lands for his own children. See N. Williams, *Thomas Howard, Fourth Duke of Norfolk* (London, 1964), pp. 116 ff., 146 ff.

[189] *Ibid.*, pp. 161 ff.

[190] The tragedy of the rising was summed up in Westmorland's denunciation of Norfolk's desertion; he said, "cursing the duke, he was the undoing of them for by that message [that is, not to rise] and breach of that day, their friends fell from them and gave them over": Sharp, *Memorials of the Rebellion of 1569*, p. 362. Cf. ". . . the said earl of Northumberland and Countesse did affirm, that the coming of the duke of Norfolk from Kenninghall was the only overthrow of the said enterprise": examination of Thomas Bishop, in *Collection of State Papers*, ed. Murdin, p. 217.

opposition role for the great lords. A period of political eclipse set in for the peerage which began to pass only with the revival of aristocratic oppositionism in the Parliaments of the 1620s.[191]

Another recurring feature, met with again and again in Tudor revolts (the Pilgrimage, the Lincolnshire rebellion, the Western rebellion and others), projects the same ambivalent and evasive aura which surrounds all manifestations of political dissidence. This was the convention whereby noblemen and gentlemen presented themselves as coerced by plebeian rioters into the leadership of revolts, which they supposedly assumed out of fear of their lives. The implausibility of such excuses was frequently transparent and recognized to be such by the government. Yet it was only in exceptional cases that they were actually given the lie by authority, which therefore played a collusive role in establishing the convention.[192] Thus it became usual for revolts to present themselves, where possible, as risings "of the commons", which their betters only unwillingly joined. The convention made it possible, in the first place, to transfer the guilt for outbreaks of disorder from the latter to their inferiors, on whom the subsequent repressive measures were mainly visited, casualties among the gentry and nobility being proportionately few. Only the most exposed and patently compromised members of the upper class who had involved themselves in seditious movements were subsequently brought to book.

But the notion that risings were necessarily "of the commons" also implied a changed attitude to dissidence on the part of those who had traditionally led rebellions and revolts: one of wariness with regard to the political viability of such movements, and of doubt as to their moral status. Only plebeians, it was now assumed, took the initiative to bring about seditious outbreaks; they alone, the inchoate, unformed social mass, outside the political community to which their betters belonged, too "brutal and ignorant" to know better, were liable to break the bonds of "obedience". Thus the dissident gentry and nobility could present themselves as the victims, not the instigators of revolts; and so a common ground remained from which a reconciliation could be sought with the

[191] For the revival, see V. F. Snow, "Essex and the Aristocratic Opposition to the Early Stuarts", *Jl Mod. Hist.*, xxxii (1960), pp. 224 ff., and below, pp. 406 ff.

[192] See above, pp. 194–5; for Henry VIII's interpretation of the Pilgrimage in similar terms, cf. *L.P.*, xi, 1175, pp. 474–5.

authority they appeared never to have defied. But now dissidence was seen no longer as a confrontation between an unworthy king and his nobility but almost as a natural calamity – the shattering of polity by insensate popular forces completely alien to it.[193] This attitude implied the abandonment of the traditional honour view as to the relationship between superior and subordinate. An "absolute" or unconditional obedience was alien to this, for "faithfulness" implied a response to "good lordship". Once again a loss of nerve is apparent. But also, it will be seen, a warning. God underwrote "order" but also punished unjust princes by unleashing a plebeian chaos against a misgoverned state.

The moralization of politics

Of course, the failure of nerve was in good part rooted in political conditions. The aristocratic generation which experienced the Tudor advent had been demoralized by civil war. After 1487, as the late K. B. McFarlane once pointed out, the nobility "had become more self-effacing, less sure of their mission to coerce incompetent or high-handed rulers, . . . congenitally wary, convinced of the benefits of passive obedience".[194] Once the Tudors had consolidated their tenure of the kingship, and eliminated the pretenders, dissidence lost the impetus which disputed claims to the succession had conferred. Those still inclined to gamble on a change of régime also had to reckon with the subtle demoralizing infiltration of households and affinities by royal agents and spies.[195] "Faithfulness" was not to be relied upon in the world of Henry VII, Wolsey and Cromwell. Hence the comment of Edward, duke of Buckingham, subsequently to be betrayed by his own servants: "it would do well enough if noblemen durst break their minds together, but some of them mistrusteth and feareth to break their minds to other, and that marreth all".[196] Few were prepared to pit the "steadfastness" of honour against the devastating dexterity with which the crown crushed opponents and asserted the reality of its claim to obedience. In the longer term there were the social changes which by the end of the sixteenth century had dissolved the kind of society in which the

[193] Cf. above, pp. 264 ff.
[194] MacFarlane, "Wars of the Roses", p. 117.
[195] *Ibid.*, p. 117 and note 3, p. 118 and note 1.
[196] *L.P.*, iii (1), Introduction, p. cxxx.

traditional politics of violence could be practised. The numerical expansion of the gentry class and changes in its structure had undermined the relationship of dependence upon, and affinity with, the nobility. The rise of the grammar school, with its humanist and religious emphasis, did away with the aristocratic household and its honour culture as the typical educational environment for lay members of the upper class.[197]

All this gradually dissolved the kind of society in which the traditional politics of violence were practised. Yet one factor remained constant – the weakness and uncertain operation of the order-keeping forces at the disposal of the state. Civil order depended, to a much greater extent than in the bureaucratized societies of a later age, on the effective internalization of obedience, the external sanctions being so often unreliable. The changed pattern of dissidence, as this expressed itself in the revolts discussed above, therefore involved shifts in mentality and attitude which prepared and fostered the new developments. These included the tendency for the obligations of honour to reshape themselves. A polity structured in terms of unconditional obedience had room only for the "nationalized" honour which Norfolk, in the context of the Pilgrimage of Grace, had represented, with its source and sanction in the king; and not for the autonomous, self-authenticating honour community of nobles which Darcy took for granted.[198] Yet even Darcy, and still more Aske and the Pilgrim leaders, were troubled by the conflict between their Pilgrim's oath and the oath of allegiance; and only a defeated minority were willing to commit themselves to the violence of civil war.

Thus a concern with obedience, conceived as unconditional, underlay the decay of honour as a code of political dissidence. But this forms part of a wider transformation, which affected many aspects of the culture of the upper class as literacy became more general. From the end of the fourteenth century, and with increasing impetus during the fifteenth, a demand for books establishes itself among the laity. Beginning with the aristocracy and the court, this spreads downward into a widening circle: the gentry, the upper merchants, professional men, mainly lawyers. A broadening of the

[197] For a discussion of this process within a specific regional setting (that of the Durham palatinate), see James, *Family, Lineage, and Civil Society*, pp. 67–107.

[198] See above, pp. 339 ff.

literacy base took place, and the new needs were met first by the production of the cheap mass-produced manuscript, then by the adoption of the printing-press. At the same time the new public involved a shift in the kind of literary material in demand. Sober country gentlemen, merchants and men of law did not confine themselves to the literary products of the courtly tradition.[199] The new readers were thirsty for information, first and foremost. It was the didactic, moralizing and encyclopaedic tradition, hitherto locked up in Latin and French, which they were eager to absorb and adapt. Everywhere we find books of instruction: how to live, how to die, how to bring up children, how to cook, how to carve, how to eat, how to stay healthy. There was the urge to understand one's place in space and time which produced the historical and geographical encyclopaedias, like the translations of Higden's *Polychronichon* and of the *De proprietatibus rerum*.[200] In his *Fall of Princes* Lydgate provided a poetized compendium of biography and history; in his *Siege of Thebes*, an encyclopaedia of mythology. The overwhelmingly didactic and practical nature of the early printed books confirms the persistence of the urge to understand and procure access to facts and information into the age of Caxton and Pynson, and beyond.[201]

Facts and the practical approach did not exclude a concern with religion, politics and history. But here too the method was pragmatic, expressing itself as far as religion was concerned in a moralization of the cult of saints and images, in place of the previous numinous and "magical" emphasis, and in a stress on the literal sense of Scripture, seen primarily as a historical source-book of moral exempla.[202] In this way a receptive audience for some of the

[199] H. S. Bennett, "The Author and his Public in the Fourteenth and Fifteenth Centuries", *Essays and Studies* [English Association], xxiii (1938), pp. 7–24; H. S. Bennett, "Caxton and his Public", *Rev. Eng. Studies*, xix (1943), pp. 113–19; D. Pearsall, *John Lydgate* (London, 1970), pp. 71 ff.

[200] H. S. Bennett, *Chaucer and the Fifteenth Century* (Oxford History of English Literature, ii (1), Oxford, 1947), pp. 105 ff.; H. S. Bennett, "Science and Information in English Writings of the Fifteenth Century", *Modern Language Rev.*, xxxix (1944), pp. 1–8.

[201] H. S. Bennett, *English Books and Readers, 1475 to 1557*, 2nd edn (Cambridge, 1969), pp. 65–151.

[202] Thus in the late fourteenth-century *The Book of the Knight of La Tour-Landry*, ed. Thomas Wright (Early English Text Soc., old ser., xxxiii, London, 1868; revised London, 1906), first translated into English in the reign of Henry VI and later by Caxton, the knight makes a book of "exemples" taken out of chronicles

ideas of the humanists and reformers was prepared. Thus the tone was set for the approach to political experience. Here too the preoccupation is with the pragmatic, and with a search for practical guide-lines. There is an attempt to map out the political environment and to seek a partial understanding of it. The measure and standard adopted is to identify correct and incorrect courses of political action with right and wrong courses of action. A moralization of politics takes place. What was the motive behind this? It was an attempt, in an age when political turmoil and party strife were never far away, to form an outlook which calmed fears, brought the passions under control, and promoted obedience, consistent political behaviour, and order. It was an attempt to exorcise the grim presence of Fate, with its incomprehensible decrees, which had always overshadowed the man of honour; and to provide an insurance against the rule of Fortuna, goddess of luck and chance. Her subjects were precisely the "worshipful" and honourable, whom she raised to greatness on her Wheel, only to cast them down again. The writings on history and politics which now found their way into the hands of the gentry and aristocracy owed their appeal to their claim to provide the "remedies" against Fortune for those whom the heroic "steadfastness" of honour did not content. The Chaucerian poet-encyclopaedist and monk of Bury St Edmunds, John Lydgate (died 1449), owed his immense popularity (which spanned the Reformation and extended far into the sixteenth century) to the thoroughness with which he met this need.[203]

The Judaeo-Christian tradition, building on that of Greece and Rome, had evolved a view of history seen as a tension between Fate, chance and free will. In spite of the capricious, incalculable turns of Fortune, her rule, so it was thought, could at least be limited by human virtue, reason and prudence; indeed, Aristotle had developed the argument that chance is necessary in order to make

and "gestes", but also out of the Bible, to be used for the education of his daughters. Caxton's edition of Jacobus de Voragine's *Golden Legend* (London, [1483], S.T.C. 24873) presented the lives of the saints as moral exempla for the instruction of the faithful. He omitted Voragine's dogmatic material and combined the lives with a series of vernacular biblical narratives. See H. C. White, *Tudor Books of Saints and Martyrs* (Madison, Wisconsin, 1963), pp. 33 ff.

203 Significantly it was at the specific request of his patron, Humphrey, duke of Gloucester, that Lydgate had added an "Envoy" to each of the chapters of his *Fall of Princes*, offering a "remedie" against Fortune and directed especially to kings and princes: Pearsall, *op. cit.*, p. 236.

room for free will. Probably the most important contribution to the Christianization of Fortune was made by Boethius. He emphasized the traditional fickleness of the goddess, but linked this with the Aristotelian idea: "Chance allows for free will". Then he went on to develop the Christian approach to the theme: "Fate is the servant of God; and Chance, growing out of hidden causes, is also subject to Divine Providence." First Augustine, and then Aquinas, provided a more rigorous and systematically logical adaptation of the Aristotelian argument to a Christian point of view; and the Christianization of Fortune was completed by Dante. For him the fickleness of Fortune is only apparent; in truth she is the minister of God's judgements.[204] It remained to apply the tradition to an impressively encyclopaedic range of historical exempla, and to make these widely available. This was the achievement of Boccaccio in his *De casibus*.[205] The lore of Fortune, as expounded in the latter work, was what Lydgate made available, in the vernacular, under the title of *The Fall of Princes*,[206] to the new English literate public. He used a French version of Boccaccio which he altered and adapted in certain important respects.

Lydgate could never hope wholly to exorcise the terrifying capriciousness of Fortune. Since the goddess was God's minister, her action reflected the mystery of the decrees of Providence, ultimately impenetrable to fallen man.[207] Nevertheless to a large measure those decrees had been revealed in Scripture, as interpreted by the church. They were made available in the law, natural, divine and positive, by which the whole world of man was governed. The essence of worldly wisdom was obedience to this law. Those who held to the straight and narrow path which it laid

204 See H. R. Patch, *The Goddess Fortuna in Mediaeval Literature* (London, 1967 edn), pp. 8–34; W. Farnham, *The Medieval Heritage of Elizabethan Tragedy* (Oxford, 1936), chs. 1–2.

205 Farnham, *op. cit.*, ch. 3.

206 John Lydgate, *The Fall of Princes*, ed. H. Bergen, 4 vols. (Early English Text Soc., extra ser., cxxi–cxxiv, London, 1924–7). See also Pearsall, *op. cit.*, pp. 223 ff.; Walter F. Schirmer, *John Lydgate: A Study in the Culture of the Fifteenth Century*, trans. by A. E. Keep (London, 1961); A. Renoir, *The Poetry of John Lydgate* (London, 1967), *passim*; Farnham, *op. cit.*, pp. 160 ff.

207 This is probably the best answer to the criticism of Schirmer that in *The Fall of Princes* "on the one hand the entire world is portrayed as a fatalistic dream of the fickleness of Fortune and the transitoriness of earthly glory; on the other hand history is seen as a manifestation of the world of divine justice. Lydgate fails to extricate himself from the toils of this contradiction": Schirmer, *op. cit.*, p. 213.

down found themselves subject not to the tyranny of Fortune but to the rule of Providence, bringing with it divine favour and protection. Thus history was structured in terms of obedience, according to Lydgate the "virtue of virtues", without which "Destroyed were all worldly policy". But rulers as well as subjects were required to obey. For them wisdom implied the moderate use of their authority, with due regard for the welfare of their subjects. Those who so governed would rule long and prosperously; the tyrant dug the pit into which he himself fell.[208] Such was the lesson Lydgate hammered home in his compendium of poetic moralizing tales, each personalized as the story, abstracted from Scripture and history, ancient and modern, of a specific individual. The originality of the collection, apart from its comprehensiveness, lay in the systematic fashion with which each tale was designed, in terms of an illustrative exemplum, to indicate the pattern of conduct which, being virtuous, removed one from the rule of Fortune; or being immoral, made one subject to Fortune's tyranny. Lydgate drove home the point of his tales by providing each with an "Envoy" in the form of a "remedy against Fortune", specifically directed to those who ruled.[209] The total emphasis was on conformity to law as the likeliest guarantee of political and social stability, and on obedience as the best insurance of personal survival.

The tradition of a moralized history and its application to political action was carried further, and given a developed sophistication, early in the sixteenth century by Polydore Vergil and Thomas More. Both wrote in the latest and most approved humanist manner, with the influence of Suetonius, Sallust and Tacitus more apparent than Lydgate's. Both abandoned Lydgate's scheme of a collection of tragic histories each containing a "remedy against Fortune". Vergil developed a continuous history of England, an *Anglica historia*, largely organized on the basis of the reign as the periodic unit. More wrote the subtle and psychologized biography of a tyrant, Richard III. But the basic attitudes of *The Fall of Princes* still provide the organizing concepts, More's King Richard being no more than an extended exemplum on a traditional theme: the fall of a

[208] See above, pp. 262 ff.; Schirmer, *op. cit.*, pp. 209–10, 213–14, 216–17; Renoir, *op. cit.*, pp. 104–8.
[209] See note 203 above, this chapter.

tyrant.[210] Vergil applied them to collectivities as well as individuals. Thus it was the house of Lancaster, and not Henry IV, which had to pay the price for the latter's unjust dethronement of Richard II, "for the kingdom could not long be held by this family, the sins of the grandfather being visited on his grandson". Similarly in the case of the fall of the house of York, and the extinction of the male line of Edward IV. This was attributed to the false oath (of loyalty to Henry VI) sworn by the latter before York in 1471, retribution for which was visited by divine justice on his children. Vergil is also remarkable for his sense of politics as an inherently dangerous activity, because of the powerful temptations and the ineluctable entanglement with sin in which its practitioners were involved. Thus, if Edward had refused the oath before York, he would have pleased God, but lost his throne. Political situations were characterized by contradictory demands and divided motivation. The implied lesson was that the wise man kept clear of them. Vergil opted for quietism as well as obedience and conformity.[211]

This was the attitude popularized by the lawyer Edward Hall, whose *Chronicle*[212] translated, adapted and continued Vergil. But he also aimed at an amalgam of the cult of Fortune and divine providentialism with a powerful sense of history as a dialectic of order versus disorder. He followed those able Lancastrian exponents of strong kingship, Hardyng, Fortescue and George Ashby (the last an admirer of Lydgate), in exalting the role of the crown as triumphantly manifested in the Tudor achievement.[213]

[210] See *The "Anglica historia" of Polydore Vergil*, ed. Hay; *Three Books of Polydore Vergil's English History, Comprising the Reigns of Henry VI, Edward IV and Richard III*, ed. Sir Henry Ellis (Camden Soc., old ser., xxix, London, 1844); St Thomas More, *The History of King Richard III*, ed. Richard S. Sylvester, in *The Complete Works of St Thomas More*, ii (Yale edn, New Haven, 1963).

[211] More, *History of King Richard III*, p. cii; Denys Hay, *Polydore Vergil* (Oxford, 1952), pp. 141–2; F. J. Levy, *Tudor Historical Thought* (San Marino, Calif., 1967), pp. 171–2. Among the new-style "histories" George Cavendish's *Life of Wolsey* most of all conforms to the pattern of the medieval moralizations on Fortune and the deaths of princes. See R. S. Sylvester, "Cavendish's *Life of Wolsey*: The Artistry of a Tudor Biographer", *Studies in Philology*, lvii (1960), pp. 44–71.

[212] Edward Hall, *The Union of . . . York and Lancaster*, ed. H. Ellis (London, 1809).

[213] For Hardyng, see C. L. Kingsford, "The First Version of Hardyng's Chronicle", *Eng. Hist. Rev.*, xxvii (1912), pp. 462–82, 740–53. It is probable that Hardyng had also read Lydgate. The reference to "Bochas" at fo. xcvii^{v} of Richard Grafton's edition of Hardyng's *Chronicle* (London, 1543, S.T.C. 12767) probably related to *The Fall of Princes*. For George Ashby's *A Prisoner's Reflections* and *Active*

Henry VII, having rescued the realm from the "troublous" times of the Wars of the Roses, prepared the way for the "triumphant" reign of Henry VIII. In the latter's person the state emerges in all its grandeur not only as the vehicle of the "order" which was God's will for men, but also as the divinely appointed instrument for the renewal of religion. Yet for Hall too politics remained the area of divine judgement, where Fortune was to be encountered in all her mysteriousness as the agent of the divine decrees. An underlying pessimism about politics persists:

> What trust is in this world, what suretie man hath of his life . . . all men may perceive and see by the ruin of this noble prince [Richard II] . . . so that all men may perceive and see that fortune wayeth princes and poor men all in one balance.[214]

The wise man was content to obey, leaving political action to those called by God to bear the burdens of governance. Already in the 1530s, in the poetry of Wyatt, the quietist joys of the countryside and the simple life were being cried up against the sinister and febrile activism of the court, with its sudden and unpredictable falls: the abrupt passage from royal favour and supreme power to the Tower and the scaffold.[215]

In the case of Hall the sense of history as the stage on which God's judgements became manifest had already been informed by the influence of the Reformation. Protestantism annexed the moralized view of history and politics and drove home the lesson of conformity and obedience, turning men's minds away from the seductive and dangerous world of politics to the quietism and inner recollection which went with Lutheran "faith". Moreover, in an even more direct and pragmatic kind of way than the poetic and historical expositors of the lore of Fortune and Providence, the Protestant divines pointed to the connection between morality and prosperity, the straight and narrow path being also the road to self-preservation

Policy of a Prince, see *George Ashby's Poems*, ed. Mary Bateson (Early English Text Soc., extra ser., lxxvi, London, 1899), pp. 1–41. In the latter work, Ashby acknowledges his debt to Chaucer, Gower and Lydgate. For Fortescue, see his *The Governance of England, Otherwise Called the Difference Between an Absolute and a Limited Monarchy*, ed. C. Plummer (Oxford, 1885), and his *De laudibus legum Anglie*, ed. S. B. Chrimes (Cambridge Studies in English Legal History, Cambridge, 1942).

214 Quoted in Levy, *op. cit.*, p. 176.

215 See R. Southall, *The Courtly Maker: An Essay on the Poetry of Wyatt and his Contemporaries* (Oxford, 1964), pp. 92 ff.

and success. From this point of view Protestantism was not innovative, but an extension of tendencies already powerfully present in the lay literate culture as this had formed itself by the end of the fifteenth century. Judging for example by the kind of religious material which Caxton and his immediate successors found it profitable to print, a powerful trend in lay religion favoured a piety which would be clear, sensible, and orientated towards practical moral issues, as well as increasingly Scriptural.[216] Colet and Erasmus had pointed to the "simplicity" of Scripture, interpreted in the literal sense, as the key to the clear, practical layman's religion, the *philosophia Christi*, which was needed.[217] Tyndale denounced the clergy as "owls" who deluded the "learned laypeople" with the "many senses" of the traditional fourfold interpretation of Scripture. For, Tyndale asserted, "it hath but one, simple, literal sense, whose light the owls cannot abide".[218] As a result Scripture was transformed, no longer exhibiting the many-layered Joycean complexity (as difficult and fascinating as *Finnegan's Wake*) in which the medieval culture had wrapped it. Instead it acquired the linear clarity of a realist novel or of a historical narrative.

This emphasis tended to highlight the moral and exemplary content of Scripture. Like history itself as presented by Lydgate, the Bible (and particularly the Old Testament) resolved itself above all into a store of moral examples, in which "the glorious and wonderful deeds of God, his terrible handling of his enemies, and merciful

216 The interest in Scripture is suggested by the vernacular biblical narratives which Caxton (in spite of the ecclesiastical ban on a vernacular Scripture) included in his *Golden Legend* (see note 202 above); also by the popularity of *The Mirrour of the Blessyd Life of Christ*, printed by Caxton in 1486 (S.T.C. 3259) with a second edition in 1490 (S.T.C. 3260); the book was also published by De Worde in 1494, 1517 and 1525 (S.T.C. 3261, 3264 and 3266), and by Pynson in 1495 and 1506 (S.T.C. 3262 and 3263). The work made frequent use of the actual words of Scripture in its relation of the Gospel stories. The thirst for an instructed religion among the literate laity emerges from the works listed by F. A. Gasquet, "The Bibliography of Some Devotional Books Printed by the Earliest English Printers", *Trans. Bibliographical Soc.* for 1902–4, vii (1904), pp. 163–89, esp. pp. 174–81, 183–8.

217 L. Miles, *John Colet and the Platonic Tradition* (London, 1962), pp. 181 ff.; F. Seebohm, *The Oxford Reformers* (Everyman Library edn, London, 1929 edn), pp. 202 ff.; J. K. McConica, *English Humanists and Reformation Politics under Henry VIII and Edward VI* (Oxford, 1965), pp. 16 ff.

218 William Tyndale, "Preface to Genesis", in *Doctrinal Treatises and Introductions to Different Portions of the Holy Scriptures, by William Tyndale, Martyr, 1536*, ed. H. Walter (Parker Soc., [xxxii], Cambridge, 1848), pp. 393–4.

entreating of them that come when he calleth them" were to be contemplated.[219] For Tyndale, Moses was not, as in the traditional exegesis, a "type" prefiguring Christ, but an exemplum "unto all princes and unto all in authority, how to rule unto God's pleasure and unto their neighbour's profit".[220] Moreover a careful study of the Scriptural examples had a practical relevance. For "as thou seest blessings or cursings follow the keeping or breaking of the laws of Moses . . . even so do blessings or cursings follow the keeping or breaking of the laws of nature, from which spring all our temporal laws"; thus "when people keep the temporal laws of their land, temporal prosperity . . . do accompany them".[221] Temporal welfare is then the reward of temporal conformity; so that the Turks, who exceed Christians in obedience, also exceed them in prosperity.[222] So Tyndale, whose theology in the 1530s acquired increasingly legalistic and contractual overtones, at the expense of his earlier Lutheran emphasis on "Christian freedom".

Thus one lesson which emerged from the new religious trends was that God, "if we care to keep his laws . . . will care for the keeping of us, for the truth of his promises". Of course, God's care did not necessarily exclude sufferings (although this aspect of the matter was less emphasized by Tyndale than by other theologians like Coverdale) which were as likely to be the lot of the righteous as of the sinful. Indeed, in the case of the former, affliction, proceeding from God's "secret" will, provided the occasion for the practice of "patience" (as will be seen below). The reassurance which providentialism made available was not of a mere temporal prosperity, but rather that all experience, however disastrous it might be, was of God. As such it could not be the product of Fate or chance; consequently, if approached in the correct disposition and correctly understood, the outcome it presented was positive – even if this should be apparent only beyond this life, in eternity. But this did not affect the issue that disobedience to God's "manifest" will, revealed in law and requiring obedience, invited catastrophe. The first condition of prosperity, both temporal and eternal, was con-

[219] William Tyndale, "Prologue to Deuteronomy", in *Doctrinal Treatises*, p. 441.
[220] William Tyndale, "Prologue to Exodus", in *Doctrinal Treatises*, p. 412.
[221] *Ibid.*, pp. 417–18.
[222] William Tyndale, "The Obedience of a Christian Man", in *Doctrinal Treatises*, p. 175.

formity to the divinely constituted order of things.[223] From this point of view Protestantism stood within and continued the tradition which Lydgate also represented, while adapting it to the new theology. But no more than the new humanist history of Vergil and More did it affect Lydgate's popularity, which spanned the Reformation.[224] Indeed, so eagerly was the bulky compendium of exempla contained in *The Fall* perused, that supplementary collections taken from later contemporary history were compiled to bring Lydgate up to date.[225] The most famous of these was William Baldwin's *Mirror for Magistrates*, first printed in 1559.[226] The attraction of this kind of storehouse of exempla, by comparison with the historical narrative or chronicle, probably lay in the readiness with which the reader could find guidance in them. For the simple stories covered a wide variety of situations, and it was easy to identify with the single hero-figure in each one. The seeker after political wisdom accepted Baldwin's invitation to the nobility, in *The Mirror*: "Here as in a looking glass you may see, if any vice be in you, how the like hath been published heretofore."[227] He flipped through such works until he came to the example appropriate to his own case, and then studied the "remedy against fortune" prescribed, as a model for subsequent conduct. Thus in *The Mirror* Richard III, duly moralized into a tyrant and murderer as Tudor propaganda required, instructs the reader in the lessons of his own fall: "Loe

[223] William Tyndale, "The Practice of Prelates", in *Expositions and Notes on Sundry Portions of the Holy Scriptures, together with The Practice of Prelates, by William Tyndale, Martyr, 1536*, ed. H. Walter (Parker Soc., [xxxvii], Cambridge, 1849), p. 323. On providence and suffering, see the comments of Perry Miller, *The New England Mind: The Seventeenth Century* (Boston, Mass., 1961 edn), pp. 38–40. See also *The Catechism of Thomas Becon, S.T.P., . . . with Other Pieces Written by Him in the Reign of King Edward the Sixth*, ed. J. Ayre (Parker Soc., [xiii], Cambridge, 1844), pp. 186–93; Roger Hutchinson, "Two Sermons of Oppression, Affliction, and Patience", in *The Works of Roger Hutchinson*, ed. J. Bruce (Parker Soc., [iv], Cambridge, 1842), pp. 289 ff.; Miles Coverdale, "Fruitful Lessons", in *Writings and Translations of Myles Coverdale, Bishop of Exeter*, ed. G. Pearson (Parker Soc., [xv], Cambridge, 1844), pp. 195 ff.

[224] For the successive prints of *The Fall*, see Lydgate, *The Fall of Princes*, ed. Bergen, iv, pp. 106 ff.

[225] Farnham, *The Medieval Heritage of Elizabethan Tragedy*, pp. 271 ff.

[226] William Baldwin, *A Myrroure for Magistrates* (London, 1559, S.T.C. 1247), repr. as *The Mirror for Magistrates*, ed. Lily B. Campbell (Cambridge, 1938); and John Higgins and Thomas Blenerhasset, *Parts Added to "The Mirror for Magistrates"*, ed. Lily B. Campbell (Cambridge, 1946).

[227] Baldwin, *The Mirror for Magistrates*, ed. Campbell, p. 65.

here you may behold the due and just reward/ Of tyranny and treason which God doth most detest." Without right he had aspired to, and murderously possessed himself of the crown. "But hasty rising threatneth sidayne fall/ Content yourselves with your estates all/ And seek not right by wrong to suppresse/ For God hath promised eche wrong to redresse."[228]

Moralized politics, as expounded by the providentialist exponents of history as the field of Fortune's fickleness, partly advanced and partly symptomized the changing conception of honour which went with the decline of the politics of honour. The lessons of Lydgate's *Fall of Princes* were after all to be driven home by half a century of misrule, political instability and civil war, followed by the disintegration and demoralization which afflicted so many of the regional honour communities under Tudor rule. The note of danger and oppression, and the sense of strain manifest in some of the private devotions of Richard III[229] are probably typical of much upper-class sentiment in the late fifteenth century. In the next generation disillusion with honour values is apparent in the circle of the fifth earl of Northumberland, the literary products of the group suggesting a concern with religion as providing a more secure moral anchorage in difficult and treacherous times. The earl's father had been assassinated by the commons of Thirsk on 28 April 1489 in the course of a tax revolt; but the murder had also been marked by treachery among his retinue.[230] The poet Skelton, in the elegy he wrote to commemorate the event, emphasized not only the fickleness of Fortune but also the unfaithfulness of his followers as responsible for the earl's death. In a play on the Percy motto, *esperaunce ma conforte*, the young heir was warned not to

[228] *Ibid.*, p. 370.

[229] Lambeth Palace MS. 474; printed and translated in Pamela Tudor-Craig, *Richard III* [Catalogue of an exhibition at the National Portrait Gallery, 1973] (London, 1973), p. 96. The following extracts are typical: "O Lord who restored the race of men into concord with the Father . . . deign to establish concord between me and my enemies . . . Deign to assuage, turn aside, extinguish and bring to nothing the hatred they bear towards me . . . Deign, O Lord Jesus Christ, to bring to nothing the evil designs which they make . . . against me. I ask you, O gentle Christ Jesus . . . to keep me thy servant King Richard, and defend me from all evil and from my evil enemy, and from all danger, present past and to come, and free me from all tribulations, griefs and anguishes which I face, and deign to console me . . . ".

[230] See M. E. James, "The Murder at Cocklodge, 28th April 1489", *Durham Univ. Jl*, lvii (1965), pp. 80–7.

place the "hope of his house in men", whose very nature implied unreliability. The fifth earl, taking the lesson to heart, changed the family motto with its honour overtones (the hope implied would have been that of royal or lordly favour) to *espèraunce en dieu*. The implications of the change appear in the poem constructed around this device which the earl had painted on the wall of a chamber in his house at Leconfield:

> Esperaunce en dyeu.
> Trust hym he is moste trewe.
>
> En dieu esperaunce.
> In hym put thyne affiaunce.
>
> Esperaunce in the worlde nay.
> The worlde variethe every day.
>
> Esperaunce in riches nay not so.
> Riches slidethe and sone will go.
>
> Esperaunce in exaltation of honoure.
> Nay it widderethe away lyke a floure.
>
> Esperaunce en dieu in him is all.
> Which is above fortunes fall.[231]

John, sixth Lord Lumley, sometime after 1570, had similar verses (but in Latin) painted up in Lumley castle. These too celebrated the transience of "the world", with its honour, fame and nobility. Just as Northumberland set "esperaunce en dieu" against "Fortune's fall", so the Lumley verses concluded with the pious exhortation: "the world passes away, Christ does not pass away; worship not that which passes away".[232]

These were attitudes pointing towards obedience and quietism, and which reacted against the assertiveness and voluntarism of honour. They conformed to the chastened mood of John, Lord Mountjoy, who within a few weeks of Bosworth advised his sons "to live rightwisely, and never to take the estate of baron upon them if they may lay it from them, nor to desire to be great about princes, for it is dangerous".[233] A disillusionment with the politics of honour

[231] See above, pp. 86 ff.
[232] James, *Family, Lineage and Civil Society*, pp. 109–10.
[233] McFarlane, "Wars of the Roses", p. 119.

received expression in the action as well as the verses of the fifth earl of Northumberland, whose obsequious approaches to Henry VIII,[234] and refusal to assume any outwardly dissident stance, would also characterize his son the sixth earl, particularly during the Pilgrimage of Grace. Similarly, Lord Lumley's disenchantment with honour, fame and nobility belong to a period in his life when, after a decade of futile involvement in the aristocratic oppositionism of the fourth duke of Norfolk and the northern earls, he turned to conformity and obedience, becoming a prop of the *regnum Cecilanum*. Thus for many of the aristocracy events no longer simply presented occasions for heroic "steadfastness" in the confrontation with Fate. *Esperaunce en dieu*, or turning from "the world" to Christ, implied the religious, and therefore moral, content imparted to them by historical providentialism. History became manifest not in terms of honour, but of law, human and divine, requiring the response of obedience. Nor could religion be cordoned off from the world, as in the honour culture, which referred it to the clergy, old age, or to an eternity only relevant to the after-world entered at death. Moralized politics required that every decision, even those with a "worldly" reference, should involve a religious response. This attitude, already implicit in much of the lay religion of the pre-Reformation period, was defined and driven home by Protestantism.

Guilt and providentialism

There was another respect in which the moralized approach to events eroded honour motivation: in the case of the defeated it added the burden of guilt to that of failure. As suggested above,[235] under the honour code defeat did not necessarily imply guilt or moral opprobrium. It was the spirit (that is, the "steadfastness") with which events were encountered, not their outcome, which mattered. Judgement on the defeated was left to God in the world to come, to which honour was irrelevant. But a providentialist history and moralized politics implied that events in themselves were vehicles of divine judgement, which became manifest in the nega-

[234] See A. G. Dickens, "The Tudor-Percy Emblem in Royal MS. 18 D ii", *Archaeol. Jl*, cxii (1955), p. 95; and above, pp. 62 ff.

[235] See above, pp. 315 ff.

tive sense through the mechanism of failure and retribution. These therefore required the response of repentance and, where appropriate, public confession. Hence the custom, which seems to have been begun early in the reign of Henry VII, for those condemned for crimes of state to admit their own guilt on the scaffold, asserting that they deserved their fate, and showing a complete disregard for the "staining" of their honour which their admissions often involved.[236]

A case in point was that of the marquess of Exeter, executed for treason in 1538. According to Richard Morison, at his trial he denied the charges made against him. But "at the scaffold . . . he either began to weigh dishonour less . . . or else to think that dishonour standeth in doing traitorously, rather than in confessing it when it is known to be so; death at hand taught him and his fellows to provide for the safety of their souls, and to leave the regard for honour on the scaffold with their bodies".[237] He and his associates acknowledged their offences towards the king, and desired all present to pray for them. Another is that of George Boleyn, Viscount Rochford, treasonably implicated in the fall of his sister Queen Anne. At his trial he maintained that he was innocent, but after his condemnation said that he would no longer do so, on the grounds that the verdict proved that he deserved death "yea, even to die with worse shame and dishonour than hath ever been heard of before". He explained the nature of his guilt, which made him a living exemplum for the edification of his hearers: "It is I who ought to be blamed for having adventured to lean on Fortune, who hath proved herself fickle and false unto me, and who now maketh me an ensample to the whole world."[238] The theme thus implied in Boleyn's submission to the law's verdict, that the judgements of the law, whether in themselves true or false, were in either case those of God, would sound out more clearly and emphatically in later instances where the influences of Protestantism was more strongly present. Lady Jane Grey called the law "a never erring judge".

236 L. B. Smith, "English Treason Trials and Confessions in the Sixteenth Century", *Jl Hist. Ideas*, xv (1954), pp. 471–98.

237 Richard Morison, *An Invective Ayenste the Great and Detestable Vice, Treason* (London, 1539, S.T.C. 18111), e. 2ᵛ.

238 *Lettre d'un gentilhomme portugais à un de ses amis de Lisbonne, sur l'exécution d'Anne Boleyn, Lord Rochford, Brereton, Norris, Smeton, et Weston*, ed. F. Michel (Paris, 1832); quoted in Smith, *op. cit.*, pp. 477, 497.

Although innocent of any "procurement and desire" of treason, she was guilty of loving herself and the world, "therefore this plague and punishment is . . . happened unto me for my sins".[239] The same point of view was asserted from the scaffold by Protector Somerset. Although he had "never offended against the king, neither by word or deed", yet he willingly came there to suffer death "to testify my obedience which I owe unto the laws"; for "it seemeth thus good to Almighty God, whose ordinance it is meet and necessary that we all be obedient unto".[240] Similarly, Thomas, fourth duke of Norfolk, in 1572: at his condemnation he had cried "I shall die as a true man to the queen as any liveth"; but on the scaffold he submitted "to this which God hath prepared for me", acknowledging that "my peers have justly judged me worthy of death; neither is it my meaning to execute myself".[241]

For what other response was possible if events were structured in terms of a law which required the response of obedience, and whose instrument was the crown, the king being "but a servant to execute the law of God"?[242] Protestantism developed the implication that the contingent element in history had been swallowed up in divine providence.[243] The theme would be a favourite one, both of the Elizabethan divines and later. For Bishop Pilkington, Nehemiah provided a "manifest example" of "God's secret providence and care that he hath for his people, how he governeth all things . . . Not by chance (for so nothing falleth out) . . . ".[244] Similarly Bishop Cooper: "that which we call Fortune is nothing but the hand of God"; and for Oliver Cromwell (at a late stage in the development of the tradition): "Fate were too paganish a word . . . what are all our histories but God manifesting himself?"[245] Thus the dissident impelled into conflict with authority had need to "beware how he taketh anything in hand against the higher powers. Unless God be prosperable to his purpose, it will never take good effect or success,

[239] N. H. Nicolas, *The Literary Remains of Lady Jane Grey: With a Memoir of Her Life* (London, 1825), p. 52; *State Trials*, i, cols. 728–9.
[240] *State Trials*, i, cols. 523–5.
[241] *Ibid.*, cols. 1032–3.
[242] Tyndale, "Obedience of a Christian Man", p. 334.
[243] See Keith Thomas, *Religion and the Decline of Magic* (London, 1971), p. 79.
[244] James Pilkington, "An Exposition upon Part of the Book of Nehemiah", in *The Works of James Pilkington, B.D., Lord Bishop of Durham*, ed. J. Scholefield (Parker Soc., [iii], Cambridge, 1842), p. 309.
[245] Thomas, *op. cit.*, p. 79.

and therefore ye may now learn of me." So Sir Thomas Wyatt the younger, presenting himself at his trial, like Boleyn, as a living exemplum and warning to his time.[246]

Such attitudes provided a powerful internal sanction for unconditional obedience. Widely diffused by the printing-press among the increasingly literate governing class, they defined the context out of which the commonplaces of the *De vera obedientia* could resound convincingly and evoke a profound response: "By me (sayeth God) kings reign . . . whosoever resisteth power, resisteth the ordinance of God"; or Tyndale's "the king is, in this world, without law, and may at his lust do right and wrong and shall give accounts but to God only".[247] Such precepts did not strike home where there had been a failure to maintain a single, unified system of religious belief, or where honour attitudes still persisted. We have no record of any scaffold repentance on the part of Lord Darcy, nor did Lord Hussey make any public admission of guilt in connection with his implication in the Lincolnshire rebellion. The seventh earl of Northumberland, at his execution at York in 1570, made his death the occasion for an outright and unprecedented condemnation of authority. He said that he died a Catholic, that the realm was in schism, and that "he accounted his offence nothing . . . he said there was neither pity nor mercy".[248] His words, reported abroad, were interpreted as a clear indication that a militant Catholic party had emerged in England.

Moralized politics implied moral unity. This was conferred by a single religion and a unified system of values. Protestant doctrine combined with the Erasmian humanism inculcated by the grammar schools provided just the amalgam needed.[249] It was within this unity that, for the majority of the political nation which belonged to it, new ways of expressing dissidence had to be found. Paradoxically, it was the new providentialized history which pointed the way.

[246] *The Chronicle of Queen Jane, and of Two Years of Queen Mary, and Especially of the Rebellion of Sir Thomas Wyat*, ed. J. G. Nichols (Camden Soc., old ser., xlviii, London, 1850), p. 73.

[247] Stephen Gardiner, *De vera obedientia: An Oration*, trans. and printed by M. Wood (London, 1553, S.T.C. 11585), fo. xvi^{v}; Tyndale, "Obedience of a Christian Man", p. 178.

[248] *Cal. of State Papers, Scotland, 1547–1603*, iv, 425, p. 383; *ibid.*, 432, p. 394.

[249] Joan Simon, *Education and Society in Tudor England* (London, 1966), pp. 291 ff.; F. Caspari, *Humanism and the Social Order in Tudor England* (New York, 1968 edn), pp. 251 ff.; James, *Family, Lineage, and Civil Society*, pp. 96 ff.

For the exempla taught that revolts, if evil in themselves, were also symptoms of the failings of princes which, just as much as those of rebels, infallibly came to manifest divine judgement and "Fortune's fall". "Look because of the fall of princes", asserted a memorandum presented to the leaders of the Pilgrimage of Grace at their council at Pontefract, "where that men may perceive that vice was the occasion thereof." It was the prince who neglected to take good counsel, who upheld unjust ministers and tolerated oppression, who had reason to fear the rebel. "In this noble realm", the Pilgrims were told, "who reads the chronicles of Edward the ij, learns in what jeopardy he was for Piers de Gaveston, Despencer, and such like councillors . . . Richard the ij was deposed for following the counsel of such like."[250] The harsh and unwise ruler brought the social order as well as political stability into question. For oppression had the effect of unleashing the blind violence of the people against their betters. In one direction, of course, the search for new ways of expressing dissidence points towards the future of parliamentary oppositionism, with its peaceful conventions and bloodless battles. But more immediately the effect was to bring pressure on the rebel to conform to a role more like that of the peaceful demonstrator than of the instigator of civil strife. As such, he seeks to be accepted, not as waging treasonable war on his prince, but rather as holding up before him the mirror of the failings of his own governance. These are reflected back in the grievances of his oppressed subjects, and in the plebeian disorders to which these gave rise. Thus dissidence, by releasing pressures and compelling attention to abuses, had its place in the structure of order itself. For William Baldwin, in *The Mirror for Magistrates*, God used rebels "although the devil raise them . . . to his glory, as part of his justice", when kings and rulers failed to "hear and remedy their people's wrongs when they complain".[251] It was in such terms, and by way of commitment to the mysterious and uncertain decrees of Providence (whose true meaning would be revealed only in the unfolding of the events themselves), that the Tudor dissident tended to see his own role.

[250] *L.P.*, xi, 1244, p. 504.
[251] Cf. above, pp. 262 ff.; Baldwin, *The Mirror for Magistrates*, p. 178.

THE CHANGING EMPHASIS OF HONOUR

Interpreters of the tradition

The emergence of a state-centred honour system and the drive of providential history brought into question important aspects of the honour culture and its code, as traditionally conceived. In the first place, the emphasis in the providentialist approach on obedience and law weakened both the claim of the honour community to be self-authenticating, and that of the man of honour to the moral autonomy which "franchise" had involved. Thus the traditional two-sidedness of honour, as a support for a dissident or oppositionist stance as well as for "faithfulness", was undermined. Treason could no longer be conceived as committed against "knighthood", that is against a community and a code to which the prince as well as his subjects "of the worship" belonged and owed obedience. The "promise of a nobleman" in Darcy's sense was correspondingly weakened in the confrontation with sovereignty. Secondly, the permeation of the community of honour by humanism and religion, itself the result of a deeper penetration of lay society by literacy and education, required a redefinition of "virtue" and "learning", and of the meaning of these concepts, in relation to honour. Thirdly, honour required adaptation to the facts of social mobility. The "prouesse" of the swordsman who had proved his worth in battle had always given admission to the honour community. But to an increasing extent the "new men" who claimed a share of the privileges of honour were not men of war, but lawyers, officials, merchants, even husbandmen and artisans. How did such claims stand in relation to honour, and how did they affect the older idea of how honour was obtained? Against these winds of intellectual mutation and waters of social change, some aspects of honour stood relatively firm. There could be no whole-hearted rejection of blood and lineage in a society for which this was still a central concept. But uncertainty about the status of heredity in relation to other aspects of honour increased, with a proneness to present honour, virtue and nobility as detachable from their anchorage in pedigree and descent. Inevitably, as the landscape of honour was slowly eroded, and the relationship between its features changed, there was a search for a new synthesis, notably in the circle of Sir Philip Sidney. But, like Hooker's synthesis of church and state, the validity claimed for this proved to be only partially and temporarily achieved.

Briefly, the modification of honour at the hands of its Tudor expositors involved a wider dissemination in England of what was in effect the Bartolan concept of what honour implied. This gave parity, or even priority, to virtue over lineage, learning over arms, and "nobility dative" conferred by the state over hereditary nobility. Its influence was increasingly felt from the 1520s and 1530s, coinciding with Henry VIII's assault on the heralds, and the first royal commission for a heraldic visitation. Half a century before, even such a prominent representative of the English *noblesse de la robe* as Chief Justice John Fortescue had rejected the Bartolan concept as unnecessary as far as English lawyers (at least those who attended the Inns of Court) were concerned. Writing at the turn of the 1460s and 1470s he maintained that "there is scarcely a man learned in the laws to be found in the realm, who . . . is not sprung of noble lineage. So they care more for their nobility and the preservation of their honour than others of like estate."[252] Fortescue plainly thought that lineage was more conducive to honour than the merely Bartolan nobility which was doubtless all that "others of like estate", presumably in other realms, could claim. Traces of the Bartolan approach are however encountered at the court of Henry VII, and can be found in the interlude *Fulgens and Lucres* (1497) written by Henry Medwall,[253] chaplain in the household of Cardinal Morton, where it was presumably performed. The piece presented a poor but virtuous humanist upstart in very favourable comparison with a debauched nobleman of long descent, both being competitors for the hand of a well-born Roman lady. She shows a decided preference for the one of her suitors who "by means of his virtue to honour doth rise", and who is moreover a loyal servant of the state.

Since Medwall derived his interlude from John Tiptoft's translation of the *De nobilitate* of the Florentine civic humanist Buonaccorso, printed by Caxton in 1481,[254] it may need reiteration

[252] Fortescue, *De laudibus legum Anglie*, p. 119.

[253] Henry Medwall, *Fulgens and Lucres*, ed. F. S. Boas and A. W. Reed (Oxford, 1926).

[254] See C. R. Baskervill, "Conventional Features of Medwall's 'Fulgens and Lucres' ", *Modern Philology*, xxiv (1926–7), pp. 419–42; H. B. Lathrap, "The Translations of John Tiptoft", *Modern Language Notes*, xli (1926), pp. 496–501.

that such ideas were not new. The trope *Generositas virtus, non sanguis* had long been familiar to the learned.[255] The theme could be pursued in Seneca, Juvenal and Boethius. Chaucer had translated the last, and had also made available in English the *Romaunt de la rose* with its critique of hereditary nobility. But it was the Erasmians and humanists who, helped by the printed book, both popularized the total spectrum of the Bartolan concept, and imparted to it a greater depth and sophistication. They rescued virtue from its undefined and uncertain relationship to lineage, and promoted "learning" from those humble outer courts of Honour's Palace to which it had been relegated by Gavin Douglas, raising it to a parity with, or even superiority to, "arms". A prime influence at work was that of the Florentine neo-Platonists, reaching England by way of Erasmus, More, Thomas Starkey and Sir Thomas Elyot, then through such Platonizing handbooks of morals and honour as those of Castiglione and Romei.[256] Plato was important because he saw wisdom as the supreme virtue, placing it above the drive of the will and urge to glory appropriate to fighters; and over the involvement with appetite characteristic of workers. Of course, scholasticism had given "understanding" or *intellectus* a like precedence over the other powers of the soul. Similarly in society, the clergy, for Thomas Aquinas, enjoyed a superiority over knights and tillers of the soil, because they represented the faculty of intellect.[257] But the Platonic stress on wisdom emerged from a culture, that of Florentine humanism, orientated towards the laity, and implied a lay governing class. Thomas More had deployed the concept in all its fascination in his *Utopia*, in the pages of which the rule of wisdom shone the more brightly against a darkly painted background: the "ignorance" of the nobility, and the "idleness" of the traditional communities of honour, which More and his associates were never tired of castigating.[258]

255 G. McG. Vogt, "Gleanings for the History of a Sentiment: *Generositas virtus, non sanguis*", *Jl Eng. and Germanic Philology*, xxiv (1925), pp. 102–24. Cf. p. 310 and note 6 above.

256 See Caspari, *Humanism and the Social Order*, pp. 14 ff.

257 Cf. Walter R. Davis, "A Map of Arcadia: Sidney's Romance in its Tradition", in Walter R. Davis and Richard A. Lanham, *Sidney's Arcadia* (Yale Studies in English, clviii, New Haven and London, 1965), pp. 138 ff.

258 St Thomas More, *Utopia*, ed. Edward Surtz and J. H. Hexter, in *The Complete Works of St Thomas More*, iv (Yale edn, New Haven, 1965), introduction by J. H. Hexter, esp. pp. l–liv, lxxxi ff., and by E. Surtz, pp. clvi ff.

But it was the more prosaic talent of Sir Thomas Elyot which successfully steered the course from the older primacy of "prouesse" in the culture of honour to a style of chivalry which also implied learning. In *The Boke named The Governour*[259] he outlined the formation of a learned knighthood. It began with logic and rhetoric, and culminated in moral philosophy, this based on Plato, Aristotle's *Ethics*, and Cicero's *De officiis*. The approach required a reversal of the state of affairs which Lull had regretted but taken for granted: that knights were unlearned. No longer were they to be content with their own specialized culture, learnt in great households and courts, not at school: the rites of courtliness and ceremony, the arts of arms and the chase. From Elyot the knighthood received a supplementary and additional directive:

> A knight hath received that honour not only to defend with the sword Christ's faith, and his proper country . . . but also, and that most chiefly . . . he should effectually with his learning and wit assail vice and error . . . having thereunto for his sword and spear his tongue and pen.[260]

Learning sharpened the weapons needed for the battle with error. But not only that: more importantly, "the liberall sciences", though they may not confer, yet "prepare the mind, and make it apt to receive virtue". Therefore "no man will deny, that they be necessary to every man that coveteth very nobility; which . . . is the having and use of virtue".[261] Elsewhere in *The Governour* Elyot had identified wisdom, virtue and nobility. It was by their "understanding" that men "ought to be set in a more high place than the residue . . . And unto men of such virtue by very equity appertaineth honour, as their just reward and duty."[262] Moreover, nobility had originated in virtue. For what was it but a grant of "private possessions and dignity . . . given by the consent of the people . . . to him at whose virtue they marvelled, and by whose labour and industry they received a common benefit . . . "?[263] Elyot is silent on "blood" and lineage as the vehicle for the transmission of honourable status. The continuance of nobility in a line for him depends on the renewal, in each generation, of the virtue which had founded it.

259 Elyot, *Boke named The Governour*.
260 Sir Thomas Elyot, *A Preservative Agaynste Deth* (London, 1545, S.T.C. 7674), fo. a.ii.b, a.iii.b.
261 Elyot, *Boke named The Governour*, ii, p. 378.
262 *Ibid.*, i, pp. 5–6, 7.
263 *Ibid.*, ii, p. 27.

This he no doubt assumed (since he was no meritocrat) would occur in the case of a noble stock whose members followed his recommended style of educational formation. The later ideal of a "mixed nobility", which added the advantages of nurture, by schooling, to those of nature, was probably Elyot's. But the importance of *The Governour* lay in its popularizing role. His compendious yet succinct exposition of the nobility of wisdom, virtue and learning to which "by very equity appertaineth honour"[264] would be echoed by a legion of expositors and moralists in the century before the Civil War. Similarly influential was his outline of the polity of a remodelled and unified community of honour: a "public weal", presided over by "one capital and sovereign governour", and administered by "inferior governours called Magistrates", which "shall be appointed or chosen by the sovereign governour".[265]

Elyot therefore provided the humanist framework of ideas within which the Bartolan view of honour could establish itself within a remodelled secular culture. His "capital and sovereign governour" corresponded to the emperor of the civil law code, and provided a secular counterpart to the "godly prince" of providential history. His "wisdom" and "understanding" could be presented as a secular preparation for the insights of Protestant "faith". In his wake an increasingly abstract and civic terminology surrounded honour, as the more personalized categories of faithfulness, lordship and lineage moved into the background. Honour now centred on the state. An anonymous author, writing on the significant theme *Civil and Uncivil Life* (1579),[266] identified honour with "the respect which is borne to any man by them of the Court and the City". It was to be obtained "by the service of our prince and country, either martially or civilly".[267] The herald Ferne in 1586 had seen "public service" as the end towards which honour strove.[268] For the herald

[264] *Ibid.*, i, p. 6.

[265] *Ibid.*, i, pp. 24–5.

[266] Anon., *Cyvile and Uncyvile Life: A Discourse Where is Disputed What Order of Lyfe Best Beseemeth a Gentleman* (London, 1579, S.T.C. 15589); another issue of this work, entitled *The English Courtier, and the Cuntrey-Gentleman: A Pleasant and Learned Disputation* (London, 1586, S.T.C. 15590), is reprinted in *Inedited Tracts: Illustrating the Manners, Opinions and Occupations of Englishmen during the Sixteenth and Seventeenth Centuries*, ed. W. C. hazlitt (London, 1868), pp. 1–93.

[267] *Ibid.*, p. 42.

[268] Sir John Ferne, *The Blazon of Gentrie* (London, 1586, S.T.C. 10824), p. 24.

Segar in 1602 it was to be achieved in "public action".[269] The latter's pronouncement that "the power and authority to bestow honour resteth only with the prince"[270] would be echoed and strengthened by Cleland in 1607, Guillim and Milles in 1610, and by Francis Markham in 1625.[271] Guillim's opinion that "all degrees of nobility are but so many beames issuing forth from Regall Maiestie" was echoed by James I himself. In 1621 he rallied to the defence of the court of chivalry on the ground that his honour was engaged, the court being "immediately derived from us, who are the fountaine of all honoure".[272] In the background, references recur to the decay of the regional honour communities. *Civil and Uncivil Life* disparaged the outmoded provincial great households, whose indiscriminate hospitality and hordes of servants needed to be pruned and rationalized. The man of honour, secure in his own virtue (whose reward came from the approval of the court, not "the admiration of the common people"), must "know what sorts of servants were superfluous, and which necessary, both for private use and the public state".[273] Mere "servingmen", another author (perhaps Gervase Markham) pointed out, though "men of valour and courage, not fearing to fight in the maintenance of their master's credit", must seek other more productive occupations. The "liberality" which had once bound servants "with this indissoluble bond of assured friendship" to their masters, was dead.[274] For Thomas Milles, writing in 1610, the household was simply the restricted nuclear family, presided over by its patriarchal head, for which Adam's provided the model. "Men for the preservation of themselves, have out of families, assembled together into Villages; out of Villages, into Cities; and out of Cities have grown together into Provinces, and so into most great Kingdomes."[275] Such a commonwealth was remote

[269] Segar, *Honor Military, and Civill*, p. 113.
[270] *Ibid.*, p. 210.
[271] Cleland, *Propaideia*, p. 4; John Guillim, *A Display of Heraldrie* (London, 1610, S.T.C. 12500), Foreword fo. b; Francis Markham, *The Booke of Honour: or, Five Decads of Epistles of Honour* (London, 1625, S.T.C. 17331), p. 11.
[272] Squibb, *High Court of Chivalry*, p. 45.
[273] *Ibid.*, pp. 42, 91.
[274] Anon., *A Health to the Gentlemanly Profession of Servingmen: or, The Servingman's Comfort* (London, 1598); reprinted in *Inedited Tracts*, ed. Hazlitt, pp. 95–167, at pp. 106, 114–15.
[275] Thomas Milles, *The Catalogue of Honor, or Tresury of True Nobility Peculiar to Great Britaine* (London, 1610, S.T.C. 17926), p. 2.

from the simple structure Lord Berners had proposed a century before, which had consisted of men and a lord.[276]

Thus the community of honour came to be that which centred on the crown, its structure that of the court and city, its service that of the state, its mark the nobility of virtue, and the dignities which this conferred. Of course, there was no explicit challenge to the hierarchical grouping of the social order, and its basis in heredity. This was taken for granted, but also, since lineage constituted the "lowest" kind of nobility, was pushed into the background. Among the intellectuals a tendency emerges to view honour due to "blood" as the result of a powerful and obsessive social convention, rather than inherent in the natural order of things. The sense of blood and lineage required acceptance because of its firm grounding in the "opinion of the vulgar". But only with a half smile on the part of those of sufficient "civility" to be aware that the "true" nobility of virtue was formed by nurture, not nature. It was in this spirit that "the learned" approached the concept of a "mixed nobility", which mingled both, as the ideal. Thus the educationist Richard Mulcaster would allow that the nobly descended who were also virtuous deserved to be doubly honoured, but only because "auncience of lineage, and derivation of nobility is in such credit amongst us, and will always be".[277] Lawrence Humphrey recognized that the common people ascribed the honour of nobility to "great line", but refused to follow them in this.[278] Sir Philip Sidney took the heralds and their trappings for granted, but nevertheless asserted that he made no inquiry of men's pedigrees: "it sufficeth to know their virtues".[279]

Paradoxically, it is in the works of the heralds themselves that, frequently behind a conservative front, the principle of blood and lineage is most liable to be questioned and qualified. But heralds benefited from social mobility. As the numbers of the gentry grew, so did their earnings from visitation fees and grants of arms. It is not therefore surprising that the heraldic order should be sympathetic, both in theory and practice, to the claims of the parvenu. Sir John

[276] See above, p. 328.
[277] Richard Mulcaster, *Positions: Wherein Those Primitive Circumstances be Examined, Necessarie for the Training Up of Children* (London, 1581, S.T.C. 18253), p. 200.
[278] Humphrey, *The Nobles, or Of Nobility*, sig. a iv^{v}.
[279] *Aphorisms of Sir Philip Sidney*, 2 vols. (London, 1807), i, p. 3.

Ferne was a case in point. Following *The Boke of St Albans* he began his *Blazon of Gentrie* (1586) conservatively enough with the biblical origins of lineage in the distinction made between noble and ignoble among the children of Adam and Noah. There were the usual natural analogies which explained nobility: the hierarchy of birds, beasts and fishes; of the stars; and of the angels. All this was very traditional. The definitions of nobility taken out of Plato and Aristotle, however, followed more recent humanist precedents. So did the quoted opinion of Cicero and Diogenes in support of the view that the only true nobility was that of virtue. Ferne concluded with the conventional compromise: "most worthy and excellent above all the rest" was "mixed noblenes". This, by adding virtue to blood, ensured that each complemented the other.[280] But he also had a special word of praise for the parvenu as "deserving rather to be called noble" than the merely noble by blood. For although lacking "the domesticall examples of his ancestors . . . [he] yet hath, through virtue, . . . prevailed against the malignitie of Fortune". To the shocked inquiry of a knightly interlocutor (the book was set out in dialogue form), "Doth your herald prefer a new gentleman, which by industrie of his virtues hath obteyned to be so called, before those of ancient blood?", Ferne's reply was that indeed "in essence" virtue constituted a superior kind of nobility to that of lineage.[281]

More novel than Ferne's views on the nature of nobility is the frankly liberal heraldic practice he recommended in the matter of grants of arms. He began with a particularly rigorous statement of the traditional exclusion of merchants, practitioners of the mechanical arts, and husbandmen from gentility. But then he proceeded to qualify his veto out of existence. This he did by distinguishing those trades and crafts which were "laudable", and so qualified for coat armour. These turn out to include agriculture, clothing manufacture, architecture, merchandizing (providing the motive was the public service, and not merely profit), the art of the chase, and "the art and skill of plays, practised in Theaters, and exposed to the spectacle of multitudes".[282] Thus few who yearned for gentility, and could pay for a coat of arms, need be excluded. But this same liberality of practice, involving the dilution of gentility by so many

[280] Ferne, *Blazon of Gentrie*, pp. 2–8, 13–14, 15.
[281] *Ibid.*, p. 18. [282] *Ibid.*, pp. 7–8, 69 ff.

"gentlemen of the first head", confused and cheapened the traditional honour system, rooted in lineage and blood. It was another herald, Sir William Segar, who quoted the contemptuous comments of Sir Thomas Smith: " . . . who so can make proof, that his Auncestors or him selfe, have had arms, or can procure them by purchase, may be called Armiger or Esquier".[283] Segar sought to turn the attention of the true gentleman away from such puerilities as crests and coats to "embrace the love of virtue, and in the actions thereof to employ the course of his whole life"; he was to employ himself in "the study of wisdom", "whereby to know good from evill, and truth from falsehood".[284] Thomas Milles, also a herald, writing in 1610, rejected outright the notion of the blood as a natural vehicle of honour. Nobility, he insisted, was merely "civill and political", and based on nurture, not nature. Rejecting the animal analogies traditionally used to explain the heredity of honour, he pointed out that human characteristics, unlike those of the lion or eagle, were not innate. For man was a rational animal, endowed with reason. The excellence of nobility arose not from the blood but because "of the great means [noblemen] have, for the best bringing up and instructing of their children". In the schools lineage could be no sure pointer to superiority. There children of lower degree "in the same studies, strive with noblemen's children . . . with greater profit and praise".[285] Such writings reflect the pressures to which a hereditary governing class was subjected as the recruitment of new elements into its ranks speeded up. The competition for honour was intensified, and assumed a variety of forms. Honour was now as much to be mastered in the bloodless combats of school and classroom as on the field of battle.

Humanism, religion and honour: the need for a synthesis

Diligently though the schools laboured to temper the weapons of the intellectual knight in the battle with error, as the sixteenth century proceeded it became more, not less, difficult "to know good from evill, and truth from falsehood",[286] as far as morals in their relation to religion and honour were concerned. The old trusted

[283] Segar, *Honor Military, and Civill*, p. 288.
[284] *Ibid.*, p. 203.
[285] Milles, *Catalogue of Honor*, p. 12.
[286] Segar, *op. cit.*, p. 203.

schema of the four cardinal and three theological virtues, on which Raymond Lull relied, had been thrown overboard. The educated layman was now confronted by vernacular translations of the moralists of antiquity, and by a variety of handbooks which purported to simplify their teaching, of which William Baldwin's *A Treatise of Moral Philosophy* (1547) was an early example. Aristotle's *Nicomachean Ethics*, translated in 1547, was immensely influential in forming the outlook of the upper class; Cicero's *De officiis* equally so, since it became a grammar-school textbook. In the 1560s and 1570s the many translations of Seneca and Plutarch, culminating in North's *Lives* (1579), Lipsius's *Two Bookes of Constancie* (1595) and Holland's *Morals* of 1603, contributed to the emergent strength of Stoic influences at the turn of the century.[287] In many respects this wider and more variegated spectrum of ideas strengthened the honour culture, confirming its basic attitudes but giving them a new subtlety and sophistication. The "magnanimity" and "highmindedness" of the Aristotelian "great soul" imparted a new grandeur to the man of honour, who "will not compete for the common objects of admiration . . . and will not engage in many undertakings, but only in such as are important and distinguished". Such a one "is always higher than his fortune; be it never so great, and be she never so contrary, she cannot overthrow him".[288] But at the other end of the scale Aristotle provided the Italian theorists of the point of honour with their technical terminology. Possevino and his like (and their English interpreters) developed the duelling code in accordance with the definitions of contempt, insolence and spite found in Aristotle's *Rhetoric*.[289] These cross-currents of ideas, pre-Christian and rooted in the European heroic tradition, imparted an

[287] William Baldwin, *A Treatise of Morall Phylosophie, Contayning the Sayinges of the Wyse* (London, 1547, S.T.C. 1253); *The Ethiques of Aristotle*, trans. by John Wilkinson (London, 1547, S.T.C. 754); Plutarch, *The Lives of the Noble Grecians and Romanes*, trans. by Sir Thomas North (London, 1579, S.T.C. 20065); Justus Lipsius, *Two Bookes of Constancie*, trans. by Sir John Stradling (London, 1594 [1595], S.T.C. 15694.7); Plutarch, *The Philosophie, Commonlie Called, the Morals*, trans. by Philemon Holland (London, 1603, S.T.C. 20063).

[288] Aristotle, *Nicomachean Ethics*, iv. 3; Lodowick Bryskett, *A Discourse of Civill Life Containing the Ethike Part of Morall Philosophie* (London, 1605, S.T.C. 3958); quoted in Watson, *Shakespeare and the Renaissance Concept of Honor*, pp. 106, 109.

[289] F. R. Bryson, *The Point of Honour in Sixteenth-Century Italy: An Aspect of the Life of the Gentleman* (New York, [1935]), pp. 27–30.

unprecedented glamour to the man of honour as, in his great enterprise, he fearlessly confronted Fate.

But the moral systems of humanism also raised once more the questionable status of the self-assertive violence of honour, and of how this was to be harnessed, controlled and brought into conformity with the "wisdom" which was the fine fruit of the teaching of the ancient philosophers. Equally there was the need for a solution to the problem of the relation between honour and religion. This now arose in a setting of Protestant Christianity, with its emphasis on a total corruption of human nature, on faith, and on a sense of complete dependence on God which allowed little place to the autonomous will. The need arose with a particular urgency because the publication of Foxe's *Book of Martyrs* in 1570 gave a new and powerful twist to the providentialist tradition.[290] Foxe carried providentialism a stage further than the anxious scanning of the exempla in Scripture and history by the solitary individual in search of reassurance and guidance. This he did by placing the exempla in the context of a historical pattern which explained the past and pointed into the future, so adumbrating a collective destiny, that of the church, with which the individual could identify. This had been prefigured in the Old Testament, its outlined revealed in the New. Its future was already symbolically present, for those with eyes to see and ears to hear, in the prophecies of the Book of Revelation. This foretold the long war between Christ and Anti-Christ (the latter in due course incarnate in the Papacy) which, passing through a fivefold periodization, entered on its final and decisive stage with the dawning of the Reformation after 1300. In the final struggle thus begun, the prominence of the role which England was called upon to play implied the conferment of a special divine favour on the English nation. This was shown by God's choice of an Englishman, John Wycliffe, as the first divine to defy the Pope; and of Henry VIII as the first king to overthrow his power. The Marian martyrdoms indicated that it was above all in England that Anti-Christ would renew his war on the Elect; and it was here too, so all the signs of Scripture and history indicated, that his power would be overthrown and God's will fulfilled. Such could be the outcome once a godly prince perfectly achieved the divine vocation of the

[290] See William Haller, *Foxe's Book of Martyrs and the Elect Nation* (London, 1963) *passim*.

office, ruling a people wholly responsive to its God-given authority; a condition almost, but not wholly, fulfilled under Queen Elizabeth. Nevertheless God's favour towards the English persisted, as the defeat both of the Armada and of the Gunpowder Plot subsequently revealed. The hope of an apocalyptic consummation of history therefore remained present.[291]

Such ideas received a wide circulation just as the new-style "spiritual" preachers like Richard Greenham and Richard Rogers emerged from the Cartwright circle at Cambridge, with their large audiences, partly professional and influential, partly popular. In this setting Foxe's imagery of the war with Anti-Christ and of spiritual striving and combat acquired a potential political significance, in terms of which public opinion could be mobilized and directed. At the same time the image of the Christian warrior and the Holy War established itself as an alternative to the remodelled heroic image which the man of honour drew from Aristotle and the Stoics.[292] The Puritan John Norden excoriated the worship of the will which he saw as the essence of secular honour, denouncing "such, as are able by their force, to strike a terror and feare into a whole army of enemies"; for "the greatest conquerors which history recorde, come short of honour without God". It was faith, not honour, which enabled a general to shake off the cowardice and "covetous desire" which hindered the winning of battles. The Israelites were unassailable because "especially in perils and wars" the people of God "have ever practised godliness".[293] Here a motivation shapes itself, capable of the aggressivity, steadfastness and even violence traditional to honour, but arising from a different source. As a result the danger arose of a fissure between the secular and religious aspects of the culture, affecting the springs of political action. A synthesis was needed which would define both what "wisdom" and "understanding" implied in relation to honour, and also what contribution "godliness" had to make.

[291] *Ibid.*, pp. 140 ff.

[292] See William Haller, *The Rise of Puritanism: or, The Way to the New Jerusalem as Set Forth in Pulpit and Press, 1570–1643* (New York, 1938), pp. 150 ff.

[293] Norden, *Mirror of Honour*, p. 13.

Honour and the Sidney–Greville circle

It is something of a paradox that the reconciliation thus required of honour with wisdom and religion should have been achieved (even if, as the outcome will show, only precariously) in the circle which centred on Sir Philip Sidney. For there can be no doubt that, in Sidney, the Old Adam of honour violence remained strongly present. He was fired by the love of glory, his disposition turned him towards the world of action, and only the queen's veto prevented him (on one occasion) from defending his honour in a duel. It was as the man of honour, prone to senseless violence, that his friend Languet saw him: "You and your fellows, I mean men of noble birth, consider that nothing brings you more honour than wholesale slaughter."[294] Against this same violence Languet sought to set before his friend the claims of "wisdom", putting this forward as the mark of the governor, whose role required a more comprehensive range of qualities than the heroic activism of honour: "Ought not you, adorned as you are by Providence with those splendid gifts of the mind, to feel otherwise than men feel, who are buried in the most profound shades of ignorance, and think that all human excellence consists in physical strength."[295] Sidney took the exhortation to heart. Like Languet he saw that his intellectual qualities and training gave him a special role, which was not only to "encourage learning and honour in the schools" but also to bring "the affection and true use thereof into the Court, and Camp".[296] Under the admiring gaze of his friend and intellectual legatee Fulke Greville he aimed to plot, in the form of a prose poem, the chart of intellectual and affective growth whereby the man of honour matured from the quest for glory, by way of the self-assertiveness of violent action, to an acceptance in "patience" of a discipline of suffering. In this way he learnt submission to "wisdom", implying the service in obedience of a just political order, this resting on the divine order which religion underwrote.

All this was implied in the immensely influential work of art,

294 *The Correspondence of Sir Philip Sidney and Hubert Languet*, ed. S. A. Pears (London, 1845), p. 154.
295 *Ibid.*, p. 147.
296 Fulke Greville, Lord Brooke, *The Life of the Renowned Sir Philip Sidney . . .* (London, 1652); *Sir Fulke Greville's Life of Sir Philip Sidney*, ed. Nowell Smith (Oxford, 1907).

Sidney's *Arcadia*,[297] which resulted, and in which a synthesis of honour, humanism and religion was achieved. The success of the achievement is reflected in the popularity which, from the start, the book enjoyed in the milieu of the courtly and well-educated. Not only were fourteen editions published between 1593 and 1674, but it became the prose stylistic model of the age, quoted and requoted in the leading textbooks of rhetoric.[298] In this respect it came to occupy the place, in a remodelled culture, which Lydgate had previously held. Indeed Sidney's purpose was identical with that of the earlier writer: to provide "remedies against Fortune". Fulke Greville tells us:

> his purpose was to limn out such exact pictures, of every posture in the minde, that any man being forced, in the straines of this life, to pass through any straights, or latitudes of good, or ill fortune, might . . . see how to set a good countenance upon all the discountenances of adversitie, and a stay upon the exorbitant smilings of chance.[299]

Like *The Fall of Princes*, *Arcadia* aimed at an audience of "governors", those who ruled. For in the work Sidney's "intent, and scope was . . . to represent the growth, state, and declination of Princes . . . with all other errors, or alterations in publique affairs".[300] This approach involved, from one point of view, a strong epic emphasis, with the stress on magnanimity and on the Aristotelian virtues. The two heroes, Musidorus and Pyrocles, are presented from the outset as formidable warriors and skilful rulers. Involved on opposite sides, and unknown to each other, in the war of the Helots and Lacedemonians, they fight a ferocious duel; then, after mutual recognition, settle the war with masterly statesman-

[297] See *The Complete Works of Sir Philip Sidney*, ed. A. Feuillerat, 4 vols. (Cambridge English Classics, Cambridge, 1912–26) as follows: i, *The Countesse of Pembroke's Arcadia* (1912); ii, *The Last Part of the Countesse of Pembroke's Arcadia* . . . (1922); iv, *The Countess of Pembroke's Arcadia, Being the Original Version* (1926). See also Sir Philip Sidney, *The Countess of Pembroke's Arcadia (The Old Arcadia)*, ed. Jean Robertson (Oxford, 1973). For a summary of the history of the text, see E. M. W. Tillyard, *The English Epic and its Background* (London, 1954), pp. 295 ff.

[298] *Complete Works of Sir Philip Sidney*, ed. Feuillerat, i, p. ix; Tillyard, *op. cit.*, p. 315. Sidney carried out Spenser's unfulfilled intention to complete the ethical formation provided in *The Faerie Queen* by a political education, making *Arcadia* the more comprehensively impressive of the two works: *ibid.*, p. 307.

[299] Fulke Greville, *Life of Sir Philip Sidney*, p. 18.

[300] *Ibid.*

ship. Their role as magnanimous supermen of honour is first established, being strongly contrasted with the retired timidity of the unworthy king of Arcadia, Basilius. The heroic emphasis of the work and its concern with war and battle is subsequently developed in the account given of the Arcadians' campaigns against Amphialus and Cecropia.[301]

But Sidney's object was to show that the magnanimity of the Aristotelian hero, admirable in itself, was ineffectual to set "a stay upon the exorbitant smilings of chance", unless transcended by wisdom and religion. For heroic virtues can effect no more than a precarious command, whether over oneself or over the constellations of events in which the self is successively involved. As these continually change in the flow of time, so the stability created by heroic command of them is constantly under threat of mutability. As a result, sooner or later a dominance of Fortune gives way to sufferance at her hands. It is then that magnanimity requires the reinforcement, first of wisdom, then of Christian "patience". The first imparts to the hero a knowledge of the finite weakness of the fallen self, converting his heroic self-sufficiency into a sense of dependence on others, and on the divine order of things. The second involves the insight that happenings do not manifest themselves solely under the aspect of a test requiring the heroic, activist response; they are as likely to present themselves in a mode requiring the passive response of sufferance. But sufferance, if encountered with patience, tempers the soul, giving it the opportunity to affirm its faith in the ultimate rightness of the divine order: "howsoever they wrong me, they cannot over-master God . . . Let calamity be the exercise, but not the overthrow of my virtue." So Pamela in Cecropia's prison.[302]

The two princely heroes of *Arcadia* attain to wisdom, then to patience, by way of the *éducation sentimentale* which was the result of their respective love affairs with the two Arcadian princesses, Musidorus with Pamela, Pyrocles with Philoclea. Love, involving a contemplative withdrawal from the world of action to the inner world of affectivity, first reveals to the princes their own weaknesses and breaks down their heroic self-sufficiency. Musidorus succumbs

[301] Tillyard, *op. cit.*, p. 314.

[302] John F. Danby, *Elizabethan and Jacobean Poets: Studies in Sidney, Shakespeare, Beaumont and Fletcher* (London, 1965 edn), pp. 52–3, 47.

to lust, Pyrocles attempts suicide. Love involves them in situations in which they no longer rule, but suffer Fortune. Their ladies become the prisoners of the villainous queen Cecropia, threatened with death in her castle. They themselves are led into the disaster of confrontation with an apparently dishonourable death. Mistakenly convicted of the murder of Basilius, in the final scene they face execution. But it is thus that they learn how to transcend necessity, and overrule Fate.[303] In prison, as death approaches, the princes assert their completion of the full circuit of wisdom through the attainment of a religious fortitude, that of patience: "O blame not the heavens, sweete Pyrocles, sayd Musidorus, as their course never alters, so there is nothing done by the unreachable ruler of them but hath an everlasting reason for it." They affirm their "radiant expectation" of the union of their minds with "that high and heavenly love of the unquenchable light". Thus "they like men indeede (fortifying courage with the true Rampier of Patience) did so endure, as they did rather appeare governours of necessitie, then servants to fortune".[304]

Sidney's men of honour progress beyond heroic virtue through human to heavenly love, completed by a religious patience. The end of the story is not death. The innocence of the two heroes is established and, married to Pamela and Philoclea, they return to the world to exercise their princely office. Such storms turn out to be "but exercises of patience and magnanimity, to make them shine the more in the near-following prosperity".[305] The death involved is rather a "death to the world" as previously understood, and an initiation into the full spectrum of wisdom required for the role of princely governance.[306] The Platonic and Stoic influences in the synthesis thus achieved are obvious; but the Puritan and Calvinist overtones at work also need to be stressed. Sidney, like his friend Fulke Greville, was critical of the introverted unworldly emphasis of Platonism and Stoicism. For him the end of knowledge was rather a Calvinist style of self-examination "with the end of well-doing,

[303] Davis, "A Map of Arcadia", pp. 69 ff.

[304] *Ibid.*, pp. 63 ff., 82; *Complete Works of Sir Philip Sidney*, ed. Feuillerat, ii, pp. 163–4, 166.

[305] Sir Philip Sidney, *A Defence of Poetry*, in *Miscellaneous Prose of Sir Philip Sidney*, ed. K. Duncan-Jones and Jan van Dorsten (Oxford, 1973), pp. 59–121, at p. 90.

[306] Davis, *op. cit.*, p. 172.

and not well-knowing only".[307] He owed much, particularly in his synthesis of patience and magnanimity, to the English covenant theologians (above all perhaps Coverdale) with their stress on the role of human effort and natural virtue as well as faith.[308] From his friend Philippe de Mornay, whose *De la vérité de la religion chrétienne* he translated,[309] he learnt a Calvinist activism which allowed a place for the free will. For Mornay, by teaching that God foresees how men will freely choose, merely ordering their choices to the end he designs, modified the determinism of Calvinist predestination.

Arcadia therefore defined the affective background for the new-style honour community: one which was romantic and positive but also humanist and Protestant. This remodelled chivalry found its appropriate symbol in the Elizabethan Accession Day Tilts,[310] in which Sidney and his circle (and subsequently Essex) played a prominent role. Honour now required the Protestant knight to extend himself "out of the limits of a man's own little world, to the government of families and maintaining of public societies"; he made "his chief ends . . . above all things the honour of his Maker, and the service of his Prince, or countrey".[311] All this went well with the political stance with which Sidney so enthusiastically identified himself – that of the Leicester–Walsingham policy of Protestant activism which was inherited by the second earl of Essex, also the legatee of Sidneian chivalric romanticism. This involved a European Protestant league, a larger investment of resources in the war with Spain, wider military commitments abroad, westward oceanic expansion, and an extended naval assault on the Spanish empire. At home the keynote of the policy was bitter opposition to the dominant Cecil faction, and alliance with Puritanism.[312]

307 Sidney, *Defence of Poetry*, pp. 82–3.

308 Ronald A. Rebholz, *The Life of Fulke Greville, First Lord Brooke* (Oxford, 1971), pp. 24–5; William A. Clebsch, *England's Earliest Protestants, 1520–1535* (Yale Pubns in Religion, xi, New Haven and London, 1964), pp. 181–204, 305–18; L. Trinterud, "The Origins of Puritanism", *Church History*, xx (1951), pp. 37 ff.

309 Philippe de Mornay, *A Woorke Concerning the Trewnesse of the Christian Religion*, trans. by Philip Sidney and Arthur Golding (London, 1587, S.T.C. 18149).

310 See Frances A. Yates, "Elizabethan Chivalry: The Romance of the Accession Day Tilts", *Jl of the Warburg and Courtauld Institutes*, xx (1957), pp. 4–25.

311 Sidney, *Defence of Poetry*, p. 83; Fulke Greville, *Life of Sir Philip Sidney*, p. 47.

312 Rebholz, *op. cit.*, pp. 94–5; Roger Howell, "The Sidney Circle and the Protestant Cause", *Renaissance and Modern Studies*, xix (1975), pp. 31–46.

Political oppositionism and the disintegration of honour

Arcadia therefore emerged from the background of an oppositionist group intensely concerned about, but excluded from, political power. This had significant implications for the development of the honour culture, leading indeed to the disintegration in due course of the honour ideal as Sidney had stated it. For the generation after his death saw, in his own politically frustrated circle, a progressive disillusion with the heroic idealism which *Arcadia* had sought to express. As will be seen below, Sidney's intellectual legatee, Fulke Greville, turned increasingly from his friend's Protestant and humanistic chivalry to a gloomy Calvinism, and later to the tradition of apocalyptic Puritanism which drew its inspiration from Foxe. His heir, Robert, Lord Brooke, combined Calvinism and Platonism with a revival of dissident, anti-authoritarian honour attitudes which were rooted in the aristocratic oppositionism of the 1620s. Ironically, Sidney's synthesis of honour, humanism and religion was to find its closest parallel in the official Stuart court ideology of heroic kingship, courtly love and Platonic idealism. This reached its culmination in the years of prerogative rule in the circle of Charles I and Henrietta Maria. It was given expression in the court masques and spectacles devised by Inigo Jones.

The Stuart masques and spectacles were linked with, and developed out of, that Elizabethan cult of chivalry with which Sidney and his friends had been connected. The Elizabethan Accession Day Tilts had been taken up and continued by James I; and much of Inigo Jones's work for the Jacobean court perpetuated, while extending and elaborating, the late Elizabethan festival conventions. In the setting of the tilts Henry, prince of Wales, presided over a revival of Arthurian chivalry, with the spectacle devised by Jones to the accompaniment of poetry written by Ben Jonson.[313] In the reign of Charles I the tilts were discontinued. It was the masque, now given a deeper intellectual content, which became the vehicle of a serious political purpose close to Sidney's heroic idealism.[314]

313 See Roy Strong, "Inigo Jones and the Revival of Chivalry", *Apollo*, lxxxvi (1967), pp. 102–7.

314 Stephen Orgel and Roy Strong, *Inigo Jones: The Theatre of the Stuart Court*, 2 vols. (London, 1973); John Harris, Stephen Orgel and Roy Strong, *The King's Arcadia: Inigo Jones and the Stuart Court . . .* [Exhibition catalogue] (London, 1973).

There is the same Platonic emphasis; the same romantic stress on "heroic love" (of which the marriage of Charles and Henrietta Maria provided a visible exemplum); the same sense of princely authority as the embodiment of power completed by wisdom, and therefore securely triumphant over the passions in the self, as over the forces of political and social disorder.[315] As in *Arcadia*, heroism, love, and wisdom culminating in the vision of heavenly beauty, were presented as the source of the benefits of royal order which Charles hoped to confer on the "empire of Great Britain".[316] In due course too Charles came to see his own troubles as the occasion for the practice of a Sidneian "patience" which would culminate in his role as the Anglican royal martyr.[317]

At the Caroline court the integration of honour into the service of

315 For example, the masques *Love's Triumph* and *Chloridia* (1631). The former celebrated the ideals of Platonic love and virtue as expressions of autocratic power. The king arrives as heroic love, to banish the evil forms of sensuality, attended by the lords as other forms of exemplary love. He floats on a seascape as the embodiment of royal maritime power: of love, sprung like Venus from the waves; and of reason triumphing over the passions. The king is cast in the masque as the embodiment of Platonic intellect and will; the queen, of virtue and beauty. *Chloridia* again celebrates the royal couple, the perfection of their union, and the true ends of love. See Harris, Orgel and Strong, *The King's Arcadia*, pp. 166–9; Orgel and Strong, *Inigo Jones*, i, pp. 54 ff., 405 ff., and ii, pp. 420 ff.

316 For example, *Coelum Britannicum* (1634). The plot banishes the wicked Ovidian constellations from the sky to replace them with the stars of the Stuart Olympus. The masque opens amid the classical ruins of a city of the ancient British; it reaches its climax as king, queen and court contemplate a princely villa with gardens in the new style: they represent the ideals of a new age to be achieved by Stuart rule over the now united empire of England, Scotland and Ireland. Religion, Truth, Wisdom, Concord, Reputation and Government hover in the clouds above the royal palace of Windsor castle. Harris, Orgel and Strong, *The King's Arcadia*, p. 176; Orgel and Strong, *Inigo Jones*, i, pp. 66–70, and ii, p. 567. *Tempe Restored* (1632) tells of the vanquishing of the evil passions by the heroic example of the king. The climax of the masque is the descent of the queen in a chariot of gold and jewels in the role of heavenly beauty. Harris, Orgel and Strong, *The King's Arcadia*, p. 171; Orgel and Strong, *Inigo Jones*, i, pp. 61–2, and ii, p. 479.

317 By the date of the performance of *Salmicidia Spolia* (1640), the last of the Caroline masques in which both king and queen took part, Charles had been forced to call Parliament. "The masque is full of wistful memories of royal power at its apogee . . . Charles is still cast as the Divine King, but this time as a monarch forced to live in adverse times. The image of the King gradually assumes the mask of martyrdom, and on the proscenium arch Innocence and Forgetfulness of Injuries, attributes of Christ, take their place side by side with more familiar virtues." Harris, Orgel and Strong, *The King's Arcadia*, p. 184; Orgel and Strong, *Inigo Jones*, i, pp. 72–5, and ii, p. 729.

the crown and the state was completed. Writers like Francis Markham insisted on the source of gentility itself (and not merely titles and dignities) in the fount of honour: "a man is not said to be borne a Gentleman, only in regard of his Ancestors, but because they from the beginning obtained that acknowledgement of vertue from the King and his edicts".[318] Brathwait warned the man of honour against "daring spirits . . . whose Ambition excite them to attempt unlawful things; as to depose those whom they ought to serve, or lay violent hands on those whom loyall fidelitie bids them obey".[319] Bacon's insistence on the need to temper the traditional "valour" of honour with the other virtues, with the prime emphasis on piety, truth, temperance and justice, was echoed by the Caroline court writers, who also followed Bacon in his denunciation of the duel. Swords, being held "of the King for his defence", were to be drawn "only in the common cause" and "to fight for the safety and peace of your country".[320] Contemplation was made by Brathwait a suitable avocation for the Caroline gentleman, Anglican and God-fearing, bringing the realization that "whatsoever is sought beside God, may possesse the mind, but cannot satisfie it". Wisdom would qualify him to censure "such factious or litigous *sectists*, as either in Churche or common-weale district the State with frivolour or fruit-lesse ambiguities".[321] The close interrelation of honour and religion carried the Anglican clergy to the summit of the honour hierarchy: "Divines, above all other subjects (not of the blood Royall) are to be preferred . . . their use is so great and sacred, that it were barbarous to deny them the first Ranke in Honour . . . and may worthily have their Chayres in the next Ranke after Princes."[322]

Thus, under the auspices of Laudianism and prerogative rule, a social order was presented which rested solidly on a monarchical foundation. In this an élite of the wise and virtuous rose out of a social structure still otherwise graduated in terms of blood and lineage, the whole being capped by the state religion and the crown.[323] In the intellectual images of this same order, as projected

[318] Markham, *Booke of Honour*, p. 58.
[319] Brathwait, *English Gentleman*, p. 68.
[320] For Bacon, see note 52 above, this chapter; Brathwait, *op. cit.*, p. 145; Cleland, *Propaideia*, p. 232.
[321] Brathwait, *op. cit.*, p. 47.
[322] Markham, *op. cit.*, pp. 13–14.
[323] In *Coelum Britannicum* the new Caroline age of the "empire of Britain" is to be achieved by the monarch with the aid of just such an élite. The concept is presented by the masque in chivalric terms, an Arthurian role being attributed to the

in the masque, its culmination was in the "heroic love" of the king and queen. This presented on earth a reflection of the vision of heavenly beauty and union to which, in the metaphysical realm, the soul ascended through the Platonic gradations of Being.[324] The point about the conception was the defined sense of hierarchical structure – the "golden chain" of Being – which it expressed. This, appropriately culminating in the One, provided a correspondence to that of the church; and to that of society and the state, which similarly centred on the unifying monarch.[325] Thus Platonism, in the milieu of an absolutist court, provided a secular counterpart to the Aristotelian rationality in terms of which Hooker had defined an episcopal ecclesiastical polity. Both points of view reflected the "order" which prerogative rule guaranteed, and under which honour, perfected by wisdom, was integrated into the service of the crown. It was this which the aristocratic oppositionists were led to challenge; but with the consequence of unleashing a style of political violence which no longer had its roots in the self-assertiveness of honour. Its thrust came instead from the dynamic providentialism of Puritanism and the sects.

One commentator on *Arcadia* has suggested that Sidney, but for his premature and appropriately heroic death at Zutphen, might well have become disillusioned with the cult-of-honour idealism he had done so much to popularize.[326] For his own experience would have made him bitterly aware of how easily the chivalric quest for renown could be nullified by the jealous exclusiveness of the domi-

king. As seen above, the culmination was a view of Windsor castle, which the commentary emphasized as the seat of the Order of the Garter. This Charles had reformed and renewed as a knightly companionship of associates in the renewal of the kingdom: Orgel and Strong, *Inigo Jones*, i, pp. 69–70, and ii, p. 579.

324 In the masques the manifestations of royalty are invariably revealed as earthly reflections of heavenly and eternal neo-Platonic ideas. Thus at the close of *Love's Triumph* the clouds part to reveal the divine concepts of which Charles and Henrietta Maria, seated below, are the earthly counterparts: Jupiter and Juno, king and queen of heaven; Hymen and Genius, gods of marriage and generation. Venus descends, the Platonic love that links heaven and earth. See Roy Strong, *Splendour at Court: Renaissance Spectacle and Illusion* (London, 1973), p. 228.

325 A. O. Lovejoy, *The Great Chain of Being* (Cambridge, Mass., 1936), pp. 61 ff.; D. J. Gordon, "*Hymenaei*: Ben Jonson's Masque of Union", *Jl of the Warburg and Courtauld Institutes*, viii (1945), pp. 107–45, at p. 119. For the use of perspective and the circle in the masque to express the unifying role of the monarchy, see Strong, *Splendour at Court*, pp. 216–18, 227.

326 Richard A. Lanham, "The Old Arcadia", in Davis and Lanham, *Sidney's Arcadia*, pp. 181–410, at p. 381 note 8.

nant Tudor ruling group, in which the Cecils increasingly monopolized the queen's favour. Even as it was, his political career was dogged by a sense of failure and frustration at his exclusion from significant action and office. This was given ample expression in his correspondence. "For what purpose", he told Languet, "should our thoughts be directed to various kinds of knowledge, unless room be afforded to put it into practice, so that public advantage may result, which in a corrupt age we cannot hope for?" On another occasion: "Our cause is withering away", he asserted, "and [I] am now meditating some [West] Indian project." But this too was vetoed by the queen.[327]

Fulke Greville, Sidney's friend, became associated with the second earl of Essex, Sidney's political legatee, after the latter's death. As a result he incurred the lasting hostility of the Cecils, which was largely responsible for a career dogged by political failure and frustration. Even under Elizabeth, and to a greater extent than Sidney, he was refused by the queen the active career in war and diplomacy to which he aspired. After James I's accession, with the Cecil predominance in the person of Robert Cecil, earl of Salisbury, now unchallenged, Greville was dismissed from the treasurership of the navy which he had held since 1598. For ten years he was relegated to the political wilderness, until Salisbury's death opened the way to his appointment as chancellor of the exchequer in 1614. The office involved dependence on the Howard faction whose head, the earl of Suffolk, was lord treasurer; and so, with the fall of the latter, Greville underwent another dismissal in 1621, this time with the consolation prize of a peerage. As Lord Brooke and as a member of the council, he subsequently supported Buckingham, hoping that the latter would eventually opt for a Protestant foreign policy in alliance with the parliamentary Puritans. In the outcome he lived to see the collapse of his hopes and the bankruptcy of the favourite's policies. Before he died (in 1628) he gave bitter expression to his disillusionment with the Stuart political system, which he had previously criticized, but nevertheless served in the spirit of providentialist obedience which he thought monarchy could demand from its servants. But his last writings show a sense of the collapse of estab-

[327] *Correspondence of Sir Philip Sidney and Hubert Languet*, ed. Pears, pp. 143, 146.

lished institutions and of some kind of impending catastrophe, seen in terms of apocalyptic religion.[328]

Greville began his career as a typically Sidneian Protestant idealist, his religion based on covenant theology and shaped by the "free will" Calvinism of Philippe de Mornay, whose influence Sidney had also felt. But after the latter's death, and as his hopes and ideals were eroded by Essex's fall and his own failures, so his outlook became more Calvinist and Stoical in a grimly deterministic kind of way. His writings increasingly emphasized the weakness and inadequacy of fallen human nature. Sometime during the 1590s he scrutinized his own political attitudes in his Senecan play *Mustapha*[329] set in the Turkish empire. One of the sensitive issues which this work raised, very relevant to Greville's own position, was the role of the good counsellor, represented by the character Achmat. Confronted with a tyrannical régime whose head, the sultan, has been perverted by an evil concubine and murders his exemplary son Mustapha, Achmat considers whether his duty does not lie in rebellion. But this possibility he rejects with the arguments of a good Tudor providentialist. Rebellion would only unleash the anarchic violence of the people, and "rage of multitudes" only "ends in confusion". Obedience is unconditional, kings being "rods or blessings of the sky;/ God [is the] only judge, and knows what they deserve".[330] This plainly represented Greville's own view, to which he subsequently held. As far as his outward bearing was concerned he served both James I and Charles I with the same loyalty as he had Elizabeth.

But his inner life, as expressed in his writings, showed a growing exasperation with the Stuart political system. This emerged partly in the critique of the dominant Cecilian clique at the Jacobean court, which he incorporated in his *Life of Sidney*, written during his enforced retirement of 1604–14.[331] In addition, under the pressure of political disillusionment, his mind showed a progressive disintegration of the synthesis of wisdom, honour and religion which, under Sidney's influence, had sustained the idealism of his youth.

328 For Greville's career, see Rebholz, *Life of Fulke Greville*, and Joan Rees, *Fulke Greville, Lord Brooke, 1554–1628: A Critical Biography* (London, 1971).

329 See *Poems and Dramas of Fulke Greville, First Lord Brooke*, ed. Geoffrey Bullough, 2 vols. (London and Edinburgh, [1939]), ii.

330 *Ibid.*, ii, pp. 34 ff.; Rebholz, *op. cit.*, p. 103. Cf. Rees, *op. cit.*, pp. 165–6.

331 Rebholz, *op. cit.*, pp. 205–6.

As he grew older Greville increasingly rejected the humanist intellectualism, whether Platonist or Aristotelian, in terms of which the Stuart court expressed its political and religious ideas. In this mood he also turned away from a society and state structured in the traditional terms of a hierarchy of lineage and honour, with the king at its head. In his *Fame and Honour* (1612–14) he rejected the motivation of honour, even when this took the form of a wise magnanimity.[332] Instead he turned for a political language to Puritan religious forms, seeing the state and kingship in biblical and charismatic terms: as a people of God ruled by an elect monarch modelled on David.[333] Church and state were to be identified, and the end of government was presented as greater holiness. The approach did not imply political idealism. Greville regarded the mass of men as "fallen" and, therefore, only to be ruled by exploiting and disciplining the base motives by which most of them were moved. Only the Calvinist élite of elect "governors" either need or could show the "holiness" without which "all states, all Governments, all Thrones/ They all alaike feele dissolution ready,/ Their owne subsistence failing, and unsteady".[334] But "holiness" did not exclude, for example, rule by the exploitation of honour motivation and the greed for titles

[332] Fulke Greville, *An Inquisition upon Fame and Honour*, in *Poems and Dramas of Fulke Greville*, ed. Bullough, i, pp. 192–213. See also *ibid.*, pp. 199–200:

For where the father of Philosophie,
Vpon the common vertues, but aboue,
Doth raise and build his *Magnanimity*,
. . .
Let Truth examine where this vertue liues
. . .
For Mans chiefe vertue is *Humilitie*;
True knowledge of his wants, his height of merit;
This pride of minde, this *magnanimity*,
His greatest vice, his first seducing spirit,
. . .
Which spirituall pride (no doubt) possesseth still
All fleshly hearts, where thirst of *Honour* raues.

[333] Fulke Greville, *A Treatie of Warres*, stanzas 60–1, in *Poems and Dramas of Fulke Greville*, ed. Bullough, i, pp. 214–30, at pp. 228–9; Fulke Greville, *A Treatie of Humane Learning*, stanzas 135–7, in *ibid.*, pp. 154–91, at pp. 187–8; Fulke Greville, *An Inquisition upon Fame and Honour*, stanzas 13, 27 (ed. Bullough, i, pp. 195, 198); Rebholz, *op. cit.*, p. 305.

[334] Fulke Greville, *An Inquisition upon Fame and Honour*, stanzas 13–14 (ed. Bullough, i, p. 195).

and rewards; wars remained legitimate, and even a machiavellian kind of "policy" was justified.[335]

It was with this kind of polity in view, translated into the terms of a strong Puritan kingship implementing an active Protestant foreign policy, that Greville in 1614 embarked on his career in James I's service. But as the failures and frustrations of the subsequent decade accumulated, so his critique of his world assumed an increasingly radical tone. In his treatise on *Humane Learning* (1622–8)[336] he developed an assault (which owed much to Francis Bacon) on the metaphysical systems of the established intellectual world.[337] These were rejected as an obfuscatory playing with words which effectively clouded any clear understanding of natural phenomena, and also hid the true end of man, which was religious: his salvation. Greville still retained a hope of strong Puritan rule which would reform church and people, although with increasing uncertainty about the form which this should assume. But the first necessity, so he asserted in *Humane Learning*, was to reject the traditions and political philosophy inherited from paganism.[338] These masked the realities of governance just as metaphysics hid those of nature and religion. Rule needed to be restored to its primal simplicity of power, and so become fitted to discipline the people and suppress their inherent rebelliousness.[339] To an increasing extent, however, his hope no longer lay in any established institution, monarchical or ecclesiastical, still less in the humanism of his youth. In the final section of *Caelica* (Sonnets CVI–CIX, 1622–8)[340] all that remained was "the heart", the possibility of a drastic change in the outlook and mentality of his age: "Arks now we look for none, nor signs to part/ Egypt from Israel; all rests in the heart."[341] Otherwise, he was increasingly drawn into a mood of gloomy anticipation of the

335 *Poems and Dramas of Fulke Greville*, ed. Bullough, i, pp. 14 ff.

336 *Ibid.*, pp. 154 ff.

337 *Ibid.*, pp. 54 ff.

338 The first sixty stanzas of *A Treatie of Humane Learning* consist largely of a critique of the inheritance of humanist and scholastic culture.

339 Fulke Greville, *A Treatie of Humane Learning*, stanzas 90–5 (ed. Bullough, i, pp. 176–7).

340 Fulke Greville, *Caelica*, Sonnets CVI–CIX (ed. Bullough, i, pp. 150–3).

341 Fulke Greville, *A Treatise of Religion*, stanza 95, in Fulke Greville, Lord Brooke, *The Remains, Being Poems of Monarchy and Religion*, ed. G. A. Wilkes (Oxford English Monographs, London, 1965), pp. 203–31, at p. 226. Greville's *Treatise of Religion* was written between 1622 and 1628, but probably later rather than earlier.

apocalyptic cataclysm which the radical Puritans also expected, clearing the ground for a fresh start: "Sion lies waste, and Thy Jerusalem/ O Lord is fallen to utter desolation . . . Sweet Jesus, fill up time and come/ To yield to sin her everlasting doom."[342]

Greville's mind showed a progression towards the rejection of the structured world, built on a foundation of Aristotelian logic and Platonic rationality, which lay behind monarchical "order" and the social and religious "order" on which this rested. His appointment at the end of his life of Isaac Dorislaus, a Tacitean who was critical in his approach to monarchy, to his endowed history lectureship at Cambridge, suggests that he may have been moving towards a position sympathetic to the parliamentary opposition.[343] His cousin and heir, Robert, second Lord Brooke, was closely identified with the latter. Son-in-law to Francis, fourth earl of Bedford, and brother-in-law of Sir Arthur Haselrig, he was linked through the Saybrook colonial venture with such Puritan magnates as the earl of Warwick, Lord Saye and Sele, Sir Nathaniel Rich, John Pym and others. In 1635 Brooke considered joining Saye and Sele and "others persons of quality" in a Puritan emigration to New England, and when the Bishops' Wars got under way in Scotland he refused to serve the king or attend him. As a result both he and Saye were taken into custody at York in the spring of 1640. In the Long Parliament he emerged, according to Clarendon, as "undoubtedly one of those who could have been with most difficulty reconciled to the government of church and state", and as an implacable enemy of the bishops. Made by parliamentary ordinance lord lieutenant of Warwickshire he "carried the militia" against the royalists and garrisoned Warwick castle for the Parliament. In March 1643 he was killed at the siege of the cathedral close at Lichfield.[344]

Brooke's alienation from the Stuart political system thus carried him into the tide of violent resistance to it, a course of action in which (as will be seen below) his commitment to the concept of honour played a part. Yet paradoxically the outlook which he defined in his two brilliant published works, *The Nature of Truth* (1640) and *A Discourse Concerning the Nature of Episcopacy*

[342] Fulke Greville, *Caelica*, Sonnet CIX, ll. 1–2, 29–30 (ed. Bullough, i, pp. 152–3).
[343] Rebholz, *Life of Fulke Greville*, pp. 293–302.
[344] Robert E. L. Strider, *Robert Greville, Lord Brooke* (Cambridge, Mass., 1958).

(1642),[345] involved a further disintegration of the world of intellectual and social hierarchy in which honour had its natural place. Brooke's debt in these to the Florentine neo-Platonism of Marsilio Ficino has often been emphasized;[346] this shows itself particularly in *The Nature of Truth*, its presence thus bringing Brooke into a proximity to the intellectual and affective world defined by the Stuart masques and spectacles. But a more decisive influence is the Puritan and Calvinist attitudes shared with his cousin.[347] It was this which gave his Platonism a twist which carried it in a very different direction from that of the court, and imparted to it a critical instead of conservative emphasis. Thus in the first place he emphatically rejected the gradations of the Platonic "chain of being", asserting that:

> The Philosophers fancy to themselves *animam mundi*, and say every parcell is a Simple contributing to the existence of that *Compositum*. But Christians know, and I have . . . evinced, that all Being is *but one emanation from above*, diversified only in our apprehension.[348]

No metaphysical ladder leading up from the Many to the One needs to be climbed if Truth is to be attained, for it is already present as the divine light directly implanted in each individual by God.[349] It is this common divine origin which also guarantees the unity of Truth, making it the same for all men and therefore consistent and harmonious. The harmony thus implanted in the nature of things also carries the consequence of a social harmony as implicit in man's social state. For Brooke the "advantage" of each individual did not contradict that of the whole: "the Good of another, being the per-

345 Robert Greville, *The Nature of Truth* (London, 1640, S.T.C. 12363), facsimile reprint, with an introduction by V. De Sola Pinto (Farnborough, 1969); Robert Greville, *A Discourse Opening the Nature of Episcopacie, which is Exercised in England* (London, 1642), repr. in *Tracts on Liberty in the Puritan Revolution, 1638–1647*, ed. William Haller, 3 vols. (New York, 1934), ii, pp. 35–163.

346 See Strider, *op. cit.*, pp. 98 ff.

347 *Ibid.*, pp. 114 ff.

348 Robert Greville, *Nature of Truth*, pp. 120–1. In the neo-Platonic hierarchy of Being, the *compositum* is the pattern of the natural order, this being maintained not directly by God but by the Soul of the World, intervening between the natural and intelligible order. See F. E. Peters, *Greek Philosophical Terms: A Historical Lexicon* (London, 1967), pp. 166 ff.; P. O. Kristeller, "Marsilio Ficino", in Paul Edwards (ed.), *The Encyclopaedia of Philosophy*, 8 vols. (London, [1967]), iii, p. 197.

349 Presumably Brooke here draws on the Augustinian tradition.

fection of the whole, is my advantage. If with this eye you view that Scripture, you will see it in its glory, *Is thine eye evill, because thy brother's good increaseth*?"[350]

Thus for Brooke's Christianized Platonism, Truth imported an insight into a cosmic and social harmony. But the insight thus attained, he insisted, was as much affective (or religious) as rational. The affections were in fact as valid a way of knowing as reason, both being equally components in the unity of Truth, which was to be attained as much by a kind of aesthetic or spiritual intuition as by ratiocination:

> How would the soule improve, if all Aristotle's *Materia prima*, Plato's *Mens Platonica* . . . were converted into some spirituall light? The soule might soare and raise it selfe up to Universall Being, bathe it selfe in those stately, deep, and glorious streames of Unity, see God in Jesus Christ.[351]

The unity of religious and philosophical apprehension meant that for Brooke reason and faith were one; and his sense of freedom as a spontaneous response to the divine harmony, rather than as the possibility of choice, was wholly compatible with his Puritan belief in predestination and perseverance in grace.[352] A way of thinking and feeling followed in which religion and philosophy merged in Truth. For Brooke, therefore, reality made sense, and the business of living could be approached in an essentially rational and optimistic setting.

But what is interesting is the way in which Brooke seeks to simplify his world. He throws down its lines of intellectual demarcation, levels its hierarchies, and insists on the need for new departures within it. With an ardour which is explicitly Baconian in emphasis he attacks Aristotelianism, and rejects the "sciences" of his day as grounded only in metaphysics and therefore merely speculative: "How doth our great Master [Aristotle] perplexe himselfe in the inquiry of causes?"; "In Metaphysicks, with what curious nets do they intangle their hearers?"; "I doe not reject an industrious search after wisedome . . . I doe only, with Sir Francis Bacon, condemne . . . a nice, unnecessary, prying into those things which profit not."[353] One of the consequences of the vision into the

350 Robert Greville, *Nature of Truth*, p. 121.
351 *Ibid.*, pp. 143–4.
352 *Ibid.*, p. 165; Strider, *op. cit.*, p. 115.
353 Robert Greville, *Nature of Truth*, pp. 140, 150, 142.

unity of Truth is the insight that to divide knowledge into many sciences and into a science of things and causes is vain, for these are matters of which wise men have little real knowledge:

> Few of the Learned, consent about the degrees of heat and cold in any Simple, and so are forced to palliate all with the gaudy mantle of *occulta qualitas*; Yet what are all these but matter of observation? manifest effects, which Sense teacheth the plowman, the Countryman . . . [354]

But, with the attainment of Truth in its unity, all falls into place; then "you will perfectly be assured how many the severall pieces that make it up, must be, what their nature, and their severall proportions".[355] Then it will appear that the true way is experimental: "to ascend to causes, before we know that there are effects, is to mount to the highest round, before we ascend to the first. And therefore . . . Sir Francis Bacon, in his naturall philosophy, bringith only experiments . . ."[356]

If the tendency of Brooke's thinking was to flatten and empiricize the intellectual world, a similar tendency is also present in his view of man and politics, at least in these two treatises. This is the more surprising since Brooke also in some contexts and for some purposes, as will be seen below, assumes the traditional stance of the man of honour, with all the emphasis on blood, lineage and inherited status which this involved. But at least as far as religion and the search for Truth were concerned he saw all men as equal, each confronted with the emanation of divine light in the soul, each equally required to come to terms with this through reason and in his conscience, and without dictation from any extraneous authority. From this starting point society could be conceived as a sum of individual souls, in which authority ultimately rested on majority decision. In the church, Brooke therefore asserted, decision lay not with the officers but with the whole body of believers.[357] But he also raised the same question in relation to Parliament:

> Why are Parliaments the representative body of the Kingdome, but because the Plough cannot stand? but because no place can containe the whole body? But if all people could meet in *Campo Martio*, should those who now are but servants then be more than servants?

[354] *Ibid.*, pp. 130–1. [355] *Ibid.*, p. 144. [356] *Ibid.*, p. 125.
[357] Robert Greville, *Discourse on Episcopacie*, pp. 29, 83 (ed. Haller, pp. 73, 127).

Might not Parliament therefore, like the church, be founded on a popular sovereignty, given that "it seemeth to me against all reason . . . that the party deputed should have power . . . The Steward of a Court Leet, or Court Baron, is annihilated, if the Lord be there."[358] Such views went with the apocalyptic Puritanism to which Brooke, like Greville, was powerfully drawn, and which permeated his thinking. This made him sympathetic to the radical sects and popular preachers on whose behalf he made his famous plea for toleration, and expectant of the advent of renovation. His view of history accorded with that of Foxe and followed the same periodization. He too held that the Light of Truth had begun to dawn with Hus and Jerome of Prague in the fourteenth century, had broadened into the wide stream of the Reformation, but had yet to reach its noon: "All men yeeld there must be an encrease of light in the world . . . Light dilating, and enlarging it selfe, seemeth to become more pure . . . and yet it seemes not to be Noone." In such times extraordinary things could come to pass: "Let it not bee said of us, that Light came . . . yet we would not use it . . . because we loved darknesse."[359]

Both Greville's charismatic Calvinism with its emphasis on a religious élite, and Brooke's religious individualism, with its Platonic stress on harmony and Truth, seem remote from the world of honour, at least as traditionally conceived. But in fact both men felt themselves very much a part of this world. Indeed, an aspect of their writings is a revival of those dissident and critical aspects of honour which had been largely submerged under the Bartolan conformist stress on honour as the reward for obedient service to the state. By contrast Greville and Brooke used the terminology of honour to develop a critique of the Stuart political system and, in the case of Brooke, to justify resistance to it. This in spite of the fact that Greville (in his *Fame and Honour*) proved himself a caustic critic of honour values, while Brooke was aware (as will be seen below) of their inadequacy to the political task of resistance to an oppressive authority. Greville's use of the concept of honour is apparent in his *Life of Sir Philip Sidney*.[360] This work presented his

[358] *Ibid.*, p. 83 (ed. Haller, p. 127).
[359] *Ibid.*, p. 116 (ed. Haller, p. 160).
[360] Fulke Greville, *Life of Sir Philip Sidney*; Rebholz, *Life of Fulke Greville*, pp. 205–6.

dead friend as an idealized exemplum of Elizabethan honour and nobility, his virtues providing a startling contrast with the degenerate servants of James I. The deficiencies of the latter were ascribed to their status as merely "creatures" of the king, "children of favour and chance", who for this reason lacked the inner freedom and sense of worth of the man of honour.[361] In this way Greville made use of the traditional honour critique of the parvenu and "new man", in which the latters deficiency in blood and lineage constituted an essential component. But he was not content with this approach, if only because he was aware that some of James's favourites were in any case amply endowed with "pedigree of fleshly kindred".[362] He therefore also presented the ideal of a religious élite formed, like Norden's Christian man of honour, by providentialist faith. Such a nobility would be endowed with a detachment which would enable them to leave "success to his will that governs the blind prosperities and unprosperities of chance, and so works out His ends by the erring frailties of human reason and affection".[363] This truly noble, yet also religious, poise and detachment was precisely what James I's courtiers and councillors lacked. Caught in the toils of Fortune their "selfness" made them fear the greatness of others; they were "lovers of themselves, without rivals", seeking to be "worshipped as idols", and brooking no opposition.[364] It was not surprising, Greville thought, given such advisers, that James should have sacrificed the Protestant foreign policy inherited from his predecessor, to "the deceiving shadow" of a peace with Spain.[365]

Brooke's sense of inherited status and of the grandeur of noble descent seems if anything to exceed that of his cousin. In 1641 he developed his polemic against episcopacy in terms of the unsuitability of the bishops for the great offices and possessions entrusted to them by the king on the grounds of their lowly birth:

> Let us begin with *Antecedents*; in them the first. Which we shall finde very unsuitable to his after acquired office. For the most part he is . . . of the lowest of the people . . . Now for such a low borne man, to be exalted high, so high . . . must needes make as great a *Chasme* in *Politiques*, as such *leapes* use to doe in *Naturals*.[366]

[361] Fulke Greville, *Life of Sir Philip Sidney*, p. 10.
[362] *Ibid.*, p. 8.
[363] *Ibid.*, p. 28.
[364] *Ibid.*, pp. 30, 37.
[365] *Ibid.*, p. 210.
[366] Robert Greville, *Discourse on Episcopacie*, p. 3 (ed. Haller, p. 47).

He could even have resort to the well-worn animal analogies: "Those horses which are designed to a lofty Ayre, and generous manage, must be of a Noble race . . . Majesty, and a Base Originall, doe not well suite, neither can they dwell together . . . "[367] Brooke aimed to revive the medieval style of honour dissidence, with its emphasis on the freedom and autonomy of the man of honour and the consequent duty of the nobility to confront oppressive kings and ministers. In such a spirit he refused the oath Charles I required of all noblemen in 1640 to support the king "to the utmost hazard" of "life and fortune" against the Scots, and he declined to attend on Charles at York unless Parliament adjudged that he should do so.[368] It was in terms of honour that he replied to the royalist ultimatum demanding the surrender of Warwick castle in August 1642: "I much wonder that men of judgement, in whose breasts true honour should remaine, should so much derogate from their Ancestors and noble Predecessors, as to seeke (for private ends) the ruine of that Kingdom they should endeavour to support . . . " According to a parliamentary pamphleteer, at his first encounter with the earl of Northampton and the Warwickshire royalists, "Heroick, Brooke, offered to deside the contraries quarrell, by a Lordly combat."[369]

An archaic tone full of a romanticizing bombast clings to these appeals to honour and lordliness. Brooke's attitudes in this respect owe much to the attempt made during the 1620s to revive the oppositionist political role of the peerage. This took place under the patronage of two descendants of leading Elizabethan aristocratic dissidents, Thomas, earl of Arundel, grandson of the fourth duke of Norfolk, and Robert, earl of Essex, the rebel's son. The earls and their supporters subsidized plays and books which stressed the more archaic aspects of honour – blood, lineage and valour. They criticized the "inflation of honours" and sale of titles by the Buckingham régime. A political role was sought for the aristocracy by reviving and extending the privileges of the house of lords, particularly that of impeachment. The claims of the lords to be the hereditary councillors of the crown was once more raised, together with their duty, assembled in the *magnum concilium* of the realm, to take the lead in confronting unjust kings and unworthy ministers. A

[367] *Ibid.*, pp. 4–5 (ed. Haller, pp. 48–9).
[368] Strider, *Robert Greville*, pp. 30 ff.
[369] *Ibid.*, pp. 55, 74.

characteristic concern of the group was with the unchallengeability of the nobleman's "word of honour" (which had been unsuccessfully claimed by the fourth duke of Norfolk at his trial in 1572). Essex, in the Parliament of 1628, secured the support of the Committees for Privileges for the exemption of peers of Parliament from all obligatory oaths.[370]

It was in this context that a markedly different content was given to the concept of honour from the predominantly Bartolan emphasis of the Jacobean and Caroline expositors of honour discussed above. This was popularized by Henry Peacham's *Complete Gentleman*,[371] first printed in 1622 and the work of a former tutor in Arundel's household who dedicated it to one of the latter's sons. Peacham developed a "high" view of honour that stressed its "inherent" and "natural" character, which was inherited not conferred. The crown's role as the fount of honour was played down, for "Honours and titles externally conferred . . . are but as apparell and the drapery to a beautifull body."[372] "Nobles" may claim social pre-eminence and political influence. They should have preference over commoners in appointment to office and ought to be near to the prince, giving him counsel, particularly in time of war. Their word ought to be given credit "before any of the inferior sort", and they "have the upper hand, and greatest respect" on all public occasions.[373] Peacham tends to extol the more aggressive aspects of honour, stressing its military aspects, and he sees competitiveness as of the essence of nobility, which "stirs up emulation in great spirits, not only of equalling others, but of exceeding them".[374] By contrast the relevance of religion to honour is, by comparison with a Puritan like Norden or a Caroline like Brathwait, very much played down; the "fear and service of God" being recommended but only in a generalized and conventional kind of way.[375] Similarly there is little interest in providential history, Peacham's historical approach being more aesthetic than moralistic: "no subject affecteth us more than history, imprinting a thousand forms upon our imagination".[376] Historians are read more for the range of stylistic models

[370] See Snow, "Essex and the Aristocratic Opposition to the Early Stuarts", pp. 224 ff.
[371] Henry Peacham, *The Compleat Gentleman* (London, 1634 edn), ed. G. S. Gordon (Oxford, 1906).
[372] *Ibid.*, pp. 2–3.
[373] *Ibid.*, pp. 13–14. [374] *Ibid.*, p. 14. [375] *Ibid.*, pp. 40–1. [376] *Ibid.*, p. 51.

they make available than for the store of moral exempla they contain.

Peacham's view of society is less inclined to favour social mobility than either the Bartolans or the providentialists. His return to "arms" as the prime source of honour left a place for "letters" but made him more grudging than, for example, Ferne in his admission of merchants to gentle status; while inevitably (and again in contrast to Ferne) those involved with the "Mechanicall Arts", who "labour for their livelihood and gaine, have no share at all in Nobility or Gentry".[377] Peacham could still see his world, after a fashion already presented in *The Boke of St Albans*, as structured by the heralds in terms of "Blazonry". The colours and shapes of heraldry present mysterious, quasi-magical correspondences with the planets, nature, times, seasons, and the virtues, so that a character may be read off from a coat of arms. Heraldry was "the most refined part of naturall philosophy", having affinities with the neo-Platonism and hermeticism which also found expression in the court masques and spectacles. The heraldic symbols built honour and nobility into the structure of the universe itself. Like John Gibbon, Peacham might conclude "that heraldry was engrafted naturally into the sense of the human race", eternalizing the social order it symbolized.[378]

The aristocratic oppositionists had their victories in the Parliaments of 1621, 1626 and 1628. Indeed, after the fall of Buckingham their ideas were in part taken up by Charles I. He stopped (at least temporarily) the sale of honours and tried to enhance the social prestige of the peerage, to which he turned for support in 1640 when the Bishops' War forced him to call a great council.[379] But the peers proved to be too divided, too conservative and too inclined to peace for a militant aristocratic dissidence of honour to establish itself. The traditional ascription to noblemen of innate qualities as men of war, which led initially to a virtual aristocratic monopoly of parliamentary army commands, disappeared with the Self-Denying Ordinance. Nor could the idea of a rigidly hierarchical community of honour, led by lords, have much appeal in a society which was still mobile, and in which easier, not more restricted, access to honour

[377] *Ibid.*, pp. 12–13.
[378] *Ibid.*, pp. 154 ff., 161; for John Gibbon, see *ibid.*, pp. xviii–xix.
[379] Stone, *The Crisis of the Aristocracy*, pp. 117 ff., 750 ff.

was most in demand; one too in which the élite of blood and lineage was increasingly confronted by the claims of a religious élite. Brooke himself was brought up against the latter when in 1635 he meditated emigration (with Lord Saye and Sele) to New England. Both peers, as a condition of settling in the colony, demanded that it should be constituted as a stratified society of gentlemen and free-holders, with a system of hereditary honours. But they were told that in New England wealth and rank depended, not on lineage, but on membership of one of the churches. Hereditary honours were acceptable, but not hereditary authority, for:

> where God blesseth any branch of any noble and generous family, with a spirit and gifts fit for government, it would be taking of God's name in vain to put such a talent under a bushel . . . But if God did not delight to furnish some of their posterity with gifts fit for magistracy, we should expose them rather to reproach and prejudice, and the commonwealth with them, if we should call them forth, when God doth not, to public authority.[380]

Brooke himself found, when he entered the controversy over the bishops, that his sense of an aristocracy of lineage "whose Birth and Breeding hath filled their veines with Heroick noble blood"[381] which could be set against the merely meritocratic episcopate, had to be qualified by a recollection that the origins of the peerage were as Bartolan as those of the bishops. For in his *Discourse on Episcopacy* he had to admit that "all the Branches of *Nobility* first sprouted out from the Roote of *Royalty*; (Honours being in all Good States, Appendices to Majesty . . .)".[382] Interestingly, as a result, he brought forward the hereditary ownership of property as the ground for the constitutional role of the lay peers in Parliament. Honours were wholly disposed of by the royal hand, "yet Estates and Revenues did not; which are the Partiments and Supporters of Noble Honours. And These also in Bishops, depend on the Prince's Will."[383] As far as the lay nobility was concerned property provided a foundation for freedom and independence and so made the deployment of the qualities of "Heroick noble blood" possible.

Thus the revival of honour in the traditional sense as a significant source of political ideas and social values proved to be a non-starter,

[380] Strider, *Robert Greville*, p. 24.
[381] Robert Greville, *Discourse on Episcopacie*, p. 34 (ed. Haller, p. 78).
[382] *Ibid.*, p. 36 (ed. Haller, p. 80). [383] *Ibid.*

as much in an oppositionist as in a court setting. Instead, the tendency was for honour to develop increasingly as a subculture, the informal personal code of military men and of the anti-Puritan spectrum of the upper class. Bacon distinguished honour in this sense, seeing it as mere "vain-glory", from the magnanimity of the man of wisdom.[384] Yet he saw that even in this debased sense its role was still, within its circumscribed field, significant, for "In military commanders and soldiers, vain-glory is an essential point; for as iron sharpens iron, so by glory one courage sharpeneth another."[385] But there is also the other side of the picture: "They that are glorious must needs be factious; for all bravery stands upon comparisons. They must needs be violent, to make good their own vaunts."[386] "Vain-glory" was close to that "false" sense of honour so remote from wisdom in which, so Bacon asserted, the duel was grounded. This made "valour" and mere "opinion" the essence of honour, leaving out religion, law and moral virtue. The latter required blood to be spilt only in just and public, not private, causes.[387]

If we can trust the evidence of the drama as a reflection of the attitudes of its patrons, it was precisely this "false" notion of honour which was applauded among the increasingly aristocratic theatre-going public of the years between the 1590s and 1640s, its popularity establishing itself decisively between 1610 and 1620.[388] Honour as depicted in the Stuart theatre is characterized by an extreme attenu-

[384] Francis Bacon, "Of Vain-Glory", in his *Essays* (Everyman Library edn, London, 1972 edn), pp. 158–9, at p. 158.

[385] *Ibid.*

[386] *Ibid.*

[387] *The Charge of Sir Francis Bacon . . . Touching Duells*. Cf. the court dramatist Ben Jonson. For Lovel in Jonson's *The New Inne* (London, 1631, S.T.C. 14780) honour conforms to reason and virtue, and is always exercised in a lawful cause:

. . . it springs out of reason,
And tends to perfect honesty, the scope
Is always honour and the public good;
It is no valour for a private cause.

(iv. 4, ll. 44–7)

By contrast the false honour involved in reputation:

That's man's idol,
Set up against God, the maker of all laws,
Who hath commanded us we should not kill;
And yet we say, we must for reputation.

(*ibid.*, ll. 48–51)

[388] C. L. Barber, *The Idea of Honour in the English Drama, 1591–1700* (Gothenburg Studies in English, vi, Gothenburg, 1957), pp. 271–2.

ation of its social dimension. "Friendship" survives, but the emphasis in the traditional code on lordship, "faithfulness", affinity and allegiance has of course vanished. Rank and blood as the mark of honour is less insisted on than adhesion to a specific style of behaviour. This allocated repute in accordance with success in the duel and in displays of sexual virility. The gap between honour, religion and virtue widens, and the concern even with military renown, if obtained not in private combat but in public causes, declines.[389] Some of these traits went into the "cavalier" culture of the Civil War period, contributing to the vain, dissolute, lecherous and violent cavalier image of the Puritan and parliamentary propagandists. Others merged with the idealized monarchism of Charles I's court to recreate a social dimension for honour as the chivalrous community of honourable men, whose loyalties centred on the king's person – the incarnation of royalism and religion. Similarly, in the context of royalism the cult of personal combat could be sublimated into the knightly individualism of the militant cavalier seeking honour in the thick of battle with the Puritan foe, as in Lovelace's well-known poem: " . . . a new Mistresse now I chase/ The first Foe in the Field/ And with a stronger Faith imbrace/ A Sword, a Horse, a Shield". The attitude contrasts with the Puritan military stress on disciplined solidarity in battle rather than individual heroism.[390]

Thus, under the divisive stress induced by a political system whose capacity to command the consent of the political and cultural community had progressively weakened, the components which had made up Sidney's synthesis of wisdom, religion and honour went their several ways. Each no longer served to stabilize the society in which, since the reign of Henry VIII, the providential rule of the godly prince had been the controlling symbol. By the 1630s, as the rift widened between court and country, the exponents of providentialism were publicly striking the note of disillusion with the established structure of royal authority and honour, the foreboding sense of an undefined, apocalyptic future, which had earlier sounded, but privately, in the writings of Fulke Greville. It was

389 *Ibid.*, pp. 272–9.

390 See William Lamont and Sybil Oldfield (eds.), *Religion and Literature in the Seventeenth Century* (London and Totowa, N.J., 1975), pp. 63 ff., 84–91, 103–8; J. G. Marston, "Gentry Honor and Royalism in Early Stuart England", *Jl Brit. Studies*, xiii (1973–4), pp. 21–43.

becoming increasingly difficult to descry in the exempla an identity between obedience to God and obedience to the prince, or a necessary affinity between honour and the prince's service. Thus Brathwait, in 1630 a Caroline conformist who had dedicated his *English Gentleman* to Wentworth, took up a different position in 1638. In his *History Surveyed*,[391] first published in that year, the standpoint is traditionally providentialist, still echoing Lydgate, history providing "Receipts or Cordialls against the maladies of Fortune".[392] But the tone is less one of participation and obedience than of alienation and of fear for the future. It is "the Tragick disasters of eminent Princes" which for Brathwait increasingly appear in "the Chrystalline Mirror" of the historical examples.[393] The lesson these now taught was one of withdrawal and non-participation in the princely world of emulation and ambition: "he enjoys sufficiently who has learnt to be a Soveraigne over his own passions: to restraine the surging billows of over-flowing will, to the command of Reason. No Principality like this . . . "[394] A mood of exasperation and downright condemnation sounds out ever more strongly: "But many have we, that we may better imitate, than Princes: as their state was eminent, so were their nature depraved. We shall read that many of them were as good Law-breakers, as Law-makers . . . they had ever virtuous pretences to shadow vice . . . " The dark clouds of divine judgement already gathered over such princely destinies, "wherein everie judicious reader may gather the admirable and inscrutable purpose of God, frustrating their devices, never bringing their designs to effect . . . No Estate is secure without the protection of a Supreme Power."[395] "Clear and imitable examples" needed to be culled from the histories wherein to discover the errors of princes, whose lives had for too long been "held Models of imitation for Inferiors. Their very behaviour, were it in some gesture never so uncomely, has ever begot followers in persons of meaner quality."[396] Brathwait's sense of honour has come to be one of composed detachment: "Nor can we esteeme any person more truely deserving Honour, than he who can with a composed mind . . . suffer himself to forgo it, and retaine still the same Spirit when in the eyes of the world he seems most dejected."[397] The sense of

[391] Richard Brathwait, *A Survey of History: or, A Nursery for Gentry* (London, 1638, S.T.C. 3583[a]).
[392] *Ibid.*, p. 63.
[393] *Ibid.*, p. 8.
[394] *Ibid.*, p. 63.
[395] *Ibid.*, pp. 402 ff.
[396] *Ibid.*, p. 73.
[397] *Ibid.*, p. 9.

approaching judgement echoes that of Cromwell's schoolmaster Thomas Beard in his *Theatre of God's Judgements*, which had taken a similarly critical view of princes.[398]

CONCLUSION

Honour, it has been suggested, had originally implied for those that professed it a consistency of public and political attitude which was summed up in "faithfulness" to lords and friends. It constituted an appropriate code of political conduct for the kind of political conflict in which lords confronted unworthy kings, and which in the last resort was resolved by the violence of war and battle. The moralization of politics involved the dissolution of honour in this sense, but reasserted its role as the reward of public service. The fruit of lineage whose virtue had been nurtured by wisdom and religion, it was dispensed by the hand of the godly prince. As the agent of a providential purpose he could both command an absolute obedience and, in so far as he "defended the Church of Christ", was assured of receiving "at God's hand great blessing and felicity".[399] Guided and ruled by Providence he escaped both the capricious regimen of Fortune and the blind faithfulness to which the man of honour was subject. But it soon became apparent that providentialism, as it merged with the beliefs and preoccupations of Puritanism, contained the possibility of a new style of dissidence. Unlike honour this was ideologically motivated, but like honour it contained within it the possibility of violence. This came increasingly to the forefront as, under the first two Stuarts, the alienation of the monarchy from significant elements, both political and intellectual, of the governing class was completed. The apocalyptic element in Puritanism made it less firmly tied to inherited political and social structures than the conservatism of honour, and more liable to generate an impulse towards change, like "that new Utopia of religion and government into which they endeavour to transform the kingdom" which Charles I thought he could already perceive in the reforms

398 Christopher Hill, *God's Englishman: Oliver Cromwell and the English Revolution* (London, 1970), pp. 39–40.

399 John Foxe, *Acts and Monuments: With a Life of the Martyrologist*, 8 vols. (London, 1843–9), iv, p. 131.

proposed in the Grand Remonstrance.[400] Its militant mood could match the stubborn irreconcilability with which authority confronted it.

No doubt the exalted mood which utopianism imparted to Puritan providentialism might not have been stretched to the point of civil war, still less to the abolition of the monarchy and the house of lords, but for the influence of fortuitous factors and the pressure of events. Yet Puritanism did provide a pattern of motivation in terms of which a response, radical and confident, to the need for extreme measures could be effectively mobilized. There was the sense of insight into, and co-operation with, the purposes of God which nerved the arm in the violence of battle, and the mind to confront a future cut loose from the familiar outlines of the past. It was precisely in such extreme situations, so John Preston (a client of Greville's) had asserted, that for the Puritan the divine creativity could be expected to manifest itself:

> Put the case all were turned upside downe, as it was in the confused Chaos . . . yet as then when the Spirit of the Lord did but moove upon the waters, many beautiful creatures were brought forth . . . even so, were the Church in never so confused a condition, yet the Lord shall so order the things that seem to undo us that they shall bring forth something of speciall use.[401]

The nature of the response of honour, and that of the Puritan motivation, to situations of stress differed. The former was sustained by a sense of the quality of inner resources with which the man of honour was endowed; shaped by nature and nurture, lineage and acquired virtue, these gave a keen edge to the will. The latter relied to a greater extent on the strength imparted by a current which was larger than the self: the "sure hope" of divine election, and the sense of cool detachment from the immediate pressures of a situation which this belief could impart. Or as Norden had put it:

> the hope which is grounded upon this firm foundation is the greatest riches and chiefest jewell that a Generall can possesse;

[400] *Puritanism and Liberty: Being the Army Debates (1647–9) from the Clarke Manuscripts, with Supplementary Documents*, ed. A. S. P. Woodhouse (London, 1938), p. 47.

[401] Christopher Hill, "The Political Sermons of John Preston", in *Puritanism and Revolution: Studies in Interpretation of the English Revolution of the 17th Century* (London, 1962), pp. 239–74, at p. 263.

> for it causeth him to shake off the clogs of cowardise and of a covetous desire, which hinder much the successe of a war.[402]

Behind such an approach there were also the new forms of community of "those that best rank with God"[403] which the religious commitment of Puritanism involved, and which could supplement or supplant the traditional solidarities of honour. Providentialism had always presented the aspect of a two-handed engine at the door, projecting before kings the possibility not only of obedience by subjects and divine favour but also of a time when "God suffereth the Rebell to rage, and to execute that part of his Justice that the partial prince would not."[404]

402 Norden, *The Mirror of Honor*, p. 17.

403 Anne Barnardiston to Sir Simonds D'Ewes concerning her step-grandson, the Suffolk Puritan Sir Nathaniel Barnardiston: "The name of Barnardiston is and ever shalbe precious to me: and if any of that name, especially the Luster of the house, should undergoe justly any tart censure or incurre an harde conceit amongst his neighbours, and those of the best ranke according to Gods account, it would even much devert me, in these my declining dayes": Brit. Lib. Harleian MS. 384/27, quoted in J. H. Hexter, "The English Aristocracy, its Crises, and the English Revolution, 1558–1660", *Jl Brit. Studies*, viii (1968–9), pp. 22–78, at p. 68.

404 Baldwin, *The Mirror for Magistrates*, ed. Campbell, p. 178.

9. *At a crossroads of the political culture: the Essex revolt, 1601*

Perhaps the most interesting feature of the Essex revolt is not so much the fact of its failure, as that it was the last of its kind. I shall argue below that the revolt was motivated by, and arose out of, a specific aspect of the political culture of Elizabethan England: the cult of honour and its code.[1] The interest of the revolt is then that it was the last honour revolt: and as such the conclusion of a series and a tradition which recedes far back into the medieval period. During the last decade of Elizabeth's reign, the ideals and goals of honour tended to centre pre-eminently on one figure: the earl of Essex.[2] His aristocratic lineage, his military career, and the tradition he inherited all helped to make the earl a paradigm of honour. At the same time, the various literary and philosophical influences which circulated in the 1590s, emphasizing the cult of the heroic, and the aristocratic megalopsyche, or great soul, added to the glamour which surrounded Essex. He was able to attract to himself a following whose influence extended to over a dozen counties, which included representatives of leading gentry families and a number of peers. Yet his revolt was not only a material but also a moral failure, which revealed itself in the behaviour of the earl and his associates when called upon to account for their treason. At first, at his trial, the earl defended himself with boldness and self-confidence, and in terms of the honour-culture with which he had always been identified. But that trial also showed that the moral front of the rebels was already crumbling. One of Essex's closest associates gave

[1] See above, pp. 270 ff.

[2] Robert Devereux, 2nd earl of Essex (1566–1601). The most readable biographical study is still Lytton Strachey, *Elizabeth and Essex* (London, 1928 and 1948). See also G. B. Harrison, *The Life and Death of Robert Devereux, Earl of Essex* (London, 1937); W. B.Devereux, *Lives and Letters of the Devereux, Earls of Essex*, 2 vols. (London, 1853), i, pp. 163 ff.; E. P. Cheyney, *History of England from the Defeat of the Armada to the Death of Elizabeth*, 2 vols. (New York, 1914–26), *passim*.

evidence against him; then the others followed suit. All the sordid details of the planned *coup d'état* to seize control of the court, to enter London, and take the Tower were exposed by the conspirators themselves. Then, after his condemnation and return to his cell in the Tower, Essex himself executed a remarkable volte-face. He admitted the falsity of the stand he had taken at the trial, denounced his associates, and made a total and abject confession of all his faults. Repudiating honour, he identified himself with the religio-providentialist view of the state on which the legitimacy of the Elizabethan régime had always rested. Then he died a model, piously religious, death on the scaffold, his execution taking place privately, at his own request, within the confines of the Tower. This paper attempts to describe some of the cultural tendencies which contributed to the political attitudes of Essex and his circle, as well as the kinds of persons and families to be found in his following; and also to indicate some of the weaknesses and inconsistencies in the outlook of the group and its leader which contributed to the collapse.

For the queen, Essex's treason was rooted in irreligion. In an interview, in August 1601, with the antiquarian Lambard,[3] when the latter had referred to the ingratitude of the late earl of Essex, the queen had replied: "He that will forget God, will also forget his benefactors." The official image of Essex the traitor, as projected by the government prosecutors at the trials which followed the revolt, similarly insisted on irreligion as the prime cause of his disloyalty. There were in fact two aspects of the picture presented, both equally discreditable. Firstly, there was Essex the atheist, of no defined and firm religious allegiance; and secondly, following from this, Essex the Cataline, devoured like the Roman conspirator, with insatiable ambition and a lust for subversion. It was in particular the earl's supposed commitment to a policy of toleration for Catholics which was emphasized as revealing his lack of any settled religious commitment. "But toleration in religion", Coke had said at one of the trials, "this of all things concerns most . . . Her Majesty having made constant profession of the religion now established, and since her reign so blessed of God in it." Rather than change religion, so showing

[3] Printed in John Nichols, *The Progresses and Public Processions of Queen Elizabeth*, 3 vols. (London, 1823), iii, pp. 552–3.

ingratitude to God for his favours to her, the queen, Coke said, "would rather lose her Crown".[4] Such words could hardly have been used without the queen's knowledge and consent. Cecil's speech on the revolt in Star Chamber had the same emphasis: "No cause more important than the cause of religion, and in this cause Her Majesty, that of the commonwealth, religion, and our particular welfare, was concerned." Essex, through his collaboration with Papists and atheists, had planned "to subvert all".[5] Yelverton told the court at Essex's own trial: " . . . as Cataline entertained the most seditious persons about all Rome to join him in his conspiracy, so the earl of Essex had none but Papists, Recusants, and Atheists for his . . . abettors".[6] Thus the issue as between the queen and Essex was seen as between the established Protestant providentialist state religion on the one hand and, on the other, irreligious Catalinarian subversion. Essex had forgotten that, as William Barlow put it in his Paul's Cross sermon on the earl's treason: "Queen Elizabeth is the chosen and beloved of God, which from heaven, by his providence over her . . . He hath demonstratively shown."[7]

What grounds were there for the antithesis: religion versus irreligion; order versus subversion? The queen's attention had focused, long before the revolt, on the sceptical, amoral approach to the political process which had characterized some of the writings associated with Essex House, and which had received particularly cogent and brilliant expression in a historical work, *The First Part of the Life and Reign of King Henry IV*, by John Hayward.[8] Published in 1599, just before Essex's departure for Ireland, and dedicated to him, this was a remarkable instance of the so-called Tacitean school of historiography, which flourished in the earl's circle.[9] The real

[4] See "The Trial of Sir Christopher Blount and Others for High Treason", in *State Trials*, i, p. 1422.

[5] *Cal. State Papers, Domestic, Eliz., 1598–1601* (London, 1869), p. 554.

[6] *State Trials*, i, p. 1337.

[7] William Barlow D.D., *A Sermon Preached at Paules Crosse, on the First Sunday of Lent, Martii i, 1600. With a short discourse of the late Earle of Essex, his confession and penitence, before and at the time of his death* (London, 1601, S.T.C. 1454), sig. c.4^{r}.

[8] *The First Parte of the Life and Raigne of King Henrie the iiii, Extending to the end of the first yeare of his raigne*. Written by I.H. (London, 1599, S.T.C. 12997); hereafter cited as *The First Part*.

[9] Among the earl's followers, Francis Bacon, Sir Henry Savile, and probably Henry Cuffe, were practitioners of the Tacitean genre. Essex himself was acquainted with Tacitus, and occasionally quoted him in his correspondence;

theme of *The First Part* was the fall of Richard II, and the role of Henry of Lancaster in bringing it about. It was a study therefore of a sensitive subject: the overthrow of an unpopular régime, followed by the deposition of a prince, which had a special interest for Essex and his friends, themselves, like Henry of Lancaster and his supporters, political dissidents. But obviously the theme of deposition would similarly arouse the attention of the wary queen. The earl's own concern with the history of Richard II was well known. He had many times patronized and applauded a play of Richard II, whether Shakespeare's or another;[10] and on the night before the revolt his followers had attended and paid for a special performance probably of Shakespeare's play.[11] The queen told Lambard, in the interview

Ben Jonson credited him with writing the foreword to Savile's *The Ende of Nero and the Beginning of Galba. Fower Books of the Histories of Tacitus* (London, 1591, S.T.C. 23642), but the evidence for this seems no more than hearsay. But a cultivation of Tacitean styles and attitudes seems nevertheless to have been a characteristic of the Essex circle. See F. J. Levy, *Tudor Historical Thought* (San Marino, Calif., 1967), p. 251. Hayward was a Cambridge civil lawyer who was not a member of the circle, but who plainly aspired to join it, and hoped that *The First Part*, both by its dedication and content, would attract the earl's patronage. The book was largely constructed out of political maxims and aphorisms taken from Savile's Tacitean translations. See S. L. Goldberg, "Sir John Hayward, 'Politic' Historian", in *Rev. Eng. Studies*, new ser., vi (1955), pp. 233 ff.; Edwin B. Benjamin, "Sir John Hayward and Tacitus", *ibid.*, new ser., viii (1957), pp. 275 ff. For some of the implications of the study of Tacitus during the period, see Peter Burke, "Tacitism", in *Tacitus*, ed. T. A. Dorey (London, 1969), pp. 149 ff.

10 The evidence which was put together in July 1600 in support of a hypothetical charge of treason against Essex (which was not proceeded with) stated: "Essex's own actions confirm the intent of the treason. His permitting underhand that treasonable book of Henry IV to be published; it being plainly deciphered, not only by the matter, but also by the earl so often being present at the playing thereof, and with great applause giving countenance to it" (*Cal. State Papers, Domestic, Eliz.*, p. 455). In the interview with Lambard cited at n. 3 above, the queen said that "this tragedy [of Richard II] was played 40tie times in open streets and houses" under Essex's auspices. It seems most likely that the "playing" referred to in the Abstract of treason evidence quoted above, and the "tragedy" mentioned by the queen, refer to the same play; and that this was not Shakespeare's, but "some kind of tragical recitation or dramatic show, based on Hayward, and full of pointed political analogies". See *The Arden Edition of the Works of William Shakespeare: Richard II*, ed. Peter Ure (London, 1966), p. lxi.

11 *Cal. State Papers, Domestic, Eliz., 1598–1601*, p. 578: Examination of Augustine Phillips, 18 Feb. 1601. Phillips was a friend and business associate of Shakespeare's and described the play of "the deposing and killing of Richard II" put on at the request of the Essexians as "old and so long out of use", as Shakespeare's would have been, having been published in 1597, and probably performed a year or two before that. See E. K. Chambers, *William Shakespeare*, 2 vols. (Oxford, 1930), i, p. 354.

already quoted, that she *was* Richard II,[12] meaning that the Essexians had seen her as such, and with the implication that, had the revolt succeeded, she would have suffered the same fate. When Hayward's book appeared, she had immediately noticed, and been angry at, the dedication to Essex; and she thought the book "a seditious prelude to put into people's hearts boldness and faction", telling Francis Bacon "she had good opinion there was treason in it".[13] According to Cecil, Hayward's history did indeed foreshadow Essex's treasons, by "making this time seem like that of Henry IV, to be reformed by him [Essex] as by Henry IV".[14] What then did Hayward say? What light does his work throw on the political attitudes of Essex and his circle, and what does it reveal about the ideology of his revolt?

In the first place, Hayward contributed to the reputation of the Essex circle as characterized by an atheistic political secularism. This was because Hayward, as an exponent of the Tacitean historical style, abandoned in his historical work the providentialist framework, and the stress on the moral *exemplum* which had been characteristic of earlier Tudor historiography.[15] Following in the

[12] *Loc. cit.*, n. 3 above.

[13] Francis Bacon, "Apology Concerning the Earl of Essex": see *Francis Bacon, Viscount St Albans, Life and Letters*, iii, p. 149, in Francis Bacon, *Collected Works, with his Letters and Life*, ed. J. Spedding, R. L. Ellis, and D. D. Heath, 14 vols. (London, 1857–74). Eager to defend Essex, whose client he then still was, Bacon did his best (but without success) to convince the queen that *The First Part* was no more than an academic rhetorical exercise in the Tacitean style. The queen persisted in her opinion that the book had political implications; its content, and the circumstances of its publication made a deep impression on her mind.

[14] *Cal. State Papers, Domestic, Eliz., 1598–1601*, p. 555. The case against Essex was that, although aware of the politically inflammatory implications of *The First Part*, he kept it for several weeks without taking any action, particularly with regard to the dedication to himself. During this time the book circulated widely, five or six hundred copies, complete with the dedication, being sold. At last Essex informed the archbishop of Canterbury that the book was dangerous, and that the dedication should be removed. A second edition, amended and without the dedication, was prepared, another five or six hundred copies being printed, "the people calling for it exceedingly", but this was impounded. See *Cal. State Papers, Domestic, Eliz., 1598–1601*, pp. 450–1. It was also regarded as suspicious that Hayward had used underhand means to steer his book through the censorship, exploiting his acquaintance with one of the bishop of London's gentlemen, and with the censor, Samuel Harsnett, to conceal its real character, presenting it as no more than "a cantel of our English chronicles phrased and flourished over, only to show the author's pretty wit" (*Cal. State Papers, Domestic, Eliz. 1598–1601*, p. 452).

[15] See Goldberg, *op. cit.*, pp. 233–4, and *passim*; Levy, *op. cit.*, pp. 237 ff.

steps of Guicciardini, Machiavelli, and the French *politique* Bodin, Hayward, using Tacitus as a stylistic model both of form and manner, aimed at realistic character-studies of the historical figures he presented. In these, actions were analysed, not as in the older historiography in terms of conformity to the moral purpose unfolded in history by providentialist design,[16] but instead in terms of the "politic" art by means of which the historical actor, his will powered by passion and interest, attained his objectives, which were understood in terms of the pursuit and preservation of dominance. As a result, the sense of history as reflecting an over-arching divine purpose, which favoured, sustained, and protected (so providing the terms in which Hall, for example, had seen Tudor England and its monarchy as sustained and protected by its Protestant and anti-Papist mission), was thrown overboard. Instead, history simply became a field for the play of the heroic energy of the autonomous politic will, seeking to dominate events by its command of the politic arts. It was an approach which, by comparison with that of the providentialist historian, could be thought of as "atheist"; for the historical actors it presented were seen as released from the sanctions and controls imposed by morality and law, and underwritten by religion. Hayward had tried in fact to meet this criticism by giving his *First Part* a somewhat incongruous providentialist conclusion, borrowed from Hall, whose tone and implications are however very different from the rest of the work.[17]

Hayward has been seen as the exponent of a new, rationalized history, freed from the moralistic and providentialist assumptions of earlier historians.[18] Yet a reading of his analysis of the fall of Richard II reveals a highly traditionalist content. For it is in fact constructed out of the categories of what the American historian Bertram Wyatt-Brown calls "primal honour", that is, the ancient, preconceptual assumptions, free from any Christian or philosophical top-dressing, in terms of which honour communities had always seen the nature of society, of political conflict, and of political motivation.[19] At the beginning of his work, Hayward presents

[16] See above, Chapter 8, pp. 360 ff.

[17] *The First Part*, p. 134.

[18] Arthur B. Ferguson, *Clio Unbound: Perception of the Social and Cultural Past in Renaissance England*, pp. 10, 26; Levy, *op. cit.*, ch. 7, *passim*.

[19] Bertram Wyatt-Brown, *Southern Honour: Ethics and Behaviour in the Old South* (New York, 1982), pp. 25 ff.

honour as the motive force of history: "Citties at the first were builded, lawes made, and many things invented . . . chiefly for the desire of glory."[20] History is written to eternize honour: "Neyther is that the least benefit of history, that it perceiveth the glory of good men, and the shame of evill."[21] Why, Hayward asks, in the reign of Richard II, did the polity become unnaturally distorted, and the king a tyrant? Because the natural political class, conceived as those qualified by lineage and inherent inherited honourable status to rule, were excluded from the king's confidence. "The King", Hayward makes Henry of Lancaster say, "regarded not the noble Princes of his blood and Peeres of the Realm . . . instead of these he was wholly governed by certaine new-found . . . favourites, vulgar in birth, and corrupt in qualities, having no sufficencie eyther of councell in peace, or of courage in war"; these exploited the state and oppressed the people to gratify their parvenu greed.[22] How was this state of affairs to be remedied? By the common action of the nobility, under their natural leader, Henry of Lancaster. What was the bond which united them in resistance to Richard's corrupt régime? It was the bond of honour. Lancaster's aristocratic associates, Hayward tells us, "bound themselves in honour" to proceed against the king's councillors.[23] What was the essential quality of the political leader, particularly of a dissident political movement? It was, Hayward said, "never to prefer abject and base safety before hazard with honour". He must always be ready for the bold, heroic initiative; and willing to stake all in the gamble with Fortune. Because Richard failed in this, seeking safety in surrender to his enemies instead of ending his life "with glory" in battle against them, he had to endure the shame of his fall and subsequent abject fate.[24] Hayward presents his picture in terms familiar to any honour culture. On the one hand, there is the natural political élite, selected by lineally inherited status; opposed to it the oppressive and cor-

20 *The First Part*, "Preface, A.P. to the Reader", but written by Hayward: see *Cal. State Papers, Domestic, Eliz., 1598–1601*, p. 539.

21 *The First Part, ibid.*

22 Thus the earl of Suffolk "was a merchant's son from London, and growing mighty of a sudden, he could not govern himself in the change . . . he made open sale of the princes honour"; similarly, "John Foorde, Bishop of Durham . . . rising from mean estate to so high a pitch of honour, he excited the more excessively his riot, avarice, and ambition, not able to moderate the lustes . . . former want had kindled." See *ibid.*, pp. 8, 10, 42, 54, 63.

23 *Ibid.*, p. 70.

24 *Ibid.*, pp. 82 ff.

rupting influence of an upstart, and therefore unnatural, régime, installed by a dishonourable and tyrannical monarch. Honour provides both the motivation and the bond of élite solidarity required for the correction of the resulting distortion in the proper political order.

The significance of *The First Part* lies in the fact that the terms of Hayward's analysis reflect, parallel, and perhaps in part suggested those in which Essex and his friends presented their relationship to the Cecilian régime, and the continued disfavour with which they were regarded by the queen. Essex too emphasized the low birth and cowardly disposition of his antagonists, qualities which Hayward had attributed to Bussy, Green, and the other favourites of Richard II. "Judge you", the earl told Sir Robert Sidney at the surrender of Essex House, " . . . whether it can be grief to a man descended as I am, to be trodden underfoot by such base upstarts",[25] whose cowardly disposition showed itself in the way in which "they keep aloof from danger, and dare not approach me".[26] Like Hayward's Ricardian favourites too, the earl's enemies were "caterpillars", devouring the resources of the state to their own profit, their avarice prompted by their "base condition", and the natural greed characteristic of the low-born. And again like Richard's favourites, the Cecilians exploited their corrupt monopoly of the queen's favour to bar the natural élite, the nobility, from access to her person,[27] which they could not approach without peril. Essex saw himself as chosen, both by lineage, and by his tenure of the office of earl marshal,[28] to be the natural leader of a community of honour, "the flower of the nobility and gentry of England",[29] against a debased régime of upstarts. As in Henry's case, so in that of Essex, the bond of faithfulness between the conspirators was informed by honour; a bond which, according to Essex himself, articulated a union of hearts so strong that no oath of secrecy or fidelity was needed between them.[30] The Essex revolt then, like that of Hayward's Henry of Lancaster, had honour as its constitutive principle.

[25] Hist. MSS. Comm., Bath *Longleat* MSS., Devereux Papers, 1533–1659, p. 280.

[26] *Ibid.*, p. 280. [27] *Ibid.*, p. 279. [28] See below, p. 450.

[29] The phrase used by one of Essex's followers to describe the peers and gentlemen who accompanied Essex in his entry into London on the day of the revolt. See Hist. MSS. Comm., *Hatfield MSS* (hereafter cited as *Hatf. MSS.*), xi, p. 61.

[30] Thomas Birch, *Memoirs of the Reign of Queen Elizabeth*, 2 vols. (London, 1754), ii, p. 481.

The same principle also pervades the attitudes, political and social, and the distinctive styles of behaviour and manners which were characteristic of the earl's followers, which I will now attempt to describe. Needless to say, the group of peers, heads of gentry families, younger sons, and army officers who circled around Essex House had few of the characteristics of the old-style "feudal" affinity, which had still played a role of some importance in the risings of the earlier part of the century. Essex lacked the landed resources from which to raise a levy of tenants considerable enough to form the basis of a regional revolt, even if he had wished to do so;[31] and during his lifetime he abandoned the practice of retainder, preferring his followers to be bound to him by the more informal bonds of friendship and honour.[32] His relationship to them conformed therefore not to the model of a feudal magnate's to his regional affinity, but rather to that of a patron to his clientele, his resources for this role deriving from his position as a prominent court peer, councillor, and military leader, who had intermittently enjoyed the favour of the queen, and who might do so again. The nature of the clientele was determined in part by the background of his own family, which had a long connection, landed and administrative, with the Welsh Border, and a more recent one with Wales itself, where the family had acquired monastic and episcopal estates, had sat on the Council in Wales, held many stewardships of crown lordships, and similar offices.[33] These factors then account for the strength of the Essex connection in the Welsh counties, and

[31] On the Devereux estate, see H. A. Lloyd, "The Essex Inheritance", in *Welsh Hist. Rev.*, viii (1974–5), pp. 13 ff.

[32] Penry Williams, *The Council in the Marches of Wales under Elizabeth I* (Cardiff, 1958), p. 286; retainder amongst Essex's following seems to have survived only in Wales. The queen's speech of June 1595 to the assembled circuit judges, urging them to enforce the statutes against maintenance and remove all unworthy magistrates (John Howarde, *Les reportes del cases in Camera Stellata*, ed. R. P. Bailey (London, 1884), p. 20) followed on a memorandum by Burghley in May. About this time, Essex wrote to Lord Keeper Puckering: "Although I am very loath to leave the name of Master to so manie honest gentlemen in Wales; yet I had rather give them libertie and free them from reteyninge than that they should lose any jot of their former reputations . . . being all of them verie able and sufficient gentlemen . . . Yt shall suffice henceforthe that I have their love without further ceremonies, praying your Lordship that they may not by the late order be subject to loss of their places for this cause." See Williams, *loc. cit.* Burghley's memorandum and the queen's speech had been followed by an order excluding retainers from the commission of the peace.

[33] Lloyd, *op. cit.*, pp. 15 ff.

amongst the gentry communities of Worcestershire, Herefordshire, and Shropshire along the Border. These were all areas where relatively archaic life-styles tended to survive, with a stress on lineage, extended family loyalties, and on violent forms of socio-political competition.[34] But of course the clientele ramified far more widely than Wales and the Border. At the other side of the country there was a significant Essex faction in Norfolk;[35] also in the midland

[34] On the Essex following in Wales, see Williams, *op. cit.*, pp. 281 ff.; David Mathew, *The Celtic Peoples and Renaissance Europe* (London, 1933), pp. 336 ff.; H. A. Lloyd, *The Gentry of South-West Wales, 1540–1640* (Cardiff, 1968), pp. 112 ff.; A. H. Dodd, "North Wales and the Essex Revolt", *Eng. Hist. Rev.*, lix (1944), pp. 348 ff.; *ibid.*, "The Earl of Essex's Faction in North Wales, c. 1593–1601", in *The National Library of Wales Journal*, vi (1949–50), pp. 190–1

Along the Border, in Herefordshire, the dominating figure was the earl's steward, Sir Gelly Meyrick, who was seated at Wigmore castle, procured for him by the earl; around him rallied Vaughans, Seabornes, Bodnams and Jameses amongst the Herefordshire squires, many of them recusants (*Hatf. MSS.*, xi, pp. 106 ff.). Sir Herbert Croft was a close, if unreliable, ally: see P. W. Hasler, *The History of Parliament: The House of Commons, 1558–1603*, 3 vols. (London, 1981), i, p. 671. In Worcestershire, the most prominent Essexians were Sir Henry Bromley of Holt castle, a Puritan, and his relative by marriage John Lyttelton of Frankley, reputedly a Catholic; together with William Walsh, sheriff 1598–9, and county M.P. 1593, a militant Protestant. On Bromley, see T. R. Nash, *Collections for the History of Worcestershire*, 2 vols. and Suppl. (London, 1781–99), i, p. 595; ii, p. 445, and Suppl., p. 35; also Hasler, *op. cit.*, i, p. 491. On Lyttelton, Nash, *op. cit.*, ii, pp. 491 ff., and Suppl., p. 35; also Hasler, *op. cit.*, ii, p. 507. On Walsh, see Hasler, *op. cit.*, iii, p. 570. In Shropshire there was Sir Robert Vernon of Hodnet, whose sister married Essex's friend the earl of Southampton, and whose family probably had a hand in the return of Sir Henry Bromley as county M.P. in 1597 (*V.C.H., Shropshire*, iii, London, 1979, p. 95). Vernon took part in the revolt. In Gloucester, Sir John Tracy was a devoted Essexian, knighted by the earl at Rouen, M.P. for the county in 1597, and married into another Essexian family, the Shirleys of Wiston in Sussex (Hasler, *op. cit.*, iii, p. 375). Richard Stephens was another Gloucestershire Essexian, belonging to the Puritan wing of the faction, and therefore with affiliations with Bromley and Walsh (Hasler, *op. cit.*, iii, p. 444).

[35] Essex's most consistent supporters in Norfolk included Edward, Lord Cromwell (who had made a Norfolk marriage, and had a house at North Elmham), and the Heydons, Sir John and Sir Christopher, together with their allies and friends, who included the formidable Sir Arthur Heveningham. Cromwell and the Heydons had served under Essex at Cadiz and in Ireland, and all three took part in his revolt. Essex, in his turn, actively intervened in Norfolk, using his influence in matters relating to the militia offices, the deputy lieutenancies, and the shrievalty, and probably supported Lord Cromwell's unsuccessful ambition to be lord lieutenant. See A. Hassell Smith, *County and Court: Government and Politics in Norfolk, 1558–1603* (Oxford, 1974), pp. 303–4, 340–1.

counties of Warwickshire, Northamptonshire, and Staffordshire.[36] Further south, there were Essex factions in Wiltshire and Sussex,[37] and an outlier in the north, in Yorkshire.[38] The clientele therefore extended to over a dozen counties, including those in Wales. In its ranks there were local families and figures of prominence and substance, like the Treshams and Catesbies in Northamptonshire, the Lytteltons and Bromleys in Worcestershire, Sir Robert Vernon in

[36] In Warwickshire, Essex had the support of his uncle, Edward Devereux of Castle Bromwich, sheriff of the county, and the youngest son of Walter, first Viscount Hereford. He was reported upon for taking part soon after the earl's execution, in a suspicious gathering of Devereux relatives and friends at Wolverhampton, which included Sir Edward Lyttelton of Pillaton, Staffs., and his Devereux wife, who was the daughter of the late Sir Walter Devereux, Edward's brother, and an important figure both in Warwickshire and Staffordshire. See *Hatf. MSS.*, xi, p. 387; Hasler, *op. cit.*, i, p. 35. The before-mentioned Sir Edward Lyttelton was Essex's most devoted supporter in Staffordshire; he accompanied Essex in his incursion into London on the day of the revolt, "with his sword drawn, and near to him" (*Hatf. MSS.*, xi, p. 34). In Northamptonshire, Essex attracted the support of two notable recusant families: the Catesbies of Ashby St Ledger, whose head, Robert Catesby, joined the earl's revolt; and the Treshams of Rushton, whose heir, Francis Tresham, also joined the revolt. On the Catesby family, see J. Bridges, *History and Antiquities of Northamptonshire*, 2 vols. (Oxford, 1791), i, pp. 16 ff.; *Dict. Nat. Biog.*, iii, p. 1191; on the Treshams, M. E. Finch, *Five Northamptonshire Families* (Northants. Record Soc., xix, 1956), pp. 66 ff.

In these three counties, Essex's influence was related to his Ferrers inheritance, which, although mainly centred on Chartley in Staffs., also had outliers in Warwicks. and Northants.

[37] For the Wiltshire scene, where Essex had the support of the Danvers family and their allies, see A. Wall, "Faction in Local Politics, 1580–1620: Struggles for Supremacy in Wiltshire", in *Wiltshire Archaeological Magazine*, lxxvii–lxxviii (1980), pp. 119 ff. Also Hasler, *op. cit.*, ii, pp. 14 ff., *sub* "Danvers, Sir Charles"; ii, pp. 487 ff., *sub* "Long, Sir Walter"; iii, p. 26, *sub* "Marvyn, James"; iii, p. 504, *sub* "Thynne, John". In Sussex the principal Essexian family was the Shirleys of Wiston; their head, Sir Thomas, was a former treasurer at war in the Netherlands, and a deputy lieutenant until 1601. Sir Thomas's son, Sir Anthony Shirley, was a devoted admirer of Essex, served under him at Rouen, and resolved to make him "the pattern of my civil life, and from him to draw a worthy model of all my actions". See Hasler, *op. cit.*, iii, p. 375, and *Dict. Nat. Biog.*, xviii, p. 121.

[38] The most prominent Yorkshire Essexians were Richard Cholmley, born 1580, heir to Sir Henry Cholmley of Whitby, of recusant stock; and Sir William Constable, head of another recusant family, the Constables of Flamborough, who was later converted to Puritanism, and became a regicide. Constable served under Essex in Ireland, was knighted by him, and joined his revolt (see J. Foster, *Yorkshire Pedigrees*, 3 vols. (London, 1874), iii, *sub* "Cholmley" and "Constable"). The great Percy interest in Yorkshire was in eclipse, following the death of the seventh earl on the scaffold, and of the eighth in the Tower, under suspicion of treason. The ninth earl did not get on well with his brother-in-law the earl of Essex. Nevertheless, Northumberland's two brothers, Sir Charles and Sir Joscelyn Percy, were devoted Essexians, served under Essex in Ireland, were knighted by him, and joined his revolt.

Shropshire, the Heydons in Norfolk, the Danvers family in Wiltshire. Some of them were in financial difficulties, but for the most part these arose either from ideological commitment – to recusancy – or political disfavour, and need not have been permanent.[39] In my view the notion that the Essex connection consisted of impoverished backwoods gentry hoping to solve their problems by a political revolution is a very exaggerated idea, which scarcely fits the facts.[40]

As a patron, Essex operated within the structure of the state honour system, as this had evolved by the end of the sixteenth century. He used his influence as a councillor, and his friendship first with Lord Keeper Puckering, then with Lord Keeper Egerton,[41] to secure the place of his followers within the relevant shire commission of the peace; and where possible he sought their advancement (which was of course also one in prestige and honour) within the order of precedence ruling within the commission.[42] But what

[39] Of these, the Heydons seem to have been a genuine "declining" family, whose extravagance and indebtedness may have been due to a streak of instability in three successive generations (Hassell Smith, *op. cit.*, pp. 163 ff.). The Treshams and Catesbies were wealthy families which owed their money troubles to the burdens of recusancy; but nevertheless were rich enough to survive the disaster of the Essex revolt, with the resulting heavy fines. Their fall was due to entanglement in the Gunpowder Plot. Sir Henry Bromley and Sir Charles Danvers represented wealthy families, the former enriched by a great legal fortune, the latter by the inheritance of extensive Neville lands in Yorkshire, as well as of the family estates in Wiltshire and Oxfordshire. Sir Edward Lyttelton of Pillaton is often cited as a notorious example of Essexian "poverty" because he was arrested for debt on the day of the revolt; but in fact he paid the debt forthwith, and was immediately released. There is no indication that either the Lytteltons or Sir Robert Vernon were in serious financial difficulties.

[40] The phrase "Seize the Queen and be our own carvers", supposedly shouted by Essex's followers on the day of the revolt, and often cited to illustrate the predatory objectives of the faction, is not reported by any eye-witness, but was included by Sir William Sanderson, a writer of a later generation, in his *Aulicus Coquinarius* (London, 1650). Sanderson was an admirer of Sir Robert Cecil, and the words were probably no more than his own opinion of Essex and his followers – which was a low one – expressed in a pungent phrase, and given historical status.

[41] These friendships seem to have developed out of the connections of Puckering and Egerton with the law courts and administrative organs of Wales and the Marches, Puckering having been a judge of the Carmarthen circuit, and Egerton a member of the Council of Wales, besides being a friend of Francis Bacon. See Williams, *The Council in the Marches*, pp. 282, 283; and *Dict. Nat. Biog.*, vi, p. 579; xii, p. 453.

[42] For his methods of working, and the sort of pressures he tried to bring to bear, see, for Wales, Williams, *op. cit.*, pp. 281 ff.; cf., for Norfolk, Hassell Smith, *County and Court*, pp. 270, 303 ff., 340 ff.

gave the Essex connection its special tone, and many of its cultural characteristics, was its strongly military orientation. This arose of course out of the earl's role as a prominent military leader in the Elizabethan state of the 1590s. This had placed at his disposal an extensive military patronage, in the form of the colonelcies, captaincies, and other offices of the armies and naval expeditions in which he had held commands.[43] The military habits of fidelity and obedience established in these campaigns between Essex and his officers helped both to extend and consolidate his local following; and also account for the considerable representation of swordsmen with a taste for violence in the ranks of his following. About a third of those who, on 8 February 1601, accompanied Essex on his foray into the City had served under him in military offices.[44] Moreover, the military relationship had been given a special aura, of a traditionalist and chivalric kind, by the lavish way in which Essex, in spite of the queen's protests, had used his military prerogative to confer the honour of knighthood on those who distinguished themselves under him in the field, in order to raise actual or potential members of his following to this status.[45] Not all Essex knights became firm members of his faction; but most in the outcome did.[46] To those who received it, knighthood implied a special relationship with Essex himself, as the one who had "dubbed" them knight, which involved mutual peace and friendship; they also, through Essex, made contact with the glamorous overtones of Tudor

[43] For the range of his patronage, and the potential extent of the clientele his military status enabled him to attract, see the many applications to serve under him in Ireland which poured in during the early months of 1599, when his likely appointment to the Irish lord lieutenancy began to be known, in *Hatf. MSS.*, viii and ix, *passim*.

[44] Of the 86 prisoners listed in *Hatf. MSS.*, xi, p. 289, as taken (or sought) after the revolt, at least 27 can be identified as having served under Essex as officers in Ireland or elsewhere. Of the 7 peers involved, the earls of Southampton, Rutland, and Sussex had similarly served, together with Lords Cromwell and Monteagle.

[45] For the knighthoods conferred by Essex, see W. A. Shaw, *The Knights of England*, 2 vols. (London, 1906), ii, pp. 89 ff.

[46] The majority of Essex's inner circle had been knighted by him. Southampton, Rutland, Sussex, and Lords Cromwell and Monteagle were Essex knights; so were Sir Gelly Meyrick, Sir John Davies, Sir William Constable, Sir Henry Carew, Sir Ferdinando Gorges, Sir Charles Percy, Sir Joscelyn Percy, Sir Henry Linley, Sir Edward Michelmore, Sir George Manners, Sir Thomas West, Sir John Heydon, Sir Christopher Heydon, Sir John Vaughan, and Sir Simon Weston. Griffin Markham and Lord Grey of Wilton were two Essex knights who joined his enemies.

monarchical chivalry, in which the earl played a prominent part, as the spiritual heir of Sir Philip Sidney, and a leading participant in the royal chivalric rituals of the Accession Day Tilts.[47] The obligations and associations of knighthood enhanced therefore the romantic glow which surrounded the earl's leadership, and so his prestige and popularity.

Of the Essexian styles of behaviour and attitude arising out of the military connection, one of the most prominent was a sense of devoted adhesion to the military calling as "the way of arms"; that is, as a distinctive social subculture which required special qualities of those who followed it – qualities which were analogous with, but in the eyes of their practitioners to be preferred above, both the way of the robe (i.e. the law and letters) and the way of religion (i.e. the priesthood). In the Essexian context the military calling stood in a kind of unstated tension with the two Tudor élite subcultures which stood closest to it: the law and religion. Essex himself, in his *Apology*,[48] distinguished between the three "professions" of arms, law, and religion, each with its distinctive characteristics, but proudly announced his own adhesion to the profession of arms. It was this alone, he said, which cultivated in its practitioners love of "pains, dangers, and difficulties", and of "the public more than themselves"; qualities which encouraged the growth in them of a heroic "greatness of mind", placing the man of arms above the "little men" whose love was for "ease, pleasure, and profit".[49] Occasionally Essex showed a sense of contrast between the simplicity, fearlessness, and noble directness of the man of arms and the guile and calculating quality characteristic of the lawyer. Thus when Francis Bacon once advised him that, if he wished for the queen's favour, he should abandon his military affiliation and seek a politically more promising civil office, Essex saw this advice as a typical expression of lawyerly guile, in this instance tempting to a dishonourable inconstancy in his profession; he rejected Bacon's pro-

47 See Frances Yates, *Astraea: The Imperial Theme in the Sixteenth Century* (Harmondsworth, 1977), pp. 88 ff. On the implications of knighting, or being knighted, for "friendship", see Malory, *The Morte Darthur, Parts Seven and Eight*, ed. D. S. Brewer (London, 1968), p. 26.

48 *An apologie of the earle of Essex against those which jealously and maliciously tax him to be the hinderer of the peace and quiet of his country; penned by himself, in anno 1598* (London, 1603, S.T.C. 6788).

49 *Ibid.*, sig. c.$^{r-v}$, see also Devereux, *Lives and Letters*, i, pp. 487–8.

posal, and told him it was his "robe" that had spoken, and not his mind.[50] Almost to the end, Essex saw himself as "a man of arms", ruled by the sanctions of the military culture and its code of honour. By comparison, in his eyes the law represented pettifogging pedantry, alien to heroic greatness. Thus, after his condemnation for treason, he could assert that he was nevertheless merely "the law's traitor", the victim of the "rigour and quirks" of the lawyers.[51] He had a true heart to Her Majesty and his country,[52] and at the bar of honour, more generous and indifferent, the condemnation had no validity.

These attitudes were echoed, though with little of the earl's sophistication, amongst many of his followers, like the Heydons in Norfolk, who distrusted the law and despised lawyers.[53] The Heydons were typical of the Essexians, whose ranks included few of the earnest, cultivated gentry. These, often of Puritan persuasion, with large libraries in their houses, had a taste for rhetorical techniques and the mastery of legal procedures which made for advancement in the commission of the peace, and success in litigation. There were a good many such on the other, Cecilian, side of the political fence, like the Bacons and Knyvetts in Norfolk, the Salusburies of Llewenni in and the Wynnes in north Wales, or the Longs in Wiltshire, all opposed to the earl's friends in their counties.[54] The latter were prone to resolve quarrels by the sword,

50 Francis Bacon, "Apology Concerning the Earl of Essex", in Spedding, *Francis Bacon . . . Life and Letters*, iii, p. 145.

51 *State Trials*, i, p. 1356; William Camden, *Historie of Elizabeth Queene of England* (London, 1630), p. 182.

52 "The Arraignment of the Earls of Essex and Southampton" (*The Farmer Chetham MS.*, ed. A. B.Grosart, pt. 1, Chetham Society, lxxxix, Manchester, 1873; hereafter cited as *The Farmer Chetham MS.*), pp. 2, 22.

53 Both the Heydons and their ally Sir Arthur Heveningham were involved in enmities with rising Norfolk families of lawyer origin: the Heydons with Sir Nathaniel Bacon, Heveningham with Edward Flowerdew, a "knavish serjeant". In addition, both the Heydons and Heveningham levied dues and impositions arising from vice-admiralty and lieutenancy jurisdictions which were not securely grounded in the common law, which could therefore be appealed to by their enemies. See Hassell Smith, *County and Court*, pp. 194 ff., 229 ff., 253 ff.

54 On the Bacons and Knyvetts, see Hassell Smith, *op. cit.*, pp. 167 ff., 173 ff., on the Salusburies of Llewenni (and their relatives and rivals, the Salesburies of Rûg) see *Calendar of Salusbury Correspondence, 1553–c. 1700*, ed. W. J. Smith (Cardiff, 1954), and Carleton Browne, *Poems by Sir John Salusbury and Robert Chester* (Early English Text Soc., extra ser., cxiii, 1914); on the Wynnes, see Sir John Wynn, *The History of the Gwydir Family*, ed. J. Ballinger (Cardiff, 1927). The Wiltshire Longs, in spite of their military ambitions and violent proclivities,

or by confrontations between bands of riotous servants. As would be expected from the military affiliation of the group, there were many duellists in its ranks, ranging from Essex himself to the earls of Rutland and Southampton[55] amongst his close associates, and further afield to the Danvers brothers in Wiltshire, the Salesburies in north Wales, and the Heydons in Norfolk.[56] The style, with its violent, domineering overtones, went well with the military offices, particularly deputy lieutenancies, which so many Essexians, as a result of their leader's influence, occupied.[57] The "arbitrary" and "prerogative" powers claimed by lieutenancy offices facilitated an overbearing military style of rule.[58]

deserve a place amongst the "earnest", if not perhaps "cultivated" gentry because of their Puritan inclinations; in addition, their Thynne alliance probably introduced this family to a certain level of sophistication apparent in the remodelling in the 1590s of the ancestral manor house at South Wraxall, with its new renaissance-style statuary illustrating moral and intellectual themes; and with Latin proverbs painted on the walls; see *V.C.H., Wiltshire*, vii (London, 1953), p. 23; N. Pevsner, *The Buildings of England: Wiltshire*, revised by B. Cherry, (Harmondsworth, 1975), pp. 475–6; W. Chitty, *Historical Account of the Family of Long* (privately printed, 1889), pp. 19–20.

55 Essex fought a duel with Charles Blount (later Lord Mountjoy), described by Sir Robert Naunton in his *Fragmenta Regalia* (London, 1870), p. 52; and afterwards with Richard Burke, later earl of Clanrickarde, supposedly his wife's lover, later her husband. When Lord Admiral Howard was created earl of Nottingham, the patent giving him credit for the taking of Cadiz, instead of Essex, the latter claimed that his honour was "touched", and challenged him, "or any of his sons or name" to a duel, unless his honour were otherwise satisfied. Southampton fought a duel with Lord Grey of Wilton (*Cal. State Papers, Domestic, Eliz., 1598–1601*, p. 477), and was involved in more than one court brawl leading to violence and challenges to duels. See *Dict. Nat. Biog.*, xxi, pp. 1058–9. For Rutland's duelling propensities, see *ibid.*, xii, pp. 940–1.

56 For the violent proclivities of the Danverses, Salesburies, and Heydons, see F. N. Macnamara, *Memorials of the Danvers Family* (London, 1895), pp. 302 ff.; *Hatf. MSS.*, iv, pp. 412, 436, 447, 449; *Acts of the Privy Council*, xviii, pp. 89–90; Dodd, "North Wales and the Essex Revolt", p. 357; Hassell Smith, *op. cit.*, pp. 203 ff.

57 The following Essexians were deputy lieutenants at the time of the revolt: John Lyttelton (Worcestershire: Hasler, *The History of Parliament*, ii, p. 507); Sir Ferdinando Gorges (Devon: *ibid.*, ii, p.200); Robert Salesbury (Merionethshire: *ibid.*, iii, p. 334); Sir Richard Trevor (Denbighshire: *ibid.*, iii, p. 529); Sir John Lloyd (Denbighshire: *ibid.*, ii, p. 482); Sir Thomas Shirley (Sussex: *ibid.*, iii, p. 375); Sir Edward Lyttelton (Staffordshire: *Hatf. MSS.*, xi, p. 34); Sir Henry Bromley (Worcestershire: Penry Williams, *The Council in the Marches of Wales*, p. 288); Sir Gelly Meyrick (Radnorshire: *ibid.*); Sir Herbert Croft (Herefordshire: *ibid.*); Roger Vaughan (Radnorshire: *ibid.*); Francis Meyrick (Pembrokeshire: *ibid.*).

58 For the arbitrary, military style of rule to which deputy lieutenants and their agents were prone, see Dodd, "North Wales and the Essex Revolt", pp. 359–60, and n. 53 above, this chapter.

Resort to violently forceful forms of self-assertiveness became indeed almost a point of principle, as well as practice, within the group. In fact John Lyttelton of Frankley in Worcestershire, perhaps the most intelligent and articulate of the grass-roots Essexians, claimed for the gentleman, where the law failed to safeguard his supposed right, that "there must of necessity be recourse to the auncientest law, the law of nature, which teacheth to resist violence with force".[59] Adhesion to this "auncientest" principle of the law of nature was a widespread belief in Essex's circle, perhaps as a result of Lyttelton's influence. Thus in the negotiations for the surrender of Essex House in the last stages of the revolt, the earl of Southampton told Sir Robert Sidney: "You are a man of arms, you know we are bound by nature to defend ourselves against our equals, still more against our inferiors", the latter being the "base-born upstarts" of the anti-Essex faction.[60] Essex himself based his defence at his trial on the same principle, asserting that "... I have done nothing but that which by the law of nature and the necessity of my case I was enforced unto". The law of nature was known to the civil law and formed the basis of the various continental codes of honour; but not to the common law.[61]

Again, another aspect of the Essexian self-image, intrinsic to any honour culture, was a sense of lineage. In the Essex circle the conviction ruled of innate qualities, particularly of rule and dominance, inherited with the blood, and conferring a "habit", or powerful tendency towards, virtue. In this respect, as in so many others, the earl himself was the admired paradigm. As Camden put it, "He was accomplished with all virtues worthy a most noble man. His Genealogy ancient and very noble."[62] Essex inherited pride of ancestry from his father, the first earl; and he was told at the beginning of his career by the latter's secretary, Edward Waterhouse, that the aristocratic qualities of fortitude, temperance, courtesy, affability, and constancy were innate in his blood, they being (as he put it) "peculiar to your house, and grafted as it were in your principles".[63] The consciousness of distinguished ancestry remained

59 Nash, *Worcestershire*, i, pp. 494–50.
60 Hist. MSS. Comm., Bath *Longleat* MSS., Devereux Papers, p. 279.
61 *The Farmer Chetham MS.*, p. 2.
62 *Op. cit.*, p. 189.
63 See his prefatory epistle to *A Funerall Sermon preached the xxv day of November ... M.D. LXXVI ... by ... Richard ... Bishoppe of Saint Davys, at the buriall of ... Walter Earl of Essex ...* (London, 1577, S.T.C. 6364).

with Essex throughout his career, and was thought even by his enemies to mark him off from other men. Yet the sense of ancestry, in the Essexian context, strikes a special note: often self-confidently arrogant, but marked by a nostalgia for past glories, and a sense of being, as it were, under siege. Essex's complaint that he had been trodden underfoot by base upstarts was echoed by his followers. For many of the latter had similarly experienced the competitive pressure of parvenu elements, and had seen their long-established place in their county hierarchies challenged by the rise of new families enriched most commonly by lawyer or courtier fortunes. Amongst them was the Danvers family in Wiltshire, their expectations recently enhanced by a grand Neville alliance, but now threatened by the intrusive courtier Thynnes, and challenged by the latter's alliance with their rivals, the Wiltshire Longs of Wraxall.[64] Or, in Northamptonshire, the Treshams and Catesbies, confronted by the new fortunes of the sheep-rearing Spencers and lawyer Montagus, and ousted by their recusancy from their due place in the

[64] The status of the Danvers family had been fairly recently enhanced by the marriage of Sir John Danvers (d. 1594) to Elizabeth Neville, one of the daughters and co-heiresses of the last Lord Latimer, the marriage bringing with it extensive Neville estates in Yorkshire, centring on the castle and lordship of Danby. See Macnamara,*op. cit.*, pp. 285–6. The marriage raised the family to peerage status, which eventuated in the next generation when Henry Danvers became earl of Danby. Inevitably Sir John Danvers dominated the Devizes "division" of Wiltshire, which was called "Danvers' division" (*V.C.H., Wiltshire*, v, London, 1957, p. 87). The Danvers–Long feud seems to have arisen out of the attempt of Sir Walter Long – recently returned from military service in Ireland, strengthened by his Thynne marriage, and with one of his houses, Draycote, only a few miles from the Danvers seat at Dauntsey – to challenge the Danvers predominance. The most plausible account of the feud is that of Lady Danvers, in *S.P. Dom., Eliz.*, vol. 219, no. 78, printed in Macnamara, *op. cit.*, pp. 302 ff. Its culmination was the death of Henry Long at the hands of the two Danvers brothers, Charles and Henry, at Corsham on 4 October 1594, followed by the outlawry and exile of Charles and Henry Danvers, who were not pardoned until 1598. Sir Charles Danvers, the elder brother, developed a close friendship with Southampton, then with Essex, and served under him in Ireland, later taking a prominent part in the revolt. On the other hand, Sir Walter Long, through his Thynne connection, developed a friendship with Sir Walter Raleigh, who was deeply hostile to Essex (John Aubrey, *Letters . . . by Eminent Persons, and Lives of Eminent Men*, 2 vols. (London, 1813), ii, pp. 509 ff.).

In Wiltshire, the Danverses were associated with a conservative, established group of gentry which included James Marvyn, Thomas Gorges, and others, who were opposed to the rival Knyvet–Long faction, backed by the Thynnes at Longleat. See the references at n. 37 above.

shire establishment.[65] In Norfolk there were the Heydons and their friends, challenged by the parvenu Bacons and theirs.[66] The sense of political frustration, of being unjustly slighted and so their honour defaced, was an experience shared with the leader by many courtier Essexians also, including such peers as the earl of Sussex, Lord Sandys, the earl of Southampton, and Lord Cromwell; or an official like Sir Henry Neville.[67]

Just as the Essex circle gave ample expression, in the self-assertive life-style of its members, to the latent violence and competitiveness of honour, so the group was also characterized by a stress on its compensatory solidarities, comprised above all in the ties of mutual loyalty and support, based on kinship and affinity, which bound together the lineage and its allies. Essexian families often inhabited fifteenth-century styles of housing, inherited from their ancestors, whose typical features were impressive fortified gatehouses and quadrangular form, furnished with large medieval-style halls, and providing many lodgings for servants and visitors. Such was the great fortified manor-house of the Heydons at Baconthorpe, the imposing Tresham house at Rushton, and the seat of the Danvers family at Dauntsey.[68] Such houses provided accom-

65 See n. 36 above, this chapter, and Hist. MSS. Comm., *Report on MSS. in Various Collections*, iii (*Tresham Papers*), p. 27, in which Sir Thomas Tresham contrasts his own ancestors, who had risen to high office in the service of many sovereigns, "and at whose feet sundry of them . . . have faithfully ended their lives in the field", with his parvenu neighbours the Spencers and Montagus, who could claim no such distinguished descent.

66 See n. 53 above, this chapter.

67 The fifth earl of Sussex (1569?–1629), his fortunes impaired (as had been Essex's own) by his father's "troubles" in Ireland and his uncle's service to the queen (*Dict. Nat. Biog.*, xv, p. 587), had not received any appointment he regarded as equal to his status and deserts; nor had Cromwell, whose discontent at being no more than a J.P. in Norfolk surfaced in a letter to Burghley (*Hatf. MSS.*, vi, p. 294) in which he unsuccessfully applied for the lord lieutenancy. Sandys (*Complete Peerage*, xi, p. 445) seems to have been in the same position. Southampton was notorious for his disfavour with the queen, who forced Essex to dismiss him as general of horse in Ireland (*Cal. Carew MSS., Ireland*, iii, 1589–1600, pp. 312 ff.; *Cal. State Papers, Ireland, 1599–1600*, pp. 100 ff.). Sir Henry Neville's standing in Berkshire had been weakened by the failure of the queen to appoint him to the High Stewardship of Windsor held by his father. He thought he was out of favour because of his failure to negotiate a peace with Spain in the Netherlands in 1599; he was dissatisfied with his Paris embassy, which involved honour without profit, and aspired to be secretary of state (Hasler, *The History of Parliament*, iii, p. 122).

68 Sir Christopher Heydon (d. 1579) had added the great gatehouse and forecourt to "the great fortified pile at Baconsthorpe"; here he entertained lavishly, and

modation for large households, and facilitated extensive hospitality for relatives and friends.[69] A web of blood relationship and alliances bound the group together, and often motivated strong loyalties to its leader. The earl of Southampton asserted at his trial, "the first occasion that made me advance into these causes was the affinity between my lord of Essex and me, I being of his blood, so that for his sake I would have hazarded my life". The earl of Rutland, whose wife was Essex's niece, "resolved to live and die with him". Sir Edward Lyttelton of Pillaton, Staffordshire, had been brought into the Essex circle by his Devereux alliance.[70] The importance of lineage solidarities in the mentality of the group emerges from a letter written after the revolt by John Lyttelton, while in prison and awaiting trial. In this he urged the victorious party to be moderate in its revenge on the vanquished, considering (as he put it) "how many families of honour and worship will be interested in the blood that shall be shed", amongst whom "there will ever remain a desire to revenge the shedding of it".[71] Thus the expectation remained that the lineage would revenge its dead, even those condemned by law of the capital crime of treason.

The tendency of the group to articulate its solidarity in terms of honour was strengthened by the fact of its religious fissiparity, and the lack of any single unifying bond of religious allegiance. The Essex connection included a few Puritans, a strong Catholic element, and a religious centre best described as made up of politique Anglicans. Thus there was little possibility of commitment

kept a household of eighty servants (Hassell Smith, *County and Court*, pp. 163 ff.). The Treshams, at Rushton, inherited a great house of the turn of the fifteenth and sixteenth centuries, built round three sides of a court, with an impressive great hall, rising to a hammer-beam roof (J. A. Gotch, *The Buildings of Sir Thomas Tresham* (London, 1883), pp. 10–12); and the Danvers house at Dauntsey, inherited from the Stradlings and Dauntseys, is likely to have been of the same sort, although all trace of it has now disappeared. If so, it would contrast with the courtier style of Longleat at the other side of the county. Sir Henry Bromley inherited Holt castle, another late-medieval house, which incorporated a massive square fortified vower (*V.C.H., Worcestershire*, iii, London, 1913, p. 401), purchased by his father.

69 For the literary tradition which denigrated sophisticated architecture in favour of antique simplicity, associating the latter with hospitality and traditional sociability, see William A. McClung, *The Country House in English Renaissance Poetry* (Los Angeles and London, 1977).

70 *State Trials*, i, p. 1353; *Cal. State Papers, Domestic, Eliz., 1598–1601*, p. 552; *ibid.*, p. 577.

71 Nash, *Worcestershire*, i, pp. 496 ff.

to a single, clear religious line. The Puritans were the weakest, and by 1601 were represented in the inner group only by Sir Henry Bromley of Holt castle in Worcestershire; who however was important because of his many connections with the City of London, and his acquaintance with Thomas Smythe, sheriff of London and supposedly a colonel of the City trained-bands.[72] By contrast, Catholics, both converts and those of recusant descent, were numerous. Thus of the seven present at, or in the secret of, the conference which, early in 1601, discussed the proposed Whitehall *coup d'état* against the court, four were Catholics (Davies, Danvers, Blount and John Lyttelton).[73] Amongst the wider following there were such moderate Catholics as the Northamptonshire Treshams, and the Yorkshire Cholmleys and Constables; but also such a dedicated ultramontane Catholic crusader as Robert Catesby, who would later finance the Gunpowder Plot.[74] What seems to have been characteristic of the broad centre however was an undogmatic religious approach with a stress on the social role of the church, particularly as expressing local solidarities and as reinforcing the traditional social hierarchy. This involved a preference for ritualistic over didactic religious forms, and therefore anti-Puritanism: the tone was Anglican, but with a touch of non-papalist crypto-Catholicism; perhaps a kind of Laudianism in the making.[75]

[72] For Bromley, see Hasler, *op. cit.*, i, p. 491, and *Dict. Nat. Biog.*, ii, pp. 1308 ff. His father, Lord Chancellor Bromley, had been recorder of London from 1566–9, and continued to live in the City till 1580. Sir Henry married, as his fourth wife, Anne Beswicke, daughter of a London alderman. He had achieved notoriety in the Parliament of 1593, when he and his fellow Worcestershire knight of the shire, William Walsh (another Essexian), were recruited by Richard Stephens (also with Puritan and Essexian connections, but who died in 1599) to support Peter Wentworth's scheme to bring the succession question before the house of commons (J. E. Neale, *Elizabeth I and her Parliaments, 1584–1601*, London, 1957, pp. 257 ff.). For Bromley's connection with Thomas Smythe, and his part in the revolt, see below, p. 451 and n. 128, this chapter.

[73] Of the four, Sir Christopher Blount had a chequered religious history, but had recently (while on service with Essex in Ireland) returned to his original Catholic beliefs; it was he who, at Dublin, converted Sir John Davies to Catholicism (Hasler, *op. cit.*, i, p. 466; *Cal. State Papers, Domestic, Eliz., 1598–1601*, p. 547). Sir Charles Danvers's Catholicism was revealed by Sir John Davies during his examination (*ibid.*, p. 581).

[74] See n. 36 and n. 38 above, this chapter.

[75] The religious approach of the Essexian centre may be illustrated by the case of the Danvers family: on the one hand anti-Puritan, and with Catholic sympathies; but on the other insisting that the church bells be rung in Dauntsey and the other

However, as said above, the lack of a strong, unifying religious commitment did tend to strengthen the centrality of primal honour, without any religious top-dressing, as the characteristic ideological orientation of the group. Of course, this in turn pointed towards the secular, politic, and Tacitean formulation of these attitudes undertaken by the intellectuals in the ambience of Essex House, of whose work Hayward's *First Part* was an outstanding instance. The scholars, writers, and dramatists who had attached themselves to the earl's circle, naturally presented the image of honour in a sophisticated and glamourized way which was remote from that of the shire Essexians. Thus the ex-Oxford professor Henry Cuffe, one of the earl's secretaries, aimed at a revival of honour through its alliance with letters, in the sense of Tacitean and humanistic scholarship, with a view to a martial society in which, as he put it, "learning and valour would have the pre-eminence".[76] In this aspiration Cuffe and his like were ably seconded by the Essexian dramatists and poets. In particular, there was George Chapman, who also aimed at a revival of honour and heroic virtue, to be effected however, he hoped, by the dissemination of his translation of Homer into English, which was then in progress. Chapman dedicated the first instalment of his *Iliad* in 1598 to Essex, describing him as "most true Achilles, whom by sacred prophecy Homer did but prefigure", and adjuring him not to allow "the peasant-common politics of the world" to divert him from "perseverance in god-like pursuit of eternity".[77] Samuel Daniel saw Essex in similar terms, and as destined to lead the chivalry of Europe in a renewed crusade against the infidel.[78] The writers and intellectuals were building up Essex into the image of the baroque charismatic hero, heightening the hopes and expectations which centred on him. It is not surprising that the French ambassador should have commented at this time that the earl was "a man of great designs, hoping to attain glory by arms, and to win renown more and more", adding that "He . . . nowise contents himself with a petty fortune, and aspires to great-

parishes where they had lands to celebrate the pardon of Sir Charles and Sir Henry Danvers, to "the great disgrace of their adversaries . . . " (Hasler, *op. cit.*, i, p. 14).

[76] *Cal. State Papers, Domestic, Eliz., 1601–3*, p. 15.

[77] See *Chapman's Homer*, ed. by Allardyce Nicoll, 2 vols. (London, 1957), ii, p. 504.

[78] Joan Rees, *Samuel Daniel: A Critical and Biographical Study* (Liverpool, 1964), pp. 125 ff.

ness."[79] "An aspiring mind to wished honour", Yelverton commented at his trial, "is like the crocodile, which is ever growing as long as he liveth."[80] With his sense of his own destiny to serve his country and achieve renown in his noble and heroic calling, Essex found it increasingly impossible to confront the possibility of failure; or to practise the virtue of religious patience, which Sidney had taught should moderate the aspiring self-assertiveness of honour.[81] However, if we take the total spectrum of politique religion, recusancy, and secular, humanistic aspiration in the earl's circle, we can see how the charge that Essex had "none but Papists, Recusants, and Atheists for his adjutors", in the same way "as Cataline entertained the most seditious persons about all Rome to join him in his conspiracy", could be made to stick.[82]

Such then was the nature of the support, and the kind of motivation, which informed the earl's circle and attracted support for the Essex cause. But the outcome was an inadequate basis for a dissident movement: both in respect of the material force which could be mobilized; and because of the inner weaknesses and inconsistencies which undermined honour as a motivating ideology. From a material point of view, the faction could not, from its own resources, provide the means by which the earl's enemies could be dislodged from power, and his own favour with the queen restored.[83] As already seen, there was no great landed connection, centred on Essex himself, which might have been made the basis of some "neo-feudal" rising; in any case an absurdly archaic option in the military conditions of the late sixteenth century.[84] Nor even in counties where the Essexians were strongly represented was a regional rising based on the militia a feasible alternative. Apart

[79] *A Journal of All that was Accomplished by Monsieur de Mausse, Ambassador in England from King Henry IV to Queen Elizabeth, A.D. 1597*, trans. by G. B. Harrison (London, 1931), pp. 7, 16.

[80] *State Trials*, i, p. 1337.

[81] See above, pp. 387 ff.

[82] *State Trials*, i, *loc. cit.*

[83] For the factional tensions at the Elizabethan court during the queen's declining years, and for Essex's difficulties, see J. Hurstfield, "The Succession Struggle in Late Elizabethan England", in J. Hurstfield, *Freedom, Corruption, and Government in Elizabethan England* (London, 1973), pp. 104 ff.

[84] Even Wales was seen, by the sophisticated planners amongst the faction, more as a possible place of flight and refuge than as a potential field for a regional revolt. See *Correspondence of King James VI of Scotland with Sir Robert Cecil and Others . . .*, ed. John Bruce, Camden Soc., London, 1860, pp. 100–1, 108.

from Essex himself,[85] the faction had no lord lieutenant in its ranks; and without a mandate from the relevant lieutenancy the militia regiments could not be mobilized without obvious treasonable intent, so arousing resistance. Nor was this attempted. Significantly enough, Essex and his associates never seriously considered a regional rebellion; for London was the controlling centre where power must be seized and the whole game played out. Essex therefore resisted advice that he should flee to France or to Wales, where his friends would protect him.[86] Thus, when the earl began to give serious consideration to the use of force as the only solution to the political problem of the apparent monopoly of favour extended by the queen to his enemies, he and his advisers fixed on three ways in which force might be applied, none of which depended on local resources or regional risings. Firstly, there was the possibility of a military revolt; secondly, of a court *coup d'état*; thirdly, a rising in the City of London, based on the earl's supposed popularity there, and the support he was presumed to possess amongst the London élite.

Each of these options reveal the tensions and contradictions in which the faction and its leader were increasingly involved. The first possibility, that of a military revolt, had a distinct plausibility. As already seen, the earl's military commands, particularly that of the army of Ireland, had provided his clientele with the organizational structure it would have otherwise lacked. In his military commands Essex was able to fit his followers into military offices, and through his conferment of knighthood also into a structure of honour which centred on himself. Military command also placed at the earl's disposal an articulation of resources and force far more effective than anything his followers could mobilize in their countries. Indeed, in the circumstances of the late sixteenth century, the military revolt could be seen as the natural successor, as the recourse of dissident politicians, to the now out-dated regional and "feudal" rising of an earlier period. The armed affinity of seigneurial retainers, tenants, and servants had been displaced by the military apparatus of the monarchical state; but at the same time the army had been infiltrated by the military clienteles of the rival court factions. For Nottingham and the Cecilians, as well as Essex, possessed, or aimed

[85] Who was lord lieutenant of Staffordshire.
[86] *Correspondence of King James VI*, p. 101.

to possess, a military following.[87] Thus the possibility of the resolution of political by armed conflict did exist.

Essex had in fact, during the last desperate weeks of his Irish lord lieutenancy, turned over in his mind the possibility of leading the army of Ireland on an invasion of Wales, to be followed by an advance on London. On this he had consulted in Dublin with his step-father, Sir Christopher Blount, and the earl of Southampton; but their advice had been unfavourable, and the project abandoned.[88] Later, after his return to London, and when in the deepest and apparently irremediable disfavour, the earl had tried again; this time to persuade his friend Lord Mountjoy, who had succeeded him in the government of Ireland, to attempt a similar invasion. This Mountjoy was prepared seriously to consider; but only on condition that material and moral support should be forthcoming from the hoped-for successor to the English throne, James VI.[89] When it became clear that James was not prepared to commit himself, except possibly in response to some initiative taken within England itself, whether by Essex or another, once again the idea was given up.[90] It was revived towards the end of 1599 or early 1601, when at

[87] Amongst Essex's enemies, Cobham (Sir Robert Cecil's brother-in-law), as warden of the Cinque Ports and lord lieutenant of Kent; Sir Walter Raleigh, as lord lieutenant of Cornwall and governor of Jersey; Nottingham, as lord admiral and lord lieutenant of Kent, controlled offices and commanded a repute sufficient to attract a military following, although in Cobham's case (who had little personal military standing) the key figure was his deputy lieutenant, Sir John Leveson, captain of Upnor castle (Hasler, *op. cit.*, ii, p. 464). According to John Chamberlain, when in August 1599 a great army was mobilized near London, with Nottingham as lord general, there were conjectures that the mobilization was intended "to show to some that are absent that others can be followed as well as they"; i.e. to demonstrate to Essex and his supporters, then in Ireland, that they did not command any monopoly of military force: *The Letters of John Chamberlain*, ed. Norman E. McClure (American Philosophical Society Memoirs, xii, pts. 1–11, 2 vols., Philadelphia, 1939), i, p. 83. The appointment, also in August 1599, of Lord Burghley, Cecil's elder brother, as president of the Council to the North, with instructions to train and re-equip the northern shire levies, while purging the officer corps of recusants and supporters of foreign princes (Essexians were liable to be recusants and/or sympathizers of James VI's claims to the English succession), strengthened the Cecilian military connection. See *Cal. State Papers, Domestic, Eliz., 1598–1601*, pp. 275–6; R. R. Reid, *The King's Council in the North* (London, 1921), pp. 275–6. Burghley subsequently was prominently involved in the suppression of Essex's revolt. So was Cobham's deputy, Sir John Leveson, who, "coming from the house of Lord Cobham", repelled the attempt of Essex's men to force their way through Ludgate (*Hatf. MSS.*, xi, p. 59).

[88] *Correspondence of King James VI*, p. 107 ff.

[89] *Ibid.*, pp. 96 ff.

[90] *Ibid.*, pp. 103–4.

the nadir of his fortunes Essex sent Southampton and later Sir Charles Danvers over to Ireland in order that Mountjoy should once more be consulted. As far as the invasion was concerned, Mountjoy now "utterly rejected it, as a thing he could no way think honest"; but he did agree that, if Essex should take any initiative, he would send a letter "wherein he should complain of the ill government of the state, and to wishe that some course mought be taken to remove from about Her Majesty's person those that were bad instrumentes", which the earl could show the queen should he secure access to her presence. He also undertook that "if any there (in Ireland) of his followers would goe over, he would not hinder them".[91] At the same time, a secret communication with James VI established that the king was willing to send to London an ambassador who would be available to support by diplomatic means any initiative taken by Essex.[92] Thus the earl could not raise support for a military revolt from his own followers, or from Ireland, or from Scotland. Moreover, both Mountjoy and James had pushed the initiative back on to Essex himself. They would move only in response to a revolution in London. Thus the earl and his advisers were forced back on to the other alternatives which were under consideration: the court *coup d'état* or the London rising; or a combination of both.

But the project of a military revolt had already revealed signs of divided minds and moral disarray in the ranks of the Essexians. In the first place, an invasion of the queen's realm implied treason, in the clearest and most obviously inexcusable sense, which nobody could mistake. Thus the Essexians, and particularly those immediately involved in the consultations, like Blount, Southampton, Mountjoy, and Danvers, were suddenly confronted by a shocking change in the image of their leader. The charismatic Essex, the preeminently successful courtier who could be relied on, by his mysterious hold over the queen, always sooner or later to seize Fortune's forelock and turn failure into success, now appeared in a different light: that of the desperate man who saw treason as the only recourse. Thus these courtiers, whose careers or whose family fortunes had been made in the Tudor service, were now being asked to join in a game of a very different sort. Moreover, while the bonds of "friendship", and the "union of minds and hearts" bound them in

[91] *Ibid.*, pp. 89, 98.

[92] *Ibid.*, pp. 85–90, 100.

honour to Essex, yet honour also raised the issue of "faithfulness" to the queen. For treason, so clearly proposed in the invasion project, constituted in terms of honour a "blot" with which no honourable lineage would wish to be stained. Thus it was precisely in these terms that Blount declared against the invasion; it was, he said, "a matter most foul, because he [Essex] was not only held a patron of his country . . . but also should have laid upon himself an irrecoverable blot, having been so deeply bound to Her Majesty". For Mountjoy, an invasion would not be "honestı", and therefore also not honourable.[93] Thus the appeal to honour, as conferring moral coherence and a motive for action on an excluded political group, revealed a contradiction within honour itself. For, as the leaders of a court faction, Southampton, Blount, Mountjoy, Essex himself were all inseparable from the court: their influence, their resources, their mode of wielding political power, their capacity to translate aspiration into the pattern of a career, even their inherited status, were all unthinkable apart from the organs of the monarchical state, and the loyalties which the latter imposed. For them the source of honour could no longer be conceived as inherent in locally orientated communities of honour centring on a lord, after the older medieval pattern. For their experience of honour was of that dispensed by the state, with the queen as its source. How then could honour subsist apart from her, still less against her? Thus the invasion project already revealed, in the simplest terms, a lesion in the self-image of the group, which was both dissident and conformist, and one which honour could not resolve.

Nor was Essex himself exempt from the divided mind and uncertain purpose. After all, as would be pointed out at his trial, he owed everything to the queen and her predecessors. The Devereux family derived their status and fortune from the rewards of service to the Tudor state: for over a century they had been courtiers. Essex's father, Walter the first earl, had been designated a paradigm of nobility and honour by the queen herself. Although she had abandoned him in Ireland, where she allowed him to ruin himself and his family in her service, Earl Walter had died an edifying Protestant death which was widely publicized as a model of religious patience and of providentialist obedience to the prince.[94] Essex had aspired

[93] *Ibid.*, pp. 108, 97.
[94] On Earl Walter, see Devereux, *Lives and Letters of the Devereux*, i, pp. 11 ff., and Lloyd, "The Essex Inheritance", *loc. cit.*

to follow in his footsteps, and had intermittently sought to practise his father's patience and resignation. Yet his relationship to the queen nevertheless became progressively charged with a tension which contained the seeds of violence. The tension, rooted in political failure and exclusion, was related to his view of their respective sexual roles, and the language in which this was expressed, which was not that of providentialist obedience, but came from the terminology of honour.

In terms of honour, Essex could admit the legitimacy of female rule in the case of women designated by lineage to be queens or princesses. In this respect the honour culture was perhaps rather more tolerant than the learned and scientific, with its mainly Aristotelian premisses.[95] Nevertheless, even in terms of honour there remained a certain unnaturalness, even absurdity, in a female magistracy. For a woman's nature could only partially and imperfectly embody the spectrum of virtues appropriate to a prince. Female rule could be expected to be strong in humility, mildness, and courtesy, all princely qualities which were natural to women; but also lacking in courage, open-handedness, and constancy of fixed purpose, these being male, not female, characteristics.[96] Essex tended to see the queen's exercise of her royal power in these terms, and therefore as characterized, on the negative side, by hesitation,

[95] Learned opinion was agreed that "Nature and convention, divine and human law, all predispose man, rather than woman, to govern, and if woman is to be involved in public life, it should only be in an emergency or because the woman in question possesses outstanding qualities of leadership": Ian Maclean, *The Renaissance Notion of Woman* (Cambridge, 1970), p. 60. In terms of honour, women whose lineage and rank place them in positions of authority, could rightly and might effectively rule; their power deriving in these cases however not from their sexuality, but simply from their status (J. Pitt-Rivers, "Honour and Social Status in Andalusia", in *The Fate of Schechem and the Politics of Sex* (Cambridge, 1977), p. 45. But the danger is always present that a woman's sexuality might adversely affect the way in which her authority is exercised.

[96] The qualities of the ideal female ruler, characterized by humility, mildness, and courtesy, may be found in the Princess Oriana, heroine of that sixteenth-century compendium of honourable styles of behaviour, the *Amadis de Gaule*. Oriana inspired her people to trust and devotion because "she was so humble, wise, and debonaire, that by her humility and courtesy, she knew how to steale the heartie affections of everyone" (John O. O'Connor, *Amadis de Gaule and its Influence on Elizabethan Literature* (New Brunswick, 1970), p. 77). In the Tudor chivalric cult, Oriana was one of the names given Elizabeth (R. C. Strong, "Queen Elizabeth I as Oriana", in *Studies in the Renaissance*, vi, pp. 251 ff.). It was no doubt these canons that Essex considered the queen had violated when, in the course of the "great quarrel", she struck him at the Council board.

inconstancy, timidity, and avarice; qualities which all tended to preclude great designs, particularly in foreign affairs, such as his own frustrated policy of a Protestant and anti-Spanish European coalition. These were the characteristic failings of the English court, Essex told de Mausse the French ambassador, and they proceeded "chiefly from the sex of the Queen".[97]

An attempt could be made to resolve this tension between the male self-assertiveness of honour, and the fact of female rule by translating the latter into the terminology of courtly love. In this way, the queen's sovereignty became that of beauty, which compelled not by princely command, but by the mild dominion of female affectivity over the male nature. Throughout his career Essex used this language to express his relationship to the queen, telling her "I do confess that, as a man, I have been more subject to your natural beauty, than as a subject to the power of a king . . . ". Needless to say, the terms had a political, not any amorous, correlation: they were used to signify devotion on the earl's part, and a hoped-for constancy in her favour on the queen's.[98] Nevertheless, Essex never wavered in the conviction that, when important decisions had to be made, the weaknesses of the queen's femininity must be overwhelmed by a rough masculine initiative, as when he told her " . . . my desires do triumph when I seem to myself, in a strong imagination, to conquer your resisting will".[99] To the end, Essex remained convinced that he had only to bring about a personal confrontation with the queen in order to get his own way. Hence his unauthorized return from Ireland in September 1599 in order to

[97] de Mausse, *A Journal* . . . , p. 114.

[98] Many of these letters, in spite of their "amorous" and high-flown phraseology, were in fact the work of Essex's secretaries. Typical uses of the language to express the earl's devotion in the queen's service, and appeals on his part for the first place in her favour, are: " . . . another in my absence would rob me of your gracious and dearest favour . . . I do conjure you, by your own worth, to be constant to him who will, for your Majesty's favour, forsake himself and the whole world besides" (Devereux, *op. cit.*, i, pp. 222, 249). From about the time of the Cadiz expedition, however, terms of humility, obedience, and feudal subordination alternate with the vocabulary of courtly love. Essex speaks of himself as "Your Majesty's humblest and most affectionate vassal", or simply "your poor servant"; no doubt in response to those of his advisers, like Francis Bacon, who recommended approaches of greater humility to the queen. Essex however scarcely ever uses religious and providentialist terms in his approaches to the queen.

[99] Devereux, *op. cit.*, i, p. 339.

force his way into the queen's presence and justify himself; hence too the form which his revolt was initially planned to assume, which was to secure the court, and so his access to the queen.[100] But this role was not one which Elizabeth was prepared to assume, and her response was that she would "pull down his great heart". The so-called "great quarrel" of July 1598, the point of no return in relations between Essex and the queen, generated so much bitterness precisely because of the earl's assessment of their respective sexual roles in terms of honour. For by striking him in the course of a Council meeting at which he had rudely turned his back on her, the queen had shown an unnatural male aggressiveness, and had thus submitted Essex to the unbearable dishonour which a publicly administered woman's blow involved.[101] He told her it was "an intolerable wrong", done he said "against the honour of your sex", whose nature precluded violence. He himself replied with a violent gesture, clapping his hand to his sword, and equally violent words, till the other councillors separated them.[102]

On this occasion Lord Keeper Egerton, a friend of Essex, urged upon him his duty of a submission, in patience, to the queen's divinely constituted authority, whose religious nature transcended both sex and honour. But the earl's reply was that obedience could not be demanded beyond the bounds of honour, for "I owe Her majesty the duty of an earl and lord marshal . . . but I can never serve as a slave or villein."[103] And in words which would reverberate into the seventeenth century, he repudiated a religious submission: "What, cannot princes err? Cannot subjects receive wrong? Is an earthly power infinite?"[104] Thus, from within the terms of arms and honour with which he primarily identified himself, Essex could not submit to the unconditional quality implicit in a religious obedience, or say with William Barlow, "he which denieth his duty to the visible God, his Prince and Sovereign, cannot perform his duty to God

[100] See for example Southampton's statement at the trial, that the objective was "the securing of my Lord of Essex's free access to the Queen" (D. Jardine, *Criminal Trials*, 2 vols. (London, 1832–3), i, pp. 335–6), and Essex's to the same effect, that he aimed to "serve my countrie and sovereigne, by making Her Majestie understand us, which we could not do for the potency of our enemyes, that were about her" (*Farmer Chetham MS.*, p. 22).

[101] Camden, *Historie of Elizabeth*, p. 126.

[102] Devereux, *op. cit.*, i, pp. 493–4.

[103] Birch, *Memoirs of the Reign of Queen Elizabeth*, ii, p. 386.

[104] *Ibid.*

invisible".[105] We see therefore the point of the queen's remark to Lambard: "he that will forget God, will also forget his benefactors",[106] and Barlow's "certainly, a mind inclined to rebellion was never well professed of religion".[107] The importance of religion, in the sense of the state providentialist cult, was that it provided a language in terms of which arms and honour could be incorporated, with letters and law, into the body of the realm, in obedience to its head. As far as Essex was concerned, the option of violence remained open, was considered in connection with the invasion project, and became inevitable when, towards the end of 1600, the queen refused to renew his farm of sweet wines, so condemning him to poverty, with its implication of political and social extinction, "forsaken by his friends", as Camden put it, "and held in scorne, triumphed over by his enemies".[108]

With the project of a military revolt therefore abandoned, the two alternatives, of the court coup or the London rising, came into the forefront. As far as the court coup was concerned, the proposal was that the palace of Whitehall should be occupied by an élite of Essexian swordsmen, led by close associates of the earl. The guards were to be disarmed, and their captain (who was Essex's enemy Sir Walter Raleigh) arrested, together with a number of councillors. Once the palace had been secured, Essex was to appear, and proceed in the company of a delegation of Essexian peers, to the queen's presence, there to tender a petition. This set out his own grievances, and those of the realm. A Parliament was to be called, the succession was to be assured to James VI, and the enemies of the realm were to be given a fair trial.[109] The Whitehall coup as thus conceived had two points to commend it. Firstly, it could be undertaken out of the resources Essex had immediately at his disposal in London; and, secondly, there was an avoidance of the direct implication of treason raised by the invasion project. The coup intended no harm or disrespect to the queen, but merely to secure for Essex access to her presence, from which he had been unjustly barred by his enemies.[110]

[105] Barlow, *A Sermon*, sig. b.3^{v}.
[106] Nichols, *Progresses and Public Processions of Queen Elizabeth*, iii, pp. 552–3.
[107] Barlow, *ibid.*
[108] *Op. cit.*, p. 170.
[109] *Hatf. MSS.*, xi, p. 69; *Cal. State Papers, Domestic, Eliz., 1598–1601*, pp. 577, 579, 581.
[110] Jardine, *op. cit.*, i, p. 363; *Farmer Chetham MS.*, p. 22.

But this project too revealed divided minds, torn by doubts and hesitations, which eventually made it impossible to put into effect. A new development was that the circle of the earl's close associates and advisers now began to polarize into two groups. On the one hand a party of activists shaped itself, a leading influence amongst them being the earl's confidential secretary Henry Cuffe, an intellectual who was one of the Taciteans and a former professor of Greek. But also identifiable as belonging to the group are the earl's sister, Penelope Rich, and his close friend the earl of Southampton. These emphasized the earl's heroic charisma, and, as Naunton said, "blew the coals of his ambition, and infused him too much with the spirit of glory", insisting that his honour required him to act before it was too late.[111] Cuffe, particularly, asserted that Essex had already shown himself too submissive to his enemies, so incurring the charge that, in Hayward's phrase, he preferred "abject and base safety, to hazard with honour"; and affirmed that the earl could recover his repute only "by attempting something worthy himself . . . by delivering his friends from servitude, and the kingdom".[112] The activists were particularly intent on breaking the mood of religious submission in patience to which Essex was intermittently inclined in the late months of 1600 and early in the new year. Cuffe told him that "his friends said that he had lost all his courage with praying, and hearing of sermons, and was now become a coward". Penelope Rich took the same line, telling the earl that he had lost all his valour.[113]

But, on the other hand, there were the exponents of caution, doubt, and hesitation; and when early in February 1601 the coup project was considered at a conference held at Essex House, it was these who carried the day. Sir Ferdinando Gorges, stirred, so he later said, to horror at the very idea of a coup, opposed it because he thought the resistance encountered would be too great. The conference could reach no decision, and everything had to be referred back to Essex. Raised again on the night before the revolt, the coup project was once more rejected on Gorges's recommendation, on the grounds of information, probably untrue, that the queen's

111 Sir Robert Naunton, *Fragmenta Regalia* (London, 1870), p. 54.

112 Camden, *op. cit.*, p. 170; on Henry Cuffe, see *Dict. Nat. Biog.*, v, pp. 272 ff.

113 Camden, *op. cit.*, p. 169; G. Goodman, *The Court of James I*, ed. J. S. Brewer, 2 vols. (London, 1839), ii, pp. 16 ff.

guards had been doubled.[114] As a result, the coup lost its main chance of success, for, according to the newswriter Vincent Hussey, had Essex "gone straight to the Court, he would have surprised it unprovided of defence, and full of his own well-wishers", an opinion which is supported by the hasty and improvised defensive measures adopted on the day of the revolt.[115] Gorges had probably already decided to leave the sinking ship he would subsequently desert. After the revolt he confessed, gave evidence against Essex at his trial, and was let off with no more than a few months' imprisonment.[116] The moral disintegration of the group, which would become evident after the revolt, had already begun.

There remained therefore the third option, the project of the City. Amongst his friends, Essex persistently affirmed that he had powerful friends in the ranks of the London élite, and that these included the wealthy merchant Thomas Smythe, of Puritan inclination, who was sheriff of London. Essex claimed that Smythe was also a colonel of the City trained-bands, with a thousand men, which he was ready to place at the earl's disposition.[117] But there was also the latter's conviction that he enjoyed a special standing with the people of London, whose affection for him was such that his mere appearance in distress in their midst, his life supposedly threatened by his enemies, would produce a rising in his favour. The theme of "popularity" had long been a prominent one in Essex's career. It had its basis in the enthusiasm aroused, particularly in London, by his military exploits and role as the Protestant champion. Essex could respond with condescension, charm, and courtesy to the plaudits of crowds; and his reputation for chivalry and high lineage owed much to the literature of chivalric romance,

[114] *Cal. State Papers, Domestic, Eliz., 1598–1601*, pp. 577–8.

[115] *Cal. State Papers, Domestic, Eliz., 1598–1601*, p. 351; *Acts of the Privy Council, 1600–1*, pp. 147 ff.

[116] Sir Ferdinando Gorges, on the day of the revolt, first released the hostages left by the earl at Essex House, then accompanied them to the court, thus becoming the first of the rebel Essexians to make contact with the government. Either he or Sir John Davies was the first to make a confession revealing all the details of the plan to seize Whitehall; so cracking the moral front of the imprisoned Essexians, and preparing the way for the spate of other confessions which followed. For Gorges's recommendation to abandon the coup, see the reference at n. 114 above, this chapter. Gorges was not brought to trial, and no fine appears against his name in the list of those fined in *Hatf. MSS.*, xi, p. 214.

[117] *Cal. State Papers, Domestic, Eliz., 1598–1601*, pp. 577–8; *Hatf. MSS.*, xi, p. 48; Camden, *op. cit.*, p. 174.

which circulated amongst the London populace in ballad chap-book, and other forms.[118] In addition, there was the more sophisticated theme of the Stoical and Plutarchian hero, who was also the idol of the people, which appealed to the Tacitean intellectuals, but was also more widely known through the popular theatre, where Shakespeare once found it worth his while to compare the earl's repute in London with that of Henry V.[119] There were also modern examples of the sway of aristocratic leaders over crowds and capitals, like that of the duke of Guise in Paris.[120] Francis Bacon had told Essex that his "popular reputation" was "one of the flowers of his greatness"; and that while "popularity" needed to be "handled tenderly", because of the queen's distrust of it, Bacon nevertheless advised the earl "to go on with your honourable commonwealth courses, as you do", that is, unobtrusively to continue his courtship of the people.[121] It was a theme which obviously generated large hopes, and also bred illusions. The means Essex adopted, after his return from Ireland and release from confinement, to follow Bacon's recommendation, consisted of a patronage of City Puritan clergy, whose preachings attracted large crowds to Essex House, which was made available for this purpose.[122] Essex therefore based

[118] Louis B. Wright, *Middle-Class Culture in Elizabethan England* (Chapel Hill, 1935), pp. 375 ff.; Ronald S. Crane, *The Vogue of Medieval Chivalric Romance during the English Renaissance* (Menasha, Wisconsin, 1919), pp. 13 ff.

[119] *Henry V*, Act v, Chorus, ll. 30–4.

[120] To which Francis Bacon referred in the course of Essex's trials: *State Trials*, i, p. 1355.

[121] Devereux, *op. cit.*, i, p. 396.

[122] H. Foley, *Records of the English Province of the Society of Jesus*, 7 vols. (London, 1877–84), i, pp. 7–8; P. Collinson, *The Elizabethan Puritan Movement* (London, 1967), pp. 444 ff. Essex's links with the London Puritans seem to have been maintained largely through the King's College, Cambridge network to which a number of his household belonged. Essex's chaplain, Anthony Wotton, lecturer at All Hallow's, Barking, had been a pupil at King's of William Temple, one of the earl's secretaries, who, like Wotton, had been a fellow of King's; Giles Fletcher, another former fellow of King's, and City Remembrancer, of Puritan affiliation, was a friend of Temple's, and had been a client of the earl. Through his religious interests and involvement through his office in City business, he also knew sheriff Thomas Smythe. See *Dict. Nat. Biog.*, xxi, p. 961; vii, p. 299; xix, p. 520. Stephen Egerton, Minister of St Anane's, Blackfriars, was another City Puritan who had a long acquaintance with the Essex faction, through Richard Stephens and Sir Henry Bromley, the latter another acquaintance of Smythe's. In 1598, when Egerton had been cited by Bancroft for nonconformity, Essex had intervened on his behalf. See *Dict. Nat. Biog.*, vi, p. 578; Hasler, *The History of Parliament*, iii, p. 444; *Hatf. MSS.*, xi, p. 154. Egerton was one of several London clergy in trouble for prayers or sermons favouring Essex, the group including

his hopes on two elements in the City: his supposed friends amongst the élite, and the people. Both in the outcome were to fail him.

The form of Essex's entry into London is perhaps clearer than its ultimate purpose, which may have been to use the City both as a base, and to mediate between himself and the court. The entry was not, at any rate in intention, a forcible fray or incursion, for the citizens were supposedly friends; rather it was to be an impressive, but peaceful, demonstration on the part of the earl and his friends, who apart from side-arms and a few pistols were not equipped for any military action. In front walked Essex, with half-a-dozen noblemen friends, earls or barons; behind them, over a hundred gentlemen with servants and followers, some of them heads of important families. The object was to dazzle the citizens with an impressive display of "the flower of the nobility and gentry of England", gathered round their natural leader, the high-born earl marshal, who was also the heroic Protestant champion. Undoubtedly, in his conception of his own role, Essex placed great emphasis on his office of earl marshal, which made him, as it were, the guardian and overseer of honour.[123] As earl marshal, Essex advanced to his encounter with the citizens as representing honour.[124] In addition, he thought that the office gave him warrant to reform the state, and probably also to judge his enemies, using the summary jurisdiction of a court of chivalry.[125] In the meanwhile, the immediate objective

Wotton, David Roberts of St Andrew by the Wardrobe, and Edward Phillips, preacher at St Saviour's, Southwark (*Cal. State Papers, Domestic, Eliz., 1598–1601*, p. 375; Collinson, *op. cit.*, p. 447).

123 Cf. the earl of Arundel's view (which was probably also that of Essex) that the earl marshal's office (to which he was appointed in 1621) involved the duty "to support ancient nobility and gentry, and to interpose on their behalfs" (B. Manning, "The Aristocracy and the Downfall of Charles I", in *Politics, Religion, and the Civil War*, ed. B. Manning (London, 1973), p. 41).

124 Like Arundel, Essex as earl marshal saw himself as personifying "the interests of the old aristocracy, and the values of honour and nobility" (K. Sharpe, "The Earl of Arundel, his Circle, and the Opposition to the Duke of Buckingham", in *Faction and Parliament: Essays in Early Stuart History*, ed. K. Sharpe (Oxford, 1978), p. 242).

125 When, during Essex's imprisonment in the Tower after the revolt, the dean of Norwich, Thomas Dove, asked him what his warrant had been to seek to "remove such evils, as the commonwealth is burthened with", and to show his authority, the earl replied "that he was earl marshal of England, and needed no other warrant" (Barlow, *op. cit.*, quoted in Birch, *Memoirs of the Reign of Queen Elizabeth*, ii, p. 475). For the summary jurisdiction of courts of chivalry, presided over by the constable and his deputy the marshal, see J. G. Bellamy, *The Law of Treason in the Later Middle Ages* (Cambridge, 1970), pp. 158 ff. Since the

was the house of a Sheriff Smythe, who was expected to stiffen the demonstration with a reinforcement of men and arms.

As the procession, setting out from Essex House in the Strand, advanced through Ludgate into the City, Essex shouted that his life was endangered by his enemies, and that the realm was sold to the Spaniard. He added "God save the Queen", and called on the citizens to bring arms and join him for his protection. But there was no motion to do so. Crowds gathered in the streets to view the spectacle, but the reaction was one of bewilderment and incomprehension.[126] Essex went straight to Thomas Smythe's house in Gracechurch Street, confronted him, and tried to induce him to supply the arms and raise the men he had supposedly promised. Again the response was one of bewilderment and evasion. Eventually, Smythe escaped, to join the lord mayor who was organizing resistance.[127] The earl's expectations of him had no better basis than a tissue of illusions and misunderstandings, mainly inculcated and encouraged by Sir Henry Bromley, probably on the instigation of Penelope Rich, who was so eager to goad her brother into action and end his evasions and delays.[128] In despair Essex now tried to force his way

Constable's office had been vacant since the death of the earl of Derby in 1504, the earl marshal, as his deputy, could claim the exercise of his powers and functions in this (as in other) respects. The legitimacy of the claim to do so was recognized by the Privy Council in favour of Earl Marshal Arundel in 1622: Sharpe, *loc. cit.*, p. 218.

126 Camden, *op. cit.*, pp. 176 ff.

127 *Cal. State Papers, Domestic, Eliz., 1598–1601*, pp. 558, 559, 560; *ibid.*, *1601–3*, pp. 3, 26.

128 Essex derived his faith in Sheriff Smythe simply from "other men's speeches" (Camden, *op. cit.*, p. 174), which convinced him that Smythe, "who had command of a thousand soldiers, would assist him upon all occasions" (*ibid.*). In fact, the "command" was no more than the captaincy of Bishopgate and Broad Street Ward trained band, which had a strength of a hundred pikes and two hundred musketeers (see J. H. Leslie, "A Survey or Muster of the Armed and Trayned Companies in London, 1588 and 1599", in *Journal of the Society of Army Historical Research*, iv (1925), pp. 62 ff.). The "speeches" came from Sir Henry Bromley, who had many City contacts (see n. 72 above, this chapter), and knew Smythe through a relative by marriage, Sir John Scott, who was also Smythe's brother-in-law. Bromley, after a conference with Penelope Rich, at which the latter had informed him of Essex's supposed danger of arrest and fear of his life from his enemies, sent the earl a message from himself and Scott that Sheriff Smythe would be ready to do him service (*Cal. State Papers, Domestic, Eliz., 1601–3*, p. 4). This was the night before the revolt, and Essex instructed Bromley to go to Smythe's house with Scott, and wait for him there; but there is no indication that they did so. Essex took the message on trust, and himself had no contact with Smythe before the encounter in Gracechurch Street. If the message was

back through Ludgate into the Strand and to his house; there was a fight and casualties, and the Essexians were repelled. Abandoning Ludgate, they eventually made their way back by river to Essex House, which was soon surrounded by government forces and forced to surrender late in the evening.[129] The revolt was over.

What had caused the failure? It arose in the first place out of a mistaken assessment of the earl's public image, particularly as this was understood by Londoners. In the highly charged, military, aristocratic, and intellectual ambience of Essex House, with its Tacitean overtones, it was possible to conceive of a kind of electric contact between the "people" and their hero, leading to a spontaneous movement of sympathy and support. But, amongst the citizens, Essex was admired not so much as the baroque hero, his virtue inherent in his own inner quality, but as the Protestant hero, whose charisma was inseparable from his providential role within the body of the Protestant realm, as the queen's devoted councillor and valiant general. So Shakespeare had seen, as in the chorus of Henry V he gave expression to the Londoner's adulation of Essex, who had just departed for Ireland: "Were now the general of our gracious empress,/ As in good time he may, from Ireland coming,/ Bringing rebellion broached on his sword,/ How many would the peaceful city quit/ To welcome him."[130] It was as "the general of our gracious empress", that the earl's heroic image as the embodiment of lineage, arms and honour acquired validity in the eyes of the citizens. Essex had tried to save the image by his shouts of "God save the Queen"; but against the background of his increasingly dis-

prompted by Penelope Rich, eager to spur her brother to action by hearsay promises and illusory hopes, Essex's subsequent bitterness against her becomes more explicable. It seems that Essex was told that Smythe would move into action upon receipt of a message from the earl "to remember his promise, and send Mr Wotton to him" (*Cal. State Papers, Domestic, Eliz., 1598–1601*, p. 560); the message was not received till 2 p.m. on the day of the revolt. Essex also sent Smythe a copy of the petition he proposed to present to the queen, which did not reach him till the revolt was over (*Cal. State Papers, Domestic, Eliz., 1601–2*, p. 16). Smythe, who maintained that he had not spoken to the earl for nine years, was imprisoned and thoroughly interrogated, but no evidence could be found against him. Tobie Matthew reported that by the end of March 1601 he was already out of danger (*ibid.*, p. 19). No fine is set against his name in the list in *Hatf. MSS.*, xi, p. 214. Smythe appeared before the Council on 5 July 1601, with Sir Henry Neville, but, whereas Neville was fined £10,000, Smythe "had little said to him" (*ibid.*, p. 89). He was probably released shortly afterwards.

129 Camden, *op. cit.*, p. 177; *Hatf. MSS.*, xi, pp. 59 ff.

130 *Henry V*, *loc. cit.*

orderly and tumultuous progress nobody was convinced. The heroic glamour on which he had relied was soon dissipated when the news circulated that he had been proclaimed a traitor. One Londoner, hearing that Essex had entered the City with two or three hundred gentlemen, their rapiers in one hand and pistol in the other, remarked that "he marvelled that they could come in that sort in a civil government, and on a Sunday".[131] There was a sense of breach both of civil order and religious propriety.

Still more marked was the earl's misjudgement of the attitude of the City élite, amongst whom he claimed so many friends; and of what he could expect from that quarter. Their views were given succinct expression by the City remembrancer, Giles Fletcher, a former Essex client, who as a Puritan was one of the earl's favourers. He stated that the earl's attempt on London had been "both ungodly and seditious", as well as foolish, reverence for the queen and Council being a religious duty, and therefore required "for conscience sake". Essex, he said, had been well looked upon by many aldermen; yet they, "being faithful subjects, and careful of their estates", would never have allowed, still less joined, "in so desperate an attempt".[132] These were characteristic attitudes of the London ruling class, whose policies of conformity and obedience involved keeping clear of damaging commitments to the court factions. For the City, the Essexian role, however glamorously heroic, was firmly contained within the ordered and religious framework of the realm; outside that framework, he could have no status or standing except that of a traitor. Essex would later bitterly denounce the Londoners as "a base and cowardly people", incapable of response to the imperatives of honour, and lament that he trusted in their "plausibility"; later still, at the nadir of his disillusionment, he would say that "all popularity is vain".[133] But in the confrontation which had thus been engineered between the claims of honour and arms, and those of providential obedience, it was the emptiness of the former which had been conclusively established.

After the failure in London, the retreat to Essex House (to find that the hostages retained there had been set free by Gorges), and its surrender later in the day, the only decision left for Essex to take was how he was to die. There may have been a faint possibility of an

[131] *Cal. State Papers, Domestic, Eliz., 1601–3*, pp. 109–10.
[132] *Ibid.*, pp. 9–10.
[133] Barlow, *op. cit.*, sig. d.4.3^r.

acquittal in the "honourable and just trial" which had been promised him in the terms of surrender; and of the queen's mercy, in the far likelier event of a condemnation. But even before the surrender the earl seemed determined on his own death: "For as to my life", he told Sir Robert Sidney in the course of the surrender negotiations, "I hate it . . . Death will end all, and death will be welcome to me."[134] The kind of death he had in mind was that of the man of honour, defying Fortune by his fearless acceptance of his fate, and by his remarkable refusal to plead to the queen for mercy, in which he persisted until the very end. In addition, this same death, fearless and honourable in its defiance of Fate, was to be adorned by that complete faithfulness to friends and followers which was a central value of the honour code. He said that he had agreed to the surrender of Essex House, instead of dying sword in hand in its ruins, for their sake; and he took the whole responsibility for the revolt upon himself, requesting the lord admiral "to desire Her Majesty to inflict all the torments upon him that could be invented, for the punishment of the rest to be diminished".[135] At his trial, he defended himself with assiduity, but claimed indifference as the outcome, saying "I would not that I went about to save my life . . . That which I speak is rather in satisfaction of . . . the rest that are engaged with me."[136]

Moreover Essex denied that his honour had been stained by treason or rebellion. His plot to seize the court by the forcible occupation of Whitehall had been only a means of access to the queen, in order that he might prostrate himself at her feet, and open his grievances to her. His entry into the City had been merely in pursuit of a private feud, and to defend himself against his enemies, who sought his life, which by the law of nature he was entitled to do.[137] Two points of law were explained to him as establishing his guilt: firstly, that any subject putting himself in such strength within the realm that the monarch could not resist him, to compel the monarch to govern other than according to his own royal authority and discretion, was in manifest rebellion; secondly, that in every rebellion the law assumed as a consequence "the encompassing the death and deposition of the king, the law foreseeing that the rebel will never

[134] Bath *Longleat* MSS., Devereux Paper, p. 280.
[135] *Ibid.*, p. 281.
[136] *Farmer Chetham MS.*, p. 8.
[137] See above, p. 432.

suffer the king to live and reign, who might punish or take revenge of his treason or rebellion". But Essex's reply was that he was willing to be accounted "the law's traitor, and would die for it".[138] Not only did the earl's honour remain intact in his own eyes, but his boldness and steadfastness created a favourable public, the newswriter Chamberlain approvingly comparing his demeanour with that of the earl of Southampton, who "descended to entreaty, and . . . was somewhat too low and submiss, and too loath to die". Chamberlain added that, from the boldness of Essex's answers to his judges, "a man might easily perceive that he had ever lived popularly, as his chief care was to leave a good opinion in people's minds now at parting".[139] Essex's stance at his trial was intended to underwrite and confirm the traditional dissidence of honour which bound men of lineage and lordship to each other in the obligation to confront unworthy ministers, or even monarchs.[140] It was from this standpoint that the earl was able to reassure Archbishop Whitgift, soon after his arrest, "that the sincerity of my conscience, and the goodness of my cause, doth comfort me"; and later tell Dr Dove that in nothing he had done was he "guilty of offending Almighty God", adding that his warrant for reforming the realm proceeded from his status as earl marshal, and therefore as chief officer of the community of honour, the guardian of its values.[141] This then was the paradigm and political style Essex saw as his legacy in the future.

Yet within twenty-four hours of his condemnation, an extraordinary change of attitude had taken place. The earl underwent a violent revulsion, and repudiated almost all the positions he had taken up at his trial. The essence of the change was an abandonment of the canons of honour; and Essex now presented himself, no longer as the stoical death-defying hero, but as an abject penitent, condemned at the bar of providentialist religion, both in his own eyes and those of the world. He drew up a self-inculpatory confession, revealing details of, and admitting responsibility for, the proposed Whitehall *coup d'état*, which he prefaced with the words: " . . . God of his mercy hath opened my eyes, and made me see my sin, my offence, and so touched my heart as I hate it, both in myself and others". The confession went on to denounce the close

138 *State Trials*, i, pp. 1355–6. Cf. above, pp. 429–30.

139 *The Letters of John Chamberlain*, i, p. 120.

140 See above, p. 413.

141 See above, p. 450 n.

associates who had been involved in planning the revolt, naming Southampton, Danvers, Lyttelton, Davies, and Blount, whose guilt however had already been established by their own confessions.[142] But Essex also went on to inculpate others previously thought to have been only marginally, if at all, involved, like Henry Cuffe; Penelope Rich; the English ambassador to France, Sir Henry Neville; and his friends Lord Mountjoy and Lord Sandys. At his trial, Essex now said, he had maintained all falsehood.[143] The earl remained firmly committed to his changed attitude to the end, performing on the scaffold before his execution all the rituals of penitent self-abasement required by the providentialist religion in whose terms he had now determined to die.[144] Only in one respect did the earl's stance at his trial survive his volte-face: till the end he remained determined to die; and till the end he refused to plead for the queen's mercy, so removing the one hope of pardon.[145]

What motivated this extraordinary reversal? It is usually attributed to the influence of the earl's Puritan chaplain, Abdy Ashton, who seemed to have been his confidant in matters of religion, and whom he had asked to be with him in the Tower for his consolation. Ashton was able, so it is said, to play effectively upon the religious and Puritan side of Essex's nature, and on his fear of the divine judgement he must soon confront. This was no doubt so; as a condemned man, about to die, Essex knew that he had already

[142] The earl's confession has not survived, and only an abstract of it remains amongst the State Papers and the *Hatfield MSS.* (*Cal. State Papers, Domestic, Eliz., 1598–1601*, pp. 587–8; *Hatf. MSS.*, xi, p. 75). The original, four pages long, was shown to Henry Cuffe at his trial, and acknowledged by him to be in the earl's handwriting (*State Trials*, i, p. 1430). The content was summarized by Nottingham in his letter to Lord Mountjoy of 31 May 1601 (Goodman, *The Court of James I*, i, pp. 16 ff.), and by Sir Robert Cecil in his letter to Ralph Winwood of 7 March 1601 in *Memorials of State in the Reigns of Queen Elizabeth and James I . . . of Sir Ralph Winwood*, ed. Edmund Sawyer, 3 vols. (London, 1725), i, p. 301. The first sentence was quoted by Barlow, *op. cit.*, sig. d.1^{r}, who affirmed that the text of the confession was available for public inspection. See also Birch, *Memoirs of the Reign of Queen Elizabeth*, ii, pp. 477 ff.

[143] Camden, *op. cit.*, pp. 186–7; Goodman, *loc. cit.*; *Cal. State Papers, Domestic, Eliz., 1598–1601*, p. 588; Bacon, *Life and Letters*, ii, pp. 236 ff.

[144] For his execution and scaffold speeches, see *Cal. State Papers, Domestic, Eliz., 1598–1601*, pp. 590–6; *Hatf. MSS.*, xi, p. 83; Birch, *op. cit.*, pp. 481 ff.

[145] Camden, *op. cit.*, pp. 187–8. The earl's refusal to ask for mercy, chronicled by Camden, is confirmed by the Council's instruction that he was to be told, the night before his execution, that "as hitherto he has always owned himself most resolute and constant to die, so now he do prepare himself accordingly" (*Cal. State Papers, Domestic, Eliz., 1598–1601*, p. 591).

quitted the world of honour, and that his first priority was to prepare himself for the next world by a full confession of his sins. But the question remained open whether his honour-motivated initiative to what he had termed "my best to remove such evils as the commonwealth is burthened with" had involved him in sin, and therefore (since the sin would be publicly confessed) in dishonour, as well as in supposed breaches of the law.[146] The fact was however that Essex's abandonment of honour, and his decision to die a providentialist, not an honourable, death, has a social, as well as personal, dimension. For the honour community of which he had been the centre had already, by the end of his trial, disintegrated under the stresses of failure and the fear of death; as a result, the persisting tension within the group between the claims made on honour by loyalty both to the queen and to their leader had surfaced to the latter's disadvantage. Consequently, at his trial Essex was confronted by confessions already made by Gorges, Blount, Davies, and others, which revealed all the details of the plans to seize the court, enter London, and take the Tower.[147] The united front of the conspirators had been broken, and by the end of the proceedings Essex's bold stance in terms of honour had already acquired an aura of brazen falsehood and absurdity. His own disillusionment followed. He conceived himself betrayed by those who he had thought, "are engaged with me, and whose hearts are purely affected . . . ", for whom he had prepared himself to die.[148] He saw himself as forced by bad advice and appeals to his honour into a hopeless and badly planned insurrection; then abandoned by those who had been most vehement in its instigation. "A man's friends" he said "will fail him; all popularity and trust in men is vain, as I have had experience."[149]

[146] On the distinction between ethical wrong-doing and dishonour, see J. Pitt-Rivers, "Honour and Social Status", in *Honour and Shame*, ed. J. G. Peristiany (London, 1965), pp. 32 ff.

[147] For the confessions, see *Cal. State Papers, Domestic, Eliz., 1598–1601*, pp. 571 ff., *Hatf. MSS.*, xi, pp. 69 ff., and *State Trials*, ii, pp. 1344 ff.

[148] Essex's resentment against his associates received expression immediately after his trial, as he was leaving Westminster Hall: "Before he went out of the hall, when he saw himself condemned, and found that Sir John Davies, Sir Ferdinando Gorges, Sir Christopher Blount, and Sir Charles Danvers, had all confessed the conferences held at Drury House for surprising the Queen and the Tower of London, he broke out to divers gentlemen that attended him in the hall, that his confederates who had now accused him had been principal inciters of him, not he of them" (*Winwood's Memorials*, i, p. 301).

[149] Barlow, *A Sermon*, sig. d.4.3^{r}.

In his final collapse, and in the confessions and declarations which expressed it, Essex almost with deliberation violated all the canons of honour. By publicly admitting that he had spoken falsehood at his trial, he gave himself the lie, and so published his own dishonour; while at the same time failing to maintain the settled steadfastness of attitude, sustained until death once publicly assumed, which honour required. His denunciation of friends like Neville and Lord Mountjoy proved his own unfaithfulness, and so disqualified him for the leadership of a society of honourable men. Particularly discreditable was his betrayal of a dependant, his secretary Henry Cuffe, and his ascription to him of such a high politic act as his revolt, which his status required him to take upon himself. When the earl taxed Cuffe that "you were the principal man that moved me to this perfidiousness", the latter in his turn "taxed briefly and sharply the earl's inconstancy, in that he had betrayed those most devoted to him".[150] Thus Essex was exposed to the disgrace of having his dishonour thrown in his face by a servant. Even more shameful, in terms of honour, were the charges he made against his sister Penelope Rich, "who did continually urge me on", so showing that he was incapable of loyalty even to his own blood. The spectacle of apparent collapse made a deep impression. Observers were bewildered, friends nonplussed, and enemies overjoyed. Amongst the latter, Lord Admiral Nottingham asked Penelope's lover, Lord Mountjoy, "Would you have thought this weakness and unnaturalness in this man?".[151] A more detached onlooker commented on the "strangeness" of the whole action, how these "noble and resolute men, assured of one another by their undoubted valour, and combined together by firm oathe", fell to "plain confessions and accusations one of another, that they seemed to strive who should draw one another in deepest . . . in which the earl exceeded all other, to all men's wonders".[152]

The outcome of the revolt displayed the insufficiency of honour as a coherent articulation of attitudes, motives, and convictions in terms of which political dissent could any longer be effectively expressed: the brittleness of its ties, the implausibility of its pretensions, the divided loyalties to which its proponents were exposed all stood revealed. Honour could still make its appeal to a sector of the

[150] Camden, *op. cit.*, p. 187.
[151] Goodman, *loc. cit.*
[152] *Correspondence of King James VI*, pp. xix–xx.

ruling élite; particularly that involved with the military apparatus of the state. But honour could no longer claim the status of an autonomous political culture, dispensing with any secure anchorage in the law and providentialist religion, in terms of which shifts in the distribution of political power could be effected. The Essexian claim to a prescriptive warrant to "reform the commonwealth", based on lineage, faithfulness, arms, the appeal to heroic and aristocratic charisma, and to popularity, had achieved nothing beyond a political and moral collapse, which compelled Essex himself into a total self-repudiation. The earl's image as the paradigm of honour, the chivalric and Protestant hero, was successfully defaced; instead he appeared as the atheistic Cataline, allied to sinister and rootless elements in the state, intent on its destruction. As his chaplain Ashton is said to have told him, " . . . you have dishonoured God, shamed your profession, and pulled upon yourself many notes of infamy . . . all your show of religion was hypocrisy . . . you are in your heart either an atheist or papist, which doth plainly appear, in that all your instruments, followers, and favourers, were of this quality . . . ".[153] By the end of the sixteenth century, honour had become too firmly integrated into the structure of the monarchical state, under the queen, the fount of honour, for its terms to provide an effective idiom of dissent.

Yet the problem of political dissidence, and of its expression, remained; but the social and ideological development of the Tudor period had altered the terms in which this could be conceived. The case of the earl of Essex, the leader with a divided mind, who in the end repudiated his own past, reveals reflected in the mentality of an individual the kind of tension intrinsic to dissident politics[154] in

[153] William Camden, *Annales rerum anglicarum et hibernicarum regnante Elizabetha*, ed. Thomas Hearne, 3 vols. (London, 1717), iii, pp. 957 ff.

[154] It is surely still Essex's many-sided individuality, which found expression in his displays of political and personal inconsistency, which makes the strongest impression against the background of a world in which convention and conformity were the rule. Cf. E. P. Cheney, *History of England*, ii, p. 544: " . . . one would have a poor comprehension of the complex character of the Earl of Essex, if he failed to perceive that it included the devotee and the dreamer, as well as the soldier, the courtier, and something of the statesman . . . "; and Lytton Strachey, *Elizabeth and Essex*, p. 248: "He rushed from opposite to opposite; he allowed the strongest contradictions to take root together, and grow up side by side in his heart." Bacon, with his usual sharp insight, observed of Essex's death that so deep was his absorption in his own inner conflicts as he stood on the scaffold, that the occasion lacked the element of social support and self-identification by means

a political order which had come to have no place for it. For there could be none in a political culture whose stress was exclusively on the creation and watchful maintenance of wholeness: i.e. on the effective incorporation of the individual into the body of the realm, under its head the queen.[155] The desire and pursuit of the whole can be seen as a dominant theme of English sixteenth-century political aspiration. In its pursuit the Reformation had played its part. Catholicism had been rejected because of its supposed tendency to promote fissiparity, not unity. For the Catholic religious order had divided secular authority from religious authority, clergy from laity. The mass, so Protestant divines insisted, had become the preserve of a sacrificing priesthood; and as a result had become the sacrament of disunity, not unity. The Reformation had been intended to correct these defects. As a result of it, sacred and secular had become two aspects of a single realm, under one head, whose unity was articulated in terms of a single law; and the new Communion service would, it was hoped, "move and stir all men to friendship, love, and concord, and to put away all hatred, variance, and discord".[156] Parliament had much the same function. As recent writers have emphasized, there were powerful resistances to the emergence of the house of commons as a platform for adversary politics; and

of which those about to die (even by execution) consoled themselves: "For he never remembered wife, children, or friend, nor took particular leave of any that were present, but wholly abstracted and sequestered himself in a state of prayer" (*Declaration of the . . . Treasons Committed by Robert, Earl of Essex*, in Bacon, *Letters and Life*, ii, p. 285). Essex's disposition attuned him to the problem of multi-culturality, as manifested during the 1590s in the conflicting claims of rival religions, and of honour, law, and providentialist obedience, which heralded the breakdown of the Tudor conformist synthesis. It is significant that the date of *Hamlet* (mid-1599–late 1601), the classic statement of the problem of choice in a multi-cultural situation, with personal decision emerging out of the conflicting claims of honour, obedience, love, and providence, coincides with the years of Essex's eclipse and fall.

155 Cf. Hooker, I, iii, 5 (*The Laws of Ecclesiastical Polity*) in which he speaks of the law which governs men in their social nature as: "a law which bindeth them each to serve each other's good, and all to prefer the good of the whole before whatsoever their own particular". But the well-known inconsistencies in, and qualifications of, Hooker's argument illustrate the fissiparous tendencies within the political culture which, by the end of the century, made the argument for an unconditional conformity to the authority, and subjection to the power, of the social whole increasingly difficult to maintain. See e.g. Peter Munz, *The Place of Hooker in the History of Thought* (London, 1952).

156 Thomas Cranmer, *The True and Catholic Doctrine . . . of the Lord's Supper*, ed. H. Wace (London, 1907), p. 10.

Parliament was conceived primarily as a unifying institution.[157] All this was seen as standing under divine providential favour, which had been extended in a special sense, particularly since the Reformation, to England, and to the Tudor monarchs in so far as they conformed to the providential purpose.[158] Thus the political order had a religious foundation; but at the same time religion was built into a synthesis which included law and humanistic wisdom, under which honour was distributed as the reward of service to the body of the realm, and its head. The result aimed at was the ordered harmony of a "civil society", an ideal which at least a representative segment of the Tudor élite could conceive as having been by and large achieved by the end of the reign of the great queen. The charisma of honour and lineage could no longer sanctify aristocratic dissidence in a society whose preconceptions were harmonist. The dissident could only suffer in "patience", or unmask himself as the rebel and traitor.

Thus the accepted modes of political conflict, and the language available for the expression of political dissent, needed to be adapted to changes in political opinion and practice: a process to which Essex's volte-face, involving a repudiation of his own political past, made its own paradoxical contribution. For his repentance, self-condemnation, and edifying death effected his own reincorporation into the body of the realm from which as a traitor he had been ejected. A reaction in his favour set in, which promoted the survival both of his faction and of the radical attitudes (in a suitably modified form) and policies (like the anti-Spanish Protestant crusade) which had been characteristic of the Essex House circle. Even his enemies were compelled, almost immediately, to accept his rehabilitation. Both Sir Robert Cecil and Nottingham admitted that Essex had died like a Christian, and in the treason trials which followed his own, Cecil refused to hear any evidence which implicated him.[159] Within a few weeks of Essex's execution, Barlow's Paul's Cross sermon, intended to complete the earl's disrepute by publicizing the details

[157] C. Russell, *Parliaments and English Politics, 1621–9* (Oxford, 1979), pp. 5 ff., 53 ff.; K. Sharpe, "Parliamentary History, 1603–1629: In or Out of Perspective?", in K. Sharpe (ed.), *Faction and Parliament*, pp. 14 ff.; M. Kishlansky, "The Emergence of Adversary Politics in the Long Parliament", *Jl Mod. Hist.*, xlix (1977), pp. 617 ff.

[158] See above, pp. 385–6.

[159] *Winwood's Memorials*, i, p. 16; Hist. MSS. Comm., *Rutland MSS.*, i, p. 370.

of his treasons, was "very offensively taken of the common sort". The earl's supporters disseminated the view that "His confession concerned only great repentance for the sins of his former life", and that Barlow had only "ript up, orator-like, the sins of his youth".[160] Essex's "popularity" revived, and after the queen's death the image of the chivalric Protestant hero, England's champion against Spain, his honour unstained, was restored, the process helped by the poets, dramatists, and ballad-writers who rallied around such survivors of the faction as Southampton and Mountjoy.[161] Essex was now once more presented as the victim of the law's pedantry and of the envy of his base-born enemies. The timorousness of the peers who had condemned him to death was excoriated, and the hard-heartedness of the queen who had withheld her mercy was deplored. At the same time, the saintliness of the earl's death was emphasized, and the errors which had led him into treason attributed to the provocations of his opponents. All this came to be the legacy of the faction, first led by Southampton and then, after the latter's death in 1624, by Essex's son and heir, the third earl.

The group had a recognizable continuity with the Elizabethan Essexians, not only in personnel, but also in attitude. There was the characteristic Essexian military orientation, cultivated both by Southampton and the third earl, Southampton dying while on military service in the Netherlands, and Essex replaying his father's legend by his prominent but characteristically unappreciated role in the Cadiz expedition of 1625. Like the Elizabethan Essex, both Southampton and the third earl developed military clienteles; and, like Essex, both were exponents of the anti-Spanish crusade. Both were also sensitive to issues to honour, although it is significant that

[160] *Rutland MSS.*, i, p. 373.

[161] A key document in the refurbishment of Essex's image was Robert Prickett's long elegiac poem, *Honour's Fame in Triumph Riding, or the Life and Death of the Late Honourable Earl of Essex* (London, 1604, S.T.C. 20339), dedicated to Southampton and Mountjoy. For examples of ballads glorifying Essex and lamenting his death, see *The Roxburghe Ballads*, ed. C. Hindley, 2 vols. (London, 1973), i, pp. 395 ff., and ii, pp. 202 ff. Cf. "The Diary of the duke of Stettin's Journey through England, 1602", ed. G. von Bulow, in *Trans. Roy. Hist. Soc.*, new ser., vi (1892), p. 13. Samuel Daniel's play *Philotas* (1605), the story of a councillor of Alexander's executed for treason, was thought to aim at Essex's rehabilitation. It was said to have been shown to Mountjoy, and its hero was depicted as an example of injured innocence. As a result, Daniel was called before the Council to account for a seditious writing. See Joan Rees, *Samuel Daniel*, pp. 98 ff.

here for both personal honour was increasingly closely associated with that of the collective constitutional group within the state to which both belonged, i.e. the peerage, or with the honour of the state itself. The former was seen as threatened by the sale of honours engineered by the favourites and their cliques; the latter by the military incompetence of the same cliques, and particularly of Buckingham and his supporters. Essex was deeply wounded in his personal honour by James I's validation of the favourite Somerset's love-intrigue with the countess of Essex, leading to a divorce suit which exposed the earl to the deeply dishonourable accusation of sexual impotence; and by his exclusion from the high civil and military office for which he considered himself entitled, by Charles I. The third earl shared with his father a sense of exclusion from his rightful place within the monarchical and court system, and developed a detached and sceptical attitude towards it which had been shared by Southampton, who was himself the largely frustrated opponent of Salisbury, Somerset, and Buckingham, and never fully received into the inner court ring, in spite of his appointment in 1619 to the Council. Thus the Essexians retained their inherited Elizabethan role of an essentially oppositionist group, a fact which accounts for the "radical" attitudes attributed to Southampton, as subsequently to the third earl, and their circle, which included a reputation both for "popularity" and even republicanism.[162] Appropriately, the alliance of "arms and letters", which in the Elizabethan days had been one of the ideals of the Essex House intellectuals, was continued particularly by Southampton, whose union of the traits of "valour" and "learning" was celebrated by George Chapman, once a client of the Elizabethan Essex, in a dedicatory sonnet included in the 1608 volume of translations from the *Iliad*.[163]

162 For Southampton's faction, and its reputation for radicalism and republicanism, see S. L. Adams, "Foreign Policy and the Parliaments of 1621 and 1624", in K. Sharpe (ed.), *op. cit.*, pp. 144–5. On the third earl of Essex, who was "heir . . . to a popular legend of heroism, royal injustice, and martyrdom . . . champion of the rights of the nobility and . . . the rights of the people", "the darling of the swordsmen" and "the most 'popular' man in the kingdom", see B. Manning, "The Aristocracy", p. 42; V. F. Snow, *Essex the Rebel; the Life of Robert Devereux, Third Earl of Essex* (Lincoln, Nebraska, 1970), and "Essex and the Aristocratic Opposition to the Early Stuarts", *Jl Mod. Hist.*, xxxii (1960), pp. 224 ff.

163 S.T.C. 13633, comprising the first twelve books.

Yet these features of the Essex tradition were no longer tied, as in the 1590s, to a community of swordsmen and men of honour prepared, in the name of honour, to disrupt the state by violence in the interest of their leader. Southampton and the third earl worked within the body of the realm, using Parliament for this purpose. As seen above, Essex's heirs, like himself, were much concerned with honour; but the vehicle of honour was no longer simply a clientele; but rather a formalized group, the peerage, which through the house of lords had a recognized place under the law, in the body politic, from which group ideals could be upheld and interests advanced. The weapons were no longer the military revolt, the *coup d'état*, or the popular rising; but the exploitation of parliamentary privilege, impeachment, and membership of the Lords Committee of Petitions to apply pressure to alter the balance of factions around the king.[164] Even "popularity" came to mean no longer the charismatic contact between the hero and the London crowd; but in the case of Southampton and the third earl, more a matter of prosaic conferences with members of the house of commons. Such modes of political action could be shared with other aristocratic connections, like those of Pembroke, Warwick, the Bedford interest, and Archbishop Abbot, all of whom had in common a strongly Protestant, anti-Spanish, and anti-favourite orientation.[165] Even Arundel, legatee of the Howards, and pro-Spanish, but ultimately anti-Buckingham, could become an ally; with his stress on honour and his tenure of the constable's and earl marshal's office, he had much in common with the inheritors of the Essex tradition. Yet it is indicative of the changed political climate that Arundel valued these offices not, like Essex, as giving warrant to reform the state and judge his enemies, but simply for the precedence they conferred in the Privy Council;[166] and that the support he received from the third earl should have been in defence of the privilege of peers to freedom from arrest in time of Parliament.

Of course, the time was not far distant when the body of the realm would prove unable to contain the irresolvable religious fears and political tensions which surfaced within it. Once this was so, the dis-

[164] Snow, "Essex and the Aristocratic Opposition", pp. 225 ff., and *Essex the Rebel*, pp. 100 ff., 148 ff., 183 ff.; A. L. Rowse, *Shakespeare's Southampton* (London, 1965), pp. 263 ff.; Russell, *op. cit.*, p. 33.

[165] Adams, *op. cit.*, pp. 142 ff.

[166] Sharpe, "Arundel", *loc. cit.*, p. 218; Snow, *Essex the Rebel*, pp. 153 ff.

ruptive features of the Essex tradition – its radicalism and appeal to popularity and the sword – could once more emerge. Yet the violence which eventually found expression in the outbreak of civil war was not, as in 1601, a matter simply of a connection woven out of kinship, lineage, and a common devotion to arms and honour confronting a tyrannical régime of the supposedly base and low-born. This theme, where it existed, was subordinate to the larger issue of the nature of the body politic, and of the relationship between its parts; together with the threat which seemed to be presented to the religious essence of the body itself. The dissidents of the Long Parliament gave precedence not to the language of honour, but of law and religion; the terminology of Tudor conformity and social wholeness had been adapted to the needs of dissidence, so that it became possible to identify the agents of royal authority, Strafford and Laud, as the rebels, traitors, and crypto-Papists who aimed to disrupt the state, and divert it from its providentially determined destiny. On 12 July 1642 it was not any community of honour but the members of the two houses of Parliament who were called on "to live and die with the earl of Essex". The politics of honour had been overshadowed by a politics of principle and ideological commitment.

Index

Past and Present Publications

General Editor: PAUL SLACK, *Exeter College, Oxford*

Family and Inheritance: Rural Society in Western Europe, 1200–1800, edited by Jack Goody, Joan Thirsk and E. P. Thompson*
French Society and the Revolution, edited by Douglas Johnson
Peasants, Knights and Heretics: Studies in Medieval English Social History, edited by R. H. Hilton*
Towns in Societies: Essays in Economic History and Historical Sociology, edited by Philip Abrams and E. A. Wrigley*
Desolation of a City: Coventry and the Urban Crisis of the Late Middle Ages, Charles Phythian-Adams
Puritanism and Theatre: Thomas Middleton and Opposition Drama under the Early Stuarts, Margot Heinemann*
Lords and Peasants in a Changing Society: The Estates of the Bishopric of Worcester 680–1540, Christopher Dyer
Life, Marriage and Death in a Medieval Parish: Economy, Society and Demography in Halesowen 1270–1400, Zvi Razi
Biology, Medicine and Society 1840–1940, edited by Charles Webster
The Invention of Tradition, edited by Eric Hobsbawm and Terence Ranger*
Industrialization before Industrialization: Rural Industry and the Genesis of Capitalism, Peter Kriedte, Hans Medick and Jürgen Schlumbohm†*
The Republic in the Village: The People of the Var from the French Revolution to the Second Republic, Maurice Agulhon†
Social Relations and Ideas: Essays in Honour of R. H. Hilton, edited by T. H. Aston, P. R. Coss, Christopher Dyer and Joan Thirsk
A Medieval Society: The West Midlands at the End of the Thirteenth Century, R. H. Hilton
Winstanley: 'The Law of Freedom' and Other Writings, edited by Christopher Hill
Crime in Seventeenth-Century England: A County Study, J. A. Sharpe†
The Crisis of Feudalism: Economy and Society in Eastern Normandy c. 1300–1550, Guy Bois†
The Development of the Family and Marriage in Europe, Jack Goody
Disputes and Settlements: Law and Human Relations in the West, edited by John Bossy
Rebellion, Popular Protest and the Social Order in Early Modern England, edited by Paul Slack
Studies on Byzantine Literature of the Eleventh and Twelfth Centuries, Alexander Kazhdan in collaboration with Simon Franklin†
The English Rising of 1381, edited by R. H. Hilton and T. H. Aston

Praise and Paradox: Merchants and Craftsmen in Elizabethan Popular Literature, Laura Caroline Stevenson
The Brenner Debate: Agrarian Class Structure and Economic Development in Pre-Industrial Europe, edited by T. H. Aston and C. H. E. Philpin
Eternal Victory: Triumphal Rulership in Late Antiquity, Byzantium, and the Early Medieval West, Michael McCormick†
East-Central Europe in Transition: From the Fourteenth to the Seventeenth Century, edited by Antoni Mączak, Henryk Samsonowicz and Peter Burke†
Small Books and Pleasant Histories: Popular Fiction and its Readership in Seventeenth-Century England, Margaret Spufford**
Society, Politics and Culture: Studies in Early Modern England, Mervyn James
Horses, Oxen and Technological Innovation: The Use of Draught Animals in English Farming 1066–1500, John Langdon

*Published also as a paperback
**Published only as a paperback
†Co-published with the Maison des Sciences de l'Homme, Paris

The 1997 Information Please Sports Almanac

Now in its 8th year as America's favorite sports reference book. Ranked as one of journalism's "50 Basic Reference Books" by *The Essential Researcher.*

With Year in Review essays by the country's top sports writers:

Mark Blaudschun
The Boston Globe
on College Football

Ron Chimelis
The Springfield [Mass.] Union-News
on College Sports

Jerry Crasnick
The Denver Post
on Baseball

Eric Duhatschek
Calgary Herald
on Hockey

Bernard Fernandez
The Philadelphia Daily News
on Boxing

Tom Gaffney
Akron Beacon Journal
on Bowling

Paul Gardner
Soccer America
on Soccer

Mike Harris
Associated Press
on Auto Racing

Philip Hersh
Chicago Tribune
on the Olympic Games and International Sports

David Moore
Dallas Morning News
on Pro Basketball

Keith Olbermann
ESPN
on Ballparks and Arenas

Scott Ostler
San Francisco Chronicle
on The Year in Sports

Marino Parascenzo
Pittsburgh Post-Gazette
on Golf

Diane Pucin
The Philadelphia Inquirer
on Tennis

Chris Raymond
ESPN Total Sports
on College Basketball

Richard Sandomir
The New York Times
on Business and Media

Sharon Smith
Author and commentator
on Horse Racing

Vito Stellino
The Baltimore Sun
on Pro Football

"This is a remarkable book—complete, accurate and interesting. After my over 60 years announcing sports, I should know a great record book. This is certainly it."
—Red Barber (1908-92)

The Champions of 1996

Auto Racing

NASCAR Circuit
- Daytona 500 .... Dale Jarrett
- Winston 500 .... Sterling Marlin
- Coca-Cola 600 .... Dale Jarrett
- Southern 500 .... Jeff Gordon

IndyCar Circuit
- U.S. 500 .... Jimmy Vasser
- PPG Cup Champion .... Jimmy Vasser

Indy Racing League Circuit
- Indianapolis 500 .... Buddy Lazier

Formula One Circuit
- World Driving Championship .... Damon Hill

Baseball

World Series .... New York def. Atlanta, 4 games to 2
- MVP .... John Wetteland, New York, P

All-Star Game .... NL 6, AL 0 in Philadelphia
- MVP .... Mike Piazza, Los Angeles, C

College World Series .... LSU
- MVP .... Pat Burrell, Miami, 3B

College Basketball

Men's NCAA Final Four
- Championship .... Kentucky 76, Syracuse 67
- MVP .... Tony Delk, Kentucky, G

Women's NCAA Final Four
- Championship .... Tennessee 83, Georgia 65
- MVP .... Michelle Marciniak, Tennessee, G

Pro Basketball

NBA Finals .... Chicago def. Seattle 4 games to 2
- MVP .... Michael Jordan, Chicago, G

Eastern Final .... Chicago def. Orlando 4 games to 0
Western Final .... Seattle def. Utah 4 games to 3
All-Star Game .... East 129, West 118 at San Antonio
- MVP .... Michael Jordan, Chicago, G

Bowling

Men's Major Championships
- PBA National .... Butch Soper
- BPAA U.S. Open .... Dave Husted
- Tournament of Champions .... Dave D'Entremont
- ABC Masters .... Ernie Schlegel

Women's Major Championships
- Sam's Town Invitational (1995) .... Michelle Mullen
- WIBC Queens .... Lisa Wagner
- BPAA U.S. Open .... Liz Johnson

College Football (1995)

National Champions
- AP and Coaches .... Nebraska (12-0)

Major Bowls
- Orange .... Florida St. 31, Notre Dame 26
- Rose .... USC 41, Northwestern 32
- Sugar .... Va. Tech 28, Texas 10
- Fiesta .... Nebraska 62, Florida 24

Heisman Trophy .... Eddie George, Ohio St., RB

Pro Football (1995)

Super Bowl XXX .... Dallas 27, Pittsburgh 17
- MVP .... Larry Brown, Dallas, CB

AFC Championship .... Pittsburgh 20, Indianapolis 16
NFC Championship .... Dallas 38, Green Bay 27
Pro Bowl .... NFC 20, AFC 13
- MVP .... Jerry Rice, San Francisco, WR

CFL Grey Cup Final .... Baltimore 37, Calgary 20
- MVP .... Tracy Ham, Baltimore, QB

Golf

Men's Major Championships
- Masters .... Nick Faldo
- U.S. Open .... Steve Jones
- British Open .... Tom Lehman
- PGA Championship .... Mark Brooks

Seniors Major Championships
- The Tradition .... Jack Nicklaus
- PGA Seniors .... Hale Irwin
- U.S. Senior Open .... Dave Stockton
- Senior Players Championship .... Ray Floyd

Women's Major Championships
- Nabisco Dinah Shore .... Patty Sheehan
- LPGA Championship .... Laura Davies
- U.S. Women's Open .... Annika Sorenstam
- du Marier Classic .... Laura Davies
- National Team Competition
- Solheim Cup (Women) .... United States 17, Europe 11

Hockey

Stanley Cup .... Colorado def. Florida 4 games to 0
- MVP .... Joe Sakic, Colorado, C

Western Final .... Colorado def. Detroit 4 games to 2
Eastern Final .... Florida def. Pittsburgh 4 games to 3
All-Star Game .... East 5, West 4 at Boston
- MVP .... Ray Bourque, Boston, D

NCAA Div. 1 Final .... Michigan 3, Colorado Col. 2 (OT)
- MVP .... Brendan Morrison, Michigan, C

World Cup .... United States def. Canada 2 games to 1
- MVP .... Mike Richter, USA, G

Horse Racing

Triple Crown Champions
- Kentucky Derby .... Grindstone (Jerry Bailey)
- Preakness .... Louis Quatorze (Pat Day)
- Belmont .... Editor's Note (Rene Douglas)

Harness Racing
- Hambletonian .... Continentalvictory (Michel Lachance)
- Little Brown Jug .... Armbro Operative (Michel Lachance)

Soccer

- MLS Champ. Game .... D.C. United 3, Los Angeles 2 (OT)
- MVP .... Marco Etcheverry, D.C. United, M
- European Championship .... Germany
- African Nations Cup .... S. Africa
- CONCACAF Gold Cup .... Mexico
- US Cup '96 .... Mexico

Tennis

Men's Grand Slam Championships
- Australian Open .... Boris Becker
- French Open .... Yevgeny Kafelnikov
- Wimbledon .... Richard Krajicek
- U.S. Open .... Pete Sampras

Women's Grand Slam Championship
- Australian Open .... Monica Seles
- French Open .... Steffi Graf
- Wimbledon .... Steffi Graf
- U.S. Open .... Steffi Graf

National Team Competition
- Fed Cup (Women) .... USA 5, Spain 0

Miscellaneous Champions

Little League World Series .... Taiwan
Tour de France .... Bjarne Riis (DEN)
Tour duPont .... Lance Armstrong (USA)
FIDE Chess Championships .... Anatoly Karpov (RUS)

THE 1997 INFORMATION PLEASE® SPORTS ALMANAC

John Hassan
EDITOR

Associate Editor
Gerry Brown
Assistant Editor
Michael Morrison

Production Coordinator, **Jennifer Sullivan**
Production Assistant, **Kate Binder**

Research Assistants,
John Gettings, Greg Kelly and **Pat Page**

HOUGHTON MIFFLIN COMPANY
Boston New York

The Information Please® Sports Almanac

ISSN: 1045-4980
ISBN: 0-395-82856-2

Front Cover photograph: **Emmitt Smith**: 1995 Mike Powell/Allsport USA .

Back cover photographs: **Ken Griffey, Jr.** : 1995 Stephen Dunn/Allsport USA. **Kerri Strug and Bela Karolyi**: 1996 Doug Pensinger/Allsport USA **Dennis Rodman and Michael Jordan**: 1996 Doug Pensinger/Allsport USA.

Comments and Suggestions

Comments and suggestions from readers are invited. Because of the many letters received, however, it's not possible to respond personally to every correspondent. Nevertheless, all letters are welcome and each will be carefully considered. **The Information Please Sports Almanac** does not rule on bets or wagers. Address all correspondence to Inso Corp., 31 St. James Avenue, Boston, Massachusetts 02116-4104.

Additional copies of The **1997 Information Please Sports Almanac** may be ordered directly by mail from:

Customer Service Department
Houghton Mifflin Company
181 Ballardvale St.
P.O. Box 7050
Wilmington, MA 01887-7050

Phone toll-free (800) 225-3362 for price and shipping information. In Massachusetts, phone (617) 272-1500.

Printed in the United States of America

WPC 10 9 8 7 6 5

PRO FOOTBALL (CONT.)

COLLEGE BASKETBALL

PRO BASKETBALL

HOCKEY

I promise that this will be the only year that this message is named after the Belmont Stakes winner. Actually, Wayne Lukas didn't even offer a modest fee to sponsor my little page here. Although, since everything in sports has to have a corporate sponsor, you might very well be reading John Hassan's "Roto-Rooter Ramblings" next year.

Sadly, avarice is our constant companion on the sports pages. Our usual lineup of the country's best sportswriters does get around to the actual games but in "College Sports" by Ron Chimelis, "Ballparks and Arenas" by Keith Olbermann, "College Basketball" by Chris Raymond and, naturally, "Business and Media" by Richard Sandomir, you'll see that the green monster has spread well beyond Fenway Park.

A lot of this book is about teams and we have a good one. I leaned heavily on Gerry Brown who was here last year. Brown, the only returning starter, not only carried his own share of the work but was always quick to help out elsewhere. Michael Morrison rose to every challenge and acted like he'd been putting out almanacs since grade school. Jennifer Sullivan got the book out the door without bloodshed, assisted by Kate Binder who came on in the top of the ninth. John Gettings, Pat Page and Greg Kelly provided excellent fact-checking and research. My transition was also made a lot easier because so many writers came back despite a change at the helm. My sincere thanks to all of you.

Outside assistance was graciously provided by Pam Reichmann of R.C. Ltd, Nat Andriani of the Associated Press, Jamie Calsyn of Allsport, Lydia Rypcinski of Bowler's Journal, Andy Mitchell of CNN Sports, Michael Shulman of Archive Photos, Dave Nagle and Judy Murrone of ESPN, Gary Johnson and Rick Campbell of the NCAA, Howard Bass of Thoroughbred Racing Communications and Paul Ramlow of the Unites States Trotting Association, Barbara Zidovsky of Nielsen Media Research, and Mike Woitalla of *Soccer America*.

The founding editor of this book, Mike Meserole, also gets a tip of the hat. With each passing day, I admire his achievement all the more. Thanks also to our friends at Houghton Mifflin.

I also wish to thank my colleagues at Inso Corporation, most especially Liz Kubik, Bill Trippe (and team), Patty Guzikowski, Robert Heywood (and crew), Michael Melody, and Steve Vana-Paxhia. Thanks also to Jeff Melvin, whose brains, heart and soul make him the great friend that he's always been.

Moving to Boston was part of the job description. I want to thank Cindy and J.D. Hale for taking me into their home and making the transition from New York an easy one. To be part of a family while I missed my own was comforting. I'll always be grateful.

Over the last few years, I have been fortunate to have worked with several people who have taken the time to help me. Glen Waggoner is a great editor and writer but, more important, a true gentleman. Geoffrey Precourt is also a master with ideas and words but he has no peer when it comes to the human side of this business. Craig Horowitz has taught me about reporting, writing and friendship. And finally, I have to thank Daniel "Tricky Sam" Okrent. For over 12 years, Dan has always had time to listen or talk or generally help me make sense of the opportunities, challenges, and responsibilities that have come my way. You may recall Dan as the guy in the red sweater in Ken Burns' "Baseball" who compared Babe Ruth to Cézanne and Beethoven and made them all seem better when he finished. I know Dan as a friend who hasn't compared me to anybody but who has made me better.

Finally, this book is dedicated to my family, especially my parents, Bill and Janet Hassan. My father has taught me all of the important things, from Cootie Williams to Ted Williams. And my mother. She drafted me in the first round, gave me a huge bonus and has yet to trade me.

My wife, Karen Mynatt, was also wonderfully supportive as I, in her words, "found a way to get paid to watch SportsCenter."

John Hassan
Boston
November 1, 1996

Major League Cities & Teams

As of Oct. 31, 1996, there were 134 major league teams playing or scheduled to play baseball, basketball, football, hockey and soccer in 53 cities in the United States and Canada. Listed below are the cities and the teams that play there.

Anaheim
AL California Angels
NHL Mighty Ducks of Anaheim

Atlanta
NL Braves
NBA Hawks
NFL Falcons

Baltimore
AL Orioles
NFL Ravens

Boston
AL Red Sox
NBA Celtics
NFL N.E. Patriots (Foxboro)
NHL Bruins
MLS N.E. Revolution (Foxboro)

Buffalo
NFL Bills (Orchard Park)
NHL Sabres

Calgary
CFL Stampeders
NHL Flames

Charlotte
NBA Hornets
NFL Carolina Panthers

Chicago
AL White Sox
NL Cubs
NBA Bulls
NFL Bears
NHL Blackhawks

Cincinnati
NL Reds
NFL Bengals

Cleveland
AL Indians
NBA Cavaliers

Columbus
MLS Crew

Dallas
AL Texas Rangers (Arlington)
NBA Mavericks
NFL Cowboys (Irving)
NHL Stars
MLS Burn

Denver
NL Colorado Rockies
NBA Nuggets
NFL Broncos
NHL Colorado Avalanche
MLS Colorado Rapids

Detroit
AL Tigers
NBA Pistons (Auburn Hills)
NFL Lions (Pontiac)
NHL Red Wings

East Rutherford
NBA New Jersey Nets
NFL New York Giants
NFL New York Jets
NHL New Jersey Devils
MLS Metrostars

Edmonton
CFL Eskimos
NHL Oilers

Green Bay
NFL Packers

Hamilton
CFL Tiger-Cats

Hartford
NHL Whalers

Houston
NL Astros
NBA Rockets
NFL Oilers

Indianapolis
NBA Pacers
NFL Colts

Jacksonville
NFL Jaguars

Kansas City
AL Royals
NFL Chiefs
MLS Wiz

Los Angeles
NL Dodgers
NBA Clippers
NBA Lakers (Inglewood)
NHL Kings (Inglewood)
MLS Galaxy (Pasadena)

Miami
NL Florida Marlins
NBA Heat
NFL Dolphins
NHL Florida Panthers

Milwaukee
AL Brewers
NBA Bucks

Minneapolis
AL Minn. Twins
NBA Minn. Timberwolves
NFL Minn. Vikings

Montreal
NL Expos
NHL Canadiens
CFL Alouettes

New Orleans
NFL Saints

New York
AL Yankees
NL Mets
NBA Knicks
NHL Rangers
NHL N.Y. Islanders (Uniondale)

Oakland
AL Athletics
NBA Golden St. Warriors
NFL Raiders

Orlando
NBA Magic

Ottawa
CFL Rough Riders
NHL Senators

Philadelphia
NL Phillies
NBA 76ers
NFL Eagles
NHL Flyers

Phoenix
NBA Suns
NFL Arizona Cardinals (Tempe)
MLB Arizona DiamondBacks (1998)
NHL Coyotes

Pittsburgh
NL Pirates
NFL Steelers
NHL Penguins

Portland
NBA Trail Blazers

Regina
CFL Saskatchewan Roughriders

Sacramento
NBA Kings

St. Louis
NL Cardinals
NFL Rams
NHL Blues

Salt Lake City
NBA Utah Jazz

San Antonio
NBA Spurs

San Diego
NL Padres
NFL Chargers

San Francisco
NL Giants
NFL 49ers

San Jose
NHL Sharks
MLS Clash

Seattle
AL Mariners
NBA SuperSonics
NFL Seahawks

Tampa
NFL Buccaneers
NHL Lightning
MLB Devil Rays (1998)
MLS Mutiny

Toronto
AL Blue Jays
CFL Argonauts
NBA Raptors
NHL Maple Leafs

Vancouver
CFL B.C. Lions
NBA Grizzlies
NHL Canucks

Washington
NBA Bullets (Landover)
NFL Redskins
NHL Capitals (Landover)
MLS United

Winnipeg
CFL Blue Bombers

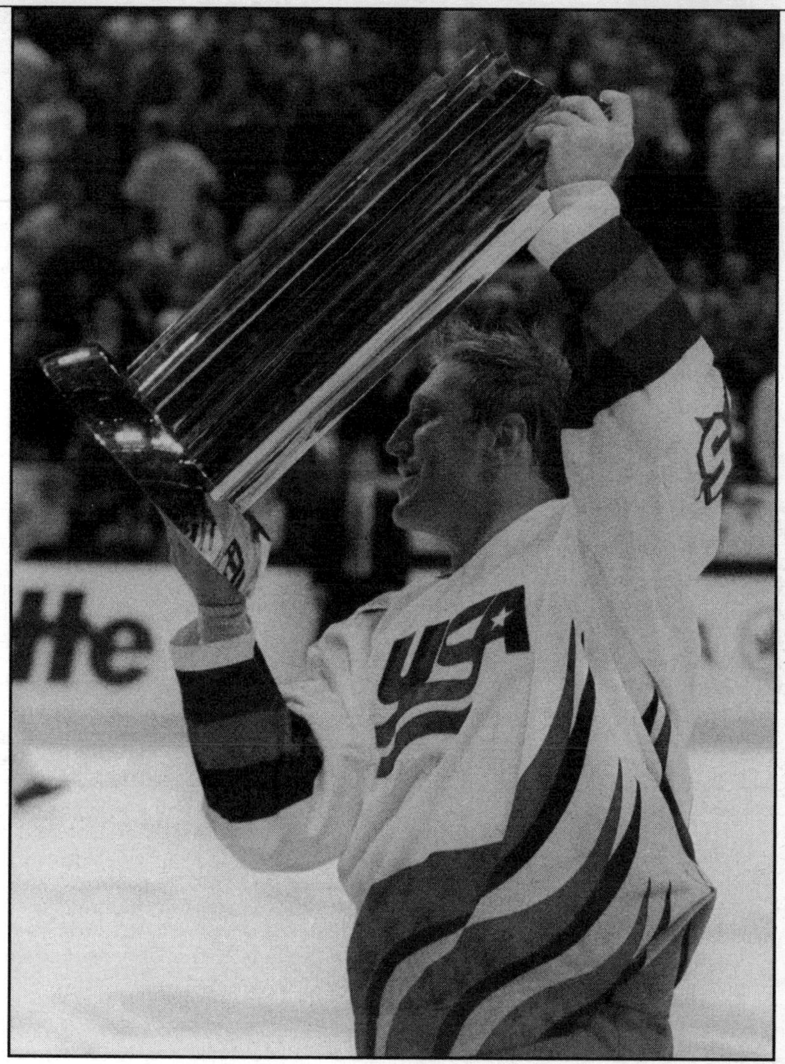

Wide World Photos

Brett Hull carries the trophy that signifies the United States' victory over Canada in the 1996 World Cup of Hockey.

UPDATES

A Hull of a Win

Brett Hull led the Unites States to victory in the World Cup of Hockey over Canada, the place of his birth

Do you believe in miracles? Well hold on. Let's not get carried away. Maybe the United States' victory in the inaugural World Cup of Hockey wasn't quite as unexpected or dramatic as the 1980 Olympic gold medal but it certainly ranks as one of the top achievements in U.S. hockey history.

The young, physical United States squad rolled through the initial three-game round-robin series unbeaten and then pasted a speedy Russian team in the semifinals (5-2) to set up a dream matchup with Canada, whose only previous loss in the tournament was at the hands of the Americans.

The championship series was supposed to be sweet revenge for Canada, the sport's originators, whose hockey ego has taken a blow in the past two years. First the Quebec Nordiques migrated to Colorado and then won the Stanley Cup, then the Winnipeg Jets moved to Phoenix, and then all five of Canada's franchises making the NHL playoffs in the 1995-96 season were defeated by American teams in the first round. Clearly, there was a score to settle.

U.S.-Canada relations were also affected by the play of one Brett Hull, one of the NHL's top snipers, who was starring for the U.S. despite being born in Canada. Hull, who has dual citizenship, had decided to play all international competition as an American after being spurned by Team Canada in 1986. Canadian fans emphasized the bitterness during the United States' semifinal round win over Russia when a majority of the 18,500 fans at the Corel Centre in Ottawa actually booed the Americans and cheered for the Russians.

It should have been a surprise to no one that these two teams would reach the finals. In fact, in 1991, the final year of the Canada Cup which eventually became the World Cup, Wayne Gretzky and goaltender Bill Ranford led the Canadians to a two-game sweep of the Americans in the championship series to capture the title. The story played out a little differently this time.

Game one was short on neither excitement nor controversy. The Canadians carried a 3-2 lead into the final minute of play when the Americans pulled goaltender Mike Richter in place of an extra attacker. With just ten seconds left, U.S. defenseman Brian Leetch blasted a 20-footer that was stopped by goalie Curtis Joseph. The rebound went to Canadian defenseman Eric Desjardins who tried to scoop the puck under his goaltender, only to see the puck trickle in with just 6.3 seconds remaining. John LeClair was given credit for the goal that sent the contest into overtime and the crowd in Philadelphia into a frenzy.

The frenzy was short-lived however, 10 minutes and 37 seconds to be exact. Canadian center Steve Yzerman fired a shot from a tough angle that was misplayed by U.S. goalie Mike Richter to give the Canadians a 4-3 victory. U.S. head coach Ron Wilson later claimed that the play was "about three feet offside" but the play stood. The Canadians won round one.

Wide World Photos

This one happened to sail by Canada's **Curtis Joseph** but **Brett Hull** of the USA still led all scorers in the World Cup of Hockey with seven goals and four assists.

At the brink of elimination, the U.S. stormed right back in game two in Montreal led by the spectacular goaltending of Richter and the hard-nosed play of wingers Keith Tkachuk, Bill Guerin, and John LeClair who recorded two goals in the American's 5-2 victory. Much to the chagrin of the Canadian fans, it was Hull, who despite the never-ending chants of "Traitor!", broke in alone and deked Joseph to tally the game winner at 15:24 of the second period and set the stage for a winner-take-all final game also in Montreal.

Despite being outshot 32-14 in the first two periods of game three, the U.S went into the second intermission tied at one. Hull and Canadian star Eric Lindros traded power-play goals and Richter was practically flawless as he single-handedly kept the Americans in the game. At 12:50 of the third stanza, Canada broke the tie on a goal not by Gretzky, Lindros, or Yzerman, but by unlikely source Adam Foote . The defenseman, who had just 13 career NHL goals, wristed a shot past a screened Richter for his first goal of the tournament. The lead stood for just under four minutes when two controversial goals gave the U.S. a 3-2 lead.

Hull scored the tying goal when he deflected a Leetch slap shot out of midair and into the net. Canada protested and the play was reviewed to see if Hull's stick was too high when the puck was tipped. Decision: Goal stands. Just 43 seconds later, Tony Amonte scored the game winner although once again, the play had to be reviewed because it appeared that Amonte may have kicked the puck into the net. Once again, the appeal went the way of the United States to give them a lead with 2:35 left to play. Canada's attempts at a comeback were snuffed out by Richter and the Americans went on to score two late goals to secure the 5-2 victory and the World Cup of Hockey championship.

Richter stopped 35 shots in the final game and was named tournament MVP for his efforts. Hull finished the tournament with seven goals and 11 points to lead all players in both categories. "There were two fantastic hockey teams out there," Hull told reporters after the win, "Both teams deserved to win but the puck was bouncing for us." The Canadians weren't full of excuses after their defeat although they could have chosen from a long list. If Mario Lemieux and Ray Bourque had decided to play, things may have been different. If Mark Messier wasn't fighting the flu during the championship series and forced to miss game two, things may have been different. But things weren't different and this was certainly no miracle. With all due respect to the Russians and the Swedes, the road to hockey success goes straight through Canada and at least for now, that road seems to be heading south.

—Michael Morrison

College Football— October 27

In an early season filled with upsets, college football was heading for an interesting bowl season. After seven weeks the USA Today/CNN poll featured some real surprises. And a pairing of number one versus number two in a bowl game looked extremely doubtful.

At number one was Florida, led by quarterback Danny Wuerffel. The Gators were undefeated and heading for a showdown with Florida State, having brushed off Tennessee, 35-29, on September 21 in Knoxville in one of the year's most anticipated games. The third-ranked Gators jumped out early and barely hung on as the second-ranked Volunteers dominated the second half. Tennessee has stayed in the top ten at 5-1 and was on the fringe of the national title picture after beating seventh-ranked Alabama 20-13 on October 26.

Later that day Arizona State provided a real shocker by defeating two-time defending national champion Nebraska, 19-0. Using that victory as a springboard, and with the emergence of quarterback Jake Plummer, the Sun Devils were undefeated at 8-0 and were poised to be a player in the national title picture.

Ohio State seems ready to be a factor too as they lead the Big Ten at 7-0 highlighted by victories over Penn State and Notre Dame. Barring any huge upsets, Ohio State will finish the season as Big Ten champs and they will be ranked one or two. The winner of the Florida-Florida State game will probably also be ranked one or two and the bowl alliance does not include the Rose Bowl this year so look for more controversy on January 2nd.

Other developments....Last year's Cinderella story, Northwestern, came back to reality with a season-opening loss to Wake Forest, but the Wildcats rebounded to beat Michigan for the second year in a row and sat atop the Big Ten at 5-0...After the loss to Ohio State, Notre Dame also lost to Air Force 20-17 in overtime on October 19th...Penn State dropped out of title contention when the Nittany Lions lost to Iowa 21-20 after also losing to the Buckeyes.....Michigan dropped Colorado 20-13 on September 14 to buffalo the Buffaloes chances at having a say on New Year's Day.

Auto Racing

Damon Hill of England won the 1996 Formula One World Driving Championship on October 13th in Suzuka, Japan. Hill clinched the title by winning the Japanese Grand Prix, the last event in the 16-race series. Hill won eight races this year and started every race in the front row. Hill and his father, Graham Hill, are the first father and son team to win the Formula One title. Graham, who also won the 1966 Indianapolis 500, won the title in 1962 and 1968. Hill won the title for the Williams team but will be racing for the TWR Arrows in 1997.

Women's Basketball

The emergence of women's basketball continued as the American Basketball League began play on October 18th. The ABL features many well-known college stars and Olympians such as Teresa Edwards, Jennifer Rizzoti, Venus Lacey, Jennifer Azzi, Nikki McCray, Saudia Roundtree, Dawn Staley and Katrina McClain. The ABL will also have renowned heptathlete Jackie Joyner-Kersee. With eight teams, the ABL will play a forty game season with playoffs to begin in March of 1997. While the ABL will start out in smaller cities like San Jose, Richmond, Columbus, Hartford-Springfield and Portland, the legue's competition, the WNBA, will begin play in June of 1997 in eight NBA cities.

The WNBA features the marketing power of the NBA, a national television contract and will start out with name players Rebecca Lobo and Sheryl Swoopes. The

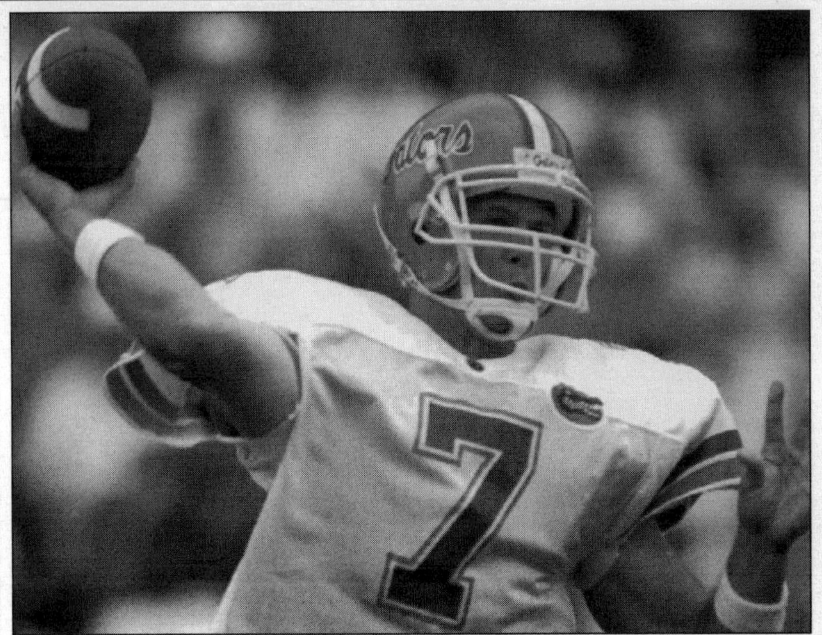

Wide World Photos

Danny Wuerffel of the Florida Gators had led his team to the number one position in the polls. Wuerffel himself was the leading candidate for the 1996 Hesiman Trophy due to his mastery of Steve Spurrier's high-powered passing offense.

league will play a 30-game schedule in the summer from June to August, a season not noted for intense television watching. Baseball will be its main competition. The ABL has a head start but is competing with professional hockey, basketball, football and college football.

Pro Football

By the end of week eight, there were no undefeated teams, though the Denver Broncos, Washington Redskins and Green Bay Packers were all 6-1. At the other end of the spectrum were the hapless Atlanta Falcons at 0-7 and the really hapless New York Jets at 0-8.

The defending Super Bowl champion Dallas Cowboys were 4-2 and struggled early on with injuries to tight end Jay Novacek, wide receiver Kevin Williams, and pass rushing specialist Charles Haley. Wide receiver Michael Irvin also sat out five games due to a suspension by the league for drug possession charges stemming from an incident in a Dallas hotel room in which Irvin and a friend were caught by police with two topless dancers, marijuana and cocaine.

Despite a loss to the Minnesota Vikings, the Green Bay Packers had emerged as the class of the league. Their key victory was a Monday night defeat of the San Francisco 49ers in a hard fought battle. The 49ers had banged-up quarterbacks in Steve Young and Elvis Grbac and might have lost WR receiver J.J. Stokes for the season with a wrist injury. On the bright side, FB William Floyd returned to action after more than a year and played extremely well in a come-from behind win against the Bengals on October 20. The surprising Carolina Panthers, powered by a stingy defense, were tied with the 49ers at the top of the NFC West Division at 5-2.

That 49er victory cost Dave Shula his job as coach of the Bengals. Bruce Coslet, former head coach of the Jets, will take over as head coach in Cincinnati. Jim Mora of the Saints also resigned the day Shula was canned. Mora will be replaced by the Saints' linebackers' coach Rick Venturi.

The AFC East was shaping up as the best

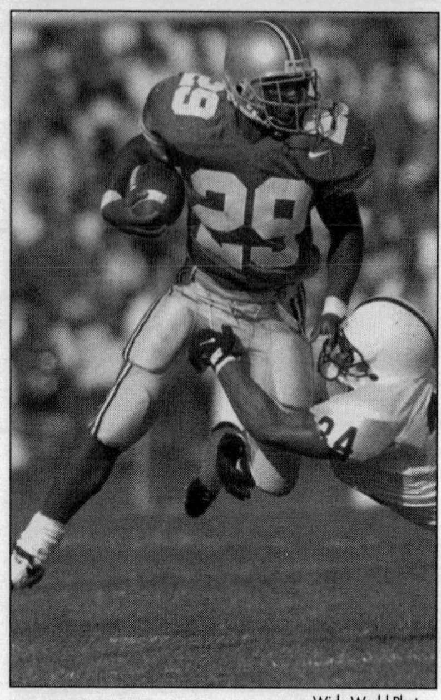

Wide World Photos

Pepe Pearson and his Ohio State Buckeyes were on a roll in the fall of 1996 with victories over Notre Dame and Michigan.

divisional race in pro football with Miami (4-3), Buffalo (5-2), New England (4-3) and Indianapolis (5-2) all playing well if not spectacularly. Quarterback Dan Marino broke his ankle and missed three weeks, making life difficult for new coach Jimmy Johnson. Bill Parcells' New England Patriots had generated some offense with Drew Bledsoe, RB Curtis Martin rookie WR Terry Glenn but the team was plagued by poor secondary play. The Pats ranked at the bottom of the league in pass defense after week 8. The Buffalo Bills were playing tough defense and winning close games despite injuries to and bad play from QB Jim Kelly. And the Indianapolis Colts were hanging tough despite the most injuries of any team in the league.

Denver's surprising season featured a good running attack led by Terrell Davis, great play from QB John Elway and, surprise, a very tough defense. The Kansas City Chiefs were also playing well, right behind the 6-1 Broncos at 5-2. And in the AFC Central, Houston and Pittsburgh were tied at 5-2. For the second year in a row, the Steelers lost a key member of their defense when All-Pro linebacker Greg Lloyd was lost for the season with a torn anterior cruciate ligament. In other player moves, the Atlanta Falcons dumped malcontent quarterback Jeff George. After he got into a heated argument with head coach June Jones on the sidelines when Jones benched him in a September 22 game against the Philadelphia Eagles, the Falcons decided they did not want him around. After trying unsuccessfully to work out a trade with Seattle, George was waived. He was not claimed by any team and became an unrestricted free agent.

In the strange world that is Tampa Bay Buccaneers football, RB Errict Rhett returned to the team after holding out for all of training camp and eight weeks of the season. Rhett, who has rushed for 1,000 yards twice, will play out the season under the original terms of his existing contract. The 1-6 Bucs got bad news when a trainer cut off the tip of star WR Alvin Harper's finger when trying to remove tape after a practice. Harper was gracious about the incident but is expected to miss at least one game.

Boxing

For reasons known only to him, Sugar Ray Leonard announced that he would be returning to the ring in February of 1997 to fight Hector "Macho" Camacho in a pay-per-view event. Leonard has not fought since being beaten badly by junior-middleweight Terry Norris in 1991. Leonard, 40 and a grandfather, is currently an official at the MGM Grand Hotel in Las Vegas. The popular Leonard rose to fame by winning a gold medal at the 1976 Olympics. His career was cut short by a detached retina in 1981 but he has retired and unretired three times since then. Camacho, 34, has continued to fight and has apparently been trying to get Leonard to come back for a while. The fight will take place somehere in the United States.

Tommy Morrison, the heavyweight fighter who announced that he was HIV positive in February of 1996, has signed to fight Anthony Cooks on November 3rd in Tokyo. Cooks is from Oklahoma City and has a 9-5 career record. The Morrison-Cooks bout will be part of the undercard for the George Foreman-Crawford Grimsley fight. The fight is considered a tune-up for a possible

Morrison-Foreman fight in 1997. There is a provision in the contract that the fight will be stopped if Morrison is cut. The decision goes to the fighter with the most points. Morrison will be donating proceeds from this and future fights to help children with AIDS. If Morrison decides on a full return to boxing, he will probably have to fight overseas as it would be difficult for him to obtain a boxing license in the United States given his medical condition.

Golf

Tiger Woods started relatively slowly but finished with a flourish in the seven PGA tournaments that he entered after turning pro in August of 1996. The remarkably long-hitting Woods finished tied for 60th at his first pro tournament, the Greater Milwaukee Open. The next week he jumped up to 11th at the Bell Canadian Open. The next two tournaments hinted at what was to come when Woods finished tied for fifth at the Quad-City Classic and tied for third at the B.C. Open.

After skipping out at the last minute at the Buick Challenge, Woods won the Las Vegas Invitational on October 6th. His goal of securing a tour card for 1997 was achieved. His next two tournaments almost mocked that goal. He finished second at the LaCantera Texas Open and won the Walt Disney World Classic.

Woods won the Walt Disney event when Taylor Smith's putter was deemed to be illegal, therefore canceling their playoff. But he had battled Payne Stewart head-to-head to force the playoff. And at Las Vegas he beat Davis Love III in a playoff. In seven tournaments Woods won $734,794 and ended up 23rd on the money list, qualifying him for the Tour Championship. In just under two months, Tiger Woods had put together the best debut season in the history of the PGA. While some tour players were rankled by all the attention Woods was getting, even the most skeptical player had to admit he was living up to the hype. As Payne Stewart told USA Today, " Tiger is a shot in the arm the Tour needs. He's created an unbelievable interest in our Tour, and that's increased interest in our jobs. That keeps corporate America looking at our Tour year-round. Hey, that's good for my business."

Tom Lehman was running away with the Tour Championship at Southern Hills in

Wide World Photos

Tiger Woods tees off during the 1996 Greater Milwaukee Open where he made his professional debut.

Tulsa, Oklahoma after 54 holes. Rain had postponed the final round but Lehman was leading by nine strokes.

In women's golf, the United States LPGA Tour team won its second consecutive Nichirei International tournament in Ibaragi-ken, Japan. The US team was led by captain (and Australian) Karrie Webb and Brandie Burton. The United States has won 16 of the 18 tournaments between the two teams.

Olympics

Federal prosecutors sent a letter to Richard Jewell's lawyer informing him that he is no longer a suspect in the bombing incident at Centennial Olympic Park. Jewell was working as a private security guard when a pipe bomb exploded just before dawn on July 27. The bomb killed one person and injured more than 100. Jewell was initially crowned a hero for spotting the bomb before it went off but he later came under intense scrutiny. Now it appears that all the investigating done by the FBI and local police turned up nothing to link Jewell to the crime. U.S.

Attorney Kent Alexander said as much in the exonerating letter, which read in part, "This is to advise you that based on evidence developed to date, your client Richard Jewell is not considered a target of the federal criminal investigation into the bombing. Barring any newly discovered evidence, this status will not change."

Tennis

Women: Gabriela Sabatini announced her retirement on October 24. In a statement released by the Corel WTA Tour at a press conference held at Madison Square Garden, Sabatini said " I have made this decision after a long and well-thought-out analysis, out of which has arisen my strong desire to pursue the development of other activities. I want to give thanks to my legion of faithful admirers and to the general public for always having inexhaustibly followed and supported me and for being a great source of motivation during every moment of my career."

Sabatini's career will probably be judged as one of moderate achievement, with one Grand Slam victory on a resume that will end in just her 26th year. A stomach injury caused her to miss both the French Open and Wimbledon this year. In the two Grand Slams she did play in 1996, she lost in the fourth round of the Australian Open and in the third round of the U.S. Open. Her last tour victory was at the New South Wales Open in January of 1995. Having been ranked as high as third in 1995, Sabatini will bow out at the 29th spot.

Her departure at Madison Square Garden was fitting because Sabatini's brightest moments came in New York City. She won the U.S. Open in 1990 over Steffi Graf in straight sets. And she won the 1988 and 1994 Virginia Slims championships in the Garden itself.

Men: In a field that contained the world's top players, sixth-seeded Boris Becker defeated top seed Pete Sampras 3-6, 6-3, 3-6, 6-3, 6-4 to win the Stuttgart Eurocard Open. Becker seemed fully recovered from the wrist injury that had been bothering him since Wimbledon. He won his fourth title of the year with an ace on his first match point. The win moved Becker up to number three on the tour rankings.

Sampras was going for what would have been his tour-leading eighth victory. Sampras had been 7 for 7 in finals in 1996 and saw his 21-Match winning streak come to an end. He hadn't lost since August 9 to Thomas Enqvist at the ATP Championships. This defeat was also Sampras' first in 22 indoor matches this year. Despite Becker's obvious talent, the victory was something of a surprise because Sampras had been playing superbly. In the quarterfinals Sampras beat Andre Agassi in straight sets, a match that Sampras called his best ever.

Horse Racing

In a disappointing end to his illustrious career, heavily favored Cigar was beaten by Alphabet Soup, a 19-1 longshot in the Breeder's Cup Classic at the Woodbine Racetrack in Toronto. Chris McCarron rode Alphabet Soup to an exciting finish and fought off challenges from Preakness winner Louis Quatorze and Cigar. Cigar lost for the third time in 20 races but all three have come in his last four starts. Alphabet Soup was a bit more rested with the Classic being just his seventh race of the year. The five-year old Soup, trained by David Hoffmans, set a course record by running the mile and quarter in two minutes and one second and he took home $2.06 million in the richest thoroughbred race in North America. In other races, Pilsudski won the Breeder's Cup Turf, Boston Harbor won the Juvenile, Da Hoss took the Mile and Storm Song won the Juvenile Fillies and defeated three horses trained by D. Wayne Lukas.

Baseball

As the baseball world basked in the glow of a thrilling World Series, the looming ugliness of the labor situation lumbered back on stage. Since the custodians of the game, the owners, do not like the game enough to give it peace, an agreement was still not in sight. Despite the fact that representatives of the owners and the players had reached an agreement and despite the fact that the players had approved it, the owners had not even scheduled a ratification meeting by the Monday after the Series ended. Donald Fehr, the head of the players union, was heading off to Japan with a team of major league All-Stars. Fehr indicated that there was nothing left for him to do. Fehr was due to return to the US the week of November 10th. What the owners would do in the meantime was anybody's guess. ❐

COLLEGE FOOTBALL

AP Top 25 Poll

(as of Oct. 27, 1996)

The October 27, 1996 Associated Press Top 25 college football poll, with number of first-place votes and this year's record in parentheses, total points and preseason ranking:

	Record	Pts	Preseason
1 Florida (59)	(7-0)	1,666	4
2 Ohio State (4)	(7-0)	1,579	9
3 Florida State (3)	(6-0)	1,563	3
4 Arizona State (1)	(8-0)	1,481	20
5 Nebraska	(6-1)	1,404	1
6 Tennessee	(5-1)	1,347	2
7 Colorado	(6-1)	1,210	5
8 North Carolina	(6-1)	1,195	—
9 Michigan	(6-1)	1,080	14
10 Alabama	(7-1)	1,065	15
11 Northwestern	(7-1)	1,037	18
12 LSU	(6-1)	868	19
13 Brigham Young	(8-1)	790	—
14 Kansas State	(7-1)	759	21
15 Penn State	(7-2)	644	11
16 Virginia	(5-2)	580	23
17 Wyoming	(8-0)	576	—
18 West Virginia	(7-1)	459	—
19 Notre Dame	(4-2)	439	6
20 Utah	(7-1)	412	—
21 Washington	(5-2)	271	—
22 Miami	(5-2)	265	12
23 Southern Miss	(7-1)	257	—
24 Auburn	(5-2)	231	17
25 Iowa	(5-2)	190	22

Others Receiving Votes: Virginia Tech 106, Syracuse 72, Army 66, East Carolina 63, Air Force 42, Michigan State 20, Navy 13, Texas Tech 13, Georgia Tech 6, California 3, Southern Cal 3.

TENNIS

Late 1996 Tournament Results

Men's Tour

Finals	Tournament	Winner	Earnings	Loser	Score
Oct. 20	IPB Czech Indoor (Ostrava)	David Prinosil	$64,000	P. Korda	61 62
Oct. 20	Toulouse Grand Prix (France)	Mark Philippoussis	54,000	M. Larsson	61 57 64
Oct. 20	Eisenberg Israel Open	Javier Sanchez	43,000	M. Ondruska	64 75
Oct. 27	Eurocard Open (Stuttgart)	Boris Becker	333,300	P. Sampras	36 63 36 63 64

Remaining ATP Events (4): Paris Open (Nov. 3); Kremlin Cup (Nov. 10); Hellmann's Cup (Nov. 10); Stockholm Open (Nov. 10).

Women's Tour

Finals	Tournament	Winner	Earnings	Loser	Score
Oct. 13	Wismilak Int'l (Surabaya)	Shi-Ting Wang	$17,700	N. Miyagi	64 60
Oct. 20	European Indoors (Zurich)	Jana Novotna	150,000	M. Hingis	62 62
Oct. 20	Nokia Open (Beijing)	Shi-Ting Wang	17,700	L. Chen	63 64
Oct. 27	Bell Challenge (Quebec)	Lisa Raymond	27,500	E. Callens	64 64
Oct. 27	Seat Open (Luxembourg)	Anke Huber	27,500	K. Habsudova	63 60

Remaining WTA Events (4): Ameritech Cup (Nov. 3); Ladies Kremlin Cup (Nov. 3); Bank of the West Classic (Nov. 10); Advanta Championships (Nov. 17).

GOLF

Late 1996 Tournament Results

PGA Tour

Last Rd	Tournament	Winner	Earnings	Runner-Up
Oct. 6	Las Vegas International	Tiger Woods (332)*	$297,000	D. Love III (332)
Oct. 13	Lacantera Texas Open	David Ogrin (275)	216,000	J. Haas (276)
Oct. 20	Disney/Oldsmobile Classic	Tiger Woods (267)	216,000	P. Stewart (268)
Oct. 27	The Tour Championship	Tom Lehman (268)	540,000	B. Faxon (274)

***Playoffs: Las Vegas**— Woods won on the first hole.

Remaining Events (10): World Open Championship (Oct. 31-Nov.3); Kapalua International (Nov. 7-10); PGA Grand Slam (Nov. 12-13); Shark Shootout (Nov. 14-17); World Cup of Golf (Nov. 21-24); Wendy's Three-Tour Challenge (Nov. 25-26); Skins Game (Nov. 28-Dec. 1); JC Penney Classic (Dec. 5-8); Diners Club Matches (Dec. 12-15); Andersen Consulting World Champ. (Jan. 4-5, 1997).

Late 1996 Tournament Results (Cont.)

European PGA Tour

Last Rd	Tournament	Winner	Earnings	Runner-Up
Oct. 6	German Masters	Darren Clarke (264)	£108,330	M. Davis (265)
Oct. 13	Oki Pro-Am	Tom Kite (273)	74,500	A. Cabrera (274)
Oct. 13	Alfred Dunhill Cup	United States (2-1)	300,000	New Zealand
Oct. 20	World Matchplay	Ernie Els (3 & 2)	170,000	Vijay Singh
Oct. 27	Volvo Masters	Mark McNulty (276)	238,000	4-way tie (283)

Remaining Events (3): World Open Championship (Oct. 31-Nov. 3); World Cup of Golf (Nov. 21-24); Andersen Consulting World Championship (Jan. 4-5, 1997).

Seniors Tour

Last Rd	Tournament	Winner	Earnings	Runner-Up
Oct. 6	Ralph's Classic	Gil Morgan (202)	$120,000	C.C. Rodriguez & Jim Colbert (203)
Oct. 13	The TransAmerica	John Bland (204)	105,000	J. Colbert (205)
Oct. 20	Raley's Gold Rush	Jim Colbert (202)	120,000	D. Stockton (207)
Oct. 27	Maui Kaanapali Classic	Bob Charles (198)	97,500	H. Irwin (199)

Remaining Events (5): Emerald Coast Classic (Nov. 1-3); Senior Tour Championship (Nov. 7-10); Wendy's Three-Tour Challenge (Nov. 25-26); Diners Club Matches (Dec. 13-15); Lexus Challenge (Dec. 19-22).

LPGA

Last Rd	Tournament	Winner	Earnings	Runner-Up
Oct. 5	JAL Big Apple Classic	Caroline Pierce (211)	$108,750	T. Barrett & K. Webb (216)
Oct. 13	CoreStates Betsy King Classic	Annika Sorenstam (270)	90,000	L. Davies (278)
Oct. 20	World Championship of Golf	Annika Sorenstam (274)	125,000	H. Alfredsson (275)
Oct. 27	Nichirei International	USA (21½)	432,000	Japan (14½)

Remaining Events (5): Toray Japan Queens Cup (Nov. 1-3); Tour Championship (Nov. 21-24); JC Penney Classic (Dec. 5-8); Diners Club Matches (Dec. 13-15); Wendy's Three-Tour Challenge (Dec. 21-22).

Team Competition

Alfred Dunhill Cup

at St. Andrews, Scotland (Oct. 10-13)
United States def. New Zealand, 2-1

Semifinals (United States def. Sweden, 2-1): Mark O'Meara (USA) def. Peter Hedblom (SWE), 68-74; Steve Stricker (USA) def. Patrick Sjoland (SWE), 70-73; Jarmo Sandelin (SWE) def. Phil Mickelson (USA), 68-71.

Semifinals (New Zealand def. South Africa, 2-1): Wayne Westner (S.AFR) def. Grant Waite (NZ), 74-74; Greg Turner (NZ) def. Retief Goosen (S.AFR), 71-72; Ernie Els (S.AFR) def. F. Nobilo (NZ), 69-72.

Finals (United States def. New Zealand, 2-1): Frank Nobilo (NZ) def. Mark O'Meara (USA), 69-72; Phil Mickelson (USA) def. Greg Turner (NZ), 69-72; Steve Stricker (USA) def. Grant Waite (NZ), 67-73.

THOROUGHBRED RACING

Breeders' Cup

Results from the seven Breeders' Cup races held Saturday, Oct. 26, 1996 at Woodbine in Toronto, Canada.

	Time	Top 3 Finishers	Jockeys	Trainers	Money Won
Sprint (6 furlongs)	1:08⅘	1 Lit de Justice	Corey Nakatani	Jenine Sahadi	$520,000
		2 Paying Dues	Pat Day	Clifford W. Sise Jr.	200,000
		3 Honour and Glory	Gary Stevens	D. Wayne Lukas	120,000
Juv. Fil (1¹⁄₁₆ miles)	1:43⅗	1 Storm Song	Craig Perret	Nick Zito	$520,000
		2 Love That Jazz	Mike Smith	Nick Zito	200,000
		3 Critical Factor	Alex Solis	Myung Kwon Cho	120,000
Distaff (1⅛ miles)	1:48⅕	1 Jewel Princess	Corey Nakatani	Wallace Dollase	$520,000
		2 Serena's Song	Gary Stevens	D. Wayne Lukas	200,000
		3 Different	Chris McCarron	Ronald McAnally	120,000
Mile	1:35⅘	1 Da Hoss	Gary Stevens	Michael W. Dickinson	$520,000
		2 Spinning World	Cash Asmussen	Jonathan Pease	200,000
		3 Same Old Wish	Shane Sellers	Robert Barbara	120,000
Juvenile (1¹⁄₁₆ miles)	1:43⅗	1 Boston Harbor	Jerry Bailey	D. Wayne Lukas	$520,000
		2 Acceptable	Shane Sellers	Nick Zito	200,000
		3 Ordway	John Velazquez	David Donk	120,000
Turf (1½ miles)	2:30⅕	1 Pilsudski	Walter Swinburn	Michael Stoute	$1,040,000
		2 Singspiel	Gary Stevens	Michael Stoute	400,000
		3 Swain	Olivier Peslier	Andre Fabre	240,000
Classic 1½ miles)	2:01	1 Alphabet Soup	Chris McCarron	David Hofmans	$2,080,000
		2 Louis Quatorze	Pat Day	Nick Zito	800,000
		3 Cigar	Jerry Bailey	Bill Mott	480,000

Other Late 1996 Major Stakes Races

Date	Race	Location	Miles	Winner	Jockey	Purse
Sept. 29	Canadian International	Woodbine	1½	Singspiel	Gary Stevens	$1,000,000
Oct. 4	Buick Meadowlands Cup	Meadowlands	1⅛	Dramatic Gold	Kent Desormeaux	750,000
Oct. 5	Goodwood Breeders' Cup	Santa Anita	1⅛	Savinio	Corey Nakatani	303,300
Oct. 5	Moet Champagne Stakes	Belmont	1¹⁄₁₆	Ordway	John Velazquez	400,000
Oct. 5	Jockey Club Gold Cup	Belmont	1½	Skip Away	Shane Sellers	1,000,000
Oct. 5	Turf Classic International	Belmont	1½ (T)	Diplomatic Jet	Jorge Chavez	500,000
Oct. 6	Frizette Stakes	Belmont	1¹⁄₁₆	Storm Song	Graig Perret	400,000
Oct. 6	Beldame Stakes	Belmont	1⅛	Yanks Music	John Velazquez	400,000
Oct. 6	Spinster Stakes	Keeneland	1⅛	Different	Chris McCarron	542,000
Oct. 6	L'Arc De Triomphe	Longchamp	Oct. 6	Helissio	Oliver Peslier	1,369,595

HARNESS RACING

Late 1996 Major Stakes Races

Date	Race	Raceway	Winner	Driver	Purse
Oct. 4	Kentucky Futurity	Lexington	Running Sea	Wally Hennessey	$125,200
Oct. 12	Messenger Stakes	Meadowlands	Go For Grins	Dave Palone	333,080
Oct. 25	BC 3-Yr-Old Filly Trot	Vernon Downs	Personal Banner	Peter Wrenn	350,000
Oct. 25	BC 3-Yr-Old Colt Trot	Vernon Downs	Running Sea	Wally Hennessey	400,000
Oct. 26	BC 3-Yr-Old C & G Pace	Yonkers Raceway	Armbro Operative	Mike Lachance	400,000
Oct. 26	BC 3-Yr-Old Filly Pace	Yonkers Raceway	Mystical Maddy	Mike Lachance	390,000

STEEPLECHASE RACING

Late 1996 Major Stakes Races

Date	Race	Location	Miles	Winner	Jockey	Purse
Oct. 26	Grand National	Far Hills, NJ	2⅝	Corneggio (IRE)	A. Kingsley Jr.	$150,000

AUTO RACING

Late 1996 Results

NASCAR

Date	Event	Location	Winner (Pos.)	Avg.mph	Earnings	Pole	Qual.mph
Oct. 20	AC Delco 400	Rockingham	Ricky Rudd (2)	122.280	$90,025	D. Jarrett	157.194
Oct. 27	Dura-Lube 500	Phoenix	Bobby Hamilton (17)	109.709*	95,550	B. Labonte	131.076

* track record

Winning Cars: Ford Thunderbird (1)—Rudd; Pontiac Grand Prix (1)—Hamilton.
Remaining Races (1): NAPA 500 in Atlanta (Nov. 10).

NHRA

Date		Event	Winner	Time	MPH	2nd Place	Time	MPH
Oct. 13	Chief Auto Parts Nationals	Top Fuel	Cory McClenathan	4.746	301.91	S. Kalitta	7.252	107.47
		Funny Car	Dale Pulde	5.009	303.95	C. Pedregon	7.838	108.17
		Pro Stock	Jim Yates	7.006	196.20	K. Johnson	7.083	195.35
Oct. 27	Winston Select Finals	Top Fuel	Joe Amato	4.664	312.93	S. Kalitta	4.698	304.36
		Funny Car	John Force	15.074	76.42	T. Pedregon	No Show	
		Pro Stock	Mike Edwards	7.010	197.19	R. Smith	7.012	196.97

BOWLING

1996 Fall Tour Results

PBA

Final	Event	Winner	Earnings	Final	Runner-Up
Sept. 22	Japan Cup	Steve Wilson	$50,000	248-244	Danny Wiseman
Oct. 4	**BPAA US Open**	Dave Husted	46,000	216-214	George Brooks
Oct. 9	Cleveland Open	George Branham III	16,000	234-194	Mark Williams
Oct. 15	Ebonite Classic	Marshall Holman	22,000	246-235	Wayne Webb
Oct. 23	Rochester Open	W.R. Williams Jr.	16,000	232-223	Pete Weber

Remaining Events (3): Touring Pro/ Senior Doubles (Oct. 26-30); Greater Harrisburg Open (Nov. 2-6); Touring Players Championship (Nov. 8-12).

1996 Fall Tour Results (Cont.)

LPBT

Final	Event	Winner	Earnings	Final	Runner-Up
Sept. 26	Rossford Gold. Triangle	Cheryl Daniels	$9,000	212-196	Kim Canady
Oct. 4	**BPAA US Open**	Liz Johnson	18,000	265-236	Marianne DiRupo
Oct. 9	Brunswick Three Rivers Open	Wendy Macpherson	10,000	212-210	Anne Marie Duggan
Oct. 15	Columbia 300 Delaware Open	Michelle Feldman	11,500	245-195	Lisa Wagner
Oct. 23	Baltimore Eastern Open	Carol Gianotti-Block	9,000	220-214	Liz Johnson

Remaining Events (3): Lady Ebonite Classic (Oct. 26-31); Hammer Players Championship (Nov. 2-7); Sam's Town Invitational (Nov. 10-17).

SOCCER

Continental Indoor Soccer League (CISL)

Championships Series (Best of 3)

Monterrey La Raza vs. Houston Hotshots

Date	Result	Site
Oct. 20	Monterrey, 10-6	at Monterrey
Oct. 26	Monterrey 6-5 (OT)	at Houston

Monterrey La Raza wins back-to-back CISL Championships

TRIATHLON

Ironman Triathlon

Results of the Ironman Triathlon Championship held Kailua-Kona, Hawaii on Oct. 26. The race consists of a 2.4-mile ocean swim, a 112-mile bike ride and a 26.2 mile run.

	Men	Swim	Bike	Run	Total Time
1	Luc Lierde, Belgium	:51:36	4:30:44	2:41:48	8:04:08
2	Thomas Hellriegel, Germany	:54:22	4:24:50	2:46:55	8:06:07
3	Greg Welch, Encinitas, Calif.	:51:23	4:35:43	2:51:51	8:18:57
4	Peter Reid, Canada	:54:22	4:30:33	2:59:42	8:24:37
5	Dave Scott, Boulder, Colo.	:53:16	4:49:55	2:45:20	8:28:31

	Women	Swim	Bike	Run	Total Time
1	Paula Newby-Fraser, Encinitas, Calif.	:55:30	5:01:34	3:09:45	9:06:49
2	Natasha Badmann, Germany	1:04:41	4:53:47	3:16:51	9:11:19
3	Karen Smyers, Lincoln, Mass.	:54:11	5:02:33	3:22:29	9:19:13
4	Wendy Ingraham, Walnut Creek, Calif.	:51:30	5:06:44	3:23:58	9:22:12
5	Ute Mueckel, Germany	:51:27	5:16:57	3:18:18	9:26:42

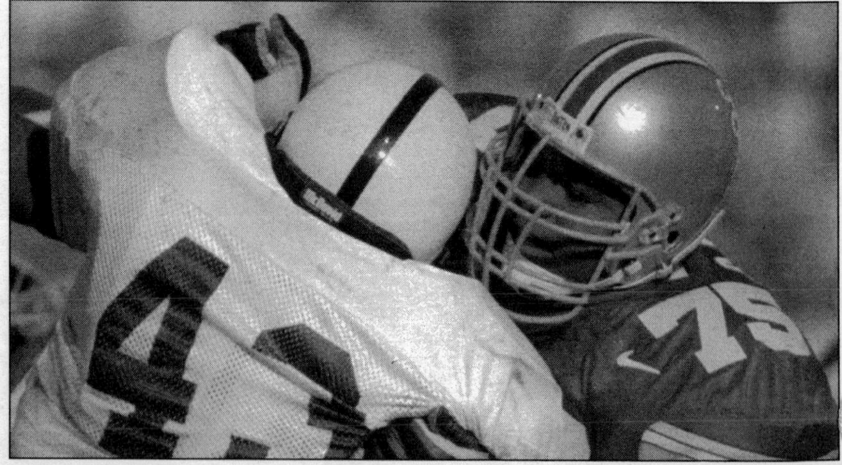

Wide World Photos

Ohio State tackle **Orlando Pace** (r), a Heisman candidate, is a big part of the reason the Buckeyes were undefeated and ranked second in the nation as of October 27.

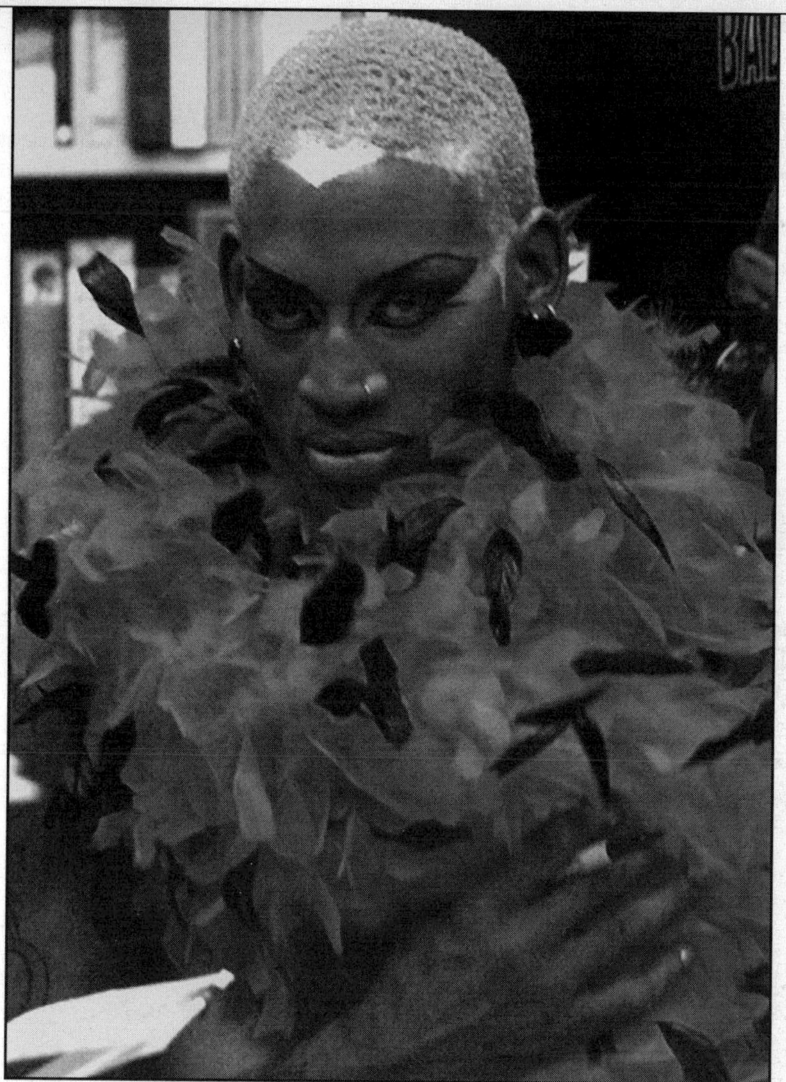

Wide World Photos

When **Dennis Rodman** appeared in the outfit pictured above to promote his book, it was not the first time he exhibited unusual behavior for a professional athlete.

THE CLASS OF '96

Top Sports Personalities of 1996

by the editors of the Information Please Sports Almanac

Distilling an entire year from the world of sports down to sixteen personalities is difficult, especially in an Olympic year. And especially today. The onslaught of sports media coverage allows many different people to emerge. Sometimes it's hard to tell if someone is a true star or a shooting star. Well, it isn't always hard; Super Bowl MVP Larry Brown wasn't even considered.

At the end of this section, you'll find a list of all the other athletes whose achievements we examined. But these fifteen people (and a horse) are the ones who defined the past year and the ones who will be remembered in the coming years. In alphabetical order, they are:

The Sports Almanac Class of '96

(in alphabetical order)

Roberto Alomar
Marcus Camby
Cigar
Jeff Gordon
Steffi Graf
Michael Johnson
Mario Lemieux
Art Modell
Eddie Murray
Marie-Jose Perec
Dennis Rodman
Alan Rothenberg
Pat Summitt
Kerri Strug
Reggie White
Tiger Woods

Baltimore Orioles

Roberto Alomar

Forget about the spitting at an umpire. It was an ugly moment and quite out of character for one of the game's nicer people. The lingering effect of this incident will be to underscore baseball's biggest problem. The American League responded with an impotent five game suspension. In response, every side involved had their lawyers ready to strike. After some empty litigation, the suspension stood. And the world was reminded, again, that the game has no leadership.

Toronto Raptors

Marcus Camby

Marcus Camby was one of the better sports stories of recent times. UMass had become a national power in men's basketball. And in Camby they finally had a star, the consensus national player of the year. Shortly after turning pro, Camby admitted that he had received some gifts from a sports agent. Camby now symbolized a lot of the bad things about college basketball: players leaving early, players receiving gifts and special treatment, and unethical agents preying on young stars.

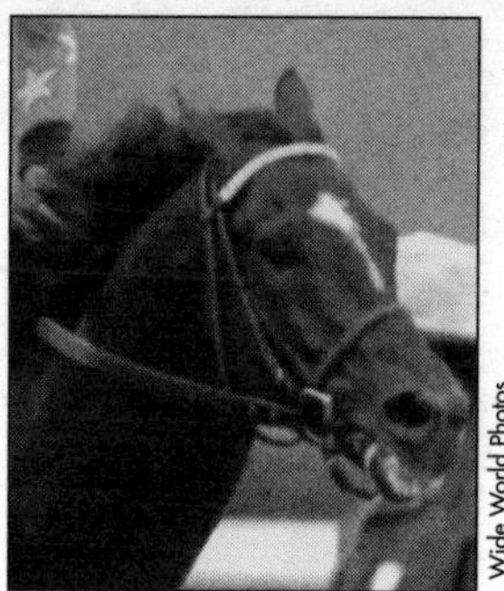
Wide World Photos

Cigar

While he's the youngest star on our list, the six-year old Cigar is at the end of his career, the most celebrated career of any horse in the last fifty years. By winning 16 consecutive races, Cigar tied a record set by Citation, a contemporary of Joe Dimaggio, Sammy Baugh and Ben Hogan. Those names also place Cigar in a larger historical perspective; one of the all-time greats.

Wide World Photos

Jeff Gordon

Normally, the Winston Cup champion would head into the next season with little to prove. But 25-year old Jeff Gordon had a mission. Gordon wants the emphasis put on his driving not his age. By October 1, Gordon had made 28 starts with 19 top five finishes, 22 top ten finishes and an amazing 10 victories. And, of course, he led in winnings with over $2 million. The Winston Cup title is still up for grabs but Jeff Gordon has already made his point.

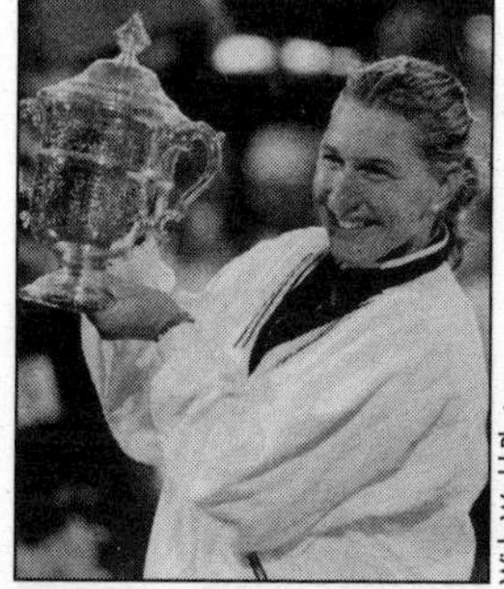
Wide World Photos

Steffi Graf

Is she the best ever? That is the only remaining question concerning Steffi Graf. In 1996, Graf won three quarters of a grand slam with victories at the French Open, Wimbledon and the U.S. Open. She now has 21 career grand slam titles, three behind Margaret Smith Court. If she wins the 1997 Australian Open, she will have at least 5 wins in each major. Maybe the question has been answered.

Allsport/Vandystadt

Michael Johnson

When Michael Johnson lined up for the medal race in both the 200 and 400 meters, he faced an unusual pressure, even for Olympic competition. Everyone assumed he would win. By becoming the first man to win those two events in the same Olympics, Johnson demonstrated that he was a remarkable athlete. By conquering the pressure of the world's assumptions, he showed that he was a remarkable man.

Pittsburgh Penguins

Mario Lemieux

Few things in sports are as celebrated as comebacks. Mario Lemieux, however, had health problems that made his return to being the best player in hockey seem remote. Hodgkin's disease and back problems presented Lemieux with a challenge to merely have a normal life. After missing a full year, Lemieux came back to play for the Pittsburgh Penguins in 1995-96. In a comeback for the ages, Lemieux led the NHL in scoring and won the MVP award. Super Mario, indeed.

Wide World Photos

Art Modell

Stripping Cleveland of a pro football team is the worst thing Art Modell has ever done. With so many other options (sell the team, run it intelligently, get a partner), Modell still took the low road to riches. Everywhere lip service is paid to the concerns of the fans. Columnists and commentators call attention whenever they feel the little guy has been done wrong. It doesn't matter. As Modell reminded us so forcefully, the big guys will always do whatever they want.

Wide World Photos

Eddie Murray

Eddie Murray's name has been showing up on the all-time baseball record lists for a while now. And in a sport that reveres records and numbers more than any other, Murray put up a very big one in 1996. When he hit his 500th home run on September 6, Murray became just the third player in history to have 3,000 hits and 500 homers. The other two? Hank Aaron and Willie Mays.

Wide World Photos

Marie-Jose Perec

Marie-Jose Perec is the first athlete to win the 200 and 400 meter events in the same Olympics with all countries represented.

Unlike Michael Johnson's, Perec's double was not heavily anticipated because she didn't even announce her intention to run the 200 until she had won the 400. But, despite her hesitation, Perec got there first. Because of her amazing talent, she beat Jamaica's Merlene Ottey by .12 seconds in the 200. Because of event scheduling, she beat Michael Johnson by fifteen minutes.

Wide World Photos

Dennis Rodman

We venerate athletes. We overpay them. And as long as they win, pretty much anything goes. Into this long-established scenario comes Dennis Rodman. In a wedding dress, with full makeup, countless piercings, tattoos and hair that changes color on a regular basis. He knows we can't ignore him. And he knows the reason. He's got three championship rings. By our own rules, we have to let him stay. So, whether we like it or not, Rodman has our attention. And he will until he stops winning.

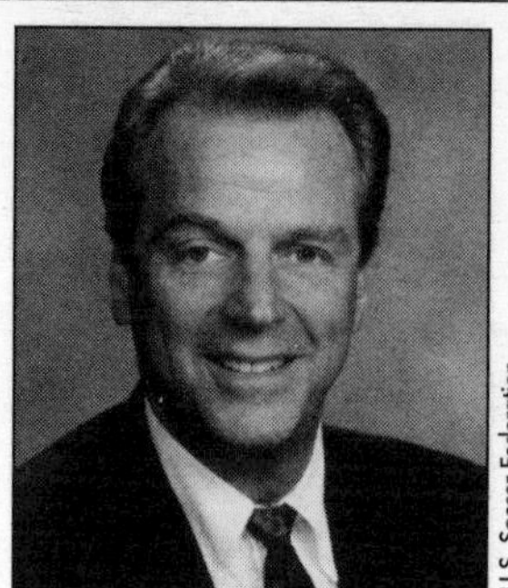

U.S. Soccer Federation

Alan Rothenberg

The credit for the triumph of Major League Soccer goes to its chairman and founder, Alan Rothenberg, who is also the president of the U.S. Soccer Federation. World Cup USA 1994 was a turning point for soccer in the US and Rothenberg headed up that effort as well. In 1996, MLS exceeded all expectations. And while the enduring success of a fifth major pro sports league is by no means assured, Alan Rothenberg has already done more than anyone dreamed possible.

Allsport/Doug Pensinger

Kerri Strug

Due to simultaneous competition, Kerri Strug didn't know that the Russians had done poorly on the beam. The US had already clinched the gold. Despite injuring her ankle on her previous vault, Strug did one more because she thought the gold medal was still on the line. In doing so she provided the most courageous moment of the year in American sports. In a sport known for daintiness and grace, Kerri Strug showed that you also need a little grit.

University of Tennessee

Pat Summitt

In 21 years as coach of the Tennessee women's basketball team, Pat Summitt has produced 596 victories and 4 NCAA titles. In 1984, she coached the first women's basketball team to win a gold medal. It is fitting, then, that the Lady Vols are the reigning NCAA champs as two women's professional leagues begin play. One of them, the American Basketball League, features eight players from Tennessee. Women's basketball has never been more popular. No one is more responsible than Pat Summitt.

Wide World Photos

Reggie White

When it comes to Reggie White, the question of whether or not athletes are role models is not relevant. When black churches were burning down throughout the south, including the Inner City Community Church in Knoxville, Tennessee where he is an associate pastor, White was never a more valuable player. By speaking out and drawing attention to the tragedies, White put his fame to use and got help for the mostly poor communities that were affected.

Stanford University

Tiger Woods

Tiger Woods might have made this list just by winning his third consecutive United States Amateur title. No one had ever done it before. Not Jack Nicklaus, not Bobby Jones. But then he turned pro. Woods admitted he was merely hoping to play well enough to get his tour card for 1997. Well, Woods won two of his first seven pro events and earned more than $700,000 overall. He landed in 23rd place on the season money list and qualified for the Tour Championship.

Also Receiving Votes

Albert Belle
Barry Bonds
Jean-Marc Bosman
Riddick Bowe
Brett Butler
Jorge Campos
Roger Clemens
Continentalvictory
Tom Dolan
Amy Van Dyken
Dale Earnhardt
Dick Ebersol
Marco Etcheverry
Nick Faldo
Salah Hissou
Michael Irvin
Dale Jarrett
Roy Jones Jr.
Michael Jordan
Garry Kasparov
Richard Krajicek
Terry Labonte
Tom Lehman
Carl Lewis
Christy Martin
Paul Molitor
Tommy Morrison
Greg Norman
Tom Osborne
Andy Pettitte
Uta Pippig
Kirby Puckett
David Reid
Mike Richter
Bjarn Riis
Patrick Roy
Joe Sakic
Pete Sampras
Monica Seles
Bud Selig/Donald Fehr
Emmitt Smith
Michelle Smith
Annika Sorenstam
Picabo Street
Alberto Tomba
Mike Tyson
Carlos Valderrama
George Weah

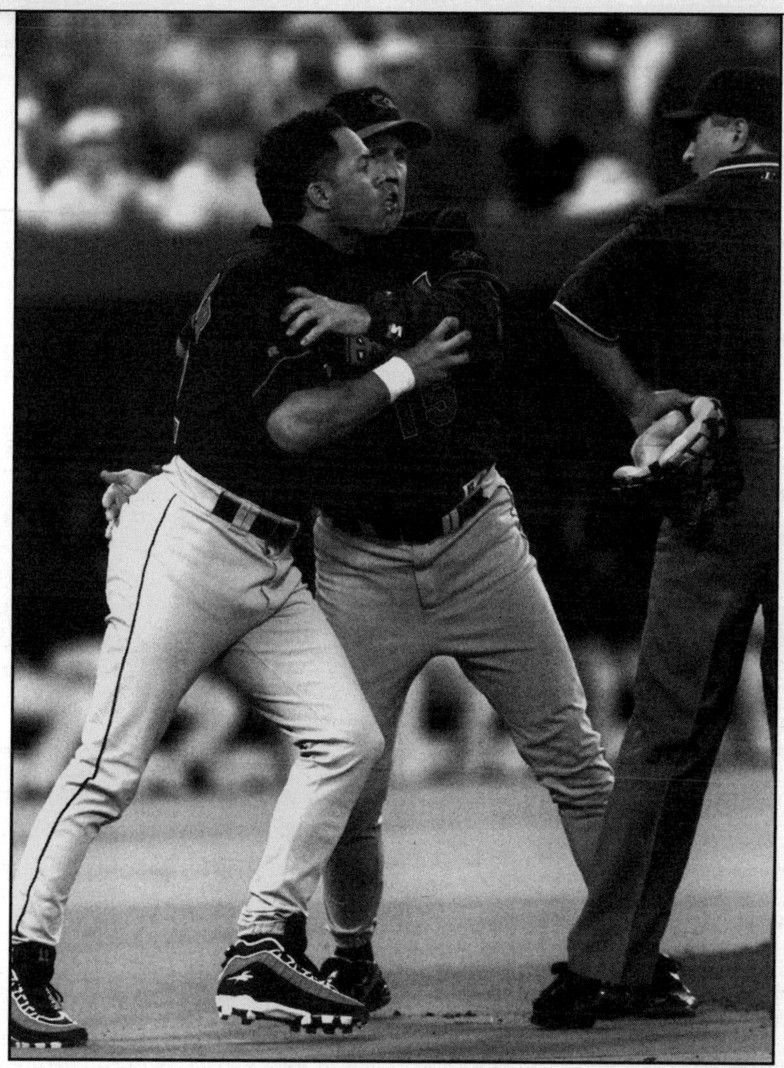

World Wide Photos

When **Roberto Alomar** spit in the face of an umpire, in the most regrettable act of 1996, he assured that his career will always have a moral asterisk.

THE YEAR IN REVIEW

by Scott Ostler

Be Like Mike

An overheard survey of the year in sports reveals that amid the boors, there are some people to cheer

They meet at the same time and place every year, these two guys, a tradition. I just happened to be there, sheer coincidence, with my tape recorder.

They always order a couple of tall ones, then they wrestle with the year in sport, trying to make sense of it, declare some winners and losers and find some cosmic order to the chaos.

They do it, they tell me, "Because it has been said that those who cannot remember the past are condemned to bet the Bills in the Super Bowl."

And, "We like to think of what we do as helping the Year find its way home to bed after a really wild night on the town."

The small guy opens the discussion by suggesting to close it.

"It wasn't really a year of sports," he says, "it was a Ken Burns-length Looney Tune, so absurd that we shouldn't dignify it with our analysis.

"Look at baseball! Fine season, no strikes, but one week in October speaks volumes. Roberto Alomar of the Orioles spits in the face of umpire John Hirschbeck over a called third strike. A 12-year-old kid, Jeff Maier, leans out of the Yankee Stadium bleachers to scoop away a fly ball about to be caught by an Orioles' outfielder, and umpire Richie Garcia somehow doesn't see the kid and rules it a Yankee homer.

"So here's what we get: Baltimore fans cheering a spitting fool, New York fans cheering a kid who cheated his team into the World Series while cutting school, Garcia signing autographs, the fan who stole the "home run" ball from Maier selling it like it's the Hope Diamond, Alomar apologizing to Hirschbeck via a phony prepared statement, and Hirschbeck forgiving Alomar via a stilted prepared statement. Abner Doubleday, wherever he is, has taken up beach volleyball.

"And it's not just baseball. Football? The big story is Michael Irvin's bimbos-'n'-drugs birthday party. More baseball? Business as usual. Marge Schott praises Hitler, Albert Belle rums amok.

"Basketball? Dennis Rodman's marriage to himself gets more national attention than Michael Jordan's fourth NBA championship."

The big guy butts in.

"My overwrought friend," he says, "you are fixated on the negative. It's a year of surpassing heroism and grandeur. Baseball has its most exciting season in decades. Mark McGwire and Brady Anderson each hit 50 homers. Brett Butler is stricken with throat cancer but battles back. Yankees vs. Braves in the Fall Classic.

"Look around! Cigar wins 16 straight races. Tiger Woods stops being golf's greatest amateur and starts being its most exciting pro. Kerri Strug vaults on one leg and wins a nation's hearts. I could go on..."

"No you can't," the small man says, "I've got to be at work Monday morning. What'a ya say, Mo?"

That's the signal for Mo the Barkeep to flip

Scott Ostler is a sports columnist for the *San Francisco Chronicle*.

The departure of **Kirby Puckett** from the baseball scene unfortunately leaves more room for **Albert Belle**, shown here moments after decking Fernando Vina in the most unsportsmanlike act of a career filled with them.

a coin and begin tossing out the categories. The big guy wins the coin flip and elects to face the jukebox and to be quoted in italics.

"This tends to degenerate in a hurry," Mo says, "so let's start on a positive note: Smartest athlete."

Cigar. He wins the 16 consecutive races before finally losing to 39-1 longshot Dare and Glow at Del Mar. Despite his fame, Cigar manages to avoid media interviews, autograph hounds and scandals. And he'll probably retire to stud by the age of seven. That's smart.

Impressive, but IQ-wise, Cigar can't carry Dennis Rodman's jock. By quitting on his team the previous season, Rodman gets traded to the Bulls, where all he has to do is collect rebounds, tattoos and a championship ring.

Then Rodman writes an autobiography, "Bad As I Wanna Be," which is three literary notches below a comic book, but features a sex romp with Madonna and cover photos of Dennis in the buff. The book is a No. 1 bestseller. The man's a knucklehead, but a genius at rebounding and marketing and hair coloring.

Not a bad start you guys. And you got sex into both of your answers. Moving along: Newcomer of the Year?

Tiger Woods. He wins his third straight U.S. Amateur title with yet another come-from-behind charge, then turns pro, and signs with Nike for $40 mil.

First PGA tournament, he sinks a hole-in-one. Fifth tournament, Las Vegas Invitational, he wins! Sixth tournament, another win. Three months after checking out of his college dorm, he's dominating the pro tour.

Maybe the sports newcomer of the decade.

Whoa, Mr. Blinded by the Hype. Did you catch Alex Rodriguez, the Mariners' shortstop? As a 20-year-old, he plays his way into the Honus Wagner class of shortstops. Hits .358 with 36 home runs and 123 RBIs. And for style, humility, attitude and flair, Rodriguez makes Tiger look like...Let's just say he's Tiger's match.

What departure leaves the biggest void?

Joe Montana retired as a TV football analyst, but we survived that blow. My vote goes to Don Shula, prodded into retirement by Dolphins ownership and by carping fans, after 33 seasons as a head coach.

Baseball takes the biggest hit. Tommy Lasorda has a heart attack and steps down as Dodger manager in the midst of his 20th season. Kirby Puckett, who is only 35 and is everything that's good about baseball, and coming off a .318 season, gets knocked out of the game for good by a sudden degeneration of his eyesight.

Choker of the year?

If we go by body of work, Andre Agassi.

Who?

Exactly. This was the year Andre would challenge Pete Sampras, the rivalry blossoms into a sports classic. But Andre does a Judge Crater. Loses to Luke Jensen in the first round of the Australian Open. At Wimbledon, loses in the semis to Michael Chang in straight sets. Suddenly, Andre is over the hill on a skateboard.

With all due disrespect to Agassi, nobody this year out-chokes the Shark, Greg Norman. He goes into the final day of the Masters leading by SIX strokes, shoots a 78 and finishes five strokes behind Nick Faldo.

It was Golfdom's all-time el foldo, and one of the Top 10 in sports, all time.

Amen.

Onward, boys. Guttiest performance?

I'll salute Kerri Strug for vaulting on a sprained ankle as the US gymnasts upset the world to win the Olympic gold. But consider: Utta Pippig wins her third straight Boston Marathon, running with an upset stomach, diarrhea and menstrual cramps. She says, "I felt not nice." Strug gutted it out for two seconds; Pippig for 2 1/2 hours.

Courageous, but Pete Sampras takes four hours, nine minutes to beat Alex Corretja in the U.S. Open quarterfinals, battling dreadful heat and fatigue.

Sampras barfs on the court! You talk about your gut-checks. Then Pete goes on to win the tournament, his eighth Grand Slam win. This victory cements his place on tennis' Mt. Olympus.

Agreed, but for courage, let's not overlook Steffi Graf winning the Open. It's her 21st Slam win, and she does it under heavy emotional stress. Her father is in jail awaiting trial for tax cheating, and the German tax cops are also breathing down Steffi's neck. Richard (The Fugitive) Kimball wasn't under that much pressure.

By the way, if we're honoring gutty performances, how about Michael Irvin? The Cowboys' wide receiver is caught in a cheap hotel room with a pal, two topless dancers and a nice assortment of recreational drugs.

When the cops barge in, Irvin pulls one aside and says, "Can I tell you who I am?" That's gutsy.

One of the ladies takes the fall for the other three, so all Irvin gets is a six-game suspension, even though he is also accused of threatening a witness. When Irvin returns to the Cowboys, Troy Aikman observes, "He's the same flamboyant, loving guy."

You sure it wasn't Irvin's wife who said that?

Hey, no cheap shots. How about the least courageous performance?

Flat-footed two-way tie.

Right. Half the trophy goes to Roberto Alomar. He spits in Hirschbeck's face after that called third strike in the Orioles' final regular-season game, then he tells the media that Hirschbeck has been crabby ever since his seven-year-old son died of a terrible disease three years ago.

And the other half of the Most Gutless trophy goes to Gene Budig, the American League President. He responds to the obvious need for swift justice by giving Alomar a five-game suspension, beginning NEXT SEASON!

Alomar bats the Orioles into the playoffs, and past the Cleveland Indians. The Orioles eventually lose to the Yankees in the ALCS, denying Mr. Spit a World Series appearance.

Moving on: Worst team in sports?

You mean, besides Alomar-Budig? Well, I would hate to overlook the Jets, because it's so darn hard to lose as consistently as they do in this age of NFL parity.

But the Tigers! They lose 109 games and their batters whiff a major league record 1,268 times, and their pitchers set an ML record for gopher balls (241). The pitching staff is held together with pine tar and paper clips.

Agreed.

Every year has its whacko nutballs, although that's probably not the technical term. Who topped the '96 crop?

Often our nominees are offensive but rel-

Wide World Photos

In one of the year's more bizarre moments, defending 100 meter Olympic champion **Linford Christie** committed two foot faults and was disqualified from competitino in Atlanta. He refused to leave the arena, partially disrobed and later came back for a victory lap.

atively harmless. This year we weren't so lucky. We had a Class A whacko in John duPont, the chemical company heir.

He gave massive financial support to U.S. amateur wrestling over the years, but in January, for no known reason, duPont, increasingly unstable in recent years, shot and killed his friend and U.S. Olympic wrestling veteran Dave Schultz, then holed up for two days before he was apprehended. He was ruled psychotic and incompetent to stand trial.

So by comparison, our other nominees are mosquitos, but let's not trivialize the damage they can inflict on people and sports.

Take Marge Schott. Please. She's not a loose cannon, she's a loose armory. In a TV interview, the Reds' owner rips several of her own players, then she soft-pedals Adolf Hitler, saying, "Everybody knows he was good at the beginning, but he just went too far."

For that statement, heaped atop her large pile of previous offensive remarks, Schott gets suspended for 2 1/2 years.

Sorry, but nutball-wise, Marge can't carry Albert Belle's jock. Belle throws a baseball at a photographer who is harassing him by snapping pictures from 300 feet away. And Belle gets suspended for a cheap-shot forearm to the chops of secondbaseman Fernando Vina.

When a fan at Arlington fetches a Belle homer and offers to give it to Belle in exchange for an autographed ball, Bell says, "I won't pay you (spit)."

Some say Belle is crude but harmless. I say, "Tick, tick, tick."

Let's not neglect Linford Christie, the British 100-meter dash star. Defending his Olympic title, Christie DQs himself with two false starts, but he refuses to leave the track, wanders like a demented Shakespearean king, holding up the race.

Finally he leaves, but returns to the track after the race to take a victory lap. It's the closest we come in '96 to seeing deployment of the large butterfly net.

Can we select a shining hero from '96?

How about NOT Jeff Maier? Kid didn't even catch the ball, just swiped it into the stands, which makes him the new Sultan of Swat.

My pick is Mahmoud Abdul-Rauf, the Denver (now Sacramento) guard who refused to stand for the Star Spangled Banner because he said it was offensive to his religious beliefs.

Boy, that zinged some nerves. A lot of people have died for that flag, but they also died defending the freedom to do irritating stuff like snub the flag.

At least Abdul-Rauf was sincere. Until he reached an agreement with the league he would stand for the song but pray he was suspended without pay.

I say he gave us a working example of the best reason of all to honor the flag and the anthem: Because you don't have to.

Gutsy choice. Wrong, but gutsy. I'll go with Brett Butler. Early in the season he's diagnosed with tonsil cancer. Near the end of the season, after surgeries and radiation treatments, the 39-year-old Butler returns to the Dodgers. Goes up to bat with tears in his eyes. Scores the winning run. That's hero stuff.

And honorable mention to J.R. Rider's mother. J.R. gets tossed from a game with two technicals, but refuses to leave the court. Maybe this is where Linford Christie got his inspiration.

Anyway, Rider's mother is at the game and she walks onto the court and orders her son to the showers. And he leaves, because he knows the next step is that mom grabs him by an ear.

Most unusual injury.

I'll go with Russian Olympic swim hero Alexander Popov getting stabbed by some Moscow watermelon vendors after an argument. I hate it when that happens.

Art Modell, who moved his Browns from Cleveland to Baltimore, is running to pick up a telephone late one night, trips over some furniture and scrapes his scrotum. He claims the injury nearly killed him. Thanks, Art, for sharing that with us.

I'm sure the folks in Cleveland feel Art's pain and in the same place.

OK boys. We have to move it along. Any nominees for weirdest story of the year?

I'm a sucker for animal stories, so I'll split my vote. Half to the Famous Chicken, who gets sued by an ex-Chicago Bulls' cheerleader for forcing her to dance, rolling her on the court and injuring her elbow and jaw. The Chicken has to pay $317,000, which, need I say, ain't chicken feed.

And the rats. Scott Mellanby of the Florida Panthers kills a rat in the locker room before the team's home opener and a fad is born. Every Panthers goal on home ice sets off a rain of plastic and rubber rats from the fans. I guess if a player scores three goals, the rats wear hats.

The Panthers make it to the Stanley Cup finals, losing to the Colorado Avalanche, proving that, in the end, you can never

Postcards From the Edge of the Olympic Games in Atlanta:

Day 1:

The Dream Team (U.S. men's basketball team for those of you just returning from a five-year alien abduction) is under heavy criticism for its grand Olympic lifestyle. The players stay in a luxury hotel, instead of the tiny dorm rooms in the Athletes' Village. But don't think our Dreamers are spoiled! Reggie Miller revealed, "People think we have it so easy. They have no idea. Our hotel isn't even a four-star hotel, and the room service is really terrible."

Day 2:

Rumor: Last night room service left the rainbow sprinkles off Reggie's chocolate mousse.

Atlanta brags that this is the most high-tech, computer-enhanced Olympics ever. Only about half the gadgetry actually works, but it's the thought that counts.

Day 3:

Most impressive star-wars venue: Boxing. The ringside computer system that coordinates the scoring five judges with "punch" buttons looks like Houston's mission control on steroids. The result, in theory: Flawlessly fair judging. In practice: Some of the judges are punchy ex-pugs, so it's like French poodles manning a nuclear reactor.

Day 4:

The Cheetah, a nude dancing club near the Olympic Centennial Park, reportedly is doing a brisk business. Magic Johnson has been seen there.

I would check the place out, but I've been working so hard that I'm simply too tired to dance nude.

Day 5:

Four fire trucks rushed to the Main Press Center today in response to a smoke alarm. The problem was a smoldering doughnut, left too long in a cafeteria microwave.

According to the *Atlanta Constitution-Journal*, "Damage was confined to the donut."

Wide World Photos

Gold medalist **Halil Mutlu** of Turkey wasn't the only guy doing some heavy lifting in Atlanta as our Correspondent weighed in with his own observations.

Day 6:

Everybody was relieved when the FBI fingered a suspect in the park bombing. But it's been several days now, and they haven't found any evidence to link this Richard Jewell guy to the crime, and their search begins to smack of desperation.

Today it was reported that the FBI found some nails in Jewell's apartment. One journalist commented, "Bet they had a hell of a time prying 'em out of his walls."

Day 7:

The Greek water polo team lost today, and a Greek journalist opened the press conference by asking the team captain, "You are a disgrace to your country. Explain yourself."

Coincidentally, that's the exact message I got from my editor after I turned in my first week's expense account. Hey, I have to take a lot of cabs. The Atlanta bus and subway systems haven't been upgraded since they were used to transport Confederate troops, so cabs are a necessity.

I actually overheard on a bus radio a driver telling his dispatcher, "My steering wheel keeps coming off."

Now even taxis aren't safe. Today my cab passed another taxi burning on the freeway shoulder, consumed in flames 20 feet high.

"Glad we weren't in that one," I said to the reporter sharing my cab.

"You know," he observed, "it's not the heat, it's the humidity."

Day 8:

Revenge of the nerd?

What motivates an Olympic champion? American swimmer Amy Van Dyken won two golds and she said, "To the girls who gave me a hard time in high school, I kind of want to say thank you."

Day 9:

I've watched some of the NBC coverage. What's up with that "plausibly live" stuff, which is actually videotape heavily edited and manipulated, no more live than a Dr. Kevorkian patient?

I know NBC is trying to make the Games more entertaining, but I think they went too far when Paavo Nurmi won yesterday's marathon.

Day 10:

Commercial notes: Under heavy pressure from the USOC, which is sponsored by Kodak, Fuji Film painted out its logo on 18 Atlanta billboards featuring Dan O'Brien... Michael Jordan declined the offer to appear in Atlanta to represent Uncle Sam. However, he did appear here representing Sara Lee... The gold shoes Michael Johnson wore in winning the 400 and 200? He donated them to (drum roll, please) the Atlanta Planet Hollywood.

Day 11:

And finally something we should all strive to avoid:

NBC's rowing analyst said of a faltering two-man team, "I watched them practice this morning, and they let their oars get sloppy."

Allsport/Jonathan Daniel

Allsport/Gary M. Prior

Making the world safe for sports fans in 1996 were the legendary **Michael Jordan** and the equally accomplished but not as celebrated **Michael Johnson.**

really count on a rat.

Cute. But the weirdest story is Magic Johnson's comeback/re-retirement. He sits out three and a half seasons after learning he is HIV-positive, but the all-time greatest point guard comes back to the Lakers in mid-season, heavier and slower, but still a force.

When he can't make the Lakers click in the playoffs, Magic retires again. Then says he will un-retire again. Then changes his mind. When Shaquille O'Neal signed with the Lakers, Magic made more noise about coming back. And he backed off from that.

Whew! Magic makes Dennis Rodman look like a bedrock of emotional stability.

Almost closing time, Gents. Who's your person of the year?

Whoever juiced the baseballs. The season-long homerfest really jacked up the game's fun quotient.

How about Bruce Seldon, who earns a million bucks in two minutes, getting knocked out cold by Mike Tyson's breath?

Seriously.

Michael Johnson. Ultimate pressure, the Olympic Games, and he delivers with the toughest gold-medal double, 200 and 400, blows away the 200 world record.

Mo said to be serious. Michael Johnson wasn't even the Michael of the Year. We've gone all night without mentioning that Jordan fellow.

Greatest basketball player of all time, wins his eighth scoring title, leads the Bulls to their fourth NBA title in the last five years he's played.

Jordan has to assimilate Rodman into the Bulls' mix, has to carry a team with no real center, continues as the ultimate go-to guy in sports. Athlete of the decade, already, no question.

The decade? Must be the beer talking.

I'm drinking soda pop.

Your brain got fizzed.

Last call, boys.

Last call? We're just getting started, Mo.

Last call.

Don't you have any pull around here?

I don't make the rules. Last call.

Can I tell you who I am? ❐

Wide World Photos

There were plenty of bridesmaids in sports during the year (the Houston Astros with their third straight second-place divisional finish come to mind), but there was only one bride. To promote a book signing in Manhattan, **Dennis Rodman** stepped out of a horse-drawn carriage straight into the history of hype in a blond wig and a body hugging, halter-top silk shantung wedding gown.

EXTRA POINTS

EXTRA POINTS

by Charles A. Monagan

Archive Photos
Halle Berry

Archive Photos
Dave Justice

ESPN/Rick LaBranche
Chris Berman

"She'd get mad when I watched ESPN."
—Atlanta Brave Dave Justice, philosophizing on his break-up with actress Halle Berry. No one at ESPN, including the ubiquitous Berman, was available for comment.

QUOTES I

"I didn't expect it, but I expected it."
—Red Sox infielder Luis Alicea, after being placed on waivers.

"We're not talking 'date' here. The whole family is going."
—Dan Beard, father of 14-year-old Olympic swimmer Amanda Beard, on her plans to go to breakfast and a ball game with Dennis Rodman.

"Maturity."
—Houston Rockets' Sam Cassell, on what Kevin Garnett, 19, brings to the Timberwolves.

"The last thing you want to do is go down in the history of All-Star Game competition as the only injury sustained during the team picture."
—Orioles' Cal Ripken Jr., after breaking his nose on Roberto Hernandez's forearm.

"It's amazing how many people beat you at golf now that you're no longer President."
—George Bush

Charles A. Monagan has been the editor of *Connecticut* magazine since 1989.

"Obviously we don't want it to smell like sweat."
—spokesman for Michael Jordan's new perfume.

MASCOT BLUES

Talk about social Siberia! After several years of high-profile stardom, Izzy, the much maligned official mascot of the Atlanta Olympics, wasn't invited to the Opening Ceremonies or the Closing Ceremonies. Formerly known as Whatizit, the mascot was left out in the cold because "there really wasn't a moment when we were trying to create a lighthearted, entertaining moment that would appeal to small children," according to an Olympics spokeswoman.

Meanwhile, things weren't much better for a mascot all the way across the country in Oregon. Benny the Beaver, the official spokesbeaver at Oregon State, was roughed up twice. Benny was punched by a University of California lineman after tapping him on the shoulder with a giant plastic hammer. Two weeks later, he was punched in the face by an Arizona U lineman for no apparent reason.

CLOTHING CORNER

Adidas produced and sold a new athletic shoe called "Hemp," a commonly used slang word for marijuana. U.S. drug czar Lee Brown accused the company of trying to "capitalize on the drug culture." Adidas America's president Steve Wynne mocked Brown, writing to him, "It's comforting to know that the war on drugs is going so well that you can afford to devote your time to writing letters to me."

If U.S. medal winners at the Olympics wanted to wear their medals around their necks in public in Atlanta, they also had to wear the team's official awards jacket—by Champion.

KEEP THE SHOES, BOB

And then for the ultimate in comfortable, hardworking athletic apparel, here's this from a Nike Olympics ad: "Right after Bob Kempainen qualified for the marathon, he crossed the finish line and puked all over his Nike running shoes. We can't tell you how proud we were."

THANKS, HARLEY. WE'LL TAKE IT FROM HERE

Harley Sheffield lived every torchbearer's worst nightmare when the Olympic torch went out during his watch. Sheffield, 32, of Redmond, Wash., was bearing the flame on the back of his bicycle while crossing the Tacoma Narrows Bridge when his rear tire slipped and so did the torch, "shattering all over the ground," as Sheffield put it. Luckily, the "mother flame" was still burning in a trailing van, and a replacement torch was soon lit and put back on the road.

BOO BOO BRAZIL

Brazilian soccer bad boy Edmundo was hauled in for a disciplinary hearing after he allegedly struck a Santos defender. His team, Corinthians, said Edmundo didn't do it and they had the tapes to prove it. Unfortunately, the tape they brought to play at the hearing turned out to be one featuring not Edmundo, but the immortal Scooby Doo.

DOPEY BOSSES? CHECK AISLE 5

A grocery store clerk in Dallas claimed he was fired after wearing a Green Bay Packers jersey to work. Sam Young said all employees of the Minyard grocery store were told by their boss to wear Cowboys shirts to work to show support for the team in their playoff game against the Packers. When Young showed up in his Packers top he was told to remove it. When he refused, he said, he was fired on the spot. The Cowboys won, 38-27, but no one mentioned the Minyard grocery store as a key element in the victory.

AND SOMEWHERE BOBBY KNIGHT IS SMILING

During a junior high school recreational league basketball game in Alexandria, Ky., the coach of one team was ejected for repeatedly cursing referee Brian Sizemore. The coach later reappeared on the court and tackled Sizemore. His players, aged 12 to 14, followed, attacking Sizemore and his partner, kicking them and hitting them with metal chairs. Criminal charges were brought against the coach. "It gets worse every year," said Sizemore.

Wide World Photos

Marge Schott

THE MARGE REPORT I

"Snow this morning and now this. I don't believe it. Why are they calling the game?" So went Cincinnati Reds owner Marge Schott's reaction when umpire John McSherry collapsed and died seven pitches into the Cincy home opener.

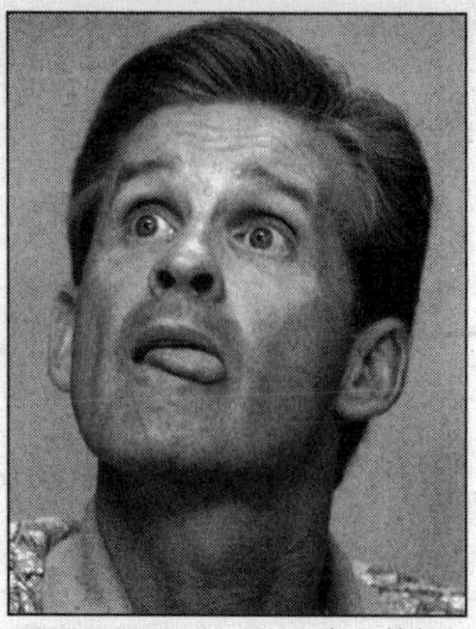

Wide World Photos

Wide World Photos

"I didn't know I looked like Marty Feldman."
—Marlins manager **John Boles** (above, l & r) on his perpetual bug-eyed look.

QUOTES II

"She's making progress."
—Patriots coach Bill Parcells, commenting on the condition of rookie wide receiver Terry Glenn.

"Everyone in our league lives where they live because they can't sell their house or they've been relocated in the witness protection program."
—Utah basketball coach Rick Majerus, on life in the Western Athletic Conference.

"I'm not going to rush it. I'm not going to force it."
—Jersey Nets center Yinka Dare, on not having even one assist after his first 45 games as a pro.

"When they asked him what country he was arriving from, he said, 'USDA.'"
—Nets forward Jayson Williams, on the difficulty of getting teammate Yinka Dare through customs to play in Canada.

"You can't compare him to Nicklaus and Palmer anymore because they never did this."
—PGA veteran Peter Jacobsen on Tiger Woods, after Woods unceremoniously blew off a dinner honoring him at the Buick Challenge.

"Anytime someone says the word 'poll' to him, he says 'Greg Norman'."
—Clinton press secretary Mike McCurry, on what it's like for the President to be so far ahead in the early election polls.

Wide World Photos

President Bill Clinton

HEAD CASES

Archive Photos

Charlie Sheen

Pinhead Actor Charlie Sheen bought out an entire section at Anaheim Stadium so he'd have a better chance at catching and keeping a ball. No ball was hit into his section.

Gearhead Shortly before announcing he'd be leaving Georgetown at the end of his sophomore year to enter the NBA draft, Allen Iverson was seen tooling around town in a $130,000 Mercedes on loan to him from a local auto dealer.

Old Head Ron Weaver, 30, passed himself off as a college student named Ron McKelvey and played 12 games for the University of Texas. "He did it because he loves football and wanted a second chance to play," said his stepsister.

Hophead After several embarrassing incidents he attributed to drinking problems and subsequent treatment for alcohol addiction, golfer John Daly said he was once again drinking beer "in moderation."

Garbagehead While refusing to apologize for using profanity on live national television after Dallas clinched the NFC championship, Michael Irvin used the same expletive at least five times.

Phonehead He can dial long distance on the basketball court—and off it, too. Villanova's Kerry Kittles was suspended for ringing up $3,100 in unauthorized phone calls on a university calling card.

Corkhead Cincinnati Reds Chris Sabo was suspended for seven games for using a corked bat. He'd shattered his bat in a game against Houston; bits of cork flew out of the bat, with a large chunk landing near third base.

Cokehead Former Red Sox manager Butch Hobson was fired as manager of Triple A Scranton Wilkes-Barre after admitting he used cocaine during the season.

Bighead After the Lakers signed Shaquille O'Neal, Magic Johnson let it be known that he might be interested in coming back yet again. The silence was deafening, so Johnson quickly dropped the idea.

Spacehead U.S. Olympic softball player Dani Tyler neglected to touch home plate with what would have been the winning run in an eventual loss to Australia.

Chokehead Greg Norman blew a seven-stroke lead on the last day in relinquishing the Masters crown to Nick Faldo. Later in the year, Norman had to withdraw from the Canon Greater Hartford Open after using a mismarked ball.

Pillhead Irish 5,000-meter runner Marie McMahon tested positive for Advil during the Atlanta Olympics. Advil is a banned substance. Fizzies may be next.

Wide World Photos

Marge Schott

THE MARGE REPORT II

Following umpire John McSherry's death at the Reds' home opener, team owner Marge Schott took some flowers that had been given to her earlier in the day, scribbled a note of sympathy and sent it down to the umpire's locker room.

Wide World Photos

Jeff Maier (top center)

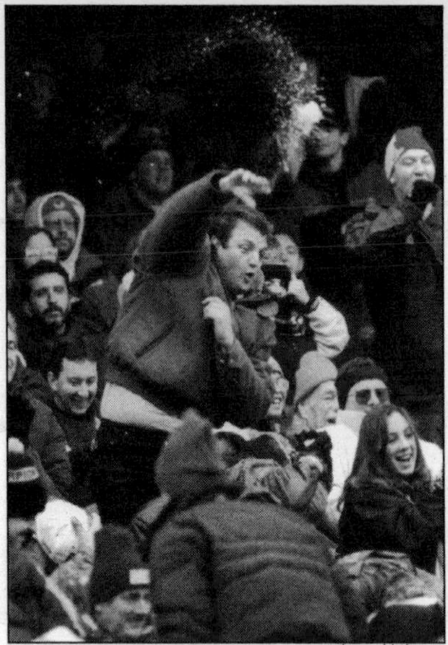

Wide World Photos

Jeffrey Lange

WE'RE NOT ROLE MODELS, EITHER, CHARLES

12-year-old Jeff Maier, from Old Tappan, N.J., turned a long fly ball by the Yankees Derek Jeter into a backbreaking home run when he reached out of the stands and swiped the ball away from Orioles outfielder Tony Tarasco.

Jeffrey Lange, of Bridgewater, N.J., was arrested on a charge of improper behavior after he was photographed—and later identified by at least 15 "friends"— throwing snowballs at the San Diego Chargers during a game at Giants Stadium.

YER OUTTA HERE!

1996 Coaching Adjustments

NHL

Pat Burns, Toronto (fired)
Rick Bowness/Dave Allison, Ottawa (fired)
Kevin Constantine, San Jose (fired)
Bob Gainey, Dallas (GM only)
Paul Holmgren, Hartford (fired)
Rick Ley, Vancouver (fired)
Terry Simpson, Win-Pho (fired)

Baseball

Terry Collins, Houston (fired)
Jim Fregosi, Philadelphia (fired)
Dallas Green, N.Y. Mets (fired)
Kevin Kennedy, Boston (fired)
Marcel Lachemann, California (quit)
Rene Lachemann, Florida (fired)
Tommy Lasorda, Los Angeles (retired)

NFL

Bill Belichick, Cleveland (fired)
Jim Mora, New Orleans (resigned)
Buddy Ryan, Arizona (fired)
David Shula, Cincinnati (fired)
Don Shula, Miami (retired)
Sam Wyche, Tampa Bay (fired)

NBA

Butch Beard, New Jersey (fired)
Allan Bristow, Charlotte (fired)
Mike Dunleavy, Milwaukee (resigned)
John Lucas, Philadelphia (fired)
Brendan Malone, Toronto (fired)
Dick Motta, Dallas (resigned)
Paul Westphal, Phoenix (fired)

THE AGE OF SHAQ HAS BEGUN

Fifty-three NBA players made fewer than 60 percent of their free throws during the 1995-96 season.

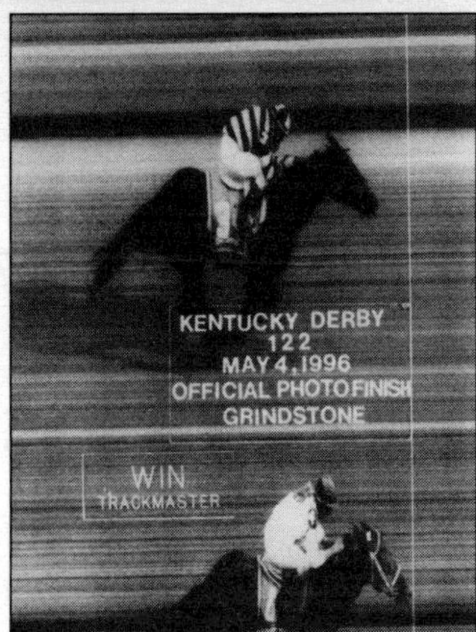

Wide World Photos

IN CASE YOU MISSED IT

Here's how they finished at the Kentucky Derby, something you might not have seen on ABC, which cut away to commercials before the results of a photo finish were made official. The network, which has in the past botched finishes of the New York City Marathon and the Indy 500, is reportedly looking for ways to cut away from game winning field goals, no-hitters, and even 300 games in bowling.

FUN COUPLES

Myra Kraft and Bill Parcells
Roberto Alomar and John Hirschbeck
Albert Belle and Hannah Storm
George Steinbrenner and Reggie Jackson
Latrell Sprewell and Tim Hardaway
Christian Peter and Womankind
Greg Norman and David Graham

WORST NEW TREND

If naming sporting events and arenas after corporations isn't bad enough, or enduring billboards placed behind home plate isn't sickening enough, or watching tennis players and golfers become human billboards isn't embarrassing enough, here come virtual ads. The ads usually involve a company's logo which will be seen (on a tennis court baseline, say, or between the goal posts at a football game) by television viewers, but not by fans at the actual event. Maybe they could throw in some virtual athletes, too. They'd be cheap, they'd be well-behaved and they probably could do really cool stuff.

MEDIA ATTACKS

The Cleveland Indian's Albert Belle, already under fire for cursing out NBC's Hannah Storm, fired two baseballs at *Sports Illustrated* photographer Tony Tomsic. Belle was upset because Tomsic tried to take his picture.

Next to show his royal displeasure was San Francisco outfielder Barry Bonds, who shoved *USA Today* reporter Rod Beaton in the Giants' clubhouse.

But the press found a way to fight back. NBC's NBA basketball analyst and *New York Post* writer Peter Vecsey was charged with assault after he allegedly attacked a man in a Toys 'R' Us in Washington. The man supposedly had called Vecsey an "idiot."

Wide World Photos

Marge Schott

THE MARGE REPORT III

Claiming she couldn't afford cash bonuses, Reds owner Marge Schott sent employees candy for 1995 holiday gifts. Once they opened the treats, the employees found coupons inviting consumers to "win a free trip to the 1991 Grammys."

OLYMPICS QUOTES

"The Dead have always represented the underdog in the struggle for freedom."

—NBC's Bill Walton, on why the Lithuanian Olympic basketball team wears tie-dye shirts in honor of the late Jerry Garcia.

"I would have gone all the way up there to light that thing."

—the impaired former heavyweight champ Joe Frazier, on why he should have been chosen to light the Olympic flame instead of impaired Muhammad Ali.

"My face got tired."

—410-pound U.S. weightlifter Mark Henry, on why he once had to stop eating steak after downing 50 ounces.

"That's a tough question."

—U.S. hoopster Karl Malone, after being asked by a Danish reporter at the Olympics why a basket is worth two points.

"My mother sent me to a sports club when I was 6. Now I am totally exhausted and that is my story."

—Russian gymnast Alexei Nemov, on being asked about his life shortly after being edged out for the gold medal.

"She's basically as guilty as O.J. Simpson."

—U.S. swimmer Ryan Berube, on Ireland's medalist Michelle Smith and the question of steroid use.

BASEBALL: WINNING BACK THE FANS

The Salem Avalanche of the Carolina League offered seats in a hot tub built into a deck along the first base line. The cost of a seat in the tub: $10. Tub capacity: 10.

Going the Avalanche one further were the Palm Springs Suns, who invited fans to attend the July 8 game nude. Nudists were to watch the game from inside a tent near the leftfield line. No nudists showed up for the game but more of the regular fans than normal brought binoculars.

Meanwhile, at the major league level there was no such currying to the fans. In fact, six big-league teams didn't even have games scheduled for Memorial Day.

Wide World Photos

Marge Schott

DER MARGE REPORT IV

During an interview with ESPN, Reds owner Marge Schott offered some praise for Adolf Hitler, saying, "Everybody knows he was good at the beginning, but he just went too far." ❐

Wide World Photos

Dwight Gooden of the New York Yankees celebrates after completing his comeback by throwing a no-hitter on May 14, 1996.

CALENDAR

NOV '95

Sun	Mon	Tue	Wed	Thu	Fri	Sat
			1	2	3	4
5	6	7	8	9	10	11
12	13	14	15	16	17	18
19	20	21	22	23	24	25
26	27	28	29	30		

Closest MVP voting

On November 16th, Red Sox slugger Mo Vaughn edged Cleveland's Albert Belle for the MVP award by a mere eight votes. Below are the closest votes since its inception in 1931.

Year			Pts.	Diff.
1979	NL	**W. Stargell, Pit.**	**216**	
		K. Hernandez, Stl.	216	0
1947	AL	**J. DiMaggio, NYY**	**202**	
		T. Williams, Bos.	201	1
1944	NL	**M. Marion, Stl.**	**190**	
		B. Nicholson, Chi.	189	1
1960	AL	**R. Maris, NYY**	**225**	
		M. Mantle, NYY	222	3
1961	AL	**R. Maris, NYY**	**202**	
		M. Mantle, NYY	198	4
1944	AL	**H. Newhouser, Det.**	**236**	
		D. Trout, Det.	232	4
1957	AL	**T. Williams, Bos.**	**209**	
		R. Sievers, Wash,	205	4
1955	NL	**R. Campanella, Bro.**	**226**	
		D. Snider, Bro.	221	5
1962	NL	**M. Wills, LA**	**209**	
		W. Mays, SF	202	7
1995	AL	**M. Vaughn, Bos.**	**308**	
		A. Belle, Cle.	300	8
1957	NL	**S. Musial, Stl**	**230**	
		R. Schoendienst, NYG Mil.	221	9
1966	NL	**R. Clemente, Pit.**	**218**	
		S. Koufax, LA	208	10

Dan's now the man

NOV. 26—Dan Marino's first touchdown pass in the Dolphins' 36-28 loss to Indianapolis is the 343rd of his illustrious career, vaulting him over the legendary Fran Tarkenton for most touchdown passes in a career. Just two weeks earlier, Marino broke Tarkenton's record for career passing yards. The list below compares the two statistically as of Nov. 26, 1995. The number in parentheses denotes their NFL rank in those categories where applicable.

	Marino	Tarkenton
Yards	47,808 (1)	47,003 (2)
Touchdowns	346 (1)	342 (2)
Completions	3820 (1)	3,686 (2)
Attempts	6,385 (2)	6,467 (1)
Super Bowl Record	0-1	0-3

1 **Deion Sanders signs** a seven year, $35 million contract with the Dallas Cowboys that includes a record $13 million dollar signing bonus. The signing ended a dispute between the players' union and the NFL, who accused the club of evading the salary cap.

2 **Joe Torre** is named manager of the New York Yankees, signing a two year contract worth $500,000 in 1996 and $550,000 in 1997. Torre joins Casey Stengel, Yogi Berra, and Dallas Green as managers of both the Mets and Yankees.

No. 2 ranked Florida State is stunned by No. 20 Virginia, 33-28, their first ACC loss after 29 wins. The game ended with Seminole back Warrick Dunn's rush from six yards out ending less than a yard from the goal line.

Marty Liquori and Florence Griffith Joyner are among six elected to the National Track And Field Hall Of Fame. They are joined by Olympic gold medalists Valerie Briscoe-Hooks and Louise Ritter, coach Mel Rosen and the late Don Lach.

3 **Charlotte Hornets** trade Alonzo Mourning, Pete Myers, and LeRon Ellis to Miami Heat for Glen Rice, Khalid Reeves, and Matt Geiger. Mourning had previously rejected a seven year, $70 million contract from the Hornets.

4 **Riddick Bowe** registers an eighth round TKO of Evander Holyfield to retain the WBO belt. In the sixth round of the see-saw battle, Bowe is knocked to the canvas for the first time in his career.

6 **Cleveland Browns owner Art Modell** announces he is moving the franchise to Baltimore for the 1996 season. Modell signs a 30 year lease with Baltimore that includes a new $200 million, natural grass stadium.

Hartford Whalers fire head coach Paul Holmgren and replace him 28-year-old assistant Paul Maurice, the league's youngest coach.

Baseball announces a five-year, $1.7 billion television deal with NBC, ESPN, Fox and Prime Liberty Cable.

Seattle Mariners skipper Lou Piniella is voted AL Manager of the Year, edging out Boston's Kevin Kennedy for the prize.

New York Rangers center Mark Messier registers three goals in a 4-2 win over Calgary to become the 21st player in the NHL to reach the 500 goal plateau.

Dallas Cowboys owner Jerry Jones, in response to a $300 million suit filed against him by the NFL, initiates a $750 million antitrust suit, claiming NFL Properties prohibits teams from free-market competition.

7 **Colorado Rockies** manager Don Baylor is voted National League Manager of the Year after leading his club to the playoffs in their third season. He joins Frank Robinson as the only former MVPs to win the award.

8 **Minnesota Twins outfielder** Marty Cordova is named American League Rookie of the Year, beating Angel Garret Anderson in the closest vote since 1979.

9 **Detroit Tigers** hire Buddy Bell to succeed Sparky Anderson as manager.

Hideo Nomo becomes the fourth consecutive Los Angeles Dodger to be voted National League Rookie of the Year.

12 **Mexico's German Silva** (2:11:00) and **Kenya's Tegla Loroupe** (2:28:06) successfully defend their New York Marathon titles.

Miami quarterback Dan Marino breaks Fran Tarkenton's career passing yardage record of 47,003 in a 34-17 loss to New England.

Jim Colbert birdies the 17th hole to take the Energizer Senior Tour Championship by one stroke over Raymond Floyd. The win makes Colbert the top money winner on the senior tour.

World Wide Photos

Tom Watson celebrates with **Fred Couples** after Couples' putt on the 18th hole forced a playoff in the Skins Game match on Sunday Nov. 26. Watson's joy was short-lived as he won no money in the end. Couples won $270,000.

Dale Earnhardt takes the checkered flag at the NASCAR NAPA 500 but Jeff Gordon's 32nd place finish is enough to give him the $1.3 million Winston Cup Championship.

3 **Braves hurler Greg Maddux** wins his unprecedented fourth consecutive NL Cy Young Award. He joins Sandy Koufax as the only pitcher to win the award unanimously in two consecutive years.

Lloyd Carr is promoted from interim to permanent head football coach at Michigan.

4 **Seattle fireballer Randy Johnson** captures 26 of 28 first place votes in winning the AL Cy Young Award.

5 **Cincinnati Reds Barry Larkin** becomes the first shortstop in 33 years to win the NL Most Valuable Player Award.

Buck Showalter inks a seven year, $7,000,000 deal to become the first manager of the 1998 expansion Arizona Diamondbacks.

6 **Houston Oilers** sign a deal to move to Nashville for the 1998 season.

Boston's Mo Vaughn edges Cleveland slugger Albert Belle (308-300) to capture the AL Most Valuable Player Award.

Art Howe signs a two-year contract to manage the Oakland Athletics.

7 **Boxing promoter Don King** is temporarily let off the hook after his trial for insurance fraud is declared a mistrial.

8 **Pernell Whitaker (WBC)** and Felix Trinidad (IBF) record 6th and 4th round knockouts, respectively, in retaining their welterweight titles.

9 **Germany captures** a tennis daily double as Steffi Graf wins the Corel WTA Tour Championships over Anke Huber and Boris Becker sweeps Michael Chang to take the IBM/ATP Tour World Championship.

Baltimore Stallions become the first U.S. team in the 83 year history of the CFL to win the Grey Cup with a 37-20 victory over Calgary.

Louisiana Tech defeats Connecticut 83-81 in women's basketball to end their 35-game winning streak

20 **Sergei Grinkov (28)**, two-time Olympic pairs figure skating champion, collapses and dies of a heart attack after a routine with wife Ekaterina Gordeeva.

Ottawa Senators fire head coach Rick Bowness after club loses eight straight.

25 **Northwestern** gains its first Rose Bowl birth since 1949 as Michigan stuns previously unbeaten and No. 2 ranked Ohio State 31-23.

26 **Dan Marino's four TD strikes** are enough to surpass Fran Tarkenton for the all-time lead (346) but not enough to defeat the Indianapolis Colts, who come from behind to win 36-28.

Conchita Martinez and Arantxa Sanchez Vicario lead Spain to its third consecutive Fed Cup tennis title.

Fred Couples sinks a ten foot birdie putt to win The Skins Game title over Corey Pavin on the fifth playoff hole. Couples earns $270,000, the richest one-hole payoff in the event's 13 year history.

27 **Baltimore Orioles** tab Pat Gillick as their general manager. Gillick had built the Toronto Blue Jays into a two-time World Series champion before retiring in 1994.

28 **UMass begins its season** by upsetting No. 1 ranked Kentucky 92-82. It marks the second consecutive season the Minutemen have kicked off their season with a win over the No. 1 team (Arkansas in 1994).

30 **New Jersey Nets** grant Derrick Coleman his wish and trades the disgruntled forward to Philadelphia for Shawn Bradley in a six-player deal.

DEC '95

Sun	Mon	Tue	Wed	Thu	Fri	Sat
					1	2
3	4	5	6	7	8	9
10	11	12	13	14	15	16
17	18	19	20	21	22	23
24/31	25	26	27	28	29	30

Consecutive NCAA Div. I Championships

DEC. 23— Notre Dame becomes the first team in the last ten years other than North Carolina to win a NCAA Division 1 women's soccer tittle. The Heels' nine year streak is tied for third, the longest in NCAA history.

No.	School	Sport	Years
12	Arkansas	Men's Indoor Track	1984-95
10	LSU	Women's Outdoor Track	1987-96
9	USC	Men's Outdoor Track	1935-43
	North Carolina	Womem's Soccer	1986-94
	Yale	Men's Golf	1905-13
	Iowa	Wrestling	1978-86
8	Colorado	Skiing	1972-79&
7	UCLA	Men's Basketball	1967-73
	Oklahoma A&M#	Wrestling	1937-46*
	USC	Outdoor Track	1949-55
	Denver	Skiing	1961-67
6	Stanford	Women's Tennis	1986-91
	Villanova	Women's Cross Country	1989-94
	West Virginia	Rifle	1988-93
	Indiana	Men's Swimming & Diving	1968-73

& - tied with Dartmouth for 1976 championship.
# - became Oklahoma St. in 1958.
* - championships not held between 1943-45.

Just Add Rice

DEC. 24— Jerry Rice continues to strengthen his label as the most prolific receiver in NFL history. The list below highlights just the regular season marks the superstar has accumulated over his illustrious career.

Career Touchdowns (156)
Career Receptions (942)
Career Receiving Yardage (15,123)
Receiving Yardage in one season (1,848 in 1995)
Touchdown receptions in one season (22 in 1987)
Touchdown receptions in one game (five on Oct. 14, 1990, at Atlanta)
Most games with 100 or more receiving yards (58)
Most seasons with 1,000 or more receiving yards (10)
Most seasons with 100 or more receptions (three)
Most consecutive seasons with 50 or more receptions (10)

1 **NCAA places** Miami football program on three yea probation for a lack of institutional control. The penalt includes a ban on bowl games for the current year an the loss of up to 24 scholarships over the next thre years.

Hall of Famer Duke Snider is sentenced to two yea probation and a $5,000 fine for failing to repo $100,000 in cash from card shows.

Azumah Nelson knocks out a distraught Gabriel Ruelc in the fifth to win the WBC Super-Featherweight title. is Ruelas' first fight since his knockout of Jimmy Garci who later died of a blood clot.

2 **San Jose Sharks fire** coach Kevin Constantine an replace him with interim coach Jim Wiley.

3 **Pete Sampras** earns his third victory in three days, straight-set sweep of Yevgeny Kafelnikov, to lead th USA past Russia for its first Davis Cup title since 1992.

Notre Dame edges Portland 1-0 to seize the NCA women's soccer championship, ending Nort Carolina's title streak at nine.

5 **Nebraska tailback Lawrence Phillips,** suspended fro the team for six games, draws a year's probatio including a domestic violence prevention class for th assault of a former girlfriend.

Paul Molitor, 39, signs a one-year, $2 million contra to play for his home-town Minnesota Twins.

6 **Montreal Canadiens deal** Patrick Roy and Mike Kean to Colorado for Jocelyn Thibault, Andrei Kovalenko an Martin Rucinsky. Roy demanded a trade after bein embarrassed in an 11-1 home loss to Detroit earlier i the week.

NBA bans Dallas' Roy Tarpley after the trouble forward tests positive for alcohol use three times.

7 **New York Yankees** acquire Tino Martinez from Seattl in a five-player deal.

9 **Ohio State's Eddie George** easily outdistances co favorites Tommie Frazier and Danny Wuerffel to win th 1995 Heisman Trophy. Iowa State's Troy Davis (5th becomes the first back to rush for 2,000 yards and nc win the prize.

Francois Botha wins the IBF heavyweight title, defeatin Axel Schulz in a 12-round decision.

10 **Wisconsin registers** its fifth consecutive shutout blanking Duke 2-0 for its first NCAA men's socce championship.

Jets kicker Nick Lowery strikes a New England ba boy after he refuses to warm up footballs on a col afternoon.

11 **Terry Donahue,** UCLA head football coach since 197 resigns to pursue a broadcasting career with CBS.

Dallas Star owner Norman Green sells the club t Dallas businessman Thomas Hicks for $84 million.

12 **Striking NBA referees** return to work after a 27-26 vot to accept the league's final contract proposal.

NBC pays $2.3 billion for the TV rights to the Olympic in 2004, 2006, and 2008.

13 **Detroit's Paul Coffey** sets up Igor Larionov in a 3-1 wi over Chicago to become the first NHL defenseman t record 1,000 career assists

14 **A $57 million free agent** spending spree in baseba sends Jack McDowell to Cleveland, Mike Stanley t Boston, and Randy Myers to the Baltimore Orioles Craig Biggio opts to stay with the Astros.

15 **Oscar De La Hoya** trounces James Leija in the secon round to retain the WBO lightweight belt.

16 **Mike Tyson KOs** Buster Mathis in the third round of hi second bout since returning from prison.

Wide World Photos

Boxing's symbol of integrity, promoter **Don King**, celebrates with **Mike Tyson** after Tyson scored a third round knockout over Buster Mathis, Jr. on Dec. 16, 1995.

Montana drives 72 yards and kicks a field goal with 39 seconds left to beat Marshall for its first Division 1-AA national title.

Nebraska wins its 31st consecutive match, topping Texas to take home the NCAA Division I women's volleyball championship.

17 **Cleveland Browns** whip Cincinnati 26-10 in their final game at Cleveland Stadium. The era ends with fans crying, hugging players, and tearing out bleachers and banners for souvenirs.

18 **Howard Schnellenberger resigns** as football coach of Oklahoma after a 5-5-1 season.

IndyCar owners and the upstart Indy Racing League continue their feud when IndyCar announces it will stage the U.S. 500 directly opposite the 1996 Indy 500.

19 **Winnipeg Jets** announce their agreement with Jerry Colangelo to move to Phoenix next season.

Jeff Tarango apologizes to the tennis world for his Wimbledon outburst. As a result, his fines are reduced by $15,000 and suspensions dropped.

Italian skiing star Alberto Tomba scores his first World Cup victory of the season after two third-place finishes.

20 **Shawn Eckardt,** former bodyguard of Tonya Harding, files a $6 million lawsuit against a minister who allegedly heard his confession and passed the information to the authorities. Eckardt is looking for compensation for his "adverse notoriety".

21 **Baltimore Orioles** ink second baseman Roberto Alomar to a three-year deal while the Yankees re-sign hurler David Cone.

NFL fines Dolphin Bryan Cox $17,500 and Buffalo's Carwell Gardner $15,000 for their altercation in the Bills' 23-20 win. Cox left the field spitting at fans.

Maine suspends hockey coach Shawn Walsh for a year without pay for NCAA rules violations. The team will also sit out of the 1996 NCAA tournament.

22 **Celtics guard Dana Barros** breaks the NBA three-point mark, canning a trey in his 80th consecutive game in a 114-113 win over Minnesota.

23 **Unruly Giant fans** shower the field with snowballs in a 27-17 loss, knocking Charger equipment manager Sid Brooks unconscious. Fifteen are arrested and 75 season tickets are subsequently revoked.

24 **Jerry Rice** catches 12 passes for 153 yards to break Charlie Hennigan's NFL single-season receiving yardage record of 1,746 yards (1961). Atlanta, however, upsets the 49ers 28-27 to secure a wild-card berth.

25 **Cowboys' Emmitt Smith** scores his 25th TD in a 37-13 win over Arizona, breaking Washington Redskin John Riggins' single-season mark.

Glen Mason changes his mind about coaching Georgia's football team, citing personal reasons, and decides to stay on at Kansas. The Jayhawks respond by blasting UCLA, 51-30 in the Aloha Bowl.

26 **Phoenix Cardinals fire** head coach Buddy Ryan after leading the club to a 4-12 record. Eagles coach Ray Rhodes is voted NFL Coach of the Year in his first year.

27 **After losing seven** of the last nine games, Sam Wyche is fired by the Tampa Bay Buccaneers. Wyche's career 36 percent winning percentage with the Bucs is the best in team history.

30 **Ottawa Senators** ink Alexei Yashin to a five-year deal, ending a bitter contract dispute in which the forward claimed he would never play for the team again.

JAN '96

Sun	Mon	Tue	Wed	Thu	Fri	Sat
	1	2	3	4	5	6
7	8	9	10	11	12	13
14	15	16	17	18	19	20
21	22	23	24	25	26	27
28	29	30	31			

On the comeback trail...

JAN. 30— Laker legend Magic Johnson made a ballyhooed, albeit brief, return to the NBA on January 30 in a 128–118 win over Golden State. Below is a breakdown of Magic's first game back compared with Michael Jordan's first game back from retirement in March of 1995.

	Jordan	Johnson
Age	32	36
Minutes	43	27
FG-FGA	7-28	7-14
3FG-3FGA	0-4	0-2
FT-FTA	5-6	5-6
Points	19	19
Rebounds	6	8
Assists	6	10
Steals	3	2
Blocks	0	0
Turnovers	3	4
Fouls	3	5
Final Score	Ind. 103 Chi. 96 (OT)	LA 128 GS 118
Length of Retirement	one year-nine mos.	four years-seven mos.

It's A Junior Mint

JAN. 31— Baseball salaries continue to escalate (although they are still dwarfed in relation to basketball) as Ken Griffey Jr. vaults to the top of the highest paid player list.

Player	Years	Avg. per year
Ken Griffey Jr., Sea.	1997-2000	$8,500,000
Barry Bonds, SF	1993-1998	7,291,667
Frank Thomas, Chi.(AL)	1995-1998	7,250,000
Cecil Fielder, NYY	1993-1997	7,237,500
Ryne Sandberg, Chi.(NL)	1993-1996	7,100,000
Jeff Bagwell, Hou.	1995-1998	6,875,000
Cal Ripken Jr., Bal.	1993-1997	6,500,000
Joe Carter, Tor.	1993-1995	6,500,000
David Cone, NYY	1996-1998	6,500,000
Len Dykstra, Phi.	1995-1998	6,225,000

1 **No. 3** Northwestern loses in its first Rose Bowl appearance in 47 years, 41-32 to No. 17 USC. In other major bowl action, No. 8 Florida State beats No. 9 Notre Dame in the Orange Bowl, Tennessee slides by Ohio State in the Citrus Bowl, and Colorado pounds Oregon in the Cotton Bowl.

Green Bay QB Brett Favre is selected AP's 1995 NFL Most Valuable Player.

2 **Nebraska becomes** the first college football team in 16 years to win two consecutive national titles with a 62-24 pasting of No. 2 Florida in the Fiesta Bowl. Tommie Frazier runs for two touchdowns and 199 of the Huskers' 524 rushing yards.

No. 4 Tennessee tops No. 18 Florida 87-67 in women's college hoops for their NCAA Division I record 69th consecutive home victory.

3 **North Korea** confirms participation in the 1996 Summer Olympics in Atlanta, making it the first time in history that all invited countries will be in attendance.

5 **Miami Dolphins' Don Shula** announces his resignation after 33 years of coaching that includes an NFL record 347 wins, two Super Bowl championships (1972-73) and the only perfect season (17-0 in 1972) in NFL history.

6 **Croatia wins** the Hopman Cup team tennis championship in Australia after Swiss star Marc Rosset injures his hand punching a billboard out of frustration.

7 **Mark O'Meara** shoots a final round 4-under-par 68 to hold off Nick Faldo and Scott Hoch and capture the PGA Tour Mercedes Championship by three strokes.

8 **Baseball Writers** Association of America fail to elect a player to the Hall of Fame for the first time since 1971. Phil Niekro, Don Sutton and slugger Tony Perez are the closest to the necessary 75 percent of the vote.

Bob Gainey, head coach of the struggling Dallas Stars, steps down to concentrate on his duties as GM. Minor league coach Ken Hitchcock is named as his successor.

Massive east coast blizzard postpones various sporting events, including the Colorado-Boston and Washington NY Rangers NHL games and the Villanova-UConn basketball tilt.

9 **CBS Sports announces** it will not use 23-year veteran golf announcer Ben Wright for the upcoming season after he allegedly made insensitive remarks about women golfers.

Dale Earnhardt agrees to a contract extension to drive on the Winston Cup series circuit through 2000.

Promoters announce the June 7th Julio Cesar Chavez - Oscar De La Hoya fight will be televised closed circuit to arenas and theaters, rather than on pay-per-view.

10 **Driver A.J. Foyt files** a federal antitrust action against CART, claiming they are monopolizing IndyCar racing and pressuring companies to refrain from sponsoring his Indy Racing League cars.

World champion sprinter Michael Johnson and World Cup downhill champ Picabo Street are named USOC Sportsman and Sportswoman of 1995.

11 **Jimmy Johnson** signs a four-year, $8 million contract to replace Don Shula as coach of the Miami Dolphins.

Boston Bruins trade Mariusz Czerkawski, Sean Brown, and a 1996 first-round draft pick to Edmonton for goaltender Bill Ranford. Edmonton signs Curtis Joseph to a three-year, $6.8 million deal.

WBO lightweight champion Oscar De La Hoya is named Boxing Writers Association of America's 1995 Fighter of the Year.

12 **Celtics' guard Dana Barros** has his consecutive game three point streak ended at 89 in a 105-92 loss to New York. Barros misses five in the last 15 seconds.

Wide World Photos

Chicago's **Ed Belfour** deflects a shot by Pittsburgh's **Mario Lemiux** in the 1996 NHL All-Star game at Boston's new FleetCenter.

Roy Jones Jr records a TKO over Merqui Sosa at 2:36 of round 2 to retain the IBF super middleweight belt.

14 **Dallas Cowboys defeat** Green Bay 38-27 in the NFC title game to advance to the Super Bowl and Pittsburgh slips by Indianapolis 20-16 after Jim Harbaugh's last second desperation pass barely rolls off Colt receiver Aaron Bailey in the end zone.

UMass star center Marcus Camby collapses minutes before the Minutemen are to play St. Boneventure. Camby spends the night in the hospital but the cause of the incident is not determined.

16 **Paul Westphal is fired** as head coach of the Phoenix Suns and replaced by Cotton Fitzsimmons.

Former NFL quarterbacks Craig Morton and Joe Kapp announce plans for a 16-team All-Star Football League to compete against the NFL.

17 **Detroit center Steve Yzerman** becomes the NHL's 22nd 500 goal scorer in a 3-2 win over Colorado.

18 **Major league baseball owners** unanimously approve the implementation of interleague play on an experimental basis in 1997. Pending approval from players and umpires, teams will play either 15 or 16 interleague games depending on their division.

19 **New Jersey Nets trade** Kenny Anderson and Willie Glass to Charlotte for guards Kendall Gill and Khalid Reeves.

20 **Boston defenseman Ray Bourque** scores with 37 seconds remaining to give the Eastern Conference a 5-4 win in the 46th NHL All-Star game.

Rudy Galindo shocks three-time champion Todd Eldredge to capture the men's title at the US Figure Skating Championships. Fifteen year old Michelle Kwan becomes the youngest women's champ since Peggy Fleming in 1964.

21 **Mexico wins** its second consecutive soccer Gold Cup with a 2-0 win over an under-23 Brazilian team.

22 **Tampa Bay Buccaneers** name Minnesota defensive coordinator Tony Dungy head coach

23 **Torono Maple Leafs acquire** Kirk Muller in a three-team, seven-player deal that sends No. 1 draft pick Bryan Berard to NY Islanders. Ottawa also fires Dave Allison, their second head coach of the season.

San Francisco 49ers hire former head coach Bill Walsh as administrative assistant to the coaching staff.

25 **Los Angeles Kings** and Boston Bruins swap veteran power forwards as Rick Tocchet goes to Boston for Kevin Stevens.

26 **Monica Seles** ousts German Anke Huber 6-4, 6-1 to win the 1996 Australian Open, her ninth major title.

27 **Former Redskins' coach** Joe Gibbs, Dan Dierdorf, and Charley Joiner head a list of five selected to the NFL Hall of Fame.

Buzz Calkins takes the checkered flag at the Indy 200 in Disney World, the Indy Racing League's inaugural event.

28 **Dallas Cowboys win** their fifth championship and their third in the last four seasons with a 27-17 triumph over the Pittsburgh Steelers in Super Bowl XXX. Cornerback Larry Brown picks off two Neil O'Donnell passes to thwart Pittsburgh's comeback bid and secure the MVP trophy.

Boris Becker handles Michael Chang in four sets to seize the men's Australian Open title.

30 **Magic Johnson returns** to the Lakers and contributes 19 points, eight rebounds, and ten assists in a 128-118 victory over Golden State.

31 **Ken Griffey Jr. signs** a four-year, $34 million contract extension with the Seattle Mariners, making him baseball's highest-paid player.

St. Louis Blues' Dale Hawerchuk becomes the 23rd player to reach 500 NHL goals and the fourth player this season in a 4-0 win at Toronto.

FEB '96

Sun	Mon	Tue	Wed	Thu	Fri	Sat
				1	2	3
4	5	6	7	8	9	10
11	12	13	14	15	16	17
18	19	20	21	22	23	24
25	26	27	28			

Quickest to 50

FEB. 27 — It's become popular to debate whether the 1995–96 Chicago Bulls are the greatest team in pro sports history but there is no denying them the record for the fastest team to win 50 games.

Season	Team	Record	Final season record
1995-96	Chicago Bulls (NBA)	50-6	72-10
1982-83	Philadelphia 76ers (NBA)	50-7	65-17
1976-77	Montreal Canadiens (NHL)	50-7-10	60-8-12
1966-67	Philadelphia 76ers	50-8	68-13
1971-72	Los Angeles Lakers (NBA)	50-8	69-13
1977-78	Montreal Canadiens	50-9-9	59-10-11
1975-76	Montreal Canadiens	50-9-10	58-11-11
1977-78	Portland Trail Blazers (NBA)	50-10	58-24
1912	NY Giants (MLB)	50-11	103-48

Bricklayers

FEB. 21 —The Miami Heat battle to a 66–57 victory over the Philadelphia 76ers for the 2nd-lowest combined total since the introduction of the 24–second clock in 1954–55.

Teams	Year	Total points
Boston 62, Milwaukee 57	1955	119
Miami 66, Philadelphia 57	**1996**	**123**
Detroit 72, New York 61	1992	133
Vancouver 69, Miami 65	1996	134
Ft. Wayne 69, Syracuse 66	1955	135

Sir Charles joins NBA royalty

FEB. 19 —Charles Barkley grabs the 10,000th rebound of his career in a 98-95 overtime win over the Vancouver Grizzlies making him only the 10th man in NBA history to amass 20,000 points and 10,000 rebounds in their career. Listed below are the NBA double threats with their career totals. Players listed in bold type were active in 1996.

	Pts	Rebs
Kareem Abdul-Jabbar	38,387	17,440
Wilt Chamberlain	31,419	23,924
Moses Malone	27,409	16,212
Elvin Hayes	27,313	16,279
Robert Parish	22,989	14,443
Elgin Baylor	23,149	11,463
Walt Bellamy	20,941	14,241
Bob Pettit	20,880	12,849
Hakeem Olajuwon	21,271	10,816
Charles Barkley	20,112	10,013

4 **Heavy California rains** wipe out the final round of the AT&T Pebble Beach National Pro-Am. With no plans for rescheduling, it marks the first PGA Tour event since 1949 to be canceled.

Jerry Rice grabs six passes for 82 yards to lead the NFC to a 20-13 victory in the Pro Bowl.

Ethiopian Haile Gebreselassie (7:30.72) shatters the 3000-meter indoor track record just eight days after setting the 5,000-meter mark.

5 **NHL reaches** a multi-year agreement in principle with Nike that includes supplying jerseys for several clubs and airing TV commercials to promote players.

Former NBA star George Gervin and women's basketball pioneer Nancy Lieberman-Cline are among six named as inductees to the Basketball Hall of Fame.

7 **Winnipeg Jets deal** superstar Teemu Selanne to the Mighty Ducks of Anaheim for former first-round picks Oleg Tverdovsky (19) and Chad Kilger (18).

Arizona Cardinals name Colts defensive coordinator Vince Tobin their fifth head coach in nine seasons.

8 **NFL approves** Browns' move from Cleveland to Baltimore but rules that the team's colors, name, and legacy must remain in Cleveland to await a future replacement. In addition, owner Art Modell must pay Cleveland $9.3 million to break his lease.

Dave Winfield retires from baseball at the age of 44 after 23 seasons and 2,973 major league games.

Dayton basketball center Chris Daniels dies at the age of 22 of natural causes due to an irregular heartbeat.

9 **Ted Marchibroda** is relieved of his duties as head coach of the Indianapolis Colts despite leading the club to the AFC title game.

Oscar De La Hoya and Julio Cesar Chavez register second-round knockouts of Darryl Tyson and Scott Walker, respectively to retain their lightweight belts and tune up for their June 7th showdown.

Donovan Bailey runs the 50-meter dash in 5.56 seconds to set the world record while Gwen Torrence sets the US women's mark with a time of 6.07 seconds.

10 **Tommy Morrison** is medically suspended by the Nevada State Athletic Commission just seven hours before his scheduled heavyweight bout. He is later confirmed to have tested positive for HIV.

Jenny Spangler is the surprise winner of the US Olympic Marathon Trials with a time of 2:29:54. Linda Somers (2nd) and Anne Marie Lauck (3rd) also qualify.

Cigar, recently named Horse of the Year, cruises to his 13th straight victory at the Donn Handicap in Florida.

11 **Michael Jordan** scores 20 points in three quarters to win the MVP award and lead the East to a 129-118 victory in the NBA All-Star game. Crowd favorite Shaquille O'Neal pumps in 25 and grabs ten rebounds.

Arizona's Miles Simon banks in a desperation 65-foot shot at the buzzer to give the Wildcats a 79-76 victory over Cincinnati.

12 **NBA owners approve** a five-year contract extension for Commissioner David Stern worth over $40 million.

Mike Aulby and Dave Husted are elected to the Professional Bowlers Association Hall of Fame on their first ballot.

13 **St. Louis Cardinals acquire** Dennis Eckersley for minor league reliever Steve Montgomery.

15 **NCAA Rules Committee** passes a vote that requires a tie-breaker in all Division 1-A football games beginning in the 1996-97 season.

Indianapolis Colts hire offensive coordinator Lindy Infante as their head coach while former Colt coach Ted Marchibroda replaces Bill Belichick as coach of the

Wide World Photos

Haile Gebreselassie of Ehtiopia is shown on the way to this record-breaking run in the 3,000 meters at a meet in Stuttgart, Germany on Feb.4, 1996. He finished with a time of 7 minutes and 30 seconds beating the old mark by 5 seconds.

Baltimore franchise.

17 **Five Michigan basketball players** and one high school recruit escape serious injury after their vehicle flips over while returning from a party.

18 **Dale Jarrett** takes the lead on Lap 176 and outduels runner-up Dale Earnhardt to take the checkered flag at the Daytona 500.

Frankie Fredericks of Namibia becomes the first man to run 200 meters under 20 seconds indoors (19.92).

19 **Charlie Finley,** former colorful owner of the Kansas City- Oakland Athletics, dies of heart disease at 77.

Charles Barkley becomes the tenth NBA player to record 20,000 points and 10,000 rebounds.

20 **Former Miami Dolphin** linebacker Bryan Cox signs a four-year deal with the Chicago Bears while Super Bowl XXX MVP Larry Brown joins the Raiders.

Utah guard John Stockton registers the 2,311th steal of his career to surpass Maurice Cheeks for the all-time NBA lead.

21 **Philadelphia 76ers** tie a 41-year-old NBA record for fewest points in a game in a 66-57 loss to the Miami Heat. The combined total is the 2nd lowest total since the inception of the shot clock in 1954.

22 **Miami Heat** gear up for the playoffs by acquiring Tim Hardaway from Golden State and Walt Williams and Ty Corbin from Sacramento. Also, Minnesota trades Christian Laettner and Sean Rooks to Atlanta for Spud Webb and Andrew Lang.

Villanova's Kerry Kittles is suspended by the NCAA for the final three games of the regular season for ringing up $3,100 in unauthorized calls using a university calling card number.

Minnesota quarterback Warren Moon is acquitted in his spousal assault case in Texas.

23 **Pittsburgh Penguins' dynamic duo** Mario Lemieux and Jaromir Jagr each score their 50th goal of the season in a 5-4 truimph over Hartford.

24 **George Washington cruises** to an 86-76 win over No. 1 UMass for the Minutemen's only regular season loss.

Michelle Kwan rallies from fourth-place to win the Champions Grand Prix women's figure skating championship in Paris. Russian Alexei Urmanov captures the men's title.

25 **Pete Sampras holds** on to his No. 1 ranking by besting Todd Martin 6-4, 7-6 (2) in the Kroger St. Jude finals.

Alberto Tomba races to victory in the slalom event to earn his second gold medal at the World Alpine Skiing Championships.

27 **Los Angeles Kings** end weeks of speculation by trading mega-star Wayne Gretzky to the St. Louis Blues for three prospects and first-round picks in '96 and '97.

Chicago Bulls (50-6) become the quickest team in North American professional sports history to reach 50 wins in a season with a 120-99 trouncing of Minnesota.

28 **San Diego Padres announce** they will play a three-game home series in August with the Mets in Monterrey, Mexico. It will be the first time the major leagues have ventured outside of the USA and Canada for non-exhibition games.

29 **Cleveland slugger Albert Belle** is fined a record $50,000 for his verbal abuse of NBC's Hannah Storm in the dugout before Game 3 of the 1995 World Series.

Quarterback Neil O'Donnell leaves the AFC Champion Pittsburgh Steelers to sign a five-year, $25 million contract with the New York Jets.

North Carolina jury convicts Daniel Green of first-degree murder in the death of Michael Jordan's father James.

MAR '96

Sun	Mon	Tue	Wed	Thu	Fri	Sat
					1	2
3	4	5	6	7	8	9
10	11	12	13	14	15	16
17	18	19	20	21	22	23
24/31	25	26	27	28	29	30

Notable Religious Incidents

MARCH 12— Nuggets guard Mahmoud Abdul Rauf's refusal to stand for the national anthem isn't the first incident regarding religion, the flag, and sporting events. Below are some of the more major ones.

Year	Incident
1996	San Francisco Giants' pitcher Mark Dewey refuses to participate in "Until There's a Cure Day" for AIDS awareness because it goes against his religious beliefs. He wears his red AIDS ribbon sideways during the game to resemble a Christian fish symbol.
1992	The Canadian flag is accidentally displayed upside-down during a World Series game between the Toronto Blue Jays and the Atlanta Braves.
1990	Roseanne Barr purposely screams the national anthem off-key, spits, and grabs her crotch in front of thousands of booing fans before a baseball game in San Diego.
1976	Chicago Cubs outfielder Rick Monday grabs the U.S. flag from two protesters who came on to the field to set it on fire.
1968	In a gesture against racism, American sprinters Tommie Smith and John Wesley Carlos wear black gloves and raise their right fists in the air on the medal podium while the national anthem is played at the Mexico City Olympics.
1965	Los Angeles Dodgers' Sandy Koufax refuses to pitch Game 1 of the World Series on Yom Kippur, the most holy day of the Jewish year.

Home Winning Streaks

MARCH 21— On March 10th, the Orlando Magic etched their name into the NBA record book by notching their 39th consecutive home win and eventually went on to set the mark at 40. Not to be outdone, the Chicago Bulls broke the record just 11 days later with their 41st consecutive home win against the NY Knicks. The Bulls' streak eventually ended at 44 on April 8th at the hands of the Charlotte Hornets. Listed are the longest home streaks in each of the major sports.

Wins	Team
129	Kentucky (1943-55), NCAA men's basketball
58	Miami (1985-94), NCAA Football
44	Chicago Bulls (1995-96), NBA
27	Miami Dolphins (1971-74), NFL
26	NY Giants (1916), MLB
24	Boston Red Sox (1988), MLB
20	Boston Bruins (1929-30), NHL
	Philadelphia Flyers (1975-76), NHL

1 **Picabo Street** caps off a tremendous season by winning her second consecutive World Cup downhill ski title.

Atlanta Falcons ink five-time Pro Bowl linebacker Cornelius Bennett to a four-year deal while the St. Louis Rams acquire defensive end Leslie O'Neal.

Atlanta Hawks' coach Lenny Wilkens, the winningest coach in NBA history, wins his 1,000th game with a 74-68 victory over Cleveland.

3 **Greg Norman fires** a 66 in the final round to finish 19-under-par and capture the Doral-Ryder Open title.

4 **Bruce Baumgartner** becomes the 2nd wrestler in 66 years to win the James E. Sullivan Award as the nation's top amateur athlete.

5 **Fiery Oriole manager Earl Weaver** and 224-game winner Jim Bunning are among four to be selected to the Baseball Hall of Fame by the Veterans Committee.

Five-time Iditarod champ Rick Swenson is ejected from the race after the death of one of his dogs causes him to break the race's new "dead dog rule".

Pat Burns is fired as coach of the Toronto Maple Leafs in the midst of an eight-game skid and replaced by director of player development Nick Beverly.

6 **Detroit's Chris Osgood** becomes the the third goalie in history to score a goal in an NHL game with an empty-netter in the Red Wings' 4-2 win over Hartford.

Filipino runner Nancy Navalta is banned from her national games when a gender test reveals she is genetically a man.

7 **Michael Jordan scores** an NBA season-high 53 points in leading the Bulls to a 102-81 thrashing of Detroit.

Tom Dolan qualifies for the US Olympic swim team by cruising to victory in the 400-meter individual medley. Kristine Quance storms back from a disqualification in the 400 to place 2nd in the 100-meter breaststroke behind 14 year old Amanda Beard.

NCAA places Mississippi State on probation for one year for various infractions in its football program.

8 **New York Knicks fire** head coach Don Nelson after a 59-game stint (34-25). He is replaced by assistant coach Jeff Van Gundy.

Chris Spielman, an eight-year veteran linebacker with the Detroit Lions, signs a four-year, $8 million contract with the Buffalo Bills.

9 **George Mason** takes home the men's NCAA Indoor Track and Field championships, ending Arkansas' 12 year reign, the longest streak in the history of Division 1 college athletics.

10 **Miami Dolphins sign** former Philadelphia receiver Fred Barnett to a five-year, $8.5 million deal.

PGA Tour rookie Tim Herron shoots an opening round 62 and never looks back, leading wire-to-wire to run away with the Honda Classic title.

Minnesota Timberwolves' Isaiah Rider is ejected in the first half against the Utah Jazz but refuses to leave until his mother walks onto the court and embarrasses Rider into the locker room.

11 **Montreal Canadiens** handle the Dallas Stars 4-1 in the final game of the 72-year-old Montreal Forum. The team will finish the season and continue their tradition in the 21,500-seat, state of the art Molson Center.

St. Johns fires head basketball coach Brian Mahoney after their worst season in 33 years.

12 **Denver Nuggets guard Mahmoud Abdul-Rauf** is suspended without pay by the NBA for refusing to stand for the national anthem due to religious beliefs. He returns after one game but not without a chorus of boos and numerous death threats.

Wide World Photos

Todd Eldredge won the gold (l) and **Rudy Galindo** (c) the bronze at the World Figure Skating Championships. The pair is shown here at the US Championships with **Dan Hollander**.

Wide World Photos

Tennessee's **Michelle Marciniak** cuts down the last of the net after the Lady Vols won the 1996 NCAA women's basketball championship. Marciniak was voted the tournament MVP.

Safety Ronnie Lott, four-time Super Bowl champion with the 49ers, retires after 15 years of NFL service.

13 **NFL announces** the return of instant replay as an experiment in 1996 but with the potential for full-time use in the 1997 season.

14 **Thirteenth-seeded Princeton shocks** the defending champion UCLA Bruins 43-41 in the opening round of the NCAA tournament, putting off the retirement of Princeton coach Pete Carril.

New York Rangers gain toughness and experience for the playoffs by acquiring Marty McSorley, Jarri Kurri, and Shane Churla from Los Angeles for Ray Ferraro and three prospects.

16 **Mike Tyson pummels** Frank Bruno in the third round to capture the WBC heavyweight belt in Las Vegas.

18 **NBA suspends** Bull's Dennis Rodman for six games and fines him $20,000 for headbutting an official after his ejection from Mar. 16th's victory in New Jersey.

19 **Florida State's football program** dodges a bullet, receiving just a one-year probation from the NCAA for a 1993 illegal Foot Locker shopping spree.

20 **Oakland A's agree** to play their first six games of the season in Las Vegas' 10,000-seat Cashman Field while waiting for the Coliseum to be renovated.

21 **Baseball owners approve** an interim revenue-sharing plan that will tax each team's revenues 15 percent. 85 percent of that amount will be divided between the 28 teams with the remaining 15 percent distributed to low-revenue clubs.

USA's Todd Eldredge and Rudy Galindo take home the gold and bronze medals, respectively at the World Figure Skating Championships in Edmonton.

22 **Pittsburgh running back Bam Morris** is arrested after being caught with more than six pounds of marijuana in the trunk of his car.

24 **Cinderellas go** to the dance this year as Mississippi State surprises Cincinnati 73-63 and Syracuse edges Kansas 60-57 to round out the Final Four.

Michelle Kwan, 15, takes the gold at the World Figure Skating Championships to become the third-youngest world champion in the past 100 years.

Michigan forward Mike Legg scores the hockey goal of the year in a victory over Minnesota as he cradles the puck on his stick lacrosse-style, swings it around the net, and deposits it over the goalie's shoulder.

25 **Tennessee, Georgia, Connecticut, and Stanford** all gain berths in the women's basketball Final Four in a repeat of last year's lineup .

26 **Mario Lemieux scores five** goals and adds two assists to lead the Pittsburgh Penguins to an 8-4 win over Wayne Gretzky and the St. Louis Blues.

27 **Cigar wins** the $4 million Dubai World Cup.

Heavyweight Francois Botha is stripped of his IBF title for testing positive for steroids after his victory over Axel Schulz in December.

29 **Minnesota center Brian Bonin** wins the Hobey Baker Award as the nation's top college hockey player.

Vancouver Grizzlies drop their 21st straight game, 105-91 to Utah to break the NBA single-season mark for futility previously held by Philadelphia ('72-73) and Dallas ('93-94).

30 **Kentucky avenges** their early season loss to UMass by whipping the Minutemen 81-74 to set up a tournament final with Syracuse who ousted Mississippi State 77-69.

Michigan scores 3:35 into overtime to beat Colorado College 3-2 and nab their first NCAA hockey championship in 32 years.

31 **Tennessee runs away** to an 83-65 victory over Georgia to win the NCAA women's basketball title.

APRIL '96

Sun	Mon	Tue	Wed	Thu	Fri	Sat
	1	2	3	4	5	6
7	8	9	10	11	12	13
14	15	16	17	18	19	20
21	22	23	24	25	26	27
28	29	30				

St. Francis 71, Robert Morris 1

APRIL 3— In a college baseball mismatch where 21 records were set, St. Francis, just three years removed from an NAIA World Series title, annihilated upstart Robert Morris College (Ill.) 71–1,in just four innings.

St. Francis	ab	r	h	rbi	Robert Morris	ab	r	h	rbi
Palermo, ss	9	7	7	5	Mann, 1b	2	1	2	0
Sanchez, 1b	6	8	4	3	Orozco, c	2	0	1	0
Mazurek, dh	8	8	6	9	Lucas, ss	2	0	0	0
Futterer, cf	7	8	5	8	Diaz, cf	1	0	0	1
Badke, rf	2	3	1	2	Caesar, ph	1	0	1	0
Biahunka, rf	5	3	4	2	Salgado, 3b	1	0	0	0
Kujawa, 3b	0	3	0	0	Madrigal, ph	1	0	0	0
Stawczyk, 3b	5	6	3	2	Zuniga, lf	1	0	0	0
Holocomb, lf	7	9	2	6	Gomez, ph	1	0	0	0
Hurry, 2b	4	6	4	6	Simmons, 1b	2	0	0	0
Hiar, 2b	2	6	2	3	Morfin, 2b	1	0	0	0
Lynch, c	9	4	6	7	Hilan, 2b	0	0	0	0
					Delgado, rf	1	0	0	0
Totals	64	71	44	53	Totals	16	1	4	1

	1	2	3	4	F
St. Francis	26	22	4	19	–71
Robert Morris	1	0	0	0	–1

St. Francis	ip	h	r	er	bb	so
Ochman (w)	4	4	1	1	0	9

Robert Morris	ip	h	r	er	bb	so
Mann (L)	1/3	4	12	6	6	0
Diaz	1	13	21	2	6	0
Simmons	2 2/3	27	38	11	10	3

Most Consecutive Playoff Appearances

APRIL 11— In 1967–68, Bobb Orr led the Boston Bruins to the Stanle Cup playoffs in his second year in the NHL. The Bruins haven't missed the postseason since. Below are the longest current playoff streaks in the four major sports.

Current

No.	Team (League)	First year
29	Boston Bruins (NHL)	1967-68
27	Chicago Blackhawks (NHL)	1969-70
17	St. Louis Blues (NHL)	1979-80
14	Portland Trail Blazers (NBA)	1982-83
13	Washington Capitals (NHL)	1982-83
13	Utah Jazz (NBA)	1983-84
12	Chicago Bulls (NBA)	1984-85
9	New York Knicks (NBA)	1987-88
8	Phoenix Suns (NBA)	1988-89

1 **Kentucky overcomes** a late Syracuse rally to forge a 76-67 victory for their sixth NCAA basketball national championship.

Tragedy strikes baseball's opening day as umpire John McSherry collapses and dies of a heart attack at the age of 51 just seven pitches into the Reds-Expos clash in Cincinnati. The game is postponed.

Dallas Cowboy receiver Michael Irvin is indicted by a grand jury on charges of cocaine and marijuana possession, stemming from his March 4th arrest.

3 **St. Louis goaltender Grant Fuhr** ends his NHL-record run of 76 consecutive starts due to a strained right knee.

Georgia Tech freshman Stephon Marbury declares his eligibility for the upcoming NBA draft.

College of St. Francis sets 21 college baseball records and ties six others in crushing Robert Morris College 71-1 in a game called after four innings.

4 **UMass center Marcus Camby** adds to his growing collection of hardware, winning the Wooden Award as the nation's top college basketball player.

6 **Charlotte center Robert Parish plays** in his 1,561st game, a 93-89 win in Cleveland, to surpass Kareem Abdul-Jabbar's record for career games played.

San Jose Clash edge the Washington, D.C. United 1-0 in the inaugural Major League Soccer game in front of a sellout crowd of 31,683 in San Jose.

8 **Chicago Bulls are upset** by Charlotte 98-97, to end the Bulls' NBA-record 44-game home winning streak.

National League umpire Eric Gregg, 6-3, 325 pounds,is granted a leave of absence to start a health and conditioning program.

Fifteen year old swimmer Jessica Foschi is ruled "innocent and without fault" after testing positive for steroid use in August of 1995. The controversial decision removes all sanctions on Foschi but many believe it undermines the authority of FINA.

Arizona Cardinals join the youth movement, releasing 37-year old quarterback Dave Kreig and inking Boomer Esiason (34) to a two-year deal.

9 **Laker guard Nick Van Exel** shoves referee Ronnie Garretson onto the scorer's table with his forearm after being ejected from the 98-91 loss to Denver. Van Exel is fined $25,000 and suspended for the remaining seven games of the season.

Heavyweight champ Mike Tyson is accused of violating his parole and sexually assaulting a woman at a bar in Chicago. Tyson is later exonerated.

11 **Mitch Richmond** and Charles Barkley are added to the 1996 U.S. Olympic Men's Basketball Team.

Greg Norman shoots a course record-tying 9-under-par 63 to jump out to a two-stroke lead over Phil Mickelson in the first round of the Masters.

Boston Bruins slip past the Hartford Whalers 3-2 to clinch a playoff birth for their professional sports record 29th consecutive year.

12 **Detroit Red Wings** register a 5-3 win over Chicago for their NHL-record 61st victory of the season, eclipsing the mark of 60 set by the 76-77 Montreal Canadiens.

13 **New Jersey Devils suffer** a 5-2 loss to Ottawa to become the first hockey team in 26 years to fail to make the playoffs the year after winning the Stanley Cup.

14 **Nick Faldo** shoots a final-round 67, storming from behind to win the Masters tournament, erasing a six-stroke lead by Greg Norman on the final day.

L.A. Laker Magic Johnson bumps referee Steve Foster after a non-call in a 118-114 win over Phoenix, just five days after criticizing teammate Nick Van Exel for shoving a referee. Johnson is fined $10,000 and suspended three games.

The Dallas Cowboys' **Michael Irvin** had a lousy off-season in 1996. He is pictured leaving a Dallas court room during a break in his drug possession trial.

5 **Uta Pippig overcomes** intestinal sickness and menstrual cramps to record an inspiring win (2:27:12) in the 100th Boston Marathon, her third consecutive Boston victory. Kenya's Moses Tanui (2:09:16) captures the men's race over three-time defending champ and fellow countryman Cosmas Ndeti.

6 **Chicago Bulls become** the first team in NBA history to win 70 games with a 86-80 come-from behind victory over the Milwaukee Bucks.

7 **Michelle Carew,** daughter of Hall of Famer and California hitting instructor Rod Carew, passes away at the age of 18 after a seven-month battle with leukemia.

Michigan State announces it will forfeit its five 1994 football wins due to the use of an ineligible player.

8 **Nebraska quarterback Brook Berringer,** expected to be taken in the upcoming NFL draft, is killed when the plane he is piloting crashes in a Nebraska farm.

9 **Texas Rangers send** 19 batters to the plate in the eighth inning and score 16 of them in a 26-7 trouncing of the Baltimore Orioles.

0 **NY Jets tab** USC wide receiver Keyshawn Johnson as the top overall pick in the NFL draft and the first of five receivers chosen in the first round. Troubled Nebraska back Lawrence Phillips slides to St. Louis at No. 6.

Pittsburgh Steelers, looking for insurance for Bam Morris' legal woes, acquire running back Jerome Bettis from St. Louis for two draft picks.

Paul Allen, Microsoft co-founder, reaches an agreement in principle to purchase the Seattle Seahawks after a 14-month trial period.

1 **Terry Labonte starts** his NASCAR-record 514th consecutive race but Rusty Wallace races to the checkered flag at the Goody's 500 in Virginia.

Controversial sports oddsmaker Jimmy "the Greek" Snyder dies of heart failure at the age of 76.

Hale Irwin cards a final round 71 to seize the PGA Senior's Championship, his first major senior tour win.

3 **Dan Marino signs** a three-year, $17.9 million contract extension with Miami, making him the third-highest NFL player behind Troy Aikman and Drew Bledsoe.

NBA owners' Board of Governers approves the concept of the Women's NBA set to play in the summer of 1997.

Petr Nedved scores with 44 seconds remaining in the fourth overtime to lift the Pittsburgh Penguins to a 3-2 playoff victory over Washington in the third-longest game in NHL history. Penguin star Mario Lemieux is uncharacteristically ejected for instigating a fight.

New England Patriots release rights to their fifth-round draft choice Christian Peter, claiming the former Nebraska star's off-the-field behavior is unacceptable.

25 **Andre Agassi and Boris Becker** are among 13 seeded players to make early exits from the Monte Carlo Open amidst a loud chorus of boos from angry spectators.

27 **San Francisco star Barry Bonds** hits the 300th homer of his career in a 6-3 win over Florida, joining his father Bobby, Willie Mays, and Andre Dawson as the only players with 300 home runs and 300 steals.

Mike Dunleavy is fired as coach of the Milwaukee Bucks but is retained as general manager of the club.

28 **Montreal Expos** join the growing 20-run club with a 21-9 whipping of Colorado at Coors Field. The outburst makes April the first month in 46 years to have three teams score 20 or more runs in a game.

29 **UMass' Marcus Camby**, college basketball's player of the year, opts to forgo his senior year and high school sensation Kobe Bryant forgoes college altogether as the two declare their eligibility for this year's NBA draft.

Monica Seles files a $16 million claim for lost income against the Citizen Cup tennis tournament in Hamburg, Germany, the sight of her 1993 stabbing.

Indiana high school administrators vote to change the country's boys basketball tournament from one to four classes, breaking an 86-year-old tradition.

30 **NFL owners vote** 23-6 to approve the Houston Oilers' move to Nashville for the 1998 season.

New York Yankees beat the Baltimore Orioles 13-10 in four hours and 21 minutes, the longest nine-inning game in baseball history.

Pittsburgh first-baseman Jeff King becomes the third player in major league history to hit two homers in one inning twice in his career.

MAY '96

Sun	Mon	Tue	Wed	Thu	Fri	Sat
			1	2	3	4
5	6	7	8	9	10	11
12	13	14	15	16	17	18
19	20	21	22	23	24	25
26	27	28	29	30	31	

Queen Steffi

MAY 12—Steffi Graf begins her 332nd week as the number one women's tennis player in the world, breaking the WTA's record for weeks as the top ranked player. Since the computer ranking system began in 1975, only six women have held the honors, while 13 men have been ranked No. 1 since the inception of the ATP rankings in 1973.

Women

Player	Weeks (No. 1)	Last Held
Steffi Graf	332	Present
Martina Navratilova	331	Aug. 16, 1987
Chris Evert	262	Nov. 25, 1985
Monica Seles	152	Present
Tracy Austin	22	Nov. 17, 1980
Arantxa Sanchez-Vicario	12	June 11, 1995

Men

Player	Weeks (No. 1)	Last Held
Ivan Lendl	270	Aug. 12, 1990
Jimmy Connors	268	July 3, 1983
John McEnroe	170	Sept. 8, 1985
Pete Sampras	121	Present
Bjorn Borg	109	Aug. 2, 1981
Stefan Edberg	72	Oct. 4, 1992
Jim Courier	58	Sept. 12, 1993
Ilie Nastase	40	June 2, 1974
Andre Agassi	32	Feb. 11, 1996
Mats Wilander	20	Jan. 28, 1989
Boris Becker	12	Sept. 8, 1991
John Newcombe	8	July 28, 1974
Thomas Muster	6	April 13, 1996

Oh! Not Again!

MAY 29—The Detroit Red Wings are ousted from the NHL playoffs by the Colorado Avalanche, marking the 41st consecutive year the Red Wings will go back to MoTown without the coveted Stanley Cup. Detroit fans aren't the longest suffering however, as seen by this list below of major sports teams with the longest current championship droughts.

Team (League)	Last Title Won	Years Ago
Chicago Cubs (NL)	1908	88
Chicago White Sox (AL)	1917	79
Boston Red Sox (AL)	1918	78
Cleveland Indians (AL)	1948	48
Chi./St.L./Ari. Cardinals (NFL)	1947	48
Roch./Cin./KC/Sac./ Kings (NBA)	1951	45
Cle./LA/St.L Rams (NFL)	1951	44
NY/SF Giants (NL)	1954	42
Detroit Red Wings (NHL)	1955	41
St.L/Atl. Hawks (NBA)	1958	38
Detroit Lions (NFL)	1957	38

1 **Georgetown sophomore Allen Iverson** declares hi eligibility for the NBA draft, making him the first Hoy in coach John Thompson's 24 years to leave early.

Dallas Mavericks are sold for $125 million to a grou of investors led by land developer Ross Perot Jr.

2 **Earthquake measuring** 4.8 on the Richter scale rock the Seattle Kingdome causing the suspension of th Mariners-Indians game in the bottom of the sevent inning. No one is reported injured.

3 **Tim Gullikson,** former tennis player and coach of Pe Sampras, dies of brain cancer at the age of 44.

NFL great Lawrence Taylor is arrested in Myrtle Beac after buying $100 worth of fake crack cocaine from a undercover officer, then swallowing it.

Kevin Greene, defensive stalwart for the AFC champio Steelers, signs a two-year deal with Carolina.

4 **Grindstone (5-1) nips Cavonnier** in a photo finish t win the 122nd running of the Kentucky Derby. Th victory gives trainer D. Wayne Lukas his sixt consecutive triumph in a triple crown race. Favorit Unbridled's Song finishes fifth.

Butch Hobson, former Red Sox manager and curre manager in the Phillies organization, is arrested aft receiving a package containing two grams of cocain between the pages of a magazine.

Dennis Rodman signs 1,400 of his books in three hou at a Chicago store while decked out in leather pants, pink feathered boa, and silver and black make-up.

5 **Reds' owner Marge Schott** causes yet another upro after praising Adolf Hitler, claiming the Nazi leader w "good in the beginning, but he just went too far".

Czech Republic beats Canada 4-2 to capture the go medal at the World Ice Hockey Championships. U. takes home the bronze for their first medal in 34 years.

7 **Dodger outfielder Brett Butler** is diagnosed with thro cancer after surgery to remove his tonsils reveals tumor in the back of his throat.

Yankee ace David Cone is place on the disabled l with a slight aneurysm in his right arm.

Brad Greenberg, former Portland Trail Blazers exe replaces John Lucas as GM of the Philadelphia 76ers.

9 **Kentucky Derby winner Grindstone** is forced to retire stud after veterinarians find a bone chip in his rig knee following a workout.

10 **Heavyweight Lennox Lewis** takes a beating b emerges victorious in a controversial decision over R Mercer. Also, Bobby Czyz succumbs to Evand Holyfield after five rounds of punishment.

11 **Al Leiter fires** the first no-hitter of the season and t first in Florida Marlins' history, with a two walk, s stikeout, 11-0 masterpiece over the Colorado Rockies.

San Diego Chargers running back Rodney Culver a his wife, Karen, are among 109 people killed in t ValuJet crash outside of Miami.

12 **Laura Davies overcomes** frigid temperatures a gusting winds to win the rain-shortened LPG championship by one stroke over Julie Piers.

Steffi Graf begins her record 332nd week as the No. tennis player in the world, eclipsing the previous ma held by Martina Navratilova.

Cyclist Lance Armstrong outdistances France's Pas Herve by over three minutes to capture the 12-day To Du Pont, becoming the race's only repeat winner.

13 **John Lucas** is fired as coach of the Philadelphia 76 after going 42-122 during his two seasons in charge.

14 **Dwight Gooden no-hits** the Seattle Mariners in leadi the Yankees to a 2-0 win. It is Gooden's second victo since his return from substance abuse.

Green Bay Packer Brett Favre announces he w

Spanish bullfighter **Christina Sanchez** is carried by fans on May 25, 1996 after a victory in Nimes, France. Sanchez is the first woman to achieve the rank of matador in Europe.

voluntarily enter himself into a rehabilitation center to cure his dependency for pain killers.

Magic Johnson announces his retirement from the NBA. The future Hall of Famer claims he has no intentions of making another comeback.

Winnipeg Jets fire coach Terry Simpson (36-40-6) as they clean house before their relocation to Phoenix.

15 **Toronto Raptors guard Damon Stoudamire** garners 76 of a possible 113 votes in grabbing the NBA Rookie of the Year award.

Whalers owner Peter Karmanos announces the team will stay in Hartford for at least two more years, despite the club's season ticket drive falling short of expectations.

Atlanta Braves lose slugger David Justice for the season after he dislocates his shoulder while swinging.

White Sox outfielder Tony Phillips changes into street clothes, enters the crowd in Milwaukee, and punches a fan who had been heckling him. The two are later fined $287 in court and Phillips is fined $5000 by the AL.

17 **Scott Brayton,** who is to be the pole sitter at the Indy 500 for the second consecutive year, is killed at the age of 37 when his car crashes into a wall during a practice session.

18 **Louis Quatorze leads** wire-to-wire and captures the 121st Preakness Stakes, ending trainer D. Wayne Lukas' Triple Crown streak at six.

19 **No surprises** in the NBA and NHL draft lotteries as the Philadelphia 76ers and Ottawa Senators draw the coveted No.1 selections.

20 **Michael Jordan wins** his fourth NBA MVP award in record fashion, receiving 96.5% of the first-place votes.

22 **Monica Seles returns** to Europe for the first time since being stabbed three years ago and whips Austria's Barbara Schett 3-6, 7-6(8), 6-2 at the Madrid Open.

24 **Seattle's Ken Griffey Jr.** cracks three homers and knocks in six to lead the Mariners to a 10-4 trouncing of New York.

26 **Buddy Lazier** takes the checkered flag at the 80th Indianapolis 500, just nine weeks after fracturing his spine in a crash in Phoenix. In racing rival IndyCar's inaugural U.S. 500, polesitter Jimmy Vasser wins despite a pre-race crash that caused him to drive his backup car.

27 **Chicago Bulls complete** their four-game sweep of the Orlando Magic with a 106-101 come-from-behind victory. Michael Jordan pumps in a game-high 45.

California Angels deal all-time saves leader Lee Smith to the Cincinnati Reds for reliever Chuck McElroy.

Princeton scores 34 seconds into overtime to edge Virginia 13-12 and win their third NCAA Division 1 lacrosse title in five years.

28 **Cal Ripken Jr.,** playing in his 2,221st consecutive game blasts three home runs for the first time in his career and drives in eight in a 12-8 win over Seattle.

29 **Hall of Fame center Dave Cowens** is named head coach of the Charlotte Hornets.

30 **Indian slugger Albert Belle** decks Milwaukee's Fernando Vina with a forearm smash, breaking the 2nd baseman's nose and igniting a bench-clearing brawl.

Dallas Mavericks announce Bulls' assistant Jim Cleamons as their new head coach

JUNE '96

Sun	Mon	Tue	Wed	Thu	Fri	Sat
						1
2	3	4	5	6	7	8
9	10	11	12	13	14	15
16	17	18	19	20	21	22
23/31	24	25	26	27	28	29

Really Big Wins

JUNE 9—Ernie Els mows down the rest of the field at the Buick Classic, finishing eight strokes ahead of the nearest compeitor Davis Love III. Below is a list of the biggest winning margins in the history of the PGA Tour.

Margin	Golfer	Event
16	Joe Kirkwood, Sr.	1924 Corpus Christie Open
	Bobby Locke	1948 Victory Nat'l. Champ.
14	Ben Hogan	1945 Portland Invitational
	Johnny Miller	1975 Phoenix Open
13	Byron Nelson	1945 Seattle Open
	Gene Littler	1955 Tourn. of Champions
12	Byron Nelson	1939 Phoenix Open
	Arnold Palmer	1962 Phoenix Open
	Jose Maria Olazabal	1990 NEC WS of Golf

Most Gold Gloves

JUNE 13—Shortstop Ozzie Smith announces his retirement from baseball after 19 years with the San Diego Padres and St. Louis Cardinals. "The Wizard" retires with 13 gold gloves to his credit, the most ever by a shortstop. The list below highlights the leading Gold Glove winner at each position since the introduction of the award in 1957.

Pos.	Player	Gold Gloves
P	Jim Kaat	16
C	Johnny Bench	10
1B	Keith Hernandez	11
2B	Ryne Sandberg	9
3B	Brooks Robinson	16
SS	Ozzie Smith	13
OF	Willie Mays	12
OF	Roberto Clemente	12
OF	Al Kaline	10

Fastest to the Finals

JUNE 1—With their 3-1 win over the Pittsburgh Penguins in game seven of the Eastern Conference finals, the Florida Panthers became the youngest NHL expansion teams to reach the Stanley Cup finals, accomplishing the feat in just their third year in existence.

Team	Year	Outcome
Florida Panthers	1996, 3rd	lost to Colorado, 4-0
Buffalo Sabres	1975, 4th	lost to Philadelphia, 4-2
Philadelphia Flyers	1974, 7th	defeated Boston, 4-2
NY Islanders	1980, 8th	defeated Philadelphia, 4-2

Note: In 1968-70, the St. Louis Blues reached the Stanley Cup finals, but were representing a division comprised entirely of expansion teams.

1 **Cigar cruises** to an easy victory at the MassCap in Boston for his 15th consecutive win, one short of Citation's modern all-time record.

Florida Panthers, in their third year in existence, shock the Pittsburgh Penguins 3-1 to win game 7 of the Eastern Conference finals and advance to the Stanley Cup finals against Colorado.

Stanford's Tiger Woods cards a 3-under 285 total to ease to the NCAA golf championship by four strokes. Arizona St. captures the team title.

2 **Annika Sorenstam** takes home the U.S. Women's Open in record fashion, firing a final round 66 for a four day total of 272, an all-time tournament low.

Seattle SuperSonics squeeze by the Utah Jazz 90-86 in a see-saw game 7 to earn the right to face the Chicago Bulls in the NBA finals.

NHL suspends Colorado bad-boy Claude Lemieux for the first two games of the Stanley Cup final for smashing Detroit's Kris Draper into the boards face first. It is Lemieux's 2nd suspension of the playoffs.

Astro pitcher Darryl Kile ties a major league record by hitting four St. Louis batters in one game.

College Football Association votes to dissolve, effective June 30, 1997, amidst declining conference support.

3 **Marcus Camby,** college basketball's player of the year, admits he accepted cash and jewelry while at UMass and claims he was blackmailed by agent Wesley Spears.

4 **Vancouver Canucks** tab Canadian national team coach Tom Renney as their new head coach.

Pittsburgh Pirates select Clemson pitcher Kris Benson with the first pick in the major league draft.

5 **UMass coach John Calipari** agrees in principle to a 5-year deal to become coach and director of basketball operations of the New Jersey Nets.

7 **Oscar De La Hoya** bloodies Julio Cesar Chavez, registering a 4th-round knockout of the aging fighter to become the WBC super lightweight champion.

8 **Editor's Note surges** to win the 128th Belmont Stakes, returning trainer D. Wayne Lukas to the spotlight with his 7th Triple Crown victory in the last eight races. Pre-race favorite Cavonnier was eased after injuring a tendon in his right leg.

Steffi Graf and Arantxa Sanchez–Vicario battle for over three hours before Graf emerges with her fifth French Open title 6-3, 6-7, 10-8.

Warren Morris blasts a dramatic, game-winning, two-run homer with two outs in the ninth inning to give LSU a 9-8 victory and the College World Series championship over Miami.

9 **Yevgeny Kafelnikov** becomes the first Russian to win a grand slam singles title with a three-set victory over Michael Stich in the French Open.

10 **Uwe Krupp scores** 4:31 into the third overtime to give the Colorado Avalanche a 1-0 win and a 4-0 sweep over Florida for their first Stanley Cup. Center Joe Sakic wins the Conn Smythe Trophy as playoff MVP.

ESPN announces the November 1 launching of ESPNEWS, a 24-hour sports news channel to compete with CNN/SI.

12 **Reds owner Marge Schott** agrees to relinquish control of day-to-day operation of the club for two years after an ultimatum by MLB threatened to suspend her indefinitely. She is replaced on an interim basis by team controller John Allen.

13 **Denver Nuggets** clean house, trading Mahmoud Abdul-Rauf to Sacramento for Sarunas Marciulionis and a pick and dishing Jalen Rose to the Pacers.

Wide World Photos

Former University of Massachusetts basketball coach **John Calipari** is introduced on June 7, 1996 as the new head coach of the New Jersey Nets.

16 **Chicago Bulls** close the book on their brilliant season with an 87-75 home victory over Seattle to win their 4th championship in the 90s. Michael Jordan is selected series MVP and leads the team to a 15-3 playoff mark.

Steve Jones holes a short par putt on the 18th hole to take home the U.S. Open golf championship by one stroke. Davis Love three putts the final hole, missing a chance at an 18-hole playoff.

Mel Allen, the"voice of the Yankees", dies at his home in Connecticut at the age of 83.

17 **Seattle Seahawk Brian Blades** is acquitted in the slaying of his cousin Charles Blades. The receiver is originally found guilty but the decision is overturned by judge Susan Lebow after a juror expressed doubts about the conviction.

Mary Slaney shows flashes of her old self, qualifying for the Olympic team with a second place finish to Lynn Jennings in the 5,000 meters.

19 **Ken Griffey Jr.** is placed on the disabled list for the second time in as many years after breaking a bone in his hand while following through on a swing.

Pittsburgh's Mario Lemieux wins the Hart Trophy as MVP of the NHL. Other winners include defenseman Chris Chelios (Norris), goaltender Jim Carey (Vezina), and rookie Daniel Alfredsson (Calder).

Ozzie Smith, future Hall of Fame shortstop for the St. Louis Cardinals, announces his plans to retire at the end of the season.

Atlanta hurler John Smoltz continues to dominate national league hitters, extending his winning streak to 14 games with a two-hit, 5-1 win over San Diego.

20 **Albert Belle's suspension** for his forearm shiver to the face of Milwaukee's Fernando Vina is reduced for the second time to two games and $25,000.

Phil Jackson signs a one-year, $2.5 million contract to remain coach of the Chicago Bulls.

22 **Michael Moorer** regains the IBF heavyweight title with a split decision over Axel Schulz. Also, Buster Douglas returns with a third round KO of Tony La Rosa.

Injured U.S. gymnasts Shannon Miller and Dominique Moceanu are given clearance to skip the Olympic Trials and vault directly onto the Olympic team.

D Chris Phillips of Alberta is selected first overall by the Ottawa Senators in the NHL entry draft.

23 **Speedster Michael Johnson** sets a 200 meter world record with a time of 19.66 to qualify for the Olympic track and field squad.

24 **Andre Agassi,** Michael Chang, and Jim Courier, three of America's top four players, are ousted on opening day at Wimbledon.

26 **Philadelphia 76ers select** Georgetown guard Allen Iverson with the first pick in the NBA draft. Top 7 players and a record 17 first round picks are underclassmen, including 2 high schoolers.

Mary Carillo, Billie Jean King and Martina Navratilova broadcast Wimbledon for HBO, making it the first time in TV history that an all-female crew has worked a sporting event.

27 **NBA and NBC** sign a five-year, revenue sharing deal for the Women's NBA beginning next June. NBC will televise 10 Saturday games and the championship. ESPN and Lifetime are later added for assorted weekday games.

30 **Fun at Coors Field** as the Colorado Rockies edge the LA Dodgers 16-15 in a 4 hour and 20 minute slugfest that boasts 38 hits, 10 out of the park. A total of 85 runs is scored in the four-game series.

JULY '96

Sun	Mon	Tue	Wed	Thu	Fri	Sat
	1	2	3	4	5	6
7	8	9	10	11	12	13
14	15	16	17	18	19	20
21	22	23	24	25	26	27
28	29	30	31			

Kirby calls it.

July 12—Kirby Puckett, his eyes ravaged by glaucoma, announces his premature retirement from baseball. The popular Twin outfielder won two World Series crowns in 12 seasons with Minnesota. His year by year numbers are listed below.

	AB	R	H	RBI	Avg
1984	557	63	165	31	.296
1985	691	80	199	74	.288
1986	680	119	223	96	.328
1987	624	96	207	99	.332
1988	657	109	234	121	.356
1989	635	75	215	85	.339
1990	551	82	164	80	.293
1991	611	92	195	89	.319
1992	639	104	210	110	.329
1993	622	89	184	89	.296
1994	439	79	139	112	.317
1995	538	83	169	99	.314
Total	7244	1071	2304	1085	.318

Cigar gets Citation

July 13—Racehorse Cigar captures the Arlington Citation Challenge to tie Citation's modern day record of 16 consecutive victories. Here is Cigar's record run:

Date	Track (Race)
Oct. 28, 1994	Aqueduct (Allowance Race)
Nov. 26, 1994	Aqueduct (NYRA Mile)
Jan. 22, 1995	Gulfstream (Allowance Race)
Feb. 11, 1995	Gulfstream (Donn Handicap)
Mar. 5, 1995	Gulfstream (Gulfstream Park Handi.)
Apr. 15, 1995	Oaklawn (Oaklawn Park Handi.)
May 13, 1995	Pimlico Race Course (Pimlico Special)
June 3, 1995	Suffolk Downs (Massachusetts Handicap)
July 2, 1995	Hollywood (Hollywood Gold Cup)
Sept. 16, 1995	Belmont (Woodward Handicap)
Oct. 7, 1995	Belmont (Jockey Club Gold Cup)
Oct. 28, 1995	Belmont (Breeders' Cup Classic)
Feb. 10, 1996	Gulfstream (Donn Handicap)
Mar. 27, 1996	Nad Al Sheba, U.A.E. (Dubai World Cup)
June 2, 1996	Suffolk Downs (Massachusetts Handicap)
July 13, 1996	Arlington Internaional (Arlington Citation Challenge.)

1 **Phoenix Coyotes name** Calgary assistant Don Hay their head coach.

3 **NY Ranger assistant Mike Murphy** is named head coach of the Toronto Maple Leafs.

6 **Steffi Graf wins** her 7th Wimbledon championship and her 20th grand slam title with a 6-3, 7-5 effort over Arantxa Sanchez Vicario.

USA College Select basketball squad gives the Dream Team their biggest challenge of the year, jumping out to a 17 point halftime lead before finally succumbing, 96-90.

7 **Unseeded Richard Krajicek** registers a staight set victory over No. 20 Malivai Washington 6-3, 6-4, 6-3 to become the first Dutch Wimbledon champ.

Dave Stockton's final round 73 is enough to hold off a late Hale Irwin charge and come away with the U.S. Senior Open title.

Darryl Strawberry returns to the Yankee lineup to a standing ovation, despite an 0 for 4 performance.

Marcel Lacheman is fired as manager of the Florida Marlins and replaced by assistant GM John Boles.

9 **L.A. catcher Mike Piazza,** playing in his native Philadelphia, blasts a 2nd-inning homer and an RBI double to lead the NL to a 6-0 win and earn the MVP award at the MLB all-star game. Iron man Cal Ripken's nose is accidentally broken during pre-game photos.

NBA locks out for two hours and 38 minutes, extending the moratorium on signings and trades for another two days.

10 **Arthur Ashe** statue is unveiled in Richmond, VA on the late tennis great's 53rrd birthday.

11 **Boxing melee erupts** in Madison Square Garden after Andrew Golota's 4th low blow disqualifies him and leaves Riddick Bowe writhing on the canvas. Riot includes Golota 's head being smashed with a walkie-talkie and trainer Lou Duva exiting on a stretcher.

NBA signs a collective bargaining agreement, opening the floodgates for trades and unprecedented free agent signings.

12 **Kirby Puckett announces** his retirement from baseball after an operation reveals irreversible damage to his eye due to glaucoma.

Michael Jordan inks a one-year pact with the Chicago Bulls worth a reported $25 million.

13 **Cigar does it again,** tying Citation's mark with his 16th consecutive victory at the Arlington (Ill) Challenge.

Slugger Andre Dawson announces this season will be his last.

14 **IndyCar rookie Jeff Krosnoff** is killed in a late crash during the Toronto Molson-Indy. The accident also takes the life of course worker Gary Arvin.

New York Knicks continue their overhaul, signing guards Allan Houston and Chris Childs, and all-star forward Larry Johnson. Juwan Howard signs a $98 million deal with Miami.

15 **Cal Ripken's streak** of 2,216 consecutive games at shortstop ends when he is shifted to 3rd base in an 8-6 Oriole win over Toronto.

Atlanta Hawks enter the free agent sweepstakes signing a five-year deal with center Dikembe Mutombo.

16 **Michael Irvin pleads** no-contest to cocaine posession in exchange for four years probation, a $10,000 fine and 800 hours of community service. He is later suspended for the first five games of the season by the NFL.

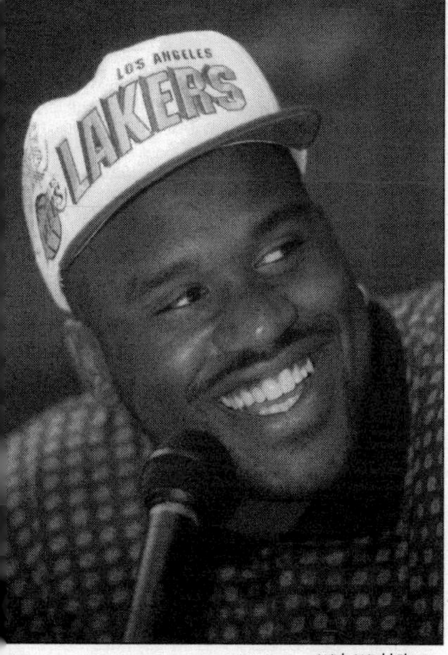

Wide World Photos

In a move that dramatically shifts the power in the NBA, **Shaquille O'Neal** greets the press to announce that he is leaving the Orlando Magic for the Los Angeles Lakers.

Wide World Photos

Seattle Mariners shortstop **Alex Rodriguez** had a breakout season in 1996 and made his first all star team in July.

17 **Marge Schott** is issued an all out ban from Riverfront Stadium after she sends a memo to Reds' employees citing her intentions to remain a major part of team decisions.

18 **Shaquille O'Neal decides** to switch coasts, signing a seven-year, $121 million deal with the Los Angeles Lakers. The center insists the decision has nothing to do with money.

19 **Summer Olympics** officially kick off as an estimated 3.5 billion watch 1960 gold medalist Muhammad Ali light the vaunted Olympic flame.

21 **US strikes gold** as swimmer Tom Dolan emerges victorious in the 400M individual medley and is later joined in the winner's circle by the men's 800M freestyle relay team.

Tom Lehman begins the day with a six -shot lead and holds on to become the 2nd American in as many years to win the British Open

Wayne Gretzky rejoins former teammate Mark Messier by agreeing to a two-year deal with the New York Rangers worth over $8 million plus incentives.

Danish cyclist Bjarne Riis pedals to victory at the Tour de France, foiling Miguel Indurain's bid for his sixth consecutive title.

23 **Gymnast Kerri Strug** becomes the darling of the '96 games by leading the U.S. squad to its first ever team gold. Strug nails her last vault on a sprained left ankle before collapsing in pain.

Rose Bowl agrees o join the bowl alliance beginning in 1998, joining three other unnamed bowls. The deal insures a matchup between the two top-ranked teams to be televised by ABC.

24 **L.A. Lakers** sign 17-year-old Kobe Bryant to an undisclosed pact, making him the youngest player in the NBA.

U.S. women add 4x100 meter medley relay gold to the growing collection of swimming medals. Ireland's Michelle Smith wins her 3rd gold and China's Li Xiaoshuang takes the men's gymnastics title.

25 **The NFL** suspended Dallas Cowboy Michael Irvin for 5 games under terms of its substance abuse policy.

28 **Dale Earnhardt and Emerson Fittipaldi** were injured in crashed, Earnhardt at the Die Hard 500 and Fittipaldi at the Marlboro 500.

30 **The US softball team** beat China 3-1 on Dot Richardson's two run homer for the Gold Medal at the Olympics

31 **The St. Louis Rams** signed tailback Lawrence Phillips of Nebraska to a 3 year, $5.6 million contract that did not have the usual bonuses associated with a high draft pick. Phillips went number 6 in the NFL draft but his off field adventures led to the unusual deal

With the Major League Baseball trading deadline approaching several teams made moves. The Red Sox traded Kevin Mitchell to Cincinnati for minor leaguers and they traded Jamie Moyer to the Seattle Mariners for Darren Bragg. The San Francisco Giants traded Mark Leiter to Montreal for pitchers Kurk Rueter and Tim Scott. The Cincinnati Reds also traded Eric Anthony to the Colorado Rockies for cash.

AUG '96

Sun	Mon	Tue	Wed	Thu	Fri	Sat
1	2	3	4	5	8	3
8	9	10	17	18	19	10
15	18	13	18	19	20	27
28	29	20	25	28	23	28
29	26	27	28	29	30	31

A Major Goal

Aug. 11—After six career PGA Tour wins, Mark Brooks wins his first major with an extra-hole victory over Kenny Perry in the PGA Championship at the Valhalla Golf Club in Louisville, Ky. Active players with the most Tour victories without a major are listed below.

	Yrs on Tour	Wins
Bruce Lietzke	21	13
Mark O'Meara	16	12
Wayne Levi	21	12
Andy Bean	20	11
Davis Love III	11	10
Mark McCumber	19	10
Jay Haas	21	9
David Frost	13	9

Falling into the history books

Aug. 28—The Detroit Tigers make history twice over in their 9-3 loss to the Cleveland Indians. The allow their major league record 11th Grand Slam of the season to Albert Belle in the sixth inning and with the loss become the seventh team in baseball history to get swept in the season series by an opponent. Note the lists below.

Season Sweeps

Year	Winner	Loser	Series
1996	Indians	Tiger	12 games
1994	Expos	Padres	12 games
1993	Braves	Rockies	13 games
1990	Athletics	Yankees	12 games
1988	Royals	Orioles	12 games
1978	Orioles	Athletics	11 games
1970	Orioles	Royals	12 games

Note: Cleveland swept Oakland in 1994 (six games) and 1995 (seven games) but both series were in strike shortened seasons.

Grand Slams Allowed

No	Team
11	1996 Detroit Tigers
10	1996 San Francisco Giants
10	1992 Seattle Mariners
9	1988 Texas Rangers
9	1950 St. Louis Browns
9	1938 St. Louis Browns
9	1933 Chicago White Sox

1 **Michael Johnson** shatters the world record in the 200 meter dash (19.32), on his way to becoming the first man in Olympic history to win both the 200 and 400 in the same Games.

Dan O'Brien finally stakes his claim as the world's greatest athlete, winning gold in the decathlon four years after failing to even make the U.S. Olympic team.

Dallas Cowboys announce a 3-year deal with AT&T worth between $5-6 million to be an official Texas Stadium Sponsor, despite the NFL's exclusive marketing agreement with Sprint as the league's telecommunications sponsor.

2 **Cuba** wins its second consecutive baseball gold medal with a 13-9 win over Japan. USA beats Nicaraga, 10-3, for the bronze.

3 **Dream Team III** beats up on Yugoslavia, 95-69, for the gold medal in men's basketball.

Canada wins the 4x100 meter relay gold, upsetting the Carl Lewis-less American team. Lewis had openly campaigned for inclusion on the team but was no selected to replaced the injured, most likely due to his poor performance at the Olympic Trials.

4 **The U.S. Women's Basketball** squad captures the gold medal, defeating Brazil 111-87.

Closing Ceremonies at the Summer Olympics in Atlanta take place. Of the record 197 nations that participate 79 took home medals.

Laura Davies wins he second major championship of the year with her two-stroke victory over Nancy Lopez and Karrie Webb at the du Maurier Classic at Edmonton Country Club. Davies started the day five strokes off the lead, but carded a final-round 66 for the win.

Dale Jarrett wins the Brickyard 400 at Indianapolis Motor Speedway, passing his Ford teammate Ernie Irvin with seven laps remaining.

U.S. Olympic boxer David Reid, way behind on points scores a final-round knockout of Cuba's Alfredo Duvergel in their light-middleweight match, giving the U.S. team it's only boxing gold medal of the 1996 Summer Olympics.

5 **Citadel football coach Charlie Taaffe** is suspended by the school after his second arrest for driving under the influence of alcohol.

Washington Bullets win the battle with Miami Heat for Juwan Howard, inking him to 7-year pact worth $100.8 million.

6 **Keyshawn Johnson,** the top overall pick in the 199 NFL college draft, ends his 24-day holdout. The wid receiver signs a 6-year deal with the N.Y. Jets wort $15 million and a $6.5 million signing bonus.

9 **Former Red Sox skipper Butch Hobson** pleads no guilty to charges of cocaine possession in Providenc (R.I.) Superior Court.

10 **Cigar's** record-tying streak of 16 consecutive victories ended when he finishes 3 lengths behind Dare and G at the Pacific Classic.

11 **Mark Brooks** bcaptions his first major when he ea Kenny Perry on the first hole of a playoff to win th PGA Championship. Brooks birdied the 18th hole t force the playoff while Perry gave interviews in the CB TV Tower instead of hitters practice balls.

12 **Emmitt Smith** re-signs with the Cowboys in an 8-yea $48 million contract, including an NFL-record $1 million signing bonus.

14 **Veteran outfielder Andre Dawson** announces he w retire from baseball following the season.

Wide World Photos

Along with the USA's Michael Johnson's victory in the men's, **Marie-Jose Perec** of France won the women's gold medal at the 1996 Olympics in both the 200 and the 400 meter races.

Tom Mees, 46, a pioneer broadcaster for ESPN, dies when he drowns in a neighbor's swimming pool in Southington, Conn.

15 **More than 3,500 physically challenged athletes** from 120 countries gather in Atlanta for the start of the Paralympics. It is the world's second largest sporting event after the Olympics.

17 **Terry Bradshaw and Walter Payton** lead a class of 14 players inducted into the College Football Hall of Fame in South Bend, Ind. It is the first time that player from smaller colleges are enshrined.

Major League Soccer announces plans to expand to 12 teams in 1998. Chicago is considered the odd-on favorite for one slot while Charlotte and Atlanta are those mentioned for the other.

18 **Emilee Klein, 22,** wins her second consecutive LPGA Tour event, capturing the Women's British Open with a 15-under 277.

19 **The Houston Rockets** acquire Charles Barkley from the Phoenix Suns in exchange for Mark Bryant, Robert Horry, Chucky Brown and Sam Cassell.

22 **Free agent guard Dan Majerle** signs with the Miami Heat, inking a three-year, $8 million deal.

24 **Taiwan** captures its 17th Little League World Series with a 13-3 victory over Cranston, R.I. in Williamsport, Pa. For more information on the Little League World Series see page 925.

25 **Tiger Woods** wins an unprecedented third straight US Amateur title with an incredible come from behind win over Univ. of Florida sophomore Steve Scott.

Phil Mickelson's takes the World Series of Golf for his fourth victory of the year and the second-highest money total in PGA Tour history.

Alexandr Popov, the world's fastest swimmer, is stabbed in the stomach during an altercation with a watermelon street vendor in Moscow. Popov, known as the Russian Rocket, won two gold and two silvers at the Summer Games in Atlanta.

26 **Dallas Green** is fired as manager of the lowly N.Y. Mets and replaced with former Texas manager Bobby Valentine.

The Tampa Bay Storm win their second consecutive Arena Bowl football title with a 42-38 victory over the Iowa Barnstormers.

27 **Tiger Woods,** three-time defending U.S. Amateur champion, announces he will turn professional immediately and join the PGA Tour.

28 **The rich get richer.** The Atlanta Braves deal pitcher Jason Schmidt and two minor leaguers to Pittsburgh for left-handed ace Denny Neagle. Jerry Rice becomes the NFL's highest paid wide receiver when he inks a 7 year deal with San Francisco worth $32 million, including a $4 million signing bonus.

29 **Randall Cunningham** is released by the Philadelphia Eagles and announces his retirement. The former Pro Bowl quarterback (1988-90) played 11 season in the NFL—all in Philly.

SEPT '96

Sun	Mon	Tue	Wed	Thu	Fri	Sat
1	2	3	4	5	6	7
8	9	10	11	12	13	14
15	16	17	18	19	20	21
22	23	24	25	26	27	28
29	30					

Steady Eddie

Sept. 6—Eddie Murray belts the 500th home run of his long career, becoming the first played to reach the milestone without hitting 40 in one season. Below is a list of players with the most home runs without a 40-homer year.

	Season High (year)	HRs
Eddie Murray	33 (1983)	500
Stan Musial	39 (1948)	475
Dave Winfield	37 (1982)	465
Al Kaline	29 (1962,.66)	399
Graig Nettles	37 (1977)	390

Rocket Launches

Sept. 18—Roger Clemens, 34, ties his own Major League Baseball record, striking out 20 batters in a 4-0 Red Sox win over the Detroit Tigers. Clemens originally set the record more than 10 years ago in April of 1986. Below is a list of pitchers with the most strikeouts in a nine-inning game.

20—Roger Clemens, Boston, Sept. 18, 1996, at Detroit
20—Roger Clemens, Boston, Apr. 29, 1986, vs. Seattle
19—David Cone, N.Y. Yankees, Oct. 6, 1991, vs. Phil.
19—Nolan Ryan, California, Aug. 12, 1974, vs. Boston
19—Tom Seaver, N.Y. Mets, Apr. 22, 1970, vs. San Diego
19—Steve Carlton, Phil., Sept. 15, 1969, vs. N.Y. Mets
18—Randy Johnson, Seattle, Sept. 27, 1992 at Texas*
18—Ron Guidry, N.Y. Yankees, June 17, 1978, vs. Cal.
*Johnson only pitched 8 innings.

Monday Night Football

Sept. 23—The Miami Dolphins make a record 52nd appearance on ABC's Monday Night Football, losing to the Indianapolis Colts, 10-6. Below is a list of NFL teams that have played the most Monday night games since 1970

Team	Record	Games
Miami Dolphins	31-21	52
Dallas Cowboys	27-21	48
Oakland Raiders	31-13-1	45
Washington Redskins	22-21	43
San Francisco 49ers	25-16	41
Chicago Bears	14-27	41

1 **Jeff Gordon** takes his seventh win of the yea defending his title in the Southern 500 at Darlington.

Kenya's Daniel Komen shatters the world record in th 3,000 meters with a time of 7:20.67 at Ruti, Italy Komen bested Algeria's Noureddine Morceli old ma of 7:25.11, set in

2 **Mike Greenwell** has the night of his life, knocking in runs on 4 hits, including two homers in a 9-8 Red So win over Seattle. It is a MLB record for driving in a your team's runs.

David Cone returns to the majors for the first time sinc having an aneurysm removed from his pitching arr and throws seven no-hit innings.

5 **All-Star forward Cam Neely,** tearfully announces hi retirement from hockey because of a degenerative hi condition. The high-scoring winger played 10 season with the Boston Bruins.

Pete Sampras battles through illness to defeat Ale Corretja, 7-6 (7-5), 5-7, 5-7, 6-4, 7-6 (9-7) in one c the most dramatic performances in U.S. Open history Sampras, who vomited several times during the match was treated for dehydration following the quarterfina victory.

6 **Baltimore's Eddie Murray** joins Hank Aaron and Willi Mays as the only players with 3,000 hits and 50 homers with a solo shot off the Tigers' Felipe Lira in th seventh inning.

Brett Butler makes his return to the LA Dodgers fror cancer treatments, scoring the go-ahead run in a 2- Dodger win over the Pirates.

7 **Mike Tyson** TKO's WBA Heavyweight champion Bruc Seldon at 1:49 of round 1 to reclaim the second o three parts of the undisputed title he lost to Buste Douglas in 1990.

8 **In the U.S. Open finals,** Pete Sampras beats Michae Chang and Steffi Graf downs Monica Seles. It is th fourth Open singles title for Sampras and the fifth fo Graf.

9 **The fastest** round of golf in history is played by 8 Massachusetts linksters spread out around a course i Worcester. The round, an even par 70, takes 9 minutes 28 seconds.

10 **College basketball's** player of the Marcus Camby, sign a three-year, $8.4 million deal with the Toronto Raptors the team that picked him second overall in the 199 NBA draft. The only person picked higher than Camby Georgetown's Allen Iverson, signs with Philadelphia fo $9.6 million, two days later.

14 **Team USA** humbles Canada with a come from behind 5-2, win in the Hockey World Cup. See page II fo more information on the World Cup of Hockey.

Bombs away! Oakland slugger Mark McGwire belts hi 50th home run of the year and Todd Hundley sets th home run record for catchers with his 41st round tripper of the season. The next day Baltimore's Brad Anderson notches his AL record 10th leadoff home besting Rickey Henderson's 1986 mark.

16 **Paul Molitor** becomes the 21st player in basebal history to collect 3,000 hits but the only one to do s with a triple. The ageless Molitor hit the milestone in th fifth inning off of Jose Rosado in a 6-5 Twins loss to th Royals.

Michigan State football program is placed on fou years probabtion by the NCAA for violations involvin recruiting, academics, ethics and institutional control.

On September 9, 1996, **Roger Clemens** of the Boston Red Sox struck out 20 Detroit Tigers in one game. Clemens is the only pitcher to accomplish this feat and he has done it twice, having struck out 20 Seattle Mariners in 1986

The Hockey Hall of Fame opens its doors to N.Y. Islander coaching legend Al Arbour, Toronto's Borje Salming and former Bruins winger Bobby Bauer.

17 **Hideo Nomo** pitches the second no-hitter of the year, blanking the Rockies at hitter-friendly Coors Field in Denver.

Defending AL champs, the Cleveland Indians, become the first team to clinch their division, doing so with a 9-4 win over the White Sox in Chicago.

Michael Lasky, a Baltimore businessman, pays fan Danny Jones an incredible $500,000 for Eddie Murray's 500th home run ball. It is the most money ever paid for a sports memorabilia item—at least until a 1910 Honus Wagner card goes for $640,000, four days later.

18 **Veteran Boston hurler,** Roger Clemens, ties his own major league record when he strikes out 20 batters in a four-hit, 4-0, win over the Detroit Tigers.

19 **Harness horse Stand Forever** sets a world record for a half-mile track, winning the Magical Mike Ivitational Pace in 1:49 2/5.

21 **Arizona St.** shutouts Nebraska, 19-0, ending their 26-game win streak and holding them scoreless in a regular season game for the first time 1973.

22 **Formula One** rookie Jacques Villeneuve wins the Portugese Grand Prix, beating teammate Damon Hill and keeping alive his hopes for the driver's title.

The U.S. comes from behind to overtake Europe and win the Solheim Cup, 17-11 at Chepstow, Wales. Solheim rookie, Michelle McGann, sparked the victory with her 3 and 2 singles win over England's Laura Davies, the top-ranked player in the world.

23 **Quarterback Jeff George** is suspended from the Atlanta Falcons following his heated exchange with head coach June Jones in Sunday's loss to Philadelphia.

24 **Millionaire** benefactor John duPont is ruled incompetent to stand trial on charges of the murder of Olympic Wrestler Dave Schultz.

26 **Earl Anthony** beats Barry Gurney, 217-211, to win the PBA Senior Classic in his first season back on the tour. The Hall of Fame kegler ended his five-year retirement in June.

27 **Roberto Alomar** spoils his nice-guy reputation when he spits in the face of umpire John Hirschbeck after he is ejected for arguing a called third strike. Alomar is quoted after the game as saying about Hirschbeck, "I think he had problems with his family after his son died...He's gotten more bitter."

Barry Bonds becomes baseball's second 40/40 man, swiping his 40th base to join Jose Canseco as the only men to collect 40 homers and 40 steals in the same season.

29 **Detroit Tiger** mainstay Alan Trammell leaves baseball after 20 years, announcing his retirement after two decades in MoTown. Trammell knocks a base-hit up the middle in his final at-bat.

Monica Seles beat Arantxa Sanchez Vicario to lift the USA to an insurmountable 3-0 lead over Spain in the finals of the Fed Cup to end the Spanish 3-year championship run.

30 **The ax falls** on two MLB managers. The Red Sox can Kevin Kennedy and the Phillies dump Jim Fregosi.

Reggie Miller signs his long-awaited deal with the Indiana Pacers, inking a 4-year pact worth a reported

OCT '96

Sun	Mon	Tue	Wed	Thu	Fri	Sat
		1	2	3	4	5
6	7	8	9	10	11	12
13	14	15	16	17	18	19
20	21	22	23	24	25	26
27	28	29	30	31		

The kid's got clout

Oct. 20—Atlanta rookie sensation Andruw Jones smashes a hanging slider off Yankee starter Andy Pettitte for a home run in his first World Series at-bat. Jones at 19 years, 6 months and 28 days is the youngest ever to hit a World Series homer. Then, in his second at-bat, Jones homers again. Below are listed the players who hit home runs in the first Series at-bat.

	Year
Joe Harris, Senator	1925
George Watkins, Cardinals	1930
Mel Ott, Giants	1933
George Selkirk, Yankees	1936
Dusty Rhodes, Giants	1954
Elston Howard, Yankees	1955
Roger Maris, Yankees	1960
Don Mincher, Twins	1965
Brooks Robinson, Orioles	1966
Jose Santiago, Red Sox	1967
Mickey Lolich, Tigers	1968
Don Buford, Orioles	1969
*Gene Tenace, A's	1972
Jim Mason, Yankees	1976
Doug DeCinces, Orioles	1979
Amos Otis, Royals	1980
Bob Watson, Yankees	1981
Jim Dwyer, Orioles	1983
Mickey Hatcher, Dodgers	1988
Jose Canseco, A's	1988
Bill Bathe, Giants	1989
Eric Davis, Reds	1990
Ed Sprague, Blue Jays	1992
Fred McGriff, Braves	1995
*Andruw Jones, Braves	1996

*homered in first two at-bats.

Show 'em you're a Tiger!

Oct. 20—PGA Tour rookie Tiger Woods gets his second professional victory when fellow rookie Taylor Smith is disqualified for using a putter with illegal grips. Here is how Woods' first year on the Tour compares with the rookie season of other PGA stars.

	Year	Sts	Wins	Top 10
Arnold Palmer	1955	28	1	7
Jack Nicklaus	1962	26	3	16
Tom Watson	1972	21	0	1
Greg Norman	1981*	9	0	3
Tiger Woods	1996	8	2	3

*Norman played two events in 1979.

1 **Major League umps,** though still upset about the wa the Roberto Alomar incident was handled by A president Gene Budig, called off the boycott planned f the divisional series.

3 **Pirates** third base coach Gene Lamont is named succeed to Jim Leyland as manager of the Pittsburg Pirates.

Nine-time all-star Dominique Wilkins makes his retu to the NBA after spending a year playing in Greec signing on with the San Antonio Spurs for the leagu minimum.

4 **The Florida Marlins** win the Jim Leyland sweepstak beating out the Angels, Red Sox and White Sox to sig the sought after former Pirate skipper.

Houston Astros manager Terry Collins is fired ar replaced by broadcaster Larry Dierker.

5 **A twelve-inning home run** by the controversial Rober Alomar lifts Baltimore past defending AL champic Cleveland and into the ALCS.

Williams College, the defending NCAA Div. III men soccer champions, loses to Bates, 2-1, ending their 4 game unbeaten streak.

6 **Tiger Woods,** on the PGA Tour just over one mont wins his first event as a pro, holding off Davis Love III a sudden-death playoff at the Las Vegas Invitational.

9 **The N.Y. Yankees** win game 1 of the AL Championsh Series, when 12-year-old Jeff Maier pulls a Derek Jet fly ball, destined for Baltimore outfielder Tony Tarasco glove, into the right-field bleachers for a home run.

Whalers Brendan Shanahan and Brad Glynn a shipped to Detroit in exchange for Keith Primeau ar veteran defenseman Paul Coffey.

10 **Justice Dept.** files suit against the nation's large architectural firm, Minneapolis-based Ellerbe Becke Inc. for designing some arenas inaccessible to disable fans. Designs in Boston, Buffalo, Clevelan Philadelphia, Portland, Ore. and Washington are und scrutiny.

12 **Darryl Strawberry's** two home runs give the Yanke the win and a 3-1 series lead over the Baltimor Orioles.

13 **New York wins** their first pennant since 1981 with a 4 win over the Orioles, taking the LCS, 4 games to Meanwhile, St. Louis pushes the defending Wor Champion Braves to the brink of elimination with come from behind win, capped by Brian Jordan's 8 inning homer.

French tennis legend Rene Lacoste, 92, dies sever days following surgery to repair his broken leg. Lacos was the last surviving member of the "Four Musketeer but will probably be best remembered for the crocodi logo, inspired by his nickname, that adorned polo shi produced by the sporting wear company he founded.

Michael Irvin returns from a five-game suspension the Dallas Cowboys defeat the Arizona Cardinals, 1 3.

14 **Atlanta,** down 3-1 to St. Louis in the NLCS, stays aliv hammering out 22 hits in a 14-0 shellacking of th Cardinals.

16 **Tragedy strikes** as more than 80 people die and ov 100 are injured when a stadium tunnel collapses at c overcrowded soccer World Cup qualifying matc between Costa Rica and Guatemala in Guatemala City

Atlanta continues their NLCS rally forcing a game with St. Louis on a 3-1 win behind strong performance by pitchers Greg Maddux and Mark Wohlers.

Wide World Photos

Roberto Alomar is alone with his thoughts a few days after his infamous spitting incident made him the object of more press attention than his considerable playing ability ever did.

17 **Braves** complete their comeback, winning th last three games of the series after falling behing 3 games to 1. beating the Cardinals ??? in game 7 after facing elimination in Game 5

19 **Game 1** of the World Series at Yankee Stadium is washed out as rain storms flood the northeast.

20 **Braves rookie Andruw Jones** hits two homers including one in his first World Series at-bat as the Braves pound the Yankees, 12-1, in game 1 of the World Series in New York.

The D.C. United stage an improbable comeback, rallying back from a two-goal second-half deficit to win the inaugural MLS Cup, 3-2, in overtime over the stunned LA Galaxy before more than 34,000 at a rain-soaked Foxboro Stadium. United midfielder Marco Etcheverry sets-up all 3 United goals.

Tiger Woods, a PGA Tour rookie, wins his second PGA Tour event with a 6 under par 66 in the final round of the Walt Disney World/Oldsmobile Classic, edging out Payne Stewart by one stroke.

The Atlanta Braves ride the winning formula of Greg Maddux and Mark Wohlers, shutting out the Yankees, 4-0 to claim a 2-0 lead in the World Series. Both wins came at Yankee Stadium.

David Shula is fired after 4 1/2 seasons as head coach of the Cincinnati Bengals. Shula compiled a 19-52 record while in Cincinnati, reaching 50 losses faster than any coach in league history. Surprisingly another coaching vacancy is created hours later when Jim Mora, longtime head coach of the New Orleans Saints quits. The day before Mora was visibly disheartened following the Saints 19-7 loss to Carolina.

22 **The Yankees** bounce back with a 5-2 win over the Braves in Game 3 of the World Series at Atlanta-Fulton County Stadium. New York outfielder Bernie Williams hits a homer and drives in three runs.

Talented but troubled quarterback Jeff George is waived by the Atlanta Falcons.

NBA steals specialist Alvin Robertson's sticky fingers land him 10 years probabtion and a $10,000 fine for the burglary of his former girlfriend's apartment.

23 **Jim Leyritz** hits a home run in the eighth inning as the Yankees climb all the way out of a six run hole and eventually pull out an 8-6 win over the Braves in 10 innings at Atlanta to even the series at two games apiece.

Sheryl Swoopes and Rebecca Lobo become the first women to sign with the upstart Women's National Basketball League, spurning offers from the American Basketball League another new women's league and rival of the WNBA.

24 **The Yankees** stay hot and take control of the series away from the Braves with a 1-0 victory in game 5 of the Series. New York starter Andy Pettitte, who struggled in game 1, scattered five hits of 8 1/3 innings.

Gabriela Sabatini hangs up her tennis racquet at age 26. Sabatini won the 1990 U.S. Open and earned $8.8 million during a career that never seemed to reach its full potential.

JANUARY

1 Major bowl games (2): Fiesta (Tempe); Rose (Pasadena).
2 Sugar Bowl (New Orleans).
4 NFL playoffs (2): AFC/NFC semifinal games.
5 NFL playoffs (2): AFC/NFC semifinal games.
11 NCAA Convention begins (Dallas).
12 NFL playoffs (2): AFC/NFC championship games.
13 Australian Open tennis begins (Melbourne).
18 NHL All-Star Game (San Jose, Calif.).
21 PBA Tournament of Champions bowling begins (Reno, Nev.).
26 Super Bowl XXXI (New Orleans).

FEBRUARY

1 24 hours of Daytona begins (Daytona Beach).
2 NFL Pro Bowl (Honolulu).
7 Davis Cup first round begins (eight sites).
8 Figure Skating Championships (Nashville).
9 NBA All-Star Game (Cleveland).
10 Westminster Dog Show begins (New York).
14 Daytona 500 (Daytona Beach).

MARCH

1 Women's Fed Cup tennis first round begins.
1 Iditarod Trail Sled Dog race begins (Anchorage to Nome).
7 NCAA Indoor Track & Field Championships begin (Indianapolis).
9 NFL Annual Meeting begins (W. Palm Beach, Fla.).
13 NCAA Men's Division I Basketball tournament begins.
14 NCAA Women's Division I Basketball tournament begins.
16 World Figure Skating Championships begin (Lausanne, Switzerland).
20 NCAA Women's Div. I Swimming & Diving finals begin. (Bloomington, Ind.)
23 PBA National Championship (Toledo).
27 LPGA Dinah Shore golf begins (Rancho Mirage, Calif.)
27 NCAA Div. I Hockey Final Four begins (Milwaukee).
27 NCAA Men's Div. I Swimming & Diving finals begin. (Minneapolis)
28 NCAA Women's Basketball Final Four begins (Cincinnati).
29 NCAA Men's Basketball Final Four begins (Indianapolis).

APRIL

4 Davis Cup second round begins (four sites).
10 Masters golf begins (Augusta).
13 NHL regular season ends.
17 NHL Stanley Cup playoffs begin.
19 NFL Draft begins (New York).
20 NBA regular season ends.
21 Boston Marathon.
24 NBA playoffs begin.
29 ABC Masters Bowling begins (Huntsville, Ala.).

MAY

1 Tour DuPont cycling race begins (Eastern U.S.).
3 Kentucky Derby (Louisville).
15 LPGA McDonald's Championship golf begins (Wilmington, Del.).
17 Preakness Stakes (Baltimore).
24 NCAA Men's Div. I Lacrosse Final Four begins (New Brunswick, N.J.).
25 Indianapolis 500.
26 French Open tennis begins (Paris).
29 U.S. Women's Open golf begins (Southern Pines, N.C.).
30 NCAA College World Series begins (Omaha, Neb.).

* tentative dates

JUNE

4 NCAA Men's and Women's Track & Field Championships begin (Bloomington, Ind.).
7 Belmont Stakes (Elmont, N.Y.).
12 U.S. Open golf begins (Bethesda, Md.).
22 NHL Draft (Pittsburgh).
23 Wimbledon tennis begins.
25 NBA Draft (Charlotte, N.C.).
26 U.S. Senior Open golf begins (Olympia Field, Ill.).

JULY

5 Tour de France cycling begins (through July 27).
8 Baseball All Star Game (Cleveland).
12 Women's Fed Cup tennis semifinals begin.
17 British Open golf begins (Scotland).
31 LPGA du Maurier Classic begins (Canada).

AUGUST

9 All-American Soap Box Derby (Akron, Ohio).
14 PGA Championship golf begins (Louisville).
13 U.S. Gymnastics Championships begin (Denver).
18 Little League World Series begins (Williamsport, Pa.).*
25 U.S. Open tennis begins (Flushing, N.Y.).
31 NFL regular season opens.

SEPTEMBER

1 World Gymnastics Team Champ. begin (Lausanne, Switzerland).
19 Davis Cup tennis semifinal round begins (two sites).
29 Baseball regular season ends.

OCTOBER

1 Baseball playoffs begin (first round).
4 U.S. Women's Open bowling.*
4 Women's Fed Cup tennis finals begins.
8 Baseball League Championship Series begin.
11 Ironman Triathlon Championship (Hawaii).
12 College Football: Oklahoma vs. Texas (Dallas).
18 USC at Notre Dame
19 World Series begins (in city of AL champion).
26 MLS World Cup '97 (Washington, D.C.)

NOVEMBER

1 Nebraska at Oklahoma.*
2 New York City Marathon.
8 Breeders' Cup horse racing (Toronto).
10 ATP Men's Tennis Championship begins (Frankfurt).
16 Triathlon World Championship (Perth, Australia).
17 WTA Tour Tennis Championships begin (New York).
22 College Football: Auburn at Alabama, Michigan at Ohio St., USC at UCLA and Yale at Harvard.
23 CFL Grey Cup (Montreal).*
28 Davis Cup tennis final begins.
29 Florida State at Miami

DECEMBER

5 National Finals Rodeo begins (Las Vegas).
6 NCAA Women's Soccer Final Four (Santa Clara, Calif.
7 College Football: SEC Championship Game (Atlanta); Army vs. Navy (Philadelphia).
12 NCAA Men's Soccer Final Four (Richmond, Va.).
13 Heisman Trophy winner announced (New York).
21 NCAA Div. I-AA Football Championship (Huntington, W.Va.)
22 NFL regular season ends.
3 (Jan.) NFL Playoffs begin.

* tentative dates

Wide World Photos

The **New York Yankees** celebrate after winning the 1996 World Series against the Atlanta Braves. After dropping the first two games at home, the Yankees won four straight.

BASEBALL

1995–96 YEAR IN REVIEW

BASEBALL

by Jerry Crasnick

The Year of the Homer

In 1996, baseballs flew out of parks at a record pace and in the post-season home teams found little advantage

Baseball's most coveted prize returned to its most hallowed site in 1996. Destiny looked quite stunning dressed in pinstripes.

The New York Yankees beat the Atlanta Braves for their 23rd World Championship, and celebrated with a Ripkenesque tour of the outfield while Frank Sinatra's "New York, New York" blared over the stadium loudspeakers.

The championship was a tribute to manager Joe Torre, who survived the loss of one brother, the medical problems of another, and the uneasy feeling of owner George Steinbrenner's hot breath down his neck from day one of spring training.

Steinbrenner shelled out big money for the franchise's first title in 18 years. But in the end the Yankees won because they played better than anyone else as a team. Even the stars checked their egos at the clubhouse door. "We're not the Bronx Bombers," Torre said. "We did whatever we needed to do to win."

In the year of the homer, the Yankees' most impressive accomplishment was winning at home. Atlanta won the first two games of the Series in New York. The Yankees responded by taking three straight in Atlanta. By holding serve at Yankee Stadium in Game 6, New York put the finishing touches on a Series that was borderline classic. "I'm in dreamland," Torre said. "This is like an out-of-body experience."

The 1996 season was notable for four-hour games, 5.00 ERAs and scoreboards on maximum-wattage alert. When your average fan postpones a trip to the nacho stand to watch Brady Anderson step to the plate, you know something is out of whack. David Vincent, a baseball statistician who specializes in longballs, christened 1996 the "Home Run Stampede Season." The final tally conjured images of 1987, when Larry Sheets, Matt Nokes and Brook Jacoby were among the one-year wonders in the 30-homer club. Even Wade Boggs hit 24 that year.

In the summer of 1996, the purported "slugger" who stopped at 30 homers could look forward to a note from management advising him to spend less time in the video room and more time in the weight room. A total of 16 players hit 40 or more homers. The previous high was eight, set in 1961. Andres Galarraga, Ellis Burks and Vinny Castilla of Colorado became the first set of three teammates to hit 40 since Davey Johnson, Darrell Evans and Hank Aaron did it for the 1973 Braves.

In early September, Florida's Gary Sheffield hit the 4,459th homer of the season to break the major-league record set in '87. Two players, Mark McGwire and Anderson, finished with at least 50 homers. Anderson hit 50 homers after coming into

Jerry Crasnick is the national baseball writer for the *Denver Post* and a columnist for *Baseball America.*

Wide World Photos

Despite missing several weeks at the beginning of the season, **Mark McGwire** of the Oakland A's led the majors with 52 homeruns in a year that featured a record number of round trippers.

the season with 72 total in an eight-year career. McGwire's 52 fell nine short of Roger Maris' single-season record of 61. But let's cut him some slack: He missed most of April with a foot injury.

For the first time in history, baseball's season opener took place in March. Chicago's Frank Thomas provided a sign of things to come when he homered— what else?— in his first at-bat against Randy Johnson.

The Cincinnati Reds' home opener was scheduled for April 1 against Montreal, and owner Marge Schott proved to be the biggest April fool. After home-plate umpire John McSherry died of a heart attack, Schott argued that the game should go on as planned. She said she felt "cheated" when McSherry's death forced a postponement. By mid-June, Schott was history. After a televised interview in which she made some intemperate remarks about Adolf Hitler, Schott agreed to relinquish day-to-day operation of the club through the 1998 season. "Mrs. Schott today has acted in the best interest of the game, the city of Cincinnati and her fans who have meant so much to her during her 11 years in baseball," acting commissioner Bud Selig said. John Allen, formerly the Reds' controller, took over as Schott's permanent successor in August.

The man generally regarded as baseball's premier goodwill ambassador left the scene shortly after Schott. Dodgers manager Tommy Lasorda was hospitalized with heart trouble in June, and announced his retirement on July 29. After taking over for Walter Alston in 1976, Lasorda had managed the Dodgers to two World Championships, four pennants and eight division titles. He did it with a Hollywood schtick all his own.

Some prominent players retired as well. The St. Louis Cardinals held a day in Ozzie Smith's honor Sept. 28 at Busch Stadium, and Smith received a standing ovation when he flied out in a pinch-hit appearance against Atlanta in Game 7 of the National League Championship Series. "My reception around baseball has been wonderful," he said. Detroit's Alan Trammell called it quits after conducting a clinic on the art of shortstop play for 20 years. And Andre Dawson, Florida's beloved Hawk, limped into the sunset after 438 homers and 12 knee operations.

Some old geezers just kept plugging along. Dennis Eckersley saved 30 games for St. Louis at age 41. Eddie Murray, a mere pup at 40, joined Hank Aaron and Willie Mays as only the third player to collect 500 homers and 3,000 hits. Paul Molitor entered the season needing 211 hits to reach 3,000. He finished with 225 hits— second most in the majors to Lance Johnson of the Mets— and made his bit of hitting history with a triple against Kansas City's Jose Rosado on Sept. 16. Molitor collected No. 3,000 with two old buddies, Robin Yount and George Brett, watching proudly from the stands.

San Diego third baseman Ken Caminiti turned in a truly inspirational performance on Aug. 16, before the Padres and Mets played the first regular-season game ever in Mexico. Caminiti, stricken with a bug, lay on the floor before the game with an intravenous tube pumping fluid into his arm. He jumped up 10 minutes before the first pitch, ate a Snicker's bar and hit two homers to lead San Diego to victory.

San Francisco left fielder Barry Bonds put up big numbers with a supporting cast that looked remarkably like the Phoenix Firebirds. Bonds joined Jose Canseco as the second player in history to hit 40 home runs and steal 40 bases in a season.

Cleveland's Albert Belle was up to his old antisocial tricks. He hit a photographer with a baseball, clashed with an autograph-seeking fan, and received a suspension after decking Milwaukee second baseman Fernando Vina with a forearm smash. But nothing could disrupt Belle's concentration at the plate. He finished with 148 RBI, the most by an American Leaguer since Boston's Ted Williams and Vern Stephens each drove in 159 runs in 1949.

The All-Star Game gave some younger players an opportunity to to show their stuff. The media swarmed Seattle shortstop Alex Rodriguez, and anointed him "Junior Jr." Los Angeles catcher Mike Piazza, a native of Norristown, Pa., was the hero in Philadelphia. He homered and won the All-Star MVP award, and the Nationals beat the Americans 6-0.

Piazza's teammate, Hideo Nomo, threw a no-hitter in a 9-0 victory over Colorado on Sept. 17 at Coors Field. Despite leading the National League with 961 runs, the Rockies were the victims of two no-hitters. Florida's

A little perspective

Some cliches are hoarier than others. But the one about life putting sports in perspective never resonated more than in the 1996 baseball season.

Baseball and tragedy were soulmates on opening day, when umpire John McSherry called timeout at Riverfront Stadium in Cincinnati, walked behind home plate, collapsed and died of a heart ailment.

The concept of baseball-as-family was drummed home when Michelle Carew, 17-year-old daughter of Hall of Famer Rod Carew, died of leukemia after an exhaustive search for a bone marrow donor. Rod Carew, so stoic and reserved as a player, showed a warm, caring side previously unseen by the public. And some of the most enduring on-field images revolved around three prominent ballplayers linked by medical misfortune and the will to keep fighting.

New York Yankees pitcher David Cone knew something was wrong when he experienced numbness in his fingers and a slight discoloration in his palm in April. When blood thinners failed to correct the problem, Cone underwent a battery of tests. They revealed an aneurysm, or a ballooning of an artery, just below his right shoulder. On May 10, doctors at Columbia Presbyterian Medical Center took a vein from Cone's leg and grafted it into the armpit area. Cone resumed throwing a baseball by mid-summer. But Yankees manager Joe Torre took pains not to expect too much. "If he makes it back, he'll be the greatest September callup in the history of baseball," Torre said. After two tuneups starts in Norwich, Conn., Cone took the mound for the Yankees on Sept. 2 in Oakland. A mere 114 days after surgery, he threw 85 pitches and seven innings of no-hit ball in a 5-0 victory over the Athletics.

From a medical standpoint, Brett Butler's comeback might have been more improbable than Cone's. In May, doctors found a tumor while performing a tonsillectomy on Butler. After a biopsy revealed cancer, Butler underwent surgery to remove 50 lymph nodes from the back of his neck and muscle tissue from behind his throat. Butler endured 32 radiation treatments. When the treatments ended in

Wide World Photos

Minnesota Twins

Brett Butler of the Los Angeles Dodgers successfully battled cancer to return to the field in September but **Kirby Puckett** had to retire due to vision problems caused by glaucoma.

July, he weighed 142 pounds and felt as if his neck were on fire.

Butler virtually willed himself back into the Los Angeles Dodgers' plans. On Sept. 6 in Los Angeles, Butler stepped in the box against Pittsburgh's Francisco Cordova to the accompaniment of 41,509 cheering fans. He waved his helmet and revealed a patch of premature gray. He felt a hitch in his throat. "It was hard for me to get my composure," Butler said. "I almost broke down. It was very moving for me."

Butler went down on a routine grounder, but christened his return to the big leagues by stomping lightly on the first-base bag. He did it with the unbridled joy of a little boy jumping in a mud puddle. Four days later, reality hit Butler full-force. While squaring to bunt against Cincinnati, he took a fastball off the left hand. He broke the fifth metacarpal bone, and missed the rest of the season. Butler still served as an example to millions just by suiting up that night in Los Angeles. A deeply religious man, he found that his ordeal helped strengthen his faith. "You don't get close to God when things are going good," Butler said. "You get close to God when things are bad."

For baseball fans, Twins outfielder Kirby Puckett had personified everything good about the game since his arrival in Minnesota in 1984. Puckett played hard, signed autographs until his hand ached, and never stopped smiling. Puckett's inherent cheerfulness was tested in 1996. He woke up one day in late March seeing spots and darkness out of his right eye. The diagnosis: Glaucoma. When Dr. Bert Glaser performed surgery on Puckett in July, he found the damage to Puckett's retina was "irreversible."

At a press conference July 12, Puckett sat at a podium with a patch over his eye and announced his retirement. Teammates cried at the sight, but Puckett handled the ordeal with dignity and self-restraint. "This is the last time you're going to see Kirby Puckett in a Twins uniform," he said. "I just want to tell you all that I love you." Puckett played in 10 All-Star Games, won six Silver Slugger Awards, led the Twins to two World Championships and made millions of friends. "If he had played in New York, they would build a five-foot, nine-inch statue of him in Times Square," said Andy MacPhail, Chicaco Cubs president and former Twins general manager. Puckett's special brand of charisma transcended small-market Minneapolis. Baseball will never replace him— never mind forget him.

Al Leiter beat them 11-0 on May 11.

The only American League no-hitter belonged to New York's Dwight Gooden. He beat Seattle 2-0 on May 14, then flew to Tampa to be with his father, Dan, who underwent open-heart surgery the next morning. "This is going to be my present to him," Gooden said. Boston Red Sox pitcher Roger Clemens certainly closed with a flourish. He tied his own major-league record with 20 strikeouts on Sept. 18 in Detroit. Amazingly, Clemens did not walk a batter in either game.

Comebacks were in vogue in 1996. Ryne Sandberg came out of retirement to hit 25 homers for the Chicago Cubs. And Eric Davis un-retired to hit 26 for Cincinnati.

Joe Torre, fired by St. Louis in June 1995, won raves for his even-tempered approach in New York. Johnny Oates, whose career had nearly unraveled in Baltimore, led Texas to its first division title since the team's inception in 1972.

Money talked. The Yankees acquired Cecil Fielder, Charlie Hayes and others for the stretch run, and finished the season with a payroll of $61 million. After adding Denny Neagle in a trade, the Atlanta Braves were pushing $50 million. Cheapskates took solace in Montreal. The peerless Felipe Alou, working with the smallest payroll in baseball, kept the Expos in contention until the final weekend.

New York, Cleveland and Texas won division titles in the American League, with Baltimore qualifying as the wild card. Atlanta, St. Louis and San Diego were the division winners in the National. The Padres swept a three-game series at Dodger Stadium on the final weekend to send Los Angeles into the postseason as a wild card.

If baseball's higher-ups hoped that the attention would be on the field in October, they were mistaken. Controversy reigned on the final weekend of the regular season, when Baltimore second baseman Roberto Alomar spit in umpire John Hirschbeck's face during an argument. AL president Gene Budig suspended Alomar for five games. When Alomar appealed the decision, umpires threatened to walk off the job unless the suspension went into effect immediately. A potential crisis was averted when a federal judge barred the umpires from striking. Alomar didn't exactly fade into the background. His 12th-inning homer off Jose Mesa gave Baltimore a 4-3 victory over Cleveland in the deciding game of the divisional playoffs.

New York eliminated Texas in the other playoff despite a monster series by Juan Gonzalez, who hit .438 with five home runs. One morning, Torre and New York coach Don Zimmer bumped into Gonzalez at breakfast. "He had already eaten," Torre said, "so it was too late to poison him."

While hitters dominated the regular season, pitchers re-asserted themselves in October. Atlanta held the Dodgers to three earned runs and a .147 batting average while sweeping the teams' series. St. Louis took three straight from San Diego, with Eckersley picking up a save in every game. Brian Jordan hit the climactic home run off reliever Trevor Hoffman in Game 3 to eliminate the Padres.

The opening game of the New York-Baltimore series featured a controversy for the ages. With the Orioles ahead 4-3 in the eighth inning, Derek Jeter hit a drive to deep right field. As Baltimore's Tony Tarasco prepared to make the catch at the wall, Jeff Maier, a 12-year old New Jersey Little Leaguer playing hooky, reached out and knocked it into the stands with his glove. Umpire Rich Garcia awarded Jeter a home run, and the Yankees went on to win 5-4 in 11 innings. Later, Garcia admitted he had made the wrong call. The Orioles were enraged, and Maier enjoyed a brief flirtation with fame. He appeared on "Good Morning America," and turned down a $1,000 offer to be interviewed by Geraldo Rivera.

The Orioles won Game 2 behind David Wells, then watched their season go down in flames. The Yankees won three straight at Camden Yards to raise their 1996 record in Baltimore to 9-0. Bernie Williams, New York's new Mr. October, hit .474 and won the series MVP award.

The Braves took a less direct route to the World Series, losing three of their first four games with St. Louis. Jordan hit the winning home run off reliever Greg McMichael in Game 4, then rushed to a local hospital to be with his 2-year-old son Bryson, who had fainted in the eighth inning. Bryson, it turns out, was fine. The Cardinals were not. Atlanta outscored St. Louis 32-1 over the next three games to advance to the World Series for the fourth time in the 1990s.

Wide World Photos

Wide World Photos

Fittingly, the two best pitchers in baseball in 1996, **Andy Pettitte** (l) of the Yankees and the Braves' **John Smoltz**, faced off in the best game of the year, Game 5 of the World Series.

Catcher Javier Lopez batted .542 to win the series MVP award.

Despite what was at stake, there wasn't much suspense in Game 7. The Braves won 15-0. Tom Glavine threw seven innings of shutout ball and cleared the bases with a triple in the first inning. "We're excited about what we've done," Glavine said. "But our goal is not to win our division. Our goal is not to be National League champions. Our goal is to be World Series champions. We know we still have a ways to go to accomplish that."

The World Series was a marketing professional's dream, with baseball's most storied franchise taking on the "team of the '90s." The Braves occasionally think of themselves that way, even though they've won one fewer championship than the Toronto Blue Jays in this decade.

The pre-Series hype focused on Ted Turner's free-spirited approach, Steinbrenner's turtlenecks, Yankee tradition and the teams' respective payrolls. And there were some sincere words of praise for Atlanta's pitching rotation.

The first two games were no contest. The Braves won the opener 12-1 behind six efficient innings from John Smoltz and the hitting of Andruw Jones, a precocious 19-year-old rookie from Curacao. Jones joined Gene Tenace of the 1972 Oakland A's as the second player to hit home runs in his first two World Series at-bats. "He's got a lot of talent," Atlanta manager Bobby Cox said. "It doesn't take a genius to figure that out."

Greg Maddux beat New York 4-0 in Game 2, and it didn't take a genius to figure out his formula for success. He threw a mere 82 pitches— 62 for strikes— before giving way to Mark Wohlers in the ninth. "This is a game I'll probably take to the grave with me," Maddux said.

The two victories in New York gave Atlanta a decided edge in the Series, but David Cone altered the storyline in Game 3. He outpitched Glavine— barely— and Bernie Williams hit a late home run off reliever Greg McMichael to give New York a 5-2 victory.

If there was a turning point in the Series, it came in Game 4. The Braves drove Kenny Rogers from the game in the third inning on the way to a 6-0 lead. But the Yankees summoned the fortitude to come back.

Jim Leyritz hit a three-run homer off Wohlers to tie the game 6-6, and pinch-hitter Wade Boggs drew a bases-loaded

Wide World Photos

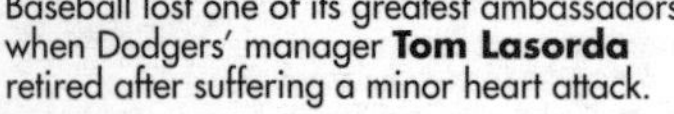

Baseball lost one of its greatest ambassadors when Dodgers' manager **Tom Lasorda** retired after suffering a minor heart attack.

Wide World Photos

One bright spot in the World Series was the emergence of **Andruw Jones** who hit a home run in his first two at bats.

walk off Steve Avery in the 10th to give New York an 8-6 victory. The loss was so disheartening for Atlanta, Cox held a clubhouse meeting before Game 5 to remind his players the Series wasn't over yet. He had to do something.

Could the Braves possibly lose three in a row at home after winning two straight on the road? Atlanta had two things working in its favor in Game 5— emotion and Smoltz. It was the final game at Atlanta-Fulton County Stadium, which will give way to a state-of-the-art new ballpark in 1997. Smoltz, the best post-season pitcher of his generation, took the mound looking for his 29th victory of the year.

Smoltz pitched with courage and guts on three day's rest, but New York's Andy Pettitte was better by a hair. He combined with John Wetteland on a five-hitter, and New York won 1-0 to take a 3-2 lead in the Series. Cecil Fielder doubled home the only run after Marquis Grissom, a Gold Glove center fielder, dropped a fly ball by Charlie Hayes. Two late season acquisitions had paid off for the Yankees.

Torre, whose brother Rocco died of a heart attack in June, received some uplifting news before Game 6 when his brother Frank underwent successful heart transplant surgery in New York.

In a stadium packed with emotion, the Yankees took a 3-0 lead against Greg Maddux, then watched Wetteland hang on by his cuticles in the ninth. Hayes caught Mark Lemke's foul pop for the final out, and the Yankees became the third team in World Series history to win four straight games after losing the first two.

The New York players took an impromptu victory lap around the field at the urging of their manager. Joe Torre wrote a wonderful script in 1996. It's only fitting that he should come up with a perfect ending.

So, aside from Roberto Alomar, once again the players, and the game itself, had done their part by providing an exciting and dramatic post-season. And during that post-season, the players had done one more thing. They had accepted the terms of a new collective bargaining agreement hammered out by representatives of the owners and the players union. It was up to the owners to put an end to the labor unrest that had plagued the sport since the disastrous strike of 1994. As the baseball world left New York, it was unclear what the owners would do. ❒

THE SEASON IN REVIEW
1996
LEAGUE LEADERS • POST SEASON

Final Major League Standings

Division champions (*) and Wild Card (†) winners are noted. Number of seasons listed after each manager refers to current tenure with club.

American League

East Division

	W	L	Pct	GB	Home	Road
* New York	92	70	.568	—	49-31	43-39
† Baltimore	88	74	.543	4	43-38	45-36
Boston	85	77	.525	7	47-34	38-43
Toronto	74	88	.457	18	35-46	39-42
Detroit	53	109	.327	39	27-54	26-55

1996 Managers: NY— Joe Torre (1st season); **Bal**— Davey Johnson (1st); **Bos**— Kevin Kennedy (2nd); **Tor**— Cito Gaston (8th); **Det**— Buddy Bell (1st).

1995 Standings: 1. Boston (86-58); 2. New York (79-65); 3. Baltimore (71-73); 4. Detroit (60-84); 5. Toronto (56-88).

Central Division

	W	L	Pct	GB	Home	Road
* Cleveland	99	62	.615	—	51-29	48-33
Chicago	85	77	.525	14½	44-37	41-40
Milwaukee	80	82	.494	19½	38-43	42-39
Minnesota	78	84	.481	21½	39-43	39-41
Kansas City	75	86	.466	24	37-43	38-43

1996 Managers: Cle— Mike Hargrove (6th season); **Chi**— Terry Bevington (2nd); **Mil**— Phil Garner (5th); **Min**— Tom Kelly (11th); **KC**— Bob Boone (2nd).

1995 Standings: 1. Cleveland (100-44); 2. Kansas City (70-74); 3. Chicago (68-76); 4. Milwaukee (65-79); 5. Minnesota (56-88).

West Division

	W	L	Pct	GB	Home	Road
* Texas	90	72	.556	—	50-31	40-41
Seattle	85	76	.528	4½	43-38	42-38
Oakland	78	84	.481	12	40-41	38-43
California	70	91	.435	19½	43-38	27-53

1996 Managers: Tex— Johnny Oates (2nd season); **Sea**— Lou Piniella (4th); **Oak**— Art Howe (1st); **Cal**— replaced Marcel Lacheman (3rd, 52-59) with John McNamara (18-32) on Aug. 6.

1995 Standings: 1. Seattle (79-66); 2. California (78-67); 3. Texas (74-70); 4. Oakland (67-77).

National League

East Division

	W	L	Pct	GB	Home	Road
* Atlanta	96	66	.593	—	56-25	40-41
Montreal	88	74	.543	8	50-31	38-43
Florida	80	82	.494	16	52-29	28-53
New York	71	91	.438	25	42-39	29-52
Philadelphia	67	95	.414	29	35-46	32-49

1996 Managers: Atl— Bobby Cox (7th season); **Mon**— Felipe Alou (5th); **Fla**— replaced Rene Lachemann (4th, 39-47) with team VP John Boles (41-35) on July 7; **NY**— replaced Dallas Green (4th, 59-72) with Bobby Valentine (12-19) on Aug. 26; **Phi**— Jim Fregosi (6th).

1995 Standings: 1. Atlanta (90-54); 2. Philadelphia (69-75); 3. New York (69-75); 4. Florida (67-76); 5. Montreal (66-78).

Central Division

	W	L	Pct	GB	Home	Road
* St. Louis	88	74	.543	—	48-33	40-41
Houston	82	80	.506	6	48-33	34-47
Cincinnati	81	81	.500	7	46-35	35-46
Chicago	76	86	.469	12	43-38	33-48
Pittsburgh	73	89	.451	15	36-44	37-45

1996 Managers: St.L— Tony La Russa (1st season); **Hou**— Terry Collins (3rd); **Cin**— Ray Knight (1st); **Chi**— Jim Riggleman (2nd); **Pit**— Jim Leyland (11th).

1995 Standings: 1. Cincinnati (85-59); 2. Houston (76-68); 3. Chicago (73-71); 4. St. Louis (62-81); Pittsburgh (58-86).

West Division

	W	L	Pct	GB	Home	Road
* San Diego	91	71	.562	—	45-36	46-35
† Los Angeles	90	72	.556	1	47-34	43-38
Colorado	83	79	.512	8	55-26	28-53
San Francisco	68	94	.420	23	38-44	30-50

1996 Managers: SD— Bruce Bochy (2nd season); **LA**— Tommy Lasorda (21st, 41-35) was replaced by Bill Russell (49-37) on June 24; **Col**— Don Baylor (4th); **SF** — Dusty Baker (4th).

1995 Standings: 1. Los Angeles (78-66); 2. Colorado (77-67); 3. San Diego (70-74); 4. San Francisco (67-77).

Baseball's Eight Work Stoppages

Year	Work Stoppage	Games Missed	Length	Dates	Issue
1972	Strike	86	13 days	April 1-13	Pensions
1973	Lockout	0	17 days	February 8-25	Salary arbitration
1976	Lockout	0	17 days	March 1-17	Free agency
1980	Strike	0	8 days	April 1-8	Free-agent compensation
1981	Strike	712	50 days	June 12-July 31	Free-agent compensation
1985	Strike	0	2 days	August 6-7	Salary arbitration
1990	Lockout	0	32 days	Feb. 15-March 18	Salary arbitration and salary cap
1994	Strike	920	232 days	Aug. 12-March 31	Salary cap and revenue sharing

Boston Red Sox
Roger Clemens
Strike Outs

Toronto Blue Jays
Pat Hentgen
Cg, Inn, ShO

Oakland A's
Mark McGwire
Home Runs, Slg. Pct.

Seattle Mariners
Alex Rodriguez
Batting

American League Leaders

Batting

	Bat	Gm	AB	R	H	Avg	TB	2B	3B	HR	RBI	BB	Int BB	SO	SB	Slg Pct	OB Pct
Alex Rodriguez, Sea	R	146	601	141	215	**.358**	379	54	1	36	123	59	1	104	15	.631	.414
Frank Thomas, Chi	R	141	527	110	184	**.349**	330	26	0	40	134	109	26	70	1	.626	.459
Chuck Knoblauch, Min	R	153	578	140	197	**.341**	299	35	14	13	72	98	6	74	45	.517	.448
Paul Molitor, Min	R	161	660	99	225	**.341**	309	41	8	9	113	56	10	72	18	.468	.390
Rusty Greer, Tex	L	139	542	96	180	**.332**	287	41	6	18	100	62	4	86	9	.530	.397
Dave Nilsson, Mil	L	123	453	81	150	**.331**	238	33	2	17	84	57	6	68	2	.525	.407
Roberto Alomar, Bal	S	153	588	132	193	**.328**	310	43	4	22	94	90	10	65	17	.527	.411
Edgar Martinez, Sea	R	139	499	121	163	**.327**	297	52	2	26	103	123	12	84	3	.595	.464
Mo Vaughn, Bos	L	161	635	118	207	**.326**	370	29	1	44	143	95	19	154	2	.583	.420
Kevin Seitzer, Mil-Cle	R	154	570	85	186	**.326**	267	35	3	13	78	87	7	79	6	.466	.416
Jeff Cirillo, Mil	R	158	566	101	184	**.325**	285	46	5	15	83	58	0	69	4	.504	.391
Julio Franco, Cle	R	112	432	72	139	**.322**	203	20	1	14	76	61	2	82	8	.470	.407
Bob Higginson, Det	L	130	440	75	141	**.320**	254	35	0	26	81	65	7	66	6	.577	.404
Kenny Lofton, Cle	L	154	662	132	210	**.317**	295	35	4	14	67	61	3	82	75	.446	.372
Juan Gonzalez, Tex	R	134	541	89	170	**.314**	348	33	2	47	144	45	12	82	2	.643	.368

Home Runs

McGwire, Oak 52
Anderson, Bal 50
Griffey Jr., Sea 49
Belle, Cle. 48
Gonzalez, Tex 47
Buhner, Sea. 44
Vaughn, Bos 44
Thomas, Chi 40
Fielder, Det-NY 39
Palmeiro, Bal 39

Triples

Knoblauch, Min 14
Vina, Mil 10
Martinez, Chi 8
Guillen, Chi 8
Molitor, Min 8
Offerman, KC 8
4 tied with 7 each.

On Base Pct.

McGwire, Oak .... .467
Martinez, Sea .... .464
Thomas, Chi .... .459
Thome, Cle .... .450
Knoblauch, Min .... .448
Vaughn, Bos .... .420
Seitzer, Mil-Cle .... .416

Runs Batted In

Belle, Cle 148
Gonzalez, Tex 144
Vaughn, Bos 143
Palmeiro, Bal 142
Griffey, Jr., Sea 140
Buhner, Sea 138
Thomas, Chi 134
Rodriguez, Sea 123
Jaha, Mil 118
Two tied with 117 each

Doubles

Rodriguez, Sea 54
Martinez, Sea 52
Rodriguez, Tex 47
Cirillo, Mil 46
Cordova, Min 46
Ramirez, Cle 45
Alomar, Bal 43
Two tied with 41 each.

Slugging Pct.

McGwire, Oak .... .730
Gonzalez, Tex .... .643
Anderson, Bal .... .637
Rodriguez, Sea .... .631
Griffey Jr., Sea .... .628
Thomas, Chi .... .626
Belle, Cle .... .623

Hits

Molitor, Min 225
Rodriguez, Sea 215
Lofton, Cle 210
Vaughn, Bos 207
Knoblauch, Min 197
Alomar, Bal 193
Rodriguez, Tex 192
Belle, Cle 187
Seitzer, Mil-Cle 186
Three tied with 184 each.

Runs

Rodriguez, Sea 141
Knoblauch, Min 140
Lofton, Cle 132
Alomar, Bal 132
Griffey Jr., Sea 125
Belle, Cle 124
Thome, Cle 122
Martinez, Sea 121

Walks

Phillips, Chi 125
Martinez, Sea 123
Thome, Cle 123
McGwire, Oak 116
Thomas, Chi 109
O'Neill, NY 102
Belle, Cle 99

Stolen Bases

	SB	CS
Lofton, Cle	75	17
Goodwin, KC	66	22
Nixon, Tor	54	13
Knoblauch, Min	45	14
Vizquel, Cle	35	9
Durham, Chi	30	4
McLemore, Tex	27	10
Amaral, Sea	25	6
Damon, KC	25	5
Listach, Mil-NY	25	5

Total Bases

Rodriguez, Sea 379
Belle, Cle 375
Vaughn, Bos 370
Anderson, Bal 369
Gonzalez, Tex 348
Griffey Jr., Sea 342
Palmeiro, Bal 342
Thomas, Chi 330

Strikeouts

Buhner, Sea 159
Nieves, Det 158
Vaughn, Bos 154
Sprague, Tor 146
Valentin, Mil 145
Palmer, Tex 145
Thome, Cle 141

Pitching

	Arm	W	L	ERA	Gm	GS	CG	ShO	Sv	IP	H	R	ER	HR	HB	BB	SO	WP
Juan Guzman, Tor	R	11	8	**2.93**	27	27	4	1	0	187.2	158	68	61	20	8	53	165	7
Pat Hentgen, Tor	R	20	10	**3.22**	35	35	10	3	0	265.2	238	105	95	20	5	94	177	8
Charles Nagy, Cle	R	17	5	**3.41**	32	32	5	0	0	222.0	217	89	84	21	3	61	167	7
Alex Fernandez, Chi	R	16	10	**3.45**	35	35	6	1	0	258.0	248	110	99	34	7	72	200	5
Kevin Appier, KC	R	14	11	**3.62**	32	32	5	1	0	211.1	192	87	85	17	5	75	207	9
Ken Hill, Tex	R	16	10	**3.63**	35	35	7	3	0	250.2	250	110	101	19	6	95	170	5
Roger Clemens, Bos	R	10	13	**3.63**	34	34	6	2	0	242.2	216	106	98	19	4	106	257	8
Andy Pettitte, NY	L	21	8	**3.87**	35	34	2	0	0	221.0	229	105	95	23	3	72	162	6
Ben McDonald, Mil	R	12	10	**3.90**	35	35	2	0	0	221.1	228	104	96	25	6	67	146	4
Tim Belcher, KC	R	15	11	**3.92**	35	35	4	1	0	238.2	262	117	104	28	6	68	112	7
Chuck Finley, Cal	L	15	16	**4.16**	35	35	4	1	0	238.0	241	124	110	27	11	94	215	17
Wilson Alvarez, Chi	L	15	10	**4.22**	35	35	0	0	0	217.1	216	106	102	21	4	97	181	2
Orel Hershiser, Cle	R	15	9	**4.24**	33	33	1	0	0	206.0	238	115	97	21	12	58	125	11
James Baldwin*, Chi	R	11	6	**4.42**	28	28	0	0	0	169.0	168	88	83	24	4	57	127	12
Brad Radke, Min	R	11	16	**4.46**	35	35	3	0	0	232.0	231	125	115	40	4	57	148	1

Wins

Pettitte, NY....21-8
Hentgen, Tor....20-10
Mussina, Bal....19-11
Nagy, Cle....17-5
Fernandez, Chi....16-10
Hill, Tex....16-10
Witt, Tex....16-12
Pavlik, Tex....15-8
Hershiser, Cle....15-9
Alvarez, Chi....15-10
Belcher, KC....15-11
Finley, Cal....15-16

Appearances

Guardado, Min....83
Myers, Det....83
Stanton, Bos-Tex....81
Slocumb, Bos....75
Jackson, Sea....73
Nelson, NY....73

Complete Games

Hentgen, Tor....10
Hill, Tex....7
Pavlik, Tex....7
Fernandez, Chi....6
Clemens, Bos....6
Erickson, Bal....6
Wakefield, Bos....6

Losses

Abbott, Cal....2-18
Robertson, Min....7-17
Hanson, Tor....13-17
Radke, Min....11-16
Finley, Cal....15-16
Quantrill, Tor....5-14
Lira, Det....6-14
Bones, Mil-NY....7-14
Haney, KC....10-14
Wells, Bal....11-14
Rodriguez, Min....13-14
Clemens, Bos....10-13
Wakefield, Bos....14-13

Innings

Hentgen, Tor....265.2
Fernandez, Chi....258.0
Hill, Tex....250.2
Mussina, Bal....243.1
Clemens, Bos....242.2
Belcher, KC....238.2
Finley, Cal....238.0
Radke, Min....232.0
Haney, KC....228.0
Tapani, Chi....225.1

Shutouts

Hentgen, Tor....3
Hill, Tex....3
Robertson, Min....3
Clemens, Bos....2
Lira, Det....2

Saves

	SV	BS
Wetteland, NY	43	4
Mesa, Cle	39	5
Hernandez, Chi	38	8
Percival, Cal	36	3
Fetters, Mil	32	7
Henneman, Tex	31	6
Myers, Bal	31	7
Slocumb, Bos	31	8
Timlin, Tor	31	7
Montgomery, KC	24	10
Charlton, Sea	20	7

HRs Given Up

Boskie, Cal....40
Radke, Min....40
Wakefield, Bos....38
Fernandez, Chi....34
Tapani, Chi....34
Wells, Bal....32
Gohr, Cal....31
Mussina, Bal....31

Wild Pitches

Finley, Cal....17
Lewis, Det....14
Abbott, Cal....13
Taponi, Chi....13
Hanson, Tor....13

Strikeouts

Clemens, Bos....257
Finley, Cal....215
Appier, KC....207
Mussina, Bal....204
Fernandez, Chi....200
Alvarez, Chi....181
Hentgen, Tor....177
Gordon, Bos....171
Hill, Tex....170
Nagy, Cle....167
Guzman, Tor....165
Pettitte, NY....162

Walks

Robertson, Min....116
Clemens, Bos....106
Gordon, Bos....105
Hamson, Tor....102
Alvarez, Chi....97
Witt, Tex....96
Hill, Tex....95

Hit Batters

Boskie, Cal....13
Grimsley, Cal....13
Wakefield, Bos....12
Hershiser, Cle....12
Karl, Mil....11
Erickson, Bal....11
Finley, Cal....11

Team Leaders

Batting

Team	Avg	AB	R	H	HR	RBI	SB
Cleveland	.293	5681	952	1665	218	904	159
Minnesota	.288	5673	877	1633	118	812	143
New York	.288	5628	871	1621	162	830	95
Seattle	.287	5668	993	1625	245	954	90
Texas	.284	5703	928	1622	221	890	83
Boston	.283	5756	928	1631	209	882	91
Chicago	.281	5644	898	1586	195	860	105
Milwaukee	.279	5659	894	1577	178	845	101
California	.276	5682	762	1571	192	727	53
Baltimore	.274	5689	949	1557	257	914	76
Kansas City	.266	5543	746	1477	123	689	195
Oakland	.265	5630	861	1492	243	822	57
Toronto	.259	5599	766	1451	177	712	116
Detroit	.256	5530	783	1413	204	741	87

Pitching

	ERA	W	Sv	CG	ShO	HR	BB	SO
Cleveland	4.35	99	46	13	9	173	484	1033
Chicago	4.53	85	43	7	5	174	616	1039
Kansas City	4.55	75	37	17	8	176	460	925
Toronto	4.58	74	35	19	7	187	610	1033
New York	4.65	92	53	6	9	143	610	1139
Texas	4.66	90	43	19	6	168	582	976
Boston	5.00	85	37	17	5	185	722	1166
Baltimore	5.15	88	44	13	2	209	597	1047
Milwaukee	5.17	80	42	6	5	213	635	846
Oakland	5.20	78	34	7	5	205	644	884
Seattle	5.21	85	34	4	4	216	605	1000
Minnesota	5.30	78	31	13	5	233	581	959
California	5.31	70	38	12	8	219	662	1052
Detroit	6.38	53	22	10	4	241	784	957

Colorado Rockies
Ellis Burks
Runs, Slg. Pct.

Colorado Rockies
Andres Galarraga
Home Runs, RBI

Atlanta Braves
John Smoltz
Wins, Strike Outs

Florida Marlins
Kevin Brown
ERA, Shut Outs

National League Leaders

Batting

	Bat	Gm	AB	R	H	Avg	TB	2B	3B	HR	RBI	BB	Int BB	SO	SB	Slg Pct	OB Pct
Tony Gwynn, SD	L	116	451	67	159	**.353**	199	27	2	3	50	39	12	17	11	.441	.400
Ellis Burks, Col	R	156	613	142	211	**.344**	392	45	8	40	128	61	2	114	32	.639	.408
Mike Piazza, LA	R	148	547	87	184	**.336**	308	16	0	36	105	81	21	93	0	.563	.422
Lance Johnson, NY	L	160	682	117	227	**.333**	327	32	21	9	69	33	8	40	50	.479	.362
Mark Grace, Chi	L	142	547	88	181	**.331**	249	39	1	9	75	62	8	41	2	.455	.396
Ken Caminiti, SD	S	146	546	109	178	**.326**	339	37	2	40	130	78	16	99	11	.621	.408
Eric Young, Col	R	141	568	113	184	**.324**	239	23	4	8	74	47	1	31	53	.421	.393
Bernard Gilkey, NY	R	153	571	108	181	**.317**	321	44	3	30	117	73	7	125	17	.562	.393
Jeff Bagwell, Hou	R	162	568	111	179	**.315**	324	48	2	31	120	135	20	114	21	.570	.451
Gary Sheffield, Fla	R	161	519	118	163	**.314**	324	33	1	42	120	142	19	66	16	.624	.465
Dante Bichette, Col	R	159	633	114	198	**.313**	336	39	3	31	141	45	4	105	31	.531	.359
Hal Morris, Cin	L	142	528	82	165	**.313**	253	32	4	16	80	50	5	76	7	.479	.374
Brian Jordan, St.L	R	140	513	82	159	**.310**	248	36	1	17	104	29	4	84	22	.483	.349
Chipper Jones, Atl	S	157	598	114	185	**.309**	317	32	5	30	110	87	0	88	14	.530	.393
Barry Bonds, SF	L	158	517	122	159	**.308**	318	27	3	42	129	151	30	76	40	.615	.461
Marquis Grissom, Atl	R	158	671	106	207	**.308**	328	32	10	23	74	41	6	73	28	.489	.349

Home Runs

Galarraga, Col	47
Bonds, SF	42
Sheffield, Fla	42
Hundley, NY	41
Caminiti, SD	40
Burks, Col	40
Sosa, Chi	40
Castilla, Col	40
Rodriguez, Mon	36
Piazza, LA	36

Triples

Johnson, NY	21
Grissom, Atl	10
Howard, Cin	10
Finley, SD	9
Deshields, LA	8
Burks, Col	8
Lankford, St.L	8

On Base Pct.

Sheffield, Fla	.465
Bonds, SF	.461
Bagwell, Hou	.451
Piazza, LA	.422
Henderson, SD	.410
Larkin, Cin	.410
Burks, Col	.408
Caminiti, SD	.408

Runs Batted In

Galarraga, Col	150
Bichette, Col	141
Caminiti, SD	130
Bonds, SF	129
Burks, Col	128
Bagwell, Hou	120
Sheffield, Fla	120
Gilkey, NY	117
Bell, Hou	113
Castilla, Col	113

Doubles

Bagwell, Hou	48
Burks, Col	45
Finley, SD	45
Gilkey, NY	44
Rodriguez, Mon	42
Lansing, Mon	40
Martin, Pit	40
Mondesi, LA	40

Slugging Pct.

Burks, Col	.639
Sheffield, Fla	.624
Caminiti, SD	.621
Bonds, SF	.615
Galarraga, Col	.601
Bagwell, Hou	.570
Larkin, Cin	.567

Hits

Johnson, NY	227
Burks, Col	211
Grissom, Atl	207
Grudzielanek, Mon	201
Bichette, Col	198
Finley, SD	195
Castilla, Col	191
Galarraga, Col	190
Martin, Pit	189
Mondesi, LA	188

Runs

Burks, Col	142
Finley, SD	126
Bonds, SF	122
Galarraga, Col	119
Sheffield, Fla	118
Johnson, NY	117
Larkin, Cin	117
Bichette, Col	114
C. Jones, Atl	114

Walks

Bonds, SF	151
Sheffield, Fla	142
Bagwell, Hou	135
Henderson, SD	125
Larkin, Cin	96
C. Jones, Atl	87
Piazza, LA	81

Stolen Bases

	SB	CS
Young, Col	53	19
Johnson, NY	50	12
Deshields, LA	48	11
Bonds, SF	40	7
Martin, Pit	38	12
McRae, Chi	37	9
Henderson, SD	37	15
Larkin, Cin	36	10
Lankford, St.L	35	7
Hunter, Hou	35	[illegible]

Total Bases

Burks, Col	392
Galarraga, Col	376
Finley, SD	348
Castilla, Col	345
Caminiti, SD	339
Bichette, Col	336
Grissom, Atl	328
Johnson, NY	327

Strikeouts

Rodriguez, Mon	160
Galarraga, Col	157
Hundley, NY	146
Sosa, Chi	134
Lankford, St.L	133
Klesko, Atl	129
Gilkey, NY	125

Pitching

	Arm	W	L	ERA	Gm	GS	CG	ShO	Sv	IP	H	R	ER	HR	HB	BB	SO	WP
evin Brown, Fla	R	17	11	**1.89**	32	32	5	3	0	233.0	187	60	49	8	16	33	159	6
reg Maddux, Atl	R	15	11	**2.72**	35	35	5	1	0	245.0	225	85	74	11	3	28	172	4
Leiter, Fla	L	16	12	**2.93**	33	33	2	1	0	215.1	153	74	70	14	11	119	200	4
hn Smoltz, Atl	R	24	8	**2.94**	35	35	6	2	0	253.2	199	93	83	19	2	55	276	10
m Glavine, Atl	L	15	10	**2.98**	36	36	1	0	0	235.1	222	91	78	14	0	85	181	4
eve Trachsel, Chi	R	13	9	**3.03**	31	31	3	2	0	205.0	181	82	69	30	8	62	132	5
deo Nomo, LA	R	16	11	**3.19**	33	33	3	2	0	228.1	180	93	81	23	2	85	234	11
ırt Schilling, Phi	R	9	10	**3.19**	26	26	8	2	0	183.1	149	69	65	16	3	50	182	5
ff Fassero, Mon	L	15	11	**3.30**	34	34	5	1	0	231.2	217	95	85	20	3	55	222	5
nael Valdes, LA	R	15	7	**3.32**	33	33	0	0	0	225.0	219	94	83	20	3	54	173	1
ımon Martinez, LA	R	15	6	**3.42**	28	27	2	2	0	168.2	153	76	64	12	8	86	134	2
ark Clark, NY	R	14	11	**3.43**	32	32	2	0	0	212.1	217	98	81	20	3	48	142	6
edro Astacio, LA	R	9	8	**3.44**	35	32	0	0	0	211.2	207	86	81	18	9	67	130	6
enny Neagle, Pit-Atl	L	16	9	**3.50**	33	33	2	0	0	221.1	226	93	86	26	3	48	149	3
onovan Osborne, St.L	L	13	9	**3.53**	30	30	2	1	0	198.2	191	87	78	22	1	57	134	6

Wins

noltz, Atl 24-8
ı. Benes, St.L....18-10
own, Fla 17-11
z, Col 17-11
eagle, Pit-Atl 16-9
ynolds, Hou....16-10
omo, LA....16-11
iter, Fla 16-12
artinez, LA....15-6
ıldes, LA 15-7
amilton, SD 15-9
avine, Atl 15-10
ssero, Mon 15-11
addux, Atl 15-11
avarro, Chi 15-12

Appearances

ontz, Atl 81
atterson, Chi....79
ewey, SF....78
aw, Cin....78
ohlers, Atl....77
en, Fla 75

Complete Games

hilling, Phi 8
noltz, Atl 6
ssero, Mon 5
addux, Atl 5
own, Fla 5
ottlemyre, St.L....5
ve tied with 4

Losses

Castillo, Chi 7-16
Rapp, Fla....8-16
Isringhausen, NY....6-14
Williams, Phi 6-14
VanLandingham, SF ..9-14
Smiley, Cin 13-14
Fernandez, SF....7-13
Burba, Cin 11-13
Wilson, NY....5-12
Watson, SF 8-12
Harnisch, NY....8-12
M. Leiter, SF-Mon....8-12
Navarro, Chi 15-12
A. Leiter, Fla 16-12

Innings

Smoltz, Atl 253.2
Maddux, Atl 245.0
Reynolds, Hou....239.0
Navarro, Chi 236.2
Glavine, Atl 235.1
Brown, Fla 233.0
Fassero, Mon 231.2
An. Benes, St.L....230.1
Nomo, LA....228.1
Valdes, LA 225.0

Shutouts

Brown, Fla 3
Schilling, Phi 2
Smiley, Cin 2
Nomo, LA....2
Martinez, LA....2
Smoltz, Atl....2
Stottlemyre, St.L....2
Trachsel, Chi 2

Saves

	SV	BS
Brantley, Cin	44	5
Worrell, LA	44	9
Hoffman, SD	42	7
Wohlers, Atl	39	5
Rojas, Mon	36	4
Beck, SF	35	7
Nen, Fla	35	7
Bottalico, Phi	34	4
Eckersley, St.L	30	4
Franco, NY	28	8
Ruffin, Col	24	5

HRs Given Up

M. Leiter, SF-Mon 37
Harnison, NY....30
Stottlemyre, St.L....30
Trachsel, Chi 30
Castillo, Chi 28
An. Benes, St.L....28
Gardner, SR....28
Watson, SF 28

Wild Pitches

Williams ....
Isringhausen....
Hamilton....
Rapp, ...
Kile, Hou ....
Freeman, Col ....

Strikeouts

Smoltz, Atl 276
Nomo, LA....234
Fassero, Mon 222
Martinez, Mon 222
Kile, Hou 219
Reynolds, Hou....204
Leiter, Fla 200
Stottlemyre, St.L....194
Hamilton, SD 184
Schilling, Phi 182
Glavine, Atl 181
Valdes, LA 173

Walks

Leiter, Fla 119
Ritz, Col 105
Burba, Cin 97
Kile, Hou 97
Stottlemyre, St.L....93
Rapp, Fla....91
Al. Benes, St.L....87

Hit Batters

Kile, Hou 16
Brown, Fla 16
M. Leiter, SF-Mon 16
Thompson, Col....13
Ritz, Col 12
Darwin, Pit-Hou 12

Team Leaders

Batting

	AVG	AB	R	H	HR	RBI	SB
Colorado	.287	5590	961	1607	221	909	201
Atlanta	.270	5614	773	1514	197	735	83
New York	.270	5618	746	1515	147	697	97
St. Louis	.267	5503	759	1468	142	711	149
Pittsburgh	.266	5665	776	1509	138	738	127
San Diego	.265	5655	771	1499	147	718	110
Houston	.262	5508	753	1445	129	703	180
Montreal	.262	5506	741	1441	148	696	108
Florida	.257	5498	688	1413	150	650	99
Cincinnati	.256	5455	778	1398	191	733	172
Philadelphia	.256	5499	650	1405	132	604	117
San Francisco	.253	5533	752	1400	153	707	113
Los Angeles	.252	5538	703	1396	150	661	123
Chicago	.251	5531	772	1388	175	725	107

Pitching

	ERA	W	SV	CG	SHO	HR	BB	SO
Los Angeles	3.48	90	50	6	9	125	534	1213
Atlanta	3.54	96	46	14	9	120	451	1245
San Diego	3.73	91	47	5	11	138	506	1194
Montreal	3.78	88	43	11	7	152	482	1204
Florida	3.95	80	41	8	13	113	598	1051
St. Louis	3.98	88	43	13	11	173	539	1050
New York	4.22	71	41	10	10	159	532	999
Cincinnati	4.33	81	52	6	8	167	591	1089
Chicago	4.36	76	34	10	11	184	546	1027
Houston	4.38	82	35	13	4	154	539	1164
Philadelphia	4.49	67	42	12	6	160	510	1043
Pittsburgh	4.64	73	37	5	7	183	479	1046
San Francisco	4.72	68	35	9	8	194	570	998
Colorado	5.60	83	34	5	5	198	624	932

1996 All-Star Game

67th Baseball All-Star Game. **Date:** July 9 at Veterans Stadium in Philadelphia, PA; **Managers:** Mike Hargrove, Clevela (AL) and Bobby Cox, Atlanta (NL); **Most Valuable Player:** C Mike Piazza (NL): 2-for-3, two-run HR and RBI double.

American League

	AB	R	H	BI	BB	SO	Avg
Kenny Lofton, Cle, cf	3	0	2	0	0	0	.667
Joe Carter, Tor, cf	1	0	1	0	0	0	1.000
Wade Boggs, NY, 3b	3	0	0	0	0	0	.000
Travis Fryman, Det, 3b	1	0	0	0	0	1	.000
Roberto Alomar, Bal, 2b	3	0	1	0	0	0	.333
Chuck Knoblauch, Min, 2b	1	0	1	0	0	0	1.000
Albert Belle, Cle, lf	4	0	0	0	0	3	.000
Mo Vaughn, Bos, 1b	3	0	1	0	0	0	.333
Mark Mcgwire, Oak, 1b	1	0	1	0	0	0	.000
Ivan Rodriguez, Tex, c	2	0	0	0	0	1	.000
Sandy Alomar, Cle, c	2	0	0	0	0	0	.000
Cal Ripken, Bal, ss	3	0	0	0	0	0	.000
Dan Wilson, Sea, ph	1	0	0	0	0	0	.000
Brady Anderson, Bal, rf	2	0	0	0	0	0	.000
Alex Rodriguez, Sea, ss	1	0	0	0	0	0	.000
Edgar Martinez, Sea, ph	1	0	0	0	0	0	.000
Jay Buhner, Sea, rf	2	0	0	0	0	0	.000
TOTALS	34	0	7	0	0	5	.206

National League

	AB	R	H	BI	BB	SO	Av
Lance Johnson, NY, cf	4	1	3	0	0	0	.7
Barry Larkin, Cin, ss	3	1	1	0	0	0	.3
Ozzie Smith, St.L, ss	1	0	0	0	0	0	.0
Barry Bonds, SF, lf	3	0	1	1	0	0	.3
Gary Sheffield, Fla, rf	1	0	0	0	0	0	.0
Fred McGriff, Atl, 1b	2	0	0	0	0	2	.0
Ken Caminiti, SD, 3b	2	1	1	1	0	1	.5
Mike Piazza, LA, c	3	1	2	2	0	1	.6
Todd Hundley, NY, c	1	0	0	0	0	0	.0
Jason Kendall, Pit, c	0	0	0	0	0	0	.0
Dante Bichette, Col, rf	3	1	1	0	0	1	.3
Mark Grudzielanek, Mon, 3b	1	0	0	0	0	0	.0
Chipper Jones, Atl, 3b	2	1	1	0	0	0	.5
Ellis Burks, Col, lf	2	0	1	0	0	1	.5
Craig Biggio, Hou, 2b	3	0	0	1	0	1	.0
Eric Young, Col, 2b	1	0	0	0	0	0	.0
Henry Rodriguez, Mon, ph	1	0	1	1	0	0	1.0
Jeff Bagwell, Hou, 1b	2	0	0	0	0	1	.0
TOTALS	35	6	12	6	0	8	.3

	1	2	3	4	5	6	7	8	9		R	H
American League	0	0	0	0	0	0	0	0	0	—	**0**	7
National League	1	2	1	0	0	2	0	0	X	—	**6**	12

LOB— American 15, National 11. **2B**—M. Vaughn (AL), Johnson (NL), Piazza (NL), Bichette (NL). **3B**—Burks (NL). **HR** Piazza (off Nagy), Caminiti (off Pavlik). **SB**— Lofton 2 (AL), Johnson (NL). **CS**— Bonds (NL), Johnson (NL). **SF**— no **GIDP**— S. Alomar (AL). **DP**— AL 1 (I. Rodriguez, Ripken), NL 1 (Smith-Young-Bagwell). **E**— Caminiti (NL).

AL Pitching	IP	H	R	ER	BB	SO	NP
Charles Nagy, Cle (L)	2.0	4	3	3	0	1	35
Chuck Finley, Cal	2.0	3	1	1	0	4	32
Roger Pavlik, Tex	2.0	3	2	2	0	2	35
Troy Percival, Cal	1.0	1	0	0	0	1	15
Roberto Hernandez, Chi	1.0	1	0	0	0	0	8
TOTALS	8.0	12	6	6	0	8	125

NL Pitching	IP	H	R	ER	BB	SO	N
John Smoltz, Atl (W)	2.0	2	0	0	0	1	
Kevin Brown, Fla	1.0	0	0	0	0	0	
Tom Glavine, Atl	1.0	0	0	0	0	1	
Ricky Bottalico, Phi	1.0	0	0	0	0	1	
Pedro Martinez, Mon	1.0	2	0	0	0	1	
Steve Trachsel, Chi	1.0	0	0	0	0	0	
Todd Worrell, LA	1.0	2	0	0	0	1	
Mark Wohlers, Atl	0.2	1	0	0	0	0	
Al Leiter, Fla	0.1	0	0	0	0	0	
TOTALS	9.0	7	0	0	0	5	1

Umpires— Randy Marsh (NL) plate; Larry McCoy (AL) 1b; Charlie Reliford (NL) 2b; Joe Brinkman (AL) 3b; Larry Ponci (NL) lf; Chuck Meriwether (AL) rf. **Attendance**— 62,670. **Time**— 2:35. **TV Rating**— 13.2/23 share (NBC).

Home Attendance

Overall 1996 regular season attendance in Major League Baseball was 60,100,715 in 2,235 games for an average pe game crowd of 26,891; numbers in parentheses indicate ranking in 1995; HD indicates home dates; Attendance base on tickets sold.

American League

		Attendance	HD	Average
1	Baltimore (1)	3,646,950	81	45,024
2	Cleveland (2)	3,318,174	79	42,002
3	Texas (5)	2,888,920	80	36,112
4	Seattle (8)	2,722,054	81	33,606
5	Toronto (3)	2,559,563	81	31,600
6	Boston (4)	2,315,233	81	28,583
7	New York (7)	2,250,124	78	28,848
8	California (6)	1,820,337	81	22,473
9	Chicago (9)	1,676,416	79	21,220
10	Minnesota (14)	1,437,352	80	17,967
11	Kansas City (10)	1,436,007	80	17,950
12	Milwaukee (13)	1,327,155	78	17,015
13	Detroit (11)	1,168,610	81	14,427
14	Oakland (12)	1,148,382	80	14,355
	AL Totals	29,715,277	1,120	26,531

National League

		Attendance	HD	Average
1	Colorado (1)	3,891,014	81	48,037
2	Los Angeles (2)	3,188,454	81	39,364
3	Atlanta (3)	2,901,242	81	35,818
4	St. Louis (7)	2,659,251	81	32,830
5	Chicago (5)	2,219,110	78	28,450
6	San Diego (13)	2,187,884	81	27,011
7	Houston (9)	1,975,888	81	24,394
8	Cincinnati (6)	1,861,428	76	24,492
9	Philadelphia (4)	1,801,677	78	23,098
10	Florida (8)	1,746,757	80	21,834
11	Montreal (10)	1,618,573	81	19,982
12	New York (11)	1,588,323	78	20,363
13	San Francisco (12)	1,413,687	80	17,671
14	Pittsburgh (14)	1,332,150	78	17,079
	NL Totals	30,385,438	1,115	27,252

AL Team by Team Statistics

.t least 135 at bats or 40 innings pitched during the regular season, unless otherwise indicated. Players who competed for ιore than one AL team are listed with their final club. Players traded from the NL are listed with AL team only if they have 35 AB or 40 IP. Note that (*) indicates rookie and PTBN indicates player to be named.

Baltimore Orioles

atting (135 AB)	**Avg**	**AB**	**R**	**H**	**HR**	**RBI**	**SB**
oberto Alomar	.328	588	132	193	22	94	17
rady Anderson	.297	579	117	172	50	110	21
.J. Surhoff	.292	537	74	157	21	82	0
afael Palmeiro	.289	626	110	181	39	142	8
obby Bonilla	.287	595	107	171	28	116	1
'al Ripken	.278	640	94	178	26	102	1
ddie Murray	.260	566	69	147	22	79	4
hris Hoiles	.258	407	64	105	25	73	0
uis Polonia	.240	175	25	42	2	14	8
ike Devereaux	.229	323	49	74	8	34	8
effrey Hammonds	.226	248	38	56	9	27	3

cquired: IF Murray from Cle. for P Kent Mercker (July 21).
igned: Free agent OF Polonia (Apr. 22); Free agent C Mark arent (Aug. 28).

itching (40 IP)	**ERA**	**W-L**	**G**	**IP**	**BB**	**SO**
esse Orosco	3.40	3-1	66	55.2	28	52
andy Myers	3.53	4-4	62	58.2	29	74
rthur Rhodes	4.08	9-1	28	53.0	23	62
oger McDowell	4.25	1-1	41	59.1	23	20
lan Mills	4.28	3-2	49	54.2	35	50
ike Mussina	4.81	19-11	36	243.1	69	204
ick Krivda	4.96	3-5	22	81.2	39	54
cott Erickson	5.02	13-12	34	222.1	66	100
avid Wells	5.14	11-14	34	224.1	51	130
ocky Coppinger*	5.18	10-6	23	125.0	60	104
mmy Haynes*	8.29	3-6	26	89.0	58	65

aves: Myers (31); Benitez and McDowell (4); Mills (3), Rhodes nd Haynes (1). **Complete games:** Erickson (6); Mussina (4); Vells (3). **Shutouts:** Mussina (1).

Boston Red Sox

atting (150 AB)	**Avg**	**AB**	**R**	**H**	**HR**	**RBI**	**SB**
eggie Jefferson	.347	386	67	134	19	74	0
o Vaughn	.326	635	118	207	44	143	2
ohn Valentin	.296	527	84	156	13	59	9
ike Greenwell	.295	295	35	87	7	44	4
ose Canseco	.289	360	68	104	28	82	3
im Naehring	.288	430	77	124	17	65	2
Vil Cordero	.288	198	29	57	3	37	2
eff Frye	.286	419	74	120	4	41	18
ill Haselman	.274	237	33	65	8	34	4
ike Stanley	.270	397	73	107	24	69	2
arren Bragg	.261	417	74	109	10	47	14
oy O'Leary	.260	497	68	129	15	81	3
ee Tinsley	.245	192	28	47	3	14	6

cquired: OF Tinsley from Phi. for minor leaguer (June 9); OF ragg from Sea. for P Jamie Moyer (July 30); P Brandenburg and P erry Lacy from Tex. for P Mike Stanton (July 31); P Mahomes from in. for PTBN (Aug. 26).
igned: Free agent IF Frye (June 26).

itching (40 IP)	**ERA**	**W-L**	**Gm**	**IP**	**BB**	**SO**
eathcliff Slocumb	3.02	5-5	75	83.1	55	88
ark Brandenburg*	3.43	5-5	55	76.0	33	66
oger Clemens	3.63	10-13	34	242.2	106	257
ike Maddux	4.48	3-2	23	64.1	27	32
ich Garces	4.91	3-2	37	44.0	33	55
im Wakefield	5.14	14-13	32	211.2	90	140
aron Sele	5.32	7-11	29	157.1	67	137
oe Hudson	5.40	3-5	36	45.0	32	19
om Gordon	5.59	12-9	34	215.2	105	171
at Mahomes	6.91	3-4	31	57.1	33	36
'aughn Eshelman	7.08	6-3	39	87.2	58	59

aves: Slocumb (31); Belinda and Mahomes (2); Hudson (1). **omplete games:** Clemens and Wakefield (6); Gordon (4); Sele). **Shutouts:** Clemens (2); Gordon (1).

California Angels

Batting (150 AB)	**Avg**	**AB**	**R**	**H**	**HR**	**RBI**	**SB**
Rex Hudler	.311	302	60	94	16	40	14
Jim Edmonds	.304	431	73	131	27	66	4
Chili Davis	.292	530	73	155	28	95	5
Jorge Fabregas	.287	254	18	73	2	26	0
Tim Salmon	.286	581	90	166	30	98	4
Garret Anderson	.285	607	79	173	12	72	7
Randy Velarde	.285	530	82	151	14	54	7
Darin Erstad*	.284	208	34	59	4	20	3
J.T. Snow	.257	575	69	148	17	67	1
Gary DiSarcina	.256	536	62	137	5	48	2
George Arias*	.238	252	19	60	6	28	2
Tim Wallach	.237	190	23	45	8	20	1

Acquired: P McElroy from Cin. for P Lee Smith (June 2); P Gohr from Det. for IF Damian Easley (July 31).

Pitching (40 IP)	**ERA**	**W-L**	**Gm**	**IP**	**BB**	**SO**
Troy Percival	2.31	0-2	62	74.0	31	100
Mike James	2.67	5-5	69	81.0	42	65
Chuck McElroy	2.95	5-1	40	36.2	13	32
Chuck Finley	4.16	15-16	35	238.0	94	215
Jason Dickson*	4.57	1-4	7	43.1	18	20
Mark Langston	4.82	6-5	18	123.1	45	83
Shawn Boskie	5.32	12-11	37	189.1	67	133
Dennis Springer	5.51	5-6	20	94.2	43	64
Jason Grimsley	6.84	5-7	35	130.1	74	82
Greg Gohr	7.24	5-9	32	115.2	44	75
Jim Abbott	7.48	2-18	27	142.0	78	58

Saves: Percival (36); Gohr and James (1). **Complete games:** Finley (4); Grimsley, Langston and Springer (2); Abbott and Boskie (1). **Shutouts:** Finley, Grimsley and Springer (1).

Chicago White Sox

Batting (150 AB)	**Avg**	**AB**	**R**	**H**	**HR**	**RBI**	**SB**
Frank Thomas	.349	527	110	184	40	134	1
Dave Martinez	.318	440	85	140	10	53	15
Don Slaught	.313	243	25	76	6	36	0
Harold Baines	.311	495	80	154	22	95	3
Lyle Mouton	.294	214	25	63	7	39	3
Robin Ventura	.287	586	96	168	34	105	1
Tony Phillips	.277	581	119	161	12	63	13
Ray Durham	.275	557	79	153	10	65	30
Domingo Cedeno	.272	301	46	82	2	20	6
Ozzie Guillen	.263	499	62	131	4	45	6
Pat Borders	.258	151	12	39	5	14	0
Danny Tartabull	.254	472	58	120	27	101	1
Darren Lewis	.228	337	55	77	4	53	21
Ron Karkovice	.220	355	44	78	10	38	0

Acquired: C Borders from Cal. for P Robert Ellis (Jul. 27); IF Cedeno and P Castillo from Tor. for P Luis Andujar and minor leaguer (Aug. 22); C Slaught from Cal. for PTBN (Aug. 31).

Pitching (40 IP)	**ERA**	**W-L**	**Gm**	**IP**	**BB**	**SO**
Roberto Hernandez	1.91	6-5	72	84.2	38	85
Alex Fernandez	3.45	16-10	35	258.0	72	200
Tony Castillo	3.60	5-4	55	95.0	24	57
Wilson Alvarez	4.22	15-10	35	217.1	97	181
James Baldwin*	4.42	11-6	28	169.0	57	127
Bill Simas*	4.58	2-8	64	72.2	39	65
Kevin Tapani	4.59	13-10	34	225.1	76	150
Brian Keyser	4.98	1-2	28	59.2	28	19
Matt Karchner	5.76	7-4	50	59.1	41	46
Joe Magrane	6.88	1-5	19	53.2	25	21
Kirk McCaskill	6.97	5-5	29	51.2	31	28

Saves: Hernandez (38); Castillo and Simas (2); Karchner and Keyser (1). **Complete games:** Fernandez (6); Tapani (1). **Shutouts:** Fernandez (1).

Cleveland Indians

Batting (135 AB)	Avg	AB	R	H	HR	RBI	SB
Kevin Seitzer	.326	573	85	187	13	78	6
Julio Franco	.322	432	72	139	14	76	8
Kenny Lofton	.317	662	132	210	14	67	75
Jim Thome	.311	505	122	157	38	116	2
Albert Belle	.311	602	124	187	48	148	11
Manny Ramirez	.309	550	94	170	33	112	8
Omar Vizquel	.297	542	98	161	9	64	35
Jose Vizcaino	.285	179	23	51	0	13	6
Carlos Baerga	.267	424	54	113	10	55	1
Sandy Alomar	.263	418	53	110	11	50	1
Tony Pena	.195	174	14	34	1	27	0

Acquired: P Mercker from Bal. for IF Eddie Murray (July 21); IF Vizcaino and IF Jeff Kent from NYM for IF Baerga and IF Alvaro Espinoza (July 29); IF Seitzer from Mil. for OF Jeremy Burnitz (Aug. 31).

Pitching (40 IP)	ERA	W-L	Gm	IP	BB	SO
Eric Plunk	2.43	3-2	56	77.2	34	85
Paul Shuey	2.85	5-2	42	53.2	26	44
Paul Assenmacher	3.09	4-2	63	46.2	14	44
Charles Nagy	3.41	17-5	32	222.0	61	167
Jose Mesa	3.73	2-7	69	72.1	28	64
Orel Hershiser	4.24	15-9	33	206.0	58	125
Dennis Martinez	4.50	9-6	20	112.0	37	48
Chad Ogea	4.79	10-6	29	146.2	42	101
Brian Anderson	4.91	3-1	10	51.1	14	21
Jack McDowell	5.11	13-9	30	192.0	67	141
Julian Tavarez	5.36	4-7	51	80.2	22	46
Albie Lopez	6.39	5-4	13	62.0	22	45
Kent Mercker	6.98	4-6	24	69.2	38	29

Saves: Mesa (39); Shuey (4); Plunk (2); Assenmacher (1). **Complete games:** McDowell and Nagy (5); Hershiser, Martinez and Ogea (1). **Shutouts:** Martinez, McDowell and Ogea (1).

Detroit Tigers

Batting (135 AB)	Avg	AB	R	H	HR	RBI	SB
Bobby Higginson	.320	440	75	141	26	81	6
Curtis Pride	.300	267	52	80	10	31	11
Mark Lewis	.270	545	69	147	11	55	6
Travis Fryman	.268	616	90	165	22	100	4
Chad Curtis	.263	400	65	105	10	37	16
Kimera Bartee*	.253	217	32	55	1	14	20
Tony Clark	.250	376	56	94	27	72	0
John Flaherty	.250	152	18	38	4	23	1
Brad Ausmus	.248	226	30	56	4	22	3
Ruben Sierra	.247	518	61	128	12	72	4
Melvin Nieves	.246	431	71	106	24	60	1
Alan Trammell	.233	193	16	45	1	16	6
Eddie Williams	.200	215	22	43	6	26	0
Andujar Cedeno	.196	179	19	35	7	20	2

Acquired: P Olson from Cin. for minor leaguer (May 2); C Ausmus and IF Cedeno from S.D. for IF Chris Gomez and C Flaherty (June 18); OF Sierra and P Matt Drews from NYY for IF Cecil Fielder (July 31). **Claimed:** P Van Poppel off waivers (Aug. 6). **Traded:** OF Curtis to Los Angeles for P Joey Eischen and P John Cummings (July 31); P Olson to Hou. for 2 PTBN (Aug. 26); IF Cedeno to Houston for PTBN (Sept. 11).

Pitching (40 IP)	ERA	W-L	Gm	IP	BB	SO
Richie Lewis	4.18	4-6	72	90.1	65	78
Justin Thompson*	4.58	1-6	11	59.0	31	44
Omar Olivares	4.89	7-11	25	160.0	75	81
Mike Myers*	5.01	1-5	83	64.2	34	69
A.J. Sager	5.01	4-5	22	79.0	29	52
Gregg Olson	5.02	3-0	43	43.0	28	29
Felipe Lira	5.22	6-14	32	194.2	66	113
Jose Lima	5.70	5-6	39	72.2	22	59
Brian Williams	6.77	3-10	40	121.0	85	72
Greg Keagle*	7.39	3-6	26	87.2	68	70
C.J. Nitkowski	8.08	2-3	11	45.2	38	36
Todd Van Poppel	9.06	3-9	37	99.1	62	53

Saves: Olson (8); Myers (6); Lima (3); Lewis and Williams (2); Van Poppel and Walker (1). **Complete games:** Olivares (4); Lira (3); Williams (2); Van Poppel (1). **Shutouts:** Lira (2); Van Poppel and Williams (1).

Kansas City Royals

Batting (135 AB)	Avg	AB	R	H	HR	RBI	SB
Jose Offerman	.303	561	85	170	5	47	24
Joe Randa	.303	337	36	102	6	47	13
Bip Roberts	.283	339	39	96	0	52	12
Tom Goodwin	.282	524	80	148	1	35	66
Mike Sweeney*	.279	165	23	46	4	24	1
Mike Macfarlane	.274	379	58	104	19	54	3
Keith Lockhart	.273	433	49	118	7	55	11
Johnny Damon	.271	517	61	140	6	50	25
Michael Tucker	.260	339	55	88	12	53	10
Craig Paquette	.259	429	61	111	22	67	5
Bob Hamelin	.255	239	31	61	9	40	5
Joe Vitiello*	.241	257	29	62	8	40	2
Dave Howard	.219	420	51	92	4	48	5
Sal Fasano*	.203	143	20	29	6	19	1

Signed: Free agent OF Paquette (April 4).

Pitching (40 IP)	ERA	W-L	Gm	IP	BB	SO
Jose Rosado*	3.21	8-6	16	106.2	26	[illegible]
Kevin Appier	3.62	14-11	32	211.1	75	[illegible]
Tim Belcher	3.92	15-11	35	238.2	68	[illegible]
Jeff Montgomery	4.26	4-6	48	63.1	19	[illegible]
Chris Haney	4.70	10-14	35	228.0	51	[illegible]
Jason Jacome	4.72	0-4	49	47.2	22	[illegible]
Doug Linton	5.02	7-9	21	104.0	26	[illegible]
Mark Gubicza	5.13	4-12	19	119.1	34	[illegible]
Hipolito Pichardo	5.43	3-5	57	68.0	26	[illegible]
Mike Magnante	5.67	2-2	38	54.0	24	[illegible]
Julio Valera	6.46	3-2	31	61.1	27	[illegible]

Saves: Montgomery (24); Bluma (5); Pichardo (3); Huisman Jacome and Valera (1). **Complete games:** Appier (5); Belcher an Haney (4); Gubicza and Rosado (2). **Shutouts:** Appier, Belche Gubicza, Haney and Rosado (1).

Milwaukee Brewers

Batting (135 AB)	Avg	AB	R	H	HR	RBI	SB
Dave Nilsson	.331	453	81	150	17	84	2
Jeff Cirillo	.325	566	101	184	15	83	4
Marc Newfield	.307	179	21	55	7	31	0
John Jaha	.300	543	108	163	34	118	3
Fernando Vina	.283	554	94	157	7	46	16
Greg Vaughn	.280	375	78	105	31	95	5
Mark Loretta*	.279	154	20	43	1	13	2
Matt Mieske	.278	374	46	104	14	64	1
Jeromy Burnitz	.265	200	38	53	9	40	4
Jose Valentin	.259	552	90	143	24	95	17
Gerald Williams	.252	325	43	82	5	34	10
Pat Listach	.240	317	51	76	1	33	25
Jesse Levis	.236	233	27	55	1	21	0
Mike Matheny	.204	313	31	64	8	46	3

Acquired: OF Newfield, P Bryce Florie and P Ron Villone from S for OF Vaughn and OF Gerald Parent (July 31); OF Williams ar P Wickman from N.Y. for P Graeme Lloyd and P Ricky Bones (Au 23); OF Burnitz from Cle. for IF Kevin Seitzer (Aug. 31).

Pitching (40 IP)	ERA	W-L	Gm	IP	BB	SO
Mike Fetters	3.38	3-3	61	61.1	26	[illegible]
Ben McDonald	3.90	12-10	35	221.1	67	[illegible]
Bob Wickman	4.42	7-1	70	95.2	44	[illegible]
Cal Eldred	4.46	4-4	15	84.2	38	[illegible]
Scott Karl	4.86	13-9	32	207.1	72	[illegible]
Angel Miranda	4.94	7-6	46	109.1	69	[illegible]
Tim VanEgmond*	5.27	3-5	12	54.2	23	[illegible]
Jeff D'Amico*	5.44	6-6	17	86.0	31	[illegible]
Steve Sparks	6.60	4-7	20	88.2	52	[illegible]
Ramon Garcia	6.66	4-4	37	75.2	21	[illegible]
Mike Potts*	7.15	1-2	24	45.1	30	[illegible]

Saves: Fetters (32); Garcia (4); Villone (2); Boze, Jones, Mirand and Potts (1). **Complete games:** Karl (3); McDonald (2); Spar (1). **Shutouts:** Karl (1).

Minnesota Twins

Batting (135 AB)	Avg	AB	R	H	HR	RBI	SB
Paul Molitor	.341	660	99	225	9	113	18
Chuck Knoblauch	.341	578	140	197	13	72	45
Roberto Kelly	.323	322	41	104	6	47	10
Marty Cordova	.309	569	97	176	16	111	11
Ron Coomer*	.296	233	34	69	12	41	3
Rich Becker	.291	525	92	153	12	71	19
Greg Myers	.286	329	37	94	6	47	0
Scott Stahoviak	.284	405	72	115	13	61	3
Pat Meares	.267	517	66	138	8	67	9
Matt Lawton*	.258	252	34	65	6	42	4
Matt Walbeck	.223	215	25	48	2	24	3
Jeff Reboulet	.222	234	20	52	0	23	4

Claimed: P Aldred off waivers (June 2).
Signed: Free agent Kelly (April 1).

Pitching (40 IP)	ERA	W-L	Gm	IP	BB	SO
Mike Trombley	3.01	5-1	43	68.2	25	57
Dan Naulty*	3.79	3-2	49	57.0	35	56
Brad Radke	4.46	11-16	35	232.0	57	148
Dave Stevens	4.66	3-3	49	58.0	25	29
Frank Rodriguez	5.05	13-14	38	206.2	78	110
Rich Robertson	5.12	7-17	36	186.1	116	114
Eddie Guardado	5.25	6-5	83	73.2	33	74
Rick Aguilera	5.42	8-6	19	111.1	27	83
Greg Hansell	5.69	3-0	50	74.1	31	46
Jose Parra	6.04	5-5	27	70.0	27	50
Scott Aldred	6.21	6-9	36	165.1	68	111

Saves: Stevens (11); Trombley (6); Guardado and Naulty (4); Hansell (3); Rodriguez (2); Bennett (1). **Complete games:** Robertson (5); Radke and Rodriguez (3); Aguilera (2). **Shutouts:** Robertson (3).

New York Yankees

Batting (135 IP)	Avg	AB	R	H	HR	RBI	SB
Mariano Duncan	.340	400	62	136	8	56	4
Derek Jeter*	.314	582	104	183	10	78	14
Wade Boggs	.311	501	80	156	2	41	1
Bernie Williams	.305	551	108	168	29	102	17
Paul O'Neill	.302	546	89	165	19	91	0
Joe Girardi	.294	422	55	124	2	45	13
Tino Martinez	.292	595	82	174	25	117	2
Tim Raines	.284	201	45	57	9	33	10
Jim Leyritz	.264	265	23	70	7	40	2
Darryl Strawberry	.262	202	35	53	11	36	6
Cecil Fielder	.252	591	85	149	39	117	2
Luis Sojo	.220	287	23	63	1	21	2
Andy Fox*	.196	189	26	37	3	13	11

Acquired: IF Fielder from Det. for OF Ruben Sierra and P Matt Drews (July 31); P Bones and P Lloyd from Mil. for OF Gerald Williams and P Bob Wickman (Aug. 23).
Signed: Free agent OF Strawberry (July 4).
Claimed: IF Sojo off waivers (Aug. 22).

Pitching (40 IP)	W-L	ERA	Gm	IP	BB	SO
Mariano Rivera	8-3	2.09	61	107.2	34	130
John Wetteland	2-3	2.83	62	63.2	21	69
David Cone	7-2	2.88	11	72.0	34	71
Andy Pettitte	21-8	3.87	35	221.0	72	162
Graeme Lloyd	2-6	4.29	65	56.2	22	30
Jeff Nelson	4-4	4.36	73	74.1	36	91
Kenny Rogers	12-8	4.68	30	179.0	83	92
Jimmy Key	12-11	4.68	30	169.1	58	116
Dwight Gooden	11-7	5.01	29	170.2	88	126
Jim Mecir*	1-1	5.13	26	40.1	23	38
Brian Boehringer*	2-4	5.44	15	46.1	21	37
Ricky Bones	7-14	6.22	36	152.0	68	63
Ramiro Mendoza*	4-5	6.79	12	53.0	10	34

Saves: Wetteland (43); M. Rivera (5); Nelson (2); Howe and Pavlas (1). **Complete games:** Pettitte and Rogers (2); Cone and Gooden (1). **Shutouts:** Gooden and Rogers (1).

Oakland Athletics

Batting (150 AB)	Avg	AB	R	H	HR	RBI	SB
Mark McGwire	.312	423	104	132	52	113	0
Scott Brosius	.304	428	73	130	22	71	7
Tony Batista*	.298	238	38	71	6	25	7
Jason Giambi	.291	536	84	156	20	79	0
Geronimo Berroa	.290	586	101	170	36	106	0
Terry Steinbach	.272	514	79	140	35	100	0
Jose Herrera*	.269	320	44	86	6	30	8
Brent Gates	.263	247	26	65	2	30	1
Ernie Young	.242	462	72	112	19	64	7
Rafael Bournigal	.242	252	33	61	0	18	4
Mike Bordick	.240	525	46	126	5	54	5
Phil Plantier	.212	231	29	49	7	31	2

Pitching (40 IP)	ERA	W-L	Gm	IP	BB	SO
Mike Mohler	3.67	6-3	72	81.0	41	64
Buddy Groom	3.84	5-0	72	77.1	34	57
Willie Adams	4.01	3-4	12	76.1	23	68
Jim Corsi	4.03	6-0	57	73.2	34	43
Ariel Prieto	4.15	6-7	21	125.2	54	75
Billy Taylor	4.33	6-3	55	60.1	25	67
Dave Telgheder	4.65	4-7	16	79.1	26	43
Carlos Reyes	4.78	7-10	46	122.1	61	78
Don Wengert	5.58	7-11	36	161.1	60	75
Steve Wojciechowski*	5.65	5-5	16	79.2	28	30
John Wasdin	5.96	8-7	25	131.1	50	75
Doug Johns	5.98	6-12	40	158.0	69	71
Bobby Chouinard*	6.10	4-2	13	59.0	32	32

Saves: Taylor (17); Mohler (7); Corsi (3); Acre and Groom (2); Briscoe and Johns (1). **Complete games:** Prieto (2); Adams, Johns, Telgheder, Wasdin and Wengert (1). **Shutouts:** Adams, Telgheder and Wengert (1).

Seattle Mariners

Batting (150 AB)	Avg	AB	R	H	HR	RBI	SB
Alex Rodriguez	.358	601	141	215	36	123	15
Edgar Martinez	.327	499	121	163	26	103	3
Ken Griffey Jr.	.303	545	125	165	49	140	16
Rich Amaral	.292	312	69	91	1	29	25
Joey Cora	.291	530	90	154	6	45	5
Paul Sorrento	.289	471	67	136	23	93	0
Dan Wilson	.285	491	51	140	18	83	1
Jay Buhner	.271	564	107	153	44	138	0
Brian Hunter	.268	198	21	53	7	28	0
Dave Hollins	.262	516	88	135	16	78	6
Doug Strange	.235	183	19	43	3	23	1
Russ Davis	.234	167	24	39	5	18	2

Acquired: P Moyer from Bos. for OF Darren Bragg (July 30); P Mulholland from Phi. for IF Desi Relaford (July 31); OF Whiten from Atl. for minor leaguer (Aug. 14); IF Hollins from Min. for PTBN (Aug. 29).

Pitching (40 IP)	ERA	W-L	Gm	IP	BB	SO
Mike Jackson	3.63	1-1	73	72.0	24	70
Randy Johnson	3.67	5-0	14	61.1	25	85
Jamie Moyer	3.98	13-3	34	160.2	46	79
Tim Davis	4.01	2-2	40	42.2	17	34
Norm Charlton	4.04	4-7	70	75.2	38	73
Rafael Carmona	4.28	8-3	53	90.1	55	62
Salomon Torres	4.59	3-3	10	49.0	23	36
Terry Mulholland	4.67	5-4	12	69.1	28	34
Bob Wells	5.30	12-7	36	130.2	46	94
Sterling Hitchcock	5.35	13-9	35	196.2	73	132
Bob Wolcott*	5.73	7-10	30	149.1	54	78
Rusty Meacham	5.74	1-1	15	42.1	13	25
Bobby Ayala	5.88	6-3	50	67.1	25	61
Chris Bosio	5.93	4-4	18	60.2	24	39
Matt Wagner*	6.86	3-5	15	80.0	38	41
Paul Menhart	7.29	2-2	11	42.0	25	18
Edwin Hurtado	7.74	2-5	16	47.2	30	36

Saves: Charlton (20); Jackson (6); Ayala (3); Hurtado (2); Carmona, Johnson and Meacham (1). **Complete games:** Torres, Wagner, Wells and Wolcott (1). **Shutouts:** Torres and Wells (1).

AL Team by Team Statistics (Cont.)

Texas Rangers

Batting (135 AB)	Avg	AB	R	H	HR	RBI	SB
Rusty Greer	.332	542	96	180	18	100	9
Juan Gonzalez	.314	541	89	170	47	144	2
Ivan Rodriguez	.300	639	116	192	19	86	5
Darryl Hamilton	.293	627	94	184	6	51	15
Mark McLemore	.290	517	84	150	5	46	27
Will Clark	.284	436	69	124	13	72	2
Damon Buford	.283	145	30	41	6	20	8
Dean Palmer	.280	582	98	163	38	107	2
Warren Newson	.255	235	34	60	10	31	3
Kevin Elster	.252	515	79	130	24	99	4
Mickey Tettleton	.246	491	78	121	24	83	2

Acquired: P Stanton from Bos. for P Mark Brandenburg and P Kerry Lacy (July 31); P Burkett from Fla. for P Rick Helling and P Ryan Dempster (Aug. 8).

Pitching (40 IP)	ERA	W-L	Gm	IP	BB	SO
Ed Vosberg	3.27	1-1	52	44.0	21	32
Jeff Russell	3.38	3-3	55	56.0	22	23
Ken Hill	3.63	16-10	35	250.2	95	170
Mike Stanton	3.66	4-4	81	78.2	27	60
John Burkett	4.06	5-2	10	68.2	16	47
Dennis Cook	4.09	5-2	60	70.1	35	64
Darren Oliver	4.66	14-6	30	173.2	76	112
Roger Pavlik	5.19	15-8	34	201.0	81	127
Kevin Gross	5.22	11-8	28	129.1	50	78
Bobby Witt	5.41	16-12	33	199.2	96	157
Mike Henneman	5.79	0-7	49	42.0	17	34
Gil Heredia	5.89	2-5	44	73.1	14	43

Saves: Henneman (31); Vosberg (8); Russell (3); Heredia and Stanton (1). **Complete games:** Hill and Pavlik (7); Witt (2); Burkett, Gross and Oliver (1). **Shutouts:** Hill (3); Burkett and Oliver (1).

Toronto Blue Jays

Batting (135 AB)	Avg	AB	R	H	HR	RBI	SB
Robert Perez*	.327	202	30	66	2	21	3
Otis Nixon	.286	496	87	142	1	29	54
Shawn Green	.280	422	52	118	11	45	5
John Olerud	.274	398	59	109	18	61	1
Carlos Delgado	.270	488	68	132	25	92	0
Jacob Brumfield	.256	308	52	79	12	52	12
Juan Samuel	.255	188	34	48	8	26	9
Joe Carter	.253	625	84	158	30	107	7
Tomas Perez	.251	295	24	74	1	19	1
Ed Sprague	.247	591	88	146	36	101	0
Charlie O'Brien	.238	324	33	77	13	44	0
Alex Gonzalez	.235	527	64	124	14	64	16
Sandy Martinez	.227	229	17	52	3	18	0

Acquired: OF Brumfield from Pit. for minor leaguer (May 18).

Pitching (40 IP)	ERA	W-L	Gm	IP	BB	SO
Tim Crabtree	2.54	5-3	53	67.1	22	57
Juan Guzman	2.93	11-8	27	187.2	53	165
Pat Hentgen	3.22	20-10	35	265.2	94	177
Mike Timlin	3.65	1-6	59	56.2	18	52
Bill Risley	3.89	0-1	25	41.2	25	29
Huck Flener*	4.58	3-2	15	70.2	33	44
Woody Williams	4.73	4-5	12	59.0	21	43
Erik Hanson	5.41	13-17	35	214.2	102	156
Paul Quantrill	5.43	5-14	38	134.1	51	86
Marty Janzen	7.33	4-6	15	73.2	38	47

Saves: Timlin (31); Bohanon, Crabtree and Spoljaric (1). **Complete games:** Hentgen (10); Guzman and Hanson (4); Williams (1). **Shutouts:** Hentgen (3); Guzman and Hanson (1).

Players Who Played in Both Leagues in 1996

While all indivdual major league statistics count on career records, players cannot transfer their stats from one league to the other if they are traded during the regular season. Here are the combined stats for batters with 400 at bats and pitchers with 80 innings pitched, who played in both leagues in 1996.

Batters (400 AB)

	Avg	AB	R	H	HR	RBI	SB
Carlos Baerga	.254	507	59	129	12	66	1
CLE.	.267	424	54	113	10	55	1
NYM.	.193	83	5	16	2	11	0
Mark Carreon	.281	434	56	122	11	65	3
S.F.	.260	292	40	76	9	51	2
CLE.	.324	142	16	46	2	14	1
Chad Curtis	.252	504	85	127	12	46	18
DET.	.263	400	65	105	10	37	16
L.A.	.212	104	20	22	2	9	2
John Flaherty	.284	416	40	118	13	64	3
DET.	.250	152	18	38	4	23	1
S.D.	.303	264	22	80	9	41	2
Chris Gomez	.257	456	53	117	4	45	3
DET.	.242	128	21	31	1	16	1
S.D.	.262	328	32	86	3	29	2
Charlie Hayes	.253	526	58	133	12	75	6
PIT.	.248	459	51	114	10	62	6
NYY.	.284	67	7	19	2	13	0
Jeff Kent	.284	437	61	124	12	55	6
NYM.	.290	335	45	97	9	39	4
CLE.	.265	102	16	27	3	16	2
Greg Vaughn	.260	516	98	134	41	117	9
MIL.	.280	375	78	105	31	95	5
S.D.	.206	141	20	29	10	22	4
Jose Vizcaino	.297	542	70	161	1	45	15
NYM.	.303	363	47	110	1	32	9
CLE.	.285	179	23	51	0	13	6
Mark Whiten	.262	412	76	108	22	71	17
PHI.	.236	182	33	43	7	21	13
ATL.	.256	90	12	23	3	17	2
SEA.	.300	140	31	42	12	33	2
Todd Zeile	.263	617	78	162	25	99	1
PHI.	.268	500	61	134	20	80	1
BAL.	.239	117	17	28	5	19	0

Pitchers (80 IP)

	ERA	W-L	Gm	IP	BB	SO
John Burkett	4.24	11-12	34	222.2	58	155
FLA.	4.32	6-10	24	154.0	42	108
TEX.	4.06	5-2	10	68.2	16	47
Marvin Freeman	6.15	7-9	27	131.2	58	72
COL.	6.04	7-9	26	129.2	57	71
CHI. (AL)	13.50	0-0	1	2.0	1	1
Mark Hutton	4.15	5-3	25	86.2	36	56
NYY.	5.04	0-2	12	30.1	18	25
FLA.	3.67	5-1	13	56.1	18	31
Terry Mulholland	4.66	13-11	33	202.2	49	86
PHI.	4.66	8-7	21	133.1	21	52
SEA.	4.67	5-4	12	69.1	28	34
David Weathers	5.48	2-4	42	88.2	42	53
FLA.	4.54	2-2	31	71.1	28	40
NYY.	9.35	0-2	11	17.1	14	13

NL Team by Team Statistics

At least 135 at bats or 40 innings pitched during the regular season unless otherwise indicated. Players who competed for more than one NL team are listed with their final club. Players traded from the AL are listed with NL team only if they have 135 AB or 40 IP. Note that (*) indicates rookie.

Atlanta Braves

Batting (135 AB)	Avg	AB	R	H	HR	RBI	SB
Dave Justice	.321	140	23	45	6	25	1
Chipper Jones	.309	598	114	185	30	110	14
Marquis Grissom	.308	671	106	207	23	74	28
Fred McGriff	.295	617	81	182	28	107	7
Javy Lopez	.282	489	56	138	23	69	1
Ryan Klesko	.282	528	90	149	34	93	6
Jermaine Dye*	.281	292	32	82	12	37	1
Eddie Perez*	.256	156	19	40	4	17	0
Mark Lemke	.255	498	64	127	5	37	5
Jeff Blauser	.245	265	48	65	10	35	6
Mark Whiten	.243	272	45	66	10	38	15
Terry Pendleton	.238	568	51	135	11	75	2
Dwight Smith	.203	153	16	31	3	16	1
Rafael Belliard	.169	142	9	24	0	3	3

Acquired: IF Pendleton from Fla. for minor leaguer (Aug. 13); P Neagle from Pit. for P Jason Schmidt and two minor leaguers (Aug. 28).
Traded: OF Whiten to Sea. for minor leaguer (Aug. 14).

Pitchers (40 IP)	ERA	W-L	Gm	IP	BB	SO
Mike Bielecki	2.63	4-3	40	75.1	33	71
Greg Maddux	2.72	15-11	35	245.0	28	172
John Smoltz	2.94	24-8	35	253.2	55	276
Terrell Wade*	2.97	5-0	44	69.2	47	79
Tom Glavine	2.98	15-10	36	235.1	85	181
Mark Wohlers	3.03	2-4	77	77.1	21	100
Greg McMichael	3.22	5-3	73	86.2	27	78
Denny Neagle	3.50	16-9	33	221.1	48	149
Steve Avery	4.47	7-10	24	131.0	40	86
Brad Clontz	5.69	6-3	81	80.2	33	49

Saves: Wohlers (39); Bielecki and McMichael (2); Borbon, Clontz and Wade (1). **Complete games:** Smoltz (6); Maddux (5); Neagle (2); Avery and Glavine (1). **Shutouts:** Smoltz (2); Maddux (1).

Chicago Cubs

Batting (135 AB)	Avg	AB	R	H	HR	RBI	SB
Mark Grace	.331	547	88	181	9	75	2
Tyler Houston*	.317	142	21	45	3	27	3
Brian McRae	.276	624	111	172	17	66	37
Sammy Sosa	.273	498	84	136	40	100	18
Luis Gonzalez	.271	483	70	131	15	79	9
Scott Servais	.265	445	42	118	11	63	0
Dave Magadan	.254	169	23	43	3	17	0
Ryne Sandberg	.244	554	85	135	25	92	12
Jose Hernandez	.242	331	52	80	10	41	4
Leo Gomez	.238	362	44	86	17	56	1
Scott Bullett	.212	165	26	35	3	16	7
Rey Sanchez	.211	289	28	61	1	12	7
Ozzie Timmons	.200	140	18	28	7	16	1

Acquired: C Houston from Atl. for minor leaguer (June 26).

Pitching (40 IP)	ERA	W-L	Gm	IP	BB	SO
Kent Bottenfield	2.63	3-5	48	61.2	19	33
Turk Wendell	2.84	4-5	70	79.1	44	75
Terry Adams*	2.94	3-6	69	101.0	49	78
Steve Trachsel	3.03	13-9	31	205.0	62	132
Bob Patterson	3.13	3-3	79	54.2	22	53
Jaime Navarro	3.92	15-12	35	236.2	72	158
Rodney Myers*	4.68	2-1	45	67.1	38	50
Frank Castillo	5.28	7-16	33	182.1	46	139
Amaury Telemaco*	5.46	5-7	25	97.1	31	64
Kevin Foster	6.21	7-6	17	87.0	35	53
Jim Bullinger	6.54	6-10	37	129.1	68	90

Saves: Wendell (18); Patterson (8); Adams (4); Jones (2); Bottenfield and Bullinger (1). **Complete games:** Navarro (4); Trachsel (3); Bullinger, Castillo and Foster (1). **Shutouts:** Trachsel (2); Bullinger, Castillo and Navarro (1).

Cincinnati Reds

Batting (140 AB)	Avg	AB	R	H	HR	RBI	SB
Hal Morris	.313	528	82	165	16	80	7
Barry Larkin	.298	517	117	154	33	89	36
Eddie Taubensee	.291	327	46	95	12	48	3
Eric Davis	.287	415	81	119	26	83	23
Lenny Harris	.285	302	33	86	5	32	14
Thomas Howard	.272	360	50	98	6	42	6
Reggie Sanders	.251	287	49	72	14	33	24
Jeff Branson	.244	311	34	76	9	37	2
Willie Greene	.244	287	48	70	19	63	0
Joe Oliver	.242	289	31	70	11	46	2
Bret Boone	.233	520	56	121	12	69	3
Eric Owens*	.200	205	26	41	0	9	16

Acquired: P Smith from Cal. for P Chuck McElroy (June 2).
Signed: Free agent P Morgan (Sept. 3).

Pitching (40 IP)	ERA	W-L	Gm	IP	BB	SO
Jeff Brantley	2.41	1-2	66	71.0	28	76
Jeff Shaw	2.49	8-6	78	104.2	29	69
John Smiley	3.64	13-14	35	217.1	54	171
Hector Carrasco	3.75	4-3	56	74.1	45	59
Dave Burba	3.83	11-13	34	195.0	97	148
Scott Service	3.94	1-0	34	48.0	18	46
Mark Portugal	3.98	8-9	27	156.0	42	93
Lee Smith	4.06	3-4	43	44.1	23	35
Mike Morgan	4.63	6-11	23	130.1	47	74
Roger Salkeld	5.20	8-5	29	116.0	54	82
Johnny Ruffin	5.49	1-3	49	62.1	37	69
Kevin Jarvis	5.98	8-9	24	120.1	43	63
Pete Schourek	6.01	4-5	12	67.1	24	54

Saves: Brantley (44); Shaw (4); Smith (2). **Complete games:** Smiley (2); Portugal and Salkeld (1). **Shutouts:** Smiley (2); Portugal and Salkeld (1).

Colorado Rockies

Batting (135 AB)	Avg	AB	R	H	HR	RBI	SB
Ellis Burks	.344	613	142	211	40	128	32
Eric Young	.324	568	113	184	8	74	53
Dante Bichette	.313	633	114	198	31	141	31
Vinny Castilla	.304	629	97	191	40	113	7
Andres Galarraga	.304	626	119	190	47	150	18
Quinton McCracken*	.290	283	50	82	3	40	17
Jeff Reed	.284	341	34	97	8	37	2
Walt Weiss	.282	517	89	146	8	48	10
Larry Walker	.276	272	58	75	18	58	18
John Vander Wal	.252	151	20	38	5	31	2
Steve Decker	.245	147	24	36	2	20	1
Eric Anthony	.243	185	32	45	12	22	0
Jayhawk Owens	.239	180	31	43	4	17	4
Jason Bates	.206	160	19	33	1	9	2

Acquired: OF Anthony from Cin. for cash (July 30); C Decker from S.F. for cash (Aug. 21).

Pitching (40 IP)	ERA	W-L	Gm	IP	BB	SO
Steve Reed	3.96	4-3	70	75.0	19	51
Darren Holmes	3.97	5-4	62	77.0	28	73
Bruce Ruffin	4.00	7-5	71	69.2	29	74
Jamey Wright*	4.93	4-4	16	91.1	41	45
Armando Reynoso	4.96	8-9	30	168.2	49	88
Kevin Ritz	5.28	17-11	35	213.0	105	105
Mark Thompson	5.30	9-11	34	169.2	74	99
Lance Painter	5.86	4-2	34	50.2	25	48
Marvin Freeman	6.04	7-9	26	129.2	57	71
Curt Leskanic	6.23	7-5	70	73.2	38	76
Roger Bailey	6.24	2-3	24	83.2	52	45
Mike Munoz	6.65	2-2	54	44.2	16	45
Bryan Rekar	8.95	2-4	14	58.1	26	25

Saves: Ruffin (24); Leskanic (6); Swift (2); Bailey and Holmes (1). **Complete games:** Ma. Thompson (3); Ritz (2). **Shutouts:** Ma. Thompson (1).

Florida Marlins

Batting (135 AB)	Avg	AB	R	H	HR	RBI	SB
Gary Sheffield	.314	519	118	163	42	120	16
Edgar Renteria*	.309	431	68	133	5	31	16
Jeff Conine	.293	597	84	175	26	95	1
Greg Colbrunn	.286	511	60	146	16	69	4
Alex Arias	.277	224	27	62	3	26	2
Devon White	.274	552	77	151	17	84	22
Luis Castillo*	.262	164	26	43	1	8	17
Kurt Abbott	.253	320	37	81	8	33	3
Quilvio Veras	.253	253	40	64	4	14	8
Joe Orsulak	.221	217	23	48	2	19	1
Charles Johnson	.218	386	34	84	13	37	1

Acquired: P Hutton from NYY for P Weathers (July 31).
Traded: P Burkett to Tex. for P Rick Helling and P Ryan Dempster (Aug. 8); P Matthews to Bal. fro PTBN (Aug. 21).

Pitching (40 IP)	ERA	W-L	Gm	IP	BB	SO
Kevin Brown	1.89	17-11	32	233.0	33	159
Robb Nen	1.95	5-1	75	83.0	21	92
Al Leiter	2.93	16-12	33	215.1	119	200
Mark Hutton*	3.67	5-1	13	56.1	18	31
John Burkett	4.32	6-10	24	154.0	42	108
Jay Powell*	4.54	4-3	67	71.1	36	52
David Weathers	4.54	2-2	31	71.1	28	40
Marc Valdes*	4.81	1-3	11	48.2	23	13
Terry Mathews	4.91	2-4	57	55.0	27	49
Pat Rapp	5.10	8-16	30	162.1	91	86
Yorkis Perez	5.29	3-4	64	47.2	31	47
Chris Hammond	6.56	5-8	38	81.0	27	50
Kurt Miller*	6.80	1-3	26	46.1	33	30

Saves: Nen (35); Mathews (4); Powell (2). **Complete games:** Brown (5); Leiter (2); Burkett (1). **Shutouts:** Brown (3); Leiter (1).

Houston Astros

Batting (135 AB)	Avg	AB	R	H	HR	RBI	SB
Jeff Bagwell	.315	568	111	179	31	120	21
Craig Biggio	.288	605	113	174	15	75	25
Ricky Gutierrez	.284	218	28	62	1	15	6
Sean Berry	.281	431	55	121	17	95	12
Brian L. Hunter	.276	526	74	145	5	35	35
Tony Eusebio	.270	152	15	41	1	19	0
John Cangelosi	.263	262	49	69	1	16	17
James Mouton	.263	300	40	79	3	34	21
Derek Bell	.263	627	84	165	17	113	29
Orlando Miller	.256	468	43	120	15	58	3
Bill Spiers	.252	218	27	55	6	26	7
Derrick May	.251	259	24	65	5	33	2
Andujar Cedeno	.231	156	11	36	3	18	3
Kirt Manwaring	.229	227	14	52	1	18	0

Acquired: P Darwin from Pit. for P Rich Loiselle (July 25); C Manwaring from S.F. for C Rick Wilkins (July 26); IF Cedeno from Det. for PTBN (Sept. 11).
Signed: Free agent P Hernandez off waivers (Apr. 24).

Pitching (40 IP)	ERA	W-L	Gm	IP	BB	SO
Billy Wagner*	2.44	2-2	37	51.2	30	67
Mike Hampton	3.59	10-10	27	160.1	49	101
Shane Reynolds	3.65	16-10	35	239.0	44	204
Danny Darwin	3.77	10-11	34	164.2	27	96
Darryl Kile	4.19	12-11	35	219.0	97	219
Todd Jones	4.40	6-3	51	57.1	32	44
Donne Wall*	4.56	9-8	26	150.0	34	99
Doug Drabek	4.57	7-9	30	175.1	60	137
Doug Brocail	4.58	1-5	23	53.0	23	34
Xavier Hernandez	4.62	5-5	61	78.0	28	81
Alvin Morman*	4.93	4-1	53	42.0	24	31

Saves: Jones (17); Wagner (9); Hernandez (6); Hudek (2); Tabaka (1). **Complete games:** Kile and Reynolds (4); Hampton and Wall (2); Drabek (1). **Shutouts:** Hampton, Reynolds and Wall (1).

Los Angeles Dodgers

Batting (135 AB)	Avg	AB	R	H	HR	RBI	SB
Mike Piazza	.336	547	87	184	36	105	0
Raul Mondesi	.297	634	98	188	24	88	14
Todd Hollandsworth*	.291	478	64	139	12	59	21
Wayne Kirby	.271	188	23	51	1	11	4
Dave Clark	.270	226	28	61	8	36	2
Mike Blowers	.265	317	31	84	6	38	0
Eric Karros	.260	608	84	158	34	111	8
Greg Gagne	.255	428	48	109	10	55	4
Roger Cedeno*	.246	211	26	52	2	18	5
Tim Wallach	.228	162	14	37	4	22	0
Delino DeShields	.224	581	75	130	5	41	48
Chad Fonville	.204	201	34	41	0	13	7

Acquired: OF Clark from Pit. for minor leaguer (Aug. 31).
Claimed: OF Kirby off waivers (June 24).
Signed: Free agent IF Wallach (July 25).
Traded: P Eischen and P John Cummings to Det. for OF Chad Curtis (July 31).

Pitching (40 IP)	ERA	W-L	Gm	IP	BB	SO
Mark Guthrie	2.22	2-3	66	73.0	22	56
Scott Radinsky	2.41	5-1	58	52.1	17	48
Antonio Osuna	3.00	9-6	73	84.0	32	85
Todd Worrell	3.03	4-6	72	65.1	15	66
Hideo Nomo	3.19	16-11	33	228.1	85	234
Ismael Valdes	3.32	15-7	33	225.0	54	173
Ramon Martinez	3.42	15-6	28	168.2	86	134
Pedro Astacio	3.44	9-8	35	211.2	67	130
Chan Ho Park*	3.64	5-5	48	108.2	71	119
Tom Candiotti	4.49	9-11	28	152.1	43	79
Joey Eischen	4.78	0-1	28	43.1	20	36

Saves: Worrell (44); Osuna (4); Guthrie and Radinsky (1). **Complete games:** Nomo (3); Martinez (2); Candiotti (1). **Shutouts:** Martinez and Nomo (2).

Montreal Expos

Batting (135 AB)	Avg	AB	R	H	HR	RBI	SB
Mark Grudzielanek	.306	657	99	201	6	49	33
Rondell White	.293	334	35	98	6	41	14
David Segui	.286	416	69	119	11	58	4
Mike Lansing	.285	641	99	183	11	53	23
Moises Alou	.281	540	87	152	21	96	9
F.P. Santangelo*	.277	393	54	109	7	56	5
Henry Rodriguez	.276	532	81	147	36	103	2
Darrin Fletcher	.266	394	41	105	12	57	0
Sherman Obando	.247	178	30	44	8	22	2
Cliff Floyd	.242	227	29	55	6	26	7
Lenny Webster	.230	174	18	40	2	17	0
Shane Andrews	.227	375	43	85	19	64	3
Dave Silvestri	.204	162	16	33	1	17	2

Acquired: P Leiter from S.F. for P Kirk Reuter and P Tim Scott (July 30).
Claimed: P Dyer off waivers (April 4); P Juden off waivers (July 11).

Pitching (40 IP)	ERA	W-L	Gm	IP	BB	SO
Mel Rojas	3.22	7-4	74	81.0	28	92
Barry Manuel*	3.24	4-1	53	86.0	26	62
Jeff Juden	3.27	5-0	58	74.1	34	61
Jeff Fassero	3.30	15-11	34	231.2	55	222
Jose Paniagua*	3.53	2-4	13	51.0	23	27
Pedro Martinez	3.70	13-10	33	216.2	70	222
Ugueth Urbina*	3.71	10-5	33	114.0	44	108
Omar Daal	4.02	4-5	64	87.1	37	82
Rheal Cormier	4.17	7-10	33	159.2	41	100
Dave Veres	4.17	6-3	68	77.2	32	81
Mike Dyer	4.40	5-5	70	75.2	34	51
Mark Leiter	4.92	8-12	35	205.0	69	164

Saves: Rojas (36); Veres (4); Dyer (2). **Complete games:** Fassero (5); Martinez (4); Leiter (2); Cormier (1). **Shutouts:** Cormier, Fassero and Martinez (1).

New York Mets

Batting (135 IP)	Avg	AB	R	H	HR	RBI	SB
Lance Johnson	.333	682	117	227	9	69	50
Bernard Gilkey	.317	571	108	181	30	117	17
Jose Vizcaino	.303	363	47	110	1	32	9
Alex Ochoa*	.294	282	37	83	4	33	4
Jeff Kent	.290	335	45	97	9	39	4
Butch Huskey	.278	414	43	115	15	60	1
Edgardo Alfonzo	.261	368	36	96	4	40	2
Todd Hundley	.259	540	85	140	41	112	1
Rey Ordonez*	.257	502	51	129	1	30	1
Rico Brogna	.255	188	18	48	7	30	0
Chris Jones	.242	149	22	36	4	18	1
Carl Everett	.240	192	29	46	1	16	6

Traded: IF Vizcaino and IF Kent to Cle. for IF Carlos Baerga and IF Alvaro Espinoza (July 29).
Acquired: P Clark from Cle. for OF Ryan Thompson and P Reid Cornelius (April 1).

Pitching (40 IP)	ERA	W-L	Gm	IP	BB	SO
John Franco	1.83	4-3	51	54.0	21	48
Dave Mlicki	3.30	6-7	51	90.0	33	83
Mark Clark	3.43	14-11	32	212.1	48	142
Jerry DiPoto	4.19	7-2	57	77.1	45	52
Pete Harnisch	4.21	8-12	31	194.2	61	114
Paul Byrd*	4.24	1-2	38	46.2	21	31
Bobby Jones	4.42	12-8	31	195.2	46	116
Robert Person*	4.52	4-5	27	89.2	35	76
Doug Henry	4.68	2-8	58	75.0	36	58
Jason Isringhausen	4.77	6-14	27	171.2	73	114
Paul Wilson*	5.38	5-12	26	149.0	71	109

Saves: Franco (28); Henry (9); Wallace (3); Mlicki (1). **Complete games:** B. Jones (3); Clark, Harnisch and Isringhausen (2); Wilson (1). **Shutouts:** Harnisch, Isringhausen and B. Jones (1).

Philadelphia Phillies

Batting (135 AB)	Avg	AB	R	H	HR	RBI	SB
Jim Eisenreich	.361	338	45	122	3	41	11
Gregg Jefferies	.292	404	59	118	7	51	20
Ricky Otero*	.273	411	54	112	2	32	16
Todd Zeile	.268	500	61	134	20	80	1
Benito Santiago	.264	481	71	127	30	85	2
Kevin Stocker	.254	394	46	100	5	41	6
Mike Lieberthal	.253	166	21	42	7	23	0
Mickey Morandini	.250	539	64	135	3	32	26
Pete Incaviglia	.234	269	33	63	16	42	2
Wendell Magee*	.204	142	9	29	2	14	0

Traded: P Mulholland to Sea.for IF Desi Relaford (July 31); OF Incaviglia and IF Zeile to Bal. for two PTBN (Aug. 30).
Signed: Free agent P Parrett (Aug. 7).

Pitching (40 IP)	ERA	W-L	Gm	IP	BB	SO
Ken Ryan	2.43	3-5	62	89.0	45	70
Curt Schilling	3.19	9-10	26	183.1	50	182
Ricky Bottalico	3.19	4-5	61	67.2	23	74
Jeff Parrett	3.39	3-3	51	66.1	31	64
Sid Fernandez	3.43	3-6	11	63.0	26	77
Mike Grace	3.49	7-2	12	80.0	16	49
Toby Borland	4.07	7-3	69	90.2	43	76
Russ Springer	4.66	3-10	51	96.2	38	94
Terry Mulholland	4.66	8-7	21	133.1	21	52
Mike Williams	5.44	6-14	32	167.0	67	103
Michael Mimbs	5.53	3-9	21	99.1	41	56
Rich Hunter*	6.49	3-7	14	69.1	33	32
Matt Beech*	6.97	1-4	8	41.1	11	33

Saves: Bottalico (34); Ryan (8). **Complete games:** Schilling (8); Mulholland (3); Grace (1). **Shutouts:** Schilling (2); Grace (1).

Pittsburgh Pirates

Batting (135 AB)	Avg	AB	R	H	HR	RBI	SB
Al Martin	.300	630	101	189	18	72	38
Jason Kendall*	.300	414	54	124	3	42	5
Keith Osik*	.293	140	18	41	1	14	1
Orlando Merced	.287	453	69	130	17	80	8
Carlos Garcia	.285	390	66	111	6	44	16
Mark Johnson	.274	343	55	94	13	47	6
Jeff King	.271	591	91	160	30	111	15
Nelson Liriano	.267	217	23	58	3	30	2
Jermaine Allensworth*	.262	229	32	60	4	31	11
John Wehner	.259	139	19	36	2	13	1
Jay Bell	.250	527	65	132	13	71	6
Charlie Hayes	.248	459	51	114	10	62	6
Mike Kingery	.246	276	32	68	3	27	2

Acquired: P Schmidt and two minor leaguers from Atl. for P Denny Neagle (Aug. 28).
Traded: IF Hayes to NYY for PTBN (Aug. 30).

Pitching (40 IP)	ERA	W-L	Gm	IP	BB	SO
Marc Wilkins*	3.84	4-3	47	75.0	36	62
Jon Lieber	3.99	9-5	51	142.0	28	94
Francisco Cordova*	4.09	4-7	59	99.0	20	95
Dan Plesac	4.09	6-5	73	70.1	24	76
Matt Ruebel*	4.60	1-1	26	58.2	25	22
Esteban Loaiza	4.96	2-3	10	52.2	19	32
Zane Smith	5.08	4-6	16	83.1	21	47
Ramon Morel*	5.36	2-1	29	42.0	19	22
Paul Wagner	5.40	4-8	16	81.2	39	81
Chris Peters*	5.63	2-4	16	64.0	25	28
Jason Schmidt*	5.70	5-6	19	96.1	53	74
Dan Miceli	5.78	2-10	44	85.2	45	66
John Ericks	5.79	4-5	28	46.2	19	46
Jason Christiansen	6.70	3-3	33	44.1	19	38

Saves: Cordova (12); Plesac (11); Boever (2); Lieber, Miceli, Ruebel and Wilkins (1). **Complete games:** Loaiza, Schmidt, Smith and Wagner (1). **Shutouts:** Loaiza and Smith (1).

St. Louis Cardinals

Batting (135 AB)	Avg	AB	R	H	HR	RBI	SB
Brian Jordan	.310	513	82	159	17	104	22
Willie McGee	.307	309	52	95	5	41	5
John Mabry	.297	543	63	161	13	74	3
Ozzie Smith	.282	227	36	64	2	18	7
Royce Clayton	.277	491	64	136	6	35	33
Ray Lankford	.275	545	100	150	21	86	35
Gary Gaetti	.274	522	71	143	23	80	2
Tom Pagnozzi	.270	407	48	110	13	55	4
Mark Sweeney*	.265	170	32	45	3	22	3
Luis Alicea	.258	380	54	98	5	42	11
Ron Gant	.246	419	74	103	30	82	13
Danny Sheaffer	.227	198	10	45	2	20	3
David Bell	.214	145	12	31	1	9	1
Mike Gallego	.210	143	12	30	0	4	0

Pitching (35 IP)	ERA	W-L	Gm	IP	BB	SO
Tony Fossas	2.68	0-4	65	47.0	21	36
Rick Honeycutt	2.85	2-1	61	47.1	7	30
Cory Bailey*	3.00	5-2	51	57.0	30	38
T.J. Mathews*	3.01	2-6	67	83.2	32	80
Dennis Eckersley	3.30	0-6	63	60.0	6	49
Donovan Osborne	3.53	13-9	30	198.2	57	134
Mark Petkovsek	3.55	11-2	48	88.2	35	45
Andy Benes	3.83	18-10	36	230.1	77	160
Todd Stottlemyre	3.87	14-11	34	223.1	93	194
Danny Jackson	4.46	1-1	13	36.1	16	27
Alan Benes*	4.90	13-10	34	191.0	87	131

Saves: Eckersley (30); Mathews (6); Honeycutt (4); Fossas (2); An. Benes (1). **Complete games:** Stottlemyre (5); Al. Benes and An. Benes (3); Osborne (2). **Shutouts:** Stottlemyre (2); Al. Benes, An. Benes and Osborne (1).

San Diego Padres

Batting (135 AB)	Avg	AB	R	H	HR	RBI	SB
Tony Gwynn	.353	451	67	159	3	50	11
Ken Caminiti	.326	546	109	178	40	130	11
John Flaherty	.303	264	22	80	9	41	2
Steve Finley	.298	655	126	195	30	95	22
Scott Livingstone	.297	172	20	51	2	20	0
Archi Cianfrocco	.281	192	21	54	2	32	1
Wally Joyner	.277	433	59	120	8	65	5
Brian Johnson	.272	243	18	66	8	35	0
Chris Gomez	.262	328	32	86	3	29	2
Marc Newfield	.251	191	27	48	5	26	1
Jody Reed	.244	495	45	121	2	49	2
Rickey Henderson	.241	465	110	112	9	29	37
Greg Vaughn	.206	141	20	29	10	22	4
Brad Ausmus	.181	149	16	27	1	13	1
Luis Lopez	.180	139	10	25	2	11	0

Acquired: IF Gomez and C Flaherty from Det. for IF Andujar Cedeno and C Ausmus (June 18); OF Vaughn and OF Gerald Parent from Mil. for OF Newfield, P Florie and P Ron Villone (July 31).

Pitching (40 IP)	ERA	W-L	Gm	IP	BB	SO
Trevor Hoffman	2.25	9-5	70	88.0	31	111
Doug Bochtler	3.02	2-4	63	65.2	39	68
Tim Worrell	3.05	9-7	50	121.0	39	99
Andy Ashby	3.23	9-5	24	150.2	34	85
Scott Sanders	3.38	9-5	46	144.0	48	157
Fernando Valenzuela	3.62	13-8	33	171.2	67	95
Bryce Florie	4.01	2-2	39	49.1	27	51
Joey Hamilton	4.17	15-9	34	211.2	83	184
Bob Tewksbury	4.31	10-10	36	206.2	43	126
Sean Bergman	4.37	6-8	41	113.1	33	85
Willie Blair	4.60	2-6	60	88.0	29	67

Saves: Hoffman (42); Bochtler (3); Blair and Worrell (1). **Complete games:** Hamilton (3); Ashby and Tewksbury (1). **Shutouts:** Hamilton (1).

San Francisco Giants

Batting (135 AB)	Avg	AB	R	H	HR	RBI	SB
Bill Mueller*	.330	200	31	66	0	19	0
Barry Bonds	.308	517	122	159	42	129	40
Matt Williams	.302	404	69	122	22	85	1
Shawon Dunston	.300	287	27	86	5	25	8
Glenallen Hill	.280	379	56	106	19	67	6
Stan Javier	.270	274	44	74	2	22	14
Mark Carreon	.260	292	40	76	9	51	2
Marvin Benard*	.248	488	89	121	5	27	25
Rick Wilkins	.243	411	53	100	14	59	0
Rich Aurilia	.239	318	27	76	3	26	4
Tom Lampkin	.232	177	26	41	6	29	1
Steve Scarsone	.219	283	28	62	5	23	2
Dave McCarty	.217	175	16	38	6	24	2
Robby Thompson	.211	227	35	48	5	21	2

Traded: IF Carreon to Cle. for P Jim Poole And PTBN (July 10).
Acquired: C Wilkins from Hou. for C Kirt Manwaring (July 26); P Reuter and P Scott from Mon. for P Mark Leiter (July 30).
Signed: Free agent P Gardner (March 31)..

Pitching (40 IP)	ERA	W-L	Gm	IP	BB	SO
Rod Beck	3.34	0-9	63	62.0	10	48
Jose Bautista	3.36	3-4	37	69.2	15	28
Shawn Estes*	3.60	3-5	11	70.0	39	60
Kirk Rueter	3.97	6-8	20	102.0	27	46
Mark Dewey	4.21	6-3	78	83.1	41	57
Mark Gardner	4.42	12-7	30	179.1	57	145
Allen Watson	4.61	8-12	29	185.2	69	128
Osvaldo Fernandez*	4.61	7-13	30	171.2	57	106
Tim Scott	4.64	5-7	65	66.0	30	47
W. VanLandingham	5.40	9-14	32	181.2	78	97
Rich DeLucia	5.84	3-6	56	61.2	31	55
Steve Bourgeois*	6.30	1-3	15	40.0	21	17
Doug Creek*	6.52	0-2	63	48.1	32	38

Saves: Beck (35); Scott (1). **Complete games:** Gardner (4); Fernandez and Watson (2). **Shutouts:** Gardner (1).

3,000 Hits

Minnesota Twins

Paul Molitor

Became the 21st player to reach the 3,000 hit plateau with a fifth-inning triple off Royals' Jose Rosado at Kansas City on Sept. 16...first player in history to reach 3,000 with a triple and first to accomplish the feat in a season where he also got 200 or more hits...Royals win game, 6-5.

500 HRs

Baltimore Orioles

Eddie Murray

Became the 15th player to hit 500 home runs with a seventh-inning blast to right field off Detroit's Felipe Lira on Sept. 6 in Baltimore...joined Hank Aaron and Willie Mays as only players to have 3,000 hits and 500 HRs...hit no. 500 while batting from left side of the plate...Tigers win game, 5-4.

20-20

Boston Red Sox

Roger Clemens

Tied his own major league record by striking out 20 batters in one game in a 4-0 win over the Detroit Tigers at Fenway Park on Sept. 18...the five-hitter was his 67th career game with 10 or more strike-outs...similar to his record-setting performance 10 years earlier, he did not walk a batter.

40-40

S. F. Giants

Barry Bonds

Stole second base in the third inning of a 9-3 win at Colorado on Sept. 27 to become the second player in history to steal 40 bases and hit 40 home runs in one season...hit his 40th homer 11 days earlier off San Diego's Scott Sanders...finished the season with 42 homers and 40 steals.

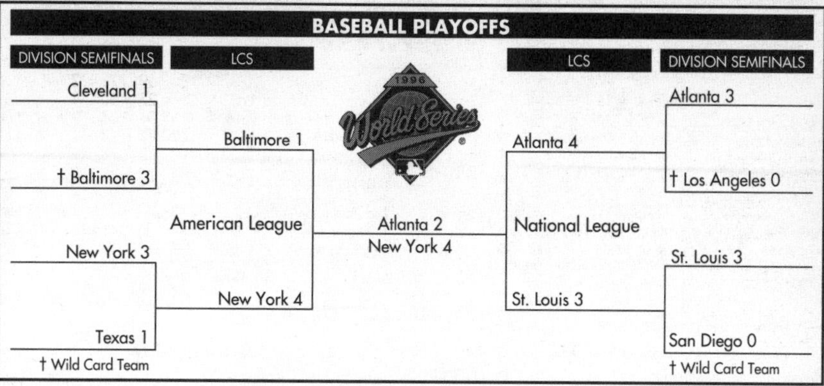

Divisional Series Summaries

AMERICAN LEAGUE

Yankees, 3-1

Date	Winner	Home Field
Oct. 1	Rangers, 6-2	at New York
Oct. 2	Yankees, 5-4 (12 inn.)	at New York
Oct. 4	Yankees, 3-2	at Texas
Oct. 5	Yankees, 6-4	at Texas

Game 1

Tuesday, Oct. 1, at New York

	1	2	3	4	5	6	7	8	9	R	H	E
Texas	0	0	0	5	0	1	0	0	0	–6	8	0
New York	1	0	0	1	0	0	0	0	0	–2	10	0

Win: Burkett, Tex. (1-0). **Loss:** Cone, N.Y. (0-1).
2B: Texas— Elster; New York— Martinez 2, Boggs. **HR:** Texas— Gonzalez (1), Palmer (1). **RBI:** Texas— Gonzalez 3, Palmer 2, Mclemore; New York— Williams, Duncan.
Attendance: 57,205. **Time:** 2:50.

Game 2

Wednesday, Oct. 2, at New York

	1	2	3	4	5	6	7	8	9	0	1	2	R	H	E
Texas	0	1	3	0	0	0	0	0	0	0	0	0	–4	8	1
New York	0	1	0	1	0	0	1	1	0	0	0	1	–5	8	0

Win: Boehringer, N.Y. (1-0). **Loss:** Stanton, Tex. (0-1).
2B: Texas— Elster; New York— Jeter. **HR:** Texas— Gonzalez 2 (3); New York— Fielder (1). **RBI:** Texas— Gonzalez 4; New York— Fielder 2, Hayes, Leyritz.
Attendance: 57,156. **Time:** 4:25.

Game 3

Friday, Oct. 4, at Texas

	1	2	3	4	5	6	7	8	9	R	H	E
New York	1	0	0	0	0	0	0	0	2	–3	7	1
Texas	0	0	0	1	1	0	0	0	0	–2	6	1

Win: Nelson, N.Y. (1-0). **Loss:** Oliver, Tex. (0-1). **Save:** Wetteland, N.Y. (1).
2B: Texas— Rodriguez. **HR:** New York— Williams (1); Texas— Gonzalez (4). **RBI:** New York— Williams 2, Duncan; Texas— Gonzalez, Rodriguez. **SB:** Texas— Elster (1).
Attendance: 50,860. **Time:** 3:09.

Game 4

Saturday, Oct. 5, at Texas

	1	2	3	4	5	6	7	8	9	R	H	E
New York	0	0	0	3	1	0	1	0	1	–6	12	1
Texas	0	2	2	0	0	0	0	0	0	–4	9	0

Win: Weathers, N.Y. (1-0). **Loss:** Pavlik, Tex. (0-1). **Save:** Wetteland, N.Y. (2).
2B: Texas— Palmer. **HR:** New York— Williams 2 (3); Texas— Gonzalez (5). **RBI:** New York— Fielder 2, Williams 2, Duncan, Jeter; Texas— Tettleton, Gonzalez, Rodriguez, Mclemore. **SB:** New York— Williams (1).
Attendance: 50,066. **Time:** 3:57.

Orioles, 3-1

Date	Winner	Home Field
Oct. 1	Orioles, 10-4	at Baltimore
Oct. 2	Orioles, 7-4	at Baltimore
Oct. 4	Indians, 9-4	at Cleveland
Oct. 5	Orioles, 4-3 (12 inn.)	at Cleveland

Game 1

Tuesday, Oct. 1, at Baltimore

	1	2	3	4	5	6	7	8	9	R	H	E
Cleveland	0	1	0	2	0	0	1	0	0	–4	10	0
Baltimore	1	1	2	0	0	5	1	0	x	–10	12	1

Win: Wells, Bal. (1-0). **Loss:** Nagy, Cle. (0-1).
2B: Cleveland— Kent, Vizquel; Baltimore— Palmeiro, Ripken. **HR:** Cleveland— Ramirez (1); Baltimore— Surhoff 2 (2), Anderson (1), Bonilla (1). **RBI:** Cleveland— S. Alomar, Lofton, Ramirez, Vizquel; Baltimore— Bonilla 4, Surhoff 2, R. Alomar, Anderson, Palmeiro, Ripken. **SB:**Cleveland— Vizquel (1).
Attendance: 47,644. **Time:** 3:25.

Game 2

Wednesday, Oct. 2, at Baltimore

	1	2	3	4	5	6	7	8	9	R	H	E
Cleveland	0	0	0	0	0	3	0	1	0	–4	8	2
Baltimore	1	0	0	0	3	0	0	3	x	–7	9	0

Win: Benitez, Bal. (1-0). **Loss:** Plunk, Cle. (0-1). **Save:** Myers, Bal. (1).
2B: Cleveland— Seitzer; Baltimore— Murray, Ripken. **HR:** Cleveland— Belle (1); Baltimore— Anderson (2). **RBI:** Cleveland— Belle 2, Franco, Seitzer; Baltimore— Anderson 2, R. Alomar, Murray, Ripken. **SB:** Cleveland— Lofton 2 (2), Vizquel (2).
Attendance: 48,970. **Time:** 3:27.

Baseball Playoffs (Cont.)

NATIONAL LEAGUE

Game 3

Friday, Oct. 4, at Cleveland

	1	2	3	4	5	6	7	8	9	R	H	E
Baltimore	0	1	0	3	0	0	0	0	0	4	8	2
Cleveland	1	2	0	1	0	0	4	1	x	9	10	0

Win: Assenmacher, Cle. (1-0). **Loss:** Orosco, Bal. (0-1).
2B: Cleveland— Vizcaino 2. **HR:** Baltimore— Surhoff (3); Cleveland— Belle (2), Ramirez (2). **RBI:** Baltimore— Surhoff 3, Anderson; Cleveland— Belle 4, Seitzer 3, Ramirez, Vizcaino. **SB:** Baltimore— Murray (1); Cleveland— Lofton 3 (5), Belle (1), Vizquel (3).
Attendance: 44,250. **Time:** 3:44.

Game 4

Saturday, Oct. 5, at Cleveland

	1	2	3	4	5	6	7	8	9	0	1	2	R	H	E
Baltimore	0	2	0	0	0	0	0	0	1	0	0	1	4	14	1
Cleveland	0	0	0	2	1	0	0	0	0	0	0	0	3	7	1

Win: Benitez, Bal. (2-0). **Loss:** Mesa, Cle. (0-1). **Save:** Myers, Bal. (2).
2B: Baltimore— Ripken, Zeile; Cleveland— Ramirez 2. **HR:** Baltimore— R. Alomar (1), Bonilla (2), Palmeiro (1). **RBI:** Baltimore— R. Alomar 2, Bonilla, Palmeiro; Cleveland— S. Alomar 2, Vizquel. **SB:** Cleveland— Seitzer (1), Vizquel (4).
Attendance: 44,280. **Time:** 4:41.

NATIONAL LEAGUE

Cardinals, 3-0

Date	Winner	Home Field
Oct. 1	Cardinals, 3-1	at St. Louis
Oct. 3	Cardinals, 5-4	at St. Louis
Oct. 5	Cardinals, 7-5	at San Diego

Game 1

Tuesday, Oct. 1, at St. Louis

	1	2	3	4	5	6	7	8	9	R	H	E
San Diego	0	0	0	0	0	1	0	0	0	1	8	1
St. Louis	3	0	0	0	0	0	0	0	x	3	6	0

Win: Stottlemyre, St.L. (1-0). **Loss:** Hamilton, S.D. (0-1). **Save:** Eckersley, St.L. (1).
2B: San Diego— T. Gwynn; St. Louis— Alicea 2. **HR:** San Diego— Henderson (1); St. Louis— Gaetti (1). **RBI:** San Diego— Henderson; St. Louis— Gaetti 3. **SB:**San Diego— T. Gwynn (1), Finley (1); St. Louis— Gant 2 (2).
Attendance: 54,193. **Time:** 2:39.

Game 2

Thursday, Oct. 3, at St. Louis

	1	2	3	4	5	6	7	8	9	R	H	E
San Diego	0	0	0	0	1	2	0	1	0	4	6	0
St. Louis	0	0	1	0	3	0	0	1	x	5	5	1

Win: Honeycutt, St.L. (1-0). **Loss:** Bochtler, S.D. (0-1). **Save:** Eckersley, St.L. (2).
2B: St. Louis— Gant. **HR:** San Diego— Caminiti (1). **RBI:** San Diego— Caminiti, Finley, T. Gwynn; St. Louis— Gant 3, McGee, Pagnozzi.
Attendance: 56,752. **Time:** 2:55.

Game 3

Saturday, Oct. 5, at San Diego

	1	2	3	4	5	6	7	8	9	R	H	E
St. Louis	1	0	0	0	0	3	1	0	2	7	13	1
San Diego	0	2	1	1	0	0	0	1	0	5	11	2

Win: Matthews, St.L. (1-0). **Loss:** Hoffman, S.D. (0-1). **Save:** Eckersley, St.L. (3).
2B: San Diego— Johnson, Reed. **3B:** St. Louis— Mabry. **HR:** St. Louis— Gant (1), Jordan (1); San Diego— Caminiti 2 (3). **RBI:** St. Louis— Jordan 3, Gant, Mabry, Pagnozzi; San Diego— Caminiti 2, Reed 2, Gomez. **SB:** St. Louis— Jordan (1).
Attendance: 53,899. **Time:** 3:32.

Playoff Series

The AL and NL League Championship Series began in 1969 with a Best of 5 format, then changed to Best of 7 in 1985. The '95 season was the first year for wild card teams and the new Best of 3 Divisional Series.

Braves, 3-0

Date	Winner	Home Field
Oct. 2	Braves, 2-1 (10 inn.)	at Los Angeles
Oct. 3	Braves, 3-2	at Los Angeles
Oct. 5	Braves, 5-2	at Atlanta

Game 1

Wednesday, Oct. 2, at Los Angeles

	1	2	3	4	5	6	7	8	9	10	R	H	E
Atlanta	0	0	0	1	0	0	0	0	0	1	2	4	1
Los Angeles	0	0	0	0	1	0	0	0	0	0	1	5	0

Win: Smoltz, Atl. (1-0). **Loss:** Osuna, L.A. (0-1). **Save:** Wohlers, Atl. (1).
2B: Los Angeles— Hollandsworth, Gagne. **HR:** Atlanta— Lopez (1). **RBI:**Atlanta— McGriff, Lopez; Los Angeles— Hollandsworth.
SB: Atlanta— Grissom (1), Klesko (1).
Attendance: 47,428. **Time:** 3:08.

Game 2

Thursday, Oct. 3, at Los Angeles

	1	2	3	4	5	6	7	8	9	R	H	E
Atlanta	0	1	0	0	0	0	2	0	0	3	5	2
Los Angeles	1	0	0	1	0	0	0	0	0	2	3	0

Win: Maddux, Atl. (1-0). **Loss:** Valdes, L.A. (0-1). **Save:** Wohlers, Atl. (2).
2B: Los Angeles— Mondesi. **HR:** Atlanta— Klesko (1), McGriff (1), Dye (1). **RBI:** Atlanta— Klesko, McGriff, Dye; Los Angeles— Piazza, Mondesi.
Attendance: 51,916. **Time:** 2:08.

Game 3

Saturday, Oct. 5, at Atlanta

	1	2	3	4	5	6	7	8	9	R	H	E
Los Angeles	0	0	0	0	0	0	1	1	0	2	6	1
Atlanta	1	0	0	4	0	0	0	0	x	5	7	0

Win: Glavine, Atl. (1-0). **Loss:** Nomo, L.A. (0-1). **Save:** Wohlers, Atl. (3).
2B: Los Angeles— Hollandsworth 2, Mondesi, Castro; Atlanta— McGriff, Glavine, Lemke. **HR:** Atlanta— C. Jones (1). **RBI:** Los Angeles— Castro, Piazza; Atlanta— Lemke 2, C. Jones 2, McGriff.
SB: Atlanta— C. Jones (1), Dye (1), Lopez (1).
Attendance: 52,529. **Time:** 3:19.

American League Championship Series

Yankees, 4-1

Date	Winner	Home Field
Oct. 9	Yankees, 5-4 (11 inn.)	at New York
Oct. 10	Orioles, 5-3	at New York
Oct. 11	Yankees, 5-2	at Baltimore
Oct. 12	Yankees, 8-4	at Baltimore
Oct. 13	Yankees, 6-4	at Baltimore

Game 1

Wednesday, Oct. 9, at New York

	1	2	3	4	5	6	7	8	9	10	11	R	H	E
Baltimore	0	1	1	1	0	1	0	0	0	0	0	4	11	1
New York	1	1	0	0	0	0	1	1	0	0	1	5	11	0

Win: M. Rivera, N.Y. (1-0). **Loss:** Myers, Bal. (0-1).
2B: Baltimore— C. Ripken, Anderson; New York— Raines, Williams. **HR:** Baltimore— Anderson (3), Palmeiro (2); New York— Jeter (1), Williams (4). **RBI:** Baltimore— Anderson, Murray, Palmeiro, Surhoff; New York— Williams 2, Leyritz, Strawberry, Jeter. **SB:** New York— Jeter (1).
Attendance: 56,495. **Time:** 4:23.

Game 2

Thursday, Oct. 10, at New York

	1	2	3	4	5	6	7	8	9	R	H	E
Baltimore	0	0	2	0	0	0	2	1	0	5	10	0
New York	2	0	0	0	0	0	1	0	0	3	11	1

Win: Wells, Bal. (2-0). **Loss:** Nelson, N.Y. (0-1). **Save:** Benitez, Bal. (1).
2B: Baltimore— Alomar; New York— Duncan. **3B:** New York— Girardi. **HR:** Baltimore— Zeile (1), Palmeiro (3). **RBI:** Baltimore— Zeile 2, Palmeiro 2, Alomar; New York— Williams, Fielder.
Attendance: 56,432. **Time:** 4:13.

Game 3

Friday, Oct. 11, at Baltimore

	1	2	3	4	5	6	7	8	9	R	H	E
New York	0	0	0	1	0	0	0	4	0	5	8	0
Baltimore	2	0	0	0	0	0	0	0	0	2	3	2

Win: Key, N.Y. (1-0). **Loss:** Mussina, Bal. (0-1). **Save:** Wetteland, N.Y. (3).
2B: New York— Jeter, Martinez. **HR:** New York— Fielder (2); Baltimore— Zeile (2). **RBI:** New York— Fielder 3, Williams; Baltimore— Zeile 2.
Attendance: 48,635. **Time:** 2:50.

Most Valuable Player

Bernie Williams, New York, CF

Avg	AB	R	H	HR	RBI	BB	SO
.474	19	6	9	2	6	5	4

Game 4

Saturday, Oct. 12, at Baltimore

	1	2	3	4	5	6	7	8	9	R	H	E
New York	2	1	0	2	0	0	0	3	0	8	9	0
Baltimore	1	0	1	2	0	0	0	0	0	4	11	0

Win: Weathers, N.Y. (2-0). **Loss:** Coppinger, Bal. (0-1).
2B: New York— Jeter, Duncan, Williams; Baltimore— Alomar. **HR:** New York— Strawberry 2 (2), Williams (5), O'Neill (1); Baltimore— Hoiles (1). **RBI:** New York— Stawberry 3, Williams 2, O'Neill 2, Fielder; Baltimore— Hoiles 2, Surhoff, Palmeiro.
Attendance: 48,974. **Time:** 3:45.

Game 5

Sunday, Oct. 13, at Baltimore

	1	2	3	4	5	6	7	8	9	R	H	E
New York	0	0	6	0	0	0	0	0	0	6	11	0
Baltimore	0	0	0	0	0	1	0	1	2	4	4	1

Win: Pettitte, N.Y. (1-0). **Loss:** Erickson, Bal. (0-1).
2B: New York— Williams. **HR:** New York— Leyritz (1), Fielder (3), Strawberry (3); Baltimore— Zeile (3), Bonilla (3), Murray (1).
RBI: New York— Fielder 3, Stawberry, Leyritz; Baltimore— Bonilla 2, Zeile, Murray. **SB:** New York— Jeter (2), Williams (2).
Attendance: 48,718. **Time:** 2:57.

ALCS Composite Box Score

New York Yankees

Batting	LCS vs. Baltimore Avg	AB	R	H	HR	RBI	BB	SO	Overall AL Playoffs Avg	AB	R	H	HR	RBI	BB	SO
Bernie Williams, cf	.474	19	6	9	2	6	5	4	.471	34	11	16	5	11	7	5
Derek Jeter, ss	.417	24	5	10	1	1	0	5	.415	41	7	17	1	2	0	7
Darryl Strawberry, rf-lf	.417	12	4	5	3	5	2	2	.294	17	4	5	3	5	2	4
Paul O'Neill, rf	.273	11	1	3	1	2	3	2	.192	26	1	5	1	2	3	4
Tim Raines, lf	.267	15	2	4	0	0	1	1	.258	31	5	8	0	0	4	2
Joe Girardi, c	.250	12	1	3	0	0	1	3	.238	21	2	5	0	0	5	4
Jim Leyritz, c-ph-rf	.250	8	1	2	1	2	1	4	.182	11	1	2	1	3	1	5
Mariano Duncan, 2b	.200	15	0	3	0	0	0	3	.258	31	0	8	0	3	0	7
Luis Sojo, 2b	.200	5	0	1	0	0	0	1	.200	5	0	1	0	0	0	1
Tino Martinez, 1b	.182	22	3	4	0	0	0	2	.216	37	6	8	0	0	3	3
Cecil Fielder, dh	.167	18	3	3	2	8	4	5	.241	29	5	7	3	12	5	7
Charlie Hayes, ph-3b	.143	7	0	1	0	0	2	2	.167	12	0	2	0	1	2	2
Wade Boggs, 3b	.133	15	1	2	0	0	1	3	.111	27	1	3	0	0	1	5
TOTALS	.273	183	27	50	10	24	20	37	.269	323	43	87	14	39	33	57

ALCS Composite Box Score (Cont.)

New York Yankees

Pitching	ERA	W-L	SV	Gm	IP	H	BB	SO	ERA	W-L	Sv	Gm	IP	H	BB	SO
Mariano Rivera	0.00	1-0	0	2	4.0	6	1	5	0.00	1-0	0	4	8.2	6	2	6
Graeme Lloyd	0.00	0-0	0	2	1.2	0	0	1	0.00	0-0	0	4	2.2	1	0	1
David Weathers	0.00	1-0	0	2	3.0	3	0	0	0.00	2-0	0	4	8.0	4	0	5
Jimmy Key	2.25	1-0	0	1	8.0	3	1	5	2.77	1-0	0	2	13.0	8	2	8
David Cone	3.00	0-0	0	1	6.0	5	5	5	6.00	0-1	0	2	12.0	13	7	13
Andy Pettitte	3.60	1-0	0	2	15.0	10	5	7	4.22	1-0	0	3	21.1	14	11	10
John Wetteland	4.50	0-0	1	4	4.0	2	1	5	2.25	0-0	3	7	8.0	4	5	9
Jeff Nelson	11.57	0-1	0	2	2.1	5	0	2	4.50	1-1	0	4	6.0	7	2	7
Kenny Rogers	12.00	0-0	0	1	3.0	5	2	3	10.80	0-0	0	3	5.0	10	4	4
Brian Boehringer	—	—	—	—	—	—	—	—	6.75	1-0	0	2	1.1	3	2	0
TOTALS	3.64	4-1	1	5	47.0	39	15	33	3.56	7-2	3	9	86.0	70	35	63

Wild Pitches— LCS (Cone, Rogers); OVERALL (Cone, Pettitte, Rogers). **Hit Batters**— LCS (none); OVERALL (none).

Baltimore Orioles

	LCS vs New York								Overall AL Playoffs							
Batting	Avg	AB	R	H	HR	RBI	BB	SO	Avg	AB	R	H	HR	RBI	BB	SO
Pete Incaviglia, dh	.500	2	1	1	0	0	0	0	.286	7	2	2	0	0	0	4
Todd Zeile, 3b	.364	22	3	8	3	5	2	1	.317	41	5	13	3	5	4	6
Eddie Murray, dh-ph	.267	15	1	4	1	2	2	2	.333	30	2	10	1	3	5	6
B.J. Surhoff, lf-ph	.267	15	0	4	0	2	1	2	.321	28	3	9	3	7	1	3
Cal Ripken, ss	.250	20	1	5	0	0	1	4	.342	38	3	13	0	2	1	7
Rafael Palmeiro, 1b	.235	17	4	4	2	4	4	4	.206	34	8	7	3	6	5	10
Roberto Alomar, 2b	.217	23	2	5	0	1	0	4	.250	40	4	10	1	5	2	7
Brady Anderson, cf	.190	21	5	4	1	1	3	5	.237	38	8	9	3	5	5	8
Chris Hoiles, c	.167	12	1	2	1	2	1	3	.158	19	2	3	1	2	4	6
Mark Parent, c	.167	6	0	1	0	0	0	2	.182	11	0	2	0	0	0	4
Bobby Bonilla, rf	.050	20	1	1	1	2	1	4	.114	35	5	4	3	7	5	10
Tony Tarasco, rf	.000	1	0	0	0	0	0	1	.000	1	0	0	0	0	0	1
Mike Devereaux, lf	.000	2	0	0	0	0	0	1	.000	3	0	0	0	0	0	1
Manny Alexander, pr	—	—	—	—	—	—	—	—	.000	0	2	0	0	0	0	0
TOTALS	.222	176	19	39	9	19	15	33	.252	325	44	82	18	42	32	73

Pitching	ERA	W-L	Sv	Gm	IP	H	BB	SO	ERA	W-L	Sv	Gm	IP	H	BB	SO
Terry Mathews	0.00	0-0	0	3	2.1	0	2	3	0.00	0-0	0	6	5.0	3	3	5
Arthur Rhodes	0.00	0-0	0	3	2	2	0	2	3.00	0-0	0	5	3.0	3	1	3
Randy Myers	2.25	0-1	0	3	4	4	3	2	1.29	0-1	2	6	7.0	4	3	5
Scott Erickson	2.38	0-1	0	2	11.1	14	4	8	3.00	0-1	0	3	18.0	20	6	14
Alan Mills	3.86	0-0	0	3	2.1	3	1	3	3.86	0-0	0	3	2.1	3	1	3
David Wells	4.05	1-0	0	1	6.2	8	3	6	4.43	2-0	0	3	20.1	23	7	12
Jesse Orosco	4.50	0-0	0	4	2	2	1	2	15.00	0-1	0	8	3.0	4	4	4
Mike Mussina	5.87	0-1	0	1	7.2	8	2	6	5.27	0-1	0	2	13.2	15	4	12
Armando Benitez	7.71	0-0	1	3	2.1	3	3	2	4.26	2-0	1	6	6.1	4	5	8
Rocky Coppinger	8.44	0-1	0	1	5.1	6	1	3	8.44	0-1	0	1	5.1	6	1	3
TOTALS	4.11	1-4	1	5	46	50	20	37	4.29	4-5	3	9	84.0	85	35	69

Wild Pitches— LCS (Rhodes); OVERALL (Mattews, Rhodes). **Hit Batters**— LCS (Matthews, Wells); OVERALL (Matthews, Orosco, Wells).

Score by Innings

	1	2	3	4	5	6	7	8	9	10	11	R	H	E
Baltimore	3	1	4	3	0	2	2	2	2	0	0	–19	39	4
New York	5	2	6	3	0	0	2	8	0	0	1	–27	50	1

DP: Baltimore 7; New York 2. **LOB:** Baltimore 34, New York 40. **2B:** Baltimore— Alomar (2), Anderson, C. Ripken; New York— Williams (3), Jeter (2), Duncan (2), Martinez, Raines. **3B:** New York— Girardi. **SB:** New York— Jeter (2), Williams. **SF:** Baltimore— Alomar, Palmeiro, Surhoff.

Umpires: Larry Barnett, Dale Scott, Mike Reilly, Dan Morrison, Rocky Roe, Rich Garcia. **Ejections:** Davey Johnson (by Garcia), Game 1— 8th inn.

National League Championship Series

Braves, 4-3

Date	Winner	Home Field
Oct. 9	Braves, 4-2	at Atlanta
Oct. 10	Cardinals, 8-3	at Atlanta
Oct. 12	Cardinals, 3-2	at St. Louis
Oct. 13	Cardinals, 4-3	at St. Louis
Oct. 14	Braves, 14-0	at St. Louis
Oct. 16	Braves, 3-1	at Atlanta
Oct. 17	Braves, 15-0	at Atlanta

Game 1

Wednesday, Oct. 9, at Atlanta

	1	2	3	4	5	6	7	8	9	R	H	E
St. Louis	0	1	0	0	0	0	1	0	0	–2	5	1
Atlanta	0	0	0	0	2	0	0	2	x	–4	9	0

Win: Smoltz, Atl. (2-0). **Loss:** Petkovsek, St.L. (0-1). **Save:** Wohlers, Atl. (4).
2B: St. Louis— An. Benes; Atlanta— Grissom. **3B:** St. Louis— Jordan. **RBI:** St. Louis— Pagnozzi; Atlanta— Lemke 2, Lopez 2. **SB:** Atlanta— C. Jones (2).
Attendance: 48,686. **Time:** 2:35.

Game 2

Thursday, Oct. 10, at Atlanta

	1	2	3	4	5	6	7	8	9	R	H	E
St. Louis	1	0	2	0	0	0	5	0	0	–8	11	2
Atlanta	0	0	2	0	0	1	0	0	0	–3	5	2

Win: Stottlemyre, St.L. (2-0). **Loss:** Maddux, Atl. (0-1).
2B: St. Louis— Gant, Jordan, Pagnozzi. **HR:** St. Louis— Gaetti (2); Atlanta— Grissom (1). **RBI:** St. Louis— Gaetti 4, Gant, Jordan, Lankford; Atlanta— Grissom 2, Klesko. **SB:** St. Louis— Clayton (1); Atlanta— Grissom (2).
Attendance: 52,067. **Time:** 2:53.

Game 3

Saturday, Oct. 12, at St. Louis

	1	2	3	4	5	6	7	8	9	R	H	E
Atlanta	1	0	0	0	0	0	0	1	0	–2	8	1
St. Louis	2	0	0	0	0	1	0	0	x	–3	7	0

Win: Osborne, St.L. (1-0). **Loss:** Glavine, Atl. (1-1). **Save:** Eckersley, St.L. (4).
2B: Atlanta— Lopez. **HR:** St. Louis— Gant 2 (3). **RBI:** Atlanta— C. Jones, Dye; St. Louis— Gant 3.
Attendance: 56,769. **Time:** 2:46.

Game 4

Sunday, Oct. 13, at St. Louis

	1	2	3	4	5	6	7	8	9	R	H	E
Atlanta	0	1	0	0	0	2	0	0	0	–3	9	1
St. Louis	0	0	0	0	0	0	3	1	x	–4	5	0

Win: Eckersley, St.L. (1-0). **Loss:** McMichael, Atl. (0-1).
2B: Atlanta— C. Jones, Dye. **3B:** St. Louis— Young. **HR:** Atlanta— Klesko (2), Lemke (1); St. Louis— Jordan (2). **RBI:** Atlanta— Klesko, Lemke, Dye; St. Louis— Young 2, Clayton, Jordan.
Attendance: 56,764. **Time:** 3:17.

Game 5

Monday, Oct. 14, at St. Louis

	1	2	3	4	5	6	7	8	9	R	H	E
Atlanta	5	2	0	3	1	0	0	1	2	–14	22	0
St. Louis	0	0	0	0	0	0	0	0	0	–0	7	0

Win: Smoltz, Atl. (3-0). **Loss:** Stottlemyre, St.L. (2-1).
2B: Atlanta— Lopez 2, Lemke, C. Jones. **3B:** Atlanta— Blauser. **HR:** Atlanta— Lopez (2), McGriff (2). **RBI:** Atlanta— C. Jones 3, McGriff 3, Blauser 2, Grissom, Lemke, Klesko, Lopez, Belliard, Smoltz. **SB:** Atlanta— Grissom (3).
Attendance: 56,782. **Time:** 2:57.

Game 6

Wednesday, Oct. 16, at Atlanta

	1	2	3	4	5	6	7	8	9	R	H	E
St. Louis	0	0	0	0	0	0	0	1	0	–1	6	1
Atlanta	0	1	0	0	1	0	0	1	x	–3	7	0

Win: Maddux, Atl. (2-1). **Loss:** Al. Benes, St.L. (0-1). **Save:** Wohlers, Atl. (5).
2B: Atlanta— Lopez. **RBI:** Atlanta— Lemke, Dye, Belliard. **SB:**Atlanta— Lopez (2).
Attendance: 52,067. **Time:** 2:41.

Game 7

Thursday, Oct. 17, at Atlanta

	1	2	3	4	5	6	7	8	9	R	H	E
St. Louis	0	0	0	0	0	0	0	0	0	–0	4	2
Atlanta	6	0	0	4	0	3	2	0	x	–15	17	0

Win: Glavine, Atl. (2-1). **Loss:** Osborne, St.L. (1-1).
2B: Atlanta— Lemke, Lopez. **3B:** Atlanta— Glavine, McGriff. **HR:**Atlanta— Lopez (3), A. Jones (1), McGriff (3). **RBI:** Atlanta— McGriff 4, Lopez 3, A. Jones 3, Glavine 3, Dye 1. **SB:** Atlanta— Lopez (2).
Attendance: 52,067. **Time:** 2:25.

Most Valuable Player

Javy Lopez, Atlanta, C

Avg	AB	R	H	HR	RBI	BB	SO
.542	24	8	13	2	6	3	1

NLCS Composite Box Score

Atlanta Braves

Batting	LCS vs St. Louis Avg	AB	R	H	HR	RBI	BB	SO	Overall NL Playoffs Avg	AB	R	H	HR	RBI	BB	SO
Rafael Belliard, ss	.667	6	0	4	0	2	0	0	.667	6	0	4	0	2	0	0
Javy Lopez, c	.542	24	8	13	2	6	3	1	.484	31	9	15	3	7	4	1
Denny Neagle, p	.500	2	0	1	0	0	0	0	.500	2	0	1	0	0	0	0
Mark Lemke, 2b	.444	27	4	12	1	5	3	2	.359	39	5	14	1	7	4	3
Chipper Jones, 3b	.440	25	6	11	0	4	4	1	.382	34	8	13	1	6	6	5
Marquis Grissom, cf	.286	35	7	10	1	3	0	8	.234	47	9	11	1	3	1	10
John Smoltz, p	.286	7	1	2	0	1	0	3	.222	9	1	2	0	1	0	3
Ryan Klesko, lf	.250	16	1	4	1	3	2	6	.208	24	2	5	2	4	5	10
Mike Mordecai, 3b	.250	4	1	1	0	0	0	1	.250	4	1	1	0	0	0	1
Fred McGriff, 1b	.250	28	6	7	2	7	3	5	.270	37	7	10	3	10	5	6
Andruw Jones, lf	.222	9	3	2	1	3	3	2	.222	9	3	2	1	3	4	2
Jermaine Dye, rf	.214	28	2	6	0	4	1	7	.205	39	3	8	1	5	1	13
Jeff Blauser, ss	.176	17	5	3	0	2	4	6	.154	26	5	4	0	2	5	9
Tom Glavine, p	.167	6	0	1	0	3	0	3	.250	8	1	2	0	3	0	3
Eddie Perez, c	.000	1	0	0	0	0	1	0	.250	4	0	1	0	0	1	0
Mark Wohlers, p	.000	1	0	0	0	0	0	1	.000	1	0	0	0	0	0	1
Luis Polonia, ph	.000	3	0	0	0	0	0	0	.000	5	0	0	0	0	0	1
Greg Maddux, p	.000	4	0	0	0	0	0	2	.000	6	0	0	0	0	0	3
Terry Pendleton, ph	.000	6	0	0	0	0	1	3	.000	7	0	0	0	0	1	4
TOTALS	.309	249	44	77	8	43	25	51	.275	338	54	93	13	53	37	75

Pitching	LCS vs St. Louis ERA	W-L	Sv	Gm	IP	H	BB	SO	Overall NL Playoffs ERA	W-L	Sv	Gm	IP	H	BB	SO
Mark Wohlers	0.00	0-0	2	3	3.0	0	0	4	0.00	0-0	5	6	6.1	1	0	8
Mike Bielecki	0.00	0-0	0	3	3.0	0	1	5	0.00	0-0	0	4	3.2	0	2	6
Steve Avery	0.00	0-0	0	2	2.0	2	1	1	0.00	0-0	0	2	2.0	2	1	1
Brad Clontz	0.00	0-0	0	1	0.2	0	0	0	0.00	0-0	0	1	0.2	0	0	0
Terrell Wade	0.00	0-0	0	1	0.1	0	0	1	0.00	0-0	0	1	0.1	0	0	1
John Smoltz	1.20	2-0	0	2	15.0	12	3	12	1.13	3-0	0	3	24.0	16	5	19
Tom Glavine	2.08	1-1	0	2	13.0	10	0	9	1.83	2-1	0	3	19.2	15	3	16
Denny Neagle	2.35	0-0	0	2	7.2	2	3	8	2.35	0-0	0	2	7.2	2	3	8
Greg Maddux	2.51	1-1	0	2	14.1	15	2	10	1.69	2-1	0	3	21.1	18	2	17
Greg McMichael	9.00	0-1	0	3	2.0	4	1	3	8.10	0-1	0	5	3.1	5	2	6
TOTALS	1.92	4-3	2	6	61.0	45	11	53	1.62	7-3	5	10	89	59	18	82

Wild Pitches— LCS (Smoltx 2, Maddux, Wohlers); OVERALL (Smoltx 2, Maddux, Wohlers). **Hit Batters**— LCS (Glavine); OVERALL (Glavine).

St. Louis Cardinals

Batting	LCS vs Atlanta Avg	AB	R	H	HR	RBI	BB	SO	Overall NL Playoffs Avg	AB	R	H	HR	RBI	BB	SO
Royce Clayton, ss	.350	20	4	7	0	1	1	4	.346	26	5	9	0	1	4	5
Willie McGee, cf	.333	15	0	5	0	0	0	3	.240	25	1	6	0	1	1	6
Gary Gaetti, 3b	.292	24	1	7	1	4	1	5	.229	35	2	8	2	7	1	8
Dmitri Young, ph-1b	.286	7	1	2	0	2	0	2	.286	7	1	2	0	2	0	2
John Mabry, 1b	.261	23	1	6	0	0	0	6	.273	33	2	9	0	1	1	7
Andy Benes, p	.250	4	0	1	0	0	1	2	.250	6	1	2	0	0	1	3
Ron Gant, lf	.240	25	3	6	2	4	2	6	.286	35	6	10	3	8	4	6
Brian Jordan, rf	.240	25	3	6	1	2	1	3	.270	37	7	10	2	5	2	6
Tom Pagnozzi, c	.158	19	1	3	0	1	1	4	.200	30	1	6	0	3	2	7
Mike Gallego, 3b	.143	14	1	2	0	0	1	3	.133	15	1	2	0	0	1	4
Miguel Mejia, cf	.000	1	1	0	0	0	0	1	.000	1	1	0	0	0	0	1
Alan Benes, p	.000	1	0	0	0	0	0	1	.000	1	0	0	0	0	0	1
Danny Jackson, p	.000	1	0	0	0	0	0	1	.000	1	0	0	0	0	0	1
Todd Stottlemyre, p	.000	2	0	0	0	0	0	0	.000	4	0	0	0	0	0	2
Donovan Osborne, p	.000	3	0	0	0	0	0	3	.000	4	0	0	0	0	0	3
Danny Sheaffer, c	.000	3	0	0	0	0	0	1	.000	3	0	0	0	0	0	1
Mark Sweeney, rf	.000	4	1	0	0	0	0	2	.200	5	1	1	0	0	0	2
Luis Alicea, 2b	.000	8	0	0	0	0	2	1	.105	19	1	2	0	0	3	5
Ozzie Smith, ss	.000	9	0	0	0	0	0	1	.083	12	1	1	0	0	2	1
Ray Lankford, cf	.000	13	1	0	0	1	1	4	.067	15	2	1	0	1	2	4
Rick Honeycutt, p	—	—	—	—	—	—	—	—	.000	1	0	0	0	0	0	1
TOTALS	.204	221	18	45	4	15	11	53	.219	315	33	69	7	29	24	76

Pitching	ERA	W-L	Sv	Gm	IP	H	BB	SO	ERA	W-L	Sv	Gm	IP	H	BB	SO
Dennis Eckersley	0.00	1-0	1	3	3.1	2	0	4	0.00	1-0	4	6	7.0	5	0	6
T.J. Mathews	0.00	0-0	0	2	0.2	2	1	2	0.00	1-0	0	3	1.2	3	1	4
Tony Fossas	2.08	0-0	0	5	4.1	1	3	1	2.08	0-0	0	5	4.1	1	3	1
Alan Benes	2.84	0-1	0	2	6.1	3	2	5	2.84	0-1	0	2	6.1	3	2	5
Andy Benes	5.28	0-0	0	3	15.1	19	3	9	5.24	0-0	0	4	22.1	25	4	18
Mark Petkovsek	7.36	0-1	0	6	7.1	11	3	7	5.79	0-1	0	7	9.1	11	3	8
Rick Honeycutt	9.00	0-0	0	5	4.0	5	3	3	6.75	1-0	0	8	6.2	8	4	5
Danny Jackson	9.00	0-0	0	1	3.0	7	3	3	9.00	0-0	0	1	3.0	7	3	3
Donovan Osborne	9.39	1-1	0	2	7.2	12	4	6	9.26	1-1	0	3	11.2	19	4	11
Todd Stottlemyre	12.38	1-1	0	3	8.0	15	3	11	7.36	2-1	0	4	14.2	20	5	18
TOTALS	6.60	3-4	1	7	60.0	77	25	51	5.59	6-4	4	10	87.0	102	29	79

Wild Pitches— LCS (Osborne, Petkovsek); OVERALL (Osborne, Petkovsek). **Hit Batters**— LCS (Al. Benes, Osborne, Stottlemyre); OVERALL (Stottlemyre 2, Al. Benes, Osborne).

Score by Innings

	1	2	3	4	5	6	7	8	9	R	H	E
St. Louis	3	1	2	0	0	1	9	2	0	–18	45	6
Atlanta	12	4	2	7	4	6	2	5	2	–44	77	4

DP: St. Louis 5, Atlanta 6. **LOB:** St. Louis 34, Atlanta 58. **2B:**. St. Louis— An. Benes, Gant, Jordan, Pagnozzi; Atlanta— Lopez (5), Lemke (2), C. Jones (2), Grissom, Dye. **3B:** St. Louis— Jordan, Young; Atlanta— Blauser, Glavine, McGriff. **HR:** St. Louis— Gant (2), Gaetti, Jordan; Atlanta— Lopez (2), McGriff (2), Grissom, A. Jones, Klesko, Lemke. **SB:** St. Louis— Clayton; Atlanta— Grissom (2), C. Jones, Lopez. **CS:** St. Louis— Clayton; Atlanta— Dye. **S:** St. Louis— Sweeney; Atlanta— Maddux, Neagle. **SF:** St. Louis— Lankford; Atlanta— Dye (2), C. Jones. **Umpires:** Paul Runge, Mark Hirschbeck, Bob Davidson, Joe West, Jerry Crawford, Ed Montague.

WORLD SERIES

Yankees, 4-2

Date	Winner	Home Field
Oct. 20	Braves, 12-1	New York
Oct. 21	Braves, 4-0	New York
Oct. 22	Yankees, 5-2	Atlanta
Oct. 23	Yankees, 8-6 (10)	Atlanta
Oct. 24	Yankees, 1-0	Atlanta
Oct. 26	Yankees, 3-2	New York

Game 1

Sunday, Oct. 20, at New York

	1	2	3	4	5	6	7	8	9	R	H	E
Atlanta	0	2	6	0	1	3	0	0	0	–12	13	0
New York	0	0	0	0	1	0	0	0	0	–1	4	1

Win: Smoltz, Atl. (1-0) Loss: Pettitte, N.Y. (0-1).
2B: New York—Boggs. **HR:** Atlanta—A. Jones (2); McGriff (1).
RBI: Atlanta—A. Jones (5), C. Jones (3), McGriff (2), Grissom , Lemke
SB: Atlanta—C. Jones. **SF:** Atlanta—C. Jones
Attendance: 56,365. **Time:** 3:02.

Game 2

Monday, Oct. 21, at New York

	1	2	3	4	5	6	7	8	9	R	H	E
Atlanta	1	0	1	0	1	1	0	0	0	–4	10	0
New York	0	0	0	0	0	0	0	0	0	–0	7	1

Win: Maddux, Atl. (1-0). Loss: Key, N.Y. (0-1).
2B: Atlanta—Grissom, Lemke, C. Jones, Pendleton; New York—O'Neill. **RBI:** Atlanta—McGriff (3), Grissom. **CS:** New York—Raines.
Attendance: 51,877. **Time:** 3:17.

Game 3

Tuesday, Oct. 22 at Atlanta

	1	2	3	4	5	6	7	8	9	R	H	E
New York	1	0	0	1	0	0	0	3	0	–5	8	1
Atlanta	0	0	0	0	0	1	0	1	0	–2	6	1

Win: Cone, N.Y. (1-0). Save: Wetteland (1). Loss: Glavine, Atl. (0-1).
2B: New York— Fielder. **3B:** Atlanta— Grissom. **HR:** New York— B. Williams. **RBI:** New York— B. Williams (3), Sojo, Strawberry; Atlanta— Klesko, Lemke. **CS:** Atlanta—Jones (1), Polonia (1).
Attendance: 51,843. **Time:** 3:22.

Game 4

Wednesday, Oct. 23, at Atlanta

	1	2	3	4	5	6	7	8	9	10	R	H	E
New York	0	0	0	0	0	3	0	3	0	2	–8	12	0
Atlanta	0	4	1	0	1	0	0	0	0	0	–6	9	2

Win: Lloyd, N.Y. (1-0). **Save:** Wetteland (2). **Loss:** Avery, Atl. (0-1).
2B: Atlanta—Grissom (2), A. Jones (1). **HR:** New York—Leyritz (1). Atlanta—McGriff (2). **RBI:** New York—Leyritz 3 (3), Boggs (2), Fielder, Hayes; Atlanta—Grissom 2 (4), A. Jones, McGriff (6), Blauser, Lopez;. **SB:** Atlanta— Grissom 2 (2).
Attendance: 51,881. **Time:** 4:19.

Game 5

Thursday, Oct. 24, at Atlanta

	1	2	3	4	5	6	7	8	9	R	H	E
New York	0	0	0	1	0	0	0	0	0	–1	4	1
Atlanta	0	0	0	0	0	0	0	0	0	–0	5	1

Win: Pettitte, N.Y. (1-1). **Save:** Wetteland, N.Y. (3). **Loss:** Smotlz, Atl. (1-1).
2B: New York—Fielder (2). Atlanta—C. Jones. **RBI:** New York—Fielder. **CS:** Atlanta—A. Jones (2)
Attendance: 51,881. **Time:** 2:54.

Game 6

Saturday, Oct. 26, at New York

	1	2	3	4	5	6	7	8	9	R	H	E
Atlanta	0	0	0	1	0	0	0	0	1	–2	8	0
New York	0	0	3	0	0	0	0	0	0	–3	8	1

Win: Key, N.Y. (1-1) **Save:** Wetteland, N.Y. (4) **Loss:** Maddux, Atl. (1-1)
2B: Atlanta—Blauser, C. Jones (3); New York—O'Neill (2), Sojo.
3B: New York— Girardi. **RBI:** Atlanta—Dye, Grissom; New York—Girardi, Jeter, Williams. **SB:** New York—Jeter, Williams. **CS:** Pendelton.
Attendance: 56,375. **Time:** 2:52.

Most Valuable Player

John Wetteland, RHP

W-L	Svs	ERA	Gm	IP	H	BB	SO
0-0	4	2.08	5	4.1	4	1	6

World Series Composite Box Score

New York Yankees

Batting	WS vs Atlanta								Overall Playoffs							
	Avg	AB	R	H	HR	RBI	BB	SO	Avg	AB	R	H	HR	RBI	BB	SO
Kenny Rogers, p	1.000	1	0	1	0	0	0	0	1.000	1	0	1	0	0	0	0
Luis Sojo, 2b	.600	5	0	3	0	1	0	0	.400	10	0	4	0	1	0	1
Cecil Fielder, dh-1b	.391	23	1	9	0	2	2	2	.308	52	6	16	3	14	7	9
Jim Leyritz, c	.375	8	1	3	1	3	3	2	.263	19	2	5	2	6	4	7
Wade Boggs, 3b	.273	11	0	3	0	2	1	0	.158	38	1	6	0	2	2	5
Derek Jeter, ss	.250	20	5	5	0	1	4	6	.361	61	12	22	1	3	4	13
Tim Raines, lf	.214	14	2	3	0	0	2	1	.244	45	7	11	0	0	6	3
Joe Girardi, c	.200	10	1	2	0	1	1	2	.226	31	3	7	0	1	6	6
Darryl Strawberry, lf-rf	.188	16	0	3	0	1	4	6	.242	33	4	8	3	6	6	10
Charlie Hayes, 3b-1b	.188	16	2	3	0	1	1	5	.179	28	2	5	0	2	3	7
Paul O'Neill, rf	.167	12	1	2	0	0	3	2	.184	38	2	7	1	2	6	6
Bernie Williams, rf	.167	24	3	4	1	4	3	6	.345	58	14	20	6	15	10	11
Tino Martinez, 1b	.091	11	0	1	0	0	2	5	.188	48	6	9	0	0	5	8
Mariano Duncan, 2b	.053	19	1	1	0	0	0	4	.180	50	1	9	0	3	0	11
Mike Aldrete, rf	.000	1	0	0	0	0	0	0	.000	1	0	0	0	0	0	0
Graeme Lloyd, p	.000	1	0	0	0	0	0	0	.000	1	0	0	0	0	0	0
David Cone, p	.000	2	0	0	0	0	0	1	.000	2	0	0	0	0	0	1
Andy Pettitte, p	.000	4	0	0	0	0	0	1	.000	4	0	0	0	0	0	1
Ruben Rivera	—	—	—	—	—	—	—	—	.000	1	0	0	0	0	0	1
TOTALS	.216	199	18	43	2	16	26	43	250	521	60	130	16	55	59	100

Pitching	ERA	W-L	Sv	Gm	IP	H	BB	SO	ERA	W-L	Sv	Gm	IP	H	BB	SO
Jeff Nelson	0.00	0-0	0	3	4.1	1	1	5	2.61	1-1	0	7	10.1	8	3	12
Graeme Lloyd	0.00	1-0	0	4	2.2	0	0	4	0.00	1-0	0	8	5.1	1	0	5
David Cone	1.50	1-0	0	1	6	4	4	3	4.50	1-1	0	3	18.0	17	11	16
Mariano Rivera	1.59	0-0	0	4	5.2	4	3	4	0.63	1-0	0	8	14.1	10	5	10
John Wetteland	2.08	0-0	4	5	4.1	4	1	6	2.19	0-0	7	12	12.1	8	3	8
David Weathers	3.00	0-0	0	3	3	2	3	3	0.82	2-0	0	7	11.0	6	6	15
Jimmy Key	3.97	1-1	0	2	11.1	15	5	1	3.33	2-1	0	4	24.1	23	7	9
Brian Boehringer	5.40	0-0	0	2	5	5	0	5	5.68	1-0	0	4	6.1	8	2	5
Andy Pettitte	5.91	1-1	0	2	10.2	11	4	5	4.78	2-1	0	5	32.0	25	15	15
Kenny Rogers	22.50	0-0	0	1	2	5	2	0	14.14	0-0	0	4	7.0	15	6	4
TOTALS	3.93	4-2	4	6	55	51	43	36	3.70	10-4	7	62	141	121	61	106

Wild Pitches— WS (none); OVERALL (Cone, Pettitte, Rogers). **Hit Batters**— WS (Key); OVERALL (Key). **Balk**— WS (Weathers); OVERALL—(Weathers, Pettitte).

Atlanta Braves

Batting	WS vs New York								Overall Playoffs							
	Avg	AB	R	H	HR	RBI	BB	SO	Avg	AB	R	H	HR	RBI	BB	SO
John Smoltz, p	.500	2	0	1	0	0	0	0	.273	11	1	3	0	1	0	3
Marquis Grissom, cf	.444	27	4	12	0	5	1	2	.311	74	13	23	1	8	2	12
Andruw Jones, lf	.400	20	4	8	2	6	3	6	.345	29	7	10	3	9	7	8
Fred McGriff, 1b	.300	20	4	6	2	6	5	4	.281	57	11	16	5	16	10	10
Chipper Jones, 3b-ss	.286	21	3	6	0	3	4	2	.345	55	11	19	1	9	10	7
Mark Lemke, 2b	.231	26	2	6	0	2	0	3	.308	65	7	20	1	9	4	6
Terry Pendleton, dh-3b	.222	9	1	2	0	0	1	1	.125	16	1	2	0	0	2	5
Javier Lopez, c	.190	21	3	4	0	1	3	4	.365	52	12	19	3	8	7	5
Jeff Blauser, ss	.167	18	2	3	0	1	1	4	.159	44	7	7	0	3	6	13
Jermaine Dye, rf	.118	17	0	2	0	1	1	1	.179	56	3	10	1	6	2	14
Ryan Klesko, dh-lf-1b	.100	10	2	1	0	1	2	4	.176	34	4	6	2	5	7	14
Mike Mordecai, ph	.000	1	0	0	0	0	0	0	.200	5	1	1	0	0	0	1
Mike Bielecki, p	.000	1	0	0	0	0	0	1	.000	1	0	0	0	0	0	1
Tom Glavine, p	.000	1	1	0	0	0	1	1	.222	9	2	2	0	3	1	3
Denny Neagle, p	.000	1	0	0	0	0	0	1	.333	3	0	1	0	0	0	1
Eddie Perez, c	.000	1	0	0	0	0	0	0	.200	5	0	1	0	0	1	0
Luis Polonia, ph	.000	5	0	0	0	0	1	2	.000	10	0	0	0	0	1	4
Mark Wohlers, p	—	—	—	—	—	—	—	—	.000	1	0	0	0	0	0	1
TOTALS	.254	201	26	51	4	26	23	36	.266	527	80	140	17	77	60	108

Pitching	ERA	W-L	Sv	Gm	IP	H	BB	SO	ERA	W-L	Sv	Gm	IP	H	BB	SO
Mike Bielecki	0.00	0-0	0	2	3	0	3	6	0.00	0-0	0	6	6.2	0	5	12
Brad Clontz	0.00	0-0	0	3	1.2	1	1	2	0.00	0-0	0	4	2.1	1	1	2
Terrell Wade	0.00	0-0	0	2	0.2	0	1	0	0.00	0-0	0	3	1.0	0	1	1
John Smoltz	0.64	1-1	0	2	14	6	8	14	0.95	4-1	0	5	38.0	22	13	33
Tom Glavine	1.29	0-1	0	1	7	4	3	8	1.69	2-2	0	4	26.2	19	6	24
Greg Maddux	1.72	1-1	0	2	15.2	14	1	5	1.70	3-2	0	5	37.0	32	3	22
Denny Neagle	3.00	0-0	0	2	6	5	4	3	2.63	0-0	0	4	13.2	7	7	11
Mark Wohlers	6.23	0-0	0	4	4.1	7	2	4	2.53	0-0	5	10	10.2	8	2	12
Steve Avery	13.50	0-1	0	1	0.2	1	3	0	3.38	0-1	0	3	2.2	3	4	1
Greg McMichael	27.00	0-0	0	2	1	5	3	1	12.46	0-1	0	7	4.1	10	2	7
TOTALS	2.33	2-4	0	6	54	43	26	43	1.92	9-7	5	51	140.2	102	44	125

Wild Pitches— WS (none); OVERALL (Smoltz 2, Wohlers 2, Maddux). **Hit Batters**—WS (Maddux); OVERALL (Maddux, Glauine). **Balk**— WS (none); OVERALL— (none).

Score by Innings

	1	2	3	4	5	6	7	8	9	10	R	H	E
Atlanta	1	6	8	1	3	5	0	1	1	0	–26	51	3
New York	1	0	3	2	1	3	0	6	0	2	–18	43	5

DP: Atlanta 6, New York 7. **LOB:** Atlanta 41, New York 48. **2B:** Atlanta—C. Jones (3), Grissom (2), Blauser, A. Jones, Lemke, Pendleton; New York— Fielder (2), O'Neill (2), Boggs, Sojo **3B:** Atlanta— Grissom; New York—Girardi. **SB:** Atlanta— C. Jones (2), Grissom, A. Jones; New York— Duncan, Leyritz, Jeter, Williams. **CS:** Atlanta— A. Jones (2), Polonia, Pendleton; New York— Raines. **S:** Atlanta— Lemke (2), Dye, Neagle; New York— Girardi, Jeter. **SF:** Atlanta— C. Jones, Lopez, McGriff.
Umpires: James Evans (AL), Terry Tata (NL), Tim Welke (AL), Steve Rippley (NL), Larry Young (AL), Gerry Davis (NL).

COLLEGE

Final *Baseball America* Top 25

Final 1996 Division I Top 25, voted on by the editors of *Baseball America* and released June 10, following the NCAA College World Series. Given are final records and winning percentage (including all postseason games); records in College World Series and team eliminated by (DNP indicates team did not play in tourney); head coach (career years and Division I record including 1996 postseason) preseason ranking and rank before start of CWS.

	Record	Pct	CWS Recap	Head Coach	Rank	Rank
1 LSU	52-15	.776	4-0	Skip Bertman (13 yrs: 626-233-1)	1	6
2 Miami	50-14	.781	3-1 (LSU)	Jim Morris (15 yrs: 651-289-1)	21	7
3 Florida	50-18	.735	2-2 (LSU)	Andy Lopez (14 yrs: 491-301-5)	NR	2
4 Alabama	50-19	.725	1-2 (CLEMSON)	Jim Wells (7 yrs: 284-131)	18	1
5 Clemson	51-17	.750	2-2 (MIAMI)	Jack Leggett (17 yrs: 539-336)	8	5
6 Florida St.	52-17	.754	1-2 (FLORIDA)	Mike Martin (17 yrs: 918-312-3)	15	4
7 USC	44-16	.733	DNP	Mike Gillespie (10 yrs: 391-230-2)	13	8
8 Wichita St.	54-11	.831	0-2 (FL. STATE)	Gene Stephenson (19 yrs: 1,058-321-3)	4	3
9 Stanford	41-19	683	DNP	Mark Marquess (20 yrs: 808-433-4)	2	9
10 CS-Northridge	52-18	.743	DNP	Mike Batesole (1 yr: 52-18)	NR	10
11 Oklahoma St.	45-21	.682	0-2 (CLEMSON)	Gary Ward (19 yrs: 953-313-1)	16	11
12 CS-Fullerton	45-16	.738	DNP	Augie Garrido (28 yrs: 1,152-523-7)	3	12
13 Tennessee	43-20	.683	DNP	Rod Delmonico (7 yrs: 298-140)	6	13
14 Virginia	44-21	.677	DNP	Dennis Womack (16 yrs:408-403-5)	NR	14
15 Texas Tech	49-15	.766	DNP	Larry Hays (26 yrs: 1,067-588-2)	19	15
16 South Florida	47-19	.712	DNP	Eddie Cardieri (13 yrs: 490-286)	20	16
17 Rice	42-23	.646	DNP	Wayne Graham (5 yrs: 185-107)	25	17
18 Texas	39-24	.619	DNP	Cliff Gustafson (29 yrs: 1466-377-2)	12	18
19 Massachusetts	40-13	.755	DNP	Mike Stone (14 yrs: 311-257-1)	NR	19
20 Tulane	43-20	.683	DNP	Rick Jones (7 yrs: 258-105)	NR	20
21 UCLA	36-28	.563	DNP	Gary Adams (27 yrs: 915-659-11)	10	21
22 Georgia Tech	40-24	.625	DNP	Danny Hall (9 yrs: 336-180)	5	22
23 UNLV	43-17	.717	DNP	Fred Dallimore (23 yrs: 794-558)	NR	23
24 Georgia Southern	46-14	.767	DNP	Jack Stallings (36 yrs: 1,173-711-5)	NR	24
25 Arizona St.	35-21	.625	DNP	Pat Murphy (12 yrs: 442-213-3)	11	25

College World Series

CWS Seeds: 1. Alabama (49-17); **2.** Florida (48-16); **3.** Wichita St. (54-9); **4.** Clemson (49-15); **5.** Miami (47-13); **6.** LSU (48-15); **7.** Florida St. (51-15); **8.** Oklahoma St. (45-19).

Bracket One

May 31— Alabama 7 .... Oklahoma St. 5
May 31— Miami 7 .... Clemson 3
June 2— Miami 15 .... Alabama 1
June 2— Clemson 8 .... Oklahoma St. 5 (out)
June 4— Clemson 14 .... Alabama 1 (out)
June 5— Miami 14 .... Clemson 5 (out)

Bracket Two

June 1— Florida 5 .... Florida St. 2
June 1— LSU 9 .... Wichita St. 8
June 3— LSU 9 .... Florida 4
June 3— Florida St. 8 .... Wichita St. 4 (out)
June 4— Florida 6 .... Florida St. 3 (out)
June 6— LSU 2 .... Florida 1 (out)

CWS Championship Game

Saturday, June 8, at Rosenblatt Stadium in Omaha.

	1 2 3	4 5 6	7 8 9	R	H	E
Miami	2 0 0	0 3 2	0 0 1	-8	14	2
LSU	0 0 3	0 0 0	2 2 2	-9	15	2

Win: LSU— Patrick Coogan (6-0). **Loss:**Miami— Robbie Morrison (4-2). **Starters:** Miami— J.D. Arteaga; LSU— Kevin Shipp. **Strikeouts:** Miami— Arteaga 7, Morrison 2; LSU— Shipp 3, Coogan 1. **WP:** Miami— Morrison.
2B: Miami— T.R. Marcinczyk, Alex Cora, Rick Saggese; LSU— Brad Wilson, Justin Bowles, Warren Morris. **3B:** Miami— Cora. **HR:** LSU— Morris (1). **RBI:** Miami— Michael DeCelle 3, Cora 3, Pat Burrell, Eddie Rivero; LSU— Nathan Dunn 2, Mike Koerner 2, Morris 2, Eddy Furniss. **SB:** Miami— Rudy Gomez (28); LSU— Tim Lanier (2). **CS:** LSU— Koerner.
Attendance: 23,905. **Time**: 3:19.

Annual Awards

Chosen by *Baseball America, Collegiate Baseball* and the American Baseball Coaches Association.

Players of the Year

Kris Benson, Clemson .... ABCA, *BA*, *CB*

Coaches of the Year

Skip Bertman, LSU .... ABCA, *BA*, co-*CB*
Andy Lopez, Florida .... co-*CB*

Most Outstanding Player

Pat Burrell, Miami, 3B

Avg	AB	R	H	2B	3B	HR	RBI	SB	BB
.500	14	6	7	2	0	2	8	1	5

All-Tournament Team

C— Tim Lanier, LSU. **1B**— Chris Moller, Alabama. **2B**— Rudy Gomez, Miami. **3B**— Pat Burrell, Miami. **SS**— Alex Cora, Miami. **OF**— Justin Bowles, LSU; Michael DeCelle, Miami; Brad Wilkerson, Florida. **DH**— Chuck Hazzard, Florida. **P**— J.D. Arteaga, Miami; Eddie Yarnall, LSU.

Consensus All-America Team

NCAA Division I players cited most frequently by the following four selectors: the American Baseball Coaches Assn. (ABCA), *Baseball America*, *Collegiate Baseball*, and the National Collegiate Baseball Writers Assn. (NCBWA). Holdover from the 1995 All-America first team are in **bold** type.

First Team

Pos		Cl	Avg	HR	RBI
C	A.J. Hinch, Stanford	Sr.	.381	11	59
1B	Eddy Furniss, LSU	So.	.374	26	103
2B	Travis Young, New Mexico	Jr.	.442	2	32
SS	Josh Klimek, Illinois	Jr.	.400	26	94
3B	Pat Burrell, Miami	Fr.	.484	23	64
OF	J.D. Drew, Florida St.	So.	.386	21	94
OF	Chad Green, Kentucky	Jr.	.352	12	44
OF	**Mark Kotsay**, CS-Fullerton	Jr.	.402	20	91
DH	Casey Blake, Wichita St.	Sr.	.360	22	101

		Cl	W-L	Sv	ERA
P	Kris Benson, Clemson	Jr.	14-2	0	2.02
P	Seth Greisinger, Virginia	Jr.	12-2	0	1.76
P	Braden Looper, Wichita St.	Jr.	4-1	12	2.09
P	Evan Thomas, Fla. Int'l	Sr.	10-3	1	1.78
P	R.A. Dickey, Tennessee	Jr.	9-4	3	2.76
P	Eddie Yarnall, LSU	Jr.	11-1	0	2.38

Second Team

Pos		Cl	Avg	HR	RBI
C	Robert Fick, CS-Northridge	Jr.	.420	25	96
1B	Travis Lee, S.D. St.	Jr.	.355	14	60
2B	Josh Kliner, Kansas	Sr.	.438	10	85
SS	Kip Harkrider, Texas	So.	.381	4	43
3B	Clint Bryant, Texas Tech	Sr.	.382	18	100
OF	Jeff Guiel, Oklahoma St.	Jr.	.394	15	80
OF	Matt Kastelic, Texas Tech	Sr.	.424	8	70
OF	Brad Wilkerson, Florida	Fr.	.407	9	68
UT	Jason Grabowski, UConn	So.	.380	18	59

		Cl	W-L	Sv	ERA
P	Brian Carmody, Santa Clara	Jr.	10-3	0	1.81
P	Jeff Weaver, Fresno St.	Fr.	11-5	1	2.34
P	Eric DuBose, Mississippi St.	So.	10-4	1	3.11
P	Seth Etherton, USC	So.	12-3	0	3.94
P	Robbie Morrison, Miami	Fr.	4-2	14	1.68

Morris Is the Cat

by Jim Callis

One swing of the bat changed Warren Morris' season from trying to unforgettable.

Miami was one out away from winning the national championship when Morris, a Louisiana State junior second baseman, strode to the plate June 8 at Rosenblatt Stadium in Omaha. Hurricanes freshman closer Robbie Morrison had an 8-7 lead and had just struck out catcher Tim Lanier to stand Brad Wilson at third base.

Morris lined Morrison's first pitch, a curveball, just over the right-field fence to become the first player in the 50-year history of the College World Series to end a tournament and win the national championship with a home run. As he ran around the bases, several Miami players lay prone on the infield as if they had been shot.

"I hadn't hit a home run in so long, I didn't know what one looked like," Morris said. "It's been a tough year, but it's all worth it now."

Morris had been bothered by wrist problems that limited him to 14 regular-season starts before doctors finally found a broken hamate bone in his right hand. He had surgery to remove the bone April 24, and missed 28 days before returning.

Morris' dramatic home run was his first of the season, and that wasn't the only improbable part of his heroics. Morris joined the Tigers in 1992 on a full academic scholarship and weighed 150 pounds when he attended his first team meeting as an unrecruited walk-on. "I looked around," he said, "and the only person I was bigger than was the equipment manager."

A self-made star, Morris redshirted for a season behind former Louisiana State great and current Minnesota Twin Todd Walker before becoming a three-year starter. He has bulked his 5-foot-11 frame up to 190 pounds, and has worked equally hard in the classroom, earning academic all-American honors. He improved so much that he earned a starting job on the U.S. Olympic team.

"Isn't it ironic that Warren Morris would be there to hit his first home run of the year?" Tigers coach Skip Bertman said. "That shows you that the kids who are the greatest always come through."

Jennifer Abelson/LSU

Louisiana State University Tiger **Warren Morris** won the NCAA baseball title with one swing of his bat.

The championship was the third in the last six seasons for Louisiana State, which also won the big prize in 1991 and 1993.

Morris' memorable blast overshadowed the CWS performance of Miami freshman third baseman Pat Burrell, who was named MVP of the tournament in a losing cause. Burrell went 7-for-14 with two homers and eight RBIs in four games. He also became the first freshman ever to lead NCAA Division I in batting, finishing at .484.

Clemson junior righthander Kris Benson was named Baseball America's College Player of the Year. Benson ranked second in Division I in strikeouts (204 in 156 innings), fourth in victories (14-2) and fifth in ERA (2.02). He also was the No. 1 overall pick in the June draft, selected by the Pittsburgh Pirates., with San Diego Staes's Travis Lee, Wichita State's Brandon Looper, Billy Koch of Clemson rounding out the top four collegiate picks.

Jim Callis is the managing editor of *Baseball America*.

NCAA Division I Leaders

Batting

Average

(At least 75 AB)	Cl	Gm	AB	H	Avg
Pat Burrell, Miami (Fla)	Fr.	60	192	93	.484
Ethan Barlow, Vermont	Sr.	29	88	40	.455
Marlon Stewart, Grambling	Sr.	41	138	62	.449
Mike Shannon, Penn	Sr.	37	142	63	.444
Travis Young, New Mexico	Jr.	51	215	95	.442

Home Runs (per game)

(At least 15)	Cl	Gm	HR	Avg
Josh Klimek, Illinois	Jr.	59	26	0.44
Tommy Peterman, Ga. South	Jr.	60	26	0.43
Ryan Roberts, Brig. Young	Sr.	56	23	0.41
Tony Hausladen, St. Louis	Jr.	48	19	0.40
Eddy Furniss, LSU	So.	66	26	0.39

Runs Batted In

(At least 50)	Cl	Gm	RBI	Avg
Aaron Jaworski, Missouri	So.	58	101	1.74
Josh Klimek, Illinois	Jr.	59	94	1.59
Clint Bryant, Texas Tech	Sr.	64	100	1.56
Eddy Furniss, LSU	So.	66	103	1.56
Casey Blake, Wichita St.	Sr.	65	101	1.55

Pitching

Earned Run Avg.

(At least 50 inn.)	Cl	Gm	IP	ERA
Seth Greisinger, Virginia	Jr.	16	123.0	1.76
Evan Thomas, Fla. Int.	Sr.	20	146.2	1.78
Brian Carmody, Santa Clara	Jr.	17	119.2	1.81
Brad Brasser, Northwestern	Jr.	11	65.1	1.93
Kris Benson, Clemson	Jr.	19	156.0	2.02

Wins

	Cl	Gm	IP	W-L
Julio Ayala, Ga. Southern	Jr.	22	152.0	15-3
Clint Weibl, Miami (Fla.)	Jr.	19	120.2	15-3
Randy Choate, Fla. St.	So.	22	150.0	15-4
Erasmo Ramirez, CS-Northridge	So.	24	122.2	14-1
Kris Benson, Clemson	Jr.	19	156.0	14-2

Strikeouts (per 9 inn.)

(At least 50 inn.)	Cl	IP	SO	Avg
Evan Thomas, Fla. Int.	Sr.	146.2	220	13.5
Jason Ramsey, NC-Wilmington	Jr.	97.2	135	12.4
Billy Koch, Clemson	Jr.	111.2	152	12.3
Eric Milton, Maryland	Jr.	90.0	118	11.8
Kris Benson, Clemson	Jr.	156.0	204	11.8

Other College World Series

Participants' final records in parentheses.

NCAA Div. II

at Montgomery, Ala. (May 25-June 1)

Participants: Adelphi, NY (29-16-1); Delta St., MS (53-8); Kennesaw St. GA (48-17); Missouri-St. Louis (37-9); Shippensburg, PA (33-19); Southern Colorado (44-23); St. Joseph's, IN (52-12); Tampa (45-16).

Championship: Kennesaw St. def. St. Joseph's, 4-0.

NAIA

at Sioux City, Iowa (May 24-May 29)

Participants: Cumberland, TN (43-21); Geneva, PA (24-21); Lewis-Clark St., ID (53-11); Ohio Dominican (36-20); Oklakoma Baptist (52-13-1); St. Ambrose, IA (41-20); St. Mary's, TX (43-14); St. Thomas, FL (47-21).

Championship: Lewis-Clark St. def. St. Ambrose, 9-0.

NCAA Div. III

at Salem, Va. (May 23-29)

Participants: Bridgewater St., MA (31-10); Cal Lutheran (34-14-1); Marietta, OH (43-13); Methodist, NC (35-9); RPI, NY (29-5); Upper Iowa (37-14); William Paterson, NJ (39-5-1); Wisconsin-Oshkosh (35-6).

Championship: Wm. Paterson def. Cal Lutheran, 6-5.

NJCAA Div. I

at Grand Junction, Colo. (May 27-June 2)

Participants: Arizona Western (45-25); Northeast Texas (48-18); Meridian, MS (50-12); St. Louis (44-14); Indian Hills, IA (46-15); Triton College, IL (37-16); Jackson St., TN (38-20); Middle Georgia College (58-9); Allegany, MD (43-6); Indian River, FL (38-16).

Championship: Northeast Texas def. Meridian, 4-3.

Wide World Photos

The **Louisiana State Tigers** commence the victory dance after beating Miami in the College World Series.

MLB Amateur Draft

Top 50 selections at the 32nd Amateur Draft held June 4-6, 1996. Selections 1-30 are first round picks, 31-35 are supplemental first round picks and 36-50 are second round picks.

Top 50 Picks

No			Pos
1	Pittsburgh	Kris Benson, Clemson	P
2	Minnesota	Travis Lee, San Diego St.	1B
3	St. Louis	Braden Looper, Wichita St.	P
4	Toronto	Billy Koch, Clemson	P
5	Montreal	John Patterson, HS—Orange Tx.	P
6	Detroit	Seth Greisinger, Virginia	P
7	San Francisco	Matt White, HS—Waynesboro, Pa.	P
8	Milwaukee	Chad Green, Kentucky	OF
9	Florida	Mark Kotsay, Cal St.-Fullerton	OF
10	Oakland	Eric Chavez, HS—San Diego, Calif.	3B
11	Philadelphia	Adam Eaton, HS—Snohomish, Wash.	P
12	Chicago-AL	Bobby Seay, HS—Sarasota, Fla.	P
13	NY Mets	Robert Stratton, HS—San Marcos, Calif.	OF
14	Kansas City	Dermal Brown, HS—Marlboro, N.Y.	OF
15	San Diego	Matt Halloran, HS—Fredricksburg, Va.	SS
16	**a-**Toronto	Joe Lawrence, HS—Lake Charles, La.	SS
17	Chicago-NL	Todd Noel, HS—Maurice, La.	P
18	Texas	R.A. Dickey, Tennessee	P
19	Houton	Mark Johnson, Hawaii	P
20	**b-**NY Yankees	Eric Milton, Maryland	P
21	Colorado	Jake Westbrook, HS—Madison County, Ga.	P
22	Seattle	Gil Meche, HS—Lafayette, La.	P
23	Los Angeles	Damian Rolls, HS—Kansas City, Ks.	3B
24	**c-**Texas	Sam Marsonek, HS—Tampa, Fla.	P
25	Cincinnati	John Oliver, HS—Dallas, Pa.	OF
26	Boston	Josh Garrett, HS—Richland, Ind.	P
27	Atlanta	A.J. Zapp, HS—Greenwood, Ind.	1B
28	Cleveland	Danny Peoples, Texas	1B
29	Tampa Bay	Paul Wilder, HS—Cary, N.C.	OF
30	Arizona	Nick Bierbrodt, HS—Long Beach, Calif.	P
31	Toronto	Pete Tucci, Providence	1B-OF
32	Texas	Corey Lee, N.C. State	P
33	Cincinnati	Matt McClendon, HS—Orlando, Fla.	P
34	Boston	Chris Reitsma, HS—Calgary, Alb.	P
35	Atlanta	Jason Marquis, HS—Staten Island, N.Y.	P
36	Pittsburgh	Andy Prater, HS—Florrisant, Mo.	P
37	Minnesota	Jacque Jones, USC	OF
38	**d-**Cincinnati	Buddy Carlyle, HS—Bellevue, Neb.	P
39	**e-**Boston	Gary LoCurto, HS—San Diego, Calif.	1B
40	Montreal	Milton Bradley, Long Beach, Calif.	OF
41	Detroit	Matt Miller, Texas Tech	P
42	San Francisco	Mike Caruso, HS—Parkland, Fla.	SS
43	Milwaukee	Jose Garcia, HS—Baldwin Park, Calif.	P
44	**f-**Toronto	Brent Abernathy, HS—Atlanta, Ga.	SS
45	Oakland	Josue Espada, U. of Mobile	SS
46	Philadelphia	Jimmy Rollins, HS—Alamada, Calif.	SS
47	Chicago-AL	Josh Paul, Vanderbilt	OF
48	NY Mets	Brendan Behn, Merced (Calif.) JC	P
49	Kansas City	Taylor Myers, HS—Henderson, Nev.	P
50	San Diego	V. Maxwell, HS—Midwest City, Okla.	OF

Acquired picks: **a**— from Baltimore for signing Roberto Alomar; **b**— from California for signing Randy Velarde; **c**— from NY Yankees for signing Kenny Rogers; **d**— from St. Louis for signing Ron Gant; **e**— from Toronto for signing Erik Hanson; **f**— from Florida for signing Devon White.

Minor League Triple A Final Standings

All playoff series are Best of 5 games.

International League

Eastern Division	W	L	Pct	GB
Pawtucket (Red Sox)	78	64	.549	—
Rochester (Orioles)	72	69	.511	5½
Scranton/W-B (Phillies)	70	72	.493	8
Syracuse (Blue Jays)	67	75	.472	11
Ottawa (Montreal)	60	82	.423	18

Western Division	W	L	Pct	GB
Columbus (Yankees)	85	57	.599	—
Norfolk (Mets)	82	59	.582	2½
Toledo (Tigers)	70	72	.493	15
Richmond (Braves)	62	79	.440	22½
Charlotte (Marlins)	62	79	.440	22½

Playoffs: FIRST ROUND— Rochester def. Pawtucket (3-1); Columbus def. Norfolk (3-0). CHAMPIONSHIP— Columbus def. Rochester (3-0).

Pacific Coast League

Northern Division	W	L	Pct	GB
*†Edmonton (Athletics)	84	58	.592	—
#Salt Lake (Twins)	78	66	.542	7
Calgary (Pirates)	74	68	.521	10
Vancouver (Angels)	68	70	.493	14
Tacoma (Mariners)	69	73	.486	15

Southern Division	W	L	Pct	GB
†Las Vegas (Padres)	73	67	.521	—
Tucson (Astros)	70	74	.486	5
* Phoenix (Giants)	69	75	.479	6
Albuquerque (Dodgers)	67	76	.469	7½
Colorado Springs (Rockies)	58	83	.411	15½

* first half divisional champion; † second half divisional champion; # wild card winner.

Playoffs: FIRST ROUND— Edmonton def. Salt Lake (3-1); Phoenix def. Las Vegas (3-0). CHAMPIONSHIP— Edmonton def. Phoenix (3-1).

American Association

Eastern Division	W	L	Pct	GB
Buffalo (Indians)	84	60	.583	—
Indianapolis (Reds)	78	66	.542	6
Nashville (White Sox)	77	67	.535	7
Louisville (St. Louis)	60	84	.417	24

Western Division	W	L	Pct	GB
Omaha (Royals)	79	65	.549	—
Oklahoma City (Rangers)	74	70	.514	5
Iowa (Cubs)	64	78	.451	14
New Orleans (Brewers)	58	84	.408	20

Playoffs: FIRST ROUND— Indianapolis def. Buffalo (3-2); Oklahoma City def. Omaha (3-1). CHAMPIONSHIP— Oklahoma City def. Indianapolis (3-1).

Japanese Leagues

Final Standings

Central League	W	L	T	Pct	GB
Yomiuri Giants	77	53	0	.592	—
Chunichi Dragons	72	58	0	.554	5
Hiroshima Carp	71	59	0	.546	6
Yakult Swallows	61	69	0	.469	16
Yokohama BayStars	55	75	0	.423	22
Hanshin Tigers	54	76	0	.415	23

Pacific League	W	L	T	Pct	GB
Orix Blue Wave	74	50	6	.597	—
Nippon Ham Fighters	68	58	4	.540	7
Seibu Lions	62	64	4	.492	13
Kintetsu Buffaloes	62	67	1	.481	14½
Chiba Lotte Marines	60	67	3	.472	15½
Fukuoka Daiei Hawks	54	74	2	.422	22

Japan Series (Best of 7): Orix def. Yomiuri (4-1).

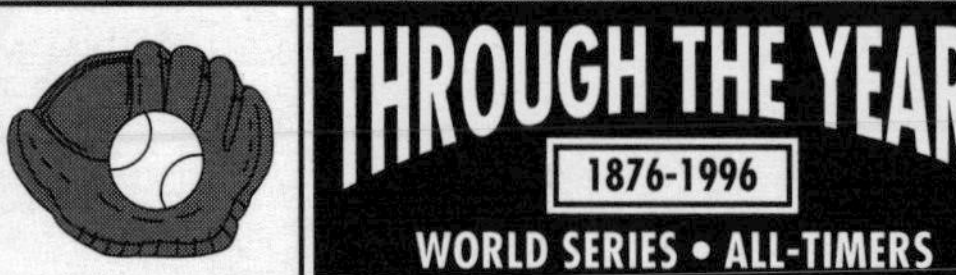

The World Series

The World Series began in 1903 when Pittsburgh of the older National League (founded in 1876) invited Boston of the American League (founded in 1901) to play a best-of-9 game series to determine which of the two league champions was the best. Boston was the surprise winner, 5 games to 3. The 1904 NL champion New York Giants refused to play Boston the following year, so there was no series. Giants' owner John T. Brush and his manager John McGraw both despised AL president Ban Johnson and considered the junior circuit to be a minor league. By the following year, however, Brush and Johnson had smoothed out their differences and the Giants agreed to play Philadelphia in a best-of-7 game series. Since then the World Series has been a best-of-7 format, except from 1919-21 when it returned to best-of-9.

After surviving two world wars and an earthquake in 1989, the World Series was cancelled for only the second time in 1994 when the players went out on strike Aug. 12 to protest the owners' call for revenue sharing and a salary cap. On Sept. 14, with no hope of reaching a labor agreement to end the 34-day strike, the owners called off the remainder of the regular season and the entire postseason. The strike ended after 232 days on Mar. 31, 1995.

In the chart below, the National League teams are listed in CAPITAL letters. Also, each World Series champion's wins and losses are noted in parentheses after the Series score in games.

Multiple champions: New York Yankees (23); Philadelphia-Oakland A's and St. Louis Cardinals (9); Brooklyn-Los Angeles Dodgers (6); Boston Red Sox, Cincinnati Reds, New York-San Francisco Giants and Pittsburgh Pirates (5); Detroit Tigers (4); Baltimore Orioles, Boston-Milwaukee-Atlanta Braves and Washington Senators-Minnesota Twins (3); Chicago Cubs, Chicago White Sox, Cleveland Indians, New York Mets and Toronto Blue Jays (2).

Year	Winner	Manager	Series	Loser	Manager
1903	Boston Red Sox	Jimmy Collins	5-3 (LWLLWWWW)	PITTSBURGH	Fred Clarke
1904	Not held				
1905	NY GIANTS	John McGraw	4-1 (WLWWW)	Philadelphia A's	Connie Mack
1906	Chicago White Sox	Fielder Jones	4-2 (WLWLWW)	CHICAGO CUBS	Frank Chance
1907	CHICAGO CUBS	Frank Chance	4-0-1 (TWWWW)	Detroit	Hughie Jennings
1908	CHICAGO CUBS	Frank Chance	4-1 (WWLWW)	Detroit	Hughie Jennings
1909	PITTSBURGH	Fred Clarke	4-3 (WLWLWLW)	Detroit	Hughie Jennings
1910	Philadelphia A's	Connie Mack	4-1 (WWWLW)	CHICAGO CUBS	Frank Chance
1911	Philadelphia A's	Connie Mack	4-2 (LWWWLW)	NY GIANTS	John McGraw
1912	Boston Red Sox	Jake Stahl	4-3-1 (WTLWWLLW)	NY GIANTS	John McGraw
1913	Philadelphia A's	Connie Mack	4-1 (WLWWW)	NY GIANTS	John McGraw
1914	BOSTON BRAVES	George Stallings	4-0	Philadelphia A's	Connie Mack
1915	Boston Red Sox	Bill Carrigan	4-1 (LWWWW)	PHILA. PHILLIES	Pat Moran
1916	Boston Red Sox	Bill Carrigan	4-1 (WWLWW)	BKLN. DODGERS	Wilbert Robinson
1917	Chicago White Sox	Pants Rowland	4-2 (WWLLWW)	NY GIANTS	John McGraw
1918	Boston Red Sox	Ed Barrow	4-2 (WLWWLW)	CHICAGO CUBS	Fred Mitchell
1919	CINCINNATI	Pat Moran	5-3 (WWLWWLLW)	Chicago White Sox	Kid Gleason
1920	Cleveland	Tris Speaker	5-2 (WLLWWWW)	BKLN. DODGERS	Wilbert Robinson
1921	NY GIANTS	John McGraw	5-3 (LLWWLWWW)	NY Yankees	Miller Huggins
1922	NY GIANTS	John McGraw	4-0-1 (WTWWW)	NY Yankees	Miller Huggins
1923	NY Yankees	Miller Huggins	4-2 (LWLWWW)	NY GIANTS	John McGraw
1924	Washington	Bucky Harris	4-3 (LWLWLWW)	NY GIANTS	John McGraw
1925	PITTSBURGH	Bill McKechnie	4-3 (LWLLWWW)	Washington	Bucky Harris
1926	ST.L. CARDINALS	Rogers Hornsby	4-3 (LWWLLWW)	NY Yankees	Miller Huggins
1927	NY Yankees	Miller Huggins	4-0	PITTSBURGH	Donie Bush
1928	NY Yankees	Miller Huggins	4-0	ST.L. CARDINALS	Bill McKechnie
1929	Philadelphia A's	Connie Mack	4-1 (WWLWW)	CHICAGO CUBS	Joe McCarthy
1930	Philadelphia A's	Connie Mack	4-2 (WWLLWW)	ST.L. CARDINALS	Gabby Street
1931	ST.L. CARDINALS	Gabby Street	4-3 (LWWLWLW)	Philadelphia A's	Connie Mack
1932	NY Yankees	Joe McCarthy	4-0	CHICAGO CUBS	Charlie Grimm
1933	NY GIANTS	Bill Terry	4-1 (WWLWW)	Washington	Joe Cronin
1934	ST.L. CARDINALS	Frankie Frisch	4-3 (WLWLLWW)	Detroit	Mickey Cochrane
1935	Detroit	Mickey Cochrane	4-2 (LWWWLW)	CHICAGO CUBS	Charlie Grimm
1936	NY Yankees	Joe McCarthy	4-2 (LWWWLW)	NY GIANTS	Bill Terry
1937	NY Yankees	Joe McCarthy	4-1 (WWWLW)	NY GIANTS	Bill Terry
1938	NY Yankees	Joe McCarthy	4-0	CHICAGO CUBS	Gabby Hartnett
1939	NY Yankees	Joe McCarthy	4-0	CINCINNATI	Bill McKechnie

World Series (Cont.)

Year	Winner	Manager	Series	Loser	Manager
1940	CINCINNATI	Bill McKechnie	4-3 (LWLWLWW)	Detroit	Del Baker
1941	NY Yankees	Joe McCarthy	4-1 (WLWWW)	BKLN. DODGERS	Leo Durocher
1942	ST.L. CARDINALS	Billy Southworth	4-1 (LWWWW)	NY Yankees	Joe McCarthy
1943	NY Yankees	Joe McCarthy	4-1 (WLWWW)	ST.L. CARDINALS	Billy Southworth
1944	ST.L. CARDINALS	Billy Southworth	4-2 (LWLWWW)	St. Louis Browns	Luke Sewell
1945	Detroit	Steve O'Neill	4-3 (LWLWWLW)	CHICAGO CUBS	Charlie Grimm
1946	ST.L. CARDINALS	Eddie Dyer	4-3 (LWLWLWW)	Boston Red Sox	Joe Cronin
1947	NY Yankees	Bucky Harris	4-3 (WWLLWLW)	BKLN. DODGERS	Burt Shotton
1948	Cleveland	Lou Boudreau	4-2 (LWWWLW)	BOSTON BRAVES	Billy Southworth
1949	NY Yankees	Casey Stengel	4-1 (WLWWW)	BKLN. DODGERS	Burt Shotton
1950	NY Yankees	Casey Stengel	4-0	PHILA. PHILLIES	Eddie Sawyer
1951	NY Yankees	Casey Stengel	4-2 (LWLWWW)	NY GIANTS	Leo Durocher
1952	NY Yankees	Casey Stengel	4-3 (LWLWLWW)	BKLN. DODGERS	Charlie Dressen
1953	NY Yankees	Casey Stengel	4-2 (WWLLWW)	BKLN. DODGERS	Charlie Dressen
1954	NY GIANTS	Leo Durocher	4-0	Cleveland	Al Lopez
1955	BKLN. DODGERS	Walter Alston	4-3 (LLWWWLW)	NY Yankees	Casey Stengel
1956	NY Yankees	Casey Stengel	4-3 (LLWWWLW	BKLN. DODGERS	Walter Alston
1957	MILW. BRAVES	Fred Haney	4-3 (LWLWWLW)	NY Yankees	Casey Stengel
1958	NY Yankees	Casey Stengel	4-3 (LLWLWWW)	MILW. BRAVES	Fred Haney
1959	LA DODGERS	Walter Alston	4-2 (LWWWLW)	Chicago White Sox	Al Lopez
1960	PITTSBURGH	Danny Murtaugh	4-3 (WLLWWLW)	NY Yankees	Casey Stengel
1961	NY Yankees	Ralph Houk	4-1 (WLWWW)	CINCINNATI	Fred Hutchinson
1962	NY Yankees	Ralph Houk	4-3 (WLWLWLW)	SF GIANTS	Alvin Dark
1963	LA DODGERS	Walter Alston	4-0	NY Yankees	Ralph Houk
1964	ST.L. CARDINALS	Johnny Keane	4-3 (WLLWWLW)	NY Yankees	Yogi Berra
1965	LA DODGERS	Walter Alston	4-3 (LLWWWLW)	Minnesota	Sam Mele
1966	Baltimore	Hank Bauer	4-0	LA DODGERS	Walter Alston
1967	ST.L. CARDINALS	Red Schoendienst	4-3 (WLWWLLW)	Boston Red Sox	Dick Williams
1968	Detroit	Mayo Smith	4-3 (LWLLWWW)	ST.L. CARDINALS	Red Schoendienst
1969	NY METS	Gil Hodges	4-1 (LWWWW)	Baltimore	Earl Weaver
1970	Baltimore	Earl Weaver	4-1 (WWWLW)	CINCINNATI	Sparky Anderson
1971	PITTSBURGH	Danny Murtaugh	4-3 (LLWWWLW)	Baltimore	Earl Weaver
1972	Oakland A's	Dick Williams	4-3 (WWLWLLW)	CINCINNATI	Sparky Anderson
1973	Oakland A's	Dick Williams	4-3 (WLWLLWW)	NY METS	Yogi Berra
1974	Oakland A's	Alvin Dark	4-1 (WLWWW)	LA DODGERS	Walter Alston
1975	CINCINNATI	Sparky Anderson	4-3 (LWWLWLW)	Boston Red Sox	Darrell Johnson
1976	CINCINNATI	Sparky Anderson	4-0	NY Yankees	Billy Martin
1977	NY Yankees	Billy Martin	4-2 (WLWWLW)	LA DODGERS	Tommy Lasorda
1978	NY Yankees	Bob Lemon	4-2 (LLWWWW)	LA DODGERS	Tommy Lasorda
1979	PITTSBURGH	Chuck Tanner	4-3 (LWLLWWW)	Baltimore	Earl Weaver
1980	PHILA. PHILLIES	Dallas Green	4-2 (WWLLWW)	Kansas City	Jim Frey
1981	LA DODGERS	Tommy Lasorda	4-2 (LLWWWW)	NY Yankees	Bob Lemon
1982	ST.L. CARDINALS	Whitey Herzog	4-3 (LWWLLWW)	Milwaukee Brewers	Harvey Kuenn
1983	Baltimore	Joe Altobelli	4-1 (LWWWW)	PHILA. PHILLIES	Paul Owens
1984	Detroit	Sparky Anderson	4-1 (WLWWW)	SAN DIEGO	Dick Williams
1985	Kansas City	Dick Howser	4-3 (LLWLWWW)	ST.L. CARDINALS	Whitey Herzog
1986	NY METS	Davey Johnson	4-3 (LLWWLWW)	Boston Red Sox	John McNamara
1987	Minnesota	Tom Kelly	4-3 (WWLLLWW)	ST.L. CARDINALS	Whitey Herzog
1988	LA DODGERS	Tommy Lasorda	4-1 (WWLWW)	Oakland A's	Tony La Russa
1989	Oakland A's	Tony La Russa	4-0	SF GIANTS	Roger Craig
1990	CINCINNATI	Lou Piniella	4-0	Oakland A's	Tony La Russa
1991	Minnesota	Tom Kelly	4-3 (WWLLLWW)	ATLANTA BRAVES	Bobby Cox
1992	Toronto	Cito Gaston	4-2 (LWWWLW)	ATLANTA BRAVES	Bobby Cox
1993	Toronto	Cito Gaston	4-2 (WLWWLW)	PHILA. PHILLIES	Jim Fregosi
1994	Not held				
1995	ATLANTA BRAVES	Bobby Cox	4-2 (WWLWLW)	Cleveland	Mike Hargrove
1996	New York Yankees	Joe Torre	4-2 (LLWWWW)	ATLANTA BRAVES	Bobby Cox

Most Valuable Players

Currently selected by media panel made up of representatives of CBS Sports, CBS Radio, AP, UPI, and World Series official scorers. Presented by *Sport* magazine from 1955-88 and by Major League Baseball since 1989. Winner who did not play for World Series champions is in **bold** type.

Multiple winners: Bob Gibson, Reggie Jackson and Sandy Koufax (2).

Year		Year		Year	
1955	Johnny Podres, Bklyn, P	1960	**Bobby Richardson**, NY, 2B	1965	Sandy Koufax, LA, P
1956	Don Larsen, NY, P	1961	Whitey Ford, NY, P	1966	Frank Robinson, Bal., OF
1957	Lew Burdette, Mil., P	1962	Ralph Terry, NY, P	1967	Bob Gibson, St.L., P
1958	Bob Turley, NY, P	1963	Sandy Koufax, LA, P	1968	Mickey Lolich, Det., P
1959	Larry Sherry, LA, P	1964	Bob Gibson, St.L., P	1969	Donn Clendenon, NY, 1B

Year		Year		Year	
1970	Brooks Robinson, Bal., 3B	1980	Mike Schmidt, Phi., 3B	1988	Orel Hershiser, LA, P
1971	Roberto Clemente, Pit., OF	1981	Pedro Guerrero, LA, OF; Ron Cey, LA, 3B; & Steve Yeager, LA, C	1989	Dave Stewart, Oak., P
1972	Gene Tenace, Oak., C	1982	Darrell Porter, St.L., C	1990	Jose Rijo, Cin., P
1973	Reggie Jackson, Oak., OF	1983	Rick Dempsey, Bal., C	1991	Jack Morris, Min., P
1974	Rollie Fingers, Oak., P	1984	Alan Trammell, Det., SS	1992	Pat Borders, Tor., C
1975	Pete Rose, Cin., 3B	1985	Bret Saberhagen, KC, P	1993	Paul Molitor, Tor., DH/1B/3B
1976	Johnny Bench, Cin., C	1986	Ray Knight, NY, 3B	1994	Series not held.
1977	Reggie Jackson, NY, OF	1987	Frank Viola, Min., P	1995	Tom Glavine, Atl., P
1978	Bucky Dent, NY, SS			1996	John Wettland, NY, P
1979	Willie Stargell, Pit., 1B				

All-Time World Series Leaders

CAREER

World Series leaders through 1996. Years listed indicate number of World Series appearances.

Hitting

Games

	Yrs	Gm
Yogi Berra, NY Yankees	14	75
Mickey Mantle, NY Yankees	12	65
Elston Howard, NY Yankees-Boston	10	54
Hank Bauer, NY Yankees	9	53
Gil McDougald, NY Yankees	8	53

At Bats

	Yrs	AB
Yogi Berra, NY Yankees	14	259
Mickey Mantle, NY Yankees	12	230
Joe DiMaggio, NY Yankees	10	199
Frankie Frisch, NY Giants-St.L. Cards	8	197
Gil McDougald, NY Yankees	8	190

Batting Avg. (minimum 50 AB)

	AB	H	Avg
Pepper Martin, St.L. Cards	55	23	.418
Paul Molitor, Mil. Brewers-Tor. Blue Jays	55	23	.418
Lou Brock, St. Louis	87	34	.391
Thurman Munson, NY Yankees	67	25	.373
George Brett, Kansas City	51	19	.373
Hank Aaron, Milw. Braves	55	20	.364

World Series Appearances

In the 92 years that the World Series has been contested, American League teams have won 54 championships while National League teams have won 38.

The following teams are ranked by number of appearances through the 1996 World Series; (*) indicates AL teams.

	App	W	L	Pct.	Last Series	Last Title
NY Yankees*	34	23	11	.676	1996	1996
Bklyn/LA Dodgers	18	6	12	.333	1988	1988
NY/SF Giants	16	5	11	.313	1989	1954
St.L. Cardinals	15	9	6	.600	1987	1982
Phi/KC/Oak.A's*	14	9	5	.643	1990	1989
Chicago Cubs	10	2	8	.200	1945	1908
Boston Red Sox*	9	5	4	.556	1986	1918
Cincinnati Reds	9	5	4	.556	1990	1990
Detroit Tigers*	9	4	5	.444	1984	1984
Bos/Mil/Atl.Braves	8	3	5	.375	1996	1995
Pittsburgh Pirates	7	5	2	.714	1979	1979
St.L/Bal.Orioles*	7	3	4	.429	1983	1983
Wash/Min.Twins*	6	3	3	.500	1991	1991
Chi.White Sox*	4	2	2	.500	1959	1917
Phi.Phillies	5	1	4	.200	1993	1980
Cle.Indians*	4	2	2	.500	1995	1948
NY Mets	3	2	1	.667	1986	1986
Tor. Blue Jays*	2	2	0	1.000	1993	1993
KC Royals*	2	1	1	.500	1985	1985
Sea/Mil.Brewers*	1	0	1	.000	1982	—
SD Padres	1	0	1	.000	1984	—

Hits

	AB	H	Avg
Yogi Berra, NY Yankees	259	71	.274
Mickey Mantle, NY Yankees	230	59	.257
Frankie Frisch, NYG-St.L. Cards	197	58	.294
Joe DiMaggio, NY Yankees	199	54	.271
Hank Bauer, NY Yankees	188	46	.245
Pee Wee Reese, Brooklyn	169	46	.272

Runs

	Gm	R
Mickey Mantle, NY Yankees	65	42
Yogi Berra, NY Yankees	75	41
Babe Ruth, Boston Red Sox-NY Yankees	41	37
Lou Gehrig, NY Yankees	34	30
Joe DiMaggio, NY Yankees	51	27

Home Runs

	AB	HR
Mickey Mantle, NY Yankees	230	18
Babe Ruth, Boston Red Sox-NY Yankees	129	15
Yogi Berra, NY Yankees	259	12
Duke Snider, Brooklyn-LA	133	11
Lou Gehrig, NY Yankees	119	10
Reggie Jackson, Oakland-NY Yankees	98	10

Runs Batted In

	Gm	RBI
Mickey Mantle, NY Yankees	65	40
Yogi Berra, NY Yankees	75	39
Lou Gehrig, NY Yankees	34	35
Babe Ruth, Boston Red Sox-NY Yankees	41	33
Joe DiMaggio, NY Yankees	51	30

Stolen Bases

	Gm	SB
Lou Brock, St. Louis	21	14
Eddie Collins, Phi. A's-Chisox	34	14
Frank Chance, Chi. Cubs	20	10
Davey Lopes, Los Angeles	23	10
Phil Rizzuto, NY Yankees	52	10

Total Bases

	Gm	TB
Mickey Mantle, NY Yankees	65	123
Yogi Berra, NY Yankees	75	117
Babe Ruth, Boston Red Sox-NY Yankees	41	96
Lou Gehrig, NY Yankees	34	87
Joe DiMaggio, NY Yankees	51	84

Slugging Pct. (50 AB)

	AB	Pct
Reggie Jackson, Oakland-NY Yankees	98	.755
Babe Ruth, Boston Red Sox-NY Yankees	129	.744
Lou Gehrig, NY Yankees	119	.731
Al Simmons, Phi. A's-Cincinnati	73	.658
Lou Brock, St. Louis	87	.655

All-Time World Series Leaders (Cont.)

Pitching

Games

	Yrs	Gm
Whitey Ford, NY Yankees	11	22
Rollie Fingers, Oakland	3	16
Allie Reynolds, NY Yankees	6	15
Bob Turley, NY Yankees	5	15
Clay Carroll, Cincinnati	3	14

Wins

	Gm	W-L
Whitey Ford, NY Yankees	22	10-8
Bob Gibson, St. Louis	9	7-2
Allie Reynolds, NY Yankees	15	7-2
Red Ruffing, NY Yankees	10	7-2
Lefty Gomez, NY Yankees	7	6-0
Chief Bender, Philadelphia A's	10	6-4
Waite Hoyt, NY Yankees-Phi. A's	12	6-4

ERA (minimum 25 IP)

	Gm	IP	ERA
Jack Billingham, Cincinnati	7	25	0.36
Harry Brecheen, St. Louis	7	33	0.83
Babe Ruth, Boston Red Sox	3	31	0.87
Sherry Smith, Brooklyn	3	30	0.89
Sandy Koufax, Los Angeles	8	57	0.95

Saves

	Gm	IP	Sv
Rollie Fingers, Oakland	16	33	6
Allie Reynolds, NY Yankees	15	77	4
Johnny Murphy, NY Yankees	8	16	4
John Wetteland, NY Yankees	5	4.1	4

Seven pitchers tied with 3 each.

Shutouts

	GS	CG	ShO
Christy Mathewson, NY Giants	11	10	4
Three Finger Brown, Chi. Cubs	7	5	3
Whitey Ford, NY Yankees	22	7	3

Seven pitchers tied with 2 each.

Innings Pitched

	Gm	IP
Whitey Ford, NY Yankees	22	146
Christy Mathewson, NY Giants	11	102
Red Ruffing, NY Yankees	10	86
Chief Bender, Philadelphia A's	10	85
Waite Hoyt, NY Yankees-Phi. A's	12	84

Complete Games

	GS	CG	W-L
Christy Mathewson, NY Giants	11	10	5-5
Chief Bender, Philadelphia A's	10	9	6-4
Bob Gibson, St. Louis	9	8	7-2
Whitey Ford, NY Yankees	22	7	10-8
Red Ruffing, NY Yankees	10	7	7-2

Strikeouts

	Gm	IP	SO
Whitey Ford, NY Yankees	22	146	94
Bob Gibson, St. Louis	9	81	92
Allie Reynolds, NY Yankees	15	77	62
Sandy Koufax, Los Angeles	8	57	61
Red Ruffing, NY Yankees	10	86	61

Bases on Balls

	Gm	IP	BB
Whitey Ford, NY Yankees	22	146	34
Allie Reynolds, NY Yankees	15	77	32
Art Nehf, NY Giants-Chi. Cubs	12	79	32
Jim Palmer, Baltimore	9	65	31
Bob Turley, NY Yankees	15	54	29

Losses

	Gm	W-L
Whitey Ford, NY Yankees	22	10-8
Christy Mathewson, NY Giants	11	5-5
Joe Bush, Phi. A's-Bosox-NY Yankees	9	2-5
Rube Marquard, NY Giants-Brooklyn	11	2-5
Eddie Plank, Philadelphia A's	7	2-5
Schoolboy Rowe, Detroit	8	2-5

League Championship Series

Division play came to the major leagues in 1969 when both the American and National Leagues expanded to 12 teams. With an East and West Division in each league, League Championship Series (LCS) became necessary to determine the NL and AL pennant winners. In 1994, teams were realigned into three divisions, the East, Central, and West with the division winners and one wildcard team playing a best-of-five series to determine the LCS competitors. In the charts below, the East Division champions are noted by the letter E, the Central Divsion champions by C and the West Division champions by W. The wild-card winner is noted by WC. Also, each playoff winner's wins and losses are noted in parentheses after the series score. The LCS changed from best-of-5 to best-of-7 in 1985. Each league's LCS was cancelled in 1994 due to the players' strike.

National League

Multiple champions: Cincinnati and LA Dodgers (5); Atlanta, NY Mets, Philadelphia and St. Louis (3); Pittsburgh (2).

Year	Winner	Manager	Series	Loser	Manager
1969	E- New York	Gil Hodges	3-0	W- Atlanta	Lum Harris
1970	W- Cincinnati	Sparky Anderson	3-0	E- Pittsburgh	Danny Murtaugh
1971	E- Pittsburgh	Danny Murtaugh	3-1 (LWWW)	W- San Francisco	Charlie Fox
1972	W- Cincinnati	Sparky Anderson	3-2 (LWLWW)	E- Pittsburgh	Bill Virdon
1973	E- New York	Yogi Berra	3-2 (LWWLW)	W- Cincinnati	Sparky Anderson
1974	W- Los Angeles	Walter Alston	3-1 (WWLW)	E- Pittsburgh	Danny Murtaugh
1975	W- Cincinnati	Sparky Anderson	3-0	E- Pittsburgh	Danny Murtaugh
1976	W- Cincinnati	Sparky Anderson	3-0	E- Philadelphia	Danny Ozark
1977	W- Los Angeles	Tommy Lasorda	3-1 (LWWW)	E- Philadelphia	Danny Ozark
1978	W- Los Angeles	Tommy Lasorda	3-1 (WWLW)	E- Philadelphia	Danny Ozark
1979	E- Pittsburgh	Chuck Tanner	3-0	W- Cincinnati	John McNamara
1980	E- Philadelphia	Dallas Green	3-2 (WLLWW)	W- Houston	Bill Virdon
1981	W- Los Angeles	Tommy Lasorda	3-2 (WLLWW)	E- Montreal	Jim Fanning

Year	Winner	Manager	Series	Loser	Manager
1982	E- St. Louis	Whitey Herzog	3-0	W- Atlanta	Joe Torre
1983	E- Philadelphia	Paul Owens	3-1 (WLWW)	W- Los Angeles	Tommy Lasorda
1984	W- San Diego	Dick Williams	3-2 (LLWWW)	E- Chicago	Jim Frey
1985	E- St. Louis	Whitey Herzog	4-2 (LLWWWW)	W- Los Angeles	Tommy Lasorda
1986	E- New York	Davey Johnson	4-2 (LWWLWW)	W- Houston	Hal Lanier
1987	E- St. Louis	Whitey Herzog	4-3 (WLWLLWW)	W- San Francisco	Roger Craig
1988	W- Los Angeles	Tommy Lasorda	4-3 (LWLWWLW)	E- New York	Davey Johnson
1989	W- San Francisco	Roger Craig	4-1 (WLWWW)	E- Chicago	Don Zimmer
1990	W- Cincinnati	Lou Piniella	4-2 (LWWWLW)	E- Pittsburgh	Jim Leyland
1991	W- Atlanta	Bobby Cox	4-3 (LWWLLWW)	E- Pittsburgh	Jim Leyland
1992	W- Atlanta	Bobby Cox	4-3 (WWLWLLW)	E- Pittsburgh	Jim Leyland
1993	E- Philadelphia	Jim Fregosi	4-2 (WLLWWW)	W- Atlanta	Bobby Cox
1994	Not held				
1995	E- Atlanta	Bobby Cox	4-0	C- Cincinnati	Davey Johnson
1996	E-Atlanta	Bobby Cox	4-3 (WLLLWWW)	C-St. Louis	Tony LaRussa

NLCS Most Valuable Players

Winners who did not play for NLCS champions are in **bold** type. **Multiple winner:** Steve Garvey (2).

Year		Year		Year	
1977	Dusty Baker, LA, OF	1985	Ozzie Smith, St.L., SS	1992	John Smoltz, Atl., P
1978	Steve Garvey, LA, 1B	1986	**Mike Scott,** Hou., P	1993	Curt Schilling, Phi., P
1979	Willie Stargell, Pit., 1B	1987	**Jeff Leonard,** SF, OF	1994	LCS not held.
1980	Manny Trillo, Phi., 2B	1988	Orel Hershiser, LA, P	1995	Mike Devereaux, Atl., OF
1981	Burt Hooton, LA, P	1989	Will Clark, SF, 1B	1996	Javy Lopez, Atl., C
1982	Darrell Porter, St.L., C	1990	Rob Dibble, Cin., P		
1983	Gary Matthews, Phi., OF		& Randy Myers, Cin., P		
1984	Steve Garvey, SD, 1B	1991	Steve Avery, Atl., P		

American League

Multiple champions: Oakland and NY Yankees (6); Baltimore (5); Boston, Kansas City, Minnesota and Toronto (2).

Year	Winner	Manager	Series	Loser	Manager
1969	E- Baltimore	Earl Weaver	3-0	W- Minnesota	Billy Martin
1970	E- Baltimore	Earl Weaver	3-0	W- Minnesota	Bill Rigney
1971	E- Baltimore	Earl Weaver	3-0	W- Oakland	Dick Williams
1972	W- Oakland	Dick Williams	3-2 (WWLLW)	E- Detroit	Billy Martin
1973	W- Oakland	Dick Williams	3-2 (LWWLW)	E- Baltimore	Earl Weaver
1974	W- Oakland	Alvin Dark	3-1 (LWWW)	E- Baltimore	Earl Weaver
1975	E- Boston	Darrell Johnson	3-0	W- Oakland	Alvin Dark
1976	E- New York	Billy Martin	3-2 (WLWLW)	W- Kansas City	Whitey Herzog
1977	E- New York	Billy Martin	3-2 (LWLWW)	W- Kansas City	Whitey Herzog
1978	E- New York	Bob Lemon	3-1 (WLWW)	W- Kansas City	Whitey Herzog
1979	E- Baltimore	Earl Weaver	3-1 (WWLW)	W- California	Jim Fregosi
1980	W- Kansas City	Jim Frey	3-0	E- New York	Dick Howser
1981	E- New York	Bob Lemon	3-0	W- Oakland	Billy Martin
1982	E- Milwaukee	Harvey Kuenn	3-2 (LLWWW)	W- California	Gene Mauch
1983	E- Baltimore	Joe Altobelli	3-1 (LWWW)	W- Chicago	Tony La Russa
1984	E- Detroit	Sparky Anderson	3-0	W- Kansas City	Dick Howser
1985	W- Kansas City	Dick Howser	4-3 (LLWLWWW)	E- Toronto	Bobby Cox
1986	E- Boston	John McNamara	4-3 (LWLLWWW)	W- California	Gene Mauch
1987	W- Minnesota	Tom Kelly	4-1 (WWLWW)	E- Detroit	Sparky Anderson
1988	W- Oakland	Tony La Russa	4-0	E- Boston	Joe Morgan
1989	W- Oakland	Tony La Russa	4-1 (WWLWW)	E- Toronto	Cito Gaston
1990	W- Oakland	Tony La Russa	4-0	E- Boston	Joe Morgan
1991	W- Minnesota	Tom Kelly	4-1 (WLWWW)	E- Toronto	Cito Gaston
1992	E- Toronto	Cito Gaston	4-2 (LWWWLW)	W- Oakland	Tony La Russa
1993	E- Toronto	Cito Gaston	4-2 (WWLLWW)	W- Chicago	Gene Lamont
1994	Not held				
1995	C- Cleveland	Mike Hargrove	4-2 (LWLWWW)	W-Seattle	Lou Piniella
1996	E-New York	Joe Torre	4-1 (WLWWW)	WC-Baltimore	Davey Johnson

ALCS Most Valuable Players

Winner who did not play for ALCS champions is in **bold** type. **Multiple winner:** Dave Stewart (2).

Year		Year		Year	
1980	Frank White, KC, 2B	1986	Marty Barrett, Bos., 2B	1992	Roberto Alomar, Tor., 2B
1981	Graig Nettles, NY, 3B	1987	Gary Gaetti, Min., 3B	1993	Dave Stewart, Tor., P
1982	**Fred Lynn,** Cal., OF	1988	Dennis Eckersley, Oak., P	1994	LCS not held.
1983	Mike Boddicker, Bal., P	1989	Rickey Henderson, Oak., OF	1995	Orel Hershiser, Cle., P
1984	Kirk Gibson, Det., OF	1990	Dave Stewart, Oak., P	1996	Bernie Williams, NY, OF
1985	George Brett, KC, 3B	1991	Kirby Puckett, Min., OF		

Other Playoffs

Seven times from 1946-80, playoffs were necessary to decide league or division championships when two teams tied for first place at the end of the regular season. In the strike year of 1981, there were playoffs between the first and second half-season champions in both leagues. In 1995, the 1994–95 players' strike shortened the regular season to 144 games.

National League

Year	NL	W	L	Manager
1946	Brooklyn	96	58	Leo Durocher
	St. Louis	96	58	Eddie Dyer
	Playoff: (Best-of-3) St. Louis, 2-0			
	NL	**W**	**L**	**Manager**
1951	Brooklyn	96	58	Charlie Dressen
	New York	96	58	Leo Durocher
	Playoff: (Best-of-3) New York, 2-1 (WLW)			
	NL	**W**	**L**	**Manager**
1959	Milwaukee	86	68	Fred Haney
	Los Angeles	86	68	Walter Alston
	Playoff: (Best-of-3) Los Angeles, 2-0			
	NL	**W**	**L**	**Manager**
1962	Los Angeles	101	61	Walter Alston
	San Francisco	101	61	Alvin Dark
	Playoff: (Best-of-3) San Francisco, 2-1 (WLW)			

Year	NL West	W	L	Manager
1980	Houston	92	70	Bill Virdon
	Los Angeles	92	70	Tommy Lasorda
	Playoff: (1 game) Houston, 7-1 (at LA)			
	NL East	**W**	**L**	**Manager**
1981	(1st Half) Phila	34	21	Dallas Green
	(2nd Half) Montreal	30	23	Jim Fanning
	Playoff: (Best-of-5) Montreal, 3-2 (WWLLW)			
	NL West	**W**	**L**	**Manager**
	(1st Half) Los Ang	36	21	Tommy Lasorda
	(2nd Half) Houston	33	20	Bill Virdon
	Playoff: (Best-of-5) Los Angeles, 3-2 (LLWWW)			

American League

Year	AL	W	L	Manager
1948	Boston	96	58	Joe McCarthy
	Cleveland	96	58	Lou Boudreau
	Playoff: (1 game) Cleveland, 8-3 (at Boston)			
	AL East	**W**	**L**	**Manager**
1978	Boston	99	63	Don Zimmer
	New York	99	63	Bob Lemon
	Playoff: (1 game) New York, 5-4 (at Boston)			

Year	AL East	W	L	Manager
1981	(1st Half) N.Y.	34	22	Bob Lemon
	(2nd Half) Milw.	31	22	Buck Rodgers
	Playoff: (Best-of-5) New York, 3-2 (WWLLW)			
	AL West	**W**	**L**	**Manager**
	(1st Half) Oakland	37	23	Billy Martin
	(2nd Half) Kan.City	30	23	Jim Frey
	Playoff: (Best-of-5), Oakland, 3-0			
	AL West	**W**	**L**	**Manager**
1995	Seattle	78	66	Lou Piniella
	California	78	66	Marcel Lachemann
	Playoff: (1 game) Seattle, 9-1 (at Seattle)			

Regular Season League & Division Winners

Regular season National and American League pennant winners from 1900-68, as well as West and East divisional champions from 1969-93. In 1994, both leagues went to three divisions—West, Central and East. However, due to the 1994 players' strike that resulted in the cancelling of the season after games played on Aug. 11, division leaders at the time of the strike are not considered official champions by either league. Note that (*) indicates 1994 divisional champion is unofficial and that **GA** column indicates games ahead of the second place club. See page 116 for NL Pennant winners before 1900.

National League

Multiple pennant winners: Brooklyn-LA (19); New York-SF Giants (17); St. Louis (15); Chicago (10); Cincinnati and Pittsburgh (9); Boston-Milwaukee-Atlanta (8); Philadelphia (5); New York Mets (3). **Multiple division winners:** WEST—Los Angeles (8); Cincinnati (7); Atlanta (5); San Francisco (3); Houston and San Diego (2). EAST—Pittsburgh (9); Philadelphia (6); NY Mets (4); St. Louis (3); Atlanta and Chicago (2).

Year		W	L	Pct	GA
1900	Brooklyn	82	54	.603	4½
1901	Pittsburgh	90	49	.647	7½
1902	Pittsburgh	103	36	.741	27½
1903	Pittsburgh	91	49	.650	6½
1904	New York	106	47	.693	13
1905	New York	105	48	.686	9
1906	Chicago	116	36	.763	20
1907	Chicago	107	45	.704	17
1908	Chicago	99	55	.643	1
1909	Pittsburgh	110	42	.724	6½
1910	Chicago	104	50	.675	13
1911	New York	99	54	.647	7½
1912	New York	103	48	.682	10
1913	New York	101	51	.664	12½
1914	Boston	94	59	.614	10½
1915	Philadelphia	90	62	.592	7
1916	Brooklyn	94	60	.610	2½
1917	New York	98	56	.636	10
1918	Chicago	84	45	.651	10½
1919	Cincinnati	96	44	.686	9

Year		W	L	Pct	GA
1920	Brooklyn	93	61	.604	7
1921	New York	94	59	.614	4
1922	New York	93	61	.604	7
1923	New York	95	58	.621	4½
1924	New York	93	60	.608	1½
1925	Pittsburgh	95	58	.621	8½
1926	St. Louis	89	65	.578	2
1927	Pittsburgh	94	60	.610	1½
1928	St. Louis	95	59	.617	2
1929	Chicago	98	54	.645	10½
1930	St. Louis	92	62	.597	2
1931	St. Louis	101	53	.656	13
1932	Chicago	90	64	.584	4
1933	New York	91	61	.599	5
1934	St. Louis	95	58	.621	2
1935	Chicago	100	54	.649	4
1936	New York	92	62	.597	5
1937	New York	95	57	.625	3
1938	Chicago	89	63	.586	2
1939	Cincinnati	97	57	.630	4½

Year		W	L	Pct	GA
1940	Cincinnati	100	53	.654	12
1941	Brooklyn	100	54	.649	2½
1942	St. Louis	106	48	.688	2
1943	St. Louis	105	49	.682	18
1944	St. Louis	105	49	.682	14½
1945	Chicago	98	56	.636	3
1946	St. Louis†	98	58	.628	2
1947	Brooklyn	94	60	.610	5
1948	Boston	91	62	.595	6½
1949	Brooklyn	97	57	.630	1
1950	Philadelphia	91	63	.591	2
1951	New York†	98	59	.624	1
1952	Brooklyn	96	57	.627	4½
1953	Brooklyn	105	49	.682	13
1954	New York	97	57	.630	5
1955	Brooklyn	98	55	.641	13½
1956	Brooklyn	93	61	.604	1
1957	Milwaukee	95	59	.617	8
1958	Milwaukee	92	62	.597	8
1959	Los Angeles†	88	68	.564	2
1960	Pittsburgh	95	59	.617	7
1961	Cincinnati	93	61	.604	4
1962	San Francisco†	103	62	.624	1
1963	Los Angeles	99	63	.611	6
1964	St. Louis	93	69	.574	1
1965	Los Angeles	97	65	.599	2
1966	Los Angeles	95	67	.586	1½
1967	St. Louis	101	60	.627	10½
1968	St. Louis	97	65	.599	9
1969	West—Atlanta	93	69	.574	3
	East—N.Y. Mets	100	62	.617	8
1970	West—Cincinnati	102	60	.630	14½
	East—Pittsburgh	89	73	.549	5
1971	West—San Francisco	90	72	.556	1
	East—Pittsburgh	97	65	.599	7
1972	West—Cincinnati	95	59	.617	10½
	East—Pittsburgh	96	59	.619	11
1973	West—Cincinnati	99	63	.611	3½
	East—N.Y. Mets	82	79	.509	1½
1974	West—Los Angeles	102	60	.630	4
	East—Pittsburgh	88	74	.543	1½
1975	West—Cincinnati	108	54	.667	20
	East—Pittsburgh	92	69	.571	6½
1976	West—Cincinnati	102	60	.630	10
	East—Philadelphia	101	61	.623	9
1977	West—Los Angeles	98	64	.605	10
	East—Philadelphia	101	61	.623	5
1978	West—Los Angeles	95	67	.586	2½
	East—Philadelphia	90	72	.556	1½
1979	West—Cincinnati	90	71	.559	1½
	East—Pittsburgh	98	64	.605	2
1980	West—Houston	93	70	.571	1
	East—Philadelphia	91	71	.562	1
1981	West—Los Angeles†	63	47	.573	—
	East—Montreal†	60	48	.556	—
1982	West—Atlanta	89	73	.549	1
	East—St. Louis	92	70	.568	3
1983	West—Los Angeles	91	71	.562	3
	East—Philadelphia	90	72	.556	6
1984	West—San Diego	92	70	.568	12
	East—Chicago	96	65	.596	6½
1985	West—Los Angeles	95	67	.586	5½
	East—St. Louis	101	61	.623	3
1986	West—Houston	96	66	.593	10
	East—N.Y. Mets	108	54	.667	21½
1987	West—San Francisco	90	72	.556	6
	East—St. Louis	95	67	.586	3
1988	West—Los Angeles	94	67	.584	7
	East—N.Y. Mets	100	60	.625	15
1989	West—San Francisco	92	70	.568	3
	East—Chicago	93	69	.574	6
1990	West—Cincinnati	91	71	.562	5
	East—Pittsburgh	95	67	.586	4
1991	West—Atlanta	94	68	.580	1
	East—Pittsburgh	98	64	.605	14
1992	West—Atlanta	98	64	.605	8
	East—Pittsburgh	96	66	.593	9
1993	West—Atlanta	104	58	.642	1
	East—Philadelphia	97	65	.599	3
1994	West—Los Angeles*	58	56	.509	3½
	Central—Cincinnati*	66	48	.579	½
	East—Montreal*	74	40	.649	6
1995	West—Los Angeles	78	66	.542	1
	Central—Cincinnati	85	59	.590	9
	East—Atlanta	90	54	.625	21
1996	West—San Diego	91	71	.562	1
	Central—St. Louis	88	74	.543	6
	East—Atlanta	96	66	.593	8

†**Regular season playoffs: 1946**—St. Louis def. Brooklyn (2 games to 1); **1951**—New York def. Brooklyn (2 games to 1); **1959**—Los Angeles def. Milwaukee (2 games to none); **1962**—San Francisco def. Los Angeles (2 games to 1); **1981**—East: Montreal def. Philadelphia (3 games to 2) and West: Los Angeles def. Houston (3 games to 2).

American League

Multiple pennant winners: NY Yankees (34); Philadelphia-Oakland A's (15); Boston (10); Detroit (9); Baltimore and Washington-Minnesota (6); Chicago (5); Cleveland (3); KC Royals and Toronto (2). **Multiple division winners:** WEST—Oakland (10); Kansas City (6); Minnesota (4); California (3); Chicago (2). EAST—Baltimore (7); NY Yankees (6); Boston and Toronto (5); Detroit (3). CENTRAL—Cleveland (2).

Year		W	L	Pct	GA
1901	Chicago	83	53	.610	4
1902	Philadelphia	83	53	.610	5
1903	Boston	91	47	.659	14½
1904	Boston	95	59	.617	1½
1905	Philadelphia	92	56	.622	2
1906	Chicago	93	58	.616	3
1907	Detroit	92	58	.613	1½
1908	Detroit	90	63	.588	½
1909	Detroit	98	54	.645	3½
1910	Philadelphia	102	48	.680	14½
1911	Philadelphia	101	50	.669	13½
1912	Boston	105	47	.691	14
1913	Philadelphia	96	57	.627	6½
1914	Philadelphia	99	53	.651	8½
1915	Boston	101	50	.669	2½
1916	Boston	91	63	.591	2
1917	Chicago	100	54	.649	9
1918	Boston	75	51	.595	2½
1919	Chicago	88	52	.629	3½
1920	Cleveland	98	56	.636	2
1921	New York	98	55	.641	4½
1922	New York	94	60	.610	1
1923	New York	98	54	.645	16
1924	Washington	92	62	.597	2
1925	Washington	96	55	.636	8½
1926	New York	91	63	.591	3
1927	New York	110	44	.714	19
1928	New York	101	53	.656	2½
1929	Philadelphia	104	46	.693	18

Regular Season League & Division Winners (Cont.)

American League

Year		W	L	Pct	GA
1930	Philadelphia	102	52	.662	8
1931	Philadelphia	107	45	.704	13½
1932	New York	107	47	.695	13
1933	Washington	99	53	.651	7
1934	Detroit	101	53	.656	7
1935	Detroit	93	58	.616	3
1936	New York	102	51	.667	19½
1937	New York	102	52	.662	13
1938	New York	99	53	.651	9½
1939	New York	106	45	.702	17
1940	Detroit	90	64	.584	1
1941	New York	101	53	.656	17
1942	New York	103	51	.669	9
1943	New York	98	56	.636	13½
1944	St. Louis	89	65	.578	1
1945	Detroit	88	65	.575	1½
1946	Boston	104	50	.675	12
1947	New York	97	57	.630	12
1948	Cleveland†	97	58	.626	1
1949	New York	97	57	.630	1
1950	New York	98	56	.636	3
1951	New York	98	56	.636	5
1952	New York	95	59	.617	2
1953	New York	99	52	.656	8½
1954	Cleveland	111	43	.721	8
1955	New York	96	58	.623	3
1956	New York	97	57	.630	9
1957	New York	98	56	.636	8
1958	New York	92	62	.597	10
1959	Chicago	94	60	.610	5
1960	New York	97	57	.630	8
1961	New York	109	53	.673	8
1962	New York	96	66	.593	5
1963	New York	104	57	.646	10½
1964	New York	99	63	.611	1
1965	Minnesota	102	60	.630	7
1966	Baltimore	97	63	.606	9
1967	Boston	92	70	.568	1
1968	Detroit	103	59	.636	12
1969	West—Minnesota	97	65	.599	9
	East—Baltimore	109	53	.673	19
1970	West—Minnesota	98	64	.605	9
	East—Baltimore	108	54	.667	15
1971	West—Oakland	101	60	.627	16
	East—Baltimore	101	57	.639	12
1972	West—Oakland	93	62	.600	5½
	East—Detroit	86	70	.551	½
1973	West—Oakland	94	68	.580	6
	East—Baltimore	97	65	.599	8

Year		W	L	Pct	GA
1974	West—Oakland	90	72	.556	5
	East—Baltimore	91	71	.562	2
1975	West—Oakland	98	64	.605	7
	East—Boston	95	65	.594	4½
1976	West—Kansas City	90	72	.556	2½
	East—New York	97	62	.610	10½
1977	West—Kansas City	102	60	.630	8
	East—New York	100	62	.617	2½
1978	West—Kansas City	92	70	.568	5
	East—New York†	100	63	.613	1
1979	West—California	88	74	.543	3
	East—Baltimore	102	57	.642	8
1980	West—Kansas City	97	65	.599	14
	East—New York	103	59	.636	3
1981	West—Oakland†	64	45	.587	—
	East—New York†	59	48	.551	—
1982	West—California	93	69	.574	3
	East—Milwaukee	95	67	.586	1
1983	West—Chicago	99	63	.611	20
	East—Baltimore	98	64	.605	6
1984	West—Kansas City	84	78	.519	3
	East—Detroit	104	58	.642	15
1985	West—Kansas City	91	71	.562	1
	East—Toronto	99	62	.615	2
1986	West—California	92	70	.568	5
	East—Boston	95	66	.590	5½
1987	West—Minnesota	85	77	.525	2
	East—Detroit	98	64	.605	2
1988	West—Oakland	104	58	.642	13
	East—Boston	89	73	.549	1
1989	West—Oakland	99	63	.611	7
	East—Toronto	89	73	.549	2
1990	West—Oakland	103	59	.636	9
	East—Boston	88	74	.543	2
1991	West—Minnesota	95	67	.586	8
	East—Toronto	91	71	.562	7
1992	West—Oakland	96	66	.593	6
	East—Toronto	96	66	.593	4
1993	West—Chicago	94	68	.580	8
	East—Toronto	95	67	.586	7
1994	West—Texas*	52	62	.456	1
	Central—Chicago*	67	46	.593	1
	East—New York*	70	43	.619	6½
1995	West—Seattle†	79	66	.545	1
	Central—Cleveland	100	44	.694	30
	East—Boston	86	58	.597	7
1996	West—Texas	90	72	.556	4½
	Central—Cleveland	99	62	.615	14½
	East—New York	92	70	.568	4½

†**Regular season playoffs: 1948**—Cleveland def. Boston, 8-3 (one game); **1978**—New York def. Boston, 5-4 (one game); **1981**—East: New York def. Milwaukee (3 games to 2) and West: Oakland def. Kansas City (3 games to none); **1995**—Seattle def. California, 9-1 (one game).

The All-Star Game

Baseball's first All-Star Game was held on July 6, 1933, before 47,595 at Comiskey Park in Chicago. From that year on, the All-Star Game has matched the best players in the American League against the best in the National. From 1959-62, two All-Star Games were played. The only year an All-Star Game wasn't played was 1945, when World War II travel restrictions made it necessary to cancel the meeting. The NL leads the series, 40-26-1. In the chart below, the American League is listed in **bold** type.

The All-Star Game MVP Award is named after Arch Ward, the *Chicago Tribune* sports editor who founded the game in 1933. First given at the two All-Star games in 1962, the name of the award was changed to the Commissioner's Trophy in 1970 and back to the Ward Memorial Award in 1985. **Multiple winners:** Gary Carter, Steve Garvey and Willie Mays (2).

Year		Host	AL Manager	NL Manager	MVP
1933	**American,** 4-2	Chicago (AL)	Connie Mack	John McGraw	No award
1934	**American,** 9-7	New York (NL)	Joe Cronin	Bill Terry	No award
1935	**American,** 4-1	Cleveland	Mickey Cochrane	Frankie Frisch	No award
1936	National, 4-3	Boston (NL)	Joe McCarthy	Charlie Grimm	No award

The All-Star Game (Cont.)

Year		Host	AL Manager	NL Manager	MVP
1937	**American,** 8-3	Washington	Joe McCarthy	Bill Terry	No award
1938	National, 4-1	Cincinnati	Joe McCarthy	Bill Terry	No award
1939	**American,** 3-1	New York (AL)	Joe McCarthy	Gabby Hartnett	No award
1940	National, 4-0	St. Louis (NL)	Joe Cronin	Bill McKechnie	No award
1941	**American,** 7-5	Detroit	Del Baker	Bill McKechnie	No award
1942	**American,** 3-1	New York (NL)	Joe McCarthy	Leo Durocher	No award
1943	**American,** 5-3	Philadelphia (AL)	Joe McCarthy	Billy Southworth	No award
1944	National, 7-1	Pittsburgh	Joe McCarthy	Billy Southworth	No award
1945	Not held				
1946	**American,** 12-0	Boston (AL)	Steve O'Neill	Charlie Grimm	No award
1947	**American,** 2-1	Chicago (NL)	Joe Cronin	Eddie Dyer	No award
1948	**American,** 5-2	St. Louis (AL)	Bucky Harris	Leo Durocher	No award
1949	**American,** 11-7	Brooklyn	Lou Boudreau	Billy Southworth	No award
1950	National, 4-3 (14)	Chicago (AL)	Casey Stengel	Burt Shotton	No award
1951	National, 8-3	Detroit	Casey Stengel	Eddie Sawyer	No award
1952	National, 3-2 (5, rain)	Philadelphia (NL)	Casey Stengel	Leo Durocher	No award
1953	National, 5-1	Cincinnati	Casey Stengel	Charlie Dressen	No award
1954	**American,** 11-9	Cleveland	Casey Stengel	Walter Alston	No award
1955	National, 6-5 (12)	Milwaukee	Al Lopez	Leo Durocher	No award
1956	National, 7-3	Washington	Casey Stengel	Walter Alston	No award
1957	**American,** 6-5	St. Louis	Casey Stengel	Walter Alston	No award
1958	**American,** 4-3	Baltimore	Casey Stengel	Fred Haney	No award
1959-a	National, 5-4	Pittsburgh	Casey Stengel	Fred Haney	No award
1959-b	**American,** 5-3	Los Angeles	Casey Stengel	Fred Haney	No award
1960-a	National, 5-3	Kansas City	Al Lopez	Walter Alston	No award
1960-b	National, 6-0	New York	Al Lopez	Walter Alston	No award
1961-a	National, 5-4 (10)	San Francisco	Paul Richards	Danny Murtaugh	No award
1961-b	TIE, 1-1 (9, rain)	Boston	Paul Richards	Danny Murtaugh	No award
1962-a	National, 3-1	Washington	Ralph Houk	Fred Hutchinson	Maury Wills, LA (NL), SS
1962-b	**American,** 9-4	Chicago (NL)	Ralph Houk	Fred Hutchinson	Leon Wagner, LA (AL), OF
1963	National, 5-3	Cleveland	Ralph Houk	Alvin Dark	Willie Mays, SF, OF
1964	National, 7-4	New York (NL)	Al Lopez	Walter Alston	Johnny Callison, Phi., OF
1965	National, 6-5	Minnesota	Al Lopez	Gene Mauch	Juan Marichal, SF, P
1966	National, 2-1 (10)	St. Louis	Sam Mele	Walter Alston	Brooks Robinson, Bal., 3B
1967	National, 2-1 (15)	California	Hank Bauer	Walter Alston	Tony Perez, Cin., 3B
1968	National, 1-0	Houston	Dick Williams	Red Schoendienst	Willie Mays, SF, OF
1969	National, 9-3	Washington	Mayo Smith	Red Schoendienst	Willie McCovey, SF, 1B
1970	National, 5-4 (12)	Cincinnati	Earl Weaver	Gil Hodges	Carl Yastrzemski, Bos., OF-1B
1971	**American,** 6-4	Detroit	Earl Weaver	Sparky Anderson	Frank Robinson, Bal., OF
1972	National, 4-3 (10)	Atlanta	Earl Weaver	Danny Murtaugh	Joe Morgan, Con., 2B
1973	National, 7-1	Kansas	Dick Williams	Sparky Anderson	Bobby Bonds, SF, OF
1974	National, 7-2	Pittsburgh	Dick Williams	Yogi Berra	Steve Garvey, LA, 1B
1975	National, 6-3	Milwaukee	Alvin Dark	Walter Alston	Bill Madlock, Chi. (NL), 3B & Jon Matlack, NY (NL), P
1976	National, 7-1	Philadelphia	Darrell Johnson	Sparky Anderson	George Foster, Cin., OF
1977	National, 7-5	New York (AL)	Billy Martin	Sparky Anderson	Don Sutton, LA, P
1978	National, 7-3	San Diego	Billy Martin	Tommy Lasorda	Steve Garvey, LA, 1B
1979	National, 7-6	Seattle	Bob Lemon	Tommy Lasorda	Dave Parker, Pit, OF
1980	National, 4-2	Los Angeles	Earl Weaver	Chuck Tanner	Ken Griffey, Cin., OF
1981	National, 5-4	Cleveland	Jim Frey	Dallas Green	Gary Carter, Mon., C
1982	National, 4-1	Montreal	Billy Martin	Tommy Lasorda	Dave Concepcion, Cin., SS
1983	**American,** 13-3	Chicago (AL)	Harvey Kuenn	Whitey Herzog	Fred Lynn, Cal., OF
1984	National, 3-1	San Francisco	Joe Altobelli	Paul Owens	Gary Carter, Mon., C
1985	National, 6-1	Minnesota	Sparky Anderson	Dick Williams	LaMarr Hoyt, SD, P
1986	**American,** 3-2	Houston	Dick Howser	Whitey Herzog	Roger Clemens, Bos., P
1987	National, 2-0 (13)	Oakland	John McNamara	Davey Johnson	Tim Raines, Mon., OF
1988	**American,** 2-1	Cincinnati	Tom Kelly	Whitey Herzog	Terry Steinbach, Oak., C
1989	**American,** 5-3	California	Tony La Russa	Tommy Lasorda	Bo Jackson, KC, OF
1990	**American,** 2-0	Chicago (NL)	Tony La Russa	Roger Craig	Julio Franco, Tex., 2B
1991	**American,** 4-2	Toronto	Tony La Russa	Lou Piniella	Cal Ripken Jr., Bal., SS
1992	**American,** 13-6	San Diego	Tom Kelly	Bobby Cox	Ken Griffey Jr., Sea., OF
1993	**American,** 9-3	Baltimore	Cito Gaston	Bobby Cox	Kirby Puckett, Min., OF
1994	National, 8-7 (10)	Pittsburgh	Cito Gaston	Jim Fregosi	Fred McGriff, Atl., 1B
1995	National, 3-2	Texas	Buck Showalter	Felipe Alou	Jeff Conine, Fla., PH
1996	National, 6-0	Philadelphia	Mike Hargrove	Bobby Cox	Mike Pizaaz, LA, C

Major League Franchise Origins

Here is what the current 28 teams in Major League Baseball have to show for the years they have put in as members of the National League (NL) and American League (AL). Pennants and World Series championships are since 1901.

National League

	1st Year	Pennants & World Series	Franchise Stops
Atlanta Braves	1876	7 NL (1914,48,57-58,91-92,95) 3 WS (1914,57,95)	• Boston (1876-1952) Milwaukee (1953-65) Atlanta (1966—)
Chicago Cubs	1876	10 NL (1906-08,10,18,29,32,35,38,45) 2 WS (1907-08)	• Chicago (1876—)
Cincinnati Reds	1876	9 NL (1919,39-40,61,70,72,75-76,90) 5 WS (1919,40,75-76,90)	• Cincinnati (1876-80) Cincinnati (1890—)
Colorado Rockies	1993	None	• Denver (1993—)
Florida Marlins	1993	None	• Miami (1993—)
Houston Astros	1962	None	• Houston (1962—)
Los Angeles Dodgers	1890	18 NL (1916,20,41,47,49,52-53,55-56,59,63, 65-66,74,77-78, 81,88) 6 WS (1955,59,63,65,81,88)	• Brooklyn (1890-1957) Los Angeles (1958—)
Montreal Expos	1969	None	• Montreal (1969—)
New York Mets	1962	3 NL (1969,73,86) 2 WS (1969,86)	• New York (1962—)
Philadelphia Phillies	1883	5 NL (1915,50,80,83,93) 1 WS (1980)	• Philadelphia (1883—)
Pittsburgh Pirates	1887	7 NL (1903,09,25,27,60,71,79) 5 WS (1909,25,60,71,79)	• Pittsburgh (1887—)
St. Louis Cardinals	1892	15 NL (1926,28,30-31,34,42-44,46,64, 67-68,82,85,87) 9 WS (1926,31,34,42,44,46,64,67,82)	• St. Louis (1892—)
San Diego Padres	1969	1 NL (1984)	• San Diego (1969—)
San Francisco Giants	1883	16 NL (1905,11-13,17,21-24,33,36-37,51, 54,62,89) 5 WS (1905,21-22,33,54)	• New York (1883–1957) San Francisco (1958—)

American League

	1st Year	Pennants & World Series	Franchise Stops
Baltimore Orioles	1901	7 AL (1944,66,69-71,79,83) 3 WS (1966,70,83)	• Milwaukee (1901) St. Louis (1902-53) Baltimore (1954—)
Boston Red Sox	1901	9 AL (1903,12,15-16,18,46,67,75,86) 5 WS (1903,12,15-16,18)	• Boston (1901—)
California Angels	1961	None	• Los Angeles (1961-65) Anaheim, CA (1966—)
Chicago White Sox	1901	4 AL (1906,17,19,59) 2 WS (1906,17)	• Chicago (1901—)
Cleveland Indians	1901	4 AL (1920,48,54,95) 2 WS (1920,48)	• Cleveland (1901—)
Detroit Tigers	1901	9 AL (1907-09,34-35,40,45,68,84) 4 WS (1935,45,68,84)	• Detroit (1901—)
Kansas City Royals	1969	2 AL (1980,85) 1 WS (1985)	• Kansas City (1969—)
Milwaukee Brewers	1969	1 AL (1982)	• Seattle (1969) Milwaukee (1970—)
Minnesota Twins	1901	6 AL (1924-25,33,65,87,91) 3 WS (1924,87,91)	• Washington, DC (1901-60) Bloomington, MN (1961-81) Minneapolis (1982—)
New York Yankees	1901	34 AL (1921-23,26-28,32,36-39,41-43,47, 49-53,55-58,60-64,76-78,81) 22 WS (1923,27-28,32,36-39,41,43,47,49-53, 56,58,61-62,77-78)	• Baltimore (1901-02) New York (1903—)
Oakland Athletics	1901	14 AL (1905,10-11,13-14,29-31,72-74,88-90) 9 WS (1910-11,13,29-30,72-74,89)	• Philadelphia (1901-54) Kansas City (1955-67) Oakland (1968—)

	1st Year	Pennants & World Series	Franchise Stops
Seattle Mariners	1977	None	• Seattle (1977—)
Texas Rangers	1961	None	• Washington, DC (1961-71) Arlington, TX (1972—)
Toronto Blue Jays	1977	2 AL (1992-93) 2 WS (1992-93)	• Toronto (1977—)

The Growth of Major League Baseball

The National League (founded in 1876) and the American League (founded in 1901) were both eight-team circuits at the tur of the century and remained that way until expansion finally came to Major League Baseball in the 1960s. The AL added twc teams in 1961 and the NL did the same a year later. Both leagues went to 12 teams and split into two divisions in 1969. Th AL then grew by two more teams in 1977, but the NL didn't follow suit until adding its 13th and 14th clubs in 1993.

Expansion Timetable (Since 1901)

1961—Los Angeles Angels (now California) and Washington Senators (now Texas Rangers) join AL; **1962**—Housto Colt .45s (now Astros) and New York Mets join NL; **1969**—Kansas City Royals and Seattle Pilots (now Milwaukee Brewers join AL, while Montreal Expos and San Diego Padres join NL; **1977**—Seattle Mariners and Toronto Blue Jays join AL **1993**—Colorado Rockies and Florida Marlins join NL; **1995**—New franchises awarded to Phoenix and St. Petersburg, Fla The Arizona Diamondbacks and Tampa Bay Devil Rays will begin play in 1998, which leagues they join will be decided later

City and Nickname Changes

National League

1953—Boston Braves move to Milwaukee; **1958**—Brooklyn Dodgers move to Los Angeles and New York Giants mov to San Francisco; **1965**—Houston Colt .45s renamed Astros; **1966**—Milwaukee Braves move to Atlanta.

Other nicknames: Boston (Beaneaters and Doves through 1908, and Bees from 1936-40); **Brooklyn** (Superba through 1926, then Robins from 1927-31; then Dodgers from 1932-57); **Cincinnati** (Red Legs from 1944-45, the Redlegs from 1954-60, then Reds since 1961); **Philadelphia** (Blue Jays from 1943-44).

American League

1902—Milwaukee Brewers move to St. Louis and become Browns; **1903**—Baltimore Orioles move to New York an become Highlanders; **1913**—NY Highlanders renamed Yankees; **1954**—St. Louis Browns move to Baltimore and becom Orioles; **1955**—Philadelphia Athletics move to Kansas City; **1961**—Washington Senators move to Bloomington, Minn and become Minnesota Twins; **1965**—LA Angels renamed California Angels; **1966**—California Angels move to Anaheim **1968**—KC Athletics move to Oakland and become A's; **1970**—Seattle Pilots move to Milwaukee and become Brewers **1972**—Washington Senators move to Arlington, Texas, and become Rangers; **1982**—Minnesota Twins move t Minneapolis; **1987**—Oakland A's renamed Athletics.

Other nicknames: Boston (Pilgrims, Puritans, Plymouth Rocks and Somersets through 1906); **Cleveland** (Broncos Blues, Naps and Molly McGuires through 1914); **Washington** (Senators through 1904, then Nationals from 1905-44 then Senators again from 1945-60).

National League Pennant Winners from 1876-99

Founded in 1876, the National League played 24 seasons before the turn of the century and its eventual rivalry with th younger American League. **Multiple winners:** Boston (8); Chicago (6); Baltimore (3); Brooklyn and New York (2).

Year		Year		Year		Year	
1876	Chicago	1882	Chicago	1888	New York	1894	Baltimore
1877	Boston	1883	Boston	1889	New York	1895	Baltimore
1878	Boston	1884	Providence	1890	Brooklyn	1896	Baltimore
1879	Providence	1885	Chicago	1891	Boston	1897	Boston
1880	Chicago	1886	Chicago	1892	Boston	1898	Boston
1881	Chicago	1887	Detroit	1893	Boston	1899	Brooklyn

Champions of Leagues That No Longer Exist

A Special Baseball Records Committee appointed by the commissioner found in 1968 that four extinct leagues qualified f major league status—the American Association (1882-91), the Union Association (1884), the Players' League (1890) and t Federal League (1914-15). The first years of the American League (1900) and Federal League (1913) were not recognize

American Association

Year	Champion	Manager	Year	Champion	Manager	Year	Champion	Manager
1882	Cincinnati	Pop Snyder	1886	St. Louis	Charlie Comiskey	1889	Brooklyn	Bill McGunnigle
1883	Philadelphia	Lew Simmons	1887	St. Louis	Charlie Comiskey	1890	Louisville	Jack Chapman
1884	New York	Jim Mutrie	1888	St. Louis	Charlie Comiskey	1891	Boston	Arthur Irwin
1885	St. Louis	Charlie Comiskey						

Union Association

Year	Champion	Manager
1884	St. Louis	Henry Lucas

Players' League

Year	Champion	Manager
1890	Boston	King Kelly

Federal League

Year	Champion	Manager
1914	Indianapolis	Bill Phillips
1915	Chicago	Joe Tinker

Annual Batting Leaders (since 1900)

Batting Average

National League

Multiple winners: Honus Wagner (8); Rogers Hornsby and Stan Musial (7); Tony Gwynn (6); Roberto Clemente and Bill Madlock (4); Pete Rose and Paul Waner (3); Hank Aaron, Richie Ashburn, Jake Daubert, Tommy Davis, Ernie Lombardi, Willie McGee, Lefty O'Doul, Dave Parker and Edd Roush (2).

Year		Avg
1900	Honus Wagner, Pit	.381
1901	Jesse Burkett, St.L	.382
1902	Ginger Beaumont, Pit	.357
1903	Honus Wagner, Pit	.355
1904	Honus Wagner, Pit	.349
1905	Cy Seymour, Cin	.377
1906	Honus Wagner, Pit	.339
1907	Honus Wagner, Pit	.350
1908	Honus Wagner, Pit	.354
1909	Honus Wagner, Pit	.339
1910	Sherry Magee, Phi	.331
1911	Honus Wagner, Pit	.334
1912	Heinie Zimmerman, Chi	.372
1913	Jake Daubert, Bklyn	.350
1914	Jake Daubert, Bklyn	.329
1915	Larry Doyle, NY	.320
1916	Hal Chase, Cin	.339
1917	Edd Roush, Cin	.341
1918	Zack Wheat, Bklyn	.335
1919	Edd Roush, Cin	.321
1920	Rogers Hornsby, St.L	.370
1921	Rogers Hornsby, St.L	.397
1922	Rogers Hornsby, St.L	.401
1923	Rogers Hornsby, St.L	.384
1924	Rogers Hornsby, St.L	.424
1925	Rogers Hornsby, St.L	.403
1926	Bubbles Hargrave, Cin	.353
1927	Paul Waner, Pit	.380
1928	Rogers Hornsby, Bos	.387
1929	Lefty O'Doul, Phi	.398
1930	Bill Terry, NY	.401
1931	Chick Hafey, St.L	.349
1932	Lefty O'Doul, Bklyn	.368

Year		Avg
1933	Chuck Klein, Phi	.368
1934	Paul Waner, Pit	.362
1935	Arky Vaughan, Pit	.385
1936	Paul Waner, Pit	.373
1937	Joe Medwick, St.L	.374
1938	Ernie Lombardi, Cin	.342
1939	Johnny Mize, St.L	.349
1940	Debs Garms, Pit	.355
1941	Pete Reiser, Bklyn	.343
1942	Ernie Lombardi, Bos	.330
1943	Stan Musial, St.L	.357
1944	Dixie Walker, Bklyn	.357
1945	Phil Cavarretta, Chi	.355
1946	Stan Musial, St.L	.365
1947	Harry Walker, St.L-Phi	.363
1948	Stan Musial, St.L	.376
1949	Jackie Robinson, Bklyn	.342
1950	Stan Musial, St.L	.346
1951	Stan Musial, St.L	.355
1952	Stan Musial, St.L	.336
1953	Carl Furillo, Bklyn	.344
1954	Willie Mays, NY	.345
1955	Richie Ashburn, Phi	.338
1956	Hank Aaron, Mil	.328
1957	Stan Musial, St.L	.351
1958	Richie Ashburn, Phi	.350
1959	Hank Aaron, Mil	.355
1960	Dick Groat, Pit	.325
1961	Roberto Clemente, Pit	.351
1962	Tommy Davis, LA	.346
1963	Tommy Davis, LA	.326
1964	Roberto Clemente, Pit	.339
1965	Roberto Clemente, Pit	.329

Year		Avg
1966	Matty Alou, Pit	.342
1967	Roberto Clemente, Pit	.357
1968	Pete Rose, Cin	.335
1969	Pete Rose, Cin	.348
1970	Rico Carty, Atl	.366
1971	Joe Torre, St.L	.363
1972	Billy Williams, Chi	.333
1973	Pete Rose, Cin	.338
1974	Ralph Garr, Atl	.353
1975	Bill Madlock, Chi	.354
1976	Bill Madlock, Chi	.339
1977	Dave Parker, Pit	.338
1978	Dave Parker, Pit	.334
1979	Keith Hernandez, St.L	.344
1980	Bill Buckner, Chi	.324
1981	Bill Madlock, Pit	.341
1982	Al Oliver, Mon	.331
1983	Bill Madlock, Pit	.323
1984	Tony Gwynn, SD	.351
1985	Willie McGee, St.L	.353
1986	Tim Raines, Mon	.334
1987	Tony Gwynn, SD	.370
1988	Tony Gwynn, SD	.313
1989	Tony Gwynn, SD	.336
1990	Willie McGee, St.L	.335
1991	Terry Pendleton, Atl	.319
1992	Gary Sheffield, SD	.330
1993	Andres Galarraga, Col	.370
1994	Tony Gwynn, SD	.394
1995	Tony Gwynn, SD	.368
1996	Tony Gwynn, SD	.353

American League

Multiple winners: Ty Cobb (12); Rod Carew (7); Ted Williams (6); Wade Boggs (5); Harry Heilmann (4); George Brett, Nap Lajoie, Tony Oliva and Carl Yastrzemski (3); Luke Appling, Joe DiMaggio, Ferris Fain, Jimmie Foxx, Edgar Martinez, Pete Runnels, Al Simmons, George Sisler and Mickey Vernon (2).

Year		Avg
1901	Nap Lajoie, Phi	.422
1902	Ed Delahanty, Wash	.376
1903	Nap Lajoie, Cle	.355
1904	Nap Lajoie, Cle	.381
1905	Elmer Flick, Cle	.306
1906	George Stone, St.L	.358
1907	Ty Cobb, Det	.350
1908	Ty Cobb, Det	.324
1909	Ty Cobb, Det	.377
1910	Ty Cobb, Det	.385
1911	Ty Cobb, Det	.420
1912	Ty Cobb, Det	.410
1913	Ty Cobb, Det	.390
1914	Ty Cobb, Det	.368
1915	Ty Cobb, Det	.369
1916	Tris Speaker, Cle	.386
1917	Ty Cobb, Det	.383
1918	Ty Cobb, Det	.382
1919	Ty Cobb, Det	.384
1920	George Sisler, St.L	.407
1921	Harry Heilmann, Det	.394
1922	George Sisler, St.L	.420
1923	Harry Heilmann, Det	.403

Year		Avg
1924	Babe Ruth, NY	.378
1925	Harry Heilmann, Det	.393
1926	Heinie Manush, Det	.378
1927	Harry Heilmann, Det	.398
1928	Goose Goslin, Wash	.379
1929	Lew Fonseca, Cle	.369
1930	Al Simmons, Phi	.381
1931	Al Simmons, Phi	.390
1932	Dale Alexander, Det-Bos	.367
1933	Jimmie Foxx, Phi	.356
1934	Lou Gehrig, NY	.363
1935	Buddy Myer, Wash	.349
1936	Luke Appling, Chi	.388
1937	Charlie Gehringer, Det	.371
1938	Jimmie Foxx, Bos	.349
1939	Joe DiMaggio, NY	.381
1940	Joe DiMaggio, NY	.352
1941	Ted Williams, Bos	.406
1942	Ted Williams, Bos	.356
1943	Luke Appling, Chi	.328
1944	Lou Boudreau, Clev	.327
1945	Snuffy Stirnweiss, NY	.309
1946	Mickey Vernon, Wash	.353

Year		Avg
1947	Ted Williams, Bos	.343
1948	Ted Williams, Bos	.369
1949	George Kell, Det	.343
1950	Billy Goodman, Bos	.354
1951	Ferris Fain, Phi	.344
1952	Ferris Fain, Phi	.327
1953	Mickey Vernon, Wash	.337
1954	Bobby Avila, Clev	.341
1955	Al Kaline, Det	.340
1956	Mickey Mantle, NY	.353
1957	Ted Williams, Bos	.388
1958	Ted Williams, Bos	.328
1959	Harvey Kuenn, Det	.353
1960	Pete Runnels, Bos	.320
1961	Norm Cash, Det	.361
1962	Pete Runnels, Bos	.326
1963	Carl Yastrzemski, Bos	.321
1964	Tony Oliva, Min	.323
1965	Tony Oliva, Min	.321
1966	Frank Robinson, Bal	.316
1967	Carl Yastrzemski, Bos	.326
1968	Carl Yastrzemski, Bos	.301
1969	Rod Carew, Min	.332

Year		Avg
1970	Alex Johnson, Cal	.329
1971	Tony Oliva, Min	.337
1972	Rod Carew, Min	.318
1973	Rod Carew, Min	.350
1974	Rod Carew, Min	.364
1975	Rod Carew, Min	.359
1976	George Brett, KC	.333
1977	Rod Carew, Min	.388
1978	Rod Carew, Min	.333
1979	Fred Lynn, Bos	.333
1980	George Brett, KC	.390
1981	Carney Lansford, Bos	.336
1982	Willie Wilson, KC	.332
1983	Wade Boggs, Bos	.361
1984	Don Mattingly, NY	.343
1985	Wade Boggs, Bos	.368
1986	Wade Boggs, Bos	.357
1987	Wade Boggs, Bos	.363
1988	Wade Boggs, Bos	.366
1989	Kirby Puckett, Min	.339
1990	George Brett, KC	.329
1991	Julio Franco, Tex	.341
1992	Edgar Martinez, Sea	.34
1993	John Olerud, Tor	.36
1994	Paul O'Neill, NY	.35
1995	Edgar Martinez, Sea	.35
1996	Alex Rodriguez, Sea	.35

Home Runs

National League

Multiple winners: Mike Schmidt (8); Ralph Kiner (7); Gavvy Cravath and Mel Ott (6); Hank Aaron, Chuck Klein, Willie Mays, Johnny Mize, Cy Williams and Hack Wilson (4); Willie McCovey (3); Ernie Banks, Johnny Bench, George Foster Rogers Hornsby, Tim Jordan, Dave Kingman, Eddie Mathews, Dale Murphy, Bill Nicholson, Dave Robertson, Wildfire Schulte and Willie Stargell (2).

Year		HR
1900	Herman Long, Bos	12
1901	Sam Crawford, Cin	16
1902	Tommy Leach, Pit	6
1903	Jimmy Sheckard, Bklyn	9
1904	Harry Lumley, Bklyn	9
1905	Fred Odwell, Cin	9
1906	Tim Jordan, Bklyn	12
1907	Dave Brain, Bos	10
1908	Tim Jordan, Bklyn	12
1909	Red Murray, NY	7
1910	Fred Beck, Bos	10
	& Wildfire Schulte, Chi	10
1911	Wildfire Schulte, Chi	21
1912	Heinie Zimmerman, Chi	14
1913	Gavvy Cravath, Phi	19
1914	Gavvy Cravath, Phi	19
1915	Gavvy Cravath, Phi	24
1916	Cy Williams, Chi	12
	& Dave Robertson, NY	12
1917	Gavvy Cravath, Phi	12
	& Dave Robertson, NY	12
1918	Gavvy Cravath, Phi	8
1919	Gavvy Cravath, Phi	12
1920	Cy Williams, Phi	15
1921	George Kelly, NY	23
1922	Rogers Hornsby, St.L	42
1923	Cy Williams, Phi	41
1924	Jack Fournier, Bklyn	27
1925	Rogers Hornsby, St.L	39
1926	Hack Wilson, Chi	21
1927	Cy Williams, Phi	30
	& Hack Wilson, Chi	30
1928	Jim Bottomley, St.L	31
	& Hack Wilson, Chi	31
1929	Chuck Klein, Phi	43
1930	Hack Wilson, Chi	56
1931	Chuck Klein, Phi	31
1932	Chuck Klein, Phi	38
	& Mel Ott, NY	38
1933	Chuck Klein, Phi	28
1934	Rip Collins, St.L	35
	& Mel Ott, NY	35
1935	Wally Berger, Bos	34
1936	Mel Ott, NY	33
1937	Joe Medwick, St.L	31
	& Mel Ott, NY	31
1938	Mel Ott, NY	36
1939	Johnny Mize, St.L	28
1940	Johnny Mize, St.L	43
1941	Dolf Camilli, Bklyn	34
1942	Mel Ott, NY	30
1943	Bill Nicholson, Chi	29
1944	Bill Nicholson, Chi	33
1945	Tommy Holmes, Bos	28
1946	Ralph Kiner, Pit	23
1947	Ralph Kiner, Pit	51
	& Johnny Mize, NY	51
1948	Ralph Kiner, Pit	40
	& Johnny Mize, NY	40
1949	Ralph Kiner, Pit	54
1950	Ralph Kiner, Pit	47
1951	Ralph Kiner, Pit	42
1952	Ralph Kiner, Pit	37
	& Hank Sauer, Chi	37
1953	Eddie Mathews, Mil	47
1954	Ted Kluszewski, Cin	49
1955	Willie Mays, NY	51
1956	Duke Snider, Bklyn	43
1957	Hank Aaron, Mil	44
1958	Ernie Banks, Chi	47
1959	Eddie Mathews, Mil	46
1960	Ernie Banks, Chi	41
1961	Orlando Cepeda, SF	46
1962	Willie Mays, SF	49
1963	Hank Aaron, Mil	4
	& Willie McCovey, SF	4
1964	Willie Mays, SF	4
1965	Willie Mays, SF	5
1966	Hank Aaron, Atl	4
1967	Hank Aaron, Atl	3
1968	Willie McCovey, SF	3
1969	Willie McCovey, SF	4
1970	Johnny Bench, Cin	4
1971	Willie Stargell, Pit	4
1972	Johnny Bench, Cin	4
1973	Willie Stargell, Pit	4
1974	Mike Schmidt, Phi	3
1975	Mike Schmidt, Phi	3
1976	Mike Schmidt, Phi	3
1977	George Foster, Cin	5
1978	George Foster, Cin	4
1979	Dave Kingman, Chi	4
1980	Mike Schmidt, Phi	4
1981	Mike Schmidt, Phi	3
1982	Dave Kingman, NY	3
1983	Mike Schmidt, Phi	4
1984	Dale Murphy, Atl	3
	& Mike Schmidt, Phi	3
1985	Dale Murphy, Atl	3
1986	Mike Schmidt, Phi	3
1987	Andre Dawson, Chi	4
1988	Darryl Strawberry, NY	3
1989	Kevin Mitchell, SF	4
1990	Ryne Sandberg, Chi	4
1991	Howard Johnson, NY	3
1992	Fred McGriff, SD	3
1993	Barry Bonds, SF	4
1994	Matt Williams, SF	4
1995	Dante Bichette, Col	4
1996	Andres Galarraga, Col	4

American League

Multiple winners: Babe Ruth (12); Harmon Killebrew (6); Home Run Baker, Harry Davis, Jimmie Foxx, Hank Greenber Reggie Jackson, Mickey Mantle and Ted Williams (4); Lou Gehrig and Jim Rice (3); Dick Allen, Tony Armas, Jose Cansec Joe DiMaggio, Larry Doby, Cecil Fielder, Juan Gonzalez, Frank Howard, Mark McGwire, Wally Pipp, Al Rosen and Gorm Thomas (2).

Year		HR
1901	Nap Lajoie, Phi	14
1902	Socks Seybold, Phi	16
1903	Buck Freeman, Bos	13
1904	Harry Davis, Phi	10
1905	Harry Davis, Phi	8
1906	Harry Davis, Phi	12
1907	Harry Davis, Phi	8
1908	Sam Crawford, Det	7
1909	Ty Cobb, Det	9
1910	Jake Stahl, Bos	10
1911	Home Run Baker, Phi	11
1912	Home Run Baker, Phi	10
	& Tris Speaker, Bos	10
1913	Home Run Baker, Phi	12
1914	Home Run Baker, Phi	
1915	Braggo Roth, Chi-Cle	
1916	Wally Pipp, NY	
1917	Wally Pipp, NY	
1918	Babe Ruth, Bos	
	& Tilly Walker, Phi	
1919	Babe Ruth, Bos	

Annual Batting Leaders (Cont.)

Home Runs

American League

Year		HR
1920	Babe Ruth, NY	54
1921	Babe Ruth, NY	59
1922	Ken Williams, St.L	39
1923	Babe Ruth, NY	41
1924	Babe Ruth, NY	46
1925	Bob Meusel, NY	33
1926	Babe Ruth, NY	47
1927	Babe Ruth, NY	60
1928	Babe Ruth, NY	54
1929	Babe Ruth, NY	46
1930	Babe Ruth, NY	49
1931	Lou Gehrig, NY	46
	& Babe Ruth, NY	46
1932	Jimmie Foxx, Phi	58
1933	Jimmie Foxx, Phi	48
1934	Lou Gehrig, NY	49
1935	Jimmie Foxx, Phi	36
	& Hank Greenberg, Det	36
1936	Lou Gehrig, NY	49
1937	Joe DiMaggio, NY	46
1938	Hank Greenberg, Det	58
1939	Jimmie Foxx, Bos	35
1940	Hank Greenberg, Det	41
1941	Ted Williams, Bos	37
1942	Ted Williams, Bos	36
1943	Rudy York, Det	34
1944	Nick Etten, NY	22
1945	Vern Stephens, St.L	24
1946	Hank Greenberg, Det	44
1947	Ted Williams, Bos	32
1948	Joe DiMaggio, NY	39
1949	Ted Williams, Bos	43
1950	Al Rosen, Cle	37
1951	Gus Zernial, Chi-Phi	33
1952	Larry Doby, Cle	32
1953	Al Rosen, Cle	43
1954	Larry Doby, Cle	32
1955	Mickey Mantle, NY	37
1956	Mickey Mantle, NY	52
1957	Roy Sievers, Wash	42
1958	Mickey Mantle, NY	42
1959	Rocky Colavito, Cle	42
	& Harmon Killebrew, Wash	42
1960	Mickey Mantle, NY	40
1961	Roger Maris, NY	61
1962	Harmon Killebrew, Min	48
1963	Harmon Killebrew, Min	45
1964	Harmon Killebrew, Min	49
1965	Tony Conigliaro, Bos	32
1966	Frank Robinson, Bal	49
1967	Harmon Killebrew, Min	44
	& Carl Yastrzemski, Bos	44
1968	Frank Howard, Wash	44
1969	Harmon Killebrew, Min	49
1970	Frank Howard, Wash	44
1971	Bill Melton, Chi	33
1972	Dick Allen, Chi	37
1973	Reggie Jackson, Oak	32
1974	Dick Allen, Chi	32
1975	Reggie Jackson, Oak	36
	& George Scott, Mil	36
1976	Graig Nettles, NY	32
1977	Jim Rice, Bos	39
1978	Jim Rice, Bos	46
1979	Gorman Thomas, Mil	45
1980	Reggie Jackson, NY	41
	& Ben Oglivie, Mil	41
1981	Tony Armas, Oak	22
	Dwight Evans, Bos	22
	Bobby Grich, Cal	22
	& Eddie Murray, Bal	22
1982	Reggie Jackson, Cal	39
	& Gorman Thomas, Mil	39
1983	Jim Rice, Bos	39
1984	Tony Armas, Bos	43
1985	Darrell Evans, Det	40
1986	Jesse Barfield, Tor	40
1987	Mark McGwire, Oak	49
1988	Jose Canseco, Oak	42
1989	Fred McGriff, Tor	36
1990	Cecil Fielder, Det	51
1991	Jose Canseco, Oak	44
	& Cecil Fielder, Det	44
1992	Juan Gonzalez, Tex	43
1993	Juan Gonzalez, Tex	46
1994	Ken Griffey Jr., Sea	40
1995	Albert Belle, Cle	50
1996	Mark McGwire, Oak	52

Runs Batted In

National League

Multiple winners: Hank Aaron, Rogers Hornsby, Sherry Magee, Mike Schmidt and Honus Wagner (4); Johnny Bench, George Foster, Joe Medwick, Johnny Mize and Heinie Zimmerman (3); Ernie Banks, Jim Bottomley, Orlando Cepeda, Gavvy Cravath, George Kelly, Chuck Klein, Willie McCovey, Dale Murphy, Stan Musial, Bill Nicholson and Hack Wilson (2).

Year		RBI
1900	Elmer Flick, Phi	110
1901	Honus Wagner, Pit	126
1902	Honus Wagner, Pit	91
1903	Sam Mertes, NY	104
1904	Bill Dahlen, NY	80
1905	Cy Seymour, Cin	121
1906	Jim Nealon, Pit	83
	& Harry Steinfeldt, Chi	83
1907	Sherry Magee, Phi	85
1908	Honus Wagner, Pit	109
1909	Honus Wagner, Pit	100
1910	Sherry Magee, Phi	123
1911	Wildfire Schulte, Chi	121
1912	Heinie Zimmerman, Chi	103
1913	Gavvy Cravath, Phi	128
1914	Sherry Magee, Phi	103
1915	Gavvy Cravath, Phi	115
1916	Heinie Zimmerman, Chi-NY	83
1917	Heinie Zimmerman, NY	102
1918	Sherry Magee, Cin	76
1919	Hy Myers, Bklyn	73
1920	Rogers Hornsby, St.L	94
	& George Kelly, NY	94
1921	Rogers Hornsby, St.L	126
1922	Rogers Hornsby, St.L	152
1923	Irish Meusel, NY	125
1924	George Kelly, NY	136
1925	Rogers Hornsby, St.L	143
1926	Jim Bottomley, St.L	120
1927	Paul Waner, Pit	131
1928	Jim Bottomley, St.L	136
1929	Hack Wilson, Chi	159
1930	Hack Wilson, Chi	190
1931	Chuck Klein, Phi	121
1932	Don Hurst, Phi	143
1933	Chuck Klein, Phi	120
1934	Mel Ott, NY	135
1935	Wally Berger, Bos	130
1936	Joe Medwick, St.L	138
1937	Joe Medwick, St.L	154
1938	Joe Medwick, St.L	122
1939	Frank McCormick, Cin	128
1940	Johnny Mize, St.L	137
1941	Dolph Camilli, Bklyn	120
1942	Johnny Mize, NY	110
1943	Bill Nicholson, Chi	128
1944	Bill Nicholson, Chi	122
1945	Dixie Walker, Bklyn	124
1946	Enos Slaughter, St.L	130
1947	Johnny Mize, NY	138
1948	Stan Musial, St.L	131
1949	Ralph Kiner, Pit	127
1950	Del Ennis, Phi	126
1951	Monte Irvin, NY	121
1952	Hank Sauer, Chi	121
1953	Roy Campanella, Bklyn	142
1954	Ted Kluszewski, Cin	141
1955	Duke Snider, Bklyn	136
1956	Stan Musial, St.L	109
1957	Hank Aaron, Mil	132
1958	Ernie Banks, Chi	129
1959	Ernie Banks, Chi	143
1960	Hank Aaron, Mil	126
1961	Orlando Cepeda, SF	142
1962	Tommy Davis, LA	153
1963	Hank Aaron, Mil	130
1964	Ken Boyer, St.L	119
1965	Deron Johnson, Cin	130
1966	Hank Aaron, Atl	127
1967	Orlando Cepeda, St.L	111
1968	Willie McCovey, SF	105
1969	Willie McCovey, SF	126
1970	Johnny Bench, Cin	148
1971	Joe Torre, St.L	137
1972	Johnny Bench, Cin	125
1973	Willie Stargell, Pit	119

Year		RBI
1974	Johnny Bench, Cin	129
1975	Greg Luzinski, Phi	120
1976	George Foster, Cin	121
1977	George Foster, Cin	149
1978	George Foster, Cin	120
1979	Dave Winfield, SD	118
1980	Mike Schmidt, Phi	121
1981	Mike Schmidt, Phi	91
1982	Dale Murphy, Atl	109
	& Al Oliver, Mon	109
1983	Dale Murphy, Atl	121
1984	Gary Carter, Mon	106
	& Mike Schmidt, Phi	106
1985	Dave Parker, Cin	125
1986	Mike Schmidt, Phi	119
1987	Andre Dawson, Chi	137
1988	Will Clark, SF	109
1989	Kevin Mitchell, SF	125
1990	Matt Williams, SF	122
1991	Howard Johnson, NY	117
1992	Darren Daulton, Phi	109
1993	Barry Bonds, SF	123
1994	Jeff Bagwell, Hou	116
1995	Dante Bichette, Col	128
1996	Andres Galarraga, Col	150

American League

Multiple winners: Babe Ruth (6); Lou Gehrig (5); Ty Cobb, Hank Greenberg and Ted Williams (4); Albert Belle, Sam Crawford, Cecil Fielder, Jimmie Foxx, Jackie Jensen, Harmon Killebrew, Vern Stephens and Bobby Veach (3); Home Run Baker, Cecil Cooper, Harry Davis, Joe DiMaggio, Buck Freeman, Nap Lajoie, Roger Maris, Jim Rice, Al Rosen, and Bobby Veach (2).

Year		RBI
1901	Nap Lajoie, Phi	125
1902	Buck Freeman, Bos	121
1903	Buck Freeman, Bos	104
1904	Nap Lajoie, Cle	102
1905	Harry Davis, Phi	83
1906	Harry Davis, Phi	96
1907	Ty Cobb, Det	116
1908	Ty Cobb, Det	108
1909	Ty Cobb, Det	107
1910	Sam Crawford, Det	120
1911	Ty Cobb, Det	144
1912	Home Run Baker, Phi	133
1913	Home Run Baker, Phi	126
1914	Sam Crawford, Det	104
1915	Sam Crawford, Det	112
	& Bobby Veach, Det	112
1916	Del Pratt, St.L	103
1917	Bobby Veach, Det	103
1918	Bobby Veach, Det	78
1919	Babe Ruth, Bos	114
1920	Babe Ruth, NY	137
1921	Babe Ruth, NY	171
1922	Ken Williams, St.L	155
1923	Babe Ruth, NY	131
1924	Goose Goslin, Wash	129
1925	Bob Meusel, NY	138
1926	Babe Ruth, NY	145
1927	Lou Gehrig, NY	175
1928	Lou Gehrig, NY	142
	& Babe Ruth, NY	142
1929	Al Simmons, Phi	157
1930	Lou Gehrig, NY	174
1931	Lou Gehrig, NY	184
1932	Jimmie Foxx, Phi	169
1933	Jimmie Foxx, Phi	163
1934	Lou Gehrig, NY	165
1935	Hank Greenberg, Det	170
1936	Hal Trosky, Cle	162
1937	Hank Greenberg, Det	183
1938	Jimmie Foxx, Bos	175
1939	Ted Williams, Bos	145
1940	Hank Greenberg, Det	150
1941	Joe DiMaggio, NY	125
1942	Ted Williams, Bos	137
1943	Rudy York, Det	118
1944	Vern Stephens, St.L	109
1945	Nick Etten, NY	111
1946	Hank Greenberg, Det	127
1947	Ted Williams, Bos	114
1948	Joe DiMaggio, NY	155
1949	Ted Williams, Bos	159
	& Vern Stephens, Bos	159
1950	Walt Dropo, Bos	144
	& Vern Stephens, Bos	144
1951	Gus Zernial, Chi-Phi	129
1952	Al Rosen, Cle	105
1953	Al Rosen, Cle	145
1954	Larry Doby, Cle	126
1955	Ray Boone, Det	116
	& Jackie Jensen, Bos	116
1956	Mickey Mantle, NY	130
1957	Roy Sievers, Wash	114
1958	Jackie Jensen, Bos	122
1959	Jackie Jensen, Bos	112
1960	Roger Maris, NY	112
1961	Roger Maris, NY	142
1962	Harmon Killebrew, Min	126
1963	Dick Stuart, Bos	118
1964	Brooks Robinson, Bal	118
1965	Rocky Colavito, Cle	108
1966	Frank Robinson, Bal	122
1967	Carl Yastrzemski, Bos	121
1968	Ken Harrelson, Bos	109
1969	Harmon Killebrew, Min	140
1970	Frank Howard, Wash	126
1971	Harmon Killebrew, Min	119
1972	Dick Allen, Chi	113
1973	Reggie Jackson, Oak	117
1974	Jeff Burroughs, Tex	118
1975	George Scott, Mil	109
1976	Lee May, Bal	109
1977	Larry Hisle, Min	119
1978	Jim Rice, Bos	139
1979	Don Baylor, Cal	139
1980	Cecil Cooper, Mil	122
1981	Eddie Murray, Bal	78
1982	Hal McRae, KC	133
1983	Cecil Cooper, Mil	126
	& Jim Rice, Bos	126
1984	Tony Armas, Bos	123
1985	Don Mattingly, NY	145
1986	Joe Carter, Cle	121
1987	George Bell, Tor	134
1988	Jose Canseco, Oak	124
1989	Ruben Sierra, Tex	119
1990	Cecil Fielder, Det	132
1991	Cecil Fielder, Det	133
1992	Cecil Fielder, Det	124
1993	Albert Belle, Cle	129
1994	Kirby Puckett, Min	112
1995	Albert Belle, Cle	126
	& Mo Vaughn, Bos	126
1996	Albert Belle, Cle	148

Batting Triple Crown Winners

Players who led either league in Batting Average, Home Runs and Runs Batted In over a single season.

National League

	Year	Avg	HR	RBI
Paul Hines, Providence	1878	.358	4	50
Hugh Duffy, Boston	1894	.438	18	145
Heinie Zimmerman, Chicago	1912	.372	14	103
Rogers Hornsby, St. Louis	1922	.401	42	152
Rogers Hornsby, St. Louis	1925	.403	39	143
Chuck Klein, Philadelphia	1933	.368	28	120
Joe Medwick, St. Louis	1937	.374	31*	154

*Tied for league lead in HRs with Mel Ott, NY.

American League

	Year	Avg	HR	RBI
Nap Lajoie, Philadelphia	1901	.422	14	125
Ty Cobb, Detroit	1909	.377	9	115
Jimmie Foxx, Philadelphia	1933	.356	48	163
Lou Gehrig, New York	1934	.363	49	165
Ted Williams, Boston	1942	.356	36	137
Ted Williams, Boston	1947	.343	32	114
Mickey Mantle, New York	1956	.353	52	130
Frank Robinson, Baltimore	1966	.316	49	122
Carl Yastrzemski, Boston	1967	.326	44*	121

*Tied for league lead in HRs with Harmon Killebrew, Min.

Annual Batting Leaders (Cont.)

Stolen Bases

National League

Multiple winners: Max Carey (10); Lou Brock (8); Vince Coleman and Maury Wills (6); Honus Wagner (5); Bob Bescher, Kiki Cuyler, Willie Mays and Tim Raines (4); Bill Bruton, Frankie Frisch and Pepper Martin (3); George Burns, Frank Chance, Augie Galan, Marquis Grissom, Stan Hack, Sam Jethroe, Davey Lopes, Omar Moreno, Pete Reiser and Jackie Robinson (2).

Year		SB
1900	Patsy Donovan, St.L	45
	& George Van Haltren, NY	45
1901	Honus Wagner, Pit	49
1902	Honus Wagner, Pit	42
1903	Frank Chance, Chi	67
	& Jimmy Sheckard, Bklyn	67
1904	Honus Wagner, Pit	53
1905	Art Devlin, NY	59
	& Billy Maloney, Chi	59
1906	Frank Chance, Chi	57
1907	Honus Wagner, Pit	61
1908	Honus Wagner, Pit	53
1909	Bob Bescher, Cin	54
1910	Bob Bescher, Cin	70
1911	Bob Bescher, Cin	81
1912	Bob Bescher, Cin	67
1913	Max Carey, Pit	61
1914	George Burns, NY	62
1915	Max Carey, Pit	36
1916	Max Carey, Pit	63
1917	Max Carey, Pit	46
1918	Max Carey, Pit	58
1919	George Burns, NY	40
1920	Max Carey, Pit	52
1921	Frankie Frisch, NY	49
1922	Max Carey, Pit	51
1923	Max Carey, Pit	51
1924	Max Carey, Pit	49
1925	Max Carey, Pit	46
1926	Kiki Cuyler, Pit	35
1927	Frankie Frisch, St.L	48
1928	Kiki Cuyler, Chi	37
1929	Kiki Cuyler, Chi	43
1930	Kiki Cuyler, Chi	37
1931	Frankie Frisch, St.L	28
1932	Chuck Klein, Phi	20
1933	Pepper Martin, St.L	26
1934	Pepper Martin, St.L	23
1935	Augie Galan, Chi	22
1936	Pepper Martin, St.L	23
1937	Augie Galan, Chi	23
1938	Stan Hack, Chi	16
1939	Stan Hack, Chi	17
	& Lee Handley, Pit	17
1940	Lonny Frey, Cin	22
1941	Danny Murtaugh, Phi	18
1942	Pete Reiser, Bklyn	20
1943	Arky Vaughan, Bklyn	20
1944	Johnny Barrett, Pit	28
1945	Red Schoendienst, St.L	26
1946	Pete Reiser, Bklyn	34
1947	Jackie Robinson, Bklyn	29
1948	Richie Ashburn, Phi	32
1949	Jackie Robinson, Bklyn	37
1950	Sam Jethroe, Bos	35
1951	Sam Jethroe, Bos	35
1952	Pee Wee Reese, Bklyn	30
1953	Bill Bruton, Mil	26
1954	Bill Bruton, Mil	34
1955	Bill Bruton, Mil	25
1956	Willie Mays, NY	40
1957	Willie Mays, NY	38
1958	Willie Mays, SF	31
1959	Willie Mays, SF	27
1960	Maury Wills, LA	50
1961	Maury Wills, LA	35
1962	Maury Wills, LA	104
1963	Maury Wills, LA	40
1964	Maury Wills, LA	53
1965	Maury Wills, LA	94
1966	Lou Brock, St.L	74
1967	Lou Brock, St.L	52
1968	Lou Brock, St.L	62
1969	Lou Brock, St.L	53
1970	Bobby Tolan, Cin	57
1971	Lou Brock, St.L	64
1972	Lou Brock, St.L	63
1973	Lou Brock, St.L	70
1974	Lou Brock, St.L	118
1975	Davey Lopes, LA	77
1976	Davey Lopes, LA	63
1977	Frank Taveras, Pit	70
1978	Omar Moreno, Pit	71
1979	Omar Moreno, Pit	77
1980	Ron LeFlore, Mon	97
1981	Tim Raines, Mon	71
1982	Tim Raines, Mon	78
1983	Tim Raines, Mon	90
1984	Tim Raines, Mon	75
1985	Vince Coleman, St.L	110
1986	Vince Coleman, St.L	107
1987	Vince Coleman, St.L	109
1988	Vince Coleman, St.L	81
1989	Vince Coleman, St.L	65
1990	Vince Coleman, St.L	77
1991	Marquis Grissom, Mon	76
1992	Marquis Grissom, Mon	78
1993	Chuck Carr, Fla	58
1994	Craig Biggio, Hou	39
1995	Quilvio Veras, Fla	56
1996	Eric Young, Col	53

American League

Multiple winners: Rickey Henderson (11); Luis Aparicio (9); Bert Campaneris, George Case and Ty Cobb (6); Kenny Lofton (5); Ben Chapman, Eddie Collins and George Sisler (4); Bob Dillinger, Minnie Minoso and Bill Werber (3); Elmer Flick, Tommy Harper, Clyde Milan, Johnny Mostil, Bill North and Snuffy Stirnweiss (2).

Year		SB
1901	Frank Isbell, Chi	52
1902	Topsy Hartsel, Phi	47
1903	Harry Bay, Cle	45
1904	Elmer Flick, Cle	42
1905	Danny Hoffman, Phi	46
1906	John Anderson, Wash	39
	& Elmer Flick, Cle	39
1907	Ty Cobb, Det	49
1908	Patsy Dougherty, Chi	47
1909	Ty Cobb, Det	76
1910	Eddie Collins, Phi	81
1911	Ty Cobb, Det	83
1912	Clyde Milan, Wash	88
1913	Clyde Milan, Wash	75
1914	Fritz Maisel, NY	74
1915	Ty Cobb, Det	96
1916	Ty Cobb, Det	68
1917	Ty Cobb, Det	55
1918	George Sisler, St.L	45
1919	Eddie Collins, Chi	33
1920	Sam Rice, Wash	63
1921	George Sisler, St.L	35
1922	George Sisler, St.L	51
1923	Eddie Collins, Chi	47
1924	Eddie Collins, Chi	42
1925	Johnny Mostil, Chi	43
1926	Johnny Mostil, Chi	35
1927	George Sisler, St.L	27
1928	Buddy Myer, Bos	30
1929	Charlie Gehringer, Det	28
1930	Marty McManus, Det	23
1931	Ben Chapman, NY	61
1932	Ben Chapman, NY	38
1933	Ben Chapman, NY	27
1934	Bill Werber, Bos	40
1935	Bill Werber, Bos	29
1936	Lyn Lary, St.L	37
1937	Ben Chapman, Wash-Bos	35
	& Bill Werber, Phi	35
1938	Frank Crosetti, NY	27
1939	George Case, Wash	51
1940	George Case, Wash	35
1941	George Case, Wash	33
1942	George Case, Wash	44
1943	George Case, Wash	61
1944	Snuffy Stirnweiss, NY	55
1945	Snuffy Stirnweiss, NY	33
1946	George Case, Cle	28
1947	Bob Dillinger, St.L	34
1948	Bob Dillinger, St.L	28
1949	Bob Dillinger, St.L	20
1950	Dom DiMaggio, Bos	15
1951	Minnie Minoso, Cle-Chi	31
1952	Minnie Minoso, Chi	22
1953	Minnie Minoso, Chi	25
1954	Jackie Jensen, Bos	22
1955	Jim Rivera, Chi	25
1956	Luis Aparicio, Chi	21
1957	Luis Aparicio, Chi	28

Year		SB
1958	Luis Aparicio, Chi	29
1959	Luis Aparicio, Chi	56
1960	Luis Aparicio, Chi	51
1961	Luis Aparicio, Chi	53
1962	Luis Aparicio, Chi	31
1963	Luis Aparicio, Bal	40
1964	Luis Aparicio, Bal	57
1965	Bert Campaneris, KC	51
1966	Bert Campaneris, KC	52
1967	Bert Campaneris, KC	55
1968	Bert Campaneris, Oak	62
1969	Tommy Harper, Sea	73
1970	Bert Campaneris, Oak	42
1971	Amos Otis, KC	52
1972	Bert Campaneris, Oak	52
1973	Tommy Harper, Bos	54
1974	Bill North, Oak	54
1975	Mickey Rivers, CA	70
1976	Bill North, Oak	75
1977	Freddie Patek, KC	53
1978	Ron LeFlore, Det	68
1979	Willie Wilson, KC	83
1980	Rickey Henderson, Oak	100
1981	Rickey Henderson, Oak	56
1982	Rickey Henderson, Oak	130
1983	Rickey Henderson, Oak	108
1984	Rickey Henderson, Oak	66
1985	Rickey Henderson, NY	80
1986	Rickey Henderson, NY	87
1987	Harold Reynolds, Sea	60
1988	Rickey Henderson, NY	93
1989	R. Henderson, NY-Oak	77
1990	Rickey Henderson, Oak	65
1991	Rickey Henderson, Oak	58
1992	Kenny Lofton, Cle	66
1993	Kenny Lofton, Cle	70
1994	Kenny Lofton, Cle	60
1995	Kenny Lofton, Cle	54
1996	Kenny Lofton, Cle	75

30 Homers & 30 Stolen Bases in One Season

National League

	Year	Gm	HR	SB
Willie Mays, NY Giants	1956	152	36	40
Willie Mays, NY Giants	1957	152	35	38
Hank Aaron, Milwaukee	1963	161	44	31
Bobby Bonds, San Francisco	1969	158	32	45
Bobby Bonds, San Francisco	1973	160	39	43
Dale Murphy, Atlanta	1983	162	36	30
Eric Davis, Cincinnati	1987	129	37	50
Howard Johnson, NY Mets	1987	157	36	32
Darryl Strawberry, NY Mets	1987	154	39	36
Howard Johnson, NY Mets	1989	153	36	41
Ron Gant, Atlanta	1990	152	32	33
Barry Bonds, Pittsburgh	1990	151	33	52
Ron Gant, Atlanta	1991	154	32	34
Howard Johnson, NY Mets	1991	156	38	30
Barry Bonds, Pittsburgh	1992	140	34	39
Sammy Sosa, Chicago	1993	159	33	36
Barry Bonds, San Francisco	1995	144	33	31
Sammy Sosa, Chicago	1995	144	36	34
Barry Bonds, San Francisco	1996	158	42	40
Ellis Burks, Colorado	1996	156	40	32
Dante Bichette, Colorado	1996	159	31	31

American League

	Year	Gm	HR	SB
Kenny Williams, St. Louis	1922	153	39	37
Tommy Harper, Milwaukee	1970	154	31	38
Bobby Bonds, New York	1975	145	32	30
Bobby Bonds, California	1977	158	37	41
Bobby Bonds, Chicago-Texas	1978	156	31	43
Joe Carter, Cleveland	1987	149	32	31
Jose Canseco, Oakland	1988	158	42	40

Consecutive Game Streaks

Regular season games through 1996.

Games Played

Active streak in **bold** type.

Gm		Dates of Streak		
2316	**Cal Ripken Jr.,** Bal	5/30/82	to	—
2130	Lou Gehrig, NY	6/1/25	to	4/30/39
1307	Everett Scott, Bos-NY	6/20/16	to	5/5/25
1207	Steve Garvey, LA-SD	9/3/75	to	7/29/83
1117	Billy Williams, Cubs	9/22/63	to	9/2/70
1103	Joe Sewell, Cle	9/13/22	to	4/30/30
895	Stan Musial, St.L	4/15/52	to	8/23/57
829	Eddie Yost, Wash	4/30/49	to	5/11/55
822	Gus Suhr, Pit	9/11/31	to	6/4/37
798	Nellie Fox, Chisox	8/8/55	to	9/3/60
745	Pete Rose, Cin-Phi	9/2/78	to	8/23/83
740	Dale Murphy, Atl	9/26/81	to	7/8/86
730	Richie Ashburn, Phi	6/7/50	to	4/13/55
717	Ernie Banks, Cubs	8/28/56	to	6/22/61
678	Pete Rose, Cin	9/28/73	to	5/7/78

Others

Gm		Gm	
673	Earl Averill	565	Aaron Ward
652	Frank McCormick	540	Candy LaChance
648	Sandy Alomar Sr.	535	Buck Freeman
618	Eddie Brown	533	Fred Luderus
585	Roy McMillan	511	Clyde Milan
577	George Pinckney	511	Charlie Gehringer
574	Steve Brodie	508	Vada Pinson

Hitting

	Gm	Year
Joe DiMaggio, New York (AL)	56	1941
Willie Keeler, Baltimore (NL)	44	1897
Pete Rose, Cincinnati (NL)	44	1978
Bill Dahlen, Chicago (NL)	42	1894
George Sisler, St. Louis (AL)	41	1922
Ty Cobb, Detroit (AL)	40	1911
Paul Molitor, Milwaukee (AL)	39	1987
Tommy Holmes, Boston (NL)	37	1945
Billy Hamilton, Philadelphia (NL)	36	1894
Fred Clarke, Louisville (NL)	35	1895
Ty Cobb, Detroit (AL)	35	1917
Ty Cobb, Detroit (AL)	34	1912
George Sisler, St. Louis (AL)	34	1925
George McQuinn, St. Louis (AL)	34	1938
Dom DiMaggio, Boston (AL)	34	1949
Benito Santiago, San Diego (NL)	34	1987
George Davis, New York (NL)	33	1893
Hal Chase, New York (AL)	33	1907
Rogers Hornsby, St. Louis (NL)	33	1922
Heinie Manush, Washington (AL)	33	1933
Ed Delahanty, Philadelphia (NL)	31	1899
Nap Lajoie, Cleveland (AL)	31	1906
Sam Rice, Washington, (AL)	31	1924
Willie Davis, Los Angeles (NL)	31	1969
Rico Carty, Atlanta (NL)	31	1970
Ken Landreaux, Minnesota (AL)	31	1980

Annual Pitching Leaders (since 1900)

Winning Percentage

At least 15 wins, except in strike years of 1981 and 1994 (when the minimum was 10).

National League

Multiple winners: Ed Reulbach and Tom Seaver (3); Larry Benton, Harry Brecheen, Jack Chesbro, Paul Derringer, Freddie Fitzsimmons, Don Bullet, Claude Hendrix, Carl Hubbell, Sandy Koufax, Bill Lee, Christy Mathewson, Don Newcombe and Preacher Roe (2).

Year		W-L	Pct
1900	Jesse Tannehill, Pittsburgh	20-6	.769
1901	Jack Chesbro, Pittsburgh	21-10	.677
1902	Jack Chesbro, Pittsburgh	28-6	.824
1903	Sam Leever, Pittsburgh	25-7	.781
1904	Joe McGinnity, New York	35-8	.814
1905	Christy Mathewson, New York	31-8	.795
1906	Ed Reulbach, Chicago	19-4	.826
1907	Ed Reulbach, Chicago	17-4	.810
1908	Ed Reulbach, Chicago	24-7	.774
1909	Howie Camnitz, Pittsburgh	25-6	.806
	& Christy Mathewson, New York	25-6	.806
1910	King Cole, Chicago	20-4	.833
1911	Rube Marquard, New York	24-7	.774
1912	Claude Hendrix, Pittsburgh	24-9	.727
1913	Bert Humphries, Chicago	16-4	.800
1914	Bill James, Boston	26-7	.788
1915	Grover Alexander, Phila.	31-10	.756
1916	Tom Hughes, Boston	16-3	.842
1917	Ferdie Schupp, New York	21-7	.750
1918	Claude Hendrix, Chicago	19-7	.731
1919	Dutch Ruether, Cincinnati	19-6	.760
1920	Burleigh Grimes, Brooklyn	23-11	.676
1921	Bill Doak, St. Louis	15-6	.714
1922	Pete Donohue, Cincinnati	18-9	.667
1923	Dolf Luque, Cincinnati	27-8	.771
1924	Emil Yde, Pittsburgh	16-3	.842
1925	Bill Sherdel, St. Louis	15-6	.714
1926	Ray Kremer, Pittsburgh	20-6	.769
1927	Larry Benton, Boston-NY	17-7	.708
1928	Larry Benton, New York	25-9	.735
1929	Charlie Root, Chicago	19-6	.760
1930	Freddie Fitzsimmons, NY	19-7	.731
1931	Paul Derringer, St. Louis	18-8	.692
1932	Lon Warneke, Chicago	22-6	.786
1933	Ben Cantwell, Boston	20-10	.667
1934	Dizzy Dean, St. Louis	30-7	.811
1935	Bill Lee, Chicago	20-6	.769
1936	Carl Hubbell, New York	26-6	.813
1937	Carl Hubbell, New York	22-8	.733
1938	Bill Lee, Chicago	22-9	.710
1939	Paul Derringer, Cincinnati	25-7	.781
1940	Freddie Fitzsimmons, Bklyn	16-2	.889
1941	Elmer Riddle, Cincinnati	19-4	.826
1942	Larry French, Brooklyn	15-4	.789
1943	Mort Cooper, St. Louis	21-8	.724
1944	Ted Wilks, St. Louis	17-4	.810
1945	Harry Brecheen, St. Louis	14-4	.778
1946	Murray Dickson, St. Louis	15-6	.714
1947	Larry Jansen, New York	21-5	.808
1948	Harry Brecheen, St. Louis	20-7	.741
1949	Preacher Roe, Brooklyn	15-6	.714
1950	Sal Maglie, New York	18-4	.818
1951	Preacher Roe, Brooklyn	22-3	.880
1952	Hoyt Wilhelm, New York	15-3	.833
1953	Carl Erskine, Brooklyn	20-6	.769
1954	Johnny Antonelli, New York	21-7	.750
1955	Don Newcombe, Brooklyn	20-5	.800
1956	Don Newcombe, Brooklyn	27-7	.794
1957	Bob Buhl, Milwaukee	18-7	.720
1958	Warren Spahn, Milwaukee	22-11	.667
	& Lew Burdette, Milwaukee	20-10	.667
1959	Roy Face, Pittsburgh	18-1	.947
1960	Ernie Broglio, St. Louis	21-9	.700
1961	Johnny Podres, Los Angeles	18-5	.783
1962	Bob Purkey, Cincinnati	23-5	.821
1963	Ron Perranoski, Los Angeles	16-3	.842
1964	Sandy Koufax, Los Angeles	19-5	.792
1965	Sandy Koufax, Los Angeles	26-8	.765
1966	Juan Marichal, San Francisco	25-6	.806
1967	Dick Hughes, St. Louis	16-6	.727
1968	Steve Blass, Pittsburgh	18-6	.750
1969	Tom Seaver, New York	25-7	.781
1970	Bob Gibson, St. Louis	23-7	.767
1971	Don Gullett, Cincinnati	16-6	.727
1972	Gary Nolan, Cincinnati	15-5	.750
1973	Tommy John, Los Angeles	16-7	.696
1974	Andy Messersmith, Los Angeles	20-6	.769
1975	Don Gullett, Cincinnati	15-4	.789
1976	Steve Carlton, Philadelphia	20-7	.741
1977	John Candelaria, Pittsburgh	20-5	.800
1978	Gaylord Perry, San Diego	21-6	.778
1979	Tom Seaver, Cincinnati	16-6	.727
1980	Jim Bibby, Pittsburgh	19-6	.760
1981	Tom Seaver, Cincinnati	14-2	.875
1982	Phil Niekro, Atlanta	17-4	.810
1983	John Denny, Philadelphia	19-6	.760
1984	Rick Sutcliffe, Chicago	16-1	.941
1985	Orel Hershiser, Los Angeles	19-3	.864
1986	Bob Ojeda, New York	18-5	.783
1987	Dwight Gooden, New York	15-7	.682
1988	David Cone, New York	20-3	.870
1989	Mike Bielecki, Chicago	18-7	.720
1990	Doug Drabek, Pittsburgh	22-6	.786
1991	John Smiley, Pittsburgh	20-8	.714
	& Jose Rijo, Cincinnati	15-6	.714
1992	Bob Tewksbury, St. Louis	16-5	.762
1993	Mark Portugal, Houston	18-4	.818
1994	Marvin Freeman, Colorado	10-2	.833
1995	Greg Maddux, Atlanta	19-2	.905
1996	John Smoltz, Atlanta	24-8	.750

Note: In 1984, Sutcliffe was also 4-5 with Cleveland for a combined AL-NL record of 20-6 (.769).

American League

Multiple winners: Lefty Grove (5); Chief Bender and Whitey Ford (3); Johnny Allen, Eddie Cicotte, Roger Clemens, Mike Cuellar, Lefty Gomez, Catfish Hunter, Walter Johnson, Jim Palmer, Pete Vuckovich and Smokey Joe Wood (2).

Year		W-L	Pct
1901	Clark Griffith, Chicago	24-7	.774
1902	Bill Bernhard, Phila-Cleve	18-5	.783
1903	Cy Young, Boston	28-9	.757
1904	Jack Chesbro, New York	41-12	.774
1905	Andy Coakley, Philadelphia	20-7	.741
1906	Eddie Plank, Philadelphia	19-6	.760

Year		W-L	Pct
1907	Wild Bill Donovan, Detroit	25-4	.862
1908	Ed Walsh, Chicago	40-15	.727
1909	George Mullin, Detroit	29-8	.784
1910	Chief Bender, Philadelphia	23-5	.821
1911	Chief Bender, Philadelphia	17-5	.773
1912	Smokey Joe Wood, Boston	34-5	.872
1913	Walter Johnson, Washington	36-7	.837
1914	Chief Bender, Philadelphia	17-3	.850
1915	Smokey Joe Wood, Boston	15-5	.750
1916	Eddie Cicotte, Chicago	15-7	.682
1917	Reb Russell, Chicago	15-5	.750
1918	Sad Sam Jones, Boston	16-5	.762
1919	Eddie Cicotte, Chicago	29-7	.806
1920	Jim Bagby, Cleveland	31-12	.721
1921	Carl Mays, New York	27-9	.750
1922	Joe Bush, New York	26-7	.788
1923	Herb Pennock, New York	19-6	.760
1924	Walter Johnson, Washington	23-7	.767
1925	Stan Coveleski, Washington	20-5	.800
1926	George Uhle, Cleveland	27-11	.711
1927	Waite Hoyt, New York	22-7	.759
1928	General Crowder, St. Louis	21-5	.808
1929	Lefty Grove, Philadelphia	20-6	.769
1930	Lefty Grove, Philadelphia	28-5	.848
1931	Lefty Grove, Philadelphia	31-4	.886
1932	Johnny Allen, New York	17-4	.810
1933	Lefty Grove, Philadelphia	24-8	.750
1934	Lefty Gomez, New York	26-5	.839
1935	Eldon Auker, Detroit	18-7	.720
1936	Monte Pearson, New York	19-7	.731
1937	Johnny Allen, Cleveland	15-1	.938
1938	Red Ruffing, New York	21-7	.750
1939	Lefty Grove, Boston	15-4	.789
1940	Schoolboy Rowe, Detroit	16-3	.842
1941	Lefty Gomez, New York	15-5	.750
1942	Ernie Bonham, New York	21-5	.808
1943	Spud Chandler, New York	20-4	.833
1944	Tex Hughson, Boston	18-5	.783
1945	Hal Newhouser, Detroit	25-9	.735
1946	Boo Ferriss, Boston	25-6	.806
1947	Allie Reynolds, New York	19-8	.704
1948	Jack Kramer, Boston	18-5	.783
1949	Ellis Kinder, Boston	23-6	.793
1950	Vic Raschi, New York	21-8	.724
1951	Bob Feller, Cleveland	22-8	.733
1952	Bobby Shantz, Philadelphia	24-7	.774
1953	Ed Lopat, New York	16-4	.800
1954	Sandy Consuegra, Chicago	16-3	.842
1955	Tommy Byrne, New York	16-5	.762
1956	Whitey Ford, New York	19-6	.760
1957	Dick Donovan, Chicago	16-6	.727
	& Tom Sturdivant, New York	16-6	.727
1958	Bob Turley, New York	21-7	.750
1959	Bob Shaw, Chicago	18-6	.750
1960	Jim Perry, Cleveland	18-10	.643
1961	Whitey Ford, New York	25-4	.862
1962	Ray Herbert, Chicago	20-9	.690
1963	Whitey Ford, New York	24-7	.774
1964	Wally Bunker, Baltimore	19-5	.792
1965	Mudcat Grant, Minnesota	21-7	.750
1966	Sonny Siebert, Cleveland	16-8	.667
1967	Joe Horlen, Chicago	19-7	.731
1968	Denny McLain, Detroit	31-6	.838
1969	Jim Palmer, Baltimore	16-4	.800
1970	Mike Cuellar, Baltimore	24-8	.750
1971	Dave McNally, Baltimore	21-5	.808
1972	Catfish Hunter, Oakland	21-7	.750
1973	Catfish Hunter, Oakland	21-5	.808
1974	Mike Cuellar, Baltimore	22-10	.688
1975	Mike Torrez, Baltimore	20-9	.690
1976	Bill Campbell, Minnesota	17-5	.773
1977	Paul Splittorff, Kansas City	16-6	.727
1978	Ron Guidry, New York	25-3	.893
1979	Mike Caldwell, Milwaukee	16-6	.727
1980	Steve Stone, Baltimore	25-7	.781
1981	Pete Vuckovich, Milwaukee	14-4	.778
1982	Pete Vuckovich, Milwaukee	18-6	.750
	& Jim Palmer, Baltimore	15-5	.750
1983	Rich Dotson, Chicago	22-7	.759
1984	Doyle Alexander, Toronto	17-6	.739
1985	Ron Guidry, New York	22-6	.786
1986	Roger Clemens, Boston	24-4	.857
1987	Roger Clemens, Boston	20-9	.690
1988	Frank Viola, Minnesota	24-7	.774
1989	Bret Saberhagen, Kansas City	23-6	.793
1990	Bob Welch, Oakland	27-6	.818
1991	Scott Erickson, Minnesota	20-8	.714
1992	Mike Mussina, Baltimore	18-5	.783
1993	Jimmy Key, New York	18-6	.750
1994	Jason Bere, Chicago	12-2	.857
1995	Randy Johnson, Seattle	18-2	.900
1996	Charles Nagy, Cleveland	17-5	.773

Earned Run Average

Earned Run Averages were based on at least 10 complete games pitched (1900-50), at least 154 innings pitched (1950-60), and at least 162 innings pitched since 1961 in the AL and 1962 in the NL. In the strike year of 1981, '94 and '95 qualifiers had to pitch at least as many innings as the total number of games their team played that season.

National League

Multiple winners: Grover Alexander, Sandy Koufax and Christy Mathewson (5); Carl Hubbell, Greg Maddux, Tom Seaver, Warren Spahn and Dazzy Vance (3); Bill Doak, Ray Kremer, Dolf Luque, Howie Pollet, Nolan Ryan, Bill Walker and Bucky Walters (2).

Year		ERA
1900	Rube Waddell, Pit	2.37
1901	Jesse Tannehill, Pit	2.18
1902	Jack Taylor, Chi	1.33
1903	Sam Leever, Pit	2.06
1904	Joe McGinnity, NY	1.61
1905	Christy Mathewson, NY	1.27
1906	Three Finger Brown, Chi	1.04
1907	Jack Pfiester, Chi	1.15
1908	Christy Mathewson, NY	1.43
1909	Christy Mathewson, NY	1.14
1910	George McQuillan, Phi	1.60
1911	Christy Mathewson, NY	1.99
1912	Jeff Tesreau, NY	1.96
1913	Christy Mathewson, NY	2.06
1914	Bill Doak, St.L	1.72
1915	Grover Alexander, Phi	1.22
1916	Grover Alexander, Phi	1.55
1917	Grover Alexander, Phi	1.86
1918	Hippo Vaughn, Chi	1.74
1919	Grover Alexander, Chi	1.72
1920	Grover Alexander, Chi	1.91
1921	Bill Doak, St.L	2.59
1922	Rosy Ryan, NY	3.01
1923	Dolf Luque, Cin	1.93
1924	Dazzy Vance, Bklyn	2.16

Annual Pitching Leaders (Cont.)

Earned Run Average

National League

Year		ERA
1925	Dolf Luque, Cin	2.63
1926	Ray Kremer, Pit	2.61
1927	Ray Kremer, Pit	2.47
1928	Dazzy Vance, Bklyn	2.09
1929	Bill Walker, NY	3.09
1930	Dazzy Vance, Bklyn	2.61
1931	Bill Walker, NY	2.26
1932	Lon Warneke, Chi	2.37
1933	Carl Hubbell, NY	1.66
1934	Carl Hubbell, NY	2.30
1935	Cy Blanton, Pit	2.58
1936	Carl Hubbell, NY	2.31
1937	Jim Turner, Bos	2.38
1938	Bill Lee, Chi	2.66
1939	Bucky Walters, Cin	2.29
1940	Bucky Walters, Cin	2.48
1941	Elmer Riddle, Cin	2.24
1942	Mort Cooper, St.L	1.78
1943	Howie Pollet, St.L	1.75
1944	Ed Heusser, Cin	2.38
1945	Hank Borowy, Chi	2.13
1946	Howie Pollet, St.L	2.10
1947	Warren Spahn, Bos	2.33
1948	Harry Brecheen, St.L	2.24
1949	Dave Koslo, NY	2.50
1950	Jim Hearn, St.L-NY	2.49
1951	Chet Nichols, Bos	2.88
1952	Hoyt Wilhelm, NY	2.43
1953	Warren Spahn, Mil	2.10
1954	Johnny Antonelli, NY	2.30
1955	Bob Friend, Pit	2.83
1956	Lew Burdette, Mil	2.70
1957	Johnny Podres, Bklyn	2.66
1958	Stu Miller, SF	2.47
1959	Sam Jones, SF	2.83
1960	Mike McCormick, SF	2.70
1961	Warren Spahn, Mil	3.02
1962	Sandy Koufax, LA	2.54
1963	Sandy Koufax, LA	1.88
1964	Sandy Koufax, LA	1.74
1965	Sandy Koufax, LA	2.04
1966	Sandy Koufax, LA	1.73
1967	Phil Niekro, Atl	1.87
1968	Bob Gibson, St.L	1.12
1969	Juan Marichal, SF	2.10
1970	Tom Seaver, NY	2.81
1971	Tom Seaver, NY	1.76
1972	Steve Carlton, Phi	1.97
1973	Tom Seaver, NY	2.08
1974	Buzz Capra, Atl	2.28
1975	Randy Jones, SD	2.24
1976	John Denny, St.L	2.52
1977	John Candelaria, Pit	2.34
1978	Craig Swan, NY	2.43
1979	J.R. Richard, Hou	2.71
1980	Don Sutton, LA	2.21
1981	Nolan Ryan, Hou	1.69
1982	Steve Rogers, Mon	2.40
1983	Atlee Hammaker, SF	2.25
1984	Alejandro Peña, LA	2.48
1985	Dwight Gooden, NY	1.53
1986	Mike Scott, Hou	2.22
1987	Nolan Ryan, Hou	2.76
1988	Joe Magrane, St.L	2.18
1989	Scott Garrelts, SF	2.28
1990	Danny Darwin, Hou	2.21
1991	Dennis Martinez, Mon	2.39
1992	Bill Swift, SF	2.08
1993	Greg Maddux, Atl	2.36
1994	Greg Maddux, Atl	1.56
1995	Greg Maddux, Atl	1.63
1996	Kevin Brown, Fla	1.89

Note: In 1945, Borowy had a 3.13 ERA in 18 games with New York (AL) for a combined ERA of 2.65.

American League

Multiple winners: Lefty Grove (9); Walter Johnson (5); Roger Clemens (4); Spud Chandler, Stan Coveleski, Red Faber, Whitey Ford, Lefty Gomez, Ron Guidry, Addie Joss, Hal Newhouser, Jim Palmer, Gary Peters, Luis Tiant and Ed Walsh (2).

Year		ERA
1901	Cy Young, Bos	1.62
1902	Ed Siever, Det	1.91
1903	Earl Moore, Cle	1.77
1904	Addie Joss, Cle	1.59
1905	Rube Waddell, Phi	1.48
1906	Doc White, Chi	1.52
1907	Ed Walsh, Chi	1.60
1908	Addie Joss, Cle	1.16
1909	Harry Krause, Phi	1.39
1910	Ed Walsh, Chi	1.27
1911	Vean Gregg, Cle	1.81
1912	Walter Johnson, Wash	1.39
1913	Walter Johnson, Wash	1.09
1914	Dutch Leonard, Bos	1.01
1915	Smokey Joe Wood, Bos	1.49
1916	Babe Ruth, Bos	1.75
1917	Eddie Cicotte, Chi	1.53
1918	Walter Johnson, Wash	1.27
1919	Walter Johnson, Wash	1.49
1920	Bob Shawkey, NY	2.45
1921	Red Faber, Chi	2.48
1922	Red Faber, Chi	2.80
1923	Stan Coveleski, Cle	2.76
1924	Walter Johnson, Wash	2.72
1925	Stan Coveleski, Wash	2.84
1926	Lefty Grove, Phi	2.51
1927	Wilcy Moore, NY	2.28
1928	Garland Braxton, Wash	2.51
1929	Lefty Grove, Phi	2.81
1930	Lefty Grove, Phi	2.54
1931	Lefty Grove, Phi	2.06
1932	Lefty Grove, Phi	2.84
1933	Monte Pearson, Cle	2.33
1934	Lefty Gomez, NY	2.33
1935	Lefty Grove, Bos	2.70
1936	Lefty Grove, Bos	2.81
1937	Lefty Gomez, NY	2.33
1938	Lefty Grove, Bos	3.08
1939	Lefty Grove, Bos	2.54
1940	Bob Feller, Cle	2.61
1941	Thornton Lee, Chi	2.37
1942	Ted Lyons, Chi	2.10
1943	Spud Chandler, NY	1.64
1944	Dizzy Trout, Det	2.12
1945	Hal Newhouser, Det	1.81
1946	Hal Newhouser, Det	1.94
1947	Spud Chandler, NY	2.46
1948	Gene Bearden, Cle	2.43
1949	Mel Parnell, Bos	2.77
1950	Early Wynn, Cle	3.20
1951	Saul Rogovin, Det-Chi	2.78
1952	Allie Reynolds, NY	2.06
1953	Ed Lopat, NY	2.42
1954	Mike Garcia, Cle	2.64
1955	Billy Pierce, Chi	1.97
1956	Whitey Ford, NY	2.47
1957	Bobby Shantz, NY	2.45
1958	Whitey Ford, NY	2.01
1959	Hoyt Wilhelm, Bal	2.19
1960	Frank Baumann, Chi	2.67
1961	Dick Donovan, Wash	2.40
1962	Hank Aguirre, Det	2.21
1963	Gary Peters, Chi	2.33
1964	Dean Chance, LA	1.65
1965	Sam McDowell, Cle	2.18
1966	Gary Peters, Chi	1.98
1967	Joe Horlen, Chi	2.06
1968	Luis Tiant, Cle	1.60
1969	Dick Bosman, Wash	2.19
1970	Diego Segui, Oak	2.56
1971	Vida Blue, Oak	1.82
1972	Luis Tiant, Bos	1.91
1973	Jim Palmer, Bal	2.40
1974	Catfish Hunter, Oak	2.49
1975	Jim Palmer, Bal	2.09
1976	Mark Fidrych, Det	2.34
1977	Frank Tanana, Cal	2.54
1978	Ron Guidry, NY	1.74
1979	Ron Guidry, NY	2.78
1980	Rudy May, NY	2.47
1981	Steve McCatty, Oak	2.32
1982	Rick Sutcliffe, Cle	2.96
1983	Rick Honeycutt, Tex	2.42
1984	Mike Boddicker, Bal	2.79
1985	Dave Stieb, Tor	2.48
1986	Roger Clemens, Bos	2.48
1987	Jimmy Key, Tor	2.76
1988	Allan Anderson, Min	2.45
1989	Bret Saberhagen, KC	2.16
1990	Roger Clemens, Bos	1.93
1991	Roger Clemens, Bos	2.62
1992	Roger Clemens, Bos	2.41
1993	Kevin Appier, KC	2.56
1994	Steve Ontiveros, Oak	2.65
1995	Randy Johnson, Sea	2.48
1996	Juan Guzman, Tor	2.93

Note: In 1940, Ernie Bonham of NY had a 1.90 ERA and 10 complete games, but appeared in only a total of 12 games and 99 innings.

Strikeouts

National League

Multiple winners: Dazzy Vance (7); Grover Alexander (6); Steve Carlton, Christy Mathewson and Tom Seaver (5); Dizzy Dean, Sandy Koufax and Warren Spahn (4); Don Drysdale, Sam Jones and Johnny Vander Meer (3); David Cone, Dwight Gooden, Bill Hallahan, J.R. Richard, Robin Roberts, Nolan Ryan, John Smoltz and Hippo Vaughn (2).

Year		SO
1900	Rube Waddell, Pit	130
1901	Noodles Hahn, Cin	239
1902	Vic Willis, Bos	225
1903	Christy Mathewson, NY	267
1904	Christy Mathewson, NY	212
1905	Christy Mathewson, NY	206
1906	Fred Beebe, Chi-St.L	171
1907	Christy Mathewson, NY	178
1908	Christy Mathewson, NY	259
1909	Orval Overall, Chi	205
1910	Earl Moore, Phi	185
1911	Rube Marquard, NY	237
1912	Grover Alexander, Phi	195
1913	Tom Seaton, Phi	168
1914	Grover Alexander, Phi	214
1915	Grover Alexander, Phi	241
1916	Grover Alexander, Phi	167
1917	Grover Alexander, Phi	201
1918	Hippo Vaughn, Chi	148
1919	Hippo Vaughn, Chi	141
1920	Grover Alexander, Chi	173
1921	Burleigh Grimes, Bklyn	136
1922	Dazzy Vance, Bklyn	134
1923	Dazzy Vance, Bklyn	197
1924	Dazzy Vance, Bklyn	262
1925	Dazzy Vance, Bklyn	221
1926	Dazzy Vance, Bklyn	140
1927	Dazzy Vance, Bklyn	184
1928	Dazzy Vance, Bklyn	200
1929	Pat Malone, Chi	166
1930	Bill Hallahan, St.L	177
1931	Bill Hallahan, St.L	159
1932	Dizzy Dean, St.L	191

Year		SO
1933	Dizzy Dean, St.L	199
1934	Dizzy Dean, St.L	195
1935	Dizzy Dean, St.L	190
1936	Van Lingle Mungo, Bklyn	238
1937	Carl Hubbell, NY	159
1938	Clay Bryant, Chi	135
1939	Claude Passeau, Phi-Chi	137
	& Bucky Walters, Cin	137
1940	Kirby Higbe, Phi	137
1941	John Vander Meer, Cin	202
1942	John Vander Meer, Cin	186
1943	John Vander Meer, Cin	174
1944	Bill Voiselle, NY	161
1945	Preacher Roe, Pit	148
1946	Johnny Schmitz, Chi	135
1947	Ewell Blackwell, Cin	193
1948	Harry Brecheen, St.L	149
1949	Warren Spahn, Bos	151
1950	Warren Spahn, Bos	191
1951	Don Newcombe, Bklyn	164
	& Warren Spahn, Bos	164
1952	Warren Spahn, Bos	183
1953	Robin Roberts, Phi	198
1954	Robin Roberts, Phi	185
1955	Sam Jones, Chi	198
1956	Sam Jones, Chi	176
1957	Jack Sanford, Phi	188
1958	Sam Jones, St.L	225
1959	Don Drysdale, LA	242
1960	Don Drysdale, LA	246
1961	Sandy Koufax, LA	269
1962	Don Drysdale, LA	232
1963	Sandy Koufax, LA	306

Year		SO
1964	Bob Veale, Pit	250
1965	Sandy Koufax, LA	382
1966	Sandy Koufax, LA	317
1967	Jim Bunning, Phi	253
1968	Bob Gibson, St.L	268
1969	Ferguson Jenkins, Chi	273
1970	Tom Seaver, NY	283
1971	Tom Seaver, NY	289
1972	Steve Carlton, Phi	310
1973	Tom Seaver, NY	251
1974	Steve Carlton, Phi	240
1975	Tom Seaver, NY	243
1976	Tom Seaver, NY	235
1977	Phil Niekro, Atl	262
1978	J.R. Richard, Hou	303
1979	J.R. Richard, Hou	313
1980	Steve Carlton, Phi	286
1981	F. Valenzuela, LA	180
1982	Steve Carlton, Phi	286
1983	Steve Carlton, Phi	275
1984	Dwight Gooden, NY	276
1985	Dwight Gooden, NY	268
1986	Mike Scott, Hou	306
1987	Nolan Ryan, Hou	270
1988	Nolan Ryan, Hou	228
1989	Jose DeLeon, St.L	201
1990	David Cone, NY	233
1991	David Cone, NY	241
1992	John Smoltz, Atl	215
1993	Jose Rijo, Cin	227
1994	Andy Benes, SD	189
1995	Hideo Nomo, LA	236
1996	John Smoltz, Atl	276

American League

Multiple winners: Walter Johnson (12); Nolan Ryan (9); Bob Feller and Lefty Grove (7); Rube Waddell (6); Sam McDowell (5); Randy Johnson (4); Roger Clemens, Lefty Gomez, Mark Langston and Camilo Pascual (3); Len Barker, Tommy Bridges, Jim Bunning, Hal Newhouser, Allie Reynolds, Herb Score, Ed Walsh and Early Wynn (2).

Year		SO
1901	Cy Young, Bos	158
1902	Rube Waddell, Phi	210
1903	Rube Waddell, Phi	302
1904	Rube Waddell, Phi	349
1905	Rube Waddell, Phi	287
1906	Rube Waddell, Phi	196
1907	Rube Waddell, Phi	232
1908	Ed Walsh, Chi	269
1909	Frank Smith, Chi	177
1910	Walter Johnson, Wash	313
1911	Ed Walsh, Chi	255
1912	Walter Johnson, Wash	303
1913	Walter Johnson, Wash	243
1914	Walter Johnson, Wash	225
1915	Walter Johnson, Wash	203
1916	Walter Johnson, Wash	228
1917	Walter Johnson, Wash	188
1918	Walter Johnson, Wash	162
1919	Walter Johnson, Wash	147

Year		SO
1920	Stan Coveleski, Cle	133
1921	Walter Johnson, Wash	143
1922	Urban Shocker, St.L	149
1923	Walter Johnson, Wash	130
1924	Walter Johnson, Wash	158
1925	Lefty Grove, Phi	116
1926	Lefty Grove, Phi	194
1927	Lefty Grove, Phi	174
1928	Lefty Grove, Phi	183
1929	Lefty Grove, Phi	170
1930	Lefty Grove, Phi	209
1931	Lefty Grove, Phi	175
1932	Red Ruffing, NY	190
1933	Lefty Gomez, NY	163
1934	Lefty Gomez, NY	158
1935	Tommy Bridges, Det	163
1936	Tommy Bridges, Det	175
1937	Lefty Gomez, NY	194
1938	Bob Feller, Cle	240

Year		SO
1939	Bob Feller, Cle	246
1940	Bob Feller, Cle	261
1941	Bob Feller, Cle	260
1942	Tex Hughson, Bos	113
	& Bobo Newsom, Wash	113
1943	Allie Reynolds, Cle	151
1944	Hal Newhouser, Det	187
1945	Hal Newhouser, Det	212
1946	Bob Feller, Cle	348
1947	Bob Feller, Cle	196
1948	Bob Feller, Cle	164
1949	Virgil Trucks, Det	153
1950	Bob Lemon, Cle	170
1951	Vic Raschi, NY	164
1952	Allie Reynolds, NY	160
1953	Billy Pierce, Chi	186
1954	Bob Turley, Bal	185
1955	Herb Score, Cle	245

Annual Pitching Leaders (Cont.)

Strikeouts

American League

Year		SO
1956	Herb Score, Cle	263
1957	Early Wynn, Cle	184
1958	Early Wynn, Chi	179
1959	Jim Bunning, Det	201
1960	Jim Bunning, Det	201
1961	Camilo Pascual, Min	221
1962	Camilo Pascual, Min	206
1963	Camilo Pascual, Min	202
1964	Al Downing, NY	217
1965	Sam McDowell, Cle	325
1966	Sam McDowell, Cle	225
1967	Jim Lonborg, Bos	246
1968	Sam McDowell, Cle	283
1969	Sam McDowell, Cle	279
1970	Sam McDowell, Cle	304
1971	Mickey Lolich, Det	308
1972	Nolan Ryan, Cal	329
1973	Nolan Ryan, Cal	383
1974	Nolan Ryan, Cal	367
1975	Frank Tanana, Cal	269
1976	Nolan Ryan, Cal	327
1977	Nolan Ryan, Cal	341
1978	Nolan Ryan, Cal	260
1979	Nolan Ryan, Cal	223
1980	Len Barker, Cle	187
1981	Len Barker, Cle	127
1982	Floyd Bannister, Sea	209
1983	Jack Morris, Det	232
1984	Mark Langston, Sea	204
1985	Bert Blyleven, Cle-Min	206
1986	Mark Langston, Sea	245
1987	Mark Langston, Sea	262
1988	Roger Clemens, Bos	291
1989	Nolan Ryan, Tex	301
1990	Nolan Ryan, Tex	232
1991	Roger Clemens, Bos	241
1992	Randy Johnson, Sea	241
1993	Randy Johnson, Sea	308
1994	Randy Johnson, Sea	204
1995	Randy Johnson, Sea	294
1996	Roger Clemens, Bos	257

Pitching Triple Crown Winners

Pitchers who led either league in Earned Run Average, Wins and Strikeouts over a single season.

National League

	Year	ERA	W-L	SO
Tommy Bond, Bos	1877	2.11	40-17	170
Hoss Radbourne, Prov	1884	1.38	60-12	441
Tim Keefe, NY	1888	1.74	35-12	333
John Clarkson, Bos	1889	2.73	49-19	284
Amos Rusie, NY	1894	2.78	36-13	195
Christy Mathewson, NY	1905	1.27	31-8	206
Christy Mathewson, NY	1908	1.43	37-11	259
Grover Alexander, Phi	1915	1.22	31-10	241
Grover Alexander, Phi	1916	1.55	33-12	167
Grover Alexander, Phi	1917	1.86	30-13	201
Hippo Vaughn, Chi	1918	1.74	22-10	148
Grover Alexander, Chi	1920	1.91	27-14	173
Dazzy Vance, Bklyn	1924	2.16	28-6	262
Bucky Walters, Cin	1939	2.29	27-11	137
Sandy Koufax, LA	1963	1.88	25-5	306
Sandy Koufax, LA	1965	2.04	26-8	382
Sandy Koufax, LA	1966	1.73	27-9	317
Steve Carlton, Phi	1972	1.97	27-10	310
Dwight Gooden, NY	1985	1.53	24-4	268

Ties: In 1894, Rusie tied for league lead in wins with Jouett Meekin, NY (36-10); in 1939, Walters tied for league lead in strikeouts with Claude Passeau, Phi-Chi; in 1963, Koufax tied for the league lead in wins with Juan Marichal, SF.

American League

	Year	ERA	W-L	SO
Cy Young, Bos	1901	1.62	33-10	158
Rube Waddell, Phi	1905	1.48	26-11	287
Walter Johnson, Wash	1913	1.09	36-7	243
Walter Johnson, Wash	1918	1.27	23-13	162
Walter Johnson, Wash	1924	2.72	23-7	158
Lefty Grove, Phi	1930	2.54	28-5	209
Lefty Grove, Phi	1931	2.06	31-4	175
Lefty Gomez, NY	1934	2.33	26-5	158
Lefty Gomez, NY	1937	2.33	21-11	194
Hal Newhouser, Det	1945	1.81	25-9	212

Perfect Games

Sixteen pitchers have thrown perfect games (27 up, 27 down) in major league history. However, the games pitched by Harvey Haddix and Ernie Shore are not considered to be official.

National League

	Game	Date	Score
Lee Richmond	Wor. vs Cle.	6/12/1880	1-0
Monte Ward	Prov. vs Bos.	6/17/1880	5-0
Harvey Haddix	Pit. at Mil.	5/26/1959	0-1*
Jim Bunning	Phi. at NY	6/21/1964	6-0
Sandy Koufax	LA vs Chi.	9/9/1965	1-0
Tom Browning	Cin. vs LA	9/16/1988	1-0
Dennis Martinez	Mon. at LA	7/28/1991	2-0

*Haddix pitched 12 perfect innings before losing in the 13th. Braves' lead-off batter Felix Mantilla reached on a throwing error by Pirates 3B Don Hoak, Eddie Mathews sacrificed Mantilla to 2nd, Hank Aaron was walked intentionally, and Joe Adcock hit a 3-run HR. Adcock, however, passed Aaron on the bases and was only credited with a 1-run double.

American League

	Game	Date	Score
Cy Young	Bos. vs Phi.	5/5/1904	3-0
Addie Joss	Cle. vs Chi.	10/2/1908	1-0
Ernie Shore	Bos. vs Wash.	6/23/1917	4-0*
Charlie Robertson	Chi. at Det.	4/30/1922	2-0
Catfish Hunter	Oak. vs Min.	5/8/1968	4-0
Len Barker	Cle. vs Tor.	5/15/1981	3-0
Mike Witt	Cal. at Tex.	9/30/1984	1-0
Kenny Rogers	Tex. vs Cal.	6/28/1994	4-0

*Babe Ruth started for Boston, walking Senators' lead-off batter Ray Morgan, then was thrown out of game by umpire Brick Owens for arguing the call. Shore came on in relief. Morgan was caught stealing and Shore retired the next 26 batters in a row. While technically not a perfect game—since he didn't start—Shore gets credit anyway.

World Series

Pitcher	Game	Date	Score
Don Larsen	NY vs Bklyn	10/8/1956	2-0

No-Hit Games

Nine innings or more, including perfect games, since 1876. Losing pitchers in **bold** type.

Multiple no-hitters: Nolan Ryan (7); Sandy Koufax (4); Larry Cocoran, Bob Feller and Cy Young (3); Jim Bunning, Steve Busby, Carl Erskine, Bob Forsch, Pud Galvin, Ken Holtzman, Addie Joss, Hub Leonard, Jim Maloney, Christy Mathewson, Allie Reynolds, Warren Spahn, Bill Stoneham, Virgil Trucks and Johnny Vander Meer (2).

National League

Year	Date	Pitcher	Result
1876	7/15	George Bradley	St.L vs Har, 2-0
1880	6/12	Lee Richmond	Wor vs Cle,1-0 (perfect game)
	6/17	Monte Ward	Prov vs Buf, 5-0 (perfect game)
	8/19	Larry Cocoran	Chi vs Bos, 6-0
	8/20	Pud Galvin	Buf at Wor, 1-0
1882	9/20	Larry Corcoran	Chi vs Wor, 1-0
1883	7/25	Old Hoss Radbourn	Prov at Cle, 8-0
	9/13	Hugh Daily	Cle at Phi, 1-0
1884	6/27	Larry Corcoran	Chi vs Prov, 6-0
	8/4	Pud Galvin	Buf at Det, 18-0
1885	7/27	John Clarkson	Chi vs Prov, 6-0
	8/29	Charlie Ferguson	Phi vs Prov, 1-0
1891	6/22	Tom Lovett	Bklyn vs NY, 4-0
	7/31	Amos Ruise	NY vs Bklyn, 11-0
1892	8/6	John Stivetts	Bos vs Bklyn, 11-0
	8/22	Ben Sanders	Lou vs Bal, 6-2
	10/22	Bumpus Jones	Cin vs Pit, 7-1 (1st major league game)
1893	8/16	Bill Hawke	Bal vs Wash, 5-0
1897	9/18	Cy Young	Cle vs Cin, 6-0
1898	4/22	Ted Breitenstein	Cin vs Pit, 11-0
	4/22	Jim Hughes	Bal vs Bos, 8-0
	7/8	Frank Donahue	Phi vs Bos, 5-0
	8/21	Walter Thornton	Chi vs Bklyn, 2-0
1899	5/25	Deacon Phillippe	Lou vs NY, 7-0
1900	7/12	Noodles Hahn	Cin vs Phi, 4-0
1901	7/15	Christy Mathewson	NY vs St.L, 5-0
1903	9/18	Chick Fraser	Phi at Chi, 10-0
1905	6/13	Christy Mathewson	NY at Chi, 1-0
1906	5/1	John Lush	Phi at Bklyn, 1-0
	7/20	Mal Eason	Bklyn at St.L, 2-0
1907	5/8	Frank Pfeffer	Bos vs Cin, 6-0
	9/20	Nick Maddox	Pit vs Bkn, 2-1
1908	7/4	Hooks Wiltse	NY vs Phi, 1-0 (10)
	9/5	Nap Rucker	Bklyn vs Bos, 6-0
1912	9/6	Jeff Tesreau	NY at Phi, 3-0
1914	9/9	George Davis	Bos vs Phi, 7-0
1915	4/15	Rube Marquard	NY vs Bklyn, 2-0
	8/31	Jimmy Lavender	Chi at N.Y, 2-0
1916	6/16	Tom Hughes	Bos vs. Pit, 2-0
1917	5/2	Fred Toney	Cin at Chi, 1-0 (10)
1919	5/11	Hod Eller	Cin at St.L, 6-0
1922	5/7	Jesse Barnes	NY vs Phi, 6-0
1924	7/17	Jesse Haines	St.L vs Bos, 5-0
1925	9/17	Dazzy Vance	Bklyn vs Phi, 10-1
1929	5/8	Carl Hubbell	NY vs Pit, 2-0
1934	9/21	Paul Dean	St.L vs Bklyn, 3-0
1938	6/11	Johnny Vander Meer	Cin vs Bos, 3-0
	6/15	Johnny Vander Meer (consecutive starts)	Cin at Bklyn, 6-0
1940	4/30	Tex Carleton	Bklyn at Cin, 3-0
1941	8/30	Lon Warneke	St.L at Cin, 2-0
1944	4/27	Jim Tobin	Bos vs Bklyn, 2-0
	5/15	Clyde Shoun	Cin vs Bos, 1-0
1946	4/23	Ed Head	Bklyn at NY, 2-0
1947	6/18	Ewell Blackwell	Cin vs Bos, 6-0
1948	9/9	Rex Barney	Bklyn at NY, 2-0
1950	8/11	Vern Bickford	Bos vs Bklyn, 7-0
1951	5/6	Cliff Chambers	Pit at Bos, 3-0
1952	6/19	Carl Erskine	Bklyn vs Chi, 5-0
1954	6/12	Jim Wilson	Mil vs Phi, 2-0
1955	5/12	Sam Jones	Chi vs Pit, 4-0

Year	Date	Pitcher	Result
1956	5/12	Carl Erskine	Bklyn vs NY, 3-0
	9/25	Sal Maglie	Bklyn vs Phi, 5-0
1960	5/15	Don Cardwell	Chi vs St.L, 4-0
	8/18	Lew Burdette	Mil vs Phi, 1-0
	9/16	Warren Spahn	Mil vs Phi, 4-0
1961	4/28	Warren Spahn	Mil vs SF, 1-0
1962	6/30	Sandy Koufax	LA vs NY, 5-0
1963	5/11	Sandy Koufax	LA vs SF, 1-0
	5/17	Don Nottebart	Hou vs Phi, 4-1
	6/15	Juan Marichal	SF vs Hou, 1-0
1964	4/23	**Ken Johnson**	Hou vs Cin, 0-1
	6/4	Sandy Koufax	LA at Phi, 3-0
	6/21	Jim Bunning	Phi at NY, 6-0 (perfect game)
1965	8/19	Jim Maloney	Cin at Chi, 1-0 (10)
	9/9	Sandy Koufax	LA vs Chi, 1-0 (perfect game)
1967	6/18	Don Wilson	Hou vs Atl, 2-0
1968	7/29	George Culver	Cin at Phi, 6-1
	9/17	Gaylord Perry	SF vs St.L, 1-0
	9/18	Ray Washburn	St.L at SF, 2-0 (next day, same park)
1969	4/17	Bill Stoneman	Mon at Phi, 7-0
	4/30	Jim Maloney	Cin vs Hou, 10-0
	5/1	Don Wilson	Hou at Cin, 4-0
	8/19	Ken Holtzman	Chi vs Atl, 3-0
	9/20	Bob Moose	Pit at NY, 4-0
1970	6/12	Dock Ellis	Pit at SD, 2-0
	7/20	Bill Singer	LA vs Phi, 5-0
1971	6/3	Ken Holtzman	Chi at Cin, 1-0
	6/23	Rick Wise	Phi at Cin, 4-0
	8/14	Bob Gibson	St.L at Pit, 11-0
1972	4/16	Burt Hooton	Chi vs Phi, 4-0
	9/2	Milt Pappas	Chi vs SD, 8-0
	10/2	Bill Stoneman	Mon vs NY, 7-0
1973	8/5	Phil Niekro	Atl vs SD, 9-0
1975	8/24	Ed Halicki	SF vs NY, 6-0
1976	7/9	Larry Dierker	Hou vs Mon, 6-0
	8/9	John Candelaria	Pit vs LA, 2-0
	9/29	John Montefusco	SF vs Atl, 9-0
1978	4/16	Bob Forsch	St.L vs Phi, 5-0
	6/16	Tom Seaver	Cin vs St.L, 4-0
1979	4/7	Ken Forsch	Hou vs Atl, 6-0
1980	6/27	Jerry Reuss	LA at SF, 4-0
1981	5/10	Charlie Lea	Mon vs SF, 4-0
	9/26	Nolan Ryan	Hou vs LA, 5-0
1983	9/26	Bob Forsch	St.L vs Mon, 3-0
1986	9/25	Mike Scott	Hou vs SF, 2-0
1988	9/16	Tom Browning	Cin vs LA, 1-0 (perfect game)
1990	6/29	Fernando Valenzuela	LA vs St.L, 6-0
	8/15	Terry Mulholland	Phi vs SF, 6-0
1991	5/23	Tommy Greene	Phi at Mon, 2-0
	7/28	Dennis Martinez	Mon at LA, 2-0 (perfect game)
	9/11	Kent Mercker (6), Mark Wohlers (2) & Alejandro Peña (1)	Atl vs SD, 1-0 (combined no-hitter)
1992	8/17	Kevin Gross	LA vs SF, 2-0
1993	9/8	Darryl Kile	Hou vs NY, 7-1
1994	4/8	Kent Mercker	Atl at LA, 6-0
1995	7/14	Ramon Martinez	LA vs Fla, 7-0
1996	5/11	Al Leiter	Fla vs Col, 11-0
	9/17	Hideo Nomo	LA at Col, 9-0

No-Hit Games (Cont.)
American League

Year	Date	Pitcher	Result
1902	9/20	Jimmy Callahan	Chi vs Det, 3-0
1904	5/5	Cy Young	Bos vs Phi, 3-0 (perfect game)
	8/17	Jesse Tannehill	Bos vs Chi, 6-0
1905	7/22	Weldon Henley	Phi at St. L, 6-0
	9/6	Frank Smith	Chi at Det, 15-0
	9/27	Bill Dinneen	Bos vs Chi, 2-0
1908	6/30	Cy Young	Bos at NY, 8-0
	9/18	Dusty Rhoades	Cle vs Bos, 2-0
	9/20	Frank Smith	Chi vs Phi, 1-0
	10/2	Addie Joss	Cle vs Chi, 1-0 (perfect game)
1910	4/20	Addie Joss	Cle at Chi, 1-0
	5/12	Chief Bender	Phi vs Cle, 4-0
1911	7/19	Smokey Joe Wood	Bos vs St. L, 5-0
	8/27	Ed Walsh	Chi vs Bos, 5-0
1912	7/4	George Mullin	Det vs St. L, 7-0
	8/30	Earl Hamilton	St. L at Det, 5-1
1914	5/31	Joe Benz	Chi vs Cle, 6-1
1916	6/16	Rube Foster	Bos vs NY, 2-0
	8/26	Joe Bush	Phi vs Cle, 5-0
	8/30	Hub Leonard	Bos vs St. L, 4-0
1917	4/14	Ed Cicotte	Chi at St. L, 11-0
	4/24	George Mogridge	NY at Bos, 2-1
	5/5	Ernie Koob	St. L vs Chi, 1-0
	5/6	Bob Groom	St. L vs Chi, 3-0
	6/23	Babe Ruth (0) & Ernie Shore (9)	Bos vs Wash, 4-0 (combined no-hitter)
1918	6/3	Hub Leonard	Bos at Det, 5-0
1919	9/10	Ray Caldwell	Cle at NY, 3-0
1920	7/1	Walter Johnson	Wash at Bos, 1-0
1922	4/30	Charlie Robertson	Chi at Det, 2-0 (perfect game)
1923	9/4	Sam Jones	NY at Phi, 2-0
	9/7	Howard Ehmke	Bos at Phi, 4-0
1926	8/21	Ted Lyons	Chi at Bos, 6-0
1931	4/29	Wes Ferrell	Cle vs St. L, 9-0
	8/8	Bob Burke	Wash vs Bos, 5-0
1935	8/31	Vern Kennedy	Chi vs Cle, 5-0
1937	6/1	Bill Dietrich	Chi vs St. L, 8-0
1938	8/27	Monte Pearson	NY vs Cle, 13-0
1940	4/16	Bob Feller	Cle at Chi, 1-0 (Opening Day)
1945	9/9	Dick Fowler	Phi vs St. L, 1-0
1946	4/30	Bob Feller	Cle vs NY, 1-0
1947	7/10	Don Black	Cle vs Phi, 3-0
	9/3	Bill McCahan	Phi vs Wash, 3-0
1948	6/30	Bob Lemon	Cle at Det, 2-0
1951	7/1	Bob Feller	Cle vs Det, 2-1
	7/12	Allie Reynolds	NY vs Cle, 1-0
	9/28	Allie Reynolds	NY vs Bos, 8-0
1952	5/15	Virgil Trucks	Det vs Wash, 1-0
	8/25	Virgil Trucks	Det at NY, 1-0
1953	5/6	Bobo Holloman	St. L vs Phi, 6-0 (first major league start)
1956	7/14	Mel Parnell	Bos vs Chi, 4-0
	10/8	Don Larsen	NY vs Bklyn, 2-0 (perfect W. Series game)
1957	8/20	Bob Keegan	Chi vs Wash, 6-0
1958	7/20	Jim Bunning	Det at Bos, 3-0
	9/2	Hoyt Wilhelm	Bal vs NY, 1-0
1962	5/5	Bo Belinsky	LA vs Bal, 2-0
	6/26	Earl Wilson	Bos vs LA, 2-0
	8/1	Bill Monbouquette	Bos at Chi, 1-0
	8/26	Jack Kralick	Min vs KC, 1-0
1965	9/16	Dave Morehead	Bos vs Cle, 2-0
1966	6/10	Sonny Siebert	Cle vs Wash, 2-0
1967	4/30	**Steve Barber** & **Stu Miller**	Bal vs Det, 1-2
	8/25	Dean Chance	Min at Cle, 2-1
	9/10	Joel Horlen	Chi vs Det, 6-0
1968	4/27	Tom Phoebus	Bal vs Bos, 6-0
	5/8	Catfish Hunter	Oak vs Min, 4-0 (perfect game)
1969	8/13	Jim Palmer	Bal vs Oak, 8-0
1970	7/3	Clyde Wright	Cal vs Oak, 4-0
	9/21	Vida Blue	Oak vs Min, 6-0
1973	4/27	Steve Busby	KC at Det, 3-0
	5/15	Nolan Ryan	Cal at KC, 3-0
	7/15	Nolan Ryan	Cal at Det, 6-0
	7/30	Jim Bibby	Tex at Oak, 6-0
1974	6/19	Steve Busby	KC at Mil, 2-0
	7/19	Dick Bosman	Cle at Oak, 4-0
	9/28	Nolan Ryan	Cal at Min, 4-0
1975	6/1	Nolan Ryan	Cal vs Bal, 1-0
	9/28	Blue (5) Abbott & Lindblad (1), and Fingers (2)	Oak vs Cal, 5-0 (combined no-hitter)
1976	7/28	John Odom (5) & Francisco Barrios (4)	Chi at Oak, 2-1 (combined no-hitter)
1977	5/14	Jim Colborn	KC vs Tex, 6-0
	5/30	Dennis Eckersley	Cle vs Cal, 1-0
	9/22	Bert Blyleven	Tex at Cal, 6-0
1981	5/15	Len Barker	Cle vs Tor, 3-0 (perfect game)
1983	7/4	Dave Righetti	NY vs Bos, 4-0
	9/29	Mike Warren	Oak vs Chi, 3-0
1984	4/7	Jack Morris	Det at Chi, 4-0
	9/30	Mike Witt	Cal at Tex, 1-0 (perfect game)
1986	9/19	Joe Cowley	Chi at Cal, 7-1
1987	4/15	Juan Nieves	Mil at Bal, 7-0
1990	6/2	Mark Langston (7) & Mike Witt (2)	Cal vs Sea, 1-0 (combined no-hitter)
	6/2	Randy Johnson	Sea vs Det, 2-0
	6/11	Nolan Ryan	Tex at Oak, 5-0
	6/29	Dave Stewart	Oak at Tor, 5-0
	9/2	Dave Stieb	Tor at Cle, 3-0
1991	5/1	Nolan Ryan	Tex vs Tor, 3-0
	7/13	Bob Milacki (6), Mike Flanagan (1), Mark Williamson (1) & Gregg Olson (1)	Bal at Oak, 2-0 (combined no-hitter)
	8/11	Wilson Alvarez	Chi at Bal, 7-0
	8/26	Bret Saberhagen	KC vs Chi, 7-0
1993	4/22	Chris Bosio	Sea vs Bos, 7-0
	9/4	Jim Abbott	NY vs Cle, 4-0
1994	4/27	Scott Erickson	Min vs Mil, 6-0
	7/28	Kenny Rogers	Tex vs Cal, 4-0 (perfect game)
1996	5/14	Dwight Gooden	NY vs Sea, 2-0

All-Time Major League Leaders

Based on statistics compiled by *The Baseball Encyclopedia* (9th ed.); through 1996 regular season.

CAREER

Players active in 1996 in **bold** type.

Batting

Note that (*) indicates left-handed hitter and (†) indicates switch-hitter.

Batting Average

	Player	Yrs	AB	H	Avg
1	Ty Cobb*	24	11,429	4191	.367
2	Rogers Hornsby	23	8,137	2930	.358
3	Joe Jackson*	13	4,981	1774	.356
4	Ed Delahanty	16	7,509	2597	.346
5	Tris Speaker*	22	10,197	3514	.345
6	Ted Williams*	19	7,706	2654	.344
7	Billy Hamilton*	14	6,284	2163	.344
8	Willie Keeler*	19	8,585	2947	.343
9	Dan Brouthers*	19	6,711	2296	.342
10	Babe Ruth*	22	8,399	2873	.342
11	Harry Heilmann	17	7,787	2660	.342
12	Pete Browning	13	4,820	1646	.341
13	Bill Terry*	14	6,428	2193	.341
14	George Sisler*	15	8,267	2812	.340
15	Lou Gehrig*	17	8,001	2721	.340
16	Jesse Burkett*	16	8,413	2853	.339
17	Nap Lajoie	21	9,592	3244	.338
18	**Tony Gwynn***	15	7,595	2560	.337
19	Riggs Stephenson	14	4,508	1515	.336
20	Al Simmons	20	8,761	2927	.334
21	**Wade Boggs***	15	8,100	2697	.333
22	Paul Waner*	20	9,459	3152	.333
23	Eddie Collins*	25	9,951	3313	.333
24	Stan Musial*	22	10,972	3630	.331
25	Sam Thompson*	14	6,005	1986	.331

Players Active in 1996

	Player	Yrs	AB	H	Avg
1	Tony Gwynn*	15	7,595	2560	.337
2	Wade Boggs*	15	8,100	2697	.333
3	Frank Thomas	7	3,291	1077	.327
4	Edgar Martinez	10	3,276	1031	.315
5	Kenny Lofton*	6	2,821	883	.313
6	Mark Grace*	9	4,903	1514	.309
7	Hal Morris*	9	2,922	902	.309
8	Paul Molitor	19	9,795	3014	.308
9	Jeff Bagwell	6	3,091	950	.307
10	Mike Piazza	5	2,002	653	.307
11	Chuck Knoblauch	6	3,328	1019	.306
12	Mike Greenwell*	12	4,623	1400	.303
13	Julio Franco	14	6,813	2061	.303

Hits

	Player	Yrs	AB	H	Avg
1	Pete Rose†	24	14,053	**4256**	.303
2	Ty Cobb*	24	11,429	**4191**	.367
3	Hank Aaron	23	12,364	**3771**	.305
4	Stan Musial*	22	10,972	**3630**	.331
5	Tris Speaker*	22	10,197	**3514**	.345
6	Carl Yastrzemski*	23	11,988	**3419**	.285
7	Honus Wagner	21	10,443	**3418**	.327
8	Eddie Collins*	25	9,951	**3313**	.333
9	Willie Mays	22	10,881	**3283**	.302
10	Nap Lajoie	21	9,592	**3244**	.338
11	**Eddie Murray†**	20	11,169	**3218**	.288
12	George Brett*	21	10,349	**3154**	.305
13	Paul Waner*	20	9,459	**3152**	.333
14	Robin Yount	20	11,008	**3142**	.285
15	Dave Winfield	22	11,003	**3110**	.283
16	Rod Carew*	19	9,315	**3053**	.328
17	Lou Brock*	19	10,332	**3023**	.293
18	**Paul Molitor**	19	9,795	**3014**	.308
19	Al Kaline	22	10,116	**3007**	.297
20	Cap Anson	22	9,108	**3000**	.329
	Roberto Clemente	18	9,454	**3000**	.317
22	Sam Rice*	20	9,269	**2987**	.322
23	Sam Crawford*	19	9,580	**2964**	.309
24	Willie Keeler*	19	8,585	**2947**	.343
25	Frank Robinson	21	10,006	**2943**	.294

Players Active in 1996

	Player	Yrs	AB	H	Avg
1	Eddie Murray+	20	11,169	**3218**	.288
2	Paul Molitor	19	9,795	**3014**	.308
3	Andre Dawson	21	9,927	**2774**	.279
4	Wade Boggs*	15	8,100	**2697**	.333
5	Tony Gwynn*	15	7,595	**2560**	.337
6	Cal Ripken Jr.	16	9,217	**2549**	.277
7	Ozzie Smith+	19	9,396	**2460**	.262
8	Rickey Henderson	18	8,558	**2450**	.286
9	Harold Baines*	17	8,366	**2425**	.290
10	Alan Trammell	20	8,288	**2365**	.285
11	Tim Raines+	18	7,967	**2352**	.295
12	Brett Butler*	16	7,837	**2278**	.291
13	Chili Davis+	16	7,617	**2089**	.274

Games Played

	Player	G
1	Pete Rose	3562
2	Carl Yastrzemski	3308
3	Hank Aaron	3298
4	Ty Cobb	3034
5	Stan Musial	3026
6	Willie Mays	2992
7	Dave Winfield	2973
8	**Eddie Murray**	2971
9	Rusty Staub	2951
10	Brooks Robinson	2896
11	Robin Yount	2856
12	Al Kaline	2834
13	Eddie Collins	2826
14	Reggie Jackson	2820
15	Frank Robinson	2808
16	Tris Speaker	2789
	Honus Wagner	2789
18	Tony Perez	2777
19	Mel Ott	2734
20	George Brett	2707

At Bats

	Player	AB
1	Pete Rose	14,053
2	Hank Aaron	12,364
3	Carl Yastrzemski	11,988
4	Ty Cobb	11,429
5	**Eddie Murray**	11,169
6	Robin Yount	11,008
7	Dave Winfield	11,003
8	Stan Musial	10,972
9	Willie Mays	10,881
10	Brooks Robinson	10,654
11	Honus Wagner	10,441
12	George Brett	10,349
13	Lou Brock	10,332
14	Luis Aparicio	10,230
15	Tris Speaker	10,197
16	Al Kaline	10,116
17	Rabbit Maranville	10,078
18	Frank Robinson	10,006
19	Eddie Collins	9,951
20	Andre Dawson	9,927

Total Bases

	Player	TB
1	Hank Aaron	6856
2	Stan Musial	6134
3	Willie Mays	6066
4	Ty Cobb	5863
5	Babe Ruth	5793
6	Pete Rose	5752
7	Carl Yastrzemski	5539
8	Frank Robinson	5373
9	**Eddie Murray**	5344
10	Dave Winfield	5219
11	Tris Speaker	5103
12	Lou Gehrig	5059
13	George Brett	5044
14	Mel Ott	5041
15	Jimmie Foxx	4956
16	Ted Williams	4884
17	Honus Wagner	4868
18	Al Kaline	4852
19	Reggie Jackson	4834
20	**Andre Dawson**	4787

All-Time Major League Leaders (Cont.)

Batting

Home Runs

		Yrs	AB	HR	AB/HR
1	Hank Aaron	23	12,364	**755**	16.4
2	Babe Ruth*	22	8,399	**714**	11.8
3	Willie Mays	22	10,881	**660**	16.5
4	Frank Robinson	21	10,006	**586**	17.1
5	Harmon Killebrew	22	8,147	**573**	14.2
6	Reggie Jackson*	21	9,864	**563**	17.5
7	Mike Schmidt	18	8,352	**548**	15.2
8	Mickey Mantle†	18	8,102	**536**	15.1
9	Jimmie Foxx	20	8,134	**534**	15.2
10	Ted Williams*	19	7,706	**521**	14.8
	Willie McCovey*	22	8,197	**521**	15.7
12	Ed Mathews*	17	8,537	**512**	16.7
	Ernie Banks	19	9,421	**512**	18.4
14	Mel Ott*	22	9,456	**511**	18.5
15	**Eddie Murray**†	20	11,169	**501**	22.3
16	Lou Gehrig*	17	8,001	**493**	16.2
17	Willie Stargell*	21	7,927	**475**	16.7
	Stan Musial*	22	10,972	**475**	23.1
19	Dave Winfield	22	11,003	**465**	23.7
20	Carl Yastrzemski*	23	11,988	**452**	26.5
21	Dave Kingman	16	6,677	**442**	15.1
22	**Andre Dawson**	21	9,927	**438**	22.7
23	Billy Williams*	18	9,350	**426**	22.0
24	Darrell Evans	21	8,973	**414**	21.7
25	Duke Snider*	18	7,161	**407**	17.6

Players Active in 1996

		Yrs	AB	HR	AB/HR
1	Eddie Murray†	20	11,169	501	22.3
2	Andre Dawson	21	9,927	438	22.7
3	Joe Carter	14	7,422	357	20.8
4	Cal Ripken Jr.	16	9,217	353	26.1
5	Barry Bonds*	11	5,537	334	16.6
6	Mark McGwire	11	4,082	329	12.4
7	Jose Canseco	12	5,071	328	15.5
8	Harold Baines*	17	8,366	323	25.9
9	Fred McGriff*	11	5,129	317	16.2
10	Gary Gaetti	16	7,725	315	24.5
11	Darryl Strawberry*	14	5,045	308	16.4
12	Chili Davis†	16	7,617	298	25.6
13	Cecil Fielder	11	4,380	289	15.2
14	Danny Tartabull	13	5,004	262	19.1
15	Tim Wallach	17	8,099	260	31.2

Runs Batted In

		Yrs	Gm	RBI	P/G
1	Hank Aaron	23	3298	**2297**	.70
2	Babe Ruth*	22	2503	**2211**	.88
3	Lou Gehrig*	17	2164	**1990**	.92
4	Ty Cobb*	24	3034	**1961**	.65
5	Stan Musial*	22	3026	**1951**	.64
6	Jimmie Foxx	20	2317	**1921**	.83
7	Willie Mays	22	2992	**1903**	.64
8	**Eddie Murray**†	20	2971	**1899**	.64
9	Mel Ott*	22	2732	**1861**	.68
10	Carl Yastrzemski*	23	3308	**1844**	.56
11	Ted Williams*	19	2292	**1839**	.80
12	Dave Winfield	22	2973	**1833**	.62
13	Al Simmons	20	2215	**1827**	.82
14	Frank Robinson	21	2808	**1812**	.65
15	Honus Wagner	21	2786	**1732**	.62
16	Cap Anson	22	2276	**1715**	.75
17	Reggie Jackson*	21	2820	**1702**	.60
18	Tony Perez	23	2777	**1652**	.59
19	Ernie Banks	19	2528	**1636**	.65
20	Goose Goslin*	18	2287	**1609**	.70
21	Nap Lajoie	21	2475	**1599**	.65
22	Mike Schmidt	18	2404	**1595**	.66
	George Brett*	21	2707	**1595**	.59
24	Andre Dawson	21	2627	**1591**	.61
25	Rogers Hornsby	23	2259	**1584**	.70
	Harmon Killebrew	22	2435	**1584**	.65

Players Active in 1996

		Yrs	Gm	RBI	P/G
1	Eddie Murray†	20	2971	**1899**	.64
2	Andre Dawson	21	2627	**1591**	.61
3	Cal Ripken Jr.	16	2381	**1369**	.57
4	Harold Baines*	17	2321	**1356**	.58
5	Joe Carter	14	1880	**1280**	.68
6	Chili Davis†	16	2113	**1195**	.57
7	Gary Gaetti	16	2105	**1155**	.55
8	Paul Molitor	19	2421	**1149**	.47
9	Tim Wallach	17	2211	**1125**	.51
10	Jose Canseco	12	1341	**1033**	.77
11	Ruben Sierra†	11	1596	**1024**	.69
12	Alan Trammell	20	2285	**1003**	.44
13	Barry Bonds*	11	1583	**993**	.63
14	Will Clark*	11	1510	**953**	.63
15	Darryl Strawberry*	14	1447	**935**	.65

Runs

1	Ty Cobb	2245
2	Babe Ruth	2174
	Hank Aaron	2174
4	Pete Rose	2165
5	Willie Mays	2062
6	Stan Musial	1949
7	Lou Gehrig	1888
8	Tris Speaker	1882
9	Mel Ott	1859
10	Frank Robinson	1829
	Rickey Henderson	1829
12	Eddie Collins	1820
13	Carl Yastrzemski	1816
14	Ted Williams	1798
15	Charlie Gehringer	1774
16	Jimmie Foxx	1751
17	**Paul Molitor**	1744
18	Honus Wagner	1735
19	Willie Keeler	1727
20	Cap Anson	1719

Extra Base Hits

1	Hank Aaron	1477
2	Stan Musial	1377
3	Babe Ruth	1356
4	Willie Mays	1323
5	Lou Gehrig	1190
6	Frank Robinson	1186
7	Carl Yastrzemski	1157
8	Ty Cobb	1139
9	Tris Speaker	1132
10	George Brett	1119
11	Ted Williams	1117
	Jimmie Foxx	1117
13	Dave Winfield	1093
14	**Eddie Murray**	1089
15	Reggie Jackson	1075
16	Mel Ott	1071
17	Pete Rose	1041
18	**Andre Dawson**	1039
19	Mike Schmidt	1015
20	Rogers Hornsby	1011

Slugging Average

1	Babe Ruth	.690
2	Ted Williams	.634
3	Lou Gehrig	.632
4	Jimmie Foxx	.609
5	Hank Greenberg	.605
6	Joe DiMaggio	.579
7	Rogers Hornsby	.577
8	Johnny Mize	.562
9	Stan Musial	.559
10	Willie Mays	.557
11	Mickey Mantle	.557
12	Hank Aaron	.555
13	Ralph Kiner	.548
14	Barry Bonds	.548
15	Hack Wilson	.545
16	Mark McGwire	.544
17	Chuck Klein	.543
18	Duke Snider	.540
19	Frank Robinson	.537
20	Al Simmons	.535

Stolen Bases

1	**Rickey Henderson**	1186
2	Lou Brock	938
3	Billy Hamilton	915
4	Ty Cobb	892
5	**Tim Raines**	787
6	**Vince Coleman**	740
7	Eddie Collins	743
7	Max Carey	738
8	Honus Wagner	720
10	Joe Morgan	689
11	Arlie Latham	679
12	Willie Wilson	668
13	Bert Campaneris	649
14	Tom Brown	627
15	George Davis	615
16	Dummy Hoy	597
17	Maury Wills	586
18	Hugh Duffy	583
	George Van Haltren	583
20	**Ozzie Smith**	580

Walks

1	Babe Ruth	2056
2	Ted Williams	2019
3	Joe Morgan	1865
4	Carl Yastrzemski	1845
5	Mickey Mantle	1734
6	Mel Ott	1708
7	**Rickey Henderson**	1675
8	Eddie Yost	1614
9	Darrell Evans	1605
10	Stan Musial	1599
11	Pete Rose	1566
12	Harmon Killebrew	1559
13	Lou Gehrig	1508
14	Mike Schmidt	1507
15	Eddie Collins	1503
16	Willie Mays	1463
17	Jimmie Foxx	1452
18	Eddie Mathews	1444
19	Frank Robinson	1420
20	Hank Aaron	1402

Strikeouts

1	Reggie Jackson	2597
2	Willie Stargell	1936
3	Mike Schmidt	1883
4	Tony Perez	1867
5	Dave Kingman	1816
6	Bobby Bonds	1757
7	Dale Murphy	1748
8	Lou Brock	1730
9	Mickey Mantle	1710
10	Harmon Killebrew	1699
11	Dwight Evans	1697
12	Dave Winfield	1686
13	Lee May	1570
14	Dick Allen	1556
15	Willie McCovey	1550
16	Dave Parker	1537
17	Frank Robinson	1532
18	Lance Parrish	1527
19	Willie Mays	1526
20	Rick Monday	1513

Pitching

Note that (*) indicates left-handed pitcher. Active pitcher leaders are listed for wins, strikeouts and saves.

Wins

		Yrs	GS	W	L	Pct
1	Cy Young	22	815	**511**	316	.618
2	Walter Johnson	21	666	**416**	279	.599
3	Christy Mathewson	17	551	**373**	188	.665
	Grover Alexander	20	598	**373**	208	.642
5	Warren Spahn*	21	665	**363**	245	.597
6	Kid Nichols	15	561	**361**	208	.634
	Pud Galvin	14	682	**361**	308	.540
8	Tim Keefe	14	594	**342**	225	.603
9	Steve Carlton*	24	709	**329**	244	.574
10	Eddie Plank*	17	527	**327**	193	.629
11	John Clarkson	12	518	**326**	177	.648
12	Don Sutton	23	756	**324**	256	.559
13	Nolan Ryan	27	773	**324**	292	.526
14	Phil Niekro	24	716	**318**	274	.537
15	Gaylord Perry	22	690	**314**	265	.542
16	Old Hoss Radbourn	12	503	**311**	194	.616
	Tom Seaver	20	647	**311**	205	.603
18	Mickey Welch	13	549	**308**	209	.596
19	Lefty Grove*	17	456	**300**	141	.680
	Early Wynn	23	612	**300**	244	.551
21	Tommy John*	26	700	**288**	231	.555
22	Bert Blyleven	22	685	**287**	250	.534
23	Robin Roberts	19	609	**286**	245	.539
24	Tony Mullane	13	505	**285**	220	.564
25	Ferguson Jenkins	19	594	**284**	226	.557
26	Jim Kaat*	25	625	**283**	237	.544
27	Red Ruffing	22	536	**273**	225	.548
28	Burleigh Grimes	19	495	**270**	212	.560
29	Jim Palmer	19	521	**268**	152	.638
30	Bob Feller	18	484	**266**	162	.621

Pitchers Active in 1996

		Yrs	GS	W	L	Pct
1	Dennis Martinez	21	547	**240**	182	.569
2	Dennis Eckersley	22	361	**192**	165	.538
3	Roger Clemens	13	382	**192**	111	.634
4	Frank Viola*	15	420	**176**	150	.540
5	Mark Langston*	13	397	**172**	145	.543
6	Fernando Valenzuela*	16	406	**171**	141	.548
7	Dwight Gooden	12	334	**168**	92	.646
8	Greg Maddux	11	332	**165**	104	.613
9	Orel Hershiser	14	362	**165**	117	.585
10	Jimmy Key*	13	344	**164**	104	.612

Strikeouts

		Yrs	IP	SO	P/9
1	Nolan Ryan	27	5387.0	**5714**	9.54
2	Steve Carlton*	24	5217.1	**4136**	7.13
3	Bert Blyleven	22	4970.1	**3701**	6.70
4	Tom Seaver	20	4782.2	**3640**	6.85
5	Don Sutton	23	5282.1	**3574**	6.09
6	Gaylord Perry	22	5350.1	**3534**	5.94
7	Walter Johnson	21	5923.2	**3508**	5.33
8	Phil Niekro	24	5404.1	**3342**	5.57
9	Ferguson Jenkins	19	4500.2	**3192**	6.38
10	Bob Gibson	17	3884.1	**3117**	7.22
11	Jim Bunning	17	3760.1	**2855**	6.83
12	Mickey Lolich*	16	3638.1	**2832**	7.01
13	Cy Young	22	7354.2	**2796**	3.42
14	Frank Tanana*	21	4186.2	**2773**	5.96
15	Roger Clemens	13	2776.0	**2590**	8.40
16	Warren Spahn*	21	5243.2	**2583**	4.43
17	Bob Feller	18	3827.0	**2581**	6.07
18	Jerry Koosman*	19	3839.1	**2556**	5.99
19	Tim Keefe	14	5061.1	**2527**	4.50
20	Christy Mathewson	17	4781.0	**2502**	4.71
21	Don Drysdale	14	3432.0	**2486**	6.52
22	Jack Morris	18	3824.2	**2478**	5.83
23	Jim Kaat*	25	4530.1	**2461**	4.89
24	Sam McDowell*	15	2492.1	**2453**	8.86
25	Luis Tiant	19	3486.1	**2416**	6.24
26	Sandy Koufax*	12	2324.1	**2396**	9.28
27	Charlie Hough	25	3799.1	**2363**	5.60
28	Robin Roberts	19	4688.2	**2357**	4.52
29	Mark Langston	13	2772.0	**2335**	7.58
	Early Wynn	23	4564.0	**2334**	4.60
30	Dennis Eckersley	22	3193.0	**2334**	6.58

Pitchers Active in 1996

		Yrs	IP	SO	P/9
1	Roger Clemens	13	2776.0	**2590**	8.40
2	Mark Langston*	13	2772.0	**2335**	7.58
3	Dennis Eckersley	22	3193.0	**2334**	6.58
4	Dennis Martinez	21	3860.1	**2070**	4.83
5	Fernando Valenzuela*	16	2841.0	**2013**	6.38
6	Dwight Gooden	12	2340.1	**2001**	7.69
7	Frank Viola*	15	2836.1	**1844**	5.85
8	David Cone	11	1944.0	**1812**	8.18
9	Danny Darwin	19	2711.1	**1769**	5.87
10	Randy Johnson*	9	1520.2	**1709**	10.11

All-Time Major League Leaders (Cont.)

Pitching

Winning Pct.

		Yrs	W-L	Pct
1	Bob Caruthers	9	218-97	.692
2	Dave Foutz	11	147-66	.690
3	Whitey Ford*	16	236-106	.690
4	Lefty Grove*	17	300-141	.680
5	Vic Raschi	10	132-66	.667
6	Christy Mathewson	17	373-188	.665
7	Larry Corcoran	8	177-90	.663
8	Sam Leever	13	194-101	.658
9	Sal Maglie	10	119-62	.657
10	Sandy Koufax*	12	165-87	.655
11	Johnny Allen	13	142-75	.654
12	Ron Guidry*	14	170-91	.651
13	**Dwight Gooden**	12	168-92	.646
14	Lefty Gomez*	14	189-102	.649
15	**Roger Clemens**	13	192-111	.634

Losses

		Yrs	GS	W	L	Pct
1	Cy Young	22	815	511	**316**	.618
2	Pud Galvin	14	682	361	**308**	.540
3	Nolan Ryan	27	773	324	**292**	.526
4	Walter Johnson	21	666	416	**279**	.599
5	Phil Niekro	24	716	318	**274**	.537
6	Gaylord Perry	22	690	314	**265**	.542
7	Jack Powell	16	517	245	**256**	.489
	Don Sutton	23	756	324	**256**	.559
9	Eppa Rixey*	21	552	266	**251**	.515
10	Bert Blyleven	22	685	287	**250**	.534
11	Robin Roberts	19	609	286	**245**	.539
	Warren Spahn*	21	665	363	**245**	.597
13	Early Wynn	23	612	300	**244**	.551
	Steve Carlton*	24	709	329	**244**	.574
15	Jim Kaat*	25	625	283	**237**	.544

Appearances

1	Hoyt Wilhelm	1070
2	Kent Tekulve	1050
3	Rich Gossage	1002
4	**Lee Smith**	997
5	Lindy McDaniel	987
6	Rollie Fingers	944
7	**Dennis Eckersley**	964
8	Gene Garber	931
9	Cy Young	906
10	Sparky Lyle	899
11	Jim Kaat	898
12	**Jesse Orosco**	885
13	Jeff Reardon	880
14	Don McMahon	874
15	Phil Niekro	864

Innings Pitched

1	Cy Young	7356.0
2	Pud Galvin	5941.1
3	Walter Johnson	5923.2
4	Phil Niekro	5403.1
5	Nolan Ryan	5387.0
6	Gaylord Perry	5350.1
7	Don Sutton	5280.1
8	Warren Spahn	5243.2
9	Steve Carlton	5217.1
10	Grover Alexander	5189.2
11	Kid Nichols	5084.0
12	Tim Keefe	5061.1
13	Bert Blyleven	4970.1
14	Mickey Welch	4802.0
15	Tom Seaver	4782.2

Earned Run Avg.

1	Ed Walsh	1.82
2	Addie Joss	1.88
3	Three Finger Brown	2.06
4	Monte Ward	2.10
5	Christy Mathewson	2.13
6	Rube Waddell	2.16
7	Walter Johnson	2.17
8	Orval Overall	2.24
9	Tommy Bond	2.25
10	Will White	2.28
11	Ed Reulbach	2.28
12	Jim Scott	2.32
13	Eddie Plank	2.34
14	Larry Corcoran	2.36
15	Eddie Cicotte	2.37

Shutouts

1	Walter Johnson	110
2	Grover Alexander	90
3	Christy Mathewson	80
4	Cy Young	76
5	Eddie Plank	69
6	Warren Spahn	63
7	Nolan Ryan	61
	Tom Seaver	61
9	Bert Blyleven	60
10	Don Sutton	58
11	Three Finger Brown	57
	Pud Galvin	57
	Ed Walsh	57
14	Bob Gibson	56
15	Steve Carlton	55

Walks Allowed

1	Nolan Ryan	2795
2	Steve Carlton	1833
3	Phil Niekro	1809
4	Early Wynn	1775
5	Bob Feller	1764
6	Bobo Newsom	1732
7	Amos Rusie	1704
8	Charlie Hough	1665
9	Gus Weyhing	1566
10	Red Ruffing	1541
11	Bump Hadley	1442
12	Warren Spahn	1434
13	Earl Whitehill	1431
14	Tony Mullane	1409
15	Sad Sam Jones	1396

HRs Allowed

1	Robin Roberts	505
2	Ferguson Jenkins	484
3	Phil Niekro	482
4	Don Sutton	472
5	Frank Tanana	448
6	Warren Spahn	434
7	Bert Blyleven	430
8	Steve Carlton	414
9	Gaylord Perry	399
10	Jim Kaat	395
11	Jack Morris	389
12	Charlie Hough	383
13	Tom Seaver	380
14	Jim Hunter	374
15	Jim Bunning	372

Saves

1	**Lee Smith**	473
2	Jeff Reardon	367
3	**Dennis Eckersley**	353
4	Rollie Fingers	341
5	**John Franco**	323
6	Tom Henke	311
7	Rich Gossage	310
8	Bruce Sutter	300
9	**Randy Myers**	274
10	Dave Righetti	252
11	Dan Quisenberry	244
12	**Jeff Montgomery**	242
	Doug Jones	242
14	Sparky Lyle	238
15	Hoyt Wilhelm	227
16	**Todd Worrell**	221
17	Gene Garber	218
18	Dave Smith	216
19	**Rick Aguilera**	211
20	Bobby Thigpen	201
21	Roy Face	193
	Mike Henneman	193
23	Mitch Williams	192
24	**Jeff Russell**	186
25	Steve Bedrosian	184
	Kent Tekulve	184
27	Tug McGraw	180
	John Wetland	180
29	Ron Perranoski	179
30	**Bryan Harvey**	177
31	Lindy McDaniel	172

SINGLE SEASON

Through 1996 regular season.

Batting

Home Runs

		Year	Gm	AB	HR
1	Roger Maris, NY-AL	1961	162	590	61
2	Babe Ruth, NY-AL	1927	151	540	60
3	Babe Ruth, NY-AL	1921	152	540	59
4	Hank Greenberg, Det	1938	155	556	58
	Jimmie Foxx, Phi-AL	1932	154	585	58
6	Hack Wilson, Chi-NL	1930	155	585	56
7	Babe Ruth, NY-AL	1920	142	458	54
	Mickey Mantle, NY-AL	1961	153	514	54
	Babe Ruth, NY-AL	1928	154	536	54
	Ralph Kiner, Pit	1949	152	549	54
11	Mickey Mantle, NY-AL	1956	150	533	52
	Willie Mays, SF	1965	157	558	52
	George Foster, Cin	1977	158	615	52
	Mark McGwire, Oak	1996	130	423	52
15	Ralph Kiner, Pit	1947	152	565	51
	Cecil Fielder, Det	1990	159	573	51
	Willie Mays, NY-NL	1955	152	580	51
	Johnny Mize, NY-NL	1947	154	586	51
19	Jimmie Foxx, Bos-AL	1938	149	565	50
	Albert Belle, Cle	1995	143	546	50
	Brady Anderson, Bal	1996	149	579	50

Hits

		Year	AB	H	Avg
1	George Sisler, StL-AL	1920	631	**257**	.407
2	Bill Terry, NY-NL	1930	633	**254**	.401
	Lefty O'Doul, Phi-NL	1929	638	**254**	.398
4	Al Simmons, Phi-AL	1925	658	**253**	.384
5	Rogers Hornsby, StL-NL	1922	623	**250**	.401
6	Chuck Klein, Phi-NL	1930	648	**250**	.386
7	Ty Cobb, Det	1911	591	**248**	.420
8	George Sisler, StL-AL	1922	586	**246**	.420
9	Babe Herman, Bklyn	1930	614	**241**	.393
	Heinie Manush, StL-AL	1928	638	**241**	.378
11	Wade Boggs, Bos	1985	653	**240**	.368
12	Rod Carew, Min	1977	616	**239**	.388
13	Don Mattingly, NY-AL	1986	677	**238**	.352
14	Harry Heilmann, Det	1921	602	**237**	.394
	Paul Waner, Pit	1927	623	**237**	.380
	Joe Medwick, StL-NL	1937	633	**237**	.374
17	Jack Tobin, StL-AL	1921	671	**236**	.352
18	Rogers Hornsby, StL-NL	1921	592	**235**	.397

Batting Average

From 1900-49

		Year	AB	H	Avg
1	Rogers Hornsby, StL-NL	1924	536	227	.424
2	Nap Lajoie, Phi-AL	1901	543	229	.422
3	George Sisler, StL-AL	1922	586	246	.420
4	Ty Cobb, Det	1911	591	248	.420
5	Ty Cobb, Det	1912	533	227	.410
6	Joe Jackson, Cle	1911	571	233	.408
7	George Sisler, StL-AL	1920	631	257	.407
8	Ted Williams, Bos-AL	1941	456	185	.406
9	Rogers Hornsby, StL-NL	1925	504	203	.403
10	Harry Heilmann, Det	1923	524	211	.403

Since 1950

		Year	AB	H	Avg
1	Tony Gwynn, SD	1994	419	175	.394
2	George Brett, KC	1980	449	175	.390
3	Ted Williams, Bos	1957	420	163	.388
4	Rod Carew, Min	1977	616	239	.388
5	Andres Galarraga, Col	1993	470	174	.370
6	Tony Gwynn, SD	1987	589	218	.370
7	Tony Gwynn, SD	1995	535	197	.368
8	Wade Boggs, Bos	1985	653	240	.368
9	Wade Boggs, Bos	1988	584	214	.366
10	Rico Carty, Atl	1970	478	175	.366

Total Bases

From 1900-49

		Year	TB
1	Babe Ruth, New York-AL	1921	457
2	Rogers Hornsby, St. Louis-NL	1922	450
3	Lou Gehrig, New York-AL	1927	447
4	Chuck Klein, Philadelphia-NL	1930	445
5	Jimmie Foxx, Philadelphia-AL	1932	438
6	Stan Musial, St. Louis-NL	1948	429
7	Hack Wilson, Chicago-NL	1930	423
8	Chuck Klein, Philadelphia-NL	1932	420
9	Lou Gehrig, New York-AL	1930	419
10	Joe DiMaggio, New York-AL	1937	418

Since 1950

		Year	TB
1	Jim Rice, Boston	1978	406
2	Hank Aaron, Milwaukee	1959	400
3	**Ellis Burks**, Colorado	1996	392
4	George Foster, Cincinnati	1977	388
	Don Mattingly, New York-AL	1986	388
6	Willie Mays, New York-NL	1955	382
	Willie Mays, San Francisco	1962	382
	Jim Rice, Boston	1977	382
9	Frank Robinson, Cincinnati	1962	380
10	Duke Snider, Brooklyn	1954	378
	Alex Rodriguez, Sea	1996	379

Runs Batted In

From 1900-49

		Year	Avg	HR	RBI
1	Hack Wilson, Chi-NL	1930	.356	56	190
2	Lou Gehrig, NY-AL	1931	.341	46	184
3	Hank Greenberg, Det	1937	.337	40	183
4	Lou Gehrig, NY-AL	1927	.373	47	175
	Jimmie Foxx, Bos-AL	1938	.349	50	175
6	Lou Gehrig, NY-AL	1930	.379	41	174
7	Babe Ruth, NY-AL	1921	.378	59	171
8	Chuck Klein, Phi-NL	1930	.386	40	170
	Hank Greenberg, Det	1935	.328	36	170
10	Jimmie Foxx, Phi-AL	1932	.364	58	169

Since 1950

		Year	Avg	HR	RBI
1	Tommy Davis, LA-NL	1962	.346	27	153
2	Andres Galarraga, Col	1996	.304	47	150
3	George Foster, Cin	1977	.320	52	149
4	Johnny Bench, Cin	1970	.293	45	148
5	**Albert Belle**, Cle	1996	.311	48	148
6	Al Rosen, Cle	1953	.336	43	145
	Don Mattingly, NY-AL	1985	.324	35	145
8	Walt Dropo, Bos-AL	1950	.322	34	144
	Juan Gonzales, Tex	1996	.314	47	144
	Vern Stephens, Bos-AL	1950	.295	30	144

All-Time Major League Leaders (Cont.)

Batting

Runs

		Year	Runs
1	Babe Ruth, New York-AL	1921	177
2	Lou Gehrig, New York-AL	1936	167
3	Babe Ruth, New York-AL	1928	163
	Lou Gehrig, New York-AL	1931	163
5	Babe Ruth, New York-AL	1920	158
	Babe Ruth, New York-AL	1927	158
	Chuck Klein, Philadelphia-NL	1930	158
8	Rogers Hornsby, Chicago-NL	1929	156
9	Kiki Cuyler, Chicago-NL	1930	155
10	Lefty O'Doul, Philadelphia-NL	1929	152
	Woody English, Chicago-NL	1930	152
	Al Simmons, Philadelphia-AL	1930	152
	Chuck Klein, Philadelphia-NL	1932	152
14	Babe Ruth, New York-AL	1923	151
	Jimmie Foxx, Philadelphia-AL	1932	151
	Joe DiMaggio, New York-AL	1937	151
17	Babe Ruth, New York-AL	1930	150
	Ted Williams, Boston-AL	1940	150
19	Lou Gehrig, New York-AL	1927	149
	Babe Ruth, New York-AL	1931	149

Walks

		Year	BB
1	Babe Ruth, New York-AL	1923	170
2	Ted Williams, Boston-AL	1947	162
	Ted Williams, Boston-AL	1949	162
4	Ted Williams, Boston-AL	1946	156
5	Barry Bonds, San Francisco	1996	151
	Eddie Yost, Washington	1956	151
7	Eddie Joost, Philadelphia-AL	1949	149
8	Babe Ruth, New York-AL	1920	148
	Eddie Stanky, Brooklyn	1945	148
	Jimmy Wynn, Houston	1969	148

Extra Base Hits

		Year	EBH
1	Babe Ruth, New York-AL	1921	119
2	Lou Gehrig, New York-AL	1927	117
3	Chuck Klein, Philadelphia-NL	1930	107
4	Chuck Klein, Philadelphia-NL	1932	103
	Hank Greenberg, Detroit	1937	103
	Stan Musial, St. Louis-NL	1948	103
	Albert Belle, Cleveland	1995	103
8	Rogers Hornsby, St. Louis-NL	1922	102
9	Lou Gehrig, New York-AL	1930	100
	Jimmie Foxx, Philadelphia-AL	1933	100

Slugging Percentage

From 1900-49

		Year	Pct
1	Babe Ruth, New York-AL	1920	.847
2	Babe Ruth, New York-AL	1921	.846
3	Babe Ruth, New York-AL	1927	.772
4	Lou Gehrig, New York-AL	1927	.765
5	Babe Ruth, New York-AL	1923	.764
6	Rogers Hornsby, St. Louis-NL	1925	.756
7	Jimmie Foxx, Philadelphia-AL	1932	.749
8	Babe Ruth, New York-AL	1924	.739
9	Babe Ruth, New York-AL	1926	.737
10	Ted Williams, Boston-AL	1941	.735

Since 1950

		Year	Pct
1	Jeff Bagwell, Houston	1994	.750
2	Ted Williams, Boston	1957	.731
3	Mark McGwire, Oakland	1996	.730
4	Frank Thomas, Chicago-AL	1994	.729
5	Albert Belle, Cleveland	1994	.714

Stolen Bases

		Year	SB
1	Rickey Henderson, Oakland	1982	130
2	Lou Brock, St. Louis	1974	118
3	Vince Coleman, St. Louis	1985	110
4	Vince Coleman, St. Louis	1987	109
5	Rickey Henderson, Oakland	1983	108
6	Vince Coleman, St. Louis	1986	107
7	Maury Wills, Los Angeles-NL	1962	104
8	Rickey Henderson, Oakland	1980	100
9	Ron LeFlore, Montreal	1980	97
10	Ty Cobb, Detroit	1915	96
11	Omar Moreno, Pittsburgh	1980	96
12	Maury Wills, Los Angeles	1965	94
13	Rickey Henderson, New York-AL	1988	93
14	Tim Raines, Montreal	1983	90
15	Clyde Milan, Washington	1912	88
16	Rickey Henderson, New York-AL	1986	87
17	Ty Cobb, Detroit	1911	83
	Willie Wilson, Kansas City	1979	83
19	Bob Bescher, Cincinnati	1911	81
	Eddie Collins, Philadelphia-AL	1910	81
	Vince Coleman, St. Louis	1988	81

Strikeouts

		Year	SO
1	Bobby Bonds, San Francisco	1970	189
2	Bobby Bonds, San Francisco	1969	187
3	Rob Deer, Milwaukee	1987	186
4	Pete Incaviglia, Texas	1986	185
5	Cecil Fielder, Detroit	1990	182
6	Mike Schmidt, Philadelphia	1975	180
7	Rob Deer, Milwaukee	1986	179
8	Dave Nicholson, Chicago-AL	1963	175
	Gorman Thomas, Milwaukee	1979	175
	Jose Canseco, Oakland	1986	175
	Rob Deer, Detroit	1991	175

Pinch Hits

Career pinch hits in parentheses.

		Year	PH	
1	John Vander Wal, Colorado	1995	28	(72)
2	Jose Morales, Montreal	1976	25	(123)
3	Dave Philley, Baltimore	1961	24	(93)
	Vic Davalillo, St. Louis	1970	24	(95)
	Rusty Staub, New York-NL	1983	24	(100)
6	Four tied with 22 each.			

Note: The all-time career pinch hit leader is Manny Mota (150).

Four Home Runs in One Game

National League

	Date	H/A	Inn
Bobby Lowe, Boston	5/30/1894	H	9
Ed Delahanty, Philadelphia	7/13/1896	A	9
Chuck Klein, Philadelphia	7/10/1936	A	10
Gil Hodges, Brooklyn	8/31/1950	H	9
Joe Adcock, Milwaukee	7/31/1954	A	9
Willie Mays, San Francisco	4/30/1961	A	9
Mike Schmidt, Philadelphia	4/17/1976	A	10
Bob Horner, Atlanta	7/6/1986	H	9
Mark Whiten, St. Louis	9/7/1993	A	9

American League

	Date	H/A	Inn
Lou Gehrig, New York	6/3/1932	A	9
Pat Seerey, Chicago	7/18/1948	A	11
Rocky Colavito, Cleveland	6/10/1959	A	9

Pitching

Wins

From 1900-49

		Year	W	L	Pct
1	Jack Chesbro, NY-AL	1904	**41**	12	.774
2	Ed Walsh, Chi-AL	1908	**40**	15	.727
3	Christy Mathewson, NY-NL	1908	**37**	11	.771
4	Walter Johnson, Wash	1913	**36**	7	.837
5	Joe McGinnity, NY-NL	1904	**35**	8	.814
6	Smokey Joe Wood, Bos-AL	1912	**34**	5	.872
7	Cy Young, Bos-AL	1901	**33**	10	.767
	Grover Alexander, Phi-NL	1916	**33**	12	.733
	Christy Mathewson, NY-NL	1904	**33**	12	.733
10	Cy Young, Bos-AL	1902	**32**	11	.744

Since 1950

		Year	W	L	Pct
1	Denny McLain, Det	1968	**31**	6	.838
2	Robin Roberts, Phi-NL	1952	**28**	7	.800
3	Bob Welch, Oak	1990	**27**	6	.818
	Don Newcombe, Bklyn	1956	**27**	7	.794
	Sandy Koufax, LA	1966	**27**	9	.750
	Steve Carlton, Phi	1972	**27**	10	.730
7	Sandy Koufax, LA	1965	**26**	8	.765
	Juan Marichal, SF	1968	**26**	9	.743

Note: 11 pitchers tied with 25 wins, including Marichal twice.

Earned Run Average

From 1900-49

		Year	ShO	ERA
1	Dutch Leonard, Bos-AL	1914	7	1.01
2	Three Finger Brown, Chi-NL	1906	10	1.04
3	Walter Johnson, Wash	1913	11	1.09
4	Christy Mathewson, NY-NL	1909	8	1.14
5	Jack Pfiester, Chi-NL	1907	3	1.15
6	Addie Joss, Cle	1908	9	1.16
7	Carl Lundgren, Chi-NL	1907	7	1.17
8	Grover Alexander, Phi-NL	1915	12	1.22
9	Cy Young, Bos-AL	1908	3	1.26
10	Three pitchers tied at 1.27			

Since 1950

		Year	ShO	ERA
1	Bob Gibson, St.L	1968	13	1.12
2	Dwight Gooden, NY-NL	1985	8	1.53
3	Greg Maddux, Atl	1994	3	1.56
4	Luis Tiant, Cle	1968	9	1.60
5	Greg Maddux, Atl	1995	3	1.63
5	Dean Chance, LA-AL	1964	11	1.65
6	Nolan Ryan, Cal	1981	3	1.69
7	Sandy Koufax, LA	1966	5	1.73
8	Sandy Koufax, LA	1964	7	1.74
9	Ron Guidry, NY-AL	1978	9	1.74
10	Tom Seaver, NY-NL	1971	4	1.76

Winning Pct.

		Year	W-L	Pct
1	Roy Face, Pit	1959	18-1	.947
2	Rick Sutcliffe, Chi-NL*	1984	16-1	.941
3	Johnny Allen, Cle	1937	15-1	.938
4	Greg Maddux, Atl	1995	19-2	.904
5	Randy Johnson, Sea	1995	18-2	.900
6	Ron Guidry, NY-AL	1978	25-3	.893
7	Freddie Fitzsimmons, Bklyn	1940	16-2	.889
8	Lefty Grove, Phi-AL	1931	31-4	.886
9	Bob Stanley, Bos	1978	15-2	.882
10	Preacher Roe, Bklyn	1951	22-3	.880
11	Tom Seaver, Cin	1981	14-2	.875
12	Smokey Joe Wood, Bos-AL	1912	34-5	.872

*Sutcliffe began 1984 with Cleveland and was 4-5 before being traded to the Cubs; his overall winning pct. was .769 (20-6).

Strikeouts

		Year	SO	P/G
1	Nolan Ryan, Cal	1973	**383**	10.57
2	Sandy Koufax, LA	1965	**382**	10.24
3	Nolan Ryan, Cal	1974	**367**	9.92
4	Rube Waddell, Phi-AL	1904	**349**	8.12
5	Bob Feller, Cle	1946	**348**	8.45
6	Nolan Ryan, Cal	1977	**341**	10.26
7	Nolan Ryan, Cal	1972	**329**	10.43
8	Nolan Ryan, Cal	1976	**327**	10.36
9	Sam McDowell, Cle	1965	**325**	10.71
10	Sandy Koufax, LA	1966	**317**	8.83

Appearances

		Year	App	Sv
1	Mike Marshall, LA	1974	**106**	21
2	Kent Tekulve, Pit	1979	**94**	31
3	Mike Marshall, LA	1973	**92**	31
4	Kent Tekulve, Pit	1978	**91**	31
5	Wayne Granger, Cin	1969	**90**	27
	Mike Marshall, Min	1979	**90**	32
	Kent Tekulve, Phi	1987	**90**	3

Saves

		Year	App	Sv
1	Bobby Thigpen, Chi-AL	1990	77	57
2	Randy Myers, Chi-NL	1993	73	53
3	Dennis Eckersley, Oak	1992	69	51
4	Dennis Eckersley, Oak	1990	63	48
	Rod Beck, SF	1993	76	48
6	Lee Smith, St.L	1991	67	47

Innings Pitched (since 1920)

		Year	IP	W-L
1	Wilbur Wood, Chi-AL	1972	**377**	24-17
2	Mickey Lolich, Det	1971	**376**	25-14
3	Bob Feller, Cle	1946	**371**	26-15
4	Grover Alexander, Chi-NL	1920	**363**	27-14
5	Wilbur Wood, Chi-AL	1973	**359**	24-20

Shutouts

		Year	ShO	ERA
1	Grover Alexander, Phi-NL	1916	**16**	1.55
2	Jack Coombs, Phi-AL	1910	**13**	1.30
	Bob Gibson, St.L	1968	**13**	1.12
4	Christy Mathewson, NY-NL	1908	**12**	1.43
	Grover Alexander, Phi-NL	1915	**12**	1.22

Walks Allowed

		Year	BB	SO
1	Bob Feller, Cle	1938	**208**	240
2	Nolan Ryan, Cal	1977	**204**	341
3	Nolan Ryan, Cal	1974	**202**	367
4	Bob Feller, Cle	1941	**194**	260
5	Bobo Newsom, St.L-AL	1938	**192**	226

Home Runs Allowed

		Year	HRs
1	Bert Blyleven, Minnesota	1986	50
2	Robin Roberts, Philadelphia	1956	46
	Bert Blyleven, Minnesota	1987	46
4	Pedro Ramos, Washington	1957	43
5	Denny McLain, Detroit	1966	42

Home Run in First Major League At-bat

*on first pitch

A.L.— Luke Stuart, St. Louis, August 8, 1921.
Earl Averill, Cleveland, April 16, 1929.
Ace Parker, Philadelphia, April 30, 1937.
Gene Hasson, Philadelphia, September 9, 1937, first game.
Bill Lefebvre, Boston, June 10, 1938.*
Hack Miller, Detroit, April 23, 1944, second game.
Eddie Pellagrini, Boston, April 22, 1946.
George Vico, Detroit, April 20, 1948.*
Bob Nieman, St. Louis, September 14, 1951.
Bob Tillman, Boston, May 19, 1962.
John Kennedy, Washington, September 5, 1962, first game.
Buster Narum, Baltimore, May 3, 1963.
Gates Brown, Detroit, June 19, 1963.
Bert Campaneris, Kansas City, July 23, 1964.*
Bill Roman, Detroit, September 30, 1964, second game.
Brant Alyea, Washington, September 12, 1965.*
John Miller, New York, September 11, 1966.
Rick Renick, Minnesota, July 11, 1968.
Joe Keough, Oakland, August 7, 1968, second game.
Gene Lamont, Detroit, September 2, 1970, second game.
Don Rose, California, May 24, 1972.*
Reggie Sanders, Detroit, September 1, 1974.
Dave McKay, Minnesota, August 22, 1975.
Al Woods, Toronto, April 7, 1977.
Dave Machemer, California, June 21, 1978.
Gary Gaetti, Minnesota, September 20, 1981.
Andre David, Minnesota, June 29, 1984, first game.
Terry Steinbach, Oakland, September 12, 1986.
Jay Bell, Cleveland, September 29, 1986.*
Junior Felix, Toronto, May 4, 1989.*
Jon Nunnally, Kansas City, April 29, 1995.
Total number of players: 31

N.L.— Joe Harrington, Boston, September 10, 1895.
Bill Duggleby, Philadelphia, April 21, 1898.
Johnny Bates, Boston, April 12, 1906.
Walter Mueller, Pittsburgh, May 7, 1922.
Clise Dudley, Brooklyn, April 27, 1929.*
Gordon Slade, Brooklyn, May 24, 1930.
Eddie Morgan, St. Louis, April 14, 1936.*
Ernie Koy, Brooklyn, April 19, 1938.
Emmett Mueller, Philadelphia, April 19, 1938.
Clyde Vollmer, Cincinnati, May 31, 1942, second game.*
Paul Gillespie, Chicago, September 11, 1942.
Buddy Kerr, New York, September 8, 1943.
Whitey Lockman, New York, July 5, 1945.
Dan Bankhead, Brooklyn, August 26, 1947.
Les Layton, New York, May 21, 1948.
Ed Sanicki, Philadelphia, September 14, 1949.
Ted Tappe, Cincinnati, September 14, 1950, first game.
Hoyt Wilhelm, New York, April 23, 1952.
Wally Moon, St. Louis, April 13, 1954.
Chuck Tanner, Milwaukee, April 12, 1955.*
Bill White, New York, May 7, 1956.
Frank Ernaga, Chicago, May 24, 1957.
Don Leppert, Pittsburgh, June 18, 1961, first game.
Cuno Barragan, Chicago, September 1, 1961.
Benny Ayala, New York, August 27, 1974.
John Montefusco, San Francisco, September 3, 1974.
Jose Sosa, Houston, July 30, 1975.
Johnnie LeMaster, San Francisco, September 2, 1975.
Tim Wallach, Montreal, September 6, 1980.
Carmelo Martinez, Chicago, August 22, 1983.
Mike Fitzgerald, New York, September 13, 1983.
Will Clark, San Francisco, April 8, 1986.
Ricky Jordan, Philadelphia, July 17, 1988
Jose Offerman, Los Angeles, August 19, 1990.
Dave Eiland, San Diego, April 10, 1992.
Jim Bullinger, Chicago, June 8, 1992, first game.
Jay Gainer, Colorado, May 14, 1993.*
Mitch Lyden, Florida, June 16, 1993.
Garey Ingram, Los Angeles, May 19, 1994.
Total number of players: 39

Hitting home runs from both sides of plate, game

(Since 1986)

A.L.— Roy Smalley, Minnesota, May 30, 1986.
Tony Bernazard, Cleveland, July 1, 1986.
Ruben Sierra, Texas, September 13, 1986.
Eddie Murray, Baltimore, May 8, 1987.
Eddie Murray, Baltimore, May 9, 1987.
Devon White, California, June 23, 1987.
Dale Sveum, Milwaukee, July 17, 1987
Dale Sveum, Milwaukee, June 12, 1988.
Mickey Tettleton, Baltimore, June 13, 1988.
Tim Raines, Chicago, August 31, 1993.
Chad Kreuter, Detroit, Deptember 7, 1993.
Eddie Murray, Cleveland, April 21, 1994.
Chili Davis, California, May 11, 1994.
Bernie Williams, New York, June 6, 1994.
Ruben Sierra, Oakland, June 7, 1994.
Chili Davis, California, July 30, 1994.
Mickey Tettleton, Texas, April 28, 1995.
Roberto Alomar, Toronto, May 3, 1995
Luis Alicea, Boston, July 28, 1995.

N.L.— Chili Davis, San Francisco, June 27, 1987.
Bobby Bonilla, Pittsburgh, July 3, 1987.
Kevin Bass, Houston, August 3, 1987, 13 innings.
Kevin Bass, Houston, September 2, 1987.
Chili Davis, San Francisco, September 15, 1987.
Bobby Bonilla, Pittsburgh, April 6, 1988, 14 innings.
Tim Raines, Montreal, July 16, 1988.
Steve Jeltz, Philadelphia, June 8, 1989.
Kevin Bass, Houston, August 20, 1989.
Eddie Murray, Los Angeles, April 18, 1990.
Eddie Murray, Los Angeles, June 9, 1990.
Bret Barberie, Montreal, August 2, 1991.
Howard Johnson, New York, August 31, 1991.
Kevin Bass, San Francisco, August 2, 1992, second game.
Bobby Bonilla, New York, April 23, 1993.
Bobby Bonilla, New York, June 10, 1993.
Todd Benzinger, San Francisco, August 30, 1993.
Mark Whiten, St. Louis, September 14, 1993.
Geronimo Pena, St. Louis, April 17, 1994.
Bobby Bonilla, New York, May 4, 1994.
Todd Hundley, New York, June 18, 1994.
Ken Caminiti, Houston, July 3, 1994.
Bobby Bonilla, New York, May 12, 1995.
Ken Caminiti, San Diego, September 16, 1995.
Ken Caminiti, San Diego, September 17, 1995.
Ken Caminiti, San Diego, September 19, 1995.

All-Time Winningest Managers

Top 20 Major League career victories through the 1996 season. Career, regular season and postseason (playoffs and World Series) records are noted along with AL and NL pennants and World Series titles won. Managers active during 1996 season in **bold** type.

	Career				Regular Season			Postseason			
	Yrs	W	L	Pct	W	L	Pct	W	L	Pct	Titles
1 Connie Mack	53	**3755**	3967	.486	3731	3948	.486	24	19	.558	9 AL, 5 WS
2 John McGraw	33	**2810**	1987	.586	2784	1959	.587	26	28	.482	10 NL, 3 WS
3 Sparky Anderson	26	**2238**	1855	.547	2194	1834	.545	34	21	.618	4 NL, 1 AL, 3 WS
4 Bucky Harris	29	**2168**	2228	.493	2157	2218	.493	11	10	.524	3 AL, 2 WS
5 Joe McCarthy	24	**2155**	1346	.616	2125	1333	.615	30	13	.698	1 NL, 8 AL, 7 WS
6 Walter Alston	23	**2063**	1634	.558	2040	1613	.558	23	21	.523	7 NL, 4 WS
7 Leo Durocher	24	**2015**	1717	.540	2008	1709	.540	7	8	.467	3 NL, 1 WS
8 Casey Stengel	25	**1942**	1868	.510	1905	1842	.508	37	26	.587	10 AL, 7 WS
9 Gene Mauch	26	**1907**	2044	.483	1902	2037	.483	5	7	.417	—None—
10 Bill McKechnie	25	**1904**	1737	.523	1896	1723	.524	8	14	.364	4 NL, 2 WS
11 **Tommy Lasorda**	21	**1630**	1469	.526	1599	1439	.526	31	30	.508	4 NL, 2 WS
12 Ralph Houk	20	**1627**	1539	.514	1619	1531	.514	8	8	.500	3 AL, 2 WS
13 Fred Clarke	19	**1609**	1189	.575	1602	1181	.576	7	8	.467	4 NL, 1 WS
14 Dick Williams	21	**1592**	1474	.519	1571	1451	.520	21	23	.477	3 AL, 1 NL, 2 WS
15 Earl Weaver	17	**1506**	1080	.582	1480	1060	.583	26	20	.565	4 AL, 1 WS
16 Clark Griffith	20	**1491**	1367	.522	1491	1367	.522	0	0	.000	1 AL (1901)
17 Miller Huggins	17	**1431**	1149	.555	1413	1134	.555	18	15	.545	6 AL, 3 WS
18 Al Lopez	17	**1412**	1012	.583	1410	1004	.584	2	8	.200	2 AL
19 Jimmy Dykes	21	**1406**	1541	.477	1406	1541	.477	0	0	.000	—None—
20 Wilbert Robertson	19	**1402**	1407	.499	1399	1398	.500	3	9	.250	2 NL

Notes: John McGraw's postseason record also includes two World Series tie games (1912,'22); Miller Huggins postseason record also includes one World Series tie game (1922).

Where They Managed

Alston—Brooklyn/Los Angeles NL (1954-76); **Anderson**—Cincinnati NL (1970-78), Detroit AL (1979-95); **Clarke**—Louisville NL (1897-99), Pittsburgh NL (1900-15); **Durocher**—Brooklyn NL (1939-46,48), New York NL (1948-55), Chicago NL (1966-72), Houston NL (1972-73); **Dykes**—Chicago AL (1934-46), Philadelphia AL (1951- 53), Baltimore AL (1954), Cincinnati NL (1958), Detroit AL (1959-60), Cleveland AL (1960-61); **Griffith**—Chicago AL (1901-02), New York AL (1903-08), Cincinnati NL (1909-11), Washington AL (1912-20); **Harris**—Washington AL (1924-28,35-42,50-54), Detroit AL (1929-33,55-56), Boston AL (1934), Philadelphia NL (1943), New York AL (1947-48); **Houk**—New York AL (1961-63,66-73), Detroit AL (1974-78), Boston AL (1981-84); **Huggins**—St. Louis NL (1913-17), New York AL (1918-29); **Lasorda**—Los Angeles NL (1976-96); **Lopez**—Cleveland AL (1951-56), Chicago AL (1957-65,68-69).

Mack—Pittsburgh NL (1894-96), Philadelphia AL (1901-50); **Mauch**—Philadelphia NL (1960-68), Montreal NL (1969-75), Minnesota AL (1976-80), California AL (1981-82,85-87); **McCarthy**—Chicago NL (1926-30), New York AL (1931-46), Boston AL (1948-50); **McGraw**—Baltimore NL (1899), Baltimore AL (1901-02), New York NL (1902-32); **McKechnie**—Newark FL (1915), Pittsburgh NL (1922-26), St. Louis NL (1928-29), Boston NL (1930- 37), Cincinnati NL (1938-46); **Robertson**—Baltimore AL (1902), Brooklyn NL (1914-31); **Stengel**—Brooklyn NL (1934-36), Boston NL (1938-43), New York AL (1949-60), New York NL (1962-65); **Weaver**—Baltimore AL (1968-82,85-86); **Williams**—Boston AL (1967-69), Oakland AL (1971-73), California AL (1974-76), Montreal NL (1977-81), San Diego NL (1982-85), Seattle AL (1986-88).

Regular Season Winning Pct.

Minimum of 750 victories.

	Yrs	W	L	Pct	Pen
1 Joe McCarthy	24	2125	1333	**.615**	9
2 Charlie Comiskey	12	838	541	**.608**	4
3 Frank Selee	16	1284	862	**.598**	5
4 Billy Southworth	13	1044	704	**.597**	4
5 Frank Chance	11	946	648	**.593**	4
6 John McGraw	33	2784	1959	**.587**	10
7 Al Lopez	17	1410	1004	**.584**	2
8 Earl Weaver	17	1480	1060	**.583**	4
9 Cap Anson	20	1296	947	**.578**	5
10 Fred Clarke	19	1602	1181	**.576**	4
11 **Davey Johnson**	11	887	663	**.572**	1
12 Steve O'Neill	14	1040	821	**.559**	1
13 Walter Alston	23	2040	1613	**.558**	7
14 Bill Terry	10	823	661	**.555**	3
15 Miller Huggins	17	1413	1134	**.555**	6
16 Billy Martin	16	1253	1013	**.553**	2
17 Harry Wright	18	1000	825	**.548**	3
18 Charlie Grimm	19	1287	1067	**.547**	3
19 Sparky Anderson	26	2194	1834	**.545**	5
20 Hugh Jennings	15	1163	984	**.542**	3

World Series Victories

	App	W	L	T	Pct	WS
1 Casey Stengel	10	**37**	26	0	.587	7
2 Joe McCarthy	9	**30**	13	0	.698	7
3 John McGraw	9	**26**	28	2	.482	2
4 Connie Mack	8	**24**	19	0	.558	5
5 Walter Alston	7	**20**	20	0	.500	4
6 Miller Huggins	6	**18**	15	1	.544	3
7 Sparky Anderson	5	**16**	12	0	.571	3
8 **Tommy Lasorda**	4	**12**	11	0	.522	2
Dick Williams	4	**12**	14	0	.462	2
10 Frank Chance	4	**11**	9	1	.548	2
Bucky Harris	3	**11**	10	0	.524	2
Billy Southworth	4	**11**	11	0	.500	2
Earl Weaver	4	**11**	13	0	.458	1
Bobby Cox	4	**11**	14	0	.440	1
15 Whitey Herzog	3	**10**	11	0	.476	1
16 Bill Carrigan	2	**8**	2	0	.800	2
Danny Murtaugh	2	**8**	6	0	.571	2
Ralph Houk	3	**8**	8	0	.500	2
Bill McKechnie	4	**8**	14	0	.364	2
Tom Kelly	2	**8**	6	0	.571	2

Active Managers' Records

Regular season games only; through 1995.

National League

		Yrs	W	L	Pct
1	Tony LaRussa, St.L.	18	**1408**	1257	.528
2	Bobby Cox, Atl.	15	**1211**	1028	.541
3	Jim Leyland, Fla.	11	**851**	863	.496
4	Bobby Valentine, NY	9	**593**	624	.487
5	Felipe Alou, Mon.	5	**384**	323	.543
6	Dusty Baker, SF	4	**293**	290	.503
7	Don Baylor, Col.	4	**280**	305	.479
8	Jim Riggleman, Chi.	5	**261**	336	.437
9	Gene Lamont, Pit.	4	**258**	210	.551
10	Bruce Bochy, SD	2	**161**	145	.526
11	Ray Knight, Cin.	1	**81**	81	.500
12	Bill Russell, LA	1	**49**	37	.570
13	Larry Dierker, Hou.	0	**0**	0	.000
14	Philadelphia				

American League

		Yrs	W	L	Pct
1	Joe Torre, NY	13	**966**	1046	.480
2	Davey Johnson, Bal.	11	**887**	663	.572
3	Tom Kelly, Min.	11	**785**	791	.498
4	Lou Piniella, Sea.	10	**774**	709	.522
5	Cito Gaston, Tor.	8	**611**	551	.526
6	Johnny Oates, Tex.	5	**455**	412	.525
7	Mike Hargrove, Cle.	6	**449**	378	.543
8	Phil Garner, Mil.	5	**359**	386	.482
9	Bob Boone, KC	2	**145**	160	.475
10	Terry Bevington, Chi.	2	**142**	133	.516
11	Art Howe, Oak.	1	**78**	84	.481
12	Buddy Bell, Det.	1	**53**	109	.327
13	Boston				
14	California				

Annual Awards

MOST VALUABLE PLAYER

There have been three different Most Valuable Player awards in baseball since 1911—the Chalmers Award (1911-14), presented by the Detroit-based automobile company; the League Award (1922-29), presented by the National and American Leagues; and the Baseball Writers' Award (since 1931), presented by the Baseball Writers' Association of America. Statistics for winning players are provided below. Stats for winning pitchers before advent of Cy Young Award are on page 142.

Multiple winners: NL—Barry Bonds, Roy Campanella, Stan Musial and Mike Schmidt (3); Ernie Banks, Johnny Bench, Rogers Hornsby, Carl Hubbell, Willie Mays, Joe Morgan and Dale Murphy (2). **AL**—Yogi Berra, Joe DiMaggio, Jimmie Foxx and Mickey Mantle (3); Mickey Cochrane, Lou Gehrig, Hank Greenberg, Walter Johnson, Roger Maris, Hal Newhouser, Cal Ripken Jr., Frank Thomas, Ted Williams and Robin Yount (2). **NL & AL**—Frank Robinson (2, one in each).

Chalmers Award

National League

Year		Pos	HR	RBI	Avg
1911	Wildfire Schulte, Chi	OF	21	121	.300
1912	Larry Doyle, NY	2B	10	90	.330
1913	Jake Daubert, Bklyn	1B	2	52	.350
1914	Johnny Evers, Bos	2B	1	40	.279

American League

Year		Pos	HR	RBI	Avg
1911	Ty Cobb, Det	OF	8	144	.420
1912	Tris Speaker, Bos	OF	10	98	.383
1913	Walter Johnson, Wash	P	—	—	—
1914	Eddie Collins, Phi	2B	2	85	.344

League Award

National League

Year		Pos	HR	RBI	Avg
1922	No selection				
1923	No selection				
1924	Dazzy Vance, Bklyn	P	—	—	—
1925	Rogers Hornsby, St.L	2B-Mgr	39	143	.403
1926	Bob O'Farrell, St.L	C	7	68	.293
1927	Paul Waner, Pit	OF	9	131	.380
1928	Jim Bottomley, St.L	1B	31	136	.325
1929	Rogers Hornsby, Chi	2B	39	149	.380

American League

Year		Pos	HR	RBI	Avg
1922	George Sisler, St.L	1B	8	105	.420
1923	Babe Ruth, NY	OF	41	131	.393
1924	Walter Johnson, Wash	P	—	—	—
1925	Roger Peckinpaugh, Wash	SS	4	64	.294
1926	George Burns, Cle	1B	4	114	.358
1927	Lou Gehrig, NY	1B	47	175	.373
1928	Mickey Cochrane, Phi	C	10	57	.293
1929	No selection				

Most Valuable Player

National League

Year		Pos	HR	RBI	Avg
1931	Frankie Frisch, St.L	2B	4	82	.311
1932	Chuck Klein, Phi	OF	38	137	.348
1933	Carl Hubbell, NY	P	—	—	—
1934	Dizzy Dean, St.L	P	—	—	—
1935	Gabby Hartnett, Chi.	C	13	91	.344
1936	Carl Hubbell, NY	P	—	—	—
1937	Joe Medwick, St.L	OF	31	154	.374
1938	Ernie Lombardi, Cin	C	19	95	.342
1939	Bucky Walters, Cin	P	—	—	—
1940	Frank McCormick, Cin	1B	19	127	.309
1941	Dolf Camilli, Bklyn	1B	34	120	.285
1942	Mort Cooper, St.L	P	—	—	—
1943	Stan Musial, St.L	OF	13	81	.357
1944	Marty Marion, St.L	SS	6	63	.267
1945	Phil Cavarretta, Chi	1B	6	97	.355

American League

Year		Pos	HR	RBI	Avg
1931	Lefty Grove, Phi	P	—	—	—
1932	Jimmie Foxx, Phi	1B	58	169	.364
1933	Jimmie Foxx, Phi	1B	48	163	.356
1934	Mickey Cochrane, Det	C-Mgr	2	76	.320
1935	Hank Greenberg, Det	1B	36	170	.328
1936	Lou Gehrig, NY	1B	49	152	.354
1937	Charlie Gehringer, Det	2B	14	96	.371
1938	Jimmie Foxx, Bos	1B	50	175	.349
1939	Joe DiMaggio, NY	OF	30	126	.381
1940	Hank Greenberg, Det	OF	41	150	.340
1941	Joe DiMaggio, NY	OF	30	125	.357
1942	Joe Gordon, NY	2B	18	103	.322
1943	Spud Chandler, NY	P	—	—	—
1944	Hal Hewhouser, Det	P	—	—	—
1945	Hal Newhouser, Det	P	—	—	—

Annual Awards (Cont.)

Most Valuable Player

National League

Year		Pos	HR	RBI	Avg
1946	Stan Musial, St.L	1B-OF	16	103	.365
1947	Bob Elliott, Bos	3B	22	113	.317
1948	Stan Musial, St.L	OF	39	131	.376
1949	Jackie Robinson, Bklyn	2B	16	124	.342
1950	Jim Konstanty, Phi	P	—	—	—
1951	Roy Campanella, Bklyn	C	33	108	.325
1952	Hank Sauer, Chi	OF	37	121	.270
1953	Roy Campanella, Bklyn	C	41	142	.312
1954	Willie Mays, NY	OF	41	110	.345
1955	Roy Campanella, Bklyn	C	32	107	.318
1956	Don Newcombe, Bklyn	P	—	—	—
1957	Hank Aaron, Mil	OF	44	132	.322
1958	Ernie Banks, Chi	SS	47	129	.313
1959	Ernie Banks, Chi	SS	45	143	.304
1960	Dick Groat, Pit	SS	2	50	.325
1961	Frank Robinson, Cin	OF	37	124	.323
1962	Maury Wills, LA	SS	6	48	.299
1963	Sandy Koufax, LA	P	—	—	—
1964	Ken Boyer, St.L	3B	24	119	.295
1965	Willie Mays, SF	OF	52	112	.317
1966	Roberto Clemente, Pit	OF	29	119	.317
1967	Orlando Cepeda, St.L	1B	25	111	.325
1968	Bob Gibson, St.L	P	—	—	—
1969	Willie McCovey, SF	1B	45	126	.320
1970	Johnny Bench, Cin	C	45	148	.293
1971	Joe Torre, St.L	3B	24	137	.363
1972	Johnny Bench, Cin	C	40	125	.270
1973	Pete Rose, Cin	OF	5	64	.338
1974	Steve Garvey, LA	1B	21	111	.312
1975	Joe Morgan, Cin	2B	17	94	.327
1976	Joe Morgan, Cin	2B	27	111	.320
1977	George Foster, Cin	OF	52	149	.320
1978	Dave Parker, Pit	OF	30	117	.334
1979	Keith Hernandez, St.L	1B	11	105	.344
	& Willie Stargell, Pit	1B	32	82	.281
1980	Mike Schmidt, Phi	3B	48	121	.286
1981	Mike Schmidt, Phi	3B	31	91	.316
1982	Dale Murphy, Atl	OF	36	109	.281
1983	Dale Murphy, Atl	OF	36	121	.302
1984	Ryne Sandberg, Chi	2B	19	84	.314
1985	Willie McGee, St.L	OF	10	82	.353
1986	Mike Schmidt, Phi	3B	37	119	.290
1987	Andre Dawson, Chi	OF	49	137	.287
1988	Kirk Gibson, LA	OF	25	76	.290
1989	Kevin Mitchell, SF	OF	47	125	.291
1990	Barry Bonds, Pit	OF	33	114	.301
1991	Terry Pendleton, Atl	3B	22	86	.319
1992	Barry Bonds, Pit	OF	34	103	.311
1993	Barry Bonds, SF	OF	46	123	.336
1994	Jeff Bagwell, Hou	1B	39	116	.368
1995	Barry Larkin, Cin	55	15	66	.319

American League

Year		Pos	HR	RBI	Avg
1946	Ted Williams, Bos	OF	38	123	.342
1947	Joe DiMaggio, NY	OF	20	97	.315
1948	Lou Boudreau, Cle	SS-Mgr	18	106	.355
1949	Ted Williams, Bos	OF	43	159	.343
1950	Phil Rizzuto, NY	SS	7	66	.324
1951	Yogi Berra, NY	C	27	88	.294
1952	Bobby Shantz, Phi	P	—	—	—
1953	Al Rosen, Cle	3B	43	145	.336
1954	Yogi Berra, NY	C	22	125	.307
1955	Yogi Berra, NY	C	27	108	.272
1956	Mickey Mantle, NY	OF	52	130	.353
1957	Mickey Mantle, NY	OF	34	94	.365
1958	Jackie Jensen, Bos	OF	35	122	.286
1959	Nellie Fox, Chi	2B	2	70	.306
1960	Roger Maris, NY	OF	39	112	.283
1961	Roger Maris, NY	OF	61	142	.269
1962	Mickey Mantle, NY	OF	30	89	.321
1963	Elston Howard, NY	C	28	85	.287
1964	Brooks Robinson, Bal	3B	28	118	.317
1965	Zoilo Versalles, Min	SS	19	77	.273
1966	Frank Robinson, Bal	OF	49	122	.316
1967	Carl Yastrzemski, Bos	OF	44	121	.326
1968	Denny McLain, Det	P	—	—	—
1969	Harmon Killebrew, Min	3B-1B	49	140	.276
1970	Boog Powell, Bal	1B	35	114	.297
1971	Vida Blue, Oak	P	—	—	—
1972	Dick Allen, Chi	1B	37	113	.308
1973	Reggie Jackson, Oak	OF	32	117	.293
1974	Jeff Burroughs, Tex	OF	25	118	.301
1975	Fred Lynn, Bos	OF	21	105	.331
1976	Thurman Munson, NY	C	17	105	.302
1977	Rod Carew, Min	1B	14	100	.388
1978	Jim Rice, Bos	OF-DH	46	139	.315
1979	Don Baylor, Cal	OF-DH	36	139	.296
1980	George Brett, KC	3B	24	118	.390
1981	Rollie Fingers, Mil	P	—	—	—
1982	Robin Yount, Mil	SS	29	114	.331
1983	Cal Ripken Jr., Bal	SS	27	102	.318
1984	Willie Hernandez, Det	P	—	—	—
1985	Don Mattingly, NY	1B	35	145	.324
1986	Roger Clemens, Bos	P	—	—	—
1987	George Bell, Tor	OF	47	134	.308
1988	Jose Canseco, Oak	OF	42	124	.307
1989	Robin Yount, Mil	OF	21	103	.318
1990	Rickey Henderson, Oak	OF	28	61	.325
1991	Cal Ripken Jr., Bal	SS	34	114	.323
1992	Dennis Eckersley, Oak	P	—	—	—
1993	Frank Thomas, Chi	1B	41	128	.317
1994	Frank Thomas, Chi	1B	38	101	.353
1995	Mo Vaughn, Bos	1B	39	126	.300

MVP Pitchers' Statistics

Pitchers have been named Most Valuable Player on 23 occasions, 10 times in the NL and 13 in the AL. Four have been relief pitchers—Jim Konstanty, Rollie Fingers, Willie Hernandez and Dennis Eckersley.

National League

Year		Gm	W-L	SV	ERA
1924	Dazzy Vance, Bklyn	35	28-6	0	2.16
1933	Carl Hubbell, NY	45	23-12	5	1.66
1934	Dizzy Dean, St.L	50	30-7	7	2.66
1936	Carl Hubbell, NY	42	26-6	3	2.31
1939	Bucky Walters, Cin	39	27-11	0	2.29
1942	Mort Cooper, St.L	37	22-7	0	1.78
1950	Jim Konstanty, Phi	74	16-7	22	2.66

American League

Year		Gm	W-L	SV	ERA
1913	Walter Johnson, Wash	47	36-7	2	1.09
1924	Walter Johnson, Wash	38	23-7	0	2.72
1931	Lefty Grove, Phi	41	31-4	5	2.06
1943	Spud Chandler, NY	30	20-4	0	1.64
1944	Hal Hewhouser, Det	47	29-9	2	2.22
1945	Hal Newhouser, Det	40	25-9	2	1.81
1952	Bobby Shantz, Phi	33	24-7	0	2.48

CY YOUNG AWARD

Voted on by the Baseball Writers Association of America. One award was presented from 1956-66, two since 1967. Pitchers who won the MVP and Cy Young awards in the same season are in **bold** type.

Multiple winners: NL—Steve Carlton and Greg Maddux (4); Sandy Koufax and Tom Seaver (3); Bob Gibson (2). **AL**—Jim Palmer and Roger Clemens (3); Denny McLain (2). **NL & AL**—Gaylord Perry (2, one in each).

NL and AL Combined

Year	National League	Gm	W-L	SV	ERA
1956	**Don Newcombe**, Bklyn	38	27-7	0	3.06
1957	Warren Spahn, Mil	39	21-11	3	2.69
1960	Vernon Law, Pit	35	20-9	0	3.08
1962	Don Drysdale, LA	43	25-9	1	2.83
1963	**Sandy Koufax**, LA	40	25-5	0	1.88
1965	Sandy Koufax, LA	43	26-8	2	2.04
1966	Sandy Koufax, LA	41	27-9	0	1.73

Year	American League	Gm	W-L	SV	ERA
1958	Bob Turley, NY	33	21-7	1	2.97
1959	Early Wynn, Chi	37	22-10	0	3.17
1961	Whitey Ford, NY	39	25-4	0	3.21
1964	Dean Chance, LA	46	20-9	4	1.65

Separate League Awards

National League

Year		Gm	W-L	SV	ERA
1967	Mike McCormick, SF	40	22-10	0	2.85
1968	**Bob Gibson**, St.L	34	22-9	0	1.12
1969	Tom Seaver, NY	36	25-7	0	2.21
1970	Bob Gibson, St.L	34	23-7	0	3.12
1971	Ferguson Jenkins, Chi	39	24-13	0	2.77
1972	Steve Carlton, Phi	41	27-10	0	1.97
1973	Tom Seaver, NY	36	19-10	0	2.08
1974	Mike Marshall, LA	106	15-12	21	2.42
1975	Tom Seaver, NY	36	22-9	0	2.38
1976	Randy Jones, SD	40	22-14	0	2.74
1977	Steve Carlton, Phi	36	23-10	0	2.64
1978	Gaylord Perry, SD	37	21-6	0	2.72
1979	Bruce Sutter, Chi	62	6-6	37	2.23
1980	Steve Carlton, Phi	38	24-9	0	2.34
1981	Fernando Valenzuela, LA	25	13-7	0	2.48
1982	Steve Carlton, Phi	38	23-11	0	3.10
1983	John Denny, Phi	36	19-6	0	2.37
1984	Rick Sutcliffe, Chi	20*	16-1	0	2.69
1985	Dwight Gooden, NY	35	24-4	0	1.53
1986	Mike Scott, Hou	37	18-10	0	2.22
1987	Steve Bedrosian, Phi	65	5-3	40	2.83
1988	Orel Hershiser, LA	35	23-8	1	2.26
1989	Mark Davis, SD	70	4-3	44	1.85
1990	Doug Drabek, Pit	33	22-6	0	2.76
1991	Tom Glavine, Atl	34	20-11	0	2.55
1992	Greg Maddux, Chi	35	20-11	0	2.18
1993	Greg Maddux, Atl	36	20-10	0	2.36
1994	Greg Maddux, Atl	25	16-6	0	1.56
1995	Greg Maddux, Atl	28	19-2	0	1.63

American League

Year		Gm	W-L	SV	ERA
1967	Jim Lonborg, Bos	39	22-9	0	3.16
1968	**Denny McLain**, Det	41	31-6	0	1.96
1969	Denny McLain, Det	42	24-9	0	2.80
	& Mike Cuellar, Bal	39	23-11	0	2.38
1970	Jim Perry, Min	40	24-12	0	3.03
1971	**Vida Blue**, Oak	39	24-8	0	1.82
1972	Gaylord Perry, Cle	41	24-16	1	1.92
1973	Jim Palmer, Bal	38	22-9	1	2.40
1974	Catfish Hunter, Oak	41	25-12	0	2.49
1975	Jim Palmer, Bal	39	23-11	1	2.09
1976	Jim Palmer, Bal	40	22-13	0	2.51
1977	Sparky Lyle, NY	72	13-5	26	2.17
1978	Ron Guidry, NY	35	25-3	0	1.74
1979	Mike Flanagan, Bal	39	23-9	0	3.08
1980	Steve Stone, Bal	37	25-7	0	3.23
1981	**Rollie Fingers**, Mil	47	6-3	28	1.04
1982	Pete Vuckovich, Mil	30	18-6	0	3.34
1983	LaMarr Hoyt, Chi	36	24-10	0	3.66
1984	**Willie Hernandez**, Det	80	9-3	32	1.92
1985	Bret Saberhagen, KC	32	20-6	0	2.87
1986	**Roger Clemens**, Bos	33	24-4	0	2.48
1987	Roger Clemens, Bos	36	20-9	0	2.97
1988	Frank Viola, Min	35	24-7	0	2.64
1989	Bret Saberhagen, KC	36	23-6	0	2.16
1990	Bob Welch, Oak	35	27-6	0	2.95
1991	Roger Clemens, Bos	35	18-10	0	2.62
1992	**Dennis Eckersley**, Oak	69	7-1	51	1.91
1993	Jack McDowell, Chi	34	22-10	0	3.37
1994	David Cone, KC	23	16-5	0	2.94
1995	Randy Johnson, Sea	30	18-2	0	248

*NL games only, Sutcliffe pitched 15 games with Cleveland before being traded to the Cubs.

ROOKIE OF THE YEAR

Voted on by the Baseball Writers Assn. of America. One award was presented from 1947-48. Two awards (one for each league) have been presented since 1949. Winner who was also named MVP is in **bold** type.

NL and AL Combined

Year		Pos
1947	Jackie Robinson, Brooklyn	1B
1948	Alvin Dark, Boston-NL	SS

National League

Year		Pos
1949	Don Newcombe, Bklyn	P
1950	Sam Jethroe, Bos	OF
1951	Willie Mays, NY	OF
1952	Joe Black, Bklyn	P
1953	Jim Gilliam, Bklyn	2B
1954	Wally Moon, St.L	OF
1955	Bill Virdon, St.L	OF
1956	Frank Robinson, Cin	OF
1957	Jack Sanford, Phi	P
1958	Orlando Cepeda, SF	1B
1959	Willie McCovey, SF	1B
1960	Frank Howard, LA	OF
1961	Billy Williams, Chi	OF
1962	Ken Hubbs, Chi	2B
1963	Pete Rose, Cin	2B
1964	Richie Allen, Phi	3B
1965	Jim Lefebvre, LA	2B

Annual Awards (Cont.)

Rookie of the Year

National League

Year		Pos
1966	Tommy Helms, Cin	3B
1967	Tom Seaver, NY	P
1968	Johnny Bench, Cin	C
1969	Ted Sizemore, LA	2B
1970	Carl Morton, Mon	P
1971	Earl Williams, Atl	C
1972	Jon Matlack, NY	P
1973	Gary Matthews, SF	OF
1974	Bake McBride, St.L	OF
1975	John Montefusco, SF	P
1976	Butch Metzger, SD	P
	& Pat Zachry, Cin	P
1977	Andre Dawson, Mon	OF
1978	Bob Horner, Atl	3B
1979	Rick Sutcliffe, LA	P
1980	Steve Howe, LA	P
1981	Fernando Valenzuela, LA	P
1982	Steve Sax, LA	2B
1983	Darryl Strawberry, NY	OF
1984	Dwight Gooden, NY	P
1985	Vince Coleman, St.L	OF
1986	Todd Worrell, St.L	P
1987	Benito Santiago, SD	C
1988	Chris Sabo, Cin	3B
1989	Jerome Walton, Chi	OF
1990	David Justice, Atl	OF
1991	Jeff Bagwell, Hou.	1B
1992	Eric Karros, LA	1B
1993	Mike Piazza, LA	C
1994	Raul Mondesi, LA	OF
1995	Hideo Nomo, LA	P

American League

Year		Pos
1949	Roy Sievers, St.L	OF
1950	Walt Dropo, Bos	1B
1951	Gil McDougald, NY	3B
1952	Harry Byrd, Phi	P
1953	Harvey Kuenn, Det	SS
1954	Bob Grim, NY	P
1955	Herb Score, Cle	P
1956	Luis Aparicio, Chi	SS
1957	Tony Kubek, NY	INF-OF
1958	Albie Pearson, Wash	OF
1959	Bob Allison, Wash	OF
1960	Ron Hansen, Bal	SS
1961	Don Schwall, Bos	P
1962	Tom Tresh, NY	SS-OF
1963	Gary Peters, Chi	P
1964	Tony Oliva, Min	OF
1965	Curt Blefary, Bal	OF
1966	Tommie Agee, Chi	OF
1967	Rod Carew, Min	2B
1968	Stan Bahnsen, NY	P
1969	Lou Piniella, KC	OF
1970	Thurman Munson, NY	C
1971	Chris Chambliss, Cle	1B
1972	Carlton Fisk, Bos	C
1973	Al Bumbry, Bal	OF
1974	Mike Hargrove, Tex	1B
1975	**Fred Lynn**, Bos	OF
1976	Mark Fidrych, Det	P
1977	Eddie Murray, Bal	DH-1B
1978	Lou Whitaker, Det	2B
1979	John Castino, Min	3B
	& Alfredo Griffin, Tor	SS
1980	Joe Charboneau, Cle	OF-DH
1981	Dave Righetti, NY	P
1982	Cal Ripken Jr., Bal	SS-3B
1983	Ron Kittle, Chi	OF
1984	Alvin Davis, Sea	1B
1985	Ozzie Guillen, Chi	SS
1986	Jose Canseco, Oak	OF
1987	Mark McGwire, Oak	1B
1988	Walt Weiss, Oak	SS
1989	Gregg Olson, Bal	P
1990	Sandy Alomar Jr., Cle	C
1991	Chuck Knoblauch, Min	2B
1992	Pat Listach, Mil	SS
1993	Tim Salmon, Cal	OF
1994	Bob Hamelin, KC	DH
1995	Marty Cordova, Min	OF

MANAGER OF THE YEAR

Voted on by the Baseball Writers Association of America. Two awards (one for each league) presented since 1983. Note that (*) indicates manager's team won division championship and (†) indicates unofficial division won in 1994.

Multiple winners: Tony La Russa (3); Sparky Anderson, Bobby Cox, Tommy Lasorda and Jim Leyland (2).

National League

Year		Improvement		
1983	Tommy Lasorda, LA	88-74	to	91-71*
1984	Jim Frey, Chi	71-91	to	96-75*
1985	Whitey Herzog, St. L	84-78	to	101-61*
1986	Hal Lanier, Hou.	83-79	to	96-66*
1987	Buck Rodgers, Mon	78-83	to	91-71
1988	Tommy Lasorda, LA	73-89	to	94-67*
1989	Don Zimmer, Chi	77-85	to	93-69*
1990	Jim Leyland, Pit	74-88	to	95-67*
1991	Bobby Cox, Atl	65-97	to	94-68*
1992	Jim Leyland, Pit	98-64*	to	96-66*
1993	Dusty Baker, SF	72-90	to	103-59
1994	Felipe Alou, Mon	94-68	to	74-40†
1995	Don Baylor, Col	53-64	to	77-67

American League

Year		Improvement		
1983	Tony La Russa, Chi	87-75	to	99-63*
1984	Sparky Anderson, Det	92-70	to	104-58*
1985	Bobby Cox, Tor	89-73	to	99-62*
1986	John McNamara, Bos	81-81	to	95-66*
1987	Sparky Anderson, Det	87-75	to	98-64*
1988	Tony La Russa, Oak	81-81	to	104-58*
1989	Frank Robinson, Bal	54-107	to	87-75
1990	Jeff Torborg, Chi	69-92	to	94-68
1991	Tom Kelly, Min	74-88	to	95-67*
1992	Tony La Russa, Oak	84-78	to	96-66*
1993	Gene Lamont, Chi.	86-76	to	94-68*
1994	Buck Showalter, NY	88-74	to	70-43†
1995	Lou Piniella, Sea	49-63	to	79-66*

George Steinbrenner's Managerial Merry-Go-Round

As managing general partner of the New York Yankees since 1973, George Steinbrenner has changed managers 21 times in 23 years. In that time, the Yankees have won four AL pennants (1976-78 and '81) and two World Series (1977-78). Note that (*) indicates interim status. Managers with multiple hitches are Billy Martin (5), and Bob Lemon, Gene Michael and Lou Piniella (2).

	Tenure	W-L
Ralph Houk	1973	80-82
Bill Virdon	1974-75	142-124
Billy Martin	1975-78*	279-192
Dick Howser	1978	0-1
Bob Lemon	1978-79	82-51
Billy Martin	1979	55-40
Dick Howser	1980	103-59
Gene Michael	1981	48-34
Bob Lemon	1981-82	17-22
Gene Michael	1982	44-42
Clyde King	1982	29-33
Billy Martin	1983	91-71
Yogi Berra	1984-85	93-85
Billy Martin	1985	91-54
Lou Piniella	1986-87	179-145
Billy Martin	1988	40-28
Lou Piniella	1988	45-48
Dallas Green	1989	56-65
Bucky Dent	1989-90	36-53
Stump Merrill	1990-91	120-155
Buck Showalter	1992-95	313-268
Joe Torre	1996—	92-70

COLLEGE BASEBALL

College World Series

The NCAA Division I College World Series has been held in Kalamazoo, Mich. (1947-48), Wichita, Kan. (1949) and Omaha, Neb. (since 1950).

Multiple winners: USC (11); Arizona St. (5); Texas (4); Arizona, CS-Fullerton, LSU and Minnesota (3); California, Miami-FL, Michigan, Oklahoma and Stanford (2).

Year	Winner	Coach	Score	Runner-up
1947	California	Clint Evans	8-7	Yale
1948	USC	Sam Barry	9-2	Yale
1949	Texas	Bibb Falk	10-3	W. Forest
1950	Texas	Bibb Falk	3-0	Wash. St.
1951	Oklahoma	Jack Baer	3-2	Tennessee
1952	Holy Cross	Jack Barry	8-4	Missouri
1953	Michigan	Ray Fisher	7-5	Texas
1954	Missouri	Hi Simmons	4-1	Rollins
1955	Wake Forest	Taylor Sanford	7-6	W. Mich.
1956	Minnesota	Dick Siebert	12-1	Arizona
1957	California	Geo. Wolfman	1-0	Penn St.
1958	USC	Rod Dedeaux	8-7	Missouri
1959	Oklahoma St.	Toby Greene	5-3	Arizona
1960	Minnesota	Dick Siebert	2-1	USC
1961	USC	Rod Dedeaux	1-0	Okla. St.
1962	Michigan	Don Lund	5-4	S. Clara
1963	USC	Rod Dedeaux	5-2	Arizona
1964	Minnesota	Dick Siebert	5-1	Missouri
1965	Arizona St.	Bobby Winkles	2-1	Ohio St.
1966	Ohio St.	Marty Karow	8-2	Okla. St.
1967	Arizona St.	Bobby Winkles	11-2	Houston
1968	USC	Rod Dedeaux	4-3	So. Ill.
1969	Arizona St.	Bobby Winkles	10-1	Tulsa
1970	USC	Rod Dedeaux	2-1	Fla. St.
1971	USC	Rod Dedeaux	7-2	So. Ill.
1972	USC	Rod Dedeaux	1-0	Ariz. St.
1973	USC	Rod Dedeaux	4-3	Ariz. St.
1974	USC	Rod Dedeaux	7-3	Miami, FL
1975	Texas	Cliff Gustafson	5-1	S. Carolina
1976	Arizona	Jerry Kindall	7-1	E. Michigan
1977	Arizona St.	Jim Brock	2-1	S. Carolina
1978	USC	Rod Dedeaux	10-3	Ariz. St.
1979	CS-Fullerton	Augie Garrido	2-1	Arkansas
1980	Arizona	Jerry Kindall	5-3	Hawaii
1981	Arizona St.	Jim Brock	7-4	Okla. St.
1982	Miami-FL	Ron Fraser	9-3	Wichita St.
1983	Texas	Cliff Gustafson	4-3	Alabama
1984	CS-Fullerton	Augie Garrido	3-1	Texas
1985	Miami-FL	Ron Fraser	10-6	Texas
1986	Arizona	Jerry Kindall	10-2	Fla. St.
1987	Stanford	M. Marquess	9-5	Okla. St.
1988	Stanford	M. Marquess	9-4	Ariz. St.
1989	Wichita St.	G.Stephenson	5-3	Texas
1990	Georgia	Steve Webber	2-1	Okla. St.
1991	LSU	Skip Bertman	6-3	Wichita St.
1992	Pepperdine	Andy Lopez	3-2	CS-Fullerton
1993	LSU	Skip Bertman	8-0	Wichita St.
1994	Oklahoma	Larry Cochell	13-5	Ga. Tech
1995	CS-Fullerton	Augie Garrido	11-5	USC
1996	LSU	Skip Bertman	9-8	Miami, FL

Most Outstanding Players

The Most Outstanding Player has been selected every year of the College World Series since 1949. Winners who did not play for the CWS champion are listed in **bold** type. No player has won the award more than once.

Year	
1949	**Charles Teague,** W. Forest, 2B
1950	**Ray VanCleef,** Rutgers, CF
1951	**Sidney Hatfield,** Tenn., P-1B
1952	James O'Neill, Holy Cross, P
1953	**J.L. Smith,** Texas, P
1954	**Tom Yewcic,** Mich. St., C
1955	**Tom Borland,** Okla. St., P
1956	Jerry Thomas, Minn., P
1957	**Cal Emery,** Penn St., P-1B
1958	Bill Thom, USC, P
1959	Jim Dobson, Okla. St., 3B
1960	John Erickson, Minn., 2B
1961	**Littleton Fowler,** Okla. St., P
1962	**Bob Garibaldi,** Santa Clara, P
1963	Bud Hollowell, USC, C
1964	**Joe Ferris,** Maine, P
1965	Sal Bando, Ariz. St., 3B
1966	Steve Arlin, Ohio St., P
1967	Ron Davini, Ariz. St., C
1968	Bill Seinsoth, USC, 1B
1969	John Dolinsek, Ariz. St., LF
1970	**Gene Ammann,** Fla. St., P
1971	**Jerry Tabb,** Tulsa, 1B
1972	Russ McQueen, USC, P
1973	**Dave Winfield,** Minn., P-OF
1974	George Milke, USC, P
1975	Mickey Reichenbach, Texas, 1B
1976	Steve Powers, Arizona, P-DH
1977	Bob Horner, Ariz. St., 3B
1978	Rod Boxberger, USC, P
1979	Tony Hudson, CS-Fullerton, P
1980	Terry Francona, Arizona, LF
1981	Stan Holmes, Ariz. St., LF
1982	Dan Smith, Miami-FL, P
1983	Calvin Schiraldi, Texas, P
1984	John Fishel, CS-Fullerton, LF
1985	Greg Ellena, Miami-FL, LF
1986	Mike Senne, Arizona, DH
1987	Paul Carey, Stanford, RF
1988	Lee Plemel, Stanford, P
1989	Greg Brummett, Wich. St., P
1990	Mike Rebhan, Georgia, P
1991	Gary Hymel, LSU, C
1992	**Phil Nevin,** CS-Fullerton, 3B
1993	Todd Walker, LSU, 2B
1994	Chip Glass, Oklahoma, OF
1995	Mark Kotsay, CS-Fullerton, OF
1996	**Pat Burrell,** Miami-FL, 3B

Annual Awards

Golden Spikes Award

First presented in 1978 by USA Baseball, honoring the nation's best amateur player. Alex Fernandez, the 1990 winner, has been the only junior college player chosen.

Year	
1978	Bob Horner, Ariz. St, 2B
1979	Tim Wallach, CS-Fullerton, 1B
1980	Terry Francona, Arizona, OF
1981	Mike Fuentes, Fla. St., OF
1982	Augie Schmidt, N. Orleans, SS
1983	Dave Magadan, Alabama, 1B
1984	Oddibe McDowell, Ariz. St., OF
1985	Will Clark, Miss. St., 1B
1986	Mike Loynd, Fla. St., P
1987	Jim Abbott, Michigan, P
1988	Robin Ventura, Okla. St., 3B
1989	Ben McDonald, LSU, P
1990	Alex Fernandez, Miami-Dade, P
1991	Mike Kelly, Ariz. St., OF
1992	Phil Nevin, CS-Fullerton, 3B
1993	Darren Dreifort, Wichita St., P
1994	Jason Varitek, Ga. Tech, C
1995	Mark Kotsay, CS-Fullerton, OF

Annual Awards (Cont.)

Baseball America Player of the Year

Presented to the College Player of the Year since 1981 by *Baseball America.*

Year		Year		Year	
1981	Mike Sodders, Ariz. St., 3B	1987	Robin Ventura, Okla. St., 3B	1993	Brooks Kieschnick, Texas, DH/P
1982	Jeff Ledbetter, Fla. St., OF/P	1988	John Olerud, Wash. St., 1B/P	1994	Jason Varitek, Ga. Tech, C
1983	Dave Magadan, Alabama, 1B	1989	Ben McDonald, LSU, P	1995	Todd Helton, Tenn., 1B/P
1984	Oddibe McDowell, Ariz. St., OF	1990	Mike Kelly, Ariz. St., OF	1996	Kris Benson, Clemson, P
1985	Pete Incaviglia, Okla. St., OF	1991	David McCarty, Stanford, 1B		
1986	Casey Close, Michigan, OF	1992	Phil Nevin, CS-Fullerton, 3B		

Dick Howser Trophy

Presented to the College Player of the Year since 1987 by the American Baseball Coaches Association. Named after the late two-time All-America shortstop and college coach at Florida St., Howser was also a major league manager with Kansas City and the New York Yankees.

Multiple winner: Brooks Kieschnick (2).

Year		Year		Year	
1987	Mike Fiore, Miami-FL, OF	1991	Bobby Jones, Fresno St., P	1995	Todd Helton, Tenn., 1B/P
1988	Robin Ventura, Okla. St., 3B	1992	Brooks Kieschnick, Texas, DH/P	1996	Kris Benson, Clemson, P
1989	Scott Bryant, Texas, DH	1993	Brooks Kieschnick, Texas, DH/P		
1990	Paul Ellis, UCLA, C	1994	Jason Varitek, Ga. Tech, C		

Baseball America Coach of the Year

Presented to the College Coach of the Year since 1981 by *Baseball America.*

Multiple winner: Skip Bertman, Dave Snow and Gene Stephenson (2).

Year		Year		Year	
1981	Ron Fraser, Miami-FL	1987	Mark Marquess, Stanford	1993	Gene Stephenson, Wichita St.
1982	Gene Stephenson, Wichita St.	1988	Jim Brock, Arizona St.	1994	Jim Morris, Miami-FL
1983	Barry Shollenberger, Alabama	1989	Dave Snow, Long Beach St.	1995	Rob Delmonico, Tennessee
1984	Augie Garrido, CS-Fullerton	1990	Steve Webber, Georgia	1996	Skip Bertman, LSU
1985	Ron Polk, Mississippi St.	1991	Jim Hendry, Creighton		
1986	Skip Bertman, LSU & Dave Snow, Loyola-CA	1992	Andy Lopez, Pepperdine		

All-Time Winningest Coaches

Coaches active in 1996 in **bold** type.

Top 10 Winning Percentage

(Minimum 10 years in Division I)

		Yrs	W	L	T	Pct
1	John Barry	40	619	147	6	.806
2	W.J. Disch	29	465	115	0	.802
3	**Cliff Gustafson**	29	1466	377	2	.795
4	Harry Carlson	17	143	41	0	.777
5	**Gene Stephenson**	19	1058	321	3	.767
6	**Gary Ward**	19	953	313	1	.753
7	George Jacobs	11	76	25	0	.752
	Bobby Winkles	13	524	173	0	.752
9	Frank Sancet	23	831	283	8	.744
10	**Mike Martin**	17	918	312	3	.726

Top 10 Victories

		Yrs	W	L	T	Pct
1	**Cliff Gustafson**	29	**1466**	377	2	.795
2	Rod Dedeaux	45	**1332**	571	11	.699
3	Ron Fraser	30	**1271**	438	9	.742
	Al Ogletree	40	**1187**	689	1	.633
5	Bobo Brayton	33	**1162**	523	8	.690
6	Bill Wilhelm	36	**1161**	536	10	.683
7	**Jack Stallings**	36	**1173**	711	5	.622
8	**Augie Garrido**	28	**1152**	523	7	.687
9	**Chuck Hartman**	37	**1138**	559	3	.670
10	Jim Brock	23	**1100**	440	0	.714

Other NCAA Champions

Division II

Multiple winner: Florida Southern (8); Cal Poly Pomona (3); CS-Northridge, Jacksonville St., Tampa, Troy St., UC-Irvine and UC-Riverside (2).

Year		Year		Year		Year	
1968	Chapman, CA	1976	Cal Poly Pomona	1984	CS-Northridge	1992	Tampa
1969	Illinois St.	1977	UC-Riverside	1985	Florida Southern	1993	Tampa
1970	CS-Northridge	1978	Florida Southern	1986	Troy St., AL	1994	Central Missouri St.
1971	Florida Southern	1979	Valdosta St., GA	1987	Troy St., AL	1995	Florida Southern
1972	Florida Southern	1980	Cal Poly Pomona	1988	Florida Southern	1996	Kennesaw St., GA
1973	UC-Irvine	1981	Florida Southern	1989	Cal Poly SLO		
1974	UC-Irvine	1982	UC-Riverside	1990	Jacksonville St., AL		
1975	Florida Southern	1983	Cal Poly Pomona	1991	Jacksonville St., AL		

Division III

Multiple winner: Marietta (3); CS-Stanislaus, Eastern Conn. St., Glassboro St., Ithaca, Montclair St. and Wm. Paterson, NJ (2).

Year		Year		Year		Year	
1976	CS-Stanislaus	1982	Eastern Conn. St.	1988	Ithaca, NY	1994	Wisconsin-Oshkosh
1977	CS-Stanislaus	1983	Marietta, OH	1989	NC-Wesleyan	1995	La Verne, CA
1978	Glassboro St., NJ	1984	Ramapo, NJ	1990	Eastern Conn. St.	1996	Wm. Paterson, NJ
1979	Glassboro St., NJ	1985	Wisconsin-Oshkosh	1991	Southern Maine		
1980	Ithaca, NY	1986	Marietta, OH	1992	Wm. Paterson, NJ		
1981	Marietta, OH	1987	Monclair St., NJ	1993	Montclair St., NJ		

Wide World Photos

Nebraska football coach **Tom Osborne** stands between his two national championship trophies, looking a bit dazed by what it takes to get to the top and stay there.

COLLEGE FOOTBALL

by Mark Blaudschun

Osborne Again

The first season of the bowl alliance delivered a second national championship to Tom Osborne's Nebraska Cornhuskers.

Can you say dynasty? Can you say Nebraska? Can you say controversy? If you can, you'll have yourself a headline news version of the 1995 college football season.

Oh, there were other plots along the way, just as there always are. Northwestern won the hearts and minds of underdog lovers by going 10-1 and earning a trip to the Rose Bowl. Miami and Alabama, two of the power brokers in the game, stayed home in the post season because the NCAA said so.

And the sport, so often looking like a confused child lost in a department store, finally brought some semblance of order to its post season system by setting up a bowl alliance that actually let the top teams in the country—this year No. 1 Nebraska and No. 2 Florida—play each other in the Fiesta Bowl.

But more about those story lines later. The main plot was Nebraska, which clearly established itself as the team of the 1990's by playing in its third consecutive national championship game and winning back to back national championships, the first team to do that since Alabama turned the trick in 1978 and 1979.

If the Huskers' ride was smooth, it would be a nice story, but lacking something. After all, how often can you talk about Nebraska racing through its Big Eight season unbeaten and winning a bowl game for the title? Been there, done that.

The meat of this story would come from off-field activities because from essentially the start of the season, the Huskers established themselves as not only America's most dominating college football team, but perhaps America's Most Wanted team.

The problem was Lawrence Phillips, the Huskers' spectacular tailback who began and ended his season playing football, but spent six weeks during the season on the sidelines, courtesy of a suspension he received after assaulting his former girlfriend, a Nebraska women's basketball player. Osborne's immediate reaction was like the rest of the country—outrage. The

Mark Blaudschun has been the national college football and basketball writer for *The Boston Globe* since 1990.

Mike Powell/Allsport

Nebraska QB **Tommie Frazier** runs all over Florida in the second quarter of the Fiesta Bowl. Frazier's outstanding but injury-plagued college football career was enough to land him a pro contract. In Canada.

incident might have quieted down if Osborne had followed his original plan of kicking Phillips off the team.

But Osborne, citing information that was unavailable to the general public and feeling a sense of obligation to help his star player while everyone else was condemning him, changed direction. Instead of booting Phillips off the team, Osborne merely suspended him. And six weeks after his suspension began, Phillips was back on the roster, remorseful and grateful for another chance.

If that had been the only incident, Nebraska's image of being squeaky clean might have survived. But all of a sudden, the police blotter seemed to be full of Nebraska players. Tailbacks Damon Benning and James Sims were arrested after arguments with former girlfriends, although the charges against Benning were quickly dropped. Receiver Riley Washington was charged with attempted second-degree murder, and cornerback Tyrone Williams was faced with a weapons charge. Defensive tackle Christian Peter had several brushes with the law.

(In fact, Peter's antics (eight arrests in six years that included charges of public urination and third-degree sexual assault) were deemed so odious that the New England Patriots drafted him in the fifth round and then rescinded their rights to him a few days later. No other NFL team bothered to claim him and his football playing days seem over.)

Back in Lincoln, the Nebraska reaction was to circle the wagons. Osborne said the national media was over-playing the stories, arguing that if Nebraska wasn't such a good team, no one would really be following the off-the-field incidents.

If the Huskers were less of a team, it might have been a problem. But nothing could stop them. Not their non-conference schedule. Not Colorado, Kansas or Kansas State, each of whom made a little bit of noise about moving the Huskers out as the top force in the Big Eight. And not the national media, which kept bringing up the Lawrence Phillips case.

All Nebraska did was win. Every week. They averaged 52 points per game and beat their opponents by an average of 39 points. With quarterback Tommie Frazier back for his senior season, the Huskers didn't even miss Phillips. They just ran their offense with other players, other bodies. Nebraska started the season as national champion and ended it the same way. While the Huskers were rolling along, other stories were developing, each with its own little twist.

The biggest change was the bowl system. With a new bowl alliance, which included the Fiesta, Sugar and Orange bowls, the conference tie-ins of past years no longer existed. Excluding the Pac-10 and Big Ten conference winners, who play in the Rose Bowl, anybody could play anybody in the Fiesta Bowl game, which paid out $8.5 million per team for the right to have No. 1 vs. No. 2 for all the marbles.

In previous years, Nebraska, which won the Big Eight title, could not have played Florida, which won the SEC title. The Huskers would have gone to the Orange Bowl, and the Gators would have gone to the Sugar Bowl. More on that later.

The season began with the Kickoff and Pigskin Classics on August 26 and 27 respectively. While Michigan beat Virginia in a thrilling Pigskin, people were watching the Kickoff more closely. Since the last two winners of the Kickoff Classic (Florida State and Nebraska) had gone on to win the national title, Ohio State's 38-6 rout of Boston College seemed like a good omen for the Buckeyes.

And it looked like the trend might hold as Ohio State climbed steadily in the polls, winning each week. Going into their final regular season game against Michigan, the Buckeyes were a solid No. 2 behind Nebraska, with unbeaten Florida No. 3.

Purple in Pasadena

It started in September and never really diminished. One upset. Then another. Then another. And another. The national championship in college football may have belonged once again to Nebraska, but the STORY of the year was Northwestern.

Opening weekend. In South Bend. Notre Dame vs. Northwestern. Just another wild Irish romp, the kind Notre Dame had been regularly putting on the Mildcats since the days when Ara Parseghian was still coaching in Evanston.

Consider: The Wildcats were picked to finish 10th in the 11 team Big Ten, ahead of only Minnesota. They hadn't had a winning season since 1971. They hadn't been to a bowl game since 1949.

But Gary Barnett knew that would change. Maybe not in this particular game, but certainly in this particular year. "I thought we would be decent," said Barnett, long after the Wildcats had stunned the college world by beating not only Notre Dame, but Michigan and Penn State. All in the same season. "I thought we had the right chemistry with this group of kids."

Chemistry, shmemistry. The Wildcats had the right talent. From running back Darnell Autry to quarterback Steve Schnur to a defense that made play after play.

The irony of it all was that their only regular season loss came against Miami of Ohio. At home. And after they seemed to have the game well in hand only to squander it with a bad punt snap inside their own 5 yard line, which set up a game-winning field goal for Miami.

That was on Sept. 16th, two weeks after their win over Notre Dame and everyone tucked the Wildcats into the discard pile as one of those one-week upset wonders.

Certainly, the oddsmakers did. In nearly every game the remainder of the season, the Wildcats were underdogs. But all they did was win. They went to Michigan and shocked everyone by winning there. They came home a couple of weeks later and beat Penn State.

And when Michigan stunned unbeaten Ohio State in the final game of the regular

Wide World Photos

Northwestern head coach **Gary Barnett** watches 1996 Rose Bowl action from the sidelines. Despite this loss, Barnett presided over the complete resurrection of the Wildcat football program in 1995.

season, the impossible had happened. Northwestern was 8-0 in its conference. As Barnett promised when he took over the seemingly dead-end job five years ago, "I'm going to bring the purple to Pasadena." Northwestern was heading to the Rose Bowl.

It was all so new. Recruits coming to town in December and the Wildcats were still practicing. Press conferences and lots of media days.

Chicago went wild. When the Wildcats left for Pasadena for their Rose Bowl date with USC, cameras followed them onto the runway. As the team plane was loading up, another plane was landing and unloading its passengers. One photographer looked over, saw the passengers getting off the plane and returned to the Wildcats. "It's only Michael (Jordan)," said the photographer, concentrating on getting pictures of Barnett and his players.

Pasadena was indeed purple for a week. And right up until game time, the town and the Rose Bowl seemed to belong to Northwestern, but then USC went out and spoiled it by outgunning the Wildcats.

In a game which had the drama of a national championship, the Wildcats and Trojans traded touchdowns for almost four quarters. Could the impossible dream season end with a Rose Bowl victory?

No. USC held on and pulled away for a 41-32 victory. As proof of how magical this season was for Northwestern, there was even a possibility that this loss could be overturned due to Pac-10 and NCCA player eligibility investigations

Still, the 1995 dream season was over. Northwestern was still 10-2. Still the Big Ten champion. Still the Cinderella team of the season, the most surprising story of the year in college football.

To show how far the Wildcats had come, Barnett was courted heavily by Georgia, UCLA and Rutgers. He turned them all down and signed a long term extension to stay at Northwestern.

Small wonder. The Wildcats have 19 of 22 starters returning.

When asked why he chose to stay, Barnett smiled. "We're still building," he said. "This is a good place. Why would you want to be anywhere else?" ❑

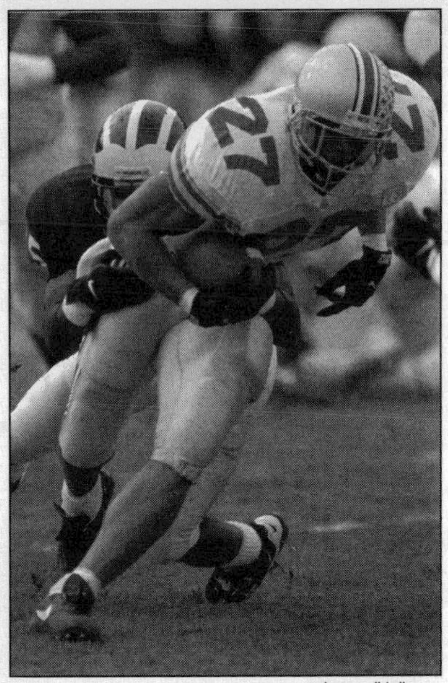

Mike Powell/Allsport

Ohio State's Heisman trophy winner **Eddie George** will carry the ball this year for the Houston/Nashville entry of the NFL.

It seemed like another controversy was brewing over No. 1 even with a bowl alliance in place because if No.2 Ohio State won the Big Ten it would play in the Rose, not the Fiesta Bowl. But then the Buckeyes were upset by Michigan, 31-23 in the final game of their regular season, a defeat which allowed Florida to slide into the No. 2 spot and set up a No. 1 vs. No. 2 game against the Huskers.

For the Buckeyes it was a bittersweet season at best. In one afternoon, they saw their chances of the Big Ten title, Rose Bowl bid and an unbeaten season all evaporate. But they did get solace when tailback Eddie George won the Heisman Trophy over Tommie Frazier and Florida's Danny Wuerffel, in what had been one of the most unpredictable Heisman races in years.

Neither the Buckeyes, nor Penn State, nor Michigan, the three favorites to win the Big Ten was the team of the year in that conference. That role belonged to once lowly Northwestern, which beat Notre Dame in its opener and never looked back until it was in the Rose Bowl for the first time in 47 years. They were also celebrating in Florida as well, as the Gators rolled through the SEC season unbeaten, winning their third consecutive SEC crown.

Perhaps the most startling game of the Gators' regular season was their meeting with Tennessee in Gainesville on Sept. 16. Trailing 30-14 near the end of the first half, the Gator offense, led by Wuerffel, who set an NCAA passing efficiency record, roared back for an astounding 62-37 victory. Wuerffel took only 24 minutes to get the Gators 48 unanswered points in a victory which clearly established the Gators as the No. 1 team in the SEC. Tennessee never lost again, though, and finished their best season in years by beating Ohio State in the Citrus Bowl and earning the number three spot in the AP and number two in the USA Today/CNN Coaches Poll.

Perhaps the unluckiest team in college football was Virginia. The Cavs, began their season by losing in the last second to Michigan in the Pigskin Classic. Then they lost to Texas on the last play of the game when Longhorn kicker Phil Dawson hit a 50 yard field goal into the wind for a 17-16 Texas victory. Then, on a Thursday night ESPN game against unbeaten and No. 1 Florida State, Virginia, which had built a 10 point half-time lead, was hanging on to a 33-28 lead over the Seminoles.

Florida State, which had rarely been behind in ACC games, and had never lost one, was staging a drive down field for the go-ahead and potential winning touchdown. With the clock ticking off the final seconds of another close Virginia game, Florida State's Warrick Dunn went from the Virginia six to the goal line before he was stopped by Virginia linebacker Anthony Poindexter and safety Adrian Blum a few inches short of the end zone. The loss to Virginia knocked the Seminoles out of the No. 1 spot and again made Coach Bobby Bowden's team a bridesmaid in the national championship derby. After the game, Virginia coach George Welsh said "I couldn't see the goal line and I thought, 'Oh, God, it's going to happen again.'"

Alas, it did, sort of. In their final regular season game against Virginia Tech, the Cavs trailed 30-29 with 47 seconds left. But then Tech cornerback Antonio Banks intercepted a Mike Groh pass and returned it 65 yards for the game-clinching touchdown in a 36-29 victory, thereby robbing Virginia of the chance to *win* a game on the last play.

While the Cavaliers were living on the edge all season, Notre Dame seemed to go over the edge a few times and kept coming back. The season began with a disaster—a home loss to Northwestern—and got worse. After five games, the Irish were 3-2, out of the national championship race, which was bad enough. But Notre Dame had other problems.

Coach Lou Holtz had been feeling worse than his team after the Northwestern game. Not only were his spirits low, but he just didn't feel right. He didn't have his usual pep. And he had a tingling sensation in his legs that would not go away. Holtz, not the type of guy to let things go unchecked, went to the doctor for a series of tests. The initial tests didn't reveal much, but sent some ominous warnings. "They came up with 19 things," said Holtz, later. "And 18 of them were fatal."

Luckily for Holtz, the other one was serious, but not life-threatening. A bulging disc in his back was bad enough for Holtz to have surgery, which was performed in mid-September at the Mayo Clinic. Three weeks later, Holtz was back on the sidelines for the Notre Dame-Ohio State game in Columbus.

The doctors had told Holtz that four to six weeks would be a more prudent course of action. But after receiving assurances from the doctor that he was not jeopardizing his health and being careful to avoid any contact with anyone on the sideline, Holtz gave it a shot. The experiment failed. Notre Dame lost to Ohio State and Holtz was exhausted. He coached for the next month from the press box and let defensive coordinator Bob Davie take the reins. Remarkably, the Irish bounced back. They won their last six games and earned an Orange Bowl bid against Florida State.

The theme of the year in the Southwest Conference was nostalgia. After 81 years, the once mighty SWC was closing its doors as a football conference, its members auctioned off to places like the Big Twelve, the Western Athletic Conference and something called Conference USA.

For the record, the final game in SWC history was played between Houston and Rice, with Houston pulling out an 18-17 win. So much for the conference which produced five Heisman winners and several volumes of lore, dating back to the days of Sammy Baugh and Bobby Layne and continuing through the time of such star players as Earl Campbell, Eric Dickerson and Craig James.

Somehow it was fitting that proud and mighty Texas, long the marquee team for the conference, won the final title, edging out Texas A&M, which began the season with plans to contend for the national championship and a Heisman Trophy candidate in running back Leeland McElroy. The Aggies received neither prize as a loss to Colorado in September effectively eliminated them from the national championship race and McElroy never quite had the year everyone expected.

The college football season saw other disappointments in other storied settings. Miami and Alabama, two of the premier programs in the country, both went on probation. The Crimson Tide argued that their

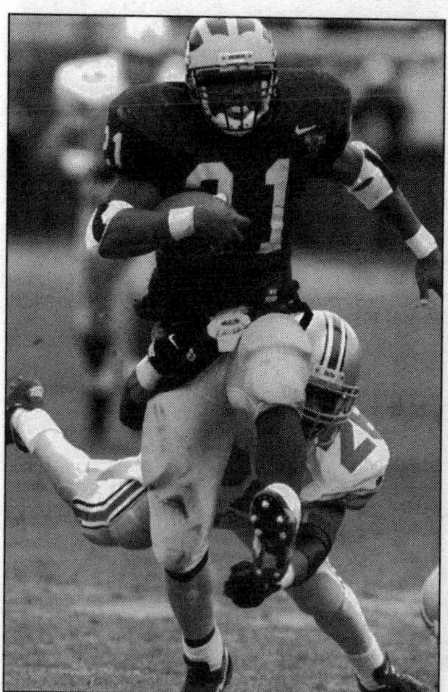

Wide World Photos

Michigan's **Tshimanga Biakabutuka** set a school record with 1,703 rushing yards in 1995. Here he gets a few of his career-high 313 yards against Ohio State.

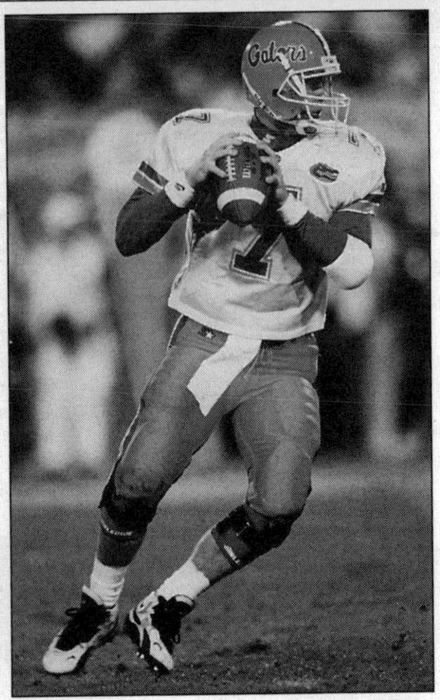

Mike Powell/Allsport

In 1995, quarterback **Danny Wuerffel** led Florida to its third straight SEC championship.

sanctions were too severe and actually won reductions on appeal. The Hurricanes accepted their probation and prepared for next year. Unfortunately for coach Butch Davis, Miami still suffers from a reputation as a program out of control. In June '96, three Hurricane players were charged with burglary and battery after they attacked Miami track star Maxwell Voce.

On the coaching front, Georgia fired Ray Goff, and UCLA's Terry Donahue quit to take a job as CBS' color commentator.

As the season went down the stretch, Florida, Ohio State and Nebraska emerged as the leading contenders for the national championship. Ohio State self-destructed with its loss to Michigan, but Florida and Nebraska each rolled through the regular season unbeaten. The Gators looked legitimate, not only going unbeaten in a tough SEC Eastern Division race, but then beating Arkansas easily in the SEC title game. This turn of events set up the '95 Gators as one of the best teams in Florida history and potentially one of the greatest teams of all time.

With the bowl alliance in place, the Fiesta Bowl became a venue for a true national championship game, contrasting two teams with different philosophies and styles. The brute strength of Tom Osborne's Nebraska vs. the "Fun and Gun" passing offense of Florida coach Steve Spurrier.

But the game turned into a Super Bowl-style rout as Nebraska quickly and convincingly thrashed the Gators with an awesome display of sheer power. Huskers quarterback Tommie Frazier was the unquestioned star as he turned in one of the most dominating offensive performances in the history of any bowl game. On one play at least six Gators had clean and direct chances to bring Frazier down and couldn't do it. It was the run of the year and might have prompted at least one NFL team to give him a shot. Unfortunately, Frazier's history of blood clots was too much to ignore and the draft ended with Frazier not in any team's plans. In June of 1996, Frazier signed a one year contract with the Montreal Alouettes and set his sights on the 1997 NFL season.

By the half, the Huskers were well on their way to a 62-24 victory, one of the most one-sided national championship games in history. But that didn't diminish the satisfaction that Osborne had in winning back-to-back national titles. Osborne said it was the best team he has had in his 23 seasons. "It was probably the most complete football team we've had," he said. "We didn't have a close call all year."

Osborne praised his team's talent and its makeup. "This team has shown great character all year," he said. "They were very focused on what they had to do."

With two in a row accomplished, the focus is now on three, which has never been done. That alone should be enough to unite the embattled Cornhuskers for another run at the history books.

Sadly, as Osborne prepared for the upcoming season, the Nebraska program was jarred by the death of QB Brook Berringer in a plane crash on April 18. Berringer's story was a positive one in a sea of bad press. Said Osborne, "If you had somebody you wanted your son to be like, it would be Brook." Even though Berringer's playing days were over, three in a row got a lot harder that day. ❐

THE SEASON IN REVIEW

1995-1996

TOP 25 • BOWLS • STANDINGS

Final AP Top 25 Poll

oted on by panel of 62 sportswriters & broadcasters and released on Jan. 3, 1996, following the Fiesta Bowl: winning team eceives the Bear Bryant Trophy, given since 1983; first place votes in parentheses, records, total points (based on 25 for 1st, 4 for 2nd, etc.) bowl game result, head coach and career record, preseason rank (released on Aug. 11, 1995) and final egular season rank (released Dec. 3, 1995).

		Final Record	Points	Bowl Game	Head Coach	Aug. 11 Rank	Dec. 3 Rank
1	Nebraska (62)	12-0-0	1550	won Fiesta	Tom Osborne (23 yrs: 231-47-3)	2	1
2	Florida	12-1-0	1474	lost Fiesta	Steve Spurrier (9 yrs: 81-26-2)	5	2
3	Tennessee	11-1-0	1428	won Citrus	Phillip Fulmer (4 yrs: 32-7-1)	8	4†
4	Florida St	10-2-0	1311	won Orange	Bobby Bowden (30 yrs: 259-81-4)	1	8
5	Colorado	10-2-0	1309	won Cotton	Rick Neuheisel (1st year: 10-2-0)	13	7
6	Ohio St	11-2-0	1161	lost Citrus	John Cooper (19 yrs: 146-69-6)	12	4†
7	Kansas St	10-2-0	1147	won Holiday	Bill Snyder (7 yrs: 46-33-1)	29	10
8	Northwestern	10-2-0	1124	lost Rose	Gary Barnett (6 yrs: 26-37-2)	NR	3
9	Kansas	10-2-0	1029	won Aloha	Glen Mason (10 yrs: 55-57-1)	NR	11
0	Virginia Tech	10-2-0	1015	won Sugar	Frank Beamer (15 yrs: 93-72-4)	24†	13
1	Notre Dame	9-3-0	931	lost Orange	Lou Holtz (26 yrs: 208-92-7)	9	6
2	USC	9-2-1	886	won Rose	John Robinson (10 yrs: 92-24-4)	7	17
3	Penn St.	9-3-0	867	won Outback	Joe Paterno (30 yrs: 278-72-3)	4	15
4	Texas	10-2-1	724	lost Sugar	John Mackovic (11 yrs: 73-52-3)	18	9
5	Texas A&M	9-3-0	661	won Alamo	R.C. Slocum (7 yrs:68-15-2)	3	19
6	Virginia	9-4-0	603	won Peach	George Welsh (23 yrs: 153-109-4)	17	18
7	Michigan	9-4-0	474½	lost Alamo	Lloyd Carr (1st year: 9-4-0)	14	14
8	Oregon	9-3-0	416	lost Cotton	Mike Bellotti (6 yrs: 30-28-2)	26†	12
9	Syracuse	9-3-0	382	won Gator	Paul Pasqualoni (10 yrs: 76-32-1)	38	26
0	Miami-FL	8-3-0	352	on probation	Butch Davis (1st year: 8-3-0)	11	22
1	Alabama	8-3-0	313	on probation	Gene Stallings (13 yrs: 87-58-2)	10	21
2	Auburn	8-4-0	276	lost Outback	Terry Bowden (12 yrs: 92-41-2)	6	16
3	Texas Tech	9-3-0	197	won Copper	Spike Dykes (9 yrs:56-47-1)	35	28
4	Toledo	11-0-1	170	won Las Vegas	Gary Pinkel (5 yrs: 34-19-3)	NR	25
5	Iowa	8-4-0	133½	won Sun	Hayden Fry (34 yrs: 213-162-10)	46†	NR

ther teams receiving votes: 26. **East Carolina** (9-3-0, 111 points, won Liberty); 27. **Washington** (7-4-1, 36 pts, lost Sun); 8. **LSU** (7-4-1, 33 pts, won Independence); 29. **North Carolina** (7-5-0, 16 pts, won Carquest); 30. **Clemson** (8-4-0, 12 pts, st Gator); 31. **Arkansas** (8-5-0, 8 pts, lost Carquest).

AP Preseason and Final Regular Season Polls

First place votes in parentheses.

Top 25 (Aug. 11, 1995)

		Pts			Pts
1	Florida St. (31)	1498	14	Michigan	642
2	Nebraska (15)	1439	15	Oklahoma	527
3	Texas A&M (6)	1366	16	UCLA	517
4	Penn St. (1)	1308	17	Virginia	516
5	Florida (6)	1299	18	Texas	368
6	Auburn (2)	1238	19	Arizona	337
7	USC	1151	20	North Carolina	290
8	Tennessee (1)	1024	21	Wisconsin	270
9	Notre Dame	1011	22	Boston College	263
0	Alabama	974	23	West Virginia	215
1	Miami-FL	893	24	Virginia Tech	196
2	Ohio St.	863	25	Washington	196
3	Colorado	689			

Top 25 (Dec. 3, 1995)

		Pts			Pts
1	Nebraska (50)	1538	14	Michigan	758
2	Florida (12)	1500	15	Penn St.	733
3	Northwestern	1413	16	Auburn	637
4	Ohio St.	1325	17	USC	536
5	Tennessee	1325	18	Virginia	420
6	Notre Dame	1203	19	Texas A&M	406
7	Colorado	1140	20	Washington	365
8	Florida St.	1128	21	Alabama	319
9	Texas	1105	22	Miami-FL	289
10	Kansas St.	963	23	Clemson	225
11	Kansas	833	24	Arkansas	111
12	Oregon	809	25	Toledo	86
13	Virginia Tech	801			

1995-96 Bowl Games

Listed by bowls matching highest-ranked teams as of final regular season AP poll (released Dec. 3, 1995). Alabama (No. 21 and Miami-FL (No. 22) were on probation and ineligible for postseason play. Attendance figures indicate tickets sold.

Bowl		Winner	Regular Season		Loser	Regular Season	Score	Date	Attendance
Fiesta	# 1	Nebraska	11-0-0	# 2	Florida	12-0-0	62-24	Jan. 2	79,864
Rose	#17	USC	8-2-1	# 3	Northwestern	10-1-0	41-32	Jan. 1	101,102
Citrus	# 4	Tennessee	11-1-0	# 4	Ohio St.	11-1-0	20-14	Jan. 1	70,797
Orange	# 8	Florida St.	9-2-0	# 6	Notre Dame	9-2-0	31-26	Jan. 1	72,198
Cotton	# 7	Colorado	9-2-0	#12	Oregon	9-2-0	38-6	Jan. 1	58,214
Sugar	#13	Virginia Tech	9-2-0	# 9	Texas	10-1-1	28-10	Dec. 31	70,283
Holiday	#10	Kansas St.	9-2-0		Colorado St.	8-3-0	54-21	Dec. 29	51,051
Aloha	#11	Kansas	9-2-0		UCLA	7-4-0	51-30	Dec. 25	41,112
Alamo	#19	Texas A&M	8-3-0	#14	Michigan	9-3-0	22-20	Dec. 28	64,597
Outback	#15	Penn St.	8-3-0	#16	Auburn	8-3-0	43-14	Jan. 1	65,313
Peach	#18	Virginia	8-4-0		Georgia	6-5-0	34-27	Dec. 30	70,825
Sun		Iowa	7-4-0	#20	Washington	7-3-1	38-18	Dec. 29	49,116
Gator		Syracuse	8-3-0	#23	Clemson	8-3-0	41-0	Jan. 1	45,202
Carquest		North Carolina	6-5-0	#24	Arkansas	8-4-0	20-10	Dec. 30	34,428
Las Vegas	#25	Toledo	10-0-1		Nevada	9-2-0	40-37 OT	Dec. 15	11,127
Copper		Texas Tech	8-3-0		Air Force	8-4-0	55-41	Dec. 27	41,004
Liberty		East Carolina	8-3-0		Stanford	7-3-1	19-13	Dec. 30	47,398
Independence		LSU	6-4-1		Michigan St.	6-4-1	45-26	Dec. 29	48,835

FAVORITES

Fiesta (Nebraska by 3½ points); **Rose** (USC by 3); **Citrus** (Ohio St. by 4½); **Orange** (Florida St. by 10½); **Cotton** (Colorad by 6½); **Sugar** (Texas by 2½); **Holiday** (Kansas St. by 9); **Aloha** (UCLA by 5); **Alamo** (Michigan by 5); **Outback** (Penn St. by 2½); **Peach** (Virginia by 6½); **Sun** (Washington by 5); **Gator** (Clemson by 2½); **Carquest** (North Carolina by 2); **Las Vega** (Even); **Copper** (Texas Tech by 4); **Liberty** (Stanford by 4); **Independence** (LSU by 6½).

PER TEAM PAYOUTS

Tostitos Fiesta ($8.58 million); **FedEx Orange** and **Nokia Sugar** ($8.33 million); **Rose** ($8.2 million); **CompUSA Florida Citru** ($3 million); **Cotton** ($2.5 million); **Plymouth Holiday** ($1.7 million); **Outback** ($1.5 million); **Toyota Gator** ($1.3 million **Peach** ($1.13 million); **Builders Square Alamo** and **Carquest** ($1 million); **Sun** ($900,000); **Jeep Eagle Aloha** ($800,000 **Weiser Lock Copper**, **Poulan/Weed Eater Independence** and **St. Jude Liberty** ($750,000); **Las Vegas** ($175,000).

Final Bowl Alliance Poll

Combined point totals of the final regular season AP media and USA Today/CNN coaches' polls to help determine bowl match-ups. Polls were released Dec. 3, 1995. Alabama (No. 21) and Miami-FL (No. 22) were officially put on NCAA probation Nov. 30 and Dec. 1, respectively, and became ineligible for the final regular season coaches' poll. AP point totals for teams on probation were doubled in the Alliance poll.

		AP Poll No.	AP Poll Pts	Coaches No.	Coaches Pts	Total Pts
1	Nebraska	1	(1538)	1	(1543)	3081
2	Florida	2	(1500)	2	(1494)	2994
3	Northwestern	3	(1413)	3	(1412)	2825
4	Tennessee	4t	(1325)	4	(1315)	2640
5	Ohio St.	4t	(1325)	5	(1305)	2630
6	Texas	9	(1105)	6	(1213)	2318
7	Colorado	7	(1140)	7	(1140)	2280
8	Notre Dame	6	(1203)	9	(1068)	2271
9	Florida St.	8	(1128)	8	(1087)	2215
10	Kansas St.	10	(963)	10	(963)	1926
11	Virginia Tech	13	(801)	11	(888)	1689
12	Oregon	12	(809)	12	(847)	1656
13	Kansas	11	(833)	13	(805)	1638
14	Michigan	14	(758)	14	(676)	1434
15	Penn St.	15	(733)	16	(651)	1384
16	Auburn	16	(637)	15	(662)	1299
17	USC	17	(536)	17	(557)	1093
18	Texas A&M	19	(406)	18	(508)	914
19	Virginia	18	(420)	19	(427)	847
20	Washington	20	(365)	20	(360)	725
21	Alabama	21	(319)		—	638
22	Miami-FL	22	(289)		—	578
23	Clemson	23	(225)	21	(344)	569
24	Syracuse	26	(57)	22	(223)	280
25	Arkansas	24	(111)	23	(143)	254

Bowl MVPs

Most Valuable Player, Offensive and Defensive Players of th Game, and Team MVP selections in all 18 bowl games fo lowing the 1995 season.

			Pos
Alamo	Off—	Kyle Bryant, Texas A&M	PK
	Def—	Keith Mitchell, Texas A&M	LB
Aloha	Team—	Karim Abdul-Jabbar, UCLA	RB
	Team—	Mark Williams, Kansas	QB
Carquest	MVP—	Leon Johnson, N. Carolina	RB
Citrus	MVP—	Jay Graham, Tennessee	RB
Copper	MVP—	Byron Hanspard, Texas Tech	RB
Cotton	Off—	Herchell Troutman, Colorado	RB
	Def—	Marcus Washington, Colorado	DB
Fiesta	Off—	Tommie Frazier, Nebraska	QB
	Def—	Michael Booker, Nebraska	DB
Gator	MVP—	Donovan McNabb, Syracuse	QB
Holiday	Off—	Brian Kavanaugh, Kansas St.	QB
	Def—	Mario Smith, Kansas St.	DB
Independence	Off—	Kevin Faulk, LSU	RB
	Def—	Gabe Northern, LSU	DE
Las Vegas	Team—	Wasean Tait, Toledo	RB
	Team—	Alex Van Dyke, Nevada	WR
Liberty	MVP—	Kwame Ellis, Stanford	DB
Orange	Team—	Andre Cooper, Florida St.	WR
	Team—	Derrick Mays, Notre Dame	WR
Outback	MVP—	Bobby Engram, Penn St.	WR
Peach	Off —	Tiki Barber, Virginia	RB
		& Hines Ward, Georgia	QB
	Def—	Skeet Jones, Virginia	LB
		& Whit Marshall, Georgia	LB
Rose	MVP—	Keyshawn Johnson, USC	WR
Sun	MVP—	Sedrick Shaw, Iowa	RB
Sugar	MVP—	Bryan Still, Va. Tech	WR

Number 1 vs. Number 2

Nebraska and Florida, who ranked first and second in the final regular season AP poll, met in the Fiesta Bowl on Jan. 2, 1996, to decide the national championship for the 1995 season. Opponents' records and AP rank listed below are day of game.

Nebraska Cornhuskers (12-0-0)

Date	AP Rank	Opponent	Result
Aug. 31	#2	at Oklahoma St. (0-0-0)	64-21
Sept. 9	#2	at Michigan St. (0-0-0)	50-10
Sept. 16	#2	Arizona St. (1-1-0)	77-28
Sept. 23	#2	Pacific (1-2-0)	49-7
Sept. 30	#2	Washington St. (2-1-0)	35-21
Oct. 7	#2	OPEN DATE	
Oct. 14	#2	Missouri (2-3-0)	57-0
Oct. 21	#2	#8 Kansas St. (6-0-0)	49-25
Oct. 28	#2	at #7 Colorado (6-1-0)	44-21
Nov. 4	#1	Iowa St. (3-5-0)	73-14
Nov. 11	#1	at #10 Kansas (8-1-0)	41-3
Nov. 18	#1	OPEN DATE	
Nov. 24	#1	Oklahoma (5-4-1)	37-0
Jan. 2	#1	vs. #2 Florida† (12-0-0)	62-24

†Fiesta Bowl (at Tempe)

Note: Four of the 11 teams on the Cornhuskers' 1995 regular season schedule went to bowl games— Colorado (won Cotton), Kansas (won Aloha), Kansas St. (won Holiday) and Michigan St. (lost Independence).

Regular Season Statistics

Passing (5 Att)	Att	Cmp	Pct.	Yds	TD	Rate
Tommie Frazier	163	92	56.4	1362	17	156.2
Brook Berringer	51	26	51.0	252	0	92.5
Matt Turman	12	4	33.3	73	1	78.6

Interceptions: Frazier 4, Turman 2.

Top Receivers	No	Yds	Avg	Long	TD
Clester Johnson	22	367	16.7	61	2
Reggie Baul	17	304	17.9	76-td	2
Mark Gilman	16	256	16.0	35-td	1
John Vedral	14	272	19.4	38-td	5
Brendan Holbein	14	151	10.8	29-td	1
Ahman Green	12	102	8.5	35	3

Top Rushers	Car	Yds	Avg	Long	TD
Ahman Green	141	1086	7.7	64-td	13
Tommie Frazier	97	604	6.2	29-td	14
Lawrence Phillips	71	547	7.7	80-td	9
Clinton Childs	55	431	7.8	65-td	3
Damon Benning	63	407	6.5	62	4
Jeff Makovicka	63	371	5.9	54	1
James Sims	30	270	9.0	80-td	3

Most Touchdowns	TD	Run	Rec	Ret	Pts
Ahman Green	16	13	3	0	96
Tommie Frazier	14	14	0	0	86*
Lawrence Phillips	9	9	0	0	54
Jon Vedral	7	1	5	0	42
Damon Benning	4	4	0	0	24

*Includes two 2-pt. conversion runs.

Kicking	FG/Att	Lg	PAT/Att	Pts
Kris Brown	13/16	47	58/61	99*
Ted Retzlaff	0/0	0	11/11	11

*Includes one 2-pt. conversion catch.

Punting	No	Yds	Long	Blk	Avg
Jesse Kosch	27	1088	74	0	40.3
Bill Lafleur	1	30	30	0	30.0

Most Interceptions	
Michael Booker	3
Terrell Farley	3

Most Sacks	
Jaren Tomich	10
Terrell Farley	5

Florida Gators (12-1-0)

Date	AP Rank	Opponent	Result
Sept. 2	#5	vs. Houston (0-0-0)	45-21
Sept. 9	#5	at Kentucky (0-1-0)	42-7
Sept. 16	#4	vs. #8 Tennessee (2-0-0)	62-37
Sept. 23	#4	OPEN DATE	
Sept. 30	#3	vs. Mississippi (2-1-0)	28-10
Oct. 7	#3	at #21 LSU (3-1-1)	28-10
Oct. 14	#3	at #7 Auburn (4-1-0)	49-38
Oct. 21	#3	OPEN DATE	
Oct. 28	#3	at Georgia (5-3-0)	52-17
Nov. 4	#3	vs. N. Illinois (3-5-0)	58-20
Nov. 11	#3	at S. Carolina (4-4-1)	63-7
Nov. 18	#3	vs. Vanderbilt (2-7-0)	38-7
Nov. 25	#3	vs. #6 Florida St. (9-1-0)	35-24
Dec. 2	#2	# 23 Arkansas (8-3-0)*	34-3
Jan. 2	#2	vs #1 Nebraska† (11-0-0)	24-62

*SEC title game at Atlanta †Fiesta Bowl (at Tempe)

Note: Six of the 12 teams on the Gators' 1995 regular season schedule went to bowl games— Arkansas (lost Carquest), Auburn (lost Outback), Florida St. (won Orange), Georgia (lost Peach), LSU (won Independence) and Tennessee (won Citrus).

Regular Season Statistics

Passing (5 Att)	Att	Cmp	Pct.	Yds	TD	Rate
Danny Wuerffel	325	210	64.6	3266	35	178.4
Eric Kresser	112	65	58.0	995	12	164.2
B. Schottenheimer	15	10	66.7	61	1	122.8

Interceptions: Wuerffel 10, Kresser 2.

Top Receivers	No	Yds	Avg	Long	TD
Chris Doering	70	1045	14.9	40-td	17
Ike Hilliard	57	1008	17.7	74-td	15
Reidel Anthony	24	366	15.3	39-td	3
Elijah Williams	22	277	12.6	30	2
Terry Jackson	20	188	9.4	45	0
Jacquez Green	19	531	28.0	96-td	5

Top Rushers	Car	Yds	Avg	Long	TD
Elijah Williams	114	858	7.5	70-td	7
Terry Jackson	122	780	6.4	66	6
Fred Taylor	48	281	5.9	24	5
Ernie Dubose	26	107	4.1	14	1
Jacquez Green	7	93	13.3	42-td	1
Dwayne Mobley	22	62	2.8	14	0
Jerome Evans	12	40	3.3	15	1

Most Touchdowns	TD	Run	Rec	Ret	Pts
Chris Doering	17	0	17	0	102
Ike Hilliard	15	0	15	0	90
Elijah Williams	9	7	2	0	54
Terry Jackson	6	6	0	0	36
Jacquez Green	6	1	5	0	36

Kicking	FG/Att	Lg	PAT/Att	Pts
Bart Edminston	6/12	47	71/71	89
Robby Stevenson	0/0	0	1/1	1
Matt Teague	0/0	0	0/1	0

Punting	No	Yds	Long	Blk	Avg
Robby Stevenson	33	1264	52	0	38.3
Matt Teague	1	33	33	0	33.0

Most Interceptions	
Michael Booker	3
Terrell Farley	3
Demetric Jackson	3
Lawrence Wright	3

Most Sacks	
Mark Campbell	4.8
Johnie Church	4.8

Fiesta Bowl

Tuesday, Jan. 2, 1996 at Sun Devil Stadium in Tempe, Ariz.

#1 **Nebraska** (Big Eight)	6	29	14	13—**62**
#2 **Florida** (SEC)	10	0	8	6—**24**

1st: FLA— Bart Edmiston 23-yd FG, 3:54. Drive: 55 yards in 11 plays. NEB— Lawrence Phillips 16-yd pass from Tommie Frazier (kick blocked), 6:50. Drive: 52 yards in 6 plays. FLA— Danny Wuerffel 1-yd run (Edmiston kick), 13:43. Drive: 54 yards in 12 plays.

2nd: NEB— Phillips 42-yd run (Kris Brown kick), 0:32. Drive: 71 yards in 5 plays. NEB— Safety (Jamel Williams tackled Wuerffel in end zone), 2:18. NEB— Ahman Green 1-yd run (Brown kick), 5:47. Drive: 51 yards in 7 plays. NEB— Brown 26-yd FG, 11:14. Drive: 33 yards in 9 plays. NEB— Michael Booker 42-yd interception return (Brown kick), 12:20. NEB— Brown 24-yd FG, 14:52. Drive: 59 yards in 8 plays.

3rd: NEB— Frazier 35-yd run (Brown kick), 12:39. Drive: 70 yards in 6 plays. FLA— Ike Hilliard 35-yd pass from Wuerffel (2-pt conversion, Reidel Anthony from Wuerffel), 14:08. Drive: 77 yards in 5 plays. NEB— Frazier 75-yd run (Brown kick), 14:59. Drive: 80 yards in 2 plays.

4th: NEB— Phillips 15-yd run (kick blocked), 6:35. Drive: 22 yards in 6 plays. NEB—Brook Berringer 1-yd run (Ted Retzlaff kick), 10:16. Drive: 53 yards in 5 plays. FLA— Anthony 93-yd kickoff return (pass failed), 10:29.

Favorite: Nebraska by 3½ **Attendance:** 79, 864
Field: Grass **Time:** 3:44
Weather: Clear, 58 degrees **TV Rating:** 18.8/31 share (CBS)

MVP: Tommie Frazier, Nebraska, QB

Team Statistics

	Nebraska	Florida
Touchdowns	8	3
Rushing	6	1
Passing	1	1
Kick returns	0	1
Interception returns	1	0
Safeties	1	0
Time of possession	35:17	24:43
First downs	27	15
Rushing	21	2
Passing	4	12
Penalties	2	1
3rd down efficiency	8-17	4-12
4th down efficiency	2-3	1-2
Total offense (net yards)	629	269
Plays	83	59
Average gain	7.6	4.6
Carries/yards (includ. sacks)	68/524	21/(-28)
Passing yards	105	297
Completions/attempts	6/15	20/38
Times sacked/yards lost	0/0	7/40
Return yardage	152	265
Punt returns/yards	4/14	1/8
Kickoff returns/yards	5/88	10/268
Interceptions/yards	3/50	2/5
Fumbles/lost	1/0	1/1
Penalties/yards	4/30	9/78
Punts/average	1/36	4/41
Punts blocked	0	0
PATs/attempts	6/8	2/3
Field goals/attempts	2/2	1/1

Individual Statistics

Nebraska

Passing	**Att**	**Cmp**	**Pct.**	**Yds**	**TD**	**Int**
Tommie Frazier	14	6	42.9	105	1	2
Lawrence Phillips	1	0	0.0	0	0	0
TOTAL	15	6	40.0	105	1	2

Receiving	**No**	**Yds**	**Avg**	**Long**	**TD**
Clester Johnson	2	43	21.5	36	0
Brendan Holbein	1	33	33.0	33	0
Lawrence Phillips	1	16	16.0	16-td	1
Jeff Makovicka	1	8	8.0	8	0
John Vedral	1	5	5.0	5	0
TOTAL	6	105	17.5	36	1

Rushing	**Car**	**Yds**	**Avg**	**Long**	**TD**
Tommie Frazier	16	199	12.4	75-td	2
Lawrence Phillips	25	165	6.6	42-td	2
Ahman Green	9	68	7.6	43	1
James Sims	2	35	17.5	32	0
Jeff Makovicka	6	32	5.3	13	0
Clinton Childs	3	14	4.7	7	0
Brian Schuster	1	4	4.0	4	0
Joel Makovicka	2	4	2.0	3	0
Damon Benning	1	3	3.0	3	0
Brook Berringer	1	1	1.0	1	1
Billy Legate	1	1	1.0	1	0
Matt Turman	1	-2	-2.0	-2	0
TOTAL	68	524	7.7	75-td	6

Field Goals	**20-29**	**30-39**	**40-49**	**50-59**	**Total**
Kris Brown	2-2	0-0	0-0	0-0	2-2

Punting	**No**	**Yds**	**Long**	**Blk**	**Avg**
Jesse Kosch	1	36	36	0	36.0

Punt Returns	**FC**	**Ret**	**Yds**	**Long**	**Avg**	**TD**
Octavius McFarlin	0	2	14	7	7.0	0
Damon Benning	0	1	0	0	0.0	0
Mike Fullman	0	1	0	0	0.0	0
TOTAL	0	4	14	7	3.5	0

Kickoff Returns	**No**	**Yds**	**Long**	**Avg**	**TD**
Clinton Childs	3	79	34	26.3	0
Tim Carpenter	1	5	5	5.0	0
Jon Hesse	1	4	4	4.0	0
TOTAL	5	88	34	17.6	0

Interceptions		**Sacks**	
Michael Booker	1	Terrell Farley	2
Eric Stokes	1	Five tied with one each.	
Tony Veland	1		

Florida

Passing	**Att**	**Cmp**	**Pct.**	**Yds**	**TD**	**Int**
Danny Wuerffel	31	17	54.8	255	1	3
Eric Kresser	7	3	42.9	42	0	0
TOTAL	38	20	52.6	297	1	3

Receiving	**No**	**Yds**	**Avg**	**Long**	**TD**
Chris Doering	8	123	15.4	30	0
Ike Hilliard	6	100	16.7	35-td	1
Reidel Anthony	2	40	20.0	26	0
Travis McGriff	2	19	9.5	10	0
Terry Jackson	1	10	10.0	10	0
Jerome Evans	1	5	5.0	5	0
TOTAL	20	297	14.9	35-td	1

Rushing	**Car**	**Yds**	**Avg**	**Long**	**TD**
Elijah Williams	6	6	1.0	3	0
Terry Jackson	4	4	1.0	3	0
Reidel Anthony	2	-1	-0.5	3	0
Danny Wuerffel	9	-37	-4-1	2	1
TOTAL	21	-28	-1.3	3	1

Field Goals	**20-29**	**30-39**	**40-49**	**50-59**	**Total**
Bart Edmiston	1-1	0-0	0-0	0-0	1-1

Punting	**No**	**Yds**	**Long**	**Blk**	**Avg**
Robby Stevenson	4	165	46	0	41.3

Punt Returns	**FC**	**Ret**	**Yds**	**Long**	**Avg**	**TD**
Octavius McFarlin	0	2	14	7	7.0	0
Reidel Anthony	0	1	-8	-8	-8.0	0

Kickoff Returns	**No**	**Yds**	**Long**	**Avg**	**TD**
Reidel Anthony	6	195	93-td	32.5	1
Jacquez Green	2	48	38	24.0	0
Ike Hilliard	2	25	23	12.5	0

Interceptions		**Sacks**
Takeo Brown	1	None.
Anthone Lott	1	

Other Final Division I-A Polls

USA Today/CNN Coaches Poll

Voted on by panel of 62 Division I-A head coaches; winning team receives the Sears Trophy (originally the McDonald's Trophy, 1991-93); first place votes in parentheses with total points (based on 25 for 1st, 24 for 2nd, etc.).

		Pts			Pts
1	Nebraska (62)	1550	14	Texas	768
2	Tennessee	1438	15	Texas A&M	703
3	Florida	1434	16	Syracuse	593
4	Colorado	1308	17	Virginia	585
5	Florida St.	1280	18	Oregon	441
6	Kansas St.	1129	19	Michigan	426
7	Northwestern	1121	20	Texas Tech	329
8	Ohio St.	1105	21	Auburn	292
9	Virginia Tech	1101	22	Iowa	205
10	Kansas	994	23	East Carolina	163
11	USC	898	24	Toledo	150
12	Penn St.	857	25	LSU	110
13	Notre Dame	813			

Other teams receiving votes: North Carolina (100 pts); Washington (98); Arkansas (54); Clemson (42); UCLA (22); Stanford (11); Colorado St. (9); Michigan St. (6); Fresno St. (5); Air Force , Baylor and Louisville (3); Georgia (1).

Teams on probation: Alabama and Miami-FL.

Winningest Teams of the 1990s

Division I-A schools with the best overall winning percentage from 1990-95, through the Jan. 1-2, 1996, bowl games.

National champions: 1990— Colorado (AP, FWAA, NFF) and Georgia Tech (UPI); 1991— Miami-FL (AP) and Washington (FWAA, NFF, USA Today/CNN); 1992— Alabama; 1993— Florida St; 1994— Nebraska; 1995— Nebraska.

		Overall Record	Bowls W-L-T	Overall Win Pct
1	Florida St.	64- 9-1	6-0-0	.872
2	Nebraska	63- 9-1	2-4-0	.870
3	Miami-FL	60-11-0	2-3-0	.845
4	Texas A&M	60-11-2	2-3-0	.836
5	Florida	61-13-1	2-3-0	.820
6	Colorado	57-12-4	4-2-0	.808
7	Penn St.	58-15-0	4-2-0	.795
8	Tennessee	56-15-2	4-2-0	.781
9	Notre Dame	55-16-2	3-3-0	.767
10	Washington	52-17-1	2-2-0	.750
11	Michigan	52-17-3	4-2-0	.743
12	Ohio St.	53-18-3	1-5-0	.736
13	Syracuse	49-19-3	4-0-0	.711
14	Alabama	52-22-0	4-1-0	.703
15	Auburn	46-19-3	1-1-0	.699
16	Bowling Green	44-19-4	2-0-0	.687
17	Virginia	48-23-1	2-3-0	.674
18	North Carolina	47-23-1	2-2-0	.669
19	BYU	49-24-2	1-3-1	.667
20	Clemson	46-23-1	2-2-0	.664
21	Toledo	43-21-3	1-0-0	.664
22	Kansas State	45-23-1	2-1-0	.659
23	Texas	44-24-2	1-2-0	.643
24	Western Michigan	41-23-2	0-0-0	.636
25	Oklahoma	42-24-3	2-1-0	.630
26	Fresno State	45-26-2	1-2-0	.630
27	N.C. State	44-27-1	2-3-0	.618
28	Iowa	42-27-2	1-2-1	.606
29	USC	42-27-4	3-2-0	.603
30	Air Force	44-30-0	2-2-0	.595

NFF/Hall of Fame Poll

Voted on by panel of 62 members of the National Football Foundation and College Hall of Fame; winning team receives the NFF's MacArthur Bowl, given since 1959; first place votes in parentheses with total points (based on 25 for 1st, 24 for 2nd, etc.).

		Pts			Pts
1	Nebraska (62)	1550	14	Texas	788
2	Florida	1447	15	Texas A&M	717
3	Tennessee	1436	16	Virginia	591
4	Florida St.	1308	17	Syracuse	508
5	Colorado	1284	18	Oregon	451
6	Northwestern	1177	19	Michigan	450
7	Ohio St.	1132	20	Auburn	297
8	Kansas St.	1114	21	Texas Tech	292
9	Virginia Tech	1027	22	Iowa	188
10	Kansas	966	23	East Carolina	177
11	USC	885	24	Toledo	113
12	Penn St.	872	25	Washington	111
13	Notre Dame	870			

Teams on probation: (and ineligible to receive votes): Alabama and Miami-FL.

FWAA Poll

Voted on by a five-man panel comprised of Bob Hammel of the *Bloomington* (Ind.) *Herald-Times*, Ed Joyce of ESPN, Blair Kerkhoff of *The Kansas City Star*, Ivan Maisel of *Newsday* and Corky Simpson of the *Tucson* (Ariz.) *Citizen*. Each selector voted for one team. Winning team receives the Grantland Rice Award, given since 1954.

Nebraska (5)

NY Times Computer Ratings

Based on an analysis of each team's scores with emphasis on three factors: who won, by what margin, and against what quality of opposition. Computer balances lop-sided scores, notes home field advantage and gives late-season games more weight than those played earlier in the schedule.
The top team is assigned a rating of 1.000, ratings of all other teams reflect their strength relative to strength of No.1 team.

		Rating			Rating
1	Nebraska	1.000	14	East Carolina	.731
2	Tennessee	.878	15	Syracuse	.730
3	Florida	.865	16	Texas Tech	.728
4	Colorado	.848	17	Texas	.722
5	Florida St.	.824	18	Miami-FL	.719
6	Virginia Tech	.801	19	Toledo	.700
7	Kansas St.	.795	20	Virginia	.700
8	Notre Dame	.770	21	USC	.696
9	Northwestern	.769	22	LSU	.682
10	Ohio St.	.767	23	Cincinnati	.669
11	Penn St.	.762	24	Utah	.664
12	Texas A&M	.750	25	Alabama	.661
13	Kansas	.745			

☞ See pages 167-169 for list of all national championship teams since 1869. Also, see pages 171-185 for every Associated Press final Top 20 poll since 1936.

NCAA Division I-A Final Standings

Standings based on conference games only; overall records include postseason games.

Atlantic Coast Conference

	Conference					Overall				
	W	L	T	PF	PA	W	L	T	PF	PA
*Virginia	7	1	0	242	156	9	4	0	378	270
*Florida St	7	1	0	421	154	10	2	0	563	246
*Clemson	6	2	0	193	133	8	4	0	303	219
Georgia Tech	5	3	0	173	198	6	5	0	260	243
Maryland	4	4	0	150	193	6	5	0	210	251
*N. Carolina	4	4	0	176	180	7	5	0	284	220
N.C. State	2	6	0	216	297	3	8	0	260	354
Duke	1	7	0	226	321	3	8	0	282	386
Wake Forest	0	8	0	129	294	1	10	0	190	360

Note: Even though Virginia beat Florida St. 33-28 on Nov. 2, the ACC has no tiebreaker to decide bowl bids, so Bowl Alliance was free to choose either team.

***Bowls (3-1):** Florida St. (won Orange), Virginia (won Peach), Clemson (lost Gator), North Carolina (won Carquest).

Big East Conference

	Conference					Overall				
	W	L	T	PF	PA	W	L	T	PF	PA
*Virginia Tech	6	1	0	194	83	10	2	0	349	165
Miami-FL	6	1	0	185	112	8	3	0	294	201
*Syracuse	5	2	0	211	136	9	3	0	375	213
West Virginia	4	3	0	147	124	5	6	0	253	210
Boston Col	4	3	0	150	167	4	8	0	207	322
Rutgers	2	5	0	184	272	4	7	0	304	412
Temple	1	6	0	113	189	1	10	0	187	358
Pittsburgh	0	7	0	93	194	2	9	0	217	329

Notes: Since the conference season ended a week before the NCAA put Miami-FL on probation (Dec. 1), the Big East considers Miami and Virginia as co-champions. Also, Tech beat Miami, 13-7 (Sept. 23).

***Bowls (2-0):** Virginia Tech (won Sugar), Syracuse (won Gator). Miami-FL was on probation and ineligible for postseason play.

Big Eight Conference

	Conference					Overall				
	W	L	T	PF	PA	W	L	T	PF	PA
*Nebraska	7	0	0	365	84	12	0	0	638	174
*Colorado	5	2	0	226	178	10	2	0	444	240
*Kansas	5	2	0	186	170	10	2	0	345	261
*Kansas St.	5	2	0	234	117	10	2	0	456	166
Oklahoma	2	5	0	96	209	5	5	1	233	275
Oklahoma St.	2	5	0	143	218	4	8	0	250	345
Iowa St.	1	6	0	151	304	3	8	0	264	409
Missouri	1	6	0	103	224	3	8	0	186	311

***Bowls (4-0):** Nebraska (won Fiesta); Colorado (won Cotton); Kansas (won Aloha); Kansas St. (won Holiday).

Big Ten Conference

	Conference					Overall				
	W	L	T	PF	PA	W	L	T	PF	PA
*Northwestern	8	0	0	204	89	10	2	0	311	181
*Ohio St	7	1	0	294	134	11	2	0	475	220
*Michigan	5	3	0	215	145	9	4	0	338	223
*Penn St	5	3	0	207	174	9	3	0	399	259
*Michigan St.	4	3	1	196	215	6	5	1	287	338
*Iowa	4	4	0	210	197	8	4	0	368	259
Illinois	3	4	1	146	157	5	5	1	193	198
Wisconsin	3	4	1	162	186	4	5	2	235	253
Purdue	2	5	1	193	197	4	6	1	282	269
Minnesota	1	7	0	169	327	3	8	0	272	368
Indiana	0	8	0	98	273	2	9	0	159	326

Note: Northwestern did not play Ohio St. during regular season.

***Bowls (2-4):** Northwestern (lost Rose); Ohio St. (lost Citrus); Michigan (lost Alamo); Penn St. (won Outback); Michigan St. (lost Independence); Iowa (won Sun).

Big West Conference

	Conference					Overall				
	W	L	T	PF	PA	W	L	T	PF	PA
*Nevada	6	0	0	262	173	9	3	0	521	375
SW Louisiana	4	2	0	199	134	6	5	0	351	275
Utah St.	4	2	0	191	94	4	7	0	293	287
Arkansas St.	3	3	0	127	134	6	5	0	265	270
N. Mexico St.	3	3	0	222	192	4	7	0	349	389
Northern Ill	3	3	0	147	184	3	8	0	220	420
Louisiana Tech	2	4	0	219	223	5	6	0	320	371
Pacific	2	4	0	170	238	3	8	0	240	439
San Jose St	2	4	0	172	167	3	8	0	271	378
UNLV	1	5	0	122	292	2	9	0	222	520

***Bowls (0-1):** Nevada (lost Las Vegas).

Mid-American Conference

	Conference					Overall				
	W	L	T	PF	PA	W	L	T	PF	PA
*Virginia	7	1	0	242	156	9	4	0	378	270
*Toledo	7	0	1	236	141	11	0	1	411	264
Miami-OH	6	1	1	254	83	8	2	1	326	165
Ball St.	6	2	0	164	114	7	4	0	204	187
Western Mich	6	2	0	202	111	7	4	0	253	190
Eastern Mich	5	3	0	258	211	6	5	0	363	335
Bowl. Green	3	5	0	151	159	5	6	0	226	228
Central Mich	2	6	0	153	190	4	7	0	255	276
Akron	2	6	0	104	260	2	9	0	141	428
Ohio	1	6	1	126	216	2	8	1	161	320
Kent	0	7	1	91	254	1	9	1	128	390

Note: Toledo tied Miami-OH, 28-28 (Oct. 14).

***Bowls (1-0):** Toledo (won Las Vegas).

Pacific 10 Conference

	Conference					Overall				
	W	L	T	PF	PA	W	L	T	PF	PA
*Virginia	7	1	0	242	156	9	4	0	378	270
*USC	6	1	1	214	125	9	2	1	355	212
*Washington	6	1	1	232	170	7	4	1	312	280
*Oregon	6	2	0	214	176	9	3	0	326	272
*Stanford	5	3	0	233	211	7	4	1	344	307
*UCLA	4	4	0	209	211	7	5	0	338	300
Arizona	4	4	0	139	162	6	5	0	207	199
Arizona St.	4	4	0	206	212	6	5	0	308	330
California	2	6	0	170	221	3	8	0	243	286
Wash. St.	2	6	0	164	201	3	8	0	236	274
Oregon St.	0	8	0	85	177	1	10	0	136	237

Rose Bowl tiebreaker: Although USC tied Washington, 21-21 (Oct. 28), the Trojans earned berth with a better overall regular season record.

***Bowls (1-4):** USC (won Rose); Washington (lost Sun); Oregon (lost Cotton); Stanford (lost Liberty); UCLA (lost Aloha).

Conference Bowling Results

Postseason records for 1995 season.

	W-L
Big Eight	4-0
ACC	3-1
Big East	2-0
Southwest	2-1
Big Ten	2-4
SEC	2-4
Mid-American	1-0
Independents	1-1
Pac-10	1-4
Big West	0-1

Southeastern Conference

Eastern	Conference W	L	T	PF	PA	Overall W	L	T	PF	PA
*Florida	8	0	0	362	133	12	1	0	558	263
*Tennessee	7	1	0	311	207	11	1	0	431	228
*Georgia	3	5	0	156	200	6	6	0	260	281
S. Carolina	2	5	1	239	320	4	6	1	401	393
Kentucky	2	6	0	163	232	4	7	0	223	269
Vanderbilt	1	7	0	90	218	2	9	0	122	281

Western	Conference W	L	T	PF	PA	Overall W	L	T	PF	PA
*Virginia	7	1	0	242	156	9	4	0	378	270
*Arkansas	6	2	0	206	179	8	5	0	284	283
Alabama	5	3	0	171	138	8	3	0	260	188
*Auburn	5	3	0	276	203	8	4	0	438	283
*LSU	4	3	1	161	113	7	4	1	324	186
Mississippi	3	5	0	99	178	6	5	0	209	208
Mississippi St	1	7	0	171	284	3	8	0	261	357

SEC championship game: Florida beat Arkansas, 34-3 (Dec. 2).
***Bowls (2-4):** Florida (lost Fiesta); Tennessee (won Citrus); Georgia (lost Peach); Arkansas (lost Carquest); Auburn (lost Outback); LSU (won Independence). Note that Alabama was on probation and ineligible for postseason play.

Southwest Conference

	Conference W	L	T	PF	PA	Overall W	L	T	PF	PA
*Virginia	7	1	0	242	156	9	4	0	378	270
*Texas	7	0	0	236	88	10	2	1	390	255
*Texas Tech	5	2	0	169	136	9	3	0	385	247
*Texas A&M	5	2	0	143	79	9	3	0	327	168
Baylor	5	2	0	187	96	7	4	0	273	166
TCU	3	4	0	138	184	6	5	0	217	246
Houston	2	5	0	137	231	2	9	0	188	360
Rice	1	6	0	134	194	2	8	1	215	284
SMU	0	7	0	103	239	1	10	0	132	352

***Bowls (2-1):** Texas (lost Sugar); Texas Tech (won Copper); Texas A&M (won Alamo).

Western Athletic Conference

	Conference W	L	T	PF	PA	Overall W	L	T	PF	PA
*Virginia	7	1	0	242	156	9	4	0	378	270
*Colorado St.	6	2	0	214	131	8	4	0	339	254
*Air Force	6	2	0	272	189	8	5	0	401	358
BYU	6	2	0	232	181	7	4	0	307	268
Utah	6	2	0	216	156	7	4	0	296	230
San Diego St.	5	3	0	267	189	8	4	0	401	283
Wyoming	4	4	0	244	184	6	5	0	322	264
Fresno St.	2	6	0	238	277	5	7	0	371	387
New Mexico	2	6	0	168	224	4	7	0	256	303
Hawaii	2	6	0	145	295	4	8	0	285	401
UTEP	1	7	0	164	334	2	10	0	263	486

Holiday Bowl tiebreaker: Colorado St. and Utah both had 2-1 records while Air Force and BYU were 1-2 in head to head games between the four co-champions. Colorado St. earned berth by beating Utah 19-14 (Oct. 14).
***Bowls (0-2):** Colorado St. (lost Holiday); Air Force (lost Copper).

I-A Independents

	W	L	T	PF	PA
*Notre Dame	9	3	0	392	247
*East Carolina	9	3	0	274	226
Louisville	7	4	0	283	165
Cincinnati	6	5	0	252	197
Southern Miss	6	5	0	284	241
Army	5	5	1	325	211
Navy	5	6	0	223	189
Tulsa	4	7	0	233	300
Memphis	3	8	0	150	240
NE Louisiana	2	9	0	233	413
North Texas	2	9	0	200	424
Tulane	2	9	0	187	303

***Bowls (1-1):** Notre Dame (lost Orange); East Carolina (won Liberty).

On Probation

Alabama of the Southeastern Conference and Miami-FL of the Big East were both on NCAA probation and ineligible for bowl games following the 1995 regular season.

NCAA Division I-A Individual Leaders
REGULAR SEASON
Total Offense

	Cl	Rushing Car	Gain	Loss	Net	Passing Att	Yds	Total Offense Plays	Yds	YdsPP	TDR	YdsPG
Mike Maxwell, Nevada	Sr.	34	91	79	12	409	3611	443	3623	8.18	34	402.56
Cody Ledbetter, N. Mex. St.	Sr.	90	405	182	223	453	3501	543	3724	6.86	32	338.55
Steve Sarkisian, BYU	Jr.	82	136	303	-167	385	3437	467	3270	7.00	22	297.27
Charlie Batch, Eastern Mich.	Jr.	61	157	105	52	421	3177	482	3229	6.70	24	293.55
Danny Wuerffel, Florida	Jr.	46	65	206	-141	325	3266	371	3125	8.42	37	284.09
Steve Taneyhill, S. Carolina	Sr.	66	203	241	-38	389	3094	455	3056	6.72	29	277.82
Billy Blanton, San Diego St.	Jr.	69	225	201	24	389	3300	458	3324	7.26	23	277.00
Tony Graziani, Oregon	Jr.	70	333	95	238	389	2491	459	2729	5.95	17	272.90
Peyton Manning, Tennessee	So.	41	90	84	6	380	2954	421	2960	7.03	27	269.09
Marcus Crandell, E. Carolina	Jr.	94	327	126	201	447	2751	541	2952	5.46	24	268.36

Games: All played 11, except Blanton (12); Graziani (10); Maxwell (9). Note that **TDR** indicates touchdowns responsible for.

All-Purpose Yards

	Cl	Gm	Rush	Rec	PR	KOR	Total Yds	YdsPG
Troy Davis, Iowa St.	So.	11	2010	159	0	297	2466	224.18
Alex Van Dyke, Nevada	Sr.	11	6	1854	0	583	2443	222.09
Wasean Tait, Toledo	Jr.	11	1905	183	0	0	2088	189.82
Eddie George, Ohio St.	Sr.	12	1826	399	0	0	2225	185.42
Abu Wilson, Utah St.	Sr.	11	1476	375	0	153	2004	182.18
Winslow Oliver, New Mexico	Sr.	11	915	228	101	666	1910	173.64
Corey Walker, Arkansas St.	Jr.	11	1013	411	0	459	1883	171.18
Leeland McElroy, Texas A&M	Jr.	10	1122	379	0	208	1709	170.90
Darnell Autry, Northwestern	So.	11	1675	130	0	45	1850	168.18
Byron Hanspard, Texas Tech	So.	11	1374	474	0	0	1848	168.00

Iowa St.
Troy Davis
Rushing, All-Purpose

Florida
Danny Wuerffel
Passing

Ohio St.
Eddie George
Scoring Total

Nevada
Mike Maxwell
Offense

NCAA Division I-A Individual Leaders (Cont.)

Passing Efficiency

(Minimum 15 attempts per game)

	Cl	Gm	Att	Cmp	Cmp Pct	Int	Int Pct	Yds	Yds/Att	TD	TD Pct	Rating Points
Danny Wuerffel, Florida	Jr.	11	325	210	64.62	10	3.08	3266	10.05	35	10.77	178.4
Bobby Hoying, Ohio St.	Sr.	12	303	192	63.37	11	3.63	3023	9.98	28	9.24	170.4
Donovan McNabb, Syracuse	Fr.	11	207	128	61.84	6	2.90	1991	9.62	16	7.73	162.3
Mike Maxwell, Nevada	Sr.	9	409	277	67.73	17	4.16	3611	8.83	33	8.07	160.2
Matt Miller, Kansas St.	Sr.	11	240	154	64.17	11	4.58	2059	8.58	22	9.17	157.3
Steve Taneyhill, S. Carolina	Sr.	11	389	261	67.10	9	2.31	3094	7.95	29	7.46	153.9
Jim Arellanes, Fresno St.	Jr.	9	172	102	59.30	6	3.49	1539	8.95	13	7.56	152.4
Donald Sellers, New Mexico	Jr.	10	195	121	62.05	3	1.54	1693	8.68	11	5.64	150.5
Steve Sarkisian, BYU	Jr.	11	385	250	64.94	14	3.64	3437	8.93	20	5.19	149.8
Josh Wallwork, Wyoming	Jr.	10	271	163	60.15	13	4.80	2363	8.72	21	7.75	149.4
Peyton Manning, Tennessee	So.	11	380	244	64.21	4	1.05	2954	7.77	22	5.79	146.5
Billy Blanton, San Diego St.	Jr.	12	389	243	62.47	14	3.60	3300	8.48	23	5.91	146.0
Danny Kanell, Florida St.	Sr.	11	402	257	63.93	13	3.23	2957	7.36	32	7.96	145.5
John Hessler, Colorado	So.	11	266	154	57.89	9	3.38	2136	8.03	20	7.52	143.4
Damon Huard, Washington	Sr.	11	287	184	64.11	6	2.09	2415	8.41	11	3.83	143.3

Rushing

	Cl	Car	Yds	TD	YdsPG
Troy Davis, Iowa St.	So.	345	2010	15	182.73
Wasean Tait, Toledo	Jr.	357	1905	20	173.18
George Jones, San Diego St.	Jr.	305	1842	23	153.50
D. Autry, Northwestern	So.	355	1675	14	152.27
Eddie George, Ohio St.	Sr.	303	1826	23	152.17
D. McCullough, Miami-OH	Sr.	321	1627	14	147.91
Moe Williams, Kentucky	Jr.	294	1600	17	145.45
Tim Biakabutuka, Mich.	Jr.	279	1724	12	143.67
Karim Abdul-Jabbar, UCLA	Jr.	270	1419	11	141.90
Charles Talley, Northern Ill.	Jr.	285	1540	7	140.00

Games: All played 11, except Biakabutuka, George and Jones (12); Abdul-Jabbar (10).

Receptions

	Cl	No	Yds	TD	P/Gm
Alex Van Dyke, Nevada	Sr.	129	1854	16	11.73
Kevin Alexander, Utah St.	Sr.	92	1400	6	8.36
Chad Mackey, La. Tech	Jr.	90	1255	9	8.18
Keyshawn Johnson, USC	Sr.	90	1218	6	8.18
W. Blackwell, San Diego St.	So.	86	1207	8	7.82
Marcus Harris, Wyoming	Jr.	78	1423	14	7.09
Brandon Stokley, SW La.	Fr.	75	1121	9	6.82
Jermaine Lewis, Maryland	Sr.	66	937	3	6.60
Andre Cooper, Florida St.	Jr.	71	1002	15	6.45
Joey Kent, Tennessee	Jr.	69	1055	9	6.27
Marco Battaglia, Rutgers	Sr.	69	894	10	6.27

Games: All played 11, except Lewis (10).

Scoring

Non-Kickers

	Cl	TD	Pts	P/Gm
Eddie George. Ohio St	Sr.	24	144	12.00
George Jones, San Diego St	Jr.	23	138	11.50
Wasean Tait, Toledo	Jr.	20	120	10.91
Scott Greene, Michigan St.	Sr.	17	104*	10.40
Byron Hanspard, Texas Tech	So.	18	108	9.82
Leeland McElroy, Texas A&M	Jr.	16	96	9.60
Baeu Morgan, Air Force	Jr.	19	114	9.50
Terry Glenn, Ohio St.	Jr.	17	104*	9.45
Stephen Davis, Auburn	Sr.	17	102	9.27
Moe Williams, Kentucky	Jr.	17	102	9.27

*Includes one 2-point conversion.

Note: Four tied with 8.73 points per game each.

Games: All played 11, except George, Jones and Morgan (12); Greene and McElroy (10).

Kickers

	Cl	FG/Att	PAT/Att	Pts
Kris Brown, Nebraska	Fr.	13/16	58/61	97
Jeff Hall, Tennessee	Fr.	16/25	47/49	95
Scott Bentley, Florida St.	Jr.	9/16	67/71	94
Rafael Garcia, Virginia	Jr.	20/27	31/36	91
Michael Reeder, TCU	So.	23/25	20/20	89
Bart Edmiston, Florida	Jr.	6/12	71/71	89
Damon Shea, Nevada	Fr.	9/11	61/63	88
Dan Pulsipher, Utah	Jr.	17/22	31/33	88*
Phil Dawson, Texas	So.	13/20	47/49	86
Brett Conway, Penn St.	Jr.	16/24	37/37	85

*Includes one touchdown.

Note: Four tied with 81 points each.

Games: All played 11, except Edmiston and Garcia (12).

Field Goals

	Cl	FG/Att	Pct	Lg
Michael Reeder, TCU	So.	23/25	.920	47*
Rafael Garcia, Virginia	Jr.	20/27	.741	56
Dan Pulsipher, Utah	Jr.	17/22	.773	48
Remy Hamilton, Michigan	Jr.	17/25	.680	49
Eric Abrams, Stanford	Sr.	16/18	.889	50
Eric Richards, Cincinnati	So.	16/24	.667	47
Brett Conway, Penn St.	Jr.	16/24	.667	57
Jeff Hall, Tennessee	Fr.	16/25	.640	53
Jeff Sauve, Clemson	Sr.	15/20	.750	47
Josh Smith, Oregon	Fr.	14/21	.667	42*
Jeremy Alexander, Oklahoma	So.	14/16	.875	43
Chris Pierce, Southern Miss.	Sr.	14/17	.824	44
Tom Cochran, Duke	Sr.	14/18	.778	45
Cory Wedel, Wyoming	So.	14/18	.778	46*
Brad Blasy, Central Mich.	Sr.	14/20	.700	42
Todd Latourette, Arkansas	Fr.	14/21	.667	44

*Did it twice.

Games: All played 11, except Garcia, Hamilton and Latourette (12); Smith (10).

Longest FGs of season: 60 yds by Derek Schorejs, Bowling Green vs Toledo (Oct. 21) and John Hall, Wisconsin vs Minnesota (Nov. 11).

Interceptions

	Cl	No	Yds	TD	Lg
Willie Smith, Louisiana Tech	Jr.	8	65	0	24
Chris Canty, Kansas St.	So.	8	117	2	39
Sean Andrews, Navy	So.	8	30	0	12
Sam Madison, Louisville	Jr.	7	136	0	60

Note: 17 tied with 6 each.

Games: All played 11, except Smith (10).

Punting

(Minimum of 3.6 per game)

	Cl	No	Yds	Avg
Brad Maynard, Ball St.	Jr.	66	3071	46.53
Brian Gragert, Wyoming	Sr.	40	1808	45.20
Greg Ivy, Oklahoma St.	Sr.	66	2947	44.65
Chad Kessler, LSU	So.	47	2072	44.09
Sean Liss, Florida St.	Jr.	49	2153	43.94

Punt Returns

(Minimum of 1.2 per game)

	Cl	No	Yds	TD	Avg
James Dye, BYU	Jr.	20	438	2	21.90
B. Roberson, Fresno St.	Jr.	19	346	1	18.21
Marvin Harrison, Syracuse	Sr.	22	369	2	16.77
Greg Myers, Colorado St.	Sr.	35	555	3	15.86
Paul Guidry, UCLA	Jr.	24	370	1	15.42

Kickoff Returns

(Minimum of 1.2 per game)

	Cl	No	Yds	TD	Avg
Robert Tate, Cincinnati	Jr.	15	515	1	34.33
Winslow Oliver, N. Mex.	Sr.	21	666	1	31.71
Damon Dunn, Stanford	So.	19	539	1	28.37
Steve Clay, Eastern Mich.	Sr.	14	395	1	28.21
Emmett Mosley, Not. Dame	Jr.	15	419	0	27.93

NCAA Division I-A Team Leaders

REGULAR SEASON

Scoring Offense

	Gm	Record	Pts	Avg
Nebraska	11	11-0-0	576	52.4
Florida St	11	9-2-0	532	48.4
Florida	12	12-0-0	534	44.5
Nevada	11	9-2-0	484	44.0
Auburn	11	8-3-0	424	38.5
Ohio St.	12	11-1-0	461	38.4
Tennessee	11	10-1-0	411	37.4
Colorado	11	9-2-0	406	36.9
Kansas St.	11	9-2-0	402	36.5
South Carolina	11	4-6-1	401	36.5

Total Offense

	Gm	Plays	Yds	Avg	TD	YdsPG
Nevada	11	917	6263	6.8	63	569.36
Nebraska	11	855	6119	7.2	69	556.27
Florida St.	11	885	6067	6.9	71	551.55
Florida	12	867	6413	7.4	72	534.42
Ohio St.	12	865	5887	6.8	60	490.58
Colorado	11	809	5353	6.6	48	486.64
San Diego St.	12	883	5785	6.6	51	482.08
New Mexico St.	11	811	5248	6.5	46	477.09
Auburn	11	788	5049	6.4	54	459.00
Fresno St.	12	899	5479	6.1	47	456.58

Note: Touchdowns scored by rushing and passing only.

Scoring Defense

	Gm	Record	Pts	Avg
Northwestern	11	10-1-0	140	12.7
Kansas St.	11	9-2-0	145	13.2
Texas A&M	11	8-3-0	148	13.5
Nebraska	11	11-0-0	150	13.6
Virginia Tech	11	9-2-0	155	14.1
LSU	11	6-4-1	160	14.5
Louisville	11	7-4-0	165	15.0
Miami-OH	11	8-2-1	165	15.0
Baylor	11	7-4-0	166	15.1
Clemson	11	8-3-0	178	16.2

Total Defense

	Gm	Plays	Yds	Avg	TD	YdsPG
Kansas St.	11	673	2759	4.1	16	250.8
Miami-OH	11	738	2764	3.7	15	251.3
Texas A&M	11	773	2835	3.7	16	257.7
Ball St.	11	712	2850	4.0	22	259.1
Baylor	11	709	2903	4.1	19	263.9
North Carolina	11	729	2940	4.0	25	267.3
Arizona	11	739	2976	4.0	19	270.5
Western Mich.	11	686	3092	4.5	23	281.1
Alabama	11	727	3125	4.3	21	284.1
Virginia Tech	11	782	3145	4.0	18	285.9

Note: Opponents' TDs scored by rushing and passing only.

Single Game Highs

INDIVIDUAL

Rushing Yards

Yds	
314	Eddie George, Ohio St. vs Illinois (Nov. 11)
313	Tim Biakabutuka, Mich. vs Ohio St. (Nov. 25)
302	Troy Davis, Iowa St. vs UNLV (Sept. 23)
299	Mo Williams, Kentucky at South Carolina (Sept. 23)
294	Chris Darkins, Minnesota vs Purdue (Oct. 7)

Rushing & Passing Yards

Yds	
559	Cody Ledbetter, New Mexico St. at UNLV (Nov. 18)
554	Rusty LaRue, Wake Forest vs N.C. State (Nov. 18)
543	Mike Maxwell, Nevada vs UNLV (Oct. 28)
541	Mike Maxwell, Nevada at La. Tech (Oct. 21)
514	Rusty LaRue, Wake Forest vs Ga. Tech (Nov. 4)

Single Game Highs (Cont.)

Passes Attempted

Att	
78	Rusty LaRue, Wake Forest at Duke (Oct. 28)
67	Danny Kanell, Florida St. at Virginia (Nov. 2)
67	Rusty LaRue, Wake Forest vs N.C. State (Nov. 18)
65	Jason Martin, La. Tech vs Nevada (Oct. 21)
65	Rusty LaRue, Wake Forest vs Georgia Tech (Nov. 4)

Receptions

No	
18	Alex Van Dyke, Nevada vs Toledo (Sept. 23)
18	Alex Van Dyke, Nevada vs UNLV (Oct. 28)
17	Chad Mackey, La. Tech vs Nevada (Oct. 21)
17	Willie Gosha, Auburn at Arkansas (Oct. 28)

Receiving Yards

Yds	
314	Alex Van Dyke, Nevada vs San Jose St. (Nov. 18)
272	Alex Van Dyke, Nevada at La. Tech (Oct. 21)
264	Stepfret Williams, NE Louisiana at Nevada (Oct. 14)
263	Chad Mackey, La. Tech at Pacific (Oct. 14)

Passing Yards

Yds	
552	Mike Maxwell, Nevada at UNLV (Oct. 28)
546	Cody Ledbetter, New Mexico St. at UNLV (Nov. 18)
545	Rusty LaRue, Wake Forest vs N.C. State (Nov. 18)
535	Mike Maxwell, Nevada at La. Tech (Oct. 21)

Passes Completed

No	
55	Rusty LaRue, Wake Forest at Duke (Oct. 28)
50	Rusty LaRue, Wake Forest vs N.C. State (Nov. 18)
46	Scott Milanovich, Maryland at Florida St. (Nov. 18)

TEAM
Points Scored

Pts	
77	Nebraska (77-28) vs Arizona St. (Sept. 16)
77	Virginia Tech (77-27) vs Akron (Oct. 14)
77	South Carolina (77-14) vs Kent (Oct. 7)
77	Florida St. (77-17) vs N.C. State (Sept. 16)
76	Auburn (76-10) vs Tenn-Chattanooga* (Sept. 9)
73	Nebraska (73-14) vs Iowa St. (Nov. 4)
72	Florida St. (72-13) vs Wake Forest (Oct. 14)
70	Florida St. (70-26) vs Duke# (Sept. 2)
68	South Carolina (68-21) vs Louisiana Tech (Sept. 16)
67	Kansas St. (67-0) vs Akron (Sept. 23)
66	Penn St. (66-14) vs Temple (Sept. 16)
66	Colorado (66-14) vs NE Louisiana (Sept. 16)
66	Pittsburgh (66-30) vs Eastern Mich. (Sept. 9)
65	Miami-OH (65-0) vs Akron (Nov. 18)
65	South Carolina (65-39) at Miss. St. (Oct. 14)

*Division I-AA opponent.
#at Orlando

Annual Awards

Players of the Year

Eddie George, Ohio St. .... Camp, Heisman, Maxwell
Tommie Frazier, Nebraska .... *The Sporting News*, UPI

Position Players of the Year

O'Brien Award (Quarterback)	Danny Wuerffel
Unitas Award (Senior QB)	Tommie Frazier
Walker Award (Running Back)	Eddie George
UPI Back of Year	Troy Davis
Biletnikoff Award (Receiver)	Terry Glenn
Groza Award (Kicker)	Michael Reeder
Outland Trophy (Interior Lineman)	Jonathan Ogden
UPI Lineman of Year	Jonathan Ogden
Lombardi Award (Lineman)	Orlando Pace
Butkus Award (Linebacker)	Kevin Hardy
Thorpe Award (Defensive Back)	Greg Myers
Nagurski Award (Defensive Player)	Pat Fitzgerald

Coach of the Year

Gary Barnett, Northwestern .... AFCA, Camp, Dodd, FWAA, *The Sporting News*, UPI

Heisman Trophy Vote

Presented since 1935 by the Downtown Athletic Club of New York City and named after former college coach and DAC athletic director John W. Heisman. Voting done by national media and former Heisman winners. Each ballot allows for three names (Pts based on 3 for 1st, 2 for 2nd and 1 for 3rd).

Top 10 Vote-Getters

	Pos	1st	2nd	3rd	Pts
Eddie George, Ohio St.	RB	268	248	160	1460
Tommie Frazier, Nebraska	QB	218	192	158	1196
Danny Wuerffel, Florida	QB	185	152	128	987
Darnell Autry, N'western	RB	87	78	118	535
Troy Davis, Iowa St.	RB	41	80	119	402
Peyton Manning, Tenn	QB	10	21	37	109
Keyshawn Johnson, USC	WR	9	10	12	59
Tim Biakabutuka, Mich	RB	1	11	6	31
Warrick Dunn, Florida St.	RB	2	3	17	29
Bobby Hoying, Ohio St.	QB	0	9	10	28

Note: All players were seniors except juniors Wuerffel, Biakabutuka and Dunn and sophomores Autry, Davis and Manning.

Consensus All-America Team

NCAA Division I-A players cited most frequently by the following six selectors: AFCA, AP, FWAA, The Sporting News, UPI and Walter Camp Foundation. Holdover from 1994 All-America team is in **bold** type; (*) indicates unanimous selection.

Offense

		Class	Hgt	Wgt
WR—	Terry Glenn, Ohio St.	Jr.	5-11	185
WR—	Keyshawn Johnson*, USC	Sr.	6-4	210
TE —	Marco Battaglia*, Rutgers	Sr.	6-3	240
L —	Jonathan Ogden*, UCLA	Sr.	6-8	310
LB —	Zach Thomas*, Texas Tech	Sr.	6-0	230
LB —	Pat Fitzgerald, Northwestern	Jr.	6-2	235
LB —	Kevin Hardy, Illinois	Sr.	6-4	240
B —	Lawyer Milloy*, Washington	Jr.	6-2	205
B —	Chris Canty, Kansas St.	So.	5-10	190
B —	Greg Myers, Colorado St.	Sr.	5-11	195
B —	Aaron Beasley, West Va.	Sr.	6-0	190
P —	Brad Maynard, Ball St.	Jr.	6-1	175

Defense

		Class	Hgt	Wgt
L —	**Tedy Bruschi***, Arizona	Sr.	6-1	255
L —	Cornell Brown, Va. Tech	Jr.	6-2	240
L —	Marcus Jones, North Carolina	Sr.	6-6	270
L —	Tony Brackens, Texas	Jr.	6-4	250
L —	Jason Odom*, Florida	Sr.	6-5	290
L —	Orlando Pace*, Ohio St.	So.	6-6	320
C —	Clay Shiver, Florida St.	Sr.	6-4	285
QB—	Tommie Frazier*, Nebraska	Sr.	6-2	205
RB—	Eddie George*, Ohio St	Sr.	6-3	230
RB—	Troy Davis, Iowa St.	So.	5-8	185
PK—	Michael Reeder, TCU	So.	6-0	160
KR—	Marvin Harrison, Syracuse	Sr.	6-1	175

Underclassmen Who Declared for 1996 NFL Draft

Twenty-five players— all juniors who have been out of high school for at least three seasons— forfeited the remainder of their college eligibility and declared for the NFL draft in 1996. NFL teams drafted 17 underclassmen. Players listed in alphabetical order; first round selections in **bold** type.

	Pos	Drafted By	Overall Pick
Karim Abdul-Jabbar, UCLA	RB	Miami	80
Willie Anderson, Auburn	OT	Cincinnati	10
Ricky Bell, N.C. State	DB	not selected	—
Tim Biakabutuka, Michigan	RB	Carolina	8
Tony Brackens, Texas	DE	Jacksonville	33
Duane Clemons, California	DE	Minnesota	16
Jamie Coleman, Appalach. St.	DB	not selected	—
Keith Drayton, Georgia	NT	not selected	—
Terry Glenn, Ohio St.	WR	New England	7
Terry Guess, Gardner-Webb	WR	New Orleans	165
Jermaine Johnson, Vanderbilt	RB	not selected	—
Eddie Kennison, LSU	WR	St. Louis	18
Jevon Langford, Okla. St.	DE	Cincinnati	108
Ray Lewis, Miami-FL	LB	Baltimore	26
Clarence Matthews, NW St.	RB	not selected	—
Leeland McElroy, Texas A&M	RB	Arizona	32
Lawyer Milloy, Washington	S	New England	36
Jerald Moore, Oklahoma	FB	St. Louis	83
Lawrence Phillips, Nebraska	RB	St. Louis	6
Jon Runyan, Michigan	OT	Houston	109
Freddie Scott, Penn St.	WR	not selected	—
Alfred Shipman, Miami	RB	not selected	—
Regan Upshaw, California	DE	Tampa Bay	12
Moe Williams, Kentucky	RB	Minnesota	75
Terrell Willis, Rutgers	RB	not selected	—

NCAA Division I-AA Final Standings

Standings based on conference games only; overall records include postseason games.

American West Conference

	Conference W	L	T	PF	PA	Overall W	L	T	PF	PA
CS-Sacramento	3	0	0	110	81	4	6	1	255	377
Cal Poly-SLO	2	1	0	120	64	5	6	0	411	271
CS-Northridge	1	2	0	57	97	2	8	0	159	355
Southern Utah	0	3	0	77	122	2	9	0	220	394

Playoffs: No teams invited.

Big Sky Conference

	Conference W	L	T	PF	PA	Overall W	L	T	PF	PA
*Montana	6	1	0	310	187	13	2	0	652	299
Boise St.	4	3	0	219	201	7	4	0	361	265
Northern Ariz.	4	3	0	190	104	7	4	0	403	163
*Idaho	4	3	0	195	147	6	5	0	287	209
Weber St.	4	3	0	160	194	6	5	0	314	318
Idaho St.	3	4	0	141	175	6	5	0	307	252
Montana St.	2	5	0	91	183	5	6	0	193	262
Eastern Wash	1	6	0	142	257	3	8	0	238	357

***Playoffs (4-1):** Montana (4-0); Idaho (0-1).

Gateway Athletic Conference

	Conference W	L	T	PF	PA	Overall W	L	T	PF	PA
*Northern Iowa	5	1	0	143	72	8	5	0	361	277
*Eastern Ill.	5	1	0	136	78	10	2	0	328	201
Indiana St.	3	3	0	114	104	7	4	0	236	186
Illinois St.	3	3	0	119	116	5	6	0	206	192
Southern Ill.	2	4	0	78	167	5	6	0	198	291
Western Ill.	2	4	0	88	130	4	7	0	267	252
SW Missouri St.	1	5	0	93	104	4	7	0	220	204

Tiebreaker: Northen Iowa beat Eastern Ill., 17-7 (Oct. 7) to gain automatic berth to IAA playoffs.

***Playoffs (1-2):** Eastern Ill. (0-1); Northern Iowa (1-1).

Ivy League

	Conference W	L	T	PF	PA	Overall W	L	T	PF	PA
Princeton	5	1	1	148	98	8	1	1	243	124
Pennsylvania	5	2	0	192	124	7	3	0	274	199
Cornell	5	2	0	203	159	6	4	0	261	222
Dartmouth	4	2	1	139	102	7	2	1	222	137
Columbia	3	4	0	142	200	3	6	1	201	281
Brown	2	5	0	193	191	5	5	0	282	239
Yale	2	5	0	114	170	3	7	0	172	247
Harvard	1	6	0	112	199	2	8	0	183	258

Playoffs: League does not play postseason games.

Metro-Atlantic Conference

	Conference W	L	T	PF	PA	Overall W	L	T	PF	PA
Duquesne	7	0	0	184	76	10	1	0	313	163
Georgetown	5	2	0	158	85	6	3	0	192	99
Marist	4	3	0	198	96	6	4	0	234	174
Canisius	4	3	0	115	112	4	6	0	130	176
St. John's	3	4	0	139	181	4	6	0	181	265
Iona	3	4	0	119	115	3	6	0	141	186
St. Peter's	2	5	0	47	185	2	7	0	81	247
Siena	0	7	0	91	201	0	9	0	98	284

Playoffs: No teams invited.

Mid-Eastern Athletic Conference

	Conference W	L	T	PF	PA	Overall W	L	T	PF	PA
†Florida A&M	6	0	0	191	72	9	3	0	324	238
Delaware St.	5	1	0	149	91	6	5	0	232	255
S.C. State	4	2	0	147	128	6	4	0	236	199
Howard	2	4	0	109	123	6	5	0	246	225
N. Car. A&T	2	4	0	116	138	4	7	0	224	247
Beth-Cookman	2	4	0	119	164	3	8	0	219	335
Morgan St	0	6	0	104	219	1	10	0	212	439

Playoffs: No teams invited.

†**Heritage Bowl:** Fla. A&M lost to SWAC champion Southern-BR, 30-25 (Dec. 29).

NCAA Division I-AA Final Standings (Cont.)

Ohio Valley Conference

	Conference					Overall				
	W	L	T	PF	PA	W	L	T	PF	PA
*Murray St.	8	0	0	295	79	11	1	0	455	149
*Eastern Ky.	7	1	0	267	110	9	3	0	363	212
Mid. Tenn. St.	6	2	0	235	98	7	4	0	303	201
SE Missouri St.	5	3	0	195	206	5	6	0	243	309
Tenn-Martin	4	4	0	202	244	5	6	0	335	302
Austin Peay	2	6	0	129	234	3	8	0	212	341
Tenn. Tech	2	6	0	147	239	3	8	0	234	311
Morehead St.	1	7	0	128	310	2	8	0	186	355
Tennessee St.	1	7	0	152	230	2	9	0	193	292

***Playoffs (0-2):** Murray St. (0-1); Eastern Ky. (0-1).

Patriot League

	Conference					Overall				
	W	L	T	PF	PA	W	L	T	PF	PA
Lehigh	5	0	0	155	83	8	3	0	306	272
Bucknell	4	1	0	123	83	7	4	0	195	174
Lafayette	3	2	0	127	114	4	6	1	176	250
Fordham	2	3	0	93	93	4	6	1	208	236
Holy Cross	1	4	0	94	136	2	9	0	180	326
Colgate	0	5	0	66	149	0	11	0	134	367

Playoffs: League does not play postseason games.

Pioneer League

	Conference					Overall				
	W	L	T	PF	PA	W	L	T	PF	PA
Drake	5	0	0	123	58	8	1	1	238	104
Dayton	4	1	0	182	74	9	2	0	422	180
San Diego	3	2	0	94	90	5	5	0	176	167
Evansville	1	4	0	53	98	5	5	0	182	139
Valparaiso	1	4	0	103	156	5	5	0	247	314
Butler	1	4	0	93	172	2	8	0	157	314

Playoffs: No teams invited.

Southern Conference

	Conference					Overall				
	W	L	T	PF	PA	W	L	T	PF	PA
*Appalachian St.	8	0	0	221	140	12	1	0	375	251
*Marshall	7	1	0	277	98	12	3	0	492	240
*Ga. Southern	5	3	0	202	127	9	4	0	294	237
Furman	5	3	0	208	183	6	5	0	274	261
East Tenn. St.	4	4	0	177	188	4	7	0	224	305
VMI	3	5	0	184	241	4	7	0	269	350
Tenn-Chatt	2	6	0	165	217	4	7	0	251	299
W. Carolina	2	6	0	113	242	3	7	0	158	311
The Citadel	0	8	0	104	215	2	9	0	165	262

***Playoffs (5-3):** Appalachian St. (1-1); Marshall (3-1); Ga. Southern (1-1).

Southland Conference

	Conference					Overall				
	W	L	T	PF	PA	W	L	T	PF	PA
*McNeese St.	5	0	0	133	39	13	1	0	444	144
*S.F. Austin St.	4	1	0	185	100	11	2	0	392	242
Northwestern St.	2	3	0	102	89	6	5	0	269	209
Sam Houston St.	2	3	0	74	119	5	5	0	193	216
SW Texas St.	2	3	0	111	143	4	7	0	274	303
Nicholls St.	0	5	0	65	180	0	11	0	142	390

***Playoffs (4-2):** McNeese St. (2-1); S.F. Austin St. (2-1).

Southwestern Athletic Conference

	Conference					Overall				
	W	L	T	PF	PA	W	L	T	PF	PA
*Jackson St.	7	0	0	225	87	9	3	0	318	206
†Southern-BR	6	1	0	294	125	11	1	0	475	220
Alabama St.	4	2	1	230	152	7	3	1	348	223
Grambling St.	4	3	0	257	134	5	6	0	340	191
Alcorn St.	3	3	1	167	187	4	6	1	244	300
Miss. Valley St.	2	5	0	137	262	2	8	0	170	383
Tex. Southern	1	6	0	137	199	2	8	0	200	259
Prairie View	0	7	0	46	347	0	11	0	79	511

***Playoffs (0-1):** Jackson St. (0-1).

†**Heritage Bowl:** Southern-BR beat MEAC champion Florida A&M, 30-25 (Dec. 29).

Yankee Conference

New England	Conference					Overall				
	W	L	T	PF	PA	W	L	T	PF	PA
Rhode Island	6	2	0	167	115	7	4	0	215	197
Connecticut	5	3	0	160	146	8	3	0	279	200
New Hampshire	4	4	0	131	124	6	5	0	206	171
Massachusetts	3	5	0	133	182	6	5	0	261	227
Boston Univ.	1	7	0	172	234	3	8	0	250	304
Maine	1	7	0	133	243	3	8	0	210	301

Mid-Atlantic	Conference					Overall				
	W	L	T	PF	PA	W	L	T	PF	PA
*Delaware	8	0	0	277	104	11	2	0	423	238
*James Madison	6	2	0	214	203	8	4	0	361	290
Richmond	5	3	0	116	142	7	3	1	187	186
Wm. & Mary	5	3	0	185	103	7	4	0	276	184
Northeastern	2	6	0	130	207	4	7	0	198	234
Villanova	2	6	0	136	151	3	8	0	194	195

***Playoffs (1-2):** Delaware (1-1); James Madison (0-1).

NCAA I-AA Independents

	W	L	T	PF	PA
*Troy St	11	1	0	446	168
*Hofstra	10	2	0	393	150
Hampton	8	3	0	343	221
St. Mary's-CA	8	2	0	334	230
Wagner	8	2	0	276	221
Liberty	8	3	0	352	203
Monmouth	7	3	0	288	118
Robert Morris	6	4	0	270	159
Jacksonville St.	7	4	0	255	256
Samford	7	4	0	263	287
Towson St.	6	4	0	234	150
Central Florida	6	5	0	283	280
Alabama-Birmingham	5	6	0	273	261
Wofford	4	7	0	191	274
Buffalo	3	8	0	198	259
Youngstown St.	3	8	0	188	236
Central Connecticut St.	2	8	0	122	284
Western Kentucky	2	8	0	229	341
Davidson	1	8	1	129	226
Charleston Southern	1	10	0	129	408
St. Francis-PA	0	10	0	125	300

***Playoffs (0-2):** Troy St. (0-1), Hofstra (0-1).

NCAA Division I-AA Regular Season Leaders

INDIVIDUALS

Passing Efficiency

(Minimum 15 attempts per game)

	Cl	Gm	Att	Cmp	Cmp Pct	Int	Int Pct	Yds	Yds/ Att	TD	TD Pct	Rating Points
Brian Kadel, Dayton	Sr.	11	183	115	62.84	6	3.28	1880	10.27	18	9.84	175.0
Dave Dickenson, Montana	Sr.	11	455	309	67.91	9	1.98	4176	9.18	38	8.35	168.6
Leo Hamlett, Delaware	Jr.	11	174	95	54.60	6	3.45	1849	10.63	15	8.62	165.4
Chris Berg, Northern Iowa	Sr.	10	206	113	54.85	6	2.91	2144	10.41	15	7.28	160.5
Jeff Lewis, Northern Ariz.	Sr.	10	313	209	66.77	3	0.96	2426	7.75	22	7.03	153.2

Total Offense

	Cl	Rush	Pass	Yds	YdsPG
D. Dickenson, Montana	Sr.	33	4176	4209	382.64
Kevin Foley, Boston Univ.	Jr.	-180	3192	3012	273.82
Kharon Brown, Hofstra	Sr.	977	1860	2837	257.91
Jason McCullough, Brown	Jr.	151	2406	2557	255.70
Bob Aylsworth, Lehigh	Sr.	-89	2899	2810	255.45

Games: All played 11, except McCullough (10).

Rushing

	Cl	Car	Yds	TD	YdsPG
Reggie Greene, Siena	So.	273	1461	11	162.33
D. Cullors, Murray St.	Sr.	269	1765	16	160.45
Tim Hall, Robert Morris	Sr.	239	1572	16	157.20
Arnold Mickens, Butler	Sr.	354	1558	11	155.80
Kito Lockwood, Wagner	Sr.	212	1018	10	145.43

Games: Cullors (11); Hall and Mickens (10); Greene (9); Lockwood (7).

Receptions

	Cl	No	Yds	TD	P/Gm
Ed Mantie, Boston Univ.	Sr.	81	943	1	7.36
Pokey Eckford, Weber St.	Sr.	77	1074	6	7.00
Brian Klingerman, Lehigh	Sr.	77	1040	10	7.00
Miles Macik, Penn	Sr.	68	816	5	6.80
Lenny Harris, Tenn-Martin	Jr.	53	790	5	6.63

Games: All played 11, except Macik (10); Harris (8).

Interceptions

	Cl	No	Yds	TD	LG
Picasso Nelson, Jackson St	Sr.	8	101	0	41
Damani Leech, Princeton	So.	8	17	0	17
Wm. Hampton, Murray St.	Jr.	8	280	4	75-td
Mark Wallrapp, Yale	Sr.	7	65	0	38
Doug Knopp, Cornell	Sr.	7	18	0	6

Games: All played 10, except Hampton (11); Nelson (9).

Scoring

Non-Kickers

	Cl	TD	XPt	Pts	P/Gm
Alcede Surtain, Alabama St.	Sr.	21	6	132	12.00
Tim Hall, Robert Morris	Sr.	20	0	120	12.00
Derrick Cullors, Murray St.	Sr.	20	0	120	10.91
William Murrell, Eastern Ky.	Jr.	18	0	108	10.80
Kito Lockwood, Wagner	Sr.	12	2	74	10.57
Rene Ingoglia, UMass	Sr.	19	0	114	10.36

Games: All played 11, except Hall and Murrell (10); Lockwood (7).

Kickers

	Cl	FG/Att	PAT/Att	Pts
David Ettinger, Hofstra	Jr.	22/33	35/38	101
Carlos Leach, Southern	Jr.	13/21	54/58	93
Chris Dill, Murray St	Sr.	9/11	56/56	89
*Tim Openlander, Marshall	Jr.	15/20	44/44	89
K. O'Leary, Northern Ariz.	Sr.	16/22	41/44	89

*Includes one touchdown.

Games: All played 11.

Field Goals

	Cl	FG/Att	Pct	LG
David Ettinger, Hofstra	Jr.	22/33	.667	54
Todd Kurz, Illinois St.	Jr.	19/25	.760	51
Tom Allison, Indiana St.	Sr.	18/23	.783	46
Gerald Carlson, Buffalo	Jr.	17/22	.773	52
David Dearmas, UConn	Sr.	17/23	.739	45

Note: Four tied with 16 each.

Games: All played 11.

Longest FG of season: 55 yds by Kevin O'Leary, No. Ariz. vs Montana (Oct. 14).

Punt/Kickoff Leaders

Punting	Cl	No	Yds	Avg
K. O'Leary, Northern Ariz.	Sr.	44	1881	42.75

Punt Returns	Cl	No	Yds	TD	Avg
R. Barlow, Alabama St.	Sr.	12	249	1	20.75

Kickoff Returns	Cl	No	Yds	TD	Avg
Josh Cole, Furman	Jr.	17	546	1	32.12

TEAMS

Scoring Offense

	Gm	Record	Pts	Avg
Montana	11	9-2-0	467	42.5
Southern-BR	11	10-1-0	445	40.5
Troy St.	11	11-0-0	425	38.6
Dayton	11	9-2-0	422	38.4
Murray St.	11	11-0-0	421	38.3
Cal Poly-SLO	11	5-6-0	411	37.4
Northern Ariz	11	7-4-0	403	36.6
Hofstra	11	10-1-0	376	34.2
Marshall	11	9-2-0	368	33.5
St. Mary's-CA	10	8-2-0	334	33.4

Scoring Defense

	Gm	Record	Pts	Avg
McNeese St.	11	11-0-0	98	8.9
Hofstra	11	10-1-0	112	10.2
Murray St.	11	11-0-0	114	10.4
Drake	10	8-1-1	104	10.4
Georgetown	9	6-3-0	99	11.0
Monmouth	10	7-3-0	118	11.8
Princeton	10	8-1-1	124	12.4
Stephen F. Austin St.	10	9-1-0	126	12.6
Troy St.	11	11-0-0	144	13.1
Dartmouth	10	7-2-1	137	13.7

NCAA Playoffs

Division I-AA

First Round (Nov. 25)

at Appalachian St. 31 .... James Madison 24
at Delaware 38 .... Hofstra 17
at Georgia Southern 24 .... Troy St. 21
at Marshall 38 .... Jackson St. 8
at McNeese St. 33 .... Idaho 3
at Montana 48 .... Eastern Kentucky 0
at Northern Iowa 35 .... Murray St. 34
at Stephen F. Austin St. 34 .... Eastern Illinois 29

Quarterfinals (Dec. 2)

at Marshall 41 .... Northern Iowa 24
at McNeese St. 52 .... Delaware 18
at Montana 45 .... Georgia Southern 0
Stephen F. Austin St. 27 .... at Appalachian St. 17

Semifinals (Dec. 9)

Marshall 25 .... at McNeese St. 13
at Montana 70 .... Stephen F. Austin St. 14

Championship Game

Dec. 16 at Huntington, W. Va. (Att: 32,106)

Montana 22 .... Marshall 20
(13-2-0) (12-3-0)

Division II

First Round (Nov. 18)

at Ferris St. (Mich.) 36 .... Millersville (Pa.) 26
at Carson-Newman (Tenn.) 37 .... West Georgia 26
at New Haven (Conn.) 27 .... Edinboro (Pa.) 12
at North Alabama 38 .... Albany St. (Ga.) 28
North Dakota St. 41 .... at North Dakota 10
at Pittsburg St. (Kan.) 36 .... Northern Colorado 17
at Texas A&M-Kingsville 59 .... Fort Hays St. (Kan.). 28
at Portland St. (Ore.) 56 .... East Texas St. 35

Quarterfinals (Nov. 25)

at Ferris St. 17 .... New Haven 9
at North Alabama 38 .... Carson-Newman 7
at Pittsburg St. 9 .... North Dakota St. 7
at Texas A&M-Kingsville 30 .... Portland St. 3

Semifinals (Dec.2)

at North Alabama 45 .... Ferris St. 7
Pittsburg St. 28 .... OT .... at Texas A&M-K'ville 25

Championship Game

Dec. 9 at Florence, Ala. (Att: 15,241)

North Alabama 27 .... Pittsburg St. 7
(14-0-0) (12-1-1)

Division I-AA, II and III Awards

Players of the Year

Payton Award (Div. I-AA) .... Dave Dickenson, QB Montana (Sr.)
Hill Trophy (Div. II) .... Ronald McKinnon, LB N. Alabama (Sr.)
Gagliardi Trophy (Div. III) .... Chris Palmer, WR St. John's-NY (Sr.)

Coaches of the Year

AFCA (NCAA Div. I-AA) .... Don Read, Montana
AFCA (College Div. II) ... Bobby Wallace, No. Alabama
AFCA (College Div. III) ... Roger Harring, WI-La Crosse

Division III

First Round (Nov. 18)

at Lycoming (Pa.) 31 .... Widener (Pa.) 27
at Mount Union (Ohio) 52 .... Hanover (Ind.) 18
Rowan (N.J.) 46 .... at Buffalo St. 7
Union (N.Y.) 24 .... at Plymouth St. (N.H.) 7
at Wash. & Jeff. (Pa.) 35 .... Emory & Henry (Va.) 16
Wheaton (Ill.) 63 .... at Wittenberg (Ohio) 41
WI-La Crosse 45 .... at Concordia-Moorhead (Minn.) 7
WI-River Falls 10 .... at Central (Iowa) 7

Quarterfinals (Nov. 25)

at Mount Union 40 .... Wheaton 14
at WI-La Crosse 28 .... WI-River Falls 14
at Wash. & Jeff. 48 .... Lycoming 0
at Rowan 38 .... Union 7

Semifinals (Dec. 2)

WI-La Crosse 20 .... at Mount Union 17
Rowan 28 .... at Wash. & Jeff. 15

Amos Alonzo Stagg Bowl

Dec. 9 at Salem, Va. (Att: 4,905)

WI-La Crosse 36 .... Rowan 7
(14-0-0) (10-3-1)

NAIA Playoffs

Division I

Semifinals (Nov. 18)

Central St. (Ohio) 49 .... Western Montana 21
Northeastern St. (Okla.) 17 .... Arkansas-Pine Bluff 14

Championship

Dec. 2 at Tahlequah, Okla. (Att: 9,500)

Central State 37 .... Northeastern St. 7
(10-1-0) (7-5-0)

Division II

First round (Nov. 18)

Findlay (Ohio) 21 .... Pacific Lutheran (Wash.) 14
Malone (Ohio) 24 .... Geneva (Pa.) 23
Sioux Falls (S.D.) 41 .... Hastings (Neb.) 23
Bethany (Kan.) 30 .... Benedictine (Kan.) 29
Lambuth (Tenn.) 49 .... Clinch Valley (Va.) 0
Mary (N.D.) 14 .... Dickinson St. (N.D.) 8
Hardin-Simmons (Tex.) 17 .... Howard Payne (Tex.) 6
Central Washington 28 .... Western Washington 21

Quarterfinals (Dec. 2)

at Findlay 15 .... Malone 7
at Lambuth 63 .... Bethany 28
Central Washington 40 .... at Hardin-Simmons 20
at Mary 42 .... Sioux Falls 17

Semifinals (Dec. 9)

Findlay 63 .... Lambuth 13
Central Washington 48 .... Mary 7

Championship

Dec. 16 at Tacoma, Wash. (Att: 5,628)

Central Washington 21 .... (TIE) .... Findlay 21
(10-3-1) (10-1-2)

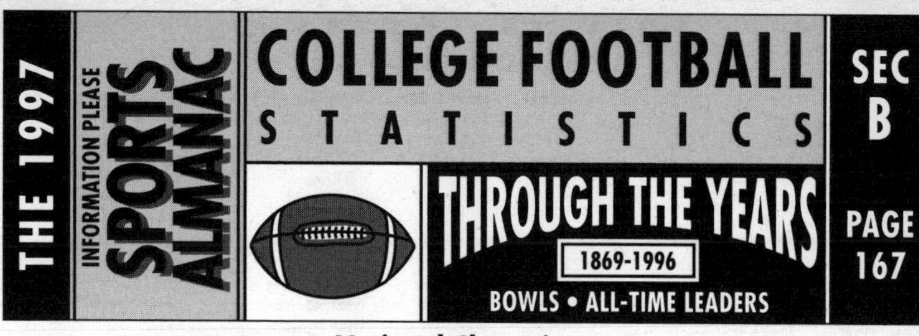

National Champions

Over the last 126 years, there have been 25 major selectors of national champions by way of polls (11), mathematical rating systems (10) and historical research (4). The best-known and most widely circulated of these surveys, the Associated Press poll of sportswriters and broadcasters, first appeared during the 1936 season. Champions prior to 1936 have been determined by retro polls, ratings and historical research.

The Early Years (1869-1935)

National champions based on the Dickinson mathematical system (DS) and three historical retro polls taken by the College Football Researchers Association (CFRA), the National Championship Foundation (NCF) and the Helms Athletic Foundation (HF). The CFRA and NCF polls start in 1869, college football's inaugural year, while the Helms poll begins in 1883, the first season the game adopted a point system for scoring. Frank Dickinson, an economics professor at Illinois, introduced his system in 1926 and retro-picked winners in 1924 and '25. Bowl game results were counted in the Helms selections, but not in the other three.

Multiple champions: Yale (18); Princeton (17); Harvard (9); Michigan (7); Notre Dame and Penn (4); Alabama, Cornell, Illinois, Pittsburgh and USC (3); California, Georgia Tech, Minnesota and Penn St. (2).

Year		Record
1869	**Princeton**	1-1-0
1870	**Princeton**	1-0-0
1871	No games played	
1872	**Princeton**	1-0-0
1873	**Princeton**	1-0-0
1874	**Yale**	3-0-0
1875	**Princeton** (CFRA)	2-0-0
	& **Harvard** (NCF)	4-0-0
1876	**Yale**	3-0-0
1877	**Yale**	3-0-1
1878	**Princeton**	6-0-0
1879	**Princeton**	4-0-1

Year		Record
1880	**Yale** (CFRA)	4-0-1
	& **Princeton** (NCF)	4-0-1
1881	**Yale**	5-0-1
1882	**Yale**	8-0-0
1883	**Yale**	8-0-0
1884	**Yale**	8-0-1
1885	**Princeton**	9-0-0
1886	**Yale**	9-0-1
1887	**Yale**	9-0-0
1888	**Yale**	13-0-0
1889	**Princeton**	10-0-0

Year		Record
1890	**Harvard**	11-0-0
1891	**Yale**	13-0-0
1892	**Yale**	13-0-0
1893	**Princeton**	11-0-0
1894	**Yale**	16-0-0
1895	**Penn**	14-0-0
1896	**Princeton** (CFRA)	10-0-1
	& **Lafayette** (NCF)	11-0-1
1897	**Penn**	15-0-0
1898	**Harvard**	11-0-0
1899	**Princeton** (CFRA)	12-1-0
	& **Harvard** (NCF, HF)	10-0-1

Year		Record	Bowl Game	Head Coach	Outstanding Player
1900	**Yale**	12-0-0	No bowl	Malcolm McBride	Perry Hale, HB
1901	**Harvard** (CFRA)	12-0-0	No bowl	Bill Reid	Bob Kernan, HB
	& **Michigan** (NCF, HF)	11-0-0	Won Rose	Hurry Up Yost	Neil Snow, E
1902	**Michigan**	11-0-0	No bowl	Hurry Up Yost	Boss Weeks, QB
1903	**Princeton**	11-0-0	No bowl	Art Hillebrand	John DeWitt, G
1904	**Penn** (CFRA, HF)	12-0-0	No bowl	Carl Williams	Andy Smith, FB
	& **Michigan** (NCF)	10-0-0	No bowl	Hurry Up Yost	Willie Heston, HB
1905	**Chicago**	10-0-0	No bowl	Amos Alonzo Stagg	Walter Eckersall, QB
1906	**Princeton**	9-0-1	No bowl	Bill Roper	Cap Wister, E
1907	**Yale**	9-0-1	No bowl	Bill Knox	Tad Jones, HB
1908	**Penn** (CFRA, HF)	11-0-1	No bowl	Sol Metzger	Hunter Scarlett, E
	& **LSU** (NCF)	10-0-0	No bowl	Edgar Wingard	Doc Fenton, QB
1909	**Yale**	12-1-0	No bowl	Howard Jones	Ted Coy, FB
1910	**Harvard** (CFRA, HF)	8-0-1	No bowl	Percy Haughton	Percy Wendell, HB
	& **Pittsburgh** (NCF)	9-0-0	No bowl	Joe Thompson	Ralph Galvin, C
1911	**Princeton** (CFRA, HF)	8-0-2	No bowl	Bill Roper	Sam White, E
	& **Penn St.** (NCF)	8-0-1	No bowl	Bill Hollenback	Dexter Very, E
1912	**Harvard** (CFRA, HF)	9-0-0	No bowl	Percy Haughton	Charley Brickley, HB
	& **Penn St.** (NCF)	8-0-0	No bowl	Bill Hollenback	Dexter Very, E
1913	**Harvard**	9-0-0	No bowl	Percy Haughton	Eddie Mahan, FB
1914	**Army**	9-0-0	No bowl	Charley Daly	John McEwan, C
1915	**Cornell**	9-0-0	No bowl	Al Sharpe	Charley Barrett, QB
1916	**Pittsburgh**	8-0-0	No bowl	Pop Warner	Bob Peck, C
1917	**Georgia Tech**	9-0-0	No bowl	John Heisman	Ev Strupper, HB
1918	**Pittsburgh** (CFRA, HF)	4-1-0	No bowl	Pop Warner	Tom Davies, HB
	& **Michigan** (NCF)	5-0-0	No bowl	Hurry Up Yost	Frank Steketee, FB
1919	**Harvard** (CFRA-tie, HF)	9-0-1	Won Rose	Bob Fisher	Eddie Casey, HB
	Illinois (CFRA-tie)	6-1-0	No bowl	Bob Zuppke	Chuck Carney, E
	& **Notre Dame** (NCF)	9-0-0	No bowl	Knute Rockne	George Gipp, HB

National Champions (Cont.)

Year		Record	Bowl Game	Head Coach	Outstanding Player
1920	**California**	9-0-0	Won Rose	Andy Smith	Dan McMillan, T
1921	**California** (CFRA)	9-0-1	Tied Rose	Andy Smith	Brick Muller, E
	& **Cornell** (NCF, HF)	8-0-0	No bowl	Gil Dobie	Eddie Kaw, HB
1922	**Princeton** (CFRA)	8-0-0	No bowl	Bill Roper	Herb Treat, T
	California (NCF)	9-0-0	No bowl	Andy Smith	Brick Muller, E
	& **Cornell** (HF)	8-0-0	No bowl	Gil Dobie	Eddie Kaw, HB
1923	**Illinois** (CFRA, HF)	8-0-0	No bowl	Bob Zuppke	Red Grange, HB
	& **Michigan** (NCF)	8-0-0	No bowl	Hurry Up Yost	Jack Blott, C
1924	**Notre Dame**	10-0-0	Won Rose	Knute Rochne	"The Four Horsemen"*
1925	**Alabama** (CFRA, HF)	10-0-0	Won Rose	Wallace Wade	Johnny Mack Brown, HB
	& **Dartmouth** (DS)	8-0-0	No bowl	Jesse Hawley	Swede Oberlander, HB
1926	**Alabama** (CFRA, HF)	9-0-1	Tied Rose	Wallace Wade	Hoyt Winslett, E
	& **Stanford** (DS)	10-0-1	Tied Rose	Pop Warner	Ted Shipkey, E
1927	**Yale** (CFRA)	7-1-0	No bowl	Tad Jones	Bill Webster, G
	& **Illinois** (NCF, HF, DS)	7-0-1	No bowl	Bob Zuppke	Bob Reitsch, C
1928	**Georgia Tech** (CFRA, NCF, HF)	10-0-0	Won Rose	Bill Alexander	Pete Pund, C
	& **USC** (DS)	9-0-1	No bowl	Howard Jones	Jesse Hibbs, T
1929	**Notre Dame**	9-0-0	No bowl	Knute Rockne	Frank Carideo, QB
1930	**Alabama** (CFRA)	10-0-0	Won Rose	Wallace Wade	Fred Sington, T
	& **Notre Dame** (NCF, HF, DS)	10-0-0	No bowl	Knute Rockne	Marchy Schwartz, HB
1931	**USC**	10-1-0	Won Rose	Howard Jones	John Baker, G
1932	**USC** (CFRA, NCF, HF)	10-0-0	Won Rose	Howard Jones	Ernie Smith, T
	& **Michigan** (DS)	8-0-0	No bowl	Harry Kipke	Harry Newman, QB
1933	**Michigan**	8-0-0	No bowl	Harry Kipke	Chuck Bernard, C
1934	**Minnesota**	8-0-0	No bowl	Bernie Bierman	Pug Lund, HB
1935	**Minnesota** (CFRA, NCF, HF)	8-0-0	No bowl	Bernie Bierman	Dick Smith, T
	& **SMU** (DS)	12-1-0	Lost Rose	Matty Bell	Bobby Wilson, HB

*Notre Dame's **Four Horsemen** were Harry Stuhldreher (QB), Jim Crowley (HB), Don Miller (HB-P) and Elmer Layden (FB).

The Media Poll Years (since 1936)

National champions according to seven media and coaches' polls: Associated Press (since 1936), United Press (1950-57), International News Service (1952-57), United Press International (1958-92), Football Writers Association of America (since 1954), National Football Foundation and Hall of Fame (since 1959) and *USA Today*/CNN (since (1991). In 1991, the American Football Coaches Association switched outlets for its poll from UPI to *USA Today*/CNN.

After 29 years of releasing its final Top 20 poll in early December, AP named its 1965 national champion following that season's bowl games. AP returned to a pre-bowls final vote in 1966 and '67, but has polled its writers and broadcasters after the bowl games since the 1968 season. The FWAA has selected its champion after the bowl games since the 1955 season, the NFF-Hall of Fame since 1971, UPI after 1974 and *USA Today*/CNN since 1982.

The Associated Press changed the name its national championship award from the AP Trophy to the Bear Bryant Trophy after the legendary Alabama coach's death in 1983. The Football Writers' trophy is called the Grantland Rice Award (after the celebrated sportswriter) and the NFF-Hall of Fame trophy is called the MacArthur Bowl (in honor of Gen. Douglas MacArthur).

Multiple champions: Notre Dame (9); Alabama (7); Ohio St. and Oklahoma (6); USC (5); Miami-FL, Minnesota and Nebraska (4); Michigan St. and Texas (3); Army, Georgia Tech, Penn St. and Pittsburgh (2).

Year		Record	Bowl Game	Head Coach	Outstanding Player
1936	**Minnesota**	7-1-0	No bowl	Bernie Bierman	Ed Widseth, T
1937	**Pittsburgh**	9-0-1	No bowl	Jock Sutherland	Marshall Goldberg, HB
1938	**TCU**	11-0-0	Won Sugar	Dutch Meyer	Davey O'Brien, QB
1939	**Texas A&M**	11-0-0	Won Sugar	Homer Norton	John Kimbrough, FB
1940	**Minnesota**	8-0-0	No Bowl	Bernie Bierman	George Franck, HB
1941	**Minnesota**	8-0-0	No bowl	Bernie Bierman	Bruce Smith, HB
1942	**Ohio St.**	9-1-0	No bowl	Paul Brown	Gene Fekete, FB
1943	**Notre Dame**	9-1-0	No bowl	Frank Leahy	Angelo Bertelli, QB
1944	**Army**	9-0-0	No bowl	Red Blaik	Glenn Davis, HB
1945	**Army**	9-0-0	No bowl	Red Blaik	Doc Blanchard, FB
1946	**Notre Dame**	8-0-1	No bowl	Frank Leahy	Johnny Lujack, QB
1947	**Notre Dame**	9-0-0	No bowl	Frank Leahy	Johnny Lujack, QB
1948	**Michigan**	9-0-0	No bowl	Bennie Oosterbaan	Dick Rifenburg, E
1949	**Notre Dame**	10-0-0	No bowl	Frank Leahy	Leon Hart, E
1950	**Oklahoma**	10-1-0	Lost Sugar	Bud Wilkinson	Leon Heath, FB
1951	**Tennessee**	10-0-0	Lost Sugar	Bob Neyland	Hank Lauricella, TB
1952	**Michigan St.** (AP, UP)	9-0-0	No bowl	Biggie Munn	Don McAuliffe, HB
	& **Georgia Tech** (INS)	12-0-0	Won Sugar	Bobby Dodd	Hal Miller, T
1953	**Maryland**	10-1-0	Lost Orange	Jim Tatum	Bernie Faloney, QB
1954	**Ohio St.** (AP, INS)	10-0-0	Won Rose	Woody Hayes	Howard Cassady, HB
	& **UCLA** (UP, FW)	9-0-0	No bowl	Red Sanders	Jack Ellena, T
1955	**Oklahoma**	11-0-0	Won Orange	Bud Wilkinson	Jerry Tubbs, C
1956	**Oklahoma**	10-0-0	No bowl	Bud Wilkinson	Tommy McDonald, HB

National Champions (Cont.)

Year		Record	Bowl Game	Head Coach	Outstanding Player
1957	**Auburn** (AP)	10-0-0	No bowl	Shug Jordan	Jimmy Phillips, E
	& **Ohio St.** (UP, FW, INS)	9-1-0	Won Rose	Woody Hayes	Bob White, FB
1958	**LSU** (AP, UPI)	11-0-0	Won Sugar	Paul Dietzel	Billy Cannon, HB
	& **Iowa** (FW)	8-1-1	Won Rose	Forest Evashevski	Randy Duncan, QB
1959	**Syracuse**	11-0-0	Won Cotton	Ben Schwartzwalder	Ernie Davis, HB
1960	**Minnesota** (AP, UPI, NFF)	8-2-0	Lost Rose	Murray Warmath	Tom Brown, G
	& **Mississippi** (FW)	10-0-1	Won Sugar	Johnny Vaught	Jake Gibbs, QB
1961	**Alabama** (AP, UPI, NFF)	11-0-0	Won Sugar	Bear Bryant	Billy Neighbors, T
	& **Ohio St.** (FW)	8-0-1	No bowl	Woody Hayes	Bob Ferguson, HB
1962	**USC**	11-0-0	Won Rose	John McKay	Hal Bedsole, E
1963	**Texas**	11-0-0	Won Cotton	Darrell Royal	Scott Appleton, T
1964	**Alabama** (AP, UPI),	10-1-0	Lost Orange	Bear Bryant	Joe Namath, QB
	Arkansas (FW)	11-0-0	Won Cotton	Frank Broyles	Ronnie Caveness, LB
	& **Notre Dame** (NFF)	9-1-0	No bowl	Ara Parseghian	John Huarte, QB
1965	**Alabama** (AP, FW-tie)	9-1-1	Won Orange	Bear Bryant	Paul Crane, C
	& **Michigan St.** (UPI, NFF, FW-tie)	10-1-0	Lost Rose	Duffy Daugherty	George Webster, LB
1966	**Notre Dame** (AP, UPI, FW, NFF-tie)	9-0-1	No bowl	Ara Parseghian	Jim Lynch, LB
	& **Michigan St.** (NFF-tie)	9-0-1	No bowl	Duffy Daugherty	Bubba Smith, DE
1967	**USC**	10-1-0	Won Rose	John McKay	O.J. Simpson, HB
1968	**Ohio St.**	10-0-0	Won Rose	Woody Hayes	Rex Kern, QB
1969	**Texas**	11-0-0	Won Cotton	Darrell Royal	James Street, QB
1970	**Nebraska** (AP, FW)	11-0-1	Won Orange	Bob Devaney	Jerry Tagge, QB
	Texas (UPI, NFF-tie),	10-1-0	Lost Cotton	Darrell Royal	Steve Worster, RB
	& **Ohio St.** (NFF-tie)	9-1-0	Lost Rose	Woody Hayes	Jim Stillwagon, MG
1971	**Nebraska**	13-0-0	Won Orange	Bob Devaney	Johnny Rodgers, WR
1972	**USC**	12-0-0	Won Rose	John McKay	Charles Young, TE
1973	**Notre Dame** (AP, FW, NFF)	11-0-0	Won Sugar	Ara Parseghian	Mike Townsend, DB
	& **Alabama** (UPI)	11-1-0	Lost Sugar	Bear Bryant	Buddy Brown, OT
1974	**Oklahoma** (AP)	11-0-0	No bowl	Barry Switzer	Joe Washington, RB
	& **USC** (UPI, FW, NFF)	10-1-1	Won Rose	John McKay	Anthony Davis, RB
1975	**Oklahoma**	11-1-0	Won Orange	Barry Switzer	Lee Roy Selmon, DT
1976	**Pittsburgh**	12-0-0	Won Sugar	Johnny Majors	Tony Dorsett, RB
1977	**Notre Dame**	11-1-0	Won Cotton	Dan Devine	Ross Browner, DE
1978	**Alabama** (AP, FW, NFF)	11-1-0	Won Sugar	Bear Bryant	Marty Lyons, DT
	& **USC** (UPI)	12-1-0	Won Rose	John Robinson	Charles White, RB
1979	**Alabama**	12-0-0	Won Sugar	Bear Bryant	Jim Bunch, OT
1980	**Georgia**	12-0-0	Won Sugar	Vince Dooley	Herschel Walker, RB
1981	**Clemson**	12-0-0	Won Orange	Danny Ford	Jeff Davis, LB
1982	**Penn St.**	11-1-0	Won Sugar	Joe Paterno	Todd Blackledge, QB
1983	**Miami-FL**	11-1-0	Won Orange	H. Schnellenberger	Bernie Kosar, QB
1984	**BYU**	13-0-0	Won Holiday	LaVell Edwards	Robbie Bosco, QB
1985	**Oklahoma**	11-1-0	Won Orange	Barry Switzer	Brian Bosworth, LB
1986	**Penn St.**	12-0-0	Won Fiesta	Joe Paterno	D.J. Dozier, RB
1987	**Miami-FL**	12-0-0	Won Orange	Jimmy Johnson	Steve Walsh, QB
1988	**Notre Dame**	12-0-0	Won Fiesta	Lou Holtz	Tony Rice, QB
1989	**Miami-FL**	11-1-0	Won Sugar	Dennis Erickson	Craig Erickson, QB
1990	**Colorado** (AP, FW, NFF)	11-1-1	Won Orange	Bill McCartney	Eric Bieniemy, RB
	& **Georgia Tech** (UPI)	11-0-1	Won Citrus	Bobby Ross	Shawn Jones, QB
1991	**Miami-FL** (AP)	12-0-0	Won Orange	Dennis Erickson	Gino Torretta, QB
	& **Washington** (USA, FW, NFF)	12-0-0	Won Rose	Don James	Steve Emtman, DT
1992	**Alabama**	13-0-0	Won Sugar	Gene Stallings	Eric Curry, DE
1993	**Florida St.**	12-1-0	Won Orange	Bobby Bowden	Charlie Ward, QB
1994	**Nebraska**	13-0-0	Won Orange	Tom Osborne	Zach Wiegert, OT
1995	**Nebraska**	12-0-0	Won Fiesta	Tom Osborne	Tommie Frazier, QB

Number 1 vs. Number 2

Since the Associated Press writers poll started keeping track of such things in 1936, the No.1 and No.2 ranked teams in the country have met 30 times; 19 during the regular season and 11 in bowl games. Since the first showdown in 1943, the No.1 team has beaten the No.2 team 18 times, lost 10 and there have been two ties. Each showdown is listed below with the date, the match-up, each team's record going into the game, the final score, the stadium and site.

Date	Match-up		Stadium
Oct. 9	**#1** Notre Dame (2-0)	35	Michigan
1943	**#2** Michigan (3-0)	12	(Ann Arbor)
Nov. 20	**#1** Notre Dame (8-0)	14	Notre Dame
1943	**#2** Iowa Pre-Flight (8-0)	13	(South Bend)
Dec. 2	**#1** Army (8-0)	23	Municipal
1944	**#2** Navy (6-2)	7	(Baltimore)
Nov. 10	**#1** Army (6-0)	48	Yankee
1945	**#2** Notre Dame (5-0-1)	0	(New York)
Dec. 1	**#1** Army (8-0)	32	Municipal
1945	**#2** Navy (7-0-1)	13	(Philadelphia)
Nov. 9	**#1** Army (7-0)	0	Yankee
1946	**#2** Notre Dame (5-0)	0	(New York)

Date	Match-up	Stadium
Jan. 1 1963	**#1** USC (10-0) ... 42 **#2** Wisconsin (8-1) ... 37	ROSE BOWL (Pasadena)
Oct. 12 1963	**#2** Texas (3-0) ... 28 **#1** Oklahoma (2-0) ... 7	Cotton Bowl (Dallas)
Jan. 1 1964	**#1** Texas (10-0) ... 28 **#2** Navy (9-1) ... 6	COTTON BOWL (Dallas)
Nov. 19 1966	**#1** Notre Dame (8-0) ... 10 **#2** Michigan St. (9-0) ... 10	Spartan (East Lansing)
Sept. 28 1968	**#1** Purdue (1-0) ... 37 **#2** Notre Dame (1-0) ... 22	Notre Dame (South Bend)
Jan. 1 1969	**#1** Ohio St. (9-0) ... 27 **#2** USC (9-0-1) ... 16	ROSE BOWL (Pasadena)
Dec. 6 1969	**#1** Texas (9-0) ... 15 **#2** Arkansas (9-0) ... 14	Razorback (Fayetteville)
Nov. 25 1971	**#1** Nebraska (10-0) ... 35 **#2** Oklahoma (9-0) ... 31	Owen Field (Norman)
Jan. 1 1972	**#1** Nebraska (12-0) ... 38 **#2** Alabama (11-0) ... 6	ORANGE BOWL (Miami)
Jan. 1 1979	**#2** Alabama (10-1) ... 14 **#1** Penn St. (11-0) ... 7	SUGAR BOWL (New Orleans)
Sept. 26 1981	**#1** USC (2-0) ... 28 **#2** Oklahoma (1-0) ... 24	Coliseum (Los Angeles)
Jan. 1 1983	**#2** Penn St. (10-1) ... 27 **#1** Georgia (11-0) ... 23	SUGAR BOWL (New Orleans)
Oct. 19 1985	**#1** Iowa (5-0) ... 12 **#2** Michigan (5-0) ... 10	Kinnick (Iowa City)
Sept. 27 1986	**#2** Miami-FL (3-0) ... 28 **#1** Oklahoma (2-0) ... 16	Orange Bowl (Miami)
Jan. 2 1987	**#2** Penn St. (11-0) ... 14 **#1** Miami-FL (11-0) ... 10	FIESTA BOWL (Tempe)
Nov. 21 1987	**#2** Oklahoma (10-0) ... 17 **#1** Nebraska (10-0) ... 7	Memorial (Lincoln)
Jan. 1 1988	**#2** Miami-FL (11-0) ... 20 **#1** Oklahoma (11-0) ... 14	ORANGE BOWL (Miami)
Nov. 26 1988	**#1** Notre Dame (10-0) ... 27 **#2** USC (10-0) ... 10	Coliseum (Los Angeles)
Sept. 16 1989	**#1** Notre Dame (1-0) ... 24 **#2** Michigan (0-0) ... 19	Michigan (Ann Arbor)
Nov. 16 1991	**#2** Miami-FL (8-0) ... 17 **#1** Florida St. (10-0) ... 16	Doak Campbell (Tallahassee)
Jan. 1 1993	**#2** Alabama (12-0-0) ... 34 **#1** Miama-FL (11-0-0) ... 13	SUGAR BOWL (New Orleans)
Nov. 13 1993	**#2** Notre Dame (9-0) ... 31 **#1** Florida St. (9-0) ... 24	Notre Dame (South Bend)
Jan. 1 1994	**#1** Florida St. (11-1) ... 18 **#2** Nebraska (11-0) ... 16	ORANGE BOWL (Miami)
Jan. 2 1996	**#1** Nebraska (11-0) ... 62 **#2** Florida (12-0) ... 24	FIESTA BOWL (Tempe)

Top 50 Rivalries

Top Division I-A and I-AA series records, including games through the 1995 season. All rivalries listed below are renewed annually with the following exceptions: **LSU-Tulane** began playing on even-numbered years only in 1995; **Michigan-Notre Dame** did not play in 1995 and will not in '96, but they are scheduled to meet in both 1997 and '98; **Penn St-Pitt** have not played since 1992, but are scheduled to meet again for four consecutive years from 1997-2000.

RECENTLY DISCONTINUED SERIES: **Arkansas vs Texas** in 1992 after 73 games (Texas ahead, 54-19-0); **Boston College vs Holy Cross** in 1986 after 79 games (BC ahead, 48-31-0); **Florida vs Miami-FL** in 1991 after 49 games (Florida ahead, 25-24); **Miami-FL vs Notre Dame** in 1990 after 23 games (ND ahead, 15-7-1);

	Gm	Series Leader
Air Force-Army	30	Air Force (18-11-1)
Air Force-Navy	28	Air Force (19-9-0)
Alabama-Auburn	60	Alabama (34-25-1)
Alabama-Tennessee	78	Alabama (42-29-7)
Arizona-Arizona St	69	Arizona (40-28-1)
Army-Navy	96	Army (46-43-7)
Auburn-Georgia	99	Auburn (47-44-8)
Baylor-TCU	102	Baylor (48-47-7)
BYU-Utah	71	Utah (43-24-4)
California-Stanford	98	Stanford (48-39-11)
Cincinnati-Miami,OH	100	Miami (54-39-7)
The Citadel-VMI	55	VMI (27-26-2)
Clemson-S. Carolina	93	Clemson (55-34-4)
Colorado-Nebraska	54	Nebraska (38-14-2)
Colo. St.-Wyoming	85	Colorado St. (44-36-5)
Duke-North Carolina	81	N. Carolina (42-35-4)
Florida-Florida St.	39	Florida (24-13-2)
Florida-Georgia	74	Georgia (44-28-2)
Florida St.-Miami,FL	39	Miami (23-16-0)
Georgia-Georgia Tech	90	Georgia (50-35-5)
Grambling-Southern	44	Grambling (23-21-0)
Harvard-Yale	112	Yale (61-43-8)
Indiana-Purdue	98	Purdue (59-33-6)
Kansas-Missouri	104	Missouri (48-47-9)
Kansas-Kansas St	93	Kansas (61-27-5)
Kentucky-Tennessee	91	Tennessee (59-23-9)
Lafayette-Lehigh	131	Lafayette (71-55-5)
LSU-Tulane	92	LSU (63-22-7)
Michigan-Michigan St	88	Michigan (57-26-5)
Michigan-Notre Dame	26	Michigan (15-10-1)
Michigan-Ohio St	92	Michigan (52-34-6)
Minnesota-Wisconsin	105	Minnesota (57-40-8)
Mississippi-Miss.St	92	Ole Miss (53-33-6)
Nebraska-Oklahoma	76	Oklahoma (39-34-3)
N. Mexico-N. Mexico St	85	New Mexico (55-25-5)
N. Carolina-N.C. State	85	N. Carolina (55-24-6)
Notre Dame-Purdue	67	Notre Dame (44-21-2)
Notre Dame-USC	67	Notre Dame (39-23-5)
Oklahoma-Okla. St	90	Oklahoma (71-12-7)
Oklahoma-Texas	90	Texas (52-33-5)
Oregon-Oregon St	99	Oregon (49-40-10)
Penn St.-Pittsburgh	92	Penn St.(47-41-4)
Pittsburgh-West Va	88	Pitt (55-30-3)
Princeton-Yale	118	Yale (64-44-10)
Richmond-Wm.& Mary	105	Wm. & Mary (53-47-5)
Tennessee-Vanderbilt	89	Tennessee (58-26-5)
Texas-Texas A&M	102	Texas (65-32-5)
UCLA-USC	65	USC (34-24-7)
Utah-Utah St	93	Utah (62-27-4)
Washington-Wash. St	88	Washington (56-26-6)

Associated Press Final Polls

The Associated Press introduced its weekly college football poll of sportswriters (later, sportswriters and broadcasters) in 1936. The final AP poll was released at the end of the regular season until 1965, when bowl results were included for one year. After a two-year return to regular season games only, the final poll has come out after the bowls since 1968.

1936

Final poll released Nov. 30. Top 20 regular season results after that: **Dec. 5**—#8 Notre Dame tied USC, 13-13; #17 Tennessee tied Ole Miss, 0-0; #18 Arkansas over Texas, 6-0. **Dec. 12**—#16 TCU over #6 Santa Clara, 9-0.

	As of Nov. 30	Head Coach	After Bowls
1 Minnesota	7-1-0	Bernie Bierman	same
2 LSU	9-0-1	Bernie Moore	9-1-1
3 Pittsburgh	7-1-1	Jock Sutherland	8-1-1
4 Alabama	8-0-1	Frank Thomas	same
5 Washington	7-1-1	Jimmy Phelan	7-2-1
6 Santa Clara	7-0-0	Buck Shaw	8-1-0
7 Northwestern	7-1-0	Pappy Waldorf	same
8 Notre Dame	6-2-0	Elmer Layden	6-2-1
9 Nebraska	7-2-0	Dana X. Bible	same
10 Penn	7-1-0	Harvey Harman	same
11 Duke	9-1-0	Wallace Wade	same
12 Yale	7-1-0	Ducky Pond	same
13 Dartmouth	7-1-1	Red Blaik	same
14 Duquesne	7-2-0	John Smith	8-2-0
15 Fordham	5-1-2	Jim Crowley	same
16 TCU	7-2-2	Dutch Meyer	9-2-2
17 Tennessee	6-2-1	Bob Neyland	6-2-2
18 Arkansas	6-3-0	Fred Thomsen	7-3-0
Navy	6-3-0	Tom Hamilton	same
20 Marquette	7-1-0	Frank Murray	7-2-0

Key Bowl Games

Sugar—#6 Santa Clara over #2 LSU, 21-14; **Rose**— #3 Pitt over #5 Washington, 21-0; **Orange**—#14 Duquesne over Mississippi St., 13-12; **Cotton**—#16 TCU over #20 Marquette, 16-6.

1937

Final poll released Nov. 29. Top 20 regular season results after that: **Dec. 4**—#18 Rice over SMU, 15-7.

	As of Nov. 29	Head Coach	After Bowls
1 Pittsburgh	9-0-1	Jock Sutherland	same
2 California	9-0-1	Stub Allison	10-0-1
3 Fordham	7-0-1	Jim Crowley	same
4 Alabama	9-0-0	Frank Thomas	9-1-0
5 Minnesota	6-2-0	Bernie Bierman	same
6 Villanova	8-0-1	Clipper Smith	same
7 Dartmouth	7-0-2	Red Blaik	same
8 LSU	9-1-0	Bernie Moore	9-2-0
9 Notre Dame	6-2-1	Elmer Layden	same
Santa Clara	8-0-0	Buck Shaw	9-0-0
11 Nebraska	6-1-2	Biff Jones	same
12 Yale	6-1-1	Ducky Pond	same
13 Ohio St.	6-2-0	Francis Schmidt	same
14 Holy Cross	8-0-2	Eddie Anderson	same
Arkansas	6-2-2	Fred Thomsen	same
16 TCU	4-2-2	Dutch Meyer	same
17 Colorado	8-0-0	Bunnie Oakes	8-1-0
18 Rice	4-3-2	Jimmy Kitts	6-3-2
19 North Carolina	7-1-1	Ray Wolf	same
20 Duke	7-2-1	Wallace Wade	same

Key Bowl Games

Rose—#2 Cal over #4 Alabama, 13-0; **Sugar**—#9 Santa Clara over #8 LSU, 6-0; **Cotton**—#18 Rice over #17 Colorado, 28-14; **Orange**—Auburn over Michigan St., 6-0.

1938

Final poll released Dec. 5. Top 20 regular season results after that: **Dec. 26**—#14 Cal over Georgia Tech, 13-7.

	As of Dec. 5	Head Coach	After Bowls
1 TCU	10-0-0	Dutch Meyer	11-0-0
2 Tennessee	10-0-0	Bob Neyland	11-0-0
3 Duke	9-0-0	Wallace Wade	9-1-0
4 Oklahoma	10-0-0	Tom Stidham	10-1-0
5 Notre Dame	8-1-0	Elmer Layden	same
6 Carnegie Tech	7-1-0	Bill Kern	7-2-0
7 USC	8-2-0	Howard Jones	9-2-0
8 Pittsburgh	8-2-0	Jock Sutherland	same
9 Holy Cross	8-1-0	Eddie Anderson	same
10 Minnesota	6-2-0	Bernie Bierman	same
11 Texas Tech	10-0-0	Pete Cawthon	10-1-0
12 Cornell	5-1-1	Carl Snavely	same
13 Alabama	7-1-1	Frank Thomas	same
14 California	9-1-0	Stub Allison	10-1-0
15 Fordham	6-1-2	Jim Crowley	same
16 Michigan	6-1-1	Fritz Crisler	same
17 Northwestern	4-2-2	Pappy Waldorf	same
18 Villanova	8-0-1	Clipper Smith	same
19 Tulane	7-2-1	Red Dawson	same
20 Dartmouth	7-2-0	Red Blaik	same

Key Bowl Games

Sugar—#1 TCU over #6 Carnegie Tech, 15-7; **Orange**—#2 Tennessee over #4 Oklahoma, 17-0; **Rose**—#7 USC over #3 Duke, 7-3; **Cotton**—St. Mary's over #11 Texas Tech 20-13.

1939

Final poll released Dec. 11. Top 20 regular season results after that: None.

	As of Dec. 11	Head Coach	After Bowls
1 Texas A&M	10-0-0	Homer Norton	11-0-0
2 Tennessee	10-0-0	Bob Neyland	10-1-0
3 USC	7-0-2	Howard Jones	8-0-2
4 Cornell	8-0-0	Carl Snavely	same
5 Tulane	8-0-1	Red Dawson	8-1-1
6 Missouri	8-1-0	Don Faurot	8-2-0
7 UCLA	6-0-4	Babe Horrell	same
8 Duke	8-1-0	Wallace Wade	same
9 Iowa	6-1-1	Eddie Anderson	same
10 Duquesne	8-0-1	Buff Donelli	same
11 Boston College	9-1-0	Frank Leahy	9-2-0
12 Clemson	8-1-0	Jess Neely	9-1-0
13 Notre Dame	7-2-0	Elmer Layden	same
14 Santa Clara	5-1-3	Buck Shaw	same
15 Ohio St.	6-2-0	Francis Schmidt	same
16 Georgia Tech	7-2-0	Bill Alexander	8-2-0
17 Fordham	6-2-0	Jim Crowley	same
18 Nebraska	7-1-1	Biff Jones	same
19 Oklahoma	6-2-1	Tom Stidham	same
20 Michigan	6-2-0	Fritz Crisler	same

Key Bowl Games

Sugar—#1 Texas A&M over #5 Tulane, 14-13; **Rose** —#3 USC over #2 Tennessee, 14-0; **Orange**—#16 Georgia Tech over #6 Missouri, 21-7; **Cotton**—#12 Clemson over #11 Boston College, 6-3.

Associated Press Final Polls (Cont.)

1940

Final poll released Dec. 2. Top 20 regular season results after that: **Dec. 7**—#16 SMU over Rice, 7-6.

	As of Dec. 2	Head Coach	After Bowls
1 Minnesota	8-0-0	Bernie Bierman	same
2 Stanford	9-0-0	Clark Shaughnessy	10-0-0
3 Michigan	7-1-0	Fritz Crisler	same
4 Tennessee	10-0-0	Bob Neyland	10-1-0
5 Boston College	10-0-0	Frank Leahy	11-0-0
6 Texas A&M	8-1-0	Homer Norton	9-1-0
7 Nebraska	8-1-0	Biff Jones	8-2-0
8 Northwestern	6-2-0	Pappy Waldorf	same
9 Mississippi St.	9-0-1	Allyn McKeen	10-0-1
10 Washington	7-2-0	Jimmy Phelan	same
11 Santa Clara	6-1-1	Buck Shaw	same
12 Fordham	7-1-0	Jim Crowley	7-2-0
13 Georgetown	8-1-0	Jack Hagerty	8-2-0
14 Penn	6-1-1	George Munger	same
15 Cornell	6-2-0	Carl Snavely	same
16 SMU	7-1-1	Matty Bell	8-1-1
17 Hardin-Simmons	9-0-0	Warren Woodson	same
18 Duke	7-2-0	Wallace Wade	same
19 Lafayette	9-0-0	Hooks Mylin	same
20 —			

Note: Only 19 teams ranked.

Key Bowl Games

Rose—#2 Stanford over #7 Nebraska, 21-13; **Sugar**—#5 Boston College over #4 Tennessee, 19-13; **Cotton**—#6 Texas A&M over #12 Fordham, 13-12; **Orange**—#9 Mississippi St. over #13 Georgetown, 14-7.

1941

Final poll released Dec. 1. Top 20 regular season results after that: **Dec. 6**—#4 Texas over Oregon, 71-7; #9 Texas A&M over #19 Washington St., 7-0; #16 Mississippi St. over San Francisco, 26-13.

	As of Dec. 1	Head Coach	After Bowls
1 Minnesota	8-0-0	Bernie Bierman	same
2 Duke	9-0-0	Wallace Wade	9-1-0
3 Notre Dame	8-0-1	Frank Leahy	same
4 Texas	7-1-1	Dana X. Bible	8-1-1
5 Michigan	6-1-1	Fritz Crisler	same
6 Fordham	7-1-0	Jim Crowley	8-1-0
7 Missouri	8-1-0	Don Faurot	8-2-0
8 Duquesne	8-0-0	Buff Donelli	same
9 Texas A&M	8-1-0	Homer Norton	9-2-0
10 Navy	7-1-1	Swede Larson	same
11 Northwestern	5-3-0	Pappy Waldorf	same
12 Oregon St.	7-2-0	Lon Stiner	8-2-0
13 Ohio St.	6-1-1	Paul Brown	same
14 Georgia	8-1-1	Wally Butts	9-1-1
15 Penn	7-1-1	George Munger	same
16 Mississippi St.	7-1-1	Allyn McKeen	8-1-1
17 Mississippi	6-2-1	Harry Mehre	same
18 Tennessee	8-2-0	John Barnhill	same
19 Washington St.	6-3-0	Babe Hollingbery	6-4-0
20 Alabama	8-2-0	Frank Thomas	9-2-0

Note: 1942 Rose Bowl moved to Durham, N.C., for one year after outbreak of World War II.

Key Bowl Games

Rose—#12 Oregon St. over #2 Duke, 20-16; **Sugar**—#6 Fordham over #7 Missouri, 2-0; **Cotton**—#20 Alabama over #9 Texas A&M, 29-21; **Orange**—#14 Georgia over TCU, 40-26.

1942

Final poll released Nov. 30. Top 20 regular season results after that: **Dec. 5**—#6 Notre Dame tied Great Lakes Naval Station, 13-13; #13 UCLA over Idaho, 40-13; #14 William & Mary over Oklahoma, 14-7; #17 Washington St. lost to Texas A&M, 21-0; #18 Mississippi St. over San Francisco, 19-7. **Dec. 12**—#13 UCLA over USC, 14-7.

	As of Nov. 30	Head Coach	After Bowls
1 Ohio St.	9-1-0	Paul Brown	same
2 Georgia	10-1-0	Wally Butts	11-1-0
3 Wisconsin	8-1-1	Harry Stuhldreher	same
4 Tulsa	10-0-0	Henry Frnka	10-1-0
5 Georgia Tech	9-1-0	Bill Alexander	9-2-0
6 Notre Dame	7-2-1	Frank Leahy	7-2-2
7 Tennessee	8-1-1	John Barnhill	9-1-1
8 Boston College	8-1-0	Denny Myers	8-2-0
9 Michigan	7-3-0	Fritz Crisler	same
10 Alabama	7-3-0	Frank Thomas	8-3-0
11 Texas	8-2-0	Dana X. Bible	9-2-0
12 Stanford	6-4-0	Marchie Schwartz	same
13 UCLA	5-3-0	Babe Horrell	7-4-0
14 William & Mary	8-1-1	Carl Voyles	9-1-1
15 Santa Clara	7-2-0	Buck Shaw	same
16 Auburn	6-4-1	Jack Meagher	same
17 Washington St.	6-1-2	Babe Hollingbery	6-2-2
18 Mississippi St.	7-2-0	Allyn McKeen	8-2-0
19 Minnesota	5-4-0	George Hauser	same
Holy Cross	5-4-1	Ank Scanlon	same
Penn St.	6-1-1	Bob Higgins	same

Key Bowl Games

Rose—#2 Georgia over #13 UCLA, 9-0; **Sugar**—#7 Tennessee over #4 Tulsa, 14-7; **Cotton**—#11 Texas over #5 Georgia Tech, 14-7; **Orange**—#10 Alabama over #8 Boston College, 37-21.

1943

Final poll released Nov. 29. Top 20 regular season results after that: **Dec. 11**—#10 March Field over #19 Pacific, 19-0.

	As of Nov. 29	Head Coach	After Bowls
1 Notre Dame	9-1-0	Frank Leahy	same
2 Iowa Pre-Flight	9-1-0	Don Faurot	same
3 Michigan	8-1-0	Fritz Crisler	same
4 Navy	8-1-0	Billick Whelchel	same
5 Purdue	9-0-0	Elmer Burnham	same
6 Great Lakes Naval Station	10-2-0	Tony Hinkle	same
7 Duke	8-1-0	Eddie Cameron	same
8 Del Monte Pre-Flight	7-1-0	Bill Kern	same
9 Northwestern	6-2-0	Pappy Waldorf	same
10 March Field	8-1-0	Paul Schissler	9-1-0
11 Army	7-2-1	Red Blaik	same
12 Washington	4-0-0	Ralph Welch	4-1-0
13 Georgia Tech	7-3-0	Bill Alexander	8-3-0
14 Texas	7-1-0	Dana X. Bible	7-1-1
15 Tulsa	6-0-1	Henry Frnka	6-1-1
16 Dartmouth	6-1-0	Earl Brown	same
17 Bainbridge Navy Training School	7-0-0	Joe Maniaci	same
18 Colorado College	7-0-0	Hal White	same
19 Pacific	7-1-0	Amos A. Stagg	7-2-0
20 Penn	6-2-1	George Munger	same

Key Bowl Games

Rose—USC over #12 Washington, 29-0; **Sugar**—#13 Georgia Tech over #15 Tulsa, 20-18; **Cotton**—#14 Texas tied Randolph Field, 7-7; **Orange**—LSU over Texas A&M, 19-14.

1944

Final poll released Dec. 4. Top 20 regular season results after that: **Dec. 10**—#3 Randolph Field over #10 March Field, 20-7; #18 Fort Pierce over Kessler Field, 34-7; Morris Field over #20 Second Air Force, 14-7.

	As of Dec. 4	Head Coach	After Bowls
1 Army	9-0-0	Red Blaik	same
2 Ohio St.	9-0-0	Carroll Widdoes	same
3 Randolph Field	10-0-0	Frank Tritico	12-0-0
4 Navy	6-3-0	Oscar Hagberg	same
5 Bainbridge Navy Training School	10-0-0	Joe Maniaci	same
6 Iowa Pre-Flight	10-1-0	Jack Meagher	same
7 USC	7-0-2	Jeff Cravath	8-0-2
8 Michigan	8-2-0	Fritz Crisler	same
9 Notre Dame	8-2-0	Ed McKeever	same
10 March Field	7-0-2	Paul Schissler	7-1-2
11 Duke	5-4-0	Eddie Cameron	6-4-0
12 Tennessee	7-0-1	John Barnhill	7-1-1
13 Georgia Tech	8-2-0	Bill Alexander	8-3-0
14 Norman Pre-Flight	6-0-0	John Gregg	same
15 Illinois	5-4-1	Ray Eliot	same
16 El Toro Marines	8-1-0	Dick Hanley	same
17 Great Lakes Naval Station	9-2-1	Paul Brown	same
18 Fort Pierce	8-0-0	Hamp Pool	9-0-0
19 St.Mary's Pre-Flight	4-4-0	Jules Sikes	same
20 Second Air Force	10-2-1	Bill Reese	10-4-1

Key Bowl Games

Treasury—#3 Randolph Field over #20 Second Air Force, 13-6; **Rose**—#7 USC over #12 Tennessee, 25-0; **Sugar**—#11 Duke over Alabama, 29-26; **Orange**—Tulsa over #13 Georgia Tech, 26-12; **Cotton**—Oklahoma A&M over TCU, 34-0.

1945

Final poll released Dec. 3. Top 20 regular season results after that: None.

	As of Dec. 3	Head Coach	After Bowls
1 Army	9-0-0	Red Blaik	same
2 Alabama	9-0-0	Frank Thomas	10-0-0
3 Navy	7-1-1	Oscar Hagberg	same
4 Indiana	9-0-1	Bo McMillan	same
5 Oklahoma A&M	8-0-0	Jim Lookabaugh	9-0-0
6 Michigan	7-3-0	Fritz Crisler	same
7 St. Mary's-CA	7-1-0	Jimmy Phelan	7-2-0
8 Penn	6-2-0	George Munger	same
9 Notre Dame	7-2-1	Hugh Devore	same
10 Texas	9-1-0	Dana X. Bible	10-1-0
11 USC	7-3-0	Jeff Cravath	7-4-0
12 Ohio St.	7-2-0	Carroll Widdoes	same
13 Duke	6-2-0	Eddie Cameron	same
14 Tennessee	8-1-0	John Barnhill	same
15 LSU	7-2-0	Bernie Moore	same
16 Holy Cross	8-1-0	John DeGrosa	8-2-0
17 Tulsa	8-2-0	Henry Frnka	8-3-0
18 Georgia	8-2-0	Wally Butts	9-2-0
19 Wake Forest	4-3-1	Peahead Walker	5-3-1
20 Columbia	8-1-0	Lou Little	same

Key Bowl Games

Rose—#2 Alabama over #11 USC, 34-14; **Sugar**— #5 Oklahoma A&M over #7 St. Mary's, 33-13; **Cotton**—#10 Texas over Missouri, 40-27; **Orange**—Miami-FL over #16 Holy Cross, 13-6.

1946

Final poll released Dec. 2. Top 20 regular season results after that: None.

	As of Dec. 2	Head Coach	After Bowls
1 Notre Dame	8-0-1	Frank Leahy	same
2 Army	9-0-1	Red Blaik	same
3 Georgia	10-0-0	Wally Butts	11-0-0
4 UCLA	10-0-0	Bert LaBrucherie	10-1-0
5 Illinois	7-2-0	Ray Eliot	8-2-0
6 Michigan	6-2-1	Fritz Crisler	same
7 Tennessee	9-1-0	Bob Neyland	9-2-0
8 LSU	9-1-0	Bernie Moore	9-1-1
9 North Carolina	8-1-1	Carl Snavely	8-2-1
10 Rice	8-2-0	Jess Neely	9-2-0
11 Georgia Tech	8-2-0	Bobby Dodd	9-2-0
12 Yale	7-1-1	Howard Odell	same
13 Penn	6-2-0	George Munger	same
14 Oklahoma	7-3-0	Jim Tatum	8-3-0
15 Texas	8-2-0	Dana X. Bible	same
16 Arkansas	6-3-1	John Barnhill	6-3-2
17 Tulsa	9-1-0	J.O. Brothers	same
18 N.C. State	8-2-0	Beattie Feathers	8-3-0
19 Delaware	9-0-0	Bill Murray	10-0-0
20 Indiana	6-3-0	Bo McMillan	same

Key Bowl Games

Sugar—#3 Georgia over #9 N.Carolina, 20-10; **Rose**— #5 Illinois over #4 UCLA, 45-14; **Orange**—#10 Rice over #7 Tennessee, 8-0; **Cotton**—#8 LSU tied #16 Arkansas, 0-0.

1947

Final poll released Dec. 8. Top 20 regular season results after that: None.

	As of Dec. 8	Head Coach	After Bowls
1 Notre Dame	9-0-0	Frank Leahy	same
2 Michigan	9-0-0	Fritz Crisler	10-0-0
3 SMU	9-0-1	Matty Bell	9-0-2
4 Penn St.	9-0-0	Bob Higgins	9-0-1
5 Texas	9-1-0	Blair Cherry	10-1-0
6 Alabama	8-2-0	Red Drew	8-3-0
7 Penn	7-0-1	George Munger	same
8 USC	7-1-1	Jeff Cravath	7-2-1
9 North Carolina	8-2-0	Carl Snavely	same
10 Georgia Tech	9-1-0	Bobby Dodd	10-1-0
11 Army	5-2-2	Red Blaik	same
12 Kansas	8-0-2	George Sauer	8-1-2
13 Mississippi	8-2-0	Johnny Vaught	9-2-0
14 William & Mary	9-1-0	Rube McCray	9-2-0
15 California	9-1-0	Pappy Waldorf	same
16 Oklahoma	7-2-1	Bud Wilkinson	same
17 N.C. State	5-3-1	Beattie Feathers	same
18 Rice	6-3-1	Jess Neely	same
19 Duke	4-3-2	Wallace Wade	same
20 Columbia	7-2-0	Lou Little	same

Key Bowl Games

Rose—#2 Michigan over #8 USC, 49-0; **Cotton**—#3 SMU tied #4 Penn St., 13-13; **Sugar**—#5 Texas over #6 Alabama, 27-7; **Orange**—#10 Georgia Tech over #12 Kansas, 20-14.

Note: An unprecedented "Who's No. 1?" poll was conducted by AP after the Rose Bowl game, pitting Notre Dame against Michigan. The Wolverines won the vote, 226-119, but AP ruled that the Irish would be the No. 1 team of record.

Associated Press Final Polls (Cont.)

1948

Final poll released Nov. 29. Top 20 regular season results after that: **Dec. 3**—#12 Vanderbilt over Miami-FL, 33-6. **Dec. 4**—#2 Notre Dame tied USC, 14-14; #11 Clemson over The Citadel, 20-0.

	As of Nov.29	Head Coach	After Bowls
1 Michigan	9-0-0	Bennie Oosterbaan	same
2 Notre Dame	9-0-0	Frank Leahy	9-0-1
3 North Carolina	9-0-1	Carl Snavely	9-1-1
4 California	10-0-0	Pappy Waldorf	10-1-0
5 Oklahoma	9-1-0	Bud Wilkinson	10-1-0
6 Army	8-0-1	Red Blaik	same
7 Northwestern	7-2-0	Bob Voigts	8-2-0
8 Georgia	9-1-0	Wally Butts	9-2-0
9 Oregon	9-1-0	Jim Aiken	9-2-0
10 SMU	8-1-1	Matty Bell	9-1-1
11 Clemson	9-0-0	Frank Howard	11-0-0
12 Vanderbilt	7-2-1	Red Sanders	8-2-1
13 Tulane	9-1-0	Henry Frnka	same
14 Michigan St.	6-2-2	Biggie Munn	same
15 Mississippi	8-1-0	Johnny Vaught	same
16 Minnesota	7-2-0	Bernie Bierman	same
17 William & Mary	6-2-2	Rube McCray	7-2-2
18 Penn St.	7-1-1	Bob Higgins	same
19 Cornell	8-1-0	Lefty James	same
20 Wake Forest	6-3-0	Peahead Walker	6-4-0

Note: Big Nine "no-repeat" rule kept Michigan from Rose Bowl.

Key Bowl Games

Sugar—#5 Oklahoma over #3 North Carolina, 14-6; **Rose**—#7 Northwestern over #4 Cal, 20-14; **Orange**—Texas over #8 Georgia, 41-28; **Cotton**—#10 SMU over #9 Oregon, 21-13.

1949

Final poll released Nov. 28. Top 20 regular season results after that: **Dec. 2**—#14 Maryland over Miami-FL, 13-0. **Dec. 3**—#1 Notre Dame over SMU, 27-20; #10 Pacific over Hawaii, 75-0.

	As of Nov. 28	Head Coach	After Bowls
1 Notre Dame	9-0-0	Frank Leahy	10-0-0
2 Oklahoma	10-0-0	Bud Wilkinson	11-0-0
3 California	10-0-0	Pappy Waldorf	10-1-0
4 Army	9-0-0	Red Blaik	same
5 Rice	9-1-0	Jess Neely	10-1-0
6 Ohio St.	6-1-2	Wes Fesler	7-1-2
7 Michigan	6-2-1	Bennie Oosterbaan	same
8 Minnesota	7-2-0	Bernie Bierman	same
9 LSU	8-2-0	Gaynell Tinsley	8-3-0
10 Pacific	10-0-0	Larry Siemering	11-0-0
11 Kentucky	9-2-0	Bear Bryant	9-3-0
12 Cornell	8-1-0	Lefty James	same
13 Villanova	8-1-0	Jim Leonard	same
14 Maryland	7-1-0	Jim Tatum	9-1-0
15 Santa Clara	7-2-1	Len Casanova	8-2-1
16 North Carolina	7-3-0	Carl Snavely	7-4-0
17 Tennessee	7-2-1	Bob Neyland	same
18 Princeton	6-3-0	Charlie Caldwell	same
19 Michigan St.	6-3-0	Biggie Munn	same
20 Missouri	7-3-0	Don Faurot	7-4-0
Baylor	8-2-0	Bob Woodruff	same

Key Bowl Games

Sugar—#2 Oklahoma over #9 LSU, 35-0; **Rose**—#6 Ohio St. over #3 Cal, 17-14; **Cotton**—#5 Rice over #16 North Carolina, 27-13; **Orange**—#15 Santa Clara over #11 Kentucky, 21-13.

1950

Final poll released Nov. 27. Top 20 regular season results after that: **Nov. 30**—#3 Texas over Texas A&M, 17-0. **Dec. 1**—#15 Miami-FL over Missouri, 27—9. **Dec. 2**—#1 Oklahoma over Okla. A&M, 41-14; Navy over #2 Army, 14-2; #4 Tennessee over Vanderbilt, 43-0; #16 Alabama over Auburn, 34-0; #19 Tulsa over Houston, 28-21; #20 Tulane tied LSU, 14-14. **Dec. 9**—#3 Texas over LSU, 21-6.

	As of Nov. 27	Head Coach	After Bowls
1 Oklahoma	9-0-0	Bud Wilkinson	10-1-0
2 Army	8-1-0	Red Blaik	same
3 Texas	7-1-0	Blair Cherry	9-2-0
4 Tennessee	9-1-0	Bob Neyland	11-1-0
5 California	9-0-1	Pappy Waldorf	9-1-1
6 Princeton	9-0-0	Charlie Caldwell	same
7 Kentucky	10-1-0	Bear Bryant	11-1-0
8 Michigan St.	8-1-0	Biggie Munn	same
9 Michigan	5-3-1	Bennie Oosterbaan	6-3-1
10 Clemson	8-0-1	Frank Howard	9-0-1
11 Washington	8-2-0	Howard Odell	same
12 Wyoming	9-0-0	Bowden Wyatt	10-0-0
13 Illinois	7-2-0	Ray Eliot	same
14 Ohio St.	6-3-0	Wes Fesler	same
15 Miami-FL	8-0-1	Andy Gustafson	9-1-1
16 Alabama	8-2-0	Red Drew	9-2-0
17 Nebraska	6-2-1	Bill Glassford	same
18 Wash. & Lee	8-2-0	George Barclay	8-3-0
19 Tulsa	8-1-1	J.O. Brothers	9-1-1
20 Tulane	6-2-0	Henry Frnka	6-2-1

Key Bowl Games

Sugar—#7 Kentucky over #1 Oklahoma, 13-7; **Cotton**—#4 Tennessee over #3 Texas, 20-14; **Rose**—#9 Michigan over #5 Cal, 14-6; **Orange**—#10 Clemson over #15 Miami-FL, 15-14.

1951

Final poll released Dec. 3. Top 20 regular season results after that: None.

	As of Dec. 3	Head Coach	After Bowls
1 Tennessee	10-0-0	Bob Neyland	10-1-0
2 Michigan St.	9-0-0	Biggie Munn	same
3 Maryland	9-0-0	Jim Tatum	10-0-0
4 Illinois	8-0-1	Ray Eliot	9-0-1
5 Georgia Tech	10-0-1	Bobby Dodd	11-0-1
6 Princeton	9-0-0	Charlie Caldwell	same
7 Stanford	9-1-0	Chuck Taylor	9-2-0
8 Wisconsin	7-1-1	Ivy Williamson	same
9 Baylor	8-1-1	George Sauer	8-2-1
10 Oklahoma	8-2-0	Bud Wilkinson	same
11 TCU	6-4-0	Dutch Meyer	6-5-0
12 California	8-2-0	Pappy Waldorf	same
13 Virginia	8-1-0	Art Guepe	same
14 San Francisco	9-0-0	Joe Kuharich	same
15 Kentucky	7-4-0	Bear Bryant	8-4-0
16 Boston Univ.	6-4-0	Buff Donelli	same
17 UCLA	5-3-1	Red Sanders	same
18 Washington St.	7-3-0	Forest Evashevski	same
19 Holy Cross	8-2-0	Eddie Anderson	same
Clemson	7-2-0	Frank Howard	7-3-0

Key Bowl Games

Sugar—#3 Maryland over #1 Tennessee, 28-13; **Rose**—#4 Illinois over #7 Stanford, 40-7; **Orange**—#5 Georgia Tech over #9 Baylor, 17-14; **Cotton**—#15 Kentucky over #11 TCU, 20-7.

1952

Final poll released Dec. 1. Top 20 regular season results after that: **Dec. 6**—#15 Florida over #20 Kentucky, 27-20.

	As of Dec. 1	Head Coach	After Bowls
1 Michigan St.	9-0-0	Biggie Munn	same
2 Georgia Tech	11-0-0	Bobby Dodd	12-0-0
3 Notre Dame	7-2-1	Frank Leahy	same
4 Oklahoma	8-1-1	Bud Wilkinson	same
5 USC	9-1-0	Jess Hill	10-1-0
6 UCLA	8-1-0	Red Sanders	same
7 Mississippi	8-0-2	Johnny Vaught	8-1-2
8 Tennessee	8-1-1	Bob Neyland	8-2-1
9 Alabama	9-2-0	Red Drew	10-2-0
10 Texas	8-2-0	Ed Price	9-2-0
11 Wisconsin	6-2-1	Ivy Williamson	6-3-1
12 Tulsa	8-1-1	J.O. Brothers	8-2-1
13 Maryland	7-2-0	Jim Tatum	same
14 Syracuse	7-2-0	Ben Schwartzwalder	7-3-0
15 Florida	6-3-0	Bob Woodruff	8-3-0
16 Duke	8-2-0	Bill Murray	same
17 Ohio St.	6-3-0	Woody Hayes	same
18 Purdue	4-3-2	Stu Holcomb	same
19 Princeton	8-1-0	Charlie Caldwell	same
20 Kentucky	5-3-2	Bear Bryant	5-4-2

Note: Michigan St. would officially join Big Ten in 1953.

Key Bowl Games

Sugar—#2 Georgia Tech over #7 Ole Miss, 24-7; **Rose**—#5 USC over #11 Wisconsin, 7-0; **Cotton**—#10 Texas over #8 Tennessee, 16-0; **Orange**—#9 Alabama over #14 Syracuse, 61-6.

1953

Final poll released Nov. 30. Top 20 regular season results after that: **Dec. 5**—#2 Notre Dame over SMU, 40-14.

	As of Nov. 30	Head Coach	After Bowls
1 Maryland	10-0-0	Jim Tatum	10-1-0
2 Notre Dame	8-0-1	Frank Leahy	9-0-1
3 Michigan St.	8-1-0	Biggie Munn	9-1-0
4 Oklahoma	8-1-1	Bud Wilkinson	9-1-1
5 UCLA	8-1-0	Red Sanders	8-2-0
6 Rice	8-2-0	Jess Neely	9-2-0
7 Illinois	7-1-1	Ray Eliot	same
8 Georgia Tech	8-2-1	Bobby Dodd	9-2-1
9 Iowa	5-3-1	Forest Evashevski	same
10 West Virginia	8-1-0	Art Lewis	8-2-0
11 Texas	7-3-0	Ed Price	same
12 Texas Tech	10-1-0	DeWitt Weaver	11-1-0
13 Alabama	6-2-3	Red Drew	6-3-3
14 Army	7-1-1	Red Blaik	same
15 Wisconsin	6-2-1	Ivy Williamson	same
16 Kentucky	7-2-1	Bear Bryant	same
17 Auburn	7-2-1	Shug Jordan	7-3-1
18 Duke	7-2-1	Bill Murray	same
19 Stanford	6-3-1	Chuck Taylor	same
20 Michigan	6-3-0	Bennie Oosterbaan	same

Key Bowl Games

Orange—#4 Oklahoma over #1 Maryland, 7-0; **Rose**—#3 Michigan St. over #5 UCLA, 28-20; **Cotton**—#6 Rice over #13 Alabama, 28-6; **Sugar**—#8 Georgia Tech over #10 West Virginia, 42-19.

1954

Final poll released Nov. 29. Top 20 regular season results after that: **Dec. 4**—#4 Notre Dame over SMU, 26-14.

	As of Nov. 29	Head Coach	After Bowls
1 Ohio St.	9-0-0	Woody Hayes	10-0-0
2 UCLA	9-0-0	Red Sanders	same
3 Oklahoma	10-0-0	Bud Wilkinson	same
4 Notre Dame	8-1-0	Terry Brennan	9-1-0
5 Navy	7-2-0	Eddie Erdelatz	8-2-0
6 Mississippi	9-1-0	Johnny Vaught	9-2-0
7 Army	7-2-0	Red Blaik	same
8 Maryland	7-2-1	Jim Tatum	same
9 Wisconsin	7-2-0	Ivy Williamson	same
10 Arkansas	8-2-0	Bowden Wyatt	8-3-0
11 Miami-FL	8-1-0	Andy Gustafson	same
12 West Virginia	8-1-0	Art Lewis	same
13 Auburn	7-3-0	Shug Jordan	8-3-0
14 Duke	7-2-1	Bill Murray	8-2-1
15 Michigan	6-3-0	Bennie Oosterbaan	same
16 Virginia Tech	8-0-1	Frank Moseley	same
17 USC	8-3-0	Jess Hill	8-4-0
18 Baylor	7-3-0	George Sauer	7-4-0
19 Rice	7-3-0	Jess Neely	same
20 Penn St.	7-2-0	Rip Engle	same

Note: PCC and Big Seven "no-repeat" rules kept UCLA and Oklahoma from Orange and Rose bowls, respectively.

Key Bowl Games

Rose—#1 Ohio St. over #17 USC, 20-7; **Sugar**—#5 Navy over #6 Ole Miss, 21-0; **Cotton**—Georgia Tech over #10 Arkansas, 14-6; **Orange**—#14 Duke over Nebraska, 34-7.

1955

Final poll released Nov. 28. Top 20 regular season results after that: None.

	As of Nov. 28	Head Coach	After Bowls
1 Oklahoma	10-0-0	Bud Wilkinson	11-0-0
2 Michigan St.	8-1-0	Duffy Daugherty	9-1-0
3 Maryland	10-0-0	Jim Tatum	10-1-0
4 UCLA	9-1-0	Red Sanders	9-2-0
5 Ohio St.	7-2-0	Woody Hayes	same
6 TCU	9-1-0	Abe Martin	9-2-0
7 Georgia Tech	8-1-1	Bobby Dodd	9-1-1
8 Auburn	8-1-1	Shug Jordan	8-2-1
9 Notre Dame	8-2-0	Terry Brennan	same
10 Mississippi	9-1-0	Johnny Vaught	10-1-0
11 Pittsburgh	7-3-0	John Michelosen	7-4-0
12 Michigan	7-2-0	Bennie Oosterbaan	same
13 USC	6-4-0	Jess Hill	same
14 Miami-FL	6-3-0	Andy Gustafson	same
15 Miami-OH	9-0-0	Ara Parseghian	same
16 Stanford	6-3-1	Chuck Taylor	same
17 Texas A&M	7-2-1	Bear Bryant	same
18 Navy	6-2-1	Eddie Erdelatz	same
19 West Virginia	8-2-0	Art Lewis	same
20 Army	6-3-0	Red Blaik	same

Note: Big Ten "no-repeat" rule kept Ohio St. from Rose Bowl.

Key Bowl Games

Orange—#1 Oklahoma over #3 Maryland, 20-6; **Rose**—#2 Michigan St. over #4 UCLA, 17-14; **Cotton**—#10 Ole Miss over #6 TCU, 14-13; **Sugar**—#7 Georgia Tech over #11 Pitt, 7-0; **Gator**—Vanderbilt over #8 Auburn, 25-13.

Associated Press Final Polls (Cont.)

1956

Final poll released Dec. 3. Top 20 regular season results after that: **Dec. 8**—#13 Pitt over #6 Miami-FL, 14-7.

	As of Dec. 3	Head Coach	After Bowls
1 Oklahoma	10-0-0	Bud Wilkinson	same
2 Tennessee	10-0-0	Bowden Wyatt	10-1-0
3 Iowa	8-1-0	Forest Evashevski	9-1-0
4 Georgia Tech	9-1-0	Bobby Dodd	10-1-0
5 Texas A&M	9-0-1	Bear Bryant	same
6 Miami-FL	8-0-1	Andy Gustafson	8-1-1
7 Michigan	7-2-0	Bennie Oosterbaan	same
8 Syracuse	7-1-0	Ben Schwartzwalder	7-2-0
9 Michigan St.	7-2-0	Duffy Daugherty	same
10 Oregon St.	7-2-1	Tommy Prothro	7-3-1
11 Baylor	8-2-0	Sam Boyd	9-2-0
12 Minnesota	6-1-2	Murray Warmath	same
13 Pittsburgh	6-2-1	John Michelosen	7-3-1
14 TCU	7-3-0	Abe Martin	8-3-0
15 Ohio St.	6-3-0	Woody Hayes	same
16 Navy	6-1-2	Eddie Erdelatz	same
17 G. Washington	7-1-1	Gene Sherman	8-1-1
18 USC	8-2-0	Jess Hill	same
19 Clemson	7-1-2	Frank Howard	7-2-2
20 Colorado	7-2-1	Dallas Ward	8-2-1

Note: Big Seven "no-repeat" rule kept Oklahoma from Orange Bowl and Texas A&M was on probation.

Key Bowl Games

Sugar—#11 Baylor over #2 Tennessee, 13-7; **Rose**— #3 Iowa over #10 Oregon St., 35-19; **Gator**—#4 Georgia Tech over #13 Pitt, 21-14; **Cotton**—#14 TCU over #8 Syracuse, 28-27; **Orange**—#20 Colorado over #19 Clemson, 27-21.

1957

Final poll released Dec. 2. Top 20 regular season results after that: **Dec. 7**—#10 Notre Dame over SMU, 54-21.

	As of Dec. 2	Head Coach	After Bowls
1 Auburn	10-0-0	Shug Jordan	same
2 Ohio St.	8-1-0	Woody Hayes	9-1-0
3 Michigan St.	8-1-0	Duffy Daugherty	same
4 Oklahoma	9-1-0	Bud Wilkinson	10-1-0
5 Navy	8-1-1	Eddie Erdelatz	9-1-1
6 Iowa	7-1-1	Forest Evashevski	same
7 Mississippi	8-1-1	Johnny Vaught	9-1-1
8 Rice	7-3-0	Jess Neely	7-4-0
9 Texas A&M	8-2-0	Bear Bryant	8-3-0
10 Notre Dame	6-3-0	Terry Brennan	7-3-0
11 Texas	6-3-1	Darrell Royal	6-4-1
12 Arizona St.	10-0-0	Dan Devine	same
13 Tennessee	7-3-0	Bowden Wyatt	8-3-0
14 Mississippi St.	6-2-1	Wade Walker	same
15 N.C. State	7-1-2	Earle Edwards	same
16 Duke	6-2-2	Bill Murray	6-3-2
17 Florida	6-2-1	Bob Woodruff	same
18 Army	7-2-0	Red Blaik	same
19 Wisconsin	6-3-0	Milt Bruhn	same
20 VMI	9-0-1	John McKenna	same

Note: Auburn on probation, ineligible for bowl game.

Key Bowl Games

Rose—#2 Ohio St. over Oregon, 10-7; **Orange**—#4 Oklahoma over #16 Duke, 48-21; **Cotton**—#5 Navy over #8 Rice, 20-7; **Sugar**—#7 Ole Miss over #11 Texas, 39-7; **Gator**—#13 Tennessee over #9 Texas A&M, 3-0.

1958

Final poll released Dec. 1. Top 20 regular season results after that: None.

	As of Dec. 1	Head Coach	After Bowls
1 LSU	10-0-0	Paul Dietzel	11-0-0
2 Iowa	7-1-1	Forest Evashevski	8-1-1
3 Army	8-0-1	Red Blaik	same
4 Auburn	9-0-1	Shug Jordan	same
5 Oklahoma	9-1-0	Bud Wilkinson	10-1-0
6 Air Force	9-0-1	Ben Martin	9-0-2
7 Wisconsin	7-1-1	Milt Bruhn	same
8 Ohio St.	6-1-2	Woody Hayes	same
9 Syracuse	8-1-0	Ben Schwartzwalder	8-2-0
10 TCU	8-2-0	Abe Martin	8-2-1
11 Mississippi	8-2-0	Johnny Vaught	9-2-0
12 Clemson	8-2-0	Frank Howard	8-3-0
13 Purdue	6-1-2	Jack Mollenkopf	same
14 Florida	6-3-1	Bob Woodruff	6-4-1
15 South Carolina	7-3-0	Warren Giese	same
16 California	7-3-0	Pete Elliott	7-4-0
17 Notre Dame	6-4-0	Terry Brennan	same
18 SMU	6-4-0	Bill Meek	same
19 Oklahoma St.	7-3-0	Cliff Speegle	8-3-0
20 Rutgers	8-1-0	John Stiegman	same

Key Bowl Games

Sugar—#1 LSU over #12 Clemson, 7-0; **Rose**—#2 Iowa over #16 Cal, 38-12; **Orange**—#5 Oklahoma over #9 Syracuse, 21-6; **Cotton**—#6 Air Force tied #10 TCU, 0-0.

1959

Final poll released Dec. 7. Top 20 regular season results after that: None.

	As of Dec. 7	Head Coach	After Bowls
1 Syracuse	10-0-0	Ben Schwartzwalder	11-0-0
2 Mississippi	9-1-0	Johnny Vaught	10-1-0
3 LSU	9-1-0	Paul Dietzel	9-2-0
4 Texas	9-1-0	Darrell Royal	9-2-0
5 Georgia	9-1-0	Wally Butts	10-1-0
6 Wisconsin	7-2-0	Milt Bruhn	7-3-0
7 TCU	8-2-0	Abe Martin	8-3-0
8 Washington	9-1-0	Jim Owens	10-1-0
9 Arkansas	8-2-0	Frank Broyles	9-2-0
10 Alabama	7-1-2	Bear Bryant	7-2-2
11 Clemson	8-2-0	Frank Howard	9-2-0
12 Penn St.	8-2-0	Rip Engle	9-2-0
13 Illinois	5-3-1	Ray Eliot	same
14 USC	8-2-0	Don Clark	same
15 Oklahoma	7-3-0	Bud Wilkinson	same
16 Wyoming	9-1-0	Bob Devaney	same
17 Notre Dame	5-5-0	Joe Kuharich	same
18 Missouri	6-4-0	Dan Devine	6-5-0
19 Florida	5-4-1	Bob Woodruff	same
20 Pittsburgh	6-4-0	John Michelosen	same

Note: Big Seven "no-repeat" rule kept Oklahoma from Orange Bowl.

Key Bowl Games

Cotton—#1 Syracuse over #4 Texas, 23-14; **Sugar**— #2 Ole Miss over #3 LSU, 21-0; **Orange**—#5 Georgia over #18 Missouri, 14-0; **Rose**—#8 Washington over #6 Wisconsin, 44-8; Bluebonnet—#11 Clemson over #7 TCU, 23-7; **Gator**—#9 Arkansas over Georgia Tech, 14-7; **Liberty**—#12 Penn St. over #10 Alabama, 7-0.

AP ranked only 10 teams from 1962-67.

1960

Final poll released Nov. 28. Top 20 regular season results after that: **Dec. 3**—UCLA over #10 Duke, 27-6.

	As of Nov. 28	Head Coach	After Bowls
1 Minnesota	8-1-0	Murray Warmath	8-2-0
2 Mississippi	9-0-1	Johnny Vaught	10-0-1
3 Iowa	8-1-0	Forest Evashevski	same
4 Navy	9-1-0	Wayne Hardin	9-2-0
5 Missouri	9-1-0	Dan Devine	10-1-0
6 Washington	9-1-0	Jim Owens	10-1-0
7 Arkansas	8-2-0	Frank Broyles	8-3-0
8 Ohio St.	7-2-0	Woody Hayes	same
9 Alabama	8-1-1	Bear Bryant	8-1-2
10 Duke	7-2-0	Bill Murray	8-3-0
11 Kansas	7-2-1	Jack Mitchell	same
12 Baylor	8-2-0	John Bridgers	8-3-0
13 Auburn	8-2-0	Shug Jordan	same
14 Yale	9-0-0	Jordan Olivar	same
15 Michigan St.	6-2-1	Duffy Daugherty	same
16 Penn St.	6-3-0	Rip Engle	7-3-0
17 New Mexico St.	10-0-0	Warren Woodson	11-0-0
18 Florida	8-2-0	Ray Graves	9-2-0
19 Syracuse	7-2-0	Ben Schwartzwalder	same
Purdue	4-4-1	Jack Mollenkopf	same

Key Bowl Games

Rose—#6 Washington over #1 Minnesota, 17-7; **Sugar**—#2 Ole Miss over Rice, 14-6; **Orange**—#5 Missouri over #4 Navy, 21-14; **Cotton**—#10 Duke over #7 Arkansas, 7-6; **Bluebonnet**—#9 Alabama tied Texas, 3-3.

1961

Final poll released Dec. 4. Top 20 regular season results after that: None.

	As of Dec. 4	Head Coach	After Bowls
1 Alabama	10-0-0	Bear Bryant	11-0-0
2 Ohio St.	8-0-1	Woody Hayes	same
3 Texas	9-1-0	Darrell Royal	10-1-0
4 LSU	9-1-0	Paul Dietzel	10-1-0
5 Mississippi	9-1-0	Johnny Vaught	9-2-0
6 Minnesota	7-2-0	Murray Warmath	8-2-0
7 Colorado	9-1-0	Sonny Grandelius	9-2-0
8 Michigan St.	7-2-0	Duffy Daugherty	same
9 Arkansas	8-2-0	Frank Broyles	8-3-0
10 Utah St.	9-0-1	John Ralston	9-1-1
11 Missouri	7-2-1	Dan Devine	same
12 Purdue	6-3-0	Jack Mollenkopf	same
13 Georgia Tech	7-3-0	Bobby Dodd	7-4-0
14 Syracuse	7-3-0	Ben Schwartzwalder	8-3-0
15 Rutgers	9-0-0	John Bateman	same
16 UCLA	7-3-0	Bill Barnes	7-4-0
17 Rice	7-3-0	Jess Neely	7-4-0
Penn St.	7-3-0	Rip Engle	8-3-0
Arizona	8-1-1	Jim LaRue	same
20 Duke	7-3-0	Bill Murray	same

Note: Ohio St. faculty council turned down Rose Bowl invitation citing concern with OSU's overemphasis on sports.

Key Bowl Games

Sugar—#1 Alabama over #9 Arkansas, 10-3; **Cotton**—#3 Texas over #5 Ole Miss, 12-7; **Orange**—#4 LSU over #7 Colorado, 25-7; **Rose**—#6 Minnesota over #16 UCLA, 21-3; **Gotham**—Baylor over #10 Utah St., 24-9.

1962

Final poll released Dec. 3. Top 10 regular season results after that: None.

	As of Dec. 3	Head Coach	After Bowls
1 USC	10-0-0	John McKay	11-0-0
2 Wisconsin	8-1-0	Milt Bruhn	8-2-0
3 Mississippi	9-0-0	Johnny Vaught	10-0-0
4 Texas	9-0-1	Darrell Royal	9-1-1
5 Alabama	9-1-0	Bear Bryant	10-1-0
6 Arkansas	9-1-0	Frank Broyles	9-2-0
7 LSU	8-1-1	Charlie McClendon	9-1-1
8 Oklahoma	8-2-0	Bud Wilkinson	8-3-0
9 Penn St.	9-1-0	Rip Engle	9-2-0
10 Minnesota	6-2-1	Murray Warmath	same

Key Bowl Games

Rose—#1 USC over #2 Wisconsin, 42-37; **Sugar**—#3 Ole Miss over #6 Arkansas, 17-13; **Cotton**—#7 LSU over #4 Texas, 13-0; **Orange**—#5 Alabama over #8 Oklahoma, 17-0; **Gator**—Florida over #9 Penn St., 17-7.

1963

Final poll released Dec. 9. Top 10 regular season results after that: **Dec.14**—#8 Alabama over Miami-FL, 17-12.

	As of Dec. 9	Head Coach	After Bowls
1 Texas	10-0-0	Darrell Royal	11-0-0
2 Navy	9-1-0	Wayne Hardin	9-2-0
3 Illinois	7-1-1	Pete Elliott	8-1-1
4 Pittsburgh	9-1-0	John Michelosen	same
5 Auburn	9-1-0	Shug Jordan	9-2-0
6 Nebraska	9-1-0	Bob Devaney	10-1-0
7 Mississippi	7-0-2	Johnny Vaught	7-1-2
8 Alabama	7-2-0	Bear Bryant	9-2-0
9 Michigan St.	6-2-1	Duffy Daugherty	same
10 Oklahoma	8-2-0	Bud Wilkinson	same

Key Bowl Games

Cotton—#1 Texas over #2 Navy, 28-6; **Rose**—#3 Illinois over Washington, 17-7; **Orange**—#6 Nebraska over #5 Auburn, 13-7; **Sugar**—#8 Alabama over #7 Ole Miss, 12-7.

1964

Final poll released Nov. 30. Top 10 regular season results after that: **Dec. 5**—Florida over #7 LSU, 20-6.

	As of Nov. 30	Head Coach	After Bowls
1 Alabama	10-0-0	Bear Bryant	10-1-0
2 Arkansas	10-0-0	Frank Broyles	11-0-0
3 Notre Dame	9-1-0	Ara Parseghian	same
4 Michigan	8-1-0	Bump Elliott	9-1-0
5 Texas	9-1-0	Darrell Royal	10-1-0
6 Nebraska	9-1-0	Bob Devaney	9-2-0
7 LSU	7-1-1	Charlie McClendon	8-2-1
8 Oregon St.	8-2-0	Tommy Prothro	8-3-0
9 Ohio St.	7-2-0	Woody Hayes	same
10 USC	7-3-0	John McKay	same

Key Bowl Games

Orange—#5 Texas over #1 Alabama, 21-17; **Cotton**—#2 Arkansas over #6 Nebraska, 10-7; **Rose**— #4 Michigan over #8 Oregon St., 34-7; **Sugar**—#7 LSU over Syracuse, 13-10.

Associated Press Final Polls (Cont.)

Final polls taken after bowl games.

1965

Final poll taken after bowl games for the first time.

	After Bowls	Head Coach	Regular Season
1 Alabama	9-1-1	Bear Bryant	8-1-1
2 Michigan St.	10-1-0	Duffy Daugherty	10-0-0
3 Arkansas	10-1-0	Frank Broyles	10-0-0
4 UCLA	8-2-1	Tommy Prothro	7-1-1
5 Nebraska	10-1-0	Bob Devaney	10-0-0
6 Missouri	8-2-1	Dan Devine	7-2-1
7 Tennessee	8-1-2	Doug Dickey	6-1-2
8 LSU	8-3-0	Charlie McClendon	7-3-0
9 Notre Dame	7-2-1	Ara Parseghian	same
10 USC	7-2-1	John McKay	same

Key Bowl Games

Rankings below reflect final regular season poll, released Nov. 29. No bowls for then #8 USC or #9 Notre Dame. **Rose**—#5 UCLA over #1 Michigan St., 14-12; **Cotton**—LSU over #2 Arkansas, 14-7; **Orange**—#4 Alabama over #3 Nebraska, 39-28; **Sugar**—#6 Missouri over Florida, 20-18; **Bluebonnet**—#7 Tennessee over Tulsa, 27-6; **Gator**—Georgia Tech over #10 Texas Tech, 31-21.

1966

Final poll released Dec. 5, returning to pre-bowl status. Top 10 regular season results after that: None.

	As of Dec. 5	Head Coach	After Bowls
1 Notre Dame	9-0-1	Ara Parseghian	same
2 Michigan St.	9-0-1	Duffy Daugherty	same
3 Alabama	10-0-0	Bear Bryant	11-0-0
4 Georgia	9-1-0	Vince Dooley	10-1-0
5 UCLA	9-1-0	Tommy Prothro	same
6 Nebraska	9-1-0	Bob Devaney	9-2-0
7 Purdue	8-2-0	Jack Mollenkopf	9-2-0
8 Georgia Tech	9-1-0	Bobby Dodd	9-2-0
9 Miami-FL	7-2-1	Charlie Tate	8-2-1
10 SMU	8-2-0	Hayden Fry	8-3-0

Key Bowl Games

Sugar—#3 Alabama over #6 Nebraska, 34-7; **Cotton**—#4 Georgia over #10 SMU, 24-9; **Rose**—#7 Purdue over USC, 14-13; **Orange**—Florida over #8 Georgia Tech, 27-12; **Liberty**—#9 Miami-FL over Virginia Tech, 14-7.

1967

Final poll released Nov. 27. Top 10 regular season results after that: **Dec. 2**—#2 Tennessee over Vanderbilt, 41-14; #3 Oklahoma over Oklahoma St., 38-14; #8 Alabama over Auburn, 7-3.

	As of Nov. 27	Head Coach	After Bowls
1 USC	9-1-0	John McKay	10-1-0
2 Tennessee	8-1-0	Doug Dickey	9-2-0
3 Oklahoma	8-1-0	Chuck Fairbanks	10-1-0
4 Indiana	9-1-0	John Pont	9-2-0
5 Notre Dame	8-2-0	Ara Parseghian	same
6 Wyoming	10-0-0	Lloyd Eaton	10-1-0
7 Oregon St.	7-2-1	Dee Andros	same
8 Alabama	7-1-1	Bear Bryant	8-2-1
9 Purdue	8-2-0	Jack Mollenkopf	same
10 Penn St.	8-2-0	Joe Paterno	8-2-1

Key Bowl Games

Rose—#1 USC over #4 Indiana, 14-3; **Orange**—#3 Oklahoma over #2 Tennessee, 26-24; **Sugar**—LSU over #6 Wyoming, 20-13; **Cotton**—Texas A&M over #8 Alabama, 20-16; **Gator**—#10 Penn St. tied Florida St. 17-17.

1968

Final poll taken after bowl games for first time since close of 1965 season.

	After Bowls	Head Coach	Regular Season
1 Ohio St.	10-0-0	Woody Hayes	9-0-0
2 Penn St.	11-0-0	Joe Paterno	10-0-0
3 Texas	9-1-1	Darrell Royal	8-1-1
4 USC	9-1-1	John McKay	9-0-1
5 Notre Dame	7-2-1	Ara Parseghian	same
6 Arkansas	10-1-0	Frank Broyles	9-1-0
7 Kansas	9-2-0	Pepper Rodgers	9-1-0
8 Georgia	8-1-2	Vince Dooley	8-0-2
9 Missouri	8-3-0	Dan Devine	7-3-0
10 Purdue	8-2-0	Jack Mollenkopf	same
11 Oklahoma	7-4-0	Chuck Fairbanks	7-3-0
12 Michigan	8-2-0	Bump Elliott	same
13 Tennessee	8-2-1	Doug Dickey	8-1-1
14 SMU	8-3-0	Hayden Fry	7-3-0
15 Oregon St.	7-3-0	Dee Andros	same
16 Auburn	7-4-0	Shug Jordan	6-4-0
17 Alabama	8-3-0	Bear Bryant	8-2-0
18 Houston	6-2-2	Bill Yeoman	same
19 LSU	8-3-0	Charlie McClendon	7-3-0
20 Ohio Univ.	10-1-0	Bill Hess	10-0-0

Key Bowl Games

Rankings below reflect final regular season poll, released Dec. 2. No bowls for then #7 Notre Dame and #11 Purdue. **Rose**—#1 Ohio St. over #2 USC, 27-16; **Orange**—#3 Penn St. over #6 Kansas, 15-14; **Sugar**—#9 Arkansas over #4 Georgia, 16-2; **Cotton**—#5 Texas over #8 Tennessee, 36-13; **Bluebonnet**—#20 SMU over #10 Oklahoma, 28-27; **Gator**—#16 Missouri over #12 Alabama, 35-10.

1969

Final poll taken after bowl games.

	After Bowls	Head Coach	Regular Season
1 Texas	11-0-0	Darrell Royal	10-0-0
2 Penn St.	11-0-0	Joe Paterno	10-0-0
3 USC	10-0-1	John McKay	9-0-1
4 Ohio St.	8-1-0	Woody Hayes	same
5 Notre Dame	8-2-1	Ara Parseghian	8-1-1
6 Missouri	9-2-0	Dan Devine	9-1-0
7 Arkansas	9-2-0	Frank Broyles	9-1-0
8 Mississippi	8-3-0	Johnny Vaught	7-3-0
9 Michigan	8-3-0	Bo Schembechler	8-2-0
10 LSU	9-1-0	Charlie McClendon	same
11 Nebraska	9-2-0	Bob Devaney	8-2-0
12 Houston	9-2-0	Bill Yeoman	8-2-0
13 UCLA	8-1-1	Tommy Prothro	same
14 Florida	9-1-1	Ray Graves	8-1-1
15 Tennessee	9-2-0	Doug Dickey	9-1-0
16 Colorado	8-3-0	Eddie Crowder	7-3-0
17 West Virginia	10-1-0	Jim Carlen	9-1-0
18 Purdue	8-2-0	Jack Mollenkopf	same
19 Stanford	7-2-1	John Ralston	same
20 Auburn	8-3-0	Shug Jordan	8-2-0

Key Bowl Games

Rankings below reflect final regular season poll, released Dec. 8. No bowls for then #4 Ohio St., #8 LSU and #10 UCLA.

Cotton—#1 Texas over #9 Notre Dame, 21-17; **Orange**—#2 Penn St. over #6 Missouri, 10-3; **Sugar**—#13 Ole Miss over #3 Arkansas, 27-22; **Rose**—#5 USC over #7 Michigan, 10-3.

1970

	Team	After Bowls	Head Coach	Regular Season
1	Nebraska	11-0-1	Bob Devaney	10-0-1
2	Notre Dame	10-1-0	Ara Parseghian	9-1-0
3	Texas	10-1-0	Darrell Royal	10-0-0
4	Tennessee	11-1-0	Bill Battle	10-1-0
5	Ohio St.	9-1-0	Woody Hayes	9-0-0
6	Arizona St.	11-0-0	Frank Kush	10-0-0
7	LSU	9-3-0	Charlie McClendon	9-2-0
8	Stanford	9-3-0	John Ralston	8-3-0
9	Michigan	9-1-0	Bo Schembechler	same
10	Auburn	9-2-0	Shug Jordan	8-2-0
11	Arkansas	9-2-0	Frank Broyles	same
12	Toledo	12-0-0	Frank Lauterbur	11-0-0
13	Georgia Tech	9-3-0	Bud Carson	8-3-0
14	Dartmouth	9-0-0	Bob Blackman	same
15	USC	6-4-1	John McKay	same
16	Air Force	9-3-0	Ben Martin	9-2-0
17	Tulane	8-4-0	Jim Pittman	7-4-0
18	Penn St.	7-3-0	Joe Paterno	same
19	Houston	8-3-0	Bill Yeoman	same
20	Oklahoma	7-4-1	Chuck Fairbanks	7-4-0
	Mississippi	7-4-0	Johnny Vaught	7-3-0

Key Bowl Games

Rankings below reflect final regular season poll, released Dec. 7. No bowls for then #4 Arkansas and #7 Michigan.

Cotton—#6 Notre Dame over #1 Texas, 24-11; **Rose**—#12 Stanford over #2 Ohio St., 27-17; **Orange**—#3 Nebraska over #8 LSU, 17-12; **Sugar**— #5 Tennessee over #11 Air Force, 34-13; **Peach**—#9 Ariz. St. over N. Carolina, 48-26.

1971

	Team	After Bowls	Head Coach	Regular Season
1	Nebraska	13-0-0	Bob Devaney	12-0-0
2	Oklahoma	11-1-0	Chuck Fairbanks	10-1-0
3	Colorado	10-2-0	Eddie Crowder	9-2-0
4	Alabama	11-1-0	Bear Bryant	11-0-0
5	Penn St.	11-1-0	Joe Paterno	10-1-0
6	Michigan	11-1-0	Bo Schembechler	11-0-0
7	Georgia	11-1-0	Vince Dooley	10-1-0
8	Arizona St.	11-1-0	Frank Kush	10-1-0
9	Tennessee	10-2-0	Bill Battle	9-2-0
10	Stanford	9-3-0	John Ralston	8-3-0
11	LSU	9-3-0	Charlie McClendon	8-3-0
12	Auburn	9-2-0	Shug Jordan	9-1-0
13	Notre Dame	8-2-0	Ara Parseghian	same
14	Toledo	12-0-0	John Murphy	11-0-0
15	Mississippi	10-2-0	Billy Kinard	9-2-0
16	Arkansas	8-3-1	Frank Broyles	8-2-1
17	Houston	9-3-0	Bill Yeoman	9-2-0
18	Texas	8-3-0	Darrell Royal	8-2-0
19	Washington	8-3-0	Jim Owens	same
20	USC	6-4-1	John McKay	same

Key Bowl Games

Rankings below reflect final regular season poll, released Dec. 6.

Orange—#1 Nebraska over #2 Alabama, 38-6; **Sugar**—#3 Oklahoma over #5 Auburn, 40-22; **Rose**—#16 Stanford over #4 Michigan, 13-12; **Gator**—#6 Georgia over N.Carolina, 7-3; **Bluebonnet**—#7 Colorado over #15 Houston, 29-17; **Fiesta**—#8 Ariz. St. over Florida St., 45-38; **Cotton**—#10 Penn St. over #12 Texas, 30-6.

1972

	Team	After Bowls	Head Coach	Regular Season
1	USC	12-0-0	John McKay	11-0-0
2	Oklahoma	11-1-0	Chuck Fairbanks	10-1-0
3	Texas	10-1-0	Darrell Royal	9-1-0
4	Nebraska	9-2-1	Bob Devaney	8-2-1
5	Auburn	10-1-0	Shug Jordan	9-1-0
6	Michigan	10-1-0	Bo Schembechler	same
7	Alabama	10-2-0	Bear Bryant	10-1-0
8	Tennessee	10-2-0	Bill Battle	9-2-0
9	Ohio St.	9-2-0	Woody Hayes	9-1-0
10	Penn St.	10-2-0	Joe Paterno	10-1-0
11	LSU	9-2-1	Charlie McClendon	9-1-1
12	North Carolina	11-1-0	Bill Dooley	10-1-0
13	Arizona St.	10-2-0	Frank Kush	9-2-0
14	Notre Dame	8-3-0	Ara Parseghian	8-2-0
15	UCLA	8-3-0	Pepper Rodgers	same
16	Colorado	8-4-0	Eddie Crowder	8-3-0
17	N.C. State	8-3-1	Lou Holtz	7-3-1
18	Louisville	9-1-0	Lee Corso	same
19	Washington St.	7-4-0	Jim Sweeney	same
20	Georgia Tech	7-4-1	Bill Fulcher	6-4-1

Key Bowl Games

Rankings below reflect final regular season poll, released Dec. 4. No bowl for then #8 Michigan.

Rose—#1 USC over #3 Ohio St., 42-17; **Sugar**—#2 Oklahoma over #5 Penn St., 14-0; **Cotton**—#7 Texas over #4 Alabama, 17-13; **Orange**—#9 Nebraska over #12 Notre Dame, 40-6; **Gator**—#6 Auburn over #13 Colorado, 24-3; **Bluebonnet**—#11 Tennessee over #10 LSU, 24-17.

1973

	Team	After Bowls	Head Coach	Regular Season
1	Notre Dame	11-0-0	Ara Parseghian	10-0-0
2	Ohio St.	10-0-1	Woody Hayes	9-0-1
3	Oklahoma	10-0-1	Barry Switzer	same
4	Alabama	11-1-0	Bear Bryant	11-0-0
5	Penn St.	12-0-0	Joe Paterno	11-0-0
6	Michigan	10-0-1	Bo Schembechler	same
7	Nebraska	9-2-1	Tom Osborne	8-2-1
8	USC	9-2-1	John McKay	9-1-1
9	Arizona St.	11-1-0	Frank Kush	10-1-0
	Houston	11-1-0	Bill Yeoman	10-1-0
11	Texas Tech	11-1-0	Jim Carlen	10-1-0
12	UCLA	9-2-0	Pepper Rodgers	same
13	LSU	9-3-0	Charlie McClendon	9-2-0
14	Texas	8-3-0	Darrell Royal	8-2-0
15	Miami-OH	11-0-0	Bill Mallory	10-0-0
16	N.C. State	9-3-0	Lou Holtz	8-3-0
17	Missouri	8-4-0	Al Onofrio	7-4-0
18	Kansas	7-4-1	Don Fambrough	7-3-1
19	Tennessee	8-4-0	Bill Battle	8-3-0
20	Maryland	8-4-0	Jerry Claiborne	8-3-0
	Tulane	9-3-0	Bennie Ellender	9-2-0

Key Bowl Games

Rankings below reflect final regular season poll, released Dec. 3. No bowls for then #2 Oklahoma (probation), #5 Michigan and #9 UCLA.

Sugar—#3 Notre Dame over #1 Alabama, 24-23; **Rose**—#4 Ohio St. over #7 USC, 42-21; **Orange**—#6 Penn St. over #13 LSU, 16-9; **Cotton**—#12 Nebraska over #8 Texas, 19-3; **Fiesta**—#10 Ariz. St. over Pitt, 28-7; **Bluebonnet**—#14 Houston over #17 Tulane, 47-7.

Associated Press Final Polls (Cont.)

Final polls taken after bowl games.

1974

	After Bowls	Head Coach	Regular Season
1 Oklahoma	11-0-0	Barry Switzer	same
2 USC	10-1-1	John McKay	9-1-1
3 Michigan	10-1-0	Bo Schembechler	same
4 Ohio St.	10-2-0	Woody Hayes	10-1-0
5 Alabama	11-1-0	Bear Bryant	11-0-0
6 Notre Dame	10-2-0	Ara Parseghian	9-2-0
7 Penn St.	10-2-0	Joe Paterno	9-2-0
8 Auburn	10-2-0	Shug Jordan	9-2-0
9 Nebraska	9-3-0	Tom Osborne	8-3-0
10 Miami-OH	10-0-1	Dick Crum	9-0-1
11 N.C. State	9-2-1	Lou Holtz	9-2-0
12 Michigan St.	7-3-1	Denny Stolz	same
13 Maryland	8-4-0	Jerry Claiborne	8-3-0
14 Baylor	8-4-0	Grant Teaff	8-3-0
15 Florida	8-4-0	Doug Dickey	8-3-0
16 Texas A&M	8-3-0	Emory Ballard	same
17 Mississippi St.	9-3-0	Bob Tyler	8-3-0
Texas	8-4-0	Darrell Royal	8-3-0
19 Houston	8-3-1	Bill Yeoman	8-3-0
20 Tennessee	7-3-2	Bill Battle	6-3-2

Key Bowl Games

Rankings below reflect final regular season poll, released Dec. 2. No bowls for #1 Oklahoma (probation) and then #4 Michigan.

Orange—#9 Notre Dame over #2 Alabama, 13-11; **Rose**—#5 USC over #3 Ohio St., 18-17; **Gator**—#6 Auburn over #11 Texas, 27-3; **Cotton**—#7 Penn St. over #12 Baylor, 41-20; **Sugar**—#8 Nebraska over #18 Florida, 13-10; **Liberty**—Tennessee over #10 Maryland, 7-3.

1975

	After Bowls	Head Coach	Regular Season
1 Oklahoma	11-1-0	Barry Switzer	10-1-0
2 Arizona St.	12-0-0	Frank Kush	11-0-0
3 Alabama	11-1-0	Bear Bryant	10-1-0
4 Ohio St.	11-1-0	Woody Hayes	11-0-0
5 UCLA	9-2-1	Dick Vermeil	8-2-1
6 Texas	10-2-0	Darrell Royal	9-2-0
7 Arkansas	10-2-0	Frank Broyles	9-2-0
8 Michigan	8-2-2	Bo Schembechler	8-1-2
9 Nebraska	10-2-0	Tom Osborne	10-1-0
10 Penn St.	9-3-0	Joe Paterno	9-2-0
11 Texas A&M	10-2-0	Emory Bellard	10-1-0
12 Miami-OH	11-1-0	Dick Crum	10-1-0
13 Maryland	9-2-1	Jerry Claiborne	8-2-1
14 California	8-3-0	Mike White	same
15 Pittsburgh	8-4-0	Johnny Majors	7-4-0
16 Colorado	9-3-0	Bill Mallory	9-2-0
17 USC	8-4-0	John McKay	7-4-0
18 Arizona	9-2-0	Jim Young	same
19 Georgia	9-3-0	Vince Dooley	9-2-0
20 West Virginia	9-3-0	Bobby Bowden	8-3-0

Key Bowl Games

Rankings below reflect final regular season poll, released Dec. 1. Texas A&M was unbeaten and ranked 2nd in that poll, but lost to #18 Arkansas, 31-6, in its final regular season game on Dec.6.

Rose—#11 UCLA over #1 Ohio St., 23-10; **Liberty**—#17 USC over #2 Texas A&M, 20-0; **Orange**—#3 Oklahoma over #5 Michigan, 14-6; **Sugar**—#4 Alabama over #8 Penn St., 13-6; **Fiesta**—#7 Ariz. St. over #6 Nebraska, 17-14; **Bluebonnet**—#9 Texas over #10 Colorado, 38-21; **Cotton**—#18 Arkansas over #12 Georgia, 31-10.

1976

	After Bowls	Head Coach	Regula Seaso
1 Pittsburgh	12-0-0	Johnny Majors	11-0-
2 USC	11-1-0	John Robinson	10-1-
3 Michigan	10-2-0	Bo Schembechler	10-1-
4 Houston	10-2-0	Bill Yeoman	9-2-
5 Oklahoma	9-2-1	Barry Switzer	8-2-
6 Ohio St.	9-2-1	Woody Hayes	8-2-
7 Texas A&M	10-2-0	Emory Bellard	9-2-
8 Maryland	11-1-0	Jerry Claiborne	11-0-
9 Nebraska	9-3-1	Tom Osborne	8-3-
10 Georgia	10-2-0	Vince Dooley	10-1-
11 Alabama	9-3-0	Bear Bryant	8-3-
12 Notre Dame	9-3-0	Dan Devine	8-3-
13 Texas Tech	10-2-0	Steve Sloan	10-1-
14 Oklahoma St.	9-3-0	Jim Stanley	8-3-
15 UCLA	9-2-1	Terry Donahue	9-1-
16 Colorado	8-4-0	Bill Mallory	8-3-
17 Rutgers	11-0-0	Frank Burns	sam
18 Kentucky	8-4-0	Fran Curci	7-4-
19 Iowa St.	8-3-0	Earle Bruce	sam
20 Mississippi St.	9-2-0	Bob Tyler	sam

Key Bowl Games

Rankings below reflect final regular season poll, release Nov. 29. No bowl for then #20 Miss. St. (probation).

Sugar—#1 Pitt over #5 Georgia, 27-3; **Rose**—#3 US over #2 Michigan, 14-6; **Cotton**—#6 Houston over # Maryland, 30-21; **Liberty**—#16 Alabama over #7 UCLA 36-6; **Fiesta**—#8 Oklahoma over Wyoming, 41-7 **Bluebonnet**—#13 Nebraska over #9 Texas Tech, 27-2 **Sun**—#10 Texas A&M over Florida, 37-14; **Orange**—#11 Ohio St. over #12 Colorado, 27-10.

1977

	After Bowls	Head Coach	Regula Season
1 Notre Dame	11-1-0	Dan Devine	10-1-
2 Alabama	11-1-0	Bear Bryant	10-1-
3 Arkansas	11-1-0	Lou Holtz	10-1-
4 Texas	11-1-0	Fred Akers	11-0-
5 Penn St.	11-1-0	Joe Paterno	10-1-
6 Kentucky	10-1-0	Fran Curci	sam
7 Oklahoma	10-2-0	Barry Switzer	10-1-
8 Pittsburgh	9-2-1	Jackie Sherrill	8-2-
9 Michigan	10-2-0	Bo Schembechler	10-1-
10 Washington	8-4-0	Don James	7-4-
11 Ohio St.	9-3-0	Woody Hayes	9-2-
12 Nebraska	9-3-0	Tom Osborne	8-3-
13 USC	8-4-0	John Robinson	7-4-
14 Florida St.	10-2-0	Bobby Bowden	9-2-
15 Stanford	9-3-0	Bill Walsh	8-3-
16 San Diego St.	10-1-0	Claude Gilbert	same
17 North Carolina	8-3-1	Bill Dooley	8-2-
18 Arizona St.	9-3-0	Frank Kush	9-2-
19 Clemson	8-3-1	Charley Pell	8-2-
20 BYU	9-2-0	LaVell Edwards	same

Key Bowl Games

Rankings below reflect final regular season poll, released Nov. 28. No bowl for then #7 Kentucky (probation).

Cotton—#5 Notre Dame over #1 Texas, 38-10 **Orange**—#6 Arkansas over #2 Oklahoma, 31-6 **Sugar**— #3 Alabama over #9 Ohio St., 35-6; **Rose**—#13 Washington over #4 Michigan, 27-20; **Fiesta**—#8 Penn St. over #15 Ariz. St., 42-30; **Gator**—#10 Pitt over #11 Clemson, 34-3.

1978

	After Bowls	Head Coach	Regular Season
1 Alabama	11-1-0	Bear Bryant	10-1-0
2 USC	12-1-0	John Robinson	11-1-0
3 Oklahoma	11-1-0	Barry Switzer	10-1-0
4 Penn St.	11-1-0	Joe Paterno	11-0-0
5 Michigan	10-2-0	Bo Schembechler	10-1-0
6 Clemson	11-1-0	Charley Pell	10-1-0
7 Notre Dame	9-3-0	Dan Devine	8-3-0
8 Nebraska	9-3-0	Tom Osborne	9-2-0
9 Texas	9-3-0	Fred Akers	8-3-0
10 Houston	9-3-0	Bill Yeoman	9-2-0
11 Arkansas	9-2-1	Lou Holtz	9-2-0
12 Michigan St.	8-3-0	Darryl Rogers	same
13 Purdue	9-2-1	Jim Young	8-2-1
14 UCLA	8-3-1	Terry Donahue	8-3-0
15 Missouri	8-4-0	Warren Powers	7-4-0
16 Georgia	9-2-1	Vince Dooley	9-1-1
17 Stanford	8-4-0	Bill Walsh	7-4-0
18 N.C. State	9-3-0	Bo Rein	8-3-0
19 Texas A&M	8-4-0	Emory Bellard (4-2) & Tom Wilson (4-2)	7-4-0
20 Maryland	9-3-0	Jerry Claiborne	9-2-0

Key Bowl Games

Rankings below reflect final regular season poll, released Dec. 4. No bowl for then #12 Michigan St. (probation).
Sugar—#2 Alabama over #1 Penn St., 14-7; **Rose**—#3 USC over #5 Michigan, 17-10; **Orange**—#4 Oklahoma over #6 Nebraska, 31-24; **Gator**—#7 Clemson over #20 Ohio St., 17-15; **Fiesta**—#8 Arkansas tied #15 UCLA, 10-10; **Cotton**—#10 Notre Dame over #9 Houston, 35-34.

1979

	After Bowls	Head Coach	Regular Season
1 Alabama	12-0-0	Bear Bryant	11-0-0
2 USC	11-0-1	John Robinson	10-0-1
3 Oklahoma	11-1-0	Barry Switzer	10-1-0
4 Ohio St.	11-1-0	Earle Bruce	11-0-0
5 Houston	11-1-0	Bill Yeoman	10-1-0
6 Florida St.	11-1-0	Bobby Bowden	11-0-0
7 Pittsburgh	11-1-0	Jackie Sherrill	10-1-0
8 Arkansas	10-2-0	Lou Holtz	10-1-0
9 Nebraska	10-2-0	Tom Osborne	10-1-0
10 Purdue	10-2-0	Jim Young	9-2-0
11 Washington	9-3-0	Don James	8-3-0
12 Texas	9-3-0	Fred Akers	9-2-0
13 BYU	11-1-0	LaVell Edwards	11-0-0
14 Baylor	8-4-0	Grant Teaff	7-4-0
15 North Carolina	8-3-1	Dick Crum	7-3-1
16 Auburn	8-3-0	Doug Barfield	same
17 Temple	10-2-0	Wayne Hardin	9-2-0
18 Michigan	8-4-0	Bo Schembechler	8-3-0
19 Indiana	8-4-0	Lee Corso	7-4-0
20 Penn St.	8-4-0	Joe Paterno	7-4-0

Key Bowl Games

Rankings below reflect final regular season poll, released Dec. 3. No bowl for then #17 Auburn (probation).
Sugar—#2 Alabama over #6 Arkansas, 24-9; **Rose**—#3 USC over #1 Ohio St., 17-16; **Orange**—#5 Oklahoma over #4 Florida St., 24-7; **Sun**—#13 Washington over #11 Texas, 14-7; **Cotton**—#8 Houston over #7 Nebraska, 17-14; **Fiesta**—#10 Pitt over Arizona, 16-10.

1980

	After Bowls	Head Coach	Regular Season
1 Georgia	12-0-0	Vince Dooley	11-0-0
2 Pittsburgh	11-1-0	Jackie Sherrill	10-1-0
3 Oklahoma	10-2-0	Barry Switzer	9-2-0
4 Michigan	10-2-0	Bo Schembechler	9-2-0
5 Florida St.	10-2-0	Bobby Bowden	10-1-0
6 Alabama	10-2-0	Bear Bryant	9-2-0
7 Nebraska	10-2-0	Tom Osborne	9-2-0
8 Penn St.	10-2-0	Joe Paterno	9-2-0
9 Notre Dame	9-2-1	Dan Devine	9-1-1
10 North Carolina	11-1-0	Dick Crum	10-1-0
11 USC	8-2-1	John Robinson	same
12 BYU	12-1-0	LaVell Edwards	11-1-0
13 UCLA	9-2-0	Terry Donahue	same
14 Baylor	10-2-0	Grant Teaff	10-1-0
15 Ohio St.	9-3-0	Earle Bruce	9-2-0
16 Washington	9-3-0	Don James	9-2-0
17 Purdue	9-3-0	Jim Young	8-3-0
18 Miami-FL	9-3-0	H. Schnellenberger	8-3-0
19 Mississippi St.	9-3-0	Emory Bellard	9-2-0
20 SMU	8-4-0	Ron Meyer	8-3-0

Key Bowl Games

Rankings below reflect final regular season poll, released Dec. 8.
Sugar—#1 Georgia over #7 Notre Dame, 17-10; **Orange**—#4 Oklahoma over #2 Florida St., 18-17; **Gator**—#3 Pitt over #18 S. Carolina, 37-9; **Rose**—#5 Michigan over #16 Washington, 23-6; **Cotton**—#9 Alabama over #6 Baylor, 30-2; **Sun**—#8 Nebraska over #17 Miss. St., 31-17; **Fiesta**—#10 Penn St. over #11 Ohio St., 31-19; **Bluebonnet**—#13 N. Carolina over Texas, 16-7.

1981

	After Bowls	Head Coach	Regular Season
1 Clemson	12-0-0	Danny Ford	11-0-0
2 Texas	10-1-1	Fred Akers	9-1-1
3 Penn St.	10-2-0	Joe Paterno	9-2-0
4 Pittsburgh	11-1-0	Jackie Sherrill	10-1-0
5 SMU	10-1-0	Ron Meyer	same
6 Georgia	10-2-0	Vince Dooley	10-1-0
7 Alabama	9-2-1	Bear Bryant	9-1-1
8 Miami-FL	9-2-0	H. Schnellenberger	same
9 North Carolina	10-2-0	Dick Crum	9-2-0
10 Washington	10-2-0	Don James	9-2-0
11 Nebraska	9-3-0	Tom Osborne	9-2-0
12 Michigan	9-3-0	Bo Schembechler	8-3-0
13 BYU	11-2-0	LaVell Edwards	10-2-0
14 USC	9-3-0	John Robinson	9-2-0
15 Ohio St.	9-3-0	Earle Bruce	8-3-0
16 Arizona St.	9-2-0	Darryl Rogers	same
17 West Virginia	9-3-0	Don Nehlen	8-3-0
18 Iowa	8-4-0	Hayden Fry	8-3-0
19 Missouri	8-4-0	Warren Powers	7-4-0
20 Oklahoma	7-4-1	Barry Switzer	6-4-1

Key Bowl Games

Rankings below reflect final regular season poll, released Nov. 30. No bowl for then #5 SMU (probation), #9 Miami-FL (probation), and #17 Ariz. St. (probation).
Orange—#1 Clemson over #4 Nebraska, 22-15; **Sugar**—#10 Pitt over #2 Georgia, 24-20; **Cotton**—#6 Texas over #3 Alabama, 14-12; **Fiesta**—#7 Penn St. over #8 USC, 26-10; **Gator**—#11 N. Carolina over Arkansas, 31-27; **Rose**—#12 Washington over #13 Iowa, 28-0.

Associated Press Final Polls (Cont.)

Final polls taken after bowl games.

1982

	After Bowls	Head Coach	Regular Season
1 Penn St.	11-1-0	Joe Paterno	10-1-0
2 SMU	11-0-1	Bobby Collins	10-0-1
3 Nebraska	12-1-0	Tom Osborne	11-1-0
4 Georgia	11-1-0	Vince Dooley	11-0-0
5 UCLA	10-1-1	Terry Donahue	9-1-1
6 Arizona St.	10-2-0	Darryl Rogers	9-2-0
7 Washington	10-2-0	Don James	9-2-0
8 Clemson	9-1-1	Danny Ford	same
9 Arkansas	9-2-1	Lou Holtz	8-2-1
10 Pittsburgh	9-3-0	Foge Fazio	9-2-0
11 LSU	8-3-1	Jerry Stovall	8-2-1
12 Ohio St.	9-3-0	Earle Bruce	8-3-0
13 Florida St.	9-3-0	Bobby Bowden	8-3-0
14 Auburn	9-3-0	Pat Dye	8-3-0
15 USC	8-3-0	John Robinson	same
16 Oklahoma	8-4-0	Barry Switzer	8-3-0
17 Texas	9-3-0	Fred Akers	9-2-0
18 North Carolina	8-4-0	Dick Crum	7-4-0
19 West Virginia	9-3-0	Don Nehlen	9-2-0
20 Maryland	8-4-0	Bobby Ross	8-3-0

Key Bowl Games

Rankings below reflect final regular season poll, released Dec. 6. No bowl for then #7 Clemson (probation) and #15 USC (probation).

Sugar—#2 Penn St. over #1 Georgia, 27-23; **Orange**—#3 Nebraska over #13 LSU, 21-20; **Cotton**—#4 SMU over #6 Pitt, 7-3; **Rose**—#5 UCLA over #19 Michigan, 24-14; **Aloha**—#9 Washington over #16 Maryland, 21-20; **Fiesta**—#11 Ariz. St. over #12 Oklahoma, 32-21; **Bluebonnet**—#14 Arkansas over Florida, 28-24.

1983

	After Bowls	Head Coach	Regular Season
1 Miami-FL	11-1-0	H. Schnellenberger	10-1-0
2 Nebraska	12-1-0	Tom Osborne	12-0-0
3 Auburn	11-1-0	Pat Dye	10-1-0
4 Georgia	10-1-1	Vince Dooley	9-1-1
5 Texas	11-1-0	Fred Akers	11-0-0
6 Florida	9-2-1	Charley Pell	8-2-1
7 BYU	11-1-0	LaVell Edwards	10-1-0
8 Michigan	9-3-0	Bo Schembechler	9-2-0
9 Ohio St.	9-3-0	Earle Bruce	8-3-0
10 Illinois	10-2-0	Mike White	10-1-0
11 Clemson	9-1-1	Danny Ford	same
12 SMU	10-2-0	Bobby Collins	10-1-0
13 Air Force	10-2-0	Ken Hatfield	9-2-0
14 Iowa	9-3-0	Hayden Fry	9-2-0
15 Alabama	8-4-0	Ray Perkins	7-4-0
16 West Virginia	9-3-0	Don Nehlen	8-3-0
17 UCLA	7-4-1	Terry Donahue	6-4-1
18 Pittsburgh	8-3-1	Foge Fazio	8-2-1
19 Boston College	9-3-0	Jack Bicknell	9-2-0
20 East Carolina	8-3-0	Ed Emory	same

Key Bowl Games

Rankings below reflect final regular season poll, released Dec. 5. No bowl for then #12 Clemson (probation).

Orange—#5 Miami-FL over #1 Nebraska, 31-30; **Cotton**—#7 Georgia over #2 Texas, 10-9; **Sugar**— #3 Auburn over #8 Michigan, 9-7; **Rose**—UCLA over #4 Illinois, 45-9; **Holiday**—#9 BYU over Missouri, 21-17; **Gator**—#11 Florida over #10 Iowa, 14-6; **Fiesta**—#14 Ohio St. over #15 Pitt, 28-23.

1984

	After Bowls	Head Coach	Regular Season
1 BYU	13-0-0	LaVell Edwards	12-0-0
2 Washington	11-1-0	Don James	10-1-0
3 Florida	9-1-1	Charley Pell (0-1-1) & Galen Hall (9-0)	same
4 Nebraska	10-2-0	Tom Osborne	9-2-0
5 Boston College	10-2-0	Jack Bicknell	9-2-0
6 Oklahoma	9-2-1	Barry Switzer	9-1-1
7 Oklahoma St.	10-2-0	Pat Jones	9-2-0
8 SMU	10-2-0	Bobby Collins	9-2-0
9 UCLA	9-3-0	Terry Donahue	8-3-0
10 USC	9-3-0	Ted Tollner	8-3-0
11 South Carolina	10-2-0	Joe Morrison	10-1-0
12 Maryland	9-3-0	Bobby Ross	8-3-0
13 Ohio St.	9-3-0	Earle Bruce	9-2-0
14 Auburn	9-4-0	Pat Dye	8-4-0
15 LSU	8-3-1	Bill Arnsparger	8-2-1
16 Iowa	8-4-1	Hayden Fry	7-4-1
17 Florida St.	7-3-2	Bobby Bowden	7-3-1
18 Miami-FL	8-5-0	Jimmy Johnson	8-4-0
19 Kentucky	9-3-0	Jerry Claiborne	8-3-0
20 Virginia	8-2-2	George Welsh	7-2-2

Key Bowl Games

Rankings below reflect final regular season poll, released Dec. 3. No bowl for then #3 Florida (probation).

Holiday—#1 BYU over Michigan, 24-17; **Orange**—#4 Washington over #2 Oklahoma, 28-17; **Sugar**—#5 Nebraska over #11 LSU, 28-10; **Rose**—#18 USC over #6 Ohio St., 20-17; **Gator**—#9 Okla. St. over #7 S. Carolina, 21-14; **Cotton**—#8 BC over Houston, 45-28; **Aloha**—#10 SMU over #17 Notre Dame, 27-20.

1985

	After Bowls	Head Coach	Regular Season
1 Oklahoma	11-1-0	Barry Switzer	10-1-0
2 Michigan	10-1-1	Bo Schembechler	9-1-1
3 Penn St.	11-1-0	Joe Paterno	11-0-0
4 Tennessee	9-1-2	Johnny Majors	8-1-2
5 Florida	9-1-1	Galen Hall	same
6 Texas A&M	10-2-0	Jackie Sherrill	9-2-0
7 UCLA	9-2-1	Terry Donahue	8-2-1
8 Air Force	12-1-0	Fisher DeBerry	11-1-0
9 Miami-FL	10-2-0	Jimmy Johnson	10-1-0
10 Iowa	10-2-0	Hayden Fry	10-1-0
11 Nebraska	9-3-0	Tom Osborne	9-2-0
12 Arkansas	10-2-0	Ken Hatfield	9-2-0
13 Alabama	9-2-1	Ray Perkins	8-2-1
14 Ohio St.	9-3-0	Earle Bruce	8-3-0
15 Florida St.	9-3-0	Bobby Bowden	8-3-0
16 BYU	11-3-0	LaVell Edwards	11-2-0
17 Baylor	9-3-0	Grant Teaff	8-3-0
18 Maryland	9-3-0	Bobby Ross	8-3-0
19 Georgia Tech	9-2-1	Bill Curry	8-2-1
20 LSU	9-2-1	Bill Arnsparger	9-1-1

Key Bowl Games

Rankings below reflect final regular season poll, released Dec. 9. No bowl for then #6 Florida (probation).

Orange—#3 Oklahoma over #1 Penn St., 25-10; **Sugar**—#8 Tennessee over #2 Miami-FL, 35-7; **Rose**—#13 UCLA over #4 Iowa, 45-28; **Fiesta**—#5 Michigan over #7 Nebraska, 27-23; **Bluebonnet**—#10 Air Force over Texas, 24-16; **Cotton**—#11 Texas A&M over #16 Auburn, 36-16.

1986

	After Bowls	Head Coach	Regular Season
1 Penn St.	12-0-0	Joe Paterno	11-0-0
2 Miami-FL	11-1-0	Jimmy Johnson	11-0-0
3 Oklahoma	11-1-0	Barry Switzer	10-1-0
4 Arizona St.	10-1-1	John Cooper	9-1-1
5 Nebraska	10-2-0	Tom Osborne	9-2-0
6 Auburn	10-2-0	Pat Dye	9-2-0
7 Ohio St.	10-3-0	Earle Bruce	9-3-0
8 Michigan	11-2-0	Bo Schembechler	11-1-0
9 Alabama	10-3-0	Ray Perkins	9-3-0
10 LSU	9-3-0	Bill Arnsparger	9-2-0
11 Arizona	9-3-0	Larry Smith	8-3-0
12 Baylor	9-3-0	Grant Teaff	8-3-0
13 Texas A&M	9-3-0	Jackie Sherrill	9-2-0
14 UCLA	8-3-1	Terry Donahue	7-3-1
15 Arkansas	9-3-0	Ken Hatfield	9-2-0
16 Iowa	9-3-0	Hayden Fry	8-3-0
17 Clemson	8-2-2	Danny Ford	7-2-2
18 Washington	8-3-1	Don James	8-2-1
19 Boston College	9-3-0	Jack Bicknell	8-3-0
20 Virginia Tech	9-2-1	Bill Dooley	8-2-1

Key Bowl Games

Rankings below reflect final regular season poll, released Dec. 1.

Fiesta—#2 Penn St. over #1 Miami-FL, 14-10; **Orange**—#3 Oklahoma over #9 Arkansas, 42-8; **Rose**— #7 Ariz. St. over #4 Michigan, 22-15; **Sugar**—#6 Nebraska over #5 LSU, 30-15; **Cotton**—#11 Ohio St. over #8 Texas A&M, 28-12; **Citrus**—#10 Auburn over USC, 16-7; **Sun**—#13 Alabama over #12 Washington, 28-6.

1987

	After Bowls	Head Coach	Regular Season
1 Miami-FL	12-0-0	Jimmy Johnson	11-0-0
2 Florida St.	11-1-0	Bobby Bowden	10-1-0
3 Oklahoma	11-1-0	Barry Switzer	11-0-0
4 Syracuse	11-0-1	Dick MacPherson	11-0-0
5 LSU	10-1-1	Mike Archer	9-1-1
6 Nebraska	10-2-0	Tom Osborne	10-1-0
7 Auburn	9-1-2	Pat Dye	9-1-1
8 Michigan St.	9-2-1	George Perles	8-2-1
9 UCLA	10-2-0	Terry Donahue	9-2-0
10 Texas A&M	10-2-0	Jackie Sherrill	9-2-0
11 Oklahoma St.	10-2-0	Pat Jones	9-2-0
12 Clemson	10-2-0	Danny Ford	9-2-0
13 Georgia	9-3-0	Vince Dooley	8-3-0
14 Tennessee	10-2-1	Johnny Majors	9-2-1
15 South Carolina	8-4-0	Joe Morrison	8-3-0
16 Iowa	10-3-0	Hayden Fry	9-3-0
17 Notre Dame	8-4-0	Lou Holtz	8-3-0
18 USC	8-4-0	Larry Smith	8-3-0
19 Michigan	8-4-0	Bo Schembechler	7-4-0
20 Arizona St.	7-4-1	John Cooper	6-4-1

Key Bowl Games

Rankings below reflect final regular season poll, released Dec. 7.

Orange—#2 Miami-FL over #1 Oklahoma, 20-14; **Fiesta**—#3 Florida St. over #5 Nebraska, 31-28; **Sugar**—#4 Syracuse tied #6 Auburn, 16-16; **Gator**—#7 LSU over #9 S.Carolina, 30-13; **Rose**—#8 Mich. St. over #16 USC, 20-17; **Aloha**—#10 UCLA over Florida, 20-16; **Cotton**—#13 Texas A&M over #12 Notre Dame, 35-10.

1988

	After Bowls	Head Coach	Regular Season
1 Notre Dame	12-0-0	Lou Holtz	11-0-0
2 Miami-FL	11-1-0	Jimmy Johnson	10-1-0
3 Florida St.	11-1-0	Bobby Bowden	10-1-0
4 Michigan	9-2-1	Bo Schembechler	8-2-1
5 West Virginia	11-1-0	Don Nehlen	11-0-0
6 UCLA	10-2-0	Terry Donahue	9-2-0
7 USC	10-2-0	Larry Smith	10-1-0
8 Auburn	10-2-0	Pat Dye	10-1-0
9 Clemson	10-2-0	Danny Ford	9-2-0
10 Nebraska	11-2-0	Tom Osborne	11-1-0
11 Oklahoma St.	10-2-0	Pat Jones	9-2-0
12 Arkansas	10-2-0	Ken Hatfield	10-1-0
13 Syracuse	10-2-0	Dick MacPherson	9-2-0
14 Oklahoma	9-3-0	Barry Switzer	9-2-0
15 Georgia	9-3-0	Vince Dooley	8-3-0
16 Washington St.	9-3-0	Dennis Erickson	8-3-0
17 Alabama	9-3-0	Bill Curry	8-3-0
18 Houston	9-3-0	Jack Pardee	9-2-0
19 LSU	8-4-0	Mike Archer	8-3-0
20 Indiana	8-3-1	Bill Mallory	7-3-1

Key Bowl Games

Rankings below reflect final regular season poll, released Dec. 5.

Fiesta—#1 Notre Dame over #3 West Va., 34-21; **Orange**—#2 Miami-FL over #6 Nebraska, 23-3; **Sugar**—#4 Florida St. over #7 Auburn, 13-7; **Rose**—#11 Michigan over #5 USC, 22-14; **Cotton**—#9 UCLA over #8 Arkansas, 17-3; **Citrus**—#13 Clemson over #10 Oklahoma, 13-6.

1989

	After Bowls	Head Coach	Regular Season
1 Miami-FL	11-1-0	Dennis Erickson	10-1-0
2 Notre Dame	12-1-0	Lou Holtz	11-1-0
3 Florida St.	10-2-0	Bobby Bowden	9-2-0
4 Colorado	11-1-0	Bill McCartney	11-0-0
5 Tennessee	11-1-0	Johnny Majors	10-1-0
6 Auburn	10-2-0	Pat Dye	9-2-0
7 Michigan	10-2-0	Bo Schembechler	10-1-0
8 USC	9-2-1	Larry Smith	8-2-1
9 Alabama	10-2-0	Bill Curry	10-1-0
10 Illinois	10-2-0	John Mackovic	9-2-0
11 Nebraska	10-2-0	Tom Osborne	10-1-0
12 Clemson	10-2-0	Danny Ford	9-2-0
13 Arkansas	10-2-0	Ken Hatfield	10-1-0
14 Houston	9-2-0	Jack Pardee	same
15 Penn St.	8-3-1	Joe Paterno	7-3-1
16 Michigan St.	8-4-0	George Perles	7-4-0
17 Pittsburgh	8-3-1	Mike Gottfried (7-3-1) & Paul Hackett (1-0)	7-3-1
18 Virginia	10-3-0	George Welsh	10-2-0
19 Texas Tech	9-3-0	Spike Dykes	8-3-0
20 Texas A&M	8-4-0	R.C. Slocum	8-3-0

Key Bowl Games

Rankings below reflect final regular season poll, released Dec. 11. No bowl for then #13 Houston (probation).

Orange—#4 Notre Dame over #1 Colorado, 21-6; **Sugar**—#2 Miami-FL over #7 Alabama, 33-25; **Rose**—#12 USC over #3 Michigan, 17-10; **Fiesta**—#5 Florida St. over #6 Nebraska, 41-17; **Cotton**—#8 Tennessee over #10 Arkansas, 31-27; **Hall of Fame**—#9 Auburn over #21 Ohio St., 31-14; **Citrus**—#11 Illinois over #15 Virginia, 31-21.

Associated Press Final Polls (Cont.)

Final poll taken after bowl games.

1990

	After Bowls	Head Coach	Regular Season
1 Colorado	11-1-1	Bill McCartney	10-1-1
2 Georgia Tech	11-0-1	Bobby Ross	10-0-1
3 Miami-FL	10-2-0	Dennis Erickson	9-2-0
4 Florida St.	10-2-0	Bobby Bowden	9-2-0
5 Washington	10-2-0	Don James	9-2-0
6 Notre Dame	9-3-0	Lou Holtz	9-2-0
7 Michigan	9-3-0	Gary Moeller	8-3-0
8 Tennessee	9-2-2	Johnny Majors	8-2-2
9 Clemson	10-2-0	Ken Hatfield	9-2-0
10 Houston	10-1-0	John Jenkins	same
11 Penn St.	9-3-0	Joe Paterno	9-2-0
12 Texas	10-2-0	David McWilliams	10-1-0
13 Florida	9-2-0	Steve Spurrier	same
14 Louisville	10-1-1	H. Schnellenberger	9-1-1
15 Texas A&M	9-3-1	R.C. Slocum	8-3-1
16 Michigan St.	8-3-1	George Perles	7-3-1
17 Oklahoma	8-3-0	Gary Gibbs	same
18 Iowa	8-4-0	Hayden Fry	8-3-0
19 Auburn	8-3-1	Pat Dye	7-3-1
20 USC	8-4-1	Larry Smith	8-3-1

Key Bowl Games

Rankings below reflect final regular season poll, released Dec. 3. No bowl for then #9 Houston (probation), #11 Florida (probation) and #20 Oklahoma (probation).

Orange—#1 Colorado over #5 Notre Dame, 10-9; **Citrus**—#2 Ga. Tech over #19 Nebraska, 45-21; **Cotton**—#4 Miami-FL over #3 Texas, 46-3; **Blockbuster**—#6 Florida St. over #7 Penn St., 24-17; **Rose**—#8 Washington over #17 Iowa, 46-34; **Sugar**—#10 Tennessee over Virginia, 23-22; **Gator**—#12 Michigan over #15 Ole Miss, 35-3.

1991

	After Bowls	Head Coach	Regular Season
1 Miami-FL	12-0-0	Dennis Erickson	11-0-0
2 Washington	12-0-0	Don James	11-0-0
3 Penn St.	11-2-0	Joe Paterno	10-2-0
4 Florida St.	11-2-0	Bobby Bowden	10-2-0
5 Alabama	11-1-0	Gene Stallings	10-1-0
6 Michigan	10-2-0	Gary Moeller	10-1-0
7 Florida	10-2-0	Steve Spurrier	10-1-0
8 California	10-2-0	Bruce Snyder	9-2-0
9 East Carolina	11-1-0	Bill Lewis	10-1-0
10 Iowa	10-1-1	Hayden Fry	10-1-0
11 Syracuse	10-2-0	Paul Pasqualoni	9-2-0
12 Texas A&M	10-2-0	R.C. Slocum	10-1-0
13 Notre Dame	10-3-0	Lou Holtz	9-3-0
14 Tennessee	9-3-0	Johnny Majors	9-2-0
15 Nebraska	9-2-1	Tom Osborne	9-1-1
16 Oklahoma	9-3-0	Gary Gibbs	8-3-0
17 Georgia	9-3-0	Ray Goff	8-3-0
18 Clemson	9-2-1	Ken Hatfield	9-1-1
19 UCLA	9-3-0	Terry Donahue	8-3-0
20 Colorado	8-3-1	Bill McCartney	8-2-1

Key Bowl Games

Rankings below reflect final regular season poll, taken Dec. 2.

Orange—#1 Miami-FL over #11 Nebraska, 22-0; **Rose**—#2 Washington over #4 Michigan, 34-14; **Sugar**—#18 Notre Dame over #3 Florida, 39-28; **Cotton**—#5 Florida St. over #9 Texas A&M, 10-2; **Fiesta**—#6 Penn St. over #10 Tennessee, 42-17; **Holiday**—#7 Iowa tied BYU, 13-13; **Blockbuster**—#8 Alabama over #15 Colorado, 30-25; **Citrus**—#14 California over #13 Clemson, 37-13; **Peach**—#12 East Carolina over #21 N.C. State, 37-34.

1992

	After Bowls	Head Coach	Regular Season
1 Alabama	13-0-0	Gene Stallings	12-0-0
2 Florida St.	11-1-0	Bobby Bowden	10-1-0
3 Miami-FL	11-1-0	Dennis Erickson	11-0-0
4 Notre Dame	10-1-1	Lou Holtz	9-1-1
5 Michigan	9-0-3	Gary Moeller	8-0-3
6 Syracuse	10-2-0	Paul Pasqualoni	9-2-0
7 Texas A&M	12-1-0	R.C. Slocum	12-0-0
8 Georgia	10-2-0	Ray Goff	9-2-0
9 Stanford	10-3-0	Bill Walsh	9-3-0
10 Florida	9-4-0	Steve Spurrier	8-4-0
11 Washington	9-3-0	Don James	9-2-0
12 Tennessee	9-3-0	Johnny Majors (5-3) & Phillip Fulmer (4-0)	8-3-0
13 Colorado	9-2-1	Bill McCartney	9-1-1
14 Nebraska	9-3-0	Tom Osborne	9-2-0
15 Washington St.	9-3-0	Mike Price	8-3-0
16 Mississippi	9-3-0	Billy Brewer	8-3-0
17 N.C. State	9-3-1	Dick Sheridan	9-2-1
18 Ohio St.	8-3-1	John Cooper	8-2-1
19 North Carolina	9-3-0	Mack Brown	8-3-0
20 Hawaii	11-2-0	Bob Wagner	10-2-0

Key Bowl Games

Rankings below reflect final regular season poll, taken Dec. 5.

Sugar—#2 Alabama over #1 Miami-FL, 34-13; **Orange**—#3 Florida St. over #11 Nebraska, 27-14; **Cotton**—#5 Notre Dame over #4 Texas A&M, 28-3; **Fiesta**—#6 Syracuse over #10 Colorado, 26-22; **Rose**—#7 Michigan over #9 Washington, 38-31; **Citrus**—#8 Georgia over #15 Ohio St., 21-14.

1993

	After Bowls	Head Coach	Regular Season
1 Florida St	12-1-0	Bobby Bowden	11-1-0
2 Notre Dame	11-1-0	Lou Holtz	10-1-0
3 Nebraska	11-1-0	Tom Osborne	11-0-0
4 Auburn	11-0-0	Terry Bowden	11-0-0
5 Florida	11-2-0	Steve Spurrier	10-2-0
6 Wisconsin	10-1-1	Barry Alvarez	9-1-1
7 West Virginia	11-1-0	Don Nehlen	11-0-0
8 Penn St	10-2-0	Joe Paterno	9-2-0
9 Texas A&M	10-2-0	R.C. Slocum	10-1-0
10 Arizona	10-2-0	Dick Tomey	9-2-0
11 Ohio St	10-1-1	John Cooper	9-1-1
12 Tennessee	9-2-1	Phillip Fulmer	9-1-1
13 Boston College	9-3-0	Tom Coughlin	8-3-0
14 Alabama	9-3-1	Gene Stallings	8-3-1
15 Miami-FL	9-3-0	Dennis Erickson	9-2-0
16 Colorado	8-3-1	Bill McCartney	7-3-1
17 Oklahoma	9-3-0	Gary Gibbs	8-3-0
18 UCLA	8-4-0	Terry Donahue	8-3-0
19 North Carolina	10-3-0	Mack Brown	10-2-0
20 Kansas St.	9-2-1	Bill Snyder	8-2-1

Key Bowl Games

Rankings below reflect final regular season poll, taken Dec. 5. No bowl for then #5 Auburn (probation).

Orange—#1 Florida St. over #2 Nebraska, 18-16; **Sugar**—#8 Florida over #3 West Virginia, 41-7; **Cotton**—#4 Notre Dame over #7 Texas A&M, 24-21; **Citrus**—#13 Penn St. over #6 Tennessee, 31-13; **Rose**—#9 Wisconsin over #14 UCLA, 21-16; **Fiesta**—#16 Arizona over #10 Miami-FL, 29-0; **Holiday**—#11 Ohio St. over BYU, 28-21; **Gator**—#18 Alabama over #12 North Carolina, 24-10; **Carquest**—#15 Boston College over Virginia, 31-13.

1994

	After Bowls	Head Coach	Regular Season
1 Nebraska	13-0-0	Tom Osborne	12-0-0
2 Penn St	12-0-0	Joe Paterno	11-0-0
3 Colorado	11-1-0	Bill McCartney	10-1-0
4 Florida St	10-1-1	Bobby Bowden	9-1-1
5 Alabama	12-1-0	Gene Stallings	11-1-0
6 Miami-FL	10-2-0	Dennis Erickson	10-1-0
7 Florida	10-2-1	Steve Spurrier	10-1-1
8 Texas A&M	10-0-1	R.C. Slocum	same
9 Auburn	9-1-1	Terry Bowden	same
10 Utah	10-2-0	Ron McBride	9-2-0
11 Oregon	9-4-0	Rich Brooks	9-3-0
12 Michigan	8-4-0	Gary Moeller	7-4-0
13 USC	8-3-1	John Robinson	7-3-1
14 Ohio St	9-4-0	John Cooper	9-3-0
15 Virginia	9-3-0	George Welsh	8-3-0
16 Colorado St	10-2-0	Sonny Lubick	10-1-0
17 N.C. State	9-3-0	Mike O'Cain	8-3-0
18 BYU	10-3-0	LaVell Edwards	9-3-0
19 Kansas St	9-3-0	Bill Snyder	9-2-0
20 Arizona	8-4-0	Dick Tomey	8-3-0

Key Bowl Games

Rankings below reflect final regular season poll, taken Dec. 4. No bowls for then #8 Texas A&M (probation) and #9 Auburn (probation).

Orange— #1 Nebraska over #3 Miami-FL, 24-17; **Rose**— #2 Penn St. over #12 Oregon, 38-20; **Fiesta**— #4 Colorado over Notre Dame, 41-24; **Sugar**— #7 Florida St. over #5 Florida, 23-17; **Citrus**— #6 Alabama over #13 Ohio St., 24-17; **Freedom**— #14 Utah over #15 Arizona, 16-13.

All-Time AP Top 20

The composite AP Top 20 from the 1936 season through the 1995 season, based on the final rankings of each year. The final AP poll has been taken after the bowl games in 1965 and since 1968. Team point totals are based on 20 points for all 1st place finishes, 19 for each 2nd, etc. Also listed are the number of times each team has been named national champion by AP and times ranked in the final Top 10 and Top 20.

		Final AP		
	Pts	No.1	Top 10	Top 20
1 Notre Dame	624	8	34	43
2 Oklahoma	558	6	29	41
3 Michigan	545	1	32	43
4 Alabama	541	6	30	40
5 Ohio St	471	3	22	38
6 Nebraska	466	4	25	35
7 USC	414	3	20	36
8 Texas	400	2	19	31
9 Tennessee	375	1	18	32
10 Penn St	370	2	20	31
11 UCLA	293	0	14	27
12 Auburn	271	1	14	25
13 LSU	260	1	14	23
14 Arkansas	259	0	13	23
15 Miami-FL	257	4	13	20
16 Georgia	238	1	13	20
Michigan St	238	1	12	19
18 Florida St.	218	1	11	15
19 Texas A&M	205	1	11	20
20 Pittsburgh	194	2	10	16
Washington	194	0	10	16

1995

	After Bowls	Head Coach	Regular Season
1 Nebraska	12-0-0	Tom Osborne	11-0-0
2 Florida	12-1-0	Steve Spurrier	12-0-0
3 Tennessee	11-1-0	Phillip Fulmer	10-1-0
4 Florida St	10-2-0	Bobby Bowden	9-2-0
5 Colorado	10-2-0	Rick Neuheisel	9-2-0
6 Ohio St.	11-2-0	John Cooper	11-1-0
7 Kansas St.	10-2-0	Bill Snyder	9-2-0
8 Northwestern	10-2-0	Gary Barnett	10-1-0
9 Kansas	10-2-0	Glen Mason	9-2-0
10 Va. Tech	10-2-0	Frank Beamer	9-2-0
11 Notre Dame	9-3-0	Lou Holtz	9-2-0
12 USC	9-2-1	John Robinson	8-2-1
13 Penn St.	9-3-0	Joe Paterno	8-3-0
14 Texas	10-2-1	John Mackovic	10-1-1
15 Texas A&M	9-3-0	R.C. Slocum	8-3-0
16 Virginia	9-4-0	George Welsh	8-4-0
17 Michigan	9-4-0	Lloyd Carr	9-3-0
18 Oregon	9-3-0	Mike Bellotti	9-2-0
19 Syracuse	9-3-0	Paul Pasqualoni	8-3-0
20 Miami-FL	8-3-0	Butch Davis	same

Key Bowl Games

Rankings below reflect final regular season poll, taken Dec. 3. No bowl for then #22 Miami-FL (probation).

Fiesta— #1 Nebraska over #2 Florida, 62-24; **Rose**— #17 USC over #3 Northwestern, 41-32; **Citrus**— #4 (tie) Tennessee over #4 (tie) Ohio St., 20-14; **Orange**— #8 Florida St. over #6 Notre Dame, 31-26; **Cotton**— #7 Colorado over #12 Oregon, 38-6; **Sugar**— #13 Va. Tech over #9 Texas, 28-10; **Holiday**— #10 Kansas St. over Colo. St., 54-21; **Aloha**— #11 Kansas over UCLA, 51-30; **Alamo**— #19 Texas A&M over #14 Michigan, 22-20; **Outback**— #15 Penn St. over #16 Auburn, 43-14; **Peach**— #18 Virginia over Georgia, 34-27; **Gator**— Syracuse over #23 Clemson, 41-0.

The Special Election That Didn't Count

There was one No. 1 vs No. 2 confrontation not noted on page 170. It came in a special election or re-vote of AP selectors following the 1948 Rose Bowl. Here's what happened: Unbeaten Notre Dame was declared 1947 national champion by AP on Dec. 8, two days after closing out an undefeated season with a 38-7 rout of then third-ranked USC in Los Angeles. Twenty-four days later, however, unbeaten Michigan, AP's final No. 2 team, clobbered now 8th-ranked USC, 49-0, in the Rose Bowl. An immediate cry went up for an unprecedented two-team, "Who's No. 1" ballot and AP gave in. Michigan won the election, 226-119, with 12 voters calling it even. However, AP ruled that the Dec. 8 final poll won by Notre Dame would be the vote of record.

Bowl Games

From Jan. 1, 1902 through Jan. 2, 1996. Corporate title sponsors and automatic berths updated through Aug. 15, 1996.

Rose Bowl

City: Pasadena, Calif. **Stadium:** Rose Bowl. **Capacity:** 100,225. **Playing surface:** Grass. **First game:** Jan. 1, 1902. **Playing sites:** Tournament Park (1902, 1916-22), Rose Bowl (1923-41 and since 1943) and Duke Stadium in Durham, N.C. (1942, due to wartime restrictions following Japan's attack at Pearl Harbor on Dec. 7, 1941).

Automatic berths: Pacific Coast Conference champion vs. opponent selected by PCC (1924-45 seasons); Big Ten champion vs. Pac-10 champion (since 1946 season).

Multiple wins: USC (20); Michigan (7); Washington (6); Ohio St., Stanford and UCLA (5); Alabama (4); Illinois and Michigan St. (3); California and Iowa (2).

Year	
1902*	Michigan 49, Stanford 0
1916	Washington St. 14, Brown 0
1917	Oregon 14, Penn 0
1918	Mare Island 19, Camp Lewis 7
1919	Great Lakes 17, Mare Island 0
1920	Harvard 7, Oregon 6
1921	California 28, Ohio St. 0
1922	0-0, California vs Wash. & Jeff.
1923	USC 14, Penn St. 3
1924	14-14, Navy vs Washington
1925	Notre Dame 27, Stanford 10
1926	Alabama 20, Washington 19
1927	7-7, Alabama vs Stanford
1928	Stanford 7, Pittsburgh 6
1929	Georgia Tech 8, California 7
1930	USC 47, Pittsburgh 14
1931	Alabama 24, Washington St. 0
1932	USC 21, Tulane 12
1933	USC 35, Pittsburgh 0
1934	Columbia 7, Stanford 0
1935	Alabama 29, Stanford 13
1936	Stanford 7, SMU 0
1937	Pittsburgh 21, Washington 0
1938	California 13, Alabama 0
1939	USC 7, Duke 3
1940	USC 14, Tennessee 0
1941	Stanford 21, Nebraska 13
1942	Oregon St. 20, Duke 16
1943	Georgia 9, UCLA 0

Year	
1944	USC 29, Washington 0
1945	USC 25, Tennessee 0
1946	Alabama 34, USC 14
1947	Illinois 45, UCLA 14
1948	Michigan 49, USC 0
1949	Northwestern 20, California 14
1950	Ohio St. 17, California 14
1951	Michigan 14, California 6
1952	Illinois 40, Stanford 7
1953	USC 7, Wisconsin 0
1954	Michigan St. 28, UCLA 20
1955	Ohio St. 20, USC 7
1956	Michigan St. 17, UCLA 14
1957	Iowa 35, Oregon St. 19
1958	Ohio St. 10, Oregon 7
1959	Iowa 38, California 12
1960	Washington 44, Wisconsin 8
1961	Washington 17, Minnesota 7
1962	Minnesota 21, UCLA 3
1963	USC 42, Wisconsin 37
1964	Illinois 17, Washington 7
1965	Michigan 34, Oregon St. 7
1966	UCLA 14, Michigan St. 12
1967	Purdue 14, USC 13
1968	USC 14, Indiana 3
1969	Ohio St. 27, USC 16
1970	USC 10, Michigan 3
1971	Stanford 27, Ohio St. 17
1972	Stanford 13, Michigan 12

Year	
1973	USC 42, Ohio St. 17
1974	Ohio St. 42, USC 21
1975	USC 18, Ohio St. 17
1976	UCLA 23, Ohio St. 10
1977	USC 14, Michigan 6
1978	Washington 27, Michigan 20
1979	USC 17, Michigan 10
1980	USC 17, Ohio St. 16
1981	Michigan 23, Washington 6
1982	Washington 28, Iowa 0
1983	UCLA 24, Michigan 14
1984	UCLA 45, Illinois 9
1985	USC 20, Ohio St. 17
1986	UCLA 45, Iowa 28
1987	Arizona St. 22, Michigan 15
1988	Michigan St. 20, USC 17
1989	Michigan 22, USC 14
1990	USC 17, Michigan 10
1991	Washington 46, Iowa 34
1992	Washington 34, Michigan 14
1993	Michigan 38, Washington 31
1994	Wisconsin 21, UCLA 16
1995	Penn St. 38, Oregon 20
1996	USC 41, Northwestern 32

*January game since 1902.

Fiesta Bowl

City: Tempe, Ariz. **Stadium:** Sun Devil. **Capacity:** 73,655. **Playing surface:** Grass. **First game:** Dec. 27, 1971. **Playing site:** Sun Devil Stadium (since 1971). **Corporate title sponsors:** Sunkist Citrus Growers (1986-91) and IBM OS/2 (1993-95) and Frito-Lay Tostitos (starting in 1996).

Automatic berths: Two of first five picks from 8-team Bowl Coalition pool (1992-94 seasons). New Bowl Alliance matchups starting with 1995 season: #1 vs. #2 on Jan. 2, 1996; #3 vs. #5 on Jan. 1, 1997; and #4 vs. #6 on Dec. 31, 1997.

Multiple wins: Arizona St. and Penn St. (5); Florida St. (2).

Year	
1971†	Arizona St. 45, Florida St. 38
1972	Arizona St. 49, Missouri 35
1973	Arizona St. 28, Pittsburgh 7
1974	Oklahoma St. 16, BYU 6
1975	Arizona St. 17, Nebraska 14
1976	Oklahoma 41, Wyoming 7
1977	Penn St. 42, Arizona St. 30
1978	10-10, Arkansas vs UCLA
1979	Pittsburgh16, Arizona 10

Year	
1980	Penn St. 31, Ohio St. 19
1982*	Penn St. 26, USC 10
1983	Arizona St. 32, Oklahoma 21
1984	Ohio St. 28, Pittsburgh 23
1985	UCLA 39, Miami-FL 37
1986	Michigan 27, Nebraska 23
1987	Penn St. 14, Miami-FL 10
1988	Florida St. 31, Nebraska 28
1989	Notre Dame 34, West Va. 21

Year	
1990	Florida St. 41, Nebraska 17
1991	Louisville 34, Alabama 7
1992	Penn St. 42, Tennessee 17
1993	Syracuse 26, Colorado 22
1994	Arizona 29, Miami-FL 0
1995	Colorado 41, Notre Dame 24
1996	Nebraska 62, Florida 24

†December game from 1971-80. *January game since 1982.

Tiebreakers in Bowl Games

The NCAA tiebreaker system was approved for Divison I-A bowl games beginning with the 1995 postseason. Unlike sudden-death overtime in the NFL, the NCAA tiebreaking procedure gives both teams a chance to score after regulation time has expired. Each team gets an offensive series beginning on the opponent's 25-yard line. A team's possession ends when it scores, turns the ball over or fails to convert a fourth-down play. This untimed procedure is repeated until the score is no longer tied at the end of an overtime period, which consists of one possession per team.

Sugar Bowl

City: New Orleans, La. **Stadium:** Louisiana Superdome. **Capacity:** 77,450. **Playing surface:** AstroTurf. **First game:** Jan. 1, 1935. **Playing sites:** Tulane Stadium (1935-74) and Superdome (since 1975). **Corporate title sponsors:** USF&G Financial Services (1987-95) and Nokia cellular telephones of Finland (starting in 1995).

Automatic berths: SEC champion vs. at-large opponent (1976-91 seasons); SEC champion vs. one of first five picks from 8-team Bowl Coalition pool (1992-94 seasons). New Bowl Alliance matchups starting with 1995 season: #4 vs. #6 on Dec. 31, 1995; #1 vs. #2 on Jan. 2, 1997; and #3 vs. #5 on Jan. 1, 1998.

Multiple wins: Alabama (8); Mississippi (5); Georgia Tech, Oklahoma and Tennessee (4); LSU and Nebraska (3); Florida St., Georgia, Notre Dame, Pittsburgh, Santa Clara and TCU (2).

Year
1935* Tulane 20, Temple 14
1936 TCU 3, LSU 2
1937 Santa Clara 21, LSU 14
1938 Santa Clara 6, LSU 0
1939 TCU 15, Carnegie Tech 7

1940 Texas A&M 14, Tulane 13
1941 Boston College 19, Tennessee 13
1942 Fordham 2, Missouri 0
1943 Tennessee 14, Tulsa 7
1944 Georgia Tech 20, Tulsa 18
1945 Duke 29, Alabama 26
1946 Okla. A&M 33, St.Mary's 13
1947 Georgia 20, N.Carolina 10
1948 Texas 27, Alabama 7
1949 Oklahoma 14, N.Carolina 6

1950 Oklahoma 35, LSU 0
1951 Kentucky 13, Oklahoma 7
1952 Maryland 28, Tennessee 13
1953 Georgia Tech 24, Mississippi 7
1954 Georgia Tech 42, West Va. 19
1955 Navy 21, Mississippi 0

Year
1956 Georgia Tech 7, Pittsburgh 0
1957 Baylor 13, Tennessee 7
1958 Mississippi 39, Texas 7
1959 LSU 7, Clemson 0

1960 Mississippi 21, LSU 0
1961 Mississippi 14, Rice 6
1962 Alabama 10, Arkansas 3
1963 Mississippi 17, Arkansas 13
1964 Alabama 12, Mississippi 7
1965 LSU 13, Syracuse 10
1966 Missouri 20, Florida 18
1967 Alabama 34, Nebraska 7
1968 LSU 20, Wyoming 13
1969 Arkansas 16, Georgia 2

1970 Mississippi 27, Arkansas 22
1971 Tennessee 34, Air Force 13
1972 Oklahoma 40, Auburn 22
1972† Oklahoma 14, Penn St. 0
1973 Notre Dame 24, Alabama 23
1974 Nebraska 13, Florida 10
1975 Alabama 13, Penn St. 6

Year
1977* Pittsburgh 27, Georgia 3
1978 Alabama 35, Ohio St. 6
1979 Alabama 14, Penn St. 7

1980 Alabama 24, Arkansas 9
1981 Georgia 17, Notre Dame 10
1982 Pittsburgh 24, Georgia 20
1983 Penn St. 27, Georgia 23
1984 Auburn 9, Michigan 7
1985 Nebraska 28, LSU 10
1986 Tennessee 35, Miami-FL 7
1987 Nebraska 30, LSU 15
1988 16-16, Syracuse vs Auburn
1989 Florida St. 13, Auburn 7

1990 Miami-FL 33, Alabama 25
1991 Tennessee 23, Virginia 22
1992 Notre Dame 39, Florida 28
1993 Alabama 34, Miami-FL 13
1994 Florida 41, West Va. 7
1995 Florida St. 23, Florida 17
1995† Va. Tech 28, Texas 10

*January game from 1935-72 and since 1977. †Game played on Dec. 31 from 1972-75 and in 1995.

Orange Bowl

City: Miami, Fla. **Stadium:** Orange Bowl. **Capacity:** 74,475. **Playing surface:** Grass. **First game:** Jan. 1, 1935. **Playing sites:** Orange Bowl (since 1935); game moves to Joe Robbie Stadium Dec. 31, 1996. **Corporate title sponsor:** Federal Express (since 1989).

Automatic berths: Big 8 champion vs. at-large opponent (1953-63 seasons and 1975-91 seasons); Big 8 champion vs. one of first five picks from 8-team Bowl Coalition pool (1992-94 seasons). New Bowl Alliance matchups starting with 1995 season: #3 vs. #5 on Jan. 1, 1996; #4 vs. #6 on Dec. 31, 1996; and #1 vs. #2 on Jan. 2, 1998.

Multiple wins: Oklahoma (11); Nebraska (6); Miami-FL (5); Alabama (4); Florida St., Georgia Tech and Penn St. (3); Clemson, Colorado, Georgia, LSU, Notre Dame and Texas (2).

Year
1935* Bucknell 26, Miami-FL 0
1936 Catholic U. 20, Mississippi 19
1937 Duquesne 13, Mississippi St. 12
1938 Auburn 6, Michigan St. 0
1939 Tennessee 17, Oklahoma 0

1940 Georgia Tech 21, Missouri 7
1941 Mississippi St. 14, Georgetown 7
1942 Georgia 40, TCU 26
1943 Alabama 37, Boston College 21
1944 LSU 19, Texas A&M 14
1945 Tulsa 26, Georgia Tech 12
1946 Miami-FL 13, Holy Cross 6
1947 Rice 8, Tennessee 0
1948 Georgia Tech 20, Kansas 14
1949 Texas 41, Georgia 28

1950 Santa Clara 21, Kentucky 13
1951 Clemson 15, Miami-FL 14
1952 Georgia Tech 17, Baylor 14
1953 Alabama 61, Syracuse 6
1954 Oklahoma 7, Maryland 0
1955 Duke 34, Nebraska 7

Year
1956 Oklahoma 20, Maryland 6
1957 Colorado 27, Clemson 21
1958 Oklahoma 48, Duke 21
1959 Oklahoma 21, Syracuse 6

1960 Georgia 14, Missouri 0
1961 Missouri 21, Navy 14
1962 LSU 25, Colorado 7
1963 Alabama 17, Oklahoma 0
1964 Nebraska 13, Auburn 7
1965† Texas 21, Alabama 17
1966 Alabama 39, Nebraska 28
1967 Florida 27, Georgia Tech 12
1968 Oklahoma 26, Tennessee 24
1969 Penn St. 15, Kansas 14

1970 Penn St. 10, Missouri 3
1971 Nebraska 17, LSU 12
1972 Nebraska 38, Alabama 6
1973 Nebraska 40, Notre Dame 6
1974 Penn St. 16, LSU 9
1975 Notre Dame 13, Alabama 11
1976 Oklahoma 14, Michigan 6

Year
1977 Ohio St. 27, Colorado 10
1978 Arkansas 31, Oklahoma 6
1979 Oklahoma 31, Nebraska 24

1980 Oklahoma 24, Florida St. 7
1981 Oklahoma 18, Florida St. 17
1982 Clemson 22, Nebraska 15
1983 Nebraska 21, LSU 20
1984 Miami-FL 31, Nebraska 30
1985 Washington 28, Oklahoma 17
1986 Oklahoma 25, Penn St. 10
1987 Oklahoma 42, Arkansas 8
1988 Miami-FL 20, Oklahoma 14
1989 Miami-FL 23, Nebraska 3

1990 Notre Dame, 21, Colorado 6
1991 Colorado 10, Notre Dame 9
1992 Miami-FL 22, Nebraska 0
1993 Florida St. 27, Nebraska 14
1994 Florida St. 18, Nebraska 16
1995 Nebraska 24, Miami-FL 17
1996 Florida St. 31, Notre Dame 26

*January game since 1935. †Night game since 1965.

Bowl Games (Cont.)

Cotton Bowl

City: Dallas, Tex. **Stadium:** Cotton Bowl. **Capacity:** 68,250. **Playing surface:** Grass. **First game:** Jan 1, 1937. **Playing sites:** Fair Park Stadium (1937) and Cotton Bowl (since 1938). **Corporate title sponsor:** Mobil Corporation (1988-95) and Southwestern Bell (starting in 1996).

Automatic berths: SWC champion vs. at-large opponent (1941-91 seasons); SWC champion vs. one of first five picks from 8-team Bowl Coalition pool (1992-1994 seasons). New Bowl Alliance matchup starting with 1995 season: first choice of WAC champion or second pick from Pac-10 vs. second pick from Big 12 (Big Eight/SWC).

Multiple wins: Texas (9); Notre Dame (5); Texas A&M (4); Rice (3); Alabama, Arkansas, Georgia, Houston, LSU, Penn St., SMU, Tennessee and TCU (2).

Year
1937* TCU 16, Marquette 6
1938 Rice 28, Colorado 14
1939 St. Mary's 20, Texas Tech 13

1940 Clemson 6, Boston College 3
1941 Texas A&M 13, Fordham 12
1942 Alabama 29, Texas A&M 21
1943 Texas 14, Georgia Tech 7
1944 7-7, Texas vs Randolph Field
1945 Oklahoma A&M 34, TCU 0
1946 Texas 40, Missouri 27
1947 0-0, Arkansas vs LSU
1948 13-13, SMU vs Penn St.
1949 SMU 21, Oregon 13

1950 Rice 27, N. Carolina 13
1951 Tennessee 20, Texas 14
1952 Kentucky 20, TCU 7
1953 Texas 16, Tennessee 0
1954 Rice 28, Alabama 6
1955 Georgia Tech 14, Arkansas 6
1956 Mississippi 14, TCU 13

Year
1957 TCU 28, Syracuse 27
1958 Navy 20, Rice 7
1959 0-0, TCU vs Air Force

1960 Syracuse 23, Texas 14
1961 Duke 7, Arkansas 6
1962 Texas 12, Mississippi 7
1963 LSU 13, Texas 0
1964 Texas 28, Navy 6
1965 Arkansas 10, Nebraska 7
1966 LSU 14, Arkansas 7
1966† Georgia 24, SMU 9
1968* Texas A&M 20, Alabama 16
1969 Texas 36, Tennessee 13

1970 Texas 21, Notre Dame 17
1971 Notre Dame 24, Texas 11
1972 Penn St. 30, Texas 6
1973 Texas 17, Alabama 13
1974 Nebraska 19, Texas 3
1975 Penn St. 41, Baylor 20
1976 Arkansas 31, Georgia 10

Year
1977 Houston 30, Maryland 21
1978 Notre Dame 38, Texas 10
1979 Notre Dame 35, Houston 34

1980 Houston 17, Nebraska 14
1981 Alabama 30, Baylor 2
1982 Texas 14, Alabama 12
1983 SMU 7, Pittsburgh 3
1984 Georgia 10, Texas 9
1985 Boston College 45, Houston 28
1986 Texas A&M 36, Auburn 16
1987 Ohio St. 28, Texas A&M 12
1988 Texas A&M 35, Notre Dame 10
1989 UCLA 17, Arkansas 3

1990 Tennessee 31, Arkansas 27
1991 Miami-FL 46, Texas 3
1992 Florida St. 10, Texas A&M 2
1993 Notre Dame 28, Texas A&M 3
1994 Notre Dame 24, Texas A&M 21
1995 USC 55, Texas Tech 14
1996 Colorado 38, Oregon 6

*January game from 1937-66 and since 1968. †Game played on Dec. 31, 1966.

Florida Citrus Bowl

City: Orlando, Fla. **Stadium:** Florida Cirtus Bowl. **Capacity:** 73,000. **Playing surface:** Grass. **First game:** Jan. 1, 1947. **Name change:** Tangerine Bowl (1947-82) and Florida Citrus Bowl (since 1983). **Playing sites:** Tangerine Bowl (1947-72, 1974-82), Ben Hill Griffin Stadium in Gainesville (1973), Orlando Stadium (1983-85) and Florida Citrus Bowl (since 1986). The Tangerine Bowl, Orlando Stadium and Florida Citrus Bowl are all the same stadium. **Corporate title sponsors:** Florida Department of Cirtus (since 1983) and CompUSA (since 1992).

Automatic berths: Championship game of Atlantic Coast Regional Conference (1964-67 seasons); Mid-American Conference champion vs. Southern Conference champion (1968-75 seasons); ACC champion vs. at-large opponent (1987-91 seasons); second pick from SEC vs. second pick from Big 10 (1992-94 seasons). New Bowl Alliance matchup starting with 1995 season: second pick from SEC vs. second pick from Big 10.

Multiple wins: East Texas St., Miami-OH and Toledo (3); Auburn, Catawba, Clemson, East Carolina and Tennessee (2).

Year
1947* Catawba 31, Maryville 6
1948 Catawba 7, Marshall 0
1949 21-21, Murray St. vs Sul Ross St.

1950 St. Vincent 7, Emory & Henry 6
1951 M. Harvey 35, Emory & Henry 14
1952 Stetson 35, Arkansas St. 20
1953 E. Texas St. 33, Tenn. Tech 0
1954 7-7, E. Texas St. vs Arkansas St.
1955 Neb.-Omaha 7, Eastern Ky. 6
1956 6-6, Juniata vs Missouri Valley
1957 W. Texas St. 20, So. Miss. 13
1958 E. Texas St. 10, So. Miss. 9
1958† E. Texas St. 26, Mo. Valley 7

1960* Mid. Tenn. 21, Presbyterian 12
1960† Citadel 27, Tenn. Tech 0
1961 Lamar 21, Middle Tenn. 14
1962 Houston 49, Miami-OH 21

Year
1963 Western Ky. 27, Coast Guard 0
1964 E. Carolina 14, Massachusetts 13
1965 E. Carolina 31, Maine 0
1966 Morgan St. 14, West Chester 6
1967 Tenn-Martin 25, West Chester 8
1968 Richmond 49, Ohio U. 42
1969 Toledo 56, Davidson 33

1970 Toledo 40, Wm. & Mary 12
1971 Toledo 28, Richmond 3
1972 Tampa 21, Kent St. 18
1973 Miami-OH 16, Florida 7
1974 Miami-OH 21, Georgia 10
1975 Miami-OH 20, S. Carolina 7
1976 Oklahoma 49, BYU 21
1977 Florida St. 40, Texas Tech 17
1978 N.C. State 30, Pittsburgh 17
1979 LSU 34, Wake Forest 10

Year
1980 Florida 35, Maryland 20
1981 Missouri 19, Southern Miss. 17
1982 Auburn 33, Boston College 26
1983 Tennessee 30, Maryland 23
1984 17-17, Florida St. vs Georgia
1985 Ohio St. 10, BYU 7
1987* Auburn 16, USC 7
1988 Clemson 35, Penn St. 10
1989 Clemson 13, Oklahoma 6

1990 Illinois 31, Virginia 21
1991 Georgia Tech 45, Nebraska 21
1992 California 37, Clemson 13
1993 Georgia 21, Ohio St. 14
1994 Penn St. 31, Tennessee 13
1995 Alabama 24, Ohio St. 17
1996 Tennessee 20, Ohio St. 14

*January game from 1947-58, in 1960 and since 1987. †December game from 1958 and 1960-85.

Gator Bowl

City: Jacksonville, Fla. **Stadium:** New Gator Bowl. **Capacity:** 73,000. **Playing surface:** Grass. **First game:** Jan. 1, 1946. **Playing sites:** Gator Bowl (1946-93), Ben Hill Griffin Stadium in Gainesville (1994) and New Gator Bowl (beginning in 1995). **Corporate title sponsors:** Mazda Motors of America, Inc. (1986-91), Outback Steakhouse, Inc. (1992-94) and Toyota Motor Co. (starting in 1995).

Automatic berths: Third pick from SEC vs. sixth pick from 8-team Bowl Coalition pool (1992-94 seasons). New Bowl Alliance matchup starting with 1995 season: second pick from ACC vs. second pick from Big East.

Multiple wins: Florida (6); Auburn and Clemson (4); Florida St., North Carolina and Tennessee (3); Georgia, Georgia Tech, Maryland, Oklahoma, Pittsburgh, and Texas Tech (2).

Year
1946* Wake Forest 26, S. Carolina 14
1947 Oklahoma 34, N.C. State 13
1948 20-20, Maryland vs Georgia
1949 Clemson 24, Missouri 23

1950 Maryland 20, Missouri 7
1951 Wyoming 20, Wash. & Lee 7
1952 Miami-FL 14, Clemson 0
1953 Florida 14, Tulsa 13
1954 Texas Tech 35, Auburn 13
1954† Auburn 33, Baylor 13
1955 Vanderbilt 25, Auburn 13
1956 Georgia Tech 21, Pittsburgh 14
1957 Tennessee 3, Texas A&M 0
1958 Mississippi 7, Florida 3

1960* Arkansas 14, Georgia Tech 7
1960† Florida 13, Baylor 12
1961 Penn St. 30, Georgia Tech 15

Year
1962 Florida 17, Penn St. 7
1963 N. Carolina 35, Air Force 0
1965* Florida St. 36, Oklahoma 19
1965† Georgia Tech 31, Texas Tech 21
1966 Tennessee 18, Syracuse 12
1967 17-17, Florida St. vs Penn St.
1968 Missouri 35, Alabama 10
1969 Florida 14, Tennessee 13

1971* Auburn 35, Mississippi 28
1971† Georgia 7, N. Carolina 3
1972 Auburn 24, Colorado 3
1973 Texas Tech 28, Tennessee 19
1974 Auburn 27, Texas 3
1975 Maryland 13, Florida 0
1976 Notre Dame 20, Penn St. 9
1977 Pittsburgh 34, Clemson 3
1978 Clemson 17, Ohio St. 15
1979 N. Carolina 17, Michigan 15

Year
1980 Pittsburgh 37, S. Carolina 9
1981 N. Carolina 31, Arkansas 27
1982 Florida St. 31, West Va. 12
1983 Florida 14, Iowa 6
1984 Oklahoma St. 21, S. Carolina 14
1985 Florida St. 34, Oklahoma St. 23
1986 Clemson 27, Stanford 21
1987 LSU 30, S. Carolina 13
1989* Georgia 34, Michigan St. 27
1989† Clemson 27, West Va. 7

1991* Michigan 35, Mississippi 3
1991† Oklahoma 48, Virginia 14
1992 Florida 27, N.C. State 10
1993 Alabama 24, N. Carolina 10
1994 Tennessee 45, Va. Tech 23
1996* Syracuse 41, Clemson 0

*January game from 1946-54, 1960, 1965, 1971, 1989, 1991 and since 1996.
†December game from 1954-58, 1960-63, 1965-69, 1971-87, 1989 and 1991-94.

Holiday Bowl

City: San Diego, Calif. **Stadium:** San Diego/Jack Murphy. **Capacity:** 62,860. **Playing surface:** Grass. **First game:** Dec. 22, 1978. **Playing sites:** San Diego/Jack Murphy Stadium (since 1978). **Corporate title sponsors:** Sea World (1986-90), Thrifty Car Rental (1991-94) and Chrysler-Plymouth Division of Chrysler Corp. (starting in 1995).

Automatic berths: WAC champion vs. at-large opponent (1978-84, 1986-90 seasons); WAC champ vs. second pick from Big 10 (1991 season); WAC champ vs. third pick from Big 10 (1992-94 seasons). New Bowl Alliance matchup starting with 1995 season: second choice of WAC champion or second pick from Pac-10 vs. third pick from Big 12 (Big Eight/SWC).

Multiple wins: BYU (4); Iowa and Ohio St. (2).

Year
1978† Navy 23, BYU 16
1979 Indiana 38, BYU 37
1980 BYU 46, SMU 45
1981 BYU 38, Washington St. 36
1982 Ohio St. 47, BYU 17
1983 BYU 21, Missouri 17

Year
1984 BYU 24, Michigan 17
1985 Arkansas 18, Arizona St. 17
1986 Iowa 39, San Diego St. 38
1987 Iowa 20, Wyoming 19
1988 Oklahoma St. 62, Wyoming 14
1989 Penn St. 50, BYU 39

Year
1990 Texas A&M 65, BYU 14
1991 13-13, Iowa vs BYU
1992 Hawaii 27, Illinois 17
1993 Ohio St. 28, BYU 21
1994 Michigan 24, Colo. St. 14
1995 Kansas St. 54, Colorado St. 21

†December game since 1978.

Bowl Matchups of Unbeaten Teams

Date	Bowl	Winner	Head Coach	Score	Loser	Head Coach
1/1/21	Rose	California (8-0)	Andy Smith	28-0	Ohio St. (7-0)	John Wilce
1/2/22	Rose	Wash. & Jeff. (10-0)	Greasy Neale	0-0	California (9-0)	Andy Smith
1/1/27	Rose	Stanford (10-0)	Pop Warner	7-7	Alabama (9-0)	Wallace Wade
1/1/31	Rose	Alabama (9-0)	Wallace Wade	24-0	Washington St. (9-0)	Babe Hollingbery
1/2/39	Orange	Tennessee (10-0)	Bob Neyland	17-0	Oklahoma (10-0)	Tom Stidham
1/1/41	Sugar	Boston College (10-0)	Frank Leahy	19-13	Tennessee (10-0)	Bob Neyland
1/1/52	Sugar	Maryland (9-0)	Jim Tatum	28-13	Tennessee (10-0)	Bob Neyland
1/2/56	Orange	Oklahoma (10-0)	Bud Wilkinson	20-6	Maryland (10-0)	Jim Tatum
1/1/72	Orange	Nebraska (12-0)	Bob Devaney	38-6	Alabama (11-0)	Bear Bryant
12/31/73	Sugar	Notre Dame (10-0)	Ara Parseghian	24-23	Alabama (11-0)	Bear Bryant
1/2/87	Fiesta	Penn St. (11-0)	Joe Paterno	14-10	Miami-FL (11-0)	Jimmy Johnson
1/1/88	Orange	Miami-FL (11-0)	Jimmy Johnson	20-14	Oklahoma (11-0)	Barry Switzer
1/2/89	Fiesta	Notre Dame (11-0)	Lou Holtz	34-21	West Va. (11-0)	Don Nehlen
1/1/93	Sugar	Alabama (12-0)	Gene Stallings	34-13	Miami-FL. (11-0)	Dennis Erickson
1/2/96	Fiesta	Nebraska (11-0)	Tom Osborne	62-24	Florida (12-0)	Steve Spurrier

Bowl Games (Cont.)

Outback Bowl

City: Tampa, Fla. **Stadium:** Tampa. **Capacity:** 74,300. **Playing surface:** Grass. **First game:** Dec. 23, 1986. **Name change:** Hall of Fame Bowl (1986-95) and Outback Bowl (starting in 1995). **Playing site:** Tampa Stadium (since 1986). **Corporate title sponsor:** Outback Steakhouse, Inc. (starting in 1995).

Automatic berths: Fourth pick from ACC vs. fourth pick from Big 10 (1993-94 seasons); New Bowl Alliance matchup starting with 1995 season: third pick from Big 10 vs. third pick from SEC.

Multiple wins: Michigan and Syracuse (2).

Year
1986† Boston College 27, Georgia 24
1988* Michigan 28, Alabama 24
1989 Syracuse 23, LSU 10
1990 Auburn 31, Ohio St. 14

Year
1991 Clemson 30, Illinois 0
1992 Syracuse 24, Ohio St. 17
1993 Tennessee 38, Boston Col. 23
1994 Michigan 42, N.C. State 7

Year
1995 Wisconsin 34, Duke 20
1996 Penn St. 43, Auburn 14

†December game in 1986. *January game since 1988.

Peach Bowl

City: Atlanta, Ga. **Stadium:** Georgia Dome. **Capacity:** 71,230. **Playing surface:** AstroTurf. **First game:** Dec. 30, 1968. **Playing sites:** Grant Field (1968-70), Atlanta-Fulton County Stadium (1971-92) and Georgia Dome (since 1993).

Automatic berths: Third pick from ACC vs. at-large opponent (1992 season); third pick from ACC vs. fourth pick from SEC (1993-94 seasons). New Bowl Alliance matchup starting with 1995 season: third pick from ACC vs. fourth pick from SEC.

Multiple wins: N.C. State (4); West Virginia (3) Virginia (2).

Year
1968† LSU 31, Florida St. 27
1969 West Va. 14, S. Carolina 3
1970 Arizona St. 48, N. Carolina 26
1971 Mississippi 41, Georgia Tech 18
1972 N.C. State 49, West Va. 13
1973 Georgia 17, Maryland 16
1974 6-6, Vanderbilt vs Texas Tech
1975 West Va. 13, N.C. State 10
1976 Kentucky 21, N. Carolina 0
1977 N.C. State 24, Iowa St. 14

Year
1978 Purdue 41, Georgia Tech 21
1979 Baylor 24, Clemson 18
1981* Miami-FL 20, Va. Tech 10
1981† West Va. 26, Florida 6
1982 Iowa 28, Tennessee 22
1983 Florida St. 28, N. Carolina 3
1984 Virginia 27, Purdue 24
1985 Army 31, Illinois 29
1986 Va. Tech 25, N.C. State 24
1988* Tennessee 27, Indiana 22

Year
1988† N.C. State 28, Iowa 23
1989 Syracuse 19, Georgia 18
1990 Auburn 27, Indiana 23
1992* E. Carolina 37, N.C. State 34
1993 N. Carolina 21, Miss. St. 17
1993† Clemson 14, Kentucky 13
1995* N.C. State 24, Miss. St. 24
1995† Virginia 34, Georgia 27

†December game from 1968-79, 1981-86, 1988-90, 1993 and since 1995. *January game in 1981, 1988, 1992-93 and 1995.

Sun Bowl

City: El Paso, Tex. **Stadium:** Sun Bowl. **Capacity:** 51,120. **Playing surface:** AstroTurf. **First game:** Jan. 1, 1936. **Name changes:** Sun Bowl (1936-85), John Hancock Sun Bowl (1986-88), John Hancock Bowl (1989-93) and Sun Bowl (since 1994). **Playing sites:** Kidd Field (1936-62) and Sun Bowl (since 1963). **Corporate title sponsor:** John Hancock Financial Services (1986-93).

Automatic berths: Eighth pick from 8-team Boal Coalition pool vs. at-large opponent (1992); Seventh and eighth picks from 8-team Bowl Coalition pool (1993-94 seasons). New Bowl Alliance matchup starting with 1995 season: third pick from Pac-10 vs. fifth pick from Big-10.

Multiple wins: Texas Western/UTEP (5); Alabama and Wyoming (3); Nebraska, New Mexico St., North Carolina, Oklahoma, Pittsburgh, Southwestern-Texas, Texas, West Texas St. and West Virginia (2).

Year
1936* 14-14, Hardin-Simmons vs New Mexico St.
1937 Hardin-Simmons 34, Texas Mines 6
1938 West Va. 7, Texas Tech 6
1939 Utah 26, New Mexico 0
1940 0-0, Catholic U. vs Arizona St.
1941 W. Reserve 26, Arizona St. 13
1942 Tulsa 6, Texas Tech 0
1943 Second Air Force 13, Hardin-Simmons 7
1944 SW Texas 7, New Mexico 0
1945 SW Texas 35, U. of Mexico 0
1946 New Mexico 34, Denver 24
1947 Cincinnati 18, Va. Tech 6
1948 Miami-OH 13, Texas Tech 12
1949 West Va. 21, Texas Mines 12
1950 Tex. Western 33, Georgetown 20
1951 West Texas 14, Cincinnati 13
1952 Texas Tech 25, Pacific 14
1953 Pacific 26, Southern Miss. 7
1954 Tex. Western 37, So. Miss. 14

Year
1955 Tex. Western 47, Florida St. 20
1956 Wyoming 21, Texas Tech 14
1957 Geo. Wash. 13, Tex. Western 0
1958 Louisville 34, Drake 20
1958* Wyoming 14, Hardin-Simmons 6
1959 New Mexico St. 28, N. Texas 8
1960 New Mexico St. 20, Utah St. 13
1961 Villanova 17, Wichita 9
1962 West Texas 15, Ohio U. 14
1963 Oregon 21, SMU 14
1964 Georgia 7, Texas Tech 0
1965 Texas Western 13, TCU 12
1966 Wyoming 28, Florida St. 20
1967 UTEP 14, Mississippi 7
1968 Auburn 34, Arizona 10
1969 Nebraska 45, Georgia 6
1970 Georgia Tech 17, Texas Tech 9
1971 LSU 33, Iowa St. 15
1972 N. Carolina 32, Texas Tech 28
1973 Missouri 34, Auburn 17
1974 Miss. St. 26, N. Carolina 24
1975 Pittsburgh 33, Kansas 19

Year
1977* Texas A&M 37, Florida 14
1977† Stanford 24, LSU 14
1978 Texas 42, Maryland 0
1979 Washington 14, Texas 7
1980 Nebraska 31, Miss. St. 17
1981 Oklahoma 40, Houston 14
1982 N. Carolina 26, Texas 10
1983 Alabama 28, SMU 7
1984 Maryland 28, Tennessee 27
1985 13-13, Georgia vs Arizona
1986 Alabama 28, Washington 6
1987 Oklahoma St. 35, West Va. 33
1988 Alabama 29, Army 28
1989 Pittsburgh 31, Texas A&M 28
1990 Michigan St. 17, USC 16
1991 UCLA 6, Illinois 3
1992 Baylor 20, Arizona 15
1993 Oklahoma 41, Texas Tech 10
1994 Texas 35, N. Carolina 31
1995 Iowa 38, Washington 18

*January game from 1936-58 and in 1977. †December game from 1958-75 and since 1977.

Alamo Bowl

City: San Antonio, Tex. **Stadium:** Alamodome. **Capacity:** 65,000. **Playing surface:** Turf. **First game:** Dec. 31, 1993. **Playing site:** Alamodome (since 1993). **Corporate title sponsor:** Builders Square (since 1993).

Automatic berths: third pick from SWC vs. fourth pick from Pac-10 (1993-94 seasons). New Bowl Alliance matchup starting with 1995 season: fourth pick from Big 10 vs. fourth pick from Big 12 (Big Eight/SWC).

Multiple wins: None.

Year
1993† California 37, Iowa 3
1994 Washington St. 10, Baylor 3
1995 Texas A&M 22, Michigan 20

†December game since 1993.

Copper Bowl

City: Tucson, Ariz. **Stadium:** Arizona. **Capacity:** 56,165. **Playing surface:** Grass. **First game:** Dec. 31, 1989. **Playing site:** Arizona Stadium (since 1989). **Corporate title sponsors:** Domino's Pizza (1990-91) and Weiser Lock (since 1992).

Automatic berths: third pick from WAC vs. at-large opponent (1992 season); third pick from WAC vs. fourth pick from Big Eight (1993-94 seasons). New Bowl Alliance matchup starting with 1995 season: second pick from WAC vs. sixth pick from Big 12 (Big Eight/SWC).

Multiple wins: None.

Year
1989† Arizona 17, N.C. State 10
1990 California 17, Wyoming 15
1991 Indiana 24, Baylor 0
1992 Washington St. 31, Utah 28
1993 Kansas St. 52, Wyoming 17
1994 BYU 31, Oklahoma 6
1995 Texas Tech 55, Air Force 41

†December game since 1989.

Liberty Bowl

City: Memphis, Tenn. **Stadium:** Liberty Bowl Memorial. **Capacity:** 62,920. **Playing surface:** Grass. **First game:** Dec. 19, 1959. **Playing sites:** Municipal Stadium in Philadelphia (1959-63), Convention Hall in Atlantic City, N.J. (1964), Memphis Memorial Stadium (1965-75) and Liberty Bowl Memorial Stadium (since 1976). Memphis Memorial Stadium renamed Liberty Bowl Memorial in 1976. **Corporate title sponsor:** St. Jude's Hospital (since 1993).

Automatic berths: Commander-in-Chief's Trophy winner (Army, Navy or Air Force) vs. at-large opponent (1989-92 seasons); none (1993 season); first pick from independent group of Cincinnati, East Carolina, Memphis, Southern Miss. and Tulane vs. at-large opponent (for the 1994 and '95 seasons).

Multiple wins: Mississippi (4); Penn St. and Tennessee (3); Air Force, Alabama and N.C. State (2).

Year
1959† Penn St. 7, Alabama 0
1960 Penn St. 41, Oregon 12
1961 Syracuse 15, Miami-FL 14
1962 Oregon St. 6, Villanova 0
1963 Mississippi St. 16, N.C. State 12
1964 Utah 32, West Virgina 6
1965 Mississippi 13, Auburn 7
1966 Miami-FL 14, Virginia Tech 7
1967 N.C. State 14, Georgia 7
1968 Mississippi 34, Virginia Tech 17
1969 Colorado 47, Alabama 33
1970 Tulane 17, Colorado 3
1971 Tennessee 14, Arkansas 13
1972 Georgia Tech 31, Iowa St. 30
1973 N.C. State 31, Kansas 18
1974 Tennessee 7, Maryland 3
1975 USC 20, Texas A&M 0
1976 Alabama 36, UCLA 6
1977 Nebraska 21, N. Carolina 17
1978 Missouri 20, LSU 15
1979 Penn St. 9, Tulane 6
1980 Purdue 28, Missouri 25
1981 Ohio St. 31, Navy 28
1982 Alabama 21, Illinois 15
1983 Notre Dame 19, Boston Col. 18
1984 Auburn 21, Arkansas 15
1985 Baylor 21, LSU 7
1986 Tennessee 21, Minnesota 14
1987 Georgia 20, Arkansas 17
1988 Indiana 34, S. Carolina 10
1989 Mississippi 42, Air Force 29
1990 Air Force 23, Ohio St. 11
1991 Air Force 38, Mississippi St. 15
1992 Mississippi 13, Air Force 0
1993 Louisville 18, Michigan St. 7
1994 Illinois 30, E. Carolina 0
1995 E. Carolina 19, Stanford 13

†December game since 1959.

Carquest Bowl

City: Miami, Fla. **Stadium:** Joe Robbie. **Capacity:** 74,915. **Playing surface:** Grass. **First game:** Dec. 28, 1990. **Name change:** Blockbuster Bowl (1990-93) and Carquest Bowl (since 1994) **Playing site:** Joe Robbie Stadium (since 1990). **Corporate title sponsors:** Blockbuster Video (1990-93) and Carquest Auto Parts (since 1993).

Automatic berths: Penn St. vs. seventh pick from 8-team Bowl Coalition pool (1992 season); third pick from Big East vs. fifth pick from SEC (1993-94 seasons). New Bowl Alliance matchup starting with 1995 season: third pick from Big East vs. fifth pick from SEC.

Year
1990† Florida St. 24, Penn St. 17
1991 Alabama 30, Colorado 25
1993* Stanford 24, Penn St. 3
1994 Boston College 31, Virginia 13
1995 S. Carolina 24, West Va. 21
1995† N. Carolina 20, Arkansas 10

†December game 1990-91 and since 1996.
*January game 1993-95.

Aloha Bowl

City: Honolulu, Hawaii. **Stadium:** Aloha. **Capacity:** 50,000. **Playing surface:** AstroTurf. **First game:** Dec. 25, 1982. **Playing site:** Aloha Stadium (since 1982). **Corporate title sponsor:** Jeep Eagle Division of Chrysler (since 1987).

Automatic berths: second pick from WAC vs. third pick from Big Eight (1992-93 seasons); third pick from Big Eight vs. at-large opponent (1994 season) New Bowl Alliance matchup starting with 1995 season: fifth pick from Big 12 (Big Eight/SWC) vs. at-large opponent

Multiple wins: Kansas (2).

Year
1982† Washington 21, Maryland 20
1983 Penn St. 13, Washington 10
1984 SMU 27, Notre Dame 20
1985 Alabama 24, USC 3
1986 Arizona 30, N. Carolina 21
1987 UCLA 20, Florida 16
1988 Washington St. 24, Houston 22
1989 Michigan St. 33, Hawaii 13
1990 Syracuse 28, Arizona 0
1991 Georgia Tech 18, Stanford 17
1992 Kansas 23, BYU 20
1993 Colorado 41, Fresno St. 30
1994 Boston Col. 12, Kansas St. 7
1995 Kansas 51, UCLA 30

†December game since 1982.

Bowl Games (Cont.)

Las Vegas Bowl

City: Las Vegas, Nev. **Stadium:** Sam Boyd Stadium. **Capacity:** 33,215. **Playing surface:** AstroTurf. **First game:** Dec. 18, 1992. **Playing site:** Sam Boyd Stadium (since 1992);

Automatic berths: Mid-American champion vs. Big West champion (since 1992 season).

Note: the MAC and Big West champs have met in a bowl game since 1981, originally in Fresno at the California Bowl (1981-88, 1992) and California Raisin Bowl (1989-91). The results from 1981-91 are included below.

Multiple wins: Fresno St. (4); Bowling Green, San Jose St. and Toledo (2).

Year	
1981†	Toledo 27, San Jose St. 25
1982	Fresno St. 29, Bowling Green 28
1983	Northern Ill. 20, CS-Fullerton 13
1984	UNLV 30, Toledo 13
1985	Fresno St. 51, Bowling Green 7
1986	San Jose St. 37, Miami-OH 7
1987	E. Michigan 30, San Jose St. 27
1988	Fresno St. 35, W. Michigan 30
1989	Fresno St. 27, Ball St. 6
1990	San Jose St. 48, C. Michigan 24
1991	Bowling Green 28, Fresno St. 21
1992	Bowling Green 35, Nevada 34
1993	Utah St. 42, Ball St. 33
1994	UNLV 52, C. Michigan 24
1995	Toledo 40, Nevada 37 (OT)

†December game since 1981. **Note:** UNLV later forfeited 1984 victory for use of ineligible players.

Independence Bowl

City: Shreveport, La. **Stadium:** Independence. **Capacity:** 50,460. **Playing surface:** Grass. **First game:** Dec. 13, 1976. **Playing sites:** Independence Stadium (since 1976). **Corporate title sponsor:** Poulan/Weed Eater (since 1990).

Automatic berths: None (since 1976 season).

Multiple wins: Air Force and Southern Miss (2).

Year	
1976†	McNeese St. 20, Tulsa 16
1977	La. Tech 24, Louisville 14
1978	E. Carolina 35, La. Tech 13
1979	Syracuse 31, McNeese St. 7
1980	Southern Miss 16, McNeese St. 14
1981	Texas A&M 33, Oklahoma St. 16
1982	Wisconsin 14, Kansas St. 3
1983	Air Force 9, Mississippi 3
1984	Air Force 23, Va. Tech 7
1985	Minnesota 20, Clemson 13
1986	Mississippi 20, Texas Tech 17
1987	Washington 24, Tulane 12
1988	Southern Miss 38, UTEP 18
1989	Oregon 27, Tulsa 24
1990	34-34, La. Tech vs Maryland
1991	Georgia 24, Arkansas 15
1992	Wake Forest 39, Oregon 35
1993	Va. Tech 45, Indiana 20
1994	Virginia 20, TCU 10
1995	LSU 45, Michigan St. 26

†December game since 1976.

The Bowl Alliance

Division I-A football remains the only NCAA sport on any level that does not have a sanctioned national champion. To that end, the Bowl Coalition was formed in 1992 in an attempt to keep the bowl system intact while forcing an annual championship game between the regular season's two top-ranked teams.

The Coalition, which lasted for three seasons, consolidated the resources of four major bowl games (the Cotton, Fiesta, Orange and Sugar), the champions of five major conferences (the ACC, Big East, Big Eight, Southeastern and Southwest) and the national following of independent Notre Dame. It worked two out of three years with No. 1 vs. No. 2 showdowns in the 1993 Sugar Bowl (#2 Alabama over #1 Miami-FL) and 1994 Orange Bowl (#1 Florida St. over #2 Nebraska). The 1995 Orange Bowl had to settle for #1 Nebraska beating #3 Miami-FL because #2 Penn St., the Big Ten champion, was obligated to play in the Rose Bowl.

The Bowl Alliance, which began a three-year run with the 1995 season, is an updated version of the Coalition. There will be a new Bowl Alliance—including the Rose Bowl— starting after the 1998 season that should guarantee a national championship (No. 1 vs. No. 2) game. The key difference in this new alliance, which is expected to run seven years (although only guaranteed for four), will be that it will include the Big Ten and Pac-10 champions. Those teams, currently locked in to playing in the Rose Bowl, would be allowed to move to another bowl if needed to create a No. 1 vs. No. 2 game. The bowls (the Fiesta, Orange and Sugar) which currently make up the Bowl Alliance must rebid to keep their spots in this new four-bowl alliance. The Rose Bowl, which is already guaranteed a spot in the new alliance, is expected to get the title game in 2002. Still yet to be determined under the new deal is whether the Bowl Alliance will continue to rely solely on the AP and *USA Today*/CNN polls to determine the teams playing in the title game.

The following is a breakdown of the *current* Bowl Alliance, set to run through the 1997 season.

Member conferences: ACC, Big East, Big 12, Big 10, Pac-10, SEC and independent Notre Dame. **Major bowls** (3): Fiesta, Orange and Sugar. **Major selection order:** *1995 season*— FIESTA (No. 1 & No. 2), ORANGE (3 & 5), SUGAR (4 & 6); *1996 season*— SUGAR (1 & 2), FIESTA (3 & 5), ORANGE (4 & 6); *1997 season*— ORANGE (1 & 2), SUGAR (3 & 5), FIESTA (4 & 6). **Annual dates:** Dec. 31 (4 vs. 6); Jan. 1 (3 vs. 5); and Jan. 2 (1 vs. 2).

Pool of teams for six slots (ranked according to combined AP media and *USA Today*/CNN coaches' polls at the end of the regular season): ACC champion, Big East champ, Big 12 champ, SEC champ, and two at-large positions open to any Division IA teams that meet one of the following requirements: a) had at least eight wins, b) is ranked in the Top 12 of the AP media or *USA Today*/CNN coaches' polls, or c) is ranked no lower in either poll than the lowest ranked conference champion.

Non-Alliance match-ups: ALAMO (fourth pick from Big 12 vs. fourth pick from Big 10); ALOHA (fourth pick from Pac-10 vs. sixth pick from Big 12); CARQUEST (third pick from Big East vs. fourth pick from ACC); CITRUS (second pick from Big 10 vs. second pick from SEC); COPPER (second pick from WAC vs. fifth pick from Big 12); COTTON (first choice of either WAC champ or second pick from Pac-10 vs. second pick from Big 12); OUTBACK (third pick from Big 10 vs. third pick from SEC); HOLIDAY (second choice of either WAC champ or second pick from Pac-10 vs. third pick from Big 12); INDEPENDENCE (fifth pick from SEC vs. at-large); LAS VEGAS (Big West champ vs. Mid-American champ); LIBERTY (Conference USA champ or East Carolina vs. fourth pick from Big East); PEACH (third pick from ACC vs. fourth pick from SEC); ROSE (Big 10 champ vs. Pac-10 champ).

All-Time Winningest Division I-A Teams

Schools classified as Divison I-A for at least 10 years; through 1995 season (including bowl games).

Top 25 Winning Percentage

	Yrs	Gm	W	L	T	Pct	—Bowls— App	Record	—1995 Season— Bowl	Record
1 Notre Dame	107	999	738	219	42	.760	21	13-8-0	lost Orange	9-3-0
2 Michigan	116	1042	756	250	36	.743	27	13-14-0	lost Alamo	9-4-0
3 Alabama	101	996	703	250	43	.727	47	27-17-3	on probation	8-3-0
4 Oklahoma	101	974	670	251	53	.715	32	20-11-1	none	5-5-1
5 Texas	103	1017	705	279	33	.709	36	17-17-2	lost Sugar	10-2-1
6 Ohio St	106	1003	679	271	53	.703	28	13-15-0	lost Citrus	11-2-0
7 USC	103	960	647	259	54	.702	38	25-13-0	won Rose	9-2-1
8 Nebraska	106	1028	698	290	40	.698	34	16-18-0	won Fiesta	12-0-0
9 Penn St	109	1030	695	294	41	.695	32	20-10-2	won Outback	9-3-0
10 Tennessee	99	989	656	281	52	.690	36	20-16-0	won Citrus	11-1-0
11 Florida St	49	532	336	179	17	.648	25	16-7-2	won Orange	10-2-0
12 Central Michigan	95	794	493	265	36	.644	5	3-2-0	none	4-7-0
13 Washington	106	944	576	318	50	.637	22	12-9-1	lost Sun	7-4-1
14 Miami-OH	107	918	559	315	44	.633	7	5-2-0	none	8-2-1
15 Army	106	987	597	339	51	.631	3	2-1-0	none	5-5-1
16 Georgia	102	998	601	343	54	.629	32	15-14-3	lost Peach	6-6-0
17 LSU	102	967	584	336	47	.628	29	12-16-1	won Independence	7-4-1
18 Arizona St	83	745	453	268	24	.624	15	9-5-1	none	6-5-0
19 Auburn	103	962	575	340	47	.622	24	12-10-2	lost Outback	8-4-0
20 Colorado	106	965	578	351	36	.618	20	8-12-0	won Cotton	10-2-0
21 Miami-FL	69	713	429	265	19	.615	21	10-11-0	on probation	8-3-0
22 Bowling Green	77	705	403	250	52	.609	5	2-3-0	none	5-6-0
23 Michigan St	99	915	532	339	44	.605	12	5-7-0	lost Independence	6-5-1
24 Texas A&M	101	980	568	364	48	.604	21	12-10-0	won Alamo	9-3-0
25 UCLA	77	777	449	291	37	.602	20	10-9-1	lost Aloha	7-5-0

Note: Alabama was forced to forfeit 11 games in 1993 in which Antonio Langham played while ineligible.

Top 50 Victories

	Wins
1 Michigan	756
2 Notre Dame	738
3 Texas	705
3 Alabama	703
5 Nebraska	698
6 Penn St	695
7 Ohio St	679
8 Oklahoma	670
9 Tennessee	656
10 USC	647
11 Georgia	601
12 Syracuse	599
13 Army	597
14 LSU	584
15 Colorado	578
16 Washington	576
17 Auburn	575
18 Pittsburgh	572
19 West Virginia	569
20 Texas A&M	568
21 North Carolina	563
22 Arkansas	563
23 Georgia Tech	562
24 Minnesota	561
25 Miami-OH	559
26 Navy	554
27 Clemson	539
Rutgers	539
29 California	537
30 Michigan St	532
31 Virginia Tech	531
32 Mississippi	524
33 Virginia	519
34 Florida	513
Missouri	513
36 Maryland	515
37 Vanderbilt	510
38 Boston College	508
Illinois	508
40 Kentucky	494
41 Central Michigan	493
Kansas	493
43 Stanford	490
Utah	490
45 Wisconsin	489
46 Baylor	482
47 Tulsa	481
48 Purdue	479
49 Iowa	478
50 Arizona	473

Note: Division I-AA schools with 500 or more wins through 1995: Yale (781); Princeton (721); Penn (710); Harvard (707); Fordham (675); Dartmouth (602); Lafayette (573); Cornell (560); Holy Cross (527); Delaware (525) and Lehigh (522).

Top 30 Bowl Appearances

	App	Record
1 Alabama	47	27-17-3
2 USC	38	25-13-0
3 Tennessee	36	20-16-0
Texas	36	17-17-2
5 Nebraska	34	16-18-0
6 Penn St	32	20-10-2
Oklahoma	32	20-11-1
Georgia	32	15-14-3
9 LSU	29	12-16-1
10 Ohio St	28	12-16-0
Arkansas	28	9-16-3
12 Michigan	27	13-14-0
13 Georgia Tech	25	17-8-0
Mississippi	25	14-11-0
15 Florida St	24	15-7-2
Auburn	24	12-10-2
17 Florida	23	10-13-0
18 Washington	22	12-9-1
Texas A&M	22	12-10-0
20 Notre Dame	21	13-8-0
Miami-FL	21	10-11-0
Texas Tech	21	5-15-1
23 Clemson	20	12-8-0
UCLA	20	10-9-1
Colorado	20	8-12-0
North Carolina	20	8-12-0
27 Missouri	19	8-11-0
BYU	19	6-12-1
Pittsburgh	18	8-10-0
30 Four teams tied with appearances each.	17	

Note: Alabama, Georgia, Georgia Tech, Notre Dame and Penn State are the only schools that have won all four of the traditional major bowl games— the Rose, Orange, Sugar and Cotton.

Major Conference Champions

Atlantic Coast Conference

Founded in 1953 when charter members all left Southern Conference to form ACC. **Charter members** (7): Clemson, Duke, Maryland, North Carolina, N.C. State, South Carolina and Wake Forest. **Admitted later** (3): Virginia in 1953 (began play in '54), Georgia Tech in 1979 (began play in '83); Florida St. in 1990 (began play in '92). **Withdrew later** (1): South Carolina in 1971 (became an independent after '70 season).

1996 playing membership (9): Clemson, Duke, Florida St., Georgia Tech, Maryland, North Carolina, N.C. State, Virginia and Wake Forest.

Multiple titles: Clemson (13); Maryland (8); Duke and N.C. State (7); North Carolina (5); Florida St. (4); Virginia (2).

Year	
1953	Duke (4-0) & Maryland (3-0)
1954	Duke (4-0)
1955	Maryland (4-0) & Duke (4-0)
1956	Clemson (4-0-1)
1957	N.C. State (5-0-1)
1958	Clemson (5-1)
1959	Clemson (6-1)
1960	Duke (5-1)
1961	Duke (5-1)
1962	Duke (6-0)
1963	North Carolina (6-1) & N.C. State (6-1)
1964	N.C. State (5-2)
1965	Clemson (5-2) & N.C. State (5-2)
1966	Clemson (6-1)
1967	Clemson (6-0)
1968	N.C. State (6-1)
1969	South Carolina (6-0)
1970	Wake Forest (5-1)
1971	North Carolina (6-0)
1972	North Carolina (6-0)
1973	N.C. State (6-0)
1974	Maryland (6-0)
1975	Maryland (5-0)
1976	Maryland (5-0)
1977	North Carolina (5-0-1)
1978	Clemson (6-0)
1979	N.C. State (5-1)
1980	North Carolina (6-0)
1981	Clemson (6-0)
1982	Clemson (6-0)
1983	Maryland (5-0)
1984	Maryland (5-0)
1985	Maryland (6-0)
1986	Clemson (5-1-1)
1987	Clemson (6-1)
1988	Clemson (6-1)
1989	Virginia (6-1) & Duke (6-1)
1990	Georgia Tech (6-0-1)
1991	Clemson (6-0-1)
1992	Florida St. (8-0)
1993	Florida St. (8-0)
1994	Florida St. (8-0)
1995	Virginia (7-1) & Florida St. (7-1)

Big East Conference

Founded in 1991 when charter members gave up independent football status to form Big East. **Charter members** (8): Boston College, Miami-FL, Pittsburgh, Rutgers, Syracuse, Temple, Virginia Tech and West Virginia. **Note:** Temple and Virginia Tech are Big East members in football only.

1996 playing membership (8): Boston College, Miami-FL, Pittsburgh, Rutgers, Syracuse, Temple, Virginia Tech and West Virginia.

Conference champion: Member schools needed two years to adjust their regular season schedules in order to begin round-robin conference play in 1993. In the meantime, the 1991 and '92 Big East titles went to the highest-ranked member in the final regular season *USA Today*/CNN coaches' poll.

Multiple titles: Miami-FL (4).

Year	
1991	Miami-FL (2-0, #1) & Syracuse (5-0, #16)
1992	Miami-FL (4-0, #1)
1993	West Virginia (7-0)
1994	Miami-FL (7-0)
1995	Virginia Tech (6-1) & Miami-FL (6-1)

Big Ten Conference

Originally founded in 1895 as the Intercollegiate Conference of Faculty Representatives, better known as the Western Conference. **Charter members** (7): Chicago, Illinois, Michigan, Minnesota, Northwestern, Purdue and Wisconsin. **Admitted later** (5): Indiana and Iowa in 1899; Ohio St. in 1912; Michigan St. in 1950 (began play in '53); Penn St. in 1990 (began play in '93). **Withdrew later** (2): Michigan in 1907 (rejoined in '17); Chicago in 1940 (dropped football after '39 season). **Note:** Iowa belonged to both the Western and Missouri Valley conferences from 1907-10.

Unofficially called the **Big Ten** from 1912 until Chicago's withdrawal in 1939, then the **Big Nine** from 1940 until Michigan St. began conference play in 1953. Formally named the **Big Ten** in 1984 and has kept the name even after adding Penn St. as its 11th member.

1996 playing membership (11): Illinois, Indiana, Iowa, Michigan, Michigan St., Minnesota, Northwestern, Ohio St., Penn St., Purdue, and Wisconsin.

Multiple titles: Michigan (37); Ohio St. (26); Minnesota (18); Illinois (14); Iowa and Wisconsin (9); Purdue (7); Chicago, Michigan St. and Northwestern (6); Indiana (2).

Year	
1896	Wisconsin (2-0-1)
1897	Wisconsin (3-0)
1898	Michigan (3-0)
1899	Chicago (4-0)
1900	Iowa (3-0-1) & Minnesota (3-0-1)
1901	Michigan (4-0) & Wisconsin (2-0)
1902	Michigan (5-0)
1903	Michigan (3-0-1), Minnesota (3-0-1) & Northwestern (1-0-2)
1904	Minnesota (3-0) & Michigan (2-0)
1905	Chicago (7-0)
1906	Wisconsin (3-0), Minnesota (2-0) & Michigan (1-0)
1907	Chicago (4-0)
1908	Chicago (5-0)
1909	Minnesota (3-0)
1910	Illinois (4-0) & Minnesota (2-0)
1911	Minnesota (3-0-1)
1912	Wisconsin (6-0)
1913	Chicago (7-0)
1914	Illinois (6-0)
1915	Minnesota (3-0-1) & Illinois (3-0-2)
1916	Ohio St. (4-0)
1917	Ohio St. (4-0)
1918	Illinois (4-0), Michigan (2-0) & Purdue (1-0)
1919	Illinois (6-1)
1920	Ohio St. (5-0)
1921	Iowa (5-0)
1922	Iowa (5-0) & Michigan (4-0)
1923	Illinois (5-0) & Michigan (4-0)
1924	Chicago (3-0-3)
1925	Michigan (5-1)
1926	Michigan (5-0) & Northwestern (5-0)
1927	Illinois (5-0) & Minnesota (3-0-1)
1928	Illinois (4-1)
1929	Purdue (5-0)
1930	Michigan (5-0) & Northwestern (5-0)
1931	Purdue (5-1), Michigan (5-1) & Northwestern (5-1)
1932	Michigan (6-0) & Purdue (5-0-1)

Year

1933 Michigan (5-0-1) & Minnesota (2-0-4)
1934 Minnesota (5-0)
1935 Minnesota (5-0) & Ohio St. (5-0)
1936 Northwestern (6-0)
1937 Minnesota (5-0)
1938 Minnesota (4-1)
1939 Ohio St. (5-1)
1940 Minnesota (6-0)
1941 Minnesota (5-0)
1942 Ohio St. (5-1)
1943 Purdue (6-0) & Michigan (6-0)
1944 Ohio St. (6-0)
1945 Indiana (5-0-1)
1946 Illinois (6-1)
1947 Michigan (6-0)
1948 Michigan (6-0)
1949 Ohio St. (4-1-1) & Michigan (4-1-1)
1950 Michigan (4-1-1)
1951 Illinois (5-0-1)

Year

1952 Wisconsin (4-1-1) & Purdue (4-1-1)
1953 Michigan St. (5-1) & Illinois (5-1)
1954 Ohio St. (7-0)
1955 Ohio St. (6-0)
1956 Iowa (5-1)
1957 Ohio St. (7-0)
1958 Iowa (5-1)
1959 Wisconsin (5-2)
1960 Minnesota (5-1) & Iowa (5-1)
1961 Ohio St. (6-0)
1962 Wisconsin (6-1)
1963 Illinois (5-1-1)
1964 Michigan (6-1)
1965 Michigan St. (7-0)
1966 Michigan St. (7-0)
1967 Indiana (6-1), Purdue (6-1) & Minnesota (6-1)
1968 Ohio St. (7-0)
1969 Ohio St. (6-1) & Michigan (6-1)

Year

1970 Ohio St. (7-0)
1971 Michigan (8-0)
1972 Ohio St. (7-1) & Michigan (7-1)
1973 Ohio St. (7-0-1) & Michigan (7-0-1)
1974 Ohio St. (7-1) & Michigan (7-1)
1975 Ohio St. (8-0)
1976 Michigan (7-1) & Ohio St. (7-1)
1977 Michigan (7-1) & Ohio St. (7-1)
1978 Michigan (7-1) & Michigan St. (7-1)
1979 Ohio St. (8-0)
1980 Michigan (8-0)
1981 Iowa (6-2) & Ohio St. (6-2)
1982 Michigan (8-1)
1983 Illinois (9-0)
1984 Ohio St. (7-2)
1985 Iowa (7-1)

Year

1986 Michigan (7-1) & Ohio St. (7-1)
1987 Michigan St. (7-0-1)
1988 Michigan (7-0-1)
1989 Michigan (8-0)
1990 Iowa (6-2), Michigan (6-2), Michigan St. (6-2) & Illinois (6-2)
1991 Michigan (8-0)
1992 Michigan (6-0-2)
1993 Wisconsin (6-1-1) & Ohio St. (6-1-1)
1994 Penn St. (8-0)
1995 Northwestern (8-0)

Big 12 Conference

Originally founded in 1907 as the Missouri Valley Intercollegiate Athletic Assn. **Charter members** (5): Iowa, Kansas, Missouri, Nebraska and Washington University of St. Louis. **Admitted later** (11): Drake and Iowa St. (then Ames College) in 1908; Kansas St. (then Kansas College of Applied Science and Agriculture) in 1913; Grinnell (Iowa) College in 1919; Oklahoma in 1920; Oklahoma A&M (now Oklahoma St.) in 1925; Colorado in 1947 (began play in '48); Baylor, Texas, Texas A&M and Texas Tech in 1994 (all four began play in '96).

Withdrew later (1): Iowa in 1911 (left for Big Ten after 1910 season); **Excluded later** (4): Drake, Grinnell, Oklahoma A&M and Washington-MO (left out when MVIAA cut membership to six teams in 1928.

Streamlined MVIAA unofficially called **Big Six** from 1928-47 with surviving members Iowa St., Kansas, Kansas St., Missouri, Nebraska and Oklahoma. Became the **Big Seven** after 1947 season when Colorado came over from the Skyline Conference, and then the **Big Eight** with the return of Oklahoma A&M in 1957. A&M, which resumed conference play in '60, became Oklahoma St. on July 10, 1957. The MVIAA was officially renamed the Big Eight in 1964 and became the **Big 12** after the 1995-96 academic year with the arrival of Baylor, Texas, Texas A&M and Texas Tech from the defunct Southwest Conference.

1996 playing membership (12): Baylor, Colorado, Iowa, St. Kansas, Kansas St., Missouri, Nebraska, Oklahoma, Oklahoma St., Texas, Texas A&M, Texas Tech,

Multiple titles: Nebraska (41); Oklahoma (33); Missouri (12); Colorado and Kansas (5); Iowa St. and Oklahoma St. (2).

Year

1907 Iowa (1-0) & Nebraska (1-0)
1908 Kansas (4-0)
1909 Missouri (4-0-1)
1910 Nebraska (2-0)
1911 Iowa St. (2-0-1) & Nebraska (2-0-1)
1912 Iowa St. (2-0) & Nebraska (2-0)
1913 Missouri (4-0) & Nebraska (3-0)
1914 Nebraska (3-0)
1915 Nebraska (4-0)
1916 Nebraska (3-1)
1917 Nebraska (2-0)
1918 Vacant (WW I)
1919 Missouri (4-0-1)
1920 Oklahoma (4-0-1)
1921 Nebraska (3-0)
1922 Nebraska (5-0)
1923 Nebraska (3-0-2)
1924 Missouri (5-1)
1925 Missouri (5-1)
1926 Okla. A&M (3-0-1)
1927 Missouri (5-1)
1928 Nebraska (4-0)
1929 Nebraska (3-0-2)

Year

1930 Kansas (4-1)
1931 Nebraska (5-0)
1932 Nebraska (5-0)
1933 Nebraska (5-0)
1934 Kansas St. (5-0)
1935 Nebraska (4-0-1)
1936 Nebraska (5-0)
1937 Nebraska (3-0-2)
1938 Oklahoma (5-0)
1939 Missouri (5-0)
1940 Nebraska (5-0)
1941 Missouri (5-0)
1942 Missouri (4-0-1)
1943 Oklahoma (5-0)
1944 Oklahoma (4-0-1)
1945 Missouri (5-0)
1946 Oklahoma (4-1) & Kansas (4-1)
1947 Kansas (4-0-1) & Oklahoma (4-0-1)
1948 Oklahoma (5-0)
1949 Oklahoma (5-0)
1950 Oklahoma (6-0)
1951 Oklahoma (6-0)
1952 Oklahoma (5-0-1)

Year

1953 Oklahoma (6-0)
1954 Oklahoma (6-0)
1955 Oklahoma (6-0)
1956 Oklahoma (6-0)
1957 Oklahoma (6-0)
1958 Oklahoma (6-0)
1959 Oklahoma (5-1)
1960 Missouri (7-0)
1961 Colorado (7-0)
1962 Oklahoma (7-0)
1963 Nebraska (7-0)
1964 Nebraska (6-1)
1965 Nebraska (7-0)
1966 Nebraska (6-1)
1967 Oklahoma (7-0)
1968 Kansas (6-1) & Oklahoma (6-1)
1969 Missouri (6-1) & Nebraska (6-1)
1970 Nebraska (7-0)
1971 Nebraska (7-0)
1972 Nebraska (5-1-1)*
1973 Oklahoma (7-0)
1974 Oklahoma (7-0)
1975 Nebraska (6-1) & Oklahoma (6-1)

Year

1976 Colorado (5-2), Oklahoma (5-2) & Oklahoma St. (5-2)
1977 Oklahoma (7-0)
1978 Nebraska (6-1) & Oklahoma (6-1)
1979 Oklahoma (7-0)
1980 Oklahoma (7-0)
1981 Nebraska (7-0)
1982 Nebraska (7-0)
1983 Nebraska (7-0)
1984 Oklahoma (6-1) & Nebraska (6-1)
1985 Oklahoma (7-0)
1986 Oklahoma (7-0)
1987 Oklahoma (7-0)
1988 Nebraska (7-0)
1989 Colorado (7-0)
1990 Colorado (7-0)
1991 Nebraska (6-0-1) & Colorado (6-0-1)
1992 Nebraska (6-1)
1993 Nebraska (7-0)
1994 Nebraska (7-0)
1995 Nebraska (7-0)

*Oklahoma (6-1) forfeited 1972 title for use of ineligible player.

Major Conference Champions (Cont.)

Big West Conference

Originally founded in 1969 as Pacific Coast Athletic Assn. **Charter members** (7): CS-Los Angeles, Fresno St., Long Beach St., Pacific, San Diego St., San Jose St. and UC-Santa Barbara. **Admitted later** (12): CS-Fullerton in 1974; Utah St. in 1977 (began play in '78); UNLV in 1982; New Mexico St. in 1983 (began play in '84); Nevada in 1991 (began play in '92); Arkansas St., Louisiana Tech, Northern Illinois and SW Louisiana in 1992 (all four began play in football only in '93); Boise St., Idaho and North Texas in 1994 (all three began play in '96).

Withdrew later (13): CS-Los Angeles and UC-Santa Barbara in 1972 (both dropped football after '71 season); San Diego St. in 1975 (became an independent after '75 season); Fresno St. in 1991 (left for WAC after '91 season); Long Beach St. in 1991 (dropped football after '91 season); CS-Fullerton in 1992 (dropped football after '92 season); San Jose St. and UNLV in 1994 (left for WAC after '95 season); Pacific in 1995 (dropped football after '95 season); Arkansas St., Louisiana Tech, Northern Illinois and SW Louisiana in 1995 (all four returned to independent football status after '95 season). Conference renamed Big West in 1988.

1996 playing membership (6): Boise St., Idaho, Nevada, New Mexico St., North Texas and Utah St.

Multiple titles: San Jose St. (8); Fresno St. (6); San Diego St. (5); Long Beach St., Nevada and Utah St. (3); CS-Fullerton and SW Louisiana (2).

Year		Year		Year		Year	
1969	San Diego St. (6-0)	1977	Fresno St. (4-0)	1985	Fresno St. (7-0)	1993	Utah St. (5-1) & SW Louisiana (5-1)
1970	Long Beach St. (5-1) & San Diego St. (5-1)	1978	San Jose St. (4-1) & Utah St. (4-1)	1986	San Jose St. (7-0)	1994	UNLV (5-1), Nevada (5-1) & SW Louisiana (5-1)
1971	Long Beach St. (5-1)	1979	Utah St. (4-0-1)*	1987	San Jose St. (7-0)	1995	Nevada (6-0)
1972	San Diego St. (4-0)	1980	Long Beach St. (5-0)	1988	Fresno St. (7-0)		
1973	San Diego St. (3-0-1)	1981	San Jose St. (5-0)	1989	Fresno St. (7-0)		
1974	San Diego St. (4-0)	1982	Fresno St. (6-0)	1990	San Jose St. (7-0)		
1975	San Jose St. (5-0)	1983	CS-Fullerton (5-1)	1991	Fresno St. (6-1) & San Jose St. (6-1)		
1976	San Jose St. (4-0)	1984	CS-Fullerton (6-1)†	1992	Nevada (5-1)		

*San Jose St. (4-0-1) forfeited share of 1979 title for use of ineligible player. †UNLV (7-0) forfeited 1984 title for use of ineligible player.

Conference USA

Founded in 1994 by six independent football schools, who began play as a conference in 1996. **Charter members** (6): Cincinnati, Houston, Louisville, Memphis, Southern Mississippi and Tulane.

Ivy League

First called the "Ivy League" in 1937 by sportswriter Caswell Adams of the *New York Herald Tribune*. Unofficial conference of 10 eastern teams was occasionally referred to as the "Old 10" and included: Army, Brown, Columbia, Cornell, Dartmouth, Harvard, Navy, Pennsylvania, Princeton and Yale. Army and Navy were dropped from the group after 1940. **League formalized** in 1954 for play beginning in 1956. **Charter members** (8): Brown, Columbia, Cornell, Dartmouth, Harvard, Pennsylvania, Princeton, and Yale. League downgraded from Division I to Division I-AA after 1977 season. **Current playing membership:** the same.

Multiple titles: Dartmouth (16); Yale (12); Penn (9); Harvard and Princeton (8); Cornell (3).

Year		Year		Year		Year	
1955	Princeton (6-1)	1967	Yale (7-0)	1977	Yale (6-1)	1988	Penn (6-1) & Cornell (6-1)
1956	Yale (7-0)	1968	Harvard (6-0-1) & Yale (6-0-1)	1978	Dartmouth (6-1)	1989	Princeton (6-1) & Yale (6-1)
1957	Princeton (6-1)	1969	Dartmouth (6-1), Yale (6-1) & Princeton (6-1)	1979	Yale (6-1)	1990	Cornell (6-1) & Dartmouth (6-1)
1958	Dartmouth (6-1)	1970	Dartmouth (7-0)	1980	Yale (6-1)	1991	Dartmouth (6-0-1)
1959	Penn (6-1)	1971	Cornell (6-1) & Dartmouth (6-1)	1981	Yale (6-1) & Dartmouth (6-1)	1992	Dartmouth (6-1) & Princeton (6-1)
1960	Yale (7-0)	1972	Dartmouth (5-1-1)	1982	Harvard (5-2), Penn (5-2) & Dartmouth (5-2)	1993	Penn (7-0)
1961	Columbia (6-1) & Harvard (6-1)	1973	Dartmouth (6-1)	1983	Harvard (5-1-1) & Penn (5-1-1)	1994	Penn (7-0)
1962	Dartmouth (7-0)	1974	Harvard (6-1) & Yale (6-1)	1984	Penn (7-0)	1995	Princeton (5-1-1)
1963	Dartmouth (5-2) & Princeton (5-2)	1975	Harvard (6-1)	1985	Penn (6-1)		
1964	Princeton (7-0)	1976	Brown (6-1) & Yale (6-1)	1986	Penn (7-0)		
1965	Dartmouth (7-0)			1987	Harvard (6-1)		
1966	Dartmouth (6-1), Harvard (6-1) & Princeton (6-1)						

Mid-American Conference

Founded in 1946. **Charter members** (6): Butler, Cincinnati, Miami-OH, Ohio University, Western Michigan and Western Reserve (Miami and WMU began play in '48). **Admitted later** (12): Kent St. (now Kent) and Toledo in 1951 (Toledo began play in '52); Bowling Green in 1952; Marshall in 1954; Central Michigan and Eastern Michigan in 1972 (CMU began play in '75 and EMU in '76); Ball St. and Northern Illinois in 1973 (both began play in '75); Akron in 1991 (began play in '92); Marshall and Northern Illinois in 1995 (both will resume play in '97); Buffalo in 1995 (will begin play in either '98 or '99). **Withdrew later** (5): Butler in 1950 (left for the Indiana Collegiate Conference); Cincinnati in 1953 (went independent); Western Reserve (now Case Western) in 1955 (left for President's Athletic Conference); Marshall in 1969 (went independent); Northern Illinois in 1986 (went independent).

1996 playing membership (10): Akron, Ball St., Bowling Green, Central Michigan, Eastern Michigan, Kent, Miami-OH, Ohio University, Toledo and Western Michigan.

Multiple titles: Miami-OH (13); Bowling Green (10); Toledo (8); Ohio University (5); Ball St., Central Michigan and Cincinnati (4); Western Michigan (2).

Year	
1947	Cincinnati (3-1)
1948	Miami-OH (4-0)
1949	Cincinnati (4-0)
1950	Miami-OH (4-0)
1951	Cincinnati (3-0)
1952	Cincinnati (3-0)
1953	Ohio Univ. (5-0-1)
1954	Miami-OH (4-0)
1955	Miami-OH (5-0)
1956	Bowling Green (5-0-1)
1957	Miami-OH (5-0)
1958	Miami-OH (5-0)
1959	Bowling Green (6-0)
1960	Ohio Univ. (6-0)
1961	Bowling Green (5-1)
1962	Bowling Green (5-0-1)
1963	Ohio Univ. (5-1)
1964	Bowling Green (5-1)
1965	Bowling Green (5-1) & Miami-OH (5-1)
1966	Miami-OH (5-1) & Western Mich. (5-1)
1967	Toledo (5-1) & Ohio Univ. (5-1)
1968	Ohio Univ. (6-0)
1969	Toledo (5-0)
1970	Toledo (5-0)
1971	Toledo (5-0)
1972	Kent St. (4-1)
1973	Miami-OH (5-0)
1974	Miami-OH (5-0)
1975	Miami-OH (6-0)
1976	Ball St. (4-1)
1977	Miami-OH (5-0)
1978	Ball St. (8-0)
1979	Central Mich. (8-0-1)
1980	Central Mich. (7-2)
1981	Toledo (8-1)
1982	Bowling Green (7-2)
1983	Northern Ill. (8-1)
1984	Toledo (7-1-1)
1985	Bowling Green (9-0)
1986	Miami-OH (6-2)
1987	Eastern Mich. (7-1)
1988	Western Mich. (7-1)
1989	Ball St. (6-1-1)
1990	Central Mich. (7-1) & Toledo (7-1)
1991	Bowling Green (8-0)
1992	Bowling Green (8-0)
1993	Ball St. (7-0-1)
1994	Central Mich. (8-1)
1995	Toledo (7-0-1)

Pacific-10 Conference

Originally founded in 1915 as Pacific Coast Conference. **Charter members** (4): California, Oregon, Oregon St. and Washington. **Admitted later** (6): Washington St. in 1917; Stanford in 1918; Idaho and USC (Southern Cal) in 1922; Montana in 1924; UCLA in 1928. **Withdrew later** (1): Montana in 1950 (left for the Mountain States Conf.).

The **PCC** dissolved in 1959 and the **AAWU** (Athletic Assn. of Western Universities) was founded. **Charter members** (5): California, Stanford, UCLA, USC and Washington. **Admitted later** (5): Washington St. in 1962; Oregon and Oregon St. in 1964; Arizona and Arizona St. in 1978. **Conference renamed** Pacific-8 in 1968 and Pacific-10 in 1978.

1996 playing membership (10): Arizona, Arizona St., California, Oregon, Oregon St., Stanford, UCLA, USC, Washington and Washington St.

Multiple titles: USC (31); UCLA (15); Washington (14); California (13); Stanford (11); Oregon (5); Oregon St. (4); Washington St. (2).

Year	
1916	Washington (3-0-1)
1917	Washington St. (3-0)
1918	California (3-0)
1919	Oregon (2-1) & Washington (2-1)
1920	California (3-0)
1921	California (5-0)
1922	California (3-0)
1923	California (5-0)
1924	Stanford (3-0-1)
1925	Washington (5-0)
1926	Stanford (4-0)
1927	USC (4-0-1) & Stanford (4-0-1)
1928	USC (4-0-1)
1929	USC (6-1)
1930	Washington St. (6-0)
1931	USC (7-0)
1932	USC (6-0)
1933	Oregon (4-1) & Stanford (4-1)
1934	Stanford (5-0)
1935	California (4-1), Stanford (4-1) & UCLA (4-1)
1936	Washington (6-0-1)
1937	California (6-0-1)
1938	USC (6-1) & California (6-1)
1939	USC (5-0-2)
1940	Stanford (7-0)
1941	Oregon St. (7-2)
1942	UCLA (6-1)
1943	USC (4-0)
1944	USC (3-0-2)
1945	USC (5-1)
1946	UCLA (7-0)
1947	USC (6-0)
1948	California (6-0) & Oregon (6-0)
1949	California (7-0)
1950	California (5-0-1)
1951	Stanford (6-1)
1952	USC (6-0)
1953	UCLA (6-1)
1954	UCLA (6-0)
1955	UCLA (6-0)
1956	Oregon St. (6-1-1)
1957	Oregon (6-2) & Oregon St. (6-2)
1958	California (6-1)
1959	Washington (3-1), USC (3-1) & UCLA (3-1)
1960	Washington (4-0)
1961	UCLA (3-1)
1962	USC (4-0)
1963	Washington (4-1)
1964	Oregon St. (3-1) & USC (3-1)
1965	UCLA (4-0)
1966	USC (4-1)
1967	USC (6-1)
1968	USC (6-0)
1969	USC (6-0)
1970	Stanford (6-1)
1971	Stanford (6-1)
1972	USC (7-0)
1973	USC (7-0)
1974	USC (6-0-1)
1975	UCLA (6-1) & California (6-1)
1976	USC (7-0)
1977	Washington (6-1)
1978	USC (6-1)
1979	USC (6-0-1)
1980	Washington (6-1)
1981	Washington (6-2)
1982	UCLA (5-1-1)
1983	UCLA (6-1-1)
1984	USC (7-1)
1985	UCLA (6-2)
1986	Arizona St. (5-1-1)
1987	USC (7-1) & UCLA (7-1)
1988	USC (8-0)
1989	USC (6-0-1)
1990	Washington (7-1)
1991	Washington (8-0)
1992	Washington (6-2) & Stanford (6-2)
1993	UCLA (6-2), Arizona (6-2) & USC (6-2)
1994	Oregon (7-1)
1995	USC (6-1-1) & Washington (6-1-1)

Southeastern Conference

Founded in 1933 when charter members all left Southern Conference to form SEC. **Charter members** (13): Alabama, Auburn, Florida, Georgia, Georgia Tech, Kentucky, LSU, Mississippi, Mississippi St., Sewanee, Tennessee, Tulane and Vanderbilt. **Admitted later** (2): Arkansas and South Carolina in 1990 (both began play in '92). **Withdrew later** (3): Sewanee in 1940 (went independent); Georgia Tech in 1964 (went independent); Tulane in 1966 (went independent).

Current playing membership (12): Alabama, Arkansas, Auburn, Florida, Georgia, Kentucky, LSU, Mississippi, Mississippi St., South Carolina, Tennessee and Vanderbilt.

Multiple titles: Alabama (20); Tennessee (11); Georgia (10); LSU (7); Mississippi (6); Auburn and Georgia Tech (5); Florida (4); Tulane (3); Kentucky (2).

Year
1933 Alabama (5-0-1)
1934 Tulane (8-0) & Alabama (7-0)
1935 LSU (5-0)
1936 LSU (6-0)
1937 Alabama (6-0)
1938 Tennessee (7-0)
1939 Tennessee (6-0), Georgia Tech (6-0) & Tulane (5-0)
1940 Tennessee (5-0)
1941 Mississippi St. (4-0-1)
1942 Georgia (6-1)
1943 Georgia Tech (3-0)
1944 Georgia Tech (4-0)
1945 Alabama (6-0)
1946 Georgia (5-0) & Tennessee (5-0)
1947 Mississippi (6-1)

Year
1948 Georgia (6-0)
1949 Tulane (5-1)
1950 Kentucky (5-1)
1951 Georgia Tech (7-0) & Tennessee (5-0)
1952 Georgia Tech (6-0)
1953 Alabama (4-0-3)
1954 Mississippi (5-1)
1955 Mississippi (5-1)
1956 Tennessee (6-0)
1957 Auburn (7-0)
1958 LSU (6-0)
1959 Georgia (7-0)
1960 Mississippi (5-0-1)
1961 Alabama (7-0) & LSU (6-0)
1962 Mississippi (6-0)
1963 Mississippi (5-0-1)

Year
1964 Alabama (8-0)
1965 Alabama (6-1-1)
1966 Alabama (6-0) & Georgia (6-0)
1967 Tennessee (6-0)
1968 Georgia (5-0-1)
1969 Tennessee (5-1)
1970 LSU (5-0)
1971 Alabama (7-0)
1972 Alabama (7-1)
1973 Alabama (8-0)
1974 Alabama (6-0)
1975 Alabama (6-0)
1976 Georgia (5-1) & Kentucky (5-1)
1977 Alabama (7-0)
1978 Alabama (6-0)
1979 Alabama (6-0)

Year
1980 Georgia (6-0)
1981 Georgia (6-0) & Alabama (6-0)
1982 Georgia (6-0)
1983 Auburn (6-0)
1984 Vacated*
1985 Tennessee (5-1)
1986 LSU (5-1)
1987 Auburn (5-0-1)
1988 Auburn (6-1) & LSU (6-1)
1989 Alabama (6-1), Tennessee (6-1) & Auburn (6-1)
1990 Tennessee (5-1-1)
1991 Florida (7-0)

*Florida (5-0-1) forced to vacate 1984 title after put on NCAA probation for recruiting violations.

SEC Championship Game

Since expanding to 12 teams and splitting into two divisions in 1992, the SEC has staged a conference championship game between the two division winners on the first Saturday in December. The game has been played at Legion Field in Birmingham, Ala., (1992-93) and the Georgia Dome in Atlanta (since 1994).

Year
1992 Alabama 28, Florida 21
1993 Florida 28, Alabama 23

Year
1994 Florida 24, Alabama 23

Year
1995 Florida 34, Arkansas 3

Southwest Conference (1914-95)

Founded in 1914 as Southwest Intercollegiate Athletic Conference. **Charter members** (8): Arkansas, Baylor, Oklahoma, Oklahoma A&M (now Oklahoma St.), Rice, Southwestern, Texas and Texas A&M. **Admitted later** (5): SMU (Southern Methodist) in 1918; Phillips University in 1920; TCU (Texas Christian) in 1923; Texas Tech in 1956 (began play in '60); Houston in 1971 (began play in '76). **Withdrew later** (9): Southwestern in 1917 (went independent); Oklahoma in 1920 (left for Missouri Valley after '19 season); Phillips in 1921; Oklahoma A&M (now Oklahoma St.) in 1925 (left for Big Six); Arkansas in 1990 (left for SEC after '91 season); Baylor, Texas, Texas A&M and Texas Tech in 1994 (all four left for Big 12 after '95 season); Rice, SMU and TCU in 1994 (all three left for WAC after '95 season); Houston in 1994 (left for Conference USA after '95 season).

1996 playing membership: Conference folded on June 30, 1996.

Multiple titles: Texas (25); Texas A&M (17); Arkansas (13); SMU (9); TCU (9); Rice (7); Baylor (5); Houston (4); Texas Tech (2).

Year
1914 No champion
1915 Oklahoma (3-0)
1916 No champion
1917 Texas A&M (2-0)
1918 Texas (4-0)
1919 Texas A&M (4-0)
1920 Texas (5-0)
1921 Texas A&M (3-0-2)
1922 Baylor (5-0)
1923 SMU (5-0)
1924 Baylor (4-0-1)
1925 Texas A&M (4-1)
1926 SMU (5-0)
1927 Texas A&M (4-0-1)
1928 Texas (5-1)
1929 TCU (4-0-1)
1930 Texas (4-1)
1931 SMU (5-0-1)
1932 TCU (6-0)
1933 No champion*
1934 Rice (5-1)
1935 SMU (6-0)
1936 Arkansas (5-1)
1937 Rice (4-1-1)

Year
1938 TCU (6-0)
1939 Texas A&M (6-0)
1940 Texas A&M (5-1)
1941 Texas A&M (5-1)
1942 Texas (5-1)
1943 Texas (5-0)
1944 TCU (3-1-1)
1945 Texas (5-1)
1946 Rice (5-1) & Arkansas (5-1)
1947 SMU (5-0-1)
1948 SMU (5-0-1)
1949 Rice (6-0)
1950 Texas (6-0)
1951 TCU (5-1)
1952 Texas (6-0)
1953 Rice (5-1) & Texas (5-1)
1954 Arkansas (5-1)
1955 TCU (5-1)
1956 Texas A&M (6-0)
1957 Rice (5-1)
1958 TCU (5-1)

Year
1959 Texas (5-1), TCU (5-1) & Arkansas (5-1)
1960 Arkansas (6-1)
1961 Texas (6-1) & Arkansas (6-1)
1962 Texas (6-0-1)
1963 Texas (7-0)
1964 Arkansas (7-0)
1965 Arkansas (7-0)
1966 SMU (6-1)
1967 Texas A&M (6-1)
1968 Arkansas (6-1) & Texas (6-1)
1969 Texas (7-0)
1970 Texas (7-0)
1971 Texas (6-1)
1972 Texas (7-0)
1973 Texas (7-0)
1974 Baylor (6-1)
1975 Arkansas (6-1), Texas (6-1) & Texas A&M (6-1)
1976 Houston (7-1) & Texas Tech (7-1)

Year
1977 Texas (8-0)
1978 Houston (7-1)
1979 Houston (7-1) & Arkansas (7-1)
1980 Baylor (8-0)
1981 SMU (7-1)*
1982 SMU (7-0-1)
1983 Texas (8-0)
1984 SMU (6-2) & Houston (6-2)
1985 Texas A&M (7-1)
1986 Texas A&M (7-1)
1987 Texas A&M (6-1)
1988 Arkansas (7-0)
1989 Arkansas (7-1)
1990 Texas (8-0)
1991 Texas A&M (8-0)
1992 Texas A&M (7-0)
1993 Texas A&M (7-0)
1994 Texas Tech (4-3), Baylor (4-3), Rice (4-3), Texas A&M* (4-3) & TCU (4-3)
1995 Texas (7-0)

*Arkansas (4-1) forced to vacate 1933 title for use of ineligible player.

Western Athletic Conference

Founded in 1962 when charter members left the Skyline and Border conferences to form the WAC. **Charter members** (6): Arizona and Arizona St. from Border; BYU (Brigham Young), New Mexico, Utah and Wyoming from Skyline. **Admitted later** (12): Colorado St. and UTEP (Texas-El Paso) in 1967 (both began play in '68); San Diego St. in 1978; Hawaii in 1979; Air Force in 1980; Fresno St. in 1991 (began play in '92); Rice, San Jose St., SMU (Southern Methodist), TCU (Texas Christian), Tulsa and UNLV (Nevada-Las Vegas)in 1994 (all began play in '96). **Withdrew later** (2): Arizona and Arizona St. in 1978 (left for Pac-10 after '77 season).

1996 playing membership (16): Air Force, BYU, Colorado St., Fresno St., Hawaii, New Mexico, Rice, San Diego St., San Jose St., SMU, TCU, Tulsa, UNLV, Utah, UTEP and Wyoming.

Multiple titles: BYU (18); Arizona St. and Wyoming (7); New Mexico (3); Air Force, Arizona, Colorado St., Fresno St. and Utah (2).

WAC Championship Game

In addition to expanding to 16 teams and splitting into two divisions in 1996, the WAC will stage a conference championship game between the two division winners on Dec. 7 in Las Vegas. The divisions: DIV. A— BYU, New Mexico, Rice, SMU, TCU, Tulsa, Utah and UTEP; DIV. B— Air Force, Colorado St., Fresno St., Hawaii, San Diego St., San Jose St., UNLV and Wyoming.

Year	
1962	New Mexico (2-1-1)
1963	New Mexico (3-1)
1964	Utah (3-1), New Mexico (3-1) & Arizona (3-1)
1965	BYU (4-1)
1966	Wyoming (5-0)
1967	Wyoming (5-0)
1968	Wyoming (6-1)
1969	Arizona St. (6-1)
1970	Arizona St. (7-0)
1971	Arizona St. (7-0)
1972	Arizona St. (5-1)
1973	Arizona St. (6-1) & Arizona (6-1)
1974	BYU (6-0-1)
1975	Arizona St. (7-0)
1976	BYU (6-1) & Wyoming (6-1)
1977	Arizona St. (6-1) & BYU (6-1)
1978	BYU (5-1)
1979	BYU (7-0)
1980	BYU (6-1)
1981	BYU (7-1)
1982	BYU (7-1)
1983	BYU (7-0)
1984	BYU (8-0)
1985	Air Force (7-1) & BYU (7-1)
1986	San Diego St. (7-1)
1987	Wyoming (8-0)
1988	Wyoming (8-0)
1989	BYU (7-1)
1990	BYU (7-1)
1991	BYU (7-0-1)
1992	Hawaii (6-2), BYU (6-2) & Fresno St. (6-2)
1993	BYU (6-2), Fresno St. (6-2) & Wyoming (6-2)
1994	Colorado St. (7-1)
1995	Colorado St. (6-2), Air Force (6-2), BYU (6-2) & Utah (6-2)

Longest Division I Streaks

Winning Streaks

(Including bowl games)

No		Seasons	Spoiler	Score
47	Oklahoma	1953-57	Notre Dame	7-0
39	Washington	1908-14	Oregon St.	0-0
37	Yale	1890-93	Princeton	6-0
37	Yale	1887-89	Princeton	10-0
35	Toledo	1969-71	Tampa	21-0
34	Penn	1894-96	Lafayette	6-4
31	Oklahoma	1948-50	Kentucky	13-7*
31	Pittsburgh	1914-18	Cleve. Naval	10-9
31	Penn	1896-98	Harvard	10-0
30	Texas	1968-70	Notre Dame	24-11*
29	Miami-FL	1990-93	Alabama	34-13*
29	Michigan	1901-03	Minnesota	6-6
28	Alabama	1978-80	Mississippi St.	6-3
28	Oklahoma	1973-75	Kansas	23-3
28	Michigan St.	1950-53	Purdue	6-0
27	Nebraska	1901-04	Colorado	6-0
26	Cornell	1921-24	Williams	14-7
26	Michigan	1903-05	Chicago	2-0
25	Nebraska	1994–	current streak	
25	BYU	1983-85	UCLA	27-24
25	Michigan	1946-49	Army	21-7
25	Army	1944-46	Notre Dame	0-0
25	USC	1931-33	Oregon St.	0-0

***Note:** Kentucky beat Oklahoma in 1951 Sugar Bowl, and Notre Dame beat Texas in 1971 Cotton Bowl.

Unbeaten Streaks

(Including bowl games)

No	W-T		Seasons	Spoiler	Score
63	59-4	Washington	1907-17	California	27-0
56	55-1	Michigan	1901-05	Chicago	2-0
50	46-4	California	1920-25	Olympic Club	15-0
48	47-1	Oklahoma	1953-57	N. Dame	7-0
48	47-1	Yale	1885-89	Princeton	10-0
47	42-5	Yale	1879-85	Princeton	6-5
44	42-2	Yale	1894-96	Princeton	24-6
42	39-3	Yale	1904-08	Harvard	4-0
39	37-2	N. Dame	1946-50	Purdue	28-14
37	36-1	Oklahoma	1972-75	Kansas	23-3
37	37-0	Yale	1890-93	Princeton	6-0
35	35-0	Toledo	1967-71	Tampa	21-0
35	34-1	Minnesota	1903-05	Wisconsin	16-12

Losing Streaks

No		Seasons	Victim	Score
57	Prairie View	1989–	current streak	
44	Columbia	1983-88	Princeton	16-14
34	Northwestern	1979-82	No. Illinois	31-6
28	Virginia	1958-60	Wm. & Mary	21-6
28	Kansas St.	1945-48	Arkansas St.	37-6
27	Eastern Mich.	1980-82	Kent St.	9-7
27	New Mexico St.	1988-90	CS-Fullerton	43-9

Note: Virginia ended its losing streak in the opening game of the 1961 season.

Annual NCAA Division I-A Leaders

Rushing

Individual title decided on Rushing Yards (1937-69), and on Yards Per Game (since 1970).

Multiple winners: Marshall Faulk, Art Luppino, Ed Marinaro, Rudy Mobley, Jim Pilot and O.J. Simpson (2).

Year		Car	Yards
1937	Byron (Whizzer) White, Colorado	181	1121
1938	Len Eshmont, Fordham	132	831
1939	John Polanski, Wake Forest	137	882
1940	Al Ghesquiere, Detroit	146	957
1941	Frank Sinkwich, Georgia	209	1103
1942	Rudy Mobley, Hardin-Simmons	187	1281
1943	Creighton Miller, Notre Dame	151	911
1944	Red Williams, Minnesota	136	911
1945	Bob Fenimore, Oklahoma A&M	142	1048
1946	Rudy Mobley, Hardin-Simmons	227	1262
1947	Wilton Davis, Hardin-Simmons	193	1173
1948	Fred Wendt, Texas Mines	184	1570
1949	John Dottley, Ole Miss	208	1312
1950	Wilford White, Arizona St	199	1502
1951	Ollie Matson, San Francisco	245	1566
1952	Howie Waugh, Tulsa	164	1372
1953	J.C. Caroline, Illinois	194	1256
1954	Art Luppino, Arizona	179	1359
1955	Art Luppino, Arizona	209	1313
1956	Jim Crawford, Wyoming	200	1104
1957	Leon Burton, Arizona St	117	1126
1958	Dick Bass, Pacific	205	1361
1959	Pervis Atkins, New Mexico St	130	971
1960	Bob Gaiters, New Mexico St	197	1338
1961	Jim Pilot, New Mexico St	191	1278
1962	Jim Pilot, New Mexico St	208	1247
1963	Dave Casinelli, Memphis St	219	1016
1964	Brian Piccolo, Wake Forest	252	1044
1965	Mike Garrett, USC	267	1440
1966	Ray McDonald, Idaho	259	1329
1967	O.J. Simpson, USC	266	1415
1968	O.J. Simpson, USC	355	1709
1969	Steve Owens, Oklahoma	358	1523

Year		Car	Yards	P/Gm
1970	Ed Marinaro, Cornell	285	1425	158.3
1971	Ed Marinaro, Cornell	356	1881	209.0
1972	Pete VanValkenburg, BYU	232	1386	138.6
1973	Mark Kellar, Northern Ill	291	1719	156.3
1974	Louie Giammona, Utah St.	329	1534	153.4
1975	Ricky Bell, USC	357	1875	170.5
1976	Tony Dorsett, Pittsburgh	338	1948	177.1
1977	Earl Campbell, Texas	267	1744	158.5
1978	Billy Sims, Oklahoma	231	1762	160.2
1979	Charles White, USC	293	1803	180.3
1980	George Rogers, S. Carolina	297	1781	161.9
1981	Marcus Allen, USC	403	2342	212.9
1982	Ernest Anderson, Okla. St.	353	1877	170.6
1983	Mike Rozier, Nebraska	275	2148	179.0
1984	Keith Byars, Ohio St.	313	1655	150.5
1985	Lorenzo White, Mich. St.	386	1908	173.5
1986	Paul Palmer, Temple	346	1866	169.6
1987	Ickey Woods, UNLV	259	1658	150.7
1988	Barry Sanders, Okla. St.	344	2628	238.9
1989	Anthony Thompson, Ind	358	1793	163.0
1990	Gerald Hudson, Okla. St.	279	1642	149.3
1991	Marshall Faulk, S. Diego St.	201	1429	158.8
1992	Marshall Faulk, S. Diego St.	265	1630	163.0
1993	LeShon Johnson, No. Ill.	327	1976	179.6
1994	Rashaan Salaam, Colorado	298	2055	186.8
1995	Troy Davis, Iowa St.	345	2010	182.7

All-Purpose Yardage

Multiple winners: Marcus Allen, Pervis Atkins, Ryan Benjamin, Louie Giammona, Tom Harmon, Art Luppino, Napolean McCallum, O.J. Simpson, Charles White and Gary Wood (2).

Year		Yards	P/Gm
1937	Byron (Whizzer) White, Colorado	1970	246.3
1938	Parker Hall, Ole Miss	1420	129.1
1939	Tom Harmon, Michigan	1208	151.0
1940	Tom Harmon, Michigan	1312	164.0
1941	Bill Dudley, Virginia	1674	186.0
1942	Complete records not available		
1943	Stan Koslowski, Holy Cross	1411	176.4
1944	Red Williams, Minnesota	1467	163.0
1945	Bob Fenimore, Oklahoma A&M	1577	197.1
1946	Rudy Mobley, Hardin-Simmons	1765	176.5
1947	Wilton Davis, Hardin-Simmons	1798	179.8
1948	Lou Kusserow, Columbia	1737	193.0
1949	Johnny Papit, Virginia	1611	179.0
1950	Wilford White, Arizona St.	2065	206.5
1951	Ollie Matson, San Francisco	2037	226.3
1952	Billy Vessels, Oklahoma	1512	151.2
1953	J.C. Caroline, Illinois	1470	163.3
1954	Art Luppino, Arizona	2193	219.3
1955	Jim Swink, TCU	1702	170.2
	& Art Luppino, Arizona	1702	170.2
1956	Jack Hill, Utah St.	1691	169.1
1957	Overton Curtis, Utah St.	1608	160.8
1958	Dick Bass, Pacific	1878	187.8
1959	Pervis Atkins, New Mexico St	1800	180.0
1960	Pervis Atkins, New Mexico St	1613	161.3
1961	Jim Pilot, New Mexico St	1606	160.6
1962	Gary Wood, Cornell	1395	155.0
1963	Gary Wood, Cornell	1508	167.6
1964	Donny Anderson, Texas Tech	1710	171.0
1965	Floyd Little, Syracuse	1990	199.0
1966	Frank Quayle, Virginia	1616	161.6
1967	O.J. Simpson, USC	1700	188.9
1968	O.J. Simpson, USC	1966	196.6
1969	Lynn Moore, Army	1795	179.5
1970	Don McCauley, North Carolina	2021	183.7
1971	Ed Marinaro, Cornell	1932	214.7
1972	Howard Stevens, Louisville	2132	213.2
1973	Willard Harrell, Pacific	1777	177.7
1974	Louie Giammona, Utah St.	1984	198.4
1975	Louie Giammona, Utah St.	2045	185.9
1976	Tony Dorsett, Pittsburgh	2021	183.7
1977	Earl Campbell, Texas	1855	168.6
1978	Charles White, USC	2096	174.7
1979	Charles White, USC	1941	194.1
1980	Marcus Allen, USC	1794	179.4
1981	Marcus Allen, USC	2559	232.6
1982	Carl Monroe, Utah	2036	185.1
1983	Napoleon McCallum, Navy	2385	216.8
1984	Keith Byars, Ohio St	2284	207.6
1985	Napoleon McCallum, Navy	2330	211.8
1986	Paul Palmer, Temple	2633	239.4
1987	Eric Wilkerson, Kent St	2074	188.6
1988	Barry Sanders, Oklahoma St.	3250	295.5
1989	Mike Pringle, CS-Fullerton	2690	244.6
1990	Glyn Milburn, Stanford	2222	202.0
1991	Ryan Benjamin, Pacific	2995	249.6
1992	Ryan Benjamin, Pacific	2597	236.1
1993	LeShon Johnson, Northern Ill.	2082	189.3
1994	Rashaan Salaam, Colorado	2349	213.5
1995	Troy Davis, Iowa St.	2466	224.2

Total Offense

Individual title decided on Total Yards (1937-69), and on Yards Per Game (since 1970).

Multiple winners: Johnny Bright, Bob Fenimore, Mike Maxwell and Jim McMahon (2).

Year		Plays	Yards
1937	Byron (Whizzer) White, Colorado	224	1596
1938	Davey O'Brien, TCU	291	1847
1939	Kenny Washington, UCLA	259	1370
1940	Johnny Knolla, Creighton	298	1420
1941	Bud Schwenk, Washington-MO	354	1928
1942	Frank Sinkwich, Georgia	341	2187
1943	Bob Hoernschemeyer, Indiana	355	1648
1944	Bob Fenimore, Oklahoma A&M	241	1758
1945	Bob Fenimore, Oklahoma A&M	203	1641
1946	Travis Bidwell, Auburn	339	1715
1947	Fred Enke, Arizona	329	1941
1948	Stan Heath, Nevada-Reno	233	1992
1949	Johnny Bright, Drake	275	1950
1950	Johnny Bright, Drake	320	2400
1951	Dick Kazmaier, Princeton	272	1827
1952	Ted Marchibroda, Detroit	305	1813
1953	Paul Larson, California	262	1572
1954	George Shaw, Oregon	276	1536
1955	George Welsh, Navy	203	1348
1956	John Brodie, Stanford	295	1642
1957	Bob Newman, Washington St	263	1444
1958	Dick Bass, Pacific	218	1440
1959	Dick Norman, Stanford	319	2018
1960	Billy Kilmer, UCLA	292	1889
1961	Dave Hoppmann, Iowa St	320	1638
1962	Terry Baker, Oregon St	318	2276
1963	George Mira, Miami-FL	394	2318
1964	Jerry Rhome, Tulsa	470	3128
1965	Bill Anderson, Tulsa	580	3343
1966	Virgil Carter, BYU	388	2545
1967	Sal Olivas, New Mexico St	368	2184
1968	Greg Cook Cincinnati	507	3210
1969	Dennis Shaw, San Diego St	388	3197

Year		Plays	Yards	P/Gm
1970	Pat Sullivan, Auburn	333	2856	285.6
1971	Gary Huff, Florida St	386	2653	241.2
1972	Don Strock, Va. Tech	480	3170	288.2
1973	Jesse Freitas, San Diego St.	410	2901	263.7
1974	Steve Joachim, Temple	331	2227	222.7
1975	Gene Swick, Toledo	490	2706	246.0
1976	Tommy Kramer, Rice	562	3272	297.5
1977	Doug Williams, Grambling	377	3229	293.5
1978	Mike Ford, SMU	459	2957	268.8
1979	Marc Wilson, BYU	488	3580	325.5
1980	Jim McMahon, BYU	540	4627	385.6
1981	Jim McMahon, BYU	487	3458	345.8
1982	Todd Dillon, Long Beach St	585	3587	326.1
1983	Steve Young, BYU	531	4346	395.1
1984	Robbie Bosco, BYU	543	3932	327.7
1985	Jim Everett, Purdue	518	3589	326.3
1986	Mike Perez, San Jose St	425	2969	329.9
1987	Todd Santos, San Diego St.	562	3688	307.3
1988	Scott Mitchell, Utah	589	4299	390.8
1989	Andre Ware, Houston	628	4661	423.7
1990	David Klingler, Houston	704	5221	474.6
1991	Ty Detmer, BYU	478	4001	333.4
1992	Jimmy Klingler, Houston	544	3768	342.6
1993	Chris Vargas, Nevada	535	4332	393.8
1994	Mike Maxwell, Nevada	477	3498	318.0
1995	Mike Maxwell, Nevada	443	3623	402.6

Passing

Individual title decided on Completions (1937-69), on Completions Per Game (1970-78), and on Passing Efficiency rating points (since 1979).

Multiple winners: Elvis Grbac, Don Heinrich, Jim McMahon, Davey O'Brien and Don Trull (2).

Year		Cmp	Pct	TD	Yds
1937	Davey O'Brien, TCU	94	.402	—	969
1938	Davey O'Brien, TCU	93	.557	—	1457
1939	Kay Eakin, Arkansas	78	.404	—	962
1940	Billy Sewell, Wash. St	86	.494	—	1023
1941	Bud Schwenk, Wash.-MO	114	.487	—	1457
1942	Ray Evans, Kansas	101	.505	—	1117
1943	Johnny Cook, Georgia	73	.465	—	1007
1944	Paul Rickards, Pittsburgh	84	.472	—	997
1945	Al Dekdebrun, Cornell	90	.464	—	1227
1946	Travis Tidwell, Auburn	79	.500	5	943
1947	Charlie Conerly, Ole Miss	133	.571	18	1367
1948	Stan Heath, Nev-Reno	126	.568	22	2005
1949	Adrian Burk, Baylor	110	.576	14	1428
1950	Don Heinrich, Washington	134	.606	14	1846
1951	Don Klosterman, Loyola-CA	159	.505	9	1843
1952	Don Heinrich, Washington	137	.507	13	1647
1953	Bob Garrett, Stanford	118	.576	17	1637
1954	Paul Larson, California	125	.641	10	1537
1955	George Welsh, Navy	94	.627	8	1319
1956	John Brodie, Stanford	139	.579	12	1633
1957	Ken Ford, H-Simmons	115	.561	14	1254
1958	Buddy Humphrey, Baylor	112	.574	7	1316
1959	Dick Norman, Stanford	152	.578	11	1963
1960	Harold Stephens, H-Simm.	145	.566	3	1254
1961	Chon Gallegos, S. Jose St	117	.594	14	1480
1962	Don Trull, Baylor	125	.546	11	1627
1963	Don Trull, Baylor	174	.565	12	2157
1964	Jerry Rhome, Tulsa	224	.687	32	2870
1965	Bill Anderson, Tulsa	296	.582	30	3464
1966	John Eckman, Wichita St	195	.426	7	2339
1967	Terry Stone, N. Mexico	160	.476	9	1946
1968	Chuck Hixson, SMU	265	.566	21	3103
1969	John Reaves, Florida	222	.561	24	2896

Year		Cmp	P/Gm	TD	Yds
1970	Sonny Sixkiller, Wash	186	18.6	15	2303
1971	Brian Sipe, S. Diego St.	196	17.8	17	2532
1972	Don Strock, Va. Tech	228	20.7	16	3243
1973	Jesse Freitas, S. Diego St.	227	20.6	21	2993
1974	Steve Bartkowski, Cal	182	16.5	12	2580
1975	Craig Penrose, S. Diego St.	198	18.0	15	2660
1976	Tommy Kramer, Rice	269	24.5	21	3317
1977	Guy Benjamin, Stanford	208	20.8	19	2521
1978	Steve Dils, Stanford	247	22.5	22	2943

Year		Cmp	TD	Yds	Rating
1979	Turk Schonert, Stanford	148	19	1922	163.0
1980	Jim McMahon, BYU	284	47	4571	176.9
1981	Jim McMahon, BYU	272	30	3555	155.0
1982	Tom Ramsey, UCLA	191	21	2824	153.5
1983	Steve Young, BYU	306	33	3902	168.5
1984	Doug Flutie, BC	233	27	3454	152.9
1985	Jim Harbaugh, Michigan	139	18	1913	163.7
1986	V. Testaverde, Miami-FL	175	26	2557	165.8
1987	Don McPherson, Syracuse	129	22	2341	164.3
1988	Timm Rosenbach, Wash. St.	199	23	2791	162.0
1989	Ty Detmer, BYU	265	32	4560	175.6
1990	Shawn Moore, Virginia	144	21	2262	160.7
1991	Elvis Grbac, Michigan	152	24	1955	169.0
1992	Elvis Grbac, Michigan	112	15	1465	154.2
1993	Trent Dilfer, Fresno St.	217	28	3276	173.1
1994	Kerry Collins, Penn St.	176	21	2679	172.9
1995	Danny Wuerffel, Florida	210	35	3266	178.4

All-Time NCAA Division I-A Leaders (Cont.)

Receptions

Title decided on Passes Caught (1937-69), and on Catches Per Game (since 1970). Touchdown totals unavailable in 1939 and 1941-45.

Multiple winners: Neil Armstrong, Hugh Campell, Manny Hazard, Reid Mosely, Jason Phillips, Howard Twilley and Alex Van Dyke (2).

Year		No	TD	Yds
1937	Jim Benton, Arkansas	47	7	754
1938	Sam Boyd, Baylor	32	5	537
1939	Ken Kavanaugh, LSU	30	—	467
1940	Eddie Bryant, Virginia	30	2	222
1941	Hank Stanton, Arizona	50	—	820
1942	Bill Rogers, Texas A&M	39	—	432
1943	Neil Armstrong, Okla. A&M	39	—	317
1944	Reid Moseley, Georgia	32	—	506
1945	Reid Moseley, Georgia	31	—	662
1946	Neil Armstrong, Okla. A&M	32	1	479
1947	Barney Poole, Ole Miss	52	8	513
1948	Red O'Quinn, Wake Forest	39	7	605
1949	Art Weiner, N. Carolina	52	7	762
1950	Gordon Cooper, Denver	46	8	569
1951	Dewey McConnell, Wyoming	47	9	725
1952	Ed Brown, Fordham	57	6	774
1953	John Carson, Georgia	45	4	663
1954	Jim Hanifan, California	44	7	569
1955	Hank Burnine, Missouri	44	2	594
1956	Art Powell, San Jose St	40	5	583
1957	Stuart Vaughan, Utah	53	5	756
1958	Dave Hibbert, Arizona	61	4	606
1959	Chris Burford, Stanford	61	6	756
1960	Hugh Campbell, Wash. St	66	10	881
1961	Hugh Campbell, Wash. St	53	5	723
1962	Vern Burke, Oregon St	69	10	1007
1963	Lawrence Elkins, Baylor	70	8	873
1964	Howard Twilley, Tulsa	95	13	1178
1965	Howard Twilley, Tulsa	134	16	1779
1966	Glenn Meltzer, Wichita St	91	4	1115
1967	Bob Goodridge, Vanderbilt	79	6	1114
1968	Ron Sellers, Florida St	86	12	1496
1969	Jerry Hendren, Idaho	95	12	1452

Year		No	P/Gm	TD	Yds
1970	Mike Mikolayunas, Davidson	87	8.7	8	1128
1971	Tom Reynolds, San Diego St	67	6.7	7	1070
1972	Tom Forzani, Utah St.	85	7.7	8	1169
1973	Jay Miller, BYU	100	9.1	8	1181
1974	D. McDonald, San Diego St	86	7.8	7	1157
1975	Bob Farnham, Brown	56	6.2	2	701
1976	Billy Ryckman, La. Tech	77	7.0	10	1382
1977	W. Tolleson, W. Carolina	73	6.6	7	1101
1978	Dave Petzke, Northern Ill	91	8.3	11	1217
1979	Rick Beasley, Appalach. St.	74	6.7	12	1205
1980	Dave Young, Purdue	67	6.1	8	917
1981	Pete Harvey, N. Texas St	57	6.3	3	743
1982	Vincent White, Stanford	68	6.8	8	677
1983	Keith Edwards, Vanderbilt	97	8.8	8	909
1984	David Williams, Illinois	101	9.2	8	1278
1985	Rodney Carter, Purdue	98	8.9	4	1099
1986	Mark Templeton, L. Beach St	99	9.0	2	688
1987	Jason Phillips, Houston	99	9.0	3	875
1988	Jason Phillips, Houston	108	9.8	15	1444
1989	Manny Hazard, Houston	142	12.9	22	1689
1990	Manny Hazard, Houston	78	7.8	9	946
1991	Fred Gilbert, Houston	106	9.6	7	957
1992	Sherman Smith, Houston	103	9.4	6	923
1993	Chris Penn, Tulsa	105	9.6	12	1578
1994	Alex Van Dyke, Nevada	98	8.9	10	1246
1995	Alex Van Dyke, Nevada	129	11.7	16	1854

Scoring

Title decided on Total Points (1937-69), and on Points Per Game (since 1970).

Multiple winners: Tom Harmon and Billy Sims (2).

Year		TD	XP	FG	Pts
1937	Byron (Whizzer) White, Colo	16	23	1	122
1938	Parker Hall, Ole Miss	11	7	0	73
1939	Tom Harmon, Michigan	14	15	1	102
1940	Tom Harmon, Michigan	16	18	1	117
1941	Bill Dudley, Virginia	18	23	1	134
1942	Bob Steuber, Missouri	18	13	0	121
1943	Steve Van Buren, LSU	14	14	0	98
1944	Glenn Davis, Army	20	0	0	120
1945	Doc Blanchard, Army	19	1	0	115
1946	Gene Roberts, Tenn-Chatt	18	9	0	117
1947	Lou Gambino, Maryland	16	0	0	96
1948	Fred Wendt, Texas Mines	20	32	0	152
1949	George Thomas, Oklahoma	19	3	0	117
1950	Bobby Reynolds, Nebraska	22	25	0	157
1951	Ollie Matson, San Francisco	21	0	0	126
1952	Jackie Parker, Miss. St.	16	24	0	120
1953	Earl Lindley, Utah St.	13	3	0	81
1954	Art Luppino, Arizona	24	22	0	166
1955	Jim Swink, TCU	20	5	0	125
1956	Clendon Thomas, Oklahoma	18	0	0	108
1957	Leon Burton, Ariz. St.	16	0	0	96
1958	Dick Bass, Pacific	18	8	0	116
1959	Pervis Atkins, N. Mexico St.	17	5	0	107
1960	Bob Gaiters, N. Mexico St.	23	7	0	145
1961	Jim Pilot, N. Mexico St.	21	12	0	138
1962	Jerry Logan, W. Texas St.	13	32	0	110
1963	Cosmo Iacavazzi, Princeton	14	0	0	84
	& Dave Casinelli, Memphis St.	14	0	0	84
1964	Brian Piccolo, Wake Forest	17	9	0	111
1965	Howard Twilley, Tulsa	16	31	0	127
1966	Ken Hebert, Houston	11	41	2	113
1967	Leroy Keyes, Purdue	19	0	0	114
1968	Jim O'Brien, Cincinnati	12	31	13	142
1969	Steve Owens, Oklahoma	23	0	0	138

Year		TD	XP	FG	Pts	P/Gm
1970	Brian Bream, Air Force	20	0	0	120	12.0
	& Gary Kosins, Dayton	18	0	0	108	12.0
1971	Ed Marinaro, Cornell	24	4	0	148	16.4
1972	Harold Henson, Ohio St.	20	0	0	120	12.0
1973	Jim Jennings, Rutgers	21	2	0	128	11.6
1974	Bill Marek, Wisconsin	19	0	0	114	12.7
1975	Pete Johnson, Ohio St.	25	0	0	150	13.6
1976	Tony Dorsett, Pitt	22	2	0	134	12.2
1977	Earl Campbell, Texas	19	0	0	114	10.4
1978	Billy Sims, Oklahoma	20	0	0	120	10.9
1979	Billy Sims, Oklahoma	22	0	0	132	12.0
1980	Sammy Winder, So. Miss.	20	0	0	120	10.9
1981	Marcus Allen, USC	23	0	0	138	12.5
1982	Greg Allen, Fla. St.	21	0	0	126	11.5
1983	Mike Rozier, Nebraska	29	0	0	174	14.5
1984	Keith Byars, Ohio St	24	0	0	144	13.1
1985	Bernard White, B. Green	19	0	0	114	10.4

Year		TD	XP	FG	Pts	P/Gm
1986	Steve Bartalo, Colo. St	19	0	0	114	10.4
1987	Paul Hewitt, S. Diego St	24	0	0	144	12.0
1988	Barry Sanders, Okla. St	39	0	0	234	21.3
1989	Anthony Thompson, Ind	25	4	0	154	14.0
1990	Stacey Robinson, No. Ill	19	6	0	120	10.9
1991	Marshall Faulk, S.D. St.	23	2	0	140	15.6
1992	Garrison Hearst, Georgia	21	0	0	126	11.5
1993	Bam Morris, Texas Tech	22	2	0	134	12.2
1994	Rashaan Salaam, Colo	24	0	0	144	13.1
1995	Eddie George, Ohio St.	24	0	0	144	12.0

All-Time NCAA Division I-A Leaders

Through the 1995 regular season. The NCAA does not recognize active players among career Per Game leaders.

CAREER

Passing

(Minimum 500 Completions)

Passing Efficiency	Years	Rating
1 Ty Detmer, BYU	1988-91	162.7
2 Jim McMahon, BYU	1977-78,80-81	156.9
3 Steve Young, BYU	1982,84-86	149.8
4 Robbie Bosco, BYU	1981-83	149.4
5 Mike Maxwell, Nevada	1993-95	148.5

Yards Gained	Years	Yards
1 Ty Detmer, BYU	1988-91	15,031
2 Todd Santos, San Diego St	1984-87	11,425
3 Eric Zeier, Georgia	1991-94	11,153
4 Alex Van Pelt, Pittsburgh	1989-92	10,913
5 Kevin Sweeney, Fresno St.	1983-86	10,623

Completions	Years	No
1 Ty Detmer, BYU	1988-91	958
2 Todd Santos, San Diego St	1984-87	910
3 Brian McClure, Bowling Green	1982-85	900
4 Erik Wilhelm, Oregon St.	1985-88	870
5 Alex Van Pelt, Pittsburgh	1989-92	845

Receptions

Catches	Years	No
1 Aaron Turner, Pacific	1989-92	266
2 Terance Mathis, New Mexico	1985-87,89	263
3 Mark Templeton, Long Beach St	1983-86	262
4 Howard Twilley, Tulsa	1963-65	261
5 David Williams, Illinois	1983-85	245

Catches Per Game	Years	No	P/Gm
1 Manny Hazard, Houston	1989-90	220	10.5
2 Alex Van Dyke, Nevada	1994-95	227	10.3
3 Howard Twilley, Tulsa	1963-65	261	10.0
4 Jason Phillips, Houston	1987-88	207	9.4
5 Bryan Reeves, Nevada	1992-93	172	8.2

Yards Gained	Years	No	Yards
1 Ryan Yarborough, Wyoming	1990-93	229	4357
2 Aaron Turner, Pacific	1989-92	266	4345
3 Terance Mathis, N. Mexico	1985-87,89	263	4254
4 Marc Zeno, Tulane	1984-87	236	3725
5 Ron Sellers, Florida St	1966-68	212	3598

Rushing

Yards Gained	Years	Yards
1 Tony Dorsett, Pittsburgh	1973-76	6082
2 Charles White, USC	1976-79	5598
3 Herschel Walker, Georgia	1980-82	5259
4 Archie Griffin, Ohio St.	1972-75	5177
5 Darren Lewis, Texas A&M	1987-90	5012

Yards Per Game	Years	Yards	P/Gm
1 Ed Marinaro, Cornell	1969-71	4715	174.6
2 O.J. Simpson, USC	1967-68	3124	164.4
3 Herschel Walker, Georgia	1980-82	5259	159.4
4 LeShon Johnson, No. Ill.	1992-93	3314	150.6
5 Marshall Faulk, S. Diego St.	1991-93	4589	148.0

Total Offense

Yards Gained	Years	Yards
1 Ty Detmer, BYU	1988-91	14,665
2 Doug Flutie, Boston College	1981-84	11,317
3 Eric Zeier, Georgia	1991-94	10,841
4 Alex Van Pelt, Pittsburgh	1989-92	10,814
5 Stoney Case, New Mexico	1991-94	10,651

Yards Per Game	Years	Yards	P/Gm
1 Chris Vargas, Nevada	1992-93	6,417	320.9
2 Ty Detmer, BYU	1988-91	14,665	318.8
3 Mike Perez, San Jose St	1986-87	6,182	309.1
4 Doug Gaynor, L. Beach St	1984-85	6,710	305.0
5 Tony Eason, Illinois	1981-82	6,589	299.5

All-Purpose Yardage

Yards Gained	Years	Yards
1 Napoleon McCallum, Navy	1981-85	7172
2 Darrin Nelson, Stanford	1977-78,80-81	6885
3 Terance Mathis, N. Mexico	1985-87,89	6691
4 Tony Dorsett, Pittsburgh	1973-76	6615
5 Paul Palmer, Temple	1983-86	6609

Yards Per Game	Years	Yards	P/Gm
1 Ryan Benjamin, Pacific	1990-92	5706	237.8
2 Sheldon Canley, S. Jose St.	1988-90	5146	205.8
3 Howard Stevens, Louisville	1971-72	3873	193.7
4 O.J. Simpson, USC	1967-68	3666	192.9
5 Ed Marinaro, Cornell	1969-71	4940	183.0

Miscellaneous

Interceptions	Years	No
1 Al Brosky, Illinois	1950-52	29
2 John Provost, Holy Cross	1972-74	27
Martin Bayless, Bowling Green	1980-83	27
4 Tom Curtis, Michigan	1967-69	25
Tony Thurman, Boston College	1981-84	25
Tracy Saul, Texas Tech	1989-92	25

Punting Average*	Years	Avg
1 Todd Sauerbrun, West Va.	1991-94	46.3
2 Reggie Roby, Iowa	1979-82	45.6
3 Greg Montgomery, Mich. St	1985-87	45.4
4 Tom Tupa, Ohio St.	1984-87	45.2
5 Barry Helton, Colorado	1984-87	44.9

*At least 150 punts kicked.

Punt Return Average*	Years	Avg
1 Jack Mitchell, Oklahoma	1946-48	23.6
2 Gene Gibson, Cincinnati	1949-50	20.5
3 Eddie Macon, Pacific	1949-51	18.9
4 Jackie Robinson, UCLA	1939-40	18.8
5 Two tied at 17.7 each.		

*Minimum 1.2 punt returns per game and 30 career returns.

Kickoff Return Average*	Years	Avg
1 Anthony Davis, USC	1972-74	35.1
2 Overton Curtis, Utah St	1957-58	31.0
3 Fred Montgomery, New Mexico St.	1991-92	30.5
4 Altie Taylor, Utah St.	1966-68	29.3
5 Two tied at 28.8 each.		

*Minimum 1.2 kickoff returns per game and 30 career returns.

All-Time NCAA Division I-A Leaders (Cont.)

Scoring

NON-KICKERS

Points	Years	TD	Xpt	FG	Pts
1 Anthony Thompson, Ind	1986-89	65	4	0	394
2 Marshall Faulk, S.D. St.	1991-93	62	4	0	376
3 Tony Dorsett, Pittsburgh	1973-76	59	2	0	356
4 Glenn Davis, Army	1943-46	59	0	0	354
5 Art Luppino, Arizona	1953-56	48	49	0	337

Points Per Game	Years	Pts	P/Gm
1 Marshall Faulk, S.Diego St.	1991-93	376	12.1
2 Ed Marinaro, Cornell	1969-71	318	11.8
3 Bill Burnett, Arkansas	1968-70	294	11.3
4 Steve Owens, Oklahoma	1967-69	336	11.2
5 Eddie Talboom, Wyoming	1948-50	303	10.8

Touchdowns Rushing	Years	No
1 Anthony Thompson, Indiana	1986-89	64
2 Marshall Faulk, S.Diego St.	1991-93	57
3 Steve Owens, Oklahoma	1967-69	56
4 Tony Dorsett, Pittsburgh	1973-76	55
5 Ed Marinaro, Cornell	1969-71	50

Touchdowns Passing	Years	No
1 Ty Detmer, BYU	1988-91	121
2 David Klingler, Houston	1988-91	91
3 Troy Kopp, Pacific	1989-92	87
4 Jim McMahon, BYU	1977-78,80-81	84
5 Joe Adams, Tenn. St	1977-80	81

Touchdown Catches	Years	No
1 Aaron Turner, Pacific	1989-92	43
2 Ryan Yarborough, Wyoming	1990-93	42
3 Clarkston Hines, Duke	1986-89	38
4 Terance Mathis, N. Mexico	1985-87,89	36
5 Elmo Wright, Houston	1968-70	34

KICKERS

Points	Years	FG	XP	Pts
1 Roman Anderson, Hou	1988-91	70	213	423
2 Carlos Huerta, Mia-FL	1988-91	73	178	397
3 J. Elam, Hawaii	1988-89, 91-92	79	158	395
4 Derek Schmidt, Fla. St	1984-87	73	174	393
5 Luis Zendejas, Ariz. St	1981-84	78	134	368
6 Jeff Jaeger, Wash	1983-86	80	118	358
7 John Lee, UCLA	1982-85	79	116	353
Max Zendejas, Arizona	1982-85	77	122	353
Kevin Butler, Georgia	1981-84	77	122	353
10 D. Mahoney, Fresno St	1990-93	45	216	351

Field Goals	Years	No
1 Jeff Jaeger, Washington	1983-86	80
2 John Lee, UCLA	1982-85	79
Jason Elam, Hawaii	1988-89, 91-92	79
4 Philip Doyle, Alabama	1987-90	78
Luis Zendejas, Arizona St	1981-84	78

SINGLE SEASON

Rushing

Yards Gained	Year	Gm	Car	Yards
Barry Sanders, Okla. St	1988	11	344	2628
Marcus Allen, USC	1981	11	403	2342
Mike Rozier, Nebraska	1983	12	275	2148
Rashaan Salaam, Colorado	1994	11	298	2055

Yards Per Game	Year	Gm	Yards	P/Gm
Barry Sanders, Okla. St	1988	11	2628	238.9
Marcus Allen, USC	1981	11	2342	212.9
Ed Marinaro, Cornell	1971	9	1881	209.0
Rashaan Salaam, Colorado	1994	11	2055	186.8

Total Offense

Yards Gained	Year	Gm	Plays	Yards
David Klingler, Houston	1990	11	704	5221
Ty Detmer, BYU	1990	12	635	5022
Andre Ware, Houston	1989	11	628	4661
Jim McMahon, BYU	1980	12	540	4627

Yards Per Game	Year	Gm	Yards	P/Gm
David Klingler, Houston	1990	11	5221	474.6
Andre Ware, Houston	1989	11	4661	423.7
Ty Detmer, BYU	1990	12	5022	418.5
Mike Maxwell, Nevada	1995	9	3623	402.6

All-Purpose Yardage

Yards Gained	Year	Yards
Barry Sanders, Okla. St	1988	3250
Ryan Benjamin, Pacific	1991	2995
Mike Pringle, CS-Fullerton	1989	2690
Paul Palmer, Temple	1986	2633

Yards Per Game	Year	Yards	P/Gm
Barry Sanders, Okla. St	1988	3250	295.5
Ryan Benjamin, Pacific	1991	2995	249.6
Byron (Whizzer) White, Colo	1937	1970	246.3
Mike Pringle, CS-Fullerton	1989	2690	244.6

Passing

(Minimum 15 Attempts Per Game)

Passing Efficiency	Year	Rating
Danny Wuerffel, Florida	1995	178.4
Jim McMahon, BYU	1980	176.9
Ty Detmer, BYU	1989	175.6
Trent Dilfer, Fresno St.	1993	173.1

Yards Gained	Year	Yards
Ty Detmer, BYU	1990	5188
David Klingler, Houston	1990	5140
Andre Ware, Houston	1989	4699
Jim McMahon, BYU	1980	4571

Completions	Year	Att	No
David Klingler, Houston	1990	643	374
Andre Ware, Houston	1989	578	365
Ty Detmer, BYU	1990	562	361
Robbie Bosco, BYU	1985	511	338

Receptions

Catches	Year	Gm	No
Manny Hazard, Houston	1989	11	142
Howard Twilley, Tulsa	1965	10	134
Alex Van Dyke, Nevada	1995	11	129
Jason Phillips, Houston	1988	11	108

Catches Per Game	Year	No	P/Gm
Howard Twilley, Tulsa	1965	134	13.4
Manny Hazard, Houston	1989	142	12.9
Alex Van Dyke, Nevada	1995	129	11.7
Jason Phillips, Houston	1988	108	9.8

Yards Gained	Year	No	Yards
Alex Van Dyke, Nevada	1995	129	1854
Howard Twilley, Tulsa	1965	134	1779
Manny Hazard, Houston	1989	142	1689
Aaron Turner, Pacific	1991	92	1604

Scoring

Points	Year	TD	Xpt	FG	Pts
Barry Sanders, Okla. St	1988	39	0	0	234
Mike Rozier, Nebraska	1983	29	0	0	174
Lydell Mitchell, Penn St	1971	29	0	0	174
Art Luppino, Arizona	1954	24	22	0	166

Points Per Game	Year	Pts	P/Gm
Barry Sanders, Okla. St	1988	234	21.3
Bobby Reynolds, Nebraska	1950	157	17.4
Art Luppino, Arizona	1954	166	16.6
Ed Marinaro, Cornell	1971	148	16.4

Touchdowns Rushing	Year	No
Barry Sanders, Okla. St	1988	37
Mike Rozier, Nebraska	1983	29
Ed Marinaro, Cornell	1971	24
Anthony Thompson, Indiana	1988	24
Anthony Thompson, Indiana	1989	24
Rashaan Salaam, Colorado	1994	24

Touchdowns Passing	Year	No
David Klingler, Houston	1990	54
Jim McMahon, BYU	1980	47
Andre Ware, Houston	1989	46
Ty Detmer, BYU	1990	41

Touchdown Catches	Year	No
Manny Hazard, Houston	1989	22
Desmond Howard, Michigan	1991	19
Tom Reynolds, San Diego St	1969	18
Dennis Smith, Utah	1989	18
Aaron Turner, Pacific	1991	18

Field Goals	Year	No
John Lee, UCLA	1984	29
Paul Woodside, West Virginia	1982	28
Luis Zendejas, Arizona St	1983	28
Fuad Reveiz, Tennessee	1982	27

Three tied with 25 each.

Miscellaneous

Interceptions	Year	No
Al Worley, Washington	1968	14
George Shaw, Oregon	1951	13

Eight tied with 12 each.

Punting Average	Year	Avg
Reggie Roby, Iowa	1981	49.8
Kirk Wilson, UCLA	1956	49.3
Todd Sauerbrun, West Virgina	1984	48.4
Zack Jordan, Colorado	1950	48.2
Ricky Anderson, Vanderbilt	1984	48.2

Punt Return Average*	Year	Avg
Bill Blackstock, Tennessee	1951	25.9
George Sims, Baylor	1948	25.0
Gene Derricotte, Michigan	1947	24.8

*At least 1.2 returns per game.

Kickoff Return Average*	Year	Avg
Paul Allen, BYU	1961	40.1
Leeland McElroy, Texas A&M	1993	39.3
Forrest Hall, San Francisco	1946	38.2

*At least 1.2 kickoff returns per game.

SINGLE GAME

Rushing

Yards Gained	Opponent	Year	Yds
Tony Sands, Kansas	Missouri	1991	396
Marshall Faulk, San Diego St	Pacific	1991	386
Anthony Thompson, Indiana	Wisconsin	1989	377
Rueben Mayes, Wash St.	Oregon	1984	357
Mike Pringle, CS-Fullerton	N. Mex. St.	1989	357

Passing

Yards Gained	Opponent	Year	Yds
David Klingler, Houston	Arizona St.	1990	716
Matt Vogler, TCU	Houston	1990	690
Scott Mitchell, Utah	Air Force	1988	631
Jeremy Leach, New Mexico	Utah	1989	622
Dave Wilson, Illinois	Ohio St.	1980	621

Completions	Opponent	Year	No
Rusty LaRue, Wake Forest	Duke	1995	55
David Klingler, Houston	SMU	1990	48
Jimmy Klingler, Houston	Rice	1992	46
Sandy Schwab, Northwestern	Michigan	1982	45

Total Offense

Yards Gained	Opponent	Year	Yds
David Klingler, Houston	Arizona St.	1990	732
Matt Vogler, TCU	Houston	1990	696
David Klingler, Houston	TCU	1990	625
Scott Mitchell, Utah	Air Force	1988	625
Jimmy Klingler, Houston	Rice	1992	612

Receptions

Catches	Opponent	Year	No
Randy Gatewood, UNLV	Idaho	1994	23
Miller, BYU	New Mexico	1973	22
Rick Eber, Tulsa	Idaho St.	1967	20

Four tied with 19 each.

Yards Gained	Opponent	Year	Yds
Randy Gatewood, UNLV	Idaho	1994	363
Chuck Hughes, UTEP*	N. Texas St.	1965	349
Rick Eber, Tulsa	Idaho St.	1967	322
Harry Wood, Tulsa	Idaho St.	1967	318

*UTEP was Texas Western in 1965.

Longest Plays (since 1941)

Rushing	Opponent	Year	Yds
Gale Sayers, Kansas	Nebraska	1963	99
Max Anderson, Ariz. St.	Wyoming	1967	99
Ralph Thompson, W. Texas St	Wich. St.	1970	99
Kelsey Finch, Tennessee	Florida	1977	99

Eleven tied at 98 each.

Passing	Opponent	Year	Yds
Fred Owens to Jack Ford, Portland	St. Mary's	1947	99
Bo Burris to Warren McVea, Houston	Wash. St.	1966	99
Colin Clapton to Eddie Jenkins, Holy Cross	Boston U.	1970	99
Terry Peel to Robert Ford, Houston	Syracuse	1970	99
Terry Peel to Robert Ford, Houston	S. Diego St.	1972	99
Cris Collinsworth to Derrick Gaffney, Florida	Rice	1977	99
Scott Ankrom to James Maness, TCU	Rice	1984	99
Gino Torretta to Horace Copeland, Miami-FL	Ark.	1991	99
John Paci to Thomas Lewis, Indiana	Penn St.	1993	99

Field Goals	Opponent	Year	Yds
Steve Little, Arkansas	Texas	1977	67
Russell Erxleben, Texas	Rice	1977	67
Joe Williams, Wichita St	So. Ill.	1978	67

All-Time NCAA Division I-A Leaders (Cont.)

Scoring

Points	Opponent	Year	Pts
Howard Griffith, Illinois	So. Ill.	1990	48
Marshall Faulk, S. Diego St.	Pacific	1991	44
Jim Brown, Syracuse	Colgate	1956	43
Showboat Boykin, Ole Miss	Miss. St.	1951	42
Fred Wendt, UTEP*	N. Mex. St.	1948	42

*UTEP was Texas Mines in 1948.

Touchdowns Rushing	Opponent	Year	No
Howard Griffith, Illinois	So. Ill	1990	8
Showboat Boykin, Ole Miss	Miss. St.	1951	7

Note: Griffith's TD runs (5-51-7-41-5-18-5-3).

Touchdowns Passing	Opponent	Year	No
David Klingler, Houston	E. Wash.	1990	11
Dennis Shaw, S. Diego St	N. Mex. St.	1969	9

Note: Klingler's TD passes (5-48-29-7-3-7-40-8-7-8-51).

Touchdown Catches	Opponent	Year	No
Tim Delaney, S. Diego St	N. Mex. St.	1969	6

Note: Delaney's TD catches (2-22-34-31-30-9).

Field Goals	Opponent	Year	No
Dale Klein, Nebraska	Missouri	1985	7
Mike Prindle, W. Mich	Marshall	1984	7

Note: Klein's FGs (32-22-43-44-29-43-43); Prindle's FGs (32-44-42-23-48-41-27).

Extra Points (Kick)	Opponent	Year	No
Terry Leiweke, Houston	Tulsa	1968	13
Derek Mahoney, Fresno St	New Mexico	1991	13

Annual Awards

Heisman Trophy

Originally presented in 1935 as the DAC Trophy by the Downtown Athletic Club of New York City to the best college football player east of the Mississippi. In 1936, players across the country were eligible and the award was renamed the Heisman Trophy following the death of former college coach and DAC athletic director John W. Heisman.

Multiple winner: Archie Griffin (2).

Winners in junior year (12): Doc Blanchard (1945), Ty Detmer (1990); Archie Griffin (1974), Desmond Howard (1991), Vic Janowicz (1950), Rashaan Salaam (1994), Barry Sanders (1988), Billy Sims (1978), Roger Staubach (1963), Doak Walker (1948), Herschel Walker (1982), Andre Ware (1989).

Winners on AP national champions (8): Angelo Bertelli (Notre Dame, 1943); Doc Blanchard (Army, 1945); Tony Dorsett (Pittsburgh, 1976); Leon Hart (Notre Dame, 1949); Johnny Lujack (Notre Dame, 1947); Davey O'Brien (TCU, 1938); Bruce Smith (Minnesota, 1941); Charlie Ward (Florida St., 1993).

Year		Points
1935	**Jay Berwanger,** Chicago, HB	84
	2nd—Monk Meyer, Army, HB	29
	3rd—Bill Shakespeare, Notre Dame, HB	23
	4th—Pepper Constable, Princeton, FB	20
1936	**Larry Kelley,** Yale, E	219
	2nd—Sam Francis, Nebraska, FB	47
	3rd—Ray Buivid, Marquette, HB	43
	4th—Sammy Baugh, TCU, HB	39
1937	**Clint Frank,** Yale, HB	524
	2nd—Byron (Whizzer) White, Colo., HB	264
	3rd—Marshall Goldberg, Pitt, HB	211
	4th—Alex Wojciechowicz, Fordham, C	85
1938	**Davey O'Brien,** TCU, QB	519
	2nd—Marshall Goldberg, Pitt, HB	294
	3rd—Sid Luckman, Columbia, QB	154
	4th—Bob MacLeod, Dartmouth, HB	78
1939	**Nile Kinnick,** Iowa, HB	651
	2nd—Tom Harmon, Michigan, HB	405
	3rd—Paul Christman, Missouri, QB	391
	4th—George Cafego, Tennessee, QB	296
1940	**Tom Harmon,** Michigan, HB	1303
	2nd—John Kimbrough, Texas A&M, FB	841
	3rd—George Franck, Minnesota, HB	102
	4th—Frankie Albert, Stanford, QB	90
1941	**Bruce Smith,** Minnesota, HB	554
	2nd—Angelo Bertelli, N.Dame, QB	345
	3rd—Frankie Albert, Stanford, QB	336
	4th—Frank Sinkwich, Georgia, HB	249
1942	**Frank Sinkwich,** Georgia, TB	1059
	2nd—Paul Governali, Columbia, QB	218
	3rd—Clint Castleberry, Ga.Tech, HB	99
	4th—Mike Holovak, Boston College, FB	95
1943	**Angelo Bertelli,** Notre Dame, QB	648
	2nd—Bob Odell, Penn, HB	177
	3rd—Otto Graham, Northwestern, QB	140
	4th—Creighton Miller, Notre Dame, HB	134
1944	**Les Horvath,** Ohio St., TB-QB	412
	2nd—Glenn Davis, Army, HB	287
	3rd—Doc Blanchard, Army, FB	237
	4th—Don Whitmire, Navy, T	115
1945	**Doc Blanchard,** Army, FB	860
	2nd—Glenn Davis, Army, HB	638
	3rd—Bob Fenimore, Oklahoma A&M, HB	187
	4th—Herman Wedemeyer, St. Mary's, HB	152
1946	**Glenn Davis,** Army, HB	792
	2nd—Charlie Trippi, Georgia, HB	435
	3rd—Johnny Lujack, Notre Dame, QB	379
	4th—Doc Blanchard, Army, FB	267
1947	**Johnny Lujack,** Notre Dame, QB	742
	2nd—Bob Chappuis, Michigan, HB	555
	3rd—Doak Walker, SMU, HB	196
	4th—Charlie Conerly, Mississippi, QB	186
1948	**Doak Walker,** SMU, HB	778
	2nd—Charlie Justice, N. Carolina, HB	443
	3rd—Chuck Bednarik, Penn, C	336
	4th—Jackie Jensen, California, HB	143
1949	**Leon Hart,** Notre Dame, E	995
	2nd—Charlie Justice, N. Carolina, HB	272
	3rd—Doak Walker, SMU, HB	229
	4th—Arnold Galiffa, Army QB	196
1950	**Vic Janowicz,** Ohio St., HB	633
	2nd—Kyle Rote, SMU, HB	280
	3rd—Reds Bagnell, Penn, HB	231
	4th—Babe Parilli, Kentucky, QB	214
1951	**Dick Kazmaier,** Princeton, TB	1777
	2nd—Hank Lauricella, Tennessee, HB	424
	3rd—Babe Parilli, Kentucky, QB	344
	4th—Bill McColl, Stanford, E	313
1952	**Billy Vessels,** Oklahoma, HB	525
	2nd—Jack Scarbath, Maryland, QB	367
	3rd—Paul Giel, Minnesota, HB	329
	4th—Donn Moomaw, UCLA, C	257
1953	**Johnny Lattner,** Notre Dame, HB	1850
	2nd—Paul Giel, Minnesota, HB	1794
	3rd—Paul Cameron, UCLA, HB	444
	4th—Bernie Faloney, Maryland, QB	258
1954	**Alan Ameche,** Wisconsin, FB	1068
	2nd—Kurt Burris, Oklahoma, C	838
	3rd—Howard Cassady, Ohio St., HB	810
	4th—Ralph Guglielmi, Notre Dame, QB	691

Annual Awards (Cont.)

Heisman Trophy

Year		Points
1955	**Howard Cassady,** Ohio St., HB	2219
	2nd—Jim Swink, TCU, HB	742
	3rd—George Welsh, Navy, QB	383
	4th—Earl Morrall, Michigan St., QB	323
1956	**Paul Hornung,** Notre Dame, QB	1066
	2nd—Johnny Majors, Tennessee, HB	994
	3rd—Tommy McDonald, Oklahoma, HB	973
	4th—Jerry Tubbs, Oklahoma, C	724
1957	**John David Crow,** Texas A&M, HB	1183
	2nd—Alex Karras, Iowa, T	693
	3rd—Walt Kowalczyk, Mich. St., HB	630
	4th—Lou Michaels, Kentucky, T	330
1958	**Pete Dawkins,** Army, HB	1394
	2nd—Randy Duncan, Iowa, QB	1021
	3rd—Billy Cannon, LSU, HB	975
	4th—Bob White, Ohio St., HB	365
1959	**Billy Cannon,** LSU, HB	1929
	2nd—Richie Lucas, Penn St., QB	613
	3rd—Don Meredith, SMU, QB	286
	4th—Bill Burrell, Illinois, G	196
1960	**Joe Bellino,** Navy, HB	1793
	2nd—Tom Brown, Minnesota, G	731
	3rd—Jake Gibbs, Mississippi, QB	453
	4th—Ed Dyas, Auburn, HB	319
1961	**Ernie Davis,** Syracuse, HB	824
	2nd—Bob Ferguson, Ohio St., HB	771
	3rd—Jimmy Saxton, Texas, HB	551
	4th—Sandy Stephens, Minnesota, QB	543
1962	**Terry Baker,** Oregon St., QB	707
	2nd—Jerry Stovall, LSU, HB	618
	3rd—Bobby Bell, Minnesota, T	429
	4th—Lee Roy Jordan, Alabama, C	321
1963	**Roger Staubach,** Navy, QB	1860
	2nd—Billy Lothridge, Ga.Tech, QB	504
	3rd—Sherman Lewis, Mich. St., HB	369
	4th—Don Trull, Baylor, QB	253
1964	**John Huarte,** Notre Dame, QB	1026
	2nd—Jerry Rhome, Tulsa, QB	952
	3rd—Dick Butkus, Illinois, C	505
	4th—Bob Timberlake, Michigan, QB	361
1965	**Mike Garrett,** USC, HB	926
	2nd—Howard Twilley, Tulsa, E	528
	3rd—Jim Grabowski, Illinois, FB	481
	4th—Donny Anderson, Texas Tech, HB	408
1966	**Steve Spurrier,** Florida, QB	1679
	2nd—Bob Griese, Purdue, QB	816
	3rd—Nick Eddy, Notre Dame, HB	456
	4th—Gary Beban, UCLA, QB	318
1967	**Gary Beban,** UCLA, QB	1968
	2nd—O.J. Simpson, USC, HB	1722
	3rd—Leroy Keyes, Purdue, HB	1366
	4th—Larry Csonka, Syracuse, FB	136
1968	**O.J. Simpson,** USC, HB	2853
	2nd—Leroy Keyes, Purdue, HB	1103
	3rd—Terry Hanratty, Notre Dame, QB	387
	4th—Ted Kwalick, Penn St., TE	254
1969	**Steve Owens,** Oklahoma, HB	1488
	2nd—Mike Phipps, Purdue, QB	1344
	3rd—Rex Kern, Ohio St., QB	856
	4th—Archie Manning, Mississippi, QB	582
1970	**Jim Plunkett,** Stanford, QB	2229
	2nd—Joe Theismann, Notre Dame, QB	1410
	3rd—Archie Manning, Mississippi, QB	849
	4th—Steve Worster, Texas, RB	398
1971	**Pat Sullivan,** Auburn, QB	1597
	2nd—Ed Marinaro, Cornell, RB	1445
	3rd—Greg Pruitt, Oklahoma, RB	586
	4th—Johnny Musso, Alabama, RB	365

Year		Points
1972	**Johnny Rodgers,** Nebraska, FL	1310
	2nd—Greg Pruitt, Oklahoma, RB	966
	3rd—Rich Glover, Nebraska, MG	652
	4th—Bert Jones, LSU, QB	351
1973	**John Cappelletti,** Penn St., RB	1057
	2nd—John Hicks, Ohio St., OT	524
	3rd—Roosevelt Leaks, Texas, RB	482
	4th—David Jaynes, Kansas, QB	394
1974	**Archie Griffin,** Ohio St., RB	1920
	2nd—Anthony Davis, USC, RB	819
	3rd—Joe Washington, Oklahoma, RB	661
	4th—Tom Clements, Notre Dame, QB	244
1975	**Archie Griffin,** Ohio St., RB	1800
	2nd—Chuck Muncie, California, RB	730
	3rd—Ricky Bell, USC, RB	708
	4th—Tony Dorsett, Pitt, RB	616
1976	**Tony Dorsett,** Pittsburgh, RB	2357
	2nd—Ricky Bell, USC, RB	1346
	3rd—Rob Lytle, Michigan, RB	413
	4th—Terry Miller, Oklahoma St., RB	197
1977	**Earl Campbell,** Texas, RB	1547
	2nd—Terry Miller, Oklahoma St., RB	812
	3rd—Ken MacAfee, Notre Dame, TE	343
	4th—Doug Williams, Grambling, QB	266
1978	**Billy Sims,** Oklahoma, RB	827
	2nd—Chuck Fusina, Penn St., QB	750
	3rd—Rick Leach, Michigan, QB	435
	4th—Charles White, USC, RB	354
1979	**Charles White,** USC, RB	1695
	2nd—Billy Sims, Oklahoma, RB	773
	3rd—Marc Wilson, BYU, QB	589
	4th—Art Schlichter, Ohio St., QB	251
1980	**George Rogers,** South Carolina, RB	1128
	2nd—Hugh Green, Pittsburgh, DE	861
	3rd—Herschel Walker, Georgia, RB	683
	4th—Mark Herrmann, Purdue, QB	405
1981	**Marcus Allen,** USC, RB	1797
	2nd—Herschel Walker, Georgia, RB	1199
	3rd—Jim McMahon, BYU, QB	706
	4th—Dan Marino, Pitt, QB	256
1982	**Herschel Walker,** Georgia, RB	1926
	2nd—John Elway, Stanford, QB	1231
	3rd—Eric Dickerson, SMU, RB	465
	4th—Anthony Carter, Michigan, WR	142
1983	**Mike Rozier,** Nebraska, RB	1801
	2nd—Steve Young, BYU, QB	1172
	3rd—Doug Flutie, Boston College, QB	253
	4th—Turner Gill, Nebraska, QB	190
1984	**Doug Flutie,** Boston College, QB	2240
	2nd—Keith Byers, Ohio St., RB	1251
	3rd—Robbie Bosco, BYU, QB	443
	4th—Bernie Kosar, Miami-FL, QB	320
1985	**Bo Jackson,** Auburn, RB	1509
	2nd—Chuck Long, Iowa, QB	1464
	3rd—Robbie Bosco, BYU, QB	459
	4th—Lorenzo White, Michigan St., RB	391
1986	**Vinny Testaverde,** Miami-FL, QB	2213
	2nd—Paul Palmer, Temple, RB	672
	3rd—Jim Harbaugh, Michigan, QB	458
	4th—Brian Bosworth, Oklahoma, LB	395
1987	**Tim Brown,** Notre Dame, WR	1442
	2nd—Don McPherson, Syracuse, QB	831
	3rd—Gordie Lockbaum, Holy Cross, WR-DB	657
	4th—Lorenzo White, Michigan St., RB	632
1988	**Barry Sanders,** Oklahoma St., RB	1878
	2nd—Rodney Peete, USC, QB	912
	3rd—Troy Aikman, UCLA, QB	582
	4th—Steve Walsh, Miami-FL, QB	341

Annual Awards (Cont.)

Year		Points
1989	**Andre Ware,** Houston, QB	1073
	2nd—Anthony Thompson, Ind., RB	1003
	3rd—Major Harris, West Va., QB	709
	4th—Tony Rice, Notre Dame, QB	523
1990	**Ty Detmer,** BYU, QB	1482
	2nd—Rocket Ismail, Notre Dame, FL	1177
	3rd—Eric Bieniemy, Colorado, RB	798
	4th—Shawn Moore, Virginia, QB	465
1991	**Desmond Howard,** Michigan, WR	2077
	2nd—Casey Weldon, Florida St., QB	503
	3rd—Ty Detmer, BYU, QB	445
	4th—Steve Emtman, Washington, DT	357
1992	**Gino Torretta,** Miami-FL, QB	1400
	2nd—Marshall Faulk, S. Diego St., RB	1080
	3rd—Garrison Hearst, Georgia, RB	982
	4th—Marvin Jones, Florida St., LB	392
1993	**Charlie Ward,** Florida St., QB	2310
	2nd—Heath Shuler, Tennessee, QB	688
	3rd—David Palmer, Alabama, RB	292
	4th—Marshall Faulk, S. Diego St., RB	250
1994	**Rashaan Salaam,** Colorado, RB	1743
	2nd—Ki-Jana Carter, Penn St., RB	901
	3rd—Steve McNair, Alcorn St., QB	655
	4th—Kerry Collins, Penn St., QB	639
1995	**Eddie George**, Ohio St., RB	1460
	2nd—Tommie Frazier, Nebraska, QB	1196
	3rd—Danny Wuerffel, Florida, QB	987
	4th—Darnell Autry, Northwestern, RB	535

Maxwell Award

First presented in 1937 by the Maxwell Memorial Football Club of Philadelphia, the award is named after Robert (Tiny) Maxwell, a Philadelphia native who was a standout lineman at the University of Chicago at the turn of the century. Like the Heisman, the Maxwell is given to the outstanding college player in the nation. Both awards have gone to the same player in the same season 31 times. Those players are preceded by (#). Glenn Davis of Army and Doak Walker of SMU won both but in different years.

Multiple winner: Johnny Lattner (2).

Year
1937 #Clint Frank, Yale, HB
1938 #Davey O'Brien, TCU, QB
1939 #Nile Kinnick, Iowa, HB

1940 #Tom Harmon, Michigan, HB
1941 Bill Dudley, Virginia, HB
1942 Paul Governali, Columbia, QB
1943 Bob Odell, Penn, HB
1944 Glenn Davis, Army, HB
1945 #Doc Blanchard, Army, FB
1946 Charley Trippi, Georgia, HB
1947 Doak Walker, SMU, HB
1948 Chuck Bednarik, Penn, C
1949 #Leon Hart, Notre Dame, E

1950 Reds Bagnell, Penn, HB
1951 #Dick Kazmaier, Princeton, TB
1952 Johnny Lattner, Notre Dame, HB
1953 #Johnny Lattner, N. Dame, HB
1954 Ron Beagle, Navy, E
1955 #Howard Cassady, Ohio St., HB
1956 Tommy McDonald, Okla., HB

Year
1957 Bob Reifsnyder, Navy, T
1958 #Pete Dawkins, Army, HB
1959 Rich Lucas, Penn St., QB

1960 #Joe Bellino, Navy, HB
1961 Bob Ferguson, Ohio St., HB
1962 #Terry Baker, Oregon St., QB
1963 #Roger Staubach, Navy, QB
1964 Glenn Ressler, Penn St., G
1965 Tommy Nobis, Texas, LB
1966 Jim Lynch, Notre Dame, LB
1967 #Gary Beban, UCLA, QB
1968 #O.J. Simpson, USC, HB
1969 Mike Reid, Penn St., DT

1970 #Jim Plunkett, Stanford, QB
1971 Ed Marinaro, Cornell, RB
1972 Brad Van Pelt, Michigan St., DB
1973 #John Cappelletti, Penn St., RB
1974 Steve Joachim, Temple, QB
1975 #Archie Griffin, Ohio St., RB
1976 #Tony Dorsett, Pitt, RB

Year
1977 Ross Browner, Notre Dame, DE
1978 Chuck Fusina, Penn St., QB
1979 #Charles White, USC, RB

1980 Hugh Green, Pitt, DE
1981 #Marcus Allen, USC, RB
1982 #Herschel Walker, Georgia, RB
1983 #Mike Rozier, Nebraska, RB
1984 #Doug Flutie, Boston Col., QB
1985 Chuck Long, Iowa, QB
1986 #V. Testaverde, Miami-FL, QB
1987 Don McPherson, Syracuse, QB
1988 #Barry Sanders, Okla. St., RB
1989 Anthony Thompson, Indiana, RB

1990 #Ty Detmer, BYU, QB
1991 #Desmond Howard, Mich., WR
1992 #Gino Torretta, Miami-FL, QB
1993 #Charlie Ward, Florida St., QB
1994 Kerry Collins, Penn St., QB
1995 #Eddie George, Ohio St., RB

Outland Trophy

First presented in 1946 by the Football Writers Association of America, honoring the the nation's outstanding interior lineman. The award is named after its benefactor, Dr. John H. Outland (Kansas, Class of 1898). Players listed in **bold** type helped lead their team to a national championship (according to AP).

Multiple winner: Dave Rimington (2). **Winners in junior year:** Ross Browner (1976), Steve Emtman (1991) and Rimington (1981).

Year
1946 **George Connor,** N. Dame, T
1947 Joe Steffy, Army, G
1948 Bill Fischer, Notre Dame, G
1949 Ed Bagdon, Michigan St., G

1950 Bob Gain, Kentucky, T
1951 Jim Weatherall, Oklahoma, T
1952 Dick Modzelewski, Maryland, T
1953 J.D. Roberts, Oklahoma, G
1954 Bill Brooks, Arkansas, G
1955 Calvin Jones, Iowa, G
1956 Jim Parker, Ohio St., G
1957 Alex Karras, Iowa, T
1958 Zeke Smith, Auburn, G
1959 Mike McGee, Duke, T

1960 **Tom Brown,** Minnesota, G
1961 Merlin Olsen, Utah St., T
1962 Bobby Bell, Minnesota, T

Year
1963 **Scott Appleton,** Texas, T
1964 Steve DeLong, Tennessee, T
1965 Tommy Nobis, Texas, G
1966 Loyd Phillips, Arkansas, T
1967 **Ron Yary,** USC, T
1968 Bill Stanfill, Georgia, T
1969 Mike Reid, Penn St., DT

1970 Jim Stillwagon, Ohio St., MG
1971 **Larry Jacobson,** Neb., DT
1972 Rich Glover, Nebraska, MG
1973 John Hicks, Ohio St., OT
1974 Randy White, Maryland, DT
1975 **Lee Roy Selmon,** Okla., DT
1976 Ross Browner, Notre Dame, DE
1977 Brad Shearer, Texas, DT
1978 Greg Roberts, Oklahoma, G
1979 Jim Richter, N.C. State, C

Year
1980 Mark May, Pittsburgh, OT
1981 Dave Rimington, Nebraska, C
1982 Dave Rimington, Nebraska, C
1983 Dean Steinkuhler, Nebraska, G
1984 Bruce Smith, Virginia Tech, DT
1985 Mike Ruth, Boston College, NG
1986 Jason Buck, BYU, DT
1987 Chad Hennings, Air Force, DT
1988 Tracy Rocker, Auburn, DT
1989 Mohammed Elewonibi, BYU, G

1990 Russell Maryland, Miami-FL, NT
1991 Steve Emtman, Washington, DT
1992 Will Shields, Nebraska, G
1993 Rob Waldrop, Arizona, NG
1994 **Zach Wiegert**, Nebraska, OT
1995 Jonathan Ogden, UCLA, OT

Butkus Award

First presented in 1985 by the Downtown Athletic Club of Orlando, Fla., to honor the nation's outstanding linebacker. The award is named after Dick Butkus, two-time consensus All-America at Illinois and six-time All-Pro with the Chicago Bears.

Multiple winner: Brian Bosworth (2).

Year
1985 Brian Bosworth, Oklahoma
1986 Brian Bosworth, Oklahoma
1987 Paul McGowan, Florida St.
1988 Derrick Thomas, Alabama

Year
1989 Percy Snow, Michigan St.
1990 Alfred Williams, Colorado
1991 Erick Anderson, Michigan
1992 Marvin Jones, Florida St.

Year
1993 Trev Alberts, Nebraska
1994 Dana Howard, Illinois
1995 Kevin Hardy, Illinois

Lombardi Award

First presented in 1970 by the Rotary Club of Houston, honoring the nation's best lineman. The award is named after pro football coach Vince Lombardi, who, as a guard, was a member of the famous "Seven Blocks of Granite" at Fordham in the 1930s. The Lombardi and Outland awards have gone to the same player in the same year nine times. Those players are preceded by (#). Ross Browner of Notre Dame won both, but in different years.

Year
1970 #Jim Stillwagon, Ohio St., MG
1971 Walt Patulski, Notre Dame, DE
1972 #Rich Glover, Nebraska, MG
1973 #John Hicks, Ohio St., OT
1974 #Randy White, Maryland, DT
1975 #Lee Roy Selmon, Okla., DT
1976 Wilson Whitley, Houston, DT
1977 Ross Browner, Notre Dame, DE
1978 Bruce Clark, Penn St., DT

Year
1979 Brad Budde, USC, G
1980 Hugh Green, Pitt, DE
1981 Kenneth Sims, Texas, DT
1982 #Dave Rimington, Neb., C
1983 #Dean Steinkuhler, Neb., G
1984 Tony Degrate, Texas, DT
1985 Tony Casillas, Oklahoma, NG
1986 Cornelius Bennett, Alabama, LB
1987 Chris Spielman, Ohio St., LB

Year
1988 #Tracy Rocker, Auburn, DT
1989 Percy Snow, Michigan St., LB
1990 Chris Zorich, Notre Dame, NT
1991 #Steve Emtman, Wash., DT
1992 Marvin Jones, Florida St., LB
1993 Aaron Taylor, Notre Dame, OT
1994 Warren Sapp, Miami-FL, DT
1995 Orlando Pace, Ohio St., OT

O'Brien Quarterback Award

First presented in 1977 as the O'Brien Memorial Trophy, the award went to the outstanding player in the Southwest. In 1981, however, the Davey O'Brien Educational and Charitable Trust of Ft. Worth renamed the prize the O'Brien National Quarterback Award and now honors the nation's best quarterback. The award is named after 1938 Heisman Trophy-winning QB Davey O'Brien of Texas Christian.

Multiple winners: Ty Detmer and Mike Singletary (2).

Memorial Trophy

Year
1977 Earl Campbell, Texas, RB
1978 Billy Sims, Oklahoma, RB

Year
1979 Mike Singletary, Baylor, LB

Year
1980 Mike Singletary, Baylor, LB

National QB Award

Year
1981 Jim McMahon, BYU
1982 Todd Blackledge, Penn St.
1983 Steve Young, BYU
1984 Doug Flutie, Boston College
1985 Chuck Long, Iowa

Year
1986 Vinny Testaverde, Miami,FL
1987 Don McPherson, Syracuse
1988 Troy Aikman, UCLA
1989 Andre Ware, Houston
1990 Ty Detmer, BYU

Year
1991 Ty Detmer, BYU
1992 Gino Torretta, Miami-FL
1993 Charlie Ward, Florida St.
1994 Kerry Collins, Penn St.
1995 Danny Wuerffel, Florida

Thorpe Award

First presented in 1986 by the Jim Thorpe Athletic Club of Oklahoma City to honor the nation's outstanding defensive back. The award is named after Jim Thorpe—Olympic champion and two-time consensus All-America HB at Carlisle.

Year
1986 Thomas Everett, Baylor
1987 Bennie Blades, Miami-FL
& Rickey Dixon, Oklahoma
1988 Deion Sanders, Florida St.

Year
1989 Mike Carrier, USC
1990 Darryl Lewis, Arizona
1991 Terrell Buckley, Florida St.
1992 Deon Figures, Colorado

Year
1993 Antonio Langham, Alabama
1994 Chris Hudson, Colorado
1995 Greg Myers, Colorado St.

Payton Award

First presented in 1987 by the Sports Network and Division I-AA sports information directors to honor the nation's outstanding Division I-AA player. The award is named after Walter Payton, the NFL's all-time leading rusher who was an All-America RB at Jackson St.

Year
1987 Kenny Gamble, Colgate, RB
1988 Dave Meggett, Towson St., RB
1989 John Friesz, Idaho, QB

Year
1990 Walter Dean, Grambling, RB
1991 Jamie Martin, Weber St., QB
1992 Michael Payton, Marshall, QB

Year
1993 Doug Nussmeier, Idaho, QB
1994 Steve McNair, Alcorn St., QB
1995 Dave Dickenson, Montana, QB

Hill Trophy

First presented in 1986 by the Harlon Hill Awards Committee in Florence, AL, to honor the nation's outstanding Division II player. The award is named after three-time NFL All-Pro Harlon Hill who played college ball at North Alabama.

Multiple winner: Johnny Bailey (3).

Year
1986 Jeff Bentrim, N.Dakota St., QB
1987 Johnny Bailey, Texas A&I, RB
1988 Johnny Bailey, Texas A&I, RB
1989 Johnny Bailey, Texas A&I, RB

Year
1990 Chris Simdorn, N. Dakota St., QB
1991 Ronnie West, Pittsburg St., WR
1992 Ronald Moore, Pittsburg St., RB
1993 Roger Graham, New Haven, RB

Year
1994 Chris Hatcher, Valdosta St., QB
1995 Ronald McKinnon, N. Ala., LB

All-Time Winningest Division I-A Coaches

Minimum of 10 years in Division I-A through 1995 season. Regular season and bowl games included. Coaches active in 1995 in **bold** type.

Top 25 Winning Percentage

		Yrs	W	L	T	Pct
1	Knute Rockne	13	105	12	5	**.881**
2	Frank Leahy	13	107	13	9	**.864**
3	George Woodruff	12	142	25	2	**.846**
4	Barry Switzer	16	157	29	4	**.837**
5	Percy Haughton	13	96	17	6	**.832**
6	Bob Neyland	21	173	31	12	**.829**
7	Hurry Up Yost	29	196	36	12	**.828**
8	**Tom Osborne**	23	231	47	3	**.827**
9	Bud Wilkinson	17	145	29	4	**.826**
10	Jock Sutherland	20	144	28	14	**.812**
11	Bob Devaney	16	136	30	7	**.806**
12	Frank Thomas	19	141	33	9	**.795**
13	**Joe Paterno**	30	278	72	3	**.792**
14	Henry Williams	23	141	34	12	**.786**
15	Gil Dobie	33	180	45	15	**.781**
16	Bear Bryant	38	323	85	17	**.780**
17	Fred Folsom	19	106	28	6	**.779**
18	Bo Schembechler	27	234	65	8	**.775**
19	Fritz Crisler	18	116	32	9	**.768**
20	Charley Moran	18	122	33	12	**.766**
21	Wallace Wade	24	171	49	10	**.765**
22	Frank Kush	22	176	54	1	**.764**
23	Dan McGugin	30	197	55	19	**.762**
24	Jim Crowley	13	78	21	10	**.761**
25	Andy Smith	17	116	32	13	**.761**

Top 25 Victories

		Yrs	W	L	T	Pct
1	Bear Bryant	38	**323**	85	17	.780
2	Pop Warner	44	**319**	106	32	.733
3	Amos Alonzo Stagg	57	**314**	199	35	.605
4	**Joe Paterno**	30	**278**	72	3	.792
5	**Bobby Bowden**	30	**259**	81	4	.759
6	Woody Hayes	33	**238**	72	10	.759
7	Bo Schembechler	27	**234**	65	8	.775
8	**Tom Osborne**	23	**231**	47	3	.827
9	**LaVell Edwards**	24	**214**	80	3	.726
10	**Hayden Fry**	34	**213**	162	10	.566
11	**Lou Holtz**	26	**208**	92	7	.689
12	Jess Neely	40	**207**	176	19	.539
13	Warren Woodson	31	**203**	95	14	.673
14	Vince Dooley	25	**201**	77	10	.715
	Eddie Anderson	39	**201**	128	15	.606
16	Dana X. Bible	33	**198**	72	23	.715
17	Dan McGugin	30	**197**	55	19	.762
18	Hurry Up Yost	29	**196**	36	12	.828
	Jim Sweeney	31	**196**	147	4	.571
20	Howard Jones	29	**194**	64	21	.733
21	Johnny Vaught	25	**190**	61	12	.745
22	John Heisman	36	**185**	70	17	.711
23	Darrell Royal	23	**184**	60	5	.749
24	**Johnny Majors**	28	**181**	130	10	.579
25	Two tied at 180 wins each.					

Note: Eddie Robinson of Division I-AA Grambling (1941-42, 1945—) is the all-time NCAA leader in coaching wins with a 402-149-15 record and .723 winning pct. over 53 seasons.

Where They Coached

Anderson—Loras (1922-24), DePaul (1925-31), Holy Cross (1933-38), Iowa (1939-42), Holy Cross (1950-64); **Bible**—Mississippi College (1913-15), LSU (1916), Texas A&M (1917, 1919-28), Nebraska (1929-36), Texas (1937-46); **Bowden**—Samford (1959-62), West Virginia (1970-75), Florida St. (1976—); **Bryant**—Maryland (1945), Kentucky (1946-53), Texas A&M (1954-57), Alabama (1958-82); **Crisler**—Minnesota (1930-31), Princeton (1932-37), Michigan (1938-47); **Crowley**—Michigan St. (1929-32), Fordham (1933-41); **Devaney**—Wyoming (1957-61), Nebraska (1962-72); **Dobie**—North Dakota St. (1906-07), Washington (1908-16), Navy (1917-19), Cornell (1920-35), Boston College (1936-38); **V. Dooley**—Georgia (1964-88); **Edwards**—BYU (1972—); **Folsom**—Colorado (1895-99, 1901-02), Dartmouth (1903-06), Colorado (1908-15).

Fry—SMU (1962-72), North Texas (1973-78), Iowa (1979—); **Haughton**—Cornell (1899-1900), Harvard (1908-16), Columbia (1923-24); **Hayes**—Denison (1946-48), Miami-OH (1949-50), Ohio St. (1951-78); **Heisman**—Oberlin (1892), Akron (1893), Oberlin (1894), Auburn (1895-99), Clemson (1900-03), Georgia Tech (1904-19), Penn (1920-22), Washington & Jefferson (1923), Rice (1924-27); **Holtz**—William & Mary (1969-71), N.C. State (1972-75), Arkansas (1977-83), Minnesota (1984-85), Notre Dame (1986—); **Jones**—Syracuse (1908), Yale (1909), Ohio St. (1910), Yale (1913), Iowa (1916-23), Duke (1924), USC (1925-40); **Kush**—Arizona St. (1958-79); **Leahy**—Boston College (1939- 40), Notre Dame (1941-43, 1946-53); **Majors**—Iowa St. (1968-72), Pittsburgh (1973-76,93—), Tennessee (1977-92); **McGugin**—Vanderbilt (1904-17, 1919-34); **Moran**—Texas A&M (1909-14), Centre (1919-23), Bucknell (1924-26), Catawba (1930-33).

Neely—Rhodes (1924-27), Clemson (1931-39), Rice (1940-66); **Neyland**—Tennessee (1926-34, 1936-40, 1946-52); **Osborne**—Nebraska (1973—); **Paterno**—Penn St. (1966—); **Rockne**—Notre Dame (1918-30); **Royal**—Mississippi St. (1954-55), Washington (1956), Texas (1957-76); **Schembechler**—Miami-OH (1963-68), Michigan (1969-89); **Smith**—Penn (1909-12), Purdue (1913-15), California (1916-25); **Stagg**—Springfield College (1890-91), Chicago (1892-1932), Pacific (1933-46); **Sutherland**—Lafayette (1919-23), Pittsburgh (1924-38); **Sweeney**—Montana St. (1963-67), Washington St. (1968-75), Fresno St. (1976—); **Switzer**—Oklahoma (1973-88).

Thomas—Chattanooga (1925-28), Alabama (1931-42, 1944-46); **Vaught**—Mississippi (1947-70); **Wade**—Alabama (1923-30), Duke (1931-41, 1946-50); **Warner**—Georgia (1895-96), Cornell (1897-98), Carlisle (1899-1903), Cornell (1904-06), Carlisle (1907-13), Pittsburgh (1915-23), Stanford (1924-32), Temple (1933-38); **Wilkinson**—Oklahoma (1947-63); **Williams**—Army (1891), Minnesota (1900-21); **Woodruff**—Penn (1892-1901), Illinois (1903), Carlisle (1905); **Woodson**—Central Arkansas (1935-39), Hardin-Simmons (1941-42, 1946-51), Arizona (1952-56), New Mexico St. (1958-67), Trinity-TX (1972-73); **Yost**—Ohio Wesleyan (1897), Nebraska (1898), Kansas (1899), Stanford (1900), Michigan (1901-23, 1925-26).

All-Time Bowl Appearances

Coaches active in 1995 in **bold** type.

		App	Overall W-L-T
1	Bear Bryant	29	15-12-2
2	**Joe Paterno**	26	17-8-1
3	**Tom Osborne**	23	10-13-0
4	**Lou Holtz**	20	10-8-2
	Vince Dooley	20	8-10-2
6	**Bobby Bowden**	19	15-3-1
	LaVell Edwards	19	6-12-1
8	Johnny Vaught	18	10-8-0
9	Bo Schembechler	17	5-12-0
10	**Johnny Majors**	16	9-7-0
	Darrell Royal	16	8-7-1
12	Don James	15	10-5-0
	Hayden Fry	15	6-8-1
14	Bobby Dodd	13	9-4-0
	Terry Donahue	13	8-4-1
	Barry Switzer	13	8-5-0
	Charlie McClendon	13	7-6-0
18	Earle Bruce	12	7-5-0
	Woody Hayes	12	6-6-0
	Shug Jordan	12	5-7-0

Active Coaches' Victories

Minimum 5 years in Division I-A.

		Yrs	W	L	T	Pct
1	Joe Paterno, Penn St.	30	**278**	72	3	.792
2	Bobby Bowden, Florida St.	30	**259**	81	4	.759
3	Tom Osborne, Nebraska	23	**231**	47	3	.827
4	LaVell Edwards, BYU	24	**214**	80	3	.726
5	Hayden Fry, Iowa	34	**213**	162	10	.566
6	Lou Holtz, Notre Dame	26	**208**	92	7	.689
7	Jim Sweeney, Fresno St.	31	**196**	147	4	.571
8	Johnny Majors, Pittsburgh	28	**181**	130	10	.579
9	Don Nehlen, West Va	25	**168**	103	8	.616
10	Al Molde, Western Mich	25	**166**	95	8	.632
11	Bill Mallory, Indiana	26	**164**	122	4	.572
12	Jim Wacker, Minnesota	25	**156**	123	3	.559
13	George Welsh, Virginia	23	**153**	109	4	.583
14	John Cooper, Ohio St	19	**146**	69	6	.674
15	Jackie Sherrill, Miss. St	18	**134**	72	4	.648
16	Jim Hess, N. Mexico St.	21	**133**	98	5	.574
17	Dick Tomey, Arizona	19	**123**	86	7	.586
18	Ken Hatfield, Rice	17	**120**	76	4	.610
19	Larry Smith, Missouri	19	**116**	96	7	.546
20	Danny Ford, Arkansas	15	**114**	45	5	.710

Note: Only four coaches— **Bill Alexander** of Georgia Tech (1920-44); **Bob Neyland** of Tennessee (1926-34,36-40,46-52); **Frank Thomas** of Alabama (1931-42,44-46) and **Joe Paterno** of Penn St. (1966—) — have taken teams to the Rose, Orange, Sugar and Cotton bowls. Paterno has won all four, while Alexander and Thomas won three and Neyland two.

AFCA Coach of the Year

First presented in 1935 by the American Football Coaches Association.

Multiple winners: Joe Paterno (4), Bear Bryant (3), John McKay and Darrell Royal (2).

Year
1935 Pappy Waldorf, Northwestern
1936 Dick Harlow, Harvard
1937 Hooks Mylin, Lafayette
1938 Bill Kern, Carnegie Tech
1939 Eddie Anderson, Iowa

1940 Clark Shaughnessy, Stanford
1941 Frank Leahy, Notre Dame
1942 Bill Alexander, Georgia Tech
1943 Amos Alonzo Stagg, Pacific
1944 Carroll Widdoes, Ohio St.
1945 Bo McMillin, Indiana
1946 Red Blaik, Army
1947 Fritz Crisler, Michigan
1948 Bennie Oosterbaan, Michigan
1949 Bud Wilkinson, Oklahoma

1950 Charlie Caldwell, Princeton
1951 Chuck Taylor, Stanford
1952 Biggie Munn, Michigan St.
1953 Jim Tatum, Maryland
1954 Red Sanders, UCLA
1955 Duffy Daugherty, Michigan St.

Year
1956 Bowden Wyatt, Tennessee
1957 Woody Hayes, Ohio St.
1958 Paul Dietzel, LSU
1959 Ben Schwartzwalder, Syracuse

1960 Murray Warmath, Minnesota
1961 Bear Bryant, Alabama
1962 John McKay, USC
1963 Darrell Royal, Texas
1964 Frank Broyles, Arkansas
& Ara Parseghian, Notre Dame
1965 Tommy Prothro, UCLA
1966 Tom Cahill, Army
1967 John Pont, Indiana
1968 Joe Paterno, Penn St.
1969 Bo Schembechler, Michigan

1970 Charlie McClendon, LSU
& Darrell Royal, Texas
1971 Bear Bryant, Alabama
1972 John McKay, USC
1973 Bear Bryant, Alabama
1974 Grant Teaff, Baylor

Year
1975 Frank Kush, Arizona St.
1976 Johnny Majors, Pittsburgh
1977 Don James, Washington
1978 Joe Paterno, Penn St.
1979 Earle Bruce, Ohio St.

1980 Vince Dooley, Georgia
1981 Danny Ford, Clemson
1982 Joe Paterno, Penn St.
1983 Ken Hatfield, Air Force
1984 LaVell Edwards, BYU
1985 Fisher DeBerry, Air Force
1986 Joe Paterno, Penn St.
1987 Dick MacPherson, Syracuse
1988 Don Nehlen, West Virginia
1989 Bill McCartney, Colorado

1990 Bobby Ross, Georgia Tech
1991 Bill Lewis, East Carolina
1992 Gene Stallings, Alabama
1993 Barry Alvarez, Wisconsin
1994 Tom Osborne, Nebraska
1995 Gary Barnett, Northwestern

FWAA Coach of the Year

First presented in 1957 by the Football Writers Association of America. The FWAA and AFCA awards have both gone to the same coach in the same season 25 times. Those double winners are preceded by (#).

Multiple winners: Woody Hayes and Joe Paterno (3); Lou Holtz, Johnny Majors and John McKay (2).

Year
1957 #Woody Hayes, Ohio St.
1958 #Paul Dietzel, LSU
1959 #Ben Schwartzwalder, Syracuse

1960 #Murray Warmath, Minnesota
1961 Darrell Royal, Texas
1962 #John McKay, USC
1963 #Darrell Royal, Texas
1964 #Ara Parseghian, Notre Dame
1965 Duffy Daugherty, Michigan St.
1966 #Tom Cahill, Army
1967 #John Pont, Indiana
1968 Woody Hayes, Ohio St.
1969 #Bo Schembechler, Michigan

Year
1970 Alex Agase, Northwestern
1971 Bob Devaney, Nebraska
1972 #John McKay, USC
1973 Johnny Majors, Pitt
1974 #Grant Teaff, Baylor
1975 Woody Hayes, Ohio St.
1976 #Johnny Majors, Pitt
1977 Lou Holtz, Arkansas
1978 #Joe Paterno, Penn St.
1979 #Earle Bruce, Ohio St.

1980 #Vince Dooley, Georgia
1981 #Danny Ford, Clemson
1982 #Joe Paterno, Penn St.

Year
1983 Howard Schnellenberger, Miami-FL
1984 #LaVell Edwards, BYU
1985 #Fisher DeBerry, Air Force
1986 #Joe Paterno, Penn St.
1987 #Dick MacPherson, Syracuse
1988 Lou Holtz, Notre Dame
1989 #Bill McCartney, Colorado

1990 #Bobby Ross, Georgia Tech
1991 Don James, Washington
1992 #Gene Stallings, Alabama
1993 Terry Bowden, Auburn
1994 Rich Brooks, Oregon
1995 #Gary Barnett, Northwestern

All-Time NCAA Division I-AA Leaders

CAREER

Total Offense

Yards Gained	Years	Yards
1 Steve McNair, Alcorn St.	1991-94	16,823
2 Willie Totten, Miss. Valley	1982-85	13,007
3 Jamie Martin, Weber St.	1989-92	12,287
4 Doug Nussmeier, Idaho	1990-93	12,054
5 Neil Lomax, Portland St.	1978-80	11,647

Yards per Game	Years	Yards	P/Gm
1 Steve McNair, Alcorn St.	1991-94	16,823	400.5
2 Neil Lomax, Portland St.	1978-80	11,647	352.9
3 Dave Dickenson, Montana	1992-95	11,523	329.2
4 Willie Totten, Miss. Valley	1982-85	13,007	325.2
5 Tom Ehrhardt, Rhode Island	1984-85	6,492	309.1

Passing

(Minimum 500 Completions)

Passing Efficiency	Years	Rating
1 Shawn Knight, William & Mary	1991-94	170.8
2 Dave Dickenson, Montana	1992-95	166.3
3 Doug Nussmeier, Idaho	1990-93	154.4
4 Jay Johnson, Northern Iowa	1989-92	148.9
5 Michael Payton, Marshall	1989-92	148.2

Yards Gained	Years	Yards
1 Steve McNair, Alcorn St.	1991-94	14,496
2 Willie Totten, Miss. Valley	1982-85	12,711
3 Jamie Martin, Weber St.	1989-92	12,207
4 Neil Lomax, Portland St.	1978-80	11,550
5 Dave Dickenson, Montan	1992-95	11,080

Receiving

Catches	Years	No
1 Jerry Rice, Miss. Valley	1981-84	301
2 Kasey Dunn, Idaho	1988-91	268
3 Brian Forster, Rhode Island	1983-85,87	245
4 Mark Didio, Connecticut	1988-91	239
5 Rennie Benn, Lehigh	1982-85	237

Yards Gained	Years	No	Yards
1 Jerry Rice, Miss. Valley	1981-84	301	4693
2 Kasey Dunn, Idaho	1988-91	268	3847
3 Rennie Benn, Lehigh	1982-85	237	3662
4 David Rhodes, Central Fla.	1991-94	213	3618
5 Mark Didio, Connecticut	1988-91	239	3535

Rushing

Yards Gained	Years	Yards
1 Frank Hawkins, Nevada	1977-80	5333
2 Kenny Gamble, Colgate	1984-87	5220
3 Markus Thomas, Eastern Ky.	1989-92	5149
4 Erik Marsh, Lafayette	1991-94	4834
5 Rene Ingoglia, Massachusetts	1992-95	4623

Yards per Game	Years	Yards	P/Gm
1 Arnold Mickens, Butler	1994-95	3813	190.7
2 Tim Hall, Robert Morris	1994-95	2908	153.1
3 Keith Elias, Princeton	1991-93	4208	140.3
4 Mike Clark, Akron	1984-86	4257	133.0
5 Michael Hicks, S. Carolina St.	1993-95	4093	127.9

Miscellaneous

Interceptions	Years	No
1 Dave Murphy, Holy Cross	1986-89	28
2 Cedric Walker, S.F. Austin	1990-93	25
3 Issiac Holt, Alcorn St.	1981-84	24
Bill McGovern, Holy Cross	1981-84	24
5 Four tied with 23 INTs each.		

Punting Average	Years	Avg
1 Pumpy Tudors, Tenn.-Chatt.	1989-91	44.4
2 Case de Brujin, Idaho St.	1978-81	43.7
3 Terry Belden, Northern Ariz.	1990-93	43.4
4 George Cimadevilla, East Tenn. St.	1983-86	43.0
5 Harold Alexander, Appalach. St.	1989-92	42.9

Punt Return Average*	Years	Avg
1 Willie Ware, Miss. Valley	1982-85	16.4
2 Buck Phillips, Western Ill.	1994-95	16.4
3 Tim Egerton, Delaware St.	1986-89	16.1
4 Mark Orlando, Towson St.	1991-94	15.7
5 John Armstrong, Richmond	1984-85	14.4

Kickoff Return Average*	Years	Avg
1 Troy Brown, Marshall	1991-92	29.7
2 Charles Swann, Indiana St.	1989-91	29.3
3 Craig Richardson, Eastern Wash.	1983-86	28.5
4 Kenyatta Sparks, Southern-BR	1992-95	28.2
5 Kerry Hayes, Western Caro.	1991-94	28.2

*(Minimum 1.2 returns per game)

Scoring

NON-KICKERS

Points	Years	TD	XP	Pts
1 Sherriden May, Idaho	1991-94	61	0	366
2 Charvez Foger, Nevada	1985-88	60	2	362
3 Kenny Gamble, Colgate	1984-87	57	0	342
4 Rene Ingoglia, UMass	1992-95	55	2	332
5 Markus Thomas, East. Ky.	1989-92	53	4	322

Touchdowns Passing	Years	No
1 Willie Totten, Miss. Valley	1982-85	139
2 Steve McNair, Alcorn St.	1991-94	119
3 Dave Dickenson, Montana	1992-95	96
4 Doug Nussmeier, Idaho	1990-93	91
5 Neil Lomax, Portland St.	1978-80	88

Touchdowns Rushing	Years	No
1 Kenny Gamble, Colgate	1984-87	55
2 Rene Ingoglia, Massachusetts	1992-95	54
3 Charvez Foger, Nevada	1985-88	52
4 Markus Thomas, Eastern Ky.	1989-92	51
5 Sherriden May, Idaho	1992-94	50
Paul Lewis, Boston Univ.	1982-84	50

Touchdown Catches	Years	No
1 Jerry Rice, Miss. Valley	1981-84	50
2 Rennie Benn, Lehigh	1982-85	44
3 Roy Banks, Easten Ill.	1983-86	38
Mike Jones, Tennessee St.	1979-92	38
5 Joe Thomas, Miss. Valley	1982-85	36

KICKERS

Points	Years	FG	XP	Pts
1 Marty Zendejas, Nevada	1984-87	72	169	385
2 B. Mitchell, Marshall/N. Iowa	1987,89-91	64	130	322
3 Thayne Doyle, Idaho	1988-91	49	160	307
4 Jose Larios, McNeese St.	1992-95	57	133	304
5 Kirk Roach, W. Carolina	1984-87	71	89	302

Field Goals	Years	No
1 Marty Zendejas, Nevada	1984-87	72
2 Kirk Roach, Western Carolina	1984-87	71
3 Tony Zendejas, Nevada	1981-83	70
4 B. Mitchell, Marshall/N. Iowa	1987,89-91	64
5 Steve Christie, William & Mary	1986-89	57
Jose Larios, McNeese St.	1992-95	57

Active Division I-AA Coaches

Minimum of 5 years as a Division I-A and/or Division I-AA through 1995 season.

Top 5 Winning Percentage

	Yrs	W	L	T	Pct
1 Roy Kidd, Eastern Ky	32	266	94	8	**.734**
2 Terry Allen, Northen Iowa	7	63	24	0	**.724**
3 Eddie Robinson, Grambling	53	402	149	15	**.723**
4 Tubby Raymond, Delaware	30	250	97	3	**.719**
5 Bobby Keasler, McNeese St.	6	53	21	2	**.711**

Top 5 Victories

	Yrs	W	L	T	Pct
1 Eddie Robinson, Grambling	53	**402**	149	15	.723
2 Roy Kidd, Eastern Ky	32	**266**	94	8	.734
3 Tubby Raymond, Delaware	30	**250**	97	3	.719
4 Carmen Cozza, Yale	31	**177**	111	5	.613
5 Ron Randleman, S.Hous.St	27	**166**	115	6	.589

Division I-AA Coach of the Year

First presented in 1983 by the American Football Coaches Association.

Multiple winners: Mark Duffner and Erk Russell (2).

Year	
1983	Rey Dempsey, Southern Ill.
1984	Dave Arnold, Montana St.
1985	Dick Sheridan, Furman
1986	Erk Russell, Ga. Southern
1987	Mark Duffner, Holy Cross
1988	Jimmy Satterfield, Furman
1989	Erk Russell, Ga. Southern
1990	Tim Stowers, Ga. Southern
1991	Mark Duffner, Holy Cross
1992	Charlie Taafe, Citadel
1993	Dan Allen, Boston Univ.
1994	Jim Tressel, Youngstown St.
1995	Don Read, Montana

NCAA PLAYOFFS

Division I-AA

Established in 1978 as a four-team playoff. Tournament field increased to eight teams in 1981, 12 teams in 1982 and 16 teams in 1986. Automatic berths have been awarded to champions of the Big Sky, Gateway, Ohio Valley, Southern, Southland and Yankee conferences since 1992.

Multiple winners: Georgia Southern (4); Youngstown St. (3); Eastern Kentucky (2).

Year	Winner	Score	Loser
1978	Florida A&M	35-28	Massachusetts
1979	Eastern Kentucky	30-7	Lehigh, PA
1980	Boise St., ID	31-29	Eastern Kentucky
1981	Idaho St.	34-23	Eastern Kentucky
1982	Eastern Kentucky	17-14	Delaware
1983	Southern Illinois	43-7	Western Carolina
1984	Montana St.	19-6	Louisiana Tech
1985	Georgia Southern	44-42	Furman, SC
1986	Georgia Southern	48-21	Arkansas St.
1987	NE Louisiana	43-42	Marshall, WV
1988	Furman, SC	17-12	Georgia Southern
1989	Georgia Southern	37-34	S.F. Austin St.
1990	Georgia Southern	36-13	Nevada-Reno
1991	Youngstown St.	25-17	Marshall
1992	Marshall	31-28	Youngstown St.
1993	Youngstown St.	17-5	Marshall
1994	Youngstown St.	28-14	Boise St.
1995	Montana	22-20	Marshall

Division II

Established in 1973 as an eight-team playoff. Tournament field increased to 16 teams in 1988. From 1964-72, eight qualifying NCAA College Division member institutions competed in four regional bowl games, but there was no tournament and no national championship until 1973.

Multiple winners: North Dakota St. (5); North Alabama (3); Southwest Texas St. and Troy St. (2).

Year	Winner	Score	Loser
1973	Louisiana Tech	34-0	Western Kentucky
1974	Central Michigan	54-14	Delaware
1975	Northern Michigan	16-14	Western Kentucky
1976	Montana St.	24-13	Akron, OH
1977	Lehigh, PA	33-0	Jacksonville St., AL
1978	Eastern Illinois	10-9	Delaware
1979	Delaware	38-21	Youngstown St., OH
1980	Cal Poly-SLO	21-13	Eastern Illinois
1981	SW Texas St.	42-13	North Dakota St.
1982	SW Texas St.	34-9	UC-Davis
1983	North Dakota St.	41-21	Central St., OH
1984	Troy St., AL	18-17	North Dakota St.
1985	North Dakota St.	35-7	North Alabama
1986	North Dakota St.	27-7	South Dakota
1987	Troy St., AL	31-17	Portland St., OR
1988	North Dakota St.	35-21	Portland St., OR
1989	Mississippi Col.	3-0	Jacksonville St., AL
1990	North Dakota St.	51-11	Indiana, PA
1991	Pittsburg St., KS	23-6	Jacksonville St., AL
1992	Jacksonville St., AL	17-13	Pittsburg St., KS
1993	North Alabama	41-34	Indiana, PA
1994	North Alabama	16-10	Tex. A&M (Kings.)
1995	North Alabama	22-7	Pittsburg St., KS

Division III

Established in 1973 as a four-team playoff. Tournament field increased to eight teams in 1975 and 16 teams in 1985. From 1969-72, four qualifying NCAA College Division member institutions competed in two regional bowl games, but there was no tournament and no national championship until 1973.

Multiple winners: Augustana (4); Ithaca (3); Dayton, Widener, WI-La Crosse and Wittenberg (2).

Year	Winner	Score	Loser
1973	Wittenberg, OH	41-0	Juniata, PA
1974	Central, IA	10-8	Ithaca, NY
1975	Wittenberg, OH	28-0	Ithaca, NY
1976	St. John's, MN	31-28	Towson St., MD
1977	Widener, PA	39-36	Wabash, IN
1978	Baldwin-Wallace	24-10	Wittenberg, OH
1979	Ithaca, NY	14-10	Wittenberg, OH
1980	Dayton, OH	63-0	Ithaca, NY
1981	Widener, PA	17-10	Dayton, OH
1982	West Georgia	14-0	Augustana, IL
1983	Augustana, IL	21-17	Union, NY
1984	Augustana, IL	21-12	Central, IA
1985	Augustana, IL	20-7	Ithaca, NY
1986	Augustana, IL	31-3	Salisbury St., MD
1987	Wagner, NY	19-3	Dayton, OH
1988	Ithaca, NY	39-24	Central, IA
1989	Dayton, OH	17-7	Union, NY
1990	Allegheny, PA*	21-14	Lycoming, PA
1991	Ithaca, NY	34-20	Dayton, OH
1992	WI-La Crosse	16-12	Wash. & Jeff., PA
1993	Mt. Union, OH	34-24	Rowan, NJ
1994	Albion, MI	38-15	Wash. & Jeff., PA
1995	WI-La Crosse	36-7	Rowan, NJ

*Overtime

NAIA PLAYOFFS

Division I

Established in 1956 as two-team playoff. Tournament field increased to four teams in 1958, eight teams in 1978 and 16 teams in 1987 before cutting back to eight teams in 1989. The title game has ended in a tie four times (1956, '64, '84 and '85).

Multiple winners: Texas A&I (7); Carson-Newman (5); Central Arkansas and Central St., OH (3); Abilene Christian, Central St-OK, Elon, Pittsburg St. and St. John's-MN (2).

Year	Winner	Score	Loser
1956	Montana St.	0-0	St. Joseph's, IN
1957	Pittsburg St., KS	27-26	Hillsdale, MI
1958	NE Oklahoma	19-13	Northern Arizona
1959	Texas A&I	20-7	Lenoir-Rhyne, NC
1960	Lenoir-Rhyne, NC	15-14	Humboldt St., CA
1961	Pittsburg St., KS	12-7	Linfield, OR
1962	Central St., OK	28-13	Lenoir-Rhyne, NC
1963	St. John's, MN	33-27	Prairie View, TX
1964	Concordia, MN	7-7	Sam Houston, TX
1965	St. John's, MN	33-0	Linfield, OR
1966	Waynesburg, PA	42-21	WI-Whitewater
1967	Fairmont St., WV	28-21	Eastern Wash.
1968	Troy St., AL	43-35	Texas A&I
1969	Texas A&I	32-7	Concordia, MN
1970	Texas A&I	48-7	Wofford, SC
1971	Livingston, AL	14-12	Arkansas Tech
1972	East Texas St.	21-18	Car-Newman, TN
1973	Abilene Christian	42-14	Elon, NC
1974	Texas A&I	34-23	Henderson St., AR
1975	Texas A&I	37-0	Salem, WV
1976	Texas A&I	26-0	Central Arkansas
1977	Abilene Christian	24-7	SW Oklahoma
1978	Angelo St., TX	34-14	Elon, NC
1979	Texas A&I	20-14	Central St., OK
1980	Elon, NC	17-10	NE Oklahoma
1981	Elon, NC	3-0	Pittsburg St., KS
1982	Central St., OK	14-11	Mesa, CO
1983	Car-Newman, TN	36-28	Mesa, CO
1984	Car-Newman, TN	19-19	Central Arkansas
1985	Hillsdale, MI	10-10	Central Arkansas
1986	Car-Newman, TN	17-0	Cameron, OK
1987	Cameron, OK	30-2	Car-Newman, TN
1988	Car-Newman, TN	56-21	Adams St., CO
1989	Car-Newman, TN	34-20	Emporia St., KS
1990	Central St., OH	38-16	Mesa, CO
1991	Central Arkansas	19-16	Central St., OH
1992	Central St., OH	19-16	Gardner-Webb, NC
1993	E. Central, OK	49-35	Glenville St., WV
1994	N'eastern St., OK	13-12	Ark-Pine Bluff
1995	Central St., OH	37-7	N'eastern St., OK

Division II

Established in 1970 as four-team playoff. Tournament field increased to eight teams in 1978 and 16 teams in 1987. The title game has ended in a tie twice (1981 and '87).

Multiple winners: Westminster (6); Findlay, Linfield and Pacific Lutheran (3); Concordia-MN, Northwestern-IA and Texas Lutheran (2).

Year	Winner	Score	Loser
1970	Westminster, PA	21-16	Anderson, IN
1971	Calif. Lutheran	20-14	Westminster, PA
1972	Missouri Southern	21-14	Northwestern, IA
1973	Northwestern, IA	10-3	Glenville St., WV
1974	Texas Lutheran	42-0	Missouri Valley
1975	Texas Lutheran	34-8	Calif.Lutheran
1976	Westminster, PA	20-13	Redlands, CA
1977	Westminster, PA	17-9	Calif.Lutheran
1978	Concordia, MN	7-0	Findlay, OH
1979	Findlay, OH	51-6	Northwestern, IA
1980	Pacific Lutheran	38-10	Wilmington, OH
1981	Austin College, TX	24-24	Concordia, MN
1982	Linfield, OR	33-15	Wm. Jewell, MO
1983	Northwestern, IA	25-21	Pacific Lutheran
1984	Linfield, OR	33-22	Northwestern, IA
1985	WI-La Crosse	24-7	Pacific Lutheran
1986	Linfield, OR	17-0	Baker, KS
1987	Pacific Lutheran	16-16	WI-Stevens Pt.*
1988	Westminster, PA	21-14	WI-La Crosse
1989	Westminster, PA	51-30	WI-La Crosse
1990	Peru St., NE	17-7	Westminster, PA
1991	Georgetown-KY	28-20	Pacific Lutheran
1992	Findlay, OH	26-13	Linfield, OR
1993	Pacific Lutheran	50-20	Westminster, PA
1994	Westminster, PA	27-7	Pacific Lutheran
1995	Findlay, OH	21-21	Central Wash.

*Wisconsin-Stevens Point forfeited its entire 1987 schedule due to its use of an ineligible player.

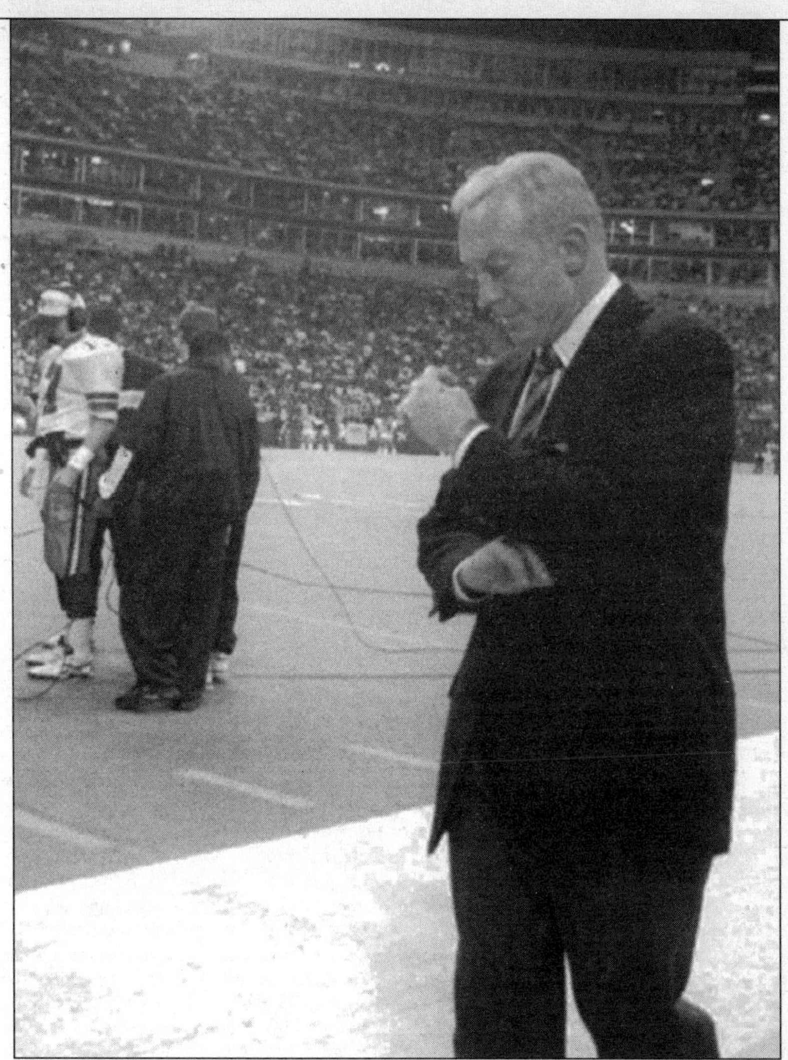

Wide World Photos

Dallas Cowboys owner and sideline showoff **Jerry Jones** quietly exults as he thinks of another way to make money that he won't share with other owners.

PRO FOOTBALL

PRO FOOTBALL

by Vito Stellino

Keeping Up With Jones

The always interesting Dallas Cowboys made history and their owner made headlines.

1995 will be remembered as the year the NFL became Planet Jerry.

Jerry Jones, the ubiquitous owner of the Dallas Cowboys, dominated the league more than any single owner since the heyday of the late George Halas, who founded and coached the Chicago Bears while virtually running the league in its early days.

Jones didn't coach the Cowboys, but he did prove his team could win the Super Bowl with a coach other than Jimmy Johnson, an obsession of Jones' since Johnson left in 1994 in a dispute over who really brought the Cowboys back to the top.

Starting in 1989 when he bought a team that went 1-15 and was losing $1 million a month, Jones oversaw the rebuilding of an historic franchise into the most profitable and successful in the sport. After winning the 1992 and 1993 Super Bowls with Johnson as his coach, Jones' Cowboys under coach Barry Switzer became the first team to win three Super Bowls in four years when they beat the Pittsburgh Steelers, 27-17, in Super Bowl XXX at Sun Devil Stadium in Tempe, Ariz. They also joined the San Francisco 49ers as the only five-time Super Bowl champions. The Super Bowl, though, was just the climax of a hectic year for Jones, who was in the headlines all year and got more attention than most players.

When Jones made his own deals with Nike and Pepsi outside the league's marketing arm, NFL Properties, his fellow owners sued him for $300 million. Naturally, Jones countersued for $700 million. He also made Deion Sanders the highest paid defensive player in league history by giving him a seven-year, $35 million deal that included a record $12.9 million signing bonus. Jones and Sanders also appeared in a pizza commercial in which Jones asked Sanders to choose between two things, like baseball and football. Sanders always answered "both".

Jones himself wanted more than both. He wanted it all.

He so infuriated his colleagues that on the morning of the Super Bowl, commissioner Paul Tagliabue said on "This Week with

Vito Stellino is the national pro football writer for *The Baltimore Sun* and has covered six Super Bowl championship teams in Pittsburgh and Washington since 1974.

Wide World Photos

The Steelers did a nice job on **Emmitt Smith** in Super Bowl XXX, holding him to 49 yards in 18 carries. Not nice enough, though, as Smith scored two crucial touchdowns. Smith now has five career Super Bowl touchdowns, second overall to Jerry Rice's seven.

David Brinkley" that Jones, in effect, is a thief. Because Jones does not want to share the revenue from his marketing deals with other owners, "He takes what does not belong to him," said Tagliabue.

About 12 hours later, Tagliabue was gracious as he presented the gleaming silver Vince Lombardi Trophy to Jones and the Cowboys "We congratulate you and your extraordinary group of players," Tagliabue said. Jones was just as gracious in accepting the trophy saying "It's wonderful just to hold this trophy."

The kind words, though, didn't change the fundamental differences between the two men, who are likely to continue the court fight that may ultimately determine the future of the league. It doesn't bother Jones that he has become an outcast in the NFL owners' lodge. Carmen Policy, the president of the San Francisco 49ers, said of Jones, "There is money and there is class and the two aren't synonymous." Jones, for his part, thinks the league would be better off if each team did its own marketing deals instead of having NFL Properties handle them. "It would be better for the league, better for the fans, better for the game," Jones said.

It'll be up to the courts to decide which side is right and it's a sign of the times for the NFL that the court fight with Jones is just one of seven major antitrust lawsuits the league is currently fighting. Al Davis, the owner of the Raiders, has filed two lawsuits over his move back from Los Angeles to Oakland. The city of St. Louis is suing to recover its $29 million relocation fee because Davis didn't pay one. And two former owners of the New England Patriots, Billy Sullivan and Victor Kiam, are contending they were forced by the league to sell the team.

On top of all that, in 1995 the NFL found itself without a team in Los Angeles, the nation's second-largest market. The Rams moved to St. Louis to replace the Cardinals, who moved to Arizona in 1988, and the Raiders, who had moved from Oakland in

1982 after Davis won yet another antitrust suit, moved back to Oakland.

But the NFL's abandonment of tinseltown didn't even register on the Richter scale compared to the seismic shock the league suffered on Nov. 6 when Art Modell announced he was moving the Cleveland Browns to Baltimore to replace the Colts, who moved to Indianapolis in 1984.

There was such a national outcry over the departure of the Cleveland team that the NFL hammered out a deal to give the city a new team that will be known as the Browns when its new stadium is built in 1999. Modell left the Browns' heritage in Cleveland. His new Baltimore team will be called the Ravens.

The league's era of franchise free agency continued when the Houston Oilers negotiated a deal to move to Nashville by 1998, when a new stadium will be constructed there, and the Seattle Seahawks announced they planned to move to Los Angeles. The Seahawks, though, have 10 years left on their lease and Seattle city officials plan a court fight to try to keep them.

Despite all the turmoil off the field, there's no indication that it is affecting the popularity of the game on the field. It continued to attract the highest TV ratings of any sport and set an attendance record for the seventh straight year. The league attracted a record average of 62,682 per game for its 240 regular season games. Spurred by the addition of two expansion teams, the league also topped the 19 million figure for the first time when 19,202,757 paid to see all the games including exhibition and playoff games.

On the field, the NFL was unpredictable as the impact of free agency spread out the talent, making it possible for a surprise team — the Colts— to come out of nowhere and nearly make the Super Bowl. Another result was that for the second straight year, the two Super Bowl teams from the previous season (the 49ers and Chargers), failed to make it back to the big game.

San Francisco was hurt early on by the erratic kicking of Doug Brien, who was released after his misses cost the club games in Detroit and Indianapolis in a three-week span. But a more costly blow was the loss of fullback William Floyd with a season-ending knee injury in midseason against New Orleans. The team had already lost Ricky Watters to free agency and the lack of a running game eventually put too much of a burden on quarterback Steve Young, who tried to carry the club after sitting out five games with a shoulder injury. The team faded badly at the end, losing its regular season finale, 28-27, in Atlanta before losing at home in the first round of the playoffs to the Green Bay Packers, 27-17.

The 49ers, who view anything less than a Super Bowl appearance as a failure, immediately started to retool when they made a surprising move by bringing back former coach Bill Walsh as a consultant to offensive coordinator Marc Trestman. Head coach George Seifert endorsed the move and Walsh said at this stage of his life, he is content to help revive the 49er offense.

San Diego's demise started in the offseason when linebacker David Griggs died in an auto accident. His loss rocked a team that never seemed to get in sync. The club rallied to win its last five games to earn a playoff berth after digging itself a 4-7 hole, but bowed meekly to Indianapolis, 30-25, in the first round of the playoffs. General manager Bobby Beathard immediately started overhauling the team in an attempt to improve its chemistry and attitude. His boldest move was cutting malcontent running back Natrone Means, who was claimed by Jacksonville. In a cruel coincidence, the Chargers endured another offseason tragedy when running back Rodney Culver and his wife perished in the Valujet crash in the Florida Everglades.

Indianapolis went on to upset the Kansas City Chiefs, 10-7, when Lin Elliott missed three field goal attempts including one that would have tied the game with 42 seconds left. It was a shattering loss for a Chiefs team that survived the retirement of Joe Montana to post the league's best regular season record — 13-3 — even though his replacement, Steve Bono, ranked 20th among NFL passers. They did it with a team that ranked No. 1 in scoring defense, No. 1 in rushing offense and No. 1 in turnovers.

"The disappointment is great when expectations are not realized," said head coach Marty Schottenheimer, who was the victim of "The Drive" and "The Fumble" in

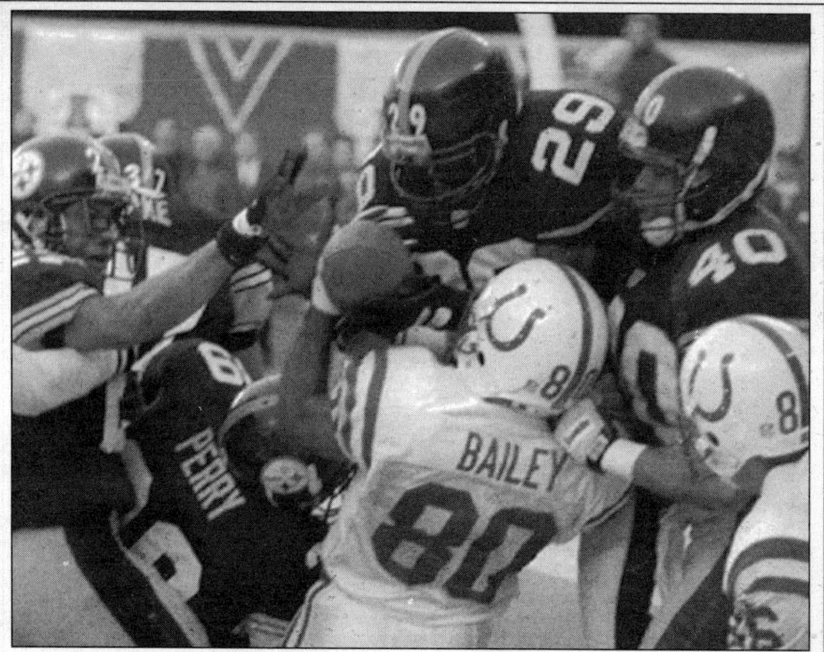

Wide World Photos

The **Pittsburgh Steelers** did not earn their Super Bowl XXX bid until this ball hit the ground, dramatically ending the AFC championship game and the surprising season of the **Indianapolis Colts.**

Cleveland when Denver twice denied him Super Bowl trips by beating his Browns in the 1986 and '87 AFC title games.

Schottenheimer's latest tormentor, the Colts, haven't been to the Super Bowl since 1971 when, as the Baltimore Colts, they beat the Cowboys. In 1996, they fell just short of returning. They lost the AFC championship game to the Steelers in Pittsburgh, 20-16, when Quentin Coryatt dropped a fourth period interception and Jim Harbaugh's Hail Mary pass on the final play landed in Aaron Bailey's lap before dribbling to the ground in the end zone.

That play ended a spectacular comeback season by Harbaugh, who became known as "Captain Comeback" when he led his team from 24-3 deficits to 27-24 victories over both the New York Jets and Miami Dolphins. Those wins enabled him to take the job from Craig Erickson while enjoying a storybook season that resurrected his previously stalled career.

Pittsburgh's survival in the AFC title game set the stage for a Super Bowl match against Dallas, which beat Green Bay, 38-27 in the NFC title game. The two teams had previously met in Super Bowls X and XIII when Pittsburgh posted 21-17 and 35-31 victories respectively, marking the first time two franchises faced each other in three Super Bowls.

This time, Dallas beat Pittsburgh but it was a game the Steelers lost more than the Cowboys won. The Steelers had the edge in first downs, 25-15, rushing yardage, 103-56, passing yardage, 207-198, and held Emmitt Smith to 49 yards rushing, Michael Irvin to five catches and Troy Aikman to one touchdown pass.

But the Cowboys won because Steeler quarterback Neil O'Donnell threw two second half passes right into the arms of Cowboy defensive back Larry Brown, who caught both of them and returned them 44 and 33 yards to set up a pair of short Smith touchdown runs that decided the game. The close victory typified the Cowboys' season.

"No matter how rocky the water was at times, we brought the ship home," Irvin said, a man who knows rocky water.

Things got rocky for the Cowboys on Nov. 12 when 49ers backup quarterback Elvis Grbac fired a quick slant on the second play of the game to Jerry Rice, who scored on an 81-yard touchdown play to start the 49ers on their way to a 38-20 rout of the Cowboys that left Switzer with an 0-3 mark against the 49ers.

A month later, Switzer decided to go for it on 4th-and-1 at the Cowboys 29 in Philadelphia with the score tied, 17-17, with just over two minutes left in the game. The Eagles stopped Emmitt Smith twice on the same play — the two-minute warning wiped out the first try — and went on to win, 20-17. That ignited another firestorm of criticism about Switzer's coaching style, but he weathered it all and shouted from the podium at the Super Bowl, "We did it our way, baby. We did it. We did it. We did it." Switzer's laid back ways are unusual in an era when coaches are intense and take themselves very seriously, but he now has the Super Bowl trophy to prove his ways can work.

Things won't get any easier for the Cowboys in the future as the salary cap continues to erode their depth. They lost four starters on defense, including Brown, who signed a $12.5 million deal with the Raiders. Still, as long as the Cowboys have the Triplets — Aikman, Smith and Irvin – they will remain contenders, but they've got to worry about Irvin's habit of getting into trouble off the field. In March, police found him in a hotel room with a former teammate and two topless dancers. Drugs were found in the room, one of the women said they belonged to her and was arrested. Irvin was also arrested and the incident could subject him to the provisions of the league's drug policy, including regular drug testing (see Updates, page XX).

The Steelers could also have a tough road back to the Super Bowl. Despite his errant passes in the Super Bowl, the New York Jets signed O'Donnell to a $25 million deal with a $7 million signing bonus that the Steelers declined to match. They'll take their chances at quarterback with untested Jim Miller, veteran Mike Tomczak and Kordell Stewart, who became known as "Slash" for

Franchise Free Fall

Do you know where your NFL team is tonight?

They're not quite asking that question on the local news yet, but they may be soon the way NFL teams are jumping around the map these days. The NFL, which had no team move from 1963 to 1982, saw three teams change addresses from April of 1995 to February of 1996. A fourth team negotiated a new deal to move and a fifth club announced its intention to move. Several others are exploring their options.

The latest round of franchise free agency started when the Rams, who had been in the Los Angeles area since 1946, struck a deal to move to St. Louis and the Raiders, who won a court fight to move from Oakland to Los Angeles in 1982, moved back to Oakland.

Even though those two moves left the league without a team in the nation's second largest market, the departure of the Rams and Raiders didn't cause much of a stir in or out of Los Angeles. After all, Los Angeles has Hollywood, Disneyland, more than one pro team in every other sport and big time college teams. Who would miss a couple of NFL teams? The owners first turned down the Rams move in March of 1995 on the grounds they didn't meet league guidelines for moving, but changed their minds less than a month later after St. Louis officials threatened to sue the league for more than $2 billion. The league has yet to fight another move.

Things got sticky for the league, though, last Nov. 6 when Cleveland owner Art Modell announced he was moving the Browns to Baltimore. Not since the Dodgers left Brooklyn for Los Angeles in 1957 has the move of a sports team caused such a national uproar. Cleveland mayor Michael White led several highly visible protest demonstrations and warned that if it could happen to Cleveland, it could happen to any city. Even though the Browns have never appeared in a Super Bowl, they have a rich heritage dating back to the days of the late Paul Brown, who took the team to 10 straight championship games in the AAFC and the NFL from 1946-55.

Wide World Photos

Art Modell, former owner of the Cleveland Browns is so deliriously happy about his stadium deal that he needs help waving to his new fans in Maryland.

The result was that the league negotiated a deal with the city of Cleveland which guaranteed the city a team by 1999 once it builds a new stadium. In return, the city dropped its lawsuits trying to fight the move. The new team — which can be an existing team or an expansion team — will be called the Browns.

Modell moved his players to Baltimore where they will be called the Ravens, a reference to the poet Edgar Allen Poe, who wrote "The Raven" and is buried in Baltimore. Poe also wrote "The Tell-Tale Heart," something Clevelanders might say Modell lacked.

The settlement, though, did little to stop the criticism about the instability in the league. Buffalo owner Ralph Wilson, one of the two owners to vote against the deal, was the most critical. He started calling the NFL the "National Floating League" and said, "This whole thing has turned into a broad comedy. Each day I wake up waiting to see who's going to throw the next pie." Wilson was particularly upset about the Cleveland move. "It was wrong. I told the owners the country will never forget this move. Never," Wilson said. Even commissioner Paul Tagliabue warned the owners at their annual March meetings that they're in danger of alienating the fans. "We are at a crossroads," he said. "The choices we make now will determine the future respect we earn from fans and the future health of the league."

But the quest for new stadiums shows no signs of abating. The league will eventually lose the fourth largest city in the country because Houston has negotiated a deal to move to Nashville in 1998 when a new stadium is constructed there. The Oilers will play lame duck seasons in Houston in 1996 and 1997.

In another development, Seattle owner Ken Behring announced he was moving to Los Angeles even though he has 10 years left on his lease in Seattle. He insisted the Kingdome is unsafe because of the danger of earthquakes even though Seattle officials presented expert reports that it could withstand an earthquake. The courts will now have to sort out the conflicting claims and decide the Seahawks' future.

Such is the state of mind in the NFL that an owner would move to Los Angeles to avoid earthquakes. ❑

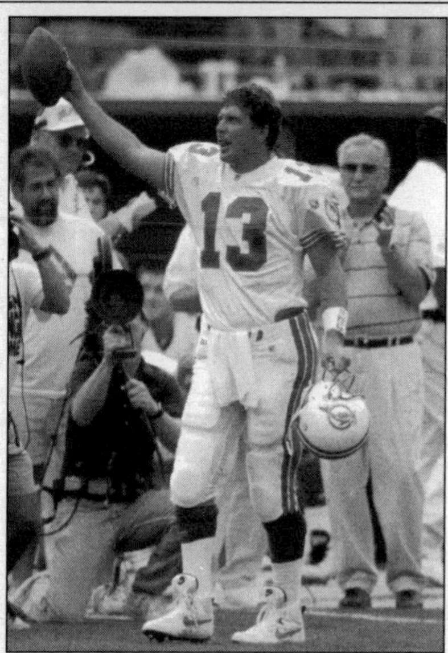

Wide World Photos

If Miami Dolphins quarterback **Dan Marino** sets any records this year, it will be Jimmy Johnson cheering from the sidelines instead of **Don Shula**.

his ability to play several positions.

It remains to be seen whether O'Donnell can make an impact on a Jets team that went 3-13 last year. Free agency has turned out to be a mixed bag for most teams. While Deion Sanders helped San Francisco and Dallas win the last two Super Bowls and Bryce Paup was the defensive player of the year for Buffalo with 17½ sacks, there have been many high profile disappointments including Andre Rison of Cleveland and Eric Green of Miami.

The most valuable player of the year was Green Bay quarterback Brett Favre, who overcame the loss of Sterling Sharpe, out for the year with a serious neck injury, and the Keith Jackson holdout to pass for 4,413 yards and take the team to the NFC title game for the first time since Vince Lombardi was a coach on the sidelines instead of a name on the Super Bowl trophy. Reggie White saluted Favre by saying, "He is 'The Man,' and we're all his supporting cast." Favre didn't disagree. "Here, they ask me to win the game. They live and die with what I do," he said. Unfortunately, Favre had been doing something against the rules. He announced on May 14 that he had become addicted to the painkiller *Vicodin*. He then entered the league's drug program on a self-referral basis.

For longevity, though, it was the year of Dan Marino. The Miami Dolphins quarterback set four all-time career marks — most touchdowns (352), most pass attempts (6,531), most passing yards (48,841) and most completions (3,913). It was a frustrating season for Marino, though, because the team lost on three of the days he set those records and was bounced out of the playoffs in the first round at Buffalo, 37-22.

The result was that Don Shula, the winningest coach in the history of the game with 347 victories decided to retire after 33 years as a head coach, 26 with the Dolphins. Although he was under fire from the impatient Miami fans who wanted Jimmy Johnson to replace him, Shula said, "I'm at peace with myself," adding "I'd be lying to you if I didn't say it will be gut-wrenching for me when the football is kicked off next September."

But when Art Modell offered him a chance to coach or run his new Baltimore team, Shula decided that at age 66, it was time for him to depart and declined. Shula had started his coaching career in Baltimore in 1963.

Besides Shula, four other coaches were let go; Ted Marchibroda in Indianapolis, Buddy Ryan in Arizona, Bill Belichick in Cleveland and Sam Wyche in Tampa Bay.

Marchibroda declined to accept a mere one-year contract offer from Indianapolis after taking his team to the AFC title game. But he wasn't unemployed for long. Once he couldn't get Shula, Modell hired Marchibroda for a second term in Baltimore. He was the Colts' coach from 1975-1979 and took the team to three straight playoff berths.

Ryan retired to his horse farm in Kentucky and Wyche will go into broadcasting. Belichick became an assistant with his old boss, Bill Parcells, in New England.

Three other coaches are taking over new head coaching jobs. Vince Tobin, a former Colt assistant, will take over the Arizona Cardinals. Lindy Infante, the former Green Bay head coach who was a Colt assistant last year, gets the top job in Indianapolis, and Tony Dungy, a former Minnesota assistant, is now the man in Tampa Bay. ❐

PRO FOOTBALL STATISTICS

THE SEASON IN REVIEW

1995-1996

STANDINGS • PLAYOFFS • DRAFTS

Final NFL Standings

Division champions (*) and Wild Card playoff qualifiers (†) are noted; division champions with two best records received first round byes. Number of seasons listed after each head coach refers to latest tenure with club through 1995 season.

American Football Conference

Eastern Division

	W	L	T	PF	PA	vs Div	vs AFC
*Buffalo	10	6	0	350	335	6-2-0	7-5-0
†Indianapolis	9	7	0	331	316	6-2-0	7-5-0
†Miami	9	7	0	398	332	3-5-0	7-5-0
New England	6	10	0	294	377	5-3-0	6-6-0
NY Jets	3	13	0	233	384	1-7-0	3-9-0

1995 Head coaches: Buf— Marv Levy (10th season); **Ind**— Ted Marchibroda (4th); **Mia**— Don Shula (26th); **NE**— Bill Parcells (3rd); **NY**— Rich Kotite (1st).
1994 Standings: 1. Miami (10-6); 2. New England (10-6); 3. Indianapolis (8-8); 4. Buffalo (7-9); 5. NY Jets (6-10).

Central Division

	W	L	T	PF	PA	vs Div	vs AFC
*Pittsburgh	11	5	0	407	327	6-2-0	9-3-0
Cincinnati	7	9	0	349	374	4-4-0	5-7-0
Houston	7	9	0	348	324	3-5-0	6-6-0
Cleveland	5	11	0	289	356	3-5-0	4-8-0
Jacksonville	4	12	0	275	404	4-4-0	4-8-0

1995 Head coaches: Pit— Bill Cowher (4th season); **Cin**— David Shula (4th); **Hou**— Jeff Fisher (2nd); **Cle**— Bill Belichick (5th); **Jax**— Tom Coughlin (1st).
1994 Standings: 1. Pittsburgh (12-4); 2. Cleveland (11-5); 3. Cincinnati (3-13); 4. Houston (2-14).

Western Division

	W	L	T	PF	PA	vs Div	vs AFC
*Kansas City	13	3	0	358	241	8-0-0	10-2-0
†San Diego	9	7	0	321	323	4-4-0	6-6-0
Denver	8	8	0	388	345	3-5-0	6-6-0
Seattle	8	8	0	363	366	3-5-0	5-7-0
Oakland	8	8	0	348	332	2-6-0	5-7-0

1995 Head coaches: KC— Marty Schottenheimer (7th season); **SD**— Bobby Ross (4th); **Den**— Mike Shanahan (1st); **Sea**— Dennis Erickson (1st); **Oak**— Mike White (1st).
1994 Standings: 1. San Diego (11-5); 2. Kansas City (9-7); 3. LA Raiders (9-7); 4. Denver (7-9); 5. Seattle (6-10).

National Football Conference

Eastern Division

	W	L	T	PF	PA	vs Div	vs NFC
*Dallas	12	4	0	435	291	5-3-0	8-4-0
†Philadelphia	10	6	0	318	338	7-1-0	9-3-0
Washington	6	10	0	326	359	3-5-0	6-6-0
NY Giants	5	11	0	290	340	4-4-0	5-7-0
Arizona	4	12	0	275	422	1-7-0	3-9-0

1995 Head coaches: Dal— Barry Switzer (2nd season); **NY**— Dan Reeves (3rd); **Ariz**— Buddy Ryan (2nd); **Phi**— Ray Rhodes (1st); **Wash**— Norv Turner (2nd).
1994 Standings: 1. Dallas (12-4); 2. NY Giants (9-7); 3. Arizona (8-8); 4. Philadelphia (7-9); 5. Washington (3-13).

Central Division

	W	L	T	PF	PA	vs Div	vs NFC
*Green Bay	11	5	0	404	314	5-3-0	7-5-0
†Detroit	10	6	0	436	336	6-2-0	7-5-0
Chicago	9	7	0	392	360	4-4-0	7-5-0
Minnesota	8	8	0	412	385	3-5-0	5-7-0
Tampa Bay	7	9	0	238	335	2-6-0	5-7-0

1995 Head Coaches: GB— Mike Holmgren (4th season); **Det**— Wayne Fontes (8th); **Chi**— Dave Wannstedt (3rd); **Min**— Dennis Green (4th); **TB**— Sam Wyche (4th).
1994 Standings: 1. Minnesota (10-6); 2. Green Bay (9-7); 3. Detroit (9-7); 4. Chicago (9-7); 5. Tampa Bay (6-10).

Western Division

	W	L	T	PF	PA	vs Div	vs NFC
*San Francisco	11	5	0	457	258	5-3-0	8-4-0
†Atlanta	9	7	0	362	349	5-3-0	7-5-0
St. Louis	7	9	0	309	418	4-4-0	6-6-0
Carolina	7	9	0	289	325	3-5-0	4-8-0
New Orleans	7	9	0	319	348	3-5-0	3-9-0

1995 Head Coaches: SF— George Seifert (7th season); **Atl**— June Jones (2nd); **St.L**— Rich Brooks (1st); **Car**— Dom Capers (1st); **NO**— Jim Mora (10th).
1994 Standings: 1. San Francisco (13-3); 2. New Orleans (7-9); 3. Atlanta (7-9); 4. LA Rams (4-12).

Playoff Tiebreakers

Wild Card berths—NFC: Atlanta (9-7) qualified over Chicago (9-7) with better record (4-2 vs. 3-3) in games against common opponents.

NFL Regular Season Individual Leaders

(* indicates rookies)

Passing Efficiency

(Minimum of 224 attempts)

AFC	Att	Cmp	Cmp Pct	Yds	Avg Gain	TD	Long	Int	Sack/Lost	Rating Points
Jim Harbaugh, Ind	314	200	63.7	2575	8.20	17	52	5	36/219	100.7
Dan Marino, Mia	482	309	64.1	3668	7.61	24	67-td	15	22/153	90.8
Vinny Testaverde, Cle	392	241	61.5	2883	7.35	17	70-td	10	17/87	87.8
Chris Chandler, Hou	356	225	63.2	2460	6.91	17	76-td	10	21/173	87.8
Neil O'Donnell, Pit	416	246	59.1	2970	7.14	17	71-td	7	15/126	87.7
John Elway, Den	542	316	58.3	3970	7.32	26	62-td	14	22/180	86.4
Mark Brunell, Jax	346	201	58.1	2168	6.27	15	45	7	39/238	82.6
Jeff Hostetler, Oak	286	172	60.1	1998	6.99	12	80-td	9	22/133	82.2
Jeff Blake, Cin	567	326	57.5	3822	6.74	28	88-td	17	24/152	82.1
Jim Kelly, Buf	458	255	55.7	3130	6.83	22	77-td	13	26/181	81.1
Stan Humphries, SD	478	282	59.0	3381	7.07	17	51-td	14	23/197	80.4
Steve Bono, KC	520	293	56.3	3121	6.00	21	60-td	10	21/158	79.5
Boomer Esiason, NY	389	221	56.8	2275	5.85	16	43-td	15	27/198	71.4
Rick Mirer, Sea	391	209	53.5	2564	6.56	13	59-td	20	42/255	63.7
Drew Bledsoe, NE	636	323	50.8	3507	5.51	13	47-td	16	23/170	63.7

NFC	Att	Cmp	Cmp Pct	Yds	Avg Gain	TD	Long	Int	Sack/Lost	Rating Points
Brett Favre, GB	570	359	63.0	4413	7.74	38	99-td	13	33/217	99.5
Troy Aikman, Dal	432	280	64.8	3304	7.65	16	50	7	14/89	93.6
Erik Kramer, Chi	522	315	60.3	3838	7.35	29	76-td	10	15/95	93.5
Steve Young, SF	447	299	66.9	3200	7.16	20	57	11	25/115	92.3
Scott Mitchell, Det	583	346	59.3	4338	7.44	32	91-td	12	31/145	92.3
Warren Moon, Min	606	377	62.2	4228	6.98	33	85-td	14	38/277	91.5
Jeff George, Atl	557	336	60.3	4143	7.44	24	62-td	11	43/270	89.5
Jim Everett, NO	567	345	60.8	3970	7.00	26	70-td	14	27/210	87.0
Chris Miller, St.L	405	232	57.3	2623	6.48	18	72	15	31/244	76.2
Dave Brown, NY	456	254	55.7	2814	6.17	11	57-td	10	44/206	73.1
Dave Krieg, Ariz	521	304	58.3	3554	6.82	16	48	21	53/380	72.6
Gus Frerotte, Wash	396	199	50.3	2751	6.95	13	73-td	13	23/192	70.2
Rodney Peete, Phi	375	215	57.3	2326	6.20	8	37-td	14	33/166	67.3
Kerry Collins*, Car	433	214	49.4	2717	6.27	14	89-td	19	24/150	61.9
Trent Dilfer, TB	415	224	54.0	2774	6.68	4	64-td	18	47/331	60.1

Receptions

AFC	No	Yds	Avg	Long	TD
Carl Pickens, Cin	99	1234	12.5	68-td	17
Tony Martin, SD	90	1224	13.6	51-td	6
Tim Brown, Oak	89	1342	15.1	80-td	10
Yancy Thigpen, Pit	85	1307	15.4	43	5
Ben Coates, NE	84	915	10.9	35	6
Brian Blades, Sea	77	1001	13.0	49	4
Adrian Murrell, NY	71	465	6.5	43	2
Joey Galloway, Sea	67	1039	15.5	59-td	7
Vincent Brisby, NE	66	974	14.8	72	3
Wayne Chrebet*, NY	66	726	11.0	32	4
Terry Kirby, Mia	66	618	9.4	46	3
Shannon Sharpe, Den	63	756	12.0	49	4

NFC	No	Yds	Avg	Long	TD
Herman Moore, Det	123	1686	13.7	69-td	14
Jerry Rice, SF	122	1848	15.1	81-td	15
Cris Carter, Min	122	1371	11.2	60-td	17
Isaac Bruce, St.L	119	1781	15.0	72	13
Michael Irvin, Dal	111	1603	14.4	50	10
Brett Perriman, Det	108	1488	13.8	91-td	9
Eric Metcalf, Atl	104	1189	11.4	62-td	8
Robert Brooks, GB	102	1497	14.7	99-td	13
Larry Centers, Ariz	101	962	9.5	32	2
Derek Loville, SF	87	662	7.6	31	3
Jeff Graham, Chi	82	1301	15.9	51	4
Quinn Early, NO	81	1087	13.4	70-td	8

Rushing

AFC	Car	Yds	Avg	Long	TD
Curtis Martin*, NE	368	1487	4.0	49	14
Chris Warren, Sea	310	1346	4.3	52	15
Terrell Davis*, Den	237	1117	4.7	60-td	7
Harvey Williams, Oak	255	1114	4.4	60	9
Marshall Faulk, Ind	289	1078	3.7	40	11
Thurman Thomas, Buf	267	1005	3.8	49	6
Rodney Thomas*, Hou	251	947	3.8	74-td	5
Marcus Allen, KC	207	890	4.3	38	5
Bernie Parmalee, Mia	236	878	3.7	40	9
Erric Pegram, Pit	213	813	3.8	38	5
Adrian Murrell, NY	192	795	4.1	30	1
Natrone Means, SD	186	730	3.9	36	5

NFC	Att	Yds	Avg	Long	TD
Emmitt Smith, Dal	377	1773	4.7	60-td	25
Barry Sanders, Det	314	1500	4.8	75-td	11
Terry Allen, Wash	338	1309	3.9	28	10
Ricky Watters, Phi	337	1273	3.8	57	11
Errict Rhett, TB	332	1207	3.6	21	11
Rodney Hampton, NY	306	1182	3.9	32	10
Craig Heyward, Atl	236	1083	4.6	31	6
Rashaan Salaam*, Chi	296	1074	3.6	42	10
Garrison Hearst, Ariz	284	1070	3.8	38	1
Edgar Bennett, GB	316	1067	3.4	23	3
Mario Bates, NO	244	951	3.9	66-td	7
Darryl Moore, Car	195	740	3.8	53-td	4

Green Bay
Brett Favre
Passing Efficiency

Detroit Lions
Herman Moore
Receptions

Dallas Cowboys
Emmitt Smith
Rushing & Touchdowns

Buffalo Bills
Bryce Paup
Sacks

All-Purpose Yardage

AFC	Rush	Rec	Ret	Total
Glyn Milburn, Den	266	191	1623	2080
Ernie Mills, Pit	39	679	1306	2024
David Meggett, NE	250	334	1347	1931
Tamarick Vanover*, KC	31	231	1635	1897
Andre Coleman, SD	0	78	1737	1815
Curtis Martin*, NE	1487	261	0	1748
Darick Holmes, Buf	698	214	799	1711
Tim Brown, Oak	0	1342	364	1706
Chris Warren, Sea	1346	247	0	1593
Joey Galloway, Sea	154	1039	390	1583
Marshall Faulk, Ind	1078	475	0	1553
O.J. McDuffie, Mia	6	819	727	1552

NFC	Rush	Rec	Ret	Total
Brian Mitchell, Wash	301	324	1723	2348
Emmitt Smith, Dal	1773	375	0	2148
Eric Metcalf, Atl	133	1189	661	1983
Kevin Williams, Dal	53	613	1274	1940
Barry Sanders, Det	1500	398	0	1898
Tyrone Hughes, NO	0	0	1898	1898
Jerry Rice, SF	36	1848	0	1884
Isaac Bruce, St.L	17	1781	52	1850
Edgar Bennett, GB	1067	648	0	1715
Ricky Watters, Phi	1273	434	0	1707
Herman Moore, Det	0	1686	0	1686
Brett Perriman, Det	48	1488	115	1651

Ret column includes all kickoff, punt, fumble and interception returns.
Note: Isaac Bruce's 52 return yards came on a lateral from St L. teammate Todd Kinchen.

Scoring

(†) point total includes 2-point conversions.

Touchdowns

AFC	TD	Rush	Rec	Ret	Pts
Carl Pickens, Cin	17	0	17	0	102
Chris Warren, Sea	16	15	1	0	96
Curtis Martin*, NE	15	14	1	0	92†
Marshall Faulk, Ind	14	11	3	0	84
Anthony Miller, Den	14	0	14	0	84
Bill Brooks, Buf	11	0	11	0	66
Tim Brown, Oak	10	0	10	0	60
Bernie Parmalee, Mia	10	9	1	0	60
Joey Galloway, Sea	9	1	7	1	54
Michael Jackson, Cle	9	0	9	0	54
Bam Morris, Pit	9	9	0	0	54
Chris Sanders, Hou	9	0	9	0	54
Harvey Williams, Oak	9	9	0	0	54
O.J. McDuffie, Mia	8	0	8	0	50†

NFC	TD	Rush	Rec	Ret	Pts
Emmitt Smith, Dal	25	25	0	0	150
Jerry Rice, SF	17	1	15	1	104†
Cris Carter, Min	17	0	17	0	102
Herman Moore, Det	14	0	14	0	84
Isaac Bruce, St.L	13	0	13	0	80†
Derek Loville, SF	13	10	3	0	80†
Robert Brooks, GB	13	0	13	0	78
Curtis Conway, Chi	12	0	12	0	72
Barry Sanders, Det	12	11	1	0	72
Ricky Watters, Phi	12	11	1	0	72
Terry Allen, Wash	11	10	1	0	66
Errict Rhett, TB	11	11	0	0	66
Rodney Hampton, NY	10	10	0	0	62†
Michael Irvin, Dal	10	0	10	0	60
Rashaan Salaam*, Chi	10	10	0	0	60
Eric Metcalf, Atl	10	1	8	1	60
Terance Mathis, Atl	9	0	9	0	60†

Kickers

AFC	PAT	FG	Long	Pts
Norm Johnson, Pit	39/39	34/41	50	141
Jason Elam, Den	39/39	31/38	56	132
Steve Christie, Buf	33/35	31/40	51	126
Doug Pelfrey, Cin	34/34	29/36	51	121
Pete Stoyanovich, Mia	37/37	27/34	51	118
Al Del Greco, Hou	33/33	27/31	53	114
Matt Stover, Cle	26/26	29/33	47	113
Todd Peterson, Sea	40/40	23/28	49	109
Lin Elliott, KC	34/37	24/30	49	106
Matt Bahr, NE	27/27	23/33	55	96
John Carney, SD	32/33	21/26	45	95
Mike Hollis, Jax	27/28	20/27	53	87
Cary Blanchard, Ind	25/25	19/24	50	82
Nick Lowery, NY	24/24	17/21	50	75

NFC	PAT	FG	Long	Pts
Jason Hanson, Det	48/48	28/34	56	132
Chris Boniol, Dal	46/48	27/28	45	127
Morten Andersen, Atl	29/30	31/37	59	122
Fuad Reveiz, Min	44/44	26/36	51	122
Kevin Butler, Chi	45/45	23/31	47	114
Eddie Murray, Wash	33/33	27/36	52	114
Greg Davis, Ariz	19/19	30/39	55	109
John Kasay, Car	27/28	26/33	52	105
Gary Anderson, Phi	32/33	22/30	43	98
Chris Jacke, GB	43/43	17/23	51	94
Doug Brien, SF-NO	35/35	19/29	51	92
Brian Daluiso, NY	28/28	20/28	51	88
Michael Husted, TB	25/25	19/26	53	82
Jeff Wilkins, SF	27/29	12/13	40	63
Steve McLaughlin, St.L	17/17	8/16	45	41
Dean Biasucci, St.L.	13/14	9/12	51	40

NFL Regular Season Individual Leaders (Cont.)

(* indicates rookies)

Interceptions

AFC	No	Yds	Long	TD
Willie Williams, Pit	7	122	63-td	1
Darryll Lewis, Hou	6	145	98-td	1
Otis Smith, NY	6	101	49-td	1
Kurt Schulz, Buf	6	48	32-td	1
Terry McDaniel, Oak	6	46	42-td	1
NFC	**No**	**Yds**	**Long**	**TD**
Orlando Thomas*, Min	9	108	45-td	1
Willie Clay, Det	8	173	39	0
William Thomas, Phi	7	104	37-td	1

Six tied with six each.

Sacks

AFC	No
Bryce Paup, Buf	17.5
Pat Swilling, Oak	13.0
Leslie O'Neal, SD	12.5
Neil Smith, KC	12.0
Willie McGinest, NE	11.0
NFC	**No**
William Fuller, Phi	13.0
Wayne Martin, NO	13.0
Reggie White, GB	12.0
D'Marco Farr, St.L	11.5

Three tied with 11 each.

Punting

AFC	No	Yds	Lg	Avg	In20
Rick Tuten, Sea	83	3735	73	**45.0**	21
Darren Bennett, SD	72	3221	66	**44.7**	28
Louie Aguiar, KC	91	3990	65	**43.8**	29
Bryan Barker, Jax	82	3591	63	**43.8**	19
Tom Tupa, Cle	65	2831	64	**43.6**	18
NFC	**No**	**Yds**	**Lg**	**Avg**	**In20**
Sean Landeta, St.L	83	3679	63	44.3	23
Jeff Feagles, Ariz	72	3150	60	43.8	20
Tom Hutton, Phi	85	3682	63	43.3	20
Reggie Roby, TB	77	3296	61	42.8	23
Mike Horan, NY	72	3063	60	42.5	15

Punt Returns

(Minimum of 20 returns)

AFC	No	FC	Yds	Avg	Long	TD
Andre Coleman, SD	28	14	326	11.6	88-td	1
Jeff Burris, Buf	20	1	229	11.5	40	0
Glyn Milburn, Den	31	17	354	11.4	44	0
Tamarick Vanover*, KC	51	4	540	10.6	86-td	1
Desmond Howard, Jax	24	8	246	10.3	40	0
NFC	**No**	**FC**	**Yds**	**Avg**	**Long**	**TD**
David Palmer, Min	26	13	342	13.2	74-td	1
Brian Mitchell, Wash	25	15	315	12.6	59-td	1
Eric Guliford, Car	43	22	475	11.0	62-td	1
Dexter Carter, NYJ-SF	30	15	309	10.3	78-td	1
Charles Jordan, GB	21	2	213	10.1	18	0

Kickoff Returns

(Minimum of 20 returns)

AFC	No	Yds	Avg	Long	TD
Glyn Milburn, Den	47	1269	27.0	86	0
Ron Carpenter, NY	21	553	26.3	58	0
Napoleon Kaufman*, Oak	22	572	26.0	84-td	1
Tamarick Vanover*, KC	43	1095	25.5	99-td	2
David Meggett, NE	38	964	25.4	62	0

NFC	No	Yds	Avg	Long	TD
Brian Mitchell, Wash	55	1408	25.6	59	0
Qadry Ismail, Min	42	1037	24.7	71	0
Tyrone Hughes, NO	66	1617	24.5	83	0
J.T. Thomas, St.L	32	752	23.5	46	0
Antonio Freeman*, GB	24	556	23.2	45	0

Single Game Highs

(*) indicates overtime game.

Passing

AFC	Att/Cmp	Yds	TD
Dan Marino, Mia at Cin (10/1)	48/33	450	2
Neil O'Donnell, Pit at Cin (11/19)	31/24	377	2
Bernie Kosar, Mia at NO (10/15)	42/29	368	3
Neil O'Donnell, Pit vs Cin (10/19)	52/30	359	0
Jeff Blake, Cin vs Hou (9/24)	46/24	356	3
NFC	**Att/Cmp**	**Yds**	**TD**
Steve Young, SF vs Min (12/18)	49/30	425	3
Dave Krieg, Ariz vs Atl (11/26)	43/27	413	4
Scott Mitchell, Det vs Min (11/23)	45/30	410	4
Jeff George, Atl at NO (9/17)	39/27	386	1
Warren Moon, Min at Det (11/23)	47/30	384	3

Reception Yards

AFC	No	Yds	TD
Shannon Sharpe, Den vs Buf (9/3)	10	180	0
Andre Rison, Cle at Cin (10/29)	7	173	1
Tony Martin, SD at Ind (12/17)	10	168	2
Tony Martin, SD vs Sea (9/10)	13	163	1
Vincent Brisby, NE at Atl (10/1)	9	161	0
Pete Mitchell, Jax at TB (11/19)	10	161	1
Tim Brown, Oak vs Dal (11/19)	12	161	1
NFC	**No**	**Yds**	**TD**
Jerry Rice, SF vs Min (12/18)	14	289	3
Isaac Bruce, St.L vs Mia (12/24)	15	210	1
Isaac Bruce, St.L vs Atl (10/12)	10	191	2
Herman Moore, Det vs Chi (12/4)	14	183	1
Isaac Bruce, St.L at Ind (10/1)	8	181	2
Jerry Rice, SF at Det (9/25)	11	181	0

Rushing

AFC	Car	Yds	TD
Marshall Faulk, Ind vs St.L (10/1)	19	177	3
Terrell Davis, Den vs SD (11/19)	30	176	1
Curtis Martin, NE at NYJ (11/5)	35	166	2
Harvey Williams, Oak vs Sea (10/8)	19	160	1
Curtis Martin, NE at Buf (11/26)	27	148	1
Curtis Martin, NE vs NYJ (12/10)	31	148	2
Thurman Thomas, Buf vs Mia (12/17)	35	148	1
NFC	**Car**	**Yds**	**TD**
Rodney Hampton, NYG at Dal (12/17)	34	187	0
Barry Sanders, Det vs GB (10/29)	22	167	0
Emmitt Smith, Dal at Atl (10/29)	26	167	1
Emmitt Smith Dal at NYG (9/4)	21	163	3
Emmitt Smith, Dal vs Phi (11/6)	27	158	2

NFL Bests

Longest Field Goal
59 yds......Morten Andersen, Atl vs SF (12/24)

Longest Run from Scrimmage
86 yds......Joey Galloway, Sea at Jax (11/12), TD

Longest Pass Play
99 yds......Brett Favre to Robert Brooks, GB at Chi (9/11), TD

Longest Interception Return
99 yds......Shaun Gayle, SD at NYG (12/23), TD

Longest Punt Return
89 yds......Joey Galloway, Sea vs NYG (11/5), TD

Longest Kickoff Return
99 yds......Tamarick Vanover, KC at Sea (9/3), TD

NFL Regular Season Team Leaders

Offensive Downs

		First Downs			3rd Downs			4th Downs		
AFC	**Tot**	**Rush**	**Pass**	**Pen**	**Made**	**Att**	**Pct**	**Made**	**Att**	**Pct**
Miami	345	98	225	22	96	209	45.9	10	13	76.9
Denver	344	114	205	25	89	207	43.0	8	18	44.4
Pittsburgh	344	117	193	34	97	230	42.2	11	20	55.0
New England	335	106	207	22	99	260	38.1	17	39	43.6
Oakland	317	104	189	24	85	213	39.9	7	14	50.0
San Diego	314	108	185	21	95	222	42.8	12	21	57.1
Seattle	311	121	171	19	82	217	37.8	9	13	69.2
Buffalo	300	130	142	28	71	225	31.6	7	13	53.8
Houston	296	109	157	30	99	228	43.4	7	12	58.3
Kansas City	295	113	164	18	82	231	35.5	15	22	68.2
Cleveland	293	83	189	21	85	211	40.3	10	21	47.6
Cincinnati	288	76	184	28	72	205	35.1	10	19	52.6
Jacksonville	283	100	154	29	74	205	36.1	6	15	40.0
Indianapolis	281	110	147	24	80	205	39.0	12	19	63.2
NY Jets	254	78	159	17	65	223	29.1	10	22	45.5

		First Downs			3rd Downs			4th Downs		
NFC	**Tot**	**Rush**	**Pass**	**Pen**	**Made**	**Att**	**Pct**	**Made**	**Att**	**Pct**
Dallas	364	141	195	28	83	186	44.6	8	13	61.5
San Francisco	355	109	231	15	109	223	48.9	11	18	61.1
Detroit	349	91	230	28	95	208	45.7	8	13	61.5
Minnesota	342	91	223	28	114	239	47.7	4	11	36.4
Chicago	340	116	201	23	88	207	42.5	13	19	68.4
Green Bay	339	84	235	20	108	220	49.1	5	8	62.5
Atlanta	317	85	216	16	80	198	40.4	7	13	53.8
Washington	297	105	169	23	93	230	40.4	10	17	58.8
New Orleans	294	75	202	17	91	215	42.3	5	11	45.5
St. Louis	292	77	199	16	87	239	36.4	15	26	57.7
Philadelphia	290	126	145	19	89	233	38.2	10	17	58.8
NY Giants	288	113	150	25	85	209	40.7	7	14	50.0
Arizona	285	65	184	36	71	205	34.6	2	13	15.4
Tampa Bay	283	101	159	23	68	195	34.9	7	13	53.8
Carolina	250	74	157	19	93	244	38.1	4	9	44.4

Takeaways/Giveaways

	Takeaways			Giveaways			Net
AFC	**Int**	**Fum**	**Tot**	**Int**	**Fum**	**Tot**	**Diff**
Kansas City	16	17	33	10	11	21	+12
Indianapolis	13	13	26	11	11	22	+4
Buffalo	17	11	28	14	12	26	+2
Pittsburgh	22	12	34	21	13	34	0
Houston	21	17	38	18	20	38	0
Oakland	11	22	33	21	13	34	-1
Miami	14	16	30	20	12	32	-2
San Diego	17	10	27	18	12	30	-3
Jacksonville	13	11	24	15	13	28	-4
New England	15	14	29	16	20	36	-7
Seattle	16	9	25	23	9	32	-7
Cleveland	17	7	24	20	11	31	-7
Cincinnati	12	12	24	18	14	32	-8
New York Jets	17	17	34	24	18	42	-8
Denver	8	13	21	14	16	30	-9

	Takeaways			Giveaways			Net
NFC	**Int**	**Fum**	**Tot**	**Int**	**Fum**	**Tot**	**Diff**
Minnesota	25	15	40	16	13	29	+11
Detroit	22	13	35	12	13	25	+10
Atlanta	18	12	30	12	9	21	+9
San Francisco	26	8	34	16	12	28	+6
Washington	16	19	35	20	10	30	+5
New Orleans	17	12	29	14	11	25	+4
New York Giants	16	15	31	13	15	28	+3
Chicago	16	13	29	10	16	26	+3
Dallas	19	6	25	10	13	23	+2
Philadelphia	19	19	38	19	17	36	+2
Arizona	19	23	42	24	19	43	-1
St. Louis	22	14	36	23	16	39	-3
Tampa Bay	14	16	30	20	14	34	-4
Carolina	21	16	37	25	16	41	-4
Green Bay	13	3	16	15	6	21	-5

Overall Club Rankings

Combined AFC and NFC rankings by yards gained on offense and yards given up on defense.

	Offense			Defense		
	Rush	**Pass**	**Rank**	**Rush**	**Pass**	**Rank**
Arizona	29	17	**24**	30	15	**26**
Atlanta	27	6	**10**	9	30	**29**
Buffalo	6	21	**20**	11	16	**13**
Carolina	20	24	**26**	10	14	**7t**
Chicago	9	12	**9**	5	27	**19**
Cincinnati	24	11	**17**	26	29	**30**
Cleveland	22	14	**21**	20	24	**24**
Dallas	2	13	**5**	16	8	**9**
Denver	5	7	**3**	23	9	**15**
Detroit	14	2	**1**	18	23	**23**
Green Bay	26	3	**7**	7	21	**14**
Houston	18	19	**23**	8	3	**5**
Indianapolis	11	23	**22**	6	20	**7t**
Jacksonville	17	27	**28**	24	17	**21**
Kansas City	1	25	**14**	3	5	**2**
Miami	21	4	**8**	12	19	**16**
Minnesota	16	5	**4**	4	28	**20**
New England	10	15	**12**	22	25	**28**
New Orleans	28	10	**19**	21	22	**22**
NY Giants	13	30	**29**	27	4	**17**
NY Jets	30	28	**30**	25	1	**6**
Oakland	8	16	**11**	17	10	**11**
Philadelphia	4	29	**25**	19	2	**4**
Pittsburgh	12	8	**6**	2	6	**3**
St. Louis	25	9	**15**	13	13	**12**
San Diego	15	18	**16**	14	12	**10**
San Francisco	23	1	**2**	1	11	**1**
Seattle	3	22	**13**	28	18	**25**
Tampa Bay	19	26	**27**	15	26	**27**
Washington	7	20	**18**	29	7	**18**

AFC Team by Team Statistics

Players with more than one team during the regular season are listed with final club; (*) indicates rookies.

Buffalo Bills

Passing (5 Att)	Att	Cmp	Pct	Yds	TD	Rate
Jim Kelly	458	255	55.7	3130	22	81.1
Todd Collins*	29	14	48.3	112	0	44.0
Alex Van Pelt	18	10	55.6	106	2	110.0

Interceptions: Kelly 13, Collins 1.

Top Receivers	No	Yds	Avg	Long	TD
Bill Brooks	53	763	14.4	51-td	11
Lonnie Johnson	49	504	10.3	52	1
Russell Copeland	42	646	15.4	77-td	1
Justin Armour*	26	300	11.5	28-td	3
Thurman Thomas	26	220	8.5	60	2
Andre Reed	24	312	13.0	41-td	3
Darick Holmes*	24	214	8.9	47	0

Top Rushers	Car	Yds	Avg	Long	TD
Thurman Thomas	267	1005	3.8	49	6
Darick Holmes*	172	698	4.1	38-td	4
Carwell Gardner	20	77	3.9	17	0
Steve Tasker	8	74	9.3	17	0

Most Touchdowns	TD	Run	Rec	Ret	Pts
Bill Brooks	11	0	11	0	66
Thurman Thomas	8	6	2	0	48
Darick Holmes*	4	4	0	0	24

Three tied with three each.

2-Pt. Conversion: Carwell Gardner.

Kicking	PAT/Att	FG/Att	Lg	Pts
Steve Christie	33/35	31/40	51	126

Punts (10 or more)	No	Yds	Long	Avg	In20
Chris Mohr	86	3473	60	40.4	23

Most Interceptions: Kurt Schulz 6
Most Sacks: Bryce Paup 17½

Cincinnati Bengals

Passing (5 Att)	Att	Cmp	Pct	Yds	TD	Rate
Jeff Blake	567	326	57.5	3822	28	82.1
David Klingler	15	7	46.7	88	1	59.9

Interceptions: Blake 17, Klingler 1.

Top Receivers	No	Yds	Avg	Long	TD
Carl Pickens	99	1234	12.5	68-td	17
Tony McGee	55	754	13.7	41	4
Darnay Scott	52	821	15.8	88-td	5
Eric Bieniemy	43	424	9.9	33	0
Harold Green	27	182	6.7	24	1
James Joseph	20	118	5.9	13	0

Top Rushers	Car	Yds	Avg	Long	TD
Harold Green	171	661	3.9	23-td	2
Eric Bieniemy	98	381	3.9	27	3
Jeff Blake	53	309	5.8	30	2
Jeff Cothran	16	62	3.9	15	0
James Joseph	16	40	2.5	8	0

Most Touchdowns	TD	Run	Rec	Ret	Pts
Carl Pickens	17	0	17	0	102
Darnay Scott	5	0	5	0	30
Tony McGee	4	0	4	0	24
Eric Bieniemy	3	3	0	0	18
Harold Green	3	2	1	0	18

2-Pt. Conversions: Jeff Blake.

Kicking	PAT/Att	FG/Att	Lg	Pts
Doug Pelfrey	34/34	29/36	51	121

Punts (10 or more)	No	Yds	Long	Avg	In20
Lee Johnson	68	2861	61	42.1	26

Most Interceptions: Bracey Walker 4
Most Sacks: John Copeland 9

Cleveland Browns

Passing (5 Att)	Att	Cmp	Pct	Yds	TD	Rate
Vinny Testaverde	392	241	61.5	2883	17	87.8
Eric Zeier*	161	82	50.9	864	4	51.9

Interceptions: Testaverde 10, Zeier 9, Michael Jackson 1.

Top Receivers	No	Yds	Avg	Long	TD
Earnest Byner	61	494	8.1	29-td	2
Keenan McCardell	56	709	12.7	36	4
Andre Rison	47	701	14.9	59	3
Michael Jackson	44	714	16.2	70-td	9
Brian Kinchen	20	216	10.8	41	0

Top Rushers	Car	Yds	Avg	Long	TD
Leroy Hoard	136	547	4.0	25	0
Earnest Byner	115	432	3.8	23	2
Lorenzo White	62	163	2.6	11	1
Ernest Hunter*	30	100	3.3	15	0
Eric Zeier*	15	80	5.3	17	0

Most Touchdowns	TD	Run	Rec	Ret	Pts
Michael Jackson	9	0	9	0	54
Earnest Byner	4	2	2	0	24
Keenan McCardell	4	0	4	0	24
Andre Rison	3	0	3	0	18
Vinny Testaverde	2	2	0	0	12

2-Pt. Conversion: Eric Zeier.

Kicking	PAT/Att	FG/Att	Lg	Pts
Matt Stover	26/26	29/33	47	113

Punts (10 or more)	No	Yds	Long	Avg	In20
Tom Tupa	65	2831	64	43.6	18

Most Interceptions: Stevon Moore 5
Most Sacks: Anthony Pleasant 8

Denver Broncos

Passing (5 Att)	Att	Cmp	Pct	Yds	TD	Rate
John Elway	542	316	58.3	3970	26	86.4
Hugh Millen	40	26	65.0	197	1	85.1
Bill Musgrave	12	8	66.7	93	0	89.9

Interceptions: Elway 14.

Top Receivers	No	Yds	Avg	Long	TD
Shannon Sharpe	63	756	12.0	49	4
Anthony Miller	59	1079	18.3	62-td	14
Terrell Davis*	49	367	7.5	31	1
Aaron Craver	43	369	8.6	32	1
Ed McCaffrey	39	477	12.2	35	2
Mike Pritchard	33	441	13.4	45-td	3

Top Rushers	Car	Yds	Avg	Long	TD
Terrell Davis*	237	1117	4.7	60-td	7
Aaron Craver	73	333	4.6	23	5
Glyn Milburn	49	266	5.4	29	0
John Elway	41	176	4.3	25	1

Most Touchdowns	TD	Run	Rec	Ret	Pts
Anthony Miller	14	0	14	0	84
Terrell Davis*	8	7	1	0	48
Aaron Craver	6	5	1	0	36
Shannon Sharpe	4	0	4	0	24
Mike Pritchard	3	0	3	0	18

2-Pt. Conversions: John Elway, Ed McCaffrey.

Kicking	PAT/Att	FG/Att	Lg	Pts
Jason Elam	39/39	31/38	56	132

Punts (10 or more)	No	Yds	Long	Avg	In20
Tom Rouen	52	2192	61	42.2	22

Most Interceptions: Steve Atwater 3
Most Sacks: Michael Dean Perry 6

Houston Oilers

Passing (5 Att)	Att	Cmp	Pct	Yds	TD	Rate
Chris Chandler	356	225	63.2	2460	17	87.8
Steve McNair*	80	41	51.3	569	3	81.7
Will Furrer	99	48	48.5	483	2	40.1

Interceptions: Chandler 10, Furrer 7, McNair 1.

Top Receivers	No	Yds	Avg	Long	TD
Haywood Jeffires	61	684	11.2	35-td	8
Todd McNair	60	501	8.4	25	1
Frank Wycheck	40	471	11.8	36-td	1
Rodney Thomas*	39	204	5.2	19	2
Chris Sanders*	35	823	23.5	76-td	9
Derek Russell	24	321	13.4	57	0

Top Rushers	Car	Yds	Avg	Long	TD
Rodney Thomas*	251	947	3.8	74-td	5
Gary Brown	86	293	3.4	21	0
Marion Butts	71	185	2.6	9	4
Todd McNair	19	136	7.2	22	0

Most Touchdowns	TD	Run	Rec	Ret	Pts
Chris Sanders	9	0	9	0	54
Haywood Jeffires	8	0	8	0	48
Rodney Thomas*	7	5	2	0	44
Marion Butts	4	4	0	0	24
Chris Chandler	2	2	0	0	14
Frank Wycheck	2	1	1	0	12

2-Pt. Conversions: Chandler, R. Thomas.

Kicking	PAT/Att	FG/Att	Lg	Pts
Al Del Greco	33/33	27/31	53	114

Punts (10 or more)	No	Yds	Long	Avg	In20
Rich Camarillo	77	3165	60	41.1	26

Most Interceptions		Most Sacks	
Darryll Lewis	6	Anthony Cook*	4½
		Henry Ford	4½

Indianapolis Colts

Passing (5 Att)	Att	Cmp	Pct	Yds	TD	Rate
Jim Harbaugh	314	200	63.7	2575	17	100.7
Craig Erickson	83	50	60.2	586	3	73.7
Paul Justin	36	20	55.6	212	0	49.8

Interceptions: Harbaugh 5, Erickson 4, Justin 2.

Top Receivers	No	Yds	Avg	Long	TD
Marshall Faulk	56	475	8.5	34	3
Sean Dawkins	52	784	15.1	52	3
Ken Dilger*	42	635	15.1	42	4
Floyd Turner	35	431	12.3	47-td	4
Aaron Bailey	21	379	18.0	45	3
Roosevelt Potts	21	228	10.9	52	1

Top Rushers	Car	Yds	Avg	Long	TD
Marshall Faulk	289	1078	3.7	40	11
Roosevelt Potts	65	309	4.8	37	0
Jim Harbaugh	52	235	4.5	21	2
Vince Workman	44	165	3.8	14	1
CAR	35	139	4.0	14	1
IND	9	26	2.9	13	0
Lamont Warren	47	152	3.2	42	1

Signed: Workman on Nov. 14 (released by Car., Nov. 7).

Most Touchdowns	TD	Run	Rec	Ret	Pts
Marshall Faulk	14	11	3	0	84
Floyd Turner	4	0	4	0	28
Aaron Bailey	4	0	3	1	24
Ken Dilger*	4	0	4	0	24
Sean Dawkins	3	0	3	0	18

2-Pt. Conversions: Turner 2.

Kicking	PAT/Att	FG/Att	Lg	Pts
Cary Blanchard	25/25	19/24	50	82
Mike Cofer	9/9	4/9	52	21

Punts (10 or more)	No	Yds	Long	Avg	In20
Chris Gardocki	63	2681	69	42.6	16

Most Interceptions		Most Sacks	
Eugene Daniel	3	Tony Bennett	10½
Ashley Ambrose	3		

Jacksonville Jaguars

Passing (5 Att)	Att	Cmp	Pct	Yds	TD	Rate
Mark Brunell	346	201	58.1	2168	15	82.6
Steve Beuerlein	142	71	50.0	952	4	60.5
Rob Johnson*	7	3	42.9	24	0	12.5

Interceptions: Brunell 7, Beuerlein 7, Johnson 1.

Top Receivers	No	Yds	Avg	Long	TD
Willie Jackson	53	589	11.1	45	5
Pete Mitchell*	41	527	12.9	35	2
Cedric Tillman	30	368	12.3	28	3
Ernest Givins	29	280	9.7	18	3
Desmond Howard	26	276	10.6	24	1
Jimmy Smith	22	288	13.1	33	3
James Stewart*	21	190	9.0	38	1

Top Rushers	Car	Yds	Avg	Long	TD
James Stewart*	137	525	3.8	22	2
Mark Brunell	67	480	7.2	27-td	4
Vaughn Dunbar	110	361	3.3	26	2
Le'Shai Maston	41	186	4.5	21	0

Claimed: Dunbar on Sept. 6 (waived by Saints, Sept. 5).

Most Touchdowns	TD	Run	Rec	Ret	Pts
Willie Jackson	5	0	5	0	32
Jimmy Smith	5	0	3	2	30
Mark Brunell	4	4	0	0	24

Three tied with three each.

2-Pt. Conversion: Jackson

Kicking	PAT/Att	FG/Att	Lg	Pts
Mike Hollis	27/28	20/27	53	87

Punts (10 or more)	No	Yds	Long	Avg	In20
Bryan Barker	82	3591	63	43.8	19

Most Interceptions		Most Sacks	
Harry Colon	3	Joel Smeenge	4

Kansas City Chiefs

Passing (5 Att)	Att	Cmp	Pct	Yds	TD	Rate
Steve Bono	520	293	56.3	3121	21	79.5
Rich Gannon	11	7	63.6	57	0	76.7

Interceptions: Bono 10.

Top Receivers	No	Yds	Avg	Long	TD
Kimble Anders	55	349	6.3	28	1
Keith Cash	42	419	10.0	38-td	1
Lake Dawson	40	513	12.8	45-td	5
Webster Slaughter	34	514	15.1	38	4
Willie Davis	33	527	16.0	60-td	5
Marcus Allen	27	210	7.8	20	0

Top Rushers	Car	Yds	Avg	Long	TD
Marcus Allen	207	890	4.3	38	5
Greg Hill	155	667	4.3	27	1
Kimble Anders	58	398	6.9	44	2
Steve Bono	28	113	4.0	76-td	5

Most Touchdowns	TD	Run	Rec	Ret	Pts
Marcus Allen	5	5	0	0	30
Steve Bono	5	5	0	0	30
Willie Davis	5	0	5	0	30
Lake Dawson	5	0	5	0	30
Tamarick Vanover*	5	0	2	3	30
Webster Slaughter	4	0	4	0	24

2-Pt. Conversions: None.

Kicking	PAT/Att	FG/Att	Lg	Pts
Lin Elliott	34/37	24/30	49	106

Punts (10 or more)	No	Yds	Long	Avg	In20
Louie Aguiar	91	3990	65	43.8	29

Most Interceptions		Most Sacks	
Dale Carter	4	Neil Smith	12

Miami Dolphins

Passing (5 Att)	Att	Cmp	Pct	Yds	TD	Rate
Dan Marino	482	309	64.1	3668	24	90.8
Bernie Kosar	108	74	68.5	699	3	76.1

Interceptions: Marino 15, Kosar 5.

Top Receivers	No	Yds	Avg	Long	TD
Terry Kirby	66	618	9.4	46	3
Irving Fryar	62	910	14.7	67-td	8
O.J. McDuffie	62	819	13.2	48	8
Keith Byars	51	362	7.1	26	2
Eric Green	43	499	11.6	31-td	3
Bernie Parmalee	39	345	8.8	35	1
Gary Clark	37	525	14.2	42-td	2

Top Rushers	Car	Yds	Avg	Long	TD
Bernie Parmalee	236	878	3.7	40	9
Terry Kirby	108	414	3.8	38	4
Irving Spikes	32	126	3.9	17-td	1
Keith Byars	15	44	2.9	15	1

Most Touchdowns	TD	Run	Rec	Ret	Pts
Bernie Parmalee	10	9	1	0	60
O.J. McDuffie	8	0	8	0	50
Irving Fryar	8	0	8	0	48
Terry Kirby	7	4	3	0	42

Two tied with three each.

2-Pt. Conversions: Eric Green, McDuffie.

Kicking	PAT/Att	FG/Att	Lg	Pts
Pete Stoyanovich	37/37	27/34	51	118

Punts (10 or more)	No	Yds	Long	Avg	In20
John Kidd	57	2433	56	42.7	15

Most Interceptions		Most Sacks	
Troy Vincent	5	Bryan Cox	7½

New England Patriots

Passing (5 Att)	Att	Cmp	Pct	Yds	TD	Rate
Drew Bledsoe	636	323	50.8	3507	13	63.7
Scott Zolak	49	28	57.1	282	1	80.5

Interceptions: Bledsoe 16.

Top Receivers	No	Yds	Avg	Long	TD
Ben Coates	84	915	10.9	35	6
Vincent Brisby	66	974	14.8	72	3
Dave Meggett	52	334	6.4	19	0
Will Moore	43	502	11.7	33	1
Curtis Martin*	30	261	8.7	27	1
Sam Gash	26	242	9.3	30	1

Top Rushers	Car	Yds	Avg	Long	TD
Curtis Martin*	368	1487	4.0	49	14
Dave Meggett	60	250	4.2	25	2
Corey Croom	13	54	4.2	12	0
Drew Bledsoe	20	28	1.4	15	0

Most Touchdowns	TD	Run	Rec	Ret	Pts
Curtis Martin*	15	14	1	0	92
Ben Coates	6	0	6	0	36
Vincent Brisby	3	0	3	0	18
Dave Meggett	2	2	0	0	16
Hason Graham*	2	0	2	0	12

2-Pt. Conversions: Meggett 2, Martin.

Kicking	PAT/Att	FG/Att	Lg	Pts
Matt Bahr	27/27	23/33	55	96

Punts (10 or more)	No	Yds	Long	Avg	In20
Bryan Wagner	37	1557	57	42.1	13

Waived: Pat O'Neill on Oct. 31 (see NY Jets).

Most Interceptions		Most Sacks	
Vincent Brown	4	Willie McGinest	11

New York Jets

Passing (5 Att)	Att	Cmp	Pct	Yds	TD	Rate
Boomer Esiason	389	221	56.8	2275	16	71.4
Bubby Brister	170	93	54.7	726	4	53.7
Glenn Foley	29	16	55.2	128	0	52.1

Interceptions: Esiason 15, Brister 8, Foley 1.

Top Receivers	No	Yds	Avg	Long	TD
Adrian Murrell	71	465	6.5	43	2
Wayne Chrebet*	66	726	11.0	32	4
Johnny Mitchell	45	497	11.0	43-td	5
Charles Wilson	41	484	11.8	24	4
Kyle Brady*	26	252	9.7	29	2
Brad Baxter	26	160	6.2	20	0

Top Rushers	Car	Yds	Avg	Long	TD
Adrian Murrell	192	795	4.1	30	1
Brad Baxter	85	296	3.5	26	1
Ron Moore	43	121	2.8	14	0

Most Touchdowns	TD	Run	Rec	Ret	Pts
Johnny Mitchell	5	0	5	0	30
Wayne Chrebet*	4	0	4	0	24
Charles Wilson	4	0	4	0	24
Adrian Murrell	3	1	2	0	18
Kyle Brady*	2	0	2	0	12
Ryan Yarborough	2	0	2	0	12

2-Pt. Conversions: None.

Kicking	PAT/Att	FG/Att	Lg	Pts
Nick Lowery	24/24	17/21	50	75

Punts (10 or more)	No	Yds	Long	Avg	In20
Brian Hansen	99	4090	67	41.3	23
Pat O'Neill	44	1603	57	36.4	14
NE	41	1514	57	36.9	14
CHI	3	89	39	29.7	0
NYJ	0	0	0	0	0

Signed: O'Neill on Dec. 12 (waived by Patriots, Oct. 31, and Bears, Dec. 5)

Most Interceptions		Most Sacks	
Otis Smith	6	Hugh Douglas	10

Oakland Raiders

Passing (5 Att)	Att	Cmp	Pct	Yds	TD	Rate
Jeff Hostetler	286	172	1998	60.1	12	82.2
Vince Evans	175	100	1236	57.1	6	71.5
Billy Joe Hobert	80	44	540	55.0	6	80.2

Interceptions: Hostetler 9, Evans 8, Hobert 4.

Top Receivers	No	Yds	Avg	Long	TD
Tim Brown	89	1342	15.1	80-td	10
Harvey Williams	54	375	6.9	28	0
Daryl Hobbs	38	612	16.1	54-td	3
Derrick Fenner	35	252	7.2	23	3
Raghib Ismail	28	491	17.5	73-td	3
Andrew Glover	26	220	8.5	25	3
Kerry Cash	25	254	10.2	23	2

Top Rushers	Car	Yds	Avg	Long	TD
Harvey Williams	255	1114	4.4	60	9
Napoleon Kaufman*	108	490	4.5	28	1
Jeff Hostetler	31	119	3.8	18	0
Derrick Fenner	39	110	2.8	10	0

Most Touchdowns	TD	Run	Rec	Ret	Pts
Tim Brown	10	0	10	0	60
Harvey Williams	9	9	0	0	54
Derrick Fenner	3	0	3	0	18
Andrew Glover	3	0	3	0	18
Daryl Hobbs	3	0	3	0	18
Raghib Ismail	3	0	3	0	18

2-Pt. Conversions: None.

Kicking	PAT/Att	FG/Att	Lg	Pts
Jeff Jaeger	22/22	13/18	46	61
Cole Ford*	17/18	8/9	46	41

Punts (10 or more)	No	Yds	Long	Avg	In20
Jeff Gossett	75	3089	60	41.2	22

Most Interceptions		Most Sacks	
Terry McDaniel	6	Pat Swilling	13

Pittsburgh Steelers

Passing (5 Att)	Att	Cmp	Pct	Yds	TD	Rate
Kordell Stewart*	7	5	60	71.4	1	136.9
Neil O'Donnell	416	246	2970	59.1	17	87.7
Jim Miller	56	32	397	57.1	2	53.9
Mike Tomczak	113	65	666	57.5	1	44.3

Interceptions: Tomczak 9, O'Donnell 7, Miller 5.

Top Receivers	No	Yds	Avg	Long	TD
Yancey Thigpen	85	1307	15.4	43	5
Andre Hastings	48	502	10.5	36	1
Ernie Mills	39	679	17.4	62-td	8
Charles Johnson	38	432	11.4	33	0
Mark Bruener*	26	238	9.2	29	3
Erric Pegram	26	206	7.9	22	1
John L. Williams	24	127	5.3	20	1

Top Rushers	Car	Yds	Avg	Long	TD
Erric Pegram	213	813	3.8	38	5
Bam Morris	148	559	3.8	30-td	9
Fred McAfee	39	156	4.0	22-td	1
John L. Williams	29	110	3.8	31	0
Kordell Stewart*	15	86	5.7	22-td	1

Most Touchdowns	TD	Run	Rec	Ret	Pts
Bam Morris	9	9	0	0	54
Ernie Mills	8	0	8	0	48
Erric Pegram	6	5	1	0	38
Yancey Thigpen	5	0	5	0	30
Mark Bruener*	3	0	3	0	18

2-Pt. Conversions: Pegram

Kicking	PAT/Att	FG/Att	Lg	Pts
Norm Johnson	39/39	34/41	50	141

Punts (10 or more)	No	Yds	Long	Avg	In20
Rohn Stark	59	2368	64	40.1	20

Most Interceptions		Most Sacks	
Willie Williams	7	Kevin Greene	9

San Diego Chargers

Passing (5 Att)	Att	Cmp	Pct	Yds	TD	Rate
Stan Humphries	478	282	59.0	3381	17	80.4
Gale Gilbert	61	36	59.0	325	0	46.1

Interceptions: Humphries 14, Gilbert 4.

Top Receivers	No	Yds	Avg	Long	TD
Tony Martin	90	1224	13.6	51-td	6
Ronnie Harmon	62	662	10.7	44	5
Shawn Jefferson	48	621	12.9	45	2
Mark Seay	45	537	11.9	38-td	3
Alfred Pupunu	35	315	9.0	26	0

Top Rushers	Car	Yds	Avg	Long	TD
Natrone Means	186	730	3.9	36	5
Aaron Hayden*	128	470	3.7	20	3
Ronnie Harmon	51	187	3.7	48-td	1
Rodney Culver	47	155	3.3	17	3
Terrell Fletcher*	26	140	5.4	46	1

Most Touchdowns	TD	Run	Rec	Ret	Pts
Ronnie Harmon	6	1	5	0	36
Tony Martin	6	0	6	0	36
Natrone Means	5	5	0	0	30
Mark Seay	3	0	3	0	20
Andre Coleman	3	0	0	3	18
Rodney Culver	3	3	0	0	18
Aaron Hayden*	3	3	0	0	18

2-Pt. Conversion: Seay.

Kicking	PAT/Att	FG/Att	Lg	Pts
John Carney	32/33	21/26	45	95

Punts (10 or more)	No	Yds	Long	Avg	In20
Darren Bennett	72	3221	66	44.7	28

Most Interceptions		Most Sacks	
Rodney Harrison	5	Leslie O'Neal	12½

Seattle Seahawks

Passing (5 Att)	Att	Cmp	Pct	Yds	TD	Rate
Rick Mirer	391	209	53.5	2564	13	63.7
John Friesz	120	64	53.3	795	6	80.4

Interceptions: Mirer 20, Friesz 3.

Top Receivers	No	Yds	Avg	Long	TD
Brian Blades	77	1001	13.0	49	4
Joey Galloway*	67	1039	15.5	59-td	7
Chris Warren	35	247	7.1	20-td	1
Carlester Crumpler	23	254	11.0	24	1
Christian Fauria*	17	181	10.6	20-td	1
Robb Thomas	12	239	19.9	50-td	1
Mack Strong	12	117	9.8	25	3

Top Rushers	Car	Yds	Avg	Long	TD
Chris Warren	310	1346	4.3	52	15
Steve Broussard	46	222	4.8	21-td	1
Lamar Smith	36	215	6.0	68	0
Rick Mirer	43	193	4.5	24	1
Joey Galloway*	11	154	14.0	86-td	1

Most Touchdowns	TD	Run	Rec	Ret	Pts
Chris Warren	16	15	1	0	96
Joey Galloway*	9	1	7	1	54
Brian Blades	4	0	4	0	24
Mack Strong	4	1	3	0	24

2-Pt.Conversions: None.

Kicking	PAT/Att	FG/Att	Lg	Pts
Todd Peterson	40/40	23/28	49	109

Punts (10 or more)	No	Yds	Long	Avg	In20
Rick Tuten	83	3735	73	45.0	21

Most Interceptions		Most Sacks	
Robert Blackmon	5	Cortez Kennedy	6½

AFC Team Leaders

Offense

	Points		Yardage			
	For	Avg	Rush	Pass	Total	Avg
Denver	388	24.3	1995	4045	6040	377.5
Pittsburgh	407	25.4	1852	3917	5769	360.6
Miami	398	24.9	1506	4210	5716	357.3
Oakland	348	21.8	1932	3573	5505	344.1
New England	294	18.4	1866	3591	5457	341.1
Seattle	363	22.7	2178	3092	5270	329.4
Kansas City	358	22.4	2222	3020	5242	327.6
San Diego	321	20.1	1747	3466	5213	325.8
Cincinnati	349	21.8	1439	3753	5192	324.5
Buffalo	350	21.9	1993	3124	5117	319.8
Cleveland	289	18.1	1482	3594	5076	317.3
Indianapolis	331	20.7	1855	3064	4919	307.4
Houston	348	21.8	1664	3241	4905	306.6
Jacksonville	275	17.2	1705	2790	4495	280.9
NY Jets	233	14.6	1279	2788	4067	254.2

Defense

	Points		Yardage			
	Opp	Avg	Rush	Pass	Total	Avg
Kansas City	241	15.1	1327	3222	4549	284.3
Pittsburgh	327	20.4	1321	3240	4561	285.1
Houston	324	20.3	1526	3125	4651	290.7
NY Jets	384	24.0	2016	2740	4756	297.3
Indianapolis	316	19.8	1457	3570	5027	314.2
San Diego	323	20.2	1691	3383	5074	317.1
Oakland	332	20.8	1794	3310	5104	319.0
Buffalo	335	20.9	1626	3502	5128	320.5
Denver	345	21.6	1895	3298	5193	324.6
Miami	332	20.8	1675	3569	5244	327.8
Jacksonville	404	25.3	2003	3512	5515	344.7
Cleveland	356	22.3	1826	3822	5648	353.0
Seattle	366	22.9	2130	3539	5669	354.3
New England	377	23.6	1878	3886	5764	360.3
Cincinnati	374	23.4	2104	4245	6349	396.8

NFC Team by Team Statistics

Players with more than one team during the regular season are listed with club they ended season with; (*) indicates rookies.

Arizona Cardinals

Passing (5 Att)	Att	Cmp	Pct	Yds	TD	Rate
Dave Krieg	521	304	58.3	3554	16	72.6
Mike Buck	32	20	62.5	271	1	99.9

Interceptions: Krieg 21.

Top Receivers	No	Yds	Avg	Long	TD
Larry Centers	101	962	9.5	32	2
Rob Moore	63	907	14.4	45	5
Frank Sanders*	52	883	17.0	48	2
Anthony Edwards	29	417	14.4	28-td	2
Garrison Hearst	29	243	8.4	39	1
Wendall Gaines	14	117	8.4	22-td	2
Oscar McBride*	13	112	8.6	24	2

Top Rushers	Car	Yds	Avg	Long	TD
Garrison Hearst	284	1070	3.8	38	1
Larry Centers	78	254	3.3	20	2
Dave Krieg	19	29	1.5	17	0

Most Touchdowns	TD	Run	Rec	Ret	Pts
Rob Moore	5	0	5	0	32
Larry Centers	4	2	2	0	24
Aeneas Williams	3	0	0	3	18

Five tied with two each.
2-Pt. Conversion: Stevie Anderson and Sanders (2), Moore.

Kicking	PAT/Att	FG/Att	Lg	Pts
Greg Davis	19/19	30/39	55	109

Punts (10 or more)	No	Yds	Long	Avg	In20
Jeff Feagles	72	3150	60	43.8	20

Most Interceptions
Aeneas Williams 6

Most Sacks
Clyde Simmons 11

Atlanta Falcons

Passing (5 Att)	Att	Cmp	Pct	Yds	TD	Rate
Jeff George	557	336	60.3	4143	24	89.5
Bobby Hebert	45	28	62.2	313	2	88.5

Interceptions: George 11, Hebert 1.

Top Receivers	No	Yds	Avg	Long	TD
Eric Metcalf	104	1189	11.4	62-td	8
Terance Mathis	78	1039	13.3	54-td	9
Bert Emanuel	74	1039	14.0	52	5
Craig Heyward	37	350	9.5	25	2
J.J. Birden	31	303	9.8	24	1
Tyrone Brown*	17	198	11.6	26	0

Top Rushers	Car	Yds	Avg	Long	TD
Craig Heyward	236	1083	4.6	31	6
Jamal Anderson	39	161	4.1	13	1
Eric Metcalf	28	133	4.8	23t	1
Jeff George	27	17	0.6	6	0

Most Touchdowns	TD	Run	Rec	Ret	Pts
Eric Metcalf	10	1	8	1	60
Terance Mathis	9	0	9	0	60
Craig Heyward	8	6	2	0	48
Bert Emanuel	5	0	5	0	30

Six tied with one each.
2-Pt. Conversions: Mathis 3.

Kicking	PAT/Att	FG/Att	Lg	Pts
Morten Andersen	29/30	31/37	59	122

Released: Tony Zendejas on Oct. 13 (see San Francisco).

Punts (10 or more)	No	Yds	Long	Avg	In20
Dan Stryzinski	67	2759	64	41.2	21

Most Interceptions
Jessie Tuggle 3
Kevin Ross 3
Terry Taylor 3

Most Sacks
Chris Doleman 9

Carolina Panthers

Passing (5 Att)	Att	Cmp	Pct	Yds	TD	Rate
Kerry Collins*	433	214	49.4	2717	14	61.9
Frank Reich	84	37	44.0	441	2	58.7
Jack Trudeau	17	11	64.7	100	0	40.9

Interceptions: Collins 19, Trudeau 3, Reich 2.

Top Receivers	No	Yds	Avg	Long	TD
Mark Carrier	66	1002	15.2	66-td	3
Willie Green	47	882	18.8	89-td	6
Eric Guliford	29	444	15.3	49	1
Bob Christian	29	255	8.8	23	1
Anthony Johnson	29	207	7.1	37	0
CHI	13	86	6.6	18	0
CAR	16	121	7.6	37	0

Claimed: Johnson on Nov. 7 (waived by Bears, Nov. 6).

Top Rushers	Car	Yds	Avg	Long	TD
Darryl Moore	195	740	3.8	53-td	4
Howard Griffith	65	197	3.0	15	1
Bob Christian	41	158	3.9	17	0
Anthony Johnson	30	140	4.7	23-td	1
CHI	6	30	5.0	11	0
CAR	24	110	4.6	23-td	1
Blair Thomas	22	90	4.1	13	0

Signed: Thomas on Nov. 7.

Most Touchdowns	TD	Run	Rec	Ret	Pts
Willie Green	6	0	6	0	36
Darryl Moore	4	4	0	0	24
Mark Carrier	3	0	3	0	18
Kerry Collins*	3	3	0	0	18
Pete Metzelaars	3	0	3	0	18

2-Pt. Conversions: Bob Christian, Walter Rasby.

Kicking	PAT/Att	FG/Att	Lg	Pts
John Kasay	27/28	26/33	52	105

Punts (10 or more)	No	Yds	Long	Avg	In20
Tommy Barnhardt	95	3906	54	41.1	27

Most Interceptions
Brett Maxie 6

Most Sacks
Lamar Lathon 8

Chicago Bears

Passing (5 Att)	Att	Cmp	Pct	Yds	TD	Rate
Erik Kramer	522	315	60.3	3838	29	93.5

Interceptions: Kramer 10.

Top Receivers	No	Yds	Avg	Long	TD
Jeff Graham	82	1301	15.9	51	4
Curtis Conway	62	1037	16.7	76-td	12
Tony Carter	40	329	8.2	27	1
Robert Green	28	246	8.8	28	0
Keith Jennings	25	217	8.7	20	6

Top Rushers	Car	Yds	Avg	Long	TD
Rashaan Salaam*	296	1074	3.6	42	10
Robert Green	107	570	5.3	38	3
Lewis Tillman	29	78	2.7	9	0
Curtis Conway	5	77	15.4	20	0
Erik Kramer	35	39	1.1	11	1

Most Touchdowns	TD	Run	Rec	Ret	Pts
Curtis Conway	12	0	12	0	72
Rashaan Salaam*	10	10	0	0	60
Keith Jennings	6	0	6	0	36
Jeff Graham	4	0	4	0	24
Robert Green	3	3	0	0	18
Michael Timpson	3	1	2	0	18

2-Pt. Conversions: None.

Kicking	PAT/Att	FG/Att	Lg	Pts
Kevin Butler	45/45	23/31	47	114

Punts (10 or more)	No	Yds	Long	Avg	In20
Todd Sauerbrun*	55	2080	61	37.8	16

Most Interceptions
Donnell Woolford...........4

Most Sacks
Jim Flanigan 11

Dallas Cowboys

Passing (5 Att)	Att	Cmp	Pct	Yds	TD	Rate
Jason Garrett	5	4	80.0	46	1	144.6
Troy Aikman	432	280	64.8	3304	16	93.6
Wade Wilson	57	38	66.7	391	1	70.1

Interceptions: Aikman 7, Wilson 3.

Top Receivers	No	Yds	Avg	Long	TD
Michael Irvin	111	1603	14.4	50	10
Jay Novacek	62	705	11.4	33-td	5
Emmitt Smith	62	375	6.0	40	0
Kevin Williams	38	613	16.1	48-td	2
Daryl Johnston	30	248	8.3	24	1

Top Rushers	Car	Yds	Avg	Long	TD
Emmitt Smith	377	1773	4.7	60-td	25
Sherman Williams*	48	205	4.3	44-td	1
Daryl Johnston	25	111	4.4	18	2
Kevin Williams	10	53	5.3	14	0
Troy Aikman	21	32	1.5	12	1

Most Touchdowns	TD	Run	Rec	Ret	Pts
Emmitt Smith	25	25	0	0	150
Michael Irvin	10	0	10	0	60
Jay Novacek	5	0	5	0	32
Daryl Johnston	3	2	1	0	18
Larry Brown	2	0	0	2	12
Kevin Williams	2	0	2	0	12

2-Pt. Conversion: Novacek.

Kicking	PAT/Att	FG/Att	Lg	Pts
Chris Boniol	46/48	27/28	45	127

Punts (10 or more)	No	Yds	Long	Avg	In20
John Jett	53	2166	58	40.9	17

Most Interceptions		Most Sacks	
Larry Brown	6	Charles Haley	10½
Brock Marion	6		

Detroit Lions

Passing (5 Att)	Att	Cmp	Pct	Yds	TD	Rate
Scott Mitchell	583	346	59.3	4338	32	92.3
Don Majkowski	20	15	75.0	161	1	114.8

Interceptions: Mitchell 12.

Top Receivers	No	Yds	Avg	Long	TD
Herman Moore	123	1686	13.7	69-td	14
Brett Perriman	108	1488	13.8	91-td	9
Barry Sanders	48	398	8.3	40	1
Johnnie Morton	44	590	13.4	32-td	8
David Sloan*	17	184	10.8	24	1

Top Rushers	Car	Yds	Avg	Long	TD
Barry Sanders	314	1500	4.8	75t	11
Scott Mitchell	36	104	2.9	18	4
Ron Rivers	18	73	4.1	19	1
Brett Perriman	5	48	9.6	16	0

Most Touchdowns	TD	Run	Rec	Ret	Pts
Herman Moore	14	0	14	0	84
Barry Sanders	12	11	1	0	72
Brett Perriman	9	0	9	0	56
Johnnie Morton	8	0	8	0	48
Scott Mitchell	4	4	0	0	24

2-Pt. Conversion: Perriman.

Kicking	PAT/Att	FG/Att	Lg	Pts
Jason Hanson	48/48	28/34	56	132

Punts (10 or more)	No	Yds	Long	Avg	In20
Mark Royals	57	2393	69	42.0	15

Most Interceptions		Most Sacks	
Willie Clay	8	Broderick Thomas	10½

Green Bay Packers

Passing (5 Att)	Att	Cmp	Pct	Yds	TD	Rate
Brett Favre	570	359	63.0	4413	38	99.5
Ty Detmer	16	8	50.0	81	1	59.6
T.J. Rubley	6	4	66.7	39	0	45.1

Interceptions: Favre 13, Detmer 1, Rubley 1.
Signed: Jim McMahon on Nov. 28 (released by Browns, Nov. 27).

Top Receivers	No	Yds	Avg	Long	TD
Robert Brooks	102	1497	14.7	99-td	13
Edgar Bennett	61	648	10.6	35	4
Mark Chmura	54	679	12.6	33	7
Dorsey Levens	48	434	9.0	27	4
Mark Ingram	39	469	12.0	29	3
Anthony Morgan	31	344	11.1	29-td	4

Top Rushers	Car	Yds	Avg	Long	TD
Edgar Bennett	316	1067	3.4	23	3
Brett Favre	39	181	4.6	40	3
Dorsey Levens	36	120	3.3	22	3

Most Touchdowns	TD	Run	Rec	Ret	Pts
Robert Brooks	13	0	13	0	78
Mark Chmura	7	0	7	0	44
Edgar Bennett	7	3	4	0	42
Dorsey Levens	7	3	4	0	42
Anthony Morgan	4	0	4	0	24
Brett Favre	3	3	0	0	18
Mark Ingram	3	0	3	0	18

2-Pt. Conversion: Chmura.

Kicking	PAT/Att	FG/Att	Lg	Pts
Chris Jacke	43/43	17/23	51	94
Craig Hentrich	5/5	3/5	49	14

Punts (10 or more)	No	Yds	Long	Avg	In20
Craig Hentrich	65	2740	61	42.2	26

Most Interceptions		Most Sacks	
LeRoy Butler	5	Reggie White	12

Minnesota Vikings

Passing (5 Att)	Att	Cmp	Pct	Yds	TD	Rate
Warren Moon	606	377	62.2	4228	33	91.5
Brad Johnson	36	25	69.4	272	0	68.3

Interceptions: Moon 14, Johnson 2.

Top Receivers	No	Yds	Avg	Long	TD
Cris Carter	122	1371	11.2	60-td	17
Jake Reed	72	1167	16.2	55-td	9
Amp Lee	71	558	7.9	33	1
Qadry Ismail	32	597	18.7	85-td	3
Andrew Jordan	27	185	6.9	17	2

Top Rushers	Car	Yds	Avg	Long	TD
Robert Smith	139	632	4.5	58-td	5
Scottie Graham	110	406	3.7	26	2
Amp Lee	69	371	5.4	66-td	2
James Stewart*	31	144	4.6	51	0
Warren Moon	33	82	2.5	16	0

Most Touchdowns	TD	Run	Rec	Ret	Pts
Cris Carter	17	0	17	0	102
Jake Reed	9	0	9	0	54
Robert Smith	5	5	0	0	32
Qadry Ismail	3	0	3	0	18
Amp Lee	3	2	1	0	18

2-Pt. Conversion: R. Smith.

Kicking	PAT/Att	FG/Att	Lg	Pts
Fuad Reveiz	44/44	26/36	51	122

Punts (10 or more)	No	Yds	Long	Avg	In20
Mike Saxon	72	2948	60	40.9	21

Most Interceptions		Most Sacks	
Orlando Thomas*	9	John Randle	10½

New Orleans Saints

Passing (5 Att)	Att	Cmp	Pct	Yds	TD	Rate
Jim Everett	567	345	60.8	3970	26	87.0
Tommy Hodson	5	3	60.0	14	0	64.6

Interceptions: Everett 14.

Top Receivers	No	Yds	Avg	Long	TD
Quinn Early	81	1087	13.4	70-td	8
Wesley Walls	57	694	12.2	29	4
Irv Smith	45	466	10.4	43	3
Michael Haynes	41	597	14.6	48	4
Torrance Small	38	461	12.1	32-td	5
Derek Brown	35	266	7.6	19	1

Top Rushers	Car	Yds	Avg	Long	TD
Mario Bates	244	951	3.9	66-td	7
Ray Zellars*	50	162	3.2	11	2
Derek Brown	49	159	3.2	35-td	1
Torrance Small	6	75	12.5	44-td	1

Most Touchdowns	TD	Run	Rec	Ret	Pts
Quinn Early	8	0	8	0	48
Mario Bates	7	7	0	0	42
Torrance Small	6	1	5	0	36
Wesley Walls	4	0	4	0	26
Michael Haynes	4	0	4	0	24
Irv Smith	3	0	3	0	20

2-Pt. Conversions: Smith, Walls.

Kicking	PAT/Att	FG/Att	Lg	Pts
Doug Brien	35/35	19/29	51	92
SF	19/19	7/12	51	40
NO	16/16	12/17	47	52
Chip Lohmiller	11/13	8/14	51	35

Signed: Brien on Oct. 31 (released by SF, Oct. 16).

Punts (10 or more)	No	Yds	Long	Avg	In20
Klaus Wilmsmeyer	73	2965	53	40.6	21

Most Interceptions		Most Sacks	
Jimmy Spencer	4	Wayne Martin	13

New York Giants

Passing (5 Att)	Att	Cmp	Pct	Yds	TD	Rate
Dave Brown	456	254	55.7	2814	11	73.1
Tommy Maddox	23	6	26.1	49	0	0.0

Interceptions: Brown 10, Maddox 3.

Top Receivers	No	Yds	Avg	Long	TD
Chris Calloway	56	796	14.2	49	3
Mike Sherrard	44	577	13.1	57-td	4
Aaron Pierce	33	310	9.4	26	0
Herschel Walker	31	234	7.5	34	1
Rodney Hampton	24	142	5.9	18	0

Top Rushers	Car	Yds	Avg	Long	TD
Rodney Hampton	306	1182	3.9	32	10
Tyrone Wheatley*	78	245	3.1	19-td	3
Dave Brown	45	228	5.1	23	4
Herschel Walker	31	126	4.1	36	0
Keith Elias	10	44	4.4	8	0

Most Touchdowns	TD	Run	Rec	Ret	Pts
Rodney Hampton	10	10	0	0	62
Dave Brown	4	4	0	0	24
Mike Sherrard	4	0	4	0	24
Chris Calloway	3	0	3	0	18
Tyrone Wheatley*	3	3	0	0	18

2-Pt. Conversion: Hampton.

Kicking	PAT/Att	FG/Att	Lg	Pts
Brad Daluiso	28/28	20/28	51	88

Punts (10 or more)	No	Yds	Long	Avg	In20
Mike Horan	72	3063	60	42.5	15

Most Interceptions		Most Sacks	
Vencie Glenn	5	Michael Strahan	7½
Phillippi Sparks	5		

Philadelphia Eagles

Passing (5 Att)	Att	Cmp	Pct	Yds	TD	Rate
Rodney Peete	375	215	57.3	2326	8	67.3
R. Cunningham	121	69	57.0	605	3	61.5

Interceptions: Peete 14, Cunningham 5.

Top Receivers	No	Yds	Avg	Long	TD
Calvin Williams	63	768	12.2	37-td	2
Ricky Watters	62	434	7.0	24	1
Fred Barnett	48	585	12.2	33	5
Rob Carpenter	29	318	11.0	29	0
Ed West	20	190	9.5	26	1
Kelvin Martin	17	206	12.1	22	0

Top Rushers	Car	Yds	Avg	Long	TD
Ricky Watters	337	1273	3.8	57	11
Charlie Garner	108	588	5.4	55-td	6
Rodney Peete	32	147	4.6	18	1
R. Cunningham	21	98	4.7	20	0

Most Touchdowns	TD	Run	Rec	Ret	Pts
Ricky Watters	12	11	1	0	72
Charlie Garner	6	6	0	0	36
Fred Barnett	5	0	5	0	32
Calvin Williams	2	0	2	0	14
Reggie Johnson	2	0	2	0	12

2-Pt. Conversions: Barnett, C. Williams.

Kicking	PAT/Att	FG/Att	Lg	Pts
Gary Anderson	32/33	22/30	43	98

Punts (10 or more)	No	Yds	Long	Avg	In20
Tom Hutton*	85	3682	63	43.3	20

Most Interceptions		Most Sacks	
William Thomas	7	William Fuller	13

St. Louis Rams

Passing (5 Att)	Att	Cmp	Pct	Yds	TD	Rate
Chris Miller	405	232	57.3	2623	18	76.2
Mark Rypien	217	129	59.4	1448	9	77.9
Dave Barr*	9	5	55.6	42	0	67.8

Interceptions: Miller 15, Rypien 8.

Top Receivers	No	Yds	Avg	Long	TD
Isaac Bruce	119	1781	15.0	72	13
Troy Drayton	47	458	9.7	31	4
Johnny Bailey	38	265	7.0	25	0
Todd Kinchen	36	419	11.6	35	4
Jessie Hester	30	399	13.3	38-td	3
Marv Cook	26	135	5.2	16	1
Alexander Wright	23	368	16.0	50	2

Top Rushers	Car	Yds	Avg	Long	TD
Jerome Bettis	183	637	3.5	41	3
Leonard Russell	66	203	3.1	18	0
Johnny Bailey	36	182	5.1	17	2
Greg Robinson	40	165	4.1	37	0

Most Touchdowns	TD	Run	Rec	Ret	Pts
Isaac Bruce	13	0	13	0	80
Troy Drayton	4	0	4	0	24
Todd Kinchen	4	0	4	0	24
Jerome Bettis	3	3	0	0	18
Jessie Hester	3	0	3	0	18

2-Pt. Conversions: Johnny Bailey, Bruce.

Kicking	PAT/Att	FG/Att	Lg	Pts
Steve McLaughlin*	17/17	8/16	45	41
Dean Biasucci	13/14	9/12	51	40

Punts (10 or more)	No	Yds	Long	Avg	In20
Sean Landeta	83	3679	63	44.3	23

Most Interceptions		Most Sacks	
Toby Wright	6	D'Marco Farr	11½

San Francisco 49ers

Passing (5 Att)	Att	Cmp	Pct	Yds	TD	Rate
Steve Young	447	299	66.9	3200	20	92.3
Elvis Grbac	183	127	69.4	1469	8	96.6
Cary Conklin	12	4	33.3	48	0	46.5

Interceptions: Young, 11, Grbac 5.

Top Receivers	No	Yds	Avg	Long	TD
Jerry Rice	122	1848	15.1	81-td	15
Derek Loville	87	662	7.6	31	3
Brent Jones	60	595	9.9	39	3
William Floyd	47	348	7.4	23	1
J.J. Stokes*	38	517	13.6	41-td	4
John Taylor	29	387	13.3	40	2

Top Rushers	Car	Yds	Avg	Long	TD
Derek Loville	218	723	3.3	27	10
Steve Young	50	250	5.0	29	3
William Floyd	64	237	3.7	23	2
Ricky Ervins	23	88	3.8	13	0

Most Touchdowns	TD	Run	Rec	Ret	Pts
Jerry Rice	17	1	15	1	104
Derek Loville	13	10	3	0	80
J.J. Stokes*	4	0	4	0	24
William Floyd	3	2	1	0	18
Brent Jones	3	0	3	0	18
Steve Young	3	3	0	0	18

2-Pt. Conversions: Loville, Rice.

Kicking	PAT/Att	FG/Att	Lg	Pts
Jeff Wilkins	27/29	12/13	40	63
Tony Zendejas	5/6	3/6	45	14
ATL	0/0	2/3	45	6
SF	5/6	1/3	38	8

Released: Doug Brien on Oct. 16 (see New Orleans).
Signed: Zendejas on Oct. 18 (released by Falcons, Oct. 13).
Waived: Zendejas (Nov. 8).

Punts (10 or more)	No	Yds	Long	Avg	In20
Tommy Thompson	57	2312	65	40.6	13

Most Interceptions		Most Sacks	
Tyronne Drakeford	5	Rickey Jackson	9½
Merton Hanks	5		

Tampa Bay Buccaneers

Passing (5 Att)	Att	Cmp	Pct	Yds	TD	Rate
Trent Dilfer	415	224	54.0	2774	4	60.1
Casey Weldon	91	42	46.2	519	1	58.8

Interceptions: Dilfer 18, Weldon 2.

Top Receivers	No	Yds	Avg	Long	TD
Jackie Harris	62	751	12.1	33	1
Alvin Harper	46	633	13.8	49	2
Courtney Hawkins	41	493	12.0	47	0
Horace Copeland	35	605	17.3	64-td	2
Lawrence Dawsey	30	372	12.4	26	0

Top Rushers	Car	Yds	Avg	Long	TD
Errict Rhett	332	1207	3.6	21	11
Jerry Ellison	26	218	8.4	75	5
Trent Dilfer	23	115	5.0	21-td	2

Most Touchdowns	TD	Run	Rec	Ret	Pts
Errict Rhett	11	11	0	0	66
Jerry Ellison	5	5	0	0	30
Horace Copeland	2	0	2	0	12
Trent Dilfer	2	2	0	0	12
Alvin Harper	2	0	2	0	12

2-Pt. Conversions: None.

Kicking	PAT/Att	FG/Att	Lg	Pts
Michael Husted	25/25	19/26	53	82

Punts (10 or more)	No	Yds	Long	Avg	In20
Reggie Roby	77	3296	61	42.8	23

Most Interceptions		Most Sacks	
Martin Mayhew	5	Santana Dotson	5

Washington Redskins

Passing (5 Att)	Att	Cmp	Pct	Yds	TD	Rate
Gus Frerotte	396	199	50.3	2751	13	70.2
Heath Shuler	125	66	52.8	745	3	55.6

Interceptions: Frerotte 13, Shuler 7.

Top Receivers	No	Yds	Avg	Long	TD
Henry Ellard	56	1005	17.9	59	5
Brian Mitchell	38	324	8.5	22-td	1
Michael Westbrook*	34	522	15.4	45	1
Terry Allen	31	232	7.5	24	1
Leslie Shepherd	29	486	16.8	73-td	2
Marc Logan	25	276	11.0	32	2

Top Rushers	Car	Yds	Avg	Long	TD
Terry Allen	338	1309	3.9	28	10
Brian Mitchell	46	301	6.5	36t	1
Michael Westbrook*	6	114	19.0	58t	1

Most Touchdowns	TD	Run	Rec	Ret	Pts
Terry Allen	11	10	1	0	66
Henry Ellard	5	0	5	0	30
Marc Logan	3	1	2	0	18
Brian Mitchell	3	1	1	1	18
Leslie Shepherd	3	1	2	0	18

2-Pt. Conversions: None.

Kicking	PAT/Att	FG/Att	Lg	Pts
Eddie Murray	33/33	27/36	52	114

Punts (10 or more)	No	Yds	Long	Avg	In20
Matt Turk	74	3140	60	42.4	29

Most Interceptions		Most Sacks	
Tom Carter	4	Ken Harvey	7½

NFC Team Leaders

Offense

	Points		Yardage			
	For	Avg	Rush	Pass	Total	Avg
Detroit	436	27.3	1753	4360	6113	382.1
San Francisco	457	28.6	1479	4608	6087	380.4
Minnesota	412	25.8	1733	4205	5938	371.1
Dallas	435	27.2	2201	3623	5824	364.0
Green Bay	404	25.3	1428	4322	5750	359.4
Chicago	392	24.5	1930	3743	5673	354.6
Atlanta	362	22.6	1393	4186	5579	348.7
St. Louis	309	19.3	1431	3805	5236	327.3
Washington	326	20.4	1956	3228	5184	324.0
New Orleans	319	19.9	1390	3788	5178	323.6
Arizona	275	17.2	1363	3503	4866	304.1
Philadelphia	318	19.9	2121	2686	4807	300.4
Carolina	289	18.1	1573	3046	4619	288.7
Tampa Bay	238	14.9	1587	2955	4542	283.9
NY Giants	290	18.1	1833	2650	4483	280.2

Defense

	Points		Yardage			
	Opp	Avg	Rush	Pass	Total	Avg
San Francisco	258	16.1	1061	3337	4398	274.9
Philadelphia	338	21.1	1822	2816	4638	289.9
Carolina	325	20.3	1576	3451	5027	314.2
Dallas	291	18.2	1772	3272	5044	315.3
St. Louis	418	26.1	1677	3441	5118	319.9
Green Bay	314	19.6	1515	3640	5155	322.2
NY Giants	340	21.3	2109	3184	5293	330.8
Washington	359	22.4	2132	3268	5400	337.5
Chicago	360	22.5	1441	4001	5442	340.1
Minnesota	385	24.1	1329	4122	5451	340.7
New Orleans	348	21.8	1838	3723	5561	347.6
Detroit	336	21.0	1795	3804	5599	349.9
Arizona	422	26.4	2249	3455	5704	356.5
Tampa Bay	335	20.9	1754	3958	5712	357.0
Atlanta	349	21.8	1547	4541	6088	380.5

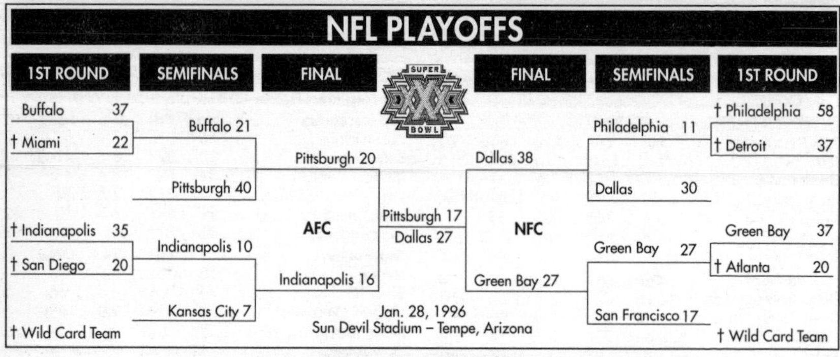

Game Summaries

Team records listed in parentheses indicate records before game.

WILD CARD ROUND

AFC

Bills, 37-22

Miami (9-7)	0	0	0	22—**22**
Buffalo (10-6)	10	14	3	10—**37**

Date— Dec. 30. **Att**— 73,103. **Time**— 3:21

1st Quarter: BUF— Thurman Thomas 1-yd run (Steve Christie kick), 5:02. BUF— Christie 48-yd FG, 7:58.

2nd Quarter: BUF— Darick Holmes 21-yd run (Christie kick), 5:06. BUF— Steve Tasker 37-yd pass from Jim Kelly (Christie kick), 7:39.

3rd Quarter: BUF— Chrisite 23-yd FG, 13:57.

4th Quarter: MIA— O.J. McDuffie 5-yd pass from Dan Marino (Pete Stoyanovich kick), 1:07. BUF— Tim Tindale 44-yd run (Christie kick), 5:29. MIA— Randal Hill 45-yd pass from Marino (Stoyanovich kick), 6:59. BUF— Christie 42-yd FG, 10:24. MIA— Terry Kirby 1-yd run (McDuffie pass from Marino), 12:51.

Colts, 35-20

Indianapolis (9-7)	0	14	7	14—**35**
San Diego (9-7)	3	7	7	3—**20**

Date— Dec. 31. **Att**— 61,182. **Time**— 3:05

1st Quarter: SD— John Carney 54-yd FG, 5:32.

2nd Quarter: IND— Ken Dilger 2-yd pass from Jim Harbaugh (Cary Blanchard kick), 0:57. SD— Alfred Pupunu 6-yd pass from Stan Humphries (Carney kick), 9:12. IND— Zack Crockett 33-yd run (Blanchard kick), 13:33.

3rd Quarter: SD— Shawn Jefferson 11-yd pass from Humphries (Carney kick), 10:40. IND— Sean Dawkins 42-yd pass from Harbaugh (Blanchard kick), 14:19.

4th Quarter: SD— Carney 30-yd FG, 3:07. IND— Crockett 66-yd run (Blanchard kick), 3:32. IND— Jim Harbaugh 3-yd run (Blanchard kick), 8:05.

NFC

Eagles, 58-37

Detroit (10-6)	7	0	14	16—**37**
Philadelphia (10-6)	7	31	13	7—**58**

Date— Dec. 30. **Att**— 66,099 **Time**— 3:22.

1st Quarter: PHI— Charlie Garner 15-yd run (Gary Anderson kick), 9:53. DET— David Sloan 32-yd pass from Scott Mitchell (Jason Hanson kick), 13:02.

2nd Quarter: PHI— Anderson 21-yd FG, 2:04. PHI— Fred Barnett 22-yd pass from Rodney Peete (Anderson kick), 4:17. PHI— Barry Wilburn 24-yd interception return (Anderson kick), 5:21. PHI— Ricky Watters 1-yd run (Anderson kick), 10:01. PHI— Rob Carpenter 43-yd pass from Peete (Anderson kick), 15:00.

3rd Quarter: PHI— Watters 45-yd pass from Peete (Anderson kick), 2:33. PHI— Anderson 31-yd FG, 6:56. PHI— Anderson 39-yd FG, 8:16. DET— Herman Moore 68-yd pass from Don Majkowski (Hanson kick), 9:16. DET— Johnnie Morton 7-yd pass from Majkowski (Hanson kick), 11:41.

4th Quarter: PHI— William Thomas 30-yd interception return (Anderson kick), 0:23. DET— Sloan 2-yd pass from Majkowski (Ron Rivers run); 9:26. DET— Rivers 1-yd run (Moore pass from Majkowski), 14:50.

Packers, 37-20

Atlanta (9-7)	7	3	0	10—**20**
Green Bay (11-5)	14	13	0	10—**37**

Date— Dec. 31 **Att**— 60,453 **Time**— 3:15

1st Quarter: ATL— Eric Metcalf 65-yd pass from Jeff George (Andersen kick), 2:59. GB— Edgar Bennett 8-yd run (Chris Jacke kick), 6:43. GB— Robert Brooks 14-yd pass from Brett Favre (Jacke kick), 11:35.

2nd Quarter: ATL— Morten Andersen 31-yd FG, 0:07. GB— Antonio Freeman 76-yd punt return (Jacke kick failed), 6:23. GB— Mark Chmura 2-yd pass from Favre (Jacke kick), 14:11.

4th Quarter: ATL— J.J. Birden 27-yd pass from George (Andersen kick), 0:53. GB— Dorsey Levens 18-yd pass from Favre (Jacke kick), 7:15. ATL— Andersen 22-yd FG, 10:54. GB- Jacke 25-yd FG, 13:04.

DIVISIONAL SEMIFINALS

AFC

Steelers, 40-21

Buffalo (11-6)	0	7	7	7— **21**
Pittsburgh (11-5)	7	16	3	14— **40**

Date— Jan. 6 **Att**— 59,072 **Time**— 3:19

1st Quarter: PIT— John L. Williams 1-yd run (Norm Johnson kick), 5:31.

2nd Quarter: PIT—Ernie Mills 10-yd pass from Neil O'Donnell (Johnson kick), 0:42. PIT— Johnson 45-yd FG, 7:29. PIT— Johnson 38-yd FG, 10:38. BUF— Thurman Thomas 1-yd run (Steve Christie kick), 14:15. PIT— Johnson 34-yd FG, 14:53.

3rd Quarter: PIT— Johnson 39-yd FG, 6:36. BUF— Tony Cline 2-yd pass from Alex Van Pelt (Christie kick), 11:33.

4th Quarter: BUF— Thomas 9-yd pass from Kelly (Christie kick), 3:37. PIT— Bam Morris 13-yd run (Johnson kick), 8:44. PIT— Morris 2-yd run (Johnson kick), 13:02.

Colts, 10-7

Indianapolis (10-7)	0	7	3	0— **10**
Kansas City (13-3)	7	0	0	0— **7**

Date—Jan.7 **Att**— 77,594 **Time**— 3:08

1st Quarter: KC— Lake Dawson 20-yd pass from Steve Bono (Lin Elliott kick), 14:31.

2nd Quarter: IND— Floyd Turner 5-yd pass from Jim Harbaugh (Cary Blanchard kick), 8:11.

3rd Quarter: IND— Blanchard 30-yd FG, 12:12.

NFC

Packers, 27-17

Green Bay (12-5)	14	7	3	3— **27**
San Francisco (11-5)	0	3	7	7— **17**

Date— Jan. 6 **Att**— 69,311 **Time**— 3:16

1st Quarter: GB— Craig Newsome 31-yd fumble return (Chris Jacke kick), 7:20. GB— Keith Jackson 3-yd pass from Brett Favre (Jacke kick), 10:47.

2nd Quarter: GB— Mark Chmura 13-yd pass from Favre (Jacke kick), 3:39. SF— Jeff Wilkins 21-yard FG, 13:04.

3rd Quarter: SF— Steve Young 1-yd run (Wilkins kick), 7:14. GB— Jacke 27-yd FG, 14:43.

4th Quarter: GB— Jacke 26-yd FG, 7:59. SF— Derek Loville 2-yd run (Wilkins kick), 14:10.

Cowboys, 30-11

Philadelphia (11-6)	0	3	0	8— **11**
Dallas (12-4)	3	14	6	7— **30**

Date—Jan. 7 **Att**— 64,371 **Time**— 2:59

1st Quarter: DAL— Chris Boniol 24-yd FG, 8:47.

2nd Quarter: PHI— Gary Anderson 26-yard FG, 0:03. DAL— Deion Sanders 21-yd run (Boniol kick), 4:35. DAL— Emmitt Smith 1-yd run (Boniol kick), 11:18.

3rd Quarter: DAL— Boniol 18-yd FG, 5:53. DAL— Boniol 51-yd FG, 12:16.

4th Quarter: DAL— Michael Irvin 9-yd pass from Troy Aikman (Boniol kick), 9:17. PHI— Randall Cunningham 4-yd run (Reggie Johnson pass from Cunningham), 12:24.

CONFERENCE CHAMPIONSHIPS

AFC

Steelers, 20-16

Indianapolis (11-7)	3	3	3	7— **16**
Pittsburgh (12-5)	3	7	3	7— **20**

Date— Jan. 14 **Att**— 61,062 **Time**— 2:59

1st Quarter: IND— Cary Blanchard 34-yd FG, 2:43. PIT— Norm Johnson 31-yd FG, 13:10.

2nd Quarter: IND— Blanchard 36-yd FG, 2:52. PIT— Kordell Stewart 5-yd pass from Neil O'Donnell (Johnson kick), 14:47.

3rd Quarter: IND—Blanchard 37-yd FG, 5:03. PIT— Johnson 36-yd FG, 14:17.

4th Quarter: IND— Floyd Turner 47-yd pass from Jim Harbaugh (Blanchard kick), 6:14. PIT— Bam Morris 1-yd run (Johnson kick), 13:26.

NFC

Cowboys, 38-27

Green Bay (13-5)	10	7	10	0— **27**
Dallas (13-4)	14	10	0	14— **38**

Date— Jan. 14 **Att**— 65,135 **Time**—3:32

1st Quarter: GB— Chris Jacke 46-yd FG, 1:10. DAL— Michael Irvin 6-yd pass from Troy Aikman (Chris Boniol kick), 7:31. DAL— Irvin 4-yd pass from Aikman (Boniol kick), 12:40. GB— Robert Brooks 73-yd pass from Brett Favre (Jacke kick), 13:01.

2nd Quarter: GB—Keith Jackson 24-yd pass from Favre (Jacke kick), 0:39. DAL— Boniol 34-yd FG, 8:19. DAL— Emmitt Smith 1-yd run (Boniol kick), 14:36.

3rd Quarter: GB— Jacke 37-yd FG, 3:31. GB— Brooks 1-yd pass from Favre (Jacke kick), 9:41.

4th Quarter: DAL— Smith 5-yd run (Boniol kick), 2:36. DAL— Smith 16-yd run (Boniol kick), 5:32.

Super Bowl XXX

Sunday, Jan. 28 at Sun Devil Stadium in Tempe, Ariz.

Dallas (14-4)	10	3	7	7—	**27**
Pittsburgh (13-5)	0	7	0	10—	**17**

1st: DAL— Chris Boniol 42-yd FG, 2:55. Drive: 47 yards in 7 plays. DAL— Jay Novacek 3-yd pass from Aikman (Boniol kick), 9:37. Drive: 75 yards in 8 plays.

2nd: DAL— Boniol 35-yd FG, 8:57. Drive: 62 yards in 14 plays. PIT— Yancey Thigpen 6-yd pass from Neil O'Donnell (Norm Johnson kick), 14:47. Drive: 54 yards in 13 plays.

3rd: DAL— Smith 1-yd run (Boniol kick), 8:18. Drive: 18 yards in 2 plays.

4th: PIT— Johnson 46-yd FG, 3:40. Drive: 52 yards in 11 plays. PIT— Morris 1-yd run (Johnson kick), 8:24. Drive: 52 yards in 9 plays. DAL— Smith 4-yd run (Boniol kick), 11:17. Drive: 6 yards in 2 plays.

Favorite: Cowboys by 13½ **Attendance:** 76,347
Field: Grass **Time:** 3:24
Weather: Clear **TV Rating:** 46.1/72 share (NBC)

Officials: Red Cashion (referee); John Keck (umpire); Paul Weidner (HL); Dale Orem (LJ); Dick Creed (BJ); Bill Carollo (SJ); Don Hakes (FJ).

Most Valuable Player—Larry Brown, Dallas, CB (2 INTS for 77 yards.)

Team Statistics

	Cowboys	Steelers
Touchdowns	3	2
Rushing	2	1
Passing	1	1
Returns	0	0
Field Goals made/attempted	2/2	1/1
Time of possession	26:11	33:49
First downs	15	25
Rushing	5	9
Passing	10	15
Penalties	0	1
3rd down efficiency	2-10	9-19
4th down efficiency	1-1	2-4
Total offense (net yards)	254	310
Plays	50	84
Average gain	5.1	3.7
Carries/yards	25/56	31/103
Yards per carry	2.2	3.3
Passing yards	198	207
Completions/attempts	15/23	28/49
Yards per pass	7.9	3.9
Times intercepted	0	3
Times sacked/yards lost	2/11	4/32
Return yardage	125	114
Punt returns/yards	1/11	2/18
Kickoff returns/yards	3/37	5/96
Interceptions/yards	3/77	0/0
Fumbles/lost	0/0	2/0
Penalties/yards	5/25	2/15
Punts/average	5/38.2	4/44.8
Punts blocked	0	0

Individual Statistics

Dallas Cowboys

Passing	Att	Cmp	Pct.	Yds	TD	Int
Troy Aikman	23	15	65.2	209	1	0

Receiving	No	Yds	Avg	Long	TD
Michael Irvin	5	76	15.2	20	0
Jay Novacek	5	50	10.0	19	1
Kevin Williams	2	29	14.5	22	0
Deion Sanders	1	47	47.0	47	0
Daryl Johnston	1	4	4.0	4	0
Emmitt Smith	1	3	3.0	3	0
TOTAL	15	209	13.9	47	1

Rushing	Car	Yds	Avg	Long	TD
Emmitt Smith	18	49	2.7	23	2
Daryl Johnston	2	8	4.0	4	0
Kevin Williams	1	2	2.0	2	0
Troy Aikman	4	-3	-0.8	0	0
TOTAL	25	56	2.2	23	2

Field Goals	20-29	30-39	40-49	50-59	Total
Chris Boniol	0-0	1-1	1-1	0-0	2-2

Punting	No	Yds	Long	Avg	In 20	TB
John Jett	5	191	51	38.2	0	1

Punt Returns	FC	Ret	Yds	Long	Avg	TD
Deion Sanders	0	1	11	11	11.0	0

Kickoff Returns	No	Yds	Long	Avg	TD
Kevin Williams	2	24	18	12.0	0
Brock Marion	1	13	13	13.0	0
TOTAL	3	37	18	12.3	0

Interceptions	No	Yds	Long	Avg	TD
Larry Brown	2	77	44	38.5	0
Brock Marion	1	0	0	0.0	0
TOTAL	3	77	44	38.5	0

Sacks		**Most Tackles**	
Chad Hennings	2	Darren Woodson	7
Tony Tolbert	1	Brock Marion	6
Charles Haley	1	Scott Case	6

Pittsburgh Steelers

Passing	Att	Cmp	Pct.	Yds	TD	Int
Neil O'Donnell	49	28	57.1	239	1	3

Receiving	No	Yds	Avg	Long	TD
Andre Hastings	10	98	9.8	19	0
Ernie Mills	8	78	9.8	17	0
Yancey Thigpen	3	19	6.3	7	1
Bam Morris	3	18	6.0	10	0
Corey Holliday	2	19	9.5	10	0
John L. Williams	2	7	3.5	5	0
TOTAL	28	239	8.5	19	1

Rushing	Car	Yds	Avg	Long	TD
Bam Morris	19	73	3.8	15	1
Erric Pegram	6	15	2.5	4	0
Kordell Stewart	4	15	3.8	7	0
Neil O'Donnell	1	0	0.0	0	0
John L. Williams	1	0	0.0	0	0
TOTAL	31	103	3.3	15	1

Field Goals	20-29	30-39	40-49	50-59	Total
Norm Johnson	0-0	0-0	1-1	0-0	1-1

Punting	No	Yds	Long	Avg	In20	TB
Rohn Stark	4	179	55	44.8	1	2

Punt Returns	FC	Ret	Yds	Long	Avg	TD
Andre Hastings	0	2	18	11	9.0	0

Kickoff Returns	No	Yds	Long	Avg	TD
Ernie Mills	4	79	22	19.8	0
Fred McAfee	1	17	17	17.0	0
TOTAL	5	96	22	19.2	0

Sacks		**Most Tackles**	
Levon Kirkland	1	Levon Kirkland	8
Ray Seals	1		

Super Bowl Finalists' Playoff Statistics

Dallas (3-0)

Passing	Att	Cmp	Pct.	Yds	TD	Int
Troy Aikman	80	53	66.3	717	4	106.1

Interceptions: Aikman 1.

Receiving	No	Yds	Avg	Long	TD
Michael Irvin	13	185	14.2	36	3
Jay Novacek	13	133	10.2	25	1
Kevin Williams	11	185	16.8	37	0
Daryl Johnston	7	59	8.4	26	0
Emmitt Smith	6	60	10.0	22	0
Deion Sanders	3	95	31.7	47	4
TOTAL	53	717	13.5	47	4

Rushing	Car	Yds	Avg	Long	TD
Emmitt Smith	74	298	4.0	25	6
Sherman Williams	11	33	3.0	10	0
Deion Sanders	3	23	7.7	21-td	1
Daryl Johnston	7	18	2.6	6	0
Troy Aikman	8	6	0.8	9	0
Kevin Williams	1	2	2.0	2	0
Wade Wilson	2	-2	-1.0	-1	0
TOTAL	106	378	3.6	25	7

Touchdowns	TD	Run	Rec	Ret	Pts
Emmitt Smith	6	6	0	0	36
Michael Irvin	3	0	3	0	18
Jay Novacek	1	0	1	0	6
Deion Sanders	1	1	0	0	6
TOTAL	11	7	4	0	66

Kicking	PAT/Att	FG/Att	Lg	Pts
Chris Boniol	11/11	6/7	51	29

Punts	No	Yds	Long	Avg	In20
John Jett	13	544	54	41.8	2
TOTAL	14	544	54	38.9	2

Most Interceptions
Larry Brown 3

Most Sacks
Tony Tolbert 5

Cowboys' 1995 Schedule

Date	Regular Season	Result	W-L
Sept. 4*	at New York Giants (0-0)	W, 35-0	1-0
Sept. 10	Denver (1-0)	W, 31-21	2-0
Sept. 17	at Minnesota (1-1)	W, 23-17 (OT)	3-0
Sept. 24	Arizona (1-2)	W, 34-20	4-0
Oct. 1	at Washington (1-3)	L, 23-27	4-1
Oct. 8	Green Bay (3-1)	W, 34-24	5-1
Oct. 15	at San Diego (3-3)	W, 23-9	6-1
Oct. 22	OPEN DATE		
Oct. 29	at Atlanta (5-2)	W, 28-13	7-1
Nov. 6*	Philadelphia (5-3)	W, 34-12	8-1
Nov. 12	San Francisco (5-4)	L, 20-38	8-2
Nov. 19	at Oakland (8-2)	W, 34-21	9-2
Nov. 23**	Kansas City (10-1)	W, 24-12	10-2
Dec. 3	Washington (3-9)	L, 17-24	10-3
Dec. 10	at Philadelphia (8-5)	L, 17-20	10-4
Dec. 17	New York Giants (5-9)	W, 21-20	11-4
Dec. 25*	at Arizona (4-11)	W, 37-13	12-4
Date	**Playoffs**	**Result**	**W-L**
Dec. 31	Bye	—	—
Jan. 7	Philadelphia (11-6)	W, 30-11	13-4
Jan. 14	Green Bay (13-5)	W, 38-27	14-4
Jan. 28	vs Pittsburgh (13-5)	W, 27-17	15-4

*(Monday); **(Thanksgiving).

Pittsburgh (2-1)

Passing	Att	Cmp	Pct.	Yds	TD	Int
Neil O'Donnell	125	72	57.6	706	3	61.6

Interceptions: O'Donnell 6.

Receiving	No	Yds	Avg	Long	TD
Ernie Mills	16	196	12.3	37	1
Andre Hastings	16	158	9.9	19	0
Yancey Thigpen	12	161	13.4	43	1
Bam Morris	9	36	4.0	10	0
John L. Williams	7	36	5.1	8	0
Kordell Stewart	4	45	11.3	19	1
Corey Holliday	3	27	9.0	10	0
Erric Pegram	3	24	8.0	23	0
Jonathan Hayes	1	17	17.0	17	0
Mark Bruener	1	6	6.0	6	0
TOTAL	72	706	9.8	43	3

Rushing	Car	Yds	Avg	Long	TD
Bam Morris	51	188	3.7	15	4
Erric Pegram	24	94	3.9	17	0
Kordell Stewart	9	32	3.6	7	0
John L. Williams	6	9	1.5	6	1
Ernie Mills	2	8	4.0	5	0
Neil O'Donnell	6	-1	-0.2	2	0
TOTAL	98	330	3.4	17	5

Touchdowns	TD	Run	Rec	Ret	Pts
Bam Morris	4	4	0	0	24
Ernie Mills	1	0	1	0	6
Kordell Stewart	1	0	1	0	6
Yancey Thigpen	1	0	1	0	6
John L. Williams	1	1	0	0	6
TOTAL	8	5	3	0	48

Kicking	PAT/Att	FG/Att	Lg	Pts
Norm Johnson	8/8	7/8	46	29

Punts	No	Yds	Long	Avg	In20
Rohn Stark	12	457	55	38.1	2
Kordell Stewart	1	41	41	41.0	0
TOTAL	13	498	55	38.3	2

Most Interceptions
Jerry Olsavsky 1
Levon Kirkland 1
Carnell Lake 1

Most Sacks
Greg Lloyd 2

Steelers' 1995 Schedule

Date	Regular Season	Result	W-L
Sept. 3	Detroit (0-0)	W, 23-20	1-0
Sept. 10	at Houston (1-0)	W, 34-17	2-0
Sept. 18*	at Miami (2-0)	L, 10-23	2-1
Sept. 24	Minnesota (1-2)	L, 24-44	2-2
Oct. 1	San Diego (3-1)	W, 31-16	3-2
Oct. 8	at Jacksonville (1-4)	L, 16-20	3-3
Oct. 15	OPEN DATE		
Oct. 19**	Cincinnati (2-4)	L, 9-27	3-4
Oct. 29	Jacksonville (3-5)	W, 24-7	4-4
Nov. 5	at Chicago (6-2)	W, 37-34 (OT)	5-4
Nov. 13*	Cleveland (4-5)	W, 20-3	6-4
Nov. 19	at Cincinnati (4-6)	W, 49-31	7-4
Nov. 26	at Cleveland (4-7)	W, 20-17	8-4
Dec. 3	Houston (5-7)	W, 21-7	9-4
Dec. 10	at Oakland (8-5)	W, 29-10	10-4
Dec. 16***	New England (6-8)	W, 41-27	11-4
Dec. 24	at Green Bay (10-5)	L, 19-24	11-5
Date	**Playoffs**	**Result**	**W-L**
Dec. 31	Bye	—	—
Jan. 6	Buffalo (11-6)	W, 40-21	12-5
Jan. 14	Indianapolis (11-7)	W, 20-16	13-5
Jan. 28	vs Dallas (14-4)	L, 17-27	13-6

*(Monday); **(Thursday); ***(Saturday).

NFL Pro Bowl

46th NFL Pro Bowl Game and 26th AFC-NFC contest (NFC leads series, 15-11). **Date:** Feb. 4 at Aloha Stadium in Honolulu. **Attendance**— 50,034. **Coaches:** Ted Marchibroda, Indianapolis (AFC) and Mike Holmgren, Green Bay (NFC). **Player of the Game:** WR Jerry Rice of San Francisco, who caught 6 passes for 82 yards and 1 touchdown.

NFC	3	17	0	0	**20**
AFC	7	0	6	0	**13**

1st: AFC— Yancey Thigpen 93-yd pass from Jeff Blake (Jason Elam kick), 2:26. Drive: 90 yards in 3 plays. NFC— Morten Andersen 36-yd FG, 9:03. Drive: 51 yards in 7 plays.

2nd: NFC— Jerry Rice 1-yd pass from Brett Favre (Andersen kick), 1:41. Drive: 80 yards in 7 plays. NFC— Ken Harvey 36-yd interception return (Andersen kick), 11:20. NFC— Andersen 24-yd FG, 15:00. Drive: 54 yards in 12 plays.

3rd: AFC— Curtis Martin 17-yd pass from Jim Harbaugh (Elam kick failed), 14:50. Drive: 87 yards in 13 plays.

Time— 3:22; **TV Rating**— 10.9/18 share (ABC).

STARTING LINEUPS

As voted on by NFL players and coaches.

American Conference

Pos	Offense	Pos	Defense
WR	Carl Pickens, Cin.	E	Bruce Smith, Buf.
WR	Tim Brown, Oak.	E	Neil Smith, KC
TE	Ben Coates, NE	T	C. McGlockton, Oak.
T	Richmond Webb, Mia.	T	Dan Saleaumua, KC
T	Bruce Armstrong, NE	LB	Bryce Paup, Buf.
G	Keith Sims, Mia.	LB	Junio Seau, SD
G	Bruce Matthews, Hou.	LB	Greg Lloyd, Pit.
C	Dermontti Dawson, Pit.	CB	Dale Carter, KC
QB	Dan Marino, Mia.	CB	Terry McDaniel, Oak.
RB	Marshall Faulk, Ind.	S	Carnell Lake, Pit.
RB	Chris Warren, Sea.	S	Steve Atwater, Den.
K	Jason Elam, Den.	P	Darren Bennett, SD
KR	Glyn Milburn, Den.	ST	Steve Tasker, Buf.

Note: OG Matthews and QB Marino were injured and unable to play.

Reserves

Offense: WR— Yancey Thigpen, Pit. and Anthony Miller, Den.; **TE**— Shannon Sharpe, Den.; **T**— Gary Zimmerman, Den.; **G**— Steve Wisniewski, Oak.; **C**— Mark Stepnoski, Hou.; **QB**— Jeff Blake, Cin. and Jim Harbaugh, Ind.; **RB**— Curtis Martin, NE; **FB**— Kimble Anders, KC.
Defense: E— Leslie O'Neal, SD; **T**— Cortez Kennedy, Sea.; **LB**— Derrick Thomas, KC; **CB**— Darryll Lewis, Hou.; **S**— Blaine Bishop, Hou.
Replacements: OFFENSE— T Will Wolford, Ind. for Gary Zimmerman, Den.; G Will Shields, KC for Matthews; QB Steve Bono, KC for Marino. DEFENSE— none. NEED PLAYER— Kevin Greene, Pit., LB.

National Conference

Pos	Offense	Pos	Defense
WR	Jerry Rice, SF	E	Reggie White, GB
WR	Herman Moore, Det.	E	Charles Haley, Dal.
TE	Jay Novacek, Dal.	T	John Randle, Min.
T	William Roaf, NO	T	Eric Swann, Ariz.
T	Lomas Brown, Det.	LB	Ken Harvey, Wash.
G	Nate Newton, Dal.	LB	Jessie Tuggle, Atl.
G	R. McDaniel, Min.	LB	Lee Woodall, SF
C	Kevin Glover, Det.	CB	Eric Davis, SF
QB	Brett Favre, GB	CB	A. Williams, Ariz.
RB	Emmitt Smith, Dal.	S	D. Woodson, Dal.
RB	Barry Sanders, Det.	S	Merton Hanks, SF
K	Morten Andersen, Atl.	P	Jeff Feagles, Ariz.
KR	Brian Mitchell, Wash.	ST	Elbert Shelley, Atl.

Note: TE Novacek was injured and unable to play.

Reserves

Offense: WR— Michael Irvin, Dal. and Cris Carter, Min; **TE**— Mark Chmura, GB and Brent Jones, SF; **T**— Mark Tuinei, Dal.; **G**— Larry Allen, Dal.; **C**— Ray Donaldson, Dal.; **QB**— Troy Aikman, Dal. and Steve Young, SF; **RB**— Ricky Watters, Phi. **FB**— Larry Centers, Ariz.
Defense: E— William Fuller, Phi.; **T**— Dana Stubblefield, SF; **LB**— William Thomas, Phi. and Ken Norton Jr., SF; **CB**— Eric Allen, NO; **S**— Tim McDonald, SF.
Replacements: OFFENSE— QB Warren Moon, Min. for Aikman; RB Craig Heyward, Atl. for Centers; TE Brent Jones, DF for Novacek; C Bart Oates, SF for Donaldson. DEFENSE— none. NEED PLAYER— Chris Doleman, Atl., DE

Annual Awards

The NFL does not sanction any of the major postseason awards for player and coaches, but many are given out. Among the presenters for the 1995 regular season were AP, UPI, The Maxwell Football Club of Philadelphia, *The Sporting News* and the Pro Football Writers of America. Conference Most Valuable Player awards were also issued by the NFL Players Association.

Most Valuable Player

NFL Brett Favre, Green Bay, QB .....AP, Max, PFWA, *TSN*
AFC Bryce Paup, Buffalo, LB ....NFLPA
NFC Brett Favre ....NFLPA

Offensive Players of the Year

NFL Brett Favre, Green Bay, QB ....AP
AFC Jim Harbaugh, Indianapolis, QB ....UPI
NFC Brett Favre ....UPI

Defensive Players of the Year

NFL Bryce Paup, Buffalo, LB................AP
AFC Bryce Paup................UPI
NFC Reggie White, Green Bay, DE ....UPI

Rookies of the Year

NFL Curtis Martin, New England, RB ....PFWA, *TSN*
AFC Curtis Martin................UPI
NFC Rashaan Salaam, Chicago, RB ....UPI
Offense Curtis Martin ....AP
Defense Hugh Douglas, NY Jets, DE ....AP

Coaches of the Year

NFL Ray Rhodes, Philadelphia................AP, Max, *TSN*
Dom Capers, Carolina................PFWA
AFC Marv Levy, Buffalo................UPI
NFC Ray Rhodes................UPI

1995 All-NFL Team

The 1995 All-NFL team combining the All-Pro selections of the Associated Press and the Pro Football Writers of America (PFWA). Holdovers from the 1994 All-NFL Team in **bold** type.

Offense

Pos	Player	Selectors
WR	**Jerry Rice**, San Francisco	AP, PFWA
WR	Herman Moore, Detroit	AP, PFWA
TE	**Ben Coates**, New England	AP, PFWA
T	**William Roaf**, New Orleans	AP, PFWA
T	Lomas Brown, Detroit	AP, PFWA
G	**Nate Newton**, Dallas	AP, PFWA
G	**Randall McDaniel**, Minnesota	AP, PFWA
C	**Dermontti Dawson**, Pittsburgh	AP, PFWA
QB	Brett Favre, Green Bay	AP, PFWA
RB	**Emmitt Smith**, Dallas	AP, PFWA
RB	**Barry Sanders**, Detroit	AP, PFWA

Defense

Pos	Player	Selectors
DE	Reggie White, Green Bay	AP, PFWA
DE	**Bruce Smith**, Buffalo	AP, PFWA
DT	**John Randle**, Minnesota	AP, PFWA
DT	**Chester McGlockton**, Oakland	AP, PFWA
LB	Bryce Paup, Buffalo	AP, PFWA
LB	**Greg Lloyd**, Pittsburgh	AP, PFWA
LB	Ken Norton, San Francisco	AP
LB	**Junior Seau**, San Diego	PFWA
CB	Eric Davis, San Francisco	AP, PFWA
CB	Aeneas Williams, Arizona	AP, PFWA
S	Merton Hanks, San Francisco	AP, PFWA
S	**Darren Woodson**, Dallas	AP, PFWA

Specialists

Pos	Player	Selectors
PK	Morten Andersen, Atlanta	AP, PFWA
P	Darren Bennett, San Diego	AP, PFWA
KR	**Brian Mitchell**, Washington	AP, PFWA
ST	**Steve Tasker**, Buffalo	PFWA

1996 College Draft

First and second round selections at the 61st annual NFL College Draft held April 20-21, 1996, in New York City. 11 underclassmen were among the first 61 players chosen and are listed in capital LETTERS.

First Round

No	Team	Player	Pos
1	NY Jets	Keyshawn Johnson, USC	WR
2	Jacksonville	Kevin Hardy, Illinois	LB
3	Arizona	Simeon Rice, Illinois	DE
4	Baltimore	Jonathan Ogden, UCLA	OT
5	NY Giants	Cedric Jones, Oklahoma	DE
6	**a**-St. Louis	LAWRENCE PHILLIPS, Nebraska	RB
7	New England	TERRY GLENN, Ohio St.	WR
8	Carolina	TIM BIAKABUTUKA, Michigan	RB
9	**b**-Oakland	Rickey Dudley, Ohio St.	TE
10	Cincinnati	WILLIE ANDERSON, Auburn	OT
11	New Orleans	Alex Molden, Oregon	CB
12	Tampa Bay	REGAN UPSHAW, California	DE
13	**c**-Chicago	Walt Harris, Mississippi St.	CB
14	**d**-Houston	Eddie George, Ohio St.	RB
15	Denver	John Mobley, Kutztown	LB
16	Minnesota	DUANE CLEMONS, California	DE
17	**e**-Detroit	Reggie Brown, Texas A&M	LB
18	**f**-St. Louis	EDDIE KENNISON, LSU	WR
19	**g**-Indianapolis	Marvin Harrison, Syracuse	WR
20	Miami	Daryl Gardener, Baylor	DT
21	**h**-Seattle	Pete Kendall, Boston College	G
22	**i**-Tampa Bay	Marcus Jones, North Carolina	DT
23	Detroit	Jeff Hartings, Penn St.	G
24	Buffalo	Eric Moulds, Mississippi St.	WR
25	Philadelphia	Jermane Mayberry, Texas A&M-Kingsville	OT
26	**j**-Baltimore	RAY LEWIS, Miami-FL	LB
27	Green Bay	John Michels, USC	OT
28	Kansas City	Jerome Woods, Memphis	S
29	Pittsburgh	Jamain Stephens, N. Carolina A&T	OT
30	**k**-Washington	Andre Johnson, Penn St.	OT

Acquired picks: a— from Washington; **b**— from Houston; **c**— from St. Louis; **d**— from Seattle; **e**— from Seattle thru Houston and Oakland; **f**— from Chicago; **g**— from Atlanta; **h**— from Detroit thru San Diego; **i**— from Indianapolis; **j**— from San Francisco; **k**— from Dallas.

Second Round

No	Team	Player	Pos
31	NY Jets	Alex Van Dyke, Nevada	WR
32	Arizona	LEELAND McELROY, Texas A&M	RB
33	Jacksonville	TONY BRACKENS, Texas	DE
34	NY Giants	Amani Toomer, Michigan	WR
35	**l**-Tampa Bay	Mike Alstott, Purdue	FB
36	New England	LAWYER MILLOY, Washington	S
37	**m**-Dallas	Kavika Pittman, McNeese St.	DE
38	Houston	Bryant Mix, Alcorn St.	DE
39	Cincinnati	Marco Battaglia, Rutgers	TE
40	New Orleans	Je'rod Cherry, California	S
41	**n**-San Diego	Bryan Still, Virigina Tech	WR
42	St. Louis	Tony Banks, Michigan St.	QB
43	Carolina	Muhsin Muhammad, Michigan St.	WR
44	Denver	Tory James, LSU	CB
45	Minnesota	James Manley, Vanderbilt	DT
46	**o**-San Francisco	Israel Ifeanyi, USC	DE
47	Seattle	Fred Thomas, Tenn.-Martin	DB
48	**p**-Houston	Jason Layman, Tennessee	G
49	**q**-Dallas	Randall Godfrey, Georgia	LB
50	San Diego	Patrick Sapp, Clemson	LB
51	Indianapolis	Dedric Mathis, Houston	DB
52	Chicago	Bobby Engram, Penn St.	WR
53	Buffalo	Gabe Northern, LSU	DE
54	Philadelphia	Jason Dunn, E. Kentucky	TE
55	**r**-Baltimore	DeRon Jenkins, Tennessee	CB
56	Green Bay	Derrick Mayes, Notre Dame	WR
57	**s**-Oakland	Lance Johnstone, Temple	LB
58	Kansas City	Reggie Tongue, Oregon St.	S
59	**t**-St. Louis	Ernie Conwell, Washington	TE
60	**u**-Jacksonville	Michael Cheever, Georgia Tech	C
61	**v**-Philadelphia	Brian Dawkins, Clemson	S

Acquired picks: l— from Baltimore; **m**— from Washington; **n**— from Tampa Bay; **o**— from Oakland; **p**— from Oakland thru Atlanta; **q**— from Miami; **r**— from Denver thru Detroit; **s**— from New England thru San Francisco; **t**— from Pittsburgh; **u**— from Miami thru Dallas; **v**— compensatory.

NFL Head Coaching Changes For 1996

As of July 1, 1996, five new head coaches were in place for the start of the '96 regular season.

AFC	Old Coach	Why Left?	New Coach	Hired	Old Job
Miami	Don Shula	Resigned (Jan. 5)	Jimmy Johnson	Jan. 12	Fox TV analyst
Indianapolis	Ted Marchibroda	Resigned (Feb. 9)	Lindy Infante	Feb. 15	Off. Coord., NFL Colts
Baltimore	Bill Belichick	Fired (Feb. 14)	Ted Marchibroda	Feb. 15	Head Coach, NFL Colts
NFC	**Old Coach**	**Why Left?**	**New Coach**	**Hired**	**Old Job**
Arizona	Buddy Ryan	Fired (Dec. 26)	Vince Tobin	Feb. 7	Def. Coord., NFL Colts
Tampa Bay	Sam Wyche	Fired (Dec. 27)	Tony Dungy	Jan. 22	Def. Coord., NFL Vikings

World League of American Football

Final 1996 Standings

	W	L	T	Pct.	PF	PA
*Scotland	7	3	0	.700	206	159
*Frankfurt	6	4	0	.600	229	251
Amsterdam	5	5	0	.500	250	210
Barcelona	5	5	0	.500	192	220
London	4	6	0	.400	161	192
Rhein	3	7	0	.300	176	195

*Clinched World Bowl berth

1st Half Standings

	W	L	T	Pct.	PF	PA
*Scotland	4	1	0	.800	102	63
Frankfurt	4	1	0	.800	137	101
Barcelona	3	2	0	.600	106	109
Amsterdam	2	3	0	.400	114	111
London	1	4	0	.200	67	118
Rhein	1	4	0	.200	82	106

Note: The team that leads the standings after week 5 hosts World Bowl '96. The team which has the best overall record at the end of the season also qualifies for the World Bowl. If the host team also leads the standings after the second half of the season, the club with the second-best overall record qualifies for the World Bowl.

World Bowl '96

June 23, 1996 at Murrayfield Stadium, Edinburgh, Scotland
(Att: 38,000)

Frankfurt (6-4)	7	12	9	4 —	32
Scotland (7-3)	7	7	6	7 —	27

MVP: Yo Murphy, Scotland, WR (7 catches, 163 yards and 3 TDs.)

Passing Efficiency

	Att	Cmp	Cmp Pct	Yds	Avg Gain	TD	TD Pct	Long	Int	Int Pct	Rating
Will Furrer, Ams	368	206	56.0	2689	7.31	20	5.4	48	13	3.5	82.6
Steve Pelluer, Fran	283	165	58.3	2136	7.55	11	3.9	90-td	12	4.2	77.4
Kelly Holcomb, Bar	319	191	59.9	2382	7.47	14	4.4	87-td	16	5.0	76.9
Andy Kelly, Rhe	245	149	60.8	1333	5.44	9	3.7	44-td	7	2.9	75.8
Steve Matthews, Sco	205	115	56.1	1560	7.61	9	4.4	52-td	10	4.9	74.9

Scoring

Touchdowns	TD	Rus	Rec	Ret	Pts
Siran Stacy, Sco	9	7	2	0	54
Byron Chamberlain, Rhe	8	0	8	0	48
Sean LaChappelle, Sco	7	0	7	0	42
Alph Browning, Bar	6	0	6	0	36
Jay Kearney, Fran	6	0	6	0	36

Rushing	Car	Yards	Avg	Long	TD
Siran Stacy, Sco	208	780	3.8	43-td	7
Tony Vinson, Lon	105	516	4.9	67	3
Char Thompson, Bar	117	410	3.5	26	1
Derrick Clark, Rhe	84	399	4.8	23	3
T.C. Wright, Ams	80	379	4.7	22	2

Kicking	PAT	FG/FGA	Lg	Pts
Scott Szeredy, Bar	15/17	9/13	47	42
Ralf Kleinmann, Fran	23/25	6/13	42	41
Paul McCallum, Sco	0/0	11/15	51	34
Adam Vinatieri, Ams	4/4	9/10	43	31
Hans Werdekker, Ams	27/28	0/0	0	27

Receptions	No	Yds	Avg	Long	TD
Byron Chamberlain, Rhe	58	685	11.8	32-td	8
Phillip Bobo, Ams	50	817	16.3	42-td	4
Jay Kearney, Fran	50	686	13.7	46-td	6
Sean LaChapelle, Sco	47	1023	21.8	76	7
Bryce Burnett, Bar	43	383	8.9	43	1
Demetri Davis, Bar	43	376	8.7	37	2

Other Individual Leaders

Yards from Scrimmage	1097	Siran Stacy, Sco
Punting Average	43.54	S. Feexico, Lon
Interceptions	5	Four tied.
Sacks	8	Jerry Drake, Lon
Punt Return Avg.	16.0	T.C. Wright, Ams
Kickoff Return Avg.	24.1	B. Bryant, Ams

Annual Awards

Offensive MVP..........Sean La Chapelle, Scoland, WR
Defensive MVP..........Ty Parten, Scotland, DT
Coach of the Year......Jim Criner, Scotland

Canadian Football League
Final 1995 Standings

Division champions (*) and other playoff qualifiers (†) are noted. Number of seasons listed after each head coach refers to latest tenure with club through 1995 season.

North Division

	W	L	T	Pts	PF	PA	vs Div
*Calgary	15	3	0	30	631	404	9-2-0
†Edmonton	13	5	0	26	599	359	9-3-0
†B.C. Lions	10	8	0	20	535	470	7-6-0
†Hamilton	8	10	0	16	427	509	5-4-0
†Winnipeg	7	11	0	14	404	653	5-7-0
Saskatchewan	6	12	0	12	422	451	5-7-0
Toronto	4	14	0	8	376	519	3-9-0
Ottawa	3	15	0	6	348	685	3-8-0

1995 Head Coaches: Calg— Wally Buono (6th season); **Edm**— Ron Lancaster (5th); **BC**— Dave Ritchie (3rd); **Ham**— Don Sutherin (2nd); **Win**— Cal Murphy (4th); **Sask** — Ray Jauch (2nd); **Tor**— replaced Mike Faragalli (1st, 2-7) with GM Bill O'Billovich (2-7) on Aug. 28; **Ott**— Jim Gilstrap (1st).

1994 Western Div. standings: 1. Calgary (15-3); 2. Edmonton (13-5); 3. B.C. Lions (11-6-1); 4. Saskatchewan (11-7); 5. Sacramento (9-8-1); 6. Las Vegas (5-13).

South Division

	W	L	T	Pts	PF	PA	vs Div
*Baltimore	15	3	0	30	541	369	7-1-0
†San Antonio	12	6	0	24	630	457	5-3-0
†Birmingham	10	8	0	20	548	518	3-4-0
Memphis	9	9	0	18	346	364	4-3-0
Shreveport	5	13	0	10	465	514	0-8-0

1995 Head Coaches: Bal— Don Matthews (2nd season); **SA**— Kay Stephenson (2nd); **Birm**— Jack Pardee (1st); **Mem**— Pepper Rodgers (1st); **Shrv**— Forrest Gregg (2nd).

1994 Eastern Div. standings: 1. Winnipeg (13-5); 2. Baltimore (12-6); 3. Toronto (7-11); 4. Ottawa (4-14) and Hamilton (4-14); 6. Shreveport (3-15).

CFL Playoffs

Division Semifinals (Nov. 4-5)

North: at Calgary 30 ... Hamilton 13
at Edmonton 26 ... B.C. Lions 15
South: at Baltimore 36 ... Winnipeg 21
at San Antonio 52 ... Birmingham 9

Division Championships (Nov. 12)

North: at Calgary 37 ... Edmonton 4
South: at Baltimore 21 ... San Antonio 11

83rd Grey Cup Championship

Nov. 19, 1995 at Taylor Field, Regina, Sask.
(Att: 52,564)

Baltimore (17-3)	7	16	8	6—	**37**
Calgary (17-3)	6	7	7	0—	**20**

Most Outstanding Player: Tracy Ham, Baltimore, QB (passing— 17 for 29, 213 yds; 0 TD, 0 Int; rushing— 7 carries for 24 yds, 1 TD). **Most Outstanding Canadian:** Dave Sapunjis, Calgary, Slot (8 catches for 113 yds).

All-CFL Team

The All-CFL team as selected by a Football Writers of Canada panel.

Pos	Offense	Pos	Defense
WR	Earl Winfield, Ham.	E	Tim Cofield, Mem.
WR	Don Narcisse, Sask.	E	Will Johnson, Calg.
T	Neal Fort, Bal.	T	Bennie Goods, Edm.
T	Rocco Romano, Calg.	T	Jearld Baylis, Bal.
G	Mike Withycombe, Bal.	LB	Willie Pless, Edm.
G	Jamie Taras, BC	LB	Alondra Johnson, Calg.
C	Mike Kiselak, SA	LB	O.J. Brigance, Bal.
QB	Matt Dunigan, Birm.	CB	Eric Carter, Ham.
FB	Mike Saunders, SA	CB	Irv Smith, Bal.
RB	Mike Pringle, Bal.	HB	Charles Anthony, Bal.
SB	Dave Sapunjis, Calg.	HB	Glenn Rogers, Edm.
SB	Allen Pitts, Calg.	SA	Drawhorn, Birm.

Specialists

PK— Roman Anderson, SA P— Josh Miller, Bal.
Special Teams— Chris Wright, Bal.

Regular Season Individual Leaders

Passing Efficiency
(Minimum of 300 attempts)

	Att	Cmp	Cmp Pct	Yds	Avg Gain	TD	Long	Int	Rating
David Archer, SA	458	281	61.4	4471	9.8	30	105-td	8	108.4
Jeff Garcia, Calg.	364	230	63.2	3358	9.2	25	60-td	7	108.1
Doug Flutie, Calg.	332	223	67.2	2788	8.4	16	63-td	5	102.8
Kerwin Bell, Edm	396	246	62.1	3064	7.7	21	98-td	13	90.1
Tracy Ham, Bal	395	232	58.7	3357	8.5	21	54	14	89.4
Matt Dunigan, Birm	643	362	56.3	4911	7.6	34	71-td	16	88.1

Rushing

	Car	Yds	Avg	Long	TD
Mike Pringle, Bal	311	1791	5.8	86	13
Cory Philpot, BC	229	1308	5.7	64-td	17
Martin Patton, Shrv	205	1040	5.1	53	12
Mike Saunders, SA	206	1030	5.0	45	8
Mike Clemons, Tor	181	836	4.6	29	7

Touchdowns

	TD	Rush	Rec	Ret	Pts
Cory Philpot, BC	22	17	4	1	132
Mike Saunders, SA	16	8	8	0	96
Martin Patton, Shrv	14	12	2	0	84
Mike Pringle, Bal	13	13	0	0	78
Earl Winfield, Ham	13	0	13	0	78

Other Individual Leaders

Points (Kicking)	235	Roman Anderson, SA
Passing Yards	4911	Matt Dunigan, Birm.
Receptions	123	Don Narcisse, Sask.
Yards from Scrimmage	2067	Mike Pringle, Bal.
Interceptions	10	Eric Carter, Ham.
Sacks	24	Tim Cofield, Mem.
Punting Average	47.7	Josh Miller, Bal.

Most Outstanding Awards

Player	Mike Pringle, Baltimore, RB
Canadian	Dave Sapunjis, Calgary, SB
Offensive Lineman	Mike Withycombe, Baltimore, OG
Defensive Player	Willie Pless, Edmonton, LB
Rookie	Shalon Baker, Edmonton, WR
Coach	Don Matthews, Baltimore

CFL Goes Retro

by Dave Supleve

For all the change the Canadian Football League has gone through, it's starting to look remarkably like it did ten years ago.

The move into the United States has proven to be an abject failure. The Baltimore Stallions, the CFL's first (and probably last) American Grey Cup champions, have been reborn as the Montreal Alouettes. The Shreveport Pirates, Birmingham Barracudas, San Antonio Texans, and Memphis Mad Dogs are now part of the CFL's inglorious past. Forced to return to its Canadian roots, the league is again in a precarious position.

Expansion was the brainchild of Larry Smith, elected as the CFL's commissioner in 1992. As a solely Canadian venture, the CFL was on the verge of collapse, having lost Montreal in 1987 and narrowly surviving numerous franchise scares in the ensuing years.

Aside from Baltimore, the Canadian game attracted little interest in the United States. The American football fans, particularly those in the southern states, proved what most Canadians already felt — once the U.S. college season began, there was no hope for other football ventures. The 1996 season, the CFL's 87th, will be a pivotal test. The league must prove it can exist in a format that failed a decade ago.

As usual, the player turnover has been extensive. Doug Flutie, the CFL's most marketable player and most outstanding player from 1992-95, has moved to the Toronto Argonauts after four seasons with the Calgary Stampeders. Flutie's move, along with the demise of the American teams, prompted an extensive shuffle of the CFL's quarterback talent. David Archer is now with the Ottawa Rough Riders, having signed for $700,000 annually after spending three seasons with the San Antonio/Sacramento franchise. The Edmonton Eskimos went after former B.C. Lions quarterback Danny McManus while Montreal lost running back Mike Pringle, the CFL's top player in 1995, to the NFL's Denver Broncos.

Smith is expected to leave the CFL once his contract expires in February of 1997. John Tory, the league's respected chairman, has announced his intention to leave in December of 1996. Bob Nicholson, president of the Toronto Argonauts, is considered the top candidate to succeed Smith. There are plans to expand to Halifax, Nova Scotia, and Windsor, Ontario in 1997. Whether that vision is shared by the new commissioner is unknown. Just saving the league might be his first priority.

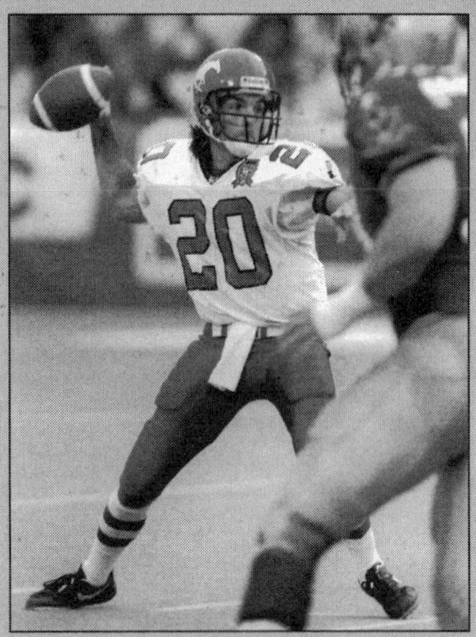

Wide World Photos

In a make-or- break year for the CFL, the league's biggest star will play in the country's biggest market as **Doug Flutie** moves from the Calgary Stampeders to the Toronto Argonauts.

Amid all this exciting business stuff, there actually was a CFL football season.

After finishing as runners-up as an expansion team with no nickname in 1994, the Baltimore Stallions finished the season with 13 consecutive wins, going 15-3 overall and whipping Flutie and the Calgary Stampeders 37-20 in the Grey Cup. For their efforts, nine Stallions were voted to the 1995 CFL All-Star team led by running back Mike Pringle, who was voted the league's Most Outstanding Player. Pringle rushed for 1,791 yards during the season, 483 more than his closest competitor. Birmingham's Matt Dunigan was the league's top quarterback, throwing for 4,911 yards and connecting for 34 touchdowns.

Dave Supleve covers the CFL for the *Winnipeg Free Press.*

The Super Bowl

The first AFL-NFL World Championship Game, as it was originally called, was played seven months after the two leagues agreed to merge in June of 1966. It became the Super Bowl (complete with roman numerals) by the third game in 1969. The Super Bowl winner has been presented the Vince Lombardi Trophy since 1971. Lombardi, whose Green Bay teams won the first two title games, died in 1970. NFL champions (1966-69) and NFC champions (since 1970) are listed in CAPITAL letters.

Multiple winners: Dallas and San Francisco (5); Pittsburgh (4); Oakland-LA Raiders and Washington (3); Green Bay, Miami and NY Giants (2).

Bowl	Date	Winner	Head Coach	Score	Loser	Head Coach	Site
I	1/15/67	GREEN BAY	Vince Lombardi	35-10	Kansas City	Hank Stram	Los Angeles
II	1/14/68	GREEN BAY	Vince Lombardi	33-14	Oakland	John Rauch	Miami
III	1/12/69	NY Jets	Weeb Ewbank	16- 7	BALTIMORE	Don Shula	Miami
IV	1/11/70	Kansas City	Hank Stram	23- 7	MINNESOTA	Bud Grant	New Orleans
V	1/17/71	Baltimore	Don McCafferty	16-13	DALLAS	Tom Landry	Miami
VI	1/16/72	DALLAS	Tom Landry	24- 3	Miami	Don Shula	New Orleans
VII	1/14/73	Miami	Don Shula	14- 7	WASHINGTON	George Allen	Los Angeles
VIII	1/13/74	Miami	Don Shula	24- 7	MINNESOTA	Bud Grant	Houston
IX	1/12/75	Pittsburgh	Chuck Noll	16- 6	MINNESOTA	Bud Grant	New Orleans
X	1/18/76	Pittsburgh	Chuck Noll	21-17	DALLAS	Tom Landry	Miami
XI	1/ 9/77	Oakland	John Madden	32-14	MINNESOTA	Bud Grant	Pasadena
XII	1/15/78	DALLAS	Tom Landry	27-10	Denver	Red Miller	New Orleans
XIII	1/21/79	Pittsburgh	Chuck Noll	35-31	DALLAS	Tom Landry	Miami
XIV	1/20/80	Pittsburgh	Chuck Noll	31-19	LA RAMS	Ray Malavasi	Pasadena
XV	1/25/81	Oakland	Tom Flores	27-10	PHILADELPHIA	Dick Vermeil	New Orleans
XVI	1/24/82	SAN FRANCISCO	Bill Walsh	26-21	Cincinnati	Forrest Gregg	Pontiac, MI
XVII	1/30/83	WASHINGTON	Joe Gibbs	27-17	Miami	Don Shula	Pasadena
XVIII	1/22/84	LA Raiders	Tom Flores	38- 9	WASHINGTON	Joe Gibbs	Tampa
XIX	1/20/85	SAN FRANCISCO	Bill Walsh	38-16	Miami	Don Shula	Stanford
XX	1/26/86	CHICAGO	Mike Ditka	46-10	New England	Raymond Berry	New Orleans
XXI	1/25/87	NY GIANTS	Bill Parcells	39-20	Denver	Dan Reeves	Pasadena
XXII	1/31/88	WASHINGTON	Joe Gibbs	42-10	Denver	Dan Reeves	San Diego
XXIII	1/22/89	SAN FRANCISCO	Bill Walsh	20-16	Cincinnati	Sam Wyche	Miami
XXIV	1/28/90	SAN FRANCISCO	George Seifert	55-10	Denver	Dan Reeves	New Orleans
XXV	1/27/91	NY GIANTS	Bill Parcells	20-19	Buffalo	Marv Levy	Tampa
XXVI	1/26/92	WASHINGTON	Joe Gibbs	37-24	Buffalo	Marv Levy	Minneapolis
XXVII	1/31/93	DALLAS	Jimmy Johnson	52-17	Buffalo	Marv Levy	Pasadena
XXVIII	1/30/94	DALLAS	Jimmy Johnson	30-13	Buffalo	Marv Levy	Atlanta
XXIX	1/29/95	SAN FRANCISCO	George Seifert	49-26	San Diego	Bobby Ross	Miami
XXX	1/28/96	DALLAS	Barry Switzer	27-17	Pittsburgh	Bill Cowher	Tempe, AZ

Pete Rozelle Award (MVP)

The Most Valuable Player in the Super Bowl. Currently selected by an 11-member panel made up of national pro football writers and broadcasters chosen by the NFL. Presented by *Sport* magazine from 1967-89 and by the NFL since 1990. Named after former NFL commissioner Pete Rozelle in 1990. Winner who did not play for Super Bowl champion is in **bold** type.

Multiple winners: Joe Montana (3); Terry Bradshaw and Bart Starr (2).

Bowl	
I	Bart Starr, Green Bay, QB
II	Bart Starr, Green Bay, QB
III	Joe Namath, NY Jets, QB
IV	Len Dawson, Kansas City, QB
V	**Chuck Howley**, Dallas, LB
VI	Roger Staubach, Dallas, QB
VII	Jake Scott, Miami, S
VIII	Larry Csonka, Miami, RB
IX	Franco Harris, Pittsburgh, RB
X	Lynn Swann, Pittsburgh, WR

Bowl	
XI	Fred Biletnikoff, Oakland, WR
XII	Harvey Martin, Dallas, DE & Randy White, Dallas, DT
XIII	Terry Bradshaw, Pittsburgh, QB
XIV	Terry Bradshaw, Pittsburgh, QB
XV	Jim Plunkett, Oakland, QB
XVI	Joe Montana, San Francisco, QB
XVII	John Riggins, Washington, RB
XVIII	Marcus Allen, LA Raiders, RB
XIX	Joe Montana, San Francisco, QB
XX	Richard Dent, Chicago, DE

Bowl	
XXI	Phil Simms, NY Giants, QB
XXII	Doug Williams, Washington, QB
XXIII	Jerry Rice, San Francisco, WR
XXIV	Joe Montana, San Francisco, QB
XXV	Ottis Anderson, NY Giants, RB
XXVI	Mark Rypien, Washington, QB
XXVII	Troy Aikman, Dallas, QB
XXVIII	Emmitt Smith, Dallas, RB
XXIX	Steve Young, San Francisco, QB
XXX	Larry Brown, Dallas, CB

All-Time Super Bowl Leaders

Through Jan. 28, 1996; participants in Super Bowl XXX in **bold** type.

CAREER

Passing Efficiency

Ratings based on performance standards established for completion percentage, average gain, touchdown percentage and interception percentage. Quarterbacks are allocated points according to how their statistics measure up to those standards. Minimum 25 passing attempts.

	Gm	Att	Cmp	Cmp%	Yards	Avg Gain	TD	TD%	Int	Int%	Rating
1 Phil Simms, NYG	1	25	22	88.0	268	10.72	3	12.0	0	0.0	150.9
2 Steve Young, SF	2	39	26	66.7	345	8.85	6	15.4	0	0.0	134.1
3 Doug Williams, Wash	1	29	18	62.1	340	11.72	4	13.8	1	3.4	128.1
4 Joe Montana, SF	4	122	83	68.0	1142	9.36	11	9.0	0	0.0	127.8
5 Jim Plunkett, Oak-LA	2	46	29	63.0	433	9.41	4	8.7	0	0.0	122.8
6 Terry Bradshaw, Pit	4	84	49	58.3	932	11.10	9	10.7	4	4.8	112.6
7 **Troy Aikman**, Dal	3	80	56	70.0	689	8.61	5	6.3	1	1.3	111.9
8 Roger Staubach, Dal	4	98	61	62.2	734	7.49	8	8.2	4	4.1	95.4
9 Ken Anderson, Cin	1	34	25	73.5	300	8.82	2	5.9	2	5.9	95.2
10 Bart Starr, GB	2	47	29	61.7	452	9.62	3	6.4	1	2.1	95.1

Passing Yards

	Gm	Att	Cmp	Pct	Yds
1 Joe Montana, SF	4	122	83	68.0	1142
2 Terry Bradshaw, Pit	4	84	49	58.3	932
3 Jim Kelly, Buf	4	145	81	55.9	829
4 Roger Staubach, Dal	4	98	61	62.2	734
5 **Troy Aikman**, Dal	3	80	56	70.0	689
6 John Elway, Den	3	101	46	45.5	669
7 Fran Tarkenton, Min	3	89	46	51.7	489
8 Bart Starr, GB	2	47	29	61.7	452
9 Jim Plunkett, Raiders	2	46	29	63.0	433
10 Joe Theismann, Wash	2	58	31	53.4	386
11 Len Dawson, KC	2	44	28	63.6	353
12 Steve Young, SF	2	26	39	66.7	345
13 Doug Williams, Wash	1	29	18	62.1	340
14 Dan Marino, Mia	1	50	29	58.0	318
15 Ken Anderson, Cin	1	34	25	73.5	300

Super Bowl Appearances

Through Super Bowl XXX, ten NFL teams have yet to play for the Vince Lombardi Trophy. In alphabetical order, they are: Arizona, Atlanta, Carolina, Cleveland, Detroit, Houston, Jacksonville, New Orleans, Seattle and Tampa Bay. Of the 20 teams that have participated, Dallas has the most appearances (8) and along with San Francisco, the most titles (5).

App		W	L	Pct	PF	PA
8	Dallas	5	3	.625	221	132
5	San Francisco	5	0	1.000	188	89
5	Pittsburgh	4	1	.800	120	100
5	Washington	3	2	.600	122	103
5	Miami	2	3	.400	74	103
4	Oak/LA Raiders	3	1	.750	111	66
4	Buffalo	0	4	.000	73	139
4	Denver	0	4	.000	50	163
4	Minnesota	0	4	.000	34	95
2	Green Bay	2	0	1.000	68	24
2	NY Giants	2	0	1.000	59	39
2	Baltimore Colts	1	1	.500	23	29
2	Kansas City	1	1	.500	33	42
2	Cincinnati	0	2	.000	37	46
1	Chicago	1	0	1.000	46	10
1	NY Jets	1	0	1.000	16	7
1	LA Rams	0	1	.000	19	31
1	New England	0	1	.000	10	46
1	Philadelphia	0	1	.000	10	27
1	San Diego	0	1	.000	26	49

Receptions

	Gm	No	Yds	Avg	TD
1 Jerry Rice, SF	3	28	512	18.3	7
2 Andre Reed, Buf	4	27	323	12.0	0
3 Roger Craig, SF	3	20	212	10.6	3
Thurman Thomas, Buf	4	20	144	7.2	0
5 **Jay Novacek**, Dal	3	17	148	8.7	2
6 Lynn Swann, Pit	4	16	364	22.8	3
7 **Michael Irvin**, Dal	3	16	256	16.0	2
8 Chuck Foreman, Min	3	15	139	9.3	0
9 Cliff Branch, Raiders	3	14	181	12.9	3
10 Don Beebe, Buf	3	12	171	14.3	2
Preston Pearson, Bal-Pit-Dal	5	12	105	8.8	0
Kenneth Davis, Buf	4	12	72	6.0	0
13 John Stallworth, Pit	4	11	268	24.4	3
Dan Ross, Cin	1	11	104	9.5	2
15 Six tied with 10 catches each.					

Rushing

	Gm	Car	Yds	Avg	TD
1 Franco Harris, Pit	4	101	354	3.5	4
2 Larry Csonka, Mia	3	57	297	5.2	2
3 **Emmitt Smith**, Dal	3	70	289	4.1	5
4 John Riggins, Wash	2	64	230	3.6	2
5 Timmy Smith, Wash	1	22	204	9.3	2
Thurman Thomas, Buf	4	52	204	3.9	4
7 Roger Craig, SF	3	52	201	3.9	2
8 Marcus Allen, Raiders	1	20	191	9.5	2
9 Tony Dorsett, Dal	2	31	162	5.2	1
10 Mark van Eeghen, Raiders	2	37	153	4.1	0
11 Kenneth Davis, Buf	4	30	145	4.8	0
12 Rocky Bleier, Pit	4	44	144	3.3	0
13 Walt Garrison, Dal	2	26	139	5.3	0
14 Clarence Davis, Raiders	1	16	137	8.6	0
15 Duane Thomas, Dal	2	37	130	3.5	1

All-Purpose Yards

	Gm	Rush	Rec	Ret	Total
1 **Jerry Rice**, SF	3	15	512	0	527
2 Franco Harris, Pit	4	354	114	0	468
3 Roger Craig, SF	3	201	212	0	413
4 Lynn Swann, Pit	4	−7	364	34	391
5 Thurman Thomas, Buf	4	204	144	0	348
6 **Emmitt Smith**, Dal	3	289	56	0	345
7 Andre Reed, Buf	3	0	323	0	323
8 Larry Csonka, Mia	3	297	17	0	314
9 Fulton Walker, Mia	2	0	0	298	298
10 Ricky Sanders, Wash	2	−3	234	46	277

Scoring

Points

		Gm	TD	FG	PAT	Pts
1	Jerry Rice, SF	3	7	0	0	42
2	**Emmitt Smith**, Dal	3	5	0	0	30
3	Roger Craig, SF	3	4	0	0	24
	Franco Harris, Pit	4	4	0	0	24
	Thurman Thomas, Buf	4	4	0	0	24
6	Ray Wersching, SF	2	0	5	7	22
7	Don Chandler, GB	2	0	4	8	20
8	Cliff Branch, Raiders	3	3	0	0	18
	John Stallworth, Pit	4	3	0	0	18
	Lynn Swann, Pit	4	3	0	0	18
	Ricky Watters, SF	1	3	0	0	18
12	Chris Bahr, Raiders	2	0	3	8	17
13	Matt Bahr, Pit-NYG	2	0	3	6	15
	Mike Cofer, SF	2	0	2	9	15
	Uwe von Schamann, Mia	2	0	4	3	15

Punting

(Minimum 10 Punts)

		Gm	No	Yds	Avg.
1	Jerrel Wilson, KC	2	11	511	46.5
2	Ray Guy, Raiders	3	14	587	41.9
3	Larry Seiple, Mia	3	15	620	41.3
4	Mike Eischeid, Oak-Min	3	17	698	41.1
5	Danny White, Dal	2	10	406	40.6

Punt Returns

(Minimum 4 returns)

		Gm	No	Yds	Avg.	TD
1	John Taylor, SF	3	6	94	15.7	0
2	Neal Colzie, Oak	1	4	43	10.8	0
3	Dana McLemore, SF	1	5	51	10.2	0
4	Mike Fuller, Cin	1	4	35	8.8	0
5	Mike Nelms, Wash	1	6	52	8.7	0

Kickoff Returns

(Minimum 4 returns)

		Gm	No	Yds	Avg.	TD
1	Fulton Walker, Mia	2	8	283	35.4	1
2	Andre Coleman, SD	1	8	242	30.3	1
3	Larry Anderson, Pit	2	8	207	25.9	0
4	Darren Carrington, Den	1	6	146	24.3	1
5	Jim Duncan, Bal	1	4	90	22.5	0

Touchdowns

		Gm	Rush	Rec	Ret	TD
1	Jerry Rice, SF	3	0	7	0	7
2	**Emmitt Smith**, Dal	3	5	0	0	5
	Roger Craig, SF	3	2	2	0	4
	Franco Harris, Pit	4	4	0	0	4
	Thurman Thomas, Buf	4	4	0	0	4
5	Cliff Branch, Raiders	3	0	3	0	3
	John Stallworth, Pit	4	0	3	0	3
	Lynn Swann, Pit	4	0	3	0	3
	Ricky Watters, SF	1	1	2	0	3
10	Twenty-three tied with 2 TDs each.					

Marcus Allen, Raiders; Ottis Anderson, NYG; Pete Banaszak, Raiders; Don Beebe, Buf.; Gary Clark, Wash.; Larry Csonka, Mia.; John Elway, Den.; **Michael Irvin,** Dal.; Butch Johnson, Dal.; Jim Kiick, Mia.; Max McGee, GB; Jim McMahon, Chi.; Bill Miller, Raiders; Joe Montana, SF; Elijah Pitts, GB; Tom Rathman, SF; John Riggins, Wash.; Gerald Riggs, Wash.; Dan Ross, Cin.; Ricky Sanders, Wash.; Timmy Smith, Wash.; John Taylor, SF and Duane Thomas, Dal.

Interceptions

		Gm	No	Yds	TD
1	**Larry Brown**, Dal	2	3	77	0
	Chuck Howley, Dal	2	3	63	0
	Rod Martin, Raiders	2	3	44	0
4	Randy Beverly, NYJ	1	2	0	0
	Mel Blount, Pit	4	2	23	0
	Brad Edwards, Wash	1	2	56	0
	Thomas Everett, Dal	1	2	22	0
	Jake Scott, Mia	3	2	63	0
	Mike Wagner, Pit	3	2	45	0
	James Washington, Dal	2	2	25	0
	Barry Wilburn, Wash	1	2	11	0
	Eric Wright, SF	4	2	25	0

Sacks

		Gm	No
1	**Charles Haley**, SF-Dal	5	4½
2	Leonard Marshall, NYG	2	3
	Danny Stubbs, SF	2	3
	Jeff Wright, Buf	4	3
5	Jim Jeffcoat, Dal	2	2½
	Dexter Manley, Wash	3	2½

Four or More Super Bowl Wins

Dallas Cowboys (5)

Year	Bowl	Head Coach	Quarterback	MVP	Opponent	Score	Site
1972	VI	Tom Landry	Roger Staubach	Staubach	Miami	24-3	New Orleans
1978	XII	Tom Landry	Roger Staubach	Harvey Martin & Randy White	Denver	27-10	New Orleans
1993	XXVII	Jimmy Johnson	Troy Aikman	Aikman	Buffalo	52-17	Pasadena
1994	XXVIII	Jimmy Johnson	Troy Aikman	Emmitt Smith	Buffalo	30-13	Atlanta
1996	XXX	Barry Switzer	Troy Aikman	Larry Brown	Pittsburgh	27-17	Tempe

San Francisco 49ers (5)

Year	Bowl	Head Coach	Quarterback	MVP	Opponent	Score	Site
1982	XVI	Bill Walsh	Joe Montana	Montana	Cincinnati	26-21	Pontiac
1985	XIX	Bill Walsh	Joe Montana	Montana	Miami	38-16	Stanford
1989	XXIII	Bill Walsh	Joe Montana	Jerry Rice	Cincinnati	20-16	Miami
1990	XXIV	George Seifert	Joe Montana	Montana	Denver	55-10	New Orleans
1995	XXIX	George Seifert	Steve Young	Young	San Diego	49-26	Miami

Pittsburgh Steelers (4)

Year	Bowl	Head Coach	Quarterback	MVP	Opponent	Score	Site
1975	IX	Chuck Noll	Terry Bradshaw	Franco Harris	Minnesota	16-6	New Orleans
1976	X	Chuck Noll	Terry Bradshaw	Lynn Swann	Dallas	21-17	Miami
1979	XIII	Chuck Noll	Terry Bradshaw	Bradshaw	Dallas	35-31	Miami
1980	XIV	Chuck Noll	Terry Bradshaw	Bradshaw	LA Rams	31-19	Pasadena

SINGLE GAME

Passing

Yards Gained	Year	Att/Cmp	Yds
Joe Montana, SF vs Cin	1989	36/23	357
Doug Williams, Wash vs Den	1988	29/18	340
Joe Montana, SF vs Mia	1985	35/24	331
Steve Young, SF vs SD	1995	24/36	325
Terry Bradshaw, Pit vs Dal	1979	30/17	318
Dan Marino, Mia vs SF	1985	50/29	318
Terry Bradshaw, Pit vs Rams	1980	21/14	309
John Elway, Den vs NYG	1987	37/22	304
Ken Anderson, Cin vs SF	1982	34/25	300
Joe Montana, SF vs Den	1990	29/22	297

Touchdown Passes	Year	TD	Int
Steve Young, SF vs SD	1995	6	0
Joe Montana, SF vs Den	1990	5	0
Terry Bradshaw, Pit vs Dal	1979	4	1
Doug Williams, Wash vs Den	1988	4	1
Troy Aikman, Dal vs Buf	1993	4	0
Roger Staubach, Dal vs Pit	1979	3	1
Jim Plunkett, Raiders vs Phi	1981	3	0
Joe Montana, SF vs Mia	1985	3	0
Phil Simms, NYG vs Den	1987	3	0

Rushing

Yards Gained	Year	Car	Yds	TD
Timmy Smith, Wash vs Den	1988	22	204	2
Marcus Allen, Raiders vs Wash	1984	20	191	2
John Riggins, Wash vs Mia	1983	38	166	1
Franco Harris, Pit vs Min	1975	34	158	1
Larry Csonka, Mia vs Min	1974	33	145	2
Clarence Davis, Raiders vs Min.	1977	16	137	0
Thurman Thomas, Buf vs NYG	1991	15	135	1
Emmitt Smith, Dal vs Buf	1994	30	132	2
Matt Snell, NYJ vs Bal	1969	30	121	1
Tom Matte, Bal vs NYJ	1969	11	116	0
Larry Csonka, Mia vs Wash	1973	15	112	1
Emmitt Smith, Dal vs Buf	1993	22	108	1
Ottis Anderson, NYG vs Buf	1991	21	102	1
Tony Dorsett, Dal vs Pit	1979	16	96	0
Duane Thomas, Dal vs Mia	1972	19	95	1

Scoring

Points	Year	TD	FG	PAT	Pts
Roger Craig, SF vs Mia	1985	3	0	0	18
Jerry Rice, SF vs Den	1990	3	0	0	18
Jerry Rice, SF vs SD	1995	3	0	0	18
Ricky Watters, SF vs SD	1995	3	0	0	18
Don Chandler, GB vs Raiders	1968	0	4	3	15

Touchdowns	Year	TD	Rush	Rec
Roger Craig, SF vs Mia	1985	3	1	2
Jerry Rice, SF vs Den	1990	3	0	3
Jerry Rice, SF vs SD	1995	3	0	3
Ricky Watters, SF vs SD	1995	3	1	2
Max McGee, GB vs KC	1967	2	0	2
Elijah Pitts, GB vs KC	1967	2	2	0
Bill Miller, Raiders vs GB	1968	2	0	2
Larry Csonka, Mia vs Min	1974	2	2	0
Pete Banaszak, Raiders vs Min.	1977	2	2	0
John Stallworth, Pit vs Dal	1979	2	0	2
Franco Harris, Pit vs Rams	1980	2	2	0
Cliff Branch, Raiders vs Phi	1981	2	0	2
Dan Ross, Cin vs SF	1982	2	0	2
Marcus Allen, Raiders vs Wash.	1984	2	2	0
Jim McMahon, Chi vs NE	1986	2	2	0
Ricky Sanders, Wash vs Den	1988	2	0	2
Timmy Smith, Wash vs Den	1988	2	2	0
Tom Rathman, SF vs Den	1990	2	2	0
Gerald Riggs, Wash vs Buf	1992	2	2	0
Michael Irvin, Dal vs Buf	1993	2	0	2
Emmitt Smith, Dal vs Buf	1994	2	2	0
Emmitt Smith, Dal vs Pitt	1996	2	2	0

Receptions

Catches	Year	No	Yds	TD
Dan Ross, Cin vs SF	1982	11	104	2
Jerry Rice, SF vs Cin	1989	11	215	1
Tony Nathan, Mia vs SF	1985	10	83	0
Jerry Rice, SF vs SD	1995	10	149	3
Andre Hastings, Pit vs Dal	1996	10	98	0
Ricky Sanders, Wash vs Den	1988	9	193	2
George Sauer, NYJ vs Bal	1969	8	133	0
Roger Craig, SF vs Cin	1989	8	101	0
Andre Reed, Buf vs NYG	1991	8	62	0
Andre Reed, Buf vs Dal	1993	8	152	0
Ronnie Harmon, SD vs SF	1995	8	68	0
Ernie Mills, Pit vs Dal	1996	8	78	0

Yards Gained	Year	No	Yds	TD
Jerry Rice, SF vs Cin	1989	11	215	1
Ricky Sanders, Wash vs Den	1988	9	193	2
Lynn Swann, Pit vs Dal	1976	4	161	1
Andre Reed, Buf vs Dal	1993	8	152	0
Jerry Rice, SF vs SD	1995	10	149	3
Jerry Rice, SF vs Den	1990	7	148	3
Max McGee, GB vs KC	1967	7	138	2
George Sauer, NYJ vs Bal	1969	8	133	0
Willie Gault, Chi vs NE	1986	4	129	0
Lynn Swann, Pit vs Dal	1979	7	124	1

All-Purpose Yards

Yards Gained	Year	Run	Rec	Tot
Andre Coleman, SD vs SF	1995	0	0	242*
Ricky Sanders, Wash vs Den	1988	−4	193	235†
Jerry Rice, SF vs Cin	1989	5	215	220
Timmy Smith, Wash vs Den	1988	204	9	213
Marcus Allen, Raiders vs Wash	1984	191	18	209
Stephen Starring, NE vs Chi	1986	0	39	192#
Fulton Walker, Mia vs Wash	1983	0	0	190$
Thurman Thomas, Buf vs NYG	1991	135	55	190
John Riggins, Wash vs Mia	1983	166	15	181
Roger Craig, SF vs Cin	1989	74	101	175

*Coleman gained all his yards on eight kickoff returns.
†Sanders also returned three kickoffs for 48 yards.
#Starring also returned seven kickoffs for 153 yards.
$Walker gained all his yards on four kickoff returns.

Interceptions

	Year	No	Yds	TD
Rod Martin, Raiders vs Phi	1981	3	44	0

Six tied with two interceptions each.

Punting

(Minimum 4 punts)

	Year	No	Yds	Avg
Bryan Wagner, SD vs SF	1995	4	195	48.8
Jerrel Wilson, KC vs Min	1970	4	194	48.5
Jim Miller, SF vs Cin	1982	4	185	46.3

Punt Returns

(Minimum 3 returns)

	Year	No	Yds	Avg
John Taylor, SF vs Cin	1989	3	56	18.7
John Taylor, SF vs Den	1990	3	38	12.7
Kelvin Martin, Dal vs Buf	1993	3	35	11.7

Kickoff Returns

(Minimum 3 returns)

	Year	No	Yds	Avg
Fulton Walker, Mia vs Wash	1983	4	190	47.5
Larry Anderson, Pit vs Rams	1980	5	162	32.4
Rick Upchurch, Den vs Dal	1978	3	94	31.3

Super Bowl Playoffs

The Super Bowl forced the NFL to set up pro football's first guaranteed multiple-game playoff format. Over the years, the NFL-AFL merger, the creation of two conferences comprised of three divisions each and the proliferation of Wild Card entries has seen the postseason field grow from four teams (1966), to six (1967-68), to eight (1969-77), to 10 (1978-81, 1983-89), to the present 12 (since 1990).

In 1968 there was a special playoff between Oakland and Kansas City who were both 12-2 and tied for first in the AFL's Western Division. In 1982, when a 57-day players' strike shortened the regular season to just nine games, playoff berths were extended to 16 teams (eight from each conference) and a 15-game tournament was played.

Note that in the following year-by-year summary, records of finalists include all games leading up to the Super Bowl; (*) indicates Wild Card teams.

1966 Season

AFL Playoffs

Championship.........................Kansas City 31, at Buffalo 7

NFL Playoffs

Championship..........................Green Bay 34, at Dallas 27

Super Bowl I

Jan. 15, 1967
Memorial Coliseum, Los Angeles
Favorite: Packers by 14 Attendance: 61,946

Kansas City (12-2-1)	0	10	0	0	**10**
Green Bay (13-2)	7	7	14	7	**35**

MVP: Green Bay QB Bart Starr (16 for 23, 250 yds, 2 TD, 1 Int)

1967 Season

AFL Playoffs

Championship ....at Oakland 40, Houston 7

NFL Playoffs

Eastern Conference....................at Dallas 52, Cleveland 14
Western Conference ....at Green Bay 28, LA Rams 7
Championship..........................at Green Bay 21, Dallas 17

Super Bowl II

Jan. 14, 1968
Orange Bowl, Miami
Favorite: Packers by 13½ Attendance: 75,546

Green Bay (11-4-1)	3	13	10	7	**33**
Oakland (14-1)	0	7	0	7	**14**

MVP: Green Bay QB Bart Starr (13 for 24, 202 yds, 1 TD)

1968 Season

AFL Playoffs

Western Div. Playoff.............at Oakland 41, Kansas City 6
AFL Championship ....at NY Jets 27, Oakland 23

NFL Playoffs

Eastern Conference....................at Cleveland 31, Dallas 20
Western Conference............at Baltimore 24, Minnesota 14
NFL Championship ....Baltimore 34, at Cleveland 0

Super Bowl III

Jan. 12, 1969
Orange Bowl, Miami
Favorite: Colts by 18 Attendance: 75,389

NY Jets (12-3)	0	7	6	3	**16**
Baltimore (15-1)	0	0	0	7	**7**

MVP: NY Jets QB Joe Namath (17 for 28, 206 yds)

1969 Season

AFL Playoffs

Inter-Division ....*Kansas City 13, at NY Jets 6
............................at Oakland 56, *Houston 7
AFL Championship................Kansas City 17, at Oakland 7

NFL Playoffs

Eastern Conference....................Cleveland 38, at Dallas 14
Western Conference..............at Minnesota 23, LA Rams 20
NFL Championship ....at Minnesota 27, Cleveland 7

Super Bowl IV

Jan. 11, 1970
Tulane Stadium, New Orleans
Favorite: Vikings by 12 Attendance: 80,562

Minnesota (14-2)	0	0	7	0	**7**
Kansas City (13-3)	3	13	7	0	**23**

MVP: KC QB Len Dawson (12 for 17, 142 yds, 1 TD, 1 Int)

1970 Season

AFC Playoffs

First Round.............................at Baltimore 17, Cincinnati 0
................................at Oakland 21, *Miami 14
Championship........................at Baltimore 27, Oakland 17

NFC Playoffs

First Round ....at Dallas 5, *Detroit 0
..................San Francisco 17, at Minnesota 14
Championship.....................Dallas 17, at San Francisco 10

Super Bowl V

Jan. 17, 1971
Orange Bowl, Miami
Favorite: Cowboys by 2½ Attendance: 79,204

Baltimore (13-2-1)	0	6	0	10	**16**
Dallas (12-4)	3	10	0	0	**13**

MVP: Dallas LB Chuck Howley (2 Interceptions for 22 yds)

1971 Season

AFC Playoffs

First Round ....Miami 27, at Kansas City 24 (OT)
............................*Baltimore 20, at Cleveland 3
Championship ....at Miami 21, Baltimore 0

NFC Playoffs

First Round..............................Dallas 20, at Minnesota 12
...............at San Francisco 24, *Washington 20
Championship......................at Dallas 14, San Francisco 3

Super Bowl VI

Jan. 16, 1972
Tulane Stadium, New Orleans
Favorite: Cowboys by 6 Attendance: 81,023

Dallas (13-3)	3	7	7	7	**24**
Miami (12-3-1)	0	3	0	0	**3**

MVP: Dallas QB Roger Staubach (12 for 19, 119 yds, 2TD)

Super Bowl Playoffs (Cont.)

1972 Season

AFC Playoffs

First Round ....at Pittsburgh 13, Oakland 7
............................at Miami 20, *Cleveland 14
Championship.........................Miami 21, at Pittsburgh 17

NFC Playoffs

First Round ....*Dallas 30, at San Francisco 28
.......................at Washington 16, Green Bay 3
Championship ....at Washington 26, Dallas 3

Super Bowl VII

Jan. 14, 1973
Memorial Coliseum, Los Angeles
Favorite: Redskins by 1½ Attendance: 90,182

Miami (16-0)	7	7	0	0—	**14**
Washington (13-3)	0	0	0	7—	**7**

MVP: Miami safety Jake Scott (2 Interceptions for 63 yds)

1973 Season

AFC Playoffs

First Round..........................at Oakland 33, *Pittsburgh 14
..............................at Miami 34, Cincinnati 16
Championship ....at Miami 27, Oakland 10

NFC Playoffs

First Round....................at Minnesota 27, *Washington 20
...............................at Dallas 27, LA Rams 16
Championship ....Minnesota 27, at Dallas 10

Super Bowl VIII

Jan. 13, 1974
Rice Stadium, Houston
Favorite: Dolphins by 6½ Attendance: 71,882

Minnesota (14-2)	0	0	0	7—	**7**
Miami (12-4)	14	3	7	0—	**24**

MVP: Miami FB Larry Csonka (33 carries, 145 yds, 2 TD)

1974 Season

AFC Playoffs

First Round ....at Oakland 28, Miami 26
.............................at Pittsburgh 32, *Buffalo 14
Championship ....Pittsburgh 24, at Oakland 13

NFC Playoffs

First Round ....at Minnesota 30, St.Louis 14
.....................at LA Rams 19, *Washington 10
Championship ....at Minnesota 14, LA Rams 10

Super Bowl IX

Jan. 12, 1975
Tulane Stadium, New Orleans
Favorite: Steelers by 3 Attendance: 80,997

Pittsburgh (12-3-1)	0	2	7	7—	**16**
Minnesota (12-4)	0	0	0	6—	**6**

MVP: Pittsburgh RB Franco Harris (34 carries, 158 yds, 1 TD)

1975 Season

AFC Playoffs

First Round ....at Pittsburgh 28, Baltimore 10
........................at Oakland 31, *Cincinnati 28
Championship ....at Pittsburgh 16, Oakland 10

NFC Playoffs

First Round..............................at LA Rams 35, St. Louis 23
..............................*Dallas 17, at Minnesota 14
Championship..............................Dallas 37, at LA Rams 7

Super Bowl X

Jan. 18, 1976
Orange Bowl, Miami
Favorite: Steelers by 6½ Attendance: 80,187

Dallas (12-4)	7	3	0	7—	**17**
Pittsburgh (14-2)	7	0	0	14—	**21**

MVP: Pittsburgh WR Lynn Swann (4 catches, 161 yds, 1 TD)

1976 Season

AFC Playoffs

First Round ....at Oakland 24, *New England 21
..........................Pittsburgh 40, at Baltimore 14
Championship ....at Oakland 24, Pittsburgh 7

NFC Playoffs

First Round....................at Minnesota 35, *Washington 20
...............................LA Rams 14, at Dallas 12
Championship ....at Minnesota 24, LA Rams 13

Super Bowl XI

Jan. 9, 1977
Rose Bowl, Pasadena
Favorite: Raiders by 4½ Attendance: 103,438

Oakland (15-1)	0	16	3	13—	**32**
Minnesota (13-2-1)	0	0	7	7—	**14**

MVP: Oakland WR Fred Biletnikoff (4 catches, 79 yds)

1977 Season

AFC Playoffs

First Round..............................at Denver 34, Pittsburgh 21
...................*Oakland 37, at Baltimore 31 (OT)
Championship ....at Denver 20, Oakland 17

NFC Playoffs

First Round ....at Dallas 37, *Chicago 7
.............................Minnesota 14, at LA Rams 7
Championship ....at Dallas 23, Minnesota 6

Super Bowl XII

Jan. 15, 1978
Louisiana Superdome, New Orleans
Favorite: Cowboys by 6 Attendance: 75,583

Dallas (14-2)	10	3	7	7—	**27**
Denver (14-2)	0	0	10	0—	**10**

MVPs: Dallas DE Harvey Martin and DT Randy White (Cowboys' defense forced 8 turnovers)

A Year Later...

Super Bowl champions who did not qualify for the playoffs the following season.

Season		Record	Finish
1968	Green Bay	6-7-1	3rd in NFL Central
1970	Kansas City	7-5-2	2nd in AFC West
1980	Pittsburgh	9-7-0	3rd in AFC Central
1981	Oakland	7-9-0	4th in AFC West
1982	San Francisco	3-6-0*	11th in overall NFC
1987	NY Giants	6-9-0*	5th in NFC East
1988	Washington	7-9-0	3rd in NFC East
1991	NY Giants	8-8-0	4th in NFC East

*Seasons when player strikes interrupted schedule.

1978 Season

AFC Playoffs

First Round ....*Houston 17, at *Miami 9
Second Round..................Houston 31, at New England 14
........................at Pittsburgh 33, Denver 10
Championship ....at Pittsburgh 34, Houston 5

NFC Playoffs

First Round........................at *Atlanta 14, *Philadelphia 13
Second Round...............................at Dallas 27, Atlanta 20
......................at LA Rams 34, Minnesota 10
Championship..............................Dallas 28, at LA Rams 0

Super Bowl XIII

Jan. 21, 1979
Orange Bowl, Miami
Favorite: Steelers by 3½ Attendance: 79,484

Pittsburgh (16-2)........................7 14 0 14— **35**
Dallas (14-4)...............................7 7 3 14— **31**
MVP: Pittsburgh QB Terry Bradshaw (17 for 30, 318 yds, 4 TD, 1 Int)

1979 Season

AFC Playoffs

First Round ....at *Houston 13, *Denver 7
Second Round ....Houston 17, at San Diego 14
..........................at Pittsburgh 34, Miami 14
Championship ....at Pittsburgh 27, Houston 13

NFC Playoffs

First Round......................at *Philadelphia 27, *Chicago 17
Second Round................at Tampa Bay 24, Philadelphia 17
.............................LA Rams 21, at Dallas 19
Championship ....LA Rams 9, at Tampa Bay 0

Super Bowl XIV

Jan. 20, 1980
Rose Bowl, Pasadena
Favorite: Steelers by 10½ Attendance: 103,985

LA Rams (11-7)..........................7 6 6 0— **19**
Pittsburgh (14-4)........................3 7 7 14— **31**
MVP: Pittsburgh QB Terry Bradshaw (14 for 21, 309 yds, 2 TD, 3 Int)

1980 Season

AFC Playoffs

First Round ....at *Oakland 27, *Houston 7
Second Round.........................at San Diego 20, Buffalo 14
......................Oakland 14, at Cleveland 12
Championship.....................Oakland 34, at San Diego 27

NFC Playoffs

First Round ....at *Dallas 34, *LA Rams 13
Second Round ....at Philadelphia 31, Minnesota 16
..............................Dallas 30, at Atlanta 27
Championship ....at Philadelphia 20, Dallas 7

Super Bowl XV

Jan. 25, 1981
Louisiana Superdome, New Orleans
Favorite: Eagles by 3 Attendance: 76,135

Oakland (14-5) ....14 0 10 3— **27**
Philadelphia (14-4) ....0 3 0 7— **10**
MVP: Oakland QB Jim Plunkett (13 for 21, 261 yds, 3 TD)

1981 Season

AFC Playoffs

First Round ....*Buffalo 31, at *NY Jets 27
Second Round ....San Diego 41, at Miami 38 (OT)
........................at Cincinnati 28, Buffalo 21
Championship ....at Cincinnati 27, San Diego 7

NFC Playoffs

First Round..................*NY Giants 27, at *Philadelphia 21
Second Round..........................at Dallas 38, Tampa Bay 0
..............at San Francisco 38, NY Giants 24
Championship....................at San Francisco 28, Dallas 27

Super Bowl XVI

Jan. 24, 1982
Pontiac Silverdome, Pontiac, Mich.
Favorite: Pick'em Attendance: 81,270

San Francisco (15-3)................7 13 0 6— **26**
Cincinnati (14-4)........................0 0 7 14— **21**
MVP: San Francisco QB Joe Montana (14 for 22, 157 yds, 1 TD; 6 carries, 18 yds, 1 TD)

1982 Season

A 57-day players' strike shortened the regular season from 16 games to nine. The playoff format was changed to a 16-team tournament open to the top eight teams in each conference.

AFC Playoffs

First Round ....at LA Raiders 27, Cleveland 10
.........................at Miami 28, New England 3
...........................NY Jets 44, at Cincinnati 17
........................San Diego 31, at Pittsburgh 28
Second Round.......................NY Jets 17, at LA Raiders 14
............................at Miami 34, San Diego 13
Championship ....at Miami 14, NY Jets 0

NFC Playoffs

First Round.............................at Washington 31, Detroit 7
...........................at Dallas 30, Tampa Bay 17
.........................at Green Bay 41, St. Louis 16
...........................at Minnesota 30, Atlanta 24
Second Round ....at Washington 21, Minnesota 7
............................at Dallas 37, Green Bay 26
Championship ....at Washington 31, Dallas 17

Super Bowl XVII

Jan. 30, 1983
Rose Bowl, Pasadena
Favorite: Dolphins by 3 Attendance: 103,667

Miami (10-2)..............................7 10 0 0— **17**
Washington (11-1) ....0 10 3 14— **27**
MVP: Washington RB John Riggins (38 carries, 166 yds, 1 TD; 1 catch, 15 yds)

Most Popular Playing Sites

Stadiums hosting more than one Super Bowl.

No		Years
5	Orange Bowl (Miami)	1968-69, 71, 76, 79
5	Rose Bowl (Pasadena)	1977, 80, 83, 87, 93
4	Superdome (N. Orleans)	1978, 81, 86, 90
3	Tulane Stadium (N. Orleans)	1970, 72, 75
2	Joe Robbie Stadium (Miami)	1989, 95
2	LA Memorial Coliseum	1967, 73
2	Tampa Stadium	1984, 91

Super Bowl Playoffs (Cont.)

1983 Season

AFC Playoffs

First Round ....at *Seattle 31, *Denver 7
Second Round ....Seattle 27, at Miami 20
.................at LA Raiders 38, Pittsburgh 10
Championship.....................at LA Raiders 30, Seattle 14

NFC Playoffs

First Round ....*LA Rams 24, at *Dallas 17
Second Round ....at San Francisco 24, Detroit 23
.................at Washington 51, LA Rams 7
Championship ....at Washington 24, San Francisco 21

Super Bowl XVIII

Jan. 22, 1984
Tampa Stadium, Tampa
Favorite: Redskins by 3 Attendance: 72,920

Washington (16-2) ....0 3 6 0— **9**
LA Raiders (14-4) ....7 14 14 3— **38**
MVP: LA Raiders RB Marcus Allen (20 carries, 191 yds, 2 TD; 2 catches, 18 yds)

1984 Season

AFC Playoffs

First Round..........................at *Seattle 13, *LA Raiders 7
Second Round ....at Miami 31, Seattle 10
......................Pittsburgh 24, at Denver 17
Championship ....at Miami 45, Pittsburgh 28

NFC Playoffs

First Round ....*NY Giants 16, at *LA Rams 13
Second Round ....at San Francisco 21, NY Giants 10
.................Chicago 23, at Washington 19
Championship ....at San Francisco 23, Chicago 0

Super Bowl XIX

Jan. 20, 1985
Stanford Stadium, Stanford, Calif.
Favorite: 49ers by 3 Attendance: 84,059

Miami (16-2)..............................10 6 0 0— **16**
San Francisco (17-1)..................7 21 10 0— **38**
MVP: San Francisco QB Joe Montana (24 for 35, 331 yds, 2 TD; 5 carries, 59 yards, 1 TD)

1985 Season

AFC Playoffs

First Round ....*New England 26, at *NY Jets 14
Second Round ....at Miami 24, Cleveland 21
............New England 27, at LA Raiders 20
Championship..................New England 31, at Miami 14

NFC Playoffs

First Round ....at *NY Giants 17, *San Francisco 3
Second Round ....at LA Rams 20, Dallas 0
......................at Chicago 21, NY Giants 0
Championship ....at Chicago 24, LA Rams 0

Super Bowl XX

Jan. 26, 1986
Louisiana Superdome, New Orleans
Favorite: Bears by 10 Attendance: 73,818

Chicago Bears (17-1) ....13 10 21 2— **46**
New England (14-5)..................3 0 0 7— **10**
MVP: Chicago DE Richard Dent (Bears defense: 7 sacks, 6 turnovers, 1 safety and gave up just 123 total yards)

1986 Season

AFC Playoffs

First Round ....at *NY Jets 35, *Kansas City 15
Second Round ....at Cleveland 23, NY Jets 20 (OT)
.................at Denver 22, New England 17
Championship ....Denver 23, at Cleveland 20 (OT)

NFC Playoffs

First Round ....at *Washington 19, *LA Rams 7
Second Round ....Washington 27, at Chicago 13
.............at NY Giants 49, San Francisco 3
Championship................at NY Giants 17, Washington 0
Super Bowl XXI

Jan. 25, 1987
Rose Bowl, Pasadena
Favorite: Giants by 9½ Attendance: 101,063

Denver (13-5) ....10 0 0 10— **20**
NY Giants (16-2)........................7 2 17 13— **39**
MVP: NY Giants QB Phil Simms (22 for 25, 268 yds, 3 TD; 3 carries, 25 yds)

1987 Season

A 24-day players' strike shortened the regular season to 15 games with replacement teams playing for three weeks.

AFC Playoffs

First Round....................at *Houston 23, *Seattle 20 (OT)
Second Round ....at Cleveland 38, Indianapolis 21
...........................at Denver 34, Houston 10
Championship ....at Denver 38, Cleveland 33

NFC Playoffs

First Round ....*Minnesota 44, at *New Orleans 10
Second Round............Minnesota 36, at San Francisco 24
..................Washington 21, at Chicago 17
Championship..............at Washington 17, Minnesota 10

Super Bowl XXII

Jan. 31, 1988
San Diego/Jack Murphy Stadium
Favorite: Broncos by 3½ Attendance: 73,302

Washington (13-4) ....0 35 0 7— **42**
Denver (12-4-1)........................10 0 0 0— **10**
MVP: Washington QB Doug Williams (18 for 29, 340 yds, 4 TD, 1 Int)

1988 Season

AFC Playoffs

First Round ....*Houston 24, at *Cleveland 23
Second Round ....at Buffalo 17, Houston 10
.......................at Cincinnati 21, Seattle 13
Championship ....at Cincinnati 21, Buffalo 10

NFC Playoffs

First Round ....at *Minnesota 28, *LA Rams 17
Second Round.............at San Francisco 34, Minnesota 9
.................at Chicago 20, Philadelphia 12
Championship ....San Francisco 28, at Chicago 3

Super Bowl XXIII

Jan. 22, 1989
Joe Robbie Stadium, Miami
Favorite: 49ers by 7 Attendance: 75,129

Cincinnati (14-4)..........................0 3 10 3— **16**
San Francisco (12-6)...................3 0 3 14— **20**
MVP: San Francisco WR Jerry Rice (11 catches, 215 yds, 1 TD; 1 carry, 5 yds)

1989 Season

AFC Playoffs

First Round ....*Pittsburgh 26, at *Houston 23
Second Round..........................at Cleveland 34, Buffalo 30
..........................at Denver 24, Pittsburgh 23
Championship ....at Denver 37, Cleveland 21

NFC Playoffs

First Round ....*LA Rams 21, at *Philadelphia 7
Second Round..........................LA Rams 19, NY Giants 13 (OT)
..........................at San Francisco 41, Minnesota 13
Championship ....at San Francisco 30, LA Rams 3

Super Bowl XXIV

Jan. 28, 1990
Louisiana Superdome, New Orleans
Favorite: 49ers by 12½ Attendance: 72,919

San Francisco (17-2)................13 14 14 14— **55**
Denver (13-6) ....3 0 7 0— **10**
MVP: San Francisco QB Joe Montana (22 for 29, 297 yds, 5 TD, 0 Int)

1990 Season

AFC Playoffs

First Round..........................at *Miami 17, *Kansas City 16
..........................at Cincinnati 41, *Houston 14
Second Round..........................at Buffalo 44, Miami 34
..........................at LA Raiders 20, Cincinnati 10
Championship ....at Buffalo 51, LA Raiders 3

NFC Playoffs

First Round ....*Washington 20, at *Philadelphia 6
..........................at Chicago 16, *New Orleans 6
Second Round ....at San Francisco 28, Washington 10
..........................at NY Giants 31, Chicago 3
Championship..............NY Giants 15, at San Francisco 13

Super Bowl XXV

Jan. 27, 1991
Tampa Stadium, Tampa
Favorite: Bills by 7 Attendance: 73,813

Buffalo (15-4) ....3 9 0 7— **19**
NY Giants (16-3).........................3 7 7 3— **20**
MVP: NY Giants RB Ottis Anderson (21 carries, 102 yds, 1 TD; 1 catch, 7 yds)

1991 Season

AFC Playoffs

First Round ....at *Kansas City 10, *LA Raiders 6
..........................at Houston 17, *NY Jets 10
Second Round ....at Denver 26, Houston 24
..........................at Buffalo 37, Kansas City 14
Championship..........................at Buffalo 10, Denver 7

NFC Playoffs

First Round..........................*Atlanta 27, at New Orleans 20
..........................*Dallas 17, at *Chicago 13
Second Round ....at Washington 24, Atlanta 7
..........................at Detroit 38, Dallas 6
Championship..........................at Washington 41, Detroit 10

Super Bowl XXVI

Jan. 26, 1992
Hubert Humphrey Metrodome, Minneapolis
Favorite: Redskins by 7 Attendance: 63,130

Washington (16-2) ....0 17 14 6— **37**
Buffalo (15-3) ....0 0 10 14— **24**
MVP: Washington QB Mark Rypien (18 for 33, 292 yds, 2 TD, 1 Int)

1992 Season

AFC Playoffs

First Round..........................at *Buffalo 41, *Houston 38 (OT)
..........................at San Diego 17, *Kansas City 0
Second Round ....Buffalo 24, at Pittsburgh 3
..........................at Miami 31, San Diego 0
Championship..........................Buffalo 29, at Miami 10

NFC Playoffs

First Round..........................*Washington 24, at Minnesota 7
..............*Philadelphia 36, at *New Orleans 20
Second Round ....at San Francisco 20, Washington 13
..........................at Dallas 34, Philadelphia 10
Championship.....................Dallas 30, at San Francisco 20

Super Bowl XXVII

Jan. 31, 1993
Rose Bowl, Pasadena
Favorite: Cowboys by 7 Attendance: 98,374

Buffalo (14-5) ....7 3 7 0— **17**
Dallas (15-3)...............................14 14 3 21— **52**
MVP: Dallas QB Troy Aikman (22 for 30, 273 yds, 4 TD, 0 Int)

1993 Season

AFC Playoffs

First Round..............at Kansas City 27, *Pittsburgh 24 (OT)
..........................at *LA Raiders 42, *Denver 24
Second Round..........................at Buffalo 29, LA Raiders 23
..........................Kansas City 28, at Houston 20
Championship ....at Buffalo 30, Kansas City 13

NFC Playoffs

First Round ....*Green Bay 28, at Detroit 24
..........................at *NY Giants 17, *Minnesota 10
Second Round................at San Francisco 44, NY Giants 3
..........................at Dallas 27, Green Bay 17
Championship.....................at Dallas 38, San Francisco 21

Super Bowl XXVIII

Jan. 30, 1994
Georgia Dome, Atlanta
Favorite: Cowboys by 10½ Attendance: 72,817

Dallas (15-4) 6 0 14 10—**30**
Buffalo (14-5) 3 10 0 0—**13**
MVP: Dallas RB Emmitt Smith (30 carries, 132 yds, 2 TDs; 4 catches, 26 yds)

Super Bowl Playoffs (Cont.)

1994 Season

AFC Playoffs

First Round ....at Miami 27, *Kansas City 17
..............at *Cleveland 20, *New England 13
Second Round ....at Pittsburgh 29, Cleveland 9
......................at San Diego 22, Miami 21
Championship ....San Diego 17, at Pittsburgh 13

NFC Playoffs

First Round........................at *Green Bay 16, *Detroit 12
......................*Chicago 25, at Minnesota 18
Second Round ....at San Francisco 44, Chicago 15
........................at Dallas 35, Green Bay 9
Championship ....at San Francisco 38, Dallas 28

Super Bowl XXIX

Jan. 29, 1995
Joe Robbie Stadium, Miami
Favorite: 49ers by 18 Attendance: 74,107

San Diego (13-5)	7	3	8	8—**26**
San Francisco (15-3)	14	14	14	7—**49**

MVP: San Francisco QB Steve Young (24 for 36, 325 yds, 6 TD, 0 Int.)

1995 Season

AFC Playoffs

First Round ....at Buffalo 37, *Miami 22
...................*Indianapolis 35, at *San Diego 20
Second Round........................at Pittsburgh 40, Buffalo 21
.............*Indianapolis 10, at Kansas City 7
Championship.............at Pittsburgh 20, *Indianapolis 16

NFC Playoffs

First Round ....at *Philadelphia 58, *Detroit 37
............................at Green Bay 37, *Atlanta 20
Second Round ....Green Bay 27, at San Francisco 17
........................at Dallas 30,*Philadelphia 11
Championship..........................at Dallas 38, Green Bay 27

Super Bowl XXX

Jan. 28, 1996
Sun Devil Stadium, Tempe, Ariz.
Favorite: Cowboys by 13½ Attendance: 76,347

Dallas (14-4)	10	3	7	7—**27**
Pittsburgh (13-5)	0	7	0	10—**17**

MVP: Larry Brown, Dallas, CB (2 Interceptions for 77 yds.)

Before the Super Bowl

The first NFL champion was the Akron Pros in 1920, when the league was called the American Professional Football Association (APFA) and the title went to the team with the best regular season record. The APFA changed its name to the National Football League in 1922.

The first playoff game with the championship at stake came in 1932, when the Chicago Bears (6-1-6) and Portsmouth (Ohio) Spartans (6-1-4) ended the regular season tied for first place. The Bears won the subsequent playoff, 9-0. Due to a snowstorm and cold weather, the game was moved from Wrigley Field to an improvised 80-yard dirt field at Chicago Stadium, making it the first indoor title game as well.

The NFL Championship Game decided the league title until the NFL merged with the AFL and the first Super Bowl was played following the 1966 season.

NFL Champions, 1920-32

Winning player-coaches noted by position.

Multiple winners: Canton-Cleveland Bulldogs and Green Bay (3); Chicago Staleys/Bears (2).

Year	Champion	Head Coach
1920	Akron Pros	Fritz Pollard, HB & Elgie Tobin, QB
1921	Chicago Staleys	George Halas, E
1922	Canton Bulldogs	Guy Chamberlin, E
1923	Canton Bulldogs	Guy Chamberlin, E
1924	Cleveland Bulldogs	Guy Chamberlin, E
1925	Chicago Cardinals	Norm Barry
1926	Frankford Yellow Jackets	Guy Chamberlin, E
1927	New York Giants	Earl Potteiger, QB
1928	Providence Steam Roller	Jimmy Conzelman, HB
1929	Green Bay Packers	Curly Lambeau, QB
1930	Green Bay Packers	Curly Lambeau
1931	Green Bay Packers	Curly Lambeau
1932	Chicago Bears (Bears beat Portsmouth-OH in playoff, 9-0)	Ralph Jones

Biggest Postseason Blowouts

(since the merger of the NFL and AFL in 1966)

Pts	Winner	Loser	Game	Date
49	at Oakland 56	Houston 7	1969 AFL Inter-Division Champ.	Dec. 21, 1969
48	at Buffalo 51	LA Raiders 3	1990 AFC Champ.	Jan. 20, 1991
46	at NY Giants 49	San Francisco 3	1986 NFC 2nd Rnd.	Jan. 4, 1987
45	San Francisco 55	Denver 10	Super Bowl XXIV	Jan. 28, 1990
44	at Washington 51	LA Rams 7	1983 NFC 2nd Rnd.	Jan. 1, 1984
41	at San Francisco 44	NY Giants 3	1993 NFC 2nd Rnd.	Jan. 15, 1994
38	at Dallas 52	Cleveland 14	1967 NFL East. Conf. Champ.	Dec. 24, 1967
38	at Dallas 38	Tampa Bay 0	1981 NFC 2nd Rnd.	Jan. 2, 1982
36	Chicago 46	New England 10	Super Bowl XX	Jan. 26, 1986
35	at Oakland 41	Kansas City 6	1968 AFL West. Div. Champ.	Dec. 22, 1968
35	Dallas 52	Buffalo 17	Super Bowl XXVII	Jan. 31, 1993
34	Minnesota 44	at New Orleans 10	1987 NFC 1st Rnd.	Jan. 3, 1988
34	Baltimore 34	at Cleveland 0	1968 NFL Champ.	Dec. 29, 1968
33	at Oakland 40	Houston 7	1967 AFL Champ.	Dec. 31, 1967
32	Washington 42	Denver 10	Super Bowl XXII	Jan. 31, 1988
32	at Detroit 38	Dallas 6	1991 NFC 2nd Rnd.	Jan. 5, 1992
31	at Washington 41	Detroit 10	1991 NFC Champ.	Jan. 12, 1992
31	at Miami 31	San Diego 0	1992 AFC 2nd Rnd.	Jan. 10, 1993
30	Dallas 37	at LA Rams 7	1975 NFC Champ.	Jan. 4, 1976
30	at Dallas 37	Chicago 7	1977 NFC 1st Rnd	Dec. 26, 1977

NFL-NFC Championship Game

NFL Championship games from 1933-69 and NFC Championship games since the completion of the NFL-AFL merger following the 1969 season.

Multiple winners: Dallas and Green Bay (8); Chicago Bears and Washington (7); NY Giants and San Francisco (5); Cleveland Browns, Detroit, Minnesota, and Philadelphia (4); Baltimore (3); Cleveland-LA Rams (2).

Season	Winner	Head Coach	Score	Loser	Head Coach	Site
1933	Chicago Bears	George Halas	23-21	New York	Steve Owen	Chicago
1934	New York	Steve Owen	30-13	Chicago Bears	George Halas	New York
1935	Detroit	Potsy Clark	26- 7	New York	Steve Owen	Detroit
1936	Green Bay	Curly Lambeau	21- 6	Boston Redskins	Ray Flaherty	New York
1937	Washington Redskins	Ray Flaherty	28-21	Chicago Bears	George Halas	Chicago
1938	New York	Steve Owen	23-17	Green Bay	Curly Lambeau	New York
1939	Green Bay	Curly Lambeau	27- 0	New York	Steve Owen	Milwaukee
1940	Chicago Bears	George Halas	73- 0	Washington	Ray Flaherty	Washington
1941	Chicago Bears	George Halas	37- 9	New York	Steve Owen	Chicago
1942	Washington	Ray Flaherty	14- 6	Chicago Bears	Hunk Anderson & Luke Johnsos	Washington
1943	Chicago Bears	Hunk Anderson & Luke Johnsos	41-21	Washington	Arthur Bergman	Chicago
1944	Green Bay	Curly Lambeau	14- 7	New York	Steve Owen	New York
1945	Cleveland Rams	Adam Walsh	15-14	Washington	Dudley DeGroot	Cleveland
1946	Chicago Bears	George Halas	24-14	New York	Steve Owen	New York
1947	Chicago Cardinals	Jimmy Conzelman	28-21	Philadelphia	Greasy Neale	Chicago
1948	Philadelphia	Greasy Neale	7- 0	Chicago Cardinals	Jimmy Conzelman	Philadelphia
1949	Philadelphia	Greasy Neale	14- 0	Los Angeles Rams	Clark Shaughnessy	Los Angeles
1950	Cleveland Browns	Paul Brown	30-28	Los Angeles	Joe Stydahar	Cleveland
1951	Los Angeles	Joe Stydahar	24-17	Cleveland	Paul Brown	Los Angeles
1952	Detroit	Buddy Parker	17- 7	Cleveland	Paul Brown	Cleveland
1953	Detroit	Buddy Parker	17-16	Cleveland	Paul Brown	Detroit
1954	Cleveland	Paul Brown	56-10	Detroit	Buddy Parker	Cleveland
1955	Cleveland	Paul Brown	38-14	Los Angeles	Sid Gillman	Los Angeles
1956	New York	Jim Lee Howell	47- 7	Chicago Bears	Paddy Driscoll	New York
1957	Detroit	George Wilson	59-14	Cleveland	Paul Brown	Detroit
1958	Baltimore	Weeb Ewbank	23-17*	New York	Jim Lee Howell	New York
1959	Baltimore	Weeb Ewbank	31-16	New York	Jim Lee Howell	Baltimore
1960	Philadelphia	Buck Shaw	17-13	Green Bay	Vince Lombardi	Philadelphia
1961	Green Bay	Vince Lombardi	37- 0	New York	Allie Sherman	Green Bay
1962	Green Bay	Vince Lombardi	16- 7	New York	Allie Sherman	New York
1963	Chicago	George Halas	14-10	New York	Allie Sherman	Chicago
1964	Cleveland	Blanton Collier	27- 0	Baltimore	Don Shula	Cleveland
1965	Green Bay	Vince Lombardi	23-12	Cleveland	Blanton Collier	Green Bay
1966	Green Bay	Vince Lombardi	34-27	Dallas	Tom Landry	Dallas
1967	Green Bay	Vince Lombardi	21-17	Dallas	Tom Landry	Green Bay
1968	Baltimore	Don Shula	34- 0	Cleveland	Blanton Collier	Cleveland
1969	Minnesota	Bud Grant	27- 7	Cleveland	Blanton Collier	Minnesota
1970	Dallas	Tom Landry	17-10	San Francisco	Dick Nolan	San Francisco
1971	Dallas	Tom Landry	14- 3	San Francisco	Dick Nolan	Dallas
1972	Washington	George Allen	26- 3	Dallas	Tom Landry	Washington
1973	Minnesota	Bud Grant	27-10	Dallas	Tom Landry	Dallas
1974	Minnesota	Bud Grant	14-10	Los Angeles	Chuck Knox	Minnesota
1975	Dallas	Tom Landry	37- 7	Los Angeles	Chuck Knox	Los Angeles
1976	Minnesota	Bud Grant	24-13	Los Angeles	Chuck Knox	Minnesota
1977	Dallas	Tom Landry	23- 6	Minnesota	Bud Grant	Dallas
1978	Dallas	Tom Landry	28- 0	Los Angeles	Ray Malavasi	Los Angeles
1979	Los Angeles	Ray Malavasi	9- 0	Tampa Bay	John McKay	Tampa Bay
1980	Philadelphia	Dick Vermeil	20- 7	Dallas	Tom Landry	Philadelphia
1981	San Francisco	Bill Walsh	28-27	Dallas	Tom Landry	San Francisco
1982	Washington	Joe Gibbs	31-17	Dallas	Tom Landry	Washington
1983	Washington	Joe Gibbs	24-21	San Francisco	Bill Walsh	Washington
1984	San Francisco	Bill Walsh	23- 0	Chicago	Mike Ditka	San Francisco
1985	Chicago	Mike Ditka	24- 0	Los Angeles	John Robinson	Chicago
1986	New York	Bill Parcells	17- 0	Washington	Joe Gibbs	New York
1987	Washington	Joe Gibbs	17-10	Minnesota	Jerry Burns	Washington
1988	San Francisco	Bill Walsh	28- 3	Chicago	Mike Ditka	Chicago
1989	San Francisco	George Seifert	30- 3	Los Angeles	John Robinson	San Francisco
1990	New York	Bill Parcells	15-13	San Francisco	George Seifert	San Francisco
1991	Washington	Joe Gibbs	41-10	Detroit	Wayne Fontes	Washington
1992	Dallas	Jimmy Johnson	30-20	San Francisco	George Seifert	San Francisco

NFL-NFC Championship Game (Cont.)

Season	Winner	Head Coach	Score	Loser	Head Coach	Site
1993	Dallas	Jimmy Johnson	38-21	San Francisco	George Seifert	Dallas
1994	San Francisco	George Seifert	38-28	Dallas	Barry Switzer	San Francisco
1995	Dallas	Barry Switzer	38-27	Green Bay	Mike Holmgren	Dallas

*Sudden death overtime

NFL-NFC Championship Game Appearances

App		W	L	Pct	PF	PA
16	Dallas Cowboys	8	8	.500	361	319
16	NY Giants	5	11	.313	240	322
13	Chicago Bears	7	6	.538	286	245
12	Boston-Wash.Redskins	7	5	.583	222	255
12	Cleveland-LA Rams	3	9	.250	123	270
11	Green Bay Packers	8	3	.727	250	154
11	San Francisco	5	6	.455	235	199
11	Cleveland Browns	4	7	.364	224	253
6	Minnesota	4	2	.667	108	80
6	Detroit	4	2	.667	139	141
5	Philadelphia	4	1	.800	79	48
4	Baltimore Colts	3	1	.750	88	60
2	Chicago Cardinals	1	1	.500	28	28
1	Tampa Bay	0	1	.000	0	9

AFL-AFC Championship Game

AFL Championship games from 1960-69 and AFC Championship games since the completion of the NFL-AFL merger following the 1969 season.

Multiple winners: Buffalo (6); Miami and Pittsburgh (5); Denver and Oakland-LA Raiders (4); Dallas Texans-KC Chiefs (3); Cincinnati, Houston and San Diego (2).

Season	Winner	Head Coach	Score	Loser	Head Coach	Site
1960	Houston	Lou Rymkus	24-16	LA Chargers	Sid Gillman	Houston
1961	Houston	Wally Lemm	10- 3	SD Chargers	Sid Gillman	San Diego
1962	Dallas	Hank Stram	20-17*	Houston	Pop Ivy	Houston
1963	San Diego	Sid Gillman	51-10	Boston Patriots	Mike Holovak	San Diego
1964	Buffalo	Lou Saban	20- 7	San Diego	Sid Gillman	Buffalo
1965	Buffalo	Lou Saban	23- 0	San Diego	Sid Gillman	San Diego
1966	Kansas City	Hank Stram	31- 7	Buffalo	Joel Collier	Buffalo
1967	Oakland	John Rauch	40- 7	Houston	Wally Lemm	Oakland
1968	NY Jets	Webb Ewbank	27-23	Oakland	John Rauch	New York
1969	Kansas City	Hank Stram	17- 7	Oakland	John Madden	Oakland
1970	Baltimore	Don McCafferty	27-17	Oakland	John Madden	Baltimore
1971	Miami	Don Shula	21- 0	Baltimore	Don McCafferty	Miami
1972	Miami	Don Shula	21-17	Pittsburgh	Chuck Noll	Pittsburgh
1973	Miami	Don Shula	27-10	Oakland	John Madden	Miami
1974	Pittsburgh	Chuck Noll	24-13	Oakland	John Madden	Oakland
1975	Pittsburgh	Chuck Noll	16-10	Oakland	John Madden	Pittsburgh
1976	Oakland	John Madden	24- 7	Pittsburgh	Chuck Noll	Oakland
1977	Denver	Red Miller	20-17	Oakland	John Madden	Denver
1978	Pittsburgh	Chuck Noll	34- 5	Houston	Bum Phillips	Pittsburgh
1979	Pittsburgh	Chuck Noll	27-13	Houston	Bum Phillips	Pittsburgh
1980	Oakland	Tom Flores	34-27	San Diego	Don Coryell	San Diego
1981	Cincinnati	Forrest Gregg	27- 7	San Diego	Don Coryell	Cincinnati
1982	Miami	Don Shula	14- 0	NY Jets	Walt Michaels	Miami
1983	LA Raiders	Tom Flores	30-14	Seattle	Chuck Knox	Los Angeles
1984	Miami	Don Shula	45-28	Pittsburgh	Chuck Noll	Miami
1985	NE Patriots	Raymond Berry	31-14	Miami	Don Shula	Miami
1986	Denver	Dan Reeves	23-20*	Cleveland	Marty Schottenheimer	Cleveland
1987	Denver	Dan Reeves	38-33	Cleveland	Marty Schottenheimer	Denver
1988	Cincinnati	Sam Wyche	21-10	Buffalo	Marv Levy	Cincinnati
1989	Denver	Dan Reeves	37-21	Cleveland	Bud Carson	Denver
1990	Buffalo	Marv Levy	51- 3	LA Raiders	Art Shell	Buffalo
1991	Buffalo	Marv Levy	10- 7	Denver	Dan Reeves	Buffalo
1992	Buffalo	Marv Levy	29-10	Miami	Don Shula	Miami
1993	Buffalo	Marv Levy	30-13	Kansas City	Marty Schottenheimer	Buffalo
1994	San Diego	Bobby Ross	17-13	Pittsburgh	Bill Cowher	Pittsburgh
1995	Pittsburgh	Bill Cowher	20-16	Indianapolis	Ted Marchibroda	Pittsburgh

*Sudden death overtime

AFL-AFC Championship Game Appearances

App		W	L	Pct	PF	PA
12	Oakland-LA Raiders	4	8	.333	228	264
8	Buffalo	6	2	.750	180	92
9	Pittsburgh Steelers	5	4	.556	186	164
8	LA-San Diego Chargers	2	6	.250	128	161
7	Miami	5	2	.714	152	115
6	Houston	2	4	.333	76	140
5	Denver	4	1	.800	125	101
4	Dallas Texans/KC Chiefs	3	1	.750	81	61
3	Baltimore-Indy Colts	1	2	.333	43	58
3	Cleveland	0	3	.000	74	98
2	Cincinnati	2	0	1.000	48	17
2	Boston-NE Patriots	1	1	.500	41	65
2	NY Jets	1	1	.500	27	37
1	Seattle	0	1	.000	14	30

NFL Divisional Champions

The NFL adopted divisional play for the first time in 1967, splitting both conferences into two four-team divisions—the Capitol and Century divisions in the East and the Central and Coastal divisions in the West. Merger with the AFL in 1970 increased NFL membership to 26 teams and made it necessary for the league to realign. Two 13-team conferences—the AFC and NFC—were formed by moving established NFL clubs in Baltimore, Cleveland and Pittsburgh to the AFC and rearranging both conferences into Eastern, Central and Western divisions.

Division champions are listed below; teams that went on to win the Super Bowl are in **bold** type. Note that in 1980, Oakland won the Super Bowl as a wild card team; and in 1982, the players' strike shortened the regular season to nine games and eliminated divisional play for one season.

Multiple champions (since 1970): **AFC**—Pittsburgh (12); Miami (11); Oakland-LA Raiders (9); Buffalo and Denver (7); Cleveland (6); Baltimore-Indianapolis Colts, Cincinnati and San Diego (5); Kansas City (3); Houston and New England (2). **NFC**—San Francisco (15); Dallas (13); Minnesota (12); LA Rams (8); Chicago (6); Washington (5); Detroit and NY Giants (3); Green Bay, Philadelphia, St. Louis Cardinals and Tampa Bay (2).

American Football League

Season	East	West
1966	Buffalo	Kansas City

Season	East	West
1967	Houston	Oakland
1968	**NY Jets**	Oakland
1969	NY Jets	Oakland

Note: Kansas City, an AFL Wild Card team, won the Super Bowl in 1969.

National Football League

Season	East	West
1966	Dallas	**Green Bay**

Season	Capitol	Century	Central	Coastal
1967	Dallas	Cleveland	**Green Bay**	LA Rams
1968	Dallas	Cleveland	Minnesota	Baltimore
1969	Dallas	Cleveland	Minnesota	LA Rams

American Football Conference

Season	East	Central	West
1970	**Baltimore**	Cincinnati	Oakland
1971	Miami	Cleveland	Kansas City
1972	**Miami**	Pittsburgh	Oakland
1973	**Miami**	Cincinnati	Oakland
1974	Miami	**Pittsburgh**	Oakland
1975	Baltimore	**Pittsburgh**	Oakland
1976	Baltimore	Pittsburgh	**Oakland**
1977	Baltimore	Pittsburgh	Denver
1978	New England	**Pittsburgh**	Denver
1979	Miami	**Pittsburgh**	San Diego
1980	Buffalo	Cleveland	San Diego
1981	Miami	Cincinnati	San Diego
1982	—	—	—
1983	Miami	Pittsburgh	**LA Raiders**
1984	Miami	Pittsburgh	Denver
1985	Miami	Cleveland	LA Raiders
1986	New England	Cleveland	Denver
1987	Indianapolis	Cleveland	Denver
1988	Buffalo	Cincinnati	Seattle
1989	Buffalo	Cleveland	Denver
1990	Buffalo	Cincinnati	LA Raiders
1991	Buffalo	Houston	Denver
1992	Miami	Pittsburgh	San Diego
1993	Buffalo	Houston	Kansas City
1994	Miami	Pittsburgh	San Diego
1995	Buffalo	Pittsburgh	Kansas City

Note: Oakland, an AFC Wild Card team, won the Super Bowl in 1980.

National Football Conference

Season	East	Central	West
1970	Dallas	Minnesota	San Francisco
1971	**Dallas**	Minnesota	San Francisco
1972	Washington	Green Bay	San Francisco
1973	Dallas	Minnesota	LA Rams
1974	St. Louis	Minnesota	LA Rams
1975	St. Louis	Minnesota	LA Rams
1976	Dallas	Minnesota	LA Rams
1977	**Dallas**	Minnesota	LA Rams
1978	Dallas	Minnesota	LA Rams
1979	Dallas	Tampa Bay	LA Rams
1980	Philadelphia	Minnesota	Atlanta
1981	Dallas	Tampa Bay	**San Francisco**
1982	—	—	—
1983	Washington	Detroit	San Francisco
1984	Washington	Chicago	**San Francisco**
1985	Dallas	**Chicago**	LA Rams
1986	**NY Giants**	Chicago	San Francisco
1987	**Washington**	Chicago	San Francisco
1988	Philadelphia	Chicago	**San Francisco**
1989	NY Giants	Minnesota	**San Francisco**
1990	**NY Giants**	Chicago	San Francisco
1991	**Washington**	Detroit	New Orleans
1992	**Dallas**	Minnesota	San Francisco
1993	**Dallas**	Detroit	San Francisco
1994	Dallas	Minnesota	**San Francisco**
1995	**Dallas**	Green Bay	San Francisco

Overall Postseason Games

The postseason records of all NFL teams, ranked by number of playoff games participated in from 1933 through the 1995 season.

Gm		W	L	Pct	PF	PA
49	Dallas Cowboys	31	18	.633	1197	891
36	Oakland-LA Raiders	21	15	.583	855	659
35	Boston-Wash. Redskins	21	14	.600	738	625
33	San Francisco 49ers	21	12	.636	860	632
33	Cleveland-LA Rams	13	20	.394	501	697
32	Pittsburgh Steelers	19	13	.594	728	635
32	New York Giants	14	18	.438	529	593
31	Miami Dolphins	17	14	.548	697	633
31	Minnesota Vikings	13	18	.419	553	646
30	Cleveland Browns	11	19	.367	596	702
28	Chicago Bears	14	14	.500	579	552
26	Buffalo Bills	14	12	.538	621	582
25	Green Bay Packers	17	8	.680	577	432
22	Houston Oilers	9	13	.409	371	533
19	Balt-Indianapolis Colts	10	9	.526	346	347
19	Denver Broncos	9	10	.474	380	502
19	Philadelphia Eagles	9	10	.474	356	355
18	Dallas Texans/KC Chiefs	8	10	.444	291	370
18	LA-San Diego Chargers	7	11	.389	332	428
15	Detroit Lions	7	8	.467	342	357
12	Cincinnati Bengals	5	7	.417	246	257
11	New York Jets	5	6	.455	216	200
11	Boston-NE Patriots	4	7	.364	208	278
7	Seattle Seahawks	3	4	.429	128	139
7	Atlanta Falcons	2	5	.286	139	181
5	Chi-St. L. Cardinals	1	4	.200	81	134
4	Tampa Bay Buccaneers	1	3	.250	41	94
4	New Orleans Saints	0	4	.000	56	123

All-Time Postseason Leaders

Through Super Bowl XXX, Jan. 28, 1996; participants in 1995 season playoffs in **bold** type.

CAREER

Passing Efficiency

Ratings based on performance standards established for completion percentage, average gain, touchdown percentage and interception percentage. Minimum 150 passing attempts.

	Gm	Cmp%	Yds	TD	Int	Rtg
1 Bart Starr	10	61.0	1753	15	3	104.8
2 **Troy Aikman**	12	68.3	3029	21	9	104.3
3 Joe Montana	23	62.7	5772	45	21	95.6
4 Kenny Anderson	6	66.3	1321	9	6	93.5
5 Joe Theismann	10	60.7	1782	11	7	91.4
6 **Steve Young**	16	62.0	2212	14	7	89.4
7 Warren Moon	10	64.3	2870	17	14	84.9
8 Ken Stabler	13	57.8	2641	19	13	84.2
9 Bernie Kosar	9	56.1	1943	16	10	83.3
10 **Dan Marino**	13	56.2	3600	29	17	83.2

Passing

Attempts	Gm	Att
1 Joe Montana, SF-KC	23	734
2 **Jim Kelly**, Buffalo	16	513
3 Terry Bradshaw, Pittsburgh	19	456

Completions	Gm	Cmp
1 Joe Montana, SF-KC	23	460
2 **Jim Kelly**, Buffalo	16	301
3 Terry Bradshaw, Pittsburgh	19	261

Yards Gained	Gm	Yds
1 Joe Montana, SF-KC	23	5772
2 Terry Bradshaw, Pittsburgh	19	3833
3 **Jim Kelly**, Buffalo	16	3624
4 John Elway, Denver	14	3321

Games

Played	Gm
1 D.D. Lewis, Dallas	27
2 Larry Cole, Dallas	26
3 Charlie Waters, Dallas	25

Coached	Gm
1 Tom Landry, Dallas	36
2 **Don Shula**, Baltimore-Miami	26
3 Chuck Noll, Pittsburgh	24

Rushing

Yards Gained	Gm	Car	Yds	Avg
1 Franco Harris	19	400	1556	3.89
2 Tony Dorsett	17	302	1383	4.58
3 **Thurman Thomas**	18	313	1349	4.31
4 **Marcus Allen**	15	255	1310	5.14
5 **Emmitt Smith**	13	279	1217	4.36

Attempts	Gm	Att
1 Franco Harris, Pittsburgh	19	400
2 **Thurman Thomas**, Buffalo.	18	313
3 Tony Dorsett, Dallas	17	302

Receiving

Catches	Gm	No	Yds	Avg
1 **Jerry Rice**	19	111	1702	15.3
2 **Andre Reed**	18	77	1137	14.8
3 **Michael Irvin**	13	74	1158	15.6

Yards Gained	Gm	Yds
1 **Jerry Rice**, San Francisco	19	1702
2 Cliff Branch, Oakland-LA	22	1289
3 Fred Biletnikoff, Oakland	19	1167

Average Gain	Gm	Avg
1 Alvin Harper, Dallas	10	27.3
2 Willie Gault, Chicago-LA	10	23.7
3 Harold Jackson, LA-NE-Minn-Sea	14	22.8

Scoring

Points	Gm	TD	FG	PAT	Pts
1 George Blanda	19	0	22	49	115
2 **Emmitt Smith**	13	18	0	0	108
Thurman Thomas	18	18	0	0	108

Touchdowns	Gm	Run	Rec	Ret	No
1 **Emmitt Smith**	13	16	2	0	18
Thurman Thomas	18	14	4	0	18
3 **Jerry Rice**	19	0	17	0	17

Field Goals	Gm	Att	FG	Pct
1 George Blanda	19	39	22	.564
2 Matt Bahr	14	25	21	.840
3 Toni Fritsch	14	28	20	.714

SINGLE GAME

Scoring

Points Scored	Year	Pts
1 Ricky Watters, SF vs. NYG	1993	30
2 Pat Harder, Det. vs. LA	1952	19
Paul Hornung, GB vs. NYG.	1961	19

Field Goals	Year	FG
1 Chuck Nelson, Min. vs. SF	1987	5
Matt Bahr, NYG vs. SF	1990	5
Steve Christie, Buf. vs. Mia	1992	5

Rushing

Yards Gained	Year	Yds
1 Eric Dickerson, LA Rams vs. Dal	1985	248
2 Keith Lincoln, SD vs. Bos	1963	206
3 Timmy Smith, Wash. vs. Den	1987	204

Most Attempts	Year	Att
1 Ricky Bell, TB vs. Phi	1979	38
John Riggins, Wash. vs. Mia.	1982	38
3 Lawrence McCutcheon, LA vs. St.L	1975	37
John Riggins, Wash. vs. Minn	1982	37

Passing

Attempts	Year	Att
1 **Steve Young**, SF vs. GB	1995	65
2 Bernie Kosar, Cle. vs. NYJ	1986	64
Dan Marino, Mia. vs. Buf.	1995	64

Completions	Year	Cmp
1 Warren Moon, Hou. vs. Buf	1992	36
2 Dan Fouts, SD vs. Mia	1981	33
Bernie Kosar, Cle. vs. NYJ	1986	33
Dan Marino, Mia. vs. Buf	1995	33

Yards Gained	Year	Yds
1 Bernie Kosar, Cle. vs. NYJ	1986	489
2 Dan Fouts, SD vs. Mia.	1981	433
3 **Dan Marino**, Mia. vs. Buf.	1995	422

Receiving

Catches	Year	Rec
1 Kellen Winslow, SD vs. Mia	1981	13
Thurman Thomas, Buf. vs. Cle.	1989	13
Shannon Sharpe, Den. vs. Raiders	1993	13

Yards Gained	Year	Yds
1 Anthony Carter, Min. vs. SF	1987	227
2 Jerry Rice, SF vs. Cin.	1988	215
3 Tom Fears, LA vs. Chi.	1950	198

Champions Of Leagues That No Longer Exist

No professional league in American sports has had to contend with more pretenders to the throne than the NFL. Seven times in as many decades a rival league has risen up to challenge the NFL and six of them went under in less than five seasons. Only the fourth American Football League (1960-69) succeeded, forcing the older league to sue for peace and a full partnership in 1966.

Of the six leagues that didn't make it, only the All-America Football Conference (1946-49) lives on—the Cleveland Browns and San Francisco 49ers joined the NFL after the AAFC folded in 1949. The champions of leagues past are listed below.

American Football League I

Year		Head Coach
1926	Philadelphia Quakers (7-2)	Bob Folwell

Note: Philadelphia was challenged to a postseason game by the 7th place New York Giants (8-4-1) of the NFL. The Giants won, 31-0, in a snowstorm.

American Football League II

Year		Head Coach
1936	Boston Shamrocks (8-3)	George Kenneally
1937	Los Angeles Bulldogs (8-0)	Gus Henderson

Note: Boston was scheduled to play 2nd place Cleveland (5-2-2) in the '36 championship game, but the Shamrock players refused to participate because they were owed pay for past games.

American Football League III

Year		Head Coach
1940	Columbus Bullies (8-1-1)	Phil Bucklew
1941	Columbus Bullies (5-1-2)	Phil Bucklew

All-America Football Conference

Year	Winner	Head Coach	Score	Loser	Head Coach	Site
1946	Cleveland Browns	Paul Brown	14-9	NY Yankees	Ray Flaherty	Cleveland
1947	Cleveland Browns	Paul Brown	14-3	NY Yankees	Ray Flaherty	New York
1948	Cleveland Browns	Paul Brown	49-7	Buffalo Bills	Red Dawson	Cleveland
1949	Cleveland Browns	Paul Brown	21-7	S.F. 49ers	Buck Shaw	Cleveland

World Football League

Year	Winner	Head Coach	Score	Loser	Head Coach	Site
1974	Birmingham Americans	Jack Gotta	22-21	Florida Blazers	Jack Pardee	Birmingham
1975	WFL folded Oct. 22.					

United States Football League

Year	Winner	Head Coach	Score	Loser	Head Coach	Site
1983	Michigan Panthers	Jim Stanley	24-22	Philadelphia Stars	Jim Mora	Denver
1984	Philadelphia Stars	Jim Mora	23- 3	Arizona Wranglers	George Allen	Tampa
1985	Baltimore Stars	Jim Mora	28-24	Oakland Invaders	Charlie Sumner	E. Rutherford

Defunct Leagues

AFL I (1926): Boston Bulldogs, Brooklyn Horseman, Chicago Bulls, Cleveland Panthers, Los Angeles Wildcats, New York Yankees, Newark Bears, Philadelphia Quakers, Rock Island Independents.

AFL II (1936-37): Boston Shamrocks (1936-37); Brooklyn Tigers (1936); Cincinnati Bengals (1937); Cleveland Rams (1936); Los Angeles Bulldogs (1937); New York Yankees (1936-37); Pittsburgh Americans (1936-37); Rochester Tigers (1936-37).

AFL III (1940-41): Boston Bears (1940); Buffalo Indians (1940-41); Cincinnati Bengals (1940-41); Columbus Bullies (1940-41); Milwaukee Chiefs (1940-41); New York Yankees (1940) renamed Americans (1941).

AAFC (1946-49): Brooklyn Dodgers (1946-48) merged to become Brooklyn-New York Yankees (1949); Buffalo Bisons (1946) renamed Bills (1947-49); Chicago Rockets (1946-48) renamed Hornets (1949); Cleveland Browns (1946-49); Los Angeles Dons (1946-49); Miami Seahawks (1946) became Baltimore Colts (1947-49); New York Yankees (1946-48) merged to become Brooklyn-New York Yankees (1949); San Francisco 49ers (1946-49).

WFL (1974-75): Birmingham Americans (1974) renamed Vulcans (1975); Chicago Fire (1974) renamed Winds (1975); Detroit Wheels (1974); Florida Blazers (1974) became San Antonio Wings (1975); The Hawaiians (1974-75); Houston Texans (1974) became Shreveport (La.) Steamer (1974-75); Jacksonville Sharks (1974) renamed Express (1975); Memphis Southmen (1974) also known as Grizzlies (1975); New York Stars (1974) became Charlotte Hornets (1974-75); Philadelphia Bell (1974-75); Portland Storm (1974) renamed Thunder (1975); Southern California Sun (1974-75).

USFL (1983-85): Arizona Wranglers (1983-84) merged with Oklahoma to become Arizona Outlaws (1985); Birmingham Stallions (1983-85); Boston Breakers (1983) became New Orleans Breakers (1984) and then Portland Breakers (1985); Chicago Blitz (1983-84); Denver Gold (1983-85); Houston Gamblers (1984-85); Jacksonville Bulls (1984-85); Los Angeles Express (1983-85); Memphis Showboats (1984-85).

Michigan Panthers (1983-84) merged with Oakland (1985); New Jersey Generals (1983-85); Oakland Invaders (1983-85); Oklahoma Outlaws (1984) merged with Arizona to become Arizona Outlaws (1985); Philadelphia Stars (1983-84) became Baltimore Stars (1985); Pittsburgh Maulers (1984); San Antonio Gunslingers (1984-85); Tampa Bay Bandits (1983-85); Washington Federals (1983-84) became Orlando Renegades (1985).

NFL Pro Bowl

A postseason All-Star game between the new league champion and a team of professional all-stars was added to the NFL schedule in 1939. In the first game at Wrigley Field in Los Angeles, the NY Giants beat a team made up of players from NFL teams and two independent clubs in Los Angeles (the LA Bulldogs and Hollywood Stars). An all-NFL All-Star team provided the opposition over the next four seasons, but the game was cancelled in 1943.

The Pro Bowl was revived in 1951 as a contest between conference all-star teams: American vs National (1951-53), Eastern vs Western (1954-70), and AFC vs NFC (since 1971). The NFC leads the current series with the AFC, 15-11.

The MVP trophy was named the Dan McGuire Award in 1984 after the late SF 49ers publicist and *Honolulu Advertiser* sports columnist.

Year	Winner	Score	Loser
1939	NY Giants	13-10	All-Stars
1940	Green Bay	16-7	All-Stars
1940	Chicago Bears	28-14	All-Stars
1942	Chcago Bears	35-24	All-Stars
1942	All-Stars	17-14	Washington
1943-50		No game	

Year	Winner	MVP
1951	American, 28-27	Otto Graham, Cle., QB
1952	National, 30-13	Dan Towler, LA, HB
1953	National, 27-7	Don Doll, Det., DB
1954	East, 20-9	Chuck Bednarik, Phi., LB
1955	West, 26-19	Billy Wilson, SF, E
1956	East, 31-30	Ollie Matson, Cards, HB
1957	West, 19-10	Back—Bert Rechichar, Bal. Line—Ernie Stautner, Pit.
1958	West, 26-7	Back—Hugh McElhenny, SF Line—Gene Brito, Wash.
1959	East, 28-21	Back—Frank Gifford, NY Line—Doug Atkins, Chi.
1960	West, 38-21	Back—Johnny Unitas, Bal. Line—Big Daddy Lipscomb, Pit.
1961	West, 35-31	Back—Johnny Unitas, Bal. Line—Sam Huff, NY
1962	West, 31-30	Back—Jim Brown, Cle. Line—Henry Jordan, GB
1963	East, 30-20	Back—Jim Brown, Cle. Line—Big Daddy Lipscomb, Pit.
1964	West, 31-17	Back—Johnny Unitas, Bal. Line—Gino Marchetti, Bal.
1965	West, 34-14	Back—Fran Tarkenton, Min. Line—Terry Barr, Det.
1966	East, 36-7	Back—Jim Brown, Cle. Line—Dale Meinhart, St.L.
1967	East, 20-10	Back—Gale Sayers, Chi. Line—Floyd Peters, Phi.
1968	West, 38-20	Back—Gale Sayers, Chi. Line—Dave Robinson, GB
1969	West, 10-7	Back—Roman Gabriel, LA Line—Merlin Olsen, LA
1970	West, 16-13	Back—Gale Sayers, Chi. Line—George Andrie, Dal.
1971	NFC, 27-6	Back—Mel Renfro, Dal. Line—Fred Carr, GB
1972	AFC, 26-13	Off—Jan Stenerud, KC Def—Willie Lanier, KC
1973	AFC, 33-28	O.J. Simpson, Buf., RB
1974	AFC, 15-13	Garo Yepremian, Mia., PK
1975	NFC, 17-10	James Harris, LA Rams, QB
1976	NFC, 23-20	Billy Johnson, Hou., KR
1977	AFC, 24-14	Mel Blount, Pit., CB
1978	NFC, 14-13	Walter Payton, Chi., RB
1979	NFC, 13-7	Ahmad Rashad, Min., WR
1980	NFC, 37-27	Chuck Muncie, NO, RB
1981	NFC, 21-7	Eddie Murray, Det., PK
1982	AFC, 16-13	Kellen Winslow, SD, WR & Lee Roy Selmon, TB, DE
1983	NFC, 20-19	Dan Fouts, SD, QB & John Jefferson, GB, WR
1984	NFC, 45-3	Joe Theismann, Wash., QB
1985	AFC, 22-14	Mark Gastineau, NYJ, DE
1986	NFC, 28-24	Phil Simms, NYG, QB
1987	AFC, 10-6	Reggie White, Phi., DE
1988	AFC, 15-6	Bruce Smith, Buf., DE
1989	NFC, 34-3	Randall Cunningham, Phi., QB
1990	NFC, 27-21	Jerry Gray, LA Rams, CB
1991	AFC, 23-21	Jim Kelly, Buf., QB
1992	NFC, 21-15	Michael Irvin, Dal., WR
1993	AFC, 23-20 (OT)	Steve Tasker, Buf., Sp. Teams
1994	NFC, 17-3	Andre Rison, Atl., WR
1995	AFC, 41-13	Marshall Faulk, Ind., RB
1996	NFC, 20-13	Jerry Rice, SF, WR

Playing sites: Wrigley Field in Los Angeles (1939); Gilmore Stadium in Los Angeles (both games); Polo Grounds in New York (Jan., 1942); Shibe Park in Philadelphia (Dec., 1942); Memorial Coliseum in Los Angeles (1951-72 and 1979); Texas Stadium in Irving, TX (1973); Arrowhead Stadium in Kansas City (1974); Orange Bowl in Miami (1975); Superdome in New Orleans (1976); Kingdome in Seattle (1977); Tampa Stadium in Tampa (1978) and Aloha Stadium in Honolulu (since 1980).

AFL All-Star Game

The AFL did not play an All-Star game after its first season in 1960 but did stage All-Star games from 1962-70. All-Star teams from the Eastern and Western divisions played each other every year except 1966 with the West winning the series, 6-2. In 1966, the league champion Buffalo Bills met an elite squad made up of the best players from the league's other eight clubs and lost, 30-19.

Year	Winner	MVP
1962	West, 47-27	Cotton Davidson, Oak., QB
1963	West, 21-14	Off—Curtis McClinton, Dal. Def—Earl Faison, SD
1964	West, 27-24	Off—Keith Lincoln, SD Def—Archie Matsos, Oak.
1965	West, 38-14	Off—Keith Lincoln, SD Def—Willie Brown, Den.
1966	All-Stars 30 Buffalo 19	Off—Joe Namath, NY Def—Frank Buncom, SD
1967	East, 30-23	Off—Babe Parilli, Bos. Def—Verlon Biggs, NY
1968	East, 25-24	Off—Joe Namath, NY & Don Maynard, NY Def—Speedy Duncan, SD
1969	West, 38-25	Off—Len Dawson, KC Def—George Webster, Hou.
1970	West, 26-3	John Hadl, SD, QB

Playing sites: Balboa Stadium in San Diego (1962-64); Jeppesen Stadium in Houston (1965); Rice Stadium in Houston (1966); Oakland Coliseum (1967); Gator Bowl in Jacksonville (1968-69) and Astrodome in Houston (1970).

NFL Franchise Origins

Here is what the current 30 teams in the National Football League have to show for the years they have put in as members of the American Professional Football Association (APFA), the NFL, the All-America Football Conference (AAFC) and the American Football League (AFL). Years given for league titles indicate seasons championships were won.

American Football Conference

	First Season	League Titles	Franchise Stops
Buffalo Bills	1960 (AFL)	2 AFL (1964-65)	• Buffalo (1960-72) Orchard Park, NY (1973—)
Cincinnati Bengals	1968 (AFL)	None	• Cincinnati (1968—)
Baltimore Ravens	1946 (AAFC)	4 AAFC (1946-49) 4 NFL (1950,54-55,64)	• Cleveland (1946-1995) Baltimore (1996—)
Denver Broncos	1960 (AFL)	None	• Denver (1960—)
Houston Oilers	1960 (AFL)	2 AFL (1960-61)	• Houston (1960—)
Indianapolis Colts	1953 (NFL)	3 NFL (1958-59,68) 1 Super Bowl (1970)	• Baltimore (1953-83) Indianapolis (1984—)
Jacksonville Jaguars	1995 (NFL)	None	• Jacksonville, FL (1995—)
Kansas City Chiefs	1960 (AFL)	3 AFL (1962,66,69) 1 Super Bowl (1969)	• Dallas (1960-62) Kansas City (1963—)
Miami Dolphins	1966 (AFL)	2 Super Bowls (1972-73)	• Miami (1966—)
New England Patriots	1960 (AFL)	None	• Boston (1960-70) Foxboro, MA (1971—)
New York Jets	1960 (AFL)	1 AFL (1968) 1 Super Bowl (1968)	• New York (1960-83) E. Rutherford, NJ (1984—)
Oakland Raiders	1960 (AFL)	1 AFL (1967) 3 Super Bowls (1976,80,83)	• Oakland (1960-81, 1995—) Los Angeles (1982-94)
Pittsburgh Steelers	1933 (NFL)	4 Super Bowls (1974-75,78-79)	• Pittsburgh (1933—)
San Diego Chargers	1960 (AFL)	1 AFL (1963)	• Los Angeles (1960) San Diego (1961—)
Seattle Seahawks	1976 (NFL)	None	• Seattle (1976—)

National Football Conference

	First Season	League Titles	Franchise Stops
Arizona Cardinals	1920 (APFA)	2 NFL (1925,47)	• Chicago (1920-59) St. Louis (1960-87) Tempe, AZ (1988—)
Atlanta Falcons	1966 (NFL)	None	• Atlanta (1966—)
Carolina Panthers	1995 (NFL)	None	• Clemson, SC (1995) Charlotte, NC (1996)
Chicago Bears	1920 (APFA)	8 NFL (1921, 32-33,40-41,43, 46,63) 1 Super Bowl (1985)	• Decatur, IL (1920) Chicago (1921—)
Dallas Cowboys	1960 (NFL)	4 Super Bowls (1971,77,92-93)	• Dallas (1960-70) Irving, TX (1971—)
Detroit Lions	1930 (NFL)	4 NFL (1935,52-53,57)	• Portsmouth, OH (1930-33) Detroit (1934-74) Pontiac, MI (1975—)
Green Bay Packers	1921 (APFA)	11 NFL (1929-31,36,39,44, 61-62,65-67) 2 Super Bowls (1966-67)	• Green Bay (1921—)
Minnesota Vikings	1961 (NFL)	1 NFL (1969)	• Bloomington, MN (1961-81) Minneapolis, MN (1982—)
New Orleans Saints	1967 (NFL)	None	• New Orleans (1967—)
New York Giants	1925 (NFL)	4 NFL (1927,34,38,56) 2 Super Bowls (1986,90)	• New York (1925-73,75) New Haven, CT (1973-74) E. Rutherford, NJ (1976—)
Philadelphia Eagles	1933 (NFL)	3 NFL (1948-49,60)	• Philadelphia (1933—)
St. Louis Rams	1937 (NFL)	2 NFL (1945,51)	• Cleveland (1937-45) Los Angeles (1946-79) Anaheim (1980-94) St. Louis (1995—)
San Francisco 49ers	1946 (AAFC)	5 Super Bowls (1981,84,88-89,94)	• San Francisco (1946—)
Tampa Bay Buccaneers	1976 (NFL)	None	• Tampa, FL (1976—)
Washington Redskins	1932 (NFL)	2 NFL (1937,42) 3 Super Bowls (1982,87,91)	• Boston (1932-36) Washington, DC (1937—)

The Growth of the NFL

Of the 14 franchises that comprised the American Professional Football Association in 1920, only two remain—the Arizona Cardinals (then the Chicago Cardinals) and the Chicago Bears (originally the Decatur-IL Staleys). Green Bay joined the APFC in 1921 and the league changed its name to the NFL in 1922. Since then, 54 NFL clubs have come and gone, five rival leagues have expired and two other leagues have been swallowed up.

The NFL merged with the **All-America Football Conference** (1946-49) following the 1949 season and adopted three of its seven clubs—the Baltimore Colts, Cleveland Browns and San Francisco 49ers. The four remaining AAFC teams—the Brooklyn/NY Yankees, Buffalo Bills, Chicago Hornets and Los Angeles Dons—did not survive. After the 1950 season, the financially troubled Colts were sold back to the NFL. The league folded the team and added its players to the 1951 college draft pool. A new Baltimore franchise, also named the Colts, joined the NFL in 1953.

The formation of the **American Football League** (1960-69) was announced in 1959 with ownership lined up in eight cities—Boston, Buffalo, Dallas, Denver, Houston, Los Angeles, Minneapolis and New York. Set to begin play in the autumn of 1960, the AFL was stunned early that year when Minneapolis withdrew to accept an offer to join the NFL as an expansion team in 1961. The new league responded by choosing Oakland to replace Minneapolis and inherit the departed team's draft picks. Since no AFL team actually played in Minneapolis, it is not considered the original home of the Oakland Raiders.

In 1966, the NFL and AFL agreed to a merger that resulted in the first Super Bowl (originally called the AFL-NFL World Championship Game) following the '66 league playoffs. In 1970, the now 10-member AFL officially joined the NFL, forming a 26-team league made up of two conferences of three divisions each.

Expansion/Merger Timetable

For teams currently in NFL.

1921—Green Bay Packers; **1925**—New York Giants; **1930**—Portsmouth-OH Spartans (now Detroit Lions); **1932**—Boston Braves (now Washington Redskins); **1933**—Philadelphia Eagles and Pittsburgh Pirates (now Steelers); **1937**—Cleveland Rams (now Los Angeles); **1950**—added AAFC's Cleveland Browns and San Francisco 49ers; **1953**—Baltimore Colts (now Indianapolis).

1960—Dallas Cowboys; **1961**—Minnesota Vikings; **1966**—Atlanta Falcons; **1967**—New Orleans Saints; **1970**—added AFL's Boston Patriots (now New England), Buffalo Bills, Cincinnati Bengals (1968 expansion team), Denver Broncos, Houston Oilers, Kansas City Chiefs, Miami Dolphins (1966 expansion team), New York Jets, Oakland Raiders and San Diego Chargers (the AFL-NFL merger divided the league into two 13-team conferences with old-line NFL clubs Baltimore, Cleveland and Pittsburgh moving to the AFC); **1976**—Seattle Seahawks and Tampa Bay Buccaneers (Seattle was originally in the NFC West and Tampa Bay in the AFC West, but were switched to their current divisions in 1977). **1995**—Carolina Panthers and Jacksonville Jaguars.

City and Nickname Changes

1921—Decatur Staleys move to Chicago; **1922**—Chicago Staleys renamed Bears; **1933**—Boston Braves renamed Redskins; **1937**—Boston Redskins move to Washington; **1934**—Portsmouth (Ohio) Spartans move to Detroit and become Lions; **1941**—Pittsburgh Pirates renamed Steelers; **1943**—Philadelphia and Pittsburgh merge for one season and become Phil-Pitt, or the "Steagles"; **1944**—Chicago Cardinals and Pittsburgh merge for one season and become Card-Pitt; **1946**—Cleveland Rams move to Los Angeles.

1960—Chicago Cardinals move to St. Louis; **1961**—Los Angeles Chargers (AFL) move to San Diego; **1963**—New York Titans (AFL) renamed Jets and Dallas Texans (AFL) move to Kansas City and become Chiefs; **1971**—Boston Patriots become New England Patriots; **1982**—Oakland Raiders move to Los Angeles; **1984**—Baltimore Colts move to Indianapolis; **1988**—St. Louis Cardinals move to Phoenix; **1994**—Phoenix Cardinals become Arizona Cardinals. **1995**—L.A. Rams move to St. Louis and L.A. Raiders move back to Oakland. **1996**—Cleveland Browns move to Baltimore and become Ravens.

Defunct NFL Teams

Teams that once played in the APFA and NFL, but no longer exist.

Akron-OH—Pros (1920-25) and Indians (1926); **Baltimore**—Colts (1950); **Boston**—Bulldogs (1926) and Yanks (1944-48); **Brooklyn**—Lions (1926), Dodgers (1930-43) and Tigers (1944); **Buffalo**—All-Americans (1921-23), Bisons (1924-25), Rangers (1926), Bisons (1927,1929); **Canton-OH**—Bulldogs (1920-23,1925-26); **Chicago**—Tigers (1920); **Cincinnati**—Celts (1921) and Reds (1933-34); **Cleveland**—Tigers (1920), Indians (1921), Indians (1923), Bulldogs (1924-25,1927) and Indians (1931); **Columbus-OH**—Panhandles (1920-22) and Tigers (1923-26); **Dallas**—Texans (1952); **Dayton-OH**—Triangles (1920-29).

Detroit—Heralds (1920-21), Panthers (1925-26) and Wolverines (1928); **Duluth-MN**—Kelleys (1923-25) and Eskimos (1926-27); **Evansville-IN**—Crimson Giants (1921-22); **Frankford-PA**—Yellow Jackets (1924-31); **Hammond-IN**—Pros (1920-26); **Hartford**—Blues (1926); **Kansas City**—Blues (1924) and Cowboys (1925-26); **Kenosha-WI**—Maroons (1924); **Los Angeles**—Buccaneers (1926); **Louisville**—Brecks (1921-23) and Colonels (1926); **Marion-OH**—Oorang Indians (1922-23); **Milwaukee**—Badgers (1922-26); **Minneapolis**—Marines (1922-24) and Red Jackets (1929-30); **Muncie-IN**—Flyers (1920-21).

New York—Giants (1921), Yankees (1927-28), Bulldogs (1949) and Yankees (1950-51); **Newark-NJ**—Tornadoes (1930); **Orange-NJ**—Tornadoes (1929); **Pottsville-PA**—Maroons (1925-28); **Providence-RI**—Steam Roller (1925-31); **Racine-WI**—Legion (1922-24) and Tornadoes (1926); **Rochester-NY**—Jeffersons (1920-25); **Rock Island-IL**—Independents (1920-26); **Staten Island-NY**—Stapletons (1929-32); **St. Louis**—All-Stars (1923) and Gunners (1934); **Toledo-OH**—Maroons (1922-23); **Tonawanda-NY**—Kardex (1921), also called Lumbermen; **Washington**—Senators (1921).

Annual NFL Leaders

Individual leaders in NFL (1932-69), NFC (since 1970), AFL (1960-69) and AFC (since 1970).

Passing

NFL-NFC

Since 1932, the NFL has used several formulas to determine passing leadership, from Total Yards alone (1932-37), to the current rating system—adopted in 1973—that takes Completions, Completion Pct., Yards Gained, TD Passes, Interceptions, Interception Pct. and other factors into account. The quarterbacks listed below all led the league according to the system in use at the time.

Multiple winners: Sammy Baugh (6); Joe Montana and Roger Staubach (5); Steve Young (4); Arnie Herber, Sonny Jurgensen, Bart Starr, and Norm Van Brocklin (3); Ed Danowski, Otto Graham, Cecil Isbell, Milt Plum and Bob Waterfield (2).

Year		Att	Cmp	Yds	TD
1932	Arnie Herber, GB	101	37	639	9
1933	Harry Newman, NY	136	53	973	11
1934	Arnie Herber, GB	115	42	799	8
1935	Ed Danowski, NY	113	57	794	10
1936	Arnie Herber, GB	173	77	1239	11
1937	Sammy Baugh, Wash	171	81	1127	8
1938	Ed Danowski, NY	129	70	848	7
1939	Parker Hall, Cle. Rams	208	106	1227	9
1940	Sammy Baugh, Wash	177	111	1367	12
1941	Cecil Isbell, GB	206	117	1479	15
1942	Cecil Isbell, GB	268	146	2021	24
1943	Sammy Baugh, Wash	239	133	1754	23
1944	Frank Filchock, Wash	147	84	1139	13
1945	Sammy Baugh, Wash	182	128	1669	11
	& Sid Luckman, Chi. Bears	217	117	1725	14
1946	Bob Waterfield, LA	251	127	1747	18
1947	Sammy Baugh, Wash	354	210	2938	25
1948	Tommy Thompson, Phi	246	141	1965	25
1949	Sammy Baugh, Wash	255	145	1903	18
1950	Norm Van Brocklin, LA	233	127	2061	18
1951	Bob Waterfield, LA	176	88	1566	13
1952	Norm Van Brocklin, LA	205	113	1736	14
1953	Otto Graham, Cle	258	167	2722	11
1954	Norm Van Brocklin, LA	260	139	2637	13
1955	Otto Graham, Cle	185	98	1721	15
1956	Ed Brown, Chi. Bears	168	96	1667	11
1957	Tommy O'Connell, Cle	110	63	1229	9
1958	Eddie LeBaron, Wash	145	79	1365	11
1959	Charlie Conerly, NY	194	113	1706	14
1960	Milt Plum, Cle	250	151	2297	21
1961	Milt Plum, Cle	302	177	2416	16
1962	Bart Starr, GB	285	178	2438	12
1963	Y.A.Tittle, NY	367	221	3145	36
1964	Bart Starr, GB	272	163	2144	15
1965	Rudy Bukich, Chi	312	176	2641	20
1966	Bart Starr, GB	251	156	2257	14
1967	Sonny Jurgensen, Wash	508	288	3747	31
1968	Earl Morrall, Bal	317	182	2909	26
1969	Sonny Jurgensen, Wash	442	274	3102	22
1970	John Brodie, SF	378	223	2941	24
1971	Roger Staubach, Dal	211	126	1882	15
1972	Norm Snead, NY	325	196	2307	17
1973	Roger Staubach, Dal	286	179	2428	23
1974	Sonny Jurgensen, Wash	167	107	1185	11
1975	Fran Tarkenton, Min	425	273	2994	25
1976	James Harris, LA	158	91	1460	8
1977	Roger Staubach, Dal	361	210	2620	18
1978	Roger Staubach, Dal	413	231	3190	25
1979	Roger Staubach, Dal	461	267	3586	27
1980	Ron Jaworski, Phi	451	257	3529	27
1981	Joe Montana, SF	488	311	3565	19
1982	Joe Theismann, Wash	252	161	2033	13
1983	Steve Bartkowski, Atl	432	274	3167	22
1984	Joe Montana, SF	432	279	3630	28
1985	Joe Montana, SF	494	303	3653	27
1986	Tommy Kramer, Min	372	208	3000	24
1987	Joe Montana, SF	398	266	3054	31
1988	Wade Wilson, Min	332	204	2746	15
1989	Don Majkowski, GB	599	353	4318	27
1990	Joe Montana, SF	520	321	3944	26
1991	Steve Young, SF	279	180	2517	17
1992	Steve Young, SF	402	268	3465	25
1993	Steve Young, SF	462	314	4023	29
1994	Steve Young, SF	461	324	3969	35
1995	Brett Favre, GB	570	359	4413	38

Note: In 1945, **Sammy Baugh** and **Sid Luckman** tied with 8 points on an inverse rating system.

AFL-AFC

Multiple winners: Dan Marino (5); Ken Anderson and Len Dawson (4); Bob Griese, Daryle Lamonica, Warren Moon and Ken Stabler (2).

Year		Att	Cmp	Yds	TD
1960	Jack Kemp, LA	406	211	3018	20
1961	George Blanda, Hou	362	187	3330	36
1962	Len Dawson, Dal	310	189	2759	29
1963	Tobin Rote, SD	286	170	2510	20
1964	Len Dawson, KC	354	199	2879	30
1965	John Hadl, SD	348	174	2798	20
1966	Len Dawson, KC	284	159	2527	26
1967	Daryle Lamonica, Oak	425	220	3228	30
1968	Len Dawson, KC	224	131	2109	17
1969	Greg Cook, Cin	197	106	1854	15
1970	Daryle Lamonica, Oak	356	179	2516	22
1971	Bob Griese, Mia	263	145	2089	19
1972	Earl Morrall, Mia	150	83	1360	11
1973	Ken Stabler, Oak	260	163	1997	14
1974	Ken Anderson, Cin	328	213	2667	18
1975	Ken Anderson, Cin	377	228	3169	21
1976	Ken Stabler, Oak	291	194	2737	27
1977	Bob Griese, Mia	307	180	2252	22
1978	Terry Bradshaw, Pit	368	207	2915	28
1979	Dan Fouts, SD	530	332	4082	24
1980	Brian Sipe, Cle	554	337	4132	30
1981	Ken Anderson, Cin	479	300	3753	29
1982	Ken Anderson, Cin	309	218	2495	12
1983	Dan Marino, Mia	296	173	2210	20
1984	Dan Marino, Mia	564	362	5084	48
1985	Ken O'Brien, NY	488	297	3888	25
1986	Dan Marino, Mia	623	378	4746	44
1987	Bernie Kosar, Cle	389	241	3033	22
1988	Boomer Esiason, Cin	388	223	3572	28
1989	Dan Marino, Mia	550	308	3997	24
1990	Warren Moon, Hou	584	362	4689	33
1991	Jim Kelly, Buf	474	304	3844	33
1992	Warren Moon, Hou	346	224	2521	18
1993	John Elway, Den	551	348	4030	25
1994	Dan Marino, Mia	615	385	4453	30
1995	Jim Harbaugh, Ind	314	200	2575	17

Annual NFL Leaders (Cont.)

Receptions

NFL-NFC

Multiple winners: Don Hutson (8); Raymond Berry, Tom Fears, Pete Pihos, Sterling Sharpe and Billy Wilson (3); Dwight Clark, Ahmad Rashad, Jerry Rice and Charley Taylor (2).

Year		No	Yds	Avg	TD
1932	Ray Flaherty, NY	21	350	16.7	3
1933	Shipwreck Kelly, Bklyn	22	246	11.2	3
1934	Joe Carter, Phi	16	238	14.9	4
	& Red Badgro, NY	16	206	12.9	1
1935	Tod Goodwin, NY	26	432	16.6	4
1936	Don Hutson, GB	34	536	15.8	8
1937	Don Hutson, GB	41	552	13.5	7
1938	Gaynell Tinsley, Chi. Cards	41	516	12.6	1
1939	Don Hutson, GB	34	846	24.9	6
1940	Don Looney, Phi	58	707	12.2	4
1941	Don Hutson, GB	58	739	12.7	10
1942	Don Hutson, GB	74	1211	16.4	17
1943	Don Hutson, GB	47	776	16.5	11
1944	Don Hutson, GB	58	866	14.9	9
1945	Don Hutson, GB	47	834	17.7	9
1946	Jim Benton, LA	63	981	15.6	6
1947	Jim Keane, Chi. Bears	64	910	14.2	10
1948	Tom Fears, LA	51	698	13.7	4
1949	Tom Fears, LA	77	1013	13.2	9
1950	Tom Fears, LA	84	1116	13.3	7
1951	Elroy Hirsch, LA	66	1495	22.7	17
1952	Mac Speedie, Cle	62	911	14.7	5
1953	Pete Pihos, Phi	63	1049	16.7	10
1954	Pete Pihos, Phi	60	872	14.5	10
	& Billy Wilson, SF	60	830	13.8	5
1955	Pete Pihos, Phi	62	864	13.9	7
1956	Billy Wilson, SF	60	889	14.8	5
1957	Billy Wilson, SF	52	757	14.6	6
1958	Raymond Berry, Bal	56	794	14.2	9
	& Pete Retzlaff, Phi	56	766	13.7	2
1959	Raymond Berry, Bal	66	959	14.5	14
1960	Raymond Berry, Bal	74	1298	17.5	10
1961	Red Phillips, LA	78	1092	14.0	5
1962	Bobby Mitchell, Wash	72	1384	19.2	11
1963	Bobby Joe Conrad, St.L	73	967	13.2	10

Year		No	Yds	Avg	TD
1964	Johnny Morris, Chi. Bears	93	1200	12.9	10
1965	Dave Parks, SF	80	1344	16.8	12
1966	Charley Taylor, Wash	72	1119	15.5	12
1967	Charley Taylor, Wash	70	990	14.1	9
1968	Clifton McNeil, SF	71	994	14.0	7
1969	Dan Abramowicz, NO	73	1015	13.9	7
1970	Dick Gordon, Chi	71	1026	14.5	13
1971	Bob Tucker, NY	59	791	13.4	4
1972	Harold Jackson, Phi	62	1048	16.9	4
1973	Harold Carmichael, Phi	67	1116	16.7	9
1974	Charles Young, Phi	63	696	11.0	3
1975	Chuck Foreman, Min	73	691	9.5	9
1976	Drew Pearson, Dal	58	806	13.9	6
1977	Ahmad Rashad, Min	51	681	13.4	2
1978	Rickey Young, Min	88	704	8.0	5
1979	Ahmad Rashad, Min	80	1156	14.5	9
1980	Earl Cooper, SF	83	567	6.8	4
1981	Dwight Clark, SF	85	1105	13.0	4
1982	Dwight Clark, SF	60	913	12.2	5
1983	Roy Green, St.L	78	1227	15.7	14
	Charlie Brown, Wash	78	1225	15.7	8
	& Earnest Gray, NY	78	1139	14.6	5
1984	Art Monk, Wash	106	1372	12.9	7
1985	Roger Craig, SF	92	1016	11.0	6
1986	Jerry Rice, SF	86	1570	18.3	15
1987	J.T. Smith, St.L	91	1117	12.3	8
1988	Henry Ellard, LA	86	1414	16.4	10
1989	Sterling Sharpe, GB	90	1423	15.8	12
1990	Jerry Rice, SF	100	1502	15.0	13
1991	Michael Irvin, Dal	93	1523	16.4	8
1992	Sterling Sharpe, GB	108	1461	13.5	13
1993	Sterling Sharpe, GB	112	1274	11.4	11
1994	Cris Carter, Min	122	1256	10.3	7
1995	Herman Moore, Det	123	1686	13.7	14

AFL-AFC

Multiple winners: Lionel Taylor (5); Lance Alworth, Haywood Jeffires, Lydell Mitchell and Kellen Winslow (3); Fred Biletnikoff, Todd Christensen and Al Toon (2).

Year		No	Yds	Avg	TD
1960	Lionel Taylor, Den	92	1235	13.4	12
1961	Lionel Taylor, Den	100	1176	11.8	4
1962	Lionel Taylor, Den	77	908	11.8	4
1963	Lionel Taylor, Den	78	1101	14.1	10
1964	Charley Hennigan, Hou	101	1546	15.3	8
1965	Lionel Taylor, Den	85	1131	13.3	6
1966	Lance Alworth, SD	73	1383	18.9	13
1967	George Sauer, NY	75	1189	15.9	6
1968	Lance Alworth, SD	68	1312	19.3	10
1969	Lance Alworth, SD	64	1003	15.7	4
1970	Marlin Briscoe, Buf	57	1036	18.2	8
1971	Fred Biletnikoff, Oak	61	929	15.2	9
1972	Fred Biletnikoff, Oak	58	802	13.8	7
1973	Fred Willis, Hou	57	371	6.5	1
1974	Lydell Mitchell, Bal	72	544	7.6	2
1975	Reggie Rucker, Cle	60	770	12.8	3
	& Lydell Mitchell, Bal	60	544	9.1	4
1976	MacArthur Lane, KC	66	686	10.4	1
1977	Lydell Mitchell, Bal	71	620	8.7	4

Year		No	Yds	Avg	TD
1978	Steve Largent, Sea	71	1168	16.5	8
1979	Joe Washington, Bal	82	750	9.1	3
1980	Kellen Winslow, SD	89	1290	14.5	9
1981	Kellen Winslow, SD	88	1075	12.2	10
1982	Kellen Winslow, SD	54	721	13.4	6
1983	Todd Christensen, LA	92	1247	13.6	12
1984	Ozzie Newsome, Cle	89	1001	11.2	5
1985	Lionel James, SD	86	1027	11.9	6
1986	Todd Christensen, LA	95	1153	12.1	8
1987	Al Toon, NY	68	976	14.4	5
1988	Al Toon, NY	93	1067	11.5	5
1989	Andre Reed, Buf	88	1312	14.9	9
1990	Haywood Jeffires, Hou	74	1048	14.2	8
	& Drew Hill, Hou	74	1019	13.8	5
1991	Haywood Jeffires, Hou	100	1181	11.8	7
1992	Haywood Jeffires, Hou	90	913	10.1	9
1993	Reggie Langhorne, Ind	85	1038	12.2	3
1994	Ben Coates, NE	96	1174	12.2	7
1995	Carl Pickens, Cin	99	1234	12.5	17

Rushing

NFL-NFC

Multiple winners: Jim Brown (8); Walter Payton (5); Emmitt Smith and Steve Van Buren (4); Eric Dickerson and Barry Sanders (3); Cliff Battles, John Brockington, Larry Brown, Bill Dudley, Leroy Kelly, Bill Paschal, Joe Perry, Gale Sayers and Whizzer White (2).

Year		Car	Yds	Avg	TD
1932	Cliff Battles, Bos	148	576	3.9	3
1933	Jim Musick, Bos	173	809	4.7	5
1934	Beattie Feathers, Chi. Bears	119	1004	8.4	8
1935	Doug Russell, Chi. Cards	140	499	3.6	0
1936	Tuffy Leemans, NY	206	830	4.0	2
1937	Cliff Battles, Wash	216	874	4.0	5
1938	Whizzer White, Pit	152	567	3.7	4
1939	Bill Osmanski, Chi. Bears	121	699	5.8	7
1940	Whizzer White, Det	146	514	3.5	5
1941	Pug Manders, Bklyn	111	486	4.4	5
1942	Bill Dudley, Pit	162	696	4.3	5
1943	Bill Paschal, NY	147	572	3.9	10
1944	Bill Paschal, NY	196	737	3.8	9
1945	Steve Van Buren, Phi	143	832	5.8	15
1946	Bill Dudley, Pit	146	604	4.1	3
1947	Steve Van Buren, Phi	217	1008	4.6	13
1948	Steve Van Buren, Phi	201	945	4.7	10
1949	Steve Van Buren, Phi	263	1146	4.4	11
1950	Marion Motley, Cle	140	810	5.8	3
1951	Eddie Price, NY Giants	271	971	3.6	7
1952	Dan Towler, LA	156	894	5.7	10
1953	Joe Perry, SF	192	1018	5.3	10
1954	Joe Perry, SF	173	1049	6.1	8
1955	Alan Ameche, Bal	213	961	4.5	9
1956	Rick Casares, Chi. Bears	234	1126	4.8	12
1957	Jim Brown, Cle	202	942	4.7	9
1958	Jim Brown, Cle	257	1527	5.9	17
1959	Jim Brown, Cle	290	1329	4.6	14
1960	Jim Brown, Cle	215	1257	5.8	9
1961	Jim Brown, Cle	305	1408	4.6	8
1962	Jim Taylor, GB	272	1474	5.4	19
1963	Jim Brown, Cle	291	1863	6.4	12

Year		Car	Yds	Avg	TD
1964	Jim Brown, Cle	280	1446	5.2	7
1965	Jim Brown, Cle	289	1544	5.3	17
1966	Gale Sayers, Chi	229	1231	5.4	8
1967	Leroy Kelly, Cle	235	1205	5.1	11
1968	Leroy Kelly, Cle	248	1239	5.0	16
1969	Gale Sayers, Chi	236	1032	4.4	8
1970	Larry Brown, Wash	237	1125	4.7	5
1971	John Brockington, GB	216	1105	5.1	4
1972	Larry Brown, Wash	285	1216	4.3	8
1973	John Brockington, GB	265	1144	4.3	3
1974	Lawrence McCutcheon, LA	236	1109	4.7	3
1975	Jim Otis, St.L	269	1076	4.0	5
1976	Walter Payton, Chi	311	1390	4.5	13
1977	Walter Payton, Chi	339	1852	5.5	14
1978	Walter Payton, Chi	333	1395	4.2	11
1979	Walter Payton, Chi	369	1610	4.4	14
1980	Walter Payton, Chi	317	1460	4.6	6
1981	George Rogers, NO	378	1674	4.4	13
1982	Tony Dorsett, Dal	177	745	4.2	5
1983	Eric Dickerson, LA	390	1808	4.6	18
1984	Eric Dickerson, LA	379	2105	5.6	14
1985	Gerald Riggs, Atl	397	1719	4.3	10
1986	Eric Dickerson, LA	404	1821	4.5	11
1987	Charles White, LA	324	1374	4.2	11
1988	Herschel Walker, Dal	361	1514	4.2	5
1989	Barry Sanders, Det	280	1470	5.3	14
1990	Barry Sanders, Det	255	1304	5.1	13
1991	Emmitt Smith, Dal	365	1563	4.3	12
1992	Emmitt Smith, Dal	373	1713	4.6	18
1993	Emmitt Smith, Dal	283	1486	5.3	9
1994	Barry Sanders, Det	331	1883	5.7	7
1995	Emmitt Smith, Dal	377	1773	4.7	25

Note: Jim Brown led the NFL in rushing eight of his nine years in the league. The one season he didn't win (1962) he finished fourth (996 yds) behind Jim Taylor, John Henry Johnson of Pittsburgh (1,141 yds) and Dick Bass of the LA Rams (1,033 yds).

AFL-AFC

Multiple winners: Earl Campbell and O.J. Simpson (4); Thurman Thomas (3); Cookie Gilchrist, Eric Dickerson, Floyd Little, Jim Nance and Curt Warner (2).

Year		Car	Yds	Avg	TD
1960	Abner Haynes, Dal	157	875	5.6	9
1961	Billy Cannon, Hou	200	948	4.7	6
1962	Cookie Gilchrist, Buf	214	1096	5.1	13
1963	Clem Daniels, Oak	215	1099	5.1	3
1964	Cookie Gilchrist, Buf	230	981	4.3	6
1965	Paul Lowe, SD	222	1121	5.0	7
1966	Jim Nance, Bos	299	1458	4.9	11
1967	Jim Nance, Bos	269	1216	4.5	7
1968	Paul Robinson, Cin	238	1023	4.3	8
1969	Dickie Post, SD	182	873	4.8	6
1970	Floyd Little, Den	209	901	4.3	3
1971	Floyd Little, Den	284	1133	4.0	6
1972	O.J. Simpson, Buf	292	1251	4.3	6
1973	O.J. Simpson, Buf	332	2003	6.0	12
1974	Otis Armstrong, Den	263	1407	5.3	9
1975	O.J. Simpson, Buf	329	1817	5.5	16
1976	O.J. Simpson, Buf	290	1503	5.2	8
1977	Mark van Eeghen, Oak	324	1273	3.9	7

Year		Car	Yds	Avg	TD
1978	Earl Campbell, Hou	302	1450	4.8	13
1979	Earl Campbell, Hou	368	1697	4.6	19
1980	Earl Campbell, Hou	373	1934	5.2	13
1981	Earl Campbell, Hou	361	1376	3.8	10
1982	Freeman McNeil, NY	151	786	5.2	6
1983	Curt Warner, Sea	335	1449	4.3	13
1984	Earnest Jackson, SD	296	1179	4.0	8
1985	Marcus Allen, LA	380	1759	4.6	11
1986	Curt Warner, Sea	319	1481	4.6	13
1987	Eric Dickerson, Ind	223	1011	4.5	5
1988	Eric Dickerson, Ind	388	1659	4.3	14
1989	Christian Okoye, KC	370	1480	4.0	12
1990	Thurman Thomas, Buf	271	1297	4.8	11
1991	Thurman Thomas, Buf	288	1407	4.9	7
1992	Barry Foster, Pit	390	1690	4.3	11
1993	Thurman Thomas, Buf	355	1315	3.7	6
1994	Chris Warren, Sea	333	1545	4.6	9
1995	Curtis Martin, NE	368	1487	4.0	14

Note: Eric Dickerson was traded to Indianapolis from the NFC's LA Rams during the 1987 season. In three games with the Rams, he carried the ball 60 times for 277 yds, a 4.6 avg and 1 TD. His official AFC statistics above came in nine games with the Colts.

Annual NFL Leaders (Cont.)

Scoring

NFL-NFC

Multiple winners: Don Hutson (5); Dutch Clark, Pat Harder, Paul Hornung, Chip Lohmiller and Mark Moseley (3); Kevin Butler, Mike Cofer, Fred Cox, Jack Manders, Chester Marcol, Eddie Murray, Emmitt Smith, Gordy Soltau and Doak Walker (2).

Year		TD	FG	PAT	Pts
1932	Dutch Clark, Portsmouth	6	3	10	55
1933	Glenn Presnell, Portsmouth	6	6	10	64
	& Ken Strong, NY	6	5	13	64
1934	Jack Manders, Chi. Bears	3	10	31	79
1935	Dutch Clark, Det	6	1	16	55
1936	Dutch Clark, Det	7	4	19	73
1937	Jack Manders, Chi. Bears	5	8	15	69
1938	Clarke Hinkle, GB	7	3	7	58
1939	Andy Farkas, Wash	11	0	2	68
1940	Don Hutson, GB	7	0	15	57
1941	Don Hutson, GB	12	1	20	95
1942	Don Hutson, GB	17	1	33	138
1943	Don Hutson, GB	12	3	26	117
1944	Don Hutson, GB	9	0	31	85
1945	Steve Van Buren, Phi	18	0	2	110
1946	Ted Fritsch, GB	10	9	13	100
1947	Pat Harder, Chi. Cards	7	7	39	102
1948	Pat Harder, Chi. Cards	6	7	53	110
1949	Gene Roberts, NY Giants	17	0	0	102
	& Pat Harder, Chi. Cards	8	3	45	102
1950	Doak Walker, Det	11	8	38	128
1951	Elroy Hirsch, LA	17	0	0	102
1952	Gordy Soltau, SF	7	6	34	94
1953	Gordy Soltau, SF	6	10	48	114
1954	Bobby Walston, Phi	11	4	36	114
1955	Doak Walker, Det	7	9	27	96
1956	Bobby Layne, Det	5	12	33	99
1957	Sam Baker, Wash	1	14	29	77
	& Lou Groza, Cle	0	15	32	77
1958	Jim Brown, Cle	18	0	0	108
1959	Paul Hornung, GB	7	7	31	94
1960	Paul Hornung, GB	15	15	41	176
1961	Paul Hornung, GB	10	15	41	146
1962	Jim Taylor, GB	19	0	0	114
1963	Don Chandler, NY	0	18	52	106
1964	Lenny Moore, Bal	20	0	0	120
1965	Gale Sayers, Chi	22	0	0	132
1966	Bruce Gossett, LA	0	28	29	113
1967	Jim Bakken, St.L	0	27	36	117
1968	Leroy Kelly, Cle	20	0	0	120
1969	Fred Cox, Min	0	26	43	121
1970	Fred Cox, Min	0	30	35	125
1971	Curt Knight, Wash	0	29	27	114
1972	Chester Marcol, GB	0	33	29	128
1973	David Ray, LA	0	30	40	130
1974	Chester Marcol, GB	0	25	19	94
1975	Chuck Foreman, Min	22	0	0	132
1976	Mark Moseley, Wash	0	22	31	97
1977	Walter Payton, Chi	16	0	0	96
1978	Frank Corral, LA	0	29	31	118
1979	Mark Moseley, Wash	0	25	39	114
1980	Eddie Murray, Det	0	27	35	116
1981	Rafael Septien, Dal	0	27	40	121
	& Eddie Murray, Det	0	25	46	121
1982	Wendell Tyler, LA	13	0	0	78
1983	Mark Moseley, Wash	0	33	62	161
1984	Ray Wersching, SF	0	25	56	131
1985	Kevin Butler, Chi	0	31	51	144
1986	Kevin Butler, Chi	0	28	36	120
1987	Jerry Rice, SF	23	0	0	138
1988	Mike Cofer, SF	0	27	40	121
1989	Mike Cofer, SF	0	29	49	136
1990	Chip Lohmiller, Wash	0	30	41	131
1991	Chip Lohmiller, Wash	0	31	56	149
1992	Chip Lohmiller, Wash	0	30	30	120
	& Morten Andersen, NO	0	29	33	120
1993	Jason Hanson, Det	0	34	28	130
1994	Emmitt Smith, Dal	22	0	0	132
	& Fuad Reveiz, Min	0	34	30	132
1995	Emmitt Smith, Dal	25	0	0	150

AFL-AFC

Multiple winners: Gino Cappelletti (5); Gary Anderson (3); Jim Breech, Roy Gerela, Gene Mingo, Nick Lowery, John Smith, Pete Stoyanovich and Jim Turner (2).

Year		TD	FG	PAT	Pts
1960	Gene Mingo, Den	6	18	33	123
1961	Gino Cappelletti, Bos	8	17	48	147
1962	Gene Mingo, Den	4	27	32	137
1963	Gino Cappelletti, Bos	2	22	35	113
1964	Gino Cappelletti, Bos	7	25	36	155
1965	Gino Cappelletti, Bos	9	17	27	132
1966	Gino Cappelletti, Bos	6	16	35	119
1967	George Blanda, Oak	0	20	56	116
1968	Jim Turner, NY	0	34	43	145
1969	Jim Turner, NY	0	32	33	129
1970	Jan Stenerud, KC	0	30	26	116
1971	Garo Yepremian, Mia	0	28	33	117
1972	Bobby Howfield, NY	0	27	40	121
1973	Roy Gerela, Pit	0	29	36	123
1974	Roy Gerela, Pit	0	20	33	93
1975	O.J. Simpson, Buf	23	0	0	138
1976	Toni Linhart, Bal	0	20	49	109
1977	Errol Mann, Oak	0	20	39	99
1978	Pat Leahy, NY	0	22	41	107
1979	John Smith, NE	0	23	46	115
1980	John Smith, NE	0	26	51	129
1981	Nick Lowery, KC	0	26	37	115
	& Jim Breech, Cin	0	22	49	115
1982	Marcus Allen, LA	14	0	0	84
1983	Gary Anderson, Pit	0	27	38	119
1984	Gary Anderson, Pit	0	24	45	117
1985	Gary Anderson, Pit	0	33	40	139
1986	Tony Franklin, NE	0	32	44	140
1987	Jim Breech, Cin	0	24	25	97
1988	Scott Norwood, Buf	0	32	33	129
1989	David Treadwell, Den	0	27	39	120
1990	Nick Lowery, KC	0	34	37	139
1991	Pete Stoyanovich, Mia	0	31	28	121
1992	Pete Stoyanovich, Mia	0	30	34	124
1993	Jeff Jaeger, LA	0	35	27	132
1994	John Carney, SD	0	34	33	135
1995	Norm Johnson, Pit	0	34	39	141

All-Time NFL Leaders

Through 1995 regular season.

CAREER

Players active in 1995 in **bold** type.

Passing Efficiency

Ratings based on performance standards established for completion percentage, average gain, touchdown percentage and interception percentage. Quarterbacks are allocated points according to how their statistics measure up to those standards. Minimum 1500 passing attempts.

		Yrs	Att	Cmp	Cmp%	Yards	Avg Gain	TD	TD%	Int	Int%	Rating
1	**Steve Young**	11	2876	1845	64.2	23,069	8.02	160	5.6	79	2.7	96.1
2	Joe Montana	15	5391	3409	63.2	40,551	7.52	273	5.1	139	2.6	92.3
3	**Dan Marino**	13	6531	3913	59.9	48,841	7.48	352	5.4	200	3.1	88.4
4	**Brett Favre**	5	2150	1342	62.4	14,825	6.90	108	5.0	66	3.1	86.8
5	**Jim Kelly**	10	4400	2652	60.3	32,657	7.42	223	5.1	156	3.5	85.4
6	**Troy Aikman**	7	2713	1704	62.8	19,607	7.23	98	3.6	85	3.1	83.5
7	Roger Staubach	11	2958	1685	57.0	22,700	7.67	153	5.2	109	3.7	83.4
8	Neil Lomax	8	3153	1817	57.6	22,771	7.22	136	4.3	90	2.9	82.7
9	Sonny Jurgensen	18	4262	2433	57.1	32,224	7.56	255	6.0	189	4.4	82.63
10	Len Dawson	19	3741	2136	57.1	28,711	7.67	239	6.4	183	4.9	82.56
11	**Dave Krieg**	16	4911	2866	58.4	35,668	7.26	247	5.0	187	3.8	81.88
12	Ken Anderson	16	4475	2654	59.3	32,838	7.34	197	4.4	160	3.6	81.86
13	**Jeff Hostetler**	10	1792	1036	57.8	12,983	7.24	66	3.7	47	2.6	81.80
14	**Neil O'Donnell**	6	1871	1069	57.1	12,867	6.88	68	3.6	37	2.0	81.78
15	Danny White	13	2950	1761	59.7	21,959	7.44	155	5.3	132	4.5	81.7
16	**Bernie Kosar**	11	3333	1970	59.1	23,093	6.91	123	3.7	87	2.6	81.6
17	**Warren Moon**	12	5753	3380	58.8	42,177	7.33	247	4.3	199	3.5	81.5
18	**Boomer Esiason**	12	4680	2661	56.9	34,149	7.30	223	4.8	168	3.6	80.8
19	Bart Starr	16	3149	1808	57.4	24,718	7.85	152	4.8	138	4.4	80.5
20	Ken O'Brien	10	3602	2110	58.6	25,094	6.97	128	3.6	98	2.7	80.44
21	Fran Tarkenton	18	6467	3686	57.0	47,003	7.27	342	5.3	266	4.1	80.35
22	Dan Fouts	15	5604	3297	58.8	43,040	7.68	254	4.5	242	4.3	80.2
23	**Jim Everett**	10	4384	2538	57.9	31,583	7.20	190	4.3	155	3.5	80.1
24	Tony Eason	8	1564	911	58.2	11,142	7.12	61	3.9	51	3.3	79.7
25	**Mark Rypien**	8	2552	1432	56.1	18,070	7.08	114	4.5	86	3.4	79.2

Note: The NFL does not recognize records from the All-American Football Conference (1946-49). If it did, **Otto Graham** would rank 5th (after Favre) with the following stats: 10 Yrs; 2,626 Att; 1,464 Comp; 55.8 Comp Pct; 23,584 Yards; 8.98 Avg Gain; 174 TD; 6.6 TD Pct; 135 Int; 5.1 Int Pct; and 86.6 Rating Pts.

Touchdown Passes

		No
1	**Dan Marino**	352
2	Fran Tarkenton	342
3	Johnny Unitas	290
4	Joe Montana	273
5	Sonny Jurgensen	255
6	Dan Fouts	254
7	**Dave Krieg**	247
	Warren Moon	247
9	John Hadl	244
10	Len Dawson	239
11	George Blanda	236
12	**John Elway**	225
13	**Boomer Esiason**	223
	Jim Kelly	223
15	John Brodie	214
6	Terry Bradshaw	212
	Y.A. Tittle	212
18	Jim Hart	209
19	Roman Gabriel	201
20	Phil Simms	199
21	Ken Anderson	197
22	Joe Ferguson	196
	Bobby Layne	196
	Norm Snead	196
25	Ken Stabler	194
26	Steve DeBerg	193
27	Bob Griese	192
28	**Jim Everett**	190
29	Sammy Baugh	187
30	Craig Morton	183
31	Steve Grogan	182
32	Ron Jaworski	179
33	Babe Parilli	178
34	Charlie Conerly	173
	Joe Namath	173
	Norm Van Brocklin	173
37	Charley Johnson	170
38	Daryle Lamonica	164
	Jim Plunkett	164
40	Earl Morrall	161
41	Joe Theismann	160
	Steve Young	160
43	Tommy Kramer	159
44	Steve Bartkowski	156
45	Danny White	155

Note: The NFL does not recognize records from the All-American Football Conference (1946-49). If it did, **Y.A. Tittle** would rank 10th (after Hadl) with 242 TDs and **Otto Graham** would rank 34th (after Parilli) with 174 TDs.

Passes Intercepted

		No
1	George Blanda	277
2	John Hadl	268
3	Fran Tarkenton	266
4	Norm Snead	253
	Johnny Unitas	253
6	Jim Hart	247
7	Bobby Layne	243
8	Dan Fouts	242
9	John Brodie	224
10	Ken Stabler	222
11	Y.A. Tittle	221
12	Joe Namath	220
	Babe Parilli	220
14	Terry Bradshaw	210
15	Joe Ferguson	209
16	Steve Grogan	208
17	Sammy Baugh	203
	Steve DeBerg	203
19	Jim Plunkett	198
20	Tobin Rote	191

All-Time NFL Leaders (Cont.)

Passing Yards

		Yrs	Att	Comp	Pct	Yards
1	**Dan Marino**	13	6531	3913	59.9	48,841
2	Fran Tarkenton	18	6467	3686	57.0	47,003
3	Dan Fouts	15	5604	3297	58.8	43,040
4	**Warren Moon**	12	5753	3380	58.8	42,177
5	**John Elway**	13	5926	3346	56.5	41,706
6	Joe Montana	15	5391	3409	63.2	40,551
7	Johnny Unitas	18	5186	2830	54.6	40,239
8	**Dave Krieg**	16	4911	2866	58.4	35,668
9	Jim Hart	19	5076	2593	51.1	34,665
10	**Boomer Esiason**	12	4680	2661	56.9	34,149
11	Steve DeBerg	16	4965	2844	57.3	33,872
12	John Hadl	16	4687	2363	50.4	33,503
13	Phil Simms	14	4647	2576	55.4	33,462
14	Ken Anderson	16	4475	2654	59.3	32,838
15	**Jim Kelly**	10	4400	2652	60.3	32,657
16	Sonny Jurgensen	18	4262	2433	57.1	32,224
17	**Jim Everett**	10	4384	2538	57.9	31,583
18	John Brodie	17	4491	2469	55.0	31,548
19	Norm Snead	15	4353	2276	52.3	30,797
20	Joe Ferguson	18	4519	2369	52.4	29,817
21	Roman Gabriel	16	4498	2366	52.6	29,444
22	Len Dawson	19	3741	2136	57.1	28,711
23	Y.A. Tittle	15	3817	2118	55.5	28,339
24	Ron Jaworski	16	4117	2187	53.1	28,190
25	Terry Bradshaw	14	3901	2025	51.9	27,989

Note: The NFL does not recognize records from the All-American Football Conference (1946-49). If it did, **Y.A. Tittle** would rank 14th (after Simms) with the following stats: 17 Yrs; 4,395 Att; 2,427 Comp; 55.2 Pct; and 33,070 Yards.

Receptions

		Yrs	No	Yards	Avg	TD
1	**Jerry Rice**	11	942	15,123	16.1	146
2	**Art Monk**	16	940	12,721	13.5	68
3	Steve Largent	14	819	13,089	16.0	100
4	James Lofton	16	764	14,004	18.3	75
5	Charlie Joiner	18	750	12,146	16.2	65
6	**Henry Ellard**	13	723	12,163	16.8	59
7	**Andre Reed**	11	700	9,848	14.1	69
8	**Gary Clark**	11	699	10,856	15.5	65
9	Ozzie Newsome	13	662	7,980	12.1	47
10	Charley Taylor	13	649	9,110	14.0	79
11	Drew Hill	15	634	9,831	15.5	60
12	Don Maynard	15	633	11,834	18.7	88
13	Raymond Berry	13	631	9,275	14.7	68
14	Sterling Sharpe	7	595	8,134	13.7	65
15	Harold Carmichael	14	590	8,985	15.2	79
16	Fred Biletnikoff	14	589	8,974	15.2	76
17	Mark Clayton	11	582	8,974	15.4	84
18	Harold Jackson	16	579	10,372	17.9	76
19	**Ernest Givins**	10	571	8,215	14.4	49
	Cris Carter	9	571	7,204	12.6	66
21	Lionel Taylor	10	567	7,195	12.7	45
22	Roger Craig	11	566	4,911	8.7	17
	Bill Brooks	10	566	7,777	13.7	46
23	**Irving Fryar**	12	562	8,916	15.9	58
24	Wes Chandler	11	559	8,966	16.0	56
	Roy Green	14	559	8,965	16.0	66

Rushing

		Yrs	Car	Yards	Avg	TD
1	Walter Payton	13	3838	16,726	4.4	110
2	Eric Dickerson	11	2996	13,259	4.4	90
3	Tony Dorsett	12	2936	12,739	4.3	77
4	Jim Brown	9	2359	12,312	5.2	106
5	Franco Harris	13	2949	12,120	4.1	91
6	John Riggins	14	2916	11,352	3.9	104
7	O.J. Simpson	11	2404	11,236	4.7	61
8	**Marcus Allen**	14	2692	10,908	4.1	103
9	Ottis Anderson	14	2562	10,273	4.0	81
10	**Barry Sanders**	7	2077	10,172	4.9	73
11	**Thurman Thomas**	8	2285	9,729	4.3	54
12	Earl Campbell	8	2187	9,407	4.3	74
13	**Emmitt Smith**	6	2007	8,956	4.5	96
14	Jim Taylor	10	1941	8,597	4.4	83
15	Joe Perry	14	1737	8,378	4.8	53
16	Roger Craig	11	1991	8,189	4.1	56
17	Gerald Riggs	10	1989	8,188	4.1	69
18	**Herschel Walker**	10	1938	8,122	4.2	60
19	Larry Csonka	11	1891	8,081	4.3	64
20	Freeman McNeil	12	1798	8,074	4.5	38
21	James Brooks	12	1685	7,962	4.7	49
22	Mike Pruitt	11	1844	7,378	4.0	51
23	**Ernest Byner**	12	1852	7,314	3.9	52
24	Leroy Kelly	10	1727	7,274	4.2	74
25	George Rogers	7	1692	7,176	4.2	54

Note: The NFL does not recognize records from the All-American Football Conference (1946-49). If it did, **Joe Perry** would rank 10th (after Allen) with the following stats: 16 Yrs; 1,929 Att; 9,723 Yards; 5.0 Avg; and 71 TD.

All-Purpose Yards

		Rush	Rec	Ret	Total
1	Walter Payton	16,726	4,538	539	21,803
2	Tony Dorsett	12,739	3,554	33	16,326
3	**Marcus Allen**	10,908	5,055	-6	15,957
4	**Herschel Walker**	8,122	4,621	3,138	15,881
5	**Jerry Rice**	547	15,123	6	15,676
6	Jim Brown	12,312	2,499	648	15,459
7	Eric Dickerson	13,259	2,137	15	15,411
8	James Brooks	7,962	3,621	3,327	14,910
9	Franco Harris	12,120	2,287	215	14,622
10	O.J. Simpson	11,236	2,142	990	14,368
11	James Lofton	246	14,004	27	14,277
12	**Henry Ellard**	50	12,163	1,891	14,104
13	Bobby Mitchell	2,735	7,954	3,389	14,078
14	John Riggins	11,352	2,090	-7	13,435
15	Steve Largent	83	13,089	224	13,396
16	Ottis Anderson	10,273	3,062	29	13,364
17	**Thurman Thomas**	9,729	3,622	0	13,351
18	Drew Hill	19	9,831	3,487	13,337
19	Greg Pruitt	5,672	3,069	4,521	13,262
20	Roger Craig	8,189	4,911	43	13,143
21	**Art Monk**	332	12,721	10	13,063
22	Ollie Matson	5,173	3,285	4,426	12,884
23	Timmy Brown	3,862	3,399	5,423	12,684
24	Lenny Moore	5,174	6,039	1,238	12,451
25	Don Maynard	70	11,834	475	12,379

Note: The NFL does not recognize records from the All-American Football Conference (1946-49). If it did, **Joe Perry** would rank 24th (after Timmy Brown) with the following stats: 9,723 Rush; 2,021 Rec; 788 Ret; 12,532 Total in 16 years.

Years played: Allen (14), Anderson (14), Brooks (12), J. Brown (9), T. Brown (10), Craig (11), Dickerson (11), Dorsett (12), Ellard (13), Harris (13), Hill (14), Largent (14), Lofton (16), Matson (14), Maynard (15), Mitchell (11), Monk (16), Moore (12), Payton (13), Pruitt (12), Rice (11), Riggins (14), Simpson (11), Thomas (8) and Walker (10).

Scoring

Points

		Yrs	TD	FG	PAT	Total
1	George Blanda	26	9	335	943	2002
2	Jan Stenerud	19	0	373	580	1699
3	**Nick Lowery**	17	0	366	536	1634
4	**Eddie Murray**	16	0	325	498	1473
5	Pat Leahy	18	0	304	558	1470
6	**Gary Anderson**	14	0	331	448	1441
7	**Morten Andersen**	14	0	333	441	1440
8	Jim Turner	16	1	304	521	1439
9	**Matt Bahr**	17	0	300	522	1422
10	Mark Moseley	16	0	300	482	1382
11	Jim Bakken	17	0	282	534	1380
12	Fred Cox	15	0	282	519	1365
13	Lou Groza	17	1	234	641	1349
14	**Norm Johnson**	14	0	277	515	1346
15	Jim Breech	14	0	243	517	1246
16	Chris Bahr	14	0	241	490	1213
17	Gino Cappelletti	11	42	176	350	1130†
18	Ray Wersching	15	0	222	456	1122
19	**Kevin Butler**	11	0	243	387	1116
20	Don Cockroft	13	0	216	432	1080
21	Garo Yepremian	14	0	210	444	1074
22	Bruce Gossett	11	0	219	374	1031
23	**Al Del Greco**	14	0	204	368	980
24	Sam Baker	15	2	179	428	977
25	Rafael Septien	10	0	180	420	960

†Cappelletti's total includes four 2-point conversions.

Note: The NFL does not recognize records from the All-American Football Conference (1946-49). If it did, **Lou Groza** would move up to 4th (after Lowery) with the following stats: 21 Yrs; 1 TD; 264 FG, 810 PAT; 1,608 Pts.

Touchdowns

		Yrs	Rush	Rec	Ret	Total
1	**Jerry Rice**	11	9	146	1	156
2	Jim Brown	9	106	20	0	126
3	Walter Payton	13	110	15	0	125
4	**Marcus Allen**	14	103	21	1	125
5	John Riggins	14	104	12	0	116
6	Lenny Moore	12	63	48	2	113
7	Don Hutson	11	3	99	3	105
8	Steve Largent	14	1	100	0	101
9	**Emmitt Smith**	6	96	4	0	100
	Franco Harris	13	91	9	0	100
11	Eric Dickerson	11	90	6	0	96
12	Jim Taylor	10	83	10	0	93
13	Tony Dorsett	12	77	13	1	91
	Bobby Mitchell	11	18	65	8	91
15	Leroy Kelly	10	74	13	3	90
	Charley Taylor	13	11	79	0	90
17	Don Maynard	15	0	88	0	88
18	Lance Alworth	11	2	85	0	87
19	Ottis Anderson	14	81	5	0	86
	Paul Warfield	13	1	85	0	86
21	Mark Clayton	11	0	84	1	85
	Tommy McDonald	12	0	84	1	85
23	Pete Johnson	8	76	6	0	82
24	Art Powell	10	0	81	1	82
25	**Herschel Walker**	10	60	19	2	81

Note: The NFL does not recognize records from the All-American Football Conference (1946-49). If it did, **Joe Perry** would rank 23rd (after Clayton and McDonald) with the following stats: 16 Yrs; 71 Rush; 12 Rec; 1 Ret; 84 TDs.

Interceptions

		Yrs	No	Yards	TD
1	Paul Krause	16	81	1185	3
2	Emlen Tunnell	14	79	1282	4
3	Dick (Night Train) Lane	14	68	1207	5
4	Ken Riley	15	65	596	5
5	Ronnie Lott	14	63	730	5

Sacks (unofficial)

		Yrs	No
1	Deacon Jones	14	172
2	**Reggie White**	11	157
3	Jack Youngblood	14	150½
4	Alan Page	15	148
5	Lawrence Taylor	13	142

Kickoff Returns

Minimum 75 returns.

		Yrs	No	Yards	Avg	TD
1	Gale Sayers	7	91	2781	30.6	6
2	Lynn Chandnois	7	92	2720	29.6	3
3	Abe Woodson	9	193	5538	28.7	5
4	Buddy Young	6	90	2514	27.9	2
5	Travis Williams	5	102	2801	27.5	6

Punting

Minimum 300 punts.

		Yrs	No	Yards	Avg
1	Sammy Baugh	16	338	15,245	45.1
2	Tommy Davis	11	511	22,833	44.7
3	Yale Lary	11	503	22,279	44.3
4	Horace Gillom	7	385	16,872	43.8
	Jerry Norton	11	358	15,671	43.8

Punt Returns

Minimum 75 returns.

		Yrs	No	Yards	Avg	TD
1	George McAfee	8	112	1431	12.8	2
	Jack Christiansen	8	85	1084	12.8	8
3	Claude Gibson	5	110	1381	12.6	3
4	Bill Dudley	9	124	1515	12.2	3
5	Rick Upchurch	9	248	3008	12.1	8

Safeties

		Yrs	No
1	Ted Hendricks	15	4
	Doug English	10	4
3	Thirteen players tied with three.		

Long-Playing Records

Seasons

		No
1	George Blanda, QB-K	26
2	Earl Morrall, QB	21
3	Jim Marshall, DE	20
	Jackie Slater, OL	20

Games

		No
1	George Blanda, QB-K	340
2	Jim Marshall, DE	282
3	Jan Stenerud, K	263

Consecutive Games

		No
1	Jim Marshall, DE	282
2	Mick Tingelhoff, C	240
3	Jim Bakken, K	234

All-Time NFL Leaders (Cont.)

SINGLE SEASON

Passing

Yards Gained	Year	Att	Cmp	Pct	Yds
Dan Marino, Mia	1984	564	362	64.2	5084
Dan Fouts, SD	1981	609	360	59.1	4802
Dan Marino, Mia	1986	623	378	60.7	4746
Dan Fouts, SD	1980	589	348	59.1	4715
Warren Moon, Hou	1991	655	404	61.7	4690
Warren Moon, Hou	1990	584	362	62.0	4689
Neil Lomax, St.L	1984	560	345	61.6	4614
Drew Bledsoe, NE	1994	691	400	57.9	4555
Lynn Dickey, GB	1983	484	286	59.7	4458
Brett Favre, GB	1995	570	359	63.0	4413

Efficiency	Year	Att/Cmp	TD	Rtg
Steve Young, SF	1994	461/324	35	112.8
Joe Montana, SF	1989	386/271	26	112.4
Milt Plum, Cle	1960	250/151	21	110.4
Sammy Baugh, Wash	1945	182/128	11	109.9
Dan Marino, Mia	1984	564/362	48	108.9
Sid Luckman, Bears	1943	202/110	28	107.5
Steve Young, SF	1992	402/268	25	107.0
Bart Starr, GB	1966	251/156	14	105.0
Y.A. Tittle, NYG	1963	367/221	36	104.8
Roger Staubach, Dal	1971	211/126	15	104.8

Receptions

Catches	Year	No	Yds
Herman Moore, Det	1995	123	1686
Jerry Rice, SF	1995	122	1848
Cris Carter, Min	1995	122	1371
Cris Carter, Min	1994	122	1256
Isaac Bruce, St.L	1995	119	1781
Jerry Rice, SF	1994	112	1499
Sterling Sharpe, GB	1993	112	1274
Michael Irvin, Dal	1995	111	1603
Terance Mathis, Atl	1994	111	1342
Brett Perriman, Det	1995	108	1488
Sterling Sharpe, GB	1992	108	1461

Rushing

Yards Gained	Year	Car	Yds	Avg
Eric Dickerson, LA Rams	1984	379	2105	5.6
O.J. Simpson, Buf	1973	332	2003	6.0
Earl Campbell, Hou	1980	373	1934	5.2
Barry Sanders, Det	1994	331	1883	5.7
Jim Brown, Cle	1963	291	1863	6.4
Walter Payton, Chi	1977	339	1852	5.5
Eric Dickerson, LA Rams	1986	404	1821	4.5
O.J. Simpson, Buf	1975	329	1817	5.5
Eric Dickerson, LA Rams	1983	390	1808	4.6
Emmitt Smith, Dal	1995	377	1773	4.7

Scoring

Points

	Year	TD	PAT	FG	Pts
Paul Hornung, GB	1960	15	41	15	176
Mark Moseley, Wash	1983	0	62	33	161
Gino Cappelletti, Bos	1964	7	38	25	155
Emmitt Smith, Dal	1995	25	0	0	150
Chip Lohmiller, Wash	1991	0	56	31	149
Gino Cappelletti, Bos	1961	8	48	17	147
Paul Hornung, GB	1961	10	41	15	146
Jim Turner, Jets	1968	0	43	34	145
John Riggins, Wash	1983	24	0	0	144
Kevin Butler, Chi	1985	0	51	31	144

Touchdowns

	Year	Rush	Rec	Ret	Total
Emmitt Smith, Dal	1995	25	0	0	25
John Riggins, Wash	1983	24	0	0	24
O.J. Simpson, Buf	1975	16	7	0	23
Jerry Rice, SF	1987	1	22	0	23
Gale Sayers, Chi	1965	14	6	2	22
Chuck Foreman, Min	1975	13	9	0	22
Emmitt Smith, Dal	1994	21	1	0	22
Jim Brown, Cle	1965	17	4	0	21
Joe Morris, NY Giants	1985	21	0	0	21

Three tied with 20 each.

Note: The NFL regular season schedule grew from 12 games (1947-60) to 14 (1961-77) to 16 (1978-present). The AFL regular season schedule was always 14 games (1960-69).

Touchdowns Passing

	Year	No
Dan Marino, Miami	1984	48
Dan Marino, Miami	1986	44
Brett Favre, Green Bay	1995	38
George Blanda, Houston	1961	36
Y.A. Tittle, NY Giants	1963	36
Steve Young, San Francisco	1994	35
Y.A. Tittle, NY Giants	1962	33
Dan Fouts, San Diego	1981	33
Warren Moon, Houston	1990	33
Jim Kelly, Buffalo	1991	33
Brett Favre, Green Bay	1994	33
Warren Moon, Minnesota	1995	33

Touchdowns Rushing

	Year	No
Emmitt Smith, Dallas	1995	25
John Riggins, Washington	1983	24
Joe Morris, NY Giants	1985	21
Emmitt Smith, Dallas	1994	21
Jim Taylor, Green Bay	1962	19
Earl Campbell, Houston	1979	19
Chuck Muncie, San Diego	1981	19
Eric Dickerson, LA Rams	1983	18
George Rogers, Washington	1986	18
Emmitt Smith, Dallas	1992	18
Jim Brown, Cleveland	1958	17
Jim Brown, Cleveland	1965	17

Touchdowns Receiving

	Year	No
Jerry Rice, San Francisco	1987	22
Mark Clayton, Miami	1984	18
Sterling Sharpe, Green Bay	1994	18
Don Hutson, Green Bay	1942	17
Elroy (Crazylegs) Hirsch, LA Rams	1951	17
Bill Groman, Houston	1961	17
Jerry Rice, San Francisco	1989	17
Cris Carter, Minnesota	1995	17
Carl Pickens, Cincinnati	1995	17
Art Powell, Oakland	1963	16

Four tied with 15 each.

Field Goals

	Year	Att	No
Ali Haji-Sheikh, NY Giants	1983	42	35
Jeff Jaeger, LA Rams	1993	44	35
Nick Lowery, Kansas City	1990	37	34
Jim Turner, NY Jets	1968	46	34
Jason Hanson, Detroit	1993	43	34
John Carney, San Diego	1994	38	34
Fuad Reveiz, Minnesota	1994	39	34
Norm Johnson, Pittsburgh	1995	41	34
Gary Anderson, Pittsburgh	1985	42	33
Mark Moseley, Washington	1983	47	33
Chester Marcol, Green Bay	1972	48	33

Interceptions

	Year	No
Dick (Night Train) Lane, Detroit	1952	14
Dan Sandifer, Washington	1948	13
Spec Sanders, NY Yanks	1950	13
Lester Hayes, Oakland	1980	13

Kickoff Returns

	Year	Avg
Travis Williams, Green Bay	1967	41.1
Gale Sayers, Chicago	1967	37.7
Ollie Matson, Chicago Cards	1958	35.5

Punting

Qualifiers	Year	Avg
Sammy Baugh, Washington	1940	51.4
Yale Lary, Detroit	1963	48.9
Sammy Baugh, Washington	1941	48.7

Punt Returns

	Year	Avg
Herb Rich, Baltimore	1950	23.0
Jack Christiansen, Detroit	1952	21.5
Dick Christy, NY Titans	1961	21.3
Bob Hayes, Dallas	1968	20.8

Sacks (unofficial)

	Year	No
Coy Bacon, Cincinnati	1976	26
Mark Gastineau, NY Jets	1984	22
Reggie White, Philadelphia	1987	21
Chris Doleman, Minnesota	1989	21

SINGLE GAME

Passing

Yards Gained	Date	Yds
Norm Van Brocklin, LA vs NY Yanks	9/28/51	554
Warren Moon, Hou at KC	12/16/90	527
Dan Marino, Mia vs NYJ	10/23/88	521
Phil Simms, NYG vs Cin	10/13/85	513
Vince Ferragamo, Rams vs Chi	12/26/82	509

Completions	Date	No
Drew Bledsoe, NE vs Min	11/13/94	45
Richard Todd, NYJ vs SF	9/21/80	42
Warren Moon, Hou vs Dal	11/10/91	41
Ken Anderson, Cin vs SD	12/20/82	40
Phil Simms, NYG vs Cin	10/13/85	40

Rushing

Yards Gained	Date	Yds
Walter Payton, Chi vs Min	11/20/77	275
O.J. Simpson, Buf vs Det	11/25/76	273
O.J. Simpson, Buf vs NE	9/16/73	250
Willie Ellison, LA Rams vs NO	12/ 5/71	247
Cookie Gilchrist, Buf vs NYJ	12/ 8/63	243

Receptions

Catches	Date	No
Tom Fears, LA vs GB	12/ 3/50	18
Clark Gaines, NYJ vs SF	9/21/80	17
Sonny Randle, St.L vs NYG	11/ 4/62	16

Seven tied with 15 each.

Yards Gained	Date	Yds
Flipper Anderson, LA Rams vs NO	11/26/89	336
Stephone Paige, KC vs SD	12/22/85	309
Jim Benton, Cle vs Det	11/22/45	303
Cloyce Box, Det vs Bal	12/ 3/50	302
Jerry Rice, SF at Det	9/25/95	289
John Taylor, SF vs LA Rams	12/11/89	286

All-Purpose Yards

	Date	Yds
Billy Cannon, Hou vs NY Titans	12/10/61	373
Lionel James, SD vs Raiders	11/10/85	345
Timmy Brown, Phi vs St.L	12/16/62	341
Gale Sayers, Chi vs Min	12/18/66	339
Gale Sayers, Chi vs SF	12/12/65	336

Scoring

Points

	Date	Pts
Ernie Nevers, Chi. Cards vs Chi. Bears	11/28/29	40
Dub Jones, Cle vs Chi. Bears	11/25/51	36
Gale Sayers, Chi vs SF	12/12/65	36
Paul Hornung, GB vs Bal	10/ 8/61	33
Bob Shaw, Chi. Cards vs Bal	10/ 2/50	30
Jim Brown, Cle vs Bal	11/ 1/59	30
Abner Haynes, Dal. Texans vs Oak	11/26/61	30
Billy Cannon, Hou vs NY Titans	12/10/61	30
Cookie Gilchrist, Buf vs NY Jets	12/ 8/63	30
Kellen Winslow, SD vs Oak	11/22/81	30
Jerry Rice, SF at Atl	10/14/90	30

Note: Nevers celebrated Thanksgiving, 1929, by scoring all the Chicago Cardinals' points on six rushing TDs and four PATs. The Cards beat Red Grange and the Chicago Bears, 40-6.

Touchdowns Passing

	Date	No
Sid Luckman, Chi. Bears vs NYG	11/14/43	7
Adrian Burk, Phi vs Wash	10/17/54	7
George Blanda, Hou vs NY Titans	11/19/61	7
Y.A. Tittle, NYG vs Wash	10/28/62	7
Joe Kapp, Min vs Bal	9/28/69	7

Touchdowns Receiving

	Date	No
Bob Shaw, Chi. Cards vs Bal	10/ 2/50	5
Kellen Winslow, SD vs Oak	11/22/81	5
Jerry Rice, SF at Atl	10/14/90	5

Touchdowns Rushing

	Date	No
Ernie Nevers, Chi. Cards vs Chi. Bears	11/28/29	6
Jim Brown, Cle vs Bal	11/ 1/59	5
Cookie Gilchrist, Buf vs NY Jets	12/ 8/63	5

Field Goals

	Date	No
Jim Bakken, St.L vs Pit	9/24/67	7
Rich Karlis, Min vs Rams	11/ 5/89	7

Twelve players tied with 6 FGs.

Note: Bakken was 7-for-9, Karlis 7-for-7.

Extra Point Kicks

	Date	No
Pat Harder, Cards vs NYG	10/17/48	9
Bob Waterfield, LA vs Bal	10/22/50	9
Charlie Gogolak, Wash vs NYG	11/27/66	9

All-Time NFL Leaders (Cont.)

LONGEST PLAYS

Passing (all for TDs)

	Date	Yds
Frank Filchock to Andy Farkas, Wash vs Pit	10/15/39	99
George Izo to Bobby Mitchell, Wash vs Cle	9/15/63	99
Karl Sweetan to Pat Studstill, Det vs Bal	10/16/66	99
Sonny Jurgensen to Gerry Allen, Wash vs Chi	9/15/68	99
Jim Plunkett to Cliff Branch, LA Raiders vs Wash	10/2/83	99
Ron Jaworski to Mike Quick, Phi vs Atl	11/10/85	99
Stan Humphries to Tony Martin, SD at Sea	9/18/94	99
Brett Favre to Robert Brooks, GB at Chi	9/11/95	99

Punt Returns (all for TDs)

	Date	Yds
Robert Bailey, Rams at NO	10/23/94	103

Four players tied with 98-yd returns.

Runs from Scrimmage (all for TDs)

	Date	Yds
Tony Dorsett, Dal vs Min	1/3/83	99
Andy Uram, GB vs Chi. Cards	10/8/39	97
Bob Gage, Pit vs Bears	12/4/49	97

Field Goals

	Date	Yds
Tom Dempsey, NO vs Det	11/8/70	63
Steve Cox, Cle vs Cin	10/21/84	60
Morten Andersen, NO vs Chi	10/27/91	60

Kickoff Returns (all for TDs)

	Date	Yds
Al Carmichael, GB vs Chi. Bears	10/7/56	106
Noland Smith, KC vs Den	12/17/67	106
Roy Green, St.L vs Dal	10/21/79	106

Interception Returns (for TDs)

	Date	Yds
Vencie Glenn, SD vs Den	11/29/87	103
Louis Oliver, Mia vs Buf	10/4/92	103

Six players tied with 102-yd returns.

Chicago College All-Star Game

On Aug. 31, 1934, a year after sponsoring Major League Baseball's first All-Star Game, *Chicago Tribune* sports editor Arch Ward presented the first Chicago College All-Star Game at Soldier Field. A crowd of 79,432 turned out to see an all-star team of graduated college seniors battle the 1933 NFL champion Chicago Bears to a scoreless tie. The preseason game was played at Soldier Field and pitted the college All-Stars against the defending NFL champions (1933-1966) or Super Bowl champions (1967-75) every year except 1935 until it was cancelled in 1977. The NFL champs won the series, 31-9-2.

Year	
1934	Chi. Bears 0, All-Stars 0
1935	Chi. Bears 5, All-Stars 0
1936	Detroit 7, All-Stars 7
1937	All-Stars 6, Green Bay 0
1938	All-Stars 28, Washington 16
1939	NY Giants 9, All-Stars 0
1940	Green Bay 45, All-Stars 28
1941	Chi. Bears 37, All-Stars 13
1942	Chi. Bears 21, All-Stars 0
1943	All-Stars 27, Washington 7
1944	Chi. Bears 24, All-Stars 21
1945	Green Bay 19, All-Stars 7
1946	All-Stars 16, LA Rams 0
1947	All-Stars 16, Chi. Bears 0
1948	Chi. Cards 28, All-Stars 0
1949	Philadelphia 38, All-Stars 0
1950	All-Stars 17, Philadelphia 7
1951	Cleveland 33, All-Stars 0
1952	LA Rams 10, All-Stars 7
1953	Detroit 24, All-Stars 10
1954	Detroit 31, All-Stars 6
1955	All-Stars 30, Cleveland 27
1956	Cleveland 26, All-Stars 0
1957	NY Giants 22, All-Stars 12
1958	All-Stars 35, Detroit 19
1959	Baltimore 29, All-Stars 0
1960	Baltimore 32, All-Stars 7
1961	Philadelphia 28, All-Stars 14
1962	Green Bay 42, All-Stars 20
1963	All-Stars 20, Green Bay 17
1964	Chi. Bears 28, All-Stars 17
1965	Cleveland 24, All-Stars 16
1966	Green Bay 38, All-Stars 0
1967	Green Bay 27, All-Stars 0
1968	Green Bay 34, All-Stars 17
1969	NY Jets 26, All-Stars 24
1970	Kansas City 24, All-Stars 3
1971	Baltimore 24, All-Stars 17
1972	Dallas 20, All-Stars 7
1973	Miami 14, All-Stars 3
1974	No Game (NFLPA Strike)
1975	Pittsburgh 21, All-Stars 14
1976	Pittsburgh 24, All-Stars 0*

*Downpour flooded field, game called with 1:22 left in 3rd quarter.

Number One Draft Choices

In an effort to blunt the dominance of the Chicago Bears and New York Giants in the 1930s and distribute talent more evenly throughout the league, the NFL established the college draft in 1936. The first player chosen in the first draft was Jay Berwanger, who was also college football's Heisman Trophy winner. In all, 16 Heisman winners have also been the NFL's No.1 draft choice. They are noted in **bold** type. The American Football League (formed in 1960) held its own draft for six years before agreeing to merge with the NFL and select players in a common draft starting in 1967.

Year	Team	
1936	Philadelphia	**Jay Berwanger**, HB, Chicago
1937	Philadelphia	Sam Francis, FB, Nebraska
1938	Cleveland Rams	Corbett Davis, FB, Indiana
1939	Chicago Cards	Ki Aldrich, C, TCU
1940	Chicago Cards	George Cafego, HB, Tennessee
1941	Chicago Bears	**Tom Harmon**, HB, Michigan
1942	Pittsburgh	Bill Dudley, HB, Viginia
1943	Detroit	**Frank Sinkwich**, HB, Georgia
1944	Boston Yanks	**Angelo Bertelli**, QB, N. Dame
1945	Chicago Cards	Charley Trippi, HB, Georgia
1946	Boston Yanks	Frank Dancewicz, QB, N. Dame
1947	Chicago Bears	Bob Fenimore, HB, Okla. A&M
1948	Washington	Harry Gilmer, QB, Alabama
1949	Philadelphia	Chuck Bednarik, C, Penn
1950	Detroit	**Leon Hart**, E, Notre Dame
1951	NY Giants	Kyle Rote, HB, SMU
1952	LA Rams	Bill Wade, QB, Vanderbilt
1953	San Francisco	Harry Babcock, E, Georgia
1954	Cleveland	Bobby Garrett, QB, Stanford
1955	Baltimore	George Shaw, QB, Oregon
1956	Pittsburgh	Gary Glick, DB, Colo. A&M
1957	Green Bay	**Paul Hornung**, QB, N. Dame
1958	Chicago Cards	King Hill, QB, Rice
1959	Green Bay	Randy Duncan, QB, Iowa
1960	NFL—LA Rams	**Billy Cannon**, HB, LSU
	AFL—No choice	
1961	NFL—Minnesota	Tommy Mason, HB, Tulane
	AFL—Buffalo	Ken Rice, G, Auburn
1962	NFL—Washington	**Ernie Davis**, HB, Syracuse
	AFL—Oakland	Roman Gabriel, QB, N.C. State
1963	NFL—LA Rams	**Terry Baker**, QB, Oregon St.
	AFL—Kan.City	Buck Buchanan, DT, Grambling
1964	NFL—San Fran	Dave Parks, E, Texas Tech
	AFL—Boston	Jack Concannon, QB, Boston Col.

Year	Team	
1965	NFL—NY Giants	Tucker Frederickson, HB, Auburn
	AFL—Houston	Lawrence Elkins, E, Baylor
1966	NFL—Atlanta	Tommy Nobis, LB, Texas
	AFL—Miami	Jim Grabowski, FB, Illinois
1967	Baltimore	Bubba Smith, DT, Michigan St.
1968	Minnesota	Ron Yary, T, USC
1969	Buffalo	**O.J. Simpson**, RB, USC
1970	Pittsburgh	Terry Bradshaw, QB, La.Tech
1971	New England	**Jim Plunkett**, QB, Stanford
1972	Buffalo	Walt Patulski, DE, Notre Dame
1973	Houston	John Matuszak, DE, Tampa
1974	Dallas	Ed (Too Tall) Jones, DE, Tenn. St.
1975	Atlanta	Steve Bartkowski, QB, Calif.
1976	Tampa Bay	Lee Roy Selmon, DE, Oklahoma
1977	Tampa Bay	Ricky Bell, RB, USC
1978	Houston	**Earl Campbell**, RB, Texas
1979	Buffalo	Tom Cousineau, LB, Ohio St.

Year	Team	
1980	Detroit	**Billy Sims**, RB, Oklahoma
1981	New Orleans	**George Rogers**, RB, S. Carolina
1982	New England	Kenneth Sims, DT, Texas
1983	Baltimore	John Elway, QB, Stanford
1984	New England	Irving Fryar, WR, Nebraska
1985	Buffalo	Bruce Smith, DE, Va. Tech
1986	Tampa Bay	**Bo Jackson**, RB, Auburn
1987	Tampa Bay	**V. Testaverde**, QB, Miami-FL
1988	Atlanta	Aundray Bruce, LB, Auburn
1989	Dallas	Troy Aikman, QB, UCLA
1990	Indianapolis	Jeff George, QB, Illinois
1991	Dallas	Russell Maryland, DL, Miami-FL
1992	Indianapolis	Steve Emtman, DL, Washington
1993	New England	Drew Bledsoe, QB, Washington St.
1994	Cincinnati	Dan Wilkinson, DT, Ohio St.
1995	Cincinnati	Ki-Jana Carter, RB, Penn St.
1996	NY Jets	Keyshawn Johnson, WR, USC

All-Time Winningest NFL Coaches

NFL career victories through the 1995 season. Career, regular season and playoff records are noted along with NFL, AFL and Super Bowl titles won. Coaches active during 1995 season in **bold** type.

		Career					Regular Season				Playoffs			
		Yrs	W	L	T	Pct	W	L	T	Pct	W	L	Pct.	League Titles
1	**Don Shula**	33	**347**	173	6	.665	328	156	6	.676	19	17	.528	2 Super Bowls and 1 NFL
2	George Halas	40	**324**	151	31	.671	318	148	31	.671	6	3	.667	5 NFL
3	Tom Landry	29	**270**	178	6	.601	250	162	6	.605	20	16	.556	2 Super Bowls
4	Curly Lambeau	33	**229**	134	22	.623	226	132	22	.624	3	2	.600	6 NFL
5	Chuck Noll	23	**209**	156	1	.572	193	148	1	.566	16	8	.667	4 Super Bowls
6	Chuck Knox	22	**193**	158	1	.550	186	147	1	.558	7	11	.389	—None—
7	Paul Brown	21	**170**	108	6	.609	166	100	6	.621	4	8	.333	3 NFL
8	Bud Grant	18	**168**	108	5	.607	158	96	5	.620	10	12	.455	1 NFL
9	Steve Owen	23	**153**	108	17	.581	151	100	17	.595	2	8	.200	2 NFL
10	**Dan Reeves**	15	**143**	103	1	.581	135	96	1	.584	8	7	.553	—None—
11	Joe Gibbs	12	**140**	65	0	.683	124	60	0	.674	16	5	.762	3 Super Bowls
12	**Marv Levy**	15	**138**	103	0	.573	127	96	0	.570	11	7	.611	—None—
13	Hank Stram	17	**136**	100	10	.573	131	97	10	.571	5	3	.625	1 Super Bowl and 3 AFL
14	Weeb Ewbank	20	**134**	130	7	.507	130	129	7	.502	4	1	.800	1 Super Bowl, 2 NFL, and 1 AFL
15	Sid Gillman	18	**123**	104	7	.541	122	99	7	.550	1	5	.167	1 AFL
16	**M. Schottenheimer**	12	**121**	76	1	.614	116	66	1	.637	5	10	.333	—None—
17	George Allen	12	**118**	54	5	.681	116	47	5	.705	2	7	.222	—None—
18	Don Coryell	14	**114**	89	1	.561	111	83	1	.572	3	6	.333	—None—
19	John Madden	10	**112**	39	7	.731	103	32	7	.750	9	7	.563	1 Super Bowl
	Mike Ditka	11	**112**	68	0	.622	106	62	0	.631	6	6	.500	1 Super Bowl
21	Buddy Parker	15	**107**	76	9	.581	104	75	9	.577	3	1	.750	2 NFL
22	**Bill Parcells**	11	**106**	80	1	.588	98	76	1	.570	8	4	.667	2 Super Bowls
23	Vince Lombardi	10	**105**	35	6	.740	96	34	6	.728	9	1	.900	2 Super Bowls and 5 NFL
	Tom Flores	12	**105**	90	0	.538	97	87	0	.527	8	3	.727	2 Super Bowls
25	Bill Walsh	10	**102**	63	1	.617	92	59	1	.609	10	4	.714	3 Super Bowls

Notes: The NFL does not recognize records from the All-American Football Conference (1946-49). If it did, **Paul Brown** (52-4-3 in four AAFC seasons) would move up to 5th on the all-time list with the following career stats— 25 Yrs; 222 Wins; 112 Losses; 9 Ties; .660 Pct; 9-8 playoff record; and 4 AAFC titles.

The NFL also considers the Playoff Bowl or "Runner-up Bowl" (officially: the Bert Bell Benefit Bowl) as a post-season exhibition game. The Playoff Bowl was contested every year from 1960-69 in Miami between Eastern and Western Conference second place teams. While the games did not count, six of the coaches above went to the Playoff Bowl at least once and came away with the following records— Allen (2-0), Brown (0-1), Grant (0-1), Landry (1-2), Lombardi (1-1) and Shula (2-0).

Where They Coached

Allen— LA Rams (1966-70), Washington (1971-77); **Brown**— Cleveland (1950-62), Cincinnati (1968-75); **Coryell**— St.Louis (1973-77), San Diego (1978-86); **Ditka**— Chicago (1982-92); **Ewbank**— Baltimore (1954-62), NY Jets (1963-73); **Flores**— Oakland-LA Raiders (1979-87), Seattle (1992-94) **Gibbs**— Washington (1981-92); **Gillman**— LA Rams (1955-59), LA-San Diego Chargers (1960-69), Houston (1973-74).

Grant— Minnesota (1967-83,1985); **Halas**— Chicago Bears (1920-29,33-42,46-55,58-67); **Knox**— LA Rams (1973-77, 1992-94); Buffalo (1978-82), Seattle (1983-91); **Lambeau**— Green Bay (1921-49), Chicago Cards (1950-51), Washington (1952-53); **Landry**— Dallas (1960-88); **Levy**— Kansas City (1978-82), Buffalo (1986—); **Lombardi**— Green Bay (1959-67), Washington (1969); **Madden**— Oakland (1969-78).

Noll— Pittsburgh (1969-91); **Owen**— NY Giants (1931-53); **Parcells**— NY Giants (1983-90), New England (1993—); **Parker**— Chicago Cards (1949), Detroit (1951-56), Pittsburgh (1957-64); **Reeves**— Denver (1981-92), NY Giants (1993—); **Schottenheimer**— Cleveland (1984-88), Kansas City (1989—); **Shula**— Baltimore (1963-69), Miami (1970-95); **Stram**— Dallas-Kansas City (1960-74), New Orleans (1976-77); **Walsh**— San Francisco (1979-88).

All-Time Winningest NFL Coaches (Cont.)

Top Winning Percentages

Minimum of 85 NFL victories, including playoffs.

		Yrs	W	L	T	Pct
1	**George Seifert**	7	95	30	0	**.760**
2	Vince Lombardi	10	105	35	6	**.740**
3	John Madden	10	112	39	7	**.731**
4	Joe Gibbs	12	140	65	0	**.683**
5	George Allen	12	118	54	5	**.681**
6	George Halas	40	324	151	31	**.671**
7	**Don Shula**	33	347	173	6	**.665**
8	Curly Lambeau	33	229	134	22	**.623**
9	Mike Ditka	11	112	68	0	**.622**
10	Bill Walsh	10	102	63	1	**.617**
11	**M. Schottenheimer**	12	121	76	1	**.614**
12	Paul Brown	21	170	108	6	**.609**
13	Bud Grant	18	168	108	5	**.607**
14	Tom Landry	29	270	178	6	**.601**
15	**Dan Reeves**	15	143	103	1	**.581**
16	Steve Owen	23	153	108	17	**.581**
17	Buddy Parker	15	107	76	9	**.581**
18	Hank Stram	17	136	100	10	**.573**
19	**Marv Levy**	15	138	103	0	**.573**
20	Chuck Noll	23	209	156	1	**.572**
21	**Bill Parcells**	11	106	80	1	**.570**
22	Don Coryell	14	114	89	1	**.561**
23	Jimmy Conzelman	15	89	68	17	**.560**
24	**Jim Mora**	10	91	72	0	**.558**
25	Chuck Knox	22	193	158	1	**.550**

Note: If AAFC records are included, **Paul Brown** moves to 8th with a percentage of .660 (25 yrs, 222-112-9) and Buck Shaw would be 10th at .619 (8 yrs, 91-55-5).

Active Coaches' Victories

Through 1995 season, including playoffs.

		Yrs	W	L	T	Pct
1	Dan Reeves, NY Giants	15	**143**	103	1	.581
2	Marv Levy, Buffalo	15	**138**	103	0	.573
3	Marty Schottenheimer, KC	12	**121**	76	1	.614
4	Bill Parcells, New England	11	**106**	80	1	.570
5	George Seifert, San Fran	7	**95**	30	0	.760
6	Jim Mora, New Orleans	10	**91**	72	0	.558
7	Ted Marchibroda, Baltimore	9	**73**	71	0	.507
8	Wayne Fontes, Detroit	8	**62**	60	0	.508
9	Jimmy Johnson, Miami	5	**51**	37	0	.580
10	Bill Cowher, Pittsburgh	4	**46**	25	0	.648
11	Bobby Ross, San Diego	4	**42**	28	0	.600
12	Mike Holmgren, Green Bay	4	**41**	29	0	.586
13	Rich Kotite, NY Jets	5	**40**	42	0	.488
14	Dennis Green, Minnesota	4	**38**	29	0	.567
15	Barry Switzer, Dallas	2	**28**	9	0	.757
16	Dave Wannstedt, Chicago	3	**26**	24	0	.520
17	Lindy Infante, Indianapolis	4	**24**	40	0	.375
18	David Shula, Cincinnati	4	**18**	46	0	.281
19	June Jones, Atlanta	2	**16**	17	0	.485
	Mike Shanahan, Denver	3	**16**	20	0	.444
21	Ray Rhodes, Philadelphia	1	**11**	7	0	.611
22	Norv Turner, Washington	2	**9**	23	0	.281
23	Dennis Erickson, Seattle	1	**8**	8	0	.500
	Mike White Oakland	1	**8**	8	0	.500
	Jeff Fisher, Houston	2	**8**	14	0	.364
26	Rich Brooks, St. Louis	1	**7**	9	0	.438
	Dom Capers, Carolina	1	**7**	9	0	.438
28	Tom Coughlin, Jacksonville	1	**4**	12	0	.250
29	Tony Dungy, Tampa Bay	0	**0**	0	0	.000
	Vince Tobin, Arizona	0	**0**	0	0	.000

Annual Awards

Most Valuable Player

Unlike other major pro team sports, the NFL does not sanction an MVP award. It gave out the Joe F. Carr Trophy (Carr was NFL president from 1921-39) for nine years but discontinued it in 1947. Since then, four principal MVP awards have been given out: UPI (1953-69), AP (since 1957), the Maxwell Club of Philadelphia's Bert Bell Trophy (since 1959) and the Pro Football Writers Assn. (since 1976). UPI switched to AFC and NFC Player of the Year awards in 1970.

Multiple winners (more than one season): Jim Brown (4); Johnny Unitas and Y.A. Tittle (3); Earl Campbell, Randall Cunningham, Otto Graham, Don Hutson, Joe Montana, Walter Payton, Ken Stabler, Joe Theismann and Steve Young (2).

Year		Awards
1938	Mel Hein, NY Giants, C	Carr
1939	Parker Hall, Cleveland Rams, HB	Carr
1940	Ace Parker, Brooklyn, HB	Carr
1941	Don Hutson, Green Bay, E	Carr
1942	Don Hutson, Green Bay, E	Carr
1943	Sid Luckman, Chicago Bears, QB	Carr
1944	Frank Sinkwich, Detroit, HB	Carr
1945	Bob Waterfield, Cleveland Rams, QB	Carr
1946	Bill Dudley, Pittsburgh, HB	Carr
1947-52	No award	
1953	Otto Graham, Cleveland Browns, QB	UPI
1954	Joe Perry, San Francisco, FB	UPI
1955	Otto Graham, Cleveland, QB	UPI
1956	Frank Gifford, NY Giants, HB	UPI
1957	Y.A. Tittle, San Francisco, QB	UPI
	& Jim Brown, Cleveland, FB	AP
1958	Jim Brown, Cleveland, FB	UPI
	& Gino Marchetti, Baltimore, DE	AP
1959	Johnny Unitas, Baltimore, QB	UPI, Bell
	& Charley Conerly, NY Giants, QB	AP
1960	Norm Van Brocklin, Phi., QB	UPI, AP (tie), Bell
	& Joe Schmidt, Detroit, LB	AP (tie)
1961	Paul Hornung, Green Bay, HB	UPI, AP, Bell
1962	Y.A. Tittle, NY Giants, QB	UPI
	Jim Taylor, Green Bay, FB	AP
	& Andy Robustelli, NY Giants, DE	Bell
1963	Jim Brown, Cleveland, FB	UPI, Bell
	& Y.A. Tittle, NY Giants, QB	AP
1964	Johnny Unitas, Baltimore, QB	UPI, AP, Bell
1965	Jim Brown, Cleveland, FB	UPI, AP
	& Pete Retzlaff, Philadelphia, TE	Bell
1966	Bart Starr, Green Bay, QB	UPI, AP
	& Don Meredith, Dallas, QB	Bell
1967	Johnny Unitas, Baltimore, QB	UPI, AP, Bell
1968	Earl Morrall, Baltimore, QB	UPI, AP
	& Leroy Kelly, Cleveland, RB	Bell
1969	Roman Gabriel, LA Rams, QB	UPI, AP, Bell
1970	John Brodie, San Francisco, QB	AP
	& George Blanda, Oakland, QB-PK	Bell
1971	Alan Page, Minnesota, DT	AP
	& Roger Staubach, Dallas, QB	Bell
1972	Larry Brown, Washington, RB	AP, Bell
1973	O.J. Simpson, Buffalo, RB	AP, Bell
1974	Ken Stabler, Oakland, QB	AP
	& Merlin Olsen, LA Rams, DT	Bell
1975	Fran Tarkenton, Minnesota, QB	AP, Bell
1976	Bert Jones, Baltimore, QB	AP, PFWA
	& Ken Stabler, Oakland, QB	Bell
1977	Walter Payton, Chicago, RB	AP, PFWA
	& Bob Griese, Miami, QB	Bell
1978	Terry Bradshaw, Pittsburgh, QB	AP, Bell
	& Earl Campbell, Houston, RB	PFWA
1979	Earl Campbell, Houston, RB	AP, Bell, PFWA

Year		Awards
1980	Brian Sipe, Cleveland, QB	AP, PFWA
	& Ron Jaworski, Philadelphia, QB	Bell
1981	Ken Anderson, Cincinnati, QB	AP, Bell, PFWA
1982	Mark Moseley, Washington, PK	AP
	Joe Theismann, Washington, QB	Bell
	& Dan Fouts, San Diego, QB	PFWA
1983	Joe Theismann, Washington, QB	AP, PFWA
	& John Riggins, Washington, RB	Bell
1984	Dan Marino, Miami, QB	AP, Bell, PFWA
1985	Marcus Allen, LA Raiders, RB	AP, PFWA
	& Walter Payton, Chicago, RB	Bell
1986	Lawrence Taylor, NY Giants, LB	AP, Bell, PFWA
1987	Jerry Rice, San Francisco, WR	Bell, PFWA
	& John Elway, Denver, QB	AP
1988	Boomer Esiason, Cincinnati, QB	AP, PFWA
	& Randall Cunningham, Phila, QB	Bell
1989	Joe Montana, San Francisco, QB	AP, Bell, PFWA
1990	Randall Cunningham, Phila., QB	Bell, PFWA
	& Joe Montana, San Francisco, QB	AP
1991	Thurman Thomas, Buffalo, RB	AP, PFWA
	& Barry Sanders, Detroit, RB	Bell
1992	Steve Young, San Francisco, QB	AP, Bell, PFWA
1993	Emmitt Smith, Dallas, RB	AP, Bell, PFWA
1994	Steve Young, San Francisco, QB	AP, Bell, PFWA
1995	Brett Favre, Green Bay, QB	AP, Bell, PFWA

NFC Player of the Year

Given out by UPI since 1970. Offensive and defensive players honored since 1983. Rookie winners are in **bold** type.

Multiple winners: Eric Dickerson and Mike Singletary (3); Charles Haley, Walter Payton, Lawrence Taylor, Reggie White and Steve Young (2).

Year		Pos
1970	John Brodie, San Francisco	QB
1971	Alan Page, Minnesota	DT
1972	Larry Brown, Washington	RB
1973	John Hadl, Los Angeles	QB
1974	Jim Hart, St. Louis	QB
1975	Fran Tarkenton, Minnesota	QB
1976	Chuck Foreman, Minnesota	RB
1977	Walter Payton, Chicago	RB
1978	Archie Manning, New Orleans	QB
1979	**Ottis Anderson**, St. Louis	RB
1980	Ron Jaworski, Philadelphia	QB
1981	Tony Dorsett, Dallas	RB
1982	Mark Moseley, Washington	PK
1983	Off—**Eric Dickerson**, Los Angeles	RB
	Def—Lawrence Taylor, New York	LB
1984	Off—Eric Dickerson, Los Angeles	RB
	Def—Mike Singletary, Chicago	LB
1985	Off—Walter Payton, Chicago	RB
	Def—Mike Singletary, Chicago	LB
1986	Off—Eric Dickerson, Los Angeles	RB
	Def—Lawrence Taylor, New York	LB
1987	Off—Jerry Rice, San Francisco	WR
	Def—Reggie White, Philadelphia	DE
1988	Off—Roger Craig, San Francisco	RB
	Def—Mike Singletary, Chicago	LB
1989	Off—Joe Montana, San Francisco	QB
	Def—Keith Millard, Minnesota	DT
1990	Off—Randall Cunningham, Philadelphia	QB
	Def—Charles Haley, San Francisco	LB
1991	Off—Mark Rypien, Washington	QB
	Def—Reggie White, Philadelphia	DE
1992	Off—Steve Young, San Francisco	QB
	Def—Chris Doleman, Minnesota	DE
1993	Off—Emmitt Smith, Dallas	RB
	Def—Eric Allen, Philadelphia	CB
1994	Off—Steve Young, San Francisco	QB
	Def—Charles Haley, Dallas	DE
1995	Off—Brett Favre, Green Bay	QB
	Def—Reggie White, Green Bay	DE

AFL-AFC Player of the Year

Presented by UPI to the top player in the AFL (1960-69) and AFC (since 1970). Offensive and defensive players have been honored since 1983. Rookie winners are in **bold** type.

Multiple winners: O.J. Simpson and Bruce Smith (3); Cornelius Bennett, George Blanda, John Elway, Dan Fouts, Daryle Lamonica, Dan Marino and Curt Warner (2).

Year		Pos
1960	**Abner Haynes**, Dallas Texans	HB
1961	George Blanda, Houston	QB
1962	Cookie Gilchrist, Buffalo	FB
1963	Lance Alworth, San Diego	FL
1964	Gino Cappelletti, Boston	FL-PK
1965	Paul Lowe, San Diego	HB
1966	Jim Nance, Boston	FB
1967	Daryle Lamonica, Oakland	QB
1968	Joe Namath, New York	QB
1969	Daryle Lamonica, Oakland	QB
1970	George Blanda, Oakland	QB-PK
1971	Otis Taylor, Kansas City	WR
1972	O.J. Simpson, Buffalo	RB
1973	O.J. Simpson, Buffalo	RB
1974	Ken Stabler, Oakland	QB
1975	O.J. Simpson, Buffalo	RB
1976	Bert Jones, Baltimore	QB
1977	Craig Morton, Denver	QB
1978	**Earl Campbell**, Houston	RB
1979	Dan Fouts, San Diego	QB
1980	Brian Sipe, Cleveland	QB
1981	Ken Anderson, Cincinnati	QB
1982	Dan Fouts, San Diego	QB
1983	Off—**Curt Warner**, Seattle	RB
	Def—Rod Martin, Los Angeles	LB
1984	Off—Dan Marino, Miami	QB
	Def—Mark Gastineau, New York	DE
1985	Off—Marcus Allen, Los Angeles	RB
	Def—Andre Tippett, New England	LB
1986	Off—Curt Warner, Seattle	RB
	Def—Rulon Jones, Denver	DE
1987	Off—John Elway, Denver	QB
	Def—Bruce Smith, Buffalo	DE
1988	Off—Boomer Esiason, Cincinnati	QB
	Def—Bruce Smith, Buffalo	DE
	& Cornelius Bennett, Buffalo	LB
1989	Off—Christian Okoye, Kansas City	RB
	Def—Michael Dean Perry, Cleveland	NT
1990	Off—Warren Moon, Houston	QB
	Def—Bruce Smith, Buffalo	DE
1991	Off—Thurman Thomas, Buffalo	RB
	Def—Cornelius Bennett, Buffalo	LB
1992	Off—Barry Foster, Pittsburgh	RB
	Def—Junior Seau, San Diego	LB
1993	Off—John Elway, Denver	QB
	Def—Rod Woodson, Pittsburgh	CB
1994	Off—Dan Marino, Miami	QB
	Def—Greg Lloyd, Pittsburgh	LB
1995	Off—Jim Harbaugh, Indianapolis	QB
	Def—Bryce Paup, Buffalo	LB

Annual Awards (Cont.)

NFL-NFC Rookie of the Year

Presented by UPI to the top rookie in the NFL (1955-69) and NFC (since 1970). Players who were the overall first pick in the NFL draft are in **bold** type.

Year		Pos
1955	Alan Ameche, Bal	FB
1956	Lenny Moore, Bal	HB
1957	Jim Brown, Cle	FB
1958	Jimmy Orr, Pit	FL
1959	Boyd Dowler, GB	FL
1960	Gail Cogdill, Det	FL
1961	Mike Ditka, Chi	TE
1962	Ronnie Bull, Chi	FB
1963	Paul Flatley, Min	FL
1964	Charley Taylor, Wash	HB
1965	Gale Sayers, Chi	HB
1966	Johnny Roland, St.L	HB
1967	Mel Farr, Det	RB
1968	Earl McCullouch, Det	FL
1969	Calvin Hill, Dal	RB
1970	Bruce Taylor, SF	DB
1971	John Brockington, GB	RB
1972	Chester Marcol, GB	PK
1973	Charle Young, Phi	TE
1974	John Hicks, NY	G
1975	Mike Thomas, Wash	RB
1976	Sammy White, Min	WR
1977	Tony Dorsett, Dal	RB
1978	Bubba Baker, Det	DE
1979	Ottis Anderson, St.L	RB
1980	**Billy Sims**, Det	RB
1981	**George Rogers**, NO	RB
1982	Jim McMahon, Chi	QB
1983	Eric Dickerson, LA	RB
1984	Paul McFadden, Phi	PK
1985	Jerry Rice, SF	WR
1986	Reuben Mayes, NO	RB
1987	Robert Awalt, St.L	TE
1988	Keith Jackson, Phi	TE
1989	Barry Sanders, Det	RB
1990	Mark Carrier, Chi	S
1991	Lawrence Dawsey, TB	WR
1992	Robert Jones, Dal	LB
1993	Jerome Bettis, LA	RB
1994	Bryant Young, SF	DT
1995	Rashaan Salaam, Oak	RB

AFL-AFC Rookie of the Year

Presented by UPI to the top rookie in the AFL (1960-69) and AFC (since 1970). Players who were the overall first pick in the AFL or NFL draft are in **bold** type.

Year		Pos
1960	Abner Haynes, Dal	HB
1961	Earl Faison, SD	DE
1962	Curtis McClinton, Dal	FB
1963	Billy Joe, Den	FB
1964	Matt Snell, NY	FB
1965	Joe Namath, NY	QB
1966	Bobby Burnett, Buf	HB
1967	George Webster, Hou	LB
1968	Paul Robinson, Cin	RB
1969	Greg Cook, Cin	QB
1970	Dennis Shaw, Buf	QB
1971	**Jim Plunkett**, NE	QB
1972	Franco Harris, Pit	RB
1973	Boobie Clark, Cin	RB
1974	Don Woods, SD	RB
1975	Robert Brazile, Hou	LB
1976	Mike Haynes, NE	DB
1977	A.J. Duhe, Mia	DE
1978	**Earl Campbell**, Hou	RB
1979	Jerry Butler, Buf	WR
1980	Joe Cribbs, Buf	RB
1981	Joe Delaney, KC	RB
1982	Marcus Allen, LA	RB
1983	Curt Warner, Sea	RB
1984	Louis Lipps, Pit	WR
1985	Kevin Mack, Cle	RB
1986	Leslie O'Neal, SD	DE
1987	Shane Conlan, Buf	LB
1988	John Stephens, NE	RB
1989	Derrick Thomas, KC	LB
1990	Richmond Webb, Mia	OT
1991	Mike Croel, Den	LB
1992	Dale Carter, KC	CB
1993	Rick Mirer, Sea	QB
1994	Marshall Faulk, Ind	RB
1995	Curtis Martin, NE	RB

NFL-NFC Coach of the Year

Presented by UPI to the top coach in the NFL (1955-69) and NFC (since 1970). Records indicate how much coach's team improved over one season.

Multiple winners: George Allen, Leeman Bennett, Mike Ditka, George Halas, Tom Landry, Jack Pardee, Allie Sherman, Don Shula and Bill Walsh (2).

Year		Improvement
1955	Joe Kuharich, Washington	3-9 to 8-4
1956	Buddy Parker, Detroit	3-9 to 9-3
1957	Paul Brown, Cleveland	5-7 to 9-2-1
1958	Weeb Ewbank, Baltimore	7-5 to 9-3
1959	Vince Lombardi, Green Bay	1-10-1 to 7-5
1960	Buck Shaw, Philadelphia	7-5 to 10-2
1961	Allie Sherman, New York	6-4-2 to 10-3-1
1962	Allie Sherman, New York	10-3-1 to 12-2
1963	George Halas, Chicago	9-5 to 11-1-2
1964	Don Shula, Baltimore	8-6 to 12-2
1965	George Halas, Chicago	5-9 to 9-5
1966	Tom Landry, Dallas	7-7 to 10-3-1
1967	George Allen, Los Angeles	8-6 to 11-1-2
1968	Don Shula, Baltimore	11-1-2 to 13-1
1969	Bud Grant, Minnesota	8-6 to 12-2
1970	Alex Webster, New York	6-8 to 9-5
1971	George Allen, Washington	6-8 to 9-4-1
1972	Dan Devine, Green Bay	4-8-2 to 10-4
1973	Chuck Knox, Los Angeles	6-7-1 to 12-2
1974	Don Coryell, St. Louis	4-9-1 to 10-4
1975	Tom Landry, Dallas	8-6 to 10-4
1976	Jack Pardee, Chicago	4-10 to 7-7
1977	Leeman Bennett, Atlanta	4-10 to 7-7
1978	Dick Vermeil, Philadelphia	5-9 to 9-7
1979	Jack Pardee, Washington	8-8 to 10-6
1980	Leeman Bennett, Atlanta	6-10 to 12-4
1981	Bill Walsh, San Francisco	6-10 to 13-3
1982	Joe Gibbs, Washington	8-8 to 8-1
1983	John Robinson, Los Angeles	2-7 to 9-7
1984	Bill Walsh, San Francisco	10-6 to 15-1
1985	Mike Ditka, Chicago	10-6 to 15-1
1986	Bill Parcells, New York	10-6 to 14-2
1987	Jim Mora, New Orleans	7-9 to 12-3
1988	Mike Ditka, Chicago	11-4 to 12-4
1989	Lindy Infante, Green Bay	4-12 to 10-6
1990	Jimmy Johnson, Dallas	1-15 to 7-9
1991	Wayne Fontes, Detroit	6-10 to 12-4
1992	Dennis Green, Minnesota	8-8 to 11-5
1993	Dan Reeves, New York	6-10 to 11-5
1994	Dave Wannstedt, Chicago	7-9 to 9-7
1995	Ray Rhodes, Philadelphia	7-9 to 10-6

AFL-AFC Coach of the Year

Presented by UPI to the top coach in the AFL (1960-69) and AFC (since 1970). Records indicate how much coach's team improved over one season. The AFC began play in 1960.

Multiple winners: Chuck Knox, Marv Levy, Dan Reeves, Sam Rutigliano, Lou Saban, and Don Shula (2)

Year	Coach	Improvement
1960	Lou Rymkus, Houston	10-4
1961	Wally Lemm, Houston	10-4 to 10-3-1
1962	Jack Faulkner, Denver	3-11 to 7-7
1963	Al Davis, Oakland	1-13 to 10-4
1964	Lou Saban, Buffalo	7-6-1 to 12-2
1965	Lou Saban, Buffalo	12-2 to 10-3-1
1966	Mike Holovak, Boston	4-8-2 to 8-4-2
1967	John Rauch, Oakland	8-5-1 to 13-1
1968	Hank Stram, Kansas City	9-5 to 12-2
1969	Paul Brown, Cincinnati	3-11 to 4-9-1
1970	Don Shula, Miami	3-10-1 to 10-4
1971	Don Shula, Miami	10-4 to 10-3-1
1972	Chuck Noll, Pittsburgh	6-8 to 11-3
1973	John Ralston, Denver	5-9 to 7-5-2
1974	Sid Gillman, Houston	1-13 to 7-7
1975	Ted Marchibroda, Baltimore	2-12 to 10-4
1976	Chuck Fairbanks, New England	3-11 to 11-3
1977	Red Miller, Denver	9-5 to 12-2
1978	Walt Michaels, New York	3-11 to 8-8
1979	Sam Rutigliano, Cleveland	8-8 to 9-7
1980	Sam Rutigliano, Cleveland	9-7 to 11-5
1981	Forrest Gregg, Cincinnati	6-10 to 12-4
1982	Tom Flores, Los Angeles	7-9 to 8-1
1983	Chuck Knox, Seattle	4-5 to 9-7
1984	Chuck Knox, Seattle	9-7 to 12-4
1985	Raymond Berry, New England	9-7 to 11-5
1986	Marty Schottenheimer, Cleveland	8-8 to 12-4
1987	Ron Meyer, Indianapolis	3-13 to 9-6
1988	Marv Levy, Buffalo	7-8 to 12-4
1989	Dan Reeves, Denver	8-8 to 11-5
1990	Art Shell, Los Angeles	8-8 to 12-4
1991	Dan Reeves, Denver	5-11 to 12-4
1992	Bobby Ross, San Diego	4-12 to 11-5
1993	Marv Levy, Buffalo	11-5 to 12-4
1994	Bill Parcells, New England	5-11 to 10-6
1995	Marty Schottenheimer, Kansas City	9-7 to 13-3

CANADIAN FOOTBALL

The Grey Cup

Earl Grey, the Governor-General of Canada (1904-11) donated a trophy in 1909 for the Rugby Football Championship of Canada. The trophy, which later became known as the Grey Cup, was originally open to competition for teams registered with the Canada Rugby Union. Since 1954, the Cup has gone to the champion of the Canadian Football League (CFL).

Overall multiple winners: Toronto Argonauts (12); Edmonton Eskimos (11); Winnipeg Blue Bombers (9); Hamilton Tiger-Cats and Ottawa Rough Riders (7); Hamilton Tigers (5); Montreal Alouettes and University of Toronto (4); B.C. Lions, Calgary Stampeders and Queen's University (3); Ottawa Senators, Sarnia Imperials, Saskatchewan Roughriders and Toronto Balmy Beach (2).

CFL multiple winners (since 1954): Edmonton (11); Winnipeg (7); Hamilton (6); Ottawa (5); B.C. Lions and Montreal (3); Calgary, Saskatchewan and Toronto (2).

Year	Cup Final
1909	Univ. of Toronto 26, Toronto Parkdale 6
1910	Univ. of Toronto 16, Hamilton Tigers 7
1911	Univ. of Toronto 14, Toronto Argonauts 7
1912	Hamilton Alerts 11, Toronto Argonauts 4
1913	Hamilton Tigers 44, Toronto Parkdale 2
1914	Toronto Argonauts 14, Univ. of Toronto 2
1915	Hamilton Tigers 13, Toronto Rowing 7
1916-19	Not held (WWI)
1920	Univ. of Toronto 16, Toronto Argonauts 3
1921	Toronto Argonauts 23, Edmonton Eskimos 0
1922	Queens Univ. 13, Edmonton Elks 1
1923	Queens Univ. 54, Regina Roughriders 0
1924	Queens Univ. 11, Toronto Balmy Beach 3
1925	Ottawa Senators 24, Winnipeg Tigers 1
1926	Ottawa Senators 10, Univ. of Toronto 7
1927	Toronto Balmy Beach 9, Hamilton Tigers 6
1928	Hamilton Tigers 30, Regina Roughriders 0
1929	Hamilton Tigers 14, Regina Roughriders 3
1930	Toronto Balmy Beach 11, Regina Roughriders 6
1931	Montreal AAA 22, Regina Roughriders 0
1932	Hamilton Tigers 25, Regina Roughriders 6
1933	Toronto Argonauts 4, Sarnia Imperials 3
1934	Sarnia Imperials 20, Regina Roughriders 12
1935	Winnipeg 'Pegs 18, Hamilton Tigers 12
1936	Sarnia Imperials 26, Ottawa Rough Riders 20
1937	Toronto Argonauts 4, Winnipeg Blue Bombers 3
1938	Toronto Argonauts 30, Winnipeg Blue Bombers 7
1939	Winnipeg Blue Bombers 8, Ottawa Rough Riders 7
1940	Gm 1: Ottawa Rough Riders 8, Toronto B-Beach 2 Gm 2: Ottawa Rough Riders 12, Toronto B-Beach 5
1941	Winnipeg Blue Bombers 18, Ottawa Rough Riders 16
1942	Toronto RACF 8, Winnipeg RACF 5
1943	Hamilton Wildcats 23, Winnipeg RACF 14
1944	Montreal HMCS 7, Hamilton Wildcats 6
1945	Toronto Argonauts 35, Winnipeg Blue Bombers 0
1946	Toronto Argonauts 28, Winnipeg Blue Bombers 6
1947	Toronto Argonauts 10, Winnipeg Blue Bombers 9
1948	Calgary Stampeders 12, Ottawa Rough Riders 7
1949	Montreal Alouettes 28, Calgary Stampeders 15
1950	Toronto Argonauts 13, Winnipeg Blue Bombers 0
1951	Ottawa Rough Riders 21, Saskatch. Roughriders 14
1952	Toronto Argonauts 21, Edmonton Eskimos 11
1953	Hamilton Tiger-Cats 12, Winnipeg Blue Bombers 6

Year	Winner	Head Coach	Score	Loser	Head Coach	Site
1954	Edmonton	Frank (Pop) Ivy	26-25	Montreal	Doug Walker	Toronto
1955	Edmonton	Frank (Pop) Ivy	34-19	Montreal	Doug Walker	Vancouver
1956	Edmonton	Frank (Pop) Ivy	50-27	Montreal	Doug Walker	Toronto
1957	Hamilton	Jim Trimble	32-7	Winnipeg	Bud Grant	Toronto
1958	Winnipeg	Bud Grant	35-28	Hamilton	Jim Trimble	Vancouver
1959	Winnipeg	Bud Grant	21-7	Hamilton	Jim Trimble	Toronto
1960	Ottawa	Frank Clair	16-6	Edmonton	Eagle Keys	Vancouver
1961	Winnipeg	Bud Grant	21-14 (OT)	Hamilton	Jim Trimble	Toronto

Canadian Football (Cont.)

The Grey Cup

Year	Winner	Head Coach	Score	Loser	Head Coach	Site
1962	Winnipeg	Bud Grant	28-27*	Hamilton	Jim Trimble	Toronto
1963	Hamilton	Ralph Sazio	21-10	B.C. Lions	Dave Skrien	Vancouver
1964	B.C. Lions	Dave Skrien	34-24	Hamilton	Ralph Sazio	Toronto
1965	Hamilton	Ralph Sazio	22-16	Winnipeg	Bud Grant	Toronto
1966	Saskatchewan	Eagle Keys	29-14	Ottawa	Frank Clair	Vancouver
1967	Hamilton	Ralph Sazio	24- 1	Saskatchewan	Eagle Keys	Ottawa
1968	Ottawa	Frank Clair	24-21	Calgary	Jerry Williams	Toronto
1969	Ottawa	Frank Clair	29-11	Saskatchewan	Eagle Keys	Montreal
1970	Montreal	Sam Etcheverry	23-10	Calgary	Jim Duncan	Toronto
1971	Calgary	Jim Duncan	14-11	Toronto	Leo Cahill	Vancouver
1972	Hamilton	Jerry Williams	13-10	Saskatchewan	Dave Skrien	Hamilton
1973	Ottawa	Jack Gotta	22-18	Edmonton	Ray Jauch	Toronto
1974	Montreal	Marv Levy	20- 7	Edmonton	Ray Jauch	Vancouver
1975	Edmonton	Ray Jauch	9- 8	Montreal	Marv Levy	Calgary
1976	Ottawa	George Brancato	23-20	Saskatchewan	John Payne	Toronto
1977	Montreal	Marv Levy	41- 6	Edmonton	Hugh Campbell	Montreal
1978	Edmonton	Hugh Campbell	20-13	Montreal	Joe Scannella	Toronto
1979	Edmonton	Hugh Campbell	17- 9	Montreal	Joe Scannella	Montrea
1980	Edmonton	Hugh Campbell	48-10	Hamilton	John Payne	Toronto
1981	Edmonton	Hugh Campbell	26-23	Ottawa	George Brancato	Montreal
1982	Edmonton	Hugh Campbell	32-16	Toronto	Bob O'Billovich	Toronto
1983	Toronto	Bob O'Billovich	18-17	B.C. Lions	Don Matthews	Vancouver
1984	Winnipeg	Cal Murphy	47-17	Hamilton	Al Bruno	Edmonton
1985	B.C. Lions	Don Matthews	37-24	Hamilton	Al Bruno	Montreal
1986	Hamilton	Al Bruno	39-15	Edmonton	Jack Parker	Vancouver
1987	Edmonton	Joe Faragalli	38-36	Toronto	Bob O'Billovich	Vancouver
1988	Winnipeg	Mike Riley	22-21	B.C. Lions	Larry Donovan	Ottawa
1989	Saskatchewan	John Gregory	43-40	Hamilton	Al Bruno	Toronto
1990	Winnipeg	Mike Riley	50-11	Edmonton	Joe Faragalli	Vancouver
1991	Toronto	Adam Rita	36-21	Calgary	Wally Buono	Winnipeg
1992	Calgary	Wally Buono	24-10	Winnipeg	Urban Bowman	Toronto
1993	Edmonton	Ron Lancaster	33-23	Winnipeg	Cal Murphy	Calgary
1994	B.C. Lions	Dave Ritchie	26-23	Baltimore	Don Matthews	Vancouver
1995	Baltimore	Don Matthews	37-20	Calgary	Wally Buono	Regina

*Halted by fog in 4th quarter, final 9:29 played the following day.

CFL Most Outstanding Player

Regular season Player of the Year as selected by The Football Reporters of Canada since 1953.
Multiple winners: Doug Flutie (4); Russ Jackson and Jackie Parker (3); Dieter Brock, Ron Lancaster (2).

Year	
1953	Billy Vessels, Edmonton, RB
1954	Sam Etcheverry, Montreal, QB
1955	Pat Abbruzzi, Montreal, RB
1956	Hal Patterson, Montreal, E-DB
1957	Jackie Parker, Edmonton, RB
1958	Jackie Parker, Edmonton, QB
1959	Johnny Bright, Edmonton, RB
1960	Jackie Parker, Edmonton, QB
1961	Bernie Faloney, Hamilton, QB
1962	George Dixon, Montreal, RB
1963	Russ Jackson, Ottawa, QB
1964	Lovell Coleman, Calgary, RB
1965	George Reed, Saskatchewan, RB
1966	Russ Jackson, Ottawa, QB
1967	Peter Liske, Calgary, QB
1968	Bill Symons, Toronto, RB
1969	Russ Jackson, Ottawa, QB
1970	Ron Lancaster, Saskatch., QB
1971	Don Jonas, Winnipeg, QB
1972	Garney Henley, Hamilton, WR
1973	Geo. McGowan, Edmonton, WR
1974	Tom Wilkinson, Edmonton, QB
1975	Willie Burden, Calgary, RB
1976	Ron Lancaster, Saskatch., QB
1977	Jimmy Edwards, Hamilton, RB
1978	Tony Gabriel, Ottawa, TE
1979	David Green, Montreal, RB
1980	Dieter Brock, Winnipeg, QB
1981	Dieter Brock, Winnipeg, QB
1982	Condredge Holloway, Tor., QB
1983	Warren Moon, Edmonton, QB
1984	Willard Reaves, Winnipeg, RB
1985	Merv Fernandez, B.C. Lions, WR
1986	James Murphy, Winnipeg, WR
1987	Tom Clements, Winnipeg, QB
1988	David Williams, B.C. Lions, WR
1989	Tracy Ham, Edmonton, QB
1990	Mike Clemons, Toronto, RB
1991	Doug Flutie, B.C. Lions, QB
1992	Doug Flutie, Calgary, QB
1993	Doug Flutie, Calgary, QB
1994	Doug Flutie, Calgary, QB
1995	Mike Pringle, Baltimore, RB

CFL Most Outstanding Rookie

Regular season Rookie of the Year as selected by The Football Reporters of Canada since 1972.

Year	
1972	Chuck Ealey, Hamilton, QB
1973	Johnny Rodgers, Montreal, WR
1974	Sam Cvijanovich, Toronto, LB
1975	Tom Clements, Ottawa, QB
1976	John Sciarra, B.C. Lions, QB
1977	Leon Bright, B.C. Lions, WR
1978	Joe Poplawski, Winnipeg, WR
1979	Brian Kelly, Edmonton, WR
1980	William Miller, Winnipeg, RB
1981	Vince Goldsmith, Saskatch., LB
1982	Chris Issac, Ottawa, QB
1983	Johnny Shepherd, Hamilton, RB
1984	Dwaine Wilson, Montreal, RB
1985	Mike Gray, B.C. Lions, DT
1986	Harold Hallman, Calgary, DT
1987	Gill Fenerty, Toronto, RB
1988	Orville Lee, Ottawa, RB
1989	Stephen Jordan, Hamilton, DB
1990	Reggie Barnes, Ottawa, RB
1991	Jon Volpe, B.C. Lions, RB
1992	Mike Richardson, Winnipeg, RB
1993	Michael O'Shea, Hamilton, DT
1994	Matt Goodwin, Baltimore, DB
1995	Shalon Baker, Edmonton, WR

Wide World Photos

Kentucky coach **Rick Pitino** faced the cameras with his daughter Jaclyn moments after his Wildcats defeated Syracuse 76-67 to win the 1995-96 NCAA Division I basketball championship.

COLLEGE BASKETBALL

by Chris Raymond

Mission Accomplished

Rick Pitino proved the experts right in guiding Kentucky to its first championship in 18 years.

Call it destiny. Call it faith. For three million hoops-happy fans in Kentucky, it was the only logical conclusion.

After 18 years of crushing disappointment—season after season of unfulfilled promise—college basketball's Late Great Empire was desperate for a champion. With a top-of-the-line coach and a boundless supply of talent, the moment of triumph was at hand.

In the end, it was Tony Delk—Kentucky's senior guard—who rescued the faithful from their madness, serving up seven three-point strikes to halt a courageous, but woefully overmatched Syracuse team, 76-67, in the NCAA championship game. At long last, the chorus of naysayers fell silent. The deafening chatter was sure to resume. Why not two in a row? But, for the moment at least, these Cats were cool. They had actually lived up to their billing.

Kentucky's season had opened five months earlier to great critical acclaim when Rick Pitino assembled in Rupp Arena arguably the most remarkable collection of college basketball talent the world had ever seen. Three Parade Magazine All-Americans. Four McDonald's High School All-Americans. Seven players who had once been the top-rated prospects in their states. Before they completed their first practice, ESPN's Dick Vitale, the game's most famous voice, had volunteered to divvy up the Wildcat roster, handing the nation's No. 1 ranking to one half of the team, No. 2 to the other.

Vitale's was but one of many voices that called out to Pitino throughout the season, making sure he always understood the score. In 18 years of coaching—in college and the pros—Pitino had demonstrated a remarkable knack for rescuing dormant programs, but he had yet to win the Big One. Until he did, he was destined to receive coaching advice daily—almost always unsolicited—by radio, television, postal service, Federal Express, word of mouth, and telephone. The consensus, it seems, was that the Wildcats' all-powerful roster was doomed to fragment much like Dean Smith's star-packed North Carolina team had in 1994. Unless, of course, Kentucky's coach was diligent.

Pitino was up to the challenge. He pushed.

Chris Raymond is an editor at *ESPN Total Sports Magazine.*

Doug Pensinger/Allsport

Last season, it seemed any three Kentucky players could have beaten any other team's starting five. Not a bad proposition if the three Wildcats are **Ron Mercer**, **Anthony Epps** and **Antoine Walker**.

He prodded. He persuaded. First, he sent the recalcitrant Roderick Rhodes, his No. 2 scorer, packing. Then he artfully convinced a busload of blue-chip teenagers that points and playing time were inconsequential when the ultimate goal was a national championship.

The Wildcats opened the season against Maryland in November with their top five athletes on the court. Delk had shifted from shooting guard to the point, Ron Mercer and Derek Anderson patrolled the perimeter, and Antoine Walker and Walter McCarty filled the low post. That left Mark Pope, Jared Prickett, Jeff Sheppard, Anthony Epps, and Wayne Turner to plug in the holes. The Cats struggled early to find their rhythm, but they managed to scratch out a victory.

Against Massachusetts, four days later, they weren't't as lucky. Marcus Camby, the Minutemen's Bill Russell, callously dismantled Pitino's game plan, scoring 32 points with nine rebounds, to relieve Kentucky of its No. 1 ranking.

No big deal.

The Wildcats simply picked up the pace, weakening their next 27 opponents with a relentless full-court press, then finishing them off with deadly precision from the three-point line. With five fresh bodies on the bench at all times, there was simply no reason to rest. Pitino's hyperactive team crushed Morehead State 96-32, brought LSU to its knees with an 86-point first half, and leveled Mississippi State 74-56 on the way to a 16-0 conference mark.

When MSU's Bulldogs ran off with the SEC championship game—dropping Kentucky from No. 1 yet again—it seemed like a stroke of good fortune. No more distractions. The Cats could now focus on the task at hand.

They were six wins away from the prize.

The truth is Kentucky reached the summit 48 hours early. In the semifinals on Saturday night—in the season's finest hour—the team clashed once again with Massachusetts. Unlike Kentucky, UMass had not needed a learning curve. Coach John Calipari's starters seemed to bond instantly the moment they stepped onto a basketball court. After humbling the Wildcats in November, they bumped off Maryland, Wake Forest, Georgia Tech, Syracuse, Memphis, Virginia Tech, Louisville, and

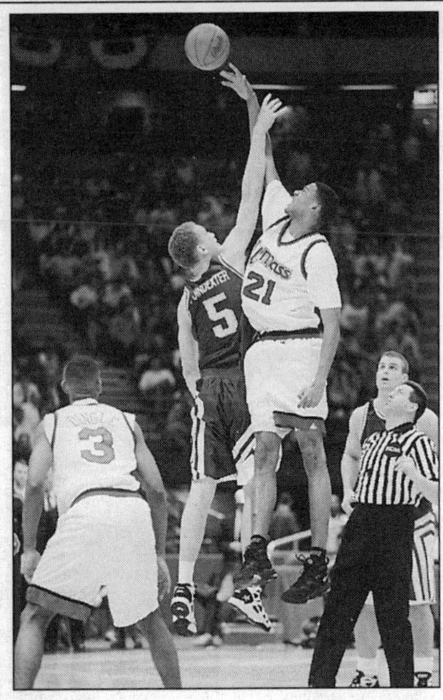

Rick Stewart/Allsport

UMass star **Marcus Camby** tarnished a stellar year by accepting gifts from an agent, including a $3,400 gold necklace (not shown).

Georgetown—nine of the nation's Top 20 teams—on their way to the Final Four.

By now, Camby was a lock for Player of the Year. And, in addition to the same birthday and the same birthplace, Edgar Padilla and Carmello Travieso—the starting backcourt—shared the same marvelous ability to step up strong in the season's biggest moments. In fact, Calipari only appeared to break a sweat once—on January 27—when he watched his star center collapse in the hallway outside the Minutemen's locker room. After four games and a battery of tests, with no conclusive diagnosis, Camby returned to the team and picked up right where he had left off.

In March, however, the Minutemen were no match for a vastly improved Kentucky team. With Epps—a former walk-on—at the point, the Wildcats easily held Massachusetts at bay. Calipari's players rallied again and again, neatly reducing a double-digit scoring margin five times, but Kentucky's all-out pressure was too much. The Wildcats advanced with a solid seven-point win.

That left Syracuse, a No. 4 seed and fourth-place finisher in the Big East, as the final obstacle. The Orangemen had made easy work of Mississippi State in the other semifinal, but they had barely survived a feisty Georgia team in the third round, escaping only on a buzzer beater from juco transfer Jason Cipolla and a last-ditch heave in overtime from senior and savior John Wallace.

In the season's final game, the Orangemen continued their surprising surge, slowing Kentucky's run-and-gun offense with a troublesome 2-3 zone, limiting the Wildcats to 38 percent shooting from the field. Syracuse's offense sputtered too, however, coughing up 24 turnovers under pressure from Kentucky's press.

Wallace's shoulders were wide enough to carry his team through the month of March, but they weren't't sufficient on the first Monday in April. The gutsy forward retired from the court in the game's waning moments with 29 points, 10 rebounds, and five fouls. With Wallace around, Syracuse had closed the gap to two points twice in the second half. Without him, the Orangemen were helpless. They couldn't muster a single bucket in the final minute of play.

Once and for all, Kentucky had closed the door. No more last-second Grant Hill to Christian Laettner stuff. No more nightmarish cold spells like the North Carolina game in 1995. Delk, the Final Four's Most Outstanding Player, wrapped up his college career with 24 points. Mercer, the team's freshman sensation, chipped in a career-high 20. The Wildcats returned to the cozy confines of Kentucky with an NCAA-record sixth national title. For the moment, at least, they were free to sit back and celebrate.

"I tried to use pressure as a motivating force for the players and the staff," Pitino admitted afterwards in the soothing glow of the championship spotlight. "Even though the players say it doesn't exist, every fan they see on campus tells them, 'Win it all, win it all, win it all'"

"It's the school's team," he explained. "But it's also a team that belongs to the state, the Commonwealth of Kentucky."

For Syracuse and Jim Boeheim, its much-maligned coach, the 1995-96 season was also a critical success. The highest accolades, of course, belonged to Wallace who passed up a mad rush to the NBA for one last run in the college ranks. His veteran leadership solidified a squad shaken by the graduation of shooting guard Lawrence Moten and the unexpected departure of point guard Michael Lloyd. In fact, Wallace had been so solid in Syracuse's hour of need, averaging 22 points and 8.8 boards per game, it was easy to forgive him for missing a team flight in the tournament's first round. Even the Big East had to bow before the future lottery pick because Wallace's heroics took some of the heat off Georgetown, UConn, and Villanova—the league's top three title contenders—when all three fell short of expectations.

The most compelling story of the tournament, however, belonged to Mississippi State. Propelled by 6'7" forward Dontae Jones, a former high-school dropout who collected 36 credits in one summer to satisfy the NCAA's eligibility requirements, the Bulldogs defeated three Top 10 teams—Kentucky (in the SEC tournament), UConn and Cincinnati—in 14 days to reach the tournament's Final Four. Though no one had overlooked the Bulldogs' talent, no one expected them to be catching a flight to the Meadowlands either. When Coach Richard Williams was presented with a baseball cap for his Final Four press conference, he was dismayed to find it was missing a few letters: S-T-A-T-E. Cross-state rival Mississippi surely snickered at the insult.

It didn't help that Williams' team crawled into the SEC tournament with a lackluster 19-7 record. But defense—the hallmark of each of the Final Four teams—became Mississippi State's saving grace. Though the Bulldogs' half-court man-to-man style looked like a throwback to the Rupp era, it worked wonders in March, wreaking havoc on the sharp shooters from UConn and Cincinnati. Once again, though, turnovers were the team's undoing: Against Syracuse, the Bulldogs had 21.

Kansas was perhaps the year's biggest disappointment. The Jayhawks, a preseason favorite, always seemed to falter when the heat was turned up. For three weeks in December, they slipped ahead of both UMass and Kentucky to hold the nation's top ranking. Then they lost to Temple in overtime. A momentary lapse right? Wrong. They lost to Oklahoma in the last game of

Doug Pensinger/Allsport

Senior **John Wallace** led a surprising Syracuse team to the championship game. However, his poor interviewing skills caused him to fall to the 18th spot in the NBA draft.

the regular season, Iowa State in the Big Eight Championship, and Syracuse in the Round of Eight.

There were some other college hoop headlines worth remembering.

Pat Summit, who can coach any team in the country—men or women—won her fourth national championship with the women's team at Tennessee. The Lady Vols ousted defending champ UConn and then defeated Georgia, 83-65, in the title game.

Western Carolina—a No. 16 seed in the men's tournament—nearly made history by advancing to the second round. But Purdue escaped with a razor-thin 73-71 win when the Catamounts' final shot—a three-point attempt—glanced off the rim.

Nolan Richardson pushed a squad of unknowns into the Sweet 16. He was joined by Tubby Smith, returning for a third straight year with his Georgia team, and Denny Crum, who hadn't been seen in those parts with Louisville in quite some time.

Gene Keady notched his third straight Big Ten title in the regular season with a faceless roster despite having to cope with his father's death and his daughter's descent into coma.

Conference USA sent four teams to the tournament in its first season: Cincinnati, Marquette, Louisville, and Memphis.

Mike Krzyzewski and Jerry Tarkanian returned to the sidelines, Krzyzewski from illness, Tarkanian from exile. Krzyzewski parted with tradition, bowing out in the tournament's first round. And Tarkanian, in accordance with tradition, was snubbed by the NCAA.

Lou Henson retired after twenty years at the University of Illinois. Lon Kruger of Florida will replace him.

Rick Majerus left his Utah team for one game in January to be with UTEP coach Don Haskins as he underwent triple-bypass surgery. "I've been there," he said. "I know about the doubts. I know about the apprehensions."

Florida State coach Pat Kennedy served a one-game suspension for arguing with officials.

Dean Smith of North Carolina and Rick Barnes of Clemson continued their war of words started the year before. Both coaches were reprimanded by the commissioner of the ACC.

St. John's fired Brian Mahoney after an 11-17 finish.

And UTEP had to forfeit a first-round victory in the WAC tournament because the school's president and athletic director failed to inform the coach that he had an ineligible player, Kevin Beal, on his team.

There were some surprises, too. Penn State and Clemson were linked with Massachusetts in December as the only undefeated teams in Division I. Maryland, with four returning starters, quickly disappeared from the Top 20. (Just for the record, the missing starter was NBA rookie Joe Smith.) And Virginia chose to disregard the preseason polls that ranked them third in the ACC, opting instead to limp across the finish line in very distant seventh place at 12-15.

There were oddball incidents.

After staging a mini-revolt in mid-season and walking out of practice to protest the policies of Coach Danny Nee, Nebraska's players pulled together to win the National Invitational Tournament. At USC, though, the players chose to collapse, closing the

Should they stay or should they go?

The announcement itself had no news value.

Long before he stepped to the podium, Allen Iverson had declared his intentions. They were clear a month earlier when he borrowed a $130,000 Mercedes from a car dealer. And they were clear when he hired David Falk to be his agent. Iverson himself may have known even as far back as 1995 when his daughter was born, or perhaps when he learned his ailing sister needed expert medical care.

No, the story on that day had nothing to do with Allen Iverson. It was about John Thompson and his reaction to losing an All-America point guard after his sophomore year. In 24 seasons, the Georgetown coach had never sent an undergraduate to the pros. Not Patrick Ewing. Not Dikembe Mutombo. Not Alonzo Mourning.

But those guys played in a bygone era.

In 1996, Iverson was simply keeping in step with the times—something he learned to do on a basketball court. Nowadays, the NCAA's best freshmen rushed for the exits. The best high school players skipped college altogether.

All totaled, 22 undergrads and two prep stars volunteered to make the leap to the NBA in the spring of 1996. The press conferences popped up everywhere: Amherst, MA, Lexington, KY, Berkeley, CA, Storrs,CT, and Brooklyn, NY.

That means Marcus Camby, Antoine Walker, Shareef Abdur-Rahim, Ray Allen,and Stephon Marbury will now join 48 other college stars who bolted early to the NBA since 1993.

And while the pros lament the slim physique and unpolished skills of high school star Kobe Bryant, they are more than happy to give him a try. "Our job has always been to look at the best available talent, regardless of age," John Gabriel, vice president of player personnel for the Orlando Magic, told one reporter after the 1995 draft.

Utah Jazz president Frank Laden agreed.

"Right now the NBA is hurting for players," he said. "That's why we're delving so deep into the colleges." All of which raises important questions for the NCAA.

With more and more talk about professional leagues and minor league systems, the future of men's college basketball is in serious doubt. College coaches are already combing the shores overseas for talent to fill their depleted

Wide World Photos

Allen Iverson (r) has more to smile about than **John Thompson** as they meet the press to announce that Iverson will leave Georgetown for the NBA, becoming the first player under Thompson to do so.

rosters. And, though they would prefer to worry about the well-being of their former student-athletes—"the 22 hours" when they aren't playing professional ball as Thompson says—their immediate concern may have more to do with money.

TV ratings for the NCAA Tournament have plunged every year since 1993, when players like Chris Webber, Jason Kidd, and Jerry Stackhouse started shuffling off to the pros. That's hardly the kind of "madness" CBS bargained for when it offered to pay $143 million a season through 2001 for the rights.

But nothing the NCAA does seems to slow the exodus. Loans to insure college superstars against career-threatening injuries don't cover declines in draft position from one year to the next. Just ask Corliss Williamson. And players rarely test the waters and return to college—as they have been permitted to do since 1990—because they are ineligible once they hire an agent and because any NBA team that drafts them continues to own their rights. Tough-love bylaws establishing minimum academic standards for student athletes only make matters worse. See Kevin Garnett, Minnesota Timberwolves.

The quick-fix solutions that are now making the rounds don't offer much hope, either. Will tinkering with freshman eligibility really convince Kobe Bryant to give college a whirl? Would a year to adjust keep Stephon Marbury on ice for one more season? And just how much good does it do Allen Iverson to up his food allowance?

While the debate raged on, fans and the media only muddied the waters with bogus diatribes on the sanctity of amateur sport and the evils of greed, though nobody ever blinked when teenagers left school to pursue professional careers in tennis and hockey.

"We didn't see it when we looked at baseball and that's been going on year after year," said John Chaney of Temple. "Now we are talking about black millionaires, and suddenly we want them to stay in school and get their educations? Hell, you can buy a university."

Meanwhile, as Georgetown's starry-eyed sophomore scoped the road ahead with his mother and his agent, Thompson tried his level best to greet the news with a smile. In the glow of the cameras recording the moment, he reflected on the NCAA's dilemma.

"I don't blame anybody but us," Thompson said. "We have the most antiquated set of rules. They're almost prehistoric. If we don't look at it very closely, there won't be one sensible reason for kids to stay in school." ❐

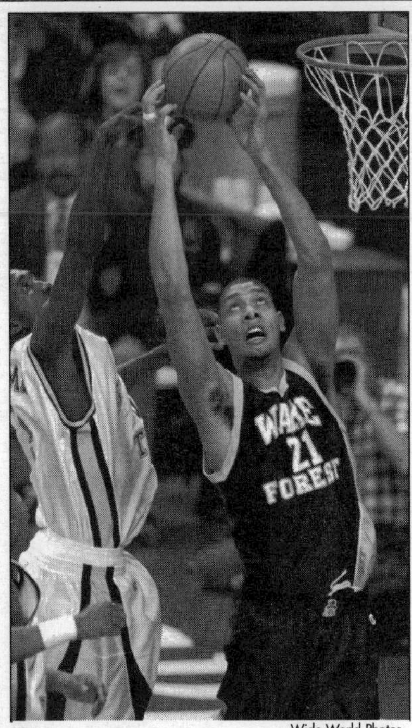

Wide World Photos

Wake Forest's **Tim Duncan** bucked the early exit trend when he decided to return to college for his senior year.

Parker got the boot in February. Colorado's Joe Harrington tried a different approach. When his players got off to a 5-9 start, he simply called it quits, taking matters into his own hands. His reason? He didn't think he was strong enough to discipline the team.

Some players put themselves in trouble.

Duane Simpkins of Maryland received a three-game suspension for accepting a loan to help pay nearly $8,000 in parking tickets. Kerry Kittles of Villanova sat three games for ringing up nearly $800 in long-distance charges on an athletic department calling card. Samaki Walker of Louisville missed 13 games for a series of NCAA violations. Michigan's Robert Traylor broke his arm when a car carrying five players and one recruit flipped on the highway at 5 a.m.

There also was tragedy. Dayton center Chris Daniels died of natural causes after collapsing on a basketball court with an irregular heartbeat.

And there were signs of trouble.

For the second straight season, the NBA sapped the college game of much of its star power, luring a slew of talented undergrads into the draft. The list includes Camby, Jones, Antoine Walker, Samaki Walker, Shareef Abdur-Rahim of California, Ray Allen of Connecticut, Erick Dampier of Mississippi State, Ronnie Henderson of Louisiana State, Allen Iverson of Georgetown, Chris Kingsbury of Iowa, Stephon Marbury of Georgia Tech, Jeff McInnis of North Carolina, Jason Osborne of Louisville, Vitaly Potapenko of Wright State, Darnell Robinson of Arkansas, Jess Settles of Iowa, Greg Simpson of West Virginia, and Lorenzen Wright of Memphis. And also for the second straight season, the NBA swiped some of the nation's top prep school talent: Kobe Bryant of Lower Merion High School in Pennsylvania and Jermaine O'Neal of Eau Claire High School in Columbia, SC.

For the most part, though, the year was short on drama. On April 6, as expected, Camby was named the nation's best player at the Naismith Award ceremonies in Atlanta. He was joined on the All-America team by Allen, Iverson, Tim Duncan of Wake Forest, and Kerry Kittles of Villanova.

With rising stars like Jason Kidd and Jerry Stackhouse strutting their stuff in the NBA, however, it was up to Texas Tech's Darvin Ham to provide us with the season's most scintillating highlight. The 6'7" forward was happy to oblige, throwing down an awkward-but-effective, backboard-shattering jam in the second round of the tournament against North Carolina. It wasn't exactly a snapshot for the ages.

Maybe that explains why CBS' tournament ratings have dropped dramatically in the last two years. With precious little star power and even less suspense—the average margin of victory in 1996 was 13.5 points—March Madness has been hard-pressed to draw a crowd.

Thanks to Pete Carril, though, the college basketball audience was left with one enduring memory, the year's brightest moment. On the eve of retirement, the Princeton coach delivered yet another master stroke. Under his guidance, the Tigers toppled mighty UCLA. When they were eliminated by Mississippi State two nights later, he walked away from the college game a coaching legend. ❐

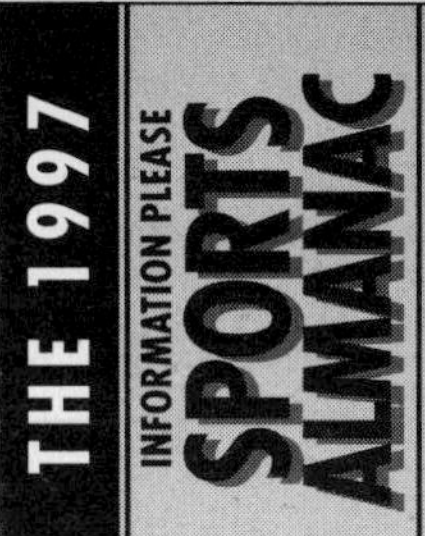

COLLEGE BASKETBALL STATISTICS

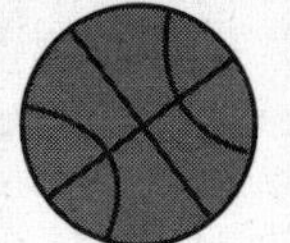

THE SEASON IN REVIEW

1995-1996

TOP 25 • NCAA'S • STANDINGS

PAGE 287

Final Regular Season AP Men's Top 25 Poll

Taken **before** start of NCAA tournament.

The sportswriters & broadcasters poll: first place votes in parentheses; records through Monday, March 11, 1996; total points (based on 25 for 1st, 24 for 2nd, etc.); record in NCAA tourney and team lost to; head coach (career years and record including 1996 postseason), and preseason ranking. Teams in **bold** type went on to reach NCAA Final Four.

		Mar. 11 Record	Points	NCAA Recap	Head Coach	Preseason Rank
1	**Massachusetts** (53)	31-1	1,587	4-1 (Kentucky)	John Calipari (8 yrs: 193-71)	7
2	**Kentucky** (2)	28-2	1,513	6-0	Rick Pitino (14 yrs: 317-119)	1
3	Connecticut (8)	30-2	1,499	2-1 (Mississippi St.)	Jim Calhoun (24 yrs: 472-236)	6
4	Georgetown	26-7	1,259	3-1 (Massachusetts)	John Thompson (24 yrs: 550-208)	5
5	Kansas	26-4	1,259	3-1 (Syracuse)	Roy Williams (8 yrs: 213-56)	2
6	Purdue	25-5	1,259	1-1 (Georgia)	Gene Keady (18 yrs: 386-167)	24
7	Cincinnati	25-4	1,248	3-1 (Mississippi St.)	Bob Huggins (15 yrs: 334-135)	21
8	Texas Tech (1)	28-1	1,231	2-1 (Georgetown)	James Dickey (5 yrs: 100-49)	NR
9	Wake Forest	23-5	1,118	3-1 (Kentucky)	Dave Odom (10 yrs: 180-114)	11
10	Villanova	25-6	995	1-1 (Louisville)	Steve Lappas (8 yrs: 135-108)	3
11	Arizona	24-6	857	2-1 (Kansas)	Lute Olson (23 yrs: 507-194)	27
12	Utah	25-6	793	2-1 (Kentucky)	Rick Majerus (12 yrs: 250-103)	10
13	Georgia Tech	22-11	693	2-1 (Cincinnati)	Bobby Cremins (21 yrs: 398-242)	30
14	UCLA	23-7	688	0-1 (Princeton)	Jim Harrick (17 yrs: 358-160)	4
15	**Syracuse**	24-8	675	5-1 (Kentucky)	Jim Boeheim (20 yrs: 483-159)	33
16	Memphis	22-7	527	0-1 (Drexel)	Larry Finch (10 yrs: 204-115)	13
17	Iowa St.	23-8	516	1-1 (Utah)	Tim Floyd (10 yrs: 209-103)	NR
18	Penn St.	21-6	497	0-1 (Arkansas)	Jerry Dunn (1 yr: 21-7)	NR
19	**Mississippi St.**	22-7	496	4-1 (Syracuse)	Richard Williams (10 yrs: 164-130)	9
20	Marquette	22-7	492	1-1 (Arkansas)	Mike Deane (12 yrs: 234-122)	NR
21	Iowa	22-8	445	1-1 (Arizona)	Tom Davis (25 yrs: 481-259)	8
22	Virginia Tech	22-5	324	1-1 (Kentucky)	Bill Foster (29 yrs: 517-309)	22
23	New Mexico	27-4	211	1-1 (Georgetown)	Dave Bliss (21 yrs: 390-246)	38
24	Louisville	20-11	157	2-1 (Wake Forest)	Denny Crum (25 yrs: 587-224)	12
25	North Carolina	20-10	151	1-1 (Texas Tech)	Dean Smith (35 yrs: 851-247)	20

Others receiving votes: 26. **Wisc.-Green Bay** (25-3, 114 pts); 27. **Stanford** (19-8, 50); 28. **E. Michigan** (24-5, 35); 29. **George Washington** (21-7, 35); 30. **Georgia** (19-9, 18); 31. **Indiana** (19-11, 11); 32. **Michigan** (20-11, 8) and **Mississippi** (12-15, 8); 34. **Bradley** (22-7, 7) and **Temple** (19-12, 7); 36. **Duke** (18-12, 6); 37. **Coll. of Charleston** (24-3, 4) and **Texas** (20-9, 4); 39. **Drexel** (26-3, 3); 40. **Boston College** (18-10, 2); 41. **Clemson** (18-10, 1), **Fresno St.** (20-10, 1), **Minnesota** (18-12, 1), **Montana St.** (21-8, 1), **Tulane** (18-9, 1) and **Tulsa** (22-7, 1).

NCAA Men's Division I Tournament Seeds

	WEST		MIDWEST		SOUTHEAST		EAST
1	Purdue (25-5)	1	Kentucky (28-2)	1	UConn (30-2)	1	UMass (31-1)
2	Kansas (26-4)	2	Wake Forest (23-5)	2	Cincinnati (25-4)	2	Georgetown (26-7)
3	Arizona (24-6)	3	Villanova (25-6)	3	Georgia Tech (22-11)	3	Texas Tech (28-1)
4	Syracuse (24-8)	4	Utah (25-6)	4	UCLA (23-7)	4	Marquette (23-6)
5	Memphis (22-7)	5	Iowa St. (23-8)	5	Mississippi St. (22-7)	5	Penn St. (21-6)
6	Iowa (22-8)	6	Louisville (20-11)	6	Indiana (19-11)	6	North Carolina (20-10)
7	Maryland (17-12)	7	Michigan (20-11)	7	Temple (19-12)	7	New Mexico (27-4)
8	Georgia (19-9)	8	WI-Green Bay (25-3)	8	Duke (81-12)	8	Bradley (22-7)
9	Clemson (18-10)	9	Virginia Tech (22-5)	9	E. Michigan (24-5)	9	Stanford (19-8)
10	Santa Clara (19-8)	10	Texas (20-9)	10	Oklahoma (17-12)	10	Kansas St. (17-11)
11	Geo. Wash. (21-7)	11	Tulsa (22-7)	11	Boston College (18-10)	11	New Orleans (21-8)
12	Drexel (26-3)	12	California (17-10)	12	VCU (24-8)	12	Arkansas (18-12)
13	Montana St. (21-8)	13	Canisius (19-10)	13	Princeton (21-6)	13	Monmouth (20-9)
14	Valparaiso (21-10)	14	Portland (19-10)	14	Austin Peay (19-10)	14	No. Illinois (20-9)
15	S.C. State (22-7)	15	NE Louisiana (16-13)	15	NC-Greensboro (20-9)	15	Miss. Valley St. (22-6)
16	W. Carolina (17-12)	16	San Jose St. (13-16)	16	Colgate (15-4)	16	Central Florida (11-18)

1996 NCAA BASKETBALL MEN'S DIVISION I

WEST (DENVER)

FIRST ROUND March 14-15

Game	Team	Score
1	1 Purdue	73
	16 W. Carolina	71
2	8 Georgia	81
	9 Clemson	74
3	5 Memphis	63
	12 Drexel	75
4	4 Syracuse	88
	13 Montana St.	55
5	6 Iowa	81
	11 G. Washington	79
6	3 Arizona	90
	14 Valparaiso	51
7	7 Maryland	79
	10 Santa Clara	91
8	2 Kansas	92
	15 S. Carolina St.	54

SECOND ROUND March 16-17

Team	Score
Purdue	69
Georgia	76
Drexel	58
Syracuse	69
Iowa	73
Arizona	87
Santa Clara	51
Kansas	76

REGIONALS March 22-24

Team	Score
Georgia	81
Syracuse (OT)	83
Arizona	80
Kansas	83
Syracuse	60
Kansas	57
Syracuse	77

SOUTHEAST (LEXINGTON)

FIRST ROUND March 14-15

Game	Team	Score
1	1 UConn	68
	16 Colgate	59
2	8 Duke	60
	9 E. Michigan	75
3	5 Mississippi St.	58
	12 VCU	51
4	4 UCLA	41
	13 Princeton	43
5	6 Indiana	51
	11 Boston Coll.	64
6	3 Georgia Tech	90
	14 Austin Peay	79
7	7 Temple	61
	10 Oklahoma	43
8	2 Cincinnati	66
	15 NC-Greensboro	61

SECOND ROUND March 16-17

Team	Score
UConn	95
E. Michigan	81
Miss. St.	63
Princeton	41
Boston Coll.	89
Ga. Tech	103
Temple	65
Cincinnati	78

REGIONALS March 22-24

Team	Score
UConn	55
Miss. St.	60
Ga. Tech	70
Cincinnati	87
Miss. St.	73
Cincinnati	63
Miss. St.	69

EAST (ATLANTA)

FIRST ROUND March 14-15

Game	Team	Score
1	1 UMass	92
	16 C. Florida	70
2	8 Bradley	58
	9 Stanford	66
3	5 Penn St.	80
	12 Arkansas	86
4	4 Marquette	68
	13 Monmouth	44
5	6 N. Carolina	83
	11 New Orleans	62
6	3 Texas Tech	74
	14 N. Illinois	73
7	7 New Mexico	69
	10 Kansas St.	48
8	2 Georgetown	93
	15 Miss Valley St.	56

SECOND ROUND March 16-17

Team	Score
UMass	79
Stanford	74
Arkansas	65
Marquette	56
N. Carolina	73
Texas Tech	92
N. Mexico	62
Georgetown	73

REGIONALS March 22-24

Team	Score
UMass	79
Arkansas	63
Texas Tech	90
Georgetown	98
UMass	86
Georgetown	62
UMass	74

MIDWEST (MINNEAPOLIS)

FIRST ROUND March 14-15

Game	Team	Score
1	1 Kentucky	110
	16 San Jose St.	72
2	8 WI-Green Bay	48
	9 Va. Tech	61
3	5 Iowa St.	74
	12 California	64
4	4 Utah	72
	13 Canisius	43
5	6 Louisville (OT)	82
	11 Tulsa	80
6	3 Villanova	92
	14 Portland	58
7	7 Michigan	76
	10 Texas	80
8	2 Wake Forest	62
	15 NE Louisiana	50

SECOND ROUND March 16-17

Team	Score
Kentucky	84
Va. Tech	60
Iowa St.	67
Utah	73
Louisville	68
Villanova	64
Texas	62
Wake Forest	65

REGIONALS March 22-24

Team	Score
Kentucky	101
Utah	70
Louisville	59
Wake Forest	60
Kentucky	83
Wake Forest	63
Kentucky	81

NATIONAL CHAMPIONSHIP

Syracuse 67

Kentucky 76

FINAL FOUR
at the Meadowlands
in E. Rutherford, N.J.
•••
Semifinals: March 30
Finals: April 1

NCAA Men's Championship Game

58th NCAA Division I Championship Game. **Date:** Monday, April 1, at the Meadowlands Arena. **Coaches:** Jim Boeheim of Syracuse and Rick Pitino of Kentucky. **Favorite:** Kentucky by 13½.
Attendance: 19,229; **Officials:** John Clougherty, Scott Thornley and David Libbey; **TV Rating:** 18.3/29 share (CBS).

Kentucky 76

	Min	FG M-A	FT M-A	Pts	Reb O-T	A	PF
Derek Anderson	16	4-8	1-1	11	3-4	1	2
Antoine Walker	32	4-12	3-6	11	4-9	4	2
Walter McCarty	19	2-6	0-0	4	5-7	3	3
Tony Delk	37	8-20	1-2	24	1-7	2	2
Anthony Epps	35	0-6	0-0	0	1-4	7	1
Mark Pope	27	1-6	2-2	4	1-3	2	3
Ron Mercer	24	8-12	1-1	20	1-2	2	3
Jeff Sheppard	7	1-2	0-1	2	1-2	0	3
Allen Edwards	3	0-1	0-0	0	0-0	1	0
TOTALS	200	28-73	8-13	76	17-38	22	19

Three-point FG: 12–27 (Delk 7–12, Mercer 3–4, Anderson 2–3, Walker 0–1, Sheppard 0–1, Edwards 0–1, Pope 0–2, Epps 0–3); **Team Rebounds:** 2; **Blocked Shots:** 1 (Delk); **Turnovers:** 15 (Pope 4, Delk 3, Sheppard 3, Anderson 2, McCarty, Epps, Edwards); **Steals:** 11 (Walker 4, Anderson 3, Delk 2, Pope, Mercer). **Percentages:** 2-Pt FG (.348), 3-Pt FG (.444), Total FG (.384), Free Throws (.615).

Syracuse 67

	Min	FG M-A	FT M-A	Pts	Reb O-T	A	PF
Todd Burgan	39	7-10	2-5	19	2-8	1	5
John Wallace	38	11-19	5-5	29	3-10	1	5
Otis Hill	28	3-9	1-1	7	2-10	1	2
Lazarus Sims	38	2-5	1-2	6	1-2	7	2
Jason Cipolla	35	3-8	0-0	6	0-1	2	1
J.B. Reafsnyder	13	0-1	0-0	0	0-4	0	0
Marius Janulis	8	0-0	0-0	0	0-2	0	2
Elimu Nelson	1	0-0	0-0	0	0-0	0	0
TOTALS	200	26-52	9-13	67	8-37	12	17

Three-point FG: 6-15 (Burgan 3–5, Wallace 2–3, Sims 1–4, Cipolla 0–3); **Team Rebounds:** 1; **Blocked Shots:** 2 (Wallace, Hill); **Turnovers:** 24 (Sims 7, Wallace 6, Burgan 5, Hill 3, Cipolla 2, Reafsnyder); **Steals:** 6 (Cipolla 4, Burgan, Sims); **Percentages:** 2-Pt FG (.541), 3-Pt FG (.400), Total FG (.500), Free Throws (.692).

	1st	2nd	Final
Syracuse (Big East)	33	34—	**67**
Kentucky (SEC)	42	34—	**76**

THE FINAL FOUR

Meadowlands Arena in East Rutherford, N.J.
(Mar. 30–Apr. 1)

Most Outstanding Player

Tony Delk, Kentucky senior guard. SEMIFINAL— 32 minutes, 20 points, 2 rebounds, 1 steal, 1 block; FINAL— 37 minutes, 24 points, 7 rebounds, 2 assists, 2 steals.

All-Tournament Team

Delk and forward Ron Mercer of Kentucky; forwards John Wallace and Todd Burgan of Syracuse; and center Marcus Camby of Massachusetts.

Semifinal—Game One

Midwest Regional champion Mississippi St. vs. West Regional champ Syracuse; Saturday, Mar. 30 (5:42 p.m. tipoff). **Coaches:** Richard Williams, Mississippi St. and Jim Boeheim, Syracuse. **Favorite:** Mississippi St. by 3½.

	1st	2nd	Final
Mississippi St. (SEC)	36	33—	**69**
Syracuse (Big East)	36	41—	**77**

High scorers— Darryl Wilson, Mississippi St. (20) and John Wallace, Syracuse (21); **Att**— 19,229; **TV rating**—11.4/25 share (CBS).

Semifinal—Game Two

East Regional champion Massachusetts vs. Midwest Regional champ Kentucky; Saturday, Mar. 30 (8:07 p.m. tipoff). **Coaches:** John Calipari, Massachusetts and Rick Pitino, Kentucky. **Favorite:** Kentucky by 7½.

	1st	2nd	Final
Kentucky (SEC)	36	45—	**81**
UMass (A-10)	28	46—	**74**

High scorers—Tony Delk, Kentucky (20) and Marcus Camby, UMass (25); **Att**— 19,229; **TV rating**—15.1/28 share (CBS).

Final *USA Today*/CNN Coaches Poll

Taken **after** NCAA Tournament.

Voted on by a panel of 32 Division I head coaches following the NCAA tournament: first place votes in parentheses with total points (based on 25 for 1st, 24 for 2nd, etc.). Schools on major probation are ineligible to be ranked.

		After NCAAs W-L	After NCAAs Pts	Before NCAAs W-L	Before NCAAs Rank
1	Kentucky (32)	34-2	800	28-2	2
2	UMass	35-2	760	31-1	1
3	Syracuse	29-9	721	24-8	14
4	Mississippi St.	26-8	658	22-7	20
5	Kansas	29-5	639	26-4	8
6	Cincinnati	28-5	610	25-4	6
7	Georgetown	29-8	606	26-7	5
8	UConn	32-3	601	30-2	3
9	Wake Forest	26-6	563	23-5	9
10	Texas Tech	30-2	478	28-1	7
11	Arizona	26-7	475	24-6	11
12	Utah	27-7	415	25-6	10
13	Georgia Tech	24-12	391	22-11	15
14	Louisville	22-12	323	20-11	23
15	Purdue	26-6	311	25-5	4
16	Georgia	21-10	299	19-9	NR
17	Villanova	26-7	269	25-6	12
18	Arkansas	20-13	172	18-12	NR
19	UCLA	23-8	155	23-7	13
20	Iowa St.	24-9	149	23-8	16
21	Virginia Tech	23-6	127	22-5	21
22	Iowa	23-9	120	22-8	19
23	Marquette	23-8	107	22-7	22
24	North Carolina	21-11	102	20-10	24
25	New Mexico	28-5	93	27-4	NR

Others receiving votes: 26. **Penn St.** (21–7, 71 pts); 27. **Stanford** (20–9, 70); 28. **Memphis** (22–8, 68); 29. **E. Michigan** (23–6, 59); 30. **Texas** (21–10, 52); 31. **Nebraska** (won NIT, 21–14, 25); 32. **Boston College** (19–11, 24); 33. **Temple** (20–13, 12); 34. **George Washington** (21–8, 10); 35. **St. Joseph's-PA** (runner-up NIT, 19–13, 10); 36. **Arkansas-LR** (21–7, 9); 37. **New Orleans** (21–9, 8) and **Santa Clara** (20–9, 8); 39. **Drexel** (26–4, 6) and **Tulane** (22–10, 6); 41. **Duke** (18–13, 4) and **Michigan** (20–12, 4); 43. **College of Charleston** (23–4, 3) and **Princeton** (21–7, 3); 45. **Davidson** (22–5, 2) and **Wisc.-Green Bay** (24–4, 2).

NCAA Finalists' Tournament and Season Statistics

At least 10 games played during the overall season.

KENTUCKY (34–2)

	NCAA TOURNAMENT			Per Game			OVERALL SEASON			Per Game		
	Gm	FG%	TPts	Pts	Reb	Ast	Gm	FG%	TPts	Pts	Reb	Ast
Tony Delk	6	47.1	113	18.8	4.0	1.3	36	49.4	639	17.8	4.2	1.8
Antoine Walker	6	43.6	88	14.7	9.0	4.3	36	46.3	547	15.2	8.4	2.9
Walter McCarty	6	60.5	67	11.2	7.2	3.3	36	54.3	407	11.3	5.7	2.6
Derek Anderson	6	56.4	65	10.8	5.2	2.3	36	50.9	337	9.4	3.4	2.4
Ron Mercer	6	55.3	51	8.5	1.7	1.3	36	45.7	288	8.0	2.9	1.4
Anthony Epps	6	39.5	46	7.7	3.5	6.3	36	42.9	241	6.7	3.1	4.9
Mark Pope	6	41.4	36	6.0	3.8	1.0	36	48.2	275	7.6	5.2	1.0
Jeff Sheppard	6	50.0	33	5.5	2.7	2.3	34	52.0	188	5.5	2.1	1.9
Allen Edwards	6	62.5	17	2.8	0.8	0.6	35	46.3	115	3.3	1.1	1.2
Wayne Turner	5	50.0	12	2.4	0.4	0.8	35	53.3	156	4.5	1.5	1.6
Nazr Mohammed	2	100.0	4	2.0	0.0	0.0	16	44.8	37	2.3	1.5	0.2
Oliver Simmons	4	60.0	7	1.8	0.3	0.3	21	48.1	37	1.8	1.1	0.1
KENTUCKY	6	49.5	535	89.2	37.0	23.8	36	48.7	3292	91.4	41.7	21.8
OPPONENTS	6	44.0	406	67.7	35.7	15.3	36	41.5	2497	69.4	35.8	13.5

Three-pointers: NCAA TOURNEY — Delk (18 for 39), Epps (7–18), McCarty (4–7), Anderson (4–8), Mercer (4–9), Pope (2–4), Sheppard (2–4), Simmons (1–1), Edwards (1–3), Walker (1–4), Team (44–97 for 45.4 pct.); OVERALL— Delk (93–210), Epps (43–105), McCarty (28–60), Anderson (23–59), Mercer (23–68), Sheppard (22–44), Pope (16–45), Walker (9–48), Edwards (7–23), Simmons (1–1), Turner (1–4), Team (266–670 for 39.7 pct.).

SYRACUSE (29–9)

	NCAA TOURNAMENT			Per Game			OVERALL SEASON			Per Game		
	Gm	FG%	TPts	Pts	Reb	Ast	Gm	FG%	TPts	Pts	Reb	Ast
John Wallace	6	48.0	131	21.8	8.7	2.0	38	48.9	845	22.2	8.7	2.4
Otis Hill	6	64.4	87	14.5	6.5	1.0	38	57.1	482	12.7	5.4	0.6
Todd Burgan	6	45.0	79	13.2	8.5	2.0	38	42.1	459	12.1	6.8	2.3
Jason Cipolla	6	43.6	62	10.3	1.7	1.5	37	38.3	284	7.7	1.9	1.4
Lazarus Sims	6	41.9	47	7.8	3.5	7.7	38	43.6	241	6.3	3.7	7.4
J.B. Reafsnyder	6	42.9	19	3.2	3.2	0.3	38	47.6	207	5.4	3.4	0.6
Marius Janulis	6	28.6	11	1.8	1.2	0.2	37	45.2	226	6.1	2.1	1.4
Bobby Lazor	2	33.3	3	1.5	0.0	0.0	21	43.8	44	2.1	1.8	0.3
David Patrick	2	100.0	2	1.0	1.0	1.5	28	40.0	24	0.9	0.6	1.0
Elvir Ovcina	2	100.0	2	1.0	1.5	0.5	16	43.5	43	2.7	2.0	0.2
Elimu Nelson	2	—	0	0.0	0.0	0.5	16	60.0	17	1.1	0.4	0.4
SYRACUSE	6	48.4	444	74.0	33.3	15.7	38	46.6	2897	76.2	38.3	17.2
OPPONENTS	6	38.0	396	66.0	36.0	15.2	38	40.8	2607	68.6	37.3	14.7

Three-pointers: NCAA TOURNEY— Burgan (9 for 22), Wallace (7–13), Cipolla (7–19), Sims (7–19), Janulis (2–4), Team (32–77 for 41.6 pct.); OVERALL— Burgan (49–144), Janulis (42–101), Cipolla (40–129), Wallace (37–88), Sims (26–72), Lazor (2–6), Patrick (1–1), Nelson (1–3), Hill (0–1), Ovcina (0–3), Team (199–553 for 36.0 pct.).

Kentucky's Schedule

Reg. Season (26-1)

W Maryland 96-84
L Massachusetts 82-92
W Indiana 89-82
W Wisc.-Green Bay 74-62
W Georgia Tech 83-60
W Morehead St. 96-32
W Marshall 118-99
W Louisville 89-66
W Rider 90-65
W Iona 106-79
W at South Carolina 89-60
W Mississippi 90-60
W at Mississippi St. 74-56
W Tennessee 61-44
W at LSU 129-97
W TCU 124-80
W at Georgia 82-77
W South Carolina 89-57
W Florida 77-63
W at Vanderbilt 120-81
W Arkansas 88-73
W Georgia 86-73
W at Tennessee 90-50
W Alabama 84-65
W at Florida 94-63
W at Auburn 88-73
W Vanderbilt 101-63

SEC Tourney (2-1)

W Florida 100-76
W Arkansas 95-75
L Mississippi St. 73-84

NCAA Tourney (6-0)

W San Jose St. 110-72
W Virginia Tech 84-60
W Utah 101-70
W Wake Forest 83-63
W UMass 81-74
W Syracuse 76-67

Syracuse's Schedule

Reg. Season (22-7)

W Lafayette 87-63
W Colgate 89-55
W at Providence 82-78
W St. Johns 97-72
W Columbia 83-60
W Washington St. 77-75
W Bowling Green 75-64
W College of Charleston 72-61
W at Arizona 79-70
W Illinois 75-64
W Rhode Island 92-66
L Massachusetts 47-65
L at Miami 66-75
W Providence 77-75
W Rutgers 81-80
L at West Virginia 78-90
L Connecticut 70-79
L at Georgetown 64-83
W Boston College 88-73
L Villanova (OT) 69-72
W Miami 72-51
W Alabama 81-68
W Pittsburgh 73-67
W Georgetown 85-64
W at Rutgers 63-54
L at Seton Hall 79-80
W Pittsburgh 77-60
W St. Johns 92-79
W Notre Dame 71-67

Big East Tourney (2-1)

W Notre Dame 76-55
W Boston College 69-61
L Connecticut 67-85

NCAA Tourney (5-1)

W Montana St. 88-55
W Drexel 69-58
W Georgia (OT) 83-81
W Kansas 60-57
W Mississippi St. 77-69
L Kentucky 67-76

Final NCAA Men's Division I Standings

Conference records include regular season games only. Overall records include all postseason tournament games.

American West Conference

	Conference W	L	Pct	Overall W	L	Pct
Cal Poly-SLO	5	1	.833	16	13	.552
So. Utah St.	3	3	.500	15	13	.536
CS-Northridge	2	4	.333	7	20	.259
CS-Sacramento	2	4	.333	7	20	.259

Conf. Tourney Final: So. Utah St. 55, Cal Poly-SLO 53.

Atlantic Coast Conference

	Conference W	L	Pct	Overall W	L	Pct
* Wake Forest	15	4	.789	26	6	.813
* Georgia Tech	15	4	.789	24	12	.667
* North Carolina	10	7	.588	21	11	.656
* Maryland	9	9	.500	17	13	.567
* Duke	8	9	.471	18	13	.581
* Clemson	8	10	.444	18	11	.621
Virginia	6	11	.353	12	15	.444
Florida St.	5	12	.294	13	14	.481
N.C. State	4	14	.222	15	16	.484

Conf. Tourney Final: Wake Forest 75, Georgia Tech 74.

* **NCAA Tourney (6-5):** Wake Forest (3-1), Georgia Tech (2-1), N. Carolina (1-1), Duke (0-1), Maryland (0-1).

Atlantic 10 Conference

East	Conference W	L	Pct	Overall W	L	Pct
* Massachusetts	15	1	.938	35	2	.946
* Temple	12	4	.750	20	12	.625
†St. Joseph's (Pa.)	9	7	.563	19	13	.594
†Rhode Island	8	8	.500	20	14	.588
St. Bonaventure	5	12	.294	10	18	.357
Fordham	2	14	.125	4	23	.148
West	**W**	**L**	**Pct**	**W**	**L**	**Pct**
* Virginia Tech	13	3	.813	23	6	.793
* Geo. Washington	13	3	.813	21	9	.700
Xavier-OH	8	8	.500	13	15	.464
Dayton	6	11	.353	15	14	.517
Duquesne	3	13	.188	9	18	.333
La Salle	3	13	.188	6	24	.200

Conf. Tourney Final: Massachusetts 75, Temple 61.

* **NCAA Tourney (6-4):** Massachusetts (4-1), Temple (1-1), Virginia Tech (1-1), Geo. Washington (0-1).

†**NIT Tourney (6-2):** St. Joseph's (4-1), Rhode Island (2-1).

Big East Conference

Big East 7	Conference W	L	Pct	Overall W	L	Pct
* Georgetown	13	5	.722	29	8	.784
* Syracuse	12	6	.667	29	9	.763
†Providence	9	9	.500	18	12	.600
Miami-FL	8	10	.444	15	13	.536
Seton Hall	7	11	.389	12	16	.428
Rutgers	6	12	.333	9	18	.333
Pittsburgh	5	13	.278	10	17	.370
Big East 6	**W**	**L**	**Pct**	**W**	**L**	**Pct**
* Connecticut	17	1	.944	32	3	.914
* Villanova	14	4	.778	26	7	.789
* Boston College	10	8	.556	19	11	.633
West Virginia	7	11	.389	12	15	.444
St. John's	5	13	.278	11	16	.407
Notre Dame	4	14	.222	9	18	.333

Conf. Tourney Final: Connecticut 75, Georgetown 74.

* **NCAA Tourney (12-5):** Syracuse (5-1), Georgetown (3-1), Connecticut (2-1), Boston College (1-1), Villanova (1-1).

†**NIT Tourney (1-1):** Providence (1-1).

Big Eight Conference

	Conference W	L	Pct	Overall W	L	Pct
* Kansas	12	2	.857	29	5	.853
* Iowa St.	9	5	.643	24	9	.727
* Oklahoma	8	6	.571	17	13	.567
Oklahoma St.	7	7	.500	17	10	.630
Kansas St.	7	7	.500	17	11	.607
†Missouri	6	8	.429	18	15	.545
†Nebraska	4	10	.286	21	14	.600
Colorado	3	11	.214	9	18	.333

Conf. Tourney Final: Iowa St. 56, Kansas 55.

* **NCAA Tourney (3-3):** Kansas (3-1), Iowa St. (0-1), Oklahoma (0-1).

†**NIT Tourney (6-1):** Nebraska (5-0), Missouri (1-1).

Big Sky Conference

	Conference W	L	Pct	Overall W	L	Pct
* Montana St.	11	3	.786	21	9	.700
Montana	10	4	.714	20	8	.714
Weber St.	10	4	.714	20	10	.667
Boise St.	10	4	.714	15	13	.536
Idaho St.	7	7	.500	11	15	.423
Idaho	5	9	.357	12	16	.429
Northern Arizona	3	11	.214	6	20	.231
Eastern Washington	0	14	.000	3	23	.115

Conf. Tourney Final: Montana St. 81, Weber St. 70.

* **NCAA Tourney (0-1):** Montana St. (0-1).

Big South Conference

	Conference W	L	Pct	Overall W	L	Pct
* NC-Greensboro	11	3	.786	19	10	.655
NC-Asheville	9	5	.643	18	10	.643
Liberty	9	5	.643	17	11	.607
Charleston Southern	9	5	.643	15	13	.536
Radford	8	6	.571	14	13	.519
Winthrop	6	8	.429	7	19	.269
MD-Balt. County	3	11	.214	5	22	.185
Coastal Carolina	1	13	.071	5	21	.192

Conf. Tourney Final: NC-Greensboro 79, Liberty 53.

* **NCAA Tourney (0-1):** NC-Greensboro (0-1).

Big Ten Conference

	Conference W	L	Pct	Overall W	L	Pct
* Purdue	15	3	.833	26	6	.813
* Penn St.	12	6	.667	21	7	.750
* Indiana	12	6	.667	19	12	.613
* Iowa	11	7	.611	23	9	.719
* Michigan	10	8	.556	20	12	.625
†Minnesota	10	8	.556	19	13	.594
†Michigan St.	9	9	.500	16	16	.500
†Wisconsin	8	10	.444	17	15	.531
†Illinois	7	11	.389	18	13	.581
Ohio St.	3	15	.167	10	17	.370
Northwestern	2	16	.111	7	20	.259

Conf. Tourney Final: Big Ten has no tournament.

* **NCAA Tourney (2-5):** Iowa (1-1), Purdue (1-1), Indiana (0-1), Michigan (0-1), Penn St. (0-1).

†**NIT Tourney (3-4):** Michigan (1-1), Minnesota (1-1), Wisconsin (1-1), Illinois (0-1).

Final NCAA Men's Division I Standings (Cont.)

Big West Conference

	Conference			Overall		
	W	L	Pct	W	L	Pct
Long Beach St	12	6	.667	17	11	.607
UC-Irvine	11	6	.647	15	11	.577
Pacific	11	7	.611	15	12	.556
Utah St	10	8	.556	18	15	.545
Nevada	9	9	.500	16	13	.552
* San Jose St	8	9	.471	12	17	.414
New Mexico St	8	10	.444	11	15	.423
UC-Santa Barbara	8	10	.444	11	15	.423
UNLV	7	11	.389	10	16	.385
CS-Fullerton	5	13	.278	6	20	.231

Conf. Tourney Final: San Jose St. 76, Utah St. 75 (OT).

* **NCAA Tourney (0-1):** San Jose St. (0-1).

Colonial Athletic Association

	Conference			Overall		
	W	L	Pct	W	L	Pct
* Va.Commonwealth	14	2	.875	24	9	.727
Old Dominion	12	4	.750	18	13	.581
NC-Wilmington	9	7	.563	13	16	.448
East Carolina	8	8	.500	17	11	.607
American	8	8	.500	12	15	.444
George Mason	6	10	.375	11	16	.407
William & Mary	6	10	.375	10	16	.385
James Madison	6	10	.375	10	20	.333
Richmond	3	13	.188	8	20	.286

Conf. Tourney Final: Va. Commonwealth 46, NC-Wilmington 43.

* **NCAA Tourney (0-1):** Va. Commonwealth (0-1).

Conference USA

	Conference			Overall		
Red Division	W	L	Pct	W	L	Pct
†Tulane	9	5	.643	22	10	.688
Ala-Birmingham	6	8	.429	16	14	.533
So. Mississippi	6	8	.429	12	15	.444
So. Florida	2	12	.143	12	16	.429
	Conference			**Overall**		
White Division	W	L	Pct	W	L	Pct
* Memphis	11	3	.786	22	8	.733
* Louisville	10	4	.714	22	12	.647
NC-Charlotte	6	8	.429	14	15	.483
	Conference			**Overall**		
Blue Division	W	L	Pct	W	L	Pct
* Cincinnati	11	3	.785	28	5	.848
* Marquette	10	4	.714	23	8	.742
†St. Louis	4	10	.286	16	14	.533
DePaul	2	12	.143	11	18	.379

Conf. Tourney Final: Cincinnati 85, Marquette 84 (OT).

***NCAA Tourney (6-4):** Cincinnati (3-1), Louisville (2-1), Marquette (1-1), Memphis (0-1).

†**NIT Tourney (4-2):** Tulane (4-1), St. Louis (0-1).

Ivy League

	Conference			Overall		
	W	L	Pct	W	L	Pct
* Princeton	12	2	.857	22	7	.759
Pennsylvania	12	2	.857	17	10	.630
Dartmouth	9	5	.643	16	10	.615
Harvard	7	7	.500	15	11	.577
Brown	5	9	.357	10	16	.385
Cornell	5	9	.357	10	16	.385
Yale	3	11	.214	8	18	.308
Columbia	3	11	.214	7	19	.269

Note: Princeton beat Penn (63–56 in OT on Mar. 9) in a one-game playoff for the Ivy League title and automatic NCAA bid.

Conf. Tourney Final: Ivy League has no tournament.

* **NCAA Tourney (1-1):** Princeton (1-1).

Metro Atlantic Conference

	Conference			Overall		
	W	L	Pct	W	L	Pct
†Iona	10	4	.714	22	7	.758
†Fairfield	10	4	.714	20	10	.667
†Manhattan	9	5	.643	17	12	.586
Loyola-MD	8	6	.571	11	16	.407
* Canisius	7	7	.500	19	11	.633
Niagara	6	8	.429	13	15	.464
St. Peter's	5	9	.357	15	12	.556
Siena	1	13	.071	5	22	.185

Conf. Tourney Final: Canisius 52, Fairfield 46.

* **NCAA Tourney (0-1):** Canisius (0-1).

†**NIT Tourney (0-3):** Fairfield (0-1), Manhattan (0-1), Iona (0-1).

Mid-American Conference

	Conference			Overall		
	W	L	Pct	W	L	Pct
* Eastern Michigan	14	4	.778	25	6	.806
Western Michigan	13	5	.722	15	12	.556
†Miami-OH	12	6	.667	21	8	.724
Ball St.	11	7	.611	16	12	.571
Ohio	11	7	.611	16	14	.533
Toledo	9	9	.500	18	14	.563
Bowling Green	9	9	.500	14	13	.519
Kent St.	8	10	.444	14	13	.519
Central Michigan	3	15	.167	6	20	.231
Akron	0	18	.000	3	23	.115

Conf. Tourney Final: Eastern Michigan 77, Toledo 63.

* **NCAA Tourney (1-1):** Eastern Michigan (1-1).

†**NIT Tourney (0-1):** Miami-OH (0-1).

Mid-Continent Conference

	Conference			Overall		
	W	L	Pct	W	L	Pct
* Valparaiso	13	5	.722	21	11	.656
Western Illinois	12	6	.667	17	12	.586
NE Illinois	10	8	.556	14	13	.519
Buffalo	10	8	.556	13	14	.481
Missouri-KC	10	8	.556	12	15	.444
Central Conn. St.	9	9	.500	13	15	.464
Eastern Illinois	9	9	.500	13	15	.464
Troy St.	8	10	.444	11	16	.407
Youngstown St.	7	11	.389	12	15	.444
Chicago St.	2	16	.111	2	25	.074

Conf. Tourney Final: Valparaiso 75, Western Illinois 52.

* **NCAA Tourney (0-1):** Valparaiso (0-1).

Mid-Eastern Athletic Conference

	Conference			Overall		
	W	L	Pct	W	L	Pct
* South Carolina St.	14	2	.875	20	8	.714
Coppin St.	14	2	.875	19	10	.655
Bethune-Cookman	8	8	.500	12	15	.444
Delaware St.	8	8	.500	11	17	.393
N. Carolina A&T	7	9	.438	10	17	.370
MD-Eastern Shore	6	10	.375	11	16	.407
Howard	6	10	.375	7	20	.259
Morgan St.	6	10	.375	7	20	.259
Florida A&M	3	13	.188	9	18	.333
Hampton	0	0	.000	9	17	.346

Conf. Tourney Final: South Carolina St. 69, Coppin St. 56.

* **NCAA Tourney (0-1):** South Carolina St. (0-1).

Midwestern Collegiate Conference

	Conference W	L	Pct	Overall W	L	Pct
*WI-Green Bay	16	0	1.000	25	4	.862
Butler	12	4	.750	19	8	.704
*No. Illinois	10	6	.625	20	10	.667
Detroit	8	8	.500	18	11	.621
Wright St	8	8	.500	14	13	.519
Ilinois-Chicago	5	11	.313	10	18	.357
WI-Milwaukee	5	11	.313	9	18	.333
Loyola-IL	5	11	.313	8	19	.296
Cleveland St	3	13	.188	5	21	.192

Conf. Tourney Final: No. Illinois 95, Detroit 63.
* **NCAA Tourney (0-2):** No. Illinois (0-1), WI-Green Bay (0-1).

Missouri Valley Conference

	Conference W	L	Pct	Overall W	L	Pct
*Bradley	15	3	.833	22	8	.733
†Illinois St	13	5	.722	22	12	.647
*Tulsa	13	6	.684	22	8	.733
SW Missouri St.	11	7	.611	16	12	.571
Creighton	9	9	.500	14	15	.483
Evansville	9	10	.474	13	14	.481
Northern Iowa	8	10	.444	14	13	.519
Drake	8	10	.444	12	15	.444
Indiana St.	6	12	.333	10	16	.385
Southern Illinois	4	14	.222	11	18	.379
Wichita St.	4	14	.222	8	21	.276

Conf. Tourney Final: Tulsa 60, Bradley 46.
* **NCAA Tourney (0-2):** Bradley (0-1), Tulsa (0-1).
† **NIT Tourney (2-1):** Illinois St. (2-1).

North Atlantic Conference

	Conference W	L	Pct	Overall W	L	Pct
*Drexel	17	1	.944	27	4	.871
Boston University	13	5	.722	18	11	.621
Towson St.	11	7	.611	16	12	.571
Delaware	11	7	.611	15	12	.556
Maine	11	7	.611	15	13	.536
Vermont	10	8	.556	12	15	.444
Hofstra	5	13	.278	9	18	.333
New Hampshire	5	13	.278	6	21	.222
Hartford	5	13	.278	6	22	.214
Northeastern	2	16	.111	4	24	.143

Conf. Tourney Final: Drexel 76, Boston University 67.
* **NCAA Tourney (1-1):** Drexel (1-1).

Northeast Conference

	Conference W	L	Pct	Overall W	L	Pct
†Mt. St. Mary's	16	2	.889	21	8	.724
†Marist	14	4	.778	22	7	.759
*Monmouth	14	4	.778	20	10	.667
Rider	12	6	.667	19	11	.633
St. Francis-PA	11	7	.611	13	14	.481
Wagner	7	11	.389	10	17	.370
Fairleigh Dickinson	6	12	.333	7	20	.259
LIU Brooklyn	5	13	.278	9	19	.321
St. Francis-NY	3	15	.167	9	18	.333
Robert Morris	2	16	.111	5	23	.179

Conf. Tourney Final: Monmouth 60, Rider 59.
* **NCAA Tourney (0-1):** Monmouth (0-1).
† **NIT Tourney (0-2):** Marist (0-1), Mount St. Mary's (0-1).

Ohio Valley Conference

	Conference W	L	Pct	Overall W	L	Pct
†Murray St	12	4	.750	19	10	.655
Tennessee St.	11	5	.688	15	13	.536
*Austin Peay	10	6	.625	19	11	.633
Middle Tenn. St	9	7	.563	15	12	.556
Tennessee-Martin	9	7	.563	13	14	.481
Eastern Kentucky	7	9	.438	13	14	.481
Tennessee Tech	7	9	.438	13	15	.464
SE Missouri St	5	11	.313	8	19	.296
Morehead St	2	14	.125	7	20	.259

Conf. Tourney Final: Austin Peay 70, Murray St. 68.
* **NCAA Tourney (0-1):** Austin Peay (0-1).
† **NIT Tourney (0-1):** Murray St. (0-1).

Pacific-10 Conference

	Conference W	L	Pct	Overall W	L	Pct
*UCLA	16	2	.889	23	8	.742
*Arizona	13	5	.722	26	7	.788
*Stanford	12	6	.667	20	9	.690
*California	11	7	.611	17	11	.607
†Washington	9	9	.500	16	12	.571
Oregon	9	9	.500	16	13	.552
†Washington St	8	10	.444	17	12	.586
Arizona St	6	12	.333	11	16	.407
USC	4	14	.222	11	19	.367
Oregon St.	2	16	.111	4	23	.148

Conf. Tourney Final: Pac-10 has no tournament.
* **NCAA Tourney (3-4):** Arizona (2-1), Stanford (1-1), California (0-1), UCLA (0-1).
† **NIT Tourney (1-2):** Washington St. (1-1), Washington (0-1).

Patriot League

	Conference W	L	Pct	Overall W	L	Pct
Navy	9	3	.750	15	12	.556
*Colgate	9	3	.750	15	15	.500
Bucknell	8	4	.667	17	11	.607
Holy Cross	8	4	.667	16	13	.551
Lafayette	4	8	.333	7	20	.259
Army	2	10	.167	7	20	.259
Lehigh	2	10	.167	4	23	.148

Tiebreaker: Three coin flips determined the conference tournament seedings after all other tiebreakers failed to break the deadlocks. Colgate got the top seed and a first round bye, winning a flip with Navy. Holy Cross won the third seed on a flip with Bucknell and Lehigh won the sixth seed on a flip with Army.

Conf. Tourney Final: Colgate 74, Holy Cross 65.
* **NCAA Tourney (0-1):** Colgate (0-1).

Best in Show

Conferences with at least two wins in 1996 NCAA's; number of tournament teams in parentheses.

	W-L		W-L
SEC (4)	14-3	Big Eight (4)	4-4
Big East (5)	12-5	Pac-10 (4)	3-4
Atlantic 10 (4)	6-4	SWC (2)	3-2
Conference USA (4)	6-4	WAC (2)	3-2
ACC (6)	6-6	Big Ten (5)	2-5

Final NCAA Men's Division I Standings (Cont.)

Southeastern Conference

Eastern Div.	Conference W	L	Pct	Overall W	L	Pct
*Kentucky	16	0	1.000	34	2	.944
*Georgia	9	7	.563	21	10	.677
†South Carolina	8	8	.500	19	12	.613
†Vanderbilt	7	9	.439	18	14	.563
†Tennessee	6	10	.375	14	15	.483
Florida	6	10	.375	12	16	.428

Western Div.	Conference W	L	Pct	Overall W	L	Pct
*Mississippi St	10	6	.625	26	8	.765
*Arkansas	9	7	.563	20	13	.606
†Alabama	9	7	.563	19	13	.594
†Auburn	6	10	.375	19	13	.594
Mississippi	6	10	.375	12	15	.444
Louisiana St	4	12	.250	12	17	.414

Conf. Tourney Final: Mississippi St. 84, Kentucky 73.
***NCAA Tourney (14-3):** Kentucky (6-0), Mississippi St. (4-1), Georgia (2-1), Arkansas (2-1).
†**NIT Tourney (6-6):** Alabama (3-2), South Carolina (2-1), Vanderbilt (1-1), Auburn (0-1), Tennessee (0-1).

Southern Conference

North Div.	Conference W	L	Pct	Overall W	L	Pct
†Davidson	14	0	1.000	25	5	.833
Virginia Military	10	4	.714	18	10	.643
Marshall	8	6	.571	17	11	.607
Appalachian St	3	11	.214	8	20	.286
East Tennessee St	3	11	.214	7	20	.259

South Div.	Conference W	L	Pct	Overall W	L	Pct
*Western Carolina	10	4	.714	17	13	.567
Tenn-Chattanooga	9	5	.643	15	12	.556
Furman	6	8	.429	10	17	.370
The Citadel	5	9	.357	10	16	.385
Georgia Southern	2	12	.143	3	23	.115

Conf. Tourney Final: Western Carolina 69, Davidson 60.
***NCAA Tourney (0-1):** Western Carolina (0-1).
†**NIT Tourney (0-1):** Davidson (0-1).

Southland Conference

	Conference W	L	Pct	Overall W	L	Pct
*NE Louisiana	13	5	.722	16	14	.533
North Texas	12	6	.667	15	13	.536
Texas-San Antonio	12	6	.667	14	14	.500
Stephen F. Austin	11	7	.611	17	11	.607
McNeese St	11	7	.611	15	12	.556
Sam Houston St	9	9	.500	11	16	.407
SW Texas St	7	11	.389	11	15	.423
Texas-Arlington	7	11	.389	11	15	.423
Nicholls St	5	13	.278	5	21	.192
Northwestern St	3	15	.167	5	21	.192

Conf. Tourney Final: NE Louisiana 71, North Texas 60.
***NCAA Tourney (0-1):** NE Louisiana (0-1).

Southwest Conference

	Conference W	L	Pct	Overall W	L	Pct
*Texas Tech	14	0	1.000	30	2	.938
Houston	11	3	.786	17	10	.630
*Texas	10	4	.714	21	10	.677
TCU	6	8	.429	15	15	.500
Rice	5	9	.357	14	14	.500
Baylor	4	10	.286	9	18	.333
Texas A&M	3	11	.214	11	16	.407
SMU	3	11	.214	8	20	.286

Conf. Tourney Final: Texas Tech 75, Texas 73.
***NCAA Tourney (3-2):** Texas Tech (2-1), Texas (1-1).

Southwestern Athletic Conference

	Conference W	L	Pct	Overall W	L	Pct
*Miss. Valley St	11	3	.786	22	7	.759
Jackson St	11	3	.786	16	13	.552
Southern	8	5	.615	16	12	.571
Texas Southern	7	7	.500	12	14	.462
Alcorn St	7	7	.500	10	15	.400
Grambling	6	7	.462	12	15	.444
Alabama St	5	9	.357	8	19	.296
Prairie View A&M	0	14	.000	4	23	.148

Conf. Tourney Final: Miss. Valley St. 111, Jackson St. 94.
***NCAA Tourney (0-1):** Miss. Valley St. (0-1).

Sun Belt Conference

	Conference W	L	Pct	Overall W	L	Pct
†Ark-Little Rock	14	4	.778	23	7	.767
*New Orleans	14	4	.778	21	9	.700
Jacksonville	10	8	.556	15	13	.536
Western Kentucky	10	8	.556	13	14	.481
SW Louisiana	9	9	.500	16	12	.571
Lamar	7	11	.389	12	15	.444
South Alabama	7	11	.389	12	15	.444
Arkansas St	7	11	.389	9	18	.333
Louisiana Tech	6	12	.333	11	17	.393
Texas-Pan Am	6	12	.333	9	19	.321

Conf. Tourney Final: New Orleans 57, Ark-Little Rock 56.
***NCAA Tourney (0-1):** New Orleans (0-1).
†**NIT Tourney (0-1):** Ark-Little Rock (0-1).

Trans America Athletic Conference

East	Conference W	L	Pct	Overall W	L	Pct
†Col. of Charleston	15	1	.938	25	4	.862
Campbell	11	5	.688	17	11	.607
*Central Florida	6	10	.375	11	19	.367
Stetson	6	10	.375	10	17	.370
Florida Int'l	6	11	.353	13	15	.464
Florida Atlantic	5	11	.313	9	18	.333

West	Conference W	L	Pct	Overall W	L	Pct
Samford	11	5	.688	16	11	.593
SE Louisiana	11	5	.688	15	12	.556
Centenary	8	8	.500	11	16	.407
Mercer	8	9	.471	15	14	.517
Georgia St	6	10	.375	10	16	.385
Jacksonville St	4	12	.250	10	17	.370

Conf. Tourney Final: Central Florida 86, Mercer 77.
***NCAA Tourney (0-1):** Central Florida (0-1).
†**NIT Tourney (1-1):** Col. of Charleston (1-1).

West Coast Conference

	Conference W	L	Pct	Overall W	L	Pct
†Gonzaga	10	4	.714	21	9	.700
* Santa Clara	10	4	.714	20	9	.690
Loyola Marymount	8	6	.571	18	11	.621
San Francisco	8	6	.571	15	13	.536
* Portland	7	7	.500	19	11	.633
San Diego	6	8	.429	14	14	.500
St. Mary's (CA)	5	9	.357	12	15	.444
Pepperdine	2	12	.143	10	18	.357

Conf. Tourney Final: Portland 76, Gonzaga 68.
* **NCAA Tourney (1-2):** Santa Clara (1-1), Portland (0-1)
†**NIT Tourney (0-1):** Gonzaga (0-1).

Division I Independents

	W	L	Pct
Oral Roberts	18	9	.667
Wofford	4	22	.154

Western Athletic Conference

	Conference W	L	Pct	Overall W	L	Pct
* Utah	15	3	.833	27	7	.794
* New Mexico	14	4	.778	28	5	.848
†Fresno St	13	5	.722	22	11	.667
†Colorado St	11	7	.611	18	12	.600
Brigham Young	9	9	.500	15	13	.536
San Diego St.	8	10	.444	15	14	.517
Wyoming	8	10	.444	14	15	.483
Hawaii	7	11	.389	10	17	.370
Texas-El Paso	4	14	.222	13	16	.448
Air Force	1	17	.056	5	23	.179

Conf. Tourney Final: New Mexico 64, Utah 60.
* **NCAA Tourney (3-2):** Utah (2-1), New Mexico (1-1).
†**NIT Tourney (2-2):** Fresno St. (2-1), Colorado St. (0-1).

Annual Awards

Players of the Year

Marcus Camby, UMass ....AP, Naismith, Wooden NABC, *TSN*, USBWA
Ray Allen, UConn ....UPI

Wooden Award Voting

Presented since 1977 by the Los Angeles Athletic Club and named after the former Purdue All-America and UCLA coach John Wooden. Voting done by 984-member panel of national media; candidates must have a cumulative college grade point average of 2.0 (out of 4.0).

		Cl	Pos	Pts
1	Marcus Camby, UMass	Jr.	C	4271
2	Ray Allen, UConn	Jr.	G	3617
3	Tim Duncan, Wake Forest	Jr.	C	3328
4	Allen Iverson, Georgetown	So.	G	3316
5	Kerry Kittles, Villanova	Sr.	F	2011
6	Tony Delk, Kentucky	Sr.	G	1581
7	Jacque Vaughn, Kansas	Jr.	G	1408
8	Keith Van Horn, Utah	Jr.	F	1285
9	Stephon Marbury, Georgia Tech	Fr.	G	1024
10	Danny Fortson, Cincinnati	So.	F	980
11	John Wallace, Syracuse	Sr.	F	932
12	Jason Sasser, Texas Tech	Sr.	F	606
13	Brian Evans, Indiana	Sr.	F	458
14	Steve Nash, Santa Clara	Sr.	G	402
15	Shareef Abdur-Rahim, Califorinia	Fr.	F	317
16	Brevin Knight, Staford	Sr.	G	311
17	Charles O'Bannon, UCLA	Jr.	F	278

Defensive Player of the Year

Formerly the Henry Iba Award, for defensive skills, sportsmanship and dedication; first presented by the Rotary Club of River Oaks in Houston in 1987 and named after the late Oklahoma St. and U.S. Olympic team coach. Voting done by NABC.

Tim Duncan, Wake Forest, C

Coaches of the Year

Gene Keady, Purdue ....AP, UPI, USBWA
John Calipari, UMass ....Naismith, NABC, *TSN*

Consensus All-America Team

The NCAA Division I players cited most frequently by the following All-America selectors: AP, U.S. Basketball Writers, National Assn. of Basketball Coaches and UPI. There were no holdovers from the 1994-95 first team; (*) indicates unanimous first team selection.

First Team

	Class	Hgt	Pos
Marcus Camby, Massachusetts*	Jr.	6-11	C
Ray Allen, Connecticut*	Jr.	6-5	G/F
Tim Duncan, Wake Forest*	Jr.	6-10	C
Allen Iverson, Georgetown*	So.	6-1	G
Tony Delk, Kentucky	Sr.	6-2	G

Second Team

	Class	Hgt	Pos
Kerry Kittles, Villanova	Sr.	6-5	G
Danny Fortson, Cincinnati	So.	6-7	F
Keith Van Horn, Utah	Jr.	6-9	C
Jacque Vaughn, Kansas	Jr.	6-1	G
John Wallace, Syracuse	Sr.	6-8	F

Third Team

	Class	Hgt	Pos
Lorenzen Wright, Memphis	So.	6-11	C
Brian Evans, Indiana	Sr.	6-8	F
Jason Sasser, Texas Tech	Sr.	6-7	F
Stephon Marbury, Georgia Tech	Fr.	6-1	G
Shareef Abdur-Rahim, California	Fr.	6-10	F

Div. II and III Annual Awards

Awarded by the National Association of Basketball Coaches.

Players of the Year

Div. II	Stand Gouard, Southern Indiana
Div. III	David Benter, Hanover College

Coaches of the Year

Div. II	Gary Garner, Fort Hays St.
Div. III	Dr. John Giannini, Rowan College
NAIA	Larry Holley, William Jewell College
JuCo	Gary Shourds, Sullivan College

NCAA Men's Division I Leaders

Includes games through NCAA and NIT tourneys.

INDIVIDUAL

Scoring

	Cl	Gm	FG%	3Pt/Att	FT%	Reb	Ast	Stl	Blk	Pts	Avg	Hi
Kevin Granger, Texas Southern	Sr.	24	49.5	30/86	79.3	168	105	35	4	648	**27.0**	38
Marcus Brown, Murray St.	Sr.	29	47.4	74/175	84.1	139	119	65	8	767	**26.4**	45
Bubba Wells, Austin Peay	Jr.	30	54.9	34/78	75.7	219	86	48	45	789	**26.3**	42
JaFonde Williams, Hampton	Sr.	26	41.2	83/228	79.8	103	66	41	0	669	**25.7**	43
Bonzi Wells, Ball St.	So.	28	49.4	31/92	70.8	246	80	87	34	712	**25.4**	41
Anquell McCollum, Western Carolina	Sr.	30	45.4	99/241	83.1	159	94	45	9	751	**25.0**	41
Allen Iverson, Georgetown	So.	37	48.0	87/238	67.8	141	173	124	16	926	**25.0**	40
Eddie Benton, Vermont	Sr.	26	37.4	69/201	84.3	86	140	27	1	636	**24.5**	45
Matt Alosa, New Hampshire	Sr.	26	41.8	76/220	83.3	79	105	28	2	624	**24.0**	39
Ray Allen, Connecticut	Jr.	35	47.2	115/247	81.0	228	117	60	18	818	**23.4**	39
Michael Hart, Tenn.-Martin	Sr.	27	56.4	1/1	71.5	248	18	23	6	616	**22.8**	38
Tunji Awojobi, Boston Univ.	Jr.	29	58.2	3/23	70.6	314	49	52	58	658	**22.7**	43
Darren McLinton, James Madison	Sr.	30	42.5	122/294	85.7	65	88	50	2	680	**22.7**	34
Reggie Elliott, Mercer	Sr.	29	40.7	54/190	79.8	186	126	57	13	656	**22.6**	36
Jeff Nordgaard, Wisc.-Green Bay	Sr.	29	55.4	8/25	71.0	183	68	29	10	655	**22.6**	38
Reggie Freeman, Texas	Jr.	31	37.6	87/270	73.2	208	120	70	10	695	**22.4**	37
Anthony Harris, Hawaii	Sr.	28	49.4	24/73	83.2	82	70	18	2	626	**22.4**	32
Jason Daisy, Northern Iowa	Jr.	27	48.9	68/162	73.0	107	62	32	7	603	**22.3**	36
Chris McGuthrie, Mt. St. Mary's	Sr.	29	43.7	102/261	80.6	70	90	56	2	647	**22.3**	41
John Wallace, Syracuse	Sr.	38	48.9	37/88	76.3	329	90	44	63	845	**22.2**	33

Rebounds

	Cl	Gm	No	Avg
Marcus Mann, Mississippi Val.	Sr.	29	394	13.6
Malik Rose, Drexel	Sr.	31	409	13.2
Adonal Foyle, Colgate	So.	29	364	12.6
Tim Duncan, Wake Forest	Jr.	32	395	12.3
Scott Farley, Mercer	Sr.	29	349	12.0
Chris Ensminger, Valparaiso	Sr.	32	368	11.5
Thaddeous DeLaney, Chas. (S.C.)	Jr.	29	330	11.4
Alan Tomidy, Marist	Sr.	29	329	11.3
Quadre Lollis, Montana St.	Sr.	30	340	11.3
Kyle Snowden, Harvard	Jr.	26	289	11.1
Tim Moore, Houston	Sr.	21	228	10.9
Tunji Awojobi, Boston Univ.	Jr.	29	314	10.8
Curtis Fincher, Eastern Ky.	Sr.	27	292	10.8
Greg Logan, Maine	Sr.	28	300	10.7
Monte O'Quinn, NE Ill.	Sr.	27	285	10.6

Assists

	Cl	Gm	No	Avg
Raimonds Miglinieks, UC-Irvine	Sr.	27	230	8.5
Curtis McCants, George Mason	Jr.	27	223	8.3
Dan Pogue, Campbell	Sr.	23	183	8.0
Pointer Williams, McNeese St.	Sr.	27	200	7.4
Lazarus Sims, Syracuse	Sr.	38	281	7.4
Brevin Knight, Stanford	Jr.	29	212	7.3
Phillip Turner, UC-Santa Barb.	Sr.	26	190	7.3
Reggie Geary, Arizona	Sr.	33	231	7.0
David Fizdale, San Diego	Sr.	28	195	7.0
Aaron Hutchins, Marquette	So.	31	215	6.9
Colby Pierce, Austin Peay	Jr.	30	205	6.8
Kyle Kessel, Texas A&M	So.	27	183	6.8
Jamar Smiley, Illinois St.	So.	34	229	6.7
Wes Flanigan, Auburn	Jr.	32	214	6.7
Edgar Padilla, Massachusetts	Jr.	37	247	6.7

Field Goal Percentage

Minimum 5 Field Goals made per game.

	Cl	Gm	FT	FTA	Pct
Quadre Lollis, Montana St.	Sr.	30	212	314	67.5
Daniel Watts, Nevada	Sr.	29	145	221	65.6
Lincoln Abrams, Centenary	Sr.	27	187	286	65.4
Alexander Koul, G. Washington	So.	29	163	254	64.2
Terquin Mott, Coppin St.	Jr.	28	208	326	63.8
Antawn Jamison, N. Carolina	Fr.	32	201	322	62.4
Stanley Caldwell, Tennessee St.	Sr.	22	110	178	61.8
Greg Smith, Delaware	Jr.	27	173	282	61.3
Marcus Mann, Mississippi Val.	Sr.	29	251	415	60.5
Curtis Fincher, Eastern Ky.	Sr.	27	148	245	60.4

3-Pt Field Goal Percentage

Minimum 1.5 Three-Point FG made per game.

	Cl	Gm	FG	FGA	Pct
Joe Stafford, Western Carolina	Jr.	30	58	110	52.7
Ricky Peral, Wake Forest	Jr.	32	51	100	51.0
Justyn Tebbs, Weber St.	Sr.	30	50	100	50.0
Aaron Brown, Central Mich.	Fr.	26	51	104	49.0
Isaac Fontaine, Washington St.	Jr.	29	66	136	48.5
Mike DeRocckis, Drexel	Fr.	31	85	178	47.8
Mike Frensley, St. Peter's	Sr.	27	58	123	47.2
Pete Lisicky, Penn St.	So.	27	89	189	47.1
Jimmy DeGraffenried, Weber St.	Sr.	30	47	100	47.0
Justin Jones, Utah St.	So.	33	77	165	46.7

Free Throw Percentage

Minimum 2.5 Free Throws made per game.

	Cl	Gm	FT	FTA	Pct
Mike Dillard, Sam Houston St.	Jr.	25	63	68	92.6
Dion Cross, Stanford	Sr.	29	81	88	92.0
Roderick Howard, NC-Charlotte	Jr.	29	93	103	90.3
Geoff Billet, Rutgers	Fr.	26	72	80	90.0
Steve Nash, Santa Clara	Sr.	29	101	113	89.4
Derek Grimm, Missouri	Jr.	33	100	113	88.5
Marcus Wilson, Evansville	Fr.	25	75	85	88.2
Nod Carter, Middle Tenn. St.	Jr.	27	104	118	88.1
Alhamisi Simms, Md.-Balt. Coun	Fr.	27	74	84	88.1

3-Pt Field Goals Per Game

	Cl	Gm	No	Avg
Dominick Young, Fresno St.	Jr.	29	120	4.1
Darren McLinton, James Madison	Sr.	30	122	4.1
Keith Veney, Marshall	Jr.	28	111	4.0
Paul Marshall, Northeast La.	Sr.	30	115	3.8
Troy Hudson, Southern Ill.	So.	25	93	3.7
Mark Lueking, Army	Sr.	27	99	3.7
Troy Green, Southeastern La.	Fr.	27	98	3.6
James Hannah, Grambling	Jr.	28	101	3.6
David Sivulich, St. Mary's (Cal.)	So.	27	96	3.6
Eric Washington, Alabama	Jr.	32	113	3.5

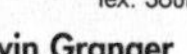
Tex. Southern
Kevin Granger
Scoring

Miss. Valley St.
Marcus Mann
Rebounds

UC Irvine
Raimonds Miglinieks
Assists

Central Conn. St.
Keith Closs
Blocked Shots

Blocked Shots

	Cl	Gm	No	Avg
Keith Closs, Central Conn. St.	So.	28	178	6.4
Adonal Foyle, Colgate	So.	29	165	5.7
Roy Rogers, Alabama	Sr.	32	156	4.9
Jerome James, Florida A&M	So.	27	119	4.4
Alan Tomidy, Marist	Sr.	29	113	3.9
Peter Aluma, Liberty	Jr.	29	113	3.9
Marcus Camby, Massachusetts	Jr.	33	128	3.9
Tim Duncan, Wake Forest	Jr.	32	120	3.8
Calvin Booth, Penn St.	Fr.	28	101	3.6
Lorenzo Coleman, Tennessee Tech	Jr.	28	96	3.4

Steals

	Cl	Gm	No	Avg
Pointer Williams, McNeese St.	Sr.	27	118	4.4
Johnny Rhodes, Maryland	Sr.	30	110	3.7
Roderick Taylor, Jackson St.	Sr.	29	106	3.7
Rasul Salahuddin, Long Beach St.	Sr.	28	101	3.6
Andrell Hoard, NE Illinois	Jr.	27	97	3.6
Ben Larson, Cal Poly-SLO	Fr.	29	100	3.4
Allen Iverson, Georgetown	So.	37	124	3.4
Bonzi Wells, Ball St.	So.	28	87	3.1
Jerry McCullough, Pittsburgh	Sr.	25	76	3.0
Edgar Padilla, Massachusetts	Jr.	37	108	2.9

Single Game Highs

Individual Points

No		Opponent	Date
46	M. Brown, Murray St.	Wash. (Mo.)	12/16
45	Eddie Benton, Vermont	Hartford	2/2
43	S. Cotright, Cal Poly SLO	Geo. Mason	1/13
43	T. Awojobi, Boston Univ.	Vermont	2/10
43	Steve Rich, Miami-FL	St. John's	2/20
42	Eddie Benton, Vermont	Hofstra	12/9
42	B. Wells, Austin Peay	Air Force	12/29
42	Eddie Benton, Vermont	Hartford	1/14
42	D. McMahan, Winthrop	Coa. Carolina	1/15
	Seven tied with 41 points each.		

Team Points

No		Opponent	Date
142	Prairie View	Bay Ridge Christ. (NCCAA)	11/27
142	Geo. Mason	Troy St. (NCAA I)	11/28
141	Tulsa	Prairie View (NCAA I)	12/17
139	Geo. Mason	Delaware St. (NCAA I)	11/25
132	Colorado	Geo. Mason (NCAA I)	12/2
129	Kentucky	LSU (NCAA I)	1/16
128	Chicago St.	Troy St. (NCAA I)	1/8

TEAM

Scoring Offense

	Gm	W-L	Pts	Avg
Troy St.	27	11-16	2551	94.5
Kentucky	36	34-2	3292	91.4
Marshall	28	17-11	2560	91.4
George Mason	27	11-16	2443	90.5
Southern-B.R.	28	17-11	2521	90.0
Mississippi Val.	29	22-7	2486	85.7
Southeastern La.	27	15-12	2296	85.0
Davidson	30	25-5	2528	84.3
Va. Military	28	18-10	2358	84.2
Weber St.	30	20-10	2524	84.1
Texas Christian	30	15-15	2519	84.0
Eastern Mich.	31	25-6	2594	83.7
Georgetown	37	29-8	3082	83.3
Drexel	31	27-4	2560	82.6
Connecticut	35	32-3	2890	82.6

Scoring Defense

	Gm	W-L	Pts	Avg
Princeton	29	22-7	1498	51.7
Wisc.-Green Bay	29	25-4	1620	55.9
South Alabama	27	12-15	1571	58.2
Temple	33	20-13	1922	58.2
NC-Wilmington	29	13-16	1694	58.4
Harvard	26	15-11	1581	60.8
Wake Forest	32	26-6	1963	61.3
Manhattan	29	17-12	1802	62.1
Charleston (S.C.)	29	25-4	1806	62.3
Massachusetts	37	35-2	2307	62.4
Virginia Tech	29	23-6	1825	62.9
Clemson	29	18-11	1826	63.0
Tennessee	29	14-15	1827	63.0
Canisius	30	19-11	1891	63.0
St. Peter's	27	15-12	1702	63.0

Scoring Margin

	Off	Def	Margin
Kentucky	91.4	69.4	+22.1
Connecticut	82.6	64.7	+17.9
Drexel	82.6	66.3	+16.3
Davidson	84.3	68.2	+16.0
Kansas	80.6	65.3	+15.4
Georgetown	83.3	68.8	+14.5
Cincinnati	79.6	65.2	+14.4
Utah	76.7	63.9	+12.9
Texas Tech	82.2	69.4	+12.8
Massachusetts	74.8	62.4	+12.5
Charleston (S.C.)	74.6	62.3	+12.3
Iowa	79.6	67.9	+11.8
Tulsa	76.4	65.0	+11.4
Georgia	79.2	68.1	+11.2
Montana St.	80.8	69.9	+10.9
Miami (Ohio)	74.8	63.9	+10.9

Underclassmen in NBA Draft

23 Division I Players (14 Juniors, 7 sophomores, 2 fresmen), one Division III player, one NAIA player, four junior college players, three high school seniors, and four players from overseas forfeited the remainder of their college eligibility and declared for the 1996 NBA Draft which took place in E. Rutherford, N.J. on June 26.

Players are listed in alphabetical order; first round selections in **bold** type.

	Cl	Drafted by	Overall Pick
Shareef Abdur-Rahim, Cal	Fr.	Vancouver	3
Ray Allen, Connecticut	Jr.	Minnesota	5
Kobe Bryant, Lower Merion HS	HS	Charlotte	13
Marcus Camby, Massachusetts	Jr.	Toronto	2
Erick Dampier, Mississippi St	Jr.	Indiana	10
Randy Edney, Mt. St. Mary's	Jr.	Not drafted	—
Eric Gingold, Williams College	Jr.	Not drafted	—
LaMarcus Golden, Tennessee	So.	Not drafted	—
Ronnie Henderson, LSU	Jr.	Washington	55
Zydrunas Ilgauskas, Lithuania	—	Cleveland	20
Allen Iverson, Georgetown	So.	Philadelphia	1
Willie Jackson, Lawson State CC	—	Not drafted	—
Dontae' Jones, Mississippi St	Jr.	New York	21
Chris Kingsbury, Iowa	Jr.	Not drafted	—
Priest Lauderdale, Peristeri Greece	—	Atlanta	28
Idris Lee, Mount Senario (Wisc.)	Jr.	Not drafted	—
Randy Livingston, LSU	So.	Houston	42
Michael Lloyd, Syracuse	Jr.	Not drafted	—
Stephon Marbury, Georgia Tech	Fr.	Milwaukee*	4
Richard Matienzo, Miami-Dade CC	Fr.	Not drafted	—
Dut Mayar Madut, Frank Phillips	So.	Not drafted	—
Taj McDavid, Palmetto HS	HS	Not drafted	—
Jeff McInnis, North Carolina	So.	Denver	37
Chris Nurse, Delaware St	Jr.	Not drafted	—
Jermaine O'Neal, Eau Claire HS	HS	Portland	17
Jason Osborne, Louisville	Jr.	Not drafted	—
Jesse Pate, Arkansas	Jr.	Not drafted	—
Vitaly Potapenko, Wright St	Jr.	Cleveland	12
Efthimios Rentzias, Paok Greece	—	Denver	23
Darnell Robinson, Arkansas	Jr.	Dallas	58
Greg Simpson, West Virginia	Jr.	Not drafted	—
Kevin Simpson, Dixie College	So.	Not drafted	—
Predrag Stojakovic, Paok Greece	—	Sacramento	14
Antoine Walker, Kentucky	So.	Boston	6
Samaki Walker, Louisville	So.	Dallas	9
Lorenzen Wright, Memphis	So.	LA Clippers	7

Note: Sunday Adebayo of Arkansas, Carlos Knox of Indiana /Purdue, Terquin Mott of Coppin St., Mark Sanford of Washington, Jess Settles of Iowa, and Kebu Stewart of Cal St. Bakersfield declared for the draft then withdrew their names before the June 24 deadline.

High School Players to enter NBA

Player	Pro career
Tony Kappen	1946-47
Connie Simmons	1946-56
Joe Graboski	1948-62
Reggie Harding	1963-68
Moses Malone	1974-95
Bill Willoughby	1975-84
Darryl Dawkins	1975-89
Kevin Garnett	1995—
Kobe Bryant	1996—
Jermaine O'Neal	1996—

Note: Kappen started out in the American Basketball League and Malone started out in the American Basketball Association. Because they enrolled in a college, Lloyd Daniels (Mount St. Antonio), Thomas Hamilton (Pittsburgh) and Shawn Kemp (Kentucky/Trinity Valley CC) were not included on this list.

Dream Team 96, USA Select 90

On Saturday, July 6, 1996 at the Palace in Auburn Hills, Mich. the U.S. 22-and-under team, made up of college all-stars and coached by Stanford's Mike Montgomery, led by 17 points at the half and nearly upset the Men's Olympic Dream Team in the first exhibition game before the Summer Games in Atlanta.

Att: 21,454; **Officials:** Lonnie Dixon and Wayne Unruh.

USA Select 90

	Min	FG M-A	FT M-A	Pts	Reb O-T	Ast	PF
Shea Seals	23	8-11	0-0	20	1-2	1	2
Austin Croshere	16	3-4	4-4	10	1-4	4	4
Tim Duncan	27	2-6	5-6	9	2-6	1	3
Anthony Parker	15	2-4	0-0	4	0-2	1	3
Brevin Knight	23	3-9	2-2	8	0-0	5	1
Toby Bailey	13	2-2	2-2	6	0-0	0	1
Maurice Taylor	17	3-8	0-0	6	3-3	0	3
Paul Pierce	10	0-5	1-2	1	0-0	0	0
Brian Skinner	8	1-3	1-3	3	2-3	0	2
Chauncey Billups	10	3-7	0-0	7	0-1	2	2
Cory Carr	9	3-3	0-0	8	0-1	0	3
Tim Young	5	0-0	0-0	0	0-1	1	0
Pete Lisicky	2	0-1	0-0	0	0-0	0	0
Louis Bullock	9	2-3	4-5	8	0-0	0	0
Sam Okey	7	0-0	0-0	0	0-4	1	0
Geno Carlisle	6	0-1	0-1	0	0-0	2	1
TOTALS	200	32-67	17-22	90	12-27	18	25

Three-point FG: 9-16 (Seals 4-6, Bailey 2-2, Pierce 0-2, Billups, 1-2, Carr 2-2, Lisicky 0-1, Bullock 0-1, Carlisle 0-1); **Team Rebounds:** 6; **Blocks:** 1 (Croshere); **Turnovers:** 20 (Knight 3, Carr 3, Lisicky 3, Seals 2, Croshere 2, Taylor 2, Pierce 2, Parker 1, Bailey 1, Billups 1; **Steals:** 12 (Knight 4, Bullock 2, Billups 2, Duncan 1, Parker 1, Pierce 1, Okey 1.); **Percentages:** 2-Pt FG (.451), 3-Pt FG: (.563), Total FG (.478), Free Throws (.773).

USA National 96

	Min	FG M-A	FT M-A	Pts	Reb O-T	Ast	PF
Grant Hill	17	3-3	0-0	6	1-2	1	1
Karl Malone	18	4-6	5-6	13	1-4	0	2
Shaquille O'Neal	9	2-7	3-4	7	2-4	0	0
Reggie Miller	26	1-6	2-2	5	0-3	2	1
John Stockton	16	2-3	0-0	4	0-0	2	3
Scottie Pippen	23	6-9	4-6	17	1-5	4	0
Charles Barkley	18	4-4	3-3	11	2-7	1	1
Gary Payton	22	2-5	1-2	5	1-2	5	3
David Robinson	14	3-4	6-7	12	1-4	1	4
Mitch Richmond	11	0-3	0-2	0	0-0	2	2
Hakeem Olajuwon	19	6-9	4-5	16	1-3	0	3
Anfernee Hardaway	7	0-2	0-0	0	0-0	1	1
TOTALS	200	33-61	28-35	96	10-35	19	21

Three-point FG: 2-11 (Miller 1-5, Pippen 1-1, Payton 0-1, Richmond 0-2, Hardaway 0-2). **Team Rebounds:** 8; **Blocks:** 7 (Olajuwon 5, Hill 1, O'Neal 1); **Turnovers:** 21 (Barkley 4, Hill 3, Stockton 3, Miller 2, Payton 2, Robinson 2, Malone 1, O'Neal 1, Pippen 1, Olajuwon 1, Hardaway 1); **Steals:** 14 (Malone 3, Miller 2, Stockton 2, Payton 2, Hill 1, Pippen 1, Barkley 1, Richmond 1, Olajuwon 1); **Percentages:** 2-Pt FG (.620), 3-Pt FG: (.182), Total FG (.541), Free Throws (.800).

USA Select	59	31	— **90**
Dream Team	42	54	— **96**

Other Men's 1996 Tournaments

NIT Tournament

The 59th annual National Invitational Tournament had a 32-team field. First three rounds played on home courts of higher seeded teams. Semifinal, Third Place and Championship games played March 26-28 at Madison Square Garden, NY.

1st Round

at Rhode Island 82 .... Marist 77
Col. of Charleston 55 .... at Tennessee 49
at South Carolina 100 .... Davidson 73
at Vanderbilt 86 .... Ark-Little Rock 80
Alabama 72 .... at Illinois 69
at Missouri 89 .... Murray St. 85
at Fresno St. 58 .... Miami-OH 57
at Michigan St. 64 .... Washington 50
Tulane 87 .... OT .... at Auburn 73
at Minnesota 68 .... St. Louis 52
at Wisconsin 55 .... Manhattan 42
at Illinois St. 73 .... Mt. St. Mary's (Md.) 49
St. Joseph's 82 .... at Iona 78
Nebraska 91 .... at Colorado St. 83
at Washington St. 92 .... Gonzaga 73
Providence 91 .... at Fairfield 79

2nd Round

at South Carolina 80 .... Vanderbilt 70
Tulane 84 .... at Minnesota 65
Illinois St. 77 .... Wisconsin 62
at Alabama 72 .... Missouri 49
St. Joseph's 82 .... at Providence 62
at Nebraska 82 .... Washington St. 73
at Fresno St. 80 .... Michigan St. 70
at Rhode Island 62 .... OT .... Col. of Charleston 58

Quarterfinals

Alabama 68 .... at South Carolina 67
at Tulane 83 .... Illinois St. 72
at St. Joseph's 76 .... Rhode Island 59
Nebraska 83 .... Fresno St. 71

Semifinals

St. Joseph's 74 .... OT .... Alabama 69
Nebraska 90 .... Tulane 78

Third Place

Tulane 87 .... Alabama 76

Championship

Nebraska 60 .... St. Joseph's 56

Most Valuable Players

NIT
Erick Strickland
Nebraska guard

NCAA Division II
Sherick Simpson
Fort Hays St. forward

NCAA Division III
Terrence Stewart
Rowan College guard

NAIA Division I
Reggie Garrett
Oklahoma City forward

NAIA Division II
Damon Archibald
Albertson (Id.) guard

NCAA Division II

The eight regional winners of the 48-team field: NORTHEAST— St. Rose, N.Y. (28-3); EAST— California, Pa. (26-5); SOUTH ATLANTIC— Virginia Union. (27-2); SOUTH— Alabama A&M (27-2); SOUTH CENTRAL— North Alabama (24-7); GREAT LAKES— Northern Kentucky (23-6); NORTH CENTRAL— Fort Hays St., Kan. (31-0); WEST— Cal St. Bakersfield (26-3).
The Elite Eight was played March 20-23, in Louisville, Ky. There was no Third Place game.

Quarterfinals

California-PA 95 .... Alabama A&M 85
Fort Hays St. 71 .... North Alabama 68
Va. Union 99 .... St. Rose 72
N. Kentucky 56 .... CS-Bakersfield 55

Semifinals

Fort Hays St. 76 .... California-PA 56
N. Kentucky 68 .... Va. Union 66

Championship

Fort Hays St. 70 .... N. Kentucky 63

NCAA Division III

Sixty-four teams played into the 32-team Division III field. The four sectional winners: ATLANTIC— Rowan, N.J. (26-6); MIDDLE ATLANTIC— Franklin & Marshall (29-1); GREAT LAKES— Hope, Mich. (26-4); SOUTH— Illinois Wesleyan (26-2).
The Final Four was played March 15-16, at Salem Civic Center in Salem, Va.

Semifinals

Hope 76 .... Franklin & Marshall 57
Rowan 79 .... Illinois Wesleyan 77

Third Place

Illinois Wesleyan 89 .... Franklin & Marshall 57

Championship

Rowan 100 .... Hope 93

NAIA Division I

The quarterfinalists, in alphabetical order, after two rounds of the 32-team NAIA tournament: Belmont, Tenn. (27-10); Birmingham-Southern, Ala. (25-4); Cumberland, Ky. (28-5); East Central, Okla. (23-5); Geneva, Pa. (24-6); Georgetown, Ky. (34-2); Lipscomb, Tenn. (32-5); Oklahoma City (29-6).
All tournament games played, March 12-18, at the Mabee Center in Tulsa, Okla. There was no Third Place game.
Quarterfinals: Lipscomb, Tenn. 93, East Central, Okla. 75; Georgetown, Ky. 93, Geneva, Pa. 77; Oklahoma City 82, Birminghan Southern 66; Belmont, Tenn. 65, Cumberland, Ky. 60.
Semifinals: Georgetown, Ky. 97, Lipscomb, Tenn. 84; Oklahoma City 80, Belmont, Tenn. 77.
Championship: Oklahoma City 86, Georgetown, Ky. 80.

NAIA Division II

The semifinalists, in alphabetical order, after three rounds of the 32-team NAIA tournament: Albertson, Idaho (29-3); Walsh, Ohio (31-4); Whitworth, Wash. (25-4); William Jewell, Mo. (30-8).
All tournament games played, March 6-12, at Nampa, Idaho. There was no Third Place game.
Semifinals: Albertson 92, Walsh 79; Whitworth 87, William Jewel 83.
Championship: Albertson 81, Whitworth 72 (OT).

Lady Vols return to the summit

by David Scott

It was déja vu all over again. Sort of. For the first time in the history of either the men's or women's Final Four, the same four teams made back-to-back appearances at the season's final weekend when Tennessee, UConn, Stanford and Georgia convened in Charlotte on the last weekend of March, just as they had done last year in Minneapolis. "The same four got there, but it was a lot harder this time," said UConn Head Coach Geno Auriemma. "The competition was improved."

Auriemma probably got his first hint of that notion during his team's opening contest of the 1995-96 season when Louisiana Tech ended the Huskies 35-game winning streak with a dramatic 83-81 overtime win during the Tipoff Classic. So much for honoring thy National Champion.

But more than showing that UConn was indeed beatable, the exciting start to the season showed there could indeed be an encore to the Bird-Magic breakthrough-type season that UConn's undefeated run in 1994-95 had provided. The Huskies storybook ride gave the sport unprecedented exposure, coverage and certainly, fan support.

Indeed, as Auriemma pointed out, the women's game has reached a point where there are more good teams ready to challenge for the titles that seemed to be the birthright of programs like Louisiana Tech, USC, Stanford and Tennessee (10 championships between them since 1982). And even though Pat Summit's Lady Volunteers stormed through a 26-4 regular season and brought the school (and Summit) its fourth national championship, the emergence of other legitimate contenders, such as San Francisco and Colorado State, should put the dominant programs on call.

Summit ran her career record to 596-133 in 22 years, which translates into an incredible .818 winning percentage. By comparison, John Wooden had a .804 winning percentage and Adolph Rupp's was .822. The woman simply knows how to win.

"It gets tougher and tougher each year," Summit. "There are more quality teams and more quality players. You have to come out and play well every night of the season."

Which is what the Lady Vols did, outscoring opponents by an average of 15.4 points, winning 23 of their 32 games by double-digits (11 wins were by 20 or more) and stomping through six NCAA Tournament games, by an average of 20.3 points.

Michelle Marciniak (center) and her Tennessee teammates celebrate their 83-65 victory over Georgia, the Lady Vols' fourth women's basketball championship.

Tennessee gained revenge for its 1995 title game loss to UConn, by eliminating the Huskies 88-83 in overtime during the national semifinals. Two days later the Lady Vols beat Georgia (who took care of Stanford to advance) for the national championship.

Even with Rebecca Lobo's graduation from UConn, the game showed the ability to generate new (and marketable) stars like Final Four Most Outstanding Player Michelle Marciniak (Tennessee), National Player of the Year Saudia Roundtree (Georgia) and one of the best freshman ever, Tennessee's Chamique Holdsclaw. In fact, interest reached such a high level that the nation's premier marketer of roundball, the NBA, announced plans to sponsor a women's basketball league and the women's Final Four for the first (and likely last) time outdrew the men's Final Four (Charlotte Coliseum holds around 4,000 more than the Meadowlands).

But it was most assuredly Tennessee's second championship this decade (also 1991) that showed no matter how much the game progresses and gains in popularity, there will be one constant, the standard set by Pat Summitt and her program in Knoxville.

David Scott is a writer for *College Sports Magazine.*

Final Regular Season AP Women's Top 25 Poll

Taken **before** start of NCAA tournament.

The sportswriters & broadcasters poll: first place votes in parentheses; records through Monday, March 11, 1996; total points (based on 25 for 1st, 24 for 2nd, etc.); record in NCAA tourney and team lost to; head coach (career years and record including 1996 postseason), and preseason ranking. Teams in **bold** type went on to reach NCAA Final Four.

		Mar. 11 Record	Points	NCAA Recap	Head Coach	Preseason Rank
1	Louisiana Tech (37)	28-1	994	3-1 (Georgia)	Leon Barmore (14 yrs: 369-58)	4
2	**UConn** (2)	30-3	945	4-1 (Tennessee)	Geno Auriemma (11 yrs: 261-85)	1
3	**Stanford** (1)	25-2	912	4-1 (Georgia)	A. Tucker & M. Stanley (1 yr: 29-3)	7
4	**Tennessee**	26-4	882	6-0	Pat Summitt (22 yrs: 596-134)	6
5	**Georgia**	23-4	854	5-1 (Tennessee)	Andy Landers (21 yrs: 499-145)	2
6	Old Dominion	27-2	780	2-1 (Virginia)	Wendy Larry (12 yrs: 238-117)	31
7	Iowa	25-3	742	2-1 (Vanderbilt)	Angie Lee (1 yr: 27-4)	19
8	Penn St.	25-6	716	2-1 (Auburn)	Rene Portland (20 yrs: 465-147)	8
9	Texas Tech	24-4	651	2-1 (La. Tech)	Marsha Sharp (14 yrs: 330-111)	11
10	Alabama	22-7	617	2-1 (Stanford)	Rick Moody (7 yrs: 150-64)	24
11	Virginia	23-6	540	3-1 (Tennessee)	Debbie Ryan (19 yrs: 439-147)	3
12	Vanderbilt	20-7	538	3-1 (UConn)	Jim Foster (18 yrs: 376-161)	5
13	Duke	25-6	500	1-1 (San Francisco)	Gail Goestenkors (4 yrs: 76-42)	17
14	Clemson	22-7	470	1-1 (S.F. Austin St.)	Jim Davis (10 yrs: 208-99)	43
15	Purdue	20-10	451	0-1 (Notre Dame)	Lin Dunn (25 yrs: 447-257)	9
16	Florida	21-8	416	0-1 (San Francisco)	Carol Ross (6 yrs: 118-59)	26
17	Colorado	25-8	319	1-1 (Auburn)	Ceal Barry (17 yrs: 349-172)	14
18	Wisconsin	20-7	290	1-1 (Vanderbilt)	Jane Albright-Dieterle (12 yrs: 208-119)	22
19	Auburn	20-8	284	3-1 (Stanford)	Joe Ciampi (19 yrs: 449-130)	34
20	Kansas	20-9	207	2-1 (Tennessee)	Marian Washington (23 yrs: 432-252)	13
21	Notre Dame	22-7	172	1-1 (Texas Tech)	Muffet McGraw (14 yrs: 270-129)	52
22	Oregon St	19-8	161	0-1 (S.F. Austin St.)	Judy Spoelstra (6 yrs: 117-77)	20
23	N.C. State	19-9	140	1-1 (Alabama)	Kay Yow (25 yrs: 508-202)	12
24	Mississippi	18-10	123	0-1 (Toledo)	Van Chancellor (18 yrs: 423-143)	21
25	Texas A&M	20-11	51	0-1 (Kent)	Candi Harvey (6 yrs: 87-89)	28

Others receiving votes: 26. **Colorado St.** (25-4, 50); 27. **Texas** (20-8, 37); 28. **Stephen F. Austin St.** (25-3, 32); 29. **George Washington** (25-6, 29); 30. **Montana** (24-4, 27); 31. **DePaul** (20-9, 22); 32. **SW Missouri St.** (25-4, 15); 33. **Northwestern** (21-10, 6); 34. **Toledo** (24-5, 5); 35. **Louisiana St.** (19-10, 4); 36. **Arkansas** (20-11, 3), **Austin Peay** (21–8, 3), **Memphis** (20-10, 3) and **Ohio St.** (20-12, 3); 40. **Oklahoma St.** (19-9, 2), 41. **Grambling** (21-6, 1), **Hawaii** (23-5, 1), **Mid. Tenn. St.** (24–6, 1) and **Tulane** (21-9, 1).

Note: Stanford head coach Tara VanDerveer took a one-year leave to coach the USA Women's Olympic Basketball team. Assistants Amy Tucker and Marianne Stanley were named interim co-head coaches.

NCAA Women's Division I Leaders

Includes games through NCAA and NIT tourneys.

Scoring

	Cl	Gm	Pts	Avg
Cindy Blodgett, Maine	So.	32	889	27.8
Gray C. Harris, SE Mo. St.	Sr.	27	713	26.4
Gina Somma, Manhattan	Sr.	30	768	25.6
Shannon Johnson, S. Carolina	Sr.	28	691	24.7
Ashley Berggren, Illinois	So.	28	689	24.6
Lara Webb, Lamar	So.	29	709	24.4
Nadine Malcolm, Providence	Jr.	26	628	24.2
Shalonda Enis, Alabama	Jr.	32	766	23.9
Anita Maxwell, N. Mexico St.	Sr.	30	711	23.7
Jenni Ruff, Washington St.	Sr.	29	685	23.6
Tanja Kostic, Oregon St.	Sr.	28	650	23.2
Charmonique Stallworth, No Ill.	Sr.	22	508	23.1
Tina Thompson, USC	Jr.	27	623	23.1
Natasha Parks, Coppin St.	Sr.	26	593	22.8
Latasha Byears, DePaul	Sr.	30	683	22.8

High-Point Games

No		Opponent	Date
50	Shannon Johnson, S. Carolina	Appalach. St.	1/31
49	Tina Thompson, USC	UCLA	1/27
49	Gray C. Harris, SE Missouri	Williams Baptist	2/26
46	Kate McAllister, Pacific	Long Beach St.	2/23
	Five tied with 44 points each.		

Rebounds

	Cl	Gm	No	Avg
Dana Wynne, Seton Hall	Jr.	29	372	12.8
Deneka Knowles, SE La.	Sr.	26	318	12.2
Felecia Autry, Campbell	So.	27	329	12.2
Erica Scott, Mississippi Val.	Sr.	28	339	12.1
Timothea Clemmer, Wright St.	Sr.	27	316	11.7
Latasha Byears, DePaul	Sr.	30	351	11.7
Natasha Rezek, Pennsylvania	Sr.	26	302	11.6
Brandy Reed, Southern Miss.	So.	26	301	11.6
Kathy Caldwell, New Hampshire	Jr.	28	323	11.5
Laphelia Doss, Eastern Ky.	So.	27	310	11.5

Assists

	Cl	Gm	No	Avg
Brenda Pantoja, Arizona	Sr.	30	278	9.3
Heather Smith, Toledo	Sr.	31	263	8.5
Tina Nicholson, Penn St.	Sr.	34	283	8.3
Dayna Smith, Rhode Island	Sr.	29	233	8.0
Eliza Sokolowska, California	Sr.	25	186	7.4
Krissy Holden, Indiana St.	Jr.	26	190	7.3
Lisa Branch, Texas A&M	Sr.	32	231	7.2
Akia Hardy, Long Beach St.	Sr.	24	171	7.1
Patricia Penicheiro, Old Dominion	Jr.	32	226	7.1
Jennifer Sutter, Eastern Wash.	Jr.	27	189	7.0

1996 NCAA BASKETBALL WOMEN'S DIVISION I

WEST — NACOGDOCHES, TX

FIRST ROUND March 15-16

Team	Score
1 Stanford	82
16 Grambling	43
8 Colorado St.	66
9 Nebraska	62
5 N.C. State	77
12 Montana	68
4 Alabama	95
13 Appalachian St.	66
6 Auburn	73
11 Hawaii	53
3 Colorado	83
14 Tulane	75
7 Texas A&M	68
10 Kent	72
2 Penn St.	94
15 Youngstown St.	71

SECOND ROUND March 17-18

Team	Score
Stanford	94
Colorado St.	63
N.C. State	68
Alabama	88
Auburn	68
Colorado	61
Kent	59
Penn St.	86

REGIONALS March 23-25

Team	Score
Stanford	78
Alabama	76
Auburn	75
Penn St.	69
Stanford	71
Auburn	57

Regional winner: Stanford 76

SOUTHEAST — CHARLOTTESVILLE, VA

FIRST ROUND March 15-16

Team	Score
1 La. Tech	98
16 Central Florida	41
8 Utah	66
9 So. Mississippi	74
5 Purdue	60
12 Notre Dame	73
4 Texas Tech	78
13 Portland	61
6 Oregon St.	65
11 S.F. Austin	67
3 Clemson	79
14 Austin Peay	52
7 Oklahoma St.	90
10 Rhode Island	82
2 Georgia	98
15 St. Francis-PA	66

SECOND ROUND March 17-18

Team	Score
La. Tech	84
So. Miss.	46
N. Dame	67
Texas Tech	82
S.F. Austin (OT)	93
Clemson	88
Oklahoma St.	55
Georgia	83

REGIONALS March 23-25

Team	Score
La. Tech	66
Texas Tech	55
S.F. Austin	64
Georgia	78
La. Tech	76
Georgia	90

Regional winner: Georgia 84

EAST — ROSEMONT, IL

FIRST ROUND March 15-16

Team	Score
1 Tennessee	97
16 Radford	56
8 Memphis	75
9 Ohio St.	97
5 Texas	73
12 SW Missouri	55
4 Kansas	72
13 Middle Tenn	57
6 G. Washington	83
11 Maine	67
3 Virginia	100
14 Manhattan	55
7 Mississippi	53
10 Toledo	65
2 Old Dominion	83
15 Holy Cross	56

SECOND ROUND March 17-18

Team	Score
Tennessee	97
Ohio St.	65
Texas	70
Kansas	77
Geo. Wash.	73
Virginia	62
Toledo	66
Old Dominion	72

REGIONALS March 23-25

Team	Score
Tennessee	92
Kansas	71
Virginia	72
Old Dominion	60
Tennessee	52
Virginia	46

Regional winner: Tenn. (OT) 88

MIDWEST — SEATTLE

FIRST ROUND March 15-16

Team	Score
1 UConn	94
16 Howard	63
8 UMass (OT)	57
9 Michigan St.	60
5 Florida	61
12 San Francisco	68
4 Duke	85
13 James Madison	53
6 Wisconsin	74
11 Oregon	60
3 Vanderbilt	100
14 Harvard	83
7 DePaul	96
10 SMU	82
2 Iowa	72
15 Butler	67

SECOND ROUND March 17-18

Team	Score
UConn	88
Michigan St.	68
San Francisco	64
Duke	60
Wisconsin	82
Vanderbilt	96
DePaul	71
Iowa	72

REGIONALS March 23-25

Team	Score
UConn	72
San Francisco	44
Vanderbilt	74
Iowa	63
UConn	67
Vanderbilt	57

Regional winner: UConn 83

NATIONAL CHAMPIONSHIP

Tennessee 83
Georgia 65

FINAL FOUR
at Charlotte Coliseum
in Charlotte, N.C.
•••
Semifinals: March 29
Finals: March 31

WOMEN'S FINAL FOUR

at Charlotte Coliseum in Charlotte, NC (March 29–31)

Semifinals

Tennessee 88 ....OT ....Connecticut 83
Georgia 86..Stanford 76

Championship

Tennessee 83 ....Georgia 65

Most Outstanding Player: Michelle Marciniak, Tennessee senior guard. SEMIFINAL— 41 minutes, 21 points, 8 rebounds, 6 assists, 0 fouls; FINAL— 37 minutes, 10 points, 4 rebounds, 5 assists, 2 steals.

All-Tournament Team: Marciniak, foward Chamique Holdsclaw and center Tiffani Johnson of Tennessee; and forward La'Keshia Frett of Georgia.

NCAA Championship Game

Georgia 65

	Min	FG M-A	FT M-A	Pts	Reb O-T	A	F
La'Keshia Frett	37	10-18	4-4	25	6-16	0	1
Kedra Holland	33	4-12	1-1	11	1-1	5	4
Tracy Henderson	36	8-15	0-1	16	4-7	0	4
Saudia Roundtree	37	3-14	1-2	8	0-5	6	1
Rachel Powell	12	0-1	0-0	0	0-0	1	1
Pam Irwin	16	1-3	0-0	3	0-2	1	0
Signe Antvorskov	3	0-0	0-0	0	0-0	0	2
Kim Thompson	1	0-0	0-0	0	0-1	1	0
Kendi Taylor	1	0-1	0-0	0	0-1	0	0
Latrese Bush	16	1-4	0-0	2	2-2	0	4
Tiffany Walker	1	0-1	0-0	0	1-2	0	0
Brandi Decker	6	0-2	0-0	0	1-2	0	4
Tracy Walls	1	0-0	0-0	0	0-0	0	1
TOTALS	200	27-71	6-8	65	15-39	14	22

Three-point FG: 5–24 (Frett 1–1, Holland 2–8, Roundtree 1–7, Powell 0–1, Irwin 1–3, Taylor 0–1, Bush 0–2, Decker 0–1); **Team Rebounds:** None; **Blocked Shots:** 2 (Henderson 2); **Turnovers:** 14 (Roundtree 6, Frett 2, Holland 2, Bush, Henderson, Irwin, Powell); **Steals:** 7 (Irwin 2, Roundtree 2, Frett, Holland, Powell). **Percentages:** 2-Pt FG (.468); 3-Pt FG (.208); Total FG (.380); Free Throws (.750).

Tennessee 83

	Min	FG M-A	FT M-A	Pts	Reb O-T	A	F
Chamique Holdsclaw	34	6-16	4-5	16	5-14	3	0
Abby Conklin	23	5-8	0-0	14	0-4	3	2
Tiffani Johnson	28	7-10	2-2	16	3-5	1	2
Michelle Marciniak	37	5-13	0-1	10	0-4	5	1
Latina Davis	32	2-10	4-8	8	5-7	8	2
Kim Smallwood	1	0-0	1-2	1	1-1	0	0
Laurie Milligan	1	0-1	0-0	0	0-0	0	0
Misty Greene	1	0-1	0-0	0	0-0	0	0
Kellie Jolly	10	1-1	0-1	2	0-0	1	2
Brynae Laxton	12	2-7	0-0	4	2-3	0	1
Pashen Thompson	21	4-6	4-6	12	5-11	0	3
TOTALS	200	32-73	15-25	83	21-49	21	13

Three-point FG: 4–9 (Conklin 4–5, Davis 0–1, Johnson 0–1, Marciniak 0–2); **Team Rebounds:** 5; **Blocked Shots:** None; **Turnovers:** 11 (Marciniak 4, Conklin 2, Thompson 2, Holdsclaw, Laxton, Johnson); **Steals:** 8 (Davis 4, Marciniak 2, Holdsclaw, Jolly). **Percentages:** 2-Pt FG (.438); 3-Pt FG (.444); Total FG (.438); Free Throws (.600).

	1st	2nd	Final
Georgia (SEC)	37	28—	**65**
Tennessee (SEC)	42	41—	**83**

Technical Fouls: None. **Officials:** Sally Bell, Dee Kantner, Violet Palmer. **Attendance:** 23,291. **TV Rating:** 3.7/6 share (ESPN).

Final *USA Today*/CNN Coaches Poll

Taken **after** NCAA tournament.

Voted on by panel of 44 women's coaches and media following the NCAA tournament: first place votes in parentheses with final overall records.

		W-L
1	Tennessee (44)	32-4
2	Georgia	28-5
3	UConn	34-4
4	Stanford	29-3
5	Lousiana Tech	31-2
6	Virginia	26-7
7	Vanderbilt	23-8
8	Auburn	23-9
9	Iowa	27-4
10	Old Dominion	29-3
11	Alabama	24-8
12	Texas Tech	27-5
13	Penn St.	27-7
14	Stephen F. Austin	27-4
15	Kansas	22-10
16	San Francisco	24-8
17	Clemson	23-8
18	Colorado	26-9
19	Duke	26-7
20	Wisconsin	21-8
21	Notre Dame	23-8
22	Florida	21-9
23	DePaul	21-10
24	Colorado St.	26-5
25	Texas	21-9

Annual Awards

Players of the Year

Saudia Roundtree, Georgia........Naismith, USBWA, WBCA
Jennifer Rizzotti, UConn.......................................AP, Wade
Michi Atkins, Texas Tech ....WBNS

Note: The Wade Trophy is awarded for academics and community service as well as player performance.

Coaches of the Year

Andy Landers, Georgia ....Naismith, WBNS
Leon Barmore, Louisiana Tech....................USBWA, WBCA
Angie Lee, Iowa ....AP

Consensus All-America Team

The NCAA Division I players cited most frequently by the Associated Press, US Basketball Writers Assn., the Women's Basketball Coaches Assn. and the Women's Basketball News Service. Holdovers from the 1994-95 All-America first team are in **bold** type; (*) indicates unanimous first team selection.

First Team

	Class	Hgt	Pos
Saudia Roundtree, Georgia*	Sr.	5-7	G
Jennifer Rizzotti, UConn*	Sr.	5-5	G
Vickie Johnson, La. Tech	Sr.	5-9	G
Chamique Holdsclaw, Tennessee	Fr.	6-2	F
Sheri Sam, Vanderbilt	Sr.	6-1	F

Second Team

	Class	Hgt	Pos
Kara Wolters, UConn	Jr.	6-7	C
Katie Smith, Ohio State	Sr.	5-11	F
Michi Atkins, Texas Tech	Sr.	6-1	C/F
Wendy Palmer, Virginia	Sr.	6-2	F
Kate Starbird, Stanford	Jr.	6-2	G/F

Other Women's Tournaments

NIT (Mar. 24 at Amarillo, Texas): Final— Arizona 79, Northwestern 63.
NCAA Division II (Mar. 23 at Fargo, N.D.): Final— North Dakota St. 105, Shippensburg, Pa. 78.
NCAA Division III (Mar. 16 at Eau Claire, Wisc.): Final— Wisconsin-Oshkosh 66, Mount Union, Ohio. 50.
NAIA Division I (Mar. 19 at Jackson, Tenn.): Final— Southern Nazarene (Okla.) 80, SE Oklahoma 79.
NAIA Division II (Mar. 12 at Angola, Ind.): Final— Western Oregon 80, Huron (S.D.) 77.

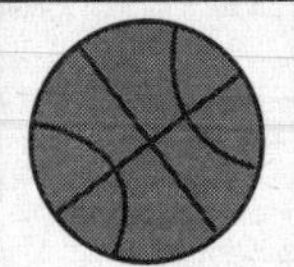

THROUGH THE YEARS

1901-1996

NCAA'S • ALL-TIME LEADERS

National Champions

The Helms Foundation of Los Angeles, under the direction of founder Bill Schroeder, selected national college basketball champions from 1942-82 and researched retroactive picks from 1901-41. The first NIT tournament and then the NCAA tournament have settled the national championship since 1938, but there are four years (1939, '40, '44 and '54) where the Helms selections differ.

Multiple champions (1901-37): Chicago, Columbia and Wisconsin (3); Kansas, Minnesota, Notre Dame, Penn, Pittsburgh, Syracuse and Yale (2).

Multiple champions (since 1938): UCLA (11); Kentucky (7); Indiana (5); North Carolina (3); Cincinnati, Duke, Kansas, Louisville, N.C. State, Oklahoma A&M (now Oklahoma St.) and San Francisco (2).

Year		Record	Head Coach	Outstanding Player
1901	**Yale**	10-4	No coach	G.M. Clark, F
1902	**Minnesota**	11-0	Louis Cooke	W.C. Deering, F
1903	**Yale**	15-1	W.H. Murphy	R.B. Hyatt, F
1904	**Columbia**	17-1	No coach	Harry Fisher, F
1905	**Columbia**	19-1	No coach	Harry Fisher, F
1906	**Dartmouth**	16-2	No coach	George Grebenstein, F
1907	**Chicago**	22-2	Joseph Raycroft	John Schommer, C
1908	**Chicago**	21-2	Joseph Raycroft	John Schommer, C
1909	**Chicago**	12-0	Joseph Raycroft	John Schommer, C
1910	**Columbia**	11-1	Harry Fisher	Ted Kiendl, F
1911	**St. John's-NY**	14-0	Claude Allen	John Keenan, F/C
1912	**Wisconsin**	15-0	Doc Meanwell	Otto Stangel, F
1913	**Navy**	9-0	Louis Wenzell	Laurence Wild, F
1914	**Wisconsin**	15-0	Doc Meanwell	Gene Van Gent, C
1915	**Illinois**	16-0	Ralph Jones	Ray Woods, G
1916	**Wisconsin**	20-1	Doc Meanwell	George Levis, F
1917	**Washington St**	25-1	Doc Bohler	Roy Bohler, G
1918	**Syracuse**	16-1	Edmund Dollard	Joe Schwarzer, G
1919	**Minnesota**	13-0	Louis Cooke	Arnold Oss, F
1920	**Penn**	22-1	Lon Jourdet	George Sweeney, F
1921	**Penn**	21-2	Edward McNichol	Danny McNichol, G
1922	**Kansas**	16-2	Phog Allen	Paul Endacott, G
1923	**Kansas**	17-1	Phog Allen	Paul Endacott, G
1924	**North Carolina**	25-0	Bo Shepard	Jack Cobb, F
1925	**Princeton**	21-2	Al Wittmer	Art Loeb, G
1926	**Syracuse**	19-1	Lew Andreas	Vic Hanson, F
1927	**Notre Dame**	19-1	George Keogan	John Nyikos, C
1928	**Pittsburgh**	21-0	Doc Carlson	Chuck Hyatt, F
1929	**Montana St.**	36-2	Schubert Dyche	John (Cat) Thompson, F
1930	**Pittsburgh**	23-2	Doc Carlson	Chuck Hyatt, F
1931	**Northwestern**	16-1	Dutch Lonborg	Joe Reiff, C
1932	**Purdue**	17-1	Piggy Lambert	John Wooden, G
1933	**Kentucky**	20-3	Adolph Rupp	Forest Sale, F
1934	**Wyoming**	26-3	Willard Witte	Les Witte, G
1935	**NYU**	19-1	Howard Cann	Sid Gross, F
1936	**Notre Dame**	22-2-1	George Keogan	John Moir, F
1937	**Stanford**	25-2	John Bunn	Hank Luisetti, F

Year		Record	Winner	Head Coach	Outstanding Player
1938	**Temple**	23-2	NIT	James Usilton	Meyer Bloom, G
1939	**Oregon**	29-5	NCAA	Howard Hobson	Slim Wintermute, C
	& **LIU-Brooklyn** (Helms)	24-0	NIT	Clair Bee	Irv Torgoff, F
1940	**Indiana**	20-3	NCAA	Branch McCracken	Marv Huffman, G
	& **USC** (Helms)	20-3	*	Sam Barry	Ralph Vaughn, F
1941	**Wisconsin**	20-3	NCAA	Bud Foster	Gene Englund, F

*USC was beaten by Kansas in the West regional of the NCAA tournament.

Year		Record	Winner	Head Coach	Outstanding Player
1942	**Stanford**	27-4	NCAA	Everett Dean	Jim Pollard, F
1943	**Wyoming**	31-2	NCAA	Everett Shelton	Kenny Sailors, G
1944	**Utah**	21-4	NCAA	Vadal Peterson	Arnie Ferrin, F
	& **Army** (Helms)	15-0	**	Ed Kelleher	Dale Hall, F
1945	**Oklahoma A&M**	27-4	NCAA	Hank Iba	Bob Kurland, C
1946	**Oklahoma A&M**	31-2	NCAA	Hank Iba	Bob Kurland, C
1947	**Holy Cross**	27-3	NCAA	Doggie Julian	George Kaftan, F
1948	**Kentucky**	36-3	NCAA	Adolph Rupp	Ralph Beard, G
1949	**Kentucky**	32-2	NCAA	Adolph Rupp	Alex Groza, C
1950	**CCNY**	24-5	NCAA & NIT	Nat Holman	Irwin Dambrot, G
1951	**Kentucky**	32-2	NCAA	Adolph Rupp	Bill Spivey, C
1952	**Kansas**	28-3	NCAA	Phog Allen	Clyde Lovellette, C
1953	**Indiana**	23-3	NCAA	Branch McCracken	Don Schlundt, C
1954	**La Salle**	26-4	NCAA	Ken Loeffler	Tom Gola, F
	& **Kentucky** (Helms)	25-0	***	Adolph Rupp	Cliff Hagan, G
1955	**San Francisco**	28-1	NCAA	Phil Woolpert	Bill Russell, C
1956	**San Francisco**	29-0	NCAA	Phil Woolpert	Bill Russell, C
1957	**North Carolina**	32-0	NCAA	Frank McGuire	Lennie Rosenbluth, F
1958	**Kentucky**	23-6	NCAA	Adolph Rupp	Vern Hatton, G
1959	**California**	25-4	NCAA	Pete Newell	Darrall Imhoff, C
1960	**Ohio St**	25-3	NCAA	Fred Taylor	Jerry Lucas, C
1961	**Cincinnati**	27-3	NCAA	Ed Jucker	Bob Wiesenhahn, F
1962	**Cincinnati**	29-2	NCAA	Ed Jucker	Paul Hogue, C
1963	**Loyola-IL**	29-2	NCAA	George Ireland	Jerry Harkness, F
1964	**UCLA**	30-0	NCAA	John Wooden	Walt Hazzard, G
1965	**UCLA**	28-2	NCAA	John Wooden	Gail Goodrich, G
1966	**Texas Western**	28-1	NCAA	Don Haskins	Bobby Joe Hill, G
1967	**UCLA**	30-0	NCAA	John Wooden	Lew Alcindor, C
1968	**UCLA**	29-1	NCAA	John Wooden	Lew Alcindor, C
1969	**UCLA**	29-1	NCAA	John Wooden	Lew Alcindor, C
1970	**UCLA**	28-2	NCAA	John Wooden	Sidney Wicks, F
1971	**UCLA**	29-1	NCAA	John Wooden	Sidney Wicks, F
1972	**UCLA**	30-0	NCAA	John Wooden	Bill Walton, C
1973	**UCLA**	30-0	NCAA	John Wooden	Bill Walton, C
1974	**N.C. State**	30-1	NCAA	Norm Sloan	David Thompson, F
1975	**UCLA**	28-3	NCAA	John Wooden	Dave Meyers, F
1976	**Indiana**	32-0	NCAA	Bob Knight	Scott May, F
1977	**Marquette**	25-7	NCAA	Al McGuire	Butch Lee, G
1978	**Kentucky**	30-2	NCAA	Joe B. Hall	Jack Givens, F
1979	**Michigan St**	26-6	NCAA	Jud Heathcote	Magic Johnson, G
1980	**Louisville**	33-3	NCAA	Denny Crum	Darrell Griffith, G
1981	**Indiana**	26-9	NCAA	Bob Knight	Isiah Thomas, G
1982	**North Carolina**	32-2	NCAA	Dean Smith	James Worthy, F
1983	**N.C. State**	26-10	NCAA	Jim Valvano	Sidney Lowe, G
1984	**Georgetown**	34-3	NCAA	John Thompson	Patrick Ewing, C
1985	**Villanova**	25-10	NCAA	Rollie Massimino	Ed Pinckney, C
1986	**Louisville**	32-7	NCAA	Denny Crum	Pervis Ellison, C
1987	**Indiana**	30-4	NCAA	Bob Knight	Steve Alford, G
1988	**Kansas**	27-11	NCAA	Larry Brown	Danny Manning, C
1989	**Michigan**	30-7	NCAA	Steve Fisher	Glen Rice, F
1990	**UNLV**	35-5	NCAA	Jerry Tarkanian	Larry Johnson, F
1991	**Duke**	32-7	NCAA	Mike Krzyzewski	Christian Laettner, F/C
1992	**Duke**	34-2	NCAA	Mike Krzyzewski	Christian Laettner, C
1993	**North Carolina**	34-4	NCAA	Dean Smith	Eric Montross, C
1994	**Arkansas**	31-3	NCAA	Nolan Richardson	Corliss Williamson, F
1995	**UCLA**	31-2	NCAA	Jim Harrick	Ed O'Bannon, F
1996	**Kentucky**	34-2	NCAA	Rick Pitino	Tony Delk, G

**Army did not lift its policy against postseason play until accepting a bid to the 1961 NIT.
***Unbeaten Kentucky turned down a bid to the 1954 NCAA tournament after the NCAA declared seniors Cliff Hagan, Frank Ramsey and Lou Tsioropoulos ineligible for postseason play.

The Red Cross Benefit Games, 1943-45

For three seasons during World War II, the NCAA and NIT champions met in a benefit game at Madison Square Garden in New York to raise money for the Red Cross. The NCAA champs won all three games.

Year	Winner	Score	Loser
1943	Wyoming (NCAA)	52-47	St. John's (NIT)
1944	Utah (NCAA)	43-36	St. John's (NIT)
1945	Oklahoma A&M (NCAA)	52-44	DePaul (NIT)

NCAA Final Four

The NCAA basketball tournament began in 1939 under the sponsorship of the National Association of Basketball Coaches, but was taken over by the NCAA in 1940. From 1939-51, the winners of the Eastern and Western Regionals played for the national championship, while regional runners-up shared third place. The concept of a Final Four originated in 1952 when four teams qualified for the first national semifinals. Consolation games to determine overall third place were held between regional finalists from 1946-51 and then national semifinalists from 1952-81. Consolation games were discontinued in 1982.

Multiple champions: UCLA (11); Kentucky (6); Indiana (5); North Carolina (3); Cincinnati, Duke, Kansas, Louisville, N.C. State, Oklahoma A&M (now Oklahoma St.) and San Francisco (2).

Year	Champion	Runner-up	Score	Final Two	Third Place	
1939	Oregon	Ohio St.	46-33	@ Evanston, IL	Oklahoma	Villanova
1940	Indiana	Kansas	60-42	@ Kansas City	Duquesne	USC
1941	Wisconsin	Washington St.	39-34	@ Kansas City	Arkansas	Pittsburgh
1942	Stanford	Dartmouth	53-38	@ Kansas City	Colorado	Kentucky
1943	Wyoming	Georgetown	46-34	@ New York	DePaul	Texas
1944	Utah	Dartmouth	42-40 (OT)	@ New York	Iowa St.	Ohio St.
1945	Oklahoma A&M	NYU	49-45	@ New York	Arkansas	Ohio St.

Year	Champion	Runner-up	Score	Final Two	Third Place	Fourth Place
1946	Oklahoma A&M	North Carolina	43-40	@ New York	Ohio St.	California
1947	Holy Cross	Oklahoma	58-47	@ New York	Texas	CCNY
1948	Kentucky	Baylor	58-42	@ New York	Holy Cross	Kansas St.
1949	Kentucky	Oklahoma A&M	46-36	@ Seattle	Illinois	Oregon St.
1950	CCNY	Bradley	71-68	@ New York	N.C. State	Baylor
1951	Kentucky	Kansas St.	68-58	@ Minneapolis	Illinois	Oklahoma A&M

Year	Champion	Runner-up	Score	Third Place	Fourth Place	Final Four
1952	Kansas	St. John's	80-63	Illinois	Santa Clara	@ Seattle
1953	Indiana	Kansas	69-68	Washington	LSU	@ Kansas City
1954	La Salle	Bradley	92-76	Penn St.	USC	@ Kansas City
1955	San Francisco	La Salle	77-63	Colorado	Iowa	@ Kansas City
1956	San Francisco	Iowa	83-71	Temple	SMU	@ Evanston, IL
1957	North Carolina	Kansas	54-53 (3OT)	San Francisco	Michigan St.	@ Kansas City
1958	Kentucky	Seattle	84-72	Temple	Kansas St.	@ Louisville
1959	California	West Virginia	71-70	Cincinnati	Louisville	@ Louisville
1960	Ohio St.	California	75-55	Cincinnati	NYU	@ San Francisco
1961	Cincinnati	Ohio St.	70-65 (OT)	St. Joseph's-PA	Utah	@ Kansas City
1962	Cincinnati	Ohio St.	71-59	Wake Forest	UCLA	@ Louisville
1963	Loyola-IL	Cincinnati	60-58 (OT)	Duke	Oregon St.	@ Louisville
1964	UCLA	Duke	98-83	Michigan	Kansas St.	@ Kansas City
1965	UCLA	Michigan	91-80	Princeton	Wichita St.	@ Portland, OR
1966	Texas Western	Kentucky	72-65	Duke	Utah	@ College Park, MD
1967	UCLA	Dayton	79-64	Houston	North Carolina	@ Louisville
1968	UCLA	North Carolina	78-55	Ohio St.	Houston	@ Los Angeles
1969	UCLA	Purdue	92-72	Drake	North Carolina	@ Louisville
1970	UCLA	Jacksonville	80-69	New Mexico St.	St. Bonaventure	@ College Park, MD
1971	UCLA	Villanova	68-62	Western Ky.	Kansas	@ Houston
1972	UCLA	Florida St.	81-76	North Carolina	Louisville	@ Los Angeles
1973	UCLA	Memphis St.	87-66	Indiana	Providence	@ St. Louis
1974	N.C. State	Marquette	76-64	UCLA	Kansas	@ Greensboro, NC
1975	UCLA	Kentucky	92-85	Louisville	Syracuse	@ San Diego
1976	Indiana	Michigan	86-68	UCLA	Rutgers	@ Philadelphia
1977	Marquette	North Carolina	67-59	UNLV	NC-Charlotte	@ Atlanta
1978	Kentucky	Duke	94-88	Arkansas	Notre Dame	@ St. Louis
1979	Michigan St.	Indiana St.	75-64	DePaul	Penn	@ Salt Lake City
1980	Louisville	UCLA	59-54	Purdue	Iowa	@ Indianapolis
1981	Indiana	North Carolina	63-50	Virginia	LSU	@ Philadelphia

Year	Champion	Runner-up	Score	Third Place		Final Four
1982	North Carolina	Georgetown	63-62	Houston	Louisville	@ New Orleans
1983	N.C. State	Houston	54-52	Georgia	Louisville	@ Albuquerque
1984	Georgetown	Houston	84-75	Kentucky	Virginia	@ Seattle
1985	Villanova	Georgetown	66-64	Memphis St.	St. John's	@ Lexington
1986	Louisville	Duke	72-69	Kansas	LSU	@ Dallas
1987	Indiana	Syracuse	74-73	Providence	UNLV	@ New Orleans
1988	Kansas	Oklahoma	83-79	Arizona	Duke	@ Kansas City
1989	Michigan	Seton Hall	80-79 (OT)	Duke	Illinois	@ Seattle
1990	UNLV	Duke	103-73	Arkansas	Georgia Tech	@ Denver
1991	Duke	Kansas	72-65	North Carolina	UNLV	@ Indianapolis
1992	Duke	Michigan	71-51	Cincinnati	Indiana	@ Minneapolis
1993	North Carolina	Michigan	77-71	Kansas	Kentucky	@ New Orleans
1994	Arkansas	Duke	76-72	Arizona	Florida	@ Charlotte
1995	UCLA	Arkansas	89-78	North Carolina	Oklahoma St.	@ Seattle
1996	Kentucky	Syracuse	76-67	UMass	Mississippi St.	@ E. Rutherford, NJ

Note: Five teams have had their standing in the Final Four vacated for using ineligible players: 1961—St. Joseph's-PA (3rd place); 1971—Villanova (Runner-up) and Western Kentucky (3rd place); 1980—UCLA (Runner-up); 1985—Memphis St. (3rd place).

Most Outstanding Player

A Most Outstanding Player has been selected every year of the NCAA tournament. Winners who did not play for the tournament champion are listed in **bold** type. The 1939 and 1951 winners are unofficial and not recognized by the NCAA.

Multiple winners: Lew Alcindor (3); Alex Groza, Bob Kurland, Jerry Lucas and Bill Walton (2).

Year		Year		Year	
1939	**Jimmy Hull**, Ohio St.	1960	Jerry Lucas, Ohio St.	1980	Darrell Griffith, Louisville
1940	Marv Huffman, Indiana	1961	**Jerry Lucas**, Ohio St.	1981	Isiah Thomas, Indiana
1941	John Kotz, Wisconsin	1962	Paul Hogue, Cincinnati	1982	James Worthy, N. Carolina
1942	Howie Dallmar, Stanford	1963	**Art Heyman**, Duke	1983	**Akeem Olajuwon**, Houston
1943	Kenny Sailors, Wyoming	1964	Walt Hazzard, UCLA	1984	Patrick Ewing, Georgetown
1944	Arnie Ferrin, Utah	1965	**Bill Bradley**, Princeton	1985	Ed Pinckney, Villanova
1945	Bob Kurland, Okla. A&M	1966	**Jerry Chambers**, Utah	1986	Pervis Ellison, Louisville
1946	Bob Kurland, Okla. A&M	1967	Lew Alcindor, UCLA	1987	Keith Smart, Indiana
1947	George Kaftan, Holy Cross	1968	Lew Alcindor, UCLA	1988	Danny Manning, Kansas
1948	Alex Groza, Kentucky	1969	Lew Alcindor, UCLA	1989	Glen Rice, Michigan
1949	Alex Groza, Kentucky	1970	Sidney Wicks, UCLA	1990	Anderson Hunt, UNLV
1950	Irwin Dambrot, CCNY	1971	**Howard Porter**, Villanova	1991	Christian Laettner, Duke
1951	Bill Spivey, Kentucky	1972	Bill Walton, UCLA	1992	Bobby Hurley, Duke
1952	Clyde Lovellette, Kansas	1973	Bill Walton, UCLA	1993	Donald Williams, N. Carolina
1953	**B.H. Born**, Kansas	1974	David Thompson, N.C. State	1994	Corliss Williamson, Arkansas
1954	Tom Gola, La Salle	1975	Richard Washington, UCLA	1995	Ed O'Bannon, UCLA
1955	Bill Russell, San Francisco	1976	Kent Benson, Indiana	1996	Tony Delk, Kentucky
1956	**Hal Lear**, Temple	1977	Butch Lee, Marquette		
1957	**Wilt Chamberlain**, Kansas	1978	Jack Givens, Kentucky		
1958	**Elgin Baylor**, Seattle	1979	Magic Johnson, Michigan St.		
1959	**Jerry West**, West Virginia				

Note: Howard Porter (1971) was declared ineligible by the NCAA after the tournament and his award was vacated.

Final Four All-Decade Teams

To celebrate the 50th anniversary of the NCAA tournament in 1989, five All-Decade teams were selected by a blue ribbon panel of coaches and administrators. An All-Time Final Four team was also chosen.

Selection panel: Vic Bubas, Denny Crum, Wayne Duke, Dave Gavitt, Joe B. Hall, Jud Heathcote, Hank Iba, Pete Newell, Dean Smith, John Thompson and John Wooden.

All-Time Team

	Years
Lew Alcindor, UCLA	1967-69
Larry Bird, Indiana St.	1979
Wilt Chamberlain, Kansas	1957
Magic Johnson, Mich. St	1979
Michael Jordan, N. Carolina	1982

All-1940s

	Years
Ralph Beard, Kentucky	1948-49
Howie Dallmar, Stanford	1942
Dwight Eddleman, Illinois	1949
Arnie Ferrin, Utah	1944
Alex Groza, Kentucky	1948-49
George Kaftan, Holy Cross	1947
Bob Kurland, Okla. A&M	1945-46
Jim Pollard, Stanford	1942
Kenny Sailors, Wyoming	1943
Gerry Tucker, Oklahoma	1947

All-1950s

	Years
Elgin Baylor, Seattle	1958
Wilt Chamberlain, Kansas	1957
Tom Gola, La Salle	1954
K.C. Jones, San Francisco	1955
Clyde Lovellette, Kansas	1952
Oscar Robertson, Cinn.	1959-60
Guy Rodgers, Temple	1958
Lennie Rosenbluth, N. Carolina	1957
Bill Russell, San Francisco	1955-56
Jerry West, West Virginia	1959

All-1960s

	Years
Lew Alcindor, UCLA	1967-69
Bill Bradley, Princeton	1965
Gail Goodrich, UCLA	1964-65
John Havlicek, Ohio St	1961-62
Elvin Hayes, Houston	1967
Walt Hazzard, UCLA	1964
Jerry Lucas, Ohio St	1960-61
Jeff Mullins, Duke	1964
Cazzie Russell, Michigan	1965
Charlie Scott, N. Carolina	1968-69

All-1970s

	Years
Kent Benson, Indiana	1976
Larry Bird, Indiana St.	1979
Jack Givens, Kentucky	1978
Magic Johnson, Mich. St.	1979
Marques Johnson, UCLA	1975-76
Scott May, Indiana	1976
David Thompson, N.C. State	1974
Bill Walton, UCLA	1972-74
Sidney Wicks, UCLA	1969-71
Keith Wilkes, UCLA	1972-74

All-1980s

	Years
Steve Alford, Indiana	1987
Johnny Dawkins, Duke	1986
Patrick Ewing, Georgetown	1982-84
Darrell Griffith, Louisville	1980
Michael Jordan, N. Carolina	1982
Rodney McCray, Louisville	1980
Akeem Olajuwon, Houston	1983-84
Ed Pinckney, Villanova	1985
Isiah Thomas, Indiana	1981
James Worthy, N. Carolina	1982

Note: Lew Alcindor later changed his name to Kareem Abdul-Jabbar; Keith Wilkes later changed his first name to Jamaal; and Akeem Olajuwon later changed the spelling of his first name to Hakeem.

Collegiate Commissioners Association Tournament

The Collegiate Commissioners Association staged an eight-team tournament for teams that didn't make the NCAA tournament in 1974 and '75.

Most Valuable Players: 1974—Kent Benson, Indiana: 1975—Bob Elliot, Arizona.

Year	Winner	Score	Loser	Site	Year	Winner	Score	Loser	Site
1974	Indiana	85-60	USC	St. Louis	1975	Drake	83-76	Arizona	Louisville

NCAA Tournament Appearances

App		W-L	F4	Championships
38	Kentucky	72-34	11	6 (1948-49,51, 58,78,96)
32	UCLA	74-25	15	11 (1964-65, 67,73,75,95)
30	North Carolina	68-30	12	3 (1957,82,93)
26	Louisville	45-28	7	2 (1980,86)
25	Indiana	50-20	7	5 (1940,53,76,81,87)
25	Kansas	54-25	10	2 (1952,88)
24	Notre Dame	25-28	1	None
23	St. John's	23-25	2	None
23	Villanova	36-23	3	1 (1985)
23	Syracuse	35-24	3	None
22	Arkansas	37-22	6	1 (1994)
22	Kansas St.	27-26	4	None
20	DePaul	20-23	2	None
20	Duke	56-18	11	2 (1991-92)
20	Marquette	28-21	2	1 (1977)
20	Georgetown	36-19	4	1 (1984)
20	Temple	23-20	2	None
19	Princeton	12-23	1	None
19	Michigan	40-18	6	1 (1989)
19	Connecticut	17-20	0	None
18	Ohio St.	31-17	8	1 (1960)
18	Houston	26-23	5	None
18	BYU	11-21	0	None
18	Utah	22-21	3	1 (1944)
17	N.C. State	27-16	3	2 (1974,83)
17	West Virginia	11-17	1	None
17	Illinois	21-18	4	None
16	Iowa	22-18	3	None
16	Missouri	13-16	0	None
16	Oregon St.	12-19	2	None
16	Pennsylvania	13-18	1	None
16	Western Ky.	15-17	1	None

Note: Although all NCAA tournament appearances are included above, the NCAA has officially voided the records of Villanova (4-1) in 1971, UCLA (5-1) in 1980, Oregon St. (2-3) from 1980-82, N.C. State (0-2) from 1987-88 and Kentucky (2-1) in 1988.

All-Time NCAA Division I Tournament Leaders

Through 1996; minimum of six games; **Last** column indicates final year played.

CAREER

Scoring

	Points	Yrs	Last	Gm	Pts
1	Christian Laettner, Duke	4	1992	23	407
2	Elvin Hayes, Houston	3	1968	13	358
3	Danny Manning, Kansas	4	1988	16	328
4	Oscar Robertson, Cincinnati	3	1960	10	324
5	Glen Rice, Michigan	4	1989	13	308
6	Lew Alcindor, UCLA	3	1969	12	304
7	Bill Bradley, Princeton	3	1965	9	303
8	Austin Carr, Notre Dame	3	1971	7	289
9	Juwan Howard, Michigan	3	1994	16	280
10	Calbert Cheaney, Indiana	4	1993	13	279

	Average	Yrs	Last	Pts	Avg
1	Austin Carr, Notre Dame	3	1971	289	41.3
2	Bill Bradley, Princeton	3	1965	303	33.7
3	Oscar Robertson, Cincinnati	3	1960	324	32.4
4	Jerry West, West Virginia	3	1960	275	30.6
5	Bob Pettit, LSU	2	1954	183	30.5
6	Dan Issel, Kentucky	3	1970	176	29.3
	Jim McDaniels, Western Ky	2	1971	176	29.3
8	Dwight Lamar, SW Louisiana	2	1973	175	29.2
9	Bo Kimble, Loyola-CA	3	1990	204	29.1
10	David Robinson, Navy	3	1987	200	28.6

Rebounds

	Total	Yrs	Last	Gm	No
1	Elvin Hayes, Houston	3	1968	13	222
2	Lew Alcindor, UCLA	3	1969	12	201
3	Jerry Lucas, Ohio St.	3	1962	12	197
4	Bill Walton, UCLA	3	1974	12	176
5	Christian Laettner, Duke	4	1992	23	169
6	Paul Hogue, Cincinnati	3	1962	12	160
7	Sam Lacey, New Mexico St.	3	1970	11	157
8	Derrick Coleman, Syracuse	4	1990	14	155
9	Akeem Olajuwon, Houston	3	1984	15	153
10	Patrick Ewing, Georgetown	4	1985	18	144

	Average	Yrs	Last	Reb	Avg
1	Johnny Green, Michigan St.	2	1959	118	19.7
2	Artis Gilmore, Jacksonville	2	1971	115	19.2
3	Paul Silas, Creighton	3	1964	111	18.5
4	Len Chappell, Wake Forest	2	1962	137	17.1
5	Elvin Hayes, Houston	3	1968	222	17.1
6	Lew Alcindor, UCLA	3	1969	201	16.8
7	Jerry Lucas, Ohio St.	3	1962	197	16.4
8	Bill Walton, UCLA	3	1974	176	14.7
9	Sam Lacey, New Mexico St.	3	1970	157	14.3
10	Bob Lanier, St. Bonaventure	3	1970	85	14.2

3-Pt Field Goals

	Total	Yrs	Last	Gm	No
1	Bobby Hurley, Duke	4	1993	20	42
2	Jeff Fryer, Loyola-CA	3	1990	7	38
3	Glen Rice, Michigan	4	1989	13	35
4	Anderson Hunt, UNLV	3	1991	15	34
5	Dennis Scott, Georgia Tech	3	1990	8	33

Assists

	Total	Yrs	Last	Gm	No
1	Bobby Hurley, Duke	4	1993	20	145
2	Sherman Douglas, Syracuse	4	1989	14	106
3	Greg Anthony, UNLV	3	1991	15	100
4	Mark Wade, UNLV	2	1987	8	93
	Rumeal Robinson, Michigan	3	1990	11	93

SINGLE TOURNAMENT

Scoring

	Points	Year	Gm	Pts
1	Glen Rice, Michigan	1989	6	184
2	Bill Bradley, Princeton	1965	5	177
3	Elvin Hayes, Houston	1968	5	167
4	Danny Manning, Kansas	1988	6	163
5	Hal Lear, Temple	1956	5	160
	Jerry West, West Virginia	1959	5	160

	Average	Year	Gm	Pts	Avg
1	Austin Carr, Notre Dame	1970	3	158	52.7
2	Austin Carr, Notre Dame	1971	3	125	41.7
3	Jerry Chambers, Utah	1966	4	143	35.8
	Bo Kimble, Loyola-CA	1990	4	143	35.8
5	Bill Bradley, Princeton	1965	5	177	35.4
6	Clyde Lovellette, Kansas	1952	4	141	35.3

Rebounds

	Total	Year	Gm	No	Avg
1	Elvin Hayes, Houston	1968	5	97	19.4
2	Artis Gilmore, Jacksonville	1970	5	93	18.6
3	Elgin Baylor, Seattle	1958	5	91	18.2
4	Sam Lacey, New Mexico St.	1970	5	90	18.0
5	Clarence Glover, Western Ky	1971	5	89	17.8

Assists

	Total	Year	Gm	No	Avg
1	Mark Wade, UNLV	1987	5	61	12.2
2	Rumeal Robinson, Michigan	1989	6	56	9.3
3	Sherman Douglas, Syracuse	1987	6	49	8.2
4	Bobby Hurley, Duke	1992	6	47	7.8
5	Michael Jackson, Georgetown	1985	6	45	7.5

SINGLE GAME

Scoring

	Points	Year	Pts
1	Austin Carr, Notre Dame vs Ohio Univ	1970	61
2	Bill Bradley, Princeton vs Wichita St.	1965	58
3	Oscar Robertson, Cincinnati vs Arkansas	1958	56
4	Austin Carr, Notre Dame vs Kentucky	1970	52
	Austin Carr, Notre Dame vs TCU	1971	52
6	David Robinson, Navy vs Michigan	1987	50
7	Elvin Hayes, Houston vs Loyola-IL	1968	49
8	Hal Lear, Temple vs SMU	1956	48
9	Austin Carr, Notre Dame vs Houston	1971	47
10	Dave Corzine, DePaul vs Louisville	1978	46
11	Bob Houbregs, Washington vs Seattle	1953	45
	Austin Carr, Notre Dame vs Iowa	1970	45
	Bo Kimble, Loyola-CA vs New Mexico St.	1990	45
14	Seven players tied with 44 each.		

Rebounds

	Total	Year	No
1	Fred Cohen, Temple vs UConn	1956	34
2	Nate Thurmond, Bowling Green vs Miss. St.	1963	31
3	Jerry Lucas, Ohio St. vs Kentucky	1961	30
4	Toby Kimball, UConn vs St. Joseph's-PA	1965	29
5	Elvin Hayes, Houston vs Pacific	1966	28

Assists

	Total	Year	No
1	Mark Wade, UNLV vs Indiana	1987	18
2	Sam Crawford, N. Mexico St. vs Nebraska	1993	16
3	Kenny Patterson, DePaul vs Syracuse	1985	15
4	Keith Smart, Indiana vs Auburn	1987	15
5	Five players tied with 14 each.		

SINGLE FINAL FOUR GAME

Letters in the **Year** column indicate the following: C for Consolation Game, F for Final and S for Semifinal.

Scoring

	Points	Year	Pts
1	Bill Bradley, Princeton vs Wichita St	1965-C	58
2	Hal Lear, Temple vs SMU	1956-C	48
3	Bill Walton, UCLA vs Memphis St	1973-F	44
4	Bob Houbregs, Washington vs LSU	1953-C	42
	Jack Egan, St. Joseph's-PA vs Utah	1961-C	42*
	Gail Goodrich, UCLA vs Michigan	1965-C	42
7	Jack Givens, Kentucky vs Duke	1978-F	41
8	Oscar Robertson, Cincinnati vs L'ville	1959-C	39
	Al Wood, N. Carolina vs Virginia	1981-S	39
10	Jerry West, West Va. vs Louisville	1959-S	38
	Jerry Chambers, Utah vs Texas Western	1966-S	38
	Freddie Banks, UNLV vs Indiana	1987-S	38

* Four overtimes.

Rebounds

	Total	Year	No
1	Bill Russell, San Francisco vs Iowa	1956-F	27
2	Elvin Hayes, Houston vs UCLA	1967-S	24
3	Bill Russell, San Francisco vs SMU	1956-S	23
4	Four players tied with 22 each.		

Assists

	Total	Year	No
1	Mark Wade, UNLV vs Indiana	1987-S	18
2	Rumeal Robinson, Michigan vs Illinois	1989-S	12
3	Michael Jackson, G'town vs St. John's	1985-S	11
4	Milt Wagner, Louisville vs LSU	1986-S	11
5	Rumeal Robinson, Mich. vs Seton Hall	1989-F	11*

*Overtime.

Teams in both NCAA and NIT

Fourteen teams played in both the NCAA and NIT tournaments from 1940-52. Colorado (1940), Utah (1944), Kentucky (1949) and BYU (1951) won one of the titles, while CCNY won two in 1950, beating Bradley in both championship games.

Year		NIT	NCAA
1940	Colorado	**Won Final**	Lost 1st Rd
	Duquesne	Lost Final	Lost 2nd Rd
1944	Utah	Lost 1st Rd	**Won Final**
1949	Kentucky	Lost 2nd Rd	**Won Final**
1950	CCNY	**Won Final**	**Won Final**
	Bradley	Lost Final	Lost Final
1951	BYU	**Won Final**	Lost 2nd Rd
	St. John's	Lost 3rd Rd	Lost 2nd Rd
	N.C. State	Lost 2nd Rd	Lost 2nd Rd
	Arizona	Lost 2nd Rd	Lost 1st Rd
1952	St. John's	Lost Final	Lost 2nd Rd
	Dayton	Lost 1st Rd	Lost Final
	Duquesne	Lost 2nd Rd	Lost 2nd Rd
	Saint Louis	Lost 2nd Rd	Lost 2nd Rd

Most Popular Final Four Sites

The NCAA has staged its Men's Division I championship—the Final Two (1939-51) and Final Four (since 1952)—at 29 different arenas and indoor stadiums in 24 different cities. The following facilities have all hosted the event more than once.

No	Arena	Years
9	Municipal Auditorium (KC)	1940-42, 53-55, 57, 61, 64
7	Madison Sq. Garden (NYC)	1943-48, 50
6	Freedom Hall (Louisville)	1958-59, 62-63, 67, 69
3	Kingdome (Seattle)	1984, 89, 95
	Superdome (New Orleans)	1982, 87, 93
2	Cole Field House (College Park, Md.)	1966, 70
	Edmundson Pavilion (Seattle)	1949, 52
	LA Sports Arena	1968, 72
	St. Louis Arena	1973, 78
	Spectrum (Philadelphia)	1976, 81

NIT Championship

The National Invitation Tournament began under the sponsorship of the Metropolitan New York Basketball Writers Association in 1938. The NIT is now administered by the Metropolitan Intercollegiate Basketball Association. All championship games have been played at Madison Square Garden.

Multiple winners: St. John's (5); Bradley (4); BYU, Dayton, Kentucky, LIU-Brooklyn, Providence, Temple, Virginia and Virginia Tech (2).

Year	Winner	Score	Loser
1938	Temple	60-36	Colorado
1939	LIU-Brooklyn	44-32	Loyola-IL
1940	Colorado	51-40	Duquesne
1941	LIU-Brooklyn	56-42	Ohio Univ.
1942	West Virginia	47-45	Western Ky.
1943	St. John's	48-27	Toledo
1944	St. John's	47-39	DePaul
1945	DePaul	71-54	Bowling Green
1946	Kentucky	46-45	Rhode Island
1947	Utah	49-45	Kentucky
1948	Saint Louis	65-52	NYU
1949	San Francisco	48-47	Loyola-IL
1950	CCNY	69-61	Bradley
1951	BYU	62-43	Dayton
1952	La Salle	75-64	Dayton
1953	Seton Hall	58-46	St. John's
1954	Holy Cross	71-62	Duquesne
1955	Duquesne	70-58	Dayton
1956	Louisville	93-80	Dayton
1957	Bradley	84-83	Memphis St.
1958	Xavier-OH	78-74 (OT)	Dayton
1959	St. John's	76-71 (OT)	Bradley
1960	Bradley	88-72	Providence
1961	Providence	62-59	Saint Louis
1962	Dayton	73-67	St. John's
1963	Providence	81-66	Canisius
1964	Bradley	86-54	New Mexico
1965	St. John's	55-51	Villanova
1966	BYU	97-84	NYU
1967	Southern Illinois	71-56	Marquette
1968	Dayton	61-48	Kansas
1969	Temple	89-76	Boston College
1970	Marquette	65-53	St. John's
1971	North Carolina	84-66	Georgia Tech
1972	Maryland	100-69	Niagara
1973	Virginia Tech	92-91 (OT)	Notre Dame
1974	Purdue	97-81	Utah
1975	Princeton	80-69	Providence
1976	Kentucky	71-67	NC-Charlotte
1977	St. Bonaventure	94-91	Houston
1978	Texas	101-93	N.C. State
1979	Indiana	53-52	Purdue
1980	Virginia	58-55	Minnesota
1981	Tulsa	86-84 (OT)	Syracuse
1982	Bradley	67-58	Purdue
1983	Fresno St.	69-60	DePaul
1984	Michigan	83-63	Notre Dame
1985	UCLA	65-62	Indiana
1986	Ohio St.	73-63	Wyoming
1987	Southern Miss.	84-80	La Salle
1988	Connecticut	72-67	Ohio St.
1989	St. John's	73-65	Saint Louis
1990	Vanderbilt	74-72	Saint Louis
1991	Stanford	78-72	Oklahoma
1992	Virginia	81-76 (OT)	Notre Dame
1993	Minnesota	62-61	Georgetown
1994	Villanova	80-73	Vanderbilt
1995	Virginia Tech	65-64 (OT)	Marquette
1996	Nebraska	60-56	St. Joseph's

Most Valuable Player

A Most Valuable Player has been selected every year of the NIT tournament. Winners who did not play for the tournament champion are listed in **bold** type.

Multiple winners: None. However, Tom Gola is the only player to be named MVP in both the NIT (1952) and NCAA (1954) tournaments.

Year	
1938	Don Shields, Temple
1939	**Bill Lloyd**, St. John's
1940	Bob Doll, Colorado
1941	**Frank Baumholtz**, Ohio U.
1942	Rudy Baric, West Virginia
1943	Harry Boykoff, St. John's
1944	Bill Kotsores, St. John's
1945	George Mikan, DePaul
1946	**Ernie Calverley**, Rhode Island
1947	Vern Gardner, Utah
1948	Ed Macauley, Saint Louis
1949	Don Lofgran, San Francisco
1950	Ed Warner, CCNY
1951	Roland Minson, BYU
1952	Tom Gola, La Salle & Norm Grekin, La Salle
1953	Walter Dukes, Seton Hall
1954	Togo Palazzi, Holy Cross
1955	**Maurice Stokes**, St. Francis-PA
1956	Charlie Tyra, Louisville
1957	**Win Wilfong**, Memphis St.
1958	Hank Stein, Xavier-OH
1959	Tony Jackson, St. John's
1960	**Lenny Wilkens**, Providence
1961	Vin Ernst, Providence
1962	Bill Chmielewski, Dayton
1963	Ray Flynn, Providence
1964	Lavern Tart, Bradley
1965	Ken McIntyre, St. John's
1966	**Bill Melchionni**, Villanova
1967	Walt Frazier, So. Illinois
1968	Don May, Dayton
1969	**Terry Driscoll**, Boston College
1970	Dean Meminger, Marquette
1971	Bill Chamberlain, N. Carolina
1972	Tom McMillen, Maryland
1973	**John Shumate**, Notre Dame
1974	**Mike Sojourner**, Utah
1975	**Ron Lee**, Oregon
1976	**Cedric Maxwell**, NC-Charlotte
1977	Greg Sanders, St. Bonaventure
1978	Ron Baxter, Texas & Jim Krivacs, Texas
1979	Clarence Carter, Indiana & Ray Tolbert, Indiana
1980	Ralph Sampson, Virginia
1981	Greg Stewart, Tulsa
1982	Mitchell Anderson, Bradley
1983	Ron Anderson, Fresno St.
1984	Tim McCormick, Michigan
1985	Reggie Miller, UCLA
1986	Brad Sellers, Ohio St.
1987	Randolph Keys, So. Miss.
1988	Phil Gamble, Connecticut
1989	Jayson Williams, St. John's
1990	Scott Draud, Vanderbilt
1991	Adam Keefe, Stanford
1992	Bryant Stith, Virginia
1993	Voshon Lenard, Minnesota
1994	**Doremus Bennerman**, Siena
1995	Shawn Smith, Va. Tech
1996	Erick Strickland, Nebraska

All-Time Winningest Division I Teams

Top 25 Winning Percentage

Division I schools with best winning percentages through 1995-96 season (including tournament games). Years in Division I only; minimum 20 years. NCAA tournament columns indicate years in tournament, record and number of championships.

		First							—NCAA Tourney—		
		Year	Yrs	Games	Won	Lost	Tied	Pct	Yrs	W-L	Titles
1	Kentucky	1903	93	2171	1650	520	1	**.760**	38	72-34	6
2	North Carolina	1911	86	2235	1647	588	0	**.737**	30	68-30	3
3	UNLV	1959	38	1073	789	284	0	**.735**	12	30-11	1
4	UCLA	1920	77	1970	1374	596	0	**.697**	32	74-25	11
5	Kansas	1899	98	2304	1596	708	0	**.693**	25	54-25	2
6	St. John's	1908	89	2201	1519	682	0	**.690**	23	23-25	0
7	Syracuse	1901	95	2102	1432	670	0	**.681**	23	35-24	0
8	Western Kentucky	1915	77	1979	1344	635	0	**.679**	16	15-17	0
9	Duke	1906	91	2232	1492	740	0	**.668**	20	56-18	2
10	DePaul	1924	73	1777	1177	600	0	**.662**	20	20-23	0
11	Arkansas	1924	73	1898	1250	648	0	**.659**	22	37-22	1
12	Louisville	1912	82	1986	1299	687	0	**.654**	26	45-28	2
13	Notre Dame	1898	91	2147	1398	748	1	**.6511**	24	25-28	0
14	Indiana	1901	96	2132	1388	744	0	**.6510**	25	50-20	5
15	Weber St.	1963	34	963	625	338	0	**.649**	11	5-12	0
16	Temple	1895	100	2247	1455	792	0	**.648**	20	23-20	0
17	Utah	1909	88	2041	1317	724	0	**.645**	18	22-21	1
18	Purdue	1897	98	2075	1337	738	0	**.644**	15	18-15	0
19	Illinois	1906	91	2025	1299	726	0	**.641**	17	21-18	0
20	Villanova	1921	76	1927	1232	695	0	**.639**	23	36-23	1
21	Penn	1897	96	2233	1425	806	2	**.6386**	16	13-18	0
22	La Salle	1931	66	1688	1075	613	0	**.637**	11	11-10	1
23	Houston	1946	51	1416	901	515	0	**.636**	18	26-23	0
24	N.C. State	1913	84	2040	1292	748	0	**.633**	17	27-16	2
25	Alabama	1913	83	1965	1234	731	1	**.628**	14	15-14	0

Top 35 Victories

Division I schools with most victories through 1995-96 (including postseason tournaments). Minimum 20 years in Division I.

		Wins
1	Kentucky	1650
2	North Carolina	1647
3	Kansas	1596
4	St. John's	1519
5	Duke	1492
6	Temple	1455
7	Oregon St.	1434
8	Syracuse	1432
9	Penn	1425
10	Notre Dame	1398
11	Indiana	1388
12	UCLA	1374
13	Washington	1348
14	Western Ky.	1344
15	Purdue	1337
16	Princeton	1335
17	Utah	1317
18	Fordham	1307
19	Bradley	1309
20	West Virginia	1304
21	Illinois	1299
22	Louisville	1299
23	N.C. State	1292
24	Washington St.	1287
25	Texas	1284
26	Arkansas	1250
27	Montana St.	1250
28	Cincinnati	1257
29	Arizona	1252
30	Ohio St.	1246
31	Alabama	1234
32	Villanova	1232
33	USC	1229
34	Kansas St.	1224
35	Iowa	1223

Top 50 Single-Season Victories

Division I schools with most victories in a single season through 1995-96 (including postseason tournaments). NCAA champions in **bold** type.

		Year	Record
1	UNLV	1987	37-2
	Duke	1986	37-3
3	**Kentucky**	1948	36-3
4	Massachusetts	1996	35-2
	Georgetown	1985	35-3
	Arizona	1988	35-3
	Kansas	1986	35-4
	Oklahoma	1988	35-4
	UNLV	1990	35-5
10	UNLV	1991	34-1
	Duke	1992	34-2
	Kentucky	1996	34-2
	Kentucky	1947	34-3
	Georgetown	1984	34-3
	Arkansas	1991	34-4
	N. Carolina	1993	34-4
15	Indiana St	1979	33-1
	Louisville	1980	33-3
	UNLV	1986	33-5
18	**N. Carolina**	1957	32-0
	Indiana	1976	32-0
	Kentucky	1949	32-2
	Kentucky	1951	32-2
	N. Carolina	1982	32-2
	Temple	1988	32-2
	Arkansas	1978	32-3
	Bradley	1986	32-3
	Connecticut	1996	32-3
	Louisville	1983	32-4
	Kentucky	1986	32-4
	N. Carolina	1987	32-4
	Temple	1987	32-4
	Bradley	1950	32-5
	Marshall	1947	32-5
	Houston	1984	32-5
	Bradley	1951	32-6
	Louisville	1986	32-7
	Duke	1991	32-7
	Arkansas	1995	32-7
37	Indiana	1975	31-1
	Wyoming	1943	31-2
	Okla. A&M	1946	31-2
	Seton Hall	1953	31-2
	Houston	1968	31-2
	Rutgers	1976	31-2
	UCLA	1995	31-2
	Houston	1983	31-3
	Arkansas	1994	31-3
	Memphis St	1985	31-4
	St. John's	1985	31-4
	Indiana	1993	31-4
	LSU	1981	31-5
	St. John's	1986	31-5
	Illinois	1989	31-5
	Michigan	1993	31-5
	Oklahoma	1985	31-6
	Connecticut	1990	31-6
	Syracuse	1987	31-7
	Seton Hall	1989	31-7

Associated Press Final Polls

The Associated Press introduced its weekly college basketball poll of sportswriters (later, sportswriters and broadcasters) during the 1948-49 season.

Since the NCAA Division I tournament has determined the national champion since 1939, the final AP poll ranks the nation's best teams through the regular season and conference tournaments.

Except for four seasons (see page 321), the final AP poll has been released prior to the NCAA and NIT tournaments and has gone from a Top 10 (1949 and 1963-67) to a Top 20 (1950-62 and 1968-89) to a Top 25 (since 1990).

Tournament champions are in **bold** type.

1949

	Before Tourns	Head Coach	Final Record
1 **Kentucky**	29-1	Adolph Rupp	32-2
2 Oklahoma A&M	21-4	Hank Iba	23-5
3 Saint Louis	22-3	Eddie Hickey	22-4
4 Illinois	19-3	Harry Combes	21-4
5 Western Ky.	25-3	Ed Diddle	25-4
6 Minnesota	18-3	Ozzie Cowles	same
7 Bradley	25-6	Forddy Anderson	27-8
8 **San Francisco**	21-5	Pete Newell	25-5
9 Tulane	24-4	Cliff Wells	same
10 Bowling Green	21-6	Harold Anderson	24-7

NCAA Final Four (at Edmundson Pavilion, Seattle): **Third Place**—Illinois 57, Oregon St. 53. **Championship**—Kentucky 46, Oklahoma A&M 36.

NIT Final Four (at Madison Square Garden): **Semifinals**—San Francisco 49, Bowling Green 39; Loyola-IL 55, Bradley 50. **Third Place**—Bowling Green 82, Bradley 77. **Championship**—San Francisco 48, Loyola-IL 47.

1950

	Before Tourns	Head Coach	Final Record
1 Bradley	28-3	Forddy Anderson	32-5
2 Ohio St.	21-3	Tippy Dye	22-4
3 Kentucky	25-4	Adolph Rupp	25-5
4 Holy Cross	27-2	Buster Sheary	27-4
5 N.C. State	25-5	Everett Case	27-6
6 Duquesne	22-5	Dudey Moore	23-6
7 UCLA	24-5	John Wooden	24-7
8 Western Ky.	24-5	Ed Diddle	25-6
9 St. John's	23-4	Frank McGuire	24-5
10 La Salle	20-3	Ken Loeffler	21-4
11 Villanova	25-4	Al Severance	same
12 San Francisco	19-6	Pete Newell	19-7
13 LIU-Brooklyn	20-4	Clair Bee	20-5
14 Kansas St.	17-7	Jack Gardner	same
15 Arizona	26-4	Fred Enke	26-5
16 Wisconsin	17-5	Bud Foster	same
17 San Jose St.	21-7	Walter McPherson	same
18 Washington St.	19-13	Jack Friel	same
19 Kansas	14-11	Phog Allen	same
20 Indiana	17-5	Branch McCracken	same

Note: Unranked **CCNY**, coached by Nat Holman, won both the NCAAs and NIT. The Beavers entered the postseason at 17-5 and had a final record of 24-5.

NCAA Final Four (at Madison Square Garden): **Third Place**—N. Carolina St. 53, Baylor 41. **Championship**—CCNY 71, Bradley 68.

NIT Final Four (at Madison Square Garden): **Semifinals**—Bradley 83, St. John's 72; CCNY 62, Duquesne 52. **Third Place**—St. John's 69, Duquesne 67 (OT). **Championship**—CCNY 69, Bradley 61.

1951

	Before Tourns	Head Coach	Final Record
1 **Kentucky**	28-2	Adolph Rupp	32-2
2 Oklahoma A&M	27-4	Hank Iba	29-6
3 Columbia	22-0	Lou Rossini	22-1
4 Kansas St.	22-3	Jack Gardner	25-4
5 Illinois	19-4	Harry Combes	22-5
6 Bradley	32-6	Forddy Anderson	same
7 Indiana	19-3	Branch McCracken	same
8 N.C. State	29-4	Everett Case	30-7
9 St. John's	22-3	Frank McGuire	26-5
10 Saint Louis	21-7	Eddie Hickey	22-8
11 **BYU**	22-8	Stan Watts	26-10
12 Arizona	24-4	Fred Enke	24-6
13 Dayton	24-4	Tom Blackburn	27-5
14 Toledo	23-8	Jerry Bush	same
15 Washington	22-5	Tippy Dye	24-6
16 Murray St.	21-6	Harlan Hodges	same
17 Cincinnati	18-3	John Wiethe	18-4
18 Siena	19-8	Dan Cunha	same
19 USC	21-6	Forrest Twogood	same
20 Villanova	25-6	Al Severance	25-7

NCAA Final Four (at Williams Arena, Minneapolis): **Third Place**—Illinois 61, Oklahoma St. 46. **Championship**—Kentucky 68, Kansas St. 58.

NIT Final Four (at Madison Sq. Garden): **Semifinals**—Dayton 69, St. John's 62 (OT); BYU 69, Seton Hall 59. **Third Place**—St. John's 70, Seton Hall 68 (2 OT). **Championship**—BYU 62, Dayton 43.

1952

	Before Tourns	Head Coach	Final Record
1 Kentucky	28-2	Adolph Rupp	29-3
2 Illinois	19-3	Harry Combes	22-4
3 Kansas St.	19-5	Jack Gardner	same
4 Duquesne	21-1	Dudey Moore	23-4
5 Saint Louis	22-6	Eddie Hickey	23-8
6 Washington	25-6	Tippy Dye	same
7 Iowa	19-3	Bucky O'Connor	same
8 **Kansas**	24-3	Phog Allen	28-3
9 West Virginia	23-4	Red Brown	same
10 St. John's	22-3	Frank McGuire	25-5
11 Dayton	24-3	Tom Blackburn	28-5
12 Duke	24-6	Harold Bradley	same
13 Holy Cross	23-3	Buster Sheary	24-4
14 Seton Hall	25-2	Honey Russell	25-3
15 St. Bonaventure	19-5	Ed Melvin	21-6
16 Wyoming	27-6	Everett Shelton	28-7
17 Louisville	20-5	Peck Hickman	20-6
18 Seattle	29-7	Al Brightman	29-8
19 UCLA	19-10	John Wooden	19-12
20 SW Texas St.	30-1	Milton Jowers	same

Note: Unranked **La Salle**, coached by Ken Loefler, won the NIT. The Explorers entered the postseason at 21-7 and had a final record of 25-7.

NCAA Final Four (at Edmundson Pavillion, Seattle): **Semifinals**—St. John's 61, Illinois 59; Kansas 74, Santa Clara 59. **Third Place**—Illinois 67, Santa Clara 64. **Championship**—Kansas 80, St. John's 63.

NIT Final Four (at Madison Sq. Garden): **Semifinals**—La Salle 59, Duquesne 46; Dayton 69, St. Bonaventure 62. **Third Place**—St. Bonaventure 48, Duquesne 34. **Championship**—La Salle 75, Dayton 64.

1953

	Before Tours	Head Coach	Final Record
1 **Indiana**	18-3	Branch McCracken	23-3
2 La Salle	25-2	Ken Loeffler	25-3
3 **Seton Hall**	28-2	Honey Russell	31-2
4 Washington	27-2	Tippy Dye	30-3
5 LSU	22-1	Harry Rabenhorst	24-3
6 Kansas	16-5	Phog Allen	19-6
7 Oklahoma A&M	22-6	Hank Iba	23-7
Kansas St.	17-4	Jack Gardner	same
9 Western Ky.	25-5	Ed Diddle	25-6
10 Illinois	18-4	Harry Combes	same
11 Oklahoma City	18-4	Doyle Parrick	18-6
12 N.C. State	26-6	Everett Case	same
13 Notre Dame	17-4	John Jordan	19-5
14 Louisville	21-5	Peck Hickman	22-6
Seattle	27-3	Al Brightman	29-4
16 Miami-OH	17-5	Bill Rohr	17-6
17 Eastern Ky.	16-8	Paul McBrayer	16-9
18 Duquesne	18-7	Dudey Moore	21-8
Navy	16-4	Ben Carnevale	16-5
20 Holy Cross	18-5	Buster Sheary	20-6

NCAA Final Four (at Municipal Auditorium, Kansas City): **Semifinals**—Indiana 80, LSU 67; Kansas 79, Washington 53. **Third Place**—Washington 88, LSU 69. **Championship**—Indiana 69, Kansas 68.

NIT Final Four (at Madison Sq. Garden): **Semifinals**—Seton Hall 74, Manhattan 56; St. John's 64, Duquesne 55. **Third Place**—Duquesne 81, Manhattan 67. **Championship**—Seton Hall 58, St. John's 46.

1954

	Before Tours	Head Coach	Final Record
1 Kentucky	25-0	Adolph Rupp	same*
2 Indiana	19-3	Branch McCracken	20-4
3 Duquesne	24-2	Dudey Moore	26-3
4 Western Ky.	28-1	Ed Diddle	29-3
5 Oklahoma A&M	23-4	Hank Iba	24-5
6 Notre Dame	20-2	John Jordan	22-3
7 Kansas	16-5	Phog Allen	same
8 **Holy Cross**	23-2	Buster Sheary	26-2
9 LSU	21-3	Harry Rabenhorst	21-5
10 **La Salle**	21-4	Ken Loeffler	26-4
11 Iowa	17-5	Bucky O'Connor	same
12 Duke	22-6	Harold Bradley	same
13 Colorado A&M	22-5	Bill Strannigan	22-7
14 Illinois	17-5	Harry Combes	same
15 Wichita	27-3	Ralph Miller	27-4
16 Seattle	26-1	Al Brightman	26-2
17 N.C. State	26-6	Everett Case	28-7
18 Dayton	24-6	Tom Blackburn	25-7
Minnesota	17-5	Ozzie Cowles	same
20 Oregon St.	19-10	Slats Gill	same
UCLA	18-7	John Wooden	same
USC	17-12	Forrest Twogood	19-14

*Kentucky turned down invitation to NCAA tournament after NCAA declared seniors Cliff Hagan, Frank Ramsey and Lou Tsioropoulos ineligible for postseason play.

NCAA Final Four (at Municipal Auditorium, Kansas City): **Semifinals**—La Salle 69, Penn St. 54; Bradley 74, USC 72. **Third Place**—Penn St. 70, USC 61. **Championship**—La Salle 92, Bradley 76.

NIT Final Four (at Madison Square Garden): **Semifinals**—Duquesne 66, Niagara 51; Holy Cross 75, Western Ky. 69. **Third Place**—Niagara 71, Western Ky. 65. **Championship**—Holy Cross 71, Duquesne 62.

1955

	Before Tours	Head Coach	Final Record
1 **San Francisco**	23-1	Phil Woolpert	28-1
2 Kentucky	22-2	Adolph Rupp	23-3
3 La Salle	22-4	Ken Loeffler	26-5
4 N.C. State	28-4	Everett Case	same
5 Iowa	17-5	Bucky O'Connor	19-7
6 **Duquesne**	19-4	Dudey Moore	22-4
7 Utah	23-3	Jack Gardner	24-4
8 Marquette	22-2	Jack Nagle	24-3
9 Dayton	23-3	Tom Blackburn	25-4
10 Oregon St.	21-7	Slats Gill	22-8
11 Minnesota	15-7	Ozzie Cowles	same
12 Alabama	19-5	Johnny Dee	same
13 UCLA	21-5	John Wooden	same
14 G. Washington	24-6	Bill Reinhart	same
15 Colorado	16-5	Bebe Lee	19-6
16 Tulsa	20-6	Clarence Iba	21-7
17 Vanderbilt	16-6	Bob Polk	same
18 Illinois	17-5	Harry Combes	same
19 West Virginia	19-10	Fred Schaus	19-11
20 Saint Louis	19-7	Eddie Hickey	20-8

NCAA Final Four (at Municipal Auditorium, Kansas City): **Semifinals**—La Salle 76, Iowa 73; San Francisco 62, Colorado 50. **Third Place**—Colorado 75, Iowa 74. **Championship**—San Francisco 77, La Salle 63.

NIT Final Four (at Madison Square Garden): **Semifinals**—Dayton 79, St. Francis-PA 73 (OT); Duquesne 65, Cincinnati 51. **Third Place**—Cincinnati 96, St. Francis-PA 91 (OT). **Championship**—Duquesne 70, Dayton 58.

1956

	Before Tours	Head Coach	Final Record
1 **San Francisco**	25-0	Phil Woolpert	29-0
2 N.C. State	24-3	Everett Case	24-4
3 Dayton	23-3	Tom Blackburn	25-4
4 Iowa	17-5	Bucky O'Connor	20-6
5 Alabama	21-3	Johnny Dee	same
6 **Louisville**	23-3	Peck Hickman	26-3
7 SMU	22-2	Doc Hayes	25-4
8 UCLA	21-5	John Wooden	22-6
9 Kentucky	19-5	Adolph Rupp	20-6
10 Illinois	18-4	Harry Combes	same
11 Oklahoma City	18-6	Abe Lemons	20-7
12 Vanderbilt	19-4	Bob Polk	same
13 North Carolina	18-5	Frank McGuire	same
14 Holy Cross	22-4	Roy Leenig	22-5
15 Temple	23-3	Harry Litwack	27-4
16 Wake Forest	19-9	Murray Greason	same
17 Duke	19-7	Harold Bradley	same
18 Utah	21-5	Jack Gardner	22-6
19 Oklahoma A&M	18-8	Hank Iba	18-9
20 West Virginia	21-8	Fred Schaus	21-9

NCAA Final Four (at McGaw Hall, Evanston, IL): **Semifinals**—Iowa 83, Temple 76; San Francisco 76, SMU 68. **Third Place**—Temple 90, SMU 81. **Championship**—San Francisco 83, Iowa 71.

NIT Final Four (at Madison Square Garden): **Semifinals**—Dayton 89, St. Francis-NY 58; Louisville 89, St. Joseph's-PA 79. **Third Place**—St. Joseph's-PA 93, St. Francis-NY 82. **Championship**—Louisville 93, Dayton 80.

Associated Press Final Polls (Cont.)

Taken **before** NCAA and NIT tournaments

1957

	Before Tourns	Head Coach	Final Record
1 **North Carolina**	27-0	Frank McGuire	32-0
2 Kansas	21-2	Dick Harp	24-3
3 Kentucky	22-4	Adolph Rupp	23-5
4 SMU	21-3	Doc Hayes	22-4
5 Seattle	24-2	John Castellani	24-3
6 Louisville	21-5	Peck Hickman	same
7 West Va.	25-4	Fred Schaus	25-5
8 Vanderbilt	17-5	Bob Polk	same
9 Oklahoma City	17-8	Abe Lemons	19-9
10 Saint Louis	19-7	Eddie Hickey	19-9
11 Michigan St.	14-8	Forddy Anderson	16-10
12 Memphis St.	21-5	Bob Vanatta	24-6
13 California	20-4	Pete Newell	21-5
14 UCLA	22-4	John Wooden	same
15 Mississippi St.	17-8	Babe McCarthy	same
16 Idaho St.	24-2	John Grayson	25-4
17 Notre Dame	18-7	John Jordan	20-8
18 Wake Forest	19-9	Murray Greason	same
19 Canisius	20-5	Joe Curran	22-6
20 Oklahoma A&M	17-9	Hank Iba	same

Note: Unranked **Bradley**, coached by Chuck Orsborn, won the NIT. The Braves entered the tourney at 19-7 and had a final record of 22-7.

NCAA Final Four (at Municipal Auditorium, Kansas City): **Semifinals**—North Carolina 74, Michigan St. 70 (3 OT); Kansas 80, San Francisco 56. **Third Place**—San Francisco 67, Michigan St. 60. **Championship**—North Carolina 54, Kansas 53 (3 OT).

NIT Final Four (at Madison Square Garden): **Semifinals**—Memphis St. 80, St. Bonaventure 78; Bradley 78, Temple 66. **Third Place**—Temple 67, St. Bonaventure 50. **Championship**—Bradley 84, Memphis St. 83.

1958

	Before Tourns	Head Coach	Final Record
1 West Virginia	26-1	Fred Schaus	26-2
2 Cincinnati	24-2	George Smith	25-3
3 Kansas St.	20-3	Tex Winter	22-5
4 San Francisco	24-1	Phil Woolpert	25-2
5 Temple	24-2	Harry Litwack	27-3
6 Maryland	20-6	Bud Millikan	22-7
7 Kansas	18-5	Dick Harp	same
8 Notre Dame	22-4	John Jordan	24-5
9 **Kentucky**	19-6	Adolph Rupp	23-6
10 Duke	18-7	Harold Bradley	same
11 Dayton	23-3	Tom Blackburn	25-4
12 Indiana	12-10	Branch McCracken	13-11
13 North Carolina	19-7	Frank McGuire	same
14 Bradley	20-6	Chuck Orsborn	20-7
15 Mississippi St.	20-5	Babe McCarthy	same
16 Auburn	16-6	Joel Eaves	same
17 Michigan St.	16-6	Forddy Anderson	same
18 Seattle	20-6	John Castellani	24-7
19 Oklahoma St.	19-7	Hank Iba	21-8
20 N.C. State	18-6	Everett Case	same

Note: Unranked **Xavier-OH**, coached by Jim McCafferty, won the NIT. The Musketeers entered the tourney at 15-11 and had a final record of 19-11.

NCAA Final Four (at Freedom Hall, Louisville): **Semifinals**—Kentucky 61, Temple 60; Seattle 73, Kansas St. 51. **Third Place**—Temple 67, Kansas St. 57. **Championship**—Kentucky 84, Seattle 72.

NIT Final Four (at Madison Square Garden): **Semifinals**—Dayton 80, St. John's 56; Xavier-OH 72, St. Bonaventure 53. **Third Place**—St. Bonaventure 84, St. John's 69. **Championship**—Xavier-OH 78, Dayton 74 (OT).

1959

	Before Tourns	Head Coach	Final Record
1 Kansas St.	24-1	Tex Winter	25-2
2 Kentucky	23-2	Adolph Rupp	24-3
3 Mississippi St.	24-1	Babe McCarthy	same*
4 Bradley	23-3	Chuck Orsborn	25-4
5 Cincinnati	23-3	George Smith	26-4
6 N.C. State	22-4	Everett Case	same
7 Michigan St.	18-3	Forddy Anderson	19-4
8 Auburn	20-2	Joel Eaves	same
9 North Carolina	20-4	Frank McGuire	20-5
10 West Virginia	25-4	Fred Schaus	29-5
11 **California**	21-4	Pete Newell	25-4
12 Saint Louis	20-5	John Benington	20-6
13 Seattle	23-6	Vince Cazzetta	same
14 St. Joseph's-PA	22-3	Jack Ramsay	22-5
15 St. Mary's-CA	18-5	Jim Weaver	19-6
16 TCU	19-5	Buster Brannon	20-6
17 Oklahoma City	20-6	Abe Lemons	20-7
18 Utah	21-5	Jack Gardner	21-7
19 St. Bonaventure	20-2	Eddie Donovan	20-3
20 Marquette	22-4	Eddie Hickey	23-6

*Mississippi St. turned down invitation to NCAA tournament because it was an integrated event.

Note: Unranked **St. John's**, coached by Joe Lapchick, won the NIT. The Redmen entered the tourney at 16-6 and had a final record of 20-6.

NCAA Final Four (at Freedom Hall, Louisville): **Semifinals**—West Virginia 94, Louisville 79; California 64, Cincinnati 58. **Third Place**—Cincinnati 98, Louisville 85. **Championship**—California 71, West Virginia 70.

NIT Final Four (at Madison Square Garden): **Semifinals**—Bradley 59, NYU 57; St. John's 76, Providence 55. **Third Place**—NYU 71, Providence 57. **Championship**—St. John's 76, Bradley 71 (OT).

1960

	Before Tourns	Head Coach	Final Record
1 Cincinnati	25-1	George Smith	28-2
2 California	24-1	Pete Newell	28-2
3 **Ohio St.**	21-3	Fred Taylor	25-3
4 **Bradley**	24-2	Chuck Orsborn	27-2
5 West Virginia	24-4	Fred Schaus	26-5
6 Utah	24-2	Jack Gardner	26-3
7 Indiana	20-4	Branch McCracken	same
8 Utah St.	22-4	Cecil Baker	24-5
9 St. Bonaventure	19-3	Eddie Donovan	21-5
10 Miami-FL	23-3	Bruce Hale	23-4
11 Auburn	19-3	Joel Eaves	same
12 NYU	19-4	Lou Rossini	22-5
13 Georgia Tech	21-5	Whack Hyder	22-6
14 Providence	21-4	Joe Mullaney	24-5
15 Saint Louis	19-7	John Benington	19-8
16 Holy Cross	20-5	Roy Leenig	20-6
17 Villanova	19-5	Al Severance	20-6
18 Duke	15-10	Vic Bubas	17-11
19 Wake Forest	21-7	Bones McKinney	same
20 St. John's	17-7	Joe Lapchick	17-8

NCAA Final Four (at the Cow Palace, San Fran.): **Semifinals**—Ohio St. 76, NYU 54; California 77, Cincinnati 69. **Third Place**—Cincinnati 95, NYU 71. **Championship**—Ohio St. 75, California 55.

NIT Final Four (at Madison Square Garden): **Semifinals**—Bradley 82, St. Bonaventure 71; Providence 68, Utah St. 62. **Third Place**—Utah St. 99, St. Bonaventure 93. **Championship**—Bradley 88, Providence 72.

1961

	Before Tourns	Head Coach	Final Record
1 Ohio St.	24-0	Fred Taylor	27-1
2 **Cincinnati**	23-3	Ed Jucker	27-3
3 St. Bonaventure	22-3	Eddie Donovan	24-4
4 Kansas St.	22-3	Tex Winter	23-4
5 North Carolina	19-4	Frank McGuire	same
6 Bradley	21-5	Chuck Orsborn	same
7 USC	20-6	Forrest Twogood	21-8
8 Iowa	18-6	S. Scheuerman	same
9 West Virginia	23-4	George King	same
10 Duke	22-6	Vic Bubas	same
11 Utah	21-6	Jack Gardner	23-8
12 Texas Tech	14-9	Polk Robison	15-10
13 Niagara	16-4	Taps Gallagher	16-5
14 Memphis St.	20-2	Bob Vanatta	20-3
15 Wake Forest	17-10	Bones McKinney	19-11
16 St. John's	20-4	Joe Lapchick	20-5
17 St. Joseph's-PA	22-4	Jack Ramsay	25-5
18 Drake	19-7	Maury John	same
19 Holy Cross	19-4	Roy Leenig	22-5
20 Kentucky	18-8	Adolph Rupp	19-9

Note: Unranked **Providence**, coached by Joe Mullaney, won the NIT. The Friars entered the tourney at 20-5 and had a final record of 24-5.

NCAA Final Four (at Municipal Auditorium, Kansas City): **Semifinals**—Ohio St. 95, St. Joseph's-PA 69; Cincinnati 82, Utah 67. **Third Place**—St. Joseph's-PA 127, Utah 120 (4 OT). **Championship**—Cincinnati 70, Ohio St. 65 (OT).

NIT Final Four (at Madison Square Garden) **Semifinals**—St. Louis 67, Dayton 60; Providence 90, Holy Cross 83 (OT). **Third Place**—Holy Cross 85, Dayton 67. **Championship**—Providence 62, St. Louis 59.

1962

	Before Tourns	Head Coach	Final Record
1 Ohio St.	23-1	Fred Taylor	26-2
2 **Cincinnati**	25-2	Ed Jucker	29-2
3 Kentucky	22-2	Adolph Rupp	23-3
4 Mississippi St.	19-6	Babe McCarthy	same
5 Bradley	21-6	Chuck Orsborn	21-7
6 Kansas St.	22-3	Tex Winter	same
7 Utah	23-3	Jack Gardner	same
8 Bowling Green	21-3	Harold Anderson	same
9 Colorado	18-6	Sox Walseth	19-7
10 Duke	20-5	Vic Bubas	same
11 Loyola-IL	21-3	George Ireland	23-4
12 St. John's	19-4	Joe Lapchick	21-5
13 Wake Forest	18-8	Bones McKinney	22-9
14 Oregon St.	22-4	Slats Gill	24-5
15 West Virginia	24-5	George King	24-6
16 Arizona St.	23-3	Ned Wulk	23-4
17 Duquesne	20-5	Red Manning	22-7
18 Utah St.	21-5	Ladell Andersen	22-7
19 UCLA	16-9	John Wooden	18-11
20 Villanova	19-6	Jack Kraft	21-7

Note: Unranked **Dayton**, coached by Tom Blackburn, won the NIT. The Flyers entered the tourney at 20-6 and had a final record of 24-6.

NCAA Final Four (at Freedom Hall, Louisville): **Semifinals**—Ohio St. 84, Wake Forest 68; Cincinnati 72, UCLA 70. **Third Place**—Wake Forest 82, UCLA 80. **Championship**—Cincinnati 71, Ohio St. 59.

NIT Final Four (at Madison Square Garden): **Semifinals**—Dayton 98, Loyola-IL 82; St. John's 76, Duquesne 65. **Third Place**—Loyola-IL 95, Duquesne 84. **Championship**—Dayton 73, St. John's 67.

1963

AP ranked only 10 teams from the 1962-63 season through 1967-68.

	Before Tourns	Head Coach	Final Record
1 Cincinnati	23-1	Ed Jucker	26-2
2 Duke	24-2	Vic Bubas	27-3
3 **Loyola-IL**	24-2	George Ireland	29-2
4 Arizona St.	24-2	Ned Wulk	26-3
5 Wichita	19-7	Ralph Miller	19-8
6 Mississippi St.	21-5	Babe McCarthy	22-6
7 Ohio St.	20-4	Fred Taylor	same
8 Illinois	19-5	Harry Combes	20-6
9 NYU	17-3	Lou Rossini	18-5
10 Colorado	18-6	Sox Walseth	19-7

Note: Unranked **Providence**, coached by Joe Mullaney, won the NIT. The Friars entered the tourney at 21-4 and had a final record of 24-4.

NCAA Final Four (at Freedom Hall, Louisville): **Semifinals**—Loyola-IL 94, Duke 75; Cincinnati 80, Oregon St. 46. **Third Place**—Duke 85, Oregon St. 63. **Championship**—Loyola-IL 60, Cincinnati 58 (OT).

NIT Final Four (at Madison Square Garden): **Semifinals**—Providence 70, Marquette 64; Canisius 61, Villanova 46. **Third Place**—Marquette 66, Villanova 58. **Championship**—Providence 81, Canisius 66.

1964

AP ranked only 10 teams from the 1962-63 season through 1967-68.

	Before Tourns	Head Coach	Final Record
1 **UCLA**	26-0	John Wooden	30-0
2 Michigan	20-4	Dave Strack	23-5
3 Duke	23-4	Vic Bubas	26-5
4 Kentucky	21-4	Adolph Rupp	21-6
5 Wichita St.	22-5	Ralph Miller	23-6
6 Oregon St.	25-3	Slats Gill	25-4
7 Villanova	22-3	Jack Kraft	24-4
8 Loyola-IL	20-5	George Ireland	22-6
9 DePaul	21-3	Ray Meyer	21-4
10 Davidson	22-4	Lefty Driesell	same

Note: Unranked **Bradley**, coached by Chuck Orsborn, won the NIT. The Braves entered the tourney at 20-6 and finished with a record of 23-6.

NCAA Final Four (at Municipal Auditorium, Kansas City): **Semifinals**—Duke 91, Michigan 80; UCLA 90, Kansas St. 84. **Third Place**—Michigan 100, Kansas St. 90. **Championship**—UCLA 98, Duke 83.

NIT Final Four (12 at Madison Square Garden): **Semifinals**—New Mexico 72, NYU 65; Bradley 67, Army 52. **Third Place**—Army 60, NYU 59. **Championship**—Bradley 86, New Mexico 54.

Undefeated National Champions

The 1964 UCLA team is one of only seven NCAA champions to win the title with an undefeated record.

Year		W-L	Year		W-L
1956	San Francisco	29-0	1972	UCLA	30-0
1957	North Carolina	32-0	1973	UCLA	30-0
1964	UCLA	30-0	1976	Indiana	32-0
1967	UCLA	30-0			

Associated Press Final Polls (Cont.)

Taken **before** NCAA and NIT tournaments

1965

AP ranked only 10 teams from the 1962-63 season through 1967-68.

	Before Tourns	Head Coach	Final Record
1 Michigan	21-3	Dave Strack	24-4
2 **UCLA**	24-2	John Wooden	28-2
3 St. Joseph's-PA	25-1	Jack Ramsay	26-3
4 Providence	22-1	Joe Mullaney	24-2
5 Vanderbilt	23-3	Roy Skinner	24-4
6 Davidson	24-2	Lefty Driesell	same
7 Minnesota	19-5	John Kundla	same
8 Villanova	21-4	Jack Kraft	23-5
9 BYU	21-5	Stan Watts	21-7
10 Duke	20-5	Vic Bubas	same

Note: Unranked **St. John's**, coached by Joe Lapchick, won the NIT. The Redmen entered the tourney at 17-8 and finished with a record of 21-8.

NCAA Final Four (at Memorial Coliseum, Portland, OR): **Semifinals**—Michigan 93, Princeton 76; UCLA 108, Wichita St. 89. **Third Place**—Princeton 118, Wichita St. 82. **Championship**—UCLA 91, Michigan 80.

NIT Final Four (at Madison Square Garden): **Semifinals**—Villanova 91, NYU 69; St. John's 67, Army 60. **Third Place**—Army 75, NYU 74. **Championship**—St. John's 55, Villanova 51.

1966

AP ranked only 10 teams from the 1962-63 season through 1967-68.

	Before Tourns	Head Coach	Final Record
1 Kentucky	24-1	Adolph Rupp	27-2
2 Duke	23-3	Vic Bubas	26-4
3 **Texas Western**	23-1	Don Haskins	28-1
4 Kansas	22-3	Ted Owens	23-4
5 St. Joseph's-PA	22-4	Jack Ramsay	24-5
6 Loyola-IL	22-2	George Ireland	22-3
7 Cincinnati	21-5	Tay Baker	21-7
8 Vanderbilt	22-4	Roy Skinner	same
9 Michigan	17-7	Dave Strack	18-8
10 Western Ky.	23-2	Johnny Oldham	25-3

Note: Unranked **BYU**, coached by Stan Watts, won the NIT. The Cougars entered the tourney at 17-5 and had a final record of 20-5.

NCAA Final Four (at Cole Fieldhouse, College Park, MD): **Semifinals**—Kentucky 83, Duke 79; Texas Western 85, Utah 78. **Third Place**—Duke 79, Utah 77. **Championship**—Texas Western 72, Kentucky 65.

NIT Final Four (at Madison Square Garden): **Semifinals**—BYU 66, Army 60; NYU 69, Villanova 63. **Third Place**—Villanova 76, Army 65. **Championship**—BYU 97, NYU 84.

1967

AP ranked only 10 teams from the 1962-63 season through 1967-68.

	Before Tourns	Head Coach	Final Record
1 **UCLA**	26-0	John Wooden	30-0
2 Louisville	23-3	Peck Hickman	23-5
3 Kansas	22-3	Ted Owens	23-4
4 North Carolina	24-4	Dean Smith	26-6
5 Princeton	23-2	B. van Breda Kolff	25-3
6 Western Ky.	23-2	Johnny Oldham	23-3
7 Houston	23-3	Guy Lewis	27-4
8 Tennessee	21-5	Ray Mears	21-7
9 Boston College	19-2	Bob Cousy	21-3
10 Texas Western	20-5	Don Haskins	22-6

Note: Unranked **Southern Illinois**, coached by Jack Hartman, won the NIT. The Salukis entered the tourney at 20-2 and had a final record of 24-2.

NCAA Final Four (at Freedom Hall, Louisville): **Semifinals**—Dayton 76, N. Carolina 62; UCLA 73, Houston 58. **Third Place**—Houston 84, N. Carolina 62. **Championship**—UCLA 79, Dayton 64.

NIT Final Four (at Madison Square Garden): **Semifinals**—Marquette 83, Marshall 78; Southern Ill. 79, Rutgers 70. **Third Place**—Rutgers 93, Marshall 76. **Championship**—Southern Ill. 71, Marquette 56.

1968

AP ranked only 10 teams from the 1962-63 season through 1967-68.

	Before Tourns	Head Coach	Final Record
1 Houston	28-0	Guy Lewis	31-2
2 **UCLA**	25-1	John Wooden	29-1
3 St. Bonaventure	22-0	Larry Weise	23-2
4 North Carolina	25-3	Dean Smith	28-4
5 Kentucky	21-4	Adolph Rupp	22-5
6 New Mexico	23-3	Bob King	23-5
7 Columbia	21-4	Jack Rohan	23-5
8 Davidson	22-4	Lefty Driesell	24-5
9 Louisville	20-6	John Dromo	21-7
10 Duke	21-5	Vic Bubas	22-6

Note: Unranked **Dayton**, coached by Don Donoher, won the NIT. The Flyers entered the tourney at 17-9 and had a final record of 21-9.

NCAA Final Four (at the Sports Arena, Los Angeles): **Semifinals**—N. Carolina 80, Ohio St. 66; UCLA 101, Houston 69. **Third Place**—Ohio St. 89, Houston 85. **Championship**—UCLA 78, N. Carolina 55.

NIT Final Four (at Madison Square Garden): **Semifinals**—Dayton 76, Notre Dame 74 (OT); Kansas 58, St. Peter's 46. **Third Place**—Notre Dame 81, St. Peter's 78. **Championship**—Dayton 61, Kansas 48.

Highest-Rated College Games on TV

The dozen highest-rated college basketball games seen on U.S. television have been NCAA tournament championship games, led by the 1979 Michigan State-Indiana State final that featured Magic Johnson and Larry Bird.

Listed below are the finalists (winning team first), date of game, TV network, and TV rating and audience share (according to Nielsen Media Research).

	Date	Net	Rtg/Sh
1 Michigan St.-Indiana St.	3/26/79	NBC	24.1/38
2 Villanova-Georgetown	4/1/85	CBS	23.3/33
3 Duke-Michigan	4/6/92	CBS	22.7/35
4 N.C. State-Houston	4/4/83	CBS	22.3/32
5 N. Carolina-Michigan	4/5/93	CBS	22.2/34
6 Arkansas-Duke	4/4/94	CBS	21.6/33
7 N. Carolina-Georgetown	3/29/82	CBS	21.6/31
8 Michigan-Seton Hall	4/3/89	CBS	21.3/33
9 UCLA-Kentucky	3/31/75	NBC	21.3/33
10 Louisville-Duke	3/32/86	CBS	20.7/31
11 Indiana-N. Carolina	3/30/81	NBC	20.7/29
12 UCLA-Memphis St.	3/26/73	NBC	20.5/32

1969

	Before Tourns	Head Coach	Final Record
1 **UCLA**	25-1	John Wooden	29-1
2 La Salle	23-1	Tom Gola	same*
3 Santa Clara	26-1	Dick Garibaldi	27-2
4 North Carolina	25-3	Dean Smith	27-5
5 Davidson	24-2	Lefty Driesell	26-3
6 Purdue	20-4	George King	23-5
7 Kentucky	22-4	Adolph Rupp	23-5
8 St. John's	22-4	Lou Carnesecca	23-6
9 Duquesne	19-4	Red Manning	21-5
10 Villanova	21-4	Jack Kraft	21-5
11 Drake	23-4	Maury John	26-5
12 New Mexico St.	23-3	Lou Henson	24-5
13 South Carolina	20-6	Frank McGuire	21-7
14 Marquette	22-4	Al McGuire	24-5
15 Louisville	20-5	John Dromo	21-6
16 Boston College	21-3	Bob Cousy	24-4
17 Notre Dame	20-6	Johnny Dee	20-7
18 Colorado	20-6	Sox Walseth	21-7
19 Kansas	20-6	Ted Owens	20-7
20 Illinois	19-5	Harvey Schmidt	same

Note: Unranked **Temple**, coached by Harry Litwak, won the NIT. The Owls entered the tourney at 18-8 and finished with a record of 22-8.

NCAA Final Four (at Freedom Hall, Louisville): **Semifinals**—Purdue 92, N. Carolina 65; UCLA 85, Drake 82. **Third Place**—Drake 104, N. Carolina 84. **Championship**—UCLA 92, Purdue 72.

NIT Final Four (at Madison Square Garden): **Semifinals**—Temple 63, Tennessee 58; Boston College 73, Army 61. **Third Place**—Tennessee 64, Army 52. **Championship**—Temple 89, Boston College 76.

1970

	Before Tourns	Head Coach	Final Record
1 Kentucky	25-1	Adolph Rupp	26-2
2 **UCLA**	24-2	John Wooden	28-2
3 St. Bonaventure	22-1	Larry Weise	25-3
4 Jacksonville	23-1	Joe Williams	27-2
5 New Mexico St.	23-2	Lou Henson	27-3
6 South Carolina	25-3	Frank McGuire	25-3
7 Iowa	19-4	Ralph Miller	20-5
8 **Marquette**	22-3	Al McGuire	26-3
9 Notre Dame	20-6	Johnny Dee	21-8
10 N.C. State	22-6	Norm Sloan	23-7
11 Florida St.	23-3	Hugh Durham	23-3
12 Houston	24-3	Guy Lewis	25-5
13 Penn	25-1	Dick Harter	25-2
14 Drake	21-6	Maury John	22-7
15 Davidson	22-4	Terry Holland	22-5
16 Utah St.	20-6	Ladell Andersen	22-7
17 Niagara	21-5	Frank Layden	22-7
18 Western Ky.	22-2	John Oldham	22-3
19 Long Beach St.	23-3	Jerry Tarkanian	24-5
20 USC	18-8	Bob Boyd	18-8

NCAA Final Four (at Cole Fieldhouse, College Park, MD): **Semifinals**—Jacksonville 91, St. Bonaventure 83; UCLA 93, New Mexico St. 77. **Third Place**—N. Mexico St. 79, St. Bonaventure 73. **Championship**—UCLA 80, Jacksonville 69.

NIT Final Four (at Madison Square Garden): **Semifinals**—St. John's 60, Army 59; Marquette 101, LSU 79. **Third Place**—Army 75, LSU 68. **Championship**—Marquette 65, St. John's 53.

1971

	Before Tourns	Head Coach	Final Record
1 **UCLA**	25-1	John Wooden	29-1
2 Marquette	26-0	Al McGuire	28-1
3 Penn	26-0	Dick Harter	28-1
4 Kansas	25-1	Ted Owens	27-3
5 USC	24-2	Bob Boyd	24-2
6 South Carolina	23-4	Frank McGuire	23-6
7 Western Ky.	20-5	John Oldham	24-6
8 Kentucky	22-4	Adolph Rupp	22-6
9 Fordham	25-1	Digger Phelps	26-3
10 Ohio St.	19-5	Fred Taylor	20-6
11 Jacksonville	22-3	Tom Wasdin	22-4
12 Notre Dame	19-7	Johnny Dee	20-9
13 **North Carolina**	22-6	Dean Smith	26-6
14 Houston	20-6	Guy Lewis	22-7
15 Duquesne	21-3	Red Manning	21-4
16 Long Beach St.	21-4	Jerry Tarkanian	23-5
17 Tennessee	20-6	Ray Mears	21-7
18 Villanova	19-5	Jack Kraft	23-6
19 Drake	20-7	Maury John	21-8
20 BYU	18-9	Stan Watts	18-11

NCAA Final Four (at the Astrodome, Houston): **Semifinals**—Villanova 92, Western Ky. 89 (2 OT); UCLA 68, Kansas 60. **Third Place**—Western Ky. 77, Kansas 75. **Championship**—UCLA 68, Villanova 62.

NIT Final Four (at Madison Square Garden): **Semifinals**—N. Carolina 73, Duke 69; Ga. Tech 76, St. Bonaventure 71 (2 OT). **Third Place**—St. Bonaventure 92, Duke 88 (OT). **Championship**—N. Carolina 84, Ga. Tech 66.

1972

	Before Tourns	Head Coach	Final Record
1 **UCLA**	26-0	John Wooden	30-0
2 North Carolina	23-4	Dean Smith	26-5
3 Penn	23-2	Chuck Daly	25-3
4 Louisville	23-4	Denny Crum	26-5
5 Long Beach St.	23-3	Jerry Tarkanian	25-4
6 South Carolina	22-4	Frank McGuire	24-5
7 Marquette	24-2	Al McGuire	25-4
8 SW Louisiana	23-3	Beryl Shipley	25-4
9 BYU	21-4	Stan Watts	21-5
10 Florida St.	23-5	Hugh Durham	27-6
11 Minnesota	17-6	Bill Musselman	18-7
12 Marshall	23-3	Carl Tacy	23-4
13 Memphis St.	21-6	Gene Bartow	21-7
14 **Maryland**	23-5	Lefty Driesell	27-5
15 Villanova	19-6	Jack Kraft	20-8
16 Oral Roberts	25-1	Ken Trickey	26-2
17 Indiana	17-7	Bob Knight	17-8
18 Kentucky	20-6	Adolph Rupp	21-7
19 Ohio St.	18-6	Fred Taylor	same
20 Virginia	21-6	Bill Gibson	21-7

NCAA Final Four (at the Sports Arena, Los Angeles): **Semifinals**—Florida St. 79, N. Carolina 75; UCLA 96, Louisville 77. **Third Place**—N. Carolina 105, Louisville 91. **Championship**—UCLA 81, Florida St. 76.

NIT Final Four (at Madison Square Garden): **Semifinals**—Maryland 91, Jacksonville 77; Niagara 69, St. John's 67. **Third Place**—Jacksonville 83, St. John's 80. **Championship**—Maryland 100, Niagara 69.

Associated Press Final Polls (Cont.)

Taken **before** NCAA, NIT and Collegiate Commissioner's Assn. (1974-75) tournaments; (*) indicates on probation.

1973

	Before Tourns	Head Coach	Final Record
1 **UCLA**	26-0	John Wooden	30-0
2 N.C. State	27-0	Norm Sloan	same*
3 Long Beach St.	24-2	Jerry Tarkanian	26-3
4 Providence	24-2	Dave Gavitt	27-4
5 Marquette	23-3	Al McGuire	25-4
6 Indiana	19-5	Bob Knight	22-6
7 SW Louisiana	23-2	Beryl Shipley	24-5
8 Maryland	22-6	Lefty Driesell	23-7
9 Kansas St.	22-4	Jack Hartman	23-5
10 Minnesota	20-4	Bill Musselman	21-5
11 North Carolina	22-7	Dean Smith	25-8
12 Memphis St.	21-5	Gene Bartow	24-6
13 Houston	23-3	Guy Lewis	23-4
14 Syracuse	22-4	Roy Danforth	24-5
15 Missouri	21-5	Norm Stewart	21-6
16 Arizona St.	18-7	Ned Wulk	19-9
17 Kentucky	19-7	Joe B. Hall	20-8
18 Penn	20-5	Chuck Daly	21-7
19 Austin Peay	21-5	Lake Kelly	22-7
20 San Francisco	22-4	Bob Gaillard	23-5

*N.C. State was ineligible for NCAA tournament for using improper methods to recruit David Thompson.

Note: Unranked **Virginia Tech**, coached by Don DeVoe, won the NIT. The Hokies entered the tourney at 18-5 and finished with a record of 22-5.

NCAA Final Four (at The Arena, St. Louis): **Semifinals**—Memphis St. 98, Providence 85; UCLA 70, Indiana 59. **Third Place**—Indiana 97, Providence 79. **Championship**—UCLA 87, Memphis St. 66.

NIT Final Four (at Madison Square Garden): **Semifinals**—Va. Tech 74, Alabama 73; Notre Dame 78, N. Carolina 71. **Third Place**—N. Carolina 88, Alabama 69. **Championship**—Va. Tech 92, Notre Dame 91 (OT).

1974

	Before Tourns	Head Coach	Final Record
1 **N.C. State**	26-1	Norm Sloan	30-1
2 UCLA	23-3	John Wooden	26-4
3 Notre Dame	24-2	Digger Phelps	26-3
4 Maryland	23-5	Lefty Driesell	same
5 Providence	26-3	Dave Gavitt	28-4
6 Vanderbilt	23-3	Roy Skinner	23-5
7 Marquette	22-4	Al McGuire	26-5
8 North Carolina	22-5	Dean Smith	22-6
9 Long Beach St.	24-2	Lute Olson	same
10 **Indiana**	20-5	Bob Knight	23-5
11 Alabama	22-4	C.M. Newton	same
12 Michigan	21-4	Johnny Orr	22-5
13 Pittsburgh	23-3	Buzz Ridl	25-4
14 Kansas	21-5	Ted Owens	23-7
15 USC	22-4	Bob Boyd	24-5
16 Louisville	21-6	Denny Crum	21-7
17 New Mexico	21-6	Norm Ellenberger	22-7
18 South Carolina	22-4	Frank McGuire	22-5
19 Creighton	22-6	Eddie Sutton	23-7
20 Dayton	19-7	Don Donoher	20-9

NCAA Final Four (at Greensboro, NC, Coliseum): **Semifinals**—N.C. State 80, UCLA 77 (2 OT); Marquette 64, Kansas 51. **Third Place**—UCLA 78, Kansas 61. **Championship**—N.C. State 76, Marquette 64.

NIT Final Four (at Madison Square Garden): **Semifinals**—Purdue 78, Jacksonville 63; Utah 117, Boston Col. 93. **Third Place**—Boston Col. 87, Jacksonville 77. **Championship**—Purdue 87, Utah 81.

CCA Final Four (at The Arena, St. Louis): **Semifinals**—Indiana 73, Toledo 72; USC 74, Bradley 73. **Championship**—Indiana 85, USC 60.

1975

	Before Tourns	Head Coach	Final Record
1 Indiana	29-0	Bob Knight	31-1
2 **UCLA**	23-3	John Wooden	28-3
3 Louisville	24-2	Denny Crum	28-3
4 Maryland	22-4	Lefty Driesell	24-5
5 Kentucky	22-4	Joe B. Hall	26-5
6 North Carolina	21-7	Dean Smith	23-8
7 Arizona St.	23-3	Ned Wulk	25-4
8 N.C. State	22-6	Norm Sloan	22-6
9 Notre Dame	18-8	Digger Phelps	19-10
10 Marquette	23-3	Al McGuire	23-4
11 Alabama	22-4	C.M. Newton	22-5
12 Cincinnati	21-5	Gale Catlett	23-6
13 Oregon St.	18-10	Ralph Miller	19-12
14 **Drake**	16-10	Bob Ortegel	19-10
15 Penn	23-4	Chuck Daly	23-5
16 UNLV	22-4	Jerry Tarkanian	24-5
17 Kansas St.	18-8	Jack Hartman	20-9
18 USC	18-7	Bob Boyd	18-8
19 Centenary	25-4	Larry Little	same
20 Syracuse	20-7	Roy Danforth	23-9

NCAA Final Four (at San Diego Sports Arena): **Semifinals**—Kentucky 95, Syracuse 79; UCLA 75, Louisville 74 (OT). **Third Place**—Louisville 96, Syracuse 88 (OT). **Championship**—UCLA 92, Kentucky 85.

NIT Championship (at Madison Sq. Garden): Princeton 80, Providence 69. No Top 20 teams played in NIT.

CCA Championship (at Freedom Hall, Louisville): Drake 83, Arizona 76. No.14 Drake and No.18 USC were only Top 20 teams in CCA.

1976

	Before Tourns	Head Coach	Final Record
1 **Indiana**	27-0	Bob Knight	32-0
2 Marquette	25-1	Al McGuire	27-2
3 UNLV	28-1	Jerry Tarkanian	29-2
4 Rutgers	28-0	Tom Young	31-2
5 UCLA	24-3	Gene Bartow	28-4
6 Alabama	22-4	C.M. Newton	23-5
7 Notre Dame	22-5	Digger Phelps	23-6
8 North Carolina	25-3	Dean Smith	25-4
9 Michigan	21-6	Johnny Orr	25-7
10 Western Mich.	24-2	Eldon Miller	25-3
11 Maryland	22-6	Lefty Driesell	same
12 Cincinnati	25-5	Gale Catlett	25-6
13 Tennessee	21-5	Ray Mears	21-6
14 Missouri	24-4	Norm Stewart	26-5
15 Arizona	22-8	Fred Snowden	24-9
16 Texas Tech	24-5	Gerald Myers	25-6
17 DePaul	19-8	Ray Meyer	20-9
18 Virginia	18-11	Terry Holland	18-12
19 Centenary	22-5	Larry Little	same
20 Pepperdine	21-5	Gary Colson	22-6

NCAA Final Four (at the Spectrum, Phila.); **Semifinals**—Michigan 86, Rutgers 70; Indiana 65, UCLA 51. **Third Place**—UCLA 106, Rutgers 92. **Championship**—Indiana 86, Michigan 68.

NIT Championship (at Madison Square Garden): Kentucky 71, NC-Charlotte 67. No Top 20 teams played in NIT.

1977

	Before Tourns	Head Coach	Final Record
1 Michigan	24-3	Johnny Orr	26-4
2 UCLA	24-3	Gene Bartow	25-4
3 Kentucky	24-3	Joe B. Hall	26-4
4 UNLV	25-2	Jerry Tarkanian	29-3
5 North Carolina	24-4	Dean Smith	28-5
6 Syracuse	25-3	Jim Boeheim	26-4
7 **Marquette**	20-7	Al McGuire	25-7
8 San Francisco	29-1	Bob Gaillard	29-2
9 Wake Forest	20-7	Carl Tacy	22-8
10 Notre Dame	21-6	Digger Phelps	22-7
11 Alabama	23-4	C.M. Newton	25-6
12 Detroit	24-3	Dick Vitale	25-4
13 Minnesota	24-3	Jim Dutcher	same*
14 Utah	22-6	Jerry Pimm	23-7
15 Tennessee	22-5	Ray Mears	22-6
16 Kansas St.	23-6	Jack Hartman	24-7
17 NC-Charlotte	25-3	Lee Rose	28-5
18 Arkansas	26-1	Eddie Sutton	26-2
19 Louisville	21-6	Denny Crum	21-7
20 VMI	25-3	Charlie Schmaus	26-4

NCAA Final Four (at the Omni, Atlanta): **Semifinals**—Marquette 51, NC-Charlotte, 49; N. Carolina 84, UNLV 83. **Third Place**—UNLV 106, NC-Charlotte 94. **Championship**—Marquette 67, N. Carolina 59.

NIT Championship (at Madison Square Garden): St. Bonaventure 94, Houston 91. No.11 Alabama was only Top 20 team in NIT.

1978

	Before Tourns	Head Coach	Final Record
1 **Kentucky**	25-2	Joe B. Hall	30-2
2 UCLA	24-2	Gary Cunningham	25-3
3 DePaul	25-2	Ray Meyer	27-3
4 Michigan St.	23-4	Jud Heathcote	25-5
5 Arkansas	28-3	Eddie Sutton	32-3
6 Notre Dame	20-6	Digger Phelps	23-8
7 Duke	23-6	Bill Foster	27-7
8 Marquette	24-3	Hank Raymonds	24-4
9 Louisville	22-6	Denny Crum	23-7
10 Kansas	24-4	Ted Owens	24-5
11 San Francisco	22-5	Bob Gaillard	23-6
12 New Mexico	24-3	Norm Ellenberger	24-4
13 Indiana	20-7	Bob Knight	21-8
14 Utah	22-5	Jerry Pimm	23-6
15 Florida St.	23-5	Hugh Durham	23-6
16 North Carolina	23-7	Dean Smith	23-8
17 **Texas**	22-5	Abe Lemons	26-5
18 Detroit	24-3	Dave Gaines	25-4
19 Miami-OH	18-8	Darrell Hedric	19-9
20 Penn	19-7	Bob Weinhauer	20-8

NCAA Final Four (at the Checkerdome, St. Louis): **Semifinals**—Kentucky 64, Arkansas 59; Duke 90, Notre Dame 86. **Third Place**—Arkansas 71, Notre Dame 69. **Championship**—Kentucky 94, Duke 88.

NIT Championship (at Madison Square Garden): Texas 101, N.C. State 93. No.17 Texas and No.18 Detroit were only Top 20 teams in NIT.

1979

	Before Tourns	Head Coach	Final Record
1 Indiana St.	29-0	Bill Hodges	33-1
2 UCLA	23-4	Gary Cunningham	25-5
3 **Michigan St.**	21-6	Jud Heathcote	26-6
4 Notre Dame	22-5	Digger Phelps	24-6
5 Arkansas	23-4	Eddie Sutton	25-5
6 DePaul	22-5	Ray Meyer	26-6
7 LSU	22-5	Dale Brown	23-6
8 Syracuse	25-3	Jim Boeheim	26-4
9 North Carolina	23-5	Dean Smith	23-6
10 Marquette	21-6	Hank Raymonds	22-7
11 Duke	22-7	Bill Foster	22-8
12 San Francisco	21-6	Dan Belluomini	22-7
13 Louisville	23-7	Denny Crum	24-8
14 Penn	21-5	Bob Weinhauer	25-7
15 Purdue	23-7	Lee Rose	27-8
16 Oklahoma	20-9	Dave Bliss	21-10
17 St. John's	18-10	Lou Carnesecca	21-11
18 Rutgers	21-8	Tom Young	22-9
19 Toledo	21-6	Bob Nichols	22-7
20 Iowa	20-7	Lute Olson	20-8

NCAA Final Four (at Special Events Center, Salt Lake City): **Semifinals**—Michigan St. 101, Penn 67; Indiana St. 76, DePaul 74. **Third Place**—DePaul 96, Penn 93. **Championship**—Michigan St. 75, Indiana St. 64.

NIT Championship (at Madison Square Garden): Indiana 53, Purdue 52. No.15 Purdue was only Top 20 team in NIT.

1980

	Before Tourns	Head Coach	Final Record
1 DePaul	26-1	Ray Meyer	26-2
2 **Louisville**	28-3	Denny Crum	33-3
3 LSU	24-5	Dale Brown	26-6
4 Kentucky	28-5	Joe B. Hall	29-6
5 Oregon St.	26-3	Ralph Miller	26-4
6 Syracuse	25-3	Jim Boeheim	26-4
7 Indiana	20-7	Bob Knight	21-8
8 Maryland	23-6	Lefty Driesell	24-7
9 Notre Dame	20-7	Digger Phelps	20-8
10 Ohio St.	24-5	Eldon Miller	21-8
11 Georgetown	24-5	John Thompson	26-6
12 BYU	24-4	Frank Arnold	24-5
13 St. John's	24-4	Lou Carnesecca	24-5
14 Duke	22-8	Bill Foster	24-9
15 North Carolina	21-7	Dean Smith	21-8
16 Missouri	23-5	Norm Stewart	25-6
17 Weber St.	26-2	Neil McCarthy	26-3
18 Arizona St.	21-6	Ned Wulk	22-7
19 Iona	28-4	Jim Valvano	29-5
20 Purdue	19-9	Lee Rose	23-10

NCAA Final Four (at Market Square Arena, Indianapolis): **Semifinals**—Louisville 80, Iowa 72; UCLA 67, Purdue 62; **Championship**—Louisville 59, UCLA 54.

NIT Championship (at Madison Square Garden): Virginia 58, Minnesota 55. No Top 20 teams played in NIT.

Associated Press Final Polls (Cont.)

Taken **before** NCAA and NIT Tournaments; (*) indicates on probation.

1981

	Before Tourns	Head Coach	Final Record
1 DePaul	27-1	Ray Meyer	27-2
2 Oregon St.	26-1	Ralph Miller	26-2
3 Arizona St.	24-3	Ned Wulk	24-4
4 LSU	28-3	Dale Brown	31-5
5 Virginia	25-3	Terry Holland	29-4
6 North Carolina	25-7	Dean Smith	29-8
7 Notre Dame	22-5	Digger Phelps	23-6
8 Kentucky	22-5	Joe B. Hall	22-6
9 **Indiana**	21-9	Bob Knight	26-9
10 UCLA	20-6	Larry Brown	20-7
11 Wake Forest	22-6	Carl Tacy	22-7
12 Louisville	21-8	Denny Crum	21-9
13 Iowa	21-6	Lute Olson	21-7
14 Utah	24-4	Jerry Pimm	25-5
15 Tennessee	20-7	Don DeVoe	21-8
16 BYU	22-6	Frank Arnold	25-7
17 Wyoming	23-5	Jim Brandenburg	24-6
18 Maryland	20-9	Lefty Driesell	21-10
19 Illinois	20-7	Lou Henson	21-8
20 Arkansas	22-7	Eddie Sutton	24-8

NCAA Final Four (at the Spectrum, Phila.): **Semifinals**—N. Carolina 78, Virginia 65; Indiana 67, LSU 49. **Third Place**—Virginia 78, LSU 74. **Championship**—Indiana 63, N. Carolina 50.

NIT Championship (at Madison Square Garden): Tulsa 86, Syracuse 84. No Top 20 teams played in NIT.

1983

	Before Tourns	Head Coach	Final Record
1 Houston	27-2	Guy Lewis	31-3
2 Louisville	29-3	Denny Crum	32-4
3 St. John's	27-4	Lou Carnesecca	28-5
4 Virginia	27-4	Terry Holland	29-5
5 Indiana	23-5	Bob Knight	24-6
6 UNLV	28-2	Jerry Tarkanian	28-3
7 UCLA	23-5	Larry Farmer	23-6
8 North Carolina	26-7	Dean Smith	28-8
9 Arkansas	25-3	Eddie Sutton	26-4
10 Missouri	26-7	Norm Stewart	26-8
11 Boston College	24-6	Gary Williams	25-7
12 Kentucky	22-7	Joe B. Hall	23-8
13 Villanova	22-7	Rollie Massimino	24-8
14 Wichita St.	25-3	Gene Smithson	same*
15 Tenn-Chatt.	26-3	Murray Arnold	26-4
16 **N.C. State**	20-10	Jim Valvano	26-10
17 Memphis St.	22-7	Dana Kirk	23-8
18 Georgia	21-9	Hugh Durham	24-10
19 Oklahoma St.	24-6	Paul Hansen	24-7
20 Georgetown	21-9	John Thompson	22-10

NCAA Final Four (at The Pit, Albuquerque, NM): **Semifinals**—N.C. State 67, Georgia 60; Houston 94, Louisville 81. **Championship**—N.C. State 54, Houston 52.

NIT Championship (at Madison Square Garden): Fresno St. 69, DePaul 60. No Top 20 teams played in NIT.

1982

	Before Tourns	Head Coach	Final Record
1 **North Carolina**	27-2	Dean Smith	32-2
2 DePaul	26-1	Ray Meyer	26-2
3 Virginia	29-3	Terry Holland	30-4
4 Oregon St.	23-4	Ralph Miller	25-5
5 Missouri	26-3	Norm Stewart	27-4
6 Georgetown	26-6	John Thompson	30-7
7 Minnesota	22-5	Jim Dutcher	23-6
8 Idaho	26-2	Don Monson	27-3
9 Memphis St.	23-4	Dana Kirk	24-5
10 Tulsa	24-5	Nolan Richardson	24-6
11 Fresno St.	26-2	Boyd Grant	27-3
12 Arkansas	23-5	Eddie Sutton	23-6
13 Alabama	23-6	Wimp Sanderson	24-7
14 West Virginia	26-3	Gale Catlett	27-4
15 Kentucky	22-7	Joe B. Hall	22-8
16 Iowa	20-7	Lute Olson	21-8
17 Ala-Birmingham	23-5	Gene Bartow	25-6
18 Wake Forest	20-8	Carl Tacy	21-9
19 UCLA	21-6	Larry Farmer	21-6
20 Louisville	20-9	Denny Crum	23-10

NCAA Final Four (at the Superdome, New Orleans): **Semifinals**—N. Carolina 68, Houston 63; Georgetown 50, Louisville 46. **Championship**—N. Carolina 63, Georgetown 62.

NIT Championship (at Madison Square Garden): Bradley 67, Purdue 58. No Top 20 teams played in NIT.

1984

	Before Tourns	Head Coach	Final Record
1 North Carolina	27-2	Dean Smith	28-3
2 **Georgetown**	29-3	John Thompson	34-3
3 Kentucky	26-4	Joe B. Hall	29-5
4 DePaul	26-2	Ray Meyer	27-3
5 Houston	28-4	Guy Lewis	32-5
6 Illinois	24-4	Lou Henson	26-5
7 Oklahoma	29-4	Billy Tubbs	29-5
8 Arkansas	25-6	Eddie Sutton	25-7
9 UTEP	27-3	Don Haskins	27-4
10 Purdue	22-6	Gene Keady	22-7
11 Maryland	23-7	Lefty Driesell	24-8
12 Tulsa	27-3	Nolan Richardson	27-4
13 UNLV	27-5	Jerry Tarkanian	29-6
14 Duke	24-9	Mike Krzyzewski	24-10
15 Washington	22-6	Marv Harshman	24-7
16 Memphis St.	24-6	Dana Kirk	26-7
17 Oregon St.	22-6	Ralph Miller	22-7
18 Syracuse	22-8	Jim Boeheim	23-9
19 Wake Forest	21-8	Carl Tacy	23-9
20 Temple	25-4	John Chaney	26-5

NCAA Final Four (at the Kingdome, Seattle): **Semifinals**—Houston 49, Virginia 47 (OT); Georgetown 53, Kentucky 40. **Championship**—Georgetown 84, Houston 75.

NIT Championship (at Madison Square Garden): Michigan 83, Notre Dame 63. No Top 20 teams played in NIT.

1985

	Before Tourns	Head Coach	Final Record
1 Georgetown	30-2	John Thompson	35-3
2 Michigan	25-3	Bill Frieder	26-4
3 St. John's	27-3	Lou Carnesecca	31-4
4 Oklahoma	28-5	Billy Tubbs	31-6
5 Memphis St.	27-3	Dana Kirk	31-4
6 Georgia Tech	24-7	Bobby Cremins	27-8
7 North Carolina	24-8	Dean Smith	27-9
8 Louisiana Tech	27-2	Andy Russo	29-3
9 UNLV	27-3	Jerry Tarkanian	28-4
10 Duke	22-7	Mike Krzyzewski	23-8
11 VCU	25-5	J.D. Barnett	26-6
12 Illinois	24-8	Lou Henson	26-9
13 Kansas	25-7	Larry Brown	26-8
14 Loyola-IL	25-5	Gene Sullivan	27-6
15 Syracuse	21-8	Jim Boeheim	22-9
16 N.C. State	20-9	Jim Valvano	23-10
17 Texas Tech	23-7	Gerald Myers	23-8
18 Tulsa	23-7	Nolan Richardson	23-8
19 Georgia	21-8	Hugh Durham	22-9
20 LSU	19-9	Dale Brown	19-10

Note: Unranked **Villanova**, coached by Rollie Massimino, won the NCAAs. The Wildcats entered the tourney at 19-10 and had a final record of 25-10.

NCAA Final Four (at Rupp Arena, Lexington, KY): **Semifinals**— Georgetown 77, St. John's 59; Villanova 52, Memphis St. 45. **Championship**—Villanova 66, Georgetown 64.

NIT Championship (at Madison Square Garden): UCLA 65, Indiana 62. No Top 20 teams played in NIT.

1986

	Before Tourns	Head Coach	Final Record
1 Duke	32-2	Mike Krzyzewski	37-3
2 Kansas	31-3	Larry Brown	35-4
3 Kentucky	29-3	Eddie Sutton	32-4
4 St. John's	30-4	Lou Carnesecca	31-5
5 Michigan	27-4	Bill Frieder	28-5
6 Georgia Tech	25-6	Bobby Cremins	27-7
7 **Louisville**	26-7	Denny Crum	32-7
8 North Carolina	26-5	Dean Smith	28-6
9 Syracuse	25-5	Jim Boeheim	26-6
10 Notre Dame	23-5	Digger Phelps	23-6
11 UNLV	31-4	Jerry Tarkanian	33-5
12 Memphis St.	27-5	Dana Kirk	28-6
13 Georgetown	23-7	John Thompson	24-8
14 Bradley	31-2	Dick Versace	32-3
15 Oklahoma	25-8	Billy Tubbs	26-9
16 Indiana	21-7	Bob Knight	21-8
17 Navy	27-4	Paul Evans	30-5
18 Michigan St.	21-7	Jud Heathcote	23-8
19 Illinois	21-9	Lou Henson	22-10
20 UTEP	27-5	Don Haskins	27-6

NCAA Final Four (at Reunion Arena, Dallas): **Semifinals**—Duke 71, Kansas 67; Louisville 88, LSU 77. **Championship**—Louisville 72, Duke 69.

NIT Championship (at Madison Square Garden): Ohio St. 73, Wyoming 63. No Top 20 teams played in NIT.

1987

	Before Tourns	Head Coach	Final Record
1 UNLV	33-1	Jerry Tarkanian	37-2
2 North Carolina	29-3	Dean Smith	32-4
3 **Indiana**	24-4	Bob Knight	30-4
4 Georgetown	26-4	John Thompson	29-5
5 DePaul	26-2	Joey Meyer	28-3
6 Iowa	27-4	Tom Davis	30-5
7 Purdue	24-4	Gene Keady	25-5
8 Temple	31-3	John Chaney	32-4
9 Alabama	26-4	Wimp Sanderson	28-5
10 Syracuse	26-6	Jim Boeheim	31-7
11 Illinois	23-7	Lou Henson	23-8
12 Pittsburgh	24-7	Paul Evans	25-8
13 Clemson	25-5	Cliff Ellis	25-6
14 Missouri	24-9	Norm Stewart	24-10
15 UCLA	24-6	Walt Hazzard	25-7
16 New Orleans	25-3	Benny Dees	26-4
17 Duke	22-8	Mike Krzyzewski	24-9
18 Notre Dame	22-7	Digger Phelps	24-8
19 TCU	23-6	Jim Killingsworth	24-7
20 Kansas	23-10	Larry Brown	25-11

NCAA Final Four (at the Superdome, New Orleans): **Semifinals**—Syracuse 77, Providence 63; Indiana 97, UNLV 93. **Championship**—Indiana 74, Syracuse 73.

NIT Championship (at Madison Square Garden): Southern Miss. 84, La Salle 80. No Top 20 teams played in NIT.

1988

	Before Tourns	Head Coach	Final Record
1 Temple	29-1	John Chaney	32-2
2 Arizona	31-2	Lute Olson	35-3
3 Purdue	27-3	Gene Keady	29-4
4 Oklahoma	30-3	Billy Tubbs	35-4
5 Duke	24-6	Mike Krzyzewski	28-7
6 Kentucky	25-5	Eddie Sutton	27-6
7 North Carolina	24-6	Dean Smith	27-7
8 Pittsburgh	23-6	Paul Evans	24-7
9 Syracuse	25-8	Jim Boeheim	26-9
10 Michigan	24-7	Bill Frieder	26-8
11 Bradley	26-4	Stan Albeck	26-5
12 UNLV	27-5	Jerry Tarkanian	28-6
13 Wyoming	26-5	Benny Dees	26-6
14 N.C. State	24-7	Jim Valvano	24-8
15 Loyola-CA	27-3	Paul Westhead	28-4
16 Illinois	22-9	Lou Henson	23-10
17 Iowa	22-9	Tom Davis	24-10
18 Xavier-OH	26-3	Pete Gillen	26-4
19 BYU	25-5	Ladell Andersen	26-6
20 Kansas St.	22-8	Lon Kruger	25-9

Note: Unranked **Kansas**, coached by Larry Brown, won the NCAAs. The Jayhawks entered the tourney at 21-11 and had a final record of 27-11.

NCAA Final Four (at Kemper Arena, Kansas City): **Semifinals**—Kansas 66, Duke 59; Oklahoma 86, Arizona 78. **Championship**—Kansas 83, Oklahoma 79.

NIT Championship (at Madison Square Garden): Connecticut 72, Ohio St. 67. No Top 20 teams played in NIT.

Associated Press Final Polls (Cont.)

Taken **before** NCAA and NIT Tournaments; (*) indicates on probation.

1989

	Before Tourns	Head Coach	Final Record
1 Arizona	27-3	Lute Olson	29-4
2 Georgetown	26-4	John Thompson	29-5
3 Illinois	27-4	Lou Henson	31-5
4 Oklahoma	28-5	Billy Tubbs	30-6
5 North Carolina	27-7	Dean Smith	29-8
6 Missouri	27-7	Norm Stewart & Rich Daly	29-8
7 Syracuse	27-7	Jim Boeheim	30-8
8 Indiana	25-7	Bob Knight	27-8
9 Duke	24-7	Mike Krzyzewski	28-8
10 **Michigan**	24-7	Bill Frieder & Steve Fisher	30-7
11 Seton Hall	26-6	P.J. Carlesimo	31-7
12 Louisville	22-8	Denny Crum	24-9
13 Stanford	26-6	Mike Montgomery	26-7
14 Iowa	22-9	Tom Davis	23-10
15 UNLV	26-7	Jerry Tarkanian	29-8
16 Florida St.	22-7	Pat Kennedy	22-8
17 West Virginia	25-4	Gale Catlett	26-5
18 Ball State	28-2	Rick Majerus	29-3
19 N.C. State	20-8	Jim Valvano	22-9
20 Alabama	23-7	Wimp Sanderson	23-8

NCAA Final Four (at The Kingdome, Seattle): **Semifinals**—Seton Hall 95, Duke 78; Michigan 83, Illinois 81. **Championship**—Michigan 80, Seton Hall 79 (OT).

NIT Championship (at Madison Square Garden): St. John's 73, St. Louis 65. No Top 20 teams played in NIT.

1990

	Before Tourns	Head Coach	Final Record
1 Oklahoma	26-4	Billy Tubbs	27-5
2 **UNLV**	29-5	Jerry Tarkanian	35-5
3 Connecticut	28-5	Jim Calhoun	31-6
4 Michigan St.	26-5	Jud Heathcote	28-6
5 Kansas	29-4	Roy Williams	30-5
6 Syracuse	24-6	Jim Boeheim	26-7
7 Arkansas	26-4	Nolan Richardson	30-5
8 Georgetown	23-6	John Thompson	24-7
9 Georgia Tech	24-6	Bobby Cremins	28-7
10 Purdue	21-7	Gene Keady	22-8
11 Missouri	26-5	Norm Stewart	26-6
12 La Salle	29-1	Speedy Morris	30-2
13 Michigan	22-7	Steve Fisher	23-8
14 Arizona	24-6	Lute Olson	25-7
15 Duke	24-8	Mike Krzyzewski	29-9
16 Louisville	26-7	Denny Crum	27-8
17 Clemson	24-8	Cliff Ellis	26-9
18 Illinois	21-7	Lou Henson	21-8
19 LSU	22-8	Dale Brown	23-9
20 Minnesota	20-8	Clem Haskins	23-9
21 Loyola-CA	23-5	Paul Westhead	26-6
22 Oregon St.	22-6	Jim Anderson	22-7
23 Alabama	24-8	Wimp Sanderson	26-9
24 New Mexico St.	26-4	Neil McCarthy	26-5
25 Xavier-OH	26-4	Pete Gillen	28-5

NCAA Final Four (at McNichols Sports Arena, Denver): **Semifinals**—Duke 97, Arkansas 83; UNLV 90, Georgia Tech 81. **Championship**—UNLV 103, Duke 73.

NIT Championship (at Madison Square Garden): Vanderbilt 74, St. Louis 72. No Top 25 teams played in NIT.

1991

	Before Tourns	Head Coach	Final Record
1 UNLV	30-0	Jerry Tarkanian	34-1
2 Arkansas	31-3	Nolan Richardson	34-4
3 Indiana	27-4	Bob Knight	29-5
4 North Carolina	25-5	Dean Smith	29-6
5 Ohio St.	25-3	Randy Ayers	27-4
6 **Duke**	26-7	Mike Krzyzewski	32-7
7 Syracuse	26-5	Jim Boeheim	26-6
8 Arizona	26-6	Lute Olson	28-7
9 Kentucky	22-6	Rick Pitino	same*
10 Utah	28-3	Rick Majerus	30-4
11 Nebraska	26-7	Danny Nee	26-8
12 Kansas	22-7	Roy Williams	27-8
13 Seton Hall	22-8	P.J. Carlesimo	25-9
14 Oklahoma St.	22-7	Eddie Sutton	24-8
15 New Mexico St.	23-5	Neil McCarthy	23-6
16 UCLA	23-8	Jim Harrick	23-9
17 E. Tennessee St.	28-4	Alan LaForce	28-5
18 Princeton	24-2	Pete Carril	24-3
19 Alabama	21-9	Wimp Sanderson	23-10
20 St. John's	20-8	Lou Carnesecca	23-9
21 Mississippi St.	20-8	Richard Williams	20-9
22 LSU	20-9	Dale Brown	20-10
23 Texas	22-8	Tom Penders	23-9
24 DePaul	20-8	Joey Meyer	20-9
25 Southern Miss	21-7	M.K. Turk	21-8

NCAA Final Four (at the Hoosier Dome, Indianapolis): **Semifinals**—Kansas 79, North Carolina 73; Duke 79, UNLV 77. **Championship**—Duke 72, Kansas 65.

NIT Championship (at Madison Square Garden): Stanford 78, Oklahoma 72. No Top 25 teams played in NIT.

1992

	Before Tourns	Head Coach	Final Record
1 **Duke**	28-2	Mike Krzyzewski	34-2
2 Kansas	26-4	Roy Williams	27-5
3 Ohio St.	23-5	Randy Ayers	26-6
4 UCLA	25-4	Jim Harrick	28-5
5 Indiana	23-6	Bob Knight	27-7
6 Kentucky	26-6	Rick Pitino	29-7
7 UNLV	26-2	Jerry Tarkanian	same*
8 USC	23-5	George Raveling	24-6
9 Arkansas	25-7	Nolan Richardson	26-8
10 Arizona	24-6	Lute Olson	24-7
11 Oklahoma St.	26-7	Eddie Sutton	28-8
12 Cincinnati	25-4	Bob Huggins	29-5
13 Alabama	25-8	Wimp Sanderson	26-9
14 Michigan St.	21-7	Jud Heathcote	22-8
15 Michigan	20-8	Steve Fisher	25-9
16 Missouri	20-8	Norm Stewart	21-9
17 Massachusetts	28-4	John Calipari	30-5
18 North Carolina	21-9	Dean Smith	23-10
19 Seton Hall	21-8	P.J. Carlesimo	23-9
20 Florida St.	20-9	Pat Kennedy	22-10
21 Syracuse	21-9	Jim Boeheim	22-10
22 Georgetown	21-9	John Thompson	22-10
23 Oklahoma	21-8	Billy Tubbs	21-9
24 DePaul	20-8	Joey Meyer	20-9
25 LSU	20-9	Dale Brown	21-10

NCAA Final Four (at the Metrodome, Minneapolis): **Semifinals**—Michigan 76, Cincinnati 72; Duke 81, Indiana 78. **Championship**—Duke 71, Michigan 51.

NIT Championship (at Madison Square Garden): Virginia 81, Notre Dame 76 (OT). No Top 25 teams played in NIT.

1993

	Before Tourns	Head Coach	Final Record
1 Indiana	28-3	Bob Knight	31-4
2 Kentucky	26-3	Rick Pitino	30-4
3 Michigan	26-4	Steve Fisher	31-5
4 **North Carolina**	28-4	Dean Smith	34-4
5 Arizona	24-3	Lute Olson	24-4
6 Seton Hall	27-6	P.J. Carlesimo	28-7
7 Cincinnati	24-4	Bob Huggins	27-5
8 Vanderbilt	26-5	Eddie Fogler	28-6
9 Kansas	25-6	Roy Williams	29-7
10 Duke	23-7	Mike Krzyzewski	24-8
11 Florida St.	22-9	Pat Kennedy	25-10
12 Arkansas	20-8	Nolan Richardson	22-9
13 Iowa	22-8	Tom Davis	23-9
14 Massachusetts	23-6	John Calipari	24-7
15 Louisville	20-8	Denny Crum	22-9
16 Wake Forest	19-8	Dave Odom	21-9
17 New Orleans	26-3	Tim Floyd	26-4
18 Georgia Tech	19-10	Bobby Cremins	19-11
19 Utah	23-6	Rick Majerus	24-7
20 Western Ky.	24-5	Ralph Willard	26-6
21 New Mexico	24-6	Dave Bliss	24-7
22 Purdue	18-9	Gene Keady	18-10
23 Oklahoma St.	19-8	Eddie Sutton	20-9
24 New Mexico St.	25-7	Neil McCarthy	26-8
25 UNLV	21-7	Rollie Massimino	21-8

NCAA Final Four (at the Superdome, New Orleans): **Semifinals**—North Carolina 78, Kansas 68; Michigan 81, Kentucky 78 (OT). **Championship**—North Carolina 77, Michigan 71.

NIT Championship (at Madison Square Garden): Minnesota 62, Georgetown 61. No. 25 UNLV was only Top 25 team played in NIT.

1994

	Before Tourns	Head Coach	Final Record
1 North Carolina	27-6	Dean Smith	28-7
2 **Arkansas**	25-3	Nolan Richardson	31-3
3 Purdue	26-4	Gene Keady	29-5
4 Connecticut	27-4	Jim Calhoun	29-5
5 Missouri	25-3	Norm Stewart	28-4
6 Duke	23-5	Mike Krzyzewski	28-6
7 Kentucky	26-6	Rick Pitino	27-7
8 Massachusetts	27-6	John Calipari	28-7
9 Arizona	25-5	Lute Olson	29-6
10 Louisville	26-5	Denny Crum	28-6
11 Michigan	21-7	Steve Fisher	24-8
12 Temple	22-7	John Chaney	23-8
13 Kansas	25-7	Roy Williams	27-8
14 Florida	25-7	Lon Kruger	29-8
15 Syracuse	21-6	Jim Boeheim	23-7
16 California	22-7	Todd Bozeman	22-8
17 UCLA	21-6	Jim Harrick	21-7
18 Indiana	19-8	Bob Knight	21-9
19 Oklahoma St.	23-9	Eddie Sutton	24-10
20 Texas	25-7	Tom Penders	26-8
21 Marquette	22-8	Kevin O'Neill	24-9
22 Nebraska	20-9	Danny Nee	20-10
23 Minnesota	20-11	Clem Haskins	21-12
24 Saint Louis	23-5	Charlie Spoonhour	23-6
25 Cincinnati	22-9	Bob Huggins	22-10

NCAA Final Four (at the Charlotte Coliseum): **Semifinals**—Arkansas 91, Arizona 82; Duke 70, Florida 65. **Championship**—Arkansas 76, Duke 72.

NIT Championship (at Madison Square Garden): Villanova 80, Vanderbilt 73. No top 25 teams played in NIT.

1995

	Before Tourns	Head Coach	Final Record
1 **UCLA**	25-2	Jim Harrick	31-2
2 Kentucky	25-4	Rick Pitino	28-5
3 Wake Forest	24-5	Dave Odom	26-6
4 North Carolina	24-5	Dean Smith	28-6
5 Kansas	23-5	Roy Williams	25-6
6 Arkansas	27-6	Nolan Richardson	32-7
7 Massachusetts	26-4	John Calipari	26-5
8 Connecticut	25-4	Jim Calhoun	28-5
9 Villanova	25-7	Steve Lappas	25-8
10 Maryland	24-7	Gary Williams	26-8
11 Michigan St.	22-5	Jud Heathcote	22-6
12 Purdue	24-6	Gene Keady	25-7
13 Virginia	22-8	Jeff Jones	25-9
14 Oklahoma St.	23-9	Eddie Sutton	27-10
15 Arizona	23-7	Lute Olson	23-8
16 Arizona St.	22-8	Bill Frieder	24-9
17 Oklahoma	23-8	Kelvin Sampson	23-9
18 Mississippi St.	20-7	Richard Williams	22-8
19 Utah	27-5	Rick Majerus	28-6
20 Alabama	22-9	David Hobbs	23-1
21 Western Ky.	26-3	Matt Kilcullen	27-4
22 Georgetown	19-9	John Thompson	21-10
23 Missouri	19-8	Norm Stewart	20-9
24 Iowa St.	22-10	Tim Floyd	23-11
25 Syracuse	19-9	Jim Boeheim	20-10

NCAA Final Four (at the Kingdome, Seattle): **Semifinals**—UCLA 74, Oklahoma St. 61; Arkansas 75, North Carolina 68. **Championship**—UCLA 89, Arkansas 78.

NIT Championship (at Madison Square Garden): Virginia Tech 65, Marquette 64 (OT). No top 25 teams played in NIT.

1996

	Before Tourns	Head Coach	Final Record
1 Massachusetts	31-1	John Calipari	35-2
2 **Kentucky**	28-2	Rick Pitino	34-2
3 Connecticut	30-2	Jim Calhoun	32-3
4 Georgetown	26-7	John Thompson	29-8
5 Kansas	26-4	Roy Williams	29-5
6 Purdue	25-5	Gene Keady	26-6
7 Cincinnati	25-4	Bob Huggins	28-5
8 Texas Tech	28-1	James Dickey	30-2
9 Wake Forest	23-5	Dave Odom	26-6
10 Villanova	25-6	Steve Lappas	26-7
11 Arizona	24-6	Lute Olson	26-7
12 Utah	25-6	Rick Majerus	27-7
13 Georgia Tech	22-11	Bobby Cremins	24-12
14 UCLA	23-7	Jim Harrick	23-8
15 Syracuse	24-8	Jim Boeheim	29-9
16 Memphis	22-7	Larry Finch	22-8
17 Iowa St.	23-8	Tim Floyd	24-9
18 Penn St.	21-6	Jerry Dunn	21-7
19 Mississippi St.	22-7	Richard Williams	26-8
20 Marquette	22-7	Mike Deane	23-8
21 Iowa	22-8	Tom Davis	23-9
22 Virginia Tech	22-5	Bill Foster	23-6
23 New Mexico	27-4	Dave Bliss	28-5
24 Louisville	20-11	Denny Crum	22-12
25 North Carolina	20-10	Dean Smith	21-11

NCAA Final Four (at the Meadowlands, E. Rutherford, N.J.): **Semifinals**—Kentucky 81, Massachusetts 74; Syracuse 77, Mississippi St. 69. **Championship**—Kentucky 76, Syracuse 67.

NIT Championship (at Madison Square Garden): Nebraska 60, St. Joseph's-PA 56. No top 25 teams in NIT.

AP Post-Tournament Final Polls

The final AP Top 20 poll has been released **after** the NCAA and NIT tournaments four times— in 1953 and '54 and again in 1974 and '75. Those four polls are listed below; teams that were not included in the last regular season polls are in *CAPITAL* italic letters.

1953

	Team	Final Record
1	Indiana	23-3
2	Seton Hall	31-2
3	Kansas	19-6
4	Washington	30-3
5	LSU	24-3
6	La Salle	25-3
7	*ST. JOHN'S*	17-6
8	Okla. A&M	23-7
9	Duquesne	21-8
10	Notre Dame	19-5
11	Illinois	18-4
12	Kansas St.	17-4
13	Holy Cross	20-6
14	Seattle	29-4
15	*WAKE FOREST*	22-7
16	*SANTA CLARA*	20-7
17	Western Ky.	25-6
18	N.C. State	26-6
19	*DEPAUL*	19-9
20	*SW MISSOURI*	24-4

1954

	Team	Final Record
1	Kentucky	25-0
2	La Salle	26-4
3	Holy Cross	26-2
4	Indiana	20-4
5	Duquesne	26-3
6	Notre Dame	22-3
7	*BRADLEY*	19-13
8	Western Ky.	29-3
9	*PENN ST.*	18-6
10	Okla. A&M	24-5
11	USC	19-14
12	*GEO. WASH.*	23-3
13	Iowa	17-5
14	LSU	21-5
15	Duke	22-6
16	*NIAGARA*	24-6
17	Seattle	26-2
18	Kansas	16-5
19	Illinois	17-5
20	*MARYLAND*	23-7

1974

	Team	Final Record
1	N.C. State	30-1
2	UCLA	26-4
3	Marquette	26-5
4	Maryland	23-5
5	Notre Dame	26-3
6	Michigan	22-5
7	Kansas	23-7
8	Providence	28-4
9	Indiana	23-5
10	Long Beach St.	24-2
11	*PURDUE*	22-8
12	North Carolina	22-6
13	Vanderbilt	23-5
14	Alabama	22-4
15	*UTAH*	22-8
16	Pittsburgh	25-4
17	USC	24-5
18	*ORAL ROBERTS*	23-6
19	South Carolina	22-5
20	Dayton	20-9

1975

	Team	Final Record
1	UCLA	28-3
2	Kentucky	26-5
3	Indiana	31-1
4	Louisville	28-3
5	Maryland	24-5
6	Syracuse	23-9
7	N.C. State	22-6
8	Arizona St.	25-4
9	North Carolina	23-8
10	Alabama	22-5
11	Marquette	23-4
12	*PRINCETON*	22-8
13	Cincinnati	23-6
14	Notre Dame	19-10
15	Kansas St.	20-9
16	Drake	19-10
17	UNLV	24-5
18	Oregon St.	19-12
19	*MICHIGAN*	19-8
20	Penn	23-5

Pre-Tournament Records

1953— St. John's (Al DeStefano, 14-5); Wake Forest (Murray Greason, 21-6); Santa Clara (Bob Feerick, 18-6); DePaul (Ray Meyer, 18-7); SW Missouri St. (Bob Vanatta, 19-4 before NAIA tourney). **1954**— Bradley (Forddy Anderson, 15-12); Penn St. (Elmer Gross, 14-5); George Washington (Bill Reinhart, 23-2); Niagara (Taps Gallagher, 22-5); Maryland (Bud Millikan, 23-7). **1974**— Purdue (Fred Schaus, 18-8); Utah (Bill Foster, 19-7); Oral Roberts (Ken Trickey, 21-5). **1975**— Princeton (Pete Carril, 18-8); Michigan (Johnny Orr, 19-7).

All Time AP Top 20

The composite AP Top 20 from the 1948-49 season through 1995-96, based on the final regular season rankings of each year. The final AP poll has been taken before the NCAA and NIT tournaments each season since 1949 except in 1953 and '54 and again in 1974 and '75 when the final poll came out after the postseason. Team point totals are based on 20 points for all 1st place finishes, 19 for each 2nd, etc.). Also listed are the number of times ranked No.1 by AP going into the tournaments, and times ranked in the pre-tournament Top 10 and Top 20.

	Team	Pts	No.1	Top10	Top20
1	Kentucky	552	7	31	36
2	North Carolina	450	4	25	32
3	UCLA	421	7	21	31
4	Duke	304	2	17	26
5	Indiana	290	4	16	22
6	Kansas	273	0	15	22
7	Louisville	233	0	11	22
8	Notre Dame	195	0	13	17
9	Michigan	191	2	10	14
10	Cincinnati	186	2	9	13
11	N.C. State	176	1	9	16
12	UNLV	173	2	8	13
13	Marquette	166	0	11	15
14	Illinois	162	0	8	17
15	Arkansas	158	0	9	13
16	Syracuse	150	0	9	15
17	Ohio St	149	2	9	10
18	Kansas St	147	1	8	12
19	DePaul	141	2	8	10
20	Bradley	139	1	7	10
	Georgetown	139	1	7	10

All Time Seeds Records

All time records of NCAA tournament seeds since tourney expanded to 64 teams in 1985. Note that 1st refers to championships, 2nd refers to runners-up and FF refers to Final Four appearances. In the 1985 tournament, 8th-seeded Villanova beat Georgetown, a No. 1-seed, 66-64, to become the lowest seed to win the NCAA tournament. In the 1986 tournament, 11th-seeded LSU beat Kentucky, a No. 1-seed, 59-57, to become the lowest seed to reach the NCAA Final Four.

Seed	W	L	Pct.	1st	2nd	FF
1	211	64	.767	9	7	16
2	162	68	.704	4	5	10
3	104	70	.598	2	3	2
4	95	72	.569	0	1	6
5	82	73	.529	0	0	2
6	98	70	.583	2	1	3
7	64	72	.471	0	0	1
8	53	71	.427	1	1	0
9	44	73	.376	0	0	1
10	38	72	.345	0	0	0
11	32	68	.320	0	0	1
12	26	68	.277	0	0	0
13	11	48	.186	0	0	0
14	11	48	.186	0	0	0
15	2	48	.040	0	0	0
16	0	48	.000	0	0	0

Division I Winning Streaks

Full Season

(Including tournaments)

No	Seasons	Broken by	Score
88 UCLA	1971-74	Notre Dame	71-70
60 San Francisco	1955-57	Illinois	62-33
47 UCLA	1966-68	Houston	71-69
45 UNLV	1990-91	Duke	79-77
44 Texas	1913-17	Rice	24-18
43 Seton Hall	1939-41	LIU-Bklyn	49-26
43 LIU-Brooklyn	1935-37	Stanford	45-31
41 UCLA	1968-69	USC	46-44
39 Marquette	1970-71	Ohio St.	60-59
37 Cincinnati	1962-63	Wichita St.	65-64
37 North Carolina	1957-58	West Virginia	75-64
36 N.C. State	1974-75	Wake Forest	83-78
35 Arkansas	1927-29	Texas	26-25

Regular Season

(Not including tournaments)

No	Seasons	Broken by	Score
76 UCLA	1971-74	Notre Dame	71-70
57 Indiana	1975-77	Toledo	59-57
56 Marquette	1970-72	Detroit	70-49
54 Kentucky	1952-55	Georgia Tech	59-58
51 San Francisco	1955-57	Illinois	62-33
48 Penn	1970-72	Temple	57-52
47 Ohio St	1960-62	Wisconsin	86-67
44 Texas	1913-17	Rice	24-18
43 UCLA	1966-68	Houston	71-69
43 LIU-Brooklyn	1935-37	Stanford	45-31
42 Seton Hall	1939-41	LIU-Bklyn	49-26

Home Court

No	Seasons	Broken By	Score
129 Kentucky	1943-55	Georgia Tech	59-58
99 St. Bonaventure	1948-61	Detroit	77-70
98 UCLA	1970-76	Oregon	65-45
86 Cincinnati	1957-64	Kansas	51-47
81 Arizona	1945-51	Kansas St.	76-57
81 Marquette	1967-73	Notre Dame	71-69
80 Lamar	1978-84	Louisiana Tech	68-65
75 Long Beach St.	1968-74	San Francisco	94-84
72 UNLV	1974-78	New Mexico	102-98
71 Arizona	1987-92	UCLA	89-87

Most Improved Teams

Since 1974

Team	Season	W-L	Previous W-L	Games Improved
N.C. A&T	1978	20-8	3-24	16.5
Murray St.	1980	23-8	4-22	16.5
Liberty	1992	22-7	5-23	16.5
North Texas	1976	22-4	6-20	16
Radford	1991	22-7	7-22	15
Tulsa	1981	26-7	8-19	15
Utah St.	1983	20-9	4-23	15
W. Michigan	1992	21-9	5-22	14.5
Tennessee St.	1993	19-10	4-24	14.5
Fresno St.	1978	21-6	7-20	14
James Madison	1987	20-10	5-23	14
Loyola Marymount	1988	28-4	12-16	14

All-Time Highest Scoring Teams

SINGLE SEASON

Scoring

	Year	Gm	Pts	Avg
Loyola-CA	1990	32	3918	122.4
Loyola-CA	1989	31	3486	112.5
UNLV	1976	31	3426	110.5
Loyola-CA	1988	32	3528	110.3
UNLV	1977	32	3426	107.1

SINGLE GAME

Scoring

	Score	Opponent	Date
Loyola-CA	186-140	US Int'l	1/5/91
Loyola-CA	181-150	US Int'l	1/31/89
Oklahoma	173-101	US Int'l	11/29/89
Oklahoma	172-112	Loyola-CA	12/15/90
Arkansas	166-101	US Int'l	12/9/89

Scoring Offense

Team	Season	Gm	Pts	Avg
Loyola Marymount	1990	32	3918	122.4
Loyola Marymount	1989	31	3486	112.5
UNLV	1976	31	3426	110.5
Loyola Marymount	1988	32	3528	110.3
UNLV	1977	32	3426	107.1
Oral Roberts	1972	28	2943	105.1
Southern-BR	1991	28	2924	104.4
Loyola Marymount	1991	31	3211	103.6
Oklahoma	1988	39	4012	102.9
Oklahoma	1989	36	3680	102.2

Scoring Defense

Before 1965

Team	Season	Gm	Pts	Avg
Oklahoma St.	1948	31	1006	32.5
Oklahoma St.	1949	28	985	35.2
Oklahoma St.	1950	27	1059	39.2
Alabama	1948	27	1070	39.6
Creighton	1948	23	925	40.2

Since 1965

Team	Season	Gm	Pts	Avg
Fresno St.	1982	30	1412	47.1
Princeton	1992	28	1349	48.2
Princeton	1991	27	1320	48.9
N.C. State	1982	32	1570	49.1
Princeton	1982	26	1277	49.1

Scoring Margin

Team	Season	Off	Def	Mar
UCLA	1972	94.6	64.3	30.3
N.C. State	1948	75.3	47.2	28.1
Kentucky	1954	87.5	60.3	27.2
Kentucky	1952	82.3	55.4	26.9
UNLV	1991	97.7	71.0	26.7
UCLA	1968	93.4	67.2	26.2
UCLA	1967	89.6	63.7	25.9
Houston	1968	97.8	72.5	25.3
Kentucky	1948	69.0	44.4	24.6
Kentucky	1949	68.2	43.9	24.3

Annual NCAA Division I Leaders

Scoring

The NCAA did not begin keeping individual scoring records until the 1947-48 season. All averages include postseason games where applicable.

Multiple winners: Pete Maravich and Oscar Robertson (3); Darrell Floyd, Harry Kelly, Frank Selvy and Freeman Williams (2).

Year		Gm	Pts	Avg
1948	Murray Wier, Iowa	19	399	21.0
1949	Tony Lavelli, Yale	30	671	22.4
1950	Paul Arizin, Villanova	29	735	25.3
1951	Bill Mlkvy, Temple	25	731	29.2
1952	Clyde Lovellette, Kansas	28	795	28.4
1953	Frank Selvy, Furman	25	738	29.5
1954	Frank Selvy, Furman	29	1209	41.7
1955	Darrell Floyd, Furman	25	897	35.9
1956	Darrell Floyd, Furman	28	946	33.8
1957	Grady Wallace, S. Carolina	29	906	31.2
1958	Oscar Robertson, Cincinnati	28	984	35.1
1959	Oscar Robertson, Cincinnati	30	978	32.6
1960	Oscar Robertson, Cincinnati	30	1011	33.7
1961	Frank Burgess, Gonzaga	26	842	32.4
1962	Billy McGill, Utah	26	1009	38.8
1963	Nick Werkman, Seton Hall	22	650	29.5
1964	Howie Komives, Bowling Green	23	844	36.7
1965	Rick Barry, Miami-FL	26	973	37.4
1966	Dave Schellhase, Purdue	24	781	32.5
1967	Jimmy Walker, Providence	28	851	30.4
1968	Pete Maravich, LSU	26	1138	43.8
1969	Pete Maravich, LSU	26	1148	44.2
1970	Pete Maravich, LSU	31	1381	44.5
1971	Johnny Neumann, Ole Miss	23	923	40.1
1972	Dwight Lamar, SW La	29	1054	36.3
1973	Bird Averitt, Pepperdine	25	848	33.9
1974	Larry Fogle, Canisius	25	835	33.4
1975	Bob McCurdy, Richmond	26	855	32.9
1976	Marshall Rodgers, Texas-Pan Am	25	919	36.8
1977	Freeman Williams, Portland St.	26	1010	38.8
1978	Freeman Williams, Portland St.	27	969	35.9
1979	Lawrence Butler, Idaho St	27	812	30.1
1980	Tony Murphy, Southern-BR	29	932	32.1
1981	Zam Fredrick, S. Carolina	27	781	28.9
1982	Harry Kelly, Texas Southern	29	862	29.7
1983	Harry Kelly, Texas Southern	29	835	28.8
1984	Joe Jakubick, Akron	27	814	30.1
1985	Xavier McDaniel, Wichita St	31	844	27.2
1986	Terrance Bailey, Wagner	29	854	29.4
1987	Kevin Houston, Army	29	953	32.9
1988	Hersey Hawkins, Bradley	31	1125	36.3
1989	Hank Gathers, Loyola-CA	31	1015	32.7
1990	Bo Kimble, Loyola-CA	32	1131	35.3
1991	Kevin Bradshaw, US Int'l	28	1054	37.6
1992	Brett Roberts, Morehead St	29	815	28.1
1993	Greg Guy, Texas-Pan Am	19	556	29.3
1994	Glenn Robinson, Purdue	34	1030	30.3
1995	Kurt Thomas, TCU	27	781	28.9
1996	Kevin Granger, Texas Southern	24	648	27.0

Note: Sixteen underclassmen have won the title. **Sophomores** (4)—Robertson (1958), Maravich (1968), Neumann (1971) and Fogle (1974); **Juniors** (12)—Selvy (1953), Floyd (1955), Robertson (1959), Werkman (1963), Maravich (1969), Lamar (1972), Williams (1977), Kelly (1982), Bailey (1986), Gathers (1989), Guy (1993) and Robinson (1994).

Rebounds

The NCAA did not begin keeping individual rebounding records until the 1950-51 season. From 1956-62, the championship was decided on highest percentage of recoveries out of all rebounds made by both teams in all games. All averages include postseason games where applicable.

Multiple winners: Artis Gilmore, Jerry Lucas, Xavier McDaniel, Kermit Washington and Leroy Wright (2).

Year		Gm	No	Avg
1951	Ernie Beck, Penn	27	556	20.6
1952	Bill Hannon, Army	17	355	20.9
1953	Ed Conlin, Fordham	26	612	23.5
1954	Art Quimby, Connecticut	26	588	22.6
1955	Charlie Slack, Marshall	21	538	25.6
1956	Joe Holup, G. Washington	26	604	.256
1957	Elgin Baylor, Seattle	25	508	.235
1958	Alex Ellis, Niagara	25	536	.262
1959	Leroy Wright, Pacific	26	652	.238
1960	Leroy Wright, Pacific	17	380	.234
1961	Jerry Lucas, Ohio St.	27	470	.198
1962	Jerry Lucas, Ohio St.	28	499	.211
1963	Paul Silas, Creighton	27	557	20.6
1964	Bob Pelkington, Xavier-OH	26	567	21.8
1965	Toby Kimball, Connecticut	23	483	21.0
1966	Jim Ware, Oklahoma City	29	607	20.9
1967	Dick Cunningham, Murray St.	22	479	21.8
1968	Neal Walk, Florida	25	494	19.8
1969	Spencer Haywood, Detroit	22	472	21.5
1970	Artis Gilmore, Jacksonville	28	621	22.2
1971	Artis Gilmore, Jacksonville	26	603	23.2
1972	Kermit Washington, American	23	455	19.8
1973	Kermit Washington, American	22	439	20.0
1974	Marvin Barnes, Providence	32	597	18.7
1975	John Irving, Hofstra	21	323	15.4
1976	Sam Pellom, Buffalo	26	420	16.2
1977	Glenn Moseley, Seton Hall	29	473	16.3
1978	Ken Williams, N. Texas	28	411	14.7
1979	Monti Davis, Tennessee St.	26	421	16.2
1980	Larry Smith, Alcorn State	26	392	15.1
1981	Darryl Watson, Miss. Valley St.	27	379	14.0
1982	LaSalle Thompson, Texas	27	365	13.5
1983	Xavier McDaniel, Wichita St.	28	403	14.4
1984	Akeem Olajuwon, Houston	37	500	13.5
1985	Xavier McDaniel, Wichita St.	31	460	14.8
1986	David Robinson, Navy	35	455	13.0
1987	Jerome Lane, Pittsburgh	33	444	13.5
1988	Kenny Miller, Loyola-IL	29	395	13.6
1989	Hank Gathers, Loyola-CA	31	426	13.7
1990	Anthony Bonner, St. Louis	33	456	13.8
1991	Shaquille O'Neal, LSU	28	411	14.7
1992	Popeye Jones, Murray St.	30	431	14.4
1993	Warren Kidd, Mid. Tenn. St.	26	386	14.8
1994	Jerome Lambert, Baylor	24	355	14.8
1995	Kurt Thomas, TCU	27	393	14.6
1996	Marcus Mann, Miss. Valley St.	29	394	13.6

Note: Only three players have ever led the NCAA in scoring and rebounding in the same season: Xavier McDaniel of Wichita St. (1985), Hank Gathers of Loyola-Marymount (1989) and Kurt Thomas of TCU (1995).

Assists

The NCAA did not begin keeping individual assist records until the 1983-84 season. All averages include postseason games where applicable.

Multiple winner: Avery Johnson (2).

Year		Gm	No	Avg
1984	Craig Lathen, IL-Chicago	29	274	9.45
1985	Rob Weingard, Hofstra	24	228	9.50
1986	Mark Jackson, St. John's	36	328	9.11
1987	Avery Johnson, Southern-BR	31	333	10.74
1988	Avery Johnson, Southern-BR	30	399	13.30
1989	Glenn Williams, Holy Cross	28	278	9.93
1990	Todd Lehmann, Drexel	28	260	9.29
1991	Chris Corchiani, N.C. State	31	299	9.65
1992	Van Usher, Tennessee Tech	29	254	8.76
1993	Sam Crawford, N. Mexico St.	34	310	9.12
1994	Jason Kidd, California	30	272	9.06
1995	Nelson Haggerty, Baylor	28	284	10.14
1996	Raimonds Miglinieks, UC-Irvine	27	230	8.52

Blocked Shots

The NCAA did not begin keeping individual blocked shots records until the 1985-86 season. All averages include postseason games where applicable.

Multiple winners: David Robinson and Keith Closs (2).

Year		Gm	No	Avg
1986	David Robinson, Navy	35	207	5.91
1987	David Robinson, Navy	32	144	4.50
1988	Rodney Blake, St. Joe's-PA	29	116	4.00
1989	Alonzo Mourning, G'town	34	169	4.97
1990	Kenny Green, Rhode Island	26	124	4.77
1991	Shawn Bradley, BYU	34	177	5.21
1992	Shaquille O'Neal, LSU	30	157	5.23
1993	Theo Ratliff, Wyoming	28	124	4.43
1994	Grady Livingston, Howard	26	115	4.42
1995	Keith Closs, Cen. Conn. St.	26	139	5.35
1996	Keith Closs, Cen. Conn. St.	28	178	6.36

All-Time NCAA Division I Individual Leaders

Through 1995-96; includes regular season and tournament games; **Last** column indicates final year played.

CAREER

Scoring

	Points	Yrs	Last	Gm	Pts
1	Pete Maravich, LSU	3	1970	83	3667
2	Freeman Williams, Port. St.	4	1978	106	3249
3	Lionel Simmons, La Salle	4	1990	131	3217
4	Alphonzo Ford, Miss. Val. St.	4	1993	109	3165
5	Harry Kelly, Texas-Southern	4	1983	110	3066
6	Hersey Hawkins, Bradley	4	1988	125	3008
7	Oscar Robertson, Cincinnati	3	1960	88	2973
8	Danny Manning, Kansas	4	1988	147	2951
9	Alfredrick Hughes, Loyola-IL	4	1985	120	2914
10	Elvin Hayes, Houston	3	1968	93	2884
11	Larry Bird, Indiana St.	3	1979	94	2850
12	Otis Birdsong, Houston	4	1977	116	2832
13	Kevin Bradshaw, US Int'l	4	1991	111	2804
14	Allan Houston, Tennessee	4	1993	128	2801
15	Hank Gathers, USC/Loyola-CA	4	1990	117	2723
16	Reggie Lewis, N'eastern	4	1987	122	2708
17	Daren Queenan, Lehigh	4	1988	118	2703
18	Byron Larkin, Xavier-OH	4	1988	121	2696
19	David Robinson, Navy	4	1987	127	2669
20	Wayman Tisdale, Oklahoma	3	1985	104	2661

	Average	Yrs	Last	Pts	Avg
1	Pete Maravich, LSU	3	1970	3667	44.2
2	Austin Carr, Notre Dame	3	1971	2560	34.6
3	Oscar Robertson, Cinn	3	1960	2973	33.8
4	Calvin Murphy, Niagara	3	1970	2548	33.1
5	Dwight Lamar, SW La	2	1973	1862	32.7
6	Frank Selvy, Furman	3	1954	2538	32.5
7	Rick Mount, Purdue	3	1970	2323	32.3
8	Darrell Floyd, Furman	3	1956	2281	32.1
9	Nick Werkman, Seton Hall	3	1964	2273	32.0
10	Willie Humes, Idaho St.	2	1971	1510	31.5
11	William Averitt, Pepperdine	2	1973	1541	31.4
12	Elgin Baylor, Idaho/Seattle	3	1958	2500	31.3
13	Elvin Hayes, Houston	3	1968	2884	31.0
14	Freeman Williams, Port. St.	4	1978	3249	30.7
15	Larry Bird, Indiana St.	3	1979	2850	30.3
16	Bill Bradley, Princeton	3	1965	2503	30.2
17	Rich Fuqua, Oral Roberts	2	1973	1617	29.9
18	Wilt Chamberlain, Kansas	2	1958	1433	29.9
19	Rick Barry, Miami-FL	3	1965	2298	29.8
20	Doug Collins, Illinois St.	3	1973	2240	29.1

	Field Goal Pct.	Yrs	Last	FG	FGA	Pct
1	Ricky Nedd, Appalach. St.	4	1994	412	597	.690
2	Stephen Scheffler, Purdue	4	1990	408	596	.685
3	Steve Johnson, Ore. St.	4	1981	828	1222	.678
4	Murray Brown, Fla. St.	4	1980	566	847	.668
5	Lee Campbell, SW Mo. St.	3	1990	411	618	.665
6	Warren Kidd, M. Tenn. St.	3	1993	496	747	.664
7	Joe Senser, West Chester	4	1979	476	719	.662
8	Kevin McGee, UC-Irvine	2	1982	552	841	.656
9	O. Phillips, Pepperdine	2	1983	404	618	.654
10	Bill Walton, UCLA	3	1974	747	1147	.651

Note: minimum 400 FGs made.

	Free Throw Pct.	Yrs	Last	FT	FTA	Pct
1	Greg Starrick, Ky/So. Ill	4	1972	341	375	.909
2	Jack Moore, Nebraska	4	1982	446	495	.901
3	Steve Henson, Kansas St.	4	1990	361	401	.900
4	Steve Alford, Indiana	4	1987	535	596	.898
5	Bob Lloyd, Rutgers	3	1967	543	605	.898
6	Jim Barton, Dartmouth	4	1989	394	440	.895
7	Tommy Boyer, Arkansas	3	1963	315	353	.892
8	Rob Robbins, N. Mexico	4	1991	309	348	.888
9	Sean Miller, Pitt	4	1992	317	358	.885
10	Ron Perry, Holy Cross	4	1980	680	768	.885
	Joe Dykstra, Western Ill	4	1983	587	663	.885

Note: minimum 300 FTs made.

	3-Pt Field Goals	Yrs	Last	Gm	3FG
1	Doug Day, Radford	4	1993	117	401
2	Ronnie Schmitz, Missouri-KC	4	1993	112	378
3	Mark Alberts, Akron	4	1993	107	375
4	Jeff Fryer, Loyola-CA	4	1990	112	363
5	Dennis Scott, Ga. Tech	3	1990	99	351

	3-Pt Field Goal Pct.	Yrs	Last	3FG	Att	Pct
1	Tony Bennett, Wisc-GB	4	1992	290	584	.497
2	Keith Jennings, E. Tenn. St.	4	1991	223	452	.493
3	Kirk Manns, Michigan St.	4	1990	212	446	.475
4	Tim Locum, Wisconsin	4	1991	227	481	.472
5	David Olson, Eastern Ill	4	1992	262	562	.466

Note: minimum 200 3FGs made.

All-Time NCAA Division I Individual Leaders (Cont.)

Rebounds

Total (before 1973)	Yrs	Last	Gm	No
1 Tom Gola, La Salle	4	1955	118	2201
2 Joe Holup, G. Washington	4	1956	104	2030
3 Charlie Slack, Marshall	4	1956	88	1916
4 Ed Conlin, Fordham	4	1955	102	1884
5 Dickie Hemric, Wake Forest	4	1955	104	1802
6 Paul Silas, Creighton	3	1964	81	1751
7 Art Quimby, Connecticut	4	1955	80	1716
8 Jerry Harper, Alabama	4	1956	93	1688
9 Jeff Cohen, Wm. & Mary	4	1961	103	1679
10 Steve Hamilton, Morehead St.	4	1958	102	1675

Total (since 1973)	Yrs	Last	Gm	No
1 Derrick Coleman, Syracuse	4	1990	143	1537
2 Malik Rose, Drexel	4	1996	120	1514
3 Ralph Sampson, Virginia	4	1983	132	1511
4 Pete Padgett, Nevada-Reno	4	1976	104	1464
5 Lionel Simmons, La Salle	4	1990	131	1429
6 Anthony Bonner, St. Louis	4	1990	133	1424
7 Tyrone Hill, Xavier-OH	4	1990	126	1380
8 Popeye Jones, Murray St.	4	1992	123	1374
9 Michael Brooks, La Salle	4	1980	114	1372
10 Xavier McDaniel, Wichita St.	4	1985	117	1359

Average (before 1973)	Yrs	Last	No	Avg
1 Artis Gilmore, Jacksonville	2	1971	1224	22.7
2 Charlie Slack, Marshall	4	1956	1916	21.8
3 Paul Silas, Creighton	3	1964	1751	21.6
4 Leroy Wright, Pacific	3	1960	1442	21.5
5 Art Quimby, Connecticut	4	1955	1716	21.5

Note: minimum 800 rebounds.

Average (since 1973)	Yrs	Last	No	Avg
1 Glenn Mosley, Seton Hall	4	1977	1263	15.2
2 Bill Campion, Manhattan	3	1975	1070	14.2
3 Pete Padgett, Nevada-Reno	4	1976	1464	14.1
4 Bob Warner, Maine	4	1976	1304	13.6
5 Shaquille O'Neal, LSU	3	1992	1217	13.5

Note: minimum 650 rebounds.

Assists

Total	Yrs	Last	Gm	No
1 Bobby Hurley, Duke	4	1993	140	1076
2 Chris Corchiani, N.C. State	4	1991	124	1038
3 Keith Jennings, E. Tenn. St.	4	1991	127	983
4 Sherman Douglas, Syracuse	4	1989	138	960
5 Tony Miller, Marquette	4	1995	123	956
6 Greg Anthony, Portland/UNLV	4	1991	138	950
7 Gary Payton, Oregon St.	4	1990	120	938
8 Orlando Smart, San Fran	4	1994	116	902
9 Andre LaFleur, N'eastern	4	1987	128	894
10 Jim Les, Bradley	4	1986	118	884

Average	Yrs	Last	No	Avg
1 A. Johnson, Cameron/Southern	3	1988	838	8.91
2 Sam Crawford, N. Mexico St.	2	1993	592	8.84
3 Mark Wade, Okla/UNLV	3	1987	693	8.77
4 Chris Corchiani, N.C. State	4	1991	1038	8.37
5 Taurence Chisholm, Delaware	4	1988	877	7.97
6 Van Usher, Tennessee Tech	3	1992	676	7.95
7 Anthony Manuel, Bradley	3	1989	855	7.92
8 Gary Payton, Oregon St.	4	1990	938	7.82
9 Orlando Smart, San Fran	4	1994	902	7.78
10 Tony Miller, Marquette	4	1995	956	7.77

Note: minimum 550 assists.

Blocked Shots

Average	Yrs	Last	No	Avg
1 David Robinson, Navy	2	1987	351	5.24
2 Shaquille O'Neal, LSU	3	1992	412	4.58
3 Theo Ratliff, Wyoming	4	1995	425	3.83
4 Alonzo Mourning, Georgetown	4	1992	453	3.78
5 Lorenzo Williams, Stetson	2	1991	234	3.71

Note: minimum 200 blocked shots.

Steals

Average	Yrs	Last	No	Avg
1 Mookie Blaylock, Oklahoma	2	1989	281	3.80
2 Ronn McMahon, Eastern Wash	3	1990	225	3.52
3 Jason Kidd, California	2	1994	204	3.46
4 Eric Murdock, Providence	4	1991	376	3.21
5 Van Usher, Tennessee Tech	3	1992	270	3.18

Note: minimum 200 steals.

2000 Points/1000 Rebounds

For a combined total of 4000 or more.

	Gm	Pts	Reb	Total
1 Tom Gola, La Salle	118	2462	2201	4663
2 Lionel Simmons, La Salle	131	3217	1429	4646
3 Elvin Hayes, Houston	93	2884	1602	4486
4 Dickie Hemric, W. Forest	104	2587	1802	4389
5 Oscar Robertson, Cinn	88	2973	1338	4311
6 Joe Holup, G. Washington	104	2226	2030	4256
7 Harry Kelly, TX-Southern	110	3066	1085	4151
8 Danny Manning, Kansas	147	2951	1187	4138
9 Larry Bird, Indiana St.	94	2850	1247	4097
10 Elgin Baylor, Col.Idaho/Seattle	80	2500	1559	4059
11 Michael Brooks, La Salle	114	2628	1372	4000

Years Played— Baylor (1956-58); **Bird** (1977-79); **Brooks** (1977-80); **Gola** (1952-55); **Hayes** (1966-68); **Hemric** (1952-55); **Holup** (1953-56); **Kelly** (1980-83); **Manning** (1985-88); **Robertson** (1958-60); **Simmons** (1987-90).

SINGLE SEASON

Scoring

Points	Year	Gm	Pts
1 Pete Maravich, LSU	1970	31	1381
2 Elvin Hayes, Houston	1968	33	1214
3 Frank Selvy, Furman	1954	29	1209
4 Pete Maravich, LSU	1969	26	1148
5 Pete Maravich, LSU	1968	26	1138
6 Bo Kimble, Loyola-CA	1990	32	1131
7 Hersey Hawkins, Bradley	1988	31	1125
8 Austin Carr, Notre Dame	1970	29	1106
9 Austin Carr, Notre Dame	1971	29	1101
10 Otis Birdsong, Houston	1977	36	1090

Average	Year	Gm	Pts	Avg
1 Pete Maravich, LSU	1970	31	1381	44.5
2 Pete Maravich, LSU	1969	26	1148	44.2
3 Pete Maravich, LSU	1968	26	1138	43.8
4 Frank Selvy, Furman	1954	29	1209	41.7
5 Johnny Neumann, Ole Miss	1971	23	923	40.1
6 Freeman Williams, Port. St.	1977	26	1010	38.8
7 Billy McGill, Utah	1962	26	1009	38.8
8 Calvin Murphy, Niagara	1968	24	916	38.2
9 Austin Carr, Notre Dame	1970	29	1106	38.1
10 Austin Carr, Notre Dame	1971	29	1101	38.0

Scoring

	Field Goal Pct.	Year	FG	FGA	Pct
1	Steve Johnson, Oregon St.	1981	235	315	.746
2	Dwayne Davis, Florida	1989	179	248	.722
3	Keith Walker, Utica	1985	154	216	.713
4	Steve Johnson, Oregon St.	1980	211	297	.710
5	Oliver Miller, Arkansas	1991	254	361	.704

	Free Throw Pct.	Year	FT	FTA	Pct
1	Craig Collins, Penn St.	1985	94	98	.959
2	Rod Foster, UCLA	1982	95	100	.950
3	Carlos Gibson, Marshall	1978	84	89	.944
4	Danny Basile, Marist	1994	84	89	.944
5	Jim Barton, Dartmouth	1986	65	69	.942

	3-Pt Field Goal Pct.	Year	3FG	Att	Pct
1	Glenn Tropf, Holy Cross	1988	52	82	.634
2	Sean Wightman, W. Mich	1992	48	76	.632
3	Keith Jennings, E. Tenn. St.	1991	84	142	.592
4	Dave Calloway, Monmouth	1989	48	82	.585
5	Steve Kerr, Arizona	1988	114	199	.573

Assists

	Average	Year	Gm	No	Avg
1	Avery Johnson, Southern-BR	1988	30	399	13.3
2	Anthony Manuel, Bradley	1988	31	373	12.0
3	Avery Johnson, Southern-BR	1987	31	333	10.7
4	Mark Wade, UNLV	1987	38	406	10.7
5	Glenn Williams, Holy Cross	1989	28	278	9.9

Rebounds

	Average (before 1973)	Year	Gm	No	Avg
1	Charlie Slack, Marshall	1955	21	538	25.6
2	Leroy Wright, Pacific	1959	26	652	25.1
3	Art Quimby, Connecticut	1955	25	611	24.4
4	Charlie Slack, Marshall	1956	22	520	23.6
5	Ed Conlin, Fordham	1953	26	612	23.5

	Average (since 1973)	Year	Gm	No	Avg
1	Kermit Washington, American	1973	25	511	20.4
2	Marvin Barnes, Providence	1973	30	571	19.0
3	Marvin Barnes, Providence	1974	32	597	18.7
4	Pete Padgett, Nevada	1973	26	462	17.8
5	Jim Bradley, Northern Ill	1973	24	426	17.8

Blocked Shots

	Average	Year	Gm	No	Avg
1	Keith Closs, Cen. Conn. St.	1996	28	178	6.36
2	David Robinson, Navy	1986	35	207	5.91
3	Shaquille O'Neal, LSU	1992	30	157	5.23
4	Shawn Bradley, BYU	1991	34	177	5.21
5	Cedric Lewis, Maryland	1991	28	143	5.11

Steals

	Average	Year	Gm	No	Avg
1	Darron Brittman, Chicago St.	1986	28	139	4.96
2	Aldwin Ware, Florida A&M	1988	29	142	4.90
3	Ronn McMahon, East Wash.	1990	29	130	4.48
4	Pointer Williams, McNeese St.	1996	27	118	4.37
5	Jim Paguaga, St. Francis-NY	1986	28	120	4.29

SINGLE GAME

Scoring

	Points vs Div. I Team	Year	Pts
1	Kevin Bradshaw, US Int'l vs Loyola-CA	1991	72
2	Pete Maravich, LSU vs Alabama	1970	69
3	Calvin Murphy, Niagara vs Syracuse	1969	68
4	Jay Handlan, Wash. & Lee vs Furman	1951	66
	Pete Maravich, LSU vs Tulane	1969	66
	Anthony Roberts, Oral Rbts vs N.C. A&T	1977	66
7	Anthony Roberts, Oral Rbts vs Ore	1977	65
	Scott Haffner, Evansville vs Dayton	1989	65
9	Pete Maravich, LSU vs Kentucky	1970	64
10	Johnny Neumann, Ole Miss vs LSU	1971	63
	Hersey Hawkins, Bradley vs Detroit	1988	63

	Points vs Non-Div. I Team	Year	Pts
1	Frank Selvy, Furman vs Newberry	1954	100
2	Paul Arizin, Villanova vs Phi. NAMC	1949	85
3	Freeman Williams, Port. St. vs Rocky Mt	1978	81
4	Bill Mlkvy, Temple vs Wilkes	1951	73
5	Freeman Williams, Port. St. vs So. Ore	1977	71

Note: Bevo Francis of Division II Rio Grande (Ohio) scored an overall collegiate record 113 points against Hillsdale in 1954. He also scored 84 against Alliance and 82 against Bluffton that same season.

Assists

		Year	No
1	Tony Fairley, Baptist vs Armstrong St.	1987	22
	Avery Johnson, Southern-BR vs TX-South	1988	22
	Sherman Douglas, Syracuse vs Providence	1989	22
4	Mark Wade, UNLV vs Navy	1986	21
	Kelvin Scarborough, N. Mexico vs Hawaii	1987	21
	Anthony Manuel, Bradley vs UC-Irvine	1987	21
	Avery Johnson, Southern-BR vs Ala. St.	1988	21

3-Pt Field Goals

		Year	No
1	Dave Jamerson, Ohio U. vs Charleston	1989	14
	Askia Jones, Kansas St. vs Fresno St.	1994	14
3	Gary Bossert, Niagara vs Siena	1987	12
	Darrin Fitzgerald, Butler vs Detroit	1987	12
	Al Dillard, Arkansas vs Delaware St.	1993	12
	Mitch Taylor, South-BR vs La. Christian	1995	12
	David McMahan, Winthrop vs Coastal Caro	1996	12

Rebounds

	Total (before 1973)	Year	No
1	Bill Chambers, Wm. & Mary vs Virginia	1953	51
2	Charlie Slack, Marshall vs M. Harvey	1954	43
3	Tom Heinsohn, Holy Cross vs BC	1955	42
4	Art Quimby, UConn vs BU	1955	40
5	Three players tied with 39 each.		

	Total (since 1973)	Year	No
1	David Vaughn, Oral Roberts vs Brandeis	1973	34
2	Robert Parish, Centenary vs So. Miss	1973	33
3	Durand Macklin, LSU vs Tulane	1976	32
	Jervaughn Scales, South-BR vs Grambling	1994	32
5	Jim Bradley, Northern Ill. vs WI-Milw	1973	31
	Calvin Natt, NE La. vs Ga. Southern	1976	31

Blocked Shots

		Year	No
1	David Robinson, Navy vs NC-Wilmington	1986	14
	Shawn Bradley, BYU vs Eastern Ky	1990	14
	Roy Rogers, Alabama vs Georgia	1996	14
4	Jim McIlvaine, Marquette vs No. Ill	1993	13
	Keith Closs, C. Conn. St. vs St. Fran-PA	1995	13

Steals

		Year	No
1	Mookie Blaylock, Oklahoma vs Centenary	1987	13
	Mookie Blaylock, Oklahoma vs Loyola-CA	1988	13
3	Kenny Robertson, Cleve. St. vs Wagner	1988	12
	Terry Evans, Oklahoma vs Florida A&M	1993	12
5	Eight players tied with 11 each.		

Annual Awards

UPI picked the first national Division I Player of the Year in 1955. Since then, the U.S. Basketball Writers Assn. (1959), the Commonwealth Athletic Club of Kentucky's Adolph Rupp Trophy (1961), the Atlanta Tip-Off Club (1969), the National Assn. of Basketball Coaches (1975), and the LA Athletic Club's John Wooden Award (1977) have joined in.

Since 1977, the first year all six awards were given out, the same player has won all of them in the same season eight times: Marques Johnson in 1977, Larry Bird in 1979, Ralph Sampson in both 1982 and '83, Michael Jordan in 1984, David Robinson in 1987, Lionel Simmons in 1990, Calbert Cheaney in 1993 and Glenn Robinson in 1994.

United Press International

Voted on by a panel of UPI college basketball writers and first presented in 1955.

Multiple winners: Oscar Robertson, Ralph Sampson and Bill Walton (3); Lew Alcindor and Jerry Lucas (2).

Year	
1955	Tom Gola, La Salle
1956	Bill Russell, San Francisco
1957	Chet Forte, Columbia
1958	Oscar Robertson, Cincinnati
1959	Oscar Robertson, Cincinnati
1960	Oscar Robertson, Cincinnati
1961	Jerry Lucas, Ohio St.
1962	Jerry Lucas, Ohio St.
1963	Art Heyman, Duke
1964	Gary Bradds, Ohio St.
1965	Bill Bradley, Princeton
1966	Cazzie Russell, Michigan
1967	Lew Alcindor, UCLA
1968	Elvin Hayes, Houston
1969	Lew Alcindor, UCLA
1970	Pete Maravich, LSU
1971	Austin Carr, Notre Dame
1972	Bill Walton, UCLA
1973	Bill Walton, UCLA
1974	Bill Walton, UCLA
1975	David Thompson, N.C. State
1976	Scott May, Indiana
1977	Marques Johnson, UCLA
1978	Butch Lee, Marquette
1979	Larry Bird, Indiana St.
1980	Mark Aguirre, DePaul
1981	Ralph Sampson, Virginia
1982	Ralph Sampson, Virginia
1983	Ralph Sampson, Virginia
1984	Michael Jordan, N. Carolina
1985	Chris Mullin, St. John's
1986	Walter Berry, St. John's
1987	David Robinson, Navy
1988	Hersey Hawkins, Bradley
1989	Danny Ferry, Duke
1990	Lionel Simmons, La Salle
1991	Shaquille O'Neal, LSU
1992	Jim Jackson, Ohio St.
1993	Calbert Cheaney, Indiana
1994	Glenn Robinson, Purdue
1995	Joe Smith, Maryland
1996	Ray Allen, UConn

U.S. Basketball Writers Association

Voted on by the USBWA and first presented in 1959.

Multiple winners: Ralph Sampson and Bill Walton (3); Lew Alcindor, Jerry Lucas and Oscar Robertson (2).

Year	
1959	Oscar Robertson, Cincinnati
1960	Oscar Robertson, Cincinnati
1961	Jerry Lucas, Ohio St.
1962	Jerry Lucas, Ohio St.
1963	Art Heyman, Duke
1964	Walt Hazzard, UCLA
1965	Bill Bradley, Princeton
1966	Cazzie Russell, Michigan
1967	Lew Alcindor, UCLA
1968	Elvin Hayes, Houston
1969	Lew Alcindor, UCLA
1970	Pete Maravich, LSU
1971	Sidney Wicks, UCLA
1972	Bill Walton, UCLA
1973	Bill Walton, UCLA
1974	Bill Walton, UCLA
1975	David Thompson, N.C. State
1976	Adrian Dantley, Notre Dame
1977	Marques Johnson, UCLA
1978	Phil Ford, North Carolina
1979	Larry Bird, Indiana St.
1980	Mark Aguirre, DePaul
1981	Ralph Sampson, Virginia
1982	Ralph Sampson, Virginia
1983	Ralph Sampson, Virginia
1984	Michael Jordan, N. Carolina
1985	Chris Mullin, St. John's
1986	Walter Berry, St. John's
1987	David Robinson, Navy
1988	Hersey Hawkins, Bradley
1989	Danny Ferry, Duke
1990	Lionel Simmons, La Salle
1991	Larry Johnson, UNLV
1992	Christian Laettner, Duke
1993	Calbert Cheaney, Indiana
1994	Glenn Robinson, Purdue
1995	Ed O'Bannon, UCLA
1996	Marcus Camby, UMass

Rupp Trophy

Voted on by AP sportswriters and broadcasters and first presented in 1961 by the Commonwealth Athletic Club of Kentucky in the name of former University of Kentucky coach Adolph Rupp.

Multiple winners: Ralph Sampson (3); Lew Alcindor, Jerry Lucas, David Thompson and Bill Walton (2).

Year	
1961	Jerry Lucas, Ohio St.
1962	Jerry Lucas, Ohio St.
1963	Art Heyman, Duke
1964	Gary Bradds, Ohio St.
1965	Bill Bradley, Princeton
1966	Cazzie Russell, Michigan
1967	Lew Alcindor, UCLA
1968	Elvin Hayes, Houston
1969	Lew Alcindor, UCLA
1970	Pete Maravich, LSU
1971	Austin Carr, Notre Dame
1972	Bill Walton, UCLA
1973	Bill Walton, UCLA
1974	David Thompson, N.C. State
1975	David Thompson, N.C. State
1976	Scott May, Indiana
1977	Marques Johnson, UCLA
1978	Butch Lee, Marquette
1979	Larry Bird, Indiana St.
1980	Mark Aguirre, DePaul
1981	Ralph Sampson, Virginia
1982	Ralph Sampson, Virginia
1983	Ralph Sampson, Virginia
1984	Michael Jordan, N. Carolina
1985	Patrick Ewing, Georgetown
1986	Walter Berry, St. John's
1987	David Robinson, Navy
1988	Hersey Hawkins, Bradley
1989	Sean Elliott, Arizona
1990	Lionel Simmons, La Salle
1991	Shaquille O'Neal, LSU
1992	Christian Laettner, Duke
1993	Calbert Cheaney, Indiana
1994	Glenn Robinson, Purdue
1995	Joe Smith, Maryland
1996	Marcus Camby, UMass

Naismith Award

Voted on by a panel of coaches, sportswriters and broadcasters and first presented in 1969 by the Atlanta Tip-Off Club in 1969 in the name of the inventor of basketball, Dr. James Naismith.

Multiple winners: Ralph Sampson and Bill Walton (3).

Year		Year		Year	
1969	Lew Alcindor, UCLA	1978	Butch Lee, Marquette	1987	David Robinson, Navy
1970	Pete Maravich, LSU	1979	Larry Bird, Indiana St.	1988	Danny Manning, Kansas
1971	Austin Carr, Notre Dame	1980	Mark Aguirre, DePaul	1989	Danny Ferry, Duke
1972	Bill Walton, UCLA	1981	Ralph Sampson, Virginia	1990	Lionel Simmons, La Salle
1973	Bill Walton, UCLA	1982	Ralph Sampson, Virginia	1991	Larry Johnson, UNLV
1974	Bill Walton, UCLA	1983	Ralph Sampson, Virginia	1992	Christian Laettner, Duke
1975	David Thompson, N.C. State	1984	Michael Jordan, N. Carolina	1993	Calbert Cheaney, Indiana
1976	Scott May, Indiana	1985	Patrick Ewing, Georgetown	1994	Glenn Robinson, Purdue
1977	Marques Johnson, UCLA	1986	Johnny Dawkins, Duke	1995	Joe Smith, Maryland
				1996	Marcus Camby, UMass

National Association of Basketball Coaches

Voted on by the National Assn. of Basketball Coaches and presented by the Eastman Kodak Co. from 1975-94.

Multiple winner: Ralph Sampson (2).

Year		Year		Year	
1975	David Thompson, N.C. State	1982	Ralph Sampson, Virginia	1990	Lionel Simmons, La Salle
1976	Scott May, Indiana	1983	Ralph Sampson, Virginia	1991	Larry Johnson, UNLV
1977	Marques Johnson, UCLA	1984	Michael Jordan, N. Carolina	1992	Christian Laettner, Duke
1978	Phil Ford, North Carolina	1985	Patrick Ewing, Georgetown	1993	Calbert Cheaney, Indiana
1979	Larry Bird, Indiana St.	1986	Walter Berry, St. John's	1994	Glenn Robinson, Purdue
1980	Michael Brooks, La Salle	1987	David Robinson, Navy	1995	Shawn Respert, Mich. St.
1981	Danny Ainge, BYU	1988	Danny Manning, Kansas	1996	Marcus Camby, UMass
		1989	Sean Elliott, Arizona		

Wooden Award

Voted on by a panel of coaches, sportswriters and broadcasters and first presented in 1977 by the Los Angeles Athletic Club in the name of former Purdue All-America and UCLA coach John Wooden. Unlike the other five Player of the Year awards, candidates for the Wooden must have a minimum grade point average of 2.00 (out of 4.00).

Multiple winner: Ralph Sampson (2).

Year		Year		Year	
1977	Marques Johnson, UCLA	1983	Ralph Sampson, Virginia	1990	Lionel Simmons, La Salle
1978	Phil Ford, North Carolina	1984	Michael Jordan, N. Carolina	1991	Larry Johnson, UNLV
1979	Larry Bird, Indiana St.	1985	Chris Mullin, St. John's	1992	Christian Laettner, Duke
1980	Darrell Griffith, Louisville	1986	Walter Berry St. John's	1993	Calbert Cheaney, Indiana
1981	Danny Ainge, BYU	1987	David Robinson, Navy	1994	Glenn Robinson, Purdue
1982	Ralph Sampson, Virginia	1988	Danny Manning, Kansas	1995	Ed O'Bannon, UCLA
		1989	Sean Elliott, Arizona	1996	Marcus Camby, UMass

Players of the Year and Top Draft Picks

Consensus college Players of the Year and first overall selections in NBA Draft since the abolition of the NBA's Territorial Draft in 1966. Top draft picks who became Rookie of the Year are in **bold** type; (*) indicates top draft pick chosen as junior and (**) indicates top draft pick chosen as sophomore.

Year	Player of the Year	Top Draft Pick
1966	Cazzie Russell, Mich.	Cazzie Russell, NY
1967	Lew Alcindor, UCLA	Jimmy Walker, Det.
1968	Elvin Hayes, Houston	Elvin Hayes, SD
1969	Lew Alcindor, UCLA	**Lew Alcindor**, Milw.
1970	Pete Maravich, LSU	Bob Lanier, Det.
1971	Sidney Wicks, UCLA	Austin Carr, Cle.
1972	Bill Walton, UCLA	LaRue Martin, Port.
1973	Bill Walton, UCLA	Doug Collins, Phi.
1974	Bill Walton, UCLA	Bill Walton, Port.
1975	David Thompson, N.C. St.	David Thompson, Atl.
1976	Scott May, Indiana	John Lucas, Hou.
1977	Marques Johnson, UCLA	Kent Benson, Ind.
1978	Butch Lee, Marquette & Phil Ford, N. Caro.	Mychal Thompson, Port.
1979	Larry Bird, Indiana St.	Magic Johnson, LAL**
1980	Mark Aguirre, DePaul	Joe Barry Carroll, G. St.
1981	Ralph Sampson, Va. & Danny Ainge, BYU	Mark Aguirre, Dal.
1982	Ralph Sampson, Va.	James Worthy, LAL*
1983	Ralph Sampson, Va.	**Ralph Sampson**, Hou.
1984	Michael Jordan, N. Caro.	Akeem Olajuwon, Hou.
1985	Patrick Ewing, G'town & Chris Mullin, St. John's	**Patrick Ewing**, NY
1986	Walter Berry, St. John's	Brad Daugherty, Cle.
1987	David Robinson, Navy	**David Robinson**, SA
1988	Hersey Hawkins, Bradley & Danny Manning, Kan.	Danny Manning, LAC
1989	Sean Elliott, Arizona & Danny Ferry, Duke	Pervis Ellison, Sac.
1990	Lionel Simmons, La Salle	**Derrick Coleman**, NJ
1991	Shaquille O'Neal, LSU	**Larry Johnson**, Char.
1992	Christian Laettner, Duke	**Shaquille O'Neal**, Orl.*
1993	Calbert Cheaney, Ind.	**Chris Webber**, Orl.**
1994	Glenn Robinson, Purdue	Glenn Robinson, Milw.*
1995	Ed O'Bannon, UCLA & Joe Smith, Maryland	Joe Smith, G. St.**
1996	Marcus Camby, UMass	Allen Iverson, Phi.**

All-Time Winningest Division I Coaches

Minimum of 10 seasons as Division I head coach; regular season and tournament games included; coaches active during 1995-96 in **bold** type.

Top 30 Winning Percentage

		Yrs	W	L	Pct
1	**Jerry Tarkanian**	25	647	133	**.829**
2	Clair Bee	21	412	87	**.826**
3	Adolph Rupp	41	876	190	**.822**
4	John Wooden	29	664	162	**.804**
5	**Dean Smith**	35	851	247	**.775**
6	Harry Fisher	13	147	44	**.770**
7	Frank Keaney	27	387	117	**.768**
8	George Keogan	24	385	117	**.767**
9	Jack Ramsay	11	231	71	**.765**
10	Vic Bubas	10	213	67	**.761**
11	**Jim Boeheim**	20	483	159	**.752**
12	**Nolan Richardson**	16	391	132	**.748**
13	Chick Davies	21	314	106	**.748**
14	Ray Mears	21	399	135	**.747**
15	**John Chaney**	24	540	187	**.743**
16	Al McGuire	20	405	143	**.739**
17	Everett Case	18	376	133	**.739**
18	Phog Allen	48	746	264	**.739**
19	Walter Meanwell	22	280	101	**.735**
20	**Bob Knight**	31	678	247	**.733**
21	**Rick Pitino**	14	317	119	**.727**
22	**John Thompson**	24	553	208	**.727**
23	Lew Andreas	25	355	134	**.726**
24	Lou Carnesecca	24	526	200	**.725**
25	**Denny Crum**	25	587	224	**.724**
26	Fred Schaus	12	251	96	**.723**
27	**Lute Olson**	23	507	194	**.723**
28	**Eddie Sutton**	26	570	219	**.722**
29	Cam Henderson	35	630	243	**.722**
30	Hugh Greer	17	290	112	**.721**

Top 30 Victories

		Yrs	W	L	Pct
1	Adolph Rupp	41	**876**	190	.822
2	**Dean Smith**	35	**851**	247	.775
3	Hank Iba	41	**767**	338	.694
4	Ed Diddle	42	**759**	302	.715
5	Phog Allen	48	**746**	264	.739
6	Ray Meyer	42	**724**	354	.672
7	**Bob Knight**	31	**678**	247	.733
	Don Haskins	35	**678**	314	.683
	Norm Stewart	35	**678**	334	.670
10	**Lefty Driesell**	34	**667**	322	.674
11	John Wooden	29	**664**	162	.804
12	**Lou Henson**	34	**663**	331	.667
13	Ralph Miller	38	**657**	382	.632
14	Marv Harshman	40	**654**	449	.593
15	**Jerry Tarkanian**	25	**647**	133	.829
	Gene Bartow	34	**647**	353	.647
17	Cam Henderson	35	**630**	243	.722
18	Norm Sloan	37	**624**	393	.614
19	Slats Gill	36	**599**	392	.604
20	Abe Lemons	34	**597**	344	.634
21	Guy Lewis	30	**592**	279	.680
22	**Denny Crum**	25	**587**	224	.724
23	**Eddie Sutton**	26	**570**	219	.722
24	Gary Colson	34	**563**	385	.594
25	Tony Hinkle	41	**557**	393	.586
26	**John Thompson**	24	**553**	208	.727
27	Glenn Wilkes	36	**551**	436	.558
28	Frank McGuire	30	**549**	236	.699
29	**Eldon Miller**	34	**542**	390	.582
30	**John Chaney**	24	**540**	187	.743

Note: Clarence (Bighouse) Gaines of Division II Winston-Salem St. (1947-93) retired after the 1992-93 season to finish his 47-year career ranked No. 2 on the all-time NCAA list of all coaches regardless of division. His record is 828-446 with a .650 winning percentage.

Where They Coached

Allen—Baker (1906-08), Kansas (1908-09), Haskell (1909), Central Mo. St. (1913-19), Kansas (1920-56); **Andreas**—Syracuse (1925-43; 45-50); **Bartow**—Central Mo. St. (1962-64), Valparaiso (1965-70), Memphis St. (1971-74), Illinois (1975), UCLA (1976-77), UAB (1979—); **Bee**—Rider (1929-31), LIU-Brooklyn (1932-45, 46-51); **Boeheim**—Syracuse (1977—); **Bubas**—Duke (1960-69); **Carnesecca**—St. John's (1966-70, 74-92); **Case**—N.C. State (1947-64); **Chaney**—Cheyney St. (1973-82), Temple (1983—); **Colson**—Valdosta St. (1959-68), Pepperdine (1969-79), New Mexico (1981-88), Fresno St. (1991—); **Crum**—Louisville (1972—); **Davies**—Duquesne (1925-43, 47-48); **Diddle**—Western Ky. (1923-64); **Driesell**—Davidson (1961-69), Maryland (1970-86), J. Madison (1989—); **Enke**—Louisville (1924-25), Arizona (1926-61); **Fisher**—Columbia (1907-16), Army (1922-23, 25).

Gill—Oregon St. (1929-64); **Greer**—Connecticut (1947-63); **Harshman**—Pacific Lutheran (1946-58), Wash. St. (1959-71), Washington (1972-85); **Haskins**—UTEP (1962—); **Henderson**—Muskingum (1920-22), Davis & Elkins (1923-35), Marshall (1936-55); **Henson**—Hardin-Simmons (1963-66), N. Mexico St. (1967-75), Illinois (1976-96); **Hinkle**—Butler (1927-42, 46-70); **Iba**—NW Missouri St. (1930-33), Colorado (1934), Oklahoma St. (1935-70); **Keaney**—Rhode Island (1921-48); **Knight**—Army (1966-71), Indiana (1972—); **Koegan**—St. Louis (1916), Allegheny (1919), Valparaiso (1920-21), Notre Dame (1924-43).

Lemons—Okla. City (1956-73), Pan American (1974-76), Texas (1977-82), Okla. City (1984-90); **Lewis**— Houston (1957-86); **A. McGuire**—Belmont Abbey (1958-64), Marquette (1965-77); **F. McGuire**—St. John's (1948-52), North Carolina (1953-61), South Carolina (1965-80); **Meanwell**—Wisconsin (1912-17, 21-34), Missouri (1918-20); **Mears**—Wittenberg (1957-62), Tennessee (1963-77); **Meyer**—DePaul (1943-84); **E. Miller**—Western Mich. (1970-75), Ohio St. (1976-1985), Northern Iowa (1986—); **R. Miller**—Wichita St. (1952-64), Iowa (1965-70), Oregon St. (1971-89); **Olson**—Long Beach St. (1974), Iowa (1975-83), Arizona (1984—).

Pitino—Boston Univ. (1979-83), Providence (1986-87), Kentucky (1990—); **Ramsay**—St. Joseph's-PA (1956-66); **Richardson**—Tulsa (1981-85), Arkansas (1986—); **Rupp**—Kentucky (1931-72); **Schaus**—West Va. (1955-60), Purdue (1973-78); **Sloan**—Presbyterian (1952-55), Citadel (1957-60), Florida (1961-66), N.C. State (1967-80), Florida (1981-89); **Smith**—North Carolina (1962—); **Stewart**—No. Iowa (1962-67), Missouri (1968—); **Sutton**—Creighton (1970-74), Arkansas (1975-85), Kentucky (1986-89), Oklahoma St. (1991—); **Tarkanian**—Long Beach St. (1969-73), UNLV (1974-92) Fresno St. (1995—); **Thompson**—Georgetown (1973—); **Wilkes**—Stetson (1958-93); **Wooden**—Indiana St. (1947-48), UCLA (1949-75).

Most NCAA Tournaments

Through 1995; listed are number of appearances, overall tournament record, times reaching Final Four, and number of NCAA championships.

App		W-L	F4	Championships
20	Adolph Rupp	30-18	6	4 (1948-49, 51, 58)
20	**Bob Knight**	40-17	5	3 (1976, 81, 87)
20	**Denny Crum**	39-20	6	2 (1980, 86)
19	**John Thompson**	34-18	3	1 (1984)
18	Lou Carnesecca	17-20	1	None
18	**Eddie Sutton**	27-18	2	None
18	**Lou Henson**	19-19	2	None
17	**Jim Boeheim**	27-17	2	None
17	**Lute Olson**	22-18	3	None
16	John Wooden	47-10	12	10 (1964-65, 67-73, 75)
16	**Jerry Tarkanian**	37-16	4	1 (1990)
15	Digger Phelps	17-17	1	None
15	**Norm Stewart**	12-15	0	None
14	**Don Haskins**	14-13	1	1 (1966)
14	Guy Lewis	26-18	5	None
13	Dale Brown	15-14	2	None
13	Ray Meyer	14-16	2	None
13	**Gene Keady**	10-13	0	None

Active Coaches' Victories

Minimum five seasons in Division I.

		Yrs	W	L	Pct
1	Dean Smith, N. Carolina	35	**851**	247	.775
2	Jim Phelan, Mt. St. Mary's	42	**758**	400	.655
3	Don Haskins, UTEP	35	**678**	314	.683
4	Norm Stewart, Missouri	35	**678**	334	.670
5	Bob Knight, Indiana	30	**678**	246	.733
6	Lefty Driesell, J. Madison	34	**667**	322	.674
7	Gene Bartow, UAB	34	**647**	353	.647
8	Jerry Tarkanian, Fresno St.	25	**647**	133	.829
9	Denny Crum, Louisville	25	**587**	224	.724
10	Eddie Sutton, Okla. St.	26	**570**	219	.722
11	John Thompson, Georgetown	24	**553**	208	.727
12	Eldon Miller, N. Iowa	34	**542**	390	.582
13	John Chaney, Temple	24	**540**	187	.743
14	Bill Foster, Va. Tech	29	**517**	309	.626
15	Lute Olson, Arizona	23	**507**	194	.723
16	Bob Hallberg, IL-Chicago	25	**484**	273	.639
17	Jim Boeheim, Syracuse	20	**483**	159	.752
18	Gale Catlett, West Va.	24	**471**	241	.661
19	Tom Davis, Iowa	25	**481**	259	.650
20	Billy Tubbs, TCU	22	**470**	228	.673

Annual Awards

UPI picked the first national Division I Coach of the Year in 1955. Since then, The U.S. Basketball Writers Assn. (1959), AP (1967), the National Assn. of Basketball Coaches (1969), and the Atlanta Tip-Off Club (1987) have joined in. Since 1987, the first year all five awards were given out, no coach has won all of them in the same season.

United Press International

Voted on by a panel of UPI college basketball writers and first presented in 1955.

Multiple winners: John Wooden (6); Bob Knight, Ray Meyer, Adolph Rupp, Norm Stewart, Fred Taylor and Phil Woolpert (2).

Year	
1955	Phil Woolpert, San Francisco
1956	Phil Woolpert, San Francisco
1957	Frank McGuire, North Carolina
1958	Tex Winter, Kansas St.
1959	Adolph Rupp, Kentucky
1960	Pete Newell, California
1961	Fred Taylor, Ohio St.
1962	Fred Taylor, Ohio St.
1963	Ed Jucker, Cincinnati
1964	John Wooden, UCLA
1965	Dave Strack, Michigan
1966	Adolph Rupp, Kentucky
1967	John Wooden, UCLA
1968	Guy Lewis, Houston
1969	John Wooden, UCLA
1970	John Wooden, UCLA
1971	Al McGuire, Marquette
1972	John Wooden, UCLA
1973	John Wooden, UCLA
1974	Digger Phelps, Notre Dame
1975	Bob Knight, Indiana
1976	Tom Young, Rutgers
1977	Bob Gaillard, San Francisco
1978	Eddie Sutton, Arkansas
1979	Bill Hodges, Indiana St.
1980	Ray Meyer, DePaul
1981	Ralph Miller, Oregon St.
1982	Norm Stewart, Missouri
1983	Jerry Tarkanian, UNLV
1984	Ray Meyer, DePaul
1985	Lou Carnesecca, St. John's
1986	Mike Krzyzewski, Duke
1987	John Thompson, Georgetown
1988	John Chaney, Temple
1989	Bob Knight, Indiana
1990	Jim Calhoun, Connecticut
1991	Rick Majerus, Utah
1992	Perry Clark, Tulane
1993	Eddie Fogler, Vanderbilt
1994	Norm Stewart, Missouri
1995	Leonard Hamilton, Miami-FL
1996	Gene Keady, Purdue

U.S. Basketball Writers Association

Voted on by the USBWA and first presented in 1959.

Multiple winners: John Wooden (5); Bob Knight (3); Lou Carnesecca, John Chaney, Gene Keady, Ray Meyer and Fred Taylor (2).

Year	
1959	Eddie Hickey, Marquette
1960	Pete Newell, California
1961	Fred Taylor, Ohio St.
1962	Fred Taylor, Ohio St.
1963	Ed Jucker, Cincinnati
1964	John Wooden, UCLA
1965	Butch van Breda Kolff, Princeton
1966	Adolph Rupp, Kentucky
1967	John Wooden, UCLA
1968	Guy Lewis, Houston
1969	Maury John, Drake
1970	John Wooden, UCLA
1971	Al McGuire, Marquette
1972	John Wooden, UCLA
1973	John Wooden, UCLA
1974	Norm Sloan, N.C. State
1975	Bob Knight, Indiana
1976	Bob Knight, Indiana
1977	Eddie Sutton, Arkansas
1978	Ray Meyer, DePaul
1979	Dean Smith, North Carolina
1980	Ray Meyer, DePaul
1981	Ralph Miller, Oregon St.
1982	John Thompson, Georgetown
1983	Lou Carnesecca, St. John's
1984	Gene Keady, Purdue
1985	Lou Carnesecca, St. John's
1986	Dick Versace, Bradley
1987	John Chaney, Temple
1988	John Chaney, Temple
1989	Bob Knight, Indiana
1990	Roy Williams, Kansas
1991	Randy Ayers, Ohio St.
1992	Perry Clark, Tulane
1993	Eddie Fogler, Vanderbilt
1994	Charlie Spoonhour, St. Louis
1995	Kelvin Sampson, Oklahoma
1996	Gene Keady, Purdue

Annual Awards (Cont.)

Associated Press

Voted on by AP sportswriters and broadcasters and first presented in 1967.

Multiple winners: John Wooden (5); Bob Knight (3); Guy Lewis, Ray Meyer, Ralph Miller and Eddie Sutton (2).

Year		Year		Year	
1967	John Wooden, UCLA	1977	Bob Gaillard, San Francisco	1987	Tom Davis, Iowa
1968	Guy Lewis, Houston	1978	Eddie Sutton, Arkansas	1988	John Chaney, Temple
1969	John Wooden, UCLA	1979	Bill Hodges, Indiana St.	1989	Bob Knight, Indiana
1970	John Wooden, UCLA	1980	Ray Meyer, DePaul	1990	Jim Calhoun, Connecticut
1971	Al McGuire, Marquette	1981	Ralph Miller, Oregon St.	1991	Randy Ayers, Ohio St.
1972	John Wooden, UCLA	1982	Ralph Miller, Oregon St.	1992	Roy Williams, Kansas
1973	John Wooden, UCLA	1983	Guy Lewis, Houston	1993	Eddie Fogler, Vanderbilt
1974	Norm Sloan, N.C. State	1984	Ray Meyer, DePaul	1994	Norm Stewart, Missouri
1975	Bob Knight, Indiana	1985	Bill Frieder, Michigan	1995	Kelvin Sampson, Oklahoma
1976	Bob Knight, Indiana	1986	Eddie Sutton, Kentucky	1996	Gene Keady, Purdue

National Association of Basketball Coaches

Voted on by NABC membership and first presented in 1969.

Multiple winner: John Wooden (3).

Year		Year		Year	
1969	John Wooden, UCLA	1979	Ray Meyer, DePaul	1989	P.J. Carlesimo, Seton Hall
1970	John Wooden, UCLA	1980	Lute Olson, Iowa	1990	Jud Heathcote, Michigan St.
1971	Jack Kraft, Villanova	1981	Ralph Miller, Oregon St. & Jack Hartman, Kansas St.	1991	Mike Krzyzewski, Duke
1972	John Wooden, UCLA			1992	George Raveling, USC
1973	Gene Bartow, Memphis St.	1982	Don Monson, Idaho	1993	Eddie Fogler, Vanderbilt
1974	Al McGuire, Marquette	1983	Lou Carnesecca, St. John's	1994	Nolan Richardson, Arkansas & Gene Keady, Purdue
1975	Bob Knight, Indiana	1984	Marv Harshman, Washington		
1976	Johnny Orr, Michigan	1985	John Thompson, Georgetown	1995	Jim Harrick, UCLA
1977	Dean Smith, North Carolina	1986	Eddie Sutton, Kentucky	1996	John Calipari, UMass
1978	Bill Foster, Duke & Abe Lemons, Texas	1987	Rick Pitino, Providence		
		1988	John Chaney, Temple		

Naismith Award

Voted on by a panel of coaches, sportswriters and broadcasters and first presented by the Atlanta Tip-Off Club in 1987.

Multiple winner: Mike Krzyzewski (2).

Year		Year		Year	
1987	Bob Knight, Indiana	1991	Randy Ayers, Ohio St.	1995	Jim Harrick, UCLA
1988	Larry Brown, Kansas	1992	Mike Krzyzewski, Duke	1996	John Calipari, UMass
1989	Mike Krzyzewski, Duke	1993	Dean Smith, North Carolina		
1990	Bobby Cremins, Georgia Tech	1994	Nolan Richardson, Arkansas		

Other Men's Champions

The NCAA has sanctioned national championship tournaments for Divison II since 1957 and Division III since 1975. The NAIA sanctioned a single tournament from 1937-91, then split into two divisions in 1992.

NCAA Div. II Finals

Multiple winners: Kentucky Wesleyan (6); Evansville (5); CS-Bakersfield, North Alabama and Virginia Union (2).

Year	Winner	Score	Loser	Year	Winner	Score	Loser
1957	Wheaton, IL	89-65	Ky. Wesleyan	1977	Tennessee-Chatt.	71-62	Randolph-Macon
1958	South Dakota	75-53	St. Michael's, VT	1978	Cheyney, PA	47-40	WI-Green Bay
1959	Evansville, IN	83-67	SW Missouri St.	1979	North Alabama	64-50	WI-Green Bay
1960	Evansville, IN	90-69	Chapman, CA	1980	Virginia Union	80-74	New York Tech
1961	Wittenberg, OH	42-38	SE Missouri St.	1981	Florida Southern	73-68	Mt. St. Mary's, MD
1962	Mt. St. Mary's, MD	58-57*	CS-Sacramento	1982	Dist. of Columbia	73-63	Florida Southern
1963	South Dakota St.	42-40	Wittenberg, OH	1983	Wright St., OH	92-73	Dist. of Columbia
1964	Evansville, IN	72-59	Akron, OH	1984	Central Mo. St.	81-77	St. Augustine's, NC
1965	Evansville, IN	85-82*	Southern Illinois	1985	Jacksonville St.	74-73	South Dakota St.
1966	Ky. Wesleyan	54-51	Southern Illinois	1986	Sacred Heart, CT	93-87	SE Missouri St.
1967	Winston-Salem, NC	77-74	SW Missouri St.	1987	Ky. Wesleyan	92-74	Gannon, PA
1968	Ky. Wesleyan	63-52	Indiana St.	1988	Lowell, MA	75-72	AK-Anchorage
1969	Ky. Wesleyan	75-71	SW Missouri St.	1989	N.C. Central	73-46	SE Missouri St.
1970	Phila. Textile	76-65	Tennessee St.	1990	Ky. Wesleyan	93-79	CS-Bakersfield
1971	Evansville, IN	97-82	Old Dominion, VA	1991	North Alabama	79-72	Bridgeport, CT
1972	Roanoke, VA	84-72	Akron, OH	1992	Virginia Union	100-75	Bridgeport, CT
1973	Ky. Wesleyan	78-76*	Tennessee St.	1993	CS-Bakersfield	85-72	Troy St., AL
1974	Morgan St., MD	67-52	SW Missouri St.	1994	CS-Bakersfield	92-86	Southern Ind.
1975	Old Dominion, VA	76-74	New Orleans	1995	Southern Indiana	71-63	CS-Riverside
1976	Puget Sound, WA	83-74	Tennessee-Chatt.	1996	Fort Hays St.	70-63	N. Kentucky

*Overtime

NCAA Div. III Finals

Multiple winners: North Park (5); Potsdam St., Scranton, WI-Platteville and WI-Whitewater (2).

Year	Winner	Score	Loser
1975	LeMoyne-Owen, TN	57-54	Glassboro St., NJ
1976	Scranton, PA	60-57	Wittenberg, OH
1977	Wittenberg, OH	79-66	Oneonta St., NY
1978	North Park, IL	69-57	Widener, PA
1979	North Park, IL	66-62	Potsdam St., NY
1980	North Park, IL	83-76	Upsala, NJ
1981	Potsdam St., NY	67-65*	Augustana, IL
1982	Wabash, IN	83-62	Potsdam St., NY
1983	Scranton, PA	64-63	Wittenberg, OH
1984	WI-Whitewater	103-86	Clark, MA
1985	North Park, IL	72-71	Potsdam St., NY
1986	Potsdam St., NY	76-73	LeMoyne-Owen, TN
1987	North Park, IL	106-100	Clark, MA
1988	Ohio Wesleyan	92-70	Scranton, PA
1989	WI-Whitewater	94-86	Trenton St., NJ
1990	Rochester, NY	43-42	DePauw, IN
1991	WI-Platteville	81-74	Franklin Marshall
1992	Calvin, MI	62-49	Rochester, NY
1993	Ohio Northern	71-68	Augustana, IL
1994	Lebanon Valley, PA	66-59*	NYU
1995	WI-Platteville	69-55	Manchester, IN
1996	Rowan, NJ	100-93	Hope, MI

*Overtime

NAIA Finals, 1937-91

Multiple winners: Grand Canyon, Hamline, Kentucky St. and Tennessee St. (3); Central Missouri, Central St., Fort Hays St., St. Benedict's, KS and SW Missouri St. (2).

Year	Winner	Score	Loser
1937	Central Missouri	35-24	Morningside, IA
1938	Central Missouri	45-30	Roanoke, VA
1939	Southwestern, KS	32-31	San Diego St.
1940	Tarkio, MO	52-31	San Diego St.
1941	San Diego St.	36-32	Murray St., KY
1942	Hamline, MN	33-31	SE Oklahoma
1943	SE Missouri St.	34-32	NW Missouri St.
1944	Not held		
1945	Loyola-LA	49-36	Pepperdine, CA
1946	Southern Illinois	49-40	Indiana St.
1947	Marshall, WV	73-59	Mankato St., MN
1948	Louisville, KY	82-70	Indiana St.
1949	Hamline, MN	57-46	Regis, CO
1950	Indiana St.	61-47	East Central, OK
1951	Hamline, MN	69-61	Millikin, IL
1952	SW Missouri St.	73-64	Murray St., KY
1953	SW Missouri St.	79-71	Hamline, MN
1954	St. Benedict's, KS	62-56	Western Illinois
1955	East Texas St.	71-54	SE Oklahoma
1956	McNeese St., LA	60-55	Texas Southern
1957	Tennessee St.	92-73	SE Oklahoma
1958	Tennessee St.	85-73	Western Illinois
1959	Tennessee St.	97-87	Pacific-Luth., WA
1960	SW Texas St.	66-44	Westminster, PA
1961	Grambling, LA	95-75	Georgetown, KY
1962	Prairie View, TX	62-53	Westminster, PA
1963	Pan American, TX	73-62	Western Carolina
1964	Rockhurst, MO	66-56	Pan American, TX
1965	Central St., OH	85-51	Oklahoma Baptist
1966	Oklahoma Baptist	88-59	Georgia Southern
1967	St. Benedict's, KS	71-65	Oklahoma Baptist
1968	Central St., OH	51-48	Fairmont St., WV
1969	Eastern New Mexico	99-76	MD-Eastern Shore
1970	Kentucky St.	79-71	Central Wash.
1971	Kentucky St.	102-82	Eastern Michigan
1972	Kentucky St.	71-62	WI-Eau Claire
1973	Guilford, NC	99-96	MD-Eastern Shore
1974	West Georgia	97-79	Alcorn St., MS
1975	Grand Canyon, AZ	65-54	M'western St., TX
1976	Coppin St., MD	96-91	Henderson St., AR
1977	Texas Southern	71-44	Campbell, NC
1978	Grand Canyon, AZ	79-75	Kearney St., NE
1979	Drury, MO	60-54	Henderson St., AR
1980	Cameron, OK	84-77	Alabama St.
1981	Beth. Nazarene, OK	86-85*	AL-Huntsville
1982	SC-Spartanburg	51-38	Biola, CA
1983	Charleston, SC	57-53	WV-Wesleyan
1984	Fort Hays St., KS	48-46*	WI-Stevens Pt.
1985	Fort Hays St., KS	82-80*	Wayland Bapt., TX
1986	David Lipscomb, TN	67-54	AR-Monticello
1987	Washburn, KS	79-77	West Virginia St.
1988	Grand Canyon, AZ	88-86*	Auburn-Montg, AL
1989	St. Mary's, TX	61-58	East Central, OK
1990	Birm-Southern, AL	88-80	WI-Eau Claire
1991	Oklahoma City	77-74	Central Arkansas

*Overtime

NAIA Div. I Finals

NAIA split tournament into two divisions in 1992.

Multiple winner: Oklahoma City (3).

Year	Winner	Score	Loser
1992	Oklahoma City	82-73*	Central Arkansas
1993	Hawaii Pacific	88-83	Okla. Baptist
1994	Oklahoma City	99-81	Life, GA
1995	Birm-Southern	92-76	Pfeiffer, NC
1996	Oklahoma City	86-80	Georgetown, KY

*Overtime

NAIA Div. II Finals

NAIA split tournament into two divisions in 1992.

Year	Winner	Score	Loser
1992	Grace, IN	85-79*	Northwestern-IA
1993	Williamette, OR	63-56	Northern St., SD
1994	Eureka, IL	98-95*	Northern St., SD
1995	Bethel, IN	103-95*	NW Nazarene, ID
1996	Albertson, ID	81-72*	Whitworth, WA

*Overtime

Player of the Year and NBA MVP

College basketball Players of the Year who have gone on to win the NBA's Most Valuable Player award.

Bill Russell: COLLEGE—San Francisco (1956); PROS—Boston Celtics (1958, 1961, 1962, 1963 and 1965).

Oscar Robertson: COLLEGE—Cincinnati (1958, 1959 and 1960); PROS—Cincinnati Royals (1964).

Kareem Abdul-Jabbar: COLLEGE—UCLA (1967 and 1968); PROS—Milwaukee Bucks (1971, 1972 and 1974) and LA Lakers (1976, 1977 and 1980).

Bill Walton: COLLEGE—UCLA (1972, 1973 and 1974); PROS—Portland Trail Blazers (1978).

Larry Bird: COLLEGE—Indiana St. (1979); PROS—Boston Celtics (1984, 1985, and 1986).

Michael Jordan: COLLEGE—North Carolina (1984); PROS—Chicago Bulls (1988, 1991, 1992 and 1996).

David Robinson: COLLEGE—Navy (1987); PROS—San Antonio Spurs (1995).

WOMEN

NCAA Final Four

Replaced the Association of Intercollegiate Athletics for Women (AIAW) tournament in 1982 as the official playoff for the national championship.

Multiple winners: Tennessee (4); Louisiana Tech, Stanford and USC (2).

Year	Champion	Head Coach	Score	Runner-up	Third Place	
1982	Louisiana Tech	Sonya Hogg	76-62	Cheyney	Maryland	Tennessee
1983	USC	Linda Sharp	69-67	Louisiana Tech	Georgia	Old Dominion
1984	USC	Linda Sharp	72-61	Tennessee	Cheyney	Louisiana Tech
1985	Old Dominion	Marianne Stanley	70-65	Georgia	NE Louisiana	Western Ky.
1986	Texas	Jody Conradt	97-81	USC	Tennessee	Western Ky.
1987	Tennessee	Pat Summitt	67-44	Louisiana Tech	Long Beach St.	Texas
1988	Louisiana Tech	Leon Barmore	56-54	Auburn	Long Beach St.	Tennessee
1989	Tennessee	Pat Summitt	76-60	Auburn	Louisiana Tech	Maryland
1990	Stanford	Tara VanDerveer	88-81	Auburn	Louisiana Tech	Virginia
1991	Tennessee	Pat Summitt	70-67 (OT)	Virginia	Connecticut	Stanford
1992	Stanford	Tara VanDerveer	78-62	Western Kentucky	SW Missouri St.	Virginia
1993	Texas Tech	Marsha Sharp	84-82	Ohio St.	Iowa	Vanderbilt
1994	North Carolina	Sylvia Hatchell	60-59	Louisiana Tech	Alabama	Purdue
1995	Connecticut	Geno Auriemma	70-64	Tennessee	Georgia	Stanford
1996	Tennessee	Pat Summitt	83-65	Georgia	Connecticut	Stanford

Final Four sites: 1982 (Norfolk, Va.), **1983** (Norfolk, Va.), **1984** (Los Angeles), **1985** (Austin), **1986** (Lexington), **1987** (Austin), **1988** (Tacoma), **1989** (Tacoma), **1990** (Knoxville), **1991** (New Orleans), **1992** (Los Angeles), **1993** (Atlanta), **1994** (Richmond), **1995** (Minneapolis), **1996** (Charlotte).

Most Outstanding Player

A Most Outstanding Player has been selected every year of the NCAA tournament. Winner who did not play for the tournament champion is listed in **bold** type.

Multiple winner: Cheryl Miller (2).

Year		Year		Year	
1982	Janice Lawrence, La. Tech	1987	Tonya Edwards, Tennessee	1992	Molly Goodenbour, Stanford
1983	Cheryl Miller, USC	1988	Erica Westbrooks, La. Tech	1993	Sheryl Swoopes, Texas Tech
1984	Cheryl Miller, USC	1989	Bridgette Gordon, Tennessee	1994	Charlotte Smith, N. Carolina
1985	Tracy Claxton, Old Dominion	1990	Jennifer Azzi, Stanford	1995	Rebecca Lobo, Connecticut
1986	Clarissa Davis, Texas	1991	**Dawn Staley,** Virginia	1996	Michelle Marciniak, Tennessee

All-Time NCAA Division I Tournament Leaders

Through 1994-95; minimum of six games; **Last** column indicates final year played

CAREER

Scoring

	Points	Yrs	Last	Pts	Avg
1	Bridgette Gordon, Tenn	4	1989	388	21.6
2	Cheryl Miller, USC	4	1986	333	20.8
3	Janice Lawrence, La. Tech	3	1984	312	22.3
4	Penny Toler, L. Beach St	4	1989	291	22.4
5	Dawn Staley, Virginia	4	1992	274	18.3
6	Cindy Brown, L. Beach St	4	1987	263	21.9
7	Venus Lacy, La. Tech	3	1990	263	18.8
8	Clarissa Davis, Texas	3	1989	261	21.8
9	Janet Harris, Georgia	4	1985	254	19.5
10	Val Whiting, Stanford	4	1993	249	15.6

Rebounds

	Average	Yrs	Last	No	Avg
1	Cheryl Miller, USC	4	1986	170	10.6
2	Sheila Frost, Tennessee	4	1989	162	9.0
3	Val Whiting, Stanford	4	1993	161	10.1
4	Venus Lacy, La. Tech	3	1990	148	10.6
5	Bridgette Gordon, Tenn	4	1989	142	7.9
6	Kirsten Cummings, L. Beach St.	4	1985	136	10.5
7	Nora Lewis, La. Tech	3	1989	130	9.3
8	Pam McGee, USC	3	1984	127	9.8
9	Daedra Charles, Tenn	3	1991	125	9.6
	Paula McGee, USC	3	1984	125	9.6

SINGLE GAME

Scoring

		Year	Pts
1	Lorri Bauman, Drake vs Maryland	1982	50
2	Sheryl Swoopes, Texas Tech vs Ohio St.	1993	47
3	Barbara Kennedy, Clemson vs Penn St.	1982	43
4	LaTaunya Pollard, L. Beach St. vs Howard	1982	40
	Cindy Brown, L. Beach St. vs Ohio St.	1987	40
6	Kerry Bascom, UConn vs Toledo	1991	39
	Portia Hill, S.F. Austin St. vs Arkansas	1990	39
	Delmonica DeHorney, Ark. vs Stanford	1990	39
9	LaTaunya Pollard, L. Beach St. vs USC	1983	37
	Teresa Edwards, Georgia vs Tennessee	1986	37

Rebounds

		Year	No
1	Cheryl Taylor, Tenn. Tech vs Georgia	1985	23
	Charlotte Smith, N. Car. vs La. Tech	1994	23
3	Daedra Charles, Tenn. vs SW Missouri	1991	22
4	Cherie Nelson, USC vs Western Ky	1987	21
5	Alison Lang, Oregon vs Missouri	1982	20
	Shelda Arceneaux, S.D. St. vs L. Beach St.	1984	20
	Tracy Claxton, ODU vs Georgia	1985	20
	Brigette Combs, West. Ky. vs West Va	1989	20
	Tandreia Green, West. Ky. vs West Va	1989	20
10	Six tied with 19 each.		

Associated Press Final Top 10 Polls

The Associated Press weekly women's college basketball poll was begun by Mel Greenberg of The Philadelphia Inquirer during the 1976-77 season. The Association of Intercollegiate Athletics for Women (AIAW) Tournament determined the Division I national champion for 1972-81. The NCAA began its women's Division I tournament in 1982. The final AP Polls were taken before the NCAA tournament. Eventual national champions are in **bold** type.

1977
1. **Delta St.**
2. Immaculata
3. St. Joseph's-PA
4. CS-Fullerton
5. Tennessee
6. Tennessee Tech
7. Wayland Baptist
8. Montclair St.
9. S.F. Austin St.
10. N.C. State

1978
1. Tennessee
2. Wayland Baptist
3. N.C. State
4. Montclair St.
5. **UCLA**
6. Maryland
7. Queens-NY
8. Valdosta St.
9. Delta St.
10. LSU

1979
1. **Old Dominion**
2. Louisiana Tech
3. Tennessee
4. Texas
5. S.F. Austin St.
6. UCLA
7. Rutgers
8. Maryland
9. Cheyney
10. Wayland Baptist

1980
1. **Old Dominion**
2. Tennessee
3. Louisiana Tech
4. South Carolina
5. S.F. Austin St.
6. Maryland
7. Texas
8. Rutgers
9. Long Beach St.
10. N.C. State

1981
1. **Louisiana Tech**
2. Tennessee
3. Old Dominion
4. USC
5. Cheyney
6. Long Beach St.
7. UCLA
8. Maryland
9. Rutgers
10. Kansas

1982
1. **Louisiana Tech**
2. Cheyney
3. Maryland
4. Tennessee
5. Texas
6. USC
7. Old Dominion
8. Rutgers
9. Long Beach St.
10. Penn St.

1983
1. **USC**
2. Louisiana Tech
3. Texas
4. Old Dominion
5. Cheyney
6. Long Beach St.
7. Maryland
8. Penn St.
9. Georgia
10. Tennessee

1984
1. Texas
2. Louisiana Tech
3. Georgia
4. Old Dominion
5. **USC**
6. Long Beach St.
7. Kansas St.
8. LSU
9. Cheyney
10. Mississippi

1985
1. Texas
2. NE Louisiana
3. Long Beach St.
4. Louisiana Tech
5. **Old Dominion**
6. Mississippi
7. Ohio St.
8. Georgia
9. Penn St.
10. Auburn

1986
1. **Texas**
2. Georgia
3. USC
4. Louisiana Tech
5. Western Ky.
6. Virginia
7. Auburn
8. Long Beach St.
9. LSU
10. Rutgers

1987
1. Texas
2. Auburn
3. Louisiana Tech
4. Long Beach St.
5. Rutgers
6. Georgia
7. **Tennessee**
8. Mississippi
9. Iowa
10. Ohio St.

1988
1. Tennessee
2. Iowa
3. Auburn
4. Texas
5. **Louisiana Tech**
6. Ohio St.
7. Long Beach St.
8. Rutgers
9. Maryland
10. Virginia

1989
1. **Tennessee**
2. Auburn
3. Louisiana Tech
4. Stanford
5. Maryland
6. Texas
7. Long Beach St.
8. Iowa
9. Colorado
10. Georgia

1990
1. **Louisiana Tech**
2. Stanford
3. Washington
4. Tennessee
5. UNLV
6. S.F. Austin St.
7. Georgia
8. Texas
9. Auburn
10. Iowa

1991
1. Penn St.
2. Virginia
3. Georgia
4. **Tennessee**
5. Purdue
6. Auburn
7. N.C. State
8. LSU
9. Arkansas
10. Western Ky.

1992
1. Virginia
2. Tennessee
3. **Stanford**
4. S.F. Austin St.
5. Mississippi
6. Miami-FL
7. Iowa
8. Maryland
9. Penn St.
10. SW Missouri St.

1993
1. Vanderbilt
2. Tennessee
3. Ohio St.
4. Iowa
5. **Texas Tech**
6. Stanford
7. Auburn
8. Penn St.
9. Virginia
10. Colorado

1994
1. Tennessee
2. Penn St.
3. Connecticut
4. **North Carolina**
5. Colorado
6. Louisiana Tech
7. USC
8. Purdue
9. Texas Tech
10. Virginia

1995
1. **Connecticut**
2. Colorado
3. Tennessee
4. Stanford
5. Texas Tech
6. Vanderbilt
7. Penn St.
8. Louisiana Tech
9. Western Ky.
10. Virginia

1996
1. Louisiana Tech
2. Connecticut
3. Stanford
4. **Tennessee**
5. Georgia
6. Old Dominion
7. Iowa
8. Penn St.
9. Texas Tech
10. Alabama

All-Time Winningest Division I Teams

Division I schools with best winning percentages and most victories through 1995-96 (including postseason tournaments).

Top 10 Winning Percentage

	Team	Yrs	W	L	Pct
1	Louisiana Tech	22	614	119	**.838**
2	Tennessee	22	596	134	**.816**
3	Texas	22	596	142	**.808**
4	Mount St. Mary's	22	448	140	**.762**
5	Montana	22	466	153	**.753**
6	S. F. Austin St.	24	566	189	**.750**
	Long Beach St.	34	603	215	**.737**
8	Mississippi	22	501	182	**.734**
9	N.C. State	22	462	169	**.732**
10	Virginia	23	486	179	**.731**

Top 10 Victories

	Team	Yrs	W	L	Pct
1	Louisiana Tech	22	**614**	119	.838
2	Long Beach St.	34	**603**	215	.737
3	James Madison	71	**597**	319	.652
4	Texas	22	**596**	142	.808
	Tennessee	22	**596**	134	.816
6	Tennessee Tech	26	**566**	233	.708
	S.F. Austin St.	24	**566**	189	.750
8	Old Dominion	27	**559**	208	.729
9	Ohio St.	31	**531**	220	.707
10	Southern Ill.	37	**511**	253	.669

Annual NCAA Division I Leaders

All averages include postseason games

Scoring

Multiple winner: Andrea Congreaves (2).

Year	Player	Gm	Pts	Avg
1982	Barbara Kennedy, Clemson	31	908	29.3
1983	LaTaunya Pollard, L. Beach St	31	907	29.3
1984	Deborah Temple, Delta St	28	873	31.2
1985	Anucha Browne, Northwestern	28	855	30.5
1986	Wanda Ford, Drake	30	919	30.6
1987	Tresa Spaulding, BYU	28	810	28.9
1988	LeChandra LeDay, Grambling	28	850	30.4
1989	Patricia Hoskins, Miss. Valley	27	908	33.6
1990	Kim Perrot, SW Louisiana	28	839	30.0
1991	Jan Jensen, Drake	30	888	29.6
1992	Andrea Congreaves, Mercer	28	925	33.0
1993	Andrea Congreaves, Mercer	26	805	31.0
1994	Kristy Ryan, CS-Sacramento	26	727	28.0
1995	Koko Lahanas, CS-Fullerton	29	778	26.8
1996	Cindy Blodgett, Maine	32	899	27.8

Rebounds

Multiple winner: Patricia Hoskins (2).

Year	Player	Gm	No	Avg
1982	Anne Donovan, Old Dominion	28	412	14.7
1983	Deborah Mitchell, Miss. Col	28	447	16.0
1984	Joy Kellog, Oklahoma City	23	373	16.2
1985	Rosina Pearson, Beth-Cookman	26	480	18.5
1986	Wanda Ford, Drake	30	506	16.9
1987	Patricia Hoskins, Miss. Valley	28	476	17.0
1988	Katie Beck, East Tenn. St.	25	441	17.6
1989	Patricia Hoskins, Miss. Valley	27	440	16.3
1990	Pam Hudson, Northwestern St.	29	438	15.1
1991	Tarcha Hollis, Grambling	29	443	15.3
1992	Christy Greis, Evansville	28	383	13.7
1993	Ann Barry, Nevada	25	355	14.2
1994	DeShawne Blocker, E. Tenn. St.	26	450	17.3
1995	Tera Sheriff, Jackson St	29	401	13.8
1996	Dana Wynne, Seton Hall	29	372	12.8

Note: Wanda Ford (1986) and Patricia Hoskins (1989) each led the country in scoring and rebounds in the same year.

All-Time NCAA Division I Individual Leaders

Through 1995-96; includes regular season and tournament games; **Last** column indicates final year played.

CAREER

Scoring

Average		Yrs	Last	Pts	Avg
1	Patricia Hoskins, Miss.Valley St.	4	1989	3122	28.4
2	Sandra Hodge, New Orleans	4	1984	2860	26.7
3	Lorri Bauman, Drake	4	1984	3115	26.0
4	Valorie Whiteside, Aplach. St.	4	1988	2944	25.4
5	Joyce Walker, LSU	4	1984	2906	24.8
6	Tarcha Hollis, Grambling	4	1991	2058	24.2
7	Karen Pelphrey, Marshall	4	1986	2746	24.1
8	Erma Jones, Bethune-Cookman	3	1984	2095	24.1
9	Cheryl Miller, USC	4	1986	3018	23.6
10	Chris Starr, Nevada	4	1986	2356	23.3

Rebounds

Average		Yrs	Last	Reb	Avg
1	Wanda Ford, Drake	4	1986	1887	16.1
2	Patricia Hoskins, Miss.Valley St.	4	1989	1662	15.1
3	Tarcha Hollis, Grambling	4	1991	1185	13.9
4	Katie Beck, East Tenn. St.	4	1988	1404	13.4
5	Marilyn Stephens, Temple	4	1984	1519	13.0
6	Cheryl Taylor, Tenn. Tech	4	1987	1532	12.8
7	Olivia Bradley, West Virginia	4	1985	1484	12.7
8	Judy Mosley, Hawaii	4	1990	1441	12.6
9	Chana Perry, NE La./S. Diego St.	4	1989	1286	12.5
10	Three players tied at 12.2 each.				

SINGLE SEASON

Scoring

Average		Year	Gm	Pts	Avg
1	Patricia Hoskins, Miss.Valley St.	1989	27	908	33.6
2	Andrea Congreaves, Mercer	1992	28	925	33.0
3	Deborah Temple, Delta St.	1984	28	873	31.2
4	Andrea Congreaves, Mercer	1993	26	805	31.0
5	Wanda Ford, Drake	1986	30	919	30.6
6	Anucha Browne, Northwestern	1985	28	855	30.5
7	LeChandra LeDay, Grambling	1988	28	850	30.4
8	Kim Perrot, SW Louisiana	1990	28	839	30.0
9	Tina Hutchinson, San Diego St.	1984	30	898	29.9
10	Jan Jensen, Drake	1991	30	888	29.6

SINGLE GAME

Scoring

Average		Year	Pts
1	Cindy Brown, Long Beach St. vs San Jose St.	1987	60
2	Lorri Bauman, Drake vs SW Missouri St.	1984	58
	Kim Perrot, SW La. vs SE La	1990	58
4	Patricia Hoskins, Miss.Valley St. vs South-BR	1989	55
	Patricia Hoskins, Miss.Valley St. vs Ala. St.	1989	55
6	Wanda Ford, Drake vs SW Missouri St.	1986	54
7	Chris Starr, Nevada vs CS-Sacramento	1983	53
	Felisha Edwards, NE La. vs Southern Miss	1991	53
	Sheryl Swoopes, Texas Tech vs Texas	1993	53
10	Three players tied at 52 points each.		

Winningest Active Division I Coaches

Minimum of five seasons as Division I head coach; regular season and tournament games included.

Top 10 Winning Percentage

		Yrs	W	L	Pct
1	Leon Barmore, La. Tech	14	397	63	**.845**
2	Pat Summit, Tennessee	22	596	134	**.816**
3	Bill Sheahan, Mt. St. Mary's	15	342	78	**.814**
4	Robin Selvig, Montana	18	432	105	**.804**
5	Sonja Hogg, Baylor	13	331	88	**.790**
6	Jody Conradt, Texas	27	675	187	**.783**
7	Tara VanDerveer, Stanford	17	403	113	**.781**
8	Vivian Stringer, Iowa	24	533	150	**.780**
9	Gary Blair, Arkansas	11	269	77	**.777**
10	Joe Ciampi, Auburn	19	449	130	**.775**

Top 11 Victories

		Yrs	W	L	Pct
1	Jody Conradt, Texas	27	**675**	187	.783
2	Pat Summitt, Tennessee	22	**596**	134	.816
3	Vivian Stringer, Iowa	24	**533**	150	.780
4	Sue Gunter, LSU	26	**522**	240	.685
5	Kay Yow, N.C. State	25	**508**	202	.715
6	Theresa Grentz, Rutgers	22	**474**	169	.737
7	Rene Portland, Penn St.	20	**465**	147	.760
8	Sylvia Hatchell, N. Carolina	21	**457**	195	.701
9	Kay James, So. Miss.	24	**450**	200	.692
10	Joe Ciampi, Auburn	19	**449**	257	.775
11	Lin Dunn, Purdue	25	**447**	257	.635

Note: Stanford coach Tara VanDerveer took the 1995-96 season off to coach the U.S. Women's Olympic team.

Annual Awards

The Broderick Award was first given out to the Women's Division I or Large School Player of the Year in 1977. Since then, the National Assn. for Girls and Women in Sports (1978), the Women's Basketball Coaches Assn. (1983) and the Atlanta Tip-Off Club (1983) and the Associated Press (1995) have joined in.

Since 1983, the first year as many as four awards were given out, the same player has won all of them in the same season twice: Cheryl Miller of USC in 1985 and Rebecca Lobo of Connecticut in 1995.

Associated Press

Voted on by AP sportswriters and broadcasters and first presented in 1995.

Year
1995 Rebecca Lobo, Connecticut
1996 Jennifer Rizzotti, Connecticut

Broderick Award

Voted on by a national panel of women's collegiate athletic directors and first presented by the late Thomas Broderick, an athletic outfitter, in 1977. Honda has presented the award since 1987. Basketball Player of the Year is one of 10 nominated for Collegiate Woman Athlete of the Year; (*) indicates player also won Athlete of the Year.

Multiple winners: Nancy Lieberman, Cheryl Miller and Dawn Staley (2).

Year
1977 Lucy Harris, Delta St.*
1978 Anne Meyers, UCLA*
1979 Nancy Lieberman, Old Dominion*
1980 Nancy Lieberman, Old Dominion*
1981 Lynette Woodward, Kansas
1982 Pam Kelly, La. Tech.
1983 Anne Donovan, Old Dominion
1984 Cheryl Miller, USC*
1985 Cheryl Miller, USC
1986 Kamie Ethridge, Texas*
1987 Katrina McClain, Georgia
1988 Teresa Weatherspoon, La. Tech*
1989 Bridgette Gordon, Tennessee
1990 Jennifer Azzi, Stanford
1991 Dawn Staley, Virginia
1992 Dawn Staley, Virginia
1993 Sheryl Swoopes, Texas Tech
1994 Lisa Leslie, USC
1995 Rebecca Lobo, Connecticut*
1996 TBA

Wade Trophy

Voted on by the National Assn. for Girls and Women in Sports (NAGWS) and awarded for academics and community service as well as player performance. First presented in 1978 in the name of former Delta St. coach Margaret Wade.

Multiple winner: Nancy Lieberman (2).

Year
1978 Carol Blazejowski, Montclair St.
1979 Nancy Lieberman, Old Dominion
1980 Nancy Lieberman, Old Dominion
1981 Lynette Woodward, Kansas
1982 Pam Kelly, La. Tech
1983 LaTaunya Pollard, L. Beach St.
1984 Janice Lawrence, La. Tech
1985 Cheryl Miller, USC
1986 Kamie Ethridge, Texas
1987 Shelly Pennefather, Villanova
1988 Teresa Weatherspoon, La. Tech
1989 Clarissa Davis, Texas
1990 Jennifer Azzi, Stanford
1991 Daedra Charles, Tennessee
1992 Susan Robinson, Penn St.
1993 Karen Jennings, Nebraska
1994 Carol Ann Shudlick, Minnesota
1995 Rebecca Lobo, Connecticut
1996 Jennifer Rizzotti, Connecticut

Naismith Trophy

Voted on by a panel of coaches, sportwriters and broadcasters and first presented in 1983 by the Atlanta Tip-Off Club in the name of the inventor of basketball, Dr. James Naismith.

Multiple winners: Cheryl Miller (3); Clarissa Davis and Dawn Staley (2).

Year
1983 Anne Donovan, Old Dominion
1984 Cheryl Miller, USC
1985 Cheryl Miller, USC
1986 Cheryl Miller, USC
1987 Clarissa Davis, Texas
1988 Sue Wicks, Rutgers
1989 Clarissa Davis, Texas
1990 Jennifer Azzi, Stanford
1991 Dawn Staley, Virgina
1992 Dawn Staley, Virginia
1993 Sheryl Swoopes, Texas Tech
1994 Lisa Leslie, USC
1995 Rebecca Lobo, Connecticut
1996 Saudia Roundtree, Georgia

Annual Awards (Cont.)

Women's Basketball Coaches Association

Voted on by the WBCA and first presented by Champion athletic outfitters in 1983.
Multiple winners: Cheryl Miller and Dawn Staley (2).

Year	Year	Year
1983 Anne Donovan, Old Dominion	1988 Michelle Edwards, Iowa	1993 Sheryl Swoopes, Texas Tech
1984 Janice Lawrence, La. Tech	1989 Clarissa Davis, Texas	1994 Lisa Leslie, USC
1985 Cheryl Miller, USC	1990 Venus Lacey, La. Tech	1995 Rebecca Lobo, Connecticut
1986 Cheryl Miller, USC	1991 Dawn Staley, Virgina	1996 Saudia Roundtree, Georgia
1987 Katrina McClain, Georgia	1992 Dawn Staley, Virginia	

Coach of the Year Award

Voted on by the Women's Basketball Coaches Assn. and first presented by Converse athletic outfitters in 1983.
Multiple winners: Jody Conradt and Vivian Stringer (2).

Year	Year	Year
1983 Pat Summitt, Tennessee	1988 Vivian Stringer, Iowa	1993 Vivian Stringer, Iowa
1984 Jody Conradt, Texas	1989 Tara VanDerveer, Stanford	1994 Marsha Sharp, Texas Tech
1985 Jim Foster, St. Joseph's-PA	1990 Kay Yow, N.C. State	1995 Gary Blair, Arkansas
1986 Jody Conradt, Texas	1991 Rene Portland, Penn St.	1996 Leon Barmore, La. Tech
1987 Theresa Grentz, Rutgers	1992 Ferne Labati, Miami-FL	

Other Women's Champions

The NCAA has sanctioned national championship tournaments for Division II and Division III since 1982. The NAIA sanctioned a single tournament from 1981-91, then split in to two divisions in 1992.

NCAA Div. II Finals

Multiple winners: North Dakota St. (5); Cal Poly Pomona (3) and Delta St. (3).

Year	Winner	Score	Loser
1982	Cal Poly Pomona	93-74	Tuskegee, AL
1983	Virginia Union	73-60	Cal Poly Pomona
1984	Central Mo. St.	80-73	Virginia Union
1985	Cal Poly Pomona	80-69	Central Mo. St.
1986	Cal Poly Pomona	70-63	North Dakota St.
1987	New Haven, CT	77-75	Cal Poly Pomona
1988	Hampton, VA	65-48	West Texas St.
1989	Delta St., MS	88-58	Cal Poly Pomona
1990	Delta St., MS	77-43	Bentley, MA
1991	North Dakota St.	81-74	SE Missouri St.
1992	Delta St., MS	65-63	North Dakota St.
1993	North Dakota St.	95-63	Delta St., MS
1994	North Dakota St.	89-56	CS-San Bernadino
1995	North Dakota St.	98-85	Portland St.
1996	North Dakota St.	105-78	Shippensburg, PA

AIAW Finals

The Association of Intercollegiate Athletics for Women Large College tournament determined the women's national champion for 10 years until supplanted by the NCAA.

In 1982, most Division I teams entered the first NCAA tournament rather than the last one staged by the AIAW.

Year	Winner	Score	Loser
1972	Immaculata, PA	52-48	West Chester, PA
1973	Immaculata, PA	59-52	Queens College, NY
1974	Immaculata, PA	68-53	Mississippi College
1975	Delta St., MS	90-81	Immaculata, PA
1976	Delta St., MS	69-64	Immaculata, PA
1977	Delta St., MS	68-55	LSU
1978	UCLA	90-74	Maryland
1979	Old Dominion	75-65	Louisiana Tech
1980	Old Dominion	68-53	Tennessee
1981	Louisiana Tech	79-59	Tennessee
1982	Rutgers	83-77	Texas

NCAA Div. III Finals

Multiple winners: Capital and Elizabethtown (2).

Year	Winner	Score	Loser
1982	Elizabethtown, PA	67-66*	NC-Greensboro
1983	North Central, IL	83-71	Elizabethtown, PA
1984	Rust College, MS	51-49	Elizabethtown, PA
1985	Scranton, PA	68-59	New Rochelle, NY
1986	Salem St., MA	89-85	Bishop, TX
1987	WI-Stevens Pt.	81-74	Concordia, MN
1988	Concordia, MN	65-57	St. John Fisher, NY
1989	Elizabethtown, PA	66-65	CS-Stanislaus
1990	Hope, MI	65-63	St. John Fisher
1991	St. Thomas, MN	73-55	Muskingum, OH
1992	Alma, MI	79-75	Moravian, PA
1993	Central Iowa	71-63	Capital, OH
1994	Capital, OH	82-63	Washington, MO
1995	Capital, OH	59-55	WI-Oshkosh
1996	WI-Oshkosh	66-50	Mt. Union, OH

*Overtime

NAIA Finals

Multiple winners: One tournament—SW Oklahoma (4); Div. I tourney—Arkansas Tech and Southern Nazarene (3); Div. II tourney—Northern St. and Western Oregon (2).

Year	Winner	Score	Loser
1981	Kentucky St.	73-67	Texas Southern
1982	SW Oklahoma	80-45	Mo. Southern
1983	SW Oklahoma	80-68	AL-Huntsville
1984	NC-Asheville	72-70*	Portland, OR
1985	SW Oklahoma	55-54	Saginaw Val., MI
1986	Francis Marion, SC	75-65	Wayland Baptist, TX
1987	SW Oklahoma	60-58	North Georgia
1988	Oklahoma City	113-95	Claflin, SC
1989	So. Nazarene	98-96	Claflin, SC
1990	SW Oklahoma	82-75	AR-Monticello
1991	Ft. Hays St., KS	57-53	SW Oklahoma
1992	I— Arkansas Tech	84-68	Wayland Baptist, TX
	II— Northern St., SD	73-56	Tarleton St., TX
1993	I— Arkansas Tech	76-75	Union, TN
	II— No. Montana	71-68	Northern St., SD
1994	I— So. Nazarene	97-74	David Lipscomb, TN
	II— Northern St., SD	48-45	Western Oregon
1995	I— So. Nazarene	78-77	SE Oklahoma
	II— Western Oregon	75-67	NW Nazarene, ID
1996	I— So. Nazarene	80-79	SE Oklahoma
	II— Western Oregon	80-77	Huron, SD

*Overtime

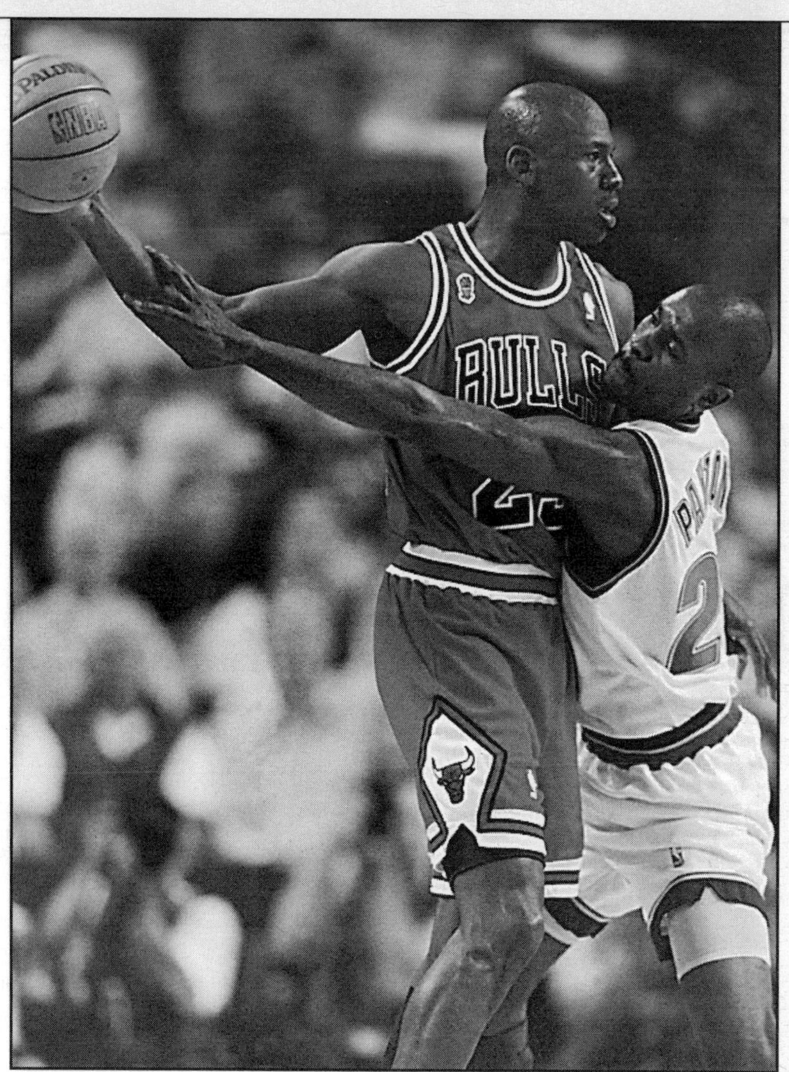

Jonathan Daniel/Allsport

The Chicago Bulls' **Michael Jordan** toys with Seattle Supersonic **Gary Payton** just like his team did with the rest of the NBA as the Bulls turned in a record-setting 72-10 regular season.

PRO BASKETBALL

by David Moore

Another Bull Run

Despite enormous pressure and cross-dressing, the Chicago Bulls staked their claim as one of the best teams in NBA history

The popularity of the world champion Chicago Bulls has officially reached absurd heights.

Defense attorney Johnnie Cochran tried to enter the Bulls locker room after a game. Apparently, his closing argument wasn't persuasive enough. He was denied access.

After Dennis Rodman was suspended for six games for head-butting a referee, Jesse Jackson offered his services. The man who has flown all over the world to mediate disputes wanted to make sure Rodman was cool and collected for the stretch run.

Technically, it is correct to call the Bulls a championship basketball team. But that description is misleading in the fact that this team evolved into something much more. With Michael Jordan's greatness, Rodman's penchant for cross-dressing and Phil Jackson's tendency to spout Lakota Sioux mysticism, the Bulls are a compelling, entertainment conglomerate.

On the court, Chicago's victory over the Seattle SuperSonics in The Finals brought an historic season to its logical conclusion. The Bulls furnished the exclamation point to a 72-10 regular season and Jordan's return to the NBA summit by disposing of the Sonics in six games.

David Moore has been the national pro basketball writer for The Dallas Morning News since 1989. He is also an NBA analyst for ESPN.

A championship was placed on our heads the first day of camp," Jackson said. "We were expected to win. Whenever you're expected to do something, the pressure is great.

"This was a relief rather than an exultation," he continued. "We knew we were good enough to win. We just had to put the nail in the coffin. We kept waiting for that game to show up."

There was a brief period when Jordan waited for *his* game to show up. Before he left the Bulls in 1993 for his fling with baseball, Jordan was considered the sport's premier player. No debate. But his return to Chicago in the second half of the 1994-95 season resulted in uncharacteristically poor games and a second round playoff exit.

Jordan started off the '95-96 season by saying at least four players—Houston's Hakeem Olajuwon, Orlando's Shaquille O'Neal, Phoenix Charles Barkley and teammate Scottie Pippen—had passed him by. He put himself in a group of five or six players who were trying to obtain the status of best player.

"When I was away from the game, other players stepped to the forefront and become stars in their own right," Jordan said of his place in the game. "I didn't have the chance to play against those stars and compete against them and see where they stand and where I stand against them.

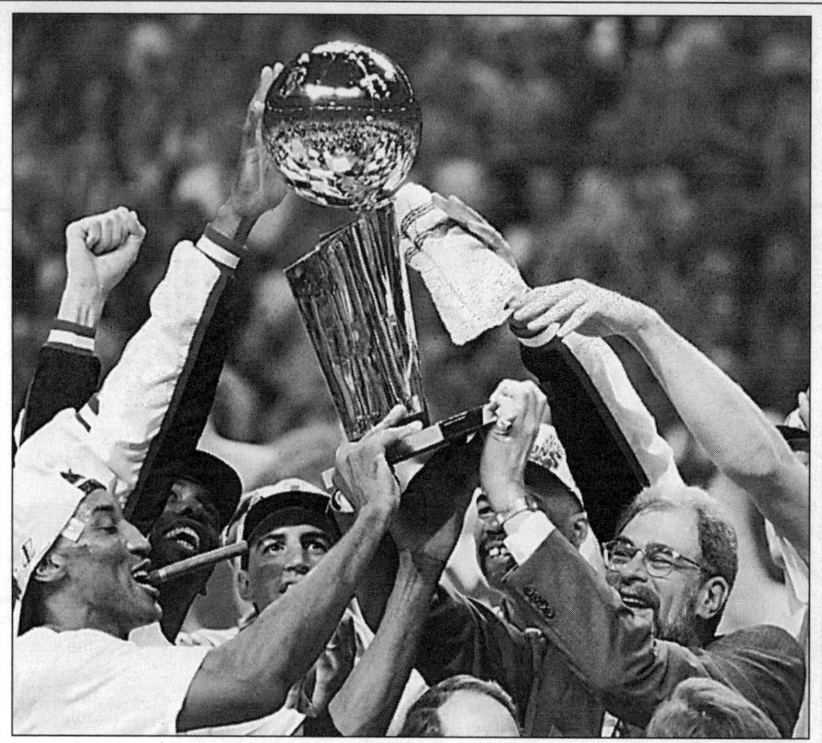

Jonathan Daniel/Allsport

Scottie Pippen (with cigar) and **Phil Jackson** (with glasses) do not get the publicity of Messrs. Jordan and Rodman but the Bulls would not have made history in the 1995-96 season without the contributions of all four men.

Those are the type of challenges that are starting to come up for me."

Those challenges - along with the drive to lift the Bulls to another championship - consumed Jordan. He finished the season with another scoring title, his fourth Most Valuable Player award and his fourth championship in the last six years.

Rodman, meanwhile, recaptured some of the respect he has lost with his volatile behavior in recent years. There were still a few ugly incidents along the way, such as the head-butt of referee Ted Bernhardt.

There were the tattoos, pierced body parts and The Hair. There was the afternoon Rodman showed up for a book signing dressed in women's clothes, sporting a pink feather boa. Still, Rodman was more comfortable and productive in his brief time in Chicago than he was at any stage of his two, tumultuous seasons in San Antonio.

"It's different," Rodman said. "Here, everyone is very mature and understands what each individual wants as far as being independent instead of trying to invent things that are wrong. They don't say we have to go and put a blanket around him like a baby, hoping that he feels secure.

"Down there (San Antonio), people wanted to accept you. They wanted one for all and all for one, which is great. There is nothing wrong with that. But here, these are men. Once we're on the floor, we fight for each other. The guys are very independent, but they are willing to go out and sacrifice and kill for each other."

Attempts to put Chicago's season in historical perspective were skirted by the Bulls. Most were content to douse themselves with champagne and let others analyze the evidence. Pippen was the only one to step forward and just say it.

"I think we can consider ourselves the greatest team ever," Pippen said.

Statistically, he is right. The Bulls were 72-10 during the regular season and lost only three games in the playoffs. Their combined record of 87-13, a winning percentage of .870, is one no other team can touch.

Momentum was building to anoint the Bulls as one of the greatest teams of all time when they jumped ahead of Seattle, 3-0. Consecutive losses stalled that discussion and sullied Chicago's credentials. Still, it would be ludicrous to allow two losses toward the end of the season - losses that occurred after Chicago had built an historically insurmountable lead - to swing the argument too much one way or the other.

"It's a new standard for NBA teams," Jackson said. "This team established a new level of play, and it's something all teams will have to chase." The standard has changed. But so has the era.

Could this Chicago team beat the Los Angeles Lakers of 1972? How would the Bulls front line match up with Boston's best of Larry Bird, Kevin McHale and Robert Parish in 1986? Are Jordan and Pippen in their prime enough to offset the 1987 Lakers team that featured Magic Johnson and Kareem Abdul-Jabbar? Could the Bulls and Luc Longley slow the Philadelphia team that stormed through the playoffs in 1983 with Moses Malone? This doesn't even include dissenting opinions concerning another Philadelphia team (1967) and the Milwaukee Bucks of 1971.

"Where we stand in history, if we're determined to be or defined to be the best team, it's not our decision," Jordan said. "I don't know. That's for you guys to decide."

While the Bulls dominated the season in terms of competition, interest and individual awards, they weren't the only story. A defending champion (Houston) fell and a talented yet scarred team (Seattle) lived up to its potential. Players were traded, coaches were fired and referees were attacked. Denver's Mahmoud Abdul-Rauf, who was later traded to Sacramento, made a stand by refusing to stand for the national anthem. A record number of underclassmen entered the NBA draft and the league barely averted its second consecutive summer of labor strife as it prepared for more than 150 players to flood the free agent market.

Still, after Chicago's remarkable ride, Johnson's return to the Los Angeles Lakers —

Let's Get Ready To Rumble!!

Nick Van Exel apologized to his teammates for charging referee Ronnie Garretson and knocking him into the scorers table. He apologized to his family, fans, sponsors and the kids who look up to him.

If the press conference had gone on much longer, the Los Angeles Lakers guard would have found a way to apologize for the ozone layer and the fragile status of the world's rain forests. But Van Exel made it clear he has no intention of telling Garretson he was sorry.

The NBA went nearly 49 years without a player assaulting an official. Then, the league office was forced to preside over two ugly episodes in three-and-a-half weeks.

First came Dennis Rodman's head-butt of Ted Bernhardt. The fine and six-game suspension cost the Chicago star $203,922. Van Exel then went after Garretson during a game in Denver. After calling Garretson, ``a little midget," Garretson hit him with a technical. Van Exel responded by hitting Garretson. The fine and seven-game suspension cost Van Exel $188,190.

The league office refused to acknowledge a trend.

``This is an aberration," said Rod Thorn, the league's vice president of basketball operations and the man responsible for meting out punishment in these matters. ``I don't think you can say we have a growing problem between the players and referees. I don't see anything along those lines.

``That is not to say we are taking this lightly. But in 49 years we have two incidents and they came three weeks apart. I really don't expect anything of this type to happen again. I'm not saying it won't happen in the history of the league. But they are both isolated incidents and neither one had anything to do with the other."

Two years ago, when there was a perception that violence was on the rise, the league office acted quickly. Fines were increased and automatic suspensions were put in place in an effort to curb confronta-

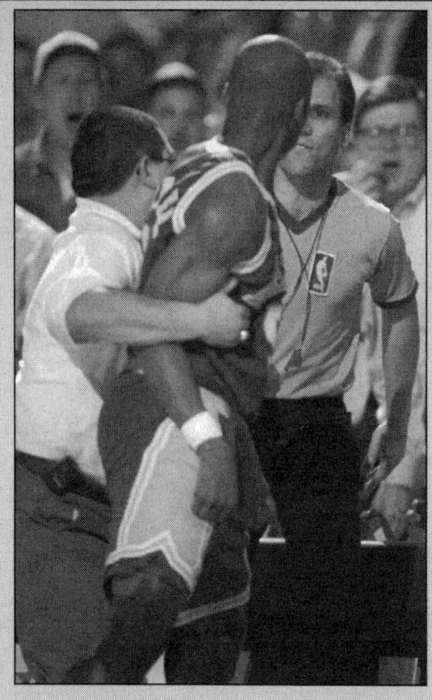

Wide World Photos (both)

Referee-baiting got out of hand during the 1995-96 NBA season. The worst incident involved **Nick Van Exel** pushing ref Ronnie Garretson over the scorers table. Teammate and peacemaker (and stern Van Exel critic) **Magic Johnson** (right) was himself later fined and suspended for bumping an official.

tions between players. Those measures helped stem the black-and-blue tide and show the league was serious about addressing its problems.

Violence against officials took on an even more disturbing air. That is one black eye the image-conscious NBA wouldn't tolerate.

``When you physically go after a referee, that's a totally different ball game,'' Thorn said. ``You allow that to happen and you have chaos. Anarchy. You can't have it.

``You can understand how some fights between players occur. But there is no provocation for hitting a referee. Say he missed a call. Big deal. Voice your displeasure and move on.

``I think Magic Johnson said it best when he was talking about the Nick Van Exel situation,'' Thorn said. ``He said, `I can't believe this. I'm upset at the refs four or five times a game, but I don't think about hitting them.'''

Shortly after that comment, Johnson lost his head and bumped an official. He was fined $10,000 and suspended for three games. That incident was a low point in a tough last year in the league for Johnson.

Some will argue the actions of Rodman, Van Exel and Johnson were part of a bigger problem. They will point to this as yet another example of the deteriorating respect players have for authority.

That may be. But the NBA is under no obligation to address societal issues. The league's obligation here is to protect its officials. The league made it clear in a directive sent to all teams before the playoffs that further violence against the officials would result in severe penalties. There were no incidents in the post-season.

``I don't think we're at the point now where we have to have something set in stone,'' Thorn said. ``These incidents depend on the situation. It depends on the people involved and their history. You look at the tape and do what you think is best.

``But I don't think it would be prudent to test us on this. If I'm a player, I don't think I would want to get involved in this kind of thing right now.''

Jonathan Daniel/Allsport

While the dresses and the cosmetics certainly help, **Dennis Rodman** garners so much attention because he is the best rebounder in the NBA. His all-out style of play often sends him spilling off the court, something that rarely happens to many other NBA stars.

and subsequent retirement—generated the most interest.

Johnson, who walked away from the NBA more than four years earlier when he tested positive for the virus that leads to AIDS, came back in January of '96. He played in 32 regular season games for the Lakers, averaging 14.6 points, 6.9 assists and 5.7 rebounds. His presence energized interest in the Lakers and made them into a much more effective halfcourt team. But the game slowed down noticeably when the ball was in his hands, and neither Johnson, 36, nor his Generation X teammates appeared comfortable as they struggled to establish an identity.

Along the way, Johnson criticized teammates Cedric Ceballos and Nick Van Exel for their unprofessional behavior. He then had to direct some of that criticism at himself after he was fined $10,000 and suspended for three games by the NBA for bumping an official. Johnson questioned his teammates, his role and the strategy of coach Del Harris during the Lakers first-round playoff series with Houston. He hinted that it might be best for him to play for another team next season, a team that would let him spend most of his time at point guard instead of power forward, and said he would test the free agent market.

Johnson struggled in the final two games of the team's first round playoff series with Houston as he averaged 7.5 points, three turnovers and was 4-of-17 from the field. But his frustrations didn't end once the Lakers were eliminated, 3-1. Three players —Van Exel, Sedale Threatt and Anthony Miller—didn't fly home with the team after their loss to the Rockets and missed the season-ending meeting. Johnson said he was disheartened with the Lakers failure to hang together and made his strongest comments yet about the lack of unity on the club.

When he went back into retirement a few weeks later, Johnson didn't focus on the negatives. He thanked everyone for their support and eluded to what he believes will be a bright future for the Lakers.

"The support generated throughout the league and from fans worldwide was tremendous and I want to thank everyone," Johnson said in his statement. "I also want to thank all Lakers fans and the entire Laker organization, who has continually supported me

"This team has a great future and I will be excited to sit courtside and root them on to a championship very soon. In announcing this decision now, I wanted to give the Lakers every advantage in planning their future and securing one of the much-talked about free agents this summer."

The future of some of the league's top players and coaches took unexpected turns during the course of the '95-96 season. It all began just hours before the season tipped off when Charlotte sent All-Star center Alonzo Mourning, LeRon Ellis and Pete Myers to Miami for Glen Rice, Matt Geiger, Khalid Reeves and the the Heat's No. 1 pick in the 1996 draft.

The Hornets made the move because they were convinced Mourning would bolt for free agency at the end of the season. Mourning wanted a seven-year, $91 million deal. Charlotte owner George Shinn eventually increased his offer to seven years at $78.4 million before dropping out. Shinn was in no position to go higher because he overextended himself several years ago when he signed forward Larry Johnson to a 12-year, $84 million contract. Even though the Charlotte Coliseum is packed to capacity (24,042) most nights, its average ticket price ranked 27th out of the 29 teams. The Coliseum isn't designed to maximize revenue in terms of luxury suites and ad signage. It was the case of a small market team having to make a concession it didn't want to make.

Neither team was finished. Before the February trading deadline, the Hornets sent Kendall Gill and Reeves to New Jersey for disgruntled guard Kenny Anderson and Gerald Glass. Miami traded five players and acquired five others —Tim Hardaway, Walt Williams, Chris Gatling, Tyrone Corbin and Tony Smith. All became free agents at the end of the season, giving the Heat plenty of cap room to be a major player in the free agent market.

"We know the direction we want to go," Miami coach Pat Riley said. "Sometimes, you have to go out on a limb and take some risks."

In other moves, Philadelphia and New Jersey swapped dilemmas when the Sixers sent Shawn Bradley to the Nets for Derrick Coleman. In another move designed to free up salary cap room in the off season, New York sent forwards Charles Smith and Monty Williams to San Antonio for two players they didn't intend to keep (J.R. Reid and Brad Lohaus) and a first round pick.

Nearly one-third of the league's coaches —Charlotte's Allan Bristow, Dallas' Dick Motta, Milwaukee's Mike Dunleavy, Minnesota's Bill Blair, New Jersey's Butch Beard, New York's Don Nelson, Philadelphia's John Lucas, Phoenix' Paul Westphal and Toronto's Brendan Malone— bit the dust by the end of the season. The most bizarre ouster belonged to Nelson, who didn't make it through an entire season with the Knicks. One day after voicing that he would understand if the club fired him, they did just that.

"This is a very difficult team to coach," Nelson said. "I've always been a flexible coach, and flexibility has always been a part of my teams. I like to trap and do some unconventional things. I think that was the wrong approach with this team.

"This team was very set in its ways," Nelson continued. "Whatever I tried to do early on was not accepted very well and wasn't given good effort, because they didn't want to do it. They wanted to continue the old way. I've never been around players who didn't like to run and score more and be in situations where they have freedom. This is a first for me."

Assistant Jeff Van Gundy replaced Nelson. He was one of seven people who landed his first NBA head coaching job. The others were Dave Cowens (Charlotte), Jim Cleamons (Dallas), Flip Saunders (Minnesota), John Calipari (New Jersey), Johnny Davis (Philadelphia) and Darrell Walker (Toronto). Cotton Fitzsimmons returned to the Suns bench after Westphal was released and former Boston coach Chris Ford resurfaced with the Bucks.

There had been speculation in Seattle about George Karl's job security. Karl had

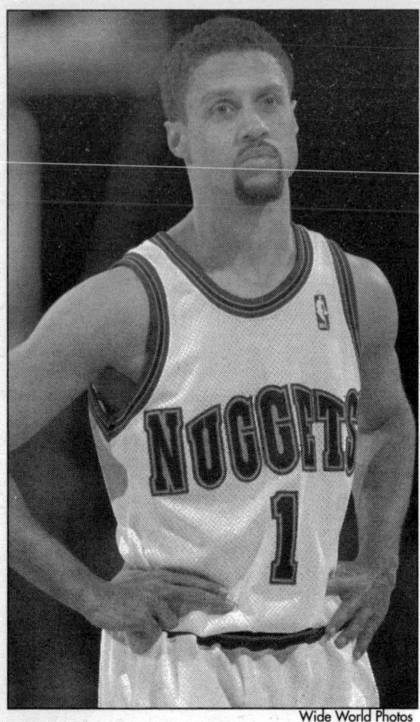

Wide World Photos

Mahmoud Abdul-Rauf caused a stir when he refused to stand for the national anthem. Eventually he came around, though not before calling the US flag a "symbol of oppression, of tyranny". Thanks, Mahmoud.

always coached with a democratic hand and a creative mind. Rather than rely on one or two stars to carry a team, he had tried to divide the responsibilities among a larger number of players. When that approach worked, the Sonics were hailed as a deep, versatile bunch. When it failed, the Sonics were dismissed as a team that lacked focus and identity.

That lingering perception, along with first round playoff losses in two consecutive years, persuaded Karl to alter his approach. Seattle was no longer run by committee. Karl put the success of the team squarely in the talented hands of Shawn Kemp and Gary Payton.

"The only real major, philosophical change is that this is Shawn's and Gary's team," Karl said of the '95-96 Sonics. "We direct not only the game, but more responsibilities in that area. They can't have excuses they are young players any more. They must show they are capable of winning not only in the regular season, but the playoffs. Shawn and Gary both know they will be judged by what we do in the playoffs. That is how we will all be judged. We have to deliver something more than we have the last two years."

The judgment was in Seattle's favor. The Sonics swept the two-time defending champion Rockets in the second round and got by Utah in the Western Conference Finals before losing to the Bulls. Cleveland, meanwhile, failed to advance past the first round of the playoffs. But then, the Cavaliers shouldn't have made the playoffs in the first place. The job coach Mike Fratello did with an undermanned, injured team was a tribute to his staff and the resolve of his players. "I think it's a great testament to words we all take for granted, like character, pride and work ethic," Fratello said.

The 95-65 season had many stories. It began with Mahmoud Abdul-Rauf choosing not to stand for the national anthem because he believe it conflicted with his Muslim religion. After a brief suspension, Abdul-Rauf chose to honor the flag and stand. It was a season in which Boston owner Paul Gaston said, "I think we know our team stinks." He was right. It was a season in which the Washington Bullets announced they will change their name to Wizards in two years and Detroit's Grant Hill received more All-Star votes (1.35 million) than Jordan.

In the June draft, an overwhelming 17 underclassmen were taken. This shattered the record of 10 taken in the '95 draft. A moratorium was imposed at the end of the season as the league and the Players Association completed the wording of the collective bargaining agreement. But on July 11, the contract was signed, the moratorium was lifted and a record free agent class of more than 150 players flooded the market. Nine days later, the third version of the Dream Team began it quest for a gold medal in the Olympics.

It was a hectic conclusion to a memorable season—a season that belonged to the Chicago Bulls.

"The historians will decide our place among the greatest teams," Jordan said. "But we certainly accomplished everything we set out to do." ❐

Final NBA Standings

Division champions (*) and playoff qualifiers (†) are noted. Number of seasons listed after each head coach refers to current tenure with club. Note that Toronto (Central) and Vancouver (Midwest) were expansion teams.

Western Conference

Midwest Division

	W	L	Pct	GB	Per Game For	Per Game Opp
* San Antonio	59	23	.720	—	103.4	97.1
† Utah	55	27	.671	4	102.5	95.9
† Houston	48	34	.585	11	102.5	100.7
† Denver	35	47	.427	24	97.7	100.4
Dallas	26	56	.317	33	102.5	107.5
Minnesota	26	56	.317	33	97.9	103.2
Vancouver	15	67	.183	44	89.8	99.8

Head Coaches: SA—Bob Hill (2nd season); **Utah**— Jerry Sloan (8th); **Hou**— Rudy Tomjanovich (5th); **Den**— Bernie Bickerstaff (2nd); **Dal**— Dick Motta (2nd); **Min**— Bill Blair (2nd); **Van**— Brian Winters (1st).

1994-95 Standings: 1. San Antonio (62–20); 2. Utah (60–22); 3. Houston (47–35); 4. Denver (41–41); 5. Dallas (36–46); 6. Minnesota (21–61).

Pacific Division

	W	L	Pct	GB	Per Game For	Per Game Opp
* Seattle	64	18	.780	—	104.5	96.7
† LA Lakers	53	29	.646	11	102.9	98.5
† Portland	44	38	.537	20	99.3	97.0
† Phoenix	41	41	.500	23	104.3	104.0
Sacramento	39	43	.476	25	99.5	102.3
Golden St.	36	46	.439	28	101.6	103.1
LA Clippers	29	53	.354	35	99.4	103.0

Head Coaches: **Sea**— George Karl (5th season); **LAL**— Del Harris (2nd); **Port**— P.J. Carlesimo (2nd); **Pho**— Paul Westphal (4th, 14–19) fired Jan. 16 and was replaced with Sr. Exec. VP Cotton Fitzsimmons (27–22); **Sac**— Garry St. Jean (4th); **G.St.**—Rick Adelman (1st); **LAC** — Bill Fitch (2nd).

1994-95 Standings: 1. Phoenix (59–23); 2. Seattle (57–25); 3. LA Lakers (48–34); 4. Portland (44–38); 5. Sacramento (39–43); 6. Golden St. (26–56); 7. LA Clippers (17–65).

Eastern Conference

Atlantic Division

	W	L	Pct	GB	Per Game For	Per Game Opp
* Orlando	60	22	.732	—	104.5	99.0
† New York	47	35	.573	13	97.2	94.9
† Miami	42	40	.512	18	96.5	95.0
Washington	39	43	.476	21	102.5	101.5
Boston	33	49	.402	27	103.6	107.0
New Jersey	30	52	.366	30	93.7	97.9
Philadelphia	18	64	.220	42	94.5	104.5

Head Coaches: Orl— Brian Hill (3rd season); **NY**— Don Nelson (1st, 34–25) fired and was replaced by assistant Jeff Van Gundy (13–10); **Mia**— Pat Riley (1st); **Wash**— Jim Lynam (2nd); **Bos**— M.L. Carr (1st); **NJ**— Butch Beard (1st); **Phi**— John Lucas (2nd).

1994-95 Standings: 1. Orlando (57–25); 2. New York (55–27); 3. Boston (35–47); 4. Miami (32-50); 5. New Jersey (30–52); 6. Philadelphia (24–58) 7. Washington (21–61).

Central Division

	W	L	Pct	GB	Per Game For	Per Game Opp
* Chicago	72	10	.878	—	105.2	92.9
† Indiana	52	30	.634	20	99.3	96.1
† Cleveland	47	35	.573	25	91.1	88.5
† Atlanta	46	36	.561	26	98.3	97.1
† Detroit	46	36	.561	26	95.4	92.9
Charlotte	41	41	.500	31	102.8	103.4
Milwaukee	25	57	.305	47	95.6	100.9
Toronto	21	61	.256	51	97.5	105.0

Head Coaches: Chi— Phil Jackson (7th season); **Ind**— Larry Brown (3rd); **Cle**— Mike Fratello (3rd); **Atl**— Lenny Wilkens (3rd); **Det**— Doug Collins (1st); **Char**— Allan Bristow (5th); **Mil**— Mike Dunleavy (4th); **Tor**— Brendan Malone (1st).

1994-95 Standings: 1. Indiana (52–30); 2. Charlotte (50–32); 3. Chicago (47–35); 4. Cleveland (43–39); 5. Atlanta (42–40); 6. Milwaukee (34–48); 7. Detroit (28-54).

Overall Conference Standings

Sixteen teams—eight from each conference—qualify for the NBA Playoffs; (*) indicates division champions.

Western Conference

	W	L	Home	Away	Div	Conf
1 Seattle*	64	18	38-3	26-15	21-3	42-10
2 San Antonio*	59	23	33-8	26-15	19-5	39-13
3 Utah	55	27	34-7	21-20	14-10	33-19
4 LA Lakers	53	29	30-11	23-18	17-7	34-18
5 Houston	48	34	27-14	21-20	15-9	31-21
6 Portland	44	38	26-15	18-23	11-13	29-23
7 Phoenix	41	41	25-16	16-25	9-15	23-29
8 Sacramento	39	43	26-15	13-28	11-13	23-29
Golden St	36	46	23-18	13-28	7-17	22-30
Denver	35	47	24-17	11-30	13-11	22-30
LA Clippers	29	53	19-22	10-31	8-16	21-31
Dallas	26	56	16-25	10-31	10-14	19-33
Minnesota	26	56	17-24	9-32	10-14	17-35
Vancouver	15	67	10-31	5-36	3-21	9-43

Eastern Conference

	W	L	Home	Away	Div	Conf
1 Chicago*	72	10	39-2	33-8	24-4	47-7
2 Orlando*	60	22	37-4	23-18	21-3	40-14
3 Indiana	52	30	32-9	20-21	19-9	36-18
4 New York	47	35	26-15	21-20	16-8	32-22
5 Cleveland	47	35	26-15	21-20	13-15	29-25
6 Atlanta	46	36	26-15	20-21	15-13	32-22
7 Detroit	46	36	30-11	16-25	15-13	27-27
8 Miami	42	40	26-15	16-25	13-12	29-25
Charlotte	41	41	25-16	16-25	13-15	26-28
Washington	39	43	25-16	14-27	10-14	21-33
Boston	33	49	18-23	15-26	12-12	23-31
New Jersey	30	52	20-21	10-31	8-17	21-33
Milwaukee	25	57	14-27	11-30	8-20	16-38
Toronto	21	61	15-26	6-35	5-23	14-40
Philadelphia	18	64	11-30	7-34	5-19	12-42

1996 NBA All-Star Game

East, 129-118

46th NBA All-Star Game. **Date:** Feb. 11, at The Alamodome in San Antonio; **Coaches:** Phil Jackson, Chicago (East) and George Karl, Seattle (West); **MVP:** Michael Jordan, Chicago (22 minutes, 20 points).

Starters chosen by fan vote, (for the second consecutive year, Detroit's Grant Hill was the leading vote-getter, receiving 1,358,004); bench chosen by conference coaches vote. **Team replacements:** none.

Eastern Conference

	Starters	Min	FG M-A	Pts	Reb	A
F	Scottie Pippen, Chi	25	4-7	**8**	8	5
F	Grant Hill, Det	26	6-10	**14**	3	2
C	Shaquille O'Neal, Orl	28	10-16	**25**	10	1
G	Michael Jordan, Chi	22	8-11	**20**	4	1
G	Anfernee Hardaway, Orl	31	6-8	**18**	3	7
	Bench					
C	Patrick Ewing, NY	12	3-7	**8**	3	1
G	Reggie Miller, Ind	18	4-8	**8**	2	2
F	Vin Baker, Mil	14	2-5	**6**	2	2
G	Terrell Brandon, Cle	20	4-10	**11**	1	3
G	Glen Rice, Char	15	1-5	**7**	1	2
C	Juwan Howard, Wash	16	1-5	**2**	6	2
C	Alonzo Mourning, Mia	13	1-6	**2**	1	0
	TOTALS	240	50-98	**129**	44	28

Three-Point FG: 4-15 (Hardaway 2-4, Rice 1-2, Brandon 1-4, Pippen 0-1, Miller 0-4); **Free Throws:** 25-31 (Hardaway 4-4, Jordan 4-4, Rice 4-4, Baker 2-2, Brandon 2-2, Ewing 2-2, Hill 2-2, O'Neal 5-11); **Percentages:** FG (.510), Three-Pt. FG (.267), Free Throws (.806); **Turnovers:** 20 (Pippen 6, Brandon 3, Hardaway 3, Hill 2, Mourning 2, Rice 2, Miller, O'Neal); **Steals:** 15 (Ewing 3, Pippen 3, Hardaway 2, Baker, Brandon, Hill, Howard, Jordan, O'Neal, Miller); **Blocked Shots:** 5 (O'Neal 2, Brandon, Ewing, Mourning); **Fouls:** 21 (Baker 4, Howard 3, O'Neal 3, Ewing 2, Mourning 2, Miller 2, Rice 2, Brandon, Hill, Jordan); **Team Rebounds:** 7.

	1	2	3	4	F
East	33	28	41	27	**129**
West	32	26	22	38	**118**

Western Conference

	Starters	Min	FG M-A	Pts	Reb	A
F	Charles Barkley, Pho	16	4-6	**8**	0	1
F	Shawn Kemp, Sea	22	6-12	**13**	4	1
C	Hakeem Olajuwon, Hou	14	2-8	**4**	3	0
G	Clyde Drexler, Hou	19	5-8	**11**	2	3
G	Jason Kidd, Dal.	22	3-4	**7**	6	10
	Bench					
C	David Robinson, SA	23	8-13	**18**	11	2
G	Gary Payton, Sea	28	6-10	**18**	5	5
F	Sean Elliott, SA	22	5-12	**13**	5	2
F	Karl Malone, Utah	20	2-6	**11**	9	2
G	Mitch Richmond, Sac	25	3-10	**7**	2	2
C	Dikembe Mutombo, Den	11	2-4	**4**	9	0
G	John Stockton, Utah	18	2-9	**4**	1	3
	TOTALS	240	48-102	**118**	57	31

Three-Point FG: 4-25 (Elliott 2-6, Kidd 1-2, Drexler 1-4, Payton 0-1, Kemp 0-2, Richmond 0-3, Stockton 0-7); **Free Throws:** 18-21 (Malone 7-8, Payton 6-6, Robinson 2-2, Elliott 1-1, Kemp 1-2, Richmond 1-2); **Percentages:** FG (.471), Three-Pt. FG (.160), Free Throws (.857); **Turnovers:** 26 (Payton 6, Drexler 3, Kemp 3, Mutombo 3, Barkley 2, Elliott 2, Kidd 2, Richmond 2, Malone, Robinson, Stockton); **Steals:** 14 (Payton 5, Drexler 3, Kidd 2, Robinson 2, Malone, Richmond); **Blocked Shots:** 3 (Robinson 2, Kemp); **Fouls:** 23 (Elliott 4, Kemp 4, Robinson 4, Mutombo 3, Olajuwon 2, Stockton 2, Barkley, Kidd, Malone, Payton); **Team Rebounds:** 3.

Halftime— East, 61-58; **Third Quarter—** East, 102-80; **Technical Fouls—** none; **Officials—** Ed T. Rush, Ronnie Nunn, Ed Middleton; **Attendance—** 36,037; **Time—** 2:15; **TV Rating—** 11.7/20 share (NBC).

1996 NBA Rookie Game

East, 94-92

Date: Feb. 10, at The Alamodome in San Antonio; **Coaches:** Bob Lanier (East) and Doug Moe (West); **MVP:** Damon Stoudamire (24 minutes, 19 points, 11 assists).

Eastern Conference: Alan Henderson, Atl. 5-1-11; Eric Williams, Bos. 6-3-15; Rasheed Wallace, Wash. 5-2-12; Jerry Stackhouse, Phi. 4-4-15; Damon Stoudamire, Tor. 8-1-19; Bob Sura, Cle. 1-1-3; George Zidek, Char. 5-0-10; Totals: 39-13-94

Western Conference: Antonio McDyess, Den. 8-1-17; Joe Smith, G.St. 6-5-20; Arvydas Sabonis, Port. 3-1-8; Tyus Edney, Sac. 6-2-14; Michael Finley, Pho. 4-0-9; Brent Barry, LAC 4-0-8; Kevin Garnett, Min. 3-2-8; Bryant Reeves, Van. 3-2-8; Totals: 37-13-92

Halftime: East, 48-45. **Officials:** Ron Olesiak, Mike Callahan and Sean Corbin. **Attendance:** 36,037.

NBA 3-point Shootout

Eight players are invited to compete in the annual three-point shooting contest during All-Star weekend, since 1986. Each shooter has 60 seconds to shoot the 25 balls in five racks outside the three-point line. Each ball is worth one point, except the last ball in each rack, which is worth two. Highest scores advance. First prize: $20,000.

First Round	Pts
Tim Legler, Wash.	23
Dennis Scott, Orl	19
Steve Kerr, Chi	18
George McCloud, Dal.	18
Failed to advance	
Dana Barros, Bos.	18
Hubert Davis, NY	18
Glen Rice, Mia	17
Cliff Robinson, Port.	11

Semifinals	Pts
Tim Legler	22
Dennis Scott	19
Failed to advance	
Steve Kerr	17
George McCloud	17
Finals	
Tim Legler	20
Dennis Scott	14

Note: Legler's three-round total of 65 set a new contest record, besting Craig Hodges' 1991 total of 61.

NBA Slam Dunk Contest

Seven players are invited to compete in the annual slam dunk contest held during All-Star weekend, since 1984. The players are selected based on "the creativity and artistry they have displayed in dunking over the course of the season." In the first round, each player has 90 seconds to attempt as many dunks as he choose with a minimum of three. Points are awarded based on "creativity, artistry and athletic ability." Only the top three scores advance to the second and final round where each player gets two dunks each. First prize: $20,000.

First Round	Pts
Brent Barry, LAC	45.5
Michael Finley, Pho.	45.0
Greg Minor, Bos.	41.0
Failed to advance	
Jerry Stackhouse, Phi.	40.0
Doug Christie, NY	39.5
Darrell Armstrong, Orl.	25.59

Finals	Pts
Brent Barry	49.0
Michael Finley	46.0
Greg Minor	40.0

Chicago Bulls
Michael Jordan
Scoring

Chicago Bulls
Dennis Rodman
Rebounds

Utah Jazz
John Stockton
Assists

Washington Bullets
Gheorghe Muresan
Field Goal Pct.

NBA Regular Season Individual Leaders

Minimum of 70 games or 1400 points, 800 rebounds, 400 assists, 100 blocked shots, 300 field goals, 125 steals, 125 free throws made, and 50 three-point field goals; (*) indicates rookie.

Scoring

	Gm	Min	FG	FG%	3pt/Att	FT	FT%	Reb	Ast	Stl	Blk	Pts	Avg	Hi
Michael Jordan, Chi	82	3090	916	.495	111/260	548	.834	543	352	180	42	2491	30.4	53
Hakeem Olajuwon, Hou	72	2797	768	.514	3/14	397	.724	784	257	113	207	1936	26.9	51
Shaquille O'Neal, Orl	54	1946	592	.573	1/2	249	.487	596	155	34	115	1434	26.6	49
Karl Malone, Utah	82	3113	789	.519	16/40	512	.723	804	345	138	56	2106	25.7	51
David Robinson, SA	82	3019	711	.516	3/9	626	.761	1000	247	111	271	2051	25.0	45
Charles Barkley, Pho	71	2632	580	.500	49/175	440	.777	821	262	114	56	1649	23.2	45
Alonzo Mourning, Mia	70	2671	563	.523	9/30	488	.685	727	159	70	189	1623	23.2	50
Mitch Richmond, Sac	81	2946	611	.447	225/515	425	.866	269	255	125	19	1872	23.1	47
Patrick Ewing, NY	76	2783	678	.466	4/28	351	.761	806	160	68	184	1711	22.5	41
Juwan Howard, Wash	81	3294	733	.489	4/13	319	.749	660	360	67	39	1789	22.1	42
Anfernee Hardaway, Orl	82	3015	623	.513	89/283	445	.767	354	582	166	41	1780	21.7	42
Glen Rice, Char	79	3142	610	.471	171/403	319	.837	378	232	91	19	1710	21.7	38
Cedric Ceballos, LAL	78	2628	638	.530	51/184	329	.804	536	119	94	22	1656	21.2	38
Reggie Miller, Ind	76	2621	504	.473	168/410	430	.863	214	253	77	13	1606	21.1	40
Vin Baker, Mil	82	3319	699	.489	10/48	321	.670	808	212	65	91	1729	21.1	41
Clifford Robinson, Port	78	2980	553	.423	178/471	360	.664	443	190	86	68	1644	21.1	41
Larry Johnson, Char	81	3274	583	.476	67/183	427	.757	683	355	55	43	1660	20.5	44
Glenn Robinson, Mil	82	3249	627	.454	90/263	316	.812	505	293	95	42	1660	20.2	39
Grant Hill, Det	80	3260	564	.462	5/26	485	.751	783	548	100	48	1618	20.2	35
Sean Elliott, SA	77	2901	525	.466	161/392	326	.771	396	211	69	33	1537	20.0	36
Allan Houston, Det	82	3072	564	.453	191/447	298	.823	362	250	61	16	1617	19.7	38
Shawn Kemp, Sea	79	2631	526	.561	5/12	493	.742	904	173	93	127	1550	19.6	32
Isaiah Rider, Min	75	2594	560	.464	102/275	248	.838	309	213	48	24	1470	19.6	33
Jim Jackson, Dal	82	2820	569	.435	121/333	345	.825	410	235	47	23	1604	19.6	38
Scottie Pippen, Chi	77	2825	563	.463	150/401	220	.679	496	452	133	57	1496	19.4	40

Rebounds

	Gm	Off	Def	Tot	Avg
Dennis Rodman, Chi	64	356	596	952	14.9
David Robinson, SA	82	319	681	1000	12.2
Dikembe Mutombo, Den	74	249	622	871	11.8
Charles Barkley, Pho	71	243	578	821	11.6
Shawn Kemp, Sea	79	276	628	904	11.4
Hakeem Olajuwon, Hou	72	176	608	784	10.9
Patrick Ewing, NY	76	157	649	806	10.6
Alonzo Mourning, Mia	70	218	509	727	10.4
Loy Vaught, LAC	80	204	604	808	10.1
Jayson Williams, NJ	80	342	461	803	10.0
Vin Baker, Mil	82	263	545	808	9.9
Karl Malone, Utah	82	175	629	804	9.8
Grant Hill, Det	80	127	656	783	9.8
C. Weatherspoon, Phi	78	237	516	753	9.7
Grant Long, Atl	82	248	540	788	9.6

Assists

	Gm	Ast	Avg
John Stockton, Utah	82	916	11.2
Jason Kidd, Dal	81	783	9.7
Avery Johnson, SA	82	789	9.6
Rod Strickland, Port	67	640	9.6
Damon Stoudamire*, Tor	70	653	9.3
Kevin Johnson, Pho	56	517	9.2
Kenny Anderson, Char	69	575	8.3
Tim Hardaway, Mia	80	640	8.0
Mark Jackson, Ind	81	635	7.8
Gary Payton, Sea	81	608	7.5
Anfernee Hardaway, Orl	82	582	7.1
Chris Childs, NJ	78	548	7.0
Greg Anthony, Van	69	476	6.9
Nick Van Exel, LAL	74	509	6.9
Grant Hill, Det	80	548	6.9

NBA Regular Season Individual Leaders (Cont.)

Field Goal Pct.

	Gm	FG	Att	Pct
Gheorghe Muresan, Wash	76	466	798	.584
Chris Gatling, Mia	71	326	567	.575
Shaquille O'Neal, Orl	54	592	1033	.573
Anthony Mason, NY	82	449	798	.563
Shawn Kemp, Sea	79	526	937	.561
Dale Davis, Ind	78	334	599	.558
Arvydas Sabonis*, Port	73	394	723	.545
Brian Williams, LAC	65	416	766	.543
Chucky Brown, Hou	82	300	555	.541
John Stockton, Utah	82	440	818	.538

Free Throw Pct.

	Gm	FT	Att	Pct
Mahmoud Abdul-Rauf, Den	57	146	157	.930
Jeff Hornacek, Utah	82	259	290	.893
Terrell Brandon, Cle	75	338	381	.887
Dana Barros, Bos	80	130	147	.884
Brent Price, Wash	81	167	191	.874
Hersey Hawkins, Sea	82	247	283	.873
Mitch Richmond, Sac	81	425	491	.866
Reggie Miller, Ind	76	430	498	.863
Tim Legler, Wash	77	132	153	.863
Spud Webb, Min	77	125	145	.862

3-Point Field Goal Pct.

	Gm	3FG	Att	Pct
Tim Legler, Wash	77	128	246	.520
Steve Kerr, Chi	82	122	237	.515
Hubert Davis, NY	74	127	267	.476
B.J. Armstrong, G.St.	82	98	207	.473
Jeff Hornacek, Utah	82	104	223	.466
Brent Price, Wash	81	139	301	.462
Bobby Phills, Cle	72	93	211	.441
Terry Dehere, LAC	82	139	316	.440
Mitch Richmond, Sac	81	225	515	.437
Allan Houston, Det	82	191	447	.427

High-Point Games

	Opp	Date	FG-FT—Pts
Michael Jordan, Chi	vs. Det.	3/7	21- 9 —53
Mahmoud Abdul-Rauf, Den	at Utah	12/7	17- 8 —51
Karl Malone, Utah	vs. G.St.	12/9	19-13 —51
Hakeem Olajuwon, Hou	vs. Bos.	1/18	20-11 —51
Alonzo Mourning, Mia	at Dal.	3/29	17-16 —50
Shaquille O'Neal, Orl	at Wash.	3/22	21- 7 —49*
Michael Jordan, Chi	at Phi.	1/13	18- 7 —48
Mitch Richmond, Sac	at Hou.	12/15	17-10 —47
Karl Malone, Utah	vs. Port.	12/26	21- 5 —47

Three tied with 45 points each.
*Overtime.

Blocked Shots

	Gm	Blk	Avg
Dikembe Mutombo, Den	74	332	4.49
Shawn Bradley, NJ	79	288	3.65
David Robinson, SA	82	271	3.30
Hakeem Olajuwon, Hou	72	207	2.88
Alonzo Mourning, Mia	70	189	2.90
Elden Campbell, LAL	82	212	2.59
Patrick Ewing, NY	76	184	2.42
Gheorghe Muresan, Wash	76	172	2.26
Shaquille O'Neal, Orl	54	115	2.13
Jim McIlvaine, Wash	80	166	2.08

Steals

	Gm	Stl	Avg
Gary Payton, Sea	81	231	2.85
Mookie Blaylock, Atl	81	212	2.62
Michael Jordan, Chi	82	180	2.20
Jason Kidd, Dal	81	175	2.16
Alvin Robertson, Tor	77	166	2.16
Anfernee Hardaway, Orl	82	166	2.02
Eric Murdock, Van	73	135	1.85
Eddie Jones, LAL	70	129	1.84
Hersey Hawkins, Sea	82	149	1.82
Tom Gugliotta, Min	78	139	1.78

Rookie Leaders

Scoring	Gm	FG	FT	Pts	Avg
Jerry Stackhouse, Phi	72	452	387	1384	19.2
Damon Stoudamire, Tor	70	481	236	1331	19.0
Joe Smith, G.St.	82	469	303	1251	15.3
Michael Finley, Pho	82	465	242	1233	15.0
Arvydas Sabonis, Port	73	394	231	1058	14.5

Field Goal Pct.	Gm	FG	Att	Pct
Arvydas Sabonis, Port	73	394	723	.545
Gary Trent, Port	69	220	429	.513
Kurt Thomas, Mia	74	274	547	.501
Kevin Garnett, Min	80	361	735	.491
Rasheed Wallace, Wash	65	275	565	.487

Rebounds	Gm	Off	Def	Tot	Avg
Joe Smith, G.St.	82	300	417	717	8.7
Arvydas Sabonis, Port	73	147	441	522	8.1
Antonio McDyess, Den	76	229	343	572	7.5
Bryant Reeves, Van	77	178	392	570	7.4
Kevin Garnett, Min	80	175	326	501	6.3
Kurt Thomas, Mia	74	122	317	439	5.9

Assists	Gm	No	Avg
Damon Stoudamire, Tor	70	653	9.3
Tyus Edney, Sac	80	491	6.1
Jerry Stackhouse, Phi	72	278	3.9
Michael Finley, Pho	82	289	3.5
Bob Sura, Cle	79	233	2.9

Personal Fouls

Otis Thorpe, Det	300
Elden Campbell, LAL	300
Shawn Kemp, Sea	299
Gheorghe Muresan, Wash	297
Rick Fox, Bos	290
Matt Geiger, Char	290

Disqualifications

Matt Geiger, Char	11
Lorenzon Williams, Dal	9
Brian Grant, Sac	9
Popeye Jones, Dal	8
Gheorghe Muresan, Wash	8

Turnovers

Jason Kidd, Dal	328
Shawn Kemp, Sea	315
Juwan Howard, Wash	303
Glenn Robinson, Mil	282
Damon Stoudamire*, Tor	267

Triple Doubles

Grant Hill, Det	10
Jason Kidd, Dal	9
Clyde Drexler, Hou	3
Hakeem Olajuwon, Hou	3
Shawn Bradley, NJ	3

Minutes Played

Anthony Mason, NY	3457
Vin Baker, Mil	3319
Juwan Howard, Wash	3294
Larry Johnson, Char	3274
Grant Hill, Det	3260

Assist/Turnover Ratio

Avery Johnson, SA	4.05
Kenny Anderson, NJ	3.94
John Stockton, Utah	3.72
Sedale Threatt, LAL	3.64
Pooh Richardson, LAC	3.58

Team by Team Statistics

At least 16 games played. Players who competed for more than one team during the regular season are listed with their final club; (*) indicates rookies.

Atlanta Hawks

	Gm	FG%	TPts	PPG	RPG	APG
Steve Smith	80	.432	1446	18.1	4.1	2.8
Christian Laettner	74	.487	1217	16.5	7.3	2.7
MIN	44	.486	792	18.0	6.9	2.9
ATL	30	.489	425	14.2	7.9	2.7
Mookie Blaylock	81	.405	1268	15.7	4.1	5.9
Grant Long	82	.471	1078	13.1	9.6	2.2
Stacey Augmon	77	.491	976	12.7	3.9	1.8
Ken Norman	34	.465	304	8.9	3.9	1.9
Craig Ehlo	79	.428	669	8.5	3.2	1.7
Sean Rooks	65	.505	424	6.5	3.9	0.7
MIN	49	.493	331	6.8	4.1	0.8
ATL	16	.552	93	5.8	3.1	0.6
Alan Henderson*	79	.442	503	6.4	4.5	0.6
Reggie Jordan	24	.507	94	3.9	2.2	1.2
Matt Bullard	46	.407	174	3.8	1.3	0.4

Triple Doubles: none. **3-pt FG leader:** Blaylock (231). **Steals leader:** Blaylock (212). **Blocks leader:** Andrew Lang (85).
Acquired: F Laettner and C Rooks for C Andrew Lang and G Spud Webb (Feb. 22). **Signed:** C Tim Kempton (Jan. 5); G/F Reggie Jordan (Mar. 6).

Boston Celtics

	Gm	FG%	TPts	PPG	RPG	APG
Dino Radja	53	.500	1043	19.7	9.8	1.6
Rick Fox	81	.454	1137	14.0	5.6	4.6
Dana Barros	80	.470	1038	13.0	2.4	3.8
David Wesley	82	.459	1009	12.3	3.2	4.8
Todd Day	79	.366	922	11.7	2.8	1.4
MIL	8	.310	73	9.1	2.8	0.6
BOS	71	.371	849	12.0	2.8	1.4
Eric Williams*	64	.441	685	10.7	3.4	1.1
Dee Brown	65	.399	695	10.7	2.1	2.2
Greg Minor	78	.500	746	9.6	3.3	1.9
Eric Montross	61	.566	442	7.2	5.8	0.7
Pervis Ellison	69	.492	365	5.3	6.5	0.9
Junior Burrough*	61	.376	189	3.1	1.8	0.3
Alton Lister	64	.486	143	2.2	4.4	0.3
MIL	7	.444	10	1.4	4.1	0.6
BOS	57	.490	133	2.3	4.4	0.3
Doug Smith	17	.359	33	1.9	1.3	0.2
Todd Mundt	33	.390	37	1.1	0.8	0.1
ATL	24	.406	31	1.3	1.0	0.1
BOS	9	.333	6	0.7	0.3	0.1

Triple Doubles: none. **3-pt FG leader:** Barros (150).
Steals leader: Fox (113). **Blocks leader:** Ellison (99).
Acquired: G/F Day and C Lister for G Sherman Douglas (Nov. 26); **Signed:** C Mundt (Mar. 23).

Individual Single Game Highs

(*) indicates overtime.

Most Field Goals Made

21 ....Shaquille O'Neal, Orl. at Wash. (3/22)
21 ....Karl Malone, Utah vs. Port. (12/26)
21 ....Michael Jordan, Chi. vs. Det. (3/7)

Most Field Goals Attempted

40* ....Shaquille O'Neal, Orl. at Wash. (3/22)

Most Assists

25* ....Jason Kidd, Dal vs. Utah (2/8)

Charlotte Hornets

	Gm	FG%	TPts	PPG	RPG	APG
Glen Rice	79	.471	1710	21.7	4.8	2.9
Larry Johnson	81	.476	1660	20.5	8.4	4.4
Kenny Anderson	69	.418	1050	15.2	2.9	8.3
NJ	31	.376	473	15.3	3.3	8.0
CHA	38	.454	577	15.2	2.7	8.6
Dell Curry	82	.453	1192	14.5	3.2	2.1
Scott Burrell	20	.447	263	13.2	4.9	2.4
Matt Geiger	77	.536	866	11.3	8.4	0.8
Anthony Goldwire*	42	.402	231	5.5	1.0	2.7
Michael Adams	21	.446	114	5.4	1.0	3.2
Darrin Hancock	63	.523	272	4.3	1.6	0.7
George Zidek*	71	.423	281	4.0	2.6	0.2
Robert Parish	74	.498	290	3.9	4.1	0.4
Pete Myers	71	.368	276	3.9	2.0	2.0
MIA	39	.388	184	4.7	1.9	2.5
CHA	32	.333	92	2.9	2.1	1.5
Rafael Addison	53	.467	171	3.2	1.7	0.6

Triple Doubles: Kendall Gill (2), Johnson (1). **3-pt FG leader:** Rice (171). **Steals leader:** Curry (108). **Blocks leader:** Geiger (63).
Acquired: F/G Rice, C Geiger, G Reeves and 1996 first round pick for C Alonzo Mourning, G Pete Myers and C LeRon Ellis (Nov. 3), G Anderson and F Glass for G Kendall Gill and G Khalid Reeves (Jan. 19). **Signed:** G Goldwire (Jan. 22), G Myers (Feb. 16) and G Hodge (Feb. 23).

Chicago Bulls

	Gm	FG%	TPts	PPG	RPG	APG
Michael Jordan	82	.495	2491	30.4	6.6	4.3
Scottie Pippen	77	.463	1496	19.4	6.4	5.9
Toni Kukoc	81	.490	1065	13.2	4.0	3.5
Luc Longley	62	.482	564	9.1	5.1	1.9
Steve Kerr	82	.506	688	8.4	1.3	2.3
Ron Harper	80	.467	594	7.4	2.7	2.6
Dennis Rodman	64	.480	351	5.5	14.9	2.5
Bill Wennington	71	.493	376	5.3	2.5	0.7
Jud Buechler	74	.463	278	3.8	1.5	0.8
Dickey Simpkins	60	.481	216	3.6	2.6	0.6
James Edwards	28	.373	98	3.5	1.4	0.4
Jason Caffey*	57	.438	182	3.2	2.0	0.4
Randy Brown	68	.406	185	2.7	1.0	1.1
John Salley	42	.450	185	4.4	3.3	1.3
TOR	25	.486	149	6.0	3.9	1.6
CHI	17	.343	36	2.1	2.5	0.9

Triple Doubles: Pippen (2), Rodman (1). **3-pt FG leader:** Pippen (150). **Steals leader:** Jordan (180). **Blocks leader:** Longley (84).
Signed: C Edwards (Oct. 26), F/C Salley (Mar. 4).

Cleveland Cavaliers

	Gm	FG%	TPts	PPG	RPG	APG
Terrell Brandon	75	.465	1449	19.3	3.3	6.5
Chris Mills	80	.468	1205	15.1	5.5	2.4
Bobby Phills	72	.467	1051	14.6	3.6	3.8
Danny Ferry	82	.459	1090	13.3	3.8	2.3
Dan Majerle	82	.405	872	10.6	3.7	2.6
Tyrone Hill	44	.512	341	7.8	5.6	0.8
Michael Cage	82	.556	490	6.0	8.9	0.7
Bob Sura*	79	.411	422	5.3	1.7	3.0
Harold Miner	19	.442	61	3.2	0.6	0.4
John Crotty	58	.447	172	3.0	0.9	1.8
Antonio Lang	41	.532	116	2.8	1.3	0.3
John Amaechi	28	.414	77	2.8	1.9	0.3
Donny Marshall*	34	.353	77	2.3	0.8	0.2
Joe Courtney	23	.429	38	1.7	2.1	0.4

Triple Doubles: none. **3-pt FG leader:** Majerle (146).
Steals leader: Brandon (132). **Blocks leader:** Cage (79).
Signed: G Crotty (Oct. 23), G Johnson (Mar. 5).

Dallas Mavericks

	Gm	FG%	TPts	PPG	RPG	APG
Jamal Mashburn	18	.379	422	23.4	5.4	2.8
Jim Jackson	82	.435	1604	19.6	5.0	2.9
George McCloud	79	.414	1497	18.9	4.8	2.7
Jason Kidd	81	.381	1348	16.6	6.8	9.7
Tony Dumas	67	.418	776	11.6	1.7	1.5
Popeye Jones	68	.446	770	11.3	10.8	1.9
Lucious Harris	61	.461	481	7.9	2.0	1.3
Scott Brooks	69	.457	352	5.1	0.6	1.4
Loren Meyer*	72	.439	363	5.0	4.4	0.8
Terry Davis	28	.509	137	4.9	4.2	0.8
Cherokee Parks*	64	.409	250	3.9	3.4	0.5
David Wood	62	.431	208	3.4	2.5	0.5
G.ST	21	.500	22	1.0	0.8	0.2
PHO	4	.167	4	1.0	1.3	0.5
DAL	37	.435	182	4.9	3.6	0.7
Lorenzo Williams	65	.407	198	3.0	8.0	1.3
PORT	4	.600	6	1.5	0.8	0.0
DEN	4	.545	14	3.5	1.8	0.5
DAL	3	.455	11	3.7	1.7	0.0

Triple Doubles: Kidd (9). **3-pt FG leader:** McCloud (257).
Steals leader: Kidd (175). **Blocks leader:** Williams (122).
Signed: F Slater (Jan. 10); F Wood (Feb. 1).

Denver Nuggets

	Gm	FG%	TPts	PPG	RPG	APG
Mahmoud Abdul-Rauf	57	.434	1095	19.2	2.4	6.8
Dale Ellis	81	.479	1204	14.9	3.9	1.7
Bryant Stith	82	.416	1119	13.6	4.9	2.9
Antonio McDyess*	76	.485	1020	13.4	7.5	1.0
Don MacLean	56	.426	625	11.2	3.7	1.6
Dikembe Mutombo	74	.499	814	11.0	11.8	1.5
LaPhonso Ellis	45	.438	471	10.5	7.2	1.6
Jalen Rose	80	.480	803	10.0	3.3	6.2
Tom Hammonds	71	.474	342	4.8	3.1	0.3
Reggie Williams	52	.370	241	4.6	2.3	1.4
Doug Overton	55	.376	182	3.3	1.1	1.9
Matt Fish	18	.583	52	2.9	1.2	0.4
NY	2	.600	12	6.0	1.5	0.5
DEN	16	.577	40	2.5	1.1	0.4
Greg Grant	31	.354	83	2.7	1.1	3.1
PHI	11	.375	45	4.1	2.0	5.5
WASH	10	.393	24	2.4	0.6	2.3
DEN	10	.261	14	1.4	0.7	1.4

Triple Doubles: Mutombo (1). **3-pt FG leader:** D. Ellis (150).
Steals leader: Stith (114). **Blocks leader:** Mutombo (332).
Signed: F Fish (Mar. 7); G Grant (Mar. 29).

Detroit Pistons

	Gm	FG%	TPts	PPG	RPG	APG
Grant Hill	80	.462	1618	20.2	9.8	6.9
Allan Houston	82	.453	1617	19.7	3.7	3.0
Otis Thorpe	82	.530	1161	14.2	8.4	1.9
Joe Dumars	67	.426	793	11.8	2.1	4.0
Terry Mills	82	.419	769	9.4	4.3	1.2
Lindsey Hunter	80	.381	679	8.5	2.4	2.4
Michael Curry*	46	.453	211	4.6	1.8	0.6
WASH	5	.300	10	2.0	1.0	0.2
DET	41	.464	201	4.9	2.0	0.6
Theo Ratliff*	75	.557	341	4.5	4.0	0.2
Don Reid*	69	.567	263	3.8	2.9	0.2
Mark Macon	23	.433	74	3.2	1.0	0.7
Mark West	47	.484	150	3.2	2.8	0.1
Eric Leckner	18	.621	44	2.4	1.9	0.1
Lou Roe	49	.356	90	1.8	1.6	0.3

Triple Doubles: Hill (10). **3-pt FG leader:** Houston (191).
Steals leader: Hill (100). **Blocks leader:** Ratliff (116).
Acquired: F Curry (Jan. 31).

Golden State Warriors

	Gm	FG%	TPts	PPG	RPG	APG
Latrell Sprewell	78	.428	1473	18.9	4.9	4.2
Joe Smith*	82	.458	1251	15.3	8.7	1.0
Chris Mullin	55	.499	734	13.3	2.9	3.5
B.J. Armstrong	82	.468	1012	12.3	2.2	4.9
Rony Seikaly	64	.502	776	12.1	7.8	1.1
Bimbo Coles	81	.409	892	11.0	3.2	5.2
Kevin Willis	75	.456	794	10.6	8.5	0.7
Jerome Kersey	76	.410	510	6.7	4.8	1.5
Donyell Marshall	62	.398	342	5.5	3.4	0.8
Jon Barry	68	.492	257	3.8	0.9	1.3
Clifford Rozier	59	.585	184	3.1	2.9	0.4
Andrew DeClercq*	22	.480	59	2.7	1.8	0.4

Triple Doubles: Mullin (1). **3-pt FG leader:** Armstrong (98).
Steals leader: Sprewell (127). **Blocks leader:** Smith (134).
Acquired: G Coles and C Willis from Miami for G Tim Hardaway and F Chris Gatling (Feb. 22).
Signed: F Kersey (Oct. 19).

Houston Rockets

	Gm	FG%	TPts	PPG	RPG	APG
Hakeem Olajuwon	72	.514	1936	26.9	10.9	3.6
Clyde Drexler	52	.433	1005	19.3	7.2	5.8
Sam Cassell	61	.439	886	14.5	3.1	4.6
Robert Horry	71	.410	853	12.0	5.8	4.0
Mario Elie	45	.504	499	11.1	3.4	3.1
Sam Mack*	31	.422	335	10.8	3.2	2.5
Mark Bryant	71	.543	611	8.6	5.0	0.7
Chucky Brown	82	.541	705	8.6	5.4	1.1
Kenny Smith	68	.433	580	8.5	1.4	3.6
Eldridge Recasner	63	.415	436	6.9	2.3	2.7
Tim Breaux	54	.366	161	3.0	1.1	0.4
Pete Chilcutt	74	.408	200	2.7	2.1	0.4
Charles Jones	46	.316	16	0.3	1.6	0.3

Triple Doubles: Drexler (3), Olajuwon (3). **3-pt FG leader:** Horry (142).
Steals leader: Horry (116). **Blocks leader:** Olajuwon (207).
Signed: F Mack (Feb. 12); G Moore (Mar. 13).

Indiana Pacers

	Gm	FG%	TPts	PPG	RPG	APG
Reggie Miller	76	.473	1606	21.1	2.8	3.3
Rik Smits	63	.521	1164	18.5	6.9	1.7
Derrick Mckey	75	.486	879	11.7	4.8	3.5
Dale Davis	78	.558	803	10.3	9.1	1.0
Mark Jackson	81	.473	806	10.0	3.8	7.8
Ricky Pierce	76	.447	737	9.7	1.8	1.3
Antonio Davis	82	.490	719	8.8	6.1	0.5
Eddie Johnson	62	.413	475	7.7	2.5	1.1
Travis Best*	59	.423	221	3.7	0.7	1.6
Duane Ferrell	54	.482	202	3.7	1.7	0.6
Haywoode Workman	77	.390	279	3.6	1.6	2.8
Dwayne Schintzius	33	.445	111	3.4	2.4	0.4
Adrian Caldwell	51	.554	110	2.2	2.2	0.1

Triple Doubles: McKey (1). **3-pt FG leader:** Miller (168).
Steals leader: Jackson (100). **Blocks leader:** D. Davis (112).
Signed: C Schintzius (Oct. 18).

More Individual Single Game Highs

(*) indicates overtime.

Most Rebounds

31*..............Dikembe Mutombo, Den vs. Char (3/26)

Most Offensive Rebounds

14 ....Joe Smith, G.St. at LAC (2/5)
14*........................Dennis Rodman, Chi at Det (2/15)

Most Defensive Rebounds

23*..............Dikembe Mutombo, Den vs. Char (3/26)

Los Angeles Clippers

	Gm	FG%	TPts	PPG	RPG	APG
Loy Vaught	80	.525	1298	16.2	10.1	1.4
Brian Williams	65	.543	1029	15.8	7.6	1.9
Terry Dehere	82	.459	1016	12.4	1.7	4.3
Pooh Richardson	63	.423	734	11.7	2.5	5.4
Rodney Rogers	67	.477	774	11.6	4.3	2.5
Malik Sealy	62	.415	712	11.5	3.9	1.9
Brent Barry*	79	.474	800	10.1	2.1	2.9
Lamond Murray	77	.447	650	8.4	3.2	1.1
Stanley Roberts	51	.464	356	7.0	3.2	0.8
Eric Piatkowski*	65	.405	301	4.6	1.6	0.7
Antonio Harvey	55	.371	204	3.7	3.6	0.3
VAN	18	.411	98	5.4	5.2	0.5
LAC	37	.341	106	2.9	2.9	0.2
Charles Outlaw	80	.575	286	3.6	2.5	0.6
Keith Tower	34	.444	82	2.4	1.5	0.1

Triple Doubles: none. **3-pt FG leader:** Dehere (139). **Steals leader:** Barry (95). **Blocks leader:** Outlaw (91). **Signed:** F/C Harvey (Jan. 3).

Los Angeles Lakers

	Gm	FG%	TPts	PPG	RPG	APG
Cedric Ceballos	78	.530	1656	21.2	6.9	1.5
Nick Van Exel	74	.417	1099	14.9	2.4	6.9
Magic Johnson	32	.466	468	14.6	5.7	6.9
Elden Campbell	82	.503	1143	13.9	7.6	2.2
Vlade Divac	79	.513	1020	12.9	8.6	3.3
Eddie Jones	70	.492	893	12.8	3.3	3.5
Anthony Peeler	73	.452	710	9.7	1.9	1.6
Sedale Threatt	82	.458	596	7.3	1.2	3.3
George Lynch	76	.430	291	3.8	2.8	0.7
Fred Roberts	33	.495	122	3.7	1.4	0.8
Derek Strong	63	.426	214	3.4	2.8	0.5
Corie Blount	57	.473	183	3.2	3.0	0.7
Anthony Miller	27	.429	36	1.3	0.9	0.1

Triple Doubles: Johnson (1), Divac (1). **3-pt FG leader:** Van Exel (144). **Steals leader:** Jones (129). **Blocks leader:** Campbell (212). **Activated:** F Johnson (Jan. 29); F Strong (Oct. 26).

Miami Heat

	Gm	FG%	TPts	PPG	RPG	APG
Alonzo Mourning	70	.523	1623	23.2	10.4	2.3
Tim Hardaway	80	.422	1217	15.2	2.9	8.0
GS	52	.421	735	14.1	2.5	6.9
MIA	28	.425	482	17.2	3.5	10.0
Rex Chapman	56	.426	786	14.0	2.6	3.0
Walt Williams	73	.444	995	13.6	4.4	3.2
SAC	45	.435	658	14.6	4.6	3.7
MIA	28	.463	337	12.0	4.0	2.3
Sasha Danilovic*	19	.451	255	13.4	2.4	2.5
Chris Gatling	71	.575	791	11.1	5.9	0.6
GS	47	.555	426	9.1	5.1	0.6
MIA	24	.598	365	15.2	7.3	0.7
Kurt Thomas*	74	.501	666	9.0	5.9	0.6
Keith Askins	75	.402	458	6.1	4.3	1.6
Voshon Lenard*	30	.376	176	5.9	1.7	1.0
Tyrone Corbin	71	.442	413	5.8	3.4	1.2
SAC	49	.452	312	6.4	3.7	1.2
MIA	22	.413	101	4.6	3.0	1.0
Jeff Malone	32	.394	186	5.8	1.3	0.8
PHI	25	.394	155	6.2	1.3	0.8
MIA	7	.394	31	4.4	1.1	1.0
Tony Smith	59	.423	298	5.1	1.6	2.6
PHO	34	.405	189	5.6	1.6	2.5
MIA	25	.455	109	4.4	1.6	2.7
Dan Schayes	32	.340	101	3.2	2.8	0.3

Triple Doubles: none. **3-pt FG leader:** Hardaway (138). **Steals leader:** Hardaway (132). **Blocks leader:** Mourning (189). **Acquired:** G Hardaway and F Gatling from Golden St. for G Bimbo Coles and C Kevin Willis; F Williams and G Corbin from Sacramento for F Billy Owens and G Kevin Gamble (Feb. 22).

Milwaukee Bucks

	Gm	FG%	TPts	PPG	RPG	APG
Vin Baker	82	.489	1729	21.1	9.9	2.6
Glenn Robinson	82	.454	1660	20.2	6.1	3.6
Sherman Douglas	79	.504	890	11.3	2.3	5.5
BOS	10	.429	98	9.8	2.3	3.9
MIL	69	.514	792	11.5	2.3	5.8
Johnny Newman	82	.495	889	10.9	2.4	1.9
Benoit Benjamin	83	.498	728	8.8	6.5	0.8
VAN	13	.441	181	13.9	7.9	1.2
MIL	70	.520	547	7.8	6.2	0.7
Terry Cummings	81	.462	645	8.0	5.5	1.1
Marty Conlon	74	.468	395	5.3	2.4	0.9
Lee Mayberry	82	.420	422	5.1	1.1	3.7
Shawn Respert*	62	.387	303	4.9	1.2	1.1
Randolph Keys	69	.418	232	3.4	1.8	0.9
Jerry Reynolds	19	.396	56	2.9	1.7	0.6

Triple Doubles: Douglas (1). **3-pt FG leader:** Robinson (90). **Steals leader:** Robinson (95). **Blocks leader:** Baker (91). **Acquired:** G Douglas from Boston for G Todd Day and C Alton Lister (Nov. 26). C Benjamin from Vancouver for G Eric Murdock and C Eric Mobley (Nov. 27). **Signed:** F Reynolds (Dec. 1).

Minnesota Timberwolves

	Gm	FG%	TPts	PPG	RPG	APG
Isaiah Rider	75	.464	1470	19.6	4.1	2.8
Tom Gugliotta	78	.471	1261	16.2	8.8	3.1
Andrew Lang	71	.447	832	11.7	6.4	0.9
ATL	51	.454	657	12.9	6.5	1.2
MIN	20	.421	175	8.8	6.1	0.2
Sam Mitchell	78	.490	844	10.8	4.3	0.9
Kevin Garnett*	80	.491	835	10.4	6.3	1.8
Terry Porter	82	.442	773	9.4	2.6	5.5
Spud Webb	77	.433	544	7.1	1.3	3.8
ATL	51	.468	300	5.9	1.2	2.7
MIN	26	.394	244	9.4	1.5	5.9
Darrick Martin	59	.406	415	7.0	1.4	3.7
VAN	24	.450	161	6.7	1.6	2.5
MIN	35	.381	254	7.3	1.3	4.5
Doug West	73	.445	465	6.4	2.2	1.6
Eric Riley	25	.473	92	3.7	3.0	0.2
Mark Davis*	57	.369	188	3.3	2.2	0.8
Jerome Allen	41	.343	108	2.6	0.6	1.2
Marques Bragg	53	.450	131	2.5	1.5	0.2

Triple Doubles: none. **3-pt FG leader:** Rider (102). **Steals leader:** Gugliotta (139). **Blocks leader:** Garnett (131). **Acquired:** C Lang and G Webb from Atlanta for F/C Christian Laettner and F/C Sean Rooks (Feb. 22); G Martin from Vancouver for 1996 second round draft choice (Jan. 12). **Signed:** G Porter (Oct. 17).

More Individual Single Game Highs

(*) indicates overtime.

Most 3-point Field Goals Made

11 ....Dennis Scott, Orl. vs. Atl. (4/18)

Most 3-point Field Goals Attempted

20 ....George McCloud, Dal. vs. N.J. (3/5)

Most Free Throws Made

22* ....Charles Barkley, Pho. vs. Wash. (12/20)

Most Free Throws Attempted

28 ....Karl Malone, Utah vs. Mia. (1/8)

Most Blocked Shots

12 ....Shawn Bradley, N.J. vs. Tor. (4/17)

Most Steals

7...Eleven tied

New Jersey Nets

	Gm	FG%	TPts	PPG	RPG	APG
Armon Gilliam	78	.474	1429	18.3	9.1	1.8
Kendall Gill	47	.469	656	14.0	4.9	5.5
CHAR	36	.481	464	12.9	5.3	6.3
NJ	11	.441	192	17.5	3.9	3.2
Chris Childs	78	.416	1002	12.8	3.1	7.0
Shawn Bradley	79	.443	944	11.9	8.1	0.8
PHI	12	.443	105	8.8	8.8	0.7
NJ	67	.443	839	12.5	7.9	0.8
Kevin Edwards	34	.364	394	11.6	2.2	2.1
PJ Brown	81	.444	915	11.3	6.9	2.0
Jayson Williams	80	.423	721	9.0	10.0	0.6
Vern Fleming	77	.433	590	7.7	2.2	3.3
Ed O'Bannon*	64	.390	399	6.2	2.6	1.0
Khalid Reeves	51	.419	279	5.5	1.5	2.3
CHAR	20	.458	162	8.1	2.0	3.6
NJ	31	.376	117	3.8	1.3	1.5
Greg Graham	53	.404	240	4.5	1.1	1.0
PHI	8	.531	56	7.0	1.9	1.4
NJ	45	.379	184	4.1	0.9	0.9
Yinka Dare	58	.438	164	2.8	3.1	0.0
Rick Mahorn	50	.352	120	2.4	2.2	0.3
Tim Perry	30	.477	71	2.4	1.6	0.3
PHI	8	.444	19	2.4	1.6	0.3
NJ	22	.489	52	2.4	1.6	0.3

Triple Doubles: Bradley (3), Childs (1). **3-pt FG leader:** Childs (95). **Steals leader:** Childs (111). **Blocks leader:** Bradley (288). **Acquired:** C Bradley, G Graham and F Perry from Philadelphia for F Derrick Coleman, F Sean Higgins and G Rex Walters (Nov. 30); G Gill and G Reeves from Charlotte for G Kenny Anderson and F Gerald Glass (Jan. 19).

New York Knickerbockers

	Gm	FG%	TPts	PPG	RPG	APG
Patrick Ewing	76	.466	1711	22.5	10.6	2.1
Anthony Mason	82	.563	1196	14.6	9.3	4.4
Derek Harper	82	.464	1149	14.0	2.5	4.3
John Starks	81	.443	1024	12.6	2.9	3.9
Charles Oakley	53	.471	604	11.4	8.7	2.6
Hubert Davis	74	.486	789	10.7	1.7	1.4
Willie Anderson	76	.436	742	9.8	3.2	2.6
TOR	49	.440	606	12.4	3.8	3.0
NY	27	.421	136	5.0	2.2	1.8
J.R. Reid	65	.494	427	6.6	3.9	0.6
S.A.	32	.439	208	6.5	3.8	0.4
NY	33	.550	219	6.6	4.0	0.8
Gary Grant	47	.486	232	4.9	1.1	1.5
Charlie Ward	62	.399	244	3.9	1.6	2.1
Brad Lohaus	55	.406	197	3.6	1.2	0.8
S.A.	32	.406	107	3.3	1.0	0.5
NY	23	.405	90	3.9	1.3	1.2
Herb Williams	44	.408	138	3.1	2.0	0.6
TOR	1	.375	6	6.0	8.0	0.0
NY	43	.410	132	3.1	1.9	0.6
Ronnie Grandison	28	.379	65	2.3	2.0	0.5
MIA	18	.333	43	2.4	2.0	0.6
ATL	4	.500	4	1.0	1.5	0.3
NY	6	.467	18	3.0	2.2	0.3

Triple Doubles: none. **3-pt FG leader:** Starks (143). **Steals leader:** Harper (131). **Blocks leader:** Ewing (184). **Acquired:** F Reid, F Lohaus and 1996 first round draft choice from San Antonio for F Charles Smith and F Monty Williams (Feb. 8); G Anderson and F/C Alexander from Toronto for F Doug Christie and C Herb Williams (Feb. 18). **Signed:** C Williams (Feb. 28); F Grandison (Mar. 12).

Orlando Magic

	Gm	FG%	TPts	PPG	RPG	APG
Shaquille O'Neal	54	.573	1434	26.6	11.0	2.9
Penny Hardaway	82	.513	1780	21.7	4.3	7.1
Dennis Scott	82	.440	1431	17.5	3.8	3.0
Nick Anderson	77	.442	1134	14.7	5.4	3.6
Horace Grant	63	.513	847	13.4	9.2	2.7
Kenny Gattison	25	.479	229	9.2	4.6	0.6
Brian Shaw	75	.374	496	6.6	3.0	4.5
Donald Royal	64	.491	337	5.3	2.4	0.7
Joe Wolf	64	.513	291	4.5	2.9	1.0
CHAR	1	.000	0	0.0	2.0	0.0
ORL	63	.515	291	4.6	2.9	1.0
Brooks Thompson	33	.466	140	4.2	0.7	0.9
Anthony Bowie	74	.471	308	4.2	1.7	1.4
Jon Koncak	67	.480	203	3.0	4.1	0.8
David Vaughn*	33	.338	64	1.9	2.4	0.2

Triple Doubles: Bowie (1). **3-pt FG leader:** Scott (267). **Steals leader:** Hardaway (166). **Blocks leader:** O'Neal (115). **Signed:** F/C Wolf (Nov. 10).

Philadelphia 76ers

	Gm	FG%	TPts	PPG	RPG	APG
Jerry Stackhouse*	72	.414	1384	19.2	3.7	3.9
C. Weatherspoon	78	.484	1300	16.7	9.7	2.0
Vernon Maxwell	75	.390	1217	16.2	3.1	4.4
Trevor Ruffin	61	.406	778	12.8	2.2	4.4
Tony Massenburg	54	.495	539	10.0	6.5	0.6
TOR	24	.510	243	10.1	6.9	0.8
PHI	30	.483	296	9.9	6.2	0.4
Sean Higgins	44	.415	351	8.0	2.1	1.3
Ed Pinckney	74	.510	478	6.5	6.2	1.0
TOR	47	.502	328	7.0	6.0	1.1
PHI	27	.529	150	5.6	6.5	0.8
Derrick Alston	73	.512	452	6.2	4.1	0.8
Richard Dumas	39	.468	241	6.2	2.5	1.1
Greg Sutton	48	.392	252	5.3	1.0	2.1
CHAR	18	.400	62	3.4	0.8	2.2
PHI	30	.389	190	6.3	1.2	2.1
Rex Walters	44	.412	186	4.2	1.3	2.4
LaSalle Thompson	44	.398	85	1.9	4.5	0.6

Triple Doubles: none. **3-pt FG leader:** Maxwell (146). **Steals leader:** Weatherspoon (112). **Blocks leader:** Weatherspoon (108). **Acquired:** F Coleman, G Higgins and G Walters from New Jersey for C Shawn Bradley, G Greg Graham and F Tim Perry (Nov. 30); F Massenburg, F Ed Pinckney and right to swap first and second round draft choices in 1996 or 1997 from Toronto for F/C Sharone Wright (Feb. 22). **Signed:** G Sutton (Jan. 10).

Phoenix Suns

	Gm	FG%	TPts	PPG	RPG	APG
Charles Barkley	71	.500	1649	23.2	11.6	3.7
Kevin Johnson	56	.507	1047	18.7	3.9	9.2
Michael Finley*	82	.476	1233	15.0	4.6	3.5
Danny Manning	33	.459	441	13.4	4.3	2.0
Chuck Person	82	.445	1045	12.7	3.9	1.7
Wayman Tisdale	63	.495	672	10.7	3.4	0.9
Elliot Perry	81	.475	697	8.6	1.7	4.4
A.C. Green	82	.484	612	7.5	6.8	0.9
John Williams	62	.453	455	7.3	6.0	1.0
Mario Bennett	19	.453	85	4.5	2.6	0.3
Chris Carr	60	.415	240	4.0	1.7	0.7
Terrence Rencher	36	.330	106	2.9	1.2	1.5
MIA	34	.323	103	3.0	1.2	1.6
PHO	2	1.000	3	1.5	1.0	0.0
Joe Kleine	56	.420	164	2.9	2.4	0.8

Triple Doubles: Barkley (1), Johnson (1). **3-pt FG leader:** Person (117). **Steals leader:** Barkley (114). **Blocks leader:** Williams (90). **Acquired:** G Rencher from Miami for G Tony Smith (Feb. 22).

Portland Trailblazers

	Gm	FG%	TPts	PPG	RPG	APG
Clifford Robinson	78	.423	1644	21.1	5.7	2.4
Rod Strickland	67	.460	1256	18.7	4.4	9.6
Aryvdas Sabonis*	73	.545	1058	14.5	8.1	1.8
Aaron McKie	81	.467	864	10.7	3.8	2.5
Harvey Grant	76	.462	709	9.3	4.8	1.5
James Robinson	76	.399	649	8.5	2.1	2.0
Gary Trent*	69	.513	518	7.5	3.4	0.7
Buck Williams	70	.500	511	7.3	5.8	0.6
Rumeal Robinson	43	.416	247	5.7	1.8	3.3
Chris Dudley	80	.453	404	5.1	9.0	0.5
Dontonio Wingfield	44	.382	165	3.8	2.4	0.6
Randolph Childress*	28	.316	85	3.0	0.7	1.1
Elmore Spencer	17	.385	14	0.8	0.8	0.1
DEN	6	.000	0	0.0	0.7	0.0
PORT	11	.417	14	1.3	0.8	0.1

Triple Doubles: none. **3-pt FG leader:** C. Robinson (178).
Steals leader: Strickland (97). **Blocks leader:** Dudley (100).
Signed: C Spencer and G Robinson (Jan. 10).

Sacramento Kings

	Gm	FG%	TPts	PPG	RPG	APG
Mitch Richmond	81	.447	1872	23.1	3.3	3.1
Brian Grant	78	.507	1120	14.4	7.0	1.6
Billy Owens	62	.480	808	13.0	6.6	3.3
MIA	40	.505	590	14.8	7.2	3.4
SAC	22	.420	218	9.9	5.7	3.2
Olden Polynice	81	.527	985	12.2	9.4	0.7
Sarunas Marciulionis	53	.452	571	10.8	1.5	2.2
Tyus Edney*	80	.412	860	10.8	2.5	6.1
Kevin Gamble	65	.401	386	5.9	1.7	1.5
MIA	44	.394	305	6.9	2.0	1.9
SAC	21	.427	81	3.9	1.3	0.9
Corliss Williamson*	53	.466	297	5.6	2.2	0.4
Michael Smith	65	.605	357	5.5	6.0	1.7
Lionel Simmons	54	.396	246	4.6	2.7	1.5
Byron Houston	25	.500	86	3.4	3.4	0.3
Duane Causwell	73	.417	250	3.4	3.4	0.3
Bobby Hurley	72	.283	220	3.1	1.0	3.0

Triple Doubles: none. **3-pt FG leader:** Richmond (225).
Steals leader: Richmond (125). **Blocks leader:** Grant (103).
Acquired: F Owens and G/F Gamble from Miami for F Walt Williams and F Tyrone Corbin (Feb. 22).

San Antonio Spurs

	Gm	FG%	TPts	PPG	RPG	APG
David Robinson	82	.516	2051	25.0	12.2	3.0
Sean Elliott	77	.466	1537	20.0	5.1	2.7
Vinny Del Negro	82	.497	1191	14.5	3.3	3.8
Avery Johnson	82	.494	1071	13.1	2.5	9.6
Chuck Person	80	.437	873	10.9	5.2	1.3
Charles Smith	73	.422	609	8.3	5.0	0.9
NY	41	.388	303	7.4	3.9	0.7
SA	32	.458	306	9.6	6.3	1.1
Will Perdue	80	.523	413	5.2	6.1	0.4
Doc Rivers	78	.372	311	4.0	1.8	1.6
Dell Demps	16	.576	53	3.3	0.6	0.5
Cory Alexander*	60	.406	168	2.8	0.7	2.0
Monty Williams	31	.397	68	2.2	1.3	0.3
NY	14	.318	19	1.4	1.2	0.3
SA	17	.435	49	2.9	1.4	0.2
Carl Herrera	44	.412	85	1.9	1.8	0.4
Greg Anderson	46	.511	54	1.2	2.2	0.2

Triple Doubles: none. **3-pt FG leader:** Person (190).
Steals leader: Johnson (119). **Blocks leader:** Robinson (271).
Acquired: F Smith and F Williams from New York for F J.R. Reid and F Brad Lohaus and 1996 first round draft choice (Feb. 8).
Signed: G Demps (Oct. 7)

Seattle Supersonics

	Gm	FG%	TPts	PPG	RPG	APG
Shawn Kemp	79	.561	1550	19.6	11.4	2.2
Gary Payton	81	.484	1563	19.3	4.2	7.5
Detlef Schrempf	63	.486	1080	17.1	5.2	4.4
Hersey Hawkins	82	.473	1279	15.6	3.6	2.7
Sam Perkins	82	.408	970	11.8	4.5	1.5
Vincent Askew	69	.493	584	8.5	3.2	2.4
Ervin Johnson	81	.511	446	5.5	5.3	0.6
Frank Brickowski	63	.488	339	5.4	2.4	0.9
Nate McMillan	55	.420	275	5.0	3.8	3.6
David Wingate	60	.415	223	3.7	0.9	1.0
Sherell Ford	28	.375	90	3.2	0.9	0.2
Eric Snow*	43	.420	115	2.7	1.0	1.7
Steve Scheffler	35	.533	58	1.7	0.9	0.1

Triple Doubles: Payton (1). **3-pt FG leader:** Hawkins (146).
Steals leader: Payton (231). **Blocks leader:** Johnson (129).

Toronto Raptors

	Gm	FG%	TPts	PPG	RPG	APG
Damon Stoudamire*	70	.426	1331	19.0	4.0	9.3
Tracy Murray	82	.454	1325	16.2	4.3	1.6
Oliver Miller	76	.526	982	12.9	7.4	2.9
Sharone Wright	57	.484	664	11.6	6.2	0.7
PHI	46	.477	483	10.5	6.5	0.6
TOR	11	.508	181	16.5	5.2	1.0
Alvin Robertson	77	.470	718	9.3	4.4	4.2
Carlos Rogers	56	.517	430	7.7	3.0	0.6
Zan Tabak	67	.543	514	7.7	4.8	0.9
Doug Christie	55	.445	415	7.5	2.8	2.1
NY	23	.479	93	4.0	1.5	1.1
TOR	32	.436	322	10.1	3.8	2.9
Acie Earl	42	.424	316	7.5	3.1	0.6
John Salley	25	.486	149	6.0	3.9	1.6
Martin Lewis	16	.483	75	4.7	1.8	0.2
Jimmy King	62	.431	279	4.5	1.8	1.4
Vincenzo Esposito	30	.360	116	3.9	0.5	0.8

Triple Doubles: Stoudamire (1). **3-pt FG leader:** Murray (151).
Steals leader: Robertson (166). **Blocks leader:** Miller (143).
Acquired: F Christie and C Williams from New York for G Willie Anderson and F/C Victor Alexander (Feb. 18); F/C Wright from Philadelphia for F Tony Massenburg, F Pinckney and the right to swap first and second round draft choices in 1996 or 1997 (Feb. 22).

Utah Jazz

	Gm	FG%	TPts	PPG	RPG	APG
Karl Malone	82	.519	2106	25.7	9.8	4.2
Jeff Hornacek	82	.502	1247	15.2	2.5	4.1
John Stockton	82	.538	1209	14.7	2.8	11.2
Chris Morris	66	.437	691	10.5	3.5	1.2
David Benoit	81	.439	661	8.2	4.7	1.0
Antoine Carr	80	.457	580	7.3	2.5	0.9
Adam Keefe	82	.520	499	6.1	5.5	0.8
Felton Spencer	71	.520	396	5.6	4.3	0.2
Howard Eisley	65	.430	287	4.4	1.2	2.2
Greg Foster	73	.439	276	3.8	2.4	0.3
Greg Ostertag*	57	.473	208	3.6	3.1	0.1
Jamie Watson	16	.419	48	3.0	1.7	1.5
Bryon Russell	59	.394	174	2.9	1.5	0.5

Triple Doubles: Malone (1). **3-pt FG leader:** Hornacek (104).
Steals leader: Stockton (140). **Blocks leader:** Carr (65).

Vancouver Grizzlies

	Gm	FG%	TPts	PPG	RPG	APG
Greg Anthony	69	.415	967	14.0	2.5	6.9
Bryant Reeves*	77	.457	1021	13.3	7.4	1.4
Blue Edwards	82	.419	1043	12.7	4.2	2.6
Byron Scott	80	.401	819	10.2	2.4	1.5
Eric Murdock	73	.416	647	8.9	2.3	4.5
MIL	9	.364	62	6.9	1.6	3.9
VAN	64	.422	585	9.1	2.4	4.6
Chris King	80	.427	634	7.9	3.6	1.3
Gerald Wilkins	28	.376	188	6.7	2.3	2.4
Lawrence Moten*	44	.453	291	6.6	1.4	1.1
Ashraf Amaya	54	.480	339	6.3	5.6	0.6
Anthony Avent	71	.384	415	5.8	5.0	1.0
Eric Mobley	39	.536	188	4.8	3.6	0.6
MIL	5	.286	6	1.2	2.4	0.0
VAN	34	.550	182	5.4	3.8	0.6
Rich Manning*	29	.434	107	3.7	1.9	0.2
Doug Edwards	31	.352	93	3.0	2.8	1.3

Triple Doubles: none. **3-pt FG leader:** Anthony (90).
Steals leader: Murdock (129). **Blocks leader:** Reeves (55).
Acquired: G Murdock and C Mobley from Milwaukee for C Benoit Benjamin (Nov. 27).
Signed: C Manning (Jan.11).

Washington Bullets

	Gm	FG%	TPts	PPG	RPG	APG
Chris Webber	15	.543	356	23.7	7.6	5.0
Juwan Howard	81	.489	1789	22.1	8.1	4.4
Robert Pack	31	.428	560	18.1	4.3	7.8
Calbert Cheaney	70	.471	1055	15.1	3.4	2.2
Gheorghe Muresan	76	.584	1104	14.5	9.6	0.7
Rasheed Wallace*	65	.487	655	10.1	4.7	1.3
Brent Price	81	.472	810	10.0	2.8	5.1
Tim Legler	77	.507	726	9.4	1.8	1.8
Ledell Eackles	55	.427	474	8.6	2.7	1.6
Chris Whitney	21	.455	150	7.1	1.6	2.4
Mitchell Butler	61	.384	237	3.9	1.9	1.1
Bob McCann	62	.497	188	3.0	2.3	0.4
Jim McIlvaine	80	.428	182	2.3	2.9	0.1

Triple Doubles: Webber (1). **3-pt FG leader:** B. Price (139).
Steals leader: B. Price (78). **Blocks leader:** Muresan (172).
Signed: G Eackles (Dec. 11); F McCann (Jan. 10); G Pritchard (Feb. 23); F Thornton (Mar. 23).

NBA Regular Season Team Leaders

Offense

WEST	Pts (Per Game)	Reb (Per Game)	Ast (Per Game)	FG%	3Pt%	FT%
Seattle	104.5	41.5	24.4	.480	.364	.760
Phoenix	104.3	42.8	24.4	.473	.332	.771
San Antonio	103.4	43.0	24.9	.477	.392	.736
LA Lakers	102.9	40.2	25.4	.479	.351	.746
Dallas	102.6	46.2	23.3	.420	.360	.722
Houston	102.5	41.1	24.2	.464	.362	.765
Utah	102.5	41.0	26.1	.48	.372	.768
Golden St.	101.6	42.2	23.0	.456	.373	.759
Sacramento	99.6	42.2	22.3	.457	.387	.731
LA Clippers	99.4	38.6	20.4	.472	.370	.702
Portland	99.3	45.6	21.5	.457	.353	.662
Minnesota	97.8	39.7	22.8	.459	.325	.777
Denver	97.7	43.2	22.6	.451	.346	.743
Vancouver	89.8	38.1	20.8	.428	.329	.724

EAST	Pts (Per Game)	Reb (Per Game)	Ast (Per Game)	FG%	3Pt%	FT%
Chicago	105.2	44.6	24.8	.478	.403	.747
Orlando	104.5	41.1	25.4	.482	.378	.691
Boston	103.6	42.4	21.9	.456	.371	.714
Charlotte	102.8	39.5	23.3	.470	.384	.770
Washington	102.5	39.7	22.1	.484	.407	.728
Indiana	99.3	39.9	23.3	.480	.373	.755
Atlanta	98.3	40.6	19.6	.448	.355	.757
Toronto	97.5	40.0	23.5	.467	.354	.723
New York	97.2	40.0	22.2	.471	.377	.757
Miami	96.5	42.6	21.4	.457	.379	.710
Milwaukee	95.6	38.2	21.4	.468	.339	.735
Detroit	95.4	40.6	19.6	.459	.404	.751
Philadelphia	94.5	38.9	19.9	.436	.342	.734
New Jersey	93.7	47.0	21.4	.427	.335	.745
Cleveland	91.1	35.6	22.2	.460	.377	.763

Defense

WEST	Pts (Per Game)	Reb (Per Game)	Ast (Per Game)	FG%	3Pt%	FT%
Utah	95.9	37.7	20.0	.445	.385	.752
Seattle	96.7	40.6	21.7	.438	.348	.717
Portland	97.0	39.6	22.2	.442	.348	.740
San Antonio	97.1	43.7	22.5	.439	.330	.730
LA Lakers	98.5	42.2	24.5	.458	.367	.738
Vancouver	99.8	44.5	24.2	.475	.374	.733
Denver	100.4	40.5	22.9	.459	.367	.760
Houston	100.7	44.2	23.7	.460	.359	.707
Sacramento	102.3	41.0	22.0	.462	.379	.751
LA Clippers	103.0	41.4	20.2	.477	.372	.746
Golden St.	103.1	41.5	25.6	.475	.365	.744
Minnesota	103.2	40.9	24.0	.469	.380	.744
Phoenix	104.0	41.3	25.5	.471	.369	.739
Dallas	107.5	46.5	24.2	.492	.394	.732

EAST	Pts (Per Game)	Reb (Per Game)	Ast (Per Game)	FG%	3Pt%	FT%
Cleveland	88.6	37.1	22.2	.462	.388	.759
Chicago	92.9	38.0	19.4	.448	.350	.717
Detroit	92.9	39.4	21.1	.442	.366	.715
New York	94.9	41.7	20.4	.442	.337	.740
Miami	95.0	40.2	20.1	.434	.361	.752
Indiana	96.1	37.3	21.0	.452	.360	.740
Atlanta	97.1	40.8	22.5	.474	.360	.746
New Jersey	97.9	41.3	22.9	.454	.384	.740
Orlando	99.0	42.1	22.8	.454	.366	.736
Milwaukee	100.9	40.2	23.6	.481	.398	.725
Washington	101.5	42.3	20.6	.460	.342	.766
Charlotte	103.4	40.4	25.0	.489	.396	.736
Philadelphia	104.5	44.4	25.6	.483	.370	.741
Toronto	105.0	41.1	24.3	.475	.367	.745
Boston	107.0	44.3	23.4	.481	.357	.747

Series Summaries

WESTERN CONFERENCE

FIRST ROUND (Best of 5)

	W-L	Avg.	Leading Scorer
Houston	3-1	96.8	Olajuwon (26.5)
Los Angeles	1-3	94.8	Ceballos (19.0)

Date	Winner	Home Court
Apr. 25	Rockets, 87-83	at Los Angeles
Apr. 27	Lakers, 104-94	at Los Angeles
Apr. 30	Rockets, 104-98	at Houston
May 2	Rockets, 102-94	at Houston

	W-L	Avg.	Leading Scorer
Utah	3-2	99.6	Malone (27.6)
Portland	2-3	89.6	Sabonis (23.6)

Date	Winner	Home Court
Apr. 25	Jazz, 110-102	at Utah
Apr. 27	Jazz, 105-90	at Utah
Apr. 29	Trail Blazers, 94-91 (OT)	at Portland
May 1	Trail Blazers, 98-90	at Portland
May 5	Jazz, 102-64	at Utah

	W-L	Avg.	Leading Scorer
San Antonio	3-1	109.8	Robinson (30.0)
Phoenix	1-3	98.8	Barkley (25.5)

Date	Winner	Home Court
Apr. 26	Spurs, 120-98	at San Antonio
Apr. 28	Spurs, 110-105	at San Antonio
May 1	Suns, 94-93	at Phoenix
May 3	Spurs, 116-98	at Phoenix

	W-L	Avg.	Leading Scorer
Seattle	3-1	93.8	Payton (20.8)
Sacramento	1-3	87.8	Richmond (21.0)

Date	Winner	Home Court
Apr. 26	SuperSonics, 97-85	at Seattle
Apr. 28	Kings, 90-81	at Seattle
Apr. 30	SuperSonics, 96-89	at Sacramento
May 2	SuperSonics, 101-87	at Sacramento

SEMIFINALS (Best of 7)

	W-L	Avg.	Leading Scorer
Seattle	4-0	110.5	Payton (24.5)
Houston	0-4	98.8	Drexler (19.3)

Date	Winner	Home Court
May 4	SuperSonics, 108-75	at Seattle
May 6	SuperSonics, 105-101	at Seattle
May 10	SuperSonics, 115-112	at Houston
May 12	SuperSonics, 114-107 (OT)	at Houston

	W-L	Avg.	Leading Scorer
Utah	4-2	95.5	Malone (25.0)
San Antonio	2-4	83.8	Robinson (19.3)

Date	Winner	Home Court
May 7	Jazz, 95-75	at San Antonio
May 9	Spurs, 88-77	at San Antonio
May 11	Jazz, 105-75	at Utah
May 12	Jazz, 101-86	at Utah
May 14	Spurs, 98-87	at San Antonio
May 16	Jazz, 108-81	at Utah

CHAMPIONSHIP (Best of 7)

	W-L	Avg.	Leading Scorer
Seattle	4-3	89.3	Payton (20.7)
Utah	3-4	91.9	Malone (27.0)

Date	Winner	Home Court
May 18	SuperSonics, 102-72	at Seattle
May 20	SuperSonics, 91-87	at Seattle
May 24	Jazz, 96-76	at Utah
May 26	SuperSonics, 88-86	at Utah
May 28	Jazz, 98-95 (OT)	at Seattle
May 30	Jazz, 118-83	at Utah
June 2	SuperSonics, 90-86	at Seattle

EASTERN CONFERENCE

FIRST ROUND (Best of 5)

	W-L	Avg.	Leading Scorer
Chicago	3-0	106.7	Jordan (30.0)
Miami	0-3	83.7	Mourning (18.0)

Date	Winner	Home Court
Apr. 26	Bulls, 102-85	at Chicago
Apr. 28	Bulls, 106-75	at Chicago
May 1	Bulls, 112-91	at Miami

	W-L	Avg.	Leading Scorer
Orlando	3-0	101.7	O'Neal (21.0)
Detroit	0-3	89.0	Houston (25.0)

Date	Winner	Home Court
Apr. 26	Magic, 112-92	at Orlando
Apr. 28	Magic, 92-77	at Orlando
Apr. 30	Magic, 101-98	at Detroit

	W-L	Avg.	Leading Scorer
Indiana	2-3	87.0	Smits (19.0)
Atlanta	3-2	88.0	Smith (22.8)

Date	Winner	Home Court
Apr. 25	Hawks, 92-80	at Indiana
Apr. 27	Pacers, 102-94 (OT)	at Indiana
Apr. 29	Hawks, 90-83	at Atlanta
May 2	Pacers, 83-75	at Atlanta
May 5	Hawks, 89-87	at Indiana

	W-L	Avg.	Leading Scorer
Cleveland	0-3	79.7	Brandon (19.3)
New York	3-0	90.3	Starks (19.7)

Date	Winner	Home Court
Apr. 25	Knicks, 106-83	at Cleveland
Apr. 29	Knicks, 84-80	at Cleveland
May 1	Knicks, 81-76	at New York

SEMIFINALS (Best of 7)

	W-L	Avg.	Leading Scorer
Chicago	4-1	93.8	Jordan (36.0)
New York	1-4	87.6	Ewing (23.4)

Date	Winner	Home Court
May 5	Bulls, 91-84	at Chicago
May 7	Bulls, 91-80	at Chicago
May 11	Knicks, 102-99 (OT)	at New York
May 12	Bulls, 94-91	at New York
May 14	Bulls, 94-81	at Chicago

	W-L	Avg.	Leading Scorer
Orlando	4-1	107.0	O'Neal (27.8)
Atlanta	1-4	97.4	Smith (20.6)

Date	Winner	Home Court
May 8	Magic, 117-105	at Orlando
May 10	Magic, 120-94	at Orlando
May 12	Magic, 103-96	at Atlanta
May 13	Hawks, 104-99	at Atlanta
May 15	Magic, 96-88	at Orlando

CHAMPIONSHIP (Best of 7)

	W-L	Avg.	Leading Scorer
Chicago	4-0	101.5	Jordan (29.5)
Orlando	0-4	84.8	O'Neal (27.0)

Date	Winner	Home Court
May 19	Bulls, 121-83	at Chicago
May 21	Bulls, 93-88	at Chicago
May 25	Bulls, 86-67	at Orlando
May 27	Bulls, 106-101	at Orlando

NBA FINALS (Best of 7)

	W-L	Avg.	Leading Scorer
Chicago	4-2	93.0	Jordan (27.3)
Seattle	2-4	89.2	Kemp (23.3)

Date	Winner	Home Court
June 5	Bulls, 107-90	At Chicago
June 7	Bulls, 92-88	At Chicago
June 9	Bulls, 108-86	At Seattle
June 12	SuperSonics, 107-86	At Seattle
June 14	SuperSonics, 89-78	At Seattle
June 16	Bulls, 87-75	At Chicago

Most Valuable Player
Michael Jordan, Chicago, G
27.3 pts, 5.3 rebs, 4.2 assists.

Final Playoff Standings

(Ranked by victories)

	Gm	W	L	Pct	–Per Game– For	Opp
Chicago	18	15	3	.833	97.4	86.8
Seattle	21	13	8	.619	94.1	92.7
Utah	16	10	6	.625	95.2	87.6
Orlando	12	7	5	.583	98.3	96.7
San Antonio	10	5	5	.500	94.2	96.8
New York	8	4	4	.500	88.6	88.5
Atlanta	10	4	6	.400	92.7	97.0
Houston	8	3	5	.375	97.8	102.6
Indiana	5	2	3	.400	87.0	88.0
Portland	5	2	3	.400	89.6	99.6
Sacramento	4	1	3	.250	87.8	93.8
Phoenix	4	1	3	.250	98.8	109.8
LA Lakers	4	1	3	.250	94.8	96.8
Cleveland	3	0	3	.000	79.7	90.3
Detroit	3	0	3	.000	89.0	101.7
Miami	3	0	3	.000	83.7	106.7

Off-Season Coaching Changes

Team	Old Coach	Why left?	New Coach	Old Job
Milwaukee Bucks	Mike Dunleavy	resigned (Apr. 27)	Chris Ford	Head Coach, Celtics
Philadelphia 76ers	John Lucas	fired (May 13)	Johnny Davis	Asst., Trailblazers
New Jersey Nets	Butch Beard	fired (Apr. 22)	John Calipari	Head Coach, UMass
Dallas Mavericks	Dick Motta	resigned (May 1)	Jim Cleamons	Asst., Bulls
Charlotte Hornets	Allan Bristow	fired (Apr. 23)	Dave Cowens	Asst., Spurs
Toronto Raptors	Brendan Malone	fired (Apr. 22)	Darrell Walker	Asst., Raptors

NBA Playoff Leaders

Scoring

	Gm	FG	FT	Pts	Avg
Michael Jordan, Chicago	18	187	153	552	30.7
Karl Malone, Utah	18	188	101	477	26.5
Shaquille O'Neal, Orlando	12	131	48	310	25.8
Charles Barkley, Phoenix	4	31	37	102	25.5
Allan Houston, Detroit	3	25	18	75	25.0
David Robinson, San Antonio	10	83	70	236	23.6
Aryvdas Sabonis, Portland	5	35	43	118	23.6
Anfernee Hardaway, Orlando	12	101	58	280	23.3
Hakeem Olajuwon, Houston	8	75	29	179	22.4
Steve Smith, Atlanta	10	75	42	217	21.7
Patrick Ewing, New York	8	65	41	172	21.5
Mitch Richmond, Sacramento	4	24	28	84	21.0
Shawn Kemp, Seattle	20	147	124	418	20.9
Gary Payton, Seattle	21	162	69	434	20.7
Rod Strickland, Portland	5	37	23	103	20.6
Terrell Brandon, Cleveland	3	21	13	58	19.3
Cedric Ceballos, LA Lakers	4	30	11	76	19.0
Grant Hill, Detroit	3	22	12	57	19.0
Rik Smits, Indiana	5	42	11	95	19.0
Alonzo Mourning, Miami	3	17	20	54	18.0

High Point Games

	Date	FG-FT—Pts
Michael Jordan, Chi at NY	5/11	17-10—46*
Michael Jordan, Chi at Orl	5/27	16-10—45
Michael Jordan, Chi vs NY	5/5	17- 9—44
Shaquille O'Neal, Orl vs Atl	5/8	18- 5—41
David Robinson, SA vs Pho	4/28	14-12—40

*Overtime.

Rebounds

	Gm	Off	Def	Tot	Avg
Dennis Rodman, Chi	18	98	149	247	13.7
Charles Barkley, Pho	4	18	36	54	13.5
Olden Polynice, Sac	4	16	32	48	12.0
Otis Thorpe, Det	3	14	21	35	11.7
Dale Davis, Ind	5	20	36	56	11.2

Assists

	Gm	No	Avg
John Stockton, Utah	18	195	10.8
Kevin Johnson, Pho	4	43	10.8
Avery Johnson, SA	10	94	9.4
Rod Strickland, Port	5	42	8.4
Terrell Brandon, Cle	3	24	8.0

NBA Finalists' Composite Box Scores

Chicago Bulls (15-3)

	Overall Playoffs			Per Game			Finals vs. Seattle			Per Game		
	Gm	FG%	TPts	Pts	Reb	Ast	Gm	FG%	TPts	Pts	Reb	Ast
Michael Jordan	18	.459	552	30.7	4.9	4.1	6	.415	164	27.3	5.3	4.2
Scottie Pippen	18	.390	305	16.9	8.5	5.9	6	.343	94	15.7	8.2	5.3
Toni Kukoc	15	.391	162	10.8	4.2	3.9	6	.423	78	13.0	4.8	3.5
Ron Harper	18	.425	158	8.8	3.7	2.5	6	.375	39	6.5	2.2	1.7
Luc Longley	18	.469	150	8.3	4.6	1.6	6	.574	70	11.7	3.8	2.2
Dennis Rodman	18	.485	135	7.5	13.7	2.1	6	.486	45	7.5	14.7	2.5
Steve Kerr	18	.448	122	6.8	1.0	1.7	6	.303	30	5.0	0.8	0.8
Bill Wennington	18	.520	54	3.0	1.7	0.5	6	.667	17	2.8	0.5	0.2
Randy Brown	16	.571	44	2.8	0.6	0.4	6	.500	17	2.8	0.3	0.8
Jud Buechler	17	.474	46	2.7	0.6	0.4	6	.222	4	0.7	0.0	0.2
James Edwards	6	.444	11	1.8	0.7	0.0	0	—	0	0.0	0.0	0.0
John Salley	16	.545	14	0.9	0.7	0.4	5	.000	0	0.0	0.2	0.4
BULLS	18	.443	1753	97.4	43.6	22.7	6	.416	558	93.0	40.8	21.7
OPPONENTS	18	.443	1563	86.8	35.7	16.1	6	.445	535	89.2	37.2	16.8

Three-pointers: PLAYOFFS—Pippen (30–for–105), Jordan (25–62), Kerr (17–53), Harper (15–47), Kukoc (13–68), Buechler (8–21), Brown (3–6), Wennington (0–1), Team (111–363 for .306 pct.); FINALS—Kukoc (10–for–32), Pippen (9–39), Jordan (6–19), Harper (4–13), Kerr (4–22), Brown (3–6), Buechler (0–6), Team (36–137 for .263 pct.).

Seattle SuperSonics (13–8)

	Overall Playoffs			Per Game			Finals vs. Chicago			Per Game		
	Gm	FG%	TPts	Pts	Reb	Ast	Gm	FG%	TPts	Pts	Reb	Ast
Shawn Kemp	20	.570	418	20.9	10.4	1.5	6	.551	140	23.3	10.0	2.2
Gary Payton	21	.485	434	20.7	5.1	6.8	6	.444	108	18.0	6.3	7.0
Detlef Shrempf	21	.475	336	16.0	5.0	3.2	6	.443	98	16.3	5.0	2.5
Hersey Hawkins	21	.452	259	12.3	3.0	2.2	6	.455	80	13.3	3.5	1.0
Sam Perkins	21	.459	258	12.3	4.3	1.7	6	.377	67	11.2	4.7	2.0
Nate McMillan	19	.406	84	4.4	3.7	2.7	4	.429	11	2.8	2.8	1.5
Vincent Askew	19	.343	71	3.7	2.2	1.4	4	.222	7	1.8	2.5	0.5
Ervin Johnson	18	.371	55	3.1	3.9	0.4	3	.333	4	1.3	2.3	0.3
Frank Brickowski	21	.421	41	2.0	1.4	0.5	6	.222	5	0.8	2.0	0.5
David Wingate	13	.438	19	1.5	0.2	0.0	6	.500	15	2.5	0.3	0.0
Eric Snow	10	.143	2	0.2	0.4	0.6	6	.000	0	0.0	0.3	0.2
Steve Scheffler	8	.000	0	0.0	0.8	0.3	4	.000	0	0.0	0.5	0.0
SUPERSONICS	21	.471	1977	94.1	38.0	20.2	6	.445	535	89.2	37.2	16.8
OPPONENTS	21	.431	1947	92.7	39.0	22.5	6	.416	558	93.0	40.8	21.7

Three-pointers: PLAYOFFS—Payton (41–for–100), Perkins (32–87), Hawkins (22–64), Schrempf (21–57), McMillan (19–40), Brickowski (6–22), Askew (6–23), Wingate (1–2), Kemp (0–3), Snow (0–2), Team (148–400 for .370 pct.); FINALS—Payton (9–for–27), Schrempf (7–18), Hawkins (6–22), Perkins (4–17), McMillan (3–5), Wingate (1–2), Askew (1–5), Brickowski (1–5), Kemp (0–1), Team (32–102 for .314 pct.).

Annual Awards

Most Valuable Player

The Maurice Podoloff Trophy; voting by 113-member panel of local and national pro basketball writers and broadcasters. Each ballot has five entries; points awarded on 10-7-5-3-1 basis.

	1st	2nd	3rd	4th	5th	Pts
Michael Jordan, Chi	109	3	0	1	0	1114
David Robinson, SA	0	54	29	14	9	574
Anfernee Hardaway, Orl	2	21	23	19	21	360
Hakeem Olajuwon, Hou	1	9	18	20	15	238
Scottie Pippen, Chi	0	11	18	14	17	226

Also receiving votes: Gary Payton, Sea. (98 pts); Karl Malone, Utah (85); Shawn Kemp, Sea. (73); Grant Hill, Det. and Shaquille O'Neal, Orl. (63); John Stockton, Utah (12); Charles Barkley, Pho. and Magic Johnson, LAL (8); Dennis Rodman, Chi. (4); Terrell Brandon, Cle. and Mitch Richmond, Sac. (3).

All-NBA Teams

Voting by a 113-member panel of local and national pro basketball writers and broadcasters. Each ballot has entries for three teams; points awarded on 5-3-1 basis. First Team repeaters from 1994-95 are in **bold** type.

First Team	**1st**	**Pts**
F **Scottie Pippen**, Chicago	91	517
F **Karl Malone**, Utah	89	509
C **David Robinson**, San Antonio	65	442
G Michael Jordan, Chicago	113	565
G **Anfernee Hardaway**, Orlando	90	516
Second Team	**1st**	**Pts**
F Shawn Kemp, Seattle	18	306
F Grant Hill, Detroit	14	266
C Hakeem Olajuwon, Houston	40	378
G Gary Payton, Seattle	14	294
G John Stockton, Utah	7	258
Third Team	**1st**	**Pts**
F Charles Barkley, Phoenix	10	236
F Juwan Howard, Washington	3	68
C Shaquille O'Neal, Orlando	8	185
G Mitch Richmond, Sacramento	1	167
G Reggie Miller, Indiana	0	90

All-Defensive Teams

Voting by NBA head coaches. Each ballot has entries for two teams; two points given for 1st team, one for 2nd. Coaches cannot vote for own players. First Team repeaters from 1994-95 are in **bold** type.

First Team	**1st**	**Pts**
F **Scottie Pippen**, Chicago	27	55
F **Dennis Rodman**, Chicago	11	30
C **David Robinson**, San Antonio	16	42
G **Gary Payton**, Seattle	20	48
G Michael Jordan, Chicago	25	53
Second Team	**1st**	**Pts**
F Horace Grant, Orlando	8	25
F Derrick McKey, Indiana	5	15
C Hakeem Olajuwon, Houston	8	27
G Mookie Blaylock, Atlanta	4	22
G Bobby Phills, Cleveland	3	12

Note: The last time three players from the same team made the All Defensive team was in 1982 when Moses Malone, Bobby Jones and Maurice Cheeks of the Philadelphia 76ers were chosen.

Coach of the Year

The Red Auerbach Trophy; voting by 113-member panel of local and national pro basketball writers and broadcasters. Each ballot has one entry.

	Votes	Improvement
Phil Jackson, Chicago	82	47-35 to 72-10
Mike Fratello, Cleveland	22	43-39 to 47-35
Doug Collins, Detroit	3	28-54 to 46-36
Bob Hill, San Antonio	3	62-20 to 59-23

Also receiving votes: Rudy Tomjanovich, Houston (2 pts); Lenny Wilkens, Atlanta (1).

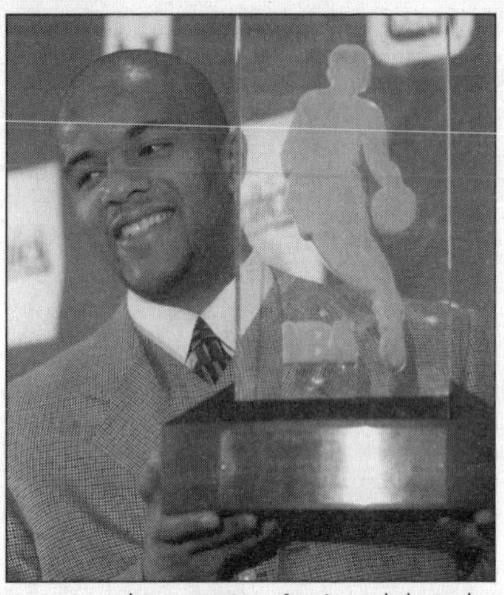

Raptors guard **Damon Stoudamire** with the Rookie of the Year award he received on May 15 in Toronto.

Rookie of the Year

The Eddie Gottlieb Trophy; voting by 113-member panel of local and national pro basketball writers and broadcasters. Each ballot has one entry.

	Pos	Votes
Damon Stoudamire, Toronto	G	76
Arvydas Sabonis, Portland	C	17
Joe Smith, Golden St.	F	15

Also receiving votes: Jerry Stackhouse, Phi (2 pts); Michael Finley, Pho (2) and Kevin Garnett, Min (1).

All-Rookie Team

Voting by NBA's 29 head coaches, who cannot vote for players on their team. Each ballot has entries for two five-man teams, regardless of position; two points given for 1st team, one for 2nd. First team votes in parentheses. Arvydas Sabonis and Michael Finley tied for the final spot on the first team. It was only the third time in NBA history that six players made the first team. Thurl Bailey tied Darrell Walker in 1984 and Wally Jones and Joe Caldwell tied in 1965.

First Team	**College**	**Pts**
Damon Stoudamire, Toronto (28)	Arizona	56
Joe Smith, Golden St. (26)	Maryland	54
Jerry Stackhouse, Philadelphia (25)	N. Carolina	52
Antonio McDyess, Denver (23)	Alabama	50
Arvydas Sabonis, Portland (17)	none	40
Michael Finley, Phoenix (15)	Wisconsin	40
Second Team	**College**	**Pts**
Kevin Garnett, Minnesota (7)	none	35
Bryant Reeves, Vancouver (2)	Oklahoma St.	28
Brent Barry, LA Clippers (1)	Oregon St.	21
Rasheed Wallace, Washington (1)	N. Carolina	15
Tyus Edney, Sacramento	UCLA	15

Other Awards

Defensive Player of the Year— Gary Payton, Seattle; **Most Improved Player**— Gheorghe Muresan, Washington; **Sixth Man Award**— Toni Kukoc, Chicago; **IBM Award** (for contributing most to team's success)— David Robinson, San Antonio; **Kennedy PBWAA Citizenship Award**—Chris Dudley, Portland; ***The Sporting News* Executive of the Year**— Jerry Krause, Chicago.

1996 College Draft

First and second round picks at the 50th annual NBA College Draft held June 26, 1996 at Continental Airlines Arena in New Jersey. The order of the first 11 positions determined by a Draft Lottery held May 19, in Secaucus, N.J. Note that Toronto and Vancouver were not eligible to receive the first pick. Positions 12 through 29 reflect regular season records in reverse order. Underclassmen selected are noted in CAPITAL letters.

First Round

	Team	Player	Pos
1	Philadelphia	ALLEN IVERSON, Georgetown	G
2	Toronto	MARCUS CAMBY, Massachusetts	C
3	Vancouver	SHAREEF ABDUR-RAHIM, California	F
4	**a**-Milwaukee	STEPHON MARBURY, Georgia Tech	G
5	**a**-Minnesota	RAY ALLEN, Connecticut	G
6	**b**-Boston	ANTOINE WALKER, Kentucky	F
7	LA Clippers	LORENZEN WRIGHT, Memphis	C
8	New Jersey	Kerry Kittles, Villanova	G
9	**c**-Dallas	SAMAKI WALKER, Louisville	C
10	**d**-Indiana	ERICK DAMPIER, Mississippi St.	C
11	Golden St.	Todd Fuller, N.C. State	C
12	**e**-Cleveland	VITALY POTAPENKO, Wright St.	C
13	Charlotte	KOBE BRYANT, Lower Merion (PA) HS	F
14	Sacramento	P. STOJAKOVIC, PAOK (Greece)	F
15	Phoenix	Steve Nash, Santa Clara	G
16	**f**-Charlotte	Tony Delk, Kentucky	G
17	Portland	JERMAINE O'NEAL, Eau Claire (SC) HS,	C
18	**g**-New York	John Wallace, Syracuse	F
19	**h**-New York	Walter McCarty, Kentucky	F
20	Cleveland	ZYDRUNAS ILGAUSKAS, Lithuania	C
21	New York	DONTAE' JONES, Mississippi St.	F
22	**i**-Vancouver	Roy Rogers, Alabama	F
23	**j**-Denver	EFTHIMIS RETZIAS, PAOK (Greece)	C
24	LA Lakers	Derek Fisher, Arkansas-Little Rock	G
25	**k**-Utah	Martin Muursepp, BC Kalev (Estonia)	F
26	**l**-Detroit	Jerome Williams, Georgetown	F
27	Orlando	Brian Evans, Indiana	G
28	**m**-Atlanta	PRIEST LAUDERDALE, Peristeri Greece	C
29	Chicago	Travis Knight, Connecticut	C

Second Round

	Team	Player	Pos
30	**n**-Houston	Othella Harrington, Georgetown	C
31	Philadelphia	Mark Hendrickson, Wash. St.	F
32	**o**-Philadelphia	Ryan Minor, Oklahoma	F
33	Milwaukee	Moochie Norris, West Florida	G
34	Dallas	Shawn Harvey, West Virginia St.	G
35	**p**-Seattle	Joseph Blair, Arizona	F
36	LA Clippers	Doron Sheffer, Connecticut	G
37	**q**-Denver	Jeff McInnis, North Carolina	G
38	Boston	Steve Hamer, Tennessee	C
39	Phoenix	Russ Millard, Iowa	C
40	Golden St.	Marcus Mann, Miss. Valley St.	F
41	Sacramento	Jason Sasser, Texas Tech	F
42	Houston	Randy Livingston, LSU	G
43	Phoenix	Ben Davis, Arizona	F
44	Charlotte	Malik Rose, Drexel	F
45	**r**-Seattle	Joe Vogel, Colorado St.	C
46	Portland	Marcus Brown, Murray St.	G
47	**s**-Seattle	Ron Riley, Arizona St.	F
48	**t**-Philadelphia	Jamie Feick, Michigan St.	C
49	Orlando	Amal McCaskill, Marquette	C
50	**u**-Houston	Terrell Bell, Georgia	C
51	**v**-Vancouver	Chris Robinson, W. Kentucky	F
52	Indiana	Mark Pope, Kentucky	F
53	Milwaukee	Jeff Nordgaard, WI-Green Bay	F
54	Utah	Shandon Anderson, Georgia	G
55	**w**-Washington	Ronnie Henderson, LSU	G
56	**x**- Cleveland	Reggie Geary, Arizona	G
57	Seattle	Drew Barry, Georgia Tech	G
58	**y**-Dallas	Darnell Robinson, Arkansas	C

Acquired Picks

FIRST ROUND: **a**- Milwaukee traded the rights to Stephon Marbury and a future first round pick to Minnesota for the rights to Ray Allen; **b**-from Dallas; **c**-from Boston; **d**-from Denver; **e**-from Washington; **f**-from Miami; **g**-from Detroit via San Antonio; **h**-from Atlanta via Miami; **i**-from Houston; **j**-from Indiana; **k**-Utah traded the rights to Muursepp to Miami for a future first-round pick; **l**-from San Antonio; **m**-from Seattle.

SECOND ROUND: **n**-from Vancouver; **o**-from Toronto; **p**-from Minnesota; **q**-from Sacramento via New Jersey; **r**-from Miami via Atlanta; **s**-from Atlanta; **t**-from Detroit; **u**-from Cleveland; **v**-from Houston; **w**-from San Antonio via Charlotte; **x**-from Orlando; **y**-from Chicago.

1996 European Clubs Championship

The European Championship of Men's Clubs was played at Bercy Arena in Paris, France from April 9-11, 1996. The Tournament is comprised of the league champions from the previous season from each Eastern and Western European country, plus Israel and Turkey. Top four teams in Groups A and B advanced to quarterfinals after preliminary round-robin.

Final Round Robin Standings

Each team plays 14 games within their group. Home and Away records are listed. Standings are based on Wins Away (WA) minus Home Loses (HL).

Group A	Country	Home	Away	WA-HL
*CSKA Moscow	Russia	7-0	3-4	3-0 = +3
*Benneton Treviso	Italy	7-0	3-4	3-0 = +3
*Olympiakos	Greece	6-1	4-3	4-1 = +3
*Ulker	Turkey	5-2	1-6	1-2 = -1
Unicaja Malaga	Spain	5-2	1-6	1-2 = -1
Olympique Antibes	France	6-1	0-7	0-1 = -1
Bayer Leverkusen	Germany	3-4	2-5	2-4 = -2
Iraklis	Greece	3-4	0-7	0-4 = -4
Group B				
*FC Barcelona	Spain	7-0	3-4	3-0 = +3
*Real Madrid	Spain	6-1	3-4	3-1 = +2
*Panathinaikos	Greece	5-2	4-3	4-2 = +2
*Pau Orthez	France	6-1	2-5	2-1 = +1
Virtus Knorr Bologna	Italy	4-3	2-5	2-3 = -1
Maccabi Tel-Aviv	Israel	4-3	2-5	2-3 = -1
Cibona Zagreb	Croatia	5-2	1-6	1-2 = -1
Benfica	Portugal	2-5	0-7	0-5 = -5

Tiebreaker: Ulker, Malaga and Antibes were all 2-2 in head-to-head meetings. Ulker advanced due to combined points scored in head-to-head games.

Quarterfinals

CSKA Moscow 2 .... Pau Orthez 1
Real Madrid 2 .... Olympiakos 1
Panathinaikos 2 .... Benneton Treviso 1
FC Barcelona 2 .... Ulker 0

Semifinals

Panathinaikos 81 .... CSKA Moscow 71
FC Barcelona 76 .... Real Madrid 66

Third Place

CSKA Moscow 74 .... Real Madrid 73

Championship Game

Panathinaikos 67 .... FC Barcelona 66

Most Valuable Player

Dominique Wilkins, Panathinaikos, forward

Continental Basketball Association

Final Standings

QW refers to quarters won. Teams get 3 points for a win, 1 point for each quarter won and 1/2 point for any quarter tied. Avg refers to average points per game played.

American Conference

Eastern Division

	W	L	QW	Pts	Avg	Home	Road
Grand Rapids	33	23	110.5	209.5	3.7	19-9	14-14
Fort Wayne	25	31	113.0	188.0	3.4	19-9	6-22
Connecticut	17	39	96.0	147.0	2.6	11-17	6-22

Mideast Division

	W	L	QW	Pts	Avg	Home	Road
Rockford	35	21	122.0	227.0	4.1	23-5	12-16
Quad City	37	19	116.0	227.0	4.1	23-5	14-14
Chicago	26	30	109.0	187.0	3.4	18-10	8-20

National Conference

Northern Division

	W	L	QW	Pts	Avg	Home	Road
Sioux Falls	32	24	127.0	223.0	4.0	21-7	11-17
Omaha	28	28	106.5	190.5	3.4	21-7	7-21
Yakima	19	37	104.5	161.5	2.9	11-17	8-20

Southern Division

	W	L	QW	Pts	Avg	Home	Road
Florida	41	15	131.5	254.5	4.5	26-2	15-13
Oklahoma City	34	22	121.5	223.5	4.0	22-6	12-16
Shreveport	17	39	99.0	150.0	2.7	11-17	6-22

Playoffs

American Conference

First Round

Fort Wayne def. Rockford, 3 games to 1
Quad City def. Grand Rapids, 3 games to 1

Second Round

Fort Wayne def. Quad City, 3 games to 2

National Conference

First Round

Florida def. Omaha, 3 games to 0
Sioux Falls def. Oklahoma City, 3 games to 1

Second Round

Sioux Falls def. Florida, 3 games to 2

Finals (Best of 7)

Sioux Falls wins series, 4 games to 1

	W-L	Avg	Leading Scorer
Sioux Falls	4-1	119.6	James (23.2)
Fort Wayne	1-4	118.0	Gray (24.6)

Date	Winner	Home Court
Apr. 17	Sioux Falls, 131-123	at Sioux Falls
Apr. 19	Fort Wayne, 113-105	at Sioux Falls
Apr. 21	Sioux Falls, 121-115	at Fort Wayne
Apr. 23	Sioux Falls, 123-122 (2 OT)	at Fort Wayne
Apr. 24	Sioux Falls, 118-117	at Fort Wayne

CBA Annual Awards

Most Valuable Player: Shelton Jones, Florida
Newcomer of the Year: Gaylon Nickerson, Okla.
Rookie of the Year: Ray Jackson, G. Rapids
Defensive Player of the Year: Emanual Davis, Rock.
Coach of the Year: Brendan Suhr, G. Rapids
Playoff MVP: Henry James, Sioux Falls

CBA Regular Season Individual Leaders

Scoring

	G	Pts	Avg
Tracy Moore, Shreveport	49	1266	25.8
Henry James, Sioux Falls	45	992	22.0
Evric Gray, Ft. Wayne	47	992	21.1
Alex Blackwell, Connecticut	56	1169	20.9
Sam Mack, Rockford	39	808	20.7
Darryl Johnson, Omaha	44	874	19.9
Reggie Jordan, Sioux Falls	38	749	19.7
Reggie Fox, Sioux Falls	42	822	19.6
Jay Taylor, Quad City	47	884	18.8
Ray Jackson, Grand Rapids	53	991	18.7
Jo Jo English, Yakima	36	572	18.7
Kelby Stuckey, Quad City	56	1019	18.2
Carl Thomas, Ft. Wayne	56	1005	17.9

Rebounding

	G	Reb	Avg
Jerome Lane, Oklahoma City	55	924	16.8
Ivano Newbill, Grand Rapids	55	565	10.3
Tracey Ware, Shreveport	40	393	9.8
Matt Fish, Ft. Wayne	30	281	9.4
Anthony Dade, Shreveport	55	479	8.7
Alex Blackwell, Connecticut	56	487	8.7
Kelby Stuckey, Quad City	56	483	8.6
Reggie Jackson, Rockford	56	475	8.5
Bruce Chubick, Omaha	56	465	8.3
Fred Lewis, Chicago	57	472	8.3

Assists

	G	Ast	Avg
Charles Smith IV, Florida	43	326	7.6
Duane Cooper, Ft. Wayne	51	381	7.5
Gerald Madkins, Rockford	39	279	7.2
Derrick Phelps, Chicago	54	360	6.7
Emanual Davis, Rockford	52	342	6.6
Reggie Jordan, Sioux Falls	38	249	6.6
Litterial Green, Quad City	56	350	6.3
Chris Whitney, Florida	34	192	5.6
Matt Maloney, Grand Rapids	56	310	5.5
Tate George, Connecticut	46	252	5.5

Blocks

	G	Blk	Avg
Kevin Salvadori, Florida	52	97	1.9
Michael McDonald, Grand Rapids	49	91	1.9
Jimmy Carruth, Ft. Wayne	47	84	1.8
Mark Strickland, Yakima	56	95	1.7
Kurt Portmann, Quad City	55	76	1.4

Steals

	G	Stl	Avg
Reggie Jordan, Sioux Falls	38	92	2.4
Emanual Davis, Rockford	52	115	2.2
Stanley Jackson, Florida	40	84	2.1
Gerald Madkins, Rockford	39	69	1.8
Keith Smart, Florida	56	95	1.7

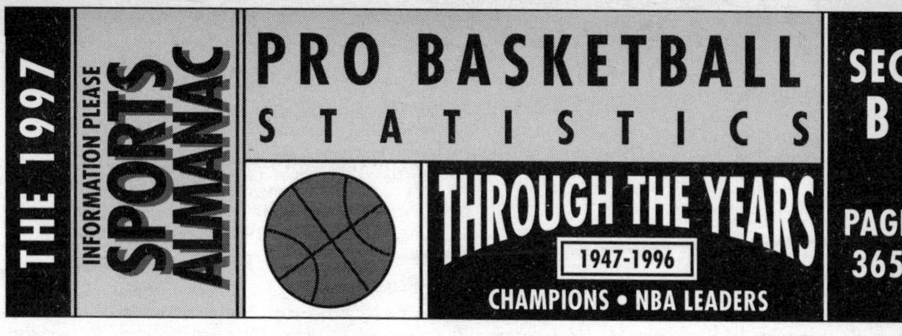

The NBA Finals

Although the National Basketball Association traces its first championship back to the 1946-47 season, the league was then called the Basketball Association of America (BAA). It did not become the NBA until after the 1948-49 season when the BAA and the National Basketball League (NBL) agreed to merge.

In the chart below, the Eastern finalists (representing the NBA Eastern Division from 1947-70, and the NBA Eastern Conference since 1971) are listed in CAPITAL letters. Also, each NBA champion's wins and losses are noted in parentheses after the series score.

Multiple winners: Boston (16); Minneapolis-LA Lakers (11); Chicago Bulls (4); Phi-SF-Golden St. Warriors and Syracuse Nationals-Phi. 76ers (3); Detroit, Houston and New York (2).

Year	Winner	Head Coach	Series	Loser	Head Coach
1947	PHILADELPHIA WARRIORS	Eddie Gottlieb	4-1 (WWWLW)	Chicago Stags	Harold Olsen
1948	Baltimore Bullets	Buddy Jeannette	4-2 (LWWWLW)	PHILA. WARRIORS	Eddie Gottlieb
1949	Minneapolis Lakers	John Kundla	4-2 (WWWLLW)	WASH. CAPITOLS	Red Auerbach
1950	Minneapolis Lakers	John Kundla	4-2 (WLWWLW)	SYRACUSE	Al Cervi
1951	Rochester	Les Harrison	4-3 (WWWLLLW)	NEW YORK	Joe Lapchick
1952	Minneapolis Lakers	John Kundla	4-3 (WLWLWLW)	NEW YORK	Joe Lapchick
1953	Minneapolis Lakers	John Kundla	4-1 (LWWWW)	NEW YORK	Joe Lapchick
1954	Minneapolis Lakers	John Kundla	4-3 (WLWLWLW)	SYRACUSE	Al Cervi
1955	SYRACUSE	Al Cervi	4-3 (WWLLLWW)	Ft. Wayne Pistons	Charley Eckman
1956	PHILADELPHIA WARRIORS	George Senesky	4-1 (WLWWW)	Ft. Wayne Pistons	Charley Eckman
1957	BOSTON	Red Auerbach	4-3 (LWLWWLW)	St. Louis Hawks	Alex Hannum
1958	St. Louis Hawks	Alex Hannum	4-2 (WLWLWW)	BOSTON	Red Auerbach
1959	BOSTON	Red Auerbach	4-0	Mpls. Lakers	John Kundla
1960	BOSTON	Red Auerbach	4-3 (WLWLWLW)	St. Louis Hawks	Ed Macauley
1961	BOSTON	Red Auerbach	4-1 (WWLWW)	St. Louis Hawks	Paul Seymour
1962	BOSTON	Red Auerbach	4-3 (WLLWLWW)	LA Lakers	Fred Schaus
1963	BOSTON	Red Auerbach	4-2 (WWLWLW)	LA Lakers	Fred Schaus
1964	BOSTON	Red Auerbach	4-1 (WWLWW)	SF Warriors	Alex Hannum
1965	BOSTON	Red Auerbach	4-1 (WWLWW)	LA Lakers	Fred Schaus
1966	BOSTON	Red Auerbach	4-3 (LWWWLLW)	LA Lakers	Fred Schaus
1967	PHILADELPHIA 76ERS	Alex Hannum	4-2 (WWLWLW)	SF Warriors	Bill Sharman
1968	BOSTON	Bill Russell	4-2 (WLWLWW)	LA Lakers	B.van Breda Kolff
1969	BOSTON	Bill Russell	4-3 (LLWWLWW)	LA Lakers	B.van Breda Kolff
1970	NEW YORK	Red Holzman	4-3 (WLWLWLW)	LA Lakers	Joe Mullaney
1971	Milwaukee	Larry Costello	4-0	BALT. BULLETS	Gene Shue
1972	LA Lakers	Bill Sharman	4-1 (LWWWW)	NEW YORK	Red Holzman
1973	NEW YORK	Red Holzman	4-1 (LWWWW)	LA Lakers	Bill Sharman
1974	BOSTON	Tommy Heinsohn	4-3 (WLWLWLW)	Milwaukee	Larry Costello
1975	Golden St. Warriors	Al Attles	4-0	WASH. BULLETS	K.C. Jones
1976	BOSTON	Tommy Heinsohn	4-2 (WWLLWW)	Phoenix	John MacLeod
1977	Portland	Jack Ramsay	4-2 (LLWWWW)	PHILA. 76ERS	Gene Shue
1978	WASHINGTON BULLETS	Dick Motta	4-3 (LWLWLWW)	Seattle	Lenny Wilkens
1979	Seattle	Lenny Wilkens	4-1 (LWWWW)	WASH. BULLETS	Dick Motta
1980	LA Lakers	Paul Westhead	4-2 (WLWLWW)	PHILA. 76ERS	Billy Cunningham
1981	BOSTON	Bill Fitch	4-2 (WLWLWW)	Houston	Del Harris
1982	LA Lakers	Pat Riley	4-2 (WLWWLW)	PHILA. 76ERS	Billy Cunningham
1983	PHILADELPHIA 76ERS	Billy Cunningham	4-0	LA Lakers	Pat Riley
1984	BOSTON	K.C. Jones	4-3 (LWLWWLW)	LA Lakers	Pat Riley
1985	LA Lakers	Pat Riley	4-2 (LWWLWW)	BOSTON	K.C. Jones
1986	BOSTON	K.C. Jones	4-2 (WWLWLW)	Houston	Bill Fitch
1987	LA Lakers	Pat Riley	4-2 (WWLWLW)	BOSTON	K.C. Jones
1988	LA Lakers	Pat Riley	4-3 (LWWLLWW)	DETROIT PISTONS	Chuck Daly
1989	DETROIT PISTONS	Chuck Daly	4-0	LA Lakers	Pat Riley

Year	Winner	Head Coach	Series	Loser	Head Coach
1990	DETROIT	Chuck Daly	4-1 (WLWWW)	Portland	Rick Adelman
1991	CHICAGO	Phil Jackson	4-1 (LWWWW)	LA Lakers	Mike Dunleavy
1992	CHICAGO	Phil Jackson	4-2 (WLWLWW)	Portland	Rick Adelman
1993	CHICAGO	Phil Jackson	4-2 (WWLWLW)	Phoenix	Paul Westphal
1994	Houston	Rudy Tomjanovich	4-3 (WLWLLWW)	NEW YORK	Pat Riley
1995	Houston	Rudy Tomjanovich	4-0	Orlando	Brian Hill
1996	CHICAGO	Phil Jackson	4-2 (WWWLLW)	Seattle	George Karl

Note: Four finalists were led by player-coaches: **1948**—Buddy Jeannette (guard) of Baltimore; **1950**—Al Cervi (guard) of Syracuse; **1968**—Bill Russell (center) of Boston; **1969**—Bill Russell (center) of Boston.

Most Valuable Player

Selected by an 11-member media panel. Winner who did not play for the NBA champion is in **bold** type.

Multiple winners: Michael Jordan (4); Magic Johnson (3); Kareem Abdul-Jabbar, Larry Bird, Hakeem Olajuwon and Willis Reed (2).

Year		Year		Year	
1969	**Jerry West**, LA Lakers, G	1979	Dennis Johnson, Seattle, G	1989	Joe Dumars, Detroit, G
1970	Willis Reed, New York, C	1980	Magic Johnson, LA Lakers, G/C	1990	Isiah Thomas, Detroit, G
1971	Lew Alcindor, Milwaukee, C	1981	Cedric Maxwell, Boston, F	1991	Michael Jordan, Chicago, G
1972	Wilt Chamberlain, LA Lakers, C	1982	Magic Johnson, LA Lakers, G	1992	Michael Jordan, Chicago, G
1973	Willis Reed, New York, C	1983	Moses Malone, Philadelphia, C	1993	Michael Jordan, Chicago, G
1974	John Havlicek, Boston, F	1984	Larry Bird, Boston, F	1994	Hakeem Olajuwon, Houston, C
1975	Rick Barry, Golden State, F	1985	K. Abdul-Jabbar, LA Lakers, C	1995	Hakeem Olajuwon, Houston, C
1976	Jo Jo White, Boston, G	1986	Larry Bird, Boston, F	1996	Michael Jordan, Chicago, G
1977	Bill Walton, Portland, C	1987	Magic Johnson, LA Lakers, G		
1978	Wes Unseld, Washington, C	1988	James Worthy, LA Lakers, F		

Note: Lew Alcindor changed his name to Kareem Abdul-Jabbar after the 1970-71 season.

All-Time NBA Playoff Leaders

Through the 1996 playoffs.

CAREER

Years listed indicate number of playoff appearances. Players active in 1996 in **bold** type.

Points

		Yrs	Gm	Pts	Avg
1	Kareem Abdul-Jabbar	18	237	5762	24.3
2	**Michael Jordan**	11	139	4717	33.9
3	Jerry West	13	153	4457	29.1
4	Larry Bird	12	164	3897	23.8
5	John Havlicek	13	172	3776	22.0
6	**Magic Johnson**	13	190	3701	19.5
7	Elgin Baylor	12	134	3623	27.0
8	Wilt Chamberlain	13	160	3607	22.5
9	**Hakeem Olajuwon**	11	115	3202	27.8
10	Kevin McHale	13	169	3182	18.8
11	Dennis Johnson	13	180	3116	17.3
12	Julius Erving	11	141	3088	21.9
13	James Worthy	9	143	3022	21.1
14	Sam Jones	12	154	2909	18.9
15	**Robert Parish**	15	182	2818	15.5
16	Bill Russell	13	165	2673	16.2
17	**Karl Malone**	11	97	2646	27.3
18	**Clyde Drexler**	13	124	2598	21.0
19	**Scottie Pippen**	9	138	2499	18.1
20	**Charles Barkley**	10	99	2417	24.4

Scoring Average

Minimum of 25 games or 700 points.

		Yrs	Gm	Pts	Avg
1	**Michael Jordan**	11	139	4717	33.9
2	Jerry West	13	153	4457	29.1
3	**Hakeem Olajuwon**	11	115	3202	27.8
4	**Karl Malone**	11	97	2646	27.3
5	Elgin Baylor	12	134	3623	27.0
6	George Gervin	9	59	1592	27.0
7	Dominique Wilkins	9	55	1421	25.8
8	Bob Pettit	9	88	2240	25.5
9	**Shaquille O'Neal**	3	36	911	25.3
10	Rick Barry	7	74	1833	24.8
11	**Reggie Miller**	7	49	1211	24.7
12	Bernard King	5	28	687	24.5
13	Alex English	10	68	1661	24.4
14	**Charles Barkley**	10	99	2417	24.4
15	Kareem Abdul-Jabbar	18	237	5762	24.3
16	Paul Arizin	8	49	1186	24.2
17	**David Robinson**	6	53	1273	24.0
18	Larry Bird	12	164	3897	23.8
19	George Mikan	9	91	2141	23.5
20	Bob Love	6	47	1076	22.9

Field Goals

		Yrs	FG	Att	Pct
1	Kareem Abdul-Jabbar	18	2356	4422	.533
2	**Michael Jordan**	11	1718	3473	.495
3	Jerry West	13	1622	3460	.469
4	Larry Bird	12	1458	3090	.472
5	John Havlicek	13	1451	3329	.436
6	Wilt Chamberlain	13	1425	2728	.522
7	Elgin Baylor	12	1388	3161	.439
8	**Magic Johnson**	13	1291	2552	.506
9	**Hakeem Olajuwon**	10	1283	2423	.530
10	James Worthy	9	1267	2329	.544

Free Throws

		Yrs	FT	Att	Pct
1	Jerry West	13	1213	1507	.805
2	Kareem Abdul-Jabbar	18	1050	1419	.740
3	**Michael Jordan**	11	1159	1395	.831
4	**Magic Johnson**	13	1068	1274	.838
5	Larry Bird	12	901	1012	.891
6	John Havlicek	13	874	1046	.836
7	Elgin Baylor	12	847	1101	.769
8	Kevin McHale	13	766	972	.788
9	Wilt Chamberlain	13	757	1627	.465
10	Dennis Johnson	13	756	943	.802

All-Time NBA Playoff Leaders (Cont.)

Assists

		Yrs	Gm	No	Avg
1	**Magic Johnson**	13	190	2346	12.3
2	**John Stockton**	12	107	1175	11.0
3	Larry Bird	12	164	1062	6.5
4	Dennis Johnson	13	180	1006	5.6
5	Isiah Thomas	9	111	987	8.9

Rebounds

		Yrs	Gm	No	Avg
1	Bill Russell	13	165	4104	24.9
2	Wilt Chamberlain	13	160	3913	24.5
3	Kareem Abdul-Jabbar	18	237	2481	10.5
4	Wes Unseld	12	119	1777	14.9
5	**Robert Parish**	15	182	1761	9.7

Appearances

	No		No
Kareem Abdul-Jabbar	18	John Havlicek	13
Robert Parish	15	Kevin McHale	13
Dolph Schayes	15	Dennis Johnson	13
Paul Silas	14	**Magic Johnson**	13
Wilt Chamberlain	13	Bill Russell	13
Maurice Cheeks	13	Chet Walker	13
Bob Cousy	13	Jerry West	13
Hal Greer	13		

Games Played

	No		No
K. Abdul-Jabbar	237	Kevin McHale	169
Danny Ainge	193	Michael Cooper	168
Magic Johnson	190	Bill Russell	165
Robert Parish	182	Larry Bird	164
Dennis Johnson	180	Paul Silas	163
Byron Scott	175	Wilt Chamberlain	160
John Havlicek	170	Sam Jones	154

SINGLE GAME

Points

	Date	FG-FT—Pts
Michael Jordan, Chi at Bos*	4/20/86	22-19—63
Elgin Baylor, LA at Bos	4/14/62	22-17—61
Wilt Chamberlain, Phi vs Syr	3/22/62	22-12—56
Michael Jordan, Chi at Mia	4/29/92	20-16—56
Charles Barkley, Pho vs G.St.	5/4/94	23- 7—56
Rick Barry, SF vs Phi	4/18/67	22-11—55
Michael Jordan, Chi vs Cle	5/1/88	24- 7—55
Michael Jordan, Chi vs Pho	4/16/93	21-13—55

*Double overtime.

Field Goals

	Date	FG	Att
Wilt Chamberlain, Phi vs Syr	3/14/60	24	42
John Havlicek, Bos vs Atl	4/1/73	24	36
Michael Jordan, Chi vs Cle	5/1/88	24	45

Seven tied with 22 each.

Appearances in NBA Finals

Standings of all NBA teams that have reached the NBA Finals since 1947.

App		Titles	Last Won
24	Minneapolis-LA Lakers	11	1988
19	Boston Celtics	16	1986
8	Syracuse Nats-Phila. 76ers	3	1983
7	New York Knicks	2	1973
6	Phila-SF-Golden St. Warriors	3	1975
5	Ft. Wayne-Detroit Pistons	2	1990
4	Houston Rockets	2	1995
4	St. Louis Hawks	1	1958
4	Baltimore-Washington Bullets	1	1978
4	Chicago Bulls	4	1996
3	Portland Trail Blazers	1	1977
2	Milwaukee Bucks	1	1971
3	Seattle SuperSonics	1	1979
2	Phoenix Suns	0	—
1	Baltimore Bullets	1	1948
1	Chicago Stags	0	—
1	Orlando Magic	0	—
1	Rochester Royals	0	—
1	Washington Capitols	0	—

Change of address: The St. Louis Hawks now play in Atlanta and the Rochester Royals are now the Sacramento Kings.

Teams now defunct: Baltimore Bullets (1947-55), Chicago Stags (1946-50) and Washington Capitols (1946-51).

Miscellaneous

3-Pt Field Goals

	Date	No
Dan Majerle, Pho vs Sea	6/1/93	8

Nine tied with 7 each.

Assists

	Date	No
Magic Johnson, LA vs Pho	5/15/84	24
John Stockton, Utah at LA Lakers	5/17/88	24
Magic Johnson, LA Lakers at Port	5/3/85	23
John Stockton, Utah vs Port	4/25/96	23
Doc Rivers, Atl vs Bos	5/16/88	22

Four tied with 21 each.

Rebounds

	Date	No
Wilt Chamberlain, Phi vs Bos	4/5/67	41
Bill Russell, Bos vs Phi	3/23/58	40
Bill Russell, Bos vs St.L	3/29/60	40
Bill Russell, Bos vs LA*	4/18/62	40

Three tied with 39 each.

*Overtime.

NBA FINALS

Points

Series		Year	Pts
4-Gm	Hakeem Olajuwon, Hou vs Orl	1995	131
5-Gm	Jerry West, LA vs Bos	1965	169
6-Gm	Michael Jordan, Chi vs Pho	1993	246
7-Gm	Elgin Baylor, LA vs Bos	1962	284

Field Goals

Series		Year	No
4-Gm	Hakeem Olajuwon, Hou vs Orl	1995	56
5-Gm	Michael Jordan, Chi vs LAL	1991	63
6-Gm	Michael Jordan, Chi vs Pho	1993	101
7-Gm	Elgin Baylor, LA vs Bos	1962	101

Assists

Series		Year	No
4-Gm	Bob Cousy, Bos vs Mpls	1959	51
5-Gm	Magic Johnson, LAL vs Chi	1991	62
6-Gm	Magic Johnson, LAL vs Bos	1985	84
7-Gm	Magic Johnson, LA vs Bos	1984	95

Rebounds

Series		Year	No
4-Gm	Bill Russell, Bos vs Mpls	1959	118
5-Gm	Bill Russell, Bos vs St.L	1961	144
6-Gm	Wilt Chamberlain, Phi vs SF	1967	171
7-Gm	Bill Russell, Bos vs LA	1962	189

The National Basketball League

Formed in 1937 by three corporations— General Electric and the Firestone and Goodyear rubber companies of Akron, Ohio— who were interested in moving up from their midwestern industrial league origins and backing a fully professional league. The NBL started with 13 previously independent teams in 1937-38 and although GE, Firestone and Goodyear were gone by late 1942, ran 12 years before merging with the three-year-old Basketball Association of America in 1949 to form the NBA.

Multiple champions: Akron Firestone Non-Skids, Fort Wayne Zollner Pistons, Oshkosh All-Stars (2).

Year	Winner	Series	Loser	Year	Winner	Series	Loser
1938	Goodyear Wingfoots	2-1	Oshkosh All-Stars	1944	Ft. Wayne Pistons	3-0	Sheboygan Redskins
1939	Firestone Non-Skids	3-2	Oshkosh All-Stars	1945	Ft. Wayne Pistons	3-2	Sheboygan Redskins
1940	Firestone Non-Skids	3-2	Oshkosh All-Stars	1946	Rochester Royals	3-0	Sheboygan Redskins
1941	Oshkosh All-Stars	3-0	Sheboygan Redskins	1947	Chicago Gears	3-2	Rochester Royals
1942	Oshkosh All-Stars	2-1	Ft. Wayne Pistons	1948	Minneapolis Lakers	3-1	Rochester Royals
1943	Sheboygan Redskins	2-1	Ft. Wayne Pistons	1949	Anderson Packers	3-0	Oshkosh All-Stars

NBA All-Star Game

The NBA staged its first All-Star Game before 10,094 at Boston Garden on March 2, 1951. From that year on, the game has matched the best players in the East against the best in the West. Winning coaches are listed first. East leads series, 29-16.

Multiple MVP winners: Bob Pettit (4); Oscar Robertson (3); Bob Cousy, Julius Erving, Magic Johnson, Michael Jordan, Karl Malone and Isiah Thomas (2).

Year		Host	Coaches	Most Valuable Player
1951	East 111, West 94	Boston	Joe Lapchick, John Kundla	Ed Macauley, Boston
1952	East 108, West 91	Boston	Al Cervi, John Kundla	Paul Arizin, Philadelphia
1953	West 79, East 75	Ft. Wayne	John Kundla, Joe Lapchick	George Mikan, Minneapolis
1954	East 98, West 93 (OT)	New York	Joe Lapchick, John Kundla	Bob Cousy, Boston
1955	East 100, West 91	New York	Al Cervi, Charley Eckman	Bill Sharman, Boston
1956	West 108, East 94	Rochester	Charley Eckman, George Senesky	Bob Pettit, St. Louis
1957	East 109, West 97	Boston	Red Auerbach, Bobby Wanzer	Bob Cousy, Boston
1958	East 130, West 118	St. Louis	Red Auerbach, Alex Hannum	Bob Pettit, St. Louis
1959	West 124, East 108	Detroit	Ed Macauley, Red Auerbach	Bob Pettit, St. Louis & Elgin Baylor, Minneapolis
1960	East 125, West 115	Philadelphia	Red Auerbach, Ed Macauley	Wilt Chamberlain, Philadelphia
1961	West 153, East 131	Syracuse	Paul Seymour, Red Auerbach	Oscar Robertson, Cincinnati
1962	West 150, East 130	St. Louis	Fred Schaus, Red Auerbach	Bob Pettit, St. Louis
1963	East 115, West 108	Los Angeles	Red Auerbach, Fred Schaus	Bill Russell, Boston
1964	East 111, West 107	Boston	Red Auerbach, Fred Schaus	Oscar Robertson, Cincinnati
1965	East 124, West 123	St. Louis	Red Auerbach, Alex Hannum	Jerry Lucas, Cincinnati
1966	East 137, West 94	Cincinnati	Red Auerbach, Fred Schaus	Adrian Smith, Cincinnati
1967	West 135, East 120	San Francisco	Fred Schaus, Red Auerbach	Rick Barry, San Francisco
1968	East 144, West 124	New York	Alex Hannum, Bill Sharman	Hal Greer, Philadelphia
1969	East 123, West 112	Baltimore	Gene Shue, Richie Guerin	Oscar Robertson, Cincinnati
1970	East 142, West 135	Philadelphia	Red Holzman, Richie Guerin	Willis Reed, New York
1971	West 108, East 107	San Diego	Larry Costello, Red Holzman	Lenny Wilkens, Seattle
1972	West 112, East 110	Los Angeles	Bill Sharman, Tom Heinsohn	Jerry West, Los Angeles
1973	East 104, West 84	Chicago	Tom Heinsohn, Bill Sharman	Dave Cowens, Boston
1974	West 134, East 123	Seattle	Larry Costello, Tom Heinsohn	Bob Lanier, Detroit
1975	East 108, West 102	Phoenix	K.C. Jones, Al Attles	Walt Frazier, New York
1976	East 123, West 109	Philadelphia	Tom Heinsohn, Al Attles	Dave Bing, Washington
1977	West 125, East 124	Milwaukee	Larry Brown, Gene Shue	Julius Erving, Philadelphia
1978	East 133, West 125	Atlanta	Billy Cunningham, Jack Ramsay	Randy Smith, Buffalo
1979	West 134, East 129	Detroit	Lenny Wilkens, Dick Motta	David Thompson, Denver
1980	East 144, West 136 (OT)	Washington	Billy Cunningham, Lenny Wilkens	George Gervin, San Antonio
1981	East 123, West 120	Cleveland	Billy Cunningham, John MacLeod	Nate Archibald, Boston
1982	East 120, West 118	New Jersey	Bill Fitch, Pat Riley	Larry Bird, Boston
1983	East 132, West 123	Los Angeles	Billy Cunningham, Pat Riley	Julius Erving, Philadelphia
1984	East 154, West 145 (OT)	Denver	K.C. Jones, Frank Layden	Isiah Thomas, Detroit
1985	West 140, East 129	Indiana	Pat Riley, K.C. Jones	Ralph Sampson, Houston
1986	East 139, West 132	Dallas	K.C. Jones, Pat Riley	Isiah Thomas, Detroit
1987	West 154, East 149 (OT)	Seattle	Pat Riley, K.C. Jones	Tom Chambers, Seattle
1988	East 138, West 133	Chicago	Mike Fratello, Pat Riley	Michael Jordan, Chicago
1989	West 143, East 134	Houston	Pat Riley, Lenny Wilkens	Karl Malone, Utah
1990	East 130, West 113	Miami	Chuck Daly, Pat Riley	Magic Johnson, LA Lakers
1991	East 116, West 114	Charlotte	Chris Ford, Rick Adelman	Charles Barkley, Philadelphia
1992	West 153, East 113	Orlando	Don Nelson, Phil Jackson	Magic Johnson, LA Lakers
1993	West 135, East 132 (OT)	Salt Lake City	Paul Westphal, Pat Riley	Karl Malone, Utah & John Stockton, Utah
1994	East 127, West 118	Minneapolis	Lenny Wilkens, George Karl	Scottie Pippen, Chicago
1995	West 139, East 112	Phoenix	Paul Westphal, Brian Hill	Mitch Richmond, Sacramento
1996	East 129, West 118	San Antonio	Phil Jackson, George Karl	Michael Jordan, Chicago

NBA Franchise Origins

Here is what the current 29 teams in the National Basketball Association have to show for the years they have put in as members of the National Basketball League (NBL), Basketball Association of America (BAA), the NBA, and the American Basketball Association (ABA). League titles are noted by year won.

Western Conference

	First Season		League Titles	Franchise Stops
Dallas Mavericks	1980-81	(NBA)	None	•Dallas (1980—)
Denver Nuggets	1967-68	(ABA)	None	•Denver (1967—)
Golden St. Warriors	1946-47	(BAA)	1 BAA (1947) 2 NBA (1956,75)	•Philadelphia (1946-62) San Francisco (1962-71) Oakland (1971—)
Houston Rockets	1967-68	(NBA)	2 NBA (1994,95)	•San Diego (1967-71) Houston (1971—)
Los Angeles Clippers	1970-71	(NBA)	None	•Buffalo (1970-78) San Diego (1978-84) Los Angeles (1984—)
Los Angeles Lakers	1947-48	(NBL)	1 NBL (1947) 1 BAA (1949) 10 NBA (1950,52-54,72, 80,82,85,87-88)	•Minneapolis (1947-60) Los Angeles (1960-67) Inglewood, CA (1967—)
Minnesota Timberwolves	1989-90	(NBA)	None	•Minneapolis (1989—)
Phoenix Suns	1968-69	(NBA)	None	•Phoenix (1968—)
Portland Trail Blazers	1970-71	(NBA)	1 NBA (1977)	•Portland (1970—)
Sacramento Kings	1945-46	(NBL)	1 NBL (1946) 1 NBA (1951)	•Rochester, NY (1945-58) Cincinnati (1958-72) KC-Omaha (1972-75) Kansas City (1975-85) Sacramento (1985—)
San Antonio Spurs	1967-68	(ABA)	None	•Dallas (1967-73) San Antonio (1973—)
Seattle SuperSonics	1967-68	(NBA)	1 NBA (1979)	•Seattle (1967—)
Utah Jazz	1974-75	(NBA)	None	•New Orleans (1974-79) Salt Lake City (1979—)
Vancouver Grizzlies	1995-96	(NBA)	None	•Vancouver (1995—)

Eastern Conference

	First Season		League Titles	Franchise Stops
Atlanta Hawks	1946-47	(NBL)	1 NBA (1958)	•Tri-Cities (1946-51) Milwaukee (1951-55) St. Louis (1955-68) Atlanta (1968—)
Boston Celtics	1946-47	(BAA)	16 NBA (1957,59-66,68-69 74,76,81,84,86)	•Boston (1946—)
Charlotte Hornets	1988-89	(NBA)	None	•Charlotte (1988—)
Chicago Bulls	1966-67	(NBA)	4 NBA (1991-93, 96)	•Chicago (1966—)
Cleveland Cavaliers	1970-71	(NBA)	None	•Cleveland (1970-74) Richfield, OH (1974-94) Cleveland (1994—)
Detroit Pistons	1941-42	(NBL)	2 NBL (1944-45) 2 NBA (1989-90)	•Ft. Wayne, IN (1941-57) Detroit (1957-78) Pontiac, MI (1978-88) Auburn Hills, MI (1988—)
Indiana Pacers	1967-68	(ABA)	3 ABA (1970,72-73)	•Indianapolis (1967—)
Miami Heat	1988-89	(NBA)	None	•Miami (1988—)
Milwaukee Bucks	1968-69	(NBA)	1 NBA (1971)	•Milwaukee (1968—)
New Jersey Nets	1967-68	(ABA)	2 ABA (1974,76)	•Teaneck, NJ (1967-68) Commack, NY (1968-69) W. Hempstead, NY (1969-71) Uniondale, NY (1971-77) Piscataway, NJ (1977-81) E. Rutherford, NJ (1981—)
New York Knicks	1946-47	(BAA)	2 NBA (1970,73)	•New York (1946—)
Orlando Magic	1989-90	(NBA)	None	•Orlando, FL (1989—)
Philadelphia 76ers	1949-50	(NBA)	3 NBA (1955,67,83)	•Syracuse, NY (1949-63) Philadelphia (1963—)
Toronto Raptors	1995-96	(NBA)	None	•Toronto (1995—)
Washington Bullets	1961-62	(NBA)	1 NBA (1978)	•Chicago (1961-63) Baltimore (1963-73) Landover, MD (1973—)

Note: The Tri-Cities Blackhawks represented Moline and Rock Island, Ill., and Davenport, Iowa.

The Growth of the NBA

Of the 11 franchises that comprised the Basketball Association of America (BAA) at the start of the 1946-47 season, only three remain—the Boston Celtics, New York Knickerbockers and Golden State Warriors (originally Philadelphia Warriors).

Just before the start of the 1948-49 season, four teams from the more established **National Basketball League** (NBL)—the Ft. Wayne Pistons (now Detroit), Indianapolis Jets, Minneapolis Lakers (now Los Angeles) and Rochester Royals (now Sacramento Kings)—joined the BAA.

A year later, the six remaining NBL franchises—Anderson (Ind.), Denver, Sheboygan (Wisc.), the Syracuse Nationals (now Philadelphia 76ers), Tri-Cities Blackhawks (now Atlanta Hawks) and Waterloo (Iowa)—joined along with the new Indianapolis Olympians and the BAA became the 17-team **National Basketball Association**.

The NBA was down to 10 teams by the 1950-51 season and slipped to eight by 1954-55 with Boston, New York, Philadelphia and Syracuse in the Eastern Division, and Ft. Wayne, Milwaukee (formerly Tri-Cities), Minneapolis and Rochester in the West.

By 1960, five of those surviving eight teams had moved to other cities but by the end of the decade the NBA was a 14-team league. It also had a rival, the **American Basketball Association**, which began play in 1967 with a red, white and blue ball, a three-point line and 11 teams. After a nine-year run, the ABA merged four clubs—the Denver Nuggets, Indiana Pacers, New York Nets and San Antonio Spurs—with the NBA following the 1975-76 season. The NBA adopted the three-point play in 1979-80.

Expansion/Merger Timetable

For teams currently in NBA.

1948—Added NBL's Ft. Wayne Pistons (now Detroit), Minneapolis Lakers (now Los Angeles) and Rochester Royals (now Sacramento Kings); **1949**—Syracuse Nationals (now Philadelphia 76ers) and Tri-Cities Blackhawks (now Atlanta Hawks).

1961—Chicago Packers (now Washington Bullets); **1966**—Chicago Bulls; **1967**—San Diego Rockets (now Houston) and Seattle SuperSonics; **1968**—Milwaukee Bucks and Phoenix Suns.

1970—Buffalo Braves (now Los Angeles Clippers), Cleveland Cavaliers and Portland Trail Blazers; **1974**—New Orleans Jazz (now Utah); **1976**—added ABA's Denver Nuggets, Indiana Pacers, New York Nets (now New Jersey) and San Antonio Spurs.

1980—Dallas Mavericks; **1988**—Charlotte Hornets and Miami Heat; **1989**—Minnesota Timberwolves and Orlando Magic.

1995—Toronto Raptors and Vancouver Grizzlies.

City and Nickname Changes

1951—Tri-Cities Blackhawks, who divided home games between Moline and Rock Island, Ill., and Davenport, Iowa, move to Milwaukee and become the Hawks; **1955**—Milwaukee Hawks move to St. Louis; **1957**—Ft. Wayne Pistons move to Detroit, while Rochester Royals move to Cincinnati.

1960—Minneapolis Lakers move to Los Angeles; **1962**—Chicago Packers renamed Zephyrs, while Philadelphia Warriors move to San Francisco; **1963**—Chicago Zephyrs move to Baltimore and become Bullets, while Syracuse Nationals move to Philadelphia and become 76ers; **1968**—St. Louis Hawks move to Atlanta.

1971—San Diego Rockets move to Houston, while San Francisco Warriors move to Oakland and become Golden State Warriors; **1972**—Cincinnati Royals move to Midwest, divide home games between Kansas City, Mo., and Omaha, Neb., and become Kings; **1973**—Baltimore Bullets move to Landover, Md., outside Washington and become Capital Bullets; **1974**—Capital Bullets renamed Washington Bullets; **1975**—KC-Omaha Kings settle in Kansas City; **1977**—New York Nets move from Uniondale, N.Y., to Piscataway, N.J. (later East Rutherford) and become New Jersey Nets; **1978**—Buffalo Braves move to San Diego and become Clippers. **1979**—New Orleans Jazz move to Salt Lake City and become Utah Jazz;

1984—San Diego Clippers move to Los Angeles; **1985**—Kansas City Kings move to Sacramento. **1997**—Washington Bullets to become Washington Wizards.

Defunct NBA Teams

Teams that once played in the BAA and NBA, but no longer exist.

Anderson (Ind.)—Packers (1949-50); **Baltimore**—Bullets (1947-55); **Chicago**—Stags (1946-50); **Cleveland**—Rebels (1946-47); **Denver**—Nuggets (1949-50); **Detroit**—Falcons (1946-47); **Indianapolis**—Jets (1948-49) and Olympians (1949-53). **Pittsburgh**—Ironmen (1946-47); **Providence**—Steamrollers (1946-49); **St. Louis**—Bombers (1946-50); **Sheboygan (Wisc.)**—Redskins (1949-50); **Toronto**—Huskies (1946-47); **Washington**—Capitols (1946-51); **Waterloo (Iowa)**—Hawks (1949-50).

ABA Teams (1967-76)

Anaheim—Amigos (1967-68, moved to LA); **Baltimore**—Claws (1975, never played); **Carolina**—Cougars (1969-74, moved to St. Louis); **Dallas**—Chaparrals (1967-73, called Texas Chaparrals in 1970-71, moved to San Antonio); **Denver**—Rockets (1967-76, renamed Nuggets in 1974-76); **Miami**—Floridians (1968-72, called simply Floridians from 1970-72).

Houston—Mavericks (1967-69, moved to North Carolina); **Indiana**—Pacers (1967-76); **Kentucky**—Colonels (1967-76); **Los Angeles**—Stars (1968-70, moved to Utah); **Memphis**—Pros (1970-75, renamed Tams in 1972 and Sounds in 1974, moved to Baltimore); **Minnesota**—Muskies (1967-68, moved to Miami) and Pipers (1968-69, moved back to Pittsburgh); **New Jersey**—Americans (1967-68, moved to New York).

New Orleans—Buccaneers (1967-70, moved to Memphis); **New York**—Nets (1968-76); **Oakland**—Oaks (1967-69, moved to Washington); **Pittsburgh**—Pipers (1967-68, moved to Minnesota), Pipers (1969-72, renamed Condors in 1970); **St. Louis**—Spirits of St. Louis (1974-76); **San Antonio**—Spurs (1973-76); **San Diego**—Conquistadors (1972-75, renamed Sails in 1975); **Utah**—Stars (1970-75); **Virginia**—Squires (1970-76); **Washington**—Caps (1969-70, moved to Virginia).

Annual NBA Leaders

Scoring

Decided by total points from 1947-69, and per game average since 1970.

Multiple winners: Michael Jordan (8); Wilt Chamberlain (7); George Gervin (4); Neil Johnston, Bob McAdoo and George Mikan (3); Kareem Abdul-Jabbar, Paul Arizin, Adrian Dantley and Bob Pettit (2).

Year		Gm	Pts	Avg
1947	Joe Fulks, Phi	60	1389	23.2
1948	Max Zaslofsky, Chi	48	1007	21.0
1949	George Mikan, Mpls	60	1698	28.3
1950	George Mikan, Mpls	68	1865	27.4
1951	George Mikan, Mpls	68	1932	28.4
1952	Paul Arizin, Phi	66	1674	25.4
1953	Neil Johnston, Phi	70	1564	22.3
1954	Neil Johnston, Phi	72	1759	24.4
1955	Neil Johnston, Phi	72	1631	22.7
1956	Bob Pettit, St.L	72	1849	25.7
1957	Paul Arizin, Phi	71	1817	25.6
1958	George Yardley, Det	72	2001	27.8
1959	Bob Pettit, St.L	72	2105	29.2
1960	Wilt Chamberlain, Phi	72	2707	37.6
1961	Wilt Chamberlain, Phi	79	3033	38.4
1962	Wilt Chamberlain, Phi	80	4029	50.4
1963	Wilt Chamberlain, SF	80	3586	44.8
1964	Wilt Chamberlain, SF	80	2948	36.9
1965	Wilt Chamberlain, SF-Phi	73	2534	34.7
1966	Wilt Chamberlain, Phi	79	2649	33.5
1967	Rick Barry, SF	78	2775	35.6
1968	Dave Bing, Det	79	2142	27.1
1969	Elvin Hayes, SD	82	2327	28.4
1970	Jerry West, LA	74	2309	31.2
1971	Lew Alcindor, Mil	82	2596	31.7
1972	Kareem Abdul-Jabbar, Mil	81	2822	34.8
1973	Nate Archibald, KC-Omaha	80	2719	34.0
1974	Bob McAdoo, Buf	74	2261	30.6
1975	Bob McAdoo, Buf	82	2831	34.5
1976	Bob McAdoo, Buf	78	2427	31.1
1977	Pete Maravich, NO	73	2273	31.1
1978	George Gervin, SA	82	2232	27.2
1979	George Gervin, SA	80	2365	29.6
1980	George Gervin, SA	78	2585	33.1
1981	Adrian Dantley, Utah	80	2452	30.7
1982	George Gervin, SA	79	2551	32.3
1983	Alex English, Den	82	2326	28.4
1984	Adrian Dantley, Utah	79	2418	30.6
1985	Bernard King, NY	55	1809	32.9
1986	Dominique Wilkins, Atl	78	2366	30.3
1987	Michael Jordan, Chi	82	3041	37.1
1988	Michael Jordan, Chi	82	2868	35.0
1989	Michael Jordan, Chi	81	2633	32.5
1990	Michael Jordan, Chi	82	2753	33.6
1991	Michael Jordan, Chi	82	2580	31.5
1992	Michael Jordan, Chi	80	2404	30.1
1993	Michael Jordan, Chi	78	2541	32.6
1994	David Robinson, SA	80	2383	29.8
1995	Shaquille O'Neal, Orl	79	2315	29.3
1996	Michael Jordan, Chi	82	2491	30.4

Note: Lew Alcindor changed his name to Kareem Abdul-Jabbar after the 1970-71 season.

Rebounds

Decided by total rebounds from 1951-69 and per game average since 1970.

Multiple winners: Wilt Chamberlain (11); Moses Malone (6); Dennis Rodman (5); Bill Russell (4); Elvin Hayes and Hakeem Olajuwon (2).

Year		Gm	No	Avg
1951	Dolph Schayes, Syr	66	1080	16.4
1952	Larry Foust, Ft. Wayne	66	880	13.3
	& Mel Hutchins, Mil	66	880	13.3
1953	George Mikan, Mpls	70	1007	14.4
1954	Harry Gallatin, NY	72	1098	15.3
1955	Neil Johnston, Phi	72	1085	15.1
1956	Bob Pettit, St.L	72	1164	16.2
1957	Maurice Stokes, Roch	72	1256	17.4
1958	Bill Russell, Bos	69	1564	22.7
1959	Bill Russell, Bos	70	1612	23.0
1960	Wilt Chamberlain, Phi	72	1941	27.0
1961	Wilt Chamberlain, Phi	79	2149	27.2
1962	Wilt Chamberlain, Phi	80	2052	25.7
1963	Wilt Chamberlain, SF	80	1946	24.3
1964	Bill Russell, Bos	78	1930	24.7
1965	Bill Russell, Bos	78	1878	24.1
1966	Wilt Chamberlain, Phi	79	1943	24.6
1967	Wilt Chamberlain, Phi	81	1957	24.2
1968	Wilt Chamberlain, Phi	82	1952	23.8
1969	Wilt Chamberlain, LA	81	1712	21.1
1970	Elvin Hayes, SD	82	1386	16.9
1971	Wilt Chamberlain, LA	82	1493	18.2
1972	Wilt Chamberlain, LA	82	1572	19.2
1973	Wilt Chamberlain, LA	82	1526	18.6
1974	Elvin Hayes, Cap*	81	1463	18.1
1975	Wes Unseld, Wash	73	1077	14.8
1976	Kareem Abdul-Jabbar, LA	82	1383	16.9
1977	Bill Walton, Port	65	934	14.4
1978	Len Robinson, NO	82	1288	15.7
1979	Moses Malone, Hou	82	1444	17.6
1980	Swen Nater, SD	81	1216	15.0
1981	Moses Malone, Hou	80	1180	14.8
1982	Moses Malone, Hou	81	1188	14.7
1983	Moses Malone, Phi	78	1194	15.3
1984	Moses Malone, Phi	71	950	13.4
1985	Moses Malone, Phi	79	1031	13.1
1986	Bill Laimbeer, Det	82	1075	13.1
1987	Charles Barkley, Phi	68	994	14.6
1988	Michael Cage, LA Clippers	72	938	13.0
1989	Hakeem Olajuwon, Hou	82	1105	13.5
1990	Hakeem Olajuwon, Hou	82	1149	14.0
1991	David Robinson, SA	82	1063	13.0
1992	Dennis Rodman, Det	82	1530	18.7
1993	Dennis Rodman, Det	62	1232	18.3
1994	Dennis Rodman, SA	79	1132	17.3
1995	Dennis Rodman, SA	49	823	16.8
1996	Dennis Rodman, Chi	64	952	14.9

*The Baltimore Bullets moved to Landover, MD in 1973-74 and became first the Capital Bullets, then the Washington Bullets in 1974-75.

Assists

Decided by total assists from 1952-69 and per game average since 1970.

Multiple winners: John Stockton (9); Bob Cousy (8); Oscar Robertson (6); Magic Johnson and Kevin Porter (4); Andy Phillip and Guy Rodgers (2).

Year		No
1947	Ernie Calverley, Prov	202
1948	Howie Dallmar, Phi	120
1949	Bob Davies, Roch	321
1950	Dick McGuire, NY	386
1951	Andy Phillip, Phi	414
1952	Andy Phillip, Phi	539
1953	Bob Cousy, Bos	547
1954	Bob Cousy, Bos	518
1955	Bob Cousy, Bos	557
1956	Bob Cousy, Bos	642
1957	Bob Cousy, Bos	478
1958	Bob Cousy, Bos	463
1959	Bob Cousy, Bos	557
1960	Bob Cousy, Bos	715
1961	Oscar Robertson, Cin	690
1962	Oscar Robertson, Cin	899
1963	Guy Rodgers, SF	825
1964	Oscar Robertson, Cin	868
1965	Oscar Robertson, Cin	861
1966	Oscar Robertson, Cin	847
1967	Guy Rodgers, Chi	908
1968	Wilt Chamberlain, Phi	702
1969	Oscar Robertson, Cin	772

Year		Avg
1970	Lenny Wilkens, Sea	9.1
1971	Norm Van Lier, Chi	10.1
1972	Jerry West, LA	9.7
1973	Nate Archibald, KC-O	11.4
1974	Ernie DiGregorio, Buf	8.2
1975	Kevin Porter, Wash	8.0
1976	Slick Watts, Sea	8.1
1977	Don Buse, Ind	8.5
1978	Kevin Porter, Det-NJ	10.2
1979	Kevin Porter, Det	13.4
1980	M.R. Richardson, NY	10.1
1981	Kevin Porter, Wash	9.1
1982	Johnny Moore, SA	9.6
1983	Magic Johnson, LA	10.5
1984	Magic Johnson, LA	13.1
1985	Isiah Thomas, Det	13.9
1986	Magic Johnson, Lakers	12.6
1987	Magic Johnson, Lakers	12.2
1988	John Stockton, Utah	13.8
1989	John Stockton, Utah	13.6
1990	John Stockton, Utah	14.5
1991	John Stockton, Utah	14.2
1992	John Stockton, Utah	13.7
1993	John Stockton, Utah	12.0
1994	John Stockton, Utah	12.6
1995	John Stockton, Utah	12.3
1996	John Stockton, Utah	11.2

Field Goal Percentage

Multiple winners: Wilt Chamberlain (9); Artis Gilmore (4); Neil Johnston (3); Bob Feerick, Johnny Green, Alex Groza, Cedric Maxwell, Kevin McHale, Ken Sears and Buck Williams (2).

Year		Pct
1947	Bob Feerick, Wash	.401
1948	Bob Feerick, Wash	.340
1949	Arnie Risen, Roch	.423
1950	Alex Groza, Indpls	.478
1951	Alex Groza, Indpls	.470
1952	Paul Arizin, Phi	.448
1953	Neil Johnston, Phi	.452
1954	Ed Macauley, Bos	.486
1955	Larry Foust, Ft.W	.487
1956	Neil Johnston, Phi.	.457
1957	Neil Johnston, Phi.	.447
1958	Jack Twyman, Cin	.452
1959	Ken Sears, NY	.490
1960	Ken Sears, NY	.477
1961	Wilt Chamberlain, Phi	.509
1962	Walt Bellamy, Chi	.519
1963	Wilt Chamberlain, SF	.528
1964	Jerry Lucas, Cin	.527
1965	W.Chamberlain, SF-Phi	.510
1966	Wilt Chamberlain, Phi	.540
1967	Wilt Chamberlain, Phi	.683
1968	Wilt Chamberlain, Phi	.595
1969	Wilt Chamberlain, LA	.583
1970	Johnny Green, Cin	.559
1971	Johnny Green, Cin	.587
1972	Wilt Chamberlain, LA	.649
1973	Wilt Chamberlain, LA	.727
1974	Bob McAdoo, Buf	.547
1975	Don Nelson, Bos	.539
1976	Wes Unseld, Wash	.561
1977	K. Abdul-Jabbar, LA	.579
1978	Bobby Jones, Den	.578
1979	Cedric Maxwell, Bos	.584
1980	Cedric Maxwell, Bos	.609
1981	Artis Gilmore, Chi.	.670
1982	Artis Gilmore, Chi.	.652
1983	Artis Gilmore, SA	.626
1984	Artis Gilmore, SA	.631
1985	James Donaldson, LAC	.637
1986	Steve Johnson, SA	.632
1987	Kevin McHale, Bos	.604
1988	Kevin McHale, Bos	.604
1989	Dennis Rodman, Det.	.595
1990	Mark West, Pho	.625
1991	Buck Williams, Port	.602
1992	Buck Williams, Port	.604
1993	Cedric Ceballos, Pho	.576
1994	Shaquille O'Neal, Orl	.599
1995	Chris Gatling, G.St	.633
1996	Gheorghe Muresan, Wash	.584

Free Throw Percentage

Multiple winners: Bill Sharman (7); Rick Barry (6); Larry Bird (4); Dolph Schayes (3); Mahmoud Abdul-Rauf, Larry Costello, Ernie DiGregorio, Bob Feerick, Kyle Macy, Calvin Murphy, Mark Price, Oscar Robertson and Larry Siegfried (2).

Year		Pct
1947	Fred Scolari, Wash	.811
1948	Bob Feerick, Wash	.788
1949	Bob Feerick, Wash	.859
1950	Max Zaslofsky, Chi	.843
1951	Joe Fulks, Phi	.855
1952	Bob Wanzer, Roch	.904
1953	Bill Sharman, Bos	.850
1954	Bill Sharman, Bos	.844
1955	Bill Sharman, Bos	.897
1956	Bill Sharman, Bos	.867
1957	Bill Sharman, Bos	.905
1958	Dolph Schayes, Syr	.904
1959	Bill Sharman, Bos	.932
1960	Dolph Schayes, Syr	.892
1961	Bill Sharman, Bos	.921
1962	Dolph Schayes, Syr	.896
1963	Larry Costello, Syr	.881
1964	Oscar Robertson, Cin	.853
1965	Larry Costello, Phi	.877
1966	Larry Siegfried, Bos	.881
1967	Adrian Smith, Cin	.903
1968	Oscar Robertson, Cin	.873
1969	Larry Siegfried, NY	.864
1970	Flynn Robinson, Mil	.898
1971	Chet Walker, Chi	.859
1972	Jack Marin, Bal	.894
1973	Rick Barry, G.St.	.902
1974	Ernie DiGregorio, Buf	.902
1975	Rick Barry, G.St.	.904
1976	Rick Barry, G.St.	.923
1977	Ernie DiGregorio, Buf	.945
1978	Rick Barry, G.St.	.924
1979	Rick Barry, Hou	.947
1980	Rick Barry, Hou	.935
1981	Calvin Murphy, Hou	.958
1982	Kyle Macy, Pho	.899
1983	Calvin Murphy, Hou	.920
1984	Larry Bird, Bos	.888
1985	Kyle Macy, Pho	.907
1986	Larry Bird, Bos	.896
1987	Larry Bird, Bos	.910
1988	Jack Sikma, Mil	.922
1989	Magic Johnson, LAL	.911
1990	Larry Bird, Bos	.930
1991	Reggie Miller, Ind	.918
1992	Mark Price, Cle	.947
1993	Mark Price, Cle	.948
1994	M. Abdul-Rauf, Den	.956
1995	Spud Webb, Sac	.934
1996	M. Abdul-Rauf, Den	.930

Annual NBA Leaders (Cont.)

Blocked Shots

Decided by per game average since 1973-74 season.

Multiple winners: Kareem Abdul-Jabbar and Mark Eaton (4); George Johnson, Dikembe Mutombo and Hakeem Olajuwon (3); Manute Bol (2).

Year		Gm	No	Avg
1974	Elmore Smith, LA	81	393	4.85
1975	Kareem Abdul-Jabbar, Mil	65	212	3.26
1976	Kareem Abdul-Jabbar, LA	82	338	4.12
1977	Bill Walton, Port	65	211	3.25
1978	George Johnson, NJ	81	274	3.38
1979	Kareem Abdul-Jabbar, LA	80	316	3.95
1980	Kareem Abdul-Jabbar, LA	82	280	3.41
1981	George Johnson, SA	82	278	3.39
1982	George Johnson, SA	75	234	3.12
1983	Tree Rollins, Atl	80	343	4.29
1984	Mark Eaton, Utah	82	351	4.28
1985	Mark Eaton, Utah	82	456	5.56
1986	Manute Bol, Wash	80	397	4.96
1987	Mark Eaton, Utah	79	321	4.06
1988	Mark Eaton, Utah	82	304	3.71
1989	Manute Bol, G.St.	80	345	4.31
1990	Akeem Olajuwon, Hou	82	376	4.59
1991	Hakeem Olajuwon, Hou	56	221	3.95
1992	David Robinson, SA	68	305	4.49
1993	Hakeem Olajuwon, Hou	82	342	4.17
1994	Dikembe Mutombo, Den	82	336	4.10
1995	Dikembe Mutombo, Den	82	321	3.91
1996	Dikembe Mutombo, Den	74	332	4.49

Steals

Decided by per game average since 1973-74 season.

Multiple winners: Michael Jordan, Micheal Ray Richardson and Alvin Robertson (3); Magic Johnson and John Stockton (2).

Year		Gm	No	Avg
1974	Larry Steele, Port	81	217	2.68
1975	Rick Barry, G.St.	80	228	2.85
1976	Slick Watts, Sea	82	261	3.18
1977	Don Buse, Ind	81	281	3.47
1978	Ron Lee, Pho	82	225	2.74
1979	M.L. Carr, Det	80	197	2.46
1980	Micheal Ray Richardson, NY	82	265	3.23
1981	Magic Johnson, LA	37	127	3.43
1982	Magic Johnson, LA	78	208	2.67
1983	Micheal Ray Richardson, G.St-NJ	64	182	2.84
1984	Rickey Green, Utah	81	215	2.65
1985	Micheal Ray Richardson, NJ	82	243	2.96
1986	Alvin Robertson, SA	82	301	3.67
1987	Alvin Robertson, SA	81	260	3.21
1988	Michael Jordan, Chi	82	259	3.16
1989	John Stockton, Utah	82	263	3.21
1990	Michael Jordan, Chi	82	227	2.77
1991	Alvin Robertson, SA	81	246	3.04
1992	John Stockton, Utah	82	244	2.98
1993	Michael Jordan, Chi	78	221	2.83
1994	Nate McMillan, Sea	73	216	2.96
1995	Scottie Pippen, Chi	79	232	2.94
1996	Gary Payton, Sea	81	231	2.85

Note: Akeem Olajuwon changed the spelling of his first name to Hakeem during the 1990-91 season.

All-Time NBA Regular Season Leaders

Through the 1995-96 regular season.

CAREER

Players active in 1995-96 in **bold** type.

Points

		Yrs	Gm	Pts	Avg
1	Kareem Abdul-Jabbar	20	1560	38,387	24.6
2	Wilt Chamberlain	14	1045	31,419	30.1
3	Moses Malone	19	1329	27,409	20.6
4	Elvin Hayes	16	1303	27,313	21.0
5	Oscar Robertson	14	1040	26,710	25.7
6	John Havlicek	16	1270	26,395	20.8
7	Alex English	15	1193	25,613	21.5
8	Dominique Wilkins	13	984	25,389	25.8
9	Jerry West	14	932	25,192	27.0
10	**Michael Jordan**	11	766	24,489	32.0
11	**Karl Malone**	11	898	23,343	26.0
12	Adrian Dantley	15	955	23,177	24.3
13	**Robert Parish**	20	1568	23,173	14.8
14	Elgin Baylor	14	846	23,149	27.4
15	**Hakeem Olajuwon**	12	900	21,840	24.3
16	Larry Bird	13	897	21,791	24.3
17	Hal Greer	15	1122	21,586	19.2
18	Walt Bellamy	14	1043	20,941	20.1
19	Bob Pettit	11	792	20,880	26.4
20	**Charles Barkley**	12	890	20,740	23.3
21	George Gervin	10	791	20,708	26.2
22	Tom Chambers	14	1094	20,024	18.3
23	**Clyde Drexler**	13	954	19,794	20.7
24	**Patrick Ewing**	11	835	19,788	23.7
25	Bernard King	14	874	19,655	22.5
26	Walter Davis	15	1033	19,521	18.9
27	Dolph Schayes	16	1059	19,249	18.2
28	Bob Lanier	14	959	19,248	20.1
29	Gail Goodrich	14	1031	19,181	18.6
30	Reggie Theus	13	1026	19,015	18.5

Scoring Average

Minimum of 400 games or 10,000 points.

		Yrs	Gm	Pts	Avg
1	**Michael Jordan**	11	766	24,489	32.0
2	Wilt Chamberlain	14	1045	31,419	30.1
3	Elgin Baylor	14	846	23,149	27.4
4	Jerry West	14	932	25,192	27.0
5	Bob Pettit	11	792	20,880	26.4
6	George Gervin	10	791	20,708	26.2
7	**Karl Malone**	11	898	23,343	26.0
8	Dominique Wilkins	13	984	25,309	25.8
9	Oscar Robertson	14	1040	26,710	25.7
10	**David Robinson**	7	557	14,260	25.6
11	Kareem Abdul-Jabbar	20	1560	38,387	24.6
12	Larry Bird	13	897	21,791	24.3
13	**Hakeem Olajuwon**	12	900	21,840	24.3
14	Adrian Dantley	15	955	23,177	24.3
15	Pete Maravich	10	658	15,948	24.2
16	**Patrick Ewing**	11	835	19,788	23.7
17	**Charles Barkley**	12	890	20,740	23.3
18	Rick Barry	10	794	18,395	23.2
19	Paul Arizin	10	713	16,266	22.8
20	**Mitch Richmond**	8	600	13,653	22.8
21	George Mikan	9	520	11,764	22.6
22	Bernard King	14	874	19,655	22.5
23	David Thompson	8	509	11,264	22.1
24	Bob McAdoo	14	852	18,787	22.1
25	Julius Erving	11	836	18,364	22.0
26	Alex English	15	1193	25,613	21.5
27	**Chris Mullin**	11	708	14,977	21.2
28	Elvin Hayes	16	1303	27,313	21.0
29	Billy Cunningham	9	654	13,626	20.8
30	John Havlicek	16	1270	26,395	20.8

NBA-ABA Top 20

Points

All-Time combined regular season scoring leaders, including ABA service (1968-76). NBA players with ABA experience are listed in CAPITAL letters. Players active during 1995-96 are in **bold** type.

		Yrs	Pts	Avg
1	Kareem Abdul-Jabbar	20	38,387	24.6
2	Wilt Chamberlain	14	31,419	30.1
3	JULIUS ERVING	16	30,026	24.2
4	MOSES MALONE	21	29,580	20.3
5	DAN ISSEL	15	27,482	22.6
6	Elvin Hayes	16	27,313	21.0
7	Oscar Robertson	14	26,710	25.7
8	GEORGE GERVIN	14	26,595	25.1
9	John Havlicek	16	26,395	20.8
10	Alex English	15	25,613	21.5
11	Dominique Wilkins	13	25,389	25.8
12	RICK BARRY	14	25,279	24.8
13	Jerry West	14	25,192	27.0
14	ARTIS GILMORE	17	24,941	18.8
15	**Michael Jordan**	11	24,489	32.0
16	**Karl Malone**	11	23,343	26.0
17	Adrian Dantley	15	23,177	24.3
18	**Robert Parish**	20	23,173	14.8
19	Elgin Baylor	14	23,149	27.4
20	**Hakeem Olajuwon**	12	21,840	24.3

ABA Totals: BARRY (4 yrs, 226 gm, 6884 pts, 30.5 avg); ERVING (5 yrs, 407 gm, 11,662 pts, 28.7 avg); GERVIN (4 yrs, 269 gm, 5887 pts, 21.9 avg); GILMORE (5 yrs, 420 gm, 9362 pts, 22.3 avg); ISSEL (6 yrs, 500 gm, 12,823 pts, 25.6 avg); MALONE (2 yrs, 126 gm, 2171 pts, 17.2 avg).

Field Goals

		Yrs	FG	Att	Pct
1	Kareem Abdul-Jabbar	20	15,837	28,307	.559
2	Wilt Chamberlain	14	12,681	23,497	.540
3	Elvin Hayes	16	10,976	24,272	.452
4	Alex English	15	10,659	21,036	.507
5	John Havlicek	16	10,513	23,930	.439
6	**Robert Parish**	20	9,544	17,771	.537
7	Dominique Wilkins	13	9,516	20,504	.464
8	Oscar Robertson	14	9,508	19,620	.485
9	Moses Malone	19	9,435	19,225	.491
10	**Michael Jordan**	11	9,157	17,901	.512

Note: If field goals made in the ABA are included, consider these NBA-ABA totals: Julius Erving (11,818), Dan Issel (10,431), George Gervin (10,368), Moses Malone (10,277), Rick Barry (9,695) and Artis Gilmore (9,403).

Free Throws

		Yrs	FT	Att	Pct
1	**Moses Malone**	19	8531	11,090	.769
2	Oscar Robertson	14	7694	9,185	.838
3	Jerry West	14	7160	8,801	.814
4	Dolph Schayes	16	6979	8,273	.844
5	Adrian Dantley	15	6832	8,351	.818
6	Kareem Abdul-Jabbar	20	6712	9,304	.721
7	Bob Pettit	11	6182	8,119	.761
8	Wilt Chamberlain	14	6057	11,862	.511
9	**Karl Malone**	11	5984	8,293	.722
10	Elgin Baylor	14	5763	7,391	.780

Note: If free throws made in the ABA are included, consider these totals: Moses Malone (9,018), Dan Issel (6,591), Julius Erving (6,256) and Artis Gilmore (6,132).

Assists

		Yrs	Gm	No	Avg
1	**John Stockton**	12	980	11,310	11.5
2	**Magic Johnson**	13	906	10,141	11.2
3	Oscar Robertson	14	1040	9,887	9.5
4	Isiah Thomas	13	979	9,061	9.3
5	Maurice Cheeks	15	1101	7,392	6.7
6	Lenny Wilkens	15	1077	7,211	6.7
7	Bob Cousy	14	924	6,955	7.5
8	Guy Rodgers	12	892	6,917	7.8
9	Nate Archibald	13	876	6,476	7.4
10	John Lucas	14	928	6,454	7.0

Rebounds

		Yrs	Gm	No	Avg
1	Wilt Chamberlain	14	1045	23,924	22.9
2	Bill Russell	13	963	21,620	22.5
3	Kareem Abdul-Jabbar	20	1560	17,440	11.2
4	Elvin Hayes	16	1303	16,279	12.5
5	Moses Malone	19	1329	16,212	12.2
6	**Robert Parish**	20	1568	14,626	9.3
7	Nate Thurmond	14	964	14,464	15.0
8	Walt Bellamy	14	1043	14,241	13.7
9	Wes Unseld	13	984	13,769	14.0
10	Jerry Lucas	11	829	12,942	15.6

Note: If rebounds pulled down in the ABA are included, consider the following totals: Moses Malone (17,834) and Artis Gilmore (16,330).

Steals

		Yrs	Gm	No
1	**John Stockton**	12	980	2365
2	Maurice Cheeks	15	1101	2310
3	**Alvin Robertson**	10	779	2112
4	**Michael Jordan**	11	766	2025
5	**Clyde Drexler**	13	954	1962

Note: Steals have only been an official stat since the 1973-74 season.

Blocked Shots

		Yrs	Gm	No
1	**Hakeem Olajuwon**	12	900	3190
2	Kareem Abdul-Jabbar	20	1560	3189
3	Mark Eaton	11	875	3064
4	Tree Rollins	18	1156	2542
5	**Robert Parish**	20	1568	2342

Note: Blocked shots have only been an official stat since the 1973-74 season.

Games Played

		Yrs	Career	Gm
1	**Robert Parish**	20	1976-96	1568
2	Kareem Abdul-Jabbar	20	1970-89	1560
3	Moses Malone	19	1976-95	1329
4	Elvin Hayes	16	1969-84	1303
5	John Havlicek	16	1963-78	1270

Note: If ABA records are included, consider the following game totals: Moses Malone (1,455); Artis Gilmore (1,329); Caldwell Jones (1,299); Julius Erving (1,243); Dan Issel (1,218); Billy Paultz (1,124).

Personal Fouls

		Yrs	Gm	Fouls	DQ
1	Kareem Abdul-Jabbar	20	1560	4657	48
2	**Robert Parish**	20	1568	4403	86
3	Elvin Hayes	16	1303	4193	53
4	**James Edwards**	19	1168	4042	96
5	Buck Williams	15	1192	3970	55

Note: If ABA records are included, consider the following personal foul totals: Artis Gilmore (4,529) and Caldwell Jones (4,436).

All-Time NBA Regular Season Leaders (Cont.)

SINGLE SEASON

Scoring Average

	Player	Season	Avg
1	Wilt Chamberlain, Phi	1961-62	50.4
2	Wilt Chamberlain, SF	1962-63	44.8
3	Wilt Chamberlain, Phi	1960-61	38.4
4	Elgin Baylor, LA	1961-62	38.3
5	Wilt Chamberlain, Phi	1959-60	37.6
6	Michael Jordan, Chi	1986-87	37.1
7	Wilt Chamberlain, SF	1963-64	36.9
8	Rick Barry, SF	1966-67	35.6
9	Michael Jordan, Chi	1987-88	35.0
10	Elgin Baylor, LA	1960-61	34.8
	Kareem Abdul-Jabbar, Mil	1971-72	34.8

Field Goal Pct.

	Player	Season	Pct
1	Wilt Chamberlain, LA	1972-73	.727
2	Wilt Chamberlain, SF	1966-67	.683
3	Artis Gilmore, Chi	1980-81	.670
4	Artis Gilmore, Chi	1981-82	.652
5	Wilt Chamberlain, LA	1971-72	.649

Free Throw Pct.

	Player	Season	Pct
1	Calvin Murphy, Hou	1980-81	.958
2	Mahmoud Abdul-Rauf, Den.	1993-94	.956
3	Mark Price, Cle	1992-93	.948
4	Mark Price, Cle	1991-92	.947
	Rick Barry, Hou	1978-79	.947

3-Pt Field Goal Pct.

	Player	Season	Pct
1	Steve Kerr, Chi	1994-95	.524
2	Jon Sundvold, Mia	1988-89	.522
3	Tim Legler, Wash	1995-96	.522
4	Steve Kerr, Chi	1995-96	.515
5	Detlef Schrempf, Sea	1994-95	.514

Assists

	Player	Season	Avg
1	John Stockton, Utah	1989-90	14.5
2	John Stockton, Utah	1990-91	14.2
3	Isiah Thomas, Det	1984-85	13.9
4	John Stockton, Utah	1987-88	13.8
5	John Stockton, Utah	1991-92	13.7
6	John Stockton, Utah	1988-89	13.6
7	Kevin Porter, Det	1978-79	13.4
8	Magic Johnson, LA Lakers	1983-84	13.1
9	Magic Johnson, LA Lakers	1988-89	12.8
10	Magic Johnson, LA Lakers	1984-85	12.6
	John Stockton, Utah	1993-94	12.6

Rebounds

	Player	Season	Avg
1	Wilt Chamberlain, Phi	1960-61	27.2
2	Wilt Chamberlain, Phi	1959-60	27.0
3	Wilt Chamberlain, Phi	1961-62	25.7
4	Bill Russell, Bos	1963-64	24.7
5	Wilt Chamberlain, Phi	1965-66	24.6

Blocked Shots

	Player	Season	Avg
1	Mark Eaton, Utah	1984-85	5.56
2	Manute Bol, Wash	1985-86	4.96
3	Elmore Smith, LA	1973-74	4.85
4	Mark Eaton, Utah	1985-86	4.61
5	Hakeem Olajuwon, Hou	1989-90	4.59

Steals

	Player	Season	Avg
1	Alvin Robertson, SA	1985-86	3.67
2	Don Buse, Ind	1976-77	3.47
3	Magic Johnson, LA Lakers	1980-81	3.43
4	Micheal Ray Richardson, NY	1979-80	3.23
5	Alvin Robertson, SA	1986-87	3.21

SINGLE GAME

Points

Player	Date	FG-FT	Pts
Wilt Chamberlain, Phi vs NY	3/2/62	36-28	100
Wilt Chamberlain, Phi vs LA***	12/8/61	31-16	78
Wilt Chamberlain, Phi vs Chi	1/13/62	29-15	73
Wilt Chamberlain, SF at NY	11/16/62	29-15	73
David Thompson, Den at Det	4/9/78	28-17	73
Wilt Chamberlain, SF at LA	11/3/62	29-14	72
Elgin Baylor, LA at NY	11/15/60	28-15	71
David Robinson, SA at LAC	4/24/94	26-18	71
Wilt Chamberlain, SF at Syr	3/10/63	27-16	70
Michael Jordan, Chi at Cle*	3/28/90	23-21	69
Wilt Chamberlain, Phi at Chi	12/16/67	30- 8	68
Pete Maravich, NO vs NYK	2/25/77	26-16	68
Wilt Chamberlain, Phi vs NY	3/9/61	27-13	67
Wilt Chamberlain, Phi at St. L	2/17/62	26-15	67
Wilt Chamberlain, Phi vs NY	2/25/62	25-17	67
Wilt Chamberlain, SF vs LA	1/11/63	28-11	67
Wilt Chamberlain, LA vs Pho	2/9/69	29- 8	66
Wilt Chamberlain, Phi at Cin	2/13/62	24-17	65
Wilt Chamberlain, Phi at St. L	2/27/62	25-15	65
Wilt Chamberlain, Phi vs LA	2/7/66	28- 9	65
Elgin Baylor, Mpls vs Bos	11/8/59	25-14	64
Rick Barry, G.St. vs Port	3/26/74	30- 4	64
Michael Jordan, Chi vs Orl	1/16/93	27- 9	64

*Overtime; ***Triple overtime.

Note: Wilt Chamberlain's 100-point game vs New York was played at Hershey, Pa.

Field Goals

Player	Date	FG	Att
Wilt Chamberlain, Phi vs NY	3/2/62	36	63
Wilt Chamberlain, Phi vs LA***	12/8/61	31	62
Wilt Chamberlain, Phi at Chi	12/16/67	30	40
Rick Barry, G.St. vs Port	3/26/74	30	45

Wilt Chamberlain made 29 four times.

***Triple overtime.

Free Throws

Player	Date	FT	Att
Wilt Chamberlain, Phi vs NY	3/2/62	28	32
Adrian Dantley, Utah vs Hou	1/4/84	28	29
Adrian Dantley, Utah vs Den	11/25/83	27	31
Adrian Dantley, Utah vs Dal	10/31/80	26	29
Michael Jordan, Chi vs NJ	2/26/87	26	27

3-Pt Field Goals

Player	Date	No
Dennis Scott, Orl vs Atl.	4/18/96	11
Brian Shaw, Mia at Mil	4/8/93	10
Joe Dumars, Det vs Min	11/8/94	10
George McCloud, Dal vs Pho	12/16/95	10*

Eight tied with 9 each.

*Overtime.

Assists

	Date	No
Scott Skiles, Orl vs Den	12/30/90	30
Kevin Porter, NJ vs Hou	2/24/78	29
Bob Cousy, Bos vs Mpls	2/27/59	28
Guy Rodgers, SF vs St.L	3/14/63	28
John Stockton, Utah vs SA	1/15/91	28

Rebounds

	Date	No
Wilt Chamberlain, Phi vs Bos	11/24/60	55
Bill Russell, Bos vs Syr	2/5/60	51
Bill Russell, Bos vs Phi	11/16/57	49
Bill Russell, Bos vs Det	3/11/65	49
Wilt Chamberlain, Phi vs Syr	2/6/60	45
Wilt Chamberlain, Phi vs LA	1/21/61	45

Blocked Shots

	Date	No
Elmore Smith, LA vs Port	10/28/73	17
Manute Bol, Wash vs Atl	1/25/86	15
Manute Bol, Wash vs Ind	2/26/87	15
Shaquille O'Neal, Orl at NJ	11/20/93	15

Steals

	Date	No
Larry Kenon, San Antonio at KC	12/26/76	11

11 different players tied with 10 each, including Alvin Robertson who had 10 steals in a game four times.

All-Time Winningest NBA Coaches

Top 25 NBA career victories through the 1995-96 season. Career, regular season and playoff records are noted along with NBA titles won. Coaches active during 1995-96 season in **bold** type.

		Career				Regular Season			Playoffs			
		Yrs	W	L	Pct	W	L	Pct	W	L	Pct	NBA Titles
1	**Lenny Wilkens**	23	**1078**	920	.540	1014	850	.544	64	70	.478	1 (1979)
2	Red Auerbach	20	**1037**	548	.654	938	479	.662	99	69	.589	9 (1957, 59-66)
3	**Dick Motta**	24	**974**	1035	.485	918	965	.488	56	70	.444	1 (1978)
4	**Bill Fitch**	23	**946**	1046	.475	891	995	.472	55	51	.519	1 (1981)
5	**Pat Riley**	14	**935**	417	.692	798	339	.702	137	78	.637	4 (1982,85,87-88)
6	Jack Ramsay	21	**908**	841	.519	864	783	.525	44	58	.431	1 (1977)
7	**Don Nelson**	19	**902**	690	.567	851	629	.575	51	61	.455	None
8	**Cotton Fitzsimmons**	20	**867**	816	.515	832	767	.520	35	49	.417	None
9	Gene Shue	22	**814**	908	.473	784	861	.477	30	47	.390	None
10	Red Holzman	18	**754**	652	.536	696	604	.535	58	48	.547	2 (1970, 73)
	John MacLeod	18	**754**	711	.515	707	657	.518	47	54	.465	None
12	Doug Moe	15	**661**	579	.533	628	529	.543	33	50	.398	None
13	Chuck Daly	12	**638**	427	.599	564	379	.598	74	48	.607	2 (1989-90)
14	**Larry Brown**	13	**626**	479	.567	585	437	.572	41	42	.494	None
15	K.C. Jones	10	**603**	309	.661	522	252	.674	81	57	.587	2 (1984,86)
16	Al Attles	14	**588**	548	.518	557	518	.518	31	30	.508	1 (1975)
17	**Jerry Sloan**	11	**552**	385	.589	513	341	.601	39	44	.470	None
18	Billy Cunningham	8	**520**	235	.689	454	196	.698	66	39	.629	1 (1983)
19	Alex Hannum	12	**518**	446	.536	471	412	.533	47	34	.580	2 (1958, 67)
20	**Phil Jackson**	7	**495**	191	.722	414	160	.721	81	31	.723	4 (1991-93, 96)
21	John Kundla	11	**485**	338	.589	423	302	.583	62	36	.633	5 (1949-50, 52-54)
22	Kevin Loughery	17	**480**	683	.413	474	662	.417	6	21	.222	None
	Mike Fratello	11	**480**	393	.550	461	362	.560	19	31	.380	None
24	Tommy Heinsohn	9	**474**	296	.616	427	263	.619	47	33	.588	2 (1974,76)
25	Larry Costello	10	**467**	323	.591	430	300	.589	37	23	.617	1 (1971)

Note: The NBA does not recognize records from the National Basketball League (1937-49), the American Basketball League (1961-62) or the American Basketball Assn. (1968-76), so the following NBL, ABL and ABA overall coaching records are not included above: NBL—**John Kundla** (51-19 and a title in 1 year). ABA— **Larry Brown** (249-129 in 4 yrs), **Alex Hannum** (194-164 and one title in 4 yrs), **K.C. Jones** (30-58 in 1 yr); **Kevin Loughery** (189-95 and one title in 3 yrs).

Where They Coached

Attles—Golden St. (1970-80,80-83); **Auerbach**—Washington (1946-49); Tri-Cities (1949-50); Boston (1950-66); **Brown**—Denver (1976-79), New Jersey (1981-83), San Antonio (1988-92), LA Clippers (1992-93), Indiana (1993—); **Costello**—Milwaukee (1968-76), Chicago (1978-79); **Cunningham**—Philadelphia (1977-85); **Daly**—Cleveland (1981-82), Detroit (1983-92), New Jersey (1992-94); **Fitch**—Cleveland (1970-79), Boston (1979-83), Houston (1983-88), New Jersey (1989-92), LA Clippers (1994—); **Fitzsimmons**—Phoenix (1970-72), Atlanta (1972-76), Buffalo (1977-78), Kansas City (1978-84), San Antonio (1984-86), Phoenix (1988-92, 95—); **Fratello**—Atlanta (1980-90), Cleveland (1993—).

Hannum—St. Louis (1957-58), Syracuse (1960-63), San Francisco (1963-66), Phila. 76ers (1966-68), Houston (1970-71); **Heinsohn**—Boston (1969-77); **Holzman**—Milwaukee-St. Louis Hawks (1954-57), NY Knicks (1968-77,78-82); **Jackson**—Chicago (1989—); **Jones**—Washington (1973-76), Boston (1983-88), Seattle (1990-92); **Kundla**—Minneapolis (1948-57,58-59); **Loughery**—Philadelphia (1972-73), NY-NJ Nets (1976-81), Atlanta (1981-83), Chicago (1983-85), Washington (1985-88), Miami (1991-95); **MacLeod**—Phoenix (1973-87), Dallas (1987-89), NY Knicks (1990-91); **Moe**—San Antonio (1976-80), Denver (1981-90), Philadelphia (1992-93).

Motta—Chicago (1968-76), Washington (1976-80), Dallas (1980-87), Sacramento (1990-91), Dallas (1994—); **Nelson**—Milwaukee (1976-87), Golden St. (1988-95), New York (1995—); **Ramsay**—Philadelphia (1968-72), Buffalo (1972-76), Portland (1976-86), Indiana (1986-89); **Riley**—LA Lakers (1981-90), New York (1991-95), Miami (1995—); **Shue**—Baltimore (1967-73), Philadelphia (1973-77), San Diego Clippers (1978-80), Washington (1980-86), LA Clippers (1987-89); **Sloan**—Chicago (1979-82), Utah (1988—); **Wilkens**—Seattle (1969-72), Portland (1974-76), Seattle (1977-85), Cleveland (1986-93), Atlanta (1993—).

All-Time Winningest NBA Coaches (Cont.)

Top Winning Percentages

Minimum of 350 victories, including playoffs; coaches active during 1995-96 season in **bold** type.

		Yrs	W	L	Pct
1	**Phil Jackson**	7	495	191	**.722**
2	**Pat Riley**	14	935	417	**.692**
3	Billy Cunningham	8	520	235	**.689**
4	K.C. Jones	10	603	309	**.661**
5	Red Auerbach	20	1037	548	**.654**
6	Tommy Heinson	9	474	296	**.616**
7	Rick Adelman	7	363	233	**.609**
8	Chuck Daly	12	638	427	**.599**
9	Larry Costello	10	467	323	**.591**
10	John Kundla	11	485	338	**.589**
11	**Jerry Sloan**	11	552	385	**.589**
12	Bill Sharman	7	368	267	**.580**
13	Al Cervi	9	359	267	**.573**
14	**George Karl**	9	420	317	**.570**
15	**Don Nelson**	19	902	690	**.567**
16	**Larry Brown**	13	626	479	**.567**
17	Joe Lapchick	9	356	277	**.562**
18	**Mike Fratello**	11	480	393	**.550**
19	Bill Russell	8	375	317	**.542**
20	**Lenny Wilkens**	23	1078	922	**.539**
21	Alex Hannum	12	518	446	**.537**
22	Red Holzman	18	754	651	**.536**
23	Doug Moe	15	661	579	**.533**
24	Richie Guerin	8	353	325	**.521**
25	Jack Ramsay	21	908	841	**.519**

Active Coaches' Victories

Through 1995-96 season, including playoffs.

		Yrs	W	L	Pct
1	Lenny Wilkens, Atlanta	23	**1078**	922	.539
2	Bill Fitch, LA Clippers	23	**946**	1046	.475
3	Pat Riley, Miami	14	**935**	417	.692
4	Cotton Fitzsimmons, Phoenix	20	**867**	816	.515
5	Larry Brown, Indiana	13	**626**	479	.567
6	Jerry Sloan, Utah	11	**552**	385	.589
7	Phil Jackson, Chicago	7	**495**	191	.722
8	Mike Fratello, Cleveland	11	**480**	393	.550
9	Del Harris, LA Lakers	11	**460**	443	.509
10	George Karl, Seattle	9	**420**	317	.570
11	Rick Adelman, Golden St.	7	**363**	233	.609
12	Jim Lynam, Washington	9	**314**	381	.452
13	Bernie Bickerstafff, Denver	7	**268**	277	.492
14	Rudy Tomjanovich, Houston	5	**263**	160	.622
15	Bob Hill, San Antonio	6	**261**	217	.546
16	Chris Ford, Milwaukee	5	**245**	204	.546
17	Doug Collins, Detroit	4	**196**	165	.543
18	Brian Hill, Orlando	3	**185**	97	.656
19	Gary St. Jean, Sacramento	4	**132**	200	.398
20	P.J. Carlesimo, Portland	2	**90**	82	.523
21	Bill Blair, Minnesota	2	**47**	117	.287
22	M.L. Carr, Boston	1	**33**	49	.402
23	Dave Cowens, Charlotte	1	**27**	41	.397
24	Jeff Van Gundy, New York	1	**18**	14	.563
25	Brian Winters, Vancouver	1	**15**	67	.183
26	John Calipari, New Jersey	0	**0**	0	.000
27	Jim Cleamons, Dallas	0	**0**	0	.000
28	Johnny Davis, Philadelphia	0	**0**	0	.000
29	Darrell Walker, Toronto	0	**0**	0	.000

Annual Awards

Most Valuable Player

The Maurice Podoloff Trophy for regular season MVP. Named after the first commissioner (then president) of the NBA. Winners first selected by the NBA players (1956-80) then a national panel of pro basketball writers and broadcasters (since 1981). Winners' scoring averages are provided; (*) indicates led league.

Multiple winners: Kareem Abdul-Jabbar (6); Bill Russell (5); Wilt Chamberlain and Michael Jordan (4); Larry Bird, Magic Johnson, and Moses Malone (3); Bob Pettit (2).

Year		Avg
1956	Bob Pettit, St. Louis, F	25.7*
1957	Bob Cousy, Boston, G	20.6
1958	Bill Russell, Boston, C	16.6
1959	Bob Pettit, St. Louis, F	29.2*
1960	Wilt Chamberlain, Philadelphia, C	37.6*
1961	Bill Russell, Boston, C	16.9
1962	Bill Russell, Boston, C	18.9
1963	Bill Russell, Boston, C	16.8
1964	Oscar Robertson, Cincinnati, G	31.4
1965	Bill Russell, Boston, C	14.1
1966	Wilt Chamberlain, Philadelphia, C	33.5*
1967	Wilt Chamberlain, Philadelphia, C	24.1
1968	Wilt Chamberlain, Philadelphia, C	24.3
1969	Wes Unseld, Baltimore, C	13.8
1970	Willis Reed, New York, C	21.7
1971	Lew Alcindor, Milwaukee, C	31.7*
1972	Kareem Abdul-Jabbar, Milwaukee, C	34.8*
1973	Dave Cowens, Boston, C	20.5
1974	Kareem Abdul-Jabbar, Milwaukee, C	27.0
1975	Bob McAdoo, Buffalo, F	34.5*
1976	Kareem Abdul-Jabbar, LA, C	27.7

Year		Avg
1977	Kareem Abdul-Jabbar, LA, C	26.2
1978	Bill Walton, Portland, C	18.9
1979	Moses Malone, Houston, C	24.8
1980	Kareem Abdul-Jabbar, LA, C	24.8
1981	Julius Erving, Philadelphia, F	24.6
1982	Moses Malone, Houston, C	31.1
1983	Moses Malone, Philadelphia, C	24.5
1984	Larry Bird, Boston, F	24.2
1985	Larry Bird, Boston, F	28.7
1986	Larry Bird, Boston, F	25.8
1987	Magic Johnson, LA Lakers, G	23.9
1988	Michael Jordan, Chicago, G	35.0*
1989	Magic Johnson, LA Lakers, G	22.5
1990	Magic Johnson, LA Lakers, G	22.3
1991	Michael Jordan, Chicago, G	31.5*
1992	Michael Jordan, Chicago, G	30.1*
1993	Charles Barkley, Phoenix, F	25.6
1994	Hakeem Olajuwon, Houston, C	27.3
1995	David Robinson, San Antonio, C	27.6
1996	Michael Jordan, Chicago, G	30.4*

Note: Lew Alcindor changed his name to Kareem Abdul-Jabbar after the 1970-71 season.

Rookie of the Year

The Eddie Gottlieb Trophy for outstanding rookie of the regular season. Named after the pro basketball pioneer and owner-coach of the first NBA champion Philadelphia Warriors. Winners selected by a national panel of pro basketball writers and broadcasters. Winners' scoring averages provided; (*) indicated led league; winners who were also named MVP are in **bold** type.

Year		Avg
1953	Don Meineke, Ft. Wayne, F	10.8
1954	Ray Felix, Baltimore, C	17.6
1955	Bob Pettit, Milwaukee Hawks, F	20.4
1956	Maurice Stokes, Rochester, F/C	16.8
1957	Tommy Heinsohn, Boston, F	16.2
1958	Woody Sauldsberry, Philadelphia, F/C	12.8
1959	Elgin Baylor, Minneapolis, F	24.9
1960	**Wilt Chamberlain**, Philadelphia, C	37.6*
1961	Oscar Robertson, Cincinnati, G	30.5
1962	Walt Bellamy, Chicago Packers, C	31.6
1963	Terry Dischinger, Chicago Zephyrs, F	25.5
1964	Jerry Lucas, Cincinnati, F/C	17.7
1965	Willis Reed, New York, C	19.5
1966	Rick Barry, San Francisco, F	25.7
1967	Dave Bing, Detroit, G	20.0
1968	Earl Monroe, Baltimore, G	24.3
1969	**Wes Unseld**, Baltimore, C	13.8
1970	Lew Alcindor, Milwaukee Bucks, C	28.8
1971	Dave Cowens, Boston, C	17.0
	& Geoff Petrie, Portland, F	24.8
1972	Sidney Wicks, Portland, F	24.5
1973	Bob McAdoo, Buffalo, C/F	18.0
1974	Ernie DiGregorio, Buffalo, G	15.2
1975	Keith Wilkes, Golden St., F	14.2
1976	Alvan Adams, Phoenix, C	19.0
1977	Adrian Dantley, Buffalo, F	20.3
1978	Walter Davis, Phoenix, G	24.2
1979	Phil Ford, Kansas City, G	15.9
1980	Larry Bird, Boston, F	21.3
1981	Darrell Griffith, Utah, G	20.6
1982	Buck Williams, New Jersey, F	15.5
1983	Terry Cummings, San Diego, F	23.7
1984	Ralph Sampson, Houston, C	21.0
1985	Michael Jordan, Chicago, G	28.2
1986	Patrick Ewing, New York, C	20.0
1987	Chuck Person, Indiana, F	18.8
1988	Mark Jackson, New York, G	13.6
1989	Mitch Richmond, Golden St., G	22.0
1990	David Robinson, San Antonio, C	24.3
1991	Derrick Coleman, New Jersey, F	18.4
1992	Larry Johnson, Charlotte, F	19.2
1993	Shaquille O'Neal, Orlando, C	23.4
1994	Chris Webber, Golden St., F	17.5
1995	Grant Hill, Detroit, F	19.9
	& Jason Kidd, Dallas, G	11.7
1996	Damon Stoudamire, Toronto, G	19.0

Note: The Chicago Packers changed their name to the Zephyrs after 1961-62 season. Also, Lew Alcindor changed his name to Kareem Abdul-Jabbar after the 1970-71 season.

Sixth Man Award

Awarded to the Best Player Off the Bench for the regular season. Winners selected by a national panel of pro basketball writers and broadcasters.

Multiple winners: Kevin McHale, Ricky Pierce and Detlef Schrempf (2).

Year	
1983	Bobby Jones, Phi., F
1984	Kevin McHale, Bos., F
1985	Kevin McHale, Bos., F
1986	Bill Walton, Bos., F/C
1987	Ricky Pierce, Mil., G/F
1988	Roy Tarpley, Dal., F
1989	Eddie Johnson, Pho., F
1990	Ricky Pierce, Mil., G/F
1991	Detlef Schrempf, Ind., F
1992	Detlef Schrempf, Ind., F
1993	Cliff Robinson, Port., F
1994	Dell Curry, Char., G
1995	Anthony Mason, NY, F
1996	Toni Kukoc, Chi., F

Number One Draft Choices

Overall first choices in the NBA draft since the abolition of the territorial draft in 1966. Players who became Rookie of the Year are in **bold** type. The draft lottery began in 1985.

Year		Overall 1st Pick
1966	New York	Cazzie Russell, Michigan
1967	Detroit	Jimmy Walker, Providence
1968	San Diego	Elvin Hayes, Houston
1969	Milwaukee	**Lew Alcindor**, UCLA
1970	Detroit	Bob Lanier, St. Bonaventure
1971	Cleveland	Austin Carr, Notre Dame
1972	Portland	LaRue Martin, Loyola-Chicago
1973	Philadelphia	Doug Collins, Illinois St.
1974	Portland	Bill Walton, UCLA
1975	Atlanta	David Thompson, N.C. State
1976	Houston	John Lucas, Maryland
1977	Milwaukee	Kent Benson, Indiana
1978	Portland	Mychal Thompson, Minnesota
1979	LA Lakers	Magic Johnson, Michigan St.
1980	Golden St	Joe Barry Carroll, Purdue
1981	Dallas	Mark Aguirre, DePaul
1982	LA Lakers	James Worthy, N. Carolina
1983	Houston	**Ralph Sampson**, Virginia
1984	Houston	Akeem Olajuwon, Houston
1985	New York	**Patrick Ewing**, Georgetown
1986	Cleveland	Brad Daugherty, N. Carolina
1987	San Antonio	**David Robinson**, Navy
1988	LA Clippers	Danny Manning, Kansas
1989	Sacramento	Pervis Ellison, Louisville
1990	New Jersey	**Derrick Coleman**, Syracuse
1991	Charlotte	**Larry Johnson**, UNLV
1992	Orlando	**Shaquille O'Neal**, LSU
1993	Orlando	**Chris Webber**, Michigan
1994	Milwaukee	Glenn Robinson, Purdue
1995	Golden St.	Joe Smith, Maryland
1996	Philadelphia	Allen Iverson, Georgetown

Note: Lew Alcindor changed his name to Kareem Abdul-Jabbar after the 1970-71 season; Akeem Olajuwon changed his first name to Hakeem in 1991; In 1975 David Thompson signed with Denver of the ABA and did not play for Atlanta; David Robinson joined NBA for 1989-90 season after fulfilling military obligation.

Defensive Player of the Year

Awarded to the Best Defensive Player for the regular season. Winners selected by a national panel of pro basketball writers and broadcasters.

Multiple winners: Mark Eaton, Sidney Moncrief, Hakeem Olajuwon and Dennis Rodman (2).

Year		Year		Year	
1983	Sidney Moncrief, Mil., G	1988	Michael Jordan, Chi., G	1993	Hakeem Olajuwon, Hou., C
1984	Sidney Moncrief, Mil., G	1989	Mark Eaton, Utah, C	1994	Hakeem Olajuwon, Hou., C
1985	Mark Eaton, Utah, C	1990	Dennis Rodman, Det., F	1995	Dikembe Mutombo, Den., C
1986	Alvin Robertson, SA, G	1991	Dennis Rodman, Det., F	1996	Gary Payton, Sea., G
1987	Michael Cooper, LAL, F	1992	David Robinson, SA, C		

Most Improved Player

Awarded to the Most Improved Player for the regular season. Winners selected by a national panel of pro basketball writers and broadcasters.

Year		Year		Year	
1986	Alvin Robertson, SA, G	1990	Rony Seikaly, Mia., C	1994	Don MacLean, Wash., F
1987	Dale Ellis, Sea., G	1991	Scott Skiles, Orl., G	1995	Dana Barros, Phi., G
1988	Kevin Duckworth, Port., C	1992	Pervis Ellison, Wash., C	1996	Gheorghe Muresan, Wash., C
1989	Kevin Johnson, Pho., G	1993	Mahmoud Abdul-Rauf, Den., G		

Coach of the Year

The Red Auerbach Trophy for outstanding coach of the year. Renamed in 1967 for the former Boston coach who led the Celtics to nine NBA titles. Winners selected by a national panel of pro basketball writers and broadcasters. Previous season and winning season records are provided; (*) indicates division title.

Multiple winners: Don Nelson (3); Bill Fitch, Cotton Fitzsimmons, Pat Riley and Gene Shue (2).

Year		Improvement		
1963	Harry Gallatin, St. L.	29-51	to	48-32
1964	Alex Hannum, SF	31-49	to	48-32*
1965	Red Auerbach, Bos	59-21*	to	61-18*
1966	Dolph Schayes, Phi	40-40	to	55-25*
1967	Johnny Kerr, Chi	Expan.	to	33-48
1968	Richie Guerin, St. L	39-42	to	56-26*
1969	Gene Shue, Balt	36-46	to	57-25*
1970	Red Holzman, NY	54-28	to	60-22*
1971	Dick Motta, Chi	39-43	to	51-31
1972	Bill Sharman, LA	48-34*	to	69-13*
1973	Tommy Heinsohn, Bos	56-26*	to	68-14*
1974	Ray Scott, Det	40-42	to	52-30
1975	Phil Johnson, KC-Omaha	33-49	to	44-38
1976	Bill Fitch, Cle	40-42	to	49-33*
1977	Tom Nissalke, Hou	40-42	to	49-33*
1978	Hubie Brown, Atl	31-51	to	41-41
1979	Cotton Fitzsimmons, KC	31-51	to	48-34*
1980	Bill Fitch, Bos	29-53	to	61-21*
1981	Jack McKinney, Ind	37-45	to	44-38
1982	Gene Shue, Wash	39-43	to	43-39
1983	Don Nelson, Mil	55-27*	to	51-31*
1984	Frank Layden, Utah	30-52	to	45-37*
1985	Don Nelson, Mil	50-32*	to	59-23*
1986	Mike Fratello, Atl	34-48	to	50-32
1987	Mike Schuler, Port	40-42	to	49-33
1988	Doug Moe, Den	37-45	to	54-28*
1989	Cotton Fitzsimmons, Pho	28-54	to	55-27
1990	Pat Riley, LA Lakers	57-25*	to	63-19*
1991	Don Chaney, Hou	41-41	to	52-30
1992	Don Nelson, GS	44-38	to	55-27
1993	Pat Riley, NY	51-31	to	60-22
1994	Lenny Wilkens, Atl	43-39	to	57-25*
1995	Del Harris, LA Lakers	33-49	to	48-34
1996	Phil Jackson, Chi	47-35	to	72-10*

World Championships

The World Basketball Championships for men and women have been played regularly at four-year intervals (give or take a year) since 1970. The men's tournament began in 1950 and the women's in 1953. The Federation Internationale de Basketball Amateur (FIBA), which governs the World and Olympic tournaments, was founded in 1932. FIBA first allowed professional players from the NBA to participate in 1994.

MEN

Multiple wins: Soviet Union, USA and Yugoslavia (3); Brazil (2).

Year	
1950	**Argentina**, United States, Chile
1954	**United States**, Brazil, Philippines
1959	**Brazil**, United States, Chile
1963	**Brazil**, Yugoslavia, Soviet Union
1967	**Soviet Union**, Yugoslavia, Brazil
1970	**Yugoslavia**, Brazil, Soviet Union
1974	**Soviet Union**, Yugoslavia, United States
1978	**Yugoslavia**, Soviet Union, Brazil
1982	**Soviet Union**, United States, Yugoslavia
1986	**United States**, Soviet Union, Yugoslavia
1990	**Yugoslavia**, Soviet Union, United States
1994	**United States**, Russia, Croatia
1998	at Athens (August)

WOMEN

Multiple wins: Soviet Union (6); USA (5).

Year	
1953	**United States**, Chile, France
1957	**United States**, Soviet Union, Czechoslovakia
1959	**Soviet Union**, Bulgaria, Czechoslovakia
1964	**Soviet Union**, Czechoslovakia, Bulgaria
1967	**Soviet Union**, South Korea, Czechoslovakia
1971	**Soviet Union**, Czechoslovakia, Brazil
1975	**Soviet Union**, Japan, Czechoslovakia
1979	**United States**, South Korea, Canada
1983	**Soviet Union**, United States, China
1986	**United States**, Soviet Union, Canada
1990	**United States**, Yugoslavia, Cuba
1994	**Brazil**, China, United States
1998	at Berlin (July)

American Basketball Association

ABA Finals

The American Basketball Assn. began play in 1967-68 as a 10-team rival of the 21-year-old NBA. The ABA, which introduced the three-point basket, a multi-colored ball and the All-Star Game Slam Dunk Contest, lasted nine seasons before folding following the 1975-76 season. Four ABA teams—Denver, Indiana, New York and San Antonio—survived to enter the NBA in 1976-77. The NBA also adopted the three-point basket (in 1979-80) and the All-Star Game Slam Dunk Contest. The older league, however, refused to take in the ABA ball.

Multiple winners: Indiana (3); New York (2).

Year	Winner	Head Coach	Series	Loser	Head Coach
1968	Pittsburgh Pipers	Vince Cazzetta	4-3 (WLLWLWW)	New Orleans Bucs	Babe McCarthy
1969	Oakland Oaks	Alex Hannum	4-1 (WLWWW)	Indiana Pacers	Bob Leonard
1970	Indiana Pacers	Bob Leonard	4-2 (WWLWLW)	Los Angeles Stars	Bill Sharman
1971	Utah Stars	Bill Sharman	4-3 (WWLLWLW)	Kentucky Colonels	Frank Ramsey
1972	Indiana Pacers	Bob Leonard	4-2 (WLWLWW)	New York Nets	Lou Carnesecca
1973	Indiana Pacers	Bob Leonard	4-3 (WLLWWLW)	Kentucky Colonels	Joe Mullaney
1974	New York Nets	Kevin Loughery	4-1 (WWWLW)	Utah Stars	Joe Mullaney
1975	Kentucky Colonels	Hubie Brown	4-1 (WWWLW)	Indiana Pacers	Bob Leonard
1976	New York Nets	Kevin Loughery	4-2 (WLWWLW)	Denver Nuggets	Larry Brown

Most Valuable Player

Winners' scoring averages provided; (*) indicates led league.

Multiple winners: Julius Erving (3); Mel Daniels (2).

Year		Avg
1968	Connie Hawkins, Pittsburgh, C	26.8*
1969	Mel Daniels, Indiana, C	24.0
1970	Spencer Haywood, Denver, C	30.0*
1971	Mel Daniels, Indiana, C	21.0
1972	Artis Gilmore, Kentucky, C	23.8
1973	Billy Cunningham, Carolina, F	24.1
1974	Julius Erving, New York, F	27.4*
1975	George McGinnis, Indiana, F	29.8*
	& Julius Erving, New York, F	27.9
1976	Julius Erving, New York, F	29.3*

Rookie of the Year

Winners' scoring averages provided; (*) indicates led league. Rookies who were also named Most Valuable Player are in **bold** type.

Year		Avg
1968	Mel Daniels, Minnesota, C	22.2
1969	Warren Armstrong, Oakland, G	21.5
1970	**Spencer Haywood**, Denver, C	30.0*
1971	Dan Issel, Kentucky, C	29.8*
	& Charlie Scott, Virginia, G	27.1
1972	**Artis Gilmore**, Kentucky, C	23.8
1973	Brian Taylor, New York, G	15.3
1974	Swen Nater, Virginia-SA, C	14.1
1975	Marvin Barnes, St. Louis, C	24.0
1976	David Thompson, Denver, F	26.0

Note: Warren Armstrong changed his name to Warren Jabali after the 1970-71 season.

Coach of the Year

Previous season and winning season records are provided; (*) indicates division title.

Multiple winner: Larry Brown (3).

Year		Improvement		
1968	Vince Cazzetta, Pittsburgh			54-24*
1969	Alex Hannum, Oakland	22-56	to	60-18*
1970	Joe Belmont, Denver	44-34	to	51-33*
	& Bill Sharman, LA Stars	33-45	to	43-41
1971	Al Bianchi, Virginia	44-40	to	55-29*
1972	Tom Nissalke, Dallas	30-54	to	42-42
1973	Larry Brown, Carolina	35-49	to	57-27*
1974	Babe McCarthy, Kentucky	56-28	to	53-31
	& Joe Mullaney, Utah	55-29*	to	51-33*
1975	Larry Brown, Denver	37-47	to	65-19*
1976	Larry Brown, Denver	65-19*	to	60-24*

Scoring Leaders

Scoring championship decided by per game point average every season.

Multiple winner: Julius Erving (3).

Year		Gm	Avg	Pts
1968	Connie Hawkins, Pittsburgh	70	1875	26.8
1969	Rick Barry, Oakland	35	1190	34.0
1970	Spencer Haywood, Denver	84	2519	30.0
1971	Dan Issel, Kentucky	83	2480	29.8
1972	Charlie Scott, Virginia	73	2524	34.6
1973	Julius Erving, Virginia	71	2268	31.9
1974	Julius Erving, New York	84	2299	27.4
1975	George McGinnis, Indiana	79	2353	29.8
1976	Julius Erving, New York	84	2462	29.3

ABA All-Star Game

The ABA All-Star Game was an Eastern Division vs Western Division contest from 1968-75. League membership had dropped to seven teams by 1976, the ABA's last season, so the team in first place at the break (Denver) played an All-Star team made up from the other six clubs.

Series: East won 5, West 3 and Denver 1.

Year	Result	Host	Coaches	Most Valuable Player
1968	East 126, West 120	Indiana	Jim Pollard, Babe McCarthy	Larry Brown, New Orleans
1969	West 133, East 127	Louisville	Alex Hannum, Gene Rhodes	John Beasley, Dallas
1970	West 128, East 98	Indiana	Babe McCarthy, Bob Leonard	Spencer Haywood, Denver
1971	East 126, West 122	Carolina	Al Bianchi, Bill Sharman	Mel Daniels, Indiana
1972	East 142, West 115	Louisville	Joe Mullaney, Ladell Andersen	Dan Issel, Kentucky
1973	West 123, East 111	Utah	Ladell Andersen, Larry Brown	Warren Jabali, Denver
1974	East 128, West 112	Virginia	Babe McCarthy, Joe Mullaney	Artis Gilmore, Kentucky
1975	East 151, West 124	San Antonio	Kevin Loughery, Larry Brown	Freddie Lewis, St. Louis
1976	Denver 144, ABA 138	Denver	Larry Brown, Kevin Loughery	David Thompson, Denver

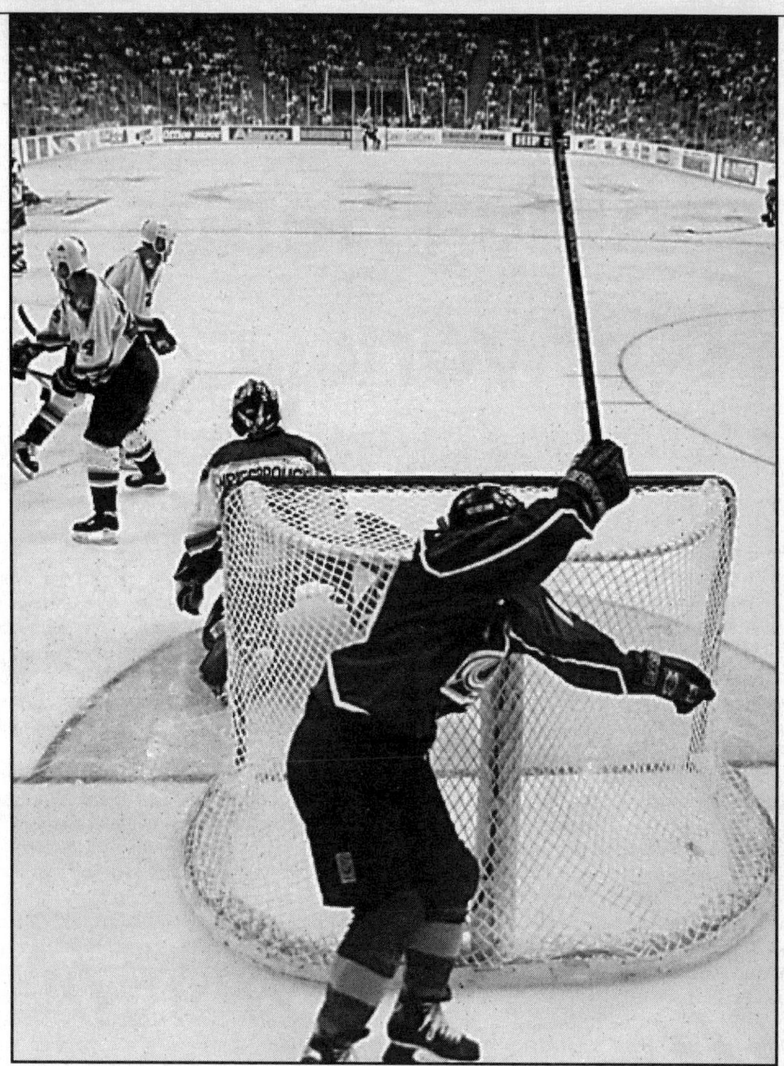

Al Bello/Allsport

Colorado's **Joe Sakic** celebrates seconds after Uwe Krupp scored the 1996 Stanley Cup winning goal, four minutes into the third overtime, capping a thrilling ride through the playoffs for the newly-transplanted Avalanche.

HOCKEY

by Eric Duhatschek

Sakic Friends Network

Joe Sakic teamed with the bounty from Quebec's Eric Lindros trade to win the Stanley Cup in Denver

The National Hockey League was set to enter its newest market, Denver, and marked the occasion by playing the 1995-96 season opener in the Mile High City. To commemorate their move from Quebec, the newly christened Colorado Avalanche raised a banner that read: Game On(e). The theory was to provide a little history to a team that boasted little history in its previous incarnation as the Quebec Nordiques. The Nordiques were sold to the COMSAT Entertainment Group on July 1, 1995 after 16 mainly fruitless years in Quebec.

Eight months after arriving in Colorado, the Avalanche had a more meaningful banner to hang - Stanley Cup champions. On a muggy June night in Miami, the Avalanche registered a stirring 1-0 triple overtime win over the Florida Panthers to capture Denver's first-ever professional sports championship.

The Nordiques had been the No. 1 team in the Eastern Conference the year before, but faltered in the first round of the playoffs against a more experienced New York Rangers' team. Five consecutive years out of the playoffs - plus the huge haul of players, draft choices and cash they received from Philadelphia Flyers in exchange for Eric Lindros - gave the Nordiques the best young talent base in the league. On paper, their requirements were clear. To get over the top, they needed players who'd previously won in the playoffs; they needed a more experienced goaltender; and they needed a strong offensive defenseman. In a 64-day span, general manager Pierre Lacroix, blessed with all that desirable talent as trade bait, completed his shopping list.

First, Lacroix acquired Claude Lemieux from the New Jersey Devils for Wendel Clark. Lemieux was the MVP of the 1995 playoffs and although reviled for his occasionally dirty play, considered one of the league's most accomplished agitators. Next, he picked up Sandis Ozolinsh from the San Jose Sharks, an exceptionally skilled offensive defenseman, with serious deficiencies in his defensive game. In the biggest gamble of all, Lacroix - a former player agent - brought in his most visible client, two-time playoff MVP Patrick Roy, in a five-player deal with the Montreal Canadiens. Accompanying Roy to Denver was Montreal's captain Mike Keane.

None of the players came cheaply, but with his team's depth, Lacroix could afford to trade younger players to add the experience his team needed. Other teams - Toronto, St. Louis, the New York Rangers - all made similar attempts to quick-fix their rosters to no avail. But in Colorado it worked. After making all the right moves on paper, the new Avalanche players all made a comparatively

Eric Duhatschek has covered the NHL for the *Calgary Herald* since 1980. He is also a columnist for *The Hockey News*.

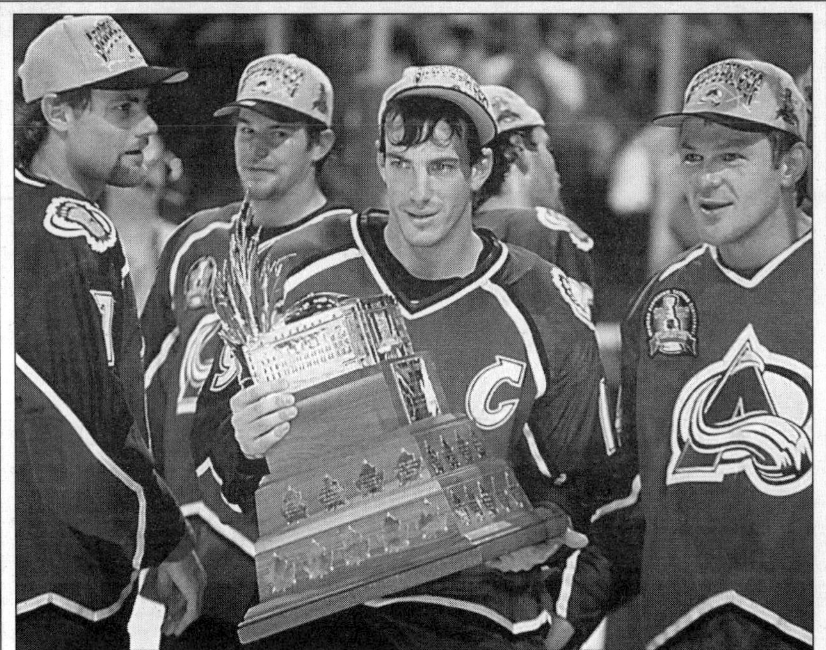

Rick Stewart/Allsport

Avalanche captain **Joe Sakic** holds the Conn Smythe trophy that will soon bear his name as MVP of the 1996 NHL playoffs. Fellow Avalanche-person, **Claude Lemieux** (right), won the award last year as a member of the New Jersey Devils.

seamless transition on the ice.

There was a real symmetry to the Avalanche season. In the aforementioned season opener against Detroit, Uwe Krupp - a player they counted on to be their No. 1 defenseman - ripped up his knee and underwent major reconstructive surgery. Krupp's injury largely precipitated the deal for Ozolinsh. Krupp wasn't supposed to come back at all last season, but diligent rehabilitation - part of it came racing dogsleds in the Colorado mountains - enabled him to get back for the final five regular-season games and playoffs. In the finals against Florida, Krupp scored two of the timeliest goals in the Colorado sweep - the insurance goal in Game 2's 3-1 win and the overtime winner in Game 4.

Ultimately, the seeds for the championship were sown back on June 30, 1992 when Pierre Page, then the Nordiques' GM, and Russ Farwell, then the Flyers' GM negotiated the complicated deal that sent the rights to Eric Lindros from Quebec to Philadelphia in exchange for six players, two No. 1 draft choices, plus $15 million U.S. in cash. Four years later on the Avalanche's championship team, the Lindros trade was evident in 11 players; three of the original six (Peter Forsberg, Mike Ricci, Chris Simon), plus varying percentages of six other players acquired in subsequent deals (Roy, Lemieux, Krupp, Keane, Adam Deadmarsh, Sylvain Lefebvre), plus two prospects (Landon Wilson and Jeff Kealty), plus the cash. For all that, the single most important piece of the puzzle was someone who'd been there all along - team captain Joe Sakic.

Sakic played for the Nordiques in their last seven years in Quebec, through all the bad times and now - finally - the good. Sakic, known as Ordinary Joe for the colorless quotes he contributed throughout four playoff rounds, is actually an extraordinary story, once you probe beneath the surface. In the summer of 1986, or exactly 10 years before he won the Stanley Cup, the 17-year-old from Burnaby, B.C., a Vancouver suburb, went to deepest, darkest

Saskatchewan to pursue a dream of playing in the National Hockey League.

That first year of junior hockey in Swift Current included its share of nightmares, however. Midway through the season, the Swift Current Broncos' team bus crashed on a lonely stretch of Saskatchewan highway, killing four of Sakic's teammates, including Brent Ruff, the younger brother of Florida Panthers' assistant coach Lindy Ruff. It was Canada's worst-ever hockey tragedy. Dealing with the death of close friends was a difficult lesson for one so young. Even now, Sakic says little about that eventful day, other than to acknowledge: "The tragedy 10 years ago changed my life quite a bit. When something like that happens to you, you just realize how fragile life is. You become more careful in the things you do and more accepting of the things that happen."

Thankfully, there were some lighter moments along the way. As a 17-year-old in Swift Current, Sakic stayed at the home of Colleen MacBean, who chose his name from a list of potential boarders because Sakic's birthday - July 7, 1969 - was the same as her daughter Karen's. In those days, Karen MacBean was the most famous teenager in the household after winning the Miss Teen Canada pageant two years earlier. It took Sakic longer to earn his place in the limelight.

After two seasons in junior, Sakic spent his first seven NHL seasons in relative obscurity. In his second year, the Nordiques won just 12 of 80 games, the low point of his NHL career. Sakic quietly produced a lot of goals and assists over time, but was usually the only bright light on a dismal team that missed the playoffs for six consecutive years. Things started to turn around in the 1994-95 season, the Nordiques' final year in Quebec. But Sakic really blossomed after the move to Denver.

Sakic posted career regular-season highs in goals (51) and points (120) and then scored 18 playoff goals, one short of the record shared by Jari Kurri (Edmonton Oilers, 1985) and Reggie Leach (Philadelphia Flyers, 1976) to win the Conn Smythe Trophy as the playoffs most valuable player. His timely scoring - six of Sakic's goals were game winners - helped the Avalanche defeat Vancouver, Chicago,

Year of the Rink Rat

Finally, the truth can be told. The hockey mania that gripped south Florida in the spring of 1996 can be blamed solely on one man, Rick Tabaracci.

Rick Tabaracci?! Yes.

The story begins hours before the Florida Panthers' home opener in early October. The previous afternoon, the Panthers had been spanked 4-0 by the defending Stanley Cup champion New Jersey Devils and the second-guessing had already started. The Panthers made one extremely unpopular off-season move, firing coach Roger Neilson and replacing him with untried Doug MacLean.

Neilson had brought the Panthers to within a point of the NHL playoffs in each of the team's first two season. Not bad. But it wasn't enough for general manager Bryan Murray, however, who wanted to see some of the Panthers' younger talent get more ice time. Florida was prepared to take a step backwards if it meant they could move two steps ahead at some vaguely promising future date.

On opening night, amid threats that the team was for sale because of owner Wayne Huizenga's inability to get a new arena built, only 12,087 spectators showed up for what became an historic night. Just before game time, winger Scott Mellanby discovered a rat in the Panthers' dressing room. Not one of the cute plastic ones that would eventually come cascading out of the stands to celebrate a goal, but the real thing. Without thinking about the consequences - SPCA be damned - Mellanby flipped the visiting rodent against a wall, killing it instantly.

Hours later, Mellanby went on the ice against the Calgary Flames and in the opening period, scored two goals against Tabaracci, the opposing goaltender. Afterwards, Panthers' goaltender John Vanbiesbrouck - demonstrating a media savvy picked up from all those years in New York - called Mellanby's feat the first "rat trick" in NHL history. As he would say later: "I was just trying to give a reporter a break on a story on opening night." No one could predict the fallout from Mellanby's actions.

The Panthers soared following their opening night win and by midseason, were the top team in the NHL's Eastern Conference, enabling MacLean to go behind the Eastern Conference bench for the 1996 All-star game.

Glenn Cratty/Allsport

Take a good look because you won't see the plastic rats after a Florida Panther goal anymore. The NHL sensibly passed a ruling that will penalize the home team for delay of game if the crowd litters the ice in celebration. Of anything.

The Panthers faltered in the final 20 games, but settled nicely into fourth place, a credible showing for a team that boasted one bonafide star - Vanbiesbrouck - plus a lot of guys who try hard.

The rat craze started slowly. First, the fans would toss the bootleg plastic rats onto the ice only when Mellanby scored. Eventually, rats were flying to celebrate every Panthers' goal. In advancing to the Stanley Cup final, Florida eliminated Boston and then two of the NHL's elite clubs, Philadelphia and Pittsburgh. As the Panthers moved on, South Florida caught the fever and from then on, the headline writers took over. From Rats to Riches. The Year of the Rat. Or when a heavily favored opponent went down to defeat, simply one word, plus punctuation: Rats !

In all his years, Vanbiesbrouck acknowledged that he'd never seen anything like it.

"The players and fans formed a kind of direct relationship I've never seen before," he said. Ten years earlier, Vanbiesbrouck won the Vezina Trophy as the NHL's top goaltender and helped the New York Rangers advance to the Stanley Cup semifinals. Eventually, he came to share the Rangers' goaltending duties with Mike Richter. Then, when expansion came around and New York could protect only one of its two prized goalies, the younger player - Richter - received the nod.

After Vanbiesbrouck, even hard-core fans would be hard pressed to name Florida's second-best player. Was it Mellanby? Or rookie defenseman Ed Jovanovski? Or promising center Rob Niedermayer. No Florida player cracked the top 45 in scoring. Fully 10 of the players on Florida's roster were chosen in the expansion draft only three years previously. Normally, teams try to dump their expansion draft acquisitions as quickly as possible. Not the Panthers. They drafted experienced professionals. In a relentless commitment to defense, based on Vanbiesbrouck's netminding, they wore down their more talented opponents - or they did until the Stanley Cup final.

All the time, the common thread was the rats. Their dressing room was the Rat Cave. Now, all that's left is to see how the rat craze plays itself out. No matter how adept the maintenance crews - clad in exterminator outfits - were at clearing the ice of debris, every Panther goal resulted in a lengthy stoppage in play. Eventually, commissioner Gary Bettman - playing the part of the Pied Piper of Hamelin - decreed that next season, the Panthers could be penalized for delay of game if the rats continued to rain down on the ice.

Detroit and then Florida in the finals. Colorado became the first team in NHL history with three Conn Smythe winners in the lineup, Roy and Lemieux being the previous winners.

Page, the architect of the Avalanche in his five years as GM, described Sakic as, "exactly what you want out of a skilled player because he wants to get better. With a lot of skilled players, first they get good, then very good, then excellent and then they don't know how to get to the next level. People are interviewing you and patting you on the back and giving you more money and you're still pushing yourself to get better? You have to be a special breed of player to do that." Sakic said the loss to New York in the opening round of the 1995 playoffs taught his team an important lesson about the value of experience. Sakic himself had played in only 12 career playoff games prior to this year.

"Last year against New York was a reality check," said Sakic. "We won a lot of games in the regular season (30 of the 48 that were played, second only to Detroit). Then came the playoffs and we were shocked. The Rangers came out and played with the desire you need to win the playoffs and we didn't have that. As players, we were frustrated in the summer. Every one of us looked forward to getting back in the playoffs and redeeming ourselves." Which they did.

On the whole, the 1995-96 season was a quantum leap forward for the NHL after 103-day lockout shortened the previous season to only 48 games. A quartet of the game's most enduring stars - Mario Lemieux, Mark Messier, Steve Yzerman and Dale Hawerchuk - all scored their 500th NHL goals, an important milestone. In the exhibition season, the NHL set out to make the game more aesthetically pleasing by reducing the amount of obstruction in the game. The league had previously tried to address extraneous hooking and holding that slowed down the game, only to ease as time passed. The standard of enforcement gradually dwindled as the season went along, but on balance, the league achieved its goal of freeing up its most highly skilled players.

From October to April, there was no better illustration of this point than the Detroit Red Wings, who established an NHL record by winning 62 games, most in league history. Among the Red Wings' star were a quintet of Russian-born players - Igor Larionov, Sergei Fedorov, Slava Kozlov, Vladimir Konstantinov and Slava Fetisov - that occasionally played together as a five-man unit, the way the powerful Soviet national teams of the 1980s did.

For all their regular-season success, however, the Red Wings extended the longest playoff drought in the NHL to 41 years by losing the conference championship to Colorado. Attrition played a significant role in the loss. Too many of their top players (Yzerman, Paul Coffey, Larionov) were too beat up to play at 100 per cent capacity. Others chose that precise moment to go into a slump (Fedorov, Keith Primeau).

In the end, Roy outplayed Detroit's Chris Osgood in goal and Sakic was better than Yzerman on offense. The sixth game was notable for a patently illegal hit from behind by Lemieux against Detroit's Kris Draper that sent the latter to the hospital with a broken jaw and fractured cheekbone and made Lemieux the first player in more than 40 years to miss a championship finals game because of suspension. "The expectations of our team, and our own expectation, was to get back to the Stanley Cup finals and win, and we didn't do that," said Yzerman. "We didn't live up to expectations. We didn't play as well as the Detroit Red Wings are expected to play, as well as we expected to play."

Individually, the brightest story was Mario Lemieux's remarkable comeback following a season on the sidelines, recovering from the twin evils of cancer treatment and back surgery. Lemieux's 161 points were enough to win him the scoring title over Pittsburgh Penguins' teammate Jaromir Jagr. His play dazzled all but his sharpest critic - himself. In the midst of the Penguins' playoff run - they made it to the semifinals before falling to the Panthers - Lemieux said: "I don't think I achieved the level that I was at before I took a year off. Over-all, it was a frustrating year for me, not to play at the level I played at all my career. I think I lost a step. Speed is a big part of my game, being able to challenge a player one-on-one and I was not able to do that on a regular basis this year. That was frustrating, because it had

Wide World Photos

Though he was wasn't a member of the St. Louis Blues for very long, future Hall of Famer **Wayne Gretzky** stayed long enough to knock a puck past Vancouver's **Kirk McLean**. The Great One will be scoring in New York in 1996-97 as the Rangers signed him after negotiations to keep Gretzky in St. Louis failed.

been part of my game since I was real young and it was something I enjoyed doing."

As part of his return, Lemieux - the Natural - started working on off-ice conditioning for the first time in his hockey-playing life, in a bid to strengthen his back and improve his cardio-vascular capacity. The result: Lemieux developed a more sculpted look, but even with that, said he lacked the stamina he had in previous years. He blamed that on the radiation treatments he received for his Hodgkin's disease.

"I get tired a lot quicker and I'm not able to recuperate like I used to, let's say, three years ago. I was able to go out for two or three minutes, come back for 30 seconds and I was ready to go again. It's been a struggle this year." Complicating matters was the fact that his wife, Nathalie, had a difficult pregnancy before giving birth to their third child, Austin, three months prematurely, in March.

So at age 30, when the NHL desperately needed his star power, Lemieux was toying with the idea of retiring again following the Penguins' playoff loss. Two factors were to determine his hockey future: if he thought the Penguins were capable of challenging for another Stanley Cup; and his health. "I'm going to sit down after the playoffs are over and see if I want to come back and play at a lower level which I'm not too comfortable with or do something else with my life," said Lemieux.

Lemieux was not the only star to crave another championship. Wayne Gretzky, the most prolific scorer in NHL history, essentially forced a Feb. 27 trade that saw him move from the also-ran Los Angeles Kings to the middle-of-the-pack St. Louis Blues. Considering Gretzky became an unrestricted free agent on July 1, the Blues sacrificed a Kings' ransom - three players, plus a No. 1 choice in the 1997 entry draft - to rent him. Gretzky struggled at times in his early days in St. Louis - a collision with the Oilers' Kelly Buchberger knocked him senseless in early March - but come playoff

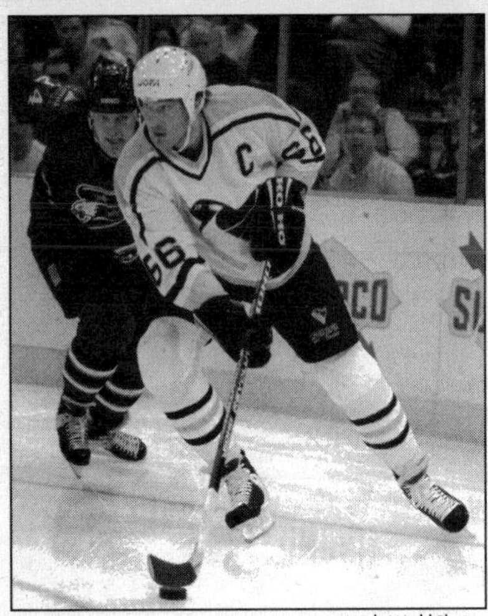

Wide World Photos

The amazing and courageous **Mario Lemieux** won his third MVP trophy and his fifth scoring title in 1996. In the spring, Lemieux openly contemplated retirement due to back problems but seemed set to return to Pittsburgh as summer ended.

time, he produced 16 points in 13 games and forced the Red Wings into double overtime before they escaped with a 1-0 win in the seventh game of their second-round series.

Blues' general manager Mike Keenan lusted after Gretzky, in part because 12 months of trades and free-agent signings did little to bring St. Louis any closer to a championship. Acquiring the highest scorer in NHL history deflected criticism from some of his previous moves - or it did until negotiations to sign Gretzky failed to bring him into the fold prior to July 1 and The Great One bolted for the Big Apple. In their inexorable quest to reproduce the great Edmonton teams of the last decade, the New York Rangers signed the aging center to a two-year deal worth approximately $8 million plus incentives, which is actually less money than he made last year. (Take *that,* Mike Keenan!) Ultimately, Gretzky was enamored with the possibility of winning at least one more championship with his close friend and former Oiler teammate Mark Messier, with whom he won four Stanley Cups in the 1980's.

The endless Edmonton reunion being staged in Madison Square Garden was apparently not as enticing to Jari Kurri as the former Oiler star left the Rangers to sign a one-year contract with the Mighty Ducks of Anaheim. Kurri will be called upon to lend his experience to the young team, especially superstars Paul Kariya and Teemu Selanne. Another west coast team, the San Jose Sharks, was possibly the most active club in the immediate off-season, adding experience and grit with the acquisition of perennial tough guys Marty McSorley (another former Oiler), Todd Ewen and Tim Hunter. The Sharks also added scoring punch by acquiring Bernie Nicholls. Winger Tony Granato and goaltender Kelly Hrudey round the list of players who will need to know the way to San Jose.

In another significant player move, the Washington Capitals made a move to bolster their defense, or at least their offense from the point, by signing the well-traveled Phil Housley to a three-year contract.

Once again, hockey's growing popularity in the Sunbelt proved to be a focal point again, especially in Canada, which lost its second NHL team in two years. After attempts to build a new arena in Winnipeg fell apart, a Minneapolis investor bought the Jets and shifted the franchise to Phoenix, where the Coyotes begin play in the 1996-97 season. (The Coyotes wasted no time in bringing in a marquee player to town when the team traded for two-way center superstar Jeremy Roenick from the Chicago for flashy Alexei Zhamnov, Craig Mills, and a first-round pick. Roenick's offensive prowess, combined with his feistiness, should make him a fan favorite in Phoenix. If he signs with them.) In all, it means there are more teams in California, Florida, Arizona and Texas (seven) than there are in all of Canada (six).

Fox TV further alienated Canadian hockey fans by introducing Fox Trax, a video enhancement of the puck that - in theory - was supposed to make it easier for viewers in regions where hockey is not indigenous to follow the game.

Perhaps the most telling blow to Canadian pride, though, was seeing all their teams ousted by the end of the first round. That gave Canada six weeks to lament the passing of the Avalanche into American hands - and then watch as Sakic made the traditional Stanley Cup skate around a Miami ice surface littered with plastic rats. ❐

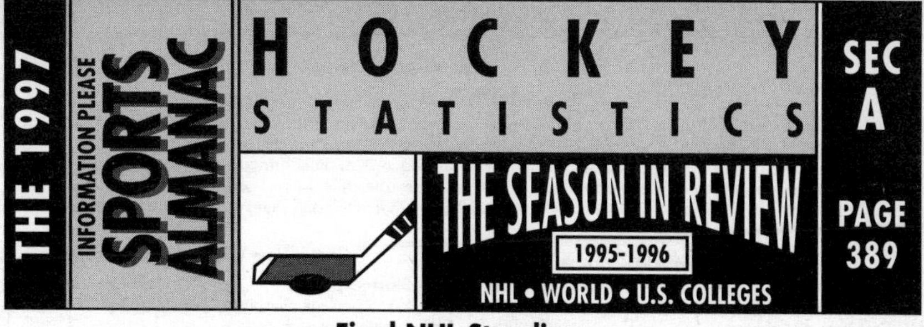

THE 1997
INFORMATION PLEASE
SPORTS ALMANAC
HOCKEY
STATISTICS
SEC
A
THE SEASON IN REVIEW
1995-1996
NHL • WORLD • U.S. COLLEGES
PAGE
389

Final NHL Standings

Division champions (*) and playoff qualifiers (†) are noted. GF and GA refer to goals for and against while Dif is the difference between the two. Number of seasons listed after each head coach refers to current tenure with club through 1995–96 season. Colorado (formerly Quebec) moved from the Northeast Division to the Pacific Division in 1995-96.

Western Conference

Central Division

	W	L	T	Pts	GF	GA	Dif
*Detroit	62	13	7	131	325	181	+144
†Chicago	40	28	14	94	273	220	+53
†Toronto	34	36	12	80	247	252	-5
†St. Louis	32	34	16	80	219	248	-29
†Winnipeg	36	40	6	78	275	291	-16
Dallas	26	42	14	66	227	280	-53

Head Coaches: Det— Scotty Bowman (3rd season); **Chi**— Craig Hartsburg (1st); **Tor**— fired Pat Burns (4th, 25–30–10) on Mar. 5 and replaced him with Nick Beverly (9–6–2); **St.L**— Mike Keenan (2nd); **Win**— Terry Simpson (2nd); **Dal**— GM-coach Bob Gainey (6th, 11-19-8) replaced himself with Ken Hitchcock (15–23–5) on Jan. 8.

1994-95 Standings: 1. Detroit (33–11–4, 70 points); 2. St. Louis (28–15–5, 61 pts); 3. Chicago (24–19–5, 53 pts); 4. Toronto (21–19–8, 50 pts); 5. Dallas (17–23–8, 42 pts); 6. Winnipeg (16–25–7, 39 pts).

Pacific Division

	W	L	T	Pts	GF	GA	Dif
*Colorado	47	25	10	104	326	240	+86
†Calgary	34	37	11	79	241	240	+1
†Vancouver	32	35	15	79	278	278	0
Anaheim	35	39	8	78	234	247	-13
Edmonton	30	44	8	68	240	304	-64
Los Angeles	24	40	18	66	256	302	-46
San Jose	20	55	7	47	252	357	-105

Head Coaches: Col— Marc Crawford (2nd season); **Cal**— Pierre Page (1st); **Van**— Fired Rick Ley (2nd, 29–32–15) and replaced him with GM Pat Quinn (3–3–0) on Mar. 28; **Ana**— Ron Wilson (3rd); **Edm**— Ron Low (2nd); **LA**— Larry Robinson (1st); **SJ**— fired Kevin Constantine (3rd, 3–18–4) and replaced him with asst. coach Jim Wiley (17–37–3) on Dec. 2.

1994-95 Standings: 1. Calgary (24–17–7, 55 points); 2. Vancouver (18–18–12, 48 pts); 3. San Jose (19–25–4, 42 pts); 4. Los Angeles (16–23–9, 41 pts); 5. Edmonton (17–27–4, 38 pts); 6. Anaheim (16–27–5, 37 pts).

Eastern Conference

Northeast Division

	W	L	T	Pts	GF	GA	Dif
*Pittsburgh	49	29	4	102	362	284	+78
†Boston	40	31	11	91	282	269	+13
†Montreal	40	32	10	90	265	248	+17
Hartford	34	39	9	77	237	259	-22
Buffalo	33	42	7	73	247	262	-15
Ottawa	18	59	5	41	191	291	-100

Head Coaches: Pit— Eddie Johnston (3rd); **Bos**— Steve Kasper (1st); **Mon**— fired Jacques Demers (4th, 0–4) on Oct. 17 and replaced him on Oct. 21 with Mario Tremblay (40–27–10); **Hart**— fired Paul Holmgren (2nd, 5–6–1) on Nov. 6 and replaced him with asst. coach Paul Maurice (29–33–8); **Buf**— Ted Nolan (1st); **Ott**— fired Rick Bowness (4th, 6–13–0) on Nov. 20 and replaced him with Dave Allison; fired Allison (2–22–1) on Jan. 23 and replaced him with Jacques Martin (10–24–4).

1994–95 Standings: 1. Quebec (30–13–5, 65 points); 2. Pittsburgh (29–16–3, 61 pts); 3. Boston (27–18–3, 57 pts); 4. Buffalo (22–19–7, 51 pts); 5. Hartford (19–24–5, 43 pts); 6. Montreal (18–23–7, 43 pts); 7. Ottawa (9–34–5, 23 pts).

Atlantic Division

	W	L	T	Pts	GF	GA	Dif
*Philadelphia	45	24	13	103	282	208	+74
†NY Rangers	41	27	14	96	272	237	+35
†Florida	41	31	10	92	254	234	+20
†Washington	39	32	11	89	234	204	+20
†Tampa Bay	38	32	12	88	238	248	-10
New Jersey	37	33	12	86	215	202	+13
NY Islanders	22	50	10	54	229	315	-86

Head Coaches: Phi— Terry Murray (2nd season); **NYR**— Colin Campbell (2nd); **Fla**— Doug MacLean (2nd); **Wash**— Jim Schoenfeld (3rd); **TB**— Terry Crisp (4th); **NJ**— Jacques Lemaire (3rd); **NYI**— Mike Milbury (1st).

1994-95 Standings: 1. Philadelphia (28–16–4, 60 points); 2. New Jersey (22–18–8, 52 pts); 3. Washington (22–18–8, 52 pts); 4. NY Rangers (22–23–3, 47 pts); 5. Florida (20–22–6, 46 pts); 6. Tampa Bay (17–28–3, 37 pts); 7. NY Islanders (15–28–5, 35 pts).

Home & Away, Division, Conference Records

Sixteen teams— eight from each conference— qualify for the Stanley Cup Playoffs; (*) indicates division champions.

Western Conference

	Pts	Home	Away	Div	Conf
1 Detroit*	131	36-3-2	26-10-5	21-3-4	43-6-7
2 Colorado*	104	24-10-7	23-15-3	20-8-4	34-17-5
3 Chicago	94	22-13-6	18-15-8	11-10-7	25-19-12
4 Toronto	80	19-15-7	15-21-5	10-14-4	27-21-8
5 St. Louis	80	15-17-9	17-17-7	11-12-5	23-23-10
6 Calgary	79	18-18-5	16-19-6	16-13-3	22-26-8
7 Vancouver	79	15-19-7	17-16-8	14-11-7	23-22-11
8 Winnipeg	78	22-16-3	14-24-3	12-12-4	25-26-5
Anaheim	78	22-15-4	13-24-4	15-16-1	22-30-4
Edmonton	68	15-21-5	15-23-3	15-12-5	19-30-7
Dallas	66	14-18-9	12-24-5	5-19-4	21-26-9
Los Angeles	66	16-16-9	8-24-9	10-14-8	15-26-15
San Jose	47	12-26-3	8-29-4	7-23-2	13-40-3

Eastern Conference

	Pts	Home	Away	Div	Conf
1 Philadelphia*	103	27-9-5	18-15-8	13-13-6	30-19-7
2 Pittsburgh*	102	32-9-0	17-20-4	16-10-2	34-19-3
3 NY Rangers	96	22-10-9	19-17-5	15-11-6	27-19-10
4 Florida	92	25-12-4	16-19-6	18-10-4	29-22-5
5 Boston	91	22-14-5	18-17-6	16-9-3	29-20-7
6 Montreal	90	23-12-6	17-20-4	19-8-1	26-23-7
7 Washington	89	21-15-5	18-17-6	12-15-5	26-23-7
8 Tampa Bay	88	22-14-5	16-18-7	13-13-6	25-23-8
New Jersey	86	22-17-2	15-16-10	19-10-3	28-20-8
Hartford	77	22-15-4	12-24-5	10-16-2	19-29-8
Buffalo	73	19-17-5	14-25-2	14-13-1	24-27-5
NY Islanders	54	14-21-6	8-29-4	6-24-2	14-34-8
Ottawa	41	8-28-5	10-31-0	3-22-3	10-43-3

1996 NHL All-Star Game

East, 5–4

46th NHL All-Star Game. **Date:** Jan. 20 at the FleetCenter in Boston; **Coaches:** Doug MacLean, Florida (East) and Scotty Bowman, Detroit (West); **MVP:** Ray Bourque, Boston defenseman (East) — game winning goal (3rd per.; 19:22).

Starters were chosen by fan vote, reserves by a 5–man panel of league GMs. Paul Kariya was promoted to the Western Conference starting lineup in place of injured Vancouver LW Pavel Bure. Larry Murphy was added to the Western Conference reserves in place of injured Chicago D Gary Suter. Senior stars Craig MacTavish and Denis Savard were selected in recognition of career accomplishments.

Western Conference

	Starters	G	A	Pts	PM
D	Paul Coffey, Detroit	1	1	2	0
LW	Paul Kariya, Anaheim	1	1	2	0
RW	Brett Hull, St. Louis	1	0	1	0
D	Chris Chelios, Chicago	0	0	0	0
C	Wayne Gretzky, Los Angeles	0	0	0	0
	Reserves				
C	Sergei Fedorov, Detroit	0	1	1	0
W	Alexander Mogilny, Vancouver	0	1	1	0
W	Teemu Selanne, Winnipeg	1	0	1	0
C	Mats Sundin, Toronto	0	1	1	0
W	Theoren Fleury, Calgary	0	0	0	0
C	Peter Forsberg, Colorado	0	0	0	0
W	Mike Gartner, Toronto	0	0	0	0
D	Kevin Hatcher, Dallas	0	0	0	0
D	Nicklas Lidstrom, Detroit	0	0	0	0
D	Al MacInnis, St. Louis	0	0	0	0
D	Larry Murphy, Toronto	0	0	0	0
W	Owen Nolan, San Jose	0	0	0	0
C	Joe Sakic, Colorado	0	0	0	0
C	Denis Savard, Chicago	0	0	0	0
C	Doug Weight, Edmonton	0	0	0	0
	TOTALS	4	5	9	2*

* Western Conference bench received a 2 minute penalty for too many men on the ice (served by Mike Gartner)

Goaltenders	Mins	Shots	Saves	GA
Ed Belfour, Chi	20:00	18	16	2
Chris Osgood, Det	20:00	15	13	2
Felix Potvin, Tor	20:00	8	7	1
TOTALS	60:00	41	36	5

Eastern Conference

	Starters	G	A	Pts	PM
C	Mario Lemieux, Pittsburgh	0	2	2	0
RW	Jaromir Jagr, Pittsburgh	1	0	1	0
LW	Brendan Shanahan, Hartford	1	0	1	0
D	Ray Bourque, Boston	1	0	1	0
D	Scott Stevens, New Jersey	0	0	0	0
	Reserves				
W	Pat Verbeek, NY Rangers	1	1	2	0
C	Ron Francis, Pittsburgh	0	1	1	0
W	John LeClair, Philadelphia	0	1	1	0
D	Brian Leetch, NY Rangers	0	1	1	0
C	Eric Lindros, Philadelphia	1	0	1	0
C	Mark Messier, NY Rangers	0	1	1	0
W	Cam Neely, Boston	0	1	1	0
D	M. Schneider, NY Islanders	0	1	1	0
C	Pierre Turgeon, Montreal	0	1	1	0
W	Daniel Alfredsson, Ottawa	0	0	0	0
W	Peter Bondra, Washington	0	0	0	0
D	Eric Desjardins, Philadelphia	0	0	0	0
D	Roman Hamrlik, Tampa Bay	0	0	0	0
C	Craig MacTavish, Philadelphia	0	0	0	0
W	Scott Mellanby, Florida	0	0	0	0
	TOTALS	5	10	15	2*

* Eastern Conference bench received a 2 minute penalty for too many men on the ice (served by Scott Mellanby)

Goaltenders	Mins	Shots	Saves	GA
Martin Brodeur, NJ	20:00	12	12	0
John Vanbiesbrouck, NYR	20:00	7	4	3
Dominik Hasek, Buf	20:00	13	12	1
TOTALS	60:00	32	28	4

Score by Periods

	1	2	3	Final
Western	0	3	1	— 4
Eastern	2	2	1	— 5

Power plays: Western — 0/1; Eastern — 0/1. **Officials:** Mark Faucette (referee), Ron Asseltine and Brad Lazarowich (linesmen). **Attendance:** 17,565. **TV Rating:** 4.1/7 share (Fox).

Hat Tricks

Players scored three or more goals in one game a total of 93 times during the 1996 regular season. Pittsburgh's Mario Lemieux led the way with six hat tricks, including one four-goal game and one five-goal game.

Five Goals	**Date**	**Score**
Mario Lemieux, Pit vs St.L	Mar. 26	Pit, 8-4
Four Goals	**Date**	**Score**
Peter Bondra, Wash vs NYI	Feb. 3	Wash, 6-5
Peter Bondra, Wash at Buf	Apr. 3	Wash, 5-1
Brett Hull, St.L vs Edm	Oct. 10	St.L, 5-3
Vyacheslav Kozlov, Det at Mon	Dec. 2	Det, 11-1
Mario Lemieux, Pit at Bos	Nov. 30	Pit, 9-6
Mike Modano, Dal vs Edm	Feb. 16	Dal, 6-1
Petr Nedved, Pit vs Win	Mar. 5	Pit, 9-4
Owen Nolan, SJ at Ana	Dec. 19	SJ, 7-4
Adam Oates, Bos vs Fla	Dec. 14	Bos, 6-4
Teemu Selanne, Win vs Edm	Dec. 15	Win, 9-4
Keith Tkachuk, Win at Dal	Mar. 26	Win, 8-2
Three Goals	**Date**	**Score**
Daniel Alfredsson*, Ott at Hart	Nov. 2	Ott, 5-0
Tony Amonte, Chi vs St.L	Feb. 22	St.L, 4-3
Niklas Andersson*, NYI vs Dal	Feb. 4	NYI, 5-3
Jason Arnott, Edm at Mon	Mar. 23	Edm, 6-5
Donald Audette, Buf vs SJ	Nov. 8	Buf, 7-2
Brian Bellows, TB at SJ	Mar. 1	TB, 7-3
Peter Bondra, Wash vs Ott	Jan. 11	Wash, 6-1
Peter Bondra, Wash at NYI	Mar. 26	Wash, 7-1
Geoff Courtnall, St.L at NYI	Nov. 11	St.L, 4-1
Russ Courtnall, Van vs Buf	Mar. 6	Van, 5-2
Jason Dawe, Buf at Mon	Jan. 6	Buf, 7-6
Ray Ferraro, NYR Vs Mon	Jan. 3	NYR, 7-4
Theoren Fleury, Calg vs LA	Dec. 11	Calg, 6-2
Theoren Fleury, Calg vs TB	Jan 2	Calg, 10-0
Theoren Fleury, Calg at LA	Jan. 16	Tied, 5-5
Peter Forsberg, Col at Phi	Feb. 11	Tied, 3-3
Peter Forsberg, Col vs Edm	Feb. 19	Col, 7-5
Ron Francis, Pit at SJ	Nov. 10	Pit, 9-1
Jeff Friesen, SJ at Win	Mar. 20	SJ, 7-1
Johan Garpenlov, Fla at Wash	Jan. 23	Fla, 5-4
Kevin Hatcher, Dal at Edm	Jan. 24	Dal, 5-3
Steve Heinze, Bos vs NYR	Mar. 23	NYR, 5-4
Brett Hull, St.L at SJ	Mar. 15	St.L, 4-2

Three Goals	Date	Score
Valeri Kamensky, Col vs SJ	Dec. 5	Col, 12-2
Valeri Kamensky, Col at LA	Mar. 20	Col, 5-2
S. Konowalchuk, Wash at Win	Dec. 10	Wash, 6-1
S. Konowalchuk, Wash vs NYR	Jan. 5	Tied, 4-4
Igor Korolev, Win vs Dal	Oct. 7	Win, 7-5
Jari Kurri, LA at Wash	Oct. 20	LA, 7-4
Pat LaFontaine, Buf vs Fla	Feb 25	Buf, 6-1
John LeClair, Phi vs SJ	Mar. 17	Phi, 8-2
John LeClair, Phi vs Pit	Mar. 31	Phi, 4-1
Claude Lemieux, Col at NYI	Nov. 28	Col, 7-3
Claude Lemieux, Col at Pot	Jan. 16	Col, 5-2
Mario Lemieux, Pit at NYI	Oct. 26	Pit, 7-5
Mario Lemieux, Pit at NJ	Oct. 28	Pit, 5-3
Mario Lemieux, Pit vs Fla	Dec. 30	Pit, 6-5
Mario Lemieux, Pit vs Phi	Jan. 27	Pit, 7-4
Trevor Linden, Van vs Col	Mar 9	Col, 7-5
Eric Lindros, Phi at St.L	Feb. 3	Phi, 7-3
Mark Messier, NYR vs Calg	Nov. 6	NYR, 4-2
Kevin Miller, SJ vs Hart	Jan. 30	SJ, 8-2
Alexander Mogilny, Van at SJ	Oct. 14	Van, 7-6
Alexander Mogilny, Van at Ana	Dec. 22	Van, 6-2
Alexander Mogilny, Van vs TB	Jan. 6	Van, 9-2
Kirk Muller, Tor vs Calg	Mar. 9	Tor, 4-3
Markus Naslund, Pit vs Ott	Nov. 28	Pit, 7-2
Markus Naslund, Van vs Calg	Apr. 13	Van, 5-0
Cam Neely, Bos vs NYI	Oct. 7	Tied, 4-4
Ed Olczyk, Win vs Mon	Dec. 12	Mon, 6-5
Zigmund Palffy, NYI vs Win	Mar. 3	Win, 7-5
Zigmund Palffy, NYI vs Bos	Mar. 5	NYI, 5-3
Dan Quinn, Ott at TB	Oct. 15	Ott, 7-4
Dave Reid, Bos vs Calg	Dec. 16	Bos, 6-3
Stephane Richer, NJ at TB	Mar. 26	NJ, 6-4
Gary Roberts, Calg vs Buf	Jan. 12	Calg, 3-1
Gary Roberts, Calg vs SJ	Feb. 20	Calg, 5-3
Gary Roberts, Calg vs Pit	Feb. 29	Calg, 7-3
Cliff Ronning, Van vs SJ	Dec. 1	Van, 7-2
Martin Rucinsky, Mon at Fla	Jan. 25	Mon, 6-2
Geoff Sanderson, Hart at Pit	Dec. 28	Pit, 9-4
Geoff Sanderson, Hart vs Fla	Mar. 2	Hart, 7-1
Brian Savage, Mon vs Chi	Oct. 28	Mon, 5-3
Teemu Selanne, Ana vs SJ	Feb. 25	Ana, 4-3
Teemu Selanne, Ana vs St.L	Mar. 17	Ana, 5-1
Brendan Shanahan, Hart at Pit	Feb. 23	Pit, 5-4
Ray Sheppard, SJ at Pit	Jan. 13	SJ, 10-8
Ray Sheppard, Fla vs NYI	Mar. 21	Fla, 3-2
Jozef Stumpel, Bos vs Win	Nov. 21	Bos, 5-4
Rick Tocchet, Bos vs Pit	Mar. 14	Bos, 4-2
Rick Tocchet, Bos vs Ott	Mar. 21	Bos, 3-1
Pierre Turgeon, Mon vs Buf	Jan. 6	Buf, 7-6
Gary Valk, Ana at St.L	Mar. 22	Ana, 6-1
Pat Verbeek, NYR vs Pit	Nov. 21	NYR, 9-4
Pat Verbeek, NYR at Ott	Dec. 2	NYR, 4-2
Doug Weight, Edm vs Col	Nov. 20	Tied, 3-3
Jason Wiemer, TB at SJ	Mar. 1	TB, 7-3
Vitali Yachmenev*, LA vs Mon	Mar. 2	LA, 5-4
Alexei Yashin, Ott at St.L	Feb. 20	Ott, 7-1
Alexei Yegorov*, SJ at Calg	Feb. 20	Calg, 5-3
Alexei Zhamnov, Win at Col	Feb. 1	Col, 6-4

Game-Winning Goals in Overtime

A total of 201 games were tied after regulation during the 1996 regular season, with 64 being resolved in overtime. Teams play one five-minute overtime period during the regular season.

	Date	Time	Score
Yanic Perreault, LA vs Chi	10/10	2:10	LA, 6-5
Mike Craig, Tor vs Calg	10/20	1:31	Tor, 4-3
Yanic Perreault, LA at Pit	10/21	0:40	LA, 3-2
Bob Sweeney, NYI at Fla	10/31	3:56	NYI, 5-4
Steve Yzerman, Det at Bos	11/2	1:50	Det, 6-5
Paul Kariya, Ana at Mon	11/8	2:35	Ana, 3-2
Jason Arnott, Edm at TB	11/10	2:41	Edm, 4-3
Shane Doan*, Win vs Chi	11/14	0:39	Win, 6-5
Benoit Hogue, Tor at TB	11/16	0:32	Tor, 5-4
Jaromir Jagr, Pit at Wash	11/17	2:48	Pit, 3-2
Peter Douris, Ana vs NYI	11/17	4:59	Ana, 2-1
Petr Klima, TB vs Van	11/18	2:06	TB, 5-4
Chris Therien, Phi vs Van	11/19	0:32	Phi, 3-2
Turner Stevenson, Mon vs Hart	11/20	3:12	Mon, 4-3
Brent Sutter, Chi at Ana	11/24	3:08	Chi, 5-4
Stephane Richer, NJ vs Col	11/29	0:57	NJ, 4-3
Kevin Haller, Phi at Fla	11/29	4:30	Phi, 2-1
Pat Verbeek, NYR vs Det	12/8	0:27	NYR, 2-1
S. Konowalchuk, Wash vs NYI	12/14	2:16	Wash, 4-3
Dave Andreychuk, Tor at Ana	12/17	2:05	Tor, 3-2
Bill Guerin, NJ vs Phi	12/19	2:13	NJ, 5-4
Ted Donato, Bos at Buf	12/22	1:37	Bos, 3-2
Miroslav Satan*, Edm vs L.A.	12/29	3:44	Edm, 5-4
Mats Sundin, Tor at St.L	12/30	0:06	Tor, 4-3
Sandy McCarthy, Calg vs Hfd	1/10	2:06	Calg, 3-2
Doug Weight, Edm vs Buf	1/13	4:48	Edm, 5-4
Mario Lemieux, Pit vs Bos	1/22	1:54	Pit, 7-6
Alex Hicks, Ana at Van	1/24	1:34	Ana, 2-1
Valeri Kamensky, Col at SJ	1/27	2:49	Col, 4-3
S. Konowalchuk, Wash vs Phi	1/28	4:20	Wash, 3-2
Mathieu Schneider, NYI vs Buf	1/30	2:19	NYI, 5-4
Theoren Fleury, Calg vs Edm	1/30	1:51	Calg, 3-2
Steve Thomas, NJ at Van	1/30	3:46	NJ, 3-2
Eric Desjardins, Phi vs Mon	2/1	4:30	Phi, 3-2
Randy McKay, NJ at Ott	2/3	0:41	NJ, 3-2
Michal Pivonka, Wash vs NYI	2/3	1:21	Wash, 6-5
Derek Plante, Buf vs Bos	2/7	0:24	Buf, 2-1
Adam Burt, Hart at Col	2/9	3:24	Hart, 3-2
Russ Courtnall, Van at Edm	2/9	0:21	Van, 3-2
Sergei Fedorov, Det at TB	2/10	0:52	Det, 3-2
Mike Keane, Col at Fla	2/16	0:55	Col, 5-4
Geoff Sanderson, Hart vs Buf	2/17	1:49	Hart, 2-1
Mark Messier, NYR at Ott	2/17	2:31	NYR, 2-1
Paul Kariya, Ana at LA	2/17	4:07	Ana, 2-1
Mario Lemieux, Pit vs NYR	2/18	2:17	Pit, 4-3
Brian Bellows, TB at Tor	2/21	1:42	TB, 3-2
Alex Hicks, Ana vs Bos	2/21	1:35	Ana, 4-3
Brian Noonan, St.L at Chi	2/22	3:14	St.L, 4-3
Rob Zamuner, TB at NYI	2/23	4:45	TB, 3-2
Dallas Drake, Win vs Chi	2/23	0:17	Win, 1-0
Mariusz Czerkawski, Edm at Bos	2/27	4:40	Edm, 4-3
Derek Plante, Buf at Ott	2/28	4:36	Buf, 3-2
Paul Kariya, Ana vs Buf	3/8	2:03	Ana, 3-2
Steve Thomas, NJ at Pit	3/9	0:21	NJ, 4-3
Bill Guerin, NJ at Phi	3/10	3:45	NJ, 3-2
Darren McCarty, Det at Tor	3/20	2:41	Det, 4-3
Ulf Dahlen, SJ at Calg	3/22	1:09	SJ, 2-1
Steve Thomas, NJ at NYI	3/23	3:38	NJ, 3-2
Tim Sweeney, Bos at Hart	3/27	3:01	Bos, 6-5
Michal Pivonka, Wash at Mon	3/27	4:14	Wash, 1-0
Marc Bureau, Mon at Bos	3/28	2:07	Mon, 4-3
Bob Corkum, Phi at Buf	3/29	3:50	Phi, 6-5
Richard Matvichuk, Dal at Calg	4/9	1:53	Dal, 4-3
Yanic Perreault, LA at Col	4/14	4:12	LA, 5-4

Pittsburgh Penguins
Mario Lemieux
Scoring

New York Rangers
Brian Leetch
Defenseman Points

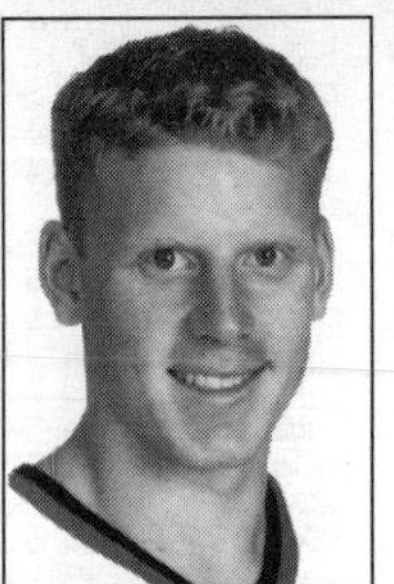
Ottawa Senators
Daniel Alfredsson
Rookie Points

Detroit Red Wings
Chris Osgood
Goaltending Wins

NHL Regular Season Individual Leaders

(*) indicates rookie eligible for Calder Trophy.

Scoring

	Pos	Gm	G	A	Pts	+/-	PM	PP	SH	GW	GT	Shots	Pct
Mario Lemieux, Pittsburgh	C	70	69	92	**161**	10	54	31	8	8	0	338	20.4
Jaromir Jagr, Pittsburgh	R	82	62	87	**149**	31	96	20	1	12	1	403	15.4
Joe Sakic, Colorado	C	82	51	69	**120**	14	44	17	6	7	1	339	15.0
Ron Francis, Pittsburgh	C	77	27	92	**119**	25	56	12	1	4	0	158	17.1
Peter Forsberg, Colorado	C	82	30	86	**116**	26	47	7	3	3	0	217	13.8
Eric Lindros, Philadelphia	C	73	47	68	**115**	26	163	15	0	4	0	294	16.0
Paul Kariya, Anaheim	L	82	50	58	**108**	9	20	20	3	9	0	349	14.3
Teemu Selanne, Win-Ana	R	79	40	68	**108**	5	22	9	1	5	0	267	15.0
Alexander Mogilny, Vancouver	R	79	55	52	**107**	14	16	10	5	6	3	292	18.8
Sergei Fedorov, Detroit	C	78	39	68	**107**	49	48	11	3	11	1	306	12.7
Doug Weight, Edmonton	C	82	25	79	**104**	19-	95	9	0	2	1	204	12.3
Wayne Gretzky, LA-St.L	C	80	23	79	**102**	13-	34	6	1	3	1	195	11.8
Mark Messier, NY Rangers	C	74	47	52	**99**	29	122	14	1	5	1	241	19.5
Petr Nedved, Pittsburgh	C	80	45	54	**99**	37	68	8	1	5	1	204	22.1
Keith Tkachuk, Winnipeg	L	76	50	48	**98**	11	156	20	2	6	0	249	20.1
John LeClair, Philadelphia	L	82	51	46	**97**	21	64	19	0	10	2	270	18.9
Theoren Fleury, Calgary	R	80	46	50	**96**	17	112	17	5	4	0	353	13.0
Pierre Turgeon, Montreal	C	80	38	58	**96**	19	44	17	1	6	0	297	12.8
Steve Yzerman, Detroit	C	80	36	59	**95**	29	64	16	2	8	0	220	16.4
Vincent Damphousse, Montreal	C	80	38	56	**94**	5	158	11	4	3	0	254	15.0

Goals

Lemieux, Pit 69
Jagr, Pit 62
Mogilny, Van 55
Bondra, Wash 52
LeClair, Phi 51
Sakic, Col 51
Tkachuk, Win 50
Kariya, Ana 50
Lindros, Phi 47
Messier, NYR 47
Fleury, Calg 46
Nedved, Pit 45

Assists

Lemieux, Pit 92
Francis, Pit 92
Jagr, Pit 87
Forsberg, Col 86
Gretzky, LA-St.L 79
Weight, Edm 79
Leetch, NYR 70
Sakic, Col 69
Lindros, Phi 68
Fedorov, Det 68
Selanne, Win-Ana 68
Oates, Bos 67

Defenseman Points

Leetch, NYR 85
Bourque, Bos 82
Coffey, Det 74
Chelios, Chi 72
Housley, Calg-NJ 68
Suter, Chi 67
Lidstrom, Det 67
Zubov, Pit 66
Hamrlik, TB 65
MacInnis, St.L 61
Murphy, Tor 61
Svehla, Fla 57

Rookie Points

Alfredsson, Ott 61
Daze, Chi 53
Yachmenev, LA 53
Koivu, Mon 45
Bure, Mon 42
Sykora, NJ 42
Bertuzzi, NYI 39
Ragnarsson, SJ 39
Satan, Edm 35
Stillman, Calg 35
Marshall, Dal 28
Lehtinen, Dal 28

Plus/Minus

Konstantinov, Det ..... +60
Fedorov, Det ..... +49
Fetisov, Det ..... +37
Nedved, Pit ..... +37
Kozlov, Det ..... +33
Leschyshyn, Col ..... +32
Larionov, Det ..... +31
Jagr, Pit ..... +31
Bourque, Bos ..... +31
Carney, Chi ..... +31

Penalty Minutes

Barnaby, Buf 335
Ciccone, TB-Chi 306
Domi, Tor 297
May, Buf 295
Ray, Buf 287
Ewen, Ana 285
Vial, Ott 276
Karpa, Ana 270
Daniels, Hart 254
Simon, Col 250

Power Play Goals

Lemieux, Pit 31
Tkachuk, Win 20
Jagr, Pit 20
Kariya, Ana 20
Mellanby, Fla 19
LeClair, Phi 19
Kamensky, Col 18
Seven tied with 17 each.

Short-Handed Goals

Lemieux, Pit 8
Reid, Bos 6
Sundin, Tor 6
Baker, SJ 6
Fitzgerald, Fla 6
Sakic, Col 6
Hull, St.L 5
Mogilny, Van 5
Fleury, Calg 5

Goaltending

(Minimum 25 games)

	Gm	Min	GAA	GA	Shots	Sv%	EN	SO	Record	Offense G	Offense A	Offense Pts	Offense PM
Ron Hextall, Philadelphia	53	3102	**2.166**	112	1292	.913	2	4	31-13-7	0	1	1	28
Chris Osgood, Detroit	50	2933	**2.168**	106	1190	.911	1	5	39-6-5	1	2	3	4
Jim Carey, Washington	71	4069	**2.26**	153	1631	.906	4	9	35-24-9	0	1	1	6
Mike Vernon, Detroit	32	1855	**2.26**	70	723	.903	1	3	21-7-2	0	0	0	2
Martin Brodeur, New Jersey	77	4434	**2.34**	173	1954	.911	8	6	34-30-12	0	1	1	6
Jeff Hackett, Chicago	35	2000	**2.40**	80	948	.916	2	4	18-11-4	0	1	1	8
Daren Puppa, Tampa Bay	57	3189	**2.46**	131	1605	.918	2	5	29-16-9	0	1	1	4
John Vanbiesbrouck, Florida	57	3178	**2.68**	142	1473	.904	2	2	26-20-7	0	2	2	10
Mike Richter, NY Rangers	41	2396	**2.68**	107	1221	.912	3	3	24-13-3	0	1	1	4
Ed Belfour, Chicago	50	2956	**2.74**	135	1373	.902	3	1	22-17-10	0	2	2	36
Damian Rhodes, Tor-Ott	47	2747	**2.77**	127	1342	.905	1	2	14-27-5	0	2	2	4
Patrick Roy, Mon-Col	61	3565	**2.78**	165	1797	.908	3	2	34-24-2	0	0	0	10
Trevor Kidd, Calgary	47	2570	**2.78**	119	1130	.895	2	3	15-21-8	0	2	2	4
Dominik Hasek, Buffalo	59	3417	**2.83**	161	2011	.920	5	2	22-30-6	0	1	1	6
Guy Hebert, Anaheim	59	3326	**2.83**	157	1820	.914	3	4	28-23-5	0	0	0	6

Wins

Osgood, Det	39
Carey, Wash	35
Roy, Mon-Col	34
Ranford, Edm-Bos	34
Brodeur, NJ	34
Hextall, Phi	31
Fuhr, St.L	30
Potvin, Tor	30
Barrasso, Pit	29
Puppa, TB	29

Shutouts

Carey, Wash	9
Brodeur, NJ	6
Osgood, Det	5
Puppa, TB	5
Hackett, Chi	4
Hextall, Phi	4
Hebert, Ana	4
Burke, Hart	4

Seven tied with 3 each.

Save Pct.

Hasek, Buf	.920
Puppa, TB	.918
Hackett, Chi	.915
Hebert, Ana	.914
Hextall, Phi	.913
Richter, NYR	.912
Brodeur, NJ	.911
Osgood, Det	.911
Potvin, Tor	.910
Roy, Mon-Col	.908
Khabibulin, Win	.908

Losses

Brodeur, NJ	30
Hasek, Buf	30
Ranford, Edm-Bos	30
Terreri, NJ-SJ	29
Beaupre, Ott-Tor	28
Burke, Hart	28
Fuhr, St.L	28
Rhodes, Tor-Ott	27
Potvin, Tor	26

Team Goaltending

WESTERN	GAA	Mins	GA	Shots	Sv%	EN	SO
Detroit	**2.19**	4961	181	1982	.909	2	9
Chicago	**2.64**	4999	220	2334	.906	5	5
Calgary	**2.89**	4984	240	2221	.892	4	6
Colorado	**2.89**	4982	240	2370	.899	6	2
Anaheim	**2.97**	4982	247	2639	.906	5	4
St. Louis	**2.97**	5003	248	2444	.899	1	3
Toronto	**3.03**	4989	252	2611	.903	5	2
Vancouver	**3.33**	5003	278	2473	.888	8	3
Dallas	**3.37**	4992	280	2526	.889	13	2
Winnipeg	**3.53**	4951	291	2763	.895	9	2
Los Angeles	**3.61**	5025	302	2905	.896	5	1
Edmonton	**3.66**	4978	304	2493	.878	8	1
San Jose	**4.32**	4959	357	2716	.869	11	0

EASTERN	GAA	Mins	GA	Shots	Sv%	EN	SO
New Jersey	**2.43**	4995	202	2173	.907	8	6
Washington	**2.45**	4990	204	2042	.900	5	9
Philadelphia	**2.49**	5009	208	2123	.902	5	5
Florida	**2.82**	4979	234	2287	.898	4	2
NY Rangers	**2.85**	4995	237	2473	.904	6	5
Montreal	**2.98**	4987	248	2656	.907	6	4
Tampa Bay	**2.98**	4993	248	2430	.898	6	5
Hartford	**3.12**	4979	259	2761	.906	6	6
Buffalo	**3.16**	4976	262	2912	.910	8	2
Boston	**3.23**	4992	269	2204	.878	3	2
Pittsburgh	**3.44**	4948	284	2840	.900	9	5
Ottawa	**3.53**	4953	291	2504	.884	11	3
NY Islanders	**3.79**	4993	315	2627	.880	6	3

Power Play/Penalty Killing

Power play and penalty killing conversions. Power play: No— number of opportunities; GF— goals for; Pct— percentage. Penalty killing: No— number of times shorthanded; GA— goals against; Pct— percentage of penalties killed; SH— shorthanded goals for.

	—Power Play—			—Penalty Killing—			
WESTERN	No	GF	Pct	No	GA	Pct	SH
Detroit	455	97	**21.3**	375	44	88.3	17
Colorado	404	86	**21.3**	439	71	83.8	21
Winnipeg	417	82	**19.7**	430	88	79.5	10
Toronto	438	83	**18.9**	403	70	82.6	11
Calgary	386	71	**18.4**	402	80	80.1	11
Los Angeles	401	72	**18.0**	381	72	81.1	12
Chicago	356	63	**17.7**	447	65	85.5	13
Vancouver	411	69	**16.8**	418	78	81.3	18
St. Louis	448	74	**16.5**	482	82	83.0	11
San Jose	383	62	**16.2**	399	93	76.7	15
Edmonton	452	72	**15.9**	417	80	80.8	10
Dallas	443	67	**15.1**	418	82	80.4	8
Anaheim	426	60	**14.1**	423	81	80.9	10

	—Power Play—			—Penalty Killing—			
EASTERN	No	GF	Pct	No	GA	Pct	SH
Pittsburgh	420	109	**26.0**	467	78	83.3	18
Tampa Bay	402	83	**20.6**	437	68	84.4	6
NY Rangers	429	85	**19.8**	495	89	82.0	6
Philadelphia	417	82	**19.7**	437	62	85.8	12
Montreal	405	77	**19.0**	382	68	82.2	15
NY Islanders	372	70	**18.8**	414	90	78.3	8
Boston	363	68	**18.7**	341	67	80.4	13
Hartford	372	67	**18.0**	429	83	80.7	8
Florida	468	81	**17.3**	370	63	83.0	11
Buffalo	477	76	**15.9**	461	74	83.9	10
Washington	403	63	**15.6**	385	67	82.6	12
New Jersey	368	55	**14.9**	319	49	84.6	11
Ottawa	430	53	**12.3**	375	83	77.9	6

Team by Team Statistics

High scorers and goaltenders with at least 10 games played. Players who competed for more than one team during the regular season are listed with their final club; (*) indicates rookies eligible for Calder Trophy.

Mighty Ducks of Anaheim

Top Scorers	Gm	G	A	Pts	+/-	PM	PP
Paul Kariya	82	50	58	108	9	20	20
Teemu Selanne	79	40	68	108	5	22	9
WIN	51	24	48	72	3	18	6
ANA	28	16	20	36	2	4	3
Roman Oksiuta	70	23	28	51	4	60	11
VAN	56	16	23	39	2	42	5
ANA	14	7	5	12	2	18	6
Steve Rucchin	64	19	25	44	3	12	8
Bobby Dollas	82	8	22	30	9	64	0
Joe Sacco	76	13	14	27	1	40	1
Anatoli Semenov	56	4	22	26	-1	24	0
PHI	44	3	13	16	3	14	0
ANA	12	1	9	10	-4	10	0
Shaun Van Allen	49	8	17	25	13	41	0
Garry Valk	79	12	12	24	8	125	1
Jason York	79	3	21	24	-7	88	0
Fredrik Olausson	56	2	22	24	-7	38	1
EDM	20	0	6	6	-14	14	0
ANA	36	2	16	18	7	24	1
Alex Hicks	64	10	11	21	11	37	0
Dave Karpa	72	3	16	19	-3	270	0

Acquired: RW Selanne, C Marc Chouinard, and '96 4th-round pick from Win. for D Oleg Tverdovsky, C Chad Kilger, and '96 3rd-round pick (Feb. 7); RW Oksiuta from Van. for RW Mike Sillinger (Mar. 17); C Semenov and D Mike Crowley from Phi. for RW Bryan Wesenberg (Mar. 19). **Claimed:** Olausson on waivers from Edm. (Jan. 16).

Goalies (10 Gm)	Gm	Min	GAA	Record	SV%
Guy Hebert	59	3326	2.83	28-23-5	.914
Mikhail Shtalenkov	30	1637	3.12	7-16-3	.896
ANAHEIM	82	4982	2.97	35-39-8	.906

Shutouts: Hebert (4). **Assists:** Shtalenkov (2). **PM:** Hebert (6) and Shtalenkov (2) .

Boston Bruins

Top Scorers	GP	G	A	Pts	+/-	PM	PP
Adam Oates	70	25	67	92	16	18	7
Ray Bourque	82	20	62	82	31	58	9
Rick Tocchet	71	29	31	60	10	181	10
LA	44	13	23	36	3	117	4
BOS	27	16	8	24	7	64	6
Jozef Stumpel	76	18	36	54	-8	14	5
Shawn McEachern	82	24	29	53	-5	34	3
Ted Donato	82	23	26	49	6	46	7
Cam Neely	49	26	20	46	3	31	7
Todd Elik	59	13	33	46	2	40	6
Dave Reid	63	23	21	44	14	4	1
Sandy Moger	80	15	14	29	-9	65	4
Steve Heinze	76	16	12	28	-3	43	0
Don Sweeney	77	4	24	28	-4	42	2
Kyle McLaren*	74	5	12	17	16	73	0
Tim Sweeney	41	8	8	16	4	14	1
Joe Mullen	37	8	7	15	-2	0	4
Rick Zombo	67	4	10	14	-7	53	0
Jon Rohloff	79	1	12	13	-8	59	1

Acquired: G Ranford from Edm. for RW Mariusz Czerkawski, D Sean Brown, and '96 1st-round pick (Jan. 11); RW Tocchet from LA for LW Kevin Stevens (Jan. 25).

Goalies (10 Gm)	Gm	Min	GAA	Record	SV%
Bill Ranford	77	4322	3.29	34-30-9	.885
EDM	37	2015	3.81	13-18-5	.875
BOS	40	2307	2.83	21-12-4	.894
Scott Bailey*	11	571	3.26	5-1-2	.883
Craig Billington	27	1380	3.43	10-13-3	.867
Blaine Lacher	12	671	3.93	3-5-2	.845
BOSTON	82	4992	3.23	40-31-11	.878

Shutouts: Ranford (2) and Billington (1). **Assists:** Ranford (3). **PM:** Lacher (4), Ranford (2) and Billington (2).

Buffalo Sabres

Top Scorers	GP	G	A	Pts	+/-	PM	PP
Pat LaFontaine	76	40	51	91	-8	36	15
Randy Burridge	74	25	33	58	0	30	6
Derek Plante	76	23	33	56	-4	28	4
Garry Galley	78	10	44	54	-2	81	7
Jason Dawe	67	25	25	50	-8	33	8
Brad May	79	15	29	44	6	295	3
Alexei Zhitnik	80	6	30	36	-25	58	5
Matthew Barnaby	73	15	16	31	-2	335	0
Mike Peca	68	11	20	31	-1	67	4
Donald Audette	23	12	13	25	0	18	8
Brian Holzinger*	58	10	10	20	-21	37	5
Mark Astley	60	2	18	20	-12	80	0
Darryl Shannon	74	4	13	17	15	92	0
WIN	48	2	7	9	5	72	0
BUF	26	2	6	8	10	20	0
Brent Hughes	76	5	10	15	-9	148	0
Mike Wilson*	58	4	8	12	13	41	1
Michal Grosek	23	6	4	10	-1	31	2
WIN	1	0	0	0	-1	0	0
BUF	22	6	4	10	0	31	2
Dane Jackson*	22	5	4	9	3	41	0
Rob Ray	71	3	6	9	-8	287	0
Rob Conn	28	2	5	7	-9	18	0

Acquired: D Shannon and LW Grosek from Win. for D Craig Muni and '96 1st-round pick (Feb. 15);

Goalies (10 Gm)	Gm	Min	GAA	Record	Sv%
Dominik Hasek	59	3417	2.83	22-30-6	.920
Andrei Trefilov	22	1094	3.51	8-8-1	.903
BUFFALO	82	4976	3.16	33-42-7	.910

Shutouts: Hasek (2). **Assists:** Hasek (1). **PM:** Hasek (6), Trefilov (4).

Calgary Flames

Top Scorers	Gm	G	A	Pts	+/-	PM	PP
Theoren Fleury	80	46	50	96	17	112	17
German Titov	82	28	39	67	9	24	13
Michael Nylander	73	17	38	55	0	20	4
Gary Roberts	35	22	20	42	15	78	9
Cory Stillman*	74	16	19	35	-5	41	4
James Patrick	80	3	32	35	3	30	1
Steve Chiasson	76	8	25	33	3	62	5
Zarley Zalapski	80	12	17	29	11	115	5
Mike Sullivan	81	9	12	21	-6	24	0
Corey Millen	44	7	14	21	8	18	2
DAL	13	3	4	7	0	8	1
CALG	31	4	10	14	8	10	1
Sandy Mccarthy	75	9	7	16	-8	173	3
Pavel Torgajev	41	6	10	16	2	14	0
Ronnie Stern	52	10	5	15	2	111	0
Paul Kruse	75	3	12	15	-5	145	0
Dean Evason	67	7	7	14	-6	38	1
Bob Sweeney	72	7	7	14	-20	65	0
NYI	66	6	6	12	-23	59	0
CALG	6	1	1	2	3	6	0
Tommy Albelin	73	1	13	14	1	18	0
NJ	53	1	12	13	0	14	0
CALG	20	0	1	1	1	4	0

Acquired: C Millen and RW Jarome Iginla from Dal. for C Joe Nieuwendyk (Dec. 20); RW Jocelyn Lemieux, D Albelin, and D Cale Hulse from NJ for D Phil Housley and D Dan Keczmer (Feb. 27); C Sweeney from NYI for LW Pat Conacher and '97 6th-round pick (Mar. 20).

Goalies (10 Gm)	Gm	Min	GAA	Record	SV%
Trevor Kidd	47	2570	2.78	15-21-8	.895
Rick Tabaracci	43	2391	2.94	19-16-3	.892
CALGARY	82	4984	2.89	34-37-11	.892

Shutouts: Kidd (3), Tabaracci (3). **Assists:** Kidd (2),Tabaracci (2). **PM:** Tabaracci (8), Kidd (4).

Chicago Blackhawks

Top Scorers	Gm	G	A	Pts	+/-	PM	PP
Chris Chelios	81	14	58	72	25	140	7
Jeremy Roenick	66	32	35	67	9	109	12
Gary Suter	82	20	47	67	3	80	12
Tony Amonte	81	31	32	63	10	62	5
Bernie Nicholls	59	19	41	60	11	60	6
Eric Daze*	80	30	23	53	16	18	2
Joe Murphy	70	22	29	51	-3	86	8
Denis Savard	69	13	35	48	20	102	2
Murray Craven	66	18	29	47	20	36	5
Bob Probert	78	19	21	40	15	237	1
Brent Sutter	80	13	27	40	14	56	0
Jeff Shantz	78	6	14	20	12	24	1
Keith Carney	82	5	14	19	31	94	1
Sergei Krivokrasov	46	6	10	16	10	32	0
Eric Weinrich	77	5	10	15	14	65	0
Steve Smith	37	0	9	9	12	71	0
James Black	13	3	3	6	1	16	0
Brent Grieve	28	2	4	6	5	28	0
Jim Cummins	52	2	4	6	-1	180	0
Enrico Ciccone	66	2	4	6	1	306	0
TB	55	2	3	5	-4	258	0
CHI	11	0	1	1	5	48	0

Acquired: D Ciccone and '96 2nd-round pick from TB for D Igor Ulanov, LW Patrick Poulin, and '96 2nd-round pick (Mar. 20).

Goalies (10 Gm)	Gm	Min	GAA	Record	SV%
Jeff Hackett	35	2000	2.40	18-11-4	.916
Ed Belfour	50	2956	2.74	22-17-10	.902
CHICAGO	82	4999	2.64	40-28-14	.906

Shutouts: Hackett (4), Belfour (1). **Assists:** Belfour (2), Hackett (1). **PM:** Belfour (36), Hackett (8).

Colorado Avalanche

Top Scorers	Gm	G	A	Pts	+/-	PM	PP
Joe Sakic	82	51	69	120	14	44	17
Peter Forsberg	82	30	86	116	26	47	7
Valeri Kamensky	81	38	47	85	14	85	18
Claude Lemieux	79	39	32	71	14	117	9
Scott Young	81	21	39	60	2	50	7
Sandis Ozolinsh	73	14	40	54	2	54	8
SJ	7	1	3	4	2	4	1
COL	66	13	37	50	0	50	7
Adam Deadmarsh	78	21	27	48	20	142	3
Chris Simon	64	16	18	34	10	250	4
Stephane Yelle*	71	13	14	27	15	30	0
Mike Keane	73	10	17	27	-5	46	0
MON	18	0	7	7	-6	6	0
COL	55	10	10	20	1	40	0
Craig Wolanin	75	7	20	27	25	50	0
Mike Ricci	62	6	21	27	1	52	3
Troy Murray	63	7	14	21	15	22	0
Alexei Gusarov	65	5	15	20	29	56	0
Curtis Leschyshyn	77	4	15	19	32	73	0
Dave Hannan	61	7	10	17	3	32	1
BUF	57	6	10	16	2	30	1
COL	4	1	0	1	1	2	0
Adam Foote	73	5	11	16	27	88	1
Sylvain Lefebvre	75	5	11	16	26	49	2
Jon Klemm*	56	3	12	15	12	20	0

Acquired: D Ozolinsh from SJ for RW Owen Nolan (Oct. 26); G Roy and RW Keane from Mon. for RW Andrei Kovalenko, LW Martin Rucinsky, and G Jocelyn Thibault (Dec. 6); C Hannan from Buf for '96 6th-round pick (Mar. 20).

Goalies (10 Gm)	Gm	Min	GAA	Record	SV%
Patrick Roy	61	3565	2.78	34-24-2	.908
MON	22	1260	2.95	12-9-1	.907
COL	39	2305	2.68	22-15-1	.909
Stephane Fiset	37	2107	2.93	22-6-7	.898
COLORADO	82	4982	2.89	47-25-10	.899

Shutouts: Roy (2) and Fiset (1). **Assists:** Fiset (1). **PM:** Roy (10) and Fiset (2).

Dallas Stars

Top Scorers	Gm	G	A	Pts	+/-	PM	PP
Mike Modano	78	36	45	81	-12	63	8
Benoit Hogue	78	19	45	64	10	104	5
TOR	44	12	25	37	6	68	3
DAL	34	7	20	27	4	36	2
Greg Adams	66	22	21	43	-21	33	11
Brent Gilchrist	77	20	22	42	-11	36	6
Kevin Hatcher	74	15	26	41	-24	58	7
Brent Fedyk	65	20	14	34	-16	54	8
PHI	24	10	5	15	1	24	4
DAL	41	10	9	19	-17	30	4
Joe Nieuwendyk	52	14	18	32	-17	41	8
Derian Hatcher	79	8	23	31	-12	129	2
Todd Harvey	69	9	20	29	-13	136	3
Grant Marshall*	70	9	19	28	0	111	0
Jere Lehtinen*	57	6	22	28	5	16	0
Mike Kennedy	61	9	17	26	-7	48	4
Grant Ledyard	73	5	19	24	-15	20	2
Guy Carbonneau	71	8	15	23	-2	38	0
Richard Matvichuk	73	6	16	22	4	71	0
Randy Wood	76	8	13	21	-15	62	1
TOR	46	7	9	16	-4	36	1
DAL	30	1	4	5	-11	26	0
Darryl Sydor	84	3	17	20	-12	75	2
LA	58	1	11	12	-11	34	1
DAL	26	2	6	8	-1	41	1

Acquired: C Nieuwendyk from Cal. for C Corey Millen and RW Jarome Iginla (Dec. 20); LW Fedyk from Phi. for RW Trent Klatt (Dec. 13); LW Wood and C Hogue from Tor. for C Dave Gagner and '96 or '97 6th-round pick (Jan. 28); D Sydor and '96 5th-round pick for D Zmolek and RW Shane Churla (Feb. 17).

Goalies (10 Gm)	Gm	Min	GAA	Record	SV%
Andy Moog	41	2228	2.99	13-19-7	.900
Allan Bester	10	601	3.00	4-5-1	.899
Darcy Wakaluk	37	1875	3.39	9-16-5	.891
DALLAS	82	4992	3.37	26-42-14	.889

Shutouts: Moog (1) and Wakaluk (1). **Assists:** none. **PM:** Moog (28), Wakaluk (6), and Bester (2).

Detroit Red Wings

Top Scorers	Gm	G	A	Pts	+/-	PM	PP
Sergei Fedorov	78	39	68	107	49	48	11
Steve Yzerman	80	36	59	95	29	64	16
Paul Coffey	76	14	60	74	19	90	3
Vyacheslav Kozlov	82	36	37	73	33	70	9
Igor Larionov	73	22	51	73	31	34	10
SJ	4	1	1	2	-6	0	1
DET	69	21	50	71	37	34	9
Nicklas Lidstrom	81	17	50	67	29	20	8
Keith Primeau	74	27	25	52	19	168	6
Dino Ciccarelli	64	22	21	43	14	99	13
Viacheslav Fetisov	69	7	35	42	37	96	1
Greg Johnson	60	18	22	40	6	30	5
Vlad. Konstantinov	81	14	20	34	60	139	3
Bob Errey	71	11	21	32	30	66	2
Darren Mccarty	63	15	14	29	14	158	8
Doug Brown	62	12	15	27	11	4	0
Tim Taylor	72	11	14	25	11	39	1
Kris Draper	52	7	9	16	2	32	0
Mathieu Dandenault*	34	5	7	12	6	6	1
Marc Bergevin	70	1	9	10	7	33	0
Martin Lapointe	58	6	3	9	0	93	1

Acquired: C Larionov and future considerations from SJ for RW Ray Sheppard (Oct. 24).

Goalies (10 Gm)	Gm	Min	GAA	Record	Sv%
Chris Osgood	50	2933	2.17	39-6-5	.911
Mike Vernon	32	1855	2.26	21-7-2	.903
DETROIT	82	4961	2.19	62-13-7	.909

Shutouts: Osgood (5), Vernon (3). **Goals:** Osgood (1). **Assists:** Osgood (2). **PM:** Osgood (4) and Vernon (2).

Edmonton Oilers

Top Scorers	Gm	G	A	Pts	+/-	PM	PP
Doug Weight	82	25	79	104	-19	95	9
Zdeno Ciger	78	31	39	70	-15	41	12
Jason Arnott	64	28	31	59	-6	87	8
Mariusz Czerkawski	70	17	23	40	-4	18	3
BOS	33	5	6	11	-11	10	1
EDM	37	12	17	29	7	8	2
David Oliver	80	20	19	39	-22	34	14
Todd Marchant	81	19	19	38	-19	66	2
Miroslav Satan*	62	18	17	35	0	22	6
Boris Mironov	78	8	24	32	-23	101	7
Jeff Norton	66	8	23	31	9	42	1
ST.L	36	4	7	11	4	26	0
EDM	30	4	16	20	5	16	1
Dean Mcammond	53	15	15	30	6	23	4
Kelly Buchberger	82	11	14	25	-20	184	0
Scott Thornton	77	9	9	18	-25	149	0
Bryan Marchment	78	3	15	18	-7	202	0
Jiri Slegr	57	4	13	17	-1	74	0
David Roberts*	34	3	10	13	-7	18	1
ST.L	28	1	6	7	-7	12	1
EDM	6	2	4	6	0	6	0
Ryan Smyth*	48	2	9	11	-10	28	1
Luke Richardson	82	2	9	11	-27	108	0

Acquired: D Norton and D Donald Dufresne from St.L for D Igor Kravchuk and D Ken Sutton (Jan. 5); RW Czerkawski, D Sean Brown, and '96 1st-round pick from Bos. for G Bill Ranford (Jan. 11); LW Roberts from St.L for future considerations (Mar. 12).

Goalies (10 Gm)	Gm	Min	GAA	Record	Sv%
Curtis Joseph	34	1936	3.44	15-16-2	.886
Joaquin Gage*	16	717	3.77	2-8-1	.871
EDMONTON	82	4978	3.66	30-44-8	.878

Shutouts: none. **Assists:** Joseph (1). **PM:** Joseph (4) and Gage (4).

Florida Panthers

Top Scorers	Gm	G	A	Pts	+/-	PM	PP
Scott Mellanby	79	32	38	70	4	160	19
Rob Niedermayer	82	26	35	61	1	107	11
Ray Sheppard	70	37	23	60	-19	16	14
DET	5	2	2	4	0	2	0
SJ	51	27	19	46	-19	10	12
FLA	14	8	2	10	0	4	2
Robert Svehla	81	8	49	57	-3	94	7
Johan Garpenlov	82	23	28	51	-10	36	8
Stu Barnes	72	19	25	44	-12	46	8
Martin Straka	77	13	30	43	-19	41	6
OTT	43	9	16	25	-14	29	5
NYI	22	2	10	12	-6	6	0
FLA	12	2	4	6	1	6	1
Jody Hull	78	20	17	37	5	25	2
Tom Fitzgerald	82	13	21	34	-3	75	1
Bill Lindsay	73	12	22	34	13	57	0
Jason Woolley	52	6	28	34	-9	32	3
Gord Murphy	70	8	22	30	5	30	4
Radek Dvorak*	77	13	14	27	5	20	0
Brian Skrudland	79	7	20	27	6	129	0
Dave Lowry	63	10	14	24	-2	36	0
Mike Hough	64	7	16	23	4	37	0
Ed Jovanovski*	70	10	11	21	-3	137	2
Terry Carkner	73	3	10	13	10	80	1
Magnus Svensson	27	2	9	11	-1	21	2
Geoff Smith	31	3	7	10	-4	20	2
Paul Laus	78	3	6	9	-2	236	0

Acquired: RW Sheppard and '96 4th-round pick from SJ for '96 2nd-round pick and '96 4th-round pick (Mar. 17).

Goalies (10 Gm)	Gm	Min	GAA	Record	Sv%
John Vanbiesbrouck	57	3178	2.68	26-20-7	.904
Mark Fitzpatrick	34	1786	2.96	15-11-3	.891
FLORIDA	82	4979	2.82	41-31-10	.898

Shutouts: Vanbiesbrouck (2). **Assists:** Vanbiesbrouck (2). **PM:** Fitzpatrick (12) and Vanbiesbrouck (10).

Hartford Whalers

Top Scorers	Gm	G	A	Pts	+/-	PM	PP
Brendan Shanahan	74	44	34	78	2	125	17
Geoff Sanderson	81	34	31	65	0	40	6
Andrew Cassels	81	20	43	63	8	39	6
Nelson Emerson	81	29	29	58	-7	78	12
Jeff Brown	76	8	47	55	8	56	5
VAN	28	1	16	17	6	18	0
HART	48	7	31	38	2	38	5
Andrei Nikolishin	61	14	37	51	-2	34	4
Robert Kron	77	22	28	50	-1	6	8
Paul Ranheim	73	10	20	30	-2	14	0
Jeff O'Neill*	65	8	19	27	-3	40	1
Glen Wesley	68	8	16	24	-9	88	6
Steven Rice	59	10	12	22	-4	47	1
Adam Burt	78	4	9	13	-4	121	0
Glen Featherstone	68	2	10	12	10	138	0
Kevin Dineen	46	2	9	11	-1	117	0
PHI	26	0	2	2	-8	50	0
HART	20	2	7	9	7	67	0
Gerald Diduck	79	1	9	10	7	88	0
Sami Kapanen*	35	5	4	9	0	6	0
Brad McCrimmon	58	3	6	9	15	62	0
Mark Janssens	81	2	7	9	-13	155	0
Scott Daniels*	53	3	4	7	-4	254	0

Acquired: D Brown and '98 3rd-round pick from Van. for C Jim Dowd, D Frank Kucera, and '97 2nd-round pick (Dec. 20); RW Dineen from Phi. for future considerations (Dec. 28). **Claimed:** G Muzzatti off waivers (Oct. 10).

Goalies (10 Gm)	Gm	Min	GAA	Record	Sv%
Jason Muzzatti*	22	1013	2.90	4-8-3	.911
Sean Burke	66	3669	3.11	28-28-6	.907
HARTFORD	82	4979	3.12	34-39-9	.906

Shutouts: Burke (4) and Muzzatti (1). **Assists:** Burke (6). **PM:** Muzzatti (33) and Burke (16).

Los Angeles Kings

Top Scorers	Gm	G	A	Pts	+/-	PM	PP
Dimitri Khristich	76	27	37	64	0	44	12
Ray Ferraro	76	29	31	60	0	92	9
NYR	65	25	29	54	13	82	8
LA	11	4	2	6	-13	10	1
Vitali Yachmenev*	80	19	34	53	-3	16	6
Yanic Perreault	78	25	24	49	-11	16	8
Kevin Todd	74	16	27	43	6	38	0
Kevin Stevens	61	13	23	36	-10	71	6
BOS	41	10	13	23	1	49	3
LA	20	3	10	13	-11	22	3
Tony Granato	49	17	18	35	-5	46	5
Eric Lacroix	72	16	16	32	-11	110	3
Craig Johnson*	60	13	11	24	-8	36	4
ST.L	49	8	7	15	-4	30	1
LA	11	5	4	9	-4	6	3
Philippe Boucher	53	7	16	23	-26	31	5
Robert Lang	68	6	16	22	-15	10	0
Jaroslav Modry	73	4	17	21	-21	44	1
OTT	64	4	14	18	-17	38	1
LA	9	0	3	3	-4	6	0
John Slaney	38	6	14	20	7	14	3
COL	7	0	3	3	2	4	0
LA	31	6	11	17	5	10	3

Acquired: D Slaney from Col. for '96 6th-round pick (Dec. 28); LW Stevens from Bos. for RW Rick Tocchet (Jan. 25); C Patrice Tardif, LW Johnson, D Roman Vopat, '97 1st-round pick, and '96 5th-round pick from St.L for C Wayne Gretzky (Feb. 27); C Ferraro, C Laperriere, C Lafayette, D Norstrom, and '97 4th-round pick from NYR for RW Jari Kurri, RW Churla, and D Marty McSorley (Mar. 14); D Modry and '96 8th-round pick from Ott. for RW Kevin Brown (Mar. 20).

Goalies (10 Gm)	Gm	Min	GAA	Record	Sv%
Kelly Hrudey	36	2077	3.26	7-15-10	.907
Byron Dafoe*	47	2666	3.87	14-24-8	.888
LOS ANGELES	82	5025	3.61	24-40-18	.896

Shutouts: Dafoe (1). **Assists:** none. **PM:** Dafoe (6) and Hrudey (4).

Montreal Canadiens

Top Scorers	Gm	G	A	Pts	+/-	PM	PP
Pierre Turgeon	80	38	58	96	19	44	17
Vincent Damphousse	80	38	56	94	5	158	11
Mark Recchi	82	28	50	78	20	69	11
Martin Rucinsky	78	29	46	75	18	68	9
COL	22	4	11	15	10	14	0
MON	56	25	35	60	8	54	9
Andrei Kovalenko	77	28	28	56	20	49	6
COL	26	11	11	22	11	16	3
MON	51	17	17	34	9	33	3
Saku Koivu*	82	20	25	45	-7	40	8
Valeri Bure*	77	22	20	42	10	28	5
Patrice Brisebois	69	9	27	36	10	65	3
Brian Savage	75	25	8	33	-8	28	4
Vladimir Malakhov	61	5	23	28	7	79	2
Turner Stevenson	80	9	16	25	-2	167	0
Lyle Odelein	79	3	14	17	8	230	0
Stephane Quintal	68	2	14	16	-4	117	0
Benoit Brunet	26	7	8	15	-4	17	3
Peter Popovic	76	2	12	14	21	69	0
Oleg Petrov	36	4	7	11	-9	23	0
Marc Bureau	65	3	7	10	-3	46	0
Chris Murray*	48	3	4	7	5	163	0

Acquired: G Jablonski from St.L for D J.J. Daigneault (Nov. 7); RW Kovalenko, LW Rucinsky, and G Thibault from Col. for G Patrick Roy and RW Mike Keane (Dec. 6).

Goalies (10 Gm)	Gm	Min	GAA	Record	Sv%
Jocelyn Thibault	50	2892	2.86	26-17-5	.907
MON	40	2334	2.83	23-13-3	.913
COL	10	558	3.01	3-4-2	.874
Pat Jablonski	24	1272	2.97	5-9-6	.907
ST.L	1	8	7.50	0-0-0	.800
MON	23	1264	2.94	5-9-6	.908
MONTREAL	82	4987	2.98	40-32-10	.907

Shutouts: Thibault (3). **Assists:** Jablonski (1). **PM:** Thibault (2), and Jablonski (2).

New Jersey Devils

Top Scorers	Gm	G	A	Pts	+/-	PM	PP
Phil Housley	81	17	51	68	-6	30	6
CALG	59	16	36	52	-2	22	6
NJ	22	1	15	16	-4	8	0
Steve Thomas	81	26	35	61	-2	98	6
Dave Andreychuk	76	28	29	57	-9	64	14
TOR	61	20	24	44	-11	54	12
NJ	15	8	5	13	2	10	2
Bill Guerin	80	23	30	53	7	116	8
John MacLean	76	20	28	48	3	91	3
Petr Sykora*	63	18	24	42	7	32	8
Scott Niedermayer	79	8	25	33	5	46	6
Stephane Richer	73	20	12	32	-8	30	3
Bobby Holik	63	13	17	30	9	58	1
Scott Stevens	82	5	23	28	7	100	2
Brian Rolston	58	13	11	24	9	8	3
Neal Broten	55	7	16	23	-3	14	1
Shawn Chambers	64	2	21	23	1	18	2
Randy McKay	76	11	10	21	7	145	3
Valeri Zelepukin	61	6	9	15	-10	107	3
Mike Peluso	57	3	8	11	4	146	0
Bob Carpenter	52	5	5	10	-10	14	0
Steve Sullivan*	16	5	4	9	3	8	2
Sergei Brylin	50	4	5	9	-2	26	0

Acquired: D Housley and D Dan Keczmer from Cal. for RW Jocelyn Lemieux, D Tommy Albelin, and D Cale Hulse (Feb. 27); LW Andreychuk from Tor. for higher of '96 2nd-round pick or Vancouver's '96 2nd-round pick, and either a '98 4th-round pick or '99 3rd-round pick (Mar. 13).

Goalies (10 Gm)	Gm	Min	GAA	Record	Sv%
Corey Schwab*	10	331	2.18	0-3-0	.899
Martin Brodeur	77	4434	2.34	34-30-12	.911
NEW JERSEY	82	4995	2.43	37-33-12	.907

Shutouts: Brodeur (6). **Assists:** Brodeur (1). **PM:** Schwab (31) and Brodeur (6).

New York Islanders

Top Scorers	Gm	G	A	Pts	+/-	PM	PP
Zigmund Palffy	81	43	44	87	-17	56	17
Travis Green	69	24	45	69	-21	42	14
Marty Mcinnis	74	12	34	46	-11	39	2
Todd Bertuzzi*	76	18	21	39	-14	83	4
Alexander Semak	69	20	14	34	-4	68	6
Derek King	61	12	20	32	-10	23	5
Kenny Jonsson	66	4	26	30	7	32	3
TOR	50	4	22	26	12	22	3
NYI	16	0	4	4	-5	10	0
Niklas Andersson*	48	14	12	26	-3	12	3
Bryan McCabe*	82	7	16	23	-24	156	3
Patrick Flatley	56	8	9	17	-24	21	0
Darby Hendrickson*	62	7	10	17	-8	80	0
TOR	46	6	6	12	-2	47	0
NYI	16	1	4	5	-6	33	0
Scott Lachance	55	3	10	13	-19	54	1
Chris Luongo	74	3	7	10	-23	55	1
Pat Conacher	55	6	3	9	-13	18	0
LA	35	5	2	7	-8	18	0
CALG	7	0	0	0	-1	0	0
NYI	13	1	1	2	-4	0	0
Brent Severyn	65	1	8	9	3	180	0
Dan Plante*	73	5	3	8	-22	50	0
Darius Kasparaitis	46	1	7	8	-12	93	0

Acquired: D Jonsson, F Hendrickson, LW Sean Haggerty, and '97 1st-round pick from Tor. for LW Wendel Clark, D Mathieu Schneider, and D Denis Smith (Mar. 13); LW Conacher and '97 6th-round pick from NYI for C Bob Sweeney (Mar. 20).

Goalies (10 Gm)	Gm	Min	GAA	Record	Sv%
Eric Fichaud*	24	1234	3.31	7-12-2	.897
Jamie McLennan	13	636	3.68	3-9-1	.886
Tommy Soderstrom	51	2590	3.87	11-22-6	.878
Tommy Salo*	10	523	4.02	1-7-1	.860
NY ISLANDERS	82	4993	3.79	22-50-10	.880

Shutouts: Soderstrom (2) and Fichaud (1). **Assists:** Fichaud (1). **PM:** Soderstrom (7) and McLennan (2).

New York Rangers

Top Scorers	Gm	G	A	Pts	+/-	PM	PP
Mark Messier	74	47	52	99	29	122	14
Brian Leetch	82	15	70	85	12	30	7
Pat Verbeek	69	41	41	82	29	129	17
Luc Robitaille	77	23	46	69	13	80	11
Alexei Kovalev	81	24	34	58	5	98	8
Adam Graves	82	22	36	58	18	100	9
Jari Kurri	71	18	27	45	-16	39	5
LA	57	17	23	40	-12	37	5
NYR	14	1	4	5	-4	2	0
Bruce Driver	66	3	34	37	2	42	3
Marty McSorley	68	10	23	33	-20	169	1
LA	59	10	21	31	-14	148	1
NYR	9	0	2	2	-6	21	0
Sergei Nemchinov	78	17	15	32	9	38	0
Sergio Momesso	73	11	12	23	-13	142	6
TOR	54	7	8	15	-11	112	4
NYR	19	4	4	8	-2	30	2
Niklas Sundstrom*	82	9	12	21	2	14	1
Ulf Samuelsson	74	1	18	19	9	122	0
Alexander Karpovtsev	40	2	16	18	12	26	1
Doug Lidster	59	5	9	14	11	50	0
Jeff Beukeboom	82	3	11	14	19	220	0

Acquired: LW Momesso and LW Bill Berg from Tor. for LW Nick Kypreos and RW Wayne Presley (Feb. 29); RW Kurri, RW Shane Churla, and D McSorley from LA for C Ray Ferraro, C Ian Laperriere, C Nathan Lafayette, D Mattias Norstrom, and '97 4th-round pick (Mar. 14).

Goalies (10 Gm)	Gm	Min	GAA	Record	Sv%
Mike Richter	41	2396	2.68	24-13-3	.912
Glenn Healy	44	2564	2.90	17-14-11	.900
NY RANGERS	82	4995	2.85	41-27-14	.904

Shutouts: Richter (3) and Healy (2). **Assists:** Healy (1) and Richter (1). **PM:** Healy (8) and Richter (4).

Ottawa Senators

Top Scorers	Gm	G	A	Pts	+/-	PM	PP
Daniel Alfredsson*	82	26	35	61	-18	28	8
Alexei Yashin	46	15	24	39	-15	28	8
Randy Cunneyworth	81	17	19	36	-31	130	4
Steve Duchesne	62	12	24	36	-23	42	7
Radek Bonk	76	16	19	35	-5	36	5
Tom Chorske	72	15	14	29	-9	21	0
Sean Hill	80	7	14	21	-26	94	2
Pavol Demitra	31	7	10	17	-3	6	2
Alexandre Daigle	50	5	12	17	-30	24	1
Ted Drury	42	9	7	16	-19	54	1
Antti Tormanen*	50	7	8	15	-15	28	0
Trent McCleary*	75	4	10	14	-15	68	0
Rob Gaudreau	52	8	5	13	-19	15	1
Stanislav Neckar	82	3	9	12	-16	54	1
David Archibald	44	6	4	10	-14	18	0
Michel Picard	17	2	6	8	-1	10	0
Lance Pitlick	28	1	6	7	-8	20	0

Acquired: G Rhodes from Tor. and D Wade Redden from NYI for G Don Beaupre (Tor.), RW Martin Straka and D Bryan Berard (NYI) (Jan. 23).

Goalies (10 Gm)	Gm	Min	GAA	Record	Sv%
Damian Rhodes	47	2747	2.77	14-27-5	.905
TOR	11	624	2.79	4-5-1	.904
OTT	36	2123	2.77	10-22-4	.906
Mike Bales*	20	1040	4.15	2-14-1	.871
OTTAWA	82	4953	3.53	18-59-5	.884

Shutouts: Rhodes (2). **Assists:** Rhodes (2). **PM:** Rhodes (4), and Bales (2).

Philadelphia Flyers

Top Scorers	Gm	G	A	Pts	+/-	PM	PP
Eric Lindros	73	47	68	115	26	163	15
John LeClair	82	51	46	97	21	64	19
Rod Brind'Amour	82	26	61	87	20	110	4
Dale Hawerchuk	82	17	44	61	15	26	6
ST.L	66	13	28	41	5	22	5
PHI	16	4	16	20	10	4	1
Pat Falloon	71	25	26	51	14	10	9
SJ	9	3	0	3	-1	4	0
PHI	62	22	26	48	15	6	9
Eric Desjardins	80	7	40	47	19	45	5
Dan Quinn	63	13	32	45	-6	46	7
OTT	28	6	18	24	-8	24	4
PHI	35	7	14	21	2	22	3
Mikael Renberg	51	23	20	43	8	45	9
Joel Otto	67	12	29	41	11	115	6
John Druce	77	13	16	29	-20	27	0
LA	64	9	12	21	-26	14	0
PHI	13	4	4	8	6	13	0
Petr Svoboda	73	1	28	29	28	105	0
Shjon Podein	79	15	10	25	25	89	0
Chris Therien	82	6	17	23	16	89	3
Rob DiMaio	59	6	15	21	0	58	1
Karl Dykhuis	82	5	15	20	12	101	1
Bob Corkum	76	9	10	19	3	34	0
ANA	48	5	7	12	0	26	0
PHI	28	4	3	7	3	8	0
Trent Klatt	71	7	12	19	2	44	0
DAL	22	4	4	8	0	23	0
PHI	49	3	8	11	2	21	0

Acquired: RW Falloon from SJ for '96 1st-round pick, '96 4th-round pick, and LW Martin Spanhel (Nov. 16); RW Klatt from Dal. for LW Brent Fedyk (Dec. 13); C Quinn from Ott. for future considerations (Jan. 23); C Corkum from Ana. for LW Chris Herpenger and '97 7th-round pick (Feb. 6); C Hawerchuk from St.L for for C Craig MacTavish (Mar. 17); RW Druce and '97 7th-round pick from LA for '96 4th-round pick (Mar. 19).

Goalies (10 Gm)	Gm	Min	GAA	Record	Sv%
Ron Hextall	53	3102	2.17	31-13-7	.913
Garth Snow	26	1437	2.88	12-8-4	.894
PHILADELPHIA	82	5009	2.49	45-24-13	.902

Shutouts: Hextall (4). **Assists:** Hextall (1). **PM:** Hextall (28) and Snow (18).

Pittsburgh Penguins

Top Scorers	Gm	G	A	Pts	+/-	PM	PP
Mario Lemieux	70	69	92	161	10	54	31
Jaromir Jagr	82	62	87	149	31	96	20
Ron Francis	77	27	92	119	25	56	12
Petr Nedved	80	45	54	99	37	68	8
Tomas Sandstrom	58	35	35	70	4	69	17
Sergei Zubov	64	11	55	66	28	22	3
Bryan Smolinski	81	24	40	64	6	69	8
Kevin Miller	81	28	25	53	-4	45	3
SJ	68	22	20	42	-8	41	2
PIT	13	6	5	11	4	4	1
Dmitri Mironov	72	3	31	34	19	88	1
Glen Murray	69	14	15	29	4	57	0
Chris Joseph	70	5	14	19	6	71	0
Neil Wilkinson	62	3	14	17	12	120	0
WIN	21	1	4	5	0	33	0
PIT	41	2	10	12	12	87	0
Dave Roche*	71	7	7	14	-5	130	0
Chris Tamer	70	4	10	14	20	153	0
J.J. Daigneault	57	4	7	11	-6	53	2
MON	7	0	1	1	0	6	0
ST.L	37	1	3	4	-6	24	0
PIT	13	3	3	6	0	23	2
Francois Leroux	66	2	9	11	2	161	0

Acquired: D Wilkinson from Win. for D Norm MacIver (Dec. 28); D Daigneault from St.L for '96 6th-round pick (Mar. 20); RW Miller from SJ for '96 5th-round pick and future considerations (Mar. 20).

Goalies (10 Gm)	Gm	Min	GAA	Record	Sv%
Ken Wregget	37	2132	3.24	20-13-2	.905
Tom Barrasso	49	2799	3.43	29-16-2	.902
PITTSBURGH	82	4948	3.44	49-29-4	.900

Shutouts: Wregget (3) and Barrasso (2). **Assists:** Barrasso (3) and Wregget (2). **PM:** Barrasso (18) and Wregget (8).

St. Louis Blues

Top Scorers	Gm	G	A	Pts	+/-	PM	PP
Wayne Gretzky	80	23	79	102	-13	34	6
LA	62	15	66	81	-7	32	5
ST.L	18	8	13	21	-6	2	1
Brett Hull	70	43	40	83	4	30	16
Al MacInnis	82	17	44	61	5	88	9
Shayne Corson	77	18	28	46	3	192	13
Geoff Courtnall	69	24	16	40	-9	101	7
Brian Noonan	81	13	22	35	2	84	3
Yuri Khmylev	73	8	21	29	-17	40	5
BUF	66	8	20	28	-12	40	5
ST.L	7	0	1	1	-5	0	0
Stephen Leach	73	11	17	28	-7	108	1
BOS	59	9	13	22	-4	86	1
ST.L	14	2	4	6	-3	22	0
Stephane Matteau	78	11	15	26	-8	87	4
NYR	32	4	2	6	-4	22	1
ST.L	46	7	13	20	-4	65	3
Chris Pronger	78	7	18	25	-18	110	3
Igor Kravchuk	66	7	16	23	-19	34	3
EDM	26	4	4	8	-13	10	3
ST.L	40	3	12	15	-6	24	0
Adam Creighton	61	11	10	21	0	78	2
Peter Zezel	57	8	13	21	-2	12	2

Acquired: LW Matteau from NYR for C Ian Laperriere (Dec. 28); D Kravchuk and D Ken Sutton from Edm. for D Jeff Norton and D Donald Dufresne (Jan. 5); C Gretzky from LA for C Patrice Tardif, LW Craig Johnson, D Roman Vopat, '97 1st-round pick, and '96 5th-round pick (Feb. 27); RW Leach from Bos. for LW Kevin Sawyer and D Steve Staios (Mar. 7); RW Khymlev and '96 8th-round pick from Buf. for D Jean-Luc Grande Pierre, '96 2nd-round pick, and '97 3rd-round pick (Mar. 20).

Goalies (10 Gm)	Gm	Min	GAA	Record	Sv%
Grant Fuhr	79	4365	2.87	30-28-16	.903
Bruce Racine	11	230	3.13	0-3-0	.881
ST. LOUIS	82	5003	2.97	32-34-16	.899

Shutouts: Fuhr (3). **Assists:** Fuhr (1). **PM:** Fuhr (8) and Racine (2).

San Jose Sharks

Top Scorers	Gm	G	A	Pts	+/-	PM	PP
Owen Nolan	81	33	36	69	-33	146	16
COL	9	4	4	8	-3	9	4
SJ	72	29	32	61	-30	137	12
Jeff Friesen	79	15	31	46	-19	42	2
Darren Turcotte	68	22	21	43	5	30	2
WIN	59	16	16	32	-3	26	2
SJ	9	6	5	11	8	4	0
Ray Whitney	60	17	24	41	-23	16	4
Marcus Ragnarsson*	71	8	31	39	-24	42	4
Jamie Baker	77	16	17	33	-19	79	2
Ulf Dahlen	59	16	12	28	-21	27	5
Doug Bodger	73	4	24	28	-24	68	3
BUF	16	0	5	5	-6	18	0
SJ	57	4	19	23	-18	50	3
Chris Tancill	45	7	16	23	-12	20	0
Shean Donovan*	74	13	8	21	-17	39	0
Michal Sykora	79	4	16	20	-14	54	1
Yves Racine	57	1	19	20	-10	54	0
MON	25	0	3	3	-7	26	0
SJ	32	1	16	17	-3	28	0
Viktor Kozlov*	62	6	13	19	-15	6	1
Jeff Odgers	78	12	4	16	-4	192	0

Acquired: RW Nolan from Col. for D Sandis Ozolinsh (Oct. 26); G Terreri from NJ for '96 2nd-round pick (Nov. 15); D Bodger from Buf for RW Vaclav Varada, LW Martin Spanhel, '96 Phi. 4th-round pick and '96 Phi. 1st-round pick (Nov. 16); C Turcotte and '96 2nd-round pick from Win. for C Craig Janney (Mar. 18).**Claimed:** D Racine on waivers from Mon. (Jan. 23).

Goalies (10 Gm)	Gm	Min	GAA	Record	Sv%
Chris Terreri	50	2726	3.61	16-29-1	.884
NJ	4	210	2.57	3-0-0	.902
SJ	46	2516	3.70	13-29-1	.883
Arturs Irbe	22	1112	4.59	4-12-4	.860
Wade Flaherty	24	1137	4.85	3-12-1	.866
SAN JOSE	82	4959	4.32	20-55-7	.869

Shutouts: none. **Assists:** Terreri (5). **PM:** Terreri (4) and Irbe (4).

Tampa Bay Lightning

Top Scorers	Gm	G	A	Pts	+/-	PM	PP
Brian Bradley	75	23	56	79	-11	77	9
Roman Hamrlik	82	16	49	65	-24	103	12
Alexander Selivanov	79	31	21	52	3	93	13
Petr Klima	67	22	30	52	-25	68	8
John Cullen	76	16	34	50	1	65	8
Brian Bellows	79	23	26	49	-14	39	13
Chris Gratton	82	17	21	38	-13	105	7
Rob Zamuner	72	15	20	35	11	62	0
Paul Ysebaert	55	16	15	31	-19	16	4
Shawn Burr	81	13	15	28	4	119	1
Bill Houlder	61	5	23	28	1	22	3
Mikael Andersson	64	8	11	19	0	2	0
Jason Wiemer	66	9	9	18	-9	81	4
Patrick Poulin	46	7	9	16	7	16	1
CHI	38	7	8	15	7	16	1
TB	8	0	1	1	0	0	0
Cory Cross	75	2	14	16	4	66	0
Aaron Gavey*	73	8	4	12	-6	56	1
Michel Petit	54	4	8	12	-11	135	0
LA	9	0	1	1	-1	27	0
TB	45	4	7	11	-10	108	0

Acquired: D Petit from LA for D Steven Finn (Nov. 13); G Reese from Hart. for '96 9th-round pick (Dec. 1); D Igor Ulanov, LW Poulin and '96 2nd-round pick from Chi for D Enrico Ciccone and '96 2nd-round pick (Mar. 20).

Goalies (10 Gm)	Gm	Min	GAA	Record	Sv%
Daren Puppa	57	3189	2.46	29-16-9	.918
Jeff Reese	26	1269	3.22	9-10-1	.891
HART	7	275	3.05	2-3-0	.918
TB	19	994	3.26	7-7-1	.884
J.C. Bergeron	12	595	4.24	2-6-2	.832
TAMPA BAY	82	4993	2.98	38-32-12	.898

Shutouts: Puppa (5) and Reese (1). **Assists:** Puppa (1). **PM:** Puppa (4).

Toronto Maple Leafs

Top Scorers	Gm	G	A	Pts	+/-	PM	PP
Mats Sundin	76	33	50	83	8	46	7
Doug Gilmour	81	32	40	72	-5	77	10
Larry Murphy	82	12	49	61	-2	34	8
Wendel Clark	71	32	26	58	-5	76	8
NYI	58	24	19	43	-12	60	6
TOR	13	8	7	15	7	16	2
Mike Gartner	82	35	19	54	5	52	15
Mathieu Schneider	78	13	41	54	-20	103	7
NYI	65	11	36	47	-18	93	7
TOR	13	2	5	7	-2	10	0
Dave Gagner	73	21	28	49	-19	103	7
DAL	45	14	13	27	-17	44	6
TOR	28	7	15	22	-2	59	1
Kirk Muller	51	13	19	32	-13	57	7
NYI	15	4	3	7	-10	15	0
TOR	36	9	16	25	-3	42	7
Todd Gill	74	7	18	25	-15	116	1
Dave Ellett	80	3	19	22	-10	59	1
Mike Craig	70	8	12	20	-8	42	1
Todd Warriner*	57	7	8	15	-11	26	1

Acquired: C Muller from NYI and G Beaupre from Ott. for RW Ken Belanger (NYI) and G Damian Rhodes (Ott.) (Jan. 23); C Gagner and '96 or '97 6th-round pick from Dal. for LW Randy Wood and C Benoit Hogue (Jan. 28); LW Nick Kypreos and RW Wayne Presley from NYR for LW Sergio Momesso and LW Bill Berg (Feb. 29); LW Clark, D Schneider, and D Denis Smith from NYI for D Kenny Jonsson, F Darby Hendrickson, LW Sean Haggerty, and '97 1st-round pick (Mar. 13).

Goalies (10 Gm)	Gm	Min	GAA	Record	Sv%
Felix Potvin	69	4009	2.87	30-26-11	.910
Don Beaupre	41	2106	3.87	6-28-0	.872
OTT	33	1770	3.73	6-23-0	.877
TOR	8	336	4.64	0-5-0	.847
TORONTO	82	4989	3.03	34-36-12	.903

Shutouts: Potvin (2) and Beaupre (1). **Assists:** Beaupre (2). **PM:** Beaupre (31) and Potvin (4).

Vancouver Canucks

Top Scorers	Gm	G	A	Pts	+/-	PM	PP
Alexander Mogilny	79	55	52	107	14	16	10
Trevor Linden	82	33	47	80	6	42	12
Cliff Ronning	79	22	45	67	16	42	5
Russ Courtnall	81	26	39	65	25	40	6
Martin Gelinas	81	30	26	56	8	59	3
Markus Naslund	76	22	33	55	20	42	4
PIT	66	19	33	52	17	36	3
VAN	10	3	0	3	3	6	1
Jyrki Lumme	80	17	37	54	-9	50	8
Esa Tikkanen	58	14	30	44	1	36	8
ST.L	11	1	4	5	1	18	0
NJ	9	0	2	2	-6	4	0
VAN	38	13	24	37	6	14	8
Jesse Belanger	72	20	21	41	-5	14	8
FLA	63	17	21	38	-5	10	7
VAN	9	3	0	3	0	4	1
Mike Sillinger	74	14	24	38	-18	38	7
ANA	62	13	21	34	-20	32	7
VAN	12	1	3	4	2	6	0
Bret Hedican	77	6	23	29	8	83	1
Dave Babych	53	3	21	24	-5	38	3
Leif Rohlin	56	6	16	22	0	32	1
Mike Ridley	37	6	15	21	-3	29	2

Acquired: LW Tikkanen from NJ for '96 2nd-round pick (Nov. 22); RW Sillinger from Ana. for RW Roman Oksiuta (Mar. 17); C Belanger from Fla. for '96 3rd-round pick and future considerations (Mar. 20); RW Naslund from Pit. for RW Alek Stojanov (Mar. 20).

Goalies (10 Gm)	Gm	Min	GAA	Record	Sv%
Corey Hirsch*	41	2338	2.93	17-14-6	.903
Kirk McLean	45	2645	3.54	15-21-9	.879
VANCOUVER	82	5003	3.33	32-35-15	.888

Shutouts: McLean (2) and Hirsch (1). **Assists:** McLean (2) and Hirsch (2). **PM:** McLean (6) and Hirsch (2).

Washington Capitals

Top Scorers	Gm	G	A	Pts	+/-	PM	PP
Michal Pivonka	73	16	65	81	18	36	6
Peter Bondra	67	52	28	80	18	40	11
Joe Juneau	80	14	50	64	-3	30	7
Todd Krygier	76	15	33	48	-1	82	3
ANA	60	9	28	37	-9	70	2
WASH	16	6	5	11	8	12	1
Steve Konowalchuk	70	23	22	45	13	92	7
Keith Jones	68	18	23	41	8	103	5
Sergei Gonchar	78	15	26	41	25	60	4
Sylvain Cote	81	5	33	38	5	40	3
Dale Hunter	82	13	24	37	5	112	4
Pat Peake	62	17	19	36	7	46	8
Calle Johansson	78	10	25	35	13	50	4
Kelly Miller	74	7	13	20	7	30	0
Stefan Ustorf*	48	7	10	17	8	14	0
Mark Tinordi	71	3	10	13	26	113	2
Craig Berube	50	2	10	12	1	151	1
Ken Klee*	66	8	3	11	-1	60	0
Mike Eagles	70	4	7	11	-1	75	0
Joe Reekie	78	3	7	10	7	149	0
Jeff Nelson*	33	0	7	7	3	16	0
Andrew Brunette*	11	3	3	6	5	0	0
Jim Johnson	66	2	4	6	-3	34	0

Acquired: LW Krygier from Ana. for G Mike Torchia (Mar. 10).

Goalies (10 Gm)	Gm	Min	GAA	Record	Sv%
Jim Carey	71	4069	2.26	35-24-9	.906
Olaf Kolzig	18	897	3.08	4-8-2	.887
WASHINGTON	82	4990	2.45	39-32-11	.900

Shutouts: Carey (9). **Assists:** Carey (1). **PM:** Carey (6) and Kolzig (2).

Winnipeg Jets

Top Scorers	Gm	G	A	Pts	+/-	PM	PP
Keith Tkachuk	76	50	48	98	11	156	20
Craig Janney	84	20	62	82	-33	26	7
SJ	71	13	49	62	-35	26	5
WIN	13	7	13	20	2	0	2
Alexei Zhamnov	58	22	37	59	-4	65	5
Teppo Numminen	74	11	43	54	-4	22	6
Norm MacIver	71	7	46	53	6	58	3
PIT	32	2	21	23	12	32	1
WIN	39	5	25	30	-6	26	2
Igor Korolev	73	22	29	51	1	42	8
Ed Olczyk	51	27	22	49	0	65	16
Dallas Drake	69	19	20	39	-7	36	4
Dave Manson	82	7	23	30	8	205	3
Oleg Tverdovsky	82	7	23	30	-7	41	2
ANA	51	7	15	22	0	35	2
WIN	31	0	8	8	-7	6	0
Mike Eastwood	80	14	14	28	-14	20	2
Mike Stapleton	58	10	14	24	-4	37	3

Acquired: D MacIver from Pit for D Neil Wilkinson (Dec. 28); C Kilger, D Tverdovsky, and '96 3rd-round pick from Ana. for RW Teemu Selanne, C Marc Chouinard, and '96 4th-round pick (Feb. 7); G Roussel from Phi for G Tim Cheveldae and '96 3rd-round pick (Feb. 27); C Janney from SJ for C Darren Turcotte and '96 2nd-round pick (Mar. 18).

Goalies (10 Gm)	Gm	Min	GAA	Record	Sv%
Nikolai Khabibulin	53	2914	3.13	26-20-3	.908
Dominic Roussel	16	741	3.08	4-5-2	.878
PHI	9	456	2.89	2-3-2	.876
WIN	7	285	3.37	2-2-0	.881
WINNIPEG	82	4951	3.53	36-40-6	.895

Shutouts: Khabibulin (2) and Roussel (1). **Assists:** none. **PM:** Khabibulin (12) and Roussel (2).

World Cup of Hockey

The inaugural World Cup of Hockey held at various sites from Aug. 26 to Sept. 14, 1996. Winners of each pool advance directly to semifinals while second and third place finishers advance to quarterfinals.

Final Round Robin Standings

European Pool	Gm	W-L-T	Pts	GF	GA
y-Sweden	3	3-0-0	6	14	3
x-Finland	3	2-1-0	4	17	11
x-Germany	3	1-2-0	2	11	15
Czech Republic	3	0-3-0	0	4	17

N. Amer. Pool	Gm	W-L-T	Pts	GF	GA
y-United States	3	3-0-0	6	19	8
x-Canada	3	2-1-0	4	11	10
x-Russia	3	1-2-0	2	12	14
Slovakia	3	0-3-0	0	10	18

y-division winner x-quarterfinalist

Quarterfinals

Canada 4 .... Germany 1
Russia 5 .... Finland 0

Semifinals

Canada 3 .... 2OT .... Sweden 2
United States 5 .... Russia 2

Championship (best of three)

Canada 4 .... OT .... United States 3
United States 5 .... Canada 2
United States 5 .... Canada 2

Leading Scorers

	Gm	G	A	Pts	PM
Brett Hull, USA	7	7	4	**11**	4
John LeClair, USA	7	6	4	**10**	6
Mats Sundin, Sweden	4	4	3	**7**	4
Wayne Gretzky, Canada	8	3	4	**7**	2
Doug Weight, USA	7	3	4	**7**	12
Paul Coffey, Canada	8	0	7	**7**	12
Brian Leetch, USA	7	0	7	**7**	4

Leading Goaltenders

	Gm	Min	W-L-T	Avg.	Sv%
T. Soderstrom, Sweden	2	120	2-0-0	**1.00**	.952
Tommy Salo, Sweden	2	160	1-1-0	**1.50**	.938
Josef Heiss, Germany	2	120	1-1-0	**2.50**	.932
Curtis Joseph, Canada	7	411	5-2-0	**2.63**	.907
Andrei Trefilov, Russia	4	200	2-1-0	**2.70**	.906
Mike Richter, USA	6	311	5-1-0	**2.89**	.923

Tournament MVP

Mike Richter, G, USA

All-Tournament Team

(Selected by media)

G— Mike Richter, USA; **D**— Calle Johansson, Sweden; Chris Chelios, USA **F**— Brett Hull, USA; John LeClair, USA; Mats Sundin, Sweden.

Final Game Box Score
United States, 5-2

Saturday, Sept. 14, 1996 at Molson Centre in Montreal; Attendance: 21,273.

Canada	0	1	1—**2**
United States	1	0	4—**5**

Scoring

1st Period: USA— Hull 6 (Leetch, Weight), 11:18 (pp).
2nd Period: CAN— Lindros 3 (Coffey, Gretzky), 19:54 (pp).
3rd Period: CAN—Foote 1 (unassisted), 12:50; USA—Hull 7 (Leetch), 16:42; USA—Amonte 2 (D. Hatcher, Smolinski), 17:25; USA—D. Hatcher 3 (unassisted), 19:18 (en); USA—Deadmarsh 2 (unassisted), 19:42.

Goaltenders

Saves: CAN— Curtis Joseph (24 shots/20 saves); USA—Mike Richter (37 shots/35 saves).

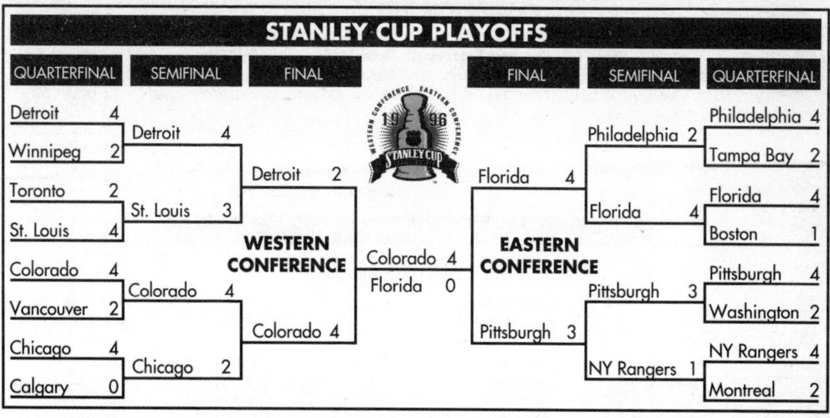

Series Summaries

WESTERN CONFERENCE

FIRST ROUND (Best of 7)

	W-L	GF	Leading Scorers
Detroit	4-2	20	Fedorov (0-7-7)
Winnipeg	2-4	10	Six tied with 3 pts

Date	Winner	Home Ice
April 17	Red Wings, 4-1	at Detroit
April 19	Red Wings, 4-0	at Detroit
April 21	Jets, 4-1	at Winnipeg
April 23	Red Wings, 6-1	at Winnipeg
April 26	Jets, 3-1	at Detroit
April 28	Red Wings, 4-1	at Winnipeg

Shutout: Osgood, Detroit

	W-L	GF	Leading Scorers
Colorado	4-2	24	Sakic (7-4-11)
Vancouver	2-4	17	Mogilny (1-8-9)

Date	Winner	Home Ice
April 16	Avalanche, 5-2	at Colorado
April 18	Canucks, 5-4	at Colorado
April 20	Avalanche, 4-0	at Vancouver
April 22	Canucks, 4-3	at Vancouver
April 25	Avalanche, 5-4 (OT)	at Colorado
April 27	Avalanche, 3-2	at Vancouver

Shutout: Roy, Colorado.

	W-L	GF	Leading Scorers
Chicago	4-0	16	Murphy (4-2-6)
Calgary	0-4	7	Chiasson (2-1-3)

Date	Winner	Home Ice
April 17	Blackhawks, 4-1	at Chicago
April 19	Blackhawks, 3-0	at Chicago
April 21	Blackhawks, 7-5	at Calgary
April 23	Blackhawks, 2-1 (3OT)	at Calgary

Shutout: Belfour, Chicago.

	W-L	GF	Leading Scorers
St. Louis	4-2	21	Gretzky (0-9-9)
Toronto	2-4	15	Gilmour (1-6-7)

Date	Winner	Home Ice
April 16	Blues, 3-1	at Toronto
April 18	Maple Leafs, 5-4 (OT)	at Toronto
April 21	Blues, 3-2 (OT)	at St. Louis
April 23	Blues, 5-1	at St. Louis
April 25	Maple Leafs, 5-4 (OT)	at Toronto
April 27	Blues, 2-1	at St. Louis

SEMIFINALS (Best of 7)

	W-L	GF	Leading Scorers
Colorado	4-2	21	Kamensky (6-3-9)
Chicago	2-4	14	Roenick (3-4-7)

Date	Winner	Home Ice
May 2	Blackhawks, 3-2 (OT)	at Colorado
May 4	Avalanche, 5-1	at Colorado
May 6	Blackhawks, 4-3 (OT)	at Chicago
May 8	Avalanche, 3-2 (3OT)	at Chicago
May 11	Avalanche, 4-1	at Colorado
May 13	Avalanche, 4-3 (2OT)	at Chicago

	W-L	GF	Leading Scorers
Detroit	4-3	22	Yzerman (6-5-11)
St. Louis	3-4	16	Hull (3-4-7)

Date	Winner	Home Ice
May 3	Red Wings, 3-2	at Detroit
May 5	Red Wings, 8-3	at Detroit
May 8	Blues, 5-4 (OT)	at St. Louis
May 10	Blues, 1-0	at St. Louis
May 12	Blues, 3-2	at Detroit
May 14	Red Wings, 4-2	at St. Louis
May 16	Red Wings, 1-0 (2OT)	at Detroit

Shutouts: Casey, St. Louis; Osgood, Detroit.

CHAMPIONSHIP (Best of 7)

	W-L	GF	Leading Scorers
Colorado	4-2	20	Sakic (4-6-10)
Detroit	2-4	16	Fedorov (1-8-9)

Date	Winner	Home Ice
May 19	Avalanche, 3-2 (OT)	at Detroit
May 21	Avalanche, 3-0	at Detroit
May 23	Red Wings, 6-4	at Colorado
May 25	Avalanche, 4-2	at Colorado
May 27	Red Wings, 5-2	at Detroit
May 29	Avalanche, 4-1	at Colorado

Shutout: Roy, Colorado

EASTERN CONFERENCE

FIRST ROUND (Best of 7)

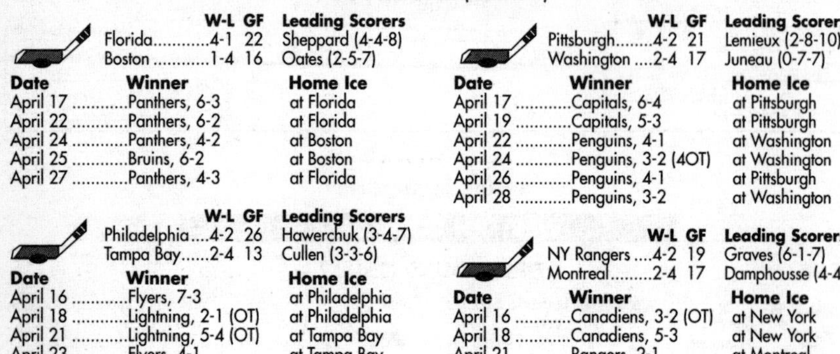

	W-L	GF	Leading Scorers
Florida	4-1	22	Sheppard (4-4-8)
Boston	1-4	16	Oates (2-5-7)

Date	Winner	Home Ice
April 17	Panthers, 6-3	at Florida
April 22	Panthers, 6-2	at Florida
April 24	Panthers, 4-2	at Boston
April 25	Bruins, 6-2	at Boston
April 27	Panthers, 4-3	at Florida

	W-L	GF	Leading Scorers
Pittsburgh	4-2	21	Lemieux (2-8-10)
Washington	2-4	17	Juneau (0-7-7)

Date	Winner	Home Ice
April 17	Capitals, 6-4	at Pittsburgh
April 19	Capitals, 5-3	at Pittsburgh
April 22	Penguins, 4-1	at Washington
April 24	Penguins, 3-2 (4OT)	at Washington
April 26	Penguins, 4-1	at Pittsburgh
April 28	Penguins, 3-2	at Washington

	W-L	GF	Leading Scorers
Philadelphia	4-2	26	Hawerchuk (3-4-7)
Tampa Bay	2-4	13	Cullen (3-3-6)

Date	Winner	Home Ice
April 16	Flyers, 7-3	at Philadelphia
April 18	Lightning, 2-1 (OT)	at Philadelphia
April 21	Lightning, 5-4 (OT)	at Tampa Bay
April 23	Flyers, 4-1	at Tampa Bay
April 25	Flyers, 4-1	at Philadelphia
April 27	Flyers, 6-1	at Tampa Bay

	W-L	GF	Leading Scorers
NY Rangers	4-2	19	Graves (6-1-7)
Montreal	2-4	17	Damphousse (4-4-8)

Date	Winner	Home Ice
April 16	Canadiens, 3-2 (OT)	at New York
April 18	Canadiens, 5-3	at New York
April 21	Rangers, 2-1	at Montreal
April 23	Rangers, 4-3	at Montreal
April 26	Rangers, 3-2	at New York
April 28	Rangers, 5-3	at Montreal

SEMIFINALS (Best of 7)

	W-L	GF	Leading Scorers
Pittsburgh	4-1	21	Lemieux (8-2-10)
NY Rangers	1-4	15	Kurri (1-5-6)

Date	Winner	Home Ice
May 3	Penguins, 4-3	at Pittsburgh
May 5	Rangers, 6-3	at Pittsburgh
May 7	Penguins, 3-2	at NY Rangers
May 9	Penguins, 4-1	at NY Rangers
May 11	Penguins, 7-3	at Pittsburgh

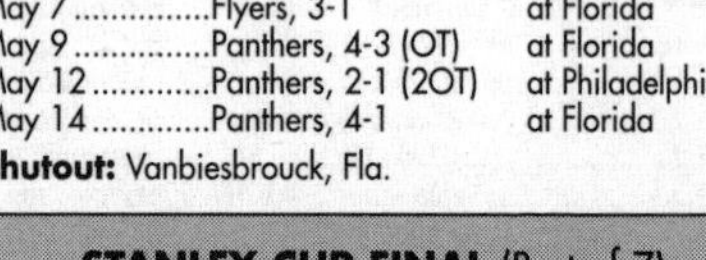

	W-L	GF	Leading Scorers
Florida	4-2	15	Barnes (3-3-6)
Philadelphia	2-4	11	Lindros (3-3-6)

Date	Winner	Home Ice
May 2	Panthers, 2-0	at Philadelphia
May 4	Flyers, 3-2	at Philadelphia
May 7	Flyers, 3-1	at Florida
May 9	Panthers, 4-3 (OT)	at Florida
May 12	Panthers, 2-1 (2OT)	at Philadelphia
May 14	Panthers, 4-1	at Florida

Shutout: Vanbiesbrouck, Fla.

CHAMPIONSHIP (Best of 7)

	W-L	GF	Leading Scorers
Florida	4-3	20	Lowry (3-4-7)
Pittsburgh	3-4	15	Lemieux (1-6-7)

Date	Winner	Home Ice
May 18	Panthers, 5-1	at Pittsburgh
May 20	Penguins, 3-2	at Pittsburgh
May 24	Panthers, 5-2	at Florida
May 26	Penguins, 2-1	at Florida
May 28	Penguins, 3-0	at Pittsburgh
May 30	Panthers, 4-3	at Florida
June 1	Panthers, 3-1	at Pittsburgh

Shutout: Barrasso, Pit.

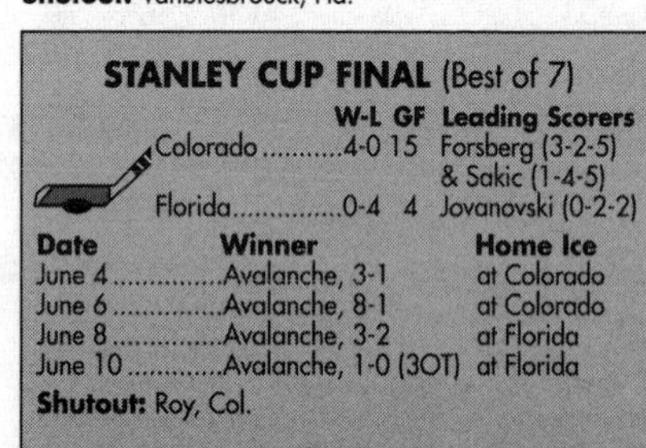

STANLEY CUP FINAL (Best of 7)

	W-L	GF	Leading Scorers
Colorado	4-0	15	Forsberg (3-2-5) & Sakic (1-4-5)
Florida	0-4	4	Jovanovski (0-2-2)

Date	Winner	Home Ice
June 4	Avalanche, 3-1	at Colorado
June 6	Avalanche, 8-1	at Colorado
June 8	Avalanche, 3-2	at Florida
June 10	Avalanche, 1-0 (3OT)	at Florida

Shutout: Roy, Col.

Conn Smythe Trophy (MVP)

Joe Sakic, Colorado, C

22 games, 18 goals, 16 assists, 34 points

Stanley Cup Leaders

Scoring

	Gm	G	A	Pts	+/-	PM	PP
Joe Sakic, Col	22	18	16	**34**	10	14	6
Mario Lemieux, Pit	18	11	16	**27**	3	33	3
Jaromir Jagr, Pit	18	11	12	**23**	7	18	5
Valeri Kamensky, Col	22	10	12	**22**	11	28	3
Peter Forsberg, Col	22	10	11	**21**	10	18	3
Petr Nedved, Pit	18	10	10	**20**	3	16	4
Steve Yzerman, Det	18	8	12	**20**	1-	4	4
Sergei Fedorov, Det	19	2	18	**20**	8	10	0
Sandis Ozolinsh, Col	22	5	14	**19**	5	16	2
Dave Lowry, Fla	22	10	7	**17**	8	39	4
Mike Ricci, Col	22	6	11	**17**	1-	18	3
Adam Deadmarsh, Col	22	5	12	**17**	8	25	1
Ray Sheppard, Fla	21	8	8	**16**	4	0	3
Stu Barnes, Fla	22	6	10	**16**	10	4	2
Uwe Krupp, Col	22	4	12	**16**	5	33	1
Wayne Gretzky, St.L	13	2	14	**16**	2	0	1

Goaltending

(Minimum 420 minutes).

	Gm	Min	W-L	ShO	GAA
Ed Belfour, Chi	9	666	6-3	1	**2.07**
Patrick Roy, Col	22	1454	16-6	3	**2.10**
Chris Osgood, Det	15	936	8-7	2	**2.12**
Ron Hextall, Phi	12	760	6-6	0	**2.13**
John Vanbiesbrouck, Fla	22	1332	12-10	1	**2.25**
Ken Wregget, Pit	9	599	7-2	0	**2.30**

Wins

Roy, Col 16-6
Vanbiesbrouck, Fla ...12-10
Osgood, Det 8-7
Wregget, Pit....7-2
Three tied with three each.

Save Pct.

Vanbiesbrouck, Fla ... .932
Wregget, Pit.... .930
Belfour, Chi .... .929
Barrasso, Pit.... .923
Roy, Col.... .921

Goals

Sakic, Col 18
Jagr, Pit....11
Lemieux, Pit....11
Nedved, Pit 10
Lowry, Fla 10
Kamensky, Col....10
Forsberg, Col 10

Assists

Fedorov, Det....18
Lemieux, Pit....16
Sakic, Col 16
Gretzky, St.L....14
Zubov, Pit....14
Ozolinsh, Col 14
Six tied with 12 each.

Power Play Goals

Graves, NYR 6
Corson, St.L....6
Ciccarelli, Det....6
Sakic, Col 6

Overtime Goals

Sakic, Col 2
17 tied with one each.

Plus/Minus

Gusarov, Col ....+13
Foote, Col ....+11
Kamensky, Col....+11
Three tied at +10.

Penalty Minutes

Laus, Fla 62
Lemieux, Col 55
Jovanovski, Fla 52
Podein, Phi....50
Mellanby, Fla 44

Final Stanley Cup Standings

	Gm	W	L	Goals For	Goals Opp	Dif
Colorado	22	16	6	80	51	+29
Florida	22	12	10	61	57	+4
Pittsburgh	18	11	7	57	52	+5
Detroit	19	10	9	58	46	+12
St. Louis	13	7	6	37	37	E
Chicago	10	6	4	30	28	+2
Philadelphia	12	6	6	37	28	+9
NY Rangers	11	5	6	34	38	-4
Montreal	6	2	4	17	19	-2
Washington	6	2	4	17	21	-4
Toronto	6	2	4	15	21	-6
Vancouver	6	2	4	17	24	-7
Winnipeg	6	2	4	10	20	-10
Tampa Bay	6	2	4	13	26	-13
Boston	5	1	4	16	22	-6
Calgary	4	0	4	7	16	-9

Finalists' Composite Box Scores

Colorado Avalanche (16–6)

Top Scorers	Pos	Overall Playoffs Gm	G	A	Pts	+/-	PM	PP	S	Finals vs Florida Gm	G	A	Pts	+/-	PM	PP	S
Joe Sakic	C	22	18	16	**34**	+10	14	6	98	4	1	4	**5**	+1	2	0	12
Valeri Kamensky	L	22	10	12	**22**	+11	28	3	56	4	1	2	**3**	+3	8	0	12
Peter Forsberg	C	22	10	11	**21**	+10	18	3	50	4	3	2	**5**	+4	0	2	13
Sandis Ozolinsh	D	22	5	14	**19**	+5	16	2	52	4	0	2	**2**	E	4	0	10
Mike Ricci	C	22	6	11	**17**	−1	18	3	31	4	1	0	**1**	+2	6	0	5
Adam Deadmarsh	C	22	5	12	**17**	+8	25	1	40	4	0	4	**4**	+4	4	0	7
Uwe Krupp	D	22	4	12	**16**	+5	33	1	38	4	2	1	**3**	+4	2	0	11
Scott Young	R	22	3	12	**15**	+6	10	0	61	4	1	1	**2**	+3	0	0	14
Claude Lemieux	R	19	5	7	**12**	+5	55	3	81	2	1	0	**1**	+1	4	0	14
Alexei Gusarov	D	21	0	9	**9**	+13	12	0	15	4	0	2	**2**	+3	2	0	1
Rene Corbet	L	8	3	2	**5**	+3	2	1	9	4	2	1	**3**	+1	0	1	8
Mike Keane	R	22	3	2	**5**	+1	16	0	22	4	1	1	**2**	+1	0	0	5
Stephane Yelle	C	22	1	4	**5**	+2	8	0	24	4	0	0	**0**	E	0	0	7
Sylvain Lefebvre	D	22	0	5	**5**	+6	12	0	22	4	0	1	**1**	+2	2	0	5
Adam Foote	D	22	1	3	**4**	+11	36	0	20	4	0	1	**1**	+4	4	0	4
Jon Klemm	D	15	2	1	**3**	+6	0	1	11	4	2	0	**2**	+2	0	1	5
Chris Simon	L	12	1	2	**3**	−2	11	0	9	0	0	0	**0**	E	0	0	0
Curtis Leschyshyn	D	17	1	2	**3**	+4	8	0	9	4	0	1	**1**	+3	4	0	3
Dave Hannan	C	13	0	2	**2**	+3	2	0	2	3	0	0	**0**	+2	0	0	0

Overtime goals— OVERALL (Sakic 2, Ozolinsh, Krupp, Keane); FINALS (Krupp). **Shorthanded goals**— OVERALL (Yelle); FINALS (none). **Power Play conversions**—OVERALL (24 for 110, 21.8%);. FINALS (4 for 16, 25%)

Goaltending	Gm	Min	GAA	GA	SA	Sv%	W-L	Gm	Min	GAA	GA	SA	Sv %	W-L
Stephane Fiset	1	1	**0.00**	0	0	.000	0-0	0	0	**0.00**	0	0	.000	0-0
Patrick Roy	22	1454	**2.10**	51	649	.921	16-6	4	285	**0.84**	4	151	.974	4-0
TOTAL	22	1460	**2.10**	51	649	.921	16-6	4	285	**0.84**	4	151	.974	4-0

Empty Net Goals— OVERALL (none); **Shutouts**— OVERALL (Roy 3), FINALS (Roy 1); **Assists**— OVERALL (none); **Penalty Minutes**— OVERALL (none).

Finalists' Composite Box Scores (cont.)

Florida Panthers (12–10)

Top Scorers	Pos	Overall Playoffs Gm	G	A	Pts	+/-	PM	PP	S	Finals vs Colorado Gm	G	A	Pts	+/-	PM	PP	S
Dave Lowry	L	22	10	7	**17**	+8	39	4	45	4	0	1	**1**	-3	2	0	7
Ray Sheppard	R	21	8	8	**16**	+4	0	3	47	4	1	0	**1**	-3	0	1	11
Stu Barnes	C	22	6	10	**16**	+10	4	2	57	4	1	0	**1**	-2	2	1	11
Bill Lindsay	L	22	5	5	**10**	+6	18	0	33	4	0	1	**1**	-1	4	0	7
Scott Mellanby	R	22	3	6	**9**	−10	44	2	57	4	0	1	**1**	-5	4	0	17
Ed Jovanovski	D	22	1	8	**9**	+2	52	0	51	4	0	2	**2**	-2	11	0	16
Rob Niedermayer	C	22	5	3	**8**	−8	12	2	48	4	1	0	**1**	-4	2	0	7
Tom Fitzgerald	R	22	4	4	**8**	+3	34	0	31	4	1	0	**1**	-1	0	0	9
Jason Woolley	D	13	2	6	**8**	+3	14	1	27	2	0	0	**0**	E	0	0	6
Paul Laus	D	21	2	6	**8**	+3	62	0	18	4	0	0	**0**	-1	2	0	6
Johan Garpenlov	L	20	4	2	**6**	−2	8	0	35	4	0	1	**1**	-1	2	0	3
Robert Svehla	D	22	0	6	**6**	+3	32	0	38	4	0	0	**0**	-1	6	0	8
Mike Hough	L	22	4	1	**5**	+5	8	0	38	4	0	0	**0**	E	0	0	4
Jody Hull	R	14	3	2	**5**	+4	0	0	18	2	0	0	**0**	E	0	0	3
Martin Straka	R	13	2	2	**4**	−2	2	0	20	4	0	1	**1**	-4	0	0	10
Radek Dvorak	L	16	1	3	**4**	+2	0	0	36	1	0	0	**0**	E	0	0	4
Brian Skrudland	C	21	1	3	**4**	+6	18	0	27	4	0	0	**0**	E	4	0	6
Gord Murphy	D	14	0	4	**4**	+1	6	0	53	4	0	0	**0**	-5	0	0	11
Terry Carkner	D	22	0	4	**4**	+8	10	0	15	4	0	0	**0**	-1	4	0	3

Overtime goals— OVERALL (Lowry, Hough); FINALS (none). **Shorthanded goals**— OVERALL (Lindsay); FINALS (none); **Power Play conversions**— OVERALL (14 for 109, 12.8%); FINALS (2 for 17, 11.8%).

Goaltending	Gm	Min	GAA	GA	SA	Sv%	W-L	Gm	Min	GAA	GA	SA	Sv%	W-L
John Vanbiesbrouck	22	1332	**2.25**	50	735	.932	12-10	4	245	**2.69**	11	119	.908	0-4
Mark Fitzpatrick	2	60	**6.00**	6	30	.800	0-0	1	40	**6.00**	4	19	.789	0-0
TOTAL	22	1397	**2.45**	57	766	.926	12-10	4	285	**3.16**	15	138	.891	0-4

Empty Net Goals— OVERALL (1), FINALS (none); **Shutouts**— OVERALL (Vanbiesbrouck 1), FINALS (none); **Assists**— OVERALL (Vanbiesbrouck 1), FINALS (none); **Penalty Minutes**— OVERALL (Vanbiesbrouck 20), FINALS (Vanbiesbrouck 6).

1996 NHL Draft

First and second round selections at the 34th NHL Entry Draft held June 22, 1996, in St. Louis. The order of the first ten positions determined by a draft lottery held May 19 in New York. Positions 11 through 26 reflect regular season records in reverse order.

First Round

	Team	Player	Pos
1	Ottawa	Chris Phillips, Prince Albert	D
2	San Jose	Andrei Zyuzin, Salavat Yulaev (RUS)	D
3	NY Islanders	Jean-Pierre Dumont, Val d'Or	L
4	**a**-Washington	Alexandre Volchkov, Barrie	R
5	Dallas	Richard Jackman, Sault Ste. Marie	D
6	Edmonton	Boyd Devereaux, Kitchener	C
7	Buffalo	Erik Rasmussen, U. of Minnesota	C
8	**b**-Boston	Johnathan Aitken, Medicine Hat	D
9	Anaheim	Ruslan Salei, Las Vegas	D
10	New Jersey	Lance Ward, Red Deer	D
11	Phoenix	Dan Focht, Tri-City	D
12	Vancouver	Josh Holden, Regina	C
13	Calgary	Derek Morris, Regina	D
14	St. Louis	Marty Reasoner, Boston College	C
15	**c**-Philadelphia	Daynus Zubrus, Caledon	R
16	Tampa Bay	Mario Larocque, Hull	D
17	Washington	Jaroslav Svejkovsky, Tri-City	R
18	Montreal	Matt Higgins, Moose Jaw	C
19	**d**-Edmonton	Mathieu Descoteaux, Shawinigan	D
20	Florida	Marcus Nilsson, Djurgarden (SWE)	R
21	**e**-San Jose	Marco Sturm, Landshut (GER)	C
22	NY Rangers	Jeff Brown, Sarnia	D
23	Pittsburgh	Craig Hillier, Ottawa	G
24	**f**-Phoenix	Daniel Briere, Drummondville	C
25	Colorado	Peter Ratchuk, Shattuck HS	D
26	Detroit	Jesse Wallin, Red Deer	D

Second Round

	Team	Player	Pos
27	**g**-Buffalo	Cory Sarich, Saskatoon	D
28	**h**-Pittsburgh	Pavel Skrbek, Kladno (CZE)	D
29	NY Islanders	Dan Lacouture, Enfield	L
30	Los Angeles	Josh Green, Medicine Hat	L
31	**i**-Chicago	Remi Royer, St. Hyacinthe	D
32	Edmonton	Chris Hajt, Guelph	D
33	Buffalo	Darren Van Oene, Brandon	L
34	Hartford	Trevor Wasyluk, Medicine Hat	L
35	Anaheim	Matt Cullen, St. Cloud State	C
36	**j**-Toronto	Marek Posmyk, Jihlava (CZE)	D
37	**k**-Los Angeles	Marian Cisar, Bratislava	R
38	**l**-New Jersey	Wesley Mason, Sarnia	L
39	Calgary	Travis Brigley, Lethbridge	L
40	**m**-Calgary	Steve Begin, Val D'Or Foreurs	C
41	**n**-New Jersey	Joshua Dewolf, Twin Cities	D
42	**o**-Chicago	Jeff Paul, Niagara Falls	R
43	Washington	Jan Bulis, Barrie	C
44	Montreal	Mathieu Garon, Victoriaville	G
45	Boston	Henry Kuster, Medicine Hat	R
46	**p**-Chicago	Geoff Peters, Niagara Falls	C
47	**q**-New Jersey	Pierre Dagenais, Moncton	L
48	NY Rangers	Daniel Goneau, Moncton	L
49	**r**-New Jersey	Colin White, Hull	D
50	**s**-Toronto	Francis Larivee, Laval	G
51	Colorado	Yuri Babenko, Krylja Sovetov	C
52	Detroit	Aren Miller, Spokane	G

Acquired picks: FIRST ROUND: **a**— from Los Angeles; **b**— from Hartford; **c**— from Toronto; **d**— from Boston; **e**— from Chicago; **f**— from Philadelphia; SECOND ROUND: **g**— from from St. Louis via Ottawa; **h**— from New Jersey via St. Louis; **i**— from San Jose via Phoenix and Dallas; **j**— from New Jersey; **k**— from Phoenix; **l**— from Vancouver; **m**— from St. Louis; **n**— from Pittsburgh via Toronto; **o**— from Tampa Bay; **p**— from San Jose via Florida; **q**— from Tampa Bay via Chicago; **r**— from Pittsburgh; **s**— from Philadelphia.

Affiliations: Czech Republic— Jihlava, Kladno; **Germany**— Landshut; **IHL** (International Hockey League)— Las Vegas; **MTJHL** (Metro Toronto Junior Hockey League)— Caledon; **OHL** (Ontario Hockey League)— Barrie, Guelph, Kitchener, Niagara Falls, Ottawa, Sarnia, Sault Ste. Marie; **QMJHL** (Quebec Major Jr. Hockey League)— Drummondville, Hull, Laval, Moncton, Shawinigan, St. Hyacinthe, Val d'Or, Victoriaville; **Russia**— Krylja Sovetov, Salavet Yulaev; **Slovakia**— Bratislava; **Sweden**— Djurgarden; **U.S. College**— Boston College, St. Cloud St., U. of Minnesota; **U.S. High School**— Shattuck-St. Mary's HS (Minn.); **U.S. Junior**— Enfield, Twin Cities; **WHL** (Western Hockey League)— Brandon, Lethbridge, Medicine Hat, Moose Jaw, Prince Albert, Red Deer, Regina, Saskatoon, Spokane,Tri-City.

Annual Awards

Except for the Vezina Trophy and Adams Award, voting is done by a 50-member panel of the Pro Hockey Writers Assn., while full PHWA membership voted for Masterton Trophy. Vezina Trophy voted on by NHL general managers and Adams Award by NHL broadcasters. Points awarded on 10–7–5–3–1 basis except for the Vezina Trophy, the Adams Award and the All-NHL team which are awarded 5-3-1.

Hart Trophy

For Most Valuable Player

	Pos	1st	2nd	3rd	4th	5th	Pts
Mario Lemieux, Pit.	C	34	10	5	1	1—	439
Mark Messier, NYR	C	10	15	10	6	2—	275
Eric Lindros, Phi.	C	2	17	7	12	3—	213
Jaromir Jagr, Pit.	R	5	3	10	10	5—	156
Sergei Fedorov, Det.	C	0	3	6	4	5—	68
Grant Fuhr, St.L	G	1	3	2	2	5—	52

Calder Trophy

For Rookie of the Year

	Pos	1st	2nd	3rd	4th	5th	Pts
D. Alfredsson, Ott	R	27	18	8	0	1—	437
Eric Daze, Chi.	L	22	20	10	2	0—	416
Ed Jovanovski, Fla	D	5	9	16	6	2—	213
Saku Koivu, Mon.	C	0	1	7	12	5—	83

Norris Trophy

For Best Defenseman

	1st	2nd	3rd	4th	5th	Pts
Chris Chelios, Chi.	22	19	9	3	1—	408
Ray Bourque, Bos.	23	16	8	7	0—	403
Brian Leetch, NYR	6	6	23	7	7—	245
Vladimir Konstantinov, Det.	2	6	7	10	4—	131
Paul Coffey, Det.	0	4	2	12	9—	83

Vezina Trophy

For Outstanding Goaltender

	1st	2nd	3rd	Pts
Jim Carey, Wash.	5	7	6—	52
Chris Osgood, Det.	5	6	3—	46
Daren Puppa, TB	4	3	5—	34
Martin Brodeur, NJ	4	3	2—	31
Ron Hextall, Phi.	2	3	4—	23

Lady Byng Trophy

For Sportsmanship and Gentlemanly Play

	Pos	1st	2nd	3rd	4th	5th	Pts
Paul Kariya, Ana.	L	12	13	6	4	2—	255
Adam Oates, Bos.	C	10	4	17	2	3—	222
Teemu Selanne, Ana	R	8	8	8	7	3—	200
A. Mogilny, Van.	R	10	8	2	6	2—	186
Joe Sakic, Col.	C	4	6	1	3	3—	99
Brian Leetch, NYR	D	2	5	1	3	4—	73

Selke Trophy

For Best Defensive Forward

	Pos	1st	2nd	3rd	4th	5th	Pts
Sergei Fedorov, Det.	C	26	10	4	1	3—	356
Ron Francis, Pit.	C	12	15	3	5	0—	255
Steve Yzerman, Det.	C	1	1	6	3	1—	57
V. Damphousse, Mon.	L	1	2	3	5	1—	55
Trevor Linden, Van.	C	1	3	3	1	5—	54
Claude Lemieux, Col.	R	2	1	3	1	0—	45

Adams Award

For Coach of the Year

	1st	2nd	3rd	Pts
Scotty Bowman, Det.	39	13	9—	243
Doug MacLean, Fla.	17	19	8—	150
Terry Crisp, TB	9	17	13—	109
Mario Tremblay, Mon.	2	2	12—	28
Craig Hartsburg, Chi.	2	2	3—	19
Terry Murray, Phi.	1	2	8—	19

World Wide Photos

Anaheim left wing **Paul Kariya** is all smiles after winning the 1996 Lady Byng Trophy for sportsmanship.

Other Awards

Lester B. Pearson Award (NHL Players Assn. MVP)— Mario Lemieux, Pittsburgh; **Jennings Trophy** (Goaltenders with a minimum of 13 games played for team with fewest goals against)— Chris Osgood & Mike Vernon, Detroit; **Masterton Trophy** (perseverance, sportsmanship,and dedication to hockey)— Gary Roberts, Calgary; **King Clancy Trophy** (leadership and humanitarian contributions to community)— Kris King, Winnipeg; **Lester Patrick Trophy** (outstanding service to hockey)— George Gund, Ken Morrow, and Milt Schmidt.

All-NHL

Voting by Pro Hockey Writers' Association (PHWA). Holdover from 1994–95 All-NHL first team in **bold** type.

	First Team	1st	2nd	3rd	Pts
G	Jim Carey, Wash	25	17	5—	181
D	**Chris Chelios** , Chi.	41	11	1—	239
D	Ray Bourque, Bos.	34	18	1—	225
C	Mario Lemieux, Pit.	50	2	0—	256
R	**Jaromir Jagr** , Pit.	49	2	1—	252
L	Paul Kariya, Ana.	25	19	6—	188

	Second Team	1st	2nd	3rd	Pts
G	Chris Osgood, Det.	7	15	8—	88
D	Brian Leetch, NYR	15	29	5—	167
D	Vladimir Konstantinov, Det.	7	18	8—	97
C	**Eric Lindros** , Phi.	2	19	3—	80
R	Alexander Mogilny, Van.	2	28	15—	109
L	**John LeClair** , Phi.	13	16	22—	135

All-Rookie Team

Voting by PHWA. Vote totals not released.

Pos		Pos	
G	Corey Hirsch, Van.	F	Daniel Alfredsson, Ott.
C	Petr Sykora, NJ	D	Kyle McLaren, Bos.
D	Ed Jovanovski, Fla.	F	Eric Daze, Chi.

U.S. Division I College Hockey

Final regular season standings; overall records, including all postseason tournament games, in parentheses.

Central Collegiate Hockey Assn.

	W	L	T	Pts	GF	GA
* Lake Superior St. (30-8-2)	22	6	2	46	136	89
* Michigan (34-7-2)	22	6	2	46	178	71
* Michigan St. (28-13-1)	22	7	1	45	115	86
* W. Michigan (27-11-3)	21	6	3	45	125	71
Bowling Green (26-14-1)	18	11	1	37	126	106
Ferris St. (13-22-3)	10	17	3	23	101	120
Miami-OH (10-22-4)	9	17	4	22	99	142
Ohio St. (10-19-5)	8	17	5	21	82	105
Notre Dame (9-23-4)	6	20	4	16	87	136
Alaska Fairbanks (10-23-1)	8	22	0	16	101	142
Illinois-Chicago (9-24-3)	6	23	1	13	73	155

Tiebreaker: Lake Superior St. and Michigan shared the regular season title but LSS was top seed in postseason tournament because of head to head record. Michigan St. finishes third because of head to head record.

Conf. Tourney Final: Michigan 4, Lake Superior St. 3.

* **NCAA Tourney (4–3):** Michigan (3–0), Lake Superior St. (1–1), Western Michigan (0–1), Michigan St. (0–1).

Eastern Collegiate Athletic Conf.

	W	L	T	Pts	GF	GA
* Vermont (27-7-4)	17	2	3	37	86	45
* Clarkson (25-10-3)	16	4	2	34	97	59
St Lawrence (20-12-3)	15	4	3	33	107	74
* Cornell (21-9-4)	14	4	4	32	94	66
Colgate (17-13-4)	13	5	4	30	95	60
Harvard (13-20-1)	9	12	1	19	76	71
Brown (9-15-8)	5	11	6	16	60	81
Rensselaer (10-21-3)	7	13	2	16	63	77
Dartmouth (7-20-3)	6	14	2	14	57	88
Princeton (7-19-4)	5	14	3	13	55	85
Union (7-19-4)	4	15	3	11	55	83
Yale (7-23-1)	4	17	1	9	53	109

Conf. Tourney Final: Cornell 2, Harvard 1.

* **NCAA Tourney (2–3):** Vermont (1–1), Clarkson (1–1), Cornell (0–1).

Hockey East Association

	W	L	T	SW	Pts	GF	GA
* Boston University (30-7-3)	17	5	2	1	90	132	79
* UMass-Lowell (26-10-4)	16	6	2	1	85	114	96
Maine (26-9-4)	14	6	4	2	80	102	75
* Providence (21-15-3)	12	9	3	0	66	83	83
Boston College (16-17-3)	12	10	2	1	65	89	102
New Hampshire (12-18-4)	8	12	4	1	49	99	103
Northeastern (10-21-5)	6	13	5	5	45	79	93
UMass-Amherst (10-19-6)	4	14	6	4	36	81	120
Merrimack (10-19-5)	4	18	2	0	24	83	111

Note: Teams receive 5 points for a win, 2 for a tie and an extra point for a shootout win (SW).

Conf. Tourney Final: Providence 3, Maine 2.

* **NCAA Tourney (2–3):** BU (1–1), UMass-Lowell (1–1), Providence (0–1).

Western Collegiate Hockey Assn.

	W	L	T	Pts	GF	GA
* Colorado College (33-5-4)	26	2	4	56	178	78
* Minnesota (30-10-2)	21	9	2	44	155	95
Denver (22-14-3)	17	12	3	37	120	112
Minnesota-Duluth (20-17-1)	16	15	1	33	116	109
North Dakota (19-18-1)	16	15	1	33	127	126
Wisconsin (17-20-3)	14	15	3	31	110	123
Michigan Tech (18-18-6)	12	14	6	30	108	118
St. Cloud State (13-22-4)	10	18	4	24	106	132
Alaska-Anchorage (9-23-5)	8	20	4	20	86	130
Northern Michigan (7-30-2)	5	25	2	12	64	147

Conf. Tourney Final: Minnesota 7, Michigan Tech 2.

* **NCAA Tourney (3–2):** Colorado College (2–1), Minnesota (1–1).

NCAA Top 10 Poll

Taken **before** final two rounds of league tournaments.

Final weekly regular season Top 10 poll conducted by The Record of Troy, N.Y. and taken March 3, before league tournaments. Voting panel made up of 20 Division I coaches, eight national media correspondents and two NHL scouts. First place votes in parentheses; teams in **bold** type went on to reach NCAA tournament Final Four.

		League	W	L	T	Pts
1	**Colorado College** (29)	WCHA	30	3	4	290
2	**Boston University**	HEA	26	5	3	249
3	Lake Superior State	CCHA	26	6	2	227
4	**Michigan**	CCHA	25	7	3	203
5	Minnesota	WCHA	27	9	2	175
6	Michigan State	CCHA	26	10	1	117
7	Western Michigan	CCHA	25	8	3	109
8	UMass-Lowell	HEA	23	7	4	101
9	**Vermont**	ECAC	23	5	4	73
10	Maine	HEA	23	8	4	19

Also receiving votes: Clarkson (17 pts); Wisconsin (8 pts); Denver (4 pts); St. Lawrence (2 pts); Bowling Green (1 pt).

Leading Scorers

Including postseason games.

	Cl	Gm	G	A	Pts	PPG
Ryan Equale, UConn	Sr.	25	21	41	62	2.48
Martin St. Louis, Vermont	Jr.	34	28	55	83	2.44
Eric Perrin, Vermont	Jr.	37	29	54	83	2.24
Pat Lyons, Iona	Sr.	25	28	26	54	2.16
Brendan Morrison, Michigan	Jr.	35	28	44	72	2.06
Teeder Wynne, North Dak.	Sr.	37	26	47	73	1.97
Brian Bonin, Minnesota	Sr.	42	34	47	81	1.93
Todd White, Clarkson	Jr.	38	29	43	72	1.89
Chris Drury, BU	So.	37	35	32	67	1.81
Josh Oort, Canisius	So.	25	15	29	44	1.76
Mike Harder, Colgate	Jr.	30	22	30	52	1.73
Jay Pandolfo, BU	Sr.	40	38	29	67	1.68
Burke Murphy, St. Lawrence	Sr.	35	33	25	58	1.66
Ian Winer, Army	Sr.	29	21	27	48	1.66
P. Geronazzo, Colorado Col.	Sr.	42	36	33	69	1.64
Eric Boguniecki, New Hamp.	Sr.	32	23	29	52	1.63
Bryan Richardson, Rensselaer	Sr.	35	20	36	56	1.60
Vin Mannetta, Iona	Sr.	25	15	25	40	1.60
B. Concannon, UMass-Lowell	Sr.	39	23	39	62	1.59
P. DiFrancesco, St. Lawrence	So.	35	16	39	55	1.57
Phil Scarinci, UConn	So.	25	18	21	39	1.56
Jason Botterill, Michigan	Jr.	36	30	25	55	1.53
Ryan Stewart, Canisius	So.	27	17	24	41	1.52
Mike Crowley, Minnesota	So.	42	17	46	63	1.50
Chris DeProfio, Colgate	Sr.	32	19	29	48	1.50

Leading Goaltenders

Including postseason games; minimum 15 games.

	Cl	Record	Sv%	GAA
Judd Lambert, Colorado Col.	Jr.	16-1-2	.912	2.14
Marty Turco, Michigan	So.	33-7-1	.896	2.20
Kevin Kreutzer, Canisius	Fr.	14-3-1	.912	2.33
Tim Thomas, Vermont	Jr.	26-7-4	.924	2.34
Jason Elliott, Cornell	So.	12-2-1	.923	2.35
Daryl Chamberlain, Army	So.	22-9-1	.904	2.37
J. Grahame, Lake Superior St.	So.	21-4-2	.904	2.42
Jeff Moen, Minnesota	Sr.	15-3-2	.891	2.59
Marc Magliarditi, Western Mich.	Fr.	21-11-2	.909	2.62
Ryan Bach, Colorado Col.	Jr.	17-4-2	.896	2.68

Big Red Won!

by Neil Koepke

For three straight seasons, the University of Michigan's dream to win a national championship ended with overtime heartbreak in the NCAA playoffs. Despite a 93-22-5 record from 1993 to 1995, each year Michigan went home without even getting to the final game. So what would go wrong in 1996 to keep Michigan from winning its first title since 1964?

Nothing.

Once again, the Wolverines found themselves in overtime in the NCAA tournament. Only this time it was the championship game. And this time, Michigan won.

Brendan Morrison, a two-time All-America forward, pounced on a rebound and flipped the puck into the upper right corner of the net at 3:35 of the first overtime to give Michigan a 3-2 victory over Colorado College.

"We needed this for people to understand just how successful this program is," said Michigan coach Red Berenson, who took over at his alma mater in 1984. "Winning a national championship isn't easy."

And a lot of standout Wolverine players have tried and tried but couldn't realize their NCAA title dreams. Players like forwards Denny Felsner, David Roberts, Brian Wiseman, Mike Knuble, defenseman David Harlock and Chris Tamer and goalie Steve Shields had great careers at U-M. But they never won. "This is for all the guys who got to the Final Four with great teams. We did it for them too," Morrison said. "Coach Berenson has taken so much criticism about how he can't win the big game, but he's the reason we've been here four of the last five years."

Morrison, a 5-11, 176 pound junior from British Columbia, was Michigan's leading scorer with 28 goals and 72 points. A talented group of forwards also included Kevin Hilton, Bill Muckalt, Jason Botterill, and John Madden. Steven Halko, Harold Schock, and Blake Sloan anchored an underrated defensive unit. Sophomore Marty Turco excelled between the posts.

The Wolverines, 34-7-2 overall and 26-6-2 in sharing the Central Collegiate Hockey Association title with Lake Superior State, had an impressive post-season run. They defeated Michigan State and LSSU in the CCHA Final Four and then edged Minnesota 4-3 in the NCAA West Regional. In the NCAA Final Four, U-M dominated defending

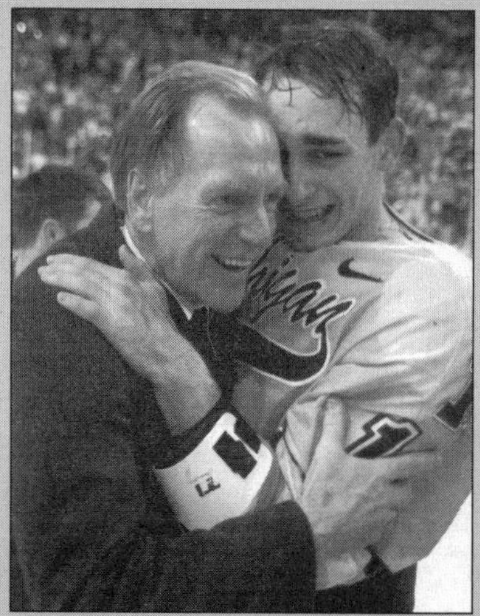

World Wide Photos

Michigan coach **Red Berenson** celebrates the Wolverine's NCAA hockey championship with star right winger **Bill Muckalt**.

NCAA champion Boston University 4-0, and then overcame a 2-1 deficit in the third period and went on to top Colorado College for the title.

"Michigan is to be congratulated. Look at the teams they've beaten in the last three weeks," Colorado College coach Don Lucia said. Lucia's Tigers won their third straight Western Collegiate Hockey Association regular season title and went 33-5-4 overall. "It's tough to take losing. But the way we lost to a great team makes it easier," said Lucia, who has developed the Tigers into a consistent national power.

Colorado College earned a berth in the championship game with a 4-3 double overtime victory over Vermont in the semifinals. A disputed goal at 9:31 of the second overtime won it for the Tigers and ended the Catamounts' (26-7-4) hopes for their first NCAA title in their first trip to the Final Four.

"Any of the four teams here could have won it." Berenson said. "I've always felt that if we did the right things, our day would come. I feel so good for our team, our school and all the kids who have played here. This is the best feeling of all. I've been on a Stanley Cup champion (with Montreal) but there's nothing close to this."

Neil Koepke is the national college hockey writer for the *Lansing* (Mich.) *State Journal.*

NCAA Division I Tournament

Regional Seeds

West	East
1 **Colorado Col.** (31-4-4)	1 **Boston U.** (29-6-3)
2 **Michigan** (31-7-2)	2 **Vermont** (26-6-4)
3 Minnesota (29-9-2)	3 Lake Superior (29-7-2)
4 UMass-Lowell (25-9-4)	4 Western Mich. (27-10-3)
5 Michigan State (28-12-1)	5 Clarkson (24-9-3)
6 Providence (21-14-3)	6 Cornell (21-8-4)

West Regional

At the Munn Ice Arena in East Lansing, Mich., March 23–24. Single elimination, two second round winners advance to Final Four.

First Round

Minnesota 5 ....Providence 1
UMass-Lowell 6 ....Michigan St. 2
(Byes: Colorado College and Michigan)

Second Round

Michigan 4 ....Minnesota 3
Colorado College 5..................................UMass-Lowell 3
(Michigan and Colorado College advance)

East Regional

At the Knickerbocker Arena in Albany, NY, March 22–23. Single elimination, two second round winners advance to Final Four.

First Round

Lake Superior State 6..Cornell 4
Clarkson 6.......................................Western Michigan 1
(Byes: Boston University and Vermont)

Second Round

Vermont 2 ....Lake Superior St. 1
Boston U. 3..Clarkson 2
(Vermont and BU advance)

Hobey Baker Award

For College Player of the Year. Presented since 1981 by the Decathlon Athletic Club of Bloomington, Minn. Voting done by 18-member panel of national media, coaches and pro scouts. Vote totals not released.

	Cl	Pos
Winner: Brian Bonin, Minnesota	Sr.	F
Runner-up: Jay Pandolfo, BU	Sr.	F

Division I All-America

Regional university first team selections as chosen by the American Hockey Coaches Association. Holdover from 1994-95 All-America first teams is in **bold** type.

West Team

Pos		Yr	Hgt	Wgt
G	Ryan Bach, Colorado Col.	Jr.	6-1	195
D	Mike Crowley, Minnesota	So.	5-11	177
D	Keith Aldridge, Lake Superior St.	Sr.	5-10	178
F	Peter Geronazzo, Colorado Col.	Sr.	5-11	185
F	**Brian Bonin**, Minnesota	Sr.	5-10	189
F	**Brendan Morrison**, Michigan	Jr.	5-11	176

East Team

Pos		Yr	Hgt	Wgt
G	Tim Thomas, Vermont	Jr.	5-11	192
D	Jeff Tory, Maine	Jr.	5-11	180
D	Dan McGillis, Northeastern	Sr.	6-2	220
F	**Martin St. Louis**, Vermont	Jr.	5-9	170
F	Eric Perrin, Vermont	Jr.	5-9	166
F	Jay Pandolfo, Boston U.	Sr.	6-1	199

THE FINAL FOUR

At Riverfront Coliseum in Cincinnati, OH, March 28 and March 30. Single elimination; no consolation game.

Semifinals

Colorado College 4..........2OT ....Vermont 3
Michigan 4 ....Boston University 0

Championship

Michigan 3 .... OT ....Colorado College 2

Final records: Boston University (30–7–3); Colorado College (33–5–4); Michigan (34–7–2); Vermont (27–7–4);.

Outstanding Player: Brendan Morrison, Michigan junior center; SEMIFINAL— 1 goal; FINAL— 1 goal, 1 assist.

All-Tournament Team: Morrison, defenseman Steven Halko, and goaltender Marty Turco of Michigan; forward Peter Geronazzo and defenseman Scott Swanson of Colorado College; forward Martin St. Louis of Vermont.

Championship Game

Michigan, 3–2 (OT)

Saturday, March 30, 1996, at Riverfront Coliseum in Cincinnati, OH; Attendance: 13,330; TV Rating: 0.9/3 share (ESPN).

Michigan (CCHA)	1	0	1	1	— **3**
Colorado College (WCHA)	0	2	0	0	— **2**

Scoring

1st Period: UM— Bill Muckalt (Brendan Morrison), 11:33.

2nd Period: CC— Peter Geronazzo (Colin Schmidt, Eric Rud), (pp) 3:52; CC— Schmidt (Geronazzo, Chad Remackel), 5:37.

3rd Period: UM— Mike Legg (Steven Halko, Harold Schock), (pp) 6:54.

Overtime: UM— Morrison (Muckalt, Greg Crozier), 3:35.

Goaltenders

Saves: UM— Marty Turco (23 shots/21 saves); CC—Ryan Bach (19 shots/16 saves).

Other NCAA Tournaments

Division II

Two teams selected from limited national field. Championship decided in two games with mini-game (one 15-minute period), if necessary.

Final Two

March 8–9 at Huntsville, AL.

Championship: GAME ONE— Alabama-Huntsville 7, Bemidji St. (Minn) 1; GAME TWO— Alabama-Huntsville 3, Bemidji St. 0.

Final records: Alabama-Huntsville (24–0–3), Bemidji St. (16–9–4).

Division III

Final Four

March 15–16 at River Falls, WI.

Semifinals— Middlebury 4, WI-Superior 3; RIT 2, WI-River Falls 1. **Third Place**— WI-River Falls 8, WI-Superior 2 **Championship**— Middlebury 3, RIT 2.

Final records: Middlebury (26–2); RIT (24–6–1); WI-River Falls (26–5–2); WI-Superior (20–11–4).

MINOR LEAGUE HOCKEY

American Hockey League

Eastern Conference

Atlantic Division

Team (Affiliate)	W	L	T	Pts
y-Prince Edward (Ottawa)	38	36(3)	6	85
x-Saint John (Calgary)	35	34(4)	11	85
x-St John's (Toronto)	31	35(4)	14	80
x-Fredericton (Montreal)	34	35	11	79
Cape Breton (Edmonton)	33	44(4)	3	73

Northern Division

Team (Affiliate)	W	L	T	Pts
yz-Springfield (Har. & Win.)	42	27(5)	11	100
x-Worcester (St. L & NYI)	36	32(4)	12	88
x-Portland (Washington)	32	38(4)	10	78
Providence (Boston)	30	40(4)	10	74

Western Conference

Central Division

Team (Affiliate)	W	L	T	Pts
yz-Albany (New Jersey)	38	34(2)	8	86
x-Rochester (Buffalo)	36	38(4)	6	83
x-Cornwall (Colorado)	34	39(5)	7	80
x-Syracuse (Vancouver)	31	44(7)	5	74

Southern Division

Team (Affiliate)	W	L	T	Pts
y-Binghamton (NY Rangers)	39	34(3)	7	88
x-Hershey (Philadelphia)	36	33(3)	11	86
x-Baltimore (Anaheim)	33	37(2)	9	77
Carolina (Florida)	28	41(3)	11	70

x-clinched playoff berth, y-clinched division title, z-clinched conference title

Note: Losses in overtime are designated in parenthesis and worth one point in the standings.

Scoring Leaders

	G	A	Pts	PM
Brad Smyth, Car	68	58	126	80
Jim Montgomery, Her	34	71	105	95
Mike Casselman, Car	35	68	103	46
Peter Ferraro, Bing	48	53	101	133
Gilbert Dionne, Car	43	58	101	29

Goaltending Leaders

	GP	GAA	Sv%	Record
Manny Legace, Spring	37	2.27	.917	20-12-4
Mike Dunham, Alb	44	2.52	.908	30-10-2
Norm Maracle, Adir	54	2.75	.905	24-18-6

Calder Cup Finals

	W-L	GF	Leading Scorers
Rochester	4-3	24	Ward (4-8-12)
Portland	3-4	22	Hulst (5-5-10)

Date	Winner	Home Ice
June 1	Rochester, 5-3	at Rochester
June 2	Rochester, 5-1	at Rochester
June 5	Portland, 3-2	at Portland
June 8	Portland, 5-4	at Portland
June 9	Rochester, 5-4 (OT)	at Portland
June 11	Portland, 5-1	at Rochester
June 13	Rochester, 2-1	at Rochester

International Hockey League

Eastern Conference

North Division

Team (Affiliate)	W	L	SoL	Pts
z-Cincinnati (Florida)	51	22	9	111
x-Michigan (Dallas)	40	24	18	98
x-Indianapolis (Chicago)	43	33	6	92
x-Fort Wayne (Independent)	39	35	8	86

Central Division

Team (Affiliate)	W	L	SoL	Pts
y-Orlando (Independent)	52	24	6	110
x-Detroit (Independent)	48	28	6	102
x-Cleveland (Pittsburgh)	43	27	12	98
x-Atlanta (Tampa Bay)	32	41	9	73
Houston (Independent)	29	45	8	66

Western Conference

Midwest Division

Team (Affiliate)	W	L	SoL	Pts
y-Milwaukee (Independent)	40	32	10	90
x-Chicago (Independent)	40	34	8	88
x-Kansas City (San Jose)	39	38	5	83
x-Peoria (St. Louis)	39	38	5	83
Minnesota (Independent)	30	45	7	67

Southwest Division

Team (Affiliate)	W	L	SoL	Pts
z-Las Vegas (Independent)	57	17	8	122
x-Utah (NY Islanders)	49	29	4	102
x-San Francisco (Independent)	40	32	10	90
x-Phoenix (Los Angeles)	36	35	11	83
Los Angeles (Independent)	32	36	14	78

x-clinched playoff berth, y-clinched division title, z-clinched conference title

Note: Two points are awarded for a victory; one for a shootout loss (SoL).

Scoring Leaders

	G	A	Pts	PM
Rob Brown, Chi	52	91	143	100
Craig Fisher, Orl	74	56	130	81
Steve Maltais, Chi	56	66	122	161
Patrice Lefebvre, LV	36	78	114	85
Todd Simon, Det	45	64	109	68
Mark Beaufait, Orl	30	79	109	87

Goaltending Leaders

	GP	GAA	Sv%	Record
Frederic Chabot, Cin	38	2.46	.921	23-9-4
Tommy Salo, Utah	45	2.65	.902	28-15-2
Bob Essensa, FW	45	2.89	.912	24-14-5

Turner Cup Finals

	W-L	GF	Leading Scorers
Utah	4-0	14	Vasilijev (5-1-6)
Orlando	0-4	9	Barr (3-1-4) & Beaufait (2-2-4)

Date	Winner	Home Ice
June 2	Grizzlies, 3-2 (OT)	at Orlando
June 4	Grizzlies, 4-3 (OT)	at Orlando
June 6	Grizzlies, 4-2	at Utah
June 8	Grizzlies, 3-2 (OT)	at Utah

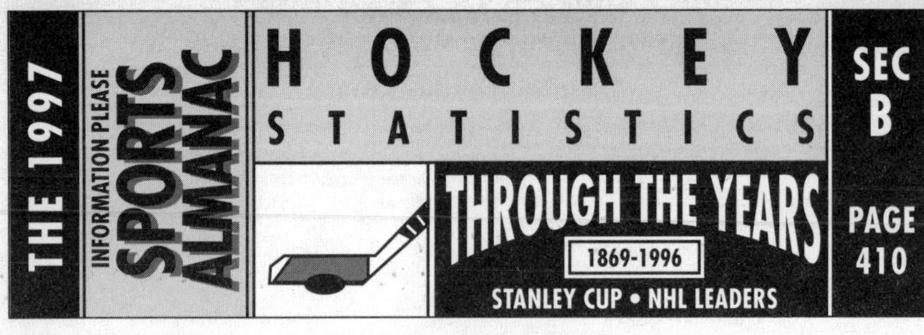

The Stanley Cup

The Stanley Cup was originally donated to the Canadian Amateur Hockey Association by Sir Frederick Arthur Stanley, Lord Stanley of Preston and 16th Earl of Derby, who had become interested in the sport while Governor General of Canada from 1888 to 1893. Stanley wanted the trophy to be a challenge cup, contested for each year by the best amateur hockey teams in Canada.

In 1893, the Cup was presented without a challenge to the AHA champion Montreal Amateur Athletic Association team. Every year since, however, there has been a playoff. In 1914, Cup trustees limited the field challenging for the trophy to the champion of the eastern professional National Hockey Association (NHA, organized in 1910) and the western professional Pacific Coast Hockey Association (PCHA, organized in 1912).

The NHA disbanded in 1917 and the National Hockey League (NHL) was formed. From 1918 to 1926, the NHL and PCHA champions played for the Cup with the Western Canada Hockey League (WCHL) champion joining in a three-way challenge in 1923 and '24. The PCHA disbanded in 1924, while the WCHL became the Western Hockey League (WHL) for the 1925-26 season and folded the following year. The NHL playoffs have decided the winner of the Stanley Cup ever since.

Champions, 1893-1917

Multiple winners: Montreal Victorias and Montreal Wanderers (4); Montreal Amateur Athletic Association and Ottawa Silver Seven (3); Montreal Shamrocks, Ottawa Senators, Quebec Bulldogs and Winnipeg Victorias (2).

Year	
1893	Montreal AAA
1894	Montreal AAA
1895	Montreal Victorias
1896	(Feb.) Winnipeg Victorias
	(Dec.) Montreal Victorias
1897	Montreal Victorias
1898	Montreal Victorias
1899	Montreal Shamrocks
1900	Montreal Shamrocks
1901	Winnipeg Victorias
1902	Montreal AAA
1903	Ottawa Silver Seven
1904	Ottawa Silver Seven
1905	Ottawa Silver Seven
1906	Montreal Wanderers
1907	(Jan.) Kenora Thistles
	(Mar.) Montreal Wanderers
1908	Montreal Wanderers
1909	Ottawa Senators
1910	Montreal Wanderers
1911	Ottawa Senators
1912	Quebec Bulldogs
1913	Quebec Bulldogs
1914	Toronto Blueshirts (NHA)
1915	Vancouver Millionaires (PCHA)
1916	Montreal Canadiens (NHA)
1917	Seattle Metropolitans (PCHA)

Champions Since 1918

Multiple winners: Montreal Canadiens (23); Toronto Arenas-St.Pats-Maple Leafs (13); Detroit Red Wings (7); Boston Bruins and Edmonton Oilers (5); NY Islanders, NY Rangers and Ottawa Senators (4); Chicago Blackhawks (3); Philadelphia Flyers, Pittsburgh Penguins and Montreal Maroons (2).

Year	Winner	Head Coach	Series	Loser	Head Coach
1918	Toronto Arenas	Dick Carroll	3-2 (WLWLW)	Vancouver (PCHA)	Frank Patrick
1919	No Decision: (see below).				
1920	Ottawa	Pete Green	3-2 (WWLLW)	Seattle (PCHA)	Pete Muldoon
1921	Ottawa	Pete Green	3-2 (LWWLW)	Vancouver (PCHA)	Frank Patrick
1922	Toronto St. Pats	Eddie Powers	3-2 (LWLWW)	Vancouver (PCHA)	Frank Patrick
1923	Ottawa	Pete Green	3-1 (WLWW)	Vancouver (PCHA)	Frank Patrick
			2-0	Edmonton (WCHL)	K.C. McKenzie
1924	Montreal	Leo Dandurand	2-0	Vancouver (PCHA)	Frank Patrick
			2-0	Calgary (WCHL)	Eddie Oatman
1925	Victoria (WCHL)	Lester Patrick	3-1 (WWLW)	Montreal	Leo Dandurand
1926	Montreal Maroons	Eddie Gerard	3-1 (WWLW)	Victoria (WHL)	Lester Patrick
1927	Ottawa	Dave Gill	2-0 (TWTW)	Boston	Art Ross
1928	NY Rangers	Lester Patrick	3-2 (LWLWW)	Montreal Maroons	Eddie Gerard
1929	Boston	Cy Denneny	2-0	NY Rangers	Lester Patrick
1930	Montreal	Cecil Hart	2-0	Boston	Art Ross
1931	Montreal	Cecil Hart	3-2 (WLLWW)	Chicago	Art Duncan
1932	Toronto	Dick Irvin	3-0	NY Rangers	Lester Patrick
1933	NY Rangers	Lester Patrick	3-1 (WWLW)	Toronto	Dick Irvin
1934	Chicago	Tommy Gorman	3-1 (WWLW)	Detroit	Jack Adams
1935	Montreal Maroons	Tommy Gorman	3-0	Toronto	Dick Irvin
1936	Detroit	Jack Adams	3-1 (WWLW)	Toronto	Dick Irvin

Note: The 1919 Finals were cancelled after five games due to an influenza epidemic with Montreal and Seattle (PCHA) tied at 2-2-1.

Year	Winner	Head Coach	Series	Loser	Head Coach
1937	Detroit	Jack Adams	3-2 (LWLWW)	NY Rangers	Lester Patrick
1938	Chicago	Bill Stewart	3-1 (WLWW)	Toronto	Dick Irvin
1939	Boston	Art Ross	4-1 (WLWWW)	Toronto	Dick Irvin
1940	NY Rangers	Frank Boucher	4-2 (WWLLWW)	Toronto	Dick Irvin
1941	Boston	Cooney Weiland	4-0	Detroit	Jack Adams
1942	Toronto	Hap Day	4-3 (LLLWWWW)	Detroit	Jack Adams
1943	Detroit	Ebbie Goodfellow	4-0	Boston	Art Ross
1944	Montreal	Dick Irvin	4-0	Chicago	Paul Thompson
1945	Toronto	Hap Day	4-3 (WWWLLLW)	Detroit	Jack Adams
1946	Montreal	Dick Irvin	4-1 (WWWLW)	Boston	Dit Clapper
1947	Toronto	Hap Day	4-2 (LWWWLW)	Montreal	Dick Irvin
1948	Toronto	Hap Day	4-0	Detroit	Tommy Ivan
1949	Toronto	Hap Day	4-0	Detroit	Tommy Ivan
1950	Detroit	Tommy Ivan	4-3 (WLWLLWW)	NY Rangers	Lynn Patrick
1951	Toronto	Joe Primeau	4-1 (WLWWW)	Montreal	Dick Irvin
1952	Detroit	Tommy Ivan	4-0	Montreal	Dick Irvin
1953	Montreal	Dick Irvin	4-1 (WLWWW)	Boston	Lynn Patrick
1954	Detroit	Tommy Ivan	4-3 (WLWWLLW)	Montreal	Dick Irvin
1955	Detroit	Jimmy Skinner	4-3 (WWLLWLW)	Montreal	Dick Irvin
1956	Montreal	Toe Blake	4-1 (WWLWW)	Detroit	Jimmy Skinner
1957	Montreal	Toe Blake	4-1 (WWWLW)	Boston	Milt Schmidt
1958	Montreal	Toe Blake	4-2 (WLWLWW)	Boston	Milt Schmidt
1959	Montreal	Toe Blake	4-1 (WWLWW)	Toronto	Punch Imlach
1960	Montreal	Toe Blake	4-0	Toronto	Punch Imlach
1961	Chicago	Rudy Pilous	4-2 (WLWLWW)	Detroit	Sid Abel
1962	Toronto	Punch Imlach	4-2 (WWLLWW)	Chicago	Rudy Pilous
1963	Toronto	Punch Imlach	4-1 (WWLWW)	Detroit	Sid Abel
1964	Toronto	Punch Imlach	4-3 (WLLWLWW)	Detroit	Sid Abel
1965	Montreal	Toe Blake	4-3 (WWLLWLW)	Chicago	Billy Reay
1966	Montreal	Toe Blake	4-2 (LLWWWW)	Detroit	Sid Abel
1967	Toronto	Punch Imlach	4-2 (LWWLWW)	Montreal	Toe Blake
1968	Montreal	Toe Blake	4-0	St. Louis	Scotty Bowman
1969	Montreal	Claude Ruel	4-0	St. Louis	Scotty Bowman
1970	Boston	Harry Sinden	4-0	St. Louis	Scotty Bowman
1971	Montreal	Al MacNeil	4-3 (LLWWLWW)	Chicago	Billy Reay
1972	Boston	Tom Johnson	4-2 (WWLWLW)	NY Rangers	Emile Francis
1973	Montreal	Scotty Bowman	4-2 (WWLWLW)	Chicago	Billy Reay
1974	Philadelphia	Fred Shero	4-2 (LWWWLW)	Boston	Bep Guidolin
1975	Philadelphia	Fred Shero	4-2 (WWLLWW)	Buffalo	Floyd Smith
1976	Montreal	Scotty Bowman	4-0	Philadelphia	Fred Shero
1977	Montreal	Scotty Bowman	4-0	Boston	Don Cherry
1978	Montreal	Scotty Bowman	4-2 (WWLLWW)	Boston	Don Cherry
1979	Montreal	Scotty Bowman	4-1 (LWWWW)	NY Rangers	Fred Shero
1980	NY Islanders	Al Arbour	4-2 (WLWWLW)	Philadelphia	Pat Quinn
1981	NY Islanders	Al Arbour	4-1 (WWWLW)	Minnesota	Glen Sonmor
1982	NY Islanders	Al Arbour	4-0	Vancouver	Roger Neilson
1983	NY Islanders	Al Arbour	4-0	Edmonton	Glen Sather
1984	Edmonton	Glen Sather	4-1 (WLWWW)	NY Islanders	Al Arbour
1985	Edmonton	Glen Sather	4-1 (LWWWW)	Philadelphia	Mike Keenan
1986	Montreal	Jean Perron	4-1 (LWWWW)	Calgary	Bob Johnson
1987	Edmonton	Glen Sather	4-3 (WWLWLLW)	Philadelphia	Mike Keenan
1988	Edmonton	Glen Sather	4-0	Boston	Terry O'Reilly
1989	Calgary	Terry Crisp	4-2 (WLLWWW)	Montreal	Pat Burns
1990	Edmonton	John Muckler	4-1 (WWLWW)	Boston	Mike Milbury
1991	Pittsburgh	Bob Johnson	4-2 (LWLWWW)	Minnesota	Bob Gainey
1992	Pittsburgh	Scotty Bowman	4-0	Chicago	Mike Keenan
1993	Montreal	Jacques Demers	4-1 (LWWWW)	Los Angeles	Barry Melrose
1994	NY Rangers	Mike Keenan	4-3 (LWWWLLW)	Vancouver	Pat Quinn
1995	New Jersey	Jacques Lemaire	4-0	Detroit	Scotty Bowman
1996	Colorado	Marc Crawford	4-0	Florida	Doug MacLean

M.J. O'Brien Trophy

Donated by Canadian mining magnate M.J. O'Brien, whose son Ambrose founded the National Hockey Association in 1910. Originally presented to the NHA champion until the league's demise in 1917, the trophy then passed to the NHL champion through 1927. It was awarded to the NHL's Canadian Division winner from 1927-38 and the Stanley Cup runner-up from 1939-50 before being retired in 1950.

NHA winners included the Montreal Wanderers (1910), original Ottawa Senators (1911 and '15), Quebec Bulldogs (1912 and '13), Toronto Blueshirts (1914) and Montreal Canadiens (1916 and '17).

Conn Smythe Trophy

The Most Valuable Player of the Stanley Cup Playoffs, as selected by the Pro Hockey Writers Assn. Presented since 1965 by Maple Leaf Gardens Limited in the name of the former Toronto coach, GM and owner, Conn Smythe. Winners who did not play for the Cup champion are in **bold** type.

Multiple winners: Wayne Gretzky, Mario Lemieux, Bobby Orr, Bernie Parent and Patrick Roy (2).

Year	
1965	Jean Beliveau, Mon., C
1966	**Roger Crozier**, Det., G
1967	Dave Keon, Tor., C
1968	**Glenn Hall**, St.L., G
1969	Serge Savard, Mon., D
1970	Bobby Orr, Bos., D
1971	Ken Dryden, Mon., G
1972	Bobby Orr, Bos., D
1973	Yvan Cournoyer, Mon., RW
1974	Bernie Parent, Phi., G
1975	Bernie Parent, Phi., G

Year	
1976	**Reggie Leach**, Phi., RW
1977	Guy Lafleur, Mon., RW
1978	Larry Robinson, Mon., D
1979	Bob Gainey, Mon., LW
1980	Bryan Trottier, NYI, C
1981	Butch Goring, NYI, C
1982	Mike Bossy, NYI, RW
1983	Billy Smith, NYI, G
1984	Mark Messier, Edm., LW
1985	Wayne Gretzky, Edm., C
1986	Patrick Roy, Mon., G

Year	
1987	**Ron Hextall**, Phi., G
1988	Wayne Gretzky, Edm., C
1989	Al MacInnis, Calg., D
1990	Bill Ranford, Edm., G
1991	Mario Lemieux, Pit., C
1992	Mario Lemieux, Pit., C
1993	Patrick Roy, Mon., G
1994	Brian Leetch, NYR, D
1995	Claude Lemieux, NJ, RW
1996	Joe Sakic, Col., C

Note: Ken Dryden (1971) and Patrick Roy (1986) are the only players to win as rookies.

All-Time Stanley Cup Playoff Leaders

CAREER

Stanley Cup Playoff leaders through 1996. Years listed indicate number of playoff appearances. Players active in 1996 in **bold** type; (DNP) indicates active player did not participate in 1996 playoffs.

Scoring

Points

	Yrs	Gm	G	A	Pts
1 **Wayne Gretzky**	15	193	112	250	362
2 **Mark Messier**	16	221	106	177	283
3 **Jari Kurri**	13	185	105	125	230
4 **Glenn Anderson**	15	225	93	121	214
5 **Paul Coffey**	14	172	58	128	186
6 Bryan Trottier	17	221	71	113	184
7 Jean Beliveau	17	162	79	97	176
8 **Denis Savard**	15	163	66	107	173
9 Denis Potvin	14	185	56	108	164
10 Mike Bossy	10	129	85	75	160
Gordie Howe	20	157	68	92	160
Bobby Smith	13	184	64	96	160
Doug Gilmour	12	136	49	111	160
14 Stan Mikita	18	155	59	91	150
15 **Mario Lemieux**	6	84	67	82	149
16 Brian Propp	13	160	64	84	148
17 **Ray Bourque**	17	162	34	112	146
18 Larry Robinson	20	227	28	116	144
19 Jacques Lemaire	11	145	61	78	139
20 Phil Esposito	15	130	61	76	137
21 Guy Lafleur	14	128	58	76	134
22 Steve Larmer	13	140	56	75	131
23 Bobby Hull	14	119	62	67	129
Henri Richard	18	180	49	80	129
25 Yvan Cournoyer	12	147	64	63	127

Goals

	Yrs	Gm	G
1 **Wayne Gretzky**	15	193	112
2 **Mark Messier**	16	221	106
3 **Jari Kurri**	13	185	105
4 **Glenn Anderson**	15	225	93
5 Mike Bossy	10	129	85
6 Maurice Richard	15	133	82
7 Jean Beliveau	17	162	79
8 **Dino Ciccarelli**	14	141	73
9 Bryan Trottier	17	221	71
10 Gordie Howe	20	157	68
11 **Mario Lemieux**	6	84	67
12 **Denis Savard**	15	163	66
13 Yvan Cournoyer	12	147	64
Brian Propp	13	160	64
Bobby Smith	13	184	64
Brett Hull	11	92	64

Assists

	Yrs	Gm	A
1 **Wayne Gretzky**	15	193	250
2 **Mark Messier**	16	221	177
3 **Paul Coffey**	14	172	128
4 **Jari Kurri**	13	185	125
5 **Glenn Anderson**	15	225	121
6 Larry Robinson	20	227	116
7 Bryan Trottier	17	221	113
8 **Ray Bourque**	17	162	112
9 **Doug Gilmour**	12	136	111
10 Denis Potvin	14	185	108
11 **Denis Savard**	15	163	107
12 Jean Beliveau	17	162	97
13 Bobby Smith	13	184	96
14 Gordie Howe	20	157	92
15 Stan Mikita	18	155	91

Goaltending

Wins

	Gm	W-L	Pct	GAA
1 Billy Smith	132	88-36	.710	2.73
2 **Patrick Roy**	136	86-48	.642	2.39
3 Ken Dryden	112	80-32	.714	2.40
4 **Grant Fuhr**	121	78-36	.684	3.04
5 Jacques Plante	112	71-37	.657	2.17
6 **Andy Moog** (DNP)	116	61-48	.560	3.05
7 Turk Broda	102	58-42	.580	1.98
8 **Mike Vernon**	103	57-41	.582	2.88
9 Terry Sawchuk	106	54-48	.529	2.54
10 **Tom Barrasso**	94	51-39	.567	3.11
11 Glenn Hall	115	49-65	.430	2.79
12 Gerry Cheevers	88	47-35	.573	2.69
13 Tony Esposito	99	45-53	.459	3.07
14 **Ron Hextall**	84	43-40	.518	3.04
15 Gump Worsley	70	41-25	.621	2.82

Shutouts

	Gm	GAA	No
1 Clint Benedict	48	1.80	15
Jacques Plante	112	2.17	15
3 Turk Broda	102	1.98	13
4 Terry Sawchuk	106	2.54	12
5 Ken Dryden	112	2.40	10

Goaltending

Goals Against Average

Minimum of 50 games played.

		Gm	Min	GA	GAA
1	George Hainsworth	52	3486	112	1.93
2	Turk Broda	101	6348	211	1.98
3	Jacques Plante	112	6651	241	2.17
4	**Patrick Roy**	136	8418	336	2.39
5	Ken Dryden	112	6846	274	2.40
6	Bernie Parent	71	4302	174	2.43
7	**Ed Belfour**	68	3942	164	2.50
8	Harry Lumley	76	4759	199	2.51
9	Johnny Bower	74	4350	184	2.54
10	Terry Sawchuk	106	6311	267	2.54

Note: Clint Benedict had an average of 1.80 but played in only 48 games.

Games Played

		Yrs	Gm
1	**Patrick Roy**, Montreal	10	136
2	Billy Smith, NY Islanders	13	132
3	**Grant Fuhr**, Edm-Buf-St.L	11	121
4	**Andy Moog**, Edm-Bos-Dal (DNP)	14	116
5	Glenn Hall, Det-Chi-St.L	17	115

Appearances in Cup Final

Standings of all teams that have reached the Stanley Cup championship round, since 1918.

App		Cups	Last Won
32	Montreal Canadiens	23*	1993
21	Toronto Maple Leafs	13†	1967
19	Detroit Red Wings	7	1955
17	Boston Bruins	5	1972
10	New York Rangers	4	1994
10	Chicago Blackhawks	3	1961
6	Edmonton Oilers	5	1990
6	Philadelphia Flyers	2	1975
5	New York Islanders	4	1983
5	Vancouver Millionaires (PCHA)	0	—
4	(original) Ottawa Senators	4	1927
3	Montreal Maroons	2	1935
3	St. Louis Blues	0	—
2	Pittsburgh Penguins	2	1992
2	Calgary Flames	1	1989
2	Victoria Cougars (WCHL-WHL)	1	1925
2	Minnesota North Stars	0	—
2	Seattle Metropolitans (PCHA)	0	—
2	Vancouver Canucks	0	—
1	Colorado Avalanche	1	1996
1	New Jersey Devils	1	1995
1	Buffalo Sabres	0	—
1	Calgary Tigers (WCHL)	0	—
1	Edmonton Eskimos (WCHL)	0	—
1	Florida Panthers	0	—
1	Los Angeles Kings	0	—

*Les Canadiens also won the Cup in 1916 for a total of 24. Also, their final with Seattle in 1919 was cancelled due to an influenza epidemic that claimed the life of the Habs' Joe Hall.

†Toronto has won the Cup under three nicknames—Arenas (1918), St. Pats (1922) and Maple Leafs (1932,42,45,47-49,51,62-64,67).

Teams now defunct (6): Calgary Tigers, Edmonton Eskimos, Montreal Maroons, (original) Ottawa Senators, Seattle, Vancouver Millionaires and Victoria. Edmonton (1923) and Calgary (1924) represented the WCHL and later the WHL, while Vancouver (1918,1921-24) and Seattle (1919-20) played out of the PCHA.

Miscellaneous

Championships

		Yrs	Cups
1	Henri Richard, Montreal	18	11
2	Yvan Cournoyer, Montreal	15	10
	Jean Beliveau, Montreal	17	10
4	Claude Provost, Montreal	14	9
5	Jacques Lemaire, Montreal	11	8
	Maurice Richard, Montreal	15	8
	Red Kelly, Detroit-Toronto	19	8

Years in Playoffs

		Yrs	Gm
1	Gordie Howe, Detroit-Hartford	20	157
	Larry Robinson, Montreal-Los Angeles	20	227
3	Red Kelly, Detroit-Toronto	19	164
4	Henri Richard, Montreal	18	180
	Stan Mikita, Chicago	18	155

Games Played

		Yrs	Gm
1	Larry Robinson, Montreal-Los Angeles	20	227
2	**Glenn Anderson**, Edm-Tor-NYR-St.L	15	225
3	Bryan Trottier, NY Isles-Pittsburgh	17	221
4	**Mark Messier**, Edm-NY Rangers	16	221
5	**Kevin Lowe**, Edm-NY Rangers	16	212

Penalty Minutes

		Yrs	Gm	Min
1	**Dale Hunter**, Que-Wash	16	146	661
2	Chris Nilan, Mon-NYR-Bos-Mon	12	111	541
3	Willi Plett, Atl-Calg-Min-Bos	10	83	466
4	Dave Williams, Tor-Van-LA	12	83	455
5	**Glenn Anderson**, Edm-Tor-NYR-St.L	15	225	442

SINGLE SEASON

Scoring

Points

		Year	Gm	G	A	Pts
1	Wayne Gretzky, Edm	1985	18	17	30	**47**
2	Mario Lemieux, Pit	1991	23	16	28	**44**
3	Wayne Gretzky, Edm	1988	19	12	31	**43**
4	Wayne Gretzky, LA	1993	24	15	25	**40**
5	Wayne Gretzky, Edm	1983	16	12	26	**38**
6	Paul Coffey, Edm	1985	18	12	25	**37**
7	Mike Bossy, NYI	1981	18	17	18	**35**
	Wayne Gretzky, Edm	1984	19	13	22	**35**
	Doug Gilmour, Tor	1993	21	10	25	**35**
10	Mario Lemieux, Pit	1992	15	16	18	**34**
	Mark Messier, Edm	1988	19	11	23	**34**
	Mark Recchi, Pit	1991	24	10	24	**34**
	Wayne Gretzky, Edm	1987	21	5	29	**34**
	Brian Leetch, NYR	1994	23	11	23	**34**
	Joe Sakic, Col	1996	22	18	16	**34**

Goals

		Year	Gm	No
1	Reggie Leach, Philadelphia	1976	16	**19**
	Jari Kurri, Edmonton	1985	18	**19**
3	Joe Sakic, Colorado	1996	22	**18**
4	Newsy Lalonde, Montreal	1919	10	**17**
	Mike Bossy, NY Islanders	1981	18	**17**
	Wayne Gretzky, Edmonton	1985	18	**17**
	Steve Payne, Minnesota	1981	19	**17**
	Mike Bossy, NY Islanders	1982	19	**17**
	Mike Bossy, NY Islanders	1983	19	**17**
	Kevin Stevens, Pittsburgh	1991	24	**17**

All-Time Stanley Cup Playoff Leaders (Cont.)

Assists

		Year	Gm	No
1	Wayne Gretzky, Edmonton	1988	19	31
2	Wayne Gretzky, Edmonton	1985	18	30
3	Wayne Gretzky, Edmonton	1987	21	29
4	Mario Lemieux, Pittsburgh	1991	23	28
5	Wayne Gretzky, Edmonton	1983	16	26
6	Paul Coffey, Edmonton	1985	18	25
	Doug Gilmour, Toronto	1993	21	25
	Wayne Gretzky, Los Angeles	1993	24	25
9	Al MacInnis, Calgary	1989	22	24
	Mark Recchi, Pittsburgh	1991	24	24

Goaltending

Wins

		Year	Gm	Min	W-L
1	Grant Fuhr, Edm	1988	19	1136	16-2
	Patrick Roy, Mon	1993	20	1293	16-4
	Martin Brodeur, NJ	1995	20	1222	16-4
	Mike Vernon, Calg	1989	22	1381	16-5
	Tom Barrasso, Pit	1992	21	1233	16-5
	Bill Ranford, Edm	1990	22	1401	16-6
	Patrick Roy, Col	1996	22	1454	16-6
	Mike Richter, NYR	1994	23	1417	16-7
9	Six tied with 15 wins each.				

Shutouts

		Year	Gm	No
1	Clint Benedict, Mon. Maroons	1926	8	4
	Terry Sawchuk, Detroit	1952	8	4
	Clint Benedict, Mon. Maroons	1928	9	4
	Dave Kerr, NY Rangers	1937	9	4
	Frank McCool, Toronto	1945	13	4
	Ken Dryden, Montreal	1977	14	4
	Bernie Parent, Philadelphia	1975	17	4
	Mike Richter, NY Rangers	1994	23	4
	Kirk McLean, Vancouver	1994	24	4

Goals Against Average

Minimum of eight games played.

		Year	Gm	Min	GA	GAA
1	Terry Sawchuk, Det	1952	8	480	5	0.63
2	Clint Benedict, Mon-M	1928	9	555	8	0.89
3	Turk Broda, Tor	1951	9	509	9	1.06
4	Dave Kerr, NYR	1937	9	553	10	1.11
5	Jacques Plante, Mon	1960	8	489	11	1.35
6	Rogie Vachon, Mon	1969	8	507	12	1.42
7	Jacques Plante, St.L	1969	10	589	14	1.43
8	Frankie Brimsek, Bos	1939	12	863	18	1.50
9	Chuck Gardiner, Chi	1934	8	602	12	1.50
10	Ken Dryden, Mon	1977	14	849	22	1.55

Note: Average determined by games played through 1942-43 season and by minutes played since then.

SINGLE SERIES

Scoring

Points

	Year	Rd	G-A—Pts
Rick Middleton, Bos vs Buf	1983	DF	5-14—19
Wayne Gretzky, Edm vs Chi	1985	CF	4-14—18
Mario Lemieux, Pit vs Wash	1992	DSF	7-10—17
Barry Pedersen, Bos vs Buf	1983	DF	7-9—16
Doug Gilmour, Tor vs SJ	1994	CSF	3-13—16
Jari Kurri, Edm vs Chi	1985	CF	12-3—15
Tim Kerr, Phi vs Pit	1989	DF	10-5—15
Mario Lemieux, Pit vs Bos	1991	CF	6-9—15
Wayne Gretzky, Edm vs LA	1987	DSF	2-13—15

Goals

	Year	Rd	No
Jari Kurri, Edm vs Chi	1985	CF	12
Newsy Lalonde, Mon vs Ott	1919	SF*	11
Tim Kerr, Phi vs Pit	1989	DF	10

Five tied with nine each.

*NHL final prior to Stanley Cup series with Seattle.

Assists

	Year	Rd	No
Rick Middleton, Bos vs Buf	1983	DF	14
Wayne Gretzky, Edm vs Chi	1985	CF	14
Wayne Gretzky, Edm vs LA	1987	DSF	13
Doug Gilmour, Tor vs SJ	1994	CSF	13

Four tied with 11 each.

SINGLE GAME

Scoring

Points

	Date	G	A	Pts
Patrik Sundstrom, NJ vs Wash	4/22/88	3	5	8
Mario Lemieux, Pit vs Phi	4/25/89	5	3	8
Wayne Gretzky, Edm at Calg	4/17/83	4	3	7
Wayne Gretzky, Edm at Win	4/25/85	3	4	7
Wayne Gretzky, Edm vs LA	4/9/87	1	6	7

Goals

	Date	No
Newsy Lalonde, Mon vs Ott	3/1/19	5
Maurice Richard, Mon vs Tor	3/23/44	5
Darryl Sittler, Tor vs Phi	4/22/76	5
Reggie Leach, Phi vs Bos	5/6/76	5
Mario Lemieux, Pit vs Phi	4/25/89	5

Assists

	Date	No
Mikko Leinonen, NYR vs Phi	4/8/82	6
Wayne Gretzky, Edm vs LA	4/9/87	6

Ten players tied with five each.

Ten Longest Playoff Overtime Games

The 10 longest overtime games in Stanley Cup history. Note the following Series initials: SF (semifinals), CQF (conference quarterfinal), DSF (division semifinal). QF (quarterfinal) and Final (Cup Final). Series winners are in **bold** type; (*) indicates deciding game of series.

		OTs	Elapsed Time	Goal Scorer	Date	Series	Location
1	**Detroit** 1, Montreal Maroons 0	6	116:30	Mud Bruneteau	3/24/36	SF, Gm 1	Montreal
2	**Toronto** 1, Boston 0	6	104:46	Ken Doraty	4/3/33	SF, Gm 5	Toronto
3	**Pittsburgh** 3 Washington 2	4	79:15	Petr Nedved	4/24/96	CQF, Gm 4	Washington
4	Toronto 3, **Detroit** 2	4	70:18	Jack McLean	3/23/43	SF, Gm 2	Detroit
5	**Montreal** 2, NY Rangers 1	4	68:52	Gus Rivers	3/28/30	SF, Gm 1	Montreal
6	**NY Islanders** 3, Washington 2	4	68:47	Pat LaFontaine	4/18/87	DSF, Gm 7*	Washington
7	Buffalo 1, **New Jersey** 0	4	65:43	Dave Hannan	4/27/94	QF, Gm 6	Buffalo
8	**Montreal** 3, Detroit 2	4	61:09	Maurice Richard	3/27/51	SF, Gm 1	Detroit
9	**NY Americans** 3, NY Rangers 2	4	60:40	Lorne Carr	3/27/38	QF, Gm 3*	New York
10	**NY Rangers** 4, Montreal 3	3	59:32	Fred Cook	3/26/32	SF, Gm 2	Montreal

NHL All-Star Game

Three benefit NHL All-Star games were staged in the 1930s for forward Ace Bailey and the families of Howie Morenz and Babe Siebert. Bailey, of Toronto, suffered a fractured skull on a career-ending check by Boston's Eddie Shore. Morenz, the Montreal Canadiens' legend, died of a heart attack at age 35 after a severely broken leg ended his career. And Siebert, who played with both Montreal teams, drowned at age 35.

The All-Star Game was revived at the start of the 1947-48 season as an annual exhibition match between the defending Stanley Cup champion and All-Stars from the league's other five teams. The game was moved to midseason in 1966-67 and became an East vs. West contest in 1968-69. The Eastern (East, 1968-74; Wales, 1975-93) Conference leads the series, 17-7-1.

Benefit Games

Date	Occasion		Host	Coaches
2/14/34	Ace Bailey Benefit	Toronto 7, All-Stars 3	Toronto	Dick Irvin, Lester Patrick
11/3/37	Howie Morenz Memorial	All-Stars 6, Montreals* 5	Montreal	Jack Adams, Cecil Hart
10/29/39	Babe Siebert Memorial	All-Stars 5, Canadiens 2	Montreal	Art Ross, Pit Lepine

*Combined squad of Montreal Canadiens and Montreal Maroons.

All-Star Games

Multiple MVP winners: Mario Lemieux (3); Wayne Gretzky, Bobby Hull and Frank Mahovlich (2).

Year		Host	Coaches	Most Valuable Player
1947	All-Stars 4, Toronto 3	Toronto	Dick Irvin, Hap Day	No award
1948	All-Stars 3, Toronto 1	Chicago	Tommy Ivan, Hap Day	No award
1949	All-Stars 3, Toronto 1	Toronto	Tommy Ivan, Hap Day	No award
1950	Detroit 7, All-Stars 1	Detroit	Tommy Ivan, Lynn Patrick	No award
1951	1st Team 2, 2nd Team 2	Toronto	Joe Primeau, Hap Day	No award
1952	1st Team 1, 2nd Team 1	Detroit	Tommy Ivan, Dick Irvin	No award
1953	All-Stars 3, Montreal 1	Montreal	Lynn Patrick, Dick Irvin	No award
1954	All-Stars 2, Detroit 2	Detroit	King Clancy, Jim Skinner	No award
1955	Detroit 3, All-Stars 1	Detroit	Jim Skinner, Dick Irvin	No award
1956	All-Stars 1, Montreal 1	Montreal	Jim Skinner, Toe Blake	No award
1957	All-Stars 5, Montreal 3	Montreal	Milt Schmidt, Toe Blake	No award
1958	Montreal 6, All-Stars 3	Montreal	Toe Blake, Milt Schmidt	No award
1959	Montreal 6, All-Stars 1	Montreal	Toe Blake, Punch Imlach	No award
1960	All-Stars 2, Montreal 1	Montreal	Punch Imlach, Toe Blake	No award
1961	All-Stars 3, Chicago 1	Chicago	Sid Abel, Rudy Pilous	No award
1962	Toronto 4, All-Stars 1	Toronto	Punch Imlach, Rudy Pilous	Eddie Shack, Tor., RW
1963	All-Stars 3, Toronto 3	Toronto	Sid Abel, Punch Imlach	Frank Mahovlich, Tor., LW
1964	All-Stars 3, Toronto 2	Toronto	Sid Abel, Punch Imlach	Jean Beliveau, Mon., C
1965	All-Stars 5, Montreal 2	Montreal	Billy Reay, Toe Blake	Gordie Howe, Det., RW
1966	No game (see below)			
1967	Montreal 3, All-Stars 0	Montreal	Toe Blake, Sid Abel	Henri Richard, Mon., C
1968	Toronto 4, All-Stars 3	Toronto	Punch Imlach, Toe Blake	Bruce Gamble, Tor., G
1969	West 3, East 3	Montreal	Scotty Bowman, Toe Blake	Frank Mahovlich, Det., LW
1970	East 4, West 1	St. Louis	Claude Ruel, Scotty Bowman	Bobby Hull, Chi., LW
1971	West 2, East 1	Boston	Scotty Bowman, Harry Sinden	Bobby Hull, Chi., LW
1972	East 3, West 2	Minnesota	Al MacNeil, Billy Reay	Bobby Orr, Bos., D
1973	East 5, West 4	NY Rangers	Tom Johnson, Billy Reay	Greg Polis, Pit., LW
1974	West 6, East 4	Chicago	Billy Reay, Scotty Bowman	Garry Unger, St.L., C
1975	Wales 7, Campbell 1	Montreal	Bep Guidolin, Fred Shero	Syl Apps Jr., Pit., C
1976	Wales 7, Campbell 5	Philadelphia	Floyd Smith, Fred Shero	Peter Mahovlich, Mon., C
1977	Wales 4, Campbell 3	Vancouver	Scotty Bowman, Fred Shero	Rick Martin, Buf., LW
1978	Wales 3, Campbell 2 (OT)	Buffalo	Scotty Bowman, Fred Shero	Billy Smith, NYI, G
1979	No game (see below)			
1980	Wales 6, Campbell 3	Detroit	Scotty Bowman, Al Arbour	Reggie Leach, Phi., RW
1981	Campbell 4, Wales 1	Los Angeles	Pat Quinn, Scotty Bowman	Mike Liut, St.L., G
1982	Wales 4, Campbell 2	Washington	Al Arbour, Glen Sonmor	Mike Bossy, NYI, RW
1983	Campbell 9, Wales 3	NY Islanders	Roger Neilson, Al Arbour	Wayne Gretzky, Edm., C
1984	Wales 7, Campbell 6	New Jersey	Al Arbour, Glen Sather	Don Maloney, NYR, LW
1985	Wales 6, Campbell 4	Calgary	Al Arbour, Glen Sather	Mario Lemieux, Pit., C
1986	Wales 4, Campbell 3 (OT)	Hartford	Mike Keenan, Glen Sather	Grant Fuhr, Edm., G
1987	No game (see below)			
1988	Wales 6, Campbell 5 (OT)	St. Louis	Mike Keenan, Glen Sather	Mario Lemieux, Pit., C
1989	Campbell 9, Wales 5	Edmonton	Glen Sather, Terry O'Reilly	Wayne Gretzky, LA, C
1990	Wales 12, Campbell 7	Pittsburgh	Pat Burns, Terry Crisp	Mario Lemieux, Pit., C
1991	Campbell 11, Wales 5	Chicago	John Muckler, Mike Milbury	Vincent Damphousse, Tor., LW
1992	Campbell 10, Wales 6	Philadelphia	Bob Gainey, Scotty Bowman	Brett Hull, St.L., RW
1993	Wales 16, Campbell 6	Montreal	Scotty Bowman, Mike Keenan	Mike Gartner, NYR, RW
1994	East 9, West 8	NY Rangers	Jacques Demers, Barry Melrose	Mike Richter, NYR, G
1995	No game (see below)			
1996	East 5, West 4	Boston	Doug MacLean, Scotty Bowman	Ray Bourque, Bos., D

No All-Star Game: in 1966 (moved from start of season to mid-season); in 1979 (replaced by Challenge Cup series with USSR); in 1987 (replaced by Rendez-Vous '87 series with USSR); and in 1995 (cancelled when NHL lockout shortened season to 48 games).

NHL Franchise Origins

Here is what the current 26 teams in the National Hockey League have to show for the years they have put in as members of the NHL, the early National Hockey Association (NHA) and the more recent World Hockey Association (WHA). League titles and Stanley Cup championships are noted by year won. The Stanley Cup has automatically gone to the NHL champion since the 1926-27 season. Following the 1992-93 season, the NHL renamed the Clarence Campbell Conference the Western Conference, while the Prince of Wales Conference became the Eastern Conference.

Western Conference

	First Season	League Titles	Franchise Stops
Anaheim, Mighty Ducks of	1993-94 (NHL)	None	•Anaheim, CA (1993—)
Calgary Flames	1972-73 (NHL)	1 Cup (1989)	•Atlanta (1972-80) Calgary (1980—)
Chicago Blackhawks	1926-27 (NHL)	3 Cups (1934,38,61)	•Chicago (1926—)
Colorado Avalanche	1972-73 (WHA)	1 WHA (1977) 1 Cup (1996)	•Quebec City (1972-95) Denver (1995—)
Dallas Stars	1967-68 (NHL)	None	•Bloomington, MN (1967-93) Dallas (1993—)
Detroit Red Wings	1926-27 (NHL)	7 Cups (1936-37,43,50, 52,54-55)	•Detroit (1926—)
Edmonton Oilers	1973-74 (WHA)	5 Cups (1984-85,87-88,90)	•Edmonton (1972—)
Los Angeles Kings	1967-68 (NHL)	None	•Inglewood, CA (1967—)
Phoenix Coyotes	1972-73 (WHA)	3 WHA (1976, 78-79)	•Winnipeg (1972-96) Phoenix (1996—)
St. Louis Blues	1967-68 (NHL)	None	•St. Louis (1967—)
San Jose Sharks	1991-92 (NHL)	None	•San Francisco (1991-93) San Jose (1993—)
Toronto Maple Leafs	1916-17 (NHA)	2 NHL (1918,22) 13 Cups (1918,22,32,42,45 47-49,51,62-64,67)	•Toronto (1916—)
Vancouver Canucks	1970-71 (NHL)	None	•Vancouver (1970—)

Eastern Conference

	First Season	League Titles	Franchise Stops
Boston Bruins	1924-25 (NHL)	5 Cups (1929,39,41,70,72)	•Boston (1924—)
Buffalo Sabres	1970-71 (NHL)	None	•Buffalo (1970—)
Florida Panthers	1993-94 (NHL)	None	•Miami (1993—)
Hartford Whalers	1972-73 (WHA)	1 WHA (1973)	•Boston (1972-74) W. Springfield, MA (1974-75) Hartford, CT (1975-78) Springfield, MA (1978-80) Hartford (1980—)
Montreal Canadiens	1909-10 (NHA)	2 NHA (1916-17) 2 NHL (1924-25) 24 Cups (1916,24,30-31,44,46, 53,56-60,65-66,68-69, 71,73,76-79,86,93)	•Montreal (1909—)
New Jersey Devils	1974-75 (NHL)	1 Cup (1995)	•Kansas City (1974-76) Denver (1976-82) E. Rutherford, NJ (1982—)
New York Islanders	1972-73 (NHL)	4 Cups (1980-83)	•Uniondale, NY (1972—)
New York Rangers	1926-27 (NHL)	4 Cups (1928,33,40,94)	•New York (1926—)
Ottawa Senators	1992-93 (NHL)	None	•Ottawa (1992-1996) Kanata, Ont. (1996—)
Philadelphia Flyers	1967-68 (NHL)	2 Cups (1974-75)	•Philadelphia (1967—)
Pittsburgh Penguins	1967-68 (NHL)	2 Cups (1991-92)	•Pittsburgh (1967—)
Tampa Bay Lightning	1992-93 (NHL)	None	•Tampa, FL (1992-93) St. Petersburg, FL (1993-96) Tampa, FL (1996—)
Washington Capitals	1974-75 (NHL)	None	•Landover, MD (1974—)

Note: The Hartford Civic Center roof collapsed after a snowstorm in January 1978, forcing the Whalers to move their home games to Springfield, Mass., for two years.

The Growth of the NHL

Of the four franchises that comprised the National Hockey League (NHL) at the start of the 1917-18 season, only two remain—the Montreal Canadiens and the Toronto Maple Leafs (originally the Toronto Arenas). From 1919-26, eight new teams joined the league, but only four—the Boston Bruins, Chicago Blackhawks (originally Black Hawks), Detroit Red Wings (originally Cougars) and New York Rangers—survived.

It was 41 years before the NHL expanded again, doubling in size for the 1967-68 season with new teams in Los Angeles, Minnesota, Oakland, Philadelphia, Pittsburgh and St. Louis. The league had 16 clubs by the start of the 1972-73 season, but it also had a rival in the **World Hockey Association**, which debuted that year with 12 teams.

The NHL added two more teams in 1974 and merged the struggling Cleveland Barons (originally the Oakland Seals) and Minnesota North Stars in 1978, before absorbing four WHA clubs—the Edmonton Oilers, Hartford Whalers, Quebec Nordiques and Winnipeg Jets—in time for the 1979-80 season. Five expansion teams have joined the league so far in the 1990s, giving the NHL its current 26-team roster.

Expansion/Merger Timetable

For teams currently in NHL.

1919—Quebec Bulldogs finally take the ice after sitting out NHL's first two seasons; **1924**—Boston Bruins and Montreal Maroons; **1925**—New York Americans and Pittsburgh Pirates; **1926**—Chicago Black Hawks (now Blackhawks), Detroit Cougars (now Red Wings) and New York Rangers; **1932**—Ottawa Senators return after sitting out 1931-32 season.

1967—California Seals (later Cleveland Barons), Los Angeles Kings, Minnesota North Stars, Philadelphia Flyers, Pittsburgh Penguins and St. Louis Blues.

1970—Buffalo Sabres and Vancouver Canucks; **1972**—Atlanta Flames (now Calgary) and New York Islanders; **1974**—Kansas City Scouts (now New Jersey Devils) and Washington Capitals; **1978**—Cleveland Barons merge with Minnesota North Stars (now Dallas Stars) and team remains in Minnesota; **1979**—added WHA's Edmonton Oilers, Hartford Whalers, Quebec Nordiques (now Colorado Avalanche) and Winnipeg Jets.

1991—San Jose Sharks; **1992**—Ottawa Senators and Tampa Bay Lightning; **1993**—Mighty Ducks of Anaheim and Florida Panthers.

City and Nickname Changes

1919—Toronto Arenas renamed St. Pats; **1920**—Quebec moves to Hamilton and becomes Tigers (will fold in 1925); **1926**—Toronto St. Pats renamed Maple Leafs; **1929**—Detroit Cougars renamed Falcons.

1930—Pittsburgh Pirates move to Philadelphia and become Quakers (will fold in 1931); **1932**—Detroit Falcons renamed Red Wings; **1934**—Ottawa Senators move to St. Louis and become Eagles (will fold in 1935); **1941**—New York Americans renamed Brooklyn Americans (will fold in 1942).

1967—California Seals renamed Oakland Seals three months into first season; **1970**—Oakland Seals renamed California Golden Seals; **1975**—California Golden Seals renamed Seals; **1976**—California Seals move to Cleveland and become Barons, while Kansas City Scouts move to Denver and become Colorado Rockies; **1978**—Cleveland Barons merge with Minnesota North Stars and become Minnesota North Stars.

1980—Atlanta Flames move to Calgary; **1982**—Colorado Rockies move to East Rutherford, N.J., and become New Jersey Devils; **1986**—Chicago Black Hawks renamed Blackhawks; **1993**—Minnesota North Stars move to Dallas and become Stars. **1995**—Quebec Nordiques move to Denver and become Colorado Avalanche; **1996**—Winnipeg Jets move to Phoenix and become Coyotes.

Defunct NHL Teams

Teams that once played in the NHL, but no longer exist.

Brooklyn—Americans (1941-42, formerly NY Americans from 1925-41); **Cleveland**—Barons (1976-78, originally California-Oakland Seals from 1967-76); **Hamilton (Ont.)**—Tigers (1920-25, originally Quebec Bulldogs from 1919-20); **Montreal**—Maroons (1924-38) and Wanderers (1917-18); **New York**—Americans (1925-42, later Brooklyn Americans for 1941-42); **Oakland**—Seals (1967-76, also known as California Seals and Golden Seals and later Cleveland Barons from 1976-78); **Ottawa**—Senators (1917-31 and 1932-34, later St. Louis Eagles for 1934-35); **Philadelphia**—Quakers (1930-31, originally Pittsburgh Pirates from 1925-30); **Pittsburgh**—Pirates (1925-30, later Philadelphia Quakers for 1930-31); **Quebec**—Bulldogs (1919-20, later Hamilton Tigers from 1920-25); **St. Louis**—Eagles (1934-35), originally Ottawa Senators (1917-31 and 1932-34).

WHA Teams (1972-79)

Baltimore—Blades (1975); **Birmingham**—Bulls (1976-78); **Calgary**—Cowboys (1975-77); **Chicago**—Cougars (1972-75); **Cincinnati**—Stingers (1975-79); **Cleveland**—Crusaders (1972-76, moved to Minnesota); **Denver**—Spurs (1975-76, moved to Ottawa); **Edmonton**—Oilers (1972-79, originally called Alberta Oilers in 1972-73); **Houston**—Aeros (1972-78); **Indianapolis**—Racers (1974-78).

Los Angeles—Sharks (1972-74, moved to Michigan); **Michigan**—Stags (1974-75, moved to Baltimore); **Minnesota**—Fighting Saints (1972-76) and New Fighting Saints (1976-77); **New England**—Whalers (1972-79, played in Boston from 1972-74, West Springfield, MA from 1974-75, Hartford from 1975-78 and Springfield, MA in 1979); **New Jersey**—Knights (1973-74, moved to San Diego); **New York**—Raiders (1972-73, renamed Golden Blades in 1973, moved to New Jersey).

Ottawa—Nationals (1972-73, moved to Toronto) and Civics (1976); **Philadelphia**—Blazers (1972-73, moved to Vancouver); **Phoenix**—Roadrunners (1974-77); **Quebec**—Nordiques (1972-79); **San Diego**—Mariners (1974-77); **Toronto**—Toros (1973-76, moved to Birmingham, AL); **Vancouver**—Blazers (1973-75, moved to Calgary); **Winnipeg**—Jets (1972-79).

Annual NHL Leaders

Art Ross Trophy (Scoring)

Given to the player who leads the league in points scored and named after the former Boston Bruins general manager-coach. First presented in 1947, names of prior leading scorers have been added retroactively. A tie for the scoring championship is broken three ways: 1. total goals; 2. fewest games played; 3. first goal scored.

Multiple winners: Wayne Gretzky (10); Gordie Howe (6); Phil Esposito and Mario Lemieux (5); Stan Mikita (4); Guy Lafleur (3); Max Bentley, Charlie Conacher, Bill Cook, Babe Dye, Bernie Geoffrion, Bobby Hull, Elmer Lach, Newsy Lalonde, Joe Malone, Dickie Moore, Howie Morenz, Bobby Orr and Sweeney Schriner (2).

Year		Gm	G	A	Pts
1918	Joe Malone, Mon	20	44	0	44
1919	Newsy Lalonde, Mon	17	23	9	32
1920	Joe Malone, Que	24	39	6	45
1921	Newsy Lalonde, Mon	24	33	8	41
1922	Punch Broadbent, Ott	24	32	14	46
1923	Babe Dye, Tor	22	26	11	37
1924	Cy Denneny, Ott	21	22	1	23
1925	Babe Dye, Tor	29	38	6	44
1926	Nels Stewart, Maroons	36	34	8	42
1927	Bill Cook, NYR	44	33	4	37
1928	Howie Morenz, Mon	43	33	18	51
1929	Ace Bailey, Tor	44	22	10	32
1930	Cooney Weiland, Bos	44	43	30	73
1931	Howie Morenz, Mon	39	28	23	51
1932	Busher Jackson, Tor	48	28	25	53
1933	Bill Cook, NYR	48	28	22	50
1934	Charlie Conacher, Tor	42	32	20	52
1935	Charlie Conacher, Tor	47	36	21	57
1936	Sweeney Schriner, NYA	48	19	26	45
1937	Sweeney Schriner, NYA	48	21	25	46
1938	Gordie Drillon, Tor	48	26	26	52
1939	Toe Blake, Mon	48	24	23	47
1940	Milt Schmidt, Bos	48	22	30	52
1941	Bill Cowley, Bos	46	17	45	62
1942	Bryan Hextall, NYR	48	24	32	56
1943	Doug Bentley, Chi	50	33	40	73
1944	Herbie Cain, Bos	48	36	46	82
1945	Elmer Lach, Mon	50	26	54	80
1946	Max Bentley, Chi	47	31	30	61
1947	Max Bentley, Chi	60	29	43	72
1948	Elmer Lach, Mon	60	30	31	61
1949	Roy Conacher, Chi	60	26	42	68
1950	Ted Lindsay, Det	69	23	55	78
1951	Gordie Howe, Det	70	43	43	86
1952	Gordie Howe, Det	70	47	39	86
1953	Gordie Howe, Det	70	49	46	95
1954	Gordie Howe, Det	70	33	48	81
1955	Bernie Geoffrion, Mon	70	38	37	75
1956	Jean Beliveau, Mon	70	47	41	88
1957	Gordie Howe, Det	70	44	45	89
1958	Dickie Moore, Mon	70	36	48	84
1959	Dickie Moore, Mon	70	41	55	96
1960	Bobby Hull, Chi	70	39	42	81
1961	Bernie Geoffrion, Mon	64	50	45	95
1962	Bobby Hull, Chi	70	50	34	84
1963	Gordie Howe, Det	70	38	48	86
1964	Stan Mikita, Chi	70	39	50	89
1965	Stan Mikita, Chi	70	28	59	87
1966	Bobby Hull, Chi	65	54	43	97
1967	Stan Mikita, Chi	70	35	62	97
1968	Stan Mikita, Chi	72	40	47	87
1969	Phil Esposito, Bos	74	49	77	126
1970	Bobby Orr, Bos	76	33	87	120
1971	Phil Esposito, Bos	78	76	76	152
1972	Phil Esposito, Bos	76	66	67	133
1973	Phil Esposito, Bos	78	55	75	130
1974	Phil Esposito, Bos	78	68	77	145
1975	Bobby Orr, Bos	80	46	89	135
1976	Guy Lafleur, Mon	80	56	69	125
1977	Guy Lafleur, Mon	80	56	80	136
1978	Guy Lafleur, Mon	79	60	72	132
1979	Bryan Trottier, NYI	76	47	87	134
1980	Marcel Dionne, LA	80	53	84	137
1981	Wayne Gretzky, Edm	80	55	109	164
1982	Wayne Gretzky, Edm	80	92	120	212
1983	Wayne Gretzky, Edm	80	71	125	196
1984	Wayne Gretzky, Edm	74	87	118	205
1985	Wayne Gretzky, Edm	80	73	135	208
1986	Wayne Gretzky, Edm	80	52	163	215
1987	Wayne Gretzky, Edm	79	62	121	183
1988	Mario Lemieux, Pit	77	70	98	168
1989	Mario Lemieux, Pit	76	85	114	199
1990	Wayne Gretzky, LA	73	40	102	142
1991	Wayne Gretzky, LA	78	41	122	163
1992	Mario Lemieux, Pit	64	44	87	131
1993	Mario Lemieux, Pit	60	69	91	160
1994	Wayne Gretzky, LA	81	38	92	130
1995	Jaromir Jagr, Pit	48	32	38	70
1996	Mario Lemieux, Pit	70	69	92	161

Note: The three times players have tied for total points in one season the player with more goals has won the trophy. In 1961-62, Hull outscored Andy Bathgate of NY Rangers, 50 goals to 28. In 1979-80, Dionne outscored Wayne Gretzky of Edmonton, 53-51. In 1995, Jagr outscored Eric Lindros of Philadelphia, 32-29.

NHL 500-Goal Scorers

Of the 500-goal scorers listed below, two (Gartner and Hull) went on to score over 600, two (Dionne and Esposito) scored over 700, and two (Gretzky and Howe) have scored over 800. Players who were active in 1996 are in **bold** type.

	Date	Game #
Maurice Richard, Mon vs Chi	10/19/57	863
Gordie Howe, Det at NYR	3/14/62	1045
Bobby Hull, Chi vs NYR	2/21/70	861
Jean Beliveau, Mon vs Min	2/11/71	1101
Frank Mahovlich, Mon vs Van	3/21/73	1105
Phil Esposito, Bos vs Det	12/22/74	803
John Bucyk, Bos vs St.L	10/30/75	1370
Stan Mikita, Chi vs Van	2/27/77	1221
Marcel Dionne, LA at Wash	12/14/82	887
Guy Lafleur, Mon at NJ	12/20/83	918
Mike Bossy, NYI vs Bos	1/2/86	647
Gilbert Perreault, Buf vs NJ	3/9/86	1159
Wayne Gretzky, Edm vs Van	11/22/86	575
Lanny McDonald, Calg vs NYI	3/21/89	1107
Bryan Trottier, NYI vs Calg	2/13/90	1104
Mike Gartner, NYR vs Wash	10/14/91	936
Michel Goulet, Chi vs Calg	2/16/92	951
Jari Kurri, LA vs Bos	10/17/92	833
Dino Ciccarelli, Det at LA	1/8/94	946
Mario Lemieux, Pit at NYI	10/26/95	605
Mark Messier, NYR vs Calg	11/6/95	1141
Steve Yzerman, Det vs Col	1/17/96	906
Dale Hawerchuk, St.L at Tor	1/31/96	1103

Goals

Multiple winners: Bobby Hull (7); Phil Esposito (6); Charlie Conacher, Wayne Gretzky, Gordie Howe and Maurice Richard (5); Bill Cook, Babe Dye, Brett Hull and Mario Lemieux (3); Jean Beliveau, Doug Bentley, Mike Bossy, Bernie Geoffrion, Bryan Hextall, Joe Malone and Nels Stewart (2).

Year		No
1918	Joe Malone, Mon	44
1919	Odie Cleghorn, Mon	23
	& Newsy Lalonde, Mon	23
1920	Joe Malone, Que	39
1921	Babe Dye, Ham-Tor	35
1922	Punch Broadbent, Ott	32
1923	Babe Dye, Tor	26
1924	Cy Denneny, Ott	22
1925	Babe Dye, Tor	38
1926	Nels Stewart, Maroons	34
1927	Bill Cook, NYR	33
1928	Howie Morenz, Mon	33
1929	Ace Bailey, Tor	22
1930	Cooney Weiland, Bos	43
1931	Charlie Conacher, Tor	31
1932	Charlie Conacher, Tor	34
	& Bill Cook, NYR	34
1933	Bill Cook, NYR	28
1934	Charlie Conacher, Tor	32
1935	Charlie Conacher, Tor	36
1936	Charlie Conacher, Tor	23
	& Bill Thoms, Tor	23
1937	Larry Aurie, Det	23
	& Nels Stewart, Bos-NYA	23
1938	Gordie Drillon, Tor	26
1939	Roy Conacher, Bos	26
1940	Bryan Hextall, NYR	24
1941	Bryan Hextall, NYR	26
1942	Lynn Patrick, NYR	32
1943	Doug Bentley, Chi	33
1944	Doug Bentley, Chi	38
1945	Maurice Richard, Mon	50
1946	Gaye Stewart, Tor	37
1947	Maurice Richard, Mon	45
1948	Ted Lindsay, Det	33
1949	Sid Abel, Det	28
1950	Maurice Richard, Mon	43
1951	Gordie Howe, Det	43
1952	Gordie Howe, Det	47
1953	Gordie Howe, Det	49
1954	Maurice Richard, Mon	37
1955	Bernie Geoffrion, Mon	38
	& Maurice Richard, Mon	38
1956	Jean Beliveau, Mon	47
1957	Gordie Howe, Det	44
1958	Dickie Moore, Mon	36
1959	Jean Beliveau, Mon	45
1960	Bronco Horvath, Bos	39
	& Bobby Hull, Chi	39
1961	Bernie Geoffrion, Mon	50
1962	Bobby Hull, Chi	50
1963	Gordie Howe, Det	38
1964	Bobby Hull, Chi	43
1965	Norm Ullman, Tor	42
1966	Bobby Hull, Chi	54
1967	Bobby Hull, Chi	52
1968	Bobby Hull, Chi	44
1969	Bobby Hull, Chi	58
1970	Phil Esposito, Bos	43
1971	Phil Esposito, Bos	76
1972	Phil Esposito, Bos	66
1973	Phil Esposito, Bos	55
1974	Phil Esposito, Bos	68
1975	Phil Esposito, Bos	61
1976	Reggie Leach, Phi	61
1977	Steve Shutt, Mon	60
1978	Guy Lafleur, Mon	60
1979	Mike Bossy, NYI	69
1980	Danny Gare, Buf	56
	Charlie Simmer, LA	56
	& Blaine Stoughton, Hart	56
1981	Mike Bossy, NYI	68
1982	Wayne Gretzky, Edm	92
1983	Wayne Gretzky, Edm	71
1984	Wayne Gretzky, Edm	87
1985	Wayne Gretzky, Edm	73
1986	Jari Kurri, Edm	68
1987	Wayne Gretzky, Edm	62
1988	Mario Lemieux, Pit	70
1989	Mario Lemieux, Pit	85
1990	Brett Hull, St.L	72
1991	Brett Hull, St.L	86
1992	Brett Hull, St.L	70
1993	Alexander Mogilny, Buf	76
	& Teemu Selanne, Win	76
1994	Pavel Bure, Van	60
1995	Peter Bondra, Wash	34
1996	Mario Lemieux, Pit	69

Assists

Multiple winners: Wayne Gretzky (14); Bobby Orr (5); Frank Boucher, Bill Cowley, Phil Esposito, Gordie Howe, Elmer Lach, Stan Mikita and Joe Primeau (3); Syl Apps, Andy Bathgate, Jean Beliveau, Doug Bentley, Art Chapman, Bobby Clarke, Ron Francis, Mario Lemieux, Ted Lindsay, Bert Olmstead, Henri Richard and Bryan Trottier (2).

Year		No
1918	No official records kept.	
1919	Newsy Lalonde, Mon	9
1920	Corbett Denneny, Tor	12
1921	Louis Berlinquette, Mon	9
	Harry Cameron, Tor	9
	& Joe Matte, Ham	9
1922	Punch Broadbent, Ott	14
	& Leo Reise, Ham	14
1923	Ed Bouchard, Ham	12
1924	King Clancy, Ott	8
1925	Cy Denneny, Ott	15
1926	Frank Nighbor, Ott	13
1927	Dick Irvin, Chi	18
1928	Howie Morenz, Mon	18
1929	Frank Boucher, NYR	16
1930	Frank Boucher, NYR	36
1931	Joe Primeau, Tor	32
1932	Joe Primeau, Tor	37
1933	Frank Boucher, NYR	28
1934	Joe Primeau, Tor	32
1935	Art Chapman, NYA	34
1936	Art Chapman, NYA	28
1937	Syl Apps, Tor	29
1938	Syl Apps, Tor	29
1939	Bill Cowley, Bos	34
1940	Milt Schmidt, Bos	30
1941	Bill Cowley, Bos	45
1942	Phil Watson, NYR	37
1943	Bill Cowley, Bos	45
1944	Clint Smith, Chi	49
1945	Elmer Lach, Mon	54
1946	Elmer Lach, Mon	34
1947	Billy Taylor, Det	46
1948	Doug Bentley, Chi	37
1949	Doug Bentley, Chi	43
1950	Ted Lindsay, Det	55
1951	Gordie Howe, Det	43
	& Teeder Kennedy, Tor	43
1952	Elmer Lach, Mon	50
1953	Gordie Howe, Det	46
1954	Gordie Howe, Det	48
1955	Bert Olmstead, Mon	48
1956	Bert Olmstead, Mon	56
1957	Ted Lindsay, Det	55
1958	Henri Richard, Mon	52
1959	Dickie Moore, Mon	55
1960	Don McKenney, Bos	49
1961	Jean Beliveau, Mon	58
1962	Andy Bathgate, NYR	56
1963	Henri Richard, Mon	50
1964	Andy Bathgate, NYR-Tor	58
1965	Stan Mikita, Chi	59
1966	Jean Beliveau, Mon	48
	Stan Mikita, Chi	48
	& Bobby Rousseau, Mon	48
1967	Stan Mikita, Chi	62
1968	Phil Esposito, Bos	49
1969	Phil Esposito, Bos	77
1970	Bobby Orr, Bos	87
1971	Bobby Orr, Bos	102
1972	Bobby Orr, Bos	80
1973	Phil Esposito, Bos	75
1974	Bobby Orr, Bos	90
1975	Bobby Clarke, Phi	89
	& Bobby Orr, Bos	89
1976	Bobby Clarke, Phi	89
1977	Guy Lafleur, Mon	80
1978	Bryan Trottier, NYI	77
1979	Bryan Trottier, NYI	87
1980	Wayne Gretzky, Edm	86
1981	Wayne Gretzky, Edm	109
1982	Wayne Gretzky, Edm	120
1983	Wayne Gretzky, Edm	125
1984	Wayne Gretzky, Edm	118
1985	Wayne Gretzky, Edm	135
1986	Wayne Gretzky, Edm	163
1987	Wayne Gretzky, Edm	121
1988	Wayne Gretzky, Edm	109
1989	Wayne Gretzky, LA	114
	& Mario Lemieux, Pit	114
1990	Wayne Gretzky, LA	102
1991	Wayne Gretzky, LA	122
1992	Wayne Gretzky, LA	90
1993	Adam Oates, Bos	97
1994	Wayne Gretzky, LA	92
1995	Ron Francis, Pit	48
1996	Ron Francis, Pit	92
	& Mario Lemieux, Pit	92

Annual NHL Leaders (Cont.)

Goals Against Average

Average determined by games played through 1942-43 season and by minutes played since then. Minimum of 15 games from 1917-18 season through 1925-26; minimum of 25 games since 1926-27 season. Not to be confused with the Vezina Trophy. Goaltenders who posted the season's lowest goals against average, but did not win the Vezina are in **bold** type.

Multiple winners: Jacques Plante (9); Clint Benedict and Bill Durnan (6); Johnny Bower, Ken Dryden and Tiny Thompson (4); Georges Vezina (3); Frankie Brimsek, Turk Broda, George Hainsworth, Dominik Hasek, Harry Lumley, Bernie Parent, Pete Peeters, Patrick Roy and Terry Sawchuk (2).

Year		GAA
1918	Georges Vezina, Mon	3.82
1919	Clint Benedict, Ott	2.94
1920	Clint Benedict, Ott	2.67
1921	Clint Benedict, Ott	3.13
1922	Clint Benedict, Ott	3.50
1923	Clint Benedict, Ott	2.25
1924	Georges Vezina, Mon	2.00
1925	Georges Vezina, Mon	1.87
1926	Alex Connell, Ott	1.17
1927	**Clint Benedict**, Mon-M	1.51
1928	Geo. Hainsworth, Mon	1.09
1929	Geo. Hainsworth, Mon	0.98
1930	Tiny Thompson, Bos	2.23
1931	Roy Worters, NYA	1.68
1932	Chuck Gardiner, Chi	1.92
1933	Tiny Thompson, Bos	1.83
1934	**Wilf Cude**, Det-Mon	1.57
1935	Lorne Chabot, Chi	1.83
1936	Tiny Thompson, Bos	1.71
1937	Norm Smith, Det	2.13
1938	Tiny Thompson, Bos	1.85
1939	Frankie Brimsek, Bos	1.58
1940	Dave Kerr, NYR	1.60
1941	Turk Broda, Tor	2.06
1942	Frankie Brimsek, Bos	2.45
1943	John Mowers, Det	2.47

Year		GAA
1944	Bill Durnan, Mon	2.18
1945	Bill Durnan, Mon	2.42
1946	Bill Durnan, Mon	2.60
1947	Bill Durnan, Mon	2.30
1948	Turk Broda, Tor	2.38
1949	Bill Durnan, Mon	2.10
1950	Bill Durnan, Mon	2.20
1951	Al Rollins, Tor	1.77
1952	Terry Sawchuk, Det	1.90
1953	Terry Sawchuk, Det	1.90
1954	Harry Lumley, Tor	1.86
1955	**Harry Lumley**, Tor	1.94
1956	Jacques Plante, Mon	1.86
1957	Jacques Plante, Mon	2.02
1958	Jacques Plante, Mon	2.11
1959	Jacques Plante, Mon	2.16
1960	Jacques Plante, Mon	2.54
1961	Johnny Bower, Tor	2.50
1962	Jacques Plante, Mon	2.37
1963	**Jacques Plante**, Mon	2.49
1964	**Johnny Bower**, Tor	2.11
1965	Johnny Bower, Tor	2.38
1966	**Johnny Bower**, Tor	2.25
1967	Glenn Hall, Chi	2.38
1968	Gump Worsley, Mon	1.98
1969	Jacques Plante, St.L	1.96

Year		GAA
1970	**Ernie Wakely**, St.L	2.11
1971	**Jacques Plante**, Tor	1.88
1972	Tony Esposito, Chi	1.77
1973	Ken Dryden, Mon	2.26
1974	Bernie Parent, Phi	1.89
1975	Bernie Parent, Phi	2.03
1976	Ken Dryden, Mon	2.03
1977	Bunny Larocque, Mon	2.09
1978	Ken Dryden, Mon	2.05
1979	Ken Dryden, Mon	2.30
1980	Bob Sauve, Buf	2.36
1981	Richard Sevigny, Mon	2.40
1982	**Denis Herron**, Mon	2.64
1983	Pete Peeters, Bos	2.36
1984	**Pat Riggin**, Wash	2.66
1985	**Tom Barrasso**, Buf	2.66
1986	**Bob Froese**, Phi	2.55
1987	**Brian Hayward**, Mon	2.81
1988	**Pete Peeters**, Wash	2.78
1989	Patrick Roy, Mon	2.47
1990	**Mike Liut**, Hart-Wash	2.53
1991	Ed Belfour, Chi	2.47
1992	Patrick Roy, Mon	2.36
1993	**Felix Potvin**, Tor	2.50
1994	Dominik Hasek, Buf	1.95
1995	Dominik Hasek, Buf	2.11
1996	**Ron Hextall**, Phi	2.17

Penalty Minutes

Multiple winners: Red Horner (8); Gus Mortson and Dave Schultz (4); Bert Corbeau, Lou Fontinato and Tiger Williams (3); Billy Boucher, Carl Brewer, Red Dutton, Pat Egan, Bill Ezinicki, Joe Hall, Tim Hunter, Keith Magnuson, Chris Nilan and Jimmy Orlando (2).

Year		Min
1918	Joe Hall, Mon	60
1919	Joe Hall, Mon	85
1920	Cully Wilson, Tor	79
1921	Bert Corbeau, Mon	86
1922	Sprague Cleghorn, Mon	63
1923	Billy Boucher, Mon	52
1924	Bert Corbeau, Tor	55
1925	Billy Boucher, Mon	92
1926	Bert Corbeau, Tor	121
1927	Nels Stewart, Mon-M	133
1928	Eddie Shore, Bos	165
1929	Red Dutton, Mon-M	139
1930	Joe Lamb, Ott	119
1931	Harvey Rockburn, Det	118
1932	Red Dutton, NYA	107
1933	Red Horner, Tor	144
1934	Red Horner, Tor	146
1935	Red Horner, Tor	125
1936	Red Horner, Tor	167
1937	Red Horner, Tor	124
1938	Red Horner, Tor	82
1939	Red Horner, Tor	85
1940	Red Horner, Tor	87
1941	Jimmy Orlando, Det	99
1942	Pat Egan, NYA	124
1943	Jimmy Orlando, Det	99

Year		Min
1944	Mike McMahon, Mon	98
1945	Pat Egan, Bos	86
1946	Jack Stewart, Det	73
1947	Gus Mortson, Tor	133
1948	Bill Barilko, Tor	147
1949	Bill Ezinicki, Tor	145
1950	Bill Ezinicki, Tor	144
1951	Gus Mortson, Tor	142
1952	Gus Kyle, Bos	127
1953	Maurice Richard, Mon	112
1954	Gus Mortson, Chi	132
1955	Fern Flaman, Bos	150
1956	Lou Fontinato, NYR	202
1957	Gus Mortson, Chi	147
1958	Lou Fontinato, NYR	152
1959	Ted Lindsay, Chi	184
1960	Carl Brewer, Tor	150
1961	Pierre Pilote, Chi	165
1962	Lou Fontinato, Mon	167
1963	Howie Young, Det	273
1964	Vic Hadfield, NYR	151
1965	Carl Brewer, Tor	177
1966	Reg Fleming, Bos-NYR	166
1967	John Ferguson, Mon	177
1968	Barclay Plager, St.L	153
1969	Forbes Kennedy, Phi-Tor	219

Year		Min
1970	Keith Magnuson, Chi	213
1971	Keith Magnuson, Chi	291
1972	Bryan Watson, Pit	212
1973	Dave Schultz, Phi	259
1974	Dave Schultz, Phi	348
1975	Dave Schultz, Phi	472
1976	Steve Durbano, Pit-KC	370
1977	Tiger Williams, Tor	338
1978	Dave Schultz, LA-Pit	405
1979	Tiger Williams, Tor	298
1980	Jimmy Mann, Win	287
1981	Tiger Williams, Van	343
1982	Paul Baxter, Pit	409
1983	Randy Holt, Wash	275
1984	Chris Nilan, Mon	338
1985	Chris Nilan, Mon	358
1986	Joey Kocur, Det	377
1987	Tim Hunter, Calg	361
1988	Bob Probert, Det	398
1989	Tim Hunter, Calg	375
1990	Basil McRae, Min	351
1991	Rob Ray, Buf	350
1992	Mike Peluso, Chi	408
1993	Marty McSorley, LA	399
1994	Tie Domi, Win	347
1995	Enrico Ciccone, TB	225
1996	Matthew Barnaby, Buf	335

All-Time NHL Regular Season Leaders

Through 1996 regular season.

CAREER

Players active during 1996 in **bold** type.

Points

		Yrs	Gm	G	A	Pts
1	**Wayne Gretzky**	17	1253	837	1771	2608
2	Gordie Howe	26	1767	801	1049	1850
3	Marcel Dionne	18	1348	731	1040	1771
4	Phil Esposito	18	1282	717	873	1590
5	**Mark Messier**	17	1201	539	929	1468
6	Stan Mikita	22	1394	541	926	1467
7	Bryan Trottier	18	1279	524	901	1425
8	**Paul Coffey**	16	1154	372	1038	1410
9	**Dale Hawerchuk**	15	1137	506	869	1375
10	**Mario Lemieux**	11	669	563	809	1372
11	John Bucyk	23	1540	556	813	1369
12	Guy Lafleur	17	1126	560	793	1353
13	**Jari Kurri**	15	1099	583	758	1341
14	Gilbert Perreault	17	1191	512	814	1326
15	**Ray Bourque**	17	1228	343	970	1313
16	**Denis Savard**	16	1132	464	847	1311
17	Alex Delvecchio	24	1549	456	825	1281
18	Jean Ratelle	21	1281	491	776	1267
19	**Ron Francis**	15	1085	376	881	1257
20	**Steve Yzerman**	13	942	517	738	1255
21	**Mike Gartner**	17	1290	664	581	1245
22	Peter Stastny	15	977	450	789	1239
23	Norm Ullman	20	1410	490	739	1229
24	Jean Beliveau	20	1125	507	712	1219
25	Bobby Clarke	15	1144	358	852	1210
26	Bobby Hull	16	1063	610	560	1170
27	Michel Goulet	15	1089	548	604	1152
28	**Bernie Nicholls**	15	992	457	677	1134
29	Bernie Federko	14	1000	369	761	1130
30	Mike Bossy	10	752	573	553	1126

Goals

		Yrs	Gm	No
1	**Wayne Gretzky**	17	1253	837
2	Gordie Howe	26	1767	801
3	Marcel Dionne	18	1348	731
4	Phil Esposito	18	1282	717
5	**Mike Gartner**	17	1290	664
6	Bobby Hull	16	1063	610
7	**Jari Kurri**	15	1099	583
8	Mike Bossy	10	752	573
9	**Mario Lemieux**	11	669	563
10	Guy Lafleur	17	1126	560
11	John Bucyk	23	1540	556
12	**Dino Ciccarelli**	16	1079	551
13	Michel Goulet	15	1089	548
14	Maurice Richard	18	978	544
15	Stan Mikita	22	1394	541
16	**Mark Messier**	17	1201	539
17	Frank Mahovlich	18	1181	533
18	Bryan Trottier	18	1279	524
19	**Steve Yzerman**	13	942	517
20	Gilbert Perreault	17	1191	512
21	Jean Beliveau	20	1125	507
22	**Dale Hawerchuk**	15	1137	506
23	Lanny McDonald	16	1111	500
24	**Glenn Anderson**	16	1128	498
25	**Joe Mullen**	16	1008	495
26	Jean Ratelle	21	1281	491
27	Norm Ullman	20	1410	490
28	**Brett Hull**	10	658	485
29	Darryl Sittler	15	1096	484
30	**Dave Andreychuk**	14	1001	476

Assists

		Yrs	Gm	No
1	**Wayne Gretzky**	17	1253	1771
2	Gordie Howe	26	1767	1049
3	Marcel Dionne	18	1348	1040
4	**Paul Coffey**	16	1154	1038
5	**Ray Bourque**	17	1228	970
6	**Mark Messier**	17	1201	929
7	Stan Mikita	22	1394	926
8	Bryan Trottier	18	1279	901
9	**Ron Francis**	15	1085	881
10	Phil Esposito	18	1281	873
11	**Dale Hawerchuk**	15	1137	869
12	Bobby Clarke	15	1144	852
13	**Denis Savard**	16	1132	847
14	Alex Delvecchio	24	1549	825
15	Gilbert Perreault	17	1191	814
16	John Bucyk	23	1540	813
17	**Mario Lemieux**	11	669	809
18	Guy Lafleur	17	1126	793
19	Peter Stastny	15	977	789
20	Jean Ratelle	21	1281	776

Penalty Minutes

		Yrs	Gm	Min
1	Tiger Williams	14	962	3966
2	**Dale Hunter**	16	1181	3218
3	Chris Nilan	13	688	3043
4	**Tim Hunter**	15	769	3011
5	**Marty McSorley**	13	775	2892
6	Willi Plett	12	834	2572
7	**Basil McRae**	15	568	2445
8	**Rick Tocchet**	12	788	2371
9	**Jay Wells**	17	1077	2346
10	**Bob Probert**	10	552	2327
11	Garth Butcher	14	897	2302
12	Dave Schultz	9	535	2294
13	**Scott Stevens**	14	1041	2290

NHL-WHA Top 15

All-Time regular season scoring leaders, including games played in World Hockey Association (1972-79). NHL players with WHA experience are listed in CAPITAL letters. Players active during 1996 are in **bold** type.

Points

		Yrs	G	A	Pts
1	**WAYNE GRETZKY**	18	883	1835	2718
2	GORDIE HOWE	32	975	1383	2358
3	BOBBY HULL	23	913	895	1808
4	Marcel Dionne	18	731	1040	1771
5	Phil Esposito	18	717	873	1590
6	**MARK MESSIER**	18	540	939	1479
7	Stan Mikita	22	541	926	1467
8	Bryan Trottier	18	524	901	1425
9	**Paul Coffey**	16	372	1038	1410
10	**Dale Hawerchuk**	15	506	869	1375
11	**Mario Lemieux**	11	563	809	1372
12	John Bucyk	23	556	813	1369
13	NORM ULLMAN	22	537	822	1359
14	Guy Lafleur	17	560	793	1353
15	**Jari Kurri**	15	583	758	1341

WHA Totals: GRETZKY (1 yr, 60 gm, 46-64—110); HOWE (6 yrs, 419 gm, 174-334—508); HULL (7 yrs, 411 gm, 303-335—638); MESSIER (1 yr, 52 gm, 1-10—11); ULLMAN (2 yrs, 144 gm, 47-83—130).

All-Time NHL Regular Season Leaders (Cont.)

Years Played

		Yrs	Career	Gm
1	Gordie Howe	26	1946-71, 79-80	1767
2	Alex Delvecchio	24	1950-74	1549
	Tim Horton	24	1949-50, 51-74	1446
4	John Bucyk	23	1955-78	1540
5	Stan Mikita	22	1958-80	1394
	Doug Mohns	22	1953-75	1390
	Dean Prentice	22	1952-74	1378
8	Harry Howell	21	1952-73	1411
	Ron Stewart	21	1952-73	1353
	Jean Ratelle	21	1960-81	1281
	Allan Stanley	21	1948-69	1244
	Eric Nesterenko	21	1951-72	1219
	Marcel Pronovost	21	1950-70	1206
	George Armstrong	21	1949-50, 51-71	1187
	Terry Sawchuk	21	1949-70	971
	Gump Worsley	21	1952-53, 54-74	862

Note: Combined NHL-WHA years played: Howe (32); Howell (24); Bobby Hull (23); Norm Ullman, Nesterenko, Frank Mahovlich and Dave Keon (22).

Games Played

		Yrs	Career	Gm
1	Gordie Howe	26	1946-71, 79-80	1767
2	Alex Delvecchio	24	1950-74	1549
3	John Bucyk	23	1955-78	1540
4	Tim Horton	24	1949-50, 51-74	1446
5	Harry Howell	21	1952-73	1411
6	Norm Ullman	20	1955-75	1410
7	Stan Mikita	22	1958-80	1394
8	Doug Mohns	22	1953-75	1390
9	Larry Robinson	20	1972-92	1384
10	Dean Prentice	22	1952-74	1378
11	Ron Stewart	21	1952-73	1353
12	Marcel Dionne	18	1971-89	1348
13	Red Kelly	20	1947-67	1316
14	Dave Keon	18	1960-75, 79-82	1296
15	**Mike Gartner**	17	1979-	1290

Note: Combined NHL-WHA games played: Howe (2,186), Keon (1,597), Howell (1,581), Ullman (1,554), Bobby Hull (1,474) and Frank Mahovlich (1,418).

Goaltending

Wins

		Yrs	Gm	W	L	T	Pct
1	Terry Sawchuk	21	971	**435**	337	188	.551
2	Jacques Plante	18	837	**434**	246	137	.615
3	Tony Esposito	16	886	**423**	307	151	.566
4	Glenn Hall	18	906	**407**	327	165	.544
5	Rogie Vachon	16	795	**355**	291	115	.542
6	Gump Worsley	21	862	**335**	353	150	.489
7	Harry Lumley	16	804	**332**	324	143	.505
8	**Andy Moog**	16	623	**326**	179	78	.626
9	**Grant Fuhr**	15	675	**320**	223	87	.577
10	**Patrick Roy**	11	590	**311**	190	67	.607
11	Billy Smith	18	680	**305**	233	105	.556
12	Turk Broda	12	629	**302**	224	101	.562
13	**Tom Barrasso**	13	597	**295**	213	63	.572
14	Mike Liut	13	663	**293**	271	74	.517
15	Ed Giacomin	13	610	**289**	206	97	.570
16	**Mike Vernon**	13	629	**288**	168	57	.617
17	Dan Bouchard	14	655	**286**	232	113	.543
18	Tiny Thompson	12	553	**284**	194	75	.581
19	Bernie Parent	13	608	**270**	197	121	.562
	Gilles Meloche	18	788	**270**	351	131	.446

Losses

		Yrs	Gm	W	L	T	Pct
1	Gump Worsley	21	862	335	**353**	150	.489
2	Gilles Meloche	18	788	270	**351**	131	.446
3	Terry Sawchuk	21	971	435	**337**	188	.551
4	Glenn Hall	18	906	407	**327**	165	.544
5	Harry Lumley	16	804	332	**324**	143	.505

Goals Against Average

Minimum of 300 games played.

Before 1950

		Gm	Min	GA	GAA
1	George Hainsworth	465	29,415	937	1.91
2	Alex Connell	416	26,030	837	2.01
3	Chuck Gardiner	316	19,687	664	2.02
4	Lorne Chabot	412	25,309	861	2.04
5	Tiny Thompson	552	34,174	1183	2.08

Since 1950

		Gm	Min	GA	GAA
1	Ken Dryden	397	23,352	870	2.24
2	Jacques Plante	837	49,633	1965	2.38
3	Glenn Hall	906	53,484	2239	2.51
4	Terry Sawchuk	971	57,205	2401	2.52
5	Johnny Bower	552	32,077	1347	2.52

Shutouts

		Yrs	Games	No
1	Terry Sawchuk	21	971	103
2	George Hainsworth	11	464	94
3	Glenn Hall	18	906	84
4	Jacques Plante	18	837	82
5	Alex Connell	12	417	81
	Tiny Thompson	12	553	81
7	Tony Esposito	16	886	76
8	Lorne Chabot	11	411	73
9	Harry Lumley	16	804	71
10	Roy Worters	12	484	66
11	Turk Broda	14	629	62
12	John Roach	14	492	58
13	Clint Benedict	13	362	57
14	Bernie Parent	13	608	55
15	Ed Giacomin	13	610	54

NHL-WHA Top 15

All-Time regular season wins leaders, including games played in World Hockey Association (1972-79). NHL goaltenders with WHA experience are listed in CAPITAL letters. Players active during 1996 are in **bold** type.

Wins

		Yrs	W	L	T	Pct
1	JACQUES PLANTE	19	449	260	138	.612
2	Terry Sawchuk	21	435	337	188	.551
3	Tony Esposito	16	423	307	151	.566
4	Glenn Hall	18	407	327	165	.544
5	Rogie Vachon	16	355	291	115	.542
6	Gump Worsley	21	335	353	150	.489
7	Harry Lumley	16	332	324	143	.505
8	GERRY CHEEVERS	16	329	172	83	.634
9	**Andy Moog**	16	326	179	78	.626
10	MIKE LIUT	15	324	310	78	.510
11	**Grant Fuhr**	15	320	223	87	.577
12	**Patrick Roy**	11	311	190	67	.607
13	Billy Smith	18	305	233	105	.556
14	BERNIE PARENT	14	303	225	121	.560
15	Turk Broda	12	302	224	101	.562

WHA Totals: CHEEVERS (4 yrs, 191 gm, 99-78-9); LIUT (2 yrs, 81 gm, 31-39-4); PARENT (1 yr, 63 gm, 33-28-0); PLANTE (1 yr, 31 gm, 15-14-1).

SINGLE SEASON

Scoring

Points

		Season	G	A	Pts
1	Wayne Gretzky, Edm	1985-86	52	163	215
2	Wayne Gretzky, Edm	1981-82	92	120	212
3	Wayne Gretzky, Edm	1984-85	73	135	208
4	Wayne Gretzky, Edm	1983-84	87	118	205
5	Mario Lemieux, Pit	1988-89	85	114	199
6	Wayne Gretzky, Edm	1982-83	71	125	196
7	Wayne Gretzky, Edm	1986-87	62	121	183
8	Mario Lemieux, Pit	1987-88	70	98	168
	Wayne Gretzky, LA	1988-89	54	114	168
10	Wayne Gretzky, Edm	1980-81	55	109	164
11	Wayne Gretzky, LA	1990-91	41	122	163
12	Mario Lemieux, Pit	1995-96	69	92	161
13	Mario Lemieux, Pit	1992-93	69	91	160
14	Steve Yzerman, Det	1988-89	65	90	155
15	Phil Esposito, Bos	1970-71	76	76	152
16	Bernie Nicholls, LA	1988-89	70	80	150
17	Jaromir Jagr, Pit	1995-96	62	87	149
	Wayne Gretzky, Edm	1987-88	40	109	149
19	Pat LaFontaine, Buf	1992-93	53	95	148
20	Mike Bossy, NYI	1981-82	64	83	147

WHA 150 points or more: 154—Marc Tardif, Que. (1977-78).

Goals

		Season	Gm	No
1	Wayne Gretzky, Edm	1981-82	80	92
2	Wayne Gretzky, Edm	1983-84	74	87
3	Brett Hull, St.L	1990-91	78	86
4	Mario Lemieux, Pit	1988-89	76	85
5	Alexander Mogilny, Buf	1992-93	77	76
	Phil Esposito, Bos	1970-71	78	76
	Teemu Selanne, Win	1992-93	84	76
8	Wayne Gretzky, Edm	1984-85	80	73
9	Brett Hull, St.L	1989-90	80	72
10	Jari Kurri, Edm	1984-85	73	71
	Wayne Gretzky, Edm	1982-83	80	71
12	Brett Hull, St.L	1991-92	73	70
	Mario Lemiuex, Pit	1987-88	77	70
	Bernie Nicholls, LA	1988-89	79	70
15	Mario Lemieux, Pit	1992-93	60	69
	Mario Lemieux, Pit	1995-96	70	69
	Mike Bossy, NYI	1978-79	80	69
18	Phil Esposito, Bos	1973-74	78	68
	Jari Kurri, Edm	1985-86	78	68
	Mike Bossy, NYI	1980-81	79	68

WHA 70 goals or more: 77—Bobby Hull, Win. (1974-75); 75—Real Cloutier, Que. (1978-79); 71—Marc Tardif, Que. (1975-76); 70—Anders Hedberg, Win. (1976-77).

Assists

		Season	Gm	No
1	Wayne Gretzky, Edm	1985-86	80	163
2	Wayne Gretzky, Edm	1984-85	80	135
3	Wayne Gretzky, Edm	1982-83	80	125
4	Wayne Gretzky, LA	1990-91	78	122
5	Wayne Gretzky, Edm	1986-87	79	121
6	Wayne Gretzky, Edm	1981-82	80	120
7	Wayne Gretzky, Edm	1983-84	74	118
8	Mario Lemieux, Pit	1988-89	76	114
	Wayne Gretzky, LA	1988-89	78	114
10	Wayne Gretzky, Edm	1987-88	64	109
	Wayne Gretzky, Edm	1980-81	80	109
12	Wayne Gretzky, LA	1989-90	73	102
	Bobby Orr, Bos	1970-71	78	102
14	Mario Lemieux, Pit	1987-88	77	98
15	Adam Oates, Bos	1992-93	84	97

WHA 95 assists or more: 106—Andre Lacroix, S.Diego 1974-75).

Goaltending

Wins

		Season	Record
1	Bernie Parent, Phi	1973-74	47-13-12
2	Bernie Parent, Phi	1974-75	44-14- 9
	Terry Sawchuk, Det	1950-51	44-13-13
	Terry Sawchuk, Det	1951-52	44-14-12
5	Tom Barrasso, Pit	1992-93	43-14- 5
	Ed Belfour, Chi	1990-91	43-19- 7
7	Jacques Plante, Mon	1955-56	42-12-10
	Jacques Plante, Mon	1961-62	42-14-14
	Ken Dryden, Mon	1975-76	42-10- 8
	Mike Richter, NYR	1993-94	42-12- 6

Most WHA wins in one season: 44—Richard Brodeur, Que. (1975-76).

Losses

		Season	Record
1	Gary Smith, Cal	1970-71	19-48- 4
2	Al Rollins, Chi	1953-54	12-47- 7
3	Peter Sidorkiewicz, Ott	1992-93	8-46- 3
4	Harry Lumley, Chi	1951-52	17-44- 9
5	Harry Lumley, Chi	1950-51	12-41-10
	Craig Billington, Ott	1993-94	11-41- 4

Most WHA losses in one season: 36—Don McLeod, Van. (1974-75) and Andy Brown, Ind. (1974-75).

Shutouts

		Season	Gm	No
1	George Hainsworth, Mon	1928-29	44	22
2	Alex Connell, Ottawa	1925-26	36	15
	Alex Connell, Ottawa	1927-28	44	15
	Hal Winkler, Bos	1927-28	44	15
	Tony Esposito, Chi	1969-70	63	15

Most WHA shutouts in one season: 5—Gerry Cheevers, Cle. (1972-73) and Joe Daly, Win. (1975-76).

Goals Against Average

Before 1950

		Season	Gm	GAA
1	George Hainsworth, Mon	1928-29	44	0.98
2	George Hainsworth, Mon	1927-28	44	1.09
3	Alex Connell, Ottawa	1925-26	36	1.17
4	Tiny Thompson, Bos	1928-29	44	1.18
5	Roy Worters, NY Americans	1928-29	38	1.21

Since 1950

		Season	Gm	GAA
1	Tony Esposito, Chi	1971-72	48	1.77
2	Al Rollins, Tor	1950-51	40	1.77
3	Harry Lumley, Tor	1953-54	69	1.86
4	Jacques Plante, Mon	1955-56	64	1.86
5	Jacques Plante, Tor	1970-71	40	1.88

Penalty Minutes

		Season	Min
1	Dave Schultz, Phi	1974-75	472
2	Paul Baxter, Pit	1981-82	409
3	Mike Peluso, Chi	1991-92	408
4	Dave Schultz, LA-Pit	1977-78	405
5	Marty McSorley, LA	1992-93	399
6	Bob Probert, Det	1987-88	398
7	Basil McRae, Min	1987-88	382
8	Joey Kocur, Det	1985-86	377
9	Tim Hunter, Calg	1988-89	375
10	Steve Durbano, Pit-KC	1975-76	370
	Gino Odjick, Van	1992-93	370

WHA 355 minutes or more: 365—Curt Brackenbury, Min-Que. (1975-76).

All-Time NHL Regular Season Leaders (Cont.)

SINGLE GAME

Scoring

Points

	Date	G-A—Pts
Darryl Sittler, Tor vs Bos	2/7/76	6-4—10
Maurice Richard, Mon vs Det	12/28/44	5-3— 8
Bert Olmstead, Mon vs Chi	1/9/54	4-4— 8
Tom Bladon, Phi vs Cle.	12/11/77	4-4— 8
Bryan Trottier, NYI vs NYR	12/23/78	5-3— 8
Peter Stastny, Que at Wash	2/22/81	4-4— 8
Anton Stastny, Que at Wash	2/22/81	3-5— 8
Wayne Gretzky, Edm vs NJ	11/19/83	3-5— 8
Wayne Gretzky, Edm vs Min	1/4/84	4-4— 8
Paul Coffey, Edm vs Det	3/14/86	2-6— 8
Mario Lemieux, Pit vs St.L	10/15/88	2-6— 8
Bernie Nicholls, LA vs Tor	12/1/88	2-6— 8
Mario Lemieux, Pit vs NJ	12/31/88	5-3— 8

Goals

	Date	No
Joe Malone, Que vs Tor	1/31/20	7
Newsy Lalonde, Mon vs Tor	1/10/20	6
Joe Malone, Que vs Ott	3/10/20	6
Corb Denneny, Tor vs Ham	1/26/21	6
Cy Denneny, Ott vs Ham	3/7/21	6
Syd Howe, Det vs NYR	2/3/44	6
Red Berenson, St.L at Phi	11/7/68	6
Darryl Sittler, Tor vs Bos	2/7/76	6

Assists

	Date	No
Billy Taylor, Det at Chi.	3/16/47	7
Wayne Gretzky, Edm vs Wash	2/15/80	7
Wayne Gretzky, Edm at Chi	12/11/85	7
Wayne Gretzky, Edm vs Que	2/14/86	7

23 players tied with 6 each.

THE GREAT ONE: FOR THE RECORD

NY Ranger center Wayne Gretzky broke Gordie Howe's all-time NHL regular season goal-scoring record with his 802nd goal on Mar. 23, 1994. The record was the 60th league mark he has either tied or set outright. Gretzky will enter the 1996-97 regular season with 837 goals, 1,771 assists and 2,608 points—all league career records.

Year by Year Statistics

			Regular Season					Playoffs					Awards
Season	Age	Club	Gm	G	A	Pts	PM	Gm	G	A	Pts	PM	
1978-79	18	Indianapolis	8	3	3	6	0	—	—	—	—	—	
		Edmonton	72	43	61	104	19	13	10*	10	20*	2	WHA Top Rookie
1979-80	19	Edmonton	79	51	86*	137†	21	3	2	1	3	0	Hart & Byng
1980-81	20	Edmonton	80	55	109*	164*	28	9	7	14	21	4	Hart & Ross
1981-82	21	Edmonton	80	92*	120*	212*	26	5	5	7	12	8	Hart & Ross
1982-83	22	Edmonton	80	71*	125*	196*	59	16	12	26*	38*	4	Hart & Ross
1983-84	23	Edmonton	74	87*	118*	205*	39	19	13	22*	35*	12	Hart & Ross
1984-85	24	Edmonton	80	73*	135*	208*	52	18	17	30*	47*	4	Hart, Ross & Smythe
1985-86	25	Edmonton	80	52	163*	215*	46	10	8	11	19	2	Hart & Ross
1986-87	26	Edmonton	79	62*	121*	183*	28	21	5	29*	34*	6	Hart & Ross
1987-88	27	Edmonton	64	40	109*	149	24	19	12	31*	43*	16	Smythe
1988-89	28	Los Angeles	78	54	114†	168	26	11	5	17	22	0	Hart
1989-90	29	Los Angeles	73	40	102*	142*	42	7	3	7	10	0	Ross
1990-91	30	Los Angeles	78	41	122*	163*	16	12	4	11	15	2	Ross & Byng
1991-92	31	Los Angeles	74	31	90*	121	34	6	2	5	7	2	Byng
1992-93	32	Los Angeles	45	16	49	65	6	24	15*	25*	40*	4	—
1993-94	33	Los Angeles	81	38	92*	130*	20	—	—	—	—	—	Byng
1995	34	Los Angeles	48	11	37	48	6	—	—	—	—	—	—
1995-96	35	LA, St. Louis	80	23	79	102	34	13	2	14	16	0	—
		WHA totals	80	46	64	110	19	13	10	10	20	2	
		NHL totals	1253	837	1771	2608	507	193	112	250	362	64	

*Led league; †Tied for league lead.

Gretzky vs. Howe

The all-time records of Wayne Gretzky and Gordie Howe, pro hockey's two most prolific scorers. Below are their career records in the NHL, the WHA and the two leagues combined. Howe played with Detroit (1946-71) and Hartford (1979-80) in the NHL and with Houston (1973-77) and New England (1977-79) in the WHA.

	Regular Season						Playoffs						
NHL	Yrs	Gm	G	A	Pts	PM	Yrs	Gm	G	A	Pts	PM	Stanley Cups
Wayne Gretzky	17	1253	837	1771	2608	507	15	193	112	250	362	64	4 (1984-85,87-88)
Gordie Howe	26	1767	801	1049	1850	1685	20	157	68	92	160	220	4 (1950,52,54-55)

	Regular Season						Playoffs						
WHA	Yrs	Gm	G	A	Pts	PM	Yrs	Gm	G	A	Pts	PM	AVCO World Cups
Gordie Howe	6	419	174	334	508	399	6	78	28	43	71	115	2 (1974-75)
Wayne Gretzky	1	80	46	64	110	19	1	13	10	10	20	2	None

	Regular Season						Playoffs					
NHL/WHA	Yrs	Gm	G	A	Pts	PM	Yrs	Gm	G	A	Pts	PM
Wayne Gretzky	18	1333	883	1835	2718	526	16	206	122	260	382	66
Gordie Howe	32	2186	975	1383	2358	2084	26	235	96	135	231	335

All-Time Winningest NHL Coaches

Top 20 NHL career victories through the 1996 season. Career, regular season and playoff records are noted along with NHL titles won. Coaches active during 1996 season in **bold** type.

		Career					Regular Season				Playoffs				
	Yrs	W	L	T	Pct	W	L	T	Pct	W	L	T	Pct	Stanley Cups
1 **Scotty Bowman**	24	**1137**	535	245	.657	975	434	245	.664	162	101	0	.616	6 (1973,76-79,92)
2 Al Arbour	22	**902**	662	246	.566	779	576	246	.563	123	86	0	.589	4 (1980-83)
3 Dick Irvin	26	**790**	609	228	.556	690	521	226	.559	100	88	2	.532	4 (1932,44,46,53)
4 Billy Reay	16	**599**	445	175	.563	542	385	175	.571	57	60	0	.487	None
5 Toe Blake	13	**582**	292	159	.640	500	255	159	.634	82	37	0	.689	8 (1956-60,65-66,68)
6 Glen Sather	11	**553**	305	110	.628	464	268	110	.616	89	37	0	.706	4 (1984-85,87-88)
7 **Mike Keenan**	11	**546**	370	98	.587	455	301	98	.590	91	69	0	.569	1 (1994)
8 Bryan Murray	12	**501**	381	115	.560	467	337	115	.571	34	44	0	.436	None
9 Punch Imlach	15	**467**	421	163	.522	423	373	163	.526	44	48	0	.478	4 (1962-64,67)
10 Jack Adams	21	**465**	442	162	.511	413	390	161	.512	52	52	1	.500	2 (1936-37)
11 Fred Shero	10	**451**	272	119	.606	390	225	119	.612	61	47	0	.565	2 (1974-75)
12 Emile Francis	13	**433**	326	112	.561	393	273	112	.577	40	53	0	.430	None
13 **Jacques Demers**	12	**430**	415	113	.508	375	372	113	.502	55	43	0	.561	1 (1993)
14 Roger Neilson	13	**418**	366	132	.528	381	326	132	.533	37	40	0	.481	None
15 Sid Abel	16	**414**	470	155	.473	382	426	155	.477	32	44	0	.421	None
16 **Pat Quinn**	12	**410**	335	102	.544	357	285	102	.548	53	50	0	.515	None
17 Bob Berry	11	**395**	377	121	.510	384	355	121	.517	11	22	0	.333	None
18 Art Ross	18	**393**	310	95	.552	361	277	90	.558	32	33	5	.493	1 (1939)
19 Michel Bergeron	10	**369**	387	104	.490	338	350	104	.492	31	37	0	.456	None
20 Bob Pulford	11	**364**	348	130	.510	336	305	130	.520	28	43	0	.394	None

Note: The NHL does not recognize records from the World Hockey Association (1972-79), so the following WHA overall coaching records are not included above: **Demers** (155-164-44 in 4 yrs); **Sather** (103-97-1 in 3 yrs).

Where They Coached

Abel—Chicago (1952-54), Detroit (1957-68,69-70), St. Louis (1971-72), Kansas City (1975-76); **Adams**—Toronto (1922-23), Detroit (1927-47); **Arbour**—St. Louis (1970-73), NY Islanders (1973-86,88-94); **Bergeron**—Quebec (1980-87), NY Rangers (1987-89), Quebec (1989-90); **Berry**—Los Angeles (1978-81), Montreal (1981-84), Pittsburgh (1984-87), St. Louis (1992-94); **Blake**—Montreal (1955-68); **Bowman**—St. Louis (1967-71), Montreal (1971-79), Buffalo (1979-87), Pittsburgh (1991-93), Detroit (1993—).

Demers—Quebec (1979-80), St. Louis (1983-86), Detroit (1986-90), Montreal (1992-95); **Francis**—NY Rangers (1965-75), St. Louis (1976-77,81-83); **Imlach**—Toronto (1958-69), Buffalo (1970-72), Toronto (1979-81); **Irvin**—Chicago (1930-31,55-56), Toronto (1931-40), Montreal (1940-55); **Keenan**—Philadelphia (1984-88), Chicago (1988-92), NY Rangers (1993-94), St. Louis (1994—); **Murray**—Washington (1982-90), Detroit (1990-93).

Neilson—Toronto (1977-79), Buffalo (1979-81), Vancouver (1982-83), Los Angeles (1984), NY Rangers (1989-93), Florida (1993-95); **Pulford**—Los Angeles (1972-77), Chicago (1977-79,81-82,85-87); **Quinn**—Philadelphia (1978-82), Los Angeles (1984-87), Vancouver (1990-94, 96); **Reay**—Toronto (1957-59), Chicago (1963-77); **Ross**—Montreal Wanderers (1917-18), Hamilton (1922-23), Boston (1924-28,29-34,36-39,41-45); **Sather**—Edmonton (1979-89, 93-94); **Shero**—Philadelphia (1971-78), NY Rangers (1978-81).

Top Winning Percentages

Minimum of 275 victories, including playoffs.

	Yrs	W	L	T	Pct
1 **Scotty Bowman**	24	1137	535	245	**.657**
2 Toe Blake	13	582	292	159	**.640**
3 Glen Sather	11	553	305	110	**.628**
4 Fred Shero	10	451	272	119	**.606**
5 Don Cherry	6	281	177	77	**.597**
6 Tommy Ivan	9	324	205	111	**.593**
7 **Mike Keenan**	11	546	370	98	**.587**
8 **Pat Burns**	8	360	260	71	**.572**
9 Al Arbour	22	902	662	246	**.566**
10 Billy Reay	16	599	445	175	**.563**
11 Emile Francis	13	433	326	112	**.561**
12 Bryan Murray	12	501	381	115	**.560**
13 Hap Day	10	308	237	81	**.557**
14 Brian Sutter	7	300	233	66	**.556**
15 Dick Irvan	26	790	609	228	**.556**
16 Lester Patrick	13	312	242	115	**.552**
17 Art Ross	18	393	310	95	**.552**
18 Bob Johnson	6	275	223	58	**.547**
19 **Pat Quinn**	12	410	335	102	**.544**
20 **Terry Crisp**	7	276	239	66	**.532**
21 Roger Neilson	13	418	366	132	**.528**
22 Punch Imlach	15	467	421	163	**.522**
23 Jack Adams	21	465	442	162	**.511**
24 Bob Berry	11	395	377	121	**.510**
25 Bob Pulford	11	364	348	130	**.510**

Active Coaches' Victories

Through 1996 season, including playoffs.

	Yrs	W	L	T	Pct
1 Scotty Bowman, Det.	24	**1137**	535	245	.657
2 Mike Keenan, St.L.	11	**546**	370	98	.587
3 Terry Crisp, TB	7	**276**	239	66	.532
4 Terry Murray, Phi	7	**270**	206	45	.561
5 Ed Johnston, Pit	7	**260**	253	74	.506
6 Pierre Page, Calg.	6	**201**	233	60	.468
7 Jacques Lemaire, NJ	5	**196**	138	44	.577
8 Jim Schoenfeld, Wash	7	**170**	163	45	.509
9 Mike Milbury, NYI	3	**135**	116	31	.534
10 Marc Crawford, Col.	2	**95**	48	15	.649
11 Ron Wilson, Ana.	3	**84**	112	18	.435
12 Jacques Martin, Ott.	3	**76**	95	27	.452
13 Colin Campbell, NYR	2	**72**	62	17	.533
14 Doug MacLean, Fla	1	**53**	41	10	.558
15 Craig Hartsburg, Chi.	1	**46**	32	14	.576
16 Mario Tremblay, Mon.	1	**42**	31	10	.566
17 Steve Kasper, Bos.	1	**41**	35	11	.534
18 Ron Low, Edm.	2	**35**	51	9	.416
19 Ted Nolan, Buf	1	**33**	42	7	.445
20 Paul Maurice, Hart.	1	**29**	33	8	.471
21 Larry Robinson, LA	1	**24**	40	18	.402
22 Mike Murphy, Tor.	2	**20**	37	8	.369
23 Ken Hitchcock, Dal.	1	**15**	23	5	.407
24 Tom Renney, Van	0	**0**	0	0	.000
Al Sims, SJ	0	**0**	0	0	.000
Don Hay, Pho.	0	**0**	0	0	.000

Annual Awards

Hart Memorial Trophy

Awarded to the player "adjudged to be the most valuable to his team" and named after Cecil Hart, the former manager-coach of the Montreal Canadiens. Winners selected by Pro Hockey Writers Assn. (PHWA). Winners' scoring statistics or goaltender W-L records and goals against average are provided; (*) indicates led or tied for league lead.

Multiple winners: Wayne Gretzky (9); Gordie Howe (6); Eddie Shore (4); Bobby Clarke, Mario Lemieux, Howie Morenz and Bobby Orr (3); Jean Beliveau, Bill Cowley, Phil Esposito, Bobby Hull, Guy Lafleur, Mark Messier, Stan Mikita and Nels Stewart (2).

Year		G	A	Pts
1924	Frank Nighbor, Ottawa, C	10	3	13
1925	Billy Burch, Hamilton, C	20	4	24
1926	Nels Stewart, Maroons, C	34	8	42*
1927	Herb Gardiner, Mon., D	6	6	12
1928	Howie Morenz, Mon., C	33	18	51*
1929	Roy Worters, NYA, G	16-13-9; 1.21		
1930	Nels Stewart, Maroons, C	39	16	55
1931	Howie Morenz, Mon., C	28	23	51*
1932	Howie Morenz, Mon., C	24	25	49
1933	Eddie Shore, Bos., D	8	27	35
1934	Aurel Joliat, Mon., LW	22	15	37
1935	Eddie Shore, Bos., D	7	26	33
1936	Eddie Shore, Bos., D	3	16	19
1937	Babe Siebert, Mon., D	8	20	28
1938	Eddie Shore, Bos., D	3	14	17
1939	Toe Blake, Mon., LW	24	23	47*
1940	Ebbie Goodfellow, Det., D	11	17	28
1941	Bill Cowley, Bos., C	17	45	62*
1942	Tommy Anderson, NYA, D	12	29	41
1943	Bill Cowley, Bos., C	27	45	72
1944	Babe Pratt, Tor., D	17	40	57
1945	Elmer Lach, Mon., C	26	54	80*
1946	Max Bentley, Chi., C	31	30	61*
1947	Maurice Richard, Mon., RW	45	26	71
1948	Buddy O'Connor, NYR, C	24	36	60
1949	Sid Abel, Det., C	28	26	54
1950	Chuck Rayner, NYR, G	28-30-11; 2.62		
1951	Milt Schmidt, Bos., C	22	39	61
1952	Gordie Howe, Det., RW	47	39	86*
1953	Gordie Howe, Det., RW	49	46	95*
1954	Al Rollins, Chi., G	12-47-7; 3.23		
1955	Ted Kennedy, Tor., C	10	42	52
1956	Jean Beliveau, Mon., C	47	41	88*
1957	Gordie Howe, Det., RW	44	45	89*
1958	Gordie Howe, Det., RW	33	44	77
1959	Andy Bathgate, NYR, RW	40	48	88
1960	Gordie Howe, Det., RW	28	45	73
1961	Bernie Geoffrion, Mon., RW	50	45	95*
1962	Jacques Plante, Mon., G	42-14-14; 2.37*		
1963	Gordie Howe, Det., RW	38	48	86*
1964	Jean Beliveau, Mon., C	28	50	78
1965	Bobby Hull, Chi., LW	39	32	71
1966	Bobby Hull, Chi., LW	54	43	97*
1967	Stan Mikita, Chi., C	35	62	97*
1968	Stan Mikita, Chi., C	40	47	87*
1969	Phil Esposito, Bos., C	49	77	126*
1970	Bobby Orr, Bos., D	33	87	120*
1971	Bobby Orr, Bos., D	37	102	139
1972	Bobby Orr, Bos., D	37	80	117
1973	Bobby Clarke, Phi., C	37	67	104
1974	Phil Esposito, Bos., C	68	77	145*
1975	Bobby Clarke, Phi., C	27	89	116
1976	Bobby Clarke, Phi., C	30	89	119
1977	Guy Lafleur, Mon., RW	56	80	136*
1978	Guy Lafleur, Mon., RW	60	72	132*
1979	Bryan Trottier, NYI., C	47	87	134*
1980	Wayne Gretzky, Edm., C	51	86	137*
1981	Wayne Gretzky, Edm., C	55	109	164*
1982	Wayne Gretzky, Edm., C	92	120	212*
1983	Wayne Gretzky, Edm., C	71	125	196*
1984	Wayne Gretzky, Edm., C	87	118	205*
1985	Wayne Gretzky, Edm., C	73	135	208*
1986	Wayne Gretzky, Edm., C	52	163	215*
1987	Wayne Gretzky, Edm., C	62	121	183*
1988	Mario Lemieux, Pit., C	70	98	168*
1989	Wayne Gretzky, LA, C	54	114	168
1990	Mark Messier, Edm., C	45	84	129
1991	Brett Hull, St. L., RW	86	45	131
1992	Mark Messier, NYR, C	35	72	107
1993	Mario Lemieux, Pit., C	69	91	160*
1994	Sergei Fedorov, Det., C	56	64	120
1995	Eric Lindros, Phi., C	29	41	70*
1996	Mario Lemieux, Pit., C	69	92	161*

Calder Memorial Trophy

Awarded to the most outstanding rookie of the year and named after Frank Calder, the late NHL president (1917-43). Since the 1990-91 season, all eligible candidates must not have attained their 26th birthday by Sept. 15 of their rookie year. Winners selected by PHWA. Winners' scoring statistics or goaltender W-L record & goals against average are provided.

Year		G	A	Pts
1933	Carl Voss, NYR-Det., C	8	15	23
1934	Russ Blinco, Maroons, C	14	9	23
1935	Sweeney Schriner, NYA, LW	18	22	40
1936	Mike Karakas, Chi., G	21-19-8;		1.92
1937	Syl Apps, Tor., C	16	29	45
1938	Cully Dahlstrom, Chi., C	10	9	19
1939	Frankie Brimsek, Bos., G	33-9-1;		1.58
1940	Kilby MacDonald, NYR, LW	15	13	28
1941	John Quilty, Mon., C	18	16	34
1942	Knobby Warwick, NYR, RW	16	17	33
1943	Gaye Stewart, Tor., LW	24	23	47
1944	Gus Bodnar, Tor., C	22	40	62
1945	Frank McCool, Tor., G	24-22-4;		3.22
1946	Edgar Laprade, NYR, C	15	19	34
1947	Howie Meeker, Tor., RW	27	18	45
1948	Jim McFadden, Det., C	24	24	48
1949	Penny Lund, NYR, RW	14	16	30
1950	Jack Gelineau, Bos., G	22-30-15; 3.28		
1951	Terry Sawchuk, Det., G	44-13-13; 1.99		
1952	Bernie Geoffrion, Mon., RW	30	24	54
1953	Gump Worsley, NYR, G	13-29-8;		3.06
1954	Camille Henry, NYR, LW	24	15	39
1955	Ed Litzenberger, Mon-Chi., RW	23	28	51
1956	Glenn Hall, Det., G	30-24-16; 2.11		
1957	Larry Regan, Bos., RW	14	19	33
1958	Frank Mahovlich, Tor., LW	20	16	36
1959	Ralph Backstrom, Mon., C	18	22	40
1960	Billy Hay, Chi., C	18	37	55
1961	Dave Keon, Tor., C	20	25	45
1962	Bobby Rousseau, Mon., RW	21	24	45
1963	Kent Douglas, Tor., D	7	15	22
1964	Jacques Laperriere, Mon., D	2	28	30
1965	Roger Crozier, Det., G	40-23-7;		2.42
1966	Brit Selby, Tor., LW	14	13	27

Year		G	A	Pts
1967	Bobby Orr, Bos., D	13	28	41
1968	Derek Sanderson, Bos., C	24	25	49
1969	Danny Grant, Min., LW	34	31	65
1970	Tony Esposito, Chi., G	38-17-8;		2.17
1971	Gilbert Perreault, Buf., C	38	34	72
1972	Ken Dryden, Mon., G	39-8-15;		2.24
1973	Steve Vickers, NYR, LW	30	23	53
1974	Denis Potvin, NYI, D	17	37	54
1975	Eric Vail, Atl., LW	39	21	60
1976	Bryan Trottier, NYI, C	32	63	95
1977	Willi Plett, Atl., RW	33	23	56
1978	Mike Bossy, NYI, RW	53	38	91
1979	Bobby Smith, Min., C	30	44	74
1980	Ray Bourque, Bos., D	17	48	65
1981	Peter Stastny, Que., C	39	70	109
1982	Dale Hawerchuk, Win., C	45	58	103
1983	Steve Larmer, Chi., RW	43	47	90
1984	Tom Barrasso, Buf., G	26-12-3;		2.84
1985	Mario Lemieux, Pit., C	43	57	100
1986	Gary Suter, Calg., D	18	50	68
1987	Luc Robitaille, LA, LW	45	39	84
1988	Joe Nieuwendyk, Calg., C	51	41	92
1989	Brian Leetch, NYR, D	23	48	71
1990	Sergei Makarov, Calg., RW	24	62	86
1991	Ed Belfour, Chi., G	43-19-7;		2.47
1992	Pavel Bure, Van., RW	34	26	60
1993	Teemu Selanne, Win., RW	76	56	132
1994	Martin Brodeur, NJ, G	27-11-8;		2.40
1995	Peter Forsberg, Que., C	15	35	50
1996	Daniel Alfredsson, Ott., RW	26	35	61

Vezina Trophy

From 1927-80, given to the principal goaltender(s) on the team allowing the fewest goals during the regular season. Trophy named after 1920's goalie Georges Vezina of the Montreal Canadiens, who died of tuberculosis in 1926. Since the 1980-81 season, the trophy has been awarded to the most outstanding goaltender of the year as selected by the league's general managers.

Multiple winners: Jacques Plante (7, one of them shared); Bill Durnan (6); Ken Dryden (5, three shared); Bunny Larocque (4, all shared); Terry Sawchuk (4, one shared); Tiny Thompson (4); Tony Esposito (3, two shared); George Hainsworth (3); Glenn Hall (3, two shared); Patrick Roy (3); Ed Belfour (2); Johnny Bower (2, one shared); Frankie Brimsek (2); Turk Broda (2); Chuck Gardiner (2); Dominik Hasek (2); Charlie Hodge (2, one shared); Bernie Parent (2, one shared); Gump Worsley (2, both shared).

Year		Record	GAA
1927	George Hainsworth, Mon	28-14-2	1.52
1928	George Hainsworth, Mon	26-11-7	1.09
1929	George Hainsworth, Mon	22-7-15	0.98
1930	Tiny Thompson, Bos	38-5-1	2.23
1931	Roy Worters, NYA	18-16-10	1.68
1932	Chuck Gardiner, Chi	18-19-11	1.92
1933	Tiny Thompson, Bos	25-15-8	1.83
1934	Chuck Gardiner, Chi	20-17-11	1.73
1935	Lorne Chabot, Chi	26-17-5	1.83
1936	Tiny Thompson, Bos	22-20-6	1.71
1937	Norm Smith, Det	25-14-9	2.13
1938	Tiny Thompson, Bos	30-11-7	1.85
1939	Frankie Brimsek, Bos	33-9-1	1.58
1940	Dave Kerr, NYR	27-11-10	1.60
1941	Turk Broda, Tor	28-14-6	2.06
1942	Frankie Brimsek, Bos	24-17-6	2.45
1943	John Mowers, Det	25-14-11	2.47
1944	Bill Durnan, Mon	38-5-7	2.18
1945	Bill Durnan, Mon	38-8-4	2.42
1946	Bill Durnan, Mon	24-11-5	2.60
1947	Bill Durnan, Mon	34-16-10	2.30
1948	Turk Broda, Tor	32-15-13	2.38
1949	Bill Durnan, Mon	28-23-9	2.10
1950	Bill Durnan, Mon	26-21-17	2.20
1951	Al Rollins, Tor	27-5-8	1.77
1952	Terry Sawchuk, Det	44-14-12	1.90
1953	Terry Sawchuk, Det	32-15-16	1.90
1954	Harry Lumley, Tor	32-24-13	1.86
1955	Terry Sawchuk, Det	40-17-11	1.96
1956	Jacques Plante, Mon	42-12-10	1.86
1957	Jacques Plante, Mon	31-18-12	2.02
1958	Jacques Plante, Mon	34-14-8	2.11
1959	Jacques Plante, Mon	38-16-13	2.16
1960	Jacques Plante, Mon	40-17-12	2.54
1961	Johnny Bower, Tor	33-15-10	2.50
1962	Jacques Plante, Mon	42-14-14	2.37
1963	Glenn Hall, Chi	30-20-16	2.55
1964	Charlie Hodge, Mon	33-18-11	2.26
1965	Johnny Bower, Tor	13-13-8	2.38
	& Terry Sawchuk, Tor	17-13-6	2.56
1966	Gump Worsley, Mon	29-14-6	2.36
	& Charlie Hodge, Mon	12-7-2	2.58
1967	Glenn Hall, Chi	19-5-5	2.38
	& Denis Dejordy, Chi	22-12-7	2.46
1968	Gump Worsley, Mon	19-9-8	1.98
	& Rogie Vachon, Mon	23-13-2	2.48
1969	Jacques Plante, St.L	18-12-6	1.96
	& Glenn Hall, St.L	19-12-8	2.17
1970	Tony Esposito, Chi	38-17-8	2.17
1971	Ed Giacomin, NYR	27-10-7	2.16
	& Gilles Villemure, NYR	22-8-4	2.30
1972	Tony Esposito, Chi	31-10-6	1.77
	& Gary Smith, Chi	14-5-6	2.42
1973	Ken Dryden, Mon	33-7-13	2.26
1974	(Tie) Bernie Parent, Phi	47-13-12	1.89
	Tony Esposito, Chi	34-14-21	2.04
1975	Bernie Parent, Phi	44-14-10	2.03
1976	Ken Dryden, Mon	42-10-8	2.03
1977	Ken Dryden, Mon	41-6-8	2.14
	& Bunny Larocque, Mon	19-2-4	2.09
1978	Ken Dryden, Mon	37-7-7	2.05
	& Bunny Larocque, Mon.	22-3-4	2.67
1979	Ken Dryden, Mon	30-10-7	2.30
	& Bunny Larocque, Mon.	22-7-4	2.84
1980	Bob Sauve, Buf	20-8-4	2.36
	& Don Edwards, Buf.	27-9-12	2.57
1981	Richard Sevigny, Mon	20-4-3	2.40
	Denis Herron, Mon	6-9-6	3.50
	& Bunny Larocque, Mon.	16-9-3	3.03
1982	Billy Smith, NYI	32-9-4	2.97
1983	Pete Peeters, Bos	40-11-9	2.36
1984	Tom Barrasso, Buf	26-12-3	2.84
1985	Pelle Lindbergh, Phi	40-17-7	3.02
1986	John Vanbiesbrouck, NYR	31-21-5	3.32
1987	Ron Hextall, Phi	37-21-6	3.00
1988	Grant Fuhr, Edm	40-24-9	3.43
1989	Patrick Roy, Mon	33-5-6	2.47
1990	Patrick Roy, Mon	31-16-5	2.53
1991	Ed Belfour, Chi	43-19-7	2.47
1992	Patrick Roy, Mon.	36-22-8	2.36
1993	Ed Belfour, Chi	41-18-11	2.59
1994	Dominik Hasek, Buf	30-20-6	1.95
1995	Dominik Hasek, Buf	19-14-7	2.11
1996	Jim Carey, Wash	35-24-9	2.26

Annual Awards (Cont.)

Lady Byng Memorial Trophy

Awarded to the player "adjudged to have exhibited the best type of sportsmanship and gentlemanly conduct combined with a high standard of playing ability" and named after Lady Evelyn Byng, the wife of former Canadian Governor General (1921-26) Baron Byng of Vimy. Winners selected by PHWA.

Multiple winners: Frank Boucher (7); Wayne Gretzky and Red Kelly (4); Bobby Bauer, Mike Bossy and Alex Delvecchio (3); Johnny Bucyk, Marcel Dionne, Dave Keon, Stan Mikita, Joey Mullen, Frank Nighbor, Jean Ratelle, Clint Smith and Sid Smith (2).

Year	
1925	Frank Nighbor, Ott., C
1926	Frank Nighbor, Ott., C
1927	Billy Burch, NYA, C
1928	Frank Boucher, NYR, C
1929	Frank Boucher, NYR, C
1930	Frank Boucher, NYR, C
1931	Frank Boucher, NYR, C
1932	Joe Primeau, Tor., C
1933	Frank Boucher, NYR, C
1934	Frank Boucher, NYR, C
1935	Frank Boucher, NYR, C
1936	Doc Romnes, Chi., F
1937	Marty Barry, Det., C
1938	Gordie Drillon, Tor., RW
1939	Clint Smith, NYR, C
1940	Bobby Bauer, Bos., RW
1941	Bobby Bauer, Bos., RW
1942	Syl Apps, Tor., C
1943	Max Bentley, Chi., C
1944	Clint Smith, Chi., C
1945	Bill Mosienko, Chi., RW
1946	Toe Blake, Mon., LW
1947	Bobby Bauer, Bos., RW
1948	Buddy O'Connor, NYR, C
1949	Bill Quackenbush, Det., D
1950	Edgar Laprade, NYR, C
1951	Red Kelly, Det., D
1952	Sid Smith, Tor., LW
1953	Red Kelly, Det., D
1954	Red Kelly, Det., D
1955	Sid Smith, Tor., LW
1956	Earl Reibel, Det., C
1957	Andy Hebenton, NYR, RW
1958	Camille Henry, NYR, LW
1959	Alex Delvecchio, Det., LW
1960	Don McKenney, Bos., C
1961	Red Kelly, Tor., D
1962	Dave Keon, Tor., C
1963	Dave Keon, Tor., C
1964	Ken Wharram, Chi., RW
1965	Bobby Hull, Chi., LW
1966	Alex Delvecchio, Det., LW
1967	Stan Mikita, Chi., C
1968	Stan Mikita, Chi., C
1969	Alex Delvecchio, Det., LW
1970	Phil Goyette, St.L., C
1971	Johnny Bucyk, Bos., LW
1972	Jean Ratelle, NYR, C
1973	Gilbert Perreault, Buf., C
1974	Johnny Bucyk, Bos., LW
1975	Marcel Dionne, Det., C
1976	Jean Ratelle, NY-Bos., C
1977	Marcel Dionne, LA, C
1978	Butch Goring, LA, C
1979	Bob MacMillan, Atl., RW
1980	Wayne Gretzky, Edm., C
1981	Rick Kehoe, Pit., RW
1982	Rick Middleton, Bos., RW
1983	Mike Bossy, NYI, RW
1984	Mike Bossy, NYI, RW
1985	Jari Kurri, Edm., RW
1986	Mike Bossy, NYI, RW
1987	Joey Mullen, Calg., RW
1988	Mats Naslund, Mon., LW
1989	Joey Mullen, Calg., RW
1990	Brett Hull, St.L., RW
1991	Wayne Gretzky, LA, C
1992	Wayne Gretzky, LA, C
1993	Pierre Turgeon, NYI, C
1994	Wayne Gretzky, LA, C
1995	Ron Francis, Pit., C
1996	Paul Kariya, Ana., LW

Note: Bill Quackenbush and Red Kelly are the only defensemen to win the Lady Byng.

James Norris Memorial Trophy

Awarded to the most outstanding defenseman of the year and named after James Norris, the late Detroit Red Wings owner-president. Winners selected by PHWA.

Multiple winners: Bobby Orr (8); Doug Harvey (7); Ray Bourque (5); Chris Chelios, Paul Coffey, Pierre Pilote and Denis Potvin (3); Rod Langway and Larry Robinson (2).

Year	
1954	Red Kelly, Detroit
1955	Doug Harvey, Montreal
1956	Doug Harvey, Montreal
1957	Doug Harvey, Montreal
1958	Doug Harvey, Montreal
1959	Tom Johnson, Montreal
1960	Doug Harvey, Montreal
1961	Doug Harvey, Montreal
1962	Doug Harvey, NY Rangers
1963	Pierre Pilote, Chicago
1964	Pierre Pilote, Chicago
1965	Pierre Pilote, Chicago
1966	Jacques Laperriere, Montreal
1967	Harry Howell, NY Rangers
1968	Bobby Orr, Boston
1969	Bobby Orr, Boston
1970	Bobby Orr, Boston
1971	Bobby Orr, Boston
1972	Bobby Orr, Boston
1973	Bobby Orr, Boston
1974	Bobby Orr, Boston
1975	Bobby Orr, Boston
1976	Denis Potvin, NY Islanders
1977	Larry Robinson, Montreal
1978	Denis Potvin, NY Islanders
1979	Denis Potvin, NY Islanders
1980	Larry Robinson, Montreal
1981	Randy Carlyle, Pittsburgh
1982	Doug Wilson, Chicago
1983	Rod Langway, Washington
1984	Rod Langway, Washington
1985	Paul Coffey, Edmonton
1986	Paul Coffey, Edmonton
1987	Ray Bourque, Boston
1988	Ray Bourque, Boston
1989	Chris Chelios, Montreal
1990	Ray Bourque, Boston
1991	Ray Bourque, Boston
1992	Brian Leetch, NY Rangers
1993	Chris Chelios, Chicago
1994	Ray Bourque, Boston
1995	Paul Coffey, Detroit
1996	Chris Chelios, Chicago

Frank Selke Trophy

Awarded to the outstanding defensive forward of the year and named after the late Montreal Canadiens general manager. Winners selected by the PHWA.

Multiple winners: Bob Gainey (4); Guy Carbonneau (3); Sergei Fedorov (2).

Year	
1978	Bob Gainey, Mon., LW
1979	Bob Gainey, Mon., LW
1980	Bob Gainey, Mon., LW
1981	Bob Gainey, Mon., LW
1982	Steve Kasper, Bos., C
1983	Bobby Clarke, Phi., C
1984	Doug Jarvis, Wash., C
1985	Craig Ramsay, Buf., LW
1986	Troy Murray, Chi., C
1987	Dave Poulin, Phi., C
1988	Guy Carbonneau, Mon., C
1989	Guy Carbonneau, Mon., C
1990	Rick Meagher, St.L., C
1991	Dirk Graham, Chi., RW
1992	Guy Carbonneau, Mon., C
1993	Doug Gilmour, Tor., C
1994	Sergei Fedorov, Det., C
1995	Ron Francis, Pit., C
1996	Sergei Fedorov, Det., C

Jack Adams Award

Awarded to the coach "adjudged to have contributed the most to his team's success" and named after the late Detroit Red Wings coach and general manager. Winners selected by NHL Broadcasters' Assn.; (*) indicates division champion.

Multiple winners: Scotty Bowman, Jacques Demers and Pat Quinn (2).

Year		Improvement		
1974	Fred Shero, Phi	37-30-11	to	50-16-12*
1975	Bob Pulford, LA	41-14-23	to	37-35- 8
1976	Don Cherry, Bos	40-26-14	to	48-15-17*
1977	Scotty Bowman, Mon	58-11-11*	to	60- 8-12*
1978	Bobby Kromm, Det	16-55- 9	to	32-34-14
1979	Al Arbour, NYI	48-17-15*	to	51-15-14*
1980	Pat Quinn, Phi	40-25-15	to	48-12-20*
1981	Red Berenson, St.L	34-34-12	to	45-18-17*
1982	Tom Watt, Win	9-57-14	to	33-33-14
1983	Orval Tessier, Chi	30-38-12	to	47-23-10*
1984	Bryan Murray, Wash	39-25-16	to	48-27- 5
1985	Mike Keenan, Phi	44-26-10	to	53-20- 7*
1986	Glen Sather, Edm	49-20-11*	to	56-17- 7*
1987	Jacques Demers, Det	17-57- 6	to	34-36-10
1988	Jacques Demers, Det	34-36-10	to	41-28-11*
1989	Pat Burns, Mon	45-22-13	to	53-18- 9*
1990	Bob Murdoch, Win	26-42-12	to	37-32-11
1991	Brian Sutter, St.L	37-34- 9	to	47-22-11
1992	Pat Quinn, Van	28-43- 9	to	42-26-12*
1993	Pat Burns, Tor	30-43-7	to	44-29-11
1994	Jacques Lemaire, NJ	40-37-7	to	47-25-12
1995	Marc Crawford, Que	34-42- 8	to	30-13-5*
1996	Scotty Bowman, Det	33-11-4*	to	62-13-7*

Lester Pearson Award

Awarded to the season's most outstanding player and named after the former diplomat, Nobel Peace Prize winner and Canadian prime minister. Winners selected by the NHL Players Assn.

Multiple winners: Wayne Gretzky (5); Mario Lemieux (4); Guy Lafleur (3); Marcel Dionne, Phil Esposito and Mark Messier (2).

Year	
1971	Phil Esposito, Bos., C
1972	Jean Ratelle, NYR, C
1973	Bobby Clarke, Phi., C
1974	Phil Esposito, Bos., C
1975	Bobby Orr, Bos., D
1976	Guy Lafleur, Mon., RW
1977	Guy Lafleur, Mon., RW
1978	Guy Lafleur, Mon., RW
1979	Marcel Dionne, LA, C
1980	Marcel Dionne, LA, C
1981	Mike Liut, St.L., G
1982	Wayne Gretzky, Edm., C
1983	Wayne Gretzky, Edm., C
1984	Wayne Gretzky, Edm., C
1985	Wayne Gretzky, Edm., C
1986	Mario Lemiuex, Pit., C
1987	Wayne Gretzky, Edm., C
1988	Mario Lemieux, Pit., C
1989	Steve Yzerman, Det., C
1990	Mark Messier, Edm., C
1991	Brett Hull, St.L., RW
1992	Mark Messier, NYR, C
1993	Mario Lemieux, Pit., C
1994	Sergei Fedorov, Det., C
1995	Eric Lindros, Phi., C
1996	Mario Lemieux, Pit., C

Bill Masterton Trophy

Awarded to the player who "best exemplifies the qualities of perseverance, sportsmanship and dedication to hockey" and named after the 29-year-old rookie center of the Minnesota North Stars who died of a head injury sustained in a 1968 NHL game. Presented by the PHWA.

Year	
1968	Claude Provost, Mon., RW
1969	Ted Hampson, Oak., C
1970	Pit Martin, Chi., C
1971	Jean Ratelle, NYR, C
1972	Bobby Clarke, Phi., C
1973	Lowell MacDonald, Pit., RW
1974	Henri Richard, Mon., C
1975	Don Luce, Buf., C
1976	Rod Gilbert, NYR, RW
1977	Ed Westfall, NYI, RW
1978	Butch Goring, LA, C
1979	Serge Savard, Mon., D
1980	Al MacAdam, Min., RW
1981	Blake Dunlop, St.L., C
1982	Chico Resch, Colo., G
1983	Lanny McDonald, Calg., RW
1984	Brad Park, Det., D
1985	Anders Hedberg, NYR, RW
1986	Charlie Simmer, Bos., LW
1987	Doug Jarvis, Hart., C
1988	Bob Bourne, LA, C
1989	Tim Kerr, Phi., C
1990	Gord Kluzak, Bos., D
1991	Dave Taylor, LA, RW
1992	Mark Fitzpatrick, NYI, G
1993	Mario Lemieux, Pit., C
1994	Cam Neely, Bos., RW
1995	Pat LaFontaine, Buf., C
1996	Gary Roberts, Calg., LW

Number One Draft Choices

Overall first choices in the NHL Draft since the league staged its first universal amateur draft in 1969. Players are listed with team that selected them; those who became Rookie of the Year are in **bold** type.

Year	
1969	Rejean Houle, Mon., LW
1970	**Gilbert Perreault,** Buf., C
1971	Guy Lafleur, Mon., RW
1972	Billy Harris, NYI, RW
1973	**Denis Potvin,** NYI, D
1974	Greg Joly, Wash., D
1975	Mel Bridgman, Phi., C
1976	Rick Green, Wash., D
1977	Dale McCourt, Det., C
1978	**Bobby Smith**, Min., C
1979	Rob Ramage, Colo., D
1980	Doug Wickenheiser, Mon., C
1981	**Dale Hawerchuk,** Win., C
1982	Gord Kluzak, Bos., D
1983	Brian Lawton, Min., C
1984	**Mario Lemieux,** Pit., C
1985	Wendel Clark, Tor., LW/D
1986	Joe Murphy, Det., C
1987	Pierre Turgeon, Buf., C
1988	Mike Modano, Min., C
1989	Mats Sundin, Que., RW
1990	Owen Nolan, Que., RW
1991	Eric Lindros, Que., C
1992	Roman Hamrlik, TB, D
1993	Alexandre Daigle, Ott., C
1994	Ed Jovanovski, Fla., D
1995	Bryan Berard, Ott., D
1996	Chris Phillips, Ott., D

World Hockey Association

WHA Finals

The World Hockey Association began play in 1972-73 as a 12-team rival of the 56-year-old NHL. The WHA played for the Avco World Trophy in its seven playoff finals (Avco Financial Services underwrote the playoffs).

Multiple winners: Winnipeg (3); Houston (2).

Year	Winner	Head Coach	Series	Loser	Head Coach
1973	New England Whalers	Jack Kelley	4-1 (WWLWW)	Winnipeg Jets	Bobby Hull
1974	Houston Aeros	Bill Dineen	4-0	Chicago Cougars	Pat Stapleton
1975	Houston Aeros	Bill Dineen	4-0	Quebec Nordiques	Jean-Guy Gendron
1976	Winnipeg Jets	Bobby Kromm	4-0	Houston Aeros	Bill Dineen
1977	Quebec Nordiques	Marc Boileau	4-3 (LWLWWLW)	Winnipeg Jets	Bobby Kromm
1978	Winnipeg Jets	Larry Hillman	4-0	NE Whalers	Harry Neale
1979	Winnipeg Jets	Larry Hillman	4-2 (WWLWLW)	Edmonton Oilers	Glen Sather

Playoff MVPs—1973—No award; **1974**—No award; **1975**—Ron Grahame, Houston, G; **1976**—Ulf Nilsson, Winnipeg, C; **1977**—Serg Bernier, Quebec, C; **1978**—Bobby Guindon, Winnipeg, C; **1979**—Rich Preston, Winnipeg, RW.

Most Valuable Player

(Gordie Howe Trophy, 1976-79)

Year		G	A	Pts
1973	Bobby Hull, Win., LW	51	52	103
1974	Gordie Howe, Hou., RW	31	69	100
1975	Bobby Hull, Win., LW	77	65	142
1976	Marc Tardif, Que., LW	71	77	148
1977	Robbie Ftorek, Pho., C	46	71	117
1978	Marc Tardif, Que., LW	65	89	154
1979	Dave Dryden, Edm., G	41-17-2; 2.89		

Scoring Leaders

Year		Gm	G	A	Pts
1973	Andre Lacroix, Phi	78	50	74	124
1974	Mike Walton, Min	78	57	60	117
1975	Andre Lacroix, S. Diego	78	41	106	147
1976	Marc Tardif, Que	81	71	77	148
1977	Real Cloutier, Que	76	66	75	141
1978	Marc Tardif, Que	78	65	89	154
1979	Real Cloutier, Que	77	75	54	129

Note: In 1979, 18 year-old Rookie of the Year Wayne Gretzky finished third in scoring (46-64—110).

Rookie of the Year

Year		G	A	Pts
1973	Terry Caffery, N. Eng., C	39	61	100
1974	Mark Howe, Hou., LW	38	41	79
1975	Anders Hedberg, Win., RW	53	47	100
1976	Mark Napier, Tor., RW	43	50	93
1977	George Lyle, N. Eng., LW	39	33	72
1978	Kent Nilsson, Win., C	42	65	107
1979	Wayne Gretzky, Ind.-Edm., C	46	64	110

Best Goaltender

Year		Record	GAA
1973	Gerry Cheevers, Cleveland	32-20-0	2.84
1974	Don McLeod, Houston	33-13-3	2.56
1975	Ron Grahame, Houston	33-10-0	3.03
1976	Michel Dion, Indianapolis	14-15-1	2.74
1977	Ron Grahame, Houston	27-10-2	2.74
1978	Al Smith, New England	30-20-3	3.22
1979	Dave Dryden, Edmonton	41-17-2	2.89

Best Defenseman

Year	
1973	J.C. Tremblay, Quebec
1974	Pat Stapleton, Chicago
1975	J.C. Tremblay, Quebec
1976	Paul Shmyr, Cleveland
1977	Ron Plumb, Cincinnati
1978	Lars-Erik Sjoberg, Winnipeg
1979	Rick Ley, New England

Coach of the Year

Year		Improvement
1973	Jack Kelley, N. Eng	46-30-2*
1974	Billy Harris, Tor	35-39-4 to 41-33-4
1975	Sandy Hucul, Pho	Expan. to 39-31-8
1976	Bobby Kromm, Win	38-35-5 to 52-27-2*
1977	Bill Dineen, Hou	53-27-0* to 50-24-6*
1978	Bill Dineen, Hou	50-24-6* to 42-34-4
1979	John Brophy, Birm	36-41-3 to 32-42-6

*Won Division.

WHA All-Star Game

The WHA All-Star Game was an Eastern Division vs Western Division contest from 1973-75. In 1976, the league's five Canadian-based teams played the nine teams in the US. Over the final three seasons—East played West in 1977; AVCO Cup champion Quebec played a WHA All-Star team in 1978; and in 1979, a full WHA All-Star team played a three-game series with Moscow Dynamo of the Soviet Union.

Year	Result	Host	Coaches	Most Valuable Player
1973	East 6, West 2	Quebec	Jack Kelley, Bobby Hull	Wayne Carleton, Ottawa
1974	East 8, West 4	St. Paul, MN	Jack Kelley, Bobby Hull	Mike Walton, Minnesota
1975	West 6, East 4	Edmonton	Bill Dineen, Ron Ryan	Rejean Houle, Quebec
1976	Canada 6, USA 1	Cleveland	Jean-Guy Gendron, Bill Dineen	Can—Real Cloutier, Que. USA—Paul Shmyr, Cleve.
1977	East 4, West 2	Hartford	Jacques Demers, Bobby Kromm	East—L. Levasseur, Min. West—W. Lindstrom, Win.
1978	Quebec 5, WHA 4	Quebec	Marc Boileau, Bill Dineen	Quebec—Marc Tardif WHA—Mark Howe, NE
1979	WHA def. Moscow Dynamo 3 games to none (4-2, 4-2, 4-3)	Edmonton	Larry Hillman, P. Iburtovich	No awards

World Championship

The World Hockey Championship tournament has been played regularly since 1930. The International Ice Hockey Federation (IIHF), which governs both the World and Winter Olympic tournaments, considers the Olympic champions from 1920-68 to also be the World champions. However the IIHF has not recognized an Olympic champion as World champion since 1968. The IIHF has sanctioned separate World Championships in Olympic years three times—in 1972, 1976 and again in 1992. The World championship is officially vacant for the three Olympic years from 1980-88.

Multiple winners: Soviet Union/Russia (23); Canada (20); Czechoslovakia and Sweden (6); USA (2).

Year		Year		Year		Year	
1920	Canada	1949	Czechoslovakia	1965	Soviet Union	1981	Soviet Union
1924	Canada	1950	Canada	1966	Soviet Union	1982	Soviet Union
1928	Canada	1951	Canada	1967	Soviet Union	1983	Soviet Union
1930	Canada	1952	Canada	1968	Soviet Union	1984	Not held
1931	Canada	1953	Sweden	1969	Soviet Union	1985	Czechoslovakia
1932	Canada	1954	Soviet Union	1970	Soviet Union	1986	Soviet Union
1933	United States	1955	Canada	1971	Soviet Union	1987	Sweden
1934	Canada	1956	Soviet Union	1972	Czechoslovakia	1988	Not held
1935	Canada	1957	Sweden	1973	Soviet Union	1989	Soviet Union
1936	Great Britain	1958	Canada	1974	Soviet Union	1990	Soviet Union
1937	Canada	1959	Canada	1975	Soviet Union	1991	Sweden
1938	Canada	1960	United States	1976	Czechoslovakia	1992	Sweden
1939	Canada	1961	Canada	1977	Czechoslovakia	1993	Russia
1940-46	Not held	1962	Sweden	1978	Soviet Union	1994	Canada
1947	Czechoslovakia	1963	Soviet Union	1979	Soviet Union	1995	Finland
1948	Canada	1964	Soviet Union	1980	Not held	1996	Czech Republic

Canada vs. USSR Summits

The first competition between the Soviet National Team and the NHL took place Sept. 2-28, 1972. A team of NHL All-Stars emerged as the winner of the heralded 8-game series, but just barely—winning with a record of 4-3-1 after trailing 1-3-1.

Two years later a WHA All-Star team played the Soviet Nationals and could win only one game and tie three others in eight contests. Two other Canada vs USSR series took place during NHL All-Star breaks: the three-game Challenge Cup at New York in 1979, and the two-game Rendez-Vous '87 in Quebec City in 1987.

The NHL All-Stars played the USSR in a three-game Challenge Cup series in 1979.

1972 Team Canada vs. USSR

NHL All-Stars vs Soviet National Team.

Date	City	Result	Goaltenders
9/2	Montreal	USSR, 7-3	Tretiak/Dryden
9/4	Toronto	Canada, 4-1	Esposito/Tretiak
9/6	Winnipeg	Tie, 4-4	Tretiak/Esposito
9/8	Vancouver	USSR, 5-3	Tretiak/Dryden
9/22	Moscow	USSR, 5-4	Tretiak/Esposito
9/24	Moscow	Canada, 3-2	Dryden/Tretiak
9/26	Moscow	Canada, 4-3	Esposito/Tretiak
9/28	Moscow	Canada, 6-5	Dryden/Tretiak

Standings

	W	L	T	Pts	GF	GA
Team Canada (NHL)	4	3	1	9	32	32
Soviet Union	3	4	1	7	32	32

Leading Scorers

1. Phil Esposito, Canada, (7-6—13); **2.** Aleksandr Yakushev, USSR (7-4—11); **3.** Paul Henderson, Canada (7-2—9); **4.** Boris Shadrin, USSR (3-5—8); **5.** Valeri Kharlamov, USSR (3-4—7) and Vladimir Petrov, USSR (3-4—7); **7.** Bobby Clarke, Canada (2-4—6) and Yuri Liapkin, USSR (1-5—6).

1974 Team Canada vs. USSR

WHA All-Stars vs Soviet National Team.

Date	City	Result	Goaltenders
9/17	Quebec City	Tie, 3-3	Tretiak/Cheevers
9/19	Toronto	Canada, 4-1	Cheevers/Tretiak
9/21	Winnipeg	USSR, 8-5	Tretiak/McLeod
9/23	Vancouver	Tie, 5-5	Tretiak/Cheevers
10/1	Moscow	USSR, 3-2	Tretiak/Cheevers
10/3	Moscow	USSR, 5-2	Tretiak/Cheevers
10/5	Moscow	Tie, 4-4	Cheevers/Tretiak
10/6	Moscow	USSR, 3-2	Sidelinkov/Cheevers

Standings

	W	L	T	Pts	GF	GA
Soviet Union	4	1	3	11	32	27
Team Canada (WHA)	1	4	3	5	27	32

Leading Scorers

1. Bobby Hull, Canada (7-2—9); **2.** Aleksandr Yakushev, USSR (6-2—8), Ralph Backstrom, Canada (4-4—8) and Valeri Kharlamov, USSR (2-6—8); **5.** Gordie Howe, Canada (3-4—7), Andre Lacroix, Canada (1-6—7) and Vladimir Petrov, USSR (1-6—7).

1979 Challenge Cup Series

NHL All-Stars vs Soviet National Team

Date	City	Result	Goaltenders
2/8	New York	NHL, 4-2	K. Dryden/Tretiak
2/10	New York	USSR, 5-4	Tretiak/K. Dryden
2/11	New York	USSR, 6-0	Myshkin/Cheevers

Rendez-Vous '87

NHL All-Stars vs Soviet National Team

Date	City	Result	Goaltenders
2/11	Quebec	NHL, 4-3	Fuhr/Belosheykhin
2/13	Quebec	USSR, 5-3	Belosheykhin/Fuhr

The Canada Cup

After organizing the historic 8-game Team Canada-Soviet Union series of 1972, NHL Players Association executive director Alan Eagleson and the NHL created the Canada Cup in 1976. For the first time, the best players from the world's six major hockey powers—Canada, Czechoslovakia, Finland, Russia, Sweden and the USA competed together in one tournament.

1976

Round Robin Standings

	W	L	T	Pts	GF	GA
Canada	4	1	0	8	22	6
Czechoslovakia	3	1	1	7	19	9
Soviet Union	2	2	1	5	23	14
Sweden	2	2	1	5	16	18
United States	1	3	1	3	14	21
Finland	1	4	0	2	16	42

Finals (Best of 3)

Date	City	Score
9/13	Toronto	Canada 6, Czechoslovakia 0
9/15	Montreal	Canada 5, Czechoslovakia 4 (OT)

Note: Darryl Sittler scored the winning goal for Canada at 11:33 in overtime to clinch the Cup, 2 games to none.

Leading Scorers

1. Victor Hluktov, USSR (5-4—9), Bobby Orr, Canada (2-7—9) and Denis Potvin, Canada (1-8—9); **4.** Bobby Hull, Canada (5-3—8) and Milan Novy, Czechoslovakia (5-3—8).

Team MVPs

Canada—Rogie Vachon
Czech.—Milan Novy
USSR—Alexandr Maltsev
Sweden—Borje Salming
USA—Robbie Ftorek
Finland—Matti Hagman

Tournament MVP—Bobby Orr, Canada

1981

Round Robin Standings

	W	L	T	Pts	GF	GA
Canada	4	0	1	9	32	13
Soviet Union	3	1	1	7	20	13
Czechoslovakia	2	1	2	6	21	13
United States	2	2	1	5	17	19
Sweden	1	4	0	2	13	20
Finland	0	4	1	1	6	31

Semifinals

Date	City	Score
9/11	Ottawa	USSR 4, Czechoslovakia 1
9/11	Montreal	Canada 4, United States 1

Finals

Date	City	Score
9/13	Montreal	USSR 8, Canada 1

Leading Scorers

1. Wayne Gretzky, Canada (5-7—12); **2.** Mike Bossy, Canada (8-3—11), Bryan Trottier, Canada (3-8—11), Guy Lafleur, Canada (2-9—11), Alexei Kasatonov, USSR (1-10—11).

All-Star Team

Goal—Vladislav Tretiak, USSR; **Defense**—Arnold Kadlec, Czech. and Alexei Kasatonov, USSR; **Forwards**—Mike Bossy, Canada, Gil Perreault, Canada, and Sergei Shepelev, USSR. **Tournament MVP**—Tretiak.

1984

Round Robin Standings

	W	L	T	Pts	GF	GA
Soviet Union	5	0	0	10	22	7
United States	3	1	1	7	21	13
Sweden	3	2	0	6	15	16
Canada	2	2	1	5	23	18
West Germany	0	4	1	1	13	29
Czechoslovakia	0	4	1	1	10	21

Semifinals

Date	City	Score
9/12	Edmonton	Sweden 9, United States 2
9/15	Montreal	Canada 3, USSR 2 (OT)

Note: Mike Bossy scored the winning goal for Canada at 12:29 in overtime.

Finals (Best of 3)

Date	City	Score
9/16	Calgary	Canada 5, Sweden 2
9/18	Edmonton	Canada 6, Sweden 5

Leading Scorers

1. Wayne Gretzky, Canada (5-7—12); **2.** Michel Goulet, Canada (5-6—11), Kent Nilsson, Sweden (3-8—11), Paul Coffey, Canada (3-8—11); **5.** Hakan Loob, Sweden (6-4—10).

All-Star Team

Goal—Vladimir Myshkin, USSR; **Defense**—Paul Coffey, Canada and Rod Langway, USA; **Forwards**—Wayne Gretzky, Canada, John Tonelli, Canada, and Sergei Makarov, USSR. **Tournament MVP**—Tonelli

1987

Round Robin Standings

	W	L	T	Pts	GF	GA
Canada	3	0	2	8	19	13
Soviet Union	3	1	1	7	22	13
Sweden	3	2	0	6	17	14
Czechoslovakia	2	2	1	5	12	15
United States	2	3	0	4	13	14
Finland	0	5	0	0	9	23

Semifinals

Date	City	Score
9/8	Hamilton	USSR 4, Sweden 2
9/9	Montreal	Canada 5, Czechoslovakia 3

Finals (Best of 3)

Date	City	Score
9/11	Montreal	USSR 6, Canada 5 (OT)
9/13	Hamilton	Canada 6, USSR 5 (2 OT)
9/15	Hamilton	Canada 6, USSR 5

Note: In Game 1, Alexander Semak of USSR scored at 5:33 in overtime. In Game 2, Mario Lemieux of Canada scored at 10:07 in the second overtime period. Lemieux also won Game 3 on a goal with 1:26 left in regulation time.

Leading Scorers

1. Wayne Gretzky, Canada (3-18—21); **2.** Mario Lemieux, Canada (11-7—18); **3.** Sergei Makarov, USSR (7-8—15); **4.** Vladimir Krutov, USSR (7-7—14); **5.** Viacheslav Bykov, USSR (2-7—9); **6.** Ray Bourque, Canada (2-6—8).

All-Star Team

Goal—Grant Fuhr, Canada; **Defense**—Ray Bourque, Canada and Viacheslav Fetisov, USSR; **Forwards**—Wayne Gretzky, Canada, Mario Lemieux, Canada, and Vladimir Krutov, USSR. **Tournament MVP**—Gretzky.

1991

Round Robin Standings

	W	L	T	Pts	GF	GA
Canada	3	0	2	8	21	11
United States	4	1	0	8	19	15
Finland	2	2	1	5	10	13
Sweden	2	3	0	4	13	17
Soviet Union	1	3	1	3	14	14
Czechoslovakia	1	4	0	2	11	18

Leading Scorers

1. Wayne Gretzky, Canada (4-8—12); **2.** Steve Larmer, Canada (6-5—11); **3.** Brett Hull, USA (2-7—9); **4.** Mike Modano, USA (2-7—9); **5.** Mark Messier, Canada (2-6—8).

Semifinals

Date	City	Score
9/11	Hamilton	United States 7, Finland 3
9/12	Toronto	Canada 4, Sweden 0

Finals (Best of 3)

Date	City	Score
9/14	Montreal	Canada 4, United States 1
9/16	Hamilton	Canada 4, United States 2

All-Star Team

Goal—Bill Ranford, Canada; **Defense**—Al MacInnis, Canada and Chris Chelios, USA; **Forwards**—Wayne Gretzky, Canada, Jeremy Roenick, USA and Mats Sundin, Sweden. **Tournament MVP**—Bill Ranford.

U.S. DIVISION I COLLEGE HOCKEY

NCAA Final Four

The NCAA Division I hockey tournament began in 1948 and was played at the Broadmoor Ice Palace in Colorado Springs from 1948-57. Since 1958, the tournament has moved around the country, stopping for consecutive years only at Boston Garden from 1972-74. Consolation games to determine third place were played from 1949-89 and discontinued in 1990.

Multiple Winners: Michigan (8); Denver, North Dakota and Wisconsin (5); Boston University (4); Lake Superior St., Michigan Tech and Minnesota (3); Colorado College, Cornell, Michigan St. and RPI (2).

Year	Champion	Head Coach	Score	Runner-up	Third Place
1948	Michigan	Vic Heyliger	8-4	Dartmouth	Colorado College and Boston College

Year	Champion	Head Coach	Score	Runner-up	Third Place	Score	Fourth Place
1949	Boston College	Snooks Kelley	4-3	Dartmouth	Michigan	10-4	Colorado Col.
1950	Colorado College	Cheddy Thompson	13-4	Boston Univ.	Michigan	10-6	Boston Col.
1951	Michigan	Vic Heyliger	7-1	Brown	Boston U.	7-4	Colorado Col.
1952	Michigan	Vic Heyliger	4-1	Colorado Col.	Yale	4-1	St. Lawrence
1953	Michigan	Vic Heyliger	7-3	Minnesota	RPI	6-3	Boston Univ.
1954	RPI	Ned Harkness	5-4*	Minnesota	Michigan	7-2	Boston Col.
1955	Michigan	Vic Heyliger	5-3	Colorado Col.	Harvard	6-3	St. Lawrence
1956	Michigan	Vic Heyliger	7-5	Michigan Tech	St. Lawrence	6-2	Boston Col.
1957	Colorado College	Tom Bedecki	13-6	Michigan	Clarkson	2-1†	Harvard
1958	Denver	Murray Armstrong	6-2	North Dakota	Clarkson	5-1	Harvard
1959	North Dakota	Bob May	4-3*	Michigan St.	Boston Col.	7-6†	St. Lawrence
1960	Denver	Murray Armstrong	5-3	Michigan Tech	Boston Univ.	7-6	St. Lawrence
1961	Denver	Murray Armstrong	12-2	St. Lawrence	Minnesota	4-3	RPI
1962	Michigan Tech	John MacInnes	7-1	Clarkson	Michigan	5-1	St. Lawrence
1963	North Dakota	Barry Thorndycraft	6-5	Denver	Clarkson	5-3	Boston Col.
1964	Michigan	Allen Renfrew	6-3	Denver	RPI	2-1	Providence
1965	Michigan Tech	John MacInnes	8-2	Boston Col.	North Dakota	9-5	Brown
1966	Michigan St.	Amo Bessone	6-1	Clarkson	Denver	4-3	Boston Univ.
1967	Cornell	Ned Harkness	4-1	Boston Univ.	Michigan St.	6-1	North Dakota
1968	Denver	Murray Armstrong	4-0	North Dakota	Cornell	6-1	Boston Col.
1969	Denver	Murray Armstrong	4-3	Cornell	Harvard	6-5†	Michigan Tech
1970	Cornell	Ned Harkness	6-4	Clarkson	Wisconsin	6-5	Michigan Tech
1971	Boston University	Jack Kelley	4-2	Minnesota	Denver	1-0	Harvard
1972	Boston University	Jack Kelley	4-0	Cornell	Wisconsin	5-2	Denver
1973	Wisconsin	Bob Johnson	4-2	Denver	Boston Col.	3-1	Cornell
1974	Minnesota	Herb Brooks	4-2	Michigan Tech	Boston Univ.	7-5	Harvard
1975	Michigan Tech	John MacInnes	6-1	Minnesota	Boston Univ.	10-5	Harvard
1976	Minnesota	Herb Brooks	6-4	Michigan Tech	Brown	8-7	Boston Univ.
1977	Wisconsin	Bob Johnson	6-5*	Michigan	Boston Univ.	6-5	New Hampshire
1978	Boston University	Jack Parker	5-3	Boston Col.	Bowling Green	4-3	Wisconsin
1979	Minnesota	Herb Brooks	4-3	North Dakota	Dartmouth	7-3	New Hampshire
1980	North Dakota	Gino Gasparini	5-2	Northern Mich.	Dartmouth	8-4	Cornell
1981	Wisconsin	Bob Johnson	6-3	Minnesota	Michigan Tech	5-2	Northern Mich.
1982	North Dakota	Gino Gasparini	5-2	Wisconsin	Northeastern	10-4	New Hampshire
1983	Wisconsin	Jeff Sauer	6-2	Harvard	Providence	4-3	Minnesota
1984	Bowling Green	Jerry York	5-4*	Minn-Duluth	North Dakota	6-5†	Michigan St.
1985	RPI	Mike Addesa	2-1	Providence	Minn-Duluth	7-6†	Boston Col.
1986	Michigan St.	Ron Mason	6-5	Harvard	Minnesota	6-4	Denver
1987	North Dakota	Gino Gasparini	5-3	Michigan St.	Minnesota	6-3	Harvard
1988	Lake Superior St.	Frank Anzalone	4-3*	St. Lawrence	Maine	5-2	Minnesota
1989	Harvard	Billy Cleary	4-3*	Minnesota	Michigan St.	7-4	Maine

†Consolation game overtimes ended in 1st OT except in 1957, '59 and '69, which all ended in 2nd OT.

NCAA Final Four (Cont.)

Year	Champion	Head Coach	Score	Runner-up	Third Place
1990	Wisconsin	Jeff Sauer	7-3	Colgate	Boston College and Boston University
1991	Northern Michigan	Rick Comley	8-7*	Boston Univ.	Maine and Clarkson
1992	Lake Superior St.	Jeff Jackson	5-3	Wisconsin	Michigan and Michigan St.
1993	Maine	Shawn Walsh	5-4	Lake Superior St.	Boston University and Michigan
1994	Lake Superior St.	Jeff Jackson	9-1	Boston Univ.	Harvard and Minnesota
1995	Boston University	Jack Parker	6-2	Maine	Michigan and Minnesota
1996	Michigan	Red Berenson	3-2*	Colorado Col.	Vermont and Boston University

***Championship game overtime goals:** **1954**—1:54; **1959**—4:22; **1977**—0: 23; **1984**—7:11 in 4th OT; **1988**—4:46; **1989**—4:16; **1991**—1:57 in 3rd OT; **1996**—3:35.

Note: Runners-up Denver (1973) and Wisconsin (1992) had participation voided by the NCAA for using ineligible players.

Most Outstanding Player

The Most Outstanding Players of each NCAA Div. I tournament since 1948. Winners of the award who did not play for the tournament champion are in **bold** type. In 1960, three players, none on the winning team, shared the award.

Multiple winners: Lou Angotti and Marc Behrend (2).

Year	
1948	**Joe Riley**, Dartmouth, F
1949	**Dick Desmond**, Dart., G
1950	**Ralph Bevins**, Boston U., G
1951	**Ed Whiston**, Brown, G
1952	**Ken Kinsley**, Colo. Col., G
1953	John Matchefts, Mich., F
1954	Abbie Moore, RPI, F
1955	**Phil Hilton**, Colo. Col., D
1956	Lorne Howes, Mich., G
1957	Bob McCusker, Colo. Col., F
1958	Murray Massier, Denver, F
1959	Reg Morelli, N. Dakota, F
1960	**Lou Angotti**, Mich. Tech, F; **Bob Marquis**, Boston U., F; & **Barry Urbanski**, Boston U., G
1961	Bill Masterton, Denver, F
1962	Lou Angotti, Mich. Tech, F
1963	Al McLean, N. Dakota, F
1964	Bob Gray, Michigan, G
1965	Gary Milroy, Mich. Tech, F
1966	Gaye Cooley, Mich. St., G
1967	Walt Stanowski, Cornell, D
1968	Gerry Powers, Denver, G
1969	Keith Magnuson, Denver, D
1970	Dan Lodboa, Cornell, D
1971	Dan Brady, Boston U., G
1972	Tim Regan, Boston, U., G
1973	Dean Talafous, Wisc., F
1974	Brad Shelstad, Minn., G
1975	Jim Warden, Mich. Tech, G
1976	Tom Vanelli, Minn., F
1977	Julian Baretta, Wisc., G
1978	Jack O'Callahan, Boston U., D
1979	Steve Janaszak, Minn., G
1980	Doug Smail, N. Dakota, F
1981	Marc Behrend, Wisc., G
1982	Phil Sykes, N. Dakota, F
1983	Marc Behrend, Wisc., G
1984	Gary Kruzich, Bowl. Green, G
1985	**Chris Terreri**, Prov., G
1986	Mike Donnelly, Mich. St., F
1987	Tony Hrkac, N. Dakota, F
1988	Bruce Hoffort, Lk. Superior, G
1989	Ted Donato, Harvard, F
1990	Chris Tancill, Wisconsin, F
1991	Scott Beattie, No. Mich., F
1992	Paul Constantin, Lk. Superior, F
1993	Jim Montgomery, Maine, F
1994	Sean Tallaire, Lk. Superior, F
1995	Chris O'Sullivan, Boston U., F
1996	Brendan Morrison, Michigan, F

Hobey Baker Award

College hockey's Player of the Year award; voted on by a national panel of sportswriters, broadcasters, college coaches and pro scouts. First presented in 1981 by the Decathlon Athletic Club of Bloomington, Minn., in the name of the Princeton collegiate hockey and football star who was killed in World War I.

Year	
1981	Neal Broten, Minnesota, F
1982	George McPhee, Bowl. Green, F
1983	Mark Fusco, Harvard, D
1984	Tom Kurvers, Minn-Duluth, D
1985	Bill Watson, Minn-Duluth, F
1986	Scott Fusco, Harvard, F
1987	Tony Hrkac, North Dakota, F
1988	Robb Stauber, Minnesota, G
1989	Lane MacDonald, Harvard, F
1990	Kip Miller, Michigan St., F
1991	Dave Emma, Boston College, F
1992	Scott Pellerin, Maine, F
1993	Paul Kariya, Maine, F
1994	Chris Marinucci, Minn-Duluth, F
1995	Brian Holzinger, Bowl. Green, F
1996	Brian Bonin, Minnesota, F

Coach of the Year

The Penrose Memorial Trophy, voted on by the American Hockey Coaches Association and first presented in 1951 in the name of Colorado gold and copper magnate Spencer T. Penrose. Penrose built the Broadmoor hotel and athletic complex in Colorado Springs, that originally hosted the NCAA hockey championship from 1948-57.

Multiple winners: Len Ceglarski and Charlie Holt (3); Rick Comley, Eddie Jeremiah, Snooks Kelly, John MacInnes, Jack Parker, Jack Riley and Cooney Weiland (2).

Year	
1951	Eddie Jeremiah, Dartmouth
1952	Cheedy Thompson, Colo. Col.
1953	John Mariucci, Minnesota
1954	Vic Heyliger, Michigan
1955	Cooney Weiland, Harvard
1956	Bill Harrison, Clarkson
1957	Jack Riley, Army
1958	Harry Cleverly, BU
1959	Snooks Kelly, BC
1960	Jack Riley, Army
1961	Murray Armstrong, Denver
1962	Jack Kelley, Colby
1963	Tony Frasca, Colorado Col.
1964	Tom Eccleston, Providence
1965	Jim Fullerton, Brown
1966	Amo Bessone, Michigan St. & Len Ceglarski, Clarkson
1967	Eddie Jeremiah, Dartmouth
1968	Ned Harkness, Cornell
1969	Charlie Holt, New Hampshire
1970	John MacInnes, Michigan Tech
1971	Cooney Weiland, Harvard
1972	Snooks Kelly, BC
1973	Len Ceglarski, BC
1974	Charlie Holt, New Hampshire
1975	Jack Parker, BU
1976	John MacInnes, Michigan Tech
1977	Jerry York, Clarkson
1978	Jack Parker, BU
1979	Charlie Holt, New Hampshire
1980	Rick Comley, No. Michigan
1981	Bill O'Flaherty, Clarkson
1982	Fern Flaman, Northeastern
1983	Bill Cleary, Harvard
1984	Mike Sertich, Minn-Duluth
1985	Len Ceglarski, BC
1986	Ralph Backstrom, Denver
1987	Gino Gasparini, N. Dakota
1988	Frank Anzalone, Lk. Superior
1989	Joe Marsh, St. Lawrence
1990	Terry Slater, Colgate
1991	Rick Comley, No. Michigan
1992	Ron Mason, Michigan St.
1993	George Gwozdecky, Miami-OH
1994	Don Lucia, Colorado Col.
1995	Shawn Walsh, Maine
1996	Bruce Crowder, UMass-Lowell

Note: 1960 winner Jack Riley won the award for coaching the USA to its first hockey gold medal in the Winter Olympics at Squaw Valley.

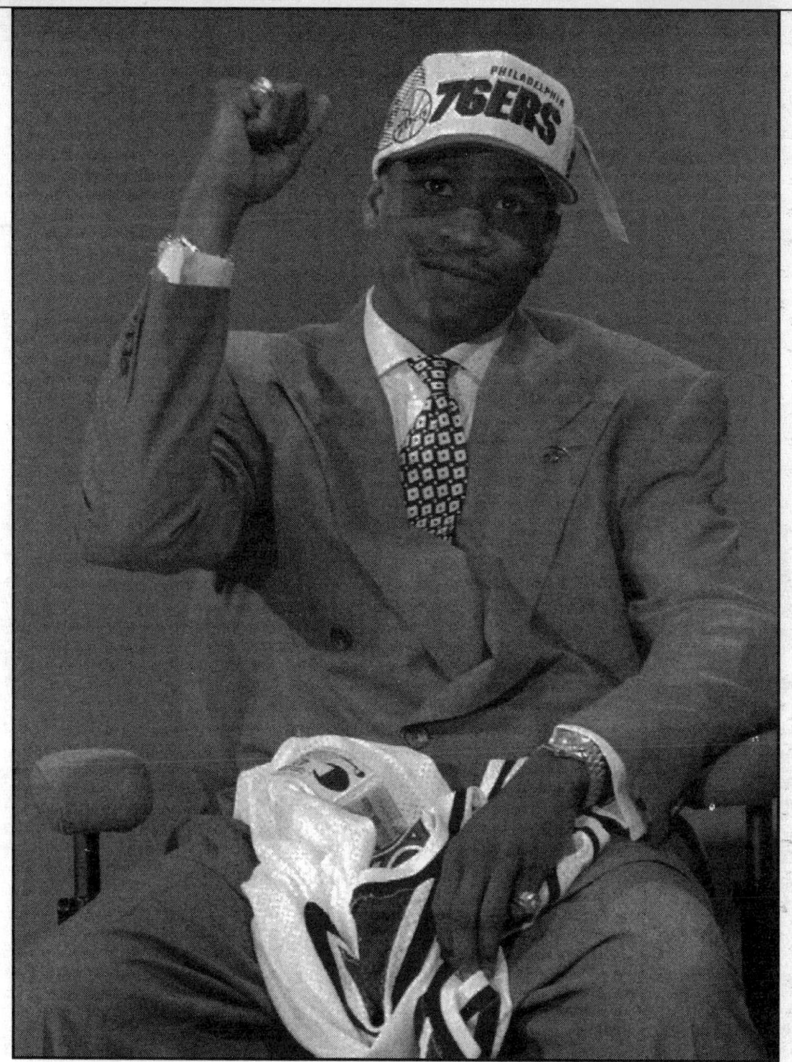

Wide World Photos

The price tag on Minnie Pearl's hat was $1.98 and it was a joke. **Allen Iverson**'s new salary cap is worth a lot more but there is nothing funny about the college game he has left behind.

COLLEGE SPORTS

1995-96 YEAR IN REVIEW

COLLEGE SPORTS

by Ron Chimelis

Time To Make The Dough

The single most important issue facing college sports is the early departure of of its marquee athletes

The academic year began with one of the classic feel-good sports stories of all time. It ended with a story that made everyone involved feel like reaching for the Alka-Seltzer.

From Northwestern football to the emergence of agents as a potent and potentially sinister force, college sports often seemed at war with itself in 1995-96. Northwestern's unlikely, unexpected run to the Rose Bowl made it look like purity in big-time college athletics was not necessarily a relic of a bygone era. But most of the other news surrounding NCAA sports was a reminder that big-time athletics involved business more than sport. The best the traditionalists could hope to do, it often seemed, was to force the business end to remain as savory as possible - and even that wasn't easy.

Speaking at a symposium at Washington State University, outgoing ABC Sports president Dennis Swanson summed up the dilemma. It wasn't a new discovery, but it still hit home. "The root of most of the problems that exist in college athletics today is money and greed - whether it's dealing with the agents or overaggressive alumni creating recruiting infractions or elimination of sports," Swanson said in comments carried by the Spokane Spokesman-Review.

Northwestern's magic carpet ride to the Rose Bowl proved one axiom: Delivering athletic success without paying the price of compromised standards could be done, at least for one season. Much of the rest of the year proved another axiom: Don't expect it to happen very often.

By June, controversy surrounding Massachusetts basketball star Marcus Camby had pushed the issue of sports agents to the forefront as one of the most problematic administrative and ethical headaches of the 1990s. Pertinent as it was, that issue competed for headlines with issues ranging from academic standards to the rising numbers of star athletes charged with felonies.

It all made Northwestern's rags-to-roses saga even more remarkable. NU coach Gary Barnett didn't allow the national doting on his team to develop into a morality play over how the Mildcats could become Wildcats without selling the university's and ethical soul, while other schools seemed unable to keep their own programs in line.

Still, the true test in Evanston, it was predicted, was whether such a best-of-both-worlds approach could stand the tests of time, temptation and a taste of success. Northwestern had won as many as four games in a season only once since 1974, and hadn't sold out 49,256-seat Dyche Stadium since 1983 until recording three sellouts in 1995. School officials promised not to stake NU's reputation or finances on sports success as other institutions had done, though they did sign

Ron Chimelis is a sportswriter for the *Springfield (Mass.) Union-News*

Al Bello/Allsport

Marcus Camby accepted gifts from a sports agent during his Player of the Year junior season at UMass. The scandal tainted Camby's accomplishments and made many wonder whether stricter limits should be placed on the activities of people seeking to cash in on the success of young athletes.

Barnett to a new contract, which indicated his belief that success with ethics was neither an aberration nor a one-year fluke. But the obvious follow-up question was why such happy marriages between academics and athletics seemed so rare. Throughout college sports, coaches and administrators insisted they were trying their best.

"I think schools are paying more attention than ever to the rules," Saint Louis University men's basketball coach Charlie Spoonhour said when asked if Camby's problems with agents was the tip of an iceberg, indicating a national lack of control. "Everybody is talking about the pitfalls these kids face, not just with cash but everything else." Camby's situation provided a perfect lab study for the agent issue because it intertwined so many elements of it: a UMass basketball program that had risen to prominence with stunning speed, a player with a solid personal reputation despite an economically disadvantaged background, and a slew of agents and go-betweens who seemed determined to entangle him whether he chose to be entangled or not. On top of everything else, Camby was the consensus national player-of-the-year. He led UMass to its first Final Four - the Land of Oz for a program once considered as inept in basketball as Northwestern had been in football. But on June 4, Camby faced the bombshell of a Hartford Courant story that he had accepted gifts from agents while still in college. Camby was later chosen by Toronto as the draft's No. 2 pick, but the story threatened not only his reputation but the credibility of the UMass basketball program.

As the tale unfolded, a seamy picture was painted of an intelligent yet naive athlete, surrounded by a collection of agents, friends and hangers-on who sought to cash in on Camby's fame and potential. Among the results of the controversy was a lawsuit filed by Camby against Wesley Spears, an agent Camby claims blackmailed him after Camby refused to let Spears represent him.

Rather than express disgust, most coaches claimed the Camby case was a symptom of the times. "If it can happen to Marcus - a good kid, a good student and role model - it can happen to anybody," UMass coach John Calipari claimed while insisting he'd done his best to monitor the agent movements around UMass. UMass would face the judgmental eye of the NCAA without Calipari, who signed a five-year, $15 million contract with the New Jersey Nets three days after the Camby controversy broke. What Camby's case did do was bring to the forefront the badly-kept secret that agents were running amok in major college sports and that there wasn't much anyone could do about it, at least under the current rules.

With Camby's case still in the headlines, the National Association of Collegiate Director of Athletics (NACDA) confronted the issue of agents at its meeting at Marco Island, Fla.

Florida State associate athletic director Robert Minnix offered some chilling figures that listed the national number of sports agents at 20,000, calling sports agency "a growth industry because of the money involved," in a report in The NCAA News. And Camby said many top players encounter agents even before they reach college, making administrative solutions at the college level even more elusive.

That fact didn't stop alarmed university officials from making suggestions ranging from a loan program for potential NBA and NFL draft choices, to eliminating the July basketball recruiting period that have made summer camps a haven for agents.

The issue of agents also loomed in women's basketball, if for no other reason than the formation of two professional leagues (the American Basketball League and the Women's NBA) expected to begin play within the next year. Big East commissioner Mike Tranghese claimed that without American-based pro leagues, top women players had not been tempted by early departure from college, or hounded by agents. That may now change. "No question, the women's game is heading into some dangerous water," said Connecticut coach Geno Auriemma, who remained generally optimistic that the women's game's comparatively clean reputation could be protected.

And there was suddenly money to be

Spencer For Hire

It is anything but a new issue, although that's how it was often treated by media and fans. It goes back to the 1971 Spencer Haywood case.

But never had the issue of college players leaving school early engulfed basketball as it did during the 1995-96 season. Its tentacles reached down to the high schools as never before and dominated the NBA Draft.

But in the spirit of concern over whether young lives were being scarred by the lure of money before maturity, the NBA and NCAA also faced questions of whether their own organizations were paying a price for early entry, too. Twenty-five years after Haywood's right to play was upheld in court, the debate over early entry was not whether it was legal, but whether it was ethical and wise.

The case of Stephon Marbury, who attended Georgia Tech with the understanding he might stay for only one year, made early entry a season-long debate. Marbury had obviously thought about using college ball as a temporary tool for some time, and he didn't understand the big fuss over it.

"If someone said they'd pay you $4 million to leave school, what would you do?" he asked on the eve of the draft, before he was picked fourth by Milwaukee and then – in a delicious reminder that basketball is indeed a business – traded to Minnesota for No. 5 pick Ray Allen before the draft was over.

"You can always go back to school," Marbury said. "But you can't always make $4 million a year."

That argument's essential truth notwithstanding, members of the college community fretted that too many players would jump into the NBA waters before they were emotionally or physically ready to do so. That didn't stop NBA teams from nearby doubling the previous record (set in 1995) of 10 first-round draftees from the early-entry pool.

"David Stern and the NBA say that players leaving college early is not their problem, it's the colleges' problem," Big East commissioner Mike Tranghese wrote in The NCAA News. "But it's about to become the NBA's problem. Because the NBA is going to be full of more and more immature, uneducated people."

At the Final Four in East Rutherford, N.J., a media seminar held with National Association of Basketball Coaches members revealed a

Wide World Photos (both)

When **Spencer Haywood** sought to turn pro in 1971, his case was rare and did not seem to be tearing at the fabric of college basketball. Today, stars like UConn's **Ray Allen** routinely hold press conferences to declare themselves eligible to be millionaires after a little success in college ball.

legitimate concern for young players. But there was also concern that the college game – and the educational experience in general – would be devalued by a new breed of player who entered school with no intention of staying for long.

"A kid could stay four years and not necessarily be ready," California coach Todd Bozeman reasoned after losing freshman Shareef Abdur-Rahim to the NBA. (The school lost Bozeman himself in August of this year when he resigned over allegations about recruiting violations.) Departing Kentucky sophomore Antoine Walker made the point that a player's rookie season would mean lifestyle adjustments no matter what his age.

But not everybody bought the argument that a handful of superstars were simply getting the early jump on their careers.

"Don't tell me that we are only talking about a few kids going to the pros – they are the example that hundreds and hundreds of children will follow," Georgetown coach John Thompson wrote in a Washington Post essay after losing sophomore guard Allen Iverson to the Philadelphia 76ers. "Hundreds of children who will believe that education is unimportant and unnecessary, that if their athletic talents are great enough, they don't need college at all – in fact they may not need high school."

Months earlier, Kentucky coach Rick Pitino had sounded a note of disapproval to Marbury's here-today, maybe-gone-tomorrow stance. Pitino said players planning on only one year of college should consider "not wasting the time" and perhaps skip college altogether, as Garnett had done.

That comment raised fair questions about whether it was not only the player's time being wasted but that of coaches investing time, money and effort into recruiting top high school players.

Not everyone followed the path of quick riches. Wake Forest junior center Tim Duncan, who would have been a serious contender for the No.1 draft pick, decided to return for his final year. And John Wallace was hailed for returning as a senior in 1995, then leading Syracuse to an unexpected trip to the national title game.

But traditionalists asking Wallace to carry their torch were disappointed. "I could have had a bad year, and it would have been a bad decision," he said, refusing to become a poster child for a four-year commitment. "For me, it worked out, but it can work both ways."

Marbury, citing hockey and baseball players who have jumped from high school to the pros for decades, didn't think an age limit was necessary.

"If someone is good enough to play tennis professionally at age 9, he should be allowed to do so," Marbury said. "Why should it be different for basketball?" Perfectly reasonable thing to ask. What about golf?

made in women's basketball. Attendance at all division levels reached 5.23 million (not including doubleheaders with men's teams), the first five-million season in history and a 5.5 percent hike from 1994-95. Women's basketball attendance figures have almost tripled since 1982, when the NCAA began keeping such statistics.

The women's numbers were in some ways more encouraging than the men's. The Kentucky-Syracuse men's basketball final, for instance, pulled an 18.3 rating - lowest ever for the telecast of a prime-time championship game.

Agents, money and TV were not the only issues in major-college sports, though they ruled the early-summer headlines. Concerns over the behavior of athletes forced some schools and coaches to harden their stances against off-the-field problems.

No one seemed to take a more noble position, against more daunting circumstances, than Miami (Fla.) football coach Butch Davis. Five Hurricane players - defensive lineman Derrick Ham, linebackers James Burgess and Jeffrey Taylor, receiver Jammi German and offensive tackle Ricky Perry - were disciplined over a two-week period in June, as the program reeled from a series of player run-ins with the law.

Miami's case was still in the news when Clemson coach Tommy West announced that Antwuan Wyatt, a receiver and one of the nation's best return men, and running back Anthony Downs were dropped from the team after being charged with intent to distribute marijuana. That made seven Tiger football players arrested over a four-month period.

In two separate, unrelated cases, Clemson football players were alleged to have been involved in rape incidents. Clemson athletic director Bobby Robinson's support of West highlighted the complexity of the problem.

"I think coach West has got a firm grip on the football program," Robinson said, the rising stack of legal matters notwithstanding. "Anytime you have a problem, it's cause for concern. But you also have to realize there are over 120 football players and 500 student-athletes, so there are things that are going to happen."

On a daily basis, issues involving police matters actually paled next to the the tamer, yet topical debate over what to expect from student-athletes in the classroom. Those issues were perhaps even more wrenching because they they raised questions of how to provide opportunity without compromising standards.

"What disturbs me is that all these rules are becoming too selective," Rhode Island basketball coach Al Skinner said in January after the NCAA Convention in Dallas, Tex. endorsed an expansion of Proposition 48 guidelines. Critics of that stance claimed it would quadruple the number of freshman-ineligible athletes, discouraging many from even trying to attend college.

"The Ivy League will always get the cream of the academic crop, but is that all the system is about?" Skinner wondered. "I hope not."

Defenders of stricter standards, however, were strengthened by figures released from the NCAA in June. Graduation rates among scholarship athletes entering in 1989 had risen 14 percent from the levels of entrants in 1985, the last year before Proposition 48 rules went into effect.

The idea of denying entry or participation to an even larger number of athletes petrified many coaches. Drake basketball coach Rudy Washington predicted that if academic standards for incoming freshmen were tightened, top athletes might bypass Division I altogether for Division II or the NAIA.

Washington spoke as executive director of the 3,000-member Black Coaches Association which nearly called a boycott over scholarship limits in 1994. He said he didn't expect such extreme measures in the future, but the disagreement within the college community over fair standards was clear.

It was also clear that the pressure on major-college football and basketball coaches to succeed was greater than even not just for their own benefit, but for the well-being of their schools' entire athletic programs.

"As we try to raise additional money, more and more pressure is going to be applied to the big-money programs to make it all work," Louisiana State athletic director Joe Dean said. "That's a sensitive issue, because you're charging someone who comes to a football or basketball game to pay for those other programs."

The cash cow known as television also underwent an examination for its role in the evolution of amateur sport as money-making big business. At the Washington State

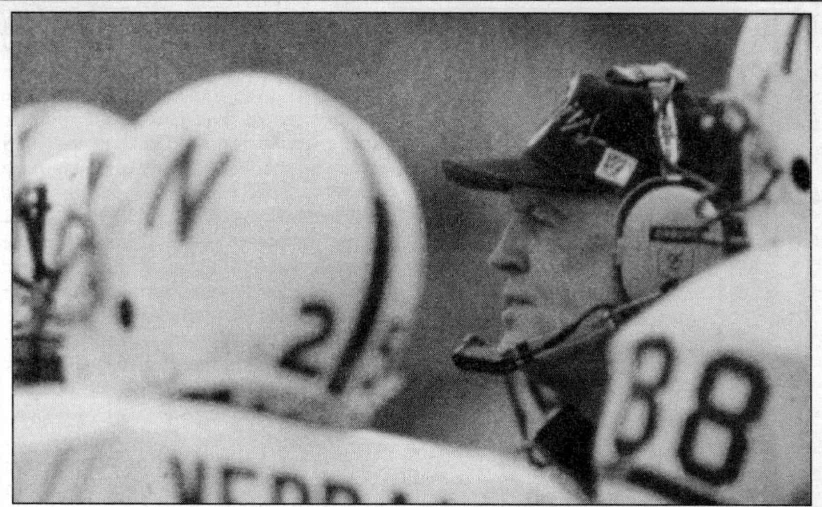

Allsport USA

In a move that all but acknowledged his program's troubles, Nebraska coach **Tom Osborne** banned all NFL personnel from his practices. Osborne was miffed at the way the New England Patriots reacted when they discovered that former Cornhusker Christian Peter had run afoul of the law several times under Osborne's watch.

were muted concerns throughout college basketball that the product might be devalued if identifiable stars kept leaving early for the NBA. CBS also prepared to begin airing Southeastern Conference and Big East football games.

At times, the CBS Eye seemed as much a symbol of intercollegiate athletics as the NCAA logo. The high-fiving in CBS headquarters was dulled only slightly when Nebraska's 62-24 Fiesta Bowl blowout win chased many viewers away early, leaving the game with an 18.8 rating and 31 share - good viewing numbers, but not the 20-something rating CBS had hoped.

The Fiesta Bowl - ahem, *Tostitos* Fiesta Bowl - showcased both the best and worst faces of college football. Nebraska running back Lawrence Phillips rushed for 165 yards and three touchdowns, but received more attention for the aftermath of a case in which he pleaded no contest to beating his former girlfriend. That charge cost Phillips a six-game suspension, and five other Cornhuskers also had legal trouble, while two Florida players were accused of hitting women in separate incidents.

With all the money riding on the games, the pressure on coaches seemed to reach viselike levels at times - even when off-field distractions were absent. Three of the nation's most renowned basketball coaches -Georgetown's John Thompson, Massachusetts' John Calipari and Cincinnati's Bob Huggins -were ejected from games by officials within a week's time in February.

Off the court, some coaches didn't take defeat without a fight. Georgia basketball coach Hugh Durham, let go in 1995 after 17 seasons, was given a settlement estimated in excess of half a million dollars. Durham had charged violation of his due process rights as a state employee, as well as an an age discrimination complaint with the U.S. Equal Employment Opportunity Commission.

Durham's case may have opened a new set of questions about the handling of coaches at state universities, whose other faculty employees often work under different work guidelines than their counterparts at private schools.

Concern over changing and rising demands placed on coaches was probably best articulated by Riley Wallace. The Hawaii men's basketball coach faced the issue -and his own school's administration-head-on at a news conference announcing a change in the Rainbows' football staff.

Citing what he considered mixed messages over what was expected of him,

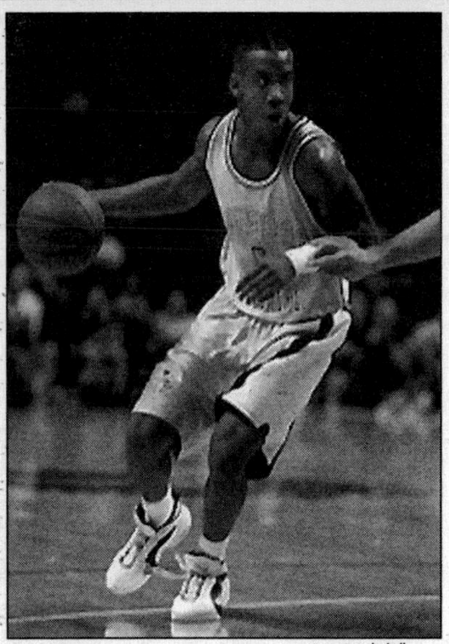

Otto Greule/Allsport

Georgia Tech's **Stephon Marbury** noted that players received "books, food and dorms" while coaches made money on shoe deals.

Wallace said that could not keep switching goals by expecting coaches to win one day, make money the next and turn out exemplary student athletes on the third.

The nation's top players, meanwhile, had their own problems. There was more concern than ever over their health after Camby's mysterious collapse and the sudden deaths of Massachusetts swimmer Greg Menton (on Jan. 10, four days before Camby's incident) and Dayton University basketball player Chris Daniels to heart-related problems.

Athletes also examined the distribution of wealth generated by big-time sports more closely than ever, and they didn't like what they saw, which was that they weren't getting any of it.

Georgia Tech freshman basketball player Stephon Marbury noted coaches were making money on endorsements and shoe contracts while the players, as he put it, received "only books, food and dorms." And clearly, Marbury and others didn't think that was enough, which helped explain why 42 underclassmen initially expressed interest in early entry to the NBA Draft and a record 17 were taken in the first round.

Even a players' strike was still whispered as a future possibility. Former University of Michigan athletic director Don Canham, speaking at the same Washington State symposium as Swanson, said such an action would devastate college sports by removing the last illusions of amateurism from the public mind, which in turn would destroy fan loyalty.

One conference with no illusions of innocence faded into history. The once-proud Southwest Conference, saddled with scandal through repeated rules violations by members in recent years, folded as scheduled at the end of the academic year. That ended a legacy dating back to its founding in 1914, and including some of the nation's best football rivalries.

While the Southwest Conference vanished, the Southeastern Conference flourished, winning nine NCAA championships. But in explaining the league's success, LSU athletic director Dean's comments reaffirmed the relationship of college sports to money.

"It becomes a financial thing," Dean said. "Because we have big football stadiums and a powerful football conference, we generate enough money to fully fund our other sports and give them an opportunity to win national championships."

As the year transpired, fans who wanted to forget about money could always cling to the football story at Northwestern, whose success had been as unexpected as it had been refreshing. While the nation's other schools scrambled to convince the public that their student-athletes were really students, Northwestern seemed determined to convince it that theirs were really athletes.

"The success story with Northwestern University's athletic programs are many and varied," began the school's message in the official Rose Bowl program, "rebutting the existing theory that NU's student-athletes are more student than athlete." As if that were bad.

Of course, Northwestern is new to big-time success, and the agents and TV executives have just begun to realize where Evanston, Ill. can be found on a map. Staying on top without getting entangled in the same myriad of legal, academic and ethical issues that other schools face may prove harder, over time, than making a bowl game every 50 years or so. ❐

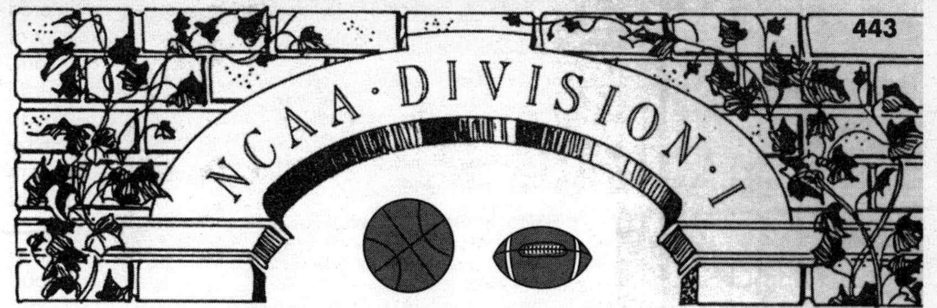

NCAA Division I Basketball Schools

1996-97 Season

Conferences and coaches as of Sept. 15, 1996.

Conference name changes as of 1996-97 season (2): Big Eight becomes Big 20; North Atlantic becomes America East.

Breakup of Southwest Conference on June 30, 1996: BAYLOR, TEXAS, TEXAS A&M and TEXAS TECH to Big 12; RICE, SMU, and TCU to WAC; HOUSTON to Conference USA.

Dissolving of American West Conference before 1996-97: CS-NORTHRIDGE and CS-SACRAMENTO to Big Sky; CAL POLY-SLO to Big West; SOUTHERN UTAH to Independent.

Joining Big 12 in 1996-97 (4): BAYLOR, TEXAS, TEXAS A&M and TEXAS TECH from Southwest.

Joining Big Sky in 1996-97 (3): CS-NORTHRIDGE and CS-SACRAMENTO from Big Sky; PORTLAND ST. from Division II.

Joining Big West in 1996-97 (4): BOISE ST. and IDAHO from Big Sky; NORTH TEXAS from Southland; CAL POLY-SLO from American West.

Joining Conference USA in 1996-97: HOUSTON from Southwest.

Joining Ohio Valley in 1996-97: EASTERN ILLINOIS from Mid-Continent.

Joining WAC in 1996-97 (6): SAN JOSE ST. and UNLV from Big West; TULSA from Mo. Valley; and RICE, SMU and TCU from Southwest.

New Division I program starting in 1996-97: PORTLAND ST. to Big Sky.

Joining Mid-American in 1997-98 (2): MARSHALL from Southern and NORTHERN ILLINOIS from Midwestern.

Joining Metro Atlantic in 1997-98 (2): MARIST and RIDER from Northeast.

Joining Mid Continent in 1997-98 (2): ORAL ROBERTS and SOUTHERN UTAH from Independent.

Joining Southern in 1997-98 (2): NC-GREENSBORO from Big South and WOFFORD from Independent.

Joining Southland in 1997-98 (2): SE LOUISIANA from Trans-America and LAMAR from Sunbelt.

Joining Trans-America in 1997-98: TROY ST. from Mid-Continent.

Joining Mid-American in 1998-99: BUFFALO from Mid-Continent.

Joining Northeast in 1998-99: MD-BALTIMORE COUNTY from Big South

Joining Southern in 1998-99: COLLEGE OF CHARLESTON from Trans-America.

	Nickname	Conference	Head Coach	Location	Colors
Air Force	Falcons	WAC	Reggie Minton	Colo. Springs, CO	Blue/Silver
Akron	Zips	Mid-American	Dan Hipsher	Akron, OH	Blue/Gold
Alabama	Crimson Tide	SEC-West	David Hobbs	Tuscaloosa, AL	Crimson/White
Alabama St.	Hornets	Southwestern	Rob Spivery	Montgomery, AL	Black/Gold
Ala-Birmingham	Blazers	USA	Murry Bartow	Birmingham, AL	Green/Gold
Alcorn St.	Braves	Southwestern	Davey Whitney	Lorman, MS	Purple/Gold
American	Eagles	Colonial	Chris Knoche	Washington, DC	Red/White/Blue
Appalachian St.	Mountaineers	Southern	Buzz Peterson	Boone,NC	Black/Gold
Arizona	Wildcats	Pac-10	Lute Olson	Tucson, AZ	Cardinal/Navy
Arizona St.	Sun Devils	Pac-10	Bill Frieder	Tempe, AZ	Maroon/Gold
Arkansas	Razorbacks	SEC-West	Nolan Richardson	Fayetteville, AR	Cardinal/White
Arkansas-Little Rock	Trojans	Sun Belt	Wimp Sanderson	Little Rock, AR	Maroon/Gold/White
Arkansas St.	Indians	Sun Belt	Dickey Nutt	State Univ., AR	Scarlet/Black
Army	Cadets, Black Knights	Patriot	Dino Gaudio	West Point, NY	Black/Gold/Gray
Auburn	Tigers	SEC-West	Cliff Ellis	Auburn, AL	Orange/Blue
Austin Peay St.	Governors	Ohio Valley	Dave Loos	Clarksville, TN	Red/White
Ball St.	Cardinals	Mid-American	Ray McCallum	Muncie, IN	Cardinal/White
Baylor	Bears	Big 12-South	Harry Miller	Waco, TX	Green/Gold
Bethune-Cookman	Wildcats	Mid-Eastern	Tony Sheals	Daytona Beach, FL	Maroon/Gold
Boise St.	Broncos	Big West	Rod Jensen	Boise, ID	Orange/Blue
Boston College	Eagles	Big East	Jim O'Brien	Chestnut Hill, MA	Maroon/Gold
Boston University	Terriers	America East	Dennis Wolff	Boston, MA	Scarlet/White
Bowling Green	Falcons	Mid-American	Jim Larranaga	Bowling Green, OH	Orange/Brown
Bradley	Braves	Mo. Valley	Jim Molinari	Peoria, IL	Red/White
BYU	Cougars	WAC	Roger Reid	Provo, UT	Royal Blue/White
Brown	Bears	Ivy	Frank Dobbs	Providence, RI	Brown/Cardinal/White
Bucknell	Bison	Patriot	Pat Flannery	Lewisburg, PA	Orange/Blue
Buffalo	Bulls	Mid-Continent	Tim Cohane	Buffalo, NY	Blue/Red/White
Butler	Bulldogs	Midwestern	Barry Collier	Indianapolis, IN	Blue/White

NCAA Division I Basketball Schools (Cont.)

	Nickname	Conference	Head Coach	Location	Colors
California	Golden Bears	Pac-10	Ben Braun	Berkeley, CA	Blue/Gold
CS-Fullerton	Titans	Big West	Bob Hawking	Fullerton, CA	Blue/Orange/White
CS-Northridge	Matadors	Big Sky	Bobby Braswell	Northridge, CA	Red/White/Black
CS-Sacramento	Hornets	Big Sky	Don Newman	Sacramento, CA	Green/Gold
Cal Poly-SLO	Mustangs	Big West	Jeff Schneider	San Luis Obispo, CA	Green/Gold
Campbell	Fighting Camels	Trans Am	Billy Lee	Buies Creek, NC	Orange/Black
Canisius	Golden Griffins	Metro Atlantic	John Beilein	Buffalo, NY	Blue/Gold
Centenary	Gentlemen	Trans Am	Tommy Vardeman	Shreveport, LA	Maroon/White
Central Conn. St.	Blue Devils	Mid-Continent	Howie Dickenman	New Britain, CT	Blue/White
Central Florida	Golden Knights	Trans Am	Kirk Speraw	Orlando, FL	Black/Gold
Central Michigan	Chippewas	Mid-American	Leonard Drake	Mt. Pleasant, MI	Maroon/Gold
Charleston So.	Buccaneers	Big South	Tom Conrad	Charleston, SC	Blue/Gold
Chicago St.	Cougars	Mid-Continent	Craig Hodges	Chicago, IL	Green/White
Cincinnati	Bearcats	USA	Bob Huggins	Cincinnati, OH	Red/Black
The Citadel	Bulldogs	Southern	Pat Dennis	Charleston, SC	Blue/White
Clemson	Tigers	ACC	Rick Barnes	Clemson, SC	Purple/Orange
Cleveland St.	Vikings	Midwestern	Rollie Massimino	Cleveland, OH	Green/White
Coastal Carolina	Chanticleers	Big South	Michael Hopkins	Myrtle Beach, SC	Scarlet/Black
Colgate	Red Raiders	Patriot	Jack Bruen	Hamilton, NY	Maroon/Gray/White
College of Charleston	Cougars	Trans Am	John Kresse	Charleston, SC	Maroon/White
Colorado	Golden Buffaloes	Big 12-North	Ricardo Patton	Boulder, CO	Silver/Gold/Black
Colorado St.	Rams	WAC	Stew Morrill	Ft. Collins, CO	Green/Gold
Columbia	Lions	Ivy	Armond Hill	New York, NY	Lt. Blue/White
Connecticut	Huskies	Big East	Jim Calhoun	Storrs, CT	Blue/White
Coppin St.	Eagles	Mid-Eastern	Ron Mitchell	Baltimore, MD	Royal Blue/Gold
Cornell	Big Red	Ivy	Scott Thompson	Ithaca, NY	Carnelian Red/White
Creighton	Bluejays	Mo. Valley	Dana Altman	Omaha, NE	Blue/White
Dartmouth	Big Green	Ivy	Dave Faucher	Hanover, NH	Green/White
Davidson	Wildcats	Southern	Bob McKillop	Davidson, NC	Red/Black
Dayton	Flyers	Atlantic 10	Oliver Purnell	Dayton, OH	Red/Blue
DePaul	Blue Demons	USA	Joey Meyer	Chicago, IL	Scarlet/Blue
Delaware	Blue Hens	America East	Mike Brey	Newark, DE	Blue/Gold
Delaware St.	Hornets	Mid-Eastern	Art Perry	Dover, DE	Red/Blue
Detroit Mercy	Titans	Midwestern	Perry Watson	Detroit, MI	Red/White/Blue
Drake	Bulldogs	Mo. Valley	Kurt Kanaskie	Des Moines, IA	Blue/White
Drexel	Dragons	America East	Bill Herrion	Philadelphia, PA	Navy Blue/Gold
Duke	Blue Devils	ACC	Mike Krzyzewski	Durham, NC	Royal Blue/White
Duquesne	Dukes	Atlantic 10	Scott Edgar	Pittsburgh, PA	Red/Blue
East Carolina	Pirates	Colonial	Joe Dooley	Greenville, NC	Purple/Gold
East Tenn. St.	Buccaneers	Southern	Ed DeChellis	Johnson City, TN	Blue/Gold
Eastern Illinois	Panthers	Ohio Valley	Rick Samuels	Charleston, IL	Blue/Gray
Eastern Kentucky	Colonels	Ohio Valley	Mike Calhoun	Richmond, KY	Maroon/White
Eastern Michigan	Eagles	Mid-American	TBA	Ypsilanti, MI	Green/White
Eastern Washington	Eagles	Big Sky	Steve Aggers	Cheney, WA	Red/White
Evansville	Aces	Mo. Valley	Jim Crews	Evansville, IN	Purple/White
Fairfield	Stags	Metro Atlantic	Paul Cormier	Fairfield, CT	Cardinal Red
Fairleigh Dickinson	Knights	Northeast	Tom Green	Teaneck, NJ	Blue/Black
Florida	Gators	SEC-East	Billy Donovan	Gainesville, FL	Orange/Blue
Florida A&M	Rattlers	Mid-Eastern	Mickey Clayton	Tallahassee, FL	Orange/Green
Florida Atlantic	Owls	Trans Am	Kevin Billerman	Boca Raton, FL	Blue/Gray
Florida Int'l	Golden Panthers	Trans Am	Shakey Rodriguez	Miami, FL	Blue/Yellow
Florida St.	Seminoles	ACC	Pat Kennedy	Tallahassee, FL	Garnet/Gold
Fordham	Rams	Atlantic 10	Nick Macarchuk	Bronx, NY	Maroon/White
Fresno St.	Bulldogs	WAC	Jerry Tarkanian	Fresno, CA	Cardinal/Blue
Furman	Paladins	Southern	Joe Cantafio	Greenville, SC	Purple/White
George Mason	Patriots	Colonial	Paul Westhead	Fairfax, VA	Green/Gold
George Washington	Colonials	Atlantic 10	Mike Jarvis	Washington, DC	Buff/Blue
Georgetown	Hoyas	Big East	John Thompson	Washington, DC	Blue/Gray
Georgia	Bulldogs, 'Dawgs	SEC-East	Tubby Smith	Athens, GA	Red/Black
Georgia Southern	Eagles	Southern	Gregg Polinsky	Statesboro, GA	Blue/White
Georgia St.	Panthers	Trans Am	Carter Wilson	Atlanta, GA	Royal Blue/Crimson
Georgia Tech	Yellow Jackets	ACC	Bobby Cremins	Atlanta, GA	Old Gold/White
Gonzaga	Bulldogs, Zags	West Coast	Dan Fitzgerald	Spokane, WA	Blue/White/Red
Grambling St.	Tigers	Southwestern	Lacey Reynolds	Grambling, LA	Black/Gold
Hampton	Pirates	Mid-Eastern	Byron Samuels	Hampton, VA	Royal Blue/White
Hartford	Hawks	America East	Paul Brazeau	W. Hartford, CT	Scarlet/White
Harvard	Crimson	Ivy	Frank Sullivan	Cambridge, MA	Crimson/Black/White
Hawaii	Rainbows	WAC	Riley Wallace	Honolulu, HI	Green/White
Hofstra	Flying Dutchmen	America East	Jay Wright	Hempstead, NY	Blue/White/Gold

	Nickname	Conference	Head Coach	Location	Colors
Holy Cross	Crusaders	Patriot	Bill Raynor	Worcester, MA	Royal Purple
Houston	Cougars	USA	Alvin Brooks	Houston, TX	Scarlet/White
Howard	Bison	Mid-Eastern	Mike McLeese	Washington, DC	Blue/White/Red
Idaho	Vandals	Big West	Kermit Davis	Moscow, ID	Silver/Gold
Idaho St.	Bengals	Big Sky	Herb Williams	Pocatello, ID	Orange/Black
Illinois	Fighting Illini	Big Ten	Lon Kruger	Champaign, IL	Orange/Blue
Illinois-Chicago	Flames	Midwestern	Jimmy Collins	Chicago, IL	Indigo/Flame
Illinois St.	Redbirds	Mo. Valley	Kevin Stallings	Normal, IL	Red/White
Indiana	Hoosiers	Big Ten	Bob Knight	Bloomington, IN	Cream/Crimson
Indiana St.	Sycamores	Mo. Valley	Sherman Dillard	Terre Haute, IN	Blue/White
Iona	Gaels	Metro Atlantic	Tim Welsh	New Rochelle, NY	Maroon/Gold
Iowa	Hawkeyes	Big Ten	Tom Davis	Iowa City, IA	Old Gold/Black
Iowa St.	Cyclones	Big 12-North	Tim Floyd	Ames, IA	Cardinal/Gold
Jackson St.	Tigers	Southwestern	Andrew Stoglin	Jackson, MS	Blue/White
Jacksonville	Dolphins	Sun Belt	George Scholtz	Jacksonville, FL	Green/Gold
Jacksonville St.	Gamecocks	Trans Am	Bill Jones	Jacksonville, AL	Red/White
James Madison	Dukes	Colonial	Lefty Driesell	Harrisonburg, VA	Purple/Gold
Kansas	Jayhawks	Big 12-North	Roy Williams	Lawrence, KS	Crimson/Blue
Kansas St.	Wildcats	Big 12-North	Tom Asbury	Manhattan, KS	Purple/White
Kent	Golden Flashes	Mid-American	Gary Waters	Kent, OH	Navy Blue/Gold
Kentucky	Wildcats	SEC-East	Rick Pitino	Lexington, KY	Blue/White
La Salle	Explorers	Atlantic 10	Speedy Morris	Philadelphia, PA	Blue/Gold
Lafayette	Leopards	Patriot	Fran O'Hanlon	Easton, PA	Maroon/White
Lamar	Cardinals	Sun Belt	Grey Giovanine	Beaumont, TX	Red/White
Lehigh	Engineers	Patriot	Sal Mentesana	Bethlehem, PA	Brown/White
Liberty	Flames	Big South	Jeff Meyer	Lynchburg, VA	Red/White/Blue
Long Beach St.	49ers	Big West	Wayne Morgan	Long Beach, CA	Black/Gold
Long Island	Blackbirds	Northeast	Ray Haskins	Brooklyn, NY	Blue/White
LSU	Fighting Tigers	SEC-West	Dale Brown	Baton Rouge, LA	Purple/Gold
Louisiana Tech	Bulldogs	Sun Belt	Jim Wooldridge	Ruston, LA	Red/Blue
Louisville	Cardinals	USA	Denny Crum	Louisville, KY	Red/Black/White
Loyola-CA	Lions	West Coast	John Olive	Los Angeles, CA	Crimson/Gray/Lt.Blue
Loyola-IL	Ramblers	Midwestern	Ken Burmeister	Chicago, IL	Maroon/Gold
Loyola-MD	Greyhounds	Metro Atlantic	Brian Ellerbe	Baltimore, MD	Green/Gray
Maine	Black Bears	America East	John Giannini	Orono, ME	Blue/White
Manhattan	Jaspers	Metro Atlantic	John Leonard	Riverdale, NY	Kelly Green/White
Marist	Red Foxes	Northeast	Dave Magarity	Poughkeepsie, NY	Red/White
Marquette	Golden Eagles	USA	Mike Deane	Milwaukee, WI	Blue/Gold
Marshall	Thundering Herd	Southern	Greg White	Huntington, WV	Green/White
Maryland	Terrapins, Terps	ACC	Gary Williams	College Park, MD	Red/White/Black/Gold
MD-Balt. County	Retrievers	Big South	Tom Sullivan	Baltimore, MD	Black/Red Gold
MD-Eastern Shore	Hawks	Mid-Eastern	Lonnie Williams	Princess Anne, MD	Maroon/Gray
Massachusetts	Minutemen	Atlantic 10	James Flint	Amherst, MA	Maroon/White
McNeese St.	Cowboys	Southland	Ron Everhart	Lake Charles, LA	Blue/Gold
Memphis	Tigers	USA	Larry Finch	Memphis, TN	Blue/Gray
Mercer	Bears	Trans Am	Bill Hodges	Macon, GA	Orange/Black
Miami-FL	Hurricanes	Big East	Leonard Hamilton	Miami, FL	Orange/Green/White
Miami-OH	Redskins	Mid-American	Charlie Coles	Oxford, OH	Red/White
Michigan	Wolverines	Big Ten	Steve Fisher	Ann Arbor, MI	Maize/Blue
Michigan St.	Spartans	Big Ten	Tom Izzo	East Lansing, MI	Green/White
Middle Tenn. St.	Blue Raiders	Ohio Valley	Randy Wiel	Murfreesboro, TN	Blue/White
Minnesota	Golden Gophers	Big Ten	Clem Haskins	Minneapolis, MN	Maroon/Gold
Mississippi	Ole Miss, Rebels	SEC-West	Rob Evans	Oxford, MS	Red/Blue
Mississippi St.	Bulldogs	SEC-West	Richard Williams	Starkville, MS	Maroon/White
Miss. Valley St.	Delta Devils	Southwestern	Lafayette Stribling	Itta Bena, MS	Green/White
Missouri	Tigers	Big 12-North	Norm Stewart	Columbia, MO	Old Gold/Black
Missouri-KC	Kangaroos	Mid-Continent	Bob Sundvold	Kansas City, MO	Blue/Gold
Monmouth	Hawks	Northeast	Wayne Szoke	W. Long Branch, NJ	Royal Blue/White
Montana	Grizzlies	Big Sky	Blaine Taylor	Missoula, MT	Copper/Silver/Gold
Montana St.	Bobcats	Big Sky	Mick Durham	Bozeman, MT	Blue/Gold
Morehead St.	Eagles	Ohio Valley	Dick Fick	Morehead, KY	Blue/Gold
Morgan St.	Bears	Mid-Eastern	Chris Fuller	Baltimore, MD	Blue/Orange
Mt. St. Mary's	Mountaineers	Northeast	Jim Phelan	Emmitsburg, MD	Blue/White
Murray St.	Racers	Ohio Valley	Mark Gottfried	Murray, KY	Blue/Gold
Navy	Midshipmen	Patriot	Don DeVoe	Annapolis, MD	Navy Blue/Gold
Nebraska	Cornhuskers	Big 12-North	Danny Nee	Lincoln, NE	Scarlet/Cream
Nevada	Wolf Pack	Big West	Pat Foster	Reno, NV	Silver/Blue
New Hampshire	Wildcats	America East	Jeff Jackson	Durham, NH	Blue/White
New Mexico	Lobos	WAC	Dave Bliss	Albuquerque, NM	Cherry/Silver

NCAA Division I Basketball Schools (Cont.)

	Nickname	Conference	Head Coach	Location	Colors
New Mexico St.	Aggies	Big West	Neil McCarthy	Las Cruces, NM	Crimson/White
New Orleans	Privateers	Sun Belt	Tic Price	New Orleans, LA	Royal Blue/Silver
Niagara	Purple Eagles	Metro Atlantic	Jack Armstrong	Lewiston, NY	Purple/White/Gold
Nicholls St.	Colonels	Southland	Rickey Broussard	Thibodaux, LA	Red/Gray
North Carolina	Tar Heels	ACC	Dean Smith	Chapel Hill, NC	Carolina Blue/White
North Carolina A&T	Aggies	Mid-Eastern	Roy Thomas	Greensboro, NC	Blue/Gold
North Carolina St.	Wolfpack	ACC	Herb Sendek	Raleigh, NC	Red/White
NC-Asheville	Bulldogs	Big South	Eddie Biedenbach	Asheville, NC	Royal Blue/White
NC-Charlotte	49ers	USA	Melvin Watkins	Charlotte, NC	Green/White
NC-Greensboro	Spartans	Big South	Randy Peele	Greensboro, NC	Gold/White/Navy
NC-Wilmington	Seahawks	Colonial	Jerry Wainwright	Wilmington, NC	Green/Gold
North Texas	Eagles	Big West	Tim Jankovich	Denton, TX	Green/White
NE Illinois	Golden Eagles	Mid-Continent	Rees Johnson	Chicago, IL	Royal Blue/Gold
NE Louisiana	Indians	Southland	Mike Vining	Monroe, LA	Maroon/Gold
Northeastern	Huskies	America East	Rudy Keeling	Boston, MA	Red/Black
Northern Arizona	Lumberjacks	Big Sky	Ben Howland	Flagstaff, AZ	Blue/Gold
Northern Illinois	Huskies	Midwestern	Brian Hammel	De Kalb, IL	Cardinal/Black
Northern Iowa	Panthers	Mo. Valley	Eldon Miller	Cedar Falls, IA	Purple/Old Gold
Northwestern	Wildcats	Big Ten	Ricky Byrdsong	Evanston, IL	Purple/White
Northwestern St.	Demons	Southland	J.D. Barnett	Natchitoches, LA	Burnt Orange/Purple
Notre Dame	Fighting Irish	Big East	John MacLeod	South Bend, IN	Gold/Blue
Ohio University	Bobcats	Mid-American	Larry Hunter	Athens, OH	Ohio Green/White
Ohio St.	Buckeyes	Big Ten	Randy Ayers	Columbus, OH	Scarlet/Gray
Oklahoma	Sooners	Big 12-South	Kelvin Sampson	Norman, OK	Crimson/Cream
Oklahoma St.	Cowboys	Big 12-South	Eddie Sutton	Stillwater, OK	Orange/Black
Old Dominion	Monarchs	Colonial	Jeff Capel	Norfolk, VA	Slate Blue/Silver
Oral Roberts	Golden Eagles	Independent	Bill Self	Tulsa, OK	Navy Blue/Gold
Oregon	Ducks	Pac-10	Jerry Green	Eugene, OR	Green/Yellow
Oregon St.	Beavers	Pac-10	Eddie Payne	Corvallis, OR	Orange/Black
Pacific	Tigers	Big West	Bob Thomason	Stockton, CA	Orange/Black
Pennylvania	Quakers	Ivy	Fran Dunphy	Philadelphia, PA	Red/Blue
Penn St.	Nittany Lions	Big Ten	Bruce Parkhill	University Park, PA	Blue/White
Pepperdine	Waves	West Coast	Lorenzo Romar	Malibu, CA	Blue/Orange
Pittsburgh	Panthers	Big East	Ralph Willard	Pittsburgh, PA	Gold/Blue
Portland	Pilots	West Coast	Rob Chavez	Portland, OR	Purple/White
Portland State	Vikings	Big Sky	Ritchie McKay	Portland, OR	Green/White
Prairie View A&M	Panthers	Southwestern	Elwood Plummer	Prairie View, TX	Purple/Gold
Princeton	Tigers	Ivy	Bill Carmody	Princeton, NJ	Orange/Black
Providence	Friars	Big East	Pete Gillen	Providence, RI	Black/White
Purdue	Boilermakers	Big Ten	Gene Keady	W. Lafayette, IN	Old Gold/Black
Radford	Highlanders	Big South	Ron Bradley	Radford, VA	Blue/Red/Green
Rhode Island	Rams	Atlantic 10	Al Skinner	Kingston, RI	Blue/White
Rice	Owls	WAC	Willis Wilson	Houston, TX	Blue/Gray
Richmond	Spiders	Colonial	Bill Dooley	Richmond, VA	Red/Blue
Rider	Broncs	Northeast	Kevin Bannon	Lawrenceville, NJ	Cranberry/White
Robert Morris	Colonials	Northeast	Jim Boone	Coraopolis, PA	Blue/White
Rutgers	Scarlet Knights	Big East	Bob Wenzel	New Brunswick, NJ	Scarlet
St. Bonaventure	Bonnies	Atlantic 10	Jim Baron	St. Bonaventure, NY	Brown/White
St. Francis-NY	Terriers	Northeast	Ron Ganulin	Brooklyn, NY	Red/Blue
St. Francis-PA	Red Flash	Northeast	Tom McConnell	Loretto, PA	Red/White
St. John's	Red Storm	Big East	Fran Fraschilla	Jamaica, NY	Red/White
St. Joseph's-PA	Hawks	Atlantic 10	Phil Martelli	Philadelphia, PA	Crimson/Gray
Saint Louis	Billikens	USA	Charlie Spoonhour	St. Louis, MO	Blue/White
St. Mary's-CA	Gaels	West Coast	Ernie Kent	Moraga, CA	Red/Blue
St. Peter's	Peacocks	Metro Atlantic	Rodger Blind	Jersey City, NJ	Blue/White
Sam Houston St.	Bearkats	Southland	Jerry Hopkins	Huntsville, TX	Orange/White
Samford	Bulldogs	Trans Am	John Brady	Birmingham, AL	Red/Blue
San Diego	Toreros	West Coast	Brad Holland	San Diego, CA	Lt. Blue/Navy/White
San Diego St.	Aztecs	WAC	Fred Trenkle	San Diego, CA	Scarlet/Black
San Francisco	Dons	West Coast	Phil Mathews	San Francisco, CA	Green/Gold
San Jose St.	Spartans	WAC	Stan Morrison	San Jose, CA	Gold/White/Blue
Santa Clara	Broncos	West Coast	Dick Davey	Santa Clara, CA	Bronco Red/White
Seton Hall	Pirates	Big East	George Blaney	South Orange, NJ	Blue/White
Siena	Saints	Metro Atlantic	Bob Beyer	Loudonville, NY	Green/Gold
South Alabama	Jaguars	Sun Belt	Bill Musselman	Mobile, AL	Red/White/Blue
South Carolina	Gamecocks	SEC-East	Eddie Fogler	Columbia, SC	Garnet/Black
South Carolina St.	Bulldogs	Mid-Eastern	Cy Alexander	Orangeburg, SC	Garnet/Blue
South Florida	Bulls	USA	Seth Greenberg	Tampa, FL	Green/Gold
SE Louisiana	Lions	Trans Am	John Lyles	Hammond, LA	Green/Gold

	Nickname	Conference	Head Coach	Location	Colors
SE Missouri St.	Indians	Ohio Valley	Ron Shumate	Cape Girardeau, MO	Red/Black
Southern Illinois	Salukis	Mo. Valley	Rich Herrin	Carbondale, IL	Maroon/White
SMU	Mustangs	WAC	Mike Dement	Dallas, TX	Red/Blue
Southern Miss.	Golden Eagles	USA	James Green	Hattiesburg, MS	Black/Gold
Southern Utah	Thunderbirds	Independent	Bill Evans	Cedar City, UT	Scarlet/Royal Blue
Southern-BR	Jaguars	Southwestern	Tommy Green	Baton Rouge, LA	Blue/Gold
SW Missouri St.	Bears	Mo. Valley	Steve Alford	Springfield, MO	Maroon/White
SW Texas St.	Bobcats	Southland	Mike Miller	San Marcos, TX	Maroon/Gold
SW Louisiana	Ragin' Cajuns	Sun Belt	Marty Fletcher	Lafayette, LA	Vermilion/White
Stanford	Cardinal	Pac-10	Mike Montgomery	Stanford, CA	Cardinal/White
S.F. Austin St.	Lumberjacks	Southland	Derek Allister	Nacogdoches, TX	Purple/White
Stetson	Hatters	Trans Am	Randy Brown	DeLand, FL	Green/White
Syracuse	Orangemen	Big East	Jim Boeheim	Syracuse, NY	Orange
Temple	Owls	Atlantic 10	John Chaney	Philadelphia, PA	Cherry/White
Tennessee	Volunteers	SEC-East	Kevin O'Neill	Knoxville, TN	Orange/White
Tenn-Chattanooga	Moccasins	Southern	Mack McCarthy	Chattanooga, TN	Navy Blue/Gold
Tenn-Martin	Skyhawks	Ohio Valley	Cal Luther	Martin, TN	Orange/White/Blue
Tennessee St.	Tigers	Ohio Valley	Frankie Allen	Nashville, TN	Blue/White
Tennessee Tech	Golden Eagles	Ohio Valley	Frank Harrell	Cookeville, TN	Purple/Gold
Texas	Longhorns	Big 12-South	Tom Penders	Austin, TX	Burnt Orange/White
Texas A&M	Aggies	Big 12-South	Tony Barone	College Station, TX	Maroon/White
TCU	Horned Frogs	WAC	Billy Tubbs	Ft. Worth, TX	Purple/White
Texas Southern	Tigers	Southwestern	Robert Moreland	Houston, TX	Maroon/Gray
Texas Tech	Red Raiders	Big 12-South	James Dickey	Lubbock, TX	Scarlet/Black
TX-Arlington	Mavericks	Southland	Eddie McCarter	Arlington, TX	Royal Blue/White
TX-Pan American	Broncs	Sun Belt	Mark Adams	Edinburg, TX	Green/White
TX-San Antonio	Roadrunners	Southland	Tim Carter	San Antonio, TX	Orange/Navy Blue
Toledo	Rockets	Mid-American	Stan Joplin	Toledo, OH	Blue/Gold
Towson St.	Tigers	America East	Terry Truax	Towson, MD	Gold/White/Black
Troy St.	Trojans	Mid-Continent	Don Maestri	Troy, AL	Cardinal/Gray/Black
Tulane	Green Wave	USA	Perry Clark	New Orleans, LA	Olive Green/Sky Blue
Tulsa	Golden Hurricane	WAC	Steve Robinson	Tulsa, OK	Blue/Red/Gold
UC-Irvine	Anteaters	Big West	Rod Baker	Irvine, CA	Blue/Gold
UCLA	Bruins	Pac-10	Jim Harrick	Los Angeles, CA	Blue/Gold
UC-Santa Barbara	Gauchos	Big West	Jerry Pimm	Santa Barbara, CA	Blue/Gold
UNLV	Runnin' Rebels	WAC	Billy Bayno	Las Vegas, NV	Scarlet/Gray
USC	Trojans	Pac-10	Henry Bibby	Los Angeles, CA	Cardinal/Gold
Utah	Utes	WAC	Rick Majerus	Salt Lake City, UT	Crimson/White
Utah St.	Aggies	Big West	Larry Eustachy	Logan, UT	Navy Blue/White
UTEP	Miners	WAC	Don Haskins	El Paso, TX	Orange/White/Blue
Valparaiso	Crusaders	Mid-Continent	Homer Drew	Valparaiso, IN	Brown/Gold
Vanderbilt	Commodores	SEC-East	Jan van Breda Kolff	Nashville, TN	Black/Gold
Vermont	Catamounts	America East	Tom Brennan	Burlington, VT	Green/Gold
Villanova	Wildcats	Big East	Steve Lappas	Villanova, PA	Blue/White
Virginia	Cavaliers	ACC	Jeff Jones	Charlottesville, VA	Orange/Blue
VCU	Rams	Colonial	Sonny Smith	Richmond, VA	Black/Gold
VMI	Keydets	Southern	Bart Bellairs	Lexington, VA	Red/White/Yellow
Virginia Tech	Hokies, Gobblers	Atlantic 10	Bill Foster	Blacksburg, VA	Orange/Maroon
Wagner	Seahawks	Northeast	Tim Capstraw	Staten Island, NY	Green/White
Wake Forest	Demon Deacons	ACC	Dave Odom	Winston-Salem, NC	Old Gold/Black
Washington	Huskies	Pac-10	Bob Bender	Seattle, WA	Purple/Gold
Washington St.	Cougars	Pac-10	Kevin Eastman	Pullman, WA	Crimson/Gray
Weber St.	Wildcats	Big Sky	Ron Abegglen	Ogden, UT	Royal Purple/White
West Virginia	Mountaineers	Big East	Gale Catlett	Morgantown, WV	Old Gold/Blue
Western Carolina	Catamounts	Southern	Phil Hopkins	Cullowhee, NC	Purple/Gold
Western Illinois	Leathernecks	Mid-Continent	Jim Kerwin	Macomb, IL	Purple/Gold
Western Kentucky	Hilltoppers	Sun Belt	Matt Kilcullen	Bowling Green, KY	Red/White
Western Michigan	Broncos	Mid-American	Bob Donewald	Kalamazoo, MI	Brown/Gold
Wichita St.	Shockers	Mo. Valley	Randy Smithson	Wichita, KS	Yellow/Black
William & Mary	Tribe	Colonial	Charlie Woollum	Williamsburg, VA	Green/Gold/Silver
Winthrop	Eagles	Big South	Dan Kenney	Rock Hill, SC	Garnet/Gold
Wisconsin	Badgers	Big Ten	Dick Bennett	Madison, WI	Cardinal/White
WI-Green Bay	Phoenix	Midwestern	Mike Heideman	Green Bay, WI	Green/White/Red
WI-Milwaukee	Panthers	Midwestern	Ric Cobb	Milwaukee, WI	Black/Gold
Wofford	Terriers	Independent	Richard Johnson	Spartanburg, SC	Old Gold/Black
Wright St.	Raiders	Midwestern	Ralph Underhill	Dayton, OH	Green/Gold
Wyoming	Cowboys	WAC	Joby Wright	Laramie, WY	Brown/Yellow
Xavier	Musketeers	Atlantic 10	Skip Prosser	Cincinnati, OH	Blue/White
Yale	Bulldogs, Elis	Ivy	Dick Kuchen	New Haven, CT	Yale Blue/White
Youngstown St.	Penguins	Mid-Continent	Dan Peters	Youngstown, OH	Red/White

NCAA Division I-A Football Schools

1996 Season

Conferences and coaches as of Sept. 15, 1996.

Changing conference name on July 1, 1996: Big Eight becomes Big 12.

Breakup of Southwest Conference on June 30, 1996: BAYLOR, TEXAS, TEXAS A&M and TEXAS TECH to Big 12; RICE, SMU and TCU to Western Athletic; HOUSTON to Conference USA.

New conference in 1996: Conference USA (6 teams)— former independents CINCINNATI, LOUISVILLE, MEMPHIS, SOUTHERN MISSISSIPPI and TULANE; HOUSTON from Southwest.

Joining Big 12 in 1996 (4): BAYLOR, TEXAS, TEXAS A&M and TEXAS TECH from Southwest.

Joining Big West in 1996 (3): independent NORTH TEXAS; BOISE ST. and IDAHO from Div. I-AA Big Sky Conference.

Joining Western Athletic in 1996 (6): SAN JOSE ST. and UNLV from Big West; RICE, SMU and TCU from Southwest; independent TULSA.

Leaving Big West in 1996 (7): ARKANSAS ST., LOUISIANA TECH, NORTHERN ILLINOIS and SOUTHWESTERN LOUISIANA to become independents; San Jose St. and UNLV to Western Athletic. PACIFIC dropped its football program.

Moving up from Division I-AA in 1996 (2): independents ALABAMA-BIRMINGHAM and CENTRAL FLORIDA.

Joining Conference USA in 1997: EAST CAROLINA from Independent.

Joining Mid-American in 1997: MARSHALL from Div. I-AA Southern Conference and independent NORTHERN ILLINOIS.

Joining Mid-American in 1998: BUFFALO from Div. I-AA Independent.

	Nickname	Conference	Head Coach	Location	Colors
Air Force	Falcons	WAC-Pac.	Fisher DeBerry	Colo. Springs, CO	Blue/Silver
Akron	Zips	Mid-American	Lee Owens	Akron, OH	Blue/Gold
Alabama	Crimson Tide	SEC-West	Gene Stallings	Tuscaloosa, AL	Crimson/White
Alabama-Birm.	Blazers	Independent	Watson Brown	Birmingham, AL	Green/Gold/White
Arizona	Wildcats	Pac-10	Dick Tomey	Tucson, AZ	Cardinal/Navy
Arizona St.	Sun Devils	Pac-10	Bruce Snyder	Tempe, AZ	Maroon/Gold
Arkansas	Razorbacks	SEC-West	Danny Ford	Fayetteville, AR	Cardinal/White
Arkansas St.	Indians	Independent	John Bobo	State Univ., AR	Scarlet/Black
Army	Cadets, Black Knights	Independent	Bob Sutton	West Point, NY	Black/Gold/Gray
Auburn	Tigers	SEC-West	Terry Bowden	Auburn, AL	Orange/Blue
Ball St.	Cardinals	Mid-American	Bill Lynch	Muncie, IN	Cardinal/White
Baylor	Bears	Big 12-South	Chuck Reedy	Waco, TX	Green/Gold
Boise St	Broncos	Big West	Tom Mason	Boise, ID	Orange/Blue
Boston College	Eagles	Big East	Dan Henning	Chestnut Hill, MA	Maroon/Gold
Bowling Green	Falcons	Mid-American	Gary Blackney	Bowling Green, OH	Orange/Brown
BYU	Cougars	WAC-Mtn.	LaVell Edwards	Provo, UT	Royal Blue/White
California	Golden Bears	Pac-10	Steve Mariucci	Berkeley, CA	Blue/Gold
Central Florida	Golden Knights	Independent	Gene McDowell	Orlando, FL	Black/Gold
Central Michigan	Chippewas	Mid-American	Dick Flynn	Mt. Pleasant, MI	Maroon/Gold
Cincinnati	Bearcats	USA	Rick Minter	Cincinnati, OH	Red/Black
Clemson	Tigers	ACC	Tommy West	Clemson, SC	Purple/Orange
Colorado	Golden Buffaloes	Big 12-North	Rick Neuheisel	Boulder, CO	Silver/Gold/Black
Colorado St.	Rams	WAC-Pac.	Sonny Lubick	Ft. Collins, CO	Green/Gold
Duke	Blue Devils	ACC	Fred Goldsmith	Durham, NC	Royal Blue/White
East Carolina	Pirates	Independent	Steve Logan	Greenville, NC	Purple/Gold
Eastern Michigan	Eagles	Mid-American	Rick Rasnick	Ypsilanti, MI	Green/White
Florida	Gators	SEC-East	Steve Spurrier	Gainesville, FL	Orange/Blue
Florida St.	Seminoles	ACC	Bobby Bowden	Tallahassee, FL	Garnet/Gold
Fresno St.	Bulldogs	WAC-Pac.	Jim Sweeney	Fresno, CA	Cardinal/Blue
Georgia	Bulldogs, 'Dawgs	SEC-East	Jim Donnan	Athens, GA	Red/Black
Georgia Tech	Yellow Jackets	ACC	George O'Leary	Atlanta, GA	Old Gold/White
Hawaii	Rainbow Warriors	WAC-Pac.	Fred von Appen	Honolulu, HI	Green/White
Houston	Cougars	USA	Kim Helton	Houston, TX	Scarlet/White
Idaho	Vandals	Big West	Chris Tormey	Moscow, ID	Silver/Gold
Illinois	Fighting Illini	Big Ten	Lou Tepper	Champaign, IL	Orange/Blue
Indiana	Hoosiers	Big Ten	Bill Mallory	Bloomington, IN	Cream/Crimson
Iowa	Hawkeyes	Big Ten	Hayden Fry	Iowa City, IA	Old Gold/Black
Iowa St.	Cyclones	Big 12-North	Dan McCarney	Ames, IA	Cardinal/Gold
Kansas	Jayhawks	Big 12-North	Glen Mason	Lawrence, KS	Crimson/Blue
Kansas St.	Wildcats	Big 12-North	Bill Snyder	Manhattan, KS	Purple/White
Kent	Golden Flashes	Mid-American	Jim Corrigall	Kent, OH	Navy Blue/Gold
Kentucky	Wildcats	SEC-East	Bill Curry	Lexington, KY	Blue/White
LSU	Fighting Tigers	SEC-West	Gerry DiNardo	Baton Rouge, LA	Purple/Gold
Louisiana Tech	Bulldogs	Independent	Gary Crowton	Ruston, LA	Red/Blue
Louisville	Cardinals	USA	Ron Cooper	Louisville, KY	Red/Black/White

	Nickname	Conference	Head Coach	Location	Colors
Maryland	Terrapins, Terps	ACC	Mark Duffner	College Park, MD	Red/White/Black/Gold
Memphis	Tigers	USA	Rip Scherer	Memphis, TN	Blue/Gray
Miami-FL	Hurricanes	Big East	Butch Davis	Miami, FL	Orange/Green/White
Miami-OH	Redskins	Mid-American	Randy Walker	Oxford, OH	Red/White
Michigan	Wolverines	Big Ten	Lloyd Carr	Ann Arbor, MI	Maize/Blue
Michigan St.	Spartans	Big Ten	Nick Saban	E. Lansing, MI	Green/White
Minnesota	Golden Gophers	Big Ten	Jim Wacker	Minneapolis, MN	Maroon/Gold
Mississippi	Ole Miss, Rebels	SEC-West	Tommy Tuberville	Oxford, MS	Cardinal/Navy Blue
Mississippi St.	Bulldogs	SEC-West	Jackie Sherrill	Starkville, MS	Maroon/White
Missouri	Tigers	Big 12-North	Larry Smith	Columbia, MO	Old Gold/Black
Navy	Midshipmen	Independent	Charlie Weatherbie	Annapolis, MD	Navy Blue/Gold
Nebraska	Cornhuskers	Big 12-North	Tom Osborne	Lincoln, NE	Scarlet/Cream
Nevada	Wolf Pack	Big West	Jeff Tisdel	Reno, NV	Silver/Blue
New Mexico	Lobos	WAC-Mtn.	Dennis Franchione	Albuquerque, NM	Cherry/Silver
New Mexico St.	Aggies	Big West	Jim Hess	Las Cruces, NM	Crimson/White
North Carolina	Tar Heels	ACC	Mack Brown	Chapel Hill, NC	Carolina Blue/White
North Carolina St.	Wolfpack	ACC	Mike O'Cain	Raleigh, NC	Red/White
North Texas	Eagles	Big West	Matt Simon	Denton, TX	Green/White
NE Louisiana	Indians	Independent	Ed Zaunbrecher	Monroe, LA	Maroon/Gold
Northern Illinois	Huskies	Independent	Joe Novak	De Kalb, IL	Cardinal/Black
Northwestern	Wildcats	Big Ten	Gary Barnett	Evanston, IL	Purple/White
Notre Dame	Fighting Irish	Independent	Lou Holtz	South Bend, IN	Gold/Blue
Ohio University	Bobcats	Mid-American	Jim Grobe	Athens, OH	Ohio Green/White
Ohio St.	Buckeyes	Big Ten	John Cooper	Columbus, OH	Scarlet/Gray
Oklahoma	Sooners	Big 12-South	John Blake	Norman, OK	Crimson/Cream
Oklahoma St.	Cowboys	Big 12-South	Bob Simmons	Stillwater, OK	Orange/Black
Oregon	Ducks	Pac-10	Mike Bellotti	Eugene, OR	Green/Yellow
Oregon St.	Beavers	Pac-10	Jerry Pettibone	Corvallis, OR	Orange/Black
Penn St.	Nittany Lions	Big Ten	Joe Paterno	University Park, PA	Blue/White
Pittsburgh	Panthers	Big East	Johnny Majors	Pittsburgh, PA	Blue/Gold
Purdue	Boilermakers	Big Ten	Jim Colletto	W. Lafayette, IN	Old Gold/Black
Rice	Owls	WAC-Mtn.	Ken Hatfield	Houston, TX	Blue/Gray
Rutgers	Scarlet Knights	Big East	Terry Shea	New Brunswick, NJ	Scarlet
San Diego St.	Aztecs	WAC-Pac.	Ted Tollner	San Diego, CA	Scarlet/Black
San Jose St.	Spartans	WAC-Pac.	John Ralston	San Jose, CA	Gold/White/Blue
South Carolina	Gamecocks	SEC-East	Brad Scott	Columbia, SC	Garnet/Black
SMU	Mustangs	WAC-Mtn.	Tom Rossley	Dallas, TX	Red/Blue
Southern Miss.	Golden Eagles	USA	Jeff Bower	Hattiesburg, MS	Black/Gold
SW Louisiana	Ragin' Cajuns	Independent	Nelson Stokley	Lafayette, LA	Vermilion/White
Stanford	Cardinal	Pac-10	Tyrone Willingham	Stanford, CA	Cardinal/White
Syracuse	Orangemen	Big East	Paul Pasqualoni	Syracuse, NY	Orange
Temple	Owls	Big East	Ron Dickerson	Philadelphia, PA	Cherry/White
Tennessee	Volunteers	SEC-East	Phillip Fulmer	Knoxville, TN	Orange/White
Texas	Longhorns	Big 12-South	John Mackovic	Austin,TX	Burnt Orange/White
Texas A&M	Aggies	Big 12-South	R.C. Slocum	College Station, TX	Maroon/White
TCU	Horned Frogs	WAC-Mtn.	Pat Sullivan	Ft. Worth, TX	Purple/White
Texas Tech	Red Raiders	Big 12-South	Spike Dykes	Lubbock, TX	Scarlet/Black
Toledo	Rockets	Mid-American	Gary Pinkel	Toledo, OH	Blue/Gold
Tulane	Green Wave	USA	Buddy Teevens	New Orleans, LA	Olive Green/Sky Blue
Tulsa	Golden Hurricane	WAC-Mtn.	Dave Rader	Tulsa, OK	Blue/Gold
UCLA	Bruins	Pac-10	Bob Toledo	Los Angeles, CA	Blue/Gold
UNLV	Runnin' Rebels	WAC-Pac.	Jeff Horton	Las Vegas, NV	Scarlet/Gray
USC	Trojans	Pac-10	John Robinson	Los Angeles, CA	Cardinal/Gold
Utah	Utes	WAC-Mtn.	Ron McBride	Salt Lake City, UT	Crimson/White
Utah St.	Aggies	Big West	John L. Smith	Logan, UT	Navy Blue/White
UTEP	Miners	WAC-Mtn.	Charlie Bailey	El Paso, TX	Orange/White/Blue
Vanderbilt	Commodores	SEC-East	Rod Dowhower	Nashville, TN	Black/Gold
Virginia	Cavaliers	ACC	George Welsh	Charlottesville, VA	Orange/Blue
Virginia Tech	Hokies, Gobblers	Big East	Frank Beamer	Blacksburg, VA	Orange/Maroon
Wake Forest	Demon Deacons	ACC	Jim Caldwell	Winston-Salem, NC	Old Gold/Black
Washington	Huskies	Pac-10	Jim Lambright	Seattle, WA	Purple/Gold
Washington St.	Cougars	Pac-10	Mike Price	Pullman, WA	Crimson/Gray
West Virginia	Mountaineers	Big East	Don Nehlen	Morgantown, WV	Old Gold/Blue
Western Michigan	Broncos	Mid-American	Al Molde	Kalamazoo, MI	Brown/Gold
Wisconsin	Badgers	Big Ten	Barry Alvarez	Madison, WI	Cardinal/White
Wyoming	Cowboys	WAC-Pac.	Joe Tiller	Laramie, WY	Brown/Yellow

NCAA Division I-AA Football Schools

1996 Season

Conferences and coaches as of Sept. 15, 1996.

New Conference in 1996: Northeast Conference (5 teams) - CENT. CONN. ST., MONMOUTH, ROBERT MORRIS, ST. FRANCIS-PA, WAGNER.

Joining Big Sky in 1996 (3): CS-NORTHRIDGE and CS-SACRAMENTO from American West; PORTLAND ST. from Division II.

Beginning play in 1996: FAIRFIELD to Metro Atlantic.

Joining Ohio Valley in 1996: EASTERN ILLINOIS from Gateway.

Joining Southland in 1996 (2): TROY ST. and JACKSONVILLE ST. from Independent (Jacksonville St. will be considered a member but can't compete for the conference championship until 1997).

Moving up from Division II in 1996: PORTLAND ST. to Big Sky.

Joining Patriot League in 1997: independent TOWSON ST.

Joining Southern in 1997: WOFFORD from Independent.

Beginning play in 1997: SOUTH FLORIDA to Independent.

	Nickname	Conference	Head Coach	Location	Colors
Alabama St.	Hornets	Southwestern	Houston Markham	Montgomery, AL	Black/Gold
Alcorn St.	Braves	Southwestern	Cardell Jones	Lorman, MS	Purple/Gold
Appalachian St.	Mountaineers	Southern	Jerry Moore	Boone, NC	Black/Gold
Austin Peay St.	Governors	Ohio Valley	Roy Gregory	Clarksville, TN	Red/White
Bethune-Cookman	Wildcats	Mid-Eastern	Jack McClairen	Daytona Beach, FL	Maroon/Gold
Boston University	Terriers	Yankee	Tom Masella	Boston, MA	Scarlet/White
Brown	Bears	Ivy	Mark Whipple	Providence, RI	Brown/Red/White
Bucknell	Bison	Patriot	Tom Gadd	Lewisburg, PA	Orange/Blue
Buffalo	Bulls	Independent	Craig Cirbus	Buffalo, NY	Blue/White
Butler	Bulldogs	Pioneer	Ken LaRose	Indianapolis, IN	Blue/White
CS-Northridge	Matadors	Big Sky	Dave Baldwin	Northridge, CA	Red/Black/White
CS-Sacramento	Hornets	Big Sky	Gregg Knapp	Sacramento, CA	Green/Gold
Cal Poly SLO	Mustangs	Independent	Andre Patterson	San Luis Obispo, CA	Green/Gold
Canisius	Golden Griffins	Metro Atlantic	Chuck Williams	Buffalo, NY	Blue/Gold
Central Conn. St.	Blue Devils	Northeast	Sal Cintorino	New Britain, CT	Blue/White
Charleston So.	Buccaneers	Independent	David Dowd	Charleston, SC	Blue/Gold
The Citadel	Bulldogs	Southern	Don Powers	Charleston, SC	Blue/White
Colgate	Red Raiders	Patriot	Dick Biddle	Hamilton, NY	Maroon/White
Columbia	Lions	Ivy	Ray Tellier	New York, NY	Lt. Blue/White
Connecticut	Huskies	Yankee	Skip Holtz	Storrs, CT	Blue/White
Cornell	Big Red	Ivy	Jim Hofher	Ithaca, NY	Red/White
Dartmouth	Big Green	Ivy	John Lyons	Hanover, NH	Green/White
Davidson	Wildcats	Independent	Tim Landis	Davidson, NC	Red/Black
Dayton	Flyers	Pioneer	Mike Kelly	Dayton, OH	Red/Blue
Delaware	Blue Hens	Yankee	Tubby Raymond	Newark, DE	Blue/Gold
Delaware St.	Hornets	Mid-Eastern	Bill Collick	Dover, DE	Red/Blue
Drake	Bulldogs	Pioneer	Rob Ash	Des Moines, IA	Blue/White
Duquesne	Dukes	Metro Atlantic	Greg Gattuso	Pittsburgh, PA	Red/Blue
East Tenn. St.	Buccaneers	Southern	Mike Cavan	Johnson City, TN	Blue/Gold
Eastern Illinois	Panthers	Ohio Valley	Bob Spoo	Charleston, IL	Blue/Gray
Eastern Kentucky	Colonels	Ohio Valley	Roy Kidd	Richmond, KY	Maroon/White
Eastern Wash.	Eagles	Big Sky	Mike Kramer	Cheney, WA	Red/White
Evansville	Aces	Pioneer	Robin Cooper	Evansville, IN	Purple/White
Fairfield	Stags	Metro Atlantic	Kevin Kiesel	Fairfield, CT	Cardinal Red
Florida A&M	Rattlers	Mid-Eastern	Billy Joe	Tallahassee, FL	Orange/Green
Fordham	Rams	Patriot	Nick Quartaro	New York, NY	Maroon/White
Furman	Paladins	Southern	Bobby Johnson	Greenville, SC	Purple/White
Georgetown	Hoyas	Metro Atlantic	Bob Benson	Washington, DC	Blue/Gray
Georgia Southern	Eagles	Southern	Frank Ellwood	Statesboro, GA	Blue/White
Grambling St.	Tigers	Southwestern	Eddie Robinson	Grambling, LA	Black/Gold
Hampton	Pirates	Mid-Eastern	Joe Taylor	Hampton, VA	Royal Blue/White
Harvard	Crimson	Ivy	Tim Murphy	Cambridge, MA	Crimson/Black/White
Hofstra	Flying Dutchmen	Independent	Joe Gardi	Hempstead, NY	Blue/White/Gold
Holy Cross	Crusaders	Patriot	Dan Allen	Worcester, MA	Royal Purple
Howard	Bison	Mid-Eastern	Steve Wilson	Washington, DC	Blue/White
Idaho St.	Bengals	Big Sky	Brian McNeely	Pocatello, ID	Orange/Black
Illinois St.	Redbirds	Gateway	Todd Berry	Normal, IL	Red/White
Indiana St.	Sycamores	Gateway	Dennis Raetz	Terre Haute, IN	Blue/White
Iona	Gaels	Metro Atlantic	Harold Crocker	New Rochelle, NY	Maroon/Gold

	Nickname	Conference	Head Coach	Location	Colors
Jackson St.	Tigers	Southwestern	James Carson	Jackson, MS	Blue/White
Jacksonville St.	Gamecocks	Southland	Bill Burgess	Jacksonville, AL	Red/White
James Madison	Dukes	Yankee	Alex Wood	Harrisonburg, VA	Purple/Gold
Lafayette	Leopards	Patriot	Bill Russo	Easton, PA	Maroon/White
Lehigh	Engineers	Patriot	Kevin Higgins	Bethlehem, PA	Brown/White
Liberty	Flames	Independent	Sam Rutigliano	Lynchburg, VA	Red/White/Blue
Maine	Black Bears	Yankee	Kirk Ferentz	Orono, ME	Blue/White
Marist	Red Foxes	Metro Atlantic	Jim Parady	Poughkeepsie, NY	Red/White
Marshall	Thundering Herd	Southern	Bob Pruett	Huntington, WV	Green/White
Massachusetts	Minutemen	Yankee	Mike Hodges	Amherst, MA	Maroon/White
McNeese St.	Cowboys	Southland	Bobby Keasler	Lake Charles, LA	Blue/Gold
Middle Tenn. St.	Blue Raiders	Ohio Valley	Boots Donnelly	Murfreesboro, TN	Blue/White
Miss. Valley St.	Delta Devils	Southwestern	Larry Dorsey	Itta Bena, MS	Green/White
Monmouth	Hawks	Northeast	Kevin Callahan	W. Long Branch, NJ	Royal Blue/White
Montana	Grizzlies	Big Sky	Mick Dennehy	Missoula, MT	Copper/Silver/Gold
Montana St.	Bobcats	Big Sky	Cliff Hysell	Bozeman, MT	Blue/Gold
Morehead St.	Eagles	Ohio Valley	Matt Ballard	Morehead, KY	Blue/Gold
Morgan St.	Bears	Mid-Eastern	Stump Mitchell	Baltimore, MD	Blue/Orange
Murray St.	Racers	Ohio Valley	Houston Nutt	Murray, KY	Blue/Gold
New Hampshire	Wildcats	Yankee	Bill Bowes	Durham, NH	Blue/White
Nicholls St.	Colonels	Southland	Darren Barbier	Thibodaux, LA	Red/Gray
North Carolina A&T	Aggies	Mid-Eastern	Bill Hayes	Greensboro, NC	Blue/Gold
Northeastern	Huskies	Yankee	Barry Gallup	Boston, MA	Red/Black
Northern Ariz.	Lumberjacks	Big Sky	Steve Axman	Flagstaff, AZ	Blue/Gold
Northern Iowa	Panthers	Gateway	Terry Allen	Cedar Falls, IA	Purple/Old Gold
Northwestern St.	Demons	Southland	Sam Goodwin	Natchitoches, LA	Purple/White
Pennsylvania	Quakers	Ivy	Al Bagnoli	Philadelphia, PA	Red/Blue
Portland State	Vikings	Big Sky	Tim Walsh	Portland, OR	Green/White
Prairie View A&M	Panthers	Southwestern	Hensley Sapenter	Prairie View, TX	Purple/Gold
Princeton	Tigers	Ivy	Steve Tosches	Princeton, NJ	Orange/Black
Rhode Island	Rams	Yankee	Floyd Keith	Kingston, RI	Lt. Blue/Dk. Blue/White
Richmond	Spiders	Yankee	Jim Reid	Richmond, VA	Red/Blue
Robert Morris	Colonials	Northeast	Joe Walton	Coraopolis, PA	Blue/White
St. Francis-PA	Red Flash	Northeast	Pete Mayock	Loretto, PA	Red/White
St. John's-NY	Red Storm	Metro Atlantic	Bob Ricca	Jamaica, NY	Red/White
St. Mary's-CA	Gaels	Independent	Mike Rasmussen	Moraga, CA	Red/Blue
St. Peter's	Peacocks	Metro Atlantic	Mark Collins	Jersey City, NJ	Blue/White
Sam Houston St.	Bearkats	Southland	Ron Randleman	Huntsville, TX	Orange/White/Blue
Samford	Bulldogs	Independent	Pete Hurt	Birmingham, AL	Red/Blue
San Diego	Toreros	Pioneer	Kevin McGarry	San Diego, CA	Lt. Blue/Navy/White
Siena	Saints	Metro Atlantic	Ed Zaloom	Loudonville, NY	Green/Gold
South Carolina St.	Bulldogs	Mid-Eastern	Willie Jeffries	Orangeburg, SC	Garnet/Blue
SE Missouri St.	Indians	Ohio Valley	John Mumford	Cape Girardeau, MO	Red/Black
Southern-BR	Jaguars	Southwestern	Pete Richardson	Baton Rouge, LA	Blue/Gold
Southern Illinois	Salukis	Gateway	Shawn Watson	Cardondale, IL	Maroon/White
Southern Utah	Thunderbirds	Independent	Rich Ellerson	Cedar City, UT	Scarlet/Blue/White
SW Missouri St.	Bears	Gateway	Del Miller	Springfield, MO	Maroon/White
SW Texas St.	Bobcats	Southland	Jim Bob Helduser	San Marcos, TX	Maroon/Gold
S.F. Austin St.	Lumberjacks	Southland	John Pearce	Nacogdoches, TX	Purple/White
Tenn-Chattanooga	Moccasins	Southern	Buddy Green	Chattanooga, TN	Navy Blue/Gold
Tenn-Martin	Skyhawks	Ohio Valley	Don McLeary	Martin, TN	Orange/White/Blue
Tennessee St.	Tigers	Ohio Valley	L.C. Cole	Nashville, TN	Blue/White
Tennessee Tech	Golden Eagles	Ohio Valley	Mike Hennigan	Cookeville, TN	Purple/Gold
Texas Southern	Tigers	Southwestern	Bill Thomas	Houston, TX	Maroon/Gray
Towson St.	Tigers	Independent	Gordy Combs	Towson, MD	Gold/White/Black
Troy St.	Trojans	Southland	Larry Blakeney	Troy, AL	Cardinal/Gray/Black
Valparaiso	Crusaders	Pioneer	Tom Horne	Valparaiso, IN	Brown/Gold
Villanova	Wildcats	Yankee	Andy Talley	Villanova, PA	Blue/White
VMI	Keydets	Southern	Bill Stewart	Lexington, VA	Red/White/Yellow
Wagner	Seahawks	Northeast	Walt Hameline	Staten Island, NY	Green/White
Weber St.	Wildcats	Big Sky	Dave Arslanian	Ogden, UT	Royal Purple/White
Western Carolina	Catamounts	Southern	Steve Hodgin	Cullowhee, NC	Purple/Gold
Western Illinois	Leathernecks	Gateway	Randy Ball	Macomb, IL	Purple/Gold
Western Kentucky	Hilltoppers	Independent	Jack Harbaugh	Bowling Green, KY	Red/White
William & Mary	Tribe	Yankee	Jimmye Laycock	Williamsburg, VA	Green/Gold
Wofford	Terriers	Independent	Mike Ayers	Spartanburg, SC	Old Gold/Black
Yale	Bulldogs, Elis	Ivy	Carmen Cozza	New Haven, CT	Yale Blue/White
Youngstown St.	Penguins	Independent	Jim Tressel	Youngstown, OH	Scarlet/White

UCLA

Bob Toledo
UCLA off. coord. to head.

Hawaii

Fred von Appen
Colorado to Hawaii

Oklahoma

John Blake
Cowboys to Oklahoma

Florida

Billy Donovan
Marshall to Florida

Coaching Changes

New head coaches were named at 20 Division I-A and 11 Division I-AA football schools while 46 Division I basketball schools changed head coaches after the 1995-96 season. Coaching changes listed below are as of Sept. 25, 1996.

Division I-A Football

	Old Coach	Record	Why Left?	New Coach	Old Job
Boise St.	Pokey Allen	7-4-0	Medical leave	Tom Mason$	Asst., Boise St.
California	Keith Gilbertson	3-8-0	Fired	Steve Mariucci	Asst., NFL Packers
Georgia	Ray Goff	6-6-0	Resigned	Jim Donnan	Coach, Marshall
Hawaii	Bob Wagner	4-8-0	Fired	Fred von Appen	Asst., Colorado
Louisiana Tech	Joe Raymond Peace	5-6-0	Fired	Gary Crowton	Off. coord., La. Tech
Nevada	Chris Ault	9-3-0	Resigned	Jeff Tisdel	Asst., Nevada
N. Illinois	Charlie Sadler	3-8-0	Fired	Joe Novak	Def. coord., Indiana
Oklahoma	H. Schnellenberger	5-5-1	Resigned	John Blake	Asst., NFL Cowboys
Rutgers	Doug Graber	4-7-0	Fired	Terry Shea	Asst., CFL BC Lions
UCLA	Terry Donahue	7-4-0	Retired	Bob Toledo	Off. coord., UCLA

Division I-AA Football

	Old Coach	Record	Why Left?	New Coach	Old Job
Boston U.	Dan Allen	3-8-0	to Holy Cross*	Tom Masella	Coach, Fairfield
The Citadel	Charlie Taafe	2-9-0	Suspended#	Don Powers$	Asst., Citadel
Colgate	Ed Sweeney	0-11-0	Fired	Dick Biddle	Asst., Colgate
Fairfield	Tom Masella	0-0-0	to Boston U*	Kevin Kiesel	Def. Coord., Albright
Georgia Southern	Tim Stowers	9-4-0	Fired	Frank Ellwood$	Sr. Assoc. AD, Georgia S.
Holy Cross	Peter Vaas	2-9-0	Fired	Dan Allen	Coach, Boston U.
Illinois St.	Jim Heacock	5-6-0	Fired	Todd Berry	Off. Coord., E. Carolina
Marshall	Jim Donnan	12-2-0	to Georgia*	Bob Pruett	Def. Coord. Florida
Montana	Don Read	12-2-0	Retired	Mick Dennehy	Off. Coord., Montana
Morgan St.	Ricky Diggs	1-10-0	Resigned	Stump Mitchell$	Off. Coord., Morgan St.
San Diego	Brian Fogarty	5-5-0	Reassigned	Kevin McGarry	Asst., San Diego
Siena	Jack Dubois	0-9-0	Reassigned	Ed Zaloom	Off. Coord., Albany
Southern Utah	Jack Bishop	2-9-0	Resigned	Rich Ellerson	Asst., Arizona
Tennessee St.	Bill Davis	2-9-0	Resigned	L.C. Cole	Asst., Cincinnati
Tennessee Tech	Jim Ragland	3-8-0	Resigned	Mike Hennigan	Def. Coord., Tenn. Tech.

* As head coach
\# Taaffe was suspended for the 1996 season on August 5, 1996 for his second DUI arrest in three years.
$ Ellwood, Mason, Mitchell, and Powers have been selected on an interim basis.

Division I Basketball

	Old Coach	Record	Why Left?	New Coach	Old Job
Alabama-Birm.	Gene Bartow	16-14	Retired	Murry Bartow	Asst., Alabama-Birm.
Alabama State	John L. Williams	9-17	Reassigned	Rob Spivery	Coach, Ashland Coll.
Alcorn State	Sam Weaver	10-15	to Iowa St.**	Davey Whitney	ex-Alcorn St. coach
Appalachian St.	Tom Apke	7-19	Fired	Buzz Peterson	Assoc. head, Vanderbilt
California	Todd Bozeman	17-11	Resigned	No Replacement named	
CS-Northridge	Pete Cassidy	7-20	Fired	Bobby Braswell	Asst., Oregon
Cent. Conn. St.	Mark Adams	13-15	Reassigned	Howie Dickenman	Asst., UConn
Charleston South.	Gary Edwards	15-13	to Indiana (Pa.)*	Tom Conrad	Assoc. head; Charles. S.
Cleveland St.	Mike Boyd	5-21	Resigned	Rollie Massimino	ex-UNLV coach
Colorado	Joe Harrington	5-9	Resigned $	Ricardo Patton	Interim coach, Colorado
Cornell	Al Walker	10-16	Resigned	Scott Thompson	Coach, Wichita St.
Delaware St.	Fred Goodman	11-17	Fired	Art Perry	Asst., Maryland
Drake	Rudy Washington	12-15	Resigned	Kurt Kanaskie	Coach, Indiana (Pa.)

E. Tennessee St.	Alan LeForce	7-20	Resigned	Ed DeChellis	Asst., Penn. St.
Eastern Wash.	Ben Braun	25-6	to California*	TBA	
Florida	Lon Kruger	12-16	to Illinois*	Billy Donovan	Coach, Marshall
Florida A&M	Ron Brown	6-13	Fired	Mickey Clayton	Wom. coach, Fla. A&M
Idaho	Joe Cravens	12-16	Fired	Kermit Davis	Asst., Utah St.
Illinois	Lou Henson	18-13	Retired	Lon Kruger	Coach, Florida
Illinois-Chicago	Bob Hallberg	10-18	Reassigned	Jimmy Collins	Asst., Illinois
Kent	Dave Grube	14-13	Fired	Gary Waters	Assoc. head, E. Michigan
Lehigh	Dave Duke	4-23	Resigned	Sal Mentesana	Coach, E. Stroudsberg
Long Beach St.	Seth Greenberg	17-11	to S. Florida*	Wayne Morgan	Asst., Syracuse
Maine	Rudy Keeling	15-13	to Northeastern*	John Giannini	Coach, Rowan
Manhattan	Fran Fraschilla	17-12	to St. John's *	John Leonard	Asst., Villanova
Marshall	Billy Donovan	17-11	to Florida*	Greg White	Asst., UCLA
MD-Eastern Shore	Jeff Menday	11-16	Fired	Lonnie Williams	Coach, Tuskegee
Massachusetts	John Calipari	35-1	to NJ Nets (NBA)*	James Flint	Asst., UMass
Miami (OH)	Herb Sendek	21-8	to N.C. State*	Charlie Coles	Asst., Miami (OH)
Middle Tenn. St.	David Farrar	15-12	Fired	Randy Wiel	Coach, N.C. Asheville
Missouri-KC	Lee Hunt	12-15	Retired	Bob Sundvold	Coach, Cent. Missouri St.
New Hampshire	Gib Chapman	6-21	Fired	Jeff Jackson	Asst., Stanford
N.C. Asheville	Randy Wiel	18-10	to Mid. Tenn. St.*	Eddie Biedenbach	Asst., N.C. State
N.C. Charlotte	Jeff Mullins	14-15	Retired	Melvin Watkins	Asst., N.C. Charlotte
N.C. State	Les Robinson	15-16	Resigned	Herb Sendek	Coach, Miami (OH)
Northeastern	Dave Leitao	4-24	to UConn**	Rudy Keeling	Coach, Maine
Pepperdine	Tony Fuller	7-8	Resigned #	Lorenzo Romar	Asst., UCLA
Princeton	Pete Carrill	22-7	Resigned	Bill Carmody	Assoc. head, Princeton
Robert Morris	Jarrett Durham	5-23	Fired	Jim Boone	Coach, California (Pa.)
St. John's (NY)	Brian Mahoney	11-16	Fired	Fran Fraschilla	Coach, Manhattan
South Florida	Bobby Paschal	12-16	Reassigned	Seth Greenberg	Coach, Long Beach St.
Southern-BR	Ben Jobe	17-11	to Tuskegee*	Tommy Green	Asst., Southern
Southern Miss.	M.K. Turk	12-15	Retired	James Green	Asst., Iowa St.
Stephen F. Austin	Ned Fowler	16-10	Fired	Derek Allister	Asst., S. F. Austin
Toledo	Larry Gipson	18-14	Resigned	Stan Joplin	Asst., Michigan St.
USC	Charlie Parker	11-10	Fired %	Henry Bibby	Interim coach, USC
Wichita St.	Scott Thompson	8-21	to Cornell*	Randy Smithson	Coach, Butler County CC

* as head coach
** as assistant coach
$ Harrington resigned on January 16, 1996 and was replaced with assistant coach Ricardo Patton (4-9) for the remainder of the season.
\# Fuller resigned on January 20, 1996 and was replaced with assistant coach Marty Wilson (3-10) for the remainder of the season.
% Parker was fired on February 7, 1996 and replaced on an interim basis with assistant coach Henry Bibby (0-9).

NCAA Division I Schools on Probation

As of Oct. 1, 1996, there were 20 division I member institutions serving NCAA probations.

School	Sport	Yrs	Penalty To End
Nevada-Las Vegas	M Basketball	3	11/9/96
Mississippi St.	Football	1	2/1/97
Southwestern La	Baseball	2	4/22/97
West Virginia	M Tennis	2	4/22/97
Alabama	Football	2	6/3/97
Washington St	Baseball	2	6/21/97
	& Football	2	6/21/97
Georgia Southern	M Basketball	2	11/11/97
Alcorn St.	M/W Basketball	3	11/13/97
	& Football	3	11/13/97
Morgan St	Football	4	2/3/98
	M/W Basketball	4	2/3/98
	M/W X-Country	4	2/3/98
	M/W Tennis	4	2/3/98
	M/W Track	4	2/3/98
	& Wrestling	4	2/3/98
New Mexico St.	M Basketball	3	8/1/98
Coastal Carolina	Basketball	4	8/12/98
Mississippi	Football	4	9/30/98
Alabama St.	W Volleyball	3	9/30/98
	W Track	3	9/30/98
	& M Basketball	3	9/30/98
Miami-FL	Football	3	11/10/98
	Baseball	3	11/10/98
	W Golf	3	11/10/98
	&M Tennis	3	11/10/98
Texas A&M	Football	5	1/6/99
Bethune-Cookman	Football	4	6/2/99
	M/W Basketball	4	6/2/99
	M Tennis	4	6/2/99
	& W Track	4	6/2/99
Maine	M Ice Hockey	4	6/3/00
	Baseball	4	6/3/00
	Football	4	6/3/00
M/W	Track and XC	4	6/3/00
	W Soccer	4	6/3/00
	Field Hockey	4	6/3/00
	M Basketball	4	6/3/00
	M Golf	4	6/3/00
Texas-Pan American	M Basketball	8	7/25/00
Alabama A&M	M Soccer	5	4/19/01

Remaining postseason and TV sanctions

1996-97 postseason ban: Alabama A&M women's track & field and cross-country; Alabama St. women's volleyball and track & field; Maine men's ice hockey; Mississippi football.

1996-97 television ban: Bethune Cookman men's basketball and football; Maine men's ice hockey.

1995-96 Directors' Cup

Officially, the Sears Directors' Cup and sponsored by the National Association of Collegiate Directors of Athletics. Introduced in 1993-94 to honor the nation's best overall NCAA Division I athletic department (combining men's and women's sports), winners in NCAA Division II and III and NAIA were named for the first time following the 1995–96 season.

Standings computed by NACDA with points awarded for each Div. I school's finish in 22 sports (9 core and two wild card sports for both men and women). Div. II schools are awarded points in 16 sports (6 core and two wild card sports for both men and women). Div III schools are awarded points in 20 sports (8 core and two wild card sports for both men and women). NAIA schools are awarded points in 16 sports (6 core and two wild card sports for both men and women). National champions in each sports get 64 points, runners-up get 63, etc., through tournament field. Division I-A football points based on final *USA Today*/CNN Coaches Top 25 poll. Listed below are team conferences (for Div. I only), combined Final Four finishes (1st thru 4th place) for men's and women's programs, overall points in **bold** type, and the previous year's ranking (for Div. I only).

Division I

	Conf	1-2-3-4	Pts	94-95 Rank
1 Stanford	Pac-10	2-1-3-2	**961½**	1
2 UCLA	Pac-10	2-2-3-1	**866**	3
3 Florida	SEC	1-0-2-1	**731½**	5
4 Texas	Big 12	1-2-2-0	**700**	10
5 Michigan	Big Ten	1-0-2-0	**689**	7
6 North Carolina	ACC	1-0-1-1	**673½**	2
7 Arizona	Pac-10	2-0-0-0	**629½**	4
8 Nebraska	Big 12	2-1-0-1	**628**	9
9 Penn St.	Big Ten	1-0-1-1	**626**	8
10 USC	Pac-10	0-0-0-1	**598½**	6
11 Georgia	SEC	0-2-1-0	**587**	14
12 Notre Dame	Independ.	1-1-0-0	**566½**	NR
13 Tennessee	SEC	1-1-0-0	**559**	11
14 Auburn	SEC	0-1-0-0	**538**	NR
15 SMU	WAC	0-1-2-0	**536½**	NR
16 LSU	SEC	3-0-0-0	**535½**	19
17 Ohio St.	Big Ten	1-0-0-0	**531½**	16
18 Wisconsin	Big Ten	1-0-0-0	**530**	17
19 Virginia	ACC	0-2-0-0	**525½**	19
20 Texas A&M	Big 12	0-0-0-0	**524½**	NR
21 Arizona St.	Pac-10	1-0-0-0	**521½**	NR
22 Minnesota	Big Ten	0-0-0-0	**494½**	NR
23 Princeton	Ivy	1-0-1-1	**482½**	NR
24 Florida St	ACC	0-0-0-0	**478½**	24
25 Colorado	Big 12	0-1-0-3	**477½**	23

Division II

	1-2-3-4	Pts
1 UC-Davis	0-0-1-1	**610**
2 Abilene Christian	4-2-1-0	**484**
3 North Dakota St.	1-0-0-1	**470½**
4 South Dakota St.	0-0-0-2	**407½**
5 CS-Bakersfield	0-1-3-0	**404**
6 N. Colorado	0-0-0-0	**376½**
7 Cent. Missouri St.	0-1-0-2	**362½**
8 North Dakota	0-0-0-0	**361½**
9 Western St., CO	1-0-2-1	**359½**
10 Lewis, IL	0-0-1-0	**341½**
11 Ashland, OH	0-0-0-1	**339½**
12 N. Florida	0-0-1-0	**335½**
13 Florida Southern	1-0-0-1	**328**
14 Nebraska-Kearney	0-0-0-1	**324**
15 Portland St.	0-0-0-0	**321½**
16 Mankato St., MN	0-0-0-1	**318**
17 Bloomsburg, PA	0-1-0-0	**311**
18 Barry, FL	1-1-0-1	**299**
19 Denver	0-1-0-0	**290½**
20 NE Missouri St.	0-0-1-0	**284½**
21 Rollins, FL	0-2-0-0	**283½**
22 Hillsdale, MI	0-0-1-0	**280**
23 Edinboro, PA	0-0-0-0	**275**
Millersville, PA	0-0-0-0	**275**
25 Kutztown, PA	0-0-0-0	**263**

Division III

	1-2-3-4	Pts
1 Williams, MA	2-1-1-1	**782**
2 UC-San Diego	1-1-2-0	**718**
3 Wisc.-Oshkosh	3-1-0-1	**593**
4 Trenton St., NJ	3-0-1-0	**543½**
5 Rowan, NJ	1-1-0-0	**490½**
6 Amherst, MA	0-0-0-0	**485½**
7 Emory, GA	1-1-0-0	**461½**
8 Claremont-Mudd-Scripps, CA	0-0-0-1	**449½**
9 Bowdoin, ME	0-0-0-0	**433**
10 Gustavus Adolphus, MN	0-0-0-1	**432½**
11 Calvin, MI	0-0-0-1	**426**
12 Binghamton, NY	0-0-0-0	**420**
13 Methodist, NC	2-1-0-0	**402½**
14 St. Thomas, MN	0-0-2-1	**389½**
15 Middlebury, VT	1-1-0-0	**380½**
16 Ithaca, NY	0-0-0-1	**375**
17 Springfield, MA	0-0-0-0	**364**
18 Wisc.-La Crosse	1-0-1-2	**363**
19 Cortland St., NY	1-0-0-0	**362½**
20 St. Olaf, MN	0-0-0-0	**336½**
21 Mt. Union, OH	0-2-1-0	**330**
22 Kenyon, OH	2-0-1-0	**329**
23 Wisc.-Whitewater	0-0-1-0	**327**
24 Rochester, NY	0-1-0-1	**324½**
25 Ohio Wesleyan	0-0-1-0	**323½**

NAIA

	1-2-3-4	Pts
1 Pacific Lutheran, WA	0-0-1-0	571
2 Simon Fraser, CA	0-2-2-0	529
3 Alabama-Mobile	0-2-0-0	526
4 Berry, GA	0-1-0-0	456
5 Azusa Pacific, CA	1-2-1-0	432½
6 Lindenwood, MO	0-1-0-0	406½
7 Ohio-Findlay	2-0-0-0	405
8 Willamette, OR	0-0-0-0	399
9 Lynn, FL	4-0-1-0	394
10 Westmont, CA	0-0-0-1	393
11 Puget Sound, WA	3-1-0-1	364½
12 Hastings, NE	0-0-0-0	345½
13 Western Washington	0-0-0-0	343
14 So. Nazarene, OK	1-0-1-0	341½
15 Doane, NE	0-0-0-0	338½
16 Oklahoma City	2-0-0-0	325
17 St. Ambrose, IA	0-1-0-0	321
18 Taylor, IN	0-0-0-0	319½
19 Central Washington	1-0-0-0	317
20 W. Oregon St.	1-0-1-0	309½
21 Belmont, TN	0-0-1-0	306½
22 Point Loma Nazarene, CA	0-0-0-0	287
23 Northwestern, IA	0-0-0-0	286
24 Life, GA	0-1-0-1	285
25 Tri-State, IN	0-0-0-1	280½

1995–96 NCAA Team Champions

Twelve schools won two or more national championships during the 1995-96 academic year, led by Division III Abilene Christian with four and two more Division III schools, Trenton-NJ and Wisconsin-Oshkosh, with three each.

Multiple winners: FOUR— Abilene Christian (Div. II men's indoor track & field, women's indoor track & field, men's outdoor track & field and women's outdoor track & field). THREE— Trenton St., NJ (Div. III field hockey, women's lacrosse and softball); Wisconsin-Oshkosh (Div. III women's basketball, women's indoor track & field and women's outdoor track & field). TWO— Kennesaw St., GA (Div. II baseball and softball); Kenyon, OH (Div. III men's swimming & diving and women's swimming & diving); Lincoln, PA (Div. III men's indoor track & field and men's outdoor track & field); LSU (Div. I baseball and women's outdoor track & field) Methodist, NC (Div. III men's golf and combined Div. II and III women's golf); Nebraska (Div. I football and women's volleyball); Stanford (Div. I women's swimming & diving and men's tennis); UCLA (National divisions of water polo and men's volleyball); Williams (Div. III men's cross country and men's soccer).

Overall titles in parentheses; (*) indicates defending champions.

FALL

Cross Country

MEN

Div.	Winner		Runner-Up	Score
I	Arkansas	(8)	N. Arizona	100-142
II	Western St., CO	(1)	Central Mo. St.	69-98
III	Williams*	(2)	N. Central, IL	83-91

Women

Div.	Winner		Runner-Up	Score
I	Providence	(1)	Colorado	88-123
II	Adams St., CO*	(4)	Abilene Chrst.	62-143
III	Cortland St., NY*	(6)	Wisc.-Oshkosh	46-83

Field Hockey

Div.	Winner		Runner-Up	Score
I	North Carolina	(2)	Maryland	5-1
II	Lock Haven, PA*	(4)	Bloomsburg, PA	1-0
III	Trenton St., NJ	(7)	Messiah	2-1

Football

Div.	Winner		Runner-Up	Score
I-A	Nebraska*	(4)	Florida	AP poll
I-AA	Montana	(1)	Marshall	22-20
II	North Alabama*	(3)	Pittsburg St., KS	27-7
III	Wisc.-La Crosse	(2)	Rowan, NJ	37-6

Note: There is no official Div. I-A playoff.

Soccer

Men

Div.	Winner		Runner-Up	Score
I	Wisconsin	(1)	Duke	2-0
II	Southern Conn. St.	(4)	S.C.-Spartanburg	2-0
III	Williams	(1)	Methodist	2-1

Women

Div.	Winner		Runner-Up	Score
I	Notre Dame	(1)	Portland	1-0 (OT)
II	Franklin Pierce, NH *	(2)	Barry	5-0
III	UC-San Diego	(2)	Methodist	3-0

Volleyball

Women

Div.	Winner		Runner-Up	Score
I	Nebraska	(1)	Texas	4 sets
II	Barry	(1)	Northern Mich.	4 sets
III	Washington, MO*	(6)	Cal Lutheran	5 sets

Water Polo

Div.	Winner		Runner-Up	Score
National	UCLA	(4)	California	10-8

WINTER

Basketball

Men

Div.	Winner		Runner-Up	Score
I	Kentucky	(6)	Syracuse	76-67
II	Fort Hays St.	(1)	N. Kentucky	70-63
III	Rowan, NJ	(1)	Hope, MI	100-93

Women

Div.	Winner		Runner-Up	Score
I	Tennessee	(4)	Georgia	83-65
II	North Dakota St.*	(5)	Shippensburg, PA	104-78
III	Wisc.-Oshkosh	(1)	Mount Union	66-50

Fencing

Div.	Winner		Runner-Up	Score
Combined	Penn St.*	(4)	Notre Dame	1500-1190

Gymnastics

Div.	Winner		Runner-Up	Score
Men	Ohio St.	(2)	California	by 0.375
Women	Alabama	(3)	UCLA	by 0.550

Ice Hockey

Div.	Winner		Runner-Up	Score
I	Michigan	(8)	Colorado College	3-2 (OT)
II	Alabama-Huntsville	(1)	Bemijidi St., MN*	7-1, 3-0†
III	Middlebury, VT*	(2)	Rochester Inst.	3-2

†Div. II championship is decided by a two-game series.

1995-96 NCAA Team Champions (Cont.)

Overall titles in parentheses; (*) indicates defending champions.

Rifle

Div.	Winner		Runner-Up	Score
Combined	West Va.*	(11)	Air Force	6179-6168

Skiing

Div.	Winner		Runner-Up	Score
Combined	Utah	(8)	Denver	719-635½

Swimming & Diving

Men

Div.	Winner		Runner-Up	Score
I	Texas	(6)	Auburn	479-443½
II	Oakland, MI*	(4)	CS-Bakersfield	869½-640
III	Kenyon, OH*	(17)	Denison, OH	572½-360

Women

Div.	Winner		Runner-Up	Score
I	Stanford*	(7)	SMU	478-397
II	Air Force*	(2)	Oakland, MI	697½-625
III	Kenyon, OH*	(13)	UC San Diego	542-380

Indoor Track

Men

Div.	Winner		Runner-Up	Score
I	George Mason	(1)	Nebraska	39-31½
II	Abilene Christian	(4)	St. Augustine's*	86⅚-46⅓
III	Lincoln, PA*	(3)	Mount Union	58-42

Women

Div.	Winner		Runner-Up	Score
I	LSU*	(7)	Georgia	52-34
II	Abilene Christian*	(8)	St. Augustine's	68-40
III	Wisc.-Oshkosh*	(3)	Lincoln, PA	41-29

Wrestling

Div.	Winner		Runner-Up	Score
I	Iowa	(15)	Oregon St.	134-77½
II	Central Oklahoma*	(4)	NE-Omaha	148-103
III	Augsburg, MN	(3)	Trenton St.	84½-76½

SPRING

Baseball

Div.	Winner		Runner-Up	Score
I	CS-Fullerton	(3)	USC	11-5
II	Fla. Southern	(8)	Georgia College	15-0
III	La Verne, CA	(1)	Methodist, NC	5-3

Golf

MEN

Div.	Winner		Runner-Up	Score
I	Oklahoma St.	(8)	Stanford	1156-1156†
II	Fla. Southern	(7)	SC-Aiken	1204-1214
III	Methodist, NC*	(5)	Otterbein	899-917

†Oklahoma St. won on 1st hole of sudden death.
Note: rain shortened Div. III tourney to 54 holes.

WOMEN

Div.	Winner		Runner-Up	Score
National	Arizona St.*	(4)	San Jose St.	1155-1181

Lacrosse

MEN

Div.	Winner		Runner-Up	Score
I	Syracuse	(6)	Maryland	13-9
II	Adelphi, NY	(4)	Springfield	12-10
III	Salisbury St., MD	(2)	Nazareth, NY	22-13

WOMEN

Div.	Winner		Runner-Up	Score
I	Maryland	(3)	Princeton* (1)	13-5
III	Trenton St., NJ*	(7)	Wm. Smith, NY	14-13

Softball

Div.	Winner		Runner-Up	Score
I	UCLA	(8)	Arizona*	4-2
II	Kennesaw St., GA	(1)	Bloomsburg, PA	3-2
III	Chapman, CA	(1)	Trenton St., NJ	4-2

Tennis

Note that both Div. II tournaments were team-only.

MEN

Div.	Winner		Runner-Up	Score
I	Stanford	(13)	Mississippi	4-0
II	Lander, SC*	(3)	North Florida	4-2
III	UC-Santa Cruz	(2)	Washington, MD	4-1

WOMEN

Div.	Winner		Runner-Up	Score
I	Texas	(2)	Florida	5-4
II	Armstrong St., GA	(1)	Grand Canyon	4-0
III	Kenyon	(2)	UC-San Diego	5-4

Outdoor Track

MEN

Div.	Winner		Runner-Up	Score
I	Arkansas*	(5)	UCLA	61½-55
II	St. Augustine's*	(7)	Abilene Chrst.	140½-95
III	Lincoln, PA	(3)	Williams	80-61

WOMEN

Div.	Winner		Runner-Up	Score
I	LSU*	(9)	UCLA	69-58
II	Abilene Christian	(5)	CS-Los Angeles	106½-71
III	WI-Oshkosh	(3)	St. Thomas-MN	58-52

Volleyball

MEN

Div.	Winner		Runner-Up	Score
National	UCLA	(15)	Penn St.	3 sets

Real Gender Equality

Schools, whose men's and women's teams won NCAA championships in the same sport, or it's equivalent, during the 1995-96 season.

School	Div.	Sports
Abilene Christain	II	Men's indoor track Women's indoor track Men's outdoor track Women's outdoor track
Kennesaw St., LA	II	baseball softball
Kenyon, OH	III	Men's swimming Women's swimming
Methodist, NC	III	Men's golf Women's golf

Arkansas
Godfrey Siamusiye
Cross-country/Track

Denver
Lisbeth Johnson
Skiing

Oregon St.
Les Gutches
Wrestling

Wisconsin
Kathy Butler
Cross-country/Track

1995-96 Division I Individual Champions

Repeat champions in **bold** type.

FALL

Cross-country

Men (10,000 meters)	**Time**
1 Godfrey Siamusiye, Arkansas	30:09
2 Mark Carroll, Providence	30:45
3 Eric Mack, Air Force	30:46

Women (5,000 meters)	**Time**
1 Kathy Butler, Wisconsin	16:51
2 Amy Skierez, Arizona	16:55
3 Jennifer Rhines, Villanova	17:02

WINTER

Fencing

MEN

Event		Record
Epee	Jeremy Kahn, Duke	20-5
Foil	Thorstein Becker, Wayne St. (MI)	22-2
Sabre	Maxim Pekarev, Princeton	19-6

WOMEN

Event		Record
Epee	Nicole Dygert, St. John's	23-2
Foil	**Olga Kalinovskaya**, Penn St.	24-1

Gymnastics

MEN

Event		Points
All-Around	Blaine Wilson, Ohio St.	58.625
Vault	Jay Thornton, Iowa	9.613
Parallel Bars (tie)	Jamie Ellis, Stanford	9.750
	& Blaine Wilson, Ohio St.	9.750
Horizonal Bar	Carl Imhauser, Temple	9.875
Floor Exercise	Ian Bachrach, Stanford	9.913
Pommel Horse	**Drew Durbin**, Ohio St.	9.875
Rings (tie)	Scott McCall, Wm. & Mary	9.825
	& Blaine Wilson, Ohio St.	9.825

WOMEN

Event		Points
All-Around	Meredith Willard, Alabama	39.450
Vault	Leah Brown, Georgia	9.950
Uneven Bars	Stephanie Woods, Alabama	9.975
Balance Beam	Summer Reid, Utah	9.925
Floor Exercise (tie)	Kim Kelly, Alabama	10.000
	& Heidi Hornbeek, Arizona	10.000

Rifle

COMBINED

Smallbore

	Pts
1 Joe Johnson, Navy	1,170
2 Trevor Gatham, West Va.	1,169
3 Mike Boggs, Kentucky	1,169

Note: Gatham placed 2nd on inner tens (69-64).

Air Rifle

	Pts
1 Trevor Gatham, West Va.	394
2 Bobbie Breyen, Air Force	391
3 Dan Pempel, Air Force	390

Skiing

MEN

Event		Time
Slalom	Matthias Erlandsson, New Mexico	1:37.31
Giant Slalom	Andre Hare, Utah	1:41.49
10-k Freestyle	Thorodd Bakken, Vermont	28:02.5
20-k Classical	Geir Skari, Denver	1:02:26.2

WOMEN

Event		Time
Slalom	Roberta Pergher, Denver	1:25.06
Giant Slalom	Jennifer Collins, Dartmouth	1:48.59
5-k Freestyle	Lisbeth Johnson, Denver	16:01.4
15-k Classical	Lisbeth Johnson, Denver	49:48.7

Wrestling

Wgt	Champion	Runner-Up
118	Sheldon Thomas, Clarion	Jason Nurre, Iowa St.
126	Sanshiro Abe, Penn St.	Dwight Hinson, Iowa St.
134	Cary Kolat, Lock Haven	Steve St. John, Ariz. St.
142	Bill Zadick, Iowa	John Hughes, Penn St.
150	Chris Bono, Iowa St.	Charlie Becks, Ohio St.
158	Joe Williams, Iowa	Ernest Benion, Illinois
167	Daryl Weber, Iowa	Mark Branch, Okla. St.
177	**Les Gutches**, Oregon St.	Reese Andy, Wyoming
190	John Kading, Oklahoma	Ryan Tobin, Nebraska
Hvy	Jeff Walter, Wisconsin	Justin Harty, N. Carolina

USC
Kristine Quance
Swimming

SMU
Ryan Berube
Swimming

Florida
Jill Craybas
Tennis

Stanford
Tiger Woods
Golf

Swimming & Diving

(*) indicates meet record.

MEN

Event (yards)		Time
50 free	Francisco Sanchez, Arizona St.	19.35
100 free	Ricky Busquets, Tennessee	42.64
200 free	Bela Szabados, Fla. Atlantic	1:34.33
500 free	**Tom Dolan**, Michigan	4:12.77
1650 free	**Tom Dolan**, Michigan	14:38.37
100 back	Ryan Berube, SMU	46.15
200 back	Ryan Berube, SMU	1:41.23
100 breast	Jeremy Linn, Tennessee	53:04
200 breast	Matthew Buck, Georgia	1:56.62
100 butterfly	Martin Pepper, Arizona	46.74
200 butterfly	**Ugur Taner**, California	1:43.22
200 IM	Ryan Berube, SMU	1:44.85
400 IM	**Tom Dolan**, Michigan	3:41.44
200 free relay	Texas	1:17.90
400 free relay	Auburn	2:52.87
800 free relay	**Michigan**	6:20.89*
200 medley relay	Tennessee	1:25.85*
400 medley relay	Tennessee	3:09.97

(*) indicates meet record.

Diving		Points
1-meter	**Pat Bogart**, Minnesota	564.90
3-meter	Chris Mantilla, Miami, FL	648.00
Platform	Bryan Gillooly, Miami, FL	789.75

WOMEN

Event (yards)		Time
50 free	Nicole deMan, Tennessee	22.59
100 free	Claudia Franco, Stanford	49.04
200 free	Martina Moravcova, SMU	1:44.64
500 free	Lindsay Benko, USC	4:42.46
1650 free	Mimosa McNerney, Florida	16:06.23
100 back	Jessica Tong, Stanford	54.40
200 back	Lindsay Benko, USC	1:55.78
100 breast	Penny Heyns, Nebraska	1:00.27
200 breast	Kristine Quance, USC	2:09.57*
100 butterfly	Lisa Coole, Georgia	54.21
200 butterfly	Annette Salmeen, UCLA	1:55.84
200 IM	Kristine Quance, USC	1:57.58
400 IM	Kristine Quance, USC	4:06.60
200 free relay	Arizona	1:31.09
400 free relay	**Stanford**	3:18.28
800 free relay	Stanford	7:11.28
200 medley relay	**Stanford**	1:40.90
400 medley relay	SMU	3:37.76

(*) indicates meet record.

Diving		Points
1-meter	Kimiki Hirai, Indiana	443.35
3-meter	Michelle Rojohn, Kansas	567.95
Platform	Becky Ruehl, Cincinnati	636.05

Indoor Track

(*) indicates meet record.

MEN

Event		Time
55 meters	Tim Harden, Kentucky	6.06
200 meters	Obadele Thompson, UTEP	20.36*
400 meters	Greg Hauton, George Mason	45.87
800 meters	Einars Tupuritis, Witchita St.	1:45.80*
Mile	Julius Achon, George Mason	4:02.83
3000 meters	Ryan Wilson, Arkansas	7:51.66
5000 meters	Jason Casiano, Wisconsin	13:50.08
55-m hurdles	Darius Pemberton, Houston	7.14
4x400-m relay	Oklahoma	3:04.46*
Distance medley relay	Nebraska	9:32.13

(*) indicates meet record.

Event		Hgt/Dist
High Jump	Michael Roberson, McNeese St.	7-5
Pole Vault	Lawrence Johnson, Tennessee	18-6½
Long Jump	Andrew Owusu, Alabama	25-11
Triple Jump	Robert Howard, Arkansas	54-10¼
Shot Put	Jonathan Ogden, UCLA	63-8¼
35-lb. Throw	Ryan Butler, Wyoming	71-1½

WOMEN

Event		Time
55 meters	D'Andre Hill, LSU	6.69
200 meters	Debbie Ferguson, Georgia	23.17
400 meters	Monique Hennagan, UNC	52.57
800 meters	Kristi Kloster, Kansas	2:04.91
Mile	Joline Staeheli, Georgetown	4:36.96
3000 meters	Melody Fairchild, Oregon	9:07.25
5000 meters	Marie McMahon, Providence	15:42.71
55-m hurdles	Kim Carson, LSU	7.44
4x400-m relay	LSU	3:32.53
Distance medley relay	Wisconsin	11:08.91

(*) indicates meet record.

Event		Hgt/Dist
High Jump	Najuma Fletcher, Pitt.	6-0¼
Long Jump	Angee Henry, Nebraska	20-11¼
Triple Jump	Nicola Martial, Nebraska	44-8¼
Shot Put	Valeyta Althouse, UCLA	57-11
20-lb. Weight	Dawn Ellerbe, S. Carolina	67-10¼

SPRING

Golf

MEN

		Total
1	Tiger Woods, Stanford	69-67-69-80—285
2	Rory Sabbatini, Arizona	70-70-74-75—289
3	Darren Angel, Arizona St.	72-74-69-76—291
	Mike Ruiz, UNLV	71-74-74-72—291

WOMEN

	Total
1 Marisa Baena, Arizona	70-75-78-73—296
2 Kellee Booth, Arizona St.	74-74-75-80—303
3 Kathy Choi, UCLA	78-74-78-74—304

Tennis

MEN

Singles—Cecil Mamiit (USC) def. Fredrik Bergh (Fresno St.), 6-2, 4-6, 6-3.

Doubles—Justin Gimelstob & Srdjan Muskatirovic (UCLA) def. Ashley Fisher & Jason Weir-Smith (TCU), 6-7 (3), 6-4, 6-4.

WOMEN

Singles—Jill Craybas (Florida) def. Kylie Hunt (Kansas), 5-7, 6-3, 6-3.

Doubles—Dawn Buth & Stephanie Nickitas (Florida) def. Christina Moros & Farley Taylor (Texas), 6-1, 6-3.

Outdoor Track

(*) indicates meet record (†) indicates American record.

MEN

Event		Time
100 meters	Tim Harden, Kentucky	10.05
100 meters	Ato Boldon, UCLA	9.92*
200 meters	Roshaan Griffin, LSU	20.24
400 meters	Davian Clarke, Miami, FL	45.29
800 meters	Einars Tupuritis, Wichita St.	1:45.08
1500 meters	Marko Koers, Illinois	3:37.57
5000 meters	Alan Culpepper, Colorado	13:47.26
10,000 meters	**Godfrey Siamusiye**, Ark.	28:56.39
110-m hurdles	Dominique Arnold, Wash. St.	13.46
400-m hurdles	Neil Gardner, Mich.	49.27
3000-m steeple	Dmitry Drozdov, Iowa St.	8:32.01
4x100-m relay	North Carolina	39.05
4x400-m relay	**Baylor**	3:01.25
Event		**Hgt/Dist**
High Jump	Eric Bishop, N. Carolina	7-6
Pole Vault	**Lawrence Johnson**, Tennessee	19-1 *
Long Jump	Richard Duncan, Texas	26-0½
Triple Jump	Robert Howard, Arkansas	56-1¼
Shot Put	Andy Bloom, Wake Forest	65-0 ½
Discus	Andy Bloom, Wake Forest	211-1
Javelin	Pal Arne Fagernes, Ariz. St.	259-8
Hammer	**Balazs Kiss**, USC	265-3 *
Decathlon	Victor Houston, Auburn	7766 pts

WOMEN

Event		Time
100 meters	**D'Andre Hill**, LSU	11.03
200 meters	Zundra Feagin, LSU	22.44
400 meters	Suziann Reid, Texas	52.16
800 meters	Monique Hennagan, UNC	2:03.27
1500 meters	Miesha Marzell, Georgetown	4:17.92
3000 meters	**Kathy Butler**, Wisconsin	9:16.19
5000 meters	**Jennifer Rhines**, Villanova	16:05.85
10,000 meters	**Katie Swords**, SMU	32:56.63
100-m hurdles	Kim Carson, LSU	12.82
400-m hurdles	**Tonya Williams**, Illinois	54.56*
4x100-m relay	**LSU**	43.03
4x400-m relay	Texas	3:27.50*
Event		**Hgt/Dist**
High Jump	**Amy Acuff**, UCLA	6- 4¼
Long Jump	Angee Henry, Nebraska	21-11½
Triple Jump	Suzette Lee, LSU	45-1
Shot Put	Teri Steer, SMU	59- 0
Discus	Anna Soderburg, N. Ariz.	195-3
Javelin	Windy Dean, SMU	186-1
Hammer	Dawn Ellerbe, S. Carolina	209-2†
Heptathlon	Corissa Yasen, Purdue	5765 pts

Most Outstanding Players

MEN

Baseball	Mark Kotsay, CS-Fullerton
Baseball	Pat Burrell, Miami-FL
Basketball	Tony Delk, Kentucky
Cross-country	Godfrey Siamusiye, Arkansas*
Golf	Tiger Woods, Stanford*
Gymnastics	Blaine Wilson, Ohio St.*
Ice Hockey	Brendan Morrison, Michigan
Lacrosse	Michael Watson, Virginia
Swimming & Diving	Ryan Berube, SMU
Tennis	Cecil Mamiit, USC*
Track: Indoor	Tim Harden, Kentucky
Outdoor	Lawrence Johnson, Tennessee
Volleyball	Yuval Katz, Hawaii
Water Polo	Jim Toring, Jeremy Braxton-Brown and Matt Swanson of UCLA and Brent Albright of California
Wrestling	Les Gutches, Oregon St.

WOMEN

Basketball	Michelle Marciniak, Tennesee
Cross-country	Kathy Butler, Wisconsin*
Golf	Marisa Baena, Arizona*
Gymnastics	Meredith Willard, Alabama*
Soccer: Offense	Cindy Dawe, Notre Dame
Soccer: Defense	Kate Sobrero, Notre Dame
Softball	Jenny Dalton, Arizona
Swimming & Diving	Kristine Quance, USC
Tennis	Jill Craybas, Florida*
Track: Indoor	Najuma Fletcher, Pittsburgh
Outdoor	D'Andre Hill, LSU

(*) indicates won individual or all-around NCAA championship; There were no official Outstanding Players in the men's and women's combined sports of fencing, riflery and skiing.

No awards: Field Hockey, Lacrosse, Men's Soccer and Volleyball.

1995-96 NAIA Team Champions

Total NAIA titles in parentheses.

FALL

Cross Country: MEN'S–Lubbock Christian, TX (6); WOMEN'S– Puget Sound, WA (4). **Football:** MEN'S– Division I: Central St., OH (3) and Division II: TIE-Central Washington (1) and Findlay, OH (3). **Soccer:** MEN'S– Lindsey Wilson, KY (1); WOMEN'S– Lynn, FL (3).**Volleyball:** WOMEN'S– BYU-Hawaii (6).

WINTER

Basketball: MEN'S– Division I: Oklahoma City (3) and Division II: Albertson, ID (1); WOMEN'S– Division I; Southern Nazarene, OK (4) and Division II: Western Oregon (2). **Swimming & Diving:**MEN'S– Puget Sound, WA (2); WOMEN'S– Puget Sound, WA (3). **Indoor Track:** MEN'S–Azusa Pacific, CA (1); WOMEN'S– Central St., OH (2). **Wrestling:** MEN'S– Missouri Valley (1).

SPRING

Baseball: MEN'S– Lewis-Clark St., ID (9); **Golf:** MEN'S– Lynn, FL (1); WOMEN'S– Lynn, FL (2); **Softball:** WOMEN'S– Oklahoma City (3); **Tennis:** MEN'S– Auburn-Montgomery, AL (3); WOMEN'S– Lynn, FL (3); **Outdoor Track:** MEN'S– Lubbock Christian, TX (1); WOMEN'S– Central St., OH (5).

Annual NCAA Division I Team Champions

Men's and Women's NCAA Division I team champions from Cross-country to Wrestling. Rowing is included, although the NCAA does not sanction championships in the sport. Team champions in baseball, basketball, football, golf, ice hockey, soccer and tennis can be found in the appropriate chapters throughout the almanac. See pages 457-459 for list of 1995-96 individual champions.

CROSS-COUNTRY

Men

Arkansas placed five runners in the top 36 to collect 100 points—42 points better than runner-up Northern Arizona and won a record-tying eighth title and its fifth in six years. The youthful Razorbacks (four freshmen, two sophomores and one senior) were paced by individual champion Godfrey Siamusiye, who covered the 10,000-meter course in 30:09— 36 seconds faster than Providence's Mark Carroll, the runner-up. *(Ames, Iowa; Nov. 20, 1995.)*

Multiple winners: Michigan St. and Arkansas (8); UTEP (7); Oregon and Villanova (4); Drake, Indiana, Penn St. and Wisconsin (3); Iowa St., San Jose St. and Western Michigan (2).

Year		Year		Year		Year		Year	
1938	Indiana	1949	Michigan St.	1961	Oregon St.	1973	Oregon	1985	Wisconsin
1939	Michigan St.	1950	Penn St.	1962	San Jose St.	1974	Oregon	1986	Arkansas
1940	Indiana	1951	Syracuse	1963	San Jose St.	1975	UTEP	1987	Arkansas
1941	Rhode Island	1952	Michigan St.	1964	Western Mich.	1976	UTEP	1988	Wisconsin
1942	Indiana & Penn St.	1953	Kansas	1965	Western Mich.	1977	Oregon	1989	Iowa St.
1943	Not held	1954	Oklahoma St.	1966	Villanova	1978	UTEP	1990	Arkansas
1944	Drake	1955	Michigan St.	1967	Villanova	1979	UTEP	1991	Arkansas
1945	Drake	1956	Michigan St.	1968	Villanova	1980	UTEP	1992	Arkansas
1946	Drake	1957	Notre Dame	1969	UTEP	1981	UTEP	1993	Arkansas
1947	Penn St.	1958	Michigan St.	1970	Villanova	1982	Wisconsin	1994	Iowa St.
1948	Michigan St.	1959	Michigan St.	1971	Oregon	1983	Vacated	1995	Arkansas
		1960	Houston	1972	Tennessee	1984	Arkansas		

Women

Providence dominated the field, earning four of the top 25 team scoring places to end Villanova's six year reign and earn their first NCAA title in any sport. The Friars were buoyed by junior Marie McMahon (17:09) and sophomore Maria McCambridge (17:22) who earned fourth and sixth-place finishes, respectively and helped them to beat second-place Colorado, 88-123. Third-place Villanova collected 151 points. Wisconsin senior Kathy Butler won the individual title, completing the 5,000-meter course in 16:51, four seconds ahead of Amy Skieresz of Arizona. *(Ames, Iowa; Nov. 20, 1995.)*

Multiple winners: Villanova (6); Oregon, Virginia and Wisconsin (2).

Year		Year		Year		Year		Year	
1981	Virginia	1984	Wisconsin	1987	Oregon	1990	Villanova	1993	Villanova
1982	Virginia	1985	Wisconsin	1988	Kentucky	1991	Villanova	1994	Villanova
1983	Oregon	1986	Texas	1989	Villanova	1992	Villanova	1995	Providence

FENCING

Men & Women

Penn St. repeated as champions behind Olga Kalinovskaya's unprecedented fourth straight title in the women's foil. Kalinovskaya defeated Notre Dame's Sara Walsh 15-4 in the championship bout to become the first woman ever to win four individual titles. The Nittany Lions (1,500 points) topped Notre Dame (1,190) and St. Johns of New York (1,130) in the first year of a new tournament format that includes a "medal round" in each of the five individual events. *(New Haven, Conn.; Mar. 29- Apr. 1, 1996.)*

Multiple winners: Penn St. (4); Columbia/Barnard (2). **Note:** Prior to 1990, men and women held separate championships. Men's multiple winners: NYU (12); Columbia (11); Wayne St. (7); Navy, Notre Dame and Penn (3); Illinois (2). Women's multiple winners: Wayne St. (3); Yale (2).

Year		Year		Year		Year		Year	
1990	Penn St.	1992	Columbia/ Barnard	1993	Columbia/ Barnard	1994	Notre Dame	1996	Penn St.
1991	Penn St.					1995	Penn St.		

FIELD HOCKEY

Women

North Carolina capped an undefeated season with a 5-1 victory over Maryland in the championship final. The Tar Heels who finished the year 24-0 and tied a championship game record for goals in a game, almost didn't make it to the game at all. The team bus never showed up to take them to the game and the players were forced to catch rides with parents. Maryland earned their spot in the final with a 3-1 win over Northeastern, while North Carolina advanced by shutting-out defending champs James Madison 3-0. *(Winston-Salem, N.C.; Nov. 18-19, 1995.)*

Multiple winners: Old Dominion (7); Connecticut, Maryland and North Carolina (2).

Year		Year		Year		Year		Year	
1981	Connecticut	1984	Old Dominion	1987	Maryland	1990	Old Dominion	1993	Maryland
1982	Old Dominion	1985	Connecticut	1988	Old Dominion	1991	Old Dominion	1994	James Madison
1983	Old Dominion	1986	Iowa	1989	North Carolina	1992	Old Dominion	1995	North Carolina

GYMNASTICS

Men

Ohio St. paid back Stanford one year after watching the Cardinal win the NCAA title at their place in Columbus, by winning the 1996 team title on Stanford's home floor. Behind performances from individual all-around champion Blaine Wilson and pommel horse winner Drew Durbin, the Buckeyes edged runners-up California 232.150 to 231.775. Stanford finished third with 229.925. *(Stanford, Calif.; Apr. 25-27, 1996.)*

Multiple winners: Illinois and Penn St. (9); Nebraska (8); So. Illinois (4); Iowa St., Oklahoma and Stanford (3); California, Florida St., Michigan, Ohio St. and UCLA (2).

Year		Year		Year		Year		Year	
1938	Chicago	1954	Penn St.	1965	Penn St.	1975	California	1986	Arizona St.
1939	Illinois	1955	Illinois	1966	So.Illinois	1976	Penn St.	1987	UCLA
1940	Illinois	1956	Illinois	1967	So.Illinois	1977	Indiana St. & Oklahoma	1988	Nebrasksa
1941	Illinois	1957	Penn St.	1968	California	1978	Oklahoma	1989	Illinois
1942	Illinois	1958	Michigan St. & Illinois	1969	Iowa & Michigan (T)	1979	Nebraska	1990	Nebraska
1943-47	Not held	1959	Penn St.	1970	Michigan & Michigan (T)	1980	Nebraska	1991	Oklahoma
1948	Penn St.	1960	Penn St.	1971	Iowa St.	1981	Nebraska	1992	Stanford
1949	Temple	1961	Penn St.	1972	So. Illinois	1982	Nebraska	1993	Stanford
1950	Illinois	1962	USC	1973	Iowa St.	1983	Nebraska	1994	Nebraska
1951	Florida St.	1963	Michigan	1974	Iowa St.	1984	UCLA	1995	Stanford
1952	Florida St.	1964	So. Illinois			1985	Ohio St.	1996	Ohio St.
1953	Penn St.								

(T) indicates won trampoline competition (1969 and '70).

Women

Alabama shed the bridesmaid role and amassed a championships record score of 198.025 points to bury the field for its third title. The Crimson Tide, runners-up the past three years before the record-setting performance on their home floor, bested second-place UCLA (197.475). Alabama dominated on the vault (49.775) and floor exercise (49.625) and Kim Kelly, Danielle McAdams and Merideth Willard were the leaders in the all-around, each scoring 39.000-plus points. *(Tuscaloosa, Ala.; Apr. 25-27, 1996.)*

Multiple winners: Utah (9); Alabama and Georgia (3).

Year		Year		Year		Year		Year	
1982	Utah	1985	Utah	1988	Alabama	1991	Alabama	1994	Utah
1983	Utah	1986	Utah	1989	Georgia	1992	Utah	1995	Utah
1984	Utah	1987	Georgia	1990	Utah	1993	Georgia	1996	Alabama

LACROSSE

Men

Princeton sophomore Jesse Hubbard bounced an underhand shot past Virginia goalie Chris Sanderson just 94 seconds into overtime to lift the Tigers to a 13-12 win and their third title in five years. Virginia's Michael Watson scored 5 goals for the Cavaliers and was named the tournament's outstanding player. In the semifinals, Princeton took the same road to the title game as they did in 1994, beating defending champion Syracuse, 11-9, while Virginia downed Johns Hopkins, 16-10. *(College Park, Md.; May 25-27, 1996.)*

Multiple winners: Johns Hopkins (7); Syracuse (6); North Carolina (4); Cornell and Princeton (3); Maryland (2).

Year		Year		Year		Year		Year	
1971	Cornell	1977	Cornell	1983	Syracuse	1989	Syracuse	1995	Syracuse
1972	Virginia	1978	Johns Hopkins	1984	Johns Hopkins	1990	Syracuse	1996	Princeton
1973	Maryland	1979	Johns Hopkins	1985	Johns Hopkins	1991	North Carolina		
1974	Johns Hopkins	1980	Johns Hopkins	1986	North Carolina	1992	Princeton		
1975	Maryland	1981	North Carolina	1987	Johns Hopkins	1993	Syracuse		
1976	Cornell	1982	North Carolina	1988	Syracuse	1994	Princeton		

Women

Maryland became the first ever repeat champion in Div. I women's lacrosse, beating Virginia 10-5. The Terrapins trailed early, 2-1, but led 5-3 at the half. In the second half, the Terps' Kelly Amonte scored three of her team's four unanswered goals to put the game away for Maryland. Amonte ended the day with five goals, finishing her career at sixth on the all-time scoring list with 319 points. In the semifinals, both teams struggled a bit to advance. Maryland squeaked by Princeton, 6-5 and Virginia edged Loyola (Md.), 10-9. *(Bethlehem, Pa.; May 18-19, 1996.)*

Multiple winners: Maryland (4); Penn St., Temple and Virginia (2).

Year		Year		Year		Year		Year	
1982	Massachusetts	1985	New Hampshire	1988	Temple	1991	Virginia	1994	Princeton
1983	Delaware	1986	Maryland	1989	Penn St.	1992	Maryland	1995	Maryland
1984	Temple	1987	Penn St.	1990	Harvard	1993	Virginia	1996	Maryland

Annual NCAA Division I Team Champions (Cont.)

RIFLE

Men & Women

West Virginia stumbled somewhat but stayed on target and won its eleventh rifle title. The Mountaineers fired its lowest air rifle score of the year (1,531 points) but made up for it in the smallbore (4,648) and tallied a combined 6,179 to runner-up Air Force's 6,168. In individual competition, West Virginia senior Trevor Gatham set a championships record for air rifle with 394 points and Navy's Joe Johnson became the first person from a service academy to win either rifle with his score of 1,170 in the smallbore. *(Colorado Springs, Colo., Mar. 8-9, 1996.)*

Multiple winners: West Virginia (11); Tennessee Tech (3); Murray St. (2).

Year		Year		Year		Year		Year	
1980	Tenn. Tech	1984	West Virginia	1988	West Virginia	1992	West Virginia	1995	West Virginia
1981	Tenn. Tech	1985	Murray St.	1989	West Virginia	1993	West Virginia	1996	West Virginia
1982	Tenn. Tech	1986	West Virginia	1990	West Virginia	1994	AK-Fairbanks		
1983	West Virginia	1987	Murray St.	1991	West Virginia				

ROWING

Intercollegiate Rowing Association Regatta
VARSITY EIGHTS
Men

Princeton overcame Washington with a late surge to win the 94th rowing of the IRA championships on Cooper River in Camden, N.J. in a course-record time of 5:29.6. The Tigers trailed with little more than 200 meters of the 2,000-meter course remaining before catching and passing the Huskies, who finished second in a time of 5:30.9. Penn was a factor early, but faded and finished third in 5:36.2. *(Camden, N.J.; June 1, 1996.)*

The IRA was formed in 1895 by several northeastern colleges after Harvard and Yale quit the Rowing Association (established in 1871) to stage an annual race of their own. Since then the IRA Regatta has been contested over courses of varing lengths in Poughkeepsie, N.Y., Marietta, Ohio, Syracuse, N.Y. and Camden, N.J.

Distances: 4 miles (1895-97,1899-1916,1925-41); 3 miles (1898,1921-24,1947-49,1952-63,1965-67); 2 miles (1920,1950-51); 2000 meters (1964, since 1968).

Multiple winners: Cornell (24); Navy (13); California and Washington (10); Penn (9); Brown and Wisconsin (7); Syracuse (6); Columbia (4); Northeastern and Princeton (2).

Year		Year		Year		Year		Year	
1895	Columbia	1915	Cornell	1937	Washington	1961	California	1981	Cornell
1896	Cornell	1916	Syracuse	1938	Navy	1962	Cornell	1982	Cornell
1897	Cornell	1917-19	Not held	1939	California	1963	Cornell	1983	Brown
1898	Penn	1920	Syracuse	1940	Washington	1964	California	1984	Navy
1899	Penn	1921	Navy	1941	Washington	1965	Navy	1985	Princeton
1900	Penn	1922	Navy	1942-46	Not held	1966	Wisconsin	1986	Brown
1901	Cornell	1923	Washington	1947	Navy	1967	Penn	1987	Brown
1902	Cornell	1924	Washington	1948	Washington	1968	Penn	1988	Northeastern
1903	Cornell	1925	Navy	1949	California	1969	Penn	1989	Penn
1904	Syracuse	1926	Washington	1950	Washington	1970	Washington	1990	Wisconsin
1905	Cornell	1927	Columbia	1951	Wisconsin	1971	Cornell	1991	Northeastern
1906	Cornell	1928	California	1952	Navy	1972	Penn	1992	Dartmouth, Navy & Penn†
1907	Cornell	1929	Columbia	1953	Navy	1973	Wisconsin	1993	Brown
1908	Syracuse	1930	Cornell	1954	Navy*	1974	Wisconsin	1994	Brown
1909	Cornell	1931	Navy	1955	Cornell	1975	Wisconsin	1995	Brown
1910	Cornell	1932	California	1956	Cornell	1976	California	1996	Princeton
1911	Cornell	1933	Not held	1957	Cornell	1977	Cornell		
1912	Cornell	1934	California	1958	Cornell	1978	Syracuse		
1913	Syracuse	1935	California	1959	Wisconsin	1979	Brown		
1914	Columbia	1936	Washington	1960	California	1980	Navy		

*In 1954, Navy was disqualified because of an ineligible coxwain; no trophies were given. †First dead heat in history of IRA Regatta.

Harvard/Yale Regatta

Yale snapped Harvard's 11-year winning streak on June 8, 1996 in the 131st Harvard/Yale Regatta for varsity eights. After over an hour delay due to high winds, Yale pulled ahead, answered every Harvard challenge and finished the four-mile course on the Thames River in New London, Conn. in 20:01.9. Harvard followed just over a length behind in 20:08.5. The Harvard/Yale Regatta is the nation's oldest intercollegiate sporting event. Harvard holds a 79-52 series edge.

National Rowing Championships

VARSITY EIGHTS

While Princeton ended Brown's three-year title run in the men's national championship race, Brown did the same to Princeton in the women's race on Lake Harsha, north of Cincinnati. In the men's race, Princeton jumped of the stake boat and built a large lead, cruising to a 1½ length victory over Penn. On the women's side, Brown became the first crew to win the Eastern Sprints, the IRA and the Ferguson Bowl, emblematic of the women's national collegiate title. The Bears took a small lead early and never broke pace to earn a near boat-length win over Princeton and a surprising Wisconsin entry. *(Lake Harsha, Bantam, Ohio; June 8, 1996.)*

Men

National championship raced annually since 1982 in Bantam, Ohio over a 2000-meter course on Lake Harsha. Winner receives Herschede Cup.

Multiple winners: Harvard (6); Brown (3); Wisconsin (2).

Year	Champion	Time	Runner-up	Time	Year	Champion	Time	Runner-up	Time
1982	Yale	5:50.8	Cornell	5:54.15	1990	Wisconsin	5:52.5	Harvard	5:56.84
1983	Harvard	5:59.6	Washington	6:00.0	1991	Penn	5:58.21	Northeastern	5:58.48
1984	Washington	5:51.1	Yale	5:55.6	1992	Harvard	5:33.97	Dartmouth	5:34.28
1985	Harvard	5:44.4	Princeton	5:44.87	1993	Brown	5:54.15	Penn	5:56.98
1986	Wisconsin	5:57.8	Brown	5:59.9	1994	Brown	5:24:52	Harvard	5:25:83
1987	Harvard	5:35.17	Brown	5:35.63	1995	Brown	5:23:40	Princeton	5:25:83
1988	Harvard	5:35.98	Northeastern	5:37.07	1996	Princeton	5:57:47	Penn	6:03.28
1989	Harvard	5:36.6	Washington	5:38.93					

Women

National championship held over various distances at 10 different venues since 1979. Distances—1000 meters (1979-81); 1500 meters (1982-83); 1000 meters (1984); 1750 meters (1985); 1852 meters (1989-90). 2000 meters (1986-88, since 1991); Winner receives Ferguson Bowl.

Multiple winners: Washington (7); Princeton (4); Boston University (2).

Year	Champion	Time	Runner-up	Time	Year	Champion	Time	Runner-up	Time
1979	Yale	3:06	California	3:08.6	1988	Washington	6:41.0	Yale	6:42.37
1980	California	3:05.4	Oregon St.	3:05.8	1989	Cornell	5:34.9	Wisconsin	5:37.5
1981	Washington	3:20.6	Yale	3:22.9	1990	Princeton	5:52.2	Radcliffe	5:54.2
1982	Washington	4:56.4	Wisconsin	4:59.83	1991	Boston Univ.	7:03.2	Cornell	7:06.21
1983	Washington	4:57.5	Dartmouth	5:03.02	1992	Boston Univ.	6:28.79	Cornell	6:32.79
1984	Washington	3:29.48	Radcliffe	3:31.08	1993	Princeton	6:40.75	Washington	6:43.86
1985	Washington	5:28.4	Wisconsin	5:32.0	1994	Princeton	6:11.38	Yale	6:14.46
1986	Wisconsin	6:53.28	Radcliffe	6:53.34	1995	Princeton	6:11.98	Washington	6:12.69
1987	Washington	6:33.8	Yale	6:37.4	1996	Brown	6:45.7	Princeton	6:49.3

SKIING

Men & Women

Utah won just one event but finished second in four and had enough depth to carry them to their eighth overall title. Utah's Andrew Hare won the giant slalom in 1:41.49 and the Utes' beat out second-place Denver, 719-635. Denver won four individual events, with Lisbeth Johnson capturing both women's cross-country crowns and Roberta Pergher winning the women's slalom. Denver's four individual titles bring its second-place total to 51 ahead of Utah's 50, but behind Colorado's 60. *(Bridger Bowl/Bohart Ranch, Bozeman, Mont.; Mar. 6-9, 1996.)*

Multiple winners: Denver (14); Colorado (13); Utah (8); Vermont (5); Dartmouth and Wyoming (2).

Year		Year		Year		Year		Year	
1954	Denver	1963	Denver	1972	Colorado	1980	Vermont	1989	Vermont
1955	Denver	1964	Denver	1973	Colorado	1981	Utah	1990	Vermont
1956	Denver	1965	Denver	1974	Colorado	1982	Colorado	1991	Colorado
1957	Denver	1966	Denver	1975	Colorado	1983	Utah	1992	Vermont
1958	Dartmouth	1967	Denver	1976	Colorado & Dartmouth	1984	Utah	1993	Utah
1959	Colorado	1968	Wyoming	1977	Colorado	1985	Wyoming	1994	Vermont
1960	Colorado	1969	Denver	1978	Colorado	1986	Utah	1995	Colorado
1961	Denver	1970	Denver	1979	Colorado	1987	Utah	1996	Utah
1962	Denver	1971	Denver			1988	Utah		

SOFTBALL

Women

Arizona jumped out early and held off Pac-10 rival and top-ranked Washington, 6-4, for its fourth title in six years. The tournament's most outstanding player, Jenny Dalton, belted a three-run homer in the top of the first inning to get things rolling for the Wildcats. Washington put up four runs in the fourth on four hits and two Wildcat errors, but Arizona pitcher Carrie Dolan shut them down the rest of the way. *(Columbus, Ga., May 23-27, 1996.)*

Multiple winners: UCLA (8); Arizona (4); Texas A&M (2).

Year		Year		Year		Year		Year	
1982	UCLA	1985	UCLA	1988	UCLA	1991	Arizona	1994	Arizona
1983	Texas A&M	1986	CS-Fullerton	1989	UCLA	1992	UCLA	1995	UCLA
1984	UCLA	1987	Texas A&M	1990	UCLA	1993	Arizona	1996	Arizona

Annual NCAA Division I Team Champions (Cont.)

SWIMMING & DIVING

Men

Host Texas, the only team to score points in all swimming events, used their depth to capture its first team title in five years. Despite winning just one event, the Longhorns beat runner-up Auburn, 479-443. Michigan's Tom Dolan and SMU's Ryan Berube were the individual standouts, winning three events, apiece. Dolan successfully defended his NCAA titles in the 500- and 1,650-yard freestyles and the 400-yard I.M., becoming the first swimmer to repeat in three events since California's Matt Biondi in 1987. Berube took the 200-yard I.M., the 100- and 200-yard backstrokes. Two American records were broken in relay events. Tennessee captured the 200-yard medley relay in a record 1:25.85 and Michigan, with Dolan swimming the anchor leg, beat a 12-year-old mark in the 800-yard freestyle relay with a time of 6:20.89. Miami (Fla.) dominated the diving events. Diver of the year Brian Gillooly won the platform event, placed second in the three-meter, behind Miami teammate Chris Mantilla, and took third in the one-meter event for the Hurricanes. *(Austin, Texas; Mar. 28-30, 1996.)*

Multiple winners: Michigan and Ohio St. (11); USC (9); Stanford (7); Indiana and Texas (6); Yale (4); California and Florida (2).

Year		Year		Year		Year		Year	
1937	Michigan	1950	Ohio St.	1963	USC	1976	USC	1989	Texas
1938	Michigan	1951	Yale	1964	USC	1977	USC	1990	Texas
1939	Michigan	1952	Ohio St.	1965	USC	1978	Tennessee	1991	Texas
1940	Michigan	1953	Yale	1966	USC	1979	California	1992	Stanford
1941	Michigan	1954	Ohio St.	1967	Stanford	1980	California	1993	Stanford
1942	Yale	1955	Ohio St.	1968	Indiana	1981	Texas	1994	Stanford
1943	Ohio St.	1956	Ohio St.	1969	Indiana	1982	UCLA	1995	Michigan
1944	Yale	1957	Michigan	1970	Indiana	1983	Florida	1996	Texas
1945	Ohio St.	1958	Michigan	1971	Indiana	1984	Florida		
1946	Ohio St.	1959	Michigan	1972	Indiana	1985	Stanford		
1947	Ohio St.	1960	USC	1973	Indiana	1986	Stanford		
1948	Michigan	1961	Michigan	1974	USC	1987	Stanford		
1949	Ohio St.	1962	Ohio St.	1975	USC	1988	Texas		

Women

Stanford won two individual events and three of five relays—all on the second day of competition—in coasting to a fifth consecutive title, 478-397, over SMU. The Cardinal got wins from Jessica Tong in the 100-yard backstroke and Claudia Franco in the 100-yard freestyle. The meet's top scorer was Swimmer of the Year Kristine Quance of Southern Cal, who won the 200- and 400-yard individual medley as well as the 200-yard breaststroke. Her teammate Lindsay Benko also gave a strong showing, winning the 500-yard freestyle and 200-yard backstroke titles and finished second in the 200-yard freestyle. Cincinnati's Becky Ruehl was named diver of the year, winning the platform event and taking second in the three-meter dive. *(Ann Arbor, Mich.; Mar. 21-23, 1996.)*

Multiple winners: Stanford and Texas (7).

Year		Year		Year		Year		Year	
1982	Florida	1985	Texas	1988	Texas	1991	Texas	1994	Stanford
1983	Stanford	1986	Texas	1989	Stanford	1992	Stanford	1995	Stanford
1984	Texas	1987	Texas	1990	Texas	1993	Stanford	1996	Stanford

INDOOR TRACK

Men

George Mason ended Arkansas 12-year national title reign, winning two individual events to edge Nebraska, 39-31. Arkansas took third place with 29 points. Several meet records were set. UTEP's Obadele Thompson smashed the 200-meter dash record with a time of 20:36, besting the previous mark of 20.59 set by Baylor's Michael Johnson in 1989. Witchita State's Einars Tupuritis turned in a record time of 1:45.80 in the 800-meters. *(RCA Dome, Indianapolis, Ind.; March 8-9, 1996.)*

Multiple winners: Arkansas (12); UTEP (7); Kansas and Villanova (3); USC (2).

Year		Year		Year		Year		Year	
1965	Missouri	1972	USC	1979	Villanova	1986	Arkansas	1993	Arkansas
1966	Kansas	1973	Manhattan	1980	UTEP	1987	Arkansas	1994	Arkansas
1967	USC	1974	UTEP	1981	UTEP	1988	Arkansas	1995	Arkansas
1968	Villanova	1975	UTEP	1982	UTEP	1989	Arkansas	1996	George Mason
1969	Kansas	1976	UTEP	1983	SMU	1990	Arkansas		
1970	Kansas	1977	Washington St.	1984	Arkansas	1991	Arkansas		
1971	Villanova	1978	UTEP	1985	Arkansas	1992	Arkansas		

Women

LSU, sparked by individual champs D'Andre Hill (55-meter dash) and Kim Carson (55-meter hurdles) and the 1,600-meter relay team, won their fourth straight national championship, over SEC rival Georgia, 52-34. Georgia earned its highest finish ever thanks largely to 200-meter dash winner Debbie Ferguson. Ferguson earned more points for her team by finishing second to Hill in the 55-meter dash. *(RCA Dome, Indianapolis, Ind.; March 8-9, 1996.)*

Mulple winners: LSU (7); Texas (3); Nebraska (2).

Year		Year		Year		Year		Year	
1983	Nebraska	1986	Texas	1989	LSU	1992	Florida	1995	LSU
1984	Nebraska	1987	LSU	1990	Texas	1993	LSU	1996	LSU
1985	Florida St.	1988	Texas	1991	LSU	1994	LSU		

Wide World Photos

Tennessee's **Lawrence Johnson** (left) is happy about clearing a meet-record 18-6 ½ in the pole vault at the NCAA Indoor Track and Field Championships, Mar. 9 in Indianapolis. Michigan's **Neil Gardner** throws his hands up in victory after winning the 400 meter hurdles in a record time of 42.97 at the NCAA Outdoor Track and Field Championships, May 31 in Eugene, Ore.

OUTDOOR TRACK

Men

Arkansas rode the performances of Godfrey Siamusiye, Jason Bunston and Robert Howard—who combined to score more points (47) than any other team in the meet—to overwhelm runner-up George Mason for its fifth consecutive title, 55-40. Siamusiye collected 18 points by coming from behind to win his second straight 10,000-meter run title and placing second in the 5,000. Southern California's Balazs Kiss became just the fourth person ever to win four consecutive individual titles, capturing the hammer throw championship for the fourth year in a row. Tennessee's Lawrence Johnson set a new standard in the pole vault, clearing a meet record 19-1. Andy Bloom of Wake Forest scored all 20 of his team's points and was the meet's only double winner, taking home the shot put and discus throw. *(Eugene, Ore.; May 29-June 1, 1996.)*

Multiple winners: USC (26); UCLA (8); Arkansas and UTEP (6); Illinois and Oregon (5); Kansas, LSU and Stanford (3); SMU and Tennessee (2).

Year		Year		Year		Year		Year	
1921	Illinois	1937	USC	1953	USC	1968	USC	1983	SMU
1922	California	1938	USC	1954	USC	1969	San Jose St.	1984	Oregon
1923	Michigan	1939	USC	1955	USC	1970	BYU, Kansas & Oregon	1985	Arkansas
1924	Not held	1940	USC	1956	UCLA	1971	UCLA	1986	SMU
1925	Stanford*	1941	USC	1957	Villanova	1972	UCLA	1987	UCLA
1926	USC*	1942	USC	1958	USC	1973	UCLA	1988	UCLA
1927	Illinois*	1943	USC	1959	Kansas	1974	Tennessee	1989	LSU
1928	Stanford	1944	Illinois	1960	Kansas	1975	UTEP	1990	LSU
1929	Ohio St.	1945	Navy	1961	USC	1976	USC	1991	Tennessee
1930	USC	1946	Illinois	1962	Oregon	1977	Arizona St.	1992	Arkansas
1931	USC	1947	Illinois	1963	USC	1978	UCLA & UTEP	1993	Arkansas
1932	Indiana	1948	Minnesota	1964	Oregon	1979	UTEP	1994	Arkansas
1933	LSU	1949	USC	1965	Oregon & USC	1980	UTEP	1995	Arkansas
1934	Stanford	1950	USC	1966	UCLA	1981	UTEP	1996	Arkansas
1935	USC	1951	USC	1967	USC	1982	UTEP		
1936	USC	1952	USC						

(*) indicates unofficial championship.

Women

LSU captured five individual titles and piled up 81 points to conquer the field, winning a women's Division I record 10th consecutive national championship. D'Andre Hill and Zundra Feagin led the way, finishing 1-2 and 2-1 in the 100- and 200-meter dashes. South Carolina's Dawn Ellerbe claimed the NCAA's first women's hammer throw championship with her hurl of 209-2, becoming the first American woman to exceed 200 feet in the event. Illinois' Tonya Williams repeated in the 400-meter hurdles with her time of 54.56, setting a meet record. Villanova's Jennifer Rhines became the first person to "three-peat" in the 5,000-meter. *(Eugene, Ore.; May 29-June 1, 1996.)*

Multiple winners: LSU (9); UCLA (2).

Year		Year		Year		Year		Year	
1982	UCLA	1985	Oregon	1988	LSU	1991	LSU	1994	LSU
1983	UCLA	1986	Texas	1989	LSU	1992	LSU	1995	LSU
1984	Florida St.	1987	LSU	1990	LSU	1993	LSU	1996	LSU

Annual NCAA Division I Team Champions (Cont.)

VOLLEYBALL

Men

UCLA, came back from a two games to one deficit and managed to hold off Hawaii in a pivotal game four, winning their record 16th national title, 15-13, 12-15, 9-15, 17-15, 15-12. Paul Nihipali led the Bruins with 23 kills and Tom Stilwell added 22, including the match-winner. Yuval Katz led Hawaii with 47 kills in 94 attempts and was named the tournament's most outstanding player. In the semifinals, Hawaii prevented Penn St. from their third straight finals appearances, winning in four games, while UCLA downed Lewis, 3-0. *(Los Angeles, Calif.; May 3-4, 1996.)*

Multiple winners: UCLA (16); Pepperdine and USC (4).

Year		Year		Year		Year		Year	
1970	UCLA	1976	UCLA	1982	UCLA	1988	USC	1994	Penn St.
1971	UCLA	1977	USC	1983	UCLA	1989	UCLA	1995	UCLA
1972	UCLA	1978	Pepperdine	1984	UCLA	1990	USC	1996	UCLA
1973	San Diego St.	1979	UCLA	1985	Pepperdine	1991	Long Beach St.		
1974	UCLA	1980	USC	1986	Pepperdine	1992	Pepperdine		
1975	UCLA	1981	UCLA	1987	UCLA	1993	UCLA		

Women

Nebraska beat Texas in four games, 11-15, 15-2, 15-7, 16-14 in the first championship contested between two non-Californian teams since 1988 when Texas beat Hawaii. Senior Billie Winsett and Junior Kate Crnich both set career-highs with 25 kills apiece for Nebraska. In the semifinals, Texas beat defending champs and top-ranked Stanford, 15-13, 0-15, 15-17, 15-6, 15-12, and Nebraska edged Michigan St. 10-15, 15-8, 15-8, 9-15, 15-8. *(Amherst, Mass., Dec. 16, 1995.)*

Multiple winners: Hawaii and UCLA (3); Long Beach St., Pacific and Stanford (2).

Year		Year		Year		Year		Year	
1981	USC	1984	UCLA	1987	Hawaii	1990	UCLA	1993	Long Beach St.
1982	Hawaii	1985	Pacific	1988	Texas	1991	UCLA	1994	Stanford
1983	Hawaii	1986	Pacific	1989	Long Beach St.	1992	Stanford	1995	Nebraska

WATER POLO

Men

UCLA's Jeremy Braxton-Brown broke an 8-8 deadlock, scoring twice in the game's final 1 minute, 44 seconds to help the Bruins edge California, 10-8 for the championship. UCLA's Jim Toring had a game-high four goals, sharing most outstanding player honors with Braxton-Brown, Bruin goalie Matt Swanson and Cal's Brent Albright. California beat Massachusetts 10-6 and UCLA knocked off UC-San Diego 21-10 in the semifinals. *(Stanford, Calif., Dec. 1 and 3, 1995.)*

Multiple winners: California (11); Stanford (8); UCLA (4); UC-Irvine (3).

Year		Year		Year		Year		Year	
1969	UCLA	1975	California	1981	Stanford	1987	California	1993	Stanford
1970	UC-Irvine	1976	Stanford	1982	UC-Irvine	1988	California	1994	Stanford
1971	UCLA	1977	California	1983	California	1989	UC-Irvine	1995	UCLA
1972	UCLA	1978	Stanford	1984	California	1990	California		
1973	California	1979	UC-S. Barbara	1985	Stanford	1991	California		
1974	California	1980	Stanford	1986	Stanford	1992	California		

WRESTLING

Men

Iowa wrestlers Bill Zadick (at 142 pounds), Joe Williams (158) and Daryl Weber (167) each won their weight classes as the Hawkeyes outscored interstate rival and runner-up Iowa St., 122-78, to win their fifth title in six years. CS-Bakersfield finished third with 66 points. Oregon State's Les Gutches (177) was the only one of seven returning champions to repeat and was named the tournament's most outstanding wrestler. *(Minneapolis, Minn.; Mar. 21-23, 1996.)*

Multiple winners: Oklahoma St. (30); Iowa (16); Iowa St. (8); Oklahoma (7).

Year		Year		Year		Year		Year	
1928	Okla. A&M*	1942	Okla. A&M	1959	Okla. St.	1974	Oklahoma	1989	Okla. St.
1929	Okla. A&M	1943-45	Not held	1960	Oklahoma	1975	Iowa	1990	Okla. St.
1930	Okla. A&M	1946	Okla. A&M	1961	Okla. St.	1976	Iowa	1991	Iowa
1931	Okla. A&M*	1947	Cornell Col.	1962	Okla. St.	1977	Iowa St.	1992	Iowa
1932	Indiana*	1948	Okla. A&M	1963	Oklahoma	1978	Iowa	1993	Iowa
1933	Okla. A&M*	1949	Okla. A&M	1964	Okla. St.	1979	Iowa	1994	Okla. St.
	& Iowa St.*	1950	Northern Iowa	1965	Iowa St.	1980	Iowa	1995	Iowa
1934	Okla. A&M	1951	Oklahoma	1966	Okla. St.	1981	Iowa	1996	Iowa
1935	Okla. A&M	1952	Oklahoma	1967	Michigan St.	1982	Iowa		
1936	Oklahoma	1953	Penn St.	1968	Okla. St.	1983	Iowa		
1937	Okla. A&M	1954	Okla. A&M	1969	Iowa St.	1984	Iowa		
1938	Okla. A&M	1955	Okla. A&M	1970	Iowa St.	1985	Iowa		
1939	Okla. A&M	1956	Okla. A&M	1971	Okla. St.	1986	Iowa		
1940	Okla. A&M	1957	Oklahoma	1972	Iowa St.	1987	Iowa St.		
1941	Okla. A&M	1958	Okla. St.	1973	Iowa St.	1988	Arizona St.		

(*) indicates unofficial champions. **Note:** Oklahoma A&M became Oklahoma St. in 1958.

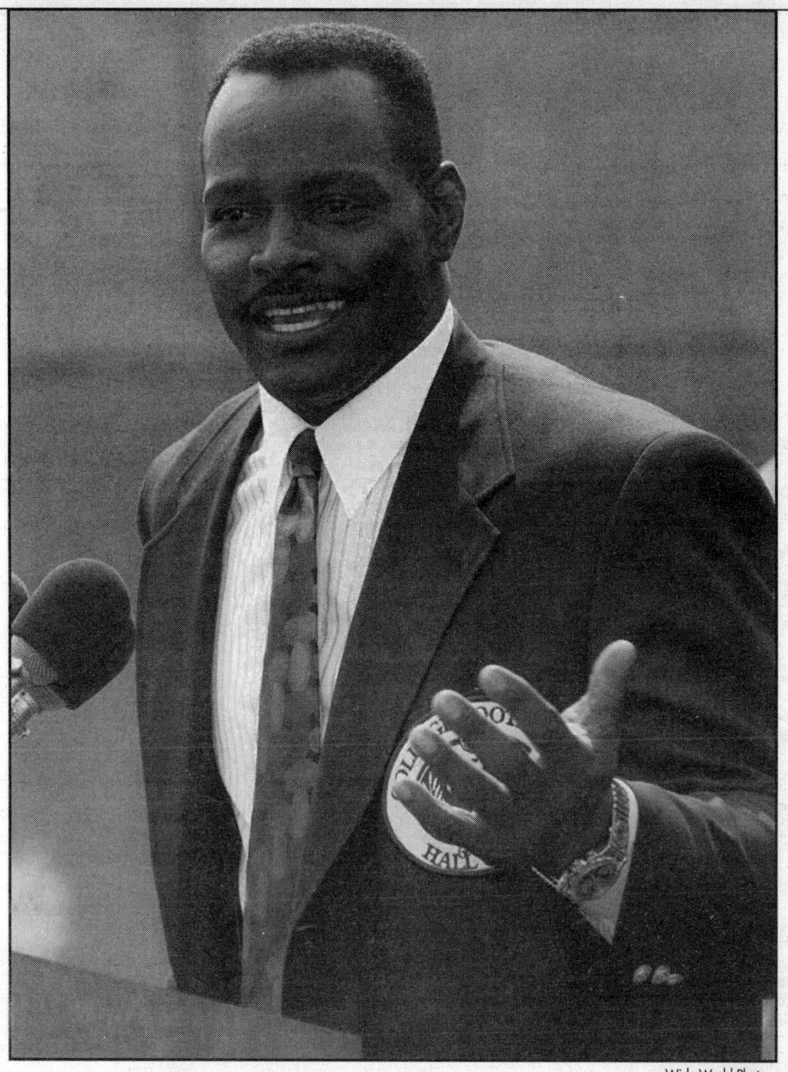

Wide World Photos

The College Football Hall of Fame honored its inaugural class of "small college" players in 1996. **Walter Payton**, who played for Jackson (Miss.) St. in the early '70s, addresses the crowd at the induction on Aug. 17 in South Bend, Ind.

HALLS OF FAME & AWARDS

BASEBALL

National Baseball Hall of Fame & Museum

Established in 1935 by Major League Baseball to celebrate the game's 100th anniversary. **Address:** P.O. Box 590, Cooperstown, NY 13326. **Telephone:** (607) 547-7200.

Eligibility: Nominated players must have played at least part of 10 seasons in the Major Leagues and be retired for at least five but no more than 20 years. Voting done by Baseball Writers' Association of America. Certain nominated players not elected by the writers can become eligible via the Veterans' Committee 23 years after retirement. The Hall of Fame board of directors voted unanimously on Feb. 4, 1991, to exclude players on baseball's ineligible list from consideration. Pete Rose is the only living ex-player on that list.

Class of 1996 (4): BBWAA vote—none. VETERAN'S COMMITTEE vote—pitcher **Jim Bunning**, Detroit (1955-63), Philadelphia (1964-67), Pittsburgh (1968-69), Los Angeles (1969), Philadelphia (1970-71); Negro Leagues pitcher **Willie Foster**, Memphis (1923-24), Chicago American Giants (1924-25), Birmingham Black Barons (1925), Chicago (1926-30), Homestead Grays (1931), Kansas City Monarchs (1931), Chicago (1932-35), Pittsburgh Crawfords (1936), Chicago (1937); manager **Ned Hanlon**, Pittsburgh-NL (1889, 1891), Pittsburgh-players league (1890), Baltimore-NL (1892-98), Brooklyn-NL (1899-1905), Cincinnati-NL (1906-07); manager **Earl Weaver**, Baltimore (1968-82, 85-86).

1996 Top 10 vote-getters (470 BBWAA ballots cast, 353 needed to elect) : 1. **Phil Niekro** (321); 2. **Tony Perez** (309); 3. **Don Sutton** (300); 4. **Steve Garvey** (175); 5. **Ron Santo** (174); 6. **Tony Oliva** (170); 7. **Jim Rice** (166); 8. **Bruce Sutter** (137); 9. **Tommy John** (102); 10. **Jim Kaat** (91).

Elected first year on ballot (31): Hank Aaron, Ernie Banks, Johnny Bench, Lou Brock, Rod Carew, Steve Carlton, Ty Cobb, Bob Feller, Bob Gibson, Reggie Jackson, Walter Johnson, Al Kaline, Sandy Koufax, Mickey Mantle, Christy Mathewson, Willie Mays, Willie McCovey, Joe Morgan, Stan Musial, Jim Palmer, Brooks Robinson, Frank Robinson, Jackie Robinson, Babe Ruth, Mike Schmidt, Tom Seaver, Warren Spahn, Willie Stargell, Honus Wagner, Ted Williams and Carl Yastrzemski.

Members are listed with years of induction; (+) indicates deceased members.

Catchers

Bench, Johnny 1989
Berra, Yogi 1972
+ Bresnahan, Roger 1945
+ Campanella, Roy 1969
+ Cochrane, Mickey 1947
+ Dickey, Bill 1954
+ Ewing, Buck 1939
+ Ferrell, Rick 1984
+ Hartnett, Gabby 1955
+ Lombardi, Ernie 1986
+ Schalk, Ray 1955

1st Basemen

+ Anson, Cap 1939
+ Beckley, Jake 1971
+ Bottomley, Jim 1974
+ Brouthers, Dan 1945
+ Chance, Frank 1946
+ Connor, Roger 1976
+ Foxx, Jimmie 1951
+ Gehrig, Lou 1939
+ Greenberg, Hank 1956
+ Kelly, George 1973
Killebrew, Harmon 1984
McCovey, Willie 1986
+ Mize, Johnny 1981
+ Sisler, George 1939
+ Terry, Bill 1954

2nd Basemen

Carew, Rod 1991
+ Collins, Eddie 1939
Doerr, Bobby 1986
+ Evers, Johnny 1946
+ Frisch, Frankie 1947
+ Gehringer, Charley 1949
+ Herman, Billy 1975
+ Hornsby, Rogers 1942
+ Lajoie, Nap 1937
+ Lazzeri, Tony 1991
Morgan, Joe 1990
+ Robinson, Jackie 1962
Schoendienst, Red 1989

Shortstops

Aparicio, Luis 1984
+ Appling, Luke 1964
+ Bancroft, Dave 1971
Banks, Ernie 1977
Boudreau, Lou 1970
+ Cronin, Joe 1956
+ Jackson, Travis 1982
+ Jennings, Hugh 1945
+ Maranville, Rabbit 1954
Reese, Pee Wee 1984
Rizzuto, Phil 1994
+ Sewell, Joe 1977
+ Tinker, Joe 1946
+ Vaughan, Arky 1985
+ Wagner, Honus 1936
+ Wallace, Bobby 1953
+ Ward, Monte 1964

3rd Basemen

+ Baker, Frank 1955
+ Collins, Jimmy 1945
Kell, George 1983
+ Lindstrom, Fred 1976
Mathews, Eddie 1978
Robinson, Brooks 1983
Schmidt, Mike 1995
+ Traynor, Pie 1948

Left Fielders

Brock, Lou 1985
+ Burkett, Jesse 1946
+ Clarke, Fred 1945
+ Delahanty, Ed 1945
+ Goslin, Goose 1968
+ Hafey, Chick 1971
+ Kelley, Joe 1971
Kiner, Ralph 1975
+ Manush, Heinie 1964
+ Medwick, Joe 1968
Musial, Stan 1969
+ O'Rourke, Jim 1945
+ Simmons, Al 1953
Stargell, Willie 1988
+ Wheat, Zack 1959
Williams, Billy 1987
Williams, Ted 1966
Yastrzemski, Carl 1989

Center Fielders

Ashburn, Richie 1995
+ Averill, Earl 1975
+ Carey, Max 1961
+ Cobb, Ty 1936
+ Combs, Earle 1970
DiMaggio, Joe 1955
+ Duffy, Hugh 1945
+ Hamilton, Billy 1961
+ Mantle, Mickey 1974
Mays, Willie 1979
+ Roush, Edd 1962
Snider, Duke 1980
+ Speaker, Tris 1937
+ Waner, Lloyd 1967
+ Wilson, Hack 1979

Wide World Photos

Newly enshrined Hall of Famers **Jim Bunning** and **Earl Weaver** pose with their plaques Aug. 4 in Cooperstown.

Right Fielders

Aaron, Hank............1982
\+ Clemente, Roberto............1973
\+ Crawford, Sam............1957
\+ Cuyler, Kiki............1968
\+ Flick, Elmer............1963
\+ Heilmann, Harry............1952
\+ Hooper, Harry............1971
Jackson, Reggie............1993
Kaline, Al............1980
\+ Keeler, Willie............1939
\+ Kelly, King............1945
\+ Klein, Chuck............1980
\+ McCarthy, Tommy............1946
\+ Ott, Mel............1951
\+ Rice, Sam............1963
Robinson, Frank............1982
\+ Ruth, Babe............1936
Slaughter, Enos............1985
\+ Thompson, Sam............1974
\+ Waner, Paul............1952
\+ Youngs, Ross............1972

Pitchers

\+ Alexander, Grover............1938
\+ Bender, Chief............1953
\+ Brown, Mordecai............1949
Bunning, Jim............1996
Carlton, Steve............1994
\+ Chesbro, Jack............1946
\+ Clarkson, John............1963
\+ Coveleski, Stan............1969
\+ Dean, Dizzy............1953
\+ Drysdale, Don............1984
\+ Faber, Red............1964
Feller, Bob............1962
Fingers, Rollie............1992
Ford, Whitey............1974
\+ Galvin, Pud............1965
Gibson, Bob............1981
\+ Gomez, Lefty............1972
\+ Grimes, Burleigh............1964
\+ Grove, Lefty............1947
\+ Haines, Jess............1970
\+ Hoyt, Waite............1969
\+ Hubbell, Carl............1947
Hunter, Catfish............1987
Jenkins, Ferguson............1991
\+ Johnson, Walter............1936
\+ Joss, Addie............1978
\+ Keefe, Tim............1964
Koufax, Sandy............1972
Lemon, Bob............1976
\+ Lyons, Ted............1955
Marichal, Juan............1983
\+ Marquard, Rube............1971
\+ Mathewson, Christy............1936
\+ McGinnity, Joe............1946
Newhouser, Hal............1992
\+ Nichols, Kid............1949
Palmer, Jim............1990
\+ Pennock, Herb............1948
Perry, Gaylord............1991
\+ Plank, Eddie............1946
\+ Radbourne, Old Hoss............1939
\+ Rixey, Eppa............1963
Roberts, Robin............1976
\+ Ruffing, Red............1967
\+ Rusie, Amos............1977
Seaver, Tom............1992
Spahn, Warren............1973
\+ Vance, Dazzy............1955
\+ Waddell, Rube............1946
\+ Walsh, Ed............1946
\+ Welch, Mickey............1973
Wilhelm, Hoyt............1985
\+ Willis, Vic............1995
Wynn, Early............1972
\+ Young, Cy............1937

Baseball Hall of Fame (Cont.)

Managers

+ Alston, Walter........................1983
+ Durocher, Leo........................1994
+ Hanlon, Ned.........................1996
+ Harris, Bucky........................1975
+ Huggins, Miller.....................1964
Lopez, Al..............................1977
+ Mack, Connie.......................1937
+ McCarthy, Joe.......................1957
+ McGraw, John......................1937
+ McKechnie, Bill.....................1962
+ Robinson, Wilbert.................1945
+ Stengel, Casey.......................1966
+ Stengel, Casey.......................1966
Weaver, Earl..........................1996

Umpires

+ Barlick, Al.............................1989
+ Conlan, Jocko.........................1974
+ Connolly, Tom........................1953
+ Evans, Billy...........................1973
+ Hubbard, Cal.........................1976
+ Klem, Bill..............................1953
+ McGowan, Bill.......................1992

From Negro Leagues

+ Bell, Cool Papa (OF)..............1974
+ Charleston, Oscar (1B-OF)......1976
+ Dandridge, Ray (3B)..............1987
+ Day, Leon (P-OF-2B)..............1995
+ Dihigo, Martin (P-OF)............1977
+ Foster, Rube (P-Mgr)..............1981
+ Foster, Willie (P)...................1996
+ Gibson, Josh (C)...................1972
Irvin, Monte (OF)...................1973
+ Johnson, Judy (3B)................1975
Leonard, Buck (1B).................1972
+ Lloyd, Pop (SS)......................1977
+ Paige, Satchel (P)..................1971

Pioneers and Executives

+ Barrow, Ed............................1953
+ Bulkeley, Morgan...................1937
+ Cartwright, Alexander...........1938
+ Chadwick, Henry...................1938
+ Chandler, Happy...................1982
+ Comiskey, Charles.................1939
+ Cummings, Candy..................1939
+ Frick, Ford............................1970
+ Giles, Warren........................1979
+ Griffith, Clark........................1946
+ Harridge, Will........................1972
+ Hulbert, William....................1995
+ Johnson, Ban.........................1937
+ Landis, Kenesaw...................1944
+ MacPhail, Larry.....................1978
+ Rickey, Branch......................1967
+ Spalding, Al..........................1939
+ Veeck, Bill.............................1991
+ Weiss, George.......................1971
+ Wright, George......................1937
+ Wright, Harry........................1953
+ Yawkey, Tom.........................1980

Ford Frick Award

First presented in 1978 by Hall of Fame for meritorious contributions by baseball broadcasters. Named in honor of the late newspaper reporter, broadcaster, National League president and commissioner, the Frick Award does not constitute induction into the Hall of Fame.

Year	
1978	Mel Allen & Red Barber
1979	Bob Elson
1980	Russ Hodges
1981	Ernie Harwell
1982	Vin Scully
1983	Jack Brickhouse
1984	Curt Gowdy
1985	Buck Canel
1986	Bob Prince
1987	Jack Buck
1988	Lindsey Nelson
1989	Harry Caray
1990	Byrum Saam
1991	Joe Garagiola
1992	Milo Hamilton
1993	Chuck Thompson
1994	Bob Murphy
1995	Bob Wolff
1996	Herb Carneal

J.G. Taylor Spink Award

First presented in 1962 by the Baseball Writers' Association of America for meritorious contributions by members of the BBWAA. Named in honor of the late publisher of *The Sporting News*, the Spink Award does not constitute induction into the Hall of Fame. Winners are honored in the year following their selection.

Year	
1962	J.G. Taylor Spink
1963	Ring Lardner
1964	Hugh Fullerton
1965	Charley Dryden
1966	Grantland Rice
1967	Damon Runyon
1968	H.G. Salsinger
1969	Sid Mercer
1970	Heywood C. Broun
1971	Frank Graham
1972	Dan Daniel, Fred Lieb & J. Roy Stockton
1973	Warren Brown, John Drebinger & John F. Kieran
1974	John Carmichael & James Isaminger
1975	Tom Meany & Shirley Povich
1976	Harold Kaese & Red Smith
1977	Gordon Cobbledick & Edgar Munzel
1978	Tim Murnane & Dick Young
1979	Bob Broeg & Tommy Holmes
1980	Joe Reichler & Milt Richman
1981	Bob Addie & Allen Lewis
1982	Si Burick
1983	Ken Smith
1984	Joe McGuff
1985	Earl Lawson
1986	Jack Lang
1987	Jim Murray
1988	Bob Hunter & Ray Kelly
1989	Jerome Holtzman
1990	Phil Collier
1991	Ritter Collett
1992	Leonard Koppett & Buzz Saidt
1993	John Wendell Smith
1994	No award
1995	Joseph Durso

Major League Baseball's 100th Anniversary All-Time Team

Selected by the Baseball Writers Assn. of America and released July 21, 1969. All-Time team members in **bold** type; vote totals not released.

C **Mickey Cockrane**, Bill Dickey, Roy Campanella
1B **Lou Gehrig**, George Sisler, Stan Musial,
2B **Rogers Hornsby**, Charley Gehringer, Eddie Collins
SS **Honus Wagner**, Joe Cronin, Ernie Banks
3B **Pie Traynor**, Brooks Robinson, Jackie Robinson
OF **Babe Ruth**, **Ty Cobb**, **Joe DiMaggio**, Ted Williams, Tris Speaker, Willie Mays
RHP **Walter Johnson**, Christy Mathewson, Cy Young
LHP **Lefty Grove**, Sandy Koufax, Carl Hubbell
Mgr. **John McGraw**, Casey Stengel, Joe McCarthy

All-Time Outstanding Player: **Ruth**, Cobb, Wagner, DiMaggio

BASKETBALL

Naismith Memorial Basketball Hall of Fame

Established in 1949 by the National Association of Basketball Coaches in memory of the sport's inventor, Dr. James Naismith. Original Hall opened in 1968 and current Hall in 1985. **Address:** 1150 West Columbus Avenue, Springfield, MA 01105. **Telephone:** (413) 781-6500.

Eligibility: Nominated players and referees must be retired for five years, coaches must have coached 25 years or be retired for five, and contributors must have already completed their noteworthy service to the game. Voting done by 24-member honors committee made up of media representatives, Hall of Fame members and trustees. Any nominee not elected after five years becomes eligible for consideration by the Veterans' Committee after a five-year wait.

Class of 1996 (6): PLAYERS—center **Kresimir Cosic**, college (Brigham Young, 1970-73), Yugoslavian National Team (1968-80); guard **George Gervin**, college (Eastern Michigan, 1970-1972), ABA (Virginia 1972-74; San Antonio 1974-76), NBA (San Antonio 1976-85, Chicago 1985-86); guard **Gail Goodrich**, college (UCLA, 1961-65), NBA (Los Angeles, 1965-68, 1970-76; Phoenix, 1968-70; New Orleans, 1976-79); guard **Nancy Lieberman-Cline**, college (Old Dominion, 1976-80), US National Team (1975-76, 1989), USBL (Springfield, 1986-87); forward **David Thompson**, college (N.C. State, 1972-75), ABA (Denver, 1975-76), NBA (Denver, 1976-82, Seattle 1982-84); forward **George Yardley**, college (Stanford, 1946-50), NBA (Fort Wayne, 1953-57; Detroit, 1957-59; Syracuse 1959-60), ABA (Los Angeles, 1961-62).

1996 finalists (nominated but not elected): PLAYERS—Dick Barnett , Roger Brown, Larry Costello, Artis Gilmore, Dennis Johnson, Arnie Risen, Jo Jo White, Jamaal Wilkes. COACHES—Don Haskins, Jerry Tarkanian, Guy Lewis, Antonio Diaz-Miguel and Tex Winter. CONTRIBUTOR—Carol Eckman.

Note: John Wooden is the only member to be honored as both a player and a coach.

Members are listed with years of induction; (+) indicates deceased members.

Men

Abdul-Jabbar, Kareem 1995
Archibald, Nate....................1991
Arizin, Paul 1977
+ Barlow, Thomas (Babe)..........1980
Barry, Rick...........................1987
Baylor, Elgin 1976
+ Beckman, John......................1972
Bellamy, Walt........................1993
Belov, Sergei.........................1992
Bing, Dave.............................1990
+ Borgmann, Benny...................1961
Bradley, Bill 1982
+ Brennan, Joe.........................1974
Cervi, Al................................1984
Chamberlain, Wilt..................1978
+ Cooper, Charles (Tarzan) 1976
+ Cosic, Kresimir......................1996
Cousy, Bob 1970
Cowens, Dave.........................1991
Cunningham, Billy..................1986
+ Davies, Bob 1969
+ DeBernardi, Forrest 1961
DeBusschere, Dave..................1982
+ Dehnert, Dutch.......................1968
Endacott, Paul........................1971
Erving, Julius (Dr. J) 1993
Foster, Bud............................1964
Frazier, Walt..........................1987
+ Friedman, Marty 1971
+ Fulks, Joe..............................1977
Gale, Laddie..........................1976
Gallatin, Harry 1991
Gates, William (Pop)...............1989
Gervin, George 1996
Gola, Tom 1975
Goodrich, Gail 1996
Greer, Hal 1981
+ Gruenig, Robert.....................1963
Hagan, Cliff..........................1977
+ Hanson, Victor......................1960
Havlicek, John 1983
Hawkins, Connie....................1992
Hayes, Elvin...........................1990
Heinsohn, Tom 1986
+ Holman, Nat..........................1964
Houbregs, Bob.......................1987
+ Hyatt, Chuck.........................1959
Issel, Dan..............................1993
Jeannette, Buddy....................1994
+ Johnson, Bill (Skinny).............1976
+ Johnston, Neil........................1990
Jones, K. C 1989
Jones, Sam 1983
+ Krause, Edward (Moose) 1975
Kurland, Bob 1961
Lanier, Bob 1992
+ Lapchick, Joe 1966
Lovellette, Clyde 1988
Lucas, Jerry 1979
Luisetti, Hank 1959
Macauley, Ed.........................1960
+ Maravich, Pete......................1987
Martin, Slater.........................1981
+ McCracken, Branch...............1960
+ McCracken, Jack...................1962
+ McDermott, Bobby 1988
McGuire, Dick 1993
Mikan, George 1959
Mikkelsen, Vern.....................1995
Monroe, Earl 1990
Murphy, Calvin 1993
+ Murphy, Charles (Stretch)........1960
+ Page, Harlan (Pat)..................1962
Pettit, Bob 1970
Phillip, Andy.........................1961
+ Pollard, Jim..........................1977
Ramsey, Frank 1981
Reed, Willis 1981
Robertson, Oscar 1979
+ Roosma, John 1961
Russell, Bill...........................1974
+ Russell, John (Honey).............1964
Schayes, Dolph 1972
+ Schmidt, Ernest J 1973
+ Schommer, John 1959
+ Sedran, Barney.....................1962
Sharman, Bill 1975
+ Steinmetz, Christian..............1961
Thompson, David 1996
+ Thompson, John (Cat)............1962
Thurmond, Nate....................1984
Twyman, Jack 1982
Unseld, Wes 1988
+ Vandivier, Robert (Fuzzy) 1974
+ Wachter, Ed..........................1961
Walton, Bill...........................1993
Wanzer, Bobby......................1987
West, Jerry 1979
Wilkens, Lenny......................1989
Wooden, John 1960
Yardley, George.....................1996

Women

Blazejowski, Carol 1994
Donovan, Anne.....................1995
Harris, Lucy 1992
Lieberman-Cline, Nancy 1996
Meyers, Ann 1993
Miller, Cheryl........................1995
Semenova, Juliana 1993
White, Nera 1992

Teams

Buffalo Germans...................1961
First Team 1959
New York Renaissance 1963
Original Celtics.....................1959

Referees

+ Enright, Jim 1978
+ Hepbron, George..................1960
+ Hoyt, George........................1961
+ Kennedy, Pat........................1959
+ Leith, Lloyd 1982
Mihalik, Red 1986
Nucatola, John 1977
+ Quigley, Ernest (Quig)...........1961
+ Shirley, J. Dallas...................1979
+ Strom, Earl 1995
Tobey, Dave..........................1961
+ Walsh, David........................1961

Basketball Hall of Fame (Cont.)

Coaches

+ Allen, Forrest (Phog)..............1959
+ Anderson, Harold (Andy)........1984
Auerbach, Red........................1968
+ Barry, Sam...........................1978
+ Blood, Ernest (Prof)................1960
+ Cann, Howard........................1967
+ Carlson, Henry (Doc)..............1959
Carnesecca, Lou.....................1992
Carnevale, Ben 1969
+ Case, Everett.........................1981
Crum, Denny 1994
Daly, Chuck 1994
+ Dean, Everett 1966
+ Diddle, Ed 1971
+ Drake, Bruce..........................1972
Gaines, Clarence (Bighouse)...1981
Gardner, Jack.........................1983
+ Gill, Amory (Slats).................1967
Gomelsky, Aleksandr..............1995
Harshman, Marv....................1984
+ Hickey, Eddie.........................1978
+ Hobson, Howard (Hobby).......1965
Holzman, Red.........................1986
+ Iba, Hank 1968
+ Julian, Alvin (Doggie) 1967
+ Keaney, Frank........................1960
+ Keogan, George 1961
Knight, Bob.............................1991
Kundla, John 1995
+ Lambert, Ward (Piggy) 1960
Litwack, Harry 1975
+ Leoffler, Ken...........................1964
+ Lonborg, Dutch 1972
+ McCutchan, Arad..................1980
McGuire, Al...........................1992
+ McGuire, Frank.......................1976
+ Meanwell, Walter (Doc)..........1959
Meyer, Ray 1978
Miller, Ralph 1988
Ramsay, Jack..........................1992
Rubini, Cesare 1994
+ Rupp, Adolph 1968
+ Sachs, Leonard 1961
+ Shelton, Everett 1979
Smith, Dean............................1982
Taylor, Fred............................1985
+ Wade, Margaret.....................1984
Watts, Stan.............................1985
Wooden, John 1972
+ Woolpert, Phil.........................1992

Contributors

+ Abbott, Senda Berenson 1984
+ Bee, Clair 1967
+ Brown, Walter A 1965
+ Bunn, John.............................1964
+ Douglas, Bob 1971
+ Duer, Al..................................1981
+ Fagen, Clifford B....................1983
+ Fisher, Harry..........................1973
+ Fleisher, Larry 1991
+ Gottlieb, Eddie.......................1971
+ Gulick, Luther.........................1959
Harrison, Les..........................1979
+ Hepp, Ferenc 1980
+ Hickox, Ed 1959
+ Hinkle, Tony...........................1965
+ Irish, Ned 1964
+ Jones, R. William 1964
+ Kennedy, Walter 1980
+ Liston, Emil (Liz) 1974
McLendon, John.....................1978
+ Mokray, Bill 1965
+ Morgan, Ralph 1959
+ Morgenweck, Frank (Pop) 1962
+ Naismith, James.....................1959
Newell, Pete 1978
+ O'Brien, John J. (Jack)............1961
+ O'Brien, Larry........................1991
+ Olsen, Harold G 1959
+ Podoloff, Maurice...................1973
+ Porter, Henry (H.V.) 1960
+ Reid, William A 1963
+ Ripley, Elmer..........................1972
+ St. John, Lynn W 1962
+ Saperstein, Abe 1970
+ Schabinger, Arthur..................1961
+ Stagg, Amos Alonzo 1959
Stankovic, Boris......................1991
+ Steitz, Ed 1983
+ Taylor, Chuck 1968
+ Teague, Bertha.......................1984
+ Tower, Oswald 1959
+ Trester, Ather (A.L.).................1961
+ Wells, Cliff..............................1971
+ Wilke, Lou 1982

Curt Gowdy Award

First presented in 1990 by the Hall of Fame Board of Trustees for meritorious contributions by the media. Named in honor of the former NBC sportscaster, the Gowdy Award does not constitute induction into the Hall of Fame.

Year	
1990	Curt Gowdy & Dick Herbert
1991	Dave Dorr & Marty Glickman
1992	Sam Goldaper & Chick Hearn
1993	Leonard Lewin & Johnny Most
1994	Leonard Koppett & Cawood Ledford
1995	Dick Enberg & Bob Hammel
1996	Billy Packer & Bob Hentzen

BOWLING

National Bowling Hall of Fame & Museum

The National Bowling Hall is one museum with separate wings for honorees of the American Bowling Congress (ABC), Professional Bowlers' Association (PBA) and Women's International Bowling Congress (WIBC). The museum does not include the new Ladies Pro Bowlers Tour Hall of Fame, which is located in Las Vegas (see page 467). **Address:** 111 Stadium Plaza, St. Louis, MO 63102. **Telephone:** (314) 231-6340.

Professional Bowlers Association

Established in 1975. **Eligibility:** Nominees must be PBA members and at least 35 years old. Voting done by 50-member panel that includes writers who have covered bowling for at least 12 years.

Class of 1996 (3): PERFORMANCE—**Mike Aulby** and **Dave Husted**. MERITORIOUS SERVICE—**Larry Lichstein**.

Members are listed with years of induction; (+) indicates deceased members.

Performance

+ Allen, Bill...............................1983
Anthony, Earl.........................1986
Aulby, Mike 1996
Berardi, Joe 1990
Bluth, Ray..............................1975
Buckley, Roy 1992
Burton, Nelson Jr 1979
Carter, Don............................1975
Colwell, Paul..........................1991
Cook, Steve 1993
Davis, Dave............................1978
Dickinson, Gary......................1988
Durbin, Mike 1984
+ Fazio, Buzz 1976
Godman, Jim..........................1987
Hardwick, Billy.......................1977
Holman, Marshall 1990
Hudson, Tommy 1989
Husted, Dave 1996
Johnson, Don.........................1977
Laub, Larry 1985
Ozio, David............................1995
Pappas, George......................1986
Petraglia, John 1982
Ritger, Dick 1978
Roth, Mark 1987
Salvino, Carmen 1975
Smith, Harry 1975
Soutar, Dave 1979
Stefanich, Jim 1980
Voss, Brian 1994
Webb, Wayne 1993
Weber, Dick...........................1975
+ Welu, Billy.............................1975
Williams, Walter Ray Jr...........1995
Zahn, Wayne.........................1981

Veterans

Allison, Glenn 1984
Asher, Barry 1988
Foremsky, Skee 1992
Guenther, Johnny 1986
+ Joseph, Joe 1985
Limongello, Mike 1994
Marzich, Andy 1990
McCune, Don 1991
McGrath, Mike 1988
+ St. John, Jim 1989
Strampe, Bob 1987

Meritorious Service

+ Antenora, Joe 1993
Archibald, John 1989
Clemens, Chuck 1994
Elias, Eddie 1976
Esposito, Frank 1975
Evans, Dick 1986
Firestone, Raymond 1987
Fisher, E.A. (Bud) 1984
+ Frantz, Lou 1978
Golden, Harry 1983
Hoffman, Ted Jr 1985
Jowdy, John 1988
Kelley, Joe 1989
Lichstein, Larry 1996
+ Nagy, Steve 1977
Pezzano, Chuck 1975
Reichert, Jack 1992
+ Richards, Joe 1976
Schenkel, Chris 1976
Stitzlein, Lorraine 1980
Thompson, Al 1991
Zeller, Roger 1995

American Bowling Congress

Established in 1941 and open to professional and amateur bowlers. **Eligibility:** Nominated bowlers must have competed in at least 20 years of ABC tournaments. Voting done by 170-member panel made up of ABC officials, Hall of Fame members and media representatives.

Class of 1996 (2): PERFORMANCE—**Robert Goike**. MERITORIOUS SERVICE—**John Archibald**.

Members are listed with years of induction; (+) indicates deceased members.

Performance

Allison, Glenn 1979
Anthony, Earl 1986
+ Asplund, Harold 1978
Baer, Gordy 1987
Beach, Bill 1991
Benkovic, Frank 1958
Berlin, Mike 1994
+ Billick, George 1982
+ Blouin, Jimmy 1953
Bluth, Ray 1973
+ Bodis, Joe 1941
+ Bomar, Buddy 1966
+ Brandt, Allie 1960
+ Brosius, Eddie 1976
+ Bujack, Fred 1967
Bunetta, Bill 1968
Burton, Nelson Jr 1981
+ Burton, Nelson Sr 1964
+ Campi, Lou 1968
+ Carlson, Adolph 1941
Carter, Don 1970
+ Caruana, Frank 1977
+ Cassio, Marty 1972
+ Castellano, Graz 1976
+ Clause, Frank 1980
Cohn, Alfred 1985
+ Crimmins, Johnny 1962
Davis, Dave 1990
+ Daw, Charlie 1941
+ Day, Ned 1952
Dickinson, Gary 1992
+ Easter, Sarge 1963
Ellis, Don 1981
+ Falcaro, Joe 1968
Faragalli, Lindy 1968
+ Fazio, Buzz 1963
Fehr, Steve 1993
+ Gersonde, Russ 1968
+ Gibson, Therm 1965
Godman, Jim 1987
Goike, Robert 1996
Golembiewski, Billy 1979
Griffo, Greg 1995
Guenther, Johnny 1988
Hardwick, Billy 1985
Hart, Bob 1994
Hennessey, Tom 1976
Hoover, Dick 1974
Horn, Bud 1992
Howard, George 1986
Jackson, Eddie 1988
Johnson, Don 1982
Johnson, Earl 1987
+ Joseph, Joe 1969
+ Jouglard, Lee 1979
+ Kartheiser, Frank 1967
+ Kawolics, Ed 1968
+ Kissoff, Joe 1976
Klares, John 1982
+ Knox, Billy 1954
+ Koster, John 1941
+ Krems, Eddie 1973
Kristof, Joe 1968
+ Krumske, Paul 1968
+ Lange, Herb 1941
+ Lauman, Hank 1976
Lillard, Bill 1972
Lindemann, Tony 1979
+ Lindsey, Mort 1941
+ Lippe, Harry 1989
Lubanski, Ed 1971
Lucci, Vince Sr 1978
+ Marino, Hank 1941
+ Martino, John 1969
Marzich, Andy 1993
McGrath, Mike 1993
+ McMahon, Junie 1967
+ Mercurio, Skang 1967
+ Meyers, Norm 1984
+ Nagy, Steve 1963
Norris, Joe 1954
O'Donnell, Chuck 1968
Pappas, George 1989
+ Patterson, Pat 1974
Ritger, Dick 1984
+ Rogoznica, Andy 1993
Salvino, Carmen 1979
Schissler, Les 1991
Schroeder, Jim 1990
+ Schwoegler, Connie 1968
Semiz, Teata 1991
+ Sielaff, Lou 1968
+ Sinke, Joe 1977
+ Sixty, Billy 1961
Smith, Harry 1978
+ Smith, Jimmy 1941
Soutar, Dave 1985
+ Sparando, Tony 1968
+ Spinella, Barney 1968
+ Steers, Harry 1941
Stefanich, Jim 1983
+ Stein, Otto Jr 1971
Stoudt, Bud 1991
Strampe, Bob 1977
+ Thoma, Sykes 1971
Toft, Rod 1991
Tountas, Pete 1989
Tucker, Bill 1988
Tuttle, Tommy 1995
+ Varipapa, Andy 1957
+ Ward, Walter 1959
Weber, Dick 1970
+ Welu, Billy 1975
+ Wilman, Joe 1951
+ Wolf, Phil 1961
Wonders, Rich 1990
+ Young, George 1959
Zahn, Wayne 1980
Zikes, Les 1983
+ Zunker, Gil 1941

Pioneers

+ Allen, Lafayette Jr. 1994
+ Carow, Rev. Charles 1995
+ Celestine, Sydney 1993
+ Curtis, Thomas 1993
de Freitas, Eric 1994
Hall, William Sr. 1994
Hirashima, Hirohito 1995
+ Karpf, Samuel 1993
+ Pasdeloup, Frank 1993
+ Satow, Masao 1994
+ Schutte, Louis 1993
+ Thompson, William V. 1993
+ Timm, Dr. Henry 1993

American Bowling Congress (Cont.)

Meritorious Service

+ Allen, Harold 1966
+ Archibald, John 1996
+ Baker, Frank 1975
+ Baumgarten, Elmer 1963
+ Bellisimo, Lou 1986
+ Bensinger, Bob 1969
+ Chase, LeRoy 1972
+ Coker, John 1980
+ Collier, Chuck 1963
+ Cruchon, Steve 1983
+ Ditzen, Walt 1973
+ Doehrman, Bill 1968
Elias, Eddie 1985
Evans, Dick 1992
Franklin, Bill 1992
+ Hagerty, Jack 1963
+ Hattstrom, H.A. (Doc) 1980
+ Hermann, Cone 1968
+ Howley, Pete 1941
+ Kennedy, Bob 1981
+ Langtry, Abe 1963
+ Levine, Sam 1971
+ Luby, David 1969
Luby, Mort Jr. 1988
+ Luby, Mort Sr. 1974
Matzelle, Al 1995
+ McCullough, Howard 1971
+ Patterson, Morehead 1985
+ Petersen, Louie 1963
Pezzano, Chuck 1982
Picchietti, Remo 1993
Pluckhahn, Bruce 1989
+ Raymer, Milt 1972
+ Reed, Elmer 1978
Rudo, Milt 1984
Schenkel, Chris 1988
+ Sweeney, Dennis 1974
Tessman, Roger 1994
+ Thum, Joe 1980
Weinstein, Sam 1970
+ Whitney, Eli 1975
Wolf, Fred 1976

Women's International Bowling Congress

Established in 1953. **Eligibility:** Performance nominees must have won at least one WIBC Championship Tournament title, a WIBC Queens tournament title or an international competition title and have bowled in at least 15 national WIBC Championship Tournaments (unless injury or illness cut career short).

Class of 1996 (3): PERFORMANCE—**Aleta Sill** and **Donna Adamek**. MERITORIOUS SERVICE—**Flora Mitchell**.

Members are listed with years of induction; (+) indicates deceased members.

Performance

Abel, Joy 1984
Adamek, Donna 1996
Ann, Patty 1995
Bolt, Mae 1978
Bouvia, Gloria 1987
Boxberger, Loa 1984
Buckner, Pam 1990
+ Burling, Catherine 1958
+ Burns, Nina 1977
Cantaline, Anita 1979
Carter, LaVerne 1977
Carter, Paula 1994
Coburn, Doris 1976
Costello, Pat 1986
Costello, Patty 1989
Dryer, Pat 1978
Duval, Helen 1970
Fellmeth, Catherine 1970
Fothergill, Dotty 1980
+ Fritz, Deane 1966
Garms, Shirley 1971
Gloor, Olga 1976
Graham, Linda 1992
Graham, Mary Lou 1989
+ Greenwald, Goldie 1953
Grinfelds, Vesma 1991
+ Harman, Janet 1985
+ Hartrick, Stella 1972
+ Hatch, Grayce 1953
Havlish, Jean 1987
+ Hoffman, Martha 1979
Holm, Joan 1974
+ Humphreys, Birdie 1979
Ignizio, Mildred 1975
Jacobson, D.D 1981
+ Jaeger, Emma 1953
Kelly, Annese 1985
+ Knechtges, Doris 1983
Kuczynski, Betty 1981
Ladewig, Marion 1964
Martin, Sylvia Wene 1966
Martorella, Millie 1975
+ Matthews, Merle 1974
+ McCutcheon, Floretta 1956
Merrick, Marge 1980
+ Mikiel, Val 1979
+ Miller, Dorothy 1954
Mivelaz, Betty 1991
Mohacsi, Mary 1994
Morris, Betty 1983
Nichols, Lorrie 1989
Norman, Edie Jo 1993
Norton, Virginia 1988
Notaro, Phyllis 1979
Ortner, Bev 1972
+ Powers, Connie 1973
Rickard, Robbie 1994
+ Robinson, Leona 1969
Romeo, Robin 1995
+ Rump, Anita 1962
+ Ruschmeyer, Addie 1961
+ Ryan, Esther 1963
+ Sablatnik, Ethel 1979
+ Schulte, Myrtle 1965
+ Shablis, Helen 1977
Sill, Aleta 1996
+ Simon, Violet (Billy) 1960
+ Small, Tess 1971
+ Smith, Grace 1968
Soutar, Judy 1976
+ Stockdale, Louise 1953
Toepfer, Elvira 1976
+ Twyford, Sally 1964
+ Warmbier, Marie 1953
Wilkinson, Dorothy 1990
+ Winandy, Cecelia 1975
Zimmerman, Donna 1982

Meritorious Service

Baetz, Helen 1977
+ Baker, Helen 1989
+ Banker, Gladys 1994
+ Bayley, Clover 1992
+ Berger, Winifred 1976
+ Bohlen, Philena 1955
Borschuk, Lo 1988
+ Botkin, Freda 1986
+ Chapman, Emily 1957
+ Crowe, Alberta 1982
+ Dornblaser, Gertrude 1979
Duffy, Agnes 1987
Finke, Gertrude 1990
+ Fisk, Rae 1983
+ Haas, Dorothy 1977
+ Higley, Margaret 1969
+ Hochstadter, Bee 1967
+ Kay, Nora 1964
+ Kelly, Ellen 1979
Kelone, Theresa 1978
+ Knepprath, Jeannette 1963
+ Lasher, Iolia 1967
Marrs, Mabel 1979
+ McBride, Bertha 1968
+ Menne, Catherine 1979
Mitchell, Flora 1996
+ Mraz, Jo 1959
O'Connor, Billie 1992
+ Phaler, Emma 1965
+ Porter, Cora 1986
+ Quin, Zoe 1979
+ Rishling, Gertrude 1972
Simone, Anne 1991
Sloan, Catherine 1985
+ Speck, Berdie 1966
Spitalnick, Mildred 1994
+ Spring, Alma 1979
+ Switzer, Pearl 1973
Todd, Trudy 1993
+ Veatch, Georgia 1974
+ White, Mildred 1975
+ Wood, Ann 1970

Ladies Pro Bowlers Tour

Established in 1995 by the Ladies Pro Bowlers Tour. **Address:** Sam's Town Hotel, Gambling Hall and Bowling Center, 5111 Boulder Highway, Las Vegas, NV 89122. **Telephone:** (815) 332-5756.

Eligibility: Nominees in performance category must have at least five titles from organizations including All-Star, World Invitational, LPBT, WPBA, PWBA, TPA and LPBA. Voting done by 10-member committee of bowling writers appointed by LPBT president John Falzone.

Class of 1996 (8): PERFORMANCE—**Nikki Gianulias**, **Lorrie Nichols**, **Robin Romeo**, **Lisa Wagner**. PIONEERS—**Doris Coburn**, **Donna Zimmerman**. BUILDERS—**Jeannette Robinson**, **Janet Buhler**.
Members are listed with year of induction; (+) indicates deceased member.

Performance

Adamek, Donna....................1995
Costello, Patty....................1995
Fothergill, Dotty....................1995
Gianulias, Nikki....................1996
Ladewig, Marion....................1995
Martorella, Millie....................1995
Morris, Betty....................1995
Nichols, Lorrie....................1996
Romeo, Robin....................1996
Wagner, Lisa....................1996

Pioneers

Carter, LaVerne....................1995
Coburn, Doris....................1996
Duval, Helen....................1995
Garms, Shirley....................1995
Zimmerman, Donna....................1996

Builders

Buhler, Janet....................1996
Robinson, Jeannette....................1996
+Veatch, Georgia....................1995

BOXING

International Boxing Hall of Fame

Established in 1989 and opened in 1990. **Address:** 1 Hall of Fame Drive, Canastota, NY 13032. **Telephone:** (315) 697-7095.

Eligibility: All nominees must be retired for five years. Voting done by 142-member panel made up of Boxing Writers' Association members and world-wide boxing historians.

Class of 1996 (13): MODERN ERA—**Wilfred Benitez** (welterweight), **Joe Brown** (lightweight), **Manuel Ortiz** (bantamweight), **Aaron Pryor** (jr. welterweight). OLD TIMERS—**Tommy Burns** (heavyweight), **Jack Delaney** (light heavyweight), **Fidel LaBarba** (flyweight), **Young Stribling** (all classes), **Kid Williams** (bantamweight). PIONEERS—**John Morrissey** (heavyweight). NON-PARTICIPANTS— **William Muldoon** (trainer-manager), **Dan Parker** (journalist), **Emanuel Steward** (trainer-manager).

Members are listed with year of induction; (+) indicates deceased member.

Modern Era

Ali, Muhammad....................1990
Arguello, Alexis....................1992
+ Armstrong, Henry....................1990
Basilio, Carmen....................1990
Benitez, Wilfred....................1996
Benvenuti, Nino....................1992
+ Berg, Jackie (Kid)....................1994
Brown, Joe....................1996
+ Burley, Charley....................1992
+ Cerdan, Marcel....................1991
+ Charles, Ezzard....................1990
+ Conn, Billy....................1990
+ Elorde, Gabriel (Flash)....................1993
Foster, Bob....................1990
Frazier, Joe....................1990
Fullmer, Gene....................1991
Gavilan, Kid....................1990
Giardello, Joey....................1993
Gomez, Wilfredo....................1995
+ Graham, Billy....................1992
+ Graziano, Rocky....................1991
Griffith, Emile....................1990
Hagler, Marvelous Marvin....................1993
Harado, Masahiko (Fighting)....................1995
Jack, Beau....................1991
Jofre, Eder....................1992
Johnson, Harold....................1993
LaMotta, Jake....................1990
+ Liston, Sonny....................1991
+ Louis, Joe....................1990
+ Marciano, Rocky....................1990
Maxim, Joey....................1994
Montgomery, Bob....................1995
+ Monzon, Carlos....................1990
Moore, Archie....................1990
Napoles, Jose....................1990
Norton, Ken....................1992
Olivares, Ruben....................1991
Ortiz, Carlos....................1991
+ Ortiz, Manuel....................1996
Patterson, Floyd....................1991
Pep, Willie....................1990
+ Perez, Pasqual....................1995
+ Pryor, Aaron....................1996
+ Robinson, Sugar Ray....................1990
Saddler, Sandy....................1990
+ Sanchez, Salvadore....................1991
Schmeling, Max....................1992
Spinks, Michael....................1994
+ Tiger, Dick....................1991
+ Walcott, Jersey Joe....................1990
+ Williams, Ike....................1990
Zale, Tony....................1991
Zarate, Carlos....................1994
+ Zivic, Fritzie....................1993

Old-Timers

Ambers, Lou....................1992
+ Attell, Abe....................1990
+ Baer, Max....................1995
+ Britton, Jack....................1990
+ Brown, Panama Al....................1992
+ Burns, Tommy....................1996
Canzoneri, Tony....................1990
+ Carpentier, Georges....................1991
+ Chocolate, Kid....................1991
+ Corbett, James J....................1990
+ Darcy, Les....................1993
+ Delaney, Jack....................1996
+ Dempsey, Jack....................1990
+ Dempsey, Jack (Nonpareil)....................1992
+ Dillon, Jack....................1995
+ Dixon, George....................1990
+ Driscoll, Jem....................1990
+ Dundee, Johnny....................1991
+ Fitzsimmons, Bob....................1990
+ Flowers, Theodore (Tiger)....................1993
+ Gans, Joe....................1990
+ Gibbons, Mike....................1992
+ Gibbons, Tommy....................1993
+ Greb, Harry....................1990
+ Griffo, Young....................1991
+ Jackson, Peter....................1990
+ Jeffries, James J....................1990
+ Johnson, Jack....................1990
+ Ketchel, Stanley....................1990
+ Kilbane, Johnny....................1995
+ LaBarba, Fidel....................1996
+ Langford, Sam....................1990
+ Leonard, Benny....................1990
+ Lewis, John Henry....................1994
+ Lewis, Ted (Kid)....................1992
+ Loughran, Tommy....................1991
+ McAuliffe, Jack....................1995
+ McCoy, Charles (Kid)....................1991
+ McFarland, Packey....................1992

Boxing Hall of Fame (Cont.)

Old-Timers (Cont.)

+ McGovern, Terry 1990
McLarnin, Jimmy 1991
+ Nelson, Battling 1992
+ O'Brien, Philadelphia Jack 1994
+ Rosenbloom, Maxie 1993
+ Ross, Barney 1990
+ Ryan, Tommy 1991
+ Sharkey, Jack 1994
+ Stribling, Young 1996
+ Tunney, Gene 1990
+ Villa, Pancho 1994
+ Walcott, Joe 1991
+ Walker, Mickey 1990
+ Wilde, Jimmy 1990
+ Williams, Kid 1996
+ Wills, Harry 1992

Pioneers

+ Belcher, Jem 1992
+ Brain, Ben 1994
+ Broughton, Jack 1990
+ Burke, James (Deaf) 1992
+ Cribb, Tom 1991
+ Duffy, Paddy 1994
+ Figg, James 1992
+ Jackson, Gentleman John 1992
+ Johnson, Tom 1995
+ King, Tom 1992
+ Langham, Nat 1992
+ Mace, Jem 1990
+ Mendoza, Daniel 1990
+ Morrisey, John 1996
+ Pearce, Henry 1993
+ Sayers, Tom 1990
Spring, Tom 1992
+ Sullivan, John L 1990
+ Thompson, William 1991
+ Ward, Jem 1995

Non-Participants

+ Andrews, Thomas S. 1992
+ Arcel, Ray 1991
+ Blackburn, Jack 1992
Brenner, Teddy 1993
+ Chambers, John Graham 1990
Clancy, Gil 1993
+ Coffroth, James W. 1991
+ D'Amato, Cus 1995
+ Donovan, Arthur 1993
Dundee, Angelo 1992
Dundee, Chris 1994
Dunphy, Don 1993
+ Egan, Pierce 1991
+ Fleischer, Nat 1990
Futch, Eddie 1994
+ Goldman, Charley 1992
+ Goldstein, Ruby 1994
+ Jacobs, Jimmy 1993
+ Jacobs, Mike 1990
+ Kearns, Jack (Doc) 1990
+ Liebling, A.J. 1992
+ Lonsdale, Lord 1990
Markson, Harry 1992
Mercante, Arthur 1995
+ Muldoon, William 1996
Odd, Gilbert 1995
+ Parker, Dan 1996
+ Parnassus, George 1991
+ Queensberry, Marquis of 1990
+ Rickard, Tex 1990
+ Siler, George 1995
+ Solomons, Jack 1995
Steward, Emanuel 1996
+ Taub, Sam 1994
+ Walker, James J. (Jimmy) 1992

Old *Ring* Hall Members Not in Int'l. Boxing Hall

Nat Fleischer, the late founder and editor-in-chief of *The Ring*, established his magazine's Boxing Hall of Fame in 1954, but it was abandoned after the 1987 inductions. One hundred members of the old *Ring* Hall have been elected to the International Hall since 1989. The 65 boxers and one sportswriter who have yet to be elected to the International Hall are listed below with their year of induction into the *Ring* Hall.

Modern Group

+ Apostoli, Fred 1978
+ Braddock, James J. 1964
+ Escobar, Sixto 1975
+ Garcia, Ceferino 1977
+ Jenkins, Lew 1976
+ Lesnevich, Gus 1973
+ Petrolle, Billy 1962
+ Shirai, Yoshio 1977
+ Tendler, Lew 1961
+ Wright, Chalky 1976

Old-Timers

+ Berlenbach, Paul 1971
+ Britt, Jimmy 1976
+ Chaney, George (K.O.) 1974
+ Choyhski, Joe 1959
+ Corbett, Young II 1965
+ Coulon, Johnny 1965
+ Fields, Jackie 1977
+ Genaro, Frankie 1973
+ Herman, Pete 1959
+ Houck, Leo 1969
+ Jeannette, Joe 1967
+ Jeffra, Harry 1982
+ Kid, The Dixie 1975
+ Klaus, Frank 1974
+ Lavigne, George (Kid) 1959
+ Levinsky, Battling 1966
+ Lynch, Benny 1986
+ Maher, Peter 1978
+ McVey, Sam 1986
+ Mitchell, Charley 1957
+ Ortiz, Manuel 1985
+ Papke, Billy 1972
+ Ritchie, Willie 1962
+ Root, Jack 1961
+ Sharkey, Tom 1959
+ Smith, Jeff 1969
+ Taylor, Bud 1986
+ Welsh, Freddie 1960
+ Willard, Jess 1977
+ Wolgast, Ad 1958

Pioneers

+ Aaron, Barney (Young) 1967
+ Chambers, Arthur 1954
+ Chandler, Tom 1972
+ Clark, Nobby 1971
+ Collyer, Sam 1964
+ Donnelly, Dan 1960
+ Donovan, Prof. Mike 1970
+ Goss, Joe 1969
+ Gully, John 1959
+ Heenan, John C 1954
+ Hyer, Jacob 1968
+ Hyer, Tom 1954
+ Jackling, Thomas 1985
+ Kilrain, Jack 1965
+ Molineaux, Tom 1958
+ Price, Ned 1962
+ Richmond, Bill 1956
+ Ryan, Paddy 1973
+ Sam, Young Dutch 1975

Non-Participant

+ Daniel, Dan (sportswriter) 1977

FOOTBALL

College Football Hall of Fame

Established in 1955 by the National Football Foundation. **Address:** 111 South St. Joseph St., South Bend, IN 46601. **Telephone:** (219) 235-9999.

Eligibility: Nominated players must be out of college 10 years and a first team All-America pick by a major selector during their careers; coaches must be retired three years. Voting done by 12-member panel of athletic directors, conference and bowl officials and media representatives. 1996 is the first year representatives from NCAA Div. I-AA, II, and III, and the NAIA are eligible for induction.

Class of 1996 (26): LARGE COLLEGE—FB **Bob Ferguson**, Ohio St. (1959-61); DE **Hugh Green**, Pittsburgh (1977-80); T **Frank Merritt**, Army (1940-43); G **John Michels**, Tennessee (1950-52); C/LB **Bob Pellegrini**, Maryland (1953-55); E **Pat Richter**, Wisconsin (1960-62); LB **Jerry Robinson**, UCLA (1975-78); RB **Jimmy Saxton**, Texas (1959-61); C/LB **Jerry Tubbs**, Oklahoma (1954-56); RB **Charles White**, USC (1976-79); QB **Marc Wilson**, BYU (1977-79). COACH—**Henry "Red" Sanders**, Vanderbilt (1940-42, '46-48) and UCLA (1949-57). SMALL COLLEGE— QB **Terry Bradshaw**, La. Tech (1966-69; OL/DL **Buck Buchanan**, Grambling (1959-62); DE **Vern Den Herder**, Central-IA (1967-70); RB **Billy "White Shoes" Johnson**, Widener-PA (1971-73); QB **Neil Lomax**, Portland St. (1977-80); OG **Tyrone McGriff**, Florida A&M (1976-79); RB **Wilbert Montgomery**, Abilene Christian (1973-76); RB **Walter Payton**, Jackson St. (1971-74); LB **Gary Reasons**, Northwestern St. (1980-83); LB **Jim Youngblood**, Tennessee Tech; (1969-72). COACHES—**Harold Burry**, Westminster-PA (1952-71); **Edgar Sherman**, Muskingum-OH (1945-66); **Gilbert Steinke**, Texas A&I (1954-76); **Lee Tressel**, Baldwin-Wallace-OH (1958-80).

Note: Bobby Dodd and **Amos Alonzo Stagg** are the only members to be honored as both players and coaches.

Players are listed with final year they played in college and coaches are listed with year of induction; (+) indicates deceased members.

Players

+ Abell, Earl-Colgate 1915
Agase, Alex-Purdue/Ill 1946
+ Agganis, Harry-Boston U........1952
Albert, Frank-Stanford............1941
+ Aldrich, Ki-TCU.....................1938
+ Aldrich, Malcolm-Yale 1921
+ Alexander, Joe-Syracuse.........1920
Alworth, Lance-Arkansas 1961
+ Ameche, Alan-Wisconsin........1954
+ Ames, Knowlton-Princeton 1889
Amling, Warren-Ohio St.........1946
Anderson, Dick-Colorado 1967
Anderson, Donny-Tex.Tech......1966
+ Anderson, Hunk-N.Dame 1921
Atkins, Doug-Tennessee 1952
Babich, Bob-Miami-OH 1968
+ Bacon, Everett-Wesleyan.........1912
+ Bagnell, Reds-Penn................1950
+ Baker, Hobey-Princeton...........1913
+ Baker, John-USC 1931
+ Baker, Moon-N'western 1926
Baker, Terry-Oregon St 1962
+ Ballin, Harold-Princeton..........1914
+ Banker, Bill-Tulane 1929
Banonis, Vince-Detroit 1941
+ Barnes, Stan-California...........1921
+ Barrett, Charles-Cornell 1915
+ Baston, Bert-Minnesota...........1916
+ Battles, Cliff-WV Wesleyan 1931
Baugh, Sammy-TCU 1936
Baughan, Maxie-Ga.Tech 1959
+ Bausch, James-Kansas...........1930
Beagle, Ron-Navy 1955
Beban, Gary-UCLA 1967
Bechtol, Hub-Texas 1946
+ Beckett, John-Oregon 1916
Bednarik, Chuck-Penn 1948
Behm, Forrest-Nebraska 1940
Bell, Bobby-Minnesota............1962
Bellino, Joe-Navy 1960
Below, Marty-Wisconsin 1923
+ Benbrook, Al-Michigan...........1910
+ Berry, Charlie-Lafayette 1924
Bertelli, Angelo-N.Dame.........1943
Berwanger, Jay-Chicago.........1935
+ Bettencourt, L.-St.Mary's 1927
Biletnikoff, Fred-Fla.St............1964
Blanchard, Doc-Army............1946
+ Blozis, Al-Georgetown............1942
Bock, Ed-Iowa St 1938
Bomar, Lynn-Vanderbilt...........1924
+ Bomeisler, Bo-Yale 1913
+ Booth, Albie-Yale 1931
+ Borries, Fred-Navy 1934
+ Bosley, Bruce-West Va 1955
Bosseler, Don-Miami,FL..........1956
Bottari, Vic-California 1938
+ Boynton, Ben-Williams............1920
+ Brewer, Charles-Harvard 1895
+ Bright, Johnny-Drake.............1951
Brodie, John-Stanford.............1956
+ Brooke, George-Penn 1895
Brown, Bob-Nebraska 1963
Brown, Geo-Navy/S.Diego St.1947
+ Brown, Gordon-Yale..............1900
Brown, Jim-Syracuse 1956
+ Brown, John, Jr.-Navy 1913
+ Brown, Johnny Mack-Ala........1925
+ Brown, Tay-USC....................1932
+ Bunker, Paul-Army.................1902
Burford, Chris-Stanford..........1959
Burton, Ron-N'western............1959
Butkus, Dick-Illinois................1964
+ Butler, Robert-Wisconsin 1912
Cafego, George-Tenn 1939
+ Cagle, Red-SWLa/Army.........1929
+ Cain, John-Alabama 1932
Cameron, Ed-Wash.& Lee.......1924
+ Campbell, David-Harvard.......1901
Campbell, Earl-Texas.............1977
+ Cannon, Jack-N.Dame 1929
Cappelletti, John-Penn St 1973
+ Carideo, Frank-N.Dame 1930
+ Carney, Charles-Illinois...........1921
Caroline, J.C.-Illinois 1954
Carpenter, Bill-Army...............1959
+ Carpenter, Hunter-Va.Tech 1905
Carroll, Chas.-Washington 1928
Casanova, Tommy-LSU 1971
+ Casey, Edward-Harvard 1919
Cassady, Howard-Ohio St 1955
+ Chamberlin, Guy-Neb. 1915
Chapman, Sam-California 1938
Chappuis, Bob-Michigan 1947
+ Christman, Paul-Missouri 1940
+ Clark, Dutch-Colo. Col...........1929
Cleary, Paul-USC 1947
+ Clevenger, Zora-Indiana 1903
Cloud, Jack-Wm. & Mary.......1948
+ Cochran, Gary-Princeton........1897
+ Cody, Josh-Vanderbilt............1919
Coleman, Don-Mich.St............1951
+ Conerly, Charlie-Miss 1947
Connor, George-HC/ND 1947
+ Corbin, William-Yale..............1888
Corbus, William-Stanford 1933
+ Cowan, Hector-Princeton 1889
+ Coy, Edward (Tad)-Yale 1909
+ Crawford, Fred-Duke..............1933
Crow, John David-Tex.A&M....1957
+ Crowley, Jim-Notre Dame.......1924
Csonka, Larry-Syracuse..........1967
Cutter, Slade-Navy 1934
+ Czarobski, Ziggie-N.Dame 1947
Dale, Carroll-Va.Tech 1959
+ Dalrymple, Gerald-Tulane.......1931
+ Dalton, John-Navy 1911
+ Daly, Chas.-Harvard/Army 1902
Daniell, Averell-Pitt 1936
+ Daniell, James-Ohio St 1941
+ Davies, Tom-Pittsburgh............1921
+ Davis, Ernie-Syracuse.............1961
Davis, Glenn-Army................1946
Davis, Robert-Ga.Tech 1947
Dawkins, Pete-Army 1958
DeLong, Steve-Tennessee........1964
+ DeRogatis, Al-Duke 1948
+ DesJardien, Paul-Chicago.......1914
+ Devine, Aubrey-Iowa.............1921
+ DeWitt, John-Princeton 1903
Dial, Buddy-Rice 1958
Ditka, Mike-Pittsburgh 1960
Dobbs, Glenn-Tulsa 1942
+ Dodd, Bobby-Tennessee..........1930
Donan, Holland-Princeton.......1950
+ Donchess, Joseph-Pitt............1929
Dorsett, Tony-Pitt 1976
+ Dougherty, Nathan-Tenn 1909
Drahos, Nick-Cornell..............1940
+ Driscoll, Paddy-N'western.......1917
+ Drury, Morley-USC................1927
Dudley, Bill-Virginia...............1941
Easley, Kenny-UCLA..............1980
+ Eckersall, Walter-Chicago.......1906

College Football Hall of Fame (Cont.)

Players

+ Edwards, Turk-Wash.St.......1931
+ Edwards, Wm.-Princeton.......1899
+ Eichenlaub, Ray-N.Dame.......1914
Eisenhauer, Steve-Navy.......1953
Elkins, Larry-Baylor.......1964
Elliott, Bump-Mich/Purdue.......1947
Elliott, Pete-Michigan.......1948
Evans, Ray-Kansas.......1947
+ Exendine, Albert-Carlisle.......1907
Falaschi, Nello-S.Clara.......1936
Fears, Tom-S.Clara/UCLA.......1947
+ Feathers, Beattie-Tenn.......1933
Fenimore, Bob-Okla.St.......1946
+ Fenton, Doc-LSU.......1909
Ferguson, Bob-Ohio St.......1961
Ferraro, John-USC.......1944
Fesler, Wes-Ohio St.......1930
+ Fincher, Bill-Ga.Tech.......1920
Fischer, Bill-Notre Dame.......1948
+ Fish, Hamilton-Harvard.......1909
+ Fisher, Robert-Harvard.......1911
+ Flowers, Allen-Ga.Tech.......1920
+ Fortmann Danny-Colgate.......1935
Francis, Sam-Nebraska.......1936
Franco, Ed-Fordham.......1937
+ Frank, Clint-Yale.......1937
Franz, Rodney-California.......1949
Frederickson, Tucker-Auburn.......1964
+ Friedman, Benny-Michigan.......1926
Gabriel, Roman-N.C. State.......1961
Gain, Bob-Kentucky.......1950
+ Galiffa, Arnold-Army.......1949
Gallarneau, Hugh-Stanford.......1940
+ Garbisch, Edgar-W.& J./Army.......1924
Garrett, Mike-USC.......1965
+ Gelbert, Charles-Penn.......1896
+ Geyer, Forest-Oklahoma.......1915
Gibbs, Jake-Miss.......1960
Giel, Paul-Minnesota.......1953
Gifford, Frank-USC.......1951
+ Gilbert, Walter-Auburn.......1936
Gilmer, Harry-Alabama.......1947
+ Gipp, George-N.Dame.......1920
+ Gladchuk, Chet-Boston Col.......1940
Glass, Bill-Baylor.......1956
Glover, Rich-Nebraska.......1972
Goldberg, Marshall-Pitt.......1938
Goodreault, Gene-BC.......1940
+ Gordon, Walter-Calif.......1918
+ Governali, Paul-Columbia.......1942
Grabowski, Jim-Illinois.......1965
Graham, Otto-N'western.......1943
+ Grange, Red-Illinois.......1925
+ Grayson, Bobby-Stanford.......1935
Green, Hugh-Pitt.......1980
+ Green, Jack-Tulane/Army.......1945
Greene, Joe-N.Texas St.......1968
Griese, Bob-Purdue.......1966
Griffin, Archie-Ohio St.......1975
Groom, Jerry-Notre Dame.......1950
+ Gulick, Merle-Toledo/Hobart.......1929
+ Guyon, Joe-Ga.Tech.......1918
Hadl, John-Kansas.......1961
+ Hale, Edwin-Miss.College.......1921
Hall, Parker-Miss.......1938
Ham, Jack-Penn St.......1970
+ Hamilton, Bob-Stanford.......1935
+ Hamilton, Tom-Navy.......1926
+ Hanson, Vic-Syracuse.......1926
+ Harder, Pat-Wisconsin.......1942
+ Hardwick, Tack-Harvard.......1914
+ Hare, T.Truxton-Penn.......1900
+ Harley, Chick-Ohio St.......1919
+ Harmon, Tom-Michigan.......1940
+ Harpster, Howard-Carnegie.......1928
+ Hart, Edward-Princeton.......1911
Hart, Leon-Notre Dame.......1949
Hartman, Bill-Georgia.......1937
+ Hazel, Homer-Rutgers.......1924
+ Hazeltine, Matt-Calif.......1954
+ Healey, Ed.-Dartmouth.......1916
+ Heffelfinger, Pudge-Yale.......1891
+ Hein, Mel-Washington St.......1930
+ Heinrich, Don-Washington.......1952
Hendricks, Ted-Miami,FL.......1968
+ Henry, Pete-Wash&Jeff.......1919
+ Herschberger, C.-Chicago.......1898
+ Herwig, Robert-Calif.......1937
+ Heston, Willie-Michigan.......1904
+ Hickman, Herman-Tenn.......1931
+ Hickok, William-Yale.......1894
Hill, Dan-Duke.......1938
+ Hillebrand, Art-Princeton.......1899
+ Hinkey, Frank-Yale.......1894
Hinkle, Carl-Vanderbilt.......1937
Hinkle, Clarke-Bucknell.......1931
Hirsch, Elroy-Wisc./Mich.......1943
+ Hitchcock, James-Auburn.......1932
Hoffmann, Frank-N.Dame.......1931
+ Hogan, James J.-Yale.......1904
+ Holland, Brud-Cornell.......1938
+ Holleder, Don-Army.......1955
+ Hollenback, Bill-Penn.......1908
Holovak, Mike-Boston Col.......1942
Holub, E.J.-Texas Tech.......1960
Hornung, Paul-N.Dame.......1956
+ Horrell, Edwin-California.......1924
+ Horvath, Les-Ohio St.......1944
+ Howe, Arthur-Yale.......1911
+ Howell, Dixie-Alabama.......1934
+ Hubbard, Cal-Centenary.......1926
+ Hubbard, John-Amherst.......1906
+ Hubert, Pooley-Ala.......1925
Huff, Sam-West Virginia.......1955
Humble, Weldon-Rice.......1946
+ Hunt, Joe-Texas A&M.......1927
Huntington, Ellery-Colgate.......1914
Hutson, Don-Alabama.......1934
+ Ingram, Jonas-Navy.......1906
+ Isbell, Cecil-Purdue.......1937
+ Jablonsky, J.-Army/Wash.......1933
+ Janowicz, Vic-Ohio St.......1951
+ Jenkins, Darold-Missouri.......1941
+ Jensen, Jackie-California.......1948
+ Joesting, Herbert-Minn.......1927
Johnson, Bob-Tennessee.......1967
+ Johnson, Jimmie-Carlisle/N'western.......1903
Johnson, Ron-Michigan.......1968
+ Jones, Calvin-Iowa.......1955
+ Jones, Gomer-Ohio St.......1935
Jordan, Lee Roy-Alabama.......1962
+ Juhan, Frank-U.of South.......1910
Justice, Charlie-N.Car.......1949
+ Kaer, Mort-USC.......1926
Karras, Alex-Iowa.......1957
Kavanaugh, Ken-LSU.......1939
+ Kaw, Edgar-Cornell.......1922
Kazmaier, Dick-Princeton.......1951
+ Keck, James-Princeton.......1921
Kelley, Larry-Yale.......1936
+ Kelly, Wild Bill-Montana.......1926
Kenna, Doug-Army.......1944
+ Kerr, George-Boston Col.......1941
+ Ketcham, Henry-Yale.......1913
Keyes, Leroy-Purdue.......1968
+ Killinger, Glenn-Penn St.......1921
+ Kilpatrick, John-Yale.......1910
Kimbrough, John-Tex A&M.......1940
+ Kinard, Frank-Mississippi.......1937
+ King, Phillip-Princeton.......1893
+ Kinnick, Nile-Iowa.......1939
+ Kipke, Harry-Michigan.......1923
+ Kirkpatrick, John-Yale.......1910
+ Kitzmiller, John-Oregon.......1930
+ Koch, Barton-Baylor.......1931
+ Koppisch, Walt-Columbia.......1924
Kramer, Ron-Michigan.......1956
Krueger, Charlie-Tex.A&M.......1957
Kutner, Malcolm-Texas.......1941
Kwalick, Ted-Penn St.......1968
+ Lach, Steve-Duke.......1941
+ Lane, Myles-Dartmouth.......1927
Lattner, Johnny-N.Dame.......1953
Lauricella, Hank-Tenn.......1952
+ Lautenschlaeger-Tulane.......1925
+ Layden, Elmer-N.Dame.......1924
+ Layne, Bobby-Texas.......1947
+ Lea, Langdon-Princeton.......1895
LeBaron, Eddie-Pacific.......1949
+ Leech, James-VMI.......1920
+ Lester, Darrell-TCU.......1935
Lilly, Bob-TCU.......1960
Little, Floyd-Syracuse.......1966
+ Lio, Augie-Georgetown.......1940
+ Locke, Gordon-Iowa.......1922
+ Lourie, Don-Princeton.......1921
Lucas, Richie-Penn St.......1959
Luckman, Sid-Columbia.......1938
Lujack, Johnny-N.Dame.......1947
+ Lund, Pug-Minnesota.......1934
Lynch, Jim-Notre Dame.......1966
+ Macomber, Bart-Illinois.......1915
MacLeod, Robert-Dart.......1938
Maegle, Dick-Rice.......1954
+ Mahan, Eddie-Harvard.......1915
Majors, John-Tennessee.......1956
+ Mallory, William-Yale.......1923
Mancha, Vaughn-Ala.......1947
+ Mann, Gerald-SMU.......1927
Manning, Archie-Miss.......1970
Manske, Edgar-N'western.......1933
Marinaro, Ed-Cornell.......1971
Markov, Vic-Washington.......1937
+ Marshall, Bobby-Minn.......1906
Martin, Jim-Notre Dame.......1949
Matson, Ollie-San Fran.......1952
Matthews, Ray-TCU.......1927
+ Maulbetsch, John-Mich.......1914
+ Mauthe, Pete-Penn St.......1912
+ Maxwell, Robert-Chicago/Swarthmore.......1906
McAfee, George-Duke.......1939
+ McClung, Thomas-Yale.......1891
McColl, Bill-Stanford.......1951
+ McCormick, Jim-Princeton.......1907
McDonald, Tommy-Okla.......1956
+ McDowall, Jack-N.C.State.......1927
McElhenny, Hugh-Wash.......1951
+ McEver, Gene-Tennessee.......1931

+ McEwan, John-Army 1916
McFadden, Banks-Clemson 1939
McFadin, Bud-Texas 1950
McGee, Mike-Duke 1959
+ McGinley, Edward-Penn 1924
+ McGovern, John-Minn 1910
McGraw, Thurman-Colo.St 1949
+ McKeever, Mike-USC 1960
+ McLaren, George-Pitt 1918
+ McMillan, Dan-USC/Calif 1922
+ McMillin, Bo-Centre 1921
+ McWhorter, Bob-Georgia 1913
+ Mercer, LeRoy-Penn 1912
Meredith, Don-SMU 1959
Merritt, Frank-Army 1943
+ Metzger, Bert-N.Dame 1930
+ Meylan, Wayne-Nebraska 1967
Michaels, Lou-Kentucky 1957
Michels, John-Tennessee 1952
Mickal, Abe-LSU 1935
Miller, Creighton-N.Dame 1943
+ Miller, Don-Notre Dame 1924
+ Miller, Eugene-Penn St 1913
+ Miller, Fred-Notre Dame 1928
Miller, Rip-Notre Dame 1924
Millner, Wayne-N.Dame 1935
+ Milstead, C.A.-Wabash/Yale 1923
+ Minds, John-Penn 1897
Minisi, Skip-Penn/Navy 1947
Modzelewski, Dick-Md. 1952
+ Moffat, Alex-Princeton 1883
+ Molinski, Ed-Tenn 1940
Montgomery, Cliff-Columbia 1933
Moomaw, Donn-UCLA 1952
+ Morley, William-Columbia 1902
Morris, George-Ga.Tech 1952
Morris, Larry-Ga.Tech 1954
Morton, Craig-California 1964
+ Morton, Bill-Dartmouth 1931
+ Moscrip, Monk-Stanford 1935
+ Muller, Brick-California 1922
+ Nagurski, Bronko-Minn 1929
+ Nevers, Ernie-Stanford 1925
+ Newell, Marshall-Harvard 1893
Newman, Harry-Michigan 1932
Newsome, Ozzie-Alabama 1977
Nielson, Gifford-BYU 1977
Nobis, Tommy-Texas 1965
Nomellini, Leo-Minnesota 1949
+ Oberlander, Andrew-Dart 1925
+ O'Brien, Davey-TCU 1938
+ O'Dea, Pat-Wisconsin 1899
Odell, Bob-Penn 1943
+ O'Hearn, Jack-Cornell 1915
Olds, Robin-Army 1942
+ Oliphant, Elmer-Army/Pur 1917
Olsen, Merlin-Utah St 1961
Onkotz, Dennis-Penn St. 1969
+ Oosterbaan, Bennie-Mich 1927
O'Rourke, Charles-BC 1940
+ Orsi, John-Colgate 1931
+ Osgood, Win-Cornell 1892
Osmanski, Bill-Holy Cross 1938
+ Owen, George-Harvard 1922
Owens, Jim-Oklahoma 1949
Owens, Steve-Oklahoma 1969
Page, Alan-Notre Dame 1966
Pardee, Jack-Texas A&M 1956
Parilli, Babe-Kentucky 1951
Parker, Ace-Duke 1936
Parker, Jackie-Miss.St 1953
Parker, Jim-Ohio St 1956
+ Pazzetti, Vince-Lehigh 1912
+ Peabody, Chub-Harvard 1941
+ Peck, Robert-Pittsburgh 1916
Pellegrini, Bob-Maryland 1955
+ Pennock, Stan-Harvard 1914
Pfann, George-Cornell 1923
+ Phillips, H.D.-U.of South 1904
Phillips, Loyd-Arkansas 1966
Pihos, Pete-Indiana 1946
Pingel, John-Michigan St 1938
+ Pinckert, Erny-USC 1931
Plunkett, Jim-Stanford 1970
+ Poe, Arthur-Princeton 1899
+ Pollard, Fritz-Brown 1916
Poole, B.-Miss/NC/Army 1947
Powell, Marvin-USC 1976
Pregulman, Merv-Michigan 1943
+ Price, Eddie-Tulane 1949
+ Pund, Peter-Georgia Tech 1928
Ramsey, G.-Wm&Mary 1942
Redman, Rick-Wash 1964
+ Reeds, Claude-Oklahoma 1913
Reid, Mike-Penn St 1969
Reid, Steve-Northwestern 1936
+ Reid, William-Harvard 1899
Renfro, Mel-Oregon 1963
+ Rentner, Pug-N'western 1932
+ Reynolds, Bobby-Nebraska 1952
+ Reynolds, Bob-Stanford 1935
Richter, Les-California 1951
Richter, Pat-Wisconsin 1962
+ Riley, Jack-Northwestern 1931
+ Rinehart, Chas.-Lafayette 1897
Roberts, J. D.-Oklahoma 1953
+ Robeson, Paul-Rutgers 1918
Robinson, Jerry-UCLA 1978
+ Rodgers, Ira-West Va 1919
+ Rogers, Ed-Carlisle/Minn 1903
Romig, Joe-Colorado 1961
+ Rosenberg, Aaron-USC 1933
Rote, Kyle-SMU 1950
+ Routt, Joe-Texas A&M 1937
+ Salmon, Red-Notre Dame 1903
+ Sauer, George-Nebraska 1933
Savitsky, George-Penn 1947
Saxton, Jimmy-Texas 1961
Sayers, Gale-Kansas 1964
Scarbath, Jack-Maryland 1952
+ Scarlett, Hunter-Penn 1908
Schloredt, Bob-Wash 1960
+ Schoonover, Wear-Ark. 1929
+ Schreiner, Dave-Wisconsin 1942
+ Schultz, Germany-Mich 1908
+ Schwab, Dutch-Lafayette 1922
+ Schwartz, Marchy-N.Dame 1931
+ Schwegler, Paul-Wash 1931
Scott, Clyde-Arkansas 1948
Scott, Richard-Navy 1947
Scott, Tom-Virginia 1953
+ Seibels, Henry-Sewanee 1899
Sellers, Ron-Florida St. 1968
Selmon, Lee Roy-Okla 1975
+ Shakespeare, Bill-N.Dame 1935
+ Shelton, Murray-Cornell 1915
+ Shevlin, Tom-Yale 1905
+ Shively, Bernie-Illinois 1926
+ Simons, Monk-Tulane 1934
Simpson, O.J.-USC 1968
Sims, Billy-Oklahoma 1979
Singletary, Mike-Baylor 1980
Sington, Fred-Alabama 1930
+ Sinkwich, Frank-Georgia 1942
+ Sitko, Emil-Notre Dame 1949
+ Skladany, Joe-Pittsburgh 1933
+ Slater, Duke-Iowa 1921
+ Smith, Bruce-Minnesota 1941
Smith, Bubba-Michigan St. 1966
+ Smith, Clipper-N.Dame 1927
+ Smith, Ernie-USC 1932
Smith, Harry-USC 1939
Smith, Jim Ray-Baylor 1954
Smith, Riley-Alabama 1935
+ Smith, Vernon-Georgia 1931
+ Snow, Neil-Michigan 1901
Sparlis, Al-UCLA 1945
+ Spears, Clarence-Dart 1915
Spears, W.D.-Vanderbilt 1927
+ Sprackling, Wm.-Brown 1911
+ Sprague, Bud-Army/Texas 1928
Spurrier, Steve-Florida 1966
Stafford, Harrison-Texas 1932
+ Stagg, Amos Alonzo-Yale 1889
+ Starcevich, Max-Wash 1936
Staubach, Roger-Navy 1964
+ Steffen, Walter-Chicago 1908
Steffy, Joe-Tenn/Army 1947
+ Stein, Herbert-Pitt 1921
Steuber, Bob-Missouri 1943
+ Stevens, Mal-Yale 1923
Stillwagon, Jim-Ohio St. 1970
+ Stinchcomb, Pete-Ohio St 1920
+ Stevenson, Vincent-Penn 1905
Strom, Brock-Air Force 1959
+ Strong, Ken-NYU 1928
+ Strupper, Ev-Ga.Tech 1917
+ Stuhldreher, Harry-N.Dame 1924
+ Sturhan, Herb-Yale 1926
+ Stydahar, Joe-West Va 1935
+ Suffridge, Bob-Tennessee 1940
+ Suhey, Steve-Penn St 1947
Sullivan, Pat-Auburn 1971
+ Sundstrom, Frank-Cornell 1923
Swann, Lynn-USC 1973
+ Swanson, Clarence-Neb 1921
+ Swiacki, Bill-Columbia/HC 1947
Swink, Jim-TCU 1956
Taliafarro, Geo.-Indiana 1948
Tarkenton, Fran-Georgia 1960
+ Tavener, John-Indiana 1944
+ Taylor, Chuck-Stanford 1942
Thomas, Aurelius-Ohio St 1957
+ Thompson, Joe-Pittsburgh 1907
+ Thorne, Samuel-Yale 1895
+ Thorpe, Jim-Carlisle 1912
+ Ticknor, Ben-Harvard 1930
+ Tigert, John-Vanderbilt 1904
Tinsley, Gaynell-LSU 1936
Tipton, Eric-Duke 1938
Tonnemaker, Clayton-Minn 1949
+ Torrey, Bob-Pennsylvania 1905
+ Travis, Brick-Missouri 1920
Trippi, Charley-Georgia 1946
+ Tryon, Edward-Colgate 1925
Tubbs, Jerry-Oklahoma 1956
Turner, Bulldog-H.Simmons 1939
Twilley, Howard-Tulsa 1965
+ Utay, Joe-Texas A&M 1907
+ Van Brocklin, Norm-Ore 1948
+ Van Sickel, Dale-Florida 1929
+ Van Surdam, H.-Wesleyan 1905
+ Very, Dexter-Penn St 1912
Vessels, Billy-Oklahoma 1952
+ Vick, Ernie-Michigan 1921
+ Wagner, Hube-Pittsburgh 1913
Walker, Doak-SMU 1949
+ Wallace, Bill-Rice 1935
+ Walsh, Adam-N.Dame 1924

College Football Hall of Fame (Cont.)

Players

+ Warburton, Cotton, USC.........1934
Ward, Bob-Maryland.............1951
+ Warner, William-Cornell.........1904
+ Washington, Kenny-UCLA......1939
+ Weatherall, Jim-Okla. 1951
Webster, George-Mich.St........1966
Wedemeyer, H.-St.Mary's.......1947
+ Weekes, Harold-Columbia......1902
Weiner, Art-N.Carolina..........1949
+ Weir, Ed-Nebraska................1925
+ Welch, Gus-Carlisle...............1914
+ Weller, John-Princeton............1935
+ Wendell, Percy-Harvard.........1912
+ West, Belford-Colgate.............1919
+ Westfall, Bob-Michigan..........1941
+ Weyand, Babe-Army.............1915
+ Wharton, Buck-Penn..............1896
+ Wheeler, Arthur-Princeton......1894
White, Byron-Colorado..........1938
White, Charles-USC...............1979
White, Randy-Maryland........1974
Whitmire, Don-Navy/Ala......1944
+ Wickhorst, Frank-Navy..........1926
Widseth, Ed-Minnesota..........1936
+ Wildung, Dick-Minnesota.......1942
Williams, Bob-N.Dame..........1950
Williams, Froggie-Rice..........1949
Willis, Bill-Ohio St.................1944
Wilson, Bobby-SMU..............1935
+ Wilson, George-Wash...........1925
+ Wilson, Harry-Army/Penn St...1926
Wilson, Marc-BYU................1979
Wilson, Mike-Lafayette...........1928
Wistert, Albert-Michigan........1942
Wistert, Alvin-Michigan.........1949
+ Wistert, Whitey-Michigan......1933
+ Wojciechowicz, Alex-Fordham.1937
+ Wood, Barry-Harvard............1931
+ Wyant, Andy-Chicago...........1894
+ Wyatt, Bowden-Tenn.............1938
+ Wyckoff, Clint-Cornell............1895
+ Yarr, Tommy-N.Dame............1931
Yary, Ron-USC......................1967
+ Yoder, Lloyd-Carnegie............1926
+ Young, Claude-Illinois..........1946
+ Young, Harry-Wash.& Lee......1916
+ Young, Waddy-Okla..............1938
Youngblood, Jack-Florida.......1970
Zarnas, Gustave-Ohio St........1937

Coaches

+ Aillet, Joe..............................1989
+ Alexander, Bill.......................1951
+ Anderson, Ed.........................1971
+ Armstrong, Ike........................1957
+ Bachman, Charlie...................1978
+ Banks, Earl............................1992
+ Baujan, Harry.........................1990
+ Bell, Matty.............................1955
+ Bezdek, Hugo.........................1954
+ Bible, Dana X.........................1951
+ Bierman, Bernie......................1955
Blackman, Bob........................1987
+ Blaik, Earl (Red).....................1965
Broyles, Frank.........................1983
+ Bryant, Paul (Bear).................1986
+ Caldwell, Charlie....................1961
+ Camp, Walter.........................1951
Casanova, Len.........................1977
+ Cavanaugh, Frank...................1954
+ Colman, Dick.........................1990
+ Crisler, Fritz..........................1954
+ Daugherty, Duffy....................1984
Devaney, Bob..........................1981
Devine, Dan............................1985
+ Dobie, Gil...............................1951
+ Dodd, Bobby..........................1993
+ Donohue, Michael...................1951
Dooley, Vince..........................1994
+ Dorais, Gus............................1954
+ Edwards, Bill..........................1986
+ Engle, Rip..............................1973
Faurot, Don............................1961
+ Gaither, Jake..........................1973
Gillman, Sid...........................1989
+ Godfrey, Ernest......................1972
Graves, Ray...........................1990
+ Gustafson, Andy.....................1985
+ Hall, Edward..........................1951
+ Harding, Jack.........................1980
+ Harlow, Richard......................1954
+ Harman, Harvey......................1981
+ Harper, Jesse..........................1971
+ Haughton, Percy.....................1951
+ Hayes, Woody........................1983
+ Heisman, John W...................1954
+ Higgins, Robert.......................1954
+ Hollingberry, Babe..................1979
+ Howard, Frank........................1989
+ Ingram, Bill.............................1973
+ Jennings, Morley.....................1973
+ Jones, Biff..............................1954
+ Jones, Howard........................1951
+ Jones, Tad..............................1958
+ Jordan, Lloyd..........................1978
+ Jordan, Ralph (Shug)...............1982
+ Kerr, Andy.............................1951
Kush, Frank............................1995
+ Leahy, Frank...........................1970
+ Little, George..........................1955
+ Little, Lou...............................1960
+ Madigan, Slip.........................1974
Maurer, Dave..........................1991
McClendon, Charley................1986
+ McCracken, Herb....................1973
+ McGugin, Dan........................1951
McKay, John..........................1988
+ McKeen, Allyn.......................1991
+ McLaughry, Tuss....................1962
+ Merritt, John..........................1994
+ Meyer, Dutch.........................1956
+ Mollenkopf, Jack....................1988
+ Moore, Bernie........................1954
+ Moore, Scrappy.....................1980
+ Morrison, Ray.......................1954
+ Munger, George.....................1976
+ Munn, Clarence (Biggie).........1959
+ Murray, Bill...........................1974
+ Murray, Frank........................1983
+ Mylin, Ed (Hooks)..................1974
+ Neale, Earle (Greasy).............1967
+ Neely, Jess............................1971
+ Nelson, David........................1987
+ Neyland, Robert......................1956
+ Norton, Homer.......................1971
+ O'Neill, Frank (Buck)..............1951
+ Owen, Bennie........................1951
Parseghian, Ara......................1980
+ Perry, Doyt............................1988
+ Phelan, Jimmy........................1973
+ Prothro, Tommy......................1991
Ralston, John..........................1992
+ Robinson, E.N.........................1955
+ Rockne, Knute.......................1951
+ Romney, Dick........................1954
+ Roper, Bill.............................1951
Royal, Darrell.........................1983
+ Sanders, Henry (Red)..............1996
+ Sanford, George....................1971
Schembechler, Bo..................1993
+ Schmidt, Francis....................1971
+ Schwartzwalder, Ben..............1982
+ Shaughnessy, Clark................1968
+ Shaw, Buck...........................1972
+ Smith, Andy...........................1951
+ Snavely, Carl.........................1965
+ Stagg, Amos Alonzo..............1951
+ Sutherland, Jock.....................1951
+ Tatum, Jim.............................1984
+ Thomas, Frank........................1951
+ Vann, Thad............................1987
Vaught, Johnny.......................1979
+ Wade, Wallace........................1955
+ Waldorf, Lynn (Pappy)............1966
+ Warner, Glenn (Pop)...............1951
+ Wieman, E.E. (Tad).................1956
+ Wilce, John............................1954
+ Wilkinson, Bud.......................1969
+ Williams, Henry.....................1951
+ Woodruff, George...................1963
Woodson, Warren...................1989
+ Yost, Fielding (Hurry Up).........1951
+ Zuppke, Bob..........................1951

Small College

Players

Brasdshaw, Terry-La. Tech......1969
+ Buchanan, Buck-Grambling....1962
Den Herder, Vern-Central IA...1970
Johnson, Billy-Widener, PA.....1973
Lomax, Neil-Portland St. 1980
McGriff, Tyrone-Jackson St.........1974
Montgomery, Wilbert-Ab. Christ...1976
Payton, Walter-Jackson St. 1974
Reasons, Gary-N'western St.......1983
Youngblood, Jim-Tenn. Tech........1972

Coaches

+ Burry, Harold.........................1996
Sherman, Edgar......................1996
+ Steinke, Gilbert......................1996
+ Tressel, Lee...........................1996

Pro Football Hall of Fame

Established in 1963 by National Football League to commemorate the sport's professional origins. **Address:** 2121 George Halas Drive NW, Canton, OH 44708. **Telephone:** (330) 456-8207.

Eligibility: Nominated players must be retired five years, coaches must be retired, and contributors can still be active. Voting done by 36-member panel made up of media representatives from all 30 NFL cities, one PFWA representative and five selectors-at-large.

Class of 1996 (6): PLAYERS—DT **Lou Creekmur**, Detroit (1950-59); OT **Dan Dierdorf**, St. Louis (1971-83); WR **Charlie Joiner**, Houston (1969-72), Cincinnati (1972-75), San Diego (1976-86); DB **Mel Renfro**, Dallas (1964-77). COACH—**Joe Gibbs**, Washington (1981-92).

1996 Finalists (nominated, but not elected): PLAYERS—Mike Haynes and Dwight Stephenson

Members are listed with year of induction; (+) indicates deceased members.

Quarterbacks

Baugh, Sammy 1963
Blanda, George (also PK) 1981
Bradshaw, Terry 1989
+ Clark, Dutch 1963
+ Conzelman, Jimmy 1964
Dawson, Len 1987
+ Driscoll, Paddy 1965
Fouts, Dan 1993
Graham, Otto 1965
Griese, Bob 1990
+ Herber, Arnie 1966
Jurgensen, Sonny 1983
+ Layne, Bobby 1967
Luckman, Sid 1965
Namath, Joe 1985
Parker, Clarence (Ace) 1972
Starr, Bart 1977
Staubach, Roger 1985
Tarkenton, Fran 1986
Tittle, Y.A 1971
Unitas, Johnny 1979
+ Van Brocklin, Norm 1971
+ Waterfield, Bob 1965

Running Backs

+ Battles, Cliff 1968
Brown, Jim 1971
Campbell, Earl 1991
Canadeo, Tony 1974
Csonka, Larry 1987
Dorsett, Tony 1994
Dudley, Bill 1966
Gifford, Frank 1977
+ Grange, Red 1963
+ Guyon, Joe 1966
Harris, Franco 1990
+ Hinkle, Clarke 1964
Hornung, Paul 1986
Johnson, John Henry 1987
Kelly, Leroy 1994
+ Leemans, Tuffy 1978
Matson, Ollie 1972
McAfee, George 1966
McElhenny, Hugh 1970
+ McNally, Johnny (Blood) 1963
Moore, Lenny 1975
Motley, Marion 1968
+ Nagurski, Bronko 1963
+ Nevers, Ernie 1963
Payton, Walter 1993
Perry, Joe 1969
Riggins, John 1992
Sayers, Gale 1977
Simpson, O.J 1985
+ Strong, Ken 1967
Taylor, Jim 1976
+ Thorpe, Jim 1963
Trippi, Charley 1968
Van Buren, Steve 1965
Walker, Doak 1986

Ends & Wide Receivers

Alworth, Lance 1978
Badgro, Red 1981
Berry, Raymond 1973
Biletnikoff, Fred 1988
+ Chamberlin, Guy 1965
Ditka, Mike 1988
Fears, Tom 1970
+ Hewitt, Bill 1971
Hirsch, Elroy (Crazylegs) 1968
Hutson, Don 1963
Joiner, Charlie 1996
Largent, Steve 1995
Lavelli, Dante 1975
Mackey, John 1992
Maynard, Don 1987
+ Millner, Wayne 1968
Mitchell, Bobby 1983
Pihos, Pete 1970
Smith, Jackie 1994
Taylor, Charley 1984
Warfield, Paul 1983
Winslow, Kellen 1995

Linemen (pre-World War II)

+ Edwards, Turk (T) 1969
+ Fortmann, Dan (G) 1985
+ Healey, Ed (T) 1964
+ Hein, Mel (C) 1963
+ Henry, Pete (T) 1963
+ Hubbard, Cal (T) 1963
+ Kiesling, Walt (G) 1966
+ Kinard, Bruiser (T) 1971
+ Lyman, Link (T) 1964
+ Michalske, Mike (G) 1964
Musso, George (T-G) 1982
+ Stydahar, Joe (T) 1967
+ Trafton, George (C) 1964
Turner, Bulldog (C) 1966
+ Wojciechowicz, Alex (C) 1968

Offensive Linemen

Bednarik, Chuck (C-LB) 1967
Brown, Roosevelt (T) 1975
Dierdorf, Dan 1996
Gatski, Frank (C) 1985
Gregg, Forrest (T-G) 1977
Groza, Lou (T-PK) 1974
Hannah, John (G) 1991
Jones, Stan (T-G-DT) 1991
Langer, Jim (C) 1987
Little, Larry (G) 1993
McCormack, Mike (T) 1984
Mix, Ron (T-G) 1979
Otto, Jim (C) 1980
Parker, Jim (G) 1973
Ringo, Jim (C) 1981
St. Clair, Bob (T) 1990
Shell, Art (T) 1989
Upshaw, Gene (G) 1987

Defensive Linemen

Atkins, Doug 1982
+ Buchanan, Buck 1990
Creekmur, Lou 1996
Davis, Willie 1981
Donovan, Art 1968
+ Ford, Len 1976
Greene, Joe 1987
Jones, Deacon 1980
+ Jordan, Henry 1995
Lilly, Bob 1980
Marchetti, Gino 1972
Nomellini, Leo 1969
Olsen, Merlin 1982
Page, Alan 1988
Robustelli, Andy 1971
Selmon, Lee Roy 1995
Stautner, Ernie 1969
Weinmeister, Arnie 1984
White, Randy 1994
Willis, Bill 1977

Linebackers

Bell, Bobby 1983
Butkus, Dick 1979
Connor, George (DT-OT) 1975
+ George, Bill 1974
Ham, Jack 1988
Hendricks, Ted 1990
Huff, Sam 1982
Lambert, Jack 1990
Lanier, Willie 1986
Nitschke, Ray 1978
Schmidt, Joe 1973

Pro Football Hall of Fame (Cont.)

Defensive Backs

Adderley, Herb 1980
Barney, Lem 1992
Blount, Mel 1989
Brown, Willie 1984
+ Christiansen, Jack 1970
Houston, Ken 1986
Johnson, Jimmy 1994
Lane, Dick (Night Train) 1974
Lary, Yale 1979
Renfro, Mel 1996
+ Tunnell, Emlen 1967
Wilson, Larry 1978
Wood, Willie 1989

Placekicker

Stenerud, Jan 1991

Coaches

+ Brown, Paul 1967
Ewbank, Weeb 1978
+ Flaherty, Ray 1976
Gibbs, Joe 1996
Gillman, Sid 1983
Grant, Bud 1994
+ Halas, George 1963
+ Lambeau, Curly 1963
Landry, Tom 1990
+ Lombardi, Vince 1971
+ Neale, Earle (Greasy) 1969
Noll, Chuck 1993
+ Owen, Steve 1966
Walsh, Bill 1993

Contributors

+ Bell, Bert 1963
+ Bidwill, Charles 1967
+ Carr, Joe 1963
Davis, Al 1992
+ Finks, Jim 1995
+ Halas, George 1963
Hunt, Lamar 1972
+ Mara, Tim 1963
+ Marshall, George 1963
+ Ray, Hugh (Shorty) 1966
+ Reeves, Dan 1967
+ Rooney, Art 1964
Rozelle, Pete 1985
Schramm, Tex 1991

Dick McCann Award

First presented in 1969 by the Pro Football Writers of America for long and distinguished reporting on pro football. Named in honor of the first director of the Hall, the McCann Award does not constitute induction into the Hall of Fame.

Year	
1969	George Strickler
1970	Arthur Daley
1971	Joe King
1972	Lewis Atchison
1973	Dave Brady
1974	Bob Oates
1975	John Steadman
1976	Jack Hand
1977	Art Daley
1978	Murray Olderman
1979	Pat Livingston
1980	Chuck Heaton
1981	Norm Miller
1982	Cameron Snyder
1983	Hugh Brown
1984	Larry Felser
1985	Cooper Rollow
1986	Bill Wallace
1987	Jerry Magee
1988	Gordon Forbes
1989	Vito Stellino
1990	Will McDonough
1991	Dick Connor
1992	Frank Luska
1993	Ira Miller
1994	Don Pierson
1995	Ray Didinger
1996	Paul Zimmerman

Pete Rozelle Award

First presented in 1989 by the Hall of Fame for exceptional longtime contributions to radio and TV in pro football. Named in honor of the former NFL commissioner, who was also a publicist and GM for the LA Rams, the Rozelle Award does not constitute induction into the Hall of Fame.

Year	
1989	Bill McPhail
1990	Lindsey Nelson
1991	Ed Sabol
1992	Chris Schenkel
1993	Curt Gowdy
1994	Pat Summerall
1995	Frank Gifford
1996	Jack Buck

NFL's 75th Anniversary All-Time Team

Selected by a 15-member panel of former players, NFL and Pro Football Hall of Fame officials and media representatives and released Sept. 1, 1994.

OFFENSE

Wide Receivers (4): Lance Alworth, Raymond Berry, Don Hutson and Jerry Rice
Tight Ends (2): Mike Ditka and Kellen Winslow
Tackles (3): Roosevelt Brown, Forrest Gregg and Anthony Munoz
Guards (3): John Hannah, Jim Parker and Gene Upshaw
Centers (2): Mel Hein and Mike Webster
Quarterbacks (4): Sammy Baugh, Otto Graham, Joe Montana and Johnny Unitas
Running Backs (6): Jim Brown, Marion Motley, Bronko Nagurski, Walter Payton, O.J. Simpson and Steve Van Buren

DEFENSE

Ends (3): Deacon Jones, Gino Marchetti and Reggie White
Tackles (3): Joe Greene, Bob Lilly and Merlin Olsen
Linebackers (7): Dick Butkus, Jack Ham, Ted Hendricks, Jack Lambert, Willie Lanier, Ray Nitschke and Lawrence Taylor
Cornerbacks (4): Mel Blount, Mike Haynes, Dick (Night Train) Lane and Rod Woodson
Safties (3): Ken Houston, Ronnie Lott and Larry Wilson

SPECIALISTS

Placekicker: Jan Stenerud
Punter: Ray Guy
Kick Returner: Gale Sayers
Punt Returner: Billy (White Shoes) Johnson

Canadian Football Hall of Fame

Established in 1963. Current Hall opened in 1972. **Address:** 58 Jackson Street West, Hamilton, Ontario, L8P 1L4. **Telephone:** (905) 528-7566.

Eligibility: Nominated players must be retired three years, but coaches and builders can still be active. Voting done by 15-member panel of Canadian pro and amateur football officials.

Class of 1996 (5): PLAYERS—OG **Al Benecick**, Saskatchewan (1959-68), Edmonton (1969); LB **Jerry "Soupy" Campbell**, Calgary (1966-68), Ottawa (1968-1975); OT/DT **Bill Clarke**, Saskatchewan (1951-64); LB **Dan Kepley**, Edmonton (1975-84). BUILDER—**Frank Gibson**, CFL Secretary-Treasurer (1962-80).

Members are listed with year of induction; (+) indicates deceased members.

Players

Atchison, Ron 1978
Bailey, Byron 1975
Baker, Bill 1994
Barrow, John 1976
+ Batstone, Harry 1963
+ Beach, Ormond 1963
Benecick, Al 1996
Box, Ab 1965
+ Breen, Joe 1963
+ Bright, Johnny 1970
Brown, Tom 1984
Brock, Dieter 1995
Campbell, Jerry "Soupy" 1996
Casey, Tom 1964
Charlton, Ken 1992
Clarke, Bill 1996
Clements, Tom 1994
Coffey, Tommy Joe 1977
+ Conacher, Lionel 1963
Copeland, Royal 1988
Corrigall, Jim 1990
+ Cox, Ernest 1963
+ Craig, Ross 1964
+ Cronin, Carl 1967
+ Cutler, Wes 1968
Dalla Riva, Peter 1993
+ Dixon, George 1974
+ Eliowitz, Abe 1969
+ Emerson, Eddie 1963
Etcheverry, Sam 1969
Evanshen, Terry 1984
Faloney, Bernie 1974
+ Fear, A.H. (Cap) 1967
Fennell, Dave 1990
+ Ferraro, John 1966
Fieldgate, Norm 1979
Fleming, Willie 1982
Gabriel, Tony 1985
Gaines, Gene 1994
+ Gall, Hugh 1963
Golab, Tony 1964
Grant, Tom 1995
Gray, Herbert 1983
Griffing, Dean 1965
Hanson, Fritz 1963
Harris, Wayne 1976
Harrison, Herm 1993
Helton, John 1986
Henley, Garney 1979
Hinton, Tom 1991
+ Huffman, Dick 1987
+ Isbister, Bob Sr 1965
Jackson, Russ 1973
+ Jacobs, Jack 1963
+ James, Eddie (Dynamite) 1963
James, Gerry 1981
+ Kabat, Greg 1966
Kapp, Joe 1984
Keeling, Jerry 1989
Kelly, Brian 1991
Kelly, Ellison 1992
Kepley, Dan 1996
Krol, Joe 1963
Kwong, Normie 1969
Lancaster, Ron 1982
+ Lawson, Smirle 1963
+ Leadlay, Frank (Pep) 1963
+ Lear, Les 1974
Lewis, Leo 1973
Lunsford, Earl 1983
Luster, Marv 1990
Luzzi, Don 1986
+ McCance, Ches 1976
+ McGill, Frank 1965
McQuarters, Ed 1988
Miles, Rollie 1980
+ Molson, Percy 1963
Morris, Frank 1983
+ Morris, Ted 1964
Mosca, Angelo 1987
Nelson, Roger 1986
Neumann, Peter 1979
O'Quinn, John (Red) 1981
Pajaczkowski, Tony 1988
Parker, Jackie 1971
Patterson, Hal 1971
Perry, Gordon 1970
+ Perry, Norm 1963
Ploen, Ken 1975
+ Quilty, S.P. (Silver) 1966
+ Rebholz, Russ 1963
Reed, George 1979
+ Reeve, Ted 1963
Rigney, Frank 1985
+ Rodden, Mike 1964
+ Rowe, Paul 1964
Ruby, Martin 1974
+ Russel, Jeff 1963
+ Scott, Vince 1982
Shatto, Dick 1975
+ Simpson, Ben 1963
Simpson, Bob 1976
+ Sprague, David 1963
Stevenson, Art 1969
Stewart, Ron 1977
+ Stirling, Hugh (Bummer) 1966
Sutherin, Don 1992
Thelen, Dave 1989
+ Timmis, Brian 1963
Tinsley, Bud 1982
+ Tommy, Andy 1989
+ Trawick, Herb 1975
+ Tubman, Joe 1968
Tucker, Whit 1993
Urness, Ted 1989
Vaughan, Kaye 1978
Wagner, Virgil 1980
+ Welch, Hawley (Huck) 1964
Wilkinson, Tom 1987
Wylie, Harvey 1980
Young, Jim 1991
+ Zock, Bill 1985

Builders

+ Back, Leonard 1971
+ Bailey, Harold 1965
+ Ballard, Harold 1987
+ Berger, Sam 1993
+ Brook, Tom 1975
+ Brown, D. Wes 1963
Chipman, Arthur 1969
Clair, Frank 1981
+ Cooper, Ralph 1992
+ Crighton, Hec 1986
+ Currie, Andrew 1974
+ Davies, Dr. Andrew 1969
+ DeGruchy, John 1963
Dojack, Paul 1978
+ Duggan, Eck 1981
+ DuMoulin, Seppi 1963
+ Foulds, William 1963
Fulton, Greg 1995
Gaudaur, J.G. (Jake) 1984
Gibson, Frank 1996
Grant, Bud 1983
+ Grey, Lord Earl 1963
+ Griffith, Dr. Harry 1963
+ Halter, Sydney 1966
+ Hannibal, Frank 1963
+ Hayman, Lew 1975
+ Hughes, W.P. (Billy) 1974
Keys, Eagle 1990
Kimball, Norman 1991
+ Kramer, R.A. (Bob) 1987
+ Lieberman, M.I. (Moe) 1973
+ McBrien, Harry 1978
+ McCaffrey, Jimmy 1967
+ McCann, Dave 1966
McNaughton, Don 1994
+ McPherson, Don 1983
+ Metras, Johnny 1980
+ Montgomery, Ken 1970
+ Newton, Jack 1964
+ Preston, Ken 1990
+ Ritchie, Alvin 1963
+ Ryan, Joe B. 1968
Sazio, Ralph 1988
+ Shaughnessy, Frank (Shag) 1963
+ Shouldice, W.T. (Hap) 1977
+ Simpson, Jimmie 1986
+ Slocomb, Karl 1989
+ Spring, Harry 1976
Stukus, Annis 1974
+ Taylor, N.J. (Piffles) 1963
+ Tindall, Frank 1985
+ Warner, Clair 1965
+ Warwick, Bert 1964
+ Wilson, Seymour 1984

GOLF

A new Golf Museum and Hall of Fame is expected to open in March 1998 at World Golf Village. Groundbreaking was Aug. 1996 at St. Johns County, Fla., between Jacksonville and St. Augustine. The new hall will incorporate the inactive PGA/World Golf Hall of Fame (formerly run by the PGA of America) and the active LPGA Hall as well as provide a role for the USGA and the Royal and Ancient Golf Club of St. Andrews. The building will feature more than 70 exhibits and a 300-seat big-screen theater. Questions concerning the new Golf Hall of Fame and Museum should be directed to the PGA Tour at (904) 273-3350.

Eligibility: Professionals will have three avenues into the WGHF. A PGA Tour player qualifies for the ballot if he has at least 10 victories in approved tournaments, or at least two victories among The Players Championship, Masters, U.S. Open, British Open and PGA Championship, is at least 40 years old and has been a member of the Tour for 10 years. Any player qualifying for the LPGA Hall automatically qualifies for the WGHF. For players not eligible for either the PGA Tour or the LPGA Hall of Fame, a body of over 300 international golf writers and historians will vote each year.

PGA/World Golf Hall of Fame

Established in 1974, but inactive since 1993. Will become part of the PGA Tour's new Golf Museum and Hall of Fame in 1997. Members are listed with year of induction; (+) indicates deceased members.

Men

+ Anderson, Willie....1975
+ Armour, Tommy....1976
+ Ball, John, Jr....1977
+ Barnes, Jim....1989
+ Boros, Julius....1982
+ Braid, James....1976
Casper, Billy....1978
Cooper, Lighthorse Harry....1992
+ Cotton, Thomas....1980
+ Demaret, Jimmy....1983
DeVicenzo, Roberto....1989
+ Evans, Chick....1975
Floyd, Ray....1989
+ Guldahl, Ralph....1981
+ Hagen, Walter....1974
+ Hilton, Harold....1978
Hogan, Ben....1974
Irwin, Hale....1992
+ Jones, Bobby....1974
+ Little, Lawson....1980
Littler, Gene....1990
+ Locke, Bobby....1977
Middlecoff, Cary....1986
+ Morris, Tom, Jr....1975
+ Morris, Tom, Sr....1976
Nelson, Byron....1974
Nicklaus, Jack....1974
+ Ouimet, Francis....1974
Palmer, Arnold....1974
Player, Gary....1974
Runyan, Paul....1990
Sarazen, Gene....1974
+ Smith, Horton....1990
Snead, Sam....1974
+ Taylor, John H....1975
Thomson, Peter....1988
+ Travers, Jerry....1976
+ Travis, Walter....1979
Trevino, Lee....1981
+ Vardon, Harry....1974
Watson, Tom....1988

Women

Berg, Patty....1974
Carner, JoAnne....1985
+ Howe, Dorothy C.H....1978
Lopez, Nancy....1989
Rawls, Betsy....1987
Suggs, Louise....1979
+ Vare, Glenna Collett....1975
+ Wethered, Joyce....1975
Whitworth, Kathy....1982
Wright, Mickey....1976
+ Zaharias, Babe Didrikson....1974

Contributors

Campbell, William....1990
+ Corcoran, Fred....1975
+ Crosby, Bing....1978
+ Dey, Joe....1975
+ Graffis, Herb....1977
+ Harlow, Robert....1988
Hope, Bob....1983
Jones, Robert Trent....1987
+ Roberts, Clifford....1978
Rodriguez, Chi Chi....1992
+ Ross, Donald....1977
+ Tufts, Richard....1992

Old PGA Hall Members Not in PGA/World Hall

The original PGA Hall of Fame was established in 1940 by the PGA of America, but abandoned after the 1982 inductions in favor of the PGA/World Hall of Fame. Twenty-seven members of the old PGA Hall have been elected to the PGA/World Hall since then. Players yet to make the cut are listed below with year of induction into old PGA Hall.

+ Brady, Mike....1960
+ Burke, Billy....1966
Burke, Jack Jr....1975
+ Cruickshank, Bobby....1967
+ Diegel, Leo....1955
+ Dudley, Ed....1964
+ Dutra, Olin....1962
+ Farroll, Johnny....1961
Ford, Doug....1975
+ Ghezzi, Vic....1965
+ Harbert, Chick....1968
Harper, Chandler....1969
+ Harrison, Dutch....1962
+ Hutchison, Jock Sr....1959
+ McDermott, John....1940
+ Mangrum, Lloyd....1964
+ McLeod, Fred....1960
+ Picard, Henry....1961
+ Revolta, Johnny....1963
+ Shute, Denny....1957
+ Smith, Alex....1940
+ Smith, Macdonald....1954
+ Wood, Craig....1956

LPGA Hall of Fame

Established in 1967 by the LPGA to replace the old Women's Golf Hall of Fame (founded in 1950). Originally located in Augusta, GA (1967-77), the Hall has been moved to Pinehurst, NC (1977-83), Sugar Land, TX (1983-89) and Daytona Beach, FL (since 1990). Will become part of the PGA Tour's new Golf Museum and Hall of Fame in 1997. **Address:** LPGA Headquarters, 2570 Volusia Ave., Suite B, Daytona Beach, FL 32114. **Telephone:** (904) 274-6200.

Eligibility: Nominees must have played 10 years on the LPGA tour and won 30 official events, including two major championships; 35 official events and one major; or 40 official events and no majors.

Latest inductee: Betsy King (30 wins, 5 majors) became the 14th player to gain entry by capturing the ShopRite Classic in Somers Point, N.J. on June 25, 1995. **Leading candidates** (through Sept. 15, 1996): Amy Alcott (29 wins, 5 majors) and Beth Daniel (32 wins, 1 major). Members are listed with year of induction; (+) indicates deceased members.

Players

Berg, Patty....1951
Bradley, Pat....1991
Carner, JoAnne....1982
Haynie, Sandra....1977
Jameson, Betty....1951
King, Betsy....1995
Lopez, Nancy....1987
Mann, Carol....1977
Rawls, Betsy....1960
Sheehan, Patty....1993
Suggs, Louise....1951
Whitworth, Kathy....1975
Wright, Mickey....1964
+ Zaharias, Babe Didrikson....1951

Contributor

+ Shore, Dinah....1994

HOCKEY

Hockey Hall of Fame

Established in 1945 by the National Hockey League and opened in 1961. **Address:** BCE Place, 30 Yonge Street, Toronto, Ontario, M5E 1X8. **Telephone:** (416) 360-7735.

Eligibility: Nominated players and referees must be retired three years. Voting done by 15-member panel made up of pro and amateur hockey personalities and media representatives. A 15-member Veterans Committee selects older players.

Class of 1996 (4): PLAYERS—forward **Bobby Bauer**, Boston (1935-42,45-47,51-52); defenseman **Borje Salming**, Toronto (1973-89), Detroit (1989-90). BUILDERS—**Al Arbour** (NHL coach from 1970-86,88-94; Islanders VP of Hockey Operations). MEDIA (not listed below)— **Bob Cole** (CBC announcer).

Members are listed with year of induction; (+) indicates deceased members.

Forwards

Abel, Sid 1969
+ Adams, Jack 1959
Apps, Syl 1961
Armstrong, George 1975
+ Bailey, Ace 1975
+ Bain, Dan 1945
+ Baker, Hobey 1945
Barber, Bill 1990
+ Barry, Marty 1965
Bathgate, Andy 1978
+ Bauer, Bobby 1996
Beliveau, Jean 1972
+ Bentley, Doug 1964
+ Bentley, Max 1966
+ Blake, Toe 1966
Bossy, Mike 1991
+ Boucher, Frank 1958
+ Bowie, Dubbie 1945
+ Broadbent, Punch 1962
Bucyk, John (Chief) 1981
+ Burch, Billy 1974
Clarke, Bobby 1987
+ Colville, Neil 1967
+ Conacher, Charlie 1961
+ Cook, Bill 1952
+ Cook, Bun 1995
Cournoyer, Yvan 1982
+ Cowley, Bill 1968
+ Crawford, Rusty 1962
+ Darragh, Jack 1962
+ Davidson, Scotty 1950
Day, Hap 1961
Delvecchio, Alex 1977
+ Denneny, Cy 1959
Dionne, Marcel 1992
+ Drillon, Gordie 1975
+ Drinkwater, Graham 1950
Dumart, Woody 1992
+ Dunderdale, Tommy 1974
+ Dye, Babe 1970
Esposito, Phil 1984
+ Farrell, Arthur 1965
+ Foyston, Frank 1958
+ Frederickson, Frank 1958
Gainey, Bob 1992
+ Gardner, Jimmy 1962
Geoffrion, Bernie 1972
+ Gerard, Eddie 1945
Gilbert, Rod 1982
+ Gilmour, Billy 1962
+ Griffis, Si 1950
+ Hay, George 1958
+ Hextall, Bryan 1969
+ Hooper, Tom 1962
Howe, Gordie 1972
+ Howe, Syd 1965
Hull, Bobby 1983
+ Hyland, Harry 1962
+ Irvin, Dick 1958
+ Jackson, Busher 1971
+ Joliat, Aurel 1947
+ Keats, Duke 1958
Kennedy, Ted (Teeder) 1966
Keon, Dave 1986
Lach, Elmer 1966
Lafleur, Guy 1988
+ Lalonde, Newsy 1950
Laprade, Edgar 1993
Lemaire, Jacques 1984
+ Lewis, Herbie 1989
Lindsay, Ted 1966
+ MacKay, Mickey 1952
Mahovlich, Frank 1981
+ Malone, Joe 1950
+ Marshall, Jack 1965
+ Maxwell, Fred 1962
McDonald, Lanny 1992
+ McGee, Frank 1945
+ McGimsie, Billy 1962
Mikita, Stan 1983
Moore, Dickie 1974
+ Morenz, Howie 1945
+ Mosienko, Bill 1965
+ Nighbor, Frank 1947
+ Noble, Reg 1962
+ O'Connor, Buddy 1988
+ Oliver, Harry 1967
Olmstead, Bert 1985
+ Patrick, Lynn 1980
Perreault, Gilbert 1990
+ Phillips, Tom 1945
+ Primeau, Joe 1963
Pulford, Bob 1991
+ Rankin, Frank 1961
Ratelle, Jean 1985
Richard, Henri 1979
Richard, Maurice (Rocket) 1961
+ Richardson, George 1950
+ Roberts, Gordie 1971
+ Russel, Blair 1965
+ Russell, Ernie 1965
+ Ruttan, Jack 1962
+ Scanlan, Fred 1965
Schmidt, Milt 1961
+ Schriner, Sweeney 1962
+ Seibert, Oliver 1961
Shutt, Steve 1993
+ Siebert, Babe 1964
Sittler, Darryl 1989
+ Smith, Alf 1962
Smith, Clint 1991
+ Smith, Hooley 1972
+ Smith, Tommy 1973
+ Stanley, Barney 1962
+ Stewart, Nels 1962
+ Stuart, Bruce 1961
+ Taylor, Fred (Cyclone) 1947
+ Trihey, Harry 1950
Ullman, Norm 1982
+ Walker, Jack 1960
+ Walsh, Marty 1962
Watson, Harry 1994
+ Watson, Harry (Moose) 1962
+ Weiland, Cooney 1971
+ Westwick, Harry (Rat) 1962
+ Whitcroft, Fred 1962

Goaltenders

+ Benedict, Clint 1965
Bower, Johnny 1976
Brimsek, Frankie 1966
+ Broda, Turk 1967
Cheevers, Gerry 1985
+ Connell, Alex 1958
Dryden, Ken 1983
+ Durnan, Bill 1964
Esposito, Tony 1988
+ Gardiner, Chuck 1945
Giacomin, Eddie 1987
+ Hainsworth, George 1961
Hall, Glenn 1975
+ Hern, Riley 1962
+ Holmes, Hap 1972
+ Hutton, J.B. (Bouse) 1962
+ Lehman, Hughie 1958
+ LeSueur, Percy 1961
Lumley, Harry 1980
+ Moran, Paddy 1958
Parent, Bernie 1984
+ Plante, Jacques 1978
Rayner, Chuck 1973
+ Sawchuk, Terry 1971
Smith, Billy 1993
+ Thompson, Tiny 1959
Tretiak, Vladislav 1989
+ Vezina, Georges 1945
Worsley, Gump 1980
+ Worters, Roy 1969

Hockey Hall of Fame (Cont.)

Defensemen

Boivin, Leo....1986
+ Boon, Dickie....1952
Bouchard, Butch....1966
+ Boucher, George....1960
+ Cameron, Harry....1962
+ Clancy, King....1958
+ Clapper, Dit....1947
+ Cleghorn, Sprague....1958
+ Conacher, Lionel....1994
Coulter, Art....1974
+ Dutton, Red....1958
Flaman, Fernie....1990
Gadsby, Bill....1970
+ Gardiner, Herb....1958
+ Goheen, F.X. (Moose)....1952
+ Goodfellow, Ebbie....1963
+ Grant, Mike....1950
+ Green, Wilf (Shorty)....1962
+ Hall, Joe....1961
+ Harvey, Doug....1973
Horner, Red....1965
+ Horton, Tim....1977
Howell, Harry....1979
+ Johnson, Ching....1958
+ Johnson, Ernie....1952
Johnson, Tom....1970
Kelly, Red....1969
Laperriere, Jacques....1987
Lapointe, Guy....1993
+ Laviolette, Jack....1962
+ Mantha, Sylvio....1960
+ McNamara, George....1958
Orr, Bobby....1979
Park, Brad....1988
+ Patrick, Lester....1947
Pilote, Pierre....1975
+ Pitre, Didier....1962
Potvin, Denis....1991
+ Pratt, Babe....1966
Pronovost, Marcel....1978
+ Pulford, Harvey....1945
Quackenbush, Bill....1976
Reardon, Kenny....1966
Robinson, Larry....1995
+ Ross, Art....1945
Salming, Borje....1996
Savard, Serge....1986
Seibert, Earl....1963
+ Shore, Eddie....1947
+ Simpson, Joe....1962
Stanley, Allan....1981
+ Stewart, Jack....1964
+ Stuart, Hod....1945
+ Wilson, Gordon (Phat)....1962

Referees & Linesmen

Armstrong, Neil....1991
Ashley, John....1981
Chadwick, Bill....1964
D'Amico, John....1993
+ Elliott, Chaucer....1961
+ Hayes, George....1988
+ Hewitson, Bobby....1963
+ Ion, Mickey....1961
Pavelich, Matt....1987
+ Rodden, Mike....1962
+ Smeaton, J. Cooper....1961
Storey, Red....1967
Udvari, Frank....1973

Builders

+ Adams, Charles....1960
+ Adams, Weston W. Sr....1972
+ Ahearn, Frank....1962
+ Ahearne, J.F. (Bunny)....1977
+ Allan, Sir Montagu....1945
Allen, Keith....1992
Arbour, Al....1996
+ Ballard, Harold....1977
+ Bauer, Fr. David....1989
+ Bickell, J.P....1978
Bowman, Scotty....1991
+ Brown, George....1961
+ Brown, Walter....1962
+ Buckland, Frank....1975
Butterfield, Jack....1980
+ Calder, Frank....1945
+ Campbell, Angus....1964
+ Campbell, Clarence....1966
+ Cattarinich, Joseph....1977
+ Dandurand, Leo....1963
Dilio, Frank....1964
+ Dudley, George....1958
+ Dunn, James....1968
Eagleson, Alan....1989
Francis, Emile....1982
+ Gibson, Jack....1976
+ Gorman, Tommy....1963
+ Griffiths, Frank A.....1993
+ Hanley, Bill....1986
+ Hay, Charles....1984
+ Hendy, Jim....1968
+ Hewitt, Foster....1965
+ Hewitt, W.A....1945
+ Hume, Fred....1962
+ Imlach, Punch....1984
Ivan, Tommy....1964
+ Jennings, Bill....1975
+ Johnson, Bob....1992
+ Juckes, Gordon....1979
+ Kilpatrick, John....1960
Knox, Seymour III....1993
+ Leader, Al....1969
LeBel, Bob....1970
+ Lockhart, Tom....1965
+ Loicq, Paul....1961
+ Mariucci, John....1985
Mathers, Frank....1992
+ McLaughlin, Frederic....1963
+ Milford, Jake....1984
Molson, Hartland....1973
+ Nelson, Francis....1945
+ Norris, Bruce....1969
+ Norris, James D....1962
+ Norris, James Sr....1958
+ Northey, William....1945
+ O'Brien, J.A....1962
O'Neill, Brian....1994
Page, Fred....1993
+ Patrick, Frank....1958
+ Pickard, Allan....1958
+ Pilous, Rudy....1985
Poile, Bud....1990
Pollock, Sam....1978
+ Raymond, Donat....1958
+ Robertson, John Ross....1945
+ Robinson, Claude....1945
+ Ross, Philip....1976
Sebetzki, Gunther....1995
+ Selke, Frank....1960
Sinden, Harry....1983
+ Smith, Frank....1962
+ Smythe, Conn....1958
Snider, Ed....1988
+ Stanley, Lord of Preston....1945
+ Sutherland, James....1945
+ Tarasov, Anatoli....1974
Torrey, Bill....1995
+ Turner, Lloyd....1958
+ Tutt, William Thayer....1978
Voss, Carl....1974
+ Waghorne, Fred....1961
+ Wirtz, Arthur....1971
Wirtz, Bill....1976
Ziegler, John....1987

Elmer Ferguson Award

First presented in 1984 by the Professional Hockey Writers' Association for meritorious contributions by members of the PHWA. Named in honor of the late Montreal newspaper reporter, the Ferguson Award does not constitute induction into the Hall of Fame and is not necessarily an annual presentation.

1984—Jacques Beauchamp, Jim Burchard, Red Burnett, Dink Carroll, Jim Coleman, Ted Damata, Marcel Desjardins, Jack Dulmage, Milt Dunnell, Elmer Ferguson, Tom Fitzgerald, Trent Frayne, Al Laney, Joe Nichols, Basil O'Meara, Jim Vipond and Lewis Walter
1985—Charlie Barton, Red Fisher, George Gross, Zotique L'Esperance, Charles Mayer & Andy O'Brien
1986—Dick Johnston, Leo Monahan & Tim Moriarty
1987—Bill Brennan, Rex MacLeod, Ben Olan & Fran Rosa
1988—Jim Proudfoot & Scott Young
1989—Claude Larochelle & Frank Orr
1990—Bertrand Raymond
1991—Hugh Delano
1992—No award
1993—Al Strachan
1994—No award
1995—Jake Gatecliff

Foster Hewitt Award

First presented in 1984 by the NHL Broadcasters' Association for meritorious contributions by members of the NHLBA. Named in honor of Canada's legendary "Voice of Hockey," the Hewitt Award does not constitute induction into the Hall of Fame and is not necessarily an annual presentation.

1984—Fred Cusick, Danny Gallivan, Foster Hewitt & Rene Lecavelier
1985—Budd Lynch & Doug Smith
1986—Wes McKnight & Lloyd Pettit
1987—Bob Wilson
1988—Dick Irvin
1989—Dan Kelly
1990—Jiggs McDonald
1991—Bruce Martyn
1992—Jim Robson
1993—Al Shaver
1994—Ted Darling
1995—Brian McFarlane
1996—Bob Cole

U.S. Hockey Hall of Fame

Established in 1968 by the Eveleth (Minn.) Civic Association Project H Committee and opened in 1973. **Address:** 801 Hat Trick Ave., P.O. Box 657, Eveleth, MN 55734. **Telephone:** (218) 744-5167.

Eligibility: Nominated players and referees must be American-born and retired five years; coaches must be American-born and must have coached predominantly American teams. Voting done by 12-member panel made up of Hall of Fame members and U.S. hockey officials.

Class of 1996 (3): PLAYER—defenseman **Reed Larson** (Univ. of Minnesota 1975-77, Detroit Red Wings 1977-86, Boston Bruins 1986-88, Edmonton Oilers, N.Y. Islanders and Minnesota North Stars 1988-89, Buffalo 1989-90) . COACH—**Sergio Gambucci** (Cathedral H.S., Crookston, Minn.; Central H.S., Grand Forks, N.D.). ADMINISTRATOR—**Craig Patrick** (exec. VP and GM of the Pittsburgh Penquins, GM of NY Rangers 1981-86 and asst. GM/asst. coach of 1980 US Olympic team.

Members are listed with year of induction; (+) indicates deceased members.

Players

+ Abel, Clarence (Taffy) ... 1973
+ Baker, Hobey ... 1973
Bartholome, Earl ... 1977
+ Bessone, Peter ... 1978
Blake, Bob ... 1985
Boucha, Henry ... 1995
Brimsek, Frankie ... 1973
Cavanaugh, Joe ... 1994
+ Chaisson, Ray ... 1974
Chase, John ... 1973
Christian, Bill ... 1984
Christian, Roger ... 1989
Cleary, Bill ... 1976
Cleary, Bob ... 1981
+ Conroy, Tony ... 1975
Dahlstrom, Carl (Cully) ... 1973
+ DesJardins, Vic ... 1974
+ Desmond, Richard ... 1988
+ Dill, Bob ... 1979
Everett, Doug ... 1974
Ftorek, Robbie ... 1991
+ Garrison, John ... 1974
Garrity, Jack ... 1986
+ Goheen, Frank (Moose) ... 1973
Grant, Wally ... 1994
+ Harding, Austie ... 1975
Iglehart, Stewart ... 1975
Ikola, Willard ... 1990
Johnson, Virgil ... 1974
+ Karakas, Mike ... 1973
Kirrane, Jack ... 1987
+ Lane, Myles ... 1973
Langevin, Dave ... 1993
Larson, Reed ... 1996
+ Linder, Joe ... 1975
+ LoPresti, Sam ... 1973
+ Mariucci, John ... 1973
Matchefts, John ... 1991
Mayasich, John ... 1976
McCartan, Jack ... 1983
Moe, Bill ... 1974
Morrow, Ken ... 1995
+ Moseley, Fred ... 1975
+ Murray, Hugh (Muzz) Sr ... 1987
+ Nelson, Hub ... 1978
Olson, Eddie ... 1977
+ Owen, George ... 1973
+ Palmer, Winthrop ... 1973
Paradise, Bob ... 1989
Purpur, Clifford (Fido) ... 1974
Riley, Bill ... 1977
+ Romnes, Elwin (Doc) ... 1973
Rondeau, Dick ... 1985
+ Williams, Tom ... 1981
+ Winters, Frank (Coddy) ... 1973
+ Yackel, Ken ... 1986

Coaches

+ Almquist, Oscar ... 1983
Bessone, Amo ... 1992
Brooks, Herb ... 1990
Ceglarski, Len ... 1992
+ Fullerton, James ... 1992
Gambucci, Sergio ... 1996
+ Gordon, Malcolm ... 1973
Harkness, Ned ... 1994
Heyliger, Vic ... 1974
Ikola, Willard ... 1990
+ Jeremiah, Eddie ... 1973
+ Johnson, Bob ... 1991
Kelley, Jack ... 1993
+ Kelly, John (Snooks) ... 1974
Pleban, Connie ... 1990
Riley, Jack ... 1979
+ Ross, Larry ... 1988
+ Thompson, Cliff ... 1973
+ Stewart, Bill ... 1982
+ Winsor, Ralph ... 1973

Referee

Chadwick, Bill ... 1974

Contributor

Schulz, Charles M. ... 1993

Administrators

+ Brown, George ... 1973
+ Brown, Walter ... 1973
Bush, Walter ... 1980
Clark, Don ... 1978
Claypool, Jim ... 1995
+ Gibson, J.L. (Doc) ... 1973
+ Jennings, Bill ... 1981
+ Kahler, Nick ... 1980
+ Lockhart, Tom ... 1973
Marvin, Cal ... 1982
Patrick, Craig ... 1996
Ridder, Bob ... 1976
Trumble, Hal ... 1970
+ Tutt, Thayer ... 1973
Wirtz, Bill ... 1967
+ Wright, Lyle ... 1973

Members of Both Hockey and U.S. Hockey Halls of Fame

(as of Sept. 15, 1996)

Players
Hobey Baker
Frankie Brimsek
Frank (Moose) Goheen
John Mariucci

Coach
Bob Johnson

Referee
Bill Chadwick

Builders
George Brown
Walter Brown
Doc Gibson
Bill Jennings
Tom Lockhart
Thayer Tutt
Bill Wirtz

HORSE RACING

National Horse Racing Hall of Fame

Established in 1950 by the Saratoga Springs Racing Association and opened in 1955. **Address:** National Museum of Racing and Hall of Fame, 191 Union Ave., Saratoga Springs, NY 12866. **Telephone:** (518) 584-0400.

Eligibility: Nominated horses must be retired five years; jockeys must be active at least 15 years; trainers must be active at least 25 years. Voting done by 100-member panel of horse racing media.

Class of 1996 (6): JOCKEYS—**Don Brumfield** and **George Barbee**. TRAINER—**James P. Conway**. HORSES—**Sunday Silence**, **Go for Wand** and **Sun Beau**.

Members are listed with year of induction; (+) indicates deceased members.

Jockeys

+ Adams, Frank (Dooley)* 1970
+ Adams, John 1965
+ Aitcheson, Joe Jr.* 1978
Arcaro, Eddie 1958
Atkinson, Ted 1957
Baeza, Braulio 1976
Bailey, Jerry 1995
+ Barbee, George 1996
+ Bassett, Carroll* 1972
+ Blum, Walter 1987
+ Bostwick, George H.* 1968
+ Boulmetis, Sam 1973
+ Brooks, Steve 1963
Brumfield, Don 1996
+ Burns, Tommy 1983
+ Butwell, Jimmy 1984
Cauthen, Steve 1994
+ Coltiletti, Frank 1970
Cordero, Angel Jr. 1988
+ Crawford, Robert (Specs)* 1973
Day, Pat 1991
Delahoussaye, Eddie 1993
+ Ensor, Lavelle (Buddy) 1962
+ Fator, Laverne 1955
Fishback, Jerry* 1992
+ Garner, Andrew (Mack) 1969
+ Garrison, Snapper 1955
+ Griffin, Henry 1956
+ Guerin, Eric 1972
Hartack, Bill 1959
Hawley, Sandy 1992
+ Johnson, Albert 1971
+ Knapp, Willie 1969
+ Kummer, Clarence 1972
+ Kurtsinger, Charley 1967
+ Loftus, Johnny 1959
Longden, Johnny 1958
Maher, Danny 1955
+ McAtee, Linus 1956
McCarron, Chris 1989
+ McCreary, Conn 1974
+ McKinney, Rigan 1968
+ McLaughlin, James 1955
+ Miller, Walter 1955
+ Murphy, Isaac 1955
+ Neves, Ralph 1960
+ Notter, Joe 1963
+ O'Connor, Winnie 1956
+ Odom, George 1955
+ O'Neill, Frank 1956
+ Parke, Ivan 1978
+ Patrick, Gil 1970
Pincay, Laffit Jr. 1975
+ Purdy, Sam 1970
+ Reiff, John 1956
+ Robertson, Alfred 1971
Rotz, John L. 1983
+ Sande, Earl 1955
+ Schilling, Carroll 1970
Shoemaker, Bill 1958
+ Simms, Willie 1977
+ Sloan, Todhunter 1955
+ Smithwick, A. Patrick* 1973
+ Stout, James 1968
+ Taral, Fred 1955
+ Tuckman, Bayard Jr.* 1973
Turcotte, Ron 1979
+ Turner, Nash 1955
Ussery, Robert 1980
Velasquez, Jorge 1990
+ Woolfe, George 1955
+ Workman, Raymond 1956
Ycaza, Manuel 1977

*Steeplechase jockey

Trainers

+ Barrera, Laz 1979
+ Bedwell, H. Guy 1971
+ Brown, Edward D. 1984
Burch, Elliot 1980
+ Burch, Preston M. 1963
+ Burch, W.P. 1955
+ Burlew, Fred 1973
+ Byers, J.D. (Dilly) 1967
+ Childs, Frank E. 1968
Cocks, W. Burling 1985
Conway, James P. 1996
Croll, Jimmy 1994
+ Duke, William 1956
+ Feustel, Louis 1964
+ Fitzsimmons, J. (Sunny Jim) 1958
Frankel, Bobby 1995
+ Gaver, John M. 1966
+ Healey, Thomas 1955
+ Hildreth, Samuel 1955
+ Hirsch, Max 1959
+ Hirsch, W.J. (Buddy) 1982
+ Hitchcock, Thomas Sr. 1973
+ Hughes, Hollie 1973
+ Hyland, John 1956
+ Jacobs, Hirsch 1958
Jerkens, H. Allen 1975
+ Johnson, William R. 1986
+ Jolley, LeRoy 1987
+ Jones, Ben A. 1958
Jones, H.A. (Jimmy) 1959
+ Joyner, Andrew 1955
Kelly, Tom 1993
Laurin, Lucien 1977
+ Lewis, J. Howard 1969
+ Luro, Horatio 1980
+ Madden, John 1983
+ Maloney, Jim 1989
Martin, Frank (Pancho) 1981
McAnally, Ron 1990
+ McDaniel, Henry 1956
+ Miller, MacKenzie 1987
+ Molter, William, Jr. 1960
+ Mulholland, Winbert 1967
+ Neloy, Eddie 1983
Nerud, John 1972
+ Parke, Burley 1986
+ Penna, Angel Sr. 1988
+ Pincus, Jacob 1988
+ Rogers, John 1955
+ Rowe, James Sr. 1955
Schulhofer, Scotty 1992
Sheppard, Jonathan 1990
+ Smith, Robert A. 1976
+ Smithwick, Mike 1976
Stephens, Woody 1976
+ Thompson, H.J. 1969
+ Trotsek, Harry 1984
Van Berg, Jack 1985
+ Van Berg, Marion 1970
+ Veitch, Sylvester 1977
+ Walden, Robert 1970
+ Ward, Sherrill 1978
Whiteley, Frank Jr. 1978
Whittingham, Charlie 1974
Winfrey, W.C. (Bill) 1971

Horses

Year foaled in parentheses.

+ Ack Ack (1966) 1986
Affectionately (1960) 1989
Affirmed (1975) 1980
All-Along (1979) 1990
+ Alsab (1939) 1976
+ Alydar (1975) 1989
Alysheba (1984) 1993
+ American Eclipse (1814) 1970
+ Armed (1941) 1963
+ Artful (1902) 1956
+ Arts and Letters (1966) 1994
+ Assault (1943) 1964
+ Battleship (1927) 1969
+ Bed O'Roses (1947) 1976
+ Beldame (1901) 1956
+ Ben Brush (1893) 1955
+ Bewitch (1945) 1977
+ Bimelech (1937) 1990
+ Black Gold (1919) 1989
+ Black Helen (1932) 1991
+ Blue Larkspur (1926) 1957

+ Bold Ruler (1954)....................1973
+ Bon Nouvel (1960)..................1976
+ Boston (1833).........................1955
+ Broomstick (1901)...................1956
+ Buckpasser (1963)..................1970
+ Busher (1942).........................1964
+ Bushranger (1930)..................1967

+ Cafe Prince (1970)..................1985
+ Carry Back (1958)...................1975
+ Cavalcade (1931)....................1993
+ Challendon (1936)...................1977
+ Chris Evert (1971)...................1988
+ Cicada (1959)..........................1967
+ Citation (1945)........................1959
+ Coaltown (1945).......................1983
+ Colin (1905).............................1956
+ Commando (1898)....................1956
+ Count Fleet (1940)....................1961
+ Crusader (1923)........................1995

+ Dahlia (1971)............................1981
+ Damascus (1964).......................1974
+ Dark Mirage (1965)...................1974
+ Davona Dale (1976)...................1985
+ Desert Vixen (1970)...................1979
+ Devil Diver (1939).....................1980
+ Discovery (1931).......................1969
+ Domino (1891)...........................1955
+ Dr. Fager (1964).........................1971
+ Eight 30 (1936)..........................1994
+ Elkridge (1938)...........................1966
+ Emperor of Norfolk (1885).....1988
+ Equipoise (1928).........................1957
+ Exterminator (1915)....................1957

+ Fairmount (1921)........................1985
+ Fair Play (1905)...........................1956
+ Firenze (1885).............................1981
Flatterer (1979)..............................1994
Foolish Pleasure (1972)..................1995
+ Forego (1971)...............................1979

+ Gallant Bloom (1966)...................1977
+ Gallant Fox (1927).......................1957
+ Gallant Man (1954)......................1987

+ Gallorette (1942)..........................1962
+ Gamely (1964)...............................1980
Genuine Risk (1977)..........................1986
+ Good and Plenty (1900).................1956
+ Go For Ward (1987)........................1996
+ Grey Lag (1918)...............................1957

+ Hamburg (1895)..............................1986
+ Hanover (1884)...............................1955
+ Henry of Navarre (1891)...............1985
+ Hill Prince (1947)............................1991
+ Hindoo (1878).................................1955

+ Imp (1894).......................................1965

+ Jay Trump (1957).............................1971
John Henry (1975)..............................1990
+ Johnstown (1936)............................1992
+ Jolly Roger (1922)............................1965

+ Kingston (1884)................................1955
+ Kelso (1957).....................................1967
+ Kentucky (1861)...............................1983

Lady's Secret (1982)...........................1992
La Prevoyante (1970)..........................1995
+ L'Escargot (1963)..............................1977
+ Lexington (1850)..............................1955
+ Longfellow (1867).............................1971
+ Luke Blackburn (1877)......................1956

+ Majestic Prince (1966).......................1988
+ Man o' War (1917)............................1957
+ Miss Woodford (1880)........................1967
+ Myrtlewood (1933).............................1979

+ Nashua (1952)....................................1965
+ Native Dancer (1950)..........................1963
+ Native Diver (1959)............................1978
+ Northern Dancer (1961).......................1976
+ Neji (1950)...1966

+ Oedipus (1941)...................................1978
+ Old Rosebud (1911).............................1968
+ Omaha (1932).....................................1965

+ Pan Zareta (1910)................................1972
+ Parole (1873).......................................1984
Personal Ensign (1984)..........................1993

+ Peter Pan (1904)..................................1956
Princess Rooney (1980)..........................1991

+ Real Delight (1949)..............................1987
+ Regret (1912)......................................1957
+ Reigh Count (1925)..............................1978
+ Roamer (1911).....................................1981
+ Roseben (1901)....................................1956
+ Round Table (1954)..............................1972
+ Ruffian (1972)......................................1976
+ Ruthless (1864).....................................1975

+ Salvator (1886)......................................1955
+ Sarazen (1921).......................................1957
+ Seabiscuit (1933)....................................1958
+ Searching (1952)....................................1978
Seattle Slew (1974)...................................1981
+ Secretariat (1970)...................................1974
+ Shuvee (1966)..1975
+ Silver Spoon (1956)................................1978
+ Sir Archy (1805).....................................1955
+ Sir Barton (1916)....................................1957
Slew o'Gold (1980)...................................1992
+ Sun Beau (1925).....................................1996
Sunday Silence (1986)...............................1996
+ Stymie (1941)..1975
+ Susan's Girl (1969)...................................1976
+ Swaps (1952)...1966
+ Sword Dancer (1956)...............................1977
+ Sysonby (1902)..1956

+ Ta Wee (1966)...1994
+ Tim Tam (1955)......................................1985
+ Tom Fool (1949)......................................1960
+ Top Flight (1929).....................................1966
+ Tosmah (1961)..1984
+ Twenty Grand (1928)...............................1957
+ Twilight Tear (1941).................................1963

+ War Admiral (1934)..................................1958
+ Whirlaway (1938).....................................1959
+ Whisk Broom II (1907)..............................1979

Zaccio (1976)...1990
+ Zev (1920)...1983

Exemplars of Racing

+ Hanes, John W..........................1982
+ Jeffords, Walter M.....................1973
Mellon, Paul................................1989
Widener, George D.......................1971

Harness Racing Living Hall of Fame

Established by the U.S. Harness Writers Association (USHWA) in 1958. **Address:** Trotting Horse Museum, 240 Main Street, P.O. Box 590, Goshen, NY 10924; **Telephone:** (914) 294-6330.

Eligibility: Open to all harness racing drivers, trainers and executives. Voting done by USHWA membership. There are 68 members of the Living Hall of Fame, but only the 37 drivers and trainer-drivers are listed below.

Class of 1996 (3): DRIVER—**Michel Lachance**. BREEDER—**J. Glen Brown**. TRAINER—**Jack Kopas**.

Members are listed with years of induction; (+) indicates deceased members.

Trainer-Drivers

Abbatiello, Carmine.............1986
Abbatiello, Tony...................1995
Ackerman, Doug...................1995
+ Avery, Earle.........................1975
+ Baldwin, Ralph.....................1972
Beissinger, Howard..............1975
Bostwick, Dunbar.................1989
+ Cameron, Del.......................1975
Campbell, John.....................1991
+ Chapman, John....................1980
Cruise, Jimmy.......................1987
Dancer, Stanley....................1970
+ Ervin, Frank.........................1969

Farrington, Bob....................1980
Filion, Herve.........................1976
+ Garnsey, Glen......................1983
Galbraith, Clint.....................1990
Gilmour, Buddy.....................1990
Harner, Levi...........................1986
+ Haughton, Billy....................1969
+ Hodgins, Clint......................1973
Insko, Del..............................1981
Kopas, Jack...........................1996
Lachance, Michel..................1996
Miller, Del..............................1969
+ O'Brien, Joe.........................1971

O'Donnell, Bill.......................1991
Patterson, John Sir................1994
+ Pownall, Harry......................1971
Riegle, Gene..........................1992
+ Russell, Sanders...................1971
+ Shively, Bion.........................1968
Sholty, George.......................1985
Simpson, John Sr...................1972
+ Smart, Curly.........................1970
Waples, Keith.........................1987
Waples, Ron...........................1994

MEDIA

National Sportscasters and Sportswriters Hall of Fame

Established in 1959 by the National Sportscasters and Sportswriters Association. **Mailing Address:** P.O. Box 559, Salisbury, NC 28144. A permanent museum is scheduled to open in the autumn of 1996. **Telephone:** (704) 633-4275.

Eligibility: Nominees must be active for at least 25 years. Voting done by NSSA membership and other media representatives.

Class of 1996 (2): sportscaster **Dick Enberg** and sportswriter **Dan Jenkins**.

Members are listed with year of induction; (+) indicates deceased members.

Sportscasters

+ Allen, Mel ... 1972
+ Barber, Walter (Red) ... 1973
Brickhouse, Jack ... 1983
Buck, Jack ... 1990
Caray, Harry ... 1989
+ Cosell, Howard ... 1993
+ Dean, Dizzy ... 1976
Dunphy, Don ... 1986
+ Elson, Bob ... 1995
Enberg, Dick ... 1996
Glickman, Marty ... 1992
Gowdy, Curt ... 1981
Harwell, Ernie ... 1989
+ Hodges, Russ ... 1975
+ Hoyt, Waite ... 1987
+ Husing, Ted ... 1963
Jackson, Keith ... 1995
+ McCarthy, Clem ... 1970
McKay, Jim ... 1987
+ McNamee, Graham ... 1964
+ Nelson, Lindsey ... 1979
+ Prince, Bob ... 1986
Schenkel, Chris ... 1981
Scott, Ray ... 1982
Scully, Vin ... 1991
+ Stern, Bill ... 1974
Summerall, Pat ... 1994

Sportswriters

Anderson, Dave ... 1990
Bisher, Furman ... 1989
Burick, Si ... 1985
+ Cannon, Jimmy ... 1986
+ Carmichael, John P. ... 1994
+ Connor, Dick ... 1992
+ Considine, Bob ... 1980
+ Daley, Arthur ... 1976
Durslag, Mel ... 1995
+ Gould, Alan ... 1990
+ Graham, Frank Sr. ... 1995
+ Grimsley, Will ... 1987
Heinz, W.C. ... 1987
Jenkins, Dan ... 1996
+ Kieran, John ... 1971
+ Lardner, Ring ... 1967
+ Murphy, Jack ... 1988
Murray, Jim ... 1978
Olderman, Murray ... 1993
+ Parker, Dan ... 1975
Pope, Edwin ... 1994
Povich, Shirley ... 1984
+ Rice, Grantland ... 1962
+ Runyon, Damon ... 1964
Russell, Fred ... 1988
Sherrod, Blackie ... 1991
+ Smith, Walter (Red) ... 1977
+ Spink, J.G. Taylor ... 1969
+ Ward, Arch ... 1973
+ Woodward, Stanley ... 1974

American Sportscasters Hall of Fame

Established in 1984 by the American Sportscasters Association. **Address:** 5 Beekman Street, Suite 814, New York, NY 10038. A permanent museum site is in the planning stages. **Telephone:** (212) 227-8080.

Eligibility: nominations made by selection committee of previous winners, voting by ASA membership.

Members are listed with year of induction; (+) indicates deceased members.

+ Allen, Mel ... 1985
+ Barber, Walter (Red) ... 1984
Brickhouse, Jack ... 1985
Buck, Jack ... 1990
Caray, Harry ... 1989
+ Cosell, Howard ... 1993
Dunphy, Don ... 1984
Glickman, Marty ... 1993
Gowdy, Curt ... 1985
Harwell, Ernie ... 1991
Hearn, Chick ... 1995
+ Husing, Ted ... 1984
Jackson, Keith ... 1994
+ McCarthy, Clem ... 1987
McKay, Jim ... 1987
+ McNamee, Graham ... 1984
+ Nelson, Lindsey ... 1986
Scully, Vin ... 1992
+ Stern, Bill ... 1984

40th Anniversary Top 40s

In 1986, *Sport* magazine celebrated its 40th anniversary by publishing a list of the 40 most significant athletes and sports figures from 1946-86. Eight years later, *Sports Illustrated* toasted its first four decades with a Top 40 of its own.

On both lists (19): Hank Aaron, Muhammad Ali, Roone Arledge, Jim Brown, Bear Bryant, Howard Cosell, Wayne Gretzky, Billie Jean King, Marvin Miller, Joe Namath, Martina Navratilova, Jack Nicklaus, Bobby Orr, Arnold Palmer, Pelé, Pete Rose, Pete Rozelle, Bill Russell and John Wooden.

Sport's "The 40 Who Changed Sports"

Selected by the editors of *Sport* for the magazine's 40th anniversary issue (December 1986). Entries were not ranked.

Aaron, Hank ... Baseball
Ali, Muhammad ... Boxing
Arledge, Roone ... Television
Auerbach, Red ... Baskteball
+ Bikila, Abebe ... Track & Field
Bouton, Jim ... Literature
Brown, Jim ... Football
+ Brown, Paul ... Football
+ Brundage, Avery ... Olympics
+ Bryant, Bear ... Football
Chamberlain, Wilt ... Basketball
+ Cosell, Howard ... Television
Cousy, Bob ... Basketball
Davis, Al ... Football
Evert, Chris ... Tennis
Flood, Curt ... Baseball
+ France, Bill Sr ... Auto Racing
Greizky, Wayne ... Hockey
King, Billie Jean ... Tennis
+ Lombardi, Vince ... Football
+ Mantle, Mickey ... Baseball
Mays, Willie ... Baseball
Miller, Marvin ... Baseball
Namath, Joe ... Football
Navratilova, Martina ... Tennis
Nicklaus, Jack ... Golf
+ Norris, James D. ... Boxing
Orr, Bobby ... Hockey
Palmer, Arnold ... Golf
Pelé ... Soccer
+ Rickey, Branch ... Baseball
+ Robinson, Jackie ... Baseball
+ Robinson, Sugar Ray ... Boxing
Rose, Pete ... Baseball
Rozelle, Pete ... Football
Russell, Bill ... Basketball
Shoemaker, Bill ... Horse Racing
+ Stengel, Casey ... Baseball
Williams, Ted ... Baseball
Wooden, John ... Basketball

Sports Illustrated's "40 For the Ages"

Selected by the editors of *Sports Illustrated* for the weekly magazie's 40th anniversary issue (Sept. 19, 1994). Entries were ranked (see below).

Aaron, Hank.....Baseball
Ali, Muhammad.....Boxing
Arledge, Roone.....Television
+ Ashe, Arthur.....Tennis
Larry Bird
& Magic Johnson.....Basketball
Brown, Jim.....Football
+ Bryant, Bear.....Football
+ Clemente, Roberto.....Baseball
+ Cosell, Howard.....Television
Davidson, Gary.....Business
Erving, Julius.....Basketball
+ Fixx, Jim.....Running
Fleming, Peggy.....Figure Skating
+ Gores, Dr. Harold.....Synthetic Turf
Gretzky, Wayne.....Hockey
Jackson, Dr. Robert.....Medicine
Jordan, Michael.....Basketball
King, Billie Jean.....Tennis
King, Don.....Boxing
Korbut, Olga.....Gymnastics
Lemond, Greg.....Cycling
Leonard, Sugar Ray.....Boxing
Lewis, Carl.....Track & Field
McCormack, Mark.....Business
Miller, Marvin.....Baseball
Montana, Joe.....Football
Namath, Joe.....Football
Navratilova, Martina.....Tennis
Nicklaus, Jack.....Golf
Orr, Bobby.....Hockey
Palmer, Arnold.....Golf
Pelé.....Soccer
Petty, Richard.....Auto Racing
Rasmussen, Bill.....Television
Rose, Pete.....Baseball
Rozelle, Pete.....Football
Russell, Bill.....Basketball
Ryan, Nolan.....Baseball
+ Secretariat.....Horse Racing
Wooden, John.....Basketball

Overall Ranking (in order of importance)

1 Muhammad Ali
2 Michael Jordan
3 Roone Arledge
4 Jim Brown
5 Billie Jean King
6 Pete Rose
7 Marvin Miller
8 Larry Bird & Magic Johnson
9 Arnold Palmer
10 Mark McCormack
11 Carl Lewis
12 Wayne Gretzky
13 Pete Rozelle
14 Martina Navratilova
15 Hank Aaron
16 John Wooden
17 Secretariat
18 Joe Namath
19 Dr. Harold Gores
20 Jack Nicklaus
21 Bill Russell
22 Howard Cosell
23 Joe Montana
24 Bear Bryant
25 Roberto Clemente
26 Olga Korbut
27 Arthur Ashe
28 Richard Petty
29 Bill Rasmussen
30 Pelé
31 Bobby Orr
32 Sugar Ray Leonard
33 Jim Fixx
34 Nolan Ryan
35 Peggy Fleming
36 Don King
37 Dr. Robert Jackson
38 Greg Lemond
39 Gary Davidson
40 Julius Erving

MOTOR SPORTS

Motorsports Hall of Fame of America

Established in 1989. **Mailing Address:** P.O. Box 194, Novi, MI 48050. **Telephone:** (810) 349-7223.

Eligibility: Nominees must be retired at least three years or engaged in their area of motor sports for at least 20 years. Areas include: open wheel, stock car, dragster, sports car, motorcycle, off road, power boat, air racing and land speed records.

Class of 1996 (9): DRIVERS—**Betty Cook** (power boats), **Bill "Grumpy" Jenkins** (dragsters), **Lee Petty** (stock cars), **Peter Revson** (sports cars), **Johnny Rutherford** (open wheel), **Malcolm Smith** (motorcycles). CONTRIBUTORS—**Henry Ford**, **Mauri Rose** and **A.J. Watson**.

Members are listed with year of induction; (+) indicates deceased members.

Drivers

Allison, Bobby.....1992
Andretti, Mario.....1990
Arfons, Art.....1991
+ Baker, Cannonball.....1989
Breedlove, Craig.....1993
+ Campbell, Sir Malcolm.....1994
Cantrell, Bill.....1992
+ Chenoweth, Dean.....1991
+ Clark, Jim.....1990
+ Cook, Betty.....1996
DeCosta, Roger.....1994
+ DePalma, Ralph.....1992
+ DePaolo, Peter.....1995
+ Donahue, Mark.....1990
Foyt, A.J.....1989
Garlits, Don.....1989
Glidden, Bob.....1994
Gurney, Dan.....1991
Hanauer, Chip.....1995
Hill, Phil.....1989
+ Holbert, Al.....1993
+ Horn, Ted.....1993
Jenkins, Bill "Grumpy".....1996
Johnson, Junior.....1991
Jones, Parnelli.....1992
Kalitta, Connie.....1992
Leonard, Joe.....1991
+ McLaren, Bruce.....1995
Mann, Dick.....1993
+ Mays, Rex.....1995
+ Meyer, Louis.....1993
Muldowney, Shirley.....1990
+ Muncy, Bill.....1989
Musson, Ron.....1993
+ Oldfield, Barney.....1989
Parks, Wally.....1993
Pearson, David.....1993
+ Petrali, Joe.....1992
Petty, Lee.....1996
Petty, Richard.....1989
Prudhomme, Don.....1991
+ Revson, Peter.....1996
+ Roberts, Fireball.....1995
Roberts, Kenny.....1990
Rutherford, Johnny.....1996
+ Shaw, Wilbur.....1991
Smith, Malcolm.....1996
+ Thompson, Mickey.....1990
Unser, Bobby.....1994
+ Vukovich, Bill Sr.....1992
Ward, Rodger.....1995
+ Wood, Gar.....1990
Yarborough, Cale.....1994

Pilots

+ Cochran, Jacqueline.....1993
+ Curtiss, Glenn.....1990
+ Doolittle, Jimmy.....1989
+ Earhart, Amelia.....1992
+ Falck, Bill.....1994
+ Turner, Roscoe.....1991

Contributors

+ Agajanian, J.C.....1992
Bignotti, George.....1993
+ Black, Keith.....1995
+ Chevrolet, Louis.....1995
Economacki, Chris.....1994
+ Ford, Henry.....1996
+ France, Bill Sr......1990
Hall, Jim.....1994
+ Hulman, Tony.....1991
Little, Bernie.....1994
Penske, Roger.....1995
+ Rickenbacker, Eddie.....1994
+ Rose, Mauri.....1996
Shelby, Carroll.....1992
Watson, A.J......1996

International Motorsports Hall of Fame

Established in 1990 by the International Motorsports Hall of Fame Commission. **Mailing Address:** P.O. Box 1018, Talladega, AL 35160. **Telephone:** (205) 362-5002.

Eligibility: Nominees must be retired from their specialty in motorsports for five years. Voting done by 150-member panel made up of the world-wide auto racing media.

Class of 1996 (6): **Richie Evans**, **Donald Haley**, **Bobby Isaac**, **Ferdinand Porsche**, **Johnny Rutherford** and **John Surtees**.

Members are listed with year of induction; (+) indicates deceased members.

Drivers

Allison, Bobby 1993
+ Ascari, Alberto 1992
Baker, Buck 1990
+ Bettenhausen, Tony 1991
Brabham, Jack 1990
+ Campbell, Sir Malcolm 1990
+ Clark, Jim 1990
+ DePalma, Ralph 1991
+ Donahue, Mark 1990
+ Evans, Richie 1996
+ Fangio, Juan Manuel 1990
Flock, Tim 1991
+ Gregg, Peter 1992
Gurney, Dan 1990
+ Haley, Donald 1996
+ Hill, Graham 1990
Hill, Phil 1991
+ Holbert, Al 1993
Isaac, Bobby 1996
Jarrett, Ned 1991
Johnson, Junior 1990
Jones, Parnelli 1990
Lauda, Niki 1993
Lorenzen, Fred 1991
+ Lund, Tiny 1994
+ Mays, Rex 1993
+ McLaren, Bruce 1991
+ Meyer, Louis 1992
Moss, Stirling 1990
+ Oldfield, Barney 1990
Parsons, Benny 1994
Pearson, David 1993
Petty, Lee 1990
+ Roberts, Fireball 1990
Roberts, Kenny 1992
Rose, Mauri 1994
Rutherford, Johnny 1996
+ Shaw, Wilbur 1991
Stewart, Jackie 1990
Surtees, John 1996
Thomas, Herb 1994
+ Turner, Curtis 1992
Unser, Bobby 1990
+ Vukovich, Bill 1991
Ward Rodger 1992
+ Weatherly, Joe 1994
Yarborough, Cale 1993

Contributors

Bignotti, George 1993
+ Chapman, Colin 1994
+ Chevrolet, Louis 1992
+ Ferrari, Enzo 1994
+ Ford, Henry 1993
+ France, Bill Sr 1990
Granatelli, Andy 1992
+ Hulman, Tony 1990
Marcum, John 1994
Moody, Ralph 1994
Parks, Wally 1992
+ Porsche, Ferdinand 1996
+ Rickenbacker, Eddie 1992
Shelby, Carroll 1991
+ Thompson, Mickey 1990
Yunick, Smokey 1990

OLYMPICS

U.S. Olympic Hall of Fame

Established in 1983 by the United States Olympic Committee. **Mailing Address:** U.S. Olympic Committee, 1750 East Boulder Street, Colorado Springs, CO 80909. Plans for a permanent museum site have been suspended due to lack of funding. **Telephone:** (719) 578-4529.

Eligibility: Nominated athletes must be five years removed from active competition.Voting done by National Sportscasters and Sportswriters Association, Hall of Fame members and the USOC board members of directors.

Voting for membership in the Hall was suspended in 1993.

Members are listed with year of induction; (+) indicates deceased members.

Teams

1956 Basketball—Dick Boushka, Carl Cain, Chuck Darling, Bill Evans, Gib Ford, Burdy Haldorson, Bill Hougland, Bob Jeangerard, K.C. Jones, Bill Russell, Ron Tomsic, +Jim Walsh and coach +Gerald Tucker.

1960 Basketball—Jay Arnette, Walt Bellamy, Bob Boozer, Terry Dischinger, Burdy Haldorson, Darrall Imhoff, Allen Kelley, +Lester Lane, Jerry Lucas, Oscar Robertson, Adrian Smith, Jerry West and coach Pete Newell.

1964 Basketball—Jim Barnes, Bill Bradley, Larry Brown, Joe Caldwell, Mel Counts, Richard Davies, Walt Hazzard, Luke Jackson, John McCaffrey, Jeff Mullins, Jerry Shipp, George Wilson and coach +Hank Iba.

1960 Ice Hockey—Billy Christian, Roger Christian, Billy Cleary, Bob Cleary, Gene Grazia, Paul Johnson, Jack Kirrane, John Mayasich, Jack McCartan, Bob McKay, Dick Meredith, Weldon Olson, Ed Owen, Rod Paavola, Larry Palmer, Dick Rodenheiser, +Tom Williams and coach Jack Riley.

1980 Ice Hockey—Bill Baker, Neal Broten, Dave Christian, Steve Christoff, Jim Craig, Mike Eruzione, John Harrington, Steve Janaszak, Mark Johnson, Ken Morrow, Rob McClanahan, Jack O'Callahan, Mark Pavelich, Mike Ramsey, Buzz Schneider, Dave Silk, Eric Strobel, Bob Suter, Phil Verchota, Mark Wells and coach Herb Brooks.

The Olympic Order

Established in 1974 by the International Olympic Committee (IOC) to honor athletes, officials and media members who have made remarkable contributions to the Olympic movement. The IOC's Council of the Olympic Order is presided over by the IOC president and active IOC members are not eligible for consideration. Through 1996, only three American officials have received the Order's highest commendation—the gold medal:

Avery Brundage, president of USOC (1928-53) and IOC (1952-72), was given the award posthumously in 1975.
Peter Ueberroth, president of Los Angeles Olympic Organizing Committee, was given the award in 1984.
Billy Payne, president of Atlanta Committee for the Olympic Games, was given the award in 1996.

Alpine Skiing

Mahre, Phil 1992

Bobsled

+ Eagan, Eddie (see Boxing) 1983

Boxing

Clay, Cassius* 1983
+ Eagan, Eddie (see Bobsled) 1983
Foreman, George 1990
Frazier, Joe 1989
Leonard, Sugar Ray 1985
Patterson, Floyd 1987

*Clay changed name to Muhammad Ali in 1964.

Cycling

Carpenter-Phinney, Connie 1992

Diving

King, Miki 1992
Lee, Sammy 1990
Louganis, Greg 1985
McCormick, Pat 1985

Figure Skating

Albright, Tenley 1988
Button, Dick 1983
Fleming, Peggy 1983
Hamill, Dorothy 1991
Hamilton, Scott 1990

Gymnastics

Conner, Bart 1991
Retton, Mary Lou 1985
Vidmar, Peter 1991

Rowing

+ Kelly, Jack Sr. 1990

Speed Skating

Heiden, Eric 1983

Swimming

Babashoff, Shirley 1987
Caulkins, Tracy 1990
+ Daniels, Charles 1988
de Varona, Donna 1987
+ Kahanamoku, Duke 1984
+ Madison, Helene 1992
Meyer, Debbie 1986
Naber, John 1984
Schollander, Don 1983
Spitz, Mark 1983
+ Weissmuller, Johnny 1983

Track & Field

Beamon, Bob 1983
Boston, Ralph 1985
+ Calhoun, Lee 1991
Campbell, Milt 1992
Davenport, Willie 1991
Davis, Glenn 1986
+ Didrikson, Babe 1983
Dillard, Harrison 1983
Evans, Lee 1989
+ Ewry, Ray 1983
Fosbury, Dick 1992
Jenner, Bruce 1986
Johnson, Rafer 1983
+ Kraenzlein, Alvin 1985
Lewis, Carl 1985
Mathias, Bob 1983
Mills, Billy 1984
Morrow, Bobby 1989
Moses, Edwin 1985
O'Brien, Parry 1984
Oerter, Al 1983
+ Owens, Jesse 1983
+ Paddock, Charley 1991
Richards, Bob 1983
+ Rudolph, Wilma 1983
+ Sheppard, Mel 1989
Shorter, Frank 1984
+ Thorpe, Jim 1983
Toomey, Bill 1984
Tyus, Wyomia 1985
Whitfield, Mal 1988
+ Wykoff, Frank 1984

Weight Lifting

+ Davis, John 1989
Kono, Tommy 1990

Wrestling

Gable, Dan 1985

Contributors

Arledge, Roone 1989
+ Brundage, Avery 1983
+ Bushnell, Asa 1990
Hull, Col. Don 1992
+ Iba, Hank 1985
+ Kane, Robert 1986
+ Kelly, Jack Jr. 1992
McKay, Jim 1988
Miller, Don 1984
Simon, William 1991
Walker, LeRoy 1987

SOCCER

National Soccer Hall of Fame

Established in 1950 by the Philadelphia Oldtimers Association. First exhibit unveiled in Oneonta, NY in 1982. Moved into present building in 1987. New Hall of Fame planned at Wright National Soccer Campus in Oneonta. **Address:** 5-11 Ford Avenue, Oneonta, NY 13820. **Telephone:** (607) 432-3351.

Eligibility: Nominated players must have represented the U.S. in international competition and be retired five years; other categories include Meritorious Service and Special Commendation.

Nominations made by state organizations and a veterans' committee. Voting done by nine-member committee made up of Hall of Famers, U.S. Soccer officials and members of the national media.

Class of 1996 (6): PLAYERS—**Nicholas Kropfelder** and **Len Oliver**. COACHES—**Gordon Bradley** and **Harry Keough** (elected previously as a player in 1976). CONTRIBUTORS—**Frank Jewell** and **Abbot Leonard**.

Members are listed with home state and year of induction; (+) indicates deceased members.

Members

Abronzino, Umberto (CA) 1971
Aimi, Milton (TX) 1991
+ Alonso, Julie (NY) 1972
+ Andersen, William (NY) 1956
+ Ardizzone, John (CA) 1971
+ Armstrong, James (NY) 1952
+ Auld, Andrew (RI) 1986

Bahr, Walter (PA) 1976
Barr, George (NY) 1983
+ Barriskill, Joe (NY) 1953
+ Beardsworth, Fred (MA) 1965
Berling, Clay (CA) 1995
Bernabei, Ray (PA) 1978
Best, John O. (CA) 1982
+ Bookie, Michael (PA) 1986
+ Booth, Joseph (CT) 1952
Borghi, Frank (MO) 1976
Boulos, Frenchy (NY) 1980
+ Boxer, Matt (CA) 1961
Bradley Gordon (Eng.) 1996
+ Briggs, Lawrence E. (MA) 1978
+ Brittan, Harold (PA) 1951
+ Brock, John (MA) 1950
+ Brown, Andrew M. (OH) 1950
+ Brown, David (NJ) 1951
Brown, George (NJ) 1995
Brown, James (NY) 1986

+ Cahill, Thomas W (NY) 1950
+ Carenza, Joe (MO) 1982
+ Caraffi, Ralph (OH) 1959
Chacurian, Chico (CT) 1992
+ Chesney, Stan (NY) 1966
+ Coll, John (NY) 1986
+ Collins, George M. (MA) 1951
+ Colombo, Charlie (MO) 1976
+ Commander, Colin (OH) 1967
+ Cordery, Ted (CA) 1975
+ Craddock, Robert (PA) 1959
+ Craggs, Edmund (WA) 1969
Craggs, George (WA) 1981
+ Cummings, Wilfred R. (IL) 1953

+ Delach, Joseph (PA) 1973
DeLuca, Enzo (NY) 1979
+ Dick, Walter (CA) 1989
Diorio, Nick (PA) 1974
+ Donaghy, Edward J. (NY) 1951
+ Donelli, Buff (PA) 1954
+ Donnelly, George (NY) 1989
+ Douglas, Jimmy (NJ) 1954
+ Dresmich, John W. (PA) 1968
+ Duff, Duncan (CA) 1972
+ Dugan, Thomas (NJ) 1951
+ Dunn, James (MO) 1974

National Soccer Hall of Fame (Cont.)

Edwards, Gene (WI)...............1985
+ Epperleim, Rudy (NJ).............1951
+ Fairfield, Harry (PA)..............1951
Feibusch, Ernst (CA)...............1984
+ Ferguson, John (PA)................1950
+ Fernley, John A. (MA).............1951
+ Ferro, Charles (NY)................1958
+ Fishwick, George E. (IL)...........1974
+ Flamhaft, Jack (NY)................1964
+ Fleming, Harry G. (PA)...........1967
+ Florie, Thomas (NJ)................1986
+ Foulds, Pal (MA)....................1953
+ Foulds, Sam (MA)...................1969
+ Fowler, Dan (NY)....................1970
+ Fowler, Peg (NY)....................1979
Fricker, Werner (PA)...............1992
+ Fryer, William J. (NJ).............1951
+ Gaetjens, Joe (NY).................1976
+ Gallagher, James (NY)............1986
+ Garcia, Pete (MO)..................1964
+ Gentle, James (PA).................1986
Getzinger, Rudy (IL)................1991
+ Giesler, Walter (MO)..............1962
Glover, Teddy (NY)..................1965
+ Gonsalves, Billy (MA).............1950
Gormley, Bob (PA)..................1989
+ Gould, David L. (PA)..............1953
+ Govier, Sheldon (IL)................1950
Greer, Don (CA).....................1985
Gryzik, Joe (IL)......................1973
+ Guelker, Bob (MO).................1980
Guennel, Joe (CO)..................1980
Harker, Al (PA).......................1979
+ Healy, George (MI).................1951
Heilpern, Herb (NY).................1988
+ Hemmings, William (IL)...........1961
+ Hudson, Maurice (CA).............1966
Hunt, Lamar (TX)....................1982
Hynes, John (NY)....................1977
+ Iglehart, Alfredda (MD)...........1951
+ Japp, John (PA)......................1953
+ Jeffrey, William (PA)..............1951
Jewell, Frank (Fla)..................1996
+ Johnson, Jack (IL)..................1952
Kabanica, Mike (WI)...............1987
Kehoe, Bob (MO)...................1990
Kelly, Frank (NJ).....................1994
+ Kempton, George (WA)...........1950
Keough, Harry (MO)...............1976
+ Klein, Paul (NJ).....................1953
Kleinaitis, Al (IN)....................1995
+ Koszma, Oscar (CA)...............1964
Kracher, Frank (IL)..................1983
Kraft, Granny (MD).................1984
+ Kraus, Harry (NY)...................1963
Kropfelder, Nicholas...............1996
+ Kunter, Rudy (NY)..................1963
+ Lamm, Kurt (NY)....................1979
Lang, Millard (MD).................1950
Larson, Bert (CT)....................1988
Leonard, Abbot (Eng)..............1996
+ Lewis, H. Edgar (PA)..............1950
Lombardo, Joe (NY)................1984
Long, Denny (MO)..................1993
+ MacEwan, John J. (MI)............1953
+ Maca, Joe (NY)......................1976
+ Magnozzi, Enzo (NY)..............1978
+ Maher, Jack (IL).....................1970
+ Manning, Dr. Randolf (NY)......1950
+ Marre, John (MO)...................1953
McBride, Pat (MO)..................1994
+ McClay, Allan (MA)................1971
+ McGhee, Bart (NY).................1986
+ McGrath, Frank (MA)..............1978
+ McGuire, Jimmy (NY)..............1951
+ McGuire, John (NY)................1951
+ McIlveney, Eddie (PA).............1976
McLaughlin, Bennie (PA).........1977
+ McSkimming, Dent (MO).........1951
Merovich, Pete (PA)................1971
+ Mieth, Werner (NJ).................1974
+ Millar, Robert (NY).................1950
Miller, Al (OH).......................1995
+ Miller, Milton (NY)..................1971
+ Mills, Jimmy (PA)...................1954
Monson, Lloyd (NY)................1994
Moore, James F. (MO).............1971
+ Moorehouse, George (NY)......1986
+ Morrison, Robert (PA).............1951
+ Morrissette, Bill (MA).............1967
Nanoski, Jukey (PA)................1993
+ Netto, Fred (IL).......................1958
Newman, Ron (CA).................1992
+ Niotis, D.J. (IL)......................1963
+ O'Brien, Shamus (NY).............1990
Olaff, Gene (NJ).....................1971
+ Oliver, Arnie (MA)..................1968
Oliver, Len (PA).....................1996
+ Palmer, William (PA)...............1952
Pariani, Gino (MO).................1976
+ Patenaude, Bert (MA).............1971
+ Pearson, Eddie (GA)...............1990
+ Peel, Peter (IL)......................1951
Pelé (Brazil)...........................1993
Peters, Wally (NJ)...................1967
Phillipson, Don (CO)...............1987
+ Piscopo, Giorgio (NY).............1978
+ Pomeroy, Edgar (CA)..............1955
+ Ramsden, Arnold (TX).............1957
+ Ratican, Harry (MO)...............1950
Reese, Doc (MD)....................1957
+ Renzulli, Pete (NY).................1951
Ringsdorf, Gene (MD).............1979
Roth, Werner (NY)..................1989
+ Rottenberg, Jack (NJ).............1971
Roy, Willy (IL)........................1989
+ Ryan, Hun (PA)......................1958
+ Sager, Tom (PA).....................1968
Saunders, Harry (NY)..............1981
Schaller, Willy (IL)..................1995
Schellscheidt, Mannie (NJ).......1990
Schillinger, Emil (PA)..............1960
+ Schroeder, Elmer (PA).............1951
+ Scwarcz, Erno (NY).................1951
+ Shields, Fred (PA)...................1968
+ Single, Erwin (NY)..................1981
+ Slone, Philip (NY)...................1986
+ Smith, Alfred (PA)...................1951
+ Souza, Ed (MA)......................1976
Souza, Clarkie (MA)................1976
+ Spalding, Dick (PA).................1951
+ Stark, Archie (NJ)...................1950
+ Steelink, Nicolaas (CA)...........1971
+ Steur, August (NY).................1969
+ Stewart, Douglas (PA).............1950
+ Stone, Robert T. (CO).............1971
+ Swords, Thomas (MA).............1976
+ Tintle, Joseph (NJ).................1952
+ Tracey, Ralph (MO)................1986
+ Triner, Joseph (IL)..................1951
+ Vaughan, Frank (MO).............1986
+ Walder, Jimmy (PA)................1971
+ Wallace, Frank (MO)...............1976
+ Washauer, Adolph (CA)...........1977
+ Webb, Tom (WA)....................1987
+ Weir, Alex (NY)......................1975
+ Weston, Victor (WA)...............1956
+ Wilson, Peter (NJ)...................1950
+ Wood, Alex (MI).....................1986
+ Woods, John W. (IL)...............1952
Yeagley, Jerry (IN)..................1989
+ Young, John (CA)...................1958
+ Zampini, Dan (PA)..................1963
Zerhusen, Al (CA)...................1978

SWIMMING

International Swimming Hall of Fame

Established in 1965 by the U.S. College Coaches' Swim Forum. **Address**: One Hall of Fame Drive, Ft. Lauderdale, FL 33316. **Telephone**: (954) 462-6536.

Categories for induction are: swimming, diving, water polo, synchronized swimming, coaching, pioneers and contributors. Of the 481 members, 266 are from the United States. Contributors are not included in the following list. Only U.S. men, women, and coaches listed below.

Members are listed with year of induction; (+) indicates deceased members.

U.S. Men

+ Anderson, Miller....................1967
Barrowman, Mike..................1997
Biondi, Matt..........................1997
+ Boggs, Phil............................1985
Brack, Walter........................1997
Breen, George.......................1975
+ Browning, Skippy..................1975
Bruner, Mike..........................1988
Burton, Mike..........................1977
+ Cann, Tedford........................1967
Carey, Rick............................1993
Clark, Earl.............................1972
Clark, Steve...........................1966
Cleveland, Dick......................1991
Clotworthy, Robert.................1980

+ Crabbe, Buster....1965
+ Daniels, Charlie....1965
Degener, Dick....1971
DeMont, Rick....1990
Dempsey, Frank....1996
+ Desjardins, Pete....1966
Edgar, David....1996
+ Faricy, John....1990
+ Farrell, Jeff....1968
+ Fick, Peter....1978
+ Flanagan, Ralph....1978
Ford, Alan....1966
Furniss, Bruce....1987
Gaines, Rowdy....1995
Garton, Tim....1997
Glancy, Harrison....1990
+ Goodwin, Budd....1971
Graef, Jed....1988
Haines, George....1977
Hall, Gary....1981
+ Harlan, Bruce....1973
+ Hebner, Harry....1968
Hencken, John....1988
Hickcox, Charles....1976
Higgins, John....1971
Holiday, Harry....1991
Irwin, Juno Stover....1980
Jastremski, Chet....1977
+ Kahanamoku, Duke....1965
+ Kealoha, Warren....1968
Kiefer, Adolph....1965
Kinsella, John....1986
Konno, Ford....1972
+ Kruger, Stubby....1986
+ Kuehn, Louis....1988
+ Langer, Ludy....1988
Larson, Lance....1980
Lee, Dr. Sammy....1968
+ LeMoyne, Harry....1988
Louganis, Greg....1993
Lundquist, Steve....1990
Mann, Thompson....1984
McCormick, Pat....1965
+ McDermott, Turk....1969
+ McGillivray, Perry....1981
McKenzie, Don....1989
McKinney, Frank....1975
McLane, Jimmy....1970
+ Medica, Jack....1966
Montgomery, Jim....1986
Mullikan, Bill....1984
Naber, John....1982
Nakama, Keo....1975
+ O'Connor, Wally....1966
Oyakawa, Yoshi....1979
+ Patnik, Al....1969
Phillips, William Berge....1997
+ Riley, Mickey....1977
+ Ris, Wally....1966
Robie, Carl....1976
Roper, Gail....1997
Ross, Clarence....1988
+ Ross, Norman....1967
Roth, Dick....1987
+ Ruddy, Joe....1986
Russell, Doug....1985
Saari, Roy....1976
+ Schaeffer, E. Carroll....1968
Scholes, Clarke....1980
Schollander, Don....1965
Shaw, Tim....1989
+ Sheldon, George....1989
+ Skelton, Robert....1988
Smith, Bill....1966
+ Smith, Dutch....1979
+ Smith, Jimmy....1992
Smith, R. Jackson....1983
Spitz, Mark....1977
Stack, Allen....1979
Stickles, Ted....1995
Stock, Tom....1989
+ Swendsen, Clyde....1991
Tobian, Gary....1978
Troy, Mike....1971
Vande Weghe, Albert....1990
Vassallo, Jesse....1997
+ Verdeur, Joe....1966
Vogel, Matt....1996
+ Vollmer, Hal....1990
Wayne, Marshall....1981
Webster, Bob....1970
+ Weissmuller, Johnny....1965
+ White, Al....1965
Wrightson, Bernie....1984
Yorzyk, Bill....1971

U.S. Women

Anderson, Terry....1986
Atwood, Sue....1992
Babashoff, Shirley....1982
Ball, Catie....1976
+ Bauer, Sybil....1967
Bean, Dawn Pawson....1996
Belote, Melissa....1983
Bleibtrey, Ethelda....1967
+ Boyle, Charlotte....1988
Burke, Lynne....1978
Bush, Lesley....1986
Callen, Gloria....1984
Caretto, Patty....1987
Carr, Cathy....1988
Caulkins, Tracy....1990
+ Chadwick, Florence....1970
Chandler, Jennifer....1987
Cohen, Tiffany....1996
+ Coleman, Georgia....1966
Cone, Carin....1984
Costie, Candy....1995
Crlenkovich, Helen....1981
Curtis, Ann....1966
Daniel, Ellie....1997
Dean, Penny....1996
de Varona, Donna....1969
+ Dorfner, Olga....1970
Draves, Vickie....1969
Duenkel, Ginny....1985
Ederle, Gertrude....1965
Ellis, Kathy....1991
Ferguson, Cathy....1978
Finneran, Sharon....1985
+ Galligan, Claire....1970
+ Garatti-Seville, Eleanor....1992
Gestring, Marjorie....1976
Gossick, Sue....1988
+ Guest, Irene....1990
Hall, Kaye....1979
Henne, Jan....1979
Holm, Eleanor....1966
Hunt-Newman, Virginia....1993
Johnson, Gail....1983
Josephson, Karen-Sarah....1997
Kane, Marion....1981
+ Kaufman, Beth....1967
Kight, Lenore....1981
King, Micki....1978
Kolb, Claudia....1975
+ Lackie, Ethel....1969
Linehan, Kim....1997
Lord-Landon, Alice....1993
+ Madison, Helene....1966
Mann, Shelly....1966
McGrath, Margo....1989
McKim, Josephine....1991
Meagher, Mary T.....1993
+ Meany, Helen....1971
Meyer, Debbie....1977
Mitchell, Michele....1995
Moe, Karen....1992
Morris, Pam....1965
Neilson, Sandra....1986
Neyer, Megan....1997
+ Norelius, Martha....1967
Olsen, Zoe-Ann....1989
O'Rourke, Heidi....1980
+ Osipowich, Albina....1986
Pedersen, Susan....1995
Pinkston, Betty Becker....1967
Pope, Paula Jean Meyers....1979
Potter, Cynthia....1987
Poynton, Dorothy....1968
+ Rawls, Katherine....1965
Redmond, Carol....1989
Riggin, Aileen....1967
Ross, Anne....1984
Rothammer, Keena....1991
Ruiz-Conforto, Tracie....1993
Ruuska, Sylvia....1976
Schuler, Carolyn....1989
Seller, Peg....1988
+ Smith, Caroline....1988
Stouder, Sharon....1972
+ Toner, Vee....1995
+ Vilen, Kay....1978
Von Saltza, Chris....1966
Wahle, Oho....1996
+ Wainwright, Helen....1972
+ Watson, Lillian (Pokey)....1984
Wehselau, Mariechen....1989
Welshons, Kim....1988
Wichman, Sharon....1991
Williams, Esther....1966
+ Woodbridge, Margaret....1989

U.S. Coaches

+ Armbruster, Dave....1966
+ Bachrach, Bill....1966
Billingsley, Hobie....1983
+ Brandsten, Ernst....1966
+ Brauninger, Stan....1972
+ Cady, Fred....1969
+ Center, George (Dad)....1991
Chavoor, Sherman....1977
+ Cody, Jack....1970
Counsilman, Dr. James....1976
+ Curtis, Katherine....1979
Daland, Peter....1977
+ Daughters, Ray....1971
Draves, Lyle....1989
Gambril, Don....1983
Haines, George....1977
Handley, L. de B.....1967
Hannula, Dick....1987

International Swimming Hall of Fame (Cont.)

U.S. Coaches (Cont.)

Kimball, Dick ... 1985
+ Kiphuth, Bob ... 1965
Mann, Matt II ... 1965
+ McCormick, Glen ... 1995
Moriarty, Phil ... 1980
Mowerson, Robert ... 1986
Muir, Bob ... 1989
+ Neuschaufer, Al ... 1967
Nitzkowski, Monte ... 1991
O'Brien, Ron ... 1988
+ Papenguth, Richard ... 1986
+ Peppe, Mike ... 1966
+ Pinkston, Clarence ... 1966
+ Robinson, Tom ... 1965
Sakamoto, Soichi ... 1966
+ Sava, Charlie ... 1970
+ Schlueter, Walt ... 1978
Schubert, Mark ... 1997
Smith, Dick ... 1979
Stager, Gus ... 1982
Thornton, Nort ... 1995
Tinkham, Stan ... 1989

TENNIS

International Tennis Hall of Fame

Originally the National Tennis Hall of Fame. Established in 1953 by James Van Alen and sanctioned by the U.S. Tennis Association in 1954. Renamed the International Tennis Hall of Fame in 1976. **Address:** 194 Bellevue Ave., Newport, RI 02840. **Telephone:** (401) 849-3990.

Eligibility: Nominated players must be five years removed from being a "significant factor" in competitive tennis. Voting done by members of the international tennis media.

Class of 1996 (2): PLAYER— **Rosie Casals**. CONTRIBUTOR— **Dan Maskell**.

Members are listed with year of induction; (+) indicates deceased members.

Men

+ Adee, George ... 1964
+ Alexander, Fred ... 1961
+ Allison, Wilmer ... 1963
+ Alonso, Manuel ... 1977
+ Ashe, Arthur ... 1985
+ Behr, Karl ... 1969
Borg, Bjorn ... 1987
+ Borotra, Jean ... 1976
Bromwich, John ... 1984
+ Brookes, Norman ... 1977
+ Brugnon, Jacques ... 1976
Budge, Don ... 1964
+ Campbell, Oliver ... 1955
+ Chace, Malcolm ... 1961
+ Clark, Clarence ... 1983
+ Clark, Joseph ... 1955
+ Clothier, William ... 1956
+ Cochet, Henri ... 1976
Cooper, Ashley ... 1991
+ Crawford, Jack ... 1979
+ Doeg, John ... 1962
+ Doherty, Lawrence ... 1980
+ Doherty, Reginald ... 1980
Drobny, Jaroslav ... 1983
+ Dwight, James ... 1955
Emerson, Roy ... 1982
+ Etchebaster, Pierre ... 1978
Falkenburg, Bob ... 1974
Fraser, Neale ... 1984
+ Garland, Chuck ... 1969
+ Gonzales, Pancho ... 1968
+ Grant, Bryan (Bitsy) ... 1972
+ Griffin, Clarence ... 1970
+ Hackett, Harold ... 1961
Hewitt, Bob ... 1992
+ Hoad, Lew ... 1980
+ Hovey, Fred ... 1974
+ Hunt, Joe ... 1966
+ Hunter, Frank ... 1961
+ Johnston, Bill ... 1958
+ Jones, Perry ... 1970
Kodes, Jan ... 1990
Kramer, Jack ... 1968
Lacoste, Rene ... 1976
+ Larned, William ... 1956
Larsen, Art ... 1969
Laver, Rod ... 1981
+ Lott, George ... 1964
Mako, Gene ... 1973
+ McKinley, Chuck ... 1986
+ McLoughlin, Maurice ... 1957
McMillan, Frew ... 1992
McNeill, Don ... 1965
Mulloy, Gardnar ... 1972
+ Murray, Lindley ... 1958
+ Myrick, Julian ... 1963
Nastase, Ilie ... 1991
Newcombe, John ... 1986
+ Nielsen, Arthur ... 1971
Olmedo, Alex ... 1987
+ Osuna, Rafael ... 1979
Parker, Frank ... 1966
+ Patterson, Gerald ... 1989
Patty, Budge ... 1977
+ Perry, Fred ... 1975
+ Pettitt, Tom ... 1982
Pietrangeli, Nicola ... 1986
+ Quist, Adrian ... 1984
Ralston, Dennis ... 1987
+ Renshaw, Ernest ... 1983
+ Renshaw, William ... 1983
+ Richards, Vincent ... 1961
+ Riggs, Bobby ... 1967
Roche, Tony ... 1986
Rosewall, Ken ... 1980
Santana, Manuel ... 1984
Savitt, Dick ... 1976
Schroeder, Ted ... 1966
+ Sears, Richard ... 1955
Sedgman, Frank ... 1979
Segura, Pancho ... 1984
Seixas, Vic ... 1971
+ Shields, Frank ... 1964
+ Slocum, Henry ... 1955
Smith, Stan ... 1987
Stolle, Fred ... 1985
Talbert, Bill ... 1967
+ Tilden, Bill ... 1959
Trabert, Tony ... 1970
Van Ryn, John ... 1963
Vilas, Guillermo ... 1991
+ Vines, Ellsworth ... 1962
+ von Cramm, Gottfried ... 1977
+ Ward, Holcombe ... 1956
+ Washburn, Watson ... 1965
+ Whitman, Malcolm ... 1955
+ Wilding, Anthony ... 1978
+ Williams, Richard 2nd ... 1957
Wood, Sidney ... 1964
+ Wrenn, Robert ... 1955
+ Wright, Beals ... 1956

Women

+ Atkinson, Juliette ... 1974
Austin, Tracy ... 1992
+ Barger-Wallach, Maud ... 1958
Betz Addie, Pauline ... 1965
+ Bjurstedt Mallory, Molla ... 1958
Brough Clapp, Louise ... 1967
+ Browne, Mary ... 1957
Bueno, Maria ... 1978
+ Cahill, Mabel ... 1976
Casals, Rosie ... 1996
+ Connolly Brinker, Maureen ... 1968
+ Dod, Charlotte (Lottie) ... 1983
+ Douglass Chambers, Dorothy .. 1981
Evert, Chris ... 1995
Fry Irvin, Shirley ... 1970
Gibson, Althea ... 1971
Goolagong Cawley, Evonne ... 1988
+ Hansell, Ellen ... 1965
Hard, Darlene ... 1973
Hart, Doris ... 1969
Haydon Jones, Ann ... 1985
Heldman, Gladys ... 1979
+ Hotchkiss Wightman, Hazel ... 1957
Jacobs, Helen Hull ... 1962
King, Billie Jean ... 1987
+ Lenglen, Suzanne ... 1978
Mandlikova, Hana ... 1994
+ Marble, Alice ... 1964
+ McKane Godfree, Kitty ... 1978
+ Moore, Elisabeth ... 1971
Mortimer Barrett, Angela ... 1993
+ Nuthall Shoemaker, Betty ... 1977
Osborne duPont, Margaret ... 1967
Palfrey Danzig, Sarah ... 1963
+ Roosevelt, Ellen ... 1975
+ Round Little, Dorothy ... 1986
+ Ryan, Elizabeth ... 1972
+ Sears, Eleanora ... 1968
Smith Court, Margaret ... 1979

+ Sutton Bundy, May 1956
+ Townsend Toulmin, Bertha 1974
Wade, Virginia 1989
+ Wagner, Marie 1969
Wills Moody Roark, Helen 1959

Contributors

+ Baker, Lawrence Sr 1975
Chatrier, Philippe 1992
Collins, Bud 1994
Cullman, Joseph F. 3rd 1990
+ Danzig, Allison 1968
+ Davis, Dwight 1956
+ Gray, David..........................1985
+ Gustaf, V (King of Sweden).....1980
+ Hester, W.E. (Slew)................1981
+ Hopman, Harry 1978
Hunt, Lamar..........................1993
+ Laney, Al 1979
Martin, Alastair......................1973
Martin, William McC.............1982
Maskell, Dan 1976
+ Outerbridge, Mary.................1981
+ Pell, Theodore.......................1966
+ Tingay, Lance.........................1982
+ Tinling, Ted 1986
+ Van Alen, James 1965

TRACK & FIELD

National Track & Field Hall of Fame

Established in 1974 by the The Athletics Congress (now USA Track & Field). Originally located in Charleston, WV, the Hall moved to Indianapolis in 1983 and reopened at the Hoosier Dome in 1986. **Address:** One RCA Dome, Indianapolis, IN 46225. **Telephone:** (317) 261-0500.

Eligibility: Nominated athletes must be retired three years and coaches must have coached at least 20 years, if retired, or 35 years, if still coaching. Voting done by 800-member panel made up of Hall of Fame and USA Track & Field officials, Hall of Fame members, current U.S. champions and members of the Track & Field Writers of America.

Class of 1995 (6): MEN— **Don Lash** and **Marty Liquori**; WOMEN— **Valerie Brisco**, **Florence Griffith-Joyner** and **Louise Ritter**; COACH— **Mel Rosen**

Members are listed with year of induction; (+) indicates deceased members.

Men

+ Albritton, Dave 1980
Ashenfelter, Horace 1975
+ Bausch, James 1979
Beamon, Bob 1977
Beatty, Jim 1990
Bell, Greg.............................1988
+ Boeckmann, Dee 1976
Boston, Ralph.........................1974
+ Calhoun, Lee..........................1974
Campbell, Milt 1989
+ Clark, Ellery..........................1991
Connolly, Harold 1984
Courtney, Tom.......................1978
+ Cunningham, Glenn 1974
+ Curtis, William.......................1979
Davenport, Willie....................1982
Davis, Glenn..........................1974
Davis, Harold 1974
Dillard, Harrison 1974
Dumas, Charley 1990
Evans, Lee 1983
Ewell, Barney.........................1986
+ Ewry, Ray 1974
+ Flanagan, John 1975
Fosbury, Dick.........................1981
+ Gordien, Fortune....................1979
Greene, Charlie 1992
+ Hahn, Archie 1983
+ Hardin, Glenn........................1978
Hayes, Bob 1976
Held, Bud 1987
Hines, Jim.............................1979
+ Houser, Bud 1979
+ Hubbard, DeHart 1979
Jenkins, Charlie......................1992
Jenner, Bruce 1980
+ Johnson, Cornelius 1994
Johnson, Rafer 1974
Jones, Hayes..........................1976
Kelley, John 1980
Kiviat, Abel...........................1985
+ Kraenzlein, Alvin 1974
Laird, Ron.............................1986
+ Lash, Don 1995
Liquori, Marty........................1995
Mathias, Bob 1974
Matson, Randy........................1984
+ Meredith, Ted........................1982
+ Metcalfe, Ralph......................1975
Milburn, Rod 1993
Mills, Billy.............................1976
Moore, Tom 1988
Morrow, Bobby.......................1975
+ Mortensen, Jess......................1992
Moses, Edwin 1994
+ Myers, Lawrence 1974
O'Brien, Parry 1974
Oerter, Al 1974
+ Osborn, Harold 1974
+ Owens, Jesse 1974
+ Paddock, Charley...................1976
Patton, Mel 1985
Peacock, Eulace 1987
+ Prefontaine, Steve..................1976
+ Ray, Joie...............................1976
+ Rice, Greg 1977
Richards, Bob 1975
+ Rose, Ralph 1976
Ryun, Jim..............................1980
+ Scholz, Jackson......................1977
Schul, Bob 1991
Seagren, Bob..........................1986
+ Sheppard, Mel.......................1976
+ Sheridan, Martin....................1988
Shorter, Frank........................1989
Sime, Dave............................1981
+ Simpson, Robert.....................1974
Smith, Tommie 1978
+ Stanfield, Andy 1977
Steers, Les.............................1974
Thomas, John.........................1985
+ Thomson, Earl 1977
+ Thorpe, Jim...........................1975
+ Tolan, Eddie..........................1982
Toomey, Bill...........................1975
+ Towns, Forrest (Spec) 1976
Warmerdam, Cornelius 1974
Whitfield, Mal........................1974
Wilkins, Mac 1993
+ Williams, Archie 1992
Wohlhuter, Rick......................1990
Woodruff, John.......................1978
Wottle, Dave..........................1982
+ Wykoff, Frank........................1977
Young, George 1981

Women

Brisco, Valerie........................1995
Coachman, Alice 1975
+ Copeland, Lillian 1994
+ Didrikson, Babe 1974
Faggs, Mae 1976
Ferrell, Barbara.......................1988
Griffith Joyner, Florence..........1995
+ Hall Adams, Evelyne 1988
Heritage, Doris Brown 1990
+ Jackson, Nell 1989
Manning, Madeline................1984
McDaniel, Mildred 1983
McGuire, Edith.......................1979
Ritter, Louise..........................1995
Robinson, Betty 1977
+ Rudolph, Wilma.....................1974
+ Schmidt, Kate 1994
Shiley Newhouse, Jean...........1993
+ Stephens, Helen 1975
Tyus, Wyomia........................1980
+ Walsh, Stella 1975
Watson, Martha......................1987
White, Willye 1981

Coaches

+ Baskin, Weems 1982
+ Beard, Percy 1981
Bell, Sam 1992
Botts, Tom 1983
Bowerman, Bill.......................1981
Bush, Jim 1987
+ Cromwell, Dean 1974
+ Doherty, Ken.........................1976
Easton, Bill............................1975
+ Elliott, Jumbo 1981
+ Giegengack, Bob 1978
+ Hamilton, Brutus....................1974

Track & Field Hall of Fame (Cont.)

Coaches

+ Haydon, Ted 1975
+ Hayes, Billy 1976
+ Haylett, Ward 1979
+ Higgins, Ralph 1982
+ Hillman, Harry 1976
+ Hurt, Edward 1975
+ Hutsell, Wilbur 1977
+ Jones, Thomas 1977
Jordan, Payton 1982
+ Littlefield, Clyde 1981
+ Moakley, Jack 1988
+ Murphy, Michael 1974
Rosen, Mel 1995
+ Snyder, Larry 1978
Temple, Ed 1989
+ Templeton, Dink 1976
Walker, LeRoy 1983
+ Wilt, Fred 1981
+ Winter, Bud 1985
Wright, Stan 1993
+ Yancy, Joseph 1984

Contributors

+ Abramson, Jesse 1981
Andersen, Roxanne 1991
+ Bakjian, Andy 1986
+ Brundage, Avery 1974
+ Ferris, Dan 1974
+ Griffith, John 1979
+ Lebow, Fred 1994
+ Nelson, Bert 1991
Nelson, Cordner 1988
+ Sullivan, James 1977

WOMEN

International Women's Sports Hall of Fame

Established in 1980 by the Women's Sports Foundation. **Address:** Women's Sports Foundation, Eisenhower Park, East Meadow, NY 11554. **Telephone:** (516) 542-4700.

Eligibility: Nominees' achievements and commitment to the development of women's sports must be internationally recognized. Athletes are elected in two categories—Pioneer (before 1960) and Contemporary (since 1960). Members are divided below by sport for the sake of easy reference; (*) indicates member inducted in Pioneer category. Coaching nominees must have coached at least 10 years.

Class of 1996 (3): PIONEER—**Florence Chadwick** (distance swimming) and sprinter **Aeriwentha Mae Faggs Star** (track & field). COACHES—**Diana Holum** (speed skating and cycling).

Members are listed with year of induction; (+) indicates deceased members.

Alpine Skiing

Cranz, Christl* 1991
Lawrence, Andrea Mead* 1983
Moser-Pröll, Annemarie 1982

Auto Racing

Guthrie, Janet 1980

Aviation

+ Coleman, Bessie* 1992
+ Earhart, Amelia* 1980
+ Marvingt, Marie* 1987

Badminton

Hashman, Judy Devlin* 1995

Baseball

Stone, Toni* 1993

Basketball

Meyers, Ann 1985
Miller, Cheryl 1991

Bowling

Ladewig, Marion* 1984

Cycling

Carpenter Phinney, Connie 1990

Diving

King, Micki 1983
McCormick, Pat* 1984
Riggin, Aileen* 1988

Equestrian

Hartel, Lis 1994

Fencing

Schacherer-Elek, Ilona* 1989

Figure Skating

Albright, Tenley* 1983
+ Blanchard, Theresa Weld* 1989
Fleming, Peggy 1981
Heiss Jenkins, Carol* 1992
+ Henie, Sonja* 1982
Protopopov, Ludmila 1992
Rodnina, Irena 1988

Golf

Berg, Patty* 1980
Carner, JoAnne 1987
Hicks, Betty* 1995
Mann, Carol 1982
Rawls, Betsy* 1986
Suggs, Louise* 1987
+ Vare, Glenna Collett* 1981
Whitworth, Kathy 1984
Wright, Mickey 1981

Golf/Track & Field

+ Zaharias, Babe Didrikson* 1980

Gymnastics

Caslavska, Vera 1991
Comaneci, Nadia 1990
Korbut, Olga 1982
Latynina, Larissa* 1985
Retton, Mary Lou 1993
Tourischeva, Lyudmila 1987

Shooting

Murdock, Margaret 1988

Softball

Joyce, Joan 1989

Speed Skating

+ Klein Outland, Kit* 1993
Young, Sheila 1981

Swimming

Caulkins, Tracy 1986
+ Chadwick, Florence* 1996
Curtis Cuneo, Ann* 1985
de Varona, Donna 1983
Ederle, Gertrude* 1980
Fraser, Dawn 1985
Holm, Eleanor* 1980
Meagher, Mary T. 1993
Meyer-Reyes, Debbie 1987

Tennis

+ Connolly, Maureen* 1987
+ Dod, Charlotte (Lottie)* 1986
Evert, Chris 1981
Gibson, Althea* 1980
Goolagong Cawley, Evonne 1989
+ Hotchkiss Wightman, Hazel* 1986
King, Billie Jean 1980
+ Lenglen, Suzanne* 1984
Navratilova, Martina 1984
+ Sears, Eleanora* 1984
Smith Court, Margaret 1986

Track & Field

Blankers-Koen, Fanny* 1982
Cheng, Chi 1994
Coachman Davis, Alice* 1991
Faggs Star, Aeriwentha Mae* 1996
Manning Mims, Madeline 1987
+ Rudolph, Wilma 1980
+ Stephens, Helen* 1983
Szewinska, Irena 1992
Tyus, Wyomia 1981
Waitz, Grete 1995
White, Willye 1988

Volleyball

+ Hyman, Flo 1986

Water Skiing

McGuire, Willa Worthington* 1990

Orienteering

Kringstad, Annichen 1995

Coaches

Applebee, Constance 1991
Backus, Sharron 1993
Conradt, Judy 1995
Grossfeld, Muriel 1991
Holum, Diana 1996
Jacket, Barbara 1995
+ Jackson, Nell 1990
Kanakogi, Rusty 1994
Summitt, Pat Head 1990
+ Wade, Margaret 1992

Wide World Photos

Pitching legend **Nolan Ryan** salutes the crowd at a ceremony to retire the number 34 he wore for four years with the Texas Rangers on Sept. 15 in Arlington, Tex. Two weeks later the Houston Astros would honor him similarly.

RETIRED NUMBERS

Major League Baseball

The New York Yankees have retired the most uniform numbers (13) in the Major Leagues; followed by Pittsburgh and the Brooklyn/Los Angeles Dodgers (8), the Chicago White Sox (7), the New York/San Francisco Giants (6) and the St. Louis Cardinals (5). **Nolan Ryan** has had his number retired by three teams—#34 by Texas and Houston and #30 by California. Four players and a manager have had their numbers retired by two teams: **Hank Aaron**—#44 by the Boston/ Milwaukee/Atlanta Braves and the Milwaukee Brewers; **Rod Carew**—#29 by Minnesota and California; **Rollie Fingers**—#34 by Milwaukee and Oakland; **Frank Robinson**—#20 by Cincinnati and Baltimore; and **Casey Stengel**—#37 by the New York Yankees and New York Mets.

Numbers retired in 1996 (3): HOUSTON—#34 worn by pitcher **Nolan Ryan** (1980-88 with Astros); ST. LOUIS—#2 worn by Hall of Fame 2nd baseman **Red Schoendienst** (1945-56, 61-63 with Cardinals); TEXAS—#34 worn by pitcher **Nolan Ryan** (1989-93 with Rangers).

American League

Two AL teams—the Seattle Mariners and Toronto Blue Jays—have not retired any numbers. Note, Baltimore unretired Eddie Murray's #33, when he returned to the team on July 22.

Baltimore
4 Earl Weaver
5 Brooks Robinson
20 Frank Robinson
22 Jim Palmer
33 Eddie Murray

Boston Red Sox
1 Bobby Doerr
4 Joe Cronin
8 Carl Yastrzemski
9 Ted Williams

California Angels
26 Gene Autry
29 Rod Carew
30 Nolan Ryan
50 Jimmie Reese

Chicago White Sox
2 Nellie Fox
3 Harold Baines
4 Luke Appling
9 Minnie Minoso
11 Luis Aparicio
16 Ted Lyons
19 Billy Pierce

Cleveland Indians
3 Earl Averill
5 Lou Boudreau
14 Larry Doby
18 Mel Harder
19 Bob Feller

Detroit Tigers
2 Charley Gehringer
5 Hank Greenberg
6 Al Kaline

Kansas City Royals
5 George Brett
10 Dick Howser
20 Frank White

Milwaukee Brewers
19 Robin Yount
34 Rollie Fingers
44 Hank Aaron

Minnesota Twins
3 Harmon Killebrew
6 Tony Oliva
14 Kent Hrbek
29 Rod Carew

New York Yankees
1 Billy Martin
3 Babe Ruth
4 Lou Gehrig
5 Joe DiMaggio
7 Mickey Mantle
8 Yogi Berra & Bill Dickey
9 Roger Maris
10 Phil Rizzuto
15 Thurman Munson
16 Whitey Ford
32 Elston Howard
37 Casey Stengel
44 Reggie Jackson

Oakland Athletics
27 Catfish Hunter
34 Rollie Fingers

Texas Rangers
34 Nolan Ryan

Retired Numbers (Cont.)

National League

San Francisco has honored former NY Giants Christy Mathewson and John McGraw even though they played before numbers were worn.

Atlanta Braves
3 Dale Murphy
21 Warren Spahn
35 Phil Niekro
41 Eddie Mathews
44 Hank Aaron

Chicago Cubs
14 Ernie Banks
26 Billy Williams

Cincinnati Reds
1 Fred Hutchinson
5 Johnny Bench

Houston Astros
25 Jose Cruz
32 Jim Umbricht
33 Mike Scott
34 Nolan Ryan
40 Don Wilson

Los Angeles Dodgers
1 Pee Wee Reese
4 Duke Snider
19 Jim Gilliam
24 Walter Alston
32 Sandy Koufax
39 Roy Campanella
42 Jackie Robinson
53 Don Drysdale

Montreal Expos
8 Gary Carter
10 Rusty Staub

New York Mets
14 Gil Hodges
37 Casey Stengel
41 Tom Seaver

Philadelphia Phillies
1 Richie Ashburn
20 Mike Schmidt
32 Steve Carlton
36 Robin Roberts

Pittsburgh Pirates
1 Billy Meyer
4 Ralph Kiner
8 Willie Stargell
9 Bill Mazeroski
20 Pie Traynor
21 Roberto Clemente
33 Honus Wagner
40 Danny Murtaugh

St. Louis Cardinals
1 Ozzie Smith
2 Red Schoendienst
6 Stan Musial
14 Ken Boyer
17 Dizzy Dean
20 Lou Brock
45 Bob Gibson
85 August (Gussie) Busch

San Diego Padres
6 Steve Garvey

San Francisco Giants
3 Bill Terry
4 Mel Ott
11 Carl Hubbell
24 Willie Mays
27 Juan Marichal
44 Willie McCovey

National Basketball Association

Boston has retired the most numbers (19) in the NBA; followed by Portland (8); the New York Knicks and the KC/Sacramento Kings have (7); Milwaukee, the Rochester/Cincinnati Royals and LA have (6); Detroit and the Syracuse Nats/Philadelphia 76ers (5). Six players have had their numbers retired by two teams: **Kareem Abdul-Jabbar**–#33 by LA Lakers and Milwaukee; **Wilt Chamberlain**—#13 by the Los Angeles Lakers and Philadelphia; **Julius Erving**—#6 by Philadelphia and #32 by New Jersey; **Bob Lanier**–#16 by Detroit and Milwaukee; **Oscar Robertson**—#1 by Milwaukee and #14 by Sacramento; and **Nate Thurmond**—#42 by Cleveland and Golden State.

Numbers retired in 1996 (9): CHARLOTTE—#6 to honor their fans, the **"sixth man"**; DETROIT—#11 worn by guard **Isiah Thomas** (1981-94 with Pistons); LOS ANGELES LAKERS—#42 worn by forward **James Worthy** (1982-94 with Lakers); PORTLAND—#1 for longtime owner **Larry Weinberg** (1970-88); SACRAMENTO—#1 worn by guard **Nate Archibald** (1970-76 with the Cincinnati Royals and K.C./Omaha Kings); SEATTLE—#43 worn by center **Jack Sikma** (1977-86 with SuperSonics) and the microphone of radio/TV announcer **Bob Blackburn** (1967-86); UTAH—#35 worn by guard **Darrell Griffith** (1980-91 with Jazz) and #53 worn by center **Mark Eaton** (1982-94 with Jazz).

Eastern Conference

Three Eastern teams—the Miami Heat, Orlando Magic, and Toronto Raptors—have not retired any numbers.

Boston Celtics
1 Walter A. Brown
2 Red Auerbach
3 Dennis Johnson
6 Bill Russell
10 Jo Jo White
14 Bob Cousy
15 Tom Heinsohn
16 Tom (Satch) Sanders
17 John Havlicek
18 Dave Cowens
19 Don Nelson
21 Bill Sharman
22 Ed Macauley
23 Frank Ramsey
24 Sam Jones
25 K.C. Jones
32 Kevin McHale
33 Larry Bird
35 Reggie Lewis
Loscy Jim Loscutoff
Radio mic. Johnny Most

Atlanta Hawks
9 Bob Pettit
23 Lou Hudson

Charlotte Hornets
6 Fans ("Sixth Man")

Chicago Bulls
4 Jerry Sloan
10 Bob Love
23 Michael Jordan

Cleveland Cavaliers
7 Bingo Smith
22 Larry Nance
34 Austin Carr
42 Nate Thurmond

Detroit Pistons
11 IsiahThomas
15 Vinnie Johnson
16 Bob Lanier
21 Dave Bing
40 Bill Laimbeer

Indiana Pacers
30 George McGinnis
34 Mel Daniels
35 Roger Brown

Milwaukee Bucks
1 Oscar Robertson
2 Junior Bridgeman
4 Sidney Moncrief
14 Jon McGlocklin
16 Bob Lanier
32 Brian Winters
33 Kareem Abdul-Jabbar

New York Knicks
10 Walt Frazier
12 Dick Barnett
15 Dick McGuire
& Earl Monroe
19 Willis Reed
22 Dave DeBusschere
24 Bill Bradley
613 Red Holzman

New Jersey Nets
3 Drazen Petrovic
4 Wendell Ladner
23 John Williamson
25 Bill Melchionni
32 Julius Erving

Philadelphia 76ers
6 Julius Erving
10 Maurice Cheeks
13 Wilt Chamberlain
15 Hal Greer
24 Bobby Jones
32 Billy Cunningham
P.A. mic. Dave Zinkoff

Washington Bullets
11 Elvin Hayes
25 Gus Johnson
41 Wes Unseld

Western Conference

Three Western teams—the Los Angeles Clippers, Minnesota Timberwolves, and Vancouver Grizzlies—have not retired any numbers.

Dallas Mavericks
15 Brad Davis

Denver Nuggets
2 Alex English
33 David Thompson
40 Byron Beck
44 Dan Issel

Golden St. Warriors
14 Tom Meschery
16 Al Attles
24 Rick Barry
42 Nate Thurmond

Houston Rockets
23 Calvin Murphy
45 Rudy Tomjanovich

Los Angeles Lakers
13 Wilt Chamberlain
22 Elgin Baylor
32 Magic Johnson
33 Kareem Abdul-Jabbar
42 James Worthy
44 Jerry West

Phoenix Suns
5 Dick Van Arsdale
6 Walter Davis
33 Alvan Adams
42 Connie Hawkins
44 Paul Westphal

Portland Trail Blazers
1 Larry Weinberg
13 Dave Twardzik
15 Larry Steele
20 Maurice Lucas
32 Bill Walton
36 Lloyd Neal
45 Geoff Petrie
77 Jack Ramsay

Sacramento Kings
1 Nate Archibald
6 Fans ("Sixth Man")
11 Bob Davies
12 Maurice Stokes
14 Oscar Robertson
27 Jack Twyman
44 Sam Lacey

San Antonio Spurs
13 James Silas
44 George Gervin

Seattle SuperSonics
19 Lenny Wilkens
32 Fred Brown
43 Jack Sikma
P.A. mic. Bob Blackburn

Utah Jazz
1 Frank Layden
7 Pete Maravich
35 Darrell Griffith
53 Mark Eaton

National Football League

The Chicago Bears have retired the most uniform numbers (13) in the NFL; followed by the New York Giants (9); the Dallas Texans/Kansas City Chiefs (8); the Baltimore-Indianapolis Colts, the Boston-New England Patriots, San Francisco (7); Detroit (6); Cleveland and Philadelphia (5). No player has ever had his number retired by more than one NFL team.

Numbers retired in 1996 (2): NEW ENGLAND—#14 worn by quarterback **Steve Grogan** and #40 worn by defensive back **Mike Haynes**.

AFC

Five AFC teams—the Baltimore Ravens, Buffalo Bills, Oakland Raiders, Pittsburgh Steelers and Jacksonville Jaguars—have not retired any numbers. The Cleveland Browns have retired five numbers— #14 Otto Graham, #32 Jim Brown, #45 Ernie Davis, #46 Don Fleming and #76 Lou Groza.

Cincinnati Bengals
54 Bob Johnson

Denver Broncos
18 Frank Tripucka
44 Floyd Little

Houston Oilers
34 Earl Campbell
43 Jim Norton
63 Mike Munchak
65 Elvin Bethea

Indianapolis Colts
19 Johnny Unitas
22 Buddy Young
24 Lenny Moore
70 Art Donovan
77 Jim Parker
82 Raymond Berry
89 Gino Marchetti

Kansas City Chiefs
3 Jan Stenerud
16 Len Dawson
28 Abner Haynes
33 Stone Johnson
36 Mack Lee Hill
63 Willie Lanier
78 Bobby Bell
86 Buck Buchanan

Miami Dolphins
12 Bob Griese

New England Patriots
14 Steve Grogan
20 Gino Cappelletti
40 Mike Haynes
57 Steve Nelson
73 John Hannah
79 Jim Hunt
89 Bob Dee

New York Jets
12 Joe Namath
13 Don Maynard

San Diego Chargers
14 Dan Fouts

Seattle Seahawks
12 Fans ("12th Man")
80 Steve Largent

NFC

Atlanta, Dallas and Carolina Panthers are the only NFC teams that haven't officially retired any numbers. The Falcons haven't issued uniforms #10 (Steve Bartowski), #31 (William Andrews) and #60 (Tommy Nobis) since those players retired; while the Cowboys have a "Ring of Honor" at Texas Stadium that includes nine players and one coach—Tony Dorsett, Chuck Howley, Lee Roy Jordan, Tom Landry, Bob Lilly, Don Meredith, Don Perkins, Mel Renfro, Roger Staubach and Randy White.

Arizona Cardinals
8 Larry Wilson
77 Stan Mauldin
88 J.V. Cain
99 Marshall Goldberg

Chicago Bears
3 Bronko Nagurski
5 George McAfee
7 George Halas
28 Willie Galimore
34 Walter Payton
40 Gale Sayers
41 Brian Piccolo
42 Sid Luckman
51 Dick Butkus
56 Bill Hewitt
61 Bill George
66 Bulldog Turner
77 Red Grange

Detroit Lions
7 Dutch Clark
22 Bobby Layne
37 Doak Walker
56 Joe Schmidt
85 Chuck Hughes
88 Charlie Sanders

Green Bay Packers
3 Tony Canadeo
14 Don Hutson
15 Bart Starr
66 Ray Nitschke

Minnesota Vikings
10 Fran Tarkenton
88 Alan Page

New Orleans Saints
31 Jim Taylor
81 Doug Atkins

New York Giants
1 Ray Flaherty
7 Mel Hein
11 Phil Simms
14 Y.A. Tittle
32 Al Blozis
40 Joe Morrison
42 Charlie Conerly
50 Ken Strong
56 Lawrence Taylor

Philadelphia Eagles
15 Steve Van Buren
40 Tom Brookshier
44 Pete Retzlaff
60 Chuck Bednarik
70 Al Wistert
99 Jerome Brown

St. Louis Rams
7 Bob Waterfield
74 Merlin Olsen

San Francisco 49ers
12 John Brodie
34 Joe Perry
37 Jimmy Johnson
39 Hugh McElhenny
70 Charlie Krueger
73 Lou Nomellini
87 Dwight Clark

Tampa Bay Bucs
63 Lee Roy Selmon

Wash. Redskins
33 Sammy Baugh

Retired Numbers (Cont.)

National Hockey League

The Boston Bruins have retired the most uniform numbers (7) in the NHL; followed by Montreal (6); Detroit (5); Buffalo, Chicago, N.Y. Islanders, St. Louis and Philadelphia (4); and the Boston-New England-Hartford Whalers, Los Angeles Kings and Quebec Nordiques-Colorado Avalanche (3). Two players have had their numbers retired by two teams: Gordie Howe—#9 by Detroit and Hartford; and Bobby Hull—#9 by Chicago and Winnipeg.

Eastern Conference

The New Jersey Devils, Ottawa Senators, Tampa Bay Lightning and Florida Panthers are the only Eastern teams that have not retired a number.

Boston Bruins
2 Eddie Shore
3 Lionel Hitchman
4 Bobby Orr
5 Dit Clapper
7 Phil Esposito
9 John Bucyk
15 Milt Schmidt

Buffalo Sabres
2 Tim Horton
7 Rick Martin
11 Gilbert Perreault
14 Rene Robert

Hartford Whalers
2 Rick Ley
9 Gordie Howe
19 John McKenzie

Montreal Canadiens
1 Jacques Plante
2 Doug Harvey
4 Jean Beliveau
7 Howie Morenz
9 Maurice Richard
10 Guy Lafleur
16 Henri Richard

New York Islanders
5 Denis Potvin
22 Mike Bossy
23 Bob Nystrom
31 Billy Smith

New York Rangers
1 Eddie Giacomin
7 Rod Gilbert

Philadelphia Flyers
1 Bernie Parent
4 Barry Ashbee
7 Bill Barber
16 Bobby Clarke

Pittsburgh Penguins
21 Michel Briere

Washington Capitals
7 Yvon Labre

Western Conference

The Colorado Avalanches, San Jose Sharks and Mighty Ducks of Anaheim are the only Western teams that have not retired a number. Note, the Quebec Nordiques retired the numbers of J.C. Tremblay (3), Marc Tardif (8) and Michel Goulet (16) but these numbers have been worn since the team moved to Colorado.

Calgary Flames
9 Lanny McDonald

Chicago Blackhawks
1 Glenn Hall
9 Bobby Hull
21 Stan Mikita
35 Tony Esposito

Dallas Stars
8 Bill Goldsworthy
19 Bill Masterton

Detroit Red Wings
1 Terry Sawchuk
7 Ted Lindsay
9 Gordie Howe
10 Alex Delvecchio
12 Sid Abel

Edmonton Oilers
3 Al Hamilton

Los Angeles Kings
16 Marcel Dionne
18 Dave Taylor
30 Rogie Vachon

Phoenix Coyotes
9 Bobby Hull
25 Thomas Steen

St. Louis Blues
3 Bob Gassoff
8 Barclay Plager
11 Brian Sutter
24 Bernie Federko

Toronto Maple Leafs
5 Bill Barilko
6 Ace Bailey

Vancouver Canucks
12 Stan Smyl

AWARDS

Sports Illustrated Sportsman of the Year

Selected annually by the editors of *Sports Illustrated* magazine since 1954.

Year	
1954	**Roger Bannister**, track
1955	**Johnny Podres**, baseball
1956	**Bobby Morrow**, track
1957	**Stan Musial**, baseball
1958	**Rafer Johnson**, track
1959	**Ingemar Johansson**, boxing
1960	**Arnold Palmer**, golf
1961	**Jerry Lucas**, basketball
1962	**Terry Baker**, football
1963	**Pete Rozelle**, pro football
1964	**Ken Venturi**, golf
1965	**Sandy Koufax**, baseball
1966	**Jim Ryun**, track
1967	**Carl Yastrzemski**, baseball
1968	**Bill Russell**, basketball
1969	**Tom Seaver**, baseball
1970	**Bobby Orr**, hockey
1971	**Lee Trevino**, golf
1972	**Billie Jean King**, tennis & **John Wooden**, basketball
1973	**Jackie Stewart**, auto racing
1974	**Muhammad Ali**, boxing
1975	**Pete Rose**, baseball
1976	**Chris Evert**, tennis
1977	**Steve Cauthen**, horse racing
1978	**Jack Nicklaus**, golf
1979	**Terry Bradshaw**, football & **Willie Stargell**, baseball
1980	**U.S. Olympic hockey team**
1981	**Sugar Ray Leonard**, boxing
1982	**Wayne Gretzky**, hockey
1983	**Mary Decker**, track
1984	**Mary Lou Retton**, gymnastics & **Edwin Moses**, track
1985	**Kareem Abdul-Jabbar**, basketball
1986	**Joe Paterno**, football
1987	**"8 Athletes Who Care"** **Bob Bourne**, hockey; **Kip Keino**, track; **Judi Brown King**, track; **Dale Murphy**, baseball; **Chip Rives**, football; **Patty Sheehan**, golf; **Rory Sparrow**, basketball; **Reggie Williams**, football
1988	**Orel Hershiser**, baseball
1989	**Greg LeMond**, cycling
1990	**Joe Montana**, football
1991	**Michael Jordan**, basketball
1992	**Arthur Ashe**, tennis
1993	**Don Shula**, football
1994	**Johan Olav Koss**, sp. skating & **Bonnie Blair**, sp. skating
1995	**Cal Ripken Jr.**, baseball

Associated Press Athletes of the Year

Selected annually by AP newspaper sports editors since 1931.

Male

Baltimore Oriole shortstop Cal Ripken Jr., who broke Lou Gehrig's streak on Sept. 6 when he played in his 2,131st consecutive game, was named the top male athlete of 1995 by Associated Press sports editors. Ripken entered the lineup for the Orioles on May 30, 1982 and has yet to leave it.

The Top 10 vote-getters (first place votes in parentheses): 1. **Cal Ripken Jr.**, baseball (192), 1110 points; 2. **Greg Maddux**, baseball (47), 501 pts; 3. **Hakeem Olajuwon**, pro basketball (19), 262 pts; 4. **Jeff Gordon**, auto racing (7), 147 pts; 5. **Brett Favre**, pro football (6), 82 pts; 6. **Jerry Rice**, pro football (2), 80 pts; 7. **Pete Sampras**, tennis (2), 79 pts; 8. **Dan Marino**, pro football (5), 73 pts; 9. **Eddie George**, college football, 67 pts, 10. **Michael Johnson**, track (6), 62 pts.

Multiple winners: Michael Jordan (3); Don Budge, Sandy Koufax, Carl Lewis, Joe Montana and Byron Nelson (2).

Year
1931 **Pepper Martin**, baseball
1932 **Gene Sarazen**, golf
1933 **Carl Hubbell**, baseball
1934 **Dizzy Dean**, baseball
1935 **Joe Louis**, boxing
1936 **Jesse Owens**, track
1937 **Don Budge**, tennis
1938 **Don Budge**, tennis
1939 **Nile Kinnick**, college football
1940 **Tom Harmon**, college football
1941 **Joe DiMaggio**, baseball
1942 **Frank Sinkwich**, college football
1943 **Gunder Haegg**, track
1944 **Byron Nelson**, golf
1945 **Byron Nelson**, golf
1946 **Glenn Davis**, college football
1947 **Johnny Lujack**, college football
1948 **Lou Boudreau**, baseball
1949 **Leon Hart**, college football
1950 **Jim Konstanty**, baseball
1951 **Dick Kazmaier**, college football
1952 **Bob Mathias**, track

Year
1953 **Ben Hogan**, golf
1954 **Willie Mays**, baseball
1955 **Hopalong Cassady**, col. football
1956 **Mickey Mantle**, baseball
1957 **Ted Williams**, baseball
1958 **Herb Elliott**, track
1959 **Ingemar Johansson**, boxing
1960 **Rafer Johnson**, track
1961 **Roger Maris**, baseball
1962 **Maury Wills**, baseball
1963 **Sandy Koufax**, baseball
1964 **Don Schollander**, swimming
1965 **Sandy Koufax**, baseball
1966 **Frank Robinson**, baseball
1967 **Carl Yastrzemski**, baseball
1968 **Denny McLain**, baseball
1969 **Tom Seaver**, baseball
1970 **George Blanda**, pro football
1971 **Lee Trevino**, golf
1972 **Mark Spitz**, swimming
1973 **O.J. Simpson**, pro football
1974 **Muhammad Ali**, boxing

Year
1975 **Fred Lynn**, baseball
1976 **Bruce Jenner**, track
1977 **Steve Cauthen**, horse racing
1978 **Ron Guidry**, baseball
1979 **Willie Stargell**, baseball
1980 **U.S. Olympic hockey team**
1981 **John McEnroe**, tennis
1982 **Wayne Gretzky**, hockey
1983 **Carl Lewis**, track
1984 **Carl Lewis**, track
1985 **Dwight Gooden**, baseball
1986 **Larry Bird**, pro basketball
1987 **Ben Johnson**, track
1988 **Orel Hershiser**, baseball
1989 **Joe Montana**, pro football
1990 **Joe Montana**, pro football
1991 **Michael Jordan**, pro basketball
1992 **Michael Jordan**, pro basketball
1993 **Michael Jordan**, pro basketball
1994 **George Foreman**, boxing
1995 **Cal Ripken Jr.**, baseball

Female

Senior forward Rebecca Lobo, who led the Connecticut Huskies to an undefeated season and the national championship, was named the top female athlete of 1995 by Associated Press sports editors. Lobo scored a NCAA Championship game-high 17 points in UConn's 70-64 win over Tennessee and was the unanimous choice for player of the year.

The Top 10 vote-getters (first place votes in parentheses): 1. **Rebecca Lobo**, college basketball (94), 774 points; 2. **Monica Seles**, tennis (86), 600 points; 3. **Steffi Graf**, tennis (43), 379 points; 4. **Bonnie Blair**, speed skating (34), 282 pts; 5. **Picabo Street**, skiing (23), 260 pts; 6. **Annika Sorenstam**, golf (13), 130 pts; 7. **Gwen Torrence**, track (6), 100 pts; 8. **Mia Hamm**, soccer (4) and **Sheryl Swoopes**, basketball (2), 55 pts; 10. **Shannon Miller**, gymnastics (3), 44 pts.

Multiple winners: Babe Didrikson Zaharias (6); Chris Evert (4); Patty Berg and Maureen Connolly (3); Tracy Austin, Althea Gibson, Billie Jean King, Nancy Lopez, Alice Marble, Martina Navratilova, Wilma Rudolph, Monica Seles, Kathy Whitworth and Mickey Wright (2).

Year
1931 **Helene Madison**, swimming
1932 **Babe Didrikson**, track
1933 **Helen Jacobs**, tennis
1934 **Virginia Van Wie**, golf
1935 **Helen Wills Moody**, tennis
1936 **Helen Stephens**, track
1937 **Katherine Rawls**, swimming
1938 **Patty Berg**, golf
1939 **Alice Marble**, tennis
1940 **Alice Marble**, tennis
1941 **Betty Hicks Newell**, golf
1942 **Gloria Callen**, swimming
1943 **Patty Berg**, golf
1944 **Ann Curtis**, swimming
1945 **Babe Didrikson Zaharias**, golf
1946 **Babe Didrikson Zaharias**, golf
1947 **Babe Didrikson Zaharias**, golf
1948 **Fanny Blankers-Koen**, track
1949 **Marlene Bauer**, golf
1950 **Babe Didrikson Zaharias**, golf
1951 **Maureen Connolly**, tennis
1952 **Maureen Connolly**, tennis

Year
1953 **Maureen Connolly**, tennis
1954 **Babe Didrikson Zaharias**, golf
1955 **Patty Berg**, golf
1956 **Pat McCormick**, diving
1957 **Althea Gibson**, tennis
1958 **Althea Gibson**, tennis
1959 **Maria Bueno**, tennis
1960 **Wilma Rudolph**, track
1961 **Wilma Rudolph**, track
1962 **Dawn Fraser**, swimming
1963 **Mickey Wright**, golf
1964 **Mickey Wright**, golf
1965 **Kathy Whitworth**, golf
1966 **Kathy Whitworth**, golf
1967 **Billie Jean King**, tennis
1968 **Peggy Fleming**, skating
1969 **Debbie Meyer**, swimming
1970 **Chi Cheng**, track
1971 **Evonne Goolagong**, tennis
1972 **Olga Korbut**, gymnastics
1973 **Billie Jean King**, tennis
1974 **Chris Evert**, tennis

Year
1975 **Chris Evert**, tennis
1976 **Nadia Comaneci**, gymnastics
1977 **Chris Evert**, tennis
1978 **Nancy Lopez**, golf
1979 **Tracy Austin**, tennis
1980 **Chris Evert Lloyd**, tennis
1981 **Tracy Austin**, tennis
1982 **Mary Decker Tabb**, track
1983 **Martina Navratilova**, tennis
1984 **Mary Lou Retton**, gymnastics
1985 **Nancy Lopez**, golf
1986 **Martina Navratilova**, tennis
1987 **Jackie Joyner-Kersee**, track
1988 **Florence Griffith Joyner**, track
1989 **Steffi Graf**, tennis
1990 **Beth Daniel**, golf
1991 **Monica Seles**, tennis
1992 **Monica Seles**, tennis
1993 **Sheryl Swoopes**, basketball
1994 **Bonnie Blair**, speed skating
1995 **Rebecca Lobo**, col. basketball

UPI International Athletes of the Year

Selected annually by United Press International's European newspaper sports editors since 1974.

Male

Multiple winners: Sebastian Coe, Alberto Juantorena and Carl Lewis (2).

Year		Year		Year	
1974	**Muhammad Ali**, boxing	1982	**Daley Thompson**, track	1990	**Stefan Edberg**, tennis
1975	**Joao Oliveira**, track	1983	**Carl Lewis**, track	1991	**Sergei Bubka**, track
1976	**Alberto Juantorena**, track	1984	**Carl Lewis**, track	1992	**Kevin Young**, track
1977	**Alberto Juantorena**, track	1985	**Steve Cram**, track	1993	**Miguel Induráin**, cycling
1978	**Henry Rono**, track	1986	**Diego Maradona**, soccer	1994	**Johan Olav Koss**, speed skating
1979	**Sebastian Coe**, track	1987	**Ben Johnson**, track	1995	**Jonathan Edwards**, track
1980	**Eric Heiden**, speed skating	1988	**Matt Biondi**, swimming		
1981	**Sebastian Coe**, track	1989	**Boris Becker**, tennis		

Female

Multiple winners: Nadia Comaneci, Steffi Graf, Marita Koch and Monica Seles (2).

Year		Year		Year	
1974	**Irena Szewinska**, track	1982	**Marita Koch**, track	1990	**Merlene Ottey**, track
1975	**Nadia Comaneci**, gymnastics	1983	**Jarmila Kratochvilova**, track	1991	**Monica Seles**, tennis
1976	**Nadia Comaneci**, gymnastics	1984	**Martina Navratilova**, tennis	1992	**Monica Seles**, tennis
1977	**Rosie Ackermann**, track	1985	**Mary Decker Slaney**, track	1993	**Wang Junxia**, track
1978	**Tracy Caulkins**, swimming	1986	**Heike Drechsler**, track	1994	**Le Jingyi**, swimming
1979	**Marita Koch**, track	1987	**Steffi Graf**, tennis	1995	**Gwen Torrence**, track
1980	**Hanni Wenzel**, alpine skiing	1988	**Florence Griffith Joyner**, track		
1981	**Chris Evert Lloyd**, tennis	1989	**Steffi Graf**, tennis		

Jesse Owens International Trophy

Presented annually by the International Amateur Athletic Association since 1981 and selected by a worldwide panel of electors. The Jesse Owens International Trophy is named after the late American Olympic champion, who won four gold medals at the 1936 Summer Games in Berlin.

Year		Year		Year	
1981	**Eric Heiden**, speed skating	1986	**Said Aouita**, track	1992	**Mike Powell**, track
1982	**Sebastian Coe**, track	1987	**Greg Louganis**, diving	1993	**Vitaly Scherbo**, gymnastics
1983	**Mary Decker**, track	1988	**Ben Johnson**, track	1994	**Wang Junxia**, track
1984	**Edwin Moses**, track	1990	**Roger Kingdom**, track	1995	**Johan Olva Koss**, speed skating
1985	**Carl Lewis**, track	1991	**Greg LeMond**, cycling	1996	**Michael Johnson**, track

James E. Sullivan Memorial Award

Presented annually by the Amateur Athletic Union since 1930. The Sullivan Award is named after the former AAU president and given to the athlete who, "by his or her performance, example and influence as an amateur, has done the most during the year to advance the cause of sportsmanship." An athlete cannot win the award more than once.

The 1995 winner was wrestler **Bruce Baumgartner**, the 1995 gold medalist at the World Freestyle Wrestling Championships. Baumgartner, who was a Sullivan Award finalist for the fifth time in '95, has won every major title in wrestling. The other nine finalists are listed alphabetically: **Tommie Frazier** (college football), **Michael Johnson** (track), **Rebecca Lobo** (college basketball), **Shannon Miller** (gymnastics), **Dominique Moceanu** (gymnastics), **Gwen Torrence** (track), **Rebecca Twigg** (cycling), **Tiger Woods** (golf) and **Lorenzen Wright** (college basketball). Vote totals were not released.

Year		Year		Year	
1930	**Bobby Jones**, golf	1952	**Horace Ashenfelter**, track	1975	**Tim Shaw**, swimming
1931	**Barney Berlinger**, track	1953	**Sammy Lee**, diving	1976	**Bruce Jenner**, track
1932	**Jim Bausch**, track	1954	**Mal Whitfield**, track	1977	**John Naber**, swimming
1933	**Glenn Cunningham**, track	1955	**Harrison Dillard**, track	1978	**Tracy Caulkins**, swimming
1934	**Bill Bonthron**, track	1956	**Pat McCormick**, diving	1979	**Kurt Thomas**, gymnastics
1935	**Lawson Little**, golf	1957	**Bobby Morrow**, track	1980	**Eric Heiden**, speed skating
1936	**Glenn Morris**, track	1958	**Glenn Davis**, track	1981	**Carl Lewis**, track
1937	**Don Budge**, tennis	1959	**Parry O'Brien**, track	1982	**Mary Decker**, track
1938	**Don Lash**, track	1960	**Rafer Johnson**, track	1983	**Edwin Moses**, track
1939	**Joe Burk**, rowing	1961	**Wilma Rudolph**, track	1984	**Greg Louganis**, diving
1940	**Greg Rice**, track	1963	**John Pennel**, track	1985	**Joan B. Samuelson**, track
1941	**Leslie MacMitchell**, track	1964	**Don Schollander**, swimming	1986	**Jackie Joyner-Kersee**, track
1942	**Cornelius Warmerdam**, track	1965	**Bill Bradley**, basketball	1987	**Jim Abbott**, baseball
1943	**Gilbert Dodds**, track	1966	**Jim Ryun**, track	1988	**Florence Griffith Joyner**, track
1944	**Ann Curtis**, swimming	1967	**Randy Matson**, track	1989	**Janet Evans**, swimming
1945	**Doc Blanchard**, football	1968	**Debbie Meyer**, swimming	1990	**John Smith**, wrestling
1946	**Arnold Tucker**, football	1969	**Bill Toomey**, track	1991	**Mike Powell**, track
1947	**John B. Kelly, Jr.**, rowing	1970	**John Kinsella**, swimming	1992	**Bonnie Blair**, speed skating
1948	**Bob Mathias**, track	1971	**Mark Spitz**, swimming	1993	**Charlie Ward**, football
1949	**Dick Button**, skating	1972	**Frank Shorter**, track	1994	**Dan Jansen**, speed skating
1950	**Fred Wilt**, track	1973	**Bill Walton**, basketball	1995	**Bruce Baumgartner**, wrest.
1951	**Bob Richards**, track	1974	**Rich Wohlhuter**, track		

USOC Sportsman & Sportswoman of the Year

To the outstanding overall male and female athletes from within the U.S. Olympic Committee member organizations. Winners are chosen from nominees of the national governing bodies for Olympic and Pan American Games and affiliated organizations. Voting is done by members of the national media, USOC board of directors and Athletes' Advisory Council.

Sportsman

Multiple winners: Eric Heiden (3); Matt Biondi, Michael Johnson and Greg Louganis (2).

Year
1974 **Jim Bolding**, track
1975 **Clint Jackson**, boxing
1976 **John Naber**, swimming
1977 **Eric Heiden**, speed skating
1978 **Bruce Davidson**, equestrian
1979 **Eric Heiden**, speed skating
1980 **Eric Heiden**, speed skating
1981 **Scott Hamilton**, fig. skating

Year
1982 **Greg Louganis**, diving
1983 **Rick McKinney**, archery
1984 **Edwin Moses**, track
1985 **Willie Banks**, track
1986 **Matt Biondi**, swimming
1987 **Greg Louganis**, diving
1988 **Matt Biondi**, swimming
1989 **Roger Kingdom**, track

Year
1990 **John Smith**, wrestling
1991 **Carl Lewis**, track
1992 **Pablo Morales**, swimming
1993 **Michael Johnson**, track
1994 **Dan Jansen**, speed skating
1995 **Michael Johnson**, track

Sportswoman

Multiple winners: Bonnie Blair, Tracy Caulkins, Jackie Joyner-Kersee and Sheila Young Ochowicz (2).

Year
1974 **Shirley Babashoff**, swimming
1975 **Kathy Heddy**, swimming
1976 **Sheila Young**, speedskating
1977 **Linda Fratianne**, fig. skating
1978 **Tracy Caulkins**, swimming
1979 **Sippy Woodhead**, swimming
1980 **Beth Heiden**, speed skating
1981 **Sheila Ochowicz**, speed skating & cycling

Year
1982 **Melanie Smith**, equestrian
1983 **Tamara McKinney**, skiing
1984 **Tracy Caulkins**, swimming
1985 **Mary Decker Slaney**, track
1986 **Jackie Joyner-Kersee**, track
1987 **Jackie Joyner-Kersee**, track
1988 **Florence Griffith Joyner**, track
1989 **Janet Evans**, swimming

Year
1990 **Lynn Jennings**, track
1991 **Kim Zmeskal**, gymnastics
1992 **Bonnie Blair**, speed skating
1993 **Gail Devers**, track
1994 **Bonnie Blair**, speed skating
1995 **Picabo Street**, skiing

Honda Broderick Cup

To the outstanding collegiate woman athlete of the year in NCAA competition. Winner is chosen from nominees in each of the NCAA's 10 competitive sports. Final voting is done by member athletic directors. Award is named after founder and sportswear manufacturer Thomas Broderick.

Multiple winner: Tracy Caulkins (2).

Year
1977 **Lucy Harris**, Delta St .... basketball
1978 **Ann Meyers**, UCLA .... basketball
1979 **Nancy Lieberman**, Old Dominion .... basketball
1980 **Julie Shea**, N.C. State .... track & field
1981 **Jill Sterkel**, Texas .... swimming
1982 **Tracy Caulkins**, Florida .... swimming
1983 **Deitre Collins**, Hawaii .... volleyball
1984 **Tracy Caulkins**, Florida .... swimming
& **Cheryl Miller**, USC .... basketball
1985 **Jackie Joyner**, UCLA .... track & field

Year
1986 **Kamie Ethridge**, Texas .... basketball
1987 **Mary T. Meagher**, California .... swimming
1988 **Teresa Weatherspoon**, La. Tech .... basketball
1989 **Vicki Huber**, Villanova .... track
1990 **Suzy Favor**, Wisconsin .... track
1991 **Dawn Staley**, Virginia .... basketball
1992 **Missy Marlowe**, Utah .... gymnastics
1993 **Lisa Fernandez**, UCLA .... softball
1994 **Mia Hamm**, North Carolina .... soccer
1995 **Rebecca Lobo**, UConn .... basketball

Flo Hyman Award

Presented annually since 1987 by the Women's Sports Foundation for "exemplifying dignity, spirit and commitment to excellence" and named in honor of the late captain of the 1984 U.S. Women's Volleyball team. Voting by WSF members.

Year
1987 **Martina Navratilova**, tennis
1988 **Jackie Joyner-Kersee**, track
1989 **Evelyn Ashford**, track
1990 **Chris Evert**, tennis

Year
1991 **Diana Golden**, skiing
1992 **Nancy Lopez**, golf
1993 **Lynette Woodward**, basketball
1994 **Patty Sheehan**, golf

Year
1995 **Mary Lou Retton**, gymnastics
1996 **Donna de Varona**, swimming

Arthur Ashe Award for Courage

Presented since 1993 on the annual ESPN "Espys" telecast. Given to a member of the sports community who has exemplified the same courage, spirit and determination to help others despite personal hardship that characterized Arthur Ashe, the late tennis champion and humanitarian. Voting done by select 26-member committee of media and sports personalities.

Year
1993 **Jim Valvano**, basketball

Year
1994 **Steve Palermo**, baseball
1995 **Howard Cosell**, TV & radio

Year
1996 **Loretta Clairborne**, special olympics

Time Man of the Year

Since Charles Lindbergh was named *Time* magazine's first Man of the Year for 1927, two individuals with significant sports credentials have won the honor.

Year
1984 **Peter Ueberroth**, president of the Los Angeles Olympic Organizing Committee.
1991 **Ted Turner**, owner-president of Turner Broadcasting System, founder of CNN cable news network, owner of the Atlanta Braves (NL) and Atlanta Hawks (NBA), and former winning America's Cup skipper.

The Hickok Belt

Officially known as the S. Rae Hickok Professional Athlete of the Year Award and presented by the Kickik Manufacturing Co. of Arlington, Texas, from 1950–76. The trophy was a large belt of gold, diamonds and other jewels, reportedly worth $30,000 in 1976, the last year it was handed out. Voting was done by 270 newspaper sports editors from around the country.

Multiple winner: Sandy Koufax (2).

Year	
1950	**Phil Rizzuto**, baseball
1951	**Allie Reynolds**, baseball
1952	**Rocky Marciano**, boxing
1953	**Ben Hogan**, golf
1954	**Willie Mays**, baseball
1955	**Otto Graham**, football
1956	**Mickey Mantle**, baseball
1957	**Carmen Basilio**, boxing
1958	**Bob Turley**, baseball
1959	**Ingemar Johansson**, boxing
1960	**Arnold Palmer**, golf
1961	**Roger Maris**, baseball
1962	**Maury Wills**, baseball
1963	**Sandy Koufax**, baseball
1964	**Jim Brown**, football
1965	**Sandy Koufax**, baseball
1966	**Frank Robinson**, baseball
1967	**Carl Yastrzemski**, baseball
1968	**Joe Namath**, football
1969	**Tom Seaver**, baseball
1970	**Brooks Robinson**, baseball
1971	**Lee Trevino**, golf
1972	**Steve Carlton**, baseball
1973	**O.J. Simpson**, football
1974	**Muhammad Ali**, boxing
1975	**Pete Rose**, baseball
1976	**Ken Stabler**, football
1977	Discontinued

ABC's "Wide World of Sports" Athlete of the Year

Selected annually by the producers of ABC Sports since 1962.

Multiple winner: Greg Lemond (2).

Year	
1962	**Jim Beatty**, track
1963	**Valery Brumel**, track
1964	**Don Schollander**, swimming
1965	**Jim Clark**, auto racing
1966	**Jim Ryun**, track
1967	**Peggy Fleming**, figure skating
1968	**Bill Toomey**, track
1969	**Mario Andretti**, auto racing
1970	**Willis Reed**, basketball
1971	**Lee Trevino**, golf
1972	**Olga Korbut**, gymnastics
1973	**O.J. Simpson**, football & **Jackie Stewart**, auto racing
1974	**Muhammad Ali**, boxing
1975	**Jack Nicklaus**, golf
1976	**Nadia Comaneci**, gymnastics
1977	**Steve Cauthen**, horse racing
1978	**Ron Guidry**, baseball
1979	**Willie Stargell**, baseball
1980	**U.S. Olympic hockey team**
1981	**Sugar Ray Leonard**, boxing
1982	**Wayne Gretzky**, hockey
1983	**Australia II**, yachting
1984	**Edwin Moses**, track
1985	**Pete Rose**, baseball
1986	**Debi Thomas**, figure skating
1987	**Dennis Conner**, yachting
1988	**Greg Louganis**, diving
1989	**Greg Lemond**, cycling
1990	**Greg Lemond**, cycling
1991	**Carl Lewis**, track & **Kim Zmeskal**, gymnastics
1992	**Bonnie Blair**, speed skating
1993	**Evander Holyfield**, boxing
1994	**Al Unser Jr.**, auto racing
1995	**Miguel Induráin**, cycling

The Sporting News Sportsman of the Year

Selected annually by the editors of *The Sporting News* since 1968. 'Man of the Year' changed to 'Sportsman' of the Year in 1993.

Year	
1968	**Denny McLain**, baseball
1969	**Tom Seaver**, baseball
1970	**John Wooden**, basketball
1971	**Lee Trevino**, golf
1972	**Charles O. Finley**, baseball
1973	**O.J. Simpson**, pro football
1974	**Lou Brock**, baseball
1975	**Archie Griffin**, football
1976	**Larry O'Brien**, basketball
1977	**Steve Cauthen**, horse racing
1978	**Ron Guidry**, baseball
1979	**Willie Stargell**, baseball
1980	**George Brett**, baseball
1981	**Wayne Gretzky**, hockey
1982	**Whitey Herzog**, baseball
1983	**Bowie Kuhn**, baseball
1984	**Peter Ueberroth**, LA Olympics
1985	**Pete Rose**, baseball
1986	**Larry Bird**, pro basketball
1987	No award
1988	**Jackie Joyner-Kersee**, track
1989	**Joe Montana**, football
1990	**Nolan Ryan**, baseball
1991	**Michael Jordan**, basketball
1992	**Mike Krzyzewski**, col. bask.
1993	**Cito Gaston** & **Pat Gillick**, baseball
1994	**Emmitt Smith**, pro football
1995	**Cal Ripken Jr.**, baseball

Presidential Medal of Freedom

Since President John F. Kennedy established the Medal of Freedom as America's highest civilian honor in 1963, only nine sports figures have won the award. Note that (*) indicates the presentation was made posthumously.

Year		President
1963	**Bob Kiphuth**, swimming	Kennedy
1976	**Jesse Owens**, track & field	Ford
1977	**Joe DiMaggio**, baseball	Ford
1983	**Paul (Bear) Bryant***, football	Reagan
1984	**Jackie Robinson***, baseball	Reagan
1986	**Earl (Red) Blaik**, football	Reagan
1991	**Ted Williams**, baseball	Bush
1992	**Richard Petty**, auto racing	Bush
1993	**Arthur Ashe***, tennis	Clinton

TROPHY CASE

From the first organized track meet at Olympia in 776 B.C., to the Atlanta Summer Olympics over 2,700 years later, championships have been officially recognized with prizes that are symbolically rich and eagerly pursued. Here are 15 of the most coveted trophies in America.

(Illustrations by Lynn Mercer Michaud.)

America's Cup

First presented by England's Royal Yacht Squadron to the winner of an invitational race around the Isle of Wight on Aug. 22, 1851 . . . . originally called the Hundred Guinea Cup . . . . renamed after the U.S. boat *America,* winner of the first race . . . . made of sterling silver and designed by London jewelers R. & G. Garrard . . . . measures 2 feet, 3 inches high and weighs 16 lbs . . . . originally cost 100 guineas ($500), now valued at $250,000 . . . . bell-shaped base added in 1958 . . . . challenged for every three to four years . . . . trophy held by yacht club sponsoring winning boat.

Vince Lombardi Trophy

First presented at the AFL-NFL World Championship Game (now Super Bowl) on Jan. 15, 1967 . . . . originally called the World Championship Game Trophy . . . . renamed in 1971 in honor of former Green Bay Packers GM-coach and two-time Super Bowl winner Vince Lombardi, who died in 1970 as coach of Washington . . . . made of sterling silver and designed by Tiffany & Co. of New York . . . . measures 21 inches high and weighs 7 lbs (football depicted is regulation size) . . . . valued at $12,500 . . . . competed for annually. . . . winning team keeps trophy.

Olympic Gold Medal

First presented by International Olympic Committee in 1908 (until then winners received silver medals) . . . . second and third place finishers also got medals of silver and bronze for first time in 1908 . . . . each medal must be at least 2.4 inches in diameter and 0.12 inches thick . . . . the gold medal is actually made of silver, but must be gilded with at least 6 grams (0.21 ounces) of pure gold . . . . the medals for the 1996 Atlanta Games were designed by Malcolm Grear Designers and produced by Reed & Barton of Taunton, Mass. . . . 604 gold, 604 silver and 630 bronze medals were made . . . . competed for every two years as Winter and Summer Games alternate . . . . winners keep medals.

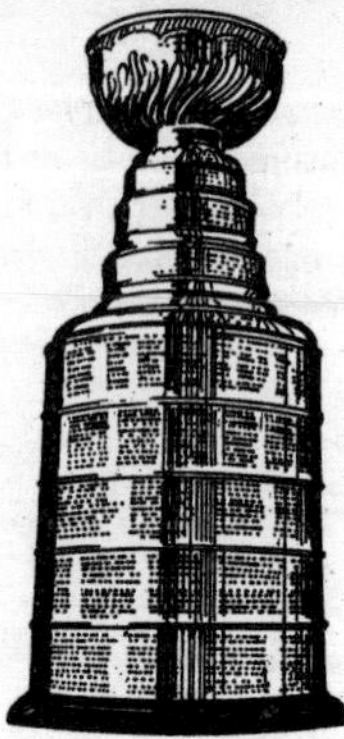

Stanley Cup

Donated by Lord Stanley of Preston, the Governor General of Canada and first presented in 1893 . . . . original cup was made of sterling silver by an unknown London silversmith and measured 7 inches high with an 11½-inch diameter . . . . in order to accommodate all the rosters of winning teams, the cup now measures 35½ inches high with a base 54 inches around and weighs 32 lbs . . . . originally bought for 10 guineas ($48.67), it is now insured for $75,000 . . . . actual cup retired to Hall of Fame and replaced in 1970 . . . . presented to NHL playoff champion since 1918 . . . . trophy loaned to winning team for one year.

World Cup

First presented by the Federation Internationale de Football Association (FIFA) . . . . originally called the World Cup Trophy . . . . renamed the Jules Rimet Cup (after the then FIFA president) in 1946, but retired by Brazil after that country's third title in 1970 . . . . new World Cup trophy created in 1974 . . . . designed by Italian sculptor Silvio Gazzaniga and made of solid 18 carat gold with two malachite rings inlaid at the base . . . . measures 14.2 inches high and weighs 11 lbs . . . . insured for $200,000 (U.S.) . . . . competed for every four years . . . . winning team gets gold-plated replica.

Commissioner's Trophy

First presented by the Commissioner of baseball to the winner of the 1967 World Series . . . . also known as the World Championship Trophy . . . . made of brass and gold plate with an ebony base and a baseball in the center made of pewter with a silver finish . . . . designed by Balfour & Co. of Attleboro, Mass . . . . 28 pennants represent 14 AL and 14 NL teams . . . . measures 30 inches high and 36 inches around at the base and weighs 30 lbs . . . . valued at $15,000 . . . . competed for annually . . . . winning team keeps trophy.

Larry O'Brien Trophy

First presented in 1978 to winner of NBA Finals . . . . originally called the Walter A. Brown Trophy after the league pioneer and Boston Celtics owner (an earlier NBA championship bowl was also named after Brown) . . . . renamed in 1984 in honor of outgoing commissioner O'Brien, who served from 1975-84 . . . . made of sterling silver with 24 carat gold overlay and designed by Tiffany & Co. of New York . . . . measures 2 feet high and weighs 14½ lbs (basketball depicted is regulation size) . . . . valued at $13,500 . . . . competed for annually . . . . winning team keeps trophy.

Heisman Trophy

First presented in 1935 to the best college football player east of the Mississippi by the Downtown Athletic Club of New York . . . . players across the entire country eligible since 1936 . . . . originally called the DAC Trophy . . . . renamed in 1936 following the death of DAC athletic director and former college coach John W. Heisman . . . . made of bronze and designed by New York sculptor Frank Eliscu, it measures 13½ in. high, 6½ in. wide and 14 in. long at the base and weighs 25 lbs . . . . valued at $2,000 . . . . voting done by national media and former Heisman winners . . . . awarded annually . . . . winner keeps trophy.

James E. Sullivan Memorial Award

First presented by the Amateur Athletic Union (AAU) in 1930 as a gold medal and given to the nation's outstanding amateur athlete . . . . trophy given since 1933 . . . . named after the amateur sports movement pioneer, who was a founder and past president of AAU and the director of the 1904 Olympic Games in St. Louis . . . . made of bronze with a marble base, it measures 17½ in. high and 11 in. wide at the base and weighs 13½ lbs . . . . valued at $2,500 . . . . voting done by AAU and USOC officials, former winners and selected media . . . . awarded annually . . . . winner keeps trophy.

Ryder Cup

Donated in 1927 by English seed merchant Samuel Ryder, who offered the gold cup for a biennial match between teams of golfing pros from Great Britain and the United States . . . . the format changed in 1977 to include the best players on the European PGA Tour . . . . made of 14 carat gold on a wood base and designed by Mappin and Webb of London . . . . the golfer depicted on the top of the trophy is Ryder's friend and teaching pro Abe Mitchell . . . . the cup measures 16 in. high and weighs 4 lbs . . . . insured for $50,000 . . . . competed for every two years at alternating British and U.S. sites . . . . the cup is held by the PGA headquarters of the winning side.

Davis Cup

Donated by American college student and U.S. doubles champion Dwight F. Davis in 1900 and presented by the International Tennis Federation (ITF) to the winner of the annual 16-team men's competition . . . . officially called the International Lawn Tennis Challenge Trophy . . . . made of sterling silver and designed by Shreve, Crump and Low of Boston, the cup has a matching tray (added in 1921) and a very heavy two-tiered base containing rosters of past winning teams . . . . it stands 34½ in. high and 108 in. around at the base and weighs 400 lbs . . . . insured for $150,000 . . . . competed for annually . . . . trophy loaned to winning country for one year.

Borg-Warner Trophy

First presented by the Borg-Warner Automotive Co. of Chicago in 1936 to the winner of the Indianapolis 500 . . . . replaced the Wheeler-Schebler Trophy which went to the 400-mile leader from 1911-32 . . . . made of sterling silver with bas-relief sculptured heads of each winning driver and a gold bas-relief head of Tony Hulman, the owner of the Indy Speedway from 1945-77 . . . . designed by Robert J. Hill and made by Gorham, Inc. of Rhode Island . . . . measures 51½ in. high and weighs over 80 lbs . . . . new base added in 1988 and the entire trophy restored in 1991 . . . . competed for annually . . . . insured for $1 million . . . . trophy stays at Speedway Hall of Fame . . . . winner gets a 14-in. high replica valued at $30,000.

NCAA Championship Trophy

First presented in 1952 by the NCAA to all 1st, 2nd and 3rd place teams in sports with sanctioned tournaments . . . . 1st place teams receive gold-plated awards, 2nd place award is silver-plated and 3rd is bronze . . . . replaced silver cup given to championship teams from 1939-1951 . . . . made of walnut, the trophy stands 24¾ in. high, 14⅛ in. wide and 4½ in. deep at the base and weighs 15 lbs . . . . designed by Medallic Art Co. of Danbury, Conn. and made by House of Usher of Kansas City since 1990 . . . . valued at $500 . . . . competed for annually . . . . winning teams keep trophies.

World Championship Belt

First presented in 1921 by the World Boxing Association, one of the three organizations (the World Boxing Council and International Boxing Federation are the others) generally accepted as sanctioning legitimate world championship fights . . . . belt weighs 8 lbs. and is made of hand tanned leather . . . . the outsized buckle measures 10½ in. high and 8 in. wide, is made of pewter with 24 carat gold plate and contains crystal and semi-precious stones . . . . side panels of polished brass are for engraving title bout results . . . . currently made by Phil Valentino Originals of Jersey City, N.J. . . . . champions keep belts even if they lose their title.

World Championship Ring

Rings decorated with gems and engraving date back to ancient Egypt where the wealthy wore heavy gold and silver rings to indicate social status . . . . championship rings in sports serve much the same purpose, indicating the wearer is a champion . . . .the Dallas Cowboys' ring for winning Super Bowl XXX on Jan. 28, 1996 was designed by Diamond Cutters International of Houston....each ring is made of 14-carat yellow gold, weighs 48-51 penny weights and features five trimmed marquis diamonds interlocking in the shape of the Cowboys' star logo as well as five more marquis diamonds (for the team's five Super Bowl wins) on a bed of 51 smaller diamonds...rings were appraised at over $30,000 each.

Wide World Photos

Wilma Rudolph of Tennessee State relaxes between events at the National Senior Women's AAU meet in Chicago on April 16, 1960. Later the same year, Rudolph would win three gold medals at the Olympics (100m, 200, and 4x100 relay).

WHO'S WHO

Sports Personalities

Eight hundred and twenty-seven entries dating back to the turn of the century. Pages updated through Sept. 20, 1996.

Hank Aaron (b. Feb. 5, 1934): Baseball OF; led NL in HRs and RBI 4 times each and batting twice with Milwaukee and Atlanta Braves; MVP in 1957; played in 24 All-Star Games, all-time leader in HRs (755) and RBI (2,297), 3rd in hits (3,771); executive with Braves and TBS, Inc.

Jim Abbott (b. Sept. 19, 1967): Baseball LHP; born without a right hand; All-America hurler at Michigan; won Sullivan Award in 1987; threw 4-0 no-hitter for NY Yankees vs. Cleveland (Sept. 4, 1993).

Kareem Abdul-Jabbar (b. Lew Alcindor, Apr. 16, 1947): Basketball C; led UCLA to 3 NCAA titles (1967-69); tourney MVP 3 times; Player of Year twice; led Milwaukee (1) and LA Lakers (5) to 6 NBA titles; playoff MVP twice (1971,85), regular season MVP 6 times (1971-72,74,76-77,80); retired in 1989 after 20 seasons as all-time leader in over 20 categories.

Andre Agassi (b. Apr. 29, 1970): Tennis; former No. 1 men's player in the world with 31 career tournament wins and 3 grand slam titles; won Wimbledon in 1992, U.S. Open as unseeded entry in '94 and Australian Open in 1996; helped U.S. win 2 Davis Cup finals (1990,92).

Troy Aikman (b. Nov. 21, 1966): Football QB; consensus All-America at UCLA (1988); 1st overall pick in 1989 NFL Draft (by Dallas); led Cowboys to 2 straight Super Bowl titles (1992 and '93 seasons); MVP in Super Bowl XXVII; entered 1996 season as second highest-paid player in NFL ($50 million over 8 years).

Tenley Albright (b. July 18, 1935): Figure skater; 2-time world champion (1953,55); won Olympic silver (1952) and gold (1956) medals; became a surgeon.

Grover Cleveland (Pete) Alexander (b. Feb. 26, 1887, d. Nov. 4, 1950): Baseball RHP; won 20 or more games 9 times; 373 career wins and 90 shutouts.

Muhammad Ali (b. Cassius Clay, Jan. 17, 1942): Boxer; 1960 Olympic light heavyweight champion; only 3-time world heavyweight champ (1964-67, 1974-78,1978-79); defeated Sonny Liston (1964), George Foreman (1974) and Leon Spinks (1978) for title; fought Joe Frazier in 3 memorable bouts (1971-75), winning twice; adopted Black Muslim faith in 1964 and changed name; stripped of title in 1967 after conviction for refusing induction into U.S. Army; verdict reversed by Supreme Court in 1971; career record of 56-5 with 37 KOs and 19 successful title defenses.

Forrest (Phog) Allen (b. Nov. 18, 1885, d. Sept. 16, 1974): Basketball; college coach 48 years; directed Kansas to NCAA title (1952); 5th on all-time list with 746 career wins.

Bobby Allison (b. Dec. 3, 1937): Auto racer; 3-time winner of Daytona 500 (1978,82,88); NASCAR national champ in 1983; father of Davey.

Davey Allison (b. Feb. 25, 1961, d. July 13, 1993): Auto racer; stock car Rookie of Year (1987); winner of 19 NASCAR races including 1992 Daytona 500; killed at age 32 in helicopter accident at Talladega Superspeedway; son of Bobby.

Roberto Alomar (b. Feb. 5, 1968) Baseball; member of two World Series champions as a Toronto Blue Jay; a switch-hitter who combines speed, power and batting average with fielding skills that have earned him five Gold Gloves; six-time All-Star; MVP of 1992 ALCS; became known well beyond baseball for spitting in the face of umpire John Hirschbeck during final weekend of 1996 season; the muddled and weak reaction (five-game suspension with pay to be served in 1997) by major league baseball underscored the vacuum that exists in the leadership of the game.

Walter Alston (b. Dec. 1, 1911, d. Oct. 1, 1984): Baseball; managed Brooklyn-LA Dodgers 23 years, won 7 pennants and 4 World Series (1955,59,63,65); retired after 1976 season with 2,060 wins (2,040 regular season and 20 postseason).

Sparky Anderson (b. Feb. 22, 1934): Baseball; only manager to win World Series in each league—Cincinnati in NL (1975-76) and Detroit in AL (1984); 3rd-ranked skipper on all-time career list with 2,168 wins (2,134 regular season and 34 postseason).

Willie Anderson (b. May 1878, d. Oct. 25, 1910): Scottish golfer; became an American citizen and won 4 U.S. Open titles, including an unmatched 3 straight from 1903-05; also won four Western Opens from 1902-09.

Mario Andretti (b. Feb. 28, 1940): Auto racer; 4-time USAC-CART national champion (1965-66,69,84); only driver to win Daytona 500 (1967), Indy 500 (1969) and Formula One world title (1978); Indy 500 Rookie of Year (1965); retired following 1994 racing season ranked 1st in poles (67) and starts (407) and 2nd in wins (52) on all-time IndyCar list; father of Michael and Jeff, uncle of John.

Michael Andretti (b. Oct. 5, 1962): Auto racer; 1991 CART national champion with single-season record 8 wins; Indy 500 Rookie of Year (1984); left IndyCar circuit for ill-fated Formula One try in 1993; returned to IndyCar in '94; entered 1995 with 29 career wins; son of Mario.

Earl Anthony (b. Apr. 27, 1938): Bowler; 6-time PBA Bowler of Year; 41 career titles; first to earn $100,000 in 1 season (1975); first to earn $1 million in career. Came out of retirement in '96.

Said Aouita (b. Nov. 2, 1959): Moroccan runner; won gold (5000m) and bronze (800m) in 1984 Olympics; won 5000m at 1987 World Championships; formerly held 2 world records recognized by IAAF—2000m and 5000m.

Luis Aparicio (b. Apr. 29, 1934): Baseball SS; all-time leader in most games, assists, chances and double plays by shortstop; led AL in stolen bases 9 times (1956-64); 506 career steals.

Al Arbour (b. Nov. 1, 1932): Hockey; coached NY Islanders to 4 straight Stanley Cup titles (1980-83); retired after 1993-94 season 2nd on all-time career list with 902 wins (779 regular season and 123 postseason).

Eddie Arcaro (b. Feb. 19, 1916): Jockey; 2-time Triple Crown winner (Whirlaway in 1941, Citation in '48); from 1938-52, he won Kentucky Derby 5 times, Preakness and Belmont 6 times each.

Roone Arledge (b. July 8, 1931): Sports TV innovator of live events, anthology shows, Olympic coverage and "Monday Night Football"; ran ABC Sports from 1968-86; has run ABC News since 1977.

Henry Armstrong (b. Dec. 12, 1912, d. Oct. 22, 1988): Boxer; held feather-, light- and welterweight titles simultaneously in 1938; pro record 145-20-9 with 98 KOs.

Arthur Ashe (b. July 10, 1943, d. Feb. 6, 1993): Tennis; first black man to win U.S. Championship (1968) and Wimbledon (1975); 1st U.S. player to earn $100,000 in 1 year (1970); won Davis Cup as player (1968-70) and captain (1981-82); wrote black sports history, *Hard Road to Glory*; announced in 1992 that he was infected with AIDS virus from a blood transfusion during 1983 heart surgery; died Feb. 6, 1993 at age 49.

Evelyn Ashford (b. Apr. 15, 1957): Track & Field; winner of 4 Olympic gold medals— 100m in 1984, and 4x100m in 1984, '88 and '92; also won silver medal in 100m in '88; member of 5 U.S. Olympic teams (1976-92).

Red Auerbach (b. Sept. 20, 1917): Basketball; 2nd winningest coach (regular season and playoffs) in NBA history; won 1,037 times in 20 years; as coach-GM, led Boston to 9 NBA titles, including 8 in a row (1959-66); also coached defunct Washington Capitols (1946-49); NBA Coach of the Year award named after him; retired as Celtics coach in 1966 and as GM in '84; club president since 1970.

Tracy Austin (b. Dec. 12, 1962): Tennis; youngest player to win U.S. Open (age 16 in 1979); won 2nd U.S. Open in '81; named AP Female Athlete of Year twice before she was 20; recurring neck and back injuries shortened career after 1983; youngest player ever inducted into Tennis Hall of Fame (age 29 in 1992).

Paul Azinger (b. Jan. 6, 1960): Golf; PGA Player of Year in 1987; entered 1996 with 11 career wins, including '93 PGA Championship; missed 1st 7 months of '94 season overcoming lymphoma (a form of cancer) in right shoulder blade.

Donovan Bailey (b. Dec. 16, 1967) Track; Jamaican-born Canadian sprinter who is currently the world's fastest human; world record holder for the 100m (9.84) set in gold medal-winning performance at 1996 Olympics; set indoor record in 50M (5.56) in 1996; member of Canadian 4x100 relay that won gold in 1996 Olympics.

Oksana Baiul (b. Feb. 26, 1977): Ukrainian figure skater; 1993 world champion at age 15; edged Nancy Kerrigan by a 5-4 judges' vote for 1994 Olympic gold medal.

Hobey Baker (b. Jan. 15, 1892, d. Dec 21, 1918): Football and hockey star at Princeton (1911-14); member of college football and pro hockey halls of fame; college hockey Player of Year award named after him; killed in WWI plane crash.

Seve Ballesteros (b. Apr. 9, 1957): Spanish golfer; has won British Open 3 times (1979,84,88) and Masters twice (1980,83); 3-time European Golfer of Year (1986,88,91); has led Europe to 3 Ryder Cup titles (1985,87,89); entered 1996 with 72 world-wide victories.

Ernie Banks (b. Jan. 31, 1931): Baseball SS-1B; led NL in home runs and RBI twice each; 2-time MVP (1958-59) with Chicago Cubs; 512 career HRs.

Roger Bannister (b. Mar. 23, 1929): British runner; first to run mile in less than 4 minutes (3:59.4 on May 6, 1954).

Walter (Red) Barber (b. Feb. 17, 1908, d. Oct. 22, 1992): Radio-TV; renowned baseball play-by-play broadcaster for Cincinnati, Brooklyn and N.Y. Yankees from 1934-66; won Peabody Award for radio commentary in 1991.

Charles Barkley (b. Feb. 20, 1963): Basketball F; 5-time All-NBA 1st team with Philadelphia and Phoenix; traded to Suns for 3 players (June 17, 1992); U.S. Olympic Dream Team member in '92; NBA regular season MVP in 1993. Traded to Houston Rockets in 1996.

Rick Barry (b. Mar. 28, 1944): Basketball F; only player to lead both NBA and ABA in scoring; 5-time All-NBA 1st team; playoff MVP with Golden St. in 1975.

Sammy Baugh (b. Mar. 17, 1914): Football QB-DB-P; led Washington to NFL titles in 1937 (his rookie year) and '42; led league in passing 6 times, punting 4 times and interceptions once.

Elgin Baylor (b. Sept. 16, 1934): Basketball F; MVP of NCAA tournament in 1958; led Minneapolis-LA Lakers to 8 NBA Finals; 10-time All-NBA 1st team (1959-65,67-69).

Bob Beamon (b. Aug. 29, 1946): Track & Field; won 1968 Olympic gold medal in long jump with world record (29-ft, 2½ in.) that shattered old mark by nearly 2 feet; record finally broken by 2 inches in 1991 by Mike Powell.

Franz Beckenbauer (b. Sept. 11, 1945): Soccer; captain of West German World Cup champions in 1974 then coached West Germany to World Cup title in 1990; invented sweeper position; played in U.S. for NY Cosmos (1977-80,83).

Boris Becker (b. Nov. 22, 1967): German tennis player; 3-time Wimbledon champ (1985-86,89); youngest male (17) to win Wimbledon; led country to 1st Davis Cup win in 1988; has also won U.S. (1989) and Australian (1991,96) Opens.

Chuck Bednarik (b. May 1, 1925): Football C-LB; 2-time All-America at Penn and 7-time All-Pro with NFL Philadelphia Eagles as both center (1950) and linebacker (1951-56); missed only 3 games in 14 seasons; led Eagles to 1960 NFL title as a 35-year-old two-way player.

Clair Bee (b. Mar. 2, 1896, d. May 20, 1983): Basketball coach who led LIU to 2 undefeated seasons (1936,39) and 2 NIT titles (1939,41); his teams won 95 percent of their games between 1931-51, including 43 in a row from 1935-37; coached NBA Baltimore Bullets from 1952-54, but was only 34-116; contributions to game include 1-3-1 zone defense, 3-second rule and NBA 24-second clock; also authored sports manuals and fictional Chip Hilton sports books for kids.

Jean Beliveau (b. Aug. 31, 1931): Hockey C; led Montreal to 10 Stanley Cups in 17 playoffs; playoff MVP (1965); 2-time regular season MVP (1956,64).

Bert Bell (b. Feb. 25, 1895, d. Oct. 11, 1959): Football; team owner and 2nd NFL commissioner (1946-59); proposed college draft in 1935 and instituted TV blackout rule.

Deane Beman (b. Apr. 22, 1938): Golf; 1st commissioner of PGA Tour (1974-94); introduced "stadium golf"; as player, won U.S. Amateur twice and British Amateur once.

Johnny Bench (b. Dec. 7, 1947): Baseball C; led NL in HRs twice and RBI 3 times; 2-time regular season MVP (1970,72) with Cincinnati, World Series MVP in 1976; 389 career HRs.

Patty Berg (b. Feb. 13, 1918): Golfer; 57 career pro wins including 15 Majors; 3-time AP Female Athlete of Year (1938,43,55).

Chris Berman (b. May 10, 1955): Radio-TV; 4-time Sportscaster of Year known for his nicknames and jovial studio anchoring on ESPN; play-by-play man only year Brown University football team won Ivy League (1976).

Yogi Berra (b. May 12, 1925): Baseball C; played on 10 World Series winners with NY Yankees; holds several WS records— games played (75), at bats (259) and hits (71); 3-time AL MVP (1951,54-55); managed both Yankees (1964) and NY Mets (1973) to pennants.

Jay Berwanger (b. Mar. 19, 1914): Football HB; University of Chicago star; won 1st Heisman Trophy in 1935.

Gary Bettman (b. June 2, 1952): Hockey; former NBA executive, who was named first commissioner of NHL on Dec. 11, 1992; took office on Feb. 1, 1993.

Abebe Bikila (b. Aug. 7, 1932, d. Oct. 25, 1973): Ethiopian runner; 1st to win consecutive Olympic marathons (1960,64).

Matt Biondi (b. Oct. 8, 1965): Swimmer; won 7 medals in 1988 Olympics, including 5 gold (2 individual, 3 relay); has won a total of 11 medals (8 gold, 2 silver and a bronze) in 3 Olympics (1984,88,92).

Larry Bird (b. Dec. 7, 1956): Basketball F; college Player of Year (1979) at Indiana St.; 1980 NBA Rookie of Year; 9-time All-NBA 1st team; 3-time regular season MVP (1984-86); led Boston to 3 NBA titles (1981,84, 86); 2-time playoff MVP (1984,86); U.S. Olympic Dream Team member in '92.

The Black Sox: Eight Chicago White Sox players who were banned from baseball for life in 1921 for allegedly throwing the 1919 World Series— RHP Eddie Cicotte (1884-1969), OF Happy Felsch (1891-1964), 1B Chick Gandil (1887-1970), OF Shoeless Joe Jackson (1889-1951), INF Fred McMullin (1891-1952), SS Swede Risberg (1894-1975), 3B-SS Buck Weaver (1890-1956), and LHP Lefty Williams (1893-1959).

Earl (Red) Blaik (b. Feb. 15, 1897, d. May 6, 1989): Football; coached Army to consecutive national titles in 1944-45; 166 career wins and 3 Heisman winners (Blanchard, Davis, Dawkins).

Bonnie Blair (b. Mar. 18, 1964): Speedskater; only American woman to win 5 Olympic gold medals in Winter or Summer Games; won 500-meters in 1988, then 500m and 1,000m in both 1992 and '94; added 1,000m bronze in 1988; Sullivan Award winner (1992); retired on 31st birthday as reigning world sprint champ.

Hector (Toe) Blake (b. Aug. 21, 1912, d. May 17, 1995): Hockey LW; led Montreal to 2 Stanley Cups as a player and 8 more as coach; regular season MVP in 1939.

Felix (Doc) Blanchard (b. Dec. 11, 1924): Football FB; 3-time All-America; led Army to national titles in 1944-45; Glenn Davis' running mate; won Heisman Trophy and Sullivan Award in 1945.

George Blanda (b. Sept. 17, 1927): Football QB-PK; NFL's all-time leading scorer (2,002 points); led Houston to 2 AFL titles (1960-61); played 26 pro seasons; retired at 48.

Fanny Blankers-Koen (b. Apr. 26, 1918): Dutch sprinter; 30-year-old mother of two, who won 4 gold medals (100m, 200m, 800m hurdles and 4x100m relay) at 1948 Olympics.

Drew Bledsoe (b. Feb. 14, 1972): Football QB; 1st overall pick in 1993 NFL draft (by New England); holds NFL single-season record for most passes attempted (691) and single-game records for most passes completed (45), attempted (70); entered 1996 season as highest-paid player in NFL ($42 million over 7 years).

Wade Boggs (b. June 15, 1958): Baseball 3B; entered 1996 season with 5 AL batting titles (1983,85-88) at Boston and .334 career average in 14 seasons.

Barry Bonds (b. July 24, 1964): Baseball OF; 3-time NL MVP, twice with Pittsburgh (1990,92) and once with San Francisco (1993); NL's HR and RBI leader in 1993; became only second player to hit 40 homers and steal 40 bases in same season in 1996; son of Bobby.

Bjorn Borg (b. June 6, 1956): Swedish tennis player; 2-time Player of Year (1979-80); won 6 French Opens and 5 straight Wimbledons (1976-80); led Sweden to 1st Davis Cup win in 1975; retired in 1983 at age 26; attempted unsuccessful comeback in 1991.

Mike Bossy (b. Jan. 22, 1957): Hockey RW; led NY Isles to 4 Stanley Cups; playoff MVP in 1982; scored 50 goals or more 9 straight years; 573 career goals.

Ralph Boston (b. May 9, 1939): Track & Field; medaled in 3 consecutive Olympic long jumps— gold (1960), silver (1964), bronze (1968).

Ray Bourque (b. Dec. 28, 1960): Hockey D; 11-time All-NHL 1st team, has won Norris Trophy 5 times (1987-88,1990-91,94) with Boston. '96 All-Star Game MVP.

Bobby Bowden (b. Nov. 8, 1929): Football; coached Florida St. to a national title in 1993; entered '95 regular season 5th on all-time career list with 249 wins, including a 14-3-1 bowl record in 29 years as coach at Samford, West Va. and FSU; father of Terry.

Terry Bowden (b. Feb. 24, 1956): Football; led Auburn to 11-0 record in his first season as Division I-A head coach in 1993; NCAA probation earned under previous staff prevented bowl appearance; son of Bobby.

Riddick Bowe (b. Aug. 10, 1967): Boxing; won world heavyweight title with unanimous decision over champion Evander Holyfield on Nov. 13, 1992; lost title to Holyfield on majority decision Nov. 6, 1993; entered 1996 with pro record of 38-1 and 32 KOs.

Scotty Bowman (b. Sept. 18, 1933): Hockey; all-time winningest NHL coach in both regular season (975 wins) and playoffs (162) over 24 seasons; led Montreal to 5 Stanley Cups (1973,76-79) and Pittsburgh to another (1992).

Jack Brabham (b. Apr. 2, 1926): Australian auto racer; 3-time Formula One champion (1959-60,66); 14 career wins.

Bill Bradley (b. July 28, 1943): Basketball F; 3-time All-America at Princeton; Player of Year and NCAA tourney MVP in 1965; captain of gold medal-winning 1964 U.S. Olympic team; Sullivan Award winner (1965); led NY Knicks to 2 NBA titles (1970,73); U.S. Senator (D, N.J.) since 1979, but announced in 1995 he would not seek re-election in '96.

Pat Bradley (b. Mar. 24, 1951): Golfer; 2-time LPGA Player of Year (1986,91); has won all four majors on LPGA tour, including 3 du Maurier Classics; inducted into the LPGA Hall of Fame on Jan. 18, 1992; entered 1995 as all-time LPGA money leader and 13th in wins (30).

Terry Bradshaw (b. Sept. 2, 1948): Football QB; led Pittsburgh to 4 Super Bowl titles (1975-76,79-80); 2-time Super Bowl MVP (1979-80).

George Brett (b. May 15, 1953): Baseball 3B-1B; AL batting champion in 3 different decades (1976,80,90); MVP in 1980; led KC to World Series title in 1985; retired after 1993 season with 3,154 hits and .305 career average.

Valerie Brisco-Hooks (b. July 6, 1960); Track and Field; won three gold medals at the 1984 Olympics (200 meters, 400 meters and 4x100 relay); first athlete to ever win the 200 and 400 in the same Olympic (note: the 1984 games were boycotted by the Soviet bloc); first American woman to break 50 seconds in the 400 meter run.

Lou Brock (b. June 18, 1939): Baseball OF; former all-time stolen base leader (938); led NL in steals 8 times; led St. Louis to 2 World Series titles (1964,67); had 3,023 career hits.

Herb Brooks (b. Aug. 5, 1937): Hockey; former U.S. Olympic player (1964,68) who coached 1980 team to gold medal; coached Minnesota to 3 NCAA titles (1974,76,78); also coached NY Rangers, Minnesota and New Jersey in NHL.

Jim Brown (b. Feb. 17, 1936): Football FB; All-America at Syracuse (1956) and NFL Rookie of Year (1957); led NFL in rushing 8 times; 8-time All-Pro (1957-61,63-65); 3-time MVP (1958,63,65) with Cleveland; ran for 12,312 yards and scored 756 points in just 9 seasons.

Larry Brown (b. Sept. 14, 1940): Basketball; played in ACC, AAU, 1964 Olympics and ABA; 3-time assist leader (1968-70) and 3-time Coach of Year (1973,75-76) in ABA; coached ABA's Carolina and Denver and NBA's Denver, New Jersey, San Antonio, LA Clippers and Indiana; also coached UCLA to Final Four (1980) and Kansas to NCAA title (1988).

Mordecai (Three-Finger) Brown (b. Oct. 18, 1876, d. Feb. 14, 1948); Baseball; nickname derived from loss of three fingers in a childhood accident; injury gave him a particularly nasty curve ball; won the decisive game of the the 1907 World Series as a Chicago Cub; in 1908, first pitcher to record 4 consecutive shutouts and his overall record was 29-9; career record of 239-130 with lifetime E.R.A. of 2.06; member of Baseball Hall of Fame.

Paul Brown (b. Sept. 7, 1908, d. Aug. 5, 1991): Football innovator; coached Ohio St. to national title in 1942; in pros, directed Cleveland Browns to 4 straight AAFC titles (1946-49) and 3 NFL titles (1950,54-55); formed Cincinnati Bengals as head coach and part-owner in 1968 (reached playoffs in '70).

Sergi Bruguera (b. Jan. 16, 1971): Spanish tennis player; won consecutive French Opens in 1993 and '94; entered 1996 as decade's winningest clay court player.

Valery Brumel (b. Apr. 14, 1942): Soviet high jumper; dominated event from 1961-64; broke world record 5 times; won silver medal in 1960 Olympics and gold in 1964; highest jump was 7-5.

Avery Brundage (b. Sept. 28, 1887, d. May 5, 1975): Amateur sports czar for over 40 years as president of AAU (1928-35), U.S. Olympic Committee (1929-53) and International Olympic Committee (1952-72).

Paul (Bear) Bryant (b. Sept. 11, 1913, d. Jan. 26, 1983): Football; coached at 4 colleges over 38 years; directed Alabama to 5 national titles (1961,64-65,78-79); 323 career wins; 15 bowl wins including 8 Sugar Bowls.

Sergey Bubka (b. Dec. 4, 1963): Ukrainian pole vaulter; 1st man to clear 20 feet both indoors and out (1991); holder of indoor (20-2) and outdoor (20-1¾) world records as of Sept. 10, 1995; 5-time world champion (1983,87,91,93,95); won Olympic gold medal in 1988, but failed to clear any height in 1992 Games.

Buck Buchanan (b. Sept. 10, 1940, d. July 16, 1992) Football; played both ways in college at Grambling; first player chosen in the first AFL draft by the Dallas Texans who later became the Kansas City Chiefs; missed one game in a 13-year pro career; played in six AFL All-Star games and two Pro Bowls at defensive tackle; defensive star of the Chiefs team that won Super Bowl IV; later coached for the New Orleans Saints and Cleveland Browns; member of Pro Football Hall of Fame.

Don Budge (b. June 13, 1915): Tennis; in 1938 became 1st player to win the Grand Slam— the French, Wimbledon, U.S. and Australian titles in 1 year; led U.S. to 2 Davis Cups (1937-38); turned pro in late '38.

Maria Bueno (b. Oct. 11, 1939): Brazilian tennis player; won 4 U.S. Championships (1959,63-64,66) and 3 Wimbledons (1959-60,64).

Leroy Burrell (b. Feb. 21, 1967): Track & Field; set former world record of 9.85 in 100 meters, July 6, 1994; previously held record (9.90) in 1991; member of 4 world record-breaking 4 x 100m relay teams.

George Bush (b. June 12, 1924): 41st President of U.S. (1989-93) and avid sportsman; played 1B on 1947 and '48 Yale baseball teams that placed 2nd in College World Series; captain of 1948 team.

Susan Butcher (b. Dec. 26, 1956): Sled Dog racer; 4-time winner of Iditarod Trail race (1986-88,90).

Dick Butkus (b. Dec. 9, 1942): Football LB; 2-time All-America at Illinois (1963-64); All-Pro 7 of 9 NFL seasons with Chicago Bears.

Dick Button (b. July 18, 1929): Figure skater; 5-time world champion (1948-52); 2-time Olympic champ (1948,52); Sullivan Award winner (1949); won Emmy Award as Best Analyst for 1980-81 TV season.

Walter Byers (b. Mar. 13, 1922): College athletics; 1st executive director of NCAA, serving from 1951-88.

Frank Calder (b. Nov. 17, 1877, d. Feb. 4, 1943): Hockey; 1st NHL president (1917-43); guided league through its formative years; NHL's Rookie of the Year award named after him.

Lee Calhoun (b. Feb. 23, 1933, d. June 22, 1989): Track & Field; won consecutive Olympic gold medals in the 110m hurdles (1956,60).

Walter Camp (b. Apr. 7, 1859, d. Mar. 14, 1925): Football coach and innovator; established scrimmage line, center snap, downs, 11 players per side; elected 1st All-America team (1889).

Roy Campanella (b. Nov. 19, 1921, d. June 26, 1993): Baseball C; 3-time NL MVP (1951,53,55); led Brooklyn to 5 pennants and 1st World Series title (1955); career cut short when 1958 car accident left him paralyzed.

Clarence Campbell (b. July 9, 1905, d. June 24, 1984): Hockey; 3rd NHL president (1946-77), league tripled in size from 6 to 18 teams during his tenure.

Earl Campbell (b. Mar. 29, 1955): Football RB; won Heisman Trophy in 1977; led NFL in rushing 3 times; 3-time All-Pro; 2-time MVP (1978-79) at Houston.

John Campbell (b. Apr. 8, 1955): Harness racing; 4-time winner of Hambletonian (1987,88,90,95); 3-time Driver of Year; first driver to go over $100 million in career winnings; entered 1996 with 7,019 career wins.

Milt Campbell (b. Dec. 9, 1933): Track & Field; won silver medal in 1952 Olympic decathlon and gold medal in '56.

Jimmy Cannon (b. 1910, d. Dec. 5, 1973): Tough, opinionated New York sportswriter and essayist who viewed sports as an extension of show business; protégé of Damon Runyon; covered World War II for *Stars & Stripes*.

Tony Canzoneri (b. Nov. 6, 1908, d. Dec. 9, 1959): Boxer; 2-time world lightweight champion (1930-33,35-36); pro record 141-24-10 with 44 KOs.

Jennifer Capriati (b. Mar. 29, 1976): Tennis; youngest Grand Slam semifinalist ever (age 14 in 1990 French Open); also youngest to win a match at Wimbledon (1990); upset Steffi Graf to win gold medal at 1992 Olympics; left tour in '94 due to personal problems including an arrest for marijuana possession.

Harry Caray (b. Mar. 1, 1917): Radio-TV; baseball play-by-play broadcaster for St. Louis Cardinals, Oakland, Chicago White Sox and Cubs since 1945; father of sportscaster Skip and grandfather of sportscaster Chip.

Rod Carew (b. Oct. 1, 1945): Baseball 2B-1B; led AL in batting 7 times (1969,72-75,77-78) with Minnesota; MVP in 1977; had 3,053 career hits.

Steve Carlton (b. Dec. 22, 1944): Baseball LHP; won 20 or more games 6 times; 4-time Cy Young winner (1972,77,80,82) with Philadelphia; 329 career wins.

JoAnne Carner (b. Apr. 4, 1939): Golfer; 5-time U.S. Amateur champion; 2-time U.S. Open champ; 3-time LPGA Player of Year (1974,81-82); 7th in career wins (42).

Cris Carter (b. Nov. 25, 1965) Football; wide receiver for the Minnesota Vikings; twice caught 122 passes in a season (1994, '95), the first time establishing an NFL record for catches in a season that was beaten by the Detroit Lions' Herman Moore the next year.

Don Carter (b. July 29, 1926): Bowler; 6-time Bowler of Year (1953-54,57-58,60-61); voted Greatest of All-Time in 1970.

Joe Carter (b. Mar. 7, 1960): Baseball OF; 3-time All-America at Wichita St. (1979-81); won 1993 World Series for Toronto with 3-run HR in bottom of the 9th of Game 6; entered 1996 season with 327 HRs and 1,173 RBI in 13 years.

Alexander Cartwright (b. Apr. 17, 1820, d. July 12, 1892): Baseball; engineer and draftsman who spread gospel of baseball from New York City to California gold fields; widely regarded as the father of modern game; his guidelines included setting 3 strikes for an out and 3 outs for each half inning.

Billy Casper (b. June 4, 1931): Golfer; 2-time PGA Player of Year (1966,70); has won U.S. Open (1959,66), Masters (1970), U.S. Senior Open (1983); compiled 51 PGA wins and 9 on Senior Tour.

Tracy Caulkins (b. Jan. 11, 1963): Swimmer; won 3 gold medals (2 individual) at 1984 Olympics; set 5 world records and won 48 U.S. national titles from 1978-84; Sullivan Award winner (1978); 2-time Honda Broderick Cup winner (1982,84).

Evonne Goolagong Cawley (b. July 31, 1951): Australian tennis player; won Australian Open 4 times, Wimbledon twice (1971,79), French once.

Florence Chadwick (b. Nov. 9, 1917, d. Mar. 15, 1995): Dominant distance swimmer of 1950's; set English Channel records from France to England (1950) and England to France (1951 and '55).

Wilt Chamberlain (b. Aug. 21, 1936): Basketball C; consensus All-America in 1957 and '58 at Kansas; Final Four MVP in 1957; led NBA in scoring 7 times and rebounding 11 times; 7-time All-NBA first team; 4-time MVP (1960,66-68) in Philadelphia; scored 100 points vs. NY Knicks in Hershey, Pa., Mar. 2, 1962; led Philadelphia 76ers (1967) and LA Lakers (1972) to NBA titles; playoff MVP in 1972.

A.B. (Happy) Chandler (b. July 14, 1898, d. June 15, 1991): Baseball; former Kentucky governor and U.S. Senator who succeeded Judge Landis as commissioner in 1945; backed Branch Rickey's move in 1947 to make Jackie Robinson 1st black player in major leagues; deemed too pro-player and ousted by owners in 1951.

Julio Cesar Chavez (b. July 12, 1962): Mexican boxer; world jr. welterweight champ; also held titles as jr. lightweight (1984-87) and lightweight (1987-89); fought Pernell Whitaker to controversial draw for welterweight title on Sept. 10, 1993; entered 1995 with 92-1-1 record with 76 KOs; 90-bout unbeaten streak ended Jan. 29, 1994 when Frankie Randall won title on split decision; Chavez won title back four months later.

Linford Christie (b. Apr. 2, 1960): British sprinter; won 100-meter gold medals at both 1992 Olympics (9.96) and '93 World Championships (9.87); set indoor world record in 200-meters (20.25) on Feb. 19, 1995 in Lievin, France.

Jim Clark (b. Mar. 14, 1936, d. Apr. 7, 1968): Scottish auto racer; 2-time Formula One world champion (1963,65); won Indy 500 in 1965; killed in car crash.

Bobby Clarke (b. Aug. 13, 1949): Hockey C; led Philadelphia Flyers to consecutive Stanley Cups in 1974-75; 3-time regular season MVP (1973,75-76).

Ron Clarke (b. Feb. 21, 1937): Australian runner; from 1963-70 set 17 world records in races from 2 miles to 20,000 meters; never won Olympic gold medal.

Roger Clemens (b. Aug. 4, 1962): Baseball RHP; twice fanned MLB record 20 batters in 9-inning game (April 29, 1986 and Sept. 18, 1996); 3 Cy Young Awards (1986-87,91) with Boston; AL MVP in 1986; entered 1996 season with 182 wins in 12 seasons.

Roberto Clemente (b. Aug. 18, 1934, d. Dec. 31, 1972): Baseball OF; hit .300 or better 13 times with Pittsburgh; led NL in batting 4 times; World Series MVP in 1971; regular season MVP in 1966; had 3,000 career hits; killed in plane crash.

Ty Cobb (b. Dec. 18, 1886, d. July 17, 1961): Baseball OF; all-time highest career batting average (.367); hit .400 or better 3 times; led AL in batting 12 times and stolen bases 6 times with Detroit; MVP in 1911; had 4,191 career hits and 892 steals.

Mickey Cochrane (b. Apr. 6, 1903, d. June 28, 1962): Baseball C; led Philadelphia A's (1929-30) and Detroit (1935) to 3 World Series titles; 2-time AL MVP (1928,34).

Sebastian Coe (b. Sept. 29, 1956): British runner; won gold medal in 1500m and silver medal in 800m at both 1980 and '84 Olympics; although retired, still holds world records in 800m and 1000m; elected to Parliament as Conservative in 1992.

Paul Coffey (b. June 1, 1961): Hockey D; holds NHL record for goals (372), assists (1,038) and points (1,410) by a defenseman; member of four Stanley Cup championship teams at Edmonton (1984-85,87) and Pittsburgh (1991).

Eddie Collins (b. May 2, 1887, d. Mar. 25, 1951): Baseball 2B; led Philadelphia A's (1910-11) and Chicago White Sox (1917) to 3 World Series titles; AL MVP in 1914; had 3,311 career hits and 743 stolen bases.

Nadia Comaneci (b. Nov. 12, 1961): Romanian gymnast; 1st to record perfect 10 in Olympics; won 3 individual gold medals at 1976 Olympics and 2 more in '80.

Lionel Conacher (b. May 24, 1901, d. May 26, 1954): Canada's greatest all-around athlete; NHL hockey (2 Stanley Cups), CFL football (1 Grey Cup), minor league baseball, soccer, lacrosse, track, amateur boxing champion; also member of Parliament (1949-54).

Gene Conley (b. Nov. 10, 1930): Baseball and Basketball played for World Series and NBA champions with Milwaukee Braves (1957) and Boston Celtics (1959-61); winning pitcher in 1954 All-Star Game; won 91 games in 11 seasons.

Billy Conn (b. Oct. 8, 1917, d. May 29, 1993): Boxer; Pittsburgh native and world light heavyweight champion from 1939-41; nearly upset heavyweight champ Joe Louis in 1941 title bout, but was knocked out in 13th round; pro record 63-11-1 with 14 KOs.

Dennis Conner (b. Sept. 16, 1942): Sailing; 3-time America's Cup-winning skipper aboard *Freedom* (1980), *Stars & Stripes* (1987) and the *Stars & Stripes* catamaran (1988); only American skipper to lose Cup, first in 1983 when *Australia II* beat *Liberty* and again in '95 when New Zealand's *Black* Magic swept Conner and his *Stars & Stripes* crew aboard the borrowed *Young America*.

Maureen Connolly (b. Sept. 17, 1934, d. June 21, 1969): Tennis; in 1953 1st woman to win Grand Slam (at age 19); riding accident ended her career in '54; won both Wimbledon and U.S. titles 3 times (1951-53); 3-time AP Female Athlete of Year (1951-53).

Jimmy Connors (b. Sept. 2, 1952): Tennis; No.1 player in world 5 times (1974-78); won 5 U.S. Opens, 2 Wimbledons and 1 Australian; rose from No. 936 at the close of 1990 to U.S. Open semifinals in 1991 at age 39; NCAA singles champ (1971); all-time leader in pro singles titles (109) and matches won at U.S. Open (98) and Wimbledon (84).

Jack Kent Cooke (b. Oct. 25, 1912): Football; sole owner of NFL Washington Redskins since 1985; teams have won 2 Super Bowls (1987,91); also owned NBA Lakers and NHL Kings in LA; built LA Forum for $12 million in 1967.

Angel Cordero Jr. (b. Nov. 8, 1942): Jockey; third on all-time list with 7,057 wins in 38,646 starts; won Kentucky Derby 3 times (1974,76,85), Preakness twice and Belmont once; 2-time Eclipse Award winner (1982-83); resumed career on Oct. 1, 1995 after retiring in 1992.

Howard Cosell (b. Mar. 25, 1920, d. Apr. 23, 1995): Radio-TV; former ABC commentator on "Monday Night Football" and "Wide World of Sports," who energized TV sports journalism with abrasive "tell it like it is" style.

Bob Costas (b. Mar. 22, 1952): Radio-TV; NBC anchor for NBA, NFL and Summer Olympics as well as baseball play-by-play man; 6-time Emmy winner and Sportscaster of Year.

James (Doc) Counsilman (b. Dec. 28, 1920): Swimming; coached Indiana men's swim team to 6 NCAA championships (1968-73); coached the 1964 and '76 U.S. men's Olympic teams that won a combined 21 of 24 gold medals; in 1979 became oldest person (59) to swim English Channel; retired in 1990 with dual meet record of 287-36-1.

Fred Couples (b. Oct. 3, 1959): Golfer; 2-time PGA Tour Player of the Year (1991,92); entered 1996 with 12 Tour victories, including 1992 Masters.

Jim Courier (b. Aug. 17, 1970): Tennis; No. 1 player in world in 1992, has won two Australian Opens (1992-93) and two French (1991-92); played on 1992 Davis Cup winner; Nick Bollettieri Academy classmate of Andre Agassi.

Margaret Smith Court (b. July 16, 1942): Australian tennis player; won Grand Slam in both singles (1970) and mixed doubles (1963 with Ken Fletcher); 26 Grand Slam singles titles— 11 Australian, 7 U.S., 5 French and 3 Wimbledon.

Bob Cousy (b. Aug. 9, 1928): Basketball G; led NBA in assists 8 times; 10-time All-NBA 1st team (1952-61); MVP in 1957; led Boston to 6 NBA titles (1957,59-63).

Buster Crabbe (b. Feb. 7, 1910, d. Apr. 23, 1983): Swimmer; 2-time Olympic freestyle medalist with bronze in 1928 (1500m) and gold in '32 (400m); became movie star and King of Serials as Flash Gordon and Buck Rogers.

Ben Crenshaw (b. Jan. 11, 1952): Golfer; co-NCAA champion with Tom Kite in 1972; battled Graves' disease in mid-1980's; entered 1996 with 19 career Tour victories; won Masters for second time on April 9, 1995 and dedicated it to 90-year-old mentor Harvey Penick, who had died on April 2.

Joe Cronin (b. Oct. 12, 1906, d. Sept. 7, 1984): Baseball SS; hit over .300 and drove in over 100 runs 8 times each; MVP in 1930; player-manager in Washington and Boston (1933-47); AL president (1959-73).

Ann Curtis (b. Mar. 6, 1926): Swimming; won 2 gold medals and 1 silver in 1948 Olympics; set 4 world and 18 U.S. records during career; 1st woman and swimmer to win Sullivan Award (1944).

Betty Cuthbert (b. Apr. 20, 1938): Australian runner; won gold medals in 100 and 200 meters and 4x100m relay at 1956 Olympics; also won 400m gold at 1964 Olympics.

Chuck Daly (b. July 20, 1930): Basketball; coached Detroit to two NBA titles (1989-90) before leaving in 1992 to coach New Jersey; retired after 1993-94 season with 638 career wins (including playoffs) in 12 years; coached NBA "Dream Team" to gold medal in 1992 Olympics.

John Daly (b. Apr. 28, 1966): Golfer; suprise winner of 1991 PGA Championship as unknown 25-year-old; battled through personal troubles in 1994 to return in '95 and win 2nd major at British Open, beating Italy's Costantino Rocca in 4-hole playoff.

Stanley Dancer (b. July 25, 1927): Harness racing; winner of 4 Hambletonians; trainer-driver of Triple Crown winners in Trotting (Nevele Pride in 1968 and Super Bowl in '72) and Pacing (Most Happy Fella in 1970); entered 1995 with 3,780 career wins.

Tamas Darnyi (b. June 3, 1967): Hungarian swimmer; 2-time double gold medal winner in 200m and 400m individual medley at 1988 and '92 Olympics; also won both events in 1986 and '91 world championships; set world records in both at '91 worlds; 1st swimmer to break 2 minutes in 200m IM (1:59:36).

Al Davis (b. July 4, 1929): Football; GM-coach of Oakland 1963-66; helped force AFL-NFL merger as AFL commissioner (April-July 1966); returned to Oakland as managing general partner and directed club to 3 Super Bowl wins (1977,81,84); defied fellow NFL owners and moved Raiders to LA in 1982; turned down owners' 1995 offer to build him a new stadium in LA and moved back to Oakland instead.

Dwight Davis (b. July 5, 1879, d. Nov. 28, 1945): Tennis; donor of Davis Cup; played for winning U.S. team in 1st two Cup finals (1900,02); won U.S. and Wimbledon doubles titles in 1901; Secretary of War (1925-29) under Coolidge.

Glenn Davis (b. Dec. 26, 1924): Football HB; 3-time All-America; led Army to national titles in 1944-45; Doc Blanchard's running mate; won Heisman Trophy in 1946.

John Davis (b. Jan. 12, 1921, d. July 13, 1984): Weightlifting; 6-time world champion; 2-time Olympic super-heavyweight champ (1948,52); undefeated from 1938-53.

Dizzy Dean (b. Jan. 16 1911, d. July 17, 1974): Baseball RHP; led NL in strikeouts and complete games 4 times; last NL pitcher to win 30 games (30-7 in 1934); MVP in 1934 with St. Louis; 150 career wins.

Dave DeBusschere (b. Oct. 16, 1940): Basketball F; 3-time All-America at Detroit; youngest coach in NBA history (24 in 1964); player-coach of Detroit Pistons (1964-67); played in 8 All-Star games; won 2 NBA titles as player with NY Knicks; ABA commissioner (1975-76); also pitched 2 seasons for Chicago White Sox (1962-63) with 3-4 record.

Pierre de Coubertin (b. Jan. 1, 1863, d. Sept. 2, 1937): French educator; father of the Modern Olympic Games; IOC president from 1896-1925.

Anita DeFrantz (b. Oct. 4, 1952): Olympics; attorney who is one of 2 American delegates to the International Olympic Committee (James Easton is the other); first woman to represent U.S. on IOC; member of USOC Executive Committee; member of bronze medal U.S. women's eight-oared shell at Montreal in 1976.

Cedric Dempsey (b. Apr. 14, 1932): College sports; named to succeed Dick Schultz as NCAA executive director on Nov. 5, 1993; served as athletic director at Pacific (1967-79), San Diego St. (1979), Houston (1979-82) and Arizona (1983-93).

Jack Dempsey (b. June 24, 1895, d. May 31, 1983): Boxer; world heavyweight champion from 1919-26; lost title to Gene Tunney, then lost "Long Count" rematch in 1927 when he floored Tunney in 7th round but failed to retreat to neutral corner; pro record 62-6-10 with 49 KOs.

Bob Devaney (b. April 13, 1915) Football; head coach at Wyoming from 1957-1961; from 1962 to 1972 built Nebraska into a college football power; won two consecutive national championships in 1970-'71; won eight Big Eight Conference titles; overall record of 136-30-11; later served as Nebraska's athletic director; College Football Hall of Fame.

Donna de Varona (b. Apr. 26, 1947): Swimming; won gold medals in 400 IM and 400 freestyle relay at 1964 Olympics; set 18 world records during career; co-founder of Women's Sports Foundation in 1974.

Gail Devers (b. Nov. 19, 1966): Track & Field; fastest-ever woman sprinter-hurdler; overcame thyroid disorder (Graves' disease) that sidelined her in 1989-90 and nearly resulted in having both feet amputated; won Olympic gold medal in 100 meters in 1992 and '96; 3-time world champion in 100 meters (1993) and 100-meter hurdles (1993,95).

Klaus Dibiasi (b. Oct. 6, 1947): Italian diver; won 3 consecutive Olympic gold medals in platform event (1968,72,76).

Eric Dickerson (b. Sept. 2, 1960): Football RB; led NFL in rushing 4 times (1983-84,86,88); ran for single-season record 2,105 yards in 1984; NFC Rookie of Year in 1983; All-Pro 5 times; traded from LA Rams to Indianapolis (Oct. 31, 1987) in 3-team, 10-player deal (including draft picks) that also involved Buffalo; 2nd on all-time career rushing list with 13,259 yards in 11 seasons.

Harrison Dillard (b. July 8, 1923): Track & Field; only man to win Olympic gold medals in both sprints (100m in 1948) and hurdles (110m in 1952).

Joe DiMaggio (b. Nov. 25, 1914): Baseball OF; hit safely in 56 straight games (1941); led AL in batting, HRs and RBI twice each; 3-time MVP (1939,41,47); hit .325 with 361 HRs over 13 seasons; led NY Yankees to 10 World Series titles.

Mike Ditka (b. Oct. 18, 1939): Football; All-America at Pitt (1960); NFL Rookie of Year (1961); 5-time Pro Bowl tight end for Chicago Bears; also played for Philadelphia and Dallas in 12-year career; returned to Chicago as head coach in 1982; won Super Bowl XX; compiled 112-68-0 record in 11 seasons with Bears.

Charlotte (Lottie) Dod (b. Sept. 24, 1871, d. June 27, 1960): British athlete; was 5-time Wimbledon singles champion (1887-88,91-93); youngest player ever to win Wimbledon (15 in 1887); archery silver medalist at 1908 Olympics; member of national field hockey team in 1899; British Amateur golf champ in 1904.

Tony Dorsett (b. Apr. 7, 1954): Football RB; won Heisman Trophy leading Pitt to national title in 1976; all-time NCAA Div. I-A rushing leader with 6,082 yards; led Dallas to Super Bowl title as NFC Rookie of Year (1977); NFC Player of Year (1981); ranks 3rd on all-time NFL list with 12,739 yards gained in 12 years; holds NFL record for run from scrimmage (99 yards vs. Min. in 1983).

James (Buster) Douglas (b. Apr. 7, 1960): Boxing; 50-1 shot who knocked out undefeated Mike Tyson in 10th round on Feb. 10, 1990 to win heavyweight title in Tokyo; 10 months later, lost only title defense to Evander Holyfield by KO in 3rd round.

The Dream Team: Head coach Chuck Daly's "Best Ever" 12-man NBA All-Star squad that headlined the 1992 Summer Olympics in Barcelona and easily won the basketball gold medal; co-captained by Larry Bird and Magic Johnson, with veterans Charles Barkley, Clyde Drexler, Patrick Ewing, Michael Jordan, Karl Malone, Chris Mullin, Scottie Pippen, David Robinson, John Stockton and rookie Christian Laettner.

Dream Team II: Head coach Don Nelson's 12-man NBA All-Star squad that cruised to gold medal at 1994 World Basketball Championships in Toronto— Derrick Coleman, Joe Dumars, Kevin Johnson, Larry Johnson, Shawn Kemp, Dan Majerle, Reggie Miller, Alonzo Mourning, Shaquille O'Neal, Mark Price, Steve Smith and Dominique Wilkins.

Dream Team III: Head coach Lenny Wilkens' 10-man NBA All-Star squad that represented the U.S. at the 1996 Summer Olympics in Atlanta— Anfernee Hardaway, Grant Hill, Karl Malone, Reggie Miller, Hakeem Olajuwon, Shaquille O'Neal, Gary Payton, Scottie Pippen, Mitch Richmond, David Robinson, Glenn Robinson and John Stockton.

Heike Drechsler (b. Dec. 16, 1964): German long jumper and sprinter; East German before reunification in 1991; set world long jump record (24-2¼) in 1988; won long jump gold medals at 1992 Olympics and 1983 and '93 World Championships; won silver medal in long jump and bronze medals in both 100- and 200-meter sprints at 1988 Olympics.

Ken Dryden (b. Aug. 8, 1947): Hockey G; led Montreal to 6 Stanley Cup titles; playoff MVP as rookie in 1971; won or shared 5 Vezina Trophies; 2.24 career GAA.

Don Drysdale (b. July 23, 1936, d. July 3, 1993): Baseball RHP; led NL in strikeouts 3 times and games started 4 straight years; pitched and won record 6 shutouts in a row in 1968; Cy Young Award winner in 1962; won 209 games and hit 29 HRs in 14 years.

Charley Dumas (b. Feb. 12, 1937): U.S. high jumper; first man to clear 7 feet (7-0 1/2) on June 29, 1956; won gold medal at 1956 Olympics.

Margaret Osborne du Pont (b. Mar. 4, 1918): Tennis; won 5 French, 7 Wimbledon and an unprecedented 24 U.S. national titles in singles, doubles and mixed doubles from 1941-62.

Roberto Duran (b. June 16, 1951): Panamanian boxer; one of only 4 fighters to hold 4 different world titles— lightweight (1972-79), welterweight (1980), junior middleweight (1983) and middleweight (1989-90); lost famous "No Mas" welterweight title bout when he quit in 8th round against Sugar Ray Leonard (1980); pro record stood at 94-11 and 65 KOs after 12-round loss to Vinny Pazienza on Jan. 14, 1995.

Leo Durocher (b. July 27, 1905, d. Oct. 7, 1991): Baseball; managed in NL 24 years; won 2,015 games, including postseason; 3 pennants with Brooklyn (1941) and NY Giants (1951,54); won World Series in 1954.

Eddie Eagan (b. Apr. 26, 1898, d. June 14, 1967): Only athlete to win gold medals in both Summer and Winter Olympics (Boxing in 1920, Bobsled in 1932).

Alan Eagleson (b. Apr. 24, 1933): Hockey; Toronto lawyer, agent and 1st executive director of NHL Players Assn. (1967-90); midwived Team Canada vs. Soviet series (1972) and Canada Cup; charged with racketeering and defrauding NHLPA in 32-count indictment handed down by U.S. grand jury on Mar. 3, 1994.

Dale Earnhardt (b. Apr. 29, 1952): Auto racer; 7-time NASCAR national champion (1980,86-87,90-91, 93-94); Rookie of Year in 1979; entered 1995 as all-time NASCAR money leader with $22,794,304 and 6th on career wins list with 63; in 21 years, has never won Daytona 500.

James Easton (b. July 26, 1935): Olympics; archer and sporting goods manufacturer (Easton softball bats); one of 2 American delegates to the International Olympic Committee; president of International Archery Federation (FITA); member of LA Olympic Organizing Committee in 1984.

Dick Ebersol (b. July 28, 1947): Radio-TV; protégé of ABC Sports czar Roone Arledge; key NBC exec in launching of "Saturday Night Live" in 1975; became president of NBC Sports in 1989, won U.S. TV rights to both 2000 Summer and 2002 Winter Olympics with unprecedented combined bid of $1.27 billion in August 1995.

Stefan Edberg (b. Jan. 19, 1966): Swedish tennis player; 2-time No.1 player (1990-91); 2-time winner of Australian Open (1985,87), Wimbledon (1988,90) and U.S. Open (1991-92); has never won French.

Gertrude Ederle (b. Oct. 23, 1906): Swimmer; 1st woman to swim English Channel, breaking men's record by 2 hours in 1926; won 3 medals in 1924 Olympics.

Krisztina Egerszegi (b. Aug. 16, 1974): Hungarian swimmer; 3-time gold medal winner (100m and 200m backstroke and 400m IM) in 1992 Olympics; also won a gold (200m back) and silver (100m back) in 1988 Games; youngest (age 14) ever to win swimming gold. Won fifth gold medal (200m back) at '96 Games.

Bill Elliott (b. Oct. 8, 1955): Auto racer; 2-time winner of Daytona 500 (1985,87); NASCAR national champ in 1988; entered 1996 with 40 NASCAR wins.

Herb Elliott (b. Feb. 25, 1938): Australian runner; undefeated from 1958-60; ran 17 sub-4:00 miles; 3 world records; won gold medal in 1500 meters at 1960 Olympics; retired at age 22.

Roy Emerson (b. Nov. 3, 1936): Australian tennis player; won 12 Majors in singles— 6 Australian, 2 French, 2 Wimbledon and 2 U.S. from 1961-67.

Kornelia Ender (b. Oct. 25, 1958): East German swimmer; 1st woman to win 4 gold medals at one Olympics (1976), all in world-record time.

Julius Erving (b. Feb. 22, 1950): Basketball F; in ABA (1972-76)— 3-time MVP, 2-time playoff MVP, led NY Nets to 2 titles (1974-76); in NBA (1977-87)— 5-time All-NBA 1st team, MVP in 1981, led Philadelphia 76ers to title in 1983.

Phil Esposito (b. Feb. 20, 1942): Hockey C; 1st NHL player to score 100 points in a season (126 in 1969); 6-time All-NHL 1st team with Boston; 2-time MVP (1969,74); 5-time scoring champ; star of 1972 Canada-Soviet series; president-GM of NHL's Tampa Bay Lightning.

Janet Evans (b. Aug. 28, 1971): Swimmer; won 3 individual gold medals (400m & 800m freestyle, 400m IM) at 1988 Olympics; 1989 Sullivan Award winner; entered 1995 as world record-holder in 400m, 800m and 1500m freestyles; won 1 gold (800m) and 1 silver (400m) at 1992 Olympics.

Lee Evans (b. Feb. 25, 1947): Track & Field; dominant quarter-miler in world from 1966-72; world record in 400m at 1968 Olympics stood 20 years.

Chris Evert (b. Dec. 21, 1954): Tennis; No.1 player in world 5 times (1975-77,80-81); won at least 1 Grand Slam singles title every year from 1974-86; 18 Majors in all— 7 French, 6 U.S., 3 Wimbledon and 2 Australian; retired after 1989 season.

Weeb Ewbank (b. May 6, 1907): Football; only coach to win NFL and AFL titles; led Baltimore to 2 NFL titles (1958-59) and NY Jets to Super Bowl III win.

Patrick Ewing (b. Aug. 5, 1962): Basketball C; 3-time All-America; led Georgetown to 3 NCAA Finals and 1984 title; tourney MVP in '84; NBA Rookie of Year with New York in '86; All-NBA in 1990; led U.S. Olympic team to gold medals in 1984 and '92.

Ray Ewry (b. Oct. 14, 1873, d. Sept. 29, 1937): Track & Field; won 10 gold medals over 4 consecutive Olympics (1900,04,06,08); all events he won (Standing HJ, LJ and TJ) were discontinued in 1912.

Nick Faldo (b. July 18, 1957): British golfer; 3-time winner of British Open (1987,90,92) and Masters (1989, 90, 96); 3-time European Golfer of Year (1989-90,92); PGA Player of Year in 1990.

Juan Manuel Fangio (b. June 24, 1911, d. July 17, 1995): Argentine auto racer; 5-time Formula One world champion (1951,54-57); 24 career wins, retired in 1958.

Sergei Fedorov (b. Dec. 13, 1969): Hockey C; first Russian to win NHL Hart Trophy as 1993-94 regular season MVP; 3-time All-Star with Detroit.

Donald Fehr (b. July 18, 1948): Baseball labor leader; protégé of Marvin Miller; executive director and general counsel of Major League Players Assn. since 1983; led players in 1994 "salary cap" strike that lasted eight months and resulted in first cancellation of World Series since 1904.

Bob Feller (b. Nov. 3, 1918): Baseball RHP; led AL in strikeouts 7 times and wins 6 times with Cleveland; threw 3 no-hitters and 12 one-hitters; 266 career wins.

Tom Ferguson (b. Dec. 20, 1950): Rodeo; 6-time All-Around champion (1974-79); 1st cowboy to win $100,000 in one season (1978); 1st to win $1 million in career (1986).

Cecil Fielder (b. Sept. 21, 1963): Baseball 1B; returned from one season with Hanshin Tigers in Japan to hit 51 HRs for Detroit Tigers in 1990; led MLB in RBI 3 straight years (1990-92); AL MVP runner-up in 1990 and '91. Entered '96 season with most homers in the '90s (219); has 250 in career.

Herve Filion (b. Feb. 1, 1940): Harness racing; 10-time Driver of Year; entered 1996 season as all-time leader in races won with 14,783 in 35 years.

Rollie Fingers (b. Aug. 25, 1946): Baseball RHP; relief ace with 341 career saves; won AL MVP and Cy Young awards in 1981 with Milwaukee; World Series MVP in 1974 with Oakland.

Charles O. Finley (b. Feb. 22, 1918): Baseball owner; moved KC A's to Oakland in 1968; won 3 straight World Series from 1972-74; also owned teams in NHL and ABA.

Bobby Fischer (b. Mar. 9, 1943): Chess; at 15, became youngest international grandmaster in chess history; only American to hold world championship (1972-75); was stripped of title in 1975 after refusing to defend against Anatoly Karpov and became recluse; re-emerged to defeat old foe and former world champion Boris Spassky in 1992.

Carlton Fisk (b. Dec. 26, 1947): Baseball C; set all-time major league record at age 45 for games caught (2,226); also all-time HR leader for catchers (376); AL Rookie of Year (1972) and 10-time All-Star; hit epic, 12th-inning Game 6 homer for Boston Red Sox in 1975 World Series.

Emerson Fittipaldi (b. Dec. 12, 1946): Brazilian auto racer; 2-time Formula One world champion (1972,74); 2-time winner of Indy 500 (1989,93); won overall IndyCar title in 1989.

Bob Fitzsimmons (b. May 26, 1863, d. Oct. 22, 1917): British boxer; held three world titles— middleweight (1881-97), heavyweight (1897-99) and light heavyweight (1903-05); pro record 40-11 with 32 KOs.

James (Sunny Jim) Fitzsimmons (b. July 23, 1874, d. Mar. 11, 1966): Horse racing; trained horses that won over 2,275 races, including 2 Triple Crown winners— Gallant Fox in 1930 and Omaha in '35.

Jim Fixx (b. Apr. 23, 1932, d. July 20, 1984): Running; author who popularized the sport of running; his 1977 bestseller *The Complete Book of Running,* is credited with helping start America's fitness revolution; died of a heart attack while running.

Larry Fleisher (b. Sept. 26, 1930, d. May 4, 1989): Basketball; led NBA players union from 1961-89; increased average yearly salary from $9,400 in 1967 to $600,000 without a strike.

Peggy Fleming (b. July 27, 1948): Figure skating; 3-time world champion (1966-68); won Olympic gold medal in 1968.

Curt Flood (b. Jan. 18, 1938): Baseball OF; played 15 years (1956-69,71) mainly with St. Louis; hit over .300 6 times with 7 gold gloves; refused trade to Phillies in 1969; lost challenge to baseball's reserve clause in Supreme Court in 1972 (see Peter Seitz).

Ray Floyd (b. Sept. 14, 1942): Golfer; entered 1995 with 22 PGA victories in 4 decades; joined Senior PGA Tour in 1992; has won Masters (1976), U.S. Open (1986), PGA twice (1969,82) and PGA Seniors Championship (1995); only player to ever win on PGA and Senior tours in same year (1992); member of 8 Ryder Cup teams and captain in 1989.

Doug Flutie (b. Oct. 23, 1962): Football QB; won Heisman Trophy with Boston College (1984); has played in USFL, NFL and CFL since then; 4-time CFL MVP with B.C. Lions (1991) and Calgary (1992-94); led Calgary to Grey Cup title in '92; missed 2nd half of 1995 season with injured right elbow.

Gerald Ford (b. July 14, 1913): 38th President of the U.S.; lettered as center on undefeated Michigan football teams in 1932 and '33; MVP on 1934 squad.

Whitey Ford (b. Oct. 21, 1928): Baseball LHP; all-time leader in World Series wins (10); led AL in wins 3 times; won both Cy Young and World Series MVP in 1961 with NY Yankees.

George Foreman (b. Jan. 10, 1949): Boxer; Olympic heavyweight champ (1968); world heavyweight champ (1973-74 and 94-95); lost title to Muhammad Ali (KO-8th) in '74; recaptured it on Nov. 5, 1994 at age 45 with a 10-round KO of WBA/IBF champ Michael Moorer, becoming the oldest man to win heavyweight crown; named AP Male Athlete of Year 20 years after losing title to Ali; stripped of WBA title on Mar. 4, 1995 after declining to fight No. 1 contender; successfully defended title at age 46 against 26-year-old Axel Schultz of Germany in controversial majority decision on Apr. 22; gave up IBF title in June after refusing rematch with Schultz; entered 1996 with pro record of 74-4 and 68 KOs.

Dick Fosbury (b. Mar. 6, 1947): Track & Field; revolutionized high jump with back-first "Fosbury Flop"; won gold medal at 1968 Olympics.

Greg Foster (b. Aug. 4, 1958): Track & Field; 3-time winner of World Championship gold medal in 110-meter hurdles (1983,87,91); best Olympic performance a silver in 1984; world indoor champion in 1991; made world Top 10 rankings 15 years (a record for running events).

The Four Horsemen: Senior backfield that led Notre Dame to national collegiate football championship in 1924; put together as sophomores by Irish coach Knute Rockne; immortalized by sportswriter Grantland Rice, whose report of the Oct. 19, 1924, Notre Dame-Army game began: "Outlined against a blue, gray October sky the Four Horsemen rode again..."; HB Jim Crowley (b. Sept. 10, 1902, d. Jan. 15, 1986), FB Elmer Layden (b. May 4, 1903, d. June 30, 1973), HB Don Miller (b. May 30, 1902, d. July 28, 1979) and QB Harry Stuhldreher (b. Oct. 14, 1901, d. Jan. 26, 1965).

The Four Musketeers: French quartet that dominated men's tennis in 1920s and '30s, winning 8 straight French singles titles (1925-32), 6 Wimbledons in a row (1924-29) and 6 consecutive Davis Cups (1927-32)— Jean Borotra (b. Aug. 13, 1898, d. July 17, 1994), Jacques Brugnon (b. May 11, 1895, d. Mar. 20, 1978), Henri Cochet (b. Dec. 14, 1901, d. Apr. 1, 1987), Rene Lacoste (b. July 2, 1905, d. Oct. 13, 1996).

Jimmie Foxx (b. Oct. 22, 1907, d. July 21, 1967): Baseball 1B; led AL in HRs 4 times and batting twice; won Triple Crown in 1933; 3-time MVP (1932-33,38) with Philadelphia and Boston; hit 30 HRs or more 12 years in a row; 534 career HRs.

A.J. Foyt (b. Jan. 16, 1935): Auto racer; 7-time USAC-CART national champion (1960-61,63-64,67,75,79); 4-time Indy 500 winner (1961,64,67,77); only driver in history to win Indy 500, Daytona 500 (1972) and 24 Hours of LeMans (1967 with Dan Gurney); retired in 1993 as all-time IndyCar wins leader with 67.

Bill France Sr. (b. Sept. 26, 1909, d. June 7, 1992): Stock car pioneer and promoter; founded NASCAR in 1948; guided race circuit through formative years; built both Daytona (Fla.) Int'l Speedway and Talladega (Ala.) Superspeedway.

Dawn Fraser (b. Sept. 4, 1937): Australian swimmer; won gold medals in 100m freestyle at 3 consecutive Olympics (1956,60,64).

Joe Frazier (b. Jan. 12, 1944): Boxer; 1964 Olympic heavyweight champion; world heavyweight champ (1970-73); fought Muhammad Ali 3 times and won once; pro record 32-4-1 with 27 KOs.

Ford Frick (b. Dec. 19, 1894, d. Apr. 8, 1978): Baseball; sportswriter and radio announcer who served as NL president (1934-51) and commissioner (1951-65); convinced record-keepers to list Roger Maris' and Babe Ruth's season records separately; major leagues moved to west coast and expanded from 16 to 20 teams during his tenure.

Frankie Frisch (b. Sept. 9, 1898, d. Mar. 12, 1973): Baseball 2B; played on 8 NL pennant winners in 19 years with NY and St. Louis; hit .300 or better 11 years in a row (1921-31); MVP in 1931; player-manager from 1933-37.

Dan Gable (b. Oct. 25, 1948): Wrestling; career college wrestling record of 118-1 at Iowa St., where he was a 2-time NCAA champ (1968,69) and tourney MVP in 1969 (137 lbs); won gold medal (149 lbs) at 1972 Olympics; coached U.S. freestyle team in 1988; coached Iowa to 9 straight NCAA titles (1978-86) and has added four more since 1991.

Eddie Gaedel (b. June 8, 1925, d. June 18, 1961): Baseball pinch hitter; St. Louis Browns' midget whose career lasted one at bat (he walked) on Aug 19, 1951.

Clarence (Bighouse) Gaines (b. May 21, 1924): Basketball; retired as coach of Div. II Winston-Salem after 1992-93 season with 828-446 record in 47 years; ranks 3rd on all-time NCAA list behind Adolph Rupp (876) and Dean Smith (830).

Alonzo (Jake) Gaither (b. Apr. 11, 1903, d. Feb. 18, 1994): Football; head coach at Florida A&M for 25 years; led Rattlers to 6 national black college titles; retired after 1969 season with record of 203-36-4 and a winning percentage of .844; coined phrase, "I like my boys agile, mobile and hostile."

Cito Gaston (b. Mar. 17, 1944): Baseball; managed Toronto to consecutive World Series titles (1992-93); first black manager to win Series; shared *The Sporting News* 1993 Man of Year award with Blue Jays GM Pat Gillick.

Lou Gehrig (b. June 19, 1903, d. June 2, 1941): Baseball 1B; played in 2,130 consecutive games from 1923-39 a major league record until Cal Ripken Jr. surpassed it in 1995; led AL in RBI 5 times and HRs 3 times; drove in 100 runs or more 13 years in a row; 2-time MVP (1927,36); hit .340 with 493 HRs over 17 seasons; led NY Yankees to 7 World Series titles; died at age 37 of Amyotrophic lateral sclerosis (ALS), a rare and incurable disease of the nervous system better known as Lou Gehrig's disease.

Charley Gehringer (b. May 11, 1903, d. Jan. 21, 1993): Baseball 2B; hit .300 or better 13 times; AL batting champion and MVP with Detroit in 1937.

A. Bartlett Giamatti (b. Apr. 14, 1938, d. Sept. 1, 1989): Scholar and 7th commissioner of baseball; banned Pete Rose for life for betting on Major League games and associating with known gamblers and drug dealers; also served as president of Yale (1978-86) and National League (1986-89).

Joe Gibbs (b. Nov. 25, 1940): Football; coached Washington to 140 victories and 3 Super Bowl titles in 12 seasons before retiring on Mar. 5, 1993; owner of NASCAR racing team that won 1993 Daytona 500.

Althea Gibson (b. Aug. 25, 1927): Tennis; won both Wimbledon and U.S. championships in 1957 and '58; 1st black to play in either tourney and 1st to win each title.

Bob Gibson (b. Nov. 9, 1935): Baseball RHP; won 20 or more games 5 times; won 2 NL Cy Young Awards (1968,70); MVP in 1968; led St. Louis to 2 World Series titles; Series MVP twice (1964,67); 251 career wins.

Josh Gibson (b. Dec. 21, 1911, d. Jan. 20, 1947): Baseball C; the "Babe Ruth of the Negro Leagues"; Satchel Paige's battery mate with Pittsburgh Crawfords. The Negro Leagues did not keep accurate records but Gibson hit 84 homeruns in one season and his Baseball Hall of Fame plaque says he hit "almost 800" homeruns in his seventeen-year career.

Kirk Gibson (b. May 28, 1957): Baseball OF; All-America flanker at Michigan St. in 1978; chose baseball career and was AL playoff MVP with Detroit in 1984 and NL regular season MVP with Los Angeles in 1988.

Frank Gifford (b. Aug. 16, 1930): Football HB; 4-time All-Pro (1955-57,59); NFL MVP in 1956; led NY Giants to 3 NFL title games; TV sportscaster since 1958, beginning career while still a player.

Sid Gillman (b. Oct. 26, 1911): Football innovator; only coach in both College and Pro Football halls of fame; led college teams at Miami-OH and Cincinnati to combined 81-19-2 record from 1944-54; coached LA Rams (1955-59) in NFL, then led LA-San Diego Chargers to 5 Western titles and 1 league championship in first six years of AFL.

George Gipp (b. Feb. 18, 1895, d. Dec. 14, 1920): Football FB; died of throat infection 2 weeks before he made All-America (Notre Dame's 1st); rushed for 2,341 yards, scored 156 points and averaged 38 yards a punt in 4 years (1917-20).

Marc Girardelli (b. July 18, 1963): Luxembourg Alpine skier; Austrian native who refused to join Austrian Ski Federation because he wanted to be coached by his father; won unprecedented 5th overall World Cup title in 1993; winless at Olympics, although he won 2 silver medals in 1992.

Tom Glavine (b. Mar 26, 1996) Baseball; Atlanta Braves' left-handed pitcher led the majors in wins from 1991-'95 with 91; won NL Cy Young award in 1991 with 20 wins and a 2.55 E.R.A.; named to three All-Star teams and was the NL starter twice; member of 1995 World Series champion Braves and won Series MVP award; pitched the first complete game shutout at Coors Field on June 16, 1995.

Tom Gola (b. Jan. 13, 1933): Basketball F; 4-time All-America and 1955 Player of Year at La Salle; MVP in 1952 NIT and '54 NCAA tournaments, leading Pioneers to both titles; won NBA title as rookie with Philadelphia Warriors in 1956; 4-time NBA All-Star.

Marshall Goldberg (b. Oct. 24, 1917): Football HB; 2-time consensus All-America at Pittsburgh (1937-38); led Pitt to national championship in 1937; played with NFL champion Chicago Cardinals 10 years later.

Lefty Gomez (b. Nov. 26, 1908, d. Feb. 17, 1989): Baseball LHP, 4-time 20-game winner with NY Yankees; holds World Series record for most wins (6) without a defeat; pitched on 5 world championship clubs in 1930s.

Pancho Gonzales (b. May 9, 1928, d. July 3, 1995): Tennis; won consecutive U.S. Championships in 1947-48 before turning pro at 21; dominated pro tour from 1950-61; in 1969 at age 41, played longest Wimbledon match ever (5:12), beating Charlie Pasarell 22-24,1-6,16-14,6-3,11-9.

Bob Goodenow (b. Oct. 29, 1952): Hockey; succeeded Alan Eagleson as executive director of NHL Players Assn. in 1990; led players out on 10-day strike (Apr. 1-10) in 1992 and during 103-day owners' lockout in 1994-95.

Jeff Gordon (b. Aug. 4, 1971): Auto racer; NASCAR Rookie of Year (1993); won inaugural Brickyard 400 in 1994; 1995 Winston Cup champion with 7 wins and 8 poles.

Dr. Harold Gores (b. Sept. 20, 1909, d. May 28, 1993): Educator and first president of Education Facilities Laboratories in New York; in 1964 hired Monsanto Co. to produce a synthetic turf that kids could play on in city schoolyards; resulting ChemGrass proved too expensive for playground use, but it was just what the Houston Astros were looking for in 1966 to cover the floor of the Astrodome where grass refused to grow; and AstroTurf was born.

Shane Gould (b. Nov. 23, 1956): Australian swimmer; set world records in 5 different freestyle events between July 1971 and Jan. 1972; won 3 gold medals, a silver and bronze in 1972 Olympics then retired at age 16.

Alf Goullet (b. Apr. 5, 1891, d. Mar. 11, 1995): Cycling; Australian who gained fame and fortune early in century as premier performer on U.S. 6-day bike race circuit; won 8 annual races at Madison Square Garden with 6 different partners from 1913-23.

Curt Gowdy (b. July 31, 1919): Radio-TV; former radio voice of NY Yankees and then Boston Red Sox from 1949-66; TV play-by-play man for AFL, NFL and major league baseball; has broadcast World Series, All-Star Games, Rose Bowls, Super Bowls, Olympics and NCAA Final Fours for all 3 networks; hosted "The American Sportsman."

Steffi Graf (b. June 14, 1969): German tennis player; won Grand Slam and Olympic gold medal in 1988 at age 19; won three of four majors in 1993, '95 and '96; has won 21 Grand Slam titles— 7 at Wimbledon, 4 Australian, 5 French, and 5 U.S. Opens.

Otto Graham (b. Dec. 6, 1921): Football QB and basketball All-America at Northwestern; in pro ball, led Cleveland Browns to 7 league titles in 10 years, winning 4 AAFC championships (1946-49) and 3 NFL (1950,54-55); 5-time All-Pro; 2-time NFL MVP (1953,55).

Red Grange (b. June 13, 1903, d. Jan. 28, 1991): Football HB; 3-time All-America at Illinois who brought 1st huge crowds to pro football when he signed with Chicago Bears in 1925; formed 1st AFL with manager-promoter C.C. Pyle in 1926, but league folded and he returned to NFL.

Bud Grant (b. May 20, 1927): Football and Basketball; only coach to win 100 games in both CFL and NFL and only member of both CFL and U.S. Pro Football halls of fame; led Winnipeg to 4 Grey Cup titles (1958-59,61-62) in 6 appearances, but his Minnesota Vikings lost all 4 Super Bowl attempts in 1970's; all-time rank of 3rd in CFL wins (122) and 8th in NFL wins (168); also All-Big Ten at Minnesota in both football and basketball in late 1940's; a 3-time CFL All-Star offensive end; also member of 1950 NBA champion Minneapolis Lakers.

Rocky Graziano (b. June 7, 1922, d. May 22, 1990): Boxer; world middleweight champion (1946-47); fought Tony Zale for title 3 times in 21 months, losing twice; pro record 67-10-6 with 52 KOs; movie "Somebody Up There Likes Me" based on his life.

Hank Greenberg (b. Jan. 1, 1911, d. Sept. 4, 1986): Baseball 1B; led AL in HRs and RBI 4 times each; 2-time MVP (1935,40) with Detroit; 331 career HRs.

Joe Greene (b. Sept. 24, 1946): Football DT; 5-time All-Pro (1972-74,77,79); led Pittsburgh to 4 Super Bowl titles in 1970s.

Bud Greenspan (b. Sept. 18, 1926): Filmmaker specializing in the Olympic Games; has won Emmy awards for 22-part "The Olympiad" (1976-77) and historical vignettes for ABC-TV's coverage of 1980 Winter Games; won 1994 Emmy award for edited special on Lillehammer Winter Olympics.

Wayne Gretzky (b. Jan. 26, 1961): Hockey C; 10-time NHL scoring champion; 9-time regular season MVP (1979-87,89) and 9-time All-NHL first team; has scored 200 points or more in a season 4 times; led Edmonton to 4 Stanley Cups (1984-85,87-88); 2-time playoff MVP (1985,88); traded to LA Kings (Aug. 9, 1988); broke Gordie Howe's all-time NHL goal scoring record of 801 on Mar. 23, 1994; entered 1996-97 regular season as all-time NHL leader in points (2,608), goals (837) and assists (1,771); also all-time Stanley Cup leader in points (346), goals (110) and assists (236).

Bob Griese (b. Feb. 3, 1945): Football QB; 2-time All-Pro (1971,77); led Miami to undefeated season (17-0) in 1972 and consecutive Super Bowl titles (1973-74).

Ken Griffey Jr. (b. Nov. 21, 1969): Baseball OF; overall 1st pick of 1987 Draft by Seattle; 5-time gold glove winner in 1st 6 seasons; MVP of 1992 All-Star game at age 23; hit home runs in 8 consecutive games in 1993; entered 1996 with 189 HRs; son of Ken Sr.

Archie Griffin (b. Aug. 21, 1954): Football RB; only college player to win two Heisman Trophies (1974-75); rushed for 5,177 yards in career at Ohio St.

Emile Griffith (b. Feb. 3, 1938): Boxer; world welterweight champion (1961,62-63,63-65); world middleweight champ (1966-67,67-68); pro record 85-24-2 with 23 KOs.

Dick Groat (b. Nov. 4, 1930): Basketball and Baseball SS; 2-time basketball All-America at Duke and college Player of Year in 1951; won NL MVP award as shortstop with Pittsburgh in 1960; won World Series with Pirates (1960) and St. Louis (1964).

Lefty Grove (b. Mar. 6, 1900, d. May 22, 1975): Baseball LHP; won 20 or more games 8 times; led AL in ERA 9 times and strikeouts 7 times; 31-4 record and MVP in 1931 with Philadelphia; 300 career wins.

Lou Groza (b. Jan. 25, 1924): Football T-PK; 6-time All-Pro; played in 13 championship games for Cleveland from 1946-67; kicked winning field goal in 1950 NFL title game; 1,608 career points (1,349 in NFL).

Janet Guthrie (b. Mar. 7, 1938): Auto racer; in 1977, became 1st woman to race in Indianapolis 500; placed 9th at Indy in 1978.

Tony Gwynn (b. May 9, 1960): Baseball OF; 6-time NL batting champion (1984,87-89,94-95) at San Diego; entered 1996 with .336 career average in 13 seasons; was hitting .394 on Aug. 12, 1994 when players' strike began.

Harvey Haddix (b. Sept. 18, 1925, d. Jan. 9, 1994): Baseball LHP; pitched 12 perfect innings for Pittsburgh, but lost to Milwaukee in the 13th, 1-0 (May 26, 1959).

Walter Hagen (b. Dec. 21, 1892, d. Oct. 5, 1969): Pro golf pioneer; won 2 U.S. Opens (1914,19), 4 British Opens (1922,24,28-29), 5 PGA Championships (1921,24-27) and 5 Western Opens; retired with 40 PGA wins; 6-time U.S. Ryder Cup captain.

Marvin Hagler (b. May 23, 1954): Boxer; world middleweight champion 1980-87; enjoyed his nickname "Marvelous Marvin" so much he would have his name legally changed; pro record 62-3-2 with 52 KOs.

George Halas (b. Feb. 2, 1895, d. Oct. 31, 1983): Football pioneer; MVP in 1919 Rose Bowl; player-coach-owner of Chicago Bears from 1920-83; signed Red Grange in 1925; coached Bears for 40 seasons and won 7 NFL titles (1932-33,40-41,43,46,63); 2nd on all-time career list with 324 wins.

Dorothy Hamill (b. July 26, 1956): Figure skater; won Olympic gold medal and world championship in 1976; Ice Capades headliner from 1977-84; bought financially-strapped Ice Capades in 1993.

Scott Hamilton (b. Aug. 28, 1958): Figure skater; 4-time world champion (1981-84); won gold medal at 1984 Olympics.

Tonya Harding (b. Nov. 12, 1970): Figure skater; 1991 U.S. women's champion; involved in bizarre plot hatched by ex-husband Jeff Gillooly to injure rival Nancy Kerrigan on Jan. 6, 1994 and keep her off Olympic team; won '94 U.S. women's title in Kerrigan's absence; denied any role in assault and sued USOC when her berth on Olympic team was threatened; finished 8th at Lillehammer (Kerrigan recovered and won silver medal); pleaded guilty on Mar. 16 to conspiracy to hinder investigation; stripped of 1994 title by U.S. Figure Skating Assn.

Tom Harmon (b. Sept. 28, 1919, d. Mar. 17, 1990): Football HB; 2-time All-America at Michigan; won Heisman Trophy in 1940; played with AFL NY Americans in 1941 and NFL LA Rams (1946-47); World War II fighter pilot who won Silver Star and Purple Heart; became radio-TV commentator.

Franco Harris (b. Mar. 7, 1950): Football RB; ran for over 1,000 yards a season 8 times; rushed for 12,120 yards in 13 years; led Pittsburgh to 4 Super Bowl titles.

Leon Hart (b. Nov. 2, 1928): Football E; only player to win 3 national championships in college and 3 more in the NFL; won his titles at Notre Dame (1946-47,49) and with Detroit Lions (1952-53,57); 3-time All-America and last lineman to win Heisman Trophy (1949); All-Pro on both offense and defense in 1951.

Bill Hartack (b. Dec. 9, 1932): Jockey; won Kentucky Derby 5 times (1957,60,62,64,69), Preakness 3 times (1956,64,69), but the Belmont only once (1960).

Doug Harvey (b. Dec. 19, 1924, d. Dec. 26, 1989): Hockey D; 10-time All-NHL 1st team; won Norris Trophy 7 times (1955-58,60-62); led Montreal to 6 Stanley Cups.

Dominik Hasek (b. Jan. 29, 1965): Czech hockey G; 2-time Vezina Trophy winner with Buffalo (1993-94,95); led NHL with a 1.95 GAA in 1993-94— the first sub-2.00 GAA since Bernie Parent in 1974.

Billy Haughton (b. Nov. 2, 1923, d. July 15, 1986): Harness racing; 4-time winner of Hambletonian; trainer-driver of one Pacing Triple Crown winner (1968); 4,910 career wins.

João Havelange (b. May 8, 1916): Soccer; Brazilian-born president of Federation Internationale de Football Assoc. (FIFA) since 1974; also member of International Olympic Committee.

John Havlicek (b. Apr. 8, 1940): Basketball; played in 3 NCAA Finals at Ohio St. (1960-62); led Boston to 8 NBA titles (1963-66,68-69,74,76); playoff MVP in 1974; 4-time All-NBA 1st team.

Bob Hayes (b. Dec. 20, 1942): Track & Field and Football; won gold medal in 100m at 1964 Olympics; All-Pro SE for Dallas in 1966; convicted of drug trafficking in 1979 and served 18 months of a 5-year sentence.

Woody Hayes (b. Feb. 14, 1913, d. Mar. 12, 1987): Football; coached Ohio St. to 3 national titles (1954,57,68) and 4 Rose Bowl victories; 238 career wins in 28 seasons at Denison, Miami-OH and OSU.

Thomas Hearns (b. Oct. 18, 1958): Boxer; has held recognized world titles as welterweight, light middleweight, middleweight and light heavyweight; four career losses have come against Sugar Ray Leonard, Marvin Hagler and twice to Iran Barkley; entered 1995 with pro record of 53-4-1 and 42 KOs.

Eric Heiden (b. June 14, 1958): Speedskater; 3-time overall world champion (1977-79); won all 5 men's gold medals at 1980 Olympics, setting new records in each; Sullivan Award winner (1980).

Mel Hein (b. Aug. 22, 1909, d. Jan. 31, 1992): Football C; NFL All-Pro 8 straight years (1933-40); MVP in 1938 with NY Giants; didn't miss a game in 15 seasons.

John W. Heisman (b. Oct. 23, 1869, d. Oct. 3, 1936): Football; coached at 9 colleges from 1892-1927; won 185 games; Director of Athletics at Downtown Athletic Club in NYC (1928-36); DAC named Heisman Trophy after him.

Carol Heiss (b. Jan. 20, 1940): Figure skater; 5-time world champion (1956-60); won Olympic silver medal in 1956 and gold in '60; married 1956 men's gold medalist Hayes Jenkins.

Rickey Henderson (b. Dec. 25, 1958): Baseball OF; AL playoff MVP (1989) and AL regular season MVP (1990); set single-season base stealing record of 130 in 1982; has led AL in steals a record 11 times; broke Lou Brock's all-time record of 938 on May 1, 1991; entered 1996 season as all-time leader in steals (1,149) and HRs as leadoff batter (67).

Sonja Henie (b. Apr. 8, 1912, d. Oct. 12, 1969): Norwegian figure skater; 10-time world champion (1927-36); won 3 consecutive Olympic gold medals (1928,32,36); became movie star.

Foster Hewitt (b. Nov. 21, 1902, d. Apr. 21, 1985): Radio-TV; Canada's premier hockey play-by-play broadcaster from 1923-81; coined phrase, "He shoots, he scores!"

Graham Hill (b. Feb. 15, 1929, d. Nov. 29, 1975): British auto racer; 2-time Formula One world champion (1962,68); won Indy 500 in 1966; killed in plane crash; father of Damon.

Phil Hill (b. Apr. 20, 1927): Auto racer; first U.S. driver to win Formula One championship (1961); 3 career wins (1958-64).

Max Hirsch (b. July 30, 1880, d. Apr. 3, 1969): Horse racing; trained 1,933 winners from 1908-68; won Triple Crown with Assault in 1946.

Tommy Hitchcock (b. Feb. 11, 1900, d. Apr. 19, 1944): Polo; world class player at 20; achieved 10-goal rating 18 times from 1922-40.

Lew Hoad (b. Nov. 23, 1934, d. July 3, 1994): Australian tennis player; 2-time Wimbledon winner (1956-57); won Australian, French and Wimbledon titles in 1956, but missed capturing Grand Slam at Forest Hills when beaten by Ken Rosewall in 4-set final.

Ben Hogan (b. Aug. 13, 1912): Golfer; 4-time PGA Player of Year; one of only four players to win all four Grand Slam titles (others are Nicklaus, Player and Sarazen); won 4 U.S. Opens, 2 Masters, 2 PGAs and 1 British Open between 1946-53; only player to win three majors in one year when he won Masters, U.S. Open and British Open in 1953; nearly killed in Feb. 13, 1949 car accident, but came back to win U.S. Open in '50; third on all-time list with 63 career wins.

Eleanor Holm (b. Dec. 6, 1913): Swimmer; won gold medal in 100m backstroke at 1932 Olympics; thrown off '36 U.S. team for drinking champagne in public and shooting craps on boat to Germany.

Nat Holman (b. Oct. 18, 1896, d. Feb. 12, 1995): Basketball pioneer; played pro with Original Celtics (1920-28); coached CCNY to both NCAA and NIT titles in 1950 (a year later, several of his players were caught up in a point-shaving scandal); 423 career wins.

Larry Holmes (b. Nov. 3, 1949): Boxer; heavyweight champion (WBC or IBF) from 1978-85; successfully defended title 20 times before losing to Michael Spinks; returned from first retirement in 1988 and was KO'd in 4th by then champ Mike Tyson; launched second comeback in 1991; fought and lost title bids against Evander Holyfield in '92 and Oliver McCall on Apr. 8, 1995; fought McCall at age 45 years and 5 months; entered 1996 with pro record of 62-5 and 40 KOs.

Lou Holtz (b. Jan. 6, 1937): Football; coached Notre Dame to national title in 1988; 2-time Coach of Year (1977,88) entered 1995 season with 199-89-7 record in 25 seasons with 5 schools— Wm. & Mary (3 years), N.C. State (4), Arkansas (7), Minnesota (2) and ND (9); also coached NFL NY Jets for 13 games (3-10) in 1976.

Evander Holyfield (b. Oct. 19, 1962): Boxer; missed shot at Olympic gold medal in 1984 when he lost controversial light heavyweight semifinal after knocking his opponent out (referee ruled it was a late hit); knocked out Buster Douglas in 3rd round to become world heavyweight champion on Oct. 25, 1990; 2 of first 4 title defenses included decisions over 42-year-old ex-champs George Foreman and Larry Holmes; lost title to Riddick Bowe by unanimous decision on Nov. 13, 1992; beat Bowe by majority decision to reclaim title on Nov. 6, 1993; lost title again to Michael Moorer by majority decision on Apr. 22, 1994; after retiring in '94 due to an apparent heart defect, he returned to the ring in 1995 with a cleaner bill of health and a pro record of 30-2 and 22 KOs.

Red Holzman (b. Aug. 10, 1920): Basketball; played for NBL and NBA champions at Rochester (1946,51); coached NY Knicks to 2 NBA titles (1970,73); Coach of Year (1970); ranks 10th on all-time NBA list with 754 wins (including playoffs).

Rogers Hornsby (b. Apr. 27, 1896, d. Jan. 5, 1963): Baseball 2B; hit .400 three times, including .424 in 1924; led NL in batting 7 times; 2-time MVP (1925,29) with St. Louis; career average of .358 over 23 years is all-time highest in NL.

Paul Hornung (b. Dec. 23, 1935): Football HB-PK; only Heisman Trophy winner to play for losing team (2-8 Notre Dame in 1956); 3-time NFL scoring leader (1959-61) at Green Bay; 176 points in 1960, an all-time record; MVP in 1961; suspended by NFL for 1963 season for betting on his own team.

Gordie Howe (b. Mar. 31, 1928): Hockey RW; played 32 seasons in NHL and WHA from 1946-80; led NHL in scoring 6 times; All-NHL 1st team 12 times; MVP 6 times in NHL (1952-53,57-58,60,63) with Detroit and once in WHA (1974) with Houston; ranks 2nd on all-time NHL list in goals (801) and points (1,850) to Wayne Gretzky; played with sons Mark and Marty at Houston (1973-77) and New England-Hartford (1977-80).

Cal Hubbard (b. Oct. 31, 1900, d. Oct. 19, 1977): Member of college football, pro football and baseball halls of fame; 9 years in NFL; 4-time All-Pro at end and tackle; AL umpire for 15 years (1936-51).

Carl Hubbell (b. June 22, 1903, d. Nov. 21, 1988): Baseball LHP; led NL in wins and ERA 3 times each; 2-time MVP (1933,36) with NY Giants; fanned Ruth, Gehrig, Foxx, Simmons and Cronin in succession in 1934 All-Star Game; 253 career wins.

Sam Huff (b. Oct. 4, 1934): Football LB; glamorized NFL's middle linebacker position with NY Giants from 1956-63; subject of "The Violent World of Sam Huff" TV special in 1961; helped lead club to 6 division titles and a world championship (1956).

Miller Huggins (b. Mar. 27, 1879, d. Sept. 25, 1929): Baseball; managed NY Yankees from 1918 until his death late in '29 season; led Yanks to 6 pennants and 3 World Series titles from 1921-28.

H. Wayne Huizenga (b. Dec. 29, 1937): Owner; vice chairman of Viacom Inc. and chairman of Blockbuster Entertainment Group; co-founded Waste Management Inc., the world's largest waste collection and disposal company in 1971; majority owner of baseball's Florida Marlins and 100-percent owner of NFL Miami Dolphins, NHL Florida Panthers and Pro Player Park, where Marlins and Dolphins play.

Bobby Hull (b. Jan. 3, 1939): Hockey LW; led NHL in scoring 3 times; 2-time MVP (1965-66) with Chicago; All-NHL first team 10 times; jumped to WHA in 1972, 2-time MVP there (1973,75) with Winnipeg; scored 913 goals in both leagues; father of Brett.

Brett Hull (b. Aug. 9, 1964): Hockey RW; named NHL MVP in 1991 with St. Louis; holds single season RW scoring record with 86 goals; he and father Bobby have both won Hart (MVP), Lady Byng (sportsmanship) and All-Star Game MVP trophies.

Jim (Catfish) Hunter (b. Apr. 8, 1946): Baseball RHP; won 20 games or more 5 times (1971-75); played on 5 World Series winners with Oakland and NY Yankees; threw perfect game in 1968; won Cy Young Award in '74.

Ibrahim Hussein (b. June 3, 1958): Kenyan distance runner; 3-time winner of Boston Marathon (1988,91-92) and 1st African runner to win in Boston; won New York Marathon in 1987.

Don Hutson (b. Jan. 31, 1913): Football E-PK; led NFL in receptions 8 times and interceptions once; 9-time All-Pro (1936,38-45) for Green Bay; 99 career TD catches.

Flo Hyman (b. July 31, 1954, d. Jan. 24, 1986): Volleyball; 3-time All-America spiker at Houston and captain of 1984 U.S. Women's Olympic team; died of heart attack caused by Marfan Syndrome during a match in Japan in 1986; Women's Sports Foundation's Hyman Award for excellence and dedication named after her.

Hank Iba (b. Aug. 6, 1904, d. Jan. 15, 1993): Basketball; coached Oklahoma A&M to 2 straight NCAA titles (1945-46); 767 career wins in 41 years; coached U.S. Olympic team to 2 gold medals (1964,68), but lost to Soviets in controversial '72 final.

Mike Ilitch (b. July 20, 1929): Baseball and Hockey owner; chairman of Little Caesar's, the international pizza chain; bought Detroit Red Wings of NHL for $8 million in 1982 and AL Detroit Tigers for $85 million in 1992.

Punch Imlach (b. Mar. 15, 1918, d. Dec. 1, 1987): Hockey; directed Toronto to 4 Stanley Cups (1962-64,67) in 11 seasons as GM-coach.

Miguel Induráin (b. July 16, 1964): Spanish cyclist; won a record 5th straight Tour de France in 1995, joining legends Jacques Anquetil and Bernard Hinault of France and Eddy Merckx of Belgium as the only 5 time winners. Won gold in time trial at '96 Olympics.

Hale Irwin (b. June 3, 1945): Golfer; oldest player ever to win U.S. Open (45 in 1990); NCAA champion in 1967; entered 1995 with 20 PGA victories, including 3 U.S. Opens (1974,79,90); 5-time Ryder Cup team member.

Bo Jackson (b. Nov. 30, 1962): Baseball OF and Football RB; won Heisman Trophy in 1985 and MVP of baseball All-Star Game in 1989; starter for both baseball's KC Royals and NFL's LA Raiders in 1988 and '89; severely injured left hip Jan. 13, 1991, in NFL playoffs; waived by Royals but signed by Chicago White Sox in 1991; missed entire 1992 season recovering from hip surgery; played for White Sox in 1993 and California in '94 before retiring.

Joe Jackson (b. July 16, 1889, d. Dec. 5, 1951): Baseball OF; hit .300 or better 11 times; nicknamed "Shoeless Joe"; career average of .356 (see Black Sox).

Phil Jackson (b. Sept. 17, 1945): Basketball; NBA champion as reserve forward with New York in 1973 (injured when Knicks won in '70); coached Chicago to three straight NBA titles (1991-93); finished 1994-95 season with 408 wins (including playoffs) in just 6 seasons.

Reggie Jackson (b. May 18, 1946): Baseball OF; led AL in HRs 4 times; MVP in 1973; played on 5 World Series winners with Oakland, NY Yankees; 1977 Series MVP with 5 HRs; 563 career HRs; all-time strikeout leader (2,597).

Dr. Robert Jackson (b. Aug. 6, 1932): Surgeon; revolutionized sports medicine by popularizing the use of othroscopic surgery to treat injuries; learned technique from Japanese physician that allowed athletes to return quickly from potentially career-ending injuries.

Helen Jacobs (b. Aug. 6, 1908): Tennis; 4-time winner of U.S. Championship (1932-35); Wimbledon winner in 1936; lost 4 Wimbledon finals to arch-rival Helen Wills Moody.

Dan Jansen (b. June 17, 1965): Speedskater; 1993 world record-holder in 500m; fell in 500m and 1,000m in 1988 Olympics at Calgary after learning of death of sister Jane; placed 4th in 500m and didn't attempt 1,000m 4 years later in Albertville; fell in 500m at '94 Games in Lillehammer, but finally won an Olympic medal with world record (1:12.43) effort in 1,000m, then took victory lap with baby daughter Jane in his arms; won 1994 Sullivan Award.

James J. Jeffries (b. Apr. 15, 1875, d. Mar. 3, 1953): Boxer; world heavyweight champion (1899-1905); retired undefeated but came back to fight Jack Johnson in 1910 and lost (KO,15th).

David Jenkins (b. June 29, 1936): Figure skater; brother of Hayes; 3-time world champion (1957-59); won gold medal at 1960 Olympics.

Hayes Jenkins (b. Mar. 23, 1933): Figure skater; 4-time world champion (1953-56); won gold medal at 1956 Olympics; married 1960 women's gold medalist Carol Heiss.

Bruce Jenner (b. Oct. 28, 1949): Track & Field; won gold medal in 1976 Olympic decathlon.

Jackie Jensen (b. Mar. 9, 1927, d. July 14, 1982): Football RB and Baseball OF; consensus All-America at California in 1948; American League MVP with Boston Red Sox in 1958.

Ben Johnson (b. Dec. 30, 1961): Canadian sprinter; set 100m world record (9.83) at 1987 World Champ-ionships; won 100m at 1988 Olympics, but flunked drug test and forfeited gold medal; 1987 world record revoked in '89 for admitted steroid use; returned drug-free in 1991, but performed poorly; banned for life by IAAF in 1993 for testing positive after a meet in Montreal.

Bob Johnson (b. Mar. 4, 1931, d. Nov. 26, 1991): Hockey; coached Pittsburgh Penguins to 1st Stanley Cup title in 1991; led Wisconsin to 3 NCAA titles (1973,77,81) in 15 years; also coached 1976 U.S. Olympic team and NHL Calgary (1982-87).

Earvin (Magic) Johnson (b. Aug. 14, 1959): Basketball G; led Michigan St. to NCAA title in 1979 and was tourney MVP; All-NBA 1st team 9 times; 3-time MVP (1987,89-90); led LA Lakers to 5 NBA titles; 3-time playoff MVP (1980, 82, 87); 2nd all-time in NBA assists with 9,921; retired on Nov. 7, 1991 after announcing he was HIV-positive; returned to score 25 points in 1992 NBA All-Star game; U.S. Olympic Dream Team member in '92; announced NBA comeback then retired again before start of 1992-93 season; named head coach of Lakers on Mar. 23, 1994, but finished season at 5-11 and quit; later named minority owner of team.

Jack Johnson (b. Mar. 31, 1878, d. June 10, 1946): Boxer; controversial heavyweight champion (1908-15) and 1st black to hold title; defeated Tommy Burns for crown at age 30; fled to Europe in 1913 after Mann Act conviction; lost title to Jess Willard in Havana, but claimed to have taken a dive; pro record 78-8-12 with 45 KOs.

Jimmy Johnson (b. July 16, 1943): Football; All-SWC defensive lineman on Arkansas' 1964 national championship team; coached Miami-FL to national title in 1987; college record of 81-34-3 in 10 years; hired by old friend and new Dallas owner Jerry Jones to succeed Tom Landry in February 1989; went 1-15 in '89, then led Cowboys to consecutive Super Bowl victories in 1992 and '93 seasons; quit on Mar. 29, 1994 after feuding with Jones; became TV analyst. Replaced Don Shula as Miami Dolphins head coach in 1996.

Judy Johnson (b. Oct. 26, 1899, d. June 13, 1989) Baseball; one of the great stars of the Negro Leagues; a great fielding third baseman who regularly batted over .300; when baseball integrated Johnson's playing days were over but he coached and scouted for the Philadelphia Athletics, Boston Braves and Philadelphia Phillies; member of Baseball Hall of Fame.

Junior Johnson (b. 1930); Auto Racing; won the second Daytona 500 in 1960; also won 13 NASCAR races in 1965 including the Rebel 300 at Darlington; retired from racing to become a highly sucessful car owner; his first driver was Bobby Allison.

Michael Johnson (b. Sep 13, 1967) Track and Field; had won 55 straight 400 meter finals going into the 1996 Olympic final which he won in an OR 43.49 seconds; in 1996, became the first man to win gold in 200 and 400 meter races in the same Olympics.

Rafer Johnson (b. Aug. 18, 1934): Track & Field; won silver medal in 1956 Olympic decathlon and gold medal in 1960.

Walter Johnson (b. Nov. 6, 1887, d. Dec. 10, 1946): Baseball RHP; won 20 games or more 10 straight years; led AL in ERA 5 times, wins 6 times and strikeouts 12 times; twice MVP (1913, 24) with Washington; all-time leader in shutouts (110) and 2nd in wins (416).

Ben A. Jones (b. Dec. 31, 1882, d. June 13, 1961): Horse racing; Calumet Farm trainer (1939-47); saddled 6 Kentucky Derby champions and 2 Triple Crown winners—Whirlaway in 1941 and Citation in '48.

Bobby Jones (b. Mar. 17, 1902, d. Dec. 18, 1971): Won U.S. and British Opens plus U.S. and British Amateurs in 1930 to become golf's only Grand Slam winner ever; from 1922-30, won 4 U.S. Opens, 5 U.S. Amateurs, 3 British Opens, and played in 6 Walker Cups; founded Masters tournament in 1934.

Deacon Jones (b. Dec. 9, 1938): Football DE; 5-time All-Pro (1965-69) with LA Rams; unofficial all-time NFL sack leader with 172 in 14 years.

Jerry Jones (b. Oct. 13, 1942): Football; owner-GM of Dallas Cowboys; maverick who bought declining team (3-13) and Texas Stadium for $140 million in 1989; hired old friend Jimmy Johnson to replace legendary Tom Landry as coach; their partnership led Cowboys to Super Bowl titles in 1992 and '93 seasons; when feud developed in 1994, Jones let Johnson go and hired Barry Switzer; defied NFL Properties by signing separate sponsorship deals with Pepsi and Nike in 1995, causing NFL to file a $300 million lawsuit against him on Sept. 19.

Roy Jones Jr. (b. Jan. 16, 1969): Boxing; robbed of gold medal at 1988 Summer Olympics due to an error in scoring; still voted Outstanding Boxer of the Games; won IBF middleweight crown by beating Bernard Hopkins in 1993; moved up to super middleweight and won IBF title from James Toney on Nov. 18, 1994; entered '96 with pro record of 30-0 with 26 KOs.

Michael Jordan (b. Feb. 17, 1963): Basketball G; College Player of Year with North Carolina in 1984; led NBA in scoring 7 years in a row (1987-93); 7-time All-NBA 1st team; 4-time regular season MVP (1988,91-92,96) and 4-time MVP of NBA Finals (1991-93,96); only 3-time AP Male Athlete of Year; led U.S. Olympic team to gold medals in 1984 and '92; stunned sports world when he retired at age 30 on Oct. 6, 1993; signed as OF with Chicago White Sox and spent summer of '94 in Double A with Birmingham; barely hit his weight with .204 average; made one of the most anticipated comebacks in sports history when he returned to the Bulls lineup on Mar. 19, 1995 and shot 7-for-28; lost first playoff series since 1990 when Bulls were eliminated by Orlando in second round.

Florence Griffith Joyner (b. Dec. 21, 1959): Track & Field; set world records in 100 and 200 meters in 1988; won 3 gold medals at '88 Olympics (100m, 200m, 4x100m relay); Sullivan Award winner (1988); retired in 1989; designed NBA Indiana Pacers uniforms (1990); named as co-chairperson of President's Council on Physical Fitness and Sports in 1993.

Jackie Joyner-Kersee (b. Mar. 3, 1962): Track & Field; 2-time world champion in both long jump (1987,91) and heptathlon (1987,93); won heptathlon gold medals at 1988 and '92 Olympics and LJ gold at '88 Games; has also won Olympic silver (1984) in heptathlon and bronze (1992) in LJ; Sullivan Award winner (1986); only woman to receive *The Sporting News* Man of Year award.

Alberto Juantorena (b. Nov. 21, 1950): Cuban runner; won both 400m and 800m gold medals at 1976 Olympics.

Sonny Jurgensen (b. Aug. 23, 1934): Football QB; played 18 seasons with Philadelphia and Washington; led NFL in passing twice (1967,69); All-Pro in 1961; 255 career TD passes.

Duke Kahanamoku (b. Aug. 24, 1890, d. Jan. 22, 1968): Swimmer; won 3 gold medals and 2 silver over 3 Olympics (1912,20,24); also surfing pioneer.

Al Kaline (b. Dec. 19, 1934): Baseball; youngest player (at age 20) to win batting title (led AL with .340 in 1955); had 3,007 hits, 399 HRs in 22 years with Detroit.

Anatoly Karpov (b. May 23, 1951): Chess; Russian world champion from 1975-85; regained International Chess Federation (FIDE) version of championship in 1993 when countryman Garry Kasparov was stripped of title after forming new Professional Chess Association.

Garry Kasparov (b. Apr. 13, 1963): Chess; Azerbaijani who became youngest player (22 years, 210 days) ever to win world championship as Russian in 1985; defeated countryman Anatoly Karpov for title; split with International Chess Federation (FIDE) to form Professional Chess Association (PCA) in 1993; stripped of FIDE title in '93 but successfully defended PCA title against Briton Nigel Short; beat IBM supercomputer "Deep Blue" 4 games to 2 in 1996 much-publicized match in New York.

Ewing Kauffman (b. Sept. 21, 1916, d. Aug. 1, 1993): Baseball; pharmaceutical billionaire and longtime owner of Kansas City Royals; Royals Stadium renamed for Kauffman on July 2, 1993, one month before his death.

Mike Keenan (b. Oct. 21, 1949): Hockey; coach who finally led NY Rangers to Stanley Cup title in 1994 after 54 unsuccessful years; quit a month later in pay dispute and signed with St. Louis as coach-GM; entered 1995-96 season with 507 wins (including playoffs); also reached Cup finals with Philadelphia (1987) and Chicago (1992); coached Team Canada to Canada Cup wins in 1987 and '91.

Kipchoge (Kip) Keino (b. Jan. 17, 1940): Kenyan runner; young policeman who beat USA's Jim Ryun to win 1,500m gold medal at 1968 Olympics; won again in steeplechase at 1972 Summer Games; his success spawned long line of international distance champions from Kenya.

Johnny Kelley (b. Sept. 6, 1907): Distance runner, ran in his 61st and final Boston Marathon at age 84 in 1992, finishing in 5:58:36; won Boston twice (1935,45) and was 2nd 7 times.

Leroy Kelly (b. May 20, 1942) Football; replaced Jim Brown in the Cleveland Brown's backfield; in 1967, Kelly led the NFL in rushing yards (1,205), rushing average (5.1 per carry) and rushing touchdowns (11); in 1968, he led the league again in yards (1,269) and touchdowns (16); played in six Pro Bowls; retired with 7,274 yards and 74 touchdowns; member of Pro Football Hall of Fame.

Jim Kelly (b. Feb. 14, 1960): Football QB; led Buffalo to four consecutive Super Bowl appearances, and is only QB to lose four times; named to AFC Pro Bowl team 5 times; entered 1995 season ranked 4th on all-time list with passer rating of 85.8.

Walter Kennedy (b. June 8, 1912, d. June 26, 1977): Basketball; 2nd NBA commissioner (1963-75), league doubled in size to 18 teams during his term of office.

Nancy Kerrigan (b. Oct. 13, 1969): Figure skating; 1993 U.S. women's champion and Olympic medalist in 1992 (bronze) and '94 (silver); victim of Jan. 6, 1994 assault at U.S. nationals in Detroit when Shane Stant clubbed her in right knee with metal baton after a practice session; conspiracy hatched by Jeff Gillooly, ex-husband of rival Tonya Harding; although unable to compete in nationals, she quickly recovered and was granted berth on Olympic team; finished 2nd in Lillehammer to Oksana Baiul of Ukraine by a 5-4 judges' vote.

Billy Kidd (b. Apr. 13, 1943) Skiing: the first great Amercian male Alpine skier; first American male to win an Olympic medal when he won a silver in the slalom and a bronze in the Alpine combined in 1964; competed respectably with the great Jean-Claude Killy; won the world Alpine combined event in 1970 which was the first world championship for an American male.

Harmon Killebrew (b. June 29, 1936): Baseball 3B-1B; led AL in HRs 6 times and RBI 3 times; MVP in 1969 with Minnesota; 573 career HRs.

Jean-Claude Killy (b. Aug. 30, 1943): French alpine skier; 2-time World Cup champion (1967-68); won 3 gold medals at 1968 Olympics in Grenoble; co-president of 1992 Winter Games in Albertville.

Ralph Kiner (b. Oct. 27, 1922): Baseball OF; led NL in home runs 7 straight years (1946-52) with Pittsburgh; 369 career HRs.

Betsy King (b. Aug. 13, 1955): Golfer; 2-time LPGA Player of Year (1984,89), who entered 1995 as Tour's all-time money winner with $4,892,873; 2-time winner of both U.S. Open (1989,90) and Dinah Shore (1987,90); became only 14th player to qualify for LPGA Hall of Fame on June 25, 1995 when she won the ShopRite Classic for her 30th career victory since 1977.

Billie Jean King (b. Nov. 22, 1943): Tennis; women's rights pioneer; Wimbledon singles champ 6 times; U.S. champ 4 times; first woman athlete to earn $100,000 in one year (1971); beat 55-year-old Bobby Riggs 6-4, 6-3, 6-3, to win $100,000 in 1973.

Don King (b. Aug. 20, 1931): Boxing promoter; controlled heavyweight title from 1978-90 while Larry Holmes and Mike Tyson were champions; 1st major promotion was Muhammad Ali's comeback fight in 1970; former numbers operator who served 4 years for manslaughter (1967-70); acquitted of tax evasion and fraud in 1985; indicted July 14, 1994 for allegedly bilking Lloyd's of London out of $350,000 on a false insurance claim involving a training injury to Julio Cesar Chavez in June 1991; regained control of heavyweight title in 1994 with wins by Oliver McCall (WBC) and Bruce Seldon (WBA); resumed role as Tyson's promoter after ex-champion's release from prison on Mar. 25, 1995.

Karch Kiraly (b. Nov. 3, 1960) Volleyball; USA's preeminent volleyball player; led UCLA to three NCAA championships (1979, '81, '82); played on US national teams that won Olympic gold medals in 1984 and '88, world championships in '82 and '86; won the inaugural gold medal for Olympic beach volleyball with Kent Steffes in 1996.

Tom Kite (b. Dec. 9, 1949): Golfer; entered 1996 as 2nd on all-time PGA Tour money list with over $9.6 million; finally won 1st major with victory in 1992 U.S. Open at Pebble Beach; co-NCAA champion with Ben Crenshaw (1972); PGA Rookie of Year (1973); PGA Player of Year (1989).

Gene Klein (b. Jan. 29, 1921, d. Mar. 12, 1990): Horseman; won 3 Eclipse awards as top owner (1985-87); filly Winning Colors won 1988 Kentucky Derby; also owned San Diego Chargers football team (1966-84).

Bob Knight (b. Oct. 25, 1940): Basketball; has coached Indiana to 3 NCAA titles (1976,81,87); 3-time Coach of Year (1975-76,89); 678 career wins in 31 years; coached 1984 U.S. Olympic team to gold medal.

Phil Knight (b. Feb. 24, 1938): Founder and chairman of Nike, Inc., the $4 billion shoe and fitness company founded in 1972 and based in Beaverton, Ore.; stable of endorsees includes Michael Jordan, Andre Agassi and Sergey Bubka; named "The Most Powerful Man in Sports" by *The Sporting News* in 1992.

Bill Koch (b. June 7, 1955) Cross-country skiing; first highly-accomplished American male in his sport; first American male to win a cross-country Olympic medal when he took home a silver in the 30-kilometer race in 1976; in 1982, he was the first American male to win the Nordic World Cup.

Olga Korbut (b. May 16, 1955): Soviet gymnast; 3 gold medals at 1972 Olympics; first to perform back somersault on balance beam.

Johann Olav Koss (b. Oct. 29, 1968): Norwegian speedskater; won three gold medals at 1994 Olympics in Lillehammer with world records in the 1,500m, 5,000m and 10,000m; also won 1,500m gold and 10,000m silver in 1992 Games; retired shortly after Olympics.

Sandy Koufax (b. Dec. 30, 1935): Baseball LHP; led NL in strikeouts 4 times and ERA 5 straight years; won 3 Cy Young Awards (1963,65,66) with LA Dodgers; MVP in 1963; 2-time World Series MVP (1963, 65); threw perfect game against Chicago Cubs (1-0, Sept. 9, 1965) and had 3 other no-hitters in 1962, '63 and '64.

Alvin Kraenzlein (b. Dec. 12, 1876, d. Jan. 6, 1928): Track & Field; won 4 individual gold medals in 1900 Olympics (60m, long jump, 110m and 200m hurdles).

Jack Kramer (b. Aug. 1, 1921): Tennis; Wimbledon singles champ 1947; U.S. champ 1946-47; promoter and Open pioneer.

Ingrid Kristiansen (b. Mar. 21, 1956): Norwegian runner; 2-time Boston Marathon winner (1986,89); won New York City Marathon in 1989; entered 1995 holding 2 world records recognized by IAAF— 5,000m and marathon.

Julie Krone (b. July 24, 1963): Jockey; only woman to ride winning horse in a Triple Crown race when she captured Belmont Stakes aboard Colonial Affair in 1993; entered 1996 as all-time winningest female jockey with 3,016 wins.

Mike Krzyzewski (b. Feb. 13, 1947): Basketball; has coached Duke to 7 Final Four appearances in last 10 years; won consecutive NCAA titles in 1991 and '92; missed most of 1994-95 season with a back injury and stress-related exhaustion; 20-year record of 431-186.

Alan Kulwicki (b. Dec. 14, 1954, d. Apr. 1, 1993): Auto racer; 1992 NASCAR national champion; 1st college grad and Northerner to win title; NASCAR Rookie of Year in 1986; famous for driving car backwards on victory lap; killed at age 38 in plane crash near Bristol, Tenn.

Marion Ladewig (b. Oct. 30, 1914): Bowler; named Woman Bowler of the Year 9 times (1950-54,57-59,63).

Guy Lafleur (b. Sept. 20, 1951): Hockey RW; led NHL in scoring 3 times (1975-78); 2-time MVP (1977-78), played for 5 Stanley Cup winners in Montreal; playoff MVP in 1977; returned to NHL as player in 1988 after election to Hall of Fame; retired again in 1991.

Napoleon (Nap) Lajoie (b. Sept. 5, 1874, d. Feb. 7, 1959): Baseball 2B; led AL in batting 3 times (1901,03-04); batted .422 in 1901; hit .338 for career with 3,244 hits.

Jack Lambert (b. July 8, 1952): Football LB; 6-time All-Pro (1975-76,79-82); led Pittsburgh to 4 Super Bowl titles.

Kenesaw Mountain Landis (b. Nov. 20, 1866, d. Nov. 25, 1944): U.S. District Court judge who became first baseball commissioner (1920-44); banned Black Sox for life.

Tom Landry (b. Sept. 11, 1924): Football; All-Pro DB for NY Giants (1954); coached Dallas for 29 years (1960-88); won 2 Super Bowls (1972,78); 3rd on NFL all-time list with 270 wins.

Steve Largent (b. Sept. 28, 1954): Football WR; retired in 1989 after 14 years in Seattle with then NFL records in passes caught (819) and TD passes caught (100); elected to U.S. House of Representatives (R, Okla.) in 1994 and Pro Football Hall of fame in '95.

Don Larsen (b. Aug. 7, 1929): Baseball RHP; NY Yankees hurler who pitched the only perfect game in World Series history— a 2-0 victory over Brooklyn in Game 5 of the 1956 Series (Oct. 8); Series MVP that year; had career record of 81-91 in 14 seasons with 6 clubs.

Tommy Lasorda (b. Sept. 22, 1927): Baseball; managed LA Dodgers to 2 World Series titles (1981,88) in 4 appearances; retired during 1996 season with 1,599 regular-season wins in 21 years.

Larissa Latynina (b. Dec. 27, 1934): Soviet gymnast; won total of 18 medals, (9 gold) in 3 Olympics (1956,60,64).

Nikki Lauda (b. Feb. 22, 1949): Austrian auto racer; 3-time world Formula One champion (1975,77,84); 25 career wins from 1971-85.

Rod Laver (b. Aug. 9, 1938): Australian tennis player; only player to win Grand Slam twice (1962,69); Wimbledon champion 4 times; 1st to earn $1 million in prize money.

Andrea Mead Lawrence (b. Apr. 19, 1932): Alpine skier; won 2 gold medals at 1952 Olympics.

Bobby Layne (b. Dec. 19, 1926, d. Dec. 1, 1986): Football QB; college star at Texas; master of 2-minute offense; led Detroit to 4 divisional titles and 3 NFL championships in 1950's.

Frank Leahy (b. Aug. 27, 1908, d. June 21, 1973): Football; coached Notre Dame to four national titles (1943,46-47,49); career record of 107-13-9 for a winning pct. of .864.

Brian Leetch (b. Mar. 3, 1968): Hockey D; NHL Rookie of Year in 1989; won Norris Trophy as top defenseman in 1992; Conn Smythe Trophy winner as playoffs' MVP in 1994 when he helped lead NY Rangers to 1st Stanley Cup title in 54 years.

Jacques Lemaire (b. Sept. 7, 1945): Hockey C; member of 8 Stanley Cup champions in Montreal; scored 366 goals in 12 seasons; coached Canadiens from 1983-85; directed New Jersey Devils to surprising 4-game sweep of Detroit to win 1995 Stanley Cup.

Claude Lemieux (b. July 16, 1965): Hockey RW; pivotal member of Stanley Cup championship teams in Montreal (1986) and New Jersey (1995); playoff MVP with Devils in '95; no relation to Mario.

Mario Lemieux (b. Oct. 5, 1965): Hockey C; 5-time NHL scoring leader (1988-89,92-93,96); Rookie of Year (1985); 4-time All-NHL 1st team (1988-89,93,96); 3-time regular season MVP (1988,93,96); 3-time All-Star Game MVP; led Pittsburgh to consecutive Stanley Cup titles (1991 and '92) and was playoff MVP both years; won 1993 scoring title despite missing 24 games to undergo radiation treatments for Hodgkin's disease; missed 62 games during 1993-94 season mostly due to back injuries; sat out 1994-95 season due to fatigue; returned in 1995-96 to lead the league in scoring and win the MVP trophy.

Greg LeMond (b. June 26, 1961): Cyclist; 3-time Tour de France winner (1986,89-90); only non-European to win the event; retired in Dec. 1994 after being diagnosed with a rare muscular disease known as mitochondrial myopathy.

Ivan Lendl (b. Mar. 7, 1960): Czech tennis player; No.1 player in world 4 times (1985-87,89); has won both French and U.S. Opens 3 times and Australian twice; owns 94 career tournament wins.

Suzanne Lenglen (b. May 24, 1899, d. July 4, 1938): French tennis player; dominated women's tennis from 1919-26; won both Wimbledon and French singles titles 6 times.

Sugar Ray Leonard (b. May 17, 1956): Boxer; light welterweight Olympic champ (1976); won world welterweight title 1979 and four more titles; retired after losing to Terry Norris on Feb. 9, 1991, with record of 36-2-1 and 25 KOs.

Marv Levy (b. Aug. 3, 1928): Football; coached Buffalo to four consecutive Super Bowls, but is one of two coaches who are 0-4 (Bud Grant is the other); won 50 games and two CFL Grey Cups with Montreal (1974,77); entered 1995 season with 127 NFL victories.

Carl Lewis (b. July 1, 1961): Track & Field; won 4 Olympic gold medals in 1984 (100m, 200m, 4x100m, LJ), 2 more in '88 (100m, LJ), 2 more in '92 (4x100m, LJ) and 1 more in '96 for a career total of 9; has record 8 World Championship titles and 9 medals in all; Sullivan Award winner (1981); entered 1996 with 71 long jumps over 28 feet.

Nancy Lieberman-Cline (b. July 1, 1958): Basketball; 3-time All-America and 2-time Player of Year (1979-80); led Old Dominion to consecutive AIAW titles in 1979 and '80; played in defunct WPBL and WABA and became 1st woman to play in men's pro league (USBL) in 1986.

Eric Lindros (b. Feb. 28, 1973): Hockey C; No. 1 pick in 1991 NHL draft by the Nordiques; sat out 1991-92 season rather than play in Quebec; traded to Philadelphia in 1992 for 6 players, 2 No. 1 picks and $15 million; elected Flyers captain at age 22; won Hart Trophy as league MVP in 1995.

Sonny Liston (b. May 8, 1932, d. Dec. 30, 1970): Boxer; heavyweight champion (1962-64), who knocked out Floyd Patterson twice in the first round, then lost title to Muhammad Ali (then Cassius Clay) in 1964; pro record of 50-4 with 39 KOs.

Rebecca Lobo (b. Oct. 6, 1973): Basketball F; women's college basketball Player of the Year in 1995; led Connecticut to undefeated season (35-0) and national title; member of 1996 U.S. Olympic team.

Vince Lombardi (b. June 11, 1913, d. Sept. 3, 1970): Football; coached Green Bay to 5 NFL titles; won first 2 Super Bowls ever played (1967-68); died as NFL's all-time winningest coach with percentage of .740 (105-35-6); Super Bowl trophy named in his honor.

Johnny Longden (b. Feb. 14, 1907): Jockey; first to win 6,000 races; rode Count Fleet to Triple Crown in 1943.

Nancy Lopez (b. Jan. 6, 1957): Golfer; 4-time LPGA Player of the Year (1978-79,85,88); Rookie of Year (1977); 3-time winner of LPGA Championship; reached Hall of Fame by age 30 with 35 victories; entered 1995 with 47 career wins.

Donna Lopiano (b. Sept. 11, 1946): Former basketball and softball star who was women's athletic director at Texas for 18 years before leaving to become executive director of Women's Sports Foundation in 1992.

Greg Louganis (b. Jan. 29, 1960): U.S. diver; won platform and springboard gold medals at both 1984 and '88 Olympics; revealed on Feb. 22, 1995 that he has AIDS.

Joe Louis (b. May 13, 1914, d. Apr. 12, 1981): Boxer; world heavyweight champion from June 22, 1937 to Mar. 1, 1949; his reign of 11 years, 8 months longest in division history; successfully defended title 25 times; retired in 1949, but returned to lose title shots against successors Ezzard Charles in 1950 and Rocky Marciano in '51; pro record of 63-3 with 49 KOs.

Sid Luckman (b. Nov. 21, 1916): Football QB; 6-time All-Pro; led Chicago Bears to 4 NFL titles (1940-41,43,46); MVP in 1943.

Hank Luisetti (b. June 16, 1916): Basketball F; 3-time All-America at Stanford (1935-38); revolutionized game with one-handed shot.

Johnny Lujack (b. Jan. 4, 1925): Football QB; led Notre Dame to three national titles (1943,46-47); won Heisman Trophy in 1947.

Darrell Wayne Lukas (b. Sept. 2, 1935): Horse racing; 4-time Eclipse Award-winning trainer who saddled Horses of Year Lady's Secret in 1988 and Criminal Type in 1990; first trainer to earn over $100 million in purses; led nation in earnings 11 times from 1983-94; Grindstone's Kentucky Derby win in 1996 gave him six Triple Crown wins in a row; also won 1996 Belmont Stakes with Editor's Note; has now won Preakness four times and Kentucky Derby and Belmont three times.

Gen. Douglas MacArthur (b. Jan. 26, 1880, d. Apr. 5, 1964): Controversial U.S. general of World War II and Korea; president of U.S. Olympic Committee (1927-28); college football devotee, National Football Foundation MacArthur Bowl (for No.1 team) named after him.

Connie Mack (b. Dec. 22, 1862, d. Feb. 8, 1956): Baseball owner; managed Philadelphia A's until he was 87 (1901-50); all-time major league wins leader with 3,755, including postseason; won 9 AL pennants and 5 World Series (1910-11,13,29-30); also finished last 18 times.

Andy MacPhail (b. Apr. 5, 1953): Baseball; Chicago Cubs president, who was GM of 2 World Series champions in Minnesota (1987,91); won first title at age 34; son of Lee, grandson of Larry.

Larry MacPhail (b. Feb. 3, 1890, d. Oct. 1, 1975): Baseball executive and innovator; introduced major leagues to night games at Cincinnati (May 24, 1935); won pennant in Brooklyn (1941) and World Series with NY Yankees (1947); father of Lee.

Lee MacPhail (b. Oct. 25, 1917): Baseball; AL president (1974-83); president of owners' Player Relations Committee (1984-85); also GM of Baltimore (1959-65) and NY Yankees (1967-74); son of Larry and father of Andy.

John Madden (b. Apr. 10, 1936): Football and Radio-TV; won 112 games and a Super Bowl (1976 season) as coach of Oakland Raiders; has won 10 Emmy Awards since 1982 as NFL analyst with CBS and Fox; signed 4-year, $32 million deal with Fox in 1994— a richer contract than any NFL player.

Greg Maddux (b. Apr. 14, 1966): Baseball RHP; won unprecedented 3 straight NL Cy Young Awards with Cubs (1992) and Atlanta (1993-94); has led NL in ERA twice (1993-94); entered 1996 with record of 150-93 in 10 seasons.

Larry Mahan (b. Nov. 21, 1943): Rodeo; 6-time All-Around world champion (1966-70,73).

Phil Mahre (b. May 10, 1957): Alpine skier; 3-time World Cup overall champ (1981-83); finished 1-2 with twin brother Steve in 1984 Olympic slalom.

Karl Malone (b. July 24, 1963): Basketball F; 7-time All-NBA 1st team (1989-95) with Utah; member of the 1992 and '96 Olympic Dream Teams.

Moses Malone (b. Mar. 23, 1955): Basketball C; signed with Utah of ABA at age 19; has led NBA in rebounding 6 times; 4-time All-NBA 1st team; 3-time NBA MVP (1979,82-83); playoff MVP with Philadelphia in 1983; played in 21st pro season in 1994-95.

Nigel Mansell (b. Aug. 8, 1953): British auto racer; won 1992 Formula One driving championship with record 9 victories and 14 poles; quit Grand Prix circuit to race Indy cars in 1993; 1st rookie to win IndyCar title; 3rd driver to win IndyCar and F1 titles; returned to F1 after 1994 IndyCar season and won '94 Australian Grand Prix; left F1 again on May 23, 1995 with 31 wins and 32 poles in 15 years.

Mickey Mantle (b. Oct. 20, 1931, d. Aug. 13, 1995): Baseball OF; named after Hall of Fame catcher Mickey Cochrane; led AL in home runs 4 times; won Triple Crown in 1956; hit 52 HRs in 1956 and 54 in '61; 3-time MVP (1956-57,62); hit 536 career HRs; played in 12 World Series with NY Yankees and won 7 times; all-time Series leader in HRs (18), RBI (40), runs (42) and strikeouts (54); underwent liver transplant on June 8, 1995 and died of cancer two months later.

Diego Maradona (b. Oct. 30, 1960): Soccer F; captain and MVP of 1986 World Cup champion Argentina; also led national team to 1990 World Cup final; consensus Player of Decade in 1980's; led Napoli to 2 Italian League titles (1987,90) and UEFA Cup (1989); tested positive for cocaine and suspended 15 months by FIFA in 1991; returned to World Cup as Argentine captain in 1994, but was kicked out of tournament after two games when doping test found 5 banned substances in his urine.

Pete Maravich (b. June 27, 1947, d. Jan. 5, 1988): Basketball; NCAA scoring leader 3 times (1968-70); averaged 44.2 points a game over career; Player of Year in 1970; NBA scoring champ in '77 with New Orleans.

Alice Marble (b. Sept. 28, 1913, d. Dec. 13, 1990): Tennis; 4-time U.S. champion (1936,38-40); won Wimbledon in 1939; swept U.S. singles, doubles and mixed doubles from 1938-40.

Gino Marchetti (b. Jan. 2, 1927): Football DE; 8-time NFL All-Pro (1957-64) with Baltimore Colts.

Rocky Marciano (b. Sept. 1, 1923, d. Aug. 31, 1969): Boxer; heavyweight champion (1952-56); retired undefeated; pro record of 49-0 with 43 KOs; killed in plane crash.

Juan Marichal (b. Oct. 20, 1938): Baseball RHP; won 21 or more games 6 times for S.F. Giants from 1963-69; ended 16-year career with 243 wins.

Dan Marino (b. Sept. 15, 1961): Football QB; 4-time leading passer in AFC (1983-84,86,89); set NFL single-season records for TD passes (48) and passing yards (5,084) with Miami in 1984; entered 1996 season as all-time leader in career TD passes (352) and passing yards (48,841).

Roger Maris (b. Sept. 10, 1934, d. Dec. 14, 1985): Baseball OF; broke Babe Ruth's single-season HR record with 61 in 1961; 2-time AL MVP (1960-61) with NY Yankees.

Billy Martin (b. May 16, 1928, d. Dec. 25, 1989): Baseball; 5-time manager of NY Yankees; won 2 pennants and 1 World Series (1977); also managed Minnesota, Detroit, Texas and Oakland; played 2B on 4 Yankee world champions in 1950's.

Eddie Mathews (b. Oct. 13, 1931): Baseball 3B; led NL in HRs twice (1953,59); hit 30 or more home runs 9 straight years; 512 career HRs.

Christy Mathewson (b. Aug. 12, 1880, d. Oct. 7, 1925): Baseball RHP; won 22 or more games 12 straight years (1903-14); 373 career wins; pitched 3 shutouts in 1905 World Series.

Bob Mathias (b. Nov. 17, 1930): Track & Field; youngest winner of decathlon with gold medal in 1948 Olympics at age 17; first to repeat as decathlon champ in 1952; Sullivan Award winner (1948); 4-term member of U.S. Congress (R, Calif.) from 1967-74.

Ollie Matson (b. May 1, 1930): Football HB; All-America at San Francisco (1951); bronze medal winner in 400m at 1952 Olympics; 4-time All-Pro for NFL Chicago Cardinals (1954-57); traded to LA Rams for 9 players in 1959; accounted for 12,884 all-purpose yards and scored 73 TDs in 14 seasons.

Willie Mays (b. May 6, 1931): Baseball OF; nicknamed the "Say Hey Kid"; led NL in HRs and stolen bases 4 times each; 2-time MVP (1954,65) with NY-SF Giants; Hall of Famer who played in 24 All-Star Games; 660 HRs and 3,283 hits in career.

Bill Mazeroski (b. Sept. 5, 1936): Baseball 2B; career .260 hitter who won the 1960 World Series for Pittsburgh with a lead-off HR in the bottom of the 9th inning of Game 7; the pitcher was Ralph Terry of the NY Yankees, the count was 1-0 and the score was tied 9-9; also a sure-fielder, Maz won 8 gold gloves in 17 seasons.

Joe McCarthy (b. Apr. 21, 1887, d. Jan. 13, 1978) Baseball; first manager to win pennants in both leagues (Chicago Cubs in 1929 and New York Yankees in 1932); greatest success came with Yankees when he won seven pennants and six World Series championships from 1936 to 1943; first manager to win four World Series in a row (1936-'39); finished his career with the Boston Red Sox (1948-'50); lifetime record of 2,125-1,333; member of Baseball Hall of Fame.

Mark McCormack (b. Nov. 6, 1930): Founder and CEO of International Management Group (IMG), the sports management conglomerate who represent, among others, Joe Montana, Wayne Gretzky, Arnold Palmer, Andre Agassi and Pete Sampras.

Pat McCormick (b. May 12, 1930): U.S. diver; won women's platform and springboard gold medals in both 1952 and '56 Olympics.

Willie McCovey (b. Jan. 10, 1938): Baseball 1B; led NL in HRs 3 times and RBI twice; MVP in 1969 with SF; 521 career HRs; indicted for tax evasion in July 1995.

John McEnroe (b. Feb. 16, 1959): Tennis; No.1 player in the world 4 times (1981-84); 4-time U.S. Open singles champ (1979-81,84); 3-time Wimbledon champ (1981,83-84); has played on 5 Davis Cup winners (1978-79,81-82,92); won NCAA singles title (1978); finished career with 77 championships in singles, 77 more in doubles (including 9 Grand Slam titles), and American Davis Cup records for years played (13) and singles matches won (41).

John McGraw (b. Apr. 7, 1873, d. Feb. 25, 1934): Baseball; managed NY Giants to 9 NL pennants between 1905-24; won World Series 3 times in 1905 and 1921-22; 2nd on all-time career list with 2,810 wins in 33 seasons (2,784 regular season and 26 postseason).

Frank McGuire (b. Nov. 8, 1916, d. Oct. 11, 1994): Basketball; winner of 731 games as high school, college and pro coach; only coach to win 100 games at 3 colleges— St. John's (103), North Carolina (164) and South Carolina (283); won 550 games in 30 college seasons; 1957 UNC team went 32-0 and beat Kansas 54-53 in triple OT to win NCAA title; coached NBA Philadelphia Warriors to 49-31 record in 1961-62 season, but refused to move with team to San Francisco.

Jim McKay (b. Sept. 24, 1921): Radio-TV; host and commentator of ABC's Olympic coverage and "Wide World of Sports" show since 1961; 12-time Emmy winner; also given Peabody Award in 1988 and Life Achievement Emmy in 1990; became part owner of Baltimore Orioles in 1993.

John McKay (b. July 5, 1923): Football; coached USC to 3 national titles (1962,67,72); won Rose Bowl 5 times; reached NFL playoffs 3 times with Tampa Bay.

Tamara McKinney (b. Oct. 16, 1962): Skiing; only American woman to win overall Alpine World Cup championship (1983); won World Cup slalom (1984) and giant slalom titles twice (1981,83).

Denny McLain (b. Mar. 29, 1944): Baseball RHP; last pitcher to win 30 games (1968); 2-time Cy Young winner (1968-69) with Detroit; convicted of racketeering, extortion and drug possession in 1985, served 29 months of 25-year jail term, sentence overturned when court ruled he had not received a fair trial.

Rick Mears (b. Dec. 3, 1951): Auto racer; 3-time CART national champ (1979,81-82); 4-time winner of Indianapolis 500 (1979,84,88,91) and only driver to win 6 Indy 500 poles; Indy 500 Rookie of Year (1978); retired after 1992 season with 29 IndyCar wins and 40 poles.

Mark Messier (b. Jan. 18, 1961): Hockey C; 2-time Hart Trophy winner as MVP with Edmonton (1990) and NY Rangers (1992); captain of Rangers team that finally won 1st Stanley Cup since 1940; entered 1996-97 season with 492 regular season goals; ranked 2nd (behind Gretzky) in all-time playoff points (283) and assists (177).

Debbie Meyer (b. Aug. 14, 1952): Swimmer; 1st swimmer to win 3 individual gold medals at one Olympics (1968).

George Mikan (b. June 18, 1924): Basketball C; 3-time All-America (1944-46); led DePaul to NIT title (1945); led Minneapolis Lakers to 5 NBA titles in 6 years (1949-54); first commissioner of ABA (1967-69).

Stan Mikita (b. May 20, 1940): Hockey C; led NHL in scoring 4 times; won both MVP and Lady Byng awards in 1967 and '68 with Chicago.

Cheryl Miller (b. Jan. 3, 1964): Basketball; 3-time college Player of Year (1984-86); led USC to NCAA title and U.S. to Olympic gold medal in 1984; coached USC to 44-14 record in 2 seasons before quitting to join Turner Sports as NBA reporter.

Del Miller (b. July 5, 1913): Harness racing; driver, trainer, owner, breeder, seller and track owner; drove to 2,441 wins from 1939-90.

Marvin Miller (b. Apr. 14, 1917): Baseball labor leader; executive director of Players' Assn. from 1966-82; increased average salary from $19,000 to over $240,000; led 13-day strike in 1972 and 50-day walkout in '81.

Shannon Miller (b. Mar. 10, 1977): Gymnast; won 5 medals in 1992 Olympics and 2 golds in '96 Games; All-Around women's world champion in 1993 and '94.

Billy Mills (b. June 30, 1938): Track & Field; upset winner of 10,000m gold medal at 1964 Olympics.

Bora Milutinovic (b. Sept. 7, 1944): Soccer; Serbian who coached United States national team from 1991-95, but was fired on Apr. 14, 1995 when he refused to accept additional duties as director of player development; hired 4 months later to revive Mexican national team; known as a miracle worker, he led Mexico, Costa Rica and the U.S. into the 2nd round of the last three World Cups.

Tommy Moe (b. Feb. 17, 1970): Alpine skier; won Downhill and placed 2nd in Super-G at 1994 Winter Olympics; 1st U.S. man to win 2 Olympic alpine medals in one year.

Paul Molitor (b. Aug. 22, 1956): Baseball DH-1B; All-America SS at Minnesota in 1976; signed as free agent by Toronto on Dec. 7, 1992, after 15 years with Milwaukee; led Blue Jays to 2nd straight World Series title as MVP (1993); has hit .418 in 2 Series appearances (1982,93); holds World Series record with five hits in one game; got career hit 3,000 with a triple on Sept. 16, 1996.

Joe Montana (b. June 11, 1956): Football QB: led Notre Dame to national title in 1977; led San Francisco to 4 Super Bowl titles in 1980s; only 3-time Super Bowl MVP; 2-time NFL MVP (1989-90); has led NFL in passing 5 times; missed all of 1991 season and nearly all of '92 after elbow surgery; traded to Kansas City in 1993; ranked 2nd in all-time passing efficiency (92.3), 4th in TD passes (273) and yards passing (40,551); announced retirement in San Francisco on Apr. 18, 1995.

Helen Wills Moody (b. Oct. 6, 1905): Tennis; won 8 Wimbledon singles titles, 7 U.S. and 4 French from 1923-38.

Warren Moon (b. Nov. 18, 1956): Football QB; MVP of 1978 Rose Bowl with Washington; MVP of CFL with Edmonton in 1983; led Eskimos to 5 consecutive Grey Cup titles (1978-82) and was playoff MVP twice (1980,82); joined Houston of NFL in 1984; led NFL in attempts, completions and yards in 1990 and '91; picked for 8 Pro Bowls; traded to Minnesota in 1994.

Archie Moore (b. Dec. 13, 1913): Boxer; world light-heavyweight champion (1952-60); pro record 199-26-8 with 145 KOs.

Herman Moore (b. Oct. 20, 1969) Football; wide receiver for the Detroit Lions; caught an NFL-record 123 passes in 1995.

Michael Moorer (b. Nov. 12, 1967): Boxer; became 1st left-hander to win heavyweight title when he scored majority decision over Evander Holyfield on Apr. 22, 1994; lost title to George Foreman on 10th round KO Nov. 5, 1994; entered 1996 with pro record of 36-1 with 30 KOs.

Noureddine Morceli (b. Feb. 28, 1970): Algerian runner; 3-time world champion at 1,500 meters (1991,93, 95); set world records at mile (3:44.39) in 1993, at 3,000m (7:25.11) in '94 and at 1,500m (3:27.37) in 1995.

Howie Morenz (b. June 21, 1902, d. Mar. 8, 1937): Hockey C; 3-time NHL MVP (1928,31-32); led Montreal Canadiens to 3 Stanley Cups; voted Outstanding Player of the Half-Century in 1950.

Joe Morgan (b. Sept. 19, 1943): Baseball 2B; led NL in walks 4 times; regular-season MVP both years he led Cincinnati to World Series titles (1975-76); 3rd behind Babe Ruth and Ted Williams in career walks with 1,865.

Bobby Morrow (b. Oct. 15, 1935): Track & Field; won 3 gold medals at 1956 Olympics (100m, 200m and 4x400m relay).

Willie Mosconi (b. June 27, 1913, d. Sept. 12, 1993): Pocket Billiards; 14-time world champion from 1941-57.

Annemarie Moser-Pröll (b. Mar. 27, 1953): Austrian alpine skier; won World Cup overall title 6 times (1971-75,79); all-time women's World Cup leader in career wins with 61; won Downhill in 1980 Olympics.

Edwin Moses (b. Aug. 31, 1955): Track & Field; won 400m hurdles at 1976 and '84 Olympics, bronze medal in '88; also winner of 122 consecutive races from 1977-87.

Stirling Moss (b. Sept. 17, 1929): Auto racer; won 194 of 466 career races and 16 Formula One events, but was never world champion.

Marion Motley (b. June 5, 1920): Football FB; all-time leading AAFC rusher; rushed for over 4,700 yards and 31 TDs for Cleveland Browns (1946-53).

Dale Murphy (b. Mar. 12, 1956): Baseball OF; led NL in RBI 3 times and HRs twice; 2-time MVP (1982-83) with Atlanta; also played with Philadelphia and Colorado; retired May 27, 1993, with 398 HRs.

Jack Murphy (b. Feb. 5, 1923, d. Sept. 24, 1980): Sports editor and columnist of *The San Diego Union* from 1951-80; instrumental in bringing AFL Chargers south from LA in 1961, landing Padres as NL expansion team in '69; and lobbying for 54,000-seat San Diego stadium that would later bear his name.

Eddie Murray (b. Feb. 24, 1956): Baseball 1B-DH; AL Rookie of Year in 1977; entered 1996 with 479 HRs and most games with switch-hit homers (11); became 20th player in history, but only 2nd switch hitter (after Pete Rose) to get 3,000 hits; belted 500th homer off Detroit's Felipe Lira on Sept. 6, 1996.

Jim Murray (b. Dec. 29, 1919): Sports columnist for *LA Times* since 1961; 14-time Sportswriter of the Year; won Pulitzer Prize for commentary in 1990.

Ty Murray (b. Oct. 11, 1969): Rodeo cowboy; 6-time All-Around world champion (1989-94); Rookie of Year in 1988; youngest (age 20) to win All-Around title; set single season earnings mark with $297,896 in 1993; missed most of 1995 season with knee injury.

Stan Musial (b. Nov. 21, 1920): Baseball OF-1B; led NL in batting 7 times; 3-time MVP (1943,46,48) with St. Louis; played in 24 All-Star Games; had 3,630 career hits and .331 average.

John Naber (b. Jan. 20, 1956): Swimmer; won 4 gold medals and a silver in 1976 Olympics.

Bronko Nagurski (b. Nov. 3, 1908, d. Jan. 7, 1990): Football FB-T; All-America at Minnesota (1929); All-Pro with Chicago Bears (1932-34); charter member of college and pro halls of fame.

James Naismith (b. Nov. 6, 1861, d. Nov. 28, 1939): Canadian physical education instructor who invented basketball in 1891 at the YMCA Training School (now Springfield College) in Springfield, Mass.

Joe Namath (b. May 31, 1943): Football QB; signed for unheard-of $400,000 as rookie with AFL's NY Jets in 1965; 2-time All-AFL (1968-69) and All-NFL (1972); led Jets to Super Bowl title as MVP in '69.

Ilie Nastase (b. July 19, 1946): Romanian tennis player; No.1 in the world twice (1972-73); won U.S. (1972) and French (1973) Opens.

Martina Navratilova (b. Oct. 18, 1956): Tennis player; No.1 player in the world 7 times (1978-79,82-86); won her record 9th Wimbledon singles title in 1990; also won 4 U.S. Opens, 3 Australian and 2 French; in all, won 18 Grand Slam singles titles and 38 Grand Slam doubles titles; all-time leader among men and women in singles titles (167) and money won ($20.3 million) over 21 years; retired from singles play after 1994 season with No. 8 ranking and appearance in 12th Wimbledon final.

Cosmas Ndeti (b. Nov. 24, 1971): Kenyan distance runner; winner of three consecutive Boston Marathons (1993-95), set course record of 2:07:15 in 1994.

Earle (Greasy) Neale (b. Nov. 5, 1891, d. Nov. 2, 1973): Baseball and Football; hit .357 for Cincinnati in 1919 World Series; also played with pre-NFL Canton Bulldogs; later coached Philadelphia Eagles to 2 NFL titles (1948-49).

Primo Nebiolo (b. July 14, 1923): Italian president of International Amateur Athletic Federation (IAAF) since 1981; also an at-large member of International Olympic Committee; regarded as dictatorial, but credited with elevating track & field to world class financial status.

Byron Nelson (b. Feb. 4, 1912): Golfer; 2-time winner of both Masters (1937,42) and PGA (1940,45); also U.S. Open champion in 1939; won 19 tournaments in 1945, including 11 in a row; also set all-time PGA stroke average with 68.33 strokes per round over 120 rounds in '45.

Lindsey Nelson (b. May 25, 1919, d. June 10, 1995): Radio-TV; all-purpose play-by-play broadcaster for CBS, NBC and others; 4-time Sportscaster of the Year (1959-62); voice of Cotton Bowl for 25 years and NY Mets from 1962-78; given Life Achievement Emmy Award in 1991.

Ernie Nevers (b. July 11, 1903, d. May 3, 1976): Football FB; earned 11 letters in four sports at Stanford; played pro football, baseball and basketball; scored 40 points for Chicago Cardinals in one NFL game (1929).

Paula Newby-Fraser (b. June 2, 1962): Zimbabwean triathlete; 7-time winner of Ironman Triathlon in Hawaii; established women's record of 8:55:28 in 1992.

John Newcombe (b. May 23, 1944): Australian tennis player; No.1 player in world 3 times (1967,70-71); won Wimbledon 3 times and U.S. and Australian championships twice each.

Pete Newell (b. Aug. 31, 1915) Basketball; coached at University of San Francisco, Michigan State and the University of California; first coach to win NIT (San Francisco -1949), NCAA (California - 1959) and Olympic gold medal (1960); later served as the general manager of the San Diego Rockets and Los Angeles Lakers in the NBA; member of Basketball Hall of Fame.

Bob Neyland (b. Feb. 17, 1892, d. Mar. 28, 1962): Football; 3-time coach at Tennessee; had 173-31-12 record in 21 years; won national title in 1951; Vols' stadium named for him; also Army general who won Distinguished Service Cross as supply officer in World War II.

Jack Nicklaus (b. Jan. 21, 1940): Golfer; all-time leader in major tournament wins with 20— including 6 Masters, 5 PGAs, 4 U.S. Opens and 3 British Opens; oldest player to win Masters (46 in 1986); PGA Player of Year 5 times (1967,72-73,75-76); named Golfer of Century by PGA in 1988; 6-time Ryder Cup player and 2-time captain (1983,87); won NCAA title (1961) and 2 U.S. Amateurs (1959,61); entered 1995 with 70 PGA Tour wins (2nd to Sam Snead's 81); 3rd win in Tradition in '95 gave him 7 majors in 6 years on Seniors Tour.

Chuck Noll (b. Jan. 5, 1932): Football; coached Pittsburgh to 4 Super Bowl titles (1975-76,79-80); retired after 1991 season ranked 5th on all-time list with 209 wins (including playoffs) in 23 years.

Greg Norman (b. Feb. 10, 1955): Australian golfer; PGA Tour's all-time money winner ($10.4 million), passing Tom Kite on Aug. 27, 1995; entered 1996 with 66 tournament wins worldwide; 2-time British Open winner (1986,93); lost Masters by a stroke in both 1986 (to Jack Nicklaus) and '87 (to Larry Mize in sudden death).

James D. Norris (b. Nov. 6, 1906, d. Feb. 25, 1966): Boxing promoter and NHL owner; president of International Boxing Club from 1949 until U.S. Supreme Court ordered its break-up (for anti-trust violations) in 1958; only NHL owner to win Stanley Cups in two cities' Detroit (1936-37,43) and Chicago (1961).

Paavo Nurmi (b. June 13, 1897, d. Oct. 2, 1973): Finnish runner; won 9 gold medals (6 individual) in 1920, '24 and '28 Olympics; from 1921-31 broke 23 world outdoor records in events ranging from 1,500 to 20,000 meters.

Dan O'Brien (b. July 18, 1966): Track & Field; set world record in decathlon (8,891 pts) on Sept. 4-5, 1992, after failing to qualify for event at U.S. Olympic Trials; three-time gold medalist at World Championships (1991,93,95).

Larry O'Brien (b. July 7, 1917, d. Sept. 27, 1990): Basketball; former U.S. Postmaster General and 3rd NBA commissioner (1975-84), league absorbed 4 ABA teams and created salary cap during his term in office.

Parry O'Brien (b. Jan. 28, 1932): Track & Field; in 4 consecutive Olympics, won two gold medals, a silver and placed 4th in the shot put (1952-64).

Al Oerter (b. Sept. 19, 1936): Track & Field; his 4 discus gold medals in consecutive Olympics from 1956-68 is an unmatched Olympic record.

Sadaharu Oh (b. May 20, 1940): Baseball 1B; led Japan League in HRs 15 times; 9-time MVP for Tokyo Giants; hit 868 HRs in 22 years.

Hakeem Olajuwon (b. Jan. 21, 1963): Basketball C; Nigerian native who was consensus All-America in 1984 and Final Four MVP in 1983 for Houston; overall 1st pick by Houston Rockets in 1984 NBA draft; led Rockets to back-to-back NBA titles (1994,95); regular season MVP ('94) and playoff MVP ('94,'95); 6-time All-NBA 1st team (1987-89,93-95). Member of Dream Team III.

José Maria Olazábal (b. Feb. 5, 1966): Spanish golfer; entered 1995 season with 13 worldwide victories; won only major at '94 Masters.

Barney Oldfield (b. Jan. 29, 1878, d. Oct. 4, 1946): Auto racing pioneer; drove cars built by Henry Ford; first man to drive car a mile per minute (1903).

Walter O'Malley (b. Oct. 9, 1903, d. Aug. 9, 1979): Baseball owner; moved Brooklyn Dodgers to Los Angeles after 1957 season; won 4 World Series (1955,59,63,65).

Shaquille O'Neal (b. Mar. 6, 1972): Basketball C; 2-time All-America at LSU (1991-92); overall 1st pick (as a junior) by Orlando in 1992 NBA draft; Rookie of Year in 1993; led NBA in scoring in 1995; member of Dream Teams II and III. Signed with LA Lakers in 1996.

Bobby Orr (b. Mar. 20, 1948): Hockey D; 8-time Norris Trophy winner as best defenseman; led NHL in scoring twice and assists 5 times; All-NHL 1st team 8 times; regular season MVP 3 times (1970-72); playoff MVP twice (1970,72) with Boston.

Tom Osborne (b. Feb. 23, 1937): Football; entered 1996 season with record of 231-47-3 in 23 seasons as coach at Nebraska; his win percentage of .827 is best of any active coach in Division I-A; finally won national championship in 1994. Won 2nd national title in '95.

Mel Ott (b. Mar. 2, 1909, d. Nov. 21, 1958): Baseball OF; joined NY Giants at age 16; led NL in HRs 6 times; had 511 HRs and 1,860 RBI in 22 years.

Kristin Otto (b. Feb. 7, 1966): East German swimmer; 1st woman to win 6 gold medals (4 individual) at one Olympics (1988).

Francis Ouimet (b. May 8, 1893, d. Sept. 3, 1967): Golfer; won 1913 U.S. Open as 20-year-old amateur playing on Brookline, Mass. course where he used to caddie; won U.S. Amateur twice; 8-time Walker Cup player.

Steve Owen (b. Apr. 21, 1898, d. May 17, 1964): Football; All-Pro guard (1927); coached NY Giants for 23 years (1931-53); won 153 career games and 2 NFL titles (1934,38).

Jesse Owens (b. Sept. 12, 1913, d. Mar. 31, 1980): Track & Field; broke 5 world records in one afternoon at Big Ten Championships (May 25, 1935); a year later, he won 4 gold medals (100m, 200m, 4x100m relay and long jump) at Berlin Summer Olympics.

Alan Page (b. Aug. 7, 1945): Football DE; consensus All-America at Notre Dame in 1966 and member of two national championship teams; 6-time NFL All-Pro and 1971 Player of Year with Minnesota Vikings; also a lawyer who was elected to Minnesota Supreme Court in 1992.

Satchel Paige (b. July 7, 1906, d. June 6, 1982): Baseball RHP; pitched 55 career no-hitters over 20 seasons in Negro Leagues, entered Major Leagues with Cleveland in 1948 at age 42; had 28-31 record in 5 years; returned to AL at age 59 to start 1 game for Kansas City in 1965; went 3 innings, gave up a hit and got a strikeout.

Arnold Palmer (b. Sept. 10, 1929): Golfer; winner of 4 Masters, 2 British Opens and a U.S. Open; 2-time PGA Player of Year (1960,62); 1st player to earn over $1 million in career (1968); annual PGA Tour money leader award named after him; entered 1995 with 60 wins on PGA Tour and 10 more on Senior Tour.

Jim Palmer (b. Oct. 15, 1945): Baseball RHP; 3-time Cy Young Award winner (1973,75-76); won 20 or more games 8 times with Baltimore; 1991 comeback attempt at age 45 scrubbed in spring training.

Bill Parcells (b. Aug. 22, 1941): Football; coached NY Giants to 2 Super Bowl titles (1986,90); retired after 1990 season then returned in '93 as coach of New England; entered 1996 season with 11-year record of 106-81-1.

Jack Pardee (b. Apr. 19, 1936): Football; All-America linebacker at Texas A&M; 2-time All-Pro with LA Rams (1963) and Washington (1971); 2-time NFL Coach of Year (1976,79) and winner of 87 games in 11 seasons; only man hired as head coach in NFL, WFL, USFL and CFL; also coached at University of Houston.

Bernie Parent (b. Apr. 3, 1945): Hockey G; led Philadelphia Flyers to 2 Stanley Cups as playoff MVP (1974,75); 2-time Vezina Trophy winner; posted 55 career shutouts and 2.55 GAA in 13 seasons.

Joe Paterno (b. Dec. 21, 1926): Football; has coached Penn State to 2 national titles (1982,86) and 16-8-1 bowl record in 29 years; also had three unbeaten teams that didn't finish No. 1; Coach of Year 4 times (1968,78,82,86); entered 1996 season leading all active Div. I-A coaches with 278 career wins (including bowls).

Craig Patrick (b. May 20, 1946): Hockey; 3rd generation Patrick to have name inscribed on Stanley Cup; GM of 2-time Cup champion Pittsburgh Penguins (1991-92); also captain of 1969 NCAA champion at Denver; assistant coach-GM of 1980 gold medal-winning U.S. Olympic team; scored 72 goals in 8 NHL seasons and won 69 games in 3 years as coach; grandson of Lester.

Lester Patrick (b. Dec. 30, 1883, d. June 1, 1960): Hockey; pro hockey pioneer as player, coach and general manager for 43 years; led NY Rangers to Stanley Cups as coach (1928,33) and GM (1940); grandfather of Craig.

Floyd Patterson (b. Jan. 4, 1935): Boxer; Olympic middleweight champ in 1952; world heavyweight champion (1956-59,60-62); 1st to regain heavyweight crown; fought Ingemar Johansson 3 times in 22 months from 1959-61 and won last two; pro record 55-8-1 with 40 KOs; jr. lightweight champion Tracy Harris Patterson is his adopted son.

Walter Payton (b. July 25, 1954): Football RB; NFL's all-time leading rusher with 16,726 yards; scored 109 career TDs; All-Pro 7 times with Chicago; MVP in 1977; led Bears to Super Bowl title in Jan. 1986.

Pelé (b. Oct. 23, 1940): Brazilian soccer F; given name— Edson Arantes do Nascimento; led Brazil to 3 World Cup titles (1958,62,70); came to U.S. in 1975 to play for NY Cosmos in NASL; scored 1,281 goals in 22 years; currently Brazil's minister of sport.

Roger Penske (b. Feb. 20, 1937): Auto racing; national sports car driving champion (1964); established racing team in 1961; co-founder of Championship Auto Racing Teams (CART); Penske Racing entered 1995 with a record 91 IndyCar victories, including 10 Indianapolis 500s and 9 IndyCar points titles; shocked racing world by failing to qualify car for 1995 Indy 500.

Willie Pep (b. Sept. 19, 1922): Boxer; 2-time world featherweight champion (1942-48,49-50); pro record 230-11-1 with 65 KOs.

Marie-Jose Perec (b. 1968) Track and field; French sprinter who became 2nd woman to win the 200m and 400m events in the same Olympics (1996); her time in the 400 (48.25) set an Olympic record; Valerie Brisco-Hooks did it in the boycotted 1984 games; also won the 400M in 1992 games.

Fred Perry (b. May 18, 1909, d. Feb. 2, 1995): British tennis player; 3-time Wimbledon champ (1934-36); fist player to win all four Grand Slam singles titles, though not simultaneously; last native to win All-England men's title.

Gaylord Perry (b. Sept. 15, 1938): Baseball RHP; only pitcher to win a Cy Young Award in both leagues; retired in 1983 with 314 wins and 3,534 strikeouts over 22 years and with 8 teams; brother Jim won 215 games for family total of 529.

Bob Pettit (b. Dec. 12, 1932): Basketball F; All-NBA 1st team 10 times (1955-64); 2-time MVP (1956,59) with St. Louis Hawks; first player to score 20,000 points.

Richard Petty (b. July 2, 1937): Auto racer; 7-time winner of Daytona 500; 7-time NASCAR national champ (1964,67,71-72,74-75,79); first stock car driver to win $1 million in career; all-time NASCAR leader in races won (200), poles (127) and wins in a single season (27 in 1967); retired after 1992 season; son of Lee (54 career wins) and father of Kyle (7 wins entering 1995).

Laffit Pincay Jr. (b. Dec. 29, 1946): Jockey; 5-time Eclipse Award winner (1971,73-74,79,85); winner of 3 Belmonts and 1 Kentucky Derby (aboard Swale in 1984); entered 1995 with 8,217 career wins, trailing only Bill Shoemaker's 8,833.

Scottie Pippen (b. Sept. 25, 1965) Basketball; Chicago Bulls forward has started on four NBA champions (1991,'92,'93, '96); All-NBA first team in '94, '95.

Nelson Piquet (b. Aug. 17, 1952): Brazilian auto racer; 3-time Formula One world champion (1981,83, 87); left circuit in 1991 with 23 career wins.

Rick Pitino (b. Sept. 18, 1952) Basketball; won 1996 NCAA championship in his seventh year at Kentucky; previously coached the New York Knicks in the NBA (96-81 overall), Providence College (42-23) and Boston University (46-24).

Jacques Plante (b. Jan. 17, 1929, d. Feb. 27, 1986): Hockey G; led Montreal to 6 Stanley Cups (1953,56-60); won 7 Vezina Trophies; MVP in 1962; first goalie to regularly wear a mask; posted 82 shutouts with 2.38 GAA.

Gary Player (b. Nov. 1, 1936): South African golfer; 3-time winner of Masters and British Open; only player in 20th century to win British Open in three different decades (1959,68,74); one of only four players to win all four Grand Slam titles (others are Hogan, Nicklaus and Sarazen); has also won 2 PGAs, a U.S. Open and 2 U.S. Senior Opens; entered 1995 with 21 wins on PGA Tour and 17 more on Senior Tour.

Jim Plunkett (b. Dec. 5, 1947): Football QB; Heisman Trophy winner in 1970; AFL Rookie of the Year in 1971; led Oakland-LA Raiders to Super Bowl wins in 1981 and '84; MVP in '81.

Maurice Podoloff (b. Aug. 18, 1890, d. Nov. 24, 1985): Basketball; engineered merger of Basketball Assn. of America and National Basketball League into NBA in 1949; NBA commissioner (1949-63); league MVP trophy named after him.

Fritz Pollard (b. Jan. 27, 1894, d. May 11, 1986): Football; 1st black All-America RB (1916 at Brown); 1st black to play in Rose Bowl; 7-year NFL pro (1920-26); 1st black NFL coach, at Milwaukee and Hammond, Ind.

Sam Pollock (b. Dec. 15, 1925): Hockey GM; managed NHL Montreal Canadiens to 9 Stanley Cups in 14 years (1965-78).

Denis Potvin (b. Oct. 29, 1953): Hockey D; won Norris Trophy 3 times (1976,78-79); 5-time All-NHL 1st-team; led NY Islanders to 4 Stanley Cups.

Mike Powell (b. Nov. 10, 1963): Track & Field; broke Bob Beamon's 23-year-old long jump world record by 2 inches with leap of 29-ft., 4½ in. at the 1991 World Championships; Sullivan Award winner (1991); won long jump silver medals in 1988 and '92 Olympics; repeated as world champ in 1993.

Steve Prefontaine (b. Jan. 25, 1951, d. June 1, 1975): Track & Field; All-America distance runner at Oregon; first athlete to win same event at NCAA championships 4 straight years (5,000 meters from 1970-73); finished 4th in 5,000 at 1972 Munich Olympics; first athlete to endorse Nike running shoes; killed in a one-car accident.

Nick Price (b. Jan. 28, 1957): Zimbabwean golfer; PGA Tour Player of Year in 1993 and '94; became 1st player since Nick Faldo in 1990 to win 2 Grand Slam titles in same year when he took British Open and PGA Championship in 1994; also won PGA in '92.

Alain Prost (b. Feb. 24, 1955): French auto racer; 4-time Formula One world champion (1985-86,89,93); sat out 1992 then returned to win 4th title in 1993; retired after '93 season as all-time F1 wins leader with 51.

Kirby Puckett (b. Mar. 14, 1961): Baseball OF; led Minnesota Twins to World Series titles in 1987 and '91; retired in 1996 with a batting title (1989), 2,304 hits and a .318 career average in 12 seasons.

C.C. Pyle (b. 1882, d. Feb. 3, 1939): Promoter; known as "Cash and Carry"; hyped Red Grange's pro football debut by arranging 1925 barnstorming tour with Chicago Bears; had Grange bolt NFL for new AFL in 1926 (AFL folded in '27); also staged 2 Transcontinental Races (1928-29), known as "Bunion Derbies."

Bobby Rahal (b. Jan. 10, 1953): Auto racer; 3-time PPG Cup champ (1986,87,92); entered 1995 with 24 career IndyCar wins, including 1986 Indy 500.

Jack Ramsay (b. Feb. 21, 1925): Basketball; coach who won 239 college games with St. Joseph's-PA in 11 seasons and 906 NBA games (including playoffs) with 4 teams over 21 years; placed 3rd in 1961 Final Four; led Portland to NBA title in 1977.

Bill Rassmussen (b. Oct. 15, 1932): Radio-TV; unemployed radio broadcaster who founded ESPN, the nation's first 24-hour all-sports cable-TV network, in 1978; bought out by Getty Oil in 1981.

Willis Reed (b. June 25, 1942): Basketball C; led NY Knicks to NBA titles in 1970 and '73, playoff MVP both years; regular season MVP 1970.

Mary Lou Retton (b. Jan. 24, 1968): Gymnast; won gold medal in women's All-Around at the 1984 Olympics, also won 2 silvers and 2 bronzes.

Butch Reynolds (b. June 8, 1964): Track & Field; set current world record in 400 meters (43.29) in 1988; banned for 2½ years for allegedly failing drug test in 1990; sued IAAF and won $27.4 million judgment in 1992, but award was voided in '94; won silver medal in 400 meters and gold as member of U.S. 4x400-meter relay team at both 1993 and '95 World Championships.

Grantland Rice (b. Nov. 1, 1880, d. July 13, 1954): First celebrated American sportswriter; chronicled the Golden Age of Sport in 1920s; immortalized Notre Dame's "Four Horsemen."

Jerry Rice (b. Oct. 13, 1962): Football WR; 2-time Div. I-AA All-America at Mississippi Valley St. (1983-84); 7-time All-Pro; regular season MVP in 1987 and Super Bowl MVP in 1989 with San Francisco; entered 1995 season as NFL all-time leader in touchdowns with 139; his 820 career receptions trail only Art Monk's 934.

Henri Richard (b. Feb. 29, 1936): Hockey C; leap year baby who played on more Stanley Cup championship teams (11) than anybody else; at 5-foot-7, known as the "Pocket Rocket"; brother of Maurice.

Maurice Richard (b. Aug. 4, 1921): Hockey RW; the "Rocket"; 8-time NHL 1st team All-Star; MVP in 1947; 1st to score 50 goals in one season (1945); 544 career goals; played on 8 Stanley Cup winners in Montreal.

Bob Richards (b. Feb. 2, 1926): Track & Field; pole vaulter, ordained minister and original *Wheaties* pitchman, who won gold medals at 1952 and '56 Olympics; remains only 2-time Olympic pole vault champ.

Nolan Richardson (b. Dec. 27, 1941): Basketball; coached Arkansas to consecutive NCAA finals, beating Duke in 1994 and losing to UCLA in '95; entered 1995-96 season with career record of 371-119 in 15 years.

Tex Rickard (b. Jan. 2, 1870, d. Jan. 6, 1929): Promoter who handled boxing's first $1 million gate (Dempsey vs. Carpentier in 1921); built Madison Square Garden in 1925; founded NY Rangers as Garden tenant in 1926 and named NHL team after himself (Tex's Rangers); also built Boston Garden in 1928.

Eddie Rickenbacker (b. Oct. 8, 1890, d. July 23, 1973): Mechanic and auto racer; became America's top flying ace (22 kills) in World War I; owned Indianapolis Speedway (1927-45) and ran Eastern Air Lines (1938-59).

Branch Rickey (b. Dec. 20, 1881, d. Dec. 9, 1965): Baseball innovator; revolutionized game with creation of modern farm system while general manager of St. Louis Cardinals (1917-42); integrated Major Leagues in 1947 as president-GM of Brooklyn Dodgers when he brought up Jackie Robinson (whom he had signed on Oct. 23, 1945); later GM of Pittsburgh Pirates.

Leni Riefenstahl (b. Aug. 22, 1902): German filmmaker of 1930's; directed classic sports documentary "Olympia" on 1936 Berlin Summer Olympics; infamous, however, for also making 1934 Hitler propaganda film "Triumph of the Will."

Roy Riegels (b. Apr. 4, 1908, d. Mar. 26, 1993): Football; California center who picked up fumble in 2nd quarter of 1929 Rose Bowl and raced 70 yards in the wrong direction to set up a 2-point safety in 8-7 loss to Georgia Tech.

Bobby Riggs (b. Feb. 25, 1918, d. Oct. 25, 1995): Tennis; won Wimbledon once (1939) and U.S. title twice (1939,41); legendary hustler who made his biggest score in 1973 as 55-year-old male chauvinist challenging the best women players; beat No. 1 Margaret Smith Court 6-2, 6-1, but was thrashed by No. 2 Billie Jean King, 6-4, 6-3, 6-3 in nationally-televised "Battle of the Sexes" on Sept. 20, before 30,492 at the Astrodome.

Pat Riley (b. Mar. 20, 1945): Basketball; coached LA Lakers to 4 of their 5 NBA titles in 1980s (1982,85,87-88); coached New York from 1991-95; 2-time Coach of Year (1990,93) and all-time NBA leader in playoff wins (137); quit Knicks after 1994-95 season with year left on contract; signed with Miami Heat on Sept. 2 as coach, team president and part-owner after Knicks agreed to drop tampering charges in exchange for $1 million and a conditional first round draft pick.

Cal Ripken Jr. (b. Aug. 24, 1960): Baseball SS; broke Lou Gehrig's major league Iron Man record of 2,130 consecutive games played on Sept. 6, 1995; record streak began on May 30, 1982; 2-time AL MVP (1983,91) for Baltimore; AL Rookie of Year (1982); AL starting SS in All-Star Game since 1984; entered 1996 season with 327 HRs in 15 seasons, the most ever by a shortstop.

Joe Robbie (b. July 7, 1916, d. Jan. 7, 1990): Football; original owner of Miami Dolphins (1966-90); won 2 Super Bowls (1972-73); built $115-million Robbie Stadium with private funds in 1987.

Oscar Robertson (b. Nov. 24, 1938): Basketball G; 3-time college Player of Year (1958-60) at Cincinnati; led 1960 U.S. Olympic team to gold medal; NBA Rookie of Year (1961); 9-time All-NBA 1st team; MVP in 1964 with Cincinnati Royals; NBA champion in 1971 with Milwaukee Bucks; 3rd in career assists with 9,887.

Paul Robeson (b. Apr. 8, 1898, d. Jan. 23, 1976): Black 4-sport star and 2-time football All-America (1917-18) at Rutgers; 3-year NFL pro; also scholar, lawyer, singer, actor and political activist; long-tainted by Communist sympathies, he was finally inducted into College Football Hall of Fame in 1995.

Brooks Robinson (b. May 18, 1937): Baseball 3B; led AL in fielding 12 times from 1960-72 with Baltimore; regular season MVP in 1964; World Series MVP in 1970.

David Robinson (b. Aug. 6, 1965): Basketball C; college Player of Year at Navy in 1987; overall 1st pick by San Antonio in 1987 NBA draft; served in military from 1987-89; NBA Rookie of Year in 1990 and regular season MVP in '95; 2-time All-NBA 1st team (1991,92); led NBA in scoring in 1994; member of 1988, '92 and '96 U.S. Olympic teams.

Eddie Robinson (b. Feb. 13, 1919): Football; head coach at Div. I-AA Grambling State for 53 years; winningest coach in college history; has led Tigers to 8 national black college titles; entered 1996 season with career record of 402-149-15.

Frank Robinson (b. Aug. 31, 1935): Baseball OF; won MVP in NL (1961) and AL (1966); Triple Crown winner and World Series MVP in 1966 with Baltimore; 1st black manager in Major Leagues with Cleveland in 1975; also managed in SF and Baltimore.

Jackie Robinson (b. Jan. 31, 1919, d. Oct. 24, 1972): Baseball 1B-2B-3B; 4-sport athlete at UCLA; hit .387 with K.C. Monarchs of Negro Leagues in 1945; signed by Brooklyn Dodgers on Oct. 23, 1945 and broke Major League baseball's color line in 1947; Rookie of Year in 1947 and NL's MVP in '49; hit .311 over 10 seasons.

Sugar Ray Robinson (b. May 3, 1921, d. Apr. 12, 1989): Boxer; world welterweight champion (1946-51); 5-time middleweight champ; retired at age 45 after 25 years in the ring; pro record 174-19-6 with 109 KOs.

Knute Rockne (b. Mar. 4, 1888, d. Mar. 31, 1931): Football; coached Notre Dame to 3 consensus national titles (1924,29,30), all-time winningest college coach (.881) with record of 105-12-5 over 13 seasons; killed in plane crash.

Bill Rodgers (b. Dec. 23, 1947): Distance runner; won Boston and New York City marathons 4 times each from 1975-80.

Irina Rodnina (b. Sept. 12, 1949): Soviet figure skater; won 10 world championships and 3 Olympic gold medals in pairs competition from 1971-80.

Alex Rodriguez (b. July 27, 1975) Baseball; highly-touted prospect exploded on the scene in 1996 with a .358 batting average (led league), 36 homeruns, 123 RBIs and 15 stolen bases.

Diann Roffe-Steinrotter (b. Mar. 24, 1967): Alpine skier; 2-time Olympic medalist in Super-G; won silver at Albertville in 1992, then gold at Lillehammer in '94.

Art Rooney (b. Jan. 27, 1901, d. Aug. 25, 1988): Race track legend and pro football pioneer; bought Pittsburgh Steelers franchise in 1933 for $2,500; finally won NFL title with 1st of 4 Super Bowls in 1974 season.

Theodore Roosevelt (b. Oct. 27, 1858, d. Jan. 6, 1919): 26th President of the U.S.; physical fitness buff who boxed as undergraduate at Harvard; credited with presidential assist in forming of Intercollegiate Athletic Assn. (now NCAA) in 1905-06.

Mauri Rose (b. May 26, 1906, d. Jan. 1, 1981): Auto racer; 3-time winner of Indy 500 (1941,47-48).

Murray Rose (b. Jan. 6, 1939): Australian swimmer; won 3 gold medals at 1956 Olympics; added a gold, silver and bronze in 1960.

Pete Rose (b. Apr. 14, 1941): Baseball OF-IF; all-time hits leader with 4,256; led NL in batting 3 times; regular-season MVP in 1973; World Series MVP in 1975; had 44-game hitting streak in '78; managed Cincinnati (1984-89); banned for life in 1989 for conduct detrimental to baseball; convicted of tax evasion in 1990 and sentenced to 5 months in prison; released Jan. 7, 1991.

Ken Rosewall (b. Nov. 2, 1934): Tennis; won French and Australian singles titles at age 18; U.S. champ twice, but never won Wimbledon.

Mark Roth (b. Apr. 10, 1951): Bowler; 4-time PBA Player of Year (1977-79,84); entered 1995 with 33 tournament wins; victory in Apr. 15, 1995 Foresters Open was first in 7 year; U.S. Open champ in 1984.

Alan Rothenberg (b. Apr. 10, 1939): Soccer; president of U.S. Soccer since 1990; surprised European skeptics by directing hugely successful 1994 World Cup tournament; successfully got oft-delayed outdoor Major League Soccer off ground in 1996.

Patrick Roy (b. Oct. 5, 1965): Hockey G; led Montreal to 2 Stanley Cup titles; playoff MVP as rookie in 1986 and again in '93; has won Vezina Trophy 3 times (1989-90,92). Won 3rd Stanley Cup with Colorado ('96).

Pete Rozelle (b. Mar. 1, 1926): Football; NFL Commissioner from 1960-89; presided over growth of league from 12 to 28 teams, merger with AFL, creation of Super Bowl and advent of huge TV rights fees.

Wilma Rudolph (b. June 23, 1940, d. Nov. 12, 1994): Track & Field; won 3 gold medals (100m, 200m and 4x400m relay) at 1960 Olympics; also won relay silver in '56 Games; 2-time AP Athlete of Year (1960-61) and Sullivan Award winner in 1961.

Damon Runyon (b. Oct. 4, 1884, d. Dec. 10, 1946): Kansas native who gained fame as New York journalist, sports columnist and short-story writer; best known for 1932 story collection, "Guys and Dolls."

Adolph Rupp (b. Sept. 2, 1901, d. Dec. 10, 1977): Basketball; all-time Div. I college wins leader with 876; coached Kentucky to 4 NCAA championships (1948-49,51,58) and an NIT title (1946).

Bill Russell (b. Feb. 12, 1934): Basketball C; won titles in college, Olympics and pros; 5-time NBA MVP; led Boston to 11 titles from 1957-69; also became first big league black head coach in 1966.

Babe Ruth (b. Feb. 6, 1895, d. Aug. 16, 1948): Baseball LHP-OF; 2-time 20-game winner with Boston Red Sox (1916-17); had a 94-46 regular season record with a 2.28 ERA, while he was 3-0 in the World Series with an ERA of 0.87; sold to NY Yankees for $100,000 in 1920; AL MVP in 1923; led AL in slugging average 13 times, HRs 12 times, RBI 6 times and batting once (.378 in 1924); hit 60 HRs in 1927 and 50 or more 3 other times; ended career with Boston Braves in 1935 with 714 HRs, 2,211 RBI and a batting average of .342; remains all-time leader in times walked (2,056) and slugging average (.690).

Johnny Rutherford (b. Mar. 12, 1938): Auto racer; 3-time winner of Indy 500 (1974,76,80); CART national champion in 1980.

Nolan Ryan (b. Jan. 31, 1947): Baseball RHP; author of record 7 no-hitters against Kansas City and Detroit (1973), Minnesota (1974), Baltimore (1975), LA Dodgers (1981), Oakland A's (1990) and Toronto (1991 at age 44); 2-time 20-game winner (1973-74); 2-time NL leader in ERA (1981,87); led AL in strikeouts 9 times and NL twice in 27 years; retired after 1993 season with 324 wins, 292 losses and all-time records for strikeouts (5,714) and walks (2,795); never won Cy Young Award.

Samuel Ryder (b. Mar. 24, 1858, d. Jan. 2, 1936): Golf; English seed merchant who donated the Ryder Cup in 1927 for competition between pro golfers from Great Britain and the U.S.; made his fortune by coming up with idea of selling seeds to public in small packages.

Toni Sailer (b. Nov. 17, 1935): Austrian skier; 1st to win 3 alpine gold medals in Winter Olympics— taking downhill, slalom and giant slalom events in 1956.

Juan Antonio Samaranch (b. July 17, 1920): Native of Barcelona, Spain; president of International Olympic Committee since 1980; reelected in 1996 after IOC's move in '95 to bump membership age limit to 80.

Pete Sampras (b. Aug. 12, 1971): Tennis; No.1 player in world in 1993 and '94; overtaken as No. 1 in 1995 by friend and arch-rival Andre Agassi; youngest ever U.S. Open men's champion (19 years, 28 days) in 1990; won Wimbledon and U.S. Open titles in 1993; Australian Open and Wimbledon in '94, and Wimbledon and U.S. Open in '95; won 5-set doubles match with John McEnroe to help win 1992 Davis Cup final.

Joan Benoit Samuelson (b. May 16, 1957): Distance runner; has won Boston Marathon twice (1979,83); won first women's Olympic marathon in 1984 Games at Los Angeles; Sullivan Award recipient in 1985.

Arantxa Sanchez Vicario (b. Dec. 18, 1971): Spanish tennis player; entered 1996 season with 22 tour victories, including 1989 French Open; won both French and U.S. Opens in 1994 and was finalist in three of four Slam finals in '95; teamed with Conchita Martinez to win 3 of 4 Federation Cups from 1991-94.

Earl Sande (b. Nov. 13, 1898, d. Aug. 19, 1968): Jockey; rode Gallant Fox to Triple Crown in 1930; won 5 Belmonts and 3 Kentucky Derbys.

Barry Sanders (b. July 16, 1968): Football RB; won 1988 Heisman Trophy as junior at Oklahoma St.; all-time NCAA single season leader in rushing (2,628 yards), scoring (234 points) and TDs (39); 2-time NFL rushing leader with Detroit (1990,94); NFC Rookie of Year (1988); 2-time NFL Player of Year (1991,94); NFC MVP (1994).

Deion Sanders (b. Aug. 9, 1967): Baseball OF and Football DB-KR-WR; 2-time All-America at Florida St. in football (1987-88); 4-time NFL All-Pro with Atlanta and San Francisco (1991-94); led Major Leagues in triples (14) with Atlanta in 1992 and hit .533 in World Series the same year; signed with San Francisco 49ers as free agent in 1994 and helped Niners win Super Bowl XXIX; only athlete to play in both World Series and Super Bowl; traded from Cincinnati to S.F. Giants on July 21, 1995 and signed a 7-year, $35 million deal with Dallas Cowboys on Sept. 9.

Abe Saperstein (b. July 4, 1901, d. Mar. 15, 1966): Basketball; founded all-black, Harlem Globetrotters barnstorming team in 1927; coached sharpshooting comedians to 1940 world pro title in Chicago and established troupe as game's foremost goodwill ambassadors; also served as 1st commissioner of American Basketball League (1961-62).

Gene Sarazen (b. Feb. 27, 1902): Golfer; one of only four players to win all four Grand Slam titles (others are Hogan, Nicklaus and Player); won Masters, British Open, 2 U.S. Opens and 3 PGA titles between 1922-35; invented sand wedge in 1930.

Glen Sather (b. Sept. 2, 1943): Hockey; GM-coach of 4 Stanley Cup winners in Edmonton (1984-85,87-88) and GM-only for another in 1990; ranks 6th on all-time NHL list with 553 wins (including playoffs).

Terry Sawchuk (b. Dec. 28, 1929, d. May 31, 1970): Hockey G; recorded 103 shutouts in 21 NHL seasons; 4-time Vezina Trophy winner; played on 4 Stanley Cup winners at Detroit and Toronto; posted career 2.52 GAA.

Gale Sayers (b. May 30, 1943): Football HB; 2-time All-America at Kansas; NFL Rookie of Year (1965) and 5-time All-Pro with Chicago; scored then-record 22 TDs in rookie year.

Chris Schenkel (b. Aug. 21, 1923): Radio-TV; 4-time Sportscaster of Year; easy-going baritone who has covered basketball, bowling, football, golf and the Olympics for ABC and CBS; host of ABC's Pro Bowlers Tour for 33 years; received lifetime achievement Emmy Award in 1993.

Vitaly Scherbo (b. Jan. 13, 1972): Russian gymnast; winner of unprecedented 6 gold medals in gymnastics, including men's All-Around, for Unified Team in 1992 Olympics; won 3 bronze in '96 Games.

Mike Schmidt (b. Sept. 27, 1949): Baseball 3B; led NL in HRs 8 times; 3-time MVP (1980,81,86) with Philadelphia; 548 career HRs and 10 gold gloves; inducted into Hall of Fame in 1995.

Don Schollander (b. Apr. 30, 1946): Swimming; won 4 gold medals at 1964 Olympics, plus one gold and one silver in 1968; won Sullivan Award in 1964.

Dick Schultz (b. Sept. 5, 1929): Reform-minded executive director of NCAA from 1988-93; announced resignation on May 11, 1993, in wake of special investigator's report citing Univ. of Virginia with improper student-athlete loan program during Schultz's tenure as athletic director (1981-87); named executive director of the USOC on June 23, 1995.

Michael Schumacher (b. Jan. 3, 1969): Auto racer; entered 1996 with 19 career Formula One wins; world champion in 1994 and '95.

Bob Seagren (b. Oct. 17, 1946): Track & Field; won gold medal in pole vault at 1968 Olympics; broke world outdoor record 5 times.

Tom Seaver (b. Nov. 17, 1944): Baseball RHP; won 3 Cy Young Awards (1969,73,75); had 311 wins, 3,640 strikeouts and 2.86 ERA over 20 years.

George Seifert (b. Jan. 22, 1940): Football; coached San Francisco to a record 17 wins in his 1st season as head coach in 1989; guided 49ers to Super Bowl-winning seasons in 1989 and '94; entered 1996 season as NFL's winningest coach ever with 95-30 record and .760 winning pct.

Peter Seitz (b. May 17, 1905, d. Oct. 17, 1983): Baseball arbitrator; ruled on Dec. 23, 1975 that players who perform for one season without a signed contract can become free agents; decision ushered in big money era for players.

Monica Seles (b. Dec. 2, 1973): Yugoslav tennis player; No.1 in the world in 1991 and '92 after winning Australian, French and U.S. Opens both years; 4-time winner of Australian and 3-time winner of French; youngest to win Grand Slam title this century when she won French at age 16 in 1990; winner of 30 singles titles in just 5 years before she was stabbed in the back by Steffi Graf fan Gunter Parche on Apr. 30, 1993 during match in Hamburg, Germany; spent remainder of 1993, all of '94 and most of '95 recovering; returned to WTA Tour with win at the Canadian Open on Aug. 20, 1995; reached U.S. Open final before losing to Graf in 3 sets.

Bud Selig (b. July 30, 1934): Baseball; Milwaukee car dealer who bought AL Seattle Pilots for $10.8 million in 1970 and moved team to Midwest; chairman of owners' executive council and de facto commissioner since he and colleagues forced Fay Vincent to resign on Sept. 7, 1992; presided over 232-day players' strike that resulted in cancellation of World Series for first time since 1904 and delayed opening of 1995 season until Apr. 25.

Frank Selke (b. May 7, 1893, d. July 3, 1985): Hockey; GM of 6 Stanley Cup champions in Montreal (1953,56-60); the annual NHL trophy for best defensive forward bears his name.

Ayrton Senna (b. Mar. 21, 1960, d. May 1, 1994): Brazilian auto racer; 3-time Formula One champion (1988,90-91); entered 1994 season as all-time F1 leader in poles (62) and 2nd in wins (41); killed in crash at Imola, Italy during '94 San Marino Grand Prix.

Wilbur Shaw (b. Oct. 13, 1902, d. Oct. 30, 1954): Auto racer; 3-time winner and 3-time runner-up of Indy 500 from 1933-1940.

Patty Sheehan (b. Oct. 27, 1956): Golfer; LPGA Player of Year in 1983; clinched entry into LPGA Hall of Fame with 30th career win in 1993; entered 1995 season with 3 LPGA titles (1983-84,93) and 2 U.S. Opens (1992, 94).

Bill Shoemaker (b. Aug. 19, 1931): Jockey; all-time career wins leader with 8,833; 3-time Eclipse Award winner as Jockey (1981) and special award recipient (1976,81); won Belmont 5 times, Kentucky Derby 4 times and Preakness twice; oldest jockey to win Kentucky Derby (age 54, aboard Ferdinand in 1986); retired in 1990 to become trainer; paralyzed in 1991 auto accident but continues to train horses.

Eddie Shore (b. Nov. 25, 1902, d. Mar. 16, 1985): Hockey D; only NHL defenseman to win Hart Trophy as MVP 4 times (1933,35-36,38); led Boston Bruins to Stanley Cup titles in 1929 and '39; had 105 goals and 1,047 penalty minuts in 14 seasons.

Frank Shorter (b. Oct. 31, 1947): Track & Field; won gold medal in marathon at 1972 Olympics, 1st American to win in 64 years.

Don Shula (b. Jan. 4, 1930): Football; one of only two NFL coaches with 300 wins (George Halas is the other); has taken 6 teams to Super Bowls and won twice with Miami (1973-74); 4-time Coach of Year, twice with Baltimore (1964,68) and twice with Miami (1970-71); retired after 1995 season with NFL-record 347 career wins (including playoffs) and a winning percentage of .670; father of Cincinnati head coach David, who entered 1996 with 4-year record of 18-46.

Al Simmons (b. May 22, 1902, d. May 26, 1956): Baseball OF; led AL in batting twice (1930-31) and knocked in 100 runs or more 11 straight years (1924-34).

O.J. Simpson (b. July 9, 1947): Football RB; won Heisman Trophy in 1968 at USC; ran for 2,003 yards in NFL in 1973; All-Pro 5 times; MVP in 1973; rushed for 11,236 career yards; TV analyst and actor after career ended; arrested June 17, 1994 as suspect in double murder of ex-wife Nicole Brown Simpson and her friend Ronald Goldman; acquitted on Oct. 3, 1995 by a Los Angeles jury.

George Sisler (b. Mar. 24, 1893, d. Mar. 26, 1973): Baseball 1B; hit over .400 twice (1920,22); 257 hits in 1920 still a major league record.

Mary Decker Slaney (b. Aug. 4, 1958): U.S. middle distance runner; has held 7 separate American track & field records from the 800 to 10,000 meters; won both 1,500 and 3,000 meters at 1983 World Championships in Helsinki, but no Olympic medals.

Raisa Smetanina (b. Feb. 29, 1952): Russian Nordic skier; all-time Winter Olympics medalist with 10 cross-country medals (4 gold, 5 silver and a bronze) in 5 appearances (1976,80,84,88,92) for USSR and Unified Team.

Billy Smith (b. Dec. 12, 1950): Hockey G; led NY Islanders to 4 consecutive Stanley Cups (1980-83); won Vezina Trophy in 1982; Stanley Cup MVP in 1983.

Dean Smith (b. Feb. 28, 1931): Basketball; has coached North Carolina to 25 NCAA tournaments in 34 years, reaching Final Four 10 times and winning championship twice (1982,93); coached U.S. Olympic team to gold medal in 1976; entered 1996-97 season with 851 wins, 2nd only to Adolph Rupp's 876 on all-time Div. I victory list.

Emmitt Smith (b. May 15, 1969): Football RB; consensus All-America (1989) at Florida; 3-time NFL rushing leader (1991-93); 3-time All-Pro (1992-94); regular season and Super Bowl MVP in 1993; played on three Super Bowl champions (1992, '93 and '96 seasons).

John Smith (b. Aug. 9, 1965): Wrestler; 2-time NCAA champion for Oklahoma St. at 134 lbs (1987-88) and Most Outstanding Wrestler of '88 championships; 3-time world champion; gold medal winner at 1988 and '92 Olympics at 137 lbs; only wrestler ever to win Sullivan Award (1990); coached Oklahoma St. to 1994 NCAA title and brother Pat was Most Outstanding Wrestler.

Lee Smith (b. Dec. 4, 1957): Baseball RHP; 3-time NL saves leader (1983,91-92); entered 1996 season as all-time major league saves leader with 471.

Michelle Smith (b. Apr. 7, 1969): Swimming; Irishwoman who won three gold medals at the 1996 Olympics; accused of using performance-enhancing drugs but passed all tests.

Ozzie Smith (b. Dec. 26, 1954): Baseball SS; won 13 straight gold gloves (1980-92); played in 12 straight All-Star Games (1981-92); MVP of 1985 NL playoffs; entered 1996 season with all-time assist record for shortstops with 8,213.

Walter (Red) Smith (b. Sept. 25, 1905, d. Jan. 15, 1982): Sportswriter for newspapers in Philadelphia and New York from 1936-82; won Pulitzer Prize for commentary in 1976.

Conn Smythe (b. Feb. 1, 1895, d. Nov. 18, 1980): Hockey pioneer; built Maple Leaf Gardens in 1931; managed Toronto to 7 Stanley Cups before retiring in 1961.

Sam Snead (b. May 27, 1912): Golfer; won both Masters and PGA 3 times and British Open once; runner-up in U.S. Open 4 times; PGA Player of Year in 1949; oldest player (52 years, 10 months) to win PGA event with Greater Greensboro Open title in 1965; all-time PGA Tour career victory leader with 81.

Peter Snell (b. Dec. 17, 1938): Track & Field; New Zealander who won gold medal in 800m at 1960 Olympics, then won both the 800m and 1,500m at 1964 Games.

Annika Sorenstam (b. Oct. 9, 1970); Golf; Swedish golfer won the 1995 U.S. Women's Open as her first LPGA victory; won the event again in 1996; College Player of the Year and NCAA champion in 1991.

Javier Sotomayor (b. Oct. 13, 1967): Cuban high jumper; first man to clear 8 feet (8-0) on July 29, 1989; won gold medal at 1992 Olympics with jump of only 7-ft, 8-in.; broke world record with leap of 8-0½ in 1993.

Warren Spahn (b. Apr. 23, 1921): Baseball LHP; led NL in wins 8 times; won 20 or more games 13 times; Cy Young winner in 1957; most career wins (363) by a left-hander.

Tris Speaker (b. Apr. 4, 1888, d. Dec. 8, 1958): Baseball OF; all-time leader in outfield assists (449) and doubles (793); had .344 career batting average and 3,515 hits.

J.G. Taylor Spink (b. Nov. 6, 1888, d. Dec. 7, 1962): Publisher of *The Sporting News* from 1914-62; Baseball Writers' Assn. annual meritorious service award named after him.

Mark Spitz (b. Feb. 10, 1950): Swimmer; set 23 world and 35 U.S. records; won all-time record 7 gold medals (4 individual, 3 relay) in 1972 Olympics; also won 4 medals (2 gold, a silver and a bronze) in 1968 Games for a total of 11; comeback attempt at age 41 foundered in 1991.

Amos Alonzo Stagg (Aug. 16, 1862, d. Mar. 17, 1965): Football innovator; coached at U. of Chicago for 41 seasons and College of the Pacific for 14 more; won 314 games; elected to both college football and basketball halls of fame.

Willie Stargell (b. Mar. 6, 1940): Baseball OF-1B; led NL in home runs twice (1971,73); 475 career HRs; regular-season and World Series MVP in 1979.

Bart Starr (b. Jan. 9, 1934): Football QB; led Green Bay to 5 NFL titles and 2 Super Bowl wins from 1961-67; regular season MVP in 1966; MVP of Super Bowls I and II.

Roger Staubach (b. Feb. 5, 1942): Football QB; Heisman Trophy winner as Navy junior in 1963; led Dallas to 2 Super Bowl titles (1972,78) and was Super Bowl MVP in 1972; 5-time leading passer in NFC (1971,73,77-79).

George Steinbrenner (b. July 4, 1930): Baseball; principal owner of NY Yankees since 1973; teams have won 4 pennants and 2 World Series (1977-78); has changed managers 21 times and GMs 10 times in 23 years; ordered by baseball commissioner Fay Vincent in 1990 to surrender control of club for dealings with small-time gambler; reinstated on Mar. 1, 1993; also serves as one of 3 VPs of U.S. Olympic Committee.

Casey Stengel (b. July 30, 1890, d. Sept. 29, 1975): Baseball; player for 14 years and manager for 25; outfielder and lifetime .284 hitter with 5 clubs (1912-25); guided NY Yankees to 10 AL pennants and 7 World Series titles from 1949-60; 1st NY Mets skipper from 1962-65.

Ingemar Stenmark (b. Mar. 18, 1956): Swedish alpine skier; 3-time World Cup overall champ (1976-78); posted 86 World Cup wins in 16 years; won 2 gold medals at 1980 Olympics.

Helen Stephens (b. Feb. 3, 1918, d. Jan. 17, 1994): Track & Field; set 3 world records in 100-yard dash and 4 more in 100 meters in 1935-36; won gold medals in 100 meters and 4x100-meter relay in 1936 Olympics; retired in 1937.

Woody Stephens (b. Sept. 1, 1913): Horse racing; trainer who saddled an unprecedented 5 straight winners in Belmont Stakes (1982-86); also had two Kentucky Derby winners (1974,84); trained 1982 Horse of Year Conquistador Cielo; won Eclipse award as nation's top trainer in 1983.

David Stern (b. Sept. 22, 1942): Basketball; marketing expert and NBA commissioner since 1984; took office the year Michael Jordan turned pro; has presided over stunning artistic and financial success of NBA both nationally and internationally, best demonstrated by reception of the Dream Team at 1992 Olympics; league has grown from 23 teams to 29 during his watch; received unprecedented 5-year, $27.5 million contract extension in 1990; imposed owners' lockout on July 1 when league and players union failed to agree on new contract; ended lockout on Sept. 18 when players voted down bid to decertify their union .

Teófilo Stevenson (b. Mar. 29, 1952): Cuban boxer; won 3 consecutive gold medals as Olympic heavyweight (1972,76,80); did not turn pro.

Jackie Stewart (b. June 11, 1939): Auto racer; won 27 Formula One races and 3 world driving titles from 1965-73.

John Stockton (b. Mar 26, 1962) Basketball; entering the 1996-97 season the point guard for the Utah Jazz is the all-time NBA leader in every major assist category, including most in a season (1,164), highest average in a season (14.4 per game) and most overall (11,310); also holds the NBA records for career steals (2,365); All-NBA team in '94 and '95; member of 1992 and '96 US Olympic basketball Dream Team; 8-time All-Star.

Curtis Strange (b. Jan. 30, 1955): Golfer; won consecutive U.S. Open titles (1988-89); 3-time leading money winner on PGA Tour (1985,87-88); first PGA player to win $1 million in one year (1988).

Picabo Street (b. Apr. 3, 1971): Skiing; won silver in women's downhill at 1994 Winter Olympics; her '95 World Cup downhill series title first-ever by U.S. women.

Kerri Strug (b. Nov. 19, 1977) Gymnastics; delivered the most dramatic moment of the 1996 summer Olympics when she completed a vault after spraining her ankle on the previous attempt; the heroic second vault assured the first all-around gold medal for a US Women's gymnastics team after poor vaulting by her teammates had put the medal in doubt; a poor performance by the Russian team on the beam had clinched the gold medal for the USA but Strug did not know that when she decided to make the second vault; second vault score was 9.712; the injury prevented her from participating in any individual events.

Louise Suggs (b. Sept. 7, 1923): Golfer; won 11 Majors and 50 LPGA events overall from 1949-62.

James E. Sullivan (b. Nov. 18, 1862, d. Sept. 16, 1914): Track & Field; pioneer who founded Amateur Athletic Union (AAU) in 1888; director of St. Louis Olympic Games in 1904; AAU's annual Sullivan Award for performance and sportsmanship named after him.

John L. Sullivan (b. Oct. 15, 1858, d. Feb. 2, 1918): Boxer; world heavyweight champion (1882-92); last of bare-knuckle champions.

Pat Summitt (b. June 14, 1952): Basketball; women's basketball coach at Tennessee (1974—); 2nd all-time with 564 career victories; coached Lady Vols to 3 national championships (1987,89,91).

Barry Switzer (b. Oct. 5, 1937): Football; coached Oklahoma to 3 national titles (1974-75,85); 4th on all-time winningest list with 157-29-4 record and .837 win percentage; resigned in 1989 after OU was slapped with 3-year NCAA probation and 5 players were brought up on criminal charges; hired as Dallas Cowboys head coach on Mar. 30, 1994 and led Dallas to a victory in Super Bowl XXX on Jan. 28, 1996.

Paul Tagliabue (b. Nov. 24, 1940): Football; NFL attorney who was elected league's 4th commissioner in 1989; ushered in salary cap in 1994; league expanded by 2 teams in 1995 for 1st time since '76; brought $300 million suit against Dallas owner Jerry Jones on Sept. 18, 1995 for Jones' rogue sponsorship deals with Pepsi and Nike.

Anatoli Tarasov (b. 1918, d. June 23, 1995): Hockey; coached Soviet Union to 9 straight world championships and 3 Olympic gold medals (1964,68,72).

Jerry Tarkanian (b. Aug. 30, 1930): Basketball; all-time winningest college coach with .837 winning pct.; had record of 625-122 in 24 years at Long Beach St. and UNLV; led UNLV to 4 Final Fours and one national title (1990); fought 16-year battle with NCAA over purity of UNLV program; quit as coach after going 26-2 in 1991-92; fired after 20 games (9-11) as coach of NBA San Antonio Spurs in 1992; left retirement on April 5, 1995 to coach his alma mater, Fresno St.

Fran Tarkenton (b. Feb. 3, 1940): Football QB; 2-time NFL All-Pro (1973,75); Player of Year (1975); threw for 47,003 yards and 342 TDs (both NFL records) in 18 seasons with Minnesota and NY Giants.

Chuck Taylor (b. June 24, 1901, d. June 23, 1969): Converse traveling salesman whose name came to grace the classic, high-top canvas basketball sneakers known as "Chucks"; over 500 million pairs have been sold since 1917; he also ran clinics worldwide and edited Converse Basketball Yearbook from 1922-68.

Lawrence Taylor (b. Feb. 4, 1959): Football LB; All-America at North Carolina (1980); only defensive player in NFL history to be consensus Player of Year (1986); led NY Giants to Super Bowl titles in 1986 and '90 seasons; played in a record 10 Pro Bowls (1981-90); retired after 1993 season with 132½ sacks.

Gustavo Thoeni (b. Feb. 28, 1951): Italian alpine skier; 4-time World Cup overall champion (1971-73,75); won giant slalom at 1972 Olympics.

Frank Thomas (b. May 27, 1968): Baseball 1B; All-America at Auburn in 1989; 2-time AL MVP with Chicago (1993,94); entered 1996 season with 182 HRs and .323 career average.

Isiah Thomas (b. Apr. 30, 1961): Basketball; led Indiana to NCAA title as sophomore and tourney MVP in 1981; consensus All-America guard in '81; led Detroit to 2 NBA titles in 1989 and '90; NBA Finals MVP in 1990; 3-time All-NBA 1st team (1984-86); retired in 1994 at age 33 after tearing right Achilles tendon; GM of expansion Toronto Raptors.

Thurman Thomas (b. May 16, 1966): Football RB; 3-time AFC rushing leader (1990-91,93); 2-time All-Pro (1990-91); NFL Player of Year (1991); led Buffalo to 4 straight Super Bowls (1991-94).

Daley Thompson (b. July 30, 1958): British Track & Field; won consecutive gold medals in decathlon at 1980 and '84 Olympics.

John Thompson (b. Sept. 2, 1941): Basketball; has coached centers Patrick Ewing, Alonzo Mourning and Dikembe Mutombo at Georgetown; reached NCAA tourney final 3 out of 4 years with Ewing, winning title in 1984; also led Hoyas to 6 Big East tourney titles; coached 1988 U.S. Olympic team to bronze medal; entered 1996-97 season with 540 wins in 24 years.

Bobby Thomson (b. Oct. 25, 1923): Baseball OF; career .270 hitter who won the 1951 NL pennant for the NY Giants with a 1-out, 3-run HR in the bottom of the 9th inning of Game 3 of a best-of-3 playoff with Brooklyn; the pitcher was Ralph Branca, the count was 0-1 and the Dodgers were ahead 4-2; the Giants had trailed Brooklyn by 13 games on Aug. 11th.

Jim Thorpe (b. May 28, 1888, d. May 28, 1953): 2-time All-America in football; won both pentathlon and decathlon at 1912 Olympics; stripped of medals a month later for playing semi-pro baseball prior to Games; medals restored in 1982; played major league baseball (1913-19) and pro football (1920-26,28); chosen "Athlete of the Half Century" by AP in 1950.

Bill Tilden (b. Feb. 10, 1893, d. June 5, 1953): Tennis; won 7 U.S. and 3 Wimbledon titles in 1920's; led U.S. to 7 straight Davis Cup victories (1920-26).

Tinker to Evers to Chance: Chicago Cubs double play combination from 1903-08; immortalized in poem by New York sportswriter Franklin P. Adams— SS Joe Tinker (1880-1948), 2B Johnny Evers (1883-1947) and 1B Frank Chance (1877-1924); all 3 managed the Cubs and made the Hall of Fame.

Y.A. Tittle (b. Oct. 24, 1926): Football QB; played 17 years in AFC and NFL; All-Pro 4 times; league MVP with San Francisco (1957) and NY Giants (1962); passed for 28,339 career yards.

Alberto Tomba (b. Dec. 19, 1966): Italian alpine skier; all-time Olympic alpine medalist with 5 (3 gold, 2 silver); became 1st alpine skier to win gold medals in 2 consecutive Winter Games when he won the slalom and giant slalom in 1988 then repeated in the GS in '92; also won silvers in slalom in 1992 and '94; won 1st overall World Cup championship along with slalom and giant slalom titles in 1995.

Vladislav Tretiak (b. Apr. 25, 1952): Hockey G; led USSR to Olympic gold medals in 1972 and '76; starred for Soviets against Team Canada in 1972, and again in 2 Canada Cups (1976,81).

Lee Trevino (b. Dec. 1, 1939): Golfer; 2-time winner of 3 Majors— U.S. Open (1968,71), British Open (1971-72) and PGA (1974,84); Player of Year once on PGA Tour (1971) and 3 times with Seniors (1990,92,94); entered 1995 with 27 PGA Tour wins and 24 on Senior Tour; all-time money leader on combined tours ($8.6 million).

Bryan Trottier (b. July 17, 1956): Hockey C; led NY Islanders to 4 straight Stanley Cups (1980-83); Rookie of Year (1976); scoring champion (134 points) and regular season MVP in 1979; playoff MVP (1980); added 5th and 6th Cups with Pittsburgh in 1991 and '92.

Gene Tunney (b. May 25, 1897, d. Nov. 7, 1978): Boxer; world heavyweight champion from 1926-28; beat 31-year-old champ Jack Dempsey in unanimous 10 round decision in 1926; beat him again in famous "long count" rematch in '27; quit while still champion in 1928 with 65-1-1 record and 47 KOs.

Ted Turner (b. Nov. 19, 1938): Sportsman and TV mogul, skippered *Courageous* to America's Cup win in 1977; owner of both Atlanta Braves and Hawks; owner of superstation WTBS, and cable stations CNN and TNT; founder of Goodwill Games; 1991 *Time* Man of Year.

Mike Tyson (b. June 30, 1966): Boxer; youngest (age 19) to win heavyweight title (WBC in 1986); undisputed champ from 1987 until upset loss to 50-1 shot Buster Douglas on Feb. 10, 1990, in Tokyo; found guilty on Feb. 10, 1992, of raping 18-year-old Miss Black America contestant Desiree Washington in Indianapolis on July 19, 1991; sentenced to 6-year prison term; released May 9, 1995 after serving 3 years; reclaimed WBC and WBA belts with wins over Frank Bruno and Bruce Seldon in 1996; see career fight record in Boxing chapter.

Wyomia Tyus (b. Aug. 29, 1945): Track & Field; 1st woman to win consecutive Olympic gold medals in 100m (1964-68).

Peter Ueberroth (b. Sept. 2, 1937): Organizer of 1984 Summer Olympics in LA; 1984 *Time* Man of Year; baseball commissioner from 1984-89; headed Rebuild Los Angeles for one year after 1992 riots.

Johnny Unitas (b. May 7, 1933): Football QB; led Baltimore Colts to 2 NFL titles (1958-59) and a Super Bowl win (1971); All-Pro 5 times; 3-time MVP (1959,64,67); passed for 40,239 career yards and 290 TDs.

Al Unser Jr. (b. Apr. 19, 1962): Auto racer; 2-time CART-IndyCar national champion (1990,94); captured Indy 500 for 2nd time in 3 years in '94, giving Unser family 9 overall titles at the Brickyard; entered 1996 with 31 IndyCar wins in 14 years; son of Al and nephew of Bobby.

Al Unser Sr. (b. May 29, 1939): Auto racer; 3-time USAC-CART national champion (1970,83,85); 4-time winner of Indy 500 (1970-71,78,87); retired in 1994 ranked 3rd on all-time IndyCar list with 39 wins; younger brother of Bobby and father of Little Al.

Bobby Unser (b. Feb. 20, 1934): Auto racer; 2-time USAC-CART national champion (1968,74); 3-time winner of Indy 500 (1968,75,81); retired after 1981 season; ranks 4th on all-time IndyCar list with 35 wins.

Gene Upshaw (b. Aug. 15, 1945): Football G; 2-time All-AFL and 3-time All-NFL selection with Oakland; helped lead Raiders to 2 Super Bowl titles in 1976 and '80 seasons; executive director of NFL Players Assn. since 1987; agreed to application of salary cap in 1994.

Norm Van Brocklin (b. Mar. 15, 1926, d. May 2, 1983): Football QB-P; led NFL in passing 3 times and punting twice; led LA Rams (1951) and Philadelphia (1960) to NFL titles; MVP in 1960.

Amy Van Dyken (b. Feb. 17, 1973): Swimming; first American woman to win four gold medals in one Olympics (1996); won the individual 50M freestyle, 100M butterfly, and was on the US team for the 4X100 freestyle and 4X50 medley; known for clapping, spitting and growling on the platform just before the start of a race.

Johnny Vander Meer (b. Nov. 2, 1914): Baseball LHP; only major leaguer to pitch consecutive no-hitters (June 11 & 15, 1938).

Harold S. Vanderbilt (b. July 6, 1884, d. July 4, 1970): Sportsman; successfully defended America's Cup 3 times (1930, 34,37); also invented contract bridge in 1926.

Glenna Collett Vare (b. June 20, 1903, d. Feb. 10, 1989): Golfer; won record 6 U.S. Women's Amateur titles from 1922-35; known as "the female Bobby Jones."

Andy Varipapa (b. Mar. 31, 1891, d. Aug. 25, 1984): Bowler; trick-shot artist; won consecutive All-Star match game titles (1947-48) at age 53.

Mo Vaughn (b. Dec. 15, 1967) Baseball; slugging first baseman for Boston Red Sox; led team to 1995 Eastern Division title and named American League MVP with 39 homeruns, 126 RBIs, .300 batting average and 11 stolen bases; two time All-Star.

Bill Veeck (b. Feb. 9, 1914, d. Jan. 2, 1986): Maverick baseball executive; owned AL teams in Cleveland, St. Louis and Chicago from 1946-80; introduced ballpark giveaways, exploding scoreboards, Wrigley Field's ivy-covered walls and midget Eddie Gaedel; won World Series with Indians (1948) and pennant with White Sox (1959).

Jacques Villeneuve (b. Apr. 9, 1971): Canadian auto racer; Indianapolis 500 runner-up and IndyCar Rookie of Year in 1994; won 500 and IndyCar driving championship in 1995; announced plans to jump to Formula One racing in 1996.

Fay Vincent (b. May 29, 1938): Baseball; became 8th commissioner after death of A. Bartlett Giamatti in 1989; presided over World Series earthquake, owners' lockout and banishment of NY Yankees owner George Steinbrenner in his first year on the job; contentious relationship with owners resulted in his resignation on Sept. 7, 1992, four days after 18-9 "no confidence" vote; office has been vacant since.

Lasse Viren (b. July 22, 1949): Finnish runner; won gold medals at 5,000 and 10,00 meters in 1972 Munich Olympics; repeated 5,000/10,000 double in 1976 Montreal Games but added a 5th place in the marathon.

Lanny Wadkins (b. Dec. 5, 1949): Golfer; member of 8 Ryder Cup teams and captain of 1995 team; entering 1995 had 21 PGA Tour wins.

Honus Wagner (b. Feb. 24, 1874, d. Dec. 6, 1955): Baseball SS; hit .300 for 17 consecutive seasons (1897-1913) with Pittsburgh; led NL in batting 8 times; ended career with 3,418 career hits, a .327 average and 722 stolen bases.

Lisa Wagner (b. May 19, 1961): Bowler; 3-time LPBT Player of Year (1983,88,93); 1980's Bowler of Decade; first woman bowler to earn $100,000 in a season; entered 1996 season with a record 29 pro titles.

Grete Waitz (b. Oct. 1, 1953): Norwegian runner; 9-time winner of New York City Marathon from 1978-88; won silver medal at 1984 Olympics.

Doak Walker (b. Jan. 1, 1927): Football HB; won Heisman Trophy as SMU junior in 1948; led Detroit to 2 NFL titles (1952-53); All-Pro 4 times in 6 years.

Herschel Walker (b. Mar. 3, 1962): Football RB; led Georgia to national title as freshman in 1980; won Heisman in 1982 then jumped to USFL in '83; signed by Dallas after USFL folded; led NFL in rushing in 1988; traded to Minnesota in 1989 for 5 players and 6 draft picks; has since played for Philadelphia and NY Giants and again with Dallas.

Bill Walsh (b. Nov. 30, 1931): Football; coached San Francisco to 3 Super Bowl titles (1982,85,89); retired after 1989 Super Bowl with 102 wins in 10 seasons; returned to college coaching in 1992 for his second stint at Stanford; retired again after 1994 season; entering 1995 NFL season, six former Walsh assistants were head coaches.

Bill Walton (b. Nov. 5, 1952): Basketball C; 3-time college Player of Year (1972-74); led UCLA to 2 national titles (1972-73); led Portland to NBA title as MVP in 1977; regular season MVP in 1978.

Arch Ward (b. Dec. 27, 1896, d. July 9, 1955): Promoter and sports editor of *Chicago Tribune* from 1930-55; founder of baseball All-Star Game (1933), Chicago College All-Star Football Game (1934) and the All-America Football Conference (1946-49).

Charlie Ward (b. Oct. 12, 1970): Football QB and Basketball G; led Florida St. to national football championship in 1993; 1st Heisman Trophy winner to play for national champs since Tony Dorsett in 1976, won Sullivan Award same year; 3-year starter for FSU basketball team; not taken in NFL Draft; 1st round pick (26th overall) of NY Knicks in 1994 NBA draft.

Glenn (Pop) Warner (b. Apr. 5, 1871, d. Sept. 7, 1954): Football innovator; coached at 7 colleges over 49 years; 319 career wins 2nd only to Bear Bryant's 323 in Div. I-A; produced 47 All-Americas, including Jim Thorpe and Ernie Nevers.

Tom Watson (b. Sept. 4, 1949): Golfer; 6-time PGA Player of the Year (1977-80,82,84); has won 5 British Opens, 2 Masters and a U.S. Open; 4-time Ryder Cup member and captain of 1993 team; entered 1995 with 32 tour wins.

Dick Weber (b. Dec. 23, 1929): Bowler; 3-time PBA Bowler of the Year (1961,63,65); won 30 PBA titles in 4 decades.

Johnny Weissmuller (b. June 2, 1904, d. Jan. 20 1984): Swimmer; won 3 gold medals at 1924 Olympics and 2 more at 1928 Games; became Hollywood's most famous Tarzan.

Jerry West (b. May 28, 1938): Basketball G; 2-time All-America and NCAA tourney MVP (1959) at West Virginia; led 1960 U.S. Olympic team to gold medal; 10-time All-NBA 1st-team; NBA finals MVP (1969); led LA Lakers to NBA title once as player (1972) and 5 times as GM in 1980's; his silhouette serves as the NBA's logo.

Pernell Whitaker (b. Jan. 2, 1964): Boxer; won Olympic gold medal as lightweight in 1984; has won 4 world championships as lightweight, jr. welterweight, welterweight and jr. middleweight; outfought but failed to beat Julio Cesar Chavez when Sept. 10, 1993 welterweight title defense ended in controversial draw; entered 1996 with pro record of 37-1-1 and 16 KOs.

Bill White (b. Jan. 28, 1934): Baseball; NL president and highest ranking black executive in sports from 1989-94; as 1st baseman, won 7 gold gloves and hit .286 with 202 HRs in 13 seasons.

Byron (Whizzer) White (b. June 8, 1917): Football; All-America HB at Colorado (1935-37); signed with Pittsburgh in 1938 for the then largest contract in pro history ($15,800); took Rhodes scholarship in 1939; returned to NFL in 1940 to lead league in rushing and retired in 1941; named to U.S. Supreme Court by President Kennedy in 1962 and stepped down in 1993.

Reggie White (b. Dec. 19, 1961): Football DE; consensus All-America in 1983 at Tennessee; 7-time All-NFL (1986-92) with Philadelphia; signed as free agent with Green Bay in 1993 for $17 million over 4 years; entered 1996 season with an official NFL-record 157 sacks.

Kathy Whitworth (b. Sept. 27, 1939): Golf; 7-time LPGA Player of the Year (1966-69,71-73); won 6 Majors; 88 tour wins, most on LPGA or PGA tour.

Hazel Hotchkiss Wightman (b. Dec. 20, 1886, d. Dec. 5, 1974): Tennis; won 16 U.S. national titles; 4-time U.S. Women's champion (1909-11,19); donor of Wightman Cup.

Hoyt Wilhelm (b. July 26, 1923): Baseball RHP; Knuckleballer who is all-time leader in games pitched (1,070), games finished (651) and games won in relief (124); had career ERA of 2.52 and 227 saves; 1st relief pitcher inducted into Hall of Fame (1985); threw no-hitter vs. NY Yankees (1958); also hit lone HR of career in first major league at bat (1952).

Lenny Wilkens (b. Oct. 28, 1937): Basketball; passed Red Auerbach as NBA's all-time winningest regular-season coach with his 939th victory on Jan. 6, 1995; entered 1996-97 season with 968 regular-season wins and 1,078 wins including playoffs. MVP of 1960 NIT as Providence guard; played 15 years in NBA, including 4 as player-coach; MVP of 1971 All-Star Game; coached Seattle to NBA title in 1979; Coach of Year in 1994 with Atlanta.

Dominique Wilkins (b. Jan. 12, 1960): Basketball F; last player to lead NBA in scoring (1986) before Michael Jordan's reign; All-NBA 1st team in '86; traded from Atlanta to LA Clippers in 1994; later signed as free agent with Boston; elder statesman of Dream Team II; signed with pro team in Greece after 1994-95 season.

Bud Wilkinson (b. Apr. 23, 1916, d. Feb. 9, 1994): Football; played on 1936 national championship team at Minnesota; coached Oklahoma to 3 national titles (1950,55,56); won 4 Orange and 2 Sugar Bowls; teams had winning streaks of 47 (1953-57) and 31 (1948-50); retired after 1963 season with 145-29-4 record in 17 years; also coached St. Louis of NFL to 9-20 record in 1978-79.

Ted Williams (b. Aug. 30, 1918): Baseball OF; led AL in batting 6 times, and HRs and RBI 4 times each; won Triple Crown twice (1942,47); 2-time MVP (1946,49); last player to bat .400 when he hit .406 in 1941; Marine Corps combat pilot who missed three full seasons during World War II (1943-45) and most of two others (1952-53) during Korean War; hit .344 lifetime with 521 HRs in 19 years with Boston Red Sox.

Walter Ray Williams Jr. (b. Oct. 6, 1959): Bowling and Horseshoes; 2-time PBA Bowler of Year (1986,93); has also won 6 World Horseshoe Pitching titles.

Hack Wilson (b. Apr. 26, 1900, d. Nov. 23, 1948) Baseball; as a Chicago Cub, he produced one of baseball's most outstanding seasons in 1930 with 56 homeruns, .356 batting average, 105 walks and, most amazingly, a major league record 190 RBIs that still stands; finished with 1,461 hits, 244 homeruns, 1,062 RBIs; member of Baseball Hall of Fame.

Dave Winfield (b. Oct. 3, 1951): Baseball OF-DH; selected in 4 major sports league drafts in 1973— NFL, NBA, ABA, and MLB; chose baseball and has played in 12 All-Star Games over 20-year career; at age 41, helped lead Toronto to World Series title in 1992; reached 3,000 hits in 1993; entered 1995 as leading active player in hits, HRs and RBI among others.

Katarina Witt (b. Dec. 3, 1965): East German figure skater; 4-time world champion (1984-85,87-88); won consecutive Olympic gold medals (1984,88).

John Wooden (b. Oct. 14, 1910): Basketball; college Player of Year at Purdue in 1932; coached UCLA to 10 national titles (1964-65,67-73,75); only member of Basketball Hall of Fame inducted as both player and coach; Bruins won first title of post-Wooden era in 1995.

Tiger Woods (b. Dec. 30, 1975): Golfer; became youngest player (age 18) and first black to win U.S. Amateur when he did it in 1994, repeated as champion in '95; has now won 5 USGA championships in as many years (Bobby Jones won 8 from 1923-30, including 4 U.S. Opens).

Mickey Wright (b. Feb. 14, 1935): Golfer; won 3 of 4 Majors (LPGA, U.S. Open, Titleholders) in 1961; 4-time winner of both U.S. Open and LPGA titles; 82 career wins including 13 Majors.

Early Wynn (b. Jan. 6, 1920): Baseball RHP; won 20 games 5 times; Cy Young winner in 1959; 300 career wins in 23 years.

Kristi Yamaguchi (b. July 12, 1971) Figure Skating; finished second in the 1991 American nationals but won the world title that year; dominated the sport in 1992 by winning the national, world and Olympic titles and then turned professional.

Cale Yarborough (b. Mar. 27, 1940): Auto racer; 3-time NASCAR national champion (1976-78); 4-time winner of Daytona 500 (1968,77,83-84); ranks 4th on NASCAR all-time list with 83 wins.

Carl Yastrzemski (b. Aug. 22, 1939): Baseball OF; led AL in batting 3 times; won Triple Crown and MVP in 1967; had 3,419 hits and 452 HRs in 23 years with Boston.

Cy Young (b. Mar. 29, 1867, d. Nov. 4, 1955): Baseball RHP; all-time leader in wins (511), losses (315), complete games (750) and innings pitched (7,355); had career 2.63 ERA in 22 years (1890-1911); 30-game winner 5 times and 20-game winner 10 other times; threw 3 no-hitters and perfect game (1904); AL and NL pitching awards named after him.

Dick Young (b. Oct. 17, 1917, d. Aug. 31, 1987): Confrontational sportswriter for 44 years with New York tabloids; as baseball beat writer and columnist, he led change from flowery prose to hard-nosed reporting.

Sheila Young (b. Oct. 14, 1950): Speed skater and cyclist; 1st U.S. athlete to win 3 medals at Winter Olympics (1976); won speed skating overall and sprint cycling world titles in 1976.

Steve Young (b. Oct. 11, 1961): Football QB; consensus All-America at BYU (1983); NFL Player of Year (1992) with S.F. 49ers; only QB to lead NFL in passer rating 4 straight years (1991-94); rating of 112.8 in 1994 was highest ever; threw NFL playoff-record 6 TD passes in MVP performance against San Diego in Super Bowl XXIX; holds NFL career records for highest passer rating (96.8) and completion percentage (63.6).

Robin Yount (b. Sept. 16, 1955): Baseball SS-OF; AL MVP at 2 positions— as SS in 1982 and OF in '89; retired after 1993 season with 3,142 hits, 251 HRs and a major league record 123 sacrifice flies after 20 seasons with Milwaukee Brewers.

Mario Zagalo (b. Aug. 9, 1931): Soccer; Brazilian forward who is one of only two men (Franz Beckenbauer is the other) to serve as both captain (1962) and coach (1970) of World Cup champion; served as advisor for Brazil's 1994 World Cup champion.

Babe Didrikson Zaharias (b. June 26, 1914, d. Sept. 27, 1956): All-around athlete who was chosen AP Female Athlete of Year 6 times from 1932-54; won 2 gold medals (javelin and 80-meter hurdles) and a silver (high jump) at 1932 Olympics; took up golf in 1935 and went on to win 55 pro and amateur events; won 10 majors, including 3 U.S. Opens (1948,50,54); helped found LPGA in 1949; chosen female "Athlete of the Half Century" by AP in 1950.

Tony Zale (b. May 29, 1913): Boxer; 2-time world middleweight champion (1941-47,48); fought Rocky Graziano for title 3 times in 21 months in 1947-48, winning twice; pro record 67-18-2 with 44 KOs.

Frank Zamboni (b. Jan. 16, 1901, d. July 27, 1988): Mechanic, ice salesman and skating rink owner in Paramount, Calif.; invented 1st ice-resurfacing machine in 1949; over 4,000 sold in more than 33 countries since then.

Emil Zatopek (b. Sept. 19, 1922): Czech distance runner; winner of 1948 Olympic gold medal at 10,000 meters; 4 years later, won unprecedented Olympic triple crown (5,000 meters, 10,000 meters and marathon) at 1952 Games in Helsinki.

John Ziegler (b. Feb. 9, 1934): Hockey; NHL president from 1977-92; negotiated settlement with rival WHA in 1979 that led to inviting four WHA teams (Edmonton, Hartford, Quebec and Winnipeg) to join NHL; stepped down June 12, 1992, 2 months after settling 10-day players' strike.

Kim Zmeskal (b. Feb 6, 1976) Gymnastics; one of the many American students of former Rumanian coach Bela Karolyi; won three U.S. all-around championships in a row (1990-'92); first American gymnast to win the all-around competition in the world championships (1991); only athlete to win two golds in the 1992 world championships (balance beam and floor exercise); despite strong expectations, finished tenth in the all-around competition in the 1992 Olympics.

Pirmin Zurbriggen (b. Feb. 4, 1963): Swiss alpine skier; 4-time World Cup overall champ (1984,87-88,90) and 3-time runner-up; 40 World Cup wins in 10 years; won gold and bronze medals at 1988 Olympics.

Wide World Photos

The defection of **Art Modell**'s NFL franchise from Cleveland to Baltimore was a spectacular betrayal of fan loyalty and a textbook display of corporate arrogance.

BALLPARKS & ARENAS

by Keith Olbermann

Pandora's Luxury Box

In 1996, team movement and stadium deals got so out of hand that the federal government took notice

Barely seven months after Art Modell became the Walter O'Malley of the 1990s, after he pulled the beloved Browns out of Cleveland for no reason other than personal financial goofiness and greed, the city of Cleveland thought it had figured out what to do with the vast cavernous bowl of Municipal Stadium that Modell had rendered obsolete. They were going to push it into Lake Erie, creating the world's largest artificial freshwater reef. And the unspoken hope was simple: when they dropped it in the drink, maybe Modell might just happen to be inside it.

Yet as loathed and infamous as Modell made himself, as much as fans in Cleveland and throughout the country might have wanted to see him sleeping with the freshwater fishies, he may have precipitated the greatest outbreak in sanity in sports in forty years. In large part because Modell yanked the lid off Pandora's Luxury Box, as far as stadium construction goes, 1996 may go down in history as the end of the free lunch. In fact, it may go down in history as the year they made the free lunch a crime.

After Modell got his shameful deal in Baltimore, and after Maryland found it had enough largesse left over to give Cooke his own cities rang with the sound of none-too-subtle threats, even the government began to sit up and take notice. Senator Daniel Patrick Moynihan (D-N.Y.) married his outrage over the stadium construction to one of his pet projects. For years Moynihan's ballpark, and after the Mariners got their deal, and Pittsburgh its, and a new Jack Kent dozen other buns have been broiling over the fact that private universities have a credit limit. Through the states in which they are located, tax-free bonds can be floated on their behalf for construction of new research facilities, new classroom buildings, new laboratories. But once the debt limit of $150,000,000 has been reached, the spigot gets turned off and no new tax-free bonds can be issued until the old ones are paid off. No new tax-free bonds means no new construction.

Why, it suddenly occurred to the white-tufted New Yorker, was spending on behalf of universities limited when such spending on behalf of sports franchises was not?

The state of Maryland was to sink $177,000,000 into Modell's new park in Baltimore alone — nevermind the state's commitment to Irascible Stadium, or whatever Cooke wanted to call his new home for the Redskins — and a large percentage of that figure was to come through tax-free bond issues.

Conceivably, Moynihan argued, Maryland could float enough tax-free bonds to build a new stadium for every club in the state ringing up billions of dollars in such issues and on top of everything else,

Keith Olbermann has been the co-anchor of ESPN's SportsCenter since 1992.

Wide World Photos

When fans like John Thompson (**Big Dawg** to his friends) are left without a football team for two years, one wonders why they play the games. Thompson takes a last stroll around Memorial Stadium after the last game in the history of the Original Cleveland Browns on December 17, 1995.

denying the federal government huge amounts of taxes (that's what a tax-free bond means). But if Johns Hopkins was at its $150 million tax-free limit, the state couldn't build them a new toilet.

Moynihan proposed, simply, to change the rules. Remove the cap on tax-free bonds for facilities of higher learning, and so the world isn't then saturated with vast armies of tax-free bond issues absolutely levelling the economy, make it illegal for a state to float a tax-free bond to build a sports stadium. Oh, you could grandfather in the projects already underway so that Senators DeWine and Glenn of Ohio wouldn't have to choose between what's right (new microscopes for Oberlin) and what's politically expedient (new stadiums for Mike Brown and Marge Schott).

Even while political pundits predicted doom for the legislation, even while Bob Dole considered opining that building new sports stadiums was not addictive, the chilling effect was immediate.

If state governments had to actually raise the money to build new stadiums, which one of them would, or even could? And if no government could build a new stadium, with what could they lure a new franchise or keep an old one? And if there suddenly were no more out-of-town ballparks to move to, what kind of blackmail gun could an owner hold at the head of his current city or its fans?

Why, the entire fabric of Franchise Free Agency would be rent asunder!

The long-term implications were astounding. Nevermind the elimination of the Modell shuffle. Nevermind the neutering of such macho games of relocation chicken as those played by the Seattle Mariners and Seahawks. Even a team with no real intention of moving (say, the New Jersey Devils) could no longer wrangle concessions out of their incumbent states and cities. And if you couldn't threaten to move out, how could you raise ticket prices year after year? And if you couldn't raise ticket prices year after year, how could you run your business with the acumen of your kid's front-yard lemonade stand, knowing that no longer would some government, somewhere, bail you out of that $15-million dollar deal you just gave this year's Matt Young?

Even short-term, would-be ballpark-builders in Florida and Arizona confessed that while they could still issue their tax-free bonds, they believed that merely the introduction of the Moynihan bill would make it more difficult to sell them. They would have to scramble.

Of course, some owners were already scrambling. As his "interim" tenure in office neared exceeding that of yet a fourth of his full-time predecessors, baseball's Acting Commissioner for Life Bud Selig proved to be far better at the out-of-the-pocket dash than he was of maintaining the fiction that he didn't want to be the boss.

First Selig managed to get the state of Wisconsin to agree to a new Brewers' stadium worth $250 million. In the liberal, quality-of-life-minded Badger State, nobody gets a completely free ballpark: the Brewers' obligation to the new palace was $90 million.

But on the eve of the consummation of the deal, Selig suddenly announced he couldn't come up with the $40 million loan he needed to secure the team's part of the pricetag. He'd have to consider moving, he said as he wandered through his nearly-empty stadium, wringing his hands like some stricken poet, listening to the support of the literally hundreds of fans to whom it made a difference. Selig hinted he might move to Charlotte, North Carolina. Nobody commented on the coincidence that the bank from which he tried to get his loan was based in Charlotte, North Carolina.

As usual, Selig got his way; local businesses and foundations anted up more than half of the Brewers' commitment. And Selig added irony to tomfoolery. The new stadium of which he dreamt was not only to be built in the first city to lure a modern baseball franchise away from its ancestral home, but moreover it would be reminiscent of Ebbets Field in Brooklyn, gone these 40 seasons precisely because cities were willing to pay taxpayers' money to lure modern baseball franchises away from their ancestral homes.

When Seattle got its second publicly-funded stadium in less than a quarter of a century, it turned up the heat in New York. George Steinbrenner figured that since the Yankees hadn't gotten a new ballpark out of the taxpayers of the Big Apple since 1976, it was time. He talked about a new facility in Manhattan and another one in the Bronx and another one in New Jersey (to which the Yankees have been threatening to move more or less since the day Mickey Mantle

Something Old, Something New

by Bill Deane

Oriole Park at Camden Yards has been witness to several historic events in its brief history: the 1993 All-Star Game, Cal Ripken's record 2131st consecutive game, and Eddie Murray's 500th career home run, to name a few. Perhaps none will have the lasting impact of the park itself, however, whose mere existence is a chapter in the history books. The stadium's opening on April 6, 1992 ushered in a new era in baseball park design.

Between the 1950s and 1980s, typical stadium design centered around practicality: maximum usage of a field with minimum maintenance. It was the age of the "multi-purpose stadium," an arena that could be used for both baseball and football (as "Green Cathedrals" author Phil Lowry says, "a marriage not made in heaven"). It spawned Astroturf and domes and round, symmetrical "cookie-cutter" stadiums, like Riverfront Stadium and Three Rivers Stadium.

Practicality notwithstanding, this trend did not set well with the baseball purists. They longed for parks with character: cozy seating capacities, oddly-shaped playing fields, and grass that a horse could eat. The mere mention of Brooklyn's Ebbets Field can mist an old-timer's eyes, while Boston's Fenway Park and Chicago's Wrigley Field represent two of the last remnants of this bygone era.

Then came Camden Yards. It melded the heart of modern park design with the soul of nostalgia. "From the brick arches to the low-raked grandstands and family picnic area in center field," said one architectural critic, "it evokes Fenway, Wrigley, and Ebbets Field without looking like any of them."

It was a hit from the start: attendance increased by more than a million in its first year, vaulting Baltimore to second place in the major leagues. The Orioles have ranked first or second in the AL attendance derby each season since. In 1994, both Cleveland (Jacobs Field) and Texas (The Ballpark at Arlington) unveiled new parks with similar appeals and results. In light of this success, several other teams are planning or discussing new arenas.

Among them:

Jerry Wachter

Oriole Park at Camden Yards is the model for all future major leage baseball stadiums. Coziness notwithstanding, the key factor in attracting and keeping fans, however, is a winning team.

Arizona. The expansion Diamondbacks plan to open their maiden season in 1998 at the Bank One Ballpark. Seating 47,000 under a retractable roof, with a grass field, the park is expected to cost $330 million.

Boston. Even the Red Sox are considering a new stadium. "It's something that's being talked about," says a Boston PR representative. "Nothing is formally set."

Detroit. After winning battles against the 10,000-member Tiger Stadium Fan Club, Detroit plans to abandon the 85-year-old park in favor of a new one in 1999. Tentatively called "New Tiger Stadium," it will be an open-air, baseball-only park with a price-tag of about $240 million.

Milwaukee. In a scramble to keep the Brewers in Sudsville, the city is proposing a $250 million, retractable roof arena called Miller Park.

New York (AL). George Steinbrenner continually threatens to move the club to New Jersey or beyond when its lease on Yankee Stadium expires in 2002. In response, New York mayor Rudolph Giuliani endorses a proposal to build a new park on the west side of Manhattan. A multi-purpose stadium with a retractable dome, the structure carries the incredible estimated price-tag of $1.1 billion.

New York (NL). The Mets are quietly completing plans for a $457 million stadium. The grass field with a capacity of 40,000 will be built a ball's throw away from Shea Stadium (set to be razed). According to Mets' General Counsel David Howard, "we're looking for a new, state-of-the-art ballpark that has an intimate, old-time feel reminiscent of Ebbets Field, with a retractable roof."

Philadelphia. The Keating Building Corporation has proposed to erect a 50,000-seat park near the west bank of the Schuylkill River. Price: a cool half-billion.

San Francisco. Giants' executive Larry Baer describes the upcoming 42,000-seat Pacific Bell Park as "Camden Yards meets Wrigley Field." Opening in 2000, it will be the first privately-funded ballfield since Dodger Stadium was built in 1962. According to Giants' president Peter Magowan, "baseball fans will have the best of both worlds: the feel and atmosphere of an old-time ballpark with modern conveniences at their fingertips."

Seattle. The city's NBBJ firm is working hard to keep the Mariners in Seattle. Their plan is to build a 45,000-seat stadium by 1999, at a cost of some $320 million.

Wide World Photos

If new legislation in congress passes, embarassing scenes like the one above featuring Houston Oilers owner **Bud Adams** and Nashville mayor **Phil Bredesen** may become rare.

retired). He talked about the bad neighborhood and the bad access. He talked about walling off the area around the park to make a 'Yankee Village.' He talked about attendance so mediocre that he'd have to fire the 76-year old guy who opened and closed the clubhouse door for the players.

He did not talk about the fact that the price of the best box seats in the house had gone from $4 each the day he bought the team to $27 each in 1996. He did not talk about what he and the city of Tampa might have been thinking when they built the Yankees a Roman Temple of a ballpark just for spring training, costing only $31 million and specially designed with the right field fence ten yards from the main drag of a city about to get a big league team so that it could never be expanded from its current capacity of barely 9,000 souls.

As cities scrambled to get their deals in place just in case the Moynihan bill became law, good taste was thrown to the wayside. The Pirates' new ownership and the mayor of Pittsburgh revealed plans for a new 37,000 seat "old-fashioned" ballpark with extensive foot access and a beatific environment visible over the outfield wall. They even pursued the facility under the nickname "Forbes Field II," apparently oblivious to the irony that previous Pirates' ownership and the past mayor of Pittsburgh had destroyed a beautiful 38,000 seat "old-fashioned" ballpark with extensive foot access and a beatific environment visible over the outfield wall in 1970 — because it was too "small" — and replaced it with one of those mail-order, cookie-cutter, paint-by-numbers giant irradiated multi-use ashtrays called Three Rivers Stadium.

The unthinkable was thought throughout the land. While anti-ballpark forces continued to fight heroically in Detroit, the future of Tiger Stadium was, in doubt. In the virtually soundproof press box of the spring training complex built for them by the city of Fort Myers, Florida, two Red Sox officials blithely mentioned — in front of several reporters — that Fenway Park had become "inadequate" and would eventually "have to come down," and the columnists of that city prepared its denizens for the holocaust.

In Baltimore, the Orioles, celebrating just their fifth season in Camden Yards, reacted with annoyance to the gelt being thrown at football teams and suggested that, at the least, they deserved some more tax breaks.

Disney took over the Angels and began to ask if Anaheim was the right place to be (uh, Mickey? Disneyland is in Anaheim). In Chicago, the White Sox had the good manners not to say that six-year old Comiskey Park was nothing more than a gaudier Three Rivers, but owner Jerry Reinsdorf had begun to Seligize — to publicly and loudly ruminate about the park's future.

The Minneapolis Metrodome, not even fifteen years old, was declared "economically infeasible" by the Twins. Oakland had to play its first homestand in Las Vegas because workers were remodeling the Coliseum as part of Al Davis's Plan Nine from Outer Space for the Raiders. Wayne Huizenga got himself a new arena for Miami's hockey and basketball teams and whispered about one for baseball.

The Astros, for whom Houston had built the largest indoor arena since they used to stretch out a tarp to keep the rain off the patrons at the Colosseum in Rome, prepared to move to Northern Virginia or Monterrey, Mexico, or Katmandu, Nepal. North Carolina, which had barely supported minor league baseball for four seasons, had no less than two separate groups hoping to get a major league team, one for the so-called "Triad" around Greensboro, the other, Charlotte, which was incidentally hindered in its pursuit of the Brewers or an expansion team because the owner of its six-year old NBA team wanted another new building there.

The late, great San Francisco sportswriter Wells Twombly had long before observed that the first law of sports was "larceny abhors a vaccuum." Even teams that neither moved nor got themselves a new arena managed to develop more virulent strains of ethics-resistant stadium folderol.

In the NHL, Hartford Whalers owner Peter Karmanos managed to enlist the local government to join him in a full-fledged attack on his own customers. Though the Whalers still had two years to go in a firm commitment to stay in Connecticut (an annoying leftover from the team's last shakedown of the state), Karmanos threatened to move the team out. He managed to hoodwink the state to name its own Lieutenant Governor to head a "Save The Whalers" campaign and establish a high-pressure, short-term deadline to boost season ticket sales from 6,500 to 11,000. In a market consisting of less than a million souls, 11,000 season tickets meant one for every 90 residents; in metropolitan New York, with three teams selling (optimistically) 40,000 season tickets, the ratio was one ticket for every 360 residents — in other words, there had to be four times as many ticket-buyers per capita in Hartford than in New York.

The real beauty of the deal, of course, was that if the fans failed to fulfill this Herculean task, the blame would not fall on the Whalers, nor the NHL, nor even politicians who refused to pony up for the sake of the fans. The villains would be the fans themselves. Connecticut Governor John Rowland said as much: "this decision will not be made by the Whalers, nor by the state. It will be made by the fans."

Owner Karmanos and the politicos might have escaped untouched, but in the middle of the six-week long marketing blitz, it was revealed that the Whalers had a deal, ready to sign, to move to Nashville. And the same day Karmanos was denying that story, he was quoted in *the New York Times*

Photo Archives

Senator **Daniel Patrick Moynihan** (D-N.Y.) has introduced a bill in congress that would put a cap on how much cities and states can go into debt to build sports arenas. Experts say just the *idea* of the bill has slowed down many projects.

Photo Archives

Being the commissioner of baseball has not prevented **Bud Selig** from begging on behalf of his financially-disadvantaged Brewers.

as saying that what he really wanted to do was move the team to his native Michigan.

As it was, the "Save The Whale" campaign fell roundly short. 8,000 season tickets were sold, not 11,000. Karmanos angrily announced that the politicians had refused to be reasonable about a buyout of his agreement to stay for two more years, and the Hartford Whalers were now lame ducks and would have to trim salaries.

Nobody mentioned that Karmanos had upped the average ticket price by $9, so that the 6,500 renewals would be paying an additional $2,340,000 for a lame duck team in 1996-97, and that the 1,500 new customers would be coughing up around $2,100,000.

Got it? The fine folks of Connecticut gave Karmanos four and a half million fish to let him break their hearts some time in 1998.

Against this kind of blinding, mind-numbing relocation not seen in this country since the premiere of the movie 'Doctor Zhivago,' the Moynihan bill loomed as a measure of titanic importance. Moreover, economists were finally beginning to speak out about the lunacy of public construction of new ballparks and arenas.

As Roger Noll of Stanford wrote in *the New York Times*, if new stadiums actually made money — for anybody — the owners would build them on their own and keep all the profits. As for building the Yankees a new park as part of an "investment" in the city, Noll suggested that New York was better off putting its billion dollars in a savings account at the corner bank.

Even the old bromide about the construction process being good for creating jobs was savaged by the Congressional Research Service. It pointed out that Maryland's own estimate was that 1,394 new jobs would spring up as a result of the state's $177 million investment in the Ravens' stadium.

Fine, said the number-crunchers from Congressional Research. That's 1,394 new jobs at $127,000 per job. But Maryland already has a job-seeding investment process called the Sunny Day Fund, which can put a man or woman to work at a state cost of $6,250. See the math yet? If the state puts $177 million in the Sunny Day Fund, it generates 28,320 jobs. If it puts $177 million in Baltimore's Modell Greedatorium, it generates 1,394 jobs. That means building this new ballpark will *prevent* 26,926 new jobs from being created.

1996 was the watershed year for the new stadium gravy train. Football had taken the first steps over the precipice in Cleveland and Houston. Add in the Rams and the Raiders and the "N" in NFL could've stood for "Nomadic."

The only baseball teams that seem to be happy with stadiums more than six years old appeared to be the Cubs, Royals, and Dodgers. New NBA and NHL facilities were seeming to pop up before the carpeting needed to be replaced in the old ones. Temples of sport ranging from the Montreal Forum to Boston Garden (even Durham Athletic Park) fell and generic "facilities" replaced them. The Canadiens now skate around the Molson Center and the Big Bad Bruins now prowl the FleetCenter. Therefore, two of the NHL's original franchises are beholden to a beer company and a bank for a place to play.

Amid all this nonsense, a bill sat on a Senator's desk which, if forgotten, could turn all the gravity off and send franchises ricocheting around the country like billiard balls after a break. A bill which, if passed, could change the concept of "complete refurbishment" of a sports stadium from millions of dollars out of the public coffers to the appropriation of $32.50 for a new can of Sherwin-Williams Rust-Proof Magenta. ❒

1996

NBA BASKETBALL

Philadelphia (East): The CoreStates Center opened on Aug. 31, 1996 with a World Cup Hockey game between the USA and Canada. The USA won, 5-3, before a capacity crowd of 19,500. Located on site of razed JFK Stadium adjacent to CoreStates Spectrum and Veterans Stadium; will seat 21,000 for basketball and 19,500 for NHL Flyers; will include 126 luxury suites; estimated cost: $210 million. Flyers home opener scheduled for October 1996.

NFL FOOTBALL

Carolina (NFC): Construction of Carolinas Stadium nearing completion. Located in downtown Charlotte; will seat 72,300 for football; open air, grass field; will include 135 luxury suites; estimated cost: $175 million. Panthers' home opener scheduled for September 1996.

Oakland (AFC): Major renovation of Oakland-Alameda County Coliseum was completed Aug. 8, 1996. New football seating increased to 62,500; rebuilding will eventually include 150 luxury suites; estimated cost: $85 million, including training and office facilities.

NHL HOCKEY

Buffalo (East): Grand Opening of Marine Midland Arena set for October 1996. Located three blocks from Buffalo Auditorium where the waterfront meets the intersection of South Park and Main St.; will seat 19,500 for hockey and 21,000 for college basketball; will include 80 luxury suites; final cost: $127.5 million.

Montreal (East): The Molson Centre opened on Mar. 16, 1996 with a game between the Montreal Canadiens and New York Rangers. The Canadiens won, 4-2, before a crowd of 21,360. Located at Windsor Station in downtown Montreal; seats 21,347 for hockey; includes 136 luxury suites; final cost: $170 million (US).

Ottawa (East): The Corel Centre opened on Jan. 15, 1996 with a concert by Canadian rocker Bryan Adams. Located in suburban Kanata, Ontario; will seat 18,500 for hockey; will include 147 luxury suites; estimated cost: $240 million (US) for arena, office tower, hotel, roads and highway interchange. The Senators, who began the season at the Ottawa Civic Center, opened the new building in January 1996.

Philadelphia (East): The CoreStates Center opened on Aug. 31, 1996 with a World Cup Hockey game between the USA and Canada. The USA won, 5-3, before a capacity crowd of 19,500. Located on site of razed JFK Stadium adjacent to CoreStates Spectrum and Veterans Stadium; will seat 19,500 for hockey and 21,000 for NBA Sixers; will include 126 luxury suites; estimated cost: $210 million. Flyers home opener scheduled for October 1996.

Tampa Bay (East): Grand opening of the Ice Palace scheduled for Oct. 20, 1996 with a Tampa Bay Lightning game against the New York Rangers. Located on waterfront site near Tampa Aquarium; will seat 19,500 for hockey; will include 72 luxury suites; estimated cost: $153 million.

1997

BASEBALL

Atlanta (NL): Reconstruction of 85,000-seat Centennial Olympic Stadium for 1996 Summer Games underway. Stadium to be converted to 49,831-seat ballpark for baseball only immediately following '96 Paralympics; Located across from Atlanta-Fulton County Stadium; open air, grass field; will include approximately 59 luxury suites; estimated cost $230 million to build Olympic stadium and convert to smaller ballpark. Braves' home opener scheduled for April 1, 1997.

NBA BASKETBALL

Golden St. (West): Complete reconstruction of Oakland Coliseum, using the existing walls, began immediately after the 1995-96 season. The new-and-improved arena will seat 19,200; will include 72 luxury suites; estimated cost: $121 million; Warriors' home opener scheduled for November 1997. Warriors will play their home games for the 1996-97 season at San Jose Arena.

Toronto (East): Construction of Air Canada Center (Air Canada is title sponsor) underway. To be located on site of Old Canada Post Building at corner of Bay Street and Lake Shore Road; will seat 22,500 for basketball and 21,325 for hockey (the NHL Maple Leafs will not be tenants); will include 124 luxury suites; estimated cost: $172 million (US). Raptors' home opener scheduled for November 1997.

Washington (East): Construction of MCI Center (MCI is title sponsor) underway. To be located above the Gallery Place Metro Station near National Mall; will seat 21,500 for basketball and 20,000 for NHL Capitals; will include 110 luxury suites; estimated cost: $175 million. Bullets' (team will be renamed the Washington Wizards) home opener scheduled for November 1997.

NFL FOOTBALL

Washington (NFC): Construction of Redskins Stadium underway. To be located on site six miles east of RFK Stadium in Landover, Md.; will seat 78,400 for football; open air, grass field; will include 280 luxury suites; estimated cost: $165 million. Redskins' home opener scheduled for September 1997.

NHL HOCKEY

Washington (East): Groundbreaking for MCI Center (MCI is title sponsor) scheduled for October 1995. To be located above the Gallery Place Metro Station near National Mall; will seat 20,000 for hockey and 21,500 for NBA Bullets; will include 110 luxury suites; estimated cost: $175 million. Capitals' home opener scheduled for October 1997.

1998

BASEBALL

Arizona (expansion team): Groundbreaking for Bank One Ballpark (Bank One is title sponsor) scheduled for October 1995. To be located one block from America West Arena and feature a retractable roof; will seat 47,350; grass field; will include 65 luxury suites; estimated cost: $280 million. Diamondbacks' major league home opener scheduled for April 1998.

Cincinnati (NL): New ballpark in planning stages. Would be part of $540 million downtown project including separate football stadium for NFL Bengals. Earliest groundbreaking would be March 1997 near Cinergy Field; would seat 47,000 for baseball; open air, grass field; to include 65 luxury suites; estimated cost: $203 million. Earliest Reds' home opener would be April 1998.

Tampa Bay (expansion team): Plans call for renovating Tropicana Field, formerly known as the Thunder Dome and the Florida Suncoast Dome when it opened in 1990. Located in St. Petersburg at the corner of 16th St. and 1st Ave. South; will seat 48,000 for baseball; indoor, artificial turf field; will include 66 luxury suites; estimated cost: $50 million. Devil Rays' major league home opener scheduled for April 1998.

NBA BASKETBALL

Denver (West): Groundbreaking for Pepsi Center (Pepsi-Cola is title sponsor) tentatively scheduled for early 1996. To be built by team owner COMSAT Inc., along with a television studio on downtown site adjacent to the new Elitch Gardens theme park; will seat 19,100 for basketball and 17,700 for NHL Avalanche; will include 84 luxury suites; estimated cost: $132 million. Nuggets' home opener planned for November 1998.

Miami (East): Groundbreaking for the as-yet-unnamed arena tentatively scheduled for late 1996/early 1997. To be located on the FEC tract next to Bayside on the Miami waterfront. Estimated cost: $165 million. Earliest Heat home opener would be late 1998.

NFL FOOTBALL

Baltimore (AFC): Broke ground for as-yet-unnamed stadium July 1996. The open-air grass field stadium will be located next to Camden Yards and cost an estimated $200 million. It will seat 68,400 and include 108 luxury suites; Earliest Ravens' home opener would be September 1998.

Cincinnati (AFC): New stadium in planning stages. Would be part of $540 million downtown project including separate baseball park for NL Reds. Earliest groundbreaking would be April 1996 near Cinergy Field; would seat 54,000 for football; open air, grass field; would include 45 luxury suites; estimated cost: $170 million. Earliest Bengals' home opener would be September 1998.

NHL HOCKEY

Colorado (West): Groundbreaking for Pepsi Center (Pepsi-Cola is title sponsor) tentatively scheduled for early 1996. To be built by team owner COMSAT Inc., along with a television studio in downtown Denver, adjacent to the new Elitch Gardens theme park; will seat 17,700 for hockey and 19,100 for NBA Nuggets; will include 84 luxury suites; estimated cost: $132 million. Avalanche home opener planned for October 1998.

Florida (East): Groundbreaking for Broward County Civic Arena scheduled for November 1996. To be located in Sunrise, Fla., west of Ft. Lauderdale; will seat between 19,000 and 20,000 for hockey; include 62 luxury suites and four larger "party suites"; estimated cost: $212 million. Earliest Panthers' home opener would be September 1998.

1999

BASEBALL

Detroit (AL): New ballpark in planning stages. To be located near a new stadium for the Detroit Lions in downtown Detroit's Foxtown Theater district. The baseball-only park would seat approximately 42,000 and have 80 luxury suites. Estimated cost: $235-240 million. Groundbreaking scheduled for early 1997 and the earliest Tigers home opener would be early 1999.

Pittsburgh (NL): New ballpark in planning stages. To be located on a site between Three Rivers Stadium and the Sixth Street bridge. The as-yet-unnamed baseball-only park would seat approximately 37,000. Earliest Pirates' home opener would be April 1999.

Seattle (AL): New Century Park in planning stages. To be located two blocks south of Kingdome; seating of 45,000 for baseball only; retractable-roof, grass field; would include 70 luxury suites; estimated cost: $320 million. Earliest Mariners' home opener would be April 1999.

NBA BASKETBALL

Los Angeles (West): New arena to house both the Lakers and NHL Kings in planning stages. Groundbreaking tenatively scheduled for September 1997. The site for the new 20,000-seat complex has been narrowed down to Inglewood and downtown Los Angeles. The project is targeted for completion in September 1999.

NFL FOOTBALL

Nashville: New stadium in planning stages to house the NFL Oilers. Groundbreaking scheduled for spring of 1997. The natural grass, open-air stadium will seat 67,000 and have 120-145 luxury suites. To be located in the East Bank area of downtown Nashville. Estimated cost: $292 million. Earliest opening would be summer of 1999.

Chicago (NFC): New stadium in planning stages. To be located next to the existing McCormick Place Exposition Center. The proposed multi-purpose domed stadium would seat approximately 75,000 and cost an estimated $465 million. Earliest opening would be fall of 1999.

NHL HOCKEY

Los Angeles (West): New arena to house both the Kings and NBA Lakers in planning stages. Groundbreaking tenatively scheduled for September 1997. The site for the new 20,000-seat complex has been narrowed down to Inglewood and downtown Los Angeles. The project is targeted for completion in September 1999.

2000

BASEBALL

Milwaukee (AL): Groundbreaking for Miller Park (Miller Brewing Co. is the title sponsor) on a site adjacent to the existing County Stadium scheduled for September 1996. The retractable-roof stadium will have natural grass and seat approximately 45,000; estimated cost: $250 million. Brewers' home opener scheduled for April 2000.

2004

NFL FOOTBALL

Detroit (NFC): New stadium in planning stages. To be located near a new stadium for AL Tigers in downtown Detroit's Foxtown Theater district. The domed stadium will seat between 65,000-72,000 for football; estimated cost: $225 million. The Lions would move to the as-yet-unnamed stadium after the lease with the Pontiac Silverdome expires in 2004.

Home, Sweet Home

The home fields, home courts and home ice of the AL, NL, NBA, NFL, CFL, NHL, NCAA Division I-A college football and Division I basketball. Also included are Formula One, IndyCar, Indy Racing League and NASCAR auto racing tracks.

Attendance figures for the 1995 NFL regular season and the 1995-96 NBA and NHL regular seasons are provided. See Baseball chapter for 1996 AL and NL attendance figures.

MAJOR LEAGUE BASEBALL

American League

				Outfield Fences					
		Built	Capacity	LF	LCF	CF	RCF	RF	Field
Baltimore Orioles	**Oriole Park at Camden Yards**	1992	**48,262**	333	410	400	373	318	Grass
Boston Red Sox	**Fenway Park**	1912	**33,871**	310	379	390	380	302	Grass
California Angels	**Anaheim Stadium**	1966	**64,593**	333	386	404	386	333	Grass
Chicago White Sox	**Comiskey Park**	1991	**44,321**	347	375	400	375	347	Grass
Cleveland Indians	**Jacobs Field**	1994	**42,865**	325	370	405	375	325	Grass
Detroit Tigers	**Tiger Stadium**	1912	**47,051**	340	365	440	375	325	Grass
Kansas City Royals	**Ewing Kauffman Stadium**	1973	**40,625**	330	375	400	375	330	Grass
Milwaukee Brewers	**County Stadium**	1953	**53,192**	315	392	402	392	315	Grass
Minnesota Twins	**Hubert H. Humphrey Metrodome**	1982	**44,457**	343	385	408	367	327	Turf
New York Yankees	**Yankee Stadium**	1923	**57,545**	318	399	408	385	314	Grass
Oakland Athletics	**Oakland-Alameda County Coliseum**	1966	**39,875**	330	362	400	362	330	Grass
Seattle Mariners	**The Kingdome**	1976	**59,856**	331	389	405	380	312	Turf
Texas Rangers	**The Ballpark in Arlington**	1994	**49,178**	332	390	400	381	325	Grass
Toronto Blue Jays	**SkyDome**	1989	**50,516**	328	375	400	375	328	Turf

National League

				Outfield Fences					
		Built	Capacity	LF	LCF	CF	RCF	RF	Field
Atlanta Braves	**Centennial Olympic Stadium***	1996	**49,831**	335	380	400	385	330	Grass
Chicago Cubs	**Wrigley Field**	1914	**38,765**	355	368	400	368	353	Grass
Cincinnati Reds	**Cinergy Field**	1970	**52,952**	330	375	404	375	330	Turf
Colorado Rockies	**Coors Field**	1995	**50,200**	347	390	415	375	350	Grass
Florida Marlins	**Pro Player Stadium**	1987	**40,585**	330	385	434	385	345	Grass
Houston Astros	**The Astrodome**	1965	**54,370**	325	375	400	375	325	Turf
Los Angeles Dodgers	**Dodger Stadium**	1962	**56,000**	330	385	395	385	330	Grass
Montreal Expos	**Olympic Stadium**	1976	**46,500**	325	375	404	375	325	Turf
New York Mets	**Shea Stadium**	1964	**55,777**	338	371	410	371	338	Grass
Philadelphia Phillies	**Veterans Stadium**	1971	**62,268**	330	371	408	371	330	Turf
Pittsburgh Pirates	**Three Rivers Stadium**	1970	**48,044**	335	375	400	375	335	Turf
St. Louis Cardinals	**Busch Stadium**	1966	**57,673**	330	372	402	375	330	Grass
San Diego Padres	**San Diego/ Jack Murphy Stadium**	1967	**59,690**	327	370	405	370	327	Grass
San Francisco Giants	**3Com Park**	1960	**62,000**	335	365	400	365	328	Grass

*Atlanta announced on Sept. 26 that they planned on renaming the rebuilt Centennial Olympic Stadium for owner Ted Turner.

1998 Expansion Teams

				Outfield Fences					
		Built	Capacity	LF	LCF	CF	RCF	RF	Field
Arizona Diamondbacks	**Bank One Ballpark**	1998	**48,500**	328	376	402	376	335	Grass
Tampa Bay Devil Rays	**Tropicana Field**	1990	**48,000**	335	385	410	385	335	Turf

Rank by Capacity

AL		NL	
California	64,593	Philadelphia	62,268
Seattle	59,158	San Francisco	62,000
New York	57,545	San Diego	59,690
Milwaukee	53,192	St. Louis	57,673
Toronto	50,516	Los Angeles	56,000
Texas	49,178	New York	55,777
Baltimore	48,262	Houston	54,370
Detroit	47,051	Cincinnati	52,952
Minnesota	44,457	Colorado	50,200
Chicago	44,321	Atlanta	49,831
Cleveland	42,865	Pittsburgh	48,044
Kansas City	40,625	Montreal	46,500
Oakland	39,875	Florida	40,585
Boston	33,871	Chicago	38,765

Rank by Age

AL		NL	
Boston	1912	Chicago	1914
Detroit	1912	San Francisco	1960
New York	1923	Los Angeles	1962
Milwaukee	1953	New York	1964
California	1966	Houston	1965
Oakland	1966	St. Louis	1966
Kansas City	1973	San Diego	1967
Seattle	1976	Cincinnati	1970
Minnesota	1982	Pittsburgh	1970
Toronto	1989	Philadelphia	1971
Chicago	1991	Montreal	1976
Baltimore	1992	Florida	1987
Cleveland	1994	Colorado	1995
Texas	1994	Atlanta	1996

Note: New York's Yankee Stadium (AL) was rebuilt in 1976.

Major League Baseball (Cont.)

Home Fields

Listed below are the principal home fields used through the years by current American and National League teams. The NL became a major league in 1876, the AL in 1901.

The capacity figures in the right-hand column indicate the largest seating capacity of the ballpark while the club played there. Capacity figures before 1915 (and the introduction of concrete grandstands) are sketchy at best and have been left blank.

American League

Baltimore Orioles

1901 Lloyd Street Grounds (Milwaukee) .... —
1902-53 Sportsman's Park II (St. Louis) 30,500
1954-91 Memorial Stadium (Baltimore) 53,371
1992— Oriole Park at Camden Yards..................48,262

Boston Red Sox

1901-11 Huntington Ave. Grounds .... —
1912— Fenway Park 33,871
(1934 capacity–27,000)

California Angels

1961 Wrigley Field (Los Angeles).....................20,457
1962-65 Dodger Stadium 56,000
1966— Anaheim Stadium..................................64,593
(1966 capacity–43,250)

Chicago White Sox

1901-10 Southside Park.................................... —
1910-90 Comiskey Park I...................................43,931
1991— Comiskey Park II..................................44,321

Cleveland Indians

1901-09 League Park I....................................... —
1910-46 League Park II 21,414
1932-93 Cleveland Stadium................................74,483
1994— Jacobs Field 42,865

Detroit Tigers

1901-11 Bennett Park .... —
1912— Tiger Stadium.......................................47,051
(1912 capacity–23,000)

Kansas City Royals

1969-72 Municipal Stadium................................35,020
1973— Ewing Kauffman Stadium........................40,625
(1973 capacity–40,762)

Milwaukee Brewers

1969 Sick's Stadium (Seattle)...........................25,420
1970— County Stadium (Milwaukee)...................53,192
(1970 capacity–46,62)

Minnesota Twins

1901-02 American League Park (Washington, DC) —
1903-60 Griffith Stadium....................................27,410
1960-81 Metropolitan Stadium (Bloomington, MN).............................45,919
1982— HHH Metrodome (Minneapolis) 44,457
(1982 capacity–54,000)

New York Yankees

1901-02 Oriole Park (Baltimore)......................... —
1903-12 Hilltop Park (New York) .... —
1913-22 Polo Grounds II 38,000
1923-73 Yankee Stadium I..................................67,224
1974-75 Shea Stadium.......................................55,101
1976— Yankee Stadium II 57,545
(1976 capacity–57,145)

Oakland Athletics

1901-08 Columbia Park (Philadelphia)................. —
1909-54 Shibe Park 33,608
1955-67 Municipal Stadium (Kansas City) 35,020
1968— Oakland Alameda County Coliseum 39,875
(1968 capacity–48,621)

Seattle Mariners

1977— The Kingdome..59,158
(1977 capacity–59,438)

Texas Rangers

1961 Griffith Stadium (Washington, DC)...........27,410
1962-71 RFK Stadium 45,016
1972-93 Arlington Stadium (Texas).......................43,521
1994— The Ballpark in Arlington........................49,178

Toronto Blue Jays

1977-89 Exhibition Stadium.................................43,737
1989— SkyDome 50,516
(1989 capacity–49,500)

Ballpark Name Changes: CHICAGO–**Comiskey Park I** originally White Sox Park (1910-12), then Comiskey Park in 1913, then White Sox Park again in 1962, then Comiskey Park again in 1976; CLEVELAND–**League Park** renamed Dunn Field in 1920, then League Park again in 1928; Cleveland Stadium originally Municipal Stadium (1932-74); DETROIT–**Tiger Stadium** originally Navin Field (1912-37), then Briggs Stadium (1938-60); KANSAS CITY—**Kauffman Stadium** originally Royals Stadium (1973-93); LOS ANGELES–**Dodger Stadium** referred to as Chavez Ravine by AL while Angels played there (1962-65); PHILADELPHIA–**Shibe Park** renamed Connie Mack Stadium in 1953; ST. LOUIS–**Sportsman's Park** renamed Busch Stadium in 1953; WASHINGTON–**Griffith Stadium** originally National Park (1892-20), **RFK Stadium** originally D.C. Stadium (1961-68).

National League

Atlanta Braves

1876-94 South End Grounds I (Boston)............... —
1894-1914 South End Grounds II.......................... —
1915-52 Braves Field 40,000
1953-65 County Stadium (Milwaukee)................43,394
1966-96 Atlanta-Fulton County Stadium 52,769
(1966 capacity–50,000)
1997— Centennial Olympic Stadium...............49,831

Chicago Cubs

1876-77 State Street Grounds............................ —
1878-84 Lakefront Park..................................... —
1885-91 West Side Park..................................... —
1891-93 Brotherhood Park .... —
1893-1915 West Side Grounds .... —
1916— Wrigley Field 38,765
(1916 capacity–16,000)

Home Fields

Cincinnati Reds

1876-79	Avenue Grounds	—
1880	Bank Street Grounds	—
1890-1901	Redland Field I	—
1902-11	Palace of the Fans	—
1912-70	Crosley Field	29,603
1970—	Cinergy Field (1970 capacity–52,000)	52,952

Colorado Rockies

1993-94	Mile High Stadium (Denver)	76,100
1995—	Coors Field	50,200

Florida Marlins

1993—	Pro Player Stadium (Miami)	40,585

Houston Astros

1962-64	Colt Stadium	32,601
1965—	The Astrodome (1965 capacity–45,011)	54,370

Los Angeles Dodgers

1890	Washington Park I (Brooklyn)	—
1891-97	Eastern Park	—
1898-1912	Washington Park II	—
1913-56	Ebbets Field	31,497
1957	Ebbets Field	31,497
	& Roosevelt Stadium (Jersey City)	24,167
1958-61	Memorial Coliseum (Los Angeles)	93,600
1962—	Dodger Stadium	56,000

Montreal Expos

1969-76	Jarry Park	28,000
1977—	Olympic Stadium (1977 capacity–58,500)	46,500

New York Mets

1962-63	Polo Grounds	55,987
1964—	Shea Stadium (1964 capacity–55,101)	55,777

Philadelphia Phillies

1883-86	Recreation Park	—
1887-94	Huntingdon Ave.Grounds	—
1895-1938	Baker Bowl	18,800
1938-70	Shibe Park	33,608
1971—	Veterans Stadium (1971 capacity–56,371)	62,268

Pittsburgh Pirates

1887-90	Recreation Park	—
1891-1909	Exposition Park	—
1909-70	Forbes Field	35,000
1970—	Three Rivers Stadium (1970 capacity–50,235)	48,044

St. Louis Cardinals

1876-77	Sportsman's Park I	—
1885-86	Vandeventer Lot	—
1892-1920	Robison Field	18,000
1920-66	Sportsman's Park II	30,500
1966—	Busch Stadium (1966 capacity–50,126)	57,673

San Diego Padres

1969—	San Diego/Jack Murphy Stadium (1969 capacity–47,634)	59,690

San Francisco Giants

1876	Union Grounds (Brooklyn)	—
1883-88	Polo Grounds I (New York)	—
1889-90	Manhattan Field	—
1891-1957	Polo Grounds II	55,987
1958-59	Seals Stadium (San Francisco)	22,900
1960—	3Com Park (1960 capacity–42,553)	63,000

Ballpark Name Changes: ATLANTA–**Atlanta-Fulton County Stadium** originally Atlanta Stadium (1966-1974); CHICAGO–**Wrigley Field** originally Weeghman Park (1914-17), then Cubs Park (1918-25); CINCINNATI–**Redland Field** originally League Park (1890-93), **Crosley Field** originally Redland Field II (1912-33) and **Cinergy Field** originally Riverfront Stadium (1970-96); FLORIDA–**Pro Player Stadium** originally Joe Robbie Stadium (1987-96); HOUSTON–**Astrodome** originally Harris County Domed Stadium before it opened in 1965; PHILADELPHIA–**Shibe Park** renamed Connie Mack Stadium in 1953; ST. LOUIS–**Robison Field** originally Vandeventer Lot, then League Park, then Cardinal Park all before becoming Robison Field in 1901, **Sportsman's Park** renamed Busch Stadium in 1953, and **Busch Stadium** originally Busch Memorial Stadium (1966-82); SAN DIEGO–**San Diego/Jack Murphy Stadium** originally San Diego Stadium (1967-81); SAN FRANCISCO–3Com Park originally Candlestick Park (1960-95).

NATIONAL BASKETBALL ASSOCIATION

Western Conference

Team	Arena	Location	Built	Capacity
Dallas Mavericks	**Reunion Arena**	Dallas, Texas	1980	**17,502**
Denver Nuggets	**McNichols Arena**	Denver, Colo.	1975	**17,171**
Golden State Warriors	**San Jose Arena**	San Jose, Calif.	1993	**18,500**
Houston Rockets	**The Summit**	Houston, Texas	1975	**16,285**
Los Angeles Clippers	**Los Angeles Sports Arena**	Los Angeles, Calif.	1959	**16,021**
	& **Arrowhead Pond**	Anaheim, Calif.	1993	**18,211**
Los Angeles Lakers	**Great Western Forum**	Inglewood, Calif.	1967	**17,505**
Minnesota Timberwolves	**Target Center**	Minneapolis, Minn.	1990	**19,006**
Phoenix Suns	**America West Arena**	Phoenix, Ariz.	1992	**19,023**
Portland Trail Blazers	**Rose Garden**	Portland, Ore.	1995	**21,400**
Sacramento Kings	**ARCO Arena**	Sacramento, Calif.	1988	**17,317**
San Antonio Spurs	**Alamodome**	San Antonio, Texas	1993	**25,666**
Seattle SuperSonics	**Key Arena at Seattle Center**	Seattle, Wash.	1962	**17,100**
Utah Jazz	**Delta Center**	Salt Lake City, Utah	1991	**19,911**
Vancouver Grizzlies	**General Motors Place**	Vancouver, B.C.	1995	**19,193**

Notes: Seattle's Key Arena was originally the Seattle Coliseum before being rebuilt in 1995; San Antonio's Alamodome seating is expandable to hold 32,500; and the Los Angeles Clippers are scheduled to play eight of 41 regular season home games at the Arrowhead Pond in Anaheim in 1996-97.

National Basketball Association (Cont.)

Eastern Conference

Team	Arena	Location	Built	Capacity
Atlanta Hawks	**The Omni**	Atlanta, Ga.	1972	**16,378**
Boston Celtics	**FleetCenter**	Boston, Mass.	1995	**18,600**
Charlotte Hornets	**Charlotte Coliseum**	Charlotte, N.C.	1988	**23,696**
Chicago Bulls	**United Center**	Chicago, Ill.	1994	**21,500**
Cleveland Cavaliers	**Gund Arena**	Cleveland, Ohio	1994	**20,562**
Detroit Pistons	**The Palace of Auburn Hills**	Auburn Hills, Mich.	1988	**21,454**
Indiana Pacers	**Market Square Arena**	Indianapolis, Ind.	1974	**16,530**
Miami Heat	**Miami Arena**	Miami, Fla.	1988	**15,200**
Milwaukee Bucks	**Bradley Center**	Milwaukee, Wisc.	1988	**18,633**
New Jersey Nets	**Byrne Meadowlands Arena**	E. Rutherford, N.J.	1981	**20,049**
New York Knicks	**Madison Square Garden**	New York, N.Y.	1968	**19,763**
Orlando Magic	**Orlando Arena**	Orlando, Fla.	1989	**17,248**
Philadelphia 76ers	**CoreStates Spectrum**	Philadelphia, Pa.	1967	**18,136**
Toronto Raptors	**SkyDome**	Toronto, Ont.	1989	**22,911**
Washington Bullets	**USAir Arena**	Landover, Md.	1973	**18,756**
	& **Baltimore Arena**	Baltimore, Md.	1962	**12,756**

Note: Washington is scheduled to play four of 41 regular season home games at Baltimore Arena in 1996-97.

Rank by Capacity

West		East	
San Antonio	25,666	Charlotte	23,696
Portland	21,400	Toronto	22,911
Utah	19,911	Chicago	21,500
Vancouver	19,193	Detroit	21,454
Phoenix	19,023	Cleveland	20,562
Minnesota	19,006	New Jersey	20,049
Golden St.	18,500	New York	19,763
LA Lakers	17,505	Washington	18,756
Dallas	17,502	Milwaukee	18,633
Sacramento	17,317	Boston	18,600
Denver	17,171	Philadelphia	18,136
Seattle	17,100	Orlando	17,248
Houston	16,285	Indiana	16,530
LA Clippers	16,005	Atlanta	16,378
		Miami	15,200

Note: Alamodome seating is expandable to 32,500.

Rank by Age

West		East	
LA Clippers	1959	Philadelphia	1967
Seattle	1962	New York	1968
LA Lakers	1967	Atlanta	1972
Denver	1975	Washington	1973
Houston	1975	Indiana	1974
Dallas	1980	New Jersey	1981
Sacramento	1988	Charlotte	1988
Minnesota	1990	Detroit	1988
Utah	1991	Miami	1988
Phoenix	1992	Milwaukee	1988
Golden St.	1993	Orlando	1989
San Antonio	1993	Toronto	1989
Portland	1995	Chicago	1994
Vancouver	1995	Cleveland	1994
		Boston	1995

Note: The Seattle Coliseum was rebuilt and renamed Key Arena in 1995.

1995-96 NBA Attendance

Official overall attendance in the NBA for the 1995-96 season was 20,513,218 for an average per game crowd of 16,689 over 1,189 games. Teams in each conference are ranked by attendance over 41 home games based on total tickets distributed; sellouts are listed in S/O column. Numbers in parentheses indicate rank in 1994-95.

Western Conference

	Team	Attendance	S/O	Average
1	Portland (12)	848,055	12	20,684
2	Utah (2)	813,073	34	19,831
3	San Antonio (1)	811,422	13	19,971
4	Phoenix (3)	779,943	41	19,023
5	Sacramento (4)	709,997	41	17,317
6	Vancouver (NR)	704,489	10	17,183
7	Seattle (8)	697,301	37	17,007
8	Dallas (6)	684,138	19	16,686
9	Denver (5)	675,426	15	16,474
10	Houston (7)	667,685	41	16,285
11	LA Lakers (11)	649,634	16	15,845
12	Golden St. (9)	616,025	41	15,025
13	Minnesota (10)	585,669	3	14,285
14	LA Clippers (13)	414,560	2	10,111
	TOTAL	9,657,417	325	16,825

Note: LA Clippers played 33 games at LA Sports Arena (one sellout and 9,074 avg.), and eight at The Arrowhead Pond in Anaheim (one sellout and 14,388 avg.)

Eastern Conference

	Team	Attendance	S/O	Average
1	Charlotte (1)	985,722	41	24,042
2	Chicago (2)	969,149	41	23,638
3	Toronto (NR)	950,330	16	23,179
4	New York (4)	810,283	41	19,763
5	Boston (11)	732,841	11	17,874
6	Detroit (5)	730,573	10	17,819
7	Cleveland (3)	730,095	9	17,807
8	Orlando (9)	707,168	41	17,248
9	Washington (6)	688,354	29	16,789
10	Indiana (10)	673,967	30	16,438
11	Milwaukee (8)	647,088	7	15,783
12	New Jersey (7)	638,144	9	15,564
13	Miami (12)	606,091	13	14,783
14	Atlanta (14)	496,669	5	12,114
15	Philadelphia (13)	489,327	4	11,935
	TOTAL	10,855,801	307	18,913

Note: Washington played 37 games at USAir Arena (27 sellouts and 16,789 avg.) and four at Baltimore Arena (2 sellouts, 12,650 avg.); Toronto played 39 games at Skydome (14 sellouts and 23,483 avg.) and two at Copps Coliseum (two sellouts and 17,242 avg.)

Home Courts

Listed below are the principal home courts used through the years by current NBA teams. The largest capacity of each arena is noted in the right-hand column. ABA arenas (1972-76) are included for Denver, Indiana, New Jersey and San Antonio.

Western Conference

Dallas Mavericks

1980— Reunion Arena 17,502

Denver Nuggets

1967-75 Auditorium Arena 6,841
1975— McNichols Sports Arena 17,171
(1975 capacity–16,700)

Golden State Warriors

1946-52 Philadelphia Arena 7,777
1952-62 Convention Hall (Philadelphia) 9,200
& Philadelphia Arena 7,777
1962-64 Cow Palace (San Francisco) 13,862
1964-66 Civic Auditorium 7,500
& (USF Memorial Gym) 6,000
1966-67 Cow Palace, Civic Auditorium
& Oakland Coliseum Arena 15,000
1967-71 Cow Palace 14,500
1971-96 Oakland Coliseum Arena 15,025
(1971 capacity–12,905)
1996-97 San Jose Arena 18,500
1997— New Oakland Coliseum 19,200

Houston Rockets

1967-71 San Diego Sports Arena 14,000
1971-72 Hofheinz Pavilion (Houston) 10,218
1972-73 Hofheinz Pavilion 10,218
& HemisFair Arena (San Antonio) 10,446
1973-75 Hofheinz Pavilion 10,218
1975— The Summit 16,285
(1975 capacity–15,600)

Los Angeles Clippers

1970-78 Memorial Auditorium (Buffalo) 17,300
1978-84 San Diego Sports Arena 12,167
1985-94 Los Angeles Sports Arena 16,005
1994— Los Angeles Sports Arena 16,021
& Arrowhead Pond 18,211

Los Angeles Lakers

1948-60 Minneapolis Auditorium 10,000
1960-67 Los Angeles Sports Arena 14,781
1967— Great Western Forum (Inglewood, CA) 17,505
(1967 capacity–17,086)

Minnesota Timberwolves

1989-90 Hubert H. Humphrey Metrodome 23,000
1990— Target Center 19,006

Phoenix Suns

1968-92 Arizona Veterans' Memorial Coliseum 14,487
1992— America West Arena 19,023

Portland Trail Blazers

1970-95 Memorial Coliseum 12,888
1995— Rose Garden 20,340

Sacramento Kings

1948-55 Edgarton Park Arena (Rochester, NY) 5,000
1955-58 Rochester War Memorial 10,000
1958-72 Cincinnati Gardens 11,438
1972-74 Municipal Auditorium (Kansas City) 9,929
& Omaha (NE) Civic Auditorium 9,136
1974-78 Kemper Arena (Kansas City) 16,785
& Omaha Civic Auditorium 9,136
1978-85 Kemper Arena 16,785
1985-88 ARCO Arena I 10,333
1988— ARCO Arena II 17,317
(1988 capacity–16,517)

San Antonio Spurs

1967-70 Memorial Auditorium (Dallas) 8,088
& Moody Coliseum (Dallas) 8,500
1970-71 Moody Coliseum 8,500
Tarrant Convention Center (Ft. Worth) 13,500
& Municipal Coliseum (Lubbock) 10,400
1971-73 Moody Coliseum 9,500
& Memorial Auditorium 8,088
1973-93 HemisFair Arena (San Antonio) 16,057
1993— The Alamodome 25,666

Seattle SuperSonics

1967-78 Seattle Center Coliseum 14,098
1978-85 Kingdome 40,192
1985-94 Seattle Center Coliseum 14,252
1994-95 Tacoma Dome 19,000
1995— Key Arena at Seattle Center 17,100

Utah Jazz

1974-75 Municipal Auditorium 7,853
& Louisiana Superdome 47,284
1975-79 Superdome 47,284
1979-83 Salt Palace (Salt Lake City) 12,519
1983-84 Salt Palace 12,519
& Thomas & Mack Center (Las Vegas) 18,500
1985-91 Salt Palace 12,616
1991— Delta Center 19,911

Vancouver Grizzlies

1995— General Motors Place 19,193

Eastern Conference

Atlanta Hawks

1949-51 Wheaton Field House (Moline, IL) 6,000
1951-55 Milwaukee Arena 11,000
1955-68 Kiel Auditorium (St. Louis) 10,000
1968-72 Alexander Mem. Coliseum (Atlanta) 7,166
1972— The Omni 16,378
(1972 capacity–16,818)

Boston Celtics

1946-95 Boston Garden 14,890
1995— FleetCenter 18,600

Note: From 1975-95 the Celtics played some regular season games at the Hartford Civic Center (15,418).

Charlotte Hornets

1988— Charlotte Coliseum 23,696
(1988 capacity–23,500)

Chicago Bulls

1966-67 Chicago Amphitheater 11,002
1967-94 Chicago Stadium 18,676
1994— United Center 21,500

Cleveland Cavaliers

1970-74 Cleveland Arena 11,000
1974-94 The Coliseum (Richfield, OH) 20,273
1994— Gund Arena 20,562

National Basketball Asociation (Cont.)

Detroit Pistons

1948-52	North Side H.S. Gym (Ft. Wayne, IN)	3,800
1952-57	Memorial Coliseum (Ft. Wayne)	9,306
1957-61	Olympia Stadium (Detroit)	14,000
1961-78	Cobo Arena	11,147
1978-88	Silverdome (Pontiac, MI)	22,366
1988—	The Palace of Auburn Hills	21,454

Indiana Pacers

1967-74	State Fairgrounds (Indianapolis)	9,479
1974—	Market Square Arena (1974 capacity–17,287)	16,530

Miami Heat

1988—	Miami Arena	15,200

Milwaukee Bucks

1968-88	Milwaukee Arena (The Mecca)	11,052
1988—	Bradley Center	18,633

New Jersey Nets

1967-68	Teaneck (NJ) Armory	3,500
1968-69	Long Island Arena (Commack, NY)	6,500
1969-71	Island Garden (W. Hempstead, NY)	5,200
1971-77	Nassau Coliseum (Uniondale, NY)	15,500
1977-81	Rutgers Ath. Center (Piscataway, NJ)	9,050
1981—	Meadowlands Arena (E. Rutherford, NJ)	20,049

New York Knicks

1946-68	Madison Sq. Garden III (50th St.)	18,496
1968—	Madison Sq. Garden IV (33rd St.) (1968 capacity–19,694)	19,763

Orlando Magic

1989—	Orlando Arena	17,248

Philadelphia 76ers

1949-51	State Fair Coliseum (Syracuse, NY)	7,500
1951-63	Onondaga County (NY) War Memorial	8,000
1963-67	Convention Hall (Philadelphia)	12,000
	& Philadelphia Arena	7,777
1967—	CoreStates Spectrum (1967 capacity–15,205)	18,136

Toronto Raptors

1995—	SkyDome	22,911

Washington Bullets

1961-62	Chicago Amphitheater	11,000
1962-63	Chicago Coliseum	7,100
1963-73	Baltimore Civic Center	12,289
1973—	USAir Arena (Landover, MD) (1973 capacity–17,500)	18,756

Note: Since 1988-89, the Bullets have played four regular season games at Baltimore Arena (12,756).

Building Name Changes: PHILADELPHIA— **CoreStates Spectrum** originally The Spectrum (1967-94); WASHINGTON—**USAir Arena** originally Capital Centre (1973–93).

NATIONAL FOOTBALL LEAGUE

American Conference

		Location	Built	Capacity	Field
Baltimore Ravens	**Memorial Stadium**	Baltimore, Md.	1954	**65,000**	Grass*
Buffalo Bills	**Rich Stadium**	Orchard Park, N.Y.	1973	**80,024**	Turf
Cincinnati Bengals	**Cinergy Field**	Cincinnati, Ohio	1970	**60,389**	Turf
Denver Broncos	**Mile High Stadium**	Denver, Colo.	1948	**76,123**	Grass
Houston Oilers	**Astrodome**	Houston, Texas	1965	**59,969**	Turf
Indianapolis Colts	**RCA Dome**	Indianapolis, Ind.	1984	**60,273**	Turf
Jacksonville Jaguars	**Jacksonville Municipal Stadium**	Jacksonville, Fla.	1995	**73,000**	Grass
Kansas City Chiefs	**Arrowhead Stadium**	Kansas City, Mo.	1972	**79,101**	Grass
Oakland Raiders	**Oakland-Alameda County Coliseum**	Oakland, Calif.	1966	**62,500**	Grass
Miami Dolphins	**Pro Player Stadium**	Miami, Fla.	1987	**74,916**	Grass
New England Patriots	**Foxboro Stadium**	Foxboro, Mass.	1971	**60,292**	Grass
New York Jets	**Giants Stadium**	E. Rutherford, N.J.	1976	**77,716**	Turf
Pittsburgh Steelers	**Three Rivers Stadium**	Pittsburgh, Pa.	1970	**59,600**	Turf
San Diego Chargers	**San Diego/Jack Murphy Stadium**	San Diego, Calif.	1967	**60,789**	Grass
Seattle Seahawks	**Kingdome**	Seattle, Wash.	1976	**66,400**	Turf

National Conference

		Location	Built	Capacity	Field
Arizona Cardinals	**Sun Devil Stadium**	Tempe, Ariz.	1958	**73,273**	Grass
Atlanta Falcons	**Georgia Dome**	Atlanta, Ga.	1992	**71,228**	Turf
Carolina Panthers	**Ericsson Stadium**	Charlotte, N.C.	1996	**72,520**	Grass
Chicago Bears	**Soldier Field**	Chicago, Ill.	1924	**66,950**	Grass
Dallas Cowboys	**Texas Stadium**	Irving, Texas	1971	**65,812**	Turf
Detroit Lions	**Pontiac Silverdome**	Pontiac, Mich.	1975	**80,368**	Turf
Green Bay Packers	**Lambeau Field**	Green Bay, Wisc.	1957	**60,790**	Grass
Minnesota Vikings	**Hubert H. Humphrey Metrodome**	Minneapolis, Minn.	1982	**63,000**	Turf
New Orleans Saints	**Louisiana Superdome**	New Orleans, La.	1975	**64,992**	Turf
New York Giants	**Giants Stadium**	E. Rutherford, N.J.	1976	**77,716**	Turf
Philadelphia Eagles	**Veterans Stadium**	Philadelphia, Pa.	1971	**65,178**	Turf
St. Louis Rams	**Trans World Dome**	St. Louis, Mo.	1995	**66,000**	Turf
San Francisco 49ers	**3Com Park**	San Francisco, Calif.	1960	**70,207**	Grass
Tampa Bay Buccaneers	**Houlihan's Stadium**	Tampa, Fla.	1967	**74,321**	Grass
Washington Redskins	**Robert F. Kennedy Stadium**	Washington, D.C.	1961	**56,454**	Grass

*The field at Memorial Stadium is Sportsgrass, a combination of natural grass turf with a below the surface system of synthetic elements to provide a more stable and durable playing surface. The grass is grown in a base of sand and is rooted through artificial grass blades and inserted into a woven backing.

Rank by Capacity

AFC		NFC	
Buffalo	80,024	Detroit	80,365
Kansas City	79,101	NY Giants	77,716
NY Jets	77,716	Tampa Bay	74,321
Denver	76,123	Arizona	73,273
Miami	74,916	Carolina	72,520
Jacksonville	73,000	Atlanta	71,228
Seattle	66,400	San Francisco	70,207
Baltimore	65,000	Chicago	66,950
Oakland	62,500	St. Louis	66,000
San Diego	60,789	Dallas	65,812
Cincinnati	60,389	Philadelphia	65,178
New England	60,292	New Orleans	64,992
Indianapolis	60,273	Minnesota	63,000
Houston	59,969	Green Bay	60,790
Pittsburgh	59,600	Washington	56,454

Rank by Age

AFC		NFC	
Denver	1948	Chicago	1924
Baltimore	1954	Green Bay	1957
Houston	1965	Arizona	1958
Oakland	1966	San Francisco	1960
San Diego	1967	Washington	1961
Cincinnati	1970	Tampa Bay	1967
Pittsburgh	1970	Dallas	1971
New England	1971	Philadelphia	1971
Kansas City	1972	Detroit	1975
Buffalo	1973	New Orleans	1975
NY Jets	1976	NY Giants	1976
Seattle	1976	Minnesota	1982
Indianapolis	1984	Atlanta	1992
Miami	1987	St. Louis	1995
Jacksonville	1995	Carolina	1996

1995 NFL Attendance

Official overall paid attendance in the NFL for the 1995 season was a record 15,047,058 for an average per game crowd of 62,636 over 240 games. Cumulative announced (day of game) attendance figures listed by *The Sporting News* in its 1996 Pro Football Guide show an overall NFL attendance of 14,196,205 for an average per game crowd of 59,151. Teams in each conference are ranked by attendance over eight home games, according to *TSN* figures. Rank column indicates rank in entire league. Numbers in parentheses indicate conference rank in 1994.

AFC

		Attendance	Rank	Average
1	Kansas City (1)	620,180	1	77,523
2	Denver (3)	583,510	2	72,939
3	Miami (5)	560,917	4	70,115
4	Jacksonville (NR)	554,814	5	69,352
5	Buffalo (2)	552,394	6	69,049
6	Cleveland (4)	512,392	10	64,049
7	San Diego (7)	469,566	16	58,696
8	New England (8)	466,743	17	58,343
9	Pittsburgh (9)	455,913	18	56,989
10	NY Jets (6)	446,337	20	55,792
11	Indianapolis (13)	440,623	22	55,078
12	Oakland (12)	414,572	24	51,822
13	Cincinnati (10)	385,071	27	48,134
14	Seattle (11)	370,870	29	46,359
15	Houston (14)	288,860	30	36,108
	TOTAL	7,122,762	—	59,356

Note: Jacksonville was an expansion team in 1995.

NFC

		Attendance	Rank	Average
1	Detroit (2)	565,234	3	70,654
2	NY Giants (1)	532,453	7	66,557
3	San Francisco (4)	518,298	8	64,866
4	Dallas (5)	518,167	9	64,771
5	Philadelphia (3)	509,695	11	63,712
6	St. Louis (14)	495,337	12	61,917
7	Green Bay (11)	481,036	13	60,130
8	Chicago (9)	476,587	14	59,573
9	Tampa Bay (13)	472,444	15	59,056
10	Minnesota (7)	448,779	19	56,097
11	Carolina (NR)	441,625	21	55,203
12	Atlanta (10)	419,105	23	52,388
13	Washington (12)	413,150	25	51,644
14	New Orleans (8)	400,589	26	50,074
15	Arizona (6)	380,314	28	47,539
	TOTAL	7,072,813	—	58,940

Note: Carolina was an expansion team in 1995.

Home Fields

Listed below are the principal home fields used through the years by current NFL teams. The largest capacity of each stadium is noted in the right-hand column. All-America Football Conference stadiums (1946-49) are included for Cleveland and San Francisco.

AFC

Baltimore Ravens

1946-95	Cleveland Stadium (1946 capacity–85,703)	78,512
1996—	Memorial Stadium (Baltimore)	65,000

Buffalo Bills

1960-72	War Memorial Stadium	45,748
1973—	Rich Stadium (Orchard Park, NY) (1973 capacity–80,020)	80,024

Cincinnati Bengals

1968-69	Nippert Stadium (Univ. of Cincinnati)	26,500
1970—	Cinergy Field (1970 capacity–56,200)	60,389

Denver Broncos

1960—	Mile High Stadium (1960 capacity–34,000)	76,123

Houston Oilers

1960-64	Jeppesen Stadium	23,500
1965-67	Rice Stadium (Rice Univ.)	70,000
1968—	Astrodome (1968 capacity–52,000)	59,969

Indianapolis Colts

1953-83	Memorial Stadium (Baltimore)	60,020
1984—	RCA Dome (Indianapolis) (1984 capacity–60,127)	60,273

Jacksonville Jaguars

1995—	Jacksonville Municipal Stadium	73,000

Kansas City Chiefs

1960-62	Cotton Bowl (Dallas)	72,000
1963-71	Municipal Stadium (Kansas City)	47,000
1972—	Arrowhead Stadium (1972 capacity–78,097)	79,101

Miami Dolphins

1966-86 Orange Bowl 75,206
1987— Pro Player Stadium 74,916
(1987 capacity–75,500)

New England Patriots

1960-62 Nickerson Field (Boston Univ.) 17,369
1963-68 Fenway Park 33,379
1969 Alumni Stadium (Boston College) 26,000
1970 Harvard Stadium 37,300
1971— Foxboro Stadium 60,292
(1971 capacity–61,114)

New York Jets

1960-63 Polo Grounds 55,987
1964-83 Shea Stadium 60,372
1984— Giants Stadium (E. Rutherford, NJ) 77,716

Oakland Raiders

1960 Kesar Stadium (San Francisco) 59,636
1961 Candlestick Park 42,500
1962-65 Frank Youell Field (Oakland) 20,000
1666-81 Oakland-Alameda County Coliseum 54,587
1982-94 Memorial Coliseum (Los Angeles) 67,800
1995— Oakland-Alameda County Coliseum 54,587

Pittsburgh Steelers

1933-57 Forbes Field 35,000
1958-63 Forbes Field 35,000
& Pitt Stadium 54,500
1964-69 Pitt Stadium 54,500
1970— Three Rivers Stadium 59,600
(1970 capacity–49,000)

San Diego Chargers

1960 Memorial Coliseum (Los Angeles) 92,604
1961-66 Balboa Stadium (San Diego) 34,000
1967— San Diego/Jack Murphy Stadium 60,789
(1967 capacity–54,000)

Seattle Seahawks

1976-94 Kingdome 66,000
1994 Kingdome 66,400
& Husky Stadium 72,500
1995— Kingdome 66,400

Ballpark Name Changes: BALTIMORE–**Cleveland Stadium** originally Municipal Stadium (1932-74); CINCINNATI–**Cinergy Field** originally Riverfront Stadium (1970-96); DENVER–**Mile High Stadium** originally Bears Stadium (1948-66); INDIANAPOLIS-**RCA Dome** originally Hoosier Dome (1984-94); NEW ENGLAND–**Foxboro Stadium** originally Schaefer Stadium (1971-82), then Sullivan Stadium (1983-89); SAN DIEGO–**San Diego/Jack Murphy Stadium** originally San Diego Stadium (1967-81).

NFC

Arizona Cardinals

1920-21 Normal Field (Chicago) 7,500
1922-25 Comiskey Park 28,000
1926-28 Normal Field 7,500
1929-59 Comiskey Park 52,000
1960-65 Busch Stadium (St. Louis) 34,000
1966-87 Busch Memorial Stadium 54,392
1988— Sun Devil Stadium (Tempe, AZ) 73,263

Atlanta Falcons

1966-91 Atlanta-Fulton County Stadium 59,643
1992— Georgia Dome 71,228

Carolina Panthers

1995 Memorial Stadium (Clemson, SC) 81,473
1996— Ericsson Stadium 72,520

Chicago Bears

1920 Staley Field (Decatur, IL) .... —
1921-70 Wrigley Field (Chicago) 37,741
1971— Soldier Field 66,950
(1971 capacity–55,049)

Dallas Cowboys

1960-70 Cotton Bowl 75,204
1971— Texas Stadium (Irving, TX) 65,812
(1971 capacity–65,101)

Detroit Lions

1930-33 Spartan Stadium (Portsmouth, OH) 8,200
1934-37 Univ. of Detroit Stadium 25,000
1938-74 Tiger Stadium 54,468
1975— Pontiac Silverdome 80,368
(1975 capacity–80,638)

Green Bay Packers

1921-22 Hagemeister Brewery Park .... —
1923-24 Bellevue Park .... —
1925-56 City Stadium I 24,800
1957— Lambeau Field 60,790
(1957 capacity–32,150)

Minnesota Vikings

1961-81 Metropolitan Stadium (Bloomington) 48,446
1982— HHH Metrodome (Minneapolis) 63,000
(1982 capacity–62,220)

New Orleans Saints

1967-74 Tulane Stadium 80,997
1975— Louisiana Superdome 64,992
(1975 capacity–74,472)

New York Giants

1925-55 Polo Grounds II 55,200
1956-73 Yankee Stadium I 63,800
1973-74 Yale Bowl (New Haven, CT) 70,896
1975 Shea Stadium 60,372
1976— Giants Stadium (E. Rutherford, NJ) 77,716
(1976 capacity–76,800)

Philadelphia Eagles

1933-35 Baker Bowl 18,800
1936-39 Municipal Stadium 73,702
1940 Shibe Park 33,608
1941 Municipal Stadium 73,702
1942 Shibe Park 33,608
1943 Forbes Field (Pittsburgh) 34,528
1944-57 Shibe Park 33,608
1958-70 Franklin Field (Univ. of Penn.) 60,546
1971— Veterans Stadium 65,178
(1971 capacity–65,000)

San Francisco 49ers

1946-70 Kezar Stadium 59,636
1971— 3Com Park 70,207
(1971 capacity–61,246)

St. Louis Rams

1937-42 Municipal Stadium (Cleveland) 85,703
1945 Suspended operations for one year.
1944-45 Municipal Stadium 85,703
1946-79 Memorial Coliseum (Los Angeles) 92,604
1980-94 Anaheim Stadium 69,008
1995— Trans World Dome 66,000

Note: The Packers played games in Milwaukee from 1933-94: at Borchert Field, State Fair Park and Marquette Stadium (1933-52), and County Stadium (1953-94).

Tampa Bay Buccaneers

1976—	Houlihan's Stadium (1976 capacity–71,951)	74,296

Washington Redskins

1932	Braves Field (Boston)	40,000
1933-36	Fenway Park	27,000
1937-60	Griffith Stadium (Washington, DC)	35,000
1961—	RFK Stadium (1961 capacity–55,004)	56,454

Ballpark Name Changes: ATLANTA–**Atlanta-Fulton County Stadium** originally Atlanta Stadium (1966-74); CHICAGO–**Wrigley Field** originally Cubs Park (1916-25), also, Comiskey Park originally White Sox Park (1910-12); DETROIT– **Tiger Stadium** originally Navin Field (1912-37), then Briggs Stadium (1938-60), also, **Pontiac Silverdome** originally Pontiac Metropolitan Stadium (1975); GREEN BAY–**Lambeau Field** originally City Stadium II (1957-64); PHILADELPHIA–**Shibe Park** renamed Connie Mack Stadium in 1953; ST. LOUIS–**Busch Memorial Stadium** renamed Busch Stadium in 1983; SAN FRANCISCO–**3Com Park** originally Candlestick Park (1960-94); TAMPA BAY–**Houlihan's Stadium** originally Tampa Stadium (1976-96); WASHINGTON–**RFK Stadium** originally D.C. Stadium (1961-68).

NATIONAL HOCKEY LEAGUE

Western Conference

Team	Arena	Location	Built	Capacity
Anaheim, Mighty Ducks of	**Arrowhead Pond**	Anaheim, Calif.	1993	**17,174**
Calgary Flames	**Canadian Airlines Saddledome**	Calgary, Alb.	1983	**20,230**
Chicago Blackhawks	**United Center**	Chicago, Ill.	1994	**20,500**
Colorado Avalanche	**McNichols Arena**	Denver, Colo.	1975	**16,061**
Dallas Stars	**Reunion Arena**	Dallas, Texas	1980	**16,924**
Detroit Red Wings	**Joe Louis Arena**	Detroit, Mich.	1979	**19,383**
Edmonton Oilers	**Edmonton Coliseum**	Edmonton, Alb.	1974	**16,439**
Los Angeles Kings	**Great Western Forum**	Inglewood, Calif.	1967	**16,005**
Phoenix Coyotes	**America West**	Phoenix, Ariz.	1992	**18,422**
St. Louis Blues	**Kiel Center**	St. Louis, Mo.	1994	**19,260**
San Jose Sharks	**San Jose Arena**	San Jose, Calif.	1993	**17,190**
Toronto Maple Leafs	**Maple Leaf Gardens**	Toronto, Ont.	1931	**15,746***
Vancouver Canucks	**General Motors Place**	Vancouver, B.C.	1995	**19,056**

*Including Standing Room.

Eastern Conference

Team	Arena	Location	Built	Capacity
Boston Bruins	**FleetCenter**	Boston, Mass.	1995	**17,565**
Buffalo Sabres	**Marine Midland Arena**	Buffalo, N.Y.	1996	**19,500**
Florida Panthers	**Miami Arena**	Miami, Fla.	1988	**14,703**
Hartford Whalers	**Civic Center Coliseum**	Hartford, Conn.	1975	**15,635**
Montreal Canadiens	**Molson Centre**	Montreal, Que.	1996	**21,347**
New Jersey Devils	**Continental Airlines Arena**	E. Rutherford, N.J.	1981	**19,040**
New York Islanders	**Veterans' Coliseum**	Uniondale, N.Y.	1972	**16,297**
New York Rangers	**Madison Square Garden**	New York, N.Y.	1968	**18,200**
Ottawa Senators	**Corel Center**	Ottawa, Ont.	1996	**18,500**
Philadelphia Flyers	**CoreStates Center**	Philadelphia, Pa.	1996	**19,500**
Pittsburgh Penguins	**Civic Arena**	Pittsburgh, Pa.	1961	**17,181**
Tampa Bay Lightning	**Ice Palace**	St. Petersburg, Fla.	1990	**19,500**
Washington Capitals	**USAir Arena**	Landover, Md.	1973	**18,130**

Note: When Buffalo closed Memorial Auditorium and moved into the new Marine Midland Arena in 1996 all the ice surfaces in the NHL became the same size (200 x 85 feet).

Rank by Capacity

Western		East	
Chicago	20,500	Montreal	21,347
Calgary	20,230	Buffalo	19,500
Detroit	19,275	Philadelphia	19,500
St. Louis	19,260	Tampa Bay	19,500
Vancouver	19,056	New Jersey	19,040
Phoenix	18,422	Ottawa	18,500
Edmonton	17,503	NY Rangers	18,200
Anaheim	17,250	Washington	18,130
San Jose	17,190	Boston	17,565
Dallas	16,924	Pittsburgh	17,181
Colorado	16,058	NY Islanders	16,297
Los Angeles	16,005	Hartford	15,635
Toronto	15,728	Florida	14,703

Rank by Age

Western		Eastern	
Toronto	1931	Pittsburgh	1961
Los Angeles	1967	NY Rangers	1968
Edmonton	1974	NY Islanders	1972
Colorado	1975	Washington	1973
Detroit	1979	Hartford	1975
Dallas	1980	New Jersey	1981
Calgary	1983	Florida	1988
Phoenix	1992	Boston	1995
Anaheim	1993	Montreal	1996
San Jose	1993	Ottawa	1996
Chicago	1994	Buffalo	1996
St. Louis	1994	Philadelphia	1996
Vancouver	1995	Tampa Bay	1996

Note: Hartford Civic Center was rebuilt in 1980.

National Hockey League (Cont.)

1996 NHL Attendance

Official overall paid attendance for the 1996 season according to the NHL accounting office was 17,041,614 (paid tickets) for an average per game crowd of 15,987 over 1,066 games. Cumulative announced (day of game) attendance figures listed by *The Hockey News* in its May 3, 1996 edition show an overall NHL attendance of 17,040,425 (including standing room) for an average per game crowd of 15,985 (an increase of 112 fans per game over 1994–95). Teams in each conference are ranked by attendance over 41 home games, according to *THN* figures. There were no neutral site games. Number of sellouts are listed in S/O column. Numbers in parentheses indicate rank in 1994–95.

Western Conference

		Attendance	S/O	Average
1	Chicago (3)	836,021	26	20,391
2	Detroit (1)	817,047	41	19,928
3	St. Louis (4)	791,053	21	19,294
4	Calgary (2)	737,996	0	18,000
5	Vancouver (10)	730,455	28	17,816
6	San Jose (5)	704,790	41	17,190
7	Anaheim (6)	703,347	38	17,155
8	Colorado (8 East)	656,695	38	16,017
9	Toronto (8)	644,888	38	15,729
10	Dallas (7)	637,303	6	15,544
11	Los Angeles (9)	555,795	5	13,556
12	Edmonton (11)	505,734	7	12,335
13	Winnipeg (12)	463,961	6	11,316
	TOTAL	8,785,085	271	16,482

Eastern Conference

		Attendance	S/O	Average
1	Tampa Bay (1)	774,389	1	18,888
2	Montreal (4)	747,557	19	18,233
3	NY Rangers (2)	746,200	41	18,200
4	Boston (10)	711,802	26	17,361
5	Philadelphia (3)	711,136	32	17,345
6	Pittsburgh (6)	665,800	20	16,239
7	New Jersey (5)	664,984	15	16,219
8	Washington (9)	621,355	24	15,155
9	Buffalo (7)	567,770	8	13,848
10	Florida (11)	544,399	15	13,278
11	Ottawa (14)	543,047	8	13,245
12	Hartford (13)	491,305	6	11,983
13	NY Islanders (12)	465,596	4	11,356
	TOTAL	8,255,350	219	15,488

Home Ice

Listed below are the principal home buildings used through the years by current NHL teams. The largest capacity of each arena is noted in the right hand column. World Hockey Association arenas (1972-76) are included for Edmonton, Hartford, Quebec (now Colorado) and Winnipeg.

Western Conference

Anaheim, Mighty Ducks of

1993— Arrowhead Pond 17,250

Calgary Flames

1972-80 The Omni (Atlanta) 15,278
1980-83 Calgary Corral 7,424
1983— Canadian Airlines Saddledome 20,230
(1983 capacity–16,674)

Chicago Blackhawks

1926-29 Chicago Coliseum 5,000
1929-94 Chicago Stadium 17,317
1994— United Center 20,500

Colorado Avalanche

1972-95 Le Colisée de Quebec 15,399
1995— McNichols Arena (Denver) 16,058

Dallas Stars

1967-93 Met Center (Bloomington, MN) 15,174
1993— Reunion Arena (Dallas) 16,942

Detroit Red Wings

1926-27 Border Cities Arena (Windsor, Ont.) 3,200
1927-79 Olympia Stadium (Detroit) 16,700
1979— Joe Louis Arena 19,275
(1979 capacity–19,275)

Edmonton Oilers

1972-74 Edmonton Gardens 7,200
1974— Edmonton Coliseum 16,437
(1974 capacity–15,513)

Los Angeles Kings

1967— Great Western Forum (Inglewood, CA) ... 16,005
(1967 capacity–15,651)

Note: The Kings played 17 games at Long Beach Sports Arena and LA Sports Arena at the start of the 1967-68 season.

Phoenix Coyotes

1972-96 Winnipeg Arena 15,393
(1972 capacity–10,177)
1996— America West (Phoenix) 18,422

St. Louis Blues

1967-94 St. Louis Arena 18,422
1994— Kiel Center 19,260

San Jose Sharks

1991-93 Cow Palace (Daly City, CA) 11,100
1993— San Jose Arena 17,190

Toronto Maple Leafs

1917-31 Mutual Street Arena 8,000
1931— Maple Leaf Gardens 15,728
(1931 capacity–13,542)

Vancouver Canucks

1970-95 Pacific Coliseum 16,150
1995— General Motors Place 19,056

Building Name Changes: DALLAS–**Met Center** in Minneapolis originally Metropolitan Sports Center (1967-82); EDMONTON–**Northlands Coliseum** renamed Edmonton Coliseum in 1994; LOS ANGELES–**Great Western Forum** originally The Forum (1967-88); ST. LOUIS–**St. Louis Arena** renamed The Checkerdome in 1977, then St. Louis Arena again in 1982.

Eastern Conference

Boston Bruins

1924-28 Boston Arena 6,200
1928-95 Boston Garden 14,448
1995— FleetCenter 17,565

Buffalo Sabres

1970-96 Memorial Auditorium (The Aud) 16,284
(1970 capacity–10,429)
1996— Marine Midland Arena 19,500

Florida Panthers

1993— Miami Arena 14,503

Hartford Whalers

1972-73 Boston Garden 14,442
1973-74 Boston Garden (regular season) 14,442
West Springfield (MA) Big E (playoffs) 5,513
1974-75 West Springfield Big E 5,513
& Hartford (CT) Civic Center 10,507
1975-77 Hartford Civic Center 10,507
1977-78 Hartford Civic Center 10,507
& Springfield (MA) Civic Center 7,725
1978-79 Springfield Civic Center 7,725
1979-80 Springfield Civic Center 7,725
& Hartford Civic Center II 14,250
1980— Hartford Civic Center II 15,635
(1980 capacity–14,460)

Note: The Hartford Civic Center roof caved in January 1978, forcing the Whalers to move their home games to Springfield, MA for two years.

Montreal Canadiens

1910-20 Jubilee Arena 3,200
1913-18 Montreal Arena (Westmount) 6,000
1918-26 Mount Royal Arena 6,750
1926-68 Montreal Forum I 15,500
1968-95 Montreal Forum II 17,959
1996— Molson Centre 21,450

New Jersey Devils

1974-76 Kemper Arena (Kansas City) 16,300
1976-82 McNichols Arena (Denver) 15,900
1982— Meadowlands Arena (E. Rutherford, NJ) 19,040
(1982 capacity–19,023)

New York Islanders

1972— Nassau Veterans' Mem. Coliseum 16,297
(1972 capacity–14,500)

New York Rangers

1925-68 Madison Square Garden III 15,925
1968— Madison Square Garden IV 18,200
(1968 capacity–17,250)

Ottawa Senators

1992-95 Ottawa Civic Center 10,755
1996— Corel Centre (Kanata) 18,500

Philadelphia Flyers

1967— CoreStates Spectrum 17,380
(1967 capacity–14,558)
1996— CoreStates Center 19,500

Pittsburgh Penguins

1967— Civic Arena 17,537
(1967 capacity–12,508)

Tampa Bay Lightning

1992-93 Expo Hall (Tampa) 10,500
1993-96 ThunderDome (St. Petersburg) 26,000
1996— Ice Palace 19,500

Washington Capitals

1974— USAir Arena (Landover, MD) 18,130

Building Name Changes: PHILADELPHIA—**CoreStates Spectrum** originally The Spectrum (1967-94); WASHINGTON—**USAir Arena** originally Capital Centre (1974-93).

AUTO RACING

Formula One, NASCAR Winston Cup, IndyCar and Indy Racing League (IRL) racing circuits. Qualifying records accurate as of Sept. 1, 1996. Capacity figures for NASCAR, IndyCar and IRL tracks are approximate and pertain to grandstand seating only. Standing room and hillside terrain seating featured at most road courses are not included.

IndyCar

	Location	Miles	Qual.mph Record	Set By	Seats
Belle Isle Park	Detroit, Mich.	2.1**	108.649	Nigel Mansell (1994)	18,000
Burke Lakefront Airport	Cleveland, Ohio	2.37**	147.512	Gil de Ferran (1995)	36,000
California Speedway	Fontana, Calif.	2.0	—	First race in 1997	69,000
Exhibition Place	Toronto, Ont.	1.78**	110.396	Jacques Villeneuve (1995)	60,000
Laguna Seca Raceway	Monterey, Calif.	2.21*	113.768	Paul Tracy (1994)	8,000
Long Beach	Long Beach, Calif.	1.59**	109.639	Gil de Ferran (1996)	45,000
Homestead Motorsports Complex	Homestead, Fla.	1.5	198.590	Paul Tracy (1996)	50,000
Michigan International Speedway	Brooklyn, Mich.	2.0	234.275	Mario Andretti (1993)	70,000
Mid-Ohio Sports Car Course	Lexington, Ohio	2.25*	119.517	Al Unser Jr. (1994)	6,000
The Milwaukee Mile	West Allis, Wisc.	1.0	176.058	Paul Tracy (1996)	36,800
Nazareth Speedway	Nazareth, Pa.	1.0	190.737	Paul Tracy (1996)	35,000
Pacific Place	Vancouver, B.C.	1.65**	110.293	Scott Goodyear (1993)	65,000
Portland International Raceway	Portland, Ore.	1.95	117.614	Jacques Villeneuve (1995)	27,000
Piquet Int'l Raceway	Rio de Janeiro, Brazil	1.6	167.084	Alex Zanardi (1996)	80,000
Road America	Elkhart Lake, Wisc.	4.0*	142.206	Jacques Villeneuve (1995)	10,000
Surfers Paradise	Gold Coast, Australia	2.804	106.053	Nigel Mansell (1994)	55,000

*Road courses (not ovals). **Temporary street circuits.

Auto Racing (Cont.)

Indy Racing League

Founded by Indianapolis Motor Speedway president Tony George, the Indy Racing League competed with the IndyCar circuit and fielded five races, anchored by the Indianapolis 500, in 1996.

	Location	Miles	Qual.mph Record	Set By	Seats
Indianapolis Motor Speedway	Indianapolis, Ind.	2.5	232.618	Arie Luyendyk (1996)	265,000
Las Vegas Motor Speedway	Las Vegas, Nev.	1.5	226.491	Arie Luyendyk (1996)	107,000
New Hampshire Intl. Speedway	Loudon, N.H.	1.06	177.436	Andre Ribeiro (1995)	72,000
Phoenix International Raceway	Phoenix, Ariz.	1.0	181.952	Bryan Herta (1995)	50,000
Pikes Peak Intl. Raceway	Fountain, Colo.	1.0	—	First race in 1997	40,000
Walt Disney World Course	Orlando, Fla.	1.1	181.388	Buddy Lazier (1996)	55,000

NASCAR

	Location	Miles	Qual.mph Record	Set By	Seats
Atlanta Motor Speedway	Hampton, Ga.	1.522	185.830	Greg Sacks (1994)	78,000
Bristol International Raceway	Bristol, Tenn.	0.533	125.093	Mark Martin (1995)	65,000
Charlotte Motor Speedway	Concord, N.C.	1.5	185.759	Ward Burton (1994)	140,000
Darlington International Raceway	Darlington, N.C.	1.37	173.797	Ward Burton (1996)	55,000
Daytona International Speedway	Daytona Beach, Fla.	2.5	210.364	Bill Elliott (1987)	97,900
Dover Downs International Speedway	Dover, Del.	1.0	154.785	Jeff Gordon (1996)	55,000
Indianapolis Motor Speedway	Indianapolis, Ind.	2.5	176.419	Jeff Gordon (1996)	265,000
Martinsville Speedway	Martinsville, Va.	0.526	94.129	Ted Musgrave (1994)	56,000
Michigan International Speedway	Brooklyn, Mich.	2.0	186.611	Jeff Gordon (1995)	70,000
New Hampshire Int'l Speedway	Loudon, N.H.	1.058	129.379	Ricky Craven (1996)	60,000
North Carolina Motor Speedway	Rockingham, N.C.	1.017	157.620	Jeff Gordon (1995)	55,000
North Wilkesboro Speedway	N. Wilkesboro, N.C.	0.625	119.016	Ernie Irvan (1994)	45,000
Phoenix International Raceway	Phoenix, Ariz.	1.0	130.020	Bill Elliott (1995)	50,000
Pocono International Raceway	Long Pond, Pa.	2.5	169.725	Jeff Gordon (1996)	77,000
Richmond International Raceway	Richmond, Va.	0.75	124.757	Jeff Gordon (1995)	71,350
Sears Point International Raceway	Sonoma, Calif.	2.52*	92.524	Terry Labonte (1996)	42,500
Talladega Superspeedway	Talladega, Ala.	2.66	212.809	Bill Elliott (1987)	85,000
Texas Motor Speedway	Ft. Worth, Tex.	1.5	—	First race in 1997	150,000
Watkins Glen	Watkins Glen, N.Y.	2.45*	120.733	Dale Earnhardt (1996)	35,000

*Road courses (not ovals). **Notes:** Richmond sells reserved seats only (no infield) for Winston Cup races. North Wilkesboro held its last NASCAR Winston Cup race in 1996.

Formula One

Race track capacity figures unavailable.

Grand Prix		Miles	Qual.mph Record	Set By
Argentine	**Oscar A. Galvez** (Buenos Aires)	2.645	105.394	Damon Hill (1996)
Australian	**Albert Park** (Melbourne)	3.274	127.598	Jacques Villeneuve (1996)
Belgian	**Spa-Francorchamps**	4.333	141.123	Nigel Mansell (1992)
Brazilian	**Interlagos** (Sao Paulo)	2.687	127.799	Nigel Mansell (1992)
British	**Silverstone** (Towcester)	3.247	148.043	Nigel Mansell (1992)
Canadian	**Circuit Gilles Villeneuve** (Montreal)	2.747	125.459	Alain Prost (1993)
European	**Nürburgring** (Nürburg/Eifel, Germany)	2.822	131.219	Teo Fabi (1985)
French	**Magny Cours** (Nevers)	2.641	128.709	Nigel Mansell (1992)
German	**Hockenheimring** (Hockenheim)	4.235	156.722	Nigel Mansell (1991)
Hungarian	**Hungaroring** (Budapest)	2.465	117.602	Riccardo Patrese (1992)
Italian	**Autodromo di Nazionale, Monza** (Milan)	3.604	159.951	Ayrton Senna (1991)
Japanese	**Suzuka** (Nagoya)	3.641	138.515	Gerhard Berger (1991)
Monaco	**Monte Carlo**	2.068	94.766	Michael Schumacher (1994)
Pacific	**TI Circuit Aida** (Japan)	2.301	117.970	Ayrton Senna (1994)
Portuguese	**Autodromo do Estoril**	2.703	133.224	Nigel Mansell (1992)
San Marino	**Ferrari Cicuit** (Imola, Italy)	3.040	138.265	Ayrton Senna (1994)
Spanish	**Catalunya** (Barcelona)	2.937	136.472	Alain Prost (1993)

SOCCER

World's Premier Soccer Stadiums

According to *The Ultimate Encyclopedia of Soccer*, compiled by the editors of *World Soccer* magazine.

Top 20 (Listed by city)

Stadium	Location	Seats	Stadium	Location	Seats
Nou Camp	Barcelona, Spain	130,000	Wembley	London, England	80,000
Olympiastadion	Berlin, Germany	76,006	Santiago Bernabeu	Madrid, Spain	105,000
Monumental	Buenos Aires, Argentina	76,000	Azteca	Mexico City, Mexico	110,000
Hampden Park	Glasgow, Scotland	50,000	Guiseppe Meazza	Milan, Italy	83,107
Estadio da Luz	Lisbon, Portugal	130,000	Centenario	Montevideo, Uruguay	76,609

Stadium	Location	Seats	Stadium	Location	Seats
Luzhniki Stadion	Moscow, Russia	100,000	Maracana	Rio de Janeiro, Brazil	120,000
Olympiastadion	Munich, Germany	74,000	Olimpico	Rome, Italy	80,000
San Paulo	Naples, Italy	85,102	Morumbi	Sao Paulo, Brazil	150,000
Parc des Princes	Paris, France	49,700	Olympic Stadium	Tokyo, Japan	62,000
Rose Bowl	Pasadena, Calif.	102,083	Prater	Vienna, Austria	62,958

Note: Construction is underway in Paris for the 80,000-seat Stade de France that will be the principle venue for the 1998 World Cup.

Major League Soccer

The long-delayed debut of Major League Soccer, the new U.S. Division I outdoor league, took place March 31, 1996. The 10-team MLS is sanctioned by FIFA and ended its first season with a championship game on Oct. 20. Note that all capacity figures are approximate given the adjustments of football stadium seating to soccer.

Western Conference

	Stadium	Built	Seats	Field
Colorado Rapids	Mile High	1948	30,000	Grass
Dallas Burn	Cotton Bowl	1935	25,425	Grass
Kansas City Wiz	Arrowhead	1972	30,554	Grass
L.A. Galaxy	Rose Bowl	1922	70,000	Grass
San Jose Clash	Spartan	1933	19,166	Grass

Eastern Conference

	Stadium	Built	Seats	Field
Columbus Crew	Ohio Stadium	1922	25,134	Grass
N.Y./N.J. Metro Stars	Giants	1976	32,000	Turf
N.E. Revolution	Foxboro	1971	22,000	Grass
Tampa Bay Mutiny	Houlihan's	1967	16,000	Grass
Washington D.C. United	RFK	1961	23,865	Grass

MISCELLANEOUS

Canadian Football League

East Division

		Location	Built	Seats	Field
Hamilton Tiger-Cats	**Ivor Wynne Stadium**	Hamilton, Ont.	1932	**29,133**	Turf
Montreal Alouettes	**Olympic Stadium**	Montreal, Que.	1976	**56,245**	Turf
Ottawa Rough Riders	**Frank Clair Stadium**	Ottawa, Ont.	1967	**30,927**	Turf
Toronto Argonauts	**SkyDome**	Toronto, Ont.	1989	**28,000**	Turf

West Division

		Location	Built	Seats	Field
British Columbia Lions	**B.C. Place**	Vancouver, B.C.	1983	**42,800**	Turf
Calgary Stampeders	**McMahon Stadium**	Calgary, Alb.	1960	**38,200**	Turf
Edmonton Eskimos	**Commonwealth Stadium**	Edmonton, Alb.	1978	**50,100**	Grass
Saskatchewan Roughriders	**Taylor Field**	Regina, Sask.	1948	**27,637**	Turf
Winnipeg Blue Bombers	**Winnipeg Stadium**	Winnipeg, Man.	1953	**33,675**	Turf

Arena Football League

American Conference

		Location	Built	Seats
Anaheim Piranhas	**Arrowhead Pond**	Anaheim, Calif.	1993	**18,000**
Arizona Rattlers	**America West Arena**	Phoenix, Ariz.	1992	**15,505**
Iowa Barnstormers	**Veterans Auditorium**	Des Moines, Iowa	1955	**11,411**
Memphis Pharaohs	**The Pyramid**	Memphis, Tenn.	1992	**18,000**
Milwaukee Mustangs	**Bradley Center**	Milwaukee, Wisc.	1988	**17,819**
Minnesota Fighting Pike	**Target Center**	Minneapolis, Minn.	1990	**16,980**
St. Louis Stampede	**Kiel Center**	St. Louis, Mo.	1994	**18,000**
San Jose SaberCats	**San Jose Arena**	San Jose, Calif.	1990	**16,929**

National Conference

		Location	Built	Seats
Albany Firebirds	**Knickerbocker Arena**	Albany, NY	1990	**13,652**
Charlotte Rage	**Charlotte Coliseum**	Charlotte, N.C.	1988	**12,500**
Connecticut Coyotes	**Hartford Civic Center**	Hartford, Conn.	1975	**16,500**
Florida Bobcats	**W. Palm Beach Auditorium**	W. Palm Beach, Fla.	1966	**4,700**
Orlando Predators	**Orlando Arena**	Orlando, Fla.	1989	**16,613**
Tampa Bay Storm	**ThunderDome**	Tampa Bay, Fla.	1990	**30,000**
Texas Terror	**The Summit**	Houston, Tex.	1975	**17,800**

Horse Racing

Triple Crown race tracks

Race	Racetrack	Seats	Infield
Kentucky Derby	Churchill Downs	48,500	100,000
Preakness	Pimlico Race Course	40,000	60,000
Belmont Sakes	Belmont Park	32,491	50,000

Record crowds: Kentucky Derby— 163,628 (1974); Preakness— 98,896 (1989); Belmont— 82,694 (1971).

Tennis

Grand Slam center courts

Event	Main Stadium	Seats
Australian Open	Flanders Park	15,000
French Open	Stade Roland Garros	16,500
Wimbledon	Centre Court	13,118
U.S. Open	Louis Armstrong Stadium	19,500

Note: the 1997 U.S. Open will be held in an as-yet-unnamed stadium with a seating capacity of 23,000.

COLLEGE BASKETBALL

The 50 Largest Arenas

The 50 largest arenas in Division I for the 1996–97 NCAA regular season. Note that (*) indicates part-time home court.

	Arena	Seats	Home Team
1	Carrier Dome	33,000	Syracuse
2	Thompson-Boling Arena	24,535	Tennessee
3	Rupp Arena	24,000	Kentucky
4	Greensboro Coliseum	23,100	NC-Greensboro
5	Marriott Center	22,700	BYU
6	Dean Smith Center	21,572	N. Carolina
7	The Rose Garden	21,401	Portland St.
8	The Pyramid	20,142	Memphis
9	Byrne Meadowlands Arena	20,029	Seton Hall*
10	Kiel Center	20,000	Saint Louis
11	Bud Walton Arena	19,200	Arkansas
	Marine Midland Arena	19,200	Canisius*
13	USAir Arena	19,035	Georgetown
14	Madison Square Garden	18,876	St. John's*
15	Freedom Hall	18,865	Louisville
16	Bradley Center	18,592	Marquette
17	Thomas & Mack Center	18,500	UNLV
18	CoreStates Spectrum	18,060	Villanova* & La Salle
19	University Arena (The Pit)	18,018	New Mexico
20	San Jose Arena	18,000	San Jose St.*
21	Assembly Hall	17,507	Indiana
22	Rosemont Horizon	17,500	DePaul*
23	ARCO Arena	17,300	CS-Sacramento
24	Pittsburgh Civic Arena	16,725	Pittsburgh*
25	UNI-Dome	16,400	Northern Iowa
26	Allen Field House	16,341	Kansas
27	Assembly Hall	16,321	Illinois
28	Hartford Civic Center	16,294	UConn*
29	Erwin Center	16,042	Texas
30	Miami Arena	15,862	Miami
31	LA Sports Arena	15,509	USC
32	Carver-Hawkeye Arena	15,500	Iowa
	Knickerbocker Arena	15,500	Siena*
34	Memorial Gymnasium	15,426	Vanderbilt
35	Breslin Events Center	15,138	Michigan St.
36	Coleman Coliseum	15,043	Alabama
37	Arena-Auditorium	15,028	Wyoming
38	Bryce Jordan Center	15,000	Penn St.
	Huntsman Center	15,000	Utah
40	Cole Fieldhouse	14,500	Maryland
41	McKale Center	14,428	Arizona
42	Joel Memorial Coliseum	14,407	Wake Forest
43	Devaney Sports Center	14,302	Nebraska
44	Williams Arena	14,300	Minnesota
45	University Activity Center	14,287	Arizona St.
46	Maravich Assembly Center	14,164	LSU
47	Mackey Arena	14,123	Purdue
48	Hilton Coliseum	14,020	Iowa St.
49	WVU Coliseum	14,000	West Va.
50	San Diego Sports Arena	13,741	San Diego St.

Division I Conference Home Courts

NCAA Division I conferences for the 1996-97 season. Teams with home games in more than one arena are noted.

America East

	Home Floor	Seats
Boston University	Case Center	2,500
Delaware	Bob Carpenter Center	5,058
Drexel	Phys. Education Center	2,300
Hartford	The Sports Center	4,475
Hofstra	Physical Fitness Center	3,500
Maine	Alfond Arena	6,000
New Hampshire	Whittemore Center	7,200
Northeastern	Cabot Gym	2,000
Towson St	Towson Center	5,000
Vermont	Patrick Gym	3,200

Note: conference changed its name from North Atlantic Conference after the 1995-96 season.

Atlantic Coast

	Home Floor	Seats
Clemson	Littlejohn Coliseum	11,020
Duke	Cameron Indoor Stadium	9,314
Florida St	Leon County Civic Center	12,500
Georgia Tech	Alexander Mem. Coliseum	10,000
Maryland	Cole Field House	14,500
North Carolina	Dean Smith Center	21,572
N.C. State	Reynolds Coliseum	12,400
Virginia	University Hall	8,457
Wake Forest	Joel Mem. Coliseum	14,407

Biggest Not Fullest

While Syracuse continues to have the largest basketball arena in the nation, it lost its claim to having the biggest nightly crowd. After 11 consecutive seasons at the top, Syracuse lost the attendance title to Kentucky, the team that beat them in the 1996 Final Four championship game. Kentucky averaged 23,895 fans over 13 home games during the 1995-96 season, while Syracuse averaged 22,728 over 16. The Big Ten had the highest average attendance for conferences with 12,769 fans per game.

Atlantic 10

	Home Floor	Seats
Dayton	Dayton Arena	13,511
Duquesne	Palumbo Center	6,200
Fordham	Rose Hill Gym	3,470
G. Washington	Smith Center	5,000
La Salle	CoreStates Spectrum	18,060
Massachusetts	Mullins Center	9,493
Rhode Island	Keaney Gymnasium	4,000
	& Providence Civic Center	13,106
St. Bonaventure	Reilly Center	6,000
St. Joseph's-PA	Alumni Mem. Fieldhouse	3,200
Temple	McGonigle Hall	3,900
Virginia Tech	Cassell Coliseum	10,052
Xavier-OH	Cincinnati Gardens	10,100

Note: There are 12 schools in the Atlantic 10.

Big East

Big East 7	Home Floor	Seats
Georgetown	USAir Arena	19,035
Miami-FL	Miami Arena	15,862
Pittsburgh	Fitzgerald Field House	6,798
Providence	Providence Civic Center	13,106
Rutgers	Brown Athletic Center	8,500
Seton Hall	Byrne Meadowlands Arena	20,029
Syracuse	Carrier Dome	33,000

Big East 6	Home Floor	Seats
Boston College	Conte Forum	8,606
Connecticut	Gampel Pavilion	8,241
	& Hartford Civic Center	16,294
Notre Dame	Joyce Center	11,418
	& Pittsburgh Civic Arena	16,725
St. John's	Alumni Hall	6,008
	& Madison Square Garden	18,876
Villanova	duPont Pavilion	6,500
	& CoreStates Spectrum	18,060
West Virginia	WVU Coliseum	14,000

Big Sky

	Home Floor	Seats
CS-Northridge	The Matadome	3,000
CS-Sacramento	Hornet Gym	1,800
	& Arco Arena	17,300
Eastern Wash	Reese Court	5,000
Idaho St	Holt Arena	7,938
Montana	Dahlberg Arena	9,029
Montana St.	Worthington Arena	7,287
Northern Ariz	Walkup Skydome	9,500
Portland St.	Rose Garden	21,401
Weber St.	Dee Events Center	12,000

Note: former American West members CS-Northridge and CS-Sacramento and former Div. II school Portland St. joined the conference after the 1995-96 season.

Big South

	Home Floor	Seats
Charleston So	CSU Fieldhouse	1,000
	& N. Charleston Coliseum	13,000
Coastal Carolina	Kimbel Gymnasium	1,800
	& Myrtle Beach Con. Center	5,000
Liberty	Vines Center	9,000
MD-Balt.County	UMBC Fieldhouse	4,024
NC-Asheville	Justice Center	2,500
	& Asheville Civic Center	6,800
NC-Greensboro	Fleming Gymnasium	2,320
	& Greensboro Coliseum	23,100
Radford	Dedmon Center	5,000
Winthrop	Winthrop Coliseum	6,100

Big Ten

	Home Floor	Seats
Illinois	Assembly Hall	16,321
Indiana	Assembly Hall	17,507
Iowa	Carver-Hawkeye Arena	15,500
Michigan	Crisler Arena	13,562
Michigan St	Breslin Events Center	15,138
Minnesota	Williams Arena	14,300
Northwestern	Welsh-Ryan Arena	8,117
Ohio St	St. John Arena	13,276
Penn St.	Bryce Jordan Center	15,000
Purdue	Mackey Arena	14,123
Wisconsin	Wisconsin Field House	11,500

Note: There are 11 schools in the Big Ten.

Big 12

North	Home Floor	Seats
Colorado	Coors Events Center	11,198
Iowa St.	Hilton Coliseum	14,020
Kansas	Allen Fieldhouse	16,341
Kansas St	Bramlage Coliseum	13,500
Missouri	Hearnes Center	13,300
Nebraska	Devaney Sports Center	14,302
South	**Home Floor**	**Seats**
Baylor	Ferrell Center	10,084
Oklahoma	Lloyd Noble Center	11,100
Oklahoma St	Gallagher-Iba Arena	6,381
Texas	Erwin Center	16,042
Texas A&M	G. Rollie White Coliseum	7,500
Texas Tech	Lubbock Muni. Coliseum	8,174

Note: The Big Eight became the Big 12 in 1996-97 with the addition of Baylor, Texas, Texas A&M and Texas Tech from the SWC which folded after the 1995-96 school year.

Independents

	Home Floor	Seats
Oral Roberts	Mabee Center	10,595
Southern Utah	Centrum	5,300
Wofford	Johnson Arena	3,500

Note: Southern Utah became independent with the break up of the American West conference after the 1995-96 season.

Big West

	Home Floor	Seats
Boise St.	BSU Pavilion	12,380
Cal Poly SLO	Mott Gym	3,500
CS-Fullerton	Titan Gym	4,000
Idaho	Kibbie Dome	10,000
Long Beach St	The Pyramid	5,000
Nevada	Lawlor Events Center	11,200
New Mexico St	Pan American Center	13,071
North Texas	The Super Pit	10,032
Pacific	Spanos Center	6,150
UC-Irvine	Bren Events Center	5,000
UC-Santa Barbara	The Thunderdome	6,000
Utah St.	The Smith Spectrum	10,270

Note: former Big Sky members Boise St. and Idaho, along with North Texas (Southland) and Cal Poly SLO (American West) joined the conference after the 1995-96 season.

Colonial

	Home Floor	Seats
American	Bender Arena	5,000
East Carolina	Minges Coliseum	7,500
George Mason	Patriot Center	10,000
James Madison	JMU Convocation Center	7,612
NC-Wilmington	Trask Coliseum	6,100
Old Dominion	Norfolk Scope	10,239
Richmond	Robins Center	9,171
VCU	Richmond Coliseum	12,500
Wm. & Mary	William & Mary Hall	10,000

Conference USA

	Home Floor	Seats
Ala-Birmingham	UAB Arena	8,500
Cincinnati	Shoemaker Center	13,176
DePaul	Rosemont Horizon	17,500
Houston	Hofheinz Pavilion	10,245
Louisville	Freedom Hall	18,865
Marquette	Bradley Center	18,592
Memphis	The Pyramid	20,142
NC-Charlotte	Halton Arena	9,200
Saint Louis	Kiel Center	20,000
South Florida	Sun Dome	10,411
Southern Miss	Green Coliseum	8,095
Tulane	Fogelman Arena	3,600

Note: former SWC member Houston joined the conference after the 1995-96 season.

Ivy League

	Home Floor	Seats
Brown	Pizzitola Sports Center	2,800
Columbia	Levien Gymnasium	3,408
Cornell	Newman Arena	4,750
Dartmouth	Berry Sports Center	2,200
Harvard	Briggs Athletic Center	3,000
Penn	The Palestra	8,700
Princeton	Jadwin Gymnasium	7,500
Yale	Payne Whitney Gymnasium	3,100

Metro Atlantic

	Home Floor	Seats
Canisius	Marine Midland Arena	19,200
	& Koessler Athletic Center	1,800
Fairfield	Alumni Hall	2,479
Iona	Mulcahy Center	3,200
Loyola-MD	Reitz Arena	3,000
Manhattan	Draddy Gymnasium	3,000
Niagara	Niagara Falls Conv. Center	6,000
	& Gallagher Center	3,200
St. Peter's	Yanitelli Center	3,200
Siena	Alumni Recreation Center	4,000
	& Knickerbocker Arena	15,500

College Basketball (Cont.)

Division I Conference Home Courts

Mid American

	Home Floor	Seats
Akron	JAR Arena	5,500
Ball St	University Arena	11,500
Bowling Green	Anderson Arena	5,000
Central Mich	Rose Arena	6,000
Eastern Mich	Bowen Field House	5,600
Kent	MAC Center	6,327
Miami-OH	Millett Hall	9,200
Ohio Univ	The Convo	13,000
Toledo	Savage Hall	9,000
Western Mich	University Arena	5,800

Mid-Continent

	Home Floor	Seats
Buffalo	Alumni Arena	10,000
Central Conn. St	Detrick Gym	4,000
Chicago St	Phys. Ed. & Athletics Bldg.	2,000
Missouri-K.C.	Municipal Auditorium	10,000
NE Illinois	Phys. Ed. Complex	2,000
Troy St.	Sartain Hall	3,500
Valparaiso	Athletics-Recreation Center	4,500
Western Ill	Western Hall	5,139
Youngstown St	Beeghly Center	8,000

Mid-Eastern

	Home Floor	Seats
Bethune-Cookman	Moore Gym	3,000
Coppin St	Pullen Gym	3,000
Delaware St.	Memorial Hall	3,000
Florida A&M	Gaither Gym	3,350
Hampton	Hampton Convocation Center	7,200
Howard	Burr Gym	3,000
MD-East.Shore	Tawes Gym	1,200
Morgan St	Hill Field House	5,500
N. Carolina A&T	Corbett Sports Center	7,500
S. Carolina St	SHM Center	3,200

Midwestern

	Home Floor	Seats
Butler	Hinkle Fieldhouse	11,043
Cleveland St	CSU Convocation Center	13,610
Detroit Mercy	Cobo Arena	11,143
IL-Chicago	UIC Pavilion	8,000
Loyola-IL	Loyola Events Center	5,200
Northern Illinois	Chick Evans Field House	6,044
WI-Green Bay	Brown County Arena	5,600
WI-Milwaukee	The Mecca	11,052
Wright St.	Nutter Center	10,632

Missouri Valley

	Home Floor	Seats
Bradley	Carver Arena	10,825
Butler	Hinkle Fieldhouse	11,043
Creighton	Omaha Civic Auditorium	9,481
Drake	Knapp Center	7,002
Evansville	Roberts Stadium	12,300
Illinois St.	Redbird Arena	10,600
Indiana St.	Hulman Center	10,200
Northern Iowa	UNI-Dome	10-20,000
Southern Ill	SIU Arena	10,014
SW Missouri St	Hammons Student Center	8,858
Wichita St	Levitt Arena	10,656

Northeast

	Home Floor	Seats
Farleigh Dickinson	Rothman Center	5,000
LIU-Brooklyn	Schwartz Athletic Center	1,700
Marist	McCann Center	3,944
Monmouth	Boylan Gym	3,000
Mt. St. Mary's	Knott Arena	3,500
Rider	Alumni Gymnasium	1,650
Robert Morris	Sewall Center	3,056
St. Francis-NY	Phys. Ed. Center	1,400
St. Francis-PA	Maurice Stokes Center	3,500
Wagner	Sutter Gym	1,650

Ohio Valley

	Home Floor	Seats
Austin Peay	Dunn Center	9,000
Eastern Illinois	Lantz Gym	6,200
Eastern Ky	McBrayer Arena	6,500
Middle Tenn. St	Murphy Center	11,520
Morehead St.	Johnson Arena	6,500
Murray St	Racer Arena	5,550
SE Missouri St	Show Me Center	7,000
Tennessee-Martin	Skyhawk Arena	6,700
Tennessee St	Gentry Complex	10,500
Tennessee Tech	Eblen Center	10,150

Note: former Mid-Continent member Eastern Illinois joined the conference after the 1995-96 season.

Pacific-10

	Home Floor	Seats
Arizona	McKale Center	14,428
Arizona St	Univ. Activity Center	14,287
California	Harmon Gym	6,578
Oregon	McArthur Court	10,063
Oregon St	Gill Coliseum	10,400
Stanford	Maples Pavilion	7,500
UCLA	Pauley Pavilion	12,819
USC	LA Sports Arena	15,509
Washington	Hec Edmundson Pavilion	8,000
Washington. St	Friel Court	12,058

Patriot League

	Home Floor	Seats
Army	Christl Arena	5,043
Bucknell	Davis Gym	2,300
Colgate	Cotterell Court	3,000
Holy Cross	Hart Recreation Center	4,000
Lafayette	Kirby Field House	3,500
Lehigh	Stabler Arena	5,600
Navy	Alumni Hall	5,710

Southeastern

Eastern	Home Floor	Seats
Florida	O'Connell Center	12,000
Georgia	Stegeman Coliseum	10,512
Kentucky	Rupp Arena	24,000
South Carolina	Carolina Coliseum	12,401
Tennessee	Thompson-Boling Arena	24,535
Vanderbilt	Memorial Gymnasium	15,426

Western	Home Floor	Seats
Alabama	Coleman Coliseum	15,043
Arkansas	Bud Walton Arena	19,200
Auburn	Eaves-Memorial Coliseum	10,108
LSU	Maravich Assembly Center	14,164
Mississippi	Tad Smith Coliseum	8,135
Mississippi St	Humphrey Coliseum	10,000

Southern

	Home Floor	Seats
Appalachian St	Varsity Gymnasium	8,000
The Citadel	McAlister Field House	6,200
Davidson	Belk Arena	6,000
E. Tenn. St	Memorial Center	12,000
Furman	Greenville Mem. Auditorium	6,000
Ga. Southern	Hanner Fieldhouse	5,500
Marshall	Henderson Center	10,250
Tenn-Chatt	UTC Arena	11,218
VMI	Cameron Hall	5,029
W. Carolina	Ramsey Center	7,826

Southland

	Home Floor	Seats
McNeese St	Burlon Coliseum	8,000
Nicholls St	Stopher Gym	3,800
NE Louisiana	Ewing Coliseum	8,000
Northwestern St	Prather Coliseum	3,900
Sam Houston St	Johnson Coliseum	6,172
SW Texas St	Strahan Coliseum	7,200
S.F. Austin St.	W.R. Johnson Coliseum	7,203
TX-Arlington	Texas Hall	4,200
TX-San Antonio	Convocation Center	5,100

Southwestern

	Home Floor	Seats
Alabama St	Joe Reed Acadome	7,000
Alcorn St	Davey L. Whitney Arena	7,500
Grambling St.	Memorial Gym	4,500
Jackson St	Williams Center	8,000
Miss.Valley	Harrison Athletic Complex	6,000
Prairie View	The Baby Dome	6,600
Southern-BR	Clark Activity Center	7,500
TX Southern	Health & P.E. Building	7,500

Sun Belt

	Home Floor	Seats
Ark-Little Rock	Barton Coliseum	8,303
Arkansas St	Convocation Center	10,563
Jacksonville	Jacksonville Coliseum	10,000
Lamar	Montagne Center	10,080
Louisiana Tech	Thomas Assembly Center	8,000
New Orleans	Lakefront Arena	10,000
South Alabama	Jaguar Gym	3,000
SW Louisiana	The Cajundome	12,000
Texas-Pan Am	UTPA Field House	5,000
Western Ky	E.A. Diddle Arena	11,300

Trans America

	Home Floor	Seats
Campbell	Carter Gym	1,050
Centenary	Gold Dome	5,000
Central Fla	UCF Arena	5,100
Charleston	Kresse Arena	3,052
Fla. Atlantic	FAU Gym	5,000
Florida Int'l	Golden Panther Arena	4,661
Georgia St	GSU Athletic Complex	5,500
Jacksonville St.	Mathews Coliseum	5,500
Mercer	Macon Coliseum	8,500
Samford	Seibert Hall	4,000
SE Louisiana	University Center	7,500
Stetson	Edmunds Center	5,000

West Coast

	Home Floor	Seats
Gonzaga	Martin Centre	4,000
Loyola-CA	Gersten Pavilion	4,156
Pepperdine	Firestone Fieldhouse	3,104
Portland	Chiles Center	5,000
St. Mary's-CA	McKeon Pavilion	3,500
San Diego	USD Sports Center	2,500
San Francisco	Memorial Gym	5,300
Santa Clara	Toso Pavilion	5,000

Western Athletic

Mountain	Home Floor	Seats
BYU	Marriott Center	22,700
New Mexico	University Arena (The Pit)	18,018
Rice	Autry Court	5,000
SMU	Moody Coliseum	8,998
TCU	Daniel-Meyer Coliseum	7,166
Tulsa	Tulsa Conv. Center	8,659
Utah	Huntsman Center	15,000
UTEP	Special Events Center	12,222
Pacific	**Home Floor**	**Seats**
Air Force	Clune Arena	6,002
Colorado St	Moby Arena	9,000
Fresno St	Selland Arena	10,159
Hawaii	Special Events Arena	10,225
San Diego St	San Diego Sports Arena	13,741
San Jose St.	The Events Center	5,000
	& San Jose Arena	18,000
UNLV	Thomas & Mack Center	18,500
Wyoming	Arena-Auditorium	15,028

Note: The WAC added six teams for the 1996-97 season with Rice, SMU and TCU coming over from the SWC; San Jose St. and UNLV from the Big West and Tulsa from the Missouri Valley Conference.

Future NCAA Final Four Sites

In 1996, the NCAA Men's Final Four was held at Byrne Meadowlands Arena (20,029 seats) in East Rutherford, N.J. It was most likely the last time the Men's Final Four will be played in anything smaller than a domed stadium. Below is a list of all future Final Four sites thus far released by the NCAA.

Men

Year	Arena	Seats	Location
1997	RCA Dome	47,100	Indianapolis
1998	Alamodome	40,000	San Antonio
1999	ThunderDome	32,351	St. Petersburg
2000	RCA Dome	47,100	Indianapolis
2001	Metrodome	50,000	Minneapolis
2002	Georgia Dome	40,000	Atlanta

Women

Year	Arena	Seats	Location
1997	Riverfront Coliseum	17,000	Cincinnati
1998	Kemper Arena	16,668	Kansas City
1999	San Jose Arena	17,500	San Jose
2000	CoreStates Spectrum	16,975	Philadelphia

COLLEGE FOOTBALL

The 40 Largest I-A Stadiums

The 40 largest stadiums in NCAA Division I-A college football heading into the 1996 season. Note that (*) indicates stadium not on campus.

		Location	Seats	Home Team	Conference	Built	Field
1	Neyland Stadium	Knoxville, Tenn.	**102,544**	Tennessee	SEC-East	1921	Grass
2	Michigan Stadium	Ann Arbor, Mich.	**102,501**	Michigan	Big Ten	1927	Grass
3	Rose Bowl*	Pasadena, Calif.	**102,083**	UCLA	Pac-10	1922	Grass
4	LA Memorial Coliseum*	Los Angeles, Calif.	**94,159**	USC	Pac-10	1923	Grass
5	Beaver Stadium	University Park, Pa.	**93,967**	Penn St.	Big Ten	1960	Grass
6	Ohio Stadium	Columbus, Ohio	**89,800**	Ohio St.	Big Ten	1922	Grass
7	Sanford Stadium	Athens, Ga.	**86,117**	Georgia	SEC-East	1929	Grass
8	Stanford Stadium	Stanford, Calif.	**85,500**	Stanford	Pac-10	1921	Grass
9	Jordan-Hare Stadium	Auburn, Ala.	**85,214**	Auburn	SEC-West	1939	Grass
10	Legion Field*	Birmingham, Ala.	**83,000**	Alabama/UAB	SEC-West/Indy	1927	Grass
	Florida Field	Gainesville, Fla.	**83,000**	Florida	SEC-East	1929	Grass
12	Memorial Stadium	Clemson, S.C.	**81,473**	Clemson	ACC	1942	Grass
13	Williams-Brice Stadium	Columbia, S.C.	**80,250**	South Carolina	SEC-East	1934	Grass
14	Tiger Stadium	Baton Rouge, La.	**79,940**	LSU	SEC-West	1924	Grass
15	Camp Randall Stadium	Madison, Wisc.	**77,745**	Wisconsin	Big Ten	1917	Turf
16	Doak Campbell Stadium	Tallahasse, Fla.	**77,500**	Florida St.	ACC	1950	Grass
17	Giants Stadium *	E. Rutherford, N.J.	**76,000**	Rutgers	Big East	1976	Turf
18	Memorial Stadium	Berkeley, Calif.	**75,662**	California	Pac-10	1923	Grass
19	Memorial Stadium	Austin, Texas	**75,512**	Texas	Big 12-South	1924	Grass
20	Owen Field	Norman, Okla.	**75,004**	Oklahoma	Big 12-South	1924	Grass
21	Orange Bowl*	Miami, Fla.	**74,476**	Miami-FL	Big East	1935	Grass
22	Sun Devil Stadium	Tempe, Ariz.	**73,656**	Arizona St.	Pac-10	1959	Grass
23	Memorial Stadium	Lincoln, Neb.	**72,700**	Nebraska	Big 12-North	1923	Turf
24	Husky Stadium	Seattle, Wash.	**72,500**	Washington	Pac-10	1920	Turf
25	Spartan Stadium	East Lansing, Mich.	**72,027**	Michigan St.	Big Ten	1957	Turf
26	Memorial Stadium	Champaign, Ill.	**70,904**	Illinois	Big Ten	1923	Turf
27	Kinnick Stadium	Iowa City, Iowa	**70,397**	Iowa	Big Ten	1929	Grass
28	Citrus Bowl*	Orlando, Fla.	**70,349**	Central Florida	Independent	1936	Grass
29	Kyle Field	College Station, Texas	**70,210**	Texas A&M	Big 12-South	1925	Grass
30	Bryant-Denny Stadium	Tuscaloosa, Ala.	**70,123**	Alabama	SEC-West	1929	Grass
31	Rice Stadium	Houston, Tex.	**70,000**	Rice	WAC-Mtn.	1950	Turf
32	Superdome*	New Orleans, La.	**69,056**	Tulane	USA	1975	Turf
33	Cotton Bowl*	Dallas, Tex.	**68,252**	SMU	WAC-Mtn.	1932	Grass
34	Ross-Ade Stadium	W. Lafayette, Ind.	**67,861**	Purdue	Big Ten	1924	Grass
35	Veterans Stadium*	Philadelphia, Pa.	**66,592**	Temple	Big East	1971	Turf
36	Cougar Stadium	Provo, Utah	**65,000**	BYU	WAC-Mtn.	1964	Grass
37	HHH Metrodome*	Minneapolis, Minn.	**63,699**	Minnesota	Big Ten	1982	Turf
38	Mountaineer Field	Morgantown, W. Va.	**63,500**	West Virginia	Big East	1980	Turf
39	Liberty Bowl *	Memphis, Tenn.	**62,380**	Memphis	USA	1965	Grass
40	Faurot Field	Columbia, Mo.	**62,000**	Missouri	Big 12-North	1926	Grass

Note: Immediately following the 1995 season, construction was scheduled to begin that would increase the capacity of Notre Dame Stadium to 80,900 by the start of the 1997 season. The $50 million renovation project will not prevent the Irish from playing there in 1996.

1996 Conference Home Fields

NCAA Division I-A conference by conference listing includes member teams heading into the 1996 season. Note that (*) indicates stadium is not on campus.

Atlantic Coast

	Stadium	Built	Seats	Field
Clemson	Memorial	1942	81,473	Grass
Duke	Wallace Wade	1929	33,941	Grass
Florida St	Doak Campbell	1950	77,500	Grass
Ga. Tech	Dodd	1913	46,000	Grass
Maryland	Byrd	1950	48,055	Grass
N. Carolina	Kenan	1927	52,000	Grass
N.C. State	Carter-Finley	1966	52,000†	Grass
Virginia	Scott	1931	40,000	Grass
Wake Forest	Groves	1968	31,500	Grass

† Grass bank holds additional 10,000.

Big East

	Stadium	Built	Seats	Field
Boston Col	Alumni	1957	44,500	Turf
Miami-FL	Orange Bowl*	1935	74,476	Grass
Pittsburgh	Pitt	1925	56,500	Turf
Rutgers	Rutgers	1994	42,000	Grass
	& Giants Stadium	1976	77,716	Turf
Syracuse	Carrier Dome	1980	50,000	Turf
Temple	Veterans*	1971	66,592	Turf
Va. Tech	Lane	1965	50,000	Grass
West Va	Mountaineer Field	1980	63,500	Turf

University of Tennessee

Tennessee's **Neyland Stadium** added over 10,000 seats in the off-season and now has a capacity of 102,544—the largest college football venue in the nation. The Tennessee-Florida game on Sept. 21 drew an NCAA on-campus record crowd of 107,608.

Big Ten

	Stadium	Built	Seats	Field
Illinois	Memorial	1923	70,904	Turf
Indiana	Memorial	1960	52,354	Turf
Iowa	Kinnick	1929	70,397	Grass
Michigan	Michigan	1927	102,501	Grass
Michigan St	Spartan	1957	72,027	Turf
Minnesota	Metrodome*	1982	63,699	Turf
Northwestern	Dyche	1926	49,256	Turf
Ohio St.	Ohio	1922	89,800	Grass
Penn St	Beaver	1960	93,967	Grass
Purdue	Ross-Ade	1924	67,861	Grass
Wisconsin	Camp Randall	1917	77,745	Turf

Big 12

With the breakup of the Southwest Conference on June 30, 1996, the Big Eight will become the Big 12 with the addition of Baylor, Texas, Texas A&M and Texas Tech from the SWC.

North	Stadium	Built	Seats	Field
Colorado	Folsom Field	1924	51,748	Turf
Iowa St	Trice Field	1975	43,000	Turf
Kansas	Memorial	1921	50,250	Turf
Kansas St	KSU	1968	42,000	Turf
Missouri	Faurot Field	1926	62,000	Grass
Nebraska	Memorial	1923	72,700	Turf

South	Stadium	Built	Seats	Field
Baylor	Floyd Casey	1950	50,000	Turf
Oklahoma	Owen Field	1924	75,004	Grass
Oklahoma St.	Lewis Field	1920	50,614	Turf
Texas	Royal Mem.	1924	75,512	Grass
Texas A&M	Kyle Field	1925	70,210	Grass
Texas Tech	Jones	1947	50,500	Turf

Note: The annual Oklahoma-Texas game has been played at the Cotton Bowl (capacity 68,252) in Dallas since 1937.

Big West

	Stadium	Built	Seats	Field
Boise St	Bronco	1970	22,600	Turf
Idaho	Kibbie Dome	1975	16,500	Turf
Nevada	Mackay	1965	31,545	Grass
New Mexico St	Aggie Memorial	1978	30,343	Grass
North Texas	Fouts Field	1952	30,500	Turf
Utah St	Romney	1968	30,257	Grass

Note: Pacific dropped its football program after the 1995 season. Also, Arkansas St., Louisiana Tech, Northern Illinois and SW Louisiana all became independent while Boise St. and Idaho moved up from I-AA.

Conference USA

	Stadium	Built	Seats	Field
Houston	Astrodome*	1965	60,000	Turf
	& Robertson	1942	22,000	Grass
Cincinnati	Nippert	1916	35,000	Turf
Louisville	Cardinal*	1956	35,500	Turf
Memphis	Liberty Bowl*	1965	62,380	Grass
Southern Miss	Roberts	1976	33,000	Grass
Tulane	Superdome*	1975	69,056	Turf

I-A Independents

	Stadium	Built	Seats	Field
Alabama-Birm.	Legion	1927	83,000	Grass
Army	Michie	1924	39,929	Turf
Arkansas St.	Indian	1974	33,410	Grass
C. Florida	Citrus Bowl	1936	70,349	Grass
E. Carolina	Dowdy-Ficklen	1963	35,000	Grass
Louisiana Tech	Joe Aillet	1968	30,600	Grass
Navy	Navy-Marine Corps Memorial	1959	30,000	Grass
NE Louisiana	Malone	1980	30,427	Grass
Northern Ill	Huskie	1965	31,000	Turf
Notre Dame	Notre Dame	1930	59,075	Grass
SW Louisiana	Cajun Field	1971	31,000	Grass

Note: Notre Dame Stadium will be enlarged to hold 80,900 by the 1997 season. The Irish will still be able to play there in '96.

College Football (Cont.)

Division I-A Conference Home Fields

Mid-American

	Stadium	Built	Seats	Field
Akron	Rubber Bowl*	1940	35,202	Turf
Ball St.	Ball State	1967	16,319	Grass
Bowling Green	Doyt Perry	1966	30,599	Grass
Central Mich	Kelly/Shorts	1972	20,086	Turf
Eastern Mich	Rynearson	1969	30,200	Turf
Kent	Dix	1969	30,520	Grass
Miami-OH	Fred Yager	1983	30,000	Grass
Ohio Univ	Peden	1929	20,000	Grass
Toledo	Glass Bowl	1937	26,248	Turf
Western Mich	Waldo	1939	30,000	Grass

Pacific-10

	Stadium	Built	Seats	Field
Arizona	Arizona	1928	56,167	Grass
Arizona St	Sun Devil	1959	73,656	Grass
California	Memorial	1923	75,662	Grass
Oregon	Autzen	1967	41,698	Turf
Oregon St.	Parker	1953	35,547	Turf
Stanford	Stanford	1921	85,500	Grass
UCLA	Rose Bowl*	1922	102,083	Grass
USC	LA Coliseum*	1923	94,159	Grass
Washington	Husky	1920	72,500	Grass
Washington St	Martin	1972	40,000	Turf

Southeastern

Eastern	Stadium	Built	Seats	Field
Florida	Florida Field	1929	83,000	Grass
Georgia	Sanford	1929	86,117	Grass
Kentucky	Commonwealth	1973	57,800	Grass
S. Carolina	Williams-Brice	1934	80,250	Grass
Tennessee	Neyland	1921	102,544	Grass
Vanderbilt	Vanderbilt	1922	41,000	Turf

Western	Stadium	Built	Seats	Field
Alabama	Bryant-Denny	1929	70,123	Grass
	& Legion Field*	1927	83,000	Grass
Arkansas	Razorback	1938	51,000	Grass
	& War Memorial*	1948	53,727	Grass
Auburn	Jordan-Hare	1939	85,214	Grass
LSU	Tiger	1924	79,940	Grass
Mississippi	Vaught-Hem'way	1941	42,577	Grass
Miss. St.	Scott Field	1915	40,656	Grass

Notes: EAST— Vanderbilt Stadium was rebuilt in 1981. WEST— at Alabama, Bryant-Denny Stadium is in Tuscaloosa and Legion Field is in Birmingham.

SEC Championship Game

The first two SEC Championship Games were played at Legion Field in Birmingham, Ala., in 1992 and 1993. The game was moved to Atlanta's 71,230-seat Georgia Dome in 1994.

Western Athletic

With the breakup of the Southwest Conference on June 30, 1996, the WAC will grow to 16 teams with the addition of SWC refugees Rice, Southern Methodist and Texas Christian, plus Nevada-Las Vegas and San Jose St. from the Big West and independent Tulsa.

Mountain	Stadium	Built	Seats	Field
BYU	Cougar	1964	65,000	Grass
New Mexico	University	1960	31,218	Grass
Rice	Rice	1950	70,000	Turf
SMU	Cotton Bowl*	1932	68,252	Grass
TCU	Amon Carter	1929	46,000	Grass
Tulsa	Skelly	1930	40,385	Turf
Utah	Robert Rice	1927	32,500	Turf
UTEP	Sun Bowl*	1963	52,000	Turf

Pacific	Stadium	Built	Seats	Field
Air Force	Falcon	1962	50,156	Grass
Colorado St	Hughes	1968	30,000	Grass
Fresno St	Bulldog	1980	41,031	Grass
Hawaii	Aloha*	1975	50,000	Turf
San Diego St.	SD/Murphy*	1967	61,121	Grass
San Jose St	Spartan	1933	31,218	Grass
UNLV	Sam Boyd*	1971	32,000	Turf
Wyoming	War Memorial	1950	33,500	Grass

Note: The field at Utah's Rice Stadium is Sportsgrass, a combination of natural grass turf with a below the surface system of synthetic elements to provide a more stable and durable playing surface. The grass is grown in a base of sand and is rooted through artificial grass blades and inserted into a woven backing.

WAC Championship Game

The first WAC championship game between division winners will take place on Dec. 7, 1996 at Sam Boyd Stadium in Las Vegas.

Bowl Games

Listed alphabetically and updated as of Aug. 1, 1996. The Bowl Alliance, which went into effect with the 1995 season, calls for the national championship game (No. 1-ranked alliance team vs. No. 2 alliance team) to rotate between the Fiesta Bowl (Jan. 2, 1996), Sugar Bowl (Jan. 2, 1997) and Orange Bowl (Jan. 2, 1998). See page 186.

	Stadium	Built	Seats	Field
Alamo	Alamodome	1993	65,000	Turf
Aloha	Aloha	1975	50,000	Turf
Carquest	Pro Player	1987	74,916	Grass
Copper	Arizona	1928	56,165	Grass
Cotton	Cotton	1932	68,252	Grass
Fiesta	Sun Devil	1958	73,655	Grass
Fla. Citrus	Fla. Citrus Bowl	1936	73,000	Grass
Gator	Municipal	1995	73,000	Grass
Haka	Eden Park	1906	50,000	Grass
Holiday	SD/Jack Murphy	1967	62,860	Grass
Independence	Independence	1936	50,460	Grass
Las Vegas	Sam Boyd	1971	33,215	Turf
Liberty	Liberty Bowl	1965	62,920	Grass
Orange	Pro Player	1987	74,916	Grass
Outback	Houlihan's	1967	74,300	Grass
Peach	Georgia Dome	1992	71,230	Turf
Rose	Rose Bowl	1922	100,225	Grass
Sugar	Superdome	1975	77,450	Turf
Sun	Sun Bowl	1963	51,120	Turf

Note: Old Gator Bowl stadium was rebuilt for NFL Jacksonville Jaguars in 1995 and renamed Jacksonville Municipal Stadium.

Playing Sites

Alamo— San Antonio; **Aloha**— Honolulu; **Carquest**— Miami; **Copper**— Tucson; **Cotton**— Dallas; **Fiesta**— Tempe; **Florida Citrus**— Orlando; **Gator**— Jacksonville; **Haka**— Aukland, New Zealand; **Holiday**— San Diego; **Independence**— Shreveport; **Sun**— El Paso; **Las Vegas**— Las Vegas; **Liberty**— Memphis; **Orange**— Miami; **Outback**— Tampa; **Peach**— Atlanta; **Rose**— Pasadena; **Sugar**— New Orleans.

NBC Sports

NBC Sports President **Dick Ebersol** spent $2.3 billion in 1996 to ensure that V of the next VI Olympiads will be tape-delayed on his network. The 1998 Winter Games will be on CBS.

BUSINESS & MEDIA

by Richard Sandomir

Let's Go To the Videotape!

NBC's profitable but controversial Olympics coverage was the sports business story of the year (unless your local sports team left town)

When the cauldron at Olympic Stadium was extinguished on Aug. 4 to mark the denouement of the Atlanta Summer Games, NBC had completed a remarkable year.

Twelve months earlier, it had acquired the rights to the 2000 Summer Games in Sydney, Australia, and the 2002 Winter Games in Salt Lake City for $1.27 billion. In December, 1995, NBC stunned its rivals with a savvy "futures deal": $2.3 billion for the 2004, 2006 and 2008 Olympics. NBC's stealthy dealmaking led its close friends at the International Olympic Committee to ask if CBS would sell it back the TV rights to the 1998 Winter Olympics so that NBC could acquire them. CBS, mindful of its 1992 and 1994 Winter successes, said no.

"We've carved out a love affair with the I.O.C.," said NBC Sports President Dick Ebersol, who suffered a heart attack in February. "In August, we got engaged. Now it seemed reasonable to get married and open up a joint checking account."

Then came Atlanta, an awesome triumph for NBC: $680 million in advertising sales; an estimated $70 million in profits; prime-time Nielsen ratings that were the best for the Summer Olympics since ABC's in Los Angeles, and 26 percent above those in Barcelona four years before; and numbers for the key 18-to-34 female demographic that rose 30 percent from Barcelona.

NBC's whopping success exposed a raw nerve for Billy Payne, the president of Atlanta's organizing committee, who had lobbied to delay bidding in order to grab more than the $456 million NBC paid.

"I said they'd sell $700 million in ads, but they said the economy was terrible," Payne said. "I was right."

The 175 hours broadcast by NBC raised a fascinating dichotomy: watched in droves against weak network competition, the critical reaction was overwhelmingly negative. Although its surveys showed 97 percent viewer satisfaction, NBC was widely excoriated for a lachrymose storytelling approach that ired some who expected more live action in these Eastern time zone Games.

NBC was scorned for not delineating what was live and what was taped (notably Kerri Strug's one-ankled vault to win the women's team gymnastics gold medal, performed at 6:40 P.M. but was not shown on tape until midnight); xenophobic jingoism that meant ignoring foreign athletes unless Americans had no chance at a medal; playing booster to Carl Lewis's efforts to join the 400-meter relay team; leading the she-must-be-taking-drugs reportorial inquisition against the Irish swimmer Michelle Smith; ignoring the U.S.A. women's soccer team's gold medal triumph over China until

---

Richard Sandomir writes the television sports column for *The New York Times.*

Wide World Photos

Billy Payne,(l) the president of the Atlanta Committee for the Olympic Games, meets the press with IOC chairman **Juan Antonio Samaranch**.

the final minute of injury time so that an ultimately meaingless Dream Team game could be seen; presenting the United States women's softball team's championship game in a short taped package, and John Tesh's melodramatic, mawkish, maudlin gymnastics commentary.

The network also took heat for lagging behind CNN and ESPN by 10 minutes to cover the fatal pipe bombing at Centennial Park, then leaving coverage of the aftermath to CNN and ESPN at noon that day to show cycling and rowing.

But NBC can take comfort in knowing that the carping came from a minority of viewers and cranky critics seeking more balanced, journalistic broadcasts; that Americans love to watch Americans win, and even when NBC time-warped events onto tape, nobody could watch any of it until it aired on NBC. But it erred in believing that all 209 million Americans who watched some part of NBC's 17-day extravaganza were fully sated. Wasn't somebody aghast that in an Olympics, the American gymnast pixies danced to "Y.M.C.A." in an exhibition?

Undoubtedly satisfied with NBC is Juan Antonio Samaranch, the I.O.C. president. NBC's deals through 2008 stabilize the cash flow that he can distribute globally to international federations and national olympic committees. But Samaranch will have to steer clear of snide, non-NBC interlocutors, like HBO's Frank Deford. In a profile that aired four days before Atlanta's opening ceremonies, Samaranch called the Olympic movement "more important than the Catholic religion" (uttered with none of the wit John Lennon applied to the Beatles-Jesus debate). He also defended his honoring of Nicolae Ceausescu, brutal Romanian dictator, and Erich Honecker, equally brutal and corrupt East German leader, for their sporting deeds, blithely ignoring their despotic ones.

NBC also played a role in another unusual deal: as a co-venturer with Fox Sports for major league baseball. At the time, last November, NBC seemed like the last network to ante up $400 million for the national passedtime. Three months before, Ebersol trashed acting Commissioner Bud Selig for not extending NBC's and ABC's tenure in The Baseball Network, vowing not to touch the sport until the next millennium.

Well, the end of the century came apace, when NBC, Fox, ESPN and Liberty Sports made a $1.7 billion deal through 2000. The deal revived the Saturday Game of the

Week on Fox, lets Fox and NBC to rotate All-Star Games and split the post-season, gave ESPN from 6 to 12 wild card games (some in daylight, too!) and gave Liberty a regular season package starting next season. Was Ebersol abashed?

"Me?" he said. "Never."

Fox hired a collection of old and new hands to call its games or man its studio show—recognizable voices like Tim McCarver, Jeff Torborg and Ken Singleton, newer ones like Dave Winfield, Steve Lyons and Bob Brenly. Fox quickly unleashed a series of amusing TV spots to help perk up baseball's antediluvian image.

Despite this good start, Fox Sports President David Hill, who introduced a blue/white glowing puck to Fox's National Hockey League broadcasts last season, offended purists with his jokey declaration: "If anybody talks about any dead guys during a broadcast, I'll sack `em!" He later said he didn't mean it.

The Fox-NBC-ESPN-Liberty deal couldn't have come too soon after the end of T.B.N.'s knuckleheaded experiment in regionalized playoff telecasts, wherein games were played simultaneously. During the wild-card series, fans could watch only one of four games available. The scheme divided Ohio, and angered fans uncomprehending of such pre-planned stupidity.

In the league championship series, viewers in markets deemed a National League city were deprived of American League games. "I'm ready to slit my wrists," said Sam Phillips, a morose fan in State College, Penn. Added Bill Giles, an owner of the Philadelphia Phillies: "We predicted there would be a lot of unhappy fans." Duh.

The "duh" factor faded a bit in baseball with the hiring in June of Greg Murphy, as president of Major League Baseball Enterprises, or, chief marketer. Baseball, far behind the N.F.L., N.B.A. and N.H.L. in promoting itself, chose the former Kraft executive who marketed Kool-Aid after the massacre in Jonestown.

"Everyone feels passionately about baseball," he said. "Even Marge Schott." Well, with Marge, Schottzie 2 is her first priority. Then the Third Reich. Then maybe baseball.

Just as overdue as marketing has been to baseball, is the arrival of a college football bowl game that would ensure the emergence of a true national champion. That's

Voice of the Yankees Stilled

Mel Allen was Alabama's homemade boy of summer whose honeyed voice became the soundtrack to baseball, from Opening Day through the chilly afternoons of the World Series, when the Yankee Stadium shadows crept ominously over the greensward. He turned "How about that!" and "Ballantine blast" into common parlance during a reign as the voice of the Bronx Bombers that spanned Lou Gehrig's final season to the final act of the Yankee dynasty in 1964.

In his post-Yankee career a new generation became familiar with him as the narrator of the syndicated program "This Week In Baseball" for 19 years.

Allen died June 16, at age 83, hours after watching a Yankee victory on TV.

"Mel Allen's life was one long, extended, exhaustive, triumphant prayer, a call to see the sublimities of the stolen sign or the first seasonal shifts of the wind," Rabbi Joshua Hammerstein said during his funeral eulogy. "To have uttered a triple play or a mammoth clout with those three words—`How about that!'—Mel Allen was able to elevate broadcasting to a prayer."

Allen started life as Melvin Allen Israel. He got a law degree from the University of Alabama and called Crimson Tide football games on radio.

But he got sidetracked from briefs and litigation forever when he auditioned for CBS Radio in New York City during Christmas vacation in 1936.

He was hired shortly after, did sports, did news, and announced for bandleaders Glenn Miller and Tommy Dorsey from Manhattan hotels. He dropped his surname when CBS executives sought to make him sound less Jewish. Allen joked about that, saying: "There was a K.K.K. guy in Alabama named Israel."

He loved baseball but harbored no ambitions to announce games. But when the assistant to announcer Arch McDonald—who called Yankees and Giants home games—mocked a sponsor, Ivory Soap, by calling it "Ovary Soap," Allen replaced him. Within weeks, Allen, only 26, introduced Gehrig in his July 4, 1939 farewell. In a story he told with choking emotion, Allen recalled a visit to the Yankee dugout by the stricken Iron Horse during the 1940 season.

Photo Archives

In a career that spanned 58 years, **Mel Allen** worked 20 World Series, 24 baseball All Star games, 15 Rose Bowls, five Orange Bowls and two Sugar Bowls. How about that!

"Lou patted me on the thigh and said, `Kid, I never listened to the broadcasts when I was playing, but now they're what keep me going,' " he recalled. Allen was 27 at the time. "I went down the steps and bawled like a baby."

Allen's garrulous style endeared him to fans but made the legions of Yankee haters detest the team more. He became as tied to the team's ups and, well, ups, as any player. He was more the emotional core of the team than Red Barber, with whom he shared the broadcast booth from 1954 to 1964.

"Some guy once said to me," he said. "`When I tune you in, I know you'll say something positive about the Yankees.' But there's a difference between partisanship and prejudice. I gave all players their due."

Allen may have been criticized for homerism but he broke in an announcer who gave new meaning to cheering from the booth: Phil Rizzuto. "His first question was about using some expression. He wanted to use `Holy cow,'" Allen recalled.

Rizzuto later became a part of a scenario that ended Allen's Yankee career. After calling 20 World Series, Allen was nixed from the 1964 Yankees-Cardinals booth, which was manned by Rizzuto and Joe Garagiola. When Allen was fired after the season, Garagiola took his place on the Yankee broadcast team.

Why was he fired? Was it for losing his voice during the 1963 Dodgers' sweep of the Yankees? Had the homerism finally caught up to him? Had he lost his talent? Was he too verbose?

"It's so simple that even Mel didn't believe it," said Len Faupel, who was advertising director of P. Ballantine & Sons, the Yankees' main beer sponsor at the time. "The team and Ballantine were falling on hard times. The team was winning, but it wasn't drawing. They were looking to find fault. Mel was vulnerable."

Red Barber, whom the Yankees would fire two years later, said: "He gave the Yankees his life and they broke his heart." Perhaps the only solace to be taken from this sad turn of events for Allen is that this is one travesty in Yankees' history that does bear the stamp of George Steinbrenner.

But Allen resurfaced. As the Indians announcer for one year. Then back to the Yankees on cable TV, from 1978 to 1985. But it was "T.W.I.B." that sustained him and renewed his professional vigor. After fighting off various illnesses into early 1996, he made plans to return to the syndicated show.

"I guess we gave him another baseball life," said Geoff Belinfante, the executive producer of Phoenix Communications, the producer of "T.W.I.B." "He was supposed to come back on June 26."

what ABC got, starting in 1999, with a $500 million deal struck in July. The existing bowl alliance does not guarantee an annual no. 1 vs. no. 2 game—as it fortuitously did on Jan. 1 for Nebraska's 68-24 trampling of Florida in the Fiesta Bowl—because the Rose Bowl preferred its splendid isolation in Pasadena, where it pits the Big 10 and Pac 10 champions.

The new four-bowl pact (the others are likely to be the Fiesta, Orange and Sugar Bowls) can last from four to seven years and will feature the Rose Bowl as the championship game's host in 2002. In the other years the three other bowls will rotate the big game while the Rose Bowl will be the Rose Bowl, unless the Big 10 or Pac 10 champions are ranked first or second.

"I don't think money is the driving force in this," said Steve Bornstein, the president of ESPN and ABC Sports. "This is the creation of the last blue-chip sports event, the delivery of a true college football championship."

Like NBC's Olympic deals, rancor over regionalized games, the national championship game, news happens. The Cleveland Browns make a sports-shaking move to Baltimore. The Chicago Bull's Dennis Rodman pens a bestselling book in the style of a ransom note. Shaquille O'Neal leaves the Orlando Magic and signs a $120 million deal with the Lakers. Fans surprisingly pack stadiums at Major League Soccer games. Steffi Graf rolls to another Wimbledon championship while dealing with tax problems in her native Germany. Another Cuban baseball player defects. Albert Belle hectors NBC's Hannah Storm at the World Series and throws a baseball at a photographer. Plus daily scores and highlights.

So, as if the current torrent of sportscasts were inadequate to the task of keeping fans overinformed, two all-sports news networks announced their existence: CNN/SI, from CNN and *Sports Illustrated*, to debut in December, and ESPNEWS, the third network created by ESPN, that was to begin operations Nov. 1. Both will shower viewers with news, but no games, the life force of sports television. Sort of like CNN without elections and wars. Both hope to capitalize on the insatiability of fans, as well as the trend in the network news world for 24-hour cable services to vie with CNN. "Our consumers have demanded more and more," said ESPN's Bornstein. Said Jim Walton, the executive producer of CNN Sports: "We don't see how it can't work. It's sports news on demand."

Sports Illustrated was also a player in the demise of Ben Wright, the CBS golf analyst who popped off intemperately in May, 1995 about lesbianism and "boobs" on the LPGA Tour. The magazine reported late in November that Wright had falsely described Valerie Helmbreck, who first reported the loutish remarks roundly denied by Wright, as probably a lesbian in a custody battle with her husband. Two months later, CBS suspended him for four years, with pay, a $1.6 million parachute, as CBS executives quietly said he'd never return. Shortly after, Wright checked in for a month of alcoholism treatment. "There've been problems," said Wright's wife, Kitty. "To say there weren't, I'd be a liar."

While CBS Sports kept trying to revive itself (starting college football in September helped but getting nixed from the bowl alliance after 1998 did not), Fox expanded (into regional sports with its takeover of Prime Sports and its local affiliates, as well as the foray into baseball), ABC Sports looked to a different future under the Walt Disney Co.

Dennis Swanson, president of the division, resigned under pressure, replaced by Bornstein. In one of his first moves, he dismissed Jack O'Hara, as executive producer. O'Hara graciously decided to oversee Tour De France coverage as his final assignment. But the next day, TWA Flight 800 to Paris crashed shortly after takeoff, killing all aboard, including O'Hara, his wife, Janet, and their daughter, Caitlin. Their twin sons were at home.

On May 26, ABC and ESPN—those Disney cousins—found themselves at opposite ends of one great news story: the blood feud between the Indianapolis 500 and the first-time U.S. 500, a rebellious creation of IndyCar. Although the upstart had the best name drivers, they drove like Mr. Magoo, punctuating the last pace lap with a messy, 12-car pileup that delayed the start for 61 minutes. The early-starting Indy 500 roundly trounced the rookie, with a 6.6 Nielsen rating, about 6.3 million homes, to a 2.8, or about 1.9 million homes.

In other TV news: ESPN's "N.F.L.

ESPN

In 1996, ESPN's entertaining and energetic **Chris Berman** took over the Monday Night Football half-time highlight show, restoring the must-see feel of original host Howard Cosell.

Gameday" expanded to 90 minutes. NBC's N.F.L. program stretched from 30 minutes to an hour; it shed Joe Montana, welcomed back former host Bob Costas as an essayist and brought in Cris Collinsworth, saving him from Marv Albert's tongue-lashings. Warren Moon was fired from TNT's football show. CBS got a huge rating for the Fiesta Bowl but low ones for analyst Terry Donahue, fresh from U.C.L.A. NBC 's resident celebrity chaser Ahmad Rashad confessed to a "private ritual" with his pal Michael Jordan. In a long overdue move, ESPN's genial Chris Berman replaced the annoying Brent Musburger as the host of "Monday Night Football's" mini-half-time show, spouting highlights.

Mike Tyson fought Buster Mathis Jr. on Fox, garnering a big rating for a lousy bout, then regained part of the heavyweight championship by whippng Frank Bruno on pay-per-view. Ronnie Lott replaced Jimmy Johnson in Fox's N.F.L. studio, over the objections of Terry Bradshaw, who wanted more time for himself. The N.F.L. toyed in the preseason with bringing back instant replay, letting coaches toss a limited number of red beanbags onto the field to signal that they wanted a play reviewed. CBS sent the wrong message about gambling by hiring Danny Sheridan as a college football analyst, the first oddsmaker in CBS's employ since Jimmy the Greek, who died this past year.

And two women's leagues—the American Basketball League and the Women's N.B.A.—got TV deals (something that eluded a new pro football league conceived by former Vikings quarterback Joe Kapp). The A.B.L., which began in October, got a regional deal from SportsChannel. The latter, a fortunate spin-off of the N.B.A. that begins operation in the summer of 1997, will be seen more broadly, on NBC, ESPN and Lifetime: one game weekly from each of the partners.

While these leagues got off to nice starts, the A.B.L., W.N.B.A. and M.L.S. teams may require decades to be worth megamillions. But when Anheuser-Busch sold the St. Louis Cardinals and Busch Stadium, it was for $150 million. When Comcast Corp., a cable TV company, acquired majority ownership of the Philadelphia 76ers, Flyers and

NBC Sports

NBC Sports president **Dick Ebersol** and **Dick Pound**, chairman of the International Olympic Committee's TV negotiation team, celebrate NBC's deal to televise all but one Olympics from now until 2008. It is not known if the other networks' bids were used to start the fire.

the old and new Spectrum Arenas, it paid upwards of $500 million. Other pricetags: The Pittsburgh Pirates, $85 million. The Los Angeles Kings, $113 million. The Winnipeg Jets, $68 million (and a new home in Phoenix). Dallas Stars, $84 million. The Dallas Mavericks, $125 million, for 67 percent acquired by H. Ross Perot Jr., who admitted he knew little about hoops but plenty about building a new arena.

"A lot of people look at a basketball team as an anchor tenant in an arena," said the son of the jug-eared billionaire. "I look at an arena as an anchor tenant for a much larger program." Red Auerbach, he's not.

There are even financial returns years after an owner has sold out. Billy Sullivan sued the N.F.L. in 1991 for $116 million claiming that the N.F.L.'s refusal to let him sell public stock in the New England Patriots forced him to sell for less than he wanted, $84 million, to electric shaver pitchman Victor Kiam, in 1988. The suit was settled for $11.5 million.

Even if you don't sell your team, there are ways to make it more valuable. Claiming huge debts, Art Modell made a secret deal in a parking lot to move his Cleveland Browns to Baltimore. A vituperative three-month drama that included death threates, Modell hung in effigy and U.S. Senate hearings concluded in February with a deal that sent the Browns (now the Ravens) to Baltimore, where by 1998, Modell will be ensconced in a new stadium with one of the N.F.L.'s sweetest leases, doubtlessly sending his net worth soaring. The Houston Oilers are expected to follow Modell's path by 1998, to Nashville, but the Seattle Seahawks' proposed fear-of-earthquake move to Los Angeles was blocked.

Stadium deals continued to make news. The San Francisco Giants plan to build a $255 million ballpark with private money. The Milwaukee Brewers continued to cobble together private and public cash for a new home, a tawdry task that began to look like raising alms for the poor (market).

Most grandly, New York City Mayor Rudolph W. Giuliani proposed that it would be easy to finance a $1 billion-plus retractable dome stadium for the Yankees on Manhattan's West Side, and suggested it would help the Big Apple in a possible 2008 Summer Olympics bid. Which would be mighty nice for NBC, which is in nearby Rockefeller Center. Better than flying everyone to Sydney, Beijing, Istanbul or Cape Town.

Eh, mate? ❒

1995-96 Top 75 TV Sports Events

Final 1995–96 network television ratings for nationally-telecast sports events, according to Nielsen Media Research. Covers period from Sept. 18, 1995 through Aug. 25, 1996. Events are listed with ratings points and audience share; each ratings point represents 959,000 households and shares indicate percentage of TV sets in use.

Multiple entries: SPORTS—NFL Football (41); Summer Olympics (15); Major League Baseball (8); NBA Basketball (6); College Football bowl games and NCAA Basketball (2). NETWORKS—NBC (35); ABC (23); FOX (14); CBS (3).

	Event	Date	Net	Rtg/Sh
1	**Super Bowl XXX** (Cowboys vs. Steelers)	1/28	NBC	46.0/68
2	**NFC Championship** (Packers at Cowboys)	1/14	FOX	33.3/58
3	**Summer Olympics** (Women's gymnastics team finals, men's/women's swim finals)	7/23	NBC	27.2/47
4	**AFC Championship** (Colts at Steelers)	1/14	NBC	27.1/57
5	**Summer Olympics** (Women's gymnastics indiv. all-around finals)	7/25	NBC	26.8/48
6	**Summer Olympics** (Men's T&F: 400m and LJ final)	7/29	NBC	26.4/47
7	**NFC Semifinal** (Eagles at Cowboys)	1/7	FOX	25.4/48
	AFC Semifinal (Colts at Chiefs)	1/7	NBC	25.4/42
9	**Summer Olympics** (Men's/Women's Gymnastics indiv. event finals)	7/28	NBC	23.4/43
10	**Summer Olympics** (Men's/Women's swim finals)	7/21	NBC	22.9/42
	Summer Olympics (Men's gymnastics team finals)	7/22	NBC	22.9/40
12	**Summer Olympics** (Men's swim finals)	7/24	NBC	22.4/41
13	**NFC Semifinal** (Packers at 49ers)	1/6	FOX	22.2/42
14	**World Series, Game 5** (Braves at Indians)	10/26	ABC	21.6/34
15	**NFL Regular Season Game** (49ers at Cowboys)	11/12	FOX	21.3/39
	Summer Olympics (Men's Dream Team vs. Brazil)	7/30	NBC	21.3/39
17	**Summer Olympics** (Women's soccer final, Men's T&F finals)	8/1	NBC	20.7/39
18	**World Series, Game 3** (Braves at Indians)	10/24	NBC	20.0/34
	World Series, Game 4 (Braves at Indians)	10/25	ABC	20.0/33
20	**Summer Olympics** (Women's springboard diving finals, T&F finals)	7/31	NBC	19.8/38
21	**World Series, Game 6** (Indians at Braves)	10/28	NBC	19.5/35
22	**World Series, Game 2** (Indians at Braves)	10/22	NBC	19.4/31
	Summer Olympics (Men's/Women's 100m finals, women's platform diving finals)	7/27	NBC	19.4/40
24	**Rose Bowl** (Northwestern vs. USC)	1/1	ABC	19.2/33
25	**Monday Night Football** (49ers at Lions)	9/25	ABC	19.1/32
26	**AFC Wildcard** (Colts at Chargers)	12/31	NBC	19.0/38
	AFC Playoff Game (Bills at Steelers)	1/6	NBC	19.0/44

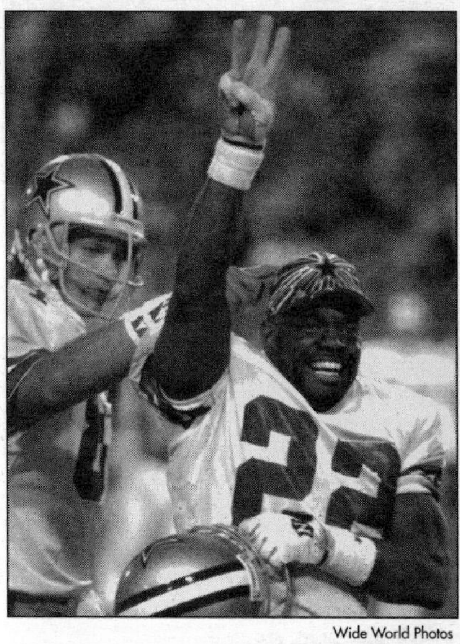

Wide World Photos

Cowboys **Emmitt Smith** and **Jay Novacek** bask in the glow of their victory over the Steelers in Superbowl XXX. The game was watched by over 44 million people.

	Event	Date	Net	Rtg/Sh
28	**NFC Wildcard** (Falcons at Green Bay)	12/31	FOX	18.9/43
29	**NBA Finals, Game 6** (SuperSonics at Bulls)	6/16	NBC	18.8/35
	Fiesta Bowl (Nebraska vs. Florida)	1/2	CBS	18.8/31
31	**Monday Night Football** (Eagles at Cowboys)	11/6	ABC	18.7/30
32	**Monday Night Football** (49ers at Dolphins)	11/20	ABC	18.5/30
33	**NFL Regular Season Game** (Chiefs at Cowboys)	11/23	NBC	18.4/48
34	**NCAA Men's Basketball Championship Game** (Syracuse vs. Kentucky)	4/1	CBS	18.3/29
35	**NBA Finals, Game 4** (Bulls at SuperSonics)	6/12	NBC	18.1/33
36	**Summer Olympics** (Men's swim finals)	7/26	NBC	17.9/37
37	**Monday Night Football** (Chiefs at Dolphins)	12/11	ABC	17.8/29
	Monday Night Football (Vikings at 49ers)	12/18	ABC	17.8/31
39	**Monday Night Football** (Raiders at Seahawks)	10/16	ABC	17.7/29
40	**NBA Finals, Game 5** (Bulls at SuperSonics)	6/14	NBC	17.2/33
	Summer Olympics (Women's swim finals)	7/20	NBC	17.2/37

1995-96 Top 75 TV Sports Events (Cont.)

Wide World Photos

College basketball needs a wake-up call. Ratings for the NCAA tournament are down and one reason is that high-profile talent, like Allen Iverson, Stephon Marbury and UMass coach **John Calipari**, is jumping to the riches of the NBA.

42 **Monday Night Football**
(Steelers at Dolphins) ....9/18 ABC 17.1/29
43 **NFC Playoff Game**
(Lions at Eagles) ....12/28 ABC 17.0/37
44 **NBA Finals, Game 1**
(SuperSonics at Bulls)...........6/5 NBC 16.8/31
Monday Night Football
(Bears at Vikings) ....10/30 ABC 16.8/28
46 **NFC Regular Season Game**
(Various teams) ....12/10 FOX 16.7/38
Monday Night Football
(Browns at Steelers) ....11/13 ABC 16.7/27
48 **Monday Night Football**
(Bills at Patriots)...............10/23 ABC 16.5/27
49 **Monday Night Football**
(Bears at Lions)..................12/4 ABC 16.4/27
World Series, Game 1
(Indians at Braves)...........10/21 ABC 16.4/30
51 **Monday Night Football**
(Chargers at Chiefs)...........10/9 ABC 16.2/28
52 **Mike Tyson vs. Buster Mathis Jr.**
....12/16 FOX 16.1/28
Summer Olympics
(Men's platform diving finals, synchro. swim final).............8/2 NBC 16.1/33
54 **NBA Finals, Game 3**
(Bulls at SuperSonics)...........6/9 NBC 15.8/28
Summer Olympics
(Men's basketball final, men's/ women's track relay finals)...8/3 NBC 15.8/34
56 **NFC Regular Season Early Game**
(Cowboys at Falcons).......10/29 FOX 15.7/37
Monday Night Football
(Raiders at Chargers).......11/27 ABC 15.7/25
58 **Monday Night Football**
(Bills at Browns).................10/2 ABC 15.6/25
59 **Monday Night Football**
(Cowboys at Cardinals) ...12/25 ABC 15.5/31
60 **NCAA Men's Basketball Semifinals**
(UMass vs. Kentucky).........3/30 CBS 15.1/28
61 **AL Championship Series, Game 6**
(Indians at Mariners) ....10/17 NBC 15.0/24
62 **NFC Regular Season Game**
(Vikings at Lions) ....11/23 FOX 14.9/39
63 **AFC Regular Season Game**
(Various Teams)...............10/22 NBC 14.7/30
64 **NL Championship Series, Game 1**
(Reds at Braves)...............10/10 ABC 14.6/24
65 **NFC Regular Season Early Game**
(Various Teams)..............11/19 FOX 14.5/35
66 **AFC Playoff Game**
(Dolphins at Bills).............12/30 ABC 14.4/38
AFC Regular Season Late Game
(Various Teams).................12/9 NBC 14.4/26
68 **AFC Regular Season Late Game**
(Various Teams)...............11/04 NBC 14.3/27
69 **NFC Regular Season Early Game**
(Various Teams).................9/24 FOX 14.2/35
NFC Regular Season Early Game
(Various Teams).................12/3 FOX 14.2/35
71 **NFC Regular Season Early Game**
(Various Teams)..............10/15 FOX 14.0/35
NL Championship Series, Game 2
(Braves at Reds)...............10/11 ABC 14.0/24
73 **NFL Post Game show**...11/19 FOX 13.9/23
NBA Finals, Game 2
(SuperSonics at Bulls)...........6/7 NBC 13.9/27
75 **AFC Regular Season Late Game**
(Various Teams).................10/8 NBC 13.7/30

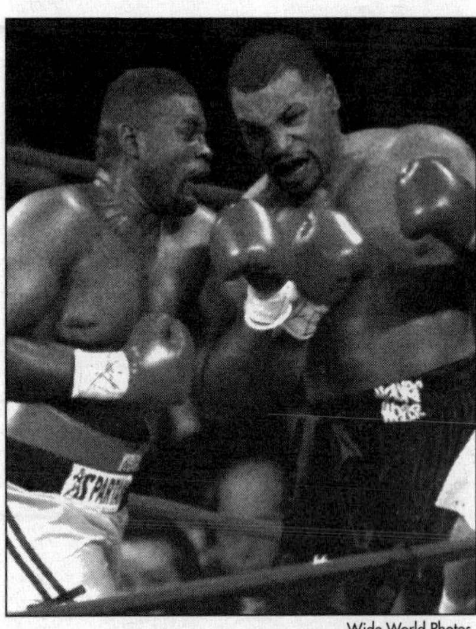

Wide World Photos

Mike Tyson made his return to free television in 1995 with a third-round TKO of **Buster Mathis Jr.** on Fox. Tyson's last fight on free TV, against Marvis Frazier in 1986, lasted just 30 seconds.

All-Time Top-Rated TV Programs

NFL Football dominates television's All-Time Top-Rated 50 Programs with 19 Super Bowls and the 1981 NFC Championship Game making the list. Rankings based on surveys taken from July 1960 through August 1996; include only sponsored programs seen on individual networks; and programs under 30 minutes scheduled duration are excluded. Programs are listed with ratings points, audience share and number of households watching, according to Nielsen Media Research.

Multiple entries: The Super Bowl (19); "Roots" (7); "The Beverly Hillbillies" and "The Thorn Birds" (3); "The Bob Hope Christmas Show," "The Ed Sullivan Show," "Gone With The Wind" and 1994 Winter Olympics (2).

	Program	Episode/Game	Net	Date	Rating	Share	Households
1	M*A*S*H (series)	Final episode	CBS	2/28/83	**60.2**	77	50,150,000
2	Dallas (series)	"Who Shot J.R.?"	CBS	11/21/80	**53.3**	76	41,470,000
3	Roots (mini-series)	Part 8	ABC	1/30/77	**51.1**	71	36,380,000
4	**Super Bowl XVI**	49ers 26, Bengals 21	CBS	1/24/82	**49.1**	73	40,020,000
5	**Super Bowl XVII**	Redskins 27, Dolphins 17	NBC	1/30/83	**48.6**	69	40,480,000
6	**XVII Winter Olympics**	Women's Figure Skating	CBS	2/23/94	**48.5**	64	45,690,000
7	**Super Bowl XX**	Bears 46, Patriots 10	NBC	1/26/86	**48.3**	70	41,490,000
8	Gone With the Wind (movie)	Part 1	NBC	11/7/76	**47.7**	65	33,960,000
9	Gone with the Wind (movie)	Part 2	NBC	11/8/76	**47.4**	64	33,750,000
10	**Super Bowl XII**	Cowboys 27, Broncos 10	CBS	1/15/78	**47.2**	67	34,410,000
11	**Super Bowl XIII**	Steelers 35, Cowboys 31	NBC	1/21/79	**47.1**	74	35,090,000
12	Bob Hope Special	Christmas Show	NBC	1/15/70	**46.6**	64	27,260,000
13	**Super Bowl XVIII**	Raiders 38, Redskins 9	CBS	1/22/84	**46.4**	71	38,800,000
	Super Bowl XIX	49ers 38, Dolphins 16	ABC	1/20/85	**46.4**	63	39,390,000
15	**Super Bowl XIV**	Steelers 31, Rams 19	CBS	1/20/80	**46.3**	67	35,330,000
16	**Super Bowl XXX**	Cowboys 27, Steelers 17	NBC	1/28/96	**46.0**	68	44,114,400
17	ABC Theater (special)	"The Day After"	ABC	11/20/83	**46.0**	62	38,550,000
18	Roots (mini-series)	Part 6	ABC	1/28/77	**45.9**	66	32,680,000
	The Fugitive (series)	Final episode	ABC	8/29/67	**45.9**	72	25,700,000
20	**Super Bowl XXI**	Giants 39, Broncos 20	CBS	1/25/87	**45.8**	66	40,030,000
21	Roots (mini-series)	Part 5	ABC	1/27/77	**45.7**	71	32,540,000
22	**Super Bowl XXVIII**	Cowboys 30, Bills 13	NBC	1/29/94	**45.5**	66	42,860,000
	Cheers	Final episode	NBC	5/20/93	**45.5**	64	42,360,500
24	The Ed Sullivan Show	Beatles' 1st appearence	CBS	2/9/64	**45.3**	60	23,240,000
25	**Super Bowl XXVII**	Cowboys 52, Bills 17	NBC	1/31/93	**45.1**	66	41,988,100
26	Bob Hope Special	Christmas Show	NBC	1/14/71	**45.0**	61	27,050,000
27	Roots (mini-series)	Part 3	ABC	1/25/77	**44.8**	68	31,900,000
28	**Super Bowl XI**	Raiders 32, Vikings 14	NBC	1/9/77	**44.4**	73	31,610,000
	Super Bowl XV	Raiders 27, Eagles 10	NBC	1/25/81	**44.4**	63	34,540,000
30	**Super Bowl VI**	Cowboys 24, Dolphins 3	CBS	1/16/72	**44.2**	74	27,450,000
31	**XVII Winter Olympics**	Women's Figure Skating	CBS	2/25/94	**44.1**	64	41,540,000
	Roots (mini-series)	Part 2	ABC	1/24/77	**44.1**	62	31,400,000
33	The Beverly Hillbillies	Regular episode	CBS	1/8/64	**44.0**	65	22,570,000
34	Roots (mini-series)	Part 4	ABC	1/26/77	**43.8**	66	31,190,000
	The Ed Sullivan Show	Beatles' 2nd appearence	CBS	2/16/64	**43.8**	60	22,445,000
36	**Super Bowl XXIII**	49ers 20, Bengals 16	NBC	1/22/89	**43.5**	68	39,320,000
37	The Academy Awards	John Wayne wins Oscar	ABC	4/7/70	**43.4**	78	25,390,000
38	The Thorn Birds (mini-series)	Part 3	ABC	3/29/83	**43.2**	62	35,990,000
39	The Thorn Birds (mini-series)	Part 4	ABC	3/30/83	**43.1**	62	35,900,000
40	**NFC Championship Game**	49ers 28, Cowboys 27	CBS	1/10/82	**42.9**	62	34,940,000
41	The Beverly Hillbillies	Regular episode	CBS	1/15/64	**42.8**	62	21,960,000
42	**Super Bowl VII**	Dolphins 14, Redskins 7	NBC	1/14/73	**42.7**	72	27,670,000
43	The Thorn Birds (mini-series)	Part 2	ABC	3/28/83	**42.5**	59	35,400,000
44	**Super Bowl IX**	Steelers 16, Vikings 6	NBC	1/12/75	**42.4**	72	29,040,000
	The Beverly Hillbillies	Regular episode	CBS	2/26/64	**42.4**	60	21,750,000
46	**Super Bowl X**	Steelers 21, Cowboys 17	CBS	1/18/76	**42.3**	78	29,440,000
	ABC Sunday Night Movie	"Airport"	ABC	11/11/73	**42.3**	63	28,000,000
	ABC Sunday Night Movie	"Love Story"	ABC	10/1/72	**42.3**	62	27,410,000
	Cinderella	Musical special	CBS	2/22/65	**42.3**	59	22,250,000
	Roots (mini-series)	Part 7	ABC	1/29/77	**42.3**	65	30,120,000

All-Time Top-Rated Cable TV Sports Events

All-time cable television for sports events, according to ESPN and Turner Sports research. Covers period from Sept. 1, 1980 through Sept. 20, 1996.

NFL Telecasts

		Date	Net	Rtg
1	Chicago at Minnesota	12/6/87	ESPN	17.6
2	Detroit at Miami	12/25/94	ESPN	15.1
3	Chicago at Minnesota	12/3/89	ESPN	14.7
4	Cleveland at San Fran	11/29/87	ESPN	14.2
5	Pittsburgh at Houston	12/30/90	ESPN	13.8

Non-NFL Telecasts

		Date	Net	Rtg
1	NBA: Detroit-Boston	6/1/88	TBS	8.8
2	NBA: Chicago-Detroit	5/31/89	TBS	8.2
3	NBA: Detroit-Boston	5/26/88	TBS	8.1
4	NCAA: G'town-St. John's	2/27/85	ESPN	8.0
5	NBA: Chicago-Orlando	5/10/95	TNT	7.9

The Rights Stuff

The roster of major 1996-97 television rights on network and cable TV as of Sept. 20, 1996.

ABC

Auto Racing— 1997 Indianapolis 500 and four other Indy Racing League races; NASCAR Brickyard 400.
College Basketball— 1997 regular season games.
Bowling— 1997 PBA Tour.
College Football— Big Ten, Big 12, Pac-10 and WAC regular season for 1996; Big 12, SEC and WAC Championship Games; Aloha, Citrus, Rose and Sugar bowls for 1996 seasons.
Cycling— weekend coverage of the 1997 Tour de France
Figure Skating— 1997 World, U.S. and European Championships.
NFL Football— ABC Monday Night Football; two 1996 season Wild Card playoff games; 1997 Pro Bowl.
Golf— 1997 British Open; British Senior Open; LPGA Dinah Shore; PGA, LPGA and Seniors Skins games.
Horse Racing— 1997 Kentucky Derby; Preakness; Belmont Stakes.
Little League Baseball— 1997 Little League World Series
Soccer— 1996 MLS championship game.

CBS

Auto Racing— 1997 Daytona 500, three other NASCAR Winston Cup races and NASCAR truck series.
College Basketball— 1996-97 Big East, Big 12 and SEC regular season games and conference tournaments; NCAA Men's tournament and Final Four through 2002.
College Football— Fiesta, Orange, Cotton and Sun bowls for 1996 seasons; Big East and SEC regular season games in 1997; 1997 Army-Navy game.
Golf— 1997 PGA Tour; Masters; PGA Championship, LPGA Championship.
Olympics— 1998 Winter Games at Nagano.
Tennis— 1997 U.S. Open.

ESPN (and ESPN2)

Auto Racing— 1997 IndyCar and NASCAR.
Major League Baseball— 1997 regular season.
College Basketball— Men's 1996-97 regular season and conference tournaments and pre- and postseason NIT; Women's 1996-97 regular season and NCAA tournament and Final Four.
Bowling— 1997 PBA and LPBT tours.
Boxing— ESPN Championship series.
Cycling— weekday coverage of the 1997 Tour de France.
College Football— ACC, Big East, Big 10, SEC and WAC regular season for '96 season; Heisman Trophy Show; Alamo, Copper, Haka, Heritage, Holiday, Independence, Liberty, Outback and Peach Bowls.
NFL Football— Sunday Night Football (2nd half of 1996 season); 1997 College Draft.
Golf— 1997 U.S. Open and British Open (early rounds); PGA, Senior and LPGA tour events.
NHL Hockey— selected regular season and Stanley Cup playoff games through 1996–97 season.
College Hockey— 1997 NCAA Final Four.
Soccer— 1997 Major League Soccer regular season and playoffs; U.S. National Team games.
Tennis— 1996–97 Davis Cup, Grand Slam Cup and Fed Cup; 1997 ATP Tour and Australian Open.

FOX

Figure Skating— 1997 Skate International Champions Series
NFL Football— NFC regular season and playoffs through 1997 season; 1997 Super Bowl.
NHL Hockey— 1997, '98 and '99 All-Star Games and selected regular season and Stanley Cup Playoff games.
Major League Baseball— 1996, 1998 and 2000 World Series, 1997 and '99 All-Star Games as well as selected playoff and regular season games through 2000.

NBC

Major League Baseball— selected playoff games through the year 2000.
NBA Basketball— regular season and playoffs, NBA finals and All-Star Games through the 1997–98 season.
College Football— Notre Dame home games through 2000.
NFL Football— AFC regular season and playoffs through 1997 season; 1998 Super Bowl.
Golf— 1997 Ryder Cup; Players Championship and PGA Seniors Championship as well as selected PGA Tour events through 1998; U.S. Open, U.S. Women's Open and U.S. Senior Open through 1999.
Horse Racing— The Breeders' Cup through 2000.
Olympics— 1996 Summer Games in Atlanta; 2000 Summer Games in Sydney; 2002 Winter Games in Salt Lake City, 2004 Summer Games; 2006 Winter Games; 2008 Summer Games.
Tennis— 1997 French Open and Wimbledon through 1999.

Turner (TBS and TNT)

Auto Racing— 1997 Coca-Cola 600 and NASCAR circuit on TBS.
Major League Baseball— 1997 Atlanta Braves regular season on TBS.
NBA Basketball— 1996-97 regular season and playoffs on TBS and TNT; NBA Draft on TNT.
College Football— Carquest and Senior bowls for 1996 season on TBS.
NFL Football— Sunday Night Football (1st half of 1996 season) on TNT.
Golf— PGA Championship (early rounds, partial 3rd and 4th), Grand Slam of Golf, Senior Slam of Golf and Sarazen World Open on TBS.

Olympics TV Rights

On Dec. 12, 1995 the IOC announced that NBC had succesfully bid a record $2.3 billion for the exclusive U.S. television rights to the 2004 and 2008 Summer Games and the 2006 Winter Games.

Year	Games	Location	Rights Fee	Net	TV Hrs
1960	Winter	Squaw Valley	$ 50,000	CBS	15
	Summer	Rome	394,000	CBS	20
1964	Winter	Innsbruck	$597,000	ABC	17¼
	Summer	Tokyo	1.5 mil.	NBC	14
1968	Winter	Grenoble	$2.5 mil.	ABC	27
	Summer	Mexico City	4.5 mil.	ABC	43¼
1972	Winter	Sapporo	$6.4 mil.	NBC	37
	Summer	Munich	7.5 mil.	ABC	62¼
1976	Winter	Innsbruck	$10 mil.	ABC	43½
	Summer	Montreal	25 mil.	ABC	76½
1980	Winter	Lake Placid	$15.5 mil.	ABC	53¼
	Summer	Moscow	87 mil.	NBC	150*
1984	Winter	Sarajevo	$91.5 mil.	ABC	63
	Summer	Los Angeles	225 mil.	ABC	180
1988	Winter	Calgary	$309 mil.	ABC	94½
	Summer	Seoul	300 mil.	NBC	179½
1992	Winter	Albertville	$243 mil.	CBS	116
	Summer	Barcelona	401 mil.	NBC	161
1994	Winter	Lillehammer	$300 mil.	CBS	120
1996	Summer	Atlanta	456 mil.	NBC	168
1998	Winter	Nagano	$375 mil.	CBS	TBD
2000	Summer	Sydney	$715 mil.	NBC	TBD
2002	Winter	Salt Lake City	$555 mil.	NBC	TBD
2004	Summer	TBD	$793 mil.	NBC	TBD
2006	Winter	TBD	$613 mil.	NBC	TBD
2008	Summer	TBD	$894 mil.	NBC	TBD

*NBC planned 150 hours of coverage for the 1980 Summer Olympics, but since the U.S. boycotted the Games, NBC did not cover them and did not pay the rights fee.

What Major League Franchises Are Worth

The estimated total market value of the 111 major league baseball, basketball, football and hockey franchises operating in the U.S. and Canada in 1994–95. Figures according to *Financial World* magazine's fourth annual survey, released in their May 20, 1996 issue. Franchise values are estimates of what a team would have been worth if put up for sale in early 1996. Values are based on gate receipts, radio and TV revenues, stadium/arena income (luxury suites, concessions, parking, etc.), operating income, player salaries and other expenses. Figures are in millions of dollars.

Avg. franchise values: NFL ($174 million), **NBA** ($127 million), **Baseball** ($115 million) and **NHL** ($74 million).

BASEBALL

	Value 1995	1994
NY Yankees	$209	$185
Baltimore	168	164
Atlanta	163	120
Toronto	152	146
LA Dodgers	147	143
Chicago-AL	144	152
Boston	143	143
Chicago-NL	143	135
Texas	140	157
Colorado	138	117
NY Mets	133	134
Cleveland	125	103
San Francisco	122	102
St. Louis	112	110
Detroit	106	83
Philadelphia	103	96
Cincinnati	99	84
Florida	98	92
Houston	97	92
Oakland	97	101
Seattle	92	76
California	90	88
Kansas City	80	96
Minnesota	74	80
Milwaukee	71	75
Montreal	68	76
San Diego	67	74
Pittsburgh	62	70

NBA

	Value 1995	1994
New York	$205	$173
Phoenix	191	156
Detroit	186	180
Chicago	178	166
LA Lakers	171	169
Cleveland	151	133
Utah	142	127
Portland	137	132
Boston	134	127
Seattle	129	119
San Antonio	126	110
Orlando	121	101
Houston	116	95
Golden St	114	93
Sacramento	114	108
Charlotte	113	110
Washington	113	96
Minnesota	110	99
New Jersey	108	92
Milwaukee	103	92
Denver	102	88
Miami	97	88
Atlanta	96	84
Indiana	94	77
Philadelphia	93	81
Dallas	89	81
LA Clippers	88	87

NFL

	Value 1995	1994
Dallas	$272	$238
Miami	214	186
Baltimore	201	163
San Francisco	196	186
St. Louis	193	153
Philadelphia	192	182
Buffalo	188	172
Kansas City	188	172
New Orleans	184	171
Washington	184	151
Chicago	184	161
NY Giants	183	168
Cincinnati	171	137
San Diego	169	153
Minnesota	167	154
Atlanta	167	156
Green Bay	166	154
Arizona	166	155
New England	165	151
Denver	164	150
Tampa Bay	164	151
Oakland	162	145
Houston	159	158
Seattle	154	152
Pittsburgh	154	144
NY Jets	153	149
Detroit	150	141
Jacksonville	145	—
Indianapolis	145	134
Carolina	133	—

NHL

	Value 1995	1994
Detroit	$126	$124
Chicago	122	102
NY Rangers	118	108
Boston	111	106
Philadelphia	102	86
Anaheim	99	108
Toronto	96	90
Vancouver	91	87
Montreal	86	86
Los Angeles	78	81
San Jose	77	66
Pittsburgh	76	75
St. Louis	74	69
Washington	70	59
Buffalo	65	60
NY Islanders	60	53
New Jersey	58	54
Ottawa	56	56
Calgary	54	50
Dallas	53	50
Tampa Bay	48	55
Colorado	47	49
Florida	45	47
Edmonton	42	42
Hartford	40	43
Winnipeg*	34	35

*The Jets were moved to Arizona and renamed the Phoenix Coyotes in 1996.

Teams Bought in 1996

Nine major league clubs acquired new majority owners or significant minority owners from Nov. 1, 1995 through Sept. 30, 1996.

Major League Baseball

St. Louis Cardinals: A group headed by Cincinnati businessman William DeWitt Jr. and including the Pultizer Publishing Co. purchased the club along with Busch Stadium and several nearby parking garages from Anheuser-Busch Inc. for $150 million. Major League Baseball owners officially approved the deal on March 21, 1996. Anheuser-Busch, the world's largest brewery, sold the club to focus on its core businesses of beer, theme parks and aluminum cans. Anheuser-Busch bought the Cardinals in February 1953 from Fred Saigh for $2.5 million.

Pittsburgh Pirates: A group named Pittsburgh Pirates Acquisition Inc., headed by 33-year-old California newspaper heir Kevin McClatchy and including Pittsburgh native and IndyCar racing team owner Chip Ganassi paid approximately $85 million for the Pirates. McClatchy and his group, which included seven of the 10 former owners, bought the club from a group including Heinz, USX, Westinghouse, Mellon Bank, PNC Bank Corp., Alcoa, PPG Industries Inc., Carnegie Mellon University and three private investors. The only owners that chose not to remain on board were PPG, Alcoa and Harvey Walken, a Chicago real estate developer. The long-awaited deal was unanimously approved by the baseball owners on Feb. 13, 1996. The former ownership purchased the Pirates from John W. Galbreath family in 1985.

NBA Basketball

Dallas Mavericks: A group of investors headed by land developer Ross Perot Jr., son of the Texas billionaire and former presidential candidate, and car dealer David McDavid purchased 67 percent of the Mavericks from owner Donald Carter for a reported $125 million on May 1, 1996. Carter and some limited partners retained 33 percent of the club. Carter was awarded the club as an expansion franchise in 1980 for $12 million.

Philadelphia 76ers: A partnership named Comcast Sports Ventures LP that includes Comcast Corp., the nation's fourth-largest cable TV company, Spectacor (owned by Philadelphia Flyers founder Ed Snider) and former 76ers conditioning coach Pat Croce purchased the 76ers from owner Harold Katz for an estimated $125 million on Mar. 19, 1996. The 76ers purchase is part of a larger deal, worth an estimated $500 million to buy the 76ers, the NHL's Philadelphia Flyers and two Philadelphia sports arenas, the CoreStates Spectrum and the new CoreStates Center. Comcast will own 66 percent of the venture, Spectacor will own 32 percent and Croce, two percent. Katz purchased the team from Fitz Dixon in July 1981.

Teams Bought in 1996 (Cont.)

NHL Hockey

Dallas Stars: North Texas investor Thomas Hicks purchased the Stars from owner Norman Green for $84 million. The NHL officially approved the sale on Jan. 19, 1996. Green, formerly part-owner of the Calgary Flames, acquired sole ownership of the then Minnesota North Stars in 1990 for approximately $36 million, moved the franchise to Dallas from Minneapolis in 1993 and renamed them the Dallas Stars.

Philadelphia Flyers: A partnership named Comcast Sports Ventures LP that includes Comcast Corp., the nation's fourth-largest cable TV company, Spectacor (owned by Philadelphia Flyers founder Ed Snider) and former Philadelphia 76ers conditioning coach Pat Croce purchased the Flyers from owner Spectacor for an estimated $85 million on Mar. 19, 1996. The Flyers purchase is part of a larger deal, worth an estimated $500 million to buy the Flyers, the NBA's Philadelphia 76ers and two Philadelphia sports arenas, the CoreStates Spectrum and the new CoreStates Center. Comcast will own 66 percent of the venture, Spectacor will own 32 percent and Croce, two percent.

Winnipeg Jets: Businessmen Steven Gluckstern and Richard Burke purchased the club from an ownership group headed by Barry Shenkarow for $68 million on July 1, 1996. The team was moved to Phoenix, Arizona and renamed the Phoenix Coyotes on July 1. Shenkarow's group brought the Jets to the NHL in 1979 after seven seasons in the World Hockey Association.

The 1995 *Forbes* Top 40

The 40 highest-paid athletes of 1995 (including salary, winnings, endorsements, etc.), according to the Dec. 18, 1995 issue of *Forbes* magazine. Nationality, birth date, and each athlete's rank on the 1994 list are also given. Age refers to athlete's age as of Dec. 31, 1995.

	Sport	Salary/ Winnings	Other Income	Total	Nat	Birthdate	Age	1994 Rank
1 Michael Jordan	Basketball	$3.9	$40.0	**$43.9**	USA	Feb. 17, 1963	32	1
2 Mike Tyson	Boxing	40.0	0.0	**40.0**	USA	June 33, 1966	29	NR
3 Deion Sanders	Football/Baseball	16.5*	6.0	**22.5**	USA	Aug. 9, 1967	28	38
4 Riddick Bowe	Boxing	22.0	0.2	**22.2**	USA	Aug. 10, 1967	28	NR
5 Shaquille O'Neal	Basketball	4.9	17.0	**21.9**	USA	Mar. 6, 1972	23	2
6 George Foreman	Boxing	10.0	8.0	**18.0**	USA	Jan 10, 1949	46	15
7 Andre Agassi	Tennis	3.0	13.0	**16.0**	USA	Apr. 29, 1970	25	9
8 Jack Nicklaus	Golf	0.6	14.5	**15.1**	USA	Jan. 20, 1940	55	3
9 Michael Schumacher	Auto Racing	10.0	5.0	**15.0**	GBR	Jan. 3, 1969	26	30
10 Wayne Gretzky	Hockey	8.5	6.0	**14.5**	CAN	Jan. 26, 1961	34	6
11 Arnold Palmer	Golf	0.1	14.0	**14.1**	USA	Sept. 10, 1929	66	4
12 Drew Bledsoe	Football	13.2*	0.7	**13.9**	USA	Feb. 14, 1972	23	NR
13 Gerhard Berger	Auto Racing	12.0	1.5	**13.5**	AUT	Aug. 27, 1959	36	5
14 Evander Holyfield	Boxing	11.0	2.0	**13.0**	USA	Oct. 19, 1962	33	8
15 Pete Sampras	Tennis	4.7	6.5	**11.2**	USA	Aug. 12, 1971	24	11
16 Cal Ripken Jr.	Baseball	6.3	4.0	**10.3**	USA	Aug. 24, 1960	35	NR
17 Greg Norman	Golf	1.7	8.0	**9.7**	AUS	Feb. 10, 1955	40	14
18 David Robinson	Basketball	7.9	1.7	**9.6**	USA	Aug. 6, 1965	30	17
19 Patrick Ewing	Basketball	7.5	2.0	**9.5**	USA	Aug. 5, 1962	33	29
20 Dale Earnhardt	Auto Racing	2.4	6.0	**8.4**	USA	Apr. 29, 1952	43	34
21 Ki-Jana Carter	Football	7.9*	0.5	**8.4**	USA	Sept. 12, 1973	22	NR
22 Jean Alesi	Auto Racing	7.0	1.0	**8.0**	FRA	June 11, 1964	31	20
23 Ken Griffey Jr.	Baseball	6.2	1.7	**7.9**	USA	Nov. 21, 1969	26	NR
24 Grant Hill	Basketall	2.8	5.0	**7.8**	USA	Oct. 5, 1972	23	NR
25 Frank Thomas	Baseball	6.3	1.5	**7.8**	USA	Mar. 27, 1968	27	NR
26 Boris Becker	Tennis	3.3	4.5	**7.8**	GER	Nov. 22, 1967	28	22
27 Hakeem Olajuwon	Basketall	5.8	2.0	**7.8**	NGR	Jan. 21, 1963	32	NR
28 Michael Chang	Tennis	2.6	5.0	**7.6**	USA	Feb. 22, 1972	23	31
29 Barry Bonds	Baseball	6.8	0.7	**7.5**	USA	July 24, 1964	31	NR
30 Steffi Graf	Tennis	2.5	5.0	**7.5**	GER	June 14, 1969	26	19
31 Greg Maddux	Baseball	6.8	0.4	**7.2**	USA	Apr. 14, 1966	29	NR
32 Charles Barkley	Basketball	4.1	3.0	**7.1**	USA	Feb. 20, 1963	32	13
33 Pernell Whitaker	Boxing	7.0	0.0	**7.0**	USA	Jan. 2, 1964	31	NR
34 Mark Messier	Hockey	6.0	1.0	**7.0**	CAN	Jan. 18, 1961	34	NR
35 Steve Young	Football	4.0	3.0	**7.0**	USA	Oct. 11, 1961	34	NR
36 Joe Carter	Baseball	6.5	0.5	**7.0**	USA	Mar. 10, 1960	35	NR
37 Jerry Rice	Football	6.0	1.0	**7.0**	USA	Oct. 13, 1962	33	NR
38 Michael Irvin	Football	6.2*	0.7	**6.9**	USA	Mar. 5, 1966	29	NR
39 Cecil Fielder	Baseball	6.4	0.3	**6.7**	USA	Sept. 21, 1963	32	NR
40 Dan Marino	Football	4.5	1.7	**6.2**	USA	Sept. 15, 1961	34	NR

* Includes signing bonus

AWARDS

The Peabody Award

Presented annually since 1940 for outstanding achievement in radio and television broadcasting. Only 13 Peabodys have been given for sports programming. Named after Georgia banker and philanthropist George Foster Peabody, the awards are administered by the Henry W. Grady College of Journalism and Mass Communication at the University of Georgia.

Television

Year
1960 **CBS** for coverage of 1960 Winter and Summer Olympic Games
1966 ABC's **"Wide World of Sports"** (for Outstanding Achievement in Promotion of International Understanding).
1968 **ABC Sports** coverage of both the 1968 Winter and Summer Olympic Games.
1972 **ABC Sports** coverage of the 1972 Summer Olympics in Munich.
1973 **Joe Garagiola** of NBC Sports (for "The Baseball World of Joe Garagiola").
1976 **ABC Sports** coverage of both the 1976 Winter and Summer Olympic Games.
1984 **Roone Arledge**, president of ABC News & Sports (for significant contributions to news and sports programming).
1986 **WFAA-TV**, Dallas for its investigation of the Southern Methodist University football program.
1988 **Jim McKay** of ABC Sports (for pioneering efforts and career accomplishments in the world of TV sports).
1991 **CBS Sports** coverage of the 1991 Masters golf tournament
& **HBO Sports** and Black Canyon Productions for the baseball special "When It Was A Game."
1995 **Kartemquin Educational Films** and **KTCA-TV** in St.Paul, MN, presented on PBS for "Hoop Dreams" & Turner Original Productions for the baseball special "Hank Aaron: Chasing the Dream."

Radio

Year
1974 **WSB** radio in Atlanta for "Henry Aaron: A Man with a Mission."
1991 **Red Barber** of National Public Radio (for his six decades as a broadcaster and his 10 years as a commentator on NPR's "Morning Edition").

National Emmy Awards
Sports Programming

Presented by the Academy of Television Arts and Sciences since 1948. Eligibility period covered the calendar year from 1948-57 and since 1988.

Multiple major award winners: ABC "Wide World of Sports" (19); ABC Olympics coverage (9); NFL Films Football coverage (8); ABC "Monday Night Football and CBS NFL Football coverage (6); CBS NCAA Basketball coverage and CBS "NFL Today" (5); ESPN "Outside the Lines" series (4); ABC "The American Sportsman," ABC Indianapolis 500 coverage, ESPN "GameDay," ESPN "SportsCenter" and NBC Olympics coverage (3); ABC Kentucky Derby coverage, ABC "Sportsbeat," Bud Greenspan Olympic specials, CBS Olympics coverage, CBS Golf coverage, MTV Sports series and NBC World Series coverage (2).

1949

Coverage—"Wrestling" (KTLA, Los Angeles)

1950

Program—"Rams Football" (KNBH-TV, Los Angeles)

1954

Program—"Gillette Cavalcade of Sports" (NBC)

1965-66

Programs—"Wide World of Sports" (ABC), "Shell's Wonderful World of Golf" (NBC) and "CBS Golf Classic" (CBS)

1966-67

Program—"Wide World of Sports" (ABC)

1967-68

Program—"Wide World of Sports" (ABC)

1968-69

Program—"1968 Summer Olympics" (ABC)

1969-70

Programs—"NFL Football" (CBS) and "Wide World of Sports" (ABC)

1970-71

Program—"Wide World of Sports" (ABC)

1971-72

Program—"Wide World of Sports" (ABC)

1972-73

News Special—"Coverage of Munich Olympic Tragedy" (ABC)
Sports Programs—"1972 Summer Olympics" (ABC) and "Wide World of Sports" (ABC)

1973-74

Program—"Wide World of Sports" (ABC)

1974-75

Non-Edited Program—"Jimmy Connors vs. Rod Laver Tennis Challenge" (CBS)
Edited Program—"Wide World of Sports" (ABC)

1975-76

Live Special—"1975 World Series: Cincinnati vs. Boston" (NBC)
Live Series—"NFL Monday Night Football" (ABC)
Edited Specials—"1976 Winter Olympics" (ABC)
and "Triumph and Tragedy: The Olympic Experience" (ABC)
Edited Series—"Wide World of Sports" (ABC)

1976-77

Live Special—"1976 Summer Olympics" (ABC)
Live Series—"The NFL Today/NFL Football" (CBS)
Edited Special—"1976 Summer Olympics Preview" (ABC)
Edited Series—"The Olympiad" (PBS)

1977-78

Live Special—"Muhammad Ali vs. Leon Spinks Heavyweight Championship Fight" (CBS)
Live Series—"The NFL Today/NFL Football" (CBS)
Edited Special—"The Impossible Dream: Ballooning Across the Atlantic" (CBS)
Edited Series—"The Way It Was" (PBS)

National Emmy Awards (Cont.)
Sports Programming

1978-79

Live Special—"Super Bowl XIII: Pittsburgh vs Dallas" (NBC)
Live Series—"NFL Monday Night Football" (ABC)
Edited Special—"Spirit of '78: The Flight of Double Eagle II" (ABC)
Edited Series—"The American Sportsman" (ABC)

1979-80

Live Special—"1980 Winter Olympics" (ABC)
Live Series—"NCAA College Football" (ABC)
Edited Special—"Gossamer Albatross: Flight of Imagination" (CBS)
Edited Series—"NFL Game of the Week" (NFL Films)

1980-81

Live Special—"1981 Kentucky Derby" (ABC)
Live Series—"PGA Golf Tour" (CBS)
Edited Special—"Wide World of Sports 20th Anniversary Show" (ABC)
Edited Series—"The American Sportsman" (ABC)

1981-82

Live Special—"1982 NCAA Basketball Final: North Carolina vs. Georgetown" (CBS)
Live Series—"NFL Football" (CBS)
Edited Special—"1982 Indianapolis 500" (ABC)
Edited Series—"Wide World of Sports" (ABC)

1982-83

Live Special—"1982 World Series: St. Louis vs Milwaukee" (NBC)
Live Series—"NFL Football" (CBS)
Edited Special—"Wimbledon '83" (NBC)
Edited Series—"Wide World of Sports" (ABC)
Journalism—"ABC Sportsbeat" (ABC)

1983-84

No awards given

1984-85

Live Special—"1984 Summer Olympics" (ABC)
Live Series—No award given
Edited Special—"Road to the Super Bowl '85" (NFL Films)
Edited Series—"The American Sportsman" (ABC)
Journalism—"ABC Sportsbeat" (ABC), "CBS Sports Sunday" (CBS), Dick Schaap features (ABC) and 1984 Summer Olympic features (ABC)

1985-86

No awards given

1986-87

Live Special—"1987 Daytona 500" (CBS)
Live Series—"NFL Football" (CBS)
Edited Special—"Wide World of Sports 25th Anniversary Special" (ABC)
Edited Series—"Wide World of Sports" (ABC)

1987-88

Live Special—"1987 Kentucky Derby" (ABC)
Live Series—"NFL Monday Night Football" (ABC)
Edited Special—"Paris-Roubaix Bike Race" (CBS)
Edited Series—"Wide World of Sports" (ABC)

1988

Live Special— "1988 Summer Olympics" (NBC)
Live Series—"1988 NCAA Basketball" (CBS)
Edited Special—"Road to the Super Bowl '88" (NFL Films)
Edited Series—"Wide World of Sports" (ABC)
Studio Show—"NFL GameDay" (ESPN)
Journalism—1988 Summer Olympic reporting (NBC)

1989

Live Special—"1989 Indianapolis 500" (ABC)
Live Series—"NFL Monday Night Football" (ABC)
Edited Special—"Trans-Antarctica! The International Expedition" (ABC)
Edited Series—"This is the NFL" (NFL Films)
Studio Show—"NFL Today" (CBS)
Journalism—1989 World Series Game 3 earthquake coverage (ABC)

1990

Live Special—"1990 Indianapolis 500" (ABC)
Live Series—"1990 NCAA Basketball Tournament" (CBS)
Edited Special—"Road to Super Bowl XXIV" (NFL Films)
Edited Series—"Wide World of Sports" (ABC)
Studio Show—"SportsCenter" (ESPN)
Journalism—"Outside the Lines: The Autograph Game" (ESPN)

1991

Live Special—"1991 NBA Finals: Chicago vs LA Lakers" (NBC)
Live Series—"1991 NCAA Basketball Tournament" (CBS)
Edited Special—"Wide World of Sports 30th Anniversary Special" (ABC)
Edited Series—"This is the NFL" (NFL Films)
Studio Show—"NFL GameDay" (ESPN) and "NFL Live" (NBC)
Journalism—"Outside the Lines: Steroids—Whatever It Takes" (ESPN)

1992

Live Special—"1992 Breeders' Cup" (NBC)
Live Series—"1992 NCAA Basketball Tournament" (CBS)
Edited Special—"1992 Summer Olympics" (NBC)
Edited Series—"MTV Sports" (MTV)
Studio Show—"The NFL Today" (CBS)
Journalism—"Outside the Lines: Portraits in Black and White" (ESPN)

1993

Live Special—"1993 World Series" (CBS)
Live Series—"Monday Night Football" (ABC)
Edited Special—"Road to the Super Bowl" (NFL Films)
Edited Series—"This is the NFL" (NFL Films)
Studio Show—"The NFL Today" (CBS)
Journalism (TIE)—"Outside the Lines: Mitch Ivey Feature" (ESPN) and "SportsCenter: University of Houston Football" (ESPN).
Feature—"Arthur Ashe: His Life, His Legacy" (NBC).

"Baseball" Wins Prime Time Emmy

Ken Burns's miniseries "Baseball" won the 1994 Emmy Award for Outstanding Informational Series. The nine-part documentary aired from Sept. 18–28, 1994 and ran more than 18 hours, drawing the largest audience in PBS history.

Sports Programming (Cont.)

1994

Live Special— "NHL Stanley Cup Finals" (ESPN)
Live Series— "Monday Night Football" (ABC)
Edited Special— "Lillehammer '94: 16 Days of Glory" (Disney/Cappy Productions)
Edited Series— "MTV Sports" (MTV)
Studio Show— "NFL GameDay" (ESPN)
Journalism— "1994 Winter Olympic Games: Mossad feature" (CBS)
Feature (TIE)— "Heroes of Telemark" on Winter Olympic Games (CBS); and "SportsCenter: Vanderbilt running back Brad Gaines" (ESPN).

1995

Live Special— "Cal Ripken 2131" (ESPN)
Live Series— "ESPN Speedworld" (ESPN)
Edited Special (quick turn-around)— "Outside the Lines: Playball— Opening Day in America" (ESPN)
Edited Special (long turn-around)— "Lillehammer, and Olympic Diary" (CBS)
Edited Series— "NFL Films Presents" (NFL Films)
Studio Show (TIE)— "NFL GameDay" (ESPN) and "Fox NFL Sunday" (Fox)
Journalism— "Real Sports with Bryant Gumbel: Broken Promises" (HBO)
Feature (TIE)— "SportsCenter: Jerry Quarry" (ESPN) and "Real Sports with Bryant Gumbel: Coach" (HBO)

Sportscasters of the Year

National Emmy Awards

An Emmy Award for Sportscasters was first introduced in 1968 and given for Outstanding Host/Commentator for the 1967-68 TV season. Two awards, one for Outstanding Host or Play-by-Play and the other for Outstanding Analyst, were first presented in 1981 for the 1980-81 season. Three awards, for Outstanding Studio Host, Play-by-Play and Analyst, have been given since the 1993 season

Multiple winners: John Madden (11); Jim McKay (9); Bob Costas (7); Dick Enberg (4); Al Michaels (3). Note that Jim McKay has won a total of 12 Emmy awards: eight for Host/Commentator, one for Host/Play-by-Play, two for Sports Writing, and one for News Commentary.

Season	Host/Commentator	Season	Host/Play-by-Play	Season	Analyst
1967-68	Jim McKay, ABC	1980-81	Dick Enberg, NBC	1980-81	Dick Button, ABC
1968-69	No award	1981-82	Jim McKay, ABC	1981-82	John Madden, CBS
1969-70	No award	1982-83	Dick Enberg, NBC	1982-83	John Madden, CBS
1970-71	Jim McKay, ABC & Don Meredith, ABC	1983-84	No award	1983-84	No award
		1984-85	George Michael, NBC	1984-85	No award
1971-72	No award	1985-86	No award	1985-86	No award
1972-73	Jim McKay, ABC	1986-87	Al Michaels, ABC	1986-87	John Madden, CBS
1973-74	Jim McKay, ABC	1987-88	Bob Costas, NBC	1987-88	John Madden, CBS
1974-75	Jim McKay, ABC	1988	Bob Costas, NBC	1988	John Madden, CBS
1975-76	Jim McKay, ABC	1989	Al Michaels, ABC	1989	John Madden, CBS
1976-77	Frank Gifford, ABC	1990	Dick Enberg, NBC	1990	John Madden, CBS
1977-78	Jack Whitaker, CBS	1991	Bob Costas, NBC	1991	John Madden, CBS
1978-79	Jim McKay, ABC	1992	Bob Costas, NBC	1992	John Madden, CBS
1979-80	Jim McKay, ABC				
Year	**Studio Host**	**Year**	**Play-by-Play**	**Year**	**Analyst**
1993	Bob Costas, NBC	1993	Dick Enberg, NBC	1993	Billy Packer, CBS
1994	Bob Costas, NBC	1994	Keith Jackson, ABC	1994	John Madden, Fox
1995	Bob Costas, NBC	1995	Al Michaels, ABC	1995	John Madden, Fox

Life Achievement Emmy Award

For outstanding work as an exemplary television sportscaster over many years.

Year	Year	Year	Year
1989 Jim McKay	1991 Curt Gowdy	1993 Pat Summerall	1995 Vin Scully
1990 Lindsey Nelson	1992 Chris Schenkel	1994 Howard Cosell	

National Sportscasters and Sportswriters Assn. Award

Sportscaster of the Year presented annually since 1959 by the National Sportcasters and Sportswriters Association, based in Salisbury, N.C. Voting is done by NSSA members and selected national media.

Multiple winners: Bob Costas (6); Keith Jackson (5); Chris Berman, Lindsey Nelson and Chris Schenkel (4); Dick Enberg, Al Michaels and Vin Scully (3); Curt Gowdy and Ray Scott (2).

Year	Year	Year	Year
1959 Lindsey Nelson	1969 Curt Gowdy	1979 Dick Enberg	1988 Bob Costas
1960 Lindsey Nelson	1970 Chris Schenkel	1980 Dick Enberg & Al Michaels	1989 Chris Berman
1961 Lindsey Nelson	1971 Ray Scott	1981 Dick Enberg	1990 Chris Berman
1962 Lindsey Nelson	1972 Keith Jackson	1982 Vin Scully	1991 Bob Costas
1963 Chris Schenkel	1973 Keith Jackson	1983 Al Michaels	1992 Bob Costas
1964 Chris Schenkel	1974 Keith Jackson	1984 John Madden	1993 Chris Berman
1965 Vin Scully	1975 Keith Jackson	1985 Bob Costas	1994 Chris Berman
1966 Curt Gowdy	1976 Keith Jackson	1986 Al Michaels	1995 Bob Costas
1967 Chris Schenkel	1977 Pat Summerall	1987 Bob Costas	
1968 Ray Scott	1978 Vin Scully		

American Sportscasters Association Award

Sportscaster of the Year presented annually from 1984-94, with the exception of 1988, by the New York-based American Sportscasters Association. Two awards presented starting in 1995 to honor top play-by-play personality and studio host. Voting done by ASA members and officials. All four-time winners become ineligible for additional awards.

Multiple winners: Bob Costas and Dick Enberg (4).

Sportscaster of the Year

Year		Year	
1984	Dick Enberg	1990	Dick Enberg
1985	Vin Scully	1991	Bob Costas
1986	Dick Enberg	1992	Bob Costas
1987	Dick Enberg	1993	Bob Costas
1988	No award	1994	Pat Summerall
1989	Bob Costas		

Play-by-Play

Year	
1995	Al Michaels

Studio Host

Year	
1995	Chris Berman

The Pulitzer Prize

The Pulitzer Prizes for journalism, letters and music have been presented annually since 1917 in the name of Joseph Pulitzer (1847-1911), the publisher of the *New York World*. Prizes are awarded by the president of Columbia University on the recommendation of a board of review. Fourteen Pulitzers have been awarded for newspaper sports reporting, sports commentary and sports photography.

News Coverage

1935 **Bill Taylor,** *NY Herald Tribune,* for his reporting on the 1934 America's Cup yacht races.

Special Citation

1952 **Max Kase,** *NY Journal-American,* for his reporting on the 1951 college basketball point-shaving scandal.

Meritorious Public Service

1954 ***Newsday*** (Garden City, N.Y.) for its exposé of New York State's race track scandals and labor racketeering.

General Reporting

1956 **Arthur Daley,** *NY Times,* for his 1955 columns.

Investigative Reporting

1981 **Clark Hallas** & **Robert Lowe,** (Tucson) *Arizona Daily Star,* for their 1980 investigation of the University of Arizona athletic department.

1986 **Jeffrey Marx** & **Michael York,** *Lexington* (Ky.) *Herald-Leader,* for their 1985 investigation of the basketball program at the University of Kentucky and other major colleges.

Specialized Reporting

1985 **Randall Savage** & **Jackie Crosby,** *Macon* (Ga.) *Telegraph and News,* for their 1984 investigation of athletics and academics at the University of Georgia and Georgia Tech.

Commentary

1976 **Red Smith,** *NY Times,* for his 1975 columns.

1981 **Dave Anderson,** *NY Times,* for his 1980 columns.

1990 **Jim Murray,** *LA Times,* for his 1989 columns.

Photography

1949 **Nat Fein,** *NY Herald Tribune,* for his photo, "Babe Ruth Bows Out."

1952 **John Robinson** & **Don Ultang,** *Des Moines* (Iowa) *Register and Tribune,* for their sequence of six pictures of the 1951 Drake-Oklahoma A&M football game, in which Drake's Johnny Bright had his jaw broken.

1985 **The Photography Staff** of the *Orange County* (Calif.) *Register,* for their coverage of the 1984 Summer Olympics in Los Angeles.

1993 **William Snyder** & **Ken Geiger,** *The Dallas Morning News,* for their coverage of the 1992 Summer Olympics in Barcelona, Spain.

Sportswriter of the Year
NSSA Award

Presented annually since 1959 by the National Sportscasters and Sportswriters Association, based in Salisbury, N.C. Voting is done by NSSA members and selected national media.

Multiple winners: Jim Murray (14); Frank Deford (6); Red Smith (5); Will Grimsley and Rick Reilly (4); Peter Gammons (3).

Year		Year		Year	
1959	Red Smith, NY *Herald-Tribune*	1972	Jim Murray, *LA Times*	1985	Frank Deford, *Sports Ill.*
1960	Red Smith, NY *Herald-Tribune*	1973	Jim Murray, *LA Times*	1986	Frank Deford, *Sports Ill.*
1961	Red Smith, NY *Herald-Tribune*	1974	Jim Murray, *LA Times*	1987	Frank Deford, *Sports Ill.*
1962	Red Smith, NY *Herald-Tribune*	1975	Jim Murray, *LA Times*	1988	Frank Deford, *Sports Ill.*
1963	Arthur Daley, *NY Times*	1976	Jim Murray, *LA Times*	1989	Peter Gammons, *Sports Ill.*
1964	Jim Murray, *LA Times*	1977	Jim Murray, *LA Times*	1990	Peter Gammons, *Boston Globe*
1965	Red Smith, NY *Herald-Tribune*	1978	Will Grimsley, AP	1991	Rick Reilly, *Sports Ill.*
1966	Jim Murray, *LA Times*	1979	Jim Murray, *LA Times*	1992	Rick Reilly, *Sports Ill.*
1967	Jim Murray, *LA Times*	1980	Will Grimsley, AP	1993	Peter Gammons, *Boston Globe*
1968	Jim Murray, *LA Times*	1981	Will Grimsley, AP	1994	Rick Reilly, *Sports Ill.*
1969	Jim Murray, *LA Times*	1982	Frank Deford, *Sports Ill.*	1995	Rick Reilly, *Sports Ill.*
1970	Jim Murray, *LA Times*	1983	Will Grimsley, AP		
1971	Jim Murray, *LA Times*	1984	Frank Deford, *Sports Ill.*		

Best Newspaper Sports Sections of 1995

Winners of the Annual Associated Press Sports Editors contest for best daily and Sunday sports sections. Awards are divided into three different categories, based on circulation figures. Selections are made by a committee of APSE members.

Circulation Over 175,000

Top 10 Daily

Atlanta Journal and Constitution
Boston Globe
Chicago Tribune
Dallas Morning News
Miami Herald
Newsday
New York Times
Philadelphia Daily News
USA Today
Washington Post

Top 10 Sunday

Atlanta Journal and Constitution
Boston Globe
Chicago Tribune
Dallas Morning News
Sun-Sentinel (Ft. Lauderdale, Fla.)
Houston Chronicle
Miami Herald
Newsday
New York Times
Palm Beach Post

Circulation 50,000-175,000

Top 10 Daily

Akron Beacon Journal
Daily Herald (Arlington Hgts., Ill.)
Asbury Park Press
The State (Columbia, S.C.)
Contra Costa Times (Walnut Creek, Calif.)
The Herald (Everett, Wash.)
The Record (Hackensack, N.J.)
The Post-Standard (Syracuse, N.Y.)
The News Tribune (Tacoma, Wash.)
Washington Times

Top 10 Sunday

Akron Beacon Journal
Asbury Park Press
Gazette Telegraph (Colorado Springs, Colo.)
The State (Columbia, S.C.)
Florida Today
Lexington (Ky.) *Herald-Leader*
The Record (Hackensack, N.J.)
San Francisco Examiner
The News Tribune (Tacoma, Wash.)
Tallahassee Democrat

Circulation Under 50,000

Top 10 Daily

Albuquerque Tribune
Journal American (Bellevue, Wash.)
The Sun Herald (Biloxi, Miss.)
Times-News (Burlington, N.C.)
Centre Daily Times (State College, Pa.)
Gaston (N.C.) *Gazette*
Journal and Courier (Lafayette, Ind.)
The Daily Times-Call (Longmont, Colo.)
Marin Independent Journal (Novata, Calif.)
Blade-Citizen (Oceanside, Calif.)

Top 10 Sunday

Beaver County (Pa.) *Times*
The Sun Herald (Biloxi, Miss.)
Casper (Wyo.) *Star-Tribune*
The Post-Star (Glens Falls, N.Y.)
Jackson (Tenn.) *Sun*
Journal and Courier (Lafayette, Ind.)
The Daily Times-Call (Longmont, Colo.)
Marin Independent Journal (Novata, Calif.)
The Times Leader (Wilkes-Barre, Pa.)
York (Pa.) *Sunday News*

Best Sportswriting of 1995

Winners of the Annual Associated Press Sports Editors contest for best sportswriting in 1995. Eventual winners were chosen from five finalists in each writing division. Selections are made by a committee of APSE members. Note the investigative writing division included all three circulation categories.

Circulation over 175,000

Column: Gary Shelton, *St. Petersburg* (Fla.) *Times*
Enterprise: Robin Romano and Larry Tye, *Boston Globe*
Feature: Mike Klingaman, *Baltimore Sun*
Game story: Larry Dorman, *New York Times*
News story: Elliott Almond and Bill Plaschke, *Los Angeles Times*

Circulation 50,000-175,000

Column: Terry Pluto, *Akron Beacon Journal*
Enterprise: Andy Boogaard, *Fresno Bee*
Feature: Adrian Wojnarowski, *Fresno Bee*
Game story: Brian Murphy, *The Press Democrat* (Santa Rosa, Calif.)
News story: Joe Weinert, *The Press of Atlantic City* (Pleasantville, N.Y.)

Circulation under 50,000

Column: Peter St. Onge, *Anniston* (Ala.) *Star*
Enterprise: Josh Peter, *Anderson* (S.C.) *Independent-Mail*
Feature: Peter St. Onge
Game story: Bob Hammel, *The Herald Times* (Bloomington, Ind.)
News story: Dan Morris, *The Jackson* (Tenn.) *Sun*

All Categories

Investigative: Dave Hyde and Randy Mell, *Sun-Sentinel* (Ft. Lauderdale, Fla.)

Directory of Organizations

Listing of the major sports organizations, teams and media addresses and officials as of Sept. 30, 1996.

AUTO RACING

IndyCar
(Championship Auto Racing Teams, Inc.)
755 W. Big Beaver Rd., Suite 800, Troy, MI 48084
(810) 362-8800
President-CEO .... Andrew Craig
Director of Publicity .... Adam Saal

Indy Racing League
4790 West 16th St., Indianapolis, ID 46222
(317) 484-6526
Exec. Director & CEO .... Jack Long
Commissioner .... Tom Binford
Director of Public Relations .... Bob Walters

FISA— Formula One
(Federation Internationale de Sport Automobile)
8 Bis Rue Boissy D'anglas 75008 Paris, France
TEL: 011-33-1-4312-4455
President .... Max Mosley
Secretary General .... Pierre de Coninck
Director of Public Relations .... Francesco Longanesi

NASCAR
(National Assn. of Stock Car Auto Racing)
P.O. Box 2875, Daytona Beach, FL 32120
(904) 253-0611
President .... Bill France Jr.
Director of Public Relations .... Andy Hall

NHRA
(National Hot Rod Association)
2035 Financial Way, Glendora, CA 91741
(818) 914-4761
President .... Dallas Gardner
Director of Communications .... Jim Trace

MAJOR LEAGUE BASEBALL

Office of the Commissioner
350 Park Ave., New York, NY 10022
(212) 339-7800
Commissioner .... vacant
(Fay Vincent resigned Sept. 7, 1992)
Chairman, Executive Council .... Bud Selig
General Counsel .... Thomas Ostertag
Executive Dir. of Public Relatons .... Rich Levin

Player Relations Committee
350 Park Ave., New York, NY 10022
(212) 339-7400
President & COO .... Randy Levine
Associate Counsels .... John Westhoff & Louis Melendez

Major League Baseball Players Association
12 East 49th St., 24th Floor, New York, NY 10017
(212) 826-0808
Exec. Director & General Counsel .... Donald Fehr
Special Assistant .... Mark Belanger

AL

American League Office
350 Park Ave., New York, NY 10022
(212) 339-7600
President .... Gene Budig
V.P., Admin. & Media Affairs .... Phyllis Merhige

Baltimore Orioles
333 West Camden St., Baltimore, MD 21201
(410) 685-9800
CEO .... Peter Angelos
Vice Chairman, Business & Finance .... Joseph Foss
General Manager .... Pat Gillick
Director of Public Relations .... John Maroon

Boston Red Sox
Fenway Park, 4 Yawkey Way, Boston, MA 02215
(617) 267-9440
General Partner .... Jean R. Yawkey Trust
President-CEO .... John Harrington
Exec. V.P. & General Manager .... Dan Duquette
V.P., Public Relations .... Dick Bresciani

California Angels
P. O. Box 2000, Anaheim, CA 92803
(714) 937-7200
Chairman .... Gene Autry
Minority Owner .... Walt Disney Co.
President & CEO .... Richard Brown
V.P. & General Manager .... Bill Bavasi
Ast. V.P., Media Relations .... John Sevano

Chicago White Sox
Comiskey Park, 333 W. 35th St., Chicago, IL 60616
(312) 924-1000
Chairman .... Jerry Reinsdorf
Vice Chairman .... Eddie Einhorn
Senior V.P. & General Manager .... Ron Schueler
Director of Public Relations .... Doug Abel

Cleveland Indians
Jacobs Field, 2401 Ontario St., Cleveland, OH 44115
(216) 420-4200
Owner-Chairman-CEO .... Richard Jacobs
Exec. V.P. & General Manager .... John Hart
V.P., Public Relations .... Bob DiBiasio

Detroit Tigers
Tiger Stadium, 2121 Trumbull Ave., Detroit, MI 48216
(313) 962-4000
Owner-Chairman .... Mike Ilitch
Owner-Secretary-Treasurer .... Marian Ilitch
President-CEO .... John McHale Jr.
General Manager-VP .... Randy Smith
Director, Public Relations .... Tyler Barnes

Kansas City Royals
P.O. Box 419969, Kansas City, MO 64141
(816) 921-2200
Owner .... Ewing Kauffman Irrevocable Trust
Chairman-CEO .... David Glass
Exec. V.P. & General Manager .... Herk Robinson
Director of Media Relations .... Steve Fink

Milwaukee Brewers
County Stadium, P.O. Box 3099, Milwaukee, WI 53201
(414) 933-4114
President-CEO .... Bud Selig
Senior V.P., Baseball Operations .... Sal Bando
V.P. & General Counsel .... Wendy Selig-Prieb
Director of Media Relations .... Jon Greenberg

Minnesota Twins
Hubert H. Humphrey Metrodome
501 Chicago Ave. South, Minneapolis, MN 55415
(612) 375-1366
Owner .... Carl Pohlad
President .... Jerry Bell
V.P. & General Manager .... Terry Ryan
Manager of Media Relations .... Sean Harlin

New York Yankees
Yankee Stadium, Bronx, NY 10451
(718) 293-4300
Principal Owner................................George Steinbrenner
General Partners................ Hal Steinbrenner & Joe Malloy
V.P. & General Manager.................................Bob Watson
Dir. of Media Relations/Publicity ....Rick Cerrone

Oakland Athletics
Oakland-Alameda County Coliseum
Oakland, CA 94621
(510) 638-4900
Co-Owners ....Steve Schott and Ken Hofmann
President & General Manager....................Sandy Alderson
Director of Baseball Information ....Jay Alves

Seattle Mariners
P.O. Box 4100, Seattle, WA 98104
(206) 628-3555
Chairman-CEO ....John Ellis
President-COO ....Chuck Armstrong
V.P., Baseball Operations ....Woody Woodward
Director of Public Relations ....Dave Aust

Texas Rangers
1000 Ballpark Way, Arlington, TX 76011
(817) 273-5222
General Partners ....Rusty Rose and Tom Schieffer
V.P., General Manager ....Doug Melvin
V.P., Public Relations...John Blake

Toronto Blue Jays
SkyDome, One Blue Jays Way, Suite 3200
Toronto, Ontario M5V 1J1
(416) 341-1000
Chairman..Sam Pollock
President-CEO..Paul Beeston
Exec. V.P. & General Manager ....Gord Ash
Director of Public Relations........................Howie Starkman

NL

National League Office
350 Park Ave., New York, NY 10022
(212) 339-7700
President & Treasurer ....Leonard Coleman
Exec. Dir. of Public Relations.........................Ricky Clemons

Atlanta Braves
P.O. Box 4064, Atlanta, GA 30302
(404) 522-7630
Owner ....Ted Turner
President...Stan Kasten
Exec. V.P. & General Manager...................John Schuerholz
Director of Public Relations ....Jim Schultz

Chicago Cubs
1060 West Addison St., Chicago, IL 60613
(312) 404-2827
Owner ....The Tribune Company
President-CEO ....Andy MacPhail
General Manager..Ed Lynch
Director of Media Relations ....Sharon Pannozzo

Cincinnati Reds
100 Cinergy Field, Cincinnati, OH 45202
(513) 421-4510
General Partner-President-CEO ....John Allen
General Manager ....Jim Bowden
Director of Publicity...................................Mike Ringering

Colorado Rockies
Coors Field, 2001 Blake St., Denver, CO 80205
(303) 292-0200
Chairman-President-CEO ....Jerry McMorris
Senior V.P. & General Manager ....Bob Gebhard
Director of Public Relations..........................Mike Swanson

Florida Marlins
2267 N.W. 199th St., Miami, FL 33056
(305) 626-7400
Owner ....Wayne Huizenga
Exec. V.P. & General Manager ....Dave Dombrowski
Director of Media Relations ....Ron Colangelo

Houston Astros
The Astrodome, P.O. Box 288, Houston, TX 77001
(713) 799-9500
Chairman-CEO ....Drayton McLane Jr.
President...Tal Smith
General Manager...................................Gerry Hunsicker
Director of Media Relations ....Rob Matwick

Los Angeles Dodgers
1000 Elysian Park Ave., Los Angeles, CA 90012
(213) 224-1500
President ....Peter O'Malley
Exec. V.P. & General Manager ....Fred Claire
Director of Publicity...Jay Lucas

Montreal Expos
P.O. Box 500, Station M, Montreal, Quebec H1V 3P2
(514) 253-3434
General Partner-President ....Claude Brochu
V.P., Baseball Operations..............................Bill Stoneman
Director of Media Relations ....Peter Loyello

New York Mets
123-01 Roosevelt Ave., Flushing, NY 11368
(718) 507-6387
Chairman ....Nelson Doubleday
President-CEO..Fred Wilpon
Exec. V.P., Baseball Operations ....Joe McIlvaine
Director of Media Relations ....Jay Horwitz

Philadelphia Phillies
P.O. Box 7575, Philadelphia, PA 19101
(215) 463-6000
Managing General Partner ....Bill Giles
Senior V.P. & General Manager ....Lee Thomas
Manager, Media Relations ....Gene Dias

Pittsburgh Pirates
P.O. Box 7000, Pittsburgh, PA 15212
(412) 323-5000
Owner..Kevin McClatchy
President...Mark Sauer
Senior V.P. & General Manager ....Cam Bonifay
Director of Media Relations ....Jim Trdinich

St. Louis Cardinals
250 Stadium Plaza, St. Louis, MO 63102
(314) 421-3060
Owner ....Frederick O. Hanser
President...Mark Lamping
V.P. & General Manager ....Walt Jocketty
Director of Public Relations ....Brian Bartow

San Diego Padres
P.O. Box 2000, San Diego, CA 92112
(619) 283-4494
Chairman...John Moores
President-CEO...Larry Lucchino
V.P., Baseball Operations & G.M....................Kevin Towers
Director, Media Relations ....Roger Riley

San Francisco Giants
3Com Park, San Francisco, CA 94124
(415) 468-3700
Managing General Partner........................Peter Magowan
Senior V.P. & General Manager ....Bob Quinn
V.P. of Communications.......................................Bob Rose

1998 Expansion Teams

Arizona Diamondbacks
P.O. Box 2095, Phoenix, AZ 85001
(602) 514-8500
Chief Executive Officer....................Jerry Colangelo
President....................Rich Dozer
V.P. & General Manager....................Joe Garagiola Jr.
Media Relations Mgr. ....Bob Crawford

Tampa Bay Devil Rays
Tropicana Field, One Stadium Dr., St. Petersburg, FL 33705
(813) 825-3137
Managing General Partner....................Vincent Naimoli
General Manager....................Chuck Lamar
VP Public Relations....................Rick Vaughn

PRO BASKETBALL

NBA

League Office
Olympic Tower, 645 Fifth Ave., New York, NY 10022
(212) 407-8000
Commissioner....................David Stern
Deputy Commissioner....................Russell Granik
V.P., Public Relations....................Brian McIntyre
Director of Media Relations....................Chris Rienza

NBA Players Association
1775 Broadway, Suite 2401, New York, NY 10019
(212) 333-7510
Exec. Dir. & Gen. Counsel....................Bill Hunter
President....................Buck Williams

Atlanta Hawks
One CNN Center, South Tower, Suite 405
Atlanta, GA 30303
(404) 827-3800
Owner....................Ted Turner
President....................Stan Kasten
General Manager....................Pete Babcock
Director of Media Relations....................Arthur Triche

Boston Celtics
151 Merrimac St., 4th Floor, Boston, MA 02114
(617) 523-6050
Chairman....................Paul Gaston
President....................Red Auerbach
Exec. V.P. & General Manager....................Jan Volk
Exec. V.P. & Head Coach....................M.L. Carr
Director of Public Relations....................Jeff Twiss

Charlotte Hornets
100 Hive Drive, Charlotte, NC 28217
(704) 357-0252
Owner....................George Shinn
V.P., Basketball Operations....................Bob Bass
Director of Media Relations....................Harold Kaufman

Chicago Bulls
United Center, 1901 West Madison St.
Chicago, IL 60612
(312) 455-4000
Chairman....................Jerry Reinsdorf
V.P., Basketball Operations....................Jerry Krause
Director of Media Services....................Tim Hallam

Cleveland Cavaliers
One Centre Court, Cleveland, OH 44115
(216) 420-2000
Owner-Chairman....................Gordon Gund
Owner-Vice Chairman....................George Gund III
President & General Manager....................Wayne Embry
Director of Media Relations....................Bob Zink

Dallas Mavericks
Reunion Arena, 777 Sports St., Dallas, TX 75207
(214) 988-0117
Owner....................Ross Perot Jr., David McDavid & Frank Zaccanelli
VP Basketball Oper. ....Keith Grant
VP Communications....................Kevin Sullivan

Denver Nuggets
1635 Clay St., Denver, CO 80204
(303) 893-6700
Owner....................Ascent Ent. Group
President-Head Coach....................Bernie Bickerstaff
General Manager....................Todd Eley
Director of Media Services....................Tommy Sheppard

Detroit Pistons
The Palace of Auburn Hills
Two Championship Dr., Auburn Hills, MI 48326
(810) 377-0100
Managing Partner....................William Davidson
President....................Tom Wilson
V.P. of Player Personnel....................Rick Sund
V.P. of Public Relations....................Matt Dobek

Golden State Warriors
1221 Broadway, 20th floor, Oakland, CA 94612
(510) 638-6300
Owner-CEO....................Chris Cohan
General Manager....................Dave Twardzik
Director of Communications....................Julie Marvel

Houston Rockets
2 Greenway Plaza, Suite 400, Houston, TX 77046
(713) 627-3865
Owner....................Les Alexander
Sr. Exec. V.P. of Basketball Affairs....................Robert Barr
Director of Public Relations....................Kathy Frietsch

Indiana Pacers
300 East Market St., Indianapolis, IN 46204
(317) 263-2100
Owners....................Melvin Simon & Herb Simon
President & General Manager....................Donnie Walsh
Director of Media Relations....................David Benner

Los Angeles Clippers
L.A. Sports Arena
3939 S. Figueroa St., Los Angeles, CA 90037
(213) 748-8000
Owner-Chairman....................Donald Sterling
V.P., Basketball Operations....................Elgin Baylor
Director of Communications....................Jill Wiggins

Los Angeles Lakers
Great Western Forum
3900 W. Manchester Blvd., Inglewood, CA 90305
(310) 419-3100
Owner....................Jerry Buss
Exec. V.P., Basketball Operations....................Jerry West
General Manager....................Mitch Kupchak
Director of Public Relations....................John Black

Miami Heat
Miami Arena, Miami, FL 33136
(305) 577-4328
Managing General Partner....................Micky Arison
President-Head Coach....................Pat Riley
Exec. V.P., Basketball Operations....................Dave Wohl
V.P. of Communications....................Mark Pray

Milwaukee Bucks
Bradley Center, 1001 N. Fourth St., Milwaukee, WI 53203
(414) 227-0500
President....................Sen. Herb Kohl (D., Wisc.)
V.P., Basketball Ops./GM....................Mike Dunleavy
Director of Publicity....................Bill King II

Minnesota Timberwolves
Target Center, 600 First Ave. North, Minneapolis, MN 55403
(612) 673-1600
Owner .... Glen Taylor
President .... Rob Moor
V.P., Basketball Operations .... Kevin McHale
Dir. of Public Relations/Communications .... Kent Wipf

New Jersey Nets
405 Murray Hill Pkwy., East Rutherford, NJ 07073
(201) 935-8888
President .... Henry Taub
COO .... Michael Rowe
Exec. V.P. of Bask. Ops .... John Calipari
Director of Public Relations .... John Mertz

New York Knickerbockers
Madison Square Garden
2 Penn Plaza, 14th Floor, New York, NY 10121
(212) 465-6471
Owner .... ITT Corp./Cablevision Systems Inc.
President (MSG) .... Dave Checketts
Pres. (Knicks) & General Manager .... Ernie Grunfeld
Director of Public Relations .... Josh Rosenfeld

Orlando Magic
Orlando Arena, 1 Magic Place, Orlando, FL 32801
(407) 649-3200
Owner .... Rich DeVos
President .... Bob Vander Weide
General Manager & COO .... John Gabriel
Dir. of Publicity/Media Relations .... Alex Martins

Philadelphia 76ers
Veterans Stadium
Broad St. and Pattison Ave., Philadelphia, PA 19148
(215) 339-7600
Owner-President .... Pat Croce
General Manager .... Brad Greenberg
Director of Public Relations .... Jody Silverman

Phoenix Suns
P.O. Box 1369, Phoenix, AZ 85001
(602) 379-7900
President-CEO .... Jerry Colangelo
V.P., Administration-G.M. .... Bryan Colangelo
V.P., Dir. of Player Personnel .... Dick Van Arsdale
Media Relations Director .... Julie Fie

Portland Trail Blazers
One Center Court, Suite 200, Portland, OR 97227
(503) 234-9291
Owner-Chairman .... Paul Allen
President & General Manager .... Bob Whitsitt
Director of Communications .... John Christensen

Sacramento Kings
One Sports Parkway, Sacramento, CA 95834
(916) 928-0000
Managing General Partner .... Jim Thomas
President .... Rick Benner
V.P., Basketball Operations .... Geoff Petrie
Director of Media Relations .... Travis Stanley

San Antonio Spurs
Alamodome, 100 Montana St., San Antonio, TX 78203
(210) 554-7700
Chairman .... Peter Holt
President-CEO .... John Diller
Exec. V.P., Basketball Operations .... Gregg Popovich
Director of Media Relations .... Tom James

Seattle SuperSonics
490 Fifth Ave. North, Seattle, WA 98109
(206) 281-5800
Owner-Chairman .... Barry Ackerley
President & General Manager .... Wally Walker
Director of Media Relations .... Cheri White

Toronto Raptors
20 Bay St., Suite 1702, Toronto, Ontario M5J 2N8
(416) 214-2255
President .... John Bitove Jr.
Exec. V.P. Basketball Operations .... Isiah Thomas
Comms. Mgr. .... Rick Kaplan

Utah Jazz
Delta Center, 301 West South Temple
Salt Lake City, UT 84101
(801) 325-2500
Owner .... Larry Miller
General Manager .... Tim Howells
President .... Frank Layden
Director of Media Relations .... Kim Turner

Vancouver Grizzlies
General Motors Place, 800 Griffiths Way
Vancouver, B.C. V6B 6G1
(604) 899-4666
Owner .... Orca Bay Sports Ent.
CEO .... Arthur Griffiths
President & GM .... Stu Jackson
Director of Media Relations .... Steve Frost

Washington Bullets
One Harry S. Truman Dr., Landover, MD 20785
(301) 773-2255
Chairman .... Abe Pollin
President .... Susan O'Malley
V.P. & General Manager .... Wes Unseld
Director of Public Relations .... Maureen Lewis

CBA

Continental Basketball Assocation
701 Market St., Suite 140, St. Louis, MO 63101
(314) 621-7222
Commissioner .... Steve Patterson
V.P. of Basketball Operations .... Clay Moser
Director of Public Relations .... Brett Meister

Member teams (12): Chicago Rockers, Connecticut Pride, Florida BeachDogs, Ft. Wayne (IN) Fury, Grand Rapids Mackers, Oklahoma City Cavalry, Omaha Racers, Quad City (IL) Thunder, Rockford (IL) Lightning, Shreveport (LA) Storm, Sioux Falls (SD) Skyforce, and Yakima (WA) Sun Kings.

BOWLING

ABC
(American Bowling Congress)
5301 South 76th St., Greendale, WI 53129
(414) 421-6400
Executive Director .... Darold Dobs
Public Relations Manager .... Dave DeLorenzo

BPAA
(Bowling Proprietors' Assn. of America)
P.O. Box 5802, Arlington, TX 76005
(817) 649-5105
Chief Exec. Officer .... Don A. Harris
President .... Charlie Brehob
Director of Public Relations .... Daniel Burgess

LPBT
(Ladies Professional Bowlers Tour)
7171 Cherryvale Blvd., Rockford, IL 61112
(815) 332-5756
President .... John Falzone
Media Director .... Angel Tucker

PBA
(Professional Bowlers Association)
1720 Merriman Road, P.O. Box 5118, Akron, OH 44334
(330) 836-5568
Commissioner .... Mark Gerberich
Public Relations Director .... Dave Schroeder

WIBC
(Women's International Bowling Congress)
5301 South 76th St., Greendale, WI 53129
(414) 421-9000
President....Joyce Deitch
Public Relations Manager....Dave DeLorenzo

BOXING

IBF
(International Boxing Federation)
134 Evergreen Place, 9th Floor,
East Orange, NJ 07018
(201) 414-0300
President....Robert (Bob) Lee
Executive Secretary....Marian Muhammad
Champs. & Ratings Chairman....Doug Beavers
P.O. Box 7577, Portsmouth, VA 23707
(804) 399-6608

WBA
(World Boxing Association)
Centro Comercial Ciudad Turmero, Local #21, Piso #2
Calle Petion Cruce Con Urdaneta,
Turmero, 2115 Estado Aragua, Venezuela
TEL: 011-58-44-63-1584
President....Gilberto Mendoza
General Counsel/U.S. Spokesman....Jimmy Binns
1735 Market St., 39th Floor, Phila., PA 19103
(215) 557-8000
Championship Chairman....Elias Cordorba
P.O. Box 87-1022, Panama 1, Rep. de Panama
TEL: 011-507-264-5363
Ratings Chairman....Bolivar Icaza
P.O. Box 1833, Panama 1, Rep. de Panama
TEL: 011-507-263-5167

WBC
(World Boxing Council)
Genova 33-503, Col. Juarez,
Delegacion Cuauhtemoc, MEXICO, 06600, D.F., Mexico
TEL: 011-525-533-6546
President....Jose Sulaiman
Executive Secretary....Eduardo Lamazon
Press Information/U.S. Spokesman....John Brister
411 Ballentine St., Bay St. Louis, MS 39520
(601) 467-3304

WBO
(World Boxing Organization)
Borinquen St. #57, Santa Rita, San Juan, P.R. 00925
(809) 765-7542
President....Francisco Valcarcel
Championship Chairman....John Montano
Phoenix, Arizona
(602) 542-1417
Ratings Chairman....Louis Perez
San Juan, P.R.
(809) 258-0340

Don King Productions, Inc.
871 West Oakland, Park Blvd., Oakland Park, FL 33311
(305) 568-3500
President....Don King
Director of Public Relations....Mike Marley

Top Rank
3900 Paradise Road, Suite 227, Las Vegas, NV 89102
(702) 732-2717
Chairman....Bob Arum
Director of Marketing....Michael Malitz

Golden Gloves Assn. of America, Inc.
8801 Princess Jeanne N.E., Albuquerque, NM 87112
(505) 298-8042
Executive Director....Stan Gallup
President....Chick Paris

COLLEGE SPORTS

CCA
(Collegiate Commissioners Association)
800 South Broadway, Suite 400, Walnut Creek, CA 94596
(510) 932-4411
President....Jim Delany (Big Ten)
Exec. V.P....Mike Gilleran (West Coast Conf.)
Secretary-Treasurer....David Price

NAIA
(National Assn. of Intercollegiate Athletics)
6120 South Yale, Suite 1450, Tulsa, OK 74136
(918) 494-8828
President-CEO....James Chasteen
Public Relations Contact....Kevin Henry

NCAA
(National Collegiate Athletic Association)
6201 College Blvd., Overland Park, KS 66211
(913) 339-1906
President....Gene Corrigan (ACC)
(term expires January, 1997)
Executive Director....Cedric Dempsey
Asst. Exec. Dir. for Enforcement....David Berst
Director of Public Information....Kathryn Reith

WSF
(Women's Sports Foundation)
Eisenhower Park, East Meadow, NY 11554
(516) 542-4700
Executive Director....Donna Lopiano
Communications Director....Lynnore Lawton

Major NCAA Conferences

See pages 443-451 for basketball coaches, football coaches, nicknames and colors of all Division I basketball schools and Division I-A and I-AA football schools.

ATLANTIC COAST CONFERENCE
P.O. Drawer ACC
Greensboro, NC 27419
(910) 854-8787 Founded: 1953
Commissioner....Gene Corrigan
Director of Media Relations....Brian Morrison

1996-97 members: BASKETBALL & FOOTBALL (9)—Clemson, Duke, Florida St., Georgia Tech, Maryland, North Carolina, North Carolina St., Virginia and Wake Forest.

Clemson University
Clemson, SC 29633 Founded: 1889
SID: (864) 656-2114 Enrollment: 16,300
President....Deno Curris
Athletic Director....Bobby Robinson
Sports Information Director....Tim Bourret

Duke University
Durham, NC 27708 Founded: 1838
SID: (919) 684-2633 Enrollment: 6,100
President....Nannerl Keohane
Athletic Director....Tom Butters
Sports Information Director....Mike Cragg

Florida State University
Tallahassee, FL 32316 Founded: 1857
SID: (904) 644-1403 Enrollment: 30,200
President....Talbot (Sandy) D'Alemberte
Athletic Director....Dave Hart Jr.
Sports Information Director....Rob Wilson

Georgia Tech
Atlanta, GA 30332 Founded: 1885
SID: (404) 894-5445 Enrollment: 13,000
President....Wayne Clough
Athletic Director....Dr. Homer Rice
Sports Information Director....Mike Finn

University of Maryland
College Park, MD 20741 — Founded: 1807
SID: (301) 314-7064 — Enrollment: 30,600
President .... William E. Kirwan
Athletic Director .... Deborah Yow
Sports Information Director .... Herb Hartnett

University of North Carolina
Chapel Hill, NC 27514 — Founded: 1789
SID: (919) 962-2123 — Enrollment: 24,439
Chancellor .... Michael K. Hooker
Athletic Director .... John Swofford
Sports Information Director .... Rick Brewer

North Carolina State University
Raleigh, NC 27695 — Founded: 1887
SID: (919) 515-2102 — Enrollment: 27,537
Chancellor .... Larry Monteith
Athletic Director .... Les Robinson (acting)
Sports Information Director .... Mark Bockelman

University of Virginia
Charlottesville, VA 22903 — Founded: 1819
SID: (804) 982-5500 — Enrollment: 18,073
President .... John T. Casteen III
Athletic Director .... Terry Holland
Sports Information Director .... Rich Murray

Wake Forest University
Winston-Salem, NC 27109 — Founded: 1834
SID: (910) 759-5640 — Enrollment: 3,620
President .... Thomas K. Hearn Jr.
Athletic Director .... Ron Wellman
Sports Information Director .... John Justus

BIG EAST CONFERENCE
56 Exchange Terrace
Providence, RI 02903
(401) 272-9108 — Founded: 1979
Commissioner .... Mike Tranghese
Asst. Commissioner/P.R .... John Paquette

1996-97 members: BASKETBALL (13)— Boston College, Connecticut, Georgetown, Miami-FL, Notre Dame, Pittsburgh, Providence, Rutgers, St. John's, Seton Hall, Syracuse, Villanova and West Virginia; FOOTBALL (8)— Boston College, Miami-FL, Pittsburgh, Rutgers, Syracuse, Temple, Virginia Tech and West Virginia.

Boston College
Chestnut Hill, MA 02167 — Founded: 1863
SID: (617) 552-3004 — Enrollment: 8,894
President .... Rev. William P. Leahy, S.J.
Athletic Director .... Chet Gladchuk
Sports Information Director .... Reid Oslin

University of Connecticut
Storrs, CT 06269 — Founded: 1881
SID: (203) 486-3531 — Enrollment: 13,629
President .... Harry J. Hartley
Athletic Director .... Lew Perkins
Sports Information Director .... Tim Tolokan

Georgetown University
Washington, DC 20057 — Founded: 1798
SID: (202) 687-2492 — Enrollment: 6,173
President .... Rev. Leo J. O'Donovan, SJ
Athletic Director .... Joseph C. Lang
Sports Information Director .... Bill Shapland

University of Miami
Coral Gables, FL 33124 — Founded: 1926
SID: (305) 284-3244 — Enrollment: 13,734
President .... Edward T. Foote II
Athletic Director .... Paul Dee
Sports Information Director .... John Hahn

University of Notre Dame
Notre Dame, IN 46556 — Founded: 1842
SID: (219) 631-7516 — Enrollment: 10,126
President .... Rev. Edward (Monk) Malloy
Athletic Director .... Michael Wadsworth
Sports Information Director .... John Heisler

University of Pittsburgh
Pittsburgh, PA 15213 — Founded: 1787
SID: (412) 648-8240 — Enrollment: 13,500
Chancellor .... Mark A. Nordenberg
Athletic Director .... TBA
Sports Information Director .... Ron Wahl

Providence College
Providence, RI 02918 — Founded: 1917
SID: (401) 865-2272 — Enrollment: 3,512
President .... Philip A. Smith, OP
Athletic Director .... John Marinatto
Sports Information Director .... Tim Connor

Rutgers University
New Brunswick, NJ 08903 — Founded: 1766
SID: (908) 445-4200 — Enrollment: 34,000
President .... Francis L. Lawrence
Athletic Director .... Fred Gruninger
Sports Information Director .... Pete Kowalski

St. John's University
Jamaica, NY 11439 — Founded: 1870
SID: (718) 990-6367 — Enrollment: 19,500
President .... Rev. Donald J. Harrington, CM
Athletic Director .... Edward J. Manetta Jr.
Sports Information Director .... Frank Racaniello

Seton Hall University
South Orange, NJ 07079 — Founded: 1856
SID: (201) 761-9493 — Enrollment: 10,538
President .... Rev. Thomas R. Peterson, OP
Athletic Director .... Larry Keating
Sports Information Director .... John Wooding

Syracuse University
Syracuse, NY 13244 — Founded: 1870
SID: (315) 443-2608 — Enrollment: 10,200
Chancellor .... Kenneth Shaw
Athletic Director .... Jake Crouthamel
Sports Information Director .... Larry Kimball

Temple University
Philadelphia, PA 19122 — Founded: 1884
SID: (215) 204-7445 — Enrollment: 32,000
President .... Peter J. Liacouras
Athletic Director .... David O'Brien
Sports Information Director .... Al Shrier

Villanova University
Villanova, PA 19085 — Founded: 1842
SID: (610) 519-4120 — Enrollment: 5,994
President .... Rev. Edmund Dobbin, OSA
Athletic Director .... Gene DeFilippo
Sports Information Director .... Karen Frascona

Virginia Tech
Blacksburg, VA 24061 — Founded: 1872
SID: (540) 231-6726 — Enrollment: 23,674
President .... Paul Torgersen
Athletic Director .... Dave Braine
Sports Information Director .... Dave Smith

West Virginia University
Morgantown, WV 26507 — Founded: 1867
SID: (304) 293-2821 — Enrollment: 23,000
President .... David Hardesty
Athletic Director .... Ed Pastilong
Sports Information Director .... Shelly Poe

BIG 12 CONFERENCE
2201 Stemmons Fwy., Dallas, TX 75207
(214) 742-1212 Founded: 1996
Commissioner ....Steve Hatchell
Service Bureau Director....................................Bo Carter

1996-97 members: BASKETBALL & FOOTBALL (12)— Baylor, Colorado, Iowa St., Kansas, Kansas St., Missouri, Nebraska, Oklahoma, Oklahoma St., Texas, Texas A&M and Texas Tech.

Baylor University
Waco, TX 76711 Founded: 1845
SID: (817) 755-2743 Enrollment: 12,500
President ....Robert B. Sloan
Athletic Director..Tom Stanton
Sports Information Director..........................Maxey Parrish

University of Colorado
Boulder, CO 80309 Founded: 1876
SID: (303) 492-5626 Enrollment: 25,000
President...Dr. John Buechner
Interim Athletic Director ....Dick Tharp
Sports Information Director ....Dave Plati

Iowa State University
Ames, IA 50011 Founded: 1858
SID: (515) 294-3372 Enrollment: 25,000
President ....Martin Jischke
Athletic Director...Eugene Smith
Sports Information Director ....Tom Kroeschell

University of Kansas
Lawrence, KS 66045 Founded: 1866
SID: (913) 864-3417 Enrollment: 25,200
Chancellor...Robert Hemenway
Athletic Director...Bob Frederick
Sports Information Director ....Dean Buchan

Kansas State University
Manhattan, KS 66502 Founded: 1863
SID: (913) 532-6735 Enrollment: 20,400
President ....Jon Wefald
Athletic Director..Max Urick
Sports Information Director ....Kent Brown

University of Missouri
Columbia, MO 65205 Founded: 1839
SID: (573) 882-3241 Enrollment: 22,168
Interim Chancellor ....Richard Wallace
Athletic Director.......................................Joe Castiglione
Sports Information Director ....Bob Brendel

University of Nebraska
Lincoln, NE 68588 Founded: 1869
SID: (402) 472-2263 Enrollment: 25,000
Chancellor...Dr. James Moeser
Athletic Director ....Bill Byrne
Sports Information Director ....Chris Anderson

University of Oklahoma
Norman, OK 73019 Founded: 1890
SID: (405) 325-8231 Enrollment: 25,000
President..David Boren
Athletic Director...Steve Owens
Sports Information Director ....Mike Prusinski

Oklahoma State University
Stillwater, OK 74078 Founded: 1890
SID: (405) 744-5749 Enrollment: 18,500
President...James Halligan
Athletic Director ....Terry Don Phillips
Sports Information Director ....Steve Buzzard

University of Texas
Austin, TX 78713 Founded: 1883
SID: (512) 471-7437 Enrollment: 47,719
President ....Robert Berdahl
Athletic Director ....De Loss Dodds
Sports Information Director..................................Dave Saba

Texas A&M University
College Station, TX 77843 Founded: 1876
SID: (409) 845-5725 Enrollment: 43,031
President...Ray Bowen
Athletic Director ....Wally Groff
Sports Information Director ....Alan Cannon

Texas Tech University
Lubbock, TX 79409 Founded: 1923
SID: (806) 742-2770 Enrollment: 25,000
President (Interim) ....Donald Haragan
Athletic Director...Gerald Myers
Sports Information Director ....Richard Kilwein

BIG TEN CONFERENCE
1500 West Higgins Road
Park Ridge, IL 60068-6300
(847) 696-1010 Founded: 1895
Commissioner...Jim Delany
Dir. of Information Services.....................Dennis LaBissonier

1996-97 members: BASKETBALL & FOOTBALL (11)— Illinois, Indiana, Iowa, Michigan, Michigan St., Minnesota, Northwestern, Ohio St., Penn St., Purdue and Wisconsin.

University of Illinois
Champaign, IL 61820 Founded: 1867
SID: (217) 333-1390 Enrollment: 36,000
President .... James J. Stukel
Athletic Director...Ron Guenther
Dir. of Communications...................................Dave Johnson

Indiana University
Bloomington, IN 47405 Founded: 1820
SID: (812) 855-9399 Enrollment: 36,000
President...Myles Brand
Athletic Director ....Clarence Doninger
Sports Information Director ....Kit Klingelhoffer

University of Iowa
Iowa City, IA 52242 Founded: 1847
SID: (319) 335-9411 Enrollment: 27,597
President..Mary Sue Coleman
Athletic Director ....Bob Bowlsby
Sports Information Director..................................Phil Haddy

University of Michigan
Ann Arbor, MI 48109 Founded: 1817
SID: (313) 763-1381 Enrollment: 36,617
Interim President..Homer A. Neal
Athletic Director ....Joe Roberson
Sports Information Director ....Bruce Madej

Michigan State University
East Lansing, MI 48824 Founded: 1855
SID: (517) 355-2271 Enrollment: 40,647
President...Peter McPherson
Athletic Director ....Merritt J. Norvell Jr.
Sports Information Director...............................Ken Hoffman

University of Minnesota
Minneapolis, MN 55455 Founded: 1851
SID: (612) 625-4090 Enrollment: 38,000
President ....Nils Hasselmo
Athletic Director ....Dr. Mark Dienhart
Sports Information Director...................................Marc Ryan

Northwestern University
Evanston, IL 60208 Founded: 1851
SID: (847) 491-7503 Enrollment: 7,400
President ....Henry S. Bienen
Athletic Director ....Rick Taylor
Sports Information Director ....Brad Hurlbut

Ohio State University
Columbus, OH 43210 Founded: 1870
SID: (614) 292-6861 Enrollment: 49,542
President....E. Gordon Gee
Athletic Director....Andy Geiger
Sports Information Director....Steve Snapp

Penn State University
University Park, PA 16802 Founded: 1855
SID: (814) 865-1757 Enrollment: 38,200
President....Graham Spanier
Athletic Director....Tim Curley
Sports Information Director....Jeff Nelson

Purdue University
West Lafayette, IN 47907 Founded: 1869
SID: (317) 494-3202 Enrollment: 34,685
President....Steven C. Beering
Athletic Director....Morgan Burke
Sports Information Director....Mark Adams

University of Wisconsin
Madison, WI 53711 Founded: 1848
SID: (608) 262-1811 Enrollment: 40,300
Chancellor....David Ward
Athletic Director....Pat Richter
Sports Information Director....Steve Malchow

BIG WEST CONFERENCE
2 Corporate Park, Suite 206
Irvine, CA 92714
(714) 261-2525 Founded: 1969
Commissioner....Dennis Farrell
Director of Information....Dennis Bickmeier

1996-97 members: BASKETBALL (12)— Boise St., CS-Fullerton, Cal Poly-SLO, Idaho, Long Beach St., Nevada, New Mexico St., North Texas, Pacific, UC-Irvine, UC-Santa Barbara, Utah St.; FOOTBALL (6)— Boise St., Idaho, Nevada, New Mexico St., North Texas, Utah St.

Boise State
Boise, ID 83725 Founded: 1932
SID: (208) 385-1515 Enrollment: 15,060
President....Charles P. Ruch
Athletic Director....Gene Bleymaier
Sports Information Director....Max Corbet

Cal State-Fullerton
Fullerton, CA 92634 Founded: 1957
SID: (714) 773-3970 Enrollment: 22,500
President....Milton A. Gordon
Athletic Director....John Easterbrook
Sports Information Director....Mel Franks

Cal Poly SLO
San Luis Obispo, CA 93407 Founded: 1901
SID: (804) 756-6531 Enrollment: 16,400
President....Dr. Warren J. Baker
Athletic Director....John McCutcheon
Sports Information Director....Eric McDowell

University of Idaho
Moscow, ID 83844 Founded: 1889
SID: (208) 885-0211 Enrollment: 13,000
President....Bob Hoover
Athletic Director....Oval Jaynes
Sports Information Director....Sean Johnson

Long Beach State
Long Beach, CA 90840 Founded: 1949
SID: (310) 985-7565 Enrollment: 27,500
President....Robert Maxson
Athletic Director....Bill Shumard
Sports Information Director....Randy Franz

University of Nevada
Reno, NV 89557 Founded: 1874
SID: (702) 784-4600 Enrollment: 12,500
President....Joe Crowley
Athletic Director....Chris Ault
Sports Information Director....Paul Stuart

New Mexico State University
Las Cruces, NM 88003 Founded: 1888
SID: (505) 646-3929 Enrollment: 15,165
President....Michael Orenduff
Athletic Director....Al Gonzales
Sports Information Director....Steve Shutt

University of North Texas
Denton, TX 76203 Founded: 1890
SID: (817) 565-2664 Enrollment: 26,400
President....Dr. Alfred F. Hurley
Athletic Director....Craig Helwig
Sports Information Director....Ann Wheelwright

University of the Pacific
Stockton, CA 95211 Founded: 1851
SID: (209) 946-2479 Enrollment: 4,000
President....Donald DeRosa
Interim Athletic Director....Cindy Spiro
Sports Information Director....Mike Millerick

University of California, Irvine
Irvine, CA 92717 Founded: 1962
SID: (714) 824-5814 Enrollment: 15,600
Chancellor....Laurel Wilkening
Athletic Director....Dan Guerrero
Sports Information Director....Bob Olson

University of California, Santa Barbara
Santa Barbara, CA 93106 Founded: 1944
SID: (805) 893-3428 Enrollment: 18,200
Chancellor....Henry Yang
Athletic Director....Gary Cunningham
Sports Information Director....Bill Mahoney

Utah State University
Logan, UT 84322 Founded: 1888
SID: (801) 797-1361 Enrollment: 19,861
President....George Emert
Athletic Director....Chuck Bell
Sports Information Director....John Lewandowski

CONFERENCE USA
35 East Wacker Drive, Suite 650, Chicago, IL 60601
(312) 553-0483 Founded: 1995
Commissioner....Mike Slive
Director of Information....Erika Amstadt

1996-97 members: BASKETBALL (12)— Alabama-Birmingham, Cincinnati, DePaul, Houston, Louisville, Marquette, Memphis, NC-Charlotte, Saint Louis, South Florida, Southern Miss and Tulane; FOOTBALL (6)— Cincinnati, Houston, Louisville, Memphis, Southern Miss and Tulane.

New in 1997-98: FOOTBALL (1)— E. Carolina

University of Alabama-Birmingham
Birmingham, AL 35294 Founded: 1969
SID: (205) 934-0722 Enrollment: 16,452
President:....J. Claude Bennett
Athletic Director....Gene Bartow
Sports Information Director....Grant Shingleton

University of Cincinnati
Cincinnati, OH 45221 Founded: 1819
SID: (513) 556-5191 Enrollment: 36,000
President....Joseph A. Steger
Athletic Director....Gerald O'Dell
Sports Information Director....Tom Hathaway

DePaul University
Chicago, IL 60614 Founded: 1898
SID: (312) 325-7525 Enrollment: 17,133
President .... Rev. John P. Minogue
Athletic Director .... Bill Bradshaw
Sports Information Director .... John Lanctot

University of Houston
Houston, TX 77204 Founded: 1927
SID: (713) 743-9404 Enrollment: 30,757
President .... Glenn Goerke
Athletic Director .... Bill Carr
Sports Information Director .... Donna Turner

University of Louisville
Louisville, KY 40292 Founded: 1798
SID: (502) 852-6581 Enrollment: 22,000
President .... John W. Shumaker
Athletic Director .... Bill Olsen
Sports Information Director .... Kenny Klein

Marquette University
Milwaukee, WI 53233 Founded: 1881
SID: (414) 288-7447 Enrollment: 10,750
President .... Rev. Robert A. Wild S.J.
Athletic Director .... Bill Cords
Sports Information Director .... Kathleen Hohl

Memphis University
Memphis, TN 38152 Founded: 1912
SID: (901) 678-2337 Enrollment: 21,500
President .... V. Lane Rawlins
Athletic Director .... R.C. Johnson
Sports Information Director .... Bob Winn

University of North Carolina-Charlotte
Charlotte, NC 28223 Founded: 1946
SID: (704) 547-4937 Enrollment: 15,895
Chancellor .... J. H. Woodward
Athletic Director .... Judy Rose
Sports Information Director .... Tom Whitestone

Saint Louis University
St. Louis, MO 63103 Founded: 1818
SID: (314) 977-2524 Enrollment: 11,300
President .... Rev. Lawrence Biondi
Athletic Director .... Doug Woolard
Sport Information Director .... Doug McIlhagga

University of South Florida
Tampa, FL 33620 Founded: 1956
SID: (813) 974-4086 Enrollment: 36,000
President .... Betty Castor
Atheltic Director .... Paul Griffin
Sports Information Director .... John Gerdes

University of Southern Mississippi
Hattiesburg, MS 39406 Founded: 1910
SID: (601) 266-4503 Enrollment: 14,000
President .... Aubrey K. Lucas
Athletic Director .... Bill McLellan
Sports Information Director .... Regiel Napier

Tulane University
New Orleans, LA 70118 Founded: 1834
SID: (504) 865-5506 Enrollment: 10,800
President .... Eamon M. Kelly
Co-Interim Athletic Directors ...... Sandy Barbour, Ian McCaw
Sports Information Director .... Lenny Vangilder

Native American Nicknames Down to 10

Miami of Ohio has discontinued the use of "Redskins" as a team nickname. So as of Sept. 30, 1996, the number of Native American nickname variations stood at 10 in Division I basketball and football: INDIANS (3)— Arkansas St., Northeast Louisiana and Southeast Missouri St.; BRAVES (2)— Alcorn St. and Bradley; CHIPPEWAS— Central Michigan; FIGHTING ILLINI— Illinois; MOCCASINS— Tennessee-Chattanooga; SEMINOLES— Florida St.; and TRIBE— William and Mary.

MID-AMERICAN CONFERENCE
Four SeaGate, Suite 102, Toledo, OH 43604
(419) 249-7177 Founded: 1946
Commissioner .... Jerry Ippoliti
Director of Communications .... Tom Lessig

1996-97 members: BASKETBALL & FOOTBALL (10)— Akron, Ball St., Bowling Green, Central Michigan, Eastern Michigan, Kent, Miami-OH, Ohio University, Toledo and Western Michigan. **New in 1997-98:** BASKETBALL & FOOTBALL (2)—Marshall and Northern Illinois.

University of Akron
Akron, OH 44325 Founded: 1870
SID: (330) 972-7468 Enrollment: 25,098
President .... Marion Ruebel
Athletic Director .... Mike Bobinski
Sports Information Director .... Jeff Brewer

Ball State University
Muncie, IN 47306 Founded: 1918
SID: (317) 285-8242 Enrollment: 19,115
President .... John Worthen
Athletic Director .... Andrea Seger
Sports Information Director .... Joe Hernandez

Bowling Green State University
Bowling Green, OH 43403 Founded: 1910
SID: (419) 372-7075 Enrollment: 17,000
President .... Sidney Ribeau
Athletic Director .... Ron Zwierlein
Sports Information Director .... Steve Barr

Central Michigan University
Mt. Pleasant, MI 48859 Founded: 1892
SID: (517) 774-3277 Enrollment: 16,435
President .... Leonard Plachta
Athletic Director .... Herb Deromedi
Sports Information Director .... Fred Stabley Jr.

Eastern Michigan University
Ypsilanti, MI 48197 Founded: 1849
SID: (313) 487-0317 Enrollment: 24,000
President .... William Shelton
Athletic Director .... Tim Weiser
Sports Information Director .... Jim Streeter

Kent State University
Kent, OH 44242 Founded: 1910
SID: (216) 672-2110 Enrollment: 29,785
President .... Carol Cartwright
Athletic Director .... Laing Kennedy
Sports Information Director .... Dale Gallagher

Miami University
Oxford, OH 45056 Founded: 1809
SID: (513) 529-4327 Enrollment: 16,000
President .... James C. Garland
Athletic Director .... Eric Hyman
Sports Information Director .... John Estes

Ohio University
Athens, OH 45701 Founded: 1804
SID: (614) 593-1298 Enrollment: 19,143
President .... Robert Glidden
Athletic Director .... Tom Boeh
Sports Information Director .... George Mauzy

University of Toledo
Toledo, OH 43606 Founded: 1872
SID: (419) 530-3790 Enrollment: 20,000
President .... Frank Horton
Athletic Director .... Pete Liske
Sports Information Director .... Rod Brandt

Western Michigan University
Kalamazoo, MI 49008 Founded: 1903
SID: (616) 387-4138 Enrollment: 26,537
President .... Diether Haenicke
Athletic Director .... Jim Weaver
Sports Information Director .... John Beatty

PACIFIC-10 CONFERENCE
800 South Broadway, Suite 400
Walnut Creek, CA 94596
(510) 932-4411 Founded: 1915
Commissioner ....Thomas Hansen
Asst. Commissioner, Public Relations................Jim Muldoon

1996-97 members: BASKETBALL & FOOTBALL (10)— Arizona, Arizona St., California, Oregon, Oregon St., Stanford, UCLA, USC, Washington and Washington St.

University of Arizona
Tucson, AZ 85721 Founded: 1885
SID: (520) 621-4163 Enrollment: 35,306
President ....Manuel Pacheco
Athletic Director ....Jim Livengood
Sports Information Director........................Tom Duddleston

Arizona State University
Tempe, AZ 85287 Founded: 1885
SID: (602) 965-6592 Enrollment: 42,600
President ....Lattie F. Coor
Athletic Director ....Kevin White
Sports Information Director ....Mark Brand

University of California
Berkeley, CA 94720 Founded: 1868
SID: (510) 642-5363 Enrollment: 31,000
Chancellor ....Chang-Lin Tien
Athletic Director ....John Kasser
Sports Information Director..........................Kevin Reneau

University of Oregon
Eugene, OR 97401 Founded: 1876
SID: (541) 346-5488 Enrollment: 16,600
President ....David Frohnmeyer
Athletic Director ....Bill Moos
Co-Sports Information Directors ....Jamie Klund
& Dave Williford

Oregon State University
Corvallis, OR 97331 Founded: 1868
SID: (541) 737-3720 Enrollment: 14,500
President ....Paul G. Risser
Athletic Director ....Dutch Bauchman
Sports Information Director ....Hal Cowan

Stanford University
Stanford, CA 94305 Founded: 1891
SID: (415) 723-4418 Enrollment: 13,075
President ....Gerhard Casper
Athletic Director ....Ted Leyland
Sports Information Director...........................Gary Migdol

UCLA— Univ. of California, Los Angeles
Los Angeles, CA 90024 Founded: 1919
SID: (310) 206-6831 Enrollment: 34,000
Chancellor ....Charles Young
Athletic Director ....Pete Dalis
Sports Information Director...........................Marc Dellins

USC— Univ. of Southern California
Los Angeles, CA 90089 Founded: 1880
SID: (213) 740-8480 Enrollment: 27,970
President ....Steven Sample
Athletic Director ....Mike Garrett
Sports Information Director..........................Tim Tessalone

University of Washington
Seattle, WA 98195 Founded: 1861
SID: (206) 543-2230 Enrollment: 35,000
President ....Richard McCormick
Athletic Director ....Barbara Hedges
Sports Information Director ....Jim Daves

Washington State University
Pullman, WA 99164 Founded: 1890
SID: (509) 335-0270 Enrollment: 17,500
President ....Samuel Smith
Athletic Director ....Rick Dickson
Sports Information Director..........................Rod Commons

SOUTHEASTERN CONFERENCE
2201 Civic Center Blvd.
Birmingham, AL 35203
(205) 458-3010 Founded: 1933
Commissioner ....Roy Kramer
Director of Communications ....Charles Bloom

1996-97 members: BASKETBALL & FOOTBALL (12)— Alabama, Arkansas, Auburn, Florida, Georgia, Kentucky, LSU, Mississippi, Mississippi St., South Carolina, Tennessee and Vanderbilt.

University of Alabama
Tuscaloosa, AL 35487 Founded: 1831
SID: (205) 348-6084 Enrollment: 20,000
President ....Dr. Andrew Sorensen
Acting Athletic Director ....Robert Bockrath
Sports Information Director ....Larry White

University of Arkansas
Fayetteville, AR 72701 Founded: 1871
SID: (501) 575-2751 Enrollment: 14,700
Chancellor ....Daniel Ferritor
Athletic Director ....Frank Broyles
Sports Information Director ....Rick Schaeffer

Auburn University
Auburn, AL 36831 Founded: 1856
SID: (334) 844-9800 Enrollment: 22,122
President ....William V. Muse
Athletic Director ....David Housel
Sports Information Director..........................Kent Partridge

University of Florida
Gainesville, FL 32604 Founded: 1853
SID: (904) 375-4683 ext. 6100 Enrollment: 39,500
President ....John Lombardi
Athletic Director ....Jeremy Foley
Sports Information Director ....John Humenik

University of Georgia
Athens, GA 30613 Founded: 1785
SID: (706) 542-1621 Enrollment: 28,383
President ....Charles Knapp
Athletic Director ....Vince Dooley
Sports Information Director...........................Claude Felton

University of Kentucky
Lexington, KY 40506 Founded: 1865
SID: (606) 257-3838 Enrollment: 24,200
President...................................Charles T. Wethington Jr.
Athletic Director ....C.M. Newton
Sports Information Director ....Rena Vicini

LSU— Louisiana State University
Baton Rouge, LA 70894 Founded: 1860
SID: (504) 388-8226 Enrollment: 24,200
Chancellor ....William (Bud) Davis
Athletic Director ....Joe Dean
Sports Information Director...........................Herb Vincent

University of Mississippi
Oxford, MS 38677 Founded: 1848
SID: (601) 232-7522 Enrollment: 12,542
Chancellor ....Dr. Robert C. Khayat
Athletic Director ....Pete Boone
Sports Information Director.......................Langston Rogers

Mississippi State University
Starkville, MS 39762 Founded: 1878
SID: (601) 325-2703 Enrollment: 13,557
President ....Donald Zacharias
Athletic Director ....Larry Templeton
Sports Information Director ....Mike Nemeth

University of South Carolina
Columbia, SC 29208 Founded: 1801
SID: (803) 777-5204 Enrollment: 25,600
President ....John Palms
Athletic Director ....Mike McGee
Sports Information Director ....Kerry Tharp

University of Tennessee
Knoxville, TN 37901 — Founded: 1794
SID: (423) 974-1212 — Enrollment: 25,489
President .... Joe Johnson
Athletic Director .... Doug Dickey
Sports Information Director .... Bud Ford

Vanderbilt University
Nashville, TN 37212 — Founded: 1873
SID: (615) 322-4121 — Enrollment: 9,300
Chancellor .... Joe B. Wyatt
Athletic Director .... Todd Turner
Sports Information Director .... Rod Williamson

WESTERN ATHLETIC CONFERENCE

14 West Dry Creek Circle
Littleton, CO 80120
(303) 795-1962 — Founded: 1962
Commissioner .... Karl Benson
Director of Communications .... Dan Willis

1996-97 members: BASKETBALL & FOOTBALL (16)— Air Force, BYU, Colorado St., Fresno St., Hawaii, New Mexico, Rice, San Diego St., San Jose St., SMU, TCU, Tulsa, UNLV, Utah, UTEP and Wyoming.

U.S. Air Force Academy
Colorado Springs, CO 80840 — Founded: 1959
SID: (719) 333-2313 — Enrollment: 4,000
Superintendent .... Lt. Gen. Paul Stein
Athletic Director .... Col. Randall W. Spetman
Sports Information Director .... Dave Kellogg

Brigham Young University
Provo, UT 84602 — Founded: 1875
SID: (801) 378-4911 — Enrollment: 27,000
President .... Merril J. Bateman
Athletic Director .... Rondo Fehlberg
Sports Information Director .... Ralph Zobell

Colorado State University
Fort Collins, CO 80523 — Founded: 1870
SID: (970) 491-5067 — Enrollment: 21,600
President .... Albert Yates
Athletic Director .... Tom Jurich
Sports Information Director .... Gary Ozzello

Fresno State University
Fresno, CA 93740 — Founded: 1911
SID: (209) 278-2509 — Enrollment: 18,900
President .... John D. Welty
Athletic Director .... Al Bohl
Sports Information Director .... Dave Haglund

University of Hawaii
Honolulu, HI 96822 — Founded: 1907
SID: (808) 956-7523 — Enrollment: 19,062
President .... Kenneth Mortimer
Athletic Director .... Hugh Yoshida
Interim Sports Information Director .... Lois Manin

University of New Mexico
Albuquerque, NM 87131 — Founded: 1889
SID: (505) 277-2026 — Enrollment: 22,890
President .... Richard Peck
Athletic Director .... Rudy Davalos
Sports Information Director .... Greg Remington

Rice University
Houston, TX 77005 — Founded: 1912
SID: (713) 527-4034 — Enrollment: 2,600
President .... Malcolm Gillis
Athletic Director .... Bobby May
Sports Information Director .... Bill Cousins

San Diego State University
San Diego, CA 92182 — Founded: 1897
SID: (619) 594-5547 — Enrollment: 29,000
President .... Stephen Weber
Athletic Director .... Rick Bay
Sports Information Director .... John Rosenthal

San Jose State University
San Jose, CA 95192 — Founded: 1857
SID: (408) 294-1217 — Enrollment: 27,000
President .... Robert Caret
Athletic Director .... Tom Brennan
Sports Information Director .... Lawrence Fan

SMU— Southern Methodist University
Dallas, TX 75275 — Founded: 1911
SID: (214) 768-2883 — Enrollment: 5,300
President .... R. Gerald Turner
Athletic Director .... Jim Copeland
Sports Information Director .... Jon Jackson

TCU— Texas Christian University
Fort Worth, TX 76129 — Founded: 1873
SID: (817) 921-7969 — Enrollment: 6,986
Chancellor .... William Tucker
Athletic Director .... Frank Windegger
Sports Information Director .... Glen Stone

University of Tulsa
Tulsa, OK 74104 — Founded: 1894
SID: (918) 631-2395 — Enrollment: 4,600
President .... Dr. Bob Lawless
Interim Athletic Director .... Judy MacLeod
Sports Information Director .... Don Tomkalski

University of Utah
Salt Lake City, UT 84112 — Founded: 1850
SID: (801) 581-3510 — Enrollment: 27,100
President .... Arthur Smith
Athletic Director .... Chris Hill
Sports Information Director .... Bruce Woodbury

UNLV— University of Nevada, Las Vegas
Las Vegas, NV 89154 — Founded: 1957
SID: (702) 895-3207 — Enrollment: 20,200
President .... Carol Hunter
Athletic Director .... Charles Cavognaro
Sports Information Director .... Jim Gemma

UTEP— University of Texas at El Paso
El Paso, TX 79968 — Founded: 1913
SID: (915) 747-5330 — Enrollment: 17,500
President .... Diana Natalicio
Athletic Director .... John Thompson
Sports Information Director .... TBA

University of Wyoming
Laramie, WY 82071 — Founded: 1886
SID: (307) 766-2256 — Enrollment: 11,200
President .... Terry Roark
Athletic Director .... Lee Moon
Sports Information Director .... Kevin McKinney

MAJOR INDEPENDENTS

Division I-A football independents in 1996.

University of Alabama Birmingham
Birmingham, AL 35294 — Founded: 1969
SID: (205) 934-0722 — Enrollment: 16,452
President .... J. Claude Bennett
Athletic Director .... Gene Bartow
Sports Information Director .... Grant Shingleton

Arkansas State University
State University, AR 72467 — Founded: 1909
SID: (501) 972-2541 — Enrollment: 9,600
President....Les Wyatt
Athletic Director....Barry Dowd
Sports Information Director....Gina Bowman

Army— U.S. Military Academy
West Point, NY 10996 — Founded: 1802
SID: (914) 938-3303 — Enrollment: 4,200
Superintendent....Lt. Gen. Howard D. Graves
Athletic Director....Al Vanderbush
Sports Information Director....Bob Beretta

University of Central Florida
Orlando, FL 32816 — Founded: 1963
SID: (407) 823-2729 — Enrollment: 28,000
President....Dr. John C. Hitt
Athletic Director....Steve Sloan
Sports Information Director....John Marini

East Carolina University
Greenville, NC 27858 — Founded: 1907
SID: (919) 328-4522 — Enrollment: 17,500
Chancellor....Richard Eakin
Athletic Director....Mike Hamrick
Sports Information Director....Norm Reilly

Louisiana Tech University
Ruston, LA 71272 — Founded: 1894
SID: (318) 257-3144 — Enrollment: 9,667
President....Dan Reneau
Athletic Director....Jim Oakes
Sports Information Director....Byron Avery

Navy— U.S. Naval Academy
Annapolis, MD 21402 — Founded: 1845
SID: (410) 268-6226 — Enrollment: 4,100
Superintendent....Adm. Charles R. Larson
Athletic Director....Jack Lengyel
Sports Information Director....Scott Strasemeier

Northeast Louisiana University
Monroe, LA 71209 — Founded: 1931
SID: (318) 342-5460 — Enrollment: 11,553
President....Lawson Swearingen, Jr.
Athletic Director....Richard Giannini
Sports Information Director....Robby Edwards

Northern Illinois University
DeKalb, IL 60115 — Founded: 1895
SID: (815) 753-1706 — Enrollment: 22,218
President....John E. LaTourette
Athletic Director....Cary Groth
Sports Information Director....Mike Korcek

University of Notre Dame
Notre Dame, IN 46556 — Founded: 1842
SID: (219) 631-7516 — Enrollment: 10,126
President....Rev. Edward (Monk) Malloy
Athletic Director....Michael Wadsworth
Sports Information Director....John Heisler

University of Southwestern Louisiana
Lafayette, LA 70506 — Founded: 1898
SID: (318) 482-6331 — Enrollment: 17,000
President....Ray Authement
Athletic Director....Nelson Schexnayder
Sports Information Director....Dan McDonald

OTHER MAJOR DIVISION I CONFERENCES

Conferences that play either Division I basketball or Division I-AA football, or both.

America East (formerly North Atlantic Conference)
P.O. Box 69 — 28 Main Street
Orono, ME 04473
(207) 866-2383 — Founded: 1979
Commissioner....Stuart Haskell
Director of Communications....Julie Power
1996-97 members: BASKETBALL (10)— Boston University, Delaware, Drexel, Hartford, Hofstra, Maine, New Hampshire, Northeastern, Towson St. and Vermont.

Atlantic 10 Conference
2 Penn Center Plaza, Suite 1410
Philadelphia, PA 19102
(215) 751-0500 — Founded: 1976
Commissioner....Linda Bruno
Director of Communications....Ray Cella
1996-97 members: BASKETBALL (12)— Dayton, Duquesne, Fordham, George Washington, La Salle, Massachusetts, Rhode Island, St. Bonaventure, St. Joseph's-PA, Temple, Virginia Tech and Xavier-OH.

Big Sky Conference
P.O. Box 1459
Ogden, UT 84402
(801) 392-1978 — Founded: 1963
Commissioner....Douglas Fullerton
Director of Information....Ron Loghry
1996-97 members: BASKETBALL & FOOTBALL (9)— Cal St. Northridge, Cal. St. Sacramento, Eastern Washington, Idaho St., Montana, Montana St., Northern Arizona, Portland St. and Weber St.

Big South Conference
Winthop Colisem
Rock Hill, SC 29733 — Founded: 1983
Commissioner....Kyle Kallander
Director of Media Relations....Angela Phelps
1996-97 members: BASKETBALL (8)— Charleston Southern, Coastal Carolina, Liberty, MD-Baltimore County, NC-Asheville, NC-Greensboro, Radford, and Winthrop.
Out in 1997-98: NC-Greensboro

Colonial Athletic Association
8625 Patterson Ave.
Richmond, VA 23229
(804) 754-1616 — Founded: 1985
Commissioner....Tom Yeager
Asst. Commisioner for Commincations....Steve Vehorn
1996-97 members: BASKETBALL (9)— American, East Carolina, George Mason, James Madison, NC-Wilmington, Old Dominion, Richmond, Virginia Commonwealth and William & Mary.

Gateway Football Conference
1000 Union Station, Suite 333
St. Louis, MO 63103
(314) 421-2268 — Founded: 1982
Commissioner....Patty Viverito
Asst. Commissioner, Information....Mike Kern
1996 members (6): Illinois St., Indiana St., Northern Iowa, Southern Illinois, SW Missouri St. and Western Illinois.

Female Athletic Directors

As of Sept. 30, 1996, there were 17 female athletics directors at the nation's 305 NCAA Div. I schools. Here they are (in alphabetical order): Eve Atkinson, Lafayette; Sandy Barbour, Tulane; Kathy Clark, Idaho; Judith Davidson, CS-Sacramento; Vivian Fuller, NE Illinois; Cary Groh, N. Illinois; Kaye Hart, Austin Peay; Barbara Hedges, Washington; Judy MacLeod, Tulsa; Marilyn McNeil, Monmouth; Patricia Meiser-McKnett, Hartford; Judith Ray, New Hampshire; Judy Rose, NC-Charlotte; Andrea Seger, Ball St.; Helen Smiley, W. Illinois; Suzanne Tyler, Maine; Debbie Yow, Maryland.

Ivy League
120 Alexander Street
Princeton, NJ 08544
(609) 258-6426 Founded: 1954
Executive Director .... Jeffrey Orleans
Director of Information .... Chuck Yrigoyen

1996-97 members: BASKETBALL & FOOTBALL (8)— Brown, Columbia, Cornell, Dartmouth, Harvard, Pennsylvania, Princeton and Yale.

Metro Atlantic Athletic Conference
1090 Amboy Avenue
Edison, NJ 08837
(908) 225-0202 Founded: 1980
Commissioner .... Richard Ensor
Director of Media Relations .... Jaye Cavallo

1996-97 members: BASKETBALL (8)— Canisius, Fairfield, Iona, Loyola-MD, Manhattan, Niagara, St. Peter's and Siena. FOOTBALL (9)— Canisius, Duquesne, Fairfield, Georgetown, Iona, Marist, St. John's, St. Peter's and Siena.

New in 1997-98: BASKETBALL— Marist and Rider

Mid-Continent Conference
40 Shuman Blvd., Suite 118
Naperville, IL 60563
(708) 416-7560 Founded: 1982
Commissioner .... Jon Steinbrecher
Director of Media Relations .... Mark Simpson

1996-97 members: BASKETBALL (9)— Buffalo, Central Connecticut St., Chicago St., Missouri/K.C., NE Illinois, Troy St., Valparaiso, Western Illinois, Youngstown St.

New in 1997-98: Southern Utah

Mid-Eastern Athletic Conference
102 North Elm St. SE Building, Suite 401
Greensboro, NC 27401
(910) 275-9961 Founded:1970
Commissioner .... Charles S. Harris
Director of Service Bureau .... Larry Barber

1996-97 members: BASKETBALL (10)— Bethune-Cookman, Coppin St., Delaware St., Florida A&M, Hampton, Howard, MD-Eastern Shore, Morgan St., North Carolina A&T and South Carolina St.; FOOTBALL (8)— all but Coppin St. and MD-Eastern Shore.

Midwestern Collegiate Conference
201 South Capitol Ave., Suite 500
Indianapolis, IN 46225
(317) 237-5622 Founded: 1979
Commissioner .... John LeCrone
Director of Communications .... Will Hancock

1996-97 members: BASKETBALL (9)— Butler, Cleveland St., Detroit Mercy, Illinois-Chicago, Loyola-IL, Northern Illinois, Wisconsin-Green Bay, Wisconsin-Milwaukee and Wright St.

Out in 1997-98: Northern Illinois

Missouri Valley Conference
1000 St. Louis Union Station, Suite 333
St. Louis, MO 63103
(314) 421-0339 Founded: 1907
Commissioner .... Doug Elgin
Asst. Commissioner .... Jack Watkins

1996-97 members: BASKETBALL (10)— Bradley, Creighton, Drake, Evansville, Illinois St., Indiana St., Northern Iowa, Southern Illinois, SW Missouri St., and Wichita St.

Division I Hockey Conferences

The four Division I hockey conferences are the Eastern Collegiate Athletic Conference (ECAC) in Centerville, Mass., (508) 771-5060; the Central Collegiate Hockey Assn. (CCHA) in Ann Arbor, Mich. (313) 764-2590; Hockey East in North Andover, Mass., (508) 837-5033; and the Western Collegiate Hockey Assn. in Madison, Wisc. (608) 829-0100.

Northeast Conference
900 Route 9, Suite 120
Woodbridge, NJ 07095
(908) 636-9119 Founded: 1981
Commissioner .... Chris Monasch
Asst. Commissiioner, Media Relations .... Dave Siroty

1996-97 members: BASKETBALL (10)— Fairleigh Dickinson, LIU-Brooklyn, Marist, Monmouth, Mount St. Mary's, Rider, Robert Morris, St. Francis-NY, St. Francis-PA and Wagner. FOOTBALL (5)—Cent. Conn. St., Monnouth, Robert Morris, St. Francis (PA) and Wagner.

Out in 1997-98: Marist and Rider

Ohio Valley Conference
278 Franklin Road, Suite 103
Brentwood, TN 37027
(615) 371-1698 Founded: 1948
Commissioner .... Dan Beebe
Director of Information .... Rob Washburn

1996-97 members: BASKETBALL & FOOTBALL (10)— Austin Peay St., Eastern Illinois, Eastern Kentucky, Middle Tennessee St., Morehead St., Murray St., SE Missouri St., Tennessee-Martin, Tennessee St. and Tennessee Tech.

Patriot League
3897 Adler Place, Building C, Suite 310
Bethlehem, PA 18017
(610) 691-2414 Founded: 1984
Executive Director .... Constance Hurlbut
Director of Information .... Todd Newcomb

1996-97 members: BASKETBALL (7)— Army, Bucknell, Colgate, Holy Cross, Lafayette, Lehigh and Navy; FOOTBALL (6)— Bucknell, Colgate, Fordham, Holy Cross, Lafayette and Lehigh.

New in 1997: Towson St. (football only).

Pioneer Football League
1000 St. Louis Union Station, Suite 333
St. Louis, MO 63103
(314) 421-0339 Founded: 1993
Commissioner .... Patty Viverito
Media Relations .... Cindy Kern

1996 members: FOOTBALL (6): Butler, Dayton, Drake, Evansville, San Diego and Valparaiso.

Southern Conference
1 West Pack Square, Suite 1508
Asheville, NC 28801
(704) 255-7872 Founded: 1921
Commissioner .... Wright Waters
Asst. Commissioner, Media Relations .... Chris Walker

1996-97 members: BASKETBALL (10)— Appalachian St., The Citadel, Davidson, East Tennessee St., Furman, Georgia Southern, Marshall, Tennessee-Chattanooga, VMI and Western Carolina; FOOTBALL (9)—all except Davidson.

New in 1997-98: NC-Greensboro (Basketball only) and Wofford.

Out in 1997-98: Marshall.

Southland Conference
8150 North Central Expressway, Suite 930
Dallas, TX 75206
(214) 750-7522 Founded: 1963
Commissioner .... Greg Sankey
Director of Media Relations .... Tommy Newsome

1996-97 members: BASKETBALL (9)— McNeese St., Nicholls St., North Texas, NE Louisiana, Northwestern St., Sam Houston St., Southwest Texas St., Stephen F. Austin St., Texas-Arlington and Texas-San Antonio; FOOTBALL (8)— Jacksonville St., McNeese St., Nicholls St., Northwestern St., Sam Houston St., Southwest Texas St., Stephen F. Austin St. and Troy St.

Southwestern Athletic Conference
1500 Sugar Bowl Drive, Superdome
New Orleans, LA 70112
(504) 523-7574 Founded: 1920
Commissioner .... James Frank
Director of Publicity .... Lonza Hardy Jr.

1996-97 members: BASKETBALL & FOOTBALL (8)— Alabama St., Alcorn St., Grambling St., Jackson St., Mississippi Valley St., Prairie View A&M, Southern-Baton Rouge and Texas Southern.

Sun Belt Conference
One Galleria Boulevard, Suite 2115
Metairie, LA 70001
(504) 834-6600 Founded: 1976
Commissioner .... Craig Thompson
Director of Media Services .... Dayna Wells

1996-97 members: BASKETBALL (10)— Arkansas-Little Rock, Arkansas St., Jacksonville, Lamar, Louisiana Tech, New Orleans, South Alabama, SW Louisiana, Texas-Pan American and Western Kentucky.

Trans America Conference
The Commons, 3370 Vineville Ave., Suite 108-B,
Macon, GA 31204
(912) 474-3394 Founded: 1978
Commissioner .... Bill Bibb
Director of Information .... Tom Snyder

1996-97 members: BASKETBALL (12)— Campbell, Centenary, Central Florida, College of Charleston, Florida Atlantic, Florida International, Georgia St., Jacksonville St., Mercer, Samford, SE Louisiana and Stetson.

West Coast Conference
400 Oyster Point Blvd., Suite 221
South San Francisco, CA 94080
(415) 873-8622 Founded: 1952
Commissioner .... Michael Gilleran
Director of Information .... Don Ott

1996-97 members: BASKETBALL (8)— Gonzaga, Loyola Marymount, Pepperdine, Portland, St. Mary's, San Diego, San Francisco and Santa Clara.

Yankee Conference
University of Richmond, P.O. Box 8
Richmond, VA 23173
(804) 289-8371 Founded: 1946
Executive Director .... Chuck Boone
Director of Information .... Pat McCarthy

1996 members: FOOTBALL (12)— Boston University, Connecticut, Delaware, James Madison, Maine, Massachusetts, New Hampshire, Northeastern, Rhode Island, Richmond, Villanova and William & Mary.

PRO FOOTBALL

National Football League

League Office
410 Park Ave., New York, NY 10022
(212) 758-1500
Commissioner .... Paul Tagliabue
President .... Neil Austrian
Exec. V.P. & League Counsel .... Jay Moyer
Director of Information, AFC .... Leslie Hammond
Director of Information, NFC .... Reggie Roberts

NFL Management Council
410 Park Ave., New York, NY 10022
(212) 758-1500
Chairman .... Harold Henderson
V.P. & General Counsel .... Dennis Curran

NFL Players Association
2021 L Street NW, Suite 600, Washington, DC 20036
(202) 463-2200
Executive Director .... Gene Upshaw
Asst. Exec. Director .... Doug Allen
General Counsel .... Richard Berthelsen
Director of Public Relations .... Frank Woschitz

AFC

Baltimore Ravens
11001 Owings Mills Blvd.
Owings Mills, MD 21117
(410) 654-6200
Owner-President .... Art Modell
Exec. V.P., Legal & Administration .... Jim Bailey
V.P., Assistant to President .... David Modell
V.P., Public Relations .... Kevin Byrne

Buffalo Bills
One Bills Drive, Orchard Park, NY 14127
(716) 648-1800
Owner-President .... Ralph Wilson
Exec. V.P. & General Manager .... John Butler
V.P. & Head Coach .... Marv Levy
Director of Media Relations .... Scott Berchtold

Cincinnati Bengals
200 Riverfront Stadium, Cincinnati, OH 45202
(513) 621-3550
Chairman .... Austin Knowlton
President & General Manager .... Mike Brown
Public Relations Director .... Jack Brennan

Denver Broncos
13655 Broncos Parkway, Englewood, CO 80112
(303) 649-9000
Owner-President-CEO .... Pat Bowlen
General Manager .... John Beake
Director of Media Relations .... Jim Saccomano

Houston Oilers
8030 el rio, Houston, TX 77054
(713) 797-9111
Owner-President .... K.S. (Bud) Adams Jr.
Exec. V.P. & General Manager .... Floyd Reese
Director of Media Services .... Dave Pearson

Indianapolis Colts
P.O. Box 535000, Indianapolis, IN 46253
(317) 297-2658
Owner-President-Treasurer .... Robert Irsay
V.P. & General Manager .... Jim Irsay
V.P., Dir. Football Operations .... Bill Tobin
Director of Public Relations .... Craig Kelley

Jacksonville Jaguars
One Stadium Place, Jacksonville, FL 32202
(904) 633-6000
Chairman-CEO .... Wayne Weaver
President-COO .... David Seldin
Sr. V.P., Football Operations .... Michael Huyghue
Exec. Director of Communications .... Dan Edwards

Kansas City Chiefs
1528 Commerce Bank Building,
1000 Walnut St., Kansas City, MO 64106
(816) 924-9300
Owner-Founder .... Lamar Hunt
Chairman .... Jack Steadman
President-CEO-General Manager .... Carl Peterson
Director of Public Relations .... Bob Moore

Miami Dolphins
7500 SW 30th St., Davie, FL 33314
(305) 452-7000
Owner-President-CEO ....Wayne Huizenga
Exec. V.P. & General Manager ....Eddie Jones
Director of Media Relations ....Harvey Greene

New England Patriots
Foxboro Stadium, Route 1, Foxboro, MA 02035
(508) 543-8200
Owner-President-CEO & General Manager ....Bob Kraft
Head Coach ....Bill Parcells
Director of Public Relations..............................Don Lowery

New York Jets
1000 Fulton Ave., Hempstead, NY 11550
(516) 560-8100
Owner-Chairman...Leon Hess
President...Steve Gutman
Director of Public Relations ....Frank Ramos

Oakland Raiders
1220 Harborbay Parkway, Alameda, CA 94502
(510) 864-5000
Managing General Partner ....Al Davis
Executive Assistant..Al LoCasale
Publications Director ....Mike Taylor

Pittsburgh Steelers
300 Stadium Circle, Pittsburgh, PA 15212
(412) 323-0300
Owner-President..Dan Rooney
Vice Presidents..................John McGinley & Art Rooney Jr.
Media Relations Coordinator.........................Rob Boulware

San Diego Chargers
Jack Murphy Stadium, Box 609609
San Diego, CA 92160
(619) 280-2111
Owner-Chairman...Alex Spanos
President -Vice Chairman..............................Dean Spanos
General Manager ....Bobby Beathard
Director of Public Relations ....Bill Johnston

Seattle Seahawks
11220 NE 53rd Street, Kirkland, WA 98033
(206) 827-9777
Owner ....Ken Behring
President ....David Behring
Public Relations Director..............................Dave Neubert

NFC

Arizona Cardinals
P.O. Box 888, Phoenix, AZ 85001
(602) 379-0101
Owner-President...Bill Bidwill
Assistants to the President...........Bob Ferguson, Joe Wooley
Public Relations Director ....Paul Jensen

Atlanta Falcons
One Falcon Place, Suwanee, GA 30174
(770) 945-1111
Owner-Chairman.....................................Rankin Smith Sr.
President ....Taylor Smith
V.P., Player Personnel ....Ken Herock
Director of Public Relations...........................Charlie Taylor

Carolina Panthers
800 South Mint St., Charlotte, NC 28202-1502
(704) 358-7000
Founder-Owner ....Jerry Richardson
President ....Mike McCormack
General Manager..Bill Polian
Director of Communications......................Charlie Dayton

Chicago Bears
Halas Hall, 250 N. Washington, Lake Forest, IL 60045
(708) 295-6600
Owner-Chairman ....Edward McCaskey
President-CEO..Mike McCaskey
V.P., Football Operations ....Ted Phillips
Director of Public Relations ....Bryan Harlan

Dallas Cowboys
Cowboys Center
One Cowboys Parkway, Irving, TX 75063
(214) 556-9900
Owner-President-GM...Jerry Jones
Public Relations Director.............................Rich Dalrymple

Detroit Lions
Pontiac Silverdome
1200 Featherstone Rd., Pontiac, MI 48342
(810) 335-4131
Owner-President..................................William Clay Ford
Executive V.P. & COO................................Chuck Schmidt
Director of Media Relations ....Mike Murray

Green Bay Packers
1265 Lombardi Ave., Green Bay, WI 54304
(414) 496-5700
President-CEO ....Bob Harlan
Exec. V.P. & General Manager ....Ron Wolf
Exec. Dir. of Public Relations.............................Lee Remmel

Minnesota Vikings
9520 Viking Drive, Eden Prairie, MN 55344
(612) 828-6500
Owner-Chairman ....John Skoglund
President-CEO ....Roger Headrick
V.P., Team Operations....................................Jeff Diamond
Director of Public Relations ....David Pelletier

New Orleans Saints
6928 Saints Drive, Metairie, LA 70003
(504) 733-0255
Owner-President..Tom Benson
Exec. VP & General Manager ....Bill Kuharich
V.P. & Head Coach ....Jim Mora
Director of Media Relations ....Rusty Kasmiersky

New York Giants
Giants Stadium, East Rutherford, NJ 07073
(201) 935-8111
President/co-CEO.................................Wellington Mara
Chairman/co-CEO ....Preston Robert Tisch
Sr. V.P. & General Manager ....George Young
Director of Public Relations ....Pat Hanlon

Philadelphia Eagles
Veterans Stadium, Broad St. & Pattison Ave.
Philadelphia, PA 19148
(215) 463-2500
Owner ....Jeff Lurie
Director of Football Administration....................Bob Ackles
Director of Public Relations..............................Ron Howard

St. Louis Rams
Matthews-Dickey Boys Club
4245 N. Kingshighway, St. Louis, MO 63115
(314) 982-7267
Owner-Chairman ....Georgia Frontiere
President ....John Shaw
V.P., Football Operations ....Steve Ortmayer
Director of Public Relations ....Rick Smith

San Francisco 49ers
4949 Centennial Blvd., Santa Clara, CA 95054
(408) 562-4949
Owner ....Edward DeBartolo Jr.
President...Carmen Policy
V.P., Football Operations ....Dwight Clark
Director of Public Relations............................Rodney Knox

Tampa Bay Buccaneers
1 Buccaneer Place, Tampa, FL 33607
(813) 870-2700
Owner-President .... Malcolm Glazer
General Manager .... Rich McKay
Director of Public Relations .... Chip Namias

Washington Redskins
Redskin Park, P.O. Box 17247, Washington D.C. 20041
(703) 478-8900
Owner-Chairman-CEO .... Jack Kent Cooke
Executive V.P. .... John Kent Cooke
General Manager .... Charley Casserly
Director of Public Relations .... Mike McCall

Canadian Football League

League Office
CFL Building, 110 Eglinton Avenue West, 5th Floor
Toronto, Ontario M4R 1A3
(416) 322-9650
Commissioner .... Larry Smith
Chairman .... John Tory
V.P., Football Operations .... Ed Chalupka
Manager of Communications .... Jim Neish

CFL Players Association
467 Speers Rd., Unit 5, Oakville, Ontario L6K 3S4
(905) 844-7852
President .... Dan Ferrone
Legal Counsel .... Ed Molstad

British Columbia Lions
10605 135th St., Surrey, B.C. V3T 4C8
(604) 930-5466
Owner .... Nelson Skalbania
President .... Mike McCarthy
Dir. of Media/Public Relations .... Jim Dorash

Calgary Stampeders
McMahon Stadium, 1817 Crowchild Trail, NW
Calgary, Alberta T2M 4R6
(403) 289-0205
Owner-President .... Sig Gutsche
General Manager & Head Coach .... Wally Buono
Media Relations Coordinator .... Ron Rooke

Edmonton Eskimos
9023 111th Ave., Edmonton, Alberta T5B 0C3
(403) 448-1525
Owner .... Community-owned
President .... Ken Bailey
General Manager .... Hugh Campbell
Asst. General Manager of Adm. .... Allan Watt

Hamilton Tiger-Cats
2 King Street West, Hamilton, Ontario L8P 1A1
(905) 521-5666
Chairman .... David M. Macdonald
General Manager .... Neil Lumsden
Communications Director .... Norm Miller

Montreal Alouettes
4545 Avenue Pierre-De Coubertin
P.O. Box 65, Station M
Montreal, Quebec H1B3L6
(514) 252-4666
Chairman/Owner .... James L. Speros
VP, Dir. of Football Ops/GM .... Jim Popp
Dir. of Media/Public Relations .... Nathalie Maurer

Ottawa Rough Riders
Landsdowne Park, Coliseum Bldg.
1015 Bank St., Ottawa, Ontario K1S 3W7
(613) 235-5554
Owner .... Horn Chen
President-CEO .... Jim Durrell
Director of Football Operations .... Leo Cahill
Director of Media Relations .... Gary Page

Saskatchewan Roughriders
2940 — 10th Avenue, P.O. Box 1277
Regina, Saskatchewan S4P 3B8
(306) 569-2323
Owner .... Community-owned
President .... Fred Wagman
COO & General Manager .... Alan Ford
Media Coordinator .... Tony Playter

Toronto Argonauts
SkyDome Gate 9, P.O. Box 2005, Station B
Toronto, Ontario M5T 3H8
(416) 341-5151
Owners .... Labatt Brewing Co.
CEO .... Paul Beesten
President .... Bob Nicholson
General Manager & Head Coach .... Don Matthews
Manager of Media Relations .... Gary Lawless

Winnipeg Blue Bombers
1465 Maroons Road, Winnipeg, Manitoba R3G 0L6
(204) 784-2583
Owner .... Community-owned
President .... Lynn Bishop
Dir. Football Operations & Head Coach .... Cal Murphy
Manager of Media Relations .... J.D. Boyd

WLAF

World League of American Football
26-A Albemarle St.
London, England W1X 3FA
TEL: 011-44-171-355-1995
President .... Oliver Luck
Public Relations Contact .... Alastair MacPhail

Member teams (6): Amsterdam Admirals, Barcelona Dragons, Frankfurt Galaxy, London Monarchs, Rhein Fire (Dusseldorf), Scottish Claymores (Edinburgh).

Arena Football League
75 E Wacker, Suite 400
Chicago, IL 60601
(312) 332-5510
Commissioner .... James Drucker
Director, Media Relations .... Nick Gandy

Member teams (16): American Conference— Anaheim Piranhas, Arizona Rattlers, Iowa Barnstormers, Memphis Pharaohs, Milwaukee Mustangs, St. Louis Stampede and San Jose Sabrecats, Texas Terror. National Conference— Albany (NY) Firebirds, Charlotte Rage, Connecticut Coyotes, Minnesota Fighting Pike, Florida Bob Cats, Orlando Predators and Tampa Bay Storm. Expansion— New Jersey

GOLF

LPGA Tour
(Ladies Professional Golf Association)
100 International Golf Drive
Daytona Beach, FL 32114
(904) 274-6200
Commissioner .... Jim Ritts
Deputy Commissioner .... Jim Webb
Director of Communications .... Elaine Scott

PGA of America
100 Avenue of the Champions
Palm Beach Gardens, FL 33410
(407) 624-8400
President .... Tom Addis III
CEO .... Jim Awtrey
Director of Communications .... Terry McSweeney

PGA European Tour
Wentworth Drive, Virginia Water
Surrey, England GU25 4LX
TEL: 011-44-1344-842881
Executive Director .... Ken Schofield
Director of Communications .... Mitchell Platts

PGA Tour
112 TPC Blvd., Ponte Vedra, FL 32082
(904) 285-3700
Commissioner .... Tim Finchem
Director of Information .... Dave Lancer

Royal & Ancient Golf Club of St. Andrews
St. Andrews, Fife, Scotland KY16 9JD
TEL: 011-44-1334-472112
Secretary .... Michael Bonallack
Deputy Secretary .... George Wilson

USGA
(United States Golf Association)
P.O. Box 708, Liberty Corner Road, Far Hills, NJ 07931
(908) 234-2300
President .... Judy Bell
Executive Director .... David Fay
Director of Communications .... Marty Parkes

PRO HOCKEY

NHL

National Hockey League
Commissioner .... Gary Bettman
Senior V.P., Hockey Operations .... Brian Burke
Senior V.P., COO .... Stephen Solomon
V.P., Public Relations .... Arthur Pincus

League Offices
Montreal .... 1800 McGill College Ave., Suite 2600
Montreal, Quebec H3A 3J6
(514) 288-9220

New York .... 1251 Sixth Ave., 47th Floor
New York, NY 10020
(212) 789-2000

Toronto .... 75 International Blvd., Suite 300
Rexdale, Ontario M9W 6L9
(416) 798-0809

NHL Players' Association
1 Dundas St. West, Suite 2300
Toronto, Ontario M5G 1Z3
(416) 408-4040
Executive Director .... Bob Goodenow
Associate Counsel .... Ian Pulver,
J.P. Barry and Jeff Citron

Anaheim, Mighty Ducks of
Arrowhead Pond of Anaheim, P.O. Box 61077
Anaheim, CA 92806
(714) 704-2700
Owner .... Walt Disney Co.
Governor .... Michael Eisner
General Manager .... Jack Ferreira
Director of Public Relations .... Bill Robertson

Boston Bruins
1 FleetCenter, Suite 250, Boston, MA 02114
(617) 624-1909
Owner .... Jeremy Jacobs
President & General Manager .... Harry Sinden
Director of Media Relations .... Heidi Holland

Buffalo Sabres
Marine Midland Arena, 1 Seymour H. Knox III Plaza,
Buffalo, NY 14203-3096
(716) 855-4100
President-CEO .... Doug Moss
General Manager .... John Muckler
Director of Public Relations .... Jeff Holbrook

Calgary Flames
Canadian Airlines Saddledome, P.O. Box 1540 Station M
Calgary, Alberta T2P 3B9
(403) 777-2177
Owners .... Harley Hotchkiss, Grant A. Bartlett,
Murray Edwards, Ronald V. Joyce, Alvin G. Libin,
Allan P. Markin, J.R. McCaig, Byron and Daryl Seamen
President & CEO .... Ron Bremner
V.P. & General Manager .... Al Coates
Director of Public Relations .... Rick Skaggs

Chicago Blackhawks
United Center, 1901 West Madison St.
Chicago, IL 60612
(312) 455-7000
Owner-President .... William Wirtz
Senior V.P. & General Manager .... Bob Pulford
V.P. of Public Relations .... Jim DeMaria

Colorado Avalanche
1635 Clay St., Denver, CO 80204
(303) 893-6700
Owner .... COMSAT Entertainment Group
President .... Charlie Lyons
Exec. V.P., Hockey Operations & GM. .... Pierre Lacroix
Director of Media Relations .... Jean Martineau

Dallas Stars
211 Cowboys Parkway, Irving, TX 75063
(214) 868-2890
Owner .... Thomas O. Hicks
General Manager .... Bob Gainey
Director of Public Relations .... Larry Kelly

Detroit Red Wings
Joe Louis Arena, 600 Civic Center Drive
Detroit, MI 48226
(313) 396-7544
Owner/President .... Mike Ilitch
Owner/Secretary-Treasurer .... Marian Ilitch
Senior V.P .... Jim Devellano
Dir. of Player Personnel & Head Coach .... Scotty Bowman
Director of Public Relations .... TBA

Edmonton Oilers
Edmonton Coliseum, 7424 118th Ave.
Edmonton, Alberta, T5B 4M9
(403) 474-8561
Owner .... Peter Pocklington
President & General Manager .... Glen Sather
Exec. V.P. & Assistant GM .... Bruce MacGregor
Director of Public Relations .... Bill Tuele

Florida Panthers
100 North East Third Ave., 10th Floor
Fort Lauderdale, FL 33301
(954) 768-1900
Owner .... Wayne Huizenga
President .... Bill Torrey
General Manager .... Bryan Murray
Dir. of Public & Media Relations .... Greg Bouris

Hartford Whalers
242 Trumbull St., 8th Floor, Hartford, CT 06103
(203) 728-3366
Owner-CEO .... Peter Karmanos Jr.
General Partner .... Thomas Thewes
President & General Manager .... Jim Rutherford
Director of Media Relations .... Chris Brown

Los Angeles Kings
Great Western Forum, 3900 West Manchester Blvd.
Inglewood, CA 90306
(310) 419-3160
Majority Owners ....Philip Anschutz and Ed Roski
President....................Jim Leiweke
General Manager....................Sam McMaster
Director of Public Relations ....Nick Salata

Montreal Canadiens
Molson Centre, 1260 Gauchetière St. West
Montreal, Quebec H3B 5E8
(514) 932-2582
Owner....................Molson Companies, Ltd.
Chairman-President ....Ronald Corey
V.P. & Managing Director ....Serge Savard
Director of Communications ....Don Beauchamp

New Jersey Devils
Continental Airlines Arena
P.O. Box 504, East Rutherford, NJ 07073
(201) 935-6050
Chairman ....John McMullen
President & General Manager ....Lou Lamoriello
Director of Public Relations ....Michael Gilbert

New York Islanders
Nassau Veterans' Memorial Coliseum
Uniondale, NY 11553
(516) 794-4100
Owners ....Paul Greenwood, Ralph Palleschi, Robert Rosenthal and Stephen Walsh
V.P. & General Manager....................Mike Milbury
Director of Media Relations....................Ginger Killian

New York Rangers
2 Penn Plaza, 14th Floor, New York, NY 10121
(212) 465-6486
Owner ....ITT Corp./Cablevision Systems Inc.
President (MSG) ....Dave Checketts
President & General Manager ....Neil Smith
Director of Communications....................John Rosasco

Ottawa Senators
301 Moodie Dr., Suite 200, Nepean, Ontario, K2H 9C4
(613) 721-0115
Chairman & Gov. ....Rod Bryden
President & CEO ....Roy MLakar
General Manager....................Pierre Gauthier
Director of Media Relations....................Phil Legault

Philadelphia Flyers
1 CoreStates Complex, Philadelphia, PA 19148
(215) 465-4500
Chairman ....Ed Snider
President & General Manager ....Bob Clarke
V.P. of Public Relations ....Mark Piazza

Phoenix Coyotes
1 Renaissance Square, 2 North Central, Suite 1930
Phoenix, AZ 85004
(602) 379-2800
Owners ....Richard Burke & Steven Gluckstern
President....................Richard Burke
General Manager....................John Paddock
Director of Media Relations....................Richard Nairn

Pittsburgh Penguins
Civic Arena, Pittsburgh, PA 15219
(412) 642-1800
Owners....................Howard Baldwin, Morris Belzberg and Thomas Ruta
Exec. V.P. & General Manager....................Craig Patrick
V.P. Communications ....Thomas McMillan

St. Louis Blues
Kiel Center, 1401 Clark Ave., St. Louis, MO 63103
(314) 622-2500
President-CEO ....Jack Quinn
General Manager & Head Coach....................Mike Keenan
Director of Public Relations ....Jeff Trammel

San Jose Sharks
525 West Santa Clara St., San Jose, CA 95113
(408) 287-7070
Owner-Chairman....................George Gund III
Co-Owner ....Gordon Gund
President-CEO ....Art Savage
Exec. V.P.& Dir. of Hockey Operations ....Dean Lombardi
Director of Media Relations....................Ken Arnold

Tampa Bay Lightning
401 Channelside Drive, Tampa, FL 33602
(813) 229-2658
Owners ....Lightning Partners, Inc.
General Manager....................Phil Esposito
Director of Hockey Development & Scouting....Tony Esposito
V.P., Communications....................Gerry Helper

Toronto Maple Leafs
Maple Leaf Gardens
60 Carlton Street, Toronto, Ontario M5B 1L1
(416) 977-1641
Chairman-CEO ....Steve Stavro
President-COO-GM....................Cliff Fletcher
Media Relations Coordinator ....Pat Park

Vancouver Canucks
General Motors Place, 800 Griffiths Way
Vancouver, B.C. V6B 6G1
(604) 899-4600
Owner-Vice Chairman ....John McCaw Jr.
Chairman-CEO ....Arthur Griffiths
President & General Manager....................Pat Quinn
Dir. of Public & Media Relations....................Steve Tambellini

Washington Capitals
USAir Arena, Landover, MD 20785
(301) 386-7000
Chairman....................Abe Pollin
President....................Susan O'Malley
V.P. & General Manager ....Dave Poile
V.P. of Communications....................Matt Williams

IIHF

International Ice Hockey Federation
Todistrasse 23
CH-8002 Zurich, Switzerland
TEL: 011-411-281-1430
President ....Rene Fasel
General Secretary ....Jan-Ake Edvinsson

HORSE RACING

Breeders' Cup Limited
2525 Harrodsburg Road, Suite 500
Lexington, KY 40504
(606) 223-5444
President ....James E. (Ted) Bassett III
Executive Director....................D.G. Van Clief, Jr.
Director of Communications ....Dan Metzger

The Jockeys' Guild
250 West Main Street, Suite 1820, Lexington, KY 40507
(606) 259-3211
President....................Jerry Bailey
National Manager....................John Giovanni

TRA
(Thoroughbred Racing Associations)
420 Fair Hill Drive, Suite 1, Elkton, MD 21921
(410) 392-9200
President....................Clifford C. Goodrich
Executive V.P ....Chris Scherf
Director of Services....................Conrad Sobkowiak

TRC
(Thoroughbred Racing Communications)
40 East 52nd Street, New York, NY 10022
(212) 371-5910
Executive Director....................Tom Merritt
Director of Media Relations ....Bob Curran

USTA
(United States Trotting Association)
750 Michigan Ave., Columbus, OH 43215
(614) 224-2291
President ....Corwin Nixon
Executive V.P ....Fred Noe
Director of Public Relations....................John Pawlak

MEDIA

PERIODICALS

Sports Illustrated
Time & Life Bldg., Rockefeller Center
New York, NY 10020
(212) 522-1212
Publisher ....David Long
Managing Editor....................William Colson
Executive Editor ....Peter Carry

The Sporting News
10176 Corporate Square Dr., Suite 200
St. Louis, MO 63132
(314) 997-7111
Editor....................John Rawlings

USA Today
1000 Wilson Blvd., Arlington, VA 22229
(703) 276-3400
Owner ....Gannett Co.
President-Publisher ....Tom Curley
Managing Editor/Sports....................Monte Morell

WIRE SERVICES

Associated Press
50 Rockefeller Plaza, New York, NY 10020
(212) 621-1630
Sports Editor....................Terry Taylor
Deputy Sports Editor....................Brian Friedman

United Press International
1400 Eye Street NW, 8th Floor, Washington, DC 20005
(202) 898-8000
Sports Editor ....Ian Love

The Sports Network
95 James Way, Suite 107 & 109
Southampton, PA 18966
(215) 947-2400
President....................Mickey Charles
Director of Operations ....Phil Sokol
Managing Editor....................Steve Abbott

Sportsticker
600 Plaza Two, Jersey City, NJ 07311
(201) 309-1200
Vice President & General Manager....................Rick Alessandri
Managing Editor ....Doug Mittler

TV NETWORKS

ABC Sports
47 West 66th St., 13th Floor, New York, NY 10023
(212) 456-4867
President....................Steve Bornstein
Senior V.P., Production ....Dennis Lewin
Director of Information ....Mark Mandel

CBC Sports
P.O. Box 500, Station A 5H 100
Toronto, Ontario M5W 1E6
(416) 205-6523
Head of Sports ....Alan Clark
Sr. Executive Producer ....Doug Sellars
Publicist ....Susan Proctor

Classic Sports Network
300 Park Ave. South, 6th Floor, New York, NY 10010
(212) 529-8000
President ....Steve Greenberg
Executive Producer....................Douglas Warshaw
V.P. Marketing....................Jerry Frantz

CBS Sports
51 West 52nd St., 25th Floor, New York, NY 10019
(212) 975-5230
President....................David Kenin
Senior V.P., Production....................Rick Gentile
V.P., Programming....................Mike Aresco
Director of Public Relations ....Leslie Ann Wade

ESPN
ESPN Plaza, Bristol, CT 06010
(203) 585-2000
President-CEO....................Steve Bornstein
Sr. V.P., Programming....................John Wildhack
Executive Editor ....John Walsh
Managing Editor, ESPN2 ....Vince Doria
Director of Communications ....Mike Soltys

FOX Sports
PO Box 900, Beverly Hills, CA 90213
(212) 556-2472
President....................David Hill
Exec. Producer ....Ed Goren
V.P., Media Relations (NYC)....................Vince Wladika

The Golf Channel
7580 Commerce Center Drive, Orlando, FL 32819
(407) 363-4653
President-CEO ....Joe Gibbs
V.P., Production....................Mike Whelan
Director of Public Relations ....Debra Sweeney

HBO Sports
1100 Ave. of the Americas, New York, NY 10036
(212) 512-1987
President-CEO....................Seth Abraham
V.P., Executive Producer ....Ross Greenburg
V.P., Programming....................Lou DiBella
Director of Publicity....................Ray Stallone

MTV Sports
1633 Broadway, 32nd Floor, New York, NY 10024
(212) 846-4684
Executive Producer ....David Byrnes
Publicity Contact ....Mike Saffran

NBC Sports
30 Rockefeller Plaza, New York, NY 10112
(212) 664-2160
President....................Dick Ebersol
Executive Producer ....Tommy Roy
Director of Public Relations ....Ed Markey

Prime SportsChannel Networks
Prime Network: 20 Crossways Park North
Houston, TX 77081
(713) 661-0078
NewSport: 3 Crossways Park West
Woodbury, NY 11797
(516) 921-3764
CEO .... James Dolan
COO .... Josh Sapan
V.P., Programming .... Michael Lardner
Dir. of Media Relations .... Craig Sanders

TSN-The Sports Network
2225 Shepherd Ave. East, Suite 100
Willowdale, Ontario, M2J-5C2
(416) 494-1212
President & General Manager .... Jim Thompson
Public Relations Manager .... Rosemary Pitfield

Turner Sports
One CNN Center, 13th Floor, Atlanta, GA 30303
(404) 827-1735
President .... Dr. Harvey Schiller
Vice President .... Mike Pearl
Sr. V.P., Programming .... Kevin O'Malley
V.P. of Public Relations .... Greg Hughes

Univision (Spanish)
9405 NW 41st St., Miami, FL 33178
(305) 471-4008
Sports Director .... Jorge Hidalgo
Publicity Coordinator .... Rosalyn Espinosa

USA Network
1230 Ave. of the Americas, New York, NY 10020
(212) 408-9100
V.P., Production in Sports .... Gordon Beck
V.P., Sports Programming .... Wayne Becker
Sports Publicist .... Dan Schoenberg

OLYMPICS

IOC
(International Olympic Committee)
Chateau de Vidy, CH-1007 Lausanne, Switzerland
TEL: 011-41-21-621-6111
President .... Juan Antonio Samaranch
Director General .... Francois Carrard
Secretary General .... Francoise Zweifel
Coordinator, Public Informartion .... Fekrou Kidane
Director of Information .... Michele Verdier

1998 WINTER GAMES

Nagano Olympic Organizing Committee
KT Building, 3109-63 Kawaishinden
Nagano City 380, Japan
TEL: 011-81-262-25-1998
Time difference: 13 hours ahead of New York (EDT)
President .... Eishiro Saito
Director General .... Makoto Kobayashi
Head of Media .... Akira Hashimoto
(XVIIIth Olympic Winter Games, Feb. 7-22)

2000 SUMMER GAMES

Sydney Olympic Organizing Committee
Level 14, Maritime Center, 207 Kent St.
Sydney, Australia NSW 2000
TEL: 011-612-931-2000
Time difference: 14 hours ahead of New York (EDT)
President .... Gary Pemberton
Director General .... Bob Elphinston
Director of Information .... Ian Dose
(Games of XXVIIth Olympiad, Sept. 16-Oct. 1)

2002 WINTER GAMES

Salt Lake Olympic Organizing Committee
215 South State, Suite 2002, Second Floor
Salt Lake City, UT 84111
(801) 322-2002
Chairman .... Frank Joklik
President & CEO .... Tom Welch
Sr. Vice Presidents .... Dave Johnson, Gordon Crabtree
Dir. of Public Information .... Mike Korologos
(XIXth Olympic Winter Games, Feb. 9-24)

COA
(Canadian Olympic Association)
2380 Avenue Pierre Dupuy, Montreal, Quebec H3C-3R4
(514) 861-3371
CEO-General Secretary .... Carol Anne Letheren
President .... Bill Warren
IOC members .... Carol Anne Letheren & Richard Pound
Manager of Media Relations .... Lorraine Lafreniere (613) 748-5647

USOC
(United States Olympic Committee)
One Olympic Plaza, Colorado Springs, CO 80909
(719) 632-5551
President .... LeRoy Walker
Director .... Dick Schultz
IOC members .... Anita DeFrantz, James Easton & George Killian
Director of Public/Media Relations .... Mike Moran

1998 GOODWILL GAMES

New York Organizing Committee
Two World Trade Center, Suite 2164
New York, NY 10048
(212) 321-1998
Chairman .... Bob Johnson
President .... Michael Rowe
V.P., Communications .... Don Smith
Project Director .... Stephen Chriss
(4th Goodwill Games, July 25-Aug. 9)

1999 PAN AMERICAN GAMES

Pan American Games Society
(Winnipeg 1999, Inc.)
500 Shaftesbury Blvd., Winninpeg, Manitoba R3P 0M1
(204) 985-1999
President-CEO .... Don MacKenzie
Media Contact .... Ernie Nairn
(XIIIth Pan American Games, July 24-Aug. 8)

U.S. OLYMPICS TRAINING CENTERS

Colorado Springs Training Center
One Olympic Plaza, Colorado Springs, CO 80909
(719) 578-4500 ext. 5500
Dir. of U.S. Training Centers .... John Smyth
Director .... Patrice Milkovich

Lake Placid Training Center
421 Old Military Road, Lake Placid, NY 12946
(518) 523-2600
Director .... Jack Favro

San Diego Training Center
c/o San Diego National Sports Training Foundation
1650 Hotel Circle N., Suite 125, San Diego, CA 92108
(619) 656-1500
Director .... Benita Fitzgerald

U.S. OLYMPIC ORGANIZATIONS

National Archery Association
One Olympic Plaza, Colorado Springs, CO 80909
(719) 578-4576
President .... Thomas Stevenson Jr.
Executive Director .... Robert C. Balink
Media Contact.................................... Coleen Walker Mar

U.S. Badminton Association
One Olympic Plaza, Colorado Springs, CO 80909
(719) 578-4808
President.. Diane Cornell
Executive Director.............................. Clifford T. McPeake
Communications Director........................... Paul Pawlaczyk

USA Baseball
2160 Greenwood Avenue, Trenton, NJ 08609
(609) 586-2381
President .... Mark Marquess
Executive Director & CEO .... Richard Case
Dir. of Media Relations.................................. George Doig

USA Basketball
5465 Mark Dabling Blvd., Colorado Springs, CO 80918
(719) 590-4800
President .... Russell Granik
Executive Director....................................... Warren Brown
Director of Public Relations............................... Craig Miller

U.S. Biathlon Association
P.O. Box 5515
Essex Junction, VT 05433
(802) 655-4524
and
421 Old Military Rd., Lake Placid, NY 12946
(518) 523-3836
President .... Maj. Gen. Donald E. Edwards
Exec. Director .... Duane (Dusty) Johnstone
Director of Summer Biathalon........................ Kyle Woodlief

U.S. Bobsled and Skeleton Federation
P.O. Box 828, 421 Old Military Road
Lake Placid, NY 12946
(518) 523-1842
President.. Jim Morris
Executive Director .... Matt Roy

USA Boxing
One Olympic Plaza, Colorado Springs, CO 80909
(719) 578-4506
President.. Jerry Dusenberry
Acting Executive Director .... David Lubf
Communications Director .... Kurt Stenerson

U.S. Canoe and Kayak Team
Pan American Plaza, Suite 610
201 South Capitol Avenue, Indianapolis, IN 46225
(317) 237-5690
Chairman.. Lamar Sims
Executive Director (Interim)................................ Rus Tippett
Communications Manager .... Lisa Fish

U.S. Cycling Federation
One Olympic Plaza, Colorado Springs, CO 80909
(719) 578-4581
President.. Mike Fraysse
Executive Director .... Lisa Voight
Managing Director....................................... Steve Penny
Director of Communications .... Cheryl Kvasnicka

United States Diving, Inc.
Pan American Plaza, Suite 430,
201 South Capitol Avenue, Indianapolis, IN 46225
(317) 237-5252
President.. Steve McFarland
Executive Director .... Todd Smith
Director of Communications .... Dave Shatkowski

U.S. Equestrian Team
Pottersville Road, Gladstone, NJ 07934
(908) 234-1251
President.. Finn Caspersen
Executive Director .... Bob Standish
Director of Public Relations .... Marty Bauman
(508) 698-6810

U.S. Fencing Association
One Olympic Plaza, Colorado Springs, CO 80909
(719) 578-4511
President .... Steve Sobel
Interim Executive Director......................... William Goering

U.S. Field Hockey Assocation
One Olympic Plaza, Colorado Springs, CO 80909
(719) 578-4567
President .... Jenepher Shillingford
Executive Director.. Jane Betts
Director of Media/Public Relations .... Marc Whitney

U.S. Figure Skating Association
20 First Street, Colorado Springs, CO 80906
(719) 635-5200
President.. Morry Stillwell
Executive Director .... Jerry Lace
Communications Coordinator...................... Heather Linhart

USA Gymnastics
Pan American Plaza, Suite 300
201 South Capitol Avenue, Indianapolis, IN 46225
(317) 237-5050
President-Exec. Director.............................. Kathy Scanlan
Director of Public Relations .... Luan Peszek

USA Hockey
4965 North 30th St., Colorado Springs, CO 80919
(719) 599-5500
President .... Walter Bush
Executive Director .... Dave Ogrean
Dir. of Public Relations & Media .... Darryl Seibel

United States Judo, Inc.
P.O. Box 10013, El Paso, TX 79991
(915) 771-6699
President & Media Contact .... Frank Fullerton

U.S. Luge Association
P.O. Box 651, Lake Placid, NY 12946
(518) 523-2071
President... Dwight Bell
Executive Director .... Ron Rossi
Public Relations Specialist .... Sandy Caligiore
Communications Manager............................. Dmitry Feld

U.S. Modern Pentathlon Association
530 McCullough, Suite 248, San Antonio, TX 78215
(210) 246-3000
President.. Robert Marbut Jr.
Executive Director .... Dean Billick

U.S. Rowing
Pan American Plaza, Suite 400
201 South Capitol Avenue, Indianapolis, IN 46225
(317) 237-5656
President .... Dave Vogel
Executive Director... Frank Coyle
Media Contact .... Terry Friel

U.S. Sailing Association
P.O. Box 1260, 5 Maritime Drive
Portsmouth, RI 02871
(401) 683-0800
President .... Dave Irish
Executive Director .... Terry D. Harper
Media Contact.................................... Barby MacGowan
(401) 849-0220

U.S. Shooting Team
One Olympic Plaza, Colorado Springs, CO 80909
(719) 578-4670
Executive Director ....Robert Jusnick
Public Relations Director................................Nancy Moore

U.S. Skiing
P.O. Box 100, 1500 Kearns Blvd., Park City, UT 84060
(801) 649-9090
Chairman..Nick Badami
CEO ....Bill Marolt
President U.S. Ski Association........................Jim McCarthy
V.P. of Communications ....Tom Kelly

U.S. Soccer Federation
U.S. Soccer House
1801-1811 South Prairie Ave., Chicago, IL 60616
(312) 808-1300
President ....Alan Rothenberg
Executive Director ....Hank Steinbrecher
Director of Communications..........................Thomas Lange

Amateur Softball Association
2801 N.E. 50th Street, Oklahoma City, OK 73111
(405) 424-5266
President...Wayne Myers
Executive Director ....Don Porter
Dir. Media Relations/PR/Hall of Fame.............Bill Plummer
Director of Communications ....Ron Babb

U.S. International Speedskating Assn.
P.O. Box 16157, Rocky River, OH 44116
(216) 899-0128
President..Bill Cushman
Executive Director...Katie Marquard
Media Relations Director..................................Wendy Day

U.S. Swimming, Inc.
One Olympic Plaza, Colorado Springs, CO 80909
(719) 578-4578
President...Carol Zaleski
Executive Director ....Ray Essick
Director of Communications.........................Charlie Snyder

U.S. Synchronized Swimming, Inc.
Pan American Plaza, Suite 510
201 South Capitol Avenue, Indianapolis, IN 46225
(317) 237-5700
President ....Laurette Longmire
Executive Director ....Debbie Hesse
Communications Coordinator ....Laura LaMarca

U.S. Table Tennis Association
One Olympic Plaza, Colorado Springs, CO 80909
(719) 578-4583
President...Terry Timmins
Executive Director...Paul Montville

U.S. Team Handball Federation
One Olympic Plaza, Colorado Springs, CO 80909
(719) 578-4582
President...Thomas P. Rosandich
Executive Director..............................Michael Cavanaugh
Media Contact ....Maureen Stone

U.S. Tennis Association
70 West Red Oak Lane, White Plains, NY 10604
(914) 696-7000
President..Lester M. Snyder Jr.
Executive Director..................................Richard D. Fermin
Dir. of Communications...........................Page Dahl Crosland

USA Track and Field
P.O. Box 120, Indianapolis, IN 46206
(317) 261-0500
President...Larry Ellis
Executive Director...Ollan Cassell
Press Information Director...................................Pete Cava

U.S. Volleyball Association
3595 East Fountain Blvd., Suite I-2
Colorado Springs, CO 80910
(719) 637-8300
President...Rebecca Howard
Director of Media Relations ....Lorene Graves

United States Water Polo
1685 W. Uintah St.
Colorado Springs, CO 80904
(719) 634-0699
President...Brett Bernard
Executive Director...Bruce Wigo
Dir. of Media/Public Relations ....Kyle Utsumi

U.S. Weightlifting Federation
One Olympic Plaza, Colorado Springs, CO 80909
(719) 578-4508
President...Brian Derwin
Executive Director...................................George Greenway
Communications Director....................Anthony Bartokowski

USA Wrestling
6155 Lehman Drive, Colorado Springs, CO 80918
(719) 598-8181
President ....Larry Sciacchetano
Executive Director ....Jim Scherr
Dir. of Communications.......................................Gary Abbott

AFFILIATED ORGANIZATIONS

U.S. Curling Association
1100 Center Point Drive, Box 866
Stevens Point, WI 54481
(715) 344-1199
President ....Winnifred Bloomquist
Exec. Dir. & Media Contact ....David Garber

U.S. Amateur Confederation of Roller Skating
P.O. Box 6579, Lincoln, NE 68506
(402) 483-7551
President ....Betty Ann Danna
Executive Director ....George Pickard
Information Director ....Andy Sealey

United States Raquetball Association
1685 West Uintah, Colorado Springs, CO 80904
(719) 635-5396
President...Van Dubolsky
Executive Director ....Luke Saint Onge
Communications Director...................................Linda Mojer

U.S. Taekwondo Union
One Olympic Plaza, Suite 405
Colorado Springs, CO 80909
(719) 578-4632
President ....Hwa Chong
Exec. Director & Media Contact.................Robert Fujimura

Triathlon Federation USA
3595 East Fountain Blvd., Suite F-1
Colorado Springs, CO 80910
(719) 597-9090
Executive Director ....Steve Locke
Media Contact and Deputy Director ....Tim Yount

American Water Ski Association
799 Overlook Drive, S.E., Winter Haven, FL 33884
(941) 324-4341
President...Andrea Plough
Executive Director...Duke Waldrop
Director of Communications..........................Don Cullimore

U.S. Windsurfing Association
P.O. Box 978
Hood River, OR 97031
(541) 386-8708
President...Bill Collins
Executive Director...................................Holly Macpherson

SOCCER

FIFA
(Federation Internationale de Football Assn.)
P.O. Box 85, 8030 Zurich, Switzerland
TEL: 011-41-1-384-9595
President .... Joao Havelange
General Secretary .... Joseph Blatter
Director of Communications .... Keith Cooper

MLS

Major League Soccer
2029 Century Park East, Suite 400
Los Angeles, CA 90067
(310) 772-2600
Chairman .... Alan I. Rothenburg
Commissioner .... Douglas G. Logan
Director of Communications .... Dan Courtemanche

Office moves to New York in January 1997
MLS
110 E. 42nd Street, Suite 1502
New York, NY 10017

Colorado Rapids
555 17th Street, Suite 3350
Denver, CO 80202
(303) 299-1570
Investor/Operator .... Philip F. Anschutz
President .... Robert Sanderman
General Manager .... Rich Levine
Director of Media Relations .... Allison Gollust

Columbus Crew
77 E. Nationwide Blvd.
Columbus, OH 43215
(614) 221-2739
Investor/Operator .... Lamar Hunt and Family
General Manager .... Jamey Rootes
Director of Public Relations .... Adam Low

Dallas Burn
2602 McKinney, Suite 200
Dallas, TX 75204
(214) 979-0303
Investor/Operator .... League-owned
President/GM .... Billy Hicks
Director of Media Relations .... Chris Ward

Kansas City Wiz
706 Broadway St., Suite 100
Kansas City, MO 64105
(816) 472-4625
Investor/Operator .... Lamar Hunt and Family
General Manager .... Tim Latta
Director of Media Relations .... Jim Moorhouse

Los Angeles Galaxy
1640 So. Sepulveda Blvd., Suite 114
Los Angeles, CA 90025
(310) 445-1260
Investor/Operator .... LA Soccer Partners
Chairman .... Mark Rapaport
General Manager .... Danny Villanueva Jr.
Director of Media Relations....Francisco Lozano/Ron Acosta

New England Revolution
Foxboro Stadium, Route 1
Foxboro, MA 02035
(508) 543-0350
Investor/Operator .... Robert Kraft and Family
General Manager .... Brian O'Donovan
Director of Media Relations .... Rafael Morffi

New York/New Jersey MetroStars
One Harmon Plaza, 8th Floor
Seacausus, NJ 07094
(201) 583-7000
Investor/Operator .... John Kluge and Stuart Subotnick
Vice President/GM .... Charlie Stillitano
Director of Media Relations .... Jeff Bradley

San Jose Clash
1265 El Camino Real, 2nd Floor
Santa Clara, CA 95050
(408) 241-9922
Investor/Operator .... League-owned
President/GM .... Peter Bridgwater
Director of Media Relations .... Rick La Plante

Tampa Bay Mutiny
1408 N. Westshore Blvd., Suite 1004
Tampa, FL 33607
(813) 288-0096
Investor/Operator .... League-owned
President/GM .... Farrukh Quraishi
Director of Media Relations .... Jim Henderson

Washington D.C. United
13832 Redskin Drive
Herndon, VA 22071
(703) 478-6600
Owner .... Washington Soccer, L.P.
President/GM .... Kevin Payne
Director of Media Relations .... Beau Wright

1998 WORLD CUP

French Organizing Committee
90 Avenue des Champs Elysees
F-75008 Paris, France
TEL: 011-33-1-44-95-1998
Time difference: five hours ahead of New York (EDT)

Co-Presidents .... Ferdnand Sastre and Michel Platini
General Director .... Jacques Lambert
Dir. of Press & Communications .... Alain Leiblang
(16th World Cup, June 10-July 12)

CONCACAF
(Confederation of North, Central American & Caribbean Association Football)
725 Fifth Ave., 17th Floor, New York, NY 10022
(212) 308-0044
President .... Jack Austin Warner
General Secretary .... Chuck Blazer

U.S. Soccer
(United States Soccer Federation)
Soccer House, 1801-1811 South Prairie Ave.
Chicago, IL 60616
(312) 808-1300
President .... Alan Rothenberg
Exec. Director/Sec. General .... Hank Steinbrecher
Director of Communications .... Tom Lange

A-League
(American Professional Soccer League)
2 Village Rd., Suite 5, Horsham, PA 19044
(215) 657-7440
Commissioner .... Richard Groff
Operations Director .... Brad Purcel
Rochester Rhinos

Member teams (7): Atlanta Ruckus, Colorado Foxes, Montreal Impact, New York Fever, Rochester Rhinos, Seattle Sounders and Vancouver 86ers.

CISL
(Continental Indoor Soccer League)
16027 Ventura Blvd., Suite 605, Encino, CA 91436
(818) 906-7627
Commissioner..Ron Weinstein
League Counsel ....Dan Grigsby
Director of Media Relations ....John Dowdy
Member teams (12): Eastern Division— Dallas Sidekicks, Detroit Neon, Houston Hotshots, Indianapolis Twisters, Monterrey La Raza, Washington Warthogs. Western Division— Anaheim Splash, Arizona Sandsharks, Portland Pride, Sacramento Knights, San Diego Sockers, Seattle SeaDogs.

NPSL
(National Professional Soccer League)
115 Dewalt Avenue, NW, Canton, OH 44702
(330) 455-4625
Commissioner ....Steve M. Paxos
Director of Operations................................Paul Luchowski
Director of Media Relations ....Chuck Murr
Member teams (15): American Conference— Baltimore Spirit, Cincinnati Silverbacks, Cleveland Crunch, Columbus Invaders, Harrisburg Heat, Philadelphia Kixx and Tamp Bay Terror. National Conference—Buffalo Blizzard, Detroit Rockers, Edmonton Drillers, Kansas City Attack, Milwaukee Wave, St. Louis Ambush, Toronto Shooting Stars and Wichita Wings.

USISL
United Systems of Independent Soccer Leagues
4322 N. Beltline Rd., Suite B-205, Irving, TX 75038
(214) 570-7575
Commissioner..Francisco Marcos
Administrative Manager ....Beverly Wright
Director of Public Relations............................Mike Agnew

TENNIS

ATP Tour
(Association of Tennis Professionals)
200 ATP Tour Blvd., Ponte Verde Beach, FL 32082
(904) 285-8000
Chief Executive Officer ....Mark Miles
V.P., Communications ....Pete Alfano

ITF
(International Tennis Federation)
Pallisert Rd., Barons Court
London, England W14 9EN
TEL: 011-44-171-3818060
President ....Brian Tobin
General Manager..Doug Mec
Media Administrator ....Ian Barnes

World TeamTennis
445 North Wells, Suite 404, Chicago, IL 60610
(312) 245-5300
Chief Executive Officer..............................Billie Jean King
Executive Director ....Ilana Kloss
Communications Director ....Kim Couch

USTA
(United States Tennis Association)
70 West Red Oak Lane, White Plains, NY 10604
(914) 696-7000
President..Lester Snyder
Executive Director...................................Richard D. Fermin
Dir. of Communications..............................Page Crosland

WTA Tour
(Women's Tennis Association)
1266 East Main St. 4th Floor, Stanford, CT 06902
(203) 978-1740
Executive Director & CEO...............Anne Person Worcester
Communications Director.................................Joe Favorito

TRACK & FIELD

IAAF
(International Ameteur Athletics Federation)
17 Rue Princesse Florestine
BP 359, MC-98007, Monaco
TEL: 011-33-93-30-7070
President..Primo Nebiolo
General Secretary ....Istvan Gyulai
Director of Information ....Giorgio Reinei

1997 WORLD CHAMPIONSHIPS

Athens Organizing Committee
Assn. Hellenique d'Athletisme Amateur (SEGAS)
137 Avenue Syngrou, Athens 17121, Greece
TEL: 011-30-1-935-8592
Time difference: Seven hours ahead of New York (EDT)
President ....Stratos Molyvas
General Secretary ....Kostis Grammatikopoulos
(6th World Championships, Aug. 1-10)

AAU
(Amateur Athletic Union)
6751 Forum Dr., Suite 200 Orlando, FL 32821
(407) 363-6170
President...Bobby Dodd
Director of Communications ....Dixie Keller

USA Track & Field
P.O. Box 120
Indianapolis, IN 46206
(317) 261-0500
Executive Director...Ollan Cassell
Director of Information ....Pete Cava

YACHTING

1999-2000 America's Cup

New Zealand Defense Committee
(Royal New Zealand Yacht Squadron)
P.O. Box 1927, Auckland, New Zealand
TEL: 011-64-9-357-6712
Time difference: 16 hours ahead of New York (EDT)
Exec. Director & Contact ....Alan Sefton
(Next America's Cup defense scheduled to begin in Oct. 1999 and run through Feb. 2000, off the coast of Auckland.)

MISCELLANEOUS

All-American Soap Box Derby
P.O. Box 7233, Akron, OH 44306
(330) 733-8723
President ....F.A. Wahl
Chairman of the Board ....John Piscitelli
Public Relations Director ....Bob Troyer

Association of Surfing Professionals
P.O. Box 309, Huntingon Beach, CA 92548
(714) 851-2774
President...George Stokes
Executive Director ....Graham Stapelberg

Association of Volleyball Professionals
15260 Ventura Blvd., Suite 2250, Sherman Oaks, CA 91403
(310) 577-0775
President...Jon Stevenson
Exec. Director ....Jerry Solomon
Media Contact ....Steve Vanderpool

BASS, Inc.
(Bass Anglers Sportsmen Society)
5845 Carmichael Road, Mongomery, AL 36117
(334) 272-9530
CEO ....Helen Sevier
Publicity Director...Ann Lewis

International Game Fish Association
1301 East Atlantic Blvd., Pompano Beach, FL 33060
(305) 941-3474
Chairman....George Matthews
President....Mike Leach
Editor....Ray Crawford

Little League Baseball Incorporated
P.O. Box 3485, Williamsport, PA 17701
(717) 326-1921
CEO....C.J. Hale
President....Steven Keener
Director of Communications....Dennis Sullivan

Major Indoor Lacrosse League
2310 West 75th St., Prairie Village, KS 66208
(913) 384-8960
Chairman-CEO....Chris Fritz
President....Russ Cline
Director of Public Relations....Mary Havel

Member teams (7): Baltimore Thunder, Boston Blazers, Buffalo Bandits, Charlotte Cobras, New York Saints, Philadelphia Wings and Rochester Knighthawks.

National Rifle Assocation
11250 Waples Mill Road, Fairfax, VA 22030
(703) 267-1000
Executive VP....Wayne LaPierre
Public Affairs Director....Bill Powers

National Sports Foundation
1314 North Hayworth Ave., Suite 402
Los Angeles, CA 90046
(770) 698-8600
Executive Director....Ed Harris

Professional Rodeo Cowboys Association
101 Pro Rodeo Drive, Colorado Springs, CO 80919
(719) 593-8840
Commissioner....Lewis Cryer
Director of Public Relations....Steve Fleming

Roller Hockey International
1388 Suttler St., Suite 710, San Francisco, CA 94109
(714) 385-1769
Commissioner....Ralph Backstrom
COO....David B. McLane
CEO....Larry King
Public Relations Director....Mike Lynch

Special Olympics
1325 G St. NW Suite 500
Washington, DC 20005
(202) 628-3630
Founder....Eunice Kennedy Shriver
COB....Sargent Shriver
COO....Kim Elliott
Public Affairs Director....Jay Emmet

Volleyball Hall of Fame
444 Dwight St.
Holyoke, MA 01040
(413) 536-0926
President....Karen S. Keirstead
Public Relations Director....John Kane

Wheelchair Sports USA
3595 East Fountain Blvd., Suite L-1
Colorado Springs, CO 80910
(719) 574-1150
Chairman....Paul DePace
Executive Director....Patricia Shepherd

Commissioners and Presidents

Chief Executives of Established Major Sports Organizations since 1876.

Major League Baseball

Commissioner	Tenure
Kanesaw Mountain Landis*	1920-44
Albert (Happy) Chandler	1945-51
Ford Frick	1951-65
William Eckert	1965-68
Bowie Kuhn	1969-84
Peter Ueberroth	1984-89
A. Bartlett Giamatti*	1989
Fay Vincent	1989-92
Bud Selig†	1992—

*Died in office.
†Chairman of Executive Committee.

National League

President	Tenure
Morgan G. Bulkeley	1876
William A. Hulbart*	1877-82
A.G. Mills	1883-84
Nicholas Young	1885-1902
Henry Pulliam*	1903-09
Thomas J. Lynch	1910-13
John K. Tener	1914-18
John A. Heydler	1918-34
Ford Frick	1935-51
Warren Giles	1951-69
Charles (Chub) Feeney	1970-86
A. Bartlett Giamatti	1987-89
Bill White	1989-94
Leonard Coleman	1994—

*Died in office.

American League

President	Tenure
Bancroft (Ban) Johnson	1901-27
Ernest Barnard*	1927-31
William Harridge	1931-59
Joe Cronin	1959-73
Lee McPhail	1974-83
Bobby Brown	1984-94
Gene Budig	1994—

*Died in office.

NBA

Commissioner	Tenure
Maurice Podoloff	1949-63
Walter Kennedy	1963-75
Larry O'Brien	1975-84
David Stern	1984—

NFL

President	Tenure
Jim Thorpe	1920
Joe Carr	1921-39
Carl Storck	1939-41
Commissioner	
Elmer Layden	1941-46
Bert Bell*	1946-59
Austin Gunsel	1959-60
Pete Rozelle	1960-89
Paul Tagliabue	1989—

*Died in office.

NHL

President	Tenure
Frank Calder*	1917-43
Red Dutton	1943-46
Clarence Campbell	1946-77
John Ziegler	1977-92
Gil Stein	1992-93
Commissioner	
Gary Bettman	1993—

*Died in office.

NCAA

Executive Director	Tenure
Walter Byers	1951-88
Dick Schultz	1988-93
Cedric Dempsey	1993—

IOC

President	Tenure
Demetrius Vikelas, Greece	1894-96
Baron Pierre de Coubertin, France	1896-1925
Count Henri de Baillet-Latour, Belgium	1925-42
Vacant	1942-46
J. Sigfried Edstrom, Sweden	1946-52
Avery Brundage, USA	1952-72
Lord Michael Killanin, Ireland	1972-80
Juan Antonio Samaranch, Spain	1980—

Wide World Photos

Muhammad Ali lowers the torch to ignite the cauldron that will signal the official beginning of the 1996 Summer Olympics in Atlanta.

OLYMPICS

by Philip Hersh

Most Exceptional Games

The Atlanta Olympiad will be remembered for stunning athletic achievement, over-commercialization and the bomb.

There could not have been a better beginning. It was perfect.

Muhammad Ali, up there on what seemed Dr. Martin Luther King's celestial mountaintop of racial equality, about to light the cauldron during the opening ceremony at Centennial Olympic Stadium in Atlanta.

Ali, the 1960 boxing gold medalist, the world's best-known sports figure of the past 50 years, showing the world that his nation, his native South, could rise above its past.

Ali, 54, his face smooth and young and his arm wobbling from a disease of age, summing up the Olympic century. It was the greatest.

Who could know the Centennial Olympics would not reach such heights again?

They eventually split into two Olympics—before and after the bombing, inside and outside of the competition venues, wondrous volunteers and inept organizers—made singular only by their global pluralism and a shared terror.

"Now, when people say 1996, they're not going to remember the medals won, they're going to remember this was the place where they had the terrorist attack," said Matt Ghaffari of Cleveland, a silver medalist in Greco-Roman wrestling.

Two months after the July 27 pipe bombing in Centennial Olympic Park, which had become the tacky soul of these Games whose ambiance only a corporate flak could have loved, no one had been charged in the 1:25 a.m. incident which left one dead and more than 100 injured.

On the 28th, after an agonizing night, the decision was made to have the Olympics continue as planned, with the mayhem acknowledged in moments of silence and Olympic flags at half mast at the start of competition in the 22 sports contested on the day of the bombing.

It was a day that began with weeping skies and hard rain and, competitively, reached its culmination when Donovan Bailey of Canada became the world's fastest man with a world record of 9.84 seconds in the quintessential Olympic event, the 100 meters.

That day summed up an Olympics of polarities in which a record 197 nations came together in a place where the city council two years before had adopted a resolution inviting "Bucharest, Hungary" to become a sister city with Atlanta.

Bailey's run encapsulated what the Olympics are to be once the cauldron is lit: a chance to see men and women athletes at their best, letting the beauty of human power and movement and will lift us briefly from our more real concerns.

There were many such moments in the Centennial Games: Kerri Strug's painful vault to ensure gymnastics team gold for the U.S.; Naim Suleymanoglu of Turkey doing a third reprise of his Pocket Hercules rou-

Philip Hersh covers international sports for the *Chicago Tribune* and has been the Tribune's full-time Olympic writer since 1986.

Wide World Photos

Michael Johnson's attempt to sweep the gold in both the 200 and 400 meter events was the most heavily anticipated performance at the 1996 Olympics. He did not disappoint.

tine; Michael Johnson making history with a time in the 200 meters so fast it nearly defied human parameters; the Nigerian soccer team captivating a continent; Carl Lewis refusing to abdicate as the king of track and field; Alexander Karelin, the Greco-Roman colossus from Russia, as infallible as ever; the duels in the pool between Alexander Popov of Russia and Gary Hall of the U.S.

With the Soviet Union having officially disintegrated as an Olympic entry, the United States topped the medal counts (44 gold, 101 total) for the first time in a non-boycotted Olympics since 1968. A record 77 nations won medals, but 10 of those were newly-minted former republics of larger nations.

These were, by popular declaration of media who had not been paying much attention in the past, the Olympics of women, particularly U.S. women, who won 19 of the 44 golds, including four of the five in team sports or events where there was a male equivalent. Truth be told, while two decades of Title IX have greatly advanced opportunities for U.S. women, the Olympics have long been a place for female stars, going back to Babe Didriksen in 1932.

Despite record crowds, cheering passionately if a bit too one-sidedly for U.S. athletes, despite the brilliance of these men and women, these Olympics will, in the words of Chicago Tribune columnist Bernie Lincicome, be remembered as "the Games of Numbers, and the most important ones were 9.712, Kerri Strug's score in the vault; 19.32, Michael Johnson's time in the 200 and, ultimately, 911."

The Greatest was at the beginning. In the end, when International Olympic Committee president Juan Antonio Samaranch usually calls the just-closed Games the greatest, he said instead they were "most exceptional."

The double meaning of exceptional—uncommon, either above or below average—hung like condemnation with faint praise. It actually was a perfect way to describe the duality of the 1996 Olympics, sweet from within, sad from without. The sport-by-sport highlights are noted below.

The Big Three:

GYMNASTICS: For the second straight "home-country" Olympics, a teenage munchkin produced what U.S. audiences would remember as the defining competitive moment in the Games. In 1984, it was Mary Lou Retton's triumph in the all-around, which she almost certainly would not have won if the Soviet Bloc had attended. In 1996, it was Kerri Strug's dramatic vault on a sprained ankle, clinching the first team gold by U.S. women and, ironically, hurting the foot so badly it kept her from the all-around, the event she most wanted to compete in.

Strug, 18, was the final vaulter in what was the final rotation for the U.S. Just before her, Dominique Moceanu had fallen on both vaults. Strug's first vault also had ended in a fall, when she heard a snap in her foot. As teammates and coaches urged her to take a second vault, not knowing exactly how far ahead the U.S. was of second-place Russia, Strug's head also was boggled by searing pain and the screams of 32,040 spectators. Thinking the gold depended on her, Strug did the vault, landed on both feet, hopped into the 90-degree turn for the ritual of saluting the judges, then collapsed onto her hands and knees, her face contorted in pain from two torn ligaments. Strug would be carried to the awards ceremony in the arms of her coach, Bela Karolyi.

The U.S. women flopped in the all-around (won by Ukraine's Lilia Podkopayeva, who also won gold in floor exercise and silver in balance beam), with Shannon Miller and Dominique Dawes unraveling to finish 8th and 18th after being 1-2 after two of the four apparatus rotations. But Miller recovered to end her stunning Olympic career (7 medals—two gold, two silver, three bronze) with a gold on balance beam, Dawes took a bronze in floor exercise and Amy Chow a silver on uneven bars. Miller, 19, won only two fewer individual Olympic medals (5) than all other U.S. women combined in Olympic history—and six of those other medals came in 1984.

Men's all-around champion Alexei Nemov of Russia was the most decorated athlete of the Olympics, with 6 medals—

Bigger Gaudier Grosser

"It is hardly imaginable that any other host could have done a worse job."

Writing in the China Daily of Aug. 22, 1996., that is the way Yi Xin saw Atlanta's role as organizer of the Centennial Olympics. While that viewpoint obviously comes filtered through a particular political perspective, it was not far from the criticism expressed in much of the non-U.S. western press. The boosterish Atlanta Journal-Constitution commissioned a national telephone poll done Aug. 4-6 in which 50 percent of Americans gave the host city an "A" for its "ambitious effort to stage the biggest Olympics in history." Another 34 percent gave it a "B." A fair grade would lie somewhere between the poll results and the China Daily's obvious "F."

It was a sad irony that Atlanta escaped even more scrutiny for its organizational failures once the deadly bomb in Centennial Olympic Park rendered massive computer glitches and late buses inconsequential. The question is how and why Atlanta, trying to create a world image for itself, gave the private Atlanta Committee for the Olympic Games such total control of planning it exposed the city to the enormous risk of being exposed as the idiot of the global village. Given its budget restraints while trying both to run the event and build venues with $1.7 billion of private funding—as opposed to Barcelona's getting hundreds of millions in government money for the 1992 Games—Atlanta was forced to put on a Wal-Mart Olympics. Even gross indulgences on the commercial side could not give ACOG much of a financial cushion. When the likes of ACOG chairman Billy Payne had the hubris to say in advance the Centennial Olympics nevertheless would be the best Games ever in the safest city on the face of the earth, anything less would attract criticism. And this time, more was less. The 1996 Atlanta Summer Games marked the Olympic Centennial by rewriting the Olympic motto from faster, higher, stronger to bigger,

Wide World Photos

Janet Evans carries the Olympic torch during the opening ceremonies in Atlanta. No one knew then that a heavily criticized and disorganized event was about to unfold.

gaudier, grosser. Whichever adjective applies, the truth is the Olympics resembled the Georgia State Fair on steroids. By refusing to take advice from anyone about potential problems, ACOG never got a grasp on what it was trying to seize. "It was like organizing 2 1/2 Olympic Games," Payne admitted just before the Aug. 4 closing ceremony. The Olympics now have found out how much is too much of a good thing. It is 3 million spectators and 8.6 million tickets sold (more people saw women's sports in Atlanta than all sports in Barcelona) in a city too small to handle those numbers. It is approximately 17,000 athletes and officials and 50,152 wondrous volunteers. It is a snowball become an avalanche. The number of spectators was ACOG's problem, because it desperately needed the $468 million realized from ticket sales. The size of the Olympics is something the International Olympic Committee must deal with as the number of athletes has burgeoned by 150 percent in the last 24 years. The IOC hardly was blameless in the Atlanta fiasco, which led rowers to hijack buses and everyone to scream at IBM's computerized information system. The IOC oversight commission, which was supposed to supervise the Games' preparations, was guilty of oversight for not insisting certain areas be imp roved. Inside the stadiums, arenas, ranges, domes and pools, everything went swimmingly and divingly. Outside went tragedy, chaos, greed, overcommercialization, rudeness, joy, celebration, courtesy and sharing.

In offering advice to 2000 Olympic host Sydney in the Aug. 10 issue of the Australian edition of *Time*, author Barry Hillebrand said, "Remember the Olympics are about sport. . .Atlanta seemed to forget that. Everyone wanted a slice of the Olympic pie. The city was transformed into one enormous tawdry bazaar with too many street vendors and beer gardens. . . the Olympic experience was debased for many by rampant commercialism." In attempting to ensure those commercial interests got maximum exposure, Centennial Olympic Park was, until July 27, left unsecured. At its best, the park allowed the hoi polloi a chance at an Olympic "experience." Atlanta turned into a street party done on the cheap, with everyone invited to eat century-old birthday cake.

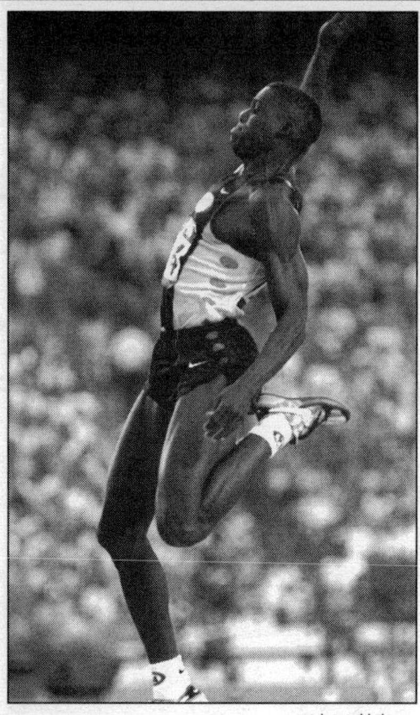

Wide World Photos

By winning his fourth straight Olympic long jump event, **Carl Lewis** tied Mark Spitz and Paavo Nurmi for second place with nine gold medals overall.

two gold, 1 silver, three bronze. Vitaly Scherbo, winner of 6 golds at Barcelona, added four bronzes. Jair Lynch became the first male African-American gymnast to win a medal with a silver on parallel bars.

SWIMMING: The U.S. dominated, sweeping the relays for the first time since 1972. The Chinese women flopped. This time the drug controversy involved the first Irish woman, Michelle Smith, to win an Olympic gold (Smith wound up with three golds and a bronze). Russia's Popov was still Alexandr the Greatest sprinter. Janet Evans, who had won gold (4) or silver (1) in all her previous Olympic races, made the final in just one of her two events, finishing sixth behind Brooke Bennett ("The Next Janet") in the 800 free. Krisztina Egerszegi of Hungary (200 backstroke) matched Australian Dawn Fraser (100 free) as the only person to win the same event three straight times. The four world records, half as many as four years ago, came from four different countries. Amy Van Dyken of the U.S., a lifetime asthmatic, was left gasping for breath after a disappointing fourth in her first event, the 100 free, then went on to win four golds (50 free, 100 butterfly, two relays). Penelope Heyns of South Africa won both breaststrokes (setting a world mark in the 100 prelims), becoming the first woman and second person from her country to win two Olympic golds; Germany's Franziska van Almsick was upset in the 200 free and her seven Olympic medals still do not include a gold.

Other world record-setters were Russia's Denis Pankratov, the Human Red October, whose submarine butterfly stroke broke his own mark while winning the 100 and also carried him to victory in the 200; Fred de Burghraeve in the 100 breaststroke, where he became the first Belgian swimmer to win an Olympic gold and the first since 1910 to have a world record; and the U.S. men's medley relay.

China's women went from dominance (12 golds in 16 events at the 1994 worlds) to mediocrity (1 gold in Atlanta, by Le Jingyi in the 100 free) so fast the only explanation was better doping control. Not only did the Chinese women win just 6 medals, but 15 of their 24 individual entrants failed to make the finals. The medals suddenly made available by Chinese failure were picked off by Ireland, Costa Rica and South Africa, among others, while the U.S. women had the same total (14) as in Barcelona.

Ireland's Smith, winner of the 400 free and both individual medleys, stirred controversy because she got a late entry to the 400 and because her progression in those events over the past two years has been so startling. Smith was judged guilty of doubt by association: her coach/husband, former Dutch discus thrower Erik de Bruin, was banned for steroid use in 1993. Smith, 26, said, "This is the culmination of 3 1/2 years hard work." All her doping controls were negative.

The best head-to-head duel of the entire Olympics was the matchup of Alexandr Popov and Gary Hall of the U.S. in the 50 and 100 freestyles. Popov won the 100 by .07 seconds and the 50 by .13, giving him back-to-back wins in both. Hall extracted a measure of revenge when he swam the anchor leg of the 4 x 100 free relay in

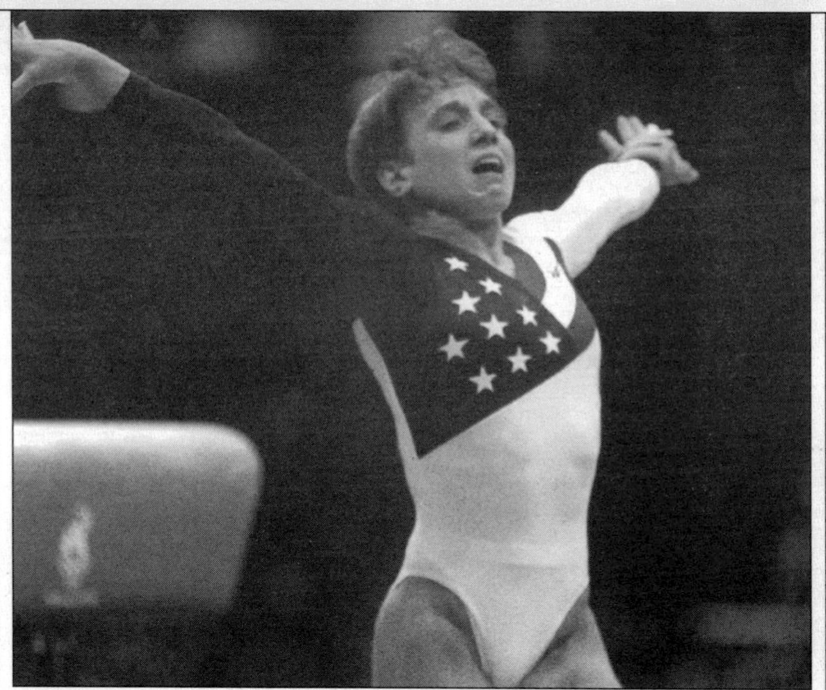

Wide World Photos

Kerri Strug's wince-seen-round-the-world (on tape delay) was the most compelling moment in an Olympics filled with amazing feats of athleticism. Strug's heroic vault assured a gold medal for her team but left her unable to compete in any individual events.

47.45 seconds, fastest relay split ever. In a sad epilogue to the Olympics, Popov was stabbed in the stomach during an Aug. 24 altercation on a Moscow street, but was released from a hospital two weeks later and expected to recover fully.

TRACK AND FIELD: A combination of the predictable and unexpected turned this into one of the most compelling Olympic track meets ever.

Everyone expected Michael Johnson of the U.S. to make history by becoming the first man to win the 200 and 400 meters in any Olympics—let alone the same Olympics. But no one could have foreseen his 19.32 in the 200 meters, lowering the 200 world record by twice as much in one fell swoop (.34 seconds) as it had dropped in the previous 28 years.

Everyone expected France's Marie-Jose Perec to become the first person to make a successful defense of a 400-meter title, but few foresaw her matching Johnson's 200-400 double. Which she did.

Everyone expected Carl Lewis to make headlines, but few expected him to do it by winning a fourth straight long jump title—and ninth Olympic gold—and then lobbying unsuccessfully for a place on the 4 x 100-meter relay.

Everyone expected U.S. sprinting to be in decline, but few gave Canada's Donovan Bailey much of a chance to win the 100, which he did in a world record 9.84 seconds, let alone anchor a Canadian 4 x 100 relay team to victory over the U.S. It was the first time the U.S. lost in the final of the sprint relay.

No one expected marathoner Josiah Thugwane to become the first black South African to win Olympic gold. Or Ukraine's Sergey Bubka, the czar of the pole vault, to withdraw before qualifying with an Achilles injury. Or two-time heptathlon champion Jackie Joyner-Kersee to withdraw after one heptathlon event with a sore leg, then end her Olympic career by earning a bronze medal on her final long jump.

Or Russia's Svetlana Masterkova, who had no track record in the 1,500, to become the second woman (after Soviet Tatiana Kazankina in 1976) to win the 800/1500 double; or Charles Austin, unranked in the world since 1992, to win the United States' first high jump gold since 1968; or oft-injured Kenny Harrison to upset world-record holder Jonathan Edwards of Great Britain in the triple jump with a U.S. and Olympic record leap of 59 feet, 4 1/4 inches—just before his girlfriend, Gail Devers, became the first woman to win back-to-back 100-meter titles since Wyomia Tyus in 1964-68.

Or Deon Hemmings to become Jamaica's first female gold medalist with an upset in the 400 hurdles; or Gwen Torrence, who went into the U.S. Olympic trials as an overwhelming Games favorite in the 100 and 200, to win just a bronze in the 100 before her hometown fans; or Chioma Ajunwa of Nigeria, whose four-year steroid ban ended in June, to win the long jump.

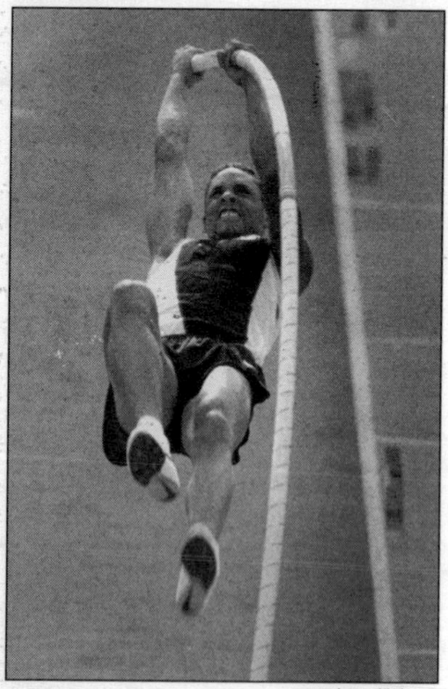

Wide World Photos

Dan O'Brien overcame the disappointment of not even making the 1992 USA Olympic team by winning the 1996 decathlon.

More predictable were: a victory by Noureddine Morceli of Algeria in the 1,500, considering his most recent defeat at the distance had been in the 1992 Olympic final; gold for world champion Allen Johnson of the U.S. in the 110-meter hurdles; Dan O'Brien of the U.S. winning the decathlon and erasing his failure to make the 1992 team; and Haile Gebrselassie of Ethiopia winning the 10,000 (but withdrawing from the 5,000 because he said the hard track made his feet too sore).

And the rest of the results worth noting, in alphabetical order:

ARCHERY: Justin Huish, a 21-year-old from Simi Valley, Calif., with a picaresque story, became the first person to win individual and team gold in the same Olympics. Huish's practice "range" forced him to shoot across a street, up his driveway, through his garage across the backyard and up a hill to have even half the Olympic distance of 90 meters. Two weeks after the Olympics, a California judge erased from Huish's record a three-year-old vandalism conviction after "KKK" had been painted on a black neighbor's property.

BADMINTON: Poul-Erik Hoyer-Larsen of Denmark, the men's champion, became the first non-Asian to win gold or silver in the sport's second Olympic appearance.

BASEBALL: Hitting 38 homers to make up for the defections to the U.S. of three players, Cuba went unbeaten (9-0) to win a second straight gold despite allowing 6.55 runs per game. With three homers and six RBI from Omar Linares, the Cubans won the final 13-9 over Japan for what it claims to be a 143rd straight victory in international tourney play dating to 1987. Japan, which lost 15-1 to the U.S. in round-robin play, stunned the Americans 11-2 in the semis. The U.S. went on to win the bronze 10-3 over Nicaragua.

BASKETBALL: While Dream Team III yawned its way to a second straight title, beating Yugoslavia 95-69 in the men's final, the first group of U.S. women to train more than a couple of months as a national team was the most impressive group of basketball players in the Olympics. By winning the final 111-87, a game in which they shot 66 percent from the field, the U.S. women finished their year of living harmoniously

Wide World Photos

South African **Penelope Heyns** set a world record in the 100 meter breaststroke preliminaries and also went on to win the gold medal in the same event. Heyns also won a gold in the 200 meter breaststroke to become the first woman from her country to win two gold medals.

with a 60-0 record, winning their eight Olympic matches by an average of 30.1 points. The team was led by four-time Olympian (and three-time gold medalist) Teresa Edwards, 32, at guard and soon-to-be supermodel Lisa Leslie at forward, where she averaged 28.7 points per game in the medal round. But, in a fitting tribute to the notion of teamwork, all 12 U.S. women scored in the final.

The men plodded to victory by an average margin of 31.8 points, 12 less than Dream Team I's dominance factor in Barcelona. Charles Barkley, David Robinson and Scottie Pippen, the team's top three scorers, and John Stockton each won a second gold.

BOXING: A dramatic third-round knockout by the last U.S. fighter in the tournament, light middleweight David Reid, kept the U.S. from a gold shutout for the first time since 1948. Reid was trailing 15-5 when he scored just the 12th final-round knockout in Olympic boxing history, keeping Cuba from a fifth gold medal in the 10 weight classes. With five bronzes, the U.S. won more than twice as many medals (6) as it had in Barcelona but won few friends with constant griping about officiating. World champion light heavyweight Antonio Tarver, who took the entire tournament too lightly, was routed in the semis and wound up only with bronze. Five-time world champion Felix Savon of Cuba, unbeaten internationally in 10 years, won the heavyweight final 20-2 for a second straight gold. Cuba also had three silver medals.

CYCLING: The United States went into the Olympics with its $30,000 "Superbikes" and hopes to approach its record nine medals in the boycotted 1984 Olympics. It was, however, the French who won nine medals, including gold (road race) and silver (time trial) by Jeannie Longo-Ciprelli, the greatest woman cyclist in history, whose resume had lacked only an Olympic triumph. The U.S. wound up with two silvers (Marty Nothstein in the match sprint, Erin Hartwell in individual pursuit), a bronze (Susan DiMattei in the new Olympic event

Wide World Photos

Michelle Smith of Ireland won three golds and a bronze while dealing with accusations of drug use because of her extraordinary progress in the time leading up to the games. Smith passed all of her drug tests and is the first Irish woman to win a gold medal.

of mountain biking) and plenty of recriminations. Leading them was pursuit world champion Rebecca Twigg, who bolted from Atlanta after losing in the quarterfinals, calling the national coaches "communists" and dropping out of the time trial. The opening of the Games to cycling pros allowed five-time Tour de France champion Miguel Indurain to win gold in the time trial, but U.S. road race favorite Lance Armstrong was a badly-beaten 12th.

CANOE-KAYAK: After winning gold and silver medals in the 1995 whitewater world meet, the U.S. men were dismally non-competitive on the Ocoee River, with no finish better than sixth. The lone U.S. medal was a silver by Dana Chadlek in slalom kayak.

DIVING: A little girl of 13 in 1992, when she became the youngest Olympic platform diving champion in history, China's Fu Mingxia at 17 became one of the sport's greatest champions by winning the springboard and platform titles. That left her only one gold behind the record four of U.S. divers Pat McCormack and Greg Louganis, but Fu announced her retirement in September. With Xiong Ni's victory on the men's springboard, China missed becoming the first country to sweep the four events for the first time since 1952 because Russia's Dmitry Sautin took the platform title. The Chinese also had a men's silver and bronze, while the U.S. missed gold for the first time since 1912. Mary Ellen Clark's bronze (platform), marking a victory over her trials with vertigo, and Mark Lenzi's bronze (springboard), marking a victory over post-Olympic depression following the 1992 gold, were the only U.S. medals.

FENCING: Russia's men won four of six gold medals, with Stanislav Pozdynakov taking individual and team titles in sabre. Laura Flessel of France (epee) was a double winner among the women. The U.S. was hopeless: only Ann Marsh (7th in foil) finished higher than 16th.

FIELD HOCKEY: While traditional powers India and Pakistan were shut out of the medals for only the second time since

1920, the Netherlands (gold men, bronze women) and Australia (gold women, bronze men) dominated. The U.S. women were a disappointing fifth while the men remained 0-for-the Olympics, losing all seven matches and making their overall Olympic record 0-26-3.

TEAM HANDBALL: Denmark, which had not qualified for the past two Olympics, stunned 1988-92 gold medalist South Korea for the women's gold. Before an Olympic handball record crowd of 32,439, Croatia beat Sweden for the men's title, giving the newly-minted nation its first Olympic gold. The U.S. women were winless, while the men finished 9th (of 12) by winning their final two matches for a 2-4 mark.

ROWING: Two of the most remarkable athletes in the sport's history, Silken Laumann of Canada and Stephen Redgrave of Great Britain, each added to their legends. Redgrave, 34, became the first to win four consecutive rowing golds—in two different boats, four with coxswain and coxless pair, and with two different partners in the pair. (He also won bronze in the 1988 pair with coxswain). Stunningly, Redgrave's was the only gold in all sports for Great Britain, its poorest performance since 1952. Single sculler Laumann, 31, was a profile in courage four years ago when she won bronze barely three months after a collision with another boat tore her right knee to shreds. She had further operations in 1993 and had to be exonerated after a doping positive (cough medicine) at the 1995 Pan Am Games. In Atlanta, she added a silver to her two previous bronzes.

The U.S. team was a big disappointment, especially its eights, each a world champion (men-1994; women-1995) in the last two years. The women's eight was 4th, the men's 5th.

SOCCER: On a ground hallowed for American football and before what is believed to be the largest crowd ever to see a women's sporting event, Team USA delighted 76,481 at Georgia's Sanford Stadium with a 2-1 victory over China for the gold medal. "It's a milestone for women's soccer and women's sports in general," said goalie Brianna Scurry, who made good on her pledge to run through the streets of Athens wearing only her medal (at 2:07 a.m.). As the standard-bearers for a U.S. women's national team program begun only 11 years ago, the veteran group had a 4-0-1 record in the tournament.

The men's tournament ended in an equally historic triumph, as Emmanuel Amunike scored in the penultimate minute of the final—his second game-winner of the tourney—to give Nigeria a 3-2 win over Argentina. The Super Eagles thus became the first African team to win a World Cup or Olympic title, and they did it with style, rallying from a 3-1 deficit against Brazil in the semifinals to win 4-3 on Nwankwu Kanu's overtime goal. "The future of football is ours," said Kanu, who also scored the tying goal against Brazil in the final minute of regulation.

The U.S. men were a bust again. With a 1-1-1 record in the first round of a tournament in which each team could add three wild-card players of any age to its 23 & Under rosters, the U.S. failed to advance past the opening round for the 10th time in 10 Olympic appearances.

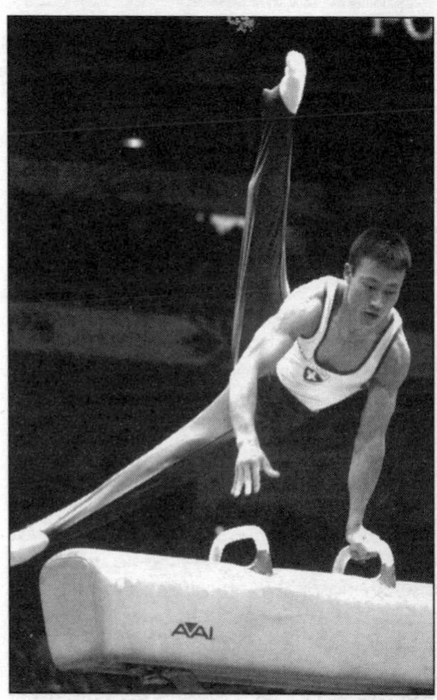

Wide World Photos

Switzerland's **Donghua Li** performs in the men's pommel horse competition. Li went on to win the gold.

Wide World Photos

Three fighters from Philly. (L to R) **Terrance Cauthen, David Reid** and **Zahir Raheem** show off their Olympic team belts. Only Reid came through, though, winning a gold in the light-middleweight division and avoiding the first gold shutout for the USA since 1948.

SOFTBALL: Despite losing 2-1 to Australia in a game forced into extra innings when Dani Tyler forgot to step on home plate after an apparent home run and then advancing to the final on a controversial 1-0 win over China, the U.S. women did exactly what was expected when they celebrated a quarter-century battle to get the sport into the Olympics by winning the gold medal. Dot Richardson, the 34-year-old shortstop and orthopedic surgeon, keyed the 3-1 win over China in the final with a two-run homer. The softball venue in Columbus, Ga., was the hidden jewel of the Olympics, with sellout crowds of 8,500 for nearly every game, plus consistently hospitable officials and volunteers.

SHOOTING: Kim Rohde, a 17-year-old high school junior from El Monte, Calif., became the youngest women's Olympic champion ever with gold in the new event of double trap (hitting two clay targets released simultaneously). For the third straight Olympics, U.S. men did not win a gold medal.

SYNCHRONIZED SWIMMING: The heavily favored U.S. team received nine perfect scores out of 10 for their optional routine to win the team competition, the only event contested. Solo and duet were dropped from the program after 1992.

TABLE TENNIS: For the first time in the sport's three Olympic appearances, one nation—China—swept the men's and women's singles and doubles golds. The return to preeminence by table tennis' traditional power was so complete the Chinese won gold and silver in three events, gold and bronze in the fourth. Liu Guoliang (men) and Dang Yaping (women) won singles and doubles golds.

TENNIS: For the second straight time, an upset in the Olympic tourney final became the career highlight for a young U.S. player—Jennifer Capriati in 1992, when she beat Steffi Graf of Germany for the gold; Lindsay Davenport in 1996, when she beat Aranxta Sanchez Vicario of Spain 7-6, 6-2. While the women's field included six of the world's top seven players (minus only

Graf), the men's was weakened by the absence of Pete Sampras, Jim Courier, Michael Chang, Thomas Muster, Michael Stich and Boris Becker. That left Andre Agassi of the U.S. an easy road to the gold, which he took with a straight-set rout of Spain's Sergi Bruguera. In doubles, Mary Joe and Gigi Fernandez won a second straight doubles title for the U.S.

VOLLEYBALL: The Dutch are no treat for Italy's men. After dominating world volleyball since 1989, with successive world titles, the Italians had their dreams of gold shattered by the Netherlands for the second straight time. In 1992, it was in the quarterfinals; this time, in a final won by the Dutch 17-15 in the fifth set. The Dutch, silver medalists in 1992, had lost 3-0 to Italy in the Atlanta preliminary round.

Cuba's women, only 3-2 in the prelims, won a second straight gold in four sets over an unbeaten Chinese team.

For the U.S., the results underscored significant decline after three Olympics in which the men had two golds and a bronze, the women silver and bronze. The men were 9th, the women 7th.

BEACH VOLLEYBALL: A sport added for its sex appeal—hard-bodied guys and dolls in skimpy bathing suits—put Karch Kiraly on a man-made beach, where he enhanced his legend as the greatest volleyballer ever. Kiraly, 35, teamed with Kent Steffes for a straight-set win over another U.S. team, Mike Dodd and Mike Whitmarsh, in the final. Kiraly, who had won indoor golds in 1984 and 1988, became the first ever to win three volleyball golds.

The highly-rated and oft-feuding U.S. women's team of Holly (Twin) McPeak, whose nickname is explained by breast enlargement surgery, and Nancy Reno was bounced in the quarters by U.S. rivals Barbara Fontana Harris and Linda Hanley. While Atlanta Beach was a far cry from Ipanema, the Brazilians obviously felt at home: the women's final was contested by

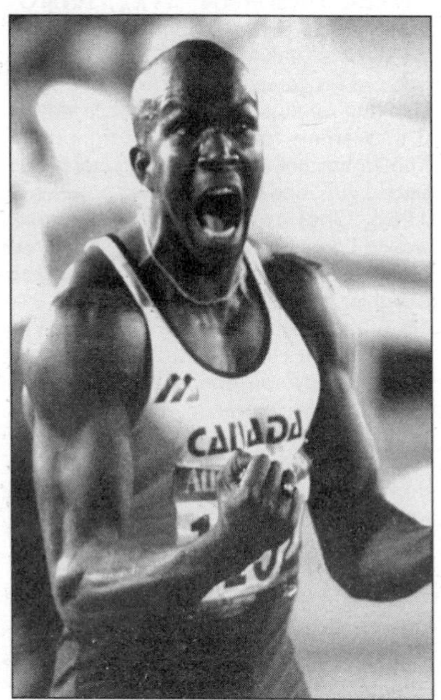

Wide World Photos

Canada's **Donovan Bailey** celebrates his gold-medal-winning performance in the 100 meters. Bailey's dash set a new world record with a time of 9.84 seconds.

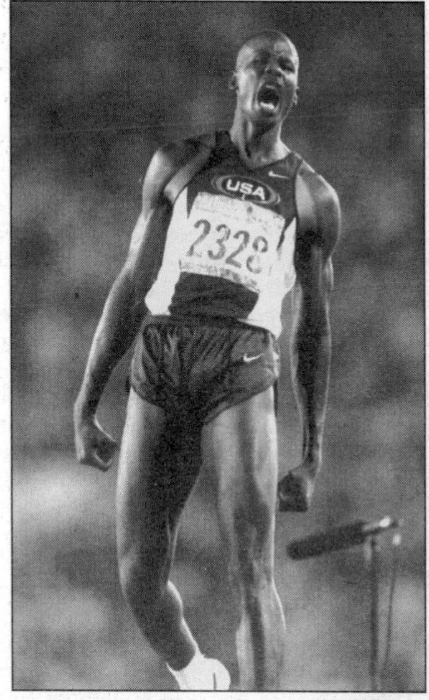

Wide World Photos

Charles Austin of the United States won the gold medal in the high jump and finished second to Bailey in the (unofficial) reaction competition.

Wide World Photos

Belgian **Fred deBurghgraeve** won the gold in men's 100 meters and set a world record in the preliminaries of the same event. He's also the first Belgian to win an Olympic medal in swimming.

two Brazilian teams, with Jackie Silva and Sandra Pires prevailing in straight sets.

WATER POLO: The U.S. men were a big disappointment, finishing with a 5-3 record and their worst finish (7th) since 1976. Manuel Estierte, a veteran of five Olympics, scored three goals as Spain beat Croatia 7-5 for its first gold in the sport after a silver in 1992.

WEIGHTLIFTING: In one of the most dramatic head-to-head duels in the Games, Naim Suleymanoglu of Turkey became the greatest weightlifter in Olympic history with a third straight gold. Suleymanoglu, known as the "Pocket Hercules" for his ability to lift nearly three times his body weight (140), needed to break world records in his final two lifts to beat Valerios Leonidis of Greece in the 141-pound class. The U.S. had just two top-10 finishers: Wes Barnett (6th) at 238 pounds and Bryan Jacob (9th) at 130. Super-hyped superheavy Mark Henry of the U.S. injured his back during the competition and placed 14th.

FREESTYLE WRESTLING: With the January murder of 1984 Olympic champion Dave Schultz haunting the proceedings, U.S. wrestlers wearing black armbands in Schultz' memory won three golds, their best showing in a nonboycotted Olympics since 1924.

Two of the U.S. champions, Kurt Angle and Tom Brands, symbolized the split in the team after Schultz was killed, allegedly by former wrestling benefactor John E. du Pont. Angle, who won a controversial decision from Iran's Abbas Jadidi at 220 pounds, represented the Dave Schultz Wrestling Club, founded by his wife, Nancy, after her husband's death. Brands, who lost only one point in five matches en route to the 136.5-pound title, still was accepting money from du Pont's Team Foxcatcher until just before the Games. Kendall Cross (125) added the third U.S. gold, while heavyweight Bruce Baumgartner's bronze made him the most medaled athlete (13) in Olympic and world championship history.

GRECO-ROMAN WRESTLING: Superheavyweight Alexander (the Great) Karelin was pushed into one of the toughest fights of his career by Matt Ghaffari of the U.S., but the Russian man mountain won 1-0 in overtime for his third straight gold. Karelin has not lost an international match since 1987; and not given up a point since 1988. Ghaffari, 34, a native of Iran, wound up as one of the Games' most visible personalities when he visited the daughter of Centennial Park bombing victim Alice Hawthorne in the hospital. With silvers from Dennis Hall (125.5) and Brandon Paulson, the U.S. had its best Olympic showing ever.

YACHTING: After winning medals in nine of 10 classes (one gold, six silver, two bronze) for the best performance by any nation in the 1992 Games, the United States was keelhauled in Savannah.

Dark horse entrant Courtenay Becker Day, who was the navigator on the all-woman crew of America's Cup entry America^3's Mighty Mary, won the bronze in the Europe Dinghy competition. And Jeff Madrigali, Kent Massey and Jim Barton brought home another bronze in the soling event after finishing a strong fourth in the 1995 Soling Worlds and fourth again in the fleet racing portion of the pre-Olympics. ❐

OLYMPICS STATISTICS

THE GAMES IN REVIEW

1996

ATLANTA

Final Medal Standings

National Medal Standings are not recognized by the IOC. The unofficial point totals are based on three points for every gold medal, two for each silver and one for each bronze.

		G	S	B	Total	Points
1	**United States**	44	32	25	101	221
2	Russia	26	21	16	63	136
3	Germany	20	18	27	65	123
4	China	16	22	12	50	104
5	France	15	7	15	37	74
6	Italy	13	10	12	35	71
7	Australia	9	9	23	41	68
8	South Korea	7	15	5	27	56
9	Cuba	9	8	8	25	51
10	Ukraine	9	2	12	23	43
11	Hungary	7	4	10	21	39
	Canada	3	11	8	22	39
13	Poland	7	5	5	17	36
14	Romania	4	7	9	20	35
15	Spain	5	6	6	17	33
16	Netherlands	4	5	10	19	32
17	Bulgaria	3	7	5	15	28
18	Japan	3	6	5	14	26
19	Great Britain	1	8	6	15	25
20	Brazil	3	3	9	15	24
21	Belarus	1	6	8	15	23
22	Czech Republic	4	3	4	11	22
23	Kazakhstan	3	4	4	11	21
24	Greece	4	4	0	8	20
25	Switzerland	4	3	0	7	18
26	Sweden	2	4	2	8	16
27	Denmark	4	1	1	6	15
	Turkey	4	1	1	6	15
29	New Zealand	3	2	1	6	14
	Kenya	1	4	3	8	14
31	Norway	2	2	3	7	13
32	South Africa	3	1	1	5	12
	Belgium	2	2	2	6	12
34	Nigeria	2	1	3	6	11
	Jamaica	1	3	2	6	11
36	Ireland	3	0	1	4	10
37	North Korea	2	1	2	5	10
38	Finland	1	2	1	4	8
39	Algeria	2	0	1	3	7
	Ethiopia	2	0	1	3	7
	Indonesia	1	1	2	4	7
	Yugloslavia	1	1	2	4	7
43	Iran	1	1	1	3	6
	Slovakia	1	1	1	3	6
45	Armenia	1	1	0	2	5
	Croatia	1	1	0	2	5
	Argentina	0	2	1	3	5
48	Portugal	1	0	1	2	4
	Thailand	1	0	1	2	4
	Namibia	0	2	0	2	4
	Slovenia	0	2	0	2	4
	Austria	0	1	2	3	4
53	Burundi	1	0	0	1	3
	Costa Rica	1	0	0	1	3
	Ecuador	1	0	0	1	3
	Hong Kong	1	0	0	1	3
	Syria	1	0	0	1	3
	Malaysia	0	1	1	2	3
	Moldova	0	1	1	2	3
	Uzbekistan	0	1	1	2	3
61	Azerbaijan	0	1	0	1	2
	Bahamas	0	1	0	1	2
	Chinese Taipei	0	1	0	1	2
	Latvia	0	1	0	1	2
	Phillipines	0	1	0	1	2
	Tonga	0	1	0	1	2
	Zambia	0	1	0	1	2
68	Georgia	0	0	2	2	2
	Morocco	0	0	2	2	2
	Trinidad and Tobago	0	0	2	2	2
71	India	0	0	1	1	1
	Israel	0	0	1	1	1
	Lithuania	0	0	1	1	1
	Mexico	0	0	1	1	1
	Mongolia	0	0	1	1	1
	Mozambique	0	0	1	1	1
	Puerto Rico	0	0	1	1	1
	Tunisia	0	0	1	1	1
	Uganda	0	0	1	1	1
	TOTALS	**271**	**273**	**298**	**842**	**1657**

Leading Medal Winners

(*) indicates at least one medal earned as preliminary member of eventual medal-winning relay team. USA medalists in **bold** type.

Men

No		Sport	G-S-B
6	Alexei Nemov, RUS	Gymnastics	2-1-3
4	**Gary Hall Jr.**, USA	Swimming	2-2-0
4	Aleksandr Popov, RUS	Swimming	2-2-0
3	**Josh Davis**, USA	Swimming	3-0-0
3	Denis Pankratov, RUS	Swimming	2-1-0
3	Daniel Kowalski, AUS	Swimming	0-1-2
3	Vitaly Scherbo, BEL	Gymnastics	0-0-3
2	Donovan Bailey, CAN	Track/Field	2-0-0
2	Martin Doktor, CZE	Canoe/Kayak	2-0-0
2	Liu Guoliang, CHN	Table Tennis	2-0-0
2	**Justin Huish**, USA	Archery	2-0-0
2	**Michael Johnson**, USA	Track/Field	2-0-0

Leading Medal Winners (Cont.)

No		Sport	G-S-B
2	Ulrich Kirchoff, GER	Equestrian	2-0-0
2	Danyon Loader, NZE	Swimming	2-0-0
2	**Jon Olsen**, USA	Swimming	2-0-0
2	Stanislav Pozdnyakov, RUS	Fencing	2-0-0
2	**Jeff Rouse**, USA	Swimming	2-0-0
2	**Brad Schumacher**, USA	Swimming	2-0-0
2	Aleksandr Beketov, RUS	Fencing	1-1-0
2	Kay Bluhm, GER	Kayak	1-1-0
2	Phillipe Ermenault, FRA	Cycling	1-1-0
2	Torsten Gutsche, GER	Canoe/Kayak	1-1-0
2	Knut Holmann, NOR	Canoe/Kayak	1-1-0
2	**Jeremy Linn**, USA	Swimming	1-1-0
2	Daniele Scarpa, ITA	Canoe/Kayak	1-1-0
2	**Tripp Schwenk**, USA	Swimming	1-1-0
2	Sergey Sharikov, RUS	Fencing	1-1-0
2	Li Xiaoshuang, CHN	Gymnastics	1-1-0
2	Jean Pierre Amat, FRA	Shooting	1-0-1
2	Robert DiDonna, ITA	Shooting	1-0-1
2	Csaba Horvath, HUN	Canoe/Kayak	1-0-1
2	Gyorgy Kolonics, HUN	Canoe/Kayak	1-0-1
2	Rustan Sharipov, UKR	Gymnastics	1-0-1
2	Sergey Beliaev, KAZ	Shooting	0-2-0
2	Roger Black, GBR	Track/Field	0-2-0
2	Beniamino Bonomi, ITA	Canoe/Kayak	0-2-0
2	Frankie Fredericks, NAM	Track/Field	0-2-0
2	Wang Tao, CHN	Table Tennis	0-2-0
2	Gustavo Borges, BRA	Swimming	0-1-1
2	Scott Miller, AUS	Swimming	0-1-1
2	Vladislav Kulikov, RUS	Swimming	0-1-1
2	Oh Kyo-moon, S.KOR	Archery	0-1-1
2	Sven Rothenberger, NET	Equestrian	0-1-1
2	Ato Bolden, TRI	Track/Field	0-0-2
2	Bradley McGee, AUS	Cycling	0-0-2
2	Stuart O'Grady, AUS	Cycling	0-0-2
2	Christian Troger, GER	Swimming	0-0-2

Amy Van Dyken

Alexei Nemov

Michelle Smith

Justin Huish

Women

No		Sport	G-S-B
4	**Amy Van Dyken**, USA	Swimming	4-0-0
4	Michelle Smith, IRE	Swimming	3-0-1
4	**Angel Martino**, USA	Swimming	2-0-2
4	Simona Amanar, ROM	Gymnastics	1-1-2
4	Dagmar Hase, GER	Swimming	0-3-1
4	Gina Gogean, ROM	Gymnastics	0-1-3
3	**Jenny Thompson**, USA	Swimming	3-0-0
3	Lilia Podkopayeva, UKR	Gymnastics	2-1-0
3	**Amanda Beard**, USA	Swimming	1-2-0
3	Le Jingyi, CHN	Swimming	1-2-0
3	**Wendy Hedgepeth**, USA	Swimming	1-2-0
3	Susan O'Neill, AUS	Swimming	1-1-1
3	Merlene Ottey, JAM	Track & Field	0-2-1
3	Franziska van Almsick, GER	Swimming	0-2-1
3	Sandra Volker, GER	Swimming	0-1-2
2	**Beth Botsford**, USA	Swimming	2-0-0
2	**Gail Devers**, USA	Track & Field	2-0-0
2	Laura Flessel, FRA	Fencing	2-0-0
2	**Catherine Fox**, USA	Swimming	2-0-0
2	Penny Heyns, S. Afr	Swimming	2-0-0
2	**Lisa Jacob**, USA	Swimming	2-0-0
2	Kim Kyung-wook, S.KOR	Archery	2-0-0
2	Svetlana Masterkova, RUS	Track & Field	2-0-0
2	**Shannon Miller**, USA	Gymnastics	2-0-0
2	Fu Mingxia, CHN	Diving	2-0-0
2	Marie-Jose Perec, FRA	Track & Field	2-0-0
2	Isabell Werth, GER	Equestrian	2-0-0
2	Deng Yaping, CHN	Table Tennis	2-0-0
2	Laura Badea, ROM	Fencing	1-1-0
2	Valerie Barlois, FRA	Fencing	1-1-0
2	Svetlana Chorkina, RUS	Gymnastics	1-1-0
2	**Amy Chow**, USA	Gymnastics	1-1-0
2	Birjit Fischer, GER	Canoe/Kayak	1-1-0
2	Wang Junxia, CHN	Track & Field	1-1-0
2	Jeannie Longo-Ciprelli, FRA	Cycling	1-1-0
2	Ramona Portwich, GER	Canoe/Kayak	1-1-0
2	Valentina Vezzali, ITA	Fencing	1-1-0
2	Gil Young-ah, S.KOR	Badminton	1-1-0
2	Agneta Andersson, SWE	Canoe/Kayak	1-0-1
2	**Dominique Dawes**, USA	Gymnastics	1-0-1
2	Krisztina Egerszegi, HUN	Swimming	1-0-1
2	Qiao Hong, CHN	Table Tennis	1-0-1
2	Aleksandra Ivosev, YUG	Shooting	1-0-1
2	Renata Mauer, POL	Shooting	1-0-1
2	Marnie McBean, CAN	Rowing	1-0-1
2	Blyth Tait, NZE	Equestrian	1-0-1
2	Giovanna Trillini, ITA	Fencing	1-0-1
2	Anky Van Grunsven, NET	Equestrian	0-2-0
2	Meike Freitag, GER	Swimming	0-1-1
2	Ingrid Haringa, NET	Cycling	0-1-1
2	Marina Logvinenko, RUS	Shooting	0-1-1
2	Jana Novotna, CZE	Tennis	0-1-1
2	Falilat Ogunkoya, NGR	Track & Field	0-1-1
2	Simone Osygus, GER	Swimming	0-1-1
2	Samantha Riley, AUS	Swimming	0-1-1
2	Arantxa Sanchez Vicario, SPA	Tennis	0-1-1
2	Shan Ying, CHN	Swimming	0-1-1
2	Clara Hughes, CAN	Cycling	0-0-2
2	Lavinia Milosvici, ROM	Gymnastics	0-0-2
2	Kirsten Vlieghuis, NET	Swimming	0-0-2

MEDAL SPORTS

Medal winners in individual sports contested at Atlanta, Georgia from July 20-Aug. 4, 1996. Team Sports summaries from Baseball to Water Polo begin on page 640.

ARCHERY

(70 meters)

MEN

Individual: 1. Justin Huish, USA def., **2.** Magnus Petersson, SWE (112-107); **3.** Oh Kyo-moon, S.KOR def. Paul Vermeiren, BEL (115-110).

Team: 1. United States (Justin Huish, Richard Johnson and Rod White) def. **2.** South Korea (251-249); **3.** Italy def. Australia (248-244).

WOMEN

Individual: 1. Kim Kyung-wook, S.KOR def., **2.** He Ying, CHN (113-107); **3.** Olena Sadovnycha def. Elif Altinkaynak, TUR (109-102).

Team: 1. South Korea (Kim Jo-sun, Yoon Hye-young and Kim Kyung-wook) def. **2.** Germany (245-235); **3.** Poland def. Turkey (244-239).

BADMINTON

MEN

Singles: 1. Poul-Erik Hoyer-Larsen, DEN def. **2.** Dong Jiong, CHN (15-12, 15-10); **3.** Rashid Sidek, MAL def. Heryanto Arbi, INA (5-15, 15-11, 15-6).

Doubles: 1. Rexy Mainaky & Ricky Subagja, INA def. **2.** Cheah Soon Kit & Yap Kim Hock, MAL (5-15, 15-13, 15-12); **3.** S. Antonius & Denny Kantono, INA def. Soo Beng Kiang & Tan Kim Her, MAS (15-4, 12-15, 15-8).

WOMEN

Singles: 1. Bang Soo Hyun, S.KOR def. **2.** Mia Audina, INA (11-6, 11-7); **3.** Susi Susanti, INA def. Ji Kim Hyun, S.KOR (11-4, 11-1).

Doubles: 1. Ge Fei & Gu Jun, CHN def. **2.** Gil Young-ah & Jang Hye-ock, S.KOR (15-5, 15-5); **3.** Qin Yiyuan & Tang Yongshu, CHN def. Helene Kirkegaard & Rikke Olsen, DEN (7-15, 15-4, 15-8).

MIXED

Doubles: 1. Kim Dong-moon & Gil Young-ah, S.KOR def. **2.** Park Joo-bong & Ra Kyung-min, S.KOR (13-15, 15-4, 15-12); **3.** Liu Jianjun & Sun Man, CHN def. Chen Xingdong & Peng Xingyong, CHN (13-15, 17-15, 15-4).

BOXING

Light Flyweight (106 lbs)**: 1.** Daniel Petrov Bojilov, BUL dec. **2.** Mansueto Velasco, PHI (19-6); **3.** Oleg Kiryukhin, UKR, and Rafael Lozano, SPA.

Flyweight (112 lbs)**: 1.** Maikro Romero, CUB dec. **2.** Bulat Dzumadilov, KAZ (12-11); **3.** Albert Pakeev, RUS, and Zoltan Lunka, GER.

Batamweight (119 lbs)**: 1.** Istvan Kovacs, HUN dec. **2.** Arnaldo Mesa, CUB (14-7); **3.** Raimkul Malakhbekov, RUS, and Vichairachanon Khadpo, THA.

Featherweight (125 lbs)**: 1.** Somluck Kamsing, THA dec. **2.** Serafim Todorov, BUL (8-5); **3.** Pablo Chacon, ARG, and Floyd Mayweather, USA.

Lightweight (132 lbs)**: 1.** Hocine Soltani, ALG dec. **2.** Tontcho Tontchev, BUL (3-3); **3.** Terrance Cauthen, USA, and Leonard Doroftei, ROM.

Light Welterweight (139 lbs)**: 1.** Hector Vinent, CUB dec. **2.** Oktay Urkal, GER (20-13); **3.** Bolat Niyazymbetov, KAZ, and Fathi Missaoui, TUN.

Welterweight (147 lbs)**: 1.** Oleg Saitov, RUS dec. **2.** Juan Hernandez, CUB (14-9); **3.** Marian Simion, ROM, and Daniel Santos, PUR.

Light Middleweight (156 lbs)**: 1.** David Reid, USA KO (00:36, Round 3) **2.** Alfredo Duvergel, CUB; **3.** Karim Tulaganov, UZB, and Ezmouhan Ibzaimov, KAZ.

Middleweight (165 lbs)**: 1.** Ariel Hernandez, CUB dec. **2.** Malik Beyleroglu, TUR (11-3); **3.** Mohamed Bahari, ALG, and Rhoshii Wells, USA.

Light Heavyweight (178 lbs)**: 1.** Vasilii Jirov, KAZ dec. **2.** Lee Seung-bao, S.KOR (17-4); **3.** Antonio Tarver, USA, and Thomas Ulrich, GER.

Heavyweight (201 lbs)**: 1.** Felix Savon, CUB dec. **2.** David Defiagbon, CAN (20-2); **3.** Nate Jones, USA, and Luan Krasniqi, GER.

Super Heavyweight (over 201 lbs)**: 1.** Vladimir Klichko, UKR dec. **2.** Paea Wolfgram, TON (7-3); **3.** Alexei Lezin, UKR, Duncan Dokiwari, NGR.

BEACH VOLLEYBALL

Men: 1. Karch Kiraly & Kent Steffes, USA def. **2.** Mike Dodd & Mike Whitmarsh, USA (12-8, 12-5); **3.** John Child & Mark Heese, CAN def. Joao Brenha & Miguel Maia, POR (12-5, 12-8).

Women: 1. Sandra Pires & Jackie Silva, BRA def. **2.** Monica Rodrigues & Adriana Samuel, BRA (12-11, 12-6); **3.** Natalie Cook & Kerri Ann Pottharst, AUS def. Fontana Harris & Linda Handley, USA (12-11, 12-7).

CANOE/KAYAK

MEN

Canoe Sprint 500m Singles: 1. Martin Doktor, CZE (1:49.93); **2.** Slavomir Knazovicky, SVK (1:50.51); **3.** Imre Pulai, HUN (1:50.75).

Canoe Sprint 1000m Singles: 1. Martin Doktor, CZE (3:54.41); **2.** Ivan Klementyev, LAT (3:54.95); **3.** Gyorgy Zala, HUN (3:56.36).

Canoe Sprint 500m Doubles: 1. Csaba Horvath & Gyorgy Kolonics, HUN (1:40.42); **2.** Nikolai Juravschi & Victor Reneischi, MOL (1:40.45); **3.** Gheorghe Andriev & Grigore Obreja, ROM (1:41.33).

Canoe Doubles 1000m Doubles: 1. Andreas Dittmer & Gunar Kirchbach, GER (3:31.87); **2.** Antonel Borsan & Marcel Glavan, ROM (3:32.29); **3.** Csaba Horvath & Gyorgy Kolonics, HUN (3:32.51).

Canoe Slalom Singles: 1. Michal Martikan, SVK (151.03 pts); **2.** Lukas Pollert, CZE (151.17); **3.** Patrice Estanguet, FRA (152.84).

Canoe Slalom Doubles: 1. Frank Adisson & Wilfrid Forgues, FRA (158.82 pts); **2.** Jiri Rohan & Miroslav Simek, CZE (160.16); **3.** Andre Ehrenberg & Michael Senft, GER (163.72).

Kayak Sprint 500m Singles: 1. Antonio Rossi, ITA (1:37.42); **2.** Knut Holmann, NOR (1:38.33); **3.** Piotr Markiewicz, POL (1:38.61).

Kayak Sprint 1000m Singles: 1. Knut Holmann, NOR (3:25.78); **2.** Beniamino Bonomi, ITA (3:27.07); **3.** Clint Robinson, AUS (3:29.71).

Kayak Sprint 500m Doubles: 1. Kay Bluhm & Torsten Gutsche, GER (1:28.69); **2.** Beniamino Bonomi & Daniele Scarpa, ITA (1:28.72); **3.** Danny Collins & Andrew Trim, AUS (1:29.40).

Kayak Sprint 1000m Doubles: 1. Antonio Rossi & Daniele Scarpa, ITA (3:09.19); **2.** Kay Bluhm & Torsten Gutsche, GER (3:10.51); **3.** Milko Kazanov & Andrian Dushev, BUL (3:11.20).

Kayak Sprint 1000m Fours: 1. Germany (2:51.52); **2.** Hungary (2:53.18); **3.** Russia (2:53.99).

Kayak Slalom Singles: 1. Oliver Fix, GER (141.22 pts); **2.** Andraz Vehova, SLO (141.65); **3.** Thomas Becker, GER (142.79).

Canoe/ Kayak (Cont.)

WOMEN

Kayak Sprint 500m Singles: 1. Rita Koban, HUN (1:47.65); **2.** Caroline Brunet, CAN (1:47.89); **3.** Josefa Idem, ITA (1:48.73).

Kayak Sprint 500m Doubles: 1. Agneta Andersson & Susanne Gunnarsson, SWE (1:39.32); **2.** Ramona Portwich & Birgit Fischer, GER (1:39.68); **3.** Katrin Borchert & Anna Wood, AUS (1:40.64).

Kayak Sprint 500m Fours: 1. Germany (1:31.07); **2.** Switzerland (1:32.70); **3.** Sweden (1:32.91).

Kayak Slalom Singles: 1. Stepanka Hilgertova, CZE (169.49 pts); **2.** Dana Chladek, USA (169.49); **3.** Myriam Fox-Jerusalmi, FRA (171.00).

CYCLING

MEN

Mountain Bike

Cross Country (47.7 km)**: 1.** Bart Jan Brentjens, NET (2:17:38); **2.** Thomas Frischknecht, SWI (2:20:14); **3.** Miguel Martinez, FRA (2:20:36).

Road

Individual Road Race (225 km)**: 1.** Pascal Richard, SWI (4:53:56); **2.** Rolf Sorensen, DEN (4:53:56); **3.** Maximilian Sciandri, GBR (4:53:58).

Individual Time Trial (52 km)**: 1.** Miguel Indurain, SPA (1:04:05); **2.** Abraham Olano, SPA (1:04:17); **3.** Chris Boardman, GBR (1:04:36).

Track

Time Trial (1 km)**: 1.** Florian Rousseau, FRA (1:02.712); **2.** Erin Hartwell, USA (1:02.940); **3.** Takanobu Jumonji, JPN (1:03.261).

Individual Match Sprint (3 laps)**: 1.** Jens Fiedler, GER; **2.** Marty Nothstein, USA; 3. Curtis Harnett, CAN.

Individual Points Race (40 km)**: 1.** Silvio Martinello, ITA (37 pts); **2.** Brian Walton, CAN (29); **3.** Stuart O'Grady, AUS (27).

Individual Pursuit (4 km)**: 1.** Andrea Collinelli, ITA (4:20.893); **2.** Philippe Ermenault, FRA (4:22.714); **3.** Bradley McGee, AUS (4:26.121).

Team Pursuit (4 km)**: 1.** France (4:05.930); **2.** Russia (4:07.730); **3.** Australia (4:07.570).

WOMEN

Mountain Bike

Cross Country (32 km)**: 1.** Paola Pezzo, ITA (1:50:51); **2.** Alison Sydor, CAN (1:51:58); **3.** Susan Demattei, USA (1:52:36).

Road

Individual Road Race (106 km)**: 1.** Jeannie Longo-Ciprelli, FRA (2:36:13); **2.** Imelda Chiappa, ITA (2:36:38); **3.** Clara Hughes, CAN (2:36:44).

Individual Time Trial (26 km)**: 1.** Zulfiya Zabirova, RUS (36:40); 2. Jeannie Longo-Ciprelli, FRA (37:00); 3. Clara Hughes, CAN (37:13).

Track

Individual Match Sprint (3 laps)**: 1.** Felicia Ballanger, FRA; **2.** Michelle Ferris, AUS; **3.** Ingrid Haringa, NET.

Individual Pursuit (3 km)**: 1.** Antonella Bellutti, ITA (3:33.595); **2.** Marion Clignet, FRA (3:38.571); **3.** Judith Arndt, GER (3:38.744).

Individual Points Race (25 km)**: 1.** Nathalie Lancien, FRA; **2.** Ingrid Haringa, NET; **3.** Lucy Tyler Sharman, AUS.

DIVING

MEN

3m Springboard: 1. Xiong Ni, CHN (701.46 pts); **2.** Yu Zhuocheng, CHN (690.93); **3.** Mark Lenzi, USA (686.49).

10m Platform: 1. Dmitri Saoutine, RUS (692.34 pts); **2.** Jan Hempel, GER (663.27); **3.** Xiao Hailiang, CHN (658.20).

WOMEN

3m Springboard: 1. Fu Mingxia, CHN (547.68 pts); **2.** Irina Lashko, RUS (512.19); **3.** Annie Pelletier, CAN (509.64).

10m Platform: 1. Fu Mingxia, CHN (521.58 pts); **2.** Annika Walter, GER (479.22); **3.** Mary Ellen Clark, USA (472.95).

EQUESTRIAN

Horses in parentheses.

Individual Dressage: 1. Isabell Werth, (Gigolo) GER (235.09); **2.** Anky Van Grunsven, (Bonfire) NET (233.02); **3.** Sven Rothenberger, (Weyden) NET (224.94).

Team Dressage: 1. Germany (5,553 pts); **2.** Netherlands (5,437); **3.** United States (5,309).

Individual Show Jumping: 1. Ulrich Kirchhoff, (Jus de Pommes) GER (1.00 pts); **2.** Willi Melliger, (Calvaro) SWI (4.00); **3.** Alexandra Ledermann, (Rochet M) FRA (4.00).

Team Show Jumping: 1. Germany (1.25 pts); **2.** United States (12.00); **3.** Brazil (17.25).

Individual 3-Day Event: 1. Blyth Tait, (Ready Teddy) NZE (56.80 pts); **2.** Sally Clark, (Squirrel Hill) NZE (60.40); **3.** Kerry Millikin, (Out and About) USA (73.70).

Team 3-Day Event: 1. Australia (203.850); **2.** United States (261.100); **3.** New Zealand (268.550).

USA Entry: Bruce Davidson, Jill Henneberg, David O'Connor, Karen O'Connor.

FENCING

MEN

Individual Epée: 1. Aleksandr Beketov, RUS, def. **2.** Ivan Trevejo Perez, CUB (15-14); **3.** Geza Imre, HUN def. Ivan Kovacs, HUN (15-9).

Team Epée: 1. Italy def. **2.** Russia (45-43); **3.** France def. Germany (45-42).

Individual Foil: 1. Alessandro Puccini, ITA, def. **2.** Lionel Plumenail, FRA (15-12); **3.** Franck Boidin, FRA def. Wolfgang Wienand, GER (15-11).

Team Foil: 1. Russia def. **2.** Poland (45-40); **3.** Cuba def. Austria (45-28).

Individual Sabre: 1. Stanislav Pozdnyakov, RUS, def. **2.** Sergey Sharikov, RUS (15-12); **3.** Damien Touya, FRA def. Jozsef Navarrete, HUN (15-7).

Team Sabre: 1. Russia def. **2.** Hungary (45-25); **3.** Italy def. Poland (45-37).

WOMEN

Individual Epée: 1. Laura Flessel, FRA, def. **2.** Valerie Barlois, FRA (15-12); **3.** Gyoengyi Szalay Horvathne, HUN def. Margherita Zalaffi, ITA, (15-13).

Team Epée: 1. France def. **2.** Italy (45-33); **3.** Russia def. Hungary (45-44).

Individual Foil: 1. Laura Badea, ROM, def. **2.** Valentina Vezzali, ITA (15-10); **3.** Giovanna Trillini, ITA, def. Laurence Modaine-Cessac, FRA (15-9).

Team Foil: 1. Italy def. **2.** Romania (45-33); **3.** Germany def. Hungary (45-42).

GYMNASTICS

MEN

All-Around

		Points
1	Li Xiaoshuang, CHN	58.423
2	Alexei Nemov, RUS	58.374
3	Vitaly Scherbo, BLR	58.197

Top 10 USA: 7th—John Roethlisberger (57.762), 10th—Blaine Wilson (57.686).

Floor Exercise

		Points
1	Ioannis Melissanidis, GRE	9.850
2	Li Xiaoshuang, CHN	9.837
3	Alexei Nemov, RUS	9.800

Horizontal Bar

		Points
1	Andreas Wecker, GER	9.850
2	Krasimir Dounev, BUL	9.825
3	(Tie) Vitaly Scherbo, BLR	9.800
	Fan Bin, CHN	9.800
	Alexei Nemov, RUS	9.800

Parallel Bars

		Points
1	Rustam Sharipov, UKR	9.837
2	Jair Lynch, USA	9.825
3	Vitaly Scherbo, BLR	9.800

Pommel Horse

		Points
1	Li Donghua, SWI	9.875
2	Marius Urzica, ROM	9.825
3	Alexei Nemov, RUS	9.787

Rings

		Points
1	Yuri Chechi, ITA	9.887
2	(Tie) Dan Burinca, ROM	9.812
	Szilveszter Csollany, HUN	9.812

Top 10 USA: 7th—Blaine Wilson (9.737).

Vault

		Points
1	Alexei Nemov, RUS	9.787
2	Yeo Hung-chul, KOR	9.756
3	Vitaly Scherbo, BLR	9.724

Team

		Points
1	Russia	576.778
2	China	575.539
3	Ukraine	571.541

USA entry: 5th— Mihai Bagiu, Jair Lynch, John Macready, John Roethlisberger, Kip Simons, Chainey Umphrey and Blaine Wilson.

WOMEN

All-Around

		Points
1	Lilia Podkopayeva, UKR	39.255
2	Gina Gogean, ROM	39.075
3	(Tie) Lavinia Milosovici, ROM	39.067
	Simona Amanar, ROM	39.067

Top 10 USA: 8th—Shannon Miller (38.811), 9th—Dominique Moceanu (38.755).

Floor Exercise

		Points
1	Lilia Podkopayeva, UKR	9.887
2	Simona Amanar, ROM	9.850
3	Dominique Dawes, USA	9.837

Other Top 8 USA: 4th—Dominque Moceanu (9.825).

Balance Beam

		Points
1	Shannon Miller, USA	9.862
2	Lilia Podkopayeva, UKR	9.825
3	Gina Gogean, ROM	9.787

Other Top 8 USA: 6th—Dominique Moceanu (9.125).

Uneven Bars

		Points
1	Svetlana Chorkina, RUS	9.850
2	(Tie) Bi Wenjiing, CHN	9.837
	Amy Chow, USA	9.837

Other Top 8 USA: 4th—Dominique Dawes (9.800).

Vault

		Points
1	Simona Amanar, ROM	9.775
2	Mo Huilan, CHN	9.768
3	Gina Gogean, ROM	9.750

Team

		Points
1	United States	389.225
2	Russia	388.404
3	Romania	388.246

USA entry: Amanda Borden, Amy Chow, Dominique Dawes, Shannon Miller, Dominique Moceanu, Jaycee Phelps and Kerri Strug.

Rythmic All-Around

		Points
1	Ekaterina Serebryanskaya, UKR	39.683
2	Ianina Batyrchina, RUS	39.382
3	Elena Vitrichenko, UKR	39.331

Rythmic Team

		Points
1	Spain	38.933
2	Bulgaria	38.866
3	Russia	38.365

JUDO

MEN

Extra Lightweight (132 lbs): **1.** Tadahiro Nomura, JPN **2.** Girolamo Giovinazzo, ITA; **3.** Dorjpalam Narmandakh, MON and Richard Trautmann, GER.

Half-Lightweight (143 lbs): **1**. Udo Quellmalz, GER; **2.** Yukimasa Nakamura, JPN; **3.** Henrique Guimares, BRA and Israel Hernandez Planas, CUB.

Lightweight (157 lbs): **1.** Kenzo Nakamura, JPN; **2.** Kwak Dae-sung, S.KOR; **3.** Christophe Gagliano, FRA and Jimmy Pedro, USA.

Half-Middleweight (172 lbs): **1.** Djamel Bouras, FRA; **2.** Toshihiko Koga, JPN; **3.** Cho In-chul, S.KOR and Soso Liparteliani, GEO.

Middleweight (190 lbs): **1.** Jeo Ki-Young, S.KOR; **2.** Armen Bagdasarov, UZB; **3.** Mark Huizinga, NET and Marko Spittka, GER.

Half-Heavyweight (209 lbs): **1.** Pawel Nastula, POL; 2. Kim Min-soo, S.KOR; 3. Miguel Fernandez, BRA and Stephane Traineau, FRA.

Heavyweight (over 209 lbs): **1.** David Douillet, FRA; **2.** Ernesto Perez, SPA; **3.** Frank Moeller, GER and Harry van Barneveld, BEL.

Judo (Cont.)

WOMEN

Extra Lightweight (106 lbs)**: 1.** Kye Sun, N.KOR; **2.** Ryoko Tamura, JPN; **3.** Amarilis Savon, CUB and Yolanda Soler, SPA.

Half-Lightweight (115 lbs)**: 1**. Marie-Claire Restoux, FRA; **2.** Hyun Suk Hee, S.KOR; **3.** Noriko Sagawara, JPN and Legna Verdecia, CUB.

Lightweight (123 lbs)**: 1.** Driulis Gonzalez, CUB; **2.** Jung Sun-Yong, S.KOR; **3.** Isabelle Fernandez, SPA and Marisbell Lomba, BEL.

Half-Middleweight (134 lbs)**: 1.** Yuko Emoto, JPN; **2.** Gella van de Caveye, BEL; **3.** Jenny Gal, NET and Jung Sung-sook, S.KOR.

Middleweight (146 lbs)**: 1.** Cho Min-sun, S.KOR; **2.** Aneta Szczepanska, POL; **3.** Wang Xianbo, CHN and Claudia Zwiers, NET.

Half-Heavyweight (159 lbs)**: 1.** Ulla Werbrouck, BEL; **2.** Yoko Tanabe, JPN; **3.** Diadenis Luna, CUB and Ylena Scapin, ITA.

Heavyweight (over 159 lbs)**: 1.** Sun Fuming, CHN; **2.** Estela Rodriguez, CUB; **3.** Johanna Hagn, GER and Christine Cicot, FRA.

MODERN PENTATHLON

Five events in one day—shooting (4.5mm air pistol), fencing (one-touch epée), swimming (300m freestyle), riding (450m stadium course with 12 jumps), and running (4,000m cross-country).

Individual: 1. Aleksandr Parygin, KAZ (5,551 pts); **2.** Eduard Zenovka, RUS (5,530); **3.** Janos Martinek, HUN (5501).

USA Entry: 16th—Michael Gostigian (5,305).

ROWING

(2000-meter course)

MEN

Single Sculls: 1. Xeno Mueller, SWI (6:44.85); **2.** Derek Porter, CAN (6:47.45); **3.** Thomas Lange, GER (6:47.72).

Lightweight Double Sculls: 1. Markus Gier & Michael Gier, SWI (6:23.47); **2.** Maarten Van Der Linden & Pepijn Aardewijn, NET (6:26.48); **3.** Anthony Edwards & Bruce Hick, AUS (6:26.69).

Double Sculls: 1. Davide Tizzano & Agostino Abbagnale, ITA (6:16.98); **2.** Kjetil Undset & Steffen Stoerseth, NOR (6:18.42); **3.** Frederic Fowal & Samuel Barathay, FRA (6:19.85).

Quadruple Sculls: 1. Germany (5:56.93); **2.** United States (5:59.10); **3.** Australia (6:01.65). **USA entry:** Tim Young, Brian Jamieson, Eric Mueller and Jason Gailes.

Coxless Pairs: 1. Steve Redgrave & Matthew Pinsent, GBR (6:20.09); **2.** David Weightman & Robert Scott, AUS (6:21.02); **3.** Michel Andrieux & Jean-Christophe Rolland, FRA (6:22.15).

Lightweight Coxless Fours: 1. Denmark (6:09.58); **2.** Canada (6:10.13); **3.** United States (6:12.29). **USA entry:** David Collins, Jeff Pfaendtner, Marc Schneider and William Carlucci.

Coxless Fours: 1. Australia (6:06.37); **2.** France (6:07.03); **3.** Great Britain (6:07.28).

Coxed Eight: 1. Netherlands (5:42.74); **2.** Germany (5:44.58); **3.** Russia (5:45.77).

USA entry: 5th—Doug Burden, Bob Kaehler, Porter Collins, Edward Murphy, Jamie Koven, Jonathan Brown, Donald Smith, Fred Honebein, Steven Segaloff (5:48.45).

WOMEN

Single Sculls: 1. Yekaterina Khodotovich, BLR (7:32.21); **2.** Silken Laumann, CAN (7:35.15); **3.** Trine Hansen, DEN (7:37.20).

Lightweight Double Sculls: 1. Constanta Burcica & Camelia Macoviciuc, ROM (7:12.78); **2.** Teresa Z. Bell & Lindsay Burns, USA (7:14.65); **3.** Rebecca Joyce & Virginia Lee, AUS (7:16.56).

Double Sculls: 1. Marnie McBean & Kathleen Heddle, CAN (6:56.84); **2.** Cao Mianying & Zhang, Xiuyun CHN (6:58.35); **3.** Irene Eijs & Eeke Van Nes, NET (6:58.72).

Quadruple Sculls: 1. Germany (6:27.44); **2.** Ukraine (6:30.36); **3.** Canada (6:30.38).

Coxless Pairs: 1. Megan Still & Kate Slatter, AUS (7:01.39); **2.** Missy Schwen & Karen Kraft, USA (7:01.78); **3.** Christine Gosse & Helene Cortin, FRA (7:03.82).

Coxed Eights: 1. Romania (6:19.73); **2.** Canada (6:24.05); **3.** Belarus (6:24.44).

USA entry: 4th— Anne Kakela, Mary McCagg, Laurel Korholz, Catriona Fallon, Betsy McCagg, Monica Tranel Michini, Amy Fuller, Jennifer Dore, Yasmin Farooq (6:26.19).

SHOOTING

MEN

50m Free Pistol: 1. Boris Kokorev, RUS (666.40 pts); **2.** Igor Basinski, BLR (662.00); **3.** Roberto DiDonna, ITA (661.80).

50m Free Rifle/3 Positions: 1. Jean Pierre Amat, FRA (1273.90 pts); **2.** Sergey Beliaev, KAZ (1272.30); **3.** Wolfram Waibel, AUT (1269.60).

50m Free Rifle/Prone: 1. Christian Klees, GER (704.80 pts); **2.** Sergei Beliaev, KAZ (703.30); **3.** Jozef Gonci, SVK (701.90).

25m Rapid Fire Pistol: 1. Ralf Schumann, GER (698.00 pts); **2.** Emil Milev, BUL (692.10); **3.** Vladimir Vokhmyanin, KAZ (691.50).

10m Running Game Target: 1. Yang Ling, CHN (685.80 pts); **2.** Xiao Jun, CHN (679.80); **3.** Miroslav Janus, CZE (678.40).

10m Air Pistol: 1. Roberto Di Donna, ITA (684.2 pts); **2.** Yifu Wang, CHN (684.1); **3.** Tanu Kiriakov, BUL (683.8).

10m Air Rifle: 1. Artem Khadzhibekov, RUS (695.70 pts); **2.** Wolfram Waibel Jr., AUT (695.20); **3.** Jean-Pierre Amat, FRA (693.10).

Trap: 1. Michael Diamond, AUS (149.0 pts); **2.** Josh Lakatos, USA (147.0, won shootoff); **3.** Lance Bade, USA (147.0).

Double Trap: 1. Russell Mark, AUS (189.00 pts); **2.** Albano Pera, ITA (183.00, won shootoff); **3.** Bing Zhang, CHN (183.00).

Skeet: 1. Ennio Falco, ITA (149.00 pts); **2.** Miroslaw Rzepkowski, POL (148.00); **3.** Andrea Benelli, ITA (147.00).

WOMEN

25m Sport Pistol: 1. Li Duihong, CHN (687.90 pts); **2.** Diana Yorgova, BUL (684.80); **3.** Marina Logvinenko, RUS (684.20).

10m Air Pistol: 1. Olga Klochneva, RUS (490.1 pts); **2.** Marina Logvinenko, RUS (488.5, won shootoff); **3.** Mariya Grozdeva, BUL (488.5 pts).

50m smallbore/3 Positions: 1. Aleksandra Ivosev, YUG (686.10 pts); **2.** Irina Gerasimenok, RUS (680.10); **3.** Renata Mauer, POL (679.80).

10m Air Rifle: 1. Renata Mauer, POL (497.6 pts); **2.** Petra Horneber, GER (497.4); **3.** Aleksandra Ivosev, YUG (497.2).

Double Trap: 1. Kim Rhode, USA (141 pts); **2.** Susanne Kiermayer, GER (139, won shootoff); **3.** Deserie Huddleston, AUS (139).

SWIMMING

MEN

50-meter Freestyle

		Time
1	Aleksandr Popov, RUS	22.13
2	Gary Hall Jr., USA	22.26
3	Fernando Scherer, BRA	22.29

100-meter Freestyle

		Time
1	Aleksandr Popov, RUS	48.74
2	Gary Hall Jr., USA	48.81
3	Gustavo Borges, BRA	49.02

200-meter Freestyle

		Time
1	Danyon Loader, NZE	1:47.63
2	Gustavo Borges, BRA	1:48.08
3	Daniel Kowalski, AUS	1:48.25

400-meter Freestyle

		Time
1	Danyon Loader, NZE	3:47.97
2	Paul Palmer, GBR	3:49.00
3	Daniel Kowalski, AUS	3:49.39

1500-meter Freestyle

		Time
1	Kieren Perkins, AUS	14:56.40
2	Daniel Kowalski, AUS	15:02.43
3	Graeme Smith, GBR	15:02.48

100-meter Backstroke

		Time
1	Jeff Rouse, USA	54.10
2	Rodolfo Falcon Cabrera, CUB	54.98
3	Niser Bent, CUB	55.02

200-meter Backstroke

		Time
1	Brad Bridgewater, USA	1:58.54
2	Tripp Schwenk, USA	1:58.99
3	Emanuele Merisi, ITA	1:59.18

100-meter Breaststroke

		Time
1	Fred Deburghgraeve, BEL	1:00.60
2	Jeremy Linn, USA	1:00.77
3	Mark Warnecke, GER	1:01.33

200-meter Breaststroke

		Time
1	Norbert Rozsa, HUN	2:12.57
2	Karoly Guttler, HUN	2:13.03
3	Andrey Korneyev, RUS	2:13.17

100-meter Butterfly

		Time
1	Denis Pankratov, RUS	52.27
2	Scott Miller, AUS	52.53
3	Vladislav Kulikov, RUS	53.13

200-meter Butterfly

		Time
1	Denis Pankratov, RUS	1:56.51
2	Tom Malchow, USA	1:57.44
3	Scott Goodman, AUS	1:57.48

200-meter Individual Medley

		Time
1	Attila Czene, HUN	1:59.91
2	Jani Sievinen, FIN	2:00.13
3	Curtis Myden, CAN	2:01.13

400-meter Individual Medley

		Time
1	Tom Dolan, USA	4:14.90
2	Eric Namesnik, USA	4:15.25
3	Curtis Myden, CAN	4:16.28

4x100-meter Freestyle Relay

		Time
1	United States	3:15.41
2	Russia	3:17.06
3	Germany	3:17.20

USA—Jon Olsen, Josh Davis, Bradley Schumacher, Gary Hall Jr.; **RUS**—Vladimir Pyshnenko, Aleksandr Popov, Roman Yegerov, Vladimir Predkin; **GER**—Mark Pinger, Bjorn Zikarsky, Chrisitan Troeger, Bengt Zikarsky.

4x200-meter Freestyle Relay

		Time
1	United States	7:14.84
2	Sweden	7:17.56
3	Germany	7:17.71

USA—Josh Davis, Joe Hudepohl, Ryan Berube, Bradley Schumacher; **SWE**—Anders Lyrbring, Anders Holmertz, Christer Wallin, Lars Frolander; **GER**—Christian Trager, Aimo Heilmann, Christian Keller, Steffen Zesner.

4x100-meter Medley Relay

		Time
1	United States	3:34.84
2	Russia	3:37.55
3	Australia	3:39.56

USA—Jeff Rouse, Mark Henderson, Gary Hall Jr., Jeremy Linn; **RUS**—Vladimir Selkov, Stanislav Lopukhov, Denis Pankratov, Aleksandr Popov; **AUS**—Philip Rogers, Michael Klim, Scott Miller, Steven Dewick.

WOMEN

50-meter Freestyle

		Time
1	Amy Van Dyken, USA	24.87
2	Le Jingyi, CHN	24.90
3	Sandra Volker, GER	25.14

100-meter Freestyle

		Time
1	Le Jingyi, CHN	54.50
2	Sandra Voelker, GER	54.88
3	Angel Martino, USA	54.93

200-meter Freestyle

		Time
1	Claudia Poll, COS	1:58.16
2	Franziska Van Almsick, GER	1:58.57
3	Dagmar Hase, GER	1:59.56

400-meter Freestyle

		Time
1	Michelle Smith, IRE	4:07.25
2	Dagmar Hase, GER	4:08.30
3	Kirsten Vlieghuis, NET	4:09.83

Swimming (Cont.)

800-meter Freestyle

		Time
1	Brooke Bennett, USA	8:27.89
2	Dagmar Hase, GER	8:29.91
3	Kirsten Vlieghuis, NET	8:30.84

100-meter Backstroke

		Time
1	Beth Botsford, USA	1:01.19
2	Whitney Hedgepeth, USA	1:01.47
3	Marianne Kriel, SAR	1:02.12

200-meter Backstroke

		Time
1	Krisztina Egerszegi, HUN	2:07.83
2	Whitney Hedgepeth, USA	2:11.98
3	Cathleen Rund, GER	2:12.06

100-meter Breaststroke

		Time
1	Penny Heyns, S. Afr	1:07.73
2	Amanda Beard, USA	1:08.09
3	Samantha Riley, AUS	1:09.18

200-meter Breaststroke

		Time
1	Penny Heyns, S. Afr	2:25.41
2	Amanda Beard, USA	2:25.75
3	Agnes Kovacs, HUN	2:26.57

100-meter Butterfly

		Time
1	Amy Van Dyken, USA	59.13
2	Liu Limin, CHN	59.14
3	Angel Martino, USA	59.23

200-meter Butterfly

		Time
1	Susan O'Neill, AUS	2:07.76
2	Petria Thomas, AUS	2:09.82
3	Michelle Smith, IRE	2:09.91

200-meter Individual Medley

		Time
1	Michelle Smith, IRE	2:13.93
2	Marianne Limpert, CAN	2:14.35
3	Lin Li, CHN	2:14.74

400-meter Individual Medley

		Time
1	Michelle Smith, IRE	4:39.18
2	Allison Wagner, USA	4:42.03
3	Krisztina Egerszegi, HUN	4:42.53

4x 100-meter Freestyle Relay

		Time
1	United States	3:39.29
2	China	3:40.48
3	Germany	3:41.48

USA—Angel Martino, Amy Van Dyken, Catherine Fox, Jenny Thompson; **CHN**—Le Jingyi, Chao Na, Nian Yun, Shan Ying; **GER**—Sandra Volker, Simone Osygus, Antje Buschschulte, Franziska van Almsick

4x 200-meter Freestyle Relay

		Time
1	United States	7:59.87
2	Germany	8:01.55
3	Australia	8:05.47

USA—Jenny Thompson, Sheila Taorima, Trina Jackson, Christina Teuscher; **GER**—Anke Scholz, Franziska van Almsick, Dagmar Hase, Kerstin Kielgass; **AUS**—Juila Greville, Emma Johnson, Nicole Stevenson, Susan O'Neill.

4x 100-meter Medley Relay

		Time
1	United States	4:02.88
2	Australia	4:05.08
3	China	4:07.34

USA—Angel Martino, Amy Van Dyken, Amanda Beard, Beth Botsford; **AUS**—Nicole Stevenson, Susan O'Neill, Samantha Riley, Sarah Ryan; **CHN**—Shan Ying, Chen Yan, Han Xue, Cai Huijue.

Synchronized Swimming

Team: 1. United States (99.720 pts); **2.** Canada (98.367); **3.** Japan (97.753).

USA Entry—Tammy Cleland, Suzannah Bianco, Heather Pease, Emily Lesueur, Becky Dyroen–Lancer, Jill Sudduth, Nathalie Schneyder, Heather Simmons-Carrasco, Jill Savery, Margot Thien.

TABLE TENNIS

MEN

Singles: 1. Liu Guoliang, CHN, def. **2.** Wang Tao, CHN (21-12, 22-24, 21-19, 15-21, 21-6); **3.** Joerg Rosskopf, GER, def. Petr Korbel, CZE (21-17, 19-21, 21-18, 21-19).

Doubles: 1. Kong Linghui & Liu Guoliang, CHN, def. **2.** Lu Lin & Wang Tao, CHN (21-8, 13-21, 21-19, 21-11); **3.** Lee Chul-Seung & Yoo Nam-Kyu, S.KOR, def. Steffen Fetzner & Joerg Rosskopf, GER (21-18, 21-13, 22-20).

WOMEN

Singles: 1. Deng Yaping, CHN, def. **2.** Chen Jing, TPE (21-14, 21-17, 20-22, 17-21, 21-5); **3.** Qiao Hong, CHN, def. Liu Wei, CHN (21-17, 15-21, 21-19, 21-11).

Doubles: 1. Deng Yaping & Qiao Hong, CHN, def. **2.** Liu Wei & Qiao Yunping, CHN (18-21, 25-23, 22-20, 21-14); **3.** Park Hae-Jung & Ryu Ji-Hae, S.KOR, def. Kim Moo-Kyo & Park Kyoung-Ae, S.KOR (21-16, 21-8, 14-21, 21-13).

TENNIS

MEN

Singles: 1. Andre Agassi, USA, def. **2.** Sergi Bruguera, SPA 6-2, 6-3, 6-1; **3.** Leander Paes, IND, def. Fernando Meligeni, BRA 3-6, 6-2, 6-4.

Doubles: 1. Todd Woodbridge & Mark Woodforde, AUS, def. **2.** Neil Broad & Tim Henman, GBR 6-4, 6-4, 6-2; **3.** Marc-Kevin Goellner & David Prinosil, GER, def. Jacco Eltingh & Paul Haarhuis, NET 6-2, 7-5.

WOMEN

Singles: 1. Lindsay Davenport, USA, def, **2.** Arantxa Sanchez Vicario, SPA 7-6 (8-6), 6-2; **3.** Jana Novotna, CZE, def. Mary Joe Fernandez, USA 7-6 (8-6), 6-4.

Doubles: 1. Gigi Fernandez & Mary Joe Fernandez, USA, def. **2.** Jana Novotna & Helena Sukova, CZE 7-6 (8-6), 6-4; **3.** Conchita Martinez & Arantxa Sanchez Vicario, SPA, def. Manon Bollegraf & Brenda Schultz-McCarthy, NET 6-1, 6-3.

TRACK & FIELD

MEN

100 meters

		Time	
1	Donovan Bailey, CAN	9.84	WR
2	Frank Fredericks, NAM	9.89	
3	Ato Boldon, TRI	9.90	

Top 10 USA—4th Dennis Mitchell (9.99); 5th Michael Marsh (10.00).

200 meters

		Time	
1	Michael Johnson, USA	19.32	WR
2	Frank Fredericks, NAM	19.68	
3	Ato Boldon, TRI	19.80	

Other Top 10 USA—5th Jeff Williams (20.17); 8th Michael Marsh (20.48).

400 meters

		Time	
1	Michael Johnson, USA	43.49	OR
2	Roger Black, GBR	44.41	
3	Davis Kamoga, UGA	44.53	

Other Top 10 USA—4th Alvin Harrison (44.62)

800 meters

		Time	
1	Vebjoern Rodal, NOR	1:42.58	OR
2	Hezekiel Sepeng, S. Afr	1:42.74	
3	Fred Onyancha, KEN	1:42.79	

Top 10 USA—7th Johnny Gray (1:44.21).

1500 meters

		Time
1	Noureddine Morceli, ALG	3:35.78
2	Fermin Cacho, SPA	3:36.40
3	Stephen Kipkorir, KEN	3:36.72

5000 meters

		Time
1	Venuste Niyongabo, BUR	13:07.96
2	Paul Bitok, KEN	13:08.16
3	Khalid Boulami, MOR	13:08.37

10,000 meters

		Time	
1	Haile Gebrselassie, ETH	27:07.34	OR
2	Paul Tergat, KEN	27:08.17	
3	Salah Hissou, MOR	27:24.67	

Marathon

		Time
1	Josia Thugwane, S. Afr	2:12:36
2	Lee Bong-Ju, S.KOR	2:12:39
3	Eric Wainaina, KEN	2:12:44

Top USA—28th Keith Brantly (2:18:17); 31st Bob Kempainen (2:18:38); 41st Mark Coogan (2:20:27).

4x100-meter Relay

		Time
1	Canada	37.69
2	United States	38.05
3	Brazil	38.41

CAN—Donovan Bailey, Robert Esmie, Glenroy Gilbert, Bruny Surin, Carlton Chambers; **USA**—Tim Harden, Jon Drummond, Michael Marsh, Dennis Mitchell, Tim Montgomery; **BRA**—Edson Ribeiro, Arnaldo Silva, Andre Silva, Robson da Silva.

4x400-meter Relay

		Time
1	United States	2:55.99
2	Great Britain	2:56.60
3	Jamaica	2:59.42

USA—Anthuan Maybank, Derek Mills, LaMont Smith, Alvin Harrison, Jason Rouser; **GBR**—Jamie Baulch, Mark Hylton, Du'aine Ladejo, Mark Richardson, Iwan Thomas, Roger Black; **JAM**—Dennis Blake, Davian Clarke; Roxbert Martin, Michael McDonald, Greg Haughton, Garth Robinson.

110-meter Hurdles

		Time	
1	Allen Johnson, USA	12.95	OR
2	Mark Crear, USA	13.09	
3	Florian Schwarthoff, GER	13.17	

Other Top 10 USA—6th Eugene Swift (13.23).

400-meter Hurdles

		Time
1	Derrick Adkins, USA	47.54
2	Samuel Matete, ZAM	47.78
3	Calvin Davis, USA	47.96

3000-meter Steeplechase

		Time
1	Joseph Keter, KEN	8:07.12
2	Moses Kiptanui, KEN	8:08.33
3	Alessandro Lambruschini, ITA	8:11.28

USA Top 12—5th Mark Croghan (8:17.84); 12th Marc Davis (9:51.96)

20-kilometer Walk

		Time
1	Jefferson Perez, ECU	1:20:07
2	Ilya Markov, RUS	1:20:16
3	Bernardo Segura, MEX	1:20:23

Top USA—50th Curt Clausen (1:31:30).

50-kilometer Walk

		Time
1	Robert Korzeniowski, POL	3:43:30
2	Mikhail Shchennikov, RUS	3:43:46
3	Valentin Massana, SPA	3:44:19

Top USA—24th Allen James (4:01:18).

High Jump

		Distance	
1	Charles Austin, USA	7-10	OR
2	Artur Partyka, POL	7-9¼	
3	Steve Smith, GBR	7-8½	

Pole Vault

		Distance	
1	Jean Galfione, FRA	19-5¼	OR
2	Igor Trandenkov, RUS	19-5¼	OR
3	Andrei Tivontchik, GER	19-5¼	OR

Note: All three cleared the same height, order of finish was decided by number of misses.

Top 10 USA—8th Lawrence Johnson (18-8¼).

Long Jump

		Distance
1	Carl Lewis, USA	27-10¾
2	James Beckford, JAM	27-2½
3	Joe Greene, USA	27-0½

Other Top 10 USA—5th Mike Powell (26-9¾)

Track & Field (Cont.)

Triple Jump

		Distance	
1	Kenny Harrison, USA	59-4¼	OR
2	Jonathan Edwards, GBR	58-8	
3	Yoelbi Quesada, CUB	57-2¾	

Other Top 10 USA—4th Mike Conley (57-1); 8th Robert Howard (55-5½)

Shot Put

		Distance
1	Randy Barnes, USA	70-11¼
2	John Godina, USA	68-2½
3	Oleksandr Bagach, UKR	68-1

Other Top 10 USA—7th C.J. Hunter (66-10¾).

Discus

		Distance
1	Lars Riedel, GER	227-8
2	Vladimir Dubrovshchik, BLR	218-6
3	Vasiliy Kaptyukh, BLR	215-10

Hammer Throw

		Distance
1	Balazs Kiss, HUN	266-6
2	Lance Deal, USA	266-2
3	Oleksiy Krykun, UKR	262-6

Javelin

		Distance
1	Jan Zelezny, CZE	289-3
2	Steve Backley, GBR	286-10
3	Seppo Raty, FIN	285-4

Decthalon

		Points
1	Dan O'Brien, USA	8824
2	Frank Busemann, GER	8706
3	Tomas Dvorak, CZE	8664

Other Top 10 USA—4th Steve Fritz (8644); 10th Chris Huffins (8300).

WOMEN

100 meters

		Time
1	Gail Devers, USA	10.94
2	Merlene Ottey, JAM	10.94
3	Gwen Torrence, USA	10.96

200 meters

		Time
1	Marie-Jose Perec, FRA	22.12
2	Merlene Ottey, JAM	22.24
3	Mary Onyali, NGR	22.38

Top 10 USA—4th Inger Miller (22.41); 8th Carlette Guidry (22.61).

400 meters

		Time	
1	Marie-Jose Perec, FRA	48.25	OR
2	Cathy Freeman, AUS	48.63	
3	Falilat Ogunkoya, NGR	49.10	

Top 10 USA—5th Jearl Miles (49.55).

800 meters

		Time
1	Svetlana Masterkova, RUS	1:57.73
2	Ana Quirot, CUB	1:58.11
3	Maria Mutola, MOZ	1:58.71

1500 meters

		Time
1	Svetlana Masterkova, RUS	4:00.83
2	Gabriela Szabo, ROM	4:01.54
3	Theresia Kiesl, AUT	4:03.02

Top 10 USA—10th Regina Jacobs (4:07.21).

5000 meters

		Time
1	Wang Junxia, CHN	14:59.88
2	Pauline Konga, KEN	15:03.49
3	Roberta Brunet, ITA	15:07.52

Top 10 USA—9th Lynn Jennings (15:17.50); 10th Amy Rudolph (15:19.77).

10,000 meters

		Time	
1	Fernanda Ribeiro, POR	31:01.63	OR
2	Wang Junxia, CHN	31:02.58	
3	Gete Wami, ETH	31:06.65	

Marathon

		Time
1	Fatuma Roba, ETH	2:26:05
2	Valentina Yegorova, RUS	2:28:05
3	Yuko Arimori, JPN	2:28:39

Top USA—10th Anne Marie Lauck (2:31:30); 31st Linda Somers (2:36:58).

4x100-meter Relay

		Time
1	United States	41.95
2	Bahamas	42.14
3	Jamaica	42.24

USA—Chryste Gaines, Gail Devers, Inger Miller, Gwen Torrence; **BAH**—Eldece Clarke, Chandra Sturrup, Sevatheda Fynes, Pauline Davis; **JAM**—Michelle Freeman, Juliet Cuthbert, Nikole Mitchell, Merlene Ottey.

4x400-meter Relay

		Time
1	United States	3:20.91
2	Nigeria	3:21.04
3	Germany	3:21.14

USA—Rochelle Stevens, Maicel Malone, Kim Graham, Jearl Miles, Linetta Wilson; **NGR**—Bisi Afolabi, Fatima Yusuf, Charity Opara, Falilat Ogunkoya; **GER**—Uta Rohlaender, Linda Kisabaka, Anja Ruecker, Grit Breuer.

100-meter Hurdles

		Time
1	Ludmila Engquist, SWE	12.58
2	Brigita Bukovec, SLO	12.59
3	Patricia Girard-Leno, FRA	12.65

Top 10 USA—4th Gail Devers (12.66).

400-meter Hurdles

		Time	
1	Deon Hemmings, JAM	52.82	OR
2	Kim Batten, USA	53.08	
3	Tonja Buford-Bailey, USA	53.22	

10-kilometer Walk

		Time
1	Yelena Ninikolayeva, RUS	41:49
2	Elisabetta Perrone, ITA	42:12
3	Wang Yan, CHN	42:19

Top USA—14th Michelle Rohl (44:29); 20th Debbie Lawrence (45:32).

High Jump

		Distance
1	Stefka Kostadinova, BUL	6-8¾ **OR**
2	Niki Bakogianni, GRE	6-8
3	Inha Babakova, UKR	6-7

Top USA—11th Tisha Waller (6-4).

Long Jump

		Distance
1	Chioma Ajunwa, NGR	23-4½
2	Fiona May, ITA	23-0½
3	Jackie Joyner-Kersee, USA	22-11¾

Triple Jump

		Distance
1	Inessa Kravets, UKR	50-3½
2	Inna Lasovskaya, RUS	49-1¾
3	Sarka Kasparkova, CZE	49-1¾

Top USA—11th Sheila Hudson, USA (46-0)

Shot Put

		Distance
1	Astrid Kumbernuss, GER	67-5½
2	Sui Xinmei, CHN	65-2¾
3	Irina Khudorozhkina, RUS	63-6

Top 10 USA—5th Connie Price-Smith (63-0¾); 9th Ramona Pagel (60-7¾).

Discus

		Distance
1	Ilke Wyludda, GER	228-6
2	Natalya Sadova, RUS	218-1
3	Elya Zvereva, BLR	215-4

Javelin

		Distance
1	Heli Rantanen, FIN	222-11
2	Louise McPaul, AUS	215-0
3	Trine Hattestad, NOR	213-2

Heptathlon

		Points
1	Ghada Shouaa, SYR	6780
2	Natasha Sazanovich, BLR	6563
3	Denise Lewis, GBR	6489

Top 10 USA—8th Kelly Blair (6307); 9th Sharon Hanson (6292).

WEIGHTLIFTING

119 lbs (54kg)**: 1.** Halil Mutlu, TUR (632.5 lbs); **2.** Zhang Xiangsen, CHN (617.29); **3.** Sevdalin Minchev, BUL (610.5).

130 lbs (59kg)**: 1.** Teng Ningsheng, CHN (677.75 lbs); **2.** Leonidas Sabanis, GRE (672.25); **3.** Nikolay Pechalov, BUL (666.75).

141 lbs (64kg)**: 1.** Naim Suleymanoglu, TUR (738.50); **2.** Valerios Leonidis, GRE (733); **3.** Jiangang Xiao, CHN (710.75).

154 lbs (70kg)**: 1.** Zhan Xugang, CHN (786.5 lbs); **2.** Kim Myong, N.KOR (759); **3.** Attila Feri, HUN (748).

168 lbs (76kg)**: 1.** Pablo Lara, CUB (807.5 lbs); **2.** Yoto Yotov, BUL (792); **3.** Jon Chol-ho, N.KOR (786.5).

183 lbs (83kg)**: 1.** Pyrros Dimas, GRE (863.5 lbs); **2.** Marc Huster, GER (841.5); **3.** Andrzej Cofalik, POL (819.5).

201 lbs (91kg)**: 1.** Aleksey Petrov, RUS (885.5 lbs); **2.** Leonidas Kokas, GRE (858); **3.** Oliver Caruso, GER (858).

218 lbs (99kg)**: 1.** Akakide Kakhiashvilis, GRE (925.75 lbs); **2.** Anatoli Khrapaty, KAZ (903.75); **3.** Denis Gotfrid, UKR (887.25).

238 lbs (108 kg)**: 1.** Timur Taimazov, UKR (946 lbs); **2.** Sergey Syrtsov, RUS (924); **3.** Nicu Vlad, ROM (924).

Over 238 lbs (108+kg)**: 1.** Andrey Chemerkin, RUS (1008 lbs); **2.** Ronny Weller, GER (1003); **3.** Stefan Botev, AUS (992).

WRESTLING

Freestyle

105.8 lbs (48 kg)**: 1.** IL Kim, N.KOR def. **2.** Armen Mkrchyan, ARM (5-4); **3.** Alexis Vila Perdomo, CUB def. Vugar Orudzhov, RUS (5-2).

114.5 lbs (52 kg)**: 1.** Valentin Dimitrov Jordanov, BUL def. **2.** Namik Abdullayev, AZB (4-3); **3.** Maulen Mamyrov, KAZ def. Chechenol Mongush, RUS (3-2).

125.5 lbs (57 kg)**: 1.** Kendall Cross, USA def. **2.** Giuvi Sissaouri, CAN (5-3); **3.** Yong Sam Ri, N.KOR def. Harun Dogan, TUR (3-0).

136.5 lbs (62 kg)**: 1.** Tom Brands, USA def. **2.** Jae-Sung Jang, S.KOR (7-0); **3.** Elbrus Tedeyev, UKR def. Takahiro Wada, JPN (3-0).

149.5 lbs (68 kg)**: 1.** Vadim Bogiyev, RUS def. **2.** Townsend Sanders, USA (1-1, ref's decision); **3.** Zaza Zazirov, UKR def. Yosvany Sanchez Larrude, CUB (8-6).

163 lbs (74 kg)**: 1.** Buvaysa Saytyev, RUS def. **2.** Jang-Soon Park, S.KOR (5-0); **3.** Takuya Ota, JPN def. Plamen Paskalev, BUL (5-3).

180.5 lbs (82 kg)**: 1.** Khadzhimurad Magomedov, RUS def. **2.** Yang Hyun-Mo, S.KOR (2-1); **3.** Amir Reza Khadem Azghadi, IRA def. Sebahattin Ozturk, TUR (0-0, ref's decision).

198 lbs (90 kg)**: 1.** Rasull Khadem Azghadi, IRA def. **2.** Makharbek Khadartsev, RUS (3-0); **3.** Eldari Kurtanidze, GEO def. Jozef Lohyna, SVK (5-0).

220 lbs (100 kg)**: 1.** Kurt Angle, USA def. **2.** Abbas Jadidi, IRA (1-1, ref's decision); **3.** Arawat Sabejew, GER def. Sergey Kovalevskiy, BLR (7-4).

286lbs (130 kg)**: 1.** Mahmut Demir, TUR def. **2.** Aleksey Medvedev, BLR (3-0); **3.** Bruce Baumgartner, USA def. Andrey Shumilin, RUS (1-1, ref's decision).

Greco-Roman

105.8 lbs (48 kg)**: 1.** Kwon-Ho Sim, S.KOR def. **2.** Aleksander Pavlov, BLR (4-0, OT, 6:16); **3.** Zafar Gulyov, RUS def. Yong Kang (4-0).

114.5 lbs (52 kg)**: 1.** Armen Nazaryan, ARM def. **2.** Brandon Paulson, USA (5-1); **3.** Andriy Kalashnikov, UKR def. Samvel Danielyan, RUS (4-1)

125.5 lbs (57 kg)**: 1.** Yuriy Melnichenko, KAZ def. **2.** Dennis Hall, USA (4-1); **3.** Zetian Sheng, CHN def. Ruslan Khakymov, UKR (4-0, OT, 6:49).

136.5 lbs (62 kg)**: 1.** Wlodzimierz Zawadzki, POL def. **2.** Juan Luis Maren Delis, CUB (3-1); **3.** Mehmet Pirim, TUR def. Koba Guliashvili, GEO (9-0).

149.5 lbs (68 kg)**: 1.** Ryszard Wolny, POL def. **2.** Ghani Yolouz, FRA (7-0); **3.** Aleksandr Tretyakov, RUS def. Kamandar Madzhidov, BLR (4-0, OT, 6:56).

163 lbs (74 kg)**: 1.** Feliberto Ascuy Aguilera, CUB def. **2.** Marko Asell, FIN (8-2); **3.** Jozef Tracz, POL def. Erik Hahn, GER (4-2).

180.5 lbs (82 kg)**: 1.** Hamza Yerlikaya, TUR def. **2.** Thomas Zander, GER (3-0); **3.** Valeriy Tsilent, BLR def. Daulet Turlykhanov, KAZ (4-0).

Wrestling (Cont.)

198 lbs (90 kg)**: 1.** Vyacheslav Oleynyk, UKR def. **2.** Jacek Fafinski, POL (6-0); **3.** Maik Bullman, GER def. Aleksandr Sidorenko, BLR (2-0).

220 lbs (100 kg)**: 1.** Andrzej Wronski, POL def. **2.** Sergey Lishtvan, BLR (ref's decision, OT, 8:00); **3.** Mikael Ljungberg, SWE def. Teymuraz Edisherashvili, RUS (pin, 1:50).

286 lbs (130 kg)**: 1.** Aleksandr Karelin, RUS def. **2.** Siamak "Matt" Ghaffari, USA (1-0); **3.** Serguei Moureiko, MDA def. Petro Kotok, UKR (1-0).

YACHTING

OPEN

Laser: 1. Robert Scheidt, BRA (26 pts); 2. Ben Ainslie, GBR (37); 3. Peer Moberg, NOR (46).

Tornado: 1. Jose Luis Ballester & Fernando Leon, SPA (30 pts); **2.** Mitch Booth & Andrew Landenberger, AUS (42); **3.** Lars Grael & Kiko Pellicano, BRA (43).

Star: 1. Torben Grael & Marcelo Ferreira, BRA (25 pts); **2.** Hans Wallen & Bobbie Lohse, SWE (29); **3.** Colin Beashel & David Giles, AUS (32).

Soling: 1. Germany (Thomas Flach, Bernd Jaekel, Jochen Schuemann) def. **2.** Russia (Georgiy Shayduko, Igor Skalin, Dmitriy Shabanov), 3-0; **3.** United States (Jim Barton, Jeff Madrigali, Kent Massey) def. Great Britain (Andrew Beadsworth, Barry Parkin, Adrian Stead), 3-1.

MEN

Finn: 1. Mateusz Kusznierewicz, POL (32 pts); **2.** Sebastien Godefroid, BEL (45); **3.** Roy Heiner, NET (50).

Mistral: 1. Nikolaos Kaklamanakis, GRE (17 pts); **2.** Carlos Espinola, ARG (19); **3.** Gal Fridman, ISR (21).

470: 1. Yevhen Braslavets & Iho Matviyenko, UKR (40 pts); **2.** John Merricks & Ian Walker, GBR (60); **3.** Vitor Rocha & Nuno Barreto, POR (62).

WOMEN

Europe: 1. Kristine Roug, DEN (24 pts); **2.** Margriet Matthijsse, NET (30); **3.** Courtenay Becker-Dey, USA (39).

Mistral: 1. Lee Lai-Shan, HKG (16 pts); **2.** Barbara Kendall, NZE (24); **3.** Alessandra Sensini, ITA (28).

470: 1. Begona Via Dufresne & Theresa Zabell, SPA (25 pts); **2.** Yumiko Shige & Alicia Kinoshita, JPN (36); **3.** Olena Pakholchik & Ruslana Taran, UKR (38).

TEAM SPORTS

BASEBALL

Round Robin Standings

Top four teams advance to medal round. Note that RF stands for Runs For and RA stands for Runs Against.

	Gm	W	L	Pct	RF	RA	Medal Round
*Cuba	7	7	0	1.000	97	49	2-0
*United States	7	6	1	.857	81	27	1-1
*Japan	7	4	3	.571	69	45	1-1
*Nicaragua	7	4	3	.571	44	30	0-2
Netherlands	7	2	5	.285	32	76	—
Italy	7	2	5	.285	33	71	—
Australia	7	2	5	.285	47	86	—
South Korea	7	1	6	.142	40	59	—

Semifinals

Cuba 8 .... Nicaragua 1
Japan 11 .... United States 2

Bronze Medal

United States 10 .... Nicaragua 3

Gold Medal

Cuba 13 .... Japan 9

Team USA Batting

	Pos	Avg	AB	R	H	HR	RBI
Warren Morris	2B	.409	22	10	9	5	11
Jacque Jones	OF	.395	38	12	15	5	13
Matt LeCroy	C	.394	33	10	13	4	10
Travis Lee	1B	.382	34	9	13	2	10
Chad Allen	OF	.375	32	9	12	3	8
Jason Williams	SS	.367	30	10	11	3	9
Mark Kotsay	OF	.303	33	10	10	3	6
Brian Loyd	C	.267	15	4	4	2	8
Kip Harkrider	IF	.250	8	0	2	0	0
A.J. Hinch	C	.238	21	6	5	1	3
Troy Glaus	IF	.219	32	9	7	4	5
Augie Ojeda	IF	.200	5	2	1	0	0
Chad Green	OF	.143	7	2	1	0	1
TOTALS		.332	310	93	103	32	84
OPPONENTS		.250	280	41	70	14	40

Team USA Pitching

	ERA	Gm	W-L	SV	IP	BB	SO
Braden Looper	0.00	2	0-0	1	6.0	1	8
R.A. Dickey	3.00	2	2-0	0	12.0	3	12
Jeff Weaver	3.68	4	0-0	1	7.1	1	3
Seth Greisinger	5.00	3	3-0	0	18.0	4	11
Kris Benson	5.82	3	2-1	0	17.0	5	17
Billy Koch	6.23	3	0-1	0	8.2	5	4
Jim Parque	9.00	4	0-0	0	4.0	1	4
TOTALS	4.68	9	7-2	2	73.0	20	57
OPPONENTS	9.76	9	2-7	2	71.0	39	75

BASKETBALL

Round Robin Standings

Top four teams advance to medal round.

MEN

Group A	Gm	W	L	Pts	Per Game For	Per Game Opp	Medal Round
*United States	5	5	0	10	104.4	69.0	3-0
*Lithuania	5	3	2	8	85.4	70.8	2-1
*Croatia	5	3	2	8	84.4	77.2	1-1
*China	5	2	3	7	72.0	100.4	0-2
Argentina	5	2	3	7	70.2	79.2	—
Angola	5	0	5	5	56.0	75.8	—

Group B	Gm	W	L	Pts	Per Game For	Per Game Opp	Medal Round
*Yugoslavia	5	5	0	10	95.6	72.8	2-1
*Australia	5	4	1	9	98.4	87.6	1-2
*Greece	5	3	2	8	80.4	83.2	1-1
*Brazil	5	2	3	7	99.6	98.8	0-2
Puerto Rico	5	1	4	6	89.4	93.0	—
South Korea	5	0	5	5	84.4	112.4	—

Quarterfinals

Lithuania 99 .... Greece 66
Yugoslavia 128 .... China 61
Australia 73 .... Croatia 71
United States 98 .... Brazil 75

Semifinals

Yugoslavia 66 .... Lithuania 58
United States 101 .... Australia 73

Bronze Medal

Lithuania 80 .... Australia 74

Gold Medal

United States 95 .... Yugoslavia 69

Team USA Scoring

	Gm	FG%	FT%	Min	Pts	Reb	Ast
				—Per Game—			
Charles Barkley	7	.816	.719	18.4	12.4	6.6	2.4
David Robinson	8	.680	.700	14.3	12.0	4.6	0.0
Reggie Miller	8	.516	.889	21.6	11.4	1.0	2.1
Scottie Pippen	8	.521	.545	21.5	11.0	3.9	3.1
Grant Hill	6	.611	.750	21.5	9.7	2.8	3.5
Mitch Richmond	8	.463	.842	19.1	9.6	1.6	1.3
Shaquille O'Neal	8	.620	.522	15.5	9.3	5.3	0.9
A. Hardaway	8	.568	.720	18.1	9.0	2.8	4.4
Karl Malone	8	.569	.529	17.5	8.4	4.5	1.5
Gary Payton	8	.378	.526	17.1	5.1	3.1	4.5
Hakeem Olajuwon	7	.448	.692	12.6	5.0	3.1	1.1
John Stockton	8	.526	.818	12.0	3.8	0.8	2.8
TOTALS	8	.560	.681	200.0	102.0	38.1	26.3
OPPONENTS	8	.420	.695	200.0	70.3	25.1	14.9

WOMEN

Group A	Gm	W	L	Pts	Per Game For	Per Game Opp	Medal Round
*Brazil	5	5	0	10	84.8	72.0	2-1
*Russia	5	4	1	9	75.6	68.4	1-1
*Italy	5	3	2	8	66.0	61.8	0-2
*Japan	5	2	3	7	73.0	79.2	1-1
China	5	1	4	6	69.4	75.6	—
Canada	5	0	5	5	58.6	70.4	—

Group B	Gm	W	L	Pts	Per Game For	Per Game Opp	Medal Round
*United States	5	5	0	10	101.4	67.8	3-0
*Ukraine	5	3	2	8	70.8	71.6	1-2
*Australia	5	3	2	8	73.8	63.8	2-1
*Cuba	5	2	3	7	73.0	75.4	0-2
South Korea	5	2	3	7	69.4	77.8	—
Zaire	5	0	5	5	57.4	89.4	—

Quarterfinals

United States 108 .... Japan 93
Australia 74 .... Russia 70
Ukraine 59 .... Italy 50
Brazil 101 .... Cuba 69

Semifinals

Brazil 81 .... Ukraine 60
United States 93 .... Australia 71

Bronze Medal

Australia 66 .... Ukraine 56

Gold Medal

United States 111 .... Brazil 87

FIELD HOCKEY

Round Robin Standings

Top two teams advance to medal round.

MEN

Group A	Gm	W	L	T	Pts	GF	GA	Medal Round
*Spain	5	4	1	0	8	14	5	1-1
*Germany	5	3	1	1	7	10	3	0-2
India	5	2	1	2	6	8	3	—
Pakistan	5	2	2	1	5	11	8	—
Argentina	5	2	3	0	4	9	13	—
United States	5	0	5	0	0	3	23	—

Group B	Gm	W	L	T	Pts	GF	GA	Medal Round
*Netherlands	5	4	0	1	9	14	6	2-0
*Australia	5	3	1	1	7	13	7	1-1
Great Britain	5	1	1	3	5	8	8	—
South Korea	5	1	2	2	4	12	13	—
South Africa	5	0	2	3	3	7	12	—
Malaysia	5	0	3	2	2	7	15	—

Semifinals

Spain 2 .... Australia 1
Netherlands 3 .... Germany 1

Bronze Medal

Australia 3 .... Germany 2

Gold Medal

Netherlands 3 .... Spain 1

WOMEN

	Gm	W	L	T	Pts	GF	GA	Medal Round
*Australia	7	6	0	1	13	24	4	1-0
*South Korea	7	4	1	2	10	18	9	0-1
*Great Britain	7	3	2	2	8	12	11	0-1
*Netherlands	7	3	2	2	8	15	15	1-0
United States	7	2	3	2	6	8	11	—
Germany	7	2	4	1	5	10	11	—
Argentina	7	2	4	1	5	7	21	—
Spain	7	0	6	1	1	5	17	—

Bronze Medal

Netherlands 0 .... Great Britain 0
Netherlands won shoot-out 4-3

Gold Medal

Australia 3 .... South Korea 1

SOCCER

MEN

Group A	Gm	W	L	T	Pts	GF	GA	Medal Round
*Argentina	3	1	0	2	5	5	3	2-1
*Portugal	3	1	0	2	5	4	2	1-2
United States	3	1	1	1	4	4	4	—
Tunisia	3	0	2	1	1	1	5	—

Group B	Gm	W	L	T	Pts	GF	GA	Medal Round
*France	3	2	0	1	7	5	2	0-1
*Spain	3	2	0	1	7	5	3	0-1
Australia	3	1	2	0	3	4	6	—
Saudi Arabia	3	0	3	0	0	2	5	—

Soccer (Cont.)

Group C	Gm	W	L	T	Pts	GF	GA	Medal Round
*Mexico	3	1	0	2	5	2	1	0-1
*Ghana	3	1	1	1	4	4	4	0-1
South Korea	3	1	1	1	4	1	1	—
Italy	3	1	2	0	3	3	4	—

Group D	Gm	W	L	T	Pts	GF	GA	Medal Round
*Brazil	3	2	1	0	6	4	2	2-1
*Nigeria	3	2	1	0	6	3	1	3-0
Japan	3	2	1	0	3	4	4	—
Hungary	3	0	3	0	0	3	7	—

Quarterfinals

Portugal 2 ... OT ... France 1
Argentina 4 ... Spain 0
Nigeria 2 ... Mexico 0
Brazil 4 ... Ghana 2

Semifinals

Argentina 2 ... Portugal 0
Nigeria 4 ... OT ... Brazil 3

Bronze Medal

Brazil 5 ... Portugal 0

Gold Medal

Nigeria 3 ... Argentina 2

WOMEN

Group E	Gm	W	L	T	Pts	GF	GA	Medal Round
*China	3	2	0	1	7	7	1	1-1
*United States	3	2	0	1	7	5	1	2-0
Sweden	3	1	2	0	3	4	5	—
Denmark	3	0	3	0	0	2	11	—

Group F	Gm	W	L	T	Pts	GF	GA	Medal Round
*Norway	3	2	0	1	7	9	4	1-1
*Brazil	3	1	0	2	5	5	3	0-2
Germany	3	1	1	1	4	6	6	—
Japan	3	0	3	0	0	2	9	—

Semifinals

China 3 ... Brazil 2
United States 2 ... OT ... Norway 1

Bronze Medal

Norway 2 ... Brazil 0

Gold Medal

United States 2 ... China 1

SOFTBALL

Top four teams advance to semifinals.

	Gm	W	L	RF	RA	Medal Round
*United States	7	6	1	35	5	2-0
*Australia	7	5	2	20	9	1-1
*China	7	5	2	27	5	1-2
*Japan	7	5	2	24	7	0-1
Canada	7	3	4	13	13	—
Taiwan	7	2	5	18	14	—
Netherlands	7	1	6	2	32	—
Puerto Rico	7	1	6	3	44	—

Semifinals

United States 1 ... China 0 (10 inn)
Australia 3 ... Japan 0

Bronze Medal

(loser gets medal)

China 4 ... Australia 2

Gold Medal

United States 3 ... China 1

TEAM HANDBALL

Top two teams in each group advance to medal round.

MEN

Group A	Gm	W	L	T	Pts	GF	GA	Medal Round
*Sweden	5	5	0	0	10	131	94	1-1
*Croatia	5	4	1	0	8	132	122	2-0
Russia	5	3	2	0	6	137	106	—
Switzerland	5	2	3	0	4	126	115	—
United States	5	1	4	0	2	111	142	—
Kuwait	5	0	5	0	0	100	158	—

Group B	Gm	W	L	T	Pts	GF	GA	Medal Round
*France	5	4	1	0	8	143	114	0-2
*Spain	5	4	1	0	8	114	103	1-1
Egypt	5	3	2	0	6	120	112	—
Germany	5	3	2	0	6	120	105	—
Algeria	5	0	4	1	1	101	124	—
Brazil	5	0	4	1	1	111	150	—

Semifinals

Sweden 25 ... Spain 20
Croatia 24 ... France 20

Bronze Medal

Spain 27 ... France 25

Gold Medal

Croatia 27 ... Sweden 26

WOMEN

Group A	Gm	W	L	T	Pts	GF	GA	Medal Round
*Denmark	3	3	0	0	6	89	62	2-0
*Hungary	3	2	1	0	4	81	70	1-1
China	3	1	2	0	2	71	83	—
United States	3	0	3	0	0	64	90	—

Group B	Gm	W	L	T	Pts	GF	GA	Medal Round
*South Korea	3	3	0	0	6	83	60	1-1
*Norway	3	2	1	0	4	79	66	0-2
Germany	3	1	2	0	2	70	73	—
Angola	3	0	3	0	0	49	82	—

Semifinals

Denmark 23 ... Norway 19
South Korea 39 ... Hungary 25

Bronze Medal

Hungary 20 ... Norway 18

Gold Medal

Denmark 37 ... 2 OT ... South Korea 33

VOLLEYBALL

Top four teams advance to quarterfinals. Note that SF stands for Sets For and SA stands for Sets Against.

MEN

Group A	Gm	W	L	Pts	SF	SA	Medal Round
*Cuba	5	4	1	9	12	5	0-1
*Argentina	5	3	2	8	9	9	0-1
*Bulgaria	5	3	2	8	10	8	0-1
*Brazil	5	3	2	8	10	6	0-1
United States	5	2	3	7	10	9	—
Poland	5	0	5	5	1	15	—

Group B	Gm	W	L	Pts	SF	SA	Medal Round
*Italy	5	5	0	10	15	0	2-1
*Netherlands	5	4	1	9	12	3	3-0
*Yugoslavia	5	3	2	8	9	8	2-1
*Russia	5	2	3	7	7	9	1-2
South Korea	5	1	4	6	3	12	—
Tunisia	5	0	5	5	1	15	—

Quarterfinals

Yugoslavia 3 .... Brazil 2
(15-6, 15-5, 8-15, 14-16, 15-10)

Netherlands 3 .... Bulgaria 1
(16-14, 9-15, 15-3, 15-13)

Italy 3 .... Argentina 1
(12-15, 15-9, 15-7, 15-4)

Russia 3 .... Cuba 0
(15-13, 17-15, 15-11)

Semifinals

Netherlands 3 .... Russia 0
(15-6, 15-6, 15-10)

Italy 3 .... Yugoslavia 1
(15-12, 8-15, 15-6, 15-7)

Bronze Medal

Yugoslavia 3 .... Russia 1
(15-8, 7-15, 15-8, 15-9)

Gold Medal

Netherlands 3 .... Italy 2
(15-12, 9-15, 16-14, 9-15, 17-15)

WOMEN

Group A	Gm	W	L	Pts	SF	SA	Medal Round
*China	5	5	0	10	15	3	2-1
*United States	5	4	1	9	13	5	0-1
Netherlands	5	3	2	8	10	7	0-1
South Korea	5	2	3	7	10	9	0-1
Japan	5	1	4	6	3	12	—
Ukraine	5	0	5	5	0	15	—

Group B	Gm	W	L	Pts	SF	SA	Medal Round
*Brazil	5	5	0	10	15	1	2-1
*Russia	5	4	1	9	12	4	1-2
*Cuba	5	3	2	8	10	6	3-0
*Germany	5	2	3	7	7	9	0-1
Canada	5	1	4	6	3	14	—
Peru	5	0	5	5	2	15	—

Quarterfinals

China 3 .... Germany 0
(15-12, 15-8, 15-8)

Russia 3 .... Netherlands 1
(10-15, 15-7, 15-9, 15-10)

Cuba 3 .... United States 0
(15-1, 15-10, 15-12)

Brazil 3 .... South Korea 0
(15-4, 15-2, 15-10)

Semifinals

China 3 .... Russia 1
(12-15, 15-5, 15-8, 15-12)

Cuba 3 .... Brazil 2
(5-15, 15-8, 10-15, 15-13, 15-12)

Bronze Medal

Brazil 3 .... Russia 2
(15-13, 4-15, 16-14, 8-15, 15-13)

Gold Medal

Cuba 3 .... China 1
(14-16, 15-12, 17-16, 15-6)

WATER POLO

Round Robin Standings

Top four teams in each group advance to quarterfinals.

Group A	Gm	W	L	T	Pts	GF	GA	Medal Round
*Hungary	5	5	0	0	10	47	38	1-1
*Yugoslavia	5	3	1	1	7	46	44	0-1
*Spain	5	3	2	0	6	39	33	3-0
*Russia	5	2	2	1	5	42	38	0-1
Germany	5	1	4	0	2	36	45	—
Netherlands	5	0	5	0	0	35	48	—

Group B	Gm	W	L	T	Pts	GF	GA	Medal Round
*Italy	5	5	0	0	10	48	38	2-1
*United States	5	4	1	0	8	45	37	0-1
*Croatia	5	3	2	0	6	51	39	2-1
*Greece	5	2	3	0	4	37	38	0-1
Romania	5	0	4	1	1	31	45	—
Ukraine	5	0	4	1	1	33	48	—

Quarterfinals

Hungary 12 .... Greece 8
Croatia 8 .... Yugoslavia 6
Spain 5 .... United States 4
Italy 11 .... Russia 9

Semifinal

Croatia 7 .... OT .... Italy 6
Spain 7 .... Hungary 6

Bronze Medal

Italy 20 .... 2OT .... Hungary 18

Gold Medal

Spain 7 .... Croatia 5

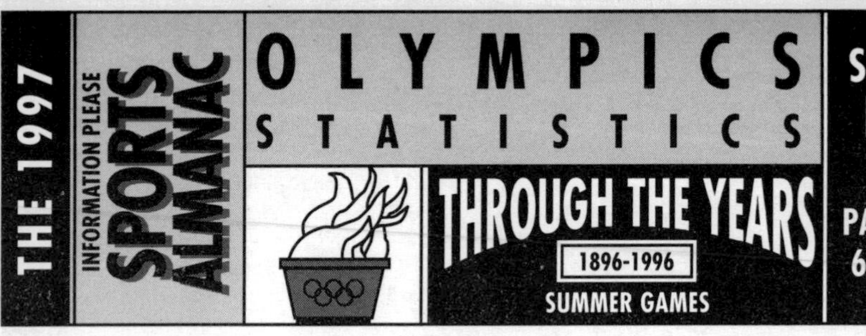

Modern Olympic Games

The original Olympic Games were celebrated as a religious festival from 776 B.C. to 393 A.D., when Roman emperor Theodosius I banned all pagan festivals (the Olympics celebrated the Greek god Zeus). On June 23, 1894, French educator Baron Pierre de Coubertin, speaking at the Sorbonne in Paris to a gathering of international sports leaders, proposed that the ancient games be revived on an international scale. The idea was enthusiastically received and the Modern Olympics were born. The first Olympics were held two years later in Athens, where 311 athletes from 14 nations competed in the ancient Panathenaic stadium to large and enthusiastic crowds. Americans captured nine out of 12 track and field events, but Greece won the most medals with 50.

The Summer Olympics

Year	No	Location	Dates	Nations	Most medals	USA Medals
1896	I	Athens, GRE	Apr. 6-15	14	Greece (10-19-18—47)	11- 6- 2— 19 (2nd)
1900	II	Paris, FRA	May 20-Oct. 28	26	France (26-37-32—95)	18-14-15— 47 (2nd)
1904	III	St. Louis, USA	July 1-Nov. 23	13	USA (78-84-82—244)	78-84-82—244 (1st)
1906-**a**	—	Athens, GRE	Apr. 22-May 2	20	France (15-9-16—40)	12- 6- 6— 24 (3rd)
1908	IV	London, GBR	Apr. 27-Oct. 31	22	Britain (54-46-38—138)	23-12-12— 47 (2nd)
1912	V	Stockholm, SWE	May 5-July 22	28	Sweden (23-24-17—64)	25-18-20— 63 (2nd)
1916	VI	Berlin, GER	Cancelled (WWI)			
1920	VII	Antwerp, BEL	Apr. 20-Sept. 12	29	USA (41-27-27—95)	41-27-27— 95 (1st)
1924	VIII	Paris, FRA	May 4-July 27	44	USA (45-27-27—99)	45-27-27— 99 (1st)
1928	IX	Amsterdam, HOL	May 17-Aug. 12	46	USA (22-18-16—56)	22-18-16— 56 (1st)
1932	X	Los Angeles, USA	July 30-Aug. 14	37	USA (41-32-30—103)	41-32-30—103 (1st)
1936	XI	Berlin, GER	Aug. 1-16	49	Germany (33-26-30-89)	24-20-12— 56 (2nd)
1940-**b**	XII	Tokyo, JPN	Cancelled (WWII)			
1944	XIII	London, GBR	Cancelled (WWII)			
1948	XIV	London, GBR	July 29-Aug. 14	59	USA (38-27-19—84)	38-27-19— 84 (1st)
1952-**cd**	XV	Helsinki, FIN	July 19-Aug. 3	69	USA (40-19-17—76)	40-19-17— 76 (1st)
1956-**e**	XVI	Melbourne, AUS	Nov. 22-Dec .8	72	USSR (37-29-32—98)	32-25-17— 74 (2nd)
1960	XVII	Rome, ITA	Aug. 25-Sept. 11	83	USSR (43-29-31—103)	34-21-16— 71 (2nd)
1964	XVIII	Tokyo, JPN	Oct. 10-24	93	USSR (30-31-35—96)	36-26-28— 90 (2nd)
1968-**f**	XIX	Mexico City, MEX	Oct. 12-27	113	USA (45-28-34—107)	45-28-34—107 (1st)
1972	XX	Munich, W. GER	Aug. 26-Sept. 10	122	USSR (50-27-22—99)	33-31-30— 94 (2nd)
1976-**g**	XXI	Montreal, CAN	July 17-Aug. 1	88	USSR (49-41-35—125)	34-35-25— 94 (3rd)
1980-**h**	XXII	Moscow, USSR	July 19-Aug. 3	81	USSR (80-69-46—195)	Boycotted Games
1984-**i**	XXIII	Los Angeles, USA	July 28-Aug. 12	140	USA (83-61-30—174)	83-61-30—174 (1st)
1988	XXIV	Seoul, S. KOR	Sept. 17-Oct. 2	160	USSR (55-31-46—132)	36-31-27— 94 (3rd)
1992-**j**	XXV	Barcelona, SPA	July 25-Aug. 9	172	UT (45-38-29—112)	37-34-37—108 (2nd)
1996	XXVI	Atlanta, USA	July 20-Aug. 4	197	USA (44-32-25—101)	44-32-25—101 (1st)
2000	XXVII	Sydney, AUS	Sept. 16-Oct. 1			

a—The 1906 Intercalated Games in Athens are considered unofficial by the IOC because they did not take place in the four-year cycle established in 1896. However, most record books include these interim games with the others.

b—The 1940 Summer Games are originally scheduled for Tokyo, but Japan resigns as host after the outbreak of the Sino-Japanese war in 1937. Helsinki is the next choice, but the IOC cancels the Games after Russian troops invade Finland in 1939.

c—Germany and Japan are allowed to rejoin Olympic community for first Summer Games since 1936. Though a divided country, the Germans send a joint East-West team.

d—The Soviet Union (USSR) participates in its first Olympics, Winter or Summer, since the Russian revolution in 1917 and takes home the second most medals (22-30-19—71).

e—Due to Australian quarantine laws, the equestrian events for the 1956 Games are held in Stockholm, June 10-17.

f—East Germany and West Germany send separate teams for the first time and will continue to do so through 1988.

g—The 1976 Games are boycotted by 32 nations, most of them from black Africa, because the IOC will not ban New Zealand. Earlier that year, a rugby team from New Zealand had toured racially-segregated South Africa.

h—The 1980 Games are boycotted by 64 nations, led by the USA, to protest the Russian invasion of Afghanistan on Dec. 27, 1979.

i—The 1984 Games are boycotted by 14 Eastern Bloc nations, led by the USSR, to protest America's overcommercialization of the Games, inadequate security and an anti-Soviet attitude by the U.S. government. Most believe, however, the communist walkout is simply revenge for 1980.

j—Germany sends a single team after East and West German reunification in 1990 and the USSR competes as the Unified Team after the breakup of the Soviet Union in 1991.

Event-by-Event

Gold medal winners from 1896-1996 in the following events: Baseball, Basketball, Boxing, Diving, Field Hockey, Gymnastics, Soccer, Swimming, Tennis, and Track & Field.

BASEBALL

Year	
1992	**Cuba**, Taiwan, Japan
1996	**Cuba**, Japan, United States

BASKETBALL

MEN

Multiple gold medals: USA (11); USSR (2).

Year	
1936	**United States**, Canada, Mexico
1948	**United States**, France, Brazil
1952	**United States**, Soviet Union, Uruguay
1956	**United States**, Soviet Union, Uruguay
1960	**United States**, Soviet Union, Brazil
1964	**United States**, Soviet Union, Brazil
1968	**United States**, Yugoslavia, Soviet Union
1972	**Soviet Union**, United States, Cuba
1976	**United States**, Yugoslavia, Soviet Union
1980	**Yugoslavia**, Italy, Soviet Union
1984	**United States**, Spain, Yugoslavia
1988	**Soviet Union**, Yugoslavia, United States
1992	**United States**, Croatia, Lithuania
1996	**United States**, Yugoslavia, Lithuania

U.S. Medal-Winning Men's Basketball Teams

1936 (gold medal): Sam Balter, Ralph Bishop, Joe Fortenberry, Tex Gibbons, Francis Johnson, Carl Knowles, Frank Lubin, Art Mollner, Don Piper, Jack Ragland, Carl Shy, Willard Schmidt, Duane Swanson and William Wheatley. Coach—Jim Needles; Assistant—Gene Johnson. Final: USA over Canada, 19-8.

1948 (gold medal): Cliff Barker, Don Barksdale, Ralph Beard, Louis Beck, Vince Boryla, Gordon Carpenter, Alex Groza, Wallace Jones, Bob Kurland, Ray Lumpp, R.C. Pitts, Jesse Renick, Robert (Jackie) Robinson and Ken Rollins. Coach—Omar Browning; Assistant—Adolph Rupp. Final: USA over France, 65-21.

1952 (gold medal): Ron Bontemps, Mark Freiberger, Wayne Glasgow, Charlie Hoag, Bill Hougland, John Keller, Dean Kelley, Bob Kenney, Bob Kurland, Bill Lienhard, Clyde Lovellette, Frank McCabe, Dan Pippin and Howie Williams. Coach—Warren Womble; Assistant—Forrest (Phog) Allen. Final: USA over USSR, 36-25.

1956 (gold medal): Dick Boushka, Carl Cain, Chuck Darling, Bill Evans, Gib Ford, Burdy Haldorson, Bill Hougland, Bob Jeangerard, K.C. Jones, Bill Russell, Ron Tomsic, Jim Walsh. Coach—Gerald Tucker; Assistant—Bruce Drake. Final: USA over USSR, 89-55.

1960 (gold medal): Jay Arnette, Walt Bellamy, Bob Boozer, Terry Dischinger, Jerry Lucas, Oscar Robertson, Adrian Smith, Burdy Haldorson, Darrall Imhoff, Allen Kelley, Lester Lane and Jerry West. Coach—Pete Newell; Assistant—Warren Womble. Final round: USA defeated USSR (81-57), Italy (112-81) and Brazil (90-63) in round robin.

1964 (gold medal): Jim (Bad News) Barnes, Bill Bradley, Larry Brown, Joe Caldwell, Mel Counts, Dick Davies, Walt Hazzard, Lucius Jackson, Pete McCaffrey, Jeff Mullins, Jerry Shipp and George Wilson. Coach—Hank Iba; Assistant—Henry Vaughn. Final: USA over USSR, 73-59.

1968 (gold medal): Mike Barrett, John Clawson, Don Dee, Cal Fowler, Spencer Haywood, Bill Hosket, Jim King, Glynn Saulters, Charlie Scott, Mike Silliman, Ken Spain, and JoJo White. Coach—Hank Iba; Assistant—Henry Vaughn. USA over Yugoslavia, 65-50.

1972 (silver medal refused): Mike Bantom, Jim Brewer, Tom Burleson, Doug Collins, Kenny Davis, Jim Forbes, Tom Henderson, Bobby Jones, Dwight Jones, Kevin Joyce, Tom McMillen and Ed Ratleff. Coach—Hank Iba; Assistants— John Bach and Don Haskins. Final: USSR over USA, 51-50.

1976 (gold medal): Tate Armstrong, Quinn Buckner, Kenny Carr, Adrian Dantley, Walter Davis, Phil Ford, Ernie Grunfeld, Phil Hubbard, Mitch Kupchak, Tommy LaGarde, Scott May and Steve Sheppard. Coach—Dean Smith; Assistants—Bill Guthridge and John Thompson. Final: USA over Yugoslavia, 95-74.

1980 (no medal): USA boycotted Moscow Games. Final: Yugoslavia over Italy, 86-77.

1984 (gold medal): Steve Alford, Patrick Ewing, Vern Fleming, Michael Jordan; Joe Kleine, Jon Koncak, Chris Mullin, Sam Perkins, Alvin Robertson, Wayman Tisdale, Jeff Turner and Leon Wood. Coach—Bobby Knight; Assistants— Don Donoher and George Raveling. Final: USA over Spain, 96-65.

1988 (bronze medal): Stacey Augmon, Willie Anderson, Bimbo Coles, Jeff Grayer, Hersey Hawkins, Dan Majerle, Danny Manning, Mitch Richmond, J.R. Reid, David Robinson, Charles D. Smith and Charles E. Smith. Coach—John Thompson; Assistants—George Raveling and Mary Fenlon. Final: USSR over Yugoslavia, 76-63.

1992 (gold medal): Charles Barkley, Larry Bird, Clyde Drexler, Patrick Ewing, Magic Johnson, Michael Jordan, Christian Laettner, Karl Malone, Chris Mullin, Scottie Pippen, David Robinson and John Stockton. Coach—Chuck Daly; Assistants—Lenny Wilkens, Mike Krzyzewski and P.J. Carlesimo. Final: USA over Croatia, 117-85.

1996 (gold medal): Charles Barkley, Anfernee Hardaway, Grant Hill, Karl Malone, Reggie Miller, Hakeem Olajuwon, Shaquille O'Neal, Gary Payton, Scottie Pippen, David Robinson and John Stockton. Coach—Lenny Wilkens; Assistants—Bobby Cremins, Clem Haskins and Jerry Sloan. Final: USA over Yugoslavia, 95-69.

WOMEN

Multiple gold medals: USSR/UT (3); USA (3).

Year	
1976	**Soviet Union**, United States, Bulgaria
1980	**Soviet Union**, Bulgaria, Yugoslavia
1984	**United States**, South Korea, China
1988	**United States**, Yugoslavia, Soviet Union
1992	**Unified Team**, China, United States
1996	**United States**, Brazil, Australia

Basketball (Cont.)

U.S. Gold Medal-Winning Women's Basketball Teams

1984: Cathy Boswell, Denise Curry, Anne Donovan, Teresa Edwards, Lea Henry, Janice Lawrence, Pamela McGee, Carol Menken-Schaudt, Cheryl Miller, Kim Mulkey, Cindy Noble, Lynette Woodard. Coach—Pat Summitt; Assistant—Kay Yow. Final: USA over South Korea, 85–55.

1988: Cindy Brown, Vicky Bullett, Cynthia Cooper, Anne Donovan, Teresa Edwards, Kamie Ethridge, Jennifer Gillom, Bridgette Gordon, Andrea Lloyd, Katrina McClain, Suzie McConnell, Teresa Weatherspoon. Coach—Kay Yow; Assistants—Sylvia Hatchell and Susan Yow. Final: USA over Yugoslavia, 77–70.

1996: Jennifer Azzi, Ruthie Bolton, Teresa Edwards, Venus Lacey, Lisa Leslie, Rebecca Lobo, Katrina McClain, Nikki McCray, Carla McGhee, Dawn Staley, Katy Steding and Sheryl Swoopes. Coach—Tara VanDerveer; Assistants—Ceal Barry, Nancy Darsch and Marian Washington. Final: USA over Brazil, 111-87.

BOXING

Multiple gold medals: László Papp and Teófilo Stevenson (3); Angel Herrera, Oliver Kirk, Jerzy Kulej, Boris Lagutin and Harry Mallin (2). All fighters won titles in consecutive Olympics, except Kirk, who won both the bantamweight and featherweight titles in 1904 (he only had to fight once in each division).

Light Flyweight (106 lbs)

Year		Final Match	Year		Final Match
1968	Francisco Rodriguez, VEN	Decision, 3-2	1984	Paul Gonzales, USA	Default
1972	György Gedó, HUN	Decision, 5-0	1988	Ivailo Hristov, BUL	Decision, 5-0
1976	Jorge Hernandez, CUB	Decision, 4-1	1992	Rogelio Marcelo, CUB	Decision, 24-10
1980	Shamil Sabyrov, USSR	Decision, 3-2	1996	Daniel Petrov Bojilov, BUL	Decision, 19-6

Flyweight (112 lbs)

Year		Final Match	Year		Final Match
1904	George Finnegan, USA	Stopped, 1st	1964	Fernando Atzori, ITA	Decision, 4-1
1920	Frank Di Gennara, USA	Decision	1968	Ricardo Delgado, MEX	Decision, 5-0
1924	Fidel LaBarba, USA	Decision	1972	Georgi Kostadinov, BUL	Decision, 5-0
1928	Antal Kocsis, HUN	Decision	1976	Leo Randolph, USA	Decision, 3-2
1932	István Énekes, HUN	Decision	1980	Peter Lessov, BUL	Stopped, 2nd
1936	Willi Kaiser, GER	Decision	1984	Steve McCrory, USA	Decision, 4-1
1948	Pascual Perez, ARG	Decision	1988	Kim Kwang-Sun, S. Kor	Decision, 4-1
1952	Nate Brooks, USA	Decision, 3-0	1992	Su Choi-Chol, N. Kor	Decision, 12-2
1956	Terence Spinks, GBR	Decision	1996	Maikro Romero, CUB	Decision 12-11
1960	Gyula Török, HUN	Decision, 3-2			

Bantamweight (119 lbs)

Year		Final Match	Year		Final Match
1904	Oliver Kirk, USA	Stopped, 3rd	1960	Oleg Grigoryev, USSR	Decision
1908	Henry Thomas, GBR	Decision	1964	Takao Sakurai, JPN	Stopped, 2nd
1920	Clarence Walker, SAF	Decision	1968	Valery Sokolov, USSR	Stopped, 2nd
1924	William Smith, SAF	Decision	1972	Orlando Martinez, CUB	Decision, 5-0
1928	Vittorio Tamagnini, ITA	Decision	1976	Gu Yong-Ju, N. Kor	Decision, 5-0
1932	Horace Gwynne, CAN	Decision	1980	Juan Hernandez, CUB	Decision, 5-0
1936	Ulderico Sergo, ITA	Decision	1984	Maurizio Stecca, ITA	Decision, 4-1
1948	Tibor Csik, HUN	Decision	1988	Kennedy McKinney, USA	Decision, 5-0
1952	Pentti Hämäläinen, FIN	Decision, 2-1	1992	Joel Casamayor, CUB	Decision, 14-8
1956	Wolfgang Behrendt, GER	Decision	1996	Istvan Kovacs, HUN	Decision, 14-7

Featherweight (125 lbs)

Year		Final Match	Year		Final Match
1904	Oliver Kirk, USA	Decision	1960	Francesco Musso, ITA	Decision, 4-1
1908	Richard Gunn, GBR	Decision	1964	Stanislav Stepashkin, USSR	Decision, 3-2
1920	Paul Fritsch, FRA	Decision	1968	Antonio Roldan, MEX	Won on Disq.
1924	John Fields, USA	Decision	1972	Boris Kousnetsov, USSR	Decision, 3-2
1928	Lambertus van Klaveren, HOL	Decision	1976	Angel Herrera, CUB	KO, 2nd
1932	Carmelo Robledo, ARG	Decision	1980	Rudi Fink, E. Ger	Decision, 4-1
1936	Oscar Casanovas, ARG	Decision	1984	Meldrick Taylor, USA	Decision, 5-0
1948	Ernesto Formenti, ITA	Decision	1988	Giovanni Parisi, ITA	Stopped, 1st
1952	Jan Zachara, CZE	Decision, 2-1	1992	Andreas Tews, GER	Decision, 16-7
1956	Vladimir Safronov, USSR	Decision	1996	Somluck Kamsing, THA	Decision, 8-5

Lightweight (132 lbs)

Year		Final Match	Year		Final Match
1904	Harry Spanger, USA	Decision	1960	Kazimierz Pazdzior, POL	Decision, 4-1
1908	Frederick Grace, GBR	Decision	1964	Józef Grudzien, POL	Decision
1920	Samuel Mosberg, USA	Decision	1968	Ronnie Harris, USA	Decision, 5-0
1924	Hans Nielsen, DEN	Decision	1972	Jan Szczepanski, POL	Decision, 5-0
1928	Carlo Orlandi, ITA	Decision	1976	Howard Davis, USA	Decision, 5-0
1932	Lawrence Stevens, SAF	Decision	1980	Angel Herrera, CUB	Stopped, 3rd
1936	Imre Harangi, HUN	Decision	1984	Pernell Whitaker, USA	Foe quit, 2nd
1948	Gerald Dreyer, SAF	Decision	1988	Andreas Zuelow, E. Ger	Decision, 5-0
1952	Aureliano Bolognesi, ITA	Decision, 2-1	1992	Oscar De La Hoya, USA	Decision, 7-2
1956	Richard McTaggart, GBR	Decision	1996	Hocine Soltani, ALG	Tiebreak, 3-3

Light Welterweight (139 lbs)

Year		Final Match	Year		Final Match
1952	Charles Adkins, USA	Decision, 2-1	1976	Ray Leonard, USA	Decision, 5-0
1956	Vladimir Yengibaryan, USSR	Decision	1980	Patrizio Oliva, ITA	Decision, 4-1
1960	Bohumil Nemecek, CZE	Decision, 5-0	1984	Jerry Page, USA	Decision, 5-0
1964	Jerzy Kulej, POL	Decision, 5-0	1988	Vyacheslav Yanovsky, USSR	Decision, 5-0
1968	Jerzy Kulej, POL	Decision, 3-2	1992	Hector Vinent, CUB	Decision, 11-1
1972	Ray Seales, USA	Decision, 3-2	1996	Hector Vinent, CUB	Decision, 20-13

Welterweight (147 lbs)

Year		Final Match	Year		Final Match
1904	Albert Young, USA	Decision	1964	Marian Kasprzyk, POL	Decision, 4-1
1920	Bert Schneider, CAN	Decision	1968	Manfred Wolke, E. Ger	Decision, 4-1
1924	Jean Delarge, BEL	Decision	1972	Emilio Correa, CUB	Decision, 5-0
1928	Edward Morgan, NZE	Decision	1976	Jochen Bachfeld, E. Ger	Decision, 3-2
1932	Edward Flynn, USA	Decision	1980	Andrés Aldama, CUB	Decision, 4-1
1936	Sten Suvio, FIN	Decision	1984	Mark Breland, USA	Decision, 5-0
1948	Julius Torma, CZE	Decision	1988	Robert Wangila, KEN	KO, 2nd
1952	Zygmunt Chychla, POL	Decision, 3-0	1992	Michael Carruth, IRE	Decision, 13-10
1956	Nicolae Linca, ROM	Decision, 3-2	1996	Oleg Saitov, RUS	Decision, 14-9
1960	Nino Benvenuti, ITA	Decision, 4-1			

Light Middleweight (156 lbs)

Year		Final Match	Year		Final Match
1952	László Papp, HUN	Decision, 3-0	1976	Jerzy Rybicki, POL	Decision, 5-0
1956	László Papp, HUN	Decision	1980	Armando Martinez, CUB	Decision, 4-1
1960	Skeeter McClure, USA	Decision, 4-1	1984	Frank Tate, USA	Decision, 5-0
1964	Boris Lagutin, USSR	Decision, 4-1	1988	Park Si-Hun, S. Kor	Decision, 3-2
1968	Boris Lagutin, USSR	Decision, 5-0	1992	Juan Lemus, CUB	Decision, 6-1
1972	Dieter Kottysch, W.Ger	Decision, 3-2	1996	David Reid, USA	KO, 3rd

Middleweight (165 lbs)

Year		Final Match	Year		Final Match
1904	Charles Mayer, USA	Stopped, 3rd	1960	Eddie Crook, USA	Decision, 3-2
1908	John Douglas, GBR	Decision	1964	Valery Popenchenko, USSR	Stopped, 1st
1920	Harry Mallin, GBR	Decision	1968	Christopher Finnegan, GBR	Decision, 3-2
1924	Harry Mallin, GBR	Decision	1972	Vyacheslav Lemechev, USSR	KO, 1st
1928	Piero Toscani, ITA	Decision	1976	Michael Spinks, USA	Stopped, 3rd
1932	Carmen Barth, USA	Decision	1980	José Gomez, CUB	Decision, 4-1
1936	Jean Despeaux, FRA	Decision	1984	Shin Joon-Sup, S. Kor	Decision, 3-2
1948	László Papp, HUN	Decision	1988	Henry Maske, E. Ger	Decision, 5-0
1952	Floyd Patterson, USA	KO, 1st	1992	Ariel Hernandez, CUB	Decision, 12-7
1956	Gennady Schatkov, USSR	KO, 1st	1996	Ariel Hernandez, CUB	Decision, 11-3

Light Heavyweight (178 lbs)

Year		Final Match	Year		Final Match
1920	Eddie Eagan, USA	Decision	1964	Cosimo Pinto, ITA	Decision, 3-2
1924	Harry Mitchell, GBR	Decision	1968	Dan Poznjak, USSR	Default
1928	Victor Avendaño, ARG	Decision	1972	Mate Parlov, YUG	Stopped, 2nd
1932	David Carstens, SAF	Decision	1976	Leon Spinks, USA	Stopped, 3rd
1936	Roger Michelot, FRA	Decision	1980	Slobodan Kacar, YUG	Decision, 4-1
1948	George Hunter, SAF	Decision	1984	Anton Josipovic, YUG	Default
1952	Norvel Lee, USA	Decision, 3-0	1988	Andrew Maynard, USA	Decision, 5-0
1956	Jim Boyd, USA	Decision	1992	Torsten May, GER	Decision, 8-3
1960	Cassius Clay, USA	Decision, 5-0	1996	Vasilii Jirov, KAZ	Decision, 17-4

Note: Cassius Clay changed his name to Muhammad Ali after winning the world heavyweight championship in 1964.

Heavyweight (201 lbs)

Year		Final Match	Year		Final Match
1984	Henry Tillman, USA	Decision, 5-0	1992	Felix Savon, CUB	Decision, 14-1
1988	Ray Mercer, USA	KO, 1st	1996	Felix Savon, CUB	Decision, 20-2

Boxing (cont.)

Super Heavyweight (Unlimited)

Year		Final Match	Year		Final Match
1904	Samuel Berger, USA	Decision	1960	Franco De Piccoli, ITA	KO, 1st
1908	Albert Oldham, GBR	KO, 1st	1964	Joe Frazier, USA	Decision, 3-2
1920	Ronald Rawson, GBR	Decision	1968	George Foreman, USA	Stopped, 2nd
1924	Otto von Porat, NOR	Decision	1972	Teófilo Stevenson, CUB	Default
1928	Arturo Rodriguez Jurado, ARG	Stopped, 1st	1976	Teófilo Stevenson, CUB	KO, 3rd
1932	Santiago Lovell, ARG	Decision	1980	Teófilo Stevenson, CUB	Decision, 4-1
1936	Herbert Runge, GER	Decision	1984	Tyrell Biggs, USA	Decision, 4-1
1948	Rafael Iglesias, ARG	KO, 2nd	1988	Lennox Lewis, CAN	Stopped, 2nd
1952	Ed Sanders, USA	Won on Disq.*	1992	Roberto Balado, CUB	Decision, 13-2
1956	Pete Rademacher, USA	Stopped, 1st	1996	Vladimir Klichko, UKR	Decision, 7-3

* Sanders' opponent, Ingemar Johansson was disqualified in 2nd round for not trying.

Future World Heavyweight Champions

Seven Olympic gold medal winners eventually went on to win the heavyweight championship of the world.

Middleweights	Light Heavyweights	Heavyweights	Super Heavyweight
Floyd Patterson	Cassius Clay	Joe Frazier	Lennox Lewis
Michael Spinks	Leon Spinks	George Foreman	

DIVING

MEN

Multiple gold medals: Greg Louganis (4); Klaus Dibiasi (3); Pete Desjardins, Sammy Lee, Bob Webster and Albert White (2).

Springboard

Year		Points	Year		Points
1908	Albert Zürner, GER	85.5	1960	Gary Tobian, USA	170.00
1912	Paul Günther, GER	79.23	1964	Ken Sitzberger, USA	159.90
1920	Louis Kuehn, USA	675.4	1968	Bernie Wrightson, USA	170.15
1924	Albert White, USA	696.4	1972	Vladimir Vasin, USSR	594.09
1928	Pete Desjardins, USA	185.04	1976	Phil Boggs, USA	619.05
1932	Michael Galitzen, USA	161.38	1980	Aleksandr Portnov, USSR	905.03
1936	Richard Degener, USA	163.57	1984	Greg Louganis, USA	754.41
1948	Bruce Harlan, USA	163.64	1988	Greg Louganis, USA	730.80
1952	David Browning, USA	205.29	1992	Mark Lenzi, USA	676.53
1956	Bob Clotworthy, USA	159.56	1996	Ni Xiong, CHN	701.46

Platform

Year		Points	Year		Points
1904	George Sheldon, USA	12.66	1956	Joaquin Capilla, MEX	152.44
1906	Gottlob Walz, GER	156.0	1960	Bob Webster, USA	165.56
1908	Hjalmar Johansson, SWE	83.75	1964	Bob Webster, USA	148.58
1912	Erik Adlerz, SWE	73.94	1968	Klaus Dibiasi, ITA	164.18
1920	Clarence Pinkston, USA	100.67	1972	Klaus Dibiasi, ITA	504.12
1924	Albert White, USA	97.46	1976	Klaus Dibiasi, ITA	600.51
1928	Pete Desjardins, USA	98.74	1980	Falk Hoffmann, E. Ger	835.65
1932	Harold Smith, USA	124.80	1984	Greg Louganis, USA	710.91
1936	Marshall Wayne, USA	113.58	1988	Greg Louganis, USA	638.61
1948	Sammy Lee, USA	130.05	1992	Sun Shuwei, CHN	677.31
1952	Sammy Lee, USA	156.28	1996	Dmitri Saoutine, RUS	692.34

WOMEN

Multiple gold medals: Pat McCormick (4); Ingrid Engel-Krämer and Fu Mingxia (3); Vicki Draves, Dorothy Poynton Hill and Gao Min (2). and Minxia Fu

Springboard

Year		Points	Year		Points
1920	Aileen Riggin, USA	539.9	1964	Ingrid Engel-Krämer, GER	145.00
1924	Elizabeth Becker, USA	474.5	1968	Sue Gossick, USA	150.77
1928	Helen Meany, USA	78.62	1972	Micki King, USA	450.03
1932	Georgia Coleman, USA	87.52	1976	Jennifer Chandler, USA	506.19
1936	Marjorie Gestring, USA	89.27	1980	Irina Kalinina, USSR	725.91
1948	Vicki Draves, USA	108.74	1984	Sylvie Bernier, CAN	530.70
1952	Pat McCormick, USA	147.30	1988	Gao Min, CHN	580.23
1956	Pat McCormick, USA	142.36	1992	Gao Min, CHN	572.40
1960	Ingrid Krämer, GER	155.81	1996	Fu Mingxia, CHN	547.68

Platform

Year		Points	Year		Points
1912	Greta Johansson, SWE	39.9	1964	Lesley Bush, USA	99.80
1920	Stefani Fryland-Clausen, DEN	34.6	1968	Milena Duchková, CZE	109.59
1924	Caroline Smith, USA	33.2	1972	Ulrika Knape, SWE	390.00
1928	Elizabeth Becker Pinkston, USA	31.6	1976	Elena Vaytsekhovskaya, USSR	406.59
1932	Dorothy Poynton, USA	40.26	1980	Martina Jäschke, E. Ger	596.25
1936	Dorothy Poynton Hill, USA	33.93	1984	Zhou Jihong, CHN	435.51
1948	Vicki Draves, USA	68.87	1988	Xu Yanmei, CHN	445.20
1952	Pat McCormick, USA	79.37	1992	Fu Mingxia, CHN	461.43
1956	Pat McCormick, USA	84.85	1996	Fu Mingxia, CHN	521.58
1960	Ingrid Krämer, GER	91.28			

FIELD HOCKEY

MEN

Multiple gold medals: India (8); Great Britain and Pakistan (3); West Germany/Germany (2).

Year		Year	
1908	**Great Britain**, Ireland, Scotland	1964	**India**, Pakistan, Australia
1920	**Great Britain**, Denmark, Belgium	1968	**Pakistan**, Australia, India
1928	**India**, Netherlands, Germany	1972	**West Germany**, Pakistan, India
1932	**India**, Japan, United States	1976	**New Zealand**, Australia, Pakistan
1936	**India**, Germany, Netherlands	1980	**India**, Spain, Soviet Union
1948	**India**, Great Britain, Netherlands	1984	**Pakistan**, West Germany, Great Britain
1952	**India**, Netherlands, Great Britain	1988	**Great Britain**, West Germany, Netherlands
1956	**India**, Pakistan, Germany	1992	**Germany**, Australia, Pakistan
1960	**Pakistan**, India, Spain	1996	**Netherlands**, Spain, Australia

WOMEN

Multiple gold medals: Australia (2).

Year		Year	
1980	**Zimbabwe**, Czechoslovakia, Soviet Union	1992	**Spain**, Germany, Great Britain
1984	**Netherlands**, West Germany, United States	1996	**Australia**, Korea, Netherlands
1988	**Australia**, South Korea, Netherlands		

GYMNASTICS

MEN

At least 4 gold medals (including team events): Sawao Kato (8); Nikolai Andrianov, Viktor Chukarin and Boris Shakhlin (7); Akinori Nakayama and Vitaly Scherbo (6); Yukio Endo, Anton Heida, Mitsuo Tsukahara and Takashi Ono (5); Vladimir Artemov, Georges Miez and Valentin Muratov (4).

All-Around

Year		Points	Year		Points
1900	Gustave Sandras, FRA	302.0	1956	Viktor Chukarin, USSR	114.25
1904	Julius Lenhart, AUT	69.80	1960	Boris Shakhlin, USSR	115.95
1906	Pierre Payssé, FRA	97.0	1964	Yukio Endo, JPN	115.95
1908	Alberto Braglia, ITA	317.0	1968	Sawao Kato, JPN	115.9
1912	Alberto Braglia, ITA	135.0	1972	Sawao Kato, JPN	114.650
1920	Giorgio Zampori, ITA	88.35	1976	Nikolai Andrianov, USSR	116.65
1924	Leon Stukelj, YUG	110.340	1980	Aleksandr Dityatin, USSR	118.65
1928	Georges Miez, SWI	247.500	1984	Koji Gushiken, JPN	118.7
1932	Romeo Neri, ITA	140.625	1988	Vladimir Artemov, USSR	119.125
1936	Alfred Schwarzmann, GER	113.100	1992	Vitaly Scherbo, UT	59.025
1948	Veikko Huhtanen, FIN	229.7	1996	Li Xiaoshuang, CHN	58.423
1952	Viktor Chukarin, USSR	115.7			

Horizontal Bar

Year		Points	Year		Points
1896	Hermann Weingartner, GER	—	1964	Boris Shakhlin, USSR	19.625
1904	(TIE) Anton Heida, USA	40.0	1968	(TIE) Akinori Nakayama, JPN	19.55
	& Edward Hennig, USA	40.0		& Mikhail Voronin, USSR	19.55
1924	Leon Stukelj, YUG	19.73	1972	Mitsuo Tsukahara, JPN	19.725
1928	Georges Miez, SWI	19.17	1976	Mitsuo Tsukahara, JPN	19.675
1932	Dallas Bixler, USA	18.33	1980	Stoyan Deltchev, BUL	19.825
1936	Aleksanteri Saarvala, FIN	19.367	1984	Shinji Morisue, JPN	20.00
1948	Josef Stalder, SWI	19.85	1988	(TIE) Vladimir Artemov, USSR	19.900
1952	Jack Günthard, SWI	19.55		& Valeri Lyukin, USSR	19.900
1956	Takashi Ono, JPN	19.60	1992	Trent Dimas, USA	9.875
1960	Takashi Ono, JPN	19.60	1996	Andreas Wecker, GER	9.850

Gymnastics (Cont.)

Parallel Bars

Year		Points	Year		Points
1896	Alfred Flatow, GER	—	1964	Yukio Endo, JPN	19.675
1904	George Eyser, USA	44.0	1968	Akinori Nakayama, JPN	19.475
1924	August Güttinger, SWI	21.63	1972	Sawao Kato, JPN	19.475
1928	Ladislav Vácha, CZE	18.83	1976	Sawao Kato, JPN	19.675
1932	Romeo Neri, ITA	18.97	1980	Aleksandr Tkachyov, USSR	19.775
1936	Konrad Frey, GER	19.067	1984	Bart Conner, USA	19.95
1948	Michael Reusch, SWI	19.75	1988	Vladimir Artemov, USSR	19.925
1952	Hans Eugster, SWI	19.65	1992	Vitaly Scherbo, UT	9.900
1956	Viktor Chukarin, USSR	19.20	1996	Rustam Sharipov, UKR	9.837
1960	Boris Shakhlin, USSR	19.40			

Vault

Year		Points	Year		Points
1896	Karl Schumann, GER	—	1960	(TIE) Takashi Ono, JPN	19.35
1904	(TIE) George Eyser, USA	36.0		& Boris Shakhlin, USSR	19.35
	& Anton Heida, USA	36.0	1964	Haruhiro Yamashita, JPN	19.60
1924	Frank Kriz, USA	9.98	1968	Mikhail Voronin, USSR	19.00
1928	Eugen Mack, SWI	9.58	1972	Klaus Köste, E. Ger	18.85
1932	Savino Guglielmetti, ITA	18.03	1976	Nikolai Andrianov, USSR	19.45
1936	Alfred Schwarzmann, GER	19.20	1980	Nikolai Andrianov, USSR	19.825
1948	Paavo Aaltonen, FIN	19.55	1984	Lou Yun, CHN	19.95
1952	Viktor Chukarin, USSR	19.20	1988	Lou Yun, CHN	19.875
1956	(TIE) Helmut Bantz, GER	18.85	1992	Vitaly Scherbo, UT	9.856
	& Valentin Muratov, USSR	18.85	1996	Alexei Nemov, RUS	9.787

Pommel Horse

Year		Points	Year		Points
1896	Louis Zutter, SWI	—	1964	Miroslav Cerar, YUG	19.525
1904	Anton Heida, USA	42	1968	Miroslav Cerar, YUG	19.325
1924	Josef Wilhelm, SWI	21.23	1972	Viktor Klimenko, SOV	19.125
1928	Hermann Hänggi, SWI	19.75	1976	Zoltán Magyar, HUN	19.70
1932	István Pelle, HUN	19.07	1980	Zoltán Magyar, HUN	19.925
1936	Konrad Frey, GER	19.333	1984	(TIE) Li Ning, CHN	19.95
1948	(TIE) Paavo Aaltonen, FIN	19.35		& Peter Vidmar, USA	19.95
	Veikko Huhtanen, FIN	19.35	1988	(TIE) Dmitri Bilozerchev, USSR	19.95
	& Heikki Savolainen, FIN	19.35		Zsolt Borkai, HUN	19.95
1952	Viktor Chukarin, USSR	19.50		& Lyubomir Geraskov, BUL	19.95
1956	Boris Shakhlin, USSR	19.25	1992	(TIE) Pae Gil-Su, N. Kor	9.925
1960	(TIE) Eugen Ekman, FIN	19.375		& Vitaly Scherbo, UT	9.925
	& Boris Shakhlin, USSR	19.375	1996	Donghua Li, SUI	9.875

Rings

Year		Points	Year		Points
1896	Ioannis Mitropoulos, GRE	—	1968	Akinori Nakayama, JPN	19.45
1904	Hermann Glass, USA	45	1972	Akinori Nakayama, JPN	19.35
1924	Francesco Martino, ITA	21.553	1976	Nikolai Andrianov, USSR	19.65
1928	Leon Stukelj, YUG	19.25	1980	Aleksandr Dityatin, USSR	19.875
1932	George Gulack, USA	18.97	1984	(TIE) Koji Gushiken, JPN	19.85
1936	Alois Hudec, CZE	19.433		& Li Ning, CHN	19.85
1948	Karl Frei, SWI	19.80	1988	(TIE) Holger Behrendt, E. Ger	19.925
1952	Grant Shaginyan, USSR	19.75		& Dmitri Bilozerchev, USSR	19.925
1956	Albert Azaryan, USSR	19.35	1992	Vitaly Scherbo, UT	9.937
1960	Albert Azaryan, USSR	19.725	1996	Yuri Chechi, ITA	9.887
1964	Takuji Haytta, JPN	19.475			

Floor Exercise

Year		Points	Year		Points
1932	István Pelle, HUN	9.60	1972	Nikolai Andrianov, USSR	19.175
1936	Georges Miez, SWI	18.666	1976	Nikolai Andrianov, USSR	19.45
1948	Ferenc Pataki, HUN	19.35	1980	Roland Brückner, E. Ger	19.75
1952	William Thoresson, SWE	19.25	1984	Li Ning, CHN	19.925
1956	Valentin Muratov, USSR	19.20	1988	Sergei Kharkov, USSR	19.925
1960	Nobuyuki Aihara, JPN	19.45	1992	Li Xiaosahuang, CHN	9.925
1964	Franco Menichelli, ITA	19.45	1996	Ioannis Melissanidis, GRE	9.850
1968	Sawao Kato, JPN	19.475			

Team Combined Exercises

Year		Points
1904	United States	374.43
1906	Norway	19.00
1908	Sweden	438
1912	Italy	265.75
1920	Italy	359.855
1924	Italy	839.058
1928	Switzerland	1718.625
1932	Italy	541.850
1936	Germany	657.430
1948	Finland	1358.30
1952	Soviet Union	574.40
1956	Soviet Union	568.25
1960	Japan	575.20
1964	Japan	577.95
1968	Japan	575.90
1972	Japan	571.25
1976	Japan	576.85
1980	Soviet Union	598.60
1984	United States	591.40
1988	Soviet Union	593.35
1992	Unified Team	585.45
1996	Russia	576.778

WOMEN

At least 4 gold medals (including team events): Larissa Latynina (9); Vera Cáslavská (7); Polina Astakhova, Nadia Comaneci, Agnes Keleti and Nelli Kim (5); Olga Korbut, Ecaterina Szabó and Lyudmila Tourischeva (4).

All-Around

Year		Points
1952	Maria Gorokhovskaya, USSR	76.78
1956	Larissa Latynina, USSR	74.933
1960	Larissa Latynina, USSR	77.031
1964	Vera Cáslavská, CZE	77.564
1968	Vera Cáslavská, CZE	78.25
1972	Lyudmila Tourischeva, USSR	77.025
1976	Nadia Comaneci, ROM	79.275
1980	Yelena Davydova, USSR	79.15
1984	Mary Lou Retton, USA	79.175
1988	Yelena Shushunova, USSR	79.662
1992	Tatiana Gutsu, UT	39.737
1996	Lilia Podkopayeva, UKR	39.255

Vault

Year		Points
1952	Yekaterina Kalinchuk, USSR	19.20
1956	Larissa Latynina, USSR	18.833
1960	Margarita Nikolayeva, USSR	19.316
1964	Vera Cáslavská, CZE	19.483
1968	Vera Cáslavská, CZE	19.775
1972	Karin Janz, E. Ger	19.525
1976	Nelli Kim, USSR	19.80
1980	Natalia Shaposhnikova, USSR	19.725
1984	Ecaterina Szabó, ROM	19.875
1988	Svetlana Boginskaya, USSR	19.905
1992	(TIE) Henrietta Onodi, HUN	9.925
	& Lavinia Milosovici, ROM	9.925
1996	Simona Amanar, ROM	9.775

Uneven Bars

Year		Points
1952	Margit Korondi, HUN	19.40
1956	Agnes Keleti, HUN	18.966
1960	Polina Astakhova, USSR	19.616
1964	Polina Astakhova, USSR	19.332
1968	Vera Cáslavská, CZE	19.65
1972	Karin Janz, E. Ger	19.675
1976	Nadia Comaneci, ROM	20.00
1980	Maxi Gnauck, E. Ger	19.875
1984	(TIE) Julianne McNamora, USA	19.95
	& Ma Yanhong, CHN	19.95
1988	Daniela Silivas, ROM	20.00
1992	Lu Li, CHN	10.00
1996	Svetlana Chorkina, RUS	9.850

Balance Beam

Year		Points
1952	Nina Bocharova, USSR	19.22
1956	Agnes Keleti, HUN	18.80
1960	Eva Bosáková, CZE	19.283
1964	Vera Cáslavská, CZE	19.449
1968	Natalya Kuchinskaya, USSR	19.65
1972	Olga Korbut, USSR	19.40
1976	Nadia Comaneci, ROM	19.95
1980	Nadia Comaneci, ROM	19.80
1984	(TIE) Simona Pauca, ROM	19.80
	& Ecaterina Szabó, ROM	19.80
1988	Daniela Silivas, ROM	19.924
1992	Tatiana Lyssenko, UT	9.975
1996	Shannon Miller, USA	9.862

Floor Exercise

Year		Points
1952	Agnes Keleti, HUN	19.36
1956	(TIE) Agnes Keleti, HUN	18.733
	& Larissa Latynina, USSR	18.733
1960	Larissa Latynina, USSR	19.583
1964	Larissa Latynina, USSR	19.599
1968	(TIE) Vera Cáslavská, CZE	19.675
	& Larissa Petrik, USSR	19.675
1972	Olga Korbut, USSR	19.575
1976	Nelli Kim, USSR	19.85
1980	(TIE) Nadia Comaneci, ROM	19.875
	& Nelli Kim, USSR	19.875
1984	Ecaterina Szabó, ROM	19.975
1988	Daniela Silivas, ROM	19.937
1992	Lavinia Milosovici, ROM	10.000
1996	Lilia Podkopayeva, UKR	9.887

Gymnastics (Cont.)

WOMEN

Team Combined Exercises

Year		Points
1928	Holland	316.75
1936	Germany	506.50
1948	Czechoslovakia	445.45
1952	Soviet Union	527.03
1956	Soviet Union	444.800
1960	Soviet Union	382.320
1964	Soviet Union	280.890
1968	Soviet Union	382.85
1972	Soviet Union	380.50
1976	Soviet Union	466.00
1980	Soviet Union	394.90
1984	Romania	392.02
1988	Soviet Union	395.475
1992	Unified Team	395.666
1996	United States	389.225

SOCCER

Multiple gold medals: Great Britain and Hungary (3); Uruguay and USSR (2).

MEN

Year	
1900	**Great Britain**, France, Belgium
1904	**Canada**, USA I, USA II
1906	**Denmark**, Smyrna (Int'l entry), Greece
1908	**Great Britain**, Denmark, Netherlands
1912	**Great Britain**, Denmark, Netherlands
1920	**Belgium**, Spain, Netherlands
1924	**Uruguay**, Switzerland, Sweden
1928	**Uruguay**, Argentina, Italy
1936	**Italy**, Austria, Norway
1948	**Sweden**, Yugoslavia, Denmark
1952	**Hungary**, Yugoslavia, Sweden
1956	**Soviet Union**, Yugoslavia, Bulgaria
1960	**Yugoslavia**, Denmark, Hungary
1964	**Hungary**, Czechoslovakia, Germany
1968	**Hungary**, Bulgaria, Japan
1972	**Poland**, Hungary, East Germany & Soviet Union
1976	**East Germany**, Poland, Soviet Union
1980	**Czechoslovakia**, East Germany, Soviet Union
1984	**France**, Brazil, Yugoslavia
1988	**Soviet Union**, Brazil, West Germany
1992	**Spain**, Poland, Ghana
1996	**Nigeria**, Argentina, Brazil

WOMEN

1996 **United States**, China, Norway

SWIMMING

World and Olympic records below that appear to be broken or equalled by winning times in subsequent years, but are not so indicated, were all broken in preliminary heats leading up to the finals. Some events were not held at every Olympics.

MEN

At least 4 gold medals (including relays): Mark Spitz (9); Matt Biondi (8); Charles Daniels, Tom Jager, Don Schollander, and Johnny Weissmuller (5); Tamás Darnyi, Roland Matthes, John Naber, Murray Rose, Vladimir Salnikov and Henry Taylor (4).

50-meter Freestyle

Year		Time	
1904	Zoltán Halmay, HUN (50 yds)	28.0	
1906-84	Not held		
1988	Matt Biondi, USA	22.14	**WR**
1992	Aleksandr Popov, UT	21.91	**OR**
1996	Aleksandr Popov, RUS	22.13	

100-meter Freestyle

Year		Time	
1896	Alfréd Hajós, HUN	1:22.2	**OR**
1904	Zoltán Halmay, HUN (100 yds)	1:02.8	
1906	Charles Daniels, USA	1:13.4	
1908	Charles Daniels, USA	1:05.6	**WR**
1912	Duke Kahanamoku, USA	1:03.4	
1920	Duke Kahanamoku, USA	1:00.4	**WR**
1924	Johnny Weissmuller, USA	59.0	**OR**
1928	Johnny Weissmuller, USA	58.6	**OR**
1932	Yasuji Miyazaki, JPN	58.2	
1936	Ferenc Csik, HUN	57.6	
1948	Wally Ris, USA	57.3	**OR**
1952	Clarke Scholes, USA	57.4	
1956	Jon Henricks, AUS	55.4	**OR**
1960	John Devitt, AUS	55.2	**OR**
1964	Don Schollander, USA	53.4	**OR**
1968	Michael Wenden, AUS	52.2	**WR**
1972	Mark Spitz, USA	51.22	**WR**
1976	Jim Montgomery, USA	49.99	**WR**
1980	Jorg Woithe, E. Ger	50.40	
1984	Rowdy Gaines, USA	49.80	**OR**
1988	Matt Biondi, USA	48.63	**OR**
1992	Aleksandr Popov, UT	49.02	
1996	Aleksandr Popov, RUS	48.74	

200-meter Freestyle

Year		Time	
1900	Frederick Lane, AUS (220 yds)	2:25.2	**OR**
1904	Charles Daniels, USA (220 yds)	2:44.2	
1968	Michael Wenden, AUS	1:55.2	**OR**
1972	Mark Spitz, USA	1:52.78	**WR**
1976	Bruce Furniss, USA	1:50.29	**WR**
1980	Sergei Kopliakov, USSR	1:49.81	**OR**
1984	Michael Gross, W. Ger	1:47.44	**WR**
1988	Duncan Armstrong, AUS	1:47.25	**WR**
1992	Yevgeny Sadovyi, UT	1:46.70	**OR**
1996	Danyon Loader, NZL	1:47.63	

400-meter Freestyle

Year		Time	
1896	Paul Neumann, AUT (550m)	8:12.6	
1904	Charles Daniels, USA (440 yds)	6:16.2	
1906	Otto Scheff, AUT	6:23.8	
1908	Henry Taylor, GBR	5:36.8	
1912	George Hodgson, CAN	5:24.4	
1920	Norman Ross, USA	5:26.8	
1924	Johnny Weissmuller, USA	5:04.2	OR
1928	Alberto Zorilla, ARG	5:01.6	OR
1932	Buster Crabbe, USA	4:48.4	OR
1936	Jack Medica, USA	4:44.5	OR
1948	Bill Smith, USA	4:41.0	OR
1952	Jean Boiteux, FRA	4:30.7	OR
1956	Murray Rose, AUS	4:27.3	OR
1960	Murray Rose, AUS	4:18.3	OR
1964	Don Schollander, USA	4:12.2	WR
1968	Mike Burton, USA	4:09.0	OR
1972	Bradford Cooper, AUS*	4:00.27	OR
1976	Brian Goodell, USA	3:51.93	WR
1980	Vladimir Salnikov, USSR	3:51.31	OR
1984	George DiCarlo, USA	3:51.23	OR
1988	Uwe Dassler, E. Ger	3:46.95	WR
1992	Yevgeny Sadovyi, UT	3:45.00	WR
1996	Danyon Loader, NZE	3:47.97	

*Australian Cooper finished second to Rick DeMont of the U.S., who was disqualified when he flunked the post-race drug test (his asthma medication was on the IOC's banned list).

1500-meter Freestyle

Year		Time	
1896	Alfréd Hajós, HUN (1200m)	18:22.2	OR
1900	John Arthur Jarvis, GBR (1000m)	13:40.2	
1904	Emil Rausch, GER (1 mile)	27:18.2	
1906	Henry Taylor, GBR (1 mile)	28:28.0	
1908	Henry Taylor, GBR	22:48.4	WR
1912	George Hodgson, CAN	22:00.0	WR
1920	Norman Ross, USA	22:23.2	
1924	Andrew (Boy) Charlton, AUS	20:06.6	WR
1928	Arne Borge, SWE	19:51.8	OR
1932	Kusuo Kitamura, JPN	19:12.4	OR
1936	Noboru Terada, JPN	19:13.7	
1948	James McLane, USA	19:18.5	
1952	Ford Konno, USA	18:30.3	OR
1956	Murray Rose, AUS	17:58.9	
1960	Jon Konrads, AUS	17:19.6	OR
1964	Robert Windle, AUS	17:01.7	OR
1968	Mike Burton, USA	16:38.9	OR
1972	Mike Burton, USA	15:52.58	WR
1976	Brian Goodell, USA	15:02.40	WR
1980	Vladimir Salnikov, USSR	14:58.27	WR
1984	Mike O'Brien, USA	15:05.20	
1988	Vladimir Salnikov, USSR	15:00.40	
1992	Kieren Perkins, AUS	14:43.48	WR
1996	Kieren Perkins, AUS	14:56.40	

100-meter Backstroke

Year		Time	
1904	Walter Brack, GER (100 yds)	1:16.8	
1908	Arno Bieberstein, GER	1:24.6	WR
1912	Harry Hebner, USA	1:21.2	
1920	Warren Kealoha, USA	1:15.2	
1924	Warren Kealoha, USA	1:13.2	OR
1928	George Kojac, USA	1:08.2	WR
1932	Masaji Kiyokawa, JPN	1:08.6	
1936	Adolf Kiefer, USA	1:05.9	OR
1948	Allen Stack, USA	1:06.4	
1952	Yoshinobu Oyakawa, USA	1:05.4	OR
1956	David Theile, AUS	1:02.2	OR
1960	David Theile, AUS	1:01.9	OR
1968	Roland Matthes, E. Ger	58.7	OR
1972	Roland Matthes, E. Ger	56.58	OR
1976	John Naber, USA	55.49	WR
1980	Bengt Baron, SWE	56.33	
1984	Rick Carey, USA	55.79	
1988	Daichi Suzuki, JPN	55.05	
1992	Mark Tewksbury, CAN	53.98	OR
1996	Jeff Rouse, USA	54.10	

200-meter Backstroke

Year		Time	
1900	Ernst Hoppenberg, GER	2:47.0	
1964	Jed Graef, USA	2:10.3	WR
1968	Roland Matthes, E. Ger	2:09.6	OR
1972	Roland Matthes, E. Ger	2:02.82	=WR
1976	John Naber, USA	1:59.19	WR
1980	Sándor Wladár, HUN	2:01.93	
1984	Rick Carey, USA	2:00.23	
1988	Igor Poliansky, USSR	1:59.37	
1992	Martin Lopez-Zubero, SPA	1:58.47	OR
1996	Brad Bridgewater, USA	1:58.54	

100-meter Breaststroke

Year		Time	
1968	Don McKenzie, USA	1:07.7	OR
1972	Nobutaka Taguchi, JPN	1:04.94	WR
1976	John Hencken, USA	1:03.11	WR
1980	Duncan Goodhew, GBR	1:03.44	
1984	Steve Lundquist, USA	1:01.65	WR
1988	Adrian Moorhouse, GBR	1:02.04	
1992	Nelson Diebel, USA	1:01.50	OR
1996	Fred Deburghgrueve, BEL	1:00.60	

200-meter Breaststroke

Year		Time	
1908	Frederick Holman, GBR	3:09.2	WR
1912	Walter Bathe, GER	3:01.8	OR
1920	Hakan Malmroth, SWE	3:04.4	
1924	Robert Skelton, USA	2:56.6	
1928	Yoshiyuki Tsuruta, JPN	2:48.8	OR
1932	Yoshiyuki Tsuruta, JPN	2:45.4	
1936	Tetsuo Hamuro, JPN	2:41.5	OR
1948	Joseph Verdeur, USA	2:39.3	OR
1952	John Davies, AUS	2:34.4	OR
1956	Masaru Furukawa, JPN	2:34.7*	OR
1960	Bill Mulliken, USA	2:37.4	
1964	Ian O'Brien, AUS	2:27.8	WR
1968	Felipe Múñoz, MEX	2:28.7	
1972	John Hencken, USA	2:21.55	WR
1976	David Wilkie, GBR	2:15.11	WR
1980	Robertas Zhulpa, USSR	2:15.85	
1984	Victor Davis, CAN	2:13.34	WR
1988	József Szabó, HUN	2:13.52	
1992	Mike Barrowman, USA	2:10.16	WR
1996	Norbert Rozsa, HUN	2:12.57	

*In 1956, the butterfly stroke and breaststroke were separated into two different events.

Swimming (Cont.)

MEN

100-meter Butterfly

Year		Time	
1968	Doug Russell, USA	55.9	OR
1972	Mark Spitz, USA	54.27	WR
1976	Matt Vogel, USA	54.35	
1980	Pär Arvidsson, SWE	54.92	
1984	Michael Gross, W. Ger	53.08	WR
1988	Anthony Nesty, SUR	53.0	OR
1992	Pablo Morales, USA	53.32	
1996	Dennis Pankratov, RUS	52.27	

200-meter Butterfly

Year		Time	
1956	Bill Yorzyk, USA	2:19.3	OR
1960	Mike Troy, USA	2:12.8	WR
1964	Kevin Berry, AUS	2:06.6	WR
1968	Carl Robie, USA	2:08.7	
1972	Mark Spitz, USA	2:00.70	WR
1976	Mike Bruner, USA	1:59.23	WR
1980	Sergei Fesenko, USSR	1:59.76	
1984	Jon Sieben, AUS	1:57.04	WR
1988	Michael Gross, W. Ger	1:56.94	OR
1992	Melvin Stewart, USA	1:56.26	OR
1996	Dennis Pankratov, RUS	1:56.51	

200-meter Individual Medley

Year		Time	
1968	Charles Hickcox, USA	2:12.0	OR
1972	Gunnar Larsson, SWE	2:07.17	WR
1984	Alex Baumann, CAN	2:01.42	WR
1988	Tamás Darnyi, HUN	2:00.17	WR
1992	Tamás Darnyi, HUN	2:00.76	
1996	Attila Czene, HUN	1:59.91	

400-meter Individual Medley

Year		Time	
1964	Richard Roth, USA	4:45.4	WR
1968	Charles Hickcox, USA	4:48.4	
1972	Gunnar Larsson, SWE	4:31.98	OR
1976	Rod Strachan, USA	4:23.68	WR
1980	Aleksandr Sidorenko, USSR	4:22.89	OR
1984	Alex Baumann, CAN	4:17.41	WR
1988	Tamás Darnyi, HUN	4:14.75	WR
1992	Tamás Darnyi, HUN	4:14.23	OR
1996	Tom Dolan, USA	4:14.90	

4x100-meter Freestyle Relay

Year		Time	
1964	United States	3:32.2	WR
1968	United States	3:31.7	WR
1972	United States	3:26.42	WR
1976-80	Not held		
1984	United States	3:19.03	WR
1988	United States	3:16.53	WR
1992	United States	3:16.74	
1996	United States	3:15.41	

4x200-meter Freestyle Relay

Year		Time	
1906	Hungary (x250m)	16:52.4	
1908	Great Britain	10:55.6	WR
1912	Australia/New Zealand	10:11.6	WR
1920	United States	10:04.4	WR
1924	United States	9:53.4	WR
1928	United States	9:36.2	WR
1932	Japan	8:58.4	WR
1936	Japan	8:51.5	WR
1948	United States	8:46.0	WR
1952	United States	8:31.1	OR
1956	Australia	8:23.6	WR
1960	United States	8:10.2	WR
1964	United States	7:52.1	WR
1968	United States	7:52.33	
1972	United States	7:35.78	WR
1976	United States	7:23.22	WR
1980	Soviet Union	7:23.50	
1984	United States	7:15.69	WR
1988	United States	7:12.51	WR
1992	Unified Team	7:11.95	WR
1996	United States	7:14.84	

4x100-meter Medley Relay

Year		Time	
1960	United States	4:05.4	WR
1964	United States	3:58.4	WR
1968	United States	3:54.9	WR
1972	United States	3:48.16	WR
1976	United States	3:42.22	WR
1980	Australia	3:45.70	
1984	United States	3:39.30	WR
1988	United States	3:36.93	WR
1992	United States	3:36.93	=WR
1996	United States	3:34.84	

WOMEN

At least 4 gold medals (including relays): Kristin Otto (6); Krisztina Egerszegi and Jenny Thompson (5); Kornelia Ender, Janet Evans, Dawn Fraser and Amy Van Dyken (4).

50-meter Freestyle

Year		Time	
1988	Kristin Otto, E. Ger	25.49	OR
1992	Yang Wenyi, CHN	24.79	WR
1996	Amy Van Dyken, USA	24.87	

100-meter Freestyle

Year		Time		Year		Time	
1912	Fanny Durack, AUS	1:22.2		1964	Dawn Fraser, AUS	59.5	OR
1920	Ethelda Bleibtrey, USA	1:13.6	WR	1968	Jan Henne, USA	1:00.0	
1924	Ethel Lackie, USA	1:12.4		1972	Sandra Neilson, USA	58.59	OR
1928	Albina Osipowich, USA	1:11.0	OR	1976	Kornelia Ender, E. Ger	55.65	WR
1932	Helene Madison, USA	1:06.8	OR	1980	Barbara Krause, E. Ger	54.79	WR
1936	Rie Mastenbroek, NET	1:05.9	OR	1984	(TIE) Nancy Hogshead, USA	55.92	
1948	Greta Andersen, DEN	1:06.3			& Carrie Steinseifer, USA	55.92	
1952	Katalin Szöke, HUN	1:06.8		1988	Kristin Otto, E. Ger	54.93	
1956	Dawn Fraser, AUS	1:02.0	WR	1992	Zhuang Yong, CHN	54.65	OR
1960	Dawn Fraser, AUS	1:01.2	OR	1996	Le Jingyi, CHN	54.50	

200-meter Freestyle

Year		Time		Year		Time	
1968	Debbie Meyer, USA	2:10.5	OR	1984	Mary Wayte, USA	1:59.23	
1972	Shane Gould, AUS	2:03.56	WR	1988	Heike Friedrich, E. Ger	1:57.65	OR
1976	Kornelia Ender, E. Ger	1:59.26	WR	1992	Nicole Haislett, USA	1:57.90	
1980	Barbara Krause, E. Ger	1:58.33	OR	1996	Claudia Poll, COS	1:58.16	

400-meter Freestyle

Year		Time		Year		Time	
1920	Ethelda Bleibtrey, USA (300m)	4:34.0	WR	1964	Ginny Duenkel, USA	4:43.3	OR
1924	Martha Norelius, USA	6:02.2	OR	1968	Debbie Meyer, USA	4:31.8	OR
1928	Martha Norelius, USA	5:42.8	WR	1972	Shane Gould, AUS	4:19.44	WR
1932	Helene Madison, USA	5:28.5	WR	1976	Petra Thümer, E. Ger	4:09.89	WR
1936	Rie Mastenbroek, NET	5:26.4	OR	1980	Ines Diers, E. Ger	4:08.76	OR
1948	Ann Curtis, USA	5:17.8	OR	1984	Tiffany Cohen, USA	4:07.10	OR
1952	Valéria Gyenge, HUN	5:12.1	OR	1988	Janet Evans, USA	4:03.85	WR
1956	Lorraine Crapp, AUS	4:54.6	OR	1992	Dagmar Hase, GER	4:07.18	
1960	Chris von Saltza, USA	4:50.6	OR	1996	Michelle Smith, IRE	4:07.25	

800-meter Freestyle

Year		Time		Year		Time	
1968	Debbie Meyer, USA	9:24.0	OR	1984	Tiffany Cohen, USA	8:24.95	OR
1972	Keena Rothhammer, USA	8:53.68	WR	1988	Janet Evans, USA	8:20.20	OR
1976	Petra Thümer, E. Ger	8:37.14	WR	1992	Janet Evans, USA	8:25.52	
1980	Michelle Ford, AUS	8:28.90	OR	1996	Brooke Bennett, USA	8:27.89	

100-meter Backstroke

Year		Time		Year		Time	
1924	Sybil Bauer, USA	1:23.2	OR	1968	Kaye Hall, USA	1:06.2	WR
1928	Maria Braun, NET	1:22.0		1972	Melissa Belote, USA	1:05.78	OR
1932	Eleanor Holm, USA	1:19.4		1976	Ulrike Richter, E. Ger	1:01.83	OR
1936	Dina Senff, NET	1:18.9		1980	Rica Reinisch, E. Ger	1:00.86	WR
1948	Karen-Margrete Harup, DEN	1:14.4	OR	1984	Theresa Andrews, USA	1:02.55	
1952	Joan Harrison, SAF	1:14.3		1988	Kristin Otto, E. Ger	1:00.89	
1956	Judy Grinham, GBR	1:12.9	OR	1992	Krisztina Egerszegi, HUN	1:00.68	OR
1960	Lynn Burke, USA	1:09.3	OR	1996	Beth Botsford, USA	1:01.19	
1964	Cathy Ferguson, USA	1:07.7	WR				

200-meter Backstroke

Year		Time		Year		Time	
1968	Pokey Watson, USA	2:24.8	OR	1984	Jolanda de Rover, NET	2:12.38	
1972	Melissa Belote, USA	2:19.19	WR	1988	Krisztina Egerszegi, HUN	2:09.29	OR
1976	Ulrike Richter, E. Ger	2:13.43	OR	1992	Krisztina Egerszegi, HUN	2:07.06	OR
1980	Rica Reinisch, E. Ger	2:11.77	WR	1996	Kristina Egerszegi, HUN	2:07.83	

100-meter Breaststroke

Year		Time		Year		Time	
1968	Djurdjica Bjedov, YUG	1:15.8	OR	1984	Petra van Staveren, NET	1:09.88	OR
1972	Cathy Carr, USA	1:13.58	WR	1988	Tania Dangalakova, BUL	1:07.95	OR
1976	Hannelore Anke, E. Ger	1:11.16		1992	Yelena Rudkovskaya, UT	1:08.00	
1980	Ute Geweniger, E. Ger	1:10.22		1996	Penny Heyns, S. Afr	1:07.73	

200-meter Breaststroke

Year		Time		Year		Time	
1924	Lucy Morton, GBR	3:33.2	OR	1968	Sharon Wichman, USA	2:44.4	OR
1928	Hilde Schrader, GER	3:12.6		1972	Beverley Whitfield, AUS	2:41.71	OR
1932	Clare Dennis, AUS	3:06.3	OR	1976	Marina Koshevaya, USSR	2:33.35	WR
1936	Hideko Maehata, JPN	3:03.6		1980	Lina Kaciusyte, USSR	2:29.54	OR
1948	Petronella van Vliet, NET	2:57.2		1984	Anne Ottenbrite, CAN	2:30.38	
1952	Éva Székely, HUN	2:51.7	OR	1988	Silke Hörner, E. Ger	2:26.71	WR
1956	Ursula Happe, GER	2:53.1	OR	1992	Kyoko Iwasaki, JPN	2:26.65	OR
1960	Anita Lonsbrough, GBR	2:49.5	WR	1996	Penny Heyns, S. Afr.	2:25.41	
1964	Galina Prozumenshikova, USSR	2:46.4	OR				

Swimming (Cont.)

WOMEN

100-meter Butterfly

Year		Time		Year		Time	
1956	Shelly Mann, USA	1:11.0	OR	1980	Caren Metschuck, E. Ger	1:00.42	
1960	Carolyn Schuler, USA	1:09.5	OR	1984	Mary T. Meagher, USA	59.26	
1964	Sharon Stouder, USA	1:04.7	WR	1988	Kristin Otto, E. Ger	59.00	OR
1968	Lynn McClements, AUS	1:05.5		1992	Qian Hong, CHN	58.62	OR
1972	Mayumi Aoki, JPN	1:03.34	WR	1996	Amy Van Dyken, USA	59.13	
1976	Kornelia Ender, E. Ger	1:00.13	=WR				

200-meter Butterfly

Year		Time		Year		Time	
1968	Ada Kok, NET	2:24.7	OR	1984	Mary T. Meagher, USA	2:06.90	OR
1972	Karen Moe, USA	2:15.57	WR	1988	Kathleen Nord, E. Ger	2:09.51	
1976	Andrea Pollack, E. Ger	2:11.41	OR	1992	Summer Sanders, USA	2:08.67	
1980	Ines Geissler, E. Ger	2:10.44	OR	1996	Susan O'Neill, AUS	2:07.76	

200-meter Individual Medley

Year		Time		Year		Time	
1968	Claudia Kolb, USA	2:24.7	OR	1988	Daniela Hunger, E. Ger	2:12.59	OR
1972	Shane Gould, AUS	2:23.07	WR	1992	Lin Li, CHN	2:11.65	WR
1984	Tracy Caulkins, USA	2:12.64	OR	1996	Michelle Smith, IRE	2:13.93	

400-meter Individual Medley

Year		Time		Year		Time
1964	Donna de Varona, USA	5:18.7	OR	1984	Tracy Caulkins, USA	4:39.24
1968	Claudia Kolb, USA	5:08.5	OR	1988	Janet Evans, USA	4:37.76
1972	Gail Neall, AUS	5:02.97	WR	1992	Krisztina Egerszegi, HUN	4:36.54
1976	Ulrike Tauber, E. Ger	4:42.77	WR	1996	Michelle Smith, IRE	4:39.18
1980	Petra Schneider, E. Ger	4:36.29	WR			

4x100-meter Freestyle Relay

Year		Time		Year		Time	
1912	Great Britain	5:52.8	WR	1964	United States	4:03.8	WR
1920	United States	5:11.6	WR	1968	United States	4:02.5	OR
1924	United States	4:58.8	WR	1972	United States	3:55.19	WR
1928	United States	4:47.6	WR	1976	United States	3:44.82	WR
1932	United States	4:38.0	WR	1980	East Germany	3:42.71	WR
1936	Netherlands	4:36.0	OR	1984	United States	3:43.43	
1948	United States	4:29.2	OR	1988	East Germany	3:40.63	OR
1952	Hungary	4:24.4	WR	1992	United States	3:39.46	WR
1956	Australia	4:17.1	WR	1996	United States	3:39.29	
1960	United States	4:08.9	WR				

4x200-meter Freestyle Relay

1996 United States 7:59.87

4x100-meter Medley Relay

Year		Time		Year		Time	
1960	United States	4:41.1	WR	1980	East Germany	4:06.67	WR
1964	United States	4:33.9	WR	1984	United States	4:08.34	
1968	United States	4:28.3	OR	1988	East Germany	4:03.74	OR
1972	United States	4:20.75	WR	1992	United States	4:02.54	WR
1976	East Germany	4:07.95	WR	1996	United States	4:02.88	

TENNIS

MEN

Multiple gold medals (including doubles): John Boland, Max Decugis, Laurie Doherty, Reggie Doherty, Arthur Gore, André Grobert, Vincent Richards, Charles Winslow and Beals Wright (2).

Singles

Year			Year		
1896	John Boland	Great Britain/Ireland	1920	Louis Raymond	South Africa
1900	Laurie Doherty,	Great Britain	1924	Vincent Richards	United States
1904	Beals Wright	United States	1928-84	Not held	
1906	Max Decugis	France	1988	Miloslav Mecir	Czechoslovakia
1908	Josiah Ritchie	Great Britain	1992	Marc Rosset	Switzerland
	(Indoor) Arthur Gore	Great Britain	1996	Andre Agassi	United States
1912	Charles Winslow	South Africa			
	(Indoor) André Gobert	France			

Doubles

Year	
1896	John Boland, IRE & Fritz Traun, GER
1900	Laurie and Reggie Doherty, GBR
1904	Edgar Leonard & Beals Wright, USA
1906	Max Decugis & Maurice Germot, FRA
1908	George Hillyard & Reggie Doherty, GBR
	(Indoor) Arthur Gore & Herbert Barrett, GBR
1912	Charles Winslow & Harold Kitson, S. Afr.
	(Indoor) André Gobert & Maurice Germot, FRA
1920	Noel Turnbull & Max Woosnam, GBR
1924	Vincent Richards & Frank Hunter, USA
1928-84	Not held
1988	Ken Flach & Robert Seguso, USA
1992	Boris Becker & Michael Stich, GER
1996	Todd Woodbridge & Mark Woodforde, AUS

WOMEN

Multiple gold medals (including doubles): Helen Wills (2).

Singles

Year		
1900	Charlotte Cooper	Great Britain
1906	Esmee Simiriotou	Greece
1908	Dorothea Chambers	Great Britain
	(Indoor) Gwen Eastlake-Smith	Great Britain
1912	Marguerite Broquedis	France
	(Indoor) Edith Hannam	Great Britain
1920	Suzanne Lenglen	France
1924	Helen Wills	United States
1928-84	Not held	
1988	Steffi Graf	West Germany
1992	Jennifer Capriati	United States
1996	Lindsay Davenport	United States

Doubles

Year	
1920	Winifred McNair & Kitty McKane, GBR
1924	Hazel Wightman & Helen Wills, USA
1928-84	Not held
1988	Pam Shriver & Zina Garrison, USA
1992	Gigi Fernandez & Mary Joe Fernandez, USA
1996	Gigi Fernandez & Mary Joe Fernandez, USA

TRACK & FIELD

World and Olympic records below that appear to be broken or equalled by winning times, heights and distances in subsequent years, but are not so indicated, were all broken in preliminary races and field events leading up to the finals. ^{W} indicates wind-aided.

MEN

At least 4 gold medals (including relays and discontinued events): Ray Ewry (10); Paavo Nurmi and Carl Lewis (9); Ville Ritola and Martin Sheridan (5); Harrison Dillard, Archie Hahn, Hannes Kolehmainen, Alvin Kraenzlein, Eric Lemming, Jim Lightbody, Al Oerter, Jesse Owens, Meyer Prinstein, Mel Sheppard, Lasse Viren and Emil Zátopek (4). Note that all of Ewry's gold medals came before 1912, in the Standing High Jump, Standing Long Jump and Standing Triple Jump.

100 meters

Year		Time	
1896	Tom Burke, USA	12.0	
1900	Frank Jarvis, USA	11.0	
1904	Archie Hahn, USA	11.0	
1906	Archie Hahn, USA	11.2	
1908	Reggie Walker, S. Afr.	10.8	**=OR**
1912	Ralph Craig, USA	10.8	
1920	Charley Paddock, USA	10.8	
1924	Harold Abrahams, GBR	10.6	**=OR**
1928	Percy Williams, CAN	10.8	
1932	Eddie Tolan, USA	10.3	**OR**
1936	Jesse Owens, USA	10.3^{W}	
1948	Harrison Dillard, USA	10.3	**=OR**
1952	Lindy Remigino, USA	10.4	
1956	Bobby Morrow, USA	10.5	
1960	Armin Hary, GER	10.2	**OR**
1964	Bob Hayes, USA	10.0	**=WR**
1968	Jim Hines, USA	9.95	**WR**
1972	Valery Borzov, USSR	10.14	
1976	Hasely Crawford, TRI	10.06	
1980	Allan Wells, GBR	10.25	
1984	Carl Lewis, USA	9.99	
1988	Carl Lewis, USA*	9.92	**WR**
1992	Linford Christie, GBR	9.96	
1996	Donovan Bailey, CAN	9.84	**WR**

*Lewis finished second to Ben Johnson of Canada, who set a world record of 9.79 seconds. A day later, Johnson was stripped of his gold medal and his record when he tested positive for steroid use in a post-race drug test.

200 meters

Year		Time	
1900	John Walter Tewksbury, USA	22.2	
1904	Archie Hahn, USA	21.6	**OR**
1908	Bobby Kerr, CAN	22.6	
1912	Ralph Craig, USA	21.7	
1920	Allen Woodring, USA	22.0	
1924	Jackson Scholz, USA	21.6	
1928	Percy Williams, CAN	21.8	
1932	Eddie Tolan, USA	21.2	**OR**
1936	Jesse Owens, USA	20.7	**OR**
1948	Mel Patton, USA	21.1	
1952	Andy Stanfield, USA	20.7	
1956	Bobby Morrow, USA	20.6	**OR**
1960	Livio Berruti, ITA	20.5	**=WR**
1964	Henry Carr, USA	20.3	**OR**
1968	Tommie Smith, USA	19.83	**WR**
1972	Valery Borzov, USSR	20.00	
1976	Donald Quarrie, JAM	20.23	
1980	Pietro Mennea, ITA	20.19	
1984	Carl Lewis, USA	19.80	**OR**
1988	Joe DeLoach, USA	19.75	**OR**
1992	Mike Marsh, USA	20.01	
1996	Michael Johnson, USA	19.32	**WR**

Track & Field (Cont.)

MEN

400 meters

Year		Time	
1896	Tom Burke, USA	54.2	
1900	Maxey Long, USA	49.4	OR
1904	Harry Hillman, USA	49.2	OR
1906	Paul Pilgrim, USA	53.2	
1908	Wyndham Halswelle, GBR	50.0	
1912	Charlie Reidpath, USA	48.2	OR
1920	Bevil Rudd, S. Afr.	49.6	
1924	Eric Liddell, GBR	47.6	OR
1928	Ray Barbuti, USA	47.8	
1932	Bill Carr, USA	46.2	WR
1936	Archie Williams, USA	46.5	
1948	Arthur Wint, JAM	46.2	
1952	George Rhoden, JAM	45.9	OR
1956	Charley Jenkins, USA	46.7	
1960	Otis Davis, USA	44.9	WR
1964	Mike Larrabee, USA	45.1	
1968	Lee Evans, USA	43.86	WR
1972	Vince Matthews, USA	44.66	
1976	Alberto Juantorena, CUB	44.26	
1980	Viktor Markin, USSR	44.60	
1984	Alonzo Babers, USA	44.27	
1988	Steve Lewis, USA	43.87	
1992	Quincy Watts, USA	43.50	OR
1996	Michael Johnson, USA	43.49	OR

800 meters

Year		Time	
1896	Teddy Flack, AUS	2:11.0	
1900	Alfred Tysoe, GBR	2:01.2	
1904	Jim Lightbody, USA	1:56.0	OR
1906	Paul Pilgrim, USA	2:01.5	
1908	Mel Sheppard, USA	1:52.8	WR
1912	Ted Meredith, USA	1:51.9	WR
1920	Albert Hill, GBR	1:53.4	
1924	Douglas Lowe, GBR	1:52.4	
1928	Douglas Lowe, GBR	1:51.8	OR
1932	Tommy Hampson, GBR	1:49.7	WR
1936	John Woodruff, USA	1:52.9	
1948	Mal Whitfield, USA	1:49.2	OR
1952	Mal Whitfield, USA	1:49.2	=OR
1956	Tom Courtney, USA	1:47.7	OR
1960	Peter Snell, NZE	1:46.3	OR
1964	Peter Snell, NZE	1:45.1	OR
1968	Ralph Doubell, AUS	1:44.3	=WR
1972	Dave Wottle, USA	1:45.9	
1976	Alberto Juantorena, CUB	1:43.50	WR
1980	Steve Ovett, GBR	1:45.4	
1984	Joaquim Cruz, BRA	1:43.00	OR
1988	Paul Ereng, KEN	1:43.45	
1992	William Tanui, KEN	1:43.66	
1996	Vebjoern Rodal, NOR	1:42.58	OR

1500 meters

Year		Time	
1896	Teddy Flack, AUS	4:33.2	
1900	Charles Bennett, GBR	4:06.2	WR
1904	Jim Lightbody, USA	4:05.4	WR
1906	Jim Lightbody, USA	4:12.0	
1908	Mel Sheppard, USA	4:03.4	OR
1912	Arnold Jackson, GBR	3:56.8	OR
1920	Albert Hill, GBR	4:01.8	
1924	Paavo Nurmi, FIN	3:53.6	OR
1928	Harry Larva, FIN	3:53.2	OR
1932	Luigi Beccali, ITA	3:51.2	OR
1936	John Lovelock, NZE	3:47.8	WR
1948	Henry Eriksson, SWE	3:49.8	
1952	Josy Barthel, LUX	3:45.1	OR
1956	Ron Delany, IRL	3:41.2	OR
1960	Herb Elliott, AUS	3:35.6	WR
1964	Peter Snell, NZE	3:38.1	
1968	Kip Keino, KEN	3:34.9	OR
1972	Pekka Vasala, FIN	3:36.3	
1976	John Walker, NZE	3:39.17	
1980	Sebastian Coe, GBR	3:38.4	
1984	Sebastian Coe, GBR	3:32.53	OR
1988	Peter Rono, KEN	3:35.96	
1992	Fermin Cacho, SPA	3:40.12	
1996	Noureddine Morceli, ALG	3:35.78	

5000 meters

Year		Time	
1912	Hannes Kolehmainen, FIN	14:36.6	WR
1920	Joseph Guillemot, FRA	14:55.6	
1924	Paavo Nurmi, FIN	14:31.2	OR
1928	Ville Ritola, FIN	14:38.0	
1932	Lauri Lehtinen, FIN	14:30.0	OR
1936	Gunnar Höckert, FIN	14:22.2	OR
1948	Gaston Reiff, BEL	14:17.6	OR
1952	Emil Zátopek, CZE	14:06.6	OR
1956	Vladimir Kuts, USSR	13:39.6	OR
1960	Murray Halberg, NZE	13:43.4	
1964	Bob Schul, USA	13:48.8	
1968	Mohamed Gammoudi, TUN	14:05.0	
1972	Lasse Viren, FIN	13:26.4	OR
1976	Lasse Viren, FIN	13:24.76	
1980	Miruts Yifter, ETH	13:21.0	
1984	Said Aouita, MOR	13:05.59	OR
1988	John Ngugi, KEN	13:11.70	
1992	Dieter Baumann, GER	13:12.52	
1996	Venuste Niyongabo, BUR	13:07.96	

10,000 meters

Year		Time	
1912	Hannes Kolehmainen, FIN	31:20.8	
1920	Paavo Nurmi, FIN	31:45.8	
1924	Ville Ritola, FIN	30:23.2	WR
1928	Paavo Nurmi, FIN	30:18.8	OR
1932	Janusz Kusocinski, POL	30:11.4	OR
1936	Ilmari Salminen, FIN	30:15.4	
1948	Emil Zátopek, CZE	29:59.6	OR
1952	Emil Zátopek, CZE	29:17.0	OR
1956	Vladimir Kuts, USSR	28:45.6	OR
1960	Pyotr Bolotnikov, USSR	28:32.2	OR
1964	Billy Mills, USA	28:24.4	OR
1968	Naftali Temu, KEN	29:27.4	
1972	Lasse Viren, FIN	27:38.4	WR
1976	Lasse Viren, FIN	27:40.38	
1980	Miruts Yifter, ETH	27:42.7	
1984	Alberto Cova, ITA	27:47.54	
1988	Brahim Boutaib, MOR	27:21.46	OR
1992	Khalid Skah, MOR	27:46.70	
1996	Haile Gebrselassie, ETH	27:07.34	OR

Marathon

Year		Time		Year		Time	
1896	Spiridon Louis, GRE	2:58:50		1952	Emil Zátopek, CZE	2:23:03.2	OR
1900	Michel Théato, FRA	2:59:45		1956	Alain Mimoun, FRA	2:25:00.0	
1904	Thomas Hicks, USA	3:28:53		1960	Abebe Bikila, ETH	2:15:16.2	WB
1906	Billy Sherring, CAN	2:51:23.6		1964	Abebe Bikila, ETH	2:12:11.2	WB
1908	Johnny Hayes, USA*	2:55:18.4	OR	1968	Mamo Wolde, ETH	2:20:26.4	
1912	Kenneth McArthur, S. Afr.	2:36:54.8		1972	Frank Shorter, USA	2:12:19.8	
1920	Hannes Kolehmainen, FIN	2:32:35.8	WB	1976	Waldemar Cierpinski, E. Ger	2:09:55.0	OR
1924	Albin Stenroos, FIN	2:41:22.6		1980	Waldemar Cierpinski, E. Ger	2:11:03.0	
1928	Boughèra El Ouafi, FRA	2:32:57.0		1984	Carlos Lopes, POR	2:09:21.0	OR
1932	Juan Carlos Zabala, ARG	2:31:36.0	OR	1988	Gelindo Bordin, ITA	2:10:32	
1936	Sohn Kee-Chung, JPN†	2:29:19.2	OR	1992	Hwang Young-Cho, S. Kor	2:13:23	
1948	Delfo Cabrera, ARG	2:34:51.6		1996	Josia Thugwane, S. Afr.	2:12:36	

*Dorando Pietri of Italy placed first, but was disqualified for being helped across the finish line.
†Sohn was a Korean, but he was forced to compete under the name Kitei Son by Japan, which occupied Korea at the time.
Note: Marathon distances—40,000 meters (1896,1904); 40,260 meters (1900); 41,860 meters (1906); 42,195 meters (1908 and since 1924); 40,200 meters (1912); 42,750 meters (1920). Current distance of 42,195 meters measures 26 miles, 385 yards.

110-meter Hurdles

Year		Time		Year		Time	
1896	Tom Curtis, USA	17.6		1952	Harrison Dillard, USA	13.7	OR
1900	Alvin Kraenzlein, USA	15.4	OR	1956	Lee Calhoun, USA	13.5	OR
1904	Frederick Schule, USA	16.0		1960	Lee Calhoun, USA	13.8	
1906	Robert Leavitt, USA	16.2		1964	Hayes Jones, USA	13.6	
1908	Forrest Smithson, USA	15.0	WR	1968	Willie Davenport, USA	13.3	OR
1912	Frederick Kelly, USA	15.1		1972	Rod Milburn, USA	13.24	=WR
1920	Earl Thomson, CAN	14.8	WR	1976	Guy Drut, FRA	13.30	
1924	Daniel Kinsey, USA	15.0		1980	Thomas Munkelt, E. Ger	13.39	
1928	Syd Atkinson, S. Afr.	14.8		1984	Roger Kingdom, USA	13.20	OR
1932	George Saling, USA	14.6		1988	Roger Kingdom, USA	12.98	OR
1936	Forrest (Spec) Towns, USA	14.2		1992	Mark McKoy, CAN	13.12	
1948	William Porter, USA	13.9	OR	1996	Allen Johnson, USA	12.95	OR

400-meter Hurdles

Year		Time		Year		Time	
1900	John Walter Tewksbury, USA	57.6		1960	Glenn Davis, USA	49.3	OR
1904	Harry Hillman, USA	53.0		1964	Rex Cawley, USA	49.6	
1908	Charley Bacon, USA	55.0	WR	1968	David Hemery, GBR	48.12	WR
1920	Frank Loomis, USA	54.0	WR	1972	John Akii-Bua, UGA	47.82	WR
1924	Morgan Taylor, USA	52.6		1976	Edwin Moses, USA	47.64	WR
1928	David Burghley, GBR	53.4	OR	1980	Volker Beck, E. Ger	48.70	
1932	Bob Tisdall, IRE	51.7		1984	Edwin Moses, USA	47.75	
1936	Glenn Hardin, USA	52.4		1988	Andre Phillips, USA	47.19	OR
1948	Roy Cochran, USA	51.1	OR	1992	Kevin Young, USA	46.78	WR
1952	Charley Moore, USA	50.8	OR	1996	Derrick Adkins, USA	47.54	
1956	Glenn Davis, USA	50.1	=OR				

3000-meter Steeplechase

Year		Time		Year		Time	
1900	George Orton, CAN	7:34.4		1960	Zdzislaw Krzyszkowiak, POL	8:34.2	OR
1904	Jim Lightbody, USA	7:39.6		1964	Gaston Roelants, BEL	8:30.8	OR
1908	Arthur Russell, GBR	10:47.8		1968	Amos Biwott, KEN	8:51.0	
1920	Percy Hodge, GBR	10:00.4	OR	1972	Kip Keino, KEN	8:23.6	OR
1924	Ville Ritola, FIN	9:33.6	OR	1976	Anders Gärderud, SWE	8:08.2	WR
1928	Toivo Loukola, FIN	9:21.8	WR	1980	Bronislaw Malinowski, POL	8:09.7	
1932	Volmari Iso-Hollo, FIN	10:33.4*		1984	Julius Korir, KEN	8:11.80	
1936	Volmari Iso-Hollo, FIN	9:03.8	WR	1988	Julius Kariuki, KEN	8:05.51	OR
1948	Thore Sjöstrand, SWE	9:04.6		1992	Matthew Birir, KEN	8:08.84	
1952	Horace Ashenfelter, USA	8:45.4	WR	1996	Joseph Keter, KEN	8:07.12	
1956	Chris Brasher, GBR	8:41.2	OR				

*Iso-Hollo ran one extra lap due to lap counter's mistake.
Note: Other steeplechase distances—2500 meters (1900); 2590 meters (1904); 3200 meters (1908) and 3460 meters (1932).

4x100-meter Relay

Year		Time		Year		Time	
1912	Great Britain	42.4		1964	United States	39.0	WR
1920	United States	42.2	WR	1968	United States	38.23	WR
1924	United States	41.0	=WR	1972	United States	38.19	WR
1928	United States	41.0	=WR	1976	United States	38.33	
1932	United States	40.0	WR	1980	Soviet Union	38.26	
1936	United States	39.8	WR	1984	United States	37.83	WR
1948	United States	40.6		1988	Soviet Union	38.19	
1952	United States	40.1		1992	United States	37.40	WR
1956	United States	39.5	WR	1996	Canada	37.69	
1960	Germany	39.5	=WR				

Track & Field (Cont.)

MEN

4x400-meter Relay

Year		Time	
1908	United States	3:29.4	
1912	United States	3:16.6	WR
1920	Great Britain	3:22.2	
1924	United States	3:16.0	WR
1928	United States	3:14.2	WR
1932	United States	3:08.2	WR
1936	Great Britain	3:09.0	
1948	United States	3:10.4	
1952	Jamaica	3:03.9	WR
1956	United States	3:04.8	
1960	United States	3:02.2	WR
1964	United States	3:00.7	WR
1968	United States	2:56.16	WR
1972	Kenya	2:59.8	
1976	United States	2:58.65	
1980	Soviet Union	3:01.1	
1984	United States	2:57.91	
1988	United States	2:56.16	=WR
1992	United States	2:55.74	WR
1996	United States	2:55.99	

20-kilometer Walk

Year		Time	
1956	Leonid Spirin, USSR	1:31:27.4	
1960	Vladimir Golubnichiy, USSR	1:34:07.2	
1964	Ken Matthews, GBR	1:29:34.0	OR
1968	Vladimir Golubnichiy, USSR	1:33:58.4	
1972	Peter Frenkel, E. Ger	1:26:42.4	OR
1976	Daniel Bautista, MEX	1:24:40.6	OR
1980	Maurizio Damilano, ITA	1:23:35.5	OR
1984	Ernesto Canto, MEX	1:23:13	OR
1988	Jozef Pribilinec, CZE	1:19:57	OR
1992	Daniel Plaza Montero, SPA	1:21:45	
1996	Jefferson Perez, ECU	1:20:07	

50-kilometer Walk

Year		Time	
1932	Thomas Green, GBR	4:50:10	
1936	Harold Whitlock, GBR	4:30:41.4	OR
1948	John Ljunggren, SWE	4:41:52	
1952	Giuseppe Dordoni, ITA	4:28:07.8	OR
1956	Norman Read, NZE	4:30:42.8	
1960	Don Thompson, GBR	4:25:30.0	OR
1964	Abdon Pamich, ITA	4:11:12.4	OR
1968	Christoph Höhne, E. Ger	4:20:13.6	
1972	Bernd Kannenberg, W. Ger	3:56:11.6	OR
1976	Not held		
1980	Hartwig Gauder, E. Ger	3:49:24.0	OR
1984	Raúl González, MEX	3:47:26	OR
1988	Vyacheslav Ivanenko, USSR	3:38:29	OR
1992	Andrei Perlov, UT	3:50:13	
1996	Robert Korzeniowski, POL	3:43:30	

High Jump

Year		Height	
1896	Ellery Clark, USA	5-11¼	
1900	Irving Baxter, USA	6- 2¾	OR
1904	Sam Jones, USA	5-11	
1906	Cornelius Leahy, GBR/IRE	5-10	
1908	Harry Porter, USA	6- 3	OR
1912	Alma Richards, USA	6- 4	OR
1920	Richmond Landon, USA	6- 4	=OR
1924	Harold Osborn, USA	6- 6	OR
1928	Bob King, USA	6- 4½	
1932	Duncan McNaughton, CAN	6- 5½	
1936	Cornelius Johnson, USA	6- 8	OR
1948	John Winter, AUS	6- 6	
1952	Walt Davis, USA	6- 8½	OR
1956	Charley Dumas, USA	6-11½	OR
1960	Robert Shavlakadze, USSR	7- 1	OR
1964	Valery Brumel, USSR	7- 1¾	OR
1968	Dick Fosbury, USA	7- 4¼	OR
1972	Yuri Tarmak, USSR	7- 3¾	
1976	Jacek Wszola, POL	7- 4½	OR
1980	Gerd Wessig, E. Ger	7- 8¾	WR
1984	Dietmar Mögenburg, W. Ger	7- 8½	
1988	Gennady Avdeyenko, USSR	7- 9¾	OR
1992	Javier Sotomayor, CUB	7- 8	
1996	Charles Austin, USA	7-10	OR

Pole Vault

Year		Height	
1896	William Hoyt, USA	10-10	
1900	Irving Baxter, USA	10-10	
1904	Charles Dvorak, USA	11- 5¾	
1906	Fernand Gonder, FRA	11- 5¾	
1908	(TIE) Edward Cooke, USA	12- 2	
	& Alfred Gilbert, USA	12- 2	OR
1912	Harry Babcock, USA	12-11½	OR
1920	Frank Foss, USA	13- 5	WR
1924	Lee Barnes, USA	12-11½	
1928	Sabin Carr, USA	13- 9¼	OR
1932	Bill Miller, USA	14- 1¾	OR
1936	Earle Meadows, USA	14- 3¼	OR
1948	Guinn Smith, USA	14- 1¼	
1952	Bob Richards, USA	14-11	OR
1956	Bob Richards, USA	14-11½	OR
1960	Don Bragg, USA	15- 5	OR
1964	Fred Hansen, USA	16- 8¾	OR
1968	Bob Seagren, USA	17- 8½	OR
1972	Wolfgang Nordwig, E. Ger	18- 0½	OR
1976	Tadeusz Slusarski, POL	18- 0½	=OR
1980	Wladyslaw Kozakiewicz, POL	18-11½	WR
1984	Pierre Quinon, FRA	18-10¼	
1988	Sergey Bubka, USSR	19- 4¼	OR
1992	Maksim Tarasov, UT	19- 0¼	
1996	Jean Galfione, FRA	19- 5¼	OR

Long Jump

Year		Distance	
1896	Ellery Clark, USA	20-10	
1900	Alvin Kraenzlein, USA	23- 6¾	OR
1904	Meyer Prinstein, USA	24- 1	OR
1906	Meyer Prinstein, USA	23- 7½	
1908	Frank Irons, USA	24- 6½	OR
1912	Albert Gutterson, USA	24-11¼	OR
1920	William Petersson, SWE	23- 5½	
1924	De Hart Hubbard, USA	24- 5	
1928	Ed Hamm, USA	25- 4½	OR
1932	Ed Gordon, USA	25- 0¾	
1936	Jesse Owens, USA	26- 5½	OR
1948	Willie Steele, USA	25- 8	
1952	Jerome Biffle, USA	24-10	
1956	Greg Bell, USA	25- 8¼	
1960	Ralph Boston, USA	26- 7¾	OR
1964	Lynn Davies, GBR	26- 5¾	
1968	Bob Beamon, USA	29- 2½	WR
1972	Randy Williams, USA	27- 0½	
1976	Arnie Robinson, USA	27- 4¾	
1980	Lutz Dombrowski, E. Ger	28- 0¼	
1984	Carl Lewis, USA	28- 0¼	
1988	Carl Lewis, USA	28- 7¼	
1992	Carl Lewis, USA	28- 5½	
1996	Carl Lewis, USA	27-10¾	

Triple Jump

Year		Distance	
1896	James Connolly, USA	44-11¾	
1900	Meyer Prinstein, USA	47- 5¾	OR
1904	Meyer Prinstein, USA	47- 1	
1906	Peter O'Connor, GBR/IRE	46- 2¼	
1908	Timothy Ahearne, GBR/IRE	48-11¼	OR
1912	Gustaf Lindblom, SWE	48- 5¼	
1920	Vilho Tuulos, FIN	47- 7	
1924	Nick Winter, AUS	50-11¼	WR
1928	Mikio Oda, JPN	49-11	
1932	Chuhei Nambu, JPN	51- 7	WR
1936	Naoto Tajima, JPN	52- 6	WR
1948	Arne Ahman, SWE	50- 6¼	
1952	Adhemar da Silva, BRA	53- 2¾	WR
1956	Adhemar da Silva, BRA	53- 7¾	OR
1960	Józef Schmidt, POL	55- 2	
1964	Józef Schmidt, POL	55- 3½	OR
1968	Viktor Saneyev, USSR	57- 0¾	WR
1972	Viktor Saneyev, USSR	56-11¼	
1976	Viktor Saneyev, USSR	56- 8¾	
1980	Jaak Uudmäe, USSR	56-11¼	
1984	Al Joyner, USA	56- 7½	
1988	Khristo Markov, BUL	57- 9¼	OR
1992	Mike Conley, USA	57-10¼	OR
1996	Kenny Harrison, USA	59- 4¼	OR

Shot Put

Year		Distance	
1896	Bob Garrett, USA	36- 9¾	
1900	Richard Sheldon, USA	46- 3¼	OR
1904	Ralph Rose, USA	48- 7	WR
1906	Martin Sheridan, USA	40- 5¼	
1908	Ralph Rose, USA	46- 7½	
1912	Patrick McDonald, USA	50- 4	OR
1920	Ville Pörhölä, FIN	48- 7¼	
1924	Bud Houser, USA	49- 2¼	
1928	John Kuck, USA	52- 0¾	WR
1932	Leo Sexton, USA	52- 6	OR
1936	Hans Woellke, GER	53- 1¾	OR
1948	Wilbur Thompson, USA	56- 2	OR
1952	Parry O'Brien, USA	57- 1½	OR
1956	Parry O'Brien, USA	60-11¼	OR
1960	Bill Nieder, USA	64- 6¾	OR
1964	Dallas Long, USA	66- 8½	OR
1968	Randy Matson, USA	67- 4¾	
1972	Wladyslaw Komar, POL	69- 6	OR
1976	Udo Beyer, E. Ger	69- 0¾	
1980	Vladimir Kiselyov, USSR	70- 0½	OR
1984	Alessandro Andrei, ITA	69- 9	
1988	Ulf Timmermann, E. Ger	73- 8¾	OR
1992	Mike Stulce, USA	71- 2½	
1996	Randy Barnes, USA	70-11¼	

Discus Throw

Year		Distance	
1896	Bob Garrett, USA	95- 7½	
1900	Rudolf Bauer, HUN	118- 3	OR
1904	Martin Sheridan, USA	128-10½	OR
1906	Martin Sheridan, USA	136- 0	
1908	Martin Sheridan, USA	134- 2	OR
1912	Armas Taipale, FIN	148- 3	OR
1920	Elmer Niklander, FIN	146- 7	
1924	Bud Houser, USA	151- 4	OR
1928	Bud Houser, USA	155- 3	OR
1932	John Anderson, USA	162- 4	OR
1936	Ken Carpenter, USA	165- 7	OR
1948	Adolfo Consolini, ITA	173- 2	OR
1952	Sim Iness, USA	180- 6	OR
1956	Al Oerter, USA	184-11	OR
1960	Al Oerter, USA	194- 2	OR
1964	Al Oerter, USA	200- 1	OR
1968	Al Oerter, USA	212- 6	OR
1972	Ludvik Danek, CZE	211- 3	
1976	Mac Wilkins, USA	221- 5	
1980	Viktor Rashchupkin, USSR	218- 8	
1984	Rolf Danneberg, W. Ger	218- 6	
1988	Jürgen Schult, E. Ger	225- 9	OR
1992	Romas Ubartas, LIT	213- 8	
1996	Lars Riedel, GER	227- 8	

Hammer Throw

Year		Distance	
1900	John Flanagan, USA	163- 1	
1904	John Flanagan, USA	168- 1	OR
1908	John Flanagan, USA	170- 4	OR
1912	Matt McGrath, USA	179- 7	OR
1920	Pat Ryan, USA	173- 5	
1924	Fred Tootell, USA	174-10	
1928	Pat O'Callaghan, IRE	168- 7	
1932	Pat O'Callaghan, IRE	176-11	
1936	Karl Hein, GER	185- 4	OR
1948	Imre Németh, HUN	183-11	
1952	József Csérmák, HUN	197-11	WR
1956	Harold Connolly, USA	207- 3	OR
1960	Vasily Rudenkov, USSR	220- 2	OR
1964	Romuald Klim, USSR	228-10	OR
1968	Gyula Zsivótzky, HUN	240- 8	OR
1972	Anatoly Bondarchuk, USSR	247- 8	OR
1976	Yuri Sedykh, USSR	254- 4	OR
1980	Yuri Sedykh, USSR	268- 4	WR
1984	Juha Tiainen, FIN	256- 2	
1988	Sergey Litvinov, USSR	278- 2	OR
1992	Andrei Abduvaliyev, UT	270- 9	
1996	Balazs Kiss, HUN	266- 6	

Track & Field (Cont.)

MEN

Javelin Throw

Year		Distance	
1908	Eric Lemming, SWE	179-10	WR
1912	Eric Lemming, SWE	198-11	WR
1920	Jonni Myyrä, FIN	215-10	OR
1924	Jonni Myyrä, FIN	206- 7	
1928	Erik Lundkvist, SWE	218- 6	OR
1932	Matti Järvinen, FIN	238- 6	OR
1936	Gerhard Stöck, GER	235- 8	
1948	Kai Tapio Rautavaara, FIN	228-10	
1952	Cy Young, USA	242- 1	OR
1956	Egil Danielson, NOR	281- 2	WR
1960	Viktor Tsibulenko, USSR	277- 8	
1964	Pauli Nevala, FIN	271- 2	
1968	Jänis Lüsis, USSR	295- 7	OR
1972	Klaus Wolfermann, W. Ger	296-10	OR
1976	Miklos Németh, HUN	310- 4	WR
1980	Dainis Kūla, USSR	299- 2	
1984	Arto Härkönen, FIN	284- 8	
1988	Tapio Korjus, FIN	276- 6	
1992	Jan Zelezny, CZE	294- 2*	OR
1996	Jan Zelezny, CZE	289- 3	

*In 1986 the balance point of the javelin was modified and new records have been kept since.

Decathlon

Year		Points	
1904	Thomas Kiely, IRL	6036	
1906-08	Not held		
1912	Jim Thrope, USA	8412	WR
1920	Helge Lövland, NOR	6803	
1924	Harold Osborn, USA	7711	WR
1928	Paavo Yrjölä, FIN	8053	WR
1932	Jim Bausch, USA	8462	WR
1936	Glenn Morris, USA	7900	WR
1948	Bob Mathias, USA	7139	
1952	Bob Mathias, USA	7887	WR
1956	Milt Campbell, USA	7937	OR
1960	Rafer Johnson, USA	8392	OR
1964	Willi Holdorf, GER	7887	
1968	Bill Toomey, USA	8193	OR
1972	Nikolai Avilov, USSR	8454	WR
1976	Bruce Jenner, USA	8617	WR
1980	Daley Thompson, GBR	8495	
1984	Daley Thompson, GBR	8798	=WR
1988	Christian Schenk, E. Ger	8488	
1992	Robert Zmelik, CZE	8611	
1996	Dan O'Brien, USA	8824	

WOMEN

At least 4 gold medals (including relays): Evelyn Ashford, Fanny Blankers-Koen, Betty Cuthbert and Bärbel Eckert Wöckel (4).

100 meters

Year		Time	
1928	Betty Robinson, USA	12.2	=WR
1932	Stella Walsh, POL*	11.9	=WR
1936	Helen Stephens, USA	11.5W	
1948	Fanny Blankers-Koen, HOL	11.9	
1952	Marjorie Jackson, AUS	11.5	=WR
1956	Betty Cuthbert, AUS	11.5	
1960	Wilma Rudolph, USA	11.0W	
1964	Wyomia Tyus, USA	11.4	
1968	Wyomia Tyus, USA	11.08	WR
1972	Renate Stecher, E. Ger	11.07	
1976	Annegret Richter, W. Ger	11.08	
1980	Lyudmila Kondratyeva, USSR	11.06	
1984	Evelyn Ashford, USA	10.97	OR
1988	Florence Griffith Joyner, USA	10.54W	
1992	Gail Devers, USA	10.82	OR
1996	Gail Devers, USA	10.94	

*An autopsy performed after Walsh's death in 1980 revealed that she was a man.

200 meters

Year		Time	
1948	Fanny Blankers-Koen, HOL	24.4	
1952	Marjorie Jackson, AUS	23.7	OR
1956	Betty Cuthbert, AUS	23.4	=OR
1960	Wilma Rudolph, USA	24.0	
1964	Edith McGuire, USA	23.0	OR
1968	Irena Szewinska, POL	22.5	WR
1972	Renate Stecher, E. Ger	22.40	=WR
1976	Bärbel Eckert, E. Ger	22.37	OR
1980	Bärbel Eckert Wöckel, E. Ger	22.03	OR
1984	Valerie Brisco-Hooks, USA	21.81	OR
1988	Florence Griffith Joyner, USA	21.34	WR
1992	Gwen Torrence, USA	21.81	
1996	Marie-Jose Perec, FRA	22.12	

400 meters

Year		Time	
1964	Betty Cuthbert, AUS	52.0	
1968	Colette Besson, FRA	52.03	=OR
1972	Monika Zehrt, E. Ger	51.08	OR
1976	Irena Szewinska, POL	49.29	WR
1980	Marita Koch, E. Ger	48.88	OR
1984	Valerie Brisco-Hooks, USA	48.83	OR
1988	Olga Bryzgina, USSR	48.65	OR
1992	Marie-Jose Perec, FRA	48.83	
1996	Marie-Jose Perec, FRA	48.25	OR

800 meters

Year		Time	
1928	Lina Radke, GER	2:16.8	WR
1932-56	Not held		
1960	Lyudmila Shevtsova, USSR	2:04.3	=WR
1964	Ann Packer, GBR	2:01.1	OR
1968	Madeline Manning, USA	2:00.9	OR
1972	Hildegard Falck, W. Ger	1:58.55	OR
1976	Tatyana Kazankina, USSR	1:54.94	WR
1980	Nadezhda Olizarenko, USSR	1:53.42	WR
1984	Doina Melinte, ROM	1:57.60	
1988	Sigrun Wodars, E. Ger	1:56.10	
1992	Ellen van Langen, HOL	1:55.54	
1996	Svetlana Masterkova, RUS	1:57.73	

1500 meters

Year		Time	
1972	Lyudmila Bragina, USSR	4:01.4	WR
1976	Tatyana Kazankina, USSR	4:05.48	
1980	Tatyana Kazankina, USSR	3:56.6	OR
1984	Gabriella Dorio, ITA	4:03.25	
1988	Paula Ivan, ROM	3:53.96	OR
1992	Hassiba Boulmerka, ALG	3:55.30	
1996	Svetlana Masterkova, RUS	4:00.83	

5000 meters

Year		Time	
1984	Maricica Puica, ROM	8:35.96	
1988	Tatyana Samolenko, USSR	8:26.53	OR
1992	Elena Romanova, UT	8:46.04	
1996	Wang Junxia, CHN	14:59.88	

Note: Event held over 3000 meters from 1984-92.

10,000 meters

Year		Time	
1988	Olga Bondarenko, USSR	31:05.21	OR
1992	Derartu Tulu, ETH	31:06.02	
1996	Fernanda Ribeiro, POR	31:01.63	OR

Marathon

Year		Time
1984	Joan Benoit, USA	2:24:52
1988	Rosa Mota, POR	2:25:40
1992	Valentina Yegorova, UT	2:32:41
1996	Fatuma Roba, ETH	2:26:05

100-meter Hurdles

Year		Time	
1932	Babe Didrikson, USA	11.7	WR
1936	Trebisonda Valla, ITA	11.7	
1948	Fanny Blankers-Koen, NET	11.2	OR
1952	Shirley Strickland, AUS	10.9	WR
1956	Shirley Strickland, AUS	10.7	OR
1960	Irina Press, USSR	10.8	
1964	Karin Balzer, GER	10.5[W]	
1968	Maureen Caird, AUS	10.3	OR
1972	Annelie Ehrhardt, E. Ger	12.59	WR
1976	Johanna Schaller, E. Ger	12.77	
1980	Vera Komisova, USSR	12.56	OR
1984	Benita Fitzgerald-Brown, USA	12.84	
1988	Yordanka Donkova, BUL	12.38	OR
1992	Paraskevi Patoulidou, GRE	12.64	
1996	Ludmila Enquist, SWE	12.58	

Note: Event held over 80 meters from 1932-68.

400-meter Hurdles

Year		Time	
1984	Nawal El Moutawakel, MOR	54.61	OR
1988	Debra Flintoff-King, AUS	53.17	OR
1992	Sally Gunnell, GBR	53.23	
1996	Deon Hemmings, JAM	52.82	OR

4x100-meter Relay

Year		Time	
1928	Canada	48.4	WR
1932	United States	46.9	WR
1936	United States	46.9	
1948	Holland	47.5	
1952	United States	45.9	WR
1956	Australia	44.5	WR
1960	United States	44.5	
1964	Poland	43.6	
1968	United States	42.87	WR
1972	West Germany	42.81	WR
1976	East Germany	42.55	OR
1980	East Germany	41.60	WR
1984	United States	41.65	
1988	United States	41.98	
1992	United States	42.11	
1996	United States	41.95	

4x400-meter Relay

Year		Time	
1972	East Germany	3:23.0	WR
1976	East Germany	3:19.23	WR
1980	Soviet Union	3:20.2	
1984	United States	3:18.29	OR
1988	Soviet Union	3:15.18	WR
1992	Unified Team	3:20.20	
1996	United States	3:20.91	

10-kilometer Walk

Year		Time
1992	Chen Yueling, CHN	44:32
1996	Yelena Ninikolayeva, RUS	41:49

High Jump

Year		Height	
1928	Ethel Catherwood, CAN	5- 2½	
1932	Jean Shiley, USA	5- 5¼	WR
1936	Ibolya Csák, HUN	5- 3	
1948	Alice Coachman, USA	5- 6	OR
1952	Esther Brand, S. Afr	5- 5¾	
1956	Mildred McDaniel, USA	5- 9¼	WR
1960	Iolanda Balas, ROM	6- 0¾	OR
1964	Iolanda Balas, ROM	6- 2¾	OR
1968	Miloslava Režková, CZE	5-11½	
1972	Ulrike Meyfarth, W. Ger	6- 3½	=WR
1976	Rosemarie Ackermann, E. Ger	6- 4	OR
1980	Sara Simeoni, ITA	6- 5½	OR
1984	Ulrike Meyfarth, W. Ger	6- 7½	OR
1988	Louise Ritter, USA	6- 8	OR
1992	Heike Henkel, GER	6- 7½	
1996	Stefka Kostadinova, BUL	6- 8¾	

Long Jump

Year		Distance	
1948	Olga Gyarmati, HUN	18- 8¼	
1952	Yvette Williams, NZE	20- 5¾	OR
1956	Elzbieta Krzesinska, POL	20-10	=WR
1960	Vyera Krepkina, USSR	20-10¾	OR
1964	Mary Rand, GBR	22- 2¼	WR
1968	Viorica Viscopoleanu, ROM	22- 4½	WR
1972	Heidemarie Rosendahl, W. Ger	22- 3	
1976	Angela Voigt, E. Ger	22- 0¾	
1980	Tatyana Kolpakova, USSR	23- 2	OR
1984	Anisoara Cusmir-Stanciu, ROM	22-10	
1988	Jackie Joyner-Kersee, USA	24- 3¼	OR
1992	Heike Drechsler, GER	23- 5¼	
1996	Chioma Ajunwa, NGR	23- 4½	

Track & Field (Cont.)

WOMEN

Triple Jump

Year		Distance
1996	Inessa Kravets, UKR	50- 3½

Shot Put

Year		Distance	
1948	Micheline Ostermeyer, FRA	45- 1½	
1952	Galina Zybina, USSR	50- 1¾	WR
1956	Tamara Tyshkevich, USSR	54- 5	OR
1960	Tamara Press, USSR	56-10	OR
1964	Tamara Press, USSR	59- 6¼	OR
1968	Margitta Gummel, E. Ger	64- 4	WR
1972	Nadezhda Chizhova, USSR	69- 0	WR
1976	Ivanka Hristova, BUL	69- 5¼	OR
1980	Ilona Slupianek, E. Ger	73- 6¼	OR
1984	Claudia Losch, W. Ger	67- 2¼	
1988	Natalia Lisovskaya, USSR	72-11¾	
1992	Svetlana Krivaleva, UT	69- 1¼	
1996	Astrid Kumbernuss, GER	67- 5½	

Discus Throw

Year		Distance	
1928	Halina Konopacka, POL	129-11¾	WR
1932	Lillian Copeland, USA	133- 2	OR
1936	Gisela Mauermayer, GER	156- 3	OR
1948	Micheline Ostermeyer, FRA	137- 6	
1952	Nina Romaschkova, USSR	168- 8	OR
1956	Olga Fikotová, CZE	176- 1	OR
1960	Nina Ponomaryeva, USSR	180- 9	OR
1964	Tamara Press, USSR	187-10	OR
1968	Lia Manoliu, ROM	191- 2	OR
1972	Faina Melnik, USSR	218- 7	OR
1976	Evelin Schlaak, E. Ger	226- 4	OR
1980	Evelin Schlaak Jahl, E. Ger	229- 6	OR
1984	Ria Stalman, HOL	214- 5	
1988	Martina Hellmann, E. Ger	237- 2½	OR
1992	Maritza Marten, CUB	229-10	
1996	Ilke Wyludda, GER	228- 6	

Javelin Throw

Year		Distance	
1932	Babe Didrikson, USA	143- 4	
1936	Tilly Fleischer, GER	148- 3	OR
1948	Herma Bauma, AUT	149- 6	OR
1952	Dana Zátopková, CZE	165- 7	OR
1956	Ineze Jaunzeme, USSR	176- 8	OR
1960	Elvira Ozolina, USSR	183- 8	OR
1964	Mihaela Penes, ROM	198- 7	OR
1968	Angéla Németh, HUN	198- 0	
1972	Ruth Fuchs, E. Ger	209- 7	OR
1976	Ruth Fuchs, E. Ger	216- 4	OR
1980	Maria Colon Rueñes, CUB	224- 5	OR
1984	Tessa Sanderson, GBR	228- 2	OR
1988	Petra Felke, E. Ger	245- 0	OR
1992	Silke Renk, GER	224- 2	
1996	Heli Rantanen, FIN	222- 11	

Heptathlon

Year		Points	
1964	Irina Press, USSR	5246	WR
1968	Ingrid Becker, W. Ger	5098	
1972	Mary Peters, GBR	4801	WR
1976	Siegrun Siegl, E. Ger	4745	
1980	Nadezhda Tkachenko, USSR	5083	WR
1984	Glynis Nunn, AUS	6390	OR
1988	Jackie Joyner-Kersee, USA	7291	WR
1992	Jackie Joyner-Kersee, USA	7044	
1996	Ghada Shouaa, SYR	6780	

Note: Seven-event Heptathlon replaced five-event Pentathlon in 1984.

All-Time Leading Medal Winners — Single Games

Athletes who have won the most medals in a single Summer Olympics through Atlanta in 1996. Note that totals include individual, relay and team medals. U.S. athletes are in **bold** type.

MEN

No		Sport	G-S-B
8	Aleksandr Dityatin, USSR (1980)	Gym	3-4-1
7	**Mark Spitz**, USA (1976)	Swim	7-0-0
7	**Willis Lee**, USA (1920)	Shoot	5-1-1
7	**Matt Biondi**, USA (1988)	Swim	5-1-1
7	Boris Shakhlin, USSR (1960)	Gym	4-2-1
7	**Lloyd Spooner**, USA (1920)	Shoot	4-1-2
7	Mikhail Voronin, USSR (1968)	Gym	2-4-1
7	Nikolai Andrianov, USSR (1976)	Gym	2-4-1
6	Vitaly Scherbo, UT (1992)	Gym	6-0-0
6	Li Ning, CHN (1984)	Gym	3-2-1
6	Akinori Nakayama, JPN (1968)	Gym	4-1-1
6	Takashi Ono, JPN (1960)	Gym	3-1-2
6	Viktor Chukarin, USSR (1956)	Gym	4-2-0
6	Konrad Frey, GER (1936)	Gym	3-1-2
6	Ville Ritola, FIN (1924)	Track	4-2-0
6	Hubert Van Innis, BEL (1920)	Arch	4-2-0
6	**Carl Osburn**, USA (1920)	Shoot	4-1-1
6	Louis Richardet, SWI (1906)	Shoot	3-3-0
6	**Anton Heida**, USA (1904)	Gym	5-1-0
6	**George Eyser**, USA (1904)	Gym	3-2-1
6	**Burton Downing**, USA (1904)	Cycle	2-3-1
6	Alexi Nemov, RUS (1996)	Gym	2-3-1

WOMEN

No		Sport	G-S-B
7	Maria Gorokhovskaya, USSR (1952)	Gym	2-5-0
6	Kristin Otto, E. Ger (1988)	Swim	6-0-0
6	Agnes Keleti, HUN (1956)	Gym	4-2-0
6	Vera Caslavska, CZE (1968)	Gym	4-2-0
6	Larisa Latynina, USSR (1956)	Gym	4-1-1
6	Larisa Latynina, USSR (1960)	Gym	3-2-1
6	Daniela Silivas, ROM (1988)	Gym	3-2-1
6	Larisa Latynina, USSR (1964)	Gym	2-2-2
6	Margit Korondi, HUN, (1956)	Gym	1-1-4
5	Kornelia Ender, E. Ger (1976)	Swim	4-1-0
5	Ecaterina Szabo, ROM (1984)	Gym	4-1-0
5	Shane Gould, AUS (1972)	Swim	3-1-1
5	Nadia Comaneci, ROM (1976)	Gym	3-1-1
5	Karin Janz, E. Ger (1972)	Gym	2-2-1
5	Ines Diers, E. Ger (1980)	Swim	2-2-1
5	**Shirley Babashoff**, USA (1976)	Swim	1-4-0
5	**Mary Lou Retton**, USA (1984)	Gym	1-2-2
5	**Shannon Miller**, USA (1992)	Gym	0-2-3

All-Time Leading Medal Winners — Career

All Nations

Most Overall Medals

MEN

No		Sport	G-S-B
15	Nikolai Andrianov, USSR	Gymnastics	7-5-3
13	Boris Shakhlin, USSR	Gymnastics	7-4-2
13	Edoardo Mangiarotti, ITA	Fencing	6-5-2
13	Takashi Ono, JPN	Gymnastics	5-4-4
12	Paavo Nurmi, FIN	Track/Field	9-3-0
12	Sawao Kato, JPN	Gymnastics	8-3-1
11	**Mark Spitz**, USA	Swimming	9-1-1
11*	**Matt Biondi**, USA	Swimming	8-2-1
11	Viktor Chukarin, USSR	Gymnastics	7-3-1
11	**Carl Osburn**, USA	Shooting	5-4-2
10	**Ray Ewry**, USA	Track/Field	10-0-0
10	**Carl Lewis**, USA	Track/Field	9-1-0
10	Aladár Gerevich, HUN	Fencing	7-1-2
10	Akinori Nakayama, JPN	Gymnastics	6-2-2
10	Aleksandr Dityatin, USSR	Gymnastics	3-6-1
9	Vitaly Scherbo, BLR	Gymnastics	6-0-3
9	**Martin Sheridan**, USA	Track/Field	5-3-1
9	Zoltán Halmay, HUN	Swimming	3-5-1
9	Giulio Gaudini, ITA	Fencing	3-4-2
9	Mikhail Voronin, USSR	Gymnastics	2-6-1
9	Heikki Savolainen, FIN	Gymnastics	2-1-6
9	Yuri Titov, USSR	Gymnastics	1-5-3

*Includes gold medal as preliminary member of 1st-place relay team.

Note: Medals won by Ewry (2-0-0), Sheridan (2-3-0) and Halmay (1-1-0) at the 1906 Intercalated games are not officially recognized by the IOC.

Games Participated In

Andrianov (1972,76,80); **Biondi** (1984,88,92); **Chukarin** (1952,56); **Dityatin** (1976,80); **Ewry** (1900,04,06,08); **Gerevich** (1932,36,48,52,56,60); **Gaudini** (1928,32,36); **Halmay** (1900,04,06,08); **Kato** (1968,72,76); **Lewis** (1984,88,92,96); **Mangiarotti** (1936,48,52,56,60); **Nakayama** (1968,72); **Nurmi** (1920,24,28); **Ono** (1952,56,60,64); **Osburn** (1912,20, 24); **Savolainen** (1928,32,36,48,52); **Shakhlin** (1956,60,64); **Sheridan** (1904,06,08); **Spitz** (1968,72); **Titov** (1956,60,64); **Voronin** (1968,72).

WOMEN

No		Sport	G-S-B
18	Larissa Latynina, USSR	Gymnastics	9-5-4
11	Vera Cáslavská, CZE	Gymnastics	7-4-0
10	Agnes Keleti, HUN	Gymnastics	5-3-2
10	Polina Astaknova, USSR	Gymnastics	5-2-3
9	Nadia Comaneci, ROM	Gymnastics	5-3-1
9	Lyudmila Tourischeva, USSR	Gymnastics	4-3-2
8	Kornelia Ender, E. Ger	Swimming	4-4-0
8	Dawn Fraser, AUS	Swimming	4-4-0
8	**Shirley Babashoff**, USA	Swimming	2-6-0
8	Sofia Muratova, USSR	Gymnastics	2-2-4
7	Krisztina Egerszegi, HUN	Swimming	5-1-1
7	Merlene Ottey, JAM	Track/Field	0-2-5
7	Irena Kirszenstein Szewinska, POL	Track/Field	3-2-2
7	Shirley Strickland, AUS	Track/Field	3-1-3
7	Maria Gorokhovskaya, USSR	Gymnastics	2-5-0
7	Ildikó Ságiné-Ujlaki-Rejtö, HUN	Fencing	2-3-2
7	**Shannon Miller**, USA	Gymnastics	2-2-3

Games Participated In

Astaknova (1956,60,64); **Babashoff** (1972,76); **Cáslavská** (1960,64,68); **Comaneci** (1976,80); **Egerszegi** (1988,92,96) **Ender** (1972,76); **Fraser** (1956,60,64); **Gorokhovskaya** (1952); **Keleti** (1952,56); **Latynina** (1956,60,64); **Miller** (1992,96); **Muratova** (1956,60); **Ottey** (1980,84,88,92,96) **Sdáginé-Ujlaki-Rejtö** (1960,64,68,72,76); **Strickland** (1948,52,56); **Szewinska** (1964,68,72,76,80); **Tourischeva** (1968, 72,76).

Most Gold Medals

MEN

No		Sport	G-S-B
10	**Ray Ewry**, USA	Track/Field	10-0-0
9	Paavo Nurmi, FIN	Track/Field	9-3-0
9	**Mark Spitz**, USA	Swimming	9-1-1
9	**Carl Lewis**, USA	Track/Field	9-1-0
8	Sawao Kato, JPN	Gymnastics	8-3-1
8*	**Matt Biondi**, USA	Swimming	8-2-1
7	Nikolai Andrianov, USSR	Gymnastics	7-5-3
7	Boris Shakhlin, USSR	Gymnastics	7-4-2
7	Viktor Chukarin, USSR	Gymnastics	7-3-1
7	Aladar Gerevich, HUN	Fencing	7-1-2

*Includes gold medal as preliminary member of 1st-place relay team.

WOMEN

No		Sport	G-S-B
9	Larissa Latynina, USSR	Gymnastics	9-5-4
7	Vera Cáslavská, CZE	Gymnastics	7-4-0
6	Kristin Otto, E. Ger	Swimming	6-0-0
5	Agnes Keleti, HUN	Gymnastics	5-3-2
5	Nadia Comaneci, ROM	Gymnastics	5-3-1
5	Polina Astaknova, USSR	Gymnastics	5-2-3
5	Krisztina Egerszegi, HUN	Swimming	5-1-1
4	Kornelia Ender, E. Ger	Swimming	4-4-0
4	Dawn Fraser, AUS	Swimming	4-4-0
4	Lyudmila Tourischeva, USSR	Gymnastics	4-3-2
4	**Evelyn Ashford**, USA	Track/Field	4-1-0
4	**Janet Evans**, USA	Swimming	4-1-0
4	Fanny Blankers-Koen, NET	Track/Field	4-0-0
4	Betty Cuthbert, AUS	Track/Field	4-0-0
4	**Pat McCormick**, USA	Diving	4-0-0
4	**Amy Van Dyken**, USA	Swimming	4-0-0
4	Bärbel Eckert Wöckel, E. Ger.	Track/Field	4-0-0

Most Silver Medals

MEN

No		Sport	G-S-B
6	Alexandr Dityatin, USSR	Gymnastics	3-6-1
6	Mikhail Voronin, USSR	Gymnastics	2-6-1
5	Nikolai Andrianov, USSR	Gymnastics	7-5-3
5	Edoardo Mangiarotti, ITA	Fencing	6-5-2
5	Zoltán Halmay, HUN	Swimming	3-5-1
5	Gustavo Marzi, ITA	Fencing	2-5-0
5	Yuri Titov, USSR	Gymnastics	1-5-3
5	Viktor Lisitsky, USSR	Gymnastics	0-5-0

WOMEN

No		Sport	G-S-B
6	**Shirley Babashoff**, USA	Swimming	2-6-0
5	Larissa Latynina, USSR	Gymnastics	9-5-4
5	Maria Gorokhovskaya, USSR	Gymnastics	2-5-0
4	Vera Cáslavská, CZE	Gymnastics	7-4-0
4	Kornelia Ender, E. Ger	Swimming	4-4-0
4	Dawn Fraser, AUS	Swimming	4-4-0
4	Erica Zuchold, E. Ger	Gymnastics	0-4-1

Most Bronze Medals

MEN

No		Sport	G-S-B
6	Heikki Savolainen, FIN	Gymnastics	2-1-6
5	Daniel Revenu, FRA	Fencing	1-0-5
5	Philip Edwards, CAN	Track/Field	0-0-5
5	Adrianus Jong, NET	Fencing	0-0-5

WOMEN

No		Sport	G-S-B
5	Merlene Ottey, JAM	Track/Field	0-2-5
4	Larissa Latynina, USSR	Gymnastics	9-5-4
4	Sofia Muratova, USSR	Gymnastics	2-2-4

All-Time Leading USA Medal Winners

Most Overall Medals

MEN

No		Sport	G-S-B
11	Mark Spitz	Swimming	9-1-1
11*	Matt Biondi	Swimming	8-2-1
11	Carl Osburn	Shooting	5-4-2
10	Ray Ewry	Track/Field	10-0-0
10	Carl Lewis	Track/Field	9-1-0
9	Martin Sheridan	Track/Field	5-3-1
8	Charles Daniels	Swimming	5-1-2
7†	Tom Jager	Swimming	5-1-1
7	Willis Lee	Shooting	5-1-1
7	Lloyd Spooner	Shooting	4-1-2
6	Anton Heida	Gymnastics	5-1-0
6	Don Schollander	Swimming	5-1-0
6	Johnny Weissmuller	Swim/Water Polo	5-0-1
6	Alfred Lane	Shooting	5-0-1
6	Jim Lightbody	Track/Field	4-2-0
6	George Eyser	Gymnastics	3-2-1
6	Michael Plumb	Equestrian	2-4-0
6	Burton Downing	Cycling	2-3-1
6	Bob Garrett	Track/Field	2-2-2

*Includes gold medal as prelim. member of 1st-place relay team.

†Includes 3 gold medals as prelim. member of 1st-place relay teams.

Note: Medals won by Ewry (2-0-0) and Sheridan (2-3-0) at the 1906 Intercalated games are not officially recognized by the IOC.

Games Participated In

Biondi (1984,88,92); **Daniels** (1904,06,08); **Downing** (1904); **Ewry** (1900,04,06,08); **Eyser** (1904); **Garrett** (1896,1900); **Heida** (1904); **Jager** (1984,88,92); **Lane** (1912,20); **Lee** (1920); **Lewis** (1984,88,92); **Lightbody** (1904,06); **Osburn** (1912,20,24); **Plumb** (1960, 64,68,72,76,84); **Schollander** (1964, 68); **Sheridan** (1904,06,08); **Spitz** (1968,72); **Spooner** (1920); **Weissmuller** (1924,28).

WOMEN

No		Sport	G-S-B
8	Shirley Babashoff	Swimming	2-6-0
7	Shannon Miller	Gymnastics	2-2-3
5	Evelyn Ashford	Track/Field	4-1-0
5	Janet Evans	Swimming	4-1-0
5*	Mary T. Meagher	Swimming	3-1-1
5	Florence Griffith Joyner	Track/Field	3-2-0
5	Jackie Joyner-Kersee	Track/Field	3-1-1
5	Mary Lou Retton	Gymnastics	1-2-2
4	Pat McCormick	Diving	4-0-0
4	Amy Van Dyken	Swimming	4-0-0
4	Valerie Brisco-Hooks	Track/Field	3-1-0
4	Nancy Hogshead	Swimming	3-1-0
4	Sharon Stouder	Swimming	3-1-0
4	Wyomia Tyus	Track/Field	3-1-0
4	Wilma Rudolph	Track/Field	3-0-1
4	Chris von Saltza	Swimming	3-1-0
4	Sue Pederson	Swimming	2-2-0
4	Jan Henne	Swimming	2-1-1
4	Dorothy Poynton Hill	Diving	2-1-1
4*	Summer Sanders	Swimming	2-1-1
4*	Dara Torres	Swimming	2-1-1
4	Kathy Ellis	Swimming	2-0-2
4	Georgia Coleman	Diving	1-2-1

*Includes silver medal as prelim. member of 2nd-place relay team.

Games Participated In

Ashford (1976,84,88,92); **Babashoff** (1972,76); **Brisco-Hooks** (1984,88); **Coleman** (1928,32); **Ellis** (1964); **Evans** (1988,92); **Griffith Joyner** (1984,88); **Henne** (1968); **Hogshead** (1984); **Joyner-Kersee** (1984,88,92); **McCormick** (1952,56); **Meagher** (1984,88); **Miller** (1992,96); **Pederson** (1968); **Poynton Hill** (1928,32,36); **Retton** (1984); **Rudolph** (1956,60); **Sanders** (1992); **Stouder** (1964); **Torres** (1984,88,92); **Tyus** (1964,68); **Van Dyken** (1996); **von Saltza** (1960).

Most Gold Medals

MEN

No		Sport	G-S-B
10	Ray Ewry	Track/Field	10-0-0
9	Mark Spitz	Swimming	9-1-1
9	Carl Lewis	Track/Field	9-1-0
8*	Matt Biondi	Swimming	8-2-1
5	Carl Osburn	Shooting	5-4-2
5	Martin Sheridan	Track/Field	5-3-1
5	Charles Daniels	Swimming	5-1-2
5†	Tom Jager	Swimming	5-1-1
5	Willis Lee	Shooting	5-1-1
5	Anton Heida	Gymnastics	5-1-0
5	Don Schollander	Swimming	5-1-0
5	Johnny Weissmuller	Swim/Water Polo	5-0-1
5	Alfred Lane	Shooting	5-0-1
5	Morris Fisher	Shooting	5-0-0
4	Jim Lightbody	Track/Field	4-2-0
4	Lloyd Spooner	Shooting	4-1-2
4	Greg Louganis	Diving	4-1-0
4	John Naber	Swimming	4-1-0
4	Meyer Prinstein	Track/Field	4-1-0
4	Mel Sheppard	Track/Field	4-1-0
4	Marcus Hurley	Cycling	4-0-1
4	Harrison Dillard	Track/Field	4-0-0
4	Archie Hahn	Track/Field	4-0-0
4	Alvin Kraenzlein	Track/Field	4-0-0
4	Al Oerter	Track/Field	4-0-0
4	Jesse Owens	Track/Field	4-0-0

*Includes gold medal as prelim. member of 1st-place relay team.

†Includes 3 gold medals as prelim. member of 1st-place relay teams.

WOMEN

No		Sport	G-S-B
4	Evelyn Ashford	Track/Field	4-1-0
4	Janet Evans	Swimming	4-1-0
4	Pat McCormick	Diving	4-0-0
3	Florence Griffith Joyner	Track/Field	3-2-0
3	Jackie Joyner-Kersee	Track/Field	3-1-1
3*	Mary T. Meagher	Swimming	3-1-1
3	Valerie Brisco-Hooks	Track/Field	3-1-0
3	Nancy Hogshead	Swimming	3-1-0
3	Sharon Stouder	Swimming	3-1-0
3	Wyomia Tyus	Track/Field	3-1-0
3	Chris von Saltza	Swimming	3-1-0
3	Wilma Rudolph	Track/Field	3-0-1
3	Melissa Belote	Swimming	3-0-0
3	Ethelda Bleibtrey	Swimming	3-0-0
3	Tracy Caulkins	Swimming	3-0-0
3*	Nicole Haislett	Swimming	3-0-0
3	Helen Madison	Swimming	3-0-0
3	Debbie Meyer	Swimming	3-0-0
3	Sandra Neilson	Swimming	3-0-0
3	Martha Norelius	Swimming	3-0-0
3*	Carrie Steinseifer	Swimming	3-0-0

*Includes gold medal as prelim. member of 1st-place relay team.

Most Silver Medals

MEN

No		Sport	G-S-B
4	Carl Osburn	Shooting	5-4-2
4	Michael Plumb	Equestrian	2-4-0
3	Martin Sheridan	Track/Field	5-3-1
3	Burton Downing	Cycling	2-3-1
3	Irving Baxter	Track/Field	2-3-0
3	Earl Thomson	Equestrian	2-3-0

WOMEN

No		Sport	G-S-B
6	Shirley Babashoff	Swimming	2-6-0

All-Time Medal Standings, 1896-1996

All-time Summer Games medal standings, according to *The Golden Book of the Olympic Games.* Medal counts include the 1906 Intercalated Games which are not recognized by the IOC.

		G	S	B	Total
1	**United States**	832	634	553	2019
2	USSR (1952-88)	395	319	296	1010
3	Great Britain	169	223	218	610
4	France	175	179	206	560
5	Sweden	132	151	174	457
6	Italy	166	135	144	445
	East Germany (1956-88)	159	150	136	445
8	Hungary	142	129	155	426
9	Germany (1896-36,92–)	124	121	134	379
10	West Germany (1952-88)	77	104	120	301
11	Finland	99	80	113	292
	Australia	86	85	121	292
13	Japan	92	8p	97	278
14	Romania	63	77	99	239
15	Poland	50	67	110	227
16	Canada	48	78	90	216
17	Netherlands	49	58	81	188
18	Bulgaria	43	76	63	182
19	Switzerland	46	69	59	174
20	China	52	63	49	164
21	Denmark	38	60	57	155
22	Czechoslovakia (1924-92)	49	49	44	142
23	Belgium	37	49	49	135
24	South Korea	38	42	46	126
25	Norway	45	41	38	124
26	Greece	28	42	43	113
27	Unified Team (1992)	45	38	29	112
28	Cuba	44	33	31	108
29	Yugoslavia (1924-88, 96-)	27	31	32	90
30	Austria	18	31	34	83
31	New Zealand	29	12	29	70
32	Russia	26	24	18	68
33	Spain	22	25	17	64
34	Turkey	30	16	13	59
35	South Africa	19	18	21	58
36	Brazil	12	13	29	54
37	Argentina	13	21	16	50
38	Kenya	14	17	16	47
39	Mexico	9	13	19	41
40	Iran	5	13	18	36
41	Jamaica	5	16	9	30
42	North Korea	8	6	12	26
43	Estonia	7	6	10	23
44	Great Britain/Ireland	6	11	3	20
45	Ireland	8	5	6	19
46	Ethiopia	8	1	7	16
	Egypt	6	5	5	16
48	India	8	3	4	15
	Portugal	3	4	8	15
50	Nigeria	2	5	7	14
	Mongolia	0	5	9	14
52	Morocco	4	2	5	11
53	Indonesia	3	4	3	10
	Pakistan	3	3	4	10
55	Uruguay	2	1	6	9
	Trinidad & Tobago	1	2	6	9
	Philippines	0	2	7	9
58	Venezuela	1	2	5	8
	Chile	0	6	2	8
60	Algeria	3	0	4	7
	Latvia	0	5	2	7
62	Uganda	1	3	2	6
	Tunisia	1	2	3	6
	Thailand	1	1	4	6
	Colombia	0	2	4	6
	Bohemia	0	1	5	6
	Puerto Rico	0	1	5	6
68	Croatia	1	2	2	5
	Chinese Taipei	0	3	2	5

		G	S	B	Total
70	Peru	1	3	0	4
	Bahamas	1	1	2	4
	Lithuania	1	0	3	4
	Namibia	0	4	0	4
	Lebanon	0	2	2	4
	Slovenia	0	2	2	4
	Ghana	0	1	3	4
	Luxenbourg	2	1	0	3
	Slovakia	1	1	1	3
	Israel	0	1	2	3
	Malaysia	0	1	2	3
81	Armenia	1	1	0	2
	Costa Rica	1	1	0	2
	Syria	1	1	0	2
	Japan/Korea	1	0	1	2
	Surinam	1	0	1	2
	Tanzania	0	2	0	2
	Cameroon	0	1	1	2
	Great Britain/USA	0	1	1	2
	Haiti	0	1	1	2
	Iceland	0	1	1	2
	Moldova	0	1	1	2
	Russia/Estonia	0	1	1	2
	United Arab Republic	0	1	1	2
	Uzbekistan	0	1	1	2
	Zambia	0	1	1	2
	The Antilles	0	0	2	2
	Georgia	0	0	2	2
	Panama	0	0	2	2
99	Australia/New Zealand	1	0	0	1
	Burundi	1	0	0	1
	Cuba/USA	1	0	0	1
	Denmark/Sweden	1	0	0	1
	Ecuador	1	0	0	1
	Gr. Britain/Ireland/Germany	1	0	0	1
	Gr. Britain/Ireland/USA	1	0	0	1
	Hong Kong	1	0	0	1
	Ireland/USA	1	0	0	1
	Zimbabwe	1	0	0	1
	Azerbaijan	0	1	0	1
	Belgium/Greece	0	1	0	1
	Ceylon	0	1	0	1
	France/USA	0	1	0	1
	France/Gr. Britain/Ireland	0	1	0	1
	Ivory Coast	0	1	0	1
	Netherlands Antilles	0	1	0	1
	Senegal	0	1	0	1
	Singapore	0	1	0	1
	Smyrna	0	1	0	1
	Tonga	0	1	0	1
	Virgin Islands	0	1	0	1
	Australia/Great Britain	0	0	1	1
	Bermuda	0	0	1	1
	Bohemia/Great Britain	0	0	1	1
	Djibouti	0	0	1	1
	Dominican Republic	0	0	1	1
	France/Great Britain	0	0	1	1
	Guyana	0	0	1	1
	Iraq	0	0	1	1
	Mexico/Spain	0	0	1	1
	Mozambique	0	0	1	1
	Niger	0	0	1	1
	Qatar	0	0	1	1
	Scotland	0	0	1	1
	Thessalonika	0	0	1	1
	Wales	0	0	1	1

Combined totals:	G	S	B	Total
USSR/UT/Russia	466	381	343	1190
Germany/E. Ger/W. Ger	360	375	390	1125

Notes: Athletes from the USSR participated in the Summer Games from 1952-88, returned as the Unified Team in 1992 after the breakup of the Soviet Union (in 1991) and then competed for the independent republics of Belarus, Kazakhstan, Russia, Ukraine, Uzbekistan and three others in the 1994 Winter Games. Yugoslavia divided into Croatia and Bosnia-Herzegovina in 1991, while Czechoslovakia split into Slovenia and the Czech Republic the same year. Germany was barred from the Olympics in 1924 and '48 following World Wars I and II. Divided into East and West Germany after WWII, both countries competed together from 1952-64, then separately from 1968-88. Germany was reunified in 1990.

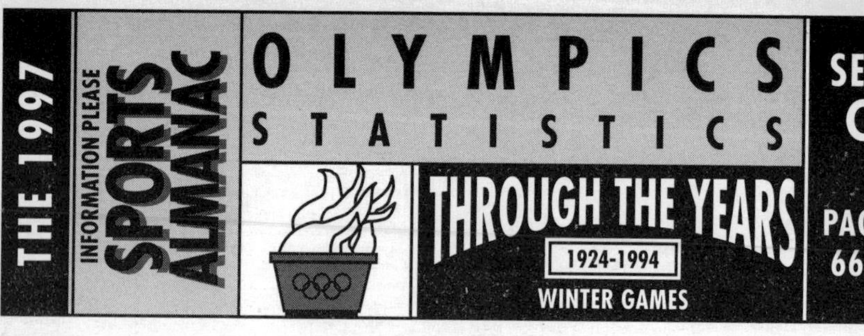

The Winter Olympics

The move toward a winter version of the Olympics began in 1908 when figure skating made an appearance at the Summer Games in London. Ten-time world champion Ulrich Salchow of Sweden, who originated the backwards, one revolution jump that bears his name, and Madge Syers of Britain were the first singles champions. Germans Anna Hubler and Heinrich Berger won the pairs competition.

Organizers of the 1916 Summer Games in Berlin planned to introduce a "Skiing Olympia," featuring nordic events in the Black Forest, but the Games were cancelled after the outbreak of World War I in 1914.

The Games resumed in 1920 at Antwerp, Belgium, where figure skating returned and ice hockey was added as a medal event. Sweden's Gillis Grafstrom and Magda Julin took individual honors, while Ludovika and Walter Jakobsson were the top pair. In hockey, Canada won the gold medal with the United States second and Czechoslovakia third.

Despite the objections of Modern Olympics' founder Baron Pierre de Coubertin and the resistance of the Scandinavian countries, which had staged their own Nordic championships every four or five years from 1901-26 in Sweden, the International Olympic Committee sanctioned an "International Winter Sports Week" at Chamonix, France, in 1924. The 11-day event, which included nordic skiing, speed skating, figure skating, ice hockey and bobsledding, was a huge success and was retroactively called the First Olympic Winter Games.

Seventy years after those first cold weather Games, the 17th edition of the Winter Olympics took place in Lillehammer, Norway, in 1994. The event ended the four-year Olympic cycle of staging both Winter and Summer Games in the same year and began a new schedule that calls for the two Games to alternate every two years.

Year	No	Location	Dates	Nations	Most medals	USA Medals
1924	I	Chamonix, FRA	Jan. 25-Feb. 4	16	Norway (4-7-6—17)	1-2-1— 4 (3rd)
1928	II	St. Moritz, SWI	Feb. 11-19	25	Norway (6-4-5—15)	2-2-2— 6 (2nd)
1932	III	Lake Placid, USA	Feb. 4-15	17	USA (6-4-2—12)	6-4-2—12 (1st)
1936	IV	Garmisch-Partenkirchen, GER	Feb. 6-16	28	Norway (7-5-3—15)	1-0-3— 4 (T-5th)
1940-**a**	—	Sapporo, JPN	Cancelled (WWII)			
1944	—	Cortina d'Ampezzo, ITA	Cancelled (WWII)			
1948	V	St. Moritz, SWI	Jan. 30-Feb. 8	28	Norway (4-3-3—10), Sweden (4-3-3—10) & Switzerland (3-4-3—10)	3-4-2— 9 (4th)
1952-**b**	VI	Oslo, NOR	Feb. 14-25	30	Norway (7-3-6—16)	4-6-1—11 (2nd)
1956-**c**	VII	Cortina d'Ampezzo, ITA	Jan. 26-Feb. 5	32	USSR (7-3-6—16)	2-3-2— 7 (T-4th)
1960	VIII	Squaw Valley, USA	Feb. 18-28	30	USSR (7-5-9—21)	3-4-3—10 (2nd)
1964	IX	Innsbruck, AUT	Jan. 29-Feb. 9	36	USSR (11-8-6—25)	1-2-3— 6 (7th)
1968-**d**	X	Grenoble, FRA	Feb. 6-18	37	Norway (6-6-2—14)	1-5-1— 7 (T-7th)
1972	XI	Sapporo, JPN	Feb. 3-13	35	USSR (8-5-3—16)	3-2-3— 8 (6th)
1976-**e**	XII	Innsbruck, AUT	Feb. 4-15	37	USSR (13-6-8—27)	3-3-4—10 (T-3rd)
1980	XIII	Lake Placid, USA	Feb. 14-23	37	E. Germany (9-7-7—23)	6-4-2—12 (3rd)
1984	XIV	Sarajevo, YUG	Feb. 7-19	49	USSR (6-10-9—25)	4-4-0— 8 (T-5th)
1988	XV	Calgary, CAN	Feb. 13-28	57	USSR (11-9-9—29)	2-1-3— 6 (T-8th)
1992-**f**	XVI	Albertville, FRA	Feb. 8-23	63	Germany (10-10-6—26)	5-4-2—11 (6th)
1994-**g**	XVII	Lillehammer, NOR	Feb. 12-27	67	Norway (10-11-5—26)	6-5-2—13 (T-5th)
1998	XVIII	Nagano, JPN	Feb. 7-22			
2002	XIX	Salt Lake City, USA	Feb. 9-24			

a—The 1940 Winter Games are originally scheduled for Sapporo, but Japan resigns as host in 1937 when the Sino-Japanese war breaks out. St. Moritz is the next choice, but the Swiss feel that ski instructors should not be considered professionals and the IOC withdraws its offer. Finally, Garmisch-Partenkirchen is asked to serve again as host, but the Germans invade Poland in 1939 and the Games are eventually cancelled.

b—Germany and Japan are allowed to rejoin the Olympic community for the first time since World War II. Though a divided country, the Germans send a joint East-West team.

c—The Soviet Union (USSR) participates in its first Winter Olympics and takes home the most medals, including the gold medal in ice hockey.

d—East Germany and West Germany officially send separate teams for the first time and will continue to do so through 1988.

e—The IOC grants the 1976 Winter Games to Denver in May 1970, but in 1972 Colorado voters reject a $5 million bond issue to finance the undertaking. Denver immediately withdraws as host and the IOC selects Innsbruck, the site of the 1964 Games, to take over.

f—Germany sends a single team after East and West German reunification in 1990 and the USSR competes as the Unified Team after the breakup of the Soviet Union in 1991.

g—The IOC moves the Winter Games' four-year cycle ahead two years in order to separate them from the Summer Games and alternate Olympics every two years.

Event-by-Event

Gold medal winners from 1924-94 in the following events: Alpine Skiing, Biathlon, Bobsled, Cross-country Skiing, Figure Skating, Ice Hockey, Luge, Nordic Combined, Ski Jumping and Speed Skating.

ALPINE SKIING

MEN

Multiple gold medals: Jean-Claude Killy, Toni Sailer and Alberto Tomba (3); Henri Oreiller, Ingemar Stenmark and Markus Wasmeier (2).

Downhill

Year		Time	Year		Time
1948	Henri Oreiller, FRA	2:55.0	1976	Franz Klammer AUT	1:45.73
1952	Zeno Colò, ITA	2:30.8	1980	Leonhard Stock, AUS	1:45.50
1956	Toni Sailer, AUT	2:52.2	1984	Bill Johnson, USA	1:45.59
1960	Jean Vuarnet, FRA	2:06.0	1988	Pirmin Zurbriggen, SWI	1:59.63
1964	Egon Zimmermann, AUT	2:18.16	1992	Patrick Ortlieb, AUT	1:50.37
1968	Jean-Claude Killy, FRA	1:59.85	1994	Tommy Moe, USA	1:45.75
1972	Bernhard Russi, SWI	1:51.43			

Slalom

Year		Time	Year		Time
1948	Edi Reinalter, SWI	2:10.3	1976	Piero Gros, ITA	2:03.29
1952	Othmar Schneider, AUT	2:00.0	1980	Ingemar Stenmark, SWE	1:44.26
1956	Toni Sailer, AUT	3:14.7	1984	Phil Mahre, USA	1:39.41
1960	Ernst Hinterseer, AUT	2:08.9	1988	Alberto Tomba, ITA	1:39.47
1964	Pepi Stiegler, AUT	2:11.13	1992	Finn Christian Jagge, NOR	1:44.39
1968	Jean-Claude Killy, FRA	1:39.73	1994	Thomas Stangassinger, AUT	2:02.02
1972	Francisco Ochoa, SPA	1:49.27			

Giant Slalom

Year		Time	Year		Time
1952	Stein Eriksen, NOR	2:25.0	1976	Heini Hemmi, SWI	3:26.97
1956	Toni Sailer, AUS	3:00.1	1980	Ingemar Stenmark, SWE	2:40.74
1960	Roger Staub, SWI	1:48.3	1984	Max Julen, SWI	2:41.18
1964	Francois Bonlieu, FRA	1:46.71	1988	Alberto Tomba, ITA	2:06.37
1968	Jean-Claude Killy, FRA	3:29.28	1992	Alberto Tomba, ITA	2:06.98
1972	Gustav Thöni, ITA	3:09.62	1994	Markus Wasmeier, GER	2:52.46

Super Giant Slalom

Year		Time	Year		Time
1988	Frank Piccard, FRA	1:39.66	1994	Markus Wasmeier, GER	1:32.53
1992	Kjetil Andre Aamadt, NOR	1:13.04			

Alpine Combined

Year		Points	Year		Points
1936	Franz Pfnür, GER	99.25	1992	Josef Polig, ITA	14.58
1948	Henri Oreiller, FRA	3.27	**Year**		**Time**
1952-84	Not held		1994	Lasse Kjus, NOR	3:17.53
1988	Hubert Strolz, AUT	36.55			

WOMEN

Multiple gold medals: Vreni Schneider (3); Deborah Compagnoni, Marielle Goitschel, Trude Jochum-Beiser, Petra Kronberger, Andrea Mead Lawrence, Rosi Mittermaier, Marie-Theres Nadig, Hanni Wenzel and Pernilla Wiberg (2).

Downhill

Year		Time	Year		Time
1948	Hedy Schlunegger, SWI	2:28.3	1976	Rosi Mittermaier, W. Ger	1:46.16
1952	Trude Jochum-Beiser, AUT	1:47.1	1980	Annemarie Moser-Pröll, AUT	1:37.52
1956	Madeleine Berthod, SWI	1:40.7	1984	Michela Figini, SWI	1:13.36
1960	Heidi Biebl, GER	1:37.6	1988	Marina Kiehl, W. Ger	1:25.86
1964	Christl Haas, AUT	1:55.39	1992	Kerrin Lee-Gartner, CAN	1:52.55
1968	Olga Pall, AUT	1:40.87	1994	Katja Seizinger, GER	1:35.93
1972	Marie-Theres Nadig, SWI	1:36.68			

Slalom

Year		Time	Year		Time
1948	Gretchen Fraser, USA	1:57.2	1976	Rosi Mittermaier, W. Ger	1:30.54
1952	Andrea Mead Lawrence, USA	2:10.6	1980	Hanni Wenzel, LIE	1:25.09
1956	Renée Colliard, SWI	1:52.3	1984	Paoletta Magoni, ITA	1:36.47
1960	Anne Heggtveit, CAN	1:49.6	1988	Vreni Schneider, SWI	1:36.69
1964	Christine Goitschel, FRA	1:29.86	1992	Petra Kronberger, AUT	1:32.68
1968	Marielle Goitschel, FRA	1:25.86	1994	Vreni Schneider, SWI	1:56.01
1972	Barbara Cochran, USA	1:31.24			

Alpine Skiing (Cont.)

WOMEN

Giant Slalom

Year		Time	Year		Time
1952	Andrea Mead Lawrence, USA	2:06.8	1976	Kathy Kreiner, CAN	1:29.13
1956	Ossi Reichert, GER	1:56.5	1980	Hanni Wenzel, LIE	2:41.66
1960	Yvonne Rügg, SWI	1:39.9	1984	Debbie Armstrong, USA	2:20.98
1964	Marielle Goitschel, FRA	1:52.24	1988	Vreni Schneider, SWI	2:06.49
1968	Nancy Greene, CAN	1:51.97	1992	Pernilla Wiberg, SWE	2:12.74
1972	Marie-Theres Nadig, SWI	1:29.90	1994	Deborah Compagnoni, ITA	2:30.97

Super Giant Slalom

Year		Time	Year		Time
1988	Sigrid Wolf, AUT	1:19.03	1994	Diann Roffe-Steinrotter, USA	1:22.15
1992	Deborah Compagnoni, ITA	1:21.22			

Alpine Combined

Year		Points	Year		Points
1936	Christl Cranz, GER	97.06	1992	Petra Kronberger, AUT	2.55
1948	Trude Beiser, AUT	6.58	**Year**		**Time**
1952-84	Not held		1994	Pernilla Wiberg, SWE	3:05.16
1988	Anita Wachter, AUT	29.25			

BIATHLON

MEN

Multiple gold medals (including relays): Aleksandr Tikhonov (4); Mark Kirchner (3); Anatoly Alyabyev, Ivan Biakov, Sergei Chepikov, Viktor Mamatov, Frank-Peter Roetsch, Magnar Solberg and Dmitri Vasilyev (2).

10 kilometers

Year		Time	Year		Time
1980	Frank Ullrich, E. Ger	32:10.69	1992	Mark Kirchner, GER	26:02.3
1984	Erik Kvalfoss, NOR	30:53.8	1994	Sergei Chepikov, RUS	28:07.0
1988	Frank-Peter Roetsch, E. Ger	25:08.1			

20 kilometers

Year		Time	Year		Time
1960	Klas Lestander, SWE	1:33:21.6	1980	Anatoly Alyabyev, USSR	1:08:16.31
1964	Vladimir Melanin, USSR	1:20:26.8	1984	Peter Angerer, W. Ger	1:11:52.7
1968	Magnar Solberg, NOR	1:13:45.9	1988	Frank-Peter Roetsch, E. Ger	56:33.3
1972	Magnar Solberg, NOR	1:15:55.50	1992	Yevgeny Redkine, UT	57:34.4
1976	Nikolai Kruglov, USSR	1:14:12.26	1994	Sergei Tarasov, RUS	57:25.3

4x7.5-kilometer Relay

Year		Time	Year		Time	Year		Time
1968	Soviet Union	2:13:02.4	1980	Soviet Union	1:34:03.27	1992	Germany	1:24:43.5
1972	Soviet Union	1:51:44.92	1984	Soviet Union	1:38:51.7	1994	Germany	1:30:22.1
1976	Soviet Union	1:57:55.64	1988	Soviet Union	1:22:30.0			

WOMEN

Multiple gold medals (including relays): Myriam Bedard and Anfisa Reztsova (2). Note that Reztsova won a third gold medal in 1988 in the Cross-country 4x5-kilometer Relay.

7.5 kilometers

Year		Time	Year		Time
1992	Anfisa Reztsova, UT	24:29.2	1994	Myriam Bedard, CAN	26:08.8

15 kilometers

Year		Time	Year		Time
1992	Antje Misersky, GER	51:47.2	1994	Myriam Bedard, CAN	52:06.6

4 x 7.5 kilometer Relay

Year		Time	Year		Time
1992	France	1:15:55.6	1994	Russia	1:47:19.5

Note: Event featured three skiers per team in 1992.

Youngest and Oldest Gold Medalists in an Individual Event

Youngest: MEN— Toni Nieminen, Finland, Large Hill Ski Jumping, 1992 (16 years, 261 days); WOMEN—Sonja Henie, Norway, Figure Skating, 1928 (15 years, 315 days).

Oldest: MEN— Magnar Solberg, NOR, 20-km Biathlon, 1972 (35 years, 4 days); WOMEN— Christina Baas-Kaiser, Holland, 3,000m Speed Skating, 1972 (33 years, 268 days).

BOBSLED

Multiple gold medals: DRIVERS—Meinhard Nehmer (3); Billy Fiske, Wolfgang Hoppe, Eugenio Monti, Andreas Ostler and Gustav Weder (2). CREW—Bernard Germeshausen (3); Donat Acklin, Luciano De Paolis, Cliff Gray, Lorenz Nieberl and Dietmar Schauerhammer (2).

Two-Man

Year		Time	Year		Time
1932	United States (Hubert Stevens)	8:14.74	1972	West Germany (Wolfgang Zimmerer)	4:57.07
1936	United States (Ivan Brown)	5:29.29	1976	East Germany (Meinhard Nehmer)	3:44.42
1948	Switzerland (Felix Endrich)	5:29.2	1980	Switzerland (Erich Schärer)	4:09.36
1952	Germany (Andreas Ostler)	5:24.54	1984	East Germany (Wolfgang Hoppe)	3:25.56
1956	Italy (Lamberto Dalla Costa)	5:30.14	1988	Soviet Union (Jānis Kipurs)	3:54.19
1960	Not held		1992	Switzerland I (Gustav Weder)	4:03.26
1964	Great Britain (Anthony Nash)	4:21.90	1994	Switzerland I (Gustav Weder)	3:30.81
1968	Italy (Eugenio Monti)	4:41.54			

Four-Man

Year		Time	Year		Time
1924	Switzerland (Eduard Scherrer)	5:45.54	1968	Italy (Eugenio Monti)	2:17.39
1928	United States (Billy Fiske)	3:20.5	1972	Switzerland (Jean Wicki)	4:43.07
1932	United States (Billy Fiske)	7:53.68	1976	East Germany (Meinhard Nehmer)	3:40.43
1936	Switzerland (Pierre Musy)	5:19.85	1980	East Germany (Meinhard Nehmer)	3:59.92
1948	United States (Francis Tyler)	5:20.1	1984	East Germany (Wolfgang Hoppe)	3:20.22
1952	Germany (Andreas Ostler)	5:07.84	1988	Switzerland (Ekkehard Fasser)	3:47.51
1956	Switzerland (Franz Kapus)	5:10.44	1992	Austria I (Ingo Appelt)	3:53.90
1960	Not held		1994	Germany II (Harald Czudaj)	3:27.78
1964	Canada (Vic Emery)	4:14.46			

Note: Five-man sleds were used in 1928.

CROSS-COUNTRY SKIING

There have been two significant changes in men's and women's Cross-country racing since the end of the 1984 Winter Games in Sarajevo. First, the classical and freestyle (i.e., skating) techniques were designated for specific events beginning in 1988, and the Pursuit race was introduced in 1992.

MEN

Multiple gold medals (including relays): Bjorn Dählie (5); Sixten Jernberg, Gunde Svan, Thomas Wassberg and Nikolai Zimyatov (4); Veikko Hakulinen, Eero Mäntyranta and Vegard Ulvang (3); Hallgeir Brenden, Harald Grönningen, Thorlief Haug, Jan Ottoson, Päl Tyldum and Vyacheslav Vedenine (2).

Multiple gold medals (including Nordic Combined): Johan Gröttumsbråten and Thorlief Haug (3).

10-kilometer Classical

Year		Time	Year		Time
1924-88	Not held		1994	Bjorn Dählie, NOR	24:20.1
1992	Vegard Ulvang, NOR	27:36.0			

15-kilometer Freestyle Pursuit

A 15-km Freestyle race in which the starting order is determined by order of finish in the 10-km Classical race. Time given is combined time of both events.

Year		Time	Year		Time
1924-88	Not held		1994	Bjorn Dählie, NOR	1:00.08.8
1992	Bjorn Dählie, NOR	1:05:37.9			

15-kilometer Classical (Discont.)

Discontinued in 1992 and replaced by 15-km Freestyle Pursuit. Event was held over 18 kilometers from 1924-52.

Year		Time	Year		Time
1924	Thorleif Haug, NOR	1:14:31.0	1964	Eero Mäntyranta, FIN	50:54.1
1928	Johan Gröttumsbråten, NOR	1:37:01.0	1968	Harald Grönningen, NOR	47:54.2
1932	Sven Utterström, SWE	1:23:07.0	1972	Sven-Ake Lundbäck, SWE	45:28.24
1936	Erik-August Larsson, SWE	1:14:38.0	1976	Nikolai Bazhukov, USSR	43:58.47
1948	Martin Lundström, SWE	1:13:50.0	1980	Thomas Wassberg, SWE	41:57.63
1952	Hallgeir Brenden, NOR	1:01:34.0	1984	Gunde Svan, SWE	41:25.6
1956	Hallgeir Brenden, NOR	49:39.0	1988	Mikhail Devyatyarov, USSR	41:18.9
1960	Håkon Brusveen NOR	51:55.5			

30-kilometer Freestyle

Year		Time	Year		Time
1924-52	Not held		1976	Sergei Saveliev, USSR	1:30:29.38
1956	Veikko Hakulinen, FIN	1:44:06.0	1980	Nikolai Zimyatov, USSR	1:27:02.80
1960	Sixten Jernberg, SWE	1:51:03.9	1984	Nikolai Zimyatov, USSR	1:28:56.3
1964	Eero Mäntyranta, FIN	1:30:50.7	1988	Alexi Prokurorov, USSR	1:24:26.3
1968	Franco Nones, ITA	1:35:39.2	1992	Vegard Ulvang, NOR	1:22:27.8
1972	Vyacheslav Vedenine, USSR	1:36:31.15	1994	Thomas Alsgaard, NOR	1:12:26.4

Cross-country Skiing (Cont.)

MEN

50-kilometer Classical

Year		Time	Year		Time
1924	Thorleif Haug, NOR	3:44:32.0	1968	Ole Ellefsaeter, NOR	2:28:45.8
1928	Per Erik Hedlund, SWE	4:52:03.0	1972	Päl Tyldum, NOR	2:43:14.75
1932	Veli Saarinen, FIN	4:28:00.0	1976	Ivar Formo, NOR	2:37:30.05
1936	Elis Wiklund, SWE	3:30:11.0	1980	Nikolai Zimyatov, USSR	2:27:24.60
1948	Nils Karlsson, SWE	3:47:48.0	1984	Thomas Wassberg, SWE	2:15:55.8
1952	Veikko Hakulinen, FIN	3:33:33.0	1988	Gunde Svan, SWE	2:04:30.9
1956	Sixten Jernberg, SWE	2:50:27.0	1992	Bjorn Dählie, NOR	2:03:41.5
1960	Kalevi Hämäläinen, FIN	2:59:06.3	1994	Vladimir Smirnov, KAZ	2:07:20.3
1964	Sixten Jernberg, SWE	2:43:52.6			

4x10-kilometer Mixed Relay

Two Classical and two Freestyle legs.

Year		Time	Year		Time	Year		Time
1936	Finland	2:41:33.0	1964	Sweden	2:18:34.6	1984	Sweden	1:55:06.3
1948	Sweden	2:32:08.0	1968	Norway	2:08:33.5	1988	Sweden	1:43:58.6
1952	Finland	2:20:16.0	1972	Soviet Union	2:04:47.94	1992	Norway	1:39:26.0
1956	Soviet Union	2:15:30.0	1976	Finland	2:07:59.72	1994	Italy	1:41:15.0
1960	Finland	2:18:45.6	1980	Soviet Union	1:57:03.46			

WOMEN

Multiple gold medals (including relays): Lyubov Egorova (6); Galina Kulakova and Raisa Smetanina (4); Claudia Boyarskikh and Marja-Liisa Hämäläinen (3); Manuela Di Centa, Toini Gustafsson, Larisa Lazutina, Barbara Petzold and Elena Valbe (2).

Multiple gold medals (including relays and Biathlon): Anfisa Reztsova (2).

5-kilometer Classical

Year		Time	Year		Time
1952-60	Not held		1980	Raisa Smetanina, USSR	15:06.92
1964	Claudia Boyarskikh, USSR	17:50.5	1984	Marja-Liisa Hämäläinen, FIN	17:04.0
1968	Toini Gustafsson, SWE	16:45.2	1988	Marjo Matikainen, FIN	15:04.0
1972	Galina Kulakova, USSR	17:00.50	1992	Marjut Lukkarinen, FIN	14:13.8
1976	Helena Takalo, FIN	15:48.69	1994	Lyubov Egorova, RUS	14:08.8

10-kilometer Freestyle Pursuit

A 10-km Freestyle race in which the starting order is determined by order of finish in the 5-km Classical race. Time given is combined time of both events.

Year		Time	Year		Time
1952-88	Not held		1994	Lyubov Egorova, RUS	41:38.1
1992	Lyubov Egorova, UT	40:07.7			

10-kilometer Classical (Discont.)

Discontinued in 1992 and replaced by 10-km Freestyle Pursuit. Event was held over 18 kilometers from 1924-52.

Year		Time	Year		Time
1952	Lydia Wideman, FIN	41:40.0	1972	Galina Kulakova, USSR	34:17.82
1956	Lyubov Kosyreva, USSR	38:11.0	1976	Raisa Smetanina, USSR	30:13.41
1960	Maria Gusakova, USSR	39:46.6	1980	Barbara Petzold, E. Ger	30:31.54
1964	Claudia Boyarskikh, USSR	40:24.3	1984	Marja-Liisa Hämäläinen, FIN	31:44.2
1968	Toini Gustafsson, SWE	36:46.5	1988	Vida Venciene, USSR	30:08.3

15-kilometer Freestyle

Year		Time	Year		Time
1952-88	Not held		1994	Manuela Di Centa, ITA	39:44.5
1992	Lyubov Egorova, UT	42:20.8			

30-kilometer Classical

Event was held over 20 kilometers from 1984-88.

Year		Time	Year		Time
1984	Marja-Liisa Hämäläinen, FIN	1:01:45.0	1992	Stefania Belmondo, ITA	1:22:30.1
1988	Tamara Tikhonova, USSR	55:53.6	1994	Manuela Di Centa, ITA	1:25:41.6

4x5-kilometer Mixed Relay

Two Classical and two Freestyle legs. Event featured three skiers per team from 1956-72.

Year		Time	Year		Time	Year		Time
1956	Finland	1:09:01.0	1972	Soviet Union	48:46.15	1988	Soviet Union	59:51.1
1960	Sweden	1:04:21.4	1976	Soviet Union	1:07:49.75	1992	Unified Team	59:34.8
1964	Soviet Union	59:20.2	1980	East Germany	1:02:11.10	1994	Russia	57:12.5
1968	Norway	57:30.0	1984	Norway	1:06:49.7			

FIGURE SKATING

MEN

Multiple gold medals: Gillis Grafström (3); Dick Button and Karl Schäfer (2).

Year		
1908	Ulrich Salchow	SWE
1912	Not held	
1920	Gillis Grafström	SWE
1924	Gillis Grafström	SWE
1928	Gillis Grafström	SWE
1932	Karl Schäfer	AUT
1936	Karl Schäfer	AUT
1948	Dick Button	USA
1952	Dick Button	USA
1956	Hayes Alan Jenkins	USA
1960	David Jenkins	USA
1964	Manfred Schnelldorfer	GER
1968	Wolfgang Schwarz	AUT
1972	Ondrej Nepela	CZE
1976	John Curry	GBR
1980	Robin Cousins	GBR
1984	Scott Hamilton	USA
1988	Brian Boitano	USA
1992	Victor Petrenko	UT
1994	Alexei Urmanov	RUS

WOMEN

Multiple gold medals: Sonja Henie (3); Katarina Witt (2).

Year		
1908	Madge Syers	GBR
1912	Not held	
1920	Magda Julin-Mauroy	SWE
1924	Herma Planck-Szabö	AUT
1928	Sonja Henie	NOR
1932	Sonja Henie	NOR
1936	Sonja Henie	NOR
1948	Barbara Ann Scott	CAN
1952	Jeanette Altwegg	GBR
1956	Tenley Albright	USA
1960	Carol Heiss	USA
1964	Sjoukje Dijkstra	NET
1968	Peggy Fleming	USA
1972	Beatrix Schuba	AUT
1976	Dorothy Hamill	USA
1980	Anett Pötzsch	E. Ger
1984	Katarina Witt	E. Ger
1988	Katarina Witt	E. Ger
1992	Kristi Yamaguchi	USA
1994	Oksana Baiul	UKR

Pairs

Multiple gold medals: MEN—Pierre Brunet, Sergei Grinkov, Oleg Protopopov and Aleksandr Zaitsev (2). WOMEN—Irina Rodnina (3); Ludmila Belousova, Ekaterina Gordeeva and Andrée Joly Brunet (2).

Year		
1908	Anna Hübler & Heinrich Burger	Germany
1912	Not held	
1920	Ludovika & Walter Jakobsson	Finland
1924	Helene Engelmann & Alfred Berger	Austria
1928	Andrée Joly & Pierre Brunet	France
1932	Andrée & Pierre Brunet	France
1936	Maxi Herber & Ernst Baier	Germany
1948	Micheline Lannoy & Pierre Baugniet	Belgium
1952	Ria & Paul Falk	Germany
1956	Elisabeth Schwartz & Kurt Oppelt	Austria
1960	Barbara Wagner & Robert Paul	Canada
1964	Ludmila Belousova & Oleg Protopopov	USSR
1968	Ludmila Belousova & Oleg Protopopov	USSR
1972	Irina Rodnina & Aleksei Ulanov	USSR
1976	Irina Rodnina & Aleksandr Zaitsev	USSR
1980	Irina Rodnina & Aleksandr Zaitsev	USSR
1984	Elena Valova & Oleg Vasiliev	USSR
1988	Ekaterina Gordeeva & Sergei Grinkov	USSR
1992	Natalya Mishkutienok & Arthur Dmitriev	UT
1994	Ekaterina Gordeeva & Sergei Grinkov	RUS

Ice Dancing

Year		
1976	Lyudmila Pakhomova & Aleksandr Gorshkov	USSR
1980	Natalia Linichuk & Gennady Karponosov	USSR
1984	Jayne Torvill & Christopher Dean	Great Britain
1988	Natalia Bestemianova & Andrei Bukin	USSR
1992	Marina Klimova & Sergei Ponomarenko	UT
1994	Oksana Gritschuk & Yevgeny Platov	RUS

ICE HOCKEY

Multiple gold medals: Soviet Union/Unified Team (8); Canada (6); United States (2).

Year	
1920	**Canada**, United States Czechoslovakia
1924	**Canada**, United States, Great Britain
1928	**Canada**, Sweden, Switzerland
1932	**Canada**, United States, Germany
1936	**Great Britain**, Canada, United States
1948	**Canada**, Czechoslovakia, Switzerland
1952	**Canada**, United States, Sweden
1956	**Soviet Union**, United States, Canada
1960	**United States**, Canada, Soviet Union
1964	**Soviet Union**, Sweden, Czechoslovakia
1968	**Soviet Union**, Czechoslovakia, Canada
1972	**Soviet Union**, United States, Czechoslovakia
1976	**Soviet Union**, Czechoslovakia, West Germany
1980	**United States**, Soviet Union, Sweden
1984	**Soviet Union**, Czechoslovakia, Sweden
1988	**Soviet Union**, Finland, Sweden
1992	**Unified Team**, Canada, Czechoslovakia
1994	**Sweden**, Canada, Finland

U.S. Gold Medal Hockey Teams

1960

Forwards: Billy Christian, Roger Christian, Billy Cleary, Gene Grazia, Paul Johnson, Bob McVey, Dick Meredith, Weldy Olson, Dick Rodenheiser and Tom Williams. **Defensemen:** Bob Cleary, Jack Kirrane (captain), John Mayasich, Bob Owen and Rod Paavola. **Goaltenders:** Jack McCartan and Larry Palmer. **Coach:** Jack Riley.

1980

Forwards: Neal Broten, Steve Christoff, Mike Eruzione (captain), John Harrington, Mark Johnson, Rob McClanahan, Mark Pavelich, Buzz Schneider, Dave Silk, Eric Strobel, Phil Verchota and Mark Wells. **Defensemen:** Bill Baker, Dave Christian, Ken Morrow, Jack O'Callahan, Mike Ramsey and Bob Suter. **Goaltenders:** Jim Craig and Steve Janaszak. **Coach:** Herb Brooks.

LUGE

MEN

Multiple gold medals: (including doubles): Norbert Hahn, Georg Hackl, Paul Hildgartner, Thomas Köhler and Hans Rinn (2).

Singles

Year		Time
1964	Thomas Köhler, GER	3:26.77
1968	Manfred Schmid, AUT	2:52.48
1972	Wolfgang Scheidel, E. Ger	3:27.58
1976	Dettlef Günther, E. Ger	3:27.688
1980	Bernhard Glass, E. Ger	2:54.796
1984	Paul Hildgartner, ITA	3:04.258
1988	Jens Müller, E. Ger	3:05.548
1992	Georg Hackl, GER	3:02.363
1994	Georg Hackl, GER	3:21.571

Doubles

Year		Time
1964	Austria	1:41.62
1968	East Germany	1:35.85
1972	(TIE) East Germany	1:28.35
	& Italy	1.28.35
1976	East Germany	1:25.604
1980	East Germany	1:19.331
1984	West Germany	1:23.620
1988	East Germany	1:31.940
1992	Germany	1:32.053
1994	Italy	1:36.720

WOMEN

Multiple gold medals: Steffi Martin Walter (2).

Singles

Year		Time
1964	Ortrun Enderlein, GER	3:24.67
1968	Erica Lechner, ITA	2:28.66
1972	Anna-Maria Müller, E. Ger	2:59.18
1976	Margit Schumann, E. Ger	2:50.621
1980	Vera Zozulya, USSR	2:36.537
1984	Steffi Martin, E. Ger	2:46.570
1988	Steffi Martin Walter, E. Ger	3:03.973
1992	Doris Neuner, AUT	3:06.696
1994	Gerda Weissensteiner, ITA	3:15.517

NORDIC COMBINED

Multiple gold medals: Ulrich Wehling (3); Johan Gröttumsbråten (2).

Individual

Year		Points
1924	Thorleif Haug, NOR	18.906
1928	Johan Gröttumsbråten, NOR	17.833
1932	Johan Gröttumsbråten, NOR	446.00
1936	Oddbjörn Hagen, NOR	430.3
1948	Heikki Hasu, FIN	448.80
1952	Simon Slattvik, NOR	451.621
1956	Sverre Stenersen, NOR	455.000
1960	Georg Thoma, GER	457.952
1964	Tormod Knutsen, NOR	469.28
1968	Franz Keller, W. Ger	449.04
1972	Ulrich Wehling, E. Ger	413.340
1976	Ulrich Wehling, E. Ger	423.39
1980	Ulrich Wehling, E. Ger	432.200
1984	Tom Sandberg, NOR	422.595
1988	Hippolyt Kempf, SWI	432.230
1992	Fabrice Guy, FRA	426.470
1994	Fred Borre Lundberg, NOR	457.970

Team

Year		Points
1924-84	Not held	
1988	West Germany	792.08
1992	Japan	1247.180
1994	Japan	1368.860

SKI JUMPING

Multiple gold medals (including team jumping): Matti Nykänen (4); Jens Weissflog (3); Birger Ruud and Toni Nieminen (2).

Normal Hill—70 Meters

Year		Points
1924-60	Not held	
1964	Veikko Kankkonen, FIN	229.9
1968	Jiri Raska, CZE	216.5
1972	Yukio Kasaya, JPN	244.2
1976	Hans-Georg Aschenbach, E. Ger	252.0
1980	Anton Innauer, AUT	266.3
1984	Jens Weissflog, E. Ger	215.2
1988	Matti Nykänen, FIN	229.1
1992	Ernst Vettori, AUT	222.8
1994	Espen Bredesen, NOR	282.0

Large Hill—90 Meters

Year		Points	Year		Points
1924	Jacob Tullin Thams, NOR	18.960	1968	Vladimir Beloussov, USSR	231.3
1928	Alf Andersen, NOR	19.208	1972	Wojciech Fortuna, POL	219.9
1932	Birger Ruud, NOR	228.1	1976	Karl Schnabl, AUT	234.8
1936	Birger Ruud, NOR	232.0	1980	Jouko Törmänen, FIN	271.0
1948	Petter Hugsted, NOR	228.1	1984	Matti Nykänen, FIN	231.2
1952	Arnfinn Bergmann, NOR	226.0	1988	Matti Nykänen, FIN	224.0
1956	Antti Hyvärinen, FIN	227.0	1992	Toni Nieminen, FIN	239.5
1960	Helmut Recknagel, GER	227.2	1994	Jens Weissflog, GER	274.5
1964	Toralf Engan, NOR	230.7			

Note: Jump held at various lengths from 1924-56; at 80 meters from 1960-64; at 90 meters from 1968-88; and at 120 meters in 1992.

Team Large Hill

Year		Points	Year		Points
1924-84	Not held		1992	Finland	644.4
1988	Finland	634.4	1994	Germany	970.1

SPEED SKATING

MEN

Multiple gold medals: Eric Heiden and Clas Thunberg (5); Ivar Ballangrud, Yevgeny Grishin and Johann Olav Koss (4); Hjalmar Andersen, Tomas Gustafson, Irving Jaffee and Ard Schenk (3); Gaétan Boucher, Knut Johannesen, Erhard Keller, Uwe-Jens Mey and Jack Shea (2). Note that Thunberg's total includes the All-Around, which was contested for the only time in 1924.

500 meters

Year		Time		Year		Time	
1924	Charles Jewtraw, USA	44.0		1964	Terry McDermott, USA	40.1	OR
1928	(TIE) Bernt Evensen, NOR	43.4	OR	1968	Erhard Keller, W. Ger	40.3	
	& Clas Thunberg, FIN	43.4	OR	1972	Erhard Keller, W. Ger	39.44	OR
1932	Jack Shea, USA	43.4	=OR	1976	Yevgeny Kulikov, USSR	39.17	OR
1936	Ivar Ballangrud, NOR	43.4	=OR	1980	Eric Heiden, USA	38.03	OR
1948	Finn Helgesen, NOR	43.1	OR	1984	Sergei Fokichev, USSR	38.19	
1952	Ken Henry, USA	43.2		1988	Uwe-Jens Mey, E. Ger	36.45	WR
1956	Yevgeny Grishin, USSR	40.2	=WR	1992	Uwe-Jens Mey, GER	37.14	
1960	Yevgeny Grishin, USSR	40.2	=WR	1994	Aleksandr Golubev, RUS	36.33	OR

1000 meters

Year		Time		Year		Time	
1924-72	Not held			1988	Nikolai Gulyaev, USSR	1:13.03	OR
1976	Peter Mueller, USA	1:19.32		1992	Olaf Zinke, GER	1:14.85	
1980	Eric Heiden, USA	1:15.18	OR	1994	Dan Jansen, USA	1:12.43	WR
1984	Gaétan Boucher, CAN	1:15.80					

1500 meters

Year		Time		Year		Time	
1924	Clas Thunberg, FIN	2:20.8		1964	Ants Antson, USSR	2:10.3	
1928	Clas Thunberg, FIN	2:21.1		1968	Kees Verkerk, NET	2:03.4	OR
1932	Jack Shea, USA	2:57.5		1972	Ard Schenk, NET	2:02.96	OR
1936	Charles Mathisen, NOR	2:19.2	OR	1976	Jan Egil Storholt, NOR	1:59.38	OR
1948	Sverre Farstad, NOR	2:17.6	OR	1980	Eric Heiden, USA	1:55.44	OR
1952	Hjalmar Andersen, NOR	2:20.4		1984	Gaétan Boucher, CAN	1:58.36	
1956	(TIE)Yevgeny Grishin, USSR	2:08.6	WR	1988	André Hoffman, E. Ger	1:52.06	WR
	& Yuri Mikhailov, USSR	2:08.6	WR	1992	Johann Olav Koss, NOR	1:54.81	
1960	(TIE) Roald Aas, NOR	2:10.4		1994	Johann Olav Koss, NOR	1:51.29	WR
	& Yevgeny Grishin, USSR	2:10.4					

5000 meters

Year		Time		Year		Time	
1924	Clas Thunberg, FIN	8:39.0		1968	Fred Anton Maier, NOR	7:22.4	WR
1928	Ivar Ballangrud, NOR	8:50.5		1972	Ard Schenk, NET	7:23.61	
1932	Irving Jaffee, USA	9:40.8		1976	Sten Stensen, NOR	7:24.48	
1936	Ivar Ballangrud, NOR	8:19.6	OR	1980	Eric Heiden, USA	7:02.29	OR
1948	Reidar Liaklev, NOR	8:29.4		1984	Tomas Gustafson, SWE	7:12.28	
1952	Hjalmar Andersen, NOR	8:10.6	OR	1988	Tomas Gustafson, SWE	6:44.63	WR
1956	Boris Shilkov, USSR	7:48.7	OR	1992	Geir Karlstad, NOR	6:59.97	
1960	Viktor Kosichkin, USSR	7:51.3		1994	Johann Olav Koss, NOR	6:34.96	WR
1964	Knut Johannesen, NOR	7:38.4	OR				

Speed Skating (Cont.)

MEN

10,000 meters

Year		Time		Year		Time	
1924	Julius Skutnabb, FIN	18:04.8		1968	Johnny Höglin, SWE	15:23.6	OR
1928	Irving Jaffee, USA*	18:36.5		1972	Ard Schenk, NET	15:01.35	OR
1932	Irving Jaffee, USA	19:13.6		1976	Piet Kleine, NET	14:50.59	OR
1936	Ivar Ballangrud, NOR	17:24.3	OR	1980	Eric Heiden, USA	14:28.13	WR
1948	Ake Seyffarth, SWE	17:26.3		1984	Igor Malkov, USSR	14:39.90	
1952	Hjalmar Andersen, NOR	16:45.8	OR	1988	Tomas Gustafson, SWE	13:48.20	WR
1956	Sigvard Ericsson, SWE	16:35.9	OR	1992	Bart Veldkamp, NET	14:12.12	
1960	Knut Johannesen, NOR	15:46.6	WR	1994	Johann Olav Koss, NOR	13:30.55	WR
1964	Jonny Nilsson, SWE	15:50.1					

*Unofficial, according to the IOC. Jaffee recorded the fastest time, but the event was called off in progress due to thawing ice.

WOMEN

Multiple gold medals: Lydia Skoblikova (6); Bonnie Blair (5); Karin Enke and Yvonne van Gennip (3); Tatiana Averina, Gunda Niemann and Christa Rothenburger (2).

500 meters

Year		Time		Year		Time	
1960	Helga Haase, GER	45.9		1980	Karin Enke, E. Ger	41.78	OR
1964	Lydia Skoblikova, USSR	45.0	OR	1984	Christa Rothenburger, E. Ger	41.02	OR
1968	Lyudmila Titova, USSR	46.1		1988	Bonnie Blair, USA	39.10	WR
1972	Anne Henning, USA	43.33	OR	1992	Bonnie Blair, USA	40.33	
1976	Sheila Young, USA	42.76	OR	1994	Bonnie Blair, USA	39.25	

1000 meters

Year		Time		Year		Time	
1960	Klara Guseva, USSR	1:34.1		1980	Natalia Petruseva, USSR	1:24.10	OR
1964	Lydia Skoblikova, USSR	1:33.2	OR	1984	Karin Enke, E. Ger	1:21.61	OR
1968	Carolina Geijssen, NET	1:32.6	OR	1988	Christa Rothenburger, E. Ger	1:17.65	WR
1972	Monika Pflug, W. Ger	1:31.40	OR	1992	Bonnie Blair, USA	1:21.90	
1976	Tatiana Averina, USSR	1:28.43	OR	1994	Bonnie Blair, USA	1:18.74	

1500 meters

Year		Time		Year		Time	
1960	Lydia Skoblikova, USSR	2:25.2	WR	1980	Annie Borckink, NET	2:10.95	OR
1964	Lydia Skoblikova, USSR	2:22.6	OR	1984	Karin Enke, E. Ger	2:03.42	WR
1968	Kaija Mustonen, FIN	2:22.4	OR	1988	Yvonne van Gennip, NET	2:00.68	OR
1972	Dianne Holum, USA	2:20.85	OR	1992	Jacqueline Börner, GER	2:05.87	
1976	Galina Stepanskaya, USSR	2:16.58	OR	1994	Emese Hunyady, AUT	2:02.19	

3000 meters

Year		Time		Year		Time	
1960	Lydia Skoblikova, USSR	5:14.3		1980	Bjorg Eva Jensen, NOR	4:32.13	OR
1964	Lydia Skoblikova, USSR	5:14.9		1984	Andrea Schöne, E. Ger	4:24.79	OR
1968	Johanna Schut, NET	4:56.2	OR	1988	Yvonne van Gennip, NET	4:11.94	WR
1972	Christina Baas-Kaiser, NET	4:52.14	OR	1992	Gunda Niemann, GER	4:19.90	
1976	Tatiana Averina, USSR	4:45.19	OR	1994	Svetlana Bazhanova, RUS	4:17.43	

5000 meters

Year		Time		Year		Time	
1960-84	Not held			1992	Gunda Niemann, GER	7:31.57	
1988	Yvonne van Gennip, NET	7:14.13	WR	1994	Claudia Pechstein, GER	7:14.37	

Athletes with Winter and Summer Medals

Only three athletes have won medals in both the Winter and Summer Olympics:

Eddie Eagan, USA— Light Heavyweight Boxing gold (1920) and Four-man Bobsled gold (1932).

Jacob Tullin Thams, Norway— Ski Jumping gold (1924) and 8-meter Yachting silver (1936).

Christa Luding-Rothenburger, East Germany— Speed Skating gold at 500 meters (1984) and 1,000m (1988), silver at 500m (1988) and bronze at 500m (1992) and Match Sprint Cycling silver (1988). Luding-Rothenburger is the only athlete to ever win medals in both Winter and Summer Games in the same year.

All-Time Leading Medal Winners

MEN

No		Sport	G-S-B
9	Sixten Jernberg, SWE	Cross-country	4-3-2
8	Bjorn Dählie, NOR	Cross-country	5-3-0
7	Clas Thunberg, FIN	Speed Skating	5-1-1
7	Ivar Ballangrud, NOR	Speed Skating	4-2-1
7	Veikko Hakulinen, FIN	Cross-country	3-3-1
7	Eero Mäntyranta, FIN	Cross-country	3-2-2
7	Bogdan Musiol, E. Ger/GER	Bobsled	1-5-1
6	Gunde Svan, SWE	Cross-country	4-1-1
6	Vegard Ulvang, NOR	Cross-country	3-2-1
6	Johan Gröttumsbraten, NOR	Nordic	3-1-2
6	Wolfgang Hoppe, E. Ger/GER	Bobsled	2-3-1
6	Eugenio Monti, ITA	Bobsled	2-2-2
6	Roald Larsen, NOR	Speed Skating	0-2-4
5	**Eric Heiden, USA**	Speed Skating	5-0-0
5	Yevgeny Grishin, USSR	Speed Skating	4-1-0
5	Johann Olav Koss, NOR	Speed Skating	4-1-0
5	Matti Nykänen, FIN	Ski Jumping	4-1-0
5	Aleksandr Tikhonov, USSR	Biathlon	4-1-0
5	Nikolai Zimyatov, USSR	Cross-country	4-1-0
5	Alberto Tomba, ITA	Alpine	3-2-0
5	Harald Grönningen, NOR	Cross-country	2-3-0
5	Pål Tyldum, NOR	Cross-country	2-3-0
5	Knut Johannesen, NOR	Speed Skating	2-2-1
5	Vladimir Smirnov, USSR/UT/KAZ	X-country	1-4-0
5	Kjetil André Aamodt, NOR	Alpine	1-2-2
5	Peter Angerer, W. Ger/GER	Biathlon	1-2-2
5	Juha Mieto, FIN	Cross-country	1-2-2
5	Fritz Feierabend, SWI	Bobsled	0-3-2

WOMEN

No		Sport	G-S-B
10	Raisa Smetanina, USSR/UT	Cross-country	4-5-1
9	Lyubov Egorova, UT/RUS	Cross-country	6-3-0
8	Galina Kulakova, USSR	Cross-country	4-2-2
8	Karin (Enke) Kania, E. Ger	Speed Skating	3-4-1
7	Marja-Liisa (Hämäläinen) Kirvesniemi, FIN	Cross-country	3-0-4
7	Andrea (Mitscherlich, Schöne) Ehrig, E. Ger	Speed Skating	1-5-1
6	Lydia Skoblikova, USSR	Speed Skating	6-0-0
6	**Bonnie Blair, USA**	Speed Skating	5-0-1
6	Manuela Di Centa, ITA	Cross-country	2-2-2
6	Elena Valbe, UT/RUS	Cross-country	2-0-4
5	Anfisa Reztsova, USSR/UT	CC/Biathlon	3-1-1
5	Vreni Schneider, SWI	Alpine	3-1-1
5	Gunda Neimann, GER	Speed Skating	2-2-1
5	Helena Takalo, FIN	Cross-country	1-3-1
5	Stefania Belmondo, ITA	Cross-country	1-1-3
5	Alevtina Kolchina, USSR	Cross-country	1-1-3

Games Medaled In

MEN— **Aamodt** (1992,94); **Angerer** (1980,84,88); **Ballangrud** (1928,32,36); **Dählie** (1992,94); **Feierabend** (1936,48,52); **Grishin** (1956,60,64); **Gröttumsbraten** (1924,28,32); **Grönningen** (1960,64,68); **Hakulinen** (1952,56,60); **Heiden** (1980); **Hoppe** (1984,88,92,94); **Jernberg** (1956,60,64); **Johannesen** (1956,60,64); **Koss** (1992,94). **Larsen** (1924,28); **Mäntyranta** (1960,64,68); **Mieto** (1976,80,84); **Monti** (1956,60,64,68); **Musiol** (1980,84,88,92); **Nykänen** (1984,88); **Smirnov** (1988,92,94); **Svan** (1984,88); **Thunberg** (1924,28); **Tikhonov** (1968,72,76,80); **Tomba** (1988,92,94); **Tyldum** (1968,72,76); **Ulvang** (1988,92,94); **Zimyatov** (1980,84).

WOMEN— **Belmondo** (1992,94); **Blair** (1988,92,94); **Di Centa** (1992,94); **Egorova** (1992,94); **Ehrig** (1976,80,84,88); **Kania** (1980,84,88); **Kirvesniemi** (1984,88,94); **Kolchina** (1956,64,68); **Kulakova** (1968,72,76,80); **Niemann** (1992-94); **Reztsova** (1988,92,94); **Schneider** (1988,92,94); **Skoblikova** (1960,64); **Smetanina** (1976,80,84,88,92); **Takalo** (1972,76,80); **Valbe** (1992,94).

Most Gold Medals

MEN

No		Sport	G-S-B
5	Bjorn Dählie, NOR	Cross-country	5-3-0
5	Clas Thunberg, FIN	Speed Skating	5-1-1
5	**Eric Heiden, USA**	Speed Skating	5-0-0
4	Sixten Jernberg, SWE	Cross-country	4-3-2
4	Ivar Ballangrud, NOR	Speed Skating	4-2-1
4	Gunde Svan, SWE	Cross-country	4-1-1
4	Yevgeny Grishin, USSR	Speed Skating	4-1-0
4	Johann Olav Koss, NOR	Speed Skating	4-1-0
4	Matti Nykänen, FIN	Ski Jumping	4-1-0
4	Aleksandr Tikhonov, USSR	Biathlon	4-1-0
4	Nikolai Zimyatov, USSR	Cross-country	4-1-0
4	Thomas Wassberg, SWE	Cross-country	4-0-0
3	Veikko Hakulinen, FIN	Cross-country	3-3-1
3	Eero Mäntyranta, FIN	Cross-country	3-2-2
3	Vegard Ulvang, NOR	Cross-country	3-2-1
3	Alberto Tomba, ITA	Alpine	3-2-0
3	Johan Gröttumsbråten, NOR	Nordic	3-1-2
3	Bernhard Germeshausen, E. Ger	Bobsled	3-1-0
3	Gillis Grafström, SWE	Figure Skating	3-1-0
3	Tomas Gustafson, SWE	Speed Skating	3-1-0
3	Vladislav Tretiak, USSR	Ice Hockey	3-1-0
3	Jens Weissflog, E. Ger/GER	Ski Jumping	3-1-0
3	Meinhard Nehmer, E. Ger	Bobsled	3-0-1
3	Hjalmar Andersen, NOR	Speed Skating	3-0-0
3	Vitaly Davydov, USSR	Ice Hockey	3-0-0
3	Anatoly Firsov, USSR	Ice Hockey	3-0-0
3	Thorleif Haug, NOR	Cross-country	3-0-0
3	**Irving Jaffee, USA**	Speed Skating	3-0-0
3	Andrei Khomoutov, USSR/UT	Ice Hockey	3-0-0
3	Jean-Claude Killy, FRA	Alpine	3-0-0
3	Viktor Kuzkin, USSR	Ice Hockey	3-0-0
3	Aleksandr Ragulin, USSR	Ice Hockey	3-0-0
3	Toni Sailer, AUT	Alpine	3-0-0
3	Ard Schenk, NET	Speed Skating	3-0-0
3	Ulrich Wehling, E. Ger	Ski Jumping	3-0-0

WOMEN

No		Sport	G-S-B
6	Lyubov Egorova, UT/RUS	Cross-country	6-3-0
6	Lydia Skoblikova, USSR	Speed Skating	6-0-0
5	**Bonnie Blair, USA**	Speed Skating	5-0-1
4	Raisa Smetanina, USSR/UT	Cross-country	4-5-1
4	Galina Kulakova, USSR	Cross-country	4-2-2
3	Karin (Enke) Kania, E. GER	Speed Skating	3-4-1
3	Anfisa Reztsova, USSR/UT	CC/Biathlon	3-1-1
3	Vreni Schneider, SWI	Alpine	3-1-1
3	Marja-Liisa (Hämäläinen) Kirvesniemi, FIN	Cross-country	3-0-4
3	Claudia Boyarskikh, USSR	Cross-country	3-0-0
3	Sonja Henie, NOR	Figure Skating	3-0-0
3	Irina Rodnina, USSR	Figure Skating	3-0-0
3	Yvonne van Gennip, NET	Speed Skating	3-0-0

All-Time Leading USA Medalists

MEN

No		Sport	G-S-B
5	Eric Heiden	Speed Skating	5-0-0
3*	Irving Jaffee	Speed Skating	3-0-0
3	Pat Martin	Bobsled	1-2-0
3	John Heaton	Bobsled/Cresta	0-2-1
2	Dick Button	Figure Skating	2-0-0
2†	Eddie Eagan	Boxing/Bobsled	2-0-0
2	Billy Fiske	Bobsled	2-0-0
2	Cliff Gray	Bobsled	2-0-0
2	Jack Shea	Speed Skating	2-0-0
2	Billy Cleary	Ice Hockey	1-1-0
2	Jennison Heaton	Bobsled/Cresta	1-1-0
2	John Mayasich	Ice Hockey	1-1-0
2	Terry McDermott	Speed Skating	1-1-0
2	Dick Meredith	Ice Hockey	1-1-0
2	Tommy Moe	Alpine	1-1-0
2	Weldy Olson	Ice Hockey	1-1-0
2	Dick Rodenheiser	Ice Hockey	1-1-0
2	David Jenkins	Figure Skating	1-1-0
2	Stan Benham	Bobsled	0-2-0
2	Herb Drury	Ice Hockey	0-2-0
2	Eric Flaim	Sp. Skate/ST Sp. Skate	0-2-0
2	Frank Synott	Ice Hockey	0-2-0
2	John Garrison	Ice Hockey	0-1-1

WOMEN

No		Sport	G-S-B
6	Bonnie Blair	Speed Skating	5-0-1
4	Cathy Turner	ST Sp. Skating	2-1-1
4	Dianne Holum	Speed Skating	1-2-1
3	Sheila Young	Speed Skating	1-1-1
3	Leah Poulos Mueller	Speed Skating	0-3-0
3	Beatrix Loughran	Figure Skating	0-2-1
3	Amy Peterson	ST Sp. Skating	0-2-1
2	Andrea Mead Lawrence	Alpine	2-0-0
2	Tenley Albright	Figure Skating	1-1-0
2	Gretchen Fraser	Alpine	1-1-0
2	Carol Heiss	Figure Skating	1-1-0
2	Diann Roffe-Steinrotter	Alpine	1-1-0
2	Anne Henning	Speed Skating	1-0-1
2	Penny Pitou	Alpine	0-2-0
2	Nancy Kerrigan	Figure Skating	0-1-1
2	Jean Saubert	Alpine	0-1-1
2	Nikki Ziegelmeyer	ST Sp. Skating	0-1-1

Notes: The Cresta run is undertaken on a heavy sled ridden head first in the prone position and has only been held at St. Moritz in 1928 and '48. Also, the term ST Sp. Skating refers to Short Track (or pack) Speed Skating.

*Jaffee is generally given credit for a third gold medal in the 10,000-meter Speed Skating race of 1928. He had the fastest time before the race was cancelled due to thawing ice. The IOC considers the race unofficial.

†Eagan won the Light Heavyweight boxing title at the 1920 Summer Games in Antwerp and the four-man Bobsled at the 1932 Winter Games in Lake Placid. He is the only athlete ever to win gold medals in both the Winter and Summer Olympics.

All-Time Medal Standings, 1924-94

All-time Winter Games medal standings, according to *The Golden Book of the Olympic Games* and updated through 1994. Medal counts include figure skating medals (1908 and '20) and hockey medals (1920) awarded at the Summer Games. National medal standings for the Winter and Summer Games are not recognized by the IOC.

		G	S	B	Total
1	Norway	73	77	64	214
2	Soviet Union (1956-88)	78	57	59	194
3	**United States**	53	56	37	146
4	Austria	36	48	44	128
5	East Germany (1956-88)	43	39	36	118
6	Finland	36	45	42	123
7	Sweden	39	26	34	99
8	Switzerland	27	29	29	85
9	Italy	25	21	21	67
10	Germany (1928-36,92—)	23	21	17	61
11	Canada	19	20	25	64
12	West Germany (1952-88)	18	20	19	57
13	France	16	16	21	53
14	Netherlands	14	19	17	50
15	Russia (1994—)	12	8	4	24
16	Unified Team (1992)	9	6	8	23
17	Great Britain	7	4	12	23
18	Czechoslovakia (1924-92)	2	8	16	26
19	Japan	3	8	8	19
20	South Korea	6	2	2	10
21	Liechtenstein	2	2	5	9
22	China	0	4	2	6
23	Hungary	0	2	4	6
24	Belgium	1	1	2	4
	Poland	1	1	2	4
	Yugoslavia (1924-88)	0	3	1	4
	Kazakhstan (1994—)	1	2	0	3
28	Spain	1	0	1	2
	Ukraine (1994—)	1	0	1	2
	Belarus (1994—)	0	2	0	2
	Luxembourg	0	2	0	2
32	Slovenia (1992—)	0	0	3	3
	North Korea	0	1	1	2
	Uzbekistan (1994—)	1	0	0	1
35	New Zealand	0	1	0	1
36	Australia	0	0	1	1
	Bulgaria	0	0	1	1
	Romania	0	0	1	1

Combined totals	G	S	B	Total
USSR/UT/Russia	99	71	71	241
Germany/E. Ger/W. Ger	84	80	72	236

Notes: Athletes from the USSR participated in the Winter Games from 1956-88, returned as the Unified Team in 1992 after the breakup of the Soviet Union (in 1991) and then competed for the independent republics of Belarus, Kazakhstan, Russia, Ukraine, Uzbekistan and three others in 1994. Yugoslavia divided into Croatia and Bosnia-Herzegovina in 1991, while Czechoslovakia split into Slovenia and the Czech Republic the same year.

Germany was barred from the Olympics in 1924 and 1948 as an aggressor nation in both World Wars I and II. Divided into East and West Germany after WWII, both countries competed under one flag from 1952-64, then as separate teams from 1968-88. Germany was reunified in 1990.

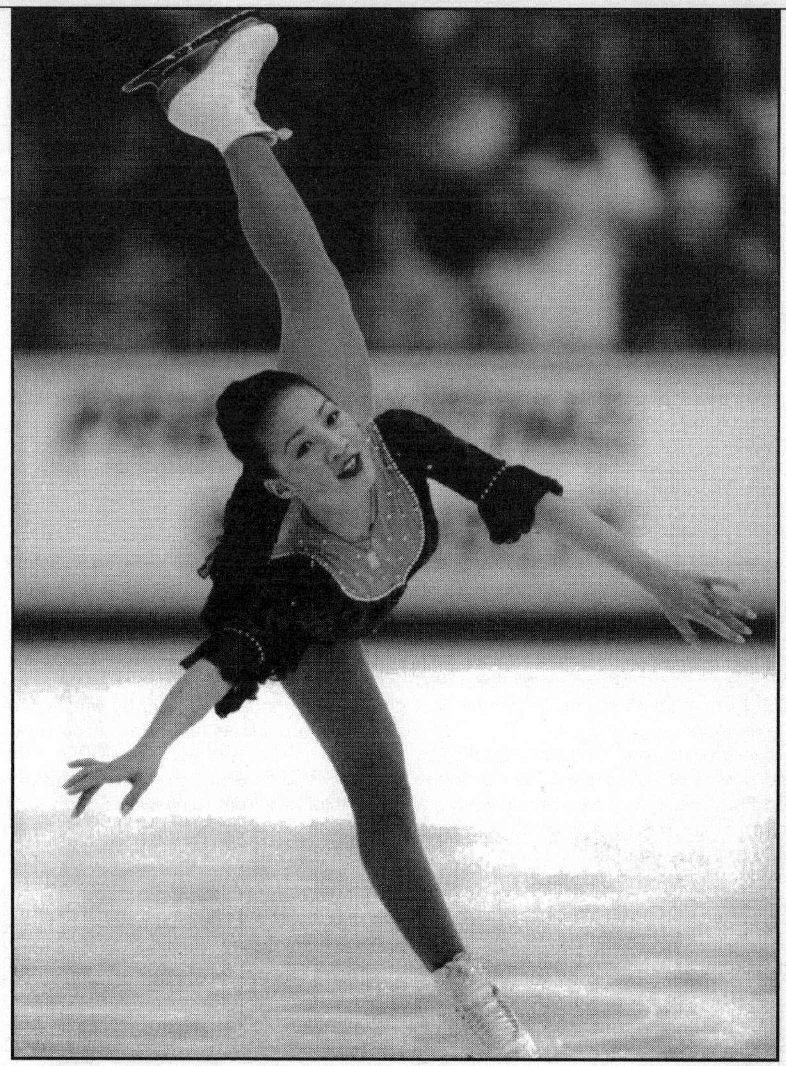

Wide World Photos

In 1996, fifteen-year old **Michelle Kwan** of the United States became the youngest American to ever win the world figure skating championship.

INTERNATIONAL SPORTS

by Philip Hersh

Ice Time

Figure skating continues to grow in popularity and Michelle Kwan and Todd Eldredge lead the way

In a Summer Olympic year, winter sports usually are put on ice in terms of attention and interest.

Not so figure skating. The sport continues to command high TV ratings, and the double victory of U.S. singles skaters Michelle Kwan and Todd Eldredge at the 1996 World Championships can only pique that interest more.

Their triumphs and the soap operatic ups and downs of U.S. skaters Nicole Bobek and Rudy Galindo were among the highlights of an international sports year dominated by the Atlanta Games. Other performances of note included Miguel Indurain's failure to win a sixth Tour de France, Alberto Tomba's first ski world titles and the continued downhill brilliance of Picabo Street.

A look at the rest, sport-by-sport:

Figure Skating. It was another boom year for the sport, which has become the No. 2 rated TV sports attraction in the United States—after the National Football League. With live, delayed and repeat shows, a person zapping through over-the-air and cable offerings was likely to find a figure skating broadcast at what seemed every hour of the day and night.

For Olympic-eligible skaters, the season offered a plethora of ways to get rich, including World (and European) Championship prize money and a new Champions Series, which linked five existing invitational events as qualifiers for a Champions Series final.

No one made more hay from the possibilities than 15-year-old Michelle Kwan of the U.S., who made $140,000 by winning the Champions Series Final and three series events, then added $50,000 as the youngest U.S. world champion in history. Her total take from competitions of all sorts, including Pro-Ams, was $315,000. Kwan also won a big prize with no financial reward—her first U.S. title.

At the world meet in Edmonton, Todd Eldredge won the men's singles, giving the U.S. its first singles sweep since 1986 and its first men's champion since 1988. Both victories came during free skate finals of surpassing quality.

In the men's event, all three medalists—Eldredge, Ilya Kulik of Russia and Rudy Galindo of the U.S.—did eight triple jumps, with Eldredge winning because he did two triple-triple jump combinations while Kulik's only combination was a triple-double. Defending champion Elvis Stojko, who dropped out of contention with a disastrous short program, landed one quad in his free skate to wind up fourth. Eldredge and Galindo gave the U.S. two men's medalists for the first time since 1981.

The women's final was even more dramatic. First defending champion Lu Chen of

Philip Hersh covers international sports for the *Chicago Tribune* and has been the Tribune's full-time Olympic writer since 1986.

Wide World Photos

In 1996, **Picabo Street**, of Triumph, ID., won her second consecutive World Cup downhill championship. In 1995, Street was the first American woman to ever win the title.

China wowed the judges with four minutes of elegant, highly romantic artistry and six triple jumps. That earned her two perfect (6.0) scores, the first for a woman at worlds since Kristi Yamaguchi got a single 6.0 in 1991. At that moment, Midori Ito of Japan was the only other woman to get 6.0 at worlds (five 6.0s in 1989).

If Chen's performance seemed like a reverse dunk for the winning basket, Kwan followed it with a 360-degree slam at the buzzer. Upgrading a double jump to a triple in the final second of her interpretation of Salome, Kwan won the judges by a 6-3 margin. Ito, returning to Olympic-style skating after a four-year absence following her 1992 Olympic silver medal, finished a disappointing seventh.

Kwan's victory at the U.S. Championships in San Jose became a foregone conclusion when defending champion Nicole Bobek withdrew because of a foot injury just prior to the free skate. Still, the way she skated, Kwan won the title on merit.

The drama at the nationals had already been created by the men's competition, when home-town skater Rudy Galindo created one of the most electric moments in the sport's history and the greatest upset in the U.S. Championships' 92-year history. Galindo, who never had been higher than fifth in seven previous nationals, became at 26 the second oldest men's champion in history, after 51-year-old Chris Christenson in 1926. He stunned the judges by finally matching his consummate artistry with technical brilliance, landing combinations of triples begun with the two most difficult jumps, axel and lutz. While two judges somehow put him below Eldredge, two others gave him scores of 6.0 and 7.0 and made Galindo the winner. Galindo announced in September he was giving up his Olympic eligibility to skate in unsanctioned pro events.

Alpine Skiing. For the second straight year, Alberto Tomba of Italy and Picabo Street of the U.S. were the star attractions on the slopes.

Although he finished fifth in the overall standings he won a year earlier and won just three races compared to 11 in 1995-96, Tomba still moved past Marc Girardelli of Luxembourg into second place on the all-time World Cup victory list with 47. Far ahead at 86 is Sweden's Ingemar Stenmark.

Tomba filled the one gap on his career resume by winning a world title—two, in fact—at the 1996 World Championships in Sierra Nevada, Spain, that had been postponed from 1995 because of a lack of snow. He won both the slalom and giant slalom, matching his Olympic double win of 1988.

Street did equally well on the World Cup circuit and in the World Championships. With three firsts, three seconds and a third in the season's nine downhills, Street repeated as World Cup downhill champion after having been the first U.S. skier to win that title a year before.

In the World Championships, Street paced an historic 1-3-5 finish in the downhill, with Hilary Lindh third and Megan Gerety fifth. For the U.S., it was: the first double-medal performance in a single world or Olympic event since 1985; the first gold since 1985; and the first downhill gold in the 65-year history of the event. Street also won a bronze medal in Super-G.

Katja Seizinger of Germany and Lasse Kjus of Norway became first-time winners of the World Cup overall titles. Seizinger won seven events in three disciplines and also won the Super-G season crown. The versatile Kjus built up a huge lead by making the top three in eight of the first 14 races and held it despite an injury that kept him out of several races.

Speedskating. After starting the season with two wins in her first two World Cup 1,000-meter races, Chris Witty of Milwaukee climaxed it by winning the World Sprint Championships in Heerenveen, the Netherlands. Witty won both 1,000s at the sprint championships and placed 8th and 11th in the 500s. Japanese skaters dominated men's sprinting on the World Cup and placed 2-3 at the World Sprints behind Sergei Klevchenya of Russia. At the final World Cup event of the season in Calgary, Japanese skaters Hiroyasu Shimizu (500 meters, 35.39 seconds), Manubu Horii (1000 meters,

The Reign of King Carl

Halfway to the stars, Michael Johnson was suddenly passed by an old man who had out-jumped time.

The life and Olympic times of Carl Lewis, a long-running soap opera, got bigger ratings than the hottest new story in the sport.

On the night Johnson won his first individual Olympic gold, setting an Olympic record of 43.49 seconds in the 400 meters, he was upstaged. Lewis' improbable fourth straight gold—and ninth overall—in the long jump was instead the more celebrated event.

Johnson, 28, of Dallas, was not pleased.

"I think as far as Carl trying to be the premier athlete in the sport, he should step down from that" Johnson said during a press conference as Lewis, 35, was taking a victory lap.

"But I'm not in any competition with Carl. I'm just trying to put my name up there with the great athletes in the history of track and field like Jesse Owens and Carl Lewis. I'm not trying to replace Carl Lewis."

Countered Lewis: "I'm too old to fight."

Too happy, as well.

"This medal, this ninth (gold), is the best," he said afterwards.

Lewis was 15th as he took his last qualifying round jump in the Olympics, and only 12 would make the final. He jumped 27 feet 2 1/5 inches, making him the leading qualifier for the next day's final.

His first jump in the final was a foul, his second 26-8 1/2, more than two feet short of Mike Powell's world record (29-4 1/2), a long way from the 28-footers that won for Lewis in the three previous Olympics.

But it was clear a 28-footer wouldn't be necessary this time, not with reigning world champion Ivan Pedroso of Cuba slow to come back from a knee injury (he placed 12th) and Powell struggling (his best jump of 26-9 3/4 earned fifth place).

Lewis was in third place as he prepared for his third jump. Suddenly he was flying longer and higher than he had in four years, landing finally at 27-10 3/4, enough to win the gold by 8 1/4 inches.

Lewis nine gold medals matched Finland's Paavo Nurmi (1920 through 28) for most in track and field, but Nurmi had twice earned two medals in the same team cross-country

World Wide Photos

Carl Lewis plays to the crowd after his surprising win in the long jump at the 1996 Olympics. Lewis has won the gold in this event four straight times.

event. Lewis was one behind the Olympic record of 10 won by Ray Ewry of the U.S. at the turn of the century,

But all of Ewry's came in standing jumps (no longer contested) and two came in the intercalcated 1906 Games, for which results are considered unofficial.

Only discus thrower Al Oerter of the U.S. had won the same track and field event in four straight Olympics.

Those stunning achievements had won over the public—80,000 people came to nearly every track and field session at Olympic Stadium—that once considered Lewis too calculated, too bizarre, too distant, too in-your-face.

"I watched the stands," two-time long jump bronze medalist Joe Greene said, "and Americans love Carl Lewis now."

That emotion changed for some when Lewis began lobbying for a place on the 4 x 100-meter relay despite being, as relay member Jon Drummond put it, "butt-naked last in the trials' 100 final."

His pursuit of a place on the relay team created a five-day controversy that ended when, after much equivocating and much media hand-wringing, coach Erv Hunt decided to stick with the athletes who had come to a pre-Olympic relay camp.

Lewis finished with 10 Olympic medals: four long jump golds, two 100-meter golds, one 200-meter gold, two relay golds, one 200-meter silver.

Without Lewis, who had anchored five world-record-breaking relays (including the 1992 gold medalists, a group he joined despite his sixth in the 100 at that Olympic trials), the U.S. relay was routed by Canada. "We got barbecued," said relay member Mike Marsh.

The night before, Johnson had the stage to himself, and he turned the inevitable into the unbelievable.

Not content merely to be the first man to win the 400 and 200 in the same Olympics, he ran a world record in the 200 so stunning it left the 82,884 who saw it even more breathless than Johnson.

His time of 19.32 crushed the 19.66 he had run on the same track at the U.S. trials, when Johnson broke what was then the oldest record in the sport: 19.72 by Italy's Pietro Mennea in 1979.

"It's an incredible thrill to run that fast," Johnson said.

He had finally outpaced Carl Lewis, if not his legend.

1:11.67) and Hiroyuki Noake (1,500 meters, 1:50.61) all set world records. Rintje Ritsma of the Netherlands and Gunda Niemann of Germany won the World All-Around Championships in Inzell, Germany, a second straight world title for both skaters.

Nordic Combined. Buoyed by support in his home town of Steamboat Springs, Colo., Todd Lodwick opened the World Cup season with the first win by a U.S. combined skier in 12 years. Lodwick would have one other top three individual finish during the season but failed to make the overall top 10, led by Knut Tore Apeland of Norway. Japan's Kenji Ojiwara, overall champion in 1993-94-95, missed several early events after wrist surgery and wound up second.

Ski Jumping. Jens Weissflog of Germany became the first to win the Four Hills Tourney four times, following victories in 1984, 1985 and 1991. The three-time Olympic gold medalist retired at the end of the season, in which Andreas Goldberger of Austria won his second straight World Cup overall title. Finland's Mika Laitinen won five of the first 10 World Cup events but missed two months after breaking his ribs and collarbone in a training accident.

Cross-Country. Early-season successes (five wins in the first six races) propelled Norway's Bjorn Daehlie to a third World Cup men's title despite a late rush by Vladimir Smirnov of Kazakhstan, who won three of the final five events. In women's racing, Manuela di Centa of Italy won seven of the final 11 events and her second overall title.

Bobsled. Christoph Langen of Germany became the first driver to win the two- and four-man events at both the European and World championships in the same year. Top U.S. finish at worlds was a fourth by Brian Shimer and Randy Jones in two-man.

Luge. Austria's Markus Prock and Germany's Jana Bode won the World Cup-World Championship double in singles, giving Prock a sixth straight World Cup overall title and a second world title. In doubles, Chris Thorpe and Gordy Sheer won their second straight world championship silver, finishing behind Austrian cousins Tobias and Markus Schlegel in 1996. Thorpe and Scheer were third in the World Cup standings.

Biathlon. Russia dominated the World Championships, going 1-2 in the men's individual events and taking four of six golds. Vladimir Dratschev, 30, was the season's big and surprising star, with two golds and a silver at the worlds and the World Cup titles in both disciplines and overall. France's Emmanuelle Claret won a world title and the World Cup overall.

Hockey. The U.S. took the bronze medal at the World Championships, its first "A" pool medal in the event since 1962. The Czech Republic won its first gold since 1985, beating Canada 4-2 in the final.

SUMMER SPORTS

Cycling. Miguel Indurain's attempt at an unprecedented sixth Tour de France victory foundered in the mountains during the race's seventh and eighth stages. In the final two miles of the climb to Les Arcs in the Savoy, the Spaniard lost more than three minutes to the man who would go on to become the first Dane to win the race, Bjarne Riis. After finishing third in 1995 and fifth in 1993, the 32-year-old Riis became the second oldest winner since 1948. Tour debutant Jan Ullrich of Germany, 22, was second, 1 minute, 41 seconds behind while Richard Virenque, third, became the first Frenchman to make the awards stand since 1989. Indurain was 11th, trailing the winner by 14:14. Later in the season, he hinted about retirement.

Doping. Jessica Foschi, 15, of Old Brookville, N.Y., still is waging a battle to overturn a doping suspension based on a positive test for steroids at the 1995 U.S. Championships. In a controversial decision, U.S. Swimming cleared Foschi to swim in the Olympic trials, in which her best finish was a fourth in the 800 meters, but the International Swimming Federation (FINA) gave her a two-year suspension from international competition. Meanwhile, FINA chose not to give Australia's Samantha Riley a mandated two-year suspension for a narcotic analgesic, reducing that ban to three months because her coach gave her the drug without apparent knowledge it was on the banned list. Riley went on to win an Olympic bronze medal.

Gymnastics. Shannon Miller regained the U.S. all-around title she had won in 1993, while defending champion Dominique

Wide World Photos

Christine Witty of Milwaukee had a great 1996 season, winning her first two World Cup 1,000 meter races and taking the 1,000 and overall titles in the World Sprint Championships.

Moceanu was third. At the Olympic trials two months later, both Miller and Moceanu were sidelined by injury but petitioned under USA Gymnastics women's team selection procedures to have their scores from nationals used again in the trials' scoring process. Both made the Olympic team. In the men's nationals, Blaine Wilson upset four-time champion John Roethlisberger for the all-around crown.

Marathons. In the 100th anniversary Boston Marathon, Uta Pippig of Germany overcame menstrual cramps and accompanying diarrhea to stage a dramatic rally for a third consecutive victory, making her the first woman to win three straight. With three miles to go, Tegla Loroupe of Kenya was 200 yards ahead, and Pippig had resigned herself to finishing second. But Loroupe's legs tightened, slowing her to a near walk, and Pippig went on to win by more than a minute in 2 hours, 27 minutes, 12 seconds. In the men's race, Cosmas Ndeti of Kenya failed to win a record fourth straight when he dropped off the pace at 22 miles and placed third, 36 seconds behind countryman Moses Tanui (2:09:15) in what would seem like the Kenyan national championships. The first five men and seven of the top eight were Kenyans.

At the 1995 New York Marathon, Loroupe won a second straight title, which she dedicated to her 33-year-old sister, Albina, who had died six days before the race. German Silva of Mexico also won a second straight and also dedicated it to a family member who had died recently—his 70-year-old father Agapito. Mexican runners have now won four of the last five New York titles.

Swimming. For the first time since 1920, the U.S. Olympic Trials produced neither a U.S. nor a world record. And they left three comebacking gold medalists from the 1992 Games—Summer Sanders, Chrissy Ahmann-Leighton and Melvin Stewart—sidelined for 1996, as each failed to qualify for Atlanta. Top performers at the trials

World Wide Photos

In 1996, Italy's **Alberto Tomba** added to his career achievements by winning his first two world titles in the slalom and giant slalom.

were Tom Dolan, winner of three events (400 free, 200 and 400 IM); and Amy Van Dyken and Angel Martino, each of whom qualified in three individual events and two relays.

Track & Field. The U.S. trials were supposed to send Michael Johnson and Gwen Torrence on their way to double victories in Atlanta. While Johnson accomplished that goal in impressive fashion, winning the 400 in the third fastest time ever (43.44 seconds) and breaking the oldest record in the sport with a 19.66 for the 200, Torrence won the 100 but failed to make the team by .001 of a second at 200, in which she was defending Olympic champion.

Johnson's time bettered the 19.72 set by Pietro Mennea of Italy at the 1979 World University Games in Mexico City. It was by far the most impressive performance of a trials in which two of the sport's biggest stars struggled: Carl Lewis, 35, was dead last in the final of the 100 and barely held onto the third and final qualifying spot in the long jump; and two-time Olympic heptathlon champion Jackie Joyner-Kersee lost a heptathlon for the first time since 1984.

Other oldies had better luck in the trials but not the Games: At 37, Mary Slaney made the team in the 5,000 meters; at 32, Mike Powell won the long jump; at 34, Lynn Jennings won the 5,000. Meanwhile, Dan O'Brien exorcised the ghosts of his dramatic 1992 trials failure and went on to collect the decathlon gold medal.

Just after the trials, Frankie Fredericks of Namibia ended Johnson's two-year, 21-race win streak at 200 meters in Oslo, but Johnson ended the season unbeaten at 400, stretching his win streak at that distance to 57 finals dating to 1989.

The rest of the post-Olympic season was dominated by African distance runners, especially one, Kenya's Daniel Komen, who did not make the Olympic team. In Rieti, Italy, Sept. 1, Komen ran the 3,000 in 7 minutes, 20.67, lowering Algerian Noureddine Morceli's world record by nearly five seconds. In Zurich, Aug. 14, Komen barely missed the 5,000 record with a season-leading 12:45.09. But the most astonishing time was the 10,000 world record of 26:38.08 by Salah Hissou of Morocco on Aug. 23 in Brussels, breaking Ethiopian Haile Gebrselassie's mark by 7.45 seconds. Among the women, the only track record-setter was double Olympic gold medalist Svetlana Masterkova of Russia, who broke marks at two distances that are rarely run by women, the mile and 1,000 meters.

Wrestling. The U.S. wrestling community was stunned by the Jan. 26 murder of 1984 Olympic champion Dave Schultz, allegedly at the hands of his and the sport's benefactor, chemical fortune heir John du Pont. Schultz, then training for the 1996 Olympics, was shot to death outside his home on Foxcatcher Farms, the du Pont estate outside Philadelphia. DuPont had been a major contributor to USA Wrestling, and his club, Team Foxcatcher, individually funded several top wrestlers, including two who went on to win 1996 Olympic golds. When several wrestlers continued to take Foxcatcher money for the first five months after Schultz's death—all eventually ceased—it caused a bitter rift within the U.S. wrestling community. That du Pont had behaved erratically for years led to unanswered questions about whether USA Wrestling should have disassociated from him far earlier. ❐

THE 1997
INFORMATION PLEASE
SPORTS ALMANAC
INT'L SPORTS
STATISTICS
THE SEASON IN REVIEW
1995-1996
CHAMPIONS • RECORDS

TRACK & FIELD

World Outdoor Records Set in 1996

World outdoor records set or equaled between Oct. 1, 1995 and Sept. 20, 1996; (p) indicates record is pending ratification by the IAAF.

MEN

Event	Name	Record	Old Mark	Former Holder
100 meters	**Donovan Bailey**, CAN	9.84p	9.85	Leroy Burell, USA (1994)
200 meters	**Michael Johnson**, USA	19.66	19.72	Pieto Mennea, ITA (1972)
200 meters	**Michael Johnson**, USA	19.32p	19.66	Michael Johnson, USA (1996)
3,000 meters	**Daniel Komen**, KEN	7:20.67	7:25.11	Noureddine Morceli, ALG (1994)
10,000 meters	**Salah Hissou**, MAR	26:38.08	26:43.63	Haile Gebreselassie, ETH (1995)
Javelin Throw	**Jan Zelezny**, CZE	323-1p	313-10	Jan Zelezny, CZE (1993)

WOMEN

Event	Name	Record	Old Mark	Former Holder
1,000 meters	**Svetlana Masterkova**, RUS	2:28.98	2:29.34	Maria Motola, MOZ (1995)
Mile	**Svetlana Masterkova**, RUS	4:12.56	4:15.61	Paula Ivan, ROM (1989)
Pole Vault	**Emma George**, AUS	14-7½	14-6	Emma George, AUS (1996)
Hammer Throw	**Mihaela Melinte**, ROM	227-9	223-7	Olga Kuzenkova, RUS (1995)
Hammer Throw	**Olga Kuzenkova**, RUS	227-11p	227-9	Mihaela Melinte, ROM (1996)

Note: The women's pole vault record was broken four times in 1996, all by Emma George of Australia. Her current mark was set on July 14, 1996.

1996 IAAF Mobil Grand Prix Final

The final meeting of the International Amateur Athletic Federation's Outdoor Grand Prix season, which includes the world's 16 leading outdoor invitational meets. Athletes earn points throughout the season with the leading point winners invited to the Grand Prix Final. The 1996 final was held Sept. 7 in Milan, Italy.

MEN

Event	Winner	Time
100m	Dennis Mitchell, USA	9.91
400m	Michael Johnson, USA	44.53
800m	Norberto Tellez, CUB	1:44.70
1500m	Hicham El Guerroudj, MOR	3:38.80
3000m Steeple	Eliud Barngetuny, KEN	8:18.45
5000m	Daniel Komen, KEN	12:52.38
400m Hurdles	Derrick Adkins, USA	48.63

Event	Winner	Hgt/Dist
High Jump	Patrik Sjoberg, SWE	7-7¾
Shot Put	John Godina, USA	69-6
Triple Jump	Jonathan Edwards, GBR	57-8½
Hammer	Lance Deal, USA	270-9
Pole Vault	Maksim Tarasov, RUS	19-4¼

WOMEN

Event	Winner	Time
100m	Merlene Ottey, JAM	10.74
400m	Cathy Freeman, AUS	49.60
1500m	Svetlana Masterkova, RUS	4:11.42
5000m	Roberta Brunet, ITA	14:54.54
100m Hurdles	Ludmilla Enquist, SWE	12.61

Event	Winner	Hgt/Dist
Long Jump	Inessa Kravets, UKR	23-2
Discus	Ilke Wyludda, GER	212-5
Javelin	Tanja Damaske, GER	217-5

Final Top 10 Standings

Overall Men's and Women's winners receive $200,000 (US) each; all ties broken by complex Grand Prix scoring system.

MEN

1. Daniel Lomen, KEN (103 points); 2. Jonathan Edwards, GBR (99); 3. Dennis Mitchell, USA (95); 4. Noureddine Morceli, ALG (93); 5. Derrick Adkins, USA (91); 6. Samuel Matete, ZAM (90); 7. Donovan Bailey, CAN (85); 8. Maksim Tarasov, RUS (79.5); 9. Igor Astapkovich, BLR (77); 10. Balazs Kiss, HUN (77).

WOMEN

1. Ludmilla Enquist, SWE (93 points); 2. Merlene Ottey, JAM (90); 3. Michelle Freeman, JAM (85); 4. Falilat Ogunkoya, NGR (83); 5. Inessa Kravets, UKR (80); 6. Oksana Ovchinnikova, RUS (78); 7. Ilke Wyludda, GER (76); 8. Cathy Freeman, AUS (75); 9. Tanja Damaske, GER (72); 10. Pauline Davis, BAH (71).

World, Olympic and American Records

As of Sept. 20, 1996

World outdoor records officially recognized by the International Amateur Athletics Federation (IAAF); (p) indicates record is pending ratification by the IAAF.

MEN

Running

Event		Time		Date Set	Location
100 meters:	**World**	9.84p	**Donovan Bailey**, Canada	July 27, 1996	Atlanta
	Olympic	9.84	Bailey (same as World)	—	—
	American	9.85	Leroy Burrell	July 6, 1994	Lausanne, SWI
200 meters:	**World**	19.32p	**Michael Johnson**, USA	Aug. 1, 1996	Atlanta
	Olympic	19.32	Johnson (same as World)	—	—
	American	19.32	Johnson (same as World)	—	—
400 meters:	**World**	43.29	**Butch Reynolds,** USA	Aug. 17, 1988	Zurich
	Olympic	43.49	Michael Johnson, USA	July 29, 1996	Atlanta
	American	43.29	Reynolds (same as World)	—	—
800 meters:	**World**	1:41.73	**Sebastian Coe,** Great Britain	June 10, 1981	Florence
	Olympic	1:42.58	Vebjoern Rodal, Norway	July 31, 1996	Atlanta
	American	1:42.60	Johnny Gray	Aug. 28, 1985	Koblenz, W. Ger.
1000 meters:	**World**	2:12.18	**Sebastian Coe,** Great Britain	July 11, 1981	Oslo
	Olympic		Not an event	—	—
	American	2:13.9	Rick Wohlhuter	July 30, 1974	Oslo
1500 meters:	**World**	3:27.37	**Noureddine Morceli,** Algeria	July 12, 1995	Nice, FRA
	Olympic	3:32.53	Sebastian Coe, Great Britain	Aug. 11, 1984	Los Angeles
	American	3:29.77	Sydney Maree	Aug. 25, 1985	Cologne
Mile:	**World**	3:44.39	**Noureddine Morceli,** Algeria	Sept. 5, 1993	Rieti, ITA
	Olympic		Not an event	—	—
	American	3:47.69	Steve Scott	July 7, 1982	Oslo
2000 meters:	**World**	4:47.88	**Noureddine Morceli,** Algeria	July 3, 1995	Paris
	Olympic		Not an event	—	—
	American	4:52.44	Jim Spivey	Sept. 15, 1987	Lausanne
3000 meters:	**World**	7:20.67	**Daniel Komen**, Kenya	Sept. 1, 1996	Riete, ITA
	Olympic		Not an event	—	—
	American	7:31.69	Bob Kennedy	Aug. 23, 1996	Brussels
5000 meters:	**World**	12:44.39	**Haile Gebrselassie,** Ethiopia	Aug. 16, 1995	Zurich
	Olympic	13:05.59	Said Aouita, Morocco	Aug. 11, 1984	Los Angeles
	American	12:58.21	Bob Kennedy	Aug. 14, 1996	Zurich
10,000 meters:	**World**	26:38.08	**Salah Hissou**, Morocco	Aug. 23, 1996	Brussels
	Olympic	27:07.34	Haile Gebrselassie, Ethiopia	July 29, 1996	Atlanta
	American	27:20.56	Mark Nenow	Sept. 5, 1986	Brussels
20,000 meters:	**World**	56:55.6	**Arturo Barrios,** Mexico	Mar. 30, 1991	La Fleche, FRA
	Olympic		Not an event	—	—
	American	58:15.0	Bill Rodgers	Aug. 9, 1977	Boston
Marathon:	**World**	2:06:50	**Belayneh Densimo,** Ethiopia	Apr. 17, 1988	Rotterdam
	Olympic	2:09:21	Carlos Lopes, Portugal	Aug. 12, 1984	Los Angeles
	American	2:10:04	Pat Petersen	Apr. 23, 1989	London
		2:08:52*	Alberto Salazar	Apr. 19, 1982	Boston

*Former American record no longer officially recognized.
Note: The Mile run is 1,609.344 meters and the Marathon is 42,194.988 meters (26 miles, 385 yards).

Walking

Event		Time		Date Set	Location
20 km:	**World**	1:17:25.5	**Bernardo Segura,** Mexico	May 7, 1994	Fana, NOR
	Olympic	1:19:57	Jozef Pribilinec, Czechoslovakia	Sept. 23, 1988	Seoul
	American	1:24:26.9	Allen James	May 7, 1994	Fana, NOR
50 km:	**World**	3:41:28.2	**Rene Piller,** France	May 7, 1994	Fana, NOR
	Olympic	3:38:29	Vyacheslav Ivanenko, USSR	Sept. 30, 1988	Seoul
	American	3:59:41.2	Herm Nelson	June 9, 1996	Seattle

Hurdles

Event		Time		Date Set	Location
110 meters:	**World**	12.91	**Colin Jackson,** Great Britain	Aug. 20, 1993	Stuttgart
	Olympic	12.95	Allen Johnson, USA	July 29, 1996	Atlanta
	American	12.92	Roger Kingdom	Aug. 16, 1989	Zurich
		12.92	Allen Johnson	June 23, 1996	Atlanta
400 meters:	**World**	46.78	**Kevin Young,** USA	Aug. 6, 1992	Barcelona
	Olympic	46.78	Young (same as World)	—	—
	American	46.78	Young (same as World)	—	—

Note: The hurdles at 110 meters are 3 feet, 6 inches high and the hurdles at 400 meters are 3 feet. There are 10 hurdles in both races.

Steeplechase

Event		Time		Date Set	Location
3000 meters:	**World**	7:59.18p	**Moses Kiptanui,** Kenya	Aug. 18, 1995	Zurich
	Olympic	8:05.51	Julius Kariuki, Kenya	Sept. 30, 1988	Seoul
	American	8:09.17	Henry Marsh	Aug. 28, 1985	Koblenz

Note: A steeplechase course consists of 28 hurdles (3 feet high) and seven water jumps (12 feet long).

Relays

Event		Time		Date Set	Location
4 x 100m:	**World**	37.40	**USA** (Marsh, Burrell, Mitchell, C. Lewis)	Aug. 8, 1992	Barcelona
		37.40	**USA** (Drummond, Cason, Mitchell, Burrell)	Aug. 21, 1993	Stuttgart
	Olympic	37.40	USA (same as World)	—	—
	American	37.40	USA (same as World)	—	—
4 x 200m:	**World**	1:18.68	**USA** (Marsh, Burrell, Heard, C. Lewis)	Apr. 17, 1994	Walnut, Calif.
	Olympic		Not an event	—	—
	American	1:18.68	USA (same as World)	—	—
4 x 400m:	**World**	2:54.29	**USA** (Valmon, Watts, Reynolds, Johnson)	Aug. 22, 1993	Stuttgart
	Olympic	2:55.74	USA (Valmon, Watts, Johnson, S. Lewis)	Aug. 8, 1992	Barcelona
	American	2:54.29	USA (same as World)	—	—
4 x 800m:	**World**	7:03.89	**Great Britain** (Elliott, Cook, Cram, Coe)	Aug. 30, 1982	London
	Olympic		Not an event	—	—
	American	7:06.5	SMTC (J. Robinson, Mack, E. Jones, Gray)	Apr. 26, 1986	Walnut, Calif.
4 x 1500m:	**World**	14:38.8	**West Germany** (Wessinghage, Hudak, Lederer, Fleschen)	Aug. 17, 1977	Cologne
	Olympic		Not an event	—	—
	American	14:46.3	USA (Aldredge, Clifford, Harbour, Duits)	June 24, 1979	Bourges, FRA

Field Events

Event		Mark		Date Set	Location
High Jump:	**World**	8- 0½	**Javier Sotomayor,** Cuba	July 27, 1993	Salamanca, SPA
	Olympic	7- 10	Charles Austin, USA	July 28, 1996	Atlanta
	American	7- 10½	Charles Austin	Aug. 7, 1991	Zurich
Pole Vault:	**World**	20- 1¾	**Sergey Bubka,** Ukraine	July 31, 1994	Sestriere, ITA
	Olympic	19- 5¼	Jean Galfione, France	Aug. 2, 1996	Atlanta
		19- 5¼	Igor Trandenkov, Russia	Aug. 2, 1996	Atlanta
		19- 5¼	Andrei Tiwontschik, Ger.	Aug. 2, 1996	Atlanta
	American	19- 7½	Lawrence Johnson	May 25, 1996	Knoxville, Tenn.
Long Jump:	**World**	29- 4¾*	**Ivan Pedroso,** Cuba	July 29, 1995	Sestriere, ITA
		29- 4½	**Mike Powell,** USA	Aug. 30, 1991	Tokyo
	Olympic	29- 2½	Bob Beamon, USA	Oct. 18, 1968	Mexico City
	American	29- 4½	Powell (same as World)	—	—
Triple Jump:	**World**	60- 0¼	**Jonathan Edwards,** GBR	Aug. 7, 1995	Göteborg
	Olympic	57- 0¼	Mike Conley, USA	Aug. 3, 1992	Barcelona
	American	58- 1½	Willie Banks	June 16, 1985	Indianapolis
Shot Put:	**World**	75- 10¼	**Randy Barnes,** USA	May 20, 1990	Los Angeles
	Olympic	73- 8¾	Ulf Timmermann, E. Ger.	Sept. 23, 1988	Seoul
	American	75- 10¼	Barnes (same as World)	—	—
Discus:	**World**	243- 0	**Jurgen Schult,** E. Ger.	June 6, 1986	Neubrandenburg
	Olympic	227- 8	Lare Reidel, Germany	July 31, 1996	Atlanta
	American	237- 4	Ben Plucknett	July 7, 1981	Stockholm
Javelin:	**World**	323- 1p	**Jan Zelezny,** Czech Rep.	May 25, 1996	Jena, GER
	Olympic	294- 2	Jan Zelezny, Czech.	Aug. 8, 1992	Barcelona
	American	284- 10	Tom Pukstys	Aug. 25, 1996	Sheffield, ENG
Hammer:	**World**	284- 7	**Yuri Sedykh,** USSR	Aug. 30, 1986	Stuttgart
	Olympic	278- 2	Sergey Litvinov, USSR	Sept. 26, 1988	Seoul
	American	270- 9	Lance Deal	Sept. 7, 1996	Milan

*Apparent world record disallowed because of interference with wind gauge at altitude.
Note: The international weights for men— **Shot** (16 lbs); **Discus** (4 lbs/6.55 oz); **Javelin** (minimum 1 lb/124¼ oz.); **Hammer** (16 lbs).

Decathlon

		Points		Date Set	Location
Ten Events:	**World**	8891	**Dan O'Brien,** USA	Sept. 4-5, 1992	Talence, FRA
	Olympic	8847	Daley Thompson, Great Britain	Aug. 8-9, 1984	Los Angeles
	American	8891	O'Brien (same as World)	—	—

Note: O'Brien's WR times and distances, in order over two days— **100m** (10.43); LJ (26- 6¼); **Shot** (54- 9¼); **HJ** (6- 9½); **400m** (48.51); **110m H** (13.98); **Discus** (159- 4); **PV** (16- 4¾); **Jav** (205-4); **1500m** (4:42.10).

World, Olympic and American Records (Cont.)

WOMEN

Running

Event		Time		Date Set	Location
100 meters:	**World**	10.49	**Florence Griffith Joyner,** USA	July 16, 1988	Indianapolis
	Olympic	10.62	Florence Griffith Joyner, USA	Sept. 24, 1988	Seoul
	American	10.49	Griffith Joyner (same as World)	—	—
200 meters:	**World**	21.34	**Florence Griffith Joyner,** USA	Sept. 29, 1988	Seoul
	Olympic	21.34	Griffith Joyner (same as World)	—	—
	American	21.34	Griffith Joyner (same as World)	—	—
400 meters:	**World**	47.60	**Marita Koch,** East Germany	Oct. 6, 1985	Canberra, AUS
	Olympic	48.65	Olga Bryzgina, USSR	Sept. 26, 1988	Seoul
	American	48.83	Valerie Brisco	Aug. 6, 1984	Los Angeles
800 meters:	**World**	1:53.28	**Jarmila Kratochvilova,** Czech.	July 26, 1983	Munich
	Olympic	1:53.42	Nadezhda Olizarenko, USSR	July 27, 1980	Moscow
	American	1:56.90	Mary Decker Slaney	Aug. 16, 1985	Bern
1000 meters:	**World**	2:28.98	**Svetlana Masterkova,** Russia	Aug. 23, 1996	Brussels
	Olympic		Not an event	—	—
	American	2:33.93	Suzy Hamilton	June 4, 1995	Eugene, Ore.
1500 meters:	**World**	3:50.46	**Qu Yunxia,** China	Sept. 11, 1993	Beijing
	Olympic	3:53.96	Paula Ivan, Romania	Oct. 1, 1988	Seoul
	American	3:57.12	Mary Decker	July 26, 1983	Stockholm
Mile:	**World**	4:12.56	**Svetlana Masterkova,** Russia	Aug. 14, 1996	Zurich
	Olympic		Not an event	—	—
	American	4:16.71	Mary Decker Slaney	Aug. 21, 1985	Zurich
2000 meters:	**World**	5:25.36	**Sonia O'Sullivan,** Ireland	July 8, 1994	Edinburgh
	Olympic		Not an event	—	—
	American	5:32.7	Mary Decker	Aug. 3, 1984	Eugene
3000 meters:	**World**	8:06.11	**Wang Junxia,** China	Sept. 13, 1993	Beijing
	Olympic	8:26.53	Tatyana Samolenko, USSR	Sept. 25, 1988	Seoul
	American	8:25.83	Mary Decker Slaney	Sept. 7, 1985	Rome
5000 meters:	**World**	14:36.45p	**Fernanda Ribiero,** Portugal	July 22, 1995	Hechtel, BEL
	Olympic		Not an event	—	—
	American	14:56.04	Amy Rudolph	July 8, 1996	Stockholm
10,000 meters:	**World**	29:31.78	**Wang Junxia,** China	Sept. 8, 1993	Beijing
	Olympic	31:05.21	Olga Bondarenko, USSR	Sept. 30, 1988	Seoul
	American	31:19.89	Lynn Jennings	Aug. 7, 1992	Barcelona
Marathon:	**World**	2:21:06	**Ingrid Kristiansen,** Norway	Apr. 21, 1985	London
	Olympic	2:24:52	Joan Benoit, USA	Aug. 5, 1984	Los Angeles
	American	2:21:21	Joan Benoit Samuelson	Oct. 20, 1985	Chicago

Note: The Mile run is 1,609.344 meters and the Marathon is 42,194.988 meters (26 miles, 385 yards).

Relays

Event		Time		Date Set	Location
4 x 100m:	**World**	41.37	**East Germany** (Gladisch, Rieger, Auerswald, Gohr);	Oct. 6, 1985	Canberra, AUS
	Olympic	41.60	East Germany (Muller, Wockel, Auerswald, Gohr)	Aug. 1, 1980	Moscow
	American	41.49	USA (Finn, Torrence, Vereen, Devers)	Aug. 22, 1993	Stuttgart
4 x 200m:	**World**	1:28.15	**East Germany** (Gohr, Muller, Wockel, Koch)	Aug. 9, 1980	Jena, E. Ger.
	Olympic		Not an event	—	—
	American	1:32.44p	Vector Sports (Jones, Taplin, Miller, Gaines)	Apr. 6, 1996	Tempe, AZ
4 x 400m:	**World**	3:15.17	**USSR** (Ledovskaya, Nazarova, Pinigina, Bryzgina)	Oct. 1, 1988	Seoul
	Olympic	3:15.17	USSR (same as World)	—	—
	American	3:15.51	USA (Howard, Dixon, Brisco, Griffith Joyner)	Oct. 1, 1988	Seoul

Hurdles

Event		Time		Date Set	Location
100 meters:	**World**	12.21	**Yordanka Donkova,** Bulgaria	Aug. 20, 1988	Stara Zagora, BUL
	Olympic	12.38	Yordanka Donkova, Bulgaria	Sept. 30, 1988	Seoul
	American	12.46	Gail Devers	Aug. 20, 1993	Stuttgart
400 meters:	**World**	52.61p	**Kim Batten,** USA	Aug. 11, 1995	Göteborg
	Olympic	53.17	Debra Flintoff-King, Australia	Sept. 28, 1988	Seoul
	American	52.61p	Batten (same as World)	—	—

Note: The hurdles at 110 meters are 3 feet, 6 inches high and the hurdles at 400 meters are 3 feet. There are 10 hurdles in both races.

Walking

Event		Time		Date Set	Location
5 km:	**World**	20:13.26	**Kerry Saxby,** Australia	Feb. 25, 1996	Hobart, AUS
	Olympic		Not an event	—	—
	American	21:28.17	Teresa Vaill	Apr. 24, 1993	Philadelphia
10 km:	**World**	41:37.9	**Gao Hongmiao,** China	Apr. 7, 1994	Beijing
	Olympic	44:32	Chen Yueling, China	Aug. 3, 1992	Barcelona
	American	44:17p	Michelle Rohl	Aug. 7, 1995	Göteborg

Field Events

Event		Mark		Date Set	Location
High Jump:	**World**	6-10¼	**Stefka Kostadinova**, Bulgaria	Aug. 30, 1987	Rome
	Olympic	6- 8	Louise Ritter, USA	Sept. 30, 1988	Seoul
	American	6- 8	Louise Ritter	July 8, 1988	Austin
		6- 8	Ritter (see Olympic)	—	—
Pole Vault:	**World**	14-7½p	**Emma George**, Australia	July 14, 1996	Sapporo
	Olympic		Not an event	—	—
	American	13- 9¼p	Stacy Dragila	June 19, 1996	Atlanta
Long Jump:	**World**	24- 8¼	**Galina Chistyakova,** USSR	June 11, 1988	Leningrad
	Olympic	24- 3¼	Jackie Joyner-Kersee, USA	Sept. 29, 1988	Seoul
	American	24- 7	Jackie Joyner-Kersee	May 22, 1994	New York
Triple Jump:	**World**	50- 0¼p	**Inessa Kravets,** Ukraine	Aug. 8, 1995	Göteborg
	Olympic		Event as of 1996	—	—
	American	47-3½	Sheila Hudson	July 8, 1996	Stockholm
Shot Put:	**World**	74- 3	**Natalya Lisovskaya,** USSR	June 7, 1987	Moscow
	Olympic	73- 6¼	Ilona Slupianek, E.Germany	July 24, 1980	Moscow
	American	66- 2½	Ramona Pagel	June 25, 1988	San Diego
Discus:	**World**	252- 0	**Gabriele Reinsch,** E. Germany	July 9, 1988	Neubrandenburg
	Olympic	237- 2½	Martina Hellmann, E. Germany	Sept. 29, 1988	Seoul
	American	216- 10	Carol Cady	May 31, 1986	San Jose
Javelin:	**World**	262- 5	**Petra Felke,** E. Germany	Sept. 9, 1988	Potsdam, E. Ger.
	Olympic	245- 0	Petra Felke, E. Germany	Sept. 26, 1988	Seoul
	American	227- 5	Kate Schmidt	Sept. 10, 1977	Furth, W. Ger.
Hammer:	**World**	227-11	**Olga Kuzenkova,** Russia	Feb. 17, 1996	Sydney
	Olympic		Not an event	—	—
	American	209-2	Dawn Ellerbe	June 1, 1996	Eugene, OR

Note: The international weights for women— **Shot** (8 lbs/13 oz); **Discus** (2 lbs/3.27 oz); **Javelin** (minimum 1 lb/5.16 oz); **Hammer** (16 lbs).

Heptathlon

		Points		Date Set	Location
Seven Events:	**World**	7291	**Jackie Joyner-Kersee,** USA	Sept. 23-24, 1988	Seoul
	Olympic	7291	Joyner-Kersee (same as World)	—	—
	American	7291	Joyner-Kersee (same as World)	—	—

Note: Joyner-Kersee's WR times and distances, in order over two days— **100m H** (12.69); **HJ** (61¼); **Shot** (51-10); **200m** (22.56); **LJ** (2310¼); **Jav** (149-10); **800m** (2:08.51).

World Indoor Records Set in 1996

World indoor records set or equaled between Oct. 1, 1995 and Sept. 20, 1996; (p) indicates record is pending.

MEN

Event		Record	Old Mark	Former Holder
50 meter	**Donovan Bailey**, CAN	5.56p	5.61	Manfred Kokot, E. GER (1973) & James Sanford, USA (1981)
200 meters	**Frankie Fredericks**, NAM	19.92	20.25	Linford Christie, GBR (1995)
3,000 meters	**Haile Gebrselassie**, ETH	7:30.72	7:35.15	Moses Kiptanui, KEN (1995)
5,000 meters	**Haile Gebrselassie**, ETH	13:10.98	13:20.40	Suleiman Nyambui, TAN (1981)

WOMEN

Event		Record	Old Mark	Former Holder
1,000 meters	**Maria Mutola**, MOZ	2:31.23	2:34.18	Lyubov Kremlyova, RUS (1995)
Pole Vault	**Sun Caiyun,** CHN	14-0½p	14-0	Sun Caiyun, CHN (1996)

Note: The women's indoor pole vault record was broken five times in 1996— four times by Sun Caiyun of China. Her current mark was set on Feb. 27, 1996.

World and American Indoor Records

As of Sept. 20, 1995

World indoor records officially recognized by the International Amateur Athletics Federation (IAAF); (p) indicates record is pending ratification by the IAAF.

MEN

Running

Event		Time		Date Set	Location
50 meters:	**World**	5.56p	**Donovan Bailey,** Canada	Feb. 9, 1996	Reno, NV
	American	5.61	James Sanford, USA	Feb. 20, 1981	San Diego
60 meters:	**World**	6.41	**Andre Cason,** USA	Feb. 14, 1992	Madrid
	American	6.41	Cason (same as World)	–	–
200 meters:	**World**	19.92	**Frankie Fredericks,** Namibia	Feb. 18, 1996	Lievin, FRA
	American	20.40	Jeff Williams	Feb. 18, 1996	Lievin, FRA
400 meters:	**World**	44.63p	**Michael Johnson,** USA	Mar. 4, 1995	Atlanta
	American	44.63p	Johnson (same as World)	—	—
800 meters:	**World**	1:44.84	**Paul Ereng,** Kenya	Mar. 4, 1989	Budapest
	American	1:45.00	Johnny Gray	Mar. 8, 1992	Sindelfingen, GER
1000 meters:	**World**	2:15.26	**Noureddine Morceli,** Algeria	Feb. 22, 1992	Birmingham, ENG
	American	2:18.19	Ocky Clark	Feb. 12, 1989	Stuttgart
1500 meters:	**World**	3:34.16	**Noureddine Morceli,** Algeria	Feb. 28, 1991	Seville
	American	3:38.12	Jeff Atkinson	Mar. 5, 1989	Budapest
Mile:	**World**	3:49.78	**Eamonn Coghlan,** Ireland	Feb. 27, 1983	E. Rutherford, N.J.
	American	3:51.8	Steve Scott	Feb. 20, 1981	San Diego
3000 meters:	World	7:30.72	**Haile Gebrselassie,** Ethiopa	Feb. 4, 1996	Stuttgart
	American	7:39.94	Steve Scott	Feb. 10, 1989	E. Rutherford, N.J.
5000 meters:	**World**	13:10.98	**Haile Gebrselassie,** Ethiopa	Jan. 27, 1996	Sindelfingen
	American	13:20.55	Doug Padilla	Feb. 12, 1982	New York

Note: The Mile run is 1,609.344 meters.

Hurdles

Event		Time		Date Set	Location
50 meters:	**World**	6.25	**Mark McKoy,** Canada	Mar. 5, 1986	Kobe, JPN
	American	6.35	Greg Foster	Jan. 27, 1985	Rosemont, Ill.
		6.35	Greg Foster	Jan. 31, 1987	Ottawa
60 meters:	**World**	7.30	**Colin Jackson,** Britain	Mar. 6, 1994	Sindelfingen, GER
	American	7.36	Greg Foster	Jan. 16, 1987	Los Angeles

Note: The hurdles for both distances are 3 feet, 6 inches high. There are four hurdles in the 50 meters and five in the 60.

Relays

Event		Time		Date Set	Location
4x200 meters:	**World**	1:22.11	**Great Britain**	Mar. 3, 1991	Glasgow
	American	1:22.71	National Team	Mar. 3, 1991	Glasgow
4x400 meters:	**World**	3:03.05	**Germany**	Mar. 10, 1991	Seville
	American	3:03.24	National Team	Mar. 10, 1991	Seville

Field Events

Event		Time		Date Set	Location
High Jump:	**World**	7- 11¼	**Javier Sotomayor,** Cuba	Mar. 4, 1989	Budapest
	American	7- 10½	Hollis Conway	Mar. 10, 1991	Seville
Pole Vault:	**World**	20- 2	**Sergey Bubka,** Ukraine	Feb. 21, 1993	Donyetsk, UKR
	American	19- 3¾	Billy Olson	Jan. 25, 1986	Albuquerque
Long Jump:	**World**	28- 10¼	**Carl Lewis,** USA	Jan. 27, 1984	New York
	American	28- 10¼	Lewis (same as World)	—	—
Triple Jump:	**World**	58- 3¾	**Leonid Voloshin,** Russia	Feb. 6, 1994	Grenoble, FRA
	American	58- 3¼	Mike Conley	Feb. 27, 1987	New York
Shot Put:	**World**	74- 4¼	**Randy Barnes,** USA	Jan. 20, 1989	Los Angeles
	American	74- 4¼	Barnes (same as World)	—	—

Note: The international shot put weight for men is 16 lbs.

Heptathlon

		Points		Date Set	Location
Seven Events:	**World**	6476	**Dan O'Brien,** USA	Mar. 13-14, 1993	Toronto
	American	6476	O'Brien (same as World)	—	—

Note: O'Brien's WR times and distances, in order over two days— **60m** (6.67); **LJ** (25-8¾); **SP** (52-6¾); **HJ** (6-11¾); **60m H** (7.85); **PV** (17-0¾); **1000m** (2:57.96).

WOMEN

Running

Event		Time		Date Set	Location
50 meters:	**World**	5.96p	**Irina Privalova,** Russia	Feb. 9, 1995	Madrid
	American	6.02	Gwen Torrence	Feb. 9, 1996	Reno, NV
60 meters:	**World**	6.92	**Irina Privalova,** Russia	Feb. 11, 1993	Madrid
		6.92	**Irina Privalova,** Russia	Feb. 9, 1995	Madrid
	American	6.95	Gail Devers	Mar. 12, 1993	Toronto
200 meters:	**World**	21.87	**Merlene Ottey,** Jamaica	Feb. 13, 1993	Lievin, FRA
	American	22.33	Gwen Torrence	Mar. 2, 1996	Atlanta
400 meters:	**World**	49.59	**Jarmila Kratochvilova,** Czech.	Mar. 7, 1982	Milan
	American	50.64	Diane Dixon	Mar. 10, 1991	Seville
800 meters:	**World**	1:56.40	**Christine Wachtel,** E. Germany	Feb. 13, 1988	Vienna
	American	1:58.9	Mary Decker	Feb. 22, 1980	San Diego
1000 meters:	**World**	2:31.23	**Maria Mutola,** Mozambique	Feb. 25, 1996	Stockholm
	American	2:37.6	Mary Decker Slaney	Jan. 21, 1989	Portland
1500 meters:	**World**	4:00.27	**Doina Melinte,** Romania	Feb. 9, 1990	E. Rutherford, N.J.
	American	4:00.8	Mary Decker	Feb. 8, 1980	New York
Mile:	**World**	4:17.13	**Doina Melinte,** Romania	Feb. 9, 1990	E. Rutherford, N.J.
	American	4:20.5	Mary Decker	Feb. 19, 1982	San Diego
3000 meters:	**World**	8:33.82	**Elly van Hulst,** Holland	Mar. 4, 1989	Budapest
	American	8:40.45	Lynn Jennings	Feb. 23, 1990	New York
5000 meters:	**World**	15:03.17	**Liz McGolgan,** Great Britain	Feb. 22, 1992	Birmingham, ENG
	American	15:22.64	Lynn Jennings	Jan. 7, 1990	Hanover, N.H.

Note: The Mile run is 1,609.344 meters.

Hurdles

Event		Time		Date Set	Location
50 meters:	**World**	6.58	**Cornelia Oschkenat,** E. Ger.	Feb. 20, 1988	East Berlin
	American	6.67	Jackie Joyner-Kersee	Feb. 10, 1995	Reno, Nev.
60 meters:	**World**	7.69	**Lyudmila Narozhilenko,** USSR	Feb. 4, 1990	Chelyabinsk, USSR
	American	7.81	Jackie Joyner-Kersee	Feb. 5, 1989	Fairfax, Va.

Note: The hurdles for both distances are 2 feet, 9 inches high. There are four hurdles in the 50 meters and five in the 60.

Walking

Event		Time		Date Set	Location
3000 meters:	**World**	11:44.00	**Alina Ivanova,** Russia	Feb. 7, 1992	Moscow
	American	12:20.79	Debbi Lawrence	Mar. 12, 1993	Toronto

Relays

Event		Time		Date Set	Location
4x200 meters:	**World**	1:32.55	**West Germany**	Feb. 20, 1988	Dortmund, W. Ger.
	American	1:33.24	National Team	Feb. 12, 1994	Glasgow
4x400 meters:	**World**	3:27.22	**Germany**	Mar. 10, 1991	Seville
	American	3:29.0	National Team	Mar. 10, 1991	Seville
4x800 meters:	**World**	8:18.71	**Russia**	Feb. 4, 1994	Moscow
	American	8:25.5	Villanova	Feb. 7, 1987	Gainesville, Fla.

Field Events

Event		Mark		Date Set	Location
High Jump:	**World**	6-9½	**Heike Henkel,** Germany	Feb. 9, 1992	Karlsruhe, GER
	American	6-6¾	Coleen Sommer	Feb. 13, 1982	Ottawa
Pole Vault:	**World**	14-0½p	**Sun Caiyun,** China	Feb. 27, 1996	Tianjin
	American	13-6¼	Melissa Price	Feb. 17, 1996	Fresno, CA
Long Jump:	**World**	24-2¼	**Heike Drechsler,** E. Germany	Feb. 13, 1988	Vienna
	American	23-4¾	Jackie Joyner-Kersee	Mar. 5, 1992	Atlanta
Triple Jump:	**World**	49-3¾p	**Yolanda Chen,** Russia	Mar. 11, 1995	Barcelona
	American	46-8¼	Sheila Hudson-Strudwick	Mar. 4, 1995	Atlanta
Shot Put:	**World**	73-10	**Helena Fibingerova,** Czech.	Feb. 19, 1977	Jablonec, CZE
	American	65-0¾	Ramona Pagel	Feb. 20, 1987	Inglewood, Calif.

Note: The international shotput weight for women is 8 lbs. and 13 oz.

Pentathlon

		Points		Date Set	Location
Five Events:	**World**	4991	**Irina Byelova,** Russia	Feb. 14-15, 1993	Berlin
	American	4632	Kym Carter	Mar. 10, 1995	Barcelona

Note: Byelova's WR times and distances, in order over two days– **60m H** (8.22); **HJ** (6-4); **SP** (43- 5¾); **LJ** (21-1¾); **800m** (2:10.26).

SWIMMING

World, Olympic and American Records

As of Sept. 20, 1996

World long course records officially recognized by the Federation Internationale de Natation Amateur (FINA). Note that (ph) indicates preliminary heat; (r) relay lead-off split; and (s) indicates split time.

MEN

Freestyle

Distance		Time		Date Set	Location
50 meters:	**World**	21.81	**Tom Jager,** USA	Mar. 24, 1990	Nashville
	Olympic	21.91	Aleksandr Popov, Unified Team	July 30, 1992	Barcelona
	American	21.81	Jager (same as World)	—	—
100 meters:	**World**	48.21	**Aleksandr Popov,** Russia	June 18, 1994	Monte Carlo
	Olympic	48.63	Matt Biondi, USA	Sept.22, 1988	Seoul
	American	48.42	Matt Biondi	Aug. 10, 1988	Austin, Tex.
200 meters:	**World**	1:46.69	**Giorgio Lamberti,** Italy	Aug. 15, 1989	Bonn, W. Ger.
	Olympic	1:46.70	Yevgeny Sadovyi, Unified Team	July 26, 1992	Barcelona
	American	1:47.72ph	Matt Biondi	Aug. 8, 1988	Austin, Tex.
400 meters:	**World**	3:43.80	**Kieren Perkins,** Australia	Sept. 9, 1994	Rome
	Olympic	3:45.00	Yevgeny Sadovyi, Unified Team	July 29, 1992	Barcelona
	American	3:48.06	Matt Cetlinski	Aug. 11, 1988	Austin, Tex.
800 meters:	**World**	7:46.00s	**Kieren Perkins,** Australia	Aug. 24, 1994	Victoria, CAN
	Olympic		Not an event	—	—
	American	7:52.45	Sean Killion	July 27, 1987	Clovis, Calif.
1500 meters:	**World**	14:41.66	**Kieren Perkins,** Australia	Aug. 24, 1994	Victoria, CAN
	Olympic	14:43.48	Kieren Perkins, Australia	July 31, 1992	Barcelona
	American	15:01.51	George DiCarlo	June 30, 1984	Indianapolis

Backstroke

Distance		Time		Date Set	Location
100 meters:	**World**	53.86r	**Jeff Rouse,** USA	July 31, 1992	Barcelona
	Olympic	53.98	Mark Tewksbury, Canada	July 30, 1992	Barcelona
	American	53.86r	Rouse (same as World)	—	—
200 meters:	**World**	1:56.57	**Martin Zubero,** Spain	Nov. 23, 1991	Tuscaloosa, Ala.
	Olympic	1:58.47	Martin Zubero, Spain	July 28, 1992	Barcelona
	American	1:58.33	Tripp Schwenk	Aug. 1, 1995	Pasadena

Breaststroke

Distance		Time		Date Set	Location
100 meters:	**World**	1:00.60p	**Fred deBurghgraeve,** Belgium	July 20, 1996	Atlanta
	Olympic	1:00.60	deBurghgraeve, BEL (same as World)	—	—
	American	1:00.77	Jeremy Linn, USA	July 20, 1996	Atlanta
200 meters:	**World**	2:10.16	**Mike Barrowman,** USA	July 29, 1992	Barcelona
	Olympic	2:10.16	Barrowman (same as World)	—	—
	American	2:10.16	Barrowman (same as World)	—	—

Butterfly

Distance		Time		Date Set	Location
100 meters:	**World**	52.27	**Denis Pankratov,** Russia	July 24, 1996	Atlanta
	Olympic	52.27	Pankratov, Russia (same as World)	—	—
	American	52.84	Pablo Morales	June 23, 1986	Orlando
200 meters:	**World**	1:55.22	**Denis Pankratov,** Russia	June 14, 1995	Canet, FRA
	Olympic	1:56.26	Melvin Stewart, USA	July 30, 1992	Barcelona
	American	1:55.69	Melvin Stewart	Jan. 12, 1991	Perth, Aus

Individual Medley

Distance		Time		Date Set	Location
200 meters:	**World**	1:58.16	**Jani Sievinen,** Finland	Sept. 11, 1994	Rome
	Olympic	1:59.91	Atilla Czene, Hungary	July 25, 1996	Atlanta
	American	2:00.11	David Wharton	Aug. 20, 1989	Tokyo
400 meters:	**World**	4:12.30	**Tom Dolan,** USA	Sept. 6, 1994	Rome
	Olympic	4:14.23	Tamas Darnyi, Hungary	July 27, 1992	Barcelona
	American	4:12.30	Dolan (same as World)	—	—

Relays

Distance		Time		Date Set	Location
4x100m medley:	**World**	3:34.84	**USA** (Rouse, Linn, Henderson, Hall Jr.)	July 26, 1996	Atlanta
	Olympic	3:34.84	USA (same as World)	—	—
	American	3:34.84	USA (same as World)	—	—
4x100m free:	**World**	3:15.11	**USA** (Fox, Hudepohl, Olsen, Hall)	Aug. 12, 1995	Atlanta
	Olympic	3:15.41	USA (Olsen, Davis, Schumacher, Hall Jr.)	July 23, 1996	Atlanta
	American	3:15.11	USA (same as World)	—	—
4x200m free:	**World**	7:11.95	**Unified Team** (Lepikov, Pychnenko, Taianovitch, Sadovyi)	July 27, 1992	Barcelona
	Olympic	7:11.95	Unified Team (same as World)	—	—
	American	7:12.51	USA (Dalbey, Cetlinski, Gjertsen, Biondi)	Sept. 21, 1988	Seoul

WOMEN

Freestyle

Distance		Time		Date Set	Location
50 meters:	**World**	24.51	**Le Jingyi,** China	Sept. 11, 1994	Rome
	Olympic	24.79	Yang Wenyi, China	July 31, 1992	Barcelona
	American	24.87	Amy Van Dyken	July 26, 1996	Atlanta
100 meters:	**World**	54.01	**Le Jingyi,** China	Sept. 5, 1994	Rome
	Olympic	54.65	Zhaung Yong, China	July 26, 1992	Barcelona
	American	54.48	Jenny Thompson	Mar. 1, 1992	Indianapolis
200 meters:	**World**	1:56.78	**Franziska Van Almsick,** Ger.	Sept. 6, 1994	Rome
	Olympic	1:57.65	Heike Friedrich, E. Germany	Sept. 21, 1988	Seoul
	American	1:57.90	Nicole Haislett	July 27, 1992	Barcelona
400 meters:	**World**	4:03.85	**Janet Evans,** USA	Sept. 22, 1988	Seoul
	Olympic	4:03.85	Evans (same as World)	—	—
	American	4:03.85	Evans (same as World)	—	—
800 meters:	**World**	8:16.22	**Janet Evans,** USA	Aug. 20, 1989	Tokyo
	Olympic	8:20.20	Janet Evans, USA	Sept. 24, 1988	Seoul
	American	8:16.22	Evans (same as World)	—	—
1500 meters:	**World**	15:52.10	**Janet Evans,** USA	Mar. 26, 1988	Orlando
	Olympic		Not an event	—	—
	American	15:52.10	Evans (same as World)	—	—

Backstroke

Distance		Time		Date Set	Location
100 meters:	**World**	1:00.16	**He Cihong,** China	Sept. 10, 1994	Rome
	Olympic	1:00.68	Krisztina Egerszegi, Hungary	July 28, 1992	Barcelona
	American	1:00.82r	Lea Loveless	July 30, 1992	Barcelona
200 meters:	**World**	2:06.62	**Krisztina Egerszegi,** Hungary	Aug. 26, 1991	Athens
	Olympic	2:07.06	Krisztina Egerszegi, Hungary	July 31, 1992	Barcelona
	American	2:08.60	Betsy Mitchell	June 27, 1986	Orlando

Breaststroke

Distance		Time		Date Set	Location
100 meters:	**World**	1:07.02p	**Penny Heyns,** South Africa	July 21, 1996	Atlanta
	Olympic	1:07.02p	Penny Heyns (same as World)	—	—
	American	1:08.09	Amanda Beard	July 21, 1996	Atlanta
200 meters:	**World**	2:24.76	**Rebecca Brown,** Australia	Mar. 16, 1994	Queensland, AUS
	Olympic	2:26.65	Kyoko Iwasaki, Japan	July 27, 1992	Barcelona
	American	2:25.35	Anita Nall	Mar. 2, 1992	Indianapolis

Swimming World Records Set in 1996

World long course records set between Oct. 1, 1995 and Sept. 20, 1996.

MEN

Event		Record	Old Mark	Former Holder
100-meter breaststroke	**Fred deBurghgraeve,** Belgium	1:00.60	1:00.95	Karoly Guttler, HUN, 1993
100-meter butterfly	**Denis Pankratov,** Russia	52.27	52.32	Pankratov, RUS, 1995
4x100m medley	**USA Olympic Team** (Jeff Rouse, Jeremy Linn, Mark Henderson, Gary Hall Jr.)	3:34.84	3:36.93	USA (Berkoff, Schroeder, Biondi, Jacobs), 1988

WOMEN

Event		Record	Old Mark	Former Holder
100-meter breaststroke	**Penny Heyns,** South Africa	1:07.02p	1:07.69	Samantha Riley, AUS, 1994

Swimming (Cont.)

WOMEN

Butterfly

Distance		Time		Date Set	Location
100 meters:	**World**	57.93	**Mary T. Meagher,** USA	Aug. 16, 1981	Brown Deer, Wisc.
	Olympic	58.62	Qian Hong, China	July 29, 1992	Barcelona
	American	57.93	Meagher (same as World)	—	—
200 meters:	**World**	2:05.96	**Mary T. Meagher,** USA	Aug. 13, 1981	Brown Deer, Wisc.
	Olympic	2:06.90	Mary T. Meagher, USA	Aug. 4, 1984	Los Angeles
	American	2:05.96	Meagher (same as World)	—	—

Individual Medley

Distance		Time		Date Set	Location
200 meters:	**World**	2:11.65	**Lin Li,** China	July 28, 1992	Barcelona
	Olympic	2:11.65	Li (same as World)	—	—
	American	2:11.91	Summer Sanders	July 28, 1992	Barcelona
400 meters:	**World**	4:36.10	**Petra Schneider,** E. Germany	Aug. 1, 1982	Guayaquil, ECU
	Olympic	4:36.29	Petra Schneider, E. Germany	July 26, 1980	Moscow
	American	4:37.58	Summer Sanders	July 26, 1992	Barcelona

Relays

Distance		Time		Date Set	Location
4x100m free:	**World**	3:37.91	**China** (Jingyi, S.Ying, L. Ying, Lu)	Sept. 7, 1994	Rome
	Olympic	3:39.29	USA (Martino, Van Dyken, Fox, Thompson)	July 22, 1996	Atlanta
	American	3:39.29	USA (same as Olympic)	—	—
4x200m free:	**World**	7:55.47	**E. Germany** (Stellmach, Strauss, Mohring, Friedrich)	Aug. 18, 1987	Strasbourg, FRA
	Olympic	7:59.87	USA (Jackson, Teuscher, Taormina, Thompson)	July 25, 1996	Atlanta
	American	7:59.87	USA (same as Olympic)	—	—
4x100m medley:	**World**	4:01.67	**China** (Cihong, Guohong, Limin, Jingyi)	Sept. 10, 1994	Rome
	Olympic	4:02.54	USA (Loveless, Nall, Ahmann-Leighton, Thompson)	July 30, 1992	Barcelona
	American	4:02.54	USA (same as Olympic)	—	—

FINA Short Course World Championships

at Rio de Janeiro, Brazil
(Nov. 29-Dec. 3, 1995)

MEN

Event		Time	
50m free	Francisco Sanchez, VEN	21.80	CR
100m free	Fernando Scherer, BRA	47.97	
200m free	Gustavo Borges, BRA	1:45.55	
400m free	Daniel Kowalski, AUS	3:45.14	
1500m free	Daniel Kowalski, AUS	14:48.51	
100m back	Rodolfo Falcon, CUB	53.12	
200m back	Rodolfo Falcon, CUB	1:55.16	
100m breast	Mark Warnecke, GER	59.89	
200m breast	Yiwu Wang, CHN	2:11.11	
100m fly	Scott Miller, AUS	52.38	CR
200m fly	Scott Goodman, AUS	1:54.79	CR
200m I.M.	Matthew Dunn, AUS	1:56.86	
400m I.M.	Matthew Dunn, AUS	4:08.02	CR

Relays

Event		Time
400m free	Brazil	3:12.42
800m free	Australia	7:07.97
400m med	New Zealand	3:35.69

WOMEN

Event		Time	
50m free	Jingyi Le, CHN	24.62	
100m free	Jingyi Le, CHN	53.23	
200m free	Claudia Poll, CRC	1:55.42	WR
400m free	Claudia Poll, CRC	4:05.18	CR
800m free	Sarah Hardcastle, GBR	8:26.46	
100m back	Misty Hyman, USA	1:00.21	
200m back	Mette Jacobsen, DEN	2:08.18	
100m breast	Samantha Riley, AUS	1:05.70	WR
200m breast	Samantha Riley, AUS	2:20.85	WR
100m fly	Limin Liu, CHN	58.68	WR
200m fly	Susan O'Neil, AUS	2:06.18	CR
200m I.M.	Ellie Overton, AUS	2:11.67	
400m I.M.	Joanne Malar, CAN	4:36.40	

Relays

Event		Time
400m free	China	3:37.00
800m free	Canada	7:58.25
400m med	Australia	4:00.46

Note: Short course world records are not included in the list above; that list is of long course world records.

WINTER SPORTS

World Hockey Championships

The 49th World Hockey Championships, held in Vienna, Austria from April 21 to May 5, 1996. Top four teams (*) in each group after preliminary round-robin advanced to quarterfinals.

Final Round Robin Standings

(Overall records in parentheses)

GROUP A	Gm	W-L-T	Pts	GF	GA
*Russia (6-1-1)	5	5-0-0	**10**	23	8
*United States (5-3-0)	5	3-2-0	**6**	15	14
*Canada (3-3-2)	5	2-2-1	**5**	17	15
*Germany (2-4-0)	5	2-3-0	**4**	11	7
Slovakia (1-3-1)	5	1-3-1	**3**	13	16
Austria (1-6-0)	5	1-4-0	**2**	3	19

GROUP B	Gm	W-L-T	Pts	GF	GA
*Czech Republic (7-0-1)	5	4-0-1	**9**	27	12
*Finland (2-2-2)	5	2-1-2	**6**	23	15
*Sweden (2-2-2)	5	2-1-2	**6**	14	12
*Italy (2-3-1)	5	2-2-1	**5**	20	26
Norway (1-2-2)	5	1-2-2	**4**	6	11
France (2-5-0)	5	0-5-0	**0**	12	25

Quarterfinals

United States 3 .... Sweden 2
Canada 3 .... Finland 1
Russia 5 .... Italy 2
Czech Republic 6 .... Germany 1

Semifinals

Czech Republic 5 .... United States 0
Canada 2 .... Russia 2
Note: Canada wins 3–2 on a penalty shootout.

Third Place: United States 4 .... OT .... Russia 3
Championship: Czech Republic 4 .... Canada 2

Leading Scorers

	Gm	G	A	Pts	PM
Yanic Perreault, Canada	8	6	3	**9**	0
Robert Lang, Czech Repub.	8	5	4	**9**	2
Sergei Berezin, Russia	8	4	5	**9**	2
Alexei Yashin, Russia	8	4	5	**9**	4
Teemu Selanne, Finland	6	5	3	**8**	8
Bruno Zarrillo, Italy	6	4	4	**8**	0
Travis Green, Canada	8	5	3	**8**	0
Robert Reichel, Czech Repub.	8	4	4	**8**	4
Dmitri Kvartalnov, Russia	8	4	4	**8**	4
Pavel Patera, Czech Repub.	8	3	5	**8**	2

Leading Goaltenders

(Minimum 100 minutes)

	Gm	Min	GA	Avg	Sv%
Andrei Trefilov, Russia	7	310	7	**1.35**	.956
Robert Schistad, Norway	5	240	6	**1.50**	.971
Curtis Joseph, Canada	8	409	12	**1.76**	.958
Roman Turek, Czech Repub.	8	480	15	**1.88**	.952
Boo Ahl, Sweden	6	300	10	**2.00**	.942
Parris Duffus, United States	7	425	18	**2.54**	.948

World All-Star Teams

(Selected by media)

First Team: G— Roman Turek, Czech Republic; **D**— Alexei Zhitnik, Russia and Michal Sykora, Czech Republic; **F**— Paul Kariya, Canada; Robert Reichel, Czech Republic; Otakar Vejvoda, Czech Republic.
Second Team: G— Curtis Joseph, Canada; **D**— Drahomor Kadlec, Czech Republic and Glen Wesley, Canada; **F**— Sergei Berezin, Russia; Alexei Yashin, Russia; Kevin Stevens, United States.

Alpine Skiing

World Alpine Championships

at Sierra Nevada, Spain (Feb. 12-25)

MEN

Slalom
1 Alberto Tomba, ITA 1:42.26
2 Mario Reiter, AUT 1:42.57
3 Michael Von Gruenigen, SWI 1:42.81

Giant Slalom
1 Alberto Tomba, ITA 1:58.63
2 Urs Kaelin, SWI 1:59.07
3 Michael Von Gruenigen, SWI 1:59.45

Super Giant Slalom
1 Atle Skaardal, NOR 1:21.80
2 Patrik Jaerbyn, SWE 1:22.09
3 Kjetil Andre Aamodt, NOR 1:22.11

Downhill
1 Patrick Ortlieb, AUT 2:00.17
2 Kristian Ghedina, ITA 2:00.44
3 Luc Alphand, FRA 2:00.45

Combined
1 Marc Girardelli, LUX 3:31.95
2 Lasse Kjus, NOR 3:32.20
3 Guenther Mader, AUT 3:32.93

WOMEN

Slalom
1 Pernilla Wiberg, SWE 1:31.46
2 Patricia Chauvet, FRA 1:32.32
3 Urska Hrovat, SLO 1:32.33

Giant Slalom
1 Deborah Compagnoni, ITA 2:10.74
2 Karin Roten, SWI 2:11.09
3 Martina Ertl, GER 2:11.44

Super Giant Slalom
1 Isolde Kostner, ITA 1:21.00
2 Heidi Zurbriggen, SWI 1:21.66
3 Picabo Street, USA 1:21.71

Downhill
1 Picabo Street, USA 1:54.06
2 Katja Seizinger, GER 1:54.63
3 Hilary Lindh, USA 1:54.70

Combined
1 Pernilla Wiberg, SWE 3:19.68
2 Anita Wachter, AUT 3:21.73
3 Marianne Kjoerstad, NOR 3:22.35

Alpine Skiing (Cont.)

World Cup Champions

MEN

Overall	Lasse Kjus, NOR
Downhill	Luc Alphand, FRA
Slalom	Sebastien Amiez, FRA
Giant Slalom	Michael von Gruenigen, SWI
Super G	Arte Skaardal, NOR
Nation's Cup	Austria

Top Five Standings

Overall: 1. Lasse Kjus, NOR (1216 pts); 2. Guenther Mader, AUT (1000); Michael von Gruenigen, SWI (880); 4. Luc Alphand, FRA (839); 5. Alberto Tomba, ITA (766). *Best USA*— Kyle Rasmussen (43rd, 188 pts).

Downhill: 1. Luc Alphand, FRA (577 pts); 2. Guenther Mader, AUT (407); 3. Patrick Ortlieb, AUT (359); 4. Lasse Kjus, NOR (343); 5. Bruno Kernen, SWI (325). *Best USA*— Kyle Rasmussen (8th, 121 pts).

Slalom: 1. Sebastien Amiez, FRA (539 pts); 2. Alberto Tomba, ITA (490); 3. Thomas Sykora, AUT (446); 4. Mario Reiter, AUT (384); 5. Jure Kosir, SLO (381). *Best USA*— Matt Grosjean (26th, 67 pts).

Giant Slalom: 1. Michael von Gruenigen, SWI (738 pts); 2. Urs Kaelin, AUT (601); 3. Lasse Kjus, NOR (475); 4. Fredrik Nyberg, SWE (338); 5. Hans Knauss, AUT (306). *Best USA*— Daron Rhalves (27th, 42 pts).

Super G: 1. Arte Skaardal, NOR (312 pts); 2. Hans Knauss, AUT (267); 3. Lasse Kjus, NOR (264); 4. Luc Alphand, FRA (262); 5. Peter Runggaldier, ITA (239). *Best USA*— Daron Rhalves (18th, 79 pts).

WOMEN

Overall	Katja Seizinger, GER
Downhill	Picabo Street, USA
Slalom	Vreni Schneider, SWI
Giant Slalom	Vreni Schneider, SWI
Super G	Katja Seizinger, GER
Nation's Cup	Austria

Top Five Standings

Overall: 1. Katja Seizinger, GER (1,472 pts); 2. Martina Ertl, GER (1,059); 3. Anita Wachter, AUT (1,044); 4. Isolde Kostner, ITA (905); 5. Alexandra Meissnitzer, AUT (894). *Best USA*— Picabo Street (6th, 837 pts).

Downhill: 1. Picabo Street, USA (640 pts); 2. Katja Seizinger, GER (485); 3. Isolde Kostner, ITA & Heidi Zurbriggen, SWI (449); 5. Warwara Zelenskaja, RUS (424).

Slalom: 1. Elfe Eder, AUT (580 pts); 2. Urska Hrovat, SLO (440); 3. Pernilla Wiberg, SWE (414); 4. Marianne Kjoerstad, NOR (398); 5. Kristina Andersson, SWE (360). *Best USA*— Kristina Koznick (40th, 29 pts).

Giant Slalom: 1. Martina Ertl, GER (485 pts); 2. Katja Seizinger, GER (410); 3. Anita Wachter, AUT (371); 4. Sabina Panzanini, ITA (313); 5. Sonja Nef, SWI (292). *Best USA*— Picabo Street (49th, 7 pts).

Super G: 1. Katja Seizinger, GER (545 pts); 2. Alexandra Meissnitzer, AUT (374); 3. Martina Ertl, GER (335); 4. Isolde Kostner, ITA (291); 5. Renate Goetschl, AUT (267). *Best USA*— Picabo Street (14th, 145 pts).

Nation's Cup: 1. Austria (11,071 pts); 2. Switzerland (7,186); 3. Italy (6,289); 4. Germany (4,602); 5. Norway (4,519); 6. France (3,867); 7. Sweden (2,905); 8. Slovenia (2,516); 9. United States (1,808); 10. Canada (982).

U.S. Championships

at Sugarloaf/USA, Maine (Mar. 21–25)

MEN

Downhill	Chad Fleischer, Vail, Colo.
Slalom	Chip Knight, New Canaan, Conn.
Giant Slalom	Daron Rahlves, Truckee, Calif.
Super G	Kyle Rasmussen, Angels Camp, Calif.
Combined	Chris Puckett, Crested Butte, Colo.

WOMEN

Downhill	Picabo Street, Sun Valley, Idaho
Slalom	Kristina Koznick, Burnsville, Minn.
Giant Slalom	Jennifer Collins, Allegany, N.Y.
Super G	Picabo Street, Sun Valley, Idaho
Combined	Kristen Clark, Raymond, Maine

Biathlon

World Cup Champions

Men's Overall	Vladimir Dratschev, RUS	Women's Overall	Emmanuelle Claret, FRA

World Championships

at Ruhpolding, Germany (Feb. 3)

MEN

10-km	Vladimir Dratshev, Russia
20-km	Sergei Tarasov, Russia

WOMEN

7.5-km	Olga Romasko, Russia
15-km	Emmanuelle Claret, France

U.S. Championships

at Lake Placid, N.Y. (Dec. 29–Jan. 4)

MEN

10-km	Curtis Schreiner, Saratoga Springs, N.Y.
20-km	Daniel Westover, Colchester, Vt.

WOMEN

7.5-km	Debbie Nordyke, Jerico, Vt.
15-km	Kristina Viljanen-Sabasteanski, Milford, N.H.

Bobsled

1996 World Championships

at Calgary, Alberta, Canada (Feb. 16–24)

Two-Man ....Christoph Langen & Markus Zimmerman, Germany I
Four-Man ....Christoph Langen, Markus Zimmerman, Sven Ruhr & Olaf Hampel, Germany II

World Cup Champion Drivers

Two-Man ....Christoph Langen, Germany I
Four-Man....................Wolfgang Hopper, Germany II
Combined ....Christoph Langen, Germany I

U.S. Championship Drivers

Lake Placid, N.Y. (Jan. 6–7)

Two-Man ....Bruce Rosselli, Terre Haute, Ind.
Four-Man....................Jim Herberich, Winchester, Mass.

Luge

World Championships

at Altenburg, Germany (Feb. 4)

Men's Singles ....Prock Markus, AUT
Men's Doubles ....Tobias Schiegl & Markus Schiegl, AUT
Women's Singles....................Jana Bode, GER
Team ....Austria

World Cup Champions

Men's Singles ....Prock Markus, AUT
Men's Doubles ....Jan Behrendt & Stefan Krause, GER
Women's Singles....................Jana Bode, GER

U.S. Championships

at Lake Placid, N.Y. (Feb. 29)

Men's Singles..............Robert Pipkins, Staten Island, N.Y.
Women's Singles............Cammy Myler, Lake Placid, N.Y.

Freestyle Skiing

World Cup Champions

MEN

Overall ....Jonny Moseley, USA
Aerials ....Sebastien Foucras, FRA
Moguls ....Jean-Luc Brassard, CAN
Dual Moguls ....Jesper Röbbnick, SWE
Acroski ....Heini Baumgartner, SWI
Combined....................Jonny Moseley, USA

WOMEN

Overall ....Katherina Kubenk, CAN
Aerials ....Colette Brand, SWI
Moguls....................Donna Weinbrecht, USA
Dual Moguls....................Candice Gilg, FRA
Acroski ....Elena Batalova, RUS

Nations Cup (Men & Women) ....USA

U.S. Championships

at Park City/Snowbird, Utah (Mar. 18–25)

MEN

Aerials ....Eric Bergoust, Missoula, Mont.
Moguls....................Garth Hager, Bothell, Wash.
Acroski ....Ian Edmondson, E. Lansing, Mich.
Uprgt. Comb......James Garland, Colorado Springs, Colo.

WOMEN

Aerials ....Stacey Blumer, Southington, Conn.
Moguls ....Donna Weinbrecht, W. Milford, N.J.
Acroski....................Laura Rosenbaum, Portsmouth, R.I.
Uprgt. Comb. ....Erin Reinhardt, Telluride, Colo.

Nordic Skiing

World Cup Champions

MEN

Cross-country ....Bjorn Daehlie, NOR
Ski Jumping....................Andreas Goldberger, AUT
Nordic Combined....................Knut Tore Apeland, NOR

WOMEN

Cross-country ....Manuela Di Centa, ITA

U.S. Championships

Cross-country

at Lake Placid, N.Y. (Jan. 10–17)

MEN

10-km classical....................John Bauer, Champlin, Minn.
15-km classical ....John Bauer
15-km freestyle ....John Bauer
50-km freestyle ....John Bauer

WOMEN

5-km classical ....Laura Wilson, Montpelier, Vt.
10-km classical....................Kerrin Petty, Townshend, Vt.
15-km freestyle ....Suzanne King, Minneapolis
30-km freestyle ....Ingrid Butts, Park City, Utah

Ski Jumping

at Lake Placid, N.Y. (Jan. 20–21)

Large Hill (120 meters) ....Randy Weber, Steamboat Springs, Colo.
Normal Hill (90 meters)....................Randy Weber

Nordic Combined

at Steamboat Springs, Colo. (Dec. 1–2, 1995)
90-meter jump/10-km cross-country ski

Individual ....Todd Lodwick, Steamboat Springs, Colo.

Snowboarding

World Championships

at Lienz, Austria (Jan. 24–28)

MEN

Halfpipe	Pts
1 Ross Powers, USA	79.3
2 Lael Gregory, USA	75.4
3 Rob Kingwill, USA	74.1

Giant Slalom	Time
1 Jeff Greenwood, USA	1:50.18
2 Mike Jacoby, USA	1:50.97
3 Helmut Pramstaller, AUT	1:51.58

Parallel Slalom
1 Ivo Rudiferia, ITA
2 Rainer Krug, GER
3 Helmut Pramstaller, AUT

WOMEN

Halfpipe	Pts
1 Carolien Van Kilsdonik, NET	49.5
2 Annemarie Uliasz, USA	44.7
3 Cammy Potter, USA	43.0

Giant Slalom	Time
1 Karine Ruby, FRA	2:11.91
2 Manuela Riegler, AUT	2:12.50
3 Sondra Van Ert, USA	2:12.87

Parallel Slalom
1 Marion Posch, ITA
2 Marcella Boerma, NET
3 Sondra Van Ert, USA

World Cup Final Standings

MEN

Overall	Pts
1 Mike Jacoby, USA	1243.33
2 Stefan Kaltschutz, AUT	956.77
3 Thedo Remmelink, NET	895.86

Halfpipe	Pts
1 Ross Powers, USA	5000
2 Rob Kingwill, USA	4760
3 Dan Smith, USA	4700

Giant Slalom	Pts
1 Mike Jacoby, USA	7900
2 Peter Pechhacker, AUT	5820
3 Harald Walder, AUT	5760

Parallel Slalom	Pts
1 Peter Pichler, ITA	6320
2 Stefan Kaltschutz, AUT	6210
3 Maxence Idesheim, FRA	5480

WOMEN

Overall	Pts
1 Karine Ruby, FRA	1760.60
2 Manuela Riegler, AUT	1024.34
3 Birgit Herbert, AUT	537.78

Halfpipe	Pts
1 Carolien Van Kilsdonk, NET	6000
2 Annemarie Uliasz, USA	4500
3 Lori Glazier, CAN	3200

Giant Slalom	Pts
1 Karine Ruby, FRA	7500
2 Sondra Van Ert, USA	5190
3 Ursula Fingerlos, AUT	4950

Parallel Slalom	Pts
1 Karine Ruby, FRA	10,200
2 Marcella Boerma, NET	5590
3 Manuela Riegler, AUT	5560

U.S. Championships

at Mammoth/June Mountain, Calif. (Mar. 27–30)

MEN

Halfpipe	Pts
1 John Summers, Lake Tahoe, Calif.	75
2 Jeff Anderson, Mammoth Lakes, Calif.	74.6
3 Lael Gregory, Eugene, Ore.	71.9

Giant Slalom	Pts
1 Mike Kildevaeld, DEN	111.80
2 Manuel Mendoza, Whitefish, Mont.	112.16
3 Thomas Lyman, Whitefish, Mont.	112.76

Slalom	Pts
1 Manuel Mendoza, Whitefish, Mont.	1:32.75
2 Anton Pogue, Hood River, Ore.	1:33.86
3 Steve Persons, Whitefish, Mont.	1:34.59

WOMEN

Halfpipe	Pts
1 Aurelie Sayres, East Haddem, Conn.	55.2
2 Cammy Potter, Park City, Utah	46.7
3 Annemarie Uliasz, Huntington Beach, Calif.	46.3

Giant Slalom	Pts
1 Sondra Van Ert, Ketchum, Idaho	117.05
2 Leslee Olson, Bend, Ore.	124.94
3 Lynn Ott, Bend, Ore.	125.22

Slalom	Pts
1 Sondra Van Ert, Ketchum, Idaho	1:38.42
2 Leslle Olson, Bend, Ore.	1:40.33
3 Kim Stacey, Stratton Mt., Vt.	1:42.12

Figure Skating

World Championships

at Edmonton, Alberta, Canada (Mar. 17–24)

Men's— 1. Todd Eldredge, USA; 2. Ilya Kulik, Russia; 3. Rudy Galindo, USA

Women's— 1. Michelle Kwan, USA; 2. Lu Chen, China; 3. Irina Slutskaya, Russia

Pairs— 1. Marina Eltsova & Andrey Bushkov, Russia; 2. Mandy Wotzel & Ingo Steuer, Germany; 3. Jenni Meno & Todd Sand, USA.

Ice Dance— 1. Oksana Gritschuk & Evgeny Platov, Russia; 2. Anjelika Krylova & Oleg Ovsiannikov, Russia; 3. Shae-Lynn Bourne & Victor Kraatz, Canada

U.S. Championships

at San Jose, Calif. (Jan. 13–20)

Men's .... Rudy Galindo, San Jose, Calif.
Women's .... Michelle Kwan, Torrance, Calif.
Pairs .... Jenni Meno, Westlake, Ohio & Todd Sand, Thousand Oaks, Calif.
Ice Dance .... Elizabeth Punsalan, Sheffield Lake, Ohio & Jerod Swallow, Northville, Mich.

European Championships

at Sofia, Bulgaria (Jan. 22–28)

Men's .... Viacheslav Zagorodniuk, Ukraine
Women's .... Irina Slutskaya, Russia
Pairs .... Oksana Kazakova & Artur Dmitriev, Russia
Ice Dance .... Oksana Grishuk & Yevgeny Platov, Russia

Speed Skating
World Cup Champions

MEN

500 meters	Manabu Horil, JPN
1000 meters	Adne Sondral, JPN
1500 meters	Hiuroyuki Noake, JPN
5000/10,000 meters	Rintje Ritsma, NET

WOMEN

500 meters	Svetlana Zhurova, RUS
1000 meters	Chris Witty, USA
1500 meters	Gunda Niemann, GER
3000/5000 meters	Gunda Niemann, GER

World Long Track Championships

at Inzell, Germany (Feb. 2–4)

MEN

500 meters	Hiroyuki Noake, JPN
1500 meters	Hiroyuki Noake, JPN
5000 meters	Bart Veldkamp, BEL
10,000 meters	Rintje Ritsma, NET
All-Around	Rintje Ritsma, NET

WOMEN

500 meters	Becky Sundstrom, USA
1500 meters	Gunda Niemann, GER
3000 meters	Gunda Niemann, GER
5000 meters	Claudia Pechstein, GER
All-Around	Gunda Niemann, GER

World Sprint Championships

at Heerenveen, Netherlands (Feb. 17–18)

MEN

500 meters	Horiyasu Shimizu, Japan
1000 meters	Sergei Klevchenja, Russia
Overall	Casey FitzRandolph, USA

WOMEN

500 meters	Svetlana Zhurova, Russia
1000 Meters	Christine Witty, USA
Overall	Christine Witty, USA

SUMMER SPORTS

Basketball
MEN

For a summary of the European Championship for Men's clubs, see page 363.

National Club Champions

English League	Birmingham Bullets def. London Towers, 78–72
French League	Pau-Orthez def. Villeurbanne, 3 games to 2
German League	Bayer-Leverkusen def. Alba Berlin, 3 games to 1
Greek League	Olympiakos def. Panathinaikos, 3 games to 2
Italian League	Stefanel Milano def. TeamSystem Bologna, 3 games to 1
Spanish League	FC Barcelona def. Caja San Fernando, 3 games to 0

WOMEN

1996 European Clubs Championship

in Sofia, Bulgaria (Mar. 19–21)

Semifinals

BTV Wuppertal (GER) def. MSK Sipox, Ruzemberok (SVK), 84–67

SFT Como (ITA) def. CJM Bourges Basket (FRA), 62–54

Third-place game

MSK Sipox, Ruzemberok def. CJM Bourges Basket, 65–59

Championship game

BTV Wuppertal def. SFT Como, 76–62

Most Valuable Player

Sandra Brondello, BTV Wuppertal

EuroLeagues Begin Inaugural Season

FIBA, the International Federation for Basketball, announced the formation of a 24-team EuroLeague for Men and a 16-team EuroLeague for Women. Each league started play in the fall of 1996 and includes professional clubs from 12 nations. The men's league will be divided into four groups of six and each team will play 16 regular season games, while the women will be divided into two groups of eight and play 14 regular season contests. The top four teams in each group will advance to the playoffs. The women's championship Final Four tournament is scheduled for Apr. 8-10, 1997 in Larissa, Greece. The men's Final Four is Apr. 22-24, 1997 in Rome.

Cross-country
IAAF World Championships

at Stellenbosch, South Africa (Mar. 23)

Men (7.54 miles)
1. Paul Tergat, KEN 33:44
2. Salah Hissou, MOR 33:56
3. Ismael Kirui, KEN 33:57

Best USA— Brian Baker, 41st 35:57

Women (3.91 miles)
1. Gete Wami, ETH 20:12
2. Rose Cheruiyot, KEN 20:18
3. Naomi Mungo, KEN 20:21

Best USA— Joan Nesbit, 25th 21:19

Cricket

World Cup

Feb. 14–Mar. 17, 1996

Group A	Gm	W	L	Pts	Run rate
Sri Lanka	3	3	0	10	+1.63
Australia	4	3	1	6	+0.88
India	5	3	2	6	+0.46
West Indies	4	2	2	4	−0.12
Zimbabwe	5	1	4	2	−0.93
Kenya	5	1	4	2	−1.03

Group B	Gm	W	L	Pts	Run rate
South Africa	5	5	0	10	+2.06
Pakistan	5	4	1	8	+0.94
New Zealand	5	3	2	6	+0.60
England	5	2	3	4	+0.07
United Arab Emirates	5	1	4	2	−1.82
Netherlands	5	0	5	0	−1.95

Note: Sri Lanka's point total includes four points awarded after Australia (Feb. 17) and West Indies (Feb. 25) forfeited their matches.

Quarterfinals

Sri Lanka def. England, by 5 wickets
India def. Pakistan, by 39 runs
West Indies def. South Africa, by 19 runs
Australia def. New Zealand, by 6 wickets

Semifinals

Sri Lanka def. India, awarded match
Australia def. West Indies, by 5 runs

Championship match

at Gaddaffi Stadium, Lahore, Pakistan (Mar. 17)
Australia 241-7 (50 overs), Sri Lanka 245-3 (47).

Sri Lanka wins Wills World Cup by 7 wickets and 22 balls.

Tournament MVP: Sanath Jayasuriya, Sri Lanka

Cycling

Tour de France

The 83rd Tour de France (June 29–July 21) was 21 stages plus a prologue, covering 2,384 miles starting at the city of Den Bosch in the Netherlands, through Belgium, Italy, Spain and France and finished a week early so as not to conflict with the Summer Olympics in Atlanta. The race began near Amsterdam in Hertogenbosch, Holland and ended in Paris. 129 out of 198 riders finished the race.

Bjarne Riis became the first Danish winner in the Tour's history with a time of 95 hours, 57 minutes and 16 seconds. Riis won $440,000 plus $400 for each of the 13 days he wore the yellow jersey. His German Telekom teammates also impressed; Jan Ullrich placed second (winning $220,000) and won the "best young rider" award ($20,000 bonus) for the top rider under 25 while Erik Zabel won the green jersey as best sprinter ($30,000). France's Richard Virenque of the Festina team took third ($120,000) and captured the red and white polka dot jersey as best climber ($30,000 bonus) for the third straight year. Virenque became the first Frenchman on the podium since Laurent Fignon took second to Greg LeMond in 1989.

		Team	Behind
1	Bjarne Riis, DEN	Telekom	—
2	Jan Ullrich, GER	Telekom	1:41
3	Richard Virenque, FRA	Festina	4:37
4	Laurent Dufaux, SWI	Festina	5:53
5	Peter Luttenberger, AUT	Carrera	7:07
6	Luc Leblanc, FRA	Polti	10:03
7	Piotyr Ugrumov, RUS	Roslotto	10:04
8	Fernando Escartin, SPA	Kelme	10:26
9	Abraham Olano, SPA	Mapei	11:00
10	Tony Rominger, SWI	Mapei	11:53
11	Miguel Indurain, SPA	Banesto	14:14
12	Patrick Jonker, AUS	ONCE	18:58
13	Bo Hamburger, DEN	TVM	22:19
14	Udo Bolts, GER	Telekom	25:56
15	Alberto Elli, ITA	MG	26:18
16	Manu Fernandez Gines,	Mapei	26:28
17	Leonardo Piepoli,	Refin	27:36
18	Laurent Brochard,	Festina	32:11
19	Michele Bartoli,	MG	37:18
20	Evgeni Berzin, RUS	Gewiss	38:00

Best USA: 111 th —Frankie Andreu, Dearborn, Mich., Motorola, 2:48:46 behind.

Other Worldwide Champions

1996 UCI (Union Cycliste Internationale) Elite Results

MEN

Race	Winner
Omloop Het Volk (BEL)	Tom Steels, BEL
Paris-Nice (FRA)	Laurent Jalabert, FRA
Tirreno-Adriatico (ITA)	Francesco Casagrande, ITA
Milan-San Remo (ITA)	Gabriele Colombo, ITA
GP Cholet-Pays de Loire (FRA)	Stephane Heulor, FRA
Semaña Catalana (SPA)	Alex Zuelle, SWI
GP H3 Harelbeke (BEL)	Carlo Bomans, BEL
Tour de Flanders (BEL)	Michele Bartoli, ITA
Vuelta al Pais Vasco (SPA)	Francesco Casagrande, ITA
Ghent-Wevelgen (BEL)	Tom Steels, BEL
Paris-Roubaix (FRA)	Johan Museeuw, BEL
Fleche Wallone (BEL)	Lance Armstrong, USA
Liege-Bastogne-Liege	Pascal Richard, SWI
GP de l'Escaut (BEL)	Franck Vandenbroucke, BEL
Amstel Gold (NET)	Stefani Zanini, ITA
Rund um den Henninger Turm (GER)	Beat Zberg, SWI
Tour du Pont (USA)	Lance Armstrong, USA
GP de Gippingen (SWI)	Fabrizio Guidi, ITA
Tour de Romandie (SWI)	Abraham Olano, SPA
Quatre Jours de Dunkerque (FRA)	Philippe Gaumont, FRA
Giro d'Italia (ITA)	Pavel Tonkov, RUS
GP du Midi Libre (FRA)	Laurent Jalabert, FRA
Dauphine Libere (FRA)	Miguel Indurain, SPA
Tour of Switzerland (SWI)	Peter Luttenberger, AUT
Clasica San Sebastian (SPA)	Udo Bolts, GER
Leeds International Classic (GB)	Andrea Ferrigato, ITA
Vuelta de Espana (SPA)	Alex Sulle, SWI

WOMEN

Race	Winner
PowerBar Challenge (USA)	Anna Wilson, AUS
Tour Cycliste Feminin (FRA)	Fabiana Luperini, ITA
Giro d'Italia Femminile (ITA)	Fabiana Luperini, ITA
CoreStates Liberty Classic (USA)	Petra Rossner, GER

1996 World Road Championships

at Lugano, Switzerland
(Oct. 9-13)

MEN

Elite Road Race (252 km)
Johan Museeuw, BEL 6:23:50
U-23 Road Race (168 km)
Giulano Figueras, ITA 4:23:50
Elite Time Trial (40.4 km)
Alex Zulle, SWI 48:13.86
U-23 Time Trial (31.6 km)
Luca Sironi, ITA 37:51.89

WOMEN

Road Race (101 km)
Barbara Heeb, SWI 2:53:05
Time Trial (26.4 km)
Jeannie Longo-Ciprelli, FRA..35:16.07

1996 World Track Championships

at Manchester Velodrome, Manchester, England
(Aug. 28–Sept. 1)

MEN

1km time trial..Shane Kelly, AUS
Keirin race..Marty Nothstein, USA
50km Madison race....Silvio Martinello & Marco Villa, ITA
4km individual pursuit ....Chris Boardman, GBR
Olympic Sprint..Australia (Darryn Hill, Shane Kelly, Gary Niewand)
4km team pursuit.....Italy (Capelli, Citton, Collinelli, Tretini)
40km points race ....Juan Llaneras, SPA
Sprint..Floria Rousseau, FRA

WOMEN

24km points race.................Svetlana Samokhvalova, RUS
Sprint..Felicia Ballanger, FRA
500m time trial..............................Felicia Ballanger, FRA
3km individual pursuit.......................Marion Clignet, FRA

Mountain Biking

1996 World Championships

at Cairns, Australia (Sept. 21–22)

MEN

Cross Country (58.4 km)	**Time**
1 Jerome Chiotti, FRA	2:37:36
2 Thomas Frischknecht, SWI	at 1:57
3 Rune Hoydahl, NOR	at 2:06

Downhill (2.5 km)	**Time**
1 Nicholas Vouilloz, FRA	4:54.79
2 Shaun Palmer, USA	at 0.15
3 Bas Be Bever, NET	at 0.33

WOMEN

Downhill (37.8 km)	**Time**
1 Alison Sydor, CAN	2:05:56
2 Ruthie Matthes, USA	at 1:52
3 Maria-Paola Turcotto, ITA	at 2:02

Downhill (2.5 km)	**Time**
1 Anne-Caroline Chausson, FRA	5:27.58
2 Leigh Donovan, USA	at 0.18
3 Missy Giove, USA	at 0.79

UCI World Cup Champions

MEN

Cross Country	**Pts**
1 Christophe Duponey, FRA	373
2 Thomas Frischknecht, SWI	357
3 Miguel Martinez, FRA	321

Downhill	**Pts**
1 Nicholas Vouilloz, FRA	201
2 Marcus Klausmann, GER	184
3 Tomas Misser, SPA	169

WOMEN

Cross Country	**Pts**
1 Alison Sydor, CAN	227
2 Gunn-Rita Dahle, NOR	161
3 Juli Furtado, USA	134
Caroline Alexander, GBR	134

Downhill	**Pts**
1 Missy Giove, USA	128
2 Anne-Caroline Chausson, FRA	125
3 Leigh Donovan, USA	100

Gymnastics

World Championships

at San Juan, Puerto Rico (April 19–20)

MEN

Vault	**Pts**
1 Alexei Nemov, Russia	9.756
2 Yeo Hong-Chul, S. Korea	9.743
Andrea Massucchi, Italy	9.743

Parallel Bars	**Pts**
1 Rustam Charipov, Ukraine	9.750
2 Vitaly Scherbo, Belarus	9.737
Alexei Nemov, Russia	9.737

Horizontal Bars	**Pts**
1 Jesus Carballo, Spain	9.800
2 Krasimir Dounev, Bulgaria	9.775
3 Vitaly Scherbo, Belarus	9.762

Floor Exercise	**Pts**
1 Vitaly Scherbo, Belarus	9.787
2 Alexei Voropaev, Russia	9.700
3 Grigory Misutin, Ukraine	9.625

Pommel Horse	**Pts**
1 Pae Gil Su, N. Korea	9.825
2 Li Donghua, Switzerland	9.812
3 Alexei Nemov, Russia	9.787

Rings	**Pts**
1 Yuri Chechi, Italy	9.825
2 Jordan Jovtchev, Bulgaria	9.737
Szilveszter Csollany, Hungary	9.737

Gymnastics (Cont.)

World Championships

WOMEN

Vault	Pts
1 Gina Gogean, Romania	9.800
2 Simona Amanar, Romania	9.787
3 Annia Portuondo, Cuba	9.756

Uneven Bars	Pts
1 Svetlana Chorkina, Russia	9.787
Yelena Piskun, Belarus	9.787
3 Isabelle Severino, France	9.775

For Olympic Gymnastic results see p. 633 in the Olympics chapter.

Balance Beam	Pts
1 Dina Kochetkova, Russia	9.887
2 Alexandra Marinescu, Romania	9.812
3 Liu Xuan, China	9.800
Dominique Dawes, USA	9.800

Floor Exercise	Pts
1 Gina Gogean, Romania	9.850
Kui Yuanyuan, China	9.850
3 Lioubov Sheremeta, Ukraine	9.800
Lavinia Milosovici, Romania	9.800

Marathons

Boston Marathon

100th edition of the Boston Marathon, held Monday, April 15, 1996 and run, as always, from Hopkinton through Ashland, Framingham, Natick, Wellesley, Newton and Brookline to Boston, Mass. Moses Tanui led the Kenyan sweep, while Germany's Uta Pippig battled physical difficulties but came from behind to win an unprecedented third-straight Boston. Heinz Frei of Switzerland won the men's wheelchair division (1:30:11) and Jean Driscoll of the United States won her seventh consecutive women's wheelchair title (1:52:54). Winners in the men's and women's divisions earned $100,000. **Distance:** 26.2 miles. **Weather:** 44 degrees, clear and sunny.

MEN

		Time
1	Moses Tanui, KEN	2:09:16
2	Ezekiel Bitok, KEN	2:09:26
3	Cosmas Ndeti, KEN	2:09:51
4	Lamek Aguta, KEN	2:10:93
5	Sammy Lelei, KEN	2:10:11
6	Abebe Mekonnen, ETH	2:10:21
7	Charles Tangus, KEN	2:10:28
8	Paul Yego, KEN	2:10:49
9	Carlos Grisales, COL	2:11:17
10	Stephen Moneghetti, AUS	2:11:17

WOMEN

		Time
1	Uta Pippig, GER	2:27:12
2	Tegla Loroupe, KEN	2:28:37
3	Nobuko Fujimura, JPN	2:29:24
4	Sonja Krolik, GER	2:29:24
5	Larisa Zouzko, RUS	2:31:06
6	Franziska Rochat-Moser, SWI	2:31:33
7	Madina Biktagirova, BEL	2:31:38
8	Lorraine Moller, NZE	2:32:02
9	Alla Jiliaeva, RUS	2:33:47
10	Valentina Enaki, MOL	2:33:58

Other 1996 Winners

Los Angeles

Mar. 3	Men	Jose Luis Molina, USA	2:13:23
	Women	Lyubov Klochko, UKR	2:30:30

London

Apr. 21	Men	Dionicio Ceron, MEX	2:10:00
	Women	Liz McClogan, GBR	2:27:54

Rotterdam

Apr. 28	Men	Belayneh Densamo, ETH	2:10:30
	Women	Lieve Slegers, BEL	2:28:06

Berlin

Sept. 29	Men	Abel Anton, SPA	2:09:15
	Women	Colleen de Reuck, S. Afr.	2:26:35

Late 1995

New York City

Nov. 12	Men	German Silva, MEX	2:11:00
	Women	Tegla Loroupe, KEN	2:28:06

Fukuoka

Dec. 3	Men	L. Antonio Dos Santos, BRA	2:09:30
	(No women's division)		

Rowing

1996 World Championships

at Strathclyde, Scotland (Aug. 11)

MEN

Lt. Eights ... 1. Germany, 5:55.06
2. Denmark, 5:56.96, 3. Canada, 5:59.47

Lt. Quad Sculls ... 1. Italy, 6:10.11
2. Germany, 6:11.53, 3. France, 6:11.82

Lt. Coxless Pairs ... 1. Denmark, 7:06.34
2. Ireland, 7:09.25, 3. Germany, 7:10.73

Lt. Single Sculls ... 1. Karsten Nielsen, DEN, 7:35.72
2. Tomas Kacovsky, CZE, 7:36.01
3. Hoikki Haavikko, FIN, 7:37.15

Coxed Fours ... 1. Romania, 6:25.74
2. Czech Republic, 6:26.76, 3. Russia, 6:28.17

Coxed Pairs ... 1. France, 7:18.26
2. Romania, 7:18.96, 3. Netherlands, 7:22.33

WOMEN

Lt. Coxless Fours ... 1. China, 7:08.56
2. Britain, 7:09.55, 3. United States (Whitney Post, Julie McCleary, Kari Green and Sarah Simmons), 7:11.10

Lt. Coxless Pairs ... 1. United States (Christine Smith & Ellen Minznar), 7:56.66
2. Great Britain, 8:02.71, 3. Romania, 8:03.31

Lt. Single Sculls ... 1. Constanta Burcica, ROM, 8:06.90
2. Benedicte Luzuy, FRA, 8:07.66
3. Saran Garner, USA, 8:09.74

Coxless Fours ... 1. United States (Emily Dickson, Sara Field, Amy Turner and Rosana Zegarra), 6:49.48
2. Romania, 6:51.36, 3. Germany, 6:55.15

INT'L SPORTS STATISTICS

THROUGH THE YEARS

1896-1996

WINNERS • RECORDS

TRACK & FIELD

IAAF World Championships

While the Summer Olympics have served as the unofficial world outdoor championships for track and field throughout the century, a separate World Championship meet was started in 1983 by the International Amateur Athletic Federation (IAAF). The meet was held every four years from 1983-91, but began an every-other-year cycle in 1993. World Championship sites include Helsinki (1983), Rome (1987), Tokyo (1991), Stuttgart (1993) and Göteborg, Sweden (1995). Note that (WR) indicates world record and (CR) indicates championship meet record.

MEN

Multiple gold medals (including relays): Carl Lewis (8); Michael Johnson (6); Sergey Bubka (5); Calvin Smith (4); Greg Foster, Werner Gunthor, Moses Kiptanui, Noureddine Morceli, Dan O'Brien, Butch Reynolds and Lars Riedel (3); Andrey Abduvaliyev, Donovan Bailey, Leroy Burrell, Andre Cason, Maurizio Damilano, Haile Gebrselassie, Ismael Kirui, Billy Konchellah, Sergey Litvinov, Dennis Mitchell, Edwin Moses, Mike Powell and Jan Zelezny (2).

100 meters

Year		Time	
1983	Carl Lewis, USA	10.07	
1987	Carl Lewis, USA	9.93	
1991	Carl Lewis, USA	9.86	WR
1993	Linford Christie, GBR	9.87	
1995	Donovan Bailey, CAN	9.97	

Note: Ben Johnson was the original winner in 1987, but was stripped of his title and world record time (9.83) following his 1989 admission of drug taking.

200 meters

Year		Time	
1983	Calvin Smith, USA	20.14	
1987	Calvin Smith, USA	20.16	
1991	Michael Johnson, USA	20.01	
1993	Frank Fredericks, NAM	19.85	
1995	Michael Johnson, USA	19.79	CR

400 meters

Year		Time	
1983	Bert Cameron, JAM	45.05	
1987	Thomas Schonlebe, E.Ger	44.33	
1991	Antonio Pettigrew, USA	44.57	
1993	Michael Johnson, USA	43.65	
1995	Michael Johnson, USA	43.39	CR

800 meters

Year		Time	
1983	Willi Wülbeck, W.Ger	1:43.65	
1987	Billy Konchellah, KEN	1:43.06	CR
1991	Billy Konchellah, KEN	1:43.99	
1993	Paul Ruto, KEN	1:44.71	
1995	Wilson Kipketer, DEN	1:45.08	

1500 meters

Year		Time	
1983	Steve Cram, GBR	3:41.59	
1987	Abdi Bile, SOM	3:36.80	
1991	Noureddine Morceli, ALG	3:32.84	CR
1993	Noureddine Morceli, ALG	3:34.24	
1995	Noureddine Morceli, ALG	3:33.73	

5000 meters

Year		Time	
1983	Eammon Coghlan, IRE	13:28.53	
1987	Said Aouita, MOR	13:26.44	
1991	Yobes Ondieki, KEN	13:14.45	
1993	Ismael Kirui, KEN	13:02.75	CR
1995	Ismael Kirui, KEN	13:16.77	

10,000 meters

Year		Time	
1983	Alberto Cova, ITA	28:01.04	
1987	Paul Kipkoech, KEN	27:38.63	
1991	Moses Tanui, KEN	27:38.74	
1993	Haile Gebrselassie, ETH	27:46.02	
1995	Haile Gebrselassie, ETH	27:12.95	CR

Marathon

Year		Time	
1983	Rob de Castella, AUS	2:10:03	CR
1987	Douglas Wakiihuri, KEN	2:11:48	
1991	Hiromi Taniguchi, JPN	2:14:57	
1993	Mark Plaatjes, USA	2:13:57	
1995	Martin Fíz, SPA	2:11:41	

110-meter Hurdles

Year		Time	
1983	Greg Foster, USA	13.42	
1987	Greg Foster, USA	13.21	
1991	Greg Foster, USA	13.06	
1993	Colin Jackson, GBR	12.91	WR
1995	Allen Johnson, USA	13.00	

400-meter Hurdles

Year		Time	
1983	Edwin Moses, USA	47.50	
1987	Edwin Moses, USA	47.46	
1991	Samuel Matete, ZAM	47.64	
1993	Kevin Young, USA	47.18	CR
1995	Derrick Adkins, USA	47.98	

Track & Field Championships (Cont.)

Men

3000-meter Steeplechase

Year		Time	
1983	Patriz Ilg, W. Ger	8:15.06	
1987	Francesco Panetta, ITA	8:08.57	
1991	Moses Kiptanui, KEN	8:12.59	
1993	Moses Kiptanui, KEN	8:06.36	
1995	Moses Kiptanui, KEN	8:04.16	CR

4x100-meter Relay

Year		Time	
1983	United States	37.86	WR
1987	United States	37.90	
1991	United States	37.50	WR
1993	United States	37.48	CR
1995	Canada	38.31	

4x400-meter Relay

Year		Time	
1983	Soviet Union	3:00.79	
1987	United States	2:57.29	
1991	Great Britain	2:57.53	
1993	United States	2:54.29	WR
1995	United States	2:57.32	

20-kilometer Walk

Year		Time	
1983	Ernesto Canto, MEX	1:20:49	
1987	Maurizio Damilano, ITA	1:20:45	
1991	Maurizio Damilano, ITA	1:19:37	CR
1993	Valentin Massana, SPA	1:22.31	
1995	Michele Didoni, ITA	1:19.59	

50-kilometer Walk

Year		Time	
1983	Ronald Weigel, E. Ger	3:43:08	
1987	Hartwig Gauder, E. Ger	3:40:53	CR
1991	Aleksandr Potashov, USSR	3:53:09	
1993	Jesus Angel Garcia, SPA	3:41:41	
1995	Valentin Kononen, FIN	3:43.42	

High Jump

Year		Height	
1983	Gennedy Avdeyenko, USSR	7- 7¼	
1987	Patrik Sjoberg, SWE	7- 9¾	
1991	Charles Austin, USA	7- 9¾	
1993	Javier Sotomayor, CUB	7-10½	CR
1995	Troy Kemp, BAH	7- 9¼	

Pole Vault

Year		Height	
1983	Sergey Bubka, USSR	18- 8¼	
1987	Sergey Bubka, USSR	19- 2¼	
1991	Sergey Bubka, USSR	19- 6¼	CR
1993	Sergey Bubka, UKR	19- 8¼	CR
1995	Sergey Bubka, UKR	19- 5	

Long Jump

Year		Distance	
1983	Carl Lewis, USA	28- 0¾	
1987	Carl Lewis, USA	28- 0¼	
1991	Mike Powell, USA	29- 4½	WR
1993	Mike Powell, USA	28- 2¼	
1995	Ivan Pedroso, CUB	28- 6½	

Triple Jump

Year		Distance	
1983	Zdzislaw Hoffmann, POL	57- 2	
1987	Khristo Markov, BUL	58- 9	
1991	Kenny Harrison, USA	58- 4	
1993	Mike Conley, USA	58- 7¼	
1995	Jonathan Edwards, GBR	60- 0¼	WR

Shot Put

Year		Distance	
1983	Edward Sarul, POL	70- 2¼	
1987	Werner Günthör, SWI	72-11¼	CR
1991	Werner Günthör, SWI	71- 1¼	
1993	Werner Günthör, SWI	72- 1	
1995	John Godina, USA	70- 5¼	

Discus

Year		Distance	
1983	Imrich Bugar, CZE	222- 2	
1987	Jurgen Schult, E. Ger	225- 6	
1991	Lars Riedel, GER	217- 2	
1993	Lars Riedel, GER	222- 2	
1995	Lars Riedel, GER	225- 7	CR

Hammer Throw

Year		Distance	
1983	Sergey Litvinov, USSR	271- 3	
1987	Sergey Litvinov, USSR	272- 6	CR
1991	Yuri Sedykh, USSR	268- 0	
1993	Andrey Abduvaliyev, TAJ	267-10	
1995	Andrey Abduvaliyev, TAJ	267- 7	

Javelin

Year		Distance	
1983	Detlef Michel, E. Ger	293- 7	
1987	Seppo Raty, FIN	274- 1	
1991	Kimmo Kinnunen, FIN	297-11	CR
1993	Jan Zelezny, CZE	282- 1	
1995	Jan Zelezny, CZE	293-11	

Decathlon

Year		Points	
1983	Daley Thompson, GBR	8714	
1987	Torsten Voss, E. Ger	8680	
1991	Dan O'Brien, USA	8812	
1993	Dan O'Brien, USA	8817	CR
1995	Dan O'Brien, USA	8695	

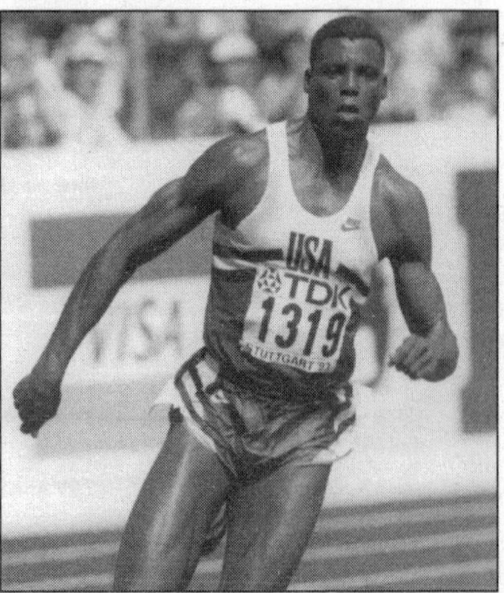

Wide World Photos

Carl Lewis of the U.S. is the all-time winningest athlete in the World Championships with five individual gold medals and three more in relays.

WOMEN

Multiple gold medals (including relays): Jackie Joyner-Kersee (4); Gail Devers, Tatyana Samolenko Dorovskikh, Silke Gladisch, Marita Koch, Jearl Miles, Merlene Ottey and Gwen Torrence (3); Hassiba Boulmerka, Olga Bryzgina, Mary Decker, Heike Daute Drechsler, Martina Optiz Hellmann, Stefka Kostadinova, Katrin Krabbe, Jarmila Kratochvilova, Marie-Rose Perec and Huang Zhihong (2).

100 meters

Year		Time	
1983	Marlies Gohr, E. Ger	10.97	
1987	Silke Gladisch, E. Ger	10.90	
1991	Katrin Krabbe, GER	10.99	
1993	Gail Devers, USA	10.81	CR
1995	Gwen Torrence, USA	10.85	

200 meters

Year		Time	
1983	Marita Koch, E. Ger	22.13	
1987	Silke Gladisch, E. Ger	21.74	CR
1991	Katrin Krabbe, GER	22.09	
1993	Merlene Ottey, JAM	21.98	
1995	Merlene Ottey, JAM	22.12	

400 meters

Year		Time	
1983	Jarmila Kratochvilova, CZE	47.99	WR
1987	Olga Bryzgina, USSR	49.38	
1991	Marie-José Pérec, FRA	49.13	
1993	Jearl Miles, USA	49.82	
1995	Marie-José Pérec, FRA	49.28	

800 meters

Year		Time	
1983	Jarmila Kratochvilova, CZE	1:54.68	CR
1987	Sigrun Wodars, E. Ger	1:55.26	
1991	Lilia Nurutdinova, USSR	1:57.50	
1993	Maria Mutola, MOZ	1:55.43	
1995	Ana Quirot, CUB	1:56.11	

1500 meters

Year		Time	
1983	Mary Decker, USA	4:00.90	
1987	Tatiana Samolenko, USSR	3:58.56	CR
1991	Hassiba Boulmerka, ALG	4:02.21	
1993	Liu Dong, CHN	4:00.50	
1995	Hassiba Boulmerka, ALG	4:02.42	

5000 meters

Held as 3000-meter race from 1983–93

Year		Time	
1983	Mary Decker, USA	8:34.62	
1987	Tatyana Samolenko, USSR	8:38.73	
1991	T. Samolenko Dorovskikh, USSR	8:35.82	
1993	Qu Yunxia, CHN	8:28.71	CR
1995	Sonia O'Sullivan, IRE	14:46.47	CR

10,000 meters

Year		Time	
1983	Not held		
1987	Ingrid Kristiansen, NOR	31:05.85	
1991	Liz McColgan, GBR	31:14.31	
1993	Wang Junxia, CHN	30:49.30	CR
1995	Fernanda Ribeiro, POR	31:04.99	

Marathon

Year		Time	
1983	Grete Waitz, NOR	2:28:09	
1987	Rose Mota, POR	2:25:17	CR
1991	Wanda Panfil, POL	2:29:53	
1993	Junko Asari, JPN	2:30:03	
1995	Manuela Machado, POR	2:25.39	

100-meter Hurdles

Year		Time	
1983	Bettine Jahn, E. Ger	12.35 w	
1987	Ginka Zagorcheva, BUL	12.34	CR
1991	Lyudmila Narozhilenko, USSR	12.59	
1993	Gail Devers, USA	12.46	
1995	Gail Devers, USA	12.68	

w indicates wind-aided.

400-meter Hurdles

Year		Time	
1983	Yekaterina Fesenko, USSR	54.14	
1987	Sabine Busch, E. Ger	53.62	
1991	Tatiana Ledovskaya, USSR	53.11	
1993	Sally Gunnell, GBR	52.74	WR
1995	Kim Batten, USA	52.61	WR

4x100-meter Relay

Year		Time	
1983	East Germany	41.76	
1987	United States	41.58	
1991	Jamaica	41.94	
1993	Russia	41.49	CR
1995	United States	42.12	

4x400-meter Relay

Year		Time	
1983	East Germany	3:19.73	
1987	East Germany	3:18.63	
1991	Soviet Union	3:18.43	
1993	United States	3:16.71	CR
1995	United States	3:22.39	

10-kilometer Walk

Year		Time	
1983	Not held		
1987	Irina Strakhova, USSR	44:12	
1991	Alina Ivanova, USSR	42:57	
1993	Sari Essayah, FIN	42:59	
1995	Irina Stankina, RUS	42:13	CR

High Jump

Year		Height	
1983	Tamara Bykova, USSR	6- 7	
1987	Stefka Kostadinova, BUL	6-10¼	WR
1991	Heike Henkel, GER	6- 8¾	
1993	Ioamnet Quintero, CUB	6- 6¼	
1995	Stefka Kostadinova, BUL	6- 7	

Long Jump

Year		Distance	
1983	Heike Daute, E. Ger	23-10¼ w	
1987	Jackie Joyner-Kersee, USA	24- 1¾	CR
1991	Jackie Joyner-Kersee, USA	24- 0¼	
1993	Heike Drechsler, GER	23- 4	
1995	Fiona May, ITA	22-10¾ w	

w indicates wind-aided.

Triple Jump

Year		Distance	
1983	Not held		
1987	Not held		
1991	Not held		
1993	Ana Biryukova, RUS	46- 6¼	WR
1995	Inessa Kravets, UKR	50-10¾	WR

Track & Field Championships (Cont.)

Women

Shot Put

Year		Distance	
1983	Helena Fibingerova, CZE	69- 0	
1987	Natalia Lisovskaya, USSR	69- 8	CR
1991	Huang Zhihong, CHN	68- 4	
1993	Huang Zhihong, CHN	67- 6	
1995	Astrid Kumbernuss, GER	69- 7½	

Javelin

Year		Distance	
1983	Tiina Lillak, FIN	232- 4	
1987	Fatima Whitbread, GBR	251- 5	CR
1991	Xu Demei, CHN	225- 8	
1993	Trine Hattestad, NOR	227- 0	
1995	Natalya Shikolenko, BLR	221- 8	

Discus

Year		Distance	
1983	Martina Opitz, E. Ger	226- 2	
1987	Martina Opitz Hellmann, E. Ger	235- 0	CR
1991	Tsvetanka Khristova, BUL	233- 0	
1993	Olga Burova, RUS	221- 1	
1995	Ellina Zvereva, BLR	225- 2	

Heptathlon

Year		Points	
1983	Ramona Neubert, E. Ger	6770	
1987	Jackie Joyner-Kersee, USA	7128	CR
1991	Sabine Braun, GER	6672	
1993	Jackie Joyner-Kersee, USA	6837	
1995	Ghada Shouaa, SYR	6651	

Marathons

Boston

America's oldest regularly contested foot race, the Boston Marathon is held on Patriots' Day every April and will be run for the 100th time in 1996. It has been run at four different distances: 24 miles, 1232 yards (1897-1923); 26 miles, 209 yards (1924-26); 26 miles, 385 yards (1927-52); 25 miles, 958 yards (1953-56); and 26 miles, 385 yards (since 1957).

MEN

Multiple winners: Clarence DeMar (7); Gerard Cote and Bill Rodgers (4); Ibrahim Hussein, Cosmas Ndeti and Leslie Pawson (3); Tarzan Brown, Jim Caffrey, John A. Kelley, John Miles, Eino Oksanen, Toshihiko Seko, Geoff Smith and Aurele Vandendriessche (2).

Year		Time
1897	John McDermott, New York	2:55:10
1898	Ronald McDonald, Massachusetts	2:42:00
1899	Lawrence Brignolia, Massachusetts	2:54:38
1900	Jim Caffrey, Canada	2:39:44
1901	Jim Caffrey, Canada	2:29:23
1902	Sam Mellor, New York	2:43:12
1903	J.C. Lorden, Massachusetts	2:41:29
1904	Mike Spring, New York	2:38:04
1905	Fred Lorz, New York	2:38:25
1906	Tim Ford, Massachusetts	2:45:45
1907	Tom Longboat, Canada	2:24:24
1908	Tom Morrissey, New York	2:25:43
1909	Henri Renaud, New Hampshire	2:53:36
1910	Fred Cameron, Nova Scotia	2:28:52
1911	Clarence DeMar, Massachusetts	2:21:39
1912	Mike Ryan, Illinois	2:21:18
1913	Fritz Carlson, Minnesota	2:25:14
1914	James Duffy, Canada	2:25:01
1915	Edouard Fabre, Canada	2:31:41
1916	Arthur Roth, Massachusetts	2:27:16
1917	Bill Kennedy, New York	2:28:37
1918	World War relay race	
1919	Carl Linder, Massachusetts	2:29:13
1920	Peter Trivoulidas, New York	2:29:31
1921	Frank Zuna, New Jersey	2:18:57
1922	Clarence DeMar, Massachusetts	2:18:10
1923	Clarence DeMar, Massachusetts	2:23:37
1924	Clarence DeMar, Massachusetts	2:29:40
1925	Charles Mellor, Illinois	2:33:00
1926	John Miles, Nova Scotia	2:25:40
1927	Clarence DeMar, Massachusetts	2:40:22
1928	Clarence DeMar, Massachusetts	2:37:07
1929	John Miles, Nova Scotia	2:33:08
1930	Clarence DeMar, Massachusetts	2:34:48
1931	James Henigan, Massachusetts	2:46:45
1932	Paul deBruyn, Germany	2:33:36
1933	Leslie Pawson, Rhode Island	2:31:01
1934	Dave Komonen, Canada	2:32:53
1935	John A. Kelley, Massachusetts	2:32:07
1936	Ellison (Tarzan) Brown, Rhode Island	2:33:40
1937	Walter Young, Canada	2:33:20
1938	Leslie Pawson, Rhode Island	2:35:34
1939	Ellison (Tarzan) Brown, Rhode Island	2:28:51
1940	Gerard Cote, Canada	2:28:28
1941	Leslie Pawson, Rhode Island	2:30:38
1942	Joe Smith, Massachusetts	2:26:51
1943	Gerard Cote, Canada	2:28:25
1944	Gerard Cote, Canada	2:31:50
1945	John A. Kelley, Massachusetts	2:30:40
1946	Stylianos Kyriakides, Greece	2:29:27
1947	Yun Bok Suh, Korea	2:25:39
1948	Gerard Cote, Canada	2:31:02
1949	Karle Leandersson, Sweden	2:31:50
1950	Kee Yonh Ham, Korea	2:32:39
1951	Shigeki Tanaka, Japan	2:27:45
1952	Doroteo Flores, Guatemala	2:31:53
1953	Keizo Yamada, Japan	2:18:51
1954	Veiko Karvonen, Finland	2:20:39
1955	Hideo Hamamura, Japan	2:18:22
1956	Antti Viskari, Finland	2:14:14
1957	John J. Kelley, Connecticut	2:20:05
1958	Franjo Mihalic, Yugoslavia	2:25:54
1959	Eino Oksanen, Finland	2:22:42
1960	Paavo Kotila, Finland	2:20:54
1961	Eino Oksanen, Finland	2:23:39
1962	Eino Oksanen, Finland	2:23:48
1963	Aurele Vandendriessche, Belgium	2:18:58
1964	Aurele Vandendriessche, Belgium	2:19:59
1965	Morio Shigematsu, Japan	2:16:33
1966	Kenji Kimihara, Japan	2:17:11
1967	David McKenzie, New Zealand	2:15:45

Year		Time
1968	Amby Burfoot, Connecticut	2:22:17
1969	Yoshiaki Unetani, Japan	2:13:49
1970	Ron Hill, England	2:10:30
1971	Alvaro Mejia, Colombia	2:18:45
1972	Olavi Suomalainen, Finland	2:15:39
1973	Jon Anderson, Oregon	2:16:03
1974	Neil Cusack, Ireland	2:13:39
1975	Bill Rodgers, Massachusetts	2:09:55
1976	Jack Fultz, Pennsylvania	2:20:19
1977	Jerome Drayton, Canada	2:14:46
1978	Bill Rodgers, Massachusetts	2:10:13
1979	Bill Rodgers, Massachusetts	2:09:27
1980	Bill Rodgers, Massachusetts	2:12:11
1981	Toshihiko Seko, Japan	2:09:26
1982	Alberto Salazar, Oregon	2:08:52
1983	Greg Meyer, New Jersey	2:09:00
1984	Geoff Smith, England	2:10:34
1985	Geoff Smith, England	2:14:05
1986	Rob de Castella, Australia	2:07:51
1987	Toshihiko Seko, Japan	2:11:50
1988	Ibrahim Hussein, Kenya	2:08:43
1989	Abebe Mekonnen, Ethiopia	2:09:06
1990	Gelindo Bordin, Italy	2:08:19
1991	Ibrahim Hussein, Kenya	2:11:06
1992	Ibrahim Hussein, Kenya	2:08:14
1993	Cosmas Ndeti, Kenya	2:09:33
1994	Cosmas Ndeti, Kenya	2:07:15*
1995	Cosmas Ndeti, Kenya	2:09:22
1996	Moses Tanui, Kenya	2:09.16

*Course record.

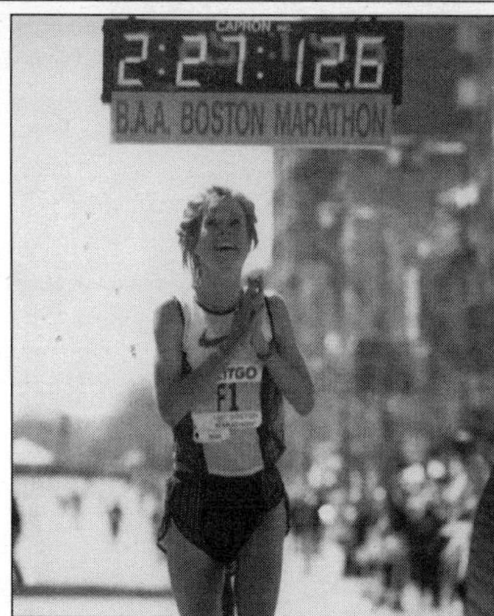

Wide World Photos

Germany's **Uta Pippig** won her third straight Boston Marathon in 1996, battling through physical difficulties to overtake Kenya's Tegla Loroupe late in the race.

WOMEN

Multiple winners: Rosa Mota and Uta Pippig (3); Joan Benoit, Miki Gorman, Ingrid Kristiansen, Olga Markova (2).

Year		Time
1972	Nina Kuscsik, New York	3:08:58
1973	Jacqueline Hansen, California	3:05:59
1974	Miki Gorman, California	2:47:11
1975	Liane Winter, West Germany	2:42:24
1976	Kim Merritt, Wisconsin	2:47:10
1977	Miki Gorman, California	2:48:33
1978	Gayle Barron, Georgia	2:44:52
1979	Joan Benoit, Maine	2:35:15
1980	Jacqueline Gareau, Canada	2:34:28
1981	Allison Roe, New Zealand	2:26:46
1982	Charlotte Teske, West Germany	2:29:33
1983	Joan Benoit, Maine	2:22:43
1984	Lorraine Moller, New Zealand	2:29:28
1985	Lisa Larsen Weidenbach, Mass	2:34:06
1986	Ingrid Kristiansen, Norway	2:24:55
1987	Rosa Mota, Portugal	2:25:21
1988	Rosa Mota, Portugal	2:24:30
1989	Ingrid Kristiansen, Norway	2:24:33
1990	Rosa Mota, Portugal	2:25:23
1991	Wanda Panfil, Poland	2:24:18
1992	Olga Markova, CIS	2:23:43
1993	Olga Markova, Russia	2:25:27
1994	Uta Pippig, Germany	2:21:45*
1995	Uta Pippig, Germany	2:25:11
1995	Uta Pippig, Germany	2:27:12

*Course record.

New York City

Started in 1970, the New York City Marathon is run in the fall, usually on the first Sunday in November. The route winds through all of the city's five boroughs and finishes in Central Park.

MEN

Multiple winners: Bill Rodgers (4); Alberto Salazar (3); Tom Fleming and Orlando Pizzolato (2).

Year		Time
1970	Gary Muhrcke, USA	2:31:38
1971	Norman Higgins, USA	2:22:54
1972	Sheldon Karlin, USA	2:27:52
1973	Tom Fleming, USA	2:21:54
1974	Norbert Sander, USA	2:26:30
1975	Tom Fleming, USA	2:19:27
1976	Bill Rodgers, USA	2:10:09
1977	Bill Rodgers, USA	2:11:28
1978	Bill Rodgers, USA	2:12:12
1979	Bill Rodgers, USA	2:11:42
1980	Alberto Salazar, USA	2:09:41
1981	Alberto Salazar, USA	2:08:13
1982	Alberto Salazar, USA	2:09:29
1983	Rod Dixon, New Zealand	2:08:59
1984	Orlando Pizzolato, Italy	2:14:53
1985	Orlando Pizzolato, Italy	2:11:34
1986	Gianni Poli, Italy	2:11:06
1987	Ibrahim Hussein, Kenya	2:11:01
1988	Steve Jones, Wales	2:08:20
1989	Juma Ikangaa, Tanzania	2:08:01*

Marathons (Cont.)

New York City

MEN

Year		Time
1990	Douglas Wakiihuri, Kenya	2:12:39
1991	Salvador Garcia, Mexico	2:09:28
1992	Willie Mtolo, South Africa	2:09:29
1993	Andres Espinosa, Mexico	2:10:04
1994	German Silva, Mexico	2:11:21
1995	German Silva, Mexico	2:11:00

*Course record.

WOMEN

Multiple winners: Grete Waitz (9); Miki Gorman and Nina Kuscsik (2).

Year		Time
1970	No Finisher	
1971	Beth Bonner, USA	2:55:22
1972	Nina Kuscsik, USA	3:08:41
1973	Nina Kuscsik, USA	2:57:07
1974	Katherine Switzer, USA	3:07:29
1975	Kim Merritt, USA	2:46:14
1976	Miki Gorman, USA	2:39:11
1977	Miki Gorman, USA	2:43:10
1978	Grete Waitz, Norway	2:32:30
1979	Grete Waitz, Norway	2:27:33
1980	Grete Waitz, Norway	2:25:41
1981	Allison Roe, New Zealand	2:25:29
1982	Grete Waitz, Norway	2:27:14
1983	Grete Waitz, Norway	2:27:00
1984	Grete Waitz, Norway	2:29:30
1985	Grete Waitz, Norway	2:28:34
1986	Grete Waitz, Norway	2:28:06
1987	Priscilla Welch, Britain	2:30:17
1988	Grete Waitz, Norway	2:28:07
1989	Ingrid Kristiansen, Norway	2:25:30
1990	Wanda Panfil, Poland	2:30:45
1991	Liz McColgan, Scotland	2:27:23
1992	Lisa Ondieki, Australia	2:24:40*
1993	Uta Pippig, Germany	2:26:24
1994	Tegla Loroupe, Kenya	2:27:37
1995	Tegla Loroupe, Kenya	2:28:06

*Course record.

Annual Awards

Track & Field News Athletes of the Year

Voted on by an international panel of track and field experts and presented since 1959 for men and 1974 for women.

MEN

Multiple winners: Carl Lewis (3); Sergey Bubka, Sebastian Coe, Alberto Juantorena, Noureddine Morceli, Jim Ryun and Peter Snell (2).

Year		Event
1959	Martin Lauer, W. Germany	110H/Decathlon
1960	Rafer Johnson, USA	Decathlon
1961	Ralph Boston, USA	Long Jump/110 Hurdles
1962	Peter Snell, New Zealand	800/1500
1963	C.K. Yang, Taiwan	Decathlon/Pole Vault
1964	Peter Snell, New Zealand	800/1500
1965	Ron Clarke, Australia	5000/10,000
1966	Jim Ryun, USA	800/1500
1967	Jim Ryun, USA	1500
1968	Bob Beamon, USA	Long Jump
1969	Bill Toomey, USA	Decathlon
1970	Randy Matson, USA	Shot Put
1971	Rod Milburn, USA	110 Hurdles
1972	Lasse Viren, Finland	5000/10,000
1973	Ben Jipcho, Kenya	1500/5000/Steeplechase
1974	Rick Wohlhuter, USA	800/1500
1975	John Walker, New Zealand	800/1500
1976	Alberto Juantorena, Cuba	400/800
1977	Alberto Juantorena, Cuba	400/800
1978	Henry Rono, Kenya	5000/10,000/Steeplechase
1979	Sebastian Coe, Great Britain	800/1500
1980	Edwin Moses, USA	400 Hurdles
1981	Sebastian Coe, Great Britain	800/1500
1982	Carl Lewis, USA	100/200/Long Jump
1983	Carl Lewis, USA	100/200/Long Jump
1984	Carl Lewis, USA	100/200/Long Jump
1985	Said Aouita, Morocco	1500/5000
1986	Yuri Sedykh, USSR	Hammer Throw
1987	Ben Johnson, Canada	100
1988	Sergey Bubka, USSR	Pole Vault
1989	Roger Kingdom, USA	110 Hurdles
1990	Michael Johnson, USA	200/400
1991	Sergey Bubka, USSR	Pole Vault
1992	Kevin Young, USA	400 Hurdles
1993	Noureddine Morceli, Algeria	Mile/1500/3000
1994	Noureddine Morceli, Algeria	Mile/1500/3000
1995	Haile Gebrselassie, ETH	5000/10,000

WOMEN

Multiple winners: Marita Koch (4); Jackie Joyner-Kersee (3); Evelyn Ashford (2).

Year		Event
1974	Irena Szewinska, Poland	100/200/400
1975	Faina Melnik, USSR	Shot Put/Discus
1976	Tatiana Kazankina, USSR	800/1500
1977	Rosemarie Ackermann, E. Germany	High Jump
1978	Marita Koch, E. Germany	100/200/400
1979	Marita Koch, E. Germany	100/200/400
1980	Ilona Briesenick, E. Germany	Shot Put
1981	Evelyn Ashford, USA	100/200
1982	Marita Koch, E. Germany	100/200/400
1983	Jarmila Kratochvilova, Czech	200/400/800
1984	Evelyn Ashford, USA	100
1985	Marita Koch, E. Germany	100/200/400
1986	Jackie Joyner-Kersee, USA	Heptathlon/Long Jump
1987	Jackie Joyner-Kersee, USA	100H/Heptathlon/LJ
1988	Florence Griffith Joyner, USA	100/200
1989	Ana Quirot, Cuba	400/800
1990	Merlene Ottey, Jamaica	100/200
1991	Heike Henkel, Germany	High Jump
1992	Heike Drechsler, Germany	Long Jump
1993	Wang Junxia, China	1500/3000/10,000
1994	Jackie Joyner-Kersee, USA	100H/Heptathlon/LJ
1995	Sonia O'Sullivan, IRE	1500/3000/5000

SWIMMING & DIVING

FINA World Championships

While the Summer Olympics have served as the unofficial world championships for swimming and diving throughout the century, a separate World Championship meet was started in 1973 by the International Amateur Swimming Federation (FINA). The meet was held three times between 1973-78, then every four years since then. Sites have included Belgrade (1973); Cali, COL (1975); West Berlin (1978); Guayaquil, ECU (1982); Madrid (1986); Perth (1991) and Rome (1994).

Swimming

MEN

Most gold medals (including relays): Jim Montgomery (7); Matt Biondi (6); Rowdy Gaines (5); Joe Bottom, Tamas Darnyi, Michael Gross, Tom Jager, David McCagg, Vladimir Salnikov and Tim Shaw (4); Billy Forrester, Andras Hargitay, Roland Matthes, John Murphy, Jeff Rouse, Norbert Rozsa and David Wilkie (3).

50-meter Freestyle

Year		Time	
1973-82	Not held		
1986	Tom Jager, USA	22.49	
1991	Tom Jager, USA	22.16	CR
1994	Aleksandr Popov, RUS	22.17	

100-meter Freestyle

Year		Time	
1973	Jim Montgomery, USA	51.70	
1975	Tim Shaw, USA	51.25	
1978	David McCagg, USA	50.24	
1982	Jorg Woithe, E. Ger	50.18	
1986	Matt Biondi, USA	48.94	CR
1991	Matt Biondi, USA	49.18	
1994	Aleksandr Popov, RUS	49.12	

200-meter Freestyle

Year		Time	
1973	Jim Montgomery, USA	1:53.02	
1975	Tim Shaw, USA	1:52.04	
1978	Billy Forrester, USA	1:51.02	
1982	Michael Gross, W. Ger	1:49.84	
1986	Michael Gross, W. Ger	1:47.92	
1991	Giorgio Lamberti, ITA	1:47.27	
1994	Antti Kasvio, FIN	1:47.32	CR

400-meter Freestyle

Year		Time	
1973	Rick DeMont, USA	3:58.18	
1975	Tim Shaw, USA	3:54.88	
1978	Vladimir Salnikov, USSR	3:51.94	
1982	Vladimir Salnikov, USSR	3:51.30	
1986	Rainer Henkel, W. Ger	3:50.05	
1991	Jorg Hoffman, GER	3:48.04	
1994	Kieren Perkins, AUS	3:43.80	WR

1500-meter Freestyle

Year		Time	
1973	Stephen Holland, AUS	15:31.85	
1975	Tim Shaw, USA	15.28.92	
1978	Vladimir Salnikov, USSR	15:03.99	
1982	Vladimir Salnikov, USSR	15:01.77	
1986	Rainer Henkel, W. Ger	15:05.31	
1991	Jorg Hoffman, GER	14:50.36	WR
1994	Kieren Perkins, AUS	14:50.52	

100-meter Backstroke

Year		Time	
1973	Roland Matthes, E. Ger	57.47	
1975	Roland Matthes, E. Ger	58.15	
1978	Bob Jackson, USA	56.36	
1982	Dirk Richter, E. Ger	55.95	
1986	Igor Polianski, USSR	55.58	
1991	Jeff Rouse, USA	55.23	
1994	Martin Lopez-Zubero, SPA	55.17	CR

200-meter Backstroke

Year		Time	
1973	Roland Matthes, E. Ger	2:01.87	
1975	Zoltan Varraszto, HUN	2:05.05	
1978	Jesse Vassallo, USA	2:02.16	
1982	Rick Carey, USA	2:00.82	
1986	Igor Polianski, USSR	1:58.78	CR
1991	Martin Zubero, SPA	1:59.52	
1994	Vladimir Selkov, RUS	1:57.42	

100-meter Breaststroke

Year		Time	
1973	John Hencken, USA	1:04.02	
1975	David Wilkie, GBR	1:04.26	
1978	Walter Kusch, W. Ger	1:03.56	
1982	Steve Lundquist, USA	1:02.75	
1986	Victor Davis, CAN	1:02.71	
1991	Norbert Rozsa, HUN	1:01.45	WR
1994	Norbert Rozsa, HUN	1:01.24	

200-meter Breaststroke

Year		Time	
1973	David Wilkie, GBR	2:19.28	
1975	David Wilkie, GBR	2:18.23	
1978	Nick Nevid, USA	2:18.37	
1982	Victor Davis, CAN	2:14.77	WR
1986	Jozsef Szabo, HUN	2:14.27	
1991	Mike Barrowman, USA	2:11.23	WR
1994	Norbert Rozsa, HUN	2:12.81	

100-meter Butterfly

Year		Time	
1973	Bruce Robertson, CAN	55.69	
1975	Greg Jagenburg, USA	55.63	
1978	Joe Bottom, USA	54.30	
1982	Matt Gribble, USA	53.88	
1986	Pablo Morales, USA	53.54	
1991	Anthony Nesty, SUR	53.29	CR
1994	Rafal Szukala, POL	53.51	

200-meter Butterfly

Year		Time	
1973	Robin Backhaus, USA	2:03.32	
1975	Billy Forrester, USA	2:01.95	
1978	Mike Bruner, USA	1:59.38	
1982	Michael Gross, W. Ger	1:58.85	
1986	Michael Gross, W. Ger	1.56.53	
1991	Melvin Stewart, USA	1:55.69	WR
1994	Denis Pankratov, RUS	1:56.54	

200-meter Individual Medley

Year		Time	
1973	Gunnar Larsson, SWE	2:08.36	
1975	Andras Hargitay, HUN	2:07.72	
1978	Graham Smith, CAN	2:03.65	WR
1982	Alexander Sidorenko, USSR	2:03.30	
1986	Tamás Darnyi, HUN	2:01.57	
1991	Tamás Darnyi, HUN	1:59.36	WR
1994	Janis Sievinen, FIN	1:58.16	WR

FINA Swimming Championships (Cont.)

MEN

400-meter Individual Medley

Year		Time	
1973	Andras Hargitay, HUN	4:31.11	
1975	Andras Hargitay, HUN	4:32.57	
1978	Jesse Vassallo, USA	4:20.05	WR
1982	Ricardo Prado, BRA	4:19.78	WR
1986	Tamás Darnyi, HUN	4.18.98	
1991	Tamás Darnyi, HUN	4:12.36	WR
1994	Tom Dolan, USA	4:12.30	WR

4 x 100-meter Freestyle Relay

Year		Time	
1973	United States	3:27.18	
1975	United States	3:24.85	
1978	United States	3:19.74	
1982	United States	3:19.26	WR
1986	United States	3:19.98	
1991	United States	3:17.15	
1994	United States	3:16.90	CR

4 x 200-meter Freestyle Relay

Year		Time	
1973	United States	7:33.22	WR
1975	West Germany	7:39.44	
1978	United States	7:20.82	
1982	United States	7:21.09	
1986	East Germany	7:15.91	
1991	Germany	7:13.50	CR
1994	Sweden	7:17.34	

4 x 100-meter Medley Relay

Year		Time	
1973	United States	3:49.49	
1975	United States	3:49.00	
1978	United States	3:44.63	
1982	United States	3:40.84	WR
1986	United States	3:41.25	
1991	United States	3:39.66	
1994	United States	3:37.74	CR

WOMEN

Most gold medals (including relays): Kornelia Ender (8); Kristin Otto (7); Tracy Caulkins, Heike Friedrich, Le Jingyi, Rosemarie Kother and Ulrike Richter (4); Hannalore Anke, Lu Bin, He Cihong, Janet Evans, Nicole Haislett, Lui Limin, Birgit Meineke, Joan Pennington, Manuela Stellmach, Renate Vogel and Cynthia Woodhead (3).

50-meter Freesstyle

Year		Time	
1973-82	Not held		
1986	Tamara Costache, ROM	25.28	WR
1991	Zhuang Yong, CHN	25.47	
1994	Le Jingyi, CHN	24.51	WR

100-meter Freestyle

Year		Time	
1973	Kornelia Ender, E. Ger	57.54	
1975	Kornelia Ender, E. Ger	56.50	
1978	Barbara Krause, E. Ger	55.68	
1982	Birgit Meineke, E. Ger	55.79	
1986	Kristin Otto, E. Ger	55.05	
1991	Nicole Haislett, USA	55.17	
1994	Le Jingyi, CHN	54.01	WR

200-meter Freestyle

Year		Time	
1973	Keena Rothhammer, USA	2:04.99	
1975	Shirley Babashoff, USA	2:02.50	
1978	Cynthia Woodhead, USA	1:58.53	WR
1982	Annemarie Verstappen, HOL	1:59.53	
1986	Heike Friedrich, E. Ger	1:58.26	
1991	Hayley Lewis, AUS	2:00.48	
1994	Franziska Van Almsick, GER	1:56.78	WR

400-meter Freestyle

Year		Time	
1973	Heather Greenwood, USA	4:20.28	
1975	Shirley Babashoff, USA	4:22.70	
1978	Tracey Wickham, AUS	4:06.28	WR
1982	Carmela Schmidt. E. Ger	4:08.98	
1986	Heike Friedrich, E. Ger	4:07.45	
1991	Janet Evans, USA	4:08.63	
1994	Yang Aihua, CHN	4:09.64	

800-meter Freestyle

Year		Time	
1973	Novella Calligaris, ITA	8:52.97	
1975	Jenny Turrall, AUS	8:44.75	
1978	Tracey Wickham, AUS	8:25.94	
1982	Kim Linehan, USA	8:27.48	
1986	Astrid Strauss, E. Ger	8:28.24	
1991	Janet Evans, USA	8:24.05	CR
1994	Janet Evans, USA	8:29.85	

100-meter Backstroke

Year		Time	
1973	Ulrike Richter, E. Ger	1:05.42	
1975	Ulrike Richter, E. Ger	1:03.30	
1978	Linda Jezek, USA	1:02.55	
1982	Kristin Otto, E. Ger	1:01.30	
1986	Betsy Mitchell, USA	1:01.74	
1991	Krisztina Egerszegi, HUN	1:01.78	
1994	He Cihong, CHN	1:00.57	WR

200-meter Backstroke

Year		Time	
1973	Melissa Belote, USA	2:20.52	
1975	Birgit Treiber, E. Ger	2:15.46	WR
1978	Linda Jezek, USA	2:11.93	WR
1982	Cornelia Sirch, E. Ger	2:09.91	WR
1986	Cornelia Sirch, E. Ger	2:11.37	
1991	Krisztina Egerszegi, HUN	2:09.15	
1994	He Cihong, CHN	2:07.40	CR

100-meter Breaststroke

Year		Time	
1973	Renate Vogel, E. Ger	1:13.74	
1975	Hannalore Anke, E. Ger	1:12.72	
1978	Julia Bogdanova, USSR	1:10.31	WR
1982	Ute Geweniger, E. Ger	1:09.14	
1986	Sylvia Gerasch, E. Ger	1:08.11	WR
1991	Linley Frame, AUS	1:08.81	
1994	Samantha Riley, AUS	1:07.69	WR

200-meter Breaststroke

Year		Time	
1973	Renate Vogel, E. Ger	2:40.01	
1975	Hannalore Anke, E. Ger	2:37.25	
1978	Lina Kachushite, USSR	2:31.42	WR
1982	Svetlana Varganova, USSR	2:28.82	
1986	Silke Hoerner, E. Ger	2:27.40	WR
1991	Elena Volkova, USSR	2:29.53	
1994	Samantha Riley, AUS	2:26.87	CR

100-meter Butterfly

Year		Time	
1973	Kornelia Ender, E. Ger	1:02.53	
1975	Kornelia Ender, E. Ger	1:01.24	WR
1978	Joan Pennington, USA	1:00.20	
1982	Mary T. Meagher, USA	59.41	
1986	Kornelai Gressler, E. Ger	59.51	
1991	Qian Hong, CHN	59.68	
1994	Liu Limin, CHN	58.98	CR

200-meter Butterfly

Year		Time	
1973	Rosemarie Kother, E. Ger	2:13.76	
1975	Rosemarie Kother, E. Ger	2:15.92	
1978	Tracy Caulkins, USA	2:09.78	WR
1982	Ines Geissler, E. Ger	2:08.66	
1986	Mary T. Meagher, USA	2:08.41	
1991	Summer Sanders, USA	2:09.24	
1994	Liu Limin, CHN	2:07.25	CR

200-meter Individual Medley

Year		Time	
1973	Andre Huebner, E. Ger	2:20.51	
1975	Kathy Heddy, USA	2:19.80	
1978	Tracy Caulkins, USA	2:19.80	WR
1982	Petra Schneider, E. Ger	2:11.79	CR
1986	Kristin Otto, E. Ger	2:15.56	
1991	Lin Li, CHN	2:13.40	
1994	Lu Bin, CHN	2:12.34	

400-meter Individual Medley

Year		Time	
1973	Gudrun Wegner, E. Ger	4:57.71	
1975	Ulrike Tauber, E. Ger	4:52.76	
1978	Tracy Caulkins, USA	4:40.83	WR
1982	Petra Schneider, E. Ger	4:36.10	WR
1986	Kathleen Nord, E. Ger	4:43.75	
1991	Lin Li, CHN	4:41.45	
1994	Dai Guohong, CHN	4:39.14	

4 x 100-meter Freestyle Relay

Year		Time	
1973	East Germany	3:52.45	
1975	East Germany	3:49.37	
1978	United States	3:43.43	WR
1982	East Germany	3:43.97	
1986	East Germany	3:40.57	
1991	United States	3:43.26	
1994	China	3:37.91	WR

4 x 200-meter Freestyle Relay

Year		Time	
1973-82	Not held		
1986	East Germany	7:59.33	WR
1991	Germany	8:02.56	
1994	China	7:57.96	CR

4 x 100-meter Medley Relay

Year		Time	
1973	East Germany	4:16.84	
1975	East Germany	4:14.74	
1978	United States	4:08.21	
1982	East Germany	4:05.8	WR
1986	East Germany	4:04.82	
1991	United States	4:06.51	
1994	China	4:01.67	CR

Diving

Multiple Gold Medals: MEN— Greg Louganis (5); Phil Boggs (3); Klaus Dibiasi (2). WOMEN— Irina Kalinina and Gao Min (3); Fu Mingxia (2).

MEN

1-meter Springboard

Year		Pts
1991	Edwin Jongejans, HOL	588.51
1994	Evan Stewart, ZIM	382.14

3-meter Springboard

Year		Pts
1973	Phil Boggs, USA	618.57
1975	Phil Boggs, USA	597.12
1978	Phil Boggs, USA	913.95
1982	Greg Louganis, USA	752.67
1986	Greg Louganis, USA	750.06
1991	Kent Ferguson, USA	650.25
1994	Yu Zhuocheng, CHN	655.44

Platform

Year		Pts
1973	Klaus Dibiasi, ITA	559.53
1975	Klaus Dibiasi, ITA	547.98
1978	Greg Louganis, USA	844.11
1982	Greg Louganis, USA	634.26
1986	Greg Louganis, USA	668.58
1991	Sun Shuwei, CHN	626.79
1994	Dmitri Sautin, RUS	634.71

WOMEN

1-meter Springboard

Year		Pts
1991	Gao Min, CHN	478.26
1994	Chen Lixia, CHN	279.30

3-meter Springboard

Year		Pts
1973	Christa Koehler, E. Ger	442.17
1975	Irina Kalinina, USSR	489.81
1978	Irina Kalinina, USSR	691.43
1982	Megan Neyer, USA	501.03
1986	Gao Min, CHN	582.90
1991	Gao Min, CHN	539.01
1994	Tan Shuping, CHN	548.49

Platform

Year		Pts
1973	Ulrike Knape, SWE	406.77
1975	Janet Ely, USA	403.89
1978	Irina Kalinina, USSR	412.71
1982	Wendy Wyland, USA	438.79
1986	Chen Lin, CHN	449.67
1991	Fu Mingxia, CHN	426.51
1994	Fu Mingxia, CHN	434.04

ALPINE SKIING

World Cup Overall Champions

World Cup Overall Champions (downhill and slalom events combined) since the tour was organized in 1967.

MEN

Multiple winners: Marc Girardelli (5), Gustavo Thoeni and Pirmin Zurbriggen (4); Phil Mahre, and Ingemar Stenmark (3); Jean-Claude Killy and Karl Schranz (2).

Year	
1967	Jean-Claude Killy, France
1968	Jean Claude Killy, France
1969	Karl Schranz, Austria
1970	Karl Schranz, Austria
1971	Gustavo Thoeni, Italy
1972	Gustavo Thoeni, Italy
1973	Gustavo Thoeni, Italy
1974	Piero Gros, Italy
1975	Gustavo Thoeni, Italy
1976	Ingemar Stenmark, Sweden
1977	Ingemar Stenmark, Sweden
1978	Ingemar Stenmark, Sweden
1979	Peter Luescher, Switzerland
1980	Andreas Wenzel, Liechtenstein
1981	Phil Mahre, USA
1982	Phil Mahre, USA
1983	Phil Mahre, USA
1984	Pirmin Zurbriggen, Switzerland
1985	Marc Girardelli, Luxembourg
1986	Marc Girardelli, Luxembourg
1987	Pirmin Zurbriggen, Switzerland
1988	Pirmin Zurbriggen, Switzerland
1989	Marc Girardelli, Luxembourg
1990	Pirmin Zurbriggen, Switzerland
1991	Marc Girardelli, Luxembourg
1992	Paul Accola, Switzerland
1993	Marc Girardelli, Luxembourg
1994	Kjetil Andre Aamodt, Norway
1995	Alberto Tomba, Italy
1996	Lasse Kjus, Norway

WOMEN

Multiple winners: Annemarie Moser-Proell (6); Petra Kronberger and Vreni Schneider (3); Michela Figini, Nancy Greene, Erika Hess, Maria Walliser and Hanni Wenzel (2).

Year	
1967	Nancy Greene, Canada
1968	Nancy Greene, Canada
1969	Gertrud Gabi, Austria
1970	Michele Jacot, France
1971	Annemarie Pröll, Austria
1972	Annemarie Pröll, Austria
1973	Annemarie Pröll, Austria
1974	Annemarie Pröll, Austria
1975	Annemarie Moser-Pröll, Austria
1976	Rosi Mittermaier, W. Germany
1977	Lise-Marie Morerod, Switzerland
1978	Hanni Wenzel, Liechtenstein
1979	Annemarie Moser-Proell, Austria
1980	Hanni Wenzel, Liechtenstein
1981	Marie-Theres Nadig, Switzerland
1982	Erika Hess, Switzerland
1983	Tamara McKinney, USA
1984	Erika Hess, Switzerland
1985	Michela Figini, Switzerland
1986	Maria Walliser, Switzerland
1987	Maria Walliser, Switzerland
1988	Michela Figini, Switzerland
1989	Vreni Schneider, Switzerland
1990	Petra Kronberger, Austria
1991	Petra Kronberger, Austria
1992	Petra Kronberger, Austria
1993	Anita Wachter, Austria
1994	Vreni Schneider, Switzerland
1995	Vreni Schneider, Switzerland
1996	Katja Seizinger, Germany

TOUR DE FRANCE

The world's premier cycling event, the Tour de France is staged throughout the country (sometimes passing through neighboring countries) over four weeks. The 1946 Tour, however, the first after World War II, was only a five-day race.

Multiple winners: Jacques Anquetil, Bernard Hinault, Miguel Induráin and Eddy Merckx (5); Louison Bobet, Greg LeMond and Philippe Thys (3); Gino Bartali, Ottavio Bottecchia, Fausto Coppi, Laurent Fignon, Nicholas Frantz, Firmin Lambot, André Leducq, Sylvere Maes, Antonin Magne, Lucien Petit-Breton and Bernard Thevenet (2).

Year	
1903	Maurice Garin, France
1904	Henri Cornet, France
1905	Louis Trousselier, France
1906	René Pottier, France
1907	Lucien Petit-Breton, France
1908	Lucien Petit-Breton, France
1909	Francois Faber, Luxembourg
1910	Octave Lapize, France
1911	Gustave Garrigou, France
1912	Odile Defraye, Belgium
1913	Philippe Thys, Belgium
1914	Philippe Thys, Belgium
1915-18	Not held
1919	Firmin Lambot, Belgium
1920	Philippe Thys, Belgium
1921	Léon Scieur, Belgium
1922	Firmin Lambot, Belgium
1923	Henri Pelissier, France
1924	Ottavio Bottecchia, Italy
1925	Ottavio Bottecchia, Italy
1926	Lucien Buysse, Belgium
1927	Nicholas Frantz, Luxembourg
1928	Nicholas Frantz, Luxembourg
1929	Maurice Dewaele, Belgium
1930	André Leducq, France
1931	Antonin Magne, France
1932	André Leducq, France
1933	Georges Speicher, France
1934	Antonin Magne, France
1935	Romain Maes, Belgium
1936	Sylvere Maes, Belgium
1937	Roger Lapebie, France
1938	Gino Bartali, Italy
1939	Sylvere Maes, Belgium
1940-45	Not held
1946	Jean Lazarides, France
1947	Jean Robic, France
1948	Gino Bartali, Italy
1949	Fausto Coppi, Italy
1950	Ferdinand Kubler, Switzerland
1951	Hugo Koblet, Switzerland
1952	Fausto Coppi, Italy
1953	Louison Bobet, France
1954	Louison Bobet, France
1955	Louison Bobet, France
1956	Roger Walkowiak, France
1957	Jacques Anquetil, France
1958	Charly Gaul, Luxembourg
1959	Federico Bahamontes, Spain
1960	Gastone Nencini, Italy
1961	Jacques Anquetil, France
1962	Jacques Anquetil, France
1963	Jacques Anquetil, France
1964	Jacques Anquetil, France
1965	Felice Gimondi, Italy
1966	Lucien Aimar, France
1967	Roger Pingeon, France
1968	Jan Janssen, Holland
1969	Eddy Merckx, Belgium
1970	Eddy Merckx, Belgium
1971	Eddy Merckx, Belgium
1972	Eddy Merckx, Belgium
1973	Luis Ocana, Spain
1974	Eddy Merckx, Belgium
1975	Bernard Thevenet, France
1976	Lucien van Impe, Belgium
1977	Bernard Thevenet, France
1978	Bernard Hinault, France
1979	Bernard Hinault, France
1980	Joop Zoetemelk, Holland
1981	Bernard Hinault, France
1982	Bernard Hinault, France
1983	Laurent Fignon, France
1984	Laurent Fignon, France
1985	Bernard Hinault, France
1986	Greg LeMond, USA
1987	Stephen Roche, Ireland
1988	Pedro Delgado, Spain
1989	Greg LeMond, USA
1990	Greg LeMond, USA
1991	Miguel Induráin, Spain
1992	Miguel Induráin, Spain
1993	Miguel Induráin, Spain
1994	Miguel Induráin, Spain
1995	Miguel Induráin, Spain
1996	Bjarne Riis, Denmark

FIGURE SKATING

World Champions

Skaters who won World and Olympic championships in the same year are listed in **bold** type.

MEN

Multiple winners: Ulrich Salchow (10); Karl Schafer (7); Dick Button (5); Willy Bockl, Kurt Browning, Scott Hamilton and Hayes Jenkins (4); Emmerich Danzer, Gillis Grafstrom, Gustav Hugel, David Jenkins, Fritz Kachler and Ondrej Nepela (3); Brian Boitano, Gilbert Fuchs, Jan Hoffmann, Felix Kaspar, Vladimir Kovalev, Elvis Stojko and Tim Wood (2).

Year	
1896	Gilbert Fuchs, Germany
1897	Gustav Hugel, Austria
1898	Henning Grenander, Sweden
1899	Gustav Hugel, Austria
1900	Gustav Hugel, Austria
1901	Ulrich Salchow, Sweden
1902	Ulrich Salchow, Sweden
1903	Ulrich Salchow, Sweden
1904	Ulrich Salchow, Sweden
1905	Ulrich Salchow, Sweden
1906	Gilbert Fuchs, Germany
1907	Ulrich Salchow, Sweden
1908	**Ulrich Salchow**, Sweden
1909	Ulrich Salchow, Sweden
1910	Ulrich Salchow, Sweden
1911	Ulrich Salchow, Sweden
1912	Fritz Kachler, Austria
1913	Fritz Kachler, Austria
1914	Gosta Sandhal, Sweden
1915-21	Not held
1922	Gillis Gräfstrom, Sweden
1923	Fritz Kachler, Austria
1924	**Gillis Gräfstrom**, Sweden
1925	Willy Bockl, Austria
1926	Willy Bockl, Austria
1927	Willy Bockl, Austria
1928	Willy Bockl, Austria
1929	Gillis Gräfstrom, Sweden
1930	Karl Schäfer, Austria
1931	Karl Schäfer, Austria
1932	**Karl Schäfer**, Austria
1933	Karl Schäfer, Austria
1934	Karl Schäfer, Austria
1935	Karl Schäfer, Austria
1936	**Karl Schäfer**, Austria
1937	Felix Kaspar, Austria
1938	Felix Kaspar, Austria
1939	Graham Sharp, Britain
1940-46	Not held
1947	Hans Gerschwiler, Switzerland
1948	**Dick Button**, USA
1949	Dick Button, USA
1950	Dick Button, USA
1951	Dick Button, USA
1952	**Dick Button**, USA
1953	Hayes Jenkins, USA
1954	Hayes Jenkins, USA
1955	Hayes Jenkins, USA
1956	**Hayes Jenkins**, USA
1957	David Jenkins, USA
1958	David Jenkins, USA
1959	David Jenkins, USA
1960	Alan Giletti, France
1961	Not held
1962	Donald Jackson, Canada
1963	Donald McPherson, Canada
1964	**Manfred Schnelldorfer**, W. Ger
1965	Alain Calmat, France
1966	Emmerich Danzer, Austria
1967	Emmerich Danzer, Austria
1968	Emmerich Danzer, Austria
1969	Tim Wood, USA
1970	Tim Wood, USA
1971	Ondrej Nepela, Czechoslovakia
1972	**Ondrej Nepela**, Czechoslovakia
1973	Ondrej Nepela, Czechoslovakia
1974	Jan Hoffmann, E. Germany
1975	Sergie Volkov, USSR
1976	**John Curry**, Britain
1977	Vladimir Kovalev, USSR
1978	Charles Tickner, USA
1979	Vladimir Kovalev, USSR
1980	Jan Hoffmann, E. Germany
1981	Scott Hamilton, USA
1982	Scott Hamilton, USA
1983	Scott Hamilton, USA
1984	**Scott Hamilton**, USA
1985	Alexander Fadeev, USSR
1986	Brian Boitano, USA
1987	Brian Orser, Canada
1988	**Brian Boitano**, USA
1989	Kurt Browning, Canada
1990	Kurt Browning, Canada
1991	Kurt Browning, Canada
1992	**Viktor Petrenko**, CIS
1993	Kurt Browning, Canada
1994	Elvis Stojko, Canada
1995	Elvis Stojko, Canada
1996	Todd Eldredge, USA

WOMEN

Multiple winners: Sonja Henie (10); Carol Heiss and Herma Planck Szabo (5); Lily Kronberger and Katarina Witt (4); Sjoukje Dijkstra, Peggy Fleming, Meray Horvath (3); Tenley Albright, Linda Fratianne, Anett Poetzsch, Beatrix Schuba, Barbara Ann Scott, Gabriele Seyfert, Megan Taylor, Alena Vrzanova, and Kristi Yamaguchi (2).

Year	
1906	Madge Syers, Britain
1907	Madge Syers, Britian
1908	Lily Kronberger, Hungary
1909	Lily Kronberger, Hungary
1910	Lily Kronberger, Hungary
1911	Lily Kronberger, Hungary
1912	Meray Horvath, Hungary
1913	Meray Horvath, Hungary
1914	Meray Horvath, Hungary
1915-21	Not held
1922	Herma Planck-Szabo, Austria
1923	Herma Planck-Szabo, Austria
1924	**Herma Planck-Szabo**, Austria
1925	Herma Planck-Szabo, Austria
1926	Herma Planck-Szabo, Austria
1927	Sonja Henie, Norway
1928	**Sonja Henie**, Norway
1929	Sonja Henie, Norway
1930	Sonja Henie, Norway
1931	Sonja Henie, Norway
1932	**Sonja Henie**, Norway
1933	Sonja Henie, Norway
1934	Sonja Henie, Norway
1935	Sonja Henie, Norway
1936	**Sonja Henie**, Norway
1937	Cecilia Colledge, Britain
1938	Megan Taylor, Britain
1939	Megan Taylor, Britain
1940-46	Not held
1947	Barbara Ann Scott, Canada
1948	**Barbara Ann Scott**, Canada
1949	Alena Vrzanova, Czechoslovakia
1950	Alena Vrzanova, Czechoslovakia
1951	Jeannette Altwegg, Britain
1952	Jacqueline Du Bief, France
1953	Tenley Albright, USA
1954	Gundi Busch, W. Germany
1955	Tenley Albright, USA
1956	Carol Heiss, USA
1957	Carol Heiss, USA
1958	Carol Heiss, USA
1959	Carol Heiss, USA
1960	**Carol Heiss**, USA
1961	Not held
1962	Sjoukje Dijkstra, Holland
1963	Sjoukje Dijkstra, Holland
1964	**Sjoukje Dijkstra**, Holland
1965	Petra Burka, Canada
1966	Peggy Fleming, USA
1967	Peggy Fleming, USA
1968	**Peggy Fleming**, USA
1969	Gabriele Seyfert, E. Germany
1970	Gabriele Seyfert, E. Germany
1971	Beatrix Schuba, Austria
1972	**Beatrix Schuba**, Austria
1973	Karen Magnussen, Canada
1974	Christine Errath, E. Germany
1975	Dianne DeLeeuw, Holland
1976	**Dorothy Hamill**, USA
1977	Linda Fratianne, USA
1978	Anett Poetzsch, E. Germany
1979	Linda Fratianne, USA
1980	**Anett Poetzsch**, E. Germany
1981	Denise Biellmann, Switzerland
1982	Elaine Zayak, USA
1983	Rosalyn Sumners, USA
1984	**Katarina Witt**, E. Germany

Figure Skating (Cont.)

World Champions

WOMEN

Year		Year		Year	
1985	Katarina Witt, E. Germany	1989	Midori Ito, Japan	1993	Oksana Baiul, Ukraine
1986	Debi Thomas, USA	1990	Jill Trenary, USA	1994	Yuka Sato, Japan
1987	Katarina Witt, E. Germany	1991	Kristi Yamaguchi, USA	1995	Lu Chen, China
1988	**Katarina Witt**, E. Germany	1992	**Kristi Yamaguchi**, USA	1996	Michelle Kwan, USA

U.S. Champions

Skaters who won U.S., World and Olympic championships in same year are in **bold** type.

MEN

Multiple winners: Dick Button and Roger Turner (7); Sherwin Badger and Robin Lee (5); Brian Boitano, Scott Hamilton, David Jenkins, Hayes Jenkins and Charles Tickner (4); Todd Eldredge, Gordon McKellen, Nathaniel Niles and Tim Wood (3); Scott Allen, Christopher Bowman, Scott Davis, Eugene Turner and Gary Visconti (2).

Year		Year		Year		Year	
1914	Norman Scott	1936	Robin Lee	1957	David Jenkins	1977	Charles Tickner
1915-17	Not held	1937	Robin Lee	1958	David Jenkins	1978	Charles Tickner
1918	Nathaniel Niles	1938	Robin Lee	1959	David Jenkins	1979	Charles Tickner
1919	Not held	1939	Robin Lee	1960	David Jenkins	1980	Charles Tickner
1920	Sherwin Badger	1940	Eugene Turner	1961	Bradley Lord	1981	Scott Hamilton
1921	Sherwin Badger	1941	Eugene Turner	1962	Monty Hoyt	1982	Scott Hamilton
1922	Sherwin Badger	1942	Robert Specht	1963	Thomas Litz	1983	Scott Hamilton
1923	Sherwin Badger	1943	Arthur Vaughn	1964	Scott Allen	1984	**Scott Hamilton**
1924	Sherwin Badger	1944-45	Not held	1965	Gary Visconti	1985	Brian Boitano
1925	Nathaniel Niles	1946	Dick Button	1966	Scott Allen	1986	Brian Boitano
1926	Chris Christenson	1947	Dick Button	1967	Gary Visconti	1987	Brian Boitano
1927	Nathaniel Niles	1948	**Dick Button**	1968	Tim Wood	1988	**Brian Boitano**
1928	Roger Turner	1949	Dick Button	1969	Tim Wood	1989	Christopher Bowman
1929	Roger Turner	1950	Dick Button	1970	Tim Wood	1990	Todd Eldredge
1930	Roger Turner	1951	Dick Button	1971	John (Misha) Petkevich	1991	Todd Eldredge
1931	Roger Turner	1952	**Dick Button**	1972	Ken Shelley	1992	Christopher Bowman
1932	Roger Turner	1953	Hayes Jenkins	1973	Gordon McKellen	1993	Scott Davis
1933	Roger Turner	1954	Hayes Jenkins	1974	Gordon McKellen	1994	Scott Davis
1934	Roger Turner	1955	Hayes Jenkins	1975	Gordon McKellen	1995	Todd Eldredge
1935	Robin Lee	1956	**Hayes Jenkins**	1976	Terry Kubicka	1996	Rudy Galindo

WOMEN

Multiple winners: Maribel Vinson (9); Theresa Weld Blanchard and Gretchen Merrill (6); Tenley Albright, Peggy Fleming, and Janet Lynn (5); Linda Fratianne and Carol Heiss (4); Dorothy Hamill, Beatrix Loughran, Rosalyn Summers, Joan Tozzer and Jill Trenary (3); Yvonne Sherman and Debi Thomas (2).

Year		Year		Year		Year	
1914	Theresa Weld	1937	Maribel Vinson	1957	Carol Heiss	1977	Linda Fratianne
1915-17	Not held	1938	Joan Tozzer	1958	Carol Heiss	1978	Linda Fratianne
1918	Rosemary Beresford	1939	Joan Tozzer	1959	Carol Heiss	1979	Linda Fratianne
1919	Not held	1940	Joan Tozzer	1960	**Carol Heiss**	1980	Linda Fratianne
1920	Theresa Weld	1941	Jane Vaughn	1961	Laurence Owen	1981	Elaine Zayak
1921	Theresa Blanchard	1942	Jane Sullivan	1962	Barbara Pursley	1982	Rosalyn Sumners
1922	Theresa Blanchard	1943	Gretchen Merrill	1963	Lorraine Hanlon	1983	Rosalyn Sumners
1923	Theresa Blanchard	1944	Gretchen Merrill	1964	Peggy Fleming	1984	Rosalyn Sumners
1924	Theresa Blanchard	1945	Gretchen Merrill	1965	Peggy Fleming	1985	Tiffany Chin
1925	Beatrix Loughran	1946	Gretchen Merrill	1966	Peggy Fleming	1986	Debi Thomas
1926	Beatrix Loughran	1947	Gretchen Merrill	1967	Peggy Fleming	1987	Jill Trenary
1927	Beatrix Loughran	1948	Gretchen Merrill	1968	**Peggy Fleming**	1988	Debi Thomas
1928	Maribel Vinson	1949	Yvonne Sherman	1969	Janet Lynn	1989	Jill Trenary
1929	Maribel Vinson	1950	Yvonne Sherman	1970	Janet Lynn	1990	Jill Trenary
1930	Maribel Vinson	1951	Sonya Klopfer	1971	Janet Lynn	1991	Tonya Harding
1931	Maribel Vinson	1952	Tenley Albright	1972	Janet Lynn	1992	**Kristi Yamaguchi**
1932	Maribel Vinson	1953	Tenley Albright	1973	Janet Lynn	1993	Nancy Kerrigan
1933	Maribel Vinson	1954	Tenley Albright	1974	Dorothy Hamill	1994	vacated*
1934	Suzanne Davis	1955	Tenley Albright	1975	Dorothy Hamill	1995	Nicole Bobek
1935	Maribel Vinson	1956	Tenley Albright	1976	**Dorothy Hamill**	1996	Michelle Kwan
1936	Maribel Vinson						

* Tonya Harding was stripped of the 1994 women's title and banned from membership in the U.S. Figure Skating Assn. for life on June 30, 1994 for violating the USFSA Code of Ethics after she pleaded guilty to a charge of conspiracy to hinder the prosecution related to the Jan. 6, 1994 attack on Nancy Kerrigan.

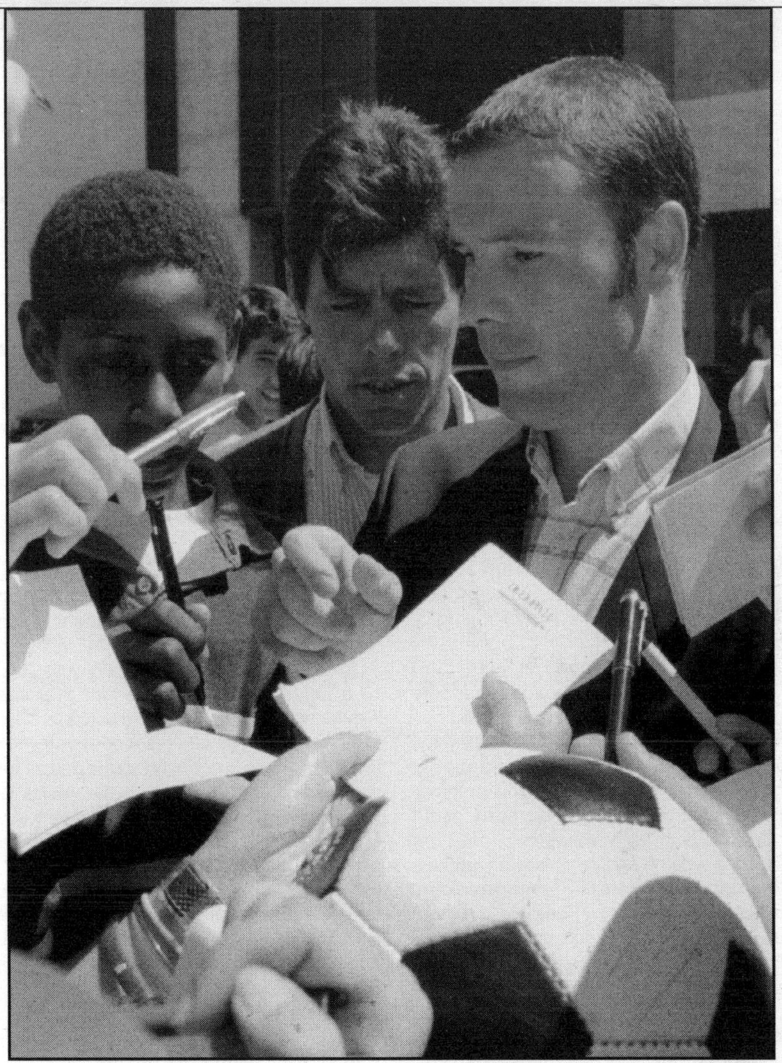

Wide World Photos

Jean Marc Bosman, an average soccer player from Belgium, won a landmark case when the European Court of Justice put an end to the reserve clause and banned all limits on foreign players per team.

SOCCER

1995–96 YEAR IN REVIEW

SOCCER

by Paul Gardner

Nigeria's Golden Moment

In the 1996 Olympic games, Nigeria became the first African country to win a major tournament

The European Championship -"Euro '96"- and the Olympic Games soccer tournament were the two big international events of 1996.

Two very different tournaments. "Euro '96", staged in England, was decidedly poor in the quality of soccer presented.

Soccer devoid of brilliant individual stars, soccer dominated by tactics, and mostly dour defensive tactics at that. "This isn't fantasy football. It's going to be hard," said England's coach Terry Venables.

Hard it was. A welter of boring games, some appalling refereeing, and occasional flashes of good soccer. Romania went out because the referee didn't see that Dorinel Munteanu's shot had crossed the Bulgarian goal-line before it was cleared. "We're going home because of some overweight, sightless imbecile," moaned a Romanian newspaper. Italy was eliminated because coach Arrigo Sacchi made no fewer than six changes to his team that had played well in beating Russia. The revamped team lost 2-1 to the Czech Republic.

The four semifinalists had not distinguished themselves with scintillating play. England made it, but then went out, on a penalty-kick tie breaker, to Germany. In the other semi-final the Czech Republic, nobody's favorite to even get out of the first round, beat France in the worst game of the tournament, also on a tie-breaker.

Having to resort to tie-breakers was seen as a failure of the new rule that overtime would be decided by the first goal, "The Golden Goal" as FIFA (soccer's international governing body) called it. The prospect of sudden-death caused teams to be ultra-cautious, and there were no Golden Goals during the four overtime games; all went to penalty kicks. The final, tied at 1-1, also went to overtime, but this time the Germans got the Golden Goal from substitute Oliver Bierhoff. The Czechs had played their usual unimaginative, cautious game, packing midfield and relying on sudden counterattacks.

The Germans were more enterprising, without ever hitting the heights. But their win was remarkable considering the plague of injuries that the team had suffered throughout the tournament.

The shaky state of European soccer was further emphasized at the Olympic Games. Despite being allocated five of the sixteen berths in the tournament, Europe was anything but dominant. Only Portugal reached the semi-finals, there to be beaten by Argentina. In the third-place game, Portugal was thrashed 5-0 by Brazil. The South Americans looked streets ahead of the pedestrian Europeans but it was to be

---

Paul Gardner has been the columnist for *Soccer America* since 1982 and is the author of four books on the sport, including *The Simplest Game* (Macmillian).

Wide World Photos

After leading Nigeria to a gold medal in the Olympics, **Nwankwo Kanu** seemed poised for a brilliant professional career. Sadly, tests revealed that Kanu has a serious heart disorder and he has been told to stop playing.

Nigeria that provided the most spectacular fireworks. There was no dull, defensive caution about Nigeria's style of play. Coming from 3-1 down, it beat Brazil with a Golden Goal in the semi-final. Then, in a sparkling final, Nigeria twice came from behind to upset Argentina 3-2. The victory marked the first major-tournament win for an African country.

Bitter tragedy quickly followed for Nigeria's brilliant captain, the 20-year-old Nwankwo Kanu. As he prepared to begin what promised to be a glittering career with Italian club Inter-Milan, medical tests revealed that he was suffering from a serious valve disorder of the heart. He was told that he should never play soccer again.

For the United States, the Olympics presented a familiar story. Bruce Arena's team could manage no better than a win, a tie and a loss in the first round. The same record as in the 1992 and 1984 Olympics. Not good enough to advance into the second round.

The Olympic tournament, basically for under-23 players, suggested an exciting future for South America, and contained a warning that, with the arrival of African soccer, the old order of soccer power was undergoing a revolution. That was bad news for the Europeans, who were already struggling with another dramatic upheaval: the Bosman Case.

This tale began in 1990, when a 25-year-old run-of-the-mill Belgian player, Jean Marc Bosman, came to the end of his contract with FC Liege. He wanted to move to the French club Dunkerque. Liege wanted to keep him, and demanded from Dunkerque an absurdly inflated transfer fee of $375,000. This effectively blocked any move, and Liege kept Bosman on their pay-

Wide World Photos

Carlos Valderrama of the Tampa Bay Mutiny acknowledges the crowd after being named the MVP of the first MLS All Star game.

roll at one quarter his previous salary.

This was the reserve clause at its most primitive, but in 1990, in Belgium, it was perfectly legal. Bosman went to court and got permission to play for Dunkerque. In 1991 the case was referred to the European Court of Justice (ECJ) for a definitive ruling. Bosman's lawyers demanded that the reserve clause be outlawed, and that once a player's contract had expired he should be a free agent. And they added another twist: they asked the Court for a ruling against restrictions imposed on foreign players.

At the time, virtually all European countries had rules limiting each major pro team to two or three foreigners per team. This, argued Bosman's lawyers, violated the Treaty of Rome, signed by all members of the European Community, which guaranteed freedom of movement for all workers within the Community. It took over four years, but on December 15 1995, Bosman's dogged persistence was rewarded. The ECJ handed him a crushing victory: it declared the reserve clause illegal, and banned all restrictions on the employment of foreign players within the European Community.

European soccer authorities - who seemed to have believed all along that nothing would come of Bosman's action - were in total panic. UEFA, the Union of European Football Associations, sent a letter to the ECJ, predicting dire consequences for the sport, and loud cries of doom echoed around European soccer. The small clubs claimed that they survived only by developing young players and selling them to the big clubs. Without the reserve clause, they would not be able to demand a transfer fee for those players.

Mike Bateson, chairman of English third-division club Torquay United, said he would disband his club's youth program: "I'm damned if I'm going to put my money into a youth system just to let the bigger clubs snaffle up the product." UEFA told its members to ignore the ruling on foreign players, and persisted in its efforts to get soccer declared a special case. The ECJ was not impressed. European Commissioner Karel Vam Miert said "negotiating with UEFA is like talking to a wall." He ordered all European countries to obey the ruling, or else...

UEFA's ill–advised resistance crumbled. The bigger problem had been the foreign-player issue, but by the beginning of the 1996-97 season, the barriers were down. The reserve clause was almost a non-issue. It had already been substantially modified in most countries. Belgium in 1990 had been an aberration, a rare feudal hold-out.

Predictions of soccer's collapse looked ridiculous. The European game had never been richer, with television money flooding into the sport. In Spain, Canal-Plus offered $1.5 billion for a seven-year deal for the rights to Spanish league games. UEFA announced that the club winning the European Champions League would get $3.6 million. And from FIFA came the news that it had accepted a bid of $2.1 billion for the television rights to the 2006 and 2010 World Cups. In England they proved that the transfer fee was far from dead when Alan Shearer changed clubs. Newcastle United paid a world record $23.3 million to the Blackburn Rovers for the striker. This was the thriving, immensely rich world of international soccer that the United States

Wide World Photos

Amid much internecine wrangling, FIFA awarded the **2002 World Cup to Korea** and **Japan** marking the first time the event will be played in Asia and with two host countries.

was striving to join. The vital move came on April 6, 1966.

With the American soccer world holding its breath and crossing its fingers, the new pro league, Major League Soccer, kicked off. Would it, could it, succeed where so many previous attempts to launch the pro sport had failed? A crucial pointer to success came quickly: the fans turned out in large numbers. The Los Angeles Galaxy recorded an astonishing 69,255 for its opening home game in the Rose Bowl, while the New York/New Jersey MetroStars drew 46,826 to Giants Stadium.

MLS officials had cautiously stated that an average crowd of 12,000 would be satisfactory. When the regular season was over, the average came in nearly 50 per cent higher at 17,416. The Galaxy topped the averages with 28,916, the MetroStars had 23,898. It no longer seemed fanciful when Commissioner Doug Logan spoke of expansion, of adding two more teams in 1998. A high proportion of the fans were Hispanic, particularly in Los Angeles, Dallas and San Jose. This fan base was a natural response to the league's policy of signing top Latin players who were considered those most likely to produce a flamboyant, exciting, attacking version of the sport.

The Tampa Bay Mutiny had Colombian Carlos Valderrama, with his blond Afro hairdo. The Galaxy had the dashing Mexican goalkeeper Jorge Campos, who could also play as a goal-scoring forward. Not that the Galaxy needed much help in that department for they had El Tanque, The Tank, the towering Eduardo Hurtado from Ecuador. At Washington DC United, the Bolivian Marco Etcheverry, El Diablo, cast a spell with his intricate left-footed skills. Colombia's Iron Man, Leonel Alvarez, ran the show for the Dallas Burn.

Unfortunately, MLS quickly began to behave like any pro league. Within two months it recorded its first coach firing. Eddie Firmani of the MetroStars "resigned", leaving the team in a shambles. Not quite what the MLS had in mind for its most important market.

The Galaxy started off by winning its first 12 games, then went mysteriously off the rails, and could manage only seven wins in its remaining 20 games. When the Columbus Crew sank to 6-16, the worst record in the league, coach Timo Liekoski

Wide World Photos

Much of the surprising success of Major League Soccer's inaugural season can be attributed to the exciting style of play favored by Latin stars like Bolivian **Marco Etcheverry** (center) of the Washington D.C. United.

was canned. Little-known assistant Tom Fitzgerald took over, and the Crew rattled off seven straight wins and sailed right into the play-offs.

Another reason for the Crew's turnaround was the arrival of outstanding goalkeeper Brad Friedel. Friedel had been playing in Turkey but, along with almost all the other members of the US national team including Tab Ramos, John Harkes, Alexi Lalas, Mike Sorber, Eric Wynalda and Joe-Max Moore - decided to join the MLS. This was another triumph for MLS. It had been feared that many top American players would prefer to continue playing overseas while they waited to see if the MLS would be successful.

By season's end, two more coaches had "resigned": Englishman Bob Houghton left the Colorado Rapids, and Irishman Frank Stapleton parted company with the New England Revolution. These were the only two clubs that failed to make the playoffs. Evidently, there was a soccer culture clash between the lively, Latin-oriented style that the MLS wanted, and the British coaching mentality. It seemed highly unlikely that MLS would feature any more imported British coaches in the near future.

The MLS inaugural season came to an extraordinary climax on October 20 in Foxboro, Ma., with the championship game between Washington D.C. United and the Los Angeles Galaxy. MLS Cup`96, they called it, and this Cup really did overflow.

Torrential rain the night before and all through the day seemed to doom the game, which was scheduled for national television on ABC. Over 43,000 tickets had been sold – there was even talk of the game being sold out. But the downpour threatened to ruin everything.

Nevertheless, postponement wasn't even considered: "There was never any doubt in our mind," said Commissioner Doug Logan, "we were going to play."

Play they did, as the rain poured down, as wind gusts of up to 50 MPH swept down the field – and, incredibly, as over 34,000 fans sat through the cold and damp ordeal.

They were rewarded with what was – considering the sloshy field conditions – a very lively and skillful game, with a highly dramatic ending. After the Galaxy had taken a 2-0 lead, on goals from Ecuadoran Eduardo Hurtado and Chris Armas, they appeared to have matters well under control. But DC United stormed back in the final 17 minutes of the game to tie the score at 2-2. Sudden death overtime lasted just over three minutes, when DC United defender American Eddie Pope rose to head home a corner kick from Bolivian midfielder Marco Etcheverry, who rebounded from a sluggish first half to dominate the second. Etcheverry who was voted the game's MVP, assisted on all three DC United Goals.

John Harkes, DC United's American captain said: "We thought maybe 15,000 fans would turn out in this weather, but this was incredible – and they stayed with us till the end! Soccer fever is alive in the United States and it's here to stay."

The triumph of DC United was also a personal triumph for coach Bruce Arena, who made the risky jump to the pros from college coach at the University of Virginia. Seven of his starting eleven were, in fact, former Cavaliers.

This fact was a decidedly encouraging note for a league that had declared that its ultimate aim was to be an American league for American players.

The bulk of the league's players were, in fact, young Americans, and the hope was that the league would help develop future national team stars.

Some highly promising players did emerge, like Jason Kreis of Dallas, Robin Fraser in Los Angeles, Brian McBride in Columbus, Roy Lassiter in Tampa Bay, and DC United's Eddie Pope. But overall, the picture was less encouraging. Far too many of the Americans fell short of the necessary pro level, and their inadequacy had an adverse effect on the overall caliber of MLS games.

Worried that the initial enthusiasm of the fans might die down if they judged the soccer sub-standard, the MLS reacted quickly. As a short-term measure to up the level of play, they requested permission from the USSF (United States Soccer Federation) to allow each team to sign five, rather than four, foreign players in 1997.

For a long-term remedy, MLS joined forces with the USSF to come up with a plan that, at last, faced up to the fact that college soccer was incapable of producing pro quality players. The gap between the college and pro games had reached crisis point. "Clearly, it's night and day," said Bruce Arena. "The pro game is a lot faster, more technical, more athletic, more competitive. In college, it's very difficult to get a good soccer environment." Said USSF President Alan Rothenberg: "The NCAA has no interest in soccer. As long as the NCAA has in place the incredibly restrictive practices that they do, we cannot look to college soccer to produce top–class talent."

Most criticism was leveled at college soccer's absurdly short three-month season, and the NCAA's ban on outside ball during the entire academic year. While young foreign talent was playing 60 or more games a year, with and against experienced pros, the college Americans were lucky to play 30 a total that, said Arena, included "very few good games."

"What development?" asked Kevin Payne, the President of DC United, "If we let our kids go into college their development will be retarded." So Project-40, the joint MLS/USSF plan, is designed to steer young players away from college soccer. Every year, starting in January 1997, forty of the country's best 18- and 19-year-olds will be assembled at a camp run by the USSF. After a period of observation and assessment, thirty will be offered pro "developmental contracts", with three being assigned to each MLS team. Players who want to continue their education will be given scholarships under the scheme.

National team coach Steve Sampson welcomed Project-40 and predicted a 90 percent positive response from players asked to participate. Project-40 has the added plus that it will open up more opportunities for inner-city players, mostly Hispanic, who have been only marginally represented in the colleges or in the USSF's own Olympic development Program. "If greater Hispanic presence is the result," said Rothenberg, "then Hallelujah! – I'll be the happiest man in the United States."

Rothenberg had, in fact, been preparing the ground to turn himself into a soccer man of the world, rather than just the United States. He announced his intention to seek a greater role in FIFA affairs. He had chosen an interesting moment.

Joao Havelange, the 80-year old Brazilian who had autocratically ruled FIFA since 1974, was coming under sustained pressure to step down. Lennart Johanssen, the Swedish president of UEFA announced that he would run against Havelange in 1998, and jumped at every opportunity to criticize him.

Havelange provided him with a beauty when he went to Nigeria and promised it the 1997 Youth Cup which had already been assigned to Malaysia. And he did it on the very day that the Nigerian government, in the face of a storm of worldwide criticism, executed seven dissidents. Johanssen accused Havelange of behaving "like a dictator." The rivalry came to a disastrous head over the awarding of the rights to stage the 2002 World Cup.

It was to be the first held in Asia, and the candidates were Japan and South Korea. Both had spent large sums of money during their campaigns, and Havelange was known to favor Japan. Which meant that Johanssen backed Korea. In fact, Johanssen built up such powerful anti-Havelange support that it became clear to Havelange that the vote would go to Korea. Havelange, humiliated, had to compromise. FIFA, going against its own rules which prohibited such a deal, agreed that Japan and Korea would jointly stage World Cup 2002. The tight lipped Japanese had no choice but to accept the arrangement. But a long history of animosity between the two countries did not suggest that co-operation was going to be easy to maintain.

FIFA General Secretary Sepp Blatter underlined the problem when 3 month slater : "I must say that the countries are not only not coming closer, it's quite the opposite. They are moving further apart. This is not the marriage we want. It has been difficult enough to arrange even a date and venue for a meeting between the representatives of the two countries ...and this is even before we come to the substantive issues. It won't be easy. They cannot even agree on the shape of the tournament. Japan wants 40 teams and Korea wants only 32."

Things went better for the United States, which got what it wanted with the rights to stage the 1999 Women's World Cup.

While the world of soccer was expanding and changing dramatically, the shrinking world of Diego Maradona continued its sad downward slide. Yet another attempted comeback this time with the Buenos Aires club Boca Juniors ended in disaster as Maradona missed a crucial penalty kick, ruining Boca's chances of winning the championship. In August, the troubled 35-year-old star flew to Switzerland to enter a clinic where he was supposed to be cured of his admitted cocaine addiction. Soon after announcing that he was ready to play for Argentina again, he stated that he would never play in Argentina again. However, he added, he was considering an offer from the Spanish club Rayo Vallecano.

Wide World Photos

Colorful Mexican goalkeeper **Jorge Campos** answers questions at an MLS press conference. Campos went on to lead the LA Galaxy into the first **MLS** title game.

Hard Luck Story of the Century:

Italy's weekly betting mania is the totocalcio a list of 13 soccer games that have to be forecast as home or away wins, or as ties. In March an anonymous better, checking the results as they came in, found that twelve of the games had ended as he had predicted. The thirteenth was within one minute of ending correctly, too when fans invaded the field and the referee abandoned the game. Which meant that the game was invalid for betting purposes...and goodbye to an estimated payout of $7.5 million! ❐

THE SEASON IN REVIEW

1995-1996

WORLD • EUROPE • AMERICA

FIFA Top 50 World Rankings

FIFA announced a new monthly world ranking system on Aug. 13, 1993 designed to "provide a constant international comparison of national team performances." The rankings are based on a mathematical formula that weighs strength of schedule, importance of matches and goals scored for and against. Games considered include World Cup qualifying and final rounds, Continental championship qualifying and final rounds, and friendly matches. At the end of the year, FIFA designates a Team of the Year. Teams of the Year so far have been Germany (1993) and Brazil (1994 and '95).

FINAL 1995

		Points	1994 Rank
1	Brazil	68.49	1
2	Germany	61.77	5
3	Italy	61.10	4
4	Spain	59.12	2
5	Russia	58.76	13
6	Netherlands	57.35	6
7	Argentina	56.88	10
8	France	56.73	19
9	Denmark	56.43	14
10	Norway	55.74	8
11	Romania	55.10	11
12	Mexico	54.81	15
13	Sweden	54.79	3
14	Czech Republic	53.40	34
15	Colombia	53.29	17
16	Portugal	53.24	20
17	Bulgaria	53.02	16
18	Switzerland	52.11	7
19	USA	51.04	23
20	Ivory Coast	48.98	25
21	England	48.86	18
22	Tunisia	48.26	30
23	Egypt	48.21	22
24	Belgium	47.99	24
25	Zambia	47.66	21
26	Scotland	47.63	32
27	Nigeria	47.44	12
28	Ireland	47.32	9
29	Ghana	47.05	26
30	Turkey	46.26	48
31	Japan	45.34	36
32	Uruguay	44.56	37
33	Poland	43.95	29
34	Greece	43.83	28
35	Slovakia	43.80	43
36	Chile	42.34	47
37	Cameroon	41.80	31
38	Morocco	41.46	33
39	Austria	41.07	49
40	South Africa	40.79	56
41	Croatia	40.45	62
42	Israel	40.24	42
43	Lithuania	38.90	59
44	Finland	38.71	38
45	No. Ireland	38.54	45
46	South Korea	38.44	35
47	Senegal	38.43	50
48	Algeria	38.39	57
49	Honduras	38.05	53
50	Iceland	37.90	39

1996 (as of Sept. 25)

		Points	1995 Rank
1	Brazil	67.86	1
2	Germany	64.43	2
3	France	61.57	8
4	Czech Republic	61.41	14
5	Russia	59.70	5
6	Italy	58.99	3
7	Netherlands	58.82	6
8	Sweden	58.43	13
9	Denmark	58.00	9
10	Spain	57.72	4
11	Colombia	57.56	15
12	England	56.01	21
13	Mexico	54.91	12
14	Portugal	54.37	16
15	Romania	53.21	11
16	Zambia	53.11	25
17	South Africa	52.95	40
18	USA	52.66	19
19	Ghana	51.59	29
20	Japan	51.31	31
21	Bulgaria	51.23	17
22	Argentina	51.22	7
23	Norway	50.77	10
24	Tunisia	50.76	22
25	Croatia	50.69	41
26	Chile	49.79	36
27	Morocco	48.24	38
28	Egypt	47.63	23
29	Ivory Coast	47.25	20
30	Greece	46.94	34
31	Ecuador	46.57	55
32	Ireland	45.93	28
33	Turkey	45.85	30
34	Trinidad & Tobago	45.52	57
35	Switzerland	44.76	18
36	Bolivia	44.53	53
37	Belgium	44.51	24
38	Jamaica	44.36	56
39	Scotland	44.14	26
40	Slovakia	44.10	35
41	South Korea	42.05	46
42	Saudi Arabia	41.77	54
43	Honduras	41.20	49
44	Algeria	41.17	48
45	Paraguay	41.03	64
46	Austria	40.75	39
47	Cameroon	40.35	37
48	Gabon	39.88	67
49	Israel	39.31	42
50	Thailand	39.23	77

Countdown to World Cup France '98

Date	Activity	Date	Activity
Nov. 16, 1997	End of preliminary competition	June 10, 1998	Final 32-team tournament begins in France
Nov. 30, 1997	Completion of any necessary playoffs	July 12, 1998	Championship game at Stade de France in Paris
Dec. 4, 1997	Draw for final competition held in Marseilles		

1996 European Championship

Contested for the tenth time since its inception in 1960. This year was the first tournament under the new "golden goal" rule which called for a "sudden death" overtime in the case of a tie. Euro '96 was held in England from June 8-June 30.

First Round

Round Robin; each team played the other three teams in its group once. Note that three points were awarded for a win and one point for a tie and (*) indicates team advanced to quarterfinals.

Group A	W	L	T	GF	GA	Pts
*England	2	0	1	4	2	7
*Holland	1	1	1	3	4	4
Scotland	1	1	1	1	2	4
Switzerland	0	2	1	1	4	1

RESULTS: **June 8**— England 1, Switzerland 1; **June 10**— Holland 0, Scotland 0; **June 13**— Holland 2, Switzerland 0; **June 15**— England 2, Scotland 0; **June 18**— England 4, Holland 1; Scotland 1, Switzerland 0.

Group B	W	L	T	GF	GA	Pts
*France	2	0	1	4	1	7
*Spain	1	0	2	3	2	5
Bulgaria	1	1	1	1	4	4
Romania	0	3	0	1	2	0

RESULTS: **June 9**— Spain 1, Bulgaria 1; **June 10**— France 1, Romania 0; **June 13**— Bulgaria 1, Romania 0; **June 15**— France 1, Spain 1; **June 18**— Spain 2, Romania 1; France 3, Bulgaria 1.

Group C	W	L	T	GF	GA	Pts
*Germany	2	0	1	5	0	7
*Czech Republic	1	1	1	5	6	4
Italy	1	1	1	3	3	4
Russia	0	2	1	4	8	1

RESULTS: **June 9**— Germany 2, Czech Republic 0; **June 11**— Italy 2, Russia 1; **June 14**— Czech Republic 2, Italy 1; **June 16**— Germany 3, Russia 0; **June 19**— Russia 3, Czech Republic 3; Italy 0, Germany 0.

Group D	W	L	T	GF	GA	Pts
*Portugal	2	0	1	5	1	7
*Croatia	2	1	0	4	3	6
Denmark	1	1	1	4	4	4
Turkey	0	3	0	0	5	0

RESULTS: **June 9**— Denmark 1, Portugal 1; **June 11**— Croatia 1, Turkey 0; **June 14**— Portugal 1, Turkey 0; **June 16**— Croatia 3, Denmark 0; **June 19**— Denmark 3, Turkey 0; Portugal 3, Croatia 0.

Quarterfinals

June 22 London (75,440) ....England 0, Spain 0*
June 22 Liverpool (37,465)...............France 0, Holland 0*
June 23 Manchester (43,412) ....Germany 2, Croatia 1
June 23 Birmingham (26,832) ....Czech Rep. 1, Portugal 0
*Shootout wins: England, 4-2; France 5-4.

Semifinals

June 26 Manchester (43,877)......Czech Rep. 0, France 0*
June 26 London (75,862).............Germany 1, England 1*
*Shootout wins: Czech Rep. 6-5, Germany 6-5.

Final

June 30 at Wembley Stadium, London
Att: 73,611

Gemany 2 ....OT ....Czech Rep. 1
Goals: GER—Oliver Bierhoff 73rd, 95th; CZE—Patrik Berger (pen.) 59th

European Championship All-Tournament Team

Selected by *Soccer America*

G—David Seamon, England
D—Matthias Sammer, Germany
M—Marcel Desailly, France
M—Dieter Eilts, Germany
M—Karel Poborsky, Czech Republic
M—Youri Djorkaeff, France
M—Steve McManaman, England
F—Rui Costa, Portugal
F—Hristo Stoichkov, Bulgaria
F—Davor Suker, Croatia
F—Alan Shearer, England

CONCACAF Gold Cup

Championship for the Confederation of North, Central American and Caribbean Association Football (CONCACAF). Contested for every two years since its revival in 1991. Held Jan. 10-21, 1996 in the United States.

First Round

Round Robin; each team plays the other two teams in its group once. Note that three points are awarded for a win and one for a tie. (*) indicates team advanced to semifinals.

Group A	W	L	T	GF	GA	Pts
*Mexico	2	0	0	6	0	6
*Guatemala	1	1	0	3	1	3
St. Vincent & Grenadines	0	0	2	0	8	0

RESULTS: **Jan. 11**—Mexico 5, St. Vincent & Grenadines 0; **Jan. 14**—Mexico 1, Guatemala 0; **Jan. 16**—Guatemala 3, St. Vincent & Grenadines 0.

Group B	W	L	T	GF	GA	Pts
*Brazil	2	0	0	9	1	6
Canada	1	1	0	4	5	3
Honduras	0	2	0	1	8	0

RESULTS: **Jan. 10**—Canada 3, Honduras 1; **Jan. 12**—Brazil 4, Canada 1; **Jan. 14**—Brazil 5, Honduras 0.

Group C	W	L	T	GF	GA	Pts
*United States	2	0	0	5	2	6
El Salvador	1	1	0	3	4	3
Trinidad & Tobago	0	2	0	4	6	0

RESULTS: **Jan. 10**—El Salvador 3, Trinidad & Tobago 2; **Jan. 13**—United States 3, Trinidad & Tobago 2; **Jan. 16**—United States 2, El Salvador 0.

Semifinals

Jan. 18 Los Angeles (22,038) ....Brazil 1, USA 0
Jan. 19 San Diego (42,221)......Mexico 1, Guatemala 0

Third Place

Jan. 21 Los Angeles (88,155)........USA 3, Guatemala 0

Final

Jan. 21 Los Angeles (88,125) ....Mexico 2, Brazil 0
Goals: MEX—Luis Garcia 55th, Cuauhtemoc Blanco 75th.

African Nations Cup

Contested for the twentieth time since its inception in 1957. Held Jan. 13-Feb. 3, 1996 in South Africa. (*) denotes team advanced to quarterfinals.

First Round

Round Robin; each team plays the other three teams in its group once. Note that three points are awarded for a win and one for a tie. (*) indicates team advanced to quarterfinals.

Group A	W	L	T	GF	GA	Pts
*South Africa	2	1	0	4	1	6
*Egypt	2	1	0	4	3	6
Cameroon	1	1	1	5	7	4
Angola	0	1	2	4	6	1

RESULTS: **Jan. 13**—South Africa 3, Cameroon 0; **Jan. 15**—Egypt 2, Angola 1; **Jan. 18**—Cameroon 2, Egypt 1; **Jan. 20**—South Africa 1, Angola 0; **Jan. 24**—Angola 3, Cameroon 3; Egypt 1, South Africa 0.

Group B	W	L	T	GF	GA	Pts
*Zambia	2	0	1	9	1	7
*Algeria	2	0	1	4	1	7
Sierra Leone	1	2	0	2	7	3
Burkina Faso	0	3	0	1	9	0

RESULTS: **Jan. 14**—Zambia 0, Algeria 0; **Jan. 15**—Sierra Leone 2, Burkina Faso 1; **Jan. 18**—Algeria 2, Sierra Leone 0; **Jan. 20**—Zambia 5, Burkina Faso 1; **Jan. 24**—Zambia 4, Sierra Leone 0; Algeria 2, Burkina Faso 1.

Group C	W	L	T	GF	GA	Pts
*Gabon	1	0	1	3	2	3
*Zaire	1	0	1	2	2	3
Liberia	1	0	1	2	3	3
†Nigeria	0	0	0	0	0	0

†defending champions Nigeria withdrew before the tournament started.

RESULTS: **Jan. 14**—Nigeria vs. Zaire (canceled); **Jan. 16**—Liberia 2, Gabon 1; **Jan. 19**—Gabon 2, Zaire 0; **Jan. 21**—Liberia vs. Nigeria (canceled); **Jan. 25**—Gabon vs. Nigeria (canceled); Zaire 2, Liberia 0.

Group D	W	L	T	GF	GA	Pts
*Ghana	3	0	0	6	1	9
*Tunisia	1	1	1	5	4	4
Ivory Coast	1	2	0	2	5	3
Mozambique	0	2	1	1	4	1

RESULTS: **Jan. 14**—Ghana 2, Ivory Coast 0; **Jan. 16**—Mozambique 1, Tunisia 1; **Jan. 19**—Ghana 2, Tunisia 1; **Jan. 21**—Ivory Coast 1, Mozambique 0; **Jan. 25**—Ghana 2, Mozambique 0; Tunisia 3, Ivory Coast 1.

Quarterfinals

Jan. 27 at Johannesburg .... South Africa 2, Algeria 1
at Bloemfontein .... Zambia 3, Egypt 1
Jan. 28 at Johannesburg .... Ghana 1, Zaire 0
at Durban .... Tunisia 1, Gabon 1
(Tunisia wins, 4-1, on penalty kicks)

Semifinals

Jan. 31 at Durban .... Tunisia 4, Zambia 2
at Johannesburg .... South Africa 3, Ghana 0

Third Place

Feb. 3 at Johannesburg .... Zambia 1, Ghana 0

Final

Feb. 3 at Johannesburg
Att: 80,000

South Africa 2 .... Tunisia 0
Goals: S. Afr—Mark Williams 73rd, 75th.

U.S. National Team

1996 Schedule and Results

Through Sept. 20, 1996. All CONCACAF Gold Cup (Jan. 10-21) and U.S. Cup '96 (June 8–16) matches are noted. Gold Cup opponents are in **bold** type. All other matches are international friendlies.

Date		Result	USA Goals	Site	Crowd
Jan. 13	**Trinidad & Tobago**	W, 3-2	Eric Wynalda (2), Joe-Max Moore	Anaheim, Calif.	12,425
Jan. 16	**El Salvador**	W, 2-0	Wynalda, Marcelo Balboa	Anaheim, Calif.	52,355
Jan. 18	**Brazil**	L, 0-1	—	Los Angeles	22,038
Jan. 21	**Guatemala**	W, 3-0	Wynalda, Jeff Agoos, Jovan Kirovski	Los Angeles	88,000
May 26	Scotland	W, 2-1	Wynalda, Cobi Jones	New Britain, Conn.	8,526
June 9	Ireland (US)	W, 2-1	Tab Ramos, Claudio Reyna	Foxboro, Mass.	25,332
June 12	Bolivia (US)	L, 0-2	—	Washington, D.C.	19,350
June 16	Mexico (US)	T, 2-2	Wynalda, Thomas Dooley	Los Angeles	92,216
Aug. 30	El Salvador	W, 3-1	Moore (2), Wynalda	Los Angeles	18,661

Note: The U.S. National team did not play in the Summer Olympics in Atlanta. Only the under-23 national teams (along with three "over-age" players) play in the Olympic Games.
Overall record: 6-2-1. **Gold Cup record:** 3-1-0. **US Cup '96 record:** 1-1-1. **Team scoring:** Goals for– 17; Goals against– 10.

1996 U.S. National Team Statistics

Individual records for entire season through Sept. 20, 1996. Note that the column labeled "Career C/G" refers to career caps and goals.

Forwards	GP	GS	Mins	G	A	Pts	Career C/G
Jovan Kirovski	5	1	141	1	0	2	16/3
Jason Kreis	1	1	45	0	0	0	1/0
Roy Lassiter	6	0	146	0	0	0	9/1
Brian McBride	3	0	78	0	1	1	4/0
Joe-Max Moore	5	5	440	3	0	6	47/14
David Wagner	1	1	45	0	0	0	1/0
Eric Wynalda	9	9	748	7	1	15	74/25

Defenders	GP	GS	Mins	G	A	Pts	Career C/G
Jeff Agoos	8	8	708	1	0	2	57/3
Marcelo Balboa	8	8	720	1	1	3	113/12
Paul Caligiuri	6	3	338	0	0	0	111/5
Frankie Hejduk	1	0	26	0	0	0	1/0
Alexi Lalas	9	9	810	0	3	3	72/7

1996 U.S. National Team (Cont.)

Midfielders	GP	GS	Mins	G	A	Pts	Career C/G
Mike Burns	8	7	642	0	0	0	43/0
Thomas Dooley	6	5	363	1	0	2	59/6
John Harkes	8	8	635	0	3	3	68/6
Cobi Jones	9	9	809	1	0	2	77/7
Tab Ramos	9	9	747	1	1	3	71/5
Claudio Reyna	8	6	597	1	2	4	36/4
Mike Sorber	3	1	103	0	0	0	57/2

Goalkeepers	GP	GS	Mins	Record	SO	Career Caps
Brad Friedel	4	4	360	2-1-1	0	39
Kasey Keller	4	4	360	3-1-0	2	16
Juergen Sommer	1	1	90	1-0-0	0	4

Yellow cards: Lalas (5), Ramos (3), Dooley and Wynalda (2); Burns, Lassiter, Reyna and Sorber. **Red cards:** none.
Head coach: Steve Sampson; **Assistant coach:** Clive Charles; **Goal coach:** Milutin Soskic; **General Manager:** Tom King; **Captain:** Marcelo Balboa.

U.S. Cup '96

Fourth U.S. Cup hosted by the United States, June 8-16, 1996. Match results listed with city and attendance.

Round Robin Standings

	Gm	W	L	T	Pts	GF	GA
Mexico	3	1	0	2	5	5	4
Ireland	3	1	1	1	4	6	4
United States	3	1	1	1	4	4	5
Bolivia	3	1	2	0	3	2	4

Match Results

Date	Site	Result
6/8	Dallas, Tex. (25,187)	Mexico 1, Bolivia 0
6/9	Foxboro, Mass. (25,332)	USA 2, Ireland 1
6/12	E. Rutherford, N.J. (21,322)	Mexico 2, Ireland 2
6/12	Wash., D.C. (19,350)	Bolivia 2, USA 0
6/15	E. Rutherford, N.J. (14,624)	Ireland 3, Bolivia 0
6/16	Pasadena, Calif. (92,216)	USA 2, Mexico 2

U.S. Women's National Team

1996 Schedule and Results

Olympic Tournament opponents are in **bold** type. Brazil Cup (BRA) and U.S. Cup '96 (US) games are all noted. All other opponents are international friendly matches.

Date	Opponent	Result	USA Goals	Site	Crowd
Jan. 14	Russia (BRA)	W, 8-1	Gabarra, Akers, Parlow (2), Foudy (2), MacMillan, Milbrett	Campinas, Brazil	1,500
Jan. 16	Brazil (BRA)	W, 3-2	Hamm, Gabarra, Milbrett	Campinas, Brazil	2,500
Jan. 18	Ukraine (BRA)	W, 6-0	Garrett (3), Grubb, MacMillan, Milbrett	Campinas, Brazil	500
Jan. 21	Brazil (BRA)	T, 1-1	Milbrett (USA wins, 3-2, on penalty kicks)	Campinas, Brazil	n/a
Feb. 2	Norway	W, 3-2	Hamm, Akers, Milbrett	Tampa, Fla.	1,879
Feb. 4	Norway	L, 1-2	Chastain	Jacksonville, Fla.	8,975
Feb. 10	Denmark	W, 2-1	Lilly, Overbeck	Orlando, Fla.	2,130
Feb. 15	Sweden	W, 3-0	MacMillan, Venturini, Hamm	San Antonio, Tex.	2,192
Feb. 17	Sweden	W, 3-0	Lilly, Milbrett, Parlow	Houston, Tex.	2,865
Mar. 14	Germany	W, 6-0	Overbeck, Parlow	Decatur, Ga.	4,212
Mar. 16	Germany	W, 2-0	Milbrett, Lilly	Davidson, N.C.	3,459
Apr. 20	Netherlands	W, 6-0	Venturini (2), Foudy, Lilly (2), Akers	Fullerton, Calif.	5,116
Apr. 26	France	W, 4-1	Akers, Lilly, Parlow	St. Louis, Mo.	6,200
Apr. 28	France	W, 8-2	Hamm (4), MacMillan, Milbrett, Akers, Gabarra	Indianapolis, Ind.	4,127
May 12	Canada (US)	W, 6-0	Foudy, Milbrett, MacMillan, Gabarra, Parlow, Roberts	Worcester, Mass.	4,312
May 16	Japan (US)	W, 4-0	Venturini, Lilly (2), Gabarra	Horsham, Penn.	5,112
May 18	China (US)	W, 1-0	Akers	Washington, D.C.	6,081
July 4	Australia	W, 2-1	Venturini, Parlow	Tampa, Fla.	5,500
July 6	Australia	W, 2-1	Venturini, Lilly	Pensacola, Fla.	5,234
July 21	Denmark	W, 3-0	Venturini, Hamm, Milbrett	Orlando, Fla.	25,303
July 23	**Sweden**	W, 2-1	Venturini, MacMillan	Orlando, Fla.	22,734
July 25	**China**	T, 0-0	—	Miami, Fla.	43,525
July 28	**Norway**	W, 2-1	Akers, MacMillan	Athens, Ga.	64,196
Aug. 1	**China**	W, 2-1	MacMillan, Milbrett	Athens, Ga.	76,481

Overall record: 21-1-2. **Olympic record:** 4-0-0. **U.S. Cup '96 record:** 3-0;
Team Scoring: Goals For— 80; Goals against— 17.

1996 U.S. Women's National Team Statistics

Individual records for entire season through Sept. 20, 1996. Note that the column labeled "Career C/G" refers to career caps and goals

Forwards	GP	GS	Mins	G	A	Pts	Career C/G
Michelle Akers	17	16	1253	7	3	17	109/92
Robin Confer	1	1	71	0	0	0	1/0
Carin Gabarra	22	9	972	5	2	12	116/53
Danielle Garrett	2	1	96	3	2	8	2/3
Mia Hamm	23	23	1840	9	18	36	120/63
Shannon MacMillan	21	18	1407	8	4	20	28/9
Tiffeny Milbrett	24	19	1524	13	3	29	65/25
Cindy Parlow	20	5	702	8	2	18	20/8
Tammy Pearman	3	0	51	0	0	0	4/1

Defenders	GP	GS	Mins	G	A	Pts	Career C/G
Brandi Chastain	23	23	1965	2	7	11	40/9
Lorrie Fair	11	2	302	0	0	0	11/0
Jen Grubb	6	4	304	1	0	2	9/1
Carla Overbeck	24	22	1984	2	0	4	100/7
Christy Rowe	1	0	8	0	0	0	1/0
Thori Staples	8	1	297	0	0	0	43/0
Staci Wilson	10	4	486	0	0	0	14/0

Midfielders	GP	GS	Mins	G	A	Pts	Career C/G
Amanda Cromwell	1	1	90	0	0	0	41/1
Joy Fawcett	20	20	1782	0	1	1	101/15
Julie Foudy	21	21	1711	4	3	11	96/17
Kristine Lilly	23	23	2007	8	6	22	121/46
Holly Manthei	5	2	195	0	1	1	19/0
Tiffany Roberts	21	6	904	1	1	3	55/6
Tisha Venturini	20	19	1716	8	4	20	71/26

Goalkeepers	GP	GS	Mins	Record	SO	Career Caps
Mary Harvey	7	7	540	4-0-1	2	27
Tracy Noonan	2	1	134	2-0-0	1	2
Briana Scurry	17	16	1495	15-1-1	8	44

Yellow cards: Foudy and Lilly (3), Chastain (2), Akers, Gabarra, Hamm, Manthei, Milbrett, Overbeck, Roberts and Scurry. Red card: Foudy.
Head coach: Tony DiCiccio
Assistant coaches: Lauren Gregg and April Heinrichs
Co-Captains: Julie Foudy and Carla Overbeck

U.S. Under-23 National Team

1996 Schedule and Results

Olympic Tournament opponents are in **bold** type. Competition against other U-23 national teams only

Date	Opponent	Result	USA Goals	Site	Crowd
Jan. 19	Jamaica	W, 4-0	Marino, Fisher, Cozier, Silvera	closed door match	—
Jan. 20	Jamaica	W, 1-0	Baumhoff	closed door match	—
Feb. 2	Norway	T, 4-4	Wood, Silvera, Baba, Vermillion	Tampa, Fla.	1,879
Feb. 4	Norway	W, 2-1	Joseph, Wood	Jacksonville, Fla.	8,975
Feb. 7	Denmark	W, 2-1	Hejduk, Wood	San Diego	1,215
Feb. 11	South Korea	T, 0-0	—	Los Angeles	1,936
Mar. 6	Mexico	L, 2-3	Baba, Wood	Fullerton, Calif.	8,116
May 1	Canada	T, 0-0	—	Vancouver, CAN	2,168
May 4	Canada	L, 1-2	Suarez	Calgary, CAN	n/a
May 19	Australia	L, 0-2	—	Indianapolis	2,211
May 25	Ireland	W, 4-1	Vargas, Hejduk (2), Wood	Decatur, Ga.	2,283
June 1	Ireland	L, 0-1	—	Davidson, N.C.	3,498
June 22	South Africa	T, 2-2	Reyna, Kirovski	Richmond, Va.	7,522
June 24	South Africa	W, 2-0	Peay, Reyna	Richmond, Va.	2,652
June 26	Mexico	W, 1-0	Kirovski	St. Louis	6,200
June 30	Saudi Arabia	W, 2-0	Kirovski (2)	Oneanta, N.Y.	4,315
July 6	Nigeria	T, 0-0	—	Pomona, N.J.	2,236
July 20	**Argentina**	L, 1-3	Reyna	Birmingham, Ala.	83,810
July 22	**Tunisia**	W, 2-0	Kirovski, Maisonneuve	Birmingham, Ala.	45,687
July 24	**Portugal**	T, 1-1	Maisonneuve	Washington, D.C.	58,012

Overall record: 9-5-6. **Olympic record:** 1-1-1. **Team Scoring:** Goals—31; Goals against—21.

1996 Under-23 Team Statistics

Forwards	Gm	GS	G	A	Pts	C
Hamisi Amani-Dove	2	2	0	0	0	0
Mac Cozier	4	1	1	1	3	0
Nate Friends	1	0	0	0	0	0
Miles Joseph	14	10	1	0	2	1
Jovan Kirovski	6	5	4	0	8	1
Pete Marino	3	2	1	1	3	0
Temoc Suarez	3	1	1	0	2	0
A.J. Wood	16	15	5	1	11	1

Defenders	Gm	GS	G	A	Pts	C
Mike DuHaney	7	7	0	0	0	1
Frankie Hejduk	16	16	3	1	7	7
Rich Kotschau	1	0	0	0	0	0
Alexi Lalas *	2	2	0	0	0	1
Clint Peay	12	11	1	1	3	1
Brandon Pollard	13	10	0	0	0	2
Eddie Pope	13	13	0	0	0	1
Scott Vermillion	7	6	1	0	2	3

Red Cards: Baba, McKeon.
Head Coach: Bruce Arena; **Assistant Coaches:** Bob Bradley, Glenn Myernick.

Midfielders	Gm	GS	G	A	Pts	C
Imad Baba	14	12	2	1	5	2
Billy Baumhoff	2	0	1	0	2	0
Mike Fisher	8	3	1	0	2	0
Brian Kelly	5	3	0	1	1	0
Brian Maisonneuve	10	10	0	0	0	0
Matt McKeon	15	13	0	2	2	5
Alberto Montoya	1	1	0	0	0	0
Claudio Reyna *	6	6	2	1	5	1
Damian Silvera	11	10	2	1	5	2
Rob Smith	5	1	0	0	0	1
Carey Talley	2	1	0	0	0	0
Nelson Vargas	9	4	1	0	2	3
Bill Walsh	8	7	0	0	0	0

Goalkeepers	W	L	T	GF	GA	SO
Jeff Cassar	2	0	1	11	4	2
Kasey Keller*	3	1	2	7	3	4
Chris Snitko	2	2	1	6	6	2
Zach Thornton	1	1	1	5	4	0

*competed as an overage player.

Club Team Competition

1995 Toyota Cup

Formerly the Intercontinental Cup; a year-end match for the World Club Championship between the European Cup and Copa Libertadores winners. Played Nov. 28, 1995, before 60,000 at Tokyo's National Stadium.

Final

Ajax Amsterdam (Holland) 0 ....Gremio (Brazil) 0

Ajax Amsterdam won, 4-3, on a penalty shoot–out after extra time. **Scoring:** Ajax— R. De Boer, F. De Boer, George, Blind; Gremio— Magno, Gelson, Adilson. **Man of the Match:** Danny Blind, Ajax

SOUTH AMERICA

1996 Liberatadores Cup

Contested by the league champions of South America's football union. Two-leg Semifinals and two-leg Final; home teams listed first. Winner River Plate of Argentina plays European Cup champion Juventus of Turin in 1996 Toyota Cup in Tokyo this December.

Final Four: America Cali (Colombia), Gremio (Brazil), River Plate (Argentina) and Univ. de Chile (Chile).

Semifinals

America Cali (COL) vs Gremio (BRA)

6/4 Porto Alegre (30,000).....Gremio 1, America Cali 0
6/12 Cali (40,000).................America Cali 3, Gremio 1
America Cali wins on aggregate, 3-2

Univ. de Chile (CHI) vs River Plate (ARG)

6/5 Santiago (70,000) ....Univ. de Chile 2, River Plate 2
6/12 Buenos Aires (70,000) ..River Plate 1, Univ. de Chile 0
River Plate wins on aggregate, 3-2

Final

6/19 Cali (45,000) ....America Cali 1, River Plate 0
6/26 Buenos Aires (76,000)...River Plate 2, America Cali 0
River Plate wins on aggregate, 2-1

EUROPE

There are three European club competitions sanctioned by the Union of European Football Associations (UEFA). The **European Cup** (officially, the Champions' Cup) is a knockout contest between national league champions of UEFA member countries; the **Cup Winners' Cup** is between winners of domestic cup competitions (note that a double winner– league and cup titles– would play for the European Cup and be replaced in the Cup Winners' Cup by the team it defeated in the domestic cup final); and the **UEFA Cup** is between the so-called "best of the rest," usually the national league runners-up. Note that home teams are listed first.

1995-96 European Cup

Champions League: Six-game double round-robin in four 4-team groups (Sept. 13-Dec. 6, 1995); top two teams in each group advance to quarterfinal round. Winner Juventus of Turin plays Libertadores Cup champion River Plate of Argentina in the 1996 Toyota Cup this December in Tokyo.

Round Robin Standings

Group A	W	L	T	Pts	GF	GA
*Panathinaikos (GRE)	3	2	1	**11**	7	3
*Nantes (FRA)	2	3	1	**9**	8	6
Porto (POR)	1	4	1	**7**	6	5
Aalborg (DEN)	1	1	4	**4**	5	12

Group B	W	L	T	Pts	GF	GA
*Spartak Moscow (RUS)	6	0	0	**18**	15	4
*Legia Warsaw (POL)	2	1	3	**7**	5	8
Roseborg (NOR)	2	0	4	**6**	11	16
Blackburn Rovers (ENG)	1	1	4	**4**	5	8

Group C	W	L	T	Pts	GF	GA
*Juventus (ITA)	4	1	1	**13**	15	4
*Borussia Dortmund (GER)	2	3	1	**9**	8	8
Steaua Bucuresti (ROM)	1	3	2	**6**	2	5
Glasgow Rangers (SCOT)	0	3	3	**3**	6	14

Group D	W	L	T	Pts	GF	GA
*Ajax Amsterdam (HOL)	5	1	0	**16**	15	1
*Real Madrid (SPA)	3	1	2	**10**	11	5
Ferencvaros (HUN)	1	2	3	**5**	9	19
Grasshoppers Zurich (SWI)	0	2	4	**2**	3	13

Quarterfinals

Two legs, total goals; home team listed first.

Legia Warsaw vs. Panathinaikos

Mar. 6 – Legia Warsaw 0.......................Panathinaikos 0
Mar. 20 – Panathinaikos 3........................Legia Warsaw 0
Panathinaikos advances on aggregate, 3-0

Nantes vs. Spartak Moscow

Mar. 6 – Nantes 2.............................Spartak Moscow 0
Mar. 20 – Spartak Moscow 2.............................Nantes 2
Nantes advances on aggregate, 4-2

Borussia Dortmund vs. Ajax Amsterdam

Mar. 6 – Borrussia Dortmund 0 ....Ajax Amsterdam 2
Mar. 20 – Ajax Amsterdam 1 ....Borrussia Dortmund 0
Ajax Amsterdam advances on aggregate, 3-0

Real Madrid vs. Juventus

Mar. 6 – Real Madrid 1..................................Juventus 0
Mar. 20 – Juventus 2..................................Real Madrid 0
Juventus advances on aggregate, 2-1

Semifinals

Two legs, total goals; home team listed first.

Ajax Amsterdam vs. Panathinaikos

Apr. 3 – Ajax Amsterdam 0 .... Panathinaikos 1
Apr. 17 – Panathinaikos 0 .... Ajax Amsterdam 3
Ajax Amsterdam advances on aggregate, 3-1

Juventus vs. Nantes

Apr. 3 – Juventus 2 .... Nantes 0
Apr. 17 – Nantes 3 .... Juventes 2
Juventus advances on aggregate, 4-3

Final

May 22 at Rome; Att– 67,000
Juventus 1 .... Ajax Amsterdam 1
Goals: Juventus— Fabrizio Ravanelli (13th) Ajax– Jari Litmanen (41st)
Juventus wins Penalty Shoot-out, 4-2

Edgar Davids (Ajax) missed, 0-0; Ciro Ferrara (Juventus) scored, 1-0; Jari Litmanen (Ajax) scored, 1-1; Gianluca Pessotto (Juventus) scored, 2-1; Arnold Scholten (Ajax) scored, 2-2; Michele Padovano (Juventus) scored, 3-2; Sonny Silooy (Ajax) missed, 3-2; Vladimir Jugovic (Juventus) scored, 4-2.

1996 Cup Winners' Cup

Final Four: Deportivo de La Coruna (Spain), Feyenoord Rotterdam (Netherlands), Paris St. Germain (France) and Rapid Vienna (Austria).

Semifinals

Two legs, total goals; home team listed first.

Feyenoord Rotterdam vs. Rapid Vienna

Apr. 4 – Feyenoord 1 .... Rapid Vienna 1
Apr. 18 – Rapid Vienna 3 .... Feyenoord 0
Rapid Vienna advances on aggregate, 4-1

Paris St. Germain vs. Deportivo de La Coruna

Apr. 4 – Deportivo de La Coruna 0 ... Paris St. Germain 1
Apr. 18 – Paris St. Germain 1 ... Deportivo de La Coruna 0
Paris SG advances on aggregate, 2-0

Final

May 8 at King Baudouin Stadium, Brussells
Att: 37,500
Paris St. Germain 1 .... Rapid Vienna 0
Goals: Paris St. Germain– Bruno N'Gotty (29th minute).

1996 UEFA Cup

Two-leg Semifinals, two-game Final; home team listed first.
Final Four: Barcelona (Spain), Bayern Munich (Germany), Bordeaux (France) and Slavia Prague (Czech Republic).

Semifinals

Barcelona vs. Bayern Munich

Apr. 2 – Bayern Munich 2 .... Barcelona 2
Apr. 16 – Barcelona 1 .... Bayern Munich 2
Bayern Munich advances on aggregate, 4-3

Bordeaux vs. Slavia Prague

Apr. 2 – Slavia Prague 0 .... Bordeaux 1
Apr. 16 – Bordeaux 1 .... Slavia Prague 0
Bordeaux advances on aggregate, 2-0

Final

May 1 (62,000) – Bayern Munich 2 .... Bordeaux 0
Goals: Bayern Munich– Thomas Helmer (35th minute), Mehmet Scholl (60th).

May 15 (36,000) – Bordeaux 1 .... Bayern Munich 3
Goals: Bayern Munich– Mehmet Scholl (53rd minute), Emil Kostadinov (65th), Juergen Klinsmann (79th); Bordeaux– Daniel Dutuel (75th).

Bayern Munich wins on aggregate, 5-1

National Champions

Twenty-six 1996 league champions and cup winners.

League Champion		Cup Winner
Rapid Vienna	**Austria**	Rapid Vienna
Club Bruges	**Belgium**	Club Bruges
Slavia Sofia	**Bulgaria**	Slovia Sofia
Zagreb	**Croatia**	Zagreb
Slavia Prague	**Czech Rep.**	S. Olomouc
Aarhus	**Denmark**	Aarhus
Manchester United	**England**	Manchester United
Auxerre	**France**	Auxerre
Borussia Dortmund	**Germany**	Kaiserslautern
Panathinaikos	**Greece**	AEK
Ajax Amsterdam	**Netherlands**	PSV Einhhoven
Ferencvaros	**Hungary**	BVSC Budapest
St. Patrick's Athletic	**Ireland**	Shelbourne
Milan	**Italy**	Fiorentina
Portadown	**No. Ireland**	Glentoran
W. Lodz	**Poland**	Legia Warsaw
Porto	**Portugal**	Sporting
Steaua Bucuresti	**Romania**	Steaua Bucuresti
Spartak Moscow*	**Russia**	Lok. Moscow
Glasgow Rangers	**Scotland**	Glasgow Rangers
Slovan Bratislava	**Slovakia**	Chemlon Humenne
Atletico Madrid	**Spain**	Valencia
IFK Göteberg	**Sweden**	AIK Solna
Grasshopper	**Switzerland**	Sion
Fenerbahce	**Turkey**	Galatasaray
Partizan	**Yugoslavia**	Red Star

*1995 champion; Russia and Sweden play spring-fall seasons.

Major League Soccer

1996 Final Regular Season Standings

Conference champions (*) and playoff qualifiers (†)are noted. SOW refers to shootout wins. Teams receive three points for a win and one point for a shootout win. SOW are included in W (win) column. The GF and GA columns refer to Goals For and Goals Against in regulation play.

Eastern Conference

Team	W	L	Pts	GF	GA	SOW
*Tampa Bay	20	12	58	66	51	1
†D.C. United	16	16	46	62	56	1
†NY/NJ	15	17	39	45	47	3
†Columbus	15	17	37	59	60	4
New England	15	17	33	43	56	6

Head Coaches: TB— Thomas Rongen; DC— Bruce Arena; NY/NJ— Eddie Firmani; Clb— Timo Liekoski; NE— Frank Stapleton.

Western Conference

Team	W	L	Pts	GF	GA	SOW
*Los Angeles	19	13	49	59	49	4
†Dallas	17	15	41	50	48	5
†Kansas City	17	15	41	61	63	5
†San Jose	15	17	39	50	50	3
Colorado	11	21	29	44	59	2

Head Coaches: LA— Lothar Osiander; Dal— David Dir; KC— Ron Newman; SJ— Laurie Calloway; Colo— Bobby Houghton.

Leading Scorers

Points

	Gm	G	A	Pts
Roy Lassiter, TB	30	27	4	58
Preki, KC	32	18	13	49
Eduardo Hurtado, LA	26	21	7	49
Raul Diaz Arce, Wash	28	23	2	48
Brian McBride, Clb	28	17	3	37
Eric Wynalda, SJ	27	10	13	33
Vitalis Takawira, KC	28	13	7	33
Steve Rammel, Wash	26	14	4	32
Paul Bravo, SJ	31	13	5	31
Jason Kreis, Dal	31	13	5	31
Giovanni Savarese, NY	26	13	1	27
Marco Etcheverry, Wash	26	4	19	27
Jean Harbor, Colo	28	11	4	26
Pete Marino, Clb	29	11	4	26
Mark Chung, KC	32	8	9	25
Missael Espinoza, SJ	26	10	5	25
Carlos Valderrama, TB	23	4	17	25
Shaun Bartlett, Colo	26	8	7	23
Joe-Max Morre, NE	14	11	1	23
Giuseppe Galderisi, TB	25	7	8	22
Adrian Paz, Clb	27	6	10	22

Goals

	Gm	No
Roy Lassiter, TB	30	27
Raul Diaz Arce, Wash	28	23
Eduardo Hurtado, LA	26	21
Preki, KC	32	18
Brian McBride, Clb	28	17
Steve Rammel, Wash	26	14
Giovanni Savarese, NY	26	13
Vitalis Takawira, KC	28	13
Paul Bravo, SJ	31	13
Jason Kreis, Dal	31	13

Assists

	Gm	No
Marco Etcheverry, Wash	26	19
Carlos Valderrama, TB	23	17
Eric Wynalda, SJ	27	13
Preki, KC	32	13
Mauricio Cienfuegos, LA	28	11
Robert Warzycha, Clb	20	10
Tab Ramos, NY	25	10
Adrian Paz, Clb	27	10
Billy Thompson, Clb	24	9
Mark Chung, KC	32	9

Leading Goaltenders

Goals Against Avg.

(minimum 1395 mins)

	Gm	Min	Shts	Svs	GAA	W-L
Jorge Campos, LA	24	2025	131	92	1.20	13-8
Tony Meola, NY	29	2610	198	143	1.31	14-15
Mark Dodd, Dal	31	2776	240	161	1.46	17-14
Mark Dougherty, TB	28	2520	192	117	1.68	17-11
Aidan Heaney, NE	19	1534	133	90	1.70	8-9
Tom Liner, SJ	20	1712	125	74	1.73	7-12
Garth Lagerwey, KC	23	1959	140	83	1.75	12-9
Chris Woods, Colo	23	2070	159	97	1.87	8-15
Jeff Causey, Wash	19	1620	114	69	1.94	9-10

Saves

	Gm	No
Mark Dodd, Dal	31	161
Tony Meola, NY	29	143
Mark Dougherty, TB	28	117
Chris Woods, Colo	23	97
Jorge Campos, LA	24	92
Aidan Heaney, NE	19	90
Garth Lagerwey, KC	23	83
Tom Liner, SJ	20	74
Jeff Causey, Wash	19	69
Bo Oshoniyi, Colo	13	64

Shutouts

	Gm	No
Tony Meola, NY	29	9
Mark Dodd, Dal	31	6
Brad Friedel, Clb	9	4
Aidan Heaney, NE	19	4
Tom Liner, SJ	10	4
Jorge Campos, LA	24	4

Seven tied with three each.

MLS Attendance

		Gm	Total	Avg.
1	Los Angeles	16	462,655	28,916
2	N.Y./N.J.	16	382,360	23,898
3	New England	16	304,392	19,025
4	Columbus	16	303,202	18,950
5	San Jose	16	275,712	17,232
6	Dallas	16	256,173	16,011
7	Wash. D.C.	16	244,489	15,281
8	Kansas City	16	206,421	12,901
9	Tampa Bay	16	186,856	11,679
10	Colorado	16	164,413	10,276
	TOTAL	160	2,786,673	17,416

MLS PLAYOFFS

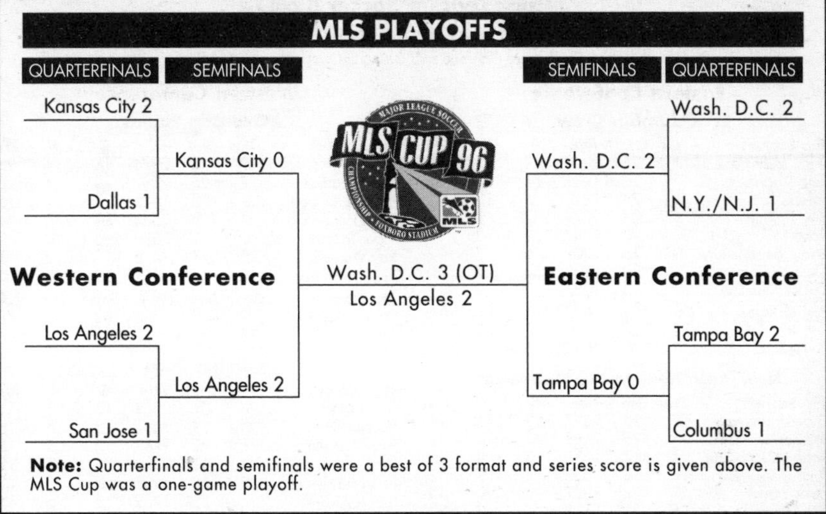

Note: Quarterfinals and semifinals were a best of 3 format and series score is given above. The MLS Cup was a one-game playoff.

Playoffs

Quarterfinals (Best of 3)

WESTERN

Kansas City Wiz vs. Dallas Burn

Date	Result	Site
Sept. 26	Wiz, 3-2	at K.C.
Sept. 29	Burn, 2-1	at Dallas
Oct. 2	Wiz, 3-2, shootout	at Dallas

Kansas City wins series, 2-1.

Los Angeles Galaxy vs. San Jose Clash

Date	Result	Site
Sept. 26	Clash, 1-0	at San Jose
Sept. 29	Galaxy, 2-0	at L.A.
Oct. 2	Galaxy, 2-0	at L.A.

Los Angeles wins series, 2-1.

EASTERN

N.Y./N.J. MetroStars vs. Washington D.C. United

Date	Result	Site
Sept. 24	MetroStars 3-2, shootout	at N.Y./N.J.
Sept. 27	United, 1-0	at D.C.
Oct. 2	United, 2-1	at D.C.

Washington, D.C. wins series, 2-1.

Tampa Bay Mutiny vs. Columbus Crew

Date	Result	Site
Sept. 25	Mutiny, 2-0	at Columbus
Sept. 28	Crew, 2-1	at Tampa
Oct. 2	Mutiny, 4-1	at Tampa

Tampa Bay wins series, 2-1.

Semifinals (Best of 3)

Los Angeles Galaxy vs. Kansas City Wiz

Date	Result	Site
Oct. 10	Galaxy, 2-1	at K.C.
Oct. 13	Galaxy, 2-1	at L.A.

Los Angeles wins series, 2-0.

Washington D.C. United vs. Tampa Bay Mutiny

Date	Result	Site
Oct. 10	United, 4-1	at D.C.
Oct. 12	United, 2-1	at Tampa

Washington, D.C. wins series, 2-0.

MLS Cup '96

Oct. 20 at Foxboro Stadium, Foxboro, Mass.
Att: 34,643

D.C. United 3-2 (OT)

Los Angeles Galaxy	1	1	0—**2**
D.C. United	0	2	1—**3**

First Half—Los Angeles, Eduardo Hurtado (Mauricio Cienfuegos) 5th.
Second Half—Los Angeles, Chris Armas (unassisted), 56th; D.C., Tony Sanneh (Marco Etcheverry), 73rd; D.C., Shawn Medved (unassisted), 82nd.
Overtime—D.C., Eddie Pope (Etcheverry), 94th.
MVP: Mario Etcheverry, D.C. United

Annual Awards

MVP: Carlos Valderrama, Tampa Bay
Coach of the Year: Thomas Rongen, Tampa Bay
Goalkeeper of the Year: Mark Dodd, Dallas
Tough Defender: John Doyle, San Jose
Rookie of the Year: Steve Ralston, Tampa Bay
Goal of the Year: Eric Wynalda (S.J. vs. D.C., April 6)

All MLS Team

G— Mark Dodd, Dallas
D— Robin Fraser, L.A.
D— John Doyle, S.J.
M— Leonel Alvarez, Dal.
M— C. Valderrama, T.B.
M— Preki, Kansas City
M— M. Cienfuegos, L.A.
M— M. Etcheverry, D.C.
M— R. Donadoni, NY/NJ
F— Eduardo Hurtado, L.A
F— Roy Lassiter, D.C.

Major League Soccer (Cont.)

Team-by-Team Statistics

Players who played with more than one club during the season are listed with final team.

Eastern Conference

Columbus Crew

Top Scorers	Pos	Gm	Min	G	A	Pts
Brian McBride	F	28	2306	17	3	37
Pete Marino	F	29	1701	11	4	26
Adrian Paz	F	27	1810	6	10	22
Billy Thompson	F	24	2074	2	9	13
Robert Warzycha	M	20	1747	2	10	14
Brian Maisonneuve	M	15	1209	5	2	12
Marcelo Carrera	F	30	1338	4	2	10
Doctor Khumalo	M	25	1937	3	3	9

Top Goalies	Gm	Min	W-L	Shts	Svs	GAA
Pat Harrington	12	924	5-6	50	22	2.05
Bo Oshoniyi	13	1170	3-10	105	64	2.54

New York/New Jersey MetroStars

Top Scorers	Pos	Gm	Min	G	A	Pts
Giovanni Savarese	F	26	1577	13	1	27
Tab Ramos	M	25	2158	3	10	16
Roberto Donadoni	M	17	1530	3	8	14
Antony De Avila	F	8	650	6	2	14
Miles Joseph	F	24	1927	4	4	12
A.J. Wood	F	21	1162	5	2	12
Rob Johnson	F	18	1132	4	3	11

Top Goalies	Gm	Min	W-L	Shts	Svs	GAA
Tony Meola	29	2610	14-15	198	143	1.31
Zach Thornton	2	180	1-1	12	6	2.50

Tampa Bay Mutiny

Top Scorers	Pos	Gm	Min	G	A	Pts
Roy Lassiter	F	30	2580	27	4	58
Carlos Valderrama	M	23	2059	4	17	25
Giuseppe Galderisi	F	21	1713	7	8	22
Steve Ralston	M	31	2762	7	2	16
Martin Vasquez	M	31	2700	5	6	16
Ivan McKinley	M	26	2168	3	6	12
Diego Viera	F	17	775	5	0	10
Steve Pittman	D	26	2252	1	6	8

Top Goalies	Gm	Min	W-L	Shts	Svs	GAA
Scott Budnick	4	360	3-1	23	18	1.00
Mark Dougherty	28	2520	17-11	192	117	1.71

New England Revolution

Top Scorers	Pos	Gm	Min	G	A	Pts
Joe-Max Moore	F	14	1238	11	1	23
Alberto Naveda	M	25	1731	6	8	20
Darren Sawatzky	F	28	1777	4	5	13
Welton	F	29	1909	3	6	12
John Kerr	M	19	1402	5	2	12
Paul Keegan	F	27	1852	4	3	11
Geoff Aunger	M	29	2397	3	3	9

Top Goalies	Gm	Min	W-L	Shts	Svs	GAA
Aidan Heaney	19	1534	8-9	133	90	1.70
Jim St. Andre	15	1346	7-8	93	57	1.81

D.C. United

Top Scorers	Pos	Gm	Min	G	A	Pts
Raul Diaz Arce	F	28	2352	23	2	48
Steve Ramell	F	26	1651	14	4	32
Marco Etcheverry	M	26	2142	4	19	27
Tony Sanneh	M	25	2046	4	8	16
John Harkes	M	29	2469	3	8	14
Jaime Moreno	F	9	700	3	4	10
Jeff Agoos	D	32	2805	1	5	7
Richie Williams	M	30	2570	1	5	7
Shawn Medved	M	27	1157	1	5	7

Top Goalies	Gm	Min	W-L	Shts	Svs	GAA
Jeff Causey	19	1620	9-10	114	69	1.94
Mark Simpson	15	1260	7-6	68	46	1.50

Western Conference

Colorado Rapids

Top Scorers	Pos	Gm	Min	G	A	Pts
Jean Harbor	F	28	2076	11	4	26
Shaun Bartlett	F	26	2252	8	7	23
Marcelo Balboa	D	18	1525	7	2	16
Chris Henderson	M	29	2544	3	8	14
Steve Trittschuh	D	32	2880	5	2	12
Roy Wegerle	F	22	1458	2	7	11
Richard Sharpe	F	17	711	2	2	6

Top Goalies	Gm	Min	W-L	Shts	Svs	GAA
Dusty Hudock	9	810	3-6	62	37	1.78
Chris Woods	23	2070	8-15	159	97	1.87

Dallas Burn

Top Scorers	Pos	Gm	Min	G	A	Pts
Jason Kreis	M	31	2564	13	5	31
Gerell Elliott	M	19	1462	5	6	16
Hugo Sanchez	F	22	1682	6	3	15
Diego Sonora	D	31	2720	2	7	11
Brian Haynes	F	26	1983	4	3	11
Leonel Alvarez	M	22	1959	3	5	11
W. Rodriguez	M	14	806	4	2	10
Ted Eck	F	25	1457	1	6	8

Top Goalies	Gm	Min	W-L	Shts	Svs	GAA
Mark Dodd	31	2776	17-14	240	161	1.46
Jeff Cassar	1	14	0-0	1	0	6.43

Kansas City Wiz

Top Scorers	Pos	Gm	Min	G	A	Pts
Preki	M	32	2880	18	13	49
Vitalis Takawira	F	28	2233	13	7	33
Mark Chung	M	32	2847	8	9	25
Mike Sorber	M	23	1960	4	8	16
Mo Johnston	F	29	2573	6	3	15
Frank Klopas	M	22	1235	2	4	8
Alan Prampin	F	15	337	3	0	6

Top Goalies	Gm	Min	W-L	Shts	Svs	GAA
Garth Lagerwey	23	1959	12-9	140	83	1.75
Pat Harrington	8	630	4-4	38	16	2.43

Los Angeles Galaxy

Top Scorers	Pos	Gm	Min	G	A	Pts
Eduardo Hurtado	F	26	2323	21	7	49
M. Cienfuegos	M	28	2405	5	11	21
Cobi Jones	M	27	2312	7	4	18
Harut Karapetyan	F	27	1813	6	6	18
Greg Vanney	M	28	2148	4	1	9
Mark Semioli	D	28	2475	3	2	8
Guillermo Jara	F	20	766	2	4	8

Top Goalies	Gm	Min	W-L	Shts	Svs	GAA
Jorge Campos	23	1962	13-8	87	72	1.24
David Kramer	14	838	5-5	87	55	2.26

San Jose Clash

Top Scorers	Pos	Gm	Min	G	A	Pts
Eric Wynalda	F	27	2336	10	13	33
Paul Bravo	M	31	2664	13	5	31
Missael Espinoza	F	26	2310	10	5	25
John Doyle	D	30	2653	3	6	12
Ben Iroha	M	29	2174	2	8	12
Troy Dayak	D	25	2232	2	3	7
Jeff Baicher	F	30	2180	3	1	7

Top Goalies	Gm	Min	W-L	Shts	Svs	GAA
Dave Salzwedel	14	1168	8-5	80	53	1.31
Tom Liner	20	1712	7-12	125	74	1.73

Other U.S. Pro Leagues

Division champions (*) and playoff qualifiers (†) are noted.

NPSL Final Standings (Indoor)

American Division

	W	L	Pct.	GB	GF	GA
* Cleveland Crunch	31	9	.775	—	775	553
†Baltimore Spirit	25	15	.625	6	604	492
†Harrisburg Heat	24	16	.600	7	604	516
†Buffalo Blizzard	21	19	.525	10	562	586
Cincinatti Silverbacks	14	26	.350	17	496	579
Tampa Bay Terror	14	26	.350	17	544	621
Canton Invaders	5	35	.125	26	425	706

National Division

	W	L	Pct.	GB	GF	GA
* Kansas City Attack	32	8	.800	—	599	430
†Milwaukee Wave	30	10	.750	2	610	438
†St. Louis Ambush	24	16	.600	8	676	560
†Wichita Wings	20	20	.500	12	547	531
Detroit Rockers	14	26	.350	18	485	607
Chicago Power	6	34	.150	26	381	689

Playoffs

Division Semifinals (Best of 3): Cleveland over Buffalo (2-1); Baltimore over Harrisburg (2-0); Kansas City over Wicita (2-0); St. Louis over Milwaukee (2-1).

Division Finals (Best of 5): Cleveland over Baltimore (3-1); Kansas City over St. Louis (3-2).

Championship (Best of 7)

	W-L	GF	GA
Cleveland	4-2	114	99
Kansas City	2-4	99	114

Date	Result	Site
Apr. 17	Kansas City, 28-18	at Kansas City
Apr. 18	Kansas City, 22-17	at Kansas City
Apr. 22	Cleveland, 24-12	at Cleveland
Apr. 24	Cleveland, 19-9	at Cleveland
Apr. 25	Cleveland, 20-16	at Kansas City
Apr. 27	Cleveland, 16-12	at Cleveland

A-League Final Standings (Outdoor)

	W	L	Pts	GF	GA
* Montreal Impact	17	6	55	40	18
†Colorado Foxes	14	11	44	55	33
†Seattle Sounders	12	11	40	35	25
†Rochester Rhinos	11	13	36	44	42
Vancouver 86ers	10	14	33	38	38
New York Fever	6	18	21	30	40
Atlanta Ruckus	3	19	9	14	60

Also: Teams earn three points for a regulation win, two points for a shootout win and one point for a shootout loss.

Playoffs

Semifinals (Best of 3)

Montreal Impact vs. Rochester Rhinos

Sept. 19	Rhinos, 3-2	at Montreal
Sept. 21	Impact, 3-0	at Rochester
Sept. 25	Rhinos, 2-1	at Montreal

Rochester wins series, 2-1

Colorado Foxes vs. Seattle Sounders

Sept. 19	Sounders, 1-0	at Colorado
Sept. 22	Foxes, 2-0	at Seattle
Sept. 25	Sounders, 3-0	at Colorado

Seattle wins series, 2-1

Final

Oct. 6 at Seattle

Seattle 2 .... Rochester 0

Goals: SEA—Joey Leonetti 72nd, 84th.

A-League Awards

Player of the Year: Wolde Harris, Colorado
Goalkeeper of the Year: Paolo Ceccarelli, Montreal
Defender of the Year: John Limniatis, Montreal
Rookie of the Year: Wolde Harris
Coach of the Year: Lorne Donaldson, Colorado

CISL Final Standings (Indoor)

Eastern Division

	W	L	Pct.	GB	GF	GA
* Monterrey La Raza	18	10	.643	—	196	159
†Houston Hotshots	18	10	.643	—	186	167
†Dallas Sidekicks	16	12	.571	2	212	181
†Washington Warthogs	13	15	.464	5	151	170
†Detroit Neon	13	15	.464	5	173	197
Indianapolis Twisters	10	18	.357	8	160	188

Western Division

	W	L	Pct.	GB	GF	GA
* San Diego Sockers	17	11	.607	—	173	156
†Anaheim Splash	15	13	.536	2	180	169
†Sacramento Knights	14	14	.500	3	143	153
Portland Pride	10	18	.357	7	156	185
Seattle SeaDogs	10	18	.357	7	143	148

Playoffs

Division Semifinals (Best of 3): Monterrey over Detroit (2-1); San Diego over Washington (2-1); Houston over Sacramento (2-1); Dallas over Anaheim (2-0).

Division Finals (Best of 3): Monterrey over Dallas (2-0); Houston over San Diego (2-1).

Finals (Best of 3)

Houston Hotshots vs. Monterrey La Raza
began Oct. 20 (see Updates).

Colleges

MEN

1995 Final *Soccer America* Top 20

Final 1995 regular season poll including games through Nov. 12. Conducted by the national weekly *Soccer America* and released in the Nov. 27th issue. Listing includes records through conference playoffs as well as NCAA tournament record and team lost to. Teams in **bold** type went on to reach NCAA Final Four. All tournament games decided by penalty kicks are considered ties.

	Nov.12 Record	NCAA Recap
1 **Virginia**	18-0-2	3-1 (Duke)
2 UCLA	17-2-1	1-1 (Santa Clara)
3 SMU	14-3-1	2-1 (Wisconsin)
4 South Carolina	15-3-0	1-1 (Duke)
5 Clemson	15-5-1	1-1 (SMU)
6 Creighton	14-2-1	0-1 (Wm.& Mary)
7 **Wisconsin**	15-4-2	5-0
8 Indiana	14-4-2	0-1 (Butler)
9 Santa Clara	13-2-2	2-1 (Portland)
10 Rhode Island	19-1-2	0-1 (Virginia)
11 **Duke**	12-6-1	4-1 (Wisconsin)
12 Penn St.	15-4-0	0-1 (Maryland)
13 Cornell	15-1-1	0-1 (Lafayette)
14 **Portland**	13-2-3	3-1 (Wisconsin)
15 Maryland	12-6-1	1-0-1 (J. Madison)
16 Saint Louis	15-5-1	0-1 (SMU)
17 William & Mary	17-5-0	1-1 (Wisconsin)
18 Brown	14-3-0	2-1 (Virginia)
19 Col. of Charleston	14-6-1	0-1 (Clemson)
20 Bowling Green	16-2-2	0-1 (Wisconsin)

NCAA Division I Tournament

First Round (Nov. 18-19)

at Brown 2		Boston University 1
Butler 1		at Indiana 0
at Clemson 2		Col. of Charleston 0
at Duke 3		NC-Greensboro 0
at Hartwick 3		St. John's 2
at James Madison 1		Princeton 0
at Lafayette 2	2 OT	Cornell 0
at Maryland 2		Penn St. 0
at Portland 1		Washington 0
at Santa Clara 4	2 OT	San Diego 1
at South Carolina 3	2 OT	Coastal Carolina 1
at SMU 4	2 OT	Saint Louis 1
at Virginia 2		Rhode Island 1
at UCLA 2		Cal Poly SLO 1
William & Mary 2	4 OT	at Creighton 1
at Wisconsin 2		Bowling Green 0

Second Round (Nov. 26)

at Brown 2		Lafayette 0
at Duke 2		South Carolina 0
at James Madison 2	4 OT	Maryland 2
		(JMU wins shootout, 4-3)
at Portland 4		Butler 1
at Santa Clara 2		UCLA 1
at SMU 3		Clemson 1
at Virginia 4		Hartwick 0
at Wisconsin 1	2 OT	William & Mary 0

Quarterfinals (Dec. 3)

at Duke 3	James Madison 2
Portland 2	at Santa Clara 1
at Virginia 4	Brown 1
Wisconsin 2	at SMU 0

FINAL FOUR

at Richmond, Va. (Dec. 8 and 10)

Semifinals

Duke 3	Virginia 2
Wisconsin 1	Portland 0

Championship

Wisconsin 2	Duke 0

Scoring: WI— Lars Hansen (Travis Roy) 8:12; Chad Cole (Scott Lamphear) 62:56.

Attendance: 21,319

Final records: Wisconsin (20-4-1); Duke (16-7-1); North Carolina (21-1-2); Portland (16-3-3).

WOMEN

1995 Final *Soccer America* Top 20

Final 1995 regular season poll including games through Nov. 5. Conducted by the national weekly *Soccer America* and released in the Nov. 20th issue. Listing includes records through conference playoffs as well as NCAA tournament record and team lost to. Teams in **bold** type went on to reach NCAA Final Four. All tournament games decided by penalty kicks are considered ties.

		Nov.5 Record	NCAA Recap
1	**North Carolina**	23-0-0	2-1 (Notre Dame)
2	**Portland**	17-0-2	3-1 (Notre Dame)
3	**SMU**	21-0-1	2-1 (Portland)
4	**Notre Dame**	17-2-2	4-0
5	Connecticut	18-2-2	1-1 (Notre Dame)
6	Duke	14-6-1	0-1 (N.C. State)
7	Santa Clara	14-3-2	2-1 (N. Carolina
8	Stanford	16-3-0	0-1 (Santa Clara)
9	Maryland	17-5-0	1-1 (Portland)
10	Texas A&M	17-5-0	1-1 (SMU)
11	Virginia	14-4-2	0-1 (Santa Clara)
12	N.C. State	17-4-0	2-1 (SMU)
13	Hartford	15-3-2	0-1 (UMass)
14	William & Mary	14-6-1	0-1 (N.C. State)
15	Clemson	14-6-0	0-1 (Texas A&M)
16	Massachusetts	13-3-2	1-1 (UConn)
17	James Madison	15-7-1	1-1 (Maryland)
18	Kentucky	17-6-0	0-1 (Vanderbilt)
19	San Diego	10-6-1	did not play
20	Minnesota	16-4-2	0-1 (Wisconsin)

NCAA Division I Tournament

First Round (Nov. 10-12)

James Madison 2		at Penn St. 1
at Massachusetts 2	OT	Hartford 1
at N.C. State 1	OT	William & Mary 0
at Santa Clara 3	OT	Stanford 2
at Texas A&M 4		Clemson 1
Vanderbilt 2		at Kentucky 0
Washington 2		at UCLA 1
at Wisconsin 1		Minnesota 0

The two dynasties end

by Mike Woitalla

The 1995 college soccer season was a pivotal one as the sport saw both the greatest men's and women's dynasties come to an end.

The Virginia Cavaliers were denied their fifth straight men's NCAA Division I title by Duke, a 3-2 semifinal winner on Dec 6, 1995, in Richmond, Va. But Wisconsin took the title by downing Duke two days later, 1-0. The Wisconsin hero was junior goalkeeper John Belskis, who had never started a game for the Badgers and played just 25 minutes before starter Todd Wilson dislocated his elbow late in the NCAA second-round win against William & Mary. With Belskis in goal, the Badgers shut out the rest of their playoff opponents to set an NCAA record. Including a red-shirt freshman year, Belskis had endured almost four years of bench-warming. "The reason I didn't quit may have had to do with my family," said Belskis. "My parents came to every game, even though I never played." Belskis' efforts were enhanced by a well-organized Badgers team that took pressure off its defense by keeping possession of the ball for long stretches. Sweeper Scott Lamphear, midfielder Mike Gentile and forward Travis Roy provided the axis.

Unfortunately, Wisconsin's first NCAA title celebrations took a bizarre turn when in January coach Jim Launder was asked to resign by Wisconsin associate athletic director Cheryl Marra. Launder refused, the university received more than 50 letters in his support from players and alumni, and the university's personnel committee signed Launder for another year.

Virginia coach Bruce Arena did leave the college game. After coaching the Cavaliers for 18 seasons, and winning five national titles, Arena took the helm of both the U.S. Olympic team and of Major League Soccer's Washington D.C. United. Arena's Cavalier teams of the 1990s were considered the best college teams ever. Using only U.S. products, they dominated the game and popularized it with their attack-minded, entertaining style. Six players from those Cavalier squads made the 18-man Olympic team roster. In addition to midfielder Billy Walsh, the other Cavaliers on the the Olympic team, defenders Clint Peay and Brandon Pollard, midfielders Claudio Reyna, Damian Silvera and striker A. J. Wood all played on Virginia's 1993 NCAA Division I champion. "Virginia winning four titles in a row created more

Wide World Photos

Notre Dame's **Shannon Boxx** rises up for a header against Portland in the women's NCAA title game, won in overtime by Notre Dame, 1-0.

interest in college soccer than we would ever have had if we had alternating champions," said Duke coach John Rennie. "It caused non-soccer people to take notice. There also wouldn't be as large a crowd at the final four or as much media." The 1995 final crowd of 21,319 almost doubled the previous record.

On the women's side, the University of North Carolina was looking for its 10th straight title. The Tar Heels had won 12 of 13 titles since the NCAA Division I championship's inception in 1982. Notre Dame ended the Tar Heels' streak with a 1-0 semifinal win Dec. 1 in Chapel Hill, N.C. Tar Heel forward Cindy Parlow accidentally headed the ball into her team's own net and the Fighting Irish hung on for the remaining 70 minutes. Notre Dame's goal in the 1-0 final win against Portland was also somewhat flukish. In the longest women's final game ever, Cindy Daws scored the sudden-death winner in the 126th minute. Portland goalkeeper Erin Fahey, apparently unaware that the free kick was about the be taken, was busy signaling to her defenders as the ball flew past her and into the net.

Mike Woitalla is a senior editor of *Soccer America.*

NCAA Division I Tournament (Cont.)

Second Round (Nov. 18-19)

at Connecticut 3		Massachusetts 0
at Maryland 6		James Madison 1
at North Carolina 3		Vanderbilt 4
N.C. State 2	3 OT	at Duke 1
at Notre Dame 5		Wisconsin 0
at Portland 1		Washington 0
Santa Clara 1		at Virginia 0
at SMU 2		Texas A&M 1

Quarterfinals (Nov. 25)

at North Carolina 2	Santa Clara 0
at Notre Dame 2	Connecticut 0
at Portland 1	Maryland 0
at SMU 4	N.C. State 3

1995 Annual Awards

Men's Players of the Year

Hermann Trophy	Mike Fisher, Virginia, F
MAC Award	Matt McKeon, Saint Louis, F
Soccer America	Mike Fisher

Women's Player of the Year

Hermann Trophy	Shannon MacMillan, Portland, F
MAC Award	Shannon MacMillan
Soccer America	Shannon MacMillan

NSCAA Coaches of the Year

Division I:	Men's	Jim Launder, Wisconsin
	Women's	Chris Petrucelli, Notre Dame

Division I All-America Teams

MEN

The combined 1995 first team All-America selections of the National Soccer Coaches Assn. of America (NSCAA) and *Soccer America*. Holdovers from the combined 1994 All-America team are in **bold** type.

Pos		Cl	Hgt	Wgt
G	Paul Grafer, Wm. & Mary	Sr.	6-3	200
G	Chris Snitko, UCLA	Sr.	6-3	200
D	Scott Lamphear, Wisconsin	Sr.	6-0	165
D	Ian McIntyre, Hartwick	Sr.	6-1	180
D	Brandon Pollard, Virginia	Sr.	5-11	168
M	Daniel Hernandez, SMU	So.	5-10	165
M	Ben Hickey, St. John's	Jr.	6-1	175
M	Jess Marsch, Princeton	Sr.	5-11	150
M	Matt McKeon, Saint Louis	Sr.	6-2	190
F	Damian Silvera, Virginia	Sr.	5-8	160
F	Mike Fisher, Virginia	Jr.	5-9	148
F	Guillermo Jara, San Diego	Sr.	5-8	145
F	Brian Kelly, Duke	Jr.	5-7	140
F	Clint Mathis, South Carolina	So.	5-10	155
F	Toni Siikala, Campbell	Sr.	6-1	180
F	Andrew Williams, Rhode Island	So.	5-8	155

WOMEN

The combined 1995 first team All-America selections of the National Soccer Coaches Assn. of America (NSCAA) and *Soccer America*. Most schools do not list heights and weights of women athletes. Holdovers from the combined 1994 All-America team are in **bold** type.

GOALKEEPER— Maja Hansen, New Hampshire, Sr.; Tracy Noonan, North Carolina, Sr. DEFENDERS— **Jessica Fischer**, Stanford, Sr.; Erin Lynch, Massachusetts; Sr.; Kate Sobrero, Notre Dame, Soph.; **Thori Staples**, N.C. State, Sr.; Sara Whalen, Connecticut, Soph.; Staci Wilson, North Carolina, Soph. MIDFIELDERS— Holly Manthei, Notre Dame, Soph.; **Jessica Reifer**, Hartford, Sr.; Emily Stauffer, Harvard, Soph. FORWARDS— Danielle Garrett, SMU, Soph.; Debbie Keller, North Carolina, Jr; **Shannon MacMillan**, Portland, Sr.; Cindy Parlow, North Carolina, Frosh.; **Kelly Walbert**, Duke, Sr.

FINAL FOUR

at Chapel Hill, N.C. (Dec. 1 and 3)

Semifinals

Notre Dame 1	North Carolina 0
Portland 4	SMU2

Championship

Notre Dame 1	3 OT	Portland 0

Scoring: ND— Cindy Daws (off direct free kick) at 125:31. Game was in sudden death overtime after two scoreless overtimes.
Attendance: 6,926.
Final records: Notre Dame (21-2-2); Portland (20-1-2); North Carolina (25-1); SMU (23-1-1).
Most Outstanding Players: OFFENSE— Cindy Daws, Notre Dame, midfielder; DEFENSE— Kate Sobrero, Notre Dame, defender.

Small College Final Fours

MEN

NCAA Division II

at Spartanburg, S.C. (Dec. 2-3)
Semifinals: Southern Conn. St. over CS-Bakerfield, 2-1 (3 OT); SC-Spartanburg over Mercyhurst (Pa.), 3-2 (3 OT).
Championship: Southern Conn. St. over SC-Spartanburg, 2-0. Final records: Southern Conn. St. (21-1-1) and SC-Spartanburg (17-5-2).

NCAA Division III

at Williamstown, Mass. (Nov. 18-19)
Semifinals: Williams (Mass.) over Muhlenberg (Pa.), 1-1 (2 OT) (Williams wins Shotout, 6-5); Methodist (N.C.) over Chapman (Calif.), 3-0.
Championship: Williams over Methodist, 2-1. Final records: Williams (17-0-2) and Methodist (21-1-0).

NAIA

National tourney at Mobile, Ala. (Nov. 20-25)
Semifinals: Lindsey Wilson (Ky.) over Birmingham-Southerm (Ala.), 2-1; Midwestern St. (Tex.) over Illinois-Springfield, 1-0.
Championship: Lindsey Wilson over Midwestern St., 2-1. Final records: Lindsey Wilson (19-4-3) and Midwestern St. (21-5-1).

WOMEN

NCAA Division II

at Rindge, N.H. (Nov. 10-12)
Semifinals: Barry (Fla.) over Quincy (Ill.), 2-1 (3OT); Franklin Pierce (N.H.) over Sonoma St. (Calif.), 3-1.
Championship: Franklin Pierce over Barry, 5-0. Final records: Franklin Pierce (20-0-0) and Barry (16-2-1).

NCAA Division III

at Pamona, N.J. (Nov. 11-12)
Semifinals: UC-San Diego over William Smith (N.Y.), 1-0; Methodist (N.C.) over Richard Stockton (N.J.), 2-0.
Championship: UC-San Diego over Methodist, 3-0. Final records: UC-San Diego (19-2-0) and Methodist (17-4-0).

NAIA

National tourney at Mt. Berry, Ga. (Nov. 20-25)
Semifinals: Lindenwood (Mo.) over So. Nazarene (Okla.), 3-1; Lynn (Fla.) over Georgian Court (N.J.), 3-1.
Championship: Lynn over Lindenwood, 4-1. Final records: Lynn (23-1-1) and Lindenwood (21-5-1).

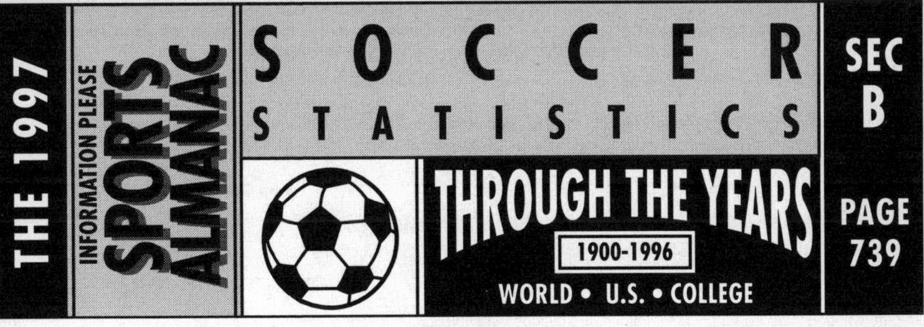

THE 1997
INFORMATION PLEASE
SPORTS ALMANAC
SOCCER
STATISTICS
THROUGH THE YEARS
1900-1996
WORLD • U.S. • COLLEGE
SEC
B
PAGE
739

The World Cup

The Federation Internationale de Football Association (FIFA) began the World Cup championship tournament in 1930 with a 13-team field in Uruguay. Sixty-four years later, 138 countries competed in qualifying rounds to fill 24 berths in the 1994 World Cup finals. FIFA has increased the World Cup '98 tournament field from 24 to 32 teams, including automatic berths for defending champion Brazil and host France. The other 30 slots are allotted by region: Europe (14), Africa (5), South America (4), CONCACAF (3), Asia (3), and the one remaining position to the winner of a playoff between the fourth place team in Asia and the champion of Oceania.

The United States hosted the World Cup for the first time in '94 and American crowds shattered tournament attendance records (see page 743). Tournaments have now been played three times in North America (Mexico 2 and U.S.), four times in South America (Argentina, Chile, Brazil and Uruguay) and eight times in Europe (Italy 2, England, France, Spain, Sweden, Switzerland and West Germany).

Brazil retired the first World Cup (called the Jules Rimet Trophy after FIFA's first president) in 1970 after winning it for the third time. The new trophy, first presented in 1974, is known as simply the World Cup.

Multiple winners: Brazil (4); Italy and West Germany (3); Argentina and Uruguay (2).

Year	Champion	Manager	Score	Runner-up	Host Country	Third Place
1930	Uruguay	Alberto Suppici	4-2	Argentina	Uruguay	No game
1934	Italy	Vittório Pozzo	2-1*	Czechoslovakia	Italy	Germany 3, Austria 2
1938	Italy	Vittório Pozzo	4-2	Hungary	France	Brazil 4, Sweden 2
1942-46	Not held					
1950	Uruguay	Juan Lopez	2-1	Brazil	Brazil	No game
1954	West Germany	Sepp Herberger	3-2	Hungary	Switzerland	Austria 3, Uruguay 1
1958	Brazil	Vicente Feola	5-2	Sweden	Sweden	France 6, W. Ger. 3
1962	Brazil	Aimoré Moreira	3-1	Czechoslovakia	Chile	Chile 1, Yugoslavia 0
1966	England	Alf Ramsey	4-2*	W. Germany	England	Portugal 2, USSR 1
1970	Brazil	Mario Zagalo	4-1	Italy	Mexico	W. Ger. 1, Uruguay 0
1974	West Germany	Helmut Schoen	2-1	Holland	W. Germany	Poland 1, Brazil 0
1978	Argentina	Cesar Menotti	3-1*	Holland	Argentina	Brazil 2, Italy 1
1982	Italy	Enzo Bearzot	3-1	W. Germany	Spain	Poland 3, France 2
1986	Argentina	Carlos Bilardo	3-2	W. Germany	Mexico	France 4, Belgium 2*
1990	West Germany	Franz Beckenbauer	1-0	Argentina	Italy	Italy 2, England 1
1994	Brazil	Carlos Parreira	0-0†	Italy	USA	Sweden 4, Bulgaria 0
1998	at France (June 10–July 12)					
2002	at Japan/South Korea					

*Winning goals scored in overtime (no sudden death); †Brazil defeated Italy in shootout (3-2) after scoreless overtime period (30 minutes).

All-Time World Cup Leaders

Career Goals

World Cup scoring leaders through 1994. Years listed are years played in World Cup.

	No
Gerd Müller, West Germany (1970, 74)	14
Just Fontaine, France (1958)	13
Pelé, Brazil (1958, 62, 66, 70)	12
Sandor Kocsis, Hungary (1954)	11
Helmut Rahn, West Germany (1954, 58)	11
Teofilo Cubillas, Peru (1970, 78)	10
Gregorz Lato, Poland (1974, 78, 82)	10
Gary Lineker, England (1986, 90)	10

Most Valuable Player

Officially, the Golden Ball Award, the Most Valuable Player of the World Cup tournament has been selected since 1982 by a panel of international soccer journalists.

Year		Year	
1982	Paolo Rossi, Italy	1990	Toto Schillaci, Italy
1986	Diego Maradona, Arg.	1994	Romario, Brazil

Single Tournament Goals

World Cup tournament scoring leaders through 1994.

Year		Gm	No
1930	Guillermo Stabile, Argentina	4	8
1934	Angelo Schiavio, Italy	3	4
	Oldrich Nejedly, Czechoslovakia	4	4
	& Edmund Conen, Germany	4	4
1938	Leônidas, Brazil	3	8
1950	Ademir, Brazil	6	7
1954	Sandor Kocsis, Hungary	5	11
1958	Just Fontaine, France	6	13
1962	Drazen Jerkovic, Yugoslavia	6	5
1966	Eusébio, Portugal	6	9
1970	Gerd Müller, West Germany	6	10
1974	Grzegorz Lato, Poland	7	7
1978	Mario Kempes, Argentina	7	6
1982	Paolo Rossi, Italy	7	6
1986	Gary Lineker, England	5	6
1990	Toto Schillaci, Italy	7	6
1994	Oleg Salenko, Russia	3	6
	Hristo Stoichkov, Bulgaria	7	6

All-Time World Cup Ranking Table

Since the first World Cup in 1930, Brazil is the only country to play in all 15 final tournaments and win the championship four times. The FIFA All-Time Table below ranks all nations that have ever qualified for a World Cup final tournament by points earned through 1994. Victories, which earned two points from 1930-90, were awarded three points starting in 1994. Note that Germany's appearances include 10 made by West Germany from 1954-90. Participants in the 1994 World Cup final are in **bold** type.

		App	Gm	W	L	T	Pts	GF	GA
1	**Brazil**	15	73	49	11	13	**111**	159	68
2	**Germany**	13	73	42	15	16	**100**	154	97
3	**Italy**	13	61	35	12	14	**84**	97	59
4	**Argentina**	11	52	26	17	9	**61**	90	65
5	England	9	41	18	11	12	**48**	55	38
6	**Spain**	9	37	15	13	9	**39**	53	44
7	Uruguay	9	37	15	14	8	**38**	61	52
	Russia	8	34	16	12	6	**38**	60	40
9	**Sweden**	9	38	14	15	9	**37**	66	60
10	France	9	34	15	14	5	**35**	71	56
	Yugoslavia	8	33	14	12	7	**35**	55	42
12	Hungary	9	32	15	14	3	**33**	87	57
13	Poland	5	25	13	7	5	**31**	39	29
14	**Holland**	6	25	11	8	6	**28**	43	29
15	Czech Rep.	8	30	11	14	5	**27**	44	45
16	Austria	6	26	12	12	2	**26**	40	43
17	**Mexico**	10	33	7	18	8	**22**	31	68
	Belgium	9	29	9	16	4	**22**	37	53
19	Chile	6	21	7	11	3	**17**	26	32
20	**Romania**	6	17	6	7	4	**16**	26	29
21	**Switzerland**	7	22	6	13	3	**15**	33	51
22	Scotland	7	20	4	10	6	**14**	23	35
23	**Bulgaria**	6	23	3	13	7	**13**	21	46
24	Portugal	2	9	6	3	0	**12**	19	12
25	Peru	4	15	4	8	3	**11**	19	31
	No. Ireland	3	13	3	5	5	**11**	13	23
27	Paraguay	4	11	3	4	4	**10**	16	25
	Cameroon	3	11	3	4	4	**10**	11	21
29	**USA**	5	14	4	9	1	**9**	17	33
30	**Ireland**	2	9	1	3	5	**7**	4	7
31	**Colombia**	3	10	2	6	2	**6**	13	20
	Denmark	1	4	3	1	0	**6**	10	6
	East Germany	1	6	2	2	2	**6**	5	5
34	**Morocco**	3	10	1	6	3	**5**	7	13
	Algeria	2	6	2	3	1	**5**	6	10
	Wales	1	5	1	1	3	**5**	4	4
37	Costa Rica	1	4	2	2	0	**4**	4	6
	Nigeria	1	4	2	2	0	**4**	7	4
	Saudi Arabia	1	4	2	2	0	**4**	5	6
40	**South Korea**	4	11	0	8	3	**3**	9	34
	Norway	2	4	1	2	1	**3**	2	3
	Cuba	1	3	1	1	1	**3**	5	12
	North Korea	1	4	1	2	1	**3**	5	9
	Tunisia	1	3	1	1	1	**3**	3	2
45	Egypt	2	4	0	2	2	**2**	3	6
	Honduras	1	3	0	1	2	**2**	2	3
	Israel	1	3	0	1	2	**2**	1	3
	Turkey	1	3	1	2	0	**2**	10	11
49	**Bolivia**	3	6	0	5	1	**1**	1	20
	Australia	1	3	0	2	1	**1**	0	5
	Iran	1	3	0	2	1	**1**	2	8
	Kuwait	1	3	0	2	1	**1**	2	6
53	El Salvador	2	6	0	6	0	**0**	1	22
	Canada	1	3	0	3	0	**0**	0	5
	East Indies	1	1	0	1	0	**0**	0	6
	Greece	1	3	0	3	0	**0**	0	10
	Haiti	1	3	0	3	0	**0**	2	14
	Iraq	1	3	0	3	0	**0**	1	4
	New Zealand	1	3	0	3	0	**0**	2	12
	UAE	1	3	0	3	0	**0**	2	11
	Zaire	1	3	0	3	0	**0**	0	14

The United States in the World Cup

While the United States has fielded a national team every year of the World Cup, only four of those teams have been able to make it past the preliminary competition and qualify for the final World Cup tournament. The 1994 national team automatically qualified because the U.S. served as host of the event for the first time. The U.S. has played in three of the first four World Cups (1930, '34 and '50) and each of the last two (1990, '94). The Americans have a record of 4-9-1 in 14 World Cup matches, with two victories in 1930, a 1-0 upset of England in 1950, and a 2-1 shocker over Colombia in 1994.

1930

1st Round Matches

United States 3 .... Belgium 0
United States 3 .... Paraguay 0

Semifinals

Argentina 6 .... United States 1

U.S. Scoring—Bert Patenaude (3), Bart McGhee (2), James Brown, Thomas Florie.

1934

1st Round Match

Italy 7 .... United States 1

U.S. Scoring—Buff Donelli (who later became a noted college and NFL football coach).

1950

1st Round Matches

Spain 3 .... United States 1
United States 1 .... England 0
Chile 5 .... United States 2

U.S. Scoring—Joe Gaetjens, Joe Maca, John Souza, Frank Wallace.

1990

1st Round Matches

Czechoslovakia 5 .... United States 1
Italy 1 .... United States 0
Austria 2 .... United States 1

U.S. Scoring—Paul Caligiuri, Bruce Murray.

1994

1st Round Matches

United States 1 .... Switzerland 1
United States 2 .... Colombia 1
Romania 1 .... United States 0

Round of 16

Brazil 1 .... United States 0

Overall U.S. Scoring— Eric Wynalda, Ernie Stewart, own goal (Colombia defender Andres Escobar).

World Cup Finals

Current World Cup champion Brazil and finalist Italy each appeared in their fifth Cup championship game in 1994 and played to the first scoreless overtime draw in the history of the Cup final. The match was also the first decided by a shootout (Brazil winning, 3-2). West Germany (now Germany) has played in the most Cup finals with six. Note that a four-team round robin determined the 1950 championship—the deciding game turned out to be the last one of the tournament between Uruguay and Brazil.

1930

Uruguay 4, Argentina 2

(at Montevideo, Uruguay)

		1	2—T
July 30	Uruguay (4-0)	1	3—4
	Argentina (4-1)	2	0—2

Goals: Uruguay—Pablo Dorado (12th minute), Pedro Cea (54th), Santos Iriarte (68th), Castro (89th); Argentina—Carlos Peucelle (20th), Guillermo Stabile (37th).

Uruguay—Ballesteros, Nasazzi, Mascheroni, Andrade, Fernandez, Gestido, Dorado, Scarone, Castro, Cea, Iriarte.

Argentina—Botasso, Della Torre, Paternoster, J. Evaristo, Monti, Suarez, Peucelle, Varallo, Stabile, Ferreira, M. Evaristo.

Attendance: 90,000. **Referee:** Langenus (Belgium).

1934

Italy 2, Czechoslovakia 1 (OT)

(at Rome)

		1	2	OT—T
June 10	Italy (4-0-1)	0	1	1—2
	Czechoslovakia (3-1)	0	1	0—1

Goals: Italy—Raimondo Orsi (80th minute), Angelo Schiavio (95th); Czechoslovakia—Puc (70th).

Italy—Combi, Monzeglio, Allemandi, Ferraris IV, Monti, Bertolini, Guaita, Meazza, Schiavio, Ferrari, Orsi.

Czechoslovakia—Planicka, Zenisek, Ctyroky, Kostalek, Cambal, Krcil, Junek, Svoboda, Sobotka, Nejedly, Puc.

Attendance: 55,000. **Referee:** Eklind (Sweden).

1938

Italy 4, Hungary 2

(at Paris)

		1	2—T
June 19	Italy (4-0)	3	1—4
	Hungary (3-1)	1	1—2

Goals: Italy—Gino Colaussi (5th minute), Silvio Piola (16th), Colassi (35th), Piola (82nd); Hungary—Titkos (7th), Georges Sarosi (70th).

Italy—Olivieri, Foni, Rava, Serantoni, Andreolo, Locatelli, Biavati, Meazza, Piola, Ferrari, Colaussi.

Hungary—Szabo, Polgar, Biro, Szalay, Szucs, Lazar, Sas, Vincze, G. Sarosi, Szengeller, Titkos.

Attendance: 65,000. **Referee:** Capdeville (France).

1950

Uruguay 2, Brazil 1

(at Rio de Janeiro)

		1	2—T
July 16	Uruguay (3-0-1)	0	2—2
	Brazil (4-1-1)	0	1—1

Goals: Uruguay—Juan Schiaffino (66th minute), Chico Ghiggia (79th); Brazil—Friaça (47th).

Uruguay—Maspoli, M. Gonzales, Tejera, Gambetta, Varela, Andrade, Ghiggia, Perez, Miguez, Schiaffino, Moran.

Brazil—Barbosa, Augusto, Juvenal, Bauer, Danilo, Bigode, Friaça, Zizinho, Ademir, Jair, Chico.

Attendance: 199,854. **Referee:** Reader (England).

1954

West Germany 3, Hungary 2

(at Berne, Switzerland)

		1	2—T
July 4	West Germany (4-1)	2	1—3
	Hungary (4-1)	2	0—2

Goals: West Germany—Max Morlock (10th minute), Helmut Rahn (18th), Rahn (84th); Hungary—Ferenc Puskas (4th), Zoltan Czibor (9th).

West Germany—Turek, Posipal, Liebrich, Kohlmeyer, Eckel, Mai, Rahn, Morlock, O. Walter, F. Walter, Schaefer.

Hungary—Grosics, Buzansky, Lorant, Lantos, Bozsik, Zakarias, Czibor, Kocsis, Hidegkuti, Puskas, J. Toth.

Attendance: 60,000. **Referee:** Ling (England).

1958

Brazil 5, Sweden 2

(at Stockholm)

		1	2—T
June 29	Brazil (5-0-1)	2	3—5
	Sweden (4-1-1)	1	1—2

Goals: Brazil—Vavà (9th minute), Vavà (32nd), Pelé (55th), Mario Zagalo (68th), Pelé (90th); Sweden—Nils Liedholm (3rd), Agne Simonsson (80th).

Brazil—Gilmar, D. Santos, N. Santos, Zito, Bellini, Orlando, Garrincha, Didi, Vavà, Pelé, Zagalo.

Sweden—Svensson, Bergmark, Axbom, Boerjesson, Gustavsson, Parling, Hamrin, Gren, Simonsson, Liedholm, Skoglund.

Attendance: 49,737. **Referee:** Guigue (France).

1962

Brazil 3, Czechoslovakia 1

(at Santiago, Chile)

		1	2—T
June 17	Brazil (5-0-1)	1	2—3
	Czechoslovakia (3-2-1)	1	0—1

Goals: Brazil—Amarildo (17th minute), Zito (68th), Vavà (77th); Czechoslovakia—Josef Masopust (15th).

Brazil—Gilmar, D. Santos, N. Santos, Zito, Mauro, Zozimo, Garrincha, Didi, Vavà, Amarildo, Zagalo.

Czechoslovakia—Schroiff, Tichy, Novak, Pluskal, Popluhar, Masopust, Pospichal, Scherer, Kvasniak, Kadraba, Jelinek.

Attendance: 68,679. **Referee:** Latishev (USSR).

1966

England 4, West Germany 2 (OT)

(at London)

		1	2	OT—T
July 30	England (5-0-1)	1	1	2—4
	West Germany (4-1-1)	1	1	0—2

Goals: England—Geoff Hurst (18th minute), Martin Peters (78th), Hurst (101st), Hurst (120th); West Germany—Helmut Haller (12th), Wolfgang Weber (90th).

England—Banks, Cohen, Wilson, Stiles, J. Charlton, Moore, Ball, Hurst, B. Charlton, Hunt, Peters.

West Germany—Tilkowski, Höttges, Schnellinger, Beckenbauer, Schulz, Weber, Haller, Seeler, Held, Overath, Emmerich.

Attendance: 93,802. **Referee:** Dienst (Switzerland).

World Cup Finals (Cont.)

1970

Brazil 4, Italy 1

(at Mexico City)

		1	2—T
June 21	Brazil (6-0)	1	3—4
	Italy (3-1-2)	1	0—1

Goals: Brazil—Pelé (18th minute), Gerson (65th), Jairzinho (70th), Carlos Alberto (86th); Italy—Roberto Boninsegna (37th).

Brazil—Felix, C. Alberto, Everaldo, Clodoaldo, Brito, Piazza, Jairzinho, Gerson, Tostão, Pelé, Rivelino.

Italy—Albertosi, Burgnich, Facchetti, Bertini (Juliano, 73rd), Rosato, Cera, Domenghini, Mazzola, Boninsegna (Rivera, 84th), De Sisti, Riva.

Attendance: 107,412. **Referee:** Glockner (E. Germany).

1974

West Germany 2, Holland 1

(at Munich)

		1	2—T
July 7	West Germany (6-1)	2	0—2
	Holland (5-1-1)	1	0—1

Goals: West Germany—Paul Breitner (25th minute, penalty kick), Gerd Müller (43rd); Holland—Johan Neeskens (1st, penalty kick).

West Germany—Maier, Beckenbauer, Vogts, Breitner, Schwarzenbeck, Overath, Bonhof, Hoeness, Grabowski, Müller, Holzenbein.

Holland—Jongbloed, Suurbier, Rijsbergen (De Jong, 58th), Krol, Haan, Jansen, Van Hanegem, Neeskens, Rep, Cruyff, Rensenbrink (R. Van de Kerkhof, 46th).

Attendance: 77,833. **Referee:** Taylor (England).

1978

Argentina 3, Holland 1 (OT)

(at Buenos Aires)

		1	2	OT—T
June 25	Argentina (5-1-1)	1	0	2—3
	Holland (3-2-2)	0	1	0—1

Goals: Argentina—Mario Kempes (37th minute), Kempes (104th), Daniel Bertoni (114th); Holland—Dirk Nanninga (81st).

Argentina—Fillol, Olguin, L. Galvan, Passarella, Tarantini, Ardiles (Larrosa, 65th), Gallego, Kempes, Luque, Bertoni, Ortiz (Houseman, 77th).

Holland—Jongbloed, Jansen (Suurbier, 72nd), Brandts, Krol, Poortvliet, Haan, Neeskens, W. Van de Kerkhof, R. Van de Kerkhof, Rep (Nanninga, 58th), Rensenbrink.

Attendance: 77,260. **Referee:** Gonella (Italy).

1982

Italy 3, West Germany 1

(at Madrid)

		1	2—T
July 11	Italy (4-0-3)	0	3—3
	West Germany (4-2-1)	0	1—1

Goals: Italy—Paolo Rossi (57th minute), Marco Tardelli (68th), Alessandro Altobelli (81st); West Germany—Paul Breitner (83rd).

Italy—Zoff, Scirea, Gentile, Cabrini, Collovati, Bergomi, Tardelli, Oriali, Conti, Rossi, Graziani (Altobelli, 8th, and Causio, 89th).

West Germany—Schumacher, Stielike, Kaltz, Briegel, K.H. Förster, B. Förster, Breitner, Dremmler (Hrubesch, 61st), Littbarski, Fischer, Rummenigge (Müller, 69th).

Attendance: 90,080. **Referee:** Coelho (Brazil).

1986

Argentina 3, West Germany 2

(at Mexico City)

		1	2—T
June 29	Argentina (6-0-1)	1	2—3
	West Germany (4-2-1)	0	2—2

Goals: Argentina—Jose Brown (22nd minute), Jorge Valdano (55th), Jorge Burruchaga (83rd); West Germany—Karl-Heinz Rummenigge (73rd), Rudi Völler (81st).

Argentina—Pumpido, Cuciuffo, Olarticoechea, Ruggeri, Brown, Batista, Burruchaga (Trobbiani, 89th), Giusti, Enrique, Maradona, Valdano.

West Germany—Schumacher, Jakobs, B. Förster, Berthold, Briegel, Eder, Brehme, Matthäus, Rummenigge, Magath (Hoeness, 61st), Allofs (Völler, 46th).

Attendance: 114,590. **Referee:** Filho (Brazil).

1990

West Germany 1, Argentina 0

(at Rome)

		1	2—T
July 8	West Germany (6-0-1)	0	1—1
	Argentina (4-2-1)	0	0—0

Goals: West Germany—Andreas Brehme (85th minute, penalty kick).

West Germany—Illgner, Berthold (Reuter, 73th), Kohler, Augenthaler, Buchwald, Brehme, Haessler, Matthäus, Littbarski, Klinsmann, Völler.

Argentina: Goycoechea, Ruggeri (Monzon, 46th), Simon, Serrizuela, Lorenzo, Basualdo, Troglio, Burruchaga (Calderon, 53rd), Sensini, Dezotti, Maradona.

Attendance: 73,603. **Referee:** Codesal (Mexico).

1994

Brazil 0, Italy 0 (SO)

(at Pasadena, Calif.)

		1	2	OT—T
July 17	Brazil (6-0-1)	0	0	0—0*
	Italy (4-2-1)	0	0	0—0

*Brazil wins shootout, 3-2.

Shootout (five shots each, alternating): ITA— Baresi (miss, 0-0); BRA— Santos (blocked, 0-0): ITA— Albertini (goal, 1-0); BRA—Romario (goal, 1-1); ITA— Evani (goal, 2-1); BRA— Branco (goal, 2-2); ITA— Massaro (blocked, 2-2); BRA— Dunga (goal, 2-3); ITA—R. Baggio (miss, 2-3).

Brazil— Taffarel, Jorginho (Cafu, 21st minute), Branco, Aldair, Santos, Mazinho, Silva, Dunga, Zinho (Viola, 106th), Bebeto, Romario.

Italy— Pagliuca, Mussi (Apolloni, 35th minute), Baresi, Benarrivo, Maldini, Albertini, D. Baggio (Evani, 95th), Berti, Donadoni, R. Baggio, Massaro.

Attendance: 94,194. **Referee:** Puhl (Hungary).

World Cup Shootouts

Introduced in 1982; winning sides in **bold** type.

Year	Round		Final	SO
1982	Semi	**W. Germany** vs France	3-3	(5-4)
1986	Quarter	**Belgium** vs Spain	1-1	(5-4)
	Quarter	**France** vs Brazil	1-1	(4-3)
	Quarter	**W. Germany** vs Mexico	0-0	(4-1)
1990	Second	**Ireland** vs Romania	0-0	(5-4)
	Quarter	**Argentina** vs Yugoslavia	0-0	(3-2)
	Semi	**Argentina** vs Italy	1-1	(4-3)
	Semi	**W. Germany** vs England	1-1	(4-3)
1994	Second	**Bulgaria** vs Mexico	1-1	(3-1)
	Quarter	**Sweden** vs Romania	2-2	(5-4)
	Final	**Brazil** vs Italy	0-0	(3-2)

Year-by-Year Comparisons

How the 15 World Cup tournaments have compared in nations qualifying, matches played, players participating, goals scored, average goals per game, overall attendance and attendance per game.

						Goals		Attendance	
Year	**Host**	**Continent**	**Nations**	**Matches**	**Players**	**Scored**	**Per Game**	**Overall**	**Per Game**
1930	Uruguay	So. America	13	18	189	70	3.8	434,500	24,138
1934	Italy	Europe	16	17	208	70	4.1	395,000	23,235
1938	France	Europe	15	18	210	84	4.7	483,000	26,833
1942-46	Not held								
1950	Brazil	So. America	13	22	192	88	4.0	1,337,000	60,772
1954	Switzerland	Europe	16	26	233	140	5.3	943,000	36,270
1958	Sweden	Europe	16	35	241	126	3.6	868,000	24,800
1962	Chile	So. America	16	32	252	89	2.8	776,000	24,250
1966	England	Europe	16	32	254	89	2.8	1,614,677	50,458
1970	Mexico	No. America	16	32	270	95	3.0	1,673,975	52,311
1974	West Germany	Europe	16	38	264	97	2.6	1,774,022	46,684
1978	Argentina	So. America	16	38	277	102	2.7	1,610,215	42,374
1982	Spain	Europe	24	52	396	146	2.8	1,856,277	33,967
1986	Mexico	No. America	24	52	414	132	2.5	2,402,951	46,211
1990	Italy	Europe	24	52	413	115	2.2	2,517,348	48,411
1994	United States	No. America	24	52	437	140	2.7	3,567,415	68,102
1998	France	Europe	32	—	—	—	—	—	—

OTHER WORLDWIDE COMPETITION

The Olympic Games

Held every four years since 1896, except during World War I (1916) and World War II (1940-44). Soccer was not a medal sport in 1896 at Athens or in 1932 at Los Angeles. By agreement between FIFA and the IOC, Olympic soccer competition is currently limited to players 23 years old and under. See pages 641-642 in the Olympics chapter for further information on soccer at the 1996 Summer Games.

Multiple winners: England and Hungary (3); Soviet Union and Uruguay (2).

MEN

Year	
1900	**England,** France, Belgium
1904	**Canada,** USA I, USA II
1906	**Denmark,** Smyrna (Int'l entry), Greece
1908	**England,** Denmark, Holland
1912	**England,** Denmark, Holland
1920	**Belgium,** Spain, Holland
1924	**Uruguay,** Switzerland, Sweden
1928	**Uruguay,** Argentina, Italy
1936	**Italy,** Austria, Norway
1948	**Sweden,** Yugoslavia, Denmark
1952	**Hungary,** Yugoslavia, Sweden
1956	**Soviet Union,** Yugoslavia, Bulgaria
1960	**Yugoslavia,** Denmark, Hungary
1964	**Hungary,** Czechoslovakia, East Germany
1968	**Hungary,** Bulgaria, Japan
1972	**Poland,** Hungary, East Germany
1976	**East Germany,** Poland, Soviet Union
1980	**Czechoslovakia,** East Germany, Soviet Union
1984	**France,** Brazil, Yugoslavia
1988	**Soviet Union,** Brazil, West Germany
1992	**Spain,** Poland, Ghana
1996	**Nigeria,** Argentia, Brazil

WOMEN

Year	
1996	**USA,** China, Norway

The Under-20 World Cup

Held every two years since 1977. Officially, The World Youth Championship for the FIFA/Coca-Cola Cup.

Multiple winners: Brazil (3); Argentina and Portugal (2).

Year	
1977	Soviet Union
1979	Argentina
1981	West Germany
1983	Brazil
1985	Brazil
1987	Yugoslavia
1989	Portugal
1991	Portugal
1993	Brazil
1995	Argentina
1997	(at Malaysia)
1999	(at South America)

The Under-17 World Cup

Held every two years since 1985. Officially, The U-17 World Tournament for the FIFA/JVC Cup.

Multiple winners: Ghana and Nigeria (2).

Year	
1985	Nigeria
1987	Soviet Union
1989	Saudi Arabia
1991	Ghana
1993	Nigeria
1995	Ghana
1997	(at Egypt)
1999	(at New Zealand)

Indoor World Championship

First held in 1989. FIFA's only Five-a-Side tournament.

Multiple winners: Brazil (2).

Year	
1989	Brazil
1992	Brazil
1996	(at Spain)

Women's World Cup

First held in 1991. Officially, the FIFA Women's World Championship.

Year	
1991	United States
1995	Norway
1999	(at United States)

Intercontinental Cup

First held in 1992. Contested by the Continental champions of Africa, Asia, Europe, North America and South America.

Year	
1992	Argentina
1995	Denmark

CONTINENTAL COMPETITION

European Championship

Held every four years since 1960. Officially, the European Football Championship. Winners receive the Henri Delaunay trophy, named for the Frenchman who first proposed the idea of a European Soccer Championship in 1927. The first one would not be played until five years after his death in 1955.

Multiple winner: West Germany (2).

Year		Year		Year		Year	
1960	Soviet Union	1972	West Germany	1984	France	1992	Denmark
1964	Spain	1976	Czechoslovakia	1988	Holland	1996	Germany
1968	Italy	1980	West Germany				

Copa America

Held irregularly since 1916. Unofficially, the Championship of South America.

Multiple winners: Argentina and Uruguay (14); Brazil (4); Paraguay and Peru (2).

Year		Year		Year		Year	
1916	Uruguay	1927	Argentina	1947	Argentina	1967	Uruguay
1917	Uruguay	1929	Argentina	1949	Brazil	1975	Peru
1919	Brazil	1935	Uruguay	1953	Paraguay	1979	Paraguay
1920	Uruguay	1937	Argentina	1955	Argentina	1983	Uruguay
1921	Argentina	1939	Peru	1956	Uruguay	1987	Uruguay
1922	Brazil	1941	Argentina	1957	Argentina	1989	Brazil
1923	Uruguay	1942	Uruguay	1958	Argentina	1991	Argentina
1924	Uruguay	1945	Argentina	1959	Uruguay	1993	Argentina
1925	Argentina	1946	Argentina	1963	Bolivia	1995	Uruguay
1926	Uruguay						

African Nations' Cup

Contested since 1957 and held every two years since 1968.

Multiple winners: Ghana (4); Congo/Zaire and Egypt (3); Cameroon and Nigeria (2).

Year		Year		Year		Year	
1957	Egypt	1968	Zaire	1978	Ghana	1988	Cameroon
1959	Egypt	1970	Sudan	1980	Nigeria	1990	Algeria
1962	Ethiopia	1972	Congo	1982	Ghana	1992	Ivory Coast
1963	Ghana	1974	Zaire	1984	Cameroon	1994	Nigeria
1965	Ghana	1976	Morocco	1986	Egypt	1996	South Africa

CONCACAF Gold Cup

The Confederation of North, Central American and Caribbean Football Championship. Contested irregularly from 1963-81 and revived as CONCACAF Gold Cup in 1991.

Multiple winners: Mexico (5); Costa Rica (2).

Year		Year		Year		Year	
1963	Costa Rica	1969	Costa Rica	1977	Mexico	1993	Mexico
1965	Mexico	1971	Mexico	1981	Honduras	1996	Mexico
1967	Guatemala	1973	Haiti	1991	United States		

CLUB COMPETITION

Toyota Cup

Also known as the World Club Championship. Contested annually in December between the winners of the European Cup and South America's Copa Libertadores. Four European Cup winners refused to participate in the championship match in the 1970s and were replaced each time by the European Cup runner-up: Panathinaikos (Greece) for Ajax Amsterdam (Holland) in 1971; Juventus (Italy) for Ajax in 1973; Atlético Madrid (Spain) for Bayern Munich (West Germany) in 1974; and Malmo (Sweden) for Nottingham Forest (England) in 1979. Another European Cup winner, Marseille of France, was prohibited by the Union of European Football Associations (UEFA) from playing for the 1993 Toyota Cup because of its involvement in the match-rigging scandal.

Best-of-three game format from 1960-68, then a two-game/total goals format from 1969-79. Toyota became Cup sponsor in 1980, changed the format to a one-game championship and moved it to Toyko.

Multiple winners: AC Milan, Nacional and Peñarol (3); Ajax Amsterdam, Independiente, Inter-Milan, Santos and São Paulo (2).

Year		Year		Year	
1960	Real Madrid (Spain)	1972	Ajax Amsterdam (Holland)	1984	Independiente (Argentina)
1961	Peñarol (Uruguay)	1973	Independiente (Argentina)	1985	Juventus (Italy)
1962	Santos (Brazil)	1974	Atlético Madrid (Spain)	1986	River Plate (Argentina)
1963	Santos (Brazil)	1975	Not held	1987	FC Porto (Portugal)
1964	Inter-Milan (Italy)	1976	Bayern Munich (W.Germany)	1988	Nacional (Uruguay)
1965	Inter-Milan (Italy)	1977	Boca Juniors (Argentina)	1989	AC Milan (Italy)
1966	Peñarol (Uruguay)	1978	Not held	1990	AC Milan (Italy)
1967	Racing Club (Argentina)	1979	Olimpia (Paraguay)	1991	Red Star (Yugoslavia)
1968	Estudiantes (Argentina)	1980	Nacional (Uruguay)	1992	São Paulo (Brazil)
1969	AC Milan (Italy)	1981	Flamengo (Brazil)	1993	São Paulo (Brazil)
1970	Feyenoord (Holland)	1982	Peñarol (Uruguay)	1994	Velez Sarsfield (Argentina)
1971	Nacional (Uruguay)	1983	Gremio (Brazil)	1995	Ajax Amsterdam (Holland)

European Cup

Contested annually since the 1955-56 season by the league champions of the member countries of the Union of European Football Associations (UEFA).

Multiple winners: Real Madrid (6); AC Milan (5); Ajax Amsterdam and Liverpool (4); Bayern Munich (3); Benfica, Inter-Milan and Nottingham Forest (2).

Year	
1956	Real Madrid (Spain)
1957	Real Madrid (Spain)
1958	Real Madrid (Spain)
1959	Real Madrid (Spain)
1960	Real Madrid (Spain)
1961	Benfica (Portugal)
1962	Benfica (Portugal)
1963	AC Milan (Italy)
1964	Inter-Milan (Italy)
1965	Inter-Milan (Italy)
1966	Real Madrid (Spain)
1967	Glasgow Celtic (Scotland)
1968	Manchester United (England)
1969	AC Milan (Italy)
1970	Feyenoord (Holland)
1971	Ajax Amsterdam (Holland)
1972	Ajax Amsterdam (Holland)
1973	Ajax Amsterdam (Holland)
1974	Bayern Munich (W. Germany)
1975	Bayern Munich (W. Germany)
1976	Bayern Munich (W. Germany)
1977	Liverpool (England)
1978	Liverpool (England)
1979	Nottingham Forest (England)
1980	Nottingham Forest (England)
1981	Liverpool (England)
1982	Aston Villa (England)
1983	SV Hamburg (W. Germany)
1984	Liverpool (England)
1985	Juventus (Italy)
1986	Steaua Bucharest (Romania)
1987	FC Porto (Portugal)
1988	PSV Eindhoven (Holland)
1989	AC Milan (Italy)
1990	AC Milan (Italy)
1991	Red Star Belgrade (Yugo.)
1992	Barcelona (Spain)
1993	Marseille (France)*
1994	AC Milan (Italy)
1995	Ajax Amsterdam (Holland)
1996	Juventus (Italy)

*title vacated

European Cup Winners' Cup

Contested annually since the 1960-61 season by the cup winners of the member countries of the Union of European Football Associations (UEFA).

Multiple winners: Barcelona (3); AC Milan, RSC Anderlecht and Dinamo Kiev (2).

Year	
1961	Fiorentina (Italy)
1962	Atlético Madrid (Spain)
1963	Tottenham Hotspur (England)
1964	Sporting Lisbon (Portugal)
1965	West Ham United (England)
1966	Borussia Dortmund (W. Germany)
1967	Bayern Munich (W. Germany)
1968	AC Milan (Italy)
1969	Slovan Bratislava (Czech.)
1970	Manchester City (England)
1971	Chelsea (England)
1972	Glasgow Rangers (Scotland)
1973	AC Milan (Italy)
1974	FC Magdeburg (E. Germany)
1975	Dinamo Kiev (USSR)
1976	RSC Anderlecht (Belgium)
1977	SV Hamburg (W. Germany)
1978	RSC Anderlecht (Belgium)
1979	Barcelona (Spain)
1980	Valencia (Spain)
1981	Dinamo Tbilisi (USSR)
1982	Barcelona (Spain)
1983	Aberdeen (Scotland)
1984	Juventus (Italy)
1985	Everton (England)
1986	Dinamo Kiev (USSR)
1987	Ajax Amsterdam (Holland)
1988	Mechelen (Belgium)
1989	Barcelona (Spain)
1990	Sampdoria (Italy)
1991	Manchester United (England)
1992	Werder Bremen (Germany)
1993	Parma (Italy)
1994	Arsenal (England)
1995	Real Zaragoza (Spain)
1996	Paris St. Germain (France)

UEFA Cup

Contested annually since the 1957-58 season by teams other than league champions and cup winners of the Union of European Football Associations (UEFA). Teams selected by UEFA based on each country's previous performance in the tournament. Teams from England were banned from UEFA Cup play from 1985-90 for the criminal behavior of their supporters.

Multiple winners: Barcelona and Juventus (3); Borussia Mönchengladbach, IFK Göteborg, Leeds United, Liverpool, Real Madrid, Tottenham Hotspur and Valencia (2).

Year	
1958	Barcelona (Spain)
1959	Not held
1960	Barcelona (Spain)
1961	AS Roma (Italy)
1962	Valencia (Spain)
1963	Valencia (Spain)
1964	Real Zaragoza (Spain)
1965	Ferencvaros (Hungary)
1966	Barcelona (Spain)
1967	Dinamo Zagreb (Yugoslavia)
1968	Leeds United (England)
1969	Newcastle United (England)
1970	Arsenal (England)
1971	Leeds United (England)
1972	Tottenham Hotspur (England)
1973	Liverpool (England)
1974	Feyenoord (Holland)
1975	Borussia Mönchengladbach (W. Germany)
1976	Liverpool (England)
1977	Juventus (Italy)
1978	PSV Eindhoven (Holland)
1979	Borussia Mönchengladbach (W. Germany)
1980	Eintracht Frankfurt (W. Germany)
1981	Ipswich Town (England)
1982	IFK Göteborg (Sweden)
1983	RSC Anderlecht (Belgium)
1984	Tottenham Hotspur (England)
1985	Real Madrid (Spain)
1986	Real Madrid (Spain)
1987	IFK Göteborg (Sweden)
1988	Bayer Leverkusen (W. Germany)
1989	Napoli (Italy)
1990	Juventus (Italy)
1991	Inter-Milan (Italy)
1992	Ajax Amsterdam (Holland)
1993	Juventus (Italy)
1994	Inter-Milan (Italy)
1995	Parma (Italy)
1996	Bayern Munich (Germany)

Club Competition (Cont.)

Copa Libertadores

Contested annually since the 1955-56 season by the league champions of South America's football union.

Multiple winners: Independiente (7); Peñarol (5); Estudiantes and Nacional-Uruguay (3); Boca Juniors, Gremio, Olimpia, River Plate, Santos and São Paulo (2).

Year	
1960	Peñarol (Uruguay)
1961	Peñarol (Uruguay)
1962	Santos (Brazil)
1963	Santos (Brazil)
1964	Independiente (Argentina)
1965	Independiente (Argentina)
1966	Peñarol (Uruguay)
1967	Racing Club (Argentina)
1968	Estudiantes de la Plata (Argentina)
1969	Estudiantes de la Plata (Argentina)
1970	Estudiantes de la Plata (Argentina)
1971	Nacional (Uruguay)
1972	Independiente (Argentina)
1973	Independiente (Argentina)
1974	Independiente (Argentina)
1975	Independiente (Argentina)
1976	Cruzeiro (Brazil)
1977	Boca Juniors (Argentina)
1978	Boca Juniors (Argentina)
1979	Olimpia (Paraguay)
1980	Nacional (Uruguay)
1981	Flamengo (Brazil)
1982	Peñarol (Uruguay)
1983	Gremio (Brazil)
1984	Independiente (Argentina)
1985	Argentinos Jrs. (Argentina)
1986	River Plate (Argentina)
1987	Peñarol (Uruguay)
1988	Nacional (Uruguay)
1989	Nacional Medellin (Colombia)
1990	Olimpia (Paraguay)
1991	Colo Colo (Chile)
1992	São Paulo (Brazil)
1993	São Paulo (Brazil)
1994	Velez Sarsfield (Argentina)
1995	Gremio (Brazil)
1996	River Plate (Argentina)

Annual Awards

World Player of the Year

Presented by FIFA, the European Sports Magazine Association (ESM) and Adidas, the sports equipment manufacturer, since 1991. Winners are selected by national team coaches from around the world.

Year		Nat'l Team
1991	Lothar Matthäus, Inter-Milan	Germany
1992	Marco Van Basten, AC Milan	Holland
1993	Roberto Baggio, Juventus	Italy
1994	Romario, Barcelona	Brazil
1995	George Weah, AC Milan	Liberia

European Player of the Year

Officially, the "Ballon d'Or" and presented by *France Football* magazine since 1956. Candidates are limited to European players in European leagues and winners are selected by a panel of 49 European soccer journalists.

Multiple winners: Johan Cruyff, Michel Platini and Marco Van Basten (3); Franz Beckenbauer, Alfredo di Stéfano, Kevin Keegan and Karl-Heinz Rummenigge (2).

Year		Nat'l Team
1956	Stanley Matthews, Blackpool	England
1957	Alfredo di Stéfano, Real Madrid	Arg./Spain
1958	Raymond Kopa, Real Madrid	France
1959	Alfredo di Stéfano, Real Madrid	Arg./Spain
1960	Luis Suarez, Barcelona	Spain
1961	Enrique Sivori, Juventus	Arg./Italy
1962	Josef Masopust, Dukla Prague	Czech.
1963	Lev Yashin, Dinamo Moscow	Soviet Union
1964	Denis Law, Manchester United	Scotland
1965	Eusébio, Benfica	Portugal
1966	Bobby Charlton, Manchester United	England
1967	Florian Albert, Ferencvaros	Hungary
1968	George Best, Manchester United	No. Ireland
1969	Gianni Rivera, AC Milan	Italy
1970	Gerd Müller, Bayern Munich	W. Ger.
1971	Johan Cruyff, Ajax Amsterdam	Holland
1972	Franz Beckenbauer, Bayern Munich	W. Ger.
1973	Johan Cruyff, Barcelona	Holland
1974	Johan Cruyff, Barcelona	Holland
1975	Oleg Blokhin, Dinamo Kiev	Soviet Union
1976	Franz Beckenbauer, Bayern Munich	W. Ger.
1977	Allan Simonsen, B. Mönchengladbach	Denmark
1978	Kevin Keegan, SV Hamburg	England
1979	Kevin Keegan, SV Hamburg	England
1980	K.H. Rummenigge, Bayern Munich	W. Ger.
1981	K.H. Rummenigge, Bayern Munich	W. Ger.
1982	Paolo Rossi, Juventus	Italy
1983	Michel Platini, Juventus	France
1984	Michel Platini, Juventus	France
1985	Michel Platini, Juventus	France
1986	Igor Belanov, Dinamo Kiev	Soviet Union
1987	Ruud Gullit, AC Milan	Holland
1988	Marco Van Basten, AC Milan	Holland
1989	Marco Van Basten, AC Milan	Holland
1990	Lothar Matthäus, Inter-Milan	W. Ger.
1991	Jean-Pierre Papin, Marseille	France
1992	Marco Van Basten, AC Milan	Holland
1993	Roberto Baggio, Juventus	Italy
1994	Hristo Stoitchkov, Barcelona	Bulgaria
1995	George Weah, AC Milan	Liberia

South American Player of the Year

Presented by *El Pais* of Uruguay since 1971. Candidates are limited to South American players in South American leagues and winners are selected by a panel of 80 Latin American sports editors.

Multiple winners: Elias Figueroa and Zico (3); Enzo Francescoli, Diego Maradona and Carlos Valderrama (2).

Year		Nat'l Team
1971	Tostão, Cruzeiro	Brazil
1972	Teofilo Cubillas, Alianza Lima	Peru
1973	Pelé, Santos	Brazil
1974	Elias Figueroa, Internacional	Chile
1975	Elias Figueroa, Internacional	Chile
1976	Elias Figueroa, Internacional	Chile
1977	Zico, Flamengo	Brazil
1978	Mario Kempes, Valencia	Argentina
1979	Diego Maradona, Argentinos Juniors	Argentina
1980	Diego Maradona, Boca Juniors	Argentina
1981	Zico, Flamengo	Brazil
1982	Zico, Flamengo	Brazil
1983	Socrates, Corinthians	Brazil
1984	Enzo Francescoli, River Plate	Uruguay

Year		Nat'l Team
1985	Julio Cesar Romero, Fluminense	Paraguay
1986	Antonio Alzamendi, River Plate	Uruguay
1987	Carlos Valderrama, Deportivo Cali	Colombia
1988	Ruben Paz, Racing Buenos Aires	Uruguay
1989	Bebeto, Vasco da Gama	Brazil
1990	Raul Amarilla, Olimpia	Paraguay
1991	Oscar Ruggeri, Velez Sarsfield	Argentina
1992	Rai, São Paulo	Brazil
1993	Carlos Valderrama, Atl. Junior	Colombia
1994	Cafu, São Paulo	Brazil
1995	Enzo Francescoli, River Plate	Uruguay

African Player of the Year

Officially, the African "Ballon d'Or" and presented by *France Football* magazine since 1970. All African players are eligible for the award and winners are selected by a panel of 52 African soccer journalists.

Multiple winners: Abedi Pele and George Weah (3); Roger Milla and Thomas N'Kono (2).

Year	
1970	Salif Keita, Mali
1971	Ibrahim Sunday, Ghana
1972	Cherif Souleymane, Guinea
1973	Tshimimu Bwanga, Zaire
1974	Paul Moukila, Congo
1975	Ahmed Faras, Morocco
1976	Roger Milla, Cameroon
1977	Dhiab Tarak, Tunisia
1978	Abdul Razak, Ghana
1979	Thomas N'Kono, Cameroon
1980	Jean Manga Onguene, Cameroon
1981	Lakhdar Belloumi, Algeria
1982	Thomas N'Kono, Cameroon
1983	Mahmoud Al-Khatib, Egypt
1984	Theophile Abega, Cameroon
1985	Mohamed Timoumi, Morocco
1986	Badou Zaki, Morocco
1987	Rabah Madjer, Algeria
1988	Kalusha Bwalya, Zambia
1989	George Weah, Liberia
1990	Roger Milla, Cameroon
1991	Abedi Pele, Ghana
1992	Abedi Pele, Ghana
1993	Abedi Pele, Ghana
1994	George Weah, Liberia
1995	George Weah, Liberia

U.S. Player of the Year

Presented by Honda and the Spanish-speaking radio show "Futbol de Primera" since 1991. Candidates are limited to American players who have played at least five games with the U.S. National Team and winners are selected by a panel of U.S. soccer journalists.

Year	
1991	Hugo Perez
1992	Eric Wynalda
1993	Thomas Dooley
1994	Marcelo Balboa
1995	Alexi Lalas

U.S. PRO LEAGUES

OUTDOOR

National Professional Soccer League (1967)

Not sanctioned by FIFA, the international soccer federation. The NPSL recruited individual players to fill the rosters of its 10 teams. The league lasted only one season.

Playoff Final				Regular Season			
Year	Winner	Score(s)	Loser	Leading Scorer	G	A	Pts
1967	Oakland Clippers	0-1, 4-1	Baltimore Bays	Yanko Daucik, Toronto	20	8	48

United Soccer Association (1967)

Sanctioned by FIFA. Originally called the North American Soccer League, it became the USA to avoid being confused with the National Professional Soccer League (see above). Instead of recruiting individual players, the USA imported 12 entire teams from Europe to represent its 12 franchises. It, too, only lasted a season. The league champion Los Angeles Wolves were actually Wolverhampton of England and the runner-up Washington Whips were Aberdeen of Scotland.

Playoff Final				Regular Season			
Year	Winner	Score	Loser	Leading Scorer	G	A	Pts
1967	Los Angeles Wolves	6-5 (OT)	Washington Whips	Roberto Boninsegna, Chicago	10	1	21

North American Soccer League (1968-84)

The NPSL and USA merged to form the NASL in 1968 and the new league lasted until 1985. The NASL championship was known as the Soccer Bowl from 1975-84. One game decided the NASL title every year but five. There were no playoffs in 1969; a two-game/aggregate goals format was used in 1968 and '70; and a best-of-three games format was used in 1971 and '84; (*) indicates overtime and (†) indicates game decided by shootout.

Multiple winners: NY Cosmos (5); Chicago (2).

Playoff Final				Regular Season			
Year	Winner	Score(s)	Loser	Leading Scorer	G	A	Pts
1968	Atlanta Chiefs	0-0,3-0	San Diego Toros	John Kowalik, Chicago	30	9	69
1969	Kansas City Spurs	No game	Atlanta Chiefs	Kaiser Motaung, Atlanta	16	4	36
1970	Rochester Lancers	3-0,1-3	Washington Darts	Kirk Apostolidis, Dallas	16	3	35
1971	Dallas Tornado	1-2*,4-1,2-0	Atlanta Chiefs	Carlos Metidieri, Rochester	19	8	46
1972	New York Cosmos	2-1	St. Louis Stars	Randy Horton, New York	9	4	22
1973	Philadelphia Atoms	2-0	Dallas Tornado	Kyle Rote, Jr., Dallas	10	10	30
1974	Los Angeles Aztecs	3-3†	Miami Toros	Paul Child, San Jose	15	6	36
1975	Tampa Bay Rowdies	2-0	Portland Timbers	Steve David, Miami	23	6	52
1976	Toronto Metros	3-0	Minnesota Kicks	Giorgio Chinaglia, New York	19	11	49

Note: In 1969, Kansas City won the NASL regular season championship with 110 points to 109 for Atlanta. There were no playoffs.

U.S. Pro Leagues (Cont.)

	Playoff Final			Regular Season			
Year	Winner	Score(s)	Loser	Leading Scorer	G	A	Pts
1977	New York Cosmos	2-1	Seattle Sounders	Steve David, Los Angeles	26	6	58
1978	New York Cosmos	3-1	Tampa Bay Rowdies	Giorgio Chinaglia, New York	34	11	79
1979	Vancouver Whitecaps	2-1	Tampa Bay Rowdies	Oscar Fabbiani, Tampa Bay	25	8	58
1980	New York Cosmos	3-0	Ft. Laud. Strikers	Giorgio Chinaglia, New York	32	13	77
1981	Chicago Sting	0-0†	New York Cosmos	Giorgio Chinaglia, New York	29	16	74
1982	New York Cosmos	1-0	Seattle Sounders	Giorgio Chinaglia, New York	20	15	55
1983	Tulsa Roughnecks	2-0	Toronto Blizzard	Roberto Cabanas, New York	25	16	66
1984	Chicago Sting	2-1,3-2	Toronto Blizzard	Steve Zungul, Golden Bay	20	10	50

Regular Season MVP

Regular season Most Valuable Player as designated by the NASL.

Multiple winner: Carlos Metidieri (2).

Year		Year		Year	
1967	Rueben Navarro, Phila (NPSL)	1973	Warren Archibald, Miami	1979	Johan Cruyff, Los Angeles
1968	John Kowalik, Chicago	1974	Peter Silvester, Baltimore	1980	Roger Davies, Seattle
1969	Cirilio Fernandez, KC	1975	Steve David, Miami	1981	Giorgio Chinaglia, New York
1970	Carlos Metidieri, Rochester	1976	Pelé, New York	1982	Peter Ward, Seattle
1971	Carlos Metidieri, Rochester	1977	Franz Beckenbauer, New York	1983	Roberto Cabanas, New York
1972	Randy Horton, New York	1978	Mike Flanagan, New England	1984	Steve Zungul, Golden Bay

A-League (American Professional Soccer League)

The American Professional Soccer League was formed in 1990 with the merger of the Western Soccer League and the New American Soccer League. The APSL was officially sanctioned as an outdoor pro league in 1992 and changed its name to the A-League in 1995.

Multiple winner: Colorado (2).

Year		Year		Year		Year	
1990	Maryland Bays	1992	Colorado Foxes	1994	Montreal Impact	1996	Seattle Sounders
1991	SF Bay Blackhawks	1993	Colorado Foxes	1995	Seattle Sounders		

INDOOR

Major Soccer League (1978-92)

Originally the Major Indoor Soccer League from 1978-79 season through 1989-90. The MISL championship was decided by one game in 1980 and 1981; a best-of-three games series in 1979, best-of-five games in 1982 and 1983; and best-of-seven games since 1984. The MSL folded after the 1991-92 season.

Multiple winners: San Diego (8); New York (4).

	Playoff Final			Regular Season			
Year	Winner	Series	Loser	Leading Scorer	G	A	Pts
1979	New York Arrows	2-0 (WW)	Philadelphia	Fred Grgurev, Philadelphia	46	28	74
1980	New York Arrows	7-4 (1 game)	Houston	Steve Zungul, New York	90	46	136
1981	New York Arrows	6-5 (1 game)	St. Louis	Steve Zungul, New York	108	44	152
1982	New York Arrows	3-2 (LWWLW)	St. Louis	Steve Zungul, New York	103	60	163
1983	San Diego Sockers	3-2 (WWLLW)	Baltimore	Steve Zungul, NY/Golden Bay	75	47	122
1984	Baltimore Blast	4-1 (LWWWW)	St. Louis	Stan Stamenkovic, Baltimore	34	63	97
1985	San Diego Sockers	4-1 (WWLWW)	Baltimore	Steve Zungul, San Diego	68	68	136
1986	San Diego Sockers	4-3 (WLLLWWW)	Minnesota	Steve Zungul, Tacoma	55	60	115
1987	Dallas Sidekicks	4-3 (LLWWLWW)	Tacoma	Tatu, Dallas	73	38	111
1988	San Diego Sockers	4-0	Cleveland	Eric Rasmussen, Wichita	55	57	112
1989	San Diego Sockers	4-3 (LWWWLLW)	Baltimore	Preki, Tacoma	51	53	104
1990	San Diego Sockers	4-2 (LWWWLW)	Baltimore	Tatu, Dallas	64	49	113
1991	San Diego Sockers	4-2 (WLWLWW)	Cleveland	Tatu, Dallas	78	66	144
1992	San Diego Sockers	4-2 (WWWLLW)	Dallas	Zoran Karic, Cleveland	39	63	102

Playoff MVPs

MSL playoff Most Valuable Players, selected by a panel of soccer media covering the playoffs.

Multiple winners: Zungul (4); Quinn (2).

Year		Year	
1979	Shep Messing, NY	1986	Brian Quinn, SD
1980	Steve Zungul, NY	1987	Tatu, Dallas
1981	Steve Zungul, NY	1988	Hugo Perez, SD
1982	Steve Zungul, NY	1989	Victor Nogueira, SD
1983	Juli Veee, SD	1990	Brian Quinn, SD
1984	Scott Manning, Bal.	1991	Ben Collins, SD
1985	Steve Zungul, SD	1992	Thompson Usiyan, SD

Regular Season MVPs

MSL regular season Most Valuable Players, selected by a panel of soccer media from every city in the league.

Multiple winner: Zungul (6); Nogueira and Tatu (2)

Year		Year	
1979	Steve Zungul, NY	1986	Steve Zungul, SD/Tac.
1980	Steve Zungul, NY	1987	Tatu, Dallas
1981	Steve Zungul, NY	1988	Erik Rasmussen, Wich.
1982	Steve Zungul, NY & Stan Terlecki, Pit.	1989	Preki, Tacoma
1983	Alan Mayer, SD	1990	Tatu, Dallas
1984	Stan Stamenkovic, Bal.	1991	Victor Nogueira, SD
1985	Steve Zungul, SD	1992	Victor Nogueira, SD

NASL Indoor Champions (1980-84)

The North American Soccer League started an indoor league in the fall of 1979. The indoor NASL, which featured many of the same teams and players who played in the outdoor NASL, crowned champions from 1980-82 before suspending play. It was revived for the 1983-84 indoor season but folded for good in 1984.

Multiple winners: San Diego (2).

Year		Year		Year		Year	
1980	Memphis Rogues	1982	San Diego Sockers	1983	Play suspended	1984	San Diego Sockers
1981	Edmonton Drillers						

National Professional Soccer League

The winter indoor NPSL began as the American Indoor Soccer Association in 1984-85, then changed its name in 1989-90.

Multiple winner: Canton (5); Cleveland (2).

Year		Year		Year		Year	
1985	Canton (OH) Invaders	1988	Canton Invaders	1991	Chicago Power	1994	Cleveland Crunch
1986	Canton Invaders	1989	Canton Invaders	1992	Detroit Rockers	1995	St. Louis Ambush
1987	Louisville Thunder	1990	Canton Invaders	1993	Kansas City Attack	1996	Cleveland Crunch

Continental Indoor Soccer League

The summer indoor CISL played its first season in 1993.

Year		Year		Year	
1993	Dallas Sidekicks	1994	Las Vegas Dustdevils	1995	Monterey La Raza

U.S. COLLEGES

NCAA Men's Division I Champions

NCAA Division I champions since the first title was contested in 1959. The championship has been shared three times—in 1967, 1968 and 1989. There was a playoff for third place from 1974-81.

Multiple winners: Saint Louis (10); San Francisco and Virginia (5); Indiana (3); Clemson, Howard, and Michigan St. (2).

Year	Winner	Head Coach	Score	Runner-up	Host/Site	Semifinalists
1959	Saint Louis	Bob Guelker	5-2	Bridgeport	UConn	West Chester, CCNY
1960	Saint Louis	Bob Guelker	3-2	Maryland	Brooklyn	West Chester, UConn
1961	West Chester	Mel Lorback	2-0	Saint Louis	Saint Louis	Bridgeport, Rutgers
1962	Saint Louis	Bob Guelker	4-3	Maryland	Saint Louis	Mich. St., Springfield
1963	Saint Louis	Bob Guelker	3-0	Navy	Rutgers	Army, Maryland
1964	Navy	F.H. Warner	1-0	Michigan St.	Brown	Army, Saint Louis
1965	Saint Louis	Bob Guelker	1-0	Michigan St.	Saint Louis	Army, Navy
1966	San Francisco	Steve Negoesco	5-2	LIU-Brooklyn	California	Army, Mich. St.
1967-**a**	Michigan St. & Saint Louis	Gene Kenney / Harry Keough	0-0	—	Saint Louis	LIU-Bklyn, Navy
1968-**b**	Michigan St. & Maryland	Gene Kenney / Doyle Royal	2-2 (2 OT)	—	Ga. Tech	Brown, San Jose St.
1969	Saint Louis	Harry Keough	4-0	San Francisco	San Jose St.	Harvard, Maryland
1970	Saint Louis	Harry Keough	1-0	UCLA	SIU-Ed'sville	Hartwick, Howard
1971-**c**	Howard	Lincoln Phillips	3-2	Saint Louis	Miami	Harvard, San Fran.
1972	Saint Louis	Harry Keough	4-2	UCLA	Miami	Cornell, Howard
1973	Saint Louis	Harry Keough	2-1 (OT)	UCLA	Miami	Brown, Clemson

Year	Winner	Head Coach	Score	Runner-up	Host/Site	Third Place
1974	Howard	Lincoln Phillips	2-1 (4OT)	Saint Louis	Saint Louis	Hartwick 3, UCLA 1
1975	San Francisco	Steve Negoesco	4-0	SIU-Ed'sville	SIU-Ed'sville	Brown 2, Howard 0
1976	San Francisco	Steve Negoesco	1-0	Indiana	Penn	Hartwick 4, Clemson 3
1977	Hartwick	Jim Lennox	2-1	San Francisco	California	SIU-Ed'sville 3, Brown 2
1978-**d**	San Francisco	Steve Negoesco	4-3 (OT)	Indiana	Tampa	Clemson 6, Phi. Textile 2
1979	SIU-Ed'sville	Bob Guelker	3-2	Clemson	Tampa	Penn St. 2, Columbia 1
1980	San Francisco	Steve Negoesco	4-3 (OT)	Indiana	Tampa	Ala. A&M 2, Hartwick 0
1981	Connecticut	Joe Morrone	2-1 (OT)	Alabama A&M	Stanford	East. Ill. 4, Phi. Textile 2

Year	Winner	Head Coach	Score	Runner-up	Host/Site	Semifinalists
1982	Indiana	Jerry Yeagley	2-1 (8 OT)	Duke	Ft. Lauderdale	UConn, SIU-Ed'sville
1983	Indiana	Jerry Yeagley	1-0 (2 OT)	Columbia	Ft. Lauderdale	UConn, Virginia
1984	Clemson	I.M. Ibrahim	2-1	Indiana	Seattle	Hartwick, UCLA
1985	UCLA	Sigi Schmid	1-0 (8 OT)	American	Seattle	Evansville, Hartwick
1986	Duke	John Rennie	1-0	Akron	Tacoma	Fresno St., Harvard
1987	Clemson	I.M. Ibrahim	2-0	San Diego St.	Clemson	Harvard, N. Carolina
1988	Indiana	Jerry Yeagley	1-0	Howard	Indiana	Portland, S. Carolina
1989-**e**	Santa Clara & Virginia	Steve Sampson / Bruce Arena	1-1 (2 OT)	—	Rutgers	Indiana, Rutgers

Notes: a—game declared a draw due to inclement weather after regulation time; **b**—game declared a draw after two overtimes; **c**—Howard vacated title for using ineligible player; **d**—San Francisco vacated title for using ineligible player; **e**—game declared a draw due to inclement weather after two overtimes.

U.S. Colleges (Cont.)

Year	Winner	Head Coach	Score	Runner-up	Host/Site	Semifinalists
1990-**f**	UCLA	Sigi Schmid	0-0 (PKs)	Rutgers	South Fla.	Evansville, N.C. State
1991-**g**	Virginia	Bruce Arena	0-0 (PKs)	Santa Clara	Tampa	Indiana, Saint Louis
1992	Virginia	Bruce Arena	2-0	San Diego	Davidson	Davidson, Duke
1993	Virginia	Bruce Arena	2-0	South Carolina	Davidson	CS-Fullerton, Princeton
1994	Virginia	Bruce Arena	1-0	Indiana	Davidson	Rutgers, UCLA
1995	Wisconsin	Jim Launder	2-0	Duke	Richmond	Portland, Virginia

Notes: f—UCLA wins on penalty kicks (4-3) after four overtimes; **g**—Virginia wins on penalty kicks (3-1) after four overtimes.

Women's NCAA Division I Champions

NCAA Division I women's champions since the first tournament was contested in 1982. Until 1995, the University of North Carolina had won the title every year but 1985 when they lost the final to George Mason.

Multiple winner: North Carolina (12).

Year	Winner	Score	Runner-up	Year	Winner	Score	Runner-up
1982	North Carolina	2-0	Central Florida	1989	North Carolina	2-0	Colorado College
1983	North Carolina	4-0	George Mason	1990	North Carolina	6-0	Connecticut
1984	North Carolina	2-0	Connecticut	1991	North Carolina	3-1	Wisconsin
1985	George Mason	2-0	North Carolina	1992	North Carolina	9-1	Duke
1986	North Carolina	2-0	Colorado College	1993	North Carolina	6-0	George Mason
1987	North Carolina	1-0	Massachusetts	1994	North Carolina	5-0	Notre Dame
1988	North Carolina	4-1	N.C. State	1995	Notre Dame	1-0 (3OT)	Portland

Annual Awards

MEN

Hermann Trophy

College Player of the Year. Voted on by Division I college coaches and selected sportswriters and first presented in 1967 in the name of Robert Hermann, one of the founders of the North American Soccer League.

Multiple winners: Mike Seerey, Ken Snow and Al Trost (2).

Year		Year		Year	
1967	Dov Markus, LIU	1977	Billy Gazonas, Hartwick	1987	Bruce Murray, Clemson
1968	Manuel Hernandez, San Jose St.	1978	Angelo DiBernardo, Indiana	1988	Ken Snow, Indiana
1969	Al Trost, Saint Louis	1979	Jim Stamatis, Penn St.	1989	Tony Meola, Virginia
1970	Al Trost, Saint Louis	1980	Joe Morrone, Jr. UConn	1990	Ken Snow, Indiana
1971	Mike Seerey, Saint Louis	1981	Armando Betancourt, Indiana	1991	Alexi Lalas, Rutgers
1972	Mike Seerey, Saint Louis	1982	Joe Ulrich, Duke	1992	Brad Friedel, UCLA
1973	Dan Counce, Saint Louis	1983	Mike Jeffries, Duke	1993	Claudio Reyna, Virginia
1974	Farrukh Quraishi, Oneonta St.	1984	Amr Aly, Columbia	1994	Brian Maisonneuve, Indiana
1975	Steve Ralbovsky, Brown	1985	Tom Kain, Duke	1995	Mike Fisher, Virginia
1976	Glenn Myernick, Hartwick	1986	John Kerr, Duke		

Missouri Athletic Club Award

College Player of the Year. Voted on by men's team coaches around the country from Division I to junior college level and first presented in 1986 by the Missouri Athletic Club of St. Louis.

Multiple winner: Claudio Reyna and Ken Snow (2).

Year		Year		Year	
1986	John Kerr, Duke	1990	Ken Snow, Indiana	1993	Claudio Reyna, Virginia
1987	John Harkes, Virginia	1991	Alexi Lalas, Rutgers	1994	Todd Yeagley, Indiana
1988	Ken Snow, Indiana	1992	Claudio Reyna, Virginia	1995	Matt McKeon, St. Louis
1989	Tony Meola, Virginia				

WOMEN

Hermann Trophy

Women's College Player of the year. Voted on by Division I college coaches and selected sportswriters and first presented in 1988 in the name of Robert Hermann, one of the founders of the North American Soccer League.

Multiple winner: Mia Hamm (2).

Year		Year		Year	
1988	Michelle Akers, Central Fla.	1991	Kristine Lilly, N. Carolina	1994	Tisha Venturini, N. Carolina
1989	Shannon Higgins, N. Carolina	1992	Mia Hamm, N. Carolina	1995	Shannon MacMillan, Portland
1990	April Kater, Massachusetts	1993	Mia Hamm, N. Carolina		

Missouri Athletic Club Award

Women's College Player of the Year. Voted on by women's team coaches around the country from Division I to junior college level and first presented in 1991 by the Missouri Athletic Club of St. Louis.

Multiple winner: Mia Hamm (2).

Year		Year		Year	
1991	Kristine Lilly, N. Carolina	1993	Mia Hamm, N. Carolina	1995	Shannon MacMillan, Portland
1992	Mia Hamm, N. Carolina	1994	Tisha Venturini, N. Carolina		

Professional Bowlers Association

In the same year that he was voted the Best Bowler Ever by the American Bowling Congress, **Earl Anthony** returned to the Senior PBA Tour in 1996 to help the sport and because he missed it.

BOWLING

by Tom Gaffney

An Early Return

In a sport yearning for good news, legendary bowler Earl Anthony comes back to the PBA Senior Tour

Bowling is a sport whose slippage and decline is often more chronicled than its successes.

So any good news is welcomed, even if it does revolve around and evolve around a 58-year-old man who has been retired for five years and whose body is losing a fight with arthritis.

Yes, in 1996, the biggest story in bowling was the un-retirement of the sport's most recognizable name, Earl Anthony. Anthony, a resident of Cornelius, Ore., left the Professional Bowlers Association Senior Tour five years ago for several reasons. He said he was burned out over the travel and the uncertainty of the purses. His right hip and left hand were beginning to feel the effects of arthritis. He had a 40-lane bowling center in Dublin, Calif., to watch over and a job as a bowling commentator on ESPN and Prime SportsChannel.

He had a house, a wife he loved and money in the bank. So he retired.

There was a problem, though. He missed bowling. And bowling missed him. So in June, he announced that he once again was going to bowl professionally.

The bowling community—one that had observed declining sponsorship and purses in tournaments and had observed stagnant television ratings—was ecstatic. And so was Earl Anthony.

"I figure bowling needs a shot in the arm. The sport isn't doing quite as well as I'd like to see and I thought if I came back it would create a little interest," Anthony said when announcing his return.

Anthony then proceeded to startle everyone by finishing second in his first PBA tournament back—the Senior Tour's Seattle Open held the first week in July. He said he had bowled about 20 games in his five years of retirement and had resumed a regular practice schedule just weeks before.

Nevertheless, he finished second in qualifying to gain the second seed in the stepladder finals. In his first finals appearance in years, he defeated John Hricsina of Franklin, Pa., by a score of 247-234. In the championship match, he was beaten by top-seeded Hobo Boothe of Canoga Park, Calif., by 225-200.

"I feel I can still compete. But I'm about 15 pounds heavier than I'd like to be and when you get to be an old man, it's a little hard to get rid of," Anthony said.

"I decided to come back and see how it goes. Mostly, I'm here to promote the game. I'm here to talk to fans and reporters."

Anthony then showed fans that Seattle was no fluke. A month later, he finished second in the Showboat Senior Invitational in Las Vegas. He lost to John Denton of

---

Tom Gaffney has covered bowling, golf and college sports for the *Akron Beacon Journal* since 1987.

Midland, Texas in the championship game by one pin, 213-212.

By returning, Anthony has a chance to add to his list of accomplishments—and that list is long. He has 41 victories on the regular PBA Tour, which is seven more than runner-up Mark Roth. He has won four Senior Tour championships, so his total of 45 is first overall in PBA annals.

Ironically, in the same year that he returned, he also earned a prestigious honor from the American Bowling Congress. In balloting by ABC members, Anthony was named the Best Bowler Ever. He received more votes than all the other candidates combined. He was named on 52.4 percent of the ballots, while Dick Weber had 13.9 percent, Don Carter 12.0, Mike Aulby 5.9 and Mark Roth 5.7.

For as many reasons as anyone can think of, bowling is glad to have Earl Anthony back among the competitive.

"He is the Jack Nicklaus of bowling," said friend and outgoing U.S. National team coach Fred Borden. "He isn't just the best there ever was, he is a straight, honest guy who understands what he means to the game. We're lucky to have him back."

Anthony joined a PBA Senior Tour that enjoyed continued growth in 1996. A total of 16 tournaments were held, up from 13 in 1995, 13 in 1994 and 14 in 1993.

Through the first 10 events on the 1996 schedule, only Gary Dickinson, 53, of Edmond, Okla., had been able to win two events. He won the Tri-City Senior Classic in Richland, Wash., on July 18 and the Pontiac Osteopathic Hospital Senior Open on Aug. 22.

Dale Eagle of Lewisville, Texas won the prestigious Senior Tour Championship tournament held in Jackson, Mich. He threw strikes in the ninth and tenth frames to beat Roy Buckley of Columbus, Ohio in the championship match 213-194 on Aug. 30.

Another milestone for the older set came in the ABC Senior Masters held at Stonehedge Place in Akron, Ohio on Aug. 12-17. The tournament offered the highest winner's purse ever for a PBA-ABC Seniors event ($60,000) and had the largest field ever for a senior tournament (500 players).

Dave Davis, while hobbling on a right knee that had recently been operated on, won by beating John Hatz of Golden, Col., in the championship match, 236-182.

Korean Bowling Journal

In the PBA tour's 20-tournament 1996 season, only one player, **Walter Ray Williams**, won more than one event and he won three.

That tournament also had another distinction—it marked the return of professional bowling to Akron, which is where the headquarters of the PBA is located. Akron had played host to the Tournament of Champions for 30 years, before the tournament was merged with the Brunswick World Open and moved to Chicago in 1995.

Late in 1995, the PBA announced that John Handegard of Las Vegas had won the 1995 Senior Tour Player of the Year award. He led in earnings with $63,133 to break Gary Dickinson's two-year stranglehold on Player of the Year honors.

Meanwhile, the struggling regular PBA Tour could have used some good news such as Earl Anthony's return to competition on the Senior Tour.

The PBA took a big hit from ABC-TV, whose "Pro Bowlers Tour" show has been a part of the ABC lineup since 1962. ABC traditionally has televised the PBA's 16-stop Winter Tour from early-January to mid-April, when the Tournament of Champions neatly concluded the season. Almost all

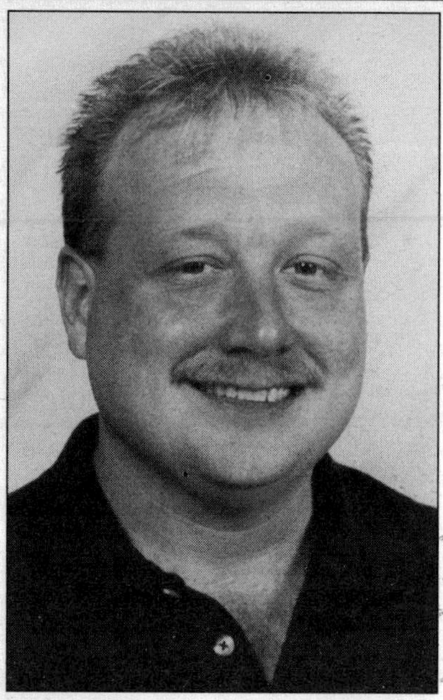

Professional Bowlers Association

Thanks to throwing a televised perfect game worth $100,00, **Bob Learn Jr.** led the PBA in earnings in 1996 with $193,998.

shows were in the well-established 3 p.m. Saturday time slot.

However, in 1996, that favorable television schedule changed as ESPN did the entire 6-stop Winter Tour from late January to early March. Unfortunately the shows ran in three different time slots and included none of the three PBA majors.

ABC then came aboard in March for the 14 tournaments of the Spring-Summer Tour. That schedule went into mid-June, which is hardly prime bowling season for viewers or players. The World Tournament of Champions came in the middle of the telecast schedule—on April 27—and another major, the PBA National Championship, was telecast on June 8.

That TV schedule, along with stagnant purses, was enough to discourage even the most avid player.

Through it all, the PBA still had one of its most exciting and competitive on-the-lanes seasons in years.

In those 20 tournaments, there were 18 different champions. Walter Ray Williams Jr., 37, of Stockton, Calif., was the only multiple winner with three titles. He won the Track Synergy Open in Kennewick, Wash., on Feb. 23, the Showboat Invitational in Las Vegas on March 16, and the Brunswick Johnny Petraglia Open in Piscataway, N.J., on April 13.

That gave Williams a definite edge in the 1996 PBA Player of the Year award. Williams, who won that honor in 1986 and 1993, was second in earnings ($155,280), first in average (226.44), first in match-play appearances (14) and first in cashes (16) through those 20 tournaments.

The only reason that Williams wasn't first in earnings was because of the $100,000 that Bob Learn Jr. won for throwing a perfect game on television at the Flagship Open in Erie, Pa., on April 6. That money and the $93,998 that Learn won in tournament play gave him a leading total of $193,998.

Perfect games are never routine — and Learn's was no exception. For one, he did it against PBA Hall of Famer Johnny Petraglia of Manalapan, N.J., who was the last man before that to throw a 300 game on television. He had performed the feat at the PBA National Championship in Toledo, Ohio, on March 5, 1994.

Secondly, Learn did it in his own home town, as a partisan crowd at the Erie Civic Center cheered wildly. Learn won four matches that day, including a 279-257 decision over Randy Pedersen of Hollywood, Fla., in the final.

"I could never do anything to match what I've done today," the 34-year-old Learn told reporters. "The 300 game, winning the title, the $100,000 and with all my family here and in my hometown. It's hard to imagine ever doing something like this."

Drama and human interest were also present at the PBA National Championship in Toledo in early June.

The winner was the remarkably courageous and persistent 46-year-old Butch Soper. The Lake Havasu, Ariz. resident had been plagued by serious health problems and inconsistent performances in the 1990s. It was the first major title of his pro career, which began in the early 1970s.

In January of 1992, Soper suffered a ruptured colon, which took two days to properly diagnose. Soper was hospitalized for 17 days in intensive care and doctors wondered if he would live.

Soper survived and faced big medical

bills since he did not have insurance. Friends and bowling colleagues held various fund raisers for him.

He also was forced to bowl with a colostomy bag until June of 1992, when he could afford a reversal operation that allowed him to live a normal life.

Soper had not won an individual PBA title since 1990 when he changed all that in the course of several amazing days in Toledo.

He was seeded second in the televised stepladder finals and he defeated Justin Hromek of Andover, Kan., 216-214 in the semifinals. That put him against Walter Ray Williams, one of the sport's best players.

The match was close all the way, but Soper got a strike in the ninth and two in the 10th to win 226-210. "What a feeling. I spent 25 years out here on Tour and I finally win a major tournament," Soper said afterward upon reflection. "Heck, I had never even made a telecast in a Triple Crown event before. I guess I paid my dues."

Another surprise came when Dave D'Entremont, 35, of Cleveland won the PBA's other major—the Brunswick World Tournament of Champions in Pallantine, Ill., a suburb of Chicago.

D'Entremont had won only four titles since joining the PBA Tour in 1982. He had been on and off the tour for years, trying to earn enough money to stay out. He had years when he won $920 and $4,713 and years when he won $185,245 and $112,175.

But he overcame those frustrations by winning four matches during the televised finals, including a 215-202 decision over Dave Arnold of Gilbert, Ariz., in the final. Arnold led the match heading into the 10th frame, but left a split while working on three strikes. D'Entremont then dazzled everyone with three strikes in the 10th frame to win.

"This is a vindication for everything bad that happened to me on TV in my career. Every bad break atoned for in one clean sweep," said D'Entremont, who earned $60,000 for the win. "It was fate. It was something that was meant to be."

Late in 1995, the PBA named Mike Aulby of Indianapolis its 1995 Player of the Year. Aulby led the tour in 1995 earnings with $219,792 and set a single-season record with an average of 225.49. Aulby also was Player of the Year in 1985.

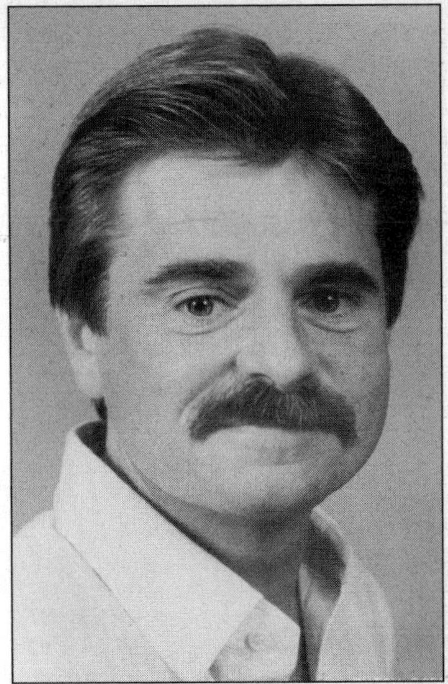

Professional Bowlers Association

Butch Soper overcame several daunting health problems to win the PBA National Championship in 1996.

The Ladies Professional Bowlers Tour, which is headquartered in Rockford, Ill., also had a competitive 1996. Of the first 14 tournaments held in 1996, there were 11 different champions.

Three players had two titles—Wendy Macpherson of Las Vegas, Tammy Turner of West Palm Beach, Fla., and Jackie Sellers of Dubois, Pa. Macpherson won the Texas Shootout and the Little Rock Classic. Turner prevailed in the Storm Doubles and the Omaha Lancers Open. Sellers won the Greater Terre Haute Open and Franklin Virginia Open.

One of the highlights of the Ladies Professional Bowlers Tour season came in the prestigious WIBC Queens tournament held in Buffalo, N.Y.

Lisa Wagner of Palmetto, Fla., has won as much money as any woman bowler anywhere. Yet she had never even made the stepladder finals in the Queens. She changed all that by winning four matches, including a 231-226 victory over Tammy Turner in the finals.

Then, during the nationally televised

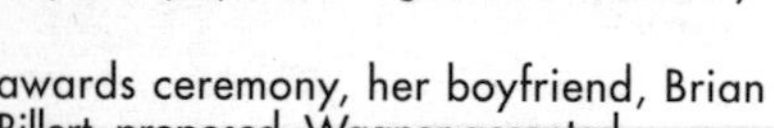

Ladies Pro Bowlers Tour

Lisa Wagner won the WIBC Queens tournament and got engaged the same day when her boyfriend proposed during the awards ceremony.

Ladies Pro Bowlers Tour

Tish Johnson earned Player of the Year Honors in 1995 by winning two tournaments and earning $123,440.

awards ceremony, her boyfriend, Brian Billert, proposed. Wagner accepted.

"We have plenty to celebrate now. It's a double whammy. The toughest tournament of the year and Brian asked me to marry him. It was perfect," said Wagner.

The 1996 LBPT Player of the Year award is shaping up as a fight until the end. Turner led in earnings ($66,255) through 13 events, and Macpherson was first in Merit points (12,070).

Tish Johnson, a left-hander from Northridge, Calif., won 1995 Player of the Year honors. She won two titles and $123,440 in 1995. Johnson also won the award in 1992.

The ABC Tournament, which was held at the Salt Palace Convention Center in Salt Lake City, drew an amazing 9,746 five-player teams competing for a $2.57 million prize fund.

Pollard's Bowl of Versailles, Ind, came away with the prestigious Team All-Events title with a tournament-record 10,425 pins. Pollard's team member Don Scudder of Cincinnati won Singles with an 823. Scott Kurtz of Somerset, N.J. was the Individual All-Events champion with a nine-game total of 2,224. Jamie Burke and Drew Hauck of Ohio won Doubles with a tournament-record 1,508 pins.

The WIBC Tournament was held in Buffalo, N.Y. and drew 37,000 competitors. Mandy Wilson and Linda Kelly, both of Dayton, Ohio, set two tournament records in winning Doubles (1,410) and also having a high game of 558.

Lorrie Nichols of Algonquin, Ill., won Individual All-Events with a 1,985 for nine games. The Naccarato Group of Tacoma, Wash., won Team All-Events with 3,185 pins. Cindy Berlanga of San Antonio was the Singles winner with a 723.

In the United States Amateur Championships in St. Louis that concluded on Aug. 21, Lucy Giovinco, 39, of Norcross, Ga., won the Women's title and Vernon Peterson of Dearborn Heights, Mich., won the Men's title.

On the college scene, Nebraska won the Men's championship and West Texas A&M took the Women's crown in the Intercollegiate Bowling Championships held in Kansas City in April. ❐

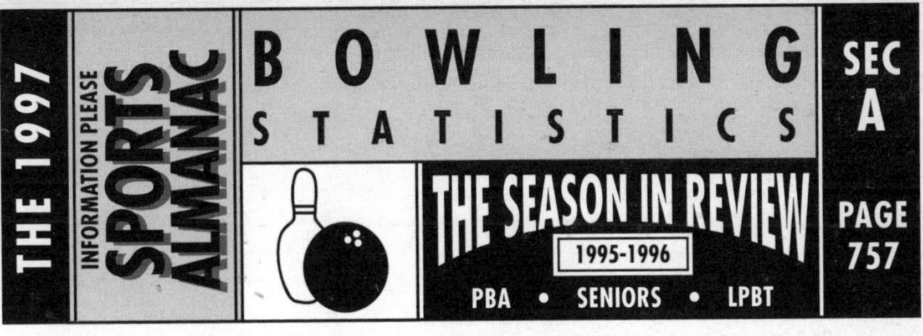

THE 1997
INFORMATION PLEASE
SPORTS ALMANAC
BOWLING
STATISTICS
THE SEASON IN REVIEW
1995-1996
PBA • SENIORS • LPBT
SEC
A
PAGE
757

Tournament Results

Winners of stepladder finals in all PBA, Seniors and LPBT tournaments from Nov. 1, 1995, through the Summer Tour of 1996; major tournaments in **bold** type. Note that (*) indicates winner was top seeded player entering championship round; and (a) indicates amateur. See Updates Chapter for later results.

PBA

Late 1995 Fall Tour

Final	Event	Winner	Earnings	Score	Runner-up
Nov. 1	AMF Dick Weber Classic	David Ozio*	$60,000	280-238	W.R. Williams Jr.
Nov. 8	Touring Players Championship	Ernie Schlegel	40,000	237-236	Randy Pederson
Dec. 10	Merit Mixed Doubles Championship	Butch Soper/	40,000	15,844-	Eric Forkel/
		Kim Canady	40,000	15,812†	Robin Romeo

†Scoring in the Merit Mixed Doubles is based on total pins.

1996 Winter/Spring Tour

Final	Event	Winner	Earnings	Score	Runner-up
Jan. 26	Peoria Open	Wayne Webb	$19,000	229-202	Bob Learn Jr.
Feb. 2	Columbia 300 Open	C.K. Moore	22,000#	214-180	Butch Soper
Feb. 9	Reno Open	Dave Arnold	16,000	241-237	W.R. Williams Jr.
Feb. 16	Oregon Open	Brian Voss	19,000	246-191	Dave Wodka
Feb. 23	Track Synergy Open	W. R. Williams Jr.	22,000	208-206	Brian LeClair
Mar. 1	Tucson Open	Bryan Goebel*	16,000	224-217	Ricky Ward
Mar. 9	AC-Delco Classic	Tom Baker*	48,000	278-247	Bob Learn Jr.
Mar. 16	Showboat Invitational	W.R. Williams Jr.	37,000	258-257	Brian LeClair
Mar. 23	Quaker State 250	Steve Wilson*	48,000	220-155	Jimmy Keeth
Mar. 30	Comfort Inn Classic	Steve Hoskins*	50,000†	250-202	Brian Voss
Apr. 6	Flagship Open	Bob Learn Jr.	30,000%	279-257	Randy Pedersen
Apr. 13	Johnny Petraglia Open	W.R. Williams Jr.	34,000	216-195	Steve Jaros
Apr. 20	Bud Light Championship	Philip Ringener*	40,000	226-224	Joe Firpo
Apr. 27	**Tournament of Champions**	Dave D'Entremont	60,000&	215-202	Dave Arnold
May 4	**ABC Masters**	Ernie Schlegel	50,600	236-200	Mike Aulby
May 18	IOF Foresters Open	David Traber	45,000	242-201	Jess Stayrook
May 25	Greater Baltimore Open	Mike Aulby*	19,000	248-237	W.R. Williams Jr.
June 1	Greater Hartford Open	Dennis Horan*	19,000	204-193	C.K. Moore
June 8	**PBA National Championship**	Butch Soper	30,000	226-210	W.R. Williams Jr.
June 15	Greater Detroit Open	Doug Kent	19,000	227-217	Jeff Zaffino
June 22	Kingpin Classic	Jess Stayrook*	27,000	228-214	Butch Soper

Note: The American Bowling Congress Masters tournament is not a PBA Tour event.
\# Does not include $25,000 bonus Moore received for rolling a 300 game on national television.
† In the "Winning Never Gets Old" Challenge match, PBA Senior Tour representative John Handegard defeated Hoskins 180–175, for a bonus of $25,000.
% Does not include $100,000 bonus Learn received for rolling a 300 game on national television.
& Does not include a $12,000 boat backage awarded as a bonus.

Higher Learning

On April 6 in front of a soldout hometown crowd in Erie, Pa., Bob Learn Jr. came closer to perfection than anyone in the history of the PBA. Learn began the ABC-televised Flagship Open with his world-record tying 52nd sanctioned perfect game, a 300-279 victory over legendary kegler Johnny Petraglia that earned him a bonus of $100,000. He went on to strike 44 times in four games, compiling three and four-game totals of 850 and 1,129, easily breaking the previous TV marks of 815 and 1,070.

SENIOR PBA

1996 Spring/Summer Tour

Final	Event	Winner	Earnings	Score	Runner-up
Mar. 15	Greater Albany Senior Open	John Handegard*	$8,000	196-188	Ron Winger
Apr. 25	Ladies and Legends	Mike Kench/ Liz Johnson	15,000	253-215	Pete Couture/ Carolyn Dorin
July 4	Seattle Senior Open	Hobo Boothe*	9,000	225-200	Earl Anthony
July 12	Northwest Senior Classic	Gary Mage*	9,000	258-256	John Handegard
July 18	Tri-Cities Senior Open	Gary Dickinson	9,000	267-258	Bruce Forsland
Aug. 3	Showboat Senior Invitational	John Denton	20,000	213-212	Earl Anthony
Aug. 9	Reno Senior Open	Pete Couture	8,500	244-204	Roger Tramp
Aug. 17	**ABC Senior Masters**	Dave Davis	60,000	236-182	John Hatz
Aug. 23	Pontiac Osteopathic Hospital Open	Gary Dickinson*	10,000	212-207	Bobby Knipple
Aug. 31	**PBA Senior Championship**	Dale Eagle	16,000	213-194	Roy Buckley
Sept. 21	St. Petersburg/Clearwater Senior Open	Jim Brenner	10,000	204-173	Teata Semiz
Sept. 26	Naples Senior Open	Earl Anthony	10,000	217-211	Barry Gurney

LPBT

Late 1995 Fall Tour

Final	Event	Winner	Earnings	Score	Runner-up
Nov. 2	Lady Ebonite Classic	Aleta Sill	$12,000	233-225	Tish Johnson
Nov. 9	Hammer Players Championship	Anne Marie Duggan	16,000	238-216	Kim Adler
Nov. 18	**Sam's Town Invitational**	Michelle Mullen*	18,000	202-189	Cheryl Daniels
Dec. 10	Merit Mixed Doubles Championship	Kim Canady/ Butch Soper	40,000	15,844-15,812†	Robin Romeo/ Eric Forkel

†Scoring in the Merit Mixed Doubles is based on total pins.

1996 Winter Tour

Final	Event	Winner	Earnings	Score	Runner-up
Feb. 8	Greater Terre Haute Open	Jackie Sellers	$10,000	214-201	Darris Street
Feb. 15	Claremore Classic	Cindy Coburn-Carroll	9,000	201-199	Tish Johnson
Feb. 22	Lubbock Open	Leanne Barrette	9,000	180-176	Cheryl Daniels
Feb. 29	Treasure Chest Classic	Sandra Jo Shiery*	10,000	227-214	Debbie McMullen
Mar. 7	South Texas Open	Dana Miller-Mackie*	9,000	246-233	Tish Johnson
Mar. 14	Texas Border Shoot-Out	Wendy Macpherson*	9,000	191-189	Jackie Sellers

1996 Spring/Summer Tour

Final	Event	Winner	Earnings	Score	Runner-up
Apr. 25	Ladies & Legends	Liz Johnson/ Mike Kench	$15,000	253-215	Carolyn Dorin/ Pete Couture
May 1	Storm Doubles	Laura Moriarty/ Tammy Turner*	14,000	247-225	Aleta Sill/ Jodi Woessner
May 9	Omaha Lancers Open	Tammy Turner	11,000	238-197	Wendy Macpherson
May 18	**WIBC Queens**	Lisa Wagner	12,675	231-226	Tammy Turner
July 18	Greater Little Rock Classic	Wendy Macpherson	9,000	180-158	Marianne DiRupo
July 25	Greater Charleston Open	Aleta Sill	9,000	257-207	Tammy Turner
Aug. 1	Franklin Virginia Open	Jackie Sellers*	9,000	266-246	Marianne DiRupo

Note: The Women's International Bowling Congress Queens tournament is not an LPBT Tour event.

1996 Fall Tour Schedules

PBA

Events (8): Japan Cup in Tokyo (Sept. 19–22); **BPAA U.S. Open** (Sept. 28-Oct. 4); Cleveland Open (Oct. 5–9); Ebonite Classic (Oct. 11–15); Rochester Open (Oct. 19–23); Touring Pro/Senior Doubles (Oct. 26–30); Greater Harrisburg Open (Nov. 2–6); Touring Players Championship (Nov. 8–12).

SENIOR PBA

Events (1): Senior/Touring Pro Doubles (Oct. 26–30).

LPBT

Events (8): Rossford Golden Triangle Open (Sept. 22–26); **BPAA U.S. Open** (Sept. 27-Oct. 4); Brunswick Three Rivers Open (Oct. 5–10); Columbia 300 Delaware Open (Oct 12–17); Baltimore Eastern Open (Oct. 19–24); Lady Ebonite Classic (Oct. 26–31); Hammer Players Championship (Nov. 2–7); **Sam's Town Invitational** (Nov. 10–17).

Tour Leaders

Official standings for 1995 and unofficial standings (through Sept. 23) for 1996. Note that (TB) indicates Tournaments Bowled; (CR) Championship Rounds as Stepladder Finalist; and (1st) Titles Won.

Final 1995

PBA

Top 10 Money Winners

		TB	CR	1st	Earnings
1	Mike Aulby	27	6	1	$219,792
2	Dave D'Entremont	30	9	2	185,245
3	W.R. Williams Jr.	26	8	1	153,170
4	Jess Stayrook	29	5	2	137,330
5	David Ozio	24	5	1	124,105
6	Mark Williams	29	5	0	123,612
7	Parker Bohn III	29	6	1	114,357
8	Amleto Monacelli	24	3	1	112,315
9	Dave Husted	14	2	2	112,015
10	Norm Duke	25	6	2	111,080

Top 10 Averages

		Gm	Pins	Avg
1	Mike Aulby	928	209,257	225.49
2	W.R. Williams Jr.	937	209,551	223.64
3	Norm Duke	831	185,014	222.64
4	Mark Williams	1017	222,250	221.48
5	Parker Bohn III	999	221,019	221.24
6	Dave D'Entremont	1003	221,818	221.15
7	Brian Voss	717	158,145	220.56
8	Bryan Goebel	864	190,485	220.47
9	Amleto Monacelli	745	164,055	220.20
10	David Ozio	742	163,380	220.19

SENIOR PBA

Top 5 Money Winners

		TB	CR	1st	Earnings
1	John Handegard	12	7	1	$63,133
2	Dave Davis	9	2	1	52,600
3	Tommy Evans	11	5	3	48,016
4	Pete Couture	10	4	0	39,875
5	Avery Le Blanc	11	3	0	39,155

Top 5 Averages

		Gm	Pins	Avg
1	Tommy Evans	400	90,000	225.00
2	John Handegard	492	109,387	222.33
3	Pete Couture	443	98,390	222.09
4	Larry Laub	441	97,840	221.86
5	Gary Dickinson	476	104,506	219.55

LPBT

Top 10 Money Winners

		TB	CR	1st	Earnings
1	Tish Johnson	22	9	2	$123,440
2	Anne Marie Duggan	22	8	2	116,847
3	Cheryl Daniels	22	9	2	112,335
4	Kim Adler	22	9	2	96,291
5	Aleta Sill	22	5	2	80,931
6	Kim Canady	22	5	2	77,111
7	Carolyn Dorin	22	7	0	74,307
8	Sandra Jo Shiery	22	6	2	70,202
9	Robin Romeo	18	5	2	69,735
10	Michelle Mullen	21	3	1	67,238

Top 5 Averages

		Gm	Pins	Avg
1	Anne Marie Duggan	787	169,827	215.79
2	Tish Johnson	836	179,957	215.26
3	Cheryl Daniels	762	162,862	213.73
4	Carol Norman	829	176,917	213.41
5	Wendy Macpherson	567	120,198	211.99

1996 (through Sept. 23)

PBA

Top 10 Money Winners

		TB	CR	1st	Earnings
1	Bob Learn Jr.	19	3	1	$199,197
2	W.R. Williams Jr.	19	6	3	159,480
3	Steve Wilson	21	2	2	126,270
4	Dave D'Entremont	21	3	1	113,200
5	David Traber	21	2	1	101,077
6	Tom Baker	20	2	1	91,947
7	Danny Wiseman	19	5	0	90,927
8	Butch Soper	20	4	1	84,237
9	Jess Stayrook	19	2	1	74,312
10	Brian Voss	16	3	1	74,302

Top 10 Averages

		Gm	Pins	Avg
1	W.R. Williams Jr.	739	166,918	225.87
2	Norm Duke	470	104,913	223.22
3	Parker Bohn III	620	138,105	222.75
4	Butch Soper	571	126,922	222.28
5	Dave Husted	357	79,311	222.16
6	Brian Voss	495	109,944	222.11
7	Bob Learn Jr.	614	136,302	221.99
8	Steve Wilson	612	135,521	221.44
9	Randy Pedersen	519	114,808	221.21
10	Dave Arnold	465	102,816	221.11

SENIOR PBA

Top 5 Money Winners

		TB	CR	1st	Earnings
1	Dave Davis	6	1	1	$63,358
2	Earl Anthony	8	5	1	35,810
3	John Hatz	2	1	0	31,000
4	Teata Semiz	11	4	0	30,802
5	Dale Eagle	9	3	1	30,780

Top 5 Averages

		Gm	Pins	Avg
1	Earl Anthony	306	69,447	226.95
2	Teata Semiz	420	94,130	224.12
3	John Handegard	440	98,437	223.72
4	Pete Couture	428	95,050	222.08
5	Dale Eagle	348	77,194	221.82

LPBT

Top 10 Money Winners

		TB	CR	1st	Earnings
1	Tammy Turner	13	5	2	$66,255
2	Wendy Macpherson	13	4	2	59,705
3	Sandra Jo Shiery	13	5	1	49,405
4	Jackie Sellers	11	3	2	46,580
5	Aleta Sill	12	4	1	42,850
6	Carolyn Dorin-Ballard	13	3	0	36,830
7	Lisa Wagner	10	2	1	36,680
8	Tish Johnson	12	2	0	35,895
9	Anne Marie Duggan	11	4	0	35,765
10	Leanne Barrette	11	3	1	33,890

Top 5 Averages

		Gm	Pins	Avg
1	Carolyn Dorin-Ballard	408	89,323	218.93
2	Wendy Macpherson	462	100,739	218.05
3	Aleta Sill	361	78,514	217.49
4	Cathy Dorin	279	60,655	217.40
5	Sandra Jo Shiery	410	89,015	217.11

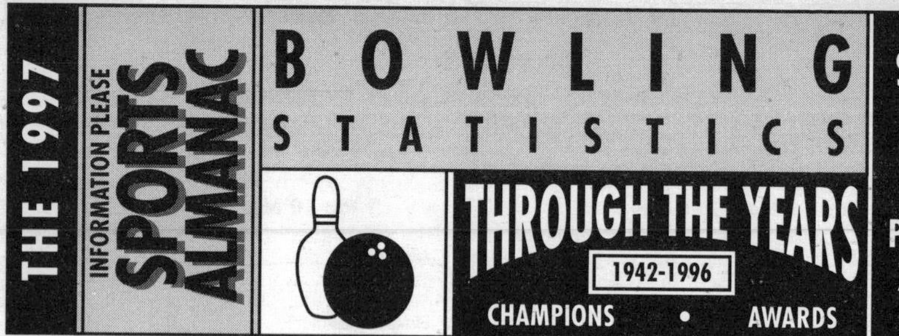

Major Championships

MEN

BPAA U.S. Open

Started in 1941 by the Bowling Proprietors' Association of America, 18 years before the founding of the Professional Bowlers Association. Originally the BPAA All-Star Tournament, it became the U.S. Open in 1971. There were two BPAA All-Star tournaments in 1955, in January and December.

Multiple winners: Don Carter and Dick Weber (4); Dave Husted (3); Del Ballard, Jr., Marshall Holman, Junie McMahon, Connie Schwoegler, Andy Varipapa and Pete Weber (2).

Year		Year		Year		Year	
1942	John Crimmons	1956	Bill Lillard	1970	Bobby Cooper	1984	Mark Roth
1943	Connie Schwoegler	1957	Don Carter	1971	Mike Limongello	1985	Marshall Holman
1944	Ned Day	1958	Don Carter	1972	Don Johnson	1986	Steve Cook
1945	Buddy Bomar	1959	Billy Welu	1973	Mike McGrath	1987	Del Ballard Jr.
1946	Joe Wilman	1960	Harry Smith	1974	Larry Laub	1988	Pete Weber
1947	Andy Varipapa	1961	Bill Tucker	1975	Steve Neff	1989	Mike Aulby
1948	Andy Varipapa	1962	Dick Weber	1976	Paul Moser	1990	Ron Palombi Jr.
1949	Connie Schwoegler	1963	Dick Weber	1977	Johnny Petraglia	1991	Pete Weber
1950	Junie McMahon	1964	Bob Strampe	1978	Nelson Burton Jr.	1992	Robert Lawrence
1951	Dick Hoover	1965	Dick Weber	1979	Joe Berardi	1993	Del Ballard Jr.
1952	Junie McMahon	1966	Dick Weber	1980	Steve Martin	1994	Justin Hromek
1953	Don Carter	1967	Les Schissler	1981	Marshall Holman	1995	Dave Husted
1954	Don Carter	1968	Jim Stefanich	1982	Dave Husted	1996	Dave Husted
1955	Steve Nagy	1969	Billy Hardwick	1983	Gary Dickinson		

PBA National Championship

The Professional Bowlers Association was formed in 1958 and its first national championship tournament was held in Memphis in 1960. The tournament has been held in Toledo, Ohio, since 1981.

Multiple winners: Earl Anthony (6); Mike Aulby, Dave Davis, Mike McGrath and Wayne Zahn (2).

Year		Year		Year		Year	
1960	Don Carter	1970	Mike McGrath	1980	Johnny Petraglia	1990	Jim Pencak
1961	Dave Soutar	1971	Mike Limongello	1981	Earl Anthony	1991	Mike Miller
1962	Carmen Salvino	1972	Johnny Guenther	1982	Earl Anthony	1992	Eric Forkel
1963	Billy Hardwick	1973	Earl Anthony	1983	Earl Anthony	1993	Ron Palombi Jr.
1964	Bob Strampe	1974	Earl Anthony	1984	Bob Chamberlain	1994	David Traber
1965	Dave Davis	1975	Earl Anthony	1985	Mike Aulby	1995	Scott Alexander
1966	Wayne Zahn	1976	Paul Colwell	1986	Tom Crites	1996	Butch Soper
1967	Dave Davis	1977	Tommy Hudson	1987	Randy Pedersen		
1968	Wayne Zahn	1978	Warren Nelson	1988	Brian Voss		
1969	Mike McGrath	1979	Mike Aulby	1989	Pete Weber		

Brunswick World Tournament of Champions

Originally the Firestone Tournament of Champions (1965-93), the tournament has also been sponsored by General Tire (1994) and Brunswick Corp. (since 1995). Held annually in Akron, Ohio from 1965-94, the T of C was moved to suburban Chicago in 1995.

Multiple winners: Mike Durbin (3); Earl Anthony, Jim Godman, Marshall Holman and Mark Williams (2).

Year		Year		Year		Year	
1965	Billy Hardwick	1973	Jim Godman	1981	Steve Cook	1990	Dave Ferraro
1966	Wayne Zahn	1974	Earl Anthony	1982	Mike Durbin	1991	David Ozio
1967	Jim Stefanich	1975	Dave Davis	1983	Joe Berardi	1992	Marc McDowell
1968	Dave Davis	1976	Marshall Holman	1984	Mike Durbin	1993	George Branham III
1969	Jim Godman	1977	Mike Berlin	1985	Mark Williams	1994	Norm Duke
1970	Don Johnson	1978	Earl Anthony	1986	Marshall Holman	1995	Mike Aulby
1971	Johnny Petraglia	1979	George Pappas	1987	Pete Weber	1996	Dave D'Entremont
1972	Mike Durbin	1980	Wayne Webb	1988	Mark Williams		
				1989	Del Ballard Jr.		

ABC Masters Tournament

Sponsored by the American Bowling Congress. The Masters is not a PBA event, but is considered one of the four major tournaments on the men's tour and is open to qualified pros and amateurs.

Multiple winners: Earl Anthony, Mike Aulby, Billy Golembiewski, Dick Hoover and Billy Welu (2).

Year		Year		Year		Year	
1951	Lee Jouglard	1963	Harry Smith	1975	Eddie Ressler	1987	Rick Steelsmith
1952	Willard Taylor	1964	Billy Welu	1976	Nelson Burton Jr.	1988	Del Ballard Jr.
1953	Rudy Habetler	1965	Billy Welu	1977	Earl Anthony	1989	Mike Aulby
1954	Red Elkins	1966	Bob Strampe	1978	Frank Ellenburg	1990	Chris Warren
1955	Buzz Fazio	1967	Lou Scalia	1979	Doug Myers	1991	Doug Kent
1956	Dick Hoover	1968	Pete Tountas	1980	Neil Burton	1992	Ken Johnson
1957	Dick Hoover	1969	Jim Chestney	1981	Randy Lightfoot	1993	Norm Duke
1958	Tom Hennessey	1970	Don Glover	1982	Joe Berardi	1994	Steve Fehr
1959	Ray Bluth	1971	Jim Godman	1983	Mike Lastowski	1995	Mike Aulby
1960	Billy Golembiewski	1972	Bill Beach	1984	Earl Anthony	1996	Ernie Schlegel
1961	Don Carter	1973	Dave Soutar	1985	Steve Wunderlich		
1962	Billy Golembiewski	1974	Paul Colwell	1986	Mark Fahy		

WOMEN

BPAA U.S. Open

Started by the Bowling Proprietors' Association of America in 1949, 11 years before the founding of the Professional Women's Bowling Association. Originally the BPAA Women's All-Star Tournament, it became the U.S. Open in 1971. There were two BPAA All-Star tournaments in 1955, in January and December. Note that (a) indicates amateur.

Multiple winners: Marion Ladewig (8); Donna Adamek, Paula Sperber Carter, Pat Costello, Dotty Fothergill, Dana Miller-Mackie and Sylvia Wene (2).

Year		Year		Year		Year	
1949	Marion Ladewig	1961	Phyllis Notaro	1974	Pat Costello	1987	Carol Norman
1950	Marion Ladewig	1962	Shirley Garms	1975	Paula Sperber Carter	1988	Lisa Wagner
1951	Marion Ladewig	1963	Marion Ladewig	1976	Patty Costello	1989	Robin Romeo
1952	Marion Ladewig	1964	LaVerne Carter	1977	Betty Morris	1990	Dana Miller-Mackie
1953	Not held	1965	Ann Slattery	1978	Donna Adamek	1991	Anne Marie Duggan
1954	Marion Ladewig	1966	Joy Abel	1979	Diana Silva	1992	Tish Johnson
1955	Sylvia Wene	1967	Gloria Simon	1980	Pat Costello	1993	Dede Davidson
1955	Anita Cantaline	1968	Dotty Fothergill	1981	Donna Adamek	1994	Aleta Sill
1956	Marion Ladewig	1969	Dotty Fothergill	1982	Shinobu Saitoh	1995	Cheryl Daniels
1957	Not held	1970	Mary Baker	1983	Dana Miller	1996	Liz Johnson
1958	Merle Matthews	1971	a-Paula Sperber	1984	Karen Ellingsworth		
1959	Marion Ladewig	1972	a-Lorrie Koch	1985	Pat Mercatanti		
1960	Sylvia Wene	1973	Millie Martorella	1986	Wendy Macpherson		

WIBC Queens

Sponsored by the Women's International Bowling Congress, the Queens is a double elimination, match play tournament. It is not an LPBT event, but is open to qualified pros and amateurs. Note that (a) indicates amateur.

Multiple winners: Millie Martorella (3); Donna Adamek, Dotty Fothergill, Aleta Sill and Katsuko Sugimoto (2).

Year		Year		Year		Year	
1961	Janet Harman	1970	Millie Martorella	1980	Donna Adamek	1990	a-Patty Ann
1962	Dorothy Wilkinson	1971	Millie Martorella	1981	Katsuko Sugimoto	1991	Dede Davidson
1963	Irene Monterosso	1972	Dotty Fothergill	1982	Katsuko Sugimoto	1992	Cindy Coburn-Carroll
1964	D.D. Jacobson	1973	Dotty Fothergill	1983	Aleta Sill	1993	Jan Schmidt
1965	Betty Kuczynski	1974	Judy Soutar	1984	Kazue Inahashi	1994	Anne Marie Duggan
1966	Judy Lee	1975	Cindy Powell	1985	Aleta Sill	1995	Sandra Postma
1967	Millie Martorella	1976	Pam Rutherford	1986	Cora Fiebig	1996	Lisa Wagner
1968	Phyllis Massey	1977	Dana Stewart	1987	Cathy Almeida		
1969	Ann Feigel	1978	Loa Boxberger	1988	Wendy Macpherson		
		1979	Donna Adamek	1989	Carol Gianotti		

Sam's Town Invitational

Originally held in Milwaukee as the Pabst Tournament of Champions, but discontinued after one year (1981). The event was revived in 1984, moved to Las Vegas and renamed the Sam's Town Tournament of Champions. Since then it has been known as the LPBT Tournament of Champions (1985), the Sam's Town National Pro/Am (1986-88) and the Sam's Town Invitational (since 1989).

Multiple winners: Tish Johnson (3); Aleta Sill (2).

Year		Year		Year		Year	
1981	Cindy Coburn	1986	Aleta Sill	1990	Wendy Macpherson	1994	Tish Johnson
1982-83	Not held	1987	Debbie Bennett	1991	Lorrie Nichols	1995	Michelle Mullen
1984	Aleta Sill	1988	Donna Adamek	1992	Tish Johnson	1996	ends Nov. 17
1985	Patty Costello	1989	Tish Johnson	1993	Robin Romeo		

Major Championships (Cont.)

WOMEN

WPBA National Championship (1960-1980)

The Women's Professional Bowling Association National Championship tournament was discontinued when the WPBA broke up in 1981. The WPBA changed its name from the Professional Women Bowlers Association (PWBA) in 1978.

Multiple winners: Patty Costello (3); Dotty Fothergill (2).

Year		Year		Year		Year	
1960	Marion Ladewig	1966	Judy Lee	1971	Patty Costello	1976	Patty Costello
1961	Shirley Garms	1967	Betty Mivelaz	1972	Patty Costello	1977	Vesma Grinfelds
1962	Stephanie Balogh	1968	Dotty Fothergill	1973	Betty Morris	1978	Toni Gillard
1963	Janet Harman	1969	Dotty Fothergill	1974	Pat Costello	1979	Cindy Coburn
1964	Betty Kuczynski	1970	Bobbe North	1975	Pam Buckner	1980	Donna Adamek
1965	Helen Duval						

Annual Leaders

Average

PBA Tour

The George Young Memorial Award, named after the late ABC Hall of Fame bowler. Based on at least 16 national PBA tournaments from 1959-78, and at least 400 games of tour competition since 1979.

Multiple winners: Mark Roth (6); Earl Anthony (5); Marshall Holman (3); Norm Duke, Billy Hardwick, Don Johnson and Wayne Zahn (2).

Year		Avg	Year		Avg	Year		Avg
1962	Don Carter	212.84	1974	Earl Anthony	219.34	1986	John Gant	214.38
1963	Bill Hardwick	210.35	1975	Earl Anthony	219.06	1987	Marshall Holman	216.80
1964	Ray Bluth	210.51	1976	Mark Roth	215.97	1988	Mark Roth	218.04
1965	Dick Weber	211.90	1977	Mark Roth	218.17	1989	Pete Weber	215.43
1966	Wayne Zahn	208.63	1978	Mark Roth	219.83	1990	Amleto Monacelli	218.16
1967	Wayne Zahn	212.14	1979	Mark Roth	221.66	1991	Norm Duke	218.21
1968	Jim Stefanich	211.90	1980	Earl Anthony	218.54	1992	Dave Ferraro	219.70
1969	Billy Hardwick	212.96	1981	Mark Roth	216.70	1993	Walter R. Williams Jr.	222.98
1970	Nelson Burton Jr	214.91	1982	Marshall Holman	216.15	1994	Norm Duke	222.83
1971	Don Johnson	213.98	1983	Earl Anthony	216.65	1995	Mike Aulby	225.49
1972	Don Johnson	215.29	1984	Marshall Holman	213.91			
1973	Earl Anthony	215.80	1985	Mark Baker	213.72			

LPBT Tour

Based on at least 282 games of tour competition.

Multiple winners: Leanne Barrette, Nikki Gianulias and Lisa Rathgeber Wagner (3); Anne Marie Duggan and Aleta Sill (2).

Year		Avg	Year		Avg	Year		Avg
1981	Nikki Gianulias	213.71	1986	Nikki Gianulias	213.89	1991	Leanne Barrette	211.48
1982	Nikki Gianulias	210.63	1987	Wendy Macpherson	211.11	1992	Leanne Barrette	211.36
1983	Lisa Rathgeber	208.50	1988	Lisa Wagner	213.02	1993	Tish Johnson	215.39
1984	Aleta Sill	210.68	1989	Lisa Wagner	211.87	1994	Anne Marie Duggan	213.47
1985	Aleta Sill	211.10	1990	Leanne Barrette	211.53	1995	Anne Marie Duggan	215.79

Money Won

PBA Tour

Multiple winners: Earl Anthony (6); Dick Weber and Mark Roth (4); Mike Aulby (3); Don Carter and Walter Ray Williams Jr. (2).

Year		Earnings	Year		Earnings	Year		Earnings
1959	Dick Weber	$ 7,672	1972	Don Johnson	$56,648	1985	Mike Aulby	$201,200
1960	Don Carter	22,525	1973	Don McCune	69,000	1986	W.R. Williams Jr.	145,550
1961	Dick Weber	26,280	1974	Earl Anthony	99,585	1987	Pete Weber	179,516
1962	Don Carter	49,972	1975	Earl Anthony	107,585	1988	Brian Voss	225,485
1963	Dick Weber	46,333	1976	Earl Anthony	110,833	1989	Mike Aulby	298,237
1964	Bob Strampe	33,592	1977	Mark Roth	105,583	1990	Amleto Monacelli	204,775
1965	Dick Weber	47,675	1978	Mark Roth	134,500	1991	David Ozio	225,585
1966	Wayne Zahn	54,720	1979	Mark Roth	124,517	1992	Marc McDowell	176,215
1967	Dave Davis	54,165	1980	Wayne Webb	116,700	1993	W.R. Williams Jr	296,370
1968	Jim Stefanich	67,375	1981	Earl Anthony	164,735	1994	Norm Duke	273,753
1969	Billy Hardwick	64,160	1982	Earl Anthony	134,760	1995	Mike Aulby	219,792
1970	Mike McGrath	52,049	1983	Earl Anthony	135,605			
1971	Johnny Petraglia	85,065	1984	Mark Roth	158,712			

WPBA and LPBT Tours

WPBA leaders through 1980; LPBT leaders since 1981.

Multiple winners: Aleta Sill (5); Donna Adamek (4); Patty Costello, Tish Johnson and Betty Morris (3); Dotty Fothergill, and Aleta Sill (2).

Year		Earnings
1965	Betty Kuczynski	$ 3,792
1966	Joy Abel	5,795
1967	Shirley Garms	4,920
1968	Dotty Fothergill	16,170
1969	Dotty Fothergill	9,220
1970	Patty Costello	9,317
1971	Vesma Grinfelds	4,925
1972	Patty Costello	11,350
1973	Judy Cook	11,200
1974	Betty Morris	30,037
1975	Judy Soutar	20,395
1976	Patty Costello	$ 39,585
1977	Betty Morris	23,802
1978	Donna Adamek	31,000
1979	Donna Adamek	26,280
1980	Donna Adamek	31,907
1981	Donna Adamek	41,270
1982	Nikki Gianulias	45,875
1983	Aleta Sill	42,525
1984	Aleta Sill	81,452
1985	Aleta Sill	52,655
1986	Aleta Sill	36,962
1987	Betty Morris	$ 63,735
1988	Lisa Wagner	105,500
1989	Robin Romeo	113,750
1990	Tish Johnson	94,420
1991	Leanne Barrette	87,618
1992	Tish Johnson	96,872
1993	Aleta Sill	57,995
1994	Aleta Sill	126,325
1995	Tish Johnson	123,440

All-Time Leaders

All-time leading money winners on the PBA and LPBT tours, through 1995. PBA figures date back to 1959, while LPBT figures include Women's Pro Bowlers Association (WPBA) earnings through 1980. National tour titles are also listed.

Money Won

PBA Top 20

		Titles	Earnings
1	Pete Weber	26	$1,746,041
2	Mike Aulby	23	1,656,805
3	Marshall Holman	21	1,655,265
4	Walter Ray Williams Jr.	16	1,590,829
5	Mark Roth	34	1,484,948
6	Amleto Monacelli	16	1,429,991
7	Brian Voss	15	1,398,082
8	Earl Anthony	41	1,361,931
9	Dave Husted	12	1,349,571
10	Wayne Webb	17	1,138,766
11	David Ozio	11	1,127,074
12	Norm Duke	11	1,084,486
13	Parker Bohn III	11	1,080,730
14	Del Ballard Jr.	12	1,048,747
15	Dave Ferraro	9	1,034,176
16	Gary Dickinson	8	1,011,192
17	Mark Williams	6	932,684
18	Dick Weber	26	904,461
19	Tom Baker	7	856,643
20	Johnny Petraglia	14	835,548

WPBA-LPBT Top 12

		Titles	Earnings
1	Aleta Sill	25	$737,862
2	Tish Johnson	21	721,886
3	Lisa Wagner	29	624,043
4	Robin Romeo	16	582,274
5	Anne Marie Duggan	13	530,776
6	Nikki Gianulias	18	505,820
7	Leanne Barrette	15	496,423
8	Donna Adamek	19	473,984
9	Cheryl Daniels	9	467,704
10	Lorrie Nichols	15	462,266
11	Jeanne Naccarato	9	415,322
12	Cindy Coburn-Carroll	14	409,101

Senior PBA Top 5

		Titles	Earnings
1	John Handegard	11	$327,195
2	Gene Stus	6	255,695
3	Teata Semiz	7	246,537
4	John Hricsina	5	222,839
5	Dick Weber	6	209,599

Annual Awards

MEN

BWAA Bowler of the Year

Winners selected by Bowling Writers Association of America.

Multiple winners: Earl Anthony and Don Carter (6); Mark Roth (4); Mike Aulby and Dick Weber (3); Buddy Bomar, Ned Day, Billy Hardwick, Don Johnson, Steve Nagy and Walter Ray Williams Jr. (2).

Year	
1942	Johnny Crimmins
1943	Ned Day
1944	Ned Day
1945	Buddy Bomar
1946	Joe Wilman
1947	Buddy Bomar
1948	Andy Varipapa
1949	Connie Schwoegler
1950	Junie McMahon
1951	Lee Jouglard
1952	Steve Nagy
1953	Don Carter
1954	Don Carter
1955	Steve Nagy
1956	Bill Lillard
1957	Don Carter
1958	Don Carter
1959	Ed Lubanski
1960	Don Carter
1961	Dick Weber
1962	Don Carter
1963	Dick Weber
1964	Billy Hardwick
1965	Dick Weber
1966	Wayne Zahn
1967	Dave Davis
1968	Jim Stefanich
1969	Billy Hardwick
1970	Nelson Burton Jr.
1971	Don Johnson
1972	Don Johnson
1973	Don McCune
1974	Earl Anthony
1975	Earl Anthony
1976	Earl Anthony
1977	Mark Roth
1978	Mark Roth
1979	Mark Roth
1980	Wayne Webb
1981	Earl Anthony
1982	Earl Anthony
1983	Earl Anthony
1984	Mark Roth
1985	Mike Aulby
1986	Walter Ray Williams Jr.
1987	Marshall Holman
1988	Brian Voss
1989	Mike Aulby
1990	Amleto Monacelli
1991	David Ozio
1992	Marc McDowell
1993	Walter Ray Williams Jr.
1994	Norm Duke
1995	Mike Aulby

Annual Awards (Cont.)

MEN

PBA Player of the Year

Winners selected by members of Professional Bowlers Association. The PBA Player of the Year has differed from the BWAA Bowler of the Year four times—in 1963, '64, '89 and '92.

Multiple winners: Earl Anthony (6); Mark Roth (4); Mike Aulby, Billy Hardwick, Don Johnson, Amleto Monacelli and Walter Ray Williams Jr. (2).

Year		Year		Year		Year	
1963	Billy Hardwick	1972	Don Johnson	1981	Earl Anthony	1990	Amleto Monacelli
1964	Bob Strampe	1973	Don McCune	1982	Earl Anthony	1991	David Ozio
1965	Dick Weber	1974	Earl Anthony	1983	Earl Anthony	1992	Dave Ferraro
1966	Wayne Zahn	1975	Earl Anthony	1984	Mark Roth	1993	Walter Ray Williams Jr.
1967	Dave Davis	1976	Earl Anthony	1985	Mike Aulby	1994	Norm Duke
1968	Jim Stefanich	1977	Mark Roth	1986	Walter Ray Williams Jr.	1995	Mike Aulby
1969	Billy Hardwick	1978	Mark Roth	1987	Marshall Holman		
1970	Nelson Burton Jr.	1979	Mark Roth	1988	Brian Voss		
1971	Don Johnson	1980	Wayne Webb	1989	Amleto Monacelli		

PBA Rookie of the Year

Winners selected by members of Professional Bowlers Association.

Year		Year		Year		Year	
1964	Jerry McCoy	1972	Tommy Hudson	1980	Pete Weber	1988	Rick Steelsmith
1965	Jim Godman	1973	Steve Neff	1981	Mark Fahy	1989	Steve Hoskins
1966	Bobby Cooper	1974	Cliff McNealy	1982	Mike Steinbach	1990	Brad Kiszewski
1967	Mike Durbin	1975	Guy Rowbury	1983	Toby Contreras	1991	Ricky Ward
1968	Bob McGregor	1976	Mike Berlin	1984	John Gant	1992	Jason Couch
1969	Larry Lichstein	1977	Steve Martin	1985	Tom Crites	1993	Mark Scroggins
1970	Denny Krick	1978	Joseph Groskind	1986	Marc McDowell	1994	Tony Ament
1971	Tye Critchlow	1979	Mike Aulby	1987	Ryan Shafer	1995	Billy Myers Jr.

WOMEN

BWAA Bowler of the Year

Winners selected by Bowling Writers Association of America.

Multiple winners: Marion Ladewig (9); Donna Adamek and Lisa Rathgeber Wagner (4); Tish Johnson and Betty Morris (3); Patty Costello, Dotty Forthergill, Shirley Garms, Val Mikiel, Aleta Sill, Judy Soutar and Sylvia Wene (2).

Year		Year		Year		Year	
1948	Val Mikiel	1960	Sylvia Wene	1972	Patty Costello	1984	Aleta Sill
1949	Val Mikiel	1961	Shirley Garms	1973	Judy Soutar	1985	Aleta Sill
1950	Marion Ladewig	1962	Shirley Garms	1974	Betty Morris	1986	Lisa Wagner
1951	Marion Ladewig	1963	Marion Ladewig	1975	Judy Soutar	1987	Betty Morris
1952	Marion Ladewig	1964	LaVerne Carter	1976	Patty Costello	1988	Lisa Wagner
1953	Marion Ladewig	1965	Betty Kuczynski	1977	Betty Morris	1989	Robin Romeo
1954	Marion Ladewig	1966	Joy Abel	1978	Donna Adamek	1990	Tish Johnson
1955	Sylvia Wene	1967	Millie Martorella	1979	Donna Adamek	1991	Leanne Barrette
1956	Anita Cantaline	1968	Dotty Fothergill	1980	Donna Adamek	1992	Tish Johnson
1957	Marion Ladewig	1969	Dotty Fothergill	1981	Donna Adamek	1993	Lisa Wagner
1958	Marion Ladewig	1970	Mary Baker	1982	Nikki Gianulias	1994	Anne Marie Duggan
1959	Marion Ladewig	1971	Paula Sperber	1983	Lisa Rathgeber	1995	Tish Johnson

LPBT Player of the Year

Winners selected by members of Ladies Professional Bowlers Tour. The LPBT Player of the Year has differed from the BWAA Bowler of the Year three times—in 1985, '86 and '90.

Multiple winners: Lisa Rathgeber Wagner (3); Leanne Barrette and Tish Johnson (2).

Year		Year		Year		Year	
1983	Lisa Rathgeber	1987	Betty Morris	1991	Leanne Barrette	1995	Tish Johnson
1984	Aleta Sill	1988	Lisa Wagner	1992	Tish Johnson		
1985	Patty Costello	1989	Robin Romeo	1993	Lisa Wagner		
1986	Jeanne Maiden	1990	Leanne Barrette	1994	Anne Marie Duggan		

WPBA and LPBT Rookie of the Year

Winners selected by members of Women's Professional Bowlers Association (1978–80) and the Ladies Professional Bowlers Tour (since 1981).

Year		Year		Year		Year	
1978	Toni Gillard	1983	Anne Marie Pike	1988	Mary Martha Cerniglia	1993	Kathy Zielke
1979	Nikki Gianulias	1984	Paula Vidad	1989	Kim Terrell	1994	Tammy Turner
1980	Lisa Rathgeber	1985	Dede Davidson	1990	Debbie McMullen	1995	Krissy Stewart
1981	Cindy Mason	1986	Wendy Macpherson	1991	Kim Kahrman		
1982	Carol Norman	1987	Paula Drake	1992	Marianne DiRupo		

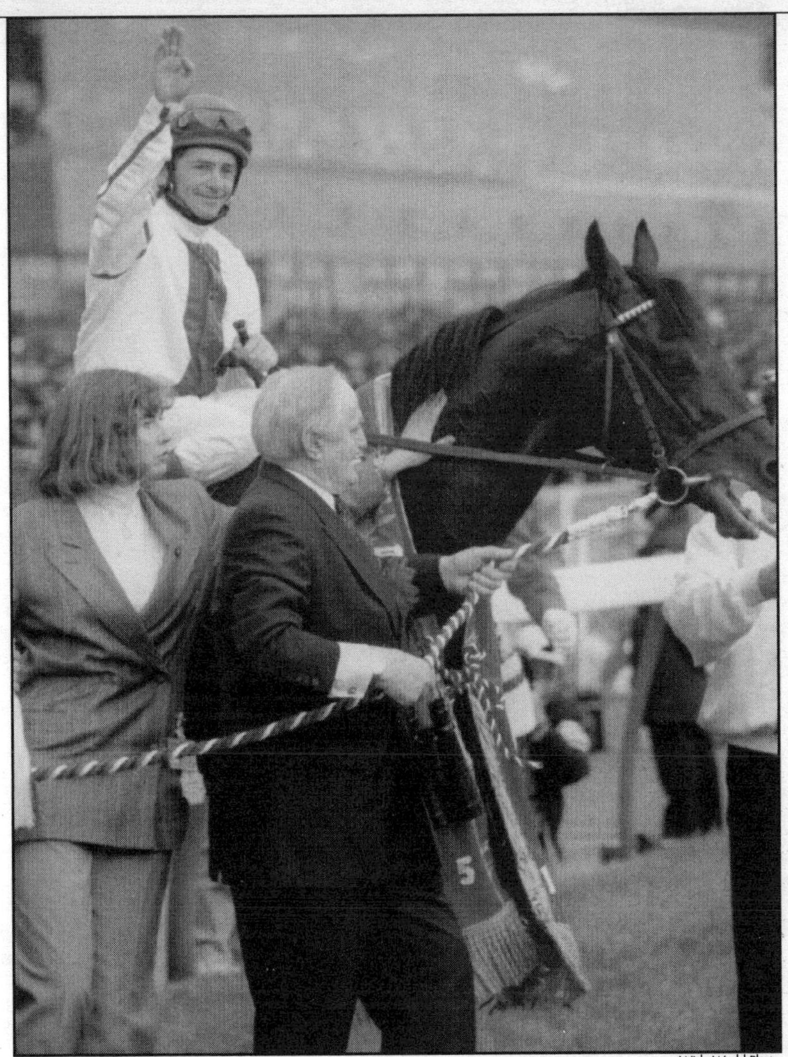

Wide World Photos

Michael Roberts, riding **Lando**, waves to fans after winning the 15th Japan Cup. With a purse of $3.9 million, the Cup is one of world's richest races, exceeded only by the new Dubai Cup whose total payout is $4 million.

HORSE RACING

by Sharon Smith

SMOKIN'

Cigar proved himself a horse for the ages by winning 16 straight races

People around the racetrack like to say that a great horse defines his times. While it sounds good, the saying is not entirely accurate. We mean instead that we remember eras by the great horses who raced during them. That's recognition enough for most horses. But in the case of Cigar, the hands-down best horse of the nineties, we all fervently wish that the original saying were true—that he really does define our times.

If Cigar were us, we could be very proud of ourselves and very optimistic about our future. Courage, determination, hard work, talent, and absolute consistency—no creature of any species could hope for more. The wins, the money, and the awards seem almost unimportant in comparison to the proof of quality.

On October 28, 1995, Cigar completed a perfect year with a win in the $3 million Breeders' Cup Classic at Belmont Park in New York. No surprise, and no trouble either—his 2-length margin of victory was the largest in Classic history. Even more extraordinary was the fact that Cigar had won his tenth straight race that year, a feat accomplished at six different racetracks. Not since the early 1950's has a handicap horse so dominated Thoroughbred racing's most difficult division, when Tom Fool was winning all the praise.

Sharon Smith has covered horse racing for ESPN, NBC and *Horse Illustrated* and is the author of *The Performance Mare* and

The surest sure thing in racing was that Cigar was going to be Horse of the Year for 1995, and indeed his name was announced on February 9, 1996 in San Diego. But he was already in Florida, preparing for his 1996 debut in the Donn Handicap at Gulfstream Park the following day. "Thank you for another year of Cigar," read the airplane sign commissioned by Gulfstream for the day of the race. It is unusual for a good horse, especially a stallion of excellent breeding, to remain in training at the age of six, and the thanks were well earned by owner Allen Paulson.

But, as usual, most thanks were owed to Cigar, whose win in the Donn was his 13th straight. It was accomplished over a good field that included the best mare then in training, Heavenly Prize. Her trainer Shug McGaughey said afterwards he had known she was probably racing for second money. Still, McGaughey said, "I was surprised by how easily he won."

They weren't all so easy. But such was the nature of Cigar's year that the harder they were, the more extraordinary the accomplishment. In March, having missed the Santa Anita Handicap with an injury, Cigar traveled 10,000 miles to Dubai for the inaugural $4-million Dubai World Cup. He pulled out a desperate half length win over fellow American Soul of the Matter for his 14th straight victory.

Soul of the Matter ran nearly as well as did Cigar on that March evening on the Arabian peninsula, but he was never to race again. Soul of the Matter was retired

World Wide Photos

Dare and Go pulls away from **Cigar** to win the Pacific Classic on August 10, 1996, ending Cigar's consecutive wins streak at 16. Citation is the only other horse to win 16 straight races.

in August with an ankle injury while preparing to challenge Cigar again.

Add sturdiness to Cigar's list of qualities. Although he took a few months off, he was able to stay sound for more travel and honor. In June, Cigar hit the highways of the Northeast for a trip to Boston and an easy win in the Massachusetts Handicap, in which he carried 130 pounds—a burden almost unheard of in modern racing.

The MassCap marked 15 straight victories at the highest level of American racing, and it also marked the moment that people realized that Cigar was no longer running against living horses. His competition now was a horse who raced nearly a half century ago.

From 1948 to 1950, the immortal Citation won 16 straight major races, a modern-day racing record. Cigar's next start would give him a chance to tie that record. Arlington International Racecourse in Chicago provided the opportunity, with the specially created Arlington Citation Challenge in July.

The track also provided an excellent field of competition, including a one-time Kentucky Derby favorite and other Grade I stakes horses. Cigar won by 3 lengths, his largest margin of the year, although he again carried 130 pounds. The streak now stood at 16, and the next win would break Citation's record.

"Records are made to be broken," said Jimmy Jones, Citation's 89-year-old trainer, a special guest at the race. But if there is one surer thing in racing than Cigar being Horse of the Year it's that a horse who starts often enough is going to lose eventually.

In August, Cigar flew to Del Mar in southern California for the Pacific Classic and his try for his 17th straight win. He faced a good field, but he also faced two other favorite sayings of racing people. "The only sure way to avoid a loss is to stay in the barn," says one. "Pace makes the race," says the other.

Cigar didn't stay in the barn, of course. He paraded to the post as the 1-9 favorite of the record crowd of 44,000. And he got

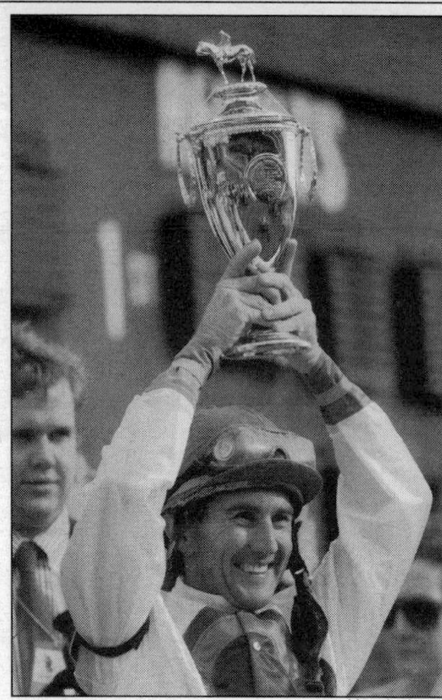

World Wide Photos

In addition to riding Cigar, **Jerry Bailey** found time to win the Kentucky Derby on Grindstone.

caught up in an early speed duel with Siphon and Dramatic Gold, two fine and fast horses. Dare and Go, a talented son of Alydar, roared past them all in the stretch to end Cigar's streak at 16 wins. Citation's had ended even less auspiciously in an obscure race at Santa Anita, in which he lost to a now forgotten horse named Miche.

Cigar's $200,000 for second place did move his lifetime earnings over the $9 million mark, a fact less important than the knowledge that he came out of the race in good shape and ready for a fall season of competition in which he would probably face Dare and Go again, as well as the superb late bloomer Smart Strike.

After the Arlington Citation Challenge, Paulson told a national television audience, "It was an honor to bring him here." It was a gracious thought, but inaccurate. It was the tracks and the sport itself who were honored by Mr. Paulson's horse in 1996, not the other way around.

If the thought of streaks dominated the older horse division during the year, they had their role in the 3-year-old story too. Trainer D. Wayne Lukas went into the 1996 season having won 5 straight Triple Crown races—each of 1995's big three, plus the Preakness and the Belmont Stakes in 1994.

For the Kentucky Derby, Lukas didn't train the favorite, Unbridled's Song, but he did have a huge contingent of prospects including Louisiana Derby winner Grindstone and four other solid contenders. The Lukas horses lacked the best credentials, but in the Derby, with huge fields the rule nowadays, luck counts as much as talent.

You get more luck of all kinds—with large fields and large entries. Lukas experienced both varieties, with his good sprinter Honor and Glory running too fast too early to beat more than one horse under the wire. The even better Editor's Note had a good trip early, but a wide trip late and finished sixth. And Lukas' Prince of Thieves got third place with a solid effort.

But the Lukas-trained Grindstone, under Cigar's jockey Jerry Bailey, got it all. He and second favorite Cavonnier each moved from just off the pace—classic Derby-winning position—to match up in a pounding stretch run. They went under the wire together in the closest Kentucky Derby finish in 37 years.

"Did we get it?" Lukas asked everybody he saw as he headed through the stands to greet his horse and rider. Then, after what must have seemed like hours to a man on a streak, "It was great to see the number come up." It was also six wins in a row in Triple Crown races.

Lukas moved on to Pimlico to try to stretch the streak in the Preakness, unfortunately not with his Derby winner Grindstone, who missed the race with an injury. He had three horses, though, and was hoping for the best. Trainer Nick Zito, whose Louis Quatorze had disappointed in the Derby, did some hoping of his own.

Zito had a more recent memory than anyone else of what it was like to beat Wayne Lukas in a Triple Crown event, having done it in the 1994 Kentucky Derby with Go for Gin. He also had an idea of how to go about it, shipping his horse to Pimlico a couple of days sooner than everyone else.

"It was like our own training center," Zito observed. The fact that Louis Quatorze, named for the Sun King of 17th century France, loved the sunny weather and fast track of Preakness day didn't hurt. Louis Quatorze led from the start, winning the

World Wide Photos

On May 4, 1996 Churchill Downs was the scene of heart-pounding action as **Jerry Bailey** (l) on **Grindstone** squeezed past **Chris McCarron** on **Cavonnier** in a photo finish, the closest Kentucky Derby in 37 years.

Preakness over Skip Away and the Lukas-trained Editor's Note. The streak had come to an end at six.

"I've been blessed on the run," Lukas told reporters after the race. "We'll see if we can start it again."

So it was off to Belmont for the three-year-olds, with Lukas now represented by Prince of Thieves and the still-promising Editor's Note. The mile-and-a-half race remains the greatest challenge in American racing, but the length of the race and the size of the Belmont Park racetrack means that luck is rarely a major contender.

But rarely doesn't mean never. Favorite Cavonnier, who had run well in both the Kentucky Derby and the Preakness, raced in close contention until the far turn. His race and probably his career ended when he took a bad step and suffered a severely bowed tendon.

A quarter mile further down the track, Editor's Note moved from promising to accomplished with a one-length win over Skip Away, with the filly My Flag in third place. Wayne Lukas had started another Triple Crown streak.

As the summer progressed, Skip Away and Louis Quatorze emerged as the best of the 3-year-olds, at least temporarily. Skip Away won the Ohio Derby and the Haskell, while Louis Quatorze took the Jim Dandy at Saratoga. But both were beaten by Will's Way in the Travers. Will's Way, as winner of the so-called Midsummer Derby, immediately became a contender for championship honors. He had been a definite Triple Crown candidate until he injured himself in a prep race, so he reached the top just a little behind schedule.

By the end of August, Will's Way was there at the top of the 3-year-old heap, alongside Skip Away and Louis Quatorze. The contenders were going to have to work out their standings under the shadow of Cigar, since 3-year-old-only races disappear along with the leaves on the trees as autumn arrives.

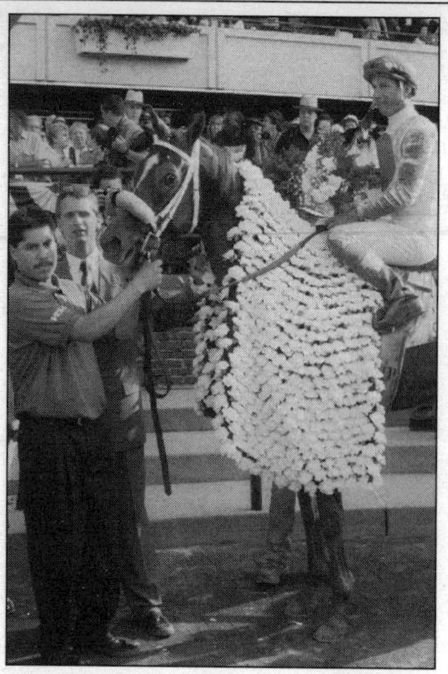

World Wide Photos

Rene Douglas won the Belmont Stakes aboard **Editor's Note** and started a new Triple Crown streak for Wayne Lukas.

1996 proved to be a good year for fillies and mares, with top quality female racehorses competing across the country. Some even performed well outside their divisions. Serena's Song nearly held off Mahogany Hall in Saratoga's prestigious Whitney Stakes, then she finished a good third to Smart Strike in the Iselin Handicap at Monmouth Park.

Among 3-year-old fillies, My Flag, placed against colts in the Belmont Stakes, won the Coaching Club American Oaks and the Gazelle, while Mother Goose winner Yanks Music turned the tables in the Alabama. Capote Belle, winner of the Test, was nearly as good as either.

But none of the 3-year-old Thoroughbred fillies could approach the accomplishments of a 3-year-old trotting filly named Continentalvictory. She didn't just sample open competition against colts; she moved into their division and stayed. She began with a victory in the Yonkers Trot, the first leg of the Trotting Triple Crown.

Then in August at the Meadowlands in New Jersey, Continentalvictory ignored the rich Hambletonian Oaks for fillies and trotted right into the Hambletonian itself, the most famous and prestigious event in harness racing. Her victory in the first heat produced a world record, and her win in the final resulted in a combined world record for two heats.

Fillies have won the big race before—twelve of them before 1996--but none had ever won the first two legs of the Triple Crown. "It's the greatest day of my life," said driver Mike Lachance after the Hambletonian. It was a great day for racing fans, too.

Lest anyone think Continentalvictory could only win at the big raceways, she moved on to DuQuoin in Illinois, the fair track that used to host the Hambletonian. On August 31, she finished an unexpected fourth in the first heat of the World Trotting Derby, proving once again that if a horse starts enough times, he or she will lose.

But harness racing sometimes offers something that Thoroughbred racing never does—a second chance in the same race.

The Trotting Derby is a heat race and in the second heat, she set a stakes record and tied the track record with a 1:52.3 mile. She then went on to win the raceoff and Derby itself. Continentalvictory was set to be Trotter of the Year for 1996, regardless of the outcome of the Kentucky Futurity, the third leg of the Trotting Triple Crown.

She may or may not be Harness Horse of the Year, because a horse she will never face in competition was just about as impressive. The 4-year-old pacing horse Jenna's Beach Boy raced the fastest mile in the history of the sport in June when he won the Driscoll at the Meadowlands in 1:47.3. By the end of the summer, Jenna's Beach Boy had paced six sub-1:50 miles, the most of any horse in history.

A milestone of another sort was reached by the harness racing sport in mid-August, when the legendary trainer-driver Delvin Miller died at the age of 83. As a driver, he won nearly 2,500 races, still competing on the track into his seventies. As a trainer, he was responsible for Dale Frost, Arndon, Countess Adios, Delmonica Hanover, and many more. His greatest accomplishment may have been his supervision of the breeding career of the great stallion Adios, whose name still appears in the pedigrees of many of today's best harness horses. ❐

HORSE RACING STATISTICS

THE SEASON IN REVIEW

1995-1996

THOROUGHBRED • HARNESS

Thoroughbred Racing

Major Stakes Races

Winners of major stakes races from Nov. 26, 1995 through Sept. 22, 1996; (T) indicates turf race course; (F) indicates furlongs. See Updates for later results.

LATE 1995

Date	Race	Track	Miles	Winner	Jockey	Purse
Nov. 26	Japan Cup	Tokyo Racecourse	1⅛ (T)	Lando	Mike Roberts	$3,900,000
Nov. 26	Matriarch Stakes	Hollywood	1¼ (T)	Duda	Jerry Bailey	700,000
Nov. 26	Hollywood Derby	Hollywood	1⅛	Labeeb (GB)	Eddie Delahoussaye	400,000
Dec. 10	Hollywood Turf Cup	Hollywood	1½ (T)	Royal Chariot	Alex Solis	500,000
Dec. 16	Hollywood Starlet Stakes	Hollywood	1 1/16	Cara Rafaela	Corey Nakatani	250,000
Dec. 17	Hollywood Futurity	Hollywood	1 1/16	Matty G	Alex Solis	500,000
Dec. 26	Malibu Stakes	Santa Anita	7 F	Afternoon Deelites	Kent Desormeaux	160,000

1996 (through Sept. 22)

Date	Race	Track	Miles	Winner	Jockey	Purse
Jan. 7	Spectacular Bid B.C. Stakes*	Gulfstream	6 F	Seacliff	Rene Douglas	$ 75,000
Jan. 15	San Pasqual Handicap	Santa Anita	1 1/16	Alphabet Soup	Chris Antley	210,000
Jan. 20	El Camino Real Derby*	Bay Meadows	1 1/16	Cavonnier	Martin Pedroza	200,000
Jan. 20	Holy Bull Stakes*	Gulfstream	1 1/16	Cobra King	Chris McCarron	75,000
Feb. 3	San Antonio Handicap	Santa Anita	1⅛	Alphabet Soup	Chris Antley	304,900
Feb. 4	Hutcheson Stakes*	Gulfstream	7 F	Appealing Skier	Rick Wilson	75,000
Feb. 4	Charles H. Strub Stakes	Santa Anita	1¼	Helmsman	Chris McCarron	500,000
Feb. 10	Donn Handicap	Gulfstream	1⅛	Cigar	Jerry Bailey	300,000
Feb. 10	San Vicente Stakes*	Santa Anita	7 F	Afleetaffair	Corey Nakatani	103,850
Feb. 11	La Cañada Stakes	Santa Anita	1⅛	Jewel Princess	Alex Solis	209,900
Feb. 17	Barbara Fritchie Handi.	Laurel	7 F	Lottsa Talc	Frank Alvarado	200,000
Feb. 19	San Luis Obispo Handi.	Santa Anita	1⅛ (T)	Windsharp	Eddie Delahoussaye	210,800
Feb. 24	Fountain of Youth Stakes*	Gulfstream	1 1/16	Built for Pleasure	Gary Boulanger	200,000
Feb. 25	Rampart Handicap	Gulfstream	1 1/16	Investalot	Shane Sellers	200,000
Mar. 2	Best Turn Stakes*	Aqueduct	6 F	Romano Gucci	Richard Migliori	80,000
Mar. 2	Southwest Stakes*	Oaklawn	1	Ide	Craig Perret	100,000
Mar. 2	Gulfstream Park Handi.	Gulfstream	1⅛	Wekiva Springs	Jerry Bailey	500,000
Mar. 2	San Rafael Stakes*	Santa Anita	1	Honour and Glory	Gary Stevens	202,000
Mar. 2	Santa Anita Handicap	Santa Anita	1¼	Mr. Purple	Eddie Delahoussaye	1,000,000
Mar. 10	Santa Margarita Invit.	Santa Anita	1⅛	Twice The Vice	Chris McCarron	300,000
Mar. 15	Cherry Hill Mile*	Garden State	1	In Contention	Tony Black	50,000
Mar. 16	Florida Derby*	Gulfstream	1⅛	Unbridled's Song	Mike Smith	500,000
Mar. 16	Swale Stakes*	Gulfstream	7 F	Roar	Mike Smith	75,000
Mar. 17	Louisiana Derby*	Fairgrounds	1 1/16	Grindstone	Jerry Bailey	370,000
Mar. 17	San Felipe Stakes*	Santa Anita	1 1/16	Odyle	Corey Nakatani	252,400
Mar. 23	Golden State Derby*	Golden Gate	1 1/16 (T)	Halo Sunshine	Eddie Delahoussaye	200,000
Mar. 23	Rebel Stakes*	Oaklawn	1 1/16	Ide	Craig Perret	100,000
Mar. 23	Remington Park Derby*	Remington	1 1/16	Semoran	Russell Baze	300,000
Mar. 24	Tampa Bay Derby*	Tampa Bay	1 1/16	Thundering Storm	Jorge Guerra	150,000
Mar. 24	San Luis Rey Stakes	Santa Anita	1½ (T)	Windsharp	Eddie Delahoussaye	261,900
Mar. 27	Dubai Classic	Nad al-Sheba	1¼	Cigar	Jerry Bailey	4,000,000
Mar. 30	Jim Beam Stakes*	Turfway	1⅛	Roar	Mike Smith	600,000
Mar. 30	Gotham Stakes*	Aqueduct	1	Romano Gucci	Julie Krone	201,200
Apr. 6	Flamingo Stakes	Hialeah	1⅛	El Amante	Ramon Perez	200,000
Apr. 6	Santa Anita Derby*	Santa Anita	1⅛	Cavonnier	Chris McCarron	1,000,000
Apr. 6	Oaklawn Handicap	Oaklawn	1⅛	Geri	Jerry Bailey	750,000
Apr. 10	Lafayette Stakes*	Keeneland	7 F	Wire Me Collect	Kristi Chapwon	75,000
Apr. 12	Apple Blossom Handicap	Oaklawn	1 1/16	Twice the Vice	Chris McCarron	500,000
Apr. 13	Blue Grass Stakes*	Keeneland	1⅛	Skip Away	Shane Sellers	700,000
Apr. 13	California Derby	Golden Gate	1⅛ (T)	Pike Place Dancer	Corey Nakatani	200,000
Apr. 13	Wood Memorial*	Aqueduct	1⅛	Unbridled's Song	Mike Smith	500,000

Thoroughbred Racing (Cont.)

1996 (through Sept. 22)

Date	Race	Track	Miles	Winner	Jockey	Purse
Apr. 13	Bay Shore Stakes*	Aqueduct	7 F	Jamies First Punch	John Velazquez	$112,000
Apr. 13	Arkansas Derby*	Oaklawn	1⅛	Zarb's Magic	Ronald Ardoin	500,000
Apr. 20	Federico Tesio Stakes*	Pimlico	1⅛	Tour's Big Red	Walter Guerra	163,000
Apr. 20	Ashland Stakes	Keeneland	1 1/16	My Flag	Jerry Bailey	540,750
Apr. 21	San Juan Capistrano	Santa Anita	1¾ (T)	Raintrap	Alex Solis	400,000
Apr. 21	Lexington Stakes*	Keeneland	1 1/16	City by Night	Shane Sellers	199,150
Apr. 27	Derby Trial*	Churchill Downs	1	Vaild Expectations	Donald Pettinger	118,500
May 3	Kentucky Oaks	Churchill Downs	1⅛	Pike Place Dancer	Corey Nakatani	500,000
May 4	**Kentucky Derby***	Churchill Downs	1¼	Grindstone	Jerry Bailey	1,000,000
May 11	Withers Stakes*	Belmont	1	Appealing Skier	Rick Wilson	111,200
May 11	Pimlico Special	Pimlico	1 3/16	Star Standard	Pat Day	582,000
May 11	Illinois Derby*	Sportsman's Prk	1⅛	Natural Selection	Randy Romero	500,000
May 17	Black-Eyed Susan Stakes	Pimlico	1⅛	Mesabi Maiden	Mike Smith	200,000
May 18	**Preakness Stakes***	Pimlico	1 3/16	Louis Quatorze	Pat Day	704,800
May 25	Sheridan Stakes*	Arlington	1	Storm Creek	Aaron Gryder	100,000
May 26	Peter Pan Stakes*	Belmont	1⅛	Jamies First Punch	John Velazquez	151,800
May 27	Metropolitan Handicap	Belmont	1	Honour and Glory	John Velazquez	400,000
May 27	Hollywood Turf Handicap	Hollywood Prk	1¼ (T)	Sandpit	Corey Nakatani	500,000
June 1	Massachusetts Handicap	Suffolk Downs	1⅛	Cigar	Jerry Bailey	500,000
June 2	Californian Stakes	Hollywood Prk	1⅛	Tinners Way	Eddie Delahoussaye	248,234
June 8	Riva Ridge Stakes*	Belmont	7 F	Gold Fever	Mike Smith	112,000
June 8	Vodafone English Derby	Epsom Downs	1½ (T)	Shaamit	Michael Hills	1,297,975
June 8	**Belmont Stakes***	Belmont	1½	Editor's Note	Rene Douglas	729,800
June 16	Shoemaker BC Mile	Hollywood	1 (T)	Fastness	Corey Nakatani	680,000
June 22	Mother Goose Stakes	Belmont	1⅛	Yanks Music	John Velazquez	200,000
June 22	Caesars Int'l Handicap	Atlantic City	1 3/16 (T)	Sandpit	Corey Nakatani	500,000
June 23	Ohio Derby*	Thistledown	1⅛	Skip Away	Jose Santos	300,000
June 28	Jersey Shore Stakes*	Atlantic City	7 F	Swing and Miss	Tom Turner	100,000
June 30	Hollywood Gold Cup	Hollywood Prk	1¼	Siphon	David Flores	1,000,000
June 30	Irish Derby	Curragh	1½ (T)	Zagreb	Pat Shanahan	£600,000
June 30	Affirmed Handicap*	Hollywood Prk	1 1/16	Hesabull	Eddie Delahoussaye	100,000
July 6	Dwyer Stakes*	Belmont	1 1/16	Victory Speech	Jerry Bailey	160,000
July 6	Round Table Stakes*	Arlington	1⅛	Slew O Mink	Donald Pettinger	150,000
July 7	Queen's Plate	Woodbine	1¼	Victor Cooley	Emile Ramsammy	425,800
July 7	Beverly Hills Handicap	Hollywood Prk	1¾	Different	Chris McCarron	273,000
July 13	Arlington Citation Chal.	Arlington	1⅛	Cigar	Jerry Bailey	1,075,000
July 20	Coaching Club Am. Oaks	Belmont	1¼	My Flag	Jerry Bailey	250,000
July 21	Swaps Stakes*	Hollywood Park	1⅛	Victory Speech	Jerry Bailey	500,000
July 27	K. George VI and Q. Elizabeth Diamond Stakes	Ascot	1½ (T)	Pentire	Michael Hills	£500,000
Aug. 3	Whitney Handicap	Saratoga	1⅛	Mahogany Hall	Jose Santos	350,000
Aug. 4	Haskell Invitational*	Monmouth	1⅛	Skip Away	Jose Santos	750,000
Aug. 4	Jim Dandy Stakes*	Saratoga	1⅛	Louis Quatorze	Pat Day	150,000
Aug. 10	Pacific Classic	Del Mar	1¼	Dare and Go	Alex Solis	1,000,000
Aug. 17	Alabama Stakes	Saratoga	1¼	Yanks Music	John Velazquez	250,000
Aug. 24	Travers Stakes*	Saratoga	1¼	Will's Way	Jorge Chavez	750,000
Aug. 24	Beverly D. Stakes	Arlington	1 3/16 (T)	Timarida	Johnny Murtagh	500,000
Aug. 25	Secretariat Stakes	Arlington	1¼ (T)	Marlin	Shane Sellers	500,000
Aug. 25	Philip H. Iselin Handicap	Monmouth	1⅛	Smart Strike	Craig Perret	300,000
Aug. 25	Arlington Million	Arlington	1¼ (T)	Mecke	Robbie Davis	1,000,000
Aug. 25	Breeders' Stakes	Woodbine	1½ (T)	Chief Bearhart	Mickey Walls	250,000
Sept. 14	Woodward Stakes	Belmont	1⅛	Cigar	Jerry Bailey	510,000
Sept. 14	Man o' War Stakes	Belmont	1⅜ (T)	Diplomatic Jet	Jorge Chavez	400,000
Sept. 14	Ruffian Handicap	Belmont	1 1/16	Yanks Music	John Velazquez	250,000
Sept. 15	Woodbine Million	Woodbine	1⅛	Skip Away	Shane Sellers	1,000,000
Sept. 21	Kentucky Cup Classic	Turfway	1⅛	Atticus	Corey Nakatani	490,000
Sept. 21	Turfway Breeders' Cup	Turfway	1 1/16	Golden Attraction	Gary Stevens	314,300
Sept. 22	Super Derby XVII	Louisiana Downs	1¼	Editor's Note	Gary Stevens	750,000

*VISA 3-yo Championship Series race (see below).

Final VISA 3-year old Series Standings

The VISA Championship Series consists of 46 stakes races to determine the VISA Three-Year-Old Champion. Points are awarded to the first, second and third-place finishers as follows: Triple Crown races are scored 15-10-7; Grade I races are scored 10-7-5; Grade II races 7-5-3; and Grade III and ungraded 5-3-1. Top 15 finishers are listed below.

	Pts
1 Skip Away	54
2 Editor's Note	35
3 Louis Quatorze	34
4 Unbridled's Song	32
5 Victory Speech	30
6 Cavonnier	28
7 Grindstone	25
8 Roar	18
9 Appealing Skier	17
Honour and Glory	17
Jamies First Punch	17
Prince of Thieves	17
13 Gold Fever	16
14 Romano Gucci	15
Will's Way	15

TRC National Thoroughbred Poll

(Sept. 22, 1996)

Through week 28 of the 1996 racing season. Poll taken by Thoroughbred Racing Communications, Inc., and based on the votes of sports and Thoroughbred racing media. Horses receive 10 points for a first place finish, nine for second, etc. First place votes are in parentheses.

	Pts	Owner (Trainer)	'96 Record Sts—1-2-3	Earnings	Last Start (Date, Distance)
1 Cigar (30)	300	Allen Paulson (Bill Mott)	6—5-1-0	$4,230,000	1st—Woodward Stakes (Sept. 14, 1⅛ mi.)
2 Dare and Go	207	La Presle Farm (Richard Mandella)	6—2-2-1	732,030	1st—Pacific Classic (Aug. 10, 1¼ mi.)
3 Skip Away	194	Carolyn Hine (Sonny Hine)	11—5-2-2	2,099,280	1st—Woodbine Million (Sept. 15, 1⅛ mi.)
4 Wekiva Springs	161	D. Dizney & J. English (Bill Mott)	8—3-3-0	1,041,000	5th—Kentucky Cup Classic (Sept. 21, 1⅛ mi.)
5 Geri	140	Allen Paulson (Bill Mott)	6—4-1-1	795,200	2nd—Hollywood Gold Cup (June 30, 1¼ mi.)
6 Siphon (BRZ)	122	Rio Claro Thoroughbreds (Richard Mandella)	6—4-1-1	919,350	3rd—Pacific Classic (Aug. 10, 1¼ mi.)
7 Fastness (IRE)	82	Evergreen Farms (Jenine Sahadi)	3—3-0-0	692,470	1st—Eddie Read Handicap (Aug. 4, 1⅛ mi.-T)
8 Mecke	69	James Lewis Jr. (Emanuel Tortora)	11—4-1-1	1,053,230	2nd—Man O' War Stakes (Sept. 14, 1⅜ mi.-T)
9 Yanks Music	67	Michael Fennessy (Leo O'Brien)	6—4-2-0	511,000	1st—Ruffian Handicap (Sept. 14, 1 1/16 mi.)
10 Serena's Song	59	Bob & Beverly Lewis (D. Wayne Lukas)	12—5-4-2	836,093	2nd—Ruffian Handicap (Sept. 14, 1 1/16 mi.)

Others receiving votes: 11. L'Carriere (51 points); **12.** Jewel Princess (35); **13.** Sandpit (22); **14.** Diplomatic Jet (19); **15.** My Flag (16); **16.** Editor's Note (15), Langfuhr (15); **18.** Grindstone (13); **19.** Smart Strike (12); **20.** Different (11); **21.** Honour and Glory (9); **22.** Soul of the Matter (8); **23.** Dramatic Gold (7); **24.** Chaposa Springs (5); **25.** Timarida (4); **26.** Louis Quatorze (3); **27.** Sharp Cat, Traitor, Will's Way, and Windsharp (1).

The 1996 Triple Crown

Thoroughbred racing's Triple Crown for 3-year-olds consists of the Kentucky Derby, Preakness Stakes and Belmont Stakes run over six weeks on May 4, May 18 and June 8, respectively.

122nd KENTUCKY DERBY

Grade I for three-year olds; 8th race at Churchill Downs in Louisville. **Date**— May 4, 1996; **Distance**— 1 ¼ miles; **Stakes Purse**— $1,169,800 ($869,800 to winner; $170,000 for 2nd; $85,000 for 3rd; $45,000 for 4th); **Track**— Fast; **Off** — 5:34 p.m. EDT; **Favorite**—Unbridled's Song (7-2 odds).
Winner— Grindstone; **Field**— 19 horses; **Time**— 2:01.06; **Start**— Good; **Won**— Driving; **Sire**— Unbridled (Fappiano); **Dam**— Buzz My Bell (Drone); **Record** (going into race)— 5 starts, 2 wins, 2 seconds; **Last start**— 2nd in Arkansas Derby (Apr. 13); **Breeder**— Overbrook Farm (Ky.).

Order of Finish	Jockey	PP	1/4	1/2	3/4	Mile	Stretch	Finish	To $1
Grindstone	Jerry Bailey	15	15-1½	15-1½	13-½	8-1½	4-½	**1**-no	5.90
Cavonnier	Chris McCarron	4	9-½	5-hd	5-1	3-2½	1-hd	**2**-3½	5.60
Prince of Thieves	Pat Day	10	12-hd	12-1	10-½	4-½	5-3	**3**-nk	7.00
Halo Sunshine	Craig Perret	5	7-1½	4-1½	4-½	2-1	3-2½	**4**-no	28.90
Unbridled's Song	Mike Smith	19	3-2½	3-1	2-½	1-2	2-1	**5**-3½	3.50
Editor's Note	Gary Stevens	17	16-1	16-½	16-1½	13-1½	8-2	**6**-hd	5.90
Blow Out	Patrick Johnson	1	19	19	15-1½	12-½	7-½	**7**-1½	10.80
Alyrob	Corey Nakatani	12	14-5	13-2½	14-hd	10-½	6-2½	**8**-1½	7.20
Diligence	Kent Desormeaux	3	17-½	17-1½	17-1	14-1	9-1½	**9**-2½	13.10
Victory Speech	Jose Santos	2	11-2½	8-1	9-hd	6-1	10-2	**10**-1¼	24.80
Corker	Corey Black	9	18-2	18-2	18-1½	16-1	13-½	**11**-2½	10.80
Skip Away	Shane Sellers	16	5-½	6-hd	8-hd	7-½	12-hd	**12**-½	7.70
Zarb's Magic	Ron Ardoin	7	8-½	9-hd	7-½	11-1	11-1	**13**-½	25.70
Semoran	Russell Baze	6	6-½	10-½	11-2	15-2	15-3	**14**-3½	5.60
In Contention	Tony Black	8	13-½	14-1	19	19	18-2½	**15**-2	19.80
Louis Quatorze	Chris Antley	11	10-hd	11-½	12-½	17-1	16-½	**16**-2½	13.10
Matty G	Alex Solis	18	2-1	2-1	3-1½	9-1	14-½	**17**-nk	10.80
Honour and Glory	Aaron Gryder	13	1-1½	1-1	1-½	5-1½	17-hd	**18**-2½	24.80
Built for Pleasure	John Velazquez	14	4-hd	7-1	6-hd	18-2½	19	**19**	10.80

Times— 22⅕; 46; 1:10; 1:35; 2:01.
$2 Mutual Prices— #4 Grindstone ($13.80, $6.00, $4.00); #3 Cavonnier ($6.20, $4.40); #8 Prince of Thieves ($4.60).
Exacta— (4–3) for $61.80; **Trifecta**— (4–3–8) for $600.60; **Pick Six**— (6–4–1–5–6–4) five correct for $341.60;
Scratched— City by Night. **Overweights**— none. **Attendance**—142,668; **TV Rating**—8.2/23 share (ABC).

Trainers & Owners (by finish): **1**— D. Wayne Lukas & W.T. Young; **2**— Bob Baffert & Robert and Barbara Walter; **3**— D. Wayne Lukas & Peter Mitchell; **4**— Richard Cross & Henry Papst; **5**— James Ryerson & Paraneck Stable; **6**— D. Wayne Lukas & W.T. Young; **7**—Jim Keefer & Bill Heiligbrodt, Buddy New, and Ted Keefer; **8**— Wally Dollase & Four Star Stable; **9**— Nick Zito & Kinsman Farm (George Steinbrenner); **10**— D. Wayne Lukas & Michael Tabor; **11**— Charlie Whittingham & Arthur B. Hancock III, Robert and Janice McNair; **12**— Hubert "Sonny" Hine & Carolyn Hine; **13**— Bret Thomas & Foxwood Plantation (La.); **14**— Bob Baffert & Donald R. Dizney and James E. English.; **15**— Cynthia Reese & Noreen Carpenito; **16**— Nick Zito & William J. Condren, Joseph M. Cornacchia, and Georgia Hofmann; **17**— Ron MacAnally & Double J Farm; **18**— D. Wayne Lukas & Michael Tabor; **19**— Thomas H. Heard Jr. & Thomas H. Heard Jr..

Thoroughbred Racing (Cont.)

The 1996 Triple Crown

121st PREAKNESS STAKES

Grade I for three-year olds; 10th race at Pimlico in Baltimore. **Date**— May 18, 1996; **Distance**— 1³⁄₁₆ miles; **Stakes Purse**— $704,800 ($458,120 to winner; $140,960 for 2nd; $70,480 for 3rd; $35,240 for 4th); **Track**— Fast; **Off**— 5:33 p.m. EDT; **Favorite**— Cavonnier (8-5).

Winner— Louis Quatorze; **Field**— 12 horses; **Time**— 1:53⅖; **Start**— Good for all but Secreto de Estado; **Won**— Driving; **Sire**—Sovereign Dancer (Northern Dancer); **Dam**— On to Royalty (On to Glory); **Record** (going into race)— 9 starts, 3 wins, 3 seconds; **Last start**— 16th in Kentucky Derby (May 4); **Breeder**— Georgia Hofmann (Ky.).

Order of Finish	Jockey	PP	1/4	1/2	3/4	Stretch	Finish	To $1
Louis Quatorze	Pat Day	6	1-1½	1-2	1-1½	1-1½	**1**-3¼	8.50
Skip Away	Shane Sellers	11	2-hd	2	2-1½	2-3½	**2**-3	3.30
Editor's Note	Gary Stevens	10	12	9	7	3	**3**-2½	6.50
Cavonnier	Chris McCarron	2	6-1	6-1½	5-2	5-2½	**4**-nk	1.70
Victory Speech	Rene Douglas	3	3-1½	3-2	3-1½	4-1	**5**-2	40.60
In Contention	Alex Solis	4	11	10-1½	10-2½	6-6	**6**-7	19.00
Prince of Thieves	Jerry Bailey	9	5-hd	4	4-1	8-6	**7**-½	4.00
Allied Forces	Richard Migliore	1	8-2	8-3½	6-2½	7-hd	**8**-5½	20.10
Secreto de Estado	Cornelio Velasquez	5	9-1½	11-2	12	9	**9**-no	103.10
Tour's Big Red	Joe Bravo	12	7-1	7-hd	8-hd	11-6	**10**-¾	48.40
Mixed Count	Edgar Prado	8	10-1½	12	11-hd	10-hd	**11**-8	99.30
Feather Box	Jorge Velasquez	7	4	5-1	9-1	12	**12**	49.60

Times—23; 46⅕; 1:09⅘; 1:34⅖; 1:53⅖.

$2 Mutual Prices— #6 Louis Quatorze ($19.00, $7.80, $5.20); #11 Skip Away ($5.60, $4.60); #10 Editor's Note ($5.00). **Exacta**— (6–11) for $104.60; **Trifecta**— (6–11–10) for $613.40; **Pick Six**— none; **Scratched**— none. **Overweights**— none. **Attendance**— 85,122; **TV Rating**— 4.1/12 share (ABC).

Trainers & Owners (by finish): **1**— Nick Zito & William J. Condren, Joseph M. Cornacchia, and Georgia Hofmann; **2**— Sonny Hine & Carolyn Hine; **3**— D. Wayne Lukas & W.T. Young; **4**— Bob Baffert & Robert and Barbara Walter; **5**— D. Wayne Lukas & Michael Tabor; **6**— Cynthia Reese & Noreen Carpenito; **7**— D. Wayne Lukas & Peter Mitchell; **8**— Kiaran McLaughlin & Ahmed al Tayer; **9**— Alfredo Callejas & Robert Perez; **10**— Enrique Alonso & William Penn; **11**— Ron Benshoff & Leonard Pearlstein; **12**— Angel Cordero & Thomas Evans.

128th BELMONT STAKES

Grade I for three-year olds; 9th race at Belmont Park in Elmont, N.Y. **Date**— June 8, 1996; **Distance**— 1½ miles; **Stakes Purse**— $729,800 ($437,880 to winner; $145,960 for 2nd; $80,278 for 3rd; $43,788 for 4th); **Track**— Fast; **Off**— 5:33 p.m. EDT; **Favorite**—Cavonnier (3–1)

Winner— Editor's Note; **Field**— 14 horses; **Time**— 2:28 ⅘; **Start**— Good; **Won**— Driving; **Sire**— Forty Niner (by Mr. Prospector); **Dam**—Beware of the Cat (by Caveat); **Record** (going into race)— 16 starts, 3 wins, 4 seconds, 3 thirds; **Last Start**— 3rd in Preakness Stakes (May 18); **Breeder**— Fawn Leap Farm (Ky.).

Order of Finish	Jockey	PP	1/4	1/2	1-Mile	1 1/4-M	Stretch	Finish	To $1
Editor's Note	Rene Douglas	7	11-½	12-2	5-hd	2-½	2-5	**1**-1	5.80
Skip Away	Jose Santos	13	5-½	6-3	2-hd	1-½	1-½	**2**-4	8.00
My Flag	Mike Smith	9	12-hd	13-2	9-2	7-2	3-½	**3**-6	7.70
Louis Quatorze	Pat Day	12	4-1½	3-2	3-2½	3-2	4-4	**4**-2	6.10
Prince of Thieves	Jerry Bailey	6	9-1	8-1½	6-1	5-½	5-3	**5**-8	6.60
Rocket Flash	Eddie Maple	4	8-½	10-hd	10-½	9-2½	8-5	**6**-1	41.50
Natural Selection	Randy Romero	2	2-hd	2-½	1-hd	4-½	7-½	**7**-2	22.50
Jamies First Punch	John Velazquez	5	7-hd	7-hd	8-2	8-3	6-2	**8**-2	5.90
In Contention	Joe Bravo	11	10-1½	9-1	11-2½	10-3	9-10	**9**-16	36.00
Traffic Circle	Jorge Chavez	10	13-1½	11-1	12-1	12-1½	11-4	**10**-6½	41.50
Saratoga Dandy	Robbie Davis	1	14	14	13-3	11-2½	10-½	**11**-nk	6.10
Appealing Skier	Richard Migliore	8	3-½	1-hd	7-½	13-16	12	**12**	37.50
South Salem	Julie Krone	3	1-hd	4-1	14	14	Eased		37.00
Cavonnier	Chris McCarron	14	6-2	5-1	4-2½	6-hd	Lame		3.50

Times— 23⅖; 46⅘; 1:10 ⅘; 1:35⅘; 2:02; 2:28⅘.

$2 Mutual Prices— #6 Editor's Note ($13.60, $6.50, $4.30); #10 Skip Away ($8.20, $6.20); #8 My Flag ($5.50). **Exacta**— (6–10) for $107.50; **Trifecta**— (6–10–8) for $914.00; **Pick Six**— none; **Scratched**— Secreto de Estado. **Overweights**— None. **Attendance**— 40,797; **TV Rating**— 3.1/9 share (ABC).

Trainers & Owners (by finish): **1**— D. Wayne Lukas & Overbrook Farm; **2**— Hubert "Sonny" Hine & Carolyn Hine; **3**— Shug McGaughey & Ogdeb Phipps; **4**— Nick Zito & William Condren, Joseph Cornacchia, and Georgia Hofmann; **5**— D. Wayne Lukas & Charles Grimm and Peter Mitchell; **6**— Bill Mott & Calumet Farm; **7**— Mohammed Moubarak & Buckram Oak Farm; **8**— Robert Barbara & Zimpom Stable; **9**— Cynthia Reese & Noreen Carpenito; **10**— John Kimmel & Caesar Kimmel, Herbert Moelis, and Philip Solondz; **11**— Nick Zito & William Condren & Joseph Cornacchia; **12**— Ben Perkins Sr. & New Farm; **13**—David Loder & Virginia Kraft Payson; **14**— Bob Baffert & Walter Family Trust.

1995-96 Money Leaders

Official Top 10 standings for 1995 and unofficial Top 10 standings for 1996, through Sept. 22, as compiled by the *Equibase Company*.

Final 1995

HORSES	Age	Sts	1-2-3	Earnings
Cigar	5	10	10-0-0	$4,819,800
Thunder Gulch	3	10	7-0-1	2,644,080
Serena's Song	3	13	9-2-0	1,524,920
Sandpit (BRA)	6	8	4-3-0	1,342,700
Peaks and Valleys	3	8	5-2-0	1,323,750
Northern Spur (IRE)	4	4	2-0-1	1,265,000
Inside Information	4	8	7-1-0	1,160,408
Awad	5	14	4-3-0	1,040,810
Mecke	3	13	2-3-4	958,750
L'Carriere	4	7	3-3-0	928,840

JOCKEYS	Mts	1st	Earnings
Jerry Bailey	1367	287	$16,311,876
Corey Nakatani	1371	298	15,025,227
Gary Stevens	929	201	13,310,095
Pat Day	1146	239	11,750,800
Mike Smith	1350	263	11,704,157
Chris McCarron	913	166	11,306,603
Kent Desormeaux	1174	235	10,757,379
Eddie Delahoussaye	1091	170	9,180,455
Alex Solis	1439	210	8,702,970
Jorge Chavez	1384	243	8,528,229

TRAINERS	Sts	1st	Earnings
D. Wayne Lukas	837	194	$12,834,483
Bill Mott	654	161	11,771,046
Ron McAnally	433	67	6,479,187
Richard Mandella	322	70	6,354,971
Bobby Frankel	336	79	5,976,094
Shug McGaughey	283	63	5,131,143
Jerry Hollendorfer	914	203	3,561,978
Gary Jones	307	52	3,297,105
Allen Jerkens	430	68	3,237,793
Nick Zito	354	46	3,224,181

1996 (through Sept. 22)

HORSES	Age	Sts	1-2-3	Earnings
Cigar	6	6	5-1-0	$4,230,000
Skip Away	3	11	5-2-2	2,099,280
Grindstone	3	4	2-2-0	1,201,000
Editor's Note	3	10	2-2-2	1,198,360
Mecke	4	11	4-1-1	1,053,230
Wekiva Springs	5	8	3-3-0	1,041,000
Cavonnier	3	7	2-1-1	949,240
Louis Quatorze	3	10	4-2-0	944,908
Siphon (BRA)	5	6	4-1-1	919,350
Soul of the Matter	5	2	0-2-0	860,000

JOCKEYS	Mts	1st	Earnings
Jerry Bailey	984	253	$15,752,238
Chris McCarron	656	150	9,835,595
Corey Nakatani	840	185	9,782,711
Pat Day	1,023	205	9,616,545
Mike Smith	1,094	196	9,338,623
Alex Solis	1,047	190	8,334,722
Shane Sellers	978	202	7,817,416
Gary Stevens	509	106	7,785,235
Jorge Chavez	1,083	182	7,240,745
Eddie Delahoussaye	781	130	6,905,025

TRAINERS	Sts	1st	Earnings
Bill Mott	571	140	$11,914,227
D. Wayne Lukas	739	143	10,842,571
Richard Mandella	244	58	6,733,908
Ron McAnally	317	59	4,142,048
Bobby Frankel	232	44	3,770,013
Bob Baffert	240	57	3,319,337
Shug McGaughey	224	49	3,200,627
Jerry Hollendorfer	634	145	3,107,456
Nick Zito	302	52	3,028,093
Hubert Hine	120	21	2,579,827

Harness Racing
1995–96 Major Stakes Races

Winners of major stakes races from Nov. 3, 1995 through Sept. 19, 1996; all paces and trots cover one mile; (BC) indicates Breeders' Crown series. See Updates for later results.

LATE 1995

Date	Race	Raceway	Winner	Time	Driver	Purse
Nov.3	BC 3-Yr-Old Filly Trot	Woodbine	Lookout Victory	1:57⅗	John Patterson	$325,000
Nov.3	BC 3-Yr-Old Filly Pace	Woodbine	Headline Hanover	1:55	Doug Brown	340,000
Nov.3	BC 3-Yr-Old C&G Pace	Woodbine	Jenna's Beach Boy	1:52⅘	Bill Fahy	440,000
Nov.3	BC 3-Yr-Old C&G Trot	Woodbine	Abundance	1:58	Bill O'Donnell	375,000
Nov. 18	Governor's Cup	Garden St.	Live Or Die	1:54⅖	Steve Condren	600,000

1996 (through Sept. 19)

Date	Race	Raceway	Winner	Time	Driver	Purse
June 22	North America Cup	Woodbine	Arizona Jack	1:55⅕	John Campbell	$1,000,000
July 6	Yonkers Trot	Yonkers	Continentalvictory	1:56⅖	Michel Lachance	334,700
July 13	Meadowlands Pace	Meadowlands	Hot Lead	1:51⅘	George Brennan	1,000,000
July 27	Budweiser Beacon Course	Meadowlands	Lindy's Lane	1:53	William O'Donnell	400,000
July 30	Peter Haughton Memorial	Meadowlands	Yankee Glide	1:57⅘	Berndt Lindstedt	500,000
July 31	Merrie Annabelle Final	Meadowlands	Vernon Blue Chip	1:56⅗	Michel Lachance	350,600
Aug. 3	**Hambletonian**	Meadowlands	Continentalvictory	1:52⅘	Michel Lachance	1,200,000
Aug. 3	Hambletonian Oaks	Meadowlands	Moni Maker	1:55⅗	Wally Hennessey	375,000
Aug. 9	BC Open Pace	Meadowlands	Jenna's Beach Boy	1:48⅘	Bill Fahy	300,000
Aug. 9	BC Open Trot	Meadowlands	CR Kay Suzie	1:52⅗	Rod Allen	500,000
Aug. 9	BC Mare Pace	Meadowlands	She's A Great Lady	1:50⅘	John Campbell	300,000
Aug. 10	Sweetheart Pace	Meadowlands	Stienam's Place	1:53⅘	Jack Moiseyev	665,400
Aug. 10	Woodrow Wilson Pace	Meadowlands	Jeremy's Gambit	1:52⅘	Michel Lachance	800,000
Aug. 10	Adios Final	Ladbroke	Electric Yankee	1:52⅕	Michel Lachance	442,844
Aug. 24	Cane Pace	Yonkers	Scoot to Power	1:55⅕	Cat Manzi	326,429
Aug. 31	World Trotting Derby	Du Quoin	Continentalvictory	1:52⅕	Michel Lachance	535,000
Sept. 19	**Little Brown Jug**	Delaware	Armbro Operative	1:52⅗	Michel Lachance	542,220

Harness Racing (Cont.)

1995–96 Money Leaders

Official Top 10 standings for 1995 and unofficial Top 10 standings for 1996 through Sept. 24, as compiled by the U.S. Trotting Association.

Final 1995

HORSES	Age	Sts	1-2-3	Earnings
David's Pass	3pc	13	5-2-1	$1,452,362
Village Connection	3pc	30	18-4-4	1,038,895
Jenna's Beach Boy	3pc	16	14-2-0	1,031,793
CR Kay Suzie	3tf	13	10-0-1	910,535
A Stud Named Sue	2pc	12	9-2-0	870,787
Tagliabue	3tc	13	5-5-2	869,600
Abundance	3tc	22	9-3-1	763,898
Pacific Rocket	4ph	27	16-4-2	724,555
Live Or Die	2pc	17	9-4-2	686,428
Ball and Chain	5ph	31	9-9-8	674,794

DRIVERS	Mts	1st	Earnings
John Campbell	1784	332	$9,469,797
Mike Lachance	2102	313	6,442,205
Jack Moiseyev	2735	457	6,282,295
Doug Brown	2205	443	5,696,611
Cat Manzi	2955	399	5,048,885
Luc Ouellette	2613	726	5,014,167
Steve Condren	1591	249	4,469,631
Tony Morgan	3421	794	4,439,134
Ron Pierce	2621	355	4,044,756
Bill Fahy	1425	203	3,950,904

1996 (through Sept. 24)

HORSES	Age	Sts	1-2-3	Earnings
Continentalvictory	3tf	11	9-0-1	$1,175,135
Hot Lead	3pg	20	11-6-1	987,687
Stout	3pc	23	10-8-3	955,776
Arizona Jack	3pc	17	4-3-0	661,273
Lindy Lane	3tc	8	4-2-0	614,720
Ball And Chain	6ph	27	9-6-4	590,400
Riyadh	6ph	22	11-7-0	521,830
Jeremy's Gambit	2pc	6	6-6-0	509,075
Misfit	7ph	28	7-4-5	502,442
Jenna's Beach Boy	4ph	14	9-1-1	459,095

DRIVERS	Mts	1st	Earnings
John Campbell	1587	291	$7,700,669
Michel Lachance	1812	272	5,219,792
Jack Moiseyev	2318	389	5,172,133
Cat Manzi	2250	299	4,088,328
Doug Brown	1626	318	4,035,672
Luc Ouellette	1835	529	3,695,801
Tony Morgan	2540	575	3,250,239
David Magee	2042	410	3,131,832
Ron Pierce	1997	255	3,029,723
Bill Fahy	1091	152	3,001,734

Hambletonian Society/Breeders Crown Standardbred Poll

(Sept. 23, 1996)

Through week 22 of the 1996 harness racing season. Number in parentheses denotes first-place votes.

		Pts	Age/Gait/Sex	'96 Sts—1-2-3	Earnings
1	Continentalvictory (28)	343	3tf	11— 9-0-1	$1,175,135
2	Jenna's Beach Boy (7)	270	4ph	14— 9-1-1	459,095
3	Riyadh	238	6ph	22—11-7-0	521,830
4	Moni Maker	225	3tf	15—15-0-0	431,574
5	Mystical Maddy	203	3pf	15—13-1-0	450,850
6	Jeremy's Gambit	191	2pc	6— 6-0-0	509,075
7	Hot Lead	123	3pg	20—11-6-1	987,687
8	Stand Forever	87	4ph	21— 8-5-1	266,725
9	Ball And Chain	68	6ph	27— 9-6-4	590,400
10	Lindy Lane	58	3tc	8— 4-2-0	614,720

Others receiving votes: 11. Stout (17 points); **12.** Armbro Operative (15); **13.** Vernon Blue Chip, The Big Boy (12); **15.** Yankee Glide (10); **16.** Act Of Grace (7); **17.** Paige Nicole Q (5); **18.** Gothic Dream, Electric Yankee, Misfit (3); **21.** Oye Vay, B Cor Pete, Western Hero (2).

Steeplechase Racing

1995-96 Major Stakes Races

Winners of major steeplechase races from Oct. 28, 1995 through Aug. 22, 1996; See Updates for later results.

LATE 1995

Date	Race	Location	Miles	Winner	Jockey	Purse
Oct. 28	Grand National	Far Hills, N.J.	2⅝	Rowdy Irishman	Jonathan Smart	$170,000
Nov. 12	Colonial Cup	Camden, S.C	2¾	Lonesome Glory	Blythe Miller	100,000

1996

Date	Race	Location	Miles	Winner	Jockey	Purse
April 6	Atlanta Cup	Cumming, Ga.	2¼	Irish Approach	Blythe Miller	$100,000
April 27	Maryland Hunt Cup	Glyndon, Md.	4 (T)	Hello Hal	Billy Meister	40,000
May 4	Virginia Gold Cup	The Plains, Va.	4 (T)	Saluter	Jack Fisher	35,000
May 11	Iroquois	Nashville, Tn.	3	To Ridley	Sean Clancy	100,000
Aug. 22	N.Y. Turf Writers	Saratoga, N.Y.	2⅜	Petroski	Keith O'Brien	110,500

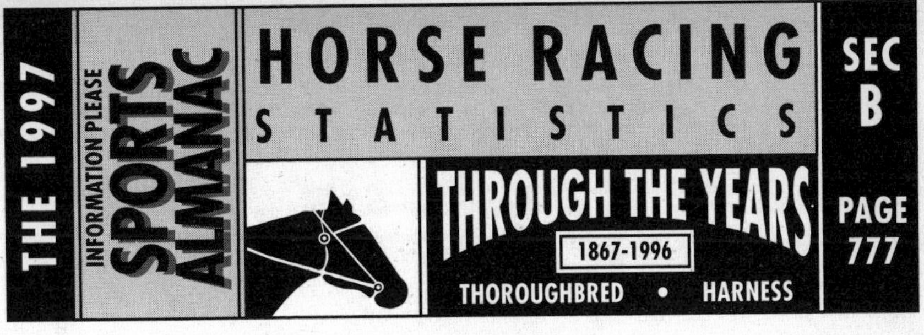

THE 1997
INFORMATION PLEASE
SPORTS ALMANAC
HORSE RACING
STATISTICS
SEC B
THROUGH THE YEARS
1867-1996
THOROUGHBRED • HARNESS
PAGE 777

Thoroughbred Racing

The Triple Crown

The term "Triple Crown" was coined by sportswriter Charles Hatton while covering the 1930 victories of Gallant Fox in the Kentucky Derby, Preakness Stakes and Belmont Stakes. Before then, only Sir Barton (1919) had won all three races in the same year. Since then, nine horses have won the Triple Crown. Two trainers, James (Sunny Jim) Fitzsimmons and Ben A. Jones, have saddled two Triple Crown champions, while Eddie Arcaro is the only jockey to ride two champions.

Year		Jockey	Trainer	Owner	Sire/Dam
1919	**Sir Barton**	Johnny Loftus	H. Guy Bedwell	J.K.L. Ross	Star Shoot/Lady Sterling
1930	**Gallant Fox**	Earl Sande	J.E. Fitzsimmons	Belair Stud	Sir Gallahad III/Marguerite
1935	**Omaha**	Willie Saunders	J.E. Fitzsimmons	Belair Stud	Gallant Fox/Flambino
1937	**War Admiral**	Charley Kurtsinger	George Conway	Samuel Riddle	Man o' War/Brushup
1941	**Whirlaway**	Eddie Arcaro	Ben A. Jones	Calumet Farm	Blenheim II/Dustwhirl
1943	**Count Fleet**	Johnny Longden	Don Cameron	Mrs. J.D. Hertz	Reigh Count/Quickly
1946	**Assault**	Warren Mehrtens	Max Hirsch	King Ranch	Bold Venture/Igual
1948	**Citation**	Eddie Arcaro	Ben A. Jones	Calumet Farm	Bull Lea/Hydroplane II
1973	**Secretariat**	Ron Turcotte	Lucien Laurin	Meadow Stable	Bold Ruler/Somethingroyal
1977	**Seattle Slew**	Jean Cruguet	Billy Turner	Karen Taylor	Bold Reasoning/My Charmer
1978	**Affirmed**	Steve Cauthen	Laz Barrera	Harbor View Farm	Exclusive Native/Won't Tell You

Note: Gallant Fox (1930) is the only Triple Crown winner to sire another Triple Crown winner, Omaha (1935). Wm. Woodward Sr., owner of Belair Stud, was breeder-owner of both horses and both were trained by Sunny Jim Fitzsimmons.

Triple Crown Near Misses

Forty-one horses have won two legs of the Triple Crown. Of those, a dozen won the Kentucky Derby (KD) and Preakness Stakes (PS) only to be beaten in the Belmont Stakes (BS). Two others, Burgoo King (1932) and Bold Venture (1936), each won the Derby and Preakness but were forced out of the Belmont with the same injury—a bowed tendon—that effectively ended their racing careers. In 1978, Alydar finished second to Affirmed in all three races, the only time that has happened. Note that the Preakness preceeded the Kentucky Derby in 1922, '23 and '31; (*) indicates won on disqualification.

Year		KD	PS	BS
1877	**Cloverbrook**	DNS	won	won
1878	**Duke of Magenta**	DNS	won	won
1880	**Grenada**	DNS	won	won
1881	**Saunterer**	DNS	won	won
1895	**Belmar**	DNS	won	won
1920	**Man o'War**	DNS	won	won
1922	**Pillory**	DNS	won	won
1923	**Zev**	won	12th	won
1931	**Twenty Grand**	won	2nd	won
1932	**Burgoo King**	won	won	DNS
1936	**Bold Venture**	won	won	DNS
1939	**Johnstown**	won	5th	won
1940	**Bimelech**	2nd	won	won
1942	**Shut Out**	won	5th	won
1944	**Pensive**	won	won	2nd
1949	**Capot**	2nd	won	won
1950	**Middleground**	won	2nd	won
1953	**Native Dancer**	2nd	won	won
1955	**Nashua**	2nd	won	won
1956	**Needles**	won	2nd	won
1958	**Tim Tam**	won	won	2nd

Year		KD	PS	BS
1961	**Carry Back**	won	won	7th
1963	**Chateaugay**	won	2nd	won
1964	**Northern Dancer**	won	won	3rd
1966	**Kauai King**	won	won	4th
1967	**Damascus**	3rd	won	won
1968	**Forward Pass**	won*	won	2nd
1969	**Majestic Prince**	won	won	2nd
1971	**Canonero II**	won	won	4th
1972	**Riva Ridge**	won	4th	won
1974	**Little Current**	5th	won	won
1976	**Bold Forbes**	won	3rd	won
1979	**Spectacular Bid**	won	won	3rd
1981	**Pleasant Colony**	won	won	3rd
1984	**Swale**	won	7th	won
1987	**Alysheba**	won	won	4th
1988	**Risen Star**	3rd	won	won
1989	**Sunday Silence**	won	won	2nd
1991	**Hansel**	10th	won	won
1994	**Tabasco Cat**	6th	won	won
1995	**Thunder Gulch**	won	3rd	won

The Triple Crown Challenge (1987-93)

Seeking to make the Triple Crown more than just a media event and to insure that owners would not be attracted to more lucrative races, officials at Churchill Downs, the Maryland Jockey Club and the New York Racing Association created Triple Crown Productions in 1985 and announced that a $1 million bonus would be given to the horse that performs best in the Kentucky Derby, Preakness Stakes and Belmont Stakes. Furthermore, a bonus of $5 million would be presented to any horse winning all three races.

Revised in 1991, the rules stated that the winning horse must: 1. finish all three races; 2. earn points by finishing first, second, third or fourth in at least one of the three races; and 3. earn the highest number of points based on the following system—10 points to win, five to place, three to show and one to finish fourth. In the event of a tie, the $1 million is distributed equally among the top point-getters. From 1987-90, the system was five points to win, three to place and one to show. The Triple Crown Challenge was discontinued in 1994.

Year		KD	PS	BS	Pts
1987	1 **Bet Twice**	2nd	2nd	1st	11
	2 Alysheba	1st	1st	4th	10
	3 Cryptoclearance	4th	3rd	2nd	4
1988	1 **Risen Star**	3rd	1st	1st	11
	2 Winning Colors	1st	3rd	6th	6
	3 Brian's Time	6th	2nd	3rd	4
1989	1 **Sunday Silence**	1st	1st	2nd	13
	2 Easy Goer	2nd	2nd	1st	11
	3 Hawkster	5th	5th	5th	0
1990	1 **Unbridled**	1st	2nd	4th	8
	2 Summer Squall	2nd	1st	DNR	8
	3 Go and Go	DNR	DNR	1st	5
	(Unbridled was only horse to run all three races.)				
1991	1 **Hansel**	10th	1st	1st	20
	2 Strike the Gold	1st	6th	2nd	15
	3 Mane Minister	3rd	3rd	3rd	9
1992	1 **Pine Bluff**	5th	1st	3rd	13
	2 Casual Lies	2nd	3rd	5th	8
	(No other horses ran all three races.)				
1993	1 **Sea Hero**	1st	5th	7th	10
	2 Wild Gale	3rd	8th	3rd	6
	(No other horses ran all three races.)				

Kentucky Derby

For three-year-olds. Held the first Saturday in May at Churchill Downs in Louisville, Ky. Inaugurated in 1875.

Originally run at 1½ miles (1875-95), shortened to present 1¼ miles in 1896.

Trainers with most wins: Ben Jones (6); Dick Thompson (4); Sunny Jim Fitzsimmons, Max Hirsch and D. Wayne Lukas (3).

Jockeys with most wins: Eddie Arcaro and Bill Hartack (5); Bill Shoemaker (4); Angel Cordero Jr., Issac Murphy and Earl Sande (3).

Winning fillies: Regret (1915), Genuine Risk (1980) and Winning Colors (1988).

Year		Time	Jockey	Trainer	2nd place	3rd place
1875	**Aristides**	2:37¾	Oliver Lewis	Ansel Anderson	Volcano	Verdigris
1876	**Vagrant**	2:38¼	Bobby Swim	James Williams	Creedmore	Harry Hill
1877	**Baden-Baden**	2:38	Billy Walker	Ed Brown	Leonard	King William
1878	**Day Star**	2:37¼	Jimmy Carter	Lee Paul	Himyar	Leveler
1879	**Lord Murphy**	2:37	Charlie Shauer	George Rice	Falsetto	Strathmore
1880	**Fonso**	2:37½	George Lewis	Tice Hutsell	Kimball	Bancroft
1881	**Hindoo**	2:40	Jim McLaughlin	James Rowe Sr.	Lelex	Alfambra
1882	**Apollo**	2:40¼	Babe Hurd	Green Morris	Runnymede	Bengal
1883	**Leonatus**	2:43	Billy Donohue	John McGinty	Drake Carter	Lord Raglan
1884	**Buchanan**	2:40¼	Isaac Murphy	William Bird	Loftin	Audrain
1885	**Joe Cotton**	2:37¼	Babe Henderson	Alex Perry	Bersan	Ten Booker
1886	**Ben Ali**	2:36½	Paul Duffy	Jim Murphy	Blue Wing	Free Knight
1887	**Montrose**	2:39¼	Isaac Lewis	John McGinty	Jim Gore	Jacobin
1888	**MacBeth II**	2:38¼	George Covington	John Campbell	Gallifet	White
1889	**Spokane**	2:34½	Thomas Kiley	John Rodegap	Proctor Knott	Once Again
1890	**Riley**	2:45	Isaac Murphy	Edward Corrigan	Bill Letcher	Robespierre
1891	**Kingman**	2:52¼	Isaac Murphy	Dud Allen	Balgowan	High Tariff
1892	**Azra**	2:41½	Lonnie Clayton	John Morris	Huron	Phil Dwyer
1893	**Lookout**	2:39¼	Eddie Kunze	Wm. McDaniel	Plutus	Boundless
1894	**Chant**	2:41	Frank Goodale	Eugene Leigh	Pearl Song	Sigurd
1895	**Halma**	2:37½	Soup Perkins	Byron McClelland	Basso	Laureate
1896	**Ben Brush**	2:07¾	Willie Simms	Hardy Campbell	Ben Eder	Semper Ego
1897	**Typhoon II**	2:12½	Buttons Garner	J.C. Cahn	Ornament	Dr. Catlett
1898	**Plaudit**	2:09	Willie Simms	John E. Madden	Lieber Karl	Isabey
1899	**Manuel**	2:12	Fred Taral	Robert Walden	Corsini	Mazo
1900	**Lieut. Gibson**	2:06¼	Jimmy Boland	Charles Hughes	Florizar	Thrive
1901	**His Eminence**	2:07¾	Jimmy Winkfield	F.B. Van Meter	Sannazarro	Driscoll
1902	**Alan-a-Dale**	2:08¾	Jimmy Winkfield	T.C. McDowell	Inventor	The Rival
1903	**Judge Himes**	2:09	Hal Booker	J.P. Mayberry	Early	Bourbon
1904	**Elwood**	2:08½	Shorty Prior	C.E. Durnell	Ed Tierney	Brancas
1905	**Agile**	2:10¾	Jack Martin	Robert Tucker	Ram's Horn	Layson
1906	**Sir Huon**	2:08⅘	Roscoe Troxler	Pete Coyne	Lady Navarre	James Reddick
1907	**Pink Star**	2:12⅗	Andy Minder	W.H. Fizer	Zal	Ovelando

Year		Time	Jockey	Trainer	2nd place	3rd place
1908	**Stone Street**	2:15⅕	Arthur Pickens	J.W. Hall	Sir Cleges	Dunvegan
1909	**Wintergreen**	2:08⅕	Vincent Powers	Charles Mack	Miami	Dr. Barkley
1910	**Donau**	2:06⅖	Fred Herbert	George Ham	Joe Morris	Fighting Bob
1911	**Meridian**	2:05	George Archibald	Albert Ewing	Governor Gray	Colston
1912	**Worth**	2:09⅖	C.H. Shilling	Frank Taylor	Duval	Flamma
1913	**Donerail**	2:04⅘	Roscoe Goose	Thomas Hayes	Ten Point	Gowell
1914	**Old Rosebud**	2:03⅖	John McCabe	F.D. Weir	Hodge	Bronzewing
1915	**Regret**	2:05⅖	Joe Notter	James Rowe Sr.	Pebbles	Sharpshooter
1916	**George Smith**	2:04	Johnny Loftus	Hollie Hughes	Star Hawk	Franklin
1917	**Omar Khayyam**	2:04⅗	Charles Borel	C.T. Patterson	Ticket	Midway
1918	**Exterminator**	2:10⅘	William Knapp	Henry McDaniel	Escoba	Viva America
1919	**SIR BARTON**	2:09⅘	Johnny Loftus	H. Guy Bedwell	Billy Kelly	Under Fire
1920	**Paul Jones**	2:09	Ted Rice	Billy Garth	Upset	On Watch
1921	**Behave Yourself**	2:04⅕	Charles Thompson	Dick Thompson	Black Servant	Prudery
1922	**Morvich**	2:04⅗	Albert Johnson	Fred Burlew	Bet Mosie	John Finn
1923	**Zev**	2:05⅖	Earl Sande	David Leary	Martingale	Vigil
1924	**Black Gold**	2:05⅕	John Mooney	Hanly Webb	Chilhowee	Beau Butler
1925	**Flying Ebony**	2:07⅗	Earl Sande	William Duke	Captain Hal	Son of John
1926	**Bubbling Over**	2:03⅘	Albert Johnson	Dick Thompson	Bagenbaggage	Rock Man
1927	**Whiskery**	2:06	Linus McAtee	Fred Hopkins	Osmand	Jock
1928	**Reigh Count**	2:10⅖	Chick Lang	Bert Michell	Misstep	Toro
1929	**Clyde Van Dusen**	2:10⅘	Linus McAtee	Clyde Van Dusen	Naishapur	Panchio
1930	**GALLANT FOX**	2:07⅗	Earl Sande	Jim Fitzsimmons	Gallant Knight	Ned O.
1931	**Twenty Grand**	2:01⅘	Charley Kurtsinger	James Rowe Jr.	Sweep All	Mate
1932	**Burgoo King**	2:05⅕	Eugene James	Dick Thompson	Economic	Stepenfetchit
1933	**Brokers Tip**	2:06⅘	Don Meade	Dick Thompson	Head Play	Charley O.
1934	**Cavalcade**	2:04	Mack Garner	Bob Smith	Discovery	Agrarian
1935	**OMAHA**	2:05	Willie Saunders	Jim Fitzsimmons	Roman Soldier	Whiskolo
1936	**Bold Venture**	2:03⅗	Ira Hanford	Max Hirsch	Brevity	Indian Broom
1937	**WAR ADMIRAL**	2:03⅕	Charley Kurtsinger	George Conway	Pompoon	Reaping Reward
1938	**Lawrin**	2:04⅘	Eddie Arcaro	Ben Jones	Dauber	Can't Wait
1939	**Johnstown**	2:03⅖	James Stout	Jim Fitzsimmons	Challedon	Heather Broom
1940	**Gallahadion**	2:05	Carroll Bierman	Roy Waldron	Bimelech	Dit
1941	**WHIRLAWAY**	2:01⅖	Eddie Arcaro	Ben Jones	Staretor	Market Wise
1942	**Shut Out**	2:04⅖	Wayne Wright	John Gaver	Alsab	Valdina Orphan
1943	**COUNT FLEET**	2:04	Johnny Longden	Don Cameron	Blue Swords	Slide Rule
1944	**Pensive**	2:04⅕	Conn McCreary	Ben Jones	Broadcloth	Stir Up
1945	**Hoop Jr**	2:07	Eddie Arcaro	Ivan Parke	Pot O'Luck	Darby Dieppe
1946	**ASSAULT**	2:06⅗	Warren Mehrtens	Max Hirsch	Spy Song	Hampden
1947	**Jet Pilot**	2:06⅘	Eric Guerin	Tom Smith	Phalanx	Faultless
1948	**CITATION**	2:05⅖	Eddie Arcaro	Ben Jones	Coaltown	My Request
1949	**Ponder**	2:04⅕	Steve Brooks	Ben Jones	Capot	Palestinian
1950	**Middleground**	2:01⅗	William Boland	Max Hirsch	Hill Prince	Mr. Trouble
1951	**Count Turf**	2:02⅗	Conn McCreary	Sol Rutchick	Royal Mustang	Ruhe
1952	**Hill Gail**	2:01⅗	Eddie Arcaro	Ben Jones	Sub Fleet	Blue Man
1953	**Dark Star**	2:02	Hank Moreno	Eddie Hayward	Native Dancer	Invigorator
1954	**Determine**	2:03	Raymond York	Willie Molter	Hasty Road	Hasseyampa
1955	**Swaps**	2:01⅘	Bill Shoemaker	Mesh Tenney	Nashua	Summer Tan
1956	**Needles**	2:03⅖	David Erb	Hugh Fontaine	Fabius	Come On Red
1957	**Iron Liege**	2:02⅕	Bill Hartack	Jimmy Jones	Gallant Man	Round Table
1958	**Tim Tam**	2:05	Ismael Valenzuela	Jimmy Jones	Lincoln Road	Noureddin
1959	**Tomy Lee**	2:02⅕	Bill Shoemaker	Frank Childs	Sword Dancer	First Landing
1960	**Venetian Way**	2:02⅖	Bill Hartack	Victor Sovinski	Bally Ache	Victoria Park
1961	**Carry Back**	2:04	John Sellers	Jack Price	Crozier	Bass Clef
1962	**Decidedly**	2:00⅖	Bill Hartack	Horatio Luro	Roman Line	Ridan
1963	**Chateaugay**	2:01⅘	Braulio Baeza	James Conway	Never Bend	Candy Spots
1964	**Northern Dancer**	2:00	Bill Hartack	Horatio Luro	Hill Rise	The Scoundrel
1965	**Lucky Debonair**	2:01⅕	Bill Shoemaker	Frank Catrone	Dapper Dan	Tom Rolfe
1966	**Kauai King**	2:02	Don Brumfield	Henry Forrest	Advocator	Blue Skyer
1967	**Proud Clarion**	2:00⅗	Bobby Ussery	Loyd Gentry	Barbs Delight	Damascus
1968	**Forward Pass***	—	Ismael Valenzuela	Henry Forrest	Francie's Hat	T.V. Commercial
1969	**Majestic Prince**	2:01⅘	Bill Hartack	Johnny Longden	Arts and Letters	Dike
1970	**Dust Commander**	2:03⅖	Mike Manganello	Don Combs	My Dad George	High Echelon
1971	**Canonero II**	2:03⅕	Gustavo Avila	Juan Arias	Jim French	Bold Reason
1972	**Riva Ridge**	2:01⅘	Ron Turcotte	Lucien Laurin	No Le Hace	Hold Your Peace

*Dancer's Image finished first (in 2:02½), but was disqualified after traces of prohibited medication were found in his system.

Kentucky Derby (Cont.)

Year		Time	Jockey	Trainer	2nd place	3rd place
1973	**SECRETARIAT**	1:59⅖	Ron Turcotte	Lucien Laurin	Sham	Our Native
1974	**Cannonade**	2:04	Angel Cordero Jr.	Woody Stephens	Hudson County	Agitate
1975	**Foolish Pleasure**	2:02	Jacinto Vasquez	LeRoy Jolley	Avatar	Diabolo
1976	**Bold Forbes**	2:01⅗	Angel Cordero Jr.	Laz Barrera	Honest Pleasure	Elocutionist
1977	**SEATTLE SLEW**	2:02⅕	Jean Cruguet	Billy Turner	Run Dusty Run	Sanhedrin
1978	**AFFIRMED**	2:01⅕	Steve Cauthen	Laz Barrera	Alydar	Believe It
1979	**Spectacular Bid**	2:02⅖	Ron Franklin	Bud Delp	General Assembly	Golden Act
1980	**Genuine Risk**	2:02	Jacinto Vasquez	LeRoy Jolley	Rumbo	Jaklin Klugman
1981	**Pleasant Colony**	2:02	Jorge Velasquez	John Campo	Woodchopper	Partez
1982	**Gato Del Sol**	2:02⅖	E. Delahoussaye	Eddie Gregson	Laser Light	Reinvested
1983	**Sunny's Halo**	2:02⅕	E. Delahoussaye	David Cross Jr.	Desert Wine	Caveat
1984	**Swale**	2:02⅖	Laffit Pincay Jr.	Woody Stephens	Coax Me Chad	At The Threshold
1985	**Spend A Buck**	2:00⅕	Angel Cordero Jr.	Cam Gambolati	Stephan's Odyssey	Chief's Crown
1986	**Ferdinand**	2:02⅘	Bill Shoemaker	Chas.Whittingham	Bold Arrangement	Broad Brush
1987	**Alysheba**	2:03⅗	Chris McCarron	Jack Van Berg	Bet Twice	Avies Copy
1988	**Winning Colors**	2:02⅕	Gary Stevens	D. Wayne Lukas	Forty Niner	Risen Star
1989	**Sunday Silence**	2:05	Pat Valenzuela	Chas. Whittingham	Easy Goer	Awe Inspiring
1990	**Unbridled**	2:02	Craig Perret	Carl Nafzger	Summer Squall	Pleasant Tap
1991	**Strike the Gold**	2:03	Chris Antley	Nick Zito	Best Pal	Mane Minister
1992	**Lil E. Tee**	2:03	Pat Day	Lynn Whiting	Casual Lies	Dance Floor
1993	**Sea Hero**	2:02⅖	Jerry Bailey	Mack Miller	Prairie Bayou	Wild Gale
1994	**Go For Gin**	2:03⅗	Chris McCarron	Nick Zito	Strodes Creek	Blumin Affair
1995	**Thunder Gulch**	2:01⅕	Gary Stevens	D. Wayne Lukas	Tejano Run	Timber Country
1996	**Grindstone**	2:01	Jerry Bailey	D. Wayne Lukas	Cavonnier	Prince of Thieves

Preakness Stakes

For three-year-olds. Held two weeks after the Kentucky Derby at Pimlico Race Course in Baltimore, Md. Inaugurated 1873. Originally run at 1½ miles (1873-88), then at 1¼ miles (1889), 1½ miles (1890), 1¹⁄₁₆ miles (1894-1900), 1 mile & 70 yards (1901-07), 1¹⁄₁₆ miles (1908), 1 mile (1909-10), 1⅛ miles (1911-24), and the present 13/16 miles since 1925

Trainers with most wins: Robert W. Walden (7); T.J. Healey (5); Sunny Jim Fitzsimmons, Jimmy Jones and D. Wayne Lukas (4); and J. Whalen (3).

Jockeys with most wins: Eddie Arcaro (6); Pat Day (5); G. Barbee, Bill Hartack and Lloyd Hughes (3).

Winning fillies: Flocarline (1903), Whimsical (1906), Rhine Maiden (1915) and Nellie Morse (1924).

Year		Time	Jockey	Trainer	2nd place	3rd place
1873	**Survivor**	2:43	G. Barbee	A.D. Pryor	John Boulger	Artist
1874	**Culpepper**	2:56½	W. Donohue	H. Gaffney	King Amadeus	Scratch
1875	**Tom Ochiltree**	2:43½	L. Hughes	R.W. Walden	Viator	Bay Final
1876	**Shirley**	2:44¾	G. Barbee	W. Brown	Rappahannock	Compliment
1877	**Cloverbrook**	2:45½	C. Holloway	J. Walden	Bombast	Lucifer
1878	**Duke of Magenta**	2:41¾	C. Holloway	R.W. Walden	Bayard	Albert
1879	**Harold**	2:40½	L. Hughes	R.W. Walden	Jericho	Rochester
1880	**Grenada**	2:40½	L. Hughes	R.W. Walden	Oden	Emily F.
1881	**Saunterer**	2:40½	T. Costello	R.W. Walden	Compensation	Baltic
1882	**Vanguard**	2:44½	T. Costello	R.W. Walden	Heck	Col. Watson
1883	**Jacobus**	2:42½	G. Barbee	R. Dwyer	Parnell	(2-horse race)
1884	**Knight of Ellerslie**	2:39½	S. Fisher	T.B. Doswell	Welcher	(2-horse race)
1885	**Tecumseh**	2:49	Jim McLaughlin	C. Littlefield	Wickham	John C.
1886	**The Bard**	2:45	S. Fisher	J. Huggins	Eurus	Elkwood
1887	**Dunboyne**	2:39½	W. Donohue	W. Jennings	Mahoney	Raymond
1888	**Refund**	2:49	F. Littlefield	R.W. Walden	Bertha B.*	Glendale
1889	**Buddhist**	2:17½	W. Anderson	J. Rogers	Japhet	(2-horse race)
1890	**Montague**	2:36¾	W. Martin	E. Feakes	Philosophy	Barrister
1891-93	Not held					
1894	**Assignee**	1:49¼	F. Taral	W. Lakeland	Potentate	Ed Kearney
1895	**Belmar**	1:50½	F. Taral	E. Feakes	April Fool	Sue Kittie
1896	**Margrave**	1:51	H. Griffin	Byron McClelland	Hamilton II	Intermission
1897	**Paul Kauvar**	1:51¼	T. Thorpe	T.P. Hayes	Elkins	On Deck
1898	**Sly Fox**	1:49¾	W. Simms	H. Campbell	The Huguenot	Nuto
1899	**Half Time**	1:47	R. Clawson	F. McCabe	Filigrane	Lackland
1900	**Hindus**	1:48⅖	H. Spencer	J.H. Morris	Sarmatian	Ten Candles
1901	**The Parader**	1:47⅕	F. Landry	T.J. Healey	Sadie S.	Dr. Barlow
1902	**Old England**	1:45⅘	L. Jackson	G.B. Morris	Maj. Daingerfield	Namtor
1903	**Flocarline**	1:44⅘	W. Gannon	H.C. Riddle	Mackey Dwyer	Rightful
1904	**Bryn Mawr**	1:44⅕	E. Hildebrand	W.F. Presgrave	Wotan	Dolly Spanker
1905	**Cairngorm**	1:45⅘	W. Davis	A.J. Joyner	Kiamesha	Coy Maid
1906	**Whimsical**	1:45	Walter Miller	T.J. Gaynor	Content	Larabie
1907	**Don Enrique**	1:45⅖	G. Mountain	J. Whalen	Ethon	Zambesi

* Later named Judge Murray.

Year		Time	Jockey	Trainer	2nd place	3rd place
1908	**Royal Tourist**	1:46⅖	Eddie Dugan	A.J. Joyner	Live Wire	Robert Cooper
1909	**Effendi**	1:39⅘	Willie Doyle	F.C. Frisbie	Fashion Plate	Hill Top
1910	**Layminster**	1:40⅗	R. Estep	J.S. Healy	Dalhousie	Sager
1911	**Watervale**	1:51	Eddie Dugan	J. Whalen	Zeus	The Nigger
1912	**Colonel Holloway**	1:56⅗	C. Turner	D. Woodford	Bwana Tumbo	Tipsand
1913	**Buskin**	1:53⅖	James Butwell	J. Whalen	Kleburne	Barnegat
1914	**Holiday**	1:53⅘	A. Schuttinger	J.S. Healy	Brave Cunarder	Defendum
1915	**Rhine Maiden**	1:58	Douglas Hoffman	F. Devers	Half Rock	Runes
1916	**Damrosch**	1:54⅘	Linus McAtee	A.G. Weston	Greenwood	Achievement
1917	**Kalitan**	1:54⅖	E. Haynes	Bill Hurley	Al M. Dick	Kentucky Boy
1918	**War Cloud**	1:53⅗	Johnny Loftus	W.B. Jennings	Sunny Slope	Lanius
1918	**Jack Hare Jr**	1:53⅖	Charles Peak	F.D. Weir	The Porter	Kate Bright
1919	**SIR BARTON**	1:53	Johnny Loftus	H. Guy Bedwell	Eternal	Sweep On
1920	**Man o' War**	1:51⅗	Clarence Kummer	L. Feustel	Upset	Wildair
1921	**Broomspun**	1:54⅕	F. Coltiletti	James Rowe Sr.	Polly Ann	Jeg
1922	**Pillory**	1:51⅗	L. Morris	Thomas Healey	Hea	June Grass
1923	**Vigil**	1:53⅗	B. Marinelli	Thomas Healey	General Thatcher	Rialto
1924	**Nellie Morse**	1:57⅕	John Merimee	A.B. Gordon	Transmute	Mad Play
1925	**Coventry**	1:59	Clarence Kummer	William Duke	Backbone	Almadel
1926	**Display**	1:59⅘	John Maiben	Thomas Healey	Blondin	Mars
1927	**Bostonian**	2:01⅗	Whitey Abel	Fred Hopkins	Sir Harry	Whiskery
1928	**Victorian**	2:00⅕	Sonny Workman	James Rowe Jr.	Toro	Solace
1929	**Dr. Freeland**	2:01⅗	Louis Schaefer	Thomas Healey	Minotaur	African
1930	**GALLANT FOX**	2:00⅗	Earl Sande	Jim Fitzsimmons	Crack Brigade	Snowflake
1931	**Mate**	1:59	George Ellis	J.W. Healy	Twenty Grand	Ladder
1932	**Burgoo King**	1:59⅘	Eugene James	Dick Thompson	Tick On	Boatswain
1933	**Head Play**	2:02	Charley Kurtsinger	Thomas Hayes	Ladysman	Utopian
1934	**High Quest**	1:58⅕	Robert Jones	Bob Smith	Cavalcade	Discovery
1935	**OMAHA**	1:58⅖	Willie Saunders	Jim Fitzsimmons	Firethorn	Psychic Bid
1936	**Bold Venture**	1:59	George Woolf	Max Hirsch	Granville	Jean Bart
1937	**WAR ADMIRAL**	1:58⅖	Charley Kurtsinger	George Conway	Pompoon	Flying Scot
1938	**Dauber**	1:59⅘	Maurice Peters	Dick Handlen	Cravat	Menow
1939	**Challedon**	1:59⅘	George Seabo	Louis Schaefer	Gilded Knight	Volitant
1940	**Bimelech**	1:58⅗	F.A. Smith	Bill Hurley	Mioland	Gallahadion
1941	**WHIRLAWAY**	1:58⅘	Eddie Arcaro	Ben Jones	King Cole	Our Boots
1942	**Alsab**	1:57	Basil James	Sarge Swenke	Requested & Sun Again (dead heat)	
1943	**COUNT FLEET**	1:57⅖	Johnny Longden	Don Cameron	Blue Swords	Vincentive
1944	**Pensive**	1:59⅕	Conn McCreary	Ben Jones	Platter	Stir Up
1945	**Polynesian**	1:58⅘	W.D. Wright	Morris Dixon	Hoop Jr.	Darby Dieppe
1946	**ASSAULT**	2:01⅖	Warren Mehrtens	Max Hirsch	Lord Boswell	Hampden
1947	**Faultless**	1:59	Doug Dodson	Jimmy Jones	On Trust	Phalanx
1948	**CITATION**	2:02⅖	Eddie Arcaro	Jimmy Jones	Vulcan's Forge	Bovard
1949	**Capot**	1:56	Ted Atkinson	J.M. Gaver	Palestinian	Noble Impulse
1950	**Hill Prince**	1:59⅕	Eddie Arcaro	Casey Hayes	Middleground	Dooly
1951	**Bold**	1:56⅖	Eddie Arcaro	Preston Burch	Counterpoint	Alerted
1952	**Blue Man**	1:57⅖	Conn McCreary	Woody Stephens	Jampol	One Count
1953	**Native Dancer**	1:57⅘	Eric Guerin	Bill Winfrey	Jamie K.	Royal Bay Gem
1954	**Hasty Road**	1:57⅖	Johnny Adams	Harry Trotsek	Correlation	Hasseyampa
1955	**Nashua**	1:54⅗	Eddie Arcaro	Jim Fitzsimmons	Saratoga	Traffic Judge
1956	**Fabius**	1:58⅖	Bill Hartack	Jimmy Jones	Needles	No Regrets
1957	**Bold Ruler**	1:56⅕	Eddie Arcaro	Jim Fitzsimmons	Iron Liege	Inside Tract
1958	**Tim Tam**	1:57⅕	Ismael Valenzuela	Jimmy Jones	Lincoln Road	Gone Fishin'
1959	**Royal Orbit**	1:57	William Harmatz	R. Cornell	Sword Dancer	Dunce
1960	**Bally Ache**	1:57⅗	Bobby Ussery	Jimmy Pitt	Victoria Park	Celtic Ash
1961	**Carry Back**	1:57⅗	Johnny Sellers	Jack Price	Globemaster	Crozier
1962	**Greek Money**	1:56⅕	John Rotz	V.W. Raines	Ridan	Roman Line
1963	**Candy Spots**	1:56⅕	Bill Shoemaker	Mesh Tenney	Chateaugay	Never Bend
1964	**Northern Dancer**	1:56⅘	Bill Hartack	Horatio Luro	The Scoundrel	Hill Rise
1965	**Tom Rolfe**	1:56⅕	Ron Turcotte	Frank Whiteley	Dapper Dan	Hail To All
1966	**Kauai King**	1:55⅖	Don Brumfield	Henry Forrest	Stupendous	Amberoid
1967	**Damascus**	1:55⅕	Bill Shoemaker	Frank Whiteley	In Reality	Proud Clarion
1968	**Forward Pass**	1:56⅘	Ismael Valenzuela	Henry Forrest	Out Of the Way	Nodouble
1969	**Majestic Prince**	1:55⅗	Bill Hartack	Johnny Longden	Arts and Letters	Jay Ray
1970	**Personality**	1:56⅕	Eddie Belmonte	John Jacobs	My Dad George	Silent Screen
1971	**Canonero II**	1:54	Gustavo Avila	Juan Arias	Eastern Fleet	Jim French
1972	**Bee Bee Bee**	1:55⅗	Eldon Nelson	Red Carroll	No Le Hace	Key To The Mint
1973	**SECRETARIAT**	1:54⅖	Ron Turcotte	Lucien Laurin	Sham	Our Native
1974	**Little Current**	1:54⅗	Miguel Rivera	Lou Rondinello	Neapolitan Way	Cannonade

Preakness Stakes (Cont.)

Year		Time	Jockey	Trainer	2nd place	3rd place
1975	**Master Derby**	1:56⅖	Darrel McHargue	Smiley Adams	Foolish Pleasure	Diabolo
1976	**Elocutionist**	1:55	John Lively	Paul Adwell	Play The Red	Bold Forbes
1977	**SEATTLE SLEW**	1:54⅖	Jean Cruguet	Billy Turner	Iron Constitution	Run Dusty Run
1978	**AFFIRMED**	1:54⅖	Steve Cauthen	Laz Barrera	Alydar	Believe It
1979	**Spectacular Bid**	1:54⅕	Ron Franklin	Bud Delp	Golden Act	Screen King
1980	**Codex**	1:54⅕	Angel Cordero Jr.	D. Wayne Lukas	Genuine Risk	Colonel Moran
1981	**Pleasant Colony**	1:54⅗	Jorge Velasquez	John Campo	Bold Ego	Paristo
1982	**Aloma's Ruler**	1:55⅖	Jack Kaenel	John Lenzini Jr.	Linkage	Cut Away
1983	**Deputed Testamony**	1:55⅖	Donald Miller Jr.	Bill Boniface	Desert Wine	High Honors
1984	**Gate Dancer**	1:53⅗	Angel Cordero Jr.	Jack Van Berg	Play On	Fight Over
1985	**Tank's Prospect**	1:53⅖	Pat Day	D. Wayne Lukas	Chief's Crown	Eternal Prince
1986	**Snow Chief**	1:54⅘	Alex Solis	Melvin Stute	Ferdinand	Broad Brush
1987	**Alysheba**	1:55⅘	Chris McCarron	Jack Van Berg	Bet Twice	Cryptoclearance
1988	**Risen Star**	1:56⅕	E. Delahoussaye	Louie Roussel III	Brian's Time	Winning Colors
1989	**Sunday Silence**	1:53⅘	Pat Valenzuela	Chas. Whittingham	Easy Goer	Rock Point
1990	**Summer Squall**	1:53⅗	Pat Day	Neil Howard	Unbridled	Mister Frisky
1991	**Hansel**	1:54	Jerry Bailey	Frank Brothers	Corporate Report	Mane Minister
1992	**Pine Bluff**	1:55⅗	Chris McCarron	Tom Bohannan	Alydeed	Casual Lies
1993	**Prairie Bayou**	1:56⅗	Mike Smith	Tom Bohannon	Cherokee Run	El Bakan
1994	**Tabasco Cat**	1:56⅖	Pat Day	D. Wayne Lukas	Go For Gin	Concern
1995	**Timber Country**	1:54⅖	Pat Day	D. Wayne Lukas	Oliver's Twist	Thunder Gulch
1996	**Louis Quatorze**	1:53⅖	Pat Day	Nick Zito	Skip Away	Editor's Note

Belmont Stakes

For three-year-olds. Held three weeks after Preakness Stakes at Belmont Park in Elmont, N.Y. Inaugurated in 1867 at Jerome Park, moved to Morris Park in 1890 and Belmont Park in 1905.

Originally run at 1 mile and 5 furlongs (1867-89), then 1¼ miles (1890-1905), 1⅜ miles (1906-25), and the present 1½ miles since 1926.

Trainers with most wins: James Rowe, Sr. (8); Sam Hildreth (7); Sunny Jim Fitzsimmons (6); Woody Stephens (5); Max Hirsch and Robert W. Walden (4); Elliott Burch, Lucien Laurin, D. Wayne Lukas, F. McCabe and D. McDaniel (3).

Jockeys with most wins: Eddie Arcaro and Jim McLaughlin (6); Earl Sande and Bill Shoemaker (5); Braulio Baeza, Laffit Pincay, Jr and James Stout (3).

Winning fillies: Ruthless (1867) and Tanya (1905).

Year		Time	Jockey	Trainer	2nd place	3rd place
1867	**Ruthless**	3:05	J. Gilpatrick	A.J. Minor	DeCourcey	Rivoli
1868	**General Duke**	3:02	Bobby Swim	A. Thompson	Northumberland	Fanny Ludlow
1869	**Fenian**	3:04¼	C. Miller	J. Pincus	Glenelg	Invercauld
1870	**Kingfisher**	2:59½	W. Dick	R. Colston	Foster	Midday
1871	**Harry Bassett**	2:56	W. Miller	D. McDaniel	Stockwood	By the Sea
1872	**Joe Daniels**	2:58¼	James Roe	D. McDaniel	Meteor	Shylock
1873	**Springbok**	3:01¾	James Roe	D. McDaniel	Count d'Orsay	Strachino
1874	**Saxon**	2:39½	G. Barbee	W. Prior	Grinstead	Aaron Pennington
1875	**Calvin**	2:42¼	Bobby Swim	A. Williams	Aristides	Milner
1876	**Algerine**	2:40½	Billy Donohue	Major Doswell	Fiddlesticks	Barricade
1877	**Cloverbrook**	2:46	C. Holloway	J. Walden	Loiterer	Baden-Baden
1878	**Duke of Magenta**	2:43½	L. Hughes	R.W. Walden	Bramble	Sparta
1879	**Spendthrift**	2:42¾	George Evans	T. Puryear	Monitor	Jericho
1880	**Grenada**	2:47	L. Hughes	R.W. Walden	Ferncliffe	Turenne
1881	**Saunterer**	2:47	T. Costello	R.W. Walden	Eole	Baltic
1882	**Forester**	2:43	Jim McLaughlin	L. Stuart	Babcock	Wyoming
1883	**George Kinney**	2:42½	Jim McLaughlin	James Rowe Sr.	Trombone	Renegade
1884	**Panique**	2:42	Jim McLaughlin	James Rowe Sr.	Knight of Ellerslie	Himalaya
1885	**Tyrant**	2:43	Paul Duffy	W. Claypool	St. Augustine	Tecumseh
1886	**Inspector B**	2:41	Jim McLaughlin	F. McCabe	The Bard	Linden
1887	**Hanover**	2:43½	Jim McLaughlin	F. McCabe	Oneko	(2-horse race)
1888	**Sir Dixon**	2:40¼	Jim McLaughlin	F. McCabe	Prince Royal	(2-horse race)
1889	**Eric**	2:47¼	W. Hayward	J. Huggins	Diablo	Zephyrus
1890	**Burlington**	2:07¾	Pike Barnes	A. Cooper	Devotee	Padishah
1891	**Foxford**	2:08¾	Ed Garrison	M. Donavan	Montana	Laurestan
1892	**Patron**	2:12	W. Hayward	L. Stuart	Shellbark	(2-horse race)
1893	**Commanche**	1:53¼	Willie Simms	G. Hannon	Dr. Rice	Rainbow
1894	**Henry of Navarre**	1:56½	Willie Simms	B. McClelland	Prig	Assignee
1895	**Belmar**	2:11½	Fred Taral	E. Feakes	Counter Tenor	Nanki Poo
1896	**Hastings**	2:24½	H. Griffin	J.J. Hyland	Handspring	Hamilton II
1897	**Scottish Chieftain**	2:23¼	J. Scherrer	M. Byrnes	On Deck	Octagon
1898	**Bowling Brook**	2:32	F. Littlefield	R.W. Walden	Previous	Hamburg
1899	**Jean Beraud**	2:23	R. Clawson	Sam Hildreth	Half Time	Glengar

Year		Time	Jockey	Trainer	2nd place	3rd place
1900	**Ildrim**	2:21¼	Nash Turner	H.E. Leigh	Petruchio	Missionary
1901	**Commando**	2:21	H. Spencer	James Rowe Sr.	The Parader	All Green
1902	**Masterman**	2:22⅗	John Bullman	J.J. Hyland	Renald	King Hanover
1903	**Africander**	2:21¾	John Bullman	R. Miller	Whorler	Red Knight
1904	**Delhi**	2:06⅗	George Odom	James Rowe Sr.	Graziallo	Rapid Water
1905	**Tanya**	2:08	E. Hildebrand	J.W. Rogers	Blandy	Hot Shot
1906	**Burgomaster**	2:20	Lucien Lyne	J.W. Rogers	The Quail	Accountant
1907	**Peter Pan**	N/A	G. Mountain	James Rowe Sr.	Superman	Frank Gill
1908	**Colin**	N/A	Joe Notter	James Rowe Sr.	Fair Play	King James
1909	**Joe Madden**	2:21⅗	E. Dugan	Sam Hildreth	Wise Mason	Donald MacDonald
1910	**Sweep**	2:22	James Butwell	James Rowe Sr.	Duke of Ormonde	(2-horse race)
1911-12	Not held					
1913	**Prince Eugene**	2:18	Roscoe Troxler	James Rowe Sr.	Rock View	Flying Fairy
1914	**Luke McLuke**	2:20	Merritt Buxton	J.F. Schorr	Gainer	Charlestonian
1915	**The Finn**	2:18⅖	George Byrne	E.W. Heffner	Half Rock	Pebbles
1916	**Friar Rock**	2:22	E. Haynes	Sam Hildreth	Spur	Churchill
1917	**Hourless**	2:17⅘	James Butwell	Sam Hildreth	Skeptic	Wonderful
1918	**Johren**	2:20⅖	Frank Robinson	A. Simons	War Cloud	Cum Sah
1919	**SIR BARTON**	2:17⅖	John Loftus	H. Guy Bedwell	Sweep On	Natural Bridge
1920	**Man o' War**	2:14⅕	Clarence Kummer	L. Feustel	Donnacona	(2-horse race)
1921	**Grey Lag**	2:16⅘	Earl Sande	Sam Hildreth	Sporting Blood	Leonardo II
1922	**Pillory**	2:18⅘	C.H. Miller	T.J. Healey	Snob II	Hea
1923	**Zev**	2:19	Earl Sande	Sam Hildreth	Chickvale	Rialto
1924	**Mad Play**	2:18⅘	Earl Sande	Sam Hildreth	Mr. Mutt	Modest
1925	**American Flag**	2:16⅘	Albert Johnson	G.R. Tompkins	Dangerous	Swope
1926	**Crusader**	2:32⅕	Albert Johnson	George Conway	Espino	Haste
1927	**Chance Shot**	2:32⅖	Earl Sande	Pete Coyne	Bois de Rose	Flambino
1928	**Vito**	2:33⅕	Clarence Kummer	Max Hirsch	Genie	Diavolo
1929	**Blue Larkspur**	2:32⅘	Mack Garner	C. Hastings	African	Jack High
1930	**GALLANT FOX**	2:31⅗	Earl Sande	Jim Fitzsimmons	Whichone	Questionnaire
1931	**Twenty Grand**	2:29⅗	Charley Kurtsinger	James Rowe Jr.	Sun Meadow	Jamestown
1932	**Faireno**	2:32⅘	Tom Malley	Jim Fitzsimmons	Osculator	Flag Pole
1933	**Hurryoff**	2:32⅗	Mack Garner	H. McDaniel	Nimbus	Union
1934	**Peace Chance**	2:29⅕	W.D. Wright	Pete Coyne	High Quest	Good Goods
1935	**OMAHA**	2:30⅗	Willie Saunders	Jim Fitzsimmons	Firethorn	Rosemont
1936	**Granville**	2:30	James Stout	Jim Fitzsimmons	Mr. Bones	Hollyrood
1937	**WAR ADMIRAL**	2:28⅗	Charley Kurtsinger	George Conway	Sceneshifter	Vamoose
1938	**Pasteurized**	2:29⅖	James Stout	George Odom	Dauber	Cravat
1939	**Johnstown**	2:29⅗	James Stout	Jim Fitzsimmons	Belay	Gilded Knight
1940	**Bimelech**	2:29⅗	Fred Smith	Bill Hurley	Your Chance	Andy K.
1941	**WHIRLAWAY**	2:31	Eddie Arcaro	Ben Jones	Robert Morris	Yankee Chance
1942	**Shut Out**	2:29⅕	Eddie Arcaro	John Gaver	Alsab	Lochinvar
1943	**COUNT FLEET**	2:28⅕	Johnny Longden	Don Cameron	Fairy Manhurst	Deseronto
1944	**Bounding Home**	2:32⅕	G.L. Smith	Matt Brady	Pensive	Bull Dandy
1945	**Pavot**	2:30⅕	Eddie Arcaro	Oscar White	Wildlife	Jeep
1946	**ASSAULT**	2:30⅘	Warren Mehrtens	Max Hirsch	Natchez	Cable
1947	**Phalanx**	2:29⅖	R. Donoso	Syl Veitch	Tide Rips	Tailspin
1948	**CITATION**	2:28⅕	Eddie Arcaro	Jimmy Jones	Better Self	Escadru
1949	**Capot**	2:30⅕	Ted Atkinson	John Gaver	Ponder	Palestinian
1950	**Middleground**	2:28⅗	William Boland	Max Hirsch	Lights Up	Mr. Trouble
1951	**Counterpoint**	2:29	David Gorman	Syl Veitch	Battlefield	Battle Morn
1952	**One Count**	2:30⅕	Eddie Arcaro	Oscar White	Blue Man	Armageddon
1953	**Native Dancer**	2:28⅗	Eric Guerin	Bill Winfrey	Jamie K.	Royal Bay Gem
1954	**High Gun**	2:30⅘	Eric Guerin	Max Hirsch	Fisherman	Limelight
1955	**Nashua**	2:29	Eddie Arcaro	Jim Fitzsimmons	Blazing Count	Portersville
1956	**Needles**	2:29⅘	David Erb	Hugh Fontaine	Career Boy	Fabius
1957	**Gallant Man**	2:26⅗	Bill Shoemaker	John Nerud	Inside Tract	Bold Ruler
1958	**Cavan**	2:30⅕	Pete Anderson	Tom Barry	Tim Tam	Flamingo
1959	**Sword Dancer**	2:28⅖	Bill Shoemaker	Elliott Burch	Bagdad	Royal Orbit
1960	**Celtic Ash**	2:29⅕	Bill Hartack	Tom Barry	Venetian Way	Disperse
1961	**Sherluck**	2:29⅕	Braulio Baeza	Harold Young	Globemaster	Guadalcanal
1962	**Jaipur**	2:28⅘	Bill Shoemaker	B. Mulholland	Admiral's Voyage	Crimson Satan
1963	**Chateaugay**	2:30⅕	Braulio Baeza	James Conway	Candy Spots	Choker
1964	**Quadrangle**	2:28⅖	Manuel Ycaza	Elliott Burch	Roman Brother	Northern Dancer
1965	**Hail to All**	2:28⅖	John Sellers	Eddie Yowell	Tom Rolfe	First Family
1966	**Amberoid**	2:29⅗	William Boland	Lucien Laurin	Buffle	Advocator
1967	**Damascus**	2:28⅘	Bill Shoemaker	F.Y. Whiteley Jr.	Cool Reception	Gentleman James

Wide World Photos

Jockey **Ron Turcotte** glances back at the field as **Secretariat** rounds the turn en route to a 31-length victory and the Triple Crown in the 1973 Belmont Stakes. The winning time of 2:24 is still a world record for a mile and a half on dirt.

Belmont Stakes (Cont.)

Year		Time	Jockey	Trainer	2nd place	3rd place
1968	**Stage Door Johnny**	2:27⅕	Gus Gustines	John Gaver	Forward Pass	Call Me Prince
1969	**Arts and Letters**	2:28⅘	Braulio Baeza	Elliott Burch	Majestic Prince	Dike
1970	**High Echelon**	2:34	John Rotz	John Jacobs	Needles N Pens	Naskra
1971	**Pass Catcher**	2:30⅖	Walter Blum	Eddie Yowell	Jim French	Bold Reason
1972	**Riva Ridge**	2:28	Ron Turcotte	Lucien Laurin	Ruritania	Cloudy Dawn
1973	**SECRETARIAT**	2:24	Ron Turcotte	Lucien Laurin	Twice A Prince	My Gallant
1974	**Little Current**	2:29⅕	Miguel Rivera	Lou Rondinello	Jolly Johu	Cannonade
1975	**Avatar**	2:28⅕	Bill Shoemaker	Tommy Doyle	Foolish Pleasure	Master Derby
1976	**Bold Forbes**	2:29	Angel Cordero Jr.	Laz Barrera	McKenzie Bridge	Great Contractor
1977	**SEATTLE SLEW**	2:29⅗	Jean Cruguet	Billy Turner	Run Dusty Run	Sanhedrin
1978	**AFFIRMED**	2:26⅘	Steve Cauthen	Laz Barrera	Alydar	Darby Creek Road
1979	**Coastal**	2:28⅗	Ruben Hernandez	David Whiteley	Golden Act	Spectacular Bid
1980	**Temperence Hill**	2:29⅘	Eddie Maple	Joseph Cantey	Genuine Risk	Rockhill Native
1981	**Summing**	2:29	George Martens	Luis Barerra	Highland Blade	Pleasant Colony
1982	**Conquistador Cielo**	2:28⅕	Laffit Pincay Jr.	Woody Stephens	Gato Del Sol	Illuminate
1983	**Caveat**	2:27⅘	Laffit Pincay Jr.	Woody Stephens	Slew o' Gold	Barberstown
1984	**Swale**	2:27⅕	Laffit Pincay Jr.	Woody Stephens	Pine Circle	Morning Bob
1985	**Creme Fraiche**	2:27	Eddie Maple	Woody Stephens	Stephan's Odyssey	Chief's Crown
1986	**Danzig Connection**	2:29⅘	Chris McCarron	Woody Stephens	Johns Treasure	Ferdinand
1987	**Bet Twice**	2:28⅕	Craig Perret	Jimmy Croll	Cryptoclearance	Gulch
1988	**Risen Star**	2:26⅖	E. Delahoussaye	Louie Roussel III	Kingpost	Brian's Time
1989	**Easy Goer**	2:26	Pat Day	Shug McGaughey	Sunday Silence	Le Voyageur
1990	**Go And Go**	2:27⅕	Michael Kinane	Dermot Weld	Thirty Six Red	Baron de Vaux
1991	**Hansel**	2:28	Jerry Bailey	Frank Brothers	Strike the Gold	Mane Minister
1992	**A.P. Indy**	2:26	E. Delahoussaye	Neil Drysdale	My Memoirs	Pine Bluff
1993	**Colonial Affair**	2:29⅘	Julie Krone	Scotty Schulhofer	Kissin Kris	Wild Gale
1994	**Tabasco Cat**	2:26⅘	Pat Day	D. Wayne Lukas	Go For Gin	Strodes Creek
1995	**Thunder Gulch**	2:32	Gary Stevens	D. Wayne Lukas	Star Standard	Citadeed
1996	**Editor's Note**	2:28⅘	Rene Douglas	D. Wayne Lukas	Skip Away	My Flag

Breeders' Cup Championship

(See Update chapter for 1996 results)

Inaugurated on Nov. 10, 1984, the Breeders' Cup Championship consists of seven races on one track on one day late in the year to determine Thoroughbred racing's principle champions.

The Breeders' Cup has been held at the following tracks (in alphabetical order): Aqueduct Racetrack (N.Y.) in 1985; Belmont Park (N.Y.) in 1990 and '95; Churchill Downs (Ky.) in 1988, '91 and '94; Gulfstream Park (Fla.) in 1989 and '92; Hollywood Park (Calif.) in 1984 and '87; Santa Anita Park (Calif.) in 1986 and '93; and Woodbine (Tor.) in 1996.

Trainers with most wins: D. Wayne Lukas (12); Shug McGaughey (7); Neil Drysdale (5); Ron McAnally (4); Francois Boutin and Bill Mott (3).

Jockeys with most wins: Pat Day (8); Eddie Delahoussaye and Laffit Pincay Jr. (7); Chris McCarron, Mike Smith and Pat Valenzuela (6); Jerry Bailey and Jose Santos (5); Angel Cordero (4); Craig Perret, Randy Romero, Mike Smith and Gary Stevens (3).

Juvenile

Distances: one mile (1984-85, 87); 1 1/16 miles (1986 and since 1988).

Year		Time	Jockey	Trainer	2nd place	3rd place
1984	**Chief's Crown**	1:36⅕	Don MacBeth	Roger Laurin	Tank's Prospect	Spend A Buck
1985	**Tasso**	1:36⅕	Laffit Pincay Jr.	Neil Drysdale	Storm Cat	Scat Dancer
1986	**Capote**	1:43⅘	Laffit Pincay Jr.	D. Wayne Lukas	Qualify	Alysheba
1987	**Success Express**	1:35⅕	Jose Santos	D. Wayne Lukas	Regal Classic	Tejano
1988	**Is It True**	1:46⅗	Laffit Pincay Jr.	D. Wayne Lukas	Easy Goer	Tagel
1989	**Rhythm**	1:43⅗	Craig Perret	Shug McGaughey	Grand Canyon	Slavic
1990	**Fly So Free**	1:43⅖	Jose Santos	Scotty Schulhofer	Take Me Out	Lost Mountain
1991	**Arazi**	1:44⅗	Pat Valenzuela	Francois Boutin	Bertrando	Snappy Landing
1992	**Gilded Time**	1:43⅖	Chris McCarron	Darrell Vienna	It'sali'lknownfact	River Special
1993	**Brocco**	1:42⅘	Gary Stevens	Randy Winick	Blumin Affair	Tabasco Cat
1994	**Timber Country**	1:44⅖	Pat Day	D. Wayne Lukas	Eltish	Tejano Run
1995	**Unbridled's Song**	1:41⅗	Mike Smith	James Ryerson	Hennessy	Editor's Note

Juvenile Fillies

Distances: one mile (1984-85, 87); 1 1/16 miles (1986 and since 1988).

Year		Time	Jockey	Trainer	2nd place	3rd place
1984	**Outstandingly**	1:37⅘	Walter Guerra	Pancho Martin	Dusty Heart	Fine Spirit
1985	**Twilight Ridge**	1:35⅘	Jorge Velasquez	D. Wayne Lukas	Family Style	Steal A Kiss
1986	**Brave Raj**	1:43⅕	Pat Valenzuela	Melvin Stute	Tappiano	Saros Brig
1987	**Epitome**	1:36⅖	Pat Day	Phil Hauswald	Jeanne Jones	Dream Team
1988	**Open Mind**	1:46⅗	Angel Cordero Jr.	D. Wayne Lukas	Darby Shuffle	Lea Lucinda
1989	**Go for Wand**	1:44⅕	Randy Romero	Wm. Badgett, Jr.	Sweet Roberta	Stella Madrid
1990	**Meadow Star**	1:44	Jose Santos	LeRoy Jolley	Private Treasure	Dance Smartly
1991	**Pleasant Stage**	1:46⅖	Eddie Delahoussaye	Chris Speckert	La Spia	Cadillac Women
1992	**Liza**	1:42⅘	Pat Valenzuela	Alex Hassingfer	Educated Risk	Boots 'n Jackie
1993	**Phone Chatter**	1:43	Laffit Pincay Jr.	Richard Mandella	Sardula	Heavenly Prize
1994	**Flanders**	1:45⅕	Pat Day	D. Wayne Lukas	Serena's Song	Stormy Blues
1995	**My Flag**	1:42⅖	Jerry Bailey	Shug McGaughey	Cara Rafaela	Golden Attraction

Note: In 1984, winner Fran's Valentine was disqualified for interference in the stretch and placed 10th.

Sprint

Distance: six furlongs (since 1984).

Year		Time	Jockey	Trainer	2nd place	3rd place
1984	**Eillo**	1:10⅕	Craig Perret	Budd Lepman	Commemorate	Fighting Fit
1985	**Precisionist**	1:08⅖	Chris McCarron	L.R. Fenstermaker	Smile	Mt. Livermore
1986	**Smile**	1:08⅖	Jacinto Vasquez	Scotty Schulhofer	Pine Tree Lane	Bedside Promise
1987	**Very Subtle**	1:08⅘	Pat Valenzuela	Melvin Stute	Groovy	Exclusive Enough
1988	**Gulch**	1:10⅖	Angel Cordero Jr.	D. Wayne Lukas	Play The King	Afleet
1989	**Dancing Spree**	1:09	Angel Cordero Jr.	Shug McGaughey	Safely Kept	Dispersal
1990	**Safely Kept**	1:09⅗	Craig Perret	Alan Goldberg	Dayjur	Black Tie Affair
1991	**Sheikh Albadou**	1:09⅕	Pat Eddery	Alexander Scott	Pleasant Tap	Robyn Dancer
1992	**Thirty Slews**	1:08⅕	Eddie Delahoussaye	Bob Baffert	Meafara	Rubiano
1993	**Cardmania**	1:08⅗	Eddie Delahoussaye	Derek Meredith	Meafara	Gilded Time
1994	**Cherokee Run**	1:09⅖	Mike Smith	Frank Alexander	Soviet Problem	Cardmania
1995	**Desert Stormer**	1:09	Kent Desormeaux	Frank Lyons	Mr. Greeley	Lit de Justice

Mile

Year		Time	Jockey	Trainer	2nd place	3rd place
1984	**Royal Heroine**	1:32⅗	Fernando Toro	John Gosden	Star Choice	Cozzene
1985	**Cozzene**	1:35	Walter Guerra	Jan Nerud	Al Mamoon	Shadeed
1986	**Last Tycoon**	1:35⅕	Yves St.-Martin	Robert Collet	Palace Music	Fred Astaire
1987	**Miesque**	1:32⅘	Freddie Head	Francois Boutin	Show Dancer	Sonic Lady
1988	**Miesque**	1:38⅗	Freddie Head	Francois Boutin	Steinlen	Simply Majestic
1989	**Steinlen**	1:37⅕	Jose Santos	D. Wayne Lukas	Sabona	Most Welcome
1990	**Royal Academy**	1:35⅕	Lester Piggott	M.V. O'Brien	Itsallgreektome	Priolo
1991	**Opening Verse**	1:37⅖	Pat Valenzuela	Dick Lundy	Val des Bois	Star of Cozzene
1992	**Lure**	1:32⅘	Mike Smith	Shug McGaughey	Paradise Creek	Brief Truce
1993	**Lure**	1:33⅖	Mike Smith	Shug McGaughey	Ski Paradise	Fourstars Allstar
1994	**Barathea**	1:34⅖	Frankie Dettori	Luca Cumani	Johann Quatz	Unfinished Symph
1995	**Ridgewood Pearl**	1:43⅗	John Murtagh	John Oxx	Fastness	Sayyedati

Note: In 1985, 2nd place finisher Palace Music was disqualified for interference and placed 9th.

Breeders' Cup Championship (Cont.)

Distaff

Distances: 1¼ miles (1984-87); 1⅛ miles (since 1988).

Year		Time	Jockey	Trainer	2nd place	3rd place
1984	**Princess Rooney**	2:02⅖	Eddie Delahoussaye	Neil Drysdale	Life's Magic	Adored
1985	**Life's Magic**	2:02	Angel Cordero Jr.	D. Wayne Lukas	Lady's Secret	DontstopThemusic
1986	**Lady's Secret**	2:01⅕	Pat Day	D. Wayne Lukas	Fran's Valentine	Outstandingly
1987	**Sacahuista**	2:02⅘	Randy Romero	D. Wayne Lukas	Clabber Girl	Oueee Bebe
1988	**Personal Ensign**	1:52	Randy Romero	Shug McGaughey	Winning Colors	Goodbye Halo
1989	**Bayakoa**	1:47⅖	Laffit Pincay Jr.	Ron McAnally	Gorgeous	Open Mind
1990	**Bayakoa**	1:49⅕	Laffit Pincay Jr.	Ron McAnally	Colonial Waters	Valay Maid
1991	**Dance Smartly**	1:50⅘	Pat Day	Jim Day	Versailles Treaty	Brought to Mind
1992	**Paseana**	1:48	Chris McCarron	Ron McAnally	Versailles Treaty	Magical Maiden
1993	Hollywood Wildcat	1:48⅕	Eddie Delahoussaye	Neil Drysdale	Paseana	Re Toss
1994	**One Dreamer**	1:50⅗	Gary Stevens	Thomas Proctor	Heavenly Prize	Miss Dominique
1995	**Inside Information**	1:46	Mike Smith	Shug McGaughey	Heavenly Prize	Lakeway

Turf

Distance: 1½ miles (since 1984).

Year		Time	Jockey	Trainer	2nd place	3rd place
1984	**Lashkari**	2:25⅕	Yves St.-Martin	de Royer-Dupre	All Along	Raami
1985	**Pebbles**	2:27	Pat Eddery	Clive Brittain	Strawberry Road II	Mourjane
1986	**Manila**	2:25⅖	Jose Santos	Leroy Jolley	Theatrical	Estrapade
1987	**Theatrical**	2:24⅖	Pat Day	Bill Mott	Trempolino	Village Star II
1988	**Gt. Communicator**	2:35⅕	Ray Sibille	Thad Ackel	Sunshine Forever	Indian Skimmer
1989	**Prized**	2:28	Eddie Delahoussaye	Neil Drysdale	Sierra Roberta	Star Lift
1990	**In The Wings**	2:29⅗	Gary Stevens	Andre Fabre	With Approval	El Senor
1991	**Miss Alleged**	2:30⅘	Eric Legrix	Pascal Bary	Itsallgreektome	Quest for Fame
1992	**Fraise**	2:24	Pat Valenzuela	Bill Mott	Sky Classic	Quest for Fame
1993	**Kotashaan**	2:25	Kent Desormeaux	Richard Mandella	Bien Bien	Luazur
1994	**Tikkanen**	2:26⅖	Mike Smith	Jonathan Pease	Hatoof	Paradise Creek
1995	**Northern Spur**	2:42	Chris McCarron	Ron McAnally	Freedom Cry	Carnegie

Classic

Distance: 1¼ miles (since 1984).

Year		Time	Jockey	Trainer	2nd place	3rd place
1984	**Wild Again**	2:03⅖	Pat Day	Vincent Timphony	Slew o' Gold	Gate Dancer
1985	**Proud Truth**	2:00⅘	Jorge Velasquez	John Veitch	Gate Dancer	Turkoman
1986	**Skywalker**	2:00⅖	Laffit Pincay Jr.	M. Whittingham	Turkoman	Precisionist
1987	**Ferdinand**	2:01⅖	Bill Shoemaker	C. Whittingham	Alysheba	Judge Angelucci
1988	**Alysheba**	2:04⅘	Chris McCarron	Jack Van Berg	Seeking the Gold	Waquoit
1989	**Sunday Silence**	2:00⅕	Chris McCarron	C. Whittingham	Easy Goer	Blushing John
1990	**Unbridled**	2:02⅕	Pat Day	Carl Nafzger	Ibn Bey	Thirty Six Red
1991	**Black Tie Affair**	2:02⅘	Jerry Bailey	Ernie Poulos	Twilight Agenda	Unbridled
1992	**A.P. Indy**	2:00⅕	Eddie Delahoussaye	Neil Drysdale	Pleasant Tap	Jolypha
1993	**Arcangues**	2:00⅘	Jerry Bailey	Andre Fabre	Bertrando	Kissin Kris
1994	**Concern**	2:02⅖	Jerry Bailey	Richard Small	Tabasco Cat	Dramatic Gold
1995	**Cigar**	1:59⅖	Jerry Bailey	Bill Mott	L'Carriere	Unaccounted For

Note: In 1984, 2nd place finisher Gate Dancer was disqualified for interference and placed 3rd.

Breeders' Cup Leaders

The all-time money-winning horses and race winning jockeys in the history of the Breeders' Cup through 1995.

Top 10 Horses

		Sts	1-2-3	Earnings
1	Alysheba	3	1-1-1	$2,133,000
2	Unbridled	2	1-0-1	1,710,000
3	Black Tie Affair (IRE)	3	1-0-1	1,668,000
4	A.P. Indy	1	1-0-0	1,560,000
	Arcangues	1	1-0-0	1,560,000
	Cigar	1	1-0-0	1,560,000
	Concern	1	1-0-0	1,560,000
8	Ferdinand	1	1-0-0	1,350,000
	Proud Truth	1	1-0-0	1,350,000
	Skywalker	2	1-0-0	1,350,000
	Sunday Silence	1	1-0-0	1,350,000
	Theatrical (IRE)	3	1-1-0	1,350,000
	Wild Again	1	1-0-0	1,350,000

Top 10 Jockeys

		Sts	1-2-3	Earnings
1	Pat Day	64	8-11-7	$12,447,000
2	Chris McCarron	66	6-11-5	10,122,000
3	Jerry Bailey	33	5-3-2	7,811,000
4	Eddie Delahoussaye	58	7-3-5	7,499,000
5	Laffit Pincay, Jr.	60	7-4-9	6,811,000
6	Angel Cordero Jr.	48	4-7-7	6,020,000
7	Gary Stevens	50	3-8-6	6,009,000
8	Mike Smith	27	6-2-2	4,605,000
9	Jose Santos	40	5-1-4	4,435,000
10	Pat Valenzuela	32	6-0-1	4,202,000

Top 10 Trainers

		Sts	1-2-3	Earnings
1	D. Wayne Lukas	94	12-15-10	$11,560,000
2	Shug McGaughey	37	7-8-1	6,423,000
3	Andre Fabre	24	2-4-4	5,144,000
4	Neil Drysdale	15	5-2-0	4,580,000
5	Bill Mott	18	3-3-1	4,562,000
6	Charlie Whittingham	23	2-2-3	$4,298,000
7	Jack Van Berg	14	1-3-3	3,600,000
8	Ron McAnally	19	4-2-1	3,156,000
9	Scotty Schulhofer	22	2-2-4	2,726,000
10	Bobby Frankel	26	0-4-3	2,463,000

Annual Money Leaders

Horses

Annual money-leading horses since 1910, according to *The American Racing Manual*.
Multiple leaders: Round Table, Buckpasser and Alysheba (2).

Year		Age	Sts	1st	Earnings
1910	Novelty	2	16	11	$72,630
1911	Worth	2	13	10	16,645
1912	Star Charter	4	17	6	14,655
1913	Old Rosebud	2	14	12	19,057
1914	Roamer	3	16	12	29,105
1915	Borrow	7	9	4	20,195
1916	Campfire	2	9	6	49,735
1917	Sun Briar	2	9	5	59,505
1918	Eternal	2	8	6	56,173
1919	Sir Barton	3	13	8	88,250
1920	Man o' War	3	11	11	166,140
1921	Morvich	2	11	11	115,234
1922	Pillory	3	7	4	95,654
1923	Zev	3	14	12	272,008
1924	Sarzen	3	12	8	95,640
1925	Pompey	2	10	7	121,630
1926	Crusader	3	15	9	166,033
1927	Anita Peabody	2	7	6	111,905
1928	High Strung	2	6	5	153,590
1929	Blue Larkspur	3	6	4	153,450
1930	Gallant Fox	3	10	9	308,275
1931	Gallant Flight	2	7	7	219,000
1932	Gusto	3	16	4	145,940
1933	Singing Wood	2	9	3	88,050
1934	Cavalcade	3	7	6	111,235
1935	Omaha	3	9	6	142,255
1936	Granville	3	11	7	110,295
1937	Seabiscuit	4	15	11	168,580
1938	Stagehand	3	15	8	189,710
1939	Challedon	3	15	9	184,535
1940	Bimelech	3	7	4	110,005
1941	Whirlaway	3	20	13	272,386
1942	Shut Out	3	12	8	238,872
1943	Count Fleet	3	6	6	174,055
1944	Pavot	2	8	8	179,040
1945	Busher	3	13	10	273,735
1946	Assault	3	15	8	424,195
1947	Armed	6	17	11	376,325
1948	Citation	3	20	19	709,470
1949	Ponder	3	21	9	321,825
1950	Noor	5	12	7	346,940
1951	Counterpoint	3	15	7	250,525
1952	Crafty Admiral	4	16	9	277,225
1953	Native Dancer	3	10	9	$513,425
1954	Determine	3	15	10	328,700
1955	Nashua	3	12	10	752,550
1956	Needles	3	8	4	440,850
1957	Round Table	3	22	15	600,383
1958	Round Table	4	20	14	662,780
1959	Sword Dancer	3	13	8	537,004
1960	Bally Ache	3	15	10	445,045
1961	Carry Back	3	16	9	565,349
1962	Never Bend	2	10	7	402,969
1963	Candy Spots	3	12	7	604,481
1964	Gun Bow	4	16	8	580,100
1965	Buckpasser	2	11	9	568,096
1966	Buckpasser	3	14	13	669,078
1967	Damascus	3	16	12	817,941
1968	Forward Pass	3	13	7	546,674
1969	Arts and Letters	3	14	8	555,604
1970	Personality	3	18	8	444,049
1971	Riva Ridge	2	9	7	503,263
1972	Droll Role	4	19	7	471,633
1973	Secretariat	3	12	9	860,404
1974	Chris Evert	3	8	5	551,063
1975	Foolish Pleasure	3	11	5	716,278
1976	Forego	6	8	6	401,701
1977	Seattle Slew	3	7	6	641,370
1978	Affirmed	3	11	8	901,541
1979	Spectacular Bid	3	12	10	1,279,334
1980	Temperence Hill	3	17	8	1,130,452
1981	John Henry	6	10	8	1,798,030
1982	Perrault (GB)	5	8	4	1,197,400
1983	All Along (FRA)	4	7	4	2,138,963
1984	Slew o' Gold	4	6	5	2,627,944
1985	Spend A Buck	3	7	5	3,552,704
1986	Snow Chief	3	9	6	1,875,200
1987	Alysheba	3	10	3	2,511,156
1988	Alysheba	4	9	7	3,808,600
1989	Sunday Silence	3	9	7	4,578,454
1990	Unbridled	3	11	4	3,718,149
1991	Dance Smartly	3	8	8	2,876,821
1992	A.P. Indy	3	7	5	2,622,560
1993	Kotashaan (FRA)	5	10	6	2,619,014
1994	Paradise Creek	5	11	8	2,610,187
1995	Cigar	5	10	10	4,819,800

Jockeys

Annual money-leading jockeys since 1910, according to *The American Racing Manual*.
Multiple leaders: Bill Shoemaker (10); Laffit Pincay Jr. (7); Eddie Arcaro (6); Braulio Baeza (5); Chris McCarron and Jose Santos (4); Angel Cordero Jr. and Earl Sande (3); Ted Atkinson, Laverne Fator, Mack Garner, Bill Hartack, Charles Kurtsinger, Johnny Longden, Mike Smith, Sonny Workman and Wayne Wright (2).

Year		Mts	Wins	Earnings
1910	Carroll Shilling	506	172	$176,030
1911	Ted Koerner	813	162	88,308
1912	Jimmy Butwell	684	144	79,843
1913	Merritt Buxton	887	146	82,552
1914	J. McCahey	824	155	121,845
1915	Mack Garner	775	151	96,628
1916	John McTaggart	832	150	155,055
1917	Frank Robinson	731	147	148,057
1918	Lucien Luke	756	178	201,864
1919	John Loftus	177	65	252,707
1920	Clarence Kummer	353	87	292,376
1921	Earl Sande	340	112	263,043
1922	Albert Johnson	297	43	345,054
1923	Earl Sande	430	122	569,394
1924	Ivan Parke	844	205	$290,395
1925	Laverne Fator	315	81	305,775
1926	Laverne Fator	511	143	361,435
1927	Earl Sande	179	49	277,877
1928	Linus McAtee	235	55	301,295
1929	Mack Garner	274	57	314,975
1930	Sonny Workman	571	152	420,438
1931	Charley Kurtsinger	519	93	392,095
1932	Sonny Workman	378	87	385,070
1933	Robert Jones	471	63	226,285
1934	Wayne Wright	919	174	287,185
1935	Silvio Coucci	749	141	319,760
1936	Wayne Wright	670	100	264,000
1937	Charley Kurtsinger	765	120	384,202

Annual Money Leaders (Cont.)

Year		Mts	Wins	Earnings	Year		Mts	Wins	Earnings
1938	Nick Wall	658	97	$ 385,161	1967	Braulio Baeza	1064	256	$3,088,888
1939	Basil James	904	191	353,333	1968	Braulio Baeza	1089	201	2,835,108
1940	Eddie Arcaro	783	132	343,661	1969	Jorge Velasquez	1442	258	2,542,315
1941	Don Meade	1164	210	398,627	1970	Laffit Pincay Jr.	1328	269	2,626,526
1942	Eddie Arcaro	687	123	481,949	1971	Laffit Pincay Jr.	1627	380	3,784,377
1943	Johnny Longden	871	173	573,276	1972	Laffit Pincay Jr.	1388	289	3,225,827
1944	Ted Atkinson	1539	287	899,101	1973	Laffit Pincay Jr.	1444	350	4,093,492
1945	Johnny Longden	778	180	981,977	1974	Laffit PincayJr.	1278	341	4,251,060
1946	Ted Atkinson	1377	233	1,036,825	1975	Braulio Baeza	1190	196	3,674,398
1947	Douglas Dodson	646	141	1,429,949	1976	Angel Cordero Jr.	1534	274	4,709,500
1948	Eddie Arcaro	726	188	1,686,230	1977	Steve Cauthen	2075	487	6,151,750
1949	Steve Brooks	906	209	1,316,817	1978	Darrel McHargue	1762	375	6,188,353
1950	Eddie Arcaro	888	195	1,410,160	1979	Laffit Pincay Jr.	1708	420	8,183,535
1951	Bill Shoemaker	1161	257	1,329,890	1980	Chris McCarron	1964	405	7,666,100
1952	Eddie Arcaro	807	188	1,859,591	1981	Chris McCarron	1494	326	8,397,604
1953	Bill Shoemaker	1683	485	1,784,187	1982	Angel Cordero Jr.	1838	397	9,702,520
1954	Bill Shoemaker	1251	380	1,876,760	1983	Angel Cordero Jr.	1792	362	10,116,807
1955	Eddie Arcaro	820	158	1,864,796	1984	Chris McCarron	1565	356	12,038,213
1956	Bill Hartack	1387	347	2,343,955	1985	Laffit Pincay Jr.	1409	289	13,415,049
1957	Bill Hartack	1238	341	3,060,501	1986	Jose Santos	1636	329	11,329,297
1958	Bill Shoemaker	1133	300	2,961,693	1987	Jose Santos	1639	305	12,407,355
1959	Bill Shoemaker	1285	347	2,843,133	1988	Jose Santos	1867	370	14,877,298
1960	Bill Shoemaker	1227	274	2,123,961	1989	Jose Santos	1459	285	13,847,003
1961	Bill Shoemaker	1256	304	2,690,819	1990	Gary Stevens	1504	283	13,881,198
1962	Bill Shoemaker	1126	311	2,916,844	1991	Chris McCarron	1440	265	14,456,073
1963	Bill Shoemaker	1203	271	2,526,925	1992	Kent Desormeaux	1568	361	14,193,006
1964	Bill Shoemaker	1056	246	2,649,553	1993	Mike Smith	1510	343	14,024,815
1965	Braulio Baeza	1245	270	2,582,702	1994	Mike Smith	1484	317	15,979,820
1966	Braulio Baeza	1341	298	2,951,022	1995	Jerry Bailey	1367	287	16,311,876

Annual Money-Leading Female Jockeys

Annual money-leading female jockeys since 1979, according to *The American Racing Manual.*

Multiple leaders: Julie Krone (11); Patty Cooksey and Karen Rogers (2).

Year		Mts	Wins	Earnings	Year		Mts	Wins	Earnings
1979	Karen Rogers	550	77	$ 590,469	1988	Julie Krone	1958	363	$7,770,314
1980	Karen Rogers	622	65	894,878	1989	Julie Krone	1673	368	8,031,445
1981	Patty Cooksey	1469	197	895,951	1990	Julie Krone	649	144	2,846,237
1982	Mary Russ	952	84	1,319,363	1991	Julie Krone	1414	230	7,748,077
1983	Julie Krone	1024	151	1,095,622	1992	Julie Krone	1462	282	9,220,824
1984	Patty Cooksey	955	116	803,189	1993	Julie Krone	1012	212	6,415,462
1985	Abby Fuller	883	145	1,452,576	1994	Julie Krone	571	101	3,968,337
1986	Julie Krone	1442	199	2,357,136	1995	Julie Krone	866	147	7,759,878
1987	Julie Krone	1698	324	4,522,191					

Trainers

Annual money-leading trainers since 1908, according to *The American Racing Manual.*

Multiple leaders: D. Wayne Lukas (12); Sam Hildreth (9), Charlie Whittingham (7); Sunny Jim Fitzsimmons and Jimmy Jones (5); Laz Barrera, Ben Jones and Willie Molter (4); Hirsch Jacobs, Eddie Neloy and James Rowe Sr. (3); H. Guy Bedwell, Jack Gaver, John Schorr, Humming Bob Smith, Silent Tom Smith, and Mesh Tenney (2).

Year		Wins	Earnings	Year		Wins	Earnings
1908	James Rowe Sr.	50	$284,335	1925	G.R. Tompkins	30	$199,245
1909	Sam Hildreth	73	123,942	1926	Scott Harlan	21	205,681
1910	Sam Hildreth	84	148,010	1927	W.H. Bringloe	63	216,563
1911	Sam Hildreth	67	49,418	1928	John Schorr	65	258,425
1912	John Schorr	63	58,110	1929	James Rowe Jr.	25	314,881
1913	James Rowe Sr.	18	45,936	1930	Sunny Jim Fitzsimmons	47	397,355
1914	R.C. Benson	45	59,315	1931	Big Jim Healy	33	297,300
1915	James Rowe Sr.	19	75,596	1932	Sunny Jim Fitzsimmons	68	266,650
1916	Sam Hildreth	39	70,950	1933	Humming Bob Smith	53	135,720
1917	Sam Hildreth	23	61,698	1934	Humming Bob Smith	43	249,938
1918	H. Guy Bedwell	53	80,296	1935	Bud Stotler	87	303,005
1919	H. Guy Bedwell	63	208,728	1936	Sunny Jim Fitzsimmons	42	193,415
1920	Louis Feustal	22	186,087	1937	Robert McGarvey	46	209,925
1921	Sam Hildreth	85	262,768	1938	Earl Sande	15	226,495
1922	Sam Hildreth	74	247,014	1939	Sunny Jim Fitzsimmons	45	266,205
1923	Sam Hildreth	75	392,124	1940	Silent Tom Smith	14	269,200
1924	Sam Hildreth	77	255,608	1941	Ben Jones	70	475,318

Trainers

Year		Wins	Earnings
1942	Jack Gaver	48	$ 406,547
1943	Ben Jones	73	267,915
1944	Ben Jones	60	601,660
1945	Silent Tom Smith	52	510,655
1946	Hirsch Jacobs	99	560,077
1947	Jimmy Jones	85	1,334,805
1948	Jimmy Jones	81	1,118,670
1949	Jimmy Jones	76	978,587
1950	Preston Burch	96	637,754
1951	Jack Gaver	42	616,392
1952	Ben Jones	29	662,137
1953	Harry Trotsek	54	1,028,873
1954	Willie Molter.	136	1,107,860
1955	Sunny Jim Fitzsimmons	66	1,270,055
1956	Willie Molter.	142	1,227,402
1957	Jimmy Jones	70	1,150,910
1958	Willie Molter	69	1,116,544
1959	Willie Molter	71	847,290
1960	Hirsch Jacobs	97	748,349
1961	Jimmy Jones	62	759,856
1962	Mesh Tenney	58	1,099,474

Year		Sts	Wins	Earnings
1963	Mesh Tenney	192	40	$ 860,703
1964	Bill Winfrey	287	61	1,350,534
1965	Hirsch Jacobs	610	91	1,331,628
1966	Eddie Neloy	282	93	2,456,250
1967	Eddie Neloy	262	72	1,776,089
1968	Eddie Neloy	212	52	1,233,101
1969	Elliott Burch	156	26	1,067,936
1970	Charlie Whittingham	551	82	$1,302,354
1971	Charlie Whittingham	393	77	1,737,115
1972	Charlie Whittingham	429	79	1,734,020
1973	Charlie Whittingham	423	85	1,865,385
1974	Pancho Martin	846	166	2,408,419
1975	Charlie Whittingham	487	3	2,437,244
1976	Jack Van Berg	2362	496	2,976,196
1977	Laz Barrera	781	127	2,715,848
1978	Laz Barrera	592	100	3,307,164
1979	Laz Barrera	492	98	3,608,517
1980	Laz Barrera	559	99	2,969,151
1981	Charlie Whittingham	376	74	3,993,302
1982	Charlie Whittingham	410	63	4,587,457
1983	D. Wayne Lukas	595	78	4,267,261
1984	D. Wayne Lukas	805	131	5,835,921
1985	D. Wayne Lukas	1140	218	11,155,188
1986	D. Wayne Lukas	1510	259	12,345,180
1987	D. Wayne Lukas	1735	343	17,502,110
1988	D. Wayne Lukas	1500	318	17,842,358
1989	D. Wayne Lukas	1398	305	16,103,998
1990	D. Wayne Lukas	1396	267	14,508,871
1991	D. Wayne Lukas	1497	289	15,942,223
1992	D. Wayne Lukas	1349	230	9,806,436
1993	Bobby Frankel	345	79	8,933,252
1994	D. Wayne Lukas	693	147	9,247,457
1995	D. Wayne Lukas	837	194	12,834,483

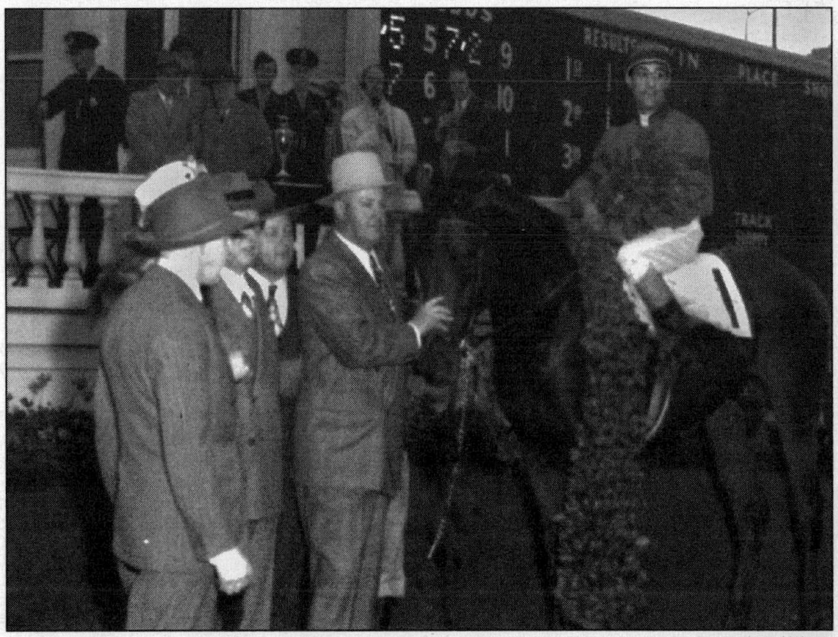

Wide World Photos

Legendary 1948 Triple Crown winner **Citation** in the winner's circle of the Kentucky Derby with jockey **Eddie Arcaro** and trainer **Jimmy Jones.** Citation was back in the headlines in 1996 as Cigar tied the horse's mark for all-time consecutive wins at 16.

All-Time Leaders

The all-time money-winning horses and race-winning jockeys of North America through 1995, according to *The American Racing Manual*. Records include all available information on races in foreign countries.

Top 35 Horses—Money Won

Note that horses who raced in 1995 are in **bold** type; and (f) indicates female.

	Sts	1st	2nd	3rd	Earnings
1 Alysheba	26	11	8	2	$6,679,242
2 John Henry	83	39	15	9	6,597,947
3 **Best Pal**	47	18	11	4	5,568,245
4 **Cigar**	25	14	2	4	5,089,015
5 Sunday Silence	14	9	5	0	4,968,554
6 Easy Goer	20	14	5	1	4,873,770
7 Unbridled	24	8	6	6	4,489,475
8 Spend A Buck	15	10	3	2	4,220,689
9 Creme Fraiche	64	17	12	13	4,024,727
10 **Devil His Due**	41	11	12	3	3,920,405
11 Ferdinand	29	8	9	6	3,777,978
12 Slew O'Gold	21	12	5	1	3,533,134
13 Precisionist	46	20	10	4	3,485,398
14 Strike the Gold	31	6	8	5	3,457,026
21 Paradise Creek	25	14	7	1	3,386,925
16 Snow Chief	24	13	4	5	3,383,210
17 Cryptoclearance	44	12	10	7	3,376,327
18 Black Tie Affair	45	18	9	6	3,370,694
19 Bet Twice	26	10	6	4	3,308,599
20 Steinlen	45	20	10	7	3,300,100
21 Dance Smartly (f)	17	12	2	3	3,263,836
22 Sky Classic	29	15	6	1	3,240,398
23 Bertrando	24	9	6	2	3,185,610
24 **Paseana** (f)	34	19	9	2	3,133,703
25 Gulch	32	13	8	4	3,095,521
26 **Concern**	29	6	7	11	3,064,350
27 Lady's Secret (f)	45	25	9	3	3,021,425
28 All Along (f)	21	9	6	2	3,015,764
29 A.P. Indy	11	8	0	1	2,979,815
30 Theatrical	22	10	4	2	2,943,627
31 Hansel	14	7	2	3	2,936,586
32 Sea Hero	24	6	3	4	2,929,869
33 Great Communicator	56	14	10	7	2,922,615
34 **Thunder Gulch**	16	9	2	2	2,915,086
35 Farma Way	23	8	5	1	2,897,176

Top 35 Jockeys—Races Won

Note that jockeys active in 1995 are in **bold** type.

	Yrs	Wins	Earnings
1 Bill Shoemaker	42	8833	$123,375,524
2 **Laffit Pincay Jr.**	30	8440	192,484,910
3 Angel Cordero Jr.	31	7057	164,561,227
4 **David Gall**	39	6910	22,431,714
5 **Jorge Velasquez**	32	6751	124,733,113
6 **Pat Day**	24	6705	168,065,509
7 Larry Snyder	35	6388	47,207,289
8 **Sandy Hawley**	28	6357	85,382,333
9 Carl Gambardella	39	6349	29,389,041
10 **Chris McCarron**	20	6338	195,660,204
11 John Longden	41	6032	24,665,800
12 **Earlie Fires**	31	5808	69,205,127
13 **E. Delahoussaye**	26	5633	152,317,592
14 **Russell Baze**	22	5434	73,933,645
21 **Jacinto Vasquez**	36	5223	80,256,130
16 Eddie Arcaro	31	4779	30,039,543
17 Don Brumfield	37	4573	43,567,861
18 Steve Brooks	34	4451	18,239,817
19 Walter Blum	22	4382	26,497,189
20 **Eddie Maple**	28	4311	101,928,775
21 **Ron Ardoin**	23	4285	41,728,827
22 Bill Hartack	22	4272	26,466,758
23 Avelino Gomez	34	4081	11,777,297
24 **Craig Perret**	30	4079	91,525,276
25 **Rodolfo Baez**	22	4004	23,475,169
26 **Gary Stevens**	18	4002	139,769,615
27 Hugo Dittfach	33	4000	13,506,052
28 **Phil Grove**	29	3977	16,344,677
29 **Randy Romero**	22	3971	67,935,394
30 **Rick Wilson**	23	3847	47,885,987
31 **Jeffrey Lloyd**	21	3829	28,049,855
32 Ted Atkinson	22	3795	17,449,360
33 David Whited	36	3784	25,469,402
34 **Jerry Bailey**	22	3772	126,419,022
Ralph Neves	21	3772	13,786,239

Retired: Arcaro (1961), Atkinson (1959), Baird (1982), Blum (1975), Brooks (1975), Brumfield (1989), Cordero (1992), Dittfach (1989), Gambardella (1994), Gomez (1980), Hartack (1974), Hansen (1993), Longden (1966), Moyers (1992), Neves (1964), Shoemaker (1990), Snyder (1994) and Whited (1993).

Horse of the Year (1936-70)

In 1971, the *Daily Racing Form,* the Thoroughbred Racing Associations, and the National Turf Writers Assn. joined forces to create the Eclipse Awards. Before then, however, the *Racing Form* (1936-70) and the TRA (1950-70) issued separate selections for Horse of the Year. Their picks differed only four times from 1950-70 and are so noted. Horses listed in CAPITAL letters are Triple Crown winners; (f) indicates female.

Multiple winners: Kelso (5); Challedon, Native Dancer and Whirlaway (2).

Year		Year		Year		Year	
1936	Granville	1946	ASSAULT	1955	Nashua	1964	Kelso
1937	WAR ADMIRAL	1947	Armed	1956	Swaps	1965	Roman Brother (DRF)
1938	Seabiscuit	1948	CITATION	1957	Bold Ruler (DRF)		Moccasin (TRA)
1939	Challedon	1949	Capot		Dedicate (TRA)	1966	Buckpasser
1940	Challedon	1950	Hill Prince	1958	Round Table	1967	Damascus
1941	WHIRLAWAY	1951	Counterpoint	1959	Sword Dancer	1968	Dr. Fager
1942	Whirlaway	1952	One Count (DRF)	1960	Kelso	1969	Arts and Letters
1943	COUNT FLEET		Native Dancer (TRA)	1961	Kelso	1970	Fort Marcy (DRF)
1944	Twilight Tear (f)	1953	Tom Fool	1962	Kelso		Personality (TRA)
1945	Busher (f)	1954	Native Dancer	1963	Kelso		

Eclipse Awards

The Eclipse Awards, honoring the Horse of the Year and other champions of the sport, are sponsored by the *Daily Racing Form*, the Thoroughbred Racing Associations and the National Turf Writers Assn.

The awards are named after the 18th century racehorse and sire, Eclipse, who began racing at age five and was unbeaten in 18 starts (eight wins were walkovers). As a stallion, Eclipse sired winners of 344 races, including three Epsom Derby champions.

Horses listed in CAPITAL letters won the Triple Crown that year. Age of horse in parentheses where necessary.

Multiple winners (horses): Forego (8); John Henry (7); Affirmed and Secretariat (5); Flatterer, Seattle Slew and Spectacular Bid (4); Ack Ack, Lonesome Glory, Susan's Girl and Zaccio (3); All Along, Alysheba, Bayakoa, Black Tie Affair, Cafe Prince, Cigar, Conquistador Cielo, Desert Vixen, Ferdinand, Flawlessly, Go for Wand, Holy Bull, Housebuster, Kotashaan, Lady's Secret, Life's Magic, Lonesome Glory, Miesque, Morley Street, Open Mind, Paseana, Riva Ridge, Slew o'Gold and Spend A Buck (2).

Multiple winners (people): Laffit Pincay Jr. (5); Laz Barrera, Pat Day, John Franks and D. Wayne Lukas (4); Steve Cauthen, Pat Day, Harbor View Farm, Fred W. Hooper, Nelson Bunker Hunt, Mr. & Mrs. Gene Klein, Dan Lasater, Ogden Phipps, Bill Shoemaker, Edward Taylor and Charlie Whittingham (3); Braulio Baeza, C.T. Chenery, Claiborne Farm, Angel Cordero Jr., Kent Desormeaux, John W. Galbreath, Chris McCarron, Paul Mellon and Mike Smith (2).

Horse of the Year

Year		Year		Year		Year	
1971	Ack Ack (5)	1978	AFFIRMED (3)	1985	Spend A Buck (3)	1992	A.P. Indy (3)
1972	Secretariat (2)	1979	Affirmed (4)	1986	Lady's Secret (4)	1993	Kotashaan (5)
1973	SECRETARIAT (3)	1980	Spectacular Bid (4)	1987	Ferdinand (4)	1994	Holy Bull (3)
1974	Forego (4)	1981	John Henry (6)	1988	Alysheba (4)	1995	Cigar (5)
1975	Forego (5)	1982	Conquistador Cielo (3)	1989	Sunday Silence (3)		
1976	Forego (6)	1983	All Along (4)	1990	Criminal Type (5)		
1977	SEATTLE SLEW (3)	1984	John Henry (9)	1991	Black Tie Affair (5)		

Older Male

Year		Year		Year		Year	
1971	Ack Ack (5)	1978	Seattle Slew (4)	1985	Vanlandingham (4)	1992	Pleasant Tap (5)
1972	Autobiography (4)	1979	Affirmed (4)	1986	Turkoman (4)	1993	Bertrando (4)
1973	Riva Ridge (4)	1980	Spectacular Bid (4)	1987	Ferdinand (4)	1994	The Wicked North (4)
1974	Forego (4)	1981	John Henry (6)	1988	Alysheba (4)	1995	Cigar (5)
1975	Forego (5)	1982	Lemhi Gold (4)	1989	Blushing John (4)		
1976	Forego (6)	1983	Bates Motel (4)	1990	Criminal Type (5)		
1977	Forego (7)	1984	Slew o' Gold (4)	1991	Black Tie Affair (5)		

Older Filly or Mare

Year		Year		Year		Year	
1971	Shuvee (5)	1978	Late Bloomer (4)	1985	Life's Magic (4)	1992	Paseana (5)
1972	Typecast (6)	1979	Waya (5)	1986	Lady's Secret (4)	1993	Paseana (6)
1973	Susan's Girl (4)	1980	Glorious Song (4)	1987	North Sider (5)	1994	Sky Beauty (4)
1974	Desert Vixen (4)	1981	Relaxing (5)	1988	Personal Ensign (4)	1995	Inside Information (4)
1975	Susan's Girl (6)	1982	Track Robbery (6)	1989	Bayakoa (5)		
1976	Proud Delta (4)	1983	Amb. of Luck (4)	1990	Bayakoa (6)		
1977	Cascapedia (4)	1984	Princess Rooney (4)	1991	Queena (5)		

3-Year-Old Colt or Gelding

Year		Year		Year		Year	
1971	Canonero II	1978	AFFIRMED	1985	Spend A Buck	1992	A.P. Indy
1972	Key to the Mint	1979	Spectacular Bid	1986	Snow Chief	1993	Prairie Bayou
1973	SECRETARIAT	1980	Temperence Hill	1987	Alysheba	1994	Holy Bull
1974	Little Current	1981	Pleasant Colony	1988	Risen Star	1995	Thunder Gulch
1975	Wajima	1982	Conquistador Cielo	1989	Sunday Silence		
1976	Bold Forbes	1983	Slew o' Gold	1990	Unbridled		
1977	SEATTLE SLEW	1984	Swale	1991	Hansel		

3-Year-Old Filly

Year		Year		Year		Year	
1971	Turkish Trousers	1978	Tempest Queen	1985	Mom's Command	1992	Saratoga Slew
1972	Susan's Girl	1979	Davona Dale	1986	Tiffany Lass	1993	Hollywood Wildcat
1973	Desert Vixen	1980	Genuine Risk	1987	Sacahuista	1994	Heavenly Prize
1974	Chris Evert	1981	Wayward Lass	1988	Winning Colors	1995	Serena's Song
1975	Ruffian	1982	Christmas Past	1989	Open Mind		
1976	Revidere	1983	Heartlight No. One	1990	Go for Wand		
1977	Our Mims	1984	Life's Magic	1991	Dance Smartly		

2-Year-Old Colt or Gelding

Year		Year		Year		Year	
1971	Riva Ridge	1978	Spectacular Bid	1985	Tasso	1992	Gilded Time
1972	Secretariat	1979	Rockhill Native	1986	Capote	1993	Dehere
1973	Protagonist	1980	Lord Avie	1987	Forty Niner	1994	Timber Country
1974	Foolish Pleasure	1981	Deputy Minister	1988	Easy Goer	1995	Maria's Mon
1975	Honest Pleasure	1982	Roving Boy	1989	Rhythm		
1976	Seattle Slew	1983	Devil's Bag	1990	Fly So Free		
1977	Affirmed	1984	Chief's Crown	1991	Arazi		

Eclipse Awards (Cont.)

2-Year-Old Filly

Year		Year		Year		Year	
1971	Numbered Account	1978	(tie) Candy Eclair	1984	Outstandingly	1991	Pleasant Stage
1972	La Prevoyante		& It's in the Air	1985	Family Style	1992	Eliza
1973	Talking Picture	1979	Smart Angle	1986	Brave Raj	1993	Phone Chatter
1974	Ruffian	1980	Heavenly Cause	1987	Epitome	1994	Flanders
1975	Dearly Precious	1981	Before Dawn	1988	Open Mind	1995	Golden Attraction
1976	Sensational	1982	Landaluce	1989	Go for Wand		
1977	Lakeville Miss	1983	Althea	1990	Meadow Star		

Champion Turf Horse

Year		Year		Year		Year	
1971	Run the Gantlet (3)	1973	SECRETARIAT (3)	1975	Snow Knight (4)	1977	Johnny D (3)
1972	Cougar II (6)	1974	Dahlia (4)	1976	Youth (3)	1978	Mac Diarmida (3)

Champion Male Turf Horse

Year		Year		Year		Year	
1979	Bowl Game (5)	1984	John Henry (9)	1989	Steinlen (6)	1994	Paradise Creek (5)
1980	John Henry (5)	1985	Cozzene (4)	1990	Itsallgreektome (3)	1995	Northern Spur (4)
1981	John Henry (6)	1986	Manila (3)	1991	Tight Spot (4)		
1982	Perrault (5)	1987	Theatrical (5)	1992	Sky Classic (5)		
1983	John Henry (8)	1988	Sunshine Forever (3)	1993	Kotashaan (5)		

Champion Female Turf Horse

Year		Year		Year		Year	
1979	Trillion (5)	1984	Royal Heroine (4)	1989	Brown Bess (7)	1994	Hatoof (5)
1980	Just A Game II (4)	1985	Pebbles (4)	1990	Laugh and Be Merry (5)	1995	Possibly Perfect (5)
1981	De La Rose (3)	1986	Estrapade (6)	1991	Miss Alleged (4)		
1982	April Run (4)	1987	Miesque (3)	1992	Flawlessly (4)		
1983	All Along (4)	1988	Miesque (4)	1993	Flawlessly (5)		

Sprinter

Year		Year		Year		Year	
1971	Ack Ack (5)	1978	(tie) Dr. Patches (4)	1984	Eillo (4)	1991	Housebuster (4)
1972	Chou Croute (4)		& J.O. Tobin (4)	1985	Precisionist (4)	1992	Rubiano (5)
1973	Shecky Greene (3)	1979	Star de Naskra (4)	1986	Smile (4)	1993	Cardmania (7)
1974	Forego (4)	1980	Plugged Nickle (3)	1987	Groovy (4)	1994	Cherokee Run (4)
1975	Gallant Bob (3)	1981	Guilty Conscience (5)	1988	Gulch (4)	1995	Not Surprising (4)
1976	My Juliet (4)	1982	Gold Beauty (3)	1989	Safely Kept (3)		
1977	What a Summer (4)	1983	Chinook Pass (4)	1990	Housebuster (3)		

Steeplechase or Hurdle Horse

Year		Year		Year		Year	
1971	Shadow Brook (7)	1978	Cafe Prince (8)	1985	Flatterer (6)	1992	Lonesome Glory (4)
1972	Soothsayer (5)	1979	Martie's Anger (4)	1986	Flatterer (7)	1993	Lonesome Glory (5)
1973	Athenian Idol (5)	1980	Zaccio (4)	1987	Inlander (6)	1994	Warm Spell (6)
1974	Gran Kan (8)	1981	Zaccio (5)	1988	Jimmy Lorenzo (6)	1995	Lonesome Glory (7)
1975	Life's Illusion (4)	1982	Zaccio (6)	1989	Highland Bud (4)		
1976	Straight and True (6)	1983	Flatterer (4)	1990	Morley Street (6)		
1977	Cafe Prince (7)	1984	Flatterer (5)	1991	Morley Street (7)		

Outstanding Jockey

Year		Year		Year		Year	
1971	Laffit Pincay Jr.	1978	Darrel McHargue	1985	Laffit Pincay Jr.	1992	Kent Desormeaux
1972	Braulio Baeza	1979	Laffit Pincay Jr.	1986	Pat Day	1993	Mike Smith
1973	Laffit Pincay Jr.	1980	Chris McCarron	1987	Pat Day	1994	Mike Smith
1974	Laffit Pincay Jr.	1981	Bill Shoemaker	1988	Jose Santos	1995	Jerry Bailey
1975	Braulio Baeza	1982	Angel Cordero Jr.	1989	Kent Desormeaux		
1976	Sandy Hawley	1983	Angel Cordero Jr.	1990	Craig Perret		
1977	Steve Cauthen	1984	Pat Day	1991	Pat Day		

Outstanding Apprentice Jockey

Year		Year		Year		Year	
1971	Gene St. Leon	1978	Ron Franklin	1985	Art Madrid Jr.	1992	Rosemary Homeister
1972	Thomas Wallis	1979	Cash Asmussen	1986	Allen Stacy	1993	Juan Umana
1973	Steve Valdez	1980	Frank Lovato Jr.	1987	Kent Desormeaux	1994	Dale Beckner
1974	Chris McCarron	1981	Richard Migliore	1988	Steve Capanas	1995	Ramon B. Perez
1975	Jimmy Edwards	1982	Alberto Delgado	1989	Michael Luzzi		
1976	George Martens	1983	Declan Murphy	1990	Mark Johnston		
1977	Steve Cauthen	1984	Wesley Ward	1991	Mickey Walls		

Outstanding Trainer

Year		Year		Year		Year	
1971	Charlie Whittingham	1978	Laz Barrera	1985	D. Wayne Lukas	1992	Ron McAnally
1972	Lucien Laurin	1979	Laz Barrera	1986	D. Wayne Lukas	1993	Bobby Frankel
1973	H. Allen Jerkens	1980	Bud Delp	1987	D. Wayne Lukas	1994	D. Wayne Lukas
1974	Sherill Ward	1981	Ron McAnally	1988	Shug McGaughey	1995	Bill Mott
1975	Steve DiMauro	1982	Charlie Whittingham	1989	Charlie Whittingham		
1976	Laz Barrera	1983	Woody Stephens	1990	Carl Nafzger		
1977	Laz Barrera	1984	Jack Van Berg	1991	Ron McAnally		

Outstanding Owner

Year		Year		Year		Year	
1971	Mr. & Mrs. E.E. Fogleson	1978	Harbor View Farm	1984	John Franks	1991	Sam-Son Farms
1972-73	No award	1979	Harbor View Farm	1985	Mr. & Mrs. Gene Klein	1992	Juddmonta Farms
1974	Dan Lasater	1980	Mr. & Mrs. Bertram Firestone	1986	Mr. & Mrs. Gene Klein	1993	John Franks
1975	Dan Lasater	1981	Dotsam Stable	1987	Mr. & Mrs. Gene Klein	1994	John Franks
1976	Dan Lasater	1982	Viola Sommer	1988	Ogden Phipps	1995	Allen Paulson
1977	Maxwell Gluck	1983	John Franks	1989	Ogden Phipps		
				1990	Frances Genter		

Outstanding Breeder

Year		Year		Year		Year	
1971	Paul Mellon	1978	Harbor View Farm	1985	Nelson Bunker Hunt	1992	William S. Farish
1972	C.T. Chenery	1979	Claiborne Farm	1986	Paul Mellon	1993	Allan Paulson
1973	C.T. Chenery	1980	Mrs. Henry Paxson	1987	Nelson Bunker Hunt	1994	William T. Young
1974	John W. Galbreath	1981	Golden Chance Farm	1988	Ogden Phipps	1995	Juddmonte Farms
1975	Fred W. Hooper	1982	Fred W. Hooper	1989	North Ridge Farm		
1976	Nelson Bunker Hunt	1983	Edward P. Taylor	1990	Calumet Farm		
1977	Edward P. Taylor	1984	Claiborne Farm	1991	Mr. & Mrs. John Mabee		

Outstanding Achievement

Year		Year	
1971	Charles Engelhard*	1972	Arthur B. Hancock Jr.*

*Awarded posthumously.

Man of the Year

Year		Year	
1972	John W. Galbreath	1974	William L. McKnight
1973	Edward P. Taylor	1975	John A. Morris

Award of Merit

Year		Year		Year		Year	
1976	Jack J. Dreyfus	1981	Bill Shoemaker	1988	John Forsythe	1992	Joe Hirsch & Robert P. Strub
1977	Steve Cauthen	1984	John Gaines	1989	Michael Sandler	1995	James E. Bassett III
1978	Dinny Phipps	1985	Keene Daingerfield	1990	Warner L. Jones		
1979	Jimmy Kilroe	1986	Herman Cohen	1991	Fred W. Hooper		
1980	John D. Shapiro	1987	J.B. Faulconer				

Special Award

Year		Year		Year		Year	
1971	Robert J. Kleberg	1980	John T. Landry & Pierre E. Bellocq	1985	Arlington Park	1988	Edward J. DeBartolo Sr.
1974	Charles Hatton	1984	C.V. Whitney	1987	Anheuser-Busch	1989	Richard Duchossois
1976	Bill Shoemaker					1995	Russell Baze

HARNESS RACING

Triple Crown Winners

PACERS

Seven 3-year-olds have won the Cane Pace, Little Brown Jug and Messenger Stakes in the same year since the Pacing Triple Crown was established in 1956. No trainer or driver has won it more than once.

Year		Driver	Trainer	Owner
1959	**Adios Butler**	Clint Hodgins	Paige West	Paige West & Angelo Pellillo
1965	**Bret Hanover**	Frank Ervin	Frank Ervin	Richard Downing
1966	**Romeo Hanover**	Bill Myer & George Sholty*	Jerry Silverman	Lucky Star Stables & Morton Finder
1968	**Rum Customer**	Billy Haughton	Billy Haughton	Kennilworth Farms & L.C. Mancuso
1970	**Most Happy Fella**	Stanley Dancer	Stanley Dancer	Egyptian Acres Stable
1980	**Niatross**	Clint Galbraith	Clint Galbraith	Niagara Acres, Niatross Stables & Clint Galbraith
1983	**Ralph Hanover**	Ron Waples	Stew Firlotte	Waples Stable, Pointsetta Stable, Grant's Direct Stable & P.J. Baugh

*Myer drove Romeo Hanover in the Cane, Sholty in the other two races.

Harness Racing (Cont.)

TROTTERS

Six 3-year-olds have won the Yonkers Trot, Hambletonian and Kentucky Futurity in the same year since the Trotting Triple Crown was established in 1955. Stanley Dancer is the only driver/trainer to win it twice.

Year		Driver/Trainer	Owner
1955	**Scott Frost**	Joe O'Brien	S.A. Camp Farms
1963	**Speedy Scot**	Ralph Baldwin	Castleton Farms
1964	**Ayres**	John Simpson Sr.	Charlotte Sheppard
1968	**Nevele Pride**	Stanley Dancer	Nevele Acres & Lou Resnick
1969	**Lindy's Pride**	Howard Beissinger	Lindy Farms
1972	**Super Bowl**	Stanley Dancer	Rachel Dancer & Rose Hild Breeding Farm

Triple Crown Near Misses

PACERS

Seven horses have won the first two legs of the Triple Crown, but not the third. The Cane Pace (CP), Little Brown Jug (LBJ), and Messenger Stakes (MS) have not always been run in the same order so numbers after races won indicate sequence for that year.

Year		CP	LBJ	MS
1957	**Torpid**	won, 1	won, 2	DNF
1960	**Countess Adios**	won, 2	NE	won, 1
1971	**Albatross**	won, 2	2nd*	won, 1
1976	**Keystone Ore**	won, 1	won, 2	2nd*
1986	**Barberry Spur**	won, 1	won, 2	2nd*
1990	**Jake and Elwood**	won, 1	NE	won, 2
1992	**Western Hanover**	won, 1	2nd*	won, 2
1993	**Rijadh**	won, 1	2nd*	won, 2

TROTTERS

Seven horses have won the first two legs of the Triple Crown—the Yonkers Trot (YT) and the Hambletonian (Ham)—but not the third. The eventual winner of the Ky. Futurity (KF) is listed.

Year		YT	Ham	KF
1962	**A.C.'s Viking**	won	won	Safe Mission
1976	**Steve Lobell**	won	won	Quick Pay
1977	**Green Speed**	won	won	Texas
1978	**Speedy Somolli**	won	won	Doublemint
1987	**Mack Lobell**	won	won	Napoletano
1993	**American Winner**	won	won	Pine Chip
1996	**Continentalvictory**	won	won	Running Sea

Note: Green Speed (1977) not eligible for Ky. Futurity; Continentalvictory (1996) was withdrawn from the Ky. Futurity due to a leg injury.

***Winning horses:** Nansemond (1971), Windshield Wiper (1976), Amity Chef (1986), Fake Left (1992), Life Sign (1993).

Note: Torpid (1957) scratched before the final heat; Countess Adios (1960) not eligible for Messenger; Jake and Elwood (1990) not eligible for Little Brown Jug.

The Hambletonian

For three-year-old trotters. Inaugurated in 1926 and has been held in Syracuse, N.Y.; Lexington, Ky.; Goshen, N.Y.; Yonkers, N.Y.; Du Quoin, Ill.; and, since 1981 at The Meadowlands in East Rutherford, N.J.

Run at one mile since 1947. Winning horse must win two heats.

Drivers with most wins: John Campbell, Stanley Dancer, Billy Haughton and Ben White (4); Howard Beissinger, Del Cameron, and Henry Thomas (3).

Year		Driver	Fastest Heat
1926	**Guy McKinney**	Nat Ray	2:04¾
1927	**Iosola's Worthy**	Marvin Childs	2:03¾
1928	**Spencer**	W.H. Lessee	2:02½
1929	**Walter Dear**	Walter Cox	2:02¾
1930	**Hanover's Bertha**	Tom Berry	2:03
1931	**Calumet Butler**	R.D. McMahon	2:03¼
1932	**The Marchioness**	Will Caton	2:01¼
1933	**Mary Reynolds**	Ben White	2:03¾
1934	**Lord Jim**	Doc Parshall	2:02¾
1935	**Greyhound**	Sep Palin	2:02¼
1936	**Rosalind**	Ben White	2:01¾
1937	**Shirley Hanover**	Henry Thomas	2:01½
1938	**McLin Hanover**	Henry Tomas	2:02¼
1939	**Peter Astra**	Doc Parshall	2:04¼
1940	**Spencer Scott**	Fred Egan	2:02
1941	**Bill Gallon**	Lee Smith	2:05
1942	**The Ambassador**	Ben White	2:04
1943	**Volo Song**	Ben White	2:02½
1944	**Yankee Maid**	Henry Thomas	2:04
1945	**Titan Hanover**	Harry Pownall Sr.	2:04
1946	**Chestertown**	Thomas Berry	2:02½
1947	**Hoot Mon**	Sep Palin	2:00
1948	**Demon Hanover**	Harrison Hoyt	2:02
1949	**Miss Tilly**	Fred Egan	2:01⅖
1950	**Lusty Song**	Del Miller	2:02
1951	**Mainliner**	Guy Crippen	2:02⅗
1952	**Sharp Note**	Bion Shively	2:02⅗
1953	**Helicopter**	Harry Harvey	2:01⅗
1954	**Newport Dream**	Del Cameron	2:02⅘
1955	**Scott Frost**	Joe O'Brien	2:00⅗
1956	**The Intruder**	Ned Bower	2:01⅖
1957	**Hickory Smoke**	John Simpson Sr.	2:00⅕
1958	**Emily's Pride**	Flave Nipe	1:59⅘
1959	**Diller Hanover**	Frank Ervin	2:01⅕
1960	**Blaze Hanover**	Joe O'Brien	1:59⅗
1961	**Harlan Dean**	James Arthur	1:58⅖
1962	**A.C.'s Viking**	Sanders Russell	1:59⅗
1963	**Speedy Scot**	Ralph Baldwin	1:57⅗
1964	**Ayres**	John Simpson Sr.	1:56⅘
1965	**Egyptian Candor**	Del Cameron	2:03⅘
1966	**Kerry Way**	Frank Ervin	1:58⅘
1967	**Speedy Streak**	Del Cameron	2:00
1968	**Nevele Pride**	Stanley Dancer	1:59⅖
1969	**Lindys Pride**	Howard Beissinger	1:57⅗
1970	**Timothy T.**	John Simpson Jr.	1:58⅖
1971	**Speedy Crown**	Howard Beissinger	1:57⅖
1972	**Super Bowl**	Stanley Dancer	1:56⅖
1973	**Flirth**	Ralph Baldwin	1:57⅕
1974	**Christopher T**	Billy Haughton	1:58⅗
1975	**Bonefish**	Stanley Dancer	1:59
1976	**Steve Lobell**	Billy Haughton	1:56⅖
1977	**Green Speed**	Billy Haughton	1:55⅗
1978	**Speedy Somolli**	Howard Beissinger	1:55
1979	**Legend Hanover**	George Sholty	1:56⅕
1980	**Burgomeister**	Billy Haughton	1:56⅗
1981	**Shiaway St. Pat**	Ray Remmen	2:01⅕
1982	**Speed Bowl**	Tommy Haughton	1:56⅘
1983	**Duenna**	Stanley Dancer	1:57⅖

Year		Driver	Fastest Heat
1984	**Historic Freight**	Ben Webster	1:56⅖
1985	**Prakas**	Bill O'Donnell	1:54⅗
1986	**Nuclear Kosmos**	Ulf Thoresen	1:55⅖
1987	**Mack Lobell**	John Campbell	1:53⅗
1988	**Armbro Goal**	John Campbell	1:54⅗
1989	**Park Avenue Joe**	Ron Waples	1:54⅗
	& **Probe**	Bill Fahy	
1990	**Harmonious**	John Campbell	1:54⅕
1991	**Giant Victory**	Jack Moiseyev	1:54⅘
1992	**Alf Palema**	Mickey McNichol	1:56⅖
1993	**American Winner**	Ron Pierce	1:53⅕
1994	**Victory Dream**	Michel Lachance	1:54⅕
1995	**Tagliabue**	John Campbell	1:54⅘
1996	**Continentalvictory**	Michel Lachance	1:52⅘

Note: In 1989, Park Avenue Joe and Probe finished in a dead heat in the race-off. They were later declared co-winners, but Park Avenue Joe was awarded 1st place money because his three-race summary (2-1-1) was better than Probe's (1-9-1).

The Little Brown Jug

Harness racing's most prestigious race for three-year-old pacers. Inaugurated in 1946 and held annually at the Delaware, Ohio County Fairgrounds. Winning horse must win two heats.

Drivers with most wins: Billy Haughton (5); Stanley Dancer (4); John Campbell, Frank Ervin, Michel Lachance and John Simpson Sr. (3); Adelbert Cameron, Herve Filion, Jack Moiseyev, Joe O'Brien, Bill O'Donnell, "Curly" Smart and Ron Waples (2).

Year		Driver	Fastest Heat
1946	**Ensign Hanover**	"Curly" Smart	2:02
1947	**Forbes Chief**	Adelbert Cameron	2:05
1948	**Knight Dream**	Frank Safford	2:07
1949	**Good Time**	Frank Ervin	2:03⅖
1950	**Dudley Hanover**	Delvin Miller	2:02⅗
1951	**Tar Heel**	Adelbert Cameron	2:00
1952	**Meadow Rice**	"Curly" Smart	2:01⅗
1953	**Keystoner**	Frank Ervin	2:02⅕
1954	**Adios Harry**	Morris MacDonald	2:02⅖
1955	**Quick Chief**	Billy Haughton	2:00
1956	**Noble Adios**	John Simpson, Sr.	2:00⅘
1957	**Torpid**	John Simpson, Sr.	2:00⅘
1958	**Shadow Wave**	Joe O'Brien	2:01
1959	**Adios Butler**	Clint Hodgkins	1:59⅖
1960	**Bullet Hanover**	John Simpson, Sr.	1:58⅗
1961	**Henry T. Adios**	Stanley Dancer	1:58⅘
1962	**Lehigh Hanover**	Stanley Dancer	1:58⅘
1963	**Overtrick**	John Patterson, Sr.	1:57⅕
1964	**Vicar Hanover**	Billy Haughton	2:00⅘
1965	**Bret Hanover**	Frank Ervin	1:57
1966	**Romeo Hanover**	George Sholty	1:59⅗
1967	**Best Of All**	Jim Hackett	1:59
1968	**Rum Customer**	Billy Haughton	1:59⅗
1969	**Laverne Hanover**	Billy Haughton	2:00⅖
1970	**Most Happy Fella**	Stanley Dancer	1:57⅕
1971	**Nansemond**	Herve Filion	1:57⅖
1972	**Strike Out**	Keith Waples	1:56⅗
1973	**Melvin's Woe**	Joe O'Brien	1:57⅗
1974	**Armbro Omaha**	Billy Haughton	1:57
1975	**Seatrain**	Ben Webster	1:56⅘
1976	**Keystone Ore**	Stanley Dancer	1:56⅘
1977	**Governor Skipper**	John Chapman	1:56⅕
1978	**Happy Escort**	Bill Popfinger	1:55⅖
1979	**Hot Hitter**	Herve Filion	1:55⅗
1980	**Niatross**	Clint Galbraith	1:54⅘
1981	**Fan Hanover** (f)	Glen Garnsey	1:56
1982	**Merger**	John Campbell	1:54⅗
1983	**Ralph Hanover**	Ron Waples	1:55⅗
1984	**Colt Fortysix**	Chris Boring	1:53⅗
1985	**Nihilator**	Bill O'Donnell	1:52⅕
1986	**Barberry Spur**	Bill O'Donnell	1:52⅘
1987	**Jaguar Spur**	Dick Stillings	1:54
1988	**B.J. Scoot**	Michel Lachance	1:52⅗
1989	**Goalie Jeff**	Michel Lachance	1:54⅕
1990	**Beach Towel**	Ray Remmen	1:53⅗
1991	**Precious Bunny**	Jack Moiseyev	1:53⅘
1992	**Fake Left**	Ron Waples	1:53⅗
1993	**Life Sign**	John Campbell	1:52
1994	**Magical Mike**	Michel Lachance	1:52⅗
1995	**Nick's Fantasy**	John Campbell	1:51⅖
1996	**Armbro Operative**	Jack Moiseyev	1:52⅗

All-Time Leaders

The all-time winning trotters, pacers and drivers through 1995 according to *The Trotting and Pacing Guide*. Purses for horses include races in foreign countries. Earnings and wins for drivers include only races held in North America.

Top 15 Horses—Money Won

Note that (*) indicates horse raced in 1995.

		T/P	Sts	1st	Earnings
1	Peace Corps	T	42	35	$4,907,307
2	Ourasi (FRA)	T	N/A	32	4,010,105
3	Mack Lobell	T	86	65	3,917,594
4	Reve d'Udon	T	23	18	3,611,351
5	Nihilator	P	38	35	3,225,653
6	Artsplace	P	49	37	3,085,083
7	Presidential Ball	P	38	26	3,021,363
8	Matt's Scooter	P	61	37	2,944,591
9	On the Road Again	P	61	44	2,819,102
10	Sea Cove*	T	N/A	N/A	2,818,693
11	Ideal du Gazeau (FRA)	T	N/A	21	2,744,777
12	Vrai Lutin (FRA)	T	N/A	N/A	2,612,429
13	Grades Singing	T	101	66	2,607,552
14	Beach Towel	P	36	29	2,570,357
15	Embassy Lobell (FRA)	T	21	8	2,566,370

Top 15 Drivers — Races Won

All drivers were active in 1995.

		Yrs	1st	Earnings
1	Herve Filion	35	14,783	$85,045,702
2	Michel Lachance	28	7,354	82,772,526
3	Carmine Abbatiello	40	7,147	49,988,504
4	Dave Magee	23	7,052	48,863,623
5	John Campbell	24	7,019	138,257,031
6	Cat Manzi	28	6,683	55,816,025
7	Walter Case Jr.	19	6,640	25,261,869
8	Jack Moiseyev	20	6,426	57,067,744
9	Doug Brown	23	6,275	55,866,564
10	Ron Waples	30	6,136	62,265,618
11	Leigh Fitch	34	6,048	6,012,775
12	Eddie Davis	32	5,992	28,682,935
13	Bill Gale	25	5,954	35,549,035
14	Joe Marsh Jr.	41	5,823	35,812,113
15	Gilles Gendron	29	5,802	25,389,625

Annual Awards

Harness Horse of the Year

Selected since 1947 by U.S. Trotting Association and the U.S. Harness Writers Association; age of winning horse is noted; (t) indicates trotter and (p) indicates pacer. USTA added Trotter and Pacer of the Year awards in 1970.

Multiple winners: Bret Hanover and Nevele Pride (3); Adios Butler, Albatross, Cam Fella, Good Time, Mack Lobell, Niatross and Scott Frost (2).

Year		Year		Year		Year	
1947	Victory Song (4t)	1960	Adios Butler (4p)	1972	Albatross (4p)	1984	Fancy Crown (3t)
1948	Rodney (4t)	1961	Adios Butler (5p)	1973	Sir Dalrai (4p)	1985	Nihilator (3p)
1949	Good Time (3p)	1962	Su Mac Lad (8t)	1974	Delmonica Hanover(5t)	1986	Forrest Skipper (4p)
1950	Proximity (8t)	1963	Speedy Scot (3t)	1975	Savoir (7t)	1987	Mack Lobell (3t)
1951	Pronto Don (6t)	1964	Bret Hanover (2p)	1976	Keystone Ore (3p)	1988	Mack Lobell (4t)
1952	Good Time (6t)	1965	Bret Hanover (3p)	1977	Green Speed (3t)	1989	Matt's Scooter (4p)
1953	Hi Lo's Forbes (5p)	1966	Bret Hanover (4p)	1978	Abercrombie (3p)	1990	Beach Towel (3p)
1954	Stenographer (3t)	1967	Nevele Pride (2t)	1979	Niatross (2p)	1991	Precious Bunny (3p)
1955	Scott Frost (3t)	1968	Nevele Pride (3t)	1980	Niatross (3p)	1992	Artsplace (4p)
1956	Scott Frost (4t)	1969	Nevele Pride (4t)	1981	Fan Hanover (3p)	1993	Staying Together (4p)
1957	Torpid (3p)	1970	Fresh Yankee (7t)	1982	Cam Fella (3p)	1994	Cam's Card Shark (3p)
1958	Emily's Pride (3t)	1971	Albatross (3p)	1983	Cam Fella (4p)	1995	CR Kay Suzie (3t)
1959	Bye Bye Byrd (4p)						

Driver of the Year

Determined by Universal Driving Rating System (UDR) and presented by the Harness Tracks of America since 1968. Eligible drivers must have at least 1,000 starts for the season.

Multiple winners: Herve Filion (10); John Campbell and Michel Lachance (3); Walter Case Jr., Bill O'Donnell and Ron Waples (2).

Year		Year		Year		Year	
1968	Stanley Dancer	1976	Herve Filion	1983	John Campbell	1991	Walter Case Jr.
1969	Herve Filion	1977	Donald Dancer	1984	Bill O'Donnell	1992	Walter Case Jr.
1970	Herve Filion	1978	Carmine Abbatiello & Herve Filion	1985	Michel Lachance	1993	Jack Moiseyeu
1971	Herve Filion	1979	Ron Waples	1986	Michel Lachance	1994	Dave Magee
1972	Herve Filion	1980	Ron Waples	1987	Michel Lachance	1995	Luc Ouellette
1973	Herve Filion	1981	Herve Filion	1988	John Campbell		
1974	Herve Filion	1982	Bill O'Donnell	1989	Herve Filion		
1975	Joe O'Brien			1990	John Campbell		

STEEPLECHASE RACING

Champion Horses

Annual horse of the year since 1956 based on vote of the National Turf Writers Association and other selected media.

Multiple Winners: Flatterer (4); Bon Nouvel, Lonesome Glory, Zaccio (3); Café Prince, Morley Street, Neji (2).

Year		Year		Year		Year	
1956	Shipboard	1967	Quick Pitch	1978	Café Prince	1990	Morley Street
1957	Neji	1968	Bon Nouvel	1979	Martie's Anger	1991	Morley Street
1958	Neji	1969	L'Escargot	1980	Zaccio	1992	Lonesome Glory
1959	Ancestor	1970	Top Bid	1981	Zaccio	1993	Lonesome Glory
1960	Benguala	1971	Shadow Brok	1982	Zaccio	1994	Warm Spell
1961	Peal	1972	Soothsayer	1983	Flatterer	1995	Lonesome Glory
1962	Barnaby's Bluff	1973	Athenian Idol	1984	Flatterer		
1963	Amber Diver	1974	Gran Kan	1985	Flatterer		
1964	Bon Nouvel	1975	Life's Illusion	1986	Flatterer		
1965	Bon Nouvel	1976	Fire Control & Straight and True	1987	Inlander		
1966	Tuscalee & Mako	1977	Café Prince	1988	Jimmy Lorenzo		
				1989	Highland Bud		

Champion Jockeys

Annual leading jockeys by races won since 1956, according to the National Steeplechase Association.

Multiple Winners: Joe Aitcheson Jr. (7); Jerry Fishback (5); John Cushman and Alfred P. Smithwick (4); Tom Skiffington and Jeff Teter (3); Ricky Hendriks, James Lawrence, Blythe Miller and Thomas Walsh (2).

Year		Year		Year		Year	
1956	Alfred P. Smithwick	1966	Thomas Walsh	1976	Tom Skiffington	1986	Ricky Hendriks
1957	Alfred P. Smithwick	1967	Joe Aitcheson Jr.	1977	Jerry Fishback	1987	Ricky Hendriks
1958	Alfred P. Smithwick	1968	Joe Aitcheson Jr.	1978	Tom Skiffington	1988	Jonathan Smart
1959	James Murphy	1969	Joe Aitcheson Jr.	1979	Tom Skiffington	1989	James Lawrence
1960	Thomas Walsh	1970	Joe Aitcheson Jr.	1980	John Cushman	1990	Jeff Teter
1961	Joe Aitcheson Jr.	1971	Jerry Fishback	1981	John Cushman	1991	Jeff Teter
1962	Alfred P. Smithwick	1972	Michael O'Brien	1982	John Cushman	1992	Craig Thornton
1963	Joe Aitcheson Jr.	1973	Jerry Fishback	1983	John Cushman	1993	James Lawrence
1964	Joe Aitcheson Jr.	1974	Jerry Fishback	1984	Jeff Teter	1994	Blythe Miller
1965	Doug Small Jr.	1975	Jerry Fishback	1985	Bernie Houghton	1995	Blythe Miller

Wide World Photos

Known affectionately as the Willie Nelson of tennis, **Steffi Graf** holds the trophy she won as winner of the 1996 U.S. Open. Graf now has 21 career Grand Slam singles titles, second only to Margaret Smith Court's 24.

TENNIS

by Diane Pucin

Tension Anyone?

Despite painful off-court problems, Steffi Graf and Pete Sampras proved they are still the top tennis players in the world

There is no way to know how much the death of his coach affected Pete Sampras and how much the legal problems and jailing of her father affected Steffi Graf.

We know that Sampras's eyes still filled with tears five months after the death of Tim Gullikson, the man who nurtured Sampras and coaxed the talented young man to realize how much history he could make. We know that Sampras couldn't talk about Gullikson, not in public. Not yet.

And we know that Graf refused to talk of her father, Peter, the man who made her a tennis player, the man who was her coach and her guru, her authority figure. We know that Graf was hardly able to return home to Germany, where Peter has been in jail since August of 1995, accused of cheating the German government out of millions of dollars in taxes supposedly owed on his daughter's earnings.

But how much Sampras and Graf hurt, we can't know. What we do know, after a topsy-turvy year of weirdness and upsets, and the emergence of some charming new stars in women's tennis, is that Sampras and Graf are still the dominant players of their respective tours.

Graf, who is 27 now, and still looks the same as she did 13 years ago when she was a tour rookie, won all three Grand Slams that she entered in 1996. After missing the Australian Open to recover from foot surgery, Graf dominated in the French Open, Wimbledon and the U.S. Open, which gives her 21 career Grand Slam titles and wins in the last six Slams in which she has played.

Sampras did not dominate in the men's season in the same way. The 25-year-old, who had won at least one Grand Slam title every year since 1992, was shut out in the first three this year.

As it became clear that Gullikson was not going to win his battle with brain cancer, Sampras became listless. He didn't win at the Australian Open, he lost his No. 1 ranking for a time and then, two weeks before the French Open, Sampras was a pallbearer at Gullikson's funeral. Gullikson, 45, had been not only Sampras's mentor, but his best friend. He had convinced Sampras to harness his talent, to realize that, yes, Sampras had a wonderful weapon in his booming serve, but also that Sampras had elegant and deadly groundstrokes. Under Gullikson's tutelage, Sampras won six Grand Slam titles.

It was at the 1995 Australian Open that Gullikson had collapsed and it was discovered that he had a brain tumor.

A year later, Sampras had become used to traveling without his coach. Paul

Diane Pucin is a columnist for the *Philadelphia Inquirer*. She has covered international tennis since 1988.

Wide World Photos

Richey Reneberg, **Todd Martin**, **Jim Courier**, **Andre Agassi**, **Pete Sampras** and team captain **Tom Gullikson** display the trophies that signify their 1995 Davis Cup championship. Only Agassi and Gullikson seem to be aware that the trophies aren't recommended as headgear.

Annacone was the interim coach but Sampras still talked often with Gullikson. Not even Annacone in person and Gullikson by phone could save Sampras from an inconsiderate whupping from the tour's most promising young star, Mark Philippoussis, an Australian with a gigantic serve and the need to find his own Gullikson, someone to teach Philippoussis the finer points of tennis.

Philippoussis didn't need the finer points in the third round at Flinders Park in Melbourne in January, though. Philippoussis stunned Sampras, winning 6-4, 7-6, 7-6 and serving 29 aces.

No, Philippoussis did not go on to win the tournament. He did not make a statement like the 19-year-old Sampras had done at the 1990 U.S. Open. Instead, the statement was made by a 28-year-old who had once been known as "Boom Boom" because of a big serve.

Boris Becker, who was supposed to be well past winning Grand Slams, who had seemed ready for retirement back in 1992 and 1993 when he was always hurt or getting upset in the early rounds of the Slams, won his sixth Grand Slam title, his second Australian Open title and his first Slam since the 1991 Australian Open, by beating Michael Chang in the finals. Becker had made it to the 1995 Wimbledon final, but that seemed just an aberration. But Becker's play in Australia, marked by some spectacular serving and amazingly steady play from the backcourt, proved that Becker, who is happily married and a doting father, was not ready for the same retirement path as his friend and Wimbledon nemesis Stefan Edberg.

Edberg, 30, had announced in December of 1995 that 1996 would be his last year on the tour, and the quiet Swede was received with standing ovations and fanatic fans everywhere he went.

With Graf missing the Australian, Monica Seles had a clear path to her first Grand Slam title since her return to the game after a 2 1/2-year hiatus, in July of 1995. Seles had been absent, recovering from physical and psychic wounds that she had suffered in 1993 when a German fan of Graf stabbed Seles in the back during a tournament in Hamburg, Germany. When Seles made it to the finals of her first Slam since her return, the 1995 U.S. Open, and played a rousing three-set final against eventual winner Graf, there was excited anticipation of a potential Graf-Seles rivalry extending over all four 1996 Slams.

But Graf didn't play in Melbourne and Seles had an easy time of it, especially in the finals, where she swept two easy sets over Anke Huber, who was a nervous participant in her first-ever Grand Slam final.

While Seles was thrilled to be a Grand Slam winner again, the Australian Open proved a costly triumph. She had aggravated a tear in her serving shoulder muscle. Seles missed most of the winter and spring season, coming back just in time for the French Open. But she returned out of shape and with her shoulder so weakened that, for the rest of the year, Seles could only serve weakly and ineffectively.

These problems would cause Seles to be eliminated in the quarterfinals of the French Open by Jana Novotna. At Wimbledon, Seles didn't even make it to the quarterfinals. Karina Studenikova, an unknown Slovakian, stunned Seles in the second round, winning 7-5, 5-7, 6-4.

That left Graf with a relatively uneventful path to her 19th and 20th Grand Slam titles. She beat plucky Spaniard Arantxa Sanchez -Vicario in both finals but admitted at Wimbledon that she would certainly like to play Seles again.

The men's results at the French and Wimbledon were not nearly so predictable.

Sampras came to the French Open emotionally wrung-out after Gullikson's death, and with nearly no clay court preparation. A terrible draw had him meeting a tough, Swedish clay court expert, Magnus Gustafsson in the first round and with possible matchups later against two-time French Open champs Sergi Bruguera and Jim Courier.

Though Sampras was the No. 1 seed, the heavy favorite was Thomas Muster, who had, as usual, dominated the clay court season and even taken the No. 1 ranking from Sampras for a time. This occurrence had caused something of an uproar. Many players on the tour, most notably Sampras and Andre Agassi, had said that Muster could not be the best player in the world because of his one-note game and because he racked up all his computer points by playing well only on clay.

On the same day that Sampras played courageously and well in beating Bruguera 6-3, 6-4, 6-7, 2-6, 6-3, Agassi played dismal and lazy tennis and was shocked by Chris Woodruff, a journeyman pro from Tennessee, 4-6, 6-4, 6-7, 6-3, 6-2. After making 69 unforced errors, Agassi bolted from Roland Garros Stadium without speaking to the press and was fined $2,000.

Meanwhile, Sampras's win over Bruguera seemed to give Sampras a mental boost. It was the first time that Sampras had beaten a true clay courter at Roland Garros. The French is the only Slam Sampras had never won. Gullikson had been trying to convince Sampras that he had groundstrokes good enough to win the event. Sampras found out that Gullikson might have been right.

"This is the best clay court victory I've had in my career," Sampras said. "I think I learned something about myself today to maybe give me some confidence here."

Sampras did have more confidence. He beat Courier in five sets and advanced to the semifinals, the farthest he had ever made it in this Slam. And Sampras wasn't the only big server to do well. Muster and Agassi and 1989 French champion Michael Chang, classic baseliners all, fell by the wayside. Michael Stich whose only Slam victory came on grass at Wimbledon upset the defending champion Muster, and big, tall, monster server Marc Rosset of Switzerland also made it to the semis.

Only 22-year-old Russian Yevgeny Kafelnikov had made it to the semis by playing from the baseline and it was Sampras's bad luck to have drawn Kafelnikov instead of Stich or Rosset. Having already played 21 sets of tennis, compared to Kafelnikov's 16, in unseasonably hot weather and with the emotions of Gullikson's recent death still tormenting him, Sampras did not have the stamina to stay with Kafelnikov and meekly lost in straight sets.

Kafelnikov was able to run past Stich 7-6, 7-5, 7-6 in the finals just as easily. It was Kafelnikov's first Grand Slam title. Many more are expected from the talented young man who said, "I don't want to be only a winner on clay. I want to win on other surfaces as well and I think I have the game to do that. But this is one of the most glorious days of my life."

Wimbledon would be just as unpredictable. There was a lot of rain. But that wasn't shocking. But a streaker on Centre Court, a naked young woman right before the Gentleman's Final? That was shocking. And so were the finalists.

MaliVai Washington, a polite 27-year-old who has been a consistent top-20 player but not much more than that, became much more during this fortnight. He became the first African-American since Arthur Ashe won Wimbledon in 1975 to make it to the finals. And he did it with class.

Washington benefited from Becker's misfortune. Becker had ruptured a tendon in his wrist in the fourth round, so the unseeded Washington needed to beat only one seed, No. 9 Thomas Enqvist, on his way to the semifinals. There, Washington found another polite, quiet American, Todd Martin, the No. 13 seed. The two proceeded to play a very impolite, tense, rain-interrupted, five-set semifinal that Washington finally won, 5-7, 6-4, 6-7, 6-3, 10-8. Martin had led the fifth set 5-1 and afterwards accused himself of "freezing up."

Standing next to Washington as that streaker struck the final was Richard Krajicek. Krajicek, a 24-year-old Dutchman who had already been labeled an underachiever for not making more use of his powerful serve and wonderful, but inconsistent forehand, produced the most notable result of the fortnight.

For it was Krajicek who had upended three-time defending champion Sampras in the quarterfinals. As had Philippoussis at the Australian, Krajicek had pretty much served Sampras off the court in fashioning a 7-5, 7-6, 6-4 upset in a match thrice delayed by rain and played over two days. "I put so much emphasis on this tournament," a distraught Sampras said. "It's going to take me some time to get over this."

Krajicek didn't let down a bit. He beat unseeded Jason Stoltenberg in the semis and then obliterated Washington, 6-3, 6-4, 6-3, in the anticlimactic championship.

Up next for some players was the Olympics. Graf, who won the gold medal in 1988 and the silver in 1992, took a pass on the Atlanta games but Seles, Sanchez-Vicario and most of the top women were entered. It was a different story for the men,

Wide World Photos

Yevgeny Kafelnikov's victory in the French Open was the highlight of a strong year for the Russian tennis star who ranked at or near the top in ATP earnings all year.

though. The only top-10 players in the draw were Agassi and Enqvist after Sampras withdrew with a leg injury at the very last moment.

While Agassi was the exuberant winner of the gold, it seemed a poor substitute for Grand Slam excellence. The women's gold medal winner, Lindsay Davenport, however, may have taken her first step toward greatness. The 20-year-old beat Sanchez-Vicario in the gold medal match, and then upset Graf a month later in a tournament just before the U.S. Open. "The Olympics gave me confidence that I can take that next step," Davenport said.

Another young women's star emerged at the U.S. Open when 15-year-old Martina Hingis, a precocious prodigy with a sweet touch and excessive smarts, marched to the semifinals. There, Hingis held five set points in the first set, then met the reality that is Graf in Grand Slams. Though her father's trial had begun only a day earlier, Graf gathered herself and played flawless tennis that extended into the championship match a day later.

Wide World Photos

With his gutsy five-set victory over Andres Correjta in the semi-finals of the U.S.Open, **Pete Sampras** made his victory over Michael Chang in the finals an afterthought.

Graf beat Hingis 7-5, 6-3 and then, with lightning flashing and a deluge of rain and thunder and wind just two minutes away, Graf finished Seles off in the finals, 7-5, 6-4, to win her third straight U.S. Open. Graf received her $600,000 winners check in the pouring rain. "But I didn't even feel the rain," Graf said afterwards, also saying she hadn't noticed the storm closing in on her final service game. It is this ability to focus on the moment, to block out everything, that has made Graf perhaps the greatest woman player in tennis history.

As well as Graf played, though, this 1996 U.S. Open will always belong to Sampras. Needing a win to save the year from being disastrous and to keep his No. 1 ranking, Sampras played perhaps the most singular match in recent memory.

In the most amazing finish ever seen at the National Tennis Center, Sampras summoned up strength from somewhere, maybe from above where he often looks to Gullikson, and beat 22-year old Alex Corretja 7-6 (7-5), 5-7, 5-7, 6-4, 7-6 (9-7) in a 4 hour, 9 minute remarkably grueling quarterfinal match that lasted through afternoon, dusk and well into the night.

The final point was a double fault by Corretja, two nervous serves that came when Sampras was barely able to stand up straight, much less swing his racket.

Sampras had been hanging his head and burying his face in a towel from the time he had his serve broken in the 12th game to lose the second set. But there was no indication of how sick Sampras must have felt until after he'd lost the second point of the fifth-set tiebreak. Sampras walked back to the wall, bent over and vomited. He staggered in a circle, vomited again. Tried to walk forward and vomited once more. A player has only 30 seconds between points, so Sampras was given a warning. One more warning and Sampras would have lost a point.

So Sampras picked up his racket, walked to the service line, served, hit a forehand, forced Corretja into a long forehand and the match continued.

From then on, Sampras leaned on his racket, propping himself up after each point, folding in half to catch his breath, then standing up and hitting shots.

After this, it seemed ordained. Sampras conquered Goran Ivanisevic in the semifinals, then he dominated Michael Chang in the final. And then Sampras broke down and cried. He won this Open on the day that would have been Gullikson's 45th birthday. Gullikson's twin, Tom, said: "The burden is off Pete. He's been trying to win one for Tim. Now he's done that. Now he can start playing for himself again."

While the Open probably capped another No. 1 season for Sampras, there were two more big team events left that would provide individual highlights.

Seles won two singles matches, including the clincher, as the United States beat two-time defending champion Spain in the KB Fed Cup finals in Atlantic City. It was the first U.S. Fed Cup championship since 1990 and the first U.S. team event ever for Seles, Yugoslavian-born and a U.S. citizen for only two years.

In the Davis Cup tournament, the U.S. team, the defending champions, lost in the second round, hardly a surprise when Sampras, Agassi, Courier and Chang all declined invitations. Sweden and France advance to the finals, to be played in Sweden in December. ❐

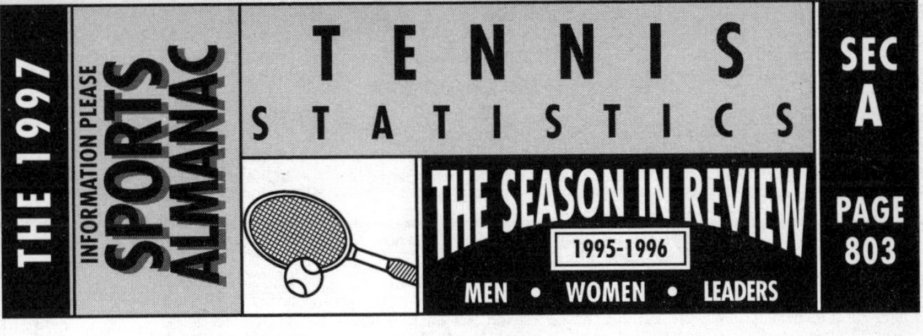

THE 1997
INFORMATION PLEASE
SPORTS ALMANAC
TENNIS
STATISTICS
THE SEASON IN REVIEW
1995-1996
MEN • WOMEN • LEADERS
SEC
A
PAGE
803

Tournament Results

Winners of men's and women's pro singles championships from Nov. 5, 1995 through Oct. 13, 1996. See Updates for later results.

Men's ATP Tour

LATE 1995

Finals	Tournament	Winner	Earnings	Runner-Up	Score
Nov. 5	Paris Indoors	Pete Sampras	$342,000	B. Becker	76 64 64
Nov. 5	Topper Open (Montevideo)	Bohdan Ulirach	29,000	A. Berasategui	62 63
Nov. 12	Stockholm Open	Thomas Enqvist	112,000	A. Boetsch	75 64
Nov. 12	Kremlin Cup (Moscow)	Carl-Uwe Steeb	157,400	D. Vacek	76 36 76
Nov. 12	South American Open (Buenos Aires)	Carlos Moya	43,000	F. Mantilla	60 63
Nov. 19	ATP World Championship (Frankfurt)	Boris Becker	1,225,000	M. Chang	76 60 76
Nov. 26	ATP Doubles Champs. (Eindhoven)	Grant Connel/ Patrick Galbraith	97,500 97,500	J. Eltingh/ P. Haarhuis	76 76 36 76
Dec. 10	ITF Grand Slam Cup (Munich)	Goran Ivanisevic	1,625,000	T. Martin	76 63 64

Note: The Grand Slam Cup, sponsored by the International Tennis Federation, is not an official ATP Tour event

1996 (through Oct. 13)

Finals	Tournament	Winner	Earnings	Runner-Up	Score
Jan. 7	Qatar Open (Doha)	Petr Korda	$84,000	Y. El Aynaoui	76 26 76
Jan. 7	Australian Hardcourt (Adelaide)	Yevgeny Kafelnikov	43,000	B. Black	76 36 61
Jan. 14	Peters International.(Sydney)	Todd Martin	43,000	G. Ivanisevic	57 63 64
Jan. 14	Indonesian Open (Jakarta)	Sjeng Schalken	43,000	Y. El Aynaoui	63 62
Jan. 14	BellSouth Open (Auckland)	Jiri Novak	43,000	B. Steven	64 64
Jan. 28	Ford **Australian Open** (Melbourne)	Boris Becker	410,260	M. Chang	62 64 26 62
Feb. 4	Croatian Indoors (Zagreb)	Goran Ivanisevic	54,000	C. Pioline	36 63 62
Feb. 4	Shanghai Open	Andrei Olhovskiy	43,000	M. Knowles	76 62
Feb. 18	Sybase Open (San Jose)	Pete Sampras	43,000	A. Agassi	62 63
Feb. 18	Open 13 (Marseille)	Guy Forget	72,000	C. Pioline	64 75
Feb. 18	Dubai Open	Goran Ivanisevic	142,000	A. Costa	64 63
Feb. 25	European Community Champ. (Antwerp)	Michael Stich	162,500	G. Ivanisevic	63 62 76
Feb. 25	Kroger/St.Jude International (Memphis)	Pete Sampras	117,000	T. Martin	64 76
Mar. 3	Italian Indoors (Milan)	Goran Ivanisevic	128,000	M. Rosset	63 76
Mar. 3	Comcast U.S. Indoor (Philadelphia)	Jim Courier	110,000	C. Woodruff	64 63
Mar. 10	ABN/AMRO World (Rotterdam)	Goran Ivanisevic	101,500	Y. Kafelnikov	64 36 63
Mar. 10	Franklin Templeton Classic (Scottsdale)	Wayne Ferreira	43,000	M. Rios	26 63 63
Mar. 10	Mexican Open (Mexico City)	Thomas Muster	43,200	J. Novak	76 62
Mar. 17	Copenhagen Open	Cedric Pioline	29,000	K. Carlsen	62 76
Mar. 17	Newsweek Champions Cup (Indian Wells)	Michael Chang	320,000	P. Haarhuis	75 61 61
Mar. 24	St. Petersburg Open (Russia)	Magnus Gustafsson	42,500	Y. Kafelnikov	62 76
Mar. 31	Lipton Championships (Key Biscayne)	Andre Agassi	338,000	G. Ivanisevic	30 (ret.)
Mar. 31	Grand Prix Hassan II (Casablanca)	Tomas Carbonell	29,000	G. Schaller	75 16 62
Apr. 14	Estoril Open (Lisbon)	Thomas Muster	84,000	A. Gaudenzi	76 64
Apr. 14	Indian Open (New Dehli)	Thomas Enqvist	58,000	B. Black	62 76
Apr. 14	Salem Open (Hong Kong)	Pete Sampras	43,000	M. Chang	64 36 64
Apr. 21	Japan Open (Tokyo)	Pete Sampras	154,000	R. Reneberg	64 75
Apr. 21	Open Seat - Godo (Barcelona)	Thomas Muster	132,000	C. Moya	46 62 64
Apr. 21	XL Bermuda Open	MaliVai Washington	43,000	M. Filippini	67 64 75
Apr. 28	Monte Carlo Open	Thomas Muster	320,000	A. Costa	63 57 46 63 62
Apr. 28	KAL Cup Korea Open (Seoul)	Byron Black	29,000	M. Damm	76 63
May 5	BMW Open (Munich)	Slava Dosedel	57,000	C. Moya	64 46 63
May 5	AT&T Challenge (Atlanta)	Karim Alami	43,000	N. Kulti	63 64
May 5	Skoda Czech Open (Prague)	Yevgeny Kafelnikov	48,200	B. Ulihrach	75 16 63
May 12	Panasonic German Open (Hamburg)	Roberto Carretero	320,000	A. Corretja	26 64 64 64

Tournament Results (Cont.)

Men's ATP Tour

Finals	Tournament	Winner	Earnings	Runner-Up	Score
May 12	US Clay Court Champ. (Pinehurst, NC)	Fernando Meligeni	$ 37,500	M. Wilander	64 62
May 19	Nokia Italian Open (Rome)	Thomas Muster	309,000	R. Krajicek	62 64 36 63
May 19	America's Red Clay Champ.	Jason Stoltenberg	34,800	C. Woodruff	76 26 75
May 26	Peugeot World Team Cup (Dusseldorf)	Switzerland	500,000	Czech Republic	2-1
May 26	Raiffeisen Grand Prix (St. Polten)	Marcelo Rios	57,000	F. Mantilla	62 64
June 9	**French Open** (Paris)	Yevgeny Kafelnikov	700,202	M. Stich	76 75 76
June 16	Stella Artois Grass Court (London)	Boris Becker	80,000	S. Edberg	64 76
June 16	Ordina Open (Rosmalen)	Richey Reneberg	66,400	S. Simian	64 60
June 16	Maia Open/Oporto Cup (Oporto)	Felix Mantilla	57,000	H. Gumy	67 64 63
June 23	The Nottingham Open	Jan Siemerink	43,000	S. Stolle	63 76
June 23	Gerry Weber Open (Halle)	Nicklas Kulti	122,000	Y. Kafelnikov	67 63 64
June 23	Internazionali di Tennis (Bologna)	Alberto Berasategui	43,000	C. Costa	63 64
July 7	**Wimbledon** (London)	Richard Krajicek	609,160	M. Washington	63 64 63
July 14	Hall of Fame Championships (Newport)	Nicolas Pereira	32,600	G. Stafford	46 64 64
July 14	Swedish Open (Bastad)	Magnus Gustafsson	43,000	A. Medvedev	61 63
July 14	Rado Swiss Open (Gstaad)	Alberto Costa	74,000	F. Mantilla	46 76 61 60
July 21	Mercedes Cup (Stuttgart)	Thomas Muster	157,000	Y. Kafelnikov	62 62 64
July 21	Legg Mason Classic (Washington, D.C.)	Michael Chang	90,000	W. Ferreira	62 64
July 28	EA Generali Open (Kitzbühel)	Alberto Berasategui	51,000	A. Corretja	62 64 64
Aug. 4	Grolsch Open (Amsterdam)	Francisco Clavet	66,400	Y. El Aynaoui	75 61 64
Aug. 4	Infiniti Open (Los Angeles)	Michael Chang	43,000	R. Krajicek	64 63
Aug. 11	San Marino Open	Alberto Costa	39,000	F. Mantilla	76 63
Aug. 11	Great American Insurance (Cincinnati)	Andre Agassi	320,000	M. Chang	76 64
Aug. 18	RCA/U.S. Hardcourts (Indianapolis)	Pete Sampras	150,000	G. Ivanisevic	76 75
Aug. 18	Pilot Pen International (New Haven)	Alex O'Brien	150,000	J. Siemerink	76 64
Aug. 18	Croatia Open (Umag)	Carlos Moya	54,000	F. Mantilla	60 76
Aug. 25	Waldbaum's Hamlet Cup (Long Island)	Andrei Medvedev	32,000	M. Damm	75 63
Aug. 25	du Maurier Open (Toronto)	Wayne Ferreira	288,000	T. Woodbridge	62 64
Sept. 8	**U.S. Open** (New York)	Pete Sampras	600,000	M. Chang	61 64 76
Sept. 15	Columbia Open (Bogota)	Thomas Muster	43,000	N. Lapentti	67 62 63
Sept. 15	Romanian Open (Bucharest)	Alberto Berasategui	66,400	C. Moya	61 76
Sept. 15	Bournemouth Open (England)	Alberto Costa	54,000	M. Goellner	67 62 62
Sept. 29	Swiss Indoors (Basel)	Pete Sampras	137,000	H. Dreekmann	75 62 60
Sept. 29	International Champ. of Sicily	Karim Alami	43,000	A. Voinea	75 21 Ret.
Oct. 6	Lyon Grand Prix	Yevgeny Kafelnikov	101,500	A. Boetsch	75 63
Oct. 6	Heinken Open (Singapore)	Jonathan Stark	55,000	M. Chang	64 64
Oct. 6	Marbella Open	Marc-Kevin Goellner	43,000	A. Corretja	76 76
Oct. 13	CA Tennis Trophy (Vienna)	Boris Becker	125,400	J. Siemerink	64 67 62 63
Oct. 13	Beijing Open	Greg Rusedski	43,000	M. Damm	76 64

Women's WTA Tour

LATE 1995

Finals	Tournament	Winner	Earnings	Runner-Up	Score
Nov. 5	Bank of the West Classic (Oakland)	Magdalena Maleeva	$79,000	A. Sugiyama	63 64
Nov. 5	Bell Challenge (Quebec City)	Brenda Schultz-McCarthy	26,500	D. Monami	76 62
Nov. 12	Advanta Championships (Philadelphia)	Steffi Graf	148,500	A. Huber	61 26 61 46 63
Nov. 19	Volvo Women's Open (Pattaya)	Barbara Paulus	17,500	J. Yi	64 63

1996 (through Oct. 13)

Finals	Tournament	Winner	Earnings	Runner-Up	Score
Jan. 6	Amway Classic (Auckland)	Sandra Cacic	$17,700	B. Paulus	63 16 64
Jan. 14	Peters International (Sydney)	Monica Seles	59,500	L. Davenport	46 76 63
Jan. 14	Tasmanian International (Hobart)	Julie Halard-Decugis	17,700	M. Endo	61 62
Jan. 28	Ford **Australian Open** (Melbourne)	Monica Seles	374,440	A. Huber	64 61
Feb. 4	Toray Pan Pacific Open (Tokyo)	Iva Majoli	150,000	A. Sanchez Vicario	64 61
Feb. 18	Open Gaz de France (Paris)	Julie Halard-Decugis	79,000	I. Majoli	75 76
Feb. 25	Faber Grand Prix (Essen)	Iva Majoli	79,000	J. Novotna	75 16 76
Feb. 25	IGA Classic (Oklahoma City)	Brenda Schultz-McCarthy	29,000	A. Coetzer	63 62
Mar. 3	EA Generali (Linz)	Sabine Appelmans	29,000	J. Halard-Decugis	62 64
Mar. 16	State Farm Evert Cup (Indian Wells)	Steffi Graf	100,000	C. Martinez	76 76
Mar. 31	Lipton Championships (Key Biscayne)	Steffi Graf	210,000	C. Rubin	61 63
April 7	Family Circle Cup (Hilton Head)	Arantxa Sanchez Vicario	200,000	B. Paulus	62 26 62
April 14	Bausch & Lomb Champs.(Amelia Island)	Irena Spirlea	450,000	M. Pierce	67 64 63
April 14	Danamon Open (Jakarta)	Linda Wild	29,000	Y. Basuki	withd.
April 21	Japan Open (Tokyo)	Kimiko Date	29,000	A. Frazier	75 64
May 5	Rexona Cup (Hamburg)	Arantxa Sanchez Vicario	79,000	C. Martinez	46 76 60
May 5	Bol Ladies Open	Gloria Pizzichini	17,700	S. Talaja	60 62

Finals	Tournament	Winner	Earnings	Runner-Up	Score
May 12	Budapest Lotto Ladies Open	Ruxandra Dragomir	$ 17,700	M. Schnell	76 61
May 12	Italian Open (Rome)	Conchita Martinez	150,000	M. Hingis	62 63
May 19	Rover Championships (Cardiff)	Dominique Van Roost	17,700	L. Courtois	64 62
May 19	German Open (Berlin)	Steffi Graf	150,000	K. Habsudova	46 62 75
May 25	Internationaux de Strasbourg	Lindsay Davenport	27,000	B. Paulus	63 76
May 25	Madrid Open	Jana Novotna	49,000	M. Maleeva	46 64 63
June 9	**French Open** (Paris)	Steffi Graf	586,898	A. Sanchez Vicario	63 67 10-8
June 16	DFS Classic (Birmingham)	Meredith McGrath	29,000	N. Tauziat	26 64 64
June 22	Direct Line Insurance Int'l. (Eastbourne)	Monica Seles	66,000	M.J. Fernandez	60 62
June 22	Wilkinson Championships (Rosmalen)	Anke Huber	27,000	H. Sukova	64 76
July 7	**Wimbledon** (London)	Steffi Graf	493,480	A. Sanchez Vicario	63 75
July 21	Torneo Internazionale (Palermo)	Barbara Schett	17,700	S. Hack	63 62
Aug. 11	Styrian Open (Austria)	Barbara Paulus	17,700	S. Cecchini	40-15 Ret.
Aug. 11	du Maurier Ltd. Open (Toronto)	Monica Seles	200,000	A. Sanchez Vicario	61 76
Aug. 18	Acura Classic (Los Angeles)	Lindsay Davenport	80,000	A. Huber	62 63
Aug. 25	Toshiba Classic (San Diego)	Kimiko Date	79,000	A. Sanchez Vicario	36 63 60
Sept. 8	**U.S. Open** (New York)	Steffi Graf	600,000	M. Seles	75 64
Sept. 22	Warsaw Cup	Henrietta Nagyova	27,000	B. Paulus	36 62 61
Sept. 22	Nichirei Open (Tokyo)	Monica Seles	79,000	A. Sanchez Vicario	61 64
Oct. 6	Sparkassen Cup (Leipzig)	Anke Huber	79,000	I. Majoli	57 63 61
Oct. 13	Porsche Tennis GP (Filderstadt)	Martina Hingis	79,000	A. Huber	62 36 63

1996 Grand Slam Tournaments

Australian Open

MEN'S SINGLES

FINAL EIGHT— #2 Andre Agassi; #4 Boris Becker; #5 Michael Chang; #6 Yevgeny Kafelnikov; #7 Thomas Enqvist; #8 Jim Courier; plus unseeded Mikael Tillstrom and Mark Woodforde.

Quarterfinals

Becker def. Kafelnikov .... 64 76(9) 61
Woodforde def. Enqvist 64 64 64
Agassi def. Courier .... 67(7) 26 63 64 62
Chang def. Tillstrom 60 62 64

Semifinals

Becker def. Woodforde 64 62 60
Chang def. Agassi .... 61 64 76(1)

Final

Becker def. Chang 62 64 26 62

WOMEN'S SINGLES

FINAL EIGHT— #1 Monica Seles; #2 Conchita Martinez; #3 Arantxa Sanchez Vicario; #7 Iva Majoli; #8 Anke Huber; #13 Chanda Rubin; #16 Amanda Coetzer; plus unseeded Martina Hingis.

Quarterfinals

Seles def. Majoli 61 62
Rubin def. Sanchez Vicario 64 26 16-14
Coetzer def. Hingis 75 46 61
Huber def. Martinez 46 62 61

Semifinals

Seles def. Rubin 67 (7-2) 61 75
Huber def. Coetzer 46 64 62

Finals

Seles def. Huber 64 61

DOUBLES FINALS

Men— Stefan Edberg & Petr Korda def. Sebastien Lareau & Alex O'Brien, 7-5, 7-5, 4-6, 6-1.
Women— #8 Chanda Rubin & A. Sanchez Vicario def. #3 Lindsay Davenport & Mary Jo Fernandez, 6-4, 2-6, 6-2.
Mixed— #1 Mark Woodforde & Larisa Neiland def. Luke Jensen & Nicole Arendt, 4-6, 7-5, 6-0.

French Open

MEN'S SINGLES

FINAL EIGHT— #1 Pete Sampras; #6 Yevgeny Kafelnikov; #7 Jim Courier; # 13 Richard Krajicek; #14 Mark Rosset; #15 Michael Stich; plus unseeded Cedric Pioline and Bernd Karbacher.

Quarterfinals

Sampras def. Courier 67 (4-7) 46 64 64 64
Kafelnikov def. Krajicek 63 64 67 (4-7) 62
Rosset def. Karbacher 46 46 63 75 60
Stich def. Pioline 64 46 63 62

Semifinals

Kafelnikov def. Sampras 76 (7-4) 60 62
Stich def. Rosset 63 64 62

Final

Kafelnikov def. Stich 76 (7-4) 75 76 (7-4)

WOMEN'S SINGLES

FINAL EIGHT— #1 Steffi Graf; # 1 Monica Seles; # 3 Conchita Martinez; #4 Aranxta Sanchez Vicario; #5 Iva Majoli; #9 Lindsay Davenport; #10 Jana Novotna; plus unseeded Karina Habsudova.

Quarterfinals

Graf def. Majoli 63 61
Martinez def. Davenport 61 63
Sanchez Vicario def. Habsudova 62 67 (4-7) 10-8
Novotna def. Seles 76 (9-7) 63

Semifinals

Graf def. Martinez 63 61
Sanchez Vicario def. Novotna 63 75

Final

Graf def. Sanchez Vicario 63 67 (4-7) 10-8

DOUBLES FINALS

Men—#7 Yevgeny Kafelnikov & Daniel Vacek def. #5 Guy Forget & Jacob Hlasek 6–2, 6–3.
Women—#4 Lindsay Davenport & Mary Joe Fernandez def. #2 Gigi Fernandez & Natasha Zvereva 6–2, 6–1.
Mixed— Javier Frana & Patricia Tarabini def. Luke Jensen & Nicole Arendt 6–2, 6–2.

1996 Grand Slam Tournaments (Cont.)

Wimbledon

MEN'S SINGLES

FINAL EIGHT— #1 Pete Sampras; #4 Goran Ivanisevic; #13 Todd Martin; plus unseeded Tim Henman, Richard Krajicek, MaliVai Washington, Alexander Radulescu, and Jason Stoltenberg.

Quarterfinals

Krajicek def. Sampras 75 76 (7-3) 64
Stoltenberg def. Ivanisevic....63 76 (7-3) 67 (3-7) 76 (7-3)
Martin def. Henman 76 (7-5) 76 (7-2) 64
Washington def. Radulescu 67 (5) 76 (1) 57 76 (3) 64

Semifinals

Washington def. Martin 57 64 67 (6-8) 63 10-8
Krajicek def. Stoltenberg....75 62 61

Final

Krajicek def. Washington 63 64 63

WOMEN'S SINGLES

FINAL EIGHT— #1 Steffi Graf; #4 Arantxa Sanchez Vicario; #6 Jana Novotna; #9 Mary Joe Fernandez; #12 Kimiko Date; #13 Mary Pierce; plus unseeded Judith Wiesner and Meredith McGrath.

Quarterfinals

Graf def. Novotna....63 62
Sanchez Vicario def. Wiesner....64 60
McGrath def. Fernandez....63 61
Date def. Pierce 36 63 61

Semifinals

Sanchez Vicario def. McGrath 62 61
Graf def. Date 62 26 63

Final

Graf def. Sanchez Vicario 63 75

DOUBLES FINALS

Men— #1 Todd Woodbridge & Mark Woodforde def. #3 Byron Black & Grant Connell 4–6, 6–1, 6–3, 6–2.

Women— #8 Martina Hingis & Helena Sukova def. #4 Meredith McGrath & Larisa Neiland 5–7, 7–5, 6–1.

Mixed— #7 Cyril Suk & Helena Sukova def. #1 Mark Woodforde & Larisa Neiland 1–6, 6–3, 6–2.

U.S. Open

MEN'S SINGLES

FINAL EIGHT— #1 Pete Sampras; #2 Michael Chang; #3 Thomas Muster; #4 Goran Ivanisevic; #6 Andre Agassi; plus unseeded Alex Corretja, Stefan Edberg, and Javier Sanchez.

Quarterfinals

Sampras def. Corretja 76 (7-5) 57 57 64 76 (9-7)
Ivanisevic def. Edberg 63 64 76 (11-9)
Agassi def. Muster 62 75 46 62
Chang def. Sanchez 75 63 67 (7-2) 63

Semifinals

Chang def. Agassi 63 62 62
Sampras def. Ivanisevic....63 64 67 (9-11) 63

Final

Sampras def. Chang 61 64 76 (7-3)

WOMEN'S SINGLES

FINAL EIGHT— #1 Steffi Graf; #2 Monica Seles; #4 Conchita Martinez; #7 Jana Novotna; #16 Martina Hingis; plus unseeded Judith Wiesner, Linda Wild, and Amanda Coetzer.

Quarterfinals

Graf def. Wiesner 75 63
Hingis def. Novotna....76 (7-1) 64
Martinez def. Wild 76 (8-6) 60
Seles def. Coetzer 60 63

Semifinals

Graf def. Hingis 75 63
Seles def. Martinez....64 63

Final

Graf def. Seles....75 64

DOUBLES FINALS

Men— #1 Todd Woodbridge & Mark Woodforde def. #8 Jacco Eltingh & Paul Haarhuis, 4–6, 7–6 (7–5), 7–6 (7–2).

Women— #2 Gigi Fernandez & Natasha Zvereva def. Jana Novotna & Arantxa Sanchez Vicario, 1-6, 6-1, 6-4.

Mixed— #3 Lisa Raymond & Patrick Galbraith def. #4 Manon Bolle-Graf & Rick Leach, 7–6 (8–6), 7–6 (7–4).

1996 Fed Cup

Originally the Federation Cup and started in 1963 by the International Tennis Federation as the Davis Cup of women's tennis. Played by 32 teams over one week at one site through 1994. Tournament changed in 1995 to Davis Cup-style format of four rounds and home sides.

Quarterfinals

(Apr. 22-28)

Winner	Loser
USA 3	at Austria 2
at Japan 3	Germany 2
at France 3	Argentina 2
at Spain 3	South Africa 2

Semifinals

United States 5, Japan 0

at Nagoya, Japan (July 13-14)

Day One— Lindsay Davenport (USA) def. Kimiko Date (JPN), 6-2, 6-1; Monica Seles (USA) def. Ai Sugiyama (JPN), 6-2, 6-2.

Day Two— Seles (USA) def. Date (JPN), 6-0, 6-2; Davenport (USA) def. Sugiyama (JPN), 7–6 (10-8), 7-5; Davenport & Wild (USA) def. Sugiyama & Kyoko Nagatsuka (JPN), 6-2, 6-1.

Spain 3, France 2

at Bayonne, Spain (July 13-14)

Day One— Conchita Martinez (SPA) def. Julie Halard-Decugis (FRA), 1-6, 6-4, 6-2; Mary Pierce (FRA) def. Arantxa Sanchez Vicario (SPA), 6-3, 6-4.

Day Two— Martinez (SPA) def. Pierce (FRA), 7-5, 6-1; Halard-Decugis (FRA) def. Sanchez Vicario (SPA), 2-6, 6-4, 7-5; Martinez & Sanchez Vicario (SPA) def. Halard-Decugis & Nathalie Tauziat (FRA), 6-4, 2-1, retired.

Finals

United States 5, Spain 0

at Atlantic City, N.J. (Sept. 28–29)

Day One— Monica Seles (USA) def. Conchita Martinez (SPA), 6-2, 6-4; Lindsay Davenport (USA) def. Arantxa Sanchez Vicario (SPA), 7-5, 6-1.

Day Two— Seles (USA) def. Sanchez Vicario (SPA), 3-6, 6-3, 6-1; Daveport (USA) def. Gala Leon Garcia (SPA), 7-5, 6-2; Mary Joe Fernandez & Davenport (USA) def. Leon Garcia & Virginia Ruano Pascual (SPA), 6-1, 6-4.

Singles Leaders

Official Top 20 computer rankings and money leaders of men's and women's tours for 1995 and unofficial rankings and money leaders for 1996 (through Oct. 14), as compiled by the ATP (Association of Tennis Professionals) and WTA (Women's Tennis Association). Note that money list includes doubles earnings.

Final 1995 Computer Rankings and Money Won

Listed are events won and times a finalist and semifinalist (Finish, 1-2-SF), match record (W-L), and earnings for the year.

MEN

		Finish 1-2-SF	W-L	Earnings
1	Pete Sampras	5-4-4	72-16	$5,415,066
2	Andre Agassi	7-4-2	73-9	2,975,738
3	Thomas Muster	12-2-0	86-18	2,887,979
4	Boris Becker	2-4-6	54-18	3,712,358
5	Michael Chang	4-4-2	65-18	2,655,870
6	Yevgeny Kafelnikov	4-1-7	73-32	1,841,561
7	Thomas Enqvist	5-1-3	63-23	1,229,646
8	Jim Courier	4-1-4	61-22	1,202,769
9	Wayne Ferreira	4-0-3	58-26	1,276,216
10	Goran Ivanisevic	1-1-7	46-24	3,777,862
11	Richard Krajicek	2-1-1	41-26	925,822
12	Michael Stich	1-3-2	47-19	853,974
13	Sergi Bruguera	0-1-4	40-19	2,058,044
14	Arnaud Boetsch	1-2-3	45-33	607,535
15	Marc Rosset	2-0-4	40-22	570,786
16	Andrei Medvedev	1-0-1	41-26	922,692
17	Magnus Larsson	0-2-3	35-15	702,245
18	Todd Martin	1-1-4	47-25	1,455,558
19	Paul Haarhuis	1-2-2	34-25	1,005,587
20	Gilbert Schaller	1-2-2	43-30	426,568

WOMEN

		Finish 1-2-SF	W-L	Earnings
1	Monica Seles	1-1-0	11-1	$ 397,010
2	Conchita Martinez	6-1-4	63-10	1,186,845
3	A. Sanchez Vicario	2-5-2	49-15	1,073,169
4	Kimiko Date	1-3-2	41-12	607,113
5	Mary Pierce	2-2-2	37-16	680,088
6	Magdalena Maleeva	3-3-4	35-11	484,951
7	Gabriela Sabatini	1-2-5	44-17	594,808
8	Mary Joe Fernandez	2-0-2	31-15	427,659
9	Iva Majoli	2-1-2	29-12	467,871
10	Anke Huber	1-1-4	42-17	607,922
11	Jana Novotna	1-0-4	30-12	394,523
12	Lindsay Davenport	1-2-1	33-13	319,914
13	B. Schultz-McCarthy	2-0-2	41-16	411,906
14	Natasha Zvereva	0-1-4	31-17	400,017
15	Chanda Rubin	2-2-2	43-19	326,523
16	Martina Hingis	0-1-0	22-13	147,154
17	Naoko Sawamatsu	0-0-1	24-13	168,407
18	Amy Frazier	1-0-1	28-15	193,139
19	Amanda Coetzer	0-2-2	34-22	263,256
20	Lisa Raymond	0-2-0	25-16	176,438

1996 Computer Rankings (through Oct. 14)

For Men's Tour, listed are tournaments won and times a finalist and semifinalist (Finish, 1-2-SF), match record (W-L), and computer points earned (Pts). For Women's Tour, listed are tournaments won and times a finalist and semifinalist (Finish, 1-2-SF), match record (W-L), and average computer points per game (Avg).

MEN

ATP Tour singles rankings based on total computer points from each player's 14 best tournaments covering the last 12 months. Tournaments, titles and match won-lost records, however, are for 1996 only.

Rank 96	(95)		Finish 1-2-SF	W-L	Pts
1	(2)	Pete Sampras	7-0-2	57-8	4740
2	(5)	Michael Chang	3-5-3	60-15	3822
3	(3)	Thomas Muster	7-0-4	67-16	3612
4	(6)	Yevgeny Kafelnikov	4-4-4	69-19	3253
5	(7)	Goran Ivanisevic	4-4-2	64-20	3165
6	(4)	Boris Becker	3-0-2	29-11	3041
7	(14)	Wayne Ferreira	2-1-2	46-24	2604
8	(13)	Richard Krajicek	1-2-0	43-22	2410
9	(1)	Andre Agassi	3-1-2	36-10	2292
10	(25)	Marcelo Rios	1-2-4	48-21	1979
11	(19)	Todd Martin	1-1-4	47-17	1951
12	(8)	Thomas Enqvist	1-0-2	44-27	1895
13	(26)	MaliVai Washington	1-1-0	27-19	1762
14	(31)	Albert Costa	3-2-1	49-25	1758
15	(9)	Jim Courier	1-0-1	25-13	1684
16	(84)	Felix Mantilla	1-4-1	42-23	1584
17	(56)	Cedric Pioline	1-2-1	40-18	1504
18	(20)	Stefan Edberg	0-1-2	42-22	1493
19	(16)	Alberto Berasategui	3-0-3	40-23	1479
20	(48)	Alex Corretja	0-3-2	37-21	1478

WOMEN

WTA Tour Media Information System singles rankings based on average computer points awarded for each tournament played during the last 12 months. Tournaments, titles and match won-lost records, however, are for 1996 only.

Rank 96	(95)		Finish 1-2-SF	W-L	Pts
1	(1)	Monica Seles	5-1-1	43-5	341.6
1	(1)	Steffi Graf	6-0-2	47-3	335.9
2	(2)	A. Sanchez Vicario	2-7-2	56-21	205.5
3	(3)	Conchita Martinez	1-2-5	46-15	197.5
4	(10)	Anke Huber	2-3-1	42-14	174.8
5	(9)	Lindsay Davenport	3-1-3	48-11	155.6
6	(13)	Iva Majoli	2-2-2	36-13	152.3
7	(6)	Kimiko Date	2-0-4	35-15	141.5
8	(4)	Jana Novotna	1-1-5	40-12	140.7
9	(16)	Martina Hingis	2-1-2	37-13	138.1
10	(11)	Mary Joe Fernandez	0-1-2	31-14	114.0
11	(14)	B. Schultz-McCarthy	1-0-2	31-15	95.6
12	(8)	Magdalena Maleeva	0-1-1	21-14	92.1
13	(19)	Amanda Coetzer	0-1-1	33-19	91.0
14	(23)	Barbara Paulus	1-5-0	34-15	87.0
15	(15)	Chanda Rubin	0-1-2	18-7	84.7
16	(51)	Julie Halard-Decugis	2-1-1	31-10	82.8
17	(21)	Irina Spirlea	1-0-1	29-15	77.6
18	(5)	Mary Pierce	0-1-1	19-13	77.2
19	(57)	Karina Habsudova	0-1-3	37-20	75.9
20	(25)	Judith Wiesner	0-0-3	35-22	72.4

Singles Leaders (Cont.)

1996 Money Winners

Amounts include singles and doubles earnings through Oct. 14, 1996.

MEN

		Earnings			Earnings			Earnings
1	Yevgeny Kafelnikov	$1,863,713	8	Todd Woodbridge	$942,738	15	Marcelo Rios	$725,248
2	Pete Sampras	1,754,922	9	Mark Woodforde	901,082	16	Paul Haarhuis	725,106
3	Thomas Muster	1,516,166	10	Wayne Ferreira	892,340	17	Todd Martin	715,186
4	Goran Ivanisevic	1,415,555	11	Boris Becker	840,827	18	Michael Stich	641,945
5	Michael Chang	1,379,916	12	Jakob Hlasek	807,128	19	Jan Siemerink	627,476
6	Richard Krajicek	1,185,511	13	Marc Rosset	806,989	20	Byron Black	625,612
7	Andre Agassi	1,045,660	14	Albert Costa	747,256			

WOMEN

		Earnings			Earnings			Earnings
1	Steffi Graf	$2,127,206	8	Iva Majoli	$541,530	15	Gigi Fernandez	$343,144
2	A. Sanchez Vicario	1,444,444	9	Anke Huber	496,060	16	Irina Spirlea	342,259
3	Monica Seles	1,066,749	10	Mary Joe Fernandez	412,606	17	Natasha Zvereva	326,280
4	Conchita Martinez	762,101	11	Kimiko Date	384,181	18	Amanda Coetzer	326,232
5	Jana Novotna	648,852	12	Helena Sukova	377,076	19	Chanda Rubin	323,339
6	Martina Hingis	643,751	13	Meredith McGrath	361,718	20	Karina Habsudova	307,387
7	Lindsay Davenport	602,663	14	Larisa Neiland	351,783			

Davis Cup

United States defeated Russia, 3-2, in Moscow to capture the 1995 Davis Cup. It was the 31st championship for the Americans, while Russia has yet to claim their first Davis Cup title. Pete Sampras won a doubles match with Todd Martin to go along with his two singles victories in the finals.

1995 Final

USA 3, Russia 2

(at Moscow, Dec. 1-3)

Day One— Pete Sampras (USA) def. Andrei Chesnokov (RUS), 3-6, 6-4, 6-3, 6-7(5), 6-4; Yevgeny Kafelnikov (RUS) def. Jim Courier (USA), 7-6(1), 7-5, 6-3.

Day Two— Todd Martin & Sampras (USA) def. Kafelnikov & Andrei Olhovskiy (RUS), 7-5, 6-4, 6-3.

Day Three— Sampras (USA) def. Kafelnikov (RUS), 6-2, 6-4, 7-6(4); Chesnokov (RUS) def. Courier, 6-7(1), 7-5, 6-0.

1996 Early Rounds

Sweden plays host to the 1996 Davis Cup final from Nov. 29-Dec. 1. The Swedes advanced to the finals as Thomas Enqvist and Stefan Edberg led them to a semifinal win over the Czech Republic. They will face France, who edged Italy, 3-2. France has won the Cup seven times since play began in 1900. Sweden has won five times.

FIRST ROUND

(Feb. 9-11)

Winner	Loser
at USA 5	Mexico 0
at Italy 3	Russia 2
at India 3	Netherlands 2
at Czech Republic 5	Hungary 0
at France 5	Denmark 0
Germany 5	at Switzerland 0
at Sweden 4	Belgium 1
at South Africa 3	Austria 2

QUARTERFINALS

(Apr. 5-7)

Winner	Loser
at Italy 4	South Africa 1
at France 5	Germany 0
Sweden 5	at India 0
at Czech Republic 3	USA 2

SEMIFINALS

Sweden 4, Czech Republic 1

at Prague, Czech Republic (Sept. 20-22)

Day One— Thomas Enqvist (SWE) def. Petr Korda (CZE), 6-4, 6-3, 7–6 (11-9); Stefan Edberg (SWE) def. Daniel Vacek (CZE), 7-6 (7-2), 7-5, 4-6, 6-3.

Day Two— Korda & Vacek (CZE) def. Nicklas Kulti & Jonas Bjorkman (SWE), 4-6, 6-3, 6-4, 6-4.

Day Three— Enqvist (SWE) def. Vacek (CZE), 6-3, 6-7 (3-7), 4-6, 7-5, 6-3; Edberg (Swe) def. Korda (CZE), 4-6, 6-2, 7-5.

France 3, Italy 2

at Nantes, France (Sept. 20-22)

Day One— Andrea Gaudenzi (ITA) def. Cedric Pioline (FRA), 5-7, 6-1, 7-6 (7-4); Renzo Furlan (ITA) def. Arnaud Boetsch (FRA), 7-5, 1-6, 6-3, 7-6 (7-5).

Day Two— Guy Forget & Guillaume Raoux (FRA) def. Gaudenzi & Diego Nargiso (ITA), 6-3, 6-4, 6-2.

Day Three— Pioline (FRA) def. Furlan (ITA), 6-3, 2-6, 6-2, 6-4; Boetsch (FRA) def. Gaudenzi (ITA), 6-4, 6-2, 7-6 (10-8).

FINAL

at Sweden (Nov. 29-Dec. 1)

Agassi vs. Sampras

From the 1992 French Open to the Feb. 18 Sybase Open, Pete Sampras and Andre Agassi met 12 times with Sampras winning seven. Sampras also leads their all-time series, 10-8.

Tourn. (Rnd.)	Winner	Score
'92 French Open (QF)	Agassi	76 62 61
'93 Wimbledon (QF)	Sampras	62 62 36 36 64
'94 Key Biscayne (F)	Sampras	57 63 63
'94 Osaka (SF)	Sampras	63 61
'94 Paris-Indoor (QF)	Agassi	76 75
'94 ATP Champ. (SF)	Sampras	46 76 63
'95 Australian Open (F)	Agassi	46 61 76 64
'95 Indian Wells (F)	Sampras	75 63 75
'95 Key Biscayne (F)	Agassi	36 62 76
'95 Canadian Open (F)	Agassi	36 62 63
'95 U.S. Open (F)	Sampras	64 63 46 75
'96 Sybase Open (F)	Sampras	62 63

1996 ATP Tour

Statistical Leaders (as of Oct. 14, 1996)

Service Game Leaders

	Aces	No	Mtchs
1	Goran Ivanisevic	1245	81
2	Richard Krajicek	799	61
3	Pete Sampras	779	65
4	Mark Philippoussis	576	43
5	Greg Rusedski	561	50
6	Yevgeny Kafelnikov	546	84
7	Todd Martin	522	60
8	Marc Rosset	484	51
9	Wayne Ferreira	478	62
10	Marc-Kevin Goellner	473	47
11	Martin Damm	472	54
12	Thomas Enqvist	443	63
13	Michael Chang	439	68
14	Boris Becker	418	40
15	Guy Forget	387	42

	2nd Serve Points Won	Pct	Mtchs
1	Thomas Muster	54%	80
2	Pete Sampras	53%	65
3	Vincent Spadea	53%	45
4	Patrick Rafter	53%	43
5	Jim Courier	53%	38
6	Yevgeny Kafelnikov	52%	84
7	Goran Ivanisevic	52%	81
8	Michael Chang	52%	68
	Albert Costa	52%	68
10	Felix Mantilla	52%	65
11	Alberto Berasategui	52%	63
12	Francisco Clavet	52%	61
13	Todd Martin	52%	60
14	Alex Corretja	52%	58
15	Richey Reneberg	52%	53

	1st Serve	Pct	Mtchs
1	Gilbert Schaller	77%	42
2	Alberto Berasategui	76%	63
3	Albert Costa	70%	68
4	Felix Mantilla	70%	65
5	Carlos Moya	66%	63
6	Tomas Carbonell	66%	45
7	Jiri Novak	65%	49
8	Magnus Gustafsson	64%	43
9	Francisco Clavet	63%	61
10	Paul Haarhuis	63%	51
11	Andrea Gaudenzi	63%	48
12	Todd Martin	62%	60
13	Javier Sanchez	62%	56
14	Renzo Furlan	62%	48
15	Vincent Spadea	62%	45

	Service Games Won	Pct	Mtchs
1	Pete Sampras	91%	65
2	Goran Ivanisevic	89%	81
3	Richard Krajicek	85%	61
4	Greg Rusedski	85%	50
5	Patrick Rafter	85%	43
6	Boris Becker	85%	40
7	Todd Martin	84%	60
8	Mark Philippoussis	84%	43
9	Yevgeny Kafelnikov	83%	84
10	Marc Rosset	83%	51
11	Thomas Muster	82%	80
12	Martin Damm	82%	54
	Jan Siemerink	82%	54
14	Cedric Pioline	82%	52
15	Marc-Kevin Goellner	82%	47

	1st Serve Points Won	Pct	Mtchs
1	Goran Ivanisevic	85%	81
2	Pete Sampras	83%	65
3	Richard Krajicek	83%	61
4	Mark Philippoussis	81%	43
5	Boris Becker	81%	40
6	Marc Rosset	80%	51
7	Greg Rusedski	80%	50
8	Michael Chang	78%	68
9	Marc-Kevin Goellner	78%	47
10	Martin Damm	77%	54
11	Thomas Enqvist	76%	63
12	Wayne Ferreira	76%	62
13	Todd Martin	76%	60
14	Patrick Rafter	76%	43
15	Guy Forget	76%	42

	Break Points Saved	Pct	Mtchs
1	Pete Sampras	73%	65
2	Goran Ivanisevic	69%	81
3	Todd Martin	68%	60
4	Thomas Muster	67%	80
5	Jan Siemerink	67%	54
6	Mark Woodforde	67%	45
7	Kenneth Carlsen	67%	37
8	Cedric Pioline	65%	52
9	Yevgeny Kafelnikov	64%	84
10	Wayne Ferreira	64%	62
11	Marc-Kevin Goellner	64%	47
12	Patrick Rafter	64%	43
13	Boris Becker	64%	40
14	Scott Draper	64%	36
15	Michael Chang	63%	68

Return Of Serve Leaders

	Returning 1st Serve	Pct	Mtchs
1	Felix Mantilla	34%	65
2	Carlos Moya	34%	63
3	Francisco Clavet	34%	61
4	Carlos Costa	34%	49
5	Magnus Gustafsson	34%	43
6	Gilbert Schaller	34%	42
7	Michael Chang	33%	68
	Albert Costa	33%	68
9	Alberto Berasategui	33%	63
10	Thomas Muster	32%	80
11	Stefan Edberg	32%	62
	Wayne Ferreira	32%	62
13	Alex Corretja	32%	58
14	Andrei Medvedev	32%	54
15	Jiri Novak	32%	49

	Returning 2nd Serve	Pct	Mtchs
1	Thomas Muster	58%	80
2	Michael Chang	58%	68
3	Alberto Berasategui	57%	63
4	Bohdan Ulihrach	57%	62
5	Felix Mantilla	56%	65
6	Jonas Bjorkman	56%	46
7	Petr Korda	56%	43
8	Andre Agassi	56%	40
9	Carlos Moya	55%	63
10	Todd Martin	55%	60
11	Byron Black	55%	52
	Cedric Pioline	55%	52
13	Carlos Costa	55%	49
14	Vincent Spadea	55%	45
15	Christian Ruud	55%	44

Statistical Leaders (Cont.)

Return of Serve Leaders

	Break Points Converted	Pct	Mtchs
1	Jiri Novak	49%	49
2	Felix Mantilla	47%	65
3	Filip Dewulf	47%	46
	Hernan Gumy	47%	46
5	Vincent Spadea	47%	45
6	Christian Ruud	47%	44
7	Michael Chang	46%	68
8	Paul Haarhuis	46%	51
9	Carlos Moya	45%	63
10	Francisco Clavet	45%	61
11	Alex Corretja	45%	58
12	Byron Black	45%	52
	Cedric Pioline	45%	52
14	Yevgeny Kafelnikov	44%	84
15	Thomas Muster	44%	80

	Return Games Won	Pct	Mtchs
1	Michael Chang	37%	68
2	Felix Mantilla	35%	65
3	Thomas Muster	34%	80
4	Carlos Costa	34%	49
5	Albert Costa	32%	68
6	Alberto Berasategui	32%	63
	Carlos Moya	32%	63
8	Francisco Clavet	32%	61
9	Christian Ruud	32%	44
10	Magnus Gustafsson	32%	43
11	Gilbert Schaller	32%	42
12	Andre Agassi	32%	40
13	Petr Korda	31%	43
14	Thomas Enqvist	30%	63
15	Stefan Edberg	30%	62

1996 Serve Speed Rankings

(as of Oct. 20, 1996)

All serves recorded by Information & Display Systems, Inc. on Stadium Court and must be in play to count.

Wide World Photos

Australian **Mark Philippoussis**, a.k.a. "Scud" for his missile-like serves, launches another one over the net into enemy territory. "Scud" recorded the fastest serve on the ATP Tour in 1996 with his blast of 137 mph in the U.S. Open.

ATP

		MPH	Site (surface)
1	Mark Philippoussis	137	U.S. Open (H)
2	Richard Krajicek	136.7	Rome (C)
3	Goran Ivanisevic	136	Indianapolis (H)
4	Greg Rusedski	135	U.S. Open (H)
5	Thomas Enqvist	134	U.S. Open (H)
	Alex Radulescu	134	Key Biscayne (H)
7	Shuzo Matsuoka	133	Wimbleton (G)
8	Pete Sampras	132	Key Biscayne (H)
9	Jordi Burillo	131.8	Milan (I)
	Marc Rosset	131.8	Davis Cup-1st RD (I)

WTA

		MPH	Site (surface)
1	B. Schultz-McCarthy	121.8	Melbourne (H)
2	Jana Novotna	115	U.S. Open (H)
3	Debbie Graham	111	U.S. Open (H)
4	Li Chen	110.6	Atlanta Olympics (H)
	Melanie Schnell	110.6	French Open (C)
6	Mariann DeSwardt	110	U.S. Open (H)
	Ludmilla Richterova	100	U.S. Open (H)
8	Kristie Boogert	109.4	Melbourne (H)
9	Steffi Graf	108	U.S. Open (H)
	Miriam Oremans	108	Wimbledon (G)
	Venus Williams	108	Amelia Island (C)

Senior Tour Unifies in 1997

The Nuveen Tour in North America, the ATP Senior Tour of Champions in Europe and the Champions Tour on other continents have formed a unified circuit which will begin play in 1997. The circuit will consist of 22 events world-wide with the top qualifying players competing in the season-ending Nuveen Masters in Naples, Fla. The tour will include former stars Bjorn Borg, Jimmy Connors, John McEnroe and Yannick Noah.

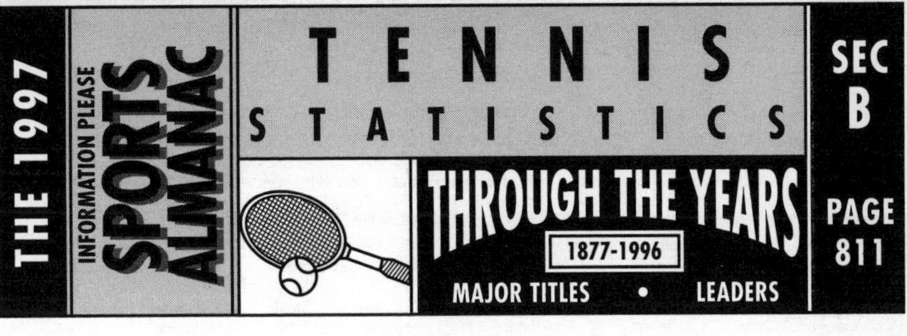

THE 1997
INFORMATION PLEASE
SPORTS ALMANAC
TENNIS
STATISTICS
THROUGH THE YEARS
1877-1996
MAJOR TITLES • LEADERS
SEC
B
PAGE
811

Grand Slam Championships

Australian Open

MEN

Became an Open Championship in 1969. Two tournaments were held in 1977; the first in January, the second in December. Tournament moved back to January in 1987, so no championship was decided in 1986.

Surface: Synpave Rebound Ace (hardcourt surface composed of polyurethane and synthetic rubber).

Multiple winners: Roy Emerson (6); Jack Crawford and Ken Rosewall (4); James Anderson, Rod Laver, Adrian Quist, Mats Wilander and Pat Wood (3); Boris Becker, Jack Bromwich, Ashley Cooper, Jim Courier, Stefan Edberg, Rodney Heath, Johan Kriek, Ivan Lendl, John Newcombe, Frank Sedgman, Guillermo Vilas and Tony Wilding (2).

Year	Winner	Loser	Score
1905	Rodney Heath	A. Curtis	46 63 64 64
1906	Tony Wilding	H. Parker	60 64 64
1907	Horace Rice	H. Parker	63 64 64
1908	Fred Alexander	A. Dunlop	36 36 60 62 63
1909	Tony Wilding	E. Parker	61 75 62
1910	Rodney Heath	H. Rice	64 63 62
1911	Norman Brookes	H. Rice	61 62 63
1912	J. Cecil Parke	A. Beamish	36 63 16 61 75
1913	Ernie Parker	H. Parker	26 61 62 63
1914	Pat Wood	G. Patterson	64 63 57 61
1915	Francis Lowe	H. Rice	46 61 61 64
1916-18	Not held	World War I	
1919	A.R.F. Kingscote	E. Pockley	64 60 63
1920	Pat Wood	R. Thomas	63 46 68 61 63
1921	Rhys Gemmell	A. Hedeman	75 61 64
1922	James Anderson	G. Patterson	60 36 36 63 62
1923	Pat Wood	C.B. St. John	61 61 63
1924	James Anderson	R. Schlesinger	63 64 36 57 63
1925	James Anderson	G. Patterson	11-9 26 62 63
1926	John Hawkes	J. Willard	61 63 61
1927	Gerald Patterson	J. Hawkes	36 64 36 18-16 63
1928	Jean Borotra	R.O. Cummings	64 61 46 57 63
1929	John Gregory	R. Schlesinger	62 62 57 75
1930	Gar Moon	H. Hopman	63 61 63
1931	Jack Crawford	H. Hopman	64 62 26 61
1932	Jack Crawford	H. Hopman	46 63 36 63 61
1933	Jack Crawford	K. Gledhill	26 75 63 62
1934	Fred Perry	J. Crawford	63 75 61
1935	Jack Crawford	F. Perry	26 64 64 64
1936	Adrian Quist	J. Crawford	62 63 46 36 97
1937	Viv McGrath	J. Bromwich	63 16 60 26 61
1938	Don Budge	J. Bromwich	64 62 61
1939	Jack Bromwich	A. Quist	64 61 63
1940	Adrian Quist	J. Crawford	63 61 62
1941-45	Not held	World War II	
1946	Jack Bromwich	D. Pails	57 63 75 36 62
1947	Dinny Pails	J. Bromwich	46 64 36 75 86
1948	Adrian Quist	J. Bromwich	64 36 63 26 63
1949	Frank Sedgman	J. Bromwich	63 63 62
1950	Frank Sedgman	K. McGregor	63 64 46 61
1951	Dick Savitt	K. McGregor	63 26 63 61
1952	Ken McGregor	F. Sedgman	75 12-10 26 62
1953	Ken Rosewall	M. Rose	60 63 64
1954	Mervyn Rose	R. Hartwig	62 06 64 62
1955	Ken Rosewall	L. Hoad	97 64 64
1956	Lew Hoad	K. Rosewall	64 36 64 75
1957	Ashley Cooper	N. Fraser	63 9-11 64 62
1958	Ashley Cooper	M. Anderson	75 63 64
1959	Alex Olmedo	N. Fraser	61 62 36 63
1960	Rod Laver	N. Fraser	57 36 63 86 86
1961	Roy Emerson	R. Laver	16 63 75 64
1962	Rod Laver	R. Emerson	86 06 64 64
1963	Roy Emerson	K. Fletcher	63 63 61
1964	Roy Emerson	F. Stolle	63 64 62
1965	Roy Emerson	F. Stolle	79 26 64 75 61
1966	Roy Emerson	A. Ashe	64 68 62 63
1967	Roy Emerson	A. Ashe	64 61 61
1968	Bill Bowrey	J. Gisbert	75 26 97 64
1969	Rod Laver	A. Gimeno	63 64 75
1970	Arthur Ashe	D. Crealy	64 97 62
1971	Ken Rosewall	A. Ashe	61 75 63
1972	Ken Rosewall	M. Anderson	76 63 75
1973	John Newcombe	O. Parun	63 67 75 61
1974	Jimmy Connors	P. Dent	76 64 46 63
1975	John Newcombe	J. Connors	75 36 64 75
1976	Mark Edmondson	J. Newcombe	67 63 76 61
1977	Roscoe Tanner	G. Vilas	63 63 63
	Vitas Gerulaitis	J. Lloyd	63 76 57 36 62
1978	Guillermo Vilas	J. Marks	64 64 36 63
1979	Guillermo Vilas	J. Sadri	76 63 62
1980	Brian Teacher	K. Warwick	75 76 63
1981	Johan Kriek	S. Denton	62 76 67 64
1982	Johan Kriek	S. Denton	63 63 62
1983	Mats Wilander	I. Lendl	61 64 64
1984	Mats Wilander	K. Curren	67 64 76 62
1985	Stefan Edberg	M. Wilander	64 63 63
1986	Not held		
1987	Stefan Edberg	P. Cash	63 64 36 57 63
1988	Mats Wilander	P. Cash	63 67 36 61 86
1989	Ivan Lendl	M. Mecir	62 62 62
1990	Ivan Lendl	S. Edberg	46 76 52 (ret.)
1991	Boris Becker	I. Lendl	16 64 64 64
1992	Jim Courier	S. Edberg	63 36 64 62
1993	Jim Courier	S. Edberg	62 61 26 75
1994	Pete Sampras	T. Martin	76 64 64
1995	Andre Agassi	P. Sampras	46 61 76 64
1996	Boris Becker	M. Chang	62 64 26 62

Grand Slam Championships (Cont.)

Australian Open

WOMEN

Became an Open Championship in 1969. Two tournaments were held in 1977, the first in January, the second in December. Tournament moved back to January in 1987, so no championship was decided in 1986.

Multiple winners: Margaret Smith Court (11); Nancye Wynne Bolton (6); Daphne Akhurst (5); Evonne Goolagong Cawley, Steffi Graf, and Monica Seles (4); Jean Hartigan and Martina Navratilova (3); Coral Buttsworth, Chris Evert Lloyd, Thelma Long, Hana Mandlikova, Mall Molesworth and Mary Carter Reitano (2).

Year	Winner	Loser	Score
1922	Mall Molesworth	E. Boyd	63 10-8
1923	Mall Molesworth	E. Boyd	61 75
1924	Sylvia Lance	E. Boyd	63 36 64
1925	Daphne Akhurst	E. Boyd	16 86 64
1926	Daphne Akhurst	E. Boyd	61 63
1927	Esna Boyd	S. Harper	57 61 62
1928	Daphne Akhurst	E. Boyd	75 62
1929	Daphne Akhurst	L. Bickerton	61 57 62
1930	Daphne Akhurst	S. Harper	10-8 26 75
1931	Coral Buttsworth	M. Crawford	16 63 64
1932	Coral Buttsworth	K. Le Messurier	97 64
1933	Joan Hartigan	C. Buttsworth	64 63
1934	Joan Hartigan	M. Molesworth	61 64
1935	Dorothy Round	N. Lyle	16 61 63
1936	Joan Hartigan	N. Bolton	64 64
1937	Nancye Wynne	E. Westacott	63 57 64
1938	Dorothy Bundy	D. Stevenson	63 62
1939	Emily Westacott	N. Hopman	61 62
1940	Nancye Wynne	T. Coyne	57 64 60
1941-45	Not held	World War II	
1946	Nancye Bolton	J. Fitch	64 64
1947	Nancye Bolton	N. Hopman	63 62
1948	Nancye Bolton	M. Toomey	63 61
1949	Doris Hart	N. Bolton	63 64
1950	Louise Brough	D. Hart	64 36 64
1951	Nancye Bolton	T. Long	61 75
1952	Thelma Long	H. Angwin	62 63
1953	Maureen Connolly	J. Sampson	63 62
1954	Thelma Long	J. Staley	63 64
1955	Beryl Penrose	T. Long	64 63
1956	Mary Carter	T. Long	36 62 97
1957	Shirley Fry	A. Gibson	63 64
1958	Angela Mortimer	L. Coghlan	63 64
1959	Mary Reitano	T. Schuurman	62 63
1960	Margaret Smith	J. Lehane	75 62
1961	Margaret Smith	J. Lehane	61 64
1962	Margaret Smith	J. Lehane	60 62
1963	Margaret Smith	J. Lehane	62 62
1964	Margaret Smith	L. Turner	63 62
1965	Margaret Smith	M. Bueno	57 64 52 (ret)
1966	Margaret Smith	N. Richey	walkover
1967	Nancy Richey	L. Turner	61 64
1968	Billie Jean King	M. Smith	61 62
1969	Margaret Court	B.J. King	64 61
1970	Margaret Court	K. Melville	61 63
1971	Margaret Court	E. Goolagong	26 76 75
1972	Virginia Wade	E. Goolagong	64 64
1973	Margaret Court	E. Goolagong	64 75
1974	Evonne Goolagong	C. Evert	76 46 60
1975	Evonne Goolagong	M. Navratilova	63 62
1976	Evonne Cawley	R. Tomanova	62 62
1977	Kerry Reid	D. Balestrat	75 62
	Evonne Cawley	H. Gourlay	63 60
1978	Chris O'Neill	B. Nagelsen	63 76
1979	Barbara Jordan	S. Walsh	63 63
1980	Hana Mandlikova	W. Turnbull	60 75
1981	Martina Navratilova	C. Evert Lloyd	67 64 75
1982	Chris Evert Lloyd	M. Navratilova	63 26 63
1983	Martina Navratilova	K. Jordan	62 76
1984	Chris Evert Lloyd	H. Sukova	67 61 63
1985	Martina Navratilova	C. Evert Lloyd	62 46 62
1986	Not held		
1987	Hana Mandlikova	M. Navratilova	75 76
1988	Steffi Graf	C. Evert	61 76
1989	Steffi Graf	H. Sukova	64 64
1990	Steffi Graf	M.J. Fernandez	63 64
1991	Monica Seles	J. Novotna	57 63 61
1992	Monica Seles	M.J. Fernandez	62 63
1993	Monica Seles	S. Graf	46 63 62
1994	Steffi Graf	A.S. Vicario	60 62
1995	Mary Pierce	A.S. Vicario	63 62
1996	Monica Seles	A. Huber	64 61

French Open

MEN

Prior to 1925, entry was restricted to members of French clubs. Became an Open Championship in 1968, but closed to contract pros in 1972.

Surface: Red clay.

First year: 1891. **Most wins:** Max Decugis (8).

Multiple winners (since 1925): Bjorn Borg (6); Henri Cochet (4); Rene Lacoste, Ivan Lendl and Mats Wilander (3); Sergi Bruguera, Jim Courier, Jaroslav Drobny, Roy Emerson, Jan Kodes, Rod Laver, Frank Parker, Nicola Pietrangeli, Ken Rosewall, Manuel Santana, Tony Trabert and Gottfried von Cramm (2).

Year	Winner	Loser	Score
1925	Rene Lacoste	J. Borotra	75 61 64
1926	Henri Cochet	R. Lacoste	62 64 63
1927	Rene Lacoste	B. Tilden	64 46 57 63 11-9
1928	Henri Cochet	R. Lacoste	57 63 61 63
1929	Rene Lacoste	J. Borotra	63 26 60 26 86
1930	Henri Cochet	B. Tilden	36 86 63 61
1931	Jean Borotra	C. Boussus	26 64 75 64
1932	Henri Cochet	G. de Stefani	60 64 46 63
1933	Jack Crawford	H. Cochet	86 61 63
1934	Gottfried von Cramm	J. Crawford	64 79 36 75 63
1935	Fred Perry	G. von Cramm	63 36 61 63
1936	Gottfried von Cramm	F. Perry	60 26 62 26 60
1937	Henner Henkel	H. Austin	61 64 63
1938	Don Budge	R. Menzel	63 62 64
1939	Don McNeill	B. Riggs	75 60 63
1940-45	Not held	World War II	
1946	Marcel Bernard	J. Drobny	36 26 61 64 63
1947	Joseph Asboth	E. Sturgess	86 75 64
1948	Frank Parker	J. Drobny	64 75 57 86
1949	Frank Parker	B. Patty	63 16 61 64

Year	Winner	Loser	Score
1950	Budge Patty	J. Drobny	61 62 36 57 75
1951	Jaroslav Drobny	E. Sturgess	63 63 63
1952	Jaroslav Drobny	F. Sedgman	62 60 36 64
1953	Ken Rosewall	V. Seixas	63 64 16 62
1954	Tony Trabert	A. Larsen	64 75 61
1955	Tony Trabert	S. Davidson	26 61 64 62
1956	Lew Hoad	S. Davidson	64 86 63
1957	Sven Davidson	H. Flam	63 64 64
1958	Mervyn Rose	L. Ayala	63 64 64
1959	Nicola Pietrangeli	I. Vermaak	36 63 64 61
1960	Nicola Pietrangeli	L. Ayala	36 63 64 46 63
1961	Manuel Santana	N. Pietrangeli	46 61 36 60 62
1962	Rod Laver	R. Emerson	36 26 63 97 62
1963	Roy Emerson	P. Darmon	36 61 64 64
1964	Manuel Santana	N. Pietrangeli	63 61 46 75
1965	Fred Stolle	T. Roche	36 60 62 63
1966	Tony Roche	I. Gulyas	61 64 75
1967	Roy Emerson	T. Roche	61 64 26 62
1968	Ken Rosewall	R. Laver	63 61 26 62
1969	Rod Laver	K. Rosewall	64 63 64
1970	Jan Kodes	Z. Franulovic	62 64 60
1971	Jan Kodes	I. Nastase	86 62 26 75
1972	Andres Gimeno	P. Proisy	46 63 61 61
1973	Ilie Nastase	N. Pilic	63 63 60
1974	Bjorn Borg	M. Orantes	26 67 60 61 61
1975	Bjorn Borg	G. Vilas	62 63 64
1976	Adriano Panatta	H. Solomon	61 64 46 76
1977	Guillermo Vilas	B. Gottfried	60 63 60
1978	Bjorn Borg	G. Vilas	61 61 63
1979	Bjorn Borg	V. Pecci	63 61 67 64
1980	Bjorn Borg	V. Gerulaitis	64 61 62
1981	Bjorn Borg	I. Lendl	61 46 62 36 61
1982	Mats Wilander	G. Vilas	16 76 60 64
1983	Yannick Noah	M. Wilander	62 75 76
1984	Ivan Lendl	J. McEnroe	36 26 64 75 75
1985	Mats Wilander	I. Lendl	36 64 62 62
1986	Ivan Lendl	M. Pernfors	63 62 64
1987	Ivan Lendl	M. Wilander	75 62 36 76
1988	Mats Wilander	H. Leconte	75 62 61
1989	Michael Chang	S. Edberg	61 36 46 64 62
1990	Andres Gomez	A. Agassi	63 26 64 64
1991	Jim Courier	A. Agassi	36 64 26 61 64
1992	Jim Courier	P. Korda	75 62 61
1993	Sergi Bruguera	J. Courier	64 26 62 36 63
1994	Sergi Bruguera	A. Berasategui	63 75 26 61
1995	Thomas Muster	M. Chang	75 62 64
1996	Yevgeny Kafelnikov	M. Stich	76 75 76

WOMEN

Prior to 1925, entry was restricted to members of French clubs. Became an Open Championship in 1968, but closed to contract pros in 1972.

First year: 1897. **Most wins:** Chris Evert Lloyd (7) and Suzanne Lenglen (6).

Multiple winners (since 1920): Chris Evert Lloyd (7); Margaret Smith Court and Steffi Graf (5); Helen Wills Moody (4); Monica Seles and Hilde Sperling (3); Maureen Connolly, Margaret Osborne duPont, Doris Hart, Ann Haydon Jones, Suzanne Lenglen, Simone Mathieu, Margaret Scriven, Martina Navratilova, Lesley Turner and Arantxa Sanchez Vicario (2).

Year	Winner	Loser	Score
1925	Suzanne Lenglen	K. McKane	61 62
1926	Suzanne Lenglen	M. Browne	61 60
1927	Kea Bouman	I. Peacock	62 64
1928	Helen Wills	E. Bennett	61 62
1929	Helen Wills	S. Mathieu	63 64
1930	Helen Moody	H. Jacobs	62 61
1931	Cilly Aussem	B. Nuthall	86 61
1932	Helen Moody	S. Mathieu	75 61
1933	Margaret Scriven	S. Mathieu	62 46 64
1934	Margaret Scriven	H. Jacobs	75 46 61
1935	Hilde Sperling	S. Mathieu	62 61
1936	Hilde Sperling	S. Mathieu	63 64
1937	Hilde Sperling	S. Mathieu	62 64
1938	Simone Mathieu	N. Landry	60 63
1939	Simone Mathieu	J. Jedrzejowska	63 86
1940-45	Not held	World War II	
1946	Margaret Osborne	P. Betz	16 86 75
1947	Patricia Todd	D. Hart	63 36 64
1948	Nelly Landry	S. Fry	62 06 60
1949	Margaret duPont	N. Adamson	75 62
1950	Doris Hart	P. Todd	64 46 62
1951	Shirley Fry	D. Hart	63 36 63
1952	Doris Hart	S. Fry	64 64
1953	Maureen Connolly	D. Hart	62 64
1954	Maureen Connolly	G. Bucaille	64 61
1955	Angela Mortimer	D. Knode	26 75 10-8
1956	Althea Gibson	A. Mortimer	60 12-10
1957	Shirley Bloomer	D. Knode	61 63
1958	Susi Kormoczi	S. Bloomer	64 16 62
1959	Christine Truman	S. Kormoczi	64 75
1960	Darlene Hard	Y. Ramirez	63 64
1961	Ann Haydon	Y. Ramirez	62 61
1962	Margaret Smith	L. Turner	63 36 75
1963	Lesley Turner	A. Jones	26 63 75
1964	Margaret Smith	M. Bueno	57 61 62
1965	Lesley Turner	M. Smith	63 64
1966	Ann Jones	N. Richey	63 61
1967	Francoise Durr	L. Turner	46 63 64
1968	Nancy Richey	A. Jones	57 64 61
1969	Margaret Court	A. Jones	61 46 63
1970	Margaret Court	H. Niessen	62 64
1971	Evonne Goolagong	H. Gourlay	63 75
1972	Billie Jean King	E. Goolagong	63 63
1973	Margaret Court	C. Evert	67 76 64
1974	Chris Evert	O. Morozova	61 62
1975	Chris Evert	M. Navratilova	26 62 61
1976	Sue Barker	R. Tomanova	62 06 62
1977	Mima Jausovec	F. Mihai	62 67 61
1978	Virginia Ruzici	M. Jausovec	62 62
1979	Chris Evert Lloyd	W. Turnbull	62 60
1980	Chris Evert Lloyd	V. Ruzici	60 63
1981	Hana Mandlikova	S. Hanika	62 64
1982	Martina Navratilova	A. Jaeger	76 61
1983	Chris Evert Lloyd	M. Jausovec	61 62
1984	Martina Navratilova	C. Evert Lloyd	63 61
1985	Chris Evert Lloyd	M. Navratilova	63 67 75
1986	Chris Evert Lloyd	M. Navratilova	26 63 63
1987	Steffi Graf	M. Navratilova	64 46 86
1988	Steffi Graf	N. Zvereva	60 60
1989	A. Sanchez Vicario	S. Graf	76 36 75
1990	Monica Seles	S. Graf	76 64
1991	Monica Seles	A.S. Vicario	63 64
1992	Monica Seles	S. Graf	62 36 10-8
1993	Steffi Graf	M.J. Fernandez	46 62 64
1994	A. Sanchez Vicario	M. Pierce	64 64
1995	Steffi Graf	A.S. Vicario	76 46 60
1996	Steffi Graf	A.S. Vicario	63 61

Grand Slam Champions (Cont.)

Wimbledon

MEN

Officially called "The Lawn Tennis Championships" at the All England Club, Wimbledon. Challenge round system (defending champion qualified for following year's final) used from 1877-1921. Became an Open Championship in 1968, but closed to contract pros in 1972.

Surface: Grass.

Multiple winners: Willie Renshaw (7); Bjorn Borg and Laurie Doherty (5); Reggie Doherty, Rod Laver and Tony Wilding (4); Wilfred Baddeley, Boris Becker, Arthur Gore, John McEnroe, John Newcombe, Fred Perry, Pete Sampras and Bill Tilden (3); Jean Borotra, Norman Brookes, Don Budge, Henri Cochet, Jimmy Connors, Stefan Edberg, Roy Emerson, John Hartley, Lew Hoad, Rene Lacoste, Gerald Patterson and Joshua Pim (2).

Year	Winner	Loser	Score
1877	Spencer Gore	W. Marshall	61 62 64
1878	Frank Hadow	S. Gore	75 61 97
1879	John Hartley	V. St. L. Gould	62 64 62
1880	John Hartley	H. Lawford	60 62 26 63
1881	Willie Renshaw	J. Hartley	60 62 61
1882	Willie Renshaw	E. Renshaw	61 26 46 62 62
1883	Willie Renshaw	E. Renshaw	26 63 63 46 63
1884	Willie Renshaw	H. Lawford	60 64 97
1885	Willie Renshaw	H. Lawford	75 62 46 75
1886	Willie Renshaw	H. Lawford	60 57 63 64
1887	Herbert Lawford	E. Renshaw	16 63 36 64 64
1888	Ernest Renshaw	H. Lawford	63 75 60
1889	Willie Renshaw	E. Renshaw	64 61 36 60
1890	William Hamilton	W. Renshaw	68 62 36 61 61
1891	Wilfred Baddeley	J. Pim	64 16 75 60
1892	Wilfred Baddeley	J. Pim	46 63 63 62
1893	Joshua Pim	W. Baddeley	36 61 63 62
1894	Joshua Pim	W. Baddeley	10-8 62 86
1895	Wilfred Baddeley	W. Eaves	46 26 86 62 63
1896	Harold Mahony	W. Baddeley	62 68 57 86 63
1897	Reggie Doherty	H. Mahony	64 64 63
1898	Reggie Doherty	L. Doherty	63 63 26 57 61
1899	Reggie Doherty	A. Gore	16 46 62 63 63
1900	Reggie Doherty	S. Smith	68 63 61 62
1901	Arthur Gore	R. Doherty	46 75 64 64
1902	Laurie Doherty	A. Gore	64 63 36 60
1903	Laurie Doherty	F. Riseley	75 63 60
1904	Laurie Doherty	F. Riseley	61 75 86
1905	Laurie Doherty	N. Brookes	86 62 64
1906	Laurie Doherty	F. Riseley	64 46 62 63
1907	Norman Brookes	A. Gore	64 62 62
1908	Arthur Gore	R. Barrett	63 62 46 36 64
1909	Arthur Gore	M. Ritchie	68 16 62 62 62
1910	Tony Wilding	A. Gore	64 75 46 62
1911	Tony Wilding	R. Barrett	64 46 26 62 (ret)
1912	Tony Wilding	A. Gore	64 64 46 64
1913	Tony Wilding	M. McLoughlin	86 63 10-8
1914	Norman Brookes	T. Wilding	64 64 75
1915-18	Not held	World War I	
1919	Gerald Patterson	N. Brookes	63 75 62
1920	Bill Tilden	G. Patterson	26 63 62 64
1921	Bill Tilden	B. Norton	46 26 61 60 75
1922	Gerald Patterson	R. Lycett	63 64 62
1923	Bill Johnston	F. Hunter	60 63 61
1924	Jean Borotra	R. Lacoste	61 36 61 36 64
1925	Rene Lacoste	J. Borotra	63 63 46 86
1926	Jean Borotra	H. Kinsey	86 61 63
1927	Henri Cochet	J. Borotra	46 46 63 64 75
1928	Rene Lacoste	H. Cochet	61 46 64 62
1929	Henri Cochet	J. Borotra	64 63 64
1930	Bill Tilden	W. Allison	63 97 64
1931	Sidney Wood	F. Shields	walkover
1932	Ellsworth Vines	H. Austin	64 62 60
1933	Jack Crawford	E. Vines	46 11-9 62 26 64
1934	Fred Perry	J. Crawford	63 60 75
1935	Fred Perry	G. von Cramm	62 64 64
1936	Fred Perry	G. von Cramm	61 61 60
1937	Don Budge	G. von Cramm	63 64 62
1938	Don Budge	H. Austin	61 60 63
1939	Bobby Riggs	E. Cooke	26 86 36 63 62
1940-45	Not held	World War II	
1946	Yvon Petra	G. Brown	62 64 79 57 64
1947	Jack Kramer	T. Brown	61 63 62
1948	Bob Falkenburg	J. Bromwich	75 06 62 36 75
1949	Ted Schroeder	J. Drobny	36 60 63 46 64
1950	Budge Patty	F. Sedgman	61 8-10 62 63
1951	Dick Savitt	K. McGregor	64 64 64
1952	Frank Sedgman	J. Drobny	46 62 63 62
1953	Vic Seixas	K. Nielsen	97 63 64
1954	Jaroslav Drobny	K. Rosewall	13-11 46 62 97
1955	Tony Trabert	K. Nielsen	63 75 61
1956	Lew Hoad	K. Rosewall	62 46 75 64
1957	Lew Hoad	A. Cooper	62 61 62
1958	Ashley Cooper	N. Fraser	36 63 64 13-11
1959	Alex Olmedo	R. Laver	64 63 64
1960	Neale Fraser	R. Laver	64 36 97 75
1961	Rod Laver	C. McKinley	63 61 64
1962	Rod Laver	M. Mulligan	62 62 61
1963	Chuck McKinley	F. Stolle	97 61 64
1964	Roy Emerson	F. Stolle	64 12-10 46 63
1965	Roy Emerson	F. Stolle	62 64 64
1966	Manuel Santana	D. Ralston	64 11-9 64
1967	John Newcombe	W. Bungert	63 61 61
1968	Rod Laver	T. Roche	63 64 62
1969	Rod Laver	J. Newcombe	64 57 64 64
1970	John Newcombe	K. Rosewall	57 63 62 36 61
1971	John Newcombe	S. Smith	63 57 26 64 64
1972	Stan Smith	I. Nastase	46 63 63 46 75
1973	Jan Kodes	A. Metreveli	61 98 63
1974	Jimmy Connors	K. Rosewall	61 61 64
1975	Arthur Ashe	J. Connors	61 61 57 64
1976	Bjorn Borg	I. Nastase	64 62 97
1977	Bjorn Borg	J. Connors	36 62 61 57 64
1978	Bjorn Borg	J. Connors	62 62 63
1979	Bjorn Borg	R. Tanner	67 61 36 63 64
1980	Bjorn Borg	J. McEnroe	16 75 63 67 86
1981	John McEnroe	B. Borg	46 76 76 64
1982	Jimmy Connors	J. McEnroe	36 63 67 76 64
1983	John McEnroe	C. Lewis	62 62 62
1984	John McEnroe	J. Connors	61 61 62
1985	Boris Becker	K. Curren	63 67 76 64
1986	Boris Becker	I. Lendl	64 63 75
1987	Pat Cash	I. Lendl	76 62 75
1988	Stefan Edberg	B. Becker	46 76 64 62
1989	Boris Becker	S. Edberg	60 76 64
1990	Stefan Edberg	B. Becker	62 62 36 36 64
1991	Michael Stich	B. Becker	64 76 64
1992	Andre Agassi	G. Ivanisevic	67 64 64 16 64
1993	Pete Sampras	J. Courier	76 76 36 63
1994	Pete Sampras	G. Ivanisevic	76 76 60
1995	Pete Sampras	B. Becker	67 62 64 62
1996	Richard Krajicek	M. Washington	63 64 63

WOMEN

Officially called "The Lawn Tennis Championships" at the All England Club, Wimbledon. Challenge round system (defending champion qualified for following year's final) used from 1886-1921. Became an Open Championship in 1968, but closed to contract pros in 1972.

Multiple winners: Martina Navratilova (9); Helen Wills Moody (8); Dorothea Douglass Chambers and Steffi Graf (7); Blanche Bingley Hillyard, Billie Jean King and Suzanne Lenglen (6); Lottie Dod and Charlotte Cooper Sterry (5); Louise Brough (4); Maria Bueno, Maureen Connolly, Margaret Smith Court and Chris Evert Lloyd (3); Evonne Goolagong Cawley, Althea Gibson, Dorothy Round, May Sutton and Maud Watson (2).

Year	Winner	Loser	Score
1884	Maud Watson	L. Watson	68 63 63
1885	Maud Watson	B. Bingley	61 75
1886	Blanche Bingley	M. Watson	63 63
1887	Lottie Dod	B. Bingley	62 60
1888	Lottie Dod	B. Hillyard	63 63
1889	Blanche Hillyard	L. Rice	46 86 64
1890	Lena Rice	M. Jacks	64 61
1891	Lottie Dod	B. Hillyard	62 61
1892	Lottie Dod	B. Hillyard	61 61
1893	Lottie Dod	B. Hillyard	68 61 64
1894	Blanche Hillyard	E. Austin	61 61
1895	Charlotte Cooper	H. Jackson	75 86
1896	Charlotte Cooper	W. Pickering	62 63
1897	Blanche Hillyard	C. Cooper	57 75 62
1898	Charlotte Cooper	L. Martin	64 64
1899	Blanche Hillyard	C. Cooper	62 63
1900	Blanche Hillyard	C. Cooper	46 64 64
1901	Charlotte Sterry	B. Hillyard	62 62
1902	Muriel Robb	C. Sterry	75 61
1903	Dorothea Douglass	E. Thomson	46 64 62
1904	Dorothea Douglass	C. Sterry	60 63
1905	May Sutton	D. Douglass	63 64
1906	Dorothea Douglass	M. Sutton	63 97
1907	May Sutton	D. Chambers	61 64
1908	Charlotte Sterry	A. Morton	64 64
1909	Dora Boothby	A. Morton	64 46 86
1910	Dorothea Chambers	D. Boothby	62 62
1911	Dorothea Chambers	D. Boothby	60 60
1912	Ethel Larcombe	C. Sterry	63 61
1913	Dorothea Chambers	R. McNair	60 64
1914	Dorothea Chambers	E. Larcombe	75 64
1915-18	Not held	World War I	
1919	Suzanne Lenglen	D. Chambers	10-8 46 97
1920	Suzanne Lenglen	D. Chambers	63 60
1921	Suzanne Lenglen	E. Ryan	62 60
1922	Suzanne Lenglen	M. Mallory	62 60
1923	Suzanne Lenglen	K. McKane	62 62
1924	Kathleen McKane	H. Wills	46 64 64
1925	Suzanne Lenglen	J. Fry	62 60
1926	Kathleen Godfree	L. de Alvarez	62 46 63
1927	Helen Wills	L. de Alvarez	62 64
1928	Helen Wills	L. de Alvarez	62 63
1929	Helen Wills	H. Jacobs	61 62
1930	Helen Moody	E. Ryan	62 62
1931	Cilly Aussem	H. Kranwinkel	62 75
1932	Helen Moody	H. Jacobs	63 61
1933	Helen Moody	D. Round	64 68 63
1934	Dorothy Round	H. Jacobs	62 57 63
1935	Helen Moody	H. Jacobs	63 36 75
1936	Helen Jacobs	H.K. Sperling	62 46 75
1937	Dorothy Round	J. Jedrzejowska	62 26 75
1938	Helen Moody	H. Jacobs	64 60
1939	Alice Marble	K. Stammers	62 60
1940-45	Not held	World War II	
1946	Pauline Betz	L. Brough	62 64
1947	Margaret Osborne	D. Hart	62 64
1948	Louise Brough	D. Hart	63 86
1949	Louise Brough	M. duPont	10-8 16 10-8
1950	Louise Brough	M. duPont	61 36 61
1951	Doris Hart	S. Fry	61 60
1952	Maureen Connolly	L. Brough	75 63
1953	Maureen Connolly	D. Hart	86 75
1954	Maureen Connolly	L. Brough	62 75
1955	Louise Brough	B. Fleitz	75 86
1956	Shirley Fry	A. Buxton	63 61
1957	Althea Gibson	D. Hard	63 62
1958	Althea Gibson	A. Mortimer	86 62
1959	Maria Bueno	D. Hard	64 63
1960	Maria Bueno	S. Reynolds	86 60
1961	Angela Mortimer	C. Truman	46 64 75
1962	Karen Susman	V. Sukova	64 64
1963	Margaret Smith	B.J. Moffitt	63 64
1964	Maria Bueno	M. Smith	64 79 63
1965	Margaret Smith	M. Bueno	64 75
1966	Billie Jean King	M. Bueno	63 36 61
1967	Billie Jean King	A. Jones	63 64
1968	Billie Jean King	J. Tegart	97 75
1969	Ann Jones	B.J. King	36 63 62
1970	Margaret Court	B.J. King	14-12 11-9
1971	Evonne Goolagong	M. Court	64 61
1972	Billie Jean King	E. Goolagong	63 63
1973	Billie Jean King	C. Evert	60 75
1974	Chris Evert	O. Morzova	60 64
1975	Billie Jean King	E. Cawley	60 61
1976	Chris Evert	E. Cawley	63 46 86
1977	Virginia Wade	B. Stove	46 63 61
1978	Martina Navratilova	C. Evert	26 64 75
1979	Martina Navratilova	C. Evert Lloyd	64 64
1980	Evonne Cawley	C. Evert Lloyd	61 76
1981	Chris Evert Lloyd	H. Mandlikova	62 62
1982	Martina Navratilova	C. Evert Lloyd	61 36 62
1983	Martina Navratilova	A. Jaeger	60 63
1984	Martina Navratilova	C. Evert Lloyd	76 62
1985	Martina Navratilova	C. Evert Lloyd	46 63 62
1986	Martina Navratilova	H. Mandlikova	76 63
1987	Martina Navratilova	S. Graf	75 63
1988	Steffi Graf	M. Navratilova	57 62 61
1989	Steffi Graf	M. Navratilova	62 67 61
1990	Martina Navratilova	Z. Garrison	64 61
1991	Steffi Graf	G. Sabatini	64 36 86
1992	Steffi Graf	M. Seles	62 61
1993	Steffi Graf	J. Novotna	76 16 64
1994	Conchita Martinez	M. Navratilova	64 36 63
1995	Steffi Graf	A.S. Vicario	46 61 75
1996	Steffi Graf	A.S. Vicario	63 75

Washington Reaches Wimbledon Finals

With his come-from-behind five-set victory over Todd Martin in the 1996 Wimbledon semifinals, MaliVai Washington became the first black men's singles finalist since the late Arthur Ashe defeated Jimmy Connors in 1975. The last black female Wimbledon finalist was Zina Garrison, beaten by Martina Navratilova in 1990.

Grand Slam Champions (Cont.)

U.S. Open

MEN

Challenge round system (defending champion qualified for following year's final) used from 1884-1911. Known as the Patriotic Tournament in 1917 during World War I. Amateur and Open Championships held in 1968 and '69. Became an exclusively Open Championship in 1970.

Surface: Decoturf II (acrylic cement).

Multiple winners: Bill Larned, Richard Sears and Bill Tilden (7); Jimmy Connors (5); John McEnroe, Pete Sampras and Robert Wrenn (4); Oliver Campbell, Ivan Lendl, Fred Perry and Malcolm Whitman (3); Don Budge, Stefan Edberg, Roy Emerson, Neale Fraser, Pancho Gonzales, Bill Johnston, Jack Kramer, Rene Lacoste, Rod Laver, Maurice McLoughlin, Lindley Murray, John Newcombe, Frank Parker, Bobby Riggs, Ken Rosewall, Frank Sedgman, Henry Slocum Jr., Tony Trabert, Ellsworth Vines and Dick Williams (2).

Year	Winner	Loser	Score
1881	Richard Sears	W. Glyn	60 63 62
1882	Richard Sears	C. Clark	61 64 60
1883	Richard Sears	J. Dwight	62 60 97
1884	Richard Sears	H. Taylor	60 16 60 62
1885	Richard Sears	G. Brinley	63 46 60 63
1886	Richard Sears	R. Beeckman	46 61 63 64
1887	Richard Sears	H. Slocum Jr.	61 63 62
1888	Henry Slocum Jr.	H. Taylor	64 61 60
1889	Henry Slocum Jr.	Q. Shaw	63 61 46 62
1890	Oliver Campbell	H. Slocum Jr.	62 46 63 61
1891	Oliver Campbell	C. Hobart	26 75 79 61 62
1892	Oliver Campbell	F. Hovey	75 36 63 75
1893	Robert Wrenn	F. Hovey	64 36 64 64
1894	Robert Wrenn	M. Goodbody	68 61 64 64
1895	Fred Hovey	R. Wrenn	63 62 64
1896	Robert Wrenn	F. Hovey	75 36 60 16 61
1897	Robert Wrenn	W. Eaves	46 86 63 26 62
1898	Malcolm Whitman	D. Davis	36 62 62 61
1899	Malcolm Whitman	P. Paret	61 62 36 75
1900	Malcolm Whitman	B. Larned	64 16 62 62
1901	Bill Larned	B. Wright	62 68 64 64
1902	Bill Larned	R. Doherty	46 62 64 86
1903	Laurie Doherty	B. Larned	60 63 10-8
1904	Holcombe Ward	B. Clothier	10-8 64 97
1905	Beals Wright	H. Ward	62 61 11-9
1906	Bill Clothier	B. Wright	63 60 64
1907	Bill Larned	R. LeRoy	62 62 64
1908	Bill Larned	B. Wright	61 62 86
1909	Bill Larned	B. Clothier	61 62 57 16 61
1910	Bill Larned	T. Bundy	61 57 60 68 61
1911	Bill Larned	M. McLoughlin	64 64 62
1912	Maurice McLoughlin	W.F. Johnson	36 26 62 64 62
1913	Maurice McLoughlin	R. Williams	64 57 63 61
1914	Dick Williams	M. McLoughlin	63 86 10-8
1915	Bill Johnston	M. McLoughlin	16 60 75 10-8
1916	Dick Williams	B. Johnston	46 64 06 62 64
1917	Lindley Murray	N. Niles	57 86 63 63
1918	Lindley Murray	B. Tilden	63 61 75
1919	Bill Johnston	B. Tilden	64 64 63
1920	Bill Tilden	B. Johnston	61 16 75 57 63
1921	Bill Tilden	W. Johnson	61 63 61
1922	Bill Tilden	B. Johnston	46 36 62 63 64
1923	Bill Tilden	B. Johnston	64 61 64
1924	Bill Tilden	B. Johnston	61 97 62
1925	Bill Tilden	B. Johnston	46 11-9 63 46 63
1926	Rene Lacoste	J. Borotra	64 60 64
1927	Rene Lacoste	B. Tilden	11-9 63 11-9
1928	Henri Cochet	F. Hunter	46 64 36 75 63
1929	Bill Tilden	F. Hunter	36 63 46 62 64
1930	John Doeg	F. Shields	10-8 16 64 16-14
1931	Ellsworth Vines	G. Lott Jr.	79 63 97 75
1932	Ellsworth Vines	H. Cochet	64 64 64
1933	Fred Perry	J. Crawford	63 11-13 46 60 61
1934	Fred Perry	W. Allison	64 63 16 86
1935	Wilmer Allison	S. Wood	62 62 63
1936	Fred Perry	D. Budge	26 62 86 16 10-8
1937	Don Budge	G. von Cramm	61 79 61 36 61
1938	Don Budge	G. Mako	63 68 62 61
1939	Bobby Riggs	S.W. van Horn	64 62 64
1940	Don McNeill	B. Riggs	46 68 63 63 75
1941	Bobby Riggs	F. Kovacs	57 61 63 63
1942	Fred Schroeder	F. Parker	86 75 36 46 62
1943	Joe Hunt	J. Kramer	63 68 10-8 60
1944	Frank Parker	B. Talbert	64 36 63 63
1945	Frank Parker	B. Talbert	14-12 61 62
1946	Jack Kramer	T. Brown, Jr.	97 63 60
1947	Jack Kramer	F. Parker	46 26 61 60 63
1948	Pancho Gonzales	E. Sturgess	62 63 14-12
1949	Pancho Gonzales	F. Schroeder	16-18 26 61 62 64
1950	Arthur Larsen	H. Flam	63 46 57 64 63
1951	Frank Sedgman	V. Seixas	64 61 61
1952	Frank Sedgman	G. Mulloy	61 62 63
1953	Tony Trabert	V. Seixas	63 62 63
1954	Vic Seixas	R. Hartwig	36 62 64 64
1955	Tony Trabert	K. Rosewall	97 63 63
1956	Ken Rosewall	L. Hoad	46 62 63 63
1957	Mal Anderson	A. Cooper	10-8 75 64
1958	Ashley Cooper	M. Anderson	62 36 46 10-8 86
1959	Neale Fraser	A. Olmedo	63 57 62 64
1960	Neale Fraser	R. Laver	64 64 97
1961	Roy Emerson	R. Laver	75 63 62
1962	Rod Laver	R. Emerson	62 64 57 64
1963	Rafael Osuna	F. Froehling	75 64 62
1964	Roy Emerson	F. Stolle	64 62 64
1965	Manuel Santana	C. Drysdale	62 79 75 61
1966	Fred Stolle	J. Newcombe	46 12-10 63 64
1967	John Newcombe	C. Graebner	64 64 86
1968	Am-Arthur Ashe	B. Lutz	46 63 8-10 60 64
	Op-Arthur Ashe	T. Okker	14-12 57 63 36 63
1969	Am-Stan Smith	B. Lutz	97 63 61
	Op-Rod Laver	T. Roche	79 61 63 62
1970	Ken Rosewall	T. Roche	26 64 76 63
1971	Stan Smith	J. Kodes	36 63 62 76
1972	Ilie Nastase	A. Ashe	36 63 67 64 63
1973	John Newcombe	J. Kodes	64 16 46 62 63
1974	Jimmy Connors	K. Rosewall	61 60 61
1975	Manuel Orantes	J. Connors	64 63 63
1976	Jimmy Connors	B. Borg	64 36 76 64
1977	Guillermo Vilas	J. Connors	26 63 76 60
1978	Jimmy Connors	B. Borg	64 62 62
1979	John McEnroe	V. Gerulaitis	75 63 63
1980	John McEnroe	B. Borg	76 61 67 57 64
1981	John McEnroe	B. Borg	46 62 64 63
1982	Jimmy Connors	I. Lendl	63 62 46 64
1983	Jimmy Connors	I. Lendl	63 67 75 60
1984	John McEnroe	I. Lendl	63 64 61
1985	Ivan Lendl	J. McEnroe	76 63 64
1986	Ivan Lendl	M. Mecir	64 62 60
1987	Ivan Lendl	M. Wilander	67 60 76 64
1988	Mats Wilander	I. Lendl	64 46 63 57 64
1989	Boris Becker	I. Lendl	76 16 63 76

Year	Winner	Loser	Score
1990	Pete Sampras	A. Agassi	64 63 62
1991	Stefan Edberg	J. Courier	62 64 60
1992	Stefan Edberg	P. Sampras	36 64 76 62
1993	Pete Sampras	C. Pioline	64 64 63
1994	Andre Agassi	M. Stich	61 76 75
1995	Pete Sampras	A. Agassi	64 63 46 75
1996	Pete Sampras	M. Chang	61 64 76

WOMEN

Challenge round system used from 1887-1918. Five set final played from 1887-1901. Amateur and Open Championships held in 1968 and '69. Became an exclusively Open Championship in 1970.

Multiple winners: Molla Mallory Bjurstedt (8); Helen Wills Moody (7); Chris Evert Lloyd (6); Margaret Smith Court and Steffi Graf (5); Pauline Betz, Mario Bueno, Helen Jacobs, Billie Jean King, Alice Marble, Elisabeth Moore, Martina Navratilova and Hazel Hotchkiss Wightman (4); Juliette Atkinson, Mary Browne, Maureen Connolly and Margaret Osborne duPont (3); Tracy Austin, Mabel Cahill, Sarah Palfrey Cooke, Darlene Hard, Doris Hart, Althea Gibson, Monica Seles and Bertha Townsend (2).

Year	Winner	Loser	Score
1887	Ellen Hansell	L. Knight	61 60
1888	Bertha Townsend	E. Hansell	63 65
1889	Bertha Townsend	L. Voorhes	75 62
1890	Ellen Roosevelt	B. Townsend	62 62
1891	Mabel Cahill	E. Roosevelt	64 61 46 63
1892	Mabel Cahill	E. Moore	57 63 64 46 62
1893	Aline Terry	A. Schultz	61 63
1894	Helen Hellwig	A. Terry	75 36 60 36 63
1895	Juliette Atkinson	H. Hellwig	64 62 61
1896	Elisabeth Moore	J. Atkinson	64 46 62 62
1897	Juliette Atkinson	E. Moore	63 63 46 36 63
1898	Juliette Atkinson	M. Jones	63 57 64 26 75
1899	Marion Jones	M. Banks	61 61 75
1900	Myrtle McAteer	E. Parker	62 62 60
1901	Elizabeth Moore	M. McAteer	64 36 75 26 62
1902	Marion Jones	E. Moore	61 10(ret)
1903	Elizabeth Moore	M. Jones	75 86
1904	May Sutton	E. Moore	61 62
1905	Elizabeth Moore	H. Homans	64 57 61
1906	Helen Homans	M. Barger-Wallach	64 63
1907	Evelyn Sears	C. Neely	63 62
1908	Maud B. Wallach	Ev. Sears	63 16 63
1909	Hazel Hotchkiss	M. Wallach	60 61
1910	Hazel Hotchkiss	L. Hammond	64 62
1911	Hazel Hotchkiss	F. Sutton	8-10 61 97
1912	Mary Browne	E. Sears	64 62
1913	Mary Browne	D. Green	62 75
1914	Mary Browne	M. Wagner	62 16 61
1915	Molla Bjurstedt	H. Wightman	46 62 60
1916	Molla Bjurstedt	L. Raymond	60 61
1917	Molla Bjurstedt	M. Vanderhoef	46 60 62
1918	Molla Bjurstedt	E. Goss	64 63
1919	Hazel Wightman	M. Zinderstein	61 62
1920	Molla Mallory	M. Zinderstein	63 61
1921	Molla Mallory	M. Browne	46 64 62
1922	Molla Mallory	H. Wills	63 61
1923	Helen Wills	M. Mallory	62 61
1924	Helen Wills	M. Mallory	61 63
1925	Helen Wills	K. McKane	36 60 62
1926	Molla Mallory	E. Ryan	46 64 97
1927	Helen Wills	B. Nuthall	61 64
1928	Helen Wills	H. Jacobs	62 61
1929	Helen Wills	P. Watson	64 62
1930	Betty Nuthall	A. Harper	61 64
1931	Helen Moody	E. Whitingstall	64 61
1932	Helen Jacobs	C. Babcock	62 62
1933	Helen Jacobs	H. Moody	86 36 30(ret)
1934	Helen Jacobs	S. Palfrey	61 64
1935	Helen Jacobs	S. Fabyan	62 64
1936	Alice Marble	H. Jacobs	46 63 62
1937	Anita Lizana	J. Jedrzejowska	64 62
1938	Alice Marble	N. Wynne	60 63
1939	Alice Marble	H. Jacobs	60 8-10 64
1940	Alice Marble	H. Jacobs	62 63
1941	Sarah Cooke	P. Betz	75 62
1942	Pauline Betz	L. Brough	46 61 64
1943	Pauline Betz	L. Brough	63 57 63
1944	Pauline Betz	M. Osborne	63 86
1945	Sarah Cooke	P. Betz	36 86 64
1946	Pauline Betz	P. Canning	11-9 63
1947	Louise Brough	M. Osborne	86 46 61
1948	Margaret duPont	L. Brough	46 64 15-13
1949	Margaret duPont	D. Hart	64 61
1950	Margaret duPont	D. Hart	64 63
1951	Maureen Connolly	S. Fry	63 16 64
1952	Maureen Connolly	D. Hart	63 75
1953	Maureen Connolly	D. Hart	62 64
1954	Doris Hart	L. Brough	68 61 86
1955	Doris Hart	P. Ward	64 62
1956	Shirley Fry	A. Gibson	63 64
1957	Althea Gibson	L. Brough	63 62
1958	Althea Gibson	D. Hard	36 61 62
1959	Maria Bueno	C. Truman	61 64
1960	Darlene Hard	M. Bueno	64 10-12 64
1961	Darlene Hard	A. Haydon	63 64
1962	Margaret Smith	D. Hard	97 64
1963	Maria Bueno	M. Smith	75 64
1964	Maria Bueno	C. Graebner	61 60
1965	Margaret Smith	B.J. Moffitt	86 75
1966	Maria Bueno	N. Richey	63 61
1967	Billie Jean King	A. Jones	11-9 64
1968	Am-Margaret Court	M. Bueno	62 62
	Op-Virginia Wade	B.J. King	64 62
1969	Am-Margaret Court	V. Wade	46 63 60
	Op-Margaret Court	N. Richey	62 62
1970	Margaret Court	R. Casals	62 26 61
1971	Billie Jean King	R. Casals	64 76
1972	Billie Jean King	K. Melville	63 75
1973	Margaret Court	E. Goolagong	76 57 62
1974	Billie Jean King	E. Goolagong	36 63 75
1975	Chris Evert	E. Cawley	57 64 62
1976	Chris Evert	E. Cawley	63 60
1977	Chris Evert	W. Turnbull	76 62
1978	Chris Evert	P. Shriver	75 64
1979	Tracy Austin	C. Evert Lloyd	64 63
1980	Chris Evert Lloyd	H. Mandlikova	57 61 61
1981	Tracy Austin	M. Navratilova	16 76 76
1982	Chris Evert Lloyd	H. Mandlikova	63 61
1983	Martina Navratilova	C. Evert Lloyd	61 63
1984	Martina Navratilova	C. Evert Lloyd	46 64 64
1985	Hana Mandlikova	M. Navratilova	76 16 76
1986	Martina Navratilova	H. Sukova	63 62
1987	Martina Navratilova	S. Graf	76 61
1988	Steffi Graf	G. Sabatini	63 36 61
1989	Steffi Graf	M. Navratilova	36 75 61
1990	Gabriela Sabatini	S. Graf	62 76
1991	Monica Seles	M. Navratilova	76 61
1992	Monica Seles	A.S. Vicario	63 63
1993	Steffi Graf	H. Sukova	63 63
1994	A. Sanchez Vicario	S. Graf	16 76 64
1995	Steffi Graf	M. Seles	76 06 63
1996	Steffi Graf	M. Seles	75 64

Grand Slam Summary

Singles winners of the four Grand Slam tournaments—Australian, French, Wimbledon and United States—since the French was opened to all comers in 1925. Note that there were two Australian Opens in 1977 and none in 1986.

MEN

Three wins in one year: Jack Crawford (1933); Fred Perry (1934); Tony Trabert (1955); Lew Hoad (1956); Ashley Cooper (1958); Roy Emerson (1964); Jimmy Connors (1974); Mats Wilander (1988).

Two wins in one year: Roy Emerson (4 times); Bjorn Borg and Pete Sampras (3 times); Rene Lacoste, Ivan Lendl, John Newcombe and Fred Perry (twice); Boris Becker, Don Budge, Henri Cochet, Jimmy Connors, Jim Courier, Neale Fraser, Jack Kramer, John McEnroe, Alex Olmedo, Budge Patty, Bobby Riggs, Ken Rosewall, Dick Savitt, Frank Sedgman and Guillermo Vilas (once).

Year	Australia	French	Wimbledon	U.S.
1925	Anderson	Lacoste	Lacoste	Tilden
1926	Hawkes	Cochet	Borotra	Lacoste
1927	Patterson	Lacoste	Cochet	Lacoste
1928	Borotra	Cochet	Lacoste	Cochet
1929	Gregory	Lacoste	Cochet	Tilden
1930	Moon	Cochet	Tilden	Doeg
1931	Crawford	Borotra	Wood	Vines
1932	Crawford	Cochet	Vines	Vines
1933	Crawford	Crawford	Crawford	Perry
1934	Perry	von Cramm	Perry	Perry
1935	Crawford	Perry	Perry	Allison
1936	Quist	von Cramm	Perry	Perry
1937	McGrath	Henkel	Budge	Budge
1938	**Budge**	**Budge**	**Budge**	**Budge**
1939	Bromwich	McNeill	Riggs	Riggs
1940	Quist	—	—	McNeill
1941	—	—	—	Riggs
1942	—	—	—	Schroeder
1943	—	—	—	Hunt
1944	—	—	—	Parker
1945	—	—	—	Parker
1946	Bromwich	Bernard	Petra	Kramer
1947	Pails	Asboth	Kramer	Kramer
1948	Quist	Parker	Falkenburg	Gonzales
1949	Sedgman	Parker	Schroeder	Gonzales
1950	Sedgman	Patty	Patty	Larsen
1951	Savitt	Drobny	Savitt	Sedgman
1952	McGregor	Drobny	Sedgman	Sedgman
1953	Rosewall	Rosewall	Seixas	Trabert
1954	Rose	Trabert	Drobny	Seixas
1955	Rosewall	Trabert	Trabert	Trabert
1956	Hoad	Hoad	Hoad	Rosewall
1957	Cooper	Davidson	Hoad	Anderson
1958	Cooper	Rose	Cooper	Cooper
1959	Olmedo	Pietrangeli	Olmedo	Fraser
1960	Laver	Pietrangeli	Fraser	Fraser
1961	Emerson	Santana	Laver	Emerson
1962	**Laver**	**Laver**	**Laver**	**Laver**
1963	Emerson	Emerson	McKinley	Osuna
1964	Emerson	Santana	Emerson	Emerson
1965	Emerson	Stolle	Emerson	Santana
1966	Emerson	Roche	Santana	Stolle
1967	Emerson	Emerson	Newcombe	Newcombe
1968	Bowrey	Rosewall	Laver	Ashe
1969	**Laver**	**Laver**	**Laver**	**Laver**
1970	Ashe	Kodes	Newcombe	Rosewall
1971	Rosewall	Kodes	Newcombe	Smith
1972	Rosewall	Gimeno	Smith	Nastase
1973	Newcombe	Nastase	Kodes	Newcombe
1974	Connors	Borg	Connors	Connors
1975	Newcombe	Borg	Ashe	Orantes
1976	Edmondson	Panatta	Borg	Connors
1977	Tanner & Gerulaitis	Vilas	Borg	Vilas
1978	Vilas	Borg	Borg	Connors
1979	Vilas	Borg	Borg	McEnroe
1980	Teacher	Borg	Borg	McEnroe
1981	Kriek	Borg	McEnroe	McEnroe
1982	Kriek	Wilander	Connors	Connors
1983	Wilander	Noah	McEnroe	Connors
1984	Wilander	Lendl	McEnroe	McEnroe
1985	Edberg	Wilander	Becker	Lendl
1986	—	Lendl	Becker	Lendl
1987	Edberg	Lendl	Cash	Lendl
1988	Wilander	Wilander	Edberg	Wilander
1989	Lendl	Chang	Becker	Becker
1990	Lendl	Gomez	Edberg	Sampras
1991	Becker	Courier	Stich	Edberg
1992	Courier	Courier	Agassi	Edberg
1993	Courier	Bruguera	Sampras	Sampras
1994	Sampras	Bruguera	Sampras	Agassi
1995	Agassi	Muster	Sampras	Sampras
1996	Becker	Kafelnikov	Krajicek	Sampras

The Calendar Year Grand Slam

The tennis Grand Slam has only been accomplished nine times in the same calendar year in either singles or doubles. And only two players have managed to do it twice— Rod Laver in singles (1962 and '69) and Margaret Smith Court in singles (1970) and doubles (1963).

Men's Singles

1938 .... Don Budge, USA
1962 .... Rod Laver, Australia
1969 .... Rod Laver, Australia

Men's Doubles

1951 .... Frank Sedgman, Australia & Ken McGregor, Australia

Mixed Doubles

1963 .... Ken Fletcher, Australia & Margaret Smith, Australia
1967 .... Owen Davidson and two partners

Women's Singles

1953 .... Maureen Connolly, USA
1970 .... Margaret Smith Court, Australia
1988 .... Steffi Graf, West Germany*

*Also won gold medal at Seoul Olympics.

Women's Doubles

1960 .... Maria Bueno, Brazil & two partners
1984 .... Martina Navratilova, USA & Pam Shriver, USA

Note: In women's doubles, Bueno won Australia with Christine Truman, then took the French, Wimbledon and the U.S. with Darlene hard. In mixed Doubles—Davidson won Australia with Lesley Turner, then took the French, Wimbledon and the U.S. with Billie Jean King.

WOMEN

Three in one year: Helen Wills Moody (1928 and '29); Margaret Smith Court (1962, '65, '69 and '73); Billie Jean King (1972); Martina Navratilova (1983 and '84); Steffi Graf (1989, '93, '95 and '96); and Monica Seles (1991 and '92).

Two in one year: Chris Evert Lloyd (5 times); Helen Wills Moody and Martina Navratilova (3 times); Maria Bueno, Maureen Connolly, Margaret Smith Court, Althea Gibson, Billie Jean King (twice); Cilly Aussem, Pauline Betz, Louise Brough, Evonne Goolagong Cawley, Shirley Fry, Darlene Hard, Margaret Osborne duPont, Suzanne Lenglen, Alice Marble and Arantxa Sanchez Vicario (once).

Year	Australia	French	Wimbledon	U.S.
1925	Akhurst	Lenglen	Lenglen	Wills
1926	Akhurst	Lenglen	Godfree	Mallory
1927	Boyd	Bouman	Wills	Wills
1928	Akhurst	Wills	Wills	Wills
1929	Akhurst	Wills	Wills	Wills
1930	Akhurst	Moody	Moody	Nuthall
1931	Buttsworth	Aussem	Aussem	Moody
1932	Buttsworth	Moody	Moody	Jacobs
1933	Hartigan	Scriven	Moody	Jacobs
1934	Hartigan	Scriven	Round	Jacobs
1935	Round	Sperling	Moody	Jacobs
1936	Hartigan	Sperling	Jacobs	Marble
1937	Bolton	Sperling	Round	Lizana
1938	Bundy	Mathieu	Moody	Marble
1939	Westacott	Mathieu	Marble	Marble
1940	Bolton	—	—	Marble
1941	—	—	—	Cooke
1942	—	—	—	Betz
1943	—	—	—	Betz
1944	—	—	—	Betz
1945	—	—	—	Cooke
1946	Bolton	Osborne	Betz	Betz
1947	Bolton	Todd	Osborne	Brough
1948	Bolton	Landry	Brough	du Pont
1949	Hart	du Pont	Brough	du Pont
1950	Brough	Hart	Brough	du Pont
1951	Bolton	Fry	Hart	Connolly
1952	Long	Hart	Connolly	Connolly
1953	**Connolly**	**Connolly**	**Connolly**	**Connolly**
1954	Long	Connolly	Connolly	Hart
1955	Penrose	Mortimer	Brough	Hart
1956	Carter	Gibson	Fry	Fry
1957	Fry	Bloomer	Gibson	Gibson
1958	Mortimer	Kormoczi	Gibson	Gibson
1959	Reitano	Truman	Bueno	Bueno
1960	Smith	Hard	Bueno	Hard
1961	Smith	Haydon	Mortimer	Hard
1962	Smith	Smith	Susman	Smith
1963	Smith	Turner	Smith	Bueno
1964	Smith	Smith	Bueno	Bueno
1965	Smith	Turner	Smith	Smith
1966	Smith	Jones	King	Bueno
1967	Richey	Durr	King	King
1968	King	Richey	King	Wade
1969	Court	Court	Jones	Court
1970	**Court**	**Court**	**Court**	**Court**
1971	Court	Goolagong	Goolagong	King
1972	Wade	King	King	King
1973	Court	Court	King	Court
1974	Goolagong	Evert	Evert	King
1975	Goolagong	Evert	King	Evert
1976	Cawley	Barker	Evert	Evert
1977	Reid & Cawley	Jausovec	Wade	Evert
1978	O'Neil	Ruzici	Navratilova	Evert
1979	Jordan	Evert Lloyd	Navratilova	Austin
1980	Mandlikova	Evert Lloyd	Cawley	Evert Lloyd
1981	Navratilova	Mandlikova	Evert Lloyd	Austin
1982	Evert Lloyd	Navratilova	Navratilova	Evert Lloyd
1983	Navratilova	Evert Lloyd	Navratilova	Navratilova
1984	Evert Lloyd	Navratilova	Navratilova	Navratilova
1985	Navratilova	Evert Lloyd	Navratilova	Mandlikova
1986	—	Evert Lloyd	Navratilova	Navratilova
1987	Mandlikova	Graf	Navratilova	Navratilova
1988	**Graf**	**Graf**	**Graf**	**Graf**
1989	Graf	Vicario	Graf	Graf
1990	Graf	Seles	Navratilova	Sabatini
1991	Seles	Seles	Graf	Seles
1992	Seles	Seles	Graf	Seles
1993	Seles	Graf	Graf	Graf
1994	Graf	Vicario	Martinez	Vicario
1995	Pierce	Graf	Graf	Graf
1996	Seles	Graf	Graf	Graf

All-Time Grand Slam Singles Titles

Men and women with the most singles championships in the Australian, French, Wimbledon and U.S. championships, through 1996. Note that (*) indicates player never played in that particular Grand Slam event; and players active in singles play in 1996 are in **bold** type.

Top 15 Men

		Aus	Fre	Wim	US	Total
1	Roy Emerson	6	2	2	2	12
2	Bjorn Borg	0	6	5	0	11
	Rod Laver	3	2	4	2	11
4	Bill Tilden	*	0	3	7	10
5	Jimmy Connors	1	0	2	5	8
	Ivan Lendl	2	3	0	3	8
	Fred Perry	1	1	3	3	8
	Ken Rosewall	4	2	0	2	8
	Pete Sampras	1	0	3	4	8
10	Henri Cochet	*	4	2	1	7
	Rene Lacoste	*	3	2	2	7
	Bill Larned	*	*	0	7	7
	John McEnroe	0	0	3	4	7
	John Newcombe	2	0	3	2	7
	Willie Renshaw	*	*	7	*	7
	Dick Sears	*	*	0	7	7

Top 15 Women

		Aus	Fre	Wim	US	Total
1	Margaret Smith Court	11	5	3	5	24
2	**Steffi Graf**	4	5	7	5	21
3	Helen Wills Moody	*	4	8	7	19
4	Chris Evert	2	7	3	6	18
	Martina Navratilova	3	2	9	4	18
6	Billie Jean King	1	1	6	4	12
	Suzanne Lenglen	*	6	6	0	12
8	Maureen Connolly	1	2	3	3	9
	Monica Seles	4	3	0	2	9
10	Molla Bjurstedt Mallory	*	*	0	8	8
11	Maria Bueno	0	0	3	4	7
	Evonne Goolagong	4	1	2	0	7
	Dorothea D. Chambers	*	*	7	0	7
14	Nancy Bolton	6	0	0	0	6
	Louise Brough	1	0	4	1	6
	Margaret duPont	*	2	1	3	6
	Doris Hart	1	2	1	2	6
	Blanche Bingley Hillyard	*	*	6	*	6

Grand Slam Summary (Cont.)

Overall Leaders

All-Time Grand Slam titlists including all singles and doubles championships at the four major tournaments. Titles listed under each heading are singles, doubles and mixed doubles. Players active in 1996 are in bold type.

MEN

		Career	Australian	French	Wimbledon	U.S.	Titles S-D-M	Titles
1	Roy Emerson	1959-71	6-3-0	2-6-0	2-3-0	2-4-0	12-16-0	28
2	John Newcombe	1965-76	2-5-0	0-3-0	3-6-0	2-3-1	7-17-1	25
3	Frank Sedgman	1949-52	2-2-2	0-2-2	1-3-2	2-2-2	5-9-8	22
4	Bill Tilden	1913-30	*	0-0-1	3-1-0	7-5-4	10-6-5	21
5	Rod Laver	1959-71	3-4-0	2-1-1	4-1-2	2-0-0	11-6-3	20
6	Jack Bromwich	1938-50	2-8-1	0-0-0	0-2-2	0-3-1	2-13-4	19
7	Ken Rosewall	1953-72	4-3-0	2-2-0	0-2-0	2-2-1	8-9-1	18
	Neale Fraser	1957-62	0-3-1	0-3-0	1-2-0	2-3-3	3-11-4	18
	Jean Borotra	1925-36	1-1-1	1-5-2	2-3-1	0-0-1	4-9-5	18
	Fred Stolle	1962-69	0-3-1	1-2-0	0-2-3	1-3-2	2-10-6	18
11	John McEnroe	1977-93	0-0-0	0-0-1	3-5-0	4-4-0	7-9-1	17
	Jack Crawford	1929-35	4-4-3	1-1-1	1-1-1	0-0-0	6-6-5	17
	Adrian Quist	1936-50	3-10-0	0-1-0	0-2-0	0-1-0	3-14-0	17
14	Laurie Doherty	1897-1906	*	*	5-8-0	1-2-0	6-10-0	16
15	Henri Cochet	1922-32	*	4-3-2	2-2-0	1-0-1	7-5-3	15
	Vic Seixas	1952-56	0-1-0	0-2-1	1-0-4	1-2-3	2-5-8	15
	Bob Hewitt	1961-79	0-2-1	0-1-2	0-5-2	0-1-1	0-9-6	15

WOMEN

		Career	Australian	French	Wimbledon	U.S.	S-D-M	Total Titles
1	Margaret Court Smith	1960-75	11-8-2	5-4-4	3-2-5	5-5-8	24-19-19	62
2	**Martina Navratilova**	1974—	3-8-0	2-7-2	9-7-3	4-9-2	18-31-7	56
3	Billie Jean King	1961-81	1-0-1	1-1-2	6-10-4	4-5-4	12-16-11	39
4	Margaret du Pont	1941-60	*	2-3-0	1-5-1	3-13-9	6-21-10	37
5	Louise Brough	1942-57	1-1-0	0-3-0	4-5-4	1-12-4	6-21-8	35
	Doris Hart	1948-55	1-1-2	2-5-3	1-4-5	2-4-5	6-14-15	35
7	Helen Wills Moody	1923-38	*	4-2-0	8-3-1	7-4-2	19-9-3	31
8	Elizabeth Ryan	1914-34	*	0-4-0	0-12-7	0-1-2	0-17-9	26
9	Suzanne Lenglen	1919-26	*	6-2-2	6-6-3	0-0-0	12-8-5	25
10	**Steffi Graf**	1982—	4-0-0	5-0-0	7-1-0	5-0-0	21-1-0	22
	Pam Shriver	1981—	0-7-0	0-4-1	0-5-0	0-5-0	0-21-1	22
12	Chris Evert	1974-89	2-0-0	7-2-0	3-1-0	6-0-0	18-3-0	21
	Darlene Hard	1958-69	*	1-3-2	0-4-3	2-6-0	3-13-5	21
14	Nancye Wynne Bolton	1935-52	6-10-4	0-0-0	0-0-0	0-0-0	6-10-4	20
15	Maria Bueno	1958-68	0-1-0	0-1-1	3-5-0	4-4-0	7-11-1	19
	Thelma Coyne Long	1936-58	2-12-4	0-0-1	0-0-0	0-0-0	2-12-5	19

Annual Number One Players

Unofficial world rankings for men and women determined by the *London Daily Telegraph* from 1914-72. Since then, official world rankings computed by men's and women's tours. Rankings included only amateur players from 1914 until the arrival of open (professional) tennis in 1968. No rankings were released during World Wars I and II.

MEN

Multiple winners: Bill Tilden (6); Jimmy Connors (5); Henri Cochet, Rod Laver, Ivan Lendl and John McEnroe (4); John Newcombe, Fred Perry and Pete Sampras (3); Bjorn Borg, Don Budge, Ashley Cooper, Stefan Edberg, Roy Emerson, Neale Fraser, Jack Kramer, Rene Lacoste, Ilie Nastase, Frank Sedgman and Tony Trabert (2).

Year	
1914	Maurice McLoughlin
1915-18	No rankings
1919	Gerald Patterson
1920	Bill Tilden
1921	Bill Tilden
1922	Bill Tilden
1923	Bill Tilden
1924	Bill Tilden
1925	Bill Tilden
1926	Rene Lacoste
1927	Rene Lacoste
1928	Henri Cochet
1929	Henri Cochet
1930	Henri Cochet
1931	Henri Cochet

Year	
1932	Ellsworth Vines
1933	Jack Crawford
1934	Fred Perry
1935	Fred Perry
1936	Fred Perry
1937	Don Budge
1938	Don Budge
1939	Bobby Riggs
1940-45	No rankings
1946	Jack Kramer
1947	Jack Kramer
1948	Frank Parker
1949	Pancho Gonzales
1950	Budge Patty
1951	Frank Sedgman

Year	
1952	Frank Sedgman
1953	Tony Trabert
1954	Jaroslav Drobny
1955	Tony Trabert
1956	Lew Hoad
1957	Ashley Cooper
1958	Ashley Cooper
1959	Neale Fraser
1960	Neale Fraser
1961	Rod Laver
1962	Rod Laver
1963	Rafael Osuna
1964	Roy Emerson
1965	Roy Emerson
1966	Manuel Santana
1967	John Newcombe

Year	
1968	Rod Laver
1969	Rod Laver
1970	John Newcombe
1971	John Newcombe
1972	Ilie Nastase
1973	Ilie Nastase
1974	Jimmy Connors
1975	Jimmy Connors
1976	Jimmy Connors
1977	Jimmy Connors
1978	Jimmy Connors
1979	Bjorn Borg
1980	Bjorn Borg
1981	John McEnroe
1982	John McEnroe

Year		Year		Year		Year	
1983	John McEnroe	1987	Ivan Lendl	1990	Stefan Edberg	1993	Pete Sampras
1984	John McEnroe	1988	Mats Wilander	1991	Stefan Edberg	1994	Pete Sampras
1985	Ivan Lendl	1989	Ivan Lendl	1992	Jim Courier	1995	Pete Sampras
1986	Ivan Lendl						

WOMEN

Multiple winners: Helen Wills Moody (9); Margaret Smith Court, Steffi Graf and Martina Navratilova (7); Chris Evert Lloyd (5); Margaret Osborne duPont and Billie Jean King (4); Maureen Connolly and Monica Seles (3); Maria Bueno, Althea Gibson and Suzanne Lenglen (2).

Year		Year		Year		Year	
1925	Suzanne Lenglen	1947	Margaret Osborne	1964	Margaret Smith	1980	Chris Evert Lloyd
1926	Suzanne Lenglen	1948	Margaret duPont	1965	Margaret Smith	1981	Chris Evert Lloyd
1927	Helen Wills	1949	Margaret duPont	1966	Billie Jean King	1982	Martina Navratilova
1928	Helen Wills	1950	Margaret duPont	1967	Billie Jean King	1983	Martina Navratilova
1929	Helen Wills Moody	1951	Doris Hart	1968	Billie Jean King	1984	Martina Navratilova
1930	Helen Wills Moody	1952	Maureen Connolly	1969	Margaret Court	1985	Martina Navratilova
1931	Helen Wills Moody	1953	Maureen Connolly	1970	Margaret Court	1986	Martina Navratilova
1932	Helen Wills Moody	1954	Maureen Connolly	1971	Evonne Goolagong	1987	Steffi Graf
1933	Helen Wills Moody	1955	Louise Brough	1972	Billie Jean King	1988	Steffi Graf
1934	Dorothy Round	1956	Shirley Fry	1973	Margaret Court	1989	Steffi Graf
1935	Helen Wills Moody	1957	Althea Gibson	1974	Billie Jean King	1990	Steffi Graf
1936	Helen Jacobs	1958	Althea Gibson	1975	Chris Evert	1991	Monica Seles
1937	Anita Lizana	1959	Maria Bueno	1976	Chris Evert	1992	Monica Seles
1938	Helen Wills Moody	1960	Maria Bueno	1977	Chris Evert	1993	Steffi Graf
1939	Alice Marble	1961	Angela Mortimer	1978	Martina Navratilova	1994	Steffi Graf
1940-45	No rankings	1962	Margaret Smith	1979	Martina Navratilova	1995	Steffi Graf & Monica Seles
1946	Pauline Betz	1963	Margaret Smith				

Annual Top 10 World Rankings (since 1968)

Year by year Top 10 world computer rankings for Men (ATP Tour) and Women (WTA Tour) since the arrival of open tennis in 1968. Rankings from 1968-72 made by Lance Tingay of the *London Daily Telegraph*. Since 1973, computerized rankings by ATP Tour (men) and WTA Tour (women).

MEN

	1968	1971	1974	1977
1	Rod Laver	John Newcombe	Jimmy Connors	Jimmy Connors
2	Arthur Ashe	Stan Smith	John Newcombe	Guillermo Vilas
3	Ken Rosewall	Rod Laver	Bjorn Borg	Bjorn Borg
4	Tom Okker	Ken Rosewall	Rod Laver	Vitas Gerulaitis
5	Tony Roche	Jan Kodes	Guillermo Vilas	Brian Gottfried
6	John Newcombe	Arthur Ashe	Tom Okker	Eddie Dibbs
7	Clark Graebner	Tom Okker	Arthur Ashe	Manuel Orantes
8	Dennis Ralston	Marty Riessen	Ken Rosewall	Raul Ramirez
9	Cliff Drysdale	Cliff Drysdale	Stan Smith	Ilie Nastase
10	Pancho Gonzales	Ilie Nastase	Ilie Nastase	Dick Stockton

	1969	1972	1975	1978
1	Rod Laver	Stan Smith	Jimmy Connors	Jimmy Connors
2	Tony Roche	Ken Rosewall	Guillermo Vilas	Bjorn Borg
3	John Newcombe	Ilie Nastase	Bjorn Borg	Guillermo Vilas
4	Tom Okker	Rod Laver	Arthur Ashe	John McEnroe
5	Ken Rosewall	Arthur Ashe	Manuel Orantes	Vitas Gerulaitis
6	Arthur Ashe	John Newcombe	Ken Rosewall	Eddie Dibbs
7	Cliff Drysdale	Bob Lutz	Ilie Nastase	Brian Gottfried
8	Pancho Gonzales	Tom Okker	John Alexander	Raul Ramirez
9	Andres Gimeno	Marty Riessen	Roscoe Tanner	Harold Solomon
10	Fred Stolle	Andres Gimeno	Rod Laver	Corrado Barazzutti

	1970	1973	1976	1979
1	John Newcombe	Ilie Nastase	Jimmy Connors	Bjorn Borg
2	Ken Rosewall	John Newcombe	Bjorn Borg	Jimmy Connors
3	Tony Roche	Jimmy Connors	Ilie Nastase	John McEnroe
4	Rod Laver	Tom Okker	Manuel Orantes	Vitas Gerulaitis
5	Arthur Ashe	Stan Smith	Raul Ramirez	Roscoe Tanner
6	Ilie Nastase	Ken Rosewall	Guillermo Vilas	Guillermo Vilas
7	Tom Okker	Manuel Orantes	Adriano Panatta	Arthur Ashe
8	Roger Taylor	Rod Laver	Harold Solomon	Harold Solomon
9	Jan Kodes	Jan Kodes	Eddie Dibbs	Jose Higueras
10	Cliff Richey	Arthur Ashe	Brian Gottfried	Eddie Dibbs

Annual Top 10 World Rankings (Cont.)

MEN

1980
1 Bjorn Borg
2 John McEnroe
3 Jimmy Connors
4 Gene Mayer
5 Guillermo Vilas
6 Ivan Lendl
7 Harold Solomon
8 Jose-Luis Clerc
9 Vitas Gerulaitis
10 Eliot Teltscher

1981
1 John McEnroe
2 Ivan Lendl
3 Jimmy Connors
4 Bjorn Borg
5 Jose-Luis Clerc
6 Guillermo Vilas
7 Gene Mayer
8 Eliot Teltscher
9 Vitas Gerulaitis
10 Peter McNamara

1982
1 John McEnroe
2 Jimmy Connors
3 Ivan Lendl
4 Guillermo Vilas
5 Vitas Gerulaitis
6 Jose-Luis Clerc
7 Mats Wilander
8 Gene Mayer
9 Yannick Noah
10 Peter McNamara

1983
1 John McEnroe
2 Ivan Lendl
3 Jimmy Connors
4 Mats Wilander
5 Yannick Noah
6 Jimmy Arias
7 Jose Higueras
8 Jose-Luis Clerc
9 Kevin Curren
10 Gene Mayer

1984
1 John McEnroe
2 Jimmy Connors
3 Ivan Lendl
4 Mats Wilander
5 Andres Gomez
6 Anders Jarryd
7 Henrik Sundstrom
8 Pat Cash
9 Eliot Teltscher
10 Yannick Noah

1985
1 Ivan Lendl
2 John McEnroe
3 Mats Wilander
4 Jimmy Connors
5 Stefan Edberg
6 Boris Becker
7 Yannick Noah
8 Anders Jarryd
9 Miloslav Mecir
10 Kevin Curren

1986
1 Ivan Lendl
2 Boris Becker
3 Mats Wilander
4 Yannick Noah
5 Stefan Edberg
6 Henri Leconte
7 Joakim Nystrom
8 Jimmy Connors
9 Miloslav Mecir
10 Andres Gomez

1987
1 Ivan Lendl
2 Stefan Edberg
3 Mats Wilander
4 Jimmy Connors
5 Boris Becker
6 Miloslav Mecir
7 Pat Cash
8 Yannick Noah
9 Tim Mayotte
10 John McEnroe

1988
1 Mats Wilander
2 Ivan Lendl
3 Andre Agassi
4 Boris Becker
5 Stefan Edberg
6 Kent Carlsson
7 Jimmy Connors
8 Jakob Hlasek
9 Henri Leconte
10 Tim Mayotte

1989
1 Ivan Lendl
2 Boris Becker
3 Stefan Edberg
4 John McEnroe
5 Michael Chang
6 Brad Gilbert
7 Andre Agassi
8 Aaron Krickstein
9 Alberto Mancini
10 Jay Berger

1990
1 Stefan Edberg
2 Boris Becker
3 Ivan Lendl
4 Andre Agassi
5 Pete Sampras
6 Andres Gomez
7 Thomas Muster
8 Emilio Sanchez
9 Goran Ivanisevic
10 Brad Gilbert

1991
1 Stefan Edberg
2 Jim Courier
3 Boris Becker
4 Michael Stich
5 Ivan Lendl
6 Pete Sampras
7 Guy Forget
8 Karel Novacek
9 Petr Korda
10 Andre Agassi

1992
1 Jim Courier
2 Stefan Edberg
3 Pete Sampras
4 Goran Ivanisevic
5 Boris Becker
6 Michael Chang
7 Petr Korda
8 Ivan Lendl
9 Andre Agassi
10 Richard Krajicek

1993
1 Pete Sampras
2 Michael Stich
3 Jim Courier
4 Sergi Bruguera
5 Stefan Edberg
6 Andrei Medvedev
7 Goran Ivanisevic
8 Michael Chang
9 Thomas Muster
10 Cedric Pioline

1994
1 Pete Sampras
2 Andre Agassi
3 Boris Becker
4 Sergi Brugera
5 Goran Ivanisevic
6 Michael Chang
7 Stefan Edberg
8 Alberto Berasategui
9 Michael Stich
10 Todd Martin

1995
1 Pete Sampras
2 Andre Agassi
3 Thomas Muster
4 Boris Becker
5 Michael Chang
6 Yevgeny Kafelnikov
7 Thomas Enqvist
8 Jim Courier
9 Wayne Ferreira
10 Goran Ivanisevic

WOMEN

1968
1 Billie Jean King
2 Virginia Wade
3 Nancy Richey
4 Maria Bueno
5 Margaret Court
6 Ann Jones
7 Judy Tegart
8 Annette du Plooy
9 Leslie Bowrey
10 Rosie Casals

1969
1 Margaret Court
2 Ann Jones
3 Billie Jean King
4 Nancy Richey
5 Julie Heldman
6 Rosie Casals
7 Kerry Melville
8 Peaches Bartkowicz
9 Virginia Wade
10 Leslie Bowrey

1970
1 Margaret Court
2 Billie Jean King
3 Rosie Casals
4 Virginia Wade
5 Helga Niessen
6 Kerry Melville
7 Julie Heldman
8 Karen Krantczke
9 Francoise Durr
10 Nancy R. Gunter

1971
1 Evonne Goolagong
2 Billie Jean King
3 Margaret Court
4 Rosie Casals
5 Kerry Melville
6 Virginia Wade
7 Judy Tagert
8 Francoise Durr
9 Helga N. Masthoff
10 Chris Evert

Connors, Graf and Navratilova Rule Top10

Jimmy Connors, Steffi Graf and Martina Navratilova have been the world's top-ranked players more often than anyone else since the advent of open tennis in 1968. Connors was the No. 1 men's player five consecutive years from 1974-78. Navratilova was the No. 1 women's player seven times from 1978 to 1986, including five years in a row from 1982-86, while Graf ruled the tennis world along with Monica Seles in 1995 for her seventh title and third consecutive.

1972
1 Billie Jean King
2 Evonne Goolagong
3 Chris Evert
4 Margaret Court
5 Kerry Melville
6 Virginia Wade
7 Rosie Casals
8 Nancy R. Gunter
9 Francoise Durr
10 Linda Tuero

1973
1 Margaret S. Court
2 Billie Jean King
3 Evonne G. Cawley
4 Chris Evert
5 Rosie Casals
6 Virginia Wade
7 Kerry Reid
8 Nancy Richey
9 Julie Heldman
10 Helga Masthoff

1974
1 Billie Jean King
2 Evonne G. Cawley
3 Chris Evert
4 Virginia Wade
5 Julie Heldman
6 Rosie Casals
7 Kerry Reid
8 Olga Morozova
9 Lesley Hunt
10 Francoise Durr

1975
1 Chris Evert
2 Billie Jean King
3 Evonne G. Cawley
4 Martina Navratilova
5 Virginia Wade
6 Margaret S. Court
7 Olga Morozova
8 Nancy Richey
9 Francoise Durr
10 Rosie Casals

1976
1 Chris Evert
2 Evonne G. Cawley
3 Virginia Wade
4 Martina Navratilova
5 Sue Barker
6 Betty Stove
7 Dianne Balestrat
8 Mima Jausovec
9 Rosie Casals
10 Francoise Durr

1977
1 Chris Evert
2 Billie Jean King
3 Martina Navratilova
4 Virginia Wade
5 Sue Barker
6 Rosie Casals
7 Betty Stove
8 Dianne Balestrat
9 Wendy Turnbull
10 Kerry Reid

1978
1 Martina Navratilova
2 Chris Evert Lloyd
3 Evonne G. Cawley
4 Virginia Wade
5 Billie Jean King
6 Tracy Austin
7 Wendy Turnbull
8 Kerry Reid
9 Betty Stove
10 Dianne Balestrat

1979
1 Martina Navratilova
2 Chris Evert Lloyd
3 Tracy Austin
4 Evonne G. Cawley
5 Billie Jean King
6 Dianne Balestrat
7 Wendy Turnbull
8 Virginia Wade
9 Kerry Reid
10 Sue Barker

1980
1 Chris Evert Lloyd
2 Tracy Austin
3 Martina Navratilova
4 Hana Mandlikova
5 Evonne G. Cawley
6 Billie Jean King
7 Andrea Jaeger
8 Wendy Turnbull
9 Pam Shriver
10 Greer Stevens

1981
1 Chris Evert Lloyd
2 Tracy Austin
3 Martina Navratilova
4 Andrea Jaeger
5 Hana Mandlikova
6 Sylvia Hanika
7 Pam Shriver
8 Wendy Turnbull
9 Bettina Bunge
10 Barbara Potter

1982
1 Martina Navratilova
2 Chris Evert Lloyd
3 Andrea Jaeger
4 Tracy Austin
5 Wendy Turnbull
6 Pam Shriver
7 Hana Mandlikova
8 Barbara Potter
9 Bettina Bunge
10 Sylvia Hanika

1983
1 Martina Navratilova
2 Chris Evert Lloyd
3 Andrea Jaeger
4 Pam Shriver
5 Sylvia Hanika
6 Jo Durie
7 Bettina Bunge
8 Wendy Turnbull
9 Tracy Austin
10 Zina Garrison

1984
1 Martina Navratilova
2 Chris Evert Lloyd
3 Hana Mandlikova
4 Pam Shriver
5 Wendy Turnbull
6 Manuela Maleeva
7 Helena Sukova
8 Claudia Kohde-Kilsch
9 Zina Garrison
10 Kathy Jordan

1985
1 Martina Navratilova
2 Chris Evert Lloyd
3 Hana Mandlikova
4 Pam Shriver
5 Claudia Kohde-Kilsch
6 Steffi Graf
7 Manuela Maleeva
8 Zina Garrison
9 Helena Sukova
10 Bonnie Gadusek

1986
1 Martina Navratilova
2 Chris Evert Lloyd
3 Steffi Graf
4 Hana Mandlikova
5 Helena Sukova
6 Pam Shriver
7 Claudia Kohde-Kilsch
8 M. Maleeva-Fragniere
9 Zina Garrison
10 Claudia Kohde-Kilsch

1987
1 Steffi Graf
2 Martina Navratilova
3 Chris Evert
4 Pam Shriver
5 Hana Mandlikova
6 Gabriela Sabatini
7 Helena Sukova
8 M. Maleeva-Fragniere
9 Zina Garrison
10 Claudia Kohde-Kilsch

1988
1 Steffi Graf
2 Martina Navratilova
3 Chris Evert
4 Gabriela Sabatini
5 Pam Shriver
6 M. Maleeva-Fragniere
7 Natalia Zvereva
8 Helena Sukova
9 Zina Garrison
10 Barbara Potter

1989
1 Steffi Graf
2 Martina Navratilova
3 Gabriela Sabatini
4 Z. Garrison-Jackson
5 A. Sanchez Vicario
6 Monica Seles
7 Conchita Martinez
8 Helena Sukova
9 M. Maleeva-Fragniere
10 Chris Evert

1990
1 Steffi Graf
2 Monica Seles
3 Martina Navratilova
4 Mary Joe Fernandez
5 Gabriela Sabatini
6 Katerina Maleeva
7 A. Sanchez Vicario
8 Jennifer Capriati
9 M. Maleeva-Fragniere
10 Z. Garrison-Jackson

1991
1 Monica Seles
2 Steffi Graf
3 Gabriela Sabatini
4 Martina Navratilova
5 A. Sanchez Vicario
6 Jennifer Capriati
7 Jana Novotna
8 Mary Joe Fernandez
9 Conchita Martinez
10 M. Maleeva-Fragniere

1992
1 Monica Seles
2 Steffi Graf
3 Gabriela Sabatini
4 A. Sanchez Vicario
5 Martina Navratilova
6 Mary Joe Fernandez
7 Jennifer Capriati
8 Conchita Martinez
9 M. Maleeva-Fragniere
10 Jana Novotna

1993
1 Steffi Graf
2 A. Sanchez Vicario
3 Martina Navratilova
4 Conchita Martinez
5 Gabriela Sabatini
6 Jana Novotna
7 Mary Joe Fernandez
8 Monica Seles
9 Jennifer Capriati
10 Anke Huber

1994
1 Steffi Graf
2 A. Sanchez Vicario
3 Conchita Martinez
4 Jana Novotna
5 Mary Pierce
6 Lindsay Davenport
7 Gabriela Sabatini
8 Martina Navratilova
9 Kimiko Date
10 Natasha Zvereva

1995
1 Steffi Graf
Monica Seles
2 Conchita Martinez
3 Arantxa Sanchez Vicario
4 Kimiko Date
5 Mary Pierce
6 Magdalena Maleeva
7 Gabriela Sabatini
8 Mary Joe Fernandez
9 Iva Majoli
10 Anke Huber

All-Time Singles Leaders

Tournaments Won

All-time tournament wins from the arrival of open tennis in 1968 through 1995. Men's totals include ATP Tour, Grand Prix and WCT tournaments. Players active in singles play in 1996 are in **bold** type.

MEN

		Total
1	Jimmy Connors	109
2	Ivan Lendl	94
3	John McEnroe	77
4	Bjorn Borg	62
	Guillermo Vilas	62
6	Ilie Nastase	57
7	Rod Laver	47
8	**Boris Becker**	44
9	**Stefan Edberg**	41
10	Stan Smith	39
11	**Pete Sampras**	36
12	**Thomas Muster**	35
13	Arthur Ashe	33
	Mats Wilander	33
15	John Newcombe	32
	Manuel Orantes	32
	Ken Rosewall	32
18	**Andre Agassi**	31
	Tom Okker	31
20	Vitas Gerulaitis	27
21	Jose-Luis Clerc	25
	Brian Gottfried	25
23	**Michael Chang**	23
	Yannick Noah	23
25	Eddie Dibbs	22
	Harold Solomon	22
27	Andres Gomez	21
28	Brad Gilbert	20
29	Raul Ramirez	17
30	Vijay Amritraj	16

WOMEN

		Total
1	Martina Navratilova	167
2	Chris Evert	157
3	**Steffi Graf**	95
4	E. Goolagong Cawley	88
5	Margaret Court	79
6	Billie Jean King	67
7	Virginia Wade	55
8	Helga Masthoff	37
9	**Monica Seles**	33
10	Olga Morozova	31
11	Tracy Austin	29
	Conchita Martinez	29
13	Hana Mandlikova	27
	Gabriela Sabatini	27
15	Nancy Richey	25
16	Kerry Melville Reid	22
	A. Sanchez Vicario	22
18	Sue Barker	21
	Pam Shriver	21
20	Julie Heldman	20
21	D. Fromholtz Balestrat	19
	M. Maleeva-Fragniere	19
23	Rosie Casals	18
24	Virginia Rizici	17
	Regina Marsikova	17
26	Sue Barker	15
27	Peaches Bartkowicz	14
	Andrea Jaeger	14
	Sandra Cecchini	14
	Z. Garrison Jackson	14

Money Won

All-time money winners from the arrival of open tennis in 1968 through 1995. Totals include doubles earnings.

MEN

		Earnings
1	Pete Sampras	$21,859,428
2	Ivan Lendl	21,262,417
3	Stefan Edberg	19,979,804
4	Boris Becker	19,528,395
5	John McEnroe	12,539,622
6	Michael Chang	11,829,210
7	Goran Ivanisevic	11,740,295
8	Jim Courier	11,655,133
9	Michael Stich	11,479,621
10	Andre Agassi	11,276,443
11	Sergi Bruguera	$9,200,060
12	Jimmy Connors	8,637,490
13	Mats Wilander	7,891,135
14	Petr Korda	6,772,865
15	Thomas Muster	6,598,568
16	Brad Gilbert	5,507,195
17	Anders Jarryd	5,303,249
18	Emilio Sanchez	5,140,371
19	Guy Forget	5,027,615
20	Guillermo Vilas	4,923,882
21	David Wheaton	$4,798.899
22	Jakob Hlasek	4,683,342
23	Wayne Ferreira	4,511,553
24	Andres Gomez	4,385,040
25	Mark Woodforde	4,228,527
26	Andrei Medvedev	3,912,339
27	Magnus Larsson	3,892,562
28	Henri Leconte	3,881,546
29	Todd Martin	3,795,063
30	Todd Woodbridge	3,753,196

WOMEN

		Earnings
1	Mart. Navratilova	$20,337,902
2	Steffi Graf	17,180,610
3	A.S. Vicario	9,774,532
4	Chris Evert	8,896,195
5	Gabriela Sabatini	8,607,800
6	Monica Seles	7,805,991
7	Helena Sukova	5,527,088
8	Pam Shriver	5,384,316
9	Conchita Martinez	5,237,865
10	Jana Novotna	5,218,358
11	Natasha Zvereva	$4,962,868
12	Z. Garrison Jackson	4,523,356
13	Gigi Fernandez	3,854,730
14	Mary Jo Fernandez	3,580,983
15	Hana Madlikova	3,340,959
16	M. Maleeva-Fragniere	3,244,811
17	Lori McNeil	3,007,491
18	Larisa Neiland	2,831,081
19	Wendy Turnbull	2,769,024
20	Claudia Kohde-Kilsch	2,226,664
21	Katerina Maleeva	$2,200,605
22	Nathalie Tauziat	2,157,082
23	Mary Pierce	2,142,300
24	Anke Huber	2,017,250
25	Tracy Austin	1,992,380
26	Billy Jean King	1,966,487
27	B. Schulz-McCarthy	1,831,248
28	Rosalyn Nideffer	1,648,991
29	Elizabeth Smylie	1,623,032
30	Kathy Jordan	1,592,111

Longest Matches

Singles

126 Games— Roger Taylor (GBR) def. Wieslaw Gasiorek (POL), 27-29, 31-29, 6-4; King's Cup, Warsaw, 1966.

Doubles

147 Games— Dick Leach and Dick Dell (USA) def. Len Schloss and and Tom Mozu (USA), 3-6, 49-47, 22-20, 2nd round, Newport Casino, Newport, R.I., 1967.

Year-end Tournaments

MEN

Masters/ATP Tour World Championship

The year-end championship of the ATP men's tour since 1970. Contested by the year's top eight players. Originally a round-robin, the Masters was revised in 1972 to include a round-robin to decide the four semifinalists then a single elimination format after that. The tournament switched from December to January in 1977–78, then back to December in 1986. Held at Madison Square Garden in New York from 1978-89. Replaced by ATP Tour World Championship in 1990 and held in Frankfurt, Germany since then.

Multiple Winners: Ivan Lendl (5); Ilie Nastase (4); Boris Becker and John McEnroe (3); Bjorn Borg and Pete Sampras (2).

Year	Winner	Runner-Up
1970	Stan Smith (4-1)	Rod Laver (4-1)
1971	Ilie Nastase (6-0)	Stan Smith (4-2)

Year	Winner	Loser	Score
1972	Ilie Nastase	S. Smith	63 62 36 26 63
1973	Ilie Nastase	T. Okker	63 75 46 63
1974	Guillermo Vilas	I. Nastase	76 62 36 36 64
1975	Ilie Nastase	B. Borg	62 62 61
1976	Manuel Orantes	W. Fibak	57 62 06 76 61
1978	Jimmy Connors	B. Borg	64 16 64
1979	John McEnroe	A. Ashe	67 63 75
1980	Bjorn Borg	V. Gerulaitis	62 62
1981	Bjorn Borg	I. Lendl	64 62 62
1982	Ivan Lendl	V. Gerulaitis	67 26 76 62 64
1983	Ivan Lendl	J. McEnroe	64 64 62
1984	John McEnroe	I. Lendl	63 64 64
1985	John McEnroe	I. Lendl	75 60 64
1986	Ivan Lendl	B. Becker	62 76 63
1986	Ivan Lendl	B. Becker	64 64 64
1987	Ivan Lendl	M. Wilander	62 62 63
1988	Boris Becker	I. Lendl	57 76 36 62 76
1989	Stefan Edberg	B. Becker	46 76 63 61
1990	Andre Agassi	S. Edberg	57 76 75 62
1991	Pete Sampras	J. Courier	36 76 63 64
1992	Boris Becker	J. Courier	64 63 75
1993	Michael Stich	P. Sampras	76 26 76 62
1994	Pete Sampras	B. Becker	46 63 75 64
1995	Boris Becker	M. Chang	76 60 76

Note: In 1970, Smith was declared the winner because he beat Laver in their round-robin match (4-6, 6-3, 6-4).

WCT Championship (1971-89)

World Championship Tennis was established in 1967 to promote professional tennis and led the way into the open era. It's major singles and doubles championships were held every May among the top eight regular season finishers on the circuit from 1971 until the WCT folded in 1989.

Mutliple winners: John McEnroe (5), Jimmy Connors, Ivan Lendl and Ken Rosewall (2).

Year	Winner	Loser	Score
1971	Ken Rosewall	R. Laver	64 16 76 76
1972	Ken Rosewall	R. Laver	46 60 63 67 76
1973	Stan Smith	A. Ashe	63 63 46 64
1974	John Newcombe	B. Borg	46 63 63 62
1975	Arthur Ashe	B. Borg	36 64 64 60
1976	Bjorn Borg	G. Vilas	16 61 75 61
1977	Jimmy Connors	D. Stockton	67 61 64 63
1978	Vitas Gerulaitis	E. Dibbs	63 62 61
1979	John McEnroe	B. Borg	75 46 62 76
1980	Jimmy Connors	J. McEnroe	26 76 61 62
1981	John McEnroe	J. Kriek	61 62 64
1982	Ivan Lendl	J. McEnroe	62 36 63 63
1983	John McEnroe	I. Lendl	62 46 63 67 76
1984	John McEnroe	J. Connors	61 62 63
1985	Ivan Lendl	T. Mayotte	76 64 61
1986	Anders Jarryd	B. Becker	67 61 61 64
1987	Miloslav Mercir	J. McEnroe	60 36 62 62
1988	Boris Becker	S. Edberg	64 16 75 62
1989	John McEnroe	B. Gilbert	63 63 76

WOMEN

WTA Tour Championship

Originally the Virginia Slims Championships from 1971-94. The WTA Tour's year-end tournament took place in March from 1972 until 1986 when the WTA decided to adopt a January-to-November playing season. Given the changeover, two championships were held in 1986. Held every year since 1979 at Madison Square Garden in New York.

Multiple winners: Martina Navratilova (8); Chris Evert and Steffi Graf (4); Monica Seles (3); Evonne Goolagong and Gabriela Sabatini (2).

Year	Winner	Loser	Score
1972	Chris Evert	K. Reid	75 64
1973	Chris Evert	N. Richey	63 63
1974	Evonne Goolagong	C. Evert	63 64
1975	Chris Evert	M. Navratilova	64 62
1976	Evonne Goolagong	C. Evert	63 57 63
1977	Chris Evert	S. Barker	26 61 61
1978	M. Navratilova	E. Goolagong	76 64
1979	M. Navratilova	T. Austin	63 36 62
1980	Tracy Austin	M. Navratilova	62 26 62
1981	M. Navratilova	A. Jaeger	63 76
1982	Sylvia Hanika	M. Navratilova	16 63 64
1983	M. Navratilova	C. Evert	62 60
1984	M. Navratilova	C. Evert	63 75 61
1985	M. Navratilova	H. Sukova	63 75 64
1986	M. Navratilova	H. Mandlikova	62 60 36 61
1986	M. Navratilova	S. Graf	76 63 62
1987	Steffi Graf	G. Sabatini	46 64 60 64
1988	Gabriela Sabatini	P. Shriver	75 62 62
1989	Steffi Graf	M. Navratilova	64 75 26 62
1990	Monica Seles	G. Sabatini	64 57 36 64 62
1991	Monica Seles	M. Navratilova	64 36 75 60
1992	Monica Seles	M. Navratilova	75 63 61
1993	Steffi Graf	A. S. Vicario	61 64 36 61
1994	Gabriela Sabatini	L. Davenport	63 62 64
1995	Steffi Graf	A. Huber	61 26 61 46 63

Mike Powell/Allsport

The 1992 U.S. Davis Cup team that beat Switzerland in the final at Fort Worth, Texas (from left to right): singles players **Andre Agassi** and **Jim Courier**, doubles partners **John McEnroe** and **Pete Sampras**, and non-playing captain **Tom Gorman**. The Americans beat the Swiss, 3–1, for their 30th Davis Cup title since 1900.

Davis Cup

Established in 1900 as an annual international tournament by American player Dwight Davis. Originally called the International Lawn Tennis Challenge Trophy. Challenge round system until 1972. Since 1981, the top 16 nations in the world have played a straight knockout tournament over the course of a year. The format is a best-of-five match of two singles, one doubles and two singles over three days. Note that from 1900–24 Australia and New Zealand competed together as Australasia.

Multiple winners: USA (31); Australia (20); France (7); Australasia (6); British Isles and Sweden (5); Britain (4); Germany (3).

Challenge Rounds

Year	Winner	Loser	Score	Site
1900	USA	British Isles	3-0	Boston
1901	Not held			
1902	USA	British Isles	3-2	New York
1903	British Isles	USA	4-1	Boston
1904	British Isles	Belgium	5-0	Wimbledon
1905	British Isles	USA	5-0	Wimbledon
1906	British Isles	USA	5-0	Wimbledon
1907	Australasia	British Isles	3-2	Wimbledon
1908	Australasia	USA	3-2	Melbourne
1909	Australasia	USA	5-0	Sydney
1910	Not held			
1911	Australasia	USA	5-0	Christchurch,NZ
1912	British Isles	Australasia	3-2	Melbourne
1913	USA	British Isles	3-2	Wimbledon
1914	Australasia	USA	3-2	New York
1915-18	Not held	World War I		
1919	Australasia	British Isles	4-1	Sydney
1920	USA	Australasia	5-0	Auckland, NZ
1921	USA	Japan	5-0	New York
1922	USA	Australasia	4-1	New York
1923	USA	Australasia	4-1	New York
1924	USA	Australia	5-0	Philadelphia
1925	USA	France	5-0	Philadelphia
1926	USA	France	4-1	Philadelphia
1927	France	USA	3-2	Philadelphia
1928	France	USA	4-1	Paris
1929	France	USA	3-2	Paris
1930	France	USA	4-1	Paris
1931	France	Britain	3-2	Paris
1932	France	USA	3-2	Paris
1933	Britain	France	3-2	Paris
1934	Britain	USA	4-1	Wimbledon
1935	Britain	USA	5-0	Wimbledon
1936	Britain	Australia	3-2	Wimbledon
1937	USA	Britain	4-1	Wimbledon
1938	USA	Australia	3-2	Philadelphia
1939	Australia	USA	3-2	Philadelphia
1940-45	Not held	World War II		
1946	USA	Australia	5-0	Melbourne
1947	USA	Australia	4-1	New York
1948	USA	Australia	5-0	New York
1949	USA	Australia	4-1	New York

Year	Winner	Loser	Score	Site
1950	Australia	USA	4-1	New York
1951	Australia	USA	3-2	Sydney
1952	Australia	USA	4-1	Adelaide
1953	Australia	USA	3-2	Melbourne
1954	USA	Australia	3-2	Sydney
1955	Australia	USA	5-0	New York
1956	Australia	USA	5-0	Adelaide
1957	Australia	USA	3-2	Melbourne
1958	USA	Australia	3-2	Brisbane
1959	Australia	USA	3-2	New York
1960	Australia	Italy	4-1	Sydney
1961	Australia	Italy	5-0	Melbourne
1962	Australia	Mexico	5-0	Brisbane
1963	USA	Australia	3-2	Adelaide
1964	Australia	USA	3-2	Cleveland
1965	Australia	Spain	4-1	Sydney
1966	Australia	India	4-1	Melbourne
1967	Australia	Spain	4-1	Brisbane

Final Rounds

Year	Winner	Loser	Score	Site
1968	USA	Australia	4-1	Adelaide
1969	USA	Romania	5-0	Cleveland
1970	USA	W. Germany	5-0	Cleveland
1971	USA	Romania	3-2	Charlotte
1972	USA	Romania	3-2	Bucharest
1973	Australia	USA	5-0	Cleveland
1974	So. Africa	India	walkover	Not held
1975	Sweden	Czech.	3-2	Stockholm
1976	Italy	Chile	4-1	Santiago
1977	Australia	Italy	3-1	Sydney
1978	USA	Britain	4-1	Palm Springs
1979	USA	Italy	5-0	San Francisco
1980	Czech.	Italy	4-1	Prague
1981	USA	Argentina	3-1	Cincinnati
1982	USA	France	4-1	Grenoble
1983	Australia	Sweden	3-2	Melbourne
1984	Sweden	USA	4-1	Göteborg
1985	Sweden	W. Germany	3-2	Munich
1986	Australia	Sweden	3-2	Melbourne
1987	Sweden	India	5-0	Göteborg
1988	W. Germany	Sweden	4-1	Göteborg
1989	W. Germany	Sweden	3-2	Stuttgart
1990	USA	Australia	3-2	St. Petersburg
1991	France	USA	3-1	Lyon
1992	USA	Switzerland	3-1	Ft. Worth
1993	Germany	Australia	4-1	Dusseldorf
1994	Sweden	Russia	4-1	Moscow
1995	USA	Russia	3-2	Moscow

Note: In 1974, India refused to play the final as a protest against the South African government's policies of apartheid.

Fed Cup

Originally the Federation Cup and started in 1963 by the International Tennis Federation as the Davis Cup of women's tennis. Played by 32 teams over one week at one site through 1994. Tournament changed in 1995 to Davis Cup-style format of four rounds and home sites.

Multiple winners: USA (15); Australia (7); Czechoslovakia (5); Spain (4); Germany (2).

Year	Winner	Loser	Score	Site
1963	USA	Australia	2-1	London
1964	Australia	USA	2-1	Philadelphia
1965	Australia	USA	2-1	Melbourne
1966	USA	W. Germany	3-0	Italy
1967	USA	Britain	2-0	W. Germany
1968	Australia	Holland	3-0	Paris
1969	USA	Australia	2-1	Athens
1970	Australia	Britain	3-0	W. Germany
1971	Australia	Britain	3-0	Perth
1972	So. Africa	Britain	2-1	Africa
1973	Australia	So. Africa	3-0	W. Germany
1974	Australia	USA	2-1	Italy
1975	Czech.	Australia	3-0	France
1976	USA	Australia	2-1	Philadelphia
1977	USA	Australia	2-1	Eastbourne
1978	USA	Australia	2-1	Melbourne
1979	USA	Australia	3-0	Spain
1980	USA	Australia	3-0	W. Germany
1981	USA	Britain	3-0	Tokyo
1982	USA	W. Germany	3-0	Santa Clara
1983	Czech.	W. Germany	2-1	Zurich
1984	Czech.	Australia	2-1	Brazil
1985	Czech.	USA	2-1	Japan
1986	USA	Czech.	3-0	Prague
1987	W. Germany	USA	2-1	Vancouver
1988	Czech.	USSR	2-1	Melbourne
1989	USA	Spain	3-0	Tokyo
1990	USA	USSR	2-1	Atlanta
1991	Spain	USA	2-1	Nottingham
1992	Germany	Spain	2-1	Frankfurt
1993	Spain	Australia	3-0	Frankfurt
1994	Spain	USA	3-0	Frankfurt
1995	Spain	USA	3-2	Valencia
1996	USA	Spain	5-0	Atlantic City, N.J.

Maiden and Married Names of Women's Champions

Maiden Name	Married Name
Blanche Bingley	Blanche Hillyard
Molla Bjurstedt	Molla Mallory
Patricia Canning	Patricia Todd
Mary Carter	Mary Raitano
Charlotte Cooper	Charlotte Sterry
Thelma Coyne	Thelma Long
Dorothea Douglass	Dorothea Lambert Chambers
Chris Evert	Chris Evert Lloyd
Evonne Goolagong	Evonne Cawley
Louise Hammond	Louise Raymond
Ann Haydon	Ann Haydon Jones
Hazel Hotchkiss	Hazel Wightman
Hilde Krahwinkel	Hilde Sperling
Kerry Melville	Kerry Reid
Kathleen McKane	Kathleen Godfrey
Billie Jean Moffitt	Billie Jean King
Margaret Osborne	Margaret duPont
Sarah Palfrey	Sarah Fabyan Cooke
Margaret Smith	Margaret Smith Court
Helen Wills	Helen Wills Moody
Nancye Wynne	Nancye Bolton

COLLEGES

NCAA team titles were not sanctioned until 1946. NCAA women's individual and team championships started in 1982.

Men's NCAA Individual Champions (1883-1945)

Multiple winners: Malcolm Chace and Pancho Segura (3); Edward Chandler, George Church, E.B. Dewhurst, Fred Hovey, Frank Guernsey, W.P. Knapp, Robert LeRoy, P.S. Sears, Cliff Sutter, Ernest Sutter and Richard Williams (2).

Year	
1883	J. Clark, Harvard (spring)
	H. Taylor, Harvard (fall)
1884	W.P. Knapp, Yale
1885	W.P. Knapp, Yale
1886	G.M. Brinley, Trinity, CT
1887	P.S. Sears, Harvard
1888	P.S. Sears, Harvard
1889	R.P. Huntington Jr, Yale
1890	Fred Hovey, Harvard
1891	Fred Hovey, Harvard
1892	William Larned, Cornell
1893	Malcolm Chace, Brown
1894	Malcolm Chace, Yale
1895	Malcolm Chace, Yale
1896	Malcolm Whitman, Harvard
1897	S.G. Thompson, Princeton
1898	Leo Ware, Harvard
1899	Dwight Davis, Harvard
1900	Ray Little, Princeton
1901	Fred Alexander, Princeton
1902	William Clothier, Harvard
1903	E.B. Dewhurst, Penn
1904	Robert LeRoy, Columbia
1905	E.B. Dewhurst, Penn
1906	Robert LeRoy, Columbia
1907	G.P. Gardner Jr, Harvard
1908	Nat Niles, Harvard
1909	Wallace Johnson, Penn
1910	R.A. Holden Jr, Yale
1911	E.H. Whitney, Harvard
1912	George Church, Princeton
1913	Richard Williams, Harv.
1914	George Church, Princeton
1915	Richard Williams, Harv.
1916	G.C. Caner, Harvard
1917-1918	Not held
1919	Charles Garland, Yale
1920	Lascelles Banks, Yale
1921	Philip Neer, Stanford
1922	Lucien Williams, Yale
1923	Carl Fischer, Phi. Osteo.
1924	Wallace Scott, Wash.
1925	Edward Chandler, Calif.
1926	Edward Chandler, Calif.
1927	Wilmer Allison, Texas
1928	Julius Seligson, Lehigh
1929	Berkeley Bell, Texas
1930	Cliff Sutter, Tulane
1931	Keith Gledhill, Stanford
1932	Cliff Sutter, Tulane
1933	Jack Tidball, UCLA
1934	Gene Mako, USC
1935	Wilbur Hess, Rice
1936	Ernest Sutter, Tulane
1937	Ernest Sutter, Tulane
1938	Frank Guernsey, Rice
1939	Frank Guernsey, Rice
1940	Don McNeill, Kenyon
1941	Joseph Hunt, Navy
1942	Fred Schroeder, Stanford
1943	Pancho Segura, Miami-FL
1944	Pancho Segura, Miami-FL
1945	Pancho Segura, Miami-FL

NCAA Men's Division I Champions

Multiple winners (Teams): UCLA and USC (15); Stanford (14); Georgia and William & Mary (2). (Players): Alex Olmedo, Mikael Pernfors, Dennis Ralston and Ham Richardson (2).

Year	Team winner	Individual Champion
1946	USC	Bob Falkenburg, USC
1947	Wm. & Mary	Garner Larned, Wm.& Mary
1948	Wm. & Mary	Harry Likas, San Francisco
1949	San Francisco	Jack Tuero, Tulane
1950	UCLA	Herbert Flam, UCLA
1951	USC	Tony Trabert, Cinncinati
1952	UCLA	Hugh Stewart, USC
1953	UCLA	Ham Richardson, Tulane
1954	UCLA	Ham Richardson, Tulane
1955	USC	Jose Aguero, Tulane
1956	UCLA	Alex Olmedo, USC
1957	Michigan	Barry MacKay, Michigan
1958	USC	Alex Olmedo, USC
1959	Tulane & Notre Dame	Whitney Reed, San Jose St.
1960	UCLA	Larry Nagler, UCLA
1961	UCLA	Allen Fox, UCLA
1962	USC	Rafael Osuna, USC
1963	USC	Dennis Ralston, USC
1964	USC	Dennis Ralston, USC
1965	UCLA	Arthur Ashe, UCLA
1966	USC	Charlie Pasarell, UCLA
1967	USC	Bob Lutz, USC
1968	USC	Stan Smith, USC
1969	USC	Joaquin Loyo-Mayo, USC
1970	UCLA	Jeff Borowiak, UCLA
1971	UCLA	Jimmy Connors, UCLA
1972	Trinity-TX	Dick Stockton, Trinity-TX
1973	Stanford	Alex Mayer, Stanford
1974	Stanford	John Whitlinger, Stanford
1975	UCLA	Bill Martin, UCLA
1976	USC & UCLA	Bill Scanlon, Trinity-TX
1977	Stanford	Matt Mitchell, Stanford
1978	Stanford	John McEnroe, Stanford
1979	UCLA	Kevin Curren, Texas
1980	Stanford	Robert Van't Hof, USC
1981	Stanford	Tim Mayotte, Stanford
1982	UCLA	Mike Leach, Michigan
1983	Stanford	Greg Holmes, Utah
1984	UCLA	Mikael Pernfors, Georgia
1985	Georgia	Mikael Pernfors, Georgia
1986	Stanford	Dan Goldie, Stanford
1987	Georgia	Andrew Burrow, Miami-FL
1988	Stanford	Robby Weiss, Pepperdine
1989	Stanford	Donni Leaycraft, LSU
1990	Stanford	Steve Bryan, Texas
1991	USC	Jared Palmer, Stanford
1992	Stanford	Alex O'Brien Stanford
1993	USC	Chris Woodruff, Tennessee
1994	USC	Mark Merklein, Florida
1995	Stanford	Sargis Sargisian, Ariz. St.
1996	Stanford	Cecil Mamiit, USC

Women's NCAA Champions

Multiple winners (Teams): Stanford (8); Texas (3); USC (2). (Players): Sandra Birch, Patty Fendick and Lisa Raymond (2).

Year	Team winner	Individual Champion
1982	Stanford	Alycia Moulton, Stanford
1983	USC	Beth Herr, USC
1984	Stanford	Lisa Spain, Georgia
1985	USC	Linda Gates, Stanford
1986	Stanford	Patty Fendick, Stanford
1987	Stanford	Patty Fendick, Stanford
1988	Stanford	Shaun Stafford, Florida
1989	Stanford	Sandra Birch, Stanford
1990	Stanford	Debbie Graham, Stanford
1991	Stanford	Sandra Birch, Stanford
1992	Florida	Lisa Raymond, Florida
1993	Texas	Lisa Raymond, Florida
1994	Georgia	Angela Lettiere, Georgia
1995	Texas	Keri Phoebus, UCLA
1996	Texas	Jill Craybas, Florida

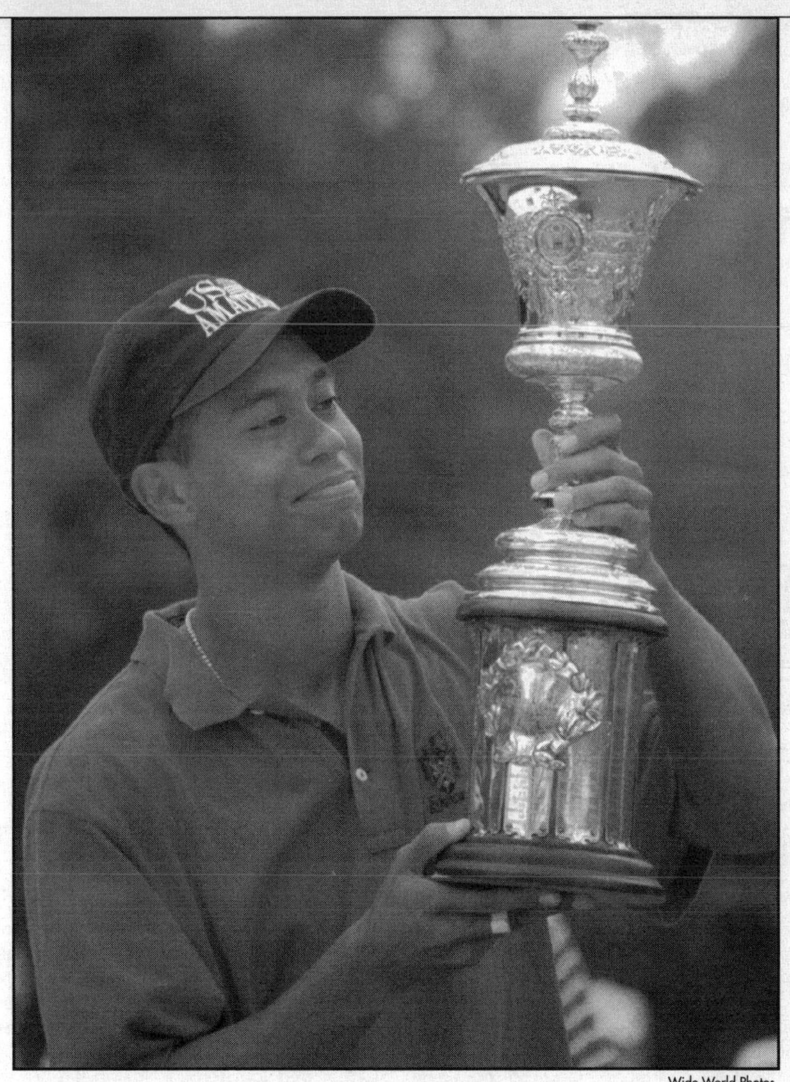

Wide World Photos

Golf sensation **Tiger Woods** holds the trophy that signifies his third consecutive U.S. Amateur title. Shortly after this unprecedented victory, Woods turned pro at the Greater Milwaukee Open.

GOLF

by Marino Parascenzo

Norman Conquest

Greg Norman blew a six shot lead on the final day and found another way to not win the Masters

Nick Faldo asked history for a break. "I hope I'm remembered for shooting a 67 on the last day, and not what happened to Greg," Faldo said.

He knew better.

"But obviously," he added, "this will be remembered for what happened to Greg."

Jim Meston, a stuttering banquet comedian from Pittsburgh, put it another way. "Y-y-y-ou rem-m-ember F-f-faldo hugging N-n-norman on the 18th at the M-m-m-asters?" he told 30 tour pros at a pro-am dinner. "Th-th-that wasn't a h-h-hug. That w-w-was the Heimlich M-m-maneuver."

Some called it the Titanic, some the Hindenburg. It was one of the greatest crashes ever in golf, even in the history of sports. Greg Norman was steaming wire-to-wire to his first Masters victory, burning the field, and he led Faldo by a huge six shots going into the final round. And he blew it all, and more. Faldo did shoot himself a 67, but Norman shot 78, and lost by five. It was an 11-shot swing in one round.

Masters, U.S. Opens, British Opens, PGAs—he'd missed another big one. It would take something like a kazoo player in a library to draw attention from this catastrophe. What timing.

Four months later, Tiger Woods won his third straight U.S. Amateur and finally turned pro, to whistles, bells, hosannas, and $60 million. Some thought there hadn't been a debut of this magnitude in about 2,000 years.

Otherwise, 1996 was quite a year in golf. Jose Maria Olazabal went in. His foot problem turned out to be rheumatoid arthritis. And Muffin Spencer-Devlin came out—the first player in the LPGA's 46-year history to reveal that she's a lesbian. Nick Faldo and his American ex-coed sweetheart, Brenna Cepelak, gradually went public, and so the British tabloids had something else to focus on besides Charles and Di halving their royal match. The mercurial Tom Weiskopf humiliated an amateur at the U.S. Senior Open.

But it was also a good time for the bible-quoting nice guys, what with Steve Jones coming from nowhere to win the U.S. Open, and Tom Lehman taking the British Open. Kenny Perry, fiddled in the TV booth while Mark Brooks burned the PGA Championship down around him, and Tom Watson resurfaced at the Memorial after nine years in the cold depths. And just when the American women thought they may regain a control of their LPGA Tour, along came a young Aussie named Karrie Webb to tell them to think again. And Phil Mickelson made the world safe for left-handers, piling up a tour-high four victories by early fall, including the rich NEC World Series of Golf.

Marino Parascenzo has been the golf writer for the *Pittsburgh Post-Gazette* since 1975. He is also a contributing writer for *Golf Digest* Magazine.

Wide World Photos

Nick Faldo slips on a particularly well-earned green jacket as the winner of the 1996 Masters tournament, his third Masters and sixth major victory overall. Faldo shot a blistering 67 in the final round to overcome Greg Norman's 6 shot lead.

But the year almost stood still at the Masters in April. They say nobody remembers who finishes second. They will now. Norman was stuffing the field. He led after the first round by two, then by four, then by six—the biggest going into the final round since Raymond Floyd's eight in 1976.

Norman was shaky starting the final round, and then it was like hitting the wall in the far turn at Indy. On a grab-bag of errors, he relentlessly bogeyed the 9th, 10th, and 11th, then watered his tee shot at the wicked little 12th and double-bogeyed.

Back in the clubhouse, Nick Price, his good friend, turned away from the television set. "I feel sick to my stomach," he said. It was like watching a puppy being beaten. In a span of four holes, Faldo had picked up five shots, and had made nothing better than par.

Norman bounced back with two birdies—Faldo matched him—then watered at the par-3 16th and double-bogeyed again. You couldn't tell from the bleeding, but Faldo was playing splendid golf. He shot a one-bogey, five-birdie 67.

At the 18th green, Faldo closed like a champ, holing a 15-footer for a birdie, then went to Norman and wrapped his arms around him, and said something. "I just said, 'I don't know what to say—I just want to give you a hug,' " Faldo said.

(It was, by the way, Faldo's third Masters, and all three were gifts. Scott Hoch blew a short putt in 1989 and Ray Floyd watered an approach shot in 1990.)

Norman put a brave face on things. He said it wasn't the end of the world. He had a good life. He would learn from this. Then he thought a moment. "I may not want to learn about this one," he said. The season was not a complete waste. Norman had won the Doral-Ryder in March. But after the Masters, he just seemed to drag himself the rest of the way.

The rest of the majors seemed almost tame. Steve Jones, still coming back from a harrowing dirt bike crash in 1991, became the most unlikely U.S. Open champ since maybe Sam Parks in 1935. He had just

Wide World Photos

After several close finishes in major tournaments, **Tom Lehman** hugs his British Open trophy after shooting a good-enough-to-win 73 at Royal Lytham and St. Annes.

made it into the Open, with last-hole heroics in the qualifier. And then at Oakland Hills, he beat his good friend Tom Lehman, who was urging him on, quoting the Book of Joshua on courage. Lehman, who led by a shot going into the final round, lost his chance when he bunkered his drive at the 18th. Davis Love's hopes fizzled in a bogey-bogey finish. Jones had to survive his own nerves. He two-putted the 18th from 12 feet for the win. His second was a one-footer coming back. "If it was one inch longer," he said, "I'm not sure where it would've gone."

Lehman was rewarded at the British Open at Royal Lytham and St. Annes. But, it was looking like a Norman for a while.

Lehman shared the lead in the second round, then led by six—over Faldo— going into the finale. Faldo frittered away his chances and dropped to fourth. Lehman shook a bit, but hung on for a 73 and a two-shot win over Mark McCumber and Ernie Els. He'd had some near misses, and now he had a winner. He could die happy. "That's always been my fear," he said. "To have on my gravestone, `Here lies, Tom Lehman— he couldn't win the big one."

The PGA Championship at Valhalla, near Louisville, Ky., ended with a thud. Kenny Perry closed with a 68 and was the leader in the clubhouse and the TV booth. He'd been invited up, and there he sat, watching one guy after another take a shot at him. The first two missed—Steve Elkington parred the 18th and Vijay Singh bogeyed. The third hit. Mark Brooks blasted from a bunker to about four feet and birdied for a tie. And suddenly Perry realized that he should have left the booth earlier to warm up. Too late. Back to the 18th for a playoff. Brooks, still loose, went from fairway to green and birdied. Perry hacked his way through the rough and lost. It was Brooks' second win of the year and the first major of his career.

How did it feel? "I don't know yet," he said. Tiger Woods, age 20, already the most famous black golfer ever, finally ended two years of speculation and turned pro right after winning a record third straight U.S. Amateur in August, and it all came from a script from some cosmic Hollywood.

First, he won the Amateur in a numbing finish. In the 36-hole final match, he was 5 down to University of Florida ace Steve Scott after the first 18, and then a near-fatal 2 down with three holes to play. But he caught Scott with birdies at the 16th and 17th—the 17th on a 40-foot putt, then beat him on the second extra hole. Two days later, at the Greater Milwaukee Open—he long ago had received a sponsor's exemption (invitiation)— Woods turned pro. He announced this at a news conference before the world, all clad in Nike swooshes, and accompanied by the hosannahs of Nike TV commercials and a three-page Nike ad in the Wall Street Journal with a totally racial theme: "Hello world... I've heard I'm not ready for you. Are you ready for me?"

He stepped into $60 million in endorsements. He signed with Nike for $40 million, and Titleist for another $20 million, both over five years. And many other endorsements were in the works. "I don't have to depend on play for my income," Woods said at Milwaukee. "I'm pretty much financially set for life." Which led some observers to wonder whether the hunger would be there.

"I'm not out just to be the best black player," Woods said. "I want to be the best golfer ever," Woods said. And two authorities, Jack Nicklaus and Arnold Palmer, say he has the stuff to do it.

In early returns, Woods tied for 60th at Milwaukee, was a solo 11th in the Canadian Open, and tied for fifth after leading the Quad City Classic. He had won $82,194 and was getting by on sponsor's exemptions. His most important task in the few '96 tour stops left was to get himself eligible for the '97 season. In the end, Woods' third place at the B.C. Open will allow him to play the entire 1997 tour on sponsor's exemptions because he had made the top 150 in earnings.

Once he got his status set for 1997, Woods pulled out of the Buick Challenge on, citing exhaustion. The move generated criticism from many tour veterans because Woods waited until Wednesday of the tournament week. They also pointed out that the tournament was there with an exemption when Woods had needed it.

The Senior PGA Tour had its own Tiger Woods, Walter Morgan, one of five blacks on the circuit. Morgan, a fifth-year man, ex-Army, took up golf at age 25, shot 79 in his first round, and got to the Senior Tour in '91. This was his biggest year. He'd won twice and was heading past $750,000.

John Bland, newcomer from South Africa, had won three times by mid-September, matching Ray Floyd and Jim Colbert, but in the majors, it was business as usual. Jack Nicklaus took the Tradition, Hale Irwin the PGA Seniors, Dave Stockton the U.S. Senior Open, and Floyd the Senior Players Championship. But they all took second billing to Tom Weiskopf.

Weiskopf, defending champion at the U.S. Senior Open at Canterbury, near Cleveland, far from mellowing with age, exceeded his own history of rage. He flew into a tirade on the course against a playing partner, Jim Stahl, the U.S. Senior Amateur champion. Among Stahl's sins: marking his ball with a shiny coin, and taking a drop where a rules official instructed. The outburst mortified Stahl and stunned officials, spectators and the media. Weiskopf said he'd rather be shopping for a horse than playing for the championship, and added that he did it all for the guy's own good. Later, he apologized.

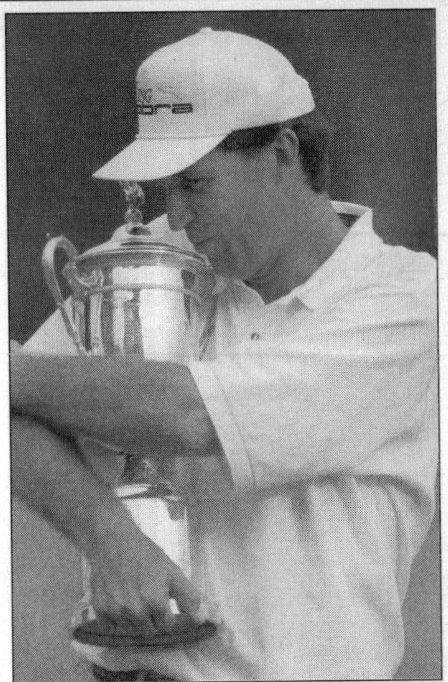

Wide World Photos

After surviving a terrible dirt bike crash, **Steve Jones** made it all the way back by winning the 1996 U.S. Open.

The U.S. Golf Association had asked Weiskopf to speak at the U.S. Junior Amateur. Then they withdrew the invitation and called in a substitute. Weiskopf was to have spoken on sportsmanship.

A new LPGA Tour was emerging in 1996. It started with Jim Ritts, 42, former advertising and cable TV executive, taking over as the tour's fifth commissioner. He inherited the post-Ben Wright Tour. Wright had been dumped by CBS after raising the issue of lesbianism in a newspaper interview. But the issue was still there, stirred up by Muffin Spencer-Devlin's coming-out.

Meanwhile, out on the golf course ...

The LPGA Tour was hit by its own Youth Revolution in the person of Karrie Webb, 21, a rookie from Australia. By mid-September, she had Rookie of the Year wrapped up and was trying to claim the money list, too, with over $750,000.

The Europeans continued to be the force on the LPGA. They took three of the four majors. England's Laura Davies got two of them herself.

Patty Sheehan—an American—led off the

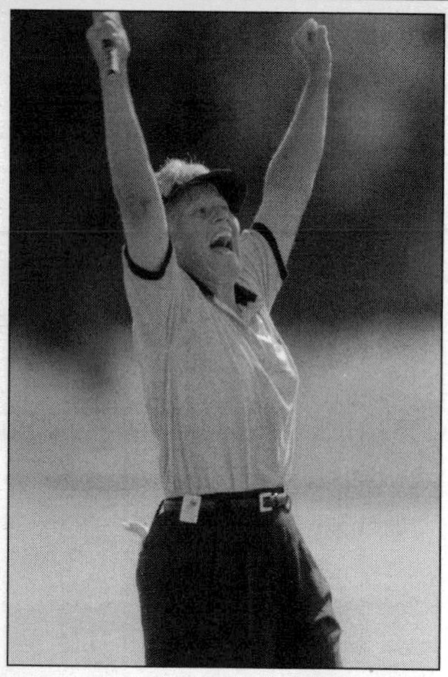

Wide World Photos

LPGA Hall of Famer **Patty Sheehan** celebrates after sinking a putt to win the Nabisco Dinah Shore, the first women's major of the year.

majors with a win in the Nabisco Dinah Shore at Mission Hills, Calif. She came to the final green facing an interesting task. "C'mon," she said, "pull yourself together. C'mon, you can do it." She had to get down in two putts from 110 feet. She did, and won by a shot.

In the McDonald's LPGA Championship, Davies ground out a closing 70 in 17 pars and a birdie in foul weather. "I seem to do well on weeks when we have a rain delay," she said. Also in the cold rain and wind, as in the final round of the du Maurier Classic in Edmonton, where she was trailing by five shots. "I thought if I could shoot 69, something would happen," she said. She shot 66 and won by two. It was her fourth victory of the year, her second major and the fourth of her career.

If it's not one Swede it's another, and this time it was the same one Annika Sorenstam, winning her second straight U.S. Women's Open, this time at Pine Needles at Southern Pines, N.C. She missed only five fairways in four rounds, broke the Open record by five shots, and won by six. Said runnerup Kris Tschetter, "I kept saying to myself, what golf course is she playing?" Said Sorenstam: "I can finally breathe. Winning once is wonderful. Winning twice is more than wonderful." The Europeans won 12 of the first 29 events, but Dottie Pepper (she dropped Mochrie after the divorce) did her part to stem the tide. She won four times in 12 tournaments by mid-September, matching England's Davies. Webb, Liselotte Neumann (a Swede), and Michelle McGann each won three each, and Meg Mallon and Emilee Klein had two.

The Europeans dominated the amateur side, too. In the biennial Curtis Cup (women amateurs), the Great Britain-Ireland team beat the Americans in June for a 4-1-1 record in the last six.

But the great Arnie Palmer, non-playing captain, squared things a bit by steering the U.S. to victory in the Presidents Cup. That's the young Ryder Cup spinoff against international players not from Europe. The gutsy Freddie Couples holed a long birdie putt on the 17th hole to beat Vijay Singh in singles and give the U.S. a one-point win, and a 2-0 record.

This stirring victory occured after the Internationals had risen in nasty public rebellion and forced out their non-playing captain, Australian David Graham. It seems Graham wasn't the touchy-feely kind of captain, and so Norman, Elkington et al. said either he goes or we'll take our clubs and go home.

On the European Tour, little Ian Woosnam returned with a bang, winning the first two tournaments and making the German Open his fourth by late summer, keeping a step ahead of Scotland's Colin Montgomerie and Australia's Robert Allenby. Jumbo Ozaki continued to rule in Japan, but a newcomer snapped heads back. In a game that adores power, Hidemichi Tanaka found a home. He's under 5-foot-6, weighs 128 pounds, has a waist of 27 inches, wrists like chopsticks, and at the World Series of Golf at brutal Firestone, he was bombing drives some 350 yards.

Golf continued to spread globally. The World Cup of Golf, which is played all over the world, broke new ground in November, 1995, by going to Shenzen, China. As in Red China. And the European Tour's developmental Challenge Tour stopped off at Moscow Country Club in September.

Yes, that Moscow. ❐

GOLF STATISTICS

THE SEASON IN REVIEW

1995-1996

PGA • SENIORS • LPGA

Tournament Results

Winners of PGA, European PGA, PGA Seniors and LPGA tournaments from Nov. 5, 1995 through Sept. 29, 1996.

PGA Tour

LATE 1995

Last Rd	Tournament	Winner	Earnings	Runner-Up
Nov. 5	Kapalua International	Jim Furyk (271)	$180,000	3-way tie (273)
Nov. 12	41st World Cup of Golf	USA— Davis Love III/ Fred Couples (543)	200,000 (each)	AUS— B. Ogle/ R. Allenby (557)
Nov. 19	Franklin Templeton Shark Shootout	Mark Calcavecchia/ Steve Elkington (184)	150,000 (each)	L. Janzen/ C. Beck (185)
Nov. 26	The Skins Game	Fred Couples (7 skins)*	270,000	C. Pavin (10 skins)
Dec. 3	JCPenney Classic	Davis Love III/ Beth Daniel (257)	162,500	R. Gamez/ H. Alfredsson (259)

World Cup teams: USA (Davis Love III 65-67-68-67—267 and Fred Couples 68-69-70-69—276), Australia (Brett Ogle 70-71-69-68—278 and Robert Allenby 68-73-68-70—279).
***Playoffs** (1): **The Skins Game**— Couples won all seven skins and $270,000 on the fifth extra hole.
Second place ties (3 players or more): 3-WAY— **Kapalua** (R. Cochran, B. Lane, J. McGovern).

1996 (through Sept. 29)

Last Rd	Tournament	Winner	Earnings	Runner-Up
Jan. 7	Mercedes Championship	Mark O'Meara (271)	$180,000	N. Faldo & S. Hoch (274)
Jan. 14	Nortel Open	Phil Mickelson (273)	225,000	B. Tway (275)
Jan. 21	Bob Hope Chrysler Classic	Mark Brooks (337)	234,000	J. Huston (338)
Jan. 28	Phoenix Open	Phil Mickelson (269)*	234,000	J. Leonard (269)
Feb. 4	AT&T Pebble Beach National Pro-Am	cancelled		
Feb. 11	Buick Invitational	Davis Love III (269)	216,000	P. Mickelson (271)
Feb. 18	United Airlines Hawaiin Open	Jim Furyk (277)*	216,000	B. Faxon (277)
Feb. 25	Nissan Open	Craig Stadler (278)	216,000	4-way tie (279)
Mar. 3	Doral-Ryder Open	Greg Norman (269)	324,000	M. Bradley & V. Singh (271)
Mar. 10	Honda Classic	Tim Herron (271)	234,000	M. McCumber (275)
Mar. 17	Bay Hill Invitational	Paul Goydos (275)	216,000	J. Maggert (276)
Mar. 24	Freeport-McDermott Classic	Scott McCarron (275)	216,000	T. Watson (280)
Mar. 31	The Players Championship	Fred Couples (270)	630,000	C. Montgomerie & T. Tolles (274)
Apr. 7	BellSouth Classic	Paul Stankowski (280)*	234,000	B. Chamblee (280)
Apr. 14	**The Masters** (Augusta)	Nick Faldo (276)	450,000	G. Norman (281)
Apr. 21	MCI Classic	Loren Roberts (265)	252,000	M. O'Meara (268)
Apr. 28	Greater Greensboro Chrysler Classic	Mark O'Meara (274)	324,000	D. Waldorf (276)
May 5	Shell Houston Open	Mark Brooks (274)*	270,000	J. Maggert (274)
May 12	GTE Byron Nelson Classic	Phil Mickelson (265)	270,000	C. Parry (267)
May 19	Mastercard Colonial	Corey Pavin (272)	270,000	J. Sluman (274)
May 26	Kemper Open	Steve Stricker (270)	270,000	4-way tie (273)
June 2	Memorial Tournament	Tom Watson (274)	324,000	D. Duval (276)
June 9	Buick Classic	Ernie Els (271)	216,000	4-way tie (279)
June 16	**U.S. Open** (Oakland Hills)	Steve Jones (278)	425,000	D. Love III & T. Lehman (279)
June 23	FedEx St. Jude Classic	John Cook (258)	243,000	J. Adams (265)
June 30	Canon Greater Hartford Open	D.A. Weibring (270)	270,000	T. Kite (274)
July 7	Motorola Western Open	Steve Stricker (270)	360,000	B. Andrade & J.D. Blake (278)
July 14	Michelob Championship at Kingsmill	Scott Hoch (265)	225,000	T. Purtzer (269)
July 21	Deposit Guaranty Golf Classic	Willie Wood (268)	180,000	K. Triplett (269)
July 21	**British Open** (Royal Lytham)	Tom Lehman (271)	310,000	M. McCumber & E. Els (273)

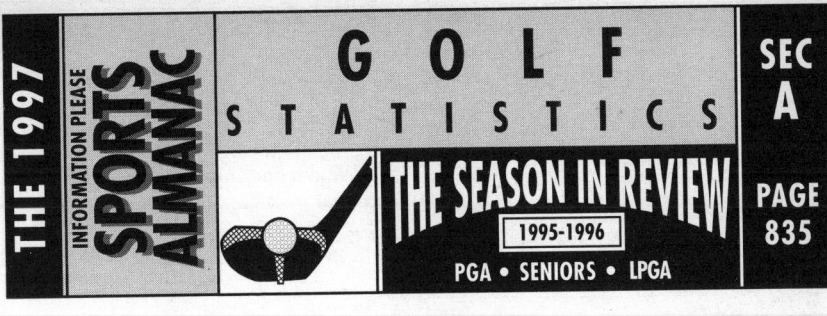

Tournament Results (Cont.)

PGA Tour

Last Rd	Tournament	Winner	Earnings	Runner-Up
July 28	CVS Charity Classic	John Cook (268)	$216,000	R. Cochran (271)
Aug. 4	Buick Open	Justin Leonard (266)	216,000	C. Beck (271)
Aug. 11	**PGA Championship** (Valhalla)	Mark Brooks (277)*	430,000	K. Perry (277)
Aug. 18	The Sprint International	Clarence Rose (31)†*	288,000	B. Faxon (31)
Aug. 25	NEC World Series of Golf	Phil Mickelson (274)	378,000	3-way tie (277)
Aug. 25	Greater Vancouver Open	Guy Boros (272)	180,000	3-way tie (273)
Sept. 1	Greater Milwaukee Open	Loren Roberts (265)*	216,000	J. Kelly (265)
Sept. 8	Bell Canadian Open	Dudley Hart (202)#	270,000	D. Duval (203)
Sept. 15	Quad City Classic	Ed Fiori (268)	216,000	A. Magee (230)
Sept. 15	The Presidents Cup	United States (16½)	none	International (15½)
Sept. 22	B.C. Open	Fred Funk (197)#*	180,000	Pete Jordan (197)
Sept. 29	Buick Challenge	Michael Bradley (134)#*	180,000	4-way tie (134)

(See Updates Chapter for later results.)
#Weather-shortened.
†The scoring for the Sprint International was based on a modified Stableford system (8 points for a double eagle, 5 for an eagle, 2 for a birdie, 0 for a par, −1 for a bogey, −3 for double bogey or worse.
% PGA Tour record.

***Playoffs** (9): **Phoenix**— Mickelson won on the 3rd hole; **Hawaiian**— Furyk won on the 3rd hole; **BellSouth**— Stankowski won on the 1st hole; **Shell Houston Open**—Brooks won on the 1st hole; **PGA Championship**— Brooks won on the 1st hole; **Sprint**— Rose won on the 3rd hole; **Milwaukee**— Roberts won on the 1st hole; **BC Open**—Funk won on the 1st hole; **Buick**— Bradley won on the 1st hole.

Second place ties (3 players or more): 4-WAY— **Nissan** (M. Brooks, F. Couples, S. Simpson, M. Wiebe), **Kemper** (B. Faxon, S. Hoch, M. O'Meara, G. Waite), **Buick** (S. Elkington, T. Lehman, J. Maggert, C. Parry), Buick (F. Funk, J Maginnes, D. Love III, L. Mattiace). 3-WAY— **NEC** (D. Waldorf, S. Stricker, B. Mayfair), **Vancouver** (E. Aubrey, L. Janzen, T. Smith).

PGA Majors

The Masters

Edition: 60th **Dates:** April 11–14
Site: Augusta National GC, Augusta, Ga.
Par: 36-36—72 (6925 yards) **Purse:** $2,500,000

		1 2 3 4 Tot	Earnings
1	Nick Faldo	69-67-73-67—276	$450,000
2	Greg Norman	63-69-71-78—281	270,000
3	Phil Mickelson	65-73-72-72—282	170,000
4	Frank Nobilo	71-71-72-69—283	120,000
5	Scott Hoch	67-73-73-71—284	95,000
	Duffy Waldorf	72-71-69-72—284	95,000
7	Corey Pavin	75-66-73-71—285	77,933
	Jeff Maggert	71-73-72-69—285	77,933
	Davis Love III	72-71-74-68—285	77,933
10	David Frost	70-68-74-74—286	65,000
	Scott McCarron	70-70-72-74—286	65,000

Early round leaders: 1st— Norman (63); 2nd— Norman (132); 3rd— Norman (203).
Top amateur: none.

U.S. Open

Edition: 96th **Dates:** June 13–16
Site: Oakland Hills CC., Bloomfield Hills, MI
Par: 35-35—70 (6974 yards) **Purse:** $2,400,000

		1 2 3 4 Tot	Earnings
1	Steve Jones	74-66-69-69—278	$425,000
2	Davis Love III	71-69-70-69—279	204,801
	Tom Lehman	71-72-65-71—279	204,801
4	John Morse	68-74-68-70—280	111,235
5	Ernie Els	72-67-72-70—281	84,965
	Jim Furyk	72-69-70-70—281	84,965
7	Scott Hoch	73-71-71-67—282	66,295
	Vijay Singh	71-72-70-69—282	66,295
	Ken Green	73-67-72-70—282	66,295
10	Lee Janzen	68-75-71-69—283	52,591
	Greg Norman	73-66-74-70—283	52,591
	Colin Montgomerie	70-72-69-72—283	52,591

Early round leaders: 1st— Woody Austin and Payne Stewart (67); 2nd— Stewart (138); 3rd— Lehman (208).
Top amateur: Randy Leen (291).

British Open

Edition: 125th **Dates:** July 18–21
Site: Royal Lytham and St. Annes, Lytham, England
Par: 35-36—71 (6892 yards) **Purse:** $2,110,000 (US)

		1 2 3 4 Tot	Earnings
1	Tom Lehman	67-67-64-73—271	$310,000
2	Mark McCumber	67-69-71-66—273	193,750
	Ernie Els	68-67-71-67—273	193,750
4	Nick Faldo	68-68-68-70—274	116,250
5	Jeff Maggert	69-70-72-65—276	77,500
	Mark Brooks	67-70-68-71—276	77,500
7	Peter Hedblom	70-65-75-67—277	54,250
	Greg Norman	71-68-71-67—277	54,250
	Greg Turner	72-69-68-68—277	54,250
	Fred Couples	67-70-69-71—277	54,250

Early round leaders: 1st— Paul Broadhurst (65); 2nd— Paul McGinley and Lehman (134); 3rd— Lehman (198).
Top amateur: Tiger Woods (281).

PGA Championship

Edition: 78th **Dates:** Aug. 8–11
Site: Valhalla GC, Louisville, Ky.
Par: 36-36—72 (7144 yards) **Purse:** $2,000,000

		1 2 3 4 Tot	Earnings
1	Mark Brooks	68-70-69-70—277	$430,000
2	Kenny Perry	66-72-71-68—277	260,000
3	Tommy Tolles	69-71-71-67—278	140,000
	Steve Elkington	67-74-67-70—278	140,000
5	Jesper Parnevik	73-67-69-70—279	86,667
	Justin Leonard	71-66-72-70—279	86,667
	Vijay Singh	69-69-69-72—279	86,667
8	Lee Janzen	68-71-71-70—280	57,500
	Per-Ulrik Johansson	73-72-66-69—280	57,500
	Frank Nobilo	69-72-71-68—280	57,500
	Nick Price	68-71-69-72—280	57,500
	Phil Mickelson	67-67-74-72—280	57,500
	Larry Mize	71-70-69-70—280	57,500

Early round leaders: 1st— Perry (66); 2nd— Mickelson (134); 3rd— Russ Cochran (205).
Top Amateur: none.

Sony World Rankings

Begun in 1986, the Sony World Rankings combine the best golfers on the PGA and European PGA tours. Rankings are based on a rolling three-year period and weighted in favor of more recent results. Points are awarded after each worldwide tournament according to finish. Final point averages are determined by dividing a player's total points by the number of tournaments played in 1996 (through Sept.29).

		Avg			Avg			Avg
1	Greg Norman	10.30	8	Corey Pavin	8.16	15	Steve Stricker	5.55
2	Ernie Els	8.85	9	Phil Mickelson	7.70	16	Loren Roberts	5.48
3	Colin Montgomerie	8.76	10	Mark O'Meara	6.94	17	David Duval	5.36
4	Nick Faldo	8.73	11	Davis Love III	6.72	18	Mark McCumber	5.34
5	Tom Lehman	8.47	12	Steve Elkington	6.55	19	Scott Hoch	5.18
6	Fred Couples	8.33	13	Nick Price	6.20	20	Vijay Singh	5.16
7	Jumbo Ozaki	8.26	14	Bernhard Langer	6.00			

European PGA Tour

Earnings listed in pounds sterling (£) unless otherwise indicated.

LATE 1995

Last Rd	Tournament	Winner	Earnings	Runner-Up
Nov. 5	Sarazen World Open	Frank Nobilo (208)	£221,518	M. McNulty & M. Jiménez (209)
Nov. 12	41st World Cup of Golf	USA— Davis Love III/ Fred Couples (543)	126,582 (each)	AUS— B. Ogle/ R. Allenby (557)
Dec. 17	Johnnie Walker World Championship	Fred Couples (279)*	358,703	L. Roberts & V. Singh (279)

***Playoffs** (1): **Johnnie Walker**— Couples won on 2nd hole.

1996 (through Sept. 29)

Last Rd	Tournament	Winner	Earnings	Runner-Up
Jan. 28	Johnny Walker Classic	Ian Woosnam (272)*	£100,000	A. Colthart (272)
Feb. 4	Heineken Classic	Ian Woosnam (277)	93,338	J. Van de Velde & P. McGinley (278)
Feb. 11	Dimenson Data Pro-Am	Mark McNulty (282)	62,491	3-way tie (286)
Feb. 18	Dunhill South Africa PGA	Sven Strüver (202)#	47,460	D. Feherty & E. Els (205)
Feb. 25	FNB Players Championship	Wayne Westner (270)	61,486	J. Coceres (271)
Mar. 3	Catalonia Open	Paul Lawrie (135)#	50,000	F. Roca (136)
Mar. 10	Moroccan Open	Peter Hedblom (281)	58,330	E. Romero (282)
Mar. 17	Dubai Desert Classic	Colin Montgomerie (270)	108,330	M. Jimenez (271)
Mar. 24	Portuguese Open	Wayne Riley (271)	54,160	M. Davis & M. Gates (273)
Mar. 31	Madeira Island Open	Jarmo Sandelin (279)	50,000	P. Affleck (280)
Apr. 21	Air France Cannes Open	Raymond Russell (272)	66,660	D. Carter (274)
Apr. 28	Turespaña Masters	Tony Johnstone (271)	55,550	P. Baker (275)
May 5	Italian Open	Jim Payne (275)	85,166	P. Sjoland (276)
May 12	Peugeot Spanish Open	Padraig Harrington (272)	91,660	G. Brand Jr. (276)
May 19	Benson & Hedges Intl. Open	Stephen Ames (283)	116,660	J. Robson (284)
May 27	Volvo PGA Championship	Constantino Rocca (274)	166,660	N. Faldo & P. Lawrie (276)
June 2	Deutsche Bank Open	Frank Nobilo (270)	120,830	C. Montgomerie (271)
June 9	Alamo English Open	Robert Allenby (278)	108,330	C. Montgomerie & R. McFarlane (279)
June 16	Slaley Hall Northumberland	Retief Goosen (277)	50,000	R. Drummond (279)
June 23	BMW International Open	Marc Farry (132)#	87,495	R. Green (133)
June 30	Peugeot French Open	Robert Allenby (272)*	100,000	B. Langher (272)
July 7	Murphy's Irish Open	Colin Montgomerie (279)	127,551	A. Oldcorn & W. Riley (280)
July 13	The Scottish Open	Ian Woosnam (289)	80,000	A. Coltart (293)
July 21	**British Open**	Tom Lehman (271)	200,000	M. McCumber & E. Els (273)
July 28	Sun Dutch Open	Mark McNulty (266)	108,330	S. Hoch (267)
Aug. 4	Volvo Scandinavian Masters	Lee Westwood (281)*	116,660	P. Broadhurst & R. Claydon (281)
Aug. 11	Hohe Brücke Open	Paul McGinley (269)	41,660	D. Lynn & J.C. Pinero (270)
Aug. 18	Chemapol Trophy Czech Open	Jonathan Lomas (272)	125,000	D. Chopra (273)
Aug. 25	Volvo German Open	Ian Woosnam (193)	116,660	4-way tie (199)
Sept. 1	Collingtree British Masters	Robert Allenby (284)*	116,660	M.A. Martin (284)
Sept. 8	Canon European Masters	Colin Montgomerie (260)	200,000	S. Torrance (264)
Sept. 15	Lancome Trophy	Jesper Parnevik (268)	108,330	C. Montgomerie (273)

European PGA Tour (Cont.)

1996 (through Sept. 29)

Last Rd	Tournament	Winner	Earnings	Runner-Up
Sept. 22	Loch Lomond World Invitational	Thomas Bjorn (277)	£125,000	J. Van de Velde
Sept. 29	Smurfit European Open	Per-Ulrik Johansson (277)	125,000	C. Rocca

(See Updates Chapter for later results.)

***Playoffs** (5): **Johnnie Walker**— Woosnam won on the 3rd hole; **Peugeot French Open**— Allenby won on the 1st hole; **Volvo Scandinavian Open**—Westwood defeated Claydon on the 2nd hole. Broadhurst was eliminated on the first hole; **British Masters**— Allenby won on the 1st hole.

#Weather-shortened

Second place ties (3 players or more): 4-way: **Volvo German Open** (I. Pyman, T. Gogele, F. Roca, R. Karlsson); 3-way: **Dimesnon Data Pro-Am** (N. Price, R. Willison, amd B. Pappas)

Note: Ryder Cup qualifying points schedule starts with Collingtree British Masters (Aug. 29-Sept. 1) through to week end Aug. 24, 1997.

Senior PGA Tour

LATE 1995

Last Rd	Tournament	Winner	Earnings	Runner-Up
Nov. 5	Emerald Coast Classic	Ray Floyd (135)*#	$150,000	T. Wargo (135)
Nov. 12	Senior Tour Championship	Jim Colbert (282)	262,000	R. Floyd (283)

#Rain-shortened

***Playoffs** (1): **Emerald Coast**— Floyd won on the 2nd hole.

1996 (through Sept. 29)

Last Rd	Tournament	Winner	Earnings	Runner-Up
Jan. 21	Senior Tournament of Champions	John Bland (207)	$151,000	J. Colbert (208)
Jan. 28	Senior Skins Game	Ray Floyd (8 skins)	240,000	J. Colbert (7)
Feb. 4	Royal Caribbean Classic	Bob Murphy (203)	127,500	H. Irwin (207)
Feb. 11	Greater Naples Intellinet Challenge	Al Geiberger (202)	90,000	I. Aoki (203)
Feb. 18	GTE Suncoast Classic	Jack Nicklaus (211)	112,500	J.C. Snead (212)
Feb. 25	American Express Inviational	Hale Irwin (197)	135,000	B. Murphy (202)
Mar. 3	FHP Health Care Classic	Walt Morgan (199)*	120,000	G. Player (199)
Mar. 5	Senior Slam at Los Cabos (Mexico)	Raymond Floyd (140)	250,000	J. Nicklaus (143)
Mar. 17	Toshiba Classic	Jim Colbert (201)	150,000	B. Eastwood (203)
Mar. 24	Liberty Mutual Legends of Golf	Trevino-Hill (198)	200,000	3-way tie (200)
Mar. 31	SBC Dominion Seniors	Tom Weiskopf (207)	97,500	3-way tie (209)
Apr. 7	**The Tradition** (Scottsdale)	Jack Nicklaus (272)	150,000	H. Irwin (275)
Apr. 21	**PGA Seniors'** (Palm Beach Gardens)	Hale Irwin (280)	198,000	I. Aoki (282)
Apr. 28	Las Vegas Senior Classic	Jim Colbert (207)*	150,000	D. Stockton & B. Charles (207)
May 5	Painewebber Invitational	Graham Marsh (206)	120,000	T. Wargo & B. Barnes (207)
May 12	Nationwide Championship	J. Colbert (206)	180,000	I. Aoki (209)
May 19	Cadillac NFL Classic	Bob Murphy (202)	142,500	J. Sigel (204)
May 26	BellSouth Classic at Opryland	Isao Aoki (202)	180,000	J. Sigel & G. Marsh (203)
June 2	Bruno's Memorial Classic	John Bland (208)*	157,500	J.P. Cain & K. Zarley (208)
June 9	Pittsburgh Classic	Tom Weiskopf (205)	165,000	B. Barnes & J.C. Snead (208)
June 16	du Maurier Champions	Charles Coody (271)	165,000	L. Mowry (272)
June 23	Bell Atlantic Classic	Dale Douglass (206)*	135,000	J. Schroeder & T. Wargo (206)
June 30	Kroger Classic	Isao Aoki (198)	135,000	R. Thompson & M. Hill (203)
July 7	**U.S. Senior Open** (Bethesda)	Dave Stockton (277)	212,500	H. Irwin (279)
July 14	**Ford Sr. Players Champs.** (Dearborn)	Ray Floyd (275)	225,000	H. Irwin (277)
July 21	Burnet Classic	Vincente Fernandez (205)	187,500	B. Crampton & J.C. Snead (206)
July 28	Ameritech Open	Walter Morgan (205)	165,000	J. Bland (207)
Aug. 4	VFW Championship	Dave Eichelberger (200)	135,000	J. Colbert (202)
Aug. 11	First of America Classic	Dave Stockton (206)	125,000	B. Murphy (207)
Aug. 18	Northville Long Island Classic	John Bland (202)	120,000	J. Colbert (205)
Aug. 25	Bank of Boston Classic	Jim Dent (204)	120,000	J. Sigel & T. Wargo (205)
Sept. 1	Franklin Quest Classic	Graham Marsh (202)	120,000	K. Zarley (204)
Spet. 8	Boone Valley Classic	Gibby Gilbert (203)*	180,000	H. Irwin (203)
Sept. 15	Bank One Classic	Mike Hill (207)	90,000	I. Aoki & G. Gilbert (208)
Sept. 22	Brickyard Crossing Championship	Jimmy Powell (134)#	£112,500	J. Jacobs (135)
Sept. 29	Vantage Championship	Jim Colbert (204)	225,000	3-way tie (205)

(See Updates Chapter for later results.)

Weather Shortened

***Playoffs** (5): **FHP Heath Care**— Morgan won on the 1st hole; **Las Vegas Senior**— Colbert defeated Stockton on the 4th hole. Charles was eliminated on the 1st hole; **Bruno's Classic**— Bland defeated Cain on the 3rd hole. Zarley was eliminated on the 2nd hole; **Bell Atlantic**— Douglass won on the 3rd hole; **Boone Valley**— Gilbert won on the 1st hole.

Second place ties (3 players or more): 3–WAY- **Liberty Mutual** (Nicklaus/Player, Henning/Rodriguez, Moody/Powell); **SBC Dominion** (G. Player, B. Dickson, G. Marsh); **Vantage** (K. Zarley, H. Irwin, G. Player).

Senior PGA Majors

The Tradition

Edition: 8th **Dates:** Apr. 1–7
Site: Desert Mt. Cochise Course, Scottsdale, Ariz.
Par: 36-36—72 (6869 yards) **Purse:** $1,000,000

	1 2 3 4 Tot	Earnings
1 Jack Nicklaus	68-74-65-65—272	$150,000
2 Hale Irwin	65-76-65-69—275	88,000
3 Ray Floyd	67-72-69-73—281	72,000
4 Bob Murphy	71-70-69-72—282	60,000
5 Walt Morgan	71-72-72-68—283	44,000
Al Geiberger	73-71-69-70—283	44,000
7 George Archer	72-74-69-69—284	34,000
John Bland	72-76-66-70—284	34,000
9 Gary Player	70-73-73-69—285	27,000
J.C. Snead	69-69-75-72—285	27,000

Early round leaders: 1st— Irwin, Ed Sneed (65); 2nd— Snead (138); 3rd— Irwin (206).

PGA Seniors' Championship

Edition: 59th **Dates:** April 18–21
Site: PGA National GC, Palm Beach Gardens, Fla.
Par: 36-36—72 (6702 yards) **Purse:** $1,100,000

	1 2 3 4 Tot	Earnings
1 Hale Irwin	66-74-69-71—280	$198,000
2 Isao Aoki	69-71-71-71—282	105,000
3 Vicente Fernandez	68-76-67-73—284	75,000
4 Chi Chi Rodriguez	71-73-71-72—287	51,666
Brian Barnes	72-71-69-75—287	51,666
Bud Allin	72-67-75-73—287	51,666
7 Bob Murphy	74-72-74-68—288	32,500
Tom Weiskopf	72-74-72-70—288	32,500
John Schroeder	69-75-71-73—288	32,500
Larry Gilbert	67-74-74-73—288	32,500

Early round leaders: 1st— Irwin (66); 2nd— Allin (139); 3rd— Irwin (209).

U.S. Senior Open

Edition: 17th **Dates:** July 4–7
Site: Canterbury GC, Beachwood, Ohio
Par: 36-36—72 (6765 yards) **Purse:** $1,200,000

	1 2 3 4 Tot	Earnings
1 Dave Stockton	70-67-67-73—277	$212,500
2 Hale Irwin	72-71-69-67—279	125,000
3 Raymond Floyd	70-73-69-68—280	79,801
4 Graham Marsh	69-74-70-69—282	55,618
5 Jay Sigel	72-69-71-72—284	42,483
Tony Jacklin	74-68-70-72—284	42,483
7 Bob Charles	66-72-73-73—285	35,863
8 Bruce Summerhays	73-69-74-70—286	30,539
Walter Morgan	73-71-72-70—286	30,539
John Bland	74-67-72-73—286	30,539

Early round leaders: 1st—Charles (66); 2nd— Stockton (137); 3rd— Stockton (204).

PGA Sr. Players Championship

Edition: 14th **Dates:** July 11–14
Site: TPC of Michigan, Dearborn, Mich.
Par: 36-36—72 (6876 yards) **Purse:** $1,500,000

	1 2 3 4 Tot	Earnings
1 Ray Floyd	71-66-65-73—275	$225,000
2 Hale Irwin	70-67-69-71—277	132,000
3 Brian Barnes	74-70-67-69—280	108,000
4 Jack Kiefer	72-74-67-68—281	81,000
Jerry McGee	70-68-69-74—281	81,000
6 Gibby Gilbert	68-72-72-70—282	57,000
Bob Charles	67-72-70-73—282	57,000
8 Rocky Thompson	74-70-71-68—283	39,600
Calvin Peete	72-68-71-72—283	39,600
Dave Stockton	74-68-69-72—283	39,600
Larry Gilbert	71-71-69-72—283	39,600
Lee Trevino	67-71-71-74—283	39,600

Early round leaders: 1st— Tom Weiskopf (66); 2nd— John Bland, Irwin, and Floyd (137); 3rd—Floyd (202).

LPGA Tour

LATE 1995

Last Rd	Tournament	Winner	Earnings	Runner-Up
Nov. 7	Toray Japan Queens Cup	Woo-Soon Ko (207)	$105,000	H. Kobayashi & T. Kimura (209)
Nov. 15	JCPenney Classic	Beth Daniel/ Davis Love III (257)	162,000	H. Alfredsson/ R. Gamez (259)

1996 (through Sept. 29)

Last Rd	Tournament	Winner	Earnings	Runner-Up
Jan. 14	Chrysler-Plymouth Tourn. of Champions	Liselotte Neumann (275)	$177,500	K. Webb (286)
Jan. 21	HealthSouth Inaugural	Karrie Webb (209)*	67,500	J. Geddes & M. Nause (209)
Feb. 24	Cup Noodles Hawaiian Open	Meg Mallon (212)	90,000	K. Webb (213)
Mar. 17	PING/Welch's Championship	Liselotte Neumann (276)	67,500	C. Johnston-Forbes (277)
Mar. 24	Standard Register PING	Laura Davies (284)	105,000	K. Parker-Gregory (285)
Mar. 31	**Nabisco Dinah Shore** (Rancho Mirage)	Patty Sheehan (281)	135,000	3-way tie (282)
Apr. 7	Twelve Bridges LPGA Classic	Kelly Robbins (273)*	75,000	V. Skinner (273)
Apr. 21	Chick-fil-A Charity Championship	Barb Mucha (208)	82,500	L. Neumann & D. Pepper (210)
Apr. 28	Sara Lee Classic	Meg Mallon (210)	90,000	S. Farwig & P. Wright (212)
May 5	Sprint Titleholders Championship	Karrie Webb (272)	180,000	K. Robbins (273)
May 12	**McDonald's LPGA Championship** (Wilmington)	Laura Davies (213)#	180,000	J. Piers (214)
May 26	Corning Classic	Rosie Jones (276)	90,000	V. Skinner (278)
May 26	JCPenney Skins Game	Laura Davies (10)	340,000	D. Pepper & A. Sorenstam (2)
June 2	**U.S. Women's Open** (So. Pines, NC)	Annika Sorenstam (272)	212,500	K. Tschetter (278)
June 9	Oldsmobile Classic	Michelle McGann (272)*	90,000	L. Neumann (272)
June 16	Edina Realty Classic	Liselotte Neumann (207)*	82,500	3-way tie (207)

LPGA Tour (Cont.)

Last Rd	Tournament	Winner	Earnings	Runner-Up
June 23	Rochester International	Dottie Pepper (206)#	$ 90,000	A. Sorenstam (208)
June 30	ShopRite Classic	Dottie Pepper (202)	112,500	A. Benz (206)
July 7	Jamie Farr Kroger Classic	Joan Pitcock (204)	86,250	M. Morris (205)
July 14	Youngstown-Warren Classic	Michelle McGann (200)	90,000	K. Saiki (203)
July 21	Friendly's Classic	Dottie Pepper (279)	75,000	B. Burton (280)
July 28	Heartland Classic	Vicki Fergon (276)	82,500	P. Liscio & P. Hurst (280)
Aug. 4	**du Maurier Ltd. Classic** (Edmonton, Alberta)	Laura Davies (277)	150,000	Nancy Lopez & K. Webb (279)
Aug. 11	PING/Welch's Championship	Emilee Klein (273)	75,000	K. Webb (275)
Aug. 18	Weetabix Women's British Open	Emilee Klein (277)	124,000	P. Hammel & A. Alcott (284)
Aug. 25	Star Bank Classic	Laura Davies (204)	82,500	M. Will & P. Hurst (207)
Sept. 2	State Farm Rail Classic	Michelle McGann (202)*	86,250	L. Davies & B. Whitehead (202)
Sept. 8	The Safeway Championship	Dottie Pepper (202)	82,500	C. Johnson (204)
Sept. 15	SAFECO Classic	Karrie Webb (277)	82,500	P. Sheehan (279)
Sept. 22	**The Solheim Cup** (Chepstow, Wales)	United States (17)	none	Europe (11)
Sept. 29	Fieldcrest Cannon Classic	Trish Johnson (270)	75,000	K. Saiki (273)

(See Updates Chapter for later results.)
Rain-shortened
***Playoffs** (5): **HealthSouth**— Webb won on the 4th hole; **Twelve Bridges**— Robbins won on the 5th hole; **Oldsmobile**— McGann won on the 3rd hole; **Edina Realty**— Neumann won on the 3rd hole; **State Farm**— McGann won on the 3rd hole
Second Place ties: (3 players or more): 3-WAY- **Nabisco Dinah Shore** (K. Robbins, M. Mallon, A. Sorenstam); **Edina Realty** (B. Burton, S. Strudwick, C. HJ Koch).

LPGA Majors

Dinah Shore

Edition: 25th **Dates:** March 28–31
Site: Mission Hills CC, Rancho Mirage, Calif.
Par: 36-36—72 (6446 yards) **Purse:** $900,000

	1 2 3 4 Tot	Earnings
1 Patty Sheehan	71-72-67-71—281	$135,000
2 Kelly Robbins	71-72-71-68—282	64,158
Meg Mallon	71-70-71-70—282	64,158
Annika Sorenstam	67-72-73-70—282	64,158
5 Amy Fruhwirth	71-73-68-71—283	32,305
Karrie Webb	72-70-70-71—283	32,305
Brandie Burton	75-67-68-73—283	32,305
8 Hollis Stacy	69-71-74-70—284	23,550
9 Kris Tschetter	71-74-70-70—285	21,285
10 Five-way tie		

Early round leaders: 1st— Sorenstam, Tracy Kerdyk (67); 2nd— Tracy Hanson (138); 3rd— Sheehan, Burton (210)
Top amateur: none

LPGA Championship

Edition: 42nd **Dates:** May 10–12
Site: Du Pont CC, Wilmington, Del.
Par: 35-36—71 (6386 yards) **Purse:** $1,200,000

	1 2 3 Tot	Earnings
1 Laura Davies	72-71-70—213	$180,000
2 Julie Piers	72-72-70—214	111,711
3 Penny Hamel	73-72-70—215	72,461
Jane Crafter	75-68-72—215	72,461
5 Judy Dickinson	71-74-71—216	37,800
Juli Inkster	70-73-73—216	37,800
Shirley Furlong	70-73-73—216	37,800
Val Skinner	73-69-74—216	37,800
Hiromi Kobayashi	71-70-75—216	37,800
10 Four-way tie		

Early round leaders: 1st—Catrin Nilsmark (67); 2nd— Kelly Robbins (140).
Top amateur: None.
Tournament was shortened to 54 holes due to rain.

U.S. Women's Open

Edition: 51st **Dates:** May 30–June 2
Site: Pine Needles Lodge & GC, Southern Pines, NC.
Par: 35-35—70 (6207 yards) **Purse:** $1,200,000

	1 2 3 4 Tot	Earnings
1 Annika Sorenstam	70-67-69-66—272	$212,500
2 Kris Tschetter	70-74-68-66—278	125,000
3 Pat Bradley	74-70-67-69—280	60,373
Jane Geddes	71-69-70-70—280	60,373
Brandie Burton	70-70-69-71—280	60,373
6 Laura Davies	74-68-70-69—281	40,077
7 Catrin Nilsmark	72-73-68-69—282	35,995
8 Cindy Rarick	73-70-72-68—283	29,584
Val Skinner	74-68-71-70—283	29,584
Liselotte Neumann	74-69-70-70—283	29,584
Tammie Green	72-70-69-72—283	29,584

Early round leaders: 1st— Kim Williams and Beth Daniel (69); 2nd—Sorenstam (137); 3rd—Sorenstam (206).
Top amateur: Cristie Kerr (291).

du Maurier Classic

Edition: 24th **Dates:** August 1–4
Site: Edmonton CC, Edmonton, Alberta, Canada
Par: 35–37—72 (6,324 yards) **Purse:** $1,000,000

	1 2 3 4 Tot	Earnings
1 Laura Davies	71–70-70-66—277	$150,000
2 Nancy Lopez	68-71-69-71—279	80,513
Karrie Webb	65-68-74-72—279	80,513
4 Meg Mallon	72-65-69-74—280	52,837
5 Pat Hurst	69-70-68-74—281	42,772
6 Liselotte Neumann	69-74-67-73—283	32,456
Annika Sorenstam	71-70-69-73—283	32,456
8 Kathy Postlewait	72-68-70-74—284	24,909
Dana Dormann	69-70-71-74—284	24,909
10 Amy Fruhwirth	70-71-71-73—285	20,128
Rosie Jones	70-71-68-76—285	20,128

Early round leaders: 1st— Webb (65); 2nd—Webb (133); 3rd— Mallon (206).
Top amateur: none.

1996 Solheim Cup

The fourth Solheim Cup Tournament, Sept. 20-22, at Marriott St. Pierre Hotel and CC in Chepstow, Wales.

ROSTERS

Selections for the 1996 United States team were determined by a special Solheim Cup points system that ranked players beginning with the 1994 Toray Japan Queens Cup through the Star Bank LPGA Classic ending on Aug. 25, 1996. The top ten players were joined by U.S. captain Judy Rankin's two selections, Brandie Burton and Beth Daniel.

The 1996 European squad was fielded via a points system that ended with the Compaq Open in Sweden ending Sept. 1. The top seven players in the points table were joined by five selections made by team captain Mickey Walker.

United States: Qualifiers— Pat Bradley, Jane Geddes, Rosie Jones, Betsy King, Meg Mallon, Michelle McGann, Dottie Pepper, Kelly Robbins, Patty Sheehan and Val Skinner; Captain's Selections— Brandie Burton and Beth Daniel.

Europe: Qualifiers— Laura Davies (England), Marie-Laure de Lorenzi (France), Lisa Hackney (England), Trish Johnson (England), Joanne Morley (England), Alison Nicholas (England) and Annika Sorenstam (Sweden); Captain's Selections— Helen Alfredsson (Sweden), Kathryn Marshall (Scotland), Liselotte Neumann (Sweden), Catrin Nilsmark (Sweden) and Dale Reid (Scotland).

First Day

Foursome Match Results

Winner	Score	Loser
Robbins/McGann	halved	Sorenstam/Nilsmark
Sheehan/Jones	1-up	Davies/Nicholas
Daniel/Skinner	1-up	de Lorenzi/Reid
Pepper/Burton	2&1	Alfredsson/Neumann

USA wins, 3½ to½

Four-Ball Match Results

Winner	Score	Loser
Davies/Johnson	6&5	Robbins/Bradley
Sorenstam/Marshall	1-up	Skinner/Geddes
Pepper/King	1-up	Neumann/Nilsmark
Mallon/Daniel	halved	Alfredsson/Nicholas

Europe wins, 2½ to 1½
(USA leads, 5-3)

Second Day

Foursome Match Results

Winner	Score	Loser
Davies/Johnson	4&3	Sheehan/Jones
Sorenstam/Nilsmark	1-up	Pepper/Burton
Mallon/Geddes	halved	Neumann/Marshall
de Lorenzi/Alfredsson	4&3	Robbins/McGann

Europe wins, 3½ to½
(Europe leads 6½-5½)

Four-Ball Match Results

Winner	Score	Loser
Davies/Hackney	6&5	Daniel/Skinner
McGann/Mallon	halved	Sorenstam/Johnson
Robbins/King	2&1	de Lorenzi/Morley
Nilsmark/Neumann	3&1	Sheehan/Geddes

Europe wins, 2½ to 1½
(Europe leads, 9-7)

Third Day

Single Match Results

Winner	Score	Loser
Annika Sorenstam	2&1	Pat Bradley
Val Skinner	2&1	Kathryn Marshall
Michelle McGann	3&2	Laura Davies
Beth Daniel	halved	Liselotte Neumann
Brandie Burton	1-up	Lisa Hackney
Dottie Pepper	3&2	Trish Johnson
Kelly Robbins	halved	Alison Nicholas
Betsy King	5&4	Marie Laure de Lorenzi
Rosie Jones	5&4	Joanne Morley
Jane Geddes	2-up	Dale Reid
Patty Sheehan	2&1	Catrin Nilsmark
Meg Mallon	4&2	Helen Alfredsson

USA wins day, 10-2

USA wins Solheim Cup, 17-11

Overall Records

Team and Individual match play combined

United States

	W-L-H	Pts
King	3-0-0	3
Pepper	3-1-0	3
Mallon	1-0-3	2½
Burton	2-1-0	2
Daniel	1-1-2	2
Jones	2-1-0	2
McGann	1-1-2	2
Robbins	1-2-2	2
Sheehan	2-2-0	2
Skinner	2-2-0	2
Geddes	1-2-1	1½
Bradley	0-2-0	0

Europe

	W-L-H	Pts
Sorenstam	3-0-2	4
Davies	3-2-0	3
Johnson	2-1-1	2½
Nilsmark	2-2-1	2½
Neumann	1-2-2	2
Alfredsson	1-2-1	1½
Marshall	1-1-1	1½
de Lorenzi	1-3-0	1
Nicholas	0-1-2	1
Hackney	1-1-0	1
Morley	0-2-0	0
Reid	0-2-0	0

Money Leaders

Official money leaders of PGA, European PGA, Senior PGA and LPGA tours for 1995 and unofficial money leaders for 1996 (through Sept. 29), as compiled by the PGA, European PGA and LPGA. All European amounts are in pound sterling (£).

PGA

Arnold Palmer Award standings: listed are tournaments played (TP); cuts made (CM); 1st, 2nd and 3rd place finishes; and earnings for the year.

Final 1995

	TP	CM	Finish 1-2-3	Earnings
1 Greg Norman	16	16	3-2-0	$1,654,959
2 Billy Mayfair	28	21	2-3-0	1,543,192
3 Lee Janzen	28	22	3-0-0	1,378,966
4 Corey Pavin	22	18	2-2-1	1,340,079
5 Steve Elkington	21	17	2-2-0	1,254,352
6 Davis Love III	24	22	1-1-1	1,111,999
7 Peter Jacobsen	25	22	2-2-1	1,075,057
8 Jim Gallagher Jr.	27	22	2-2-1	1,057,241
9 Vijay Singh	22	17	2-0-0	1,018,713
10 Mark O'Meara	27	22	2-0-0	914,129

1996 (through Sept. 29)

	TP	CM	Finish 1-2-3	Earnings
1 Phil Mickelson	21	17	4-1-1	$1,574,799
2 Mark Brooks	28	20	3-1-0	1,370,862
3 Tom Lehman	23	19	1-2-1	1,240,159
4 Mark O'Meara	22	18	2-2-2	1,196,949
5 Steve Stricker	23	18	2-1-3	1,176,739
6 Fred Couples	17	14	1-1-0	1,082,494
7 Davis Love III	22	17	1-2-0	959,739
8 Scott Hoch	25	21	1-2-3	958,924
9 David Duval	23	14	0-2-3	909,849
10 Greg Norman	17	11	1-1-0	891,237

EUROPEAN PGA

Volvo Order of Merit standings: listed are tournaments played (TP); cuts made (CM); 1st, 2nd and 3rd place finishes; and earnings for the year.

Final 1995

	TP	CM	Finish 1-2-3	Earnings
1 Colin Montgomerie	20	18	2-4-2	£835,051
2 Sam Torrance	26	23	3-4-1	755,706
3 Bernhard Langer	15	15	3-2-0	655,854
4 Costantino Rocca	24	24	0-5-1	516,320
5 Michael Campbell	21	18	0-2-2	400,977
6 Alexander Cejka	23	17	3-0-0	308,144
7 Mark James	26	22	1-1-0	297,377
8 Barry Lane	24	23	0-2-0	284,406
9 Anders Forsbrand	20	15	1-1-0	281,726
10 Peter O'Malley	21	19	1-0-0	260,726

1996 (through Sept. 29)

	TP	CM	Finish 1-2-3	Earnings
1 Colin Montgomerie	16	13	3-3-0	£684,646
2 Ian Woosnam	19	17	4-0-0	541,299
3 Robert Allenby	16	16	3-0-1	456,804
4 Costantino Rocca	20	15	1-2-1	414,352
5 Lee Westwood	31	22	1-0-1	333,306
6 Andrew Coltart	26	21	0-2-1	305,718
7 Mark McNulty	11	9	2-0-0	271,077
8 Padraig Harrington	26	19	1-0-1	247,094
9 Thomas Bjorn	25	15	1-0-0	246,605
10 Raymond Russell	24	18	1-0-2	245,580

SENIOR PGA

Final 1995

	TP	CM	Finish 1-2-3	Earnings
1 Jim Colbert	34	33	4-3-2	$1,444,386
2 Ray Floyd	21	21	3-7-1	1,419,545
3 Dave Stockton	34	33	2-6-3	1,415,847
4 Bob Murphy	28	28	4-3-3	1,241,524
5 Isao Aoki	23	23	1-4-2	1,041,766
6 J.C. Snead	28	28	2-3-2	978,137
7 Lee Trevino	29	29	2-3-1	943,993
8 Graham Marsh	27	27	1-1-2	849,350
9 Tom Wargo	33	33	1-2-2	844,687
10 Hale Irwin	12	12	2-3-0	799,175

1996 (through Sept. 29)

	TP	CM	Finish 1-2-3	Earnings
1 Hale Irwin	19	19	2-6-2	$1,441,594
2 Jim Colbert	26	26	4-4-0	1,245,395
3 Isao Aoki	24	23	2-4-1	1,089,231
4 John Bland	30	30	3-1-1	1,080,250
5 Bob Murphy	25	25	2-2-2	1,014,263
6 Ray Floyd	20	20	1-0-4	956,696
7 Graham Marsh	24	24	2-2-2	903,965
8 Dave Stockton	23	23	2-1-1	896,175
9 Walter Morgan	32	32	2-0-0	769,573
10 Jay Sigel	28	28	0-3-0	736,530

LPGA

Final 1995

	TP	CM	Finish 1-2-3	Earnings
1 Annika Sorenstam	19	19	3-3-1	$666,533
2 Laura Davies	17	16	2-3-1	530,349
3 Kelly Robbins	24	18	1-5-0	527,655
4 Dottie Mochrie	25	21	2-2-1	521,000
5 Betsy King	26	24	1-0-3	481,149
6 Beth Daniel	25	24	1-4-0	480,124
7 Michelle McGann	23	20	2-1-3	449,296
8 Meg Mallon	25	23	0-3-0	434,986
9 Val Skinner	26	24	1-0-1	430,248
10 Rosie Jones	26	23	1-1-1	426,957

1996 (through Sept. 29)

	TP	CM	Finish 1-2-3	Earnings
1 Laura Davies	16	16	4-1-1	$771,628
2 Karrie Webb	21	20	3-4-1	769,532
3 Annika Sorenstam	16	16	1-2-0	572,034
4 Dottie Pepper	20	18	4-1-1	546,047
5 Liselotte Neumann	20	19	2-2-1	542,527
6 Meg Mallon	21	20	2-1-3	495,522
7 Kelly Robbins	22	19	1-2-2	487,587
8 Michelle McGann	23	22	3-0-2	450,618
9 Emilee Klein	26	23	2-0-1	376,640
10 Val Skinner	23	22	0-1-1	376,116

1996 Tour Statistics (as of Oct. 6, 1996)

All-Around— Combined ranks in the other statistical categories; **Scoring Leaders**— The number is not a pure scoring average. It is adjusted to the average score of the field each week. If the field is under par, each player's score is adjusted upward a corresponding amount and vice versa if the field is above par. This keeps a player from receiving an advantage for playing easier-than-average courses. **Putting Leaders**— An average of the number of putts taken on greens hit in regulation. By using only greens hit in regulation, the stat no longer allows players who regularly miss greens to get up-and-down and then dominate the stat. **Eagle Leaders**— frequency that a player makes an eagle (every x number of holes). **Greens in Regulation**— A statistic based on number of greens reached in regulation out of total holes played. A hole is considered hit in regulation if any portion of the ball rest on the putting surface in two shots less than the par. A par five hit in two shots does not increase the statistic; it merely counts as one green hit in regulation. **Sand Saves**— a percentage of up-and-down efforts from greenside sand traps only. Fairway bunkers are not included. **Driving Distance**— Average computed by charting exact distances of two tee shots on the most open par four or five holes on both front and back nine. **Drive Accuracy**— Percentage of fairways hit on par four and five holes. Par threes are excluded. **Total Driving**— Drive distance rank + Drive Accuracy rank

PGA TOUR

Scoring Leaders

All-Around

		rank
1	Fred Couples	191
2	Mark Calcavecchia	248
3	Payne Stewart	281
4	David Duval	284
5	Davis Love, III	290
6	Tom Watson	308
7	Nick Faldo	322
8	Jesper Parnevik	327
9	Vijay Singh	329
10	Mark O'Meara	334
11	Michael Bradley	336
12	Jeff Maggert	338
13	Phil Mickelson	340
14	Larry Nelson	376
15	Glen Day	378
16	Tommy Tolles	391
17	Nick Price	402
18	Scott Hoch	418
19	Ernie Els	434
20	Larry Mize	436
21	Kenny Perry	437
22	Justin Leonard	453
23	John Huston	468
24	Jay Haas	476
	David Ogrin	476

Scoring Leaders

		Rnds	Avg
1	Tom Lehman	75	69.50
2	Mark O'Meara	76	69.63
3	Fred Couples	62	69.64
4	Corey Pavin	77	69.72
5	Nick Faldo	52	69.78
6	Davis Love, III	76	69.80
7	Tom Watson	50	69.81
8	Ernie Els	61	69.84
9	Scott Hoch	92	69.99
10	Brad Faxon	78	70.06

Top Tens

		Events	Top 10
1	Tom Lehman	23	12
2	Davis Love, III	24	11
3	Jeff Maggert	26	9
	Corey Pavin	22	9
5	Mark Brooks	30	8
	Fred Couples	18	8
	Brad Faxon	22	8
	Fred Funk	31	8
	Scott Hoch	27	8
	Phil Mickelson	22	8
	Mark O'Meara	22	8
	Kenny Perry	26	8
	Vijay Singh	25	8

Consecutive Cuts Made

		Cuts
1	Vijay Singh	26
2	Brad Faxon	21
3	Ernie Els	17
4	Phil Mickelson	14
5	Jeff Sluman	13
	Steve Stricker	13
7	Ronnie Black	12
8	David Ogrin	11
9	Ray Floyd	10
	Jim Furyk	10
	Tom Lehman	10
	Corey Pavin	10
	Chris Perry	10

Putting Leaders

		Putts
1	Brad Faxon	1.712
2	Mark O'Meara	1.736
3	Steve Stricker	1.742
4	Nick Faldo	1.743
5	Glen Day	1.744
6	Nolan Henke	1.746
7	Paul Azinger	1.747
	Lee Janzen	1.747
9	Gil Morgan	1.749
10	Payne Stewart	1.751

Eagle Leaders

		holes
1	Tom Watson	90.0
2	Davis Love III	114.0
3	Vijay Singh	119.1
4	Carl Paulson	120.5
5	Curt Byrum	126.0
6	Nick Price	133.7
7	Mark Calcavecchia	136.8
8	Fred Couples	139.5
9	John Adams	140.4
10	Omar Uresti	141.0

Greens in Regulation

		Pct
1	Fred Couples	73.0
2	Mark O'Meara	72.5
3	Jesper Parnevik	71.6
4	Mark Calcavecchia	71.3
5	Tom Lehman	70.9
6	David Duval	70.7
	Bob Tway	70.7
	Fuzzy Zoeller	70.7
9	Brad Bryant	70.6
10	John Cook	70.5

Tour Statistics (cont.)

Sand Saves

		Pct
1	Gary Rusnak	64.0
2	Greg Kraft	63.3
3	Glen Day	63.2
4	Jeff Sluman	62.8
5	Justin Leonard	62.1
6	Brad Faxon	61.7
	Wayne Grady	61.7
8	Jesper Parnevik	61.4
9	Jerry Kelly	61.2
10	David Frost	60.8

Birdies per Round Leaders

		Avg.
1	Fred Couples	4.27
2	Mark O'Meara	4.26
3	Brad Faxon	4.00
4	Jeff Maggert	3.98
5	David Duval	3.96
	Davis Love III	3.96
	Larry Nelson	3.96
8	Lee Janzen	3.93
9	Gil Morgan	3.92
10	Nick Faldo	3.90

Drive Accuracy

		Pct
1	Fred Funk	79.1
2	Nick Faldo	78.6
3	David Edwards	77.5
4	Tom Byrum	77.0
5	Fulton Allem	76.8
6	John Morse	76.7
7	Lennie Clements	76.2
	Nick Price	76.2
9	Jeff Hart	76.0
10	Olin Browne	75.9
	Ed Fiori	75.9

Driving Distance

		Yds
1	John Daly	288.8
2	John Adams	286.7
3	Fred Couples	285.9
4	Davis Love, III	285.8
5	Tim Herron	283.5
6	Steve Stricker	282.8
7	Kelly Gibson	280.8
8	Carl Paulson	280.4
9	Steve Jones	280.0
	Phil Mickelson	280.0
	Vijay Singh	280.0

Total Driving

		rank
1	David Duval	42
2	Nick Price	60
3	Kenny Perry	74
4	Mark Calcavecchia	78
	Davis Love, III	78
6	Tom Purtzer	96
7	Woody Austin	99
8	Keith Fergus	101
9	Craig Parry	104
10	Clarence Rose	105

SENIORS

All-Around

		Rank
1	Hale Irwin	75
2	Bob Murphy	84
3	Isao Aoki	108
4	Ray Floyd	119
5	John Bland	120
6	Vicente Fernandez	142
7	Brian Barnes	155
	Dave Stockton	155
9	Kermit Zarley	158
10	Graham Marsh	166
11	Jim Colbert	181
	Mike Hill	181
13	J.C. Snead	186
14	Lee Trevino	189
15	Jay Sigel	194
	Tom Weiskopf	194
17	Larry Gilbert	195
18	Walter Morgan	211
19	Bob Charles	228
20	Jim Dent	230

Scoring Leaders

		Rnds	Avg
1	Hale Irwin	64	69.47
2	Isao Aoki	74	69.95
3	Ray Floyd	67	70.01
4	Dave Stockton	81	70.23
5	Bob Murphy	84	70.31
6	Graham Marsh	78	70.36
7	John Bland	103	70.37
8	Jim Colbert	91	70.52
9	Jay Sigel	93	70.54
10	Vicente Fernandez	53	70.79

Putting Leaders

		Putts
1	Vicente Fernandez	1.743
2	Bob Murphy	1.750
3	Hale Irwin	1.758
4	Dave Stockton	1.765
5	Rocky Thompson	1.767
6	John Bland	1.769
7	Isao Aoki	1.770
	Jim Colbert	1.770
	Ray Floyd	1.770
	Jimmy Powell	1.770

Eagle Leaders

		Holes
1	Brian Barnes	124.0
2	David Graham	126.0
	Kermit Zarley	126.0
4	Lee Trevino	138.6
5	Tom Weiskopf	141.4
6	John Jacobs	145.5
7	Isao Aoki	148.0
8	Terry Dill	157.1
9	Mike Hill	183.6
10	John Bland	185.4

All Hail Hale

Senior Tour sophomore Hale Irwin had no second-year slump in 1996. As of Oct. 6, he was on top of the Senior money list with over $1.4 million in earnings. He also was leading the Senior circuit in three statistical categories: Birdies per round, Greens in regulation, and Scoring.

Greens in Regulations Leaders

		Avg
1	Hale Irwin	75.3
2	Brian Barnes	73.2
3	Graham Marsh	72.7
4	Ray Floyd	72.4
5	Jay Sigel	71.9
6	Isao Aoki	71.4
7	John Bland	71.3
8	Dave Stockton	70.1
9	Bob Murphy	69.7
	J.C. Snead	69.7

Sand Saves Leaders

		Pct
1	Tom Weiskopf	60.5
2	Bob Murphy	60.4
3	Ray Floyd	59.8
4	Jimmy Powell	57.6
5	Bob Dickson	57.5
6	Dave Stockton	57.0
7	Kermit Zarley	56.9
8	Vicente Fernandez	56.3
	Jerry Mcgee	56.3
10	Mike Mccullough	56.0

Birdies per Round Leaders

		Avg
1	Hale Irwin	4.06
2	Isao Aoki	3.97
3	Ray Floyd	3.88
4	Bob Murphy	3.86
5	Vicente Fernandez	3.85
6	Graham Marsh	3.78
7	Jay Sigel	3.74
8	Jim Dent	3.65
9	Jim Colbert	3.64
10	Dave Stockton	3.59

Driving Distance

		Yds
1	Terry Dill	287.0
2	John Jacobs	286.7
3	Jay Sigel	284.4
4	Jim Dent	279.2
5	Tom Weiskopf	278.4
6	David Graham	276.9
7	Dewitt Weaver	275.7
8	Brian Barnes	273.3
9	Jim Wilkinson	272.6
10	Bruce Summerhays	272.4

Driving Accuracy

		Stat
1	Calvin Peete	79.8
2	Hale Irwin	79.3
3	Deane Beman	78.8
4	John Bland	77.7
	Graham Marsh	77.7
	Bob Murphy	77.7
7	Bud Allin	77.3
8	Bob E. Smith	77.1
9	Isao Aoki	77.0
10	Bruce Crampton	76.4

Total Driving

		Stat
1	Brian Barnes	25
2	Graham Marsh	27
3	J.C. Snead	33
4	Isao Aoki	46
	Hale Irwin	46
	Walter Morgan	46
7	Jack Kiefer	48
8	Bob Murphy	51
	Jay Sigel	51
10	Ray Floyd	52

EUROPEAN

Scoring Leaders

		Avg
1	Colin Montgomerie (Scotland)	70.08
2	Mark McNulty (Zimbabwe)	70.24
3	Costantino Rocca (Italy)	70.68
4	Bernhard Langer (Germany)	70.80
5	Ian Woosnam (Wales)	70.90
6	Andrew Coltart (Scotland)	71.08
7	Robert Allenby (Australia)	71.10
8	Paul Broadhurst (England)	71.14
9	Paul McGinley (Ireland)	71.15
10	Alexander Cejka (Germany)	71.18
11	Miguel A. Jimenez (Spain)	71.23
12	Francisco Cea (Spain)	71.24
13	Jean van de Velde (France)	71.27
14	Padraig Harrington (Ireland)	71.32
15	Peter Mitchell (England)	71.38
	Darren Clarke (No. Ireland)	71.38
	Lee Westwood (England)	71.38
18	Frank Nobilo (New Zealand)	71.39
19	Greg Turner (New Zealand)	71.41
20	Miguel A. Martin (Spain)	71.44

Eagle Leaders

		No
1	Thomas Bjorn (Denmark)	19
2	Roger Chapman (England)	14
3	Ignacio Garrido (Spain)	13
4	Ian Woosnam (Wales)	12
	Paul Broadhurst (England)	12
	Colin Montgomerie (Scotland)	12
7	Derrick Cooper (England)	11
	Peter Mitchell (England)	11
	Peter Baker (England)	11
	Miguel Angel Martin (Spain)	11
	Santiago Luna (Spain)	11

Birdie Leaders

		No
1	Lee Westwood (England)	366
2	Paul Broadhurst (England)	365
3	Andrew Coltart (Scotland)	355
4	Paul McGinley (Ireland)	338
5	Peter Mitchell (England)	335
6	Padraig Harrington (Ireland)	321
7	David Carter (England)	308
8	Gary Orr (Scotland)	303
9	Peter Baker (England)	302
	Stuart Cage (England)	302

Tour Statistics (cont.)

LPGA

Scoring Average (Vare Trophy)

1	Laura Davies	70.38
2	Annika Sorenstam	70.48
3	Liselotte Neumann	70.84
4	Karrie Webb	70.89
5	Meg Mallon	71.30
6	Dottie Pepper	71.35
7	Patty Sheehan	71.47
8	Michelle McGann	71.51
9	Kelly Robbins	71.54
10	Kris Tschetter	71.60

Driving Accuracy

		Pct
1	Rosie Jones	82.4
2	Marta Figueras-Dotti	81.6
3	Nancy Ramsbottom	81.2
4	Jody Anschutz	80.6
5	Amy Fruhwirth	80.5
6	Tracy Kerdyk	80.2
7	Emilee Klein	79.4
8	Tina Barrett	79.1
9	Leta Lindley	78.3
10	Penny Hammel	78.2

Driving Distance

		Yds
1	Laura Davies	262.3
2	Michelle McGann	255.8
3	Jean Bartholomew	255.6
4	Kelly Robbins	254.7
5	Jane Geddes	253.5
6	Tania Abitbol	249.9
	Karrie Webb	249.9
8	Beth Daniel	249.6
9	Annette DeLuca	249.3
10	Helen Alfredsson	249.0

Total Eagles

		No
1	Laura Davies	12
2	Kelly Robbins	8
	Jean Zedlitz	8
4	Vicki Fergon	7
	Barb Mucha	7
6	Helen Alfredsson	6
	Tracy Hanson	6
	Catrin Nilsmark	6
	Cindy Schreyer	6
10	14 tied with 5 each	

Top 10s

		Events	Top 10
1	Karrie Webb	23	14
2	Annika Sorenstam	19	13
3	Liselotte Neumann	22	12
4	Laura Davies	17	11
	Dottie Pepper	22	11
6	Jane Geddes	25	10
	Kelly Robbins	24	10
8	Rosie Jones	24	9
	Meg Mallon	23	9
10	Four tied with 8 each		

Greens In Regulation

		Pct
1	Kelly Robbins	73.2
2	Annika Sorenstam	72.0
3	Karrie Webb	71.6
4	Marianne Morris	70.8
	Donna Andrews	70.8
6	Beth Daniel	70.5
7	Meg Mallon	70.3
8	Nancy Lopez	70.1
9	Michelle McGann	69.9
10	Laura Davies	69.4

Putting Average

		Per round
1	Liselotte Neumann	29.23
2	Dottie Pepper	29.27
3	Cindy Schreyer	29.38
4	Danielle Ammaccapane	29.45
5	Brandie Burton	29.50
6	Barb Whitehead	29.65
7	Carolyn Hill	29.68
8	Jennifer Wyatt	29.70
9	Jenny Lidback	29.72
10	Tammie Green	29.74

Rounds Under Par/Number of Rounds

1	Karrie Webb	46/82
2	Liselotte Neumann	45/80
3	Meg Mallon	43/77
4	Laura Davies	42/61
	Barb Mucha	42/91
6	Dottie Pepper	41/72
	Annika Sorenstam	41/71
8	Tracy Kerdyk	40/93
	Emilee Klein	40/94
	Kelly Robbins	40/78
	Val Skinner	40/92

Sand Saves

		Pct
1	Caroline Pierce	56.7
2	Danielle Ammaccapane	56.1
3	Carolyn Hill	53.4
4	Jennifer Wyatt	53.1
5	Martha Nause	52.7
6	Missie McGeorge	51.9
7	Alice Miller	51.7
8	Patti Liscio	51.5
9	Hollis Stacy	50.7
10	Barb Whitehead	50.5

Total Birdies

		Birds
1	Michelle McGann	309
2	Liselotte Neumann	304
3	Karrie Webb	297
4	Val Skinner	294
5	Brandie Burton	289
6	Kris Tschetter	287
7	Barb Mucha	280
8	Marianne Morris	272
9	Tracy Kerdyk	270
10	Kelly Robbins	269

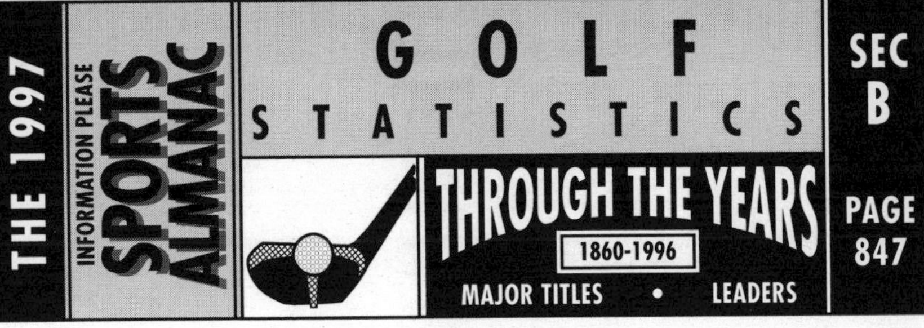

THE 1997
INFORMATION PLEASE
SPORTS ALMANAC
GOLF
STATISTICS
THROUGH THE YEARS
1860-1996
MAJOR TITLES • LEADERS
SEC B
PAGE 847

Major Championships

MEN

The Masters

The Masters has been played every year since 1934 at the Augusta National Golf Club in Augusta, Ga. Both the course (6905 yards, par 72) and the tournament were created by Bobby Jones; (*) indicates playoff winner.

Multiple winners: Jack Nicklaus (6); Arnold Palmer (4); Jimmy Demaret, Nick Faldo, Gary Player and Sam Snead (3); Seve Ballesteros, Ben Crenshaw, Ben Hogan, Bernhard Langer, Byron Nelson, Horton Smith and Tom Watson (2).

Year	Winner	Score	Runner-up
1934	Horton Smith	284	Craig Wood (285)
1935	Gene Sarazen*	282	Craig Wood (282)
1936	Horton Smith	285	Harry Cooper (286)
1937	Byron Nelson	283	Ralph Guldahl (285)
1938	Henry Picard	285	Ralph Guldahl & Harry Cooper (287)
1939	Ralph Guldahl	279	Sam Snead (280)
1940	Jimmy Demaret	280	Lloyd Mangrum (284)
1941	Craig Wood	280	Byron Nelson (283)
1942	Byron Nelson*	280	Ben Hogan (280)
1943-45	Not held		World War II
1946	Herman Keiser	282	Ben Hogan (283)
1947	Jimmy Demaret	281	Frank Stranahan & Byron Nelson (283)
1948	Claude Harmon	279	Cary Middlecoff (284)
1949	Sam Snead	282	Lloyd Mangrum & Johnny Bulla (285)
1950	Jimmy Demaret	283	Jim Ferrier (285)
1951	Ben Hogan	280	Skee Riegel (282)
1952	Sam Snead	286	Jack Burke Jr. (290)
1953	Ben Hogan	274	Ed Oliver (279)
1954	Sam Snead*	289	Ben Hogan (289)
1955	Cary Middlecoff	279	Ben Hogan (286)
1956	Jack Burke Jr.	289	Ken Venturi (290)
1957	Doug Ford	283	Sam Snead (286)
1958	Arnold Palmer	284	Doug Ford, & Fred Hawkins (285)
1959	Art Wall Jr.	284	Cary Middlecoff (285)
1960	Arnold Palmer	282	Ken Venturi (283)
1961	Gary Player	280	Arnold Palmer & Charles R. Coe (281)
1962	Arnold Palmer*	280	Dow Finsterwald & Gary Player (280)
1963	Jack Nicklaus	286	Tony Lema (287)
1964	Arnold Palmer	276	Jack Nicklaus & Dave Marr (282)
1965	Jack Nicklaus	271	Arnold Palmer & Gary Player (280)
1966	Jack Nicklaus*	288	Gay Brewer Jr. & Tommy Jacobs (288)
1967	Gay Brewer Jr.	280	Bobby Nichols (281)
1968	Bob Goalby	277	Roberto DeVicenzo (278)
1969	George Archer	281	Billy Casper, George Knudson & Tom Weiskopf (282)
1970	Billy Casper*	279	Gene Littler (279)
1971	Charles Coody	279	Jack Nicklaus & Johnny Miller (281)
1972	Jack Nicklaus	286	Bruce Crampton, Bobby Mitchell & Tom Weiskopf (289)
1973	Tommy Aaron	283	J.C. Snead (284)
1974	Gary Player	278	Tom Weiskopf, & Dave Stockton (280)
1975	Jack Nicklaus	276	Johnny Miller & Tom Weiskopf (277)
1976	Ray Floyd	271	Ben Crenshaw (279)
1977	Tom Watson	276	Jack Nicklaus (278)
1978	Gary Player	277	Hubert Green, Rod Funseth & Tom Watson (278)
1979	Fuzzy Zoeller*	280	Ed Sneed & Tom Watson (280)
1980	Seve Ballesteros	275	Gibby Gilbert & Jack Newton (279)
1981	Tom Watson	280	Jack Nicklaus & Johnny Miller (282)
1982	Craig Stadler*	284	Dan Pohl (284)
1983	Seve Ballesteros	280	Ben Crenshaw, & Tom Kite (284)
1984	Ben Crenshaw	277	Tom Watson (279)
1985	Bernhard Langer	282	Curtis Strange, Seve Ballesteros & Ray Floyd (284)
1986	Jack Nicklaus	279	Greg Norman (280)
1987	Larry Mize*	285	Seve Ballesteros & Greg Norman (285)
1988	Sandy Lyle	281	Mark Calcavecchia (282)
1989	Nick Faldo*	283	Scott Hoch (283)
1990	Nick Faldo*	278	Ray Floyd (278)
1991	Ian Woosnam	277	J.M. Olazabal (278)
1992	Fred Couples	275	Ray Floyd (277)
1993	Bernhard Langer	277	Chip Beck (281)
1994	J.M. Olazabal	279	Tom Lehman (281)
1995	Ben Crenshaw	274	Davis Love III (275)
1996	Nick Faldo	276	Greg Norman (281)

Major Championships (Cont.)

The Masters

*PLAYOFFS

1935: Gene Sarazen (144) def. Craig Wood (149) in 36 holes. **1942:** Byron Nelson (69) def. Ben Hogan (70) in 18 holes. **1954:** Sam Snead (70) def. Ben Hogan (71) in 18 holes. **1962:** Arnold Palmer (68) def. Gary Player (71) and Dow Finsterwald (77) in 18 holes. **1966:** Jack Nicklaus (70) def. Tommy Jacobs (72) and Gay Brewer (78) in 18 holes. **1970:** Billy Casper (69) def. Gene Littler (74) in 18 holes. **1979:** Fuzzy Zoeller (4-3) def. Ed Sneed (4-4) and Tom Watson (4-4) on 2nd hole of sudden death. **1982:** Craig Stadler (4) def. Dan Pohl (5) on 1st hole of sudden death. **1987:** Larry Mize (4-3) def. Greg Norman (4-4) and Seve Ballesteros (5) on 2nd hole of sudden death. **1989:** Nick Faldo (5-3) def. Scott Hoch (5-4) on 2nd hole of sudden death. **1990:** Nick Faldo (4-4) def. Raymond Floyd (4-x) on second hole of sudden death.

U.S. Open

Played at a different course each year, the U.S. Open was launched by the new U.S. Golf Association in 1895. The Open was a 36-hole event from 1895-97 and has been 72 holes since then. It switched from a 3-day, 36-hole Saturday finish to 4 days of play in 1965. Note that (*) indicates playoff winner and (a) indicates amateur winner.

Multiple winners: Willie Anderson, Ben Hogan, Bobby Jones and Jack Nicklaus (4); Hale Irwin (3); Julius Boros, Billy Casper, Ralph Guldahl, Walter Hagen, John McDermott, Cary Middlecoff, Andy North, Gene Sarazen, Alex Smith, Curtis Strange and Lee Trevino (2).

Year	Winner	Score	Runner-up	Course	Location
1895	Horace Rawlins	173	Willie Dunn (175)	Newport GC	Newport, R.I.
1896	James Foulis	152	Horace Rawlins (155)	Shinnecock Hills GC	Southampton, N.Y.
1897	Joe Lloyd	162	Willie Anderson (163)	Chicago GC	Wheaton, Ill.
1898	Fred Herd	328	Alex Smith (335)	Myopia Hunt Club	Hamilton, Mass.
1899	Willie Smith	315	George Low, W.H. Way & Val Fitzjohn (326)	Baltimore CC	Baltimore
1900	Harry Vardon	313	J.H. Taylor (315)	Chicago GC	Wheaton, Ill.
1901	Willie Anderson*	331	Alex Smith (331)	Myopia Hunt Club	Hamilton, Mass.
1902	Laurie Auchterlonie	307	Stewart Gardner (313)	Garden City GC	Garden City, N.Y.
1903	Willie Anderson*	307	David Brown (307)	Baltusrol GC	Springfield, N.J.
1904	Willie Anderson	303	Gil Nicholls (308)	Glen View Club	Golf, Ill.
1905	Willie Anderson	314	Alex Smith (316)	Myopia Hunt Club	Hamilton, Mass.
1906	Alex Smith	295	Willie Smith (302)	Onwentsia Club	Lake Forest, Ill.
1907	Alec Ross	302	Gil Nicholls (304)	Phila. Cricket Club	Chestnut Hill, Pa.
1908	Fred McLeod*	322	Willie Smith (322)	Myopia Hunt Club	Hamilton, Mass.
1909	George Sargent	290	Tom McNamara (294)	Englewood GC	Englewood, N.J.
1910	Alex Smith*	298	Macdonald Smith & John McDermott (298)	Phila. Cricket Club	Chestnut Hill, Pa.
1911	John McDermott*	307	George Simpson & Mike Brady (307)	Chicago GC	Wheaton, Ill.
1912	John McDermott	294	Tom McNamara (296)	CC of Buffalo	Buffalo
1913	a-Francis Ouimet*	304	Harry Vardon & Ted Ray (304)	The Country Club	Brookline, Mass.
1914	Walter Hagen	290	a-Chick Evans (291)	Midlothian CC	Blue Island, Ill.
1915	a-John Travers	297	Tom McNamara (298)	Baltusrol GC	Springfield, N.J.
1916	a-Chick Evans	286	Jock Hutchinson (288)	Minikahda Club	Minneapolis
1917-18	Not held		World War I		
1919	Walter Hagen*	301	Mike Brady (301)	Brae Burn CC	West Newton, Mass.
1920	Ted Ray	295	Jock Hutchison, Jack Burke, Leo Diegel & Harry Vardon (296)	Inverness Club	Toledo, Ohio
1921	Jim Barnes	289	Walter Hagen & Fred McLeod (298)	Columbia CC	Chevy Chase, Md.
1922	Gene Sarazen	288	a-Bobby Jones & John Black (289)	Skokie CC	Glencoe, Ill.
1923	a-Bobby Jones*	296	Bobby Cruickshank (296)	Inwood CC	Far Rockaway, N.Y.
1924	Cyril Walker	297	a-Bobby Jones (300)	Oakland Hills CC	Birmingham, Mich.
1925	Willie Macfarlane*	291	a-Bobby Jones (291)	Worcester CC	Worcester, Mass.
1926	a-Bobby Jones	293	Joe Turnesa (294)	Scioto CC	Columbus, Ohio
1927	Tommy Armour*	301	Harry Cooper (301)	Oakmont CC	Oakmont, Pa.
1928	Johnny Farrell*	294	a-Bobby Jones (294)	Olympia Fields CC	Matteson, Ill.
1929	a-Bobby Jones*	294	Al Espinosa (294)	Winged Foot CC	Mamaroneck, N.Y.
1930	a-Bobby Jones	287	Macdonald Smith (289)	Interlachen CC	Hopkins, Minn.
1931	Billy Burke*	292	George Von Elm (292)	Inverness Club	Toledo, Ohio
1932	Gene Sarazen	286	Bobby Cruickshank & Phil Perkins (289)	Fresh Meadow CC	Flushing, N.Y.
1933	a-Johnny Goodman	287	Ralph Guldahl (288)	North Shore GC	Glenview, Ill.
1934	Olin Dutra	293	Gene Sarazen (294)	Merion Cricket Club	Ardmore, Pa.
1935	Sam Parks Jr.	299	Jimmy Thomson (301)	Oakmont CC	Oakmont, Pa.

Year	Winner	Score	Runner-up	Course	Location
1936	Tony Manero	282	Harry E. Cooper (284)	Baltusrol GC	Springfield, N.J.
1937	Ralph Guldahl	281	Sam Snead (283)	Oakland Hills CC	Birmingham, Mich.
1938	Ralph Guldahl	284	Dick Metz (290)	Cherry Hills CC	Denver
1939	Byron Nelson*	284	Craig Wood & Denny Shute (284)	Philadelphia CC	Philadelphia
1940	Lawson Little*	287	Gene Sarazen (287)	Canterbury GC	Cleveland
1941	Craig Wood	284	Denny Shute (287)	Colonial Club	Ft. Worth
1942-45	Not held		World War II		
1946	Lloyd Mangrum*	284	Byron Nelson & Vic Ghezzi (284)	Canterbury GC	Cleveland
1947	Lew Worsham*	282	Sam Snead (282)	St. Louis CC	Clayton, Mo.
1948	Ben Hogan	276	Jimmy Demaret (278)	Riviera CC	Los Angeles
1949	Cary Middlecoff	286	Clayton Heafner & Sam Snead (287)	Medinah CC	Medinah, Ill.
1950	Ben Hogan*	287	Lloyd Mangrum & George Fazio (287)	Merion Golf Club	Ardmore, Pa.
1951	Ben Hogan	287	Clayton Heafner (289)	Oakland Hills CC	Birmingham, Mich.
1952	Julius Boros	281	Ed Oliver (285)	Northwood Club	Dallas
1953	Ben Hogan	283	Sam Snead (289)	Oakmont CC	Oakmont, Pa.
1954	Ed Furgol	284	Gene Littler (285)	Baltusrol GC	Springfield, N.J.
1955	Jack Fleck*	287	Ben Hogan (287)	Olympic CC	San Francisco
1956	Cary Middlecoff	281	Ben Hogan & Julius Boros (282)	Oak Hill CC	Rochester, N.Y.
1957	Dick Mayer*	282	Cary Middlecoff (282)	Inverness Club	Toledo, Ohio
1958	Tommy Bolt	283	Gary Player (287)	Southern Hills CC	Tulsa
1959	Billy Casper	282	Bob Rosburg (283)	Winged Foot GC	Marmaroneck, N.Y.
1960	Arnold Palmer	280	Jack Nicklaus (282)	Cherry Hills CC	Denver
1961	Gene Littler	281	Doug Sanders & Bob Goalby (282)	Oakland Hills CC	Birmingham, Mich.
1962	Jack Nicklaus*	283	Arnold Palmer (283)	Oakmont CC	Oakmont, Pa.
1963	Julius Boros*	293	Arnold Palmer & Jacky Cupit (293)	The Country Club	Brookline, Mass.
1964	Ken Venturi	278	Tommy Jacobs (282)	Congressional CC	Bethesda, Md.
1965	Gary Player*	282	Kel Nagle (282)	Bellerive CC	St. Louis
1966	Billy Casper*	278	Arnold Palmer (278)	Olympic CC	San Francisco
1967	Jack Nicklaus	275	Arnold Palmer (279)	Baltusrol GC	Springfield, N.J.
1968	Lee Trevino	275	Jack Nicklaus (279)	Oak Hill CC	Rochester, N.Y.
1969	Orville Moody	281	Al Geiberger, Deane Beman & Bob Rosburg (282)	Champions GC	Houston
1970	Tony Jacklin	281	Dave Hill (288)	Hazeltine National GC	Chaska, Minn.
1971	Lee Trevino*	280	Jack Nicklaus (280)	Merion GC	Ardmore, Pa.
1972	Jack Nicklaus	290	Bruce Crampton (293)	Pebble Beach GL	Pebble Beach, Calif.
1973	Johnny Miller	279	John Schlee (280)	Oakmont CC	Oakmont, Pa.
1974	Hale Irwin	287	Forest Fezler (289)	Winged Foot GC	Mamaroneck, N.Y.
1975	Lou Graham*	287	John Mahaffey (287)	Medinah CC	Medinah, Ill.
1976	Jerry Pate	277	Al Geiberger & Tom Weiskopf (279)	Atlanta AC	Duluth, Ga.
1977	Hubert Green	278	Lou Graham (279)	Southern Hills CC	Tulsa
1978	Andy North	285	Dave Stockton & J.C. Snead (286)	Cherry Hills CC	Denver
1979	Hale Irwin	284	Gary Player & Jerry Pate (286)	Inverness Club	Toledo, Ohio
1980	Jack Nicklaus	272	Isao Aoki (274)	Baltusrol GC	Springfield, N.J.
1981	David Graham	273	George Burns & Bill Rogers (276)	Merion GC	Ardmore, Pa.
1982	Tom Watson	282	Jack Nicklaus (284)	Pebble Beach GL	Pebble Beach, Calif.
1983	Larry Nelson	280	Tom Watson (281)	Oakmont CC	Oakmont, Pa.
1984	Fuzzy Zoeller*	276	Greg Norman (276)	Winged Foot GC	Mamaroneck, N.Y.
1985	Andy North	279	Dave Barr, T.C. Chen & Denis Watson (280)	Oakland Hills CC	Birmingham, Mich.
1986	Ray Floyd	279	Lanny Wadkins & Chip Beck (281)	Shinnecock Hills GC	Southampton, N.Y.
1987	Scott Simpson	277	Tom Watson (278)	Olympic Club	San Francisco
1988	Curtis Strange*	278	Nick Faldo (278)	The Country Club	Brookline, Mass.
1989	Curtis Strange	278	Chip Beck, Ian Woosnam & Mark McCumber (279)	Oak Hill CC	Rochester, N.Y.

Major Championships (Cont.)

U.S. Open

Year	Winner	Score	Runner-up	Course	Location
1990	Hale Irwin*	280	Mike Donald (280)	Medinah CC	Medinah, Ill.
1991	Payne Stewart*	282	Scott Simpson (282)	Hazeline National GC	Chaska, Minn.
1992	Tom Kite	285	Jeff Sluman (287)	Pebble Beach GL	Pebble Beach, Calif.
1993	Lee Janzen	272	Payne Stewart (274)	Baltusrol GC	Springfield, N.J.
1994	Ernie Els*	279	Colin Montgomerie (279) & Loren Roberts (279)	Oakmont CC	Oakmont, Pa.
1995	Corey Pavin	280	Greg Norman (282)	Shinnecock Hills GC	Southampton, N.Y.
1996	Steve Jones	278	Davis Love III (279) & Tom Lehman (279)	Oakland Hills CC	Bloomfield Hills, Mich.

***PLAYOFFS**

1901: Willie Anderson (85) def. Alex Smith (86) in 18 holes. **1903:** Willie Anderson (82) def. David Brown (84) in 18 holes. **1908:** Fred McLeod (77) def. Willie Smith (83) in 18 holes. **1910:** Alex Smith (71) def. John McDermott (75) and Macdonald Smith (77) in 18 holes. **1911:** John McDermott (80) def. Mike Brady (82) and George Simpson (85) in 18 holes. **1913:** Francis Ouimet (72) def. Harry Vardon (77) and Ted Ray (78) in 18 holes. **1919:** Walter Hagen (77) def. Mike Brady (78) in 18 holes. **1923:** Bobby Jones (76) def. Bobby Cruickshank (78) in 18 holes. **1925:** Willie Macfarlane (75-72—147) def. Bobby Jones (75-73—148) in 36 holes. **1927:** Tommy Armour (76) def. Harry Cooper (79) in 18 holes. **1928:** Johnny Farrell (70-73—143) def. Bobby Jones (73-71—144) in 36 holes. **1929:** Bobby Jones (141) def. Al Espinosa (164) in 36 holes. **1931:** Billy Burke (149-148) def. George Von Elm (149-149) in 72 holes. **1939:** Byron Nelson (68-70) def. Craig Wood (68-73) and Denny Shute (76) in 36 holes. **1940:** Lawson Little (70) def. Gene Sarazen (73) in 18 holes. **1946:** Lloyd Mangrum (72-72—144) def. Byron Nelson (72-73—145) and Vic Ghezzi (72-73—145) in 36 holes. **1947:** Lew Worsham (69) def. Sam Snead (70) in 18 holes. **1950:** Ben Hogan (69) def. Lloyd Mangrum (73) and George Fazio (75) in 18 holes. **1955:** Jack Fleck (69) def. Ben Hogan (72) in 18 holes. **1957:** Dick Mayer (72) def. Cary Middlecoff (79) in 18 holes. **1962:** Jack Nicklaus (71) def. Arnold Palmer (74) in 18 holes. **1963:** Julius Boros (70) def. Jacky Cupit (73) and Arnold Palmer (76) in 18 holes. **1965:** Gary Player (71) def. Kel Nagle (74) in 18 holes. **1966:** Billy Casper (69) def. Arnold Palmer (73) in 18 holes. **1971:** Lee Trevino (68) def. Jack Nicklaus (71) in 18 holes. **1975:** Lou Graham (71) def. John Mahaffey (73) in 18 holes. **1984:** Fuzzy Zoeller (67) def. Greg Norman (75) in 18 holes. **1988:** Curtis Strange (71) def. Nick Faldo (75) in 18 holes. **1990:** Hale Irwin (74-3) def. Mike Donald (74-4) on 1st hole of sudden death after 18 holes. **1991:** Payne Stewart (75) def. Scott Simpson (77) in 18 holes. **1994:** Ernie Els (74-4-4) def. Loren Roberts (74-4-5) and Colin Montgomerie (78-x-x) on 2nd hole of sudden death after 18 holes.

British Open

The oldest of the Majors, The Open began in 1860 to determine "the champion golfer of the world." While only professional golfers participated in the first year of the tournament, amateurs have been invited ever since. Competition was extended from 36 to 72 holes in 1892. Conducted by the Royal and Ancient Golf Club of St. Andrews, The Open is rotated among select golf courses in England and Scotland. Note that (*) indicates playoff winner and (a) indicates amateur winner.

Multiple winners: Harry Vardon (6); James Braid, J.H. Taylor, Peter Thomson and Tom Watson (5); Walter Hagen, Bobby Locke, Tom Morris Sr., Tom Morris Jr., and Willie Park (4); Jamie Anderson, Seve Ballesteros, Henry Cotton, Nick Faldo, Robert Ferguson, Bobby Jones, Jack Nicklaus and Gary Player (3); Harold Hilton, Bob Martin, Greg Norman, Arnold Palmer, Willie Park Jr., and Lee Trevino (2).

Year	Winner	Score	Runner-up	Course	Location
1860	Willie Park	174	Tom Morris Sr. (176)	Prestwick Club	Ayrshire, Scotland
1861	Tom Morris Sr.	163	Willie Park (167)	Prestwick Club	Ayrshire, Scotland
1862	Tom Morris Sr.	163	Willie Park (176)	Prestwick Club	Ayrshire, Scotland
1863	Willie Park	168	Tom Morris Sr. (170)	Prestwick Club	Ayrshire, Scotland
1864	Tom Morris Sr.	167	Andrew Strath (169)	Prestwick Club	Ayrshire, Scotland
1865	Andrew Strath	162	Willie Park (164)	Prestwick Club	Ayrshire, Scotland
1866	Willie Park	169	David Park (171)	Prestwick Club	Ayrshire, Scotland
1867	Tom Morris Sr.	170	Willie Park (172)	Prestwick Club	Ayrshire, Scotland
1868	Tom Morris Jr.	157	Robert Andrew (159)	Prestwick Club	Ayrshire, Scotland
1869	Tom Morris Jr.	154	Tom Morris Sr. (157)	Prestwick Club	Ayrshire, Scotland
1870	Tom Morris Jr.	149	Bob Kirk (161)	Prestwick Club	Ayrshire, Scotland
1871	Not held				
1872	Tom Morris Jr.	166	David Strath (169)	Prestwick Club	Ayrshire, Scotland
1873	Tom Kidd	179	Jamie Anderson (180)	St. Andrews	St. Andrews, Scotland
1874	Mungo Park	159	Tom Morris Jr. (161)	Musselburgh	Musselburgh, Scotland
1875	Willie Park	166	Bob Martin (168)	Prestwick Club	Ayrshire, Scotland
1876	Bob Martin*	176	David Strath (176)	St. Andrews	St. Andrews, Scotland
1877	Jamie Anderson	160	Bob Pringle (162)	Musselburgh	Musselburgh, Scotland
1878	Jamie Anderson	157	Bob Kirk (159)	Prestwick Club	Ayrshire, Scotland
1879	Jamie Anderson	169	Andrew Kirkaldy & James Allan (172)	St. Andrews	St. Andrews, Scotland
1880	Bob Ferguson	162	Peter Paxton (167)	Musselburgh	Musselburgh, Scotland
1881	Bob Ferguson	170	Jamie Anderson (173)	Prestwick Club	Ayrshire, Scotland
1882	Bob Ferguson	171	Willie Fernie (174)	St. Andrews	St. Andrews, Scotland
1883	Willie Fernie*	159	Bob Ferguson (159)	Musselburgh	Musselburgh, Scotland
1884	Jack Simpson	160	David Rollan & Willie Fernie (164)	Prestwick Club	Ayrshire, Scotland

Year	Winner	Score	Runner-up	Course	Location
1885	Bob Martin	171	Archie Simpson (172)	St. Andrews	St. Andrews, Scotland
1886	David Brown	157	Willie Campbell (159)	Musselburgh	Musselburgh, Scotland
1887	Willie Park Jr.	161	Bob Martin (162)	Prestwick Club	Ayrshire, Scotland
1888	Jack Burns	171	David Anderson & Ben Sayers (172)	St. Andrews	St. Andrews, Scotland
1889	Willie Park Jr.*	155	Andrew Kirkaldy (155)	Musselburgh	Musselburgh, Scotland
1890	a-John Ball	164	Willie Fernie (167) & A. Simpson (167)	Prestwick Club	Ayrshire, Scotland
1891	Hugh Kirkaldy	166	Andrew Kirkaldy & Willie Fernie (168)	St. Andrews	St. Andrews, Scotland
1892	a-Harold Hilton	305	John Ball, Sandy Herd & Hugh Kirkaldy (308)	Muirfield	Gullane, Scotland
1893	Willie Auchterlonie	322	Johnny Laidlay (324)	Prestwick Club	Ayrshire, Scotland
1894	J.H. Taylor	326	Douglas Rolland (331)	Royal St. George's	Sandwich, England
1895	J.H. Taylor	322	Sandy Herd (326)	St. Andrews	St. Andrews, Scotland
1896	Harry Vardon*	316	J.H. Taylor (316)	Muirfield	Gullane, Scotland
1897	a-Harold Hilton	314	James Braid (315)	Hoylake	Hoylake, England
1898	Harry Vardon	307	Willie Park Jr. (308)	Prestwick Club	Ayrshire, Scotland
1899	Harry Vardon	310	Jack White (315)	Royal St. George's	Sandwich, England
1900	J.H. Taylor	309	Harry Vardon (317)	St. Andrews	St. Andrews, Scotland
1901	James Braid	309	Harry Vardon (312)	Muirfield	Gullane, Scotland
1902	Sandy Herd	307	Harry Vardon (308)	Hoylake	Hoylake, England
1903	Harry Vardon	300	Tom Vardon (306)	Prestwick Club	Ayrshire, Scotland
1904	Jack White	296	James Braid (297)	Royal St. George's	Sandwich, England
1905	James Braid	318	J.H. Taylor (323) & Rolland Jones (323)	St. Andrews	St. Andrews, Scotland
1906	James Braid	300	J.H. Taylor (304)	Muirfield	Gullane, Scotland
1907	Arnaud Massy	312	J.H. Taylor (314)	Hoylake	Hoylake, England
1908	James Braid	291	Tom Ball (299)	Prestwick Club	Ayrshire, Scotland
1909	J.H. Taylor	295	James Braid (299)	Deal	Deal, England
1910	James Braid	299	Sandy Herd (303)	St. Andrews	St. Andrews, Scotland
1911	Harry Vardon*	303	Arnaud Massy (303)	Royal St. George's	Sandwich, England
1912	Ted Ray	295	Harry Vardon (299)	Muirfield	Gullane, Scotland
1913	J.H. Taylor	304	Ted Ray (312)	Hoylake	Hoylake, England
1914	Harry Vardon	306	J.H. Taylor (309)	Prestwick Club	Ayrshire, Scotland
1915-19	Not held		World War I		
1920	George Duncan	303	Sandy Herd (305)	Deal	Deal, England
1921	Jock Hutchison*	296	Roger Wethered (296)	St. Andrews	St. Andrews, Scotland
1922	Walter Hagen	300	George Duncan & Jim Barnes (301)	Royal St. George's	Sandwich, England
1923	Arthur Havers	295	Walter Hagen (296)	Troon	Troon, Scotland
1924	Walter Hagen	301	Ernest Whitcombe (302)	Hoylake	Hoylake, England
1925	Jim Barnes	300	Archie Compston & Ted Ray (301)	Prestwick Club	Ayrshire, Scotland
1926	a-Bobby Jones	291	Al Watrous (293)	Royal Lytham	Lytham, England
1927	a-Bobby Jones	285	Aubrey Boomer (291)	St. Andrews	St. Andrews, Scotland
1928	Walter Hagen	292	Gene Sarazen (294)	Royal St. George's	Sandwich, England
1929	Walter Hagen	292	Johnny Farrell (298)	Muirfield	Gullane, Scotland
1930	a-Bobby Jones	291	Macdonald Smith & Leo Diegel (293)	Hoylake	Hoylake, England
1931	Tommy Armour	296	Jose Jurado (297)	Carnoustie	Carnoustie, Scotland
1932	Gene Sarazen	283	Macdonald Smith (288)	Prince's	Prince's, England
1933	Denny Shute*	292	Craig Wood (292)	St. Andrews	St. Andrews, Scotland
1934	Henry Cotton	283	Sid Brews (288)	Royal St. George's	Sandwich, England
1935	Alf Perry	283	Alf Padgham (287)	Muirfield	Gullane, Scotland
1936	Alf Padgham	287	Jimmy Adams (288)	Hoylake	Hoylake, England
1937	Henry Cotton	290	Reg Whitcombe (292)	Carnoustie	Carnoustie, Scotland
1938	Reg Whitcombe	295	Jimmy Adams (297)	Royal St. George's	Sandwich, England
1939	Dick Burton	290	Johnny Bulla (292)	St. Andrews	St. Andrews, Scotland
1940-45	Not held		World War II		
1946	Sam Snead	290	Bobby Locke (294) & Johnny Bulla (294)	St. Andrews	St. Andrews, Scotland
1947	Fred Daly	293	Frank Stranahan & Reg Horne (294)	Hoylake	Hoylake, England
1948	Henry Cotton	284	Fred Daly (289)	Muirfield	Gullane, Scotland
1949	Bobby Locke*	283	Harry Bradshaw (283)	Royal St. George's	Sandwich, England

Major Championships (Cont.)

British Open

Year	Winner	Score	Runner-up	Course	Location
1950	Bobby Locke	279	Roberto de Vicenzo (281)	Royal Troon	Troon, Scotland
1951	Max Faulkner	285	Tony Cerda (287)	Royal Portrush	Portrush, Ireland
1952	Bobby Locke	287	Peter Thomson (288)	Royal Lytham	Lytham, England
1953	Ben Hogan	282	Frank Stranahan Dai Rees, Tony Cerda & Peter Thomson (286)	Carnoustie	Carnoustie, Scotland
1954	Peter Thomson	283	Sid Scott, Dai Rees & Bobby Locke (284)	Royal Birkdale	Southport, England
1955	Peter Thomson	281	Johny Fallon (283)	St. Andrews	St. Andrews, Scotland
1956	Peter Thomson	286	Flory Van Donck (289)	Hoylake	Hoylake, England
1957	Bobby Locke	279	Peter Thomson (282)	St. Andrews	St. Andrews, Scotland
1958	Peter Thomson*	278	Dave Thomas (278)	Royal Lytham	Lytham, England
1959	Gary Player	284	Flory Van Donck & Fred Bullock (286)	Muirfield	Gullane, Scotland
1960	Kel Nagle	278	Arnold Palmer (279)	St. Andrews	St. Andrews, Scotland
1961	Arnold Palmer	284	Dai Rees (285)	Royal Birkdale	Southport, England
1962	Arnold Palmer	276	Kel Nagle (282)	Royal Troon	Troon, Scotland
1963	Bob Charles*	277	Phil Rodgers (277)	Royal Lytham	Lytham, England
1964	Tony Lema	279	Jack Nicklaus (284)	St. Andrews	St. Andrews, Scotland
1965	Peter Thomson	285	Christy O'Connor & Brian Huggett (287)	Royal Birkdale	Southport, England
1966	Jack Nicklaus	282	Doug Sanders & Dave Thomas (283)	Muirfield	Gullane, Scotland
1967	Roberto de Vicenzo	278	Jack Nicklaus (280)	Hoylake	Hoylake, England
1968	Gary Player	289	Jack Nicklaus & Bob Charles (291)	Carnoustie	Carnoustie, Scotland
1969	Tony Jacklin	280	Bob Charles (282)	Royal Lytham	Lytham, England
1970	Jack Nicklaus*	283	Doug Sanders (283)	St. Andrews	St. Andrews, Scotland
1971	Lee Trevino	278	Lu Liang Huan (279)	Royal Birkdale	Southport, England
1972	Lee Trevino	278	Jack Nicklaus (279)	Muirfield	Gullane, Scotland
1973	Tom Weiskopf	276	Johnny Miller & Neil Coles (279)	Royal Troon	Troon, Scotland
1974	Gary Player	282	Peter Oosterhuis (286)	Royal Lytham	Lytham, England
1975	Tom Watson*	279	Jack Newton (279)	Carnoustie	Carnoustie, Scotland
1976	Johnny Miller	279	Seve Ballesteros & Jack Nicklaus (285)	Royal Birkdale	Southport, England
1977	Tom Watson	268	Jack Nicklaus (269)	Turnberry	Turnberry, Scotland
1978	Jack Nicklaus	281	Tom Kite, Ray Floyd, Ben Crenshaw & Simon Owen (283)	St. Andrews	St. Andrews, Scotland
1979	Seve Ballesteros	283	Jack Nicklaus & Ben Crenshaw (286)	Royal Lytham	Lytham, England
1980	Tom Watson	271	Lee Trevino (275)	Muirfield	Gullane, Scotland
1981	Bill Rogers	276	Bernhard Langer (280)	Royal St. George's	Sandwich, England
1982	Tom Watson	284	Peter Oosterhuis & Nick Price (285)	Royal Troon	Troon, Scotland
1983	Tom Watson	275	Hale Irwin & Andy Bean (276)	Royal Birkdale	Southport, England
1984	Seve Ballesteros	276	Bernhard Langer & Tom Watson (278)	St. Andrews	St. Andrews, Scotland
1985	Sandy Lyle	282	Payne Stewart (283)	Royal St. George's	Sandwich, England
1986	Greg Norman	280	Gordon J. Brand (285)	Turnberry	Turnberry, Scotland
1987	Nick Faldo	279	Paul Azinger & Rodger Davis (280)	Muirfield	Gullane, Scotland
1988	Seve Ballesteros	273	Nick Price (275)	Royal Lytham	Lytham, England
1989	Mark Calcavecchia*	275	Greg Norman & Wayne Grady (275)	Royal Troon	Troon, Scotland
1990	Nick Faldo	270	Payne Stewart & Mark McNulty (275)	St. Andrews	St. Andrews, Scotland
1991	Ian Baker-Finch	272	Mike Harwood (274)	Royal Birkdale	Southport, England
1992	Nick Faldo	272	John Cook (273)	Muirfield	Gullane, Scotland
1993	Greg Norman	267	Nick Faldo (269)	Royal St. George's	Sandwich, England
1994	Nick Price	268	Jesper Parnevik (269)	Turnberry	Turnberry, Scotland
1995	John Daly*	282	Costantino Rocca (282)	St. Andrews	St. Andrews, Scotland
1996	Tom Lehman	271	Mark McCumber & Ernie Els (273)	Royal Lytham	Lytham, England

*PLAYOFFS

1876: Bob Martin awarded title when David Strath refused playoff. **1883:** Willie Fernie (158) def. Bob Ferguson (159) in 36 holes. **1889:** Willie Park Jr. (158) def. Andrew Kirkaldy (163) in 36 holes. **1896:** Harry Vardon (157) def. John H.

Taylor (161) in 36 holes. **1911:** Harry Vardon won when Arnaud Massy conceded at 35th hole. **1921:** Jock Hutchison (150) def. Roger Wethered (159) in 36 holes. **1933:** Denny Shute (149) def. Craig Wood (154) in 36 holes. **1949:** Bobby Locke (135) def. Harry Bradshaw (147) in 36 holes. **1958:** Peter Thomson (139) def. Dave Thomas (143) in 36 holes. **1963:** Bob Charles (140) def. Phil Rodgers (148) in 36 holes. **1970:** Jack Nicklaus (72) def. Doug Sanders (73) in 18 holes. **1975:** Tom Watson (71) def. Jack Newton (72) in 18 holes. **1989:** Mark Calcavecchia (4-3-3-3—13) def. Wayne Grady (4-4-4-4—16) and Greg Norman (3-3-4-x) in 4 holes. **1995:** John Daly (3-4-4-4—15) def. Costantino Rocca (4-5-7-3—19) in 4 holes.

PGA Championship

The PGA Championship began in 1916 as a professional golfers match play tournament, but switched to stroke play in 1958. Conducted by the PGA of America, the tournament is played on a different course each year.

Multiple winners: Walter Hagen and Jack Nicklaus (5); Gene Sarazen and Sam Snead (3); Jim Barnes, Leo Diegel, Raymond Floyd, Ben Hogan, Byron Nelson, Larry Nelson, Gary Player, Paul Runyan, Denny Shute, Dave Stockton and Lee Trevino (2).

Year	Winner	Score	Runner-up	Course	Location
1916	Jim Barnes	1-up	Jock Hutchison	Siwanoy CC	Bronxville, N.Y.
1917-18	Not held		World War I		
1919	Jim Barnes	6 & 5	Fred McLeod	Engineers CC	Roslyn, N.Y.
1920	Jock Hutchison	1-up	J. Douglas Edgar	Flossmoor CC	Flossmoor, Ill.
1921	Walter Hagen	3 & 2	Jim Barnes	Inwood CC	Far Rockaway, N.Y.
1922	Gene Sarazen	4 & 3	Emmet French	Oakmont CC	Oakmont, Pa.
1923	Gene Sarazen*	1-up/38	Walter Hagen	Pelham CC	Pelham, N.Y.
1924	Walter Hagen	2-up	Jim Barnes	French Lick CC	French Lick, Ind.
1925	Walter Hagen	6 & 5	Bill Mehlhorn	Olympia Fields CC	Matteson, Ill.
1926	Walter Hagen	5 & 3	Leo Diegel	Salisbury GC	Westbury, N.Y.
1927	Water Hagen	1-up	Joe Turnesa	Cedar Crest CC	Dallas
1928	Leo Diegel	6 & 5	Al Espinosa	Five Farms CC	Baltimore
1929	Leo Diegel	6 & 4	John Farrell	Hillcrest CC	Los Angeles
1930	Tommy Armour	1-up	Gene Sarazen	Fresh Meadow CC	Flushing, N.Y.
1931	Tom Creavy	2 & 1	Denny Shute	Wannamoisett CC	Rumford, R.I.
1932	Olin Dutra	4 & 3	Frank Walsh	Keller GC	St. Paul, Minn.
1933	Gene Sarazen	5 & 4	Willie Goggin	Blue Mound CC	Milwaukee
1934	Paul Runyan*	1-up/38	Craig Wood	Park CC	Williamsville, N.Y.
1935	Johnny Revolta	5 & 4	Tommy Armour	Twin Hills CC	Oklahoma City
1936	Denny Shute	3 & 2	Jimmy Thomson	Pinehurst CC	Pinehurst, N.C.
1937	Denny Shute*	1-up/37	Harold McSpaden	Pittsburgh FC	Aspinwall, Pa.
1938	Paul Runyan	8 & 7	Sam Snead	Shawnee CC	Shawnee-on-Del, Pa.
1939	Henry Picard*	1-up/37	Byron Nelson	Pomonok CC	Flushing, N.Y.
1940	Byron Nelson	1-up	Sam Snead	Hershey CC	Hershey, Pa.
1941	Vic Ghezzi*	1-up/38	Byron Nelson	Cherry Hills CC	Denver
1942	Sam Snead	2 & 1	Jim Turnesa	Seaview CC	Atlantic City, N.J.
1943	Not held		World War II		
1944	Bob Hamilton	1-up	Byron Nelson	Manito G & CC	Spokane, Wash.
1945	Byron Nelson	4 & 3	Sam Byrd	Morraine CC	Dayton, Ohio
1946	Ben Hogan	6 & 4	Porky Oliver	Portland GC	Portland, Ore.
1947	Jim Ferrier	2 & 1	Chick Harbert	Plum Hollow CC	Detroit
1948	Ben Hogan	7 & 6	Mike Turnesa	Norwood Hills CC	St. Louis
1949	Sam Snead	3 & 2	John Palmer	Hermitage CC	Richmond, Va.
1950	Chandler Harper	4 & 3	Henry Williams Jr.	Scioto CC	Columbus, Ohio
1951	Sam Snead	7 & 6	Walter Burkemo	Oakmont CC	Oakmont, Pa.
1952	Jim Turnesa	1-up	Chick Harbert	Big Spring CC	Louisville
1953	Walter Burkemo	2 & 1	Felice Torza	Birmingham CC	Birmingham, Mich.
1954	Chick Harbert	4 & 3	Walter Burkemo	Keller GC	St. Paul, Minn.
1955	Doug Ford	4 & 3	Cary Middlecoff	Meadowbrook CC	Detroit
1956	Jack Burke	3 & 2	Ted Kroll	Blue Hill CC	Boston
1957	Lionel Hebert	2 & 1	Dow Finsterwald	Miami Valley GC	Dayton, Ohio
1958	Dow Finsterwald	276	Billy Casper (278)	Llanerch CC	Havertown, Pa.
1959	Bob Rosburg	277	Jerry Barber & Doug Sanders (278)	Minneapolis GC	St. Louis Park, Minn.
1960	Jay Hebert	281	Jim Ferrier (282)	Firestone CC	Akron, Ohio
1961	Jerry Barber**	277	Don January (277)	Olympia Fields CC	Matteson, Ill.
1962	Gary Player	278	Bob Goalby (279)	Aronimink GC	Newtown Square, Pa.
1963	Jack Nicklaus	279	Dave Ragan (281)	Dallas AC	Dallas
1964	Bobby Nichols	271	Jack Nicklaus & Arnold Palmer (274)	Columbus CC	Columbus, Ohio
1965	Dave Marr	280	Jack Nicklaus & Billy Casper (282)	Laurel Valley GC	Ligonier, Pa.

*While the PGA Championship was a match play tournament from 1916–57, the two finalists played 36 holes for the title. In the five years that a playoff was necessary, the match was decided on the 37th or 38th hole.

Major Championships (Cont.)

PGA Championship

Year	Winner	Score	Runner-up	Course	Location
1966	Al Geiberger	280	Dudley Wysong (284)	Firestone CC	Akron, Ohio
1967	Don January**	281	Don Massengale (281)	Columbine CC	Littleton, Colo.
1968	Julius Boros	281	Arnold Palmer & Bob Charles (282)	Pecan Valley CC	San Antonio
1969	Ray Floyd	276	Gary Player (277)	NCR GC	Dayton, Ohio
1970	Dave Stockton	279	Arnold Palmer & Bob Murphy (281)	Southern Hills CC	Tulsa
1971	Jack Nicklaus	281	Billy Casper (283)	PGA National GC	Palm Beach Gardens, Fla.
1972	Gary Player	281	Jim Jamieson & Tommy Aaron (283)	Oakland Hills GC	Birmingham, Mich.
1973	Jack Nicklaus	277	Bruce Crampton (281)	Canterbury GC	Cleveland
1974	Lee Trevino	276	Jack Nicklaus (277)	Tanglewood GC	Winston-Salem, N.C.
1975	Jack Nicklaus	276	Bruce Crampton (278)	Firestone CC	Akron, Ohio
1976	Dave Stockton	281	Don January & Ray Floyd (282)	Congressional CC	Bethesda, Md.
1977	Lanny Wadkins**	282	Gene Littler (282)	Pebble Beach GL	Pebble Beach, Calif.
1978	John Mahaffey**	276	Jerry Pate & Tom Watson (276)	Oakmont CC	Oakmont, Pa.
1979	David Graham**	272	Ben Crenshaw (272)	Oakland Hills CC	Birmingham, Mich.
1980	Jack Nicklaus	274	Andy Bean (281)	Oak Hill CC	Rochester, N.Y.
1981	Larry Nelson	273	Fuzzy Zoeller (277)	Atlanta AC	Duluth, Ga.
1982	Ray Floyd	272	Lanny Wadkins (275)	Southern Hills CC	Tulsa
1983	Hal Sutton	274	Jack Nicklaus (275)	Riviera CC	Los Angeles
1984	Lee Trevino	273	Lanny Wadkins & Gary Player (277)	Shoal Creek	Birmingham, Ala.
1985	Hubert Green	278	Lee Trevino (280)	Cherry Hills CC	Denver
1986	Bob Tway	276	Greg Norman (278)	Inverness Club	Toledo, Ohio
1987	Larry Nelson**	287	Lanny Wadkins (287)	PGA National	Palm Beach Gardens, Fla.
1988	Jeff Sluman	272	Paul Azinger 275)	Oak Tree GC	Edmond, Okla.
1989	Payne Stewart	276	Andy Bean, Mike Reid & Curtis Strange (277)	Kemper Lakes GC	Hawthorn Woods, Ill.
1990	Wayne Grady	282	Fred Couples (285)	Shoal Creek	Birmingham, Ala.
1991	John Daly	276	Bruce Lietzke (279)	Crooked Stick GC	Carmel, Ind.
1992	Nick Price	278	Nick Faldo, John Cook, Jim Gallagher & Gene Sauers (281)	Bellerive CC	St. Louis
1993	Paul Azinger**	272	Greg Norman (272)	Inverness Club	Toledo, Ohio
1994	Nick Price	269	Corey Pavin (275)	Southern Hills CC	Tulsa
1995	Steve Elkington**	267	Colin Montgomerie	Riviera CC	Pacific Palisades, Calif.
1996	Mark Brooks**	277	Kenny Perry	Valhalla GC	Louisville, Ky.

**PLAYOFFS

1961: Jerry Barber (67) def. Don January (68) in 18 holes. **1967:** Don January (69) def. Don Massengale (71) in 18 holes. **1977:** Lanny Wadkins (4-4-4) def. Gene Littler (4-4-5) on 3rd hole of sudden death. **1978:** John Mahaffey (4-3) def. Jerry Pate (4-4) and Tom Watson (4-5) on 2nd hole of sudden death. **1979:** David Graham (4-4-2) def. Ben Crenshaw (4-4-4) on 3rd hole of sudden death. **1987:** Larry Nelson (4) def. Lanny Wadkins (5) on 1st hole of sudden death. **1993:** Paul Azinger (4-4) def. Greg Norman (4-5) on 2nd hole of sudden death. **1995:** Steve Elkington (3) def. Colin Montgomerie (4) on 1st hole of sudden death. **1996:** Mark Brooks (4) def. Kenny Perry (5) on 1st hole of sudden death.

Major Championship Leaders

Through 1996; active players in **bold** type.

	US Open	British Open	PGA	Masters	US Am	British Am	Total
Jack Nicklaus	4	3	5	6	2	0	**20**
Bobby Jones	4	3	0	0	5	1	**13**
Walter Hagen	2	4	5	0	0	0	**11**
Ben Hogan	4	1	2	2	0	0	**9**
Gary Player	1	3	2	3	0	0	**9**
John Ball	0	1	0	0	0	8	**9**
Arnold Palmer	1	2	0	4	1	0	**8**
Tom Watson	1	5	0	2	0	0	**8**
Harold Hilton	0	2	0	0	1	4	**7**
Gene Sarazen	2	1	3	1	0	0	**7**
Sam Snead	0	1	3	3	0	0	**7**
Harry Vardon	1	6	0	0	0	0	**7**
Nick Faldo	0	3	0	3	0	0	**6**
Lee Trevino	2	2	2	0	0	0	**6**

Tournaments: U.S. Open, British Open, PGA Championship, Masters, U.S. Amateur, and British Amateur.

Grand Slam Summary

The only golfer ever to win a recognized Grand Slam—four major championships in a single season—was Bobby Jones in 1930. That year, Jones won the U.S. and British Opens as well as the U.S. and British Amateurs.

The men's professional Grand Slam—the Masters, U.S. Open, British Open and PGA Championship—did not gain acceptance until 30 years later when Arnold Palmer won the 1960 Masters and U.S. Open. The media wrote that the popular Palmer was chasing the "new" Grand Slam and would have to win the British Open and the PGA to claim it. He did not, but then nobody has before or since.

Three wins in one year: Ben Hogan (1953). **Two wins in one year** (15): Jack Nicklaus (5 times); Ben Hogan, Arnold Palmer and Tom Watson (twice); Nick Faldo, Gary Player, Nick Price, Sam Snead, Lee Trevino and Craig Wood (once).

Year	Masters	US Open	Brit.Open	PGA
1934	H. Smith	Dutra	Cotton	Runyan
1935	Sarazen	Parks	Perry	Revolta
1936	H. Smith	Manero	Padgham	Shute
1937	B. Nelson	Guldahl	Cotton	Shute
1938	Picard	Guldahl	Whitcombe	Runyan
1939	Guldahl	B. Nelson	Burton	Picard
1940	Demaret	Little	—	B. Nelson
1941	Wood	Wood	—	Ghezzi
1942	B. Nelson	—	—	Snead
1943	—	—	—	—
1944	—	—	—	Hamilton
1945	—	—	—	B. Nelson
1946	Keiser	Mangrum	Snead	Hogan
1947	Demaret	Worsham	F. Daly	Ferrier
1948	Harmon	Hogan	Cotton	Hogan
1949	Snead	Middlecoff	Locke	Snead
1950	Demaret	Hogan	Locke	Harper
1951	Hogan	Hogan	Faulkner	Snead
1952	Snead	Boros	Locke	Turnesa
1953	Hogan	Hogan	Hogan	Burkemo
1954	Snead	Furgol	Thomson	Harbert
1955	Middlecoff	Fleck	Thomson	Ford
1956	Burke	Middlecoff	Thomson	Burke
1957	Ford	Mayer	Locke	L. Hebert
1958	Palmer	Bolt	Thomson	Finsterwald
1959	Wall	Casper	Player	Rosburg
1960	Palmer	Palmer	Nagle	J. Hebert
1961	Player	Littler	Palmer	J. Barber
1962	Palmer	Nicklaus	Palmer	Player
1963	Nicklaus	Boros	Charles	Nicklaus
1964	Palmer	Venturi	Lema	Nichols
1965	Nicklaus	Player	Thomson	Marr
1966	Nicklaus	Casper	Nicklaus	Geiberger
1967	Brewer	Nicklaus	DeVicenzo	January
1968	Goalby	Trevino	Player	Boros
1969	Archer	Moody	Jacklin	Floyd
1970	Casper	Jacklin	Nicklaus	Stockton
1971	Coody	Trevino	Trevino	Nicklaus
1972	Nicklaus	Nicklaus	Trevino	Player
1973	Aaron	J. Miller	Weiskopf	Nicklaus
1974	Player	Irwin	Player	Trevino
1975	Nicklaus	L. Graham	T. Watson	Nicklaus
1976	Floyd	J. Pate	Miller	Stockton
1977	T. Watson	H. Green	T. Watson	L. Wadkins
1978	Player	North	Nicklaus	Mahaffey
1979	Zoeller	Irwin	Ballesteros	D. Graham
1980	Ballesteros	Nicklaus	T. Watson	Nicklaus
1981	T. Watson	D. Graham	Rogers	L. Nelson
1982	Stadler	T. Watson	T. Watson	Floyd
1983	Ballesteros	L. Nelson	T. Watson	Sutton
1984	Crenshaw	Zoeller	Ballesteros	Trevino
1985	Langer	North	Lyle	H. Green
1986	Nicklaus	Floyd	Norman	Tway
1987	Mize	S. Simpson	Faldo	L. Nelson
1988	Lyle	Strange	Ballesteros	Sluman
1989	Faldo	Strange	Calcavecchia	Stewart
1990	Faldo	Irwin	Faldo	Grady
1991	Woosnam	Stewart	Baker-Finch	J. Daly
1992	Couples	Kite	Faldo	Price
1993	Langer	Janzen	Norman	Azinger
1994	Olazabal	Els	Price	Price
1995	Crenshaw	Pavin	Daly	Elkington
1996	Faldo	S. Jones	Lehman	Brooks

Vardon Trophy

Awarded since 1937 by the PGA of America to the PGA Tour regular with the lowest scoring average. The award is named after Harry Vardon, the six-time British Open champion, who won the U.S. Open in 1900. A point system was used from 1937-41.

Multiple winners: Billy Casper and Lee Trevino (5); Arnold Palmer and Sam Snead (4); Ben Hogan, Greg Norman and Tom Watson (3); Fred Couples, Bruce Crampton, Tom Kite and Lloyd Mangrum (2).

Year		Pts
1937	Harry Cooper	500
1938	Sam Snead	520
1939	Byron Nelson	473
1940	Ben Hogan	423
1941	Ben Hogan	494
1942-46	No award	

Year		Avg
1947	Jimmy Demaret	69.90
1948	Ben Hogan	69.30
1949	Sam Snead	69.37
1950	Sam Snead	69.23
1951	Lloyd Mangrum	70.05
1952	Jack Burke	70.54
1953	Lloyd Mangrum	70.22
1954	E.J. Harrison	70.41
1955	Sam Snead	69.86
1956	Cary Middlecoff	70.35
1957	Dow Finsterwald	70.30
1958	Bob Rosburg	70.11
1959	Art Wall	70.35
1960	Billy Casper	69.95
1961	Arnold Palmer	69.85
1962	Arnold Palmer	70.27
1963	Billy Casper	70.58
1964	Arnold Palmer	70.01
1965	Billy Casper	70.85
1966	Billy Casper	70.27
1967	Arnold Palmer	70.18
1968	Billy Casper	69.82
1969	Dave Hill	70.34
1970	Lee Trevino	70.64
1971	Lee Trevino	70.27
1972	Lee Trevino	70.89
1973	Bruce Crampton	70.57
1974	Lee Trevino	70.53
1975	Bruce Crampton	70.51
1976	Don January	70.56
1977	Tom Watson	70.32
1978	Tom Watson	70.16
1979	Tom Watson	70.27
1980	Lee Trevino	69.73
1981	Tom Kite	69.80
1982	Tom Kite	70.21
1983	Ray Floyd	70.61
1984	Calvin Peete	70.56
1985	Don Pooley	70.36
1986	Scott Hoch	70.08
1987	Dan Pohl	70.25
1988	Chip Beck	69.46
1989	Greg Norman	69.49
1990	Greg Norman	69.10
1991	Fred Couples	69.59
1992	Fred Couples	69.38
1993	Nick Price	69.11
1994	Greg Norman	68.81
1995	Steve Elkington	69.62

U.S. Amateur

Match play from 1895-64, stroke play from 1965-72, match play since 1972.

Multiple winners: Bobby Jones (5); Jerry Travers (4); Walter Travis and Tiger Woods (3); Deane Beman, Charles Coe, Gary Cowan, H. Chandler Egan, Chick Evans, Lawson Little, Jack Nicklaus, Francis Ouimet, Jay Sigel, William Turnesa, Bud Ward, Harvie Ward, and H.J. Whigham (2).

Year	
1895	Charles Macdonald
1896	H.J. Whigham
1897	H.J. Whigham
1898	Findlay Douglas
1899	H.M. Harriman
1900	Walter Travis
1901	Walter Travis
1902	Louis James
1903	Walter Travis
1904	H. Chandler Egan
1905	H. Chandler Egan
1906	Eben Byers
1907	Jerry Travers
1908	Jerry Travers
1909	Robert Gardner
1910	W.C. Fownes Jr.
1911	Harold Hilton
1912	Jerry Travers
1913	Jerry Travers
1914	Francis Ouimet
1915	Robert Gardner
1916	Chick Evans
1917-18	Not held
1919	Davidson Herron
1920	Chick Evans
1921	Jesse Guilford
1922	Jess Sweetser
1923	Max Marston
1924	Bobby Jones
1925	Bobby Jones
1926	George Von Elm
1927	Bobby Jones
1928	Bobby Jones
1929	Harrison Johnston
1930	Bobby Jones
1931	Francis Ouimet
1932	Ross Somerville
1933	George Dunlap
1934	Lawson Little
1935	Lawson Little
1936	John Fischer
1937	John Goodman
1938	William Turnesa
1939	Bud Ward
1940	Richard Chapman
1941	Bud Ward
1942-45	Not held
1946	Ted Bishop
1947	Skee Riegel
1948	William Turnesa
1949	Charles Coe
1950	Sam Urzetta
1951	Billy Maxwell
1952	Jack Westland
1953	Gene Littler
1954	Arnold Palmer
1955	Harvie Ward
1956	Harvie Ward
1957	Hillman Robbins
1958	Charles Coe
1959	Jack Nicklaus
1960	Deane Beman
1961	Jack Nicklaus
1962	Labron Harris
1963	Deane Beman
1964	Bill Campbell
1965	Bob Murphy
1966	Gary Cowan
1967	Bob Dickson
1968	Bruce Fleisher
1969	Steve Melnyk
1970	Lanny Wadkins
1971	Gary Cowan
1972	Vinny Giles
1973	Craig Stadler
1974	Jerry Pate
1975	Fred Ridley
1976	Bill Sander
1977	John Fought
1978	John Cook
1979	Mark O'Meara
1980	Hal Sutton
1981	Nathaniel Crosby
1982	Jay Sigel
1983	Jay Sigel
1984	Scott Verplank
1985	Sam Randolph
1986	Buddy Alexander
1987	Billy Mayfair
1988	Eric Meeks
1989	Chris Patton
1990	Phil Mickelson
1991	Mitch Voges
1992	Justin Leonard
1993	John Harris
1994	Tiger Woods
1995	Tiger Woods
1996	Tiger Woods

British Amateur

Match play since 1885.

Multiple winners: John Ball (8); Michael Bonallack (5); Harold Hilton (4); Joe Carr (3); Horace Hutchinson, Ernest Holderness, Trevor Homer, Johnny Laidley, Lawson Little, Peter McEvoy, Dick Siderowf, Frank Stranahan, Freddie Tait and Cyril Tolley (2).

Year	
1885	Allen MacFie
1886	Horace Hutchinson
1887	Horace Hutchinson
1888	John Ball
1889	Johnny Laidley
1890	John Ball
1891	Johnny Laidley
1892	John Ball
1893	Peter Anderson
1894	John Ball
1895	Leslie Balfour-Melville
1896	Freddie Tait
1897	Jack Allan
1898	Freddie Tait
1899	John Ball
1900	Harold Hilton
1901	Harold Hilton
1902	Charles Hutchings
1903	Robert Maxwell
1904	Walter Travis
1905	Arthur Barry
1906	James Robb
1907	John Ball
1908	E.A. Lassen
1909	Robert Maxwell
1910	John Ball
1911	Harold Hilton
1912	John Ball
1913	Harold Hilton
1914	J.L.C. Jenkins
1915-19	Not held
1920	Cyril Tolley
1921	William Hunter
1922	Ernest Holderness
1923	Roger Wethered
1924	Ernest Holderness
1925	Robert Harris
1926	Jesse Sweetser
1927	William Tweddell
1928	Thomas Perkins
1929	Cyril Tolley
1930	Bobby Jones
1931	Eric Smith
1932	John deForest
1933	Michael Scott
1934	Lawson Little
1935	Lawson Little
1936	Hector Thomson
1937	Robert Sweeny Jr.
1938	Charles Yates
1939	Alexander Kyle
1940-45	Not held
1946	James Bruen
1947	William Turnesa
1948	Frank Stranahan
1949	Samuel McCready
1950	Frank Stranahan
1951	Richard Chapman
1952	Harvie Ward
1953	Joe Carr
1954	Douglas Bachli
1955	Joe Conrad
1956	John Beharrell
1957	Reid Jack
1958	Joe Carr
1959	Deane Beman
1960	Joe Carr
1961	Michael Bonallack
1962	Richard Davies
1963	Michael Lunt
1964	Gordon Clark
1965	Michael Bonallack
1966	Bobby Cole
1967	Bob Dickson
1968	Michael Bonallack
1969	Michael Bonallack
1970	Michael Bonallack
1971	Steve Melnyk
1972	Trevor Homer
1973	Dick Siderowf
1974	Trevor Homer
1975	Vinny Giles
1976	Dick Siderowf
1977	Peter McEvoy
1978	Peter McEvoy
1979	Jay Sigel
1980	Duncan Evans
1981	Phillipe Ploujoux
1982	Martin Thompson
1983	Philip Parkin
1984	Jose-Maria Olazabal
1985	Garth McGimpsey
1986	David Curry
1987	Paul Mayo
1988	Christian Hardin
1989	Stephen Dodd
1990	Rolf Muntz
1991	Gary Wolstenholme
1992	Stephen Dundas
1993	Ian Pyman
1994	Lee James
1995	Gordon Sherry
1996	Warren Bledon

Major Championships

WOMEN

U.S. Women's Open

The U.S. Women's Open began under the direction of the defunct Women's Professional Golfers Assn. in 1946, passed to the LPGA in 1949 and to the USGA in 1953. The tournament used a match play format its first year then switched to stroke play; (*) indicates playoff winner and (a) indicates amateur winner.

Multiple winners: Betsy Rawls and Mickey Wright (4); Susie Maxwell Berning, Hollis Stacy and Babe Zaharias (3); JoAnne Carner, Donna Caponi, Betsy King, Patty Sheehan, Annika Sorenstam and Louise Suggs (2).

Year		Year		Year		Year	
1946	Patty Berg	1959	Mickey Wright	1972	Susie M. Berning	1985	Kathy Baker
1947	Betty Jameson	1960	Betsy Rawls	1973	Susie M. Berning	1986	Jane Geddes*
1948	Babe Zaharias	1961	Mickey Wright	1974	Sandra Haynie	1987	Laura Davies*
1949	Louise Suggs	1962	Murle Lindstrom	1975	Sandra Palmer	1988	Liselotte Neumann
1950	Babe Zaharias	1963	Mary Mills	1976	JoAnne Carner*	1989	Betsy King
1951	Betsy Rawls	1964	Mickey Wright*	1977	Hollis Stacy	1990	Betsy King
1952	Louise Suggs	1965	Carol Mann	1978	Hollis Stacy	1991	Meg Mallon
1953	Betsy Rawls*	1966	Sandra Spuzich	1979	Jerilyn Britz	1992	Patty Sheehan*
1954	Babe Zaharias	1967	a-Catherine Lacoste	1980	Amy Alcott	1993	Lauri Merten
1955	Fay Crocker	1968	Susie M. Berning	1981	Pat Bradley	1994	Patty Sheehan
1956	Kathy Cornelius*	1969	Donna Caponi	1982	Janet Anderson	1995	Annika Sorenstam
1957	Betsy Rawls	1970	Donna Caponi	1983	Jan Stephenson	1996	Annika Sorenstam
1958	Mickey Wright	1971	JoAnne Carner	1984	Hollis Stacy		

*PLAYOFFS

1953: Betsy Rawls (71) def. Jackie Pung (77) in 18 holes. **1956:** Kathy Cornelius (75) def. Barbara McIntire (82) in 18 holes. **1964:** Mickey Wright (70) def. Ruth Jessen (72) in 18 holes. **1976:** JoAnne Carner (76) def. Sandra Palmer (78) in 18 holes. **1986:** Jane Geddes (71) def. Sally Little (73) in 18 holes. **1987:** Laura Davies (71) def. Ayako Okamoto (73) and JoAnne Carner (74) in 18 holes. **1992:** Patty Sheehan (72) def. Juli Inkster (74) in 18 holes.

LPGA Championship

Officially the McDonald's LPGA Championship since 1994 (Mazda sponsored from 1987-93), the tournament began in 1955 and has had extended stays at the Stardust CC in Las Vegas (1961-66), Pleasant Valley CC in Sutton, Mass. (1967-68, 70-74); the Jack Nicklaus Sports Center at Kings Island, Ohio (1978-89) and Bethesda CC in Maryland (since 1990); (*) indicates playoff winner.

Multiple winners: Mickey Wright (4); Nancy Lopez, Patty Sheehan and Kathy Whitworth (3); Donna Caponi, Laura Davies, Sandra Haynie, Mary Mills and Betsy Rawls (2).

Year		Year		Year		Year	
1955	Beverly Hanson	1966	Gloria Ehret	1977	Chako Higuchi	1988	Sherri Turner
1956	Marlene Hagge*	1967	Kathy Whitworth	1978	Nancy Lopez	1989	Nancy Lopez
1957	Louise Suggs	1968	Sandra Post*	1979	Donna Caponi	1990	Beth Daniel
1958	Mickey Wright	1969	Betsy Rawls	1980	Sally Little	1991	Meg Mallon
1959	Betsy Rawls	1970	Shirley Englehorn*	1981	Donna Caponi	1992	Betsy King
1960	Mickey Wright	1971	Kathy Whitworth	1982	Jan Stephenson	1993	Patty Sheehan
1961	Mickey Wright	1972	Kathy Ahern	1983	Patty Sheehan	1994	Laura Davies
1962	Judy Kimball	1973	Mary Mills	1984	Patty Sheehan	1995	Kelly Robbins
1963	Mickey Wright	1974	Sandra Haynie	1985	Nancy Lopez	1996	Laura Davies
1964	Mary Mills	1975	Kathy Whitworth	1986	Pat Bradley		
1965	Sandra Haynie	1976	Betty Burfeindt	1987	Jane Geddes		

*PLAYOFFS

1956: Marlene Hagge def. Patti Berg in sudden death. **1968:** Sandra Post (68) def. Kathy Whitworth (75) in 18-holes. **1970:** Shirley Englehorn def. Kathy Whitworth in sudden death.

Nabisco Dinah Shore

Formerly known as the Colgate Dinah Shore from 1972-81, the tournament become the LPGA's fourth designated major championship in 1983. Named after the entertainer, this tourney has been played at Mission Hills CC in Rancho Mirage, Calif., since it began; (*) indicates playoff winner.

Multiple winners (as a major): Amy Alcott (3); Juli Inkster and Betsy King (2).

Year		Year		Year		Year	
1972	Jane Blalock	1979	Sandra Post	1986	Pat Bradley	1993	Helen Alfredsson
1973	Mickey Wright	1980	Donna Caponi	1987	Betsy King*	1994	Donna Andrews
1974	Jo Ann Prentice	1981	Nancy Lopez	1988	Amy Alcott	1995	Nanci Bowen
1975	Sandra Palmer	1982	Sally Little	1989	Juli Inkster	1996	Patty Sheehan
1976	Judy Rankin	1983	Amy Alcott	1990	Betsy King		
1977	Kathy Whitworth	1984	Juli Inkster*	1991	Amy Alcott		
1978	Sandra Post	1985	Alice Miller	1992	Dottie Mochrie*		

*PLAYOFFS

1984: Juli Inkster def. Pat Bradley in sudden death. **1987:** Betsy King def. Patty Sheehan in sudden death. **1992:** Dottie Mochrie def. Juli Inkster in sudden death.

Major Championships (Cont.)

WOMEN

du Maurier Classic

Formerly known as La Canadienne in 1973 and the Peter Jackson Classic from 1974-83, this Canadian stop on the LPGA Tour became the third designated major championship in 1979; (*) indicates playoff winner.

Multiple winners (as a major): Pat Bradley (3); JoAnne Carner (2).

Year	
1973	Jocelyne Bourassa
1974	Carole Jo Skala
1975	JoAnne Carner
1976	Donna Caponi
1977	Judy Rankin
1978	JoAnne Carner
1979	Amy Alcott
1980	Pat Bradley
1981	Jan Stephenson
1982	Sandra Haynie
1983	Hollis Stacy
1984	Juli Inkster
1986	Pat Bradley*
1985	Pat Bradley
1987	Jody Rosenthal
1988	Sally Little
1989	Tammie Green
1990	Cathy Johnston
1991	Nancy Scranton
1992	Sherri Steinhaur
1993	Brandie Burton*
1994	Martha Nause
1995	Jenny Lidback
1996	Laura Davies

***PLAYOFF**

1986: Pat Bradley def. Ayako Okamoto in sudden death. **1993:** Brandie Burton def. Betsy King in sudden death.

Titleholders Championship (1937-72)

The Titleholders was considered a major title on the women's tour until it was discontinued after the 1972 tournament.

Multiple winners: Patty Berg (7); Louise Suggs (4); Babe Zaharias (3); Dorothy Kirby, Marilynn Smith, Kathy Whitworth and Mickey Wright (2).

Year	
1937	Patty Berg
1938	Patty Berg
1939	Patty Berg
1940	Betty Hicks
1941	Dorothy Kirby
1942	Dorothy Kirby
1943-45	Not held
1946	Louise Suggs
1947	Babe Zaharias
1948	Patty Berg
1949	Peggy Kirk
1950	Babe Zaharias
1951	Pat O'Sullivan
1952	Babe Zaharias
1953	Patty Berg
1954	Louise Suggs
1955	Patty Berg
1956	Louise Suggs
1957	Patty Berg
1958	Beverly Hanson
1959	Louise Suggs
1960	Fay Crocker
1961	Mickey Wright
1962	Mickey Wright
1963	Marilynn Smith
1964	Marilynn Smith
1965	Kathy Whitworth
1966	Kathy Whitworth
1967-71	Not held
1972	Sandra Palmer

Western Open (1930-67)

The Western Open was considered a major title on the women's tour until it was discontinued after the 1967 tournament.

Multiple winners: Patty Berg (7); Louise Suggs and Babe Zaharias (4); Mickey Wright (3); June Beebe; Opal Hill; Betty Jameson and Betsy Rawls (2).

Year	
1930	Mrs. Lee Mida
1931	June Beebe
1932	Jane Weiller
1933	June Beebe
1934	Marian McDougall
1935	Opal Hill
1936	Opal Hill
1937	Betty Hicks
1938	Bea Barrett
1939	Helen Dettweiler
1940	Babe Zaharias
1941	Patty Berg
1942	Betty Jameson
1943	Patty Berg
1944	Babe Zaharias
1945	Babe Zaharias
1946	Louise Suggs
1947	Louise Suggs
1948	Patty Berg
1949	Louise Suggs
1950	Babe Zaharias
1951	Patty Berg
1952	Betsy Rawls
1953	Louise Suggs
1954	Betty Jameson
1955	Patty Berg
1956	Beverly Hanson
1957	Patty Berg
1958	Patty Berg
1959	Betsy Rawls
1960	Joyce Ziske
1961	Mary Lena Faulk
1962	Mickey Wright
1963	Mickey Wright
1964	Carol Mann
1965	Susie Maxwell
1966	Mickey Wright
1967	Kathy Whitworth

Major Championship Leaders

Through 1996; active players in **bold** type.

	US Open	LPGA	duM	Dinah	Title-holders	Western	US Am	Brit Am	Total
Patty Berg	1	0	0	0	7	7	1	0	**16**
Mickey Wright	4	4	0	0	2	3	0	0	**13**
Louise Suggs	2	1	0	0	4	4	1	1	**13**
Babe Zaharias	3	0	0	0	3	4	1	1	**12**
Betsy Rawls	4	2	0	0	0	2	0	0	**8**
JoAnne Carner	2	0	0	0	0	0	5	0	**7**
Kathy Whitworth	0	3	0	0	2	1	0	0	**6**
Pat Bradley	1	1	3	1	0	0	0	0	**6**
Juli Inkster	0	0	1	2	0	0	3	0	**6**
Patty Sheehan	2	3	0	1	0	0	0	0	**6**
Glenna C. Vare	0	0	0	0	0	0	6	0	**6**

Tournaments: U.S. Open, LPGA Championship, du Maurier Classic, Nabisco Dinah Shore, Titleholders (1937-72), Western Open (1937-67), U.S. Amateur, and British Amateur.

Grand Slam Summary

The Women's Grand Slam has consisted of four tournaments only 19 years. From 1955-66, the U.S. Open, LPGA Championship, Western Open and Titleholders tournaments served as the major events. Since 1983, the U.S. Open, LPGA, du Maurier Classic in Canada and Nabisco Dinah Shore have been the major events. No one has won a four-event Grand Slam on the women's tour.

Three wins in one year (3): Babe Zaharias (1950), Mickey Wright (1961) and Pat Bradley (1986).

Two wins in one year (14): Patty Berg and Mickey Wright (3 times); Louise Suggs (twice); Laura Davies, Sandra Haynie, Juli Inkster, Betsy King, Meg Mallon, Betsy Rawls and Kathy Whitworth (once).

Year	LPGA	US Open	T'holders	Western
1937	—	—	Berg	Hicks
1938	—	—	Berg	Barrett
1939	—	—	Berg	Dettweiler
1940	—	—	Hicks	Zaharias
1941	—	—	Kirby	Berg
1942	—	—	Kirby	Jameson
1943	—	—	—	Berg`
1944	—	—	—	Zaharias
1945	—	—	—	Zaharias
1946	—	Berg	Suggs	Suggs
1947	—	Jameson	Zaharias	Suggs
1948	—	Zaharias	Berg	Berg
1949	—	Suggs	Kirk	Suggs
1950	—	Zaharias	Zaharias	Zaharias
1951	—	Rawls	O'Sullivan	Berg
1952	—	Suggs	Zaharias	Rawls
1953	—	Rawls	Berg	Suggs
1954	—	Zaharias	Suggs	Jameson
1955	Hanson	Crocker	Berg	Berg
1956	Hagge	Cornelius	Suggs	Hanson
1957	Suggs	Rawls	Berg	Berg
1958	Wright	Wright	Hanson	Berg
1959	Rawls	Wright	Suggs	Rawls
1960	Wright	Rawls	Crocker	Ziske
1961	Wright	Wright	Wright	Faulk
1962	Kimball	Lindstrom	Wright	Wright
1963	Wright	Mills	M.Smith	Wright
1964	Mills	Wright	M.Smith	Mann
1965	Haynie	Mann	Whitworth	Maxwell
1966	Ehret	Spuzich	Whitworth	Wright
1967	Whitworth	a-LaCoste	—	Whitworth
1968	Post	Berning	—	—
1969	Rawls	Caponi	—	—
1970	Englehorn	Caponi	—	—
1971	Whitworth	Carner	—	—
1972	Ahern	Berning	Palmer	—
1973	Mills	Berning	—	—
1974	Haynie	Haynie	—	—
1975	Whitworth	Palmer	—	—
1976	Burfeindt	Carner	—	—
1977	Higuchi	Stacy	—	—
1978	Lopez	Stacy	—	—

Year	LPGA	US Open	duMaurier	D. Shore
1979	Caponi	Britz	Alcott	—
1980	Little	Alcott	Bradley	—
1981	Caponi	Bradley	Stephenson	—
1982	Stephenson	Anderson	Haynie	—
1983	Sheehan	Stephenson	Stacy	Alcott
1984	Sheehan	Stacy	Inkster	Inkster
1985	Lopez	Baker	Bradley	Miller
1986	Bradley	Geddes	Bradley	Bradley
1987	Geddes	Davies	Rosenthal	King
1988	Turner	Neumann	Little	Alcott
1989	Lopez	King	Green	Inkster
1990	Daniel	King	Johnston	King
1991	Mallon	Mallon	Scranton	Alcott
1992	King	Sheehan	Steinhaur	Mochrie
1993	Sheehan	Merten	Burton	Alfredsson
1994	Davies	Sheehan	Nause	Andrews
1995	Robbins	Sorenstam	Lidback	Bowen
1996	Davies	Sorenstam	Davies	Sheehan

Vare Trophy

The Vare Trophy for best scoring average by a player on the LPGA Tour has been awarded since 1937 by the LPGA. The award is named after Glenna Collett Vare, winner of six U.S. women's amateur titles from 1922-35.

Multiple winners: Kathy Whitworth (7); JoAnne Carner and Mickey Wright (5); Patty Berg, Beth Daniel, Nancy Lopez and Judy Rankin (3); Pat Bradley and Betsy King (2).

Year		Avg
1953	Patty Berg	75.00
1954	Babe Zaharias	75.48
1955	Patty Berg	74.47
1956	Patty Berg	74.57
1957	Louise Suggs	74.64
1958	Beverly Hanson	74.92
1959	Betsy Rawls	74.03
1960	Mickey Wright	73.25
1961	Mickey Wright	73.55
1962	Mickey Wright	73.67
1963	Mickey Wright	72.81
1964	Mickey Wright	72.46
1965	Kathy Whitworth	72.61
1966	Kathy Whitworth	72.60
1967	Kathy Whitworth	72.74
1968	Carol Mann	72.04
1969	Kathy Whitworth	72.38
1970	Kathy Whitworth	72.26
1971	Kathy Whitworth	72.88
1972	Kathy Whitworth	72.38
1973	Judy Rankin	73.08
1974	JoAnne Carner	72.87
1975	JoAnne Carner	72.40
1976	Judy Rankin	72.25
1977	Judy Rankin	72.16
1978	Nancy Lopez	71.76
1979	Nancy Lopez	71.20
1980	Amy Alcott	71.51
1981	JoAnne Carner	71.75
1982	JoAnne Carner	71.49
1983	JoAnne Carner	71.41
1984	Patty Sheehan	71.40
1985	Nancy Lopez	70.73
1986	Pat Bradley	71.10
1987	Betsy King	71.14
1988	Colleen Walker	71.26
1989	Beth Daniel	70.38
1990	Beth Daniel	70.54
1991	Pat Bradley	70.66
1992	Dottie Mochrie	70.80
1993	Betsy King	70.85
1994	Beth Daniel	70.90
1995	Annika Sorenstam	71.00

U.S. Women's Amateur

Stroke play in 1895, match play since 1896.

Multiple winners: Glenna Collett Vare (6); JoAnne Gunderson Carner (5); Margaret Curtis, Beatrix Hoyt, Dorothy Campbell Hurd, Juli Inkster, Alexa Stirling, Virginia Van Wie, Anne Quast Decker Welts (3); Kay Cockerill, Beth Daniel, Vicki Goetze, Katherine Harley, Genevieve Hecker, Betty Jameson, Kelli Kuehne and Barbara McIntire (2).

Year	
1895	Mrs. C.S. Brown
1896	Beatrix Hoyt
1897	Beatrix Hoyt
1898	Beatrix Hoyt
1899	Ruth Underhill
1900	Frances Griscom
1901	Genevieve Hecker
1902	Genevieve Hecker
1903	Bessie Anthony
1904	Georgianna Bishop
1905	Pauline Mackay
1906	Harriot Curtis
1907	Margaret Curtis
1908	Katherine Harley
1909	Dorothy Campbell
1910	Dorothy Campbell
1911	Margaret Curtis
1912	Margaret Curtis
1913	Gladys Ravenscroft
1914	Katherine Harley
1915	Florence Vanderbeck
1916	Alexa Stirling
1917-18	Not held
1919	Alexa Stirling
1920	Alexa Stirling
1921	Marion Hollins
1922	Glenna Collett
1923	Edith Cummings
1924	Dorothy C. Hurd
1925	Glenna Collett
1926	Helen Stetson
1927	Miriam Burns Horn
1928	Glenna Collett
1929	Glenna Collett
1930	Glenna Collett
1931	Helen Hicks
1932	Virginia Van Wie
1933	Virginia Van Wie
1934	Virginia Van Wie
1935	Glenna Collett Vare
1936	Pamela Barton
1937	Estelle Lawson
1938	Patty Berg
1939	Betty Jameson
1940	Betty Jameson
1941	Elizabeth Hicks
1942-45	Not held
1946	Babe D. Zaharias
1947	Louise Suggs
1948	Grace Lenczyk
1949	Dorothy Porter
1950	Beverly Hanson
1951	Dorothy Kirby
1952	Jacqueline Pung
1953	Mary Lena Faulk
1954	Barbara Romack
1955	Patricia Lesser
1956	Marlene Stewart
1957	JoAnne Gunderson
1958	Anne Quast
1959	Barbara McIntire
1960	JoAnne Gunderson
1961	Anne Quast Decker
1962	JoAnne Gunderson
1963	Anne Quast Welts
1964	Barbara McIntire
1965	Jean Ashley
1966	JoAnne G. Carner
1967	Mary Lou Dill
1968	JoAnne G. Carner
1969	Catherine Lacoste
1970	Martha Wilkinson
1971	Laura Baugh
1972	Mary Budke
1973	Carol Semple
1974	Cynthia Hill
1975	Beth Daniel
1976	Donna Horton
1977	Beth Daniel
1978	Cathy Sherk
1979	Carolyn Hill
1980	Juli Inkster
1981	Juli Inkster
1982	Juli Inkster
1983	Joanne Pacillo
1984	Deb Richard
1985	Michiko Hattori
1986	Kay Cockerill
1987	Kay Cockerill
1988	Pearl Sinn
1989	Vicki Goetze
1990	Pat Hurst
1991	Amy Fruhwirth
1992	Vicki Goetze
1993	Jill McGill
1994	Wendy Ward
1995	Kelli Kuehne
1996	Kelli Kuehne

British Women's Amateur Championship

Match play since 1893.

Multiple winners: Cecil Leitch and Joyce Wethered (4); May Hezlet, Lady Margaret Scott, Brigitte Varangot and Enid Wilson (3); Rhona Adair, Pam Barton, Dorothy Campbell, Elizabeth Chadwick, Julie Wade Hall, Helen Holm, Marley Spearman, Frances Stephens, Jessie Valentine and Michelle Walker (2).

Year	
1893	Lady Margaret Scott
1894	Lady Margaret Scott
1895	Lady Maraaret Scott
1896	Amy Pascoe
1897	Edith Orr
1898	Lena Thomson
1899	May Hezlet
1900	Rhona Adair
1901	Mary Graham
1902	May Hezlet
1903	Rhona Adair
1904	Lottie Dod
1905	Bertha Thompson
1906	Mrs. W. Kennion
1907	May Hezlet
1908	Maud Titterton
1909	Dorothy Campbell
1910	Elsie Grant-Suttie
1911	Dorothy Campbell
1912	Gladys Ravenscroft
1913	Muriel Dodd
1914	Cecil Leitch
1915-19	Not held
1920	Cecil Leitch
1921	Cecil Leitch
1922	Joyce Wethered
1923	Doris Chambers
1924	Joyce Wethered
1925	Joyce Wethered
1926	Cecil Leitch
1927	Simone de la Chaume
1928	Nanette le Blan
1929	Joyce Wethered
1930	Diana Fishwick
1931	Enid Wilson
1932	Enid Wilson
1933	Enid Wilson
1934	Helen Holm
1935	Wanda Morgan
1936	Pam Barton
1937	Jessie Anderson
1938	Helen Holm
1939	Pam Barton
1940-45	Not held
1946	Jean Hetherington
1947	Babe Zaharias
1948	Louise Suggs
1949	Frances Stephens
1950	Lally de St. Sauveur
1951	Catherine MacCann
1952	Moira Paterson
1953	Marlene Stewart
1954	Frances Stephens
1955	Jessie Valentine
1956	Wiffi Smith
1957	Philomena Garvey
1958	Jessie Valentine
1959	Elizabeth Price
1960	Barbara McIntire
1961	Marley Spearman
1962	Marley Spearman
1963	Brigitte Varangot
1964	Carol Sorenson
1965	Brigitte Varangot
1966	Elizabeth Chadwick
1967	Elizabeth Chadwick
1968	Brigitte Varangot
1969	Catherine Lacoste
1970	Dinah Oxley
1971	Michelle Walker
1972	Michelle Walker
1973	Ann Irvin
1974	Carol Semple
1975	Nancy Roth Syms
1976	Cathy Panton
1977	Angela Uzielli
1978	Edwina Kennedy
1979	Maureen Madill
1980	Anne Quast Sander
1981	Belle Robertson
1982	Kitrina Douglas
1983	Jill Thornhill
1984	Jody Rosenthal
1985	Lillian Behan
1986	Marnie McGuire
1987	Janet Collingham
1988	Joanne Furby
1989	Helen Dobson
1990	Julie Wade Hall
1991	Valerie Michaud
1992	Bernille Pedersen
1993	Catriona Lambert
1994	Emma Duggleby
1995	Julie Wade Hall
1996	Kelli Kuehne

Senior PGA

PGA Seniors' Championship

First played in 1937. Two championships played in 1979 and 1984.

Multiple winners: Sam Snead (6); Gary Player, Al Watrous and Eddie Williams (3); Julius Boros, Jock Hutchison, Don January, Arnold Palmer, Paul Runyan, Gene Sarazen and Lee Trevino (2).

Year		Year		Year		Year	
1937	Jock Hutchison	1953	Harry Schwab	1969	Tommy Bolt	1983	Not held
1938	Fred McLeod*	1954	Gene Sarazen	1970	Sam Snead	1984	Arnold Palmer
1939	Not held	1955	Mortie Dutra	1971	Julius Boros	1984	Peter Thomson
1940	Otto Hackbarth*	1956	Pete Burke	1972	Sam Snead	1985	Not held
1941	Jack Burke	1957	Al Watrous	1973	Sam Snead	1986	Gary Player
1942	Eddie Williams	1958	Gene Sarazen	1974	Robert de Vicenzo	1987	Chi Chi Rodriguez
1943-44	Not held	1959	Willie Goggin	1975	Charlie Sifford*	1988	Gary Player
1945	Eddie Williams	1960	Dick Metz	1976	Pete Cooper	1989	Larry Mowry
1946	Eddie Williams*	1961	Paul Runyan	1977	Julius Boros	1990	Gary Player
1947	Jock Hutchison	1962	Paul Runyan	1978	Joe Jiminez*	1991	Jack Nicklaus
1948	Charles McKenna	1963	Herman Barron	1979	Jack Fleck*	1992	Lee Trevino
1949	Marshall Crichton	1964	Sam Snead	1979	Don January	1993	Tom Wargo*
1950	Al Watrous	1965	Sam Snead	1980	Arnold Palmer*	1994	Lee Trevino
1951	Al Watrous*	1966	Fred Haas	1981	Miller Barber	1995	Ray Floyd
1952	Ernest Newnham	1967	Sam Snead	1982	Don January	1996	Hale Irwin
		1968	Chandler Harper				

***PLAYOFFS**

1938: Fred McLeod def. Otto Hackbarth in 18 holes. **1940:** Otto Hackbarth def. Jock Hutchison in 36 holes. **1946:** Eddie Williams def. Jock Hutchison in 18 holes. **1951:** Al Watrous def. Jock Hutchison in 18 holes. **1975:** Charlie Sifford def. Fred Wampler on 1st extra hole. **1978:** Joe Jiminez def. Joe Cheves and Manuel de la Torre on 1st extra hole. **1979:** Jack Fleck def. Bill Johnston on 1st extra hole. **1980:** Arnold Palmer def. Paul Harney on 1st extra hole. **1993:** Tom Wargo def. Bruce Crampton on 2nd extra hole.

U.S. Senior Open

Established in 1980 for senior players 55 years old and over, the minimum age was dropped to 50 (the PGA Seniors Tour entry age) in 1981. Arnold Palmer, Billy Casper, Orville Moody, Jack Nicklaus and Lee Trevino are the only golfers who have won both the U.S. Open and U.S. Senior Open.

Multiple winners: Miller Barber (3); Jack Nicklaus and Gary Player (2).

Year		Year		Year		Year	
1980	Roberto deVicenzo	1985	Miller Barber	1990	Lee Trevino	1995	Tom Weiskopf
1981	Arnold Palmer*	1986	Dale Douglass	1991	Jack Nicklaus*	1996	Dave Stockton
1982	Miller Barber	1987	Gary Player	1992	Larry Laoretti		
1983	Bill Casper*	1988	Gary Player*	1993	Jack Nicklaus		
1984	Miller Barber	1989	Orville Moody	1994	Simon Hobday		

***PLAYOFFS**

1981: Arnold Palmer (70) def. Bob Stone (74) and Billy Casper (77) in 18 holes. **1983:** Tied at 75 after 18-hole playoff, Casper def. Rod Funseth with a birdie on the 1st extra hole. **1988:** Gary Player (68) def. Bob Charles (70) in 18 holes. **1991:** Jack Nicklaus (65) def. Chi Chi Rodriguez (69) in 18 holes.

Senior Players Championship

First played in 1983 and contested in Cleveland (1983-86), Ponte Vedra, Fla. (1987-89), and Dearborn, Mich. (since 1990).

Multiple winner: Arnold Palmer and Dave Stockton (3).

Year		Year		Year		Year	
1983	Miller Barber	1987	Gary Player	1991	Jim Albus	1995	J.C. Snead*
1984	Arnold Palmer	1988	Billy Casper	1992	Dave Stockton	1996	Ray Floyd
1985	Arnold Palmer	1989	Orville Moody	1993	Jim Colbert		
1986	Chi Chi Rodriguez	1990	Jack Nicklaus	1994	Dave Stockton		

***PLAYOFF**

1995: J.C. Snead def. Jack Nicklaus on 1st extra hole.

The Tradition

First played in 1989 and played every year since at the Golf Club at Desert Mountain in Scottsdale, Ariz.

Multiple winner: Jack Nicklaus (4).

Year		Year		Year		Year	
1989	Don Bies	1991	Jack Nicklaus	1993	Tom Shaw	1995	Jack Nicklaus*
1990	Jack Nicklaus	1992	Lee Trevino	1994	Ray Floyd*	1996	Jack Nicklaus

***PLAYOFF**

1994: Ray Floyd def. Dale Douglass on 1st extra hole. **1995:** Jack Nicklaus def. Isao Aoki on 3rd extra hole.

Major Senior Championship Leaders

Through 1996. All players are still active.

	PGA Sr.	US Open	Senior Players	Trad	Total
1 Jack Nicklaus	1	2	1	4	**8**
2 Gary Player	3	2	1	0	**6**
3 Lee Trevino	2	1	0	1	**4**
4 Arnold Palmer	1	0	2	0	**3**
Miller Barber	0	2	1	0	**3**
Ray Floyd	1	0	1	1	**3**
7 Billy Casper	0	1	1	0	**2**
Orville Moody	0	1	1	0	**2**
Chi Chi Rodriquez	1	0	1	0	**2**
Dave Stockton	0	0	2	0	**2**

Grand Slam Summary

The Senior Grand Slam has officially consisted of The Tradition, the PGA Senior Championship, the Senior Players Championship and the U.S. Senior Open since 1990. Jack Nicklaus won three of the four events in 1991, but no one has won all four in one season.

Three wins in one year: Jack Nicklaus (1991).

Two wins in one year: Gary Player (twice); Orville Moody, Jack Nicklaus, Arnold Palmer and Lee Trevino (once).

Year	Tradition	PGA Sr.	Players	US Open
1983	—	—	M. Barber	Casper
1984	—	Palmer	Palmer	M. Barber
1985	—	Thomson	Palmer	M. Barber
1986	—	Player	Rodriguez	Douglass
1987	—	Rodriguez	Player	Player
1988	—	Player	Casper	Player
1989	Bies	Mowry	Moody	Moody
1990	Nicklaus	Player	Nicklaus	Trevino
1991	Nicklaus	Nicklaus	Albus	Nicklaus
1992	Trevino	Trevino	Stockton	Laoretti
1993	Shaw	Wargo	Colbert	Nicklaus
1994	Floyd	Trevino	Stockton	Hobday
1995	Nicklaus	Floyd	Snead	Weiskopf
1996	Nicklaus	Irwin	Floyd	Stockton

Annual Money Leaders

Official annual money leaders on the PGA, European PGA, Senior PGA and LPGA tours. European PGA earnings listed in pounds sterling (£).

PGA

Multiple leaders: Jack Nicklaus (8); Ben Hogan and Tom Watson (5); Arnold Palmer (4); Greg Norman, Sam Snead and Curtis Strange (3); Julius Boros, Billy Casper, Tom Kite, Byron Nelson and Nick Price (2).

Year		Earnings
1934	Paul Runyan	$ 6,767
1935	Johnny Revolta	9,543
1936	Horton Smith	7,682
1937	Harry Cooper	14,139
1938	Sam Snead	19,534
1939	Henry Picard	10,303
1940	Ben Hogan	10,655
1941	Ben Hogan	18,358
1942	Ben Hogan	13,143
1943	No records kept	
1944	Byron Nelson	37,968
1945	Byron Nelson	63,336
1946	Ben Hogan	42,556
1947	Jimmy Demaret	27,937
1948	Ben Hogan	32,112
1949	Sam Snead	31,594
1950	Sam Snead	35,759
1951	Lloyd Mangrum	26,089
1952	Julius Boros	37,033
1953	Lew Worsham	34,002
1954	Bob Toski	65,820
1955	Julius Boros	$ 63,122
1956	Ted Kroll	72,836
1957	Dick Mayer	65,835
1958	Arnold Palmer	42,608
1959	Art Wall	53,168
1960	Arnold Palmer	75,263
1961	Gary Player	64,540
1962	Arnold Palmer	81,448
1963	Arnold Palmer	128,230
1964	Jack Nicklaus	113,285
1965	Jack Nicklaus	140,752
1966	Billy Casper	121,945
1967	Jack Nicklaus	188,998
1968	Billy Casper	205,169
1969	Frank Beard	164,707
1970	Lee Trevino	157,037
1971	Jack Nicklaus	244,491
1972	Jack Nicklaus	320,542
1973	Jack Nicklaus	308,362
1974	Johnny Miller	353,022
1975	Jack Nicklaus	298,149
1976	Jack Nicklaus	$ 266,439
1977	Tom Watson	310,653
1978	Tom Watson	362,429
1979	Tom Watson	462,636
1980	Tom Watson	530,808
1981	Tom Kite	375,699
1982	Craig Stadler	446,462
1983	Hal Sutton	426,668
1984	Tom Watson	476,260
1985	Curtis Strange	542,321
1986	Greg Norman	653,296
1987	Curtis Strange	925,941
1988	Curtis Strange	1,147,644
1989	Tom Kite	1,395,278
1990	Greg Norman	1,165,477
1991	Corey Pavin	979,430
1992	Fred Couples	1,344,188
1993	Nick Price	1,478,557
1994	Nick Price	1,499,927
1995	Greg Norman	1,654,959

Note: In 1944-45, Nelson's winnings were in War Bonds.

Senior PGA

Multiple leaders: Don January (3); Miller Barber, Bob Charles, Dave Stockton and Lee Trevino (2).

Year		Earnings
1980	Don January	$44,100
1981	Miller Barber	83,136
1982	Miller Barber	106,890
1983	Don January	237,571
1984	Don January	328,597
1985	Peter Thomson	386,724
1986	Bruce Crampton	$454,299
1987	Chi Chi Rodriguez	509,145
1988	Bob Charles	533,929
1989	Bob Charles	725,887
1990	Lee Trevino	1,190,518
1991	Mike Hill	1,065,657
1992	Lee Trevino	$1,027,002
1993	Dave Stockton	1,175,944
1994	Dave Stockton	1,402,519
1995	Jim Colbert	1,444,386

European PGA

Multiple leaders: Seve Ballesteros (6); Sandy Lyle and Colin Montgomerie (3); Gay Brewer, Nick Faldo, Bernard Hunt, Bernhard Langer, Peter Thomson and Ian Woosnam (2).

Year		Earnings
1961	Bernard Hunt	£ 4,492
1962	Peter Thomson	5,764
1963	Bernard Hunt	7,209
1964	Neil Coles	7,890
1965	Peter Thomson	7,011
1966	Bruce Devlin	13,205
1967	Gay Brewer	20,235
1968	Gay Brewer	23,107
1969	Billy Casper	23,483
1970	Christy O'Connor	31,532
1971	Gary Player	11,281
1972	Bob Charles	18,538
1973	Tony Jacklin	£ 24,839
1974	Peter Oosterhuis	32,127
1975	Dale Hayes	20,507
1976	Seve Ballesteros	39,504
1977	Seve Ballesteros	46,436
1978	Seve Ballesteros	54,348
1979	Sandy Lyle	49,233
1980	Greg Norman	74,829
1981	Bernhard Langer	95,991
1982	Sandy Lyle	86,141
1983	Nick Faldo	140,761
1984	Bernhard Langer	160,883
1985	Sandy Lyle	£ 254,711
1986	Seve Ballesteros	259,275
1987	Ian Woosnam	439,075
1988	Seve Ballesteros	502,000
1989	Ronan Rafferty	465,981
1990	Ian Woosnam	737,977
1991	Seve Ballesteros	790,811
1992	Nick Faldo	1,220,540
1993	Colin Montgomerie	798,145
1994	Colin Montgomerie	920,647
1995	Colin Montgomerie	999,260

LPGA

Multiple leaders: Kathy Whitworth (8); Mickey Wright (4); Patty Berg, JoAnne Carner, Betsy King and Nancy Lopez (3); Pat Bradley, Beth Daniel, Judy Rankin, Betsy Rawls, Louise Suggs and Babe Zaharias (2).

Year		Earnings
1950	Babe Zaharias	$ 14,800
1951	Babe Zaharias	15,087
1952	Betsy Rawls	14,505
1953	Louise Suggs	19,816
1954	Patty Berg	16,011
1955	Patty Berg	16,492
1956	Marlene Hagge	20,235
1957	Patty Berg	16,272
1958	Beverly Hanson	12,639
1959	Betsy Rawls	26,774
1960	Louise Suggs	16,892
1961	Mickey Wright	22,236
1962	Mickey Wright	21,641
1963	Mickey Wright	31,269
1964	Mickey Wright	29,800
1965	Kathy Whitworth	28,658
1966	Kathy Whitworth	$ 33,517
1967	Kathy Whitworth	32,937
1968	Kathy Whitworth	48,379
1969	Carol Mann	49,152
1970	Kathy Whitworth	30,235
1971	Kathy Whitworth	41,181
1972	Kathy Whitworth	65,063
1973	Kathy Whitworth	82,864
1974	JoAnne Carner	87,094
1975	Sandra Palmer	76,374
1976	Judy Rankin	150,734
1977	Judy Rankin	122,890
1978	Nancy Lopez	189,814
1979	Nancy Lopez	197,489
1980	Beth Daniel	231,000
1981	Beth Daniel	206,998
1982	JoAnne Carner	$310,400
1983	JoAnne Carner	291,404
1984	Betsy King	266,771
1985	Nancy Lopez	416,472
1986	Pat Bradley	492,021
1987	Ayako Okamoto	466,034
1988	Sherri Turner	350,851
1989	Betsy King	654,132
1990	Beth Daniel	863,578
1991	Pat Bradley	763,118
1992	Dottie Mochrie	693,335
1993	Betsy King	595,992
1994	Laura Davies	687,201
1995	Annika Sorenstam	666,533

All-Time Leaders

PGA, Senior PGA and LPGA leaders through 1995.

Tournaments Won

PGA

		No
1	Sam Snead	81
2	Jack Nicklaus	70
3	Ben Hogan	63
4	Arnold Palmer	60
5	Byron Nelson	52
6	Billy Casper	51
7	Walter Hagan	40
	Cary Middlecoff	40
9	Gene Sarazen	38
10	Lloyd Mangrum	36
11	Horton Smith	32
	Tom Watson	32
13	Harry Cooper	31
	Jimmy Demaret	31
15	Leo Diegel	30
16	Gene Littler	29
	Paul Runyan	29
18	Lee Trevino	27
19	Henry Picard	26
20	Tommy Armour	24
	Macdonald Smith	24
	Johnny Miller	24
23	Johnny Farrell	22
	Ray Floyd	22
25	Four tied with 21.	

Senior PGA

		No
1	Lee Trevino	26
2	Miller Barber	24
3	Bob Charles	22
	Don January	22
	Chi Chi Rodriguez	22
6	Bruce Crampton	19
7	Gary Player	18
8	George Archer	17
	Mike Hill	17
10	Jim Colbert	13
11	Raymond Floyd	12
12	Orville Moody	11
	Dave Stockton	11
	Peter Thomson	11
15	Dale Douglass	10
	Arnold Palmer	10
17	Billy Casper	9
	Jim Dent	9
	Al Geiberger	9
20	Lee Elder	8
	Gene Littler	8
	Bob Murphy	8
	Jack Nicklaus	8
24	Don Bies	7
25	Dave Hill	6

LPGA

		No
1	Kathy Whitworth	88
2	Mickey Wright	82
3	Patty Berg	57
4	Betsy Rawls	55
5	Louise Suggs	50
6	Nancy Lopez	47
7	JoAnne Carner	42
	Sandra Haynie	42
9	Carol Mann	38
10	Patty Sheehan	34
11	Beth Daniel	32
12	Pat Bradley	31
	Babe Zaharias	31
14	Betsy King	30
15	Amy Alcott	29
	Jane Blalock	29
17	Judy Rankin	26
18	Marlene Hagge	25
19	Donna Caponi	24
20	Marilynn Smith	22
21	Sandra Palmer	21
22	Hollis Stacey	18
23	Ayako Okamoto	17
24	Jan Stephenson	16
25	Juli Inkster	15
	Sally Little	15

Note: Patty Berg's total includes 13 official pro wins prior to formation of LPGA in 1950.

All-Time Leaders (Cont.)

Money Won

PGA

		Earnings
1	Greg Norman	$9,592,829
2	Tom Kite	9,337,998
3	Payne Stewart	7,389,479
4	Nick Price	7,338,119
5	Fred Couples	7,188,408
6	Corey Pavin	7,175,523
7	Tom Watson	7,072,113
8	Paul Azinger	6,957,324
9	Ben Crenshaw	6,845,235
10	Curtis Strange	6,791,618
11	Mark O'Meara	6,126,466
12	Lanny Wadkins	6,028,855
13	Craig Stadler	6,008,753
14	Mark Calcavecchia	5,866,716
15	Hale Irwin	5,845,024
16	Chip Beck	5,755,844
17	Bruce Lietzke	5,710,262
18	Davis Love III	5,623,890
19	Scott Hoch	5,465,898
20	David Frost	5,458,172
21	Jack Nicklaus	5,440,357
22	Jay Haas	5,426,821
23	Ray Floyd	5,194,044
24	Gil Morgan	4,991,433
25	Fuzzy Zoeller	4,918,771

Senior PGA

		Earnings
1	Lee Trevino	$6,052,896
2	Bob Charles	5,861,028
3	Chi Chi Rodriguez	5,305,644
4	Mike Hill	5,130,135
5	George Archer	5,104,172
6	Jim Colbert	4,942,907
7	Dave Stockton	4,663,732
8	Dale Douglass	4,455,322
9	Jim Dent	4,194,208
10	Ray Floyd	3,952,465
11	Gary Player	3,775,278
12	Bruce Crampton	3,678,668
13	Miller Barber	3,524,010
14	Al Geigerger	3,471,066
15	Jim Albus	3,330,478
16	Harold Henning	3,178,520
17	Orville Moody	3,128,094
18	Rocky Thompson	2,962,225
19	Don January	2,918,909
20	Bob Murphy	2,866,129
21	Charles Coody	2,855,181
22	J.C. Snead	2,783,980
23	Walter Zembriski	2,570,594
24	Isao Aoki	2,557,057
25	Simon Hobday	2,517,063

PGA/Seniors Combined

		Earnings
1	Lee Trevino	$9,531,346
2	Ray Floyd	9,146,509
3	Jack Nicklaus	7,222,744
4	George Archer	6,986,414
5	Hale Irwin	6,644,199
6	Jim Colbert	6,496,042
7	Bob Charles	6,400,146
8	Chi Chi Rodriguez	6,342,749
9	Dave Stockton	5,946,153
10	Mike Hill	5,703,859
11	Gary Player	5,598,163
12	Miller Barber	5,126,418
13	Bruce Crampton	5,054,861
14	Dale Douglass	5,033,273
15	J.C. Snead	5,003,151
16	Jim Dent	4,759,453
17	Al Geiberger	4,736,254
18	Bob Murphy	4,508,990
19	Charles Coody	4,067,170
20	Don January	4,059,835
21	Gene Littler	3,665,123
22	Orville Moody	3,518,010
23	Arnold Palmer	3,491,442
24	Tom Weiskopf	3,433,376
25	Isao Aoki	3,429,514

European PGA

		Earnings
1	Bernhard Langer	£4,973,452
2	Nick Faldo	4,838,929
3	Seve Ballasteros	4,246,088
4	Ian Woosnam	4,176,787
5	Colin Montgomerie	4,120,498
6	Sam Torrance	3,387,646
7	Jose Maria Olazabal	3,140,347
8	Mark McNulty	2,510,450
9	Ronan Rafferty	2,491,672
10	Sandy Lyle	£2,467,627
11	Mark James	2,456,839
12	Anders Forsbrand	2,288,227
13	Gordon Brand Jr.	2,230,980
14	Barry Lane	1,966,018
15	Rodger Davis	1,956,217
16	Howard Clark	1,951,420
17	Fred Couples	1,924,917
18	Jose Rivero	1,785,513
19	Costantino Rocca	£1,780,404
20	Frank Nobilo	1,730,565
21	Greg Norman	1,685,928
22	Vijay Singh	1,668,013
23	David Gilford	1,597,233
24	David Feherty	1,585,774
25	Eduardo Romero	1,511,766

LPGA

		Earnings
1	Betsy King	$5,374,023
2	Pat Bradley	5,141,019
3	Beth Daniel	4,972,216
4	Patty Sheehan	4,788,546
5	Nancy Lopez	4,275,685
6	Amy Alcott	3,135,772
7	Dottie Mochrie	3,095,716
8	JoAnne Carner	2,878,105
9	Ayako Okamoto	2,735,630
10	Rosie Jones	$2,620,006
11	Jane Geddes	2,601,295
12	Jan Stephenson	2,347,897
13	Meg Mallon	2,297,045
14	Juli Inkster	2,266,157
15	Colleen Walker	2,265,000
16	Laura Davies	2,216,006
17	Hollis Stacy	2,081,928
18	Tammie Green	2,049,880
19	Judy Dickinson	$2,014,410
20	D. Ammaccapane	1,813,396
21	Dawn Coe-Jones	1,797,841
22	Chris Johnson	1,760,394
23	Deb Richard	1,737,348
24	Kathy Whitworth	1,731,770
25	Sally Little	1,704,397

The Skins Game

The Skins Game is a made-for-TV, $540,000 shootout between four premier golfers playing 18 holes over two days (nine each day). Each hole is counted as a skin with the first six skins worth $20,000 apiece, the second six worth $30,000, and the last six worth $40,000. If a hole is tied, the money is added to the worth of the next hole. The PGA Skins Game was started in late November 1983, followed by the Senior Skins in late January 1988 and the LPGA Skins in late May 1990. Due to scheduling conflicts, the LPGA Skins was not played in 1991.

PGA Skins

Total Winnings: 1. Fred Couples ($910,000); 2. Payne Stewart ($840,000); 3. Fuzzy Zoeller ($695,000); 4. Jack Nicklaus ($650,000); 5. Curtis Strange ($605,000); 6. Tom Watson ($440,000); 7. Lee Trevino ($435,000); 8. Ray Floyd ($350,000); 9. Arnold Palmer ($245,000); 10. Corey Pavin ($240,000); 11. Greg Norman ($200,000); 12. Gary Player ($170,000); 13. John Daly ($160,000); 14. Paul Azinger ($80,000); 15. Nick Faldo ($70,000); 16. Peter Jacobsen ($30,000); 17. Tom Kite ($0).

Year	Winner	Earnings	Outskinned	
1983	Gary Player	$170,000	Palmer	$140,000
			Nicklaus	40,000
			Watson	10,000
1984	Jack Nicklaus	$240,000	Watson	$120,000
			Palmer	0
			Player	0
1985	Fuzzy Zoeller	$255,000	Watson	$100,000
			Palmer	80,000
			Nicklaus	15,000
1986	Fuzzy Zoeller	$370,000	Trevino	$55,000
			Palmer	25,000
			Nicklaus	0

Year	Winner	Earnings	Outskinned	
1987	Lee Trevino	$310,000	Nicklaus	$70,000
			Zoeller	70,000
			Palmer	0
1988	Ray Floyd	$290,000	Nicklaus	$125,000
			Trevino	35,000
			Strange	0
1989	Curtis Strange	$265,000	Nicklaus	$90,000
			Floyd	60,000
			Trevino	35,000
1990	Curtis Strange	$220,000	Norman	$90,000
			Faldo	70,000
			Nicklaus	70,000
1991	Payne Stewart	$260,000	Daly	$160,000
			Strange	120,000
			Nicklaus	0
1992	Payne Stewart	$220,000	Couples	$210,000
			Norman	110,000
			Kite	0
1993	Payne Stewart	$280,000	Couples	$260,000
			Palmer	0
			Azinger	0
1994	Tom Watson	$210,000	Couples	$170,000
			Azinger	80,000
			Stewart	80,000
1995	Fred Couples	$270,000	Pavin	$240,000
			Jacobsen	30,000
			Watson	0

Senior Skins

Total Winnings: 1. Ray Floyd ($960,000); 2. Arnold Palmer ($895,000); 3. Jack Nicklaus ($815,000); 4. Chi Chi Rodriguez ($685,000); 5. Lee Trevino ($305,000); 6. Jim Colbert ($180,000); 7. Gary Player ($180,000); 8. Billy Casper ($80,000); 9. Sam Snead ($0).

Year	Winner	Earnings	Outskinned	
1988	C.C. Rodriguez	$300,000	Player	$40,000
			Palmer	20,000
			Snead	0
1989	C.C. Rodriguez	$120,000	Player	$90,000
			Casper	80,000
			Palmer	70,000
1990	Arnold Palmer	$240,000	Nicklaus	$140,000
			Trevino	70,000
			Player	0
1991	Jack Nicklaus	$310,000	Trevino	$125,000
			Palmer	15,000
			Player	0
			Rodriguez	0
1992	Arnold Palmer	$205,000	Rodriguez	$120,000
			Nicklaus	95,000
			Trevino	30,000
1993	Arnold Palmer	$190,000	Rodriguez	$145,000
			Floyd	60,000
			Nicklaus	55,000
1994	Ray Floyd	$240,000	Palmer	$115,000
			Trevino	80,000
			Nicklaus	15,000
1995	Ray Floyd	$420,000	Nicklaus	$120,000
			Trevino	0
			Palmer	0
1996	Ray Floyd	$240,000	Colbert	$180,000
			Nicklaus	80,000
			Palmer	40,000

LPGA Skins

Total winnings: 1. Laura Davies ($480,000); 2. Betsy King and Patty Sheehan ($395,000); 4. Dottie Mochrie ($360,000); 5. Nancy Lopez ($320,000); 6. Pat Bradley ($285,000); 7. Jan Stephenson ($270,000); 8. JoAnne Carner ($110,000); 9. Dottie Pepper and Annika Sorenstam ($100,000); 11. Meg Mallon ($65,000); 12. Brandie Burton ($0).

Year	Winner	Earnings	Outskinned	
1990	Jan Stephenson	$200,000	Carner	$110,000
			Lopez	95,000
			King	45,000
1991	Not held			
1992	Pat Bradley	$200,000	Lopez	$115,000
			Stephenson	70,000
			Mallon	65,000
1993	Betsy King	$185,000	Lopez	$110,000
			Bradley	85,000
			Mochrie	70,000
1994	Patty Sheehan	$285,000	King	$165,000
			Burton	0
			Lopez	0
1995	Dottie Mochrie	$290,000	Davies	$140,000
			Sheehan	110,000
			Lopez	0
1996	Laura Davies	$340,000	Pepper	$100,000
			Sorenstam	100,000
			Daniel	0

Annual Awards

PGA of America Player of the Year

Awarded by the PGA of America; based on points scale that weighs performance in major tournaments, regular events, money earned and scoring average.

Multiple winners: Tom Watson (6); Jack Nicklaus (5); Ben Hogan (4); Julius Boros, Billy Casper, Arnold Palmer and Nick Price (2).

Year		Year		Year		Year	
1948	Ben Hogan	1960	Arnold Palmer	1972	Jack Nicklaus	1984	Tom Watson
1949	Sam Snead	1961	Jerry Barber	1973	Jack Nicklaus	1985	Lanny Wadkins
1950	Ben Hogan	1962	Arnold Palmer	1974	Johnny Miller	1986	Bob Tway
1951	Ben Hogan	1963	Julius Boros	1975	Jack Nicklaus	1987	Paul Azinger
1952	Julius Boros	1964	Ken Venturi	1976	Jack Nicklaus	1988	Curtis Strange
1953	Ben Hogan	1965	Dave Marr	1977	Tom Watson	1989	Tom Kite
1954	Ed Furgol	1966	Billy Casper	1978	Tom Watson	1990	Nick Faldo
1955	Doug Ford	1967	Jack Nicklaus	1979	Tom Watson	1991	Corey Pavin
1956	Jack Burke	1968	No award	1980	Tom Watson	1992	Fred Couples
1957	Dick Mayer	1969	Orville Moody	1981	Bill Rogers	1993	Nick Price
1958	Dow Finsterwald	1970	Billy Casper	1982	Tom Watson	1994	Nick Price
1959	Art Wall	1971	Lee Trevino	1983	Hal Sutton	1995	Greg Norman

Annual Awards (Cont.)

PGA Tour Player of the Year

Awarded by the PGA Tour starting in 1990. Winner voted on by tour members from list of nominees.
Multiple winner: Fred Couples and Nick Price (2).

Year	Year	Year	Year
1990 Wayne Levi	1992 Fred Couples	1994 Nick Price	1995 Greg Norman
1991 Fred Couples	1993 Nick Price		

PGA Tour Rookie of the Year

Awarded by the PGA Tour starting in 1990. Winner voted on by tour members from list of first-year nominees.

Year	Year	Year	Year
1990 Robert Gamez	1992 Mark Carnevale	1994 Ernie Els	1995 Woody Austin
1991 John Daly	1993 Vijay Singh		

PGA Senior Player of the Year

Awarded by the PGA Seniors Tour starting in 1990. Winner voted on by tour members from list of nominees.
Multiple winner: Lee Trevino (3).

Year	Year	Year	Year
1990 Lee Trevino	1991 George Archer & Mike Hill	1992 Lee Trevino	1994 Lee Trevino
		1993 Dave Stockton	1995 Jim Colbert

PGA Senior Tour Rookie of the Year

Awarded by the PGA Tour starting in 1990. Winner voted on by tour members from list of first-year nominees.

Year	Year	Year	Year
1990 Lee Trevino	1992 Dave Stockton	1994 Jay Sigel	1995 Hale Irwin
1991 Jim Colbert	1993 Bob Murphy		

European Golfer of the Year

Officially, the Johnnie Walker Trophy; voting done by panel of European golf writers and tour members.
Multiple winners: Seve Ballesteros and Nick Faldo (3); Bernhard Langer (2).

Year	Year	Year	Year
1985 Bernhard Langer	1988 Seve Ballesteros	1991 Seve Ballesteros	1994 Ernie Els
1986 Seve Ballesteros	1989 Nick Faldo	1992 Nick Faldo	1995 Colin Montgomerie
1987 Ian Woosnam	1990 Nick Faldo	1993 Bernhard Langer	

LPGA Player of the Year

Awarded by the LPGA; based on performance points accumulated during the year.
Multiple winners: Kathy Whitworth (7); Nancy Lopez (4); JoAnne Carner, Beth Daniel and Betsy King (3); Pat Bradley, Beth Daniel and Judy Rankin (2).

Year	Year	Year	Year
1966 Kathy Whitworth	1974 JoAnne Carner	1982 JoAnne Carner	1990 Beth Daniel
1967 Kathy Whitworth	1975 Sandra Palmer	1983 Patty Sheehan	1991 Pat Bradley
1968 Kathy Whitworth	1976 Judy Rankin	1984 Betsy King	1992 Dottie Mochrie
1969 Kathy Whitworth	1977 Judy Rankin	1985 Nancy Lopez	1993 Betsy King
1970 Sandra Haynie	1978 Nancy Lopez	1986 Pat Bradley	1994 Beth Daniel
1971 Kathy Whitworth	1979 Nancy Lopez	1987 Ayako Okamoto	1995 Annika Sorenstam
1972 Kathy Whitworth	1980 Beth Daniel	1988 Nancy Lopez	
1973 Kathy Whitworth	1981 JoAnne Carner	1989 Betsy King	

Sony World Rankings

Begun in 1986, the Sony World Rankings combine the best golfers on the PGA and European PGA tours. Rankings are based on a rolling three-year period and weighed in favor of more recent results. While annual winners are not announced, certain players reaching No. 1 have dominated each year.
Multiple winners (at year's end): Greg Norman (5); Nick Faldo (3); Seve Ballesteros (2).

Year	Year	Year	Year
1986 Seve Ballesteros	1989 Seve Ballesteros & Greg Norman	1991 Ian Woosnam	1993 Nick Faldo
1987 Greg Norman	1990 Nick Faldo & Greg Norman	1992 Fred Couples & Nick Faldo	1994 Nick Price
1988 Greg Norman			1995 Greg Norman

National Team Competition

MEN

Ryder Cup

The Ryder Cup was presented by British seed merchant and businessman Samuel Ryder in 1927 for competition between professional golfers from Great Britain and the United States. The British team was expanded to include Irish players in 1973 and the rest of Europe in 1979. The United States leads the series 23-6-2 after 31 matches.

Year
1927 United States, 9½-2½
1929 Great Britain, 7-5
1931 United States, 9-3
1933 Great Britain, 6½-5½
1935 United States, 9-3
1937 United States, 8-4
1939-45 Not held
1947 United States, 11-1
1949 United States, 7-5
1951 United States, 9½-2½
1953 United States, 6½-5½

Year
1955 United States, 8-4
1957 Great Britain, 7½-4½
1959 United States, 8½-3½
1961 United States, 14½-9½
1963 United States, 23-9
1965 United States, 19½-12½
1967 United States, 23½-8½
1969 Draw, 16-16
1971 United States, 18½-13½
1973 United States, 19-13
1975 United States, 21-11

Year
1977 United States, 12½-7½
1979 United States, 17-11
1981 United States, 18½-9½
1983 United States, 14½-13½
1985 Europe, 16½-11½
1987 Europe, 15-13
1989 Draw, 14-14
1991 United States, 14½-13½
1993 United States, 15-13
1995 Europe, 14½-13½

Playing Sites

1927—Worcester CC (Mass.); **1929**—Moortown, England; **1931**—Scioto CC (Ohio); **1933**—Southport & Ainsdale, England; **1935**—Ridgewood CC (N.J.); **1937**—Southport & Ainsdale, England; **1939-45**—Not held.

1947—Portland CC (Ore.); **1949**—Ganton GC, England; **1951**—Pinehurst CC (N.C.); **1953**—Wentworth, England; **1955**—Thunderbird Ranch & CC (Calif.); **1957**—Lindrick GC, England; **1959**—Eldorado CC (Calif.).

1961—Royal Lytham & St. Annes, England; **1963**—East Lake CC (Ga.); **1965**—Royal Birkdale, England; **1967**—Champions GC (Tex.); **1969**—Royal Birkdale, England; **1971**—Old Warson CC (Mo.); **1973**—Muirfield, Scotland; **1975**—Laurel Valley GC (Pa.); **1977**—Royal Lytham & St. Annes, England; **1979**—Greenbrier (W.Va.).

1981—Walton Heath GC, England; **1983**—PGA National GC (Fla.); **1985**—The Belfry, England; **1987**—Muirfield Village GC (Ohio); **1989**—The Belfry, England; **1991**—Ocean Course (S.C.); **1993**—The Belfry, England; **1995**—Oak Hill CC (N.Y.); **1997**—Valderrama, Costa del Sol, Spain.

Walker Cup

The Walker Cup was presented by American businessman George Herbert Walker in 1922 for competition between amateur golfers from Great Britain and the United States. The U.S. leads the series with a 30-4-1 record after 35 matches.

Year
1922 United States, 8-4
1923 United States, 6½-5½
1924 United States, 9-3
1926 United States, 6½-5½
1928 United States, 11-1
1930 United States, 10-2
1932 United States, 9½-2½
1934 United States, 9½-2½
1936 United States, 10½-1½
1938 Britain-Ireland, 7½-4½
1940-46 Not held
1947 United States, 8-4

Year
1949 United States, 10-2
1951 United States, 7½-4½
1953 United States, 9-3
1955 United States, 10-2
1957 United States, 8½-3½
1959 United States, 9-3
1961 United States, 11-1
1963 United States, 14-10
1965 Draw, 12-12
1967 United States, 15-9
1969 United States, 13-11
1971 Britain-Ireland, 13-11

Year
1973 United States, 14-10
1975 United States, 15½-8½
1977 United States, 16-8
1979 United States, 15½-8½
1981 United States, 15-9
1983 United States, 13½-10½
1985 United States, 13-11
1987 United States, 16½-7½
1989 Britain-Ireland, 12½-11½
1991 United States, 14-10
1993 United States, 19-5
1995 Britain-Ireland, 14-10

WOMEN

Solheim Cup

The Solheim Cup was presented by the Karsten Manufacturing Co. in 1990 for competition between women professional golfers from Europe and the United States. The U.S. leads the series with a 3-1 record after four matches.

Year
1990 United States, 11½-4½
1992 Europe, 11½-6½

Year
1994 United States, 13-7

Year
1996 United States, 17-11

Curtis Cup

Named after British golfing sisters Harriot and Margaret Curtis, the Curtis Cup was first contested in 1932 between teams of women amateurs from the United States and the British Isles.

Competed for every other year since 1932 (except during World War II). The U.S. leads the series with a 20-6-3 record after 29 matches.

Year
1932 United States, 5½-3½
1934 United States, 6½-2½
1936 Draw, 4½-4½
1938 United States, 5½-3½
1940-46 Not held
1948 United States, 6½-2½
1950 United States, 7½-1½
1952 British Isles, 5-4
1954 United States, 6-3
1956 British Isles, 5-4

Year
1958 Draw, 4½-4½
1960 United States, 6½-2½
1962 United States, 8-1
1964 United States, 10½-7½
1966 United States, 13-5
1968 United States, 10½-7½
1970 United States, 11½-6½
1972 United States, 10-8
1974 United States, 13-5
1976 United States, 11½-6½

Year
1978 United States, 12-6
1980 United States, 13-5
1982 United States, 14½-3½
1984 United States, 9½-8½
1986 British Isles, 13-5
1988 British Isles, 11-7
1990 United States, 14-4
1992 British Isles, 10-8
1994 Draw, 9-9
1996 British Isles, 11½-6½

COLLEGES

Men's NCAA Division I Champions

College championships decided by match play from 1897-1964, and stroke play since 1965.

Multiple winners (Teams): Yale (21); Houston (16); Princeton (12); Oklahoma St. (8); Stanford (7); Harvard (6); LSU and North Texas (4); Florida and Wake Forest (3); Arizona St., Michigan, Ohio St. and Texas (2). (Individuals): Ben Crenshaw and Phil Mickelson (3); Dick Crawford, Dexter Cummings, G.T. Dunlop, Fred Lamprecht, and Scott Simpson (2).

Year	Team winner	Individual champion
1897	Yale	Louis Bayard, Princeton
1898	Harvard (spring)	John Reid, Yale
1898	Yale (fall)	James Curtis, Harvard
1899	Harvard	Percy Pyne, Princeton
1900	Not held	
1901	Harvard	H. Lindsley, Harvard
1902	Yale (spring)	Chas. Hitchcock Jr., Yale
1902	Harvard (fall)	Chandler Egan, Harvard
1903	Harvard	F.O. Reinhart, Princeton
1904	Harvard	A.L. White, Harvard
1905	Yale	Robert Abbott, Yale
1906	Yale	W.E. Clow Jr., Yale
1907	Yale	Ellis Knowles, Yale
1908	Yale	H.H. Wilder, Harvard
1909	Yale	Albert Seckel, Princeton
1910	Yale	Robert Hunter, Yale
1911	Yale	George Stanley, Yale
1912	Yale	F.C. Davison, Harvard
1913	Yale	Nathaniel Wheeler, Yale
1914	Princeton	Edward Allis, Harvard
1915	Yale	Francis Blossom, Yale
1916	Princeton	J.W. Hubbell, Harvard
1917-18	Not held	
1919	Princeton	A.L. Walker Jr., Columbia
1920	Princeton	Jess Sweetster, Yale
1921	Dartmouth	Simpson Dean, Princeton
1922	Princeton	Pollack Boyd, Dartmouth
1923	Princeton	Dexter Cummings, Yale
1924	Yale	Dexter Cummings, Yale
1925	Yale	Fred Lamprecht, Tulane
1926	Yale	Fred Lamprecht, Tulane
1927	Princeton	Watts Gunn, Georgia Tech
1928	Princeton	Maurice McCarthy, G'town
1929	Princeton	Tom Aycock, Yale
1930	Princeton	G.T. Dunlap Jr., Princeton
1931	Yale	G.T. Dunlap Jr., Princeton
1932	Yale	J.W. Fischer, Michigan
1933	Yale	Walter Emery, Oklahoma
1934	Michigan	Charles Yates, Ga.Tech
1935	Michigan	Ed White, Texas
1936	Yale	Charles Kocsis, Michigan
1937	Princeton	Fred Haas Jr., LSU
1938	Stanford	John Burke, Georgetown
1939	Stanford	Vincent D'Antoni, Tulane
1940	Princeton & LSU	Dixon Brooke, Virginia
1941	Stanford	Earl Stewart, LSU
1942	LSU & Stanford	Frank Tatum Jr., Stanford
1943	Yale	Wallace Ulrich, Carleton
1944	Notre Dame	Louis Lick, Minnesota
1945	Ohio State	John Lorms, Ohio St.
1946	Stanford	George Hamer, Georgia
1947	LSU	Dave Barclay, Michigan
1948	San Jose St.	Bob Harris, San Jose St.
1949	North Texas	Harvie Ward, N.Carolina
1950	North Texas	Fred Wampler, Purdue
1951	North Texas	Tom Nieporte, Ohio St.
1952	North Texas	Jim Vichers, Oklahoma
1953	Stanford	Earl Moeller, Oklahoma St.
1954	SMU	Hillman Robbins, Memphis St.
1955	LSU	Joe Campbell, Purdue
1956	Houston	Rick Jones, Ohio St.
1957	Houston	Rex Baxter Jr., Houston
1958	Houston	Phil Rodgers, Houston
1959	Houston	Dick Crawford, Houston
1960	Houston	Dick Crawford, Houston
1961	Purdue	Jack Nicklaus, Ohio St.
1962	Houston	Kermit Zarley, Houston
1963	Oklahoma St.	R.H. Sikes, Arkansas
1964	Houston	Terry Small, San Jose St.
1965	Houston	Marty Fleckman, Houston
1966	Houston	Bob Murphy, Florida
1967	Houston	Hale Irwin, Colorado
1968	Florida	Grier Jones, Oklahoma St.
1969	Houston	Bob Clark, Cal St.-LA
1970	Houston	John Mahaffey, Houston
1971	Texas	Ben Crenshaw, Texas
1972	Texas	Ben Crenshaw, Texas & Tom Kite, Texas
1973	Florida	Ben Crenshaw, Texas
1974	Wake Forest	Curtis Strange, W.Forest
1975	Wake Forest	Jay Haas, Wake Forest
1976	Oklahoma St.	Scott Simpson, U.S.C
1977	Houston	Scott Simpson, U.S.C
1978	Oklahoma St.	David Edwards, Okla. St.
1979	Ohio St.	Gary Hallberg, Wake Forest
1980	Oklahoma St.	Jay Don Blake, Utah St.
1981	Brigham Young	Ron Commans, U.S.C
1982	Houston	Billy Ray Brown, Houston
1983	Oklahoma St.	Jim Carter, Arizona St.
1984	Houston	John Inman, N.Carolina
1985	Houston	Clark Burroughs, Ohio St.
1986	Wake Forest	Scott Verplank, Okla. St.
1987	Oklahoma St.	Brian Watts, Oklahoma St.
1988	UCLA	E.J. Pfister, Oklahoma St.
1989	Oklahoma	Phil Mickelson, Ariz. St.
1990	Arizona St.	Phil Mickelson, Ariz. St.
1991	Oklahoma St.	Warren Schuette, UNLV
1992	Arizona	Phil Mickelson, Ariz. St.
1993	Florida	Todd Demsey, Ariz. St.
1994	Stanford	Justin Leonard, Texas
1995	Oklahoma St.	Chip Spratlin, Auburn
1996	Arizona St.	Tiger Woods, Stanford

Women's NCAA Champions

Decided by stroke play since 1982. **Multiple winners** (Teams): Arizona St. (4); Florida, San Jose St. and Tulsa (2).

Year	Team winner	Individual champion
1982	Tulsa	Kathy Baker, Tulsa
1983	TCU	Penny Hammel, Miami
1984	Miami-FL	Cindy Schreyer, Georgia
1985	Florida	Danielle Ammaccapane, Ariz.St.
1986	Florida	Page Dunlap, Florida
1987	San Jose St.	Caroline Keggi, New Mexico
1988	Tulsa	Melissa McNamara, Tulsa
1989	San Jose St.	Pat Hurst, San Jose St.
1990	Arizona St.	Susan Slaughter, Arizona
1991	UCLA	Annika Sorenstam, Arizona
1992	San Jose St.	Vicki Goetze, Georgia
1993	Arizona St.	Charlotta Sorenstam, Ariz. St.
1994	Arizona St.	Emilee Klein, Ariz. St.
1995	Arizona St.	K. Mourgue d'Algue, Ariz. St.
1996	Arizona	Marisa Baena, Arizona

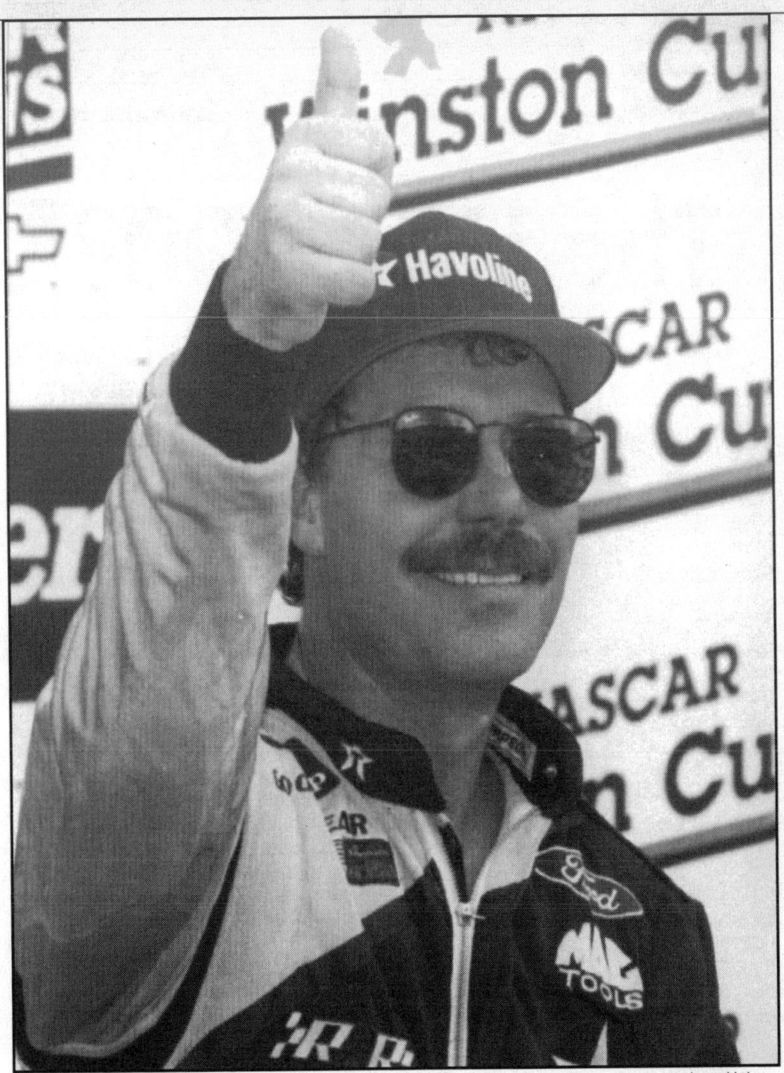

Wide World Photos

Ernie Irvan celebrates his first Winston Cup victory since his 1994 crash. Irvan won the Jiffy Lube 300 at the New Hampshire International Speedway in Loudon, N.H.

AUTO RACING

by Mike Harris

The U.S. 500?

In a move right out of baseball's PR handbook, CART and the IRL squabbled and the result was a watered-down Indy 500 and something called the U.S. 500

The auto racing scene in 1996 can be painted as an unfinished canvas, with the future of the 80-year-old Indianapolis 500 a little unclear, a record eighth Winston Cup title for Dale Earnhardt still only a hope and Formula One star Damon Hill apparently about to find out what life with the have-nots is like again.

Not that the season wasn't generally an artistic success, with both the established PPG Indy Car World Series and the fledgling Indy Racing League finding things to brag about, Jeff Gordon proving once again that he is probably going to dominate stock car racing for years to come and Formula One finding out what the people in Indy-car already knew, that Jacques Villeneuve is a real racing talent.

Indy was thrown into a tizzy in 1996 by the split between the team-owner run PPG series, also known as Championship Auto Racing Teams (CART), and the IRL, dreamed up by Tony George, president of the Indianapolis Motor Speedway as a less-expensive, all-oval alternative.

With George in charge, the first, abbreviated IRL season began in January with a virtually unknown lineup at the new Walt Disney World Speedway, just inside the main entrance to the Orlando, Fla., amusement park, and ended on May 26 with upstart Buddy Lazier winning the Indy 500.

Mike Harris covered his first Indianapolis 500 in 1969 and has been Motorsports Editor for the Associated Press since 1980.

It was a truly dramatic story, with Lazier still in considerable pain from a crash in March at Phoenix in which his lower back was shattered, as the driver put it, "like the shell of an egg when it's dropped."

The big question among racing people was whether the field that Lazier beat was truly representative, with 1990 winner Arie Luyendyk the only former winner in the 33-car lineup and virtually all of the biggest names in the open-wheel division about 300 miles away at Michigan International Speedway that day running in the inaugural U.S. 500.

"As good as our car was today, we could have beaten whoever was here," said Lazier, a 28-year-old who never had finished better than sixth in a CART event.

"The pain actually helps me keep my concentration because I don't want to go through it again," said the youngster who had to use a cane to walk to and from his car and use a back brace and special seat while in it.

Indy was also marred by two accidents, the most serious and tragic nine days before the event when two-time pole-winner Scott Brayton died in a crash during a practice session when a punctured tire sent him hurtling into the wall.

The popular Brayton, whose second pole win at Indy had come the previous weekend, was the first driver to die in an Indy-car accident since rookie Jovy Marcelo was killed during a practice at Indy in 1992.

Alessandro Zampedri of Italy, who led just

Wide World Photos

Soccer legend **Pele**, in his role as Brazil's Minister of Sports, delivers the winner's cup to **Damon Hill** after the running of the Brazilian Grand Prix while **Michael Schumacher** looks on.

11 laps from the end, was a victim of a last-lap crash in which veteran Roberto Guerrero lost control at high speed in the final turn and caught Zampedri and Eliseo Salazar in the tangle.

Zampedri sustained serious foot and leg injuries and came close to having his right foot amputated because of lack of circulation. Fortunately, however, the foot was saved and Zampedri was insisting by late in the season that he would be back in a race car for the 1997 Indy 500.

At the controversial U.S. 500, which was born after CART officials refused to go along with George's idea of reserving 25 of the starting positions at Indy for IRL regulars, things did not go smoothly either.

Before the green flag could even fly, the three-abreast start went wrong. Pole-winner Jimmy Vasser and fellow front row starters Adrian Fernandez and Bryan Herta got caught up in a melee in the fourth turn of the pace lap that brought out a red flag.

Since the race had not officially begun, all the teams that needed them were allowed to use backup cars, leaving only Fernandez without a working car when the event finally did get under way.

Vasser, whose first Indy-car win had come in the season-opener at Homestead, Fla., two months earlier, won in his backup car for his fourth win in six races. That win was a key to his eventually locking up the PPG Cup title in a close season-ending battle with Michael Andretti, Vasser's Rookie of the Year teammate Alex Zanardi of Italy and Al Unser Jr.

"The way we won that race, in our backup car after the accident at the start, says so much for the Target Chip Ganassi Team," Vasser said. "The guys prepared one car good enough to win the pole and another good enough to win the race. That's a real tribute to them."

While Lazier was collecting $1,367,854 for the win at Indy, Vasser was picking up $1,157,750 for the victory at Michigan.

Rookie Buzz Calkins and Scott Sharp, driving for longtime Indy-car star A.J. Foyt, shared the first IRL championship. The second season, which was to run through the Indy 500 next May, began in August in New Hampshire with a victory by Sharp, which was Foyt's first as just a team-owner.

Wide World Photos

Buddy Lazier came back from injury to win a less-than-competitive 1996 Indianapolis 500.

The season went on a hiatus after Richie Hearn won the next event at the new Las Vegas, Nev., track in September. It will not resume until Jan. 25 in Orlando. When it does get going again, the IRL will have switched from the year-old race cars and turbocharged engines it had been using to brand new, specially-built chassies powered by non-turbocharged engines.

"What that's going to do is slow the cars down, although we really don't know how much, yet, and keep the costs within reason," George said. "It's going to allow new teams to keep coming into our sport and it's going to be a big change."

There was more tragedy for the Indy-car people later in the season at Toronto, where rookie Jeff Krosnoff and corner worker Gary Avrin were killed when the 31-year-old driver made wheel-to-wheel contact with the car driven by Stefan Johansson and soared high into the air. The car flew above a concrete barrier lining the course, hit Avrin in its flight, then smashed hard into a huge tree. Both men were killed instantly and the race was flagged to a halt four laps early.

NASCAR's Winston Cup stock car series was a considerably more upbeat circuit, with plenty of positive stories emerging on and off the track in 1996.

The only real negative was Earnhardt, who started the season by failing for the 18th time in his illustrious career to win the season-opening Daytona 500, considered the most prestigious race in the series.

Just as he did three years earlier, Dale Jarrett, the younger son of two-time Winston Cup champion and now TV commentator Ned Jarrett, kept Earnhardt from his most coveted win.

Jarrett passed Earnhardt 24 laps from the end and stayed ahead the rest of the way, barely holding off the desperate Dale on the final trip around the 2.5-mile Daytona International Speedway oval.

"Winning this race a second time when Dale hasn't won his first yet really tells me how special it is," Jarrett said. "I was really worried that he and [Ken] Schrader would gang up on me at the end, but they didn't have a Robert and Doug Yates engine, and that was the difference."

That, however, was not the low point of the season for Earnhardt, who matched Richard Petty's record of seven Winston Cup titles with his championship in 1994.

Earnhardt spent the first half of the season battling Jarrett, Gordon and Terry Labonte at the top of the standings. Then, at Talladega Superspeedway in July, Earnhardt was involved in a spectacular crash in which his Chevrolet was virtually destroyed and he was left with fractures to his left shoulder blade and sternum.

Despite the 45-year-old driver's courageous efforts, qualifying and starting his car the next week at Indianapolis before giving way to relief driver Mike Skinner, then winning the pole and finishing sixth in a miraculous drive the following week on the road course at Watkins Glen, N.Y., the crash wrecked his season.

For the first time in his career, Earnhardt went 11 consecutive races without a top-five finish, finally breaking through with a second-place on Sept. 29 at North Wilkesboro Speedway. By that time, though, he had faded to a distant fourth in the points, apparently leaving the title battle to the other three.

"There's no question that the accident and those injuries set us back some," Earnhardt admitted afterwards. "But we've just made some mistakes on the handling at some of these races, too. We need to finish this season with some wins, and I don't give anything away while there's still a mathematical chance."

Meanwhile, the 25-year-old Gordon, whose climb to stardom in NASCAR has been meteoric, continued to show why he may eventually equal or top some of the records of Petty and Earnhardt.

After a miserable start, finishing 42nd and 40th because of handling and mechanical problems, the Kid showed his mettle by bouncing back to win at Richmond International Raceway in the season's third race.

With only three races remaining in the 31-race season, Gordon had racked up 10 wins—three more than in his 1995 championship season and more than anyone since Rusty Wallace won 10 in 1993. Even with all those wins, though, Gordon still found himself in a tough championship battle with Hendrick Motorsports teammate Labonte and Jarrett.

After Labonte won on Oct. 7 at Charlotte and Jarrett finished third while Gordon was suffering a 31st-place finish because of an overheating problem, The Kid was only one point ahead of his teammate and 92 in front of Jarrett.

"Coming back from a start like that shows what kind of a team this is," Gordon said. "They don't panic and they don't give up. And now that we're in the championship battle again, we know what to expect."

A year ago, Gordon beat Earnhardt by 34 points after leading late in the season by more than 300.

"Last year, everything was new and there was a lot of pressure and we lost a lot of our lead to Earnhardt at the end of the season," Gordon explained. "I think we're ready to handle the pressure better this time because we've been through it. We're just going to have to show some toughness."

Jarrett and new teammate Ernie Irvan both had solid seasons, with Jarrett establishing himself as a big race kind of guy and Irvan finalizing his comeback from near-fatal injuries.

Following his win at Daytona, Jarrett also won the Coca-Cola 600 at Charlotte Motor Speedway and the Brickyard 400 at Indy, giving him a sweep of NASCAR's top big money events. He also got the opportunity to try to match Bill Elliott's 1985 Winston Million performance with a win in September at Darlington Raceway. But Jarrett, who would have won a $1 million bonus by winning that race, slipped through some oil, hit the wall and wound up 14th as Gordon won on NASCAR's oldest superspeedway.

"Heck, it just wasn't our day," Jarrett said. "But we've had a pretty good year, and this team is going to really be good next year with what we've learned in our first year together."

A year ago, Jarrett filled in for Irvan, who was nearly killed in a crash at Michigan on Aug. 20, 1994. Irvan, recovering from terrible head and chest injuries, returned to racing in October of 1995 as Jarrett's teammate at Robert Yates Racing and made his comeback complete at Loudon, N.H., on July 14 with a victory. He later added another win at Richmond.

"I never even thought about quitting," Irvan said. "But the comeback won't be complete for me until we're challenging for the championship again. Hopefully, that will be next year."

The other big news in NASCAR in 1996 was the continued growth of the series, which will move into new venues next season in Fort Worth, Tex., and Fontana, Calif., expanding the circuit to 32 races.

The expansion took its toll on history, though, with the demise of 40,000-seat North Wilkesboro Speedway, which held its first race of what is now the Winston Cup series in NASCAR's inaugural season of 1949. With the death of track founder and family patriarch Enoch Staley in 1995, the Staleys sold the speedway.

Fifty percent went to Bruton Smith, chairman of Speedway Motorsports Inc., which operates tracks in Charlotte, Atlanta and Bristol, Tenn., as well as building the track in Texas and having part ownership of North Carolina Motor Speedway in Rockingham.

The other 50 percent was bought by Bob Bahre, owner of the New Hampshire track that held its first Winston Cup race in 1993.

The new owners split the 1997 North Wilkesboro dates between them, with the spring date going to the 150,000-seat Texas track and the fall race to 70,000-seat New Hampshire International Speedway as its second Winston Cup event.

Wide World Photos

Dale Jarrett raises his arms in celebration after winning the 1996 Daytona 500, which he also won in 1993.

With other new racing palaces already open or being built in places like Homestead, Las Vegas, Colorado Springs, Colo., and St. Louis, Mo., more schedule changes could be coming to Winston Cup.

In Formula One, the season started off like a Damon Hill rout, with the son of the late Graham Hill, killed in an air crash in 1975, winning the first three races and four of the first five. In fact, he had won seven times in 15 starts going into the season-finale in Japan in Mid-October.

Meanwhile, though, new teammate Villeneuve, a 25-year-old who came to Formula One in 1996 after winning both the Indianapolis 500 and the PPG Cup title the previous year, was establishing himself in his new series.

The son of the late Gilles Villeneuve, a Formula One star who was killed in 1982 in a crash during qualifying for the Belgian Grand Prix, won his first race in his fourth start and wound up winning three more while moving within nine points of his older Williams-Renault teammate going into the final event.

Elsewhere on the track, Hill, who gets little respect despite 18 wins in 66 career starts, asked for a big raise and was told by team owner Frank Williams his services would not be required in 1997. (See "Updates" on page 11).

After signing late in the season with the unheralded Arrows team, Hill said, "I have no bitterness. Frank Williams allowed me an opportunity to win a world championship. But I have to go on with my career and, hopefully, continue to win races with Arrows as it grows in stature."

Next year, the battle could well be between Villeneuve and two-time Formula One champion Michael Schumacher, whose move from Benetton to Ferrari this season took him out of the running for a third-straight title

But Ferrari, with a new car design, new gearbox and other changes, improved considerably late in the year as Schumacher won both the Belgian and Italian Grand Prix for his second and third wins of the season.

"I think Ferrari will be a force next year," Schumacher said. "I can't wait."

In other racing news in 1996, Winston Cup star Mark Martin joined Earnhardt and Unser as the only two-time winners of the International Race of Champions Series. Martin earned this title by winning the last two races—at Charlotte and Michigan—in the four-race series.

He then endeared himself to his Winston Cup team by splitting the $225,000 first-place money in IROC with his Jack Roush Racing crew.

Davy Jones, who finished second to Lazier at Indy, went to France a week later and helped Porsche teammates Manuel Reuter of Germany and Alexander Wurtz of Austria win the 24 Hours of LeMans.

Fellow IRL driver Sharp co-drove an all-American Riley & Scott MK III World Sports Car powered by an Oldsmobile Aurora V8 with Wayne Taylor of South Africa and fellow American Jim Pace to win both the Daytona 24 Hours and the 12 Hours of Sebring for a sweep of America's classic sports car endurance races.

In the second year of NASCAR's popular Craftsman Truck Series, defending champion Skinner, who will become Earnhardt's Winston Cup teammate next season, was locked in a late-season battle with point leader Ron Hornaday Jr. and third-place Jack Sprague for the title. ❒

AUTO RACING STATISTICS

THE SEASON IN REVIEW

1995-1996

NASCAR • INDYCAR • IRL • F1

NASCAR Results

Winston Cup Series

Winners of NASCAR Winston Cup races from Nov. 12, 1995 through Oct. 6, 1996 (see Updates chapter for later results).

LATE 1995

Date	Event	Location	Winner (Pos.)	Avg.mph	Earnings	Pole	Qual.mph
Nov. 12	NAPA 500	Atlanta	Dale Earnhardt (11)	163.632†	$141,850	D. Waltrip	185.046

Winning cars (for entire season): CHEVY MONTE CARLO (21)— Jeff Gordon 7, Earnhardt 5, Sterling Marlin 3, Bobby Labonte 3, Terry Labonte 3; FORD THUNDERBIRD (8)— Mark Martin 4, Rusty Wallace 2, Dale Jarrett 1, Ricky Rudd 1; PONTIAC GRAND PRIX (2)— Kyle Petty 1, Ward Burton 1.

1996 SEASON (through Oct. 6)

Date	Event	Location	Winner (Pos.)	Avg.mph	Earnings	Pole	Qual.mph
Feb. 18	**Daytona 500**	Daytona	Dale Jarrett (7)	154.308	$360,775	D. Earnhardt	189.510
Feb. 25	Goodwrench 400	Rockingham	Dale Earnhardt (18)	109.230	83,840	T. Labonte	156.870
Mar. 3	Pontiac 400	Richmond	Jeff Gordon (2)	102.750	92,400	T. Labonte	123.728
Mar. 10	Purolator 500	Atlanta	Dale Earnhardt (18)	161.257	91,050	J. Benson#	105.434
Mar. 24	TranSouth 400	Darlington	Jeff Gordon (2)	124.793	97,310	W. Burton	173.797†
Mar. 31	Food City 500	Bristol	Jeff Gordon (8)	91.308	93,765	M. Martin	123.578
Apr. 14	First Union 400	N.Wilkesboro	Terry Labonte (1)	96.370	229,025*	T. Labonte	116.659
Apr. 21	Goody's 500	Martinsville	Rusty Wallace (5)	81.410$	59,245	R. Craven	93.079
Apr. 28	**Winston 500**	Talladega	Sterling Marlin (4)	149.999	109,845	E. Irvan	192.855
May 5	Save Mart 300	Sonoma	Rusty Wallace (7)	77.673	58,395	T. Labonte	92.524†
May 18	*The Winston Select*	Charlotte	Michael Waltrip (6)	162.721	200,000	L. Speed	180.977
May 26	**Coca-Cola 600**	Charlotte	Dale Jarrett (15)	147.581	165,250	J. Gordon	183.773
June 2	Miller 500	Dover	Jeff Gordon (1)	122.741	138,730*	J. Gordon	154.785†
June 16	UAW-GM 500	Pocono	Jeff Gordon (1)	139.104	96,980*	J. Gordon	169.725†
June 23	Miller 400	Michigan	Rusty Wallace (18)	166.033$	71,380	B. Hamilton	185.166
July 6	Pepsi 400	Daytona	Sterling Marlin (2)	161.602	106,565	J. Gordon	188.869
July 14	Jiffy Lube 300	Loudon	Ernie Irvan (6)	98.930	112,625	R. Craven	129.379†
July 21	Miller 500	Pocono	Rusty Wallace (13)	144.892$	59,165	M. Martin	168.410
July 28	DieHard 500	Talladega	Jeff Gordon (2)	133.387	272,550	J. Mayfield	192.370
Aug. 3	Brickyard 400	Indianapolis	Dale Jarrett (24)	139.508	564,035	J. Gordon	176.419†
Aug. 11	The Bud at the Glen	Watkins Glen	Geoff Bodine (13)	92.304	88,740	D. Earnhardt	120.733†
Aug. 18	GM Goodwrench 400	Michigan	Dale Jarrett (11)	139.792	83,195	J. Burton	185.395
Aug. 24	Goody's 500	Bristol	Rusty Wallace (5)	91.267	77,090	M. Martin	124.857
Sept. 1	**Southern 500**	Darlington	Jeff Gordon (2)	135.757	99,630	D. Jarrett	170.934
Sept. 7	Miller 400	Richmond	Ernie Irvan (16)	105.469	86,665	M. Martin	122.744
Sept. 15	MBNA 500	Dover	Jeff Gordon (3)	105.646	153,630	B. Labonte	155.086†
Sept. 22	Hanes 500	Martinsville	Jeff Gordon (10)	82.223$	93,825	B. Hamilton	94.120
Sept. 29	Tyson Holly Fms 400	N.Wilkesboro	Jeff Gordon (2)	96.837	91,350	T. Musgrave	118.054
Oct. 6	UAW-GM 500	Charlotte	Terry Labonte (16)	143.143	133,950	B. Labonte	184.068

Note: *The Winston Select* (May 18) is a 105-mile, non-points race.

†Track record. $Race record.

#Benson won the pole but crashed in his final practice Saturday, was forced to use a back up car and had to drop to the rear of the field. He finished 38th, one of 11 drivers forced out of the race with engine-related trouble.

*Includes carryover Unocal 76 bonus for winning race from the pole: **First Union 400**— Labonte ($129,200); **Miller 500**— Gordon ($38,000); **UAW–GM 500**— Gordon ($7,600).

Winning Cars: CHEVY MONTE CARLO (16)— Gordon 10, Earnhardt 2, Marlin 2, T. Labonte 2 ; FORD THUNDERBIRD (12)— Wallace 5, Jarrett 4, Irvan 2, Bodine 1.

Remaining Races (3): AC-Delco 400 in Rockingham, N.C. (Oct. 20); Dura-Lube 500 in Phoenix (Oct. 27); NAPA 500 in Atlanta (Nov. 10).

NASCAR Results (Cont.)

1996 Race Locations

February— DAYTONA 500 at Daytona International Speedway in Daytona Beach, Fla.; GOODWRENCH 400 at North Carolina Motor Speedway in Rockingham, N.C. **March**— PONTIAC EXCITEMENT 400 at Richmond (Va.) International Raceway; PUROLATOR 500 at Atlanta International Speedway in Atlanta, Ga.; TRANSOUTH FINANCIAL 400 at Darlington (S.C.) International Raceway; FOOD CITY 500 at Bristol (Tenn.) International Raceway. **April**— FIRST UNION 400 at North Wilkesboro (N.C.) Speedway; GOODY'S HEADACHE POWDERS 500 at Martinsville (Va.) Speedway; WINSTON SELECT 500 at Talladega (Ala.) Superspeedway. **May**— SAVE MART SUPERMARKETS 300 at Sears Point International Raceway in Sonoma, Calif.; THE WINSTON SELECT at Charlotte Motor Speedway in Concord, N.C.; COCA-COLA 600 at Charlotte.

June— Miller 500 at Dover (Del.) Downs International Speedway; UAW-GM TEAMWORK 500 at Pocono (Pa.) International Raceway; MILLER 400 at Michigan International Speedway in Brooklyn, Mich. **July**— PEPSI 400 at Daytona; JIFFY LUBE 300 at New Hampshire International Speedway in Loudon, N.H.; MILLER 500 at Pocono; DIEHARD 500 at Talladega. **August**— BRICKYARD 400 at Indianapolis Motor Speedway; THE BUD AT THE GLEN at Watkins Glen, (N.Y.) International; GM GOODWRENCH DEALER 400 at Brooklyn, Mich.; GOODY'S HEADACHE POWDER 500 at Bristol. **September**— MOUNTAIN DEW SOUTHERN 500 at Darlington; MILLER 400 at Richmond; MBNA 500 at Dover; HANES 500 at Martinsville. **October**— TYSON HOLLY FARMS 400 at North Wilkesboro; UAW-GM QUALITY 500 at Charlotte.

1996 Daytona 500

Date— Sunday, Feb. 18, 1996, at Daytona International Speedway. **Distance**— 500 miles; **Course**— 2.5 miles; **Field**— 43 cars; **Average speed**— 154.308 mph; **Margin of victory**— 0.12 seconds; **Time of race**— 3 hours, 14 minutes, 25 seconds; **Caution flags**— 6 for 26 laps; **Lead changes**— 32 among 15 drivers; **Lap leaders** — T. Labonte (44 laps), D. Jarrett (40), D. Earnhardt (32), B. Elliott (29), J. Andretti (23), K. Schrader (12), R. Craven (6), R. Pressley (4), S. Marlin (3), E. Irvin (2), B. Bodine (1), J. Mayfield (1), J. Spencer (1), H. Stricklin (1), M. Waltrip (1); **Pole sitter**— Dale Earnhardt at 189.510 mph; **Attendance**— 150,000 (estimated); **TV Rating**— 9.2/24 share (CBS). Note that (r) indicates circuit rookie driver.

	Driver (start pos.)	Team	Car	Laps	Ended	Earnings
1	Dale Jarrett (7)	Qual.Care/Ford Credit	Ford Thunderbird	200	Running	$360,775
2	Dale Earnhardt (1)	GM Goodwrench Serv.	Chevrolet Monte Carlo	200	Running	215,065
3	Ken Schrader (4)	Budweiser	Chevrolet Monte Carlo	200	Running	169,547
4	Mark Martin (15)	Valvoline	Ford Thunderbird	200	Running	118,840
5	Jeff Burton (16)	Exide Batteries	Ford Thunderbird	200	Running	91,702
6	Wally Dallenbach (9)	Hayes Modems	Ford Thunderbird	200	Running	96,720
7	Ted Musgrave (20)	Family Ch./PRIMESTAR	Ford Thunderbird	200	Running	82,712
8	Bill Elliott (21)	McDonald's	Ford Thunderbird	200	Running	78,155
9	Ricky Rudd (10)	Tide	Ford Thunderbird	200	Running	79,987
10	Michael Waltrip (11)	Citgo	Ford Thunderbird	200	Running	74,255
11	Jimmy Spencer (19)	Camel Cigarettes	Ford Thunderbird	200	Running	66,105
12	Jeff Purvis (34)	MCA Records	Chevrolet Monte Carlo	200	Running	52,262
13	Ricky Craven (36)	Kodiak	Chevrolet Monte Carlo	200	Running	63,167
14	Lake Speed (32)	Spam	Ford Thunderbird	200	Running	60,445
15	Dave Marcis (23)	Prodigy	Chevrolet Monte Carlo	200	Running	52,230
16	Rusty Wallace (43)	Miller	Ford Thunderbird	200	Running	60,142
17	Bobby Labonte (35)	Interstate Batteries	Chevrolet Monte Carlo	200	Running	59,715
18	Kyle Petty (29)	Coors Light	Pontiac Grand Prix	199	Running	53,870
19	Jeremy Mayfield (14)	RCA	Ford Thunderbird	199	Running	46,482
20	Bobby Hamilton (39)	STP	Pontiac Grand Prix	199	Running	53,740
21	Kenny Wallace (33)	Square D/T.I.C.	Ford Thunderbird	199	Running	40,685
22	Hut Stricklin (42)	Circuit City	Ford Thunderbird	199	Running	43,675
23	r-Johnny Benson (27)	Pennzoil	Pontiac Grand Prix	197	Running	51,775
24	Terry Labonte (5)	Kellogg's Corn Flakes	Chevrolet Monte Carlo	196	Running	68,570
25	Elton Sawyer (18)	David Blair Motorsports	Ford Thunderbird	196	Running	40,572
26	Ward Burton (13)	MBNA America	Pontiac Grand Prix	195	Running	54,860
27	Steve Grissom (26)	Cartoon Network	Chevrolet Monte Carlo	191	Running	49,437
28	Rick Mast (31)	Hooters	Pontiac Grand Prix	190	Running	48,782
29	Darrell Waltrip (40)	Parts America	Chevrolet Monte Carlo	180	Handling	48,220
30	Robert Pressley (25)	Skoal Bandit	Chevrolet Monte Carlo	171	Handling	48,265
31	Morgan Shepherd (12)	Remington Arms	Ford Thunderbird	164	Handling	43,192
32	Brett Bodine (41)	Lowe's	Ford Thunderbird	162	Handling	44,405
33	Chad Little (30)	Sterling Cowboy	Pontiac Grand Prix	158	Accident	37,687
34	Geoff Bodine (38)	QVC	Ford Thunderbird	157	Accident	44,120
35	Ernie Irvan (2)	Texaco Havoline	Ford Thunderbird	145	Running	85,847
36	Loy Allen (24)	Healthsource	Ford Thunderbird	135	Accident	37,192
37	Mike Wallace (17)	Heilig-Meyers	Ford Thunderbird	135	Accident	37,237
38	John Andretti (6)	Kmart/Little Caesars	Ford Thunderbird	128	Accident	57,152
39	Joe Nemechek (37)	Burger King	Chevrolet Monte Carlo	86	Handling	43,302
40	Sterling Marlin (3)	Kodak Film	Chevrolet Monte Carlo	81	Engine	70,120
41	Derrike Cope (22)	Mane 'N Tail	Ford Thunderbird	53	Accident	43,752
42	Jeff Gordon (8)	DuPont Refinishes	Chevrolet Monte Carlo	13	Handling	59,052
43	Dick Trickle (28)	Purina Hi Pro	Ford Thunderbird	9	Engine	36,552

Winston Cup Point Standings

Official Top 10 NASCAR Winston Cup point leaders and Top 15 money leaders for 1995 and unofficial Top 10 point leaders and Top 15 money leaders for 1996 (through Oct. 6). Points awarded for all qualifying drivers (winner receives 175) and lap leaders. Earnings include bonuses. Listed are starts (Sts), Top 5 finishes (1-2-3-4-5), poles won (PW) and points (Pts).

FINAL 1995

	Sts	Finishes 1-2-3-4-5	PW	Pts
1 Jeff Gordon	31	7-4-5-0-1	8*	4614
2 Dale Earnhardt	31	5-6-5-1-2	3	4580
3 Sterling Marlin	31	3-2-0-2-1	1	4361
4 Mark Martin	31	4-1-4-1-3	0	4320
5 Rusty Wallace	31	2-4-5-2-1	1	4240
6 Terry Labonte	31	3-4-2-3-2	1	4146
7 Ted Musgrave	31	0-2-2-2-1	1	3949
8 Bill Elliott	31	0-0-0-2-2	2	3746
9 Ricky Rudd	31	1-0-1-4-4	2	3734
10 Bobby Labonte	31	3-3-0-0-1	2	3718

*Does not include pole awarded at Sept. 24 Goody's 500 because time trials were not held due to inclement weather.

1996 SEASON (through Oct. 6)

	Sts	Finishes 1-2-3-4-5	PW	Pts
1 Jeff Gordon	28	10-3-3-2-1	5	4163
2 Terry Labonte	28	2-7-3-1-5	4	4162
3 Dale Jarrett	28	4-5-4-2-0	1	4071
4 Dale Earnhardt	28	2-3-3-3-1	2	3892
5 Mark Martin	28	0-3-5-3-2	4	3801
6 Ricky Rudd	28	0-2-1-1-0	0	3402
7 Rusty Wallace	28	5-1-0-1-1	0	3398
8 Sterling Marlin	28	2-0-1-1-1	0	3358
9 Ken Schrader	28	0-0-1-1-1	0	3315
10 Ernie Irvan	28	2-2-0-5-2	1	3261

Top 5 Finishing Order + Pole

1996 SEASON (through Oct. 6)

No.	Event	Winner	2nd	3rd	4th	5th	Pole
1	Daytona 500	D. Jarrett	D. Earnhardt	K. Schrader	M. Martin	J. Burton	D. Earnhardt
2	Goodwrench 500	D. Earnhardt	D. Jarrett	R. Craven	R. Rudd	S. Grissom	T. Labonte
3	Pontiac 400	J. Gordon	D. Jarrett	T. Musgrave	J. Burton	M. Martin	T. Labonte
4	Purolator 500	D. Earnhardt	T. Labonte	J. Gordon	E. Irvan	J. Mayfield	J. Benson
5	TranSouth 400	J. Gordon	B. Labonte	R. Craven	R. Wallace	T. Labonte	W. Burton
6	Food City 500	J. Gordon	T. Labonte	M. Martin	D. Earnhardt	R. Wallace	M. Martin
7	First Union 400	T. Labonte	J. Gordon	D. Earnhardt	R. Pressley	S. Marlin	T. Labonte
8	Goody's 500	R. Wallace	E. Irvan	J. Gordon	J. Mayfield	D. Earnhardt	R. Craven
9	Winston 500	S. Marlin	D. Jarrett	D. Earnhardt	T. Labonte	M. Waltrip	E. Irvan
10	Save Mart 300	R. Wallace	M. Martin	W. Dallenbach	D. Earnhardt	T. Labonte	T. Labonte
11	Coca-Cola 600	D. Jarrett	D. Earnhardt	T. Labonte	J. Gordon	K. Schrader	J. Gordon
12	Miller 500	J. Gordon	T. Labonte	D. Earnhardt	E. Irvan	B. Labonte	J. Gordon
13	UAW-GM 500	J. Gordon	R. Rudd	G. Bodine	M. Martin	B. Hamilton	J. Gordon
14	Miller 400	R. Wallace	T. Labonte	S. Marlin	J. Spencer	E. Irvan	B. Hamilton
15	Pepsi 400	S. Marlin	T. Labonte	J. Gordon	D. Earnhardt	E. Irvan	J. Gordon
16	Jiffy Lube 300	E. Irvan	D. Jarrett	R. Rudd	J. Burton	R. Pressley	R. Craven
17	Miller 500	R. Wallace	R. Rudd	D. Jarrett	E. Irvan	J. Benson	M. Martin
18	DieHard 500	J. Gordon	D. Jarrett	M. Martin	E. Irvan	J. Spencer	J. Mayfield
19	Brickyard 400	D. Jarrett	E. Irvan	T. Labonte	M. Martin	M. Shepherd	J. Gordon
20	Bud at the Glen	G. Bodine	T. Labonte	M. Martin	J. Gordon	B. Labonte	D. Earnhardt
21	GM 400	D. Jarrett	M. Martin	T. Labonte	E. Irvan	J. Gordon	J. Burton
22	Goody's 500	R. Wallace	J. Gordon	M. Martin	D. Jarrett	T. Labonte	M. Martin
23	Southern 500	J. Gordon	H. Stricklin	M. Martin	K. Schrader	J. Andretti	D. Jarrett
24	Miller 400	E. Irvan	J. Gordon	J. Burton	D. Jarrett	T. Labonte	M. Martin
25	MBNA 500	J. Gordon	R. Wallace	D. Jarrett	B. Labonte	M. Martin	B. Labonte
26	Hanes 500	J. Gordon	T. Labonte	B. Hamilton	R. Mast	J. Andretti	B. Hamilton
27	Holly Farms 400	J. Gordon	D. Earnhardt	D. Jarrett	J. Burton	T. Labonte	T. Musgrave
28	UAW-GM 500	T. Labonte	M. Martin	D. Jarrett	S. Marlin	R. Craven	B. Labonte

Money Leaders

FINAL 1995

	Earnings
1 Jeff Gordon	$2,430,460
2 Dale Earnhardt	2,378,300
3 Sterling Marlin	1,712,155
4 Mark Martin	1,534,966
5 Rusty Wallace	1,375,878
6 Terry Labonte	1,328,295
7 Bobby Labonte	1,293,200
8 Dale Jarrett	1,259,224
9 Ricky Rudd	1,153,874
10 Ted Musgrave	943,675
11 Geoff Bodine	931,505
12 Morgan Shepherd	862,041
13 Brett Bodine	830,041
14 Ken Schrader	810,430
15 Michael Waltrip	809,155

1996 SEASON (through Oct. 6)

	Earnings
1 Jeff Gordon	$2,332,853
2 Dale Jarrett	2,200,070
3 Terry Labonte	1,782,098
4 Dale Earnhardt	1,618,241
5 Mark Martin	1,423,780
6 Ernie Irvan	1,368,447
7 Sterling Marlin	1,225,230
8 Rusty Wallace	1,209,547
9 Ricky Rudd	1,062,393
10 Bobby Labonte	1,019,660
11 Michael Waltrip	988,945
12 Ken Schrader	918,067
13 Jimmy Spencer	858,875
14 Geoff Bodine	850,745
15 Johnny Benson	832,555

INDYCAR Results

Winners of IndyCar races from Mar. 3 through Sept. 8, 1996.

1996 SEASON

Date	Event	Location	Winner (Pos.)	Time	Avg.mph	Pole	Qual.mph
Mar. 3	GP of Miami	Miami	Jimmy Vasser (3)	1:51:23.100	109.399	P. Tracy	198.590
Mar. 17	Rio 400	Rio de Janeiro	Andre Ribeiro (3)	2:06:08.100	117.927	A. Zanardi	167.084†
Mar. 31	IndyCar Australia	Queensland	Jimmy Vasser (1)	2:00:46.856	90.218	J. Vasser	105.583
Apr. 14	GP of Long Beach	Long Beach	Jimmy Vasser (3)	1:44:02.363	96.281	G. de Ferran	109.310
Apr. 28	Bosch GP	Nazareth	Michael Andretti (5)	1:25:08.074	140.953	P. Tracy	190.737
May. 26	**U.S. 500**	Michigan	Jimmy Vasser (1)	3:11:48.000	156.403	J. Vasser	232.025
June 2	Miller 200	Milwaukee	Michael Andretti (5)	1:33:32.649	128.282	P. Tracy*	176.058
June 9	Detroit GP	Belle Isle	Michael Andretti (9)	2:00:45.451	75.136	S. Pruett	105.290
June 23	Bud/G.I. Joe's 200	Portland	Alex Zanardi (1)	1:50:25.401	103.837	A. Zanardi	117.209
June 30	GP of Cleveland	Cleveland	Gil de Ferran (7)	1:35:39.326	133.736	J. Vasser	146.194
July 14	Molson Indy	Toronto	Adrian Fernandez (3)	1:41:59.809	97.598	A. Ribeiro	110.616
July 28	Marlboro 500	Michigan	Andre Ribeiro (8)	3:16:33.425	152.627	J. Vasser	234.665†
Aug. 11	Miller 200	Mid-Ohio	Alex Zanardi (1)	1:46:49.448	104.358	A. Zanardi	122.100†
Aug. 18	Texaco/Havoline 200	Elkhart Lake	Michael Andretti (3)	1:56:33.859	102.947	A. Zanardi	141.179
Sept. 1	Molson Indy	Vancouver	Michael Andretti (2)	1:48:16.253	94.374	A. Zanardi	113.576
Sept. 8	Bank of America 300	Monterey	Alex Zanardi (5)	1:48:32.157	102.687	B. Herta	118.449

Note: IndyCar does not release per race winnings.
†Track record.
* Tracy sat on the pole because he had the fastest time in practice prior to the qualifyer being rained out.

Winning cars: REYNARD/HONDA (8)— Vasser 4, Zanardi 3, de Ferran 1; LOLA/FORD COSWORTH (5)— Andretti; LOLA/HONDA (3)— Ribeiro 2, Fernandez 1.

1996 Race Locations

March— MARLBORO GRAND PRIX OF MIAMI Presented by Toyota at Metro-Dade Homestead Motorsports Complex; RIO 400 at Nelson Piquet International Raceway; INDYCAR AUSTRALIA at Surfers Paradise, Queensland. **April**—TOYOTA GP OF LONG BEACH at Long Beach, Calif.; BOSCH SPARK PLUG GP at Nazareth (Pa.) Speedway. **May**—U.S. 500 at Michigan International Speedway. **June**— MILLER GENUINE DRAFT 200 at Wisconsin State Fair Park Speedway in West Allis; ITT AUTOMOTIVE DETROIT GP at The Raceway at Belle Isle Park; BUDWEISER/G.I. JOE'S 200 Presented by Texaco/Havoline at Portland (Ore.) International Raceway; MEDIC DRUG GRAND PRIX OF CLEVELAND at Cleveland, Ohio.

July— MOLSON INDY TORONTO at Exhibition Place; MARLBORO 500 at Michigan International Speedway; **August**— MILLER GENUINE DRAFT 200 at Mid-Ohio Sports Car Course in Lexington; TEXACO/HAVOLINE 200 at Road America in Elkart Lake, Wisc. **September**— MOLSON INDY VANCOUVER at Pacific Place; TOYOTA GRAND PRIX OF MONTEREY Featuring the Bank of America 300 at Laguna Seca (Calif.) Raceway.

1996 U.S. 500

Date— Sunday, May 26, 1996, at Michigan International Speedway. **Distance**— 500 miles; **Course**— 2 mile oval; **Field**—27 cars; **Winner's average speed**— 156.403 mph; **Margin of victory**— 10.995 seconds; **Time of race**— 3 hours, 11 minutes, 48 seconds; **Caution flags** — 12 for 78 laps; **Lead changes**— 11 by 7 drivers; **Lap leaders**— Zanardi (134 laps), Johnstone (35), Vasser (35), Ribeiro (33), Gugelmin (9), Moreno (2), Moore (2); **Pole Sitter**—Jimmy Vasser at 232.025 mph; **Attendance**—110,879; **TV Rating**—2.8/7 share (ESPN). Note that (r) indicates rookie driver.

	Driver (start Pos.)	Residence	Car	Laps	Ended	Earnings
1	Jimmy Vasser (1)	San Francisco, Calif.	Reynard-Honda	250	Running	$1,157,750
2	Mauricio Gugelmin (14)	Brazil	Reynard-Ford Cosworth	250	Running	262,850
3	Roberto Moreno (20)	Brazil	Lola-Ford Cosworth	249	Running	104,000
4	Andre Ribeiro (6)	Brazil	Lola-Honda	249	Running	–
5	r-Mark Blundell (19)	England	Reynard-Ford Cosworth	249	Running	–
6	r-Eddie Lawson (18)	Lk. Havasu City, Ar.	Lola-Mercedes	249	Running	–
7	Paul Tracy (7)	Canada	Penske-Mercedes	248	Running	–
8	Al Unser Jr. (5)	Albuquerque, NM	Penske-Mercedes	246	Running	–
9	Gil de Ferran (13)	Brazil	Reynard-Honda	245	Running	–
10	Emerson Fittipaldi (8)	Brazil	Penske-Mercedes	241	Running	–
11	Parker Johnstone (16)	Redmond, Ore.	Reynard-Honda	236	Gearbox	–
12	Christian Fittipaldi (12)	Brazil	Lola-Ford Cosworth	232	Engine	–
13	r-Greg Moore (17)	Canada	Reynard-Mercedes	225	Engine	–
14	Hiro Matsushita (25)	Japan	Lola-Ford Cosworth	217	Running	–
15	Bryan Herta (3)	Dublin, Ohio	Reynard-Mercedes	216	Engine	–
16	Stefan Johansson (22)	Sweden	Reynard-Mercedes	195	Engine	–
17	r-Alex Zanardi (4)	Italy	Reynard-Honda	175	Engine	–
18	r-Jeff Krosnoff (24)	La Canada, Calif.	Reynard-Toyota	143	Engine	–
19	Bobby Rahal (15)	New Albany, Ohio	Reynard-Mercedes	130	Accident	–
20	Robby Gordon (21)	Orange, Calif.	Reynard-Ford Cosworth	94	Engine	–
21	Gary Bettenhausen (27)	Martinsville, Ind.	Penske-Mercedes	79	Accident	–
22	Juan Manuel Fangio II (26)	Argentina	Eagle-Toyota	69	Engine	–
23	Michael Andretti (11)	Nazareth, Pa.	Lola-Ford Cosworth	67	C.V. joint	–
24	Raul Boesel (10)	Brazil	Reynard-Ford Cosworth	54	Electrical	–
25	Fredrik Ekblom (23)	Sweden	Reynard-Ford Cosworth	11	Engine	–
26	Scott Pruett (9)	Crystal Bay, Nev.	Lola-Ford Cosworth	3	Engine	–
27	Adrian Fernandez (2)	Mexico	Lola-Honda	0	Accident	–

Note: IndyCar does not release earnings on a per-race basis. Aside from the top three finishers which were released, the remaining 24 teams each received a minimum of $75,000 for competing, plus assorted bonuses.

IndyCar Point Standings

Official Top 10 PPG Cup point leaders and Top 15 money leaders for 1995 and 1996. Points awarded for places 1 to 12, fastest qualifier and overall lap leader. Listed are starts (Sts), Top 5 finishes, poles won (PW) and points (Pts).

FINAL 1995

		Sts	Finishes 1-2-3-4-5	PW	Pts
1	Jacques Villeneuve	17	4-1-2-1-1	6	172
2	Al Unser Jr.	16	4-2-1-0-1	0	161
3	Bobby Rahal	17	0-2-3-1-2	0	128
4	Michael Andretti	17	1-2-1-3-0	3	123
5	Robby Gordon	16	2-0-1-1-3	2	121
6	Paul Tracy	17	2-3-0-1-0	0	115
7	Scott Pruett	17	1-1-2-1-0	0	112
8	Jimmy Vasser	17	0-2-2-0-0	0	92
9	Teo Fabi	17	0-0-1-3-0	1	83
10	Mauricio Gugelmin	17	0-1-1-1-2	0	80

FINAL 1996

		Sts	Finishes 1-2-3-4-5	PW	Pts
1	Jimmy Vasser	16	4-1-0-1-0	4	154
2	Michael Andretti	16	5-0-1-0-0	0	132
3	Alex Zanardi	16	3-2-1-1-0	6	132
4	Al Unser Jr.	16	0-2-2-3-1	0	125
5	Christian Fittipaldi	16	0-1-2-0-2	0	110
6	Gil de Ferran	16	1-2-1-1-1	1	104
7	Bobby Rahal	16	0-2-1-0-1	0	102
8	Bryan Herta	16	0-2-0-1-2	0	86
9	Greg Moore	16	0-1-2-1-1	0	84
10	Scott Pruett	16	0-1-2-1-0	1	82

Top 5 Finishing Order + Pole

1996 Season

No.	Event	Winner	2nd	3rd	4th	5th	Pole
1	Miami GP	J. Vasser	G. de Ferran	R. Gordon	S. Pruett	B. Rahal	P. Tracy
2	Rio 400	A. Ribeiro	A. Unser Jr.	S. Pruett	A. Zanardi	C. Fittipaldi	A. Zanardi
3	Australian GP	J. Vasser	S. Pruett	G. Moore	M. Gugelmin	C. Fittipaldi	J. Vasser
4	Long Beach	J. Vasser	P. Johnstone	A. Unser Jr.	P. Tracy	G. de Ferran	G. de Ferran
5	Bosch GP	M. Andretti	G. Moore	A. Unser Jr.	E. Fittipaldi	P. Tracy	P. Tracy
6	**U.S. 500**	J. Vasser	M. Gugelmin	R. Moreno	A. Ribeiro	M. Blundell	J. Vasser
7	Milwaukee	M. Andretti	A. Unser Jr.	P. Tracy	E. Fittipaldi	G. Moorre	P. Tracy
8	Detroit	M. Andretti	C. Fittipaldi	G. de Ferran	A. Fernandez	M. Blundell	S. Pruett
9	Portland	A. Zanardi	G. de Ferran	C. Fittipaldi	A. Unser Jr.	P. Johnstone	A. Zanardi
10	Cleveland	G. de Ferran	A. Zanardi	G. Moore	A. Unser Jr.	B. Herta	J. Vasser
11	Toronto	A. Fernandez	A. Zanardi	B. Rahal	G. Moore	P. Tracy	A. Ribeiro
12	Michigan	A. Ribeiro	B. Herta	M. Gugelmin	A. Unser Jr.	S. Johansson	J. Vasser
13	Mid-Ohio	A. Zanardi	J. Vasser	M. Andretti	B. Herta	B. Rahal	A. Zanardi
14	Road America	M. Andretti	B. Rahal	A. Zanardi	S. Johansson	B. Herta	A. Zanardi
15	Vancouver	M. Andretti	B. Rahal	C. Fittipaldi	G. de Ferran	A. Unser Jr.	A. Zanardi
16	Monterey	A. Zanardi	B. Herta	S. Pruett	J. Vasser	M. Gugelmin	B. Herta

Money Leaders

FINAL 1995

		Earnings
1	Jacques Villeneuve	$2,996,269
2	Bobby Rahal	1,390,017
3	Al Unser Jr.	1,369,000
4	Robby Gordon	1,235,667
5	Michael Andretti	1,143,303
6	Christian Fittipaldi	$1,109,918
7	Mauricio Gugelmin	1,022,667
8	Paul Tracy	1,012,953
9	Teo Fabi	991,603
10	Jimmy Vasser	940,003
11	Gil de Ferran	$800,453
12	Eliseo Salazar	790,417
13	Adrain Fernandez	782,903
14	Stefan Johansson	749,453
15	Raul Boesel	724,303

FINAL 1996

		Earnings
1	Jimmy Vasser	$3,061,500
2	Alex Zanardi	1,408,250
3	Michael Andretti	1,386,750
4	Al Unser Jr.	987,000
5	Christian Fittipaldi	913,750
6	Greg Moore	$789,750
7	Mauricio Gugelmin	742,500
8	Gil de Ferran	694,000
9	Andre Ribiero	675,250
10	Bobby Rahal	670,500
11	Bryan Herta	$642,250
12	Scott Pruett	604,500
13	Stefan Johansson	592,500
14	Paul Tracey	588,000
15	Robby Gordon	583,000

INDY RACING LEAGUE Results

Winners of Indy Racing League events from Jan. 27 through Sept. 15, 1996 (see Updates chapter for later results). The inaugural IRL season began in January and ended with the Indianapolis 500 in May. The 1996–97 season began in August with the True Value 200 and will end at the end of the 1997 calendar year. Beginning in 1998, the IRL will run on a calendar-year basis.

1996 SEASON

Date	Event	Location	Winner (Pos.)	Time	Avg.mph	Pole	Qual.mph
Jan. 27	Indy 200	Orlando	Buzz Calkins (5)	1:33:30.748	128.325	B. Lazier	181.388
Mar. 24	Dura Lube 200	Phoenix	Arie Luyendyk (1)	1:42:14.528	117.368	A. Luyendyk	183.599
May 26	Indianapolis 500	Indianapolis	Buddy Lazier (5)	3:22:45.753	147.956	T. Stewart*	233.100

* Scott Brayton earned the pole position with a 233.718 qualifying time but was killed in a practice run before race day. His teammate Stewart was given the spot.

Winning cars: REYNARD/FORD (3)— Calkins, Lazier, Luyendyk.

Indy Racing League (Cont.)

1996–97 SEASON (through Sept. 15, 1996)

Date	Event	Location	Winner (Pos)	Time	Avg.mph	Pole	Qual.mph
Aug. 18	True Value 200	Loudon	Scott Sharp (12)	1:36:57.912	130.934	R. Hearn	175.367
Sept. 15	Las Vegas 500K	Las Vegas	Richie Hearn (8)	2:36:17.345	115.171	A. Luyendyk	226.491

Winning cars: REYNARD/FORD (1)—Hearn; LOLA/FORD (1)— Sharp.

IRL Race Locations: **January**— INDY 200 presented by Aurora at Walt Disney World, Orlando, Fla. **March**—DURA LUBE 200 at Phoenix (Ari.) International Raceway. **May**—INDIANAPOLIS 500 at Indianapolis (Ind.) Motor Speedway. **August**—TRUE VALUE 200 at New Hampshire International Speedway in Louden, NH. **September**—LAS VEGAS 500K at Las Vegas (Nev.) Motor Speedway.

1996–97 Remaining Races: (7): INDY 200 at Walt Disney World, Orlando, Fla. (Jan. 25, 1997); Phoenix 200 at Phoenix International Raceway (March 23); INDIANAPOLIS 500 at Indianapolis (Ind.) Motor Speedway (May 25); Texas International Raceway (June 7); Pikes Peak International Raceway (June 29). Races at New Hampshire and Las Vegas have been confirmed with dates to be announced.

1996 Indianapolis 500

Date— Sunday, May 26, 1996, at Indianapolis Motor Speedway. **Distance**— 500 miles; **Course**— 2.5 mile oval; **Field**—33 cars; **Winner's average speed**—147.956 mph; **Margin of victory**— 0.695 seconds; **Time of race** — 3 hours, 22 minutes, 45.753 seconds; **Caution flags**— 10 for 59 laps; **Lead changes**— 15 by 5 drivers; **Lap leaders** —Guerrero (47 laps), Jones (46), Stewart (44), Lazier (43), Zampedri (20); **Pole Sitter**—Scott Brayton earned the pole position with a qualifying time of 233.718 but was killed in practice. Stewart assumed the pole position with a time of 233.100; **Attendance**—400,000 (est.); **TV Rating**— 6.6/21 share (ABC). Note that (r) indicates rookie driver.

	Driver (pos.)	Residence	Car	Laps	Ended	Earnings
1	Buddy Lazier (5)	Vail, Colo.	Reynard-Ford	200	Running	$1,367,854
2	Davy Jones (2)	Lake Tahoe, Nev.	Lola-Mercedes	200	Running	632,503
3	r-Richie Hearn (15)	Canyon Country, Calif.	Reynard-Ford	200	Running	375,203
4	Alessandro Zampedri	Italy	Lola-Ford	199	Crash	270,853
5	Roberto Guerrero (6)	San Juan Capistrano, Calif.	Reynard-Ford	198	Crash	315,503
6	Eliseo Salazar (3)	Chile	Lola-Ford	197	Crash	226,653
7	Danny Ongais (33)	Long Beach, Calif.	Lola-Menard	197	Running	228,253
8	Hideshi Matsuda (30)	Japan	Lola-Ford	197	Running	233,953
9	r-Robbie Buhl (23)	Grosse Pointe, Mich.	Lola-Ford	197	Running	195,403
10	Scott Sharp (21)	Danville, Calif.	Lola-Ford	194	Crash	202,053
11	Eddie Cheever (4)	Aspen, Col.	Lola-Menard	189	Engine	206,103
12	r-Davey Hamilton (10)	Boise, Idaho	Lola-Ford	181	Transmission	184,003
13	r-Michael Jourdain Jr. (8)	Mexico	Lola-Ford	177	Engine	193,653
14	Lyn St. James (18)	Daytona Beach, Fla.	Lola-Ford	153	Crash	182,603
15	r-Scott Harrington (32)	Indianapolis, Ind.	Reynard-Ford	150	Crash	190,753
16	Arie Luyendyk (20)	Netherlands	Reynard-Ford	149	Crash	216,503
17	r-Buzz Calkins (9)	Denver, Col.	Reynard-Ford	148	Brakes	173,553
18	r-Jim Guthrie (19)	Albuquerque, N.M.	Lola-Menard	144	Engine	168,453
19	r-Mark Dismore (14)	Greenfield, Ind.	Lola-Menard	129	Engine	161,253
20	Mike Groff (11)	Palm Desert, Calif.	Reynard-Ford	122	Fire	158,503
21	r-Fermin Velez (28)	Spain	Lola-Ford	107	Fire	176,653
22	r-Joe Gosek (31)	Oswego, N.Y.	Lola-Ford	106	Radiator	169,653
23	r-Brad Murphey (26)	Tucson, Ariz.	Reynard-Ford	91	Suspension	177,853
24	r-Tony Stewart (1)	Rushville, Ind.	Lola-Menard	82	Engine	222,053
25	r-Racin Gardner (25)	Buellton, Calif.	Lola-Ford	76	Suspension	149,853
26	Marco Greco (22)	Brazil	Lola-Ford	64	Engine	153,303
27	Stephan Gregoire (13)	France	Reynard-Ford	59	Fire	147,103
28	Johnny Parsons (27)	Indianapolis, Ind.	Lola-Menard	48	Radiator	161,203
29	r-Johnny O'Connell (29)	Chandler, Ariz.	Reynard-Ford	47	Fuel Pickup	145,553
30	r-Michele Alboreto (12)	Italy	Reynard-Ford	43	Gearbox	144,953
31	John Paul Jr. (17)	West Palm Beach, Fla.	Lola-Menard	10	Ignition	144,203
32	r-Paul Durant (24)	Manteca, Calif.	Lola-Buick	9	Engine	149,153
33	r-Johnny Unser	Sun Valley, Idaho	Reynard-Ford	0	Transmission	143,953

Indy Racing League Point Standings

FINAL 1996

		Sts	Finishes 1-2-3-4-5	PW	Pts
1	Buzz Calkins	3	1-0-0-0-0	0	246
	Scott Sharp	3	0-1-0-0-0	0	246
3	Robbie Buhl	3	0-0-1-0-0	0	240
4	Richie Hearn	3	0-0-1-1-0	0	237
	Roberto Guerrero	3	0-0-0-0-2	0	237
6	Mike Groff	3	0-0-1-0-0	0	228
7	Arie Luyendyk	3	1-0-0-0-0	1	225
8	Tony Stewart	3	0-1-0-0-0	0	204
9	Davey Hamilton	3	0-0-0-0-0	0	192
	Johnny O'Connell	3	0-0-0-0-1	0	192

1996–97 SEASON (through Sept. 15)

		Sts	Finishes 1-2-3-4-5	PW	Pts
1	Mike Groff	2	0-0-1-1-0	0	63
2	Michele Alboreto	2	0-0-1-0-1	0	62
	Buzz Calkins	2	0-1-0-0-0	0	62
4	Roberto Guerrero	2	0-0-0-1-0	0	60
5	Richie Hearn	2	1-0-0-0-0	1	59
6	Eliseo Salazar	2	0-0-0-0-0	0	54
	Marco Greco	2	0-0-0-0-0	0	54
	Davey Hamilton	2	0-0-0-0-1	0	54
	Scott Sharp	2	1-0-0-0-0	0	54
10	John Paul Jr.	2	0-0-0-0-0	0	45

Top 5 Finishing Order + Pole

1996 Season

No.		Winner	2nd	3rd	4th	5th	Pole
1	Indy 200	B. Calkins	T. Stewart	R. Buhl	M. Alboreto	R. Guerrero	B. Lazier
2	Dura-Lube 200	A. Luyendyk	S. Sharp	M. Groff	R. Hearn	J. O'Connell	A. Luyendyk
3	Indianapolis 500	B. Lazier	D. Jones	R. Hearn	A. Zampedri	R. Guerrero	S. Brayton

1996–97 Season (through Sept. 15)

No.		Winner	2nd	3rd	4th	5th	Pole
1	True Value 200	S. Sharp	B. Calkins	M. Alboreto	M. Groff	D. Hamilton	R. Hearn
2	Las Vegas 500K	R. Hearn	M. Jourdain Jr.	M. Groff	R. Guerrero	M. Alboreto	A. Luyendyk

Money Leaders

FINAL 1996

		Earnings
1	Buddy Lazier	$1,446,854
2	Davy Jones	632,503
3	Richie Hearn	512,203
4	Roberto Guerrero	439,503
5	Arie Luyendyk	414,003
6	Buzz Calkins	$376,553
7	Tony Stewart	375,303
8	Scott Sharp	361,303
9	Robbie Buhl	351.153
10	Mike Groff	306,253
11	Davey Hamilton	$286,503
12	Michele Alboreto	283,703
13	Eddie Cheever	281,353
14	Alessandro Zampedri	270,853
15	Johnny O'Connell	269,303

Note: Totals include season-ending $500,000 championship fund payout to the series' top 20 drivers.

1996–97 SEASON (through Sept. 15)

		Earnings
1	Richie Hearn	$181,000
2	Scott Sharp	155,000
3	Mike Groff	144,750
4	Michele Alboreto	137,250
5	Buzz Calkins	134,750
6	Roberto Guerrero	$132,000
7	Davey Hamilton	99,250
8	Michel Jourdain Jr.	95,250
9	John Paul Jr.	94,250
10	Marco Greco	93,500
11	Arie Luyendyk	$93,000
12	Tyce Carlson	91,000
13	Eliseo Salazar	90,750
14	Tony Stewart	73,000
15	Stan Wattles	72,000

FORMULA ONE Results

Winners of Formula One Grand Prix races from Nov. 12, 1995 through Oct 13, 1996.

LATE 1995

Date	Grand Prix	Location	Winner (Pos)	Time	Avg.mph	Pole	Qual. mph
Nov. 12	Australia	Adelaide	Damon Hill (1)	1:49:15.946	104.4700	D. Hill	117.495

Winning Constructors (for the entire season)**:** BENETTON-FORD (10)— Schumacher (8), Hebert (2); WILLIAMS-RENAULT (4)— Hill (4); FERRARI (1)— Alesi (1);

1996 SEASON (through Oct. 13)

Date	Grand Prix	Location	Winner (Pos.)	Time	Avg.mph	Pole	Qual. mph
Mar. 10	Australia	Melbourne	Damon Hill (2)	1:32:50.491	123.492	J. Villeneuve	127.598
Mar. 31	Brazilian	Interlagos	Damon Hill (1)	1:49:52.976	104.171	D. Hill	123.839
Apr. 7	Argentine	Buenos Aires	Damon Hill (1)	1:54.55.322	99.428	D. Hill	105.394
Apr. 28	European	Nurburgring	Jacques Villeneuve (2)	1:33.26.473	121.794	D. Hill	129.104
May 5	San Marino	Imola	Damon Hill (2)	1:35.26.156	120.408	M. Schumacher	125.952
May 19	Monaco	Monte Carlo	Olivier Panis (14)	2:00.45.629	77.058	M. Schumacher	92.648
June 2	Spanish	Barcelona	Michael Schumacher (3)	1:59:49.307	95.558	D. Hill	131.099
June 16	Canadian	Montreal	Damon Hill (1)	1:36:03.465	118.397	D. Hill	122.000
June 30	French	Magny-Cours	Damon Hill (2)	1:36:28.795	118.199	M. Schumacher	
July 14	British	Silverstone	Jacques Villeneuve (2)	1:33:00.874	124.027	D. Hill	130.613
July 28	German	Hockenheim	Damon Hill (1)	1:21:43.417	140.100	D. Hill	140.063
Aug. 11	Hungarian	Budapest	Jacques Villeneuve (3)	1:46:21.134	106.870	M. Schumacher	115.101
Aug. 25	Belgian	Spa-Fran'champs	Michael Schumacher (3)	1:28:15.125	129.234	J.Villeneuve	141.071
Sept. 8	Italian	Monza	Michael Schumacher (3)	1:17:43.632	146.665	D. Hill	153.271
Sept. 22	Portuguese	Estoril	Jacques Villeneuve (2)	1:40:22.915	113.352	D.Hill	121.404
Oct. 13	Japan	Suzuka	Damon Hill (2)	1:32:33.791	123.450	J. Villeneuve	132.327

†Track record.

Winning Constructors: WILLIAMS-RENAULT (12)— Hill 8, Villeneuve 4; FERRARI (3)— Schumacher 3; LIBIER-HONDA (1)—Panis 1.

1996 Race Locations

March— AUSTRALIAN GRAND PRIX at Melbourne; BRAZILIAN GP at Interlagos in Sao Paulo. **April**— ARGENTINE GP at Buenos Aires; EUROPEAN GP at Nurburgring, Germany. **May**— SAN MARINO GP at Imola, Italy; GP of MONACO at Monte Carlo. **June**— CANADIAN GP at Circuit Gilles Villenueve in Montreal. **July**—FRENCH GP at Magny-Cours; BRITISH GP at Silverstone in Towcester; GERMAN GP at Hockenheimring in Hockenheim. **August**— HUNGARIAN GP at Hungaroring in Budapest; BELGIAN GP at Spa-Francorchamps. **September**— ITALIAN GP at Monza in Milan; PORTUGUESE GP at Estoril. **October**— EUROPEAN GP at Nurburgring in Germany; JAPANESE GP at Suzuka.

Formula One Point Standings

Official Top 10 Formula One World Championship point leaders for 1995 and unofficial Top 10 point leaders for 1996. Points awarded for places 1 through 6 only (i.e., 10-6-4-3-2-1). Listed are starts (Sts), Top 6 finishes, poles won (PW) and points (Pts).

Note: Formula One does not keep Money Leader standings.

1995 SEASON

	Sts	Finishes 1-2-3-4-5-6	PW	Pts
1 Michael Schumacher	17	9-1-1-0-1-0	4	102
2 Damon Hill	17	4-3-2-1-0-0	7	69
3 David Coulthard	17	1-4-3-1-0-0	5	49
4 Johnny Hebert	17	2-1-1-4-1-1	0	45
5 Jean Alesi	17	1-4-0-0-4-0	0	42
6 Gerhard Berger	17	0-0-6-2-0-1	1	31
7 Mika Hakkinen	15	0-2-0-1-1-0	0	17
8 Oliver Panis	17	0-1-0-2-1-2	0	16
9 Heinz-Harald Frentzen	17	0-0-1-1-2-4	0	15
10 Mark Bludell	15	0-0-0-2-3-1	0	13

1996 SEASON (thru Oct. 13)

	Sts	Finishes 1-2-3-4-5-6	PW	Pts
1 Damon Hill	16	8-2-0-1-1-0	9	97
2 Jacques Villeneuve	16	4-5-2-0-0-0	3	78
3 Michael Schumacher	16	3-3-2-1-0-0	4	59
4 Jean Alesi	16	0-4-4-2-0-1	0	47
5 Mika Hakkinen	16	0-0-4-2-4-1	0	31
6 Gerhard Berger	16	0-1-1-3-0-2	0	21
7 David Coulthard	16	0-1-1-1-2-1	0	18
8 Rubens Barrichello	16	0-0-0-2-3-2	0	14
9 Olivier Panis	16	1-0-0-0-1-1	0	13
10 Eddie Irvine	16	0-0-1-1-2-0	0	11

Top 5 Finishing Order + Pole

No.	Event	Winner	2nd	3rd	4th	5th	Pole
1	Australia	D. Hill	J. Villeneuve	E. Irvine	G. Berger	M. Hakkinen	J. Villeneuve
2	Brazil	D. Hill	J. Alesi	M. Schumacher	M. Hakkinen	M. Salo	D. Hill
3	Argentina	D. Hill	J. Villeneuve	J. Alesi	R. Barrichello	E. Irvine	D. Hill
4	European	J. Villeneuve	M. Schumacher	D. Coulthard	D. Hill	R. Barrichello	D. Hill
5	San Marino	D. Hill	M. Schumacher	G. Berger	E. Irvine	R. Barrichello	M. Schumacher
6	Monaco	O. Panis	D. Coulthard	J. Herbert	H. Frentzen	M. Salo	M. Schumacher
7	Spain	M. Schumacher	J. Alesi	J. Villeneuve	H. Frentzen	M. Hakkinen	D. Hill
8	Canada	D. Hill	J. Villeneuve	J. Alesi	D. Coulthard	M. Hakkinen	D. Hill
9	France	D. Hill	J. Villeneuve	J. Alesi	G. Berger	M. Hakkinen	M. Schumacher
10	Britain	J. Villeneuve	G. Berger	M. Hakkinen	R. Barrichello	D. Coulthard	D. Hill
11	Germany	D. Hill	J. Alesi	J. Villeneuve	M. Schumacher	D. Coulthard	D. Hill
12	Hungary	J. Villeneuve	D. Hill	J. Alesi	M. Hakkinen	O. Panis	M. Schumacher
13	Belgium	M. Schumacher	J. Villeneuve	M. Hakkinen	J. Alesi	D. Hill	J. Villeneuve
14	Italy	M. Schumacher	J. Alesi	M. Hakkinen	M. Brundle	R. Barrichello	D. Hill
15	Portugal	J. Villeneuve	D. Hill	M. Schumacher	J. Alesi	E. Irvine	D. Hill
16	Japan	D. Hill	M. Schumacher	M. Hakkinen	G. Berger	M. Brundle	J. Villeneuve

Major 1996 Endurance Races

24 Hours of Daytona

Feb. 3–4, at Daytona Beach, Fla.
Officially the Rolex 24 at Daytona and first held in 1962 (as a 3-hour race). An IMSA Camel GT race for exotic prototype sports cars and contested over a 3.56-mile road course at Daytona International Speedway. Listed are qualifying position, drivers, chassis, class and laps completed.

1 (2) Wayne Taylor, Scott Sharp and Jim Pace; OLDSMOBILE R&S MK-III; WSC; 697 laps (2481.32 miles) at 103.32 mph; 1:05.518 margin of victory.
2 (1) Massimiliano Papis, Gianpiero Moretti, Bob Wollek and Didier Theys; FERRARI 333SP; WSC; 697 laps.
3 (10) Tim McAdam, Barry Waddell, Butch Hamlet and Jim Downing; MAZDA KUDZU DLM; WSC; 649 laps.
4 (40) Enzo Calderari, Ferdinand de Lesseps, Lilian Bryner and Ulrich Richter; PORSCHE 911; GTS-2; 649 laps.
5 (8) Ross Bentley, Franck Freon and Lee Payne; OLDSMOBILE R&S MK-III; WSC; 645 laps.
Fastest lap: Massimiliano Papis (lap #691), FERRARI 333SP; 125.707 mph. **Top qualifier:** Didier Theys, FERRARI 333SP; 126.610 mph (1:41.224).
Weather: cold and windy. **Attendance:** 40,000 (est.).

24 Hours of Le Mans

June 15–16, at LeMans, France
Officially the Le Mans Grand Prix d'Endurance and first held in 1923. Contested over the 8.451-mile Circuit de la Sarthe in Le Mans, France. Listed are drivers, countries, car, and laps completed.

1 (7) Davy Jones (USA), Manuel Reuter (GER) and Alexander Wurz (AUS); TWR Porsche; 354 laps (2,991.6 miles) at 124.65 mph
2 (4) Hans-Joachim Stuck (GER), Thierry Boutsen (BEL) and Bob Wollek (FRA); Porsche AG GT1; 353 laps.
3 (2) Karl Wendlinger (AUS), Yannick Dalmas (FRA) and Scott Goodyear (CAN); Porsche AG GT1; 341 laps.
4 (22) John Nielsen (DEN), Thomas Bscher (GER), Peter Kox (NET); McLaren BMW F1 GTR; 338 laps.
5 (10) Lindsay Owen Jones (GBR), Pierre Henri Raphanel (FRA), David Brabham (AUSL); McLaren BMW F1 GTR; 335 laps.
Fastest lap: Eric van de Poele, Ferrari 333 SP; mph (3:46.958), lap 213. **Top qualifier:** Pierluigi Martini; Joest Porsche WSC; (3:46.682).
Weather: clear. **Attendance:** 180,000 (est.).

NHRA Results

National Hot Rod Association Drag Racing champions in the Top Fuel, Funny Car and Pro Stock divisions from Feb. 4 through Oct. 13, 1996. All times are based on two cars racing head-to-head from a standing start over a straight line, quarter-mile course. Differences in reaction time account for apparently faster losing times. See updates for later results.

1996 Season (through Sept 29)

Date		Event	Winner	Time	MPH	2nd Place	Time	MPH
Feb. 4	Winternationals	Top Fuel	Blaine Johnson	4.736	299.70	S. Kalitta	4.821	297.32
		Funny Car	Al Hofmann	5.054	302.72	J. Force	5.401	228.94
		Pro Stock	J. Yates	7.041	195.48	B. Huff	7.147	194.88
Feb. 25	ATSCO Nationals	Top Fuel	Kenny Bernstein	4.705	305.39	C. McClenathan	13.407	71.48
		Funny Car	John Force	5.196	295.85	C. Etchells	5.755	186.48
		Pro Stock	Jim Yates	7.057	194.51	T. Martino	7.745	134.67
Mar. 17	Gatornationals	Top Fuel	Blaine Johnson	10.408	81.34	S. Kalitta	crashed	—
		Funny Car	John Force	4.999	301.40	C. Etchells	5.232	302.01
		Pro Stock	Jim Yates	7.024	195.99	S. Schmidt	foul	—
Mar. 31	Slick 50 Nationals	Top Fuel	Kenny Bernstein	4.663	306.95	J. Amato	5.721	158.50
		Funny Car	John Force	5.055	294.98	A. Hofmann	9.816	82.84
		Pro Stock	Mike Edwards	7.029	196.46	R. Franks	7.074	195.10
Apr. 21	Fram Nationals	Top Fuel	Larry Dixon	6.043	232.73	M. Dunn	6.494	141.26
		Funny Car	Tony Pedregon	5.108	294.59	J. Force	5.318	276.83
		Pro Stock	Kurt Johnson	7.068	195.82	J. Yates	7.039	195.69
May 5	Pennzoil Nationals (VA)	Top Fuel	Shelly Anderson	4.779	298.90	S. Kalitta	7.426	101.82
		Funny Car	John Force	5.071	285.17	C. Pedregon	5.307	218.12
		Pro Stock	Warren Johnson	7.018	196.03	M. Edwards	7.048	196.50
May 19	Mopar Nationals	Top Fuel	Joe Amato	4.782	301.30	L. Dixon	4.854	286.89
		Funny Car	John Force	5.087	298.80	G. Densham	5.270	287.08
		Pro Stock	Jim Yates	7.134	193.00	W. Johnson	7.149	193.13
June 9	Pontiac Nationals	Top Fuel	Cory McClenathan	4.817	306.43	L. Dixon	4.937	275.98
		Funny Car	Chuck Etchells	5.178	287.63	M. Oswald	6.406	141.08
		Pro Stock	Chuck Harris	7.168	193.09	W. Johnson	7.266	192.84
June 23	Pennzoil Nationals (TN)	Top Fuel	Mike Dunn	4.897	295.85	J. Amato	4.804	306.22
		Funny Car	John Force	5.302	296.54	T. Pedregon	5.550	265.40
		Pro Stock	Warren Johnson	7.221	192.84	J. Yates	7.270	191.53
July 7	West. Auto Nationals	Top Fuel	Scott Kalitta	4.664	314.68	K.Bernstein	14.146	77.03
		Funny Car	John Force	4.930	303.54	C. Pedregon	4.942	304.36
		Pro Stock	Warren Johnson	7.104	193.34	J. Yates	7.114	194.38
July 21	Mile-High Nationals	Top Fuel	Eddie Hill	4.845	288.92	B. Johnson	4.903	290.88
		Funny Car	John Force	5.221	294.31	C. Etchells	5.433	249.23
		Pro Stock	Jim Yates	7.476	183.41	S. Schmidt	7.495	183.74
July 28	Autolite Nationals	Top Fuel	Blaine Johnson	4.671	306.01	K. Bernstein	5.003	219.88
		Funny Car	Cruz Pedregon	5.058	291.45	J. Force	5.076	301.10
		Pro Stock	Warren Johnson	7.067	194.84	M. Edwards	7.200	178.99
Aug. 5	N.W. Nationals	Top Fuel	Shelly Anderson	4.663	308.00	M. Dunn	4.710	308.85
		Funny Car	John Force	4.965	302.11	T. Pedregon	5.028	292.01
		Pro Stock	Mike Edwards	7.046	196.24	K. Johnson	7.042	194.76
Aug. 18	Champion Nationals	Top Fuel	Kenny Bernstein	4.733	302.82	E. Hill	9.552	76.07
		Funny Car	John Force	5.120	303.13	T. Pedregon	5.260	243.17
		Pro Stock	Warren Johnson	7.110	193.38	S. Schmidt	7.153	193.00
Sept. 2	U.S. Nationals	Top Fuel	Cory McClenathan	4.734	306.53	T. Schumacher	5.742	161.49
		Funny Car	John Force	5.139	301.10	A. Hofmann	8.517	96.34
		Pro Stock	Kurt Johnson	7.070	195.14	R. Smith	7.083	195.01
Sept. 15	Keystone Nationals	Top Fuel	Kenny Bernstein	4.675	305.81	C. Kalitta	4.833	300.10
		Funny Car	Jeff Arend	5.187	291.16	T. Pedregon	5.209	298.40
		Pro Stock	Jim Yates	6.957	197.45	W. Johnson	10.789	82.28
Sept. 29	Sears Nationals	Top Fuel	Jim Head	4.713	302.82	K. Bernstein	7.039	109.48
		Funny Car	John Force	4.970	304.67	T. Pedregon	11.927	69.88
		Pro Stock	Jim Yates	7.068	195.22	R. Franks	7.092	193.46

Winston Point Standings

1996 (through Oct. 13)

First place finishes in parentheses.

Top Fuel

		Pts
1	Kenny Bernstein (4)	1361
2	Blaine Johnson (3)	1161
3	Cory McClenathan (3)	1136
4	Larry Dixon (1)	1121
5	Scott Kalitta (1)	1102

Funny Car

		Pts
1	John Force (12)	1909
2	Tony Pedregon (1)	1291
3	Cruz Pedregon (1)	1255
4	Al Hofmann (1)	1067
5	Chuck Etchells (1)	991

Pro Stock

		Pts
1	Jim Yates (8)	1348
2	Warren Johnson (5)	1341
3	Mike Edwards (2)	988
4	Kurt Johnson (2)	955
5	Steve Schmidt	930

AUTO RACING STATISTICS

THROUGH THE YEARS

1911-1996

MAJOR RACES • LEADERS

NASCAR Circuit

The Crown Jewels

The four biggest races on the NASCAR circuit are the Daytona 500, the Winston Select 500, the Coca-Cola 600 and the Mountain Dew Southern 500. The Winston Cup Media Guide lists them as the richest (Daytona), the fastest (Winston), the longest (Coca-Cola) and the oldest (Southern). Winston has offered a $1 million bonus since 1985 to any driver who can win three of the four races. The only drivers to win three of the races in a single year are Lee Roy Yarbrough (1969), David Pearson (1976) and Bill Elliott (1985).

Daytona 500

Held early in the NASCAR season; 200 laps around a 2.5-mile high-banked oval at Daytona International Speedway in Daytona Beach, FL. First race in 1959, although stock car racing at Daytona dates back to 1936. Winning drivers who started from pole positions are in **bold** type.

Multiple winners: Richard Petty (7); Cale Yarborough (4); Bobby Allison (3); Bill Elliott, Dale Jarrett and Sterling Marlin (2).

Multiple poles: Buddy Baker and Cale Yarborough (4); Bill Elliott, Fireball Roberts and Ken Schrader (3); Donnie Allison (2).

Year	Winner	Car	Owner	MPH	Pole Sitter	MPH
1959	Lee Petty	Oldsmobile	Petty Enterprises	135.521	Bob Welborn	140.121
1960	Junior Johnson	Chevrolet	Ray Fox	124.740	Cotton Owens	149.892
1961	Marvin Panch	Pontiac	Smokey Yunick	149.601	Fireball Roberts	155.709
1962	**Fireball Roberts**	Pontiac	Smokey Yunick	152.529	Fireball Roberts	156.999
1963	Tiny Lund	Ford	Wood Brothers	151.566	Fireball Roberts	160.943
1964	Richard Petty	Plymouth	Petty Enterprises	154.334	Paul Goldsmith	174.910
1965-**a**	Fred Lorenzen	Ford	Holman-Moody	141.539	Darel Dieringer	171.151
1966-**b**	**Richard Petty**	Plymouth	Petty Enterprises	160.627	Richard Petty	175.165
1967	Mario Andretti	Ford	Holman-Moody	149.926	Curtis Turner	180.831
1968	**Cale Yarborough**	Mercury	Wood Brothers	143.251	Cale Yarborough	189.222
1969	Lee Roy Yarbrough	Ford	Junior Johnson	157.950	Buddy Baker	188.901
1970	Pete Hamilton	Plymouth	Petty Enterprises	149.601	Cale Yarborough	194.015
1971	Richard Petty	Plymouth	Petty Enterprises	144.462	A.J. Foyt	182.744
1972	A.J. Foyt	Mercury	Wood Brothers	161.550	Bobby Issac	186.632
1973	Richard Petty	Dodge	Petty Enterprises	157.205	Buddy Baker	185.662
1974-**c**	Richard Petty	Dodge	Petty Enterprises	140.894	David Pearson	185.017
1975	Benny Parsons	Chevrolet	L.G. DeWitt	153.649	Donnie Allison	185.827
1976	David Pearson	Mercury	Wood Brothers	152.181	Ramo Stott	183.456
1977	Cale Yarborough	Chevrolet	Junior Johnson	153.218	Donnie Allison	188.048
1978	Bobby Allison	Ford	Bud Moore	159.730	Cale Yarborough	187.536
1979	Richard Petty	Oldsmobile	Petty Enterprises	143.977	Buddy Baker	196.049
1980	**Buddy Baker**	Oldsmobile	Ranier Racing	177.602*	Buddy Baker	194.099
1981	Richard Petty	Buick	Petty Enterprises	169.651	Bobby Allison	194.624
1982	Bobby Allison	Buick	DiGard Racing	153.991	Benny Parsons	196.317
1983	Cale Yarborough	Pontiac	Ranier Racing	155.979	Ricky Rudd	198.864
1984	**Cale Yarborough**	Chevrolet	Ranier Racing	150.994	Cale Yarborough	201.848
1985	**Bill Elliott**	Ford	Melling Racing	172.265	Bill Elliott	205.114
1986	Geoff Bodine	Chevrolet	Hendrick Motorsports	148.124	Bill Elliott	205.039
1987	**Bill Elliott**	Ford	Melling Racing	176.263	Bill Elliott	210.364†
1988	Bobby Allison	Buick	Stavola Brothers	137.531	Ken Schrader	198.823
1989	Darrell Waltrip	Chevrolet	Hendrick Motorsports	148.466	Ken Schrader	196.996
1990	Derrike Cope	Chevrolet	Bob Whitcomb	165.761	Ken Schrader	196.515
1991	Ernie Irvan	Chevrolet	Morgan-McClure	148.148	Davey Allison	195.955
1992	Davey Allison	Ford	Robert Yates	160.256	Sterling Martin	192.213
1993	Dale Jarrett	Chevrolet	Joe Gibbs Racing	154.972	Kyle Petty	189.426
1994	Sterling Marlin	Chevrolet	Morgan-McClure	156.931	Loy Allen	190.158
1995	Sterling Marlin	Chevrolet	Morgan-McClure	141.710	Dale Jarrett	193.498
1996	Dale Jarrett	Ford	Robert Yates	154.308	Dale Earnhardt	189.510

*Track and race record for Winning Speed. †Track and race record for Qualifying Speed.

Notes: a—rain shortened 1965 to 332+ miles; **b**—rain shortened 1966 race to 495 miles; **c**—in 1974, race shortened 50 miles due to energy crisis. **Also:** Pole sitters determined by pole qualifying race (1959-65); by two-lap average (1966-68); by fastest single lap (since 1969).

Winston Select 500

Held at Talladega (Ala.) Superspeedway. **Multiple winners:** Bobby Allison, Davey Allison, Buddy Baker and David Pearson (3); Dale Earnhardt, Darrell Waltrip and Cale Yarborough (2).

Year		Year		Year		Year	
1970	Pete Hamilton	1977	Darrell Waltrip	1983	Richard Petty	1990	Dale Earnhardt
1971	Donnie Allison	1978	Cale Yarborough	1984	Cale Yarborough	1991	Harry Gant
1972	David Pearson	1979	Bobby Allison	1985	Bill Elliott	1992	Davey Allison
1973	David Pearson	1980	Buddy Baker	1986	Bobby Allison	1993	Ernie Irvan
1974	David Pearson	1981	Bobby Allison	1987	Davey Allison	1994	Dale Earnhardt
1975	Buddy Baker	1982	Darrell Waltrip	1988	Phil Parsons	1995	Mark Martin
1976	Buddy Baker			1989	Davey Allison	1996	Sterling Marlin

Coca-Cola 600

Held at Charlotte (N.C.) Motor Speedway. **Multiple winners:** Darrell Waltrip (5); Bobby Allison, Buddy Baker, Dale Earnhardt and David Pearson (3); Neil Bonnett, Fred Lorenzen, Jim Paschal and Richard Petty (2).

Year		Year		Year		Year	
1960	Joe Lee Johnson	1970	Donnie Allison	1980	Benny Parsons	1990	Rusty Wallace
1961	David Pearson	1971	Bobby Allison	1981	Bobby Allison	1991	Davey Allison
1962	Nelson Stacy	1972	Buddy Baker	1982	Neil Bonnett	1992	Dale Earnhardt
1963	Fred Lorenzen	1973	Buddy Baker	1983	Neil Bonnett	1993	Dale Earnhardt
1964	Jim Paschal	1974	David Pearson	1984	Bobby Allison	1994	Jeff Gordon
1965	Fred Lorenzen	1975	Richard Petty	1985	Darrell Waltrip	1995	Bobby Labonte
1966	Marvin Panch	1976	David Pearson	1986	Dale Earnhardt	1996	Dale Jarrett
1967	Jim Paschal	1977	Richard Petty	1987	Kyle Petty		
1968	Buddy Baker	1978	Darrell Waltrip	1988	Darrell Waltrip		
1969	Lee Roy Yarbrough	1979	Darrell Waltrip	1989	Darrell Waltrip		

Southern 500

Held at Darlington (S.C.) International Raceway. **Multiple winners:** Cale Yarborough (5); Bobby Allison (4); Buck Baker, Dale Earnhardt, Bill Elliott, David Pearson and Herb Thomas (3); Harry Gant, Jeff Gordon and Fireball Roberts (2).

Year		Year		Year		Year	
1950	Johnny Mantz	1962	Larry Frank	1974	Cale Yarborough	1986	Tim Richmond
1951	Herb Thomas	1963	Fireball Roberts	1975	Bobby Allison	1987	Dale Earnhardt
1952	Fonty Flock	1964	Buck Baker	1976	David Pearson	1988	Bill Elliott
1953	Buck Baker	1965	Ned Jarrett	1977	David Pearson	1989	Dale Earnhardt
1954	Herb Thomas	1966	Darel Dieringer	1978	Cale Yarborough	1990	Dale Earnhardt
1955	Herb Thomas	1967	Richard Petty	1979	David Pearson	1991	Harry Gant
1956	Curtis Turner	1968	Cale Yarborough	1980	Terry Labonte	1992	Darrell Waltrip
1957	Speedy Thompson	1969	Lee Roy Yarbrough	1981	Neil Bonnett	1993	Mark Martin
1958	Fireball Roberts	1970	Buddy Baker	1982	Cale Yarborough	1994	Bill Elliott
1959	Jim Reed	1971	Bobby Allison	1983	Bobby Allison	1995	Jeff Gordon
1960	Buck Baker	1972	Bobby Allison	1984	Harry Gant	1996	Jeff Gordon
1961	Nelson Stacy	1973	Cale Yarborough	1985	Bill Elliott		

All-Time Leaders

NASCAR's all-time Top 20 drivers in victories, pole positions and earnings based on records through 1995. Drivers active in 1996 are in **bold** type.

Victories

1	Richard Petty	200
2	David Pearson	105
3	**Darrell Waltrip**	84
	Bobby Allison	84
5	Cale Yarborough	83
6	**Dale Earnhardt**	68
7	Lee Petty	54
8	Ned Jarrett	50
	Junior Johnson	50
10	Herb Thomas	48
11	Buck Baker	46
12	**Rusty Wallace**	41
13	**Bill Elliott**	40
	Tim Flock	40
15	Bobby Isaac	37
16	Fireball Roberts	34
17	Rex White	28
18	Fred Lorenzen	26
19	Jim Paschal	25
20	Joe Weatherly	24

Pole Positions

1	Richard Petty	127
2	David Pearson	113
3	Cale Yarborough	70
4	**Darrell Waltrip**	59
5	Bobby Allison	57
6	Bobby Isaac	51
7	**Bill Elliott**	48
8	Junior Johnson	47
9	Buck Baker	44
10	Buddy Baker	40
11	Herb Thomas	38
12	Tim Flock	37
	Fireball Roberts	37
14	Ned Jarrett	36
	Rex White	36
16	**Geoff Bodine**	35
17	Fred Lorenzen	33
18	Fonty Flock	30
19	**Mark Martin**	28
20	Marvin Panch	25

Earnings

1	**Dale Earnhardt**	$25,948,545
2	**Bill Elliott**	15,540,479
3	**Darrell Waltrip**	14,441,866
4	**Rusty Wallace**	12,754,720
5	**Terry Labonte**	10,454,755
6	**Mark Martin**	10,030,812
7	**Ricky Rudd**	10,023,314
8	**Geoff Bodine**	9,412,788
9	Harry Gant	8,438,104
10	Richard Petty	7,755,409
11	**Ken Schrader**	7,703,183
12	**Sterling Marlin**	7,354,232
13	Kyle Petty	7,187,699
14	Bobby Allison	7,102,233
15	**Jeff Gordon**	6,898,319
16	Davey Allison	6,726,974
17	**Morgan Shepard**	6,682,190
18	**Ernie Irvan**	5,653,996
19	**Dale Jarrett**	5,067,402
20	Alan Kulwicki	5,061,202

Wide World Photos

Wide World Photos

Richard Petty (left) and **Dale Earnhardt** are both NASCAR Rookies of the Year who went on to win a record seven Winston Cup driving championships. Earnhardt, who claimed his seventh title in 1994, is also the circuit's all-time money winner. Petty retired in 1992 with a record 200 victories, including seven wins in the Daytona 500.

NASCAR Circuit (Cont.)

Winston Cup Champions

Originally the Grand National Championship, 1949-70, and based on official NASCAR (National Association for Stock Car Auto Racing) records.

Multiple winners: Dale Earnhardt and Richard Petty (7); David Pearson, Lee Petty, Darrell Waltrip and Cale Yarborough (3); Buck Baker, Tim Flock, Ned Jarrett, Herb Thomas and Joe Weatherly (2).

Year		Year		Year		Year	
1949	Red Byron	1961	Ned Jarrett	1973	Benny Parsons	1985	Darrell Waltrip
1950	Bill Rexford	1962	Joe Weatherly	1974	Richard Petty	1986	Dale Earnhardt
1951	Herb Thomas	1963	Joe Weatherly	1975	Richard Petty	1987	Dale Earnhardt
1952	Tim Flock	1964	Richard Petty	1976	Cale Yarborough	1988	Bill Elliott
1953	Herb Thomas	1965	Ned Jarrett	1977	Cale Yarborough	1989	Rusty Wallace
1954	Lee Petty	1966	David Pearson	1978	Cale Yarborough	1990	Dale Earnhardt
1955	Tim Flock	1967	Richard Petty	1979	Richard Petty	1991	Dale Earnhardt
1956	Buck Baker	1968	David Pearson	1980	Dale Earnhardt	1992	Alan Kulwicki
1957	Buck Baker	1969	David Pearson	1981	Darrell Waltrip	1993	Dale Earnhardt
1958	Lee Petty	1970	Bobby Issac	1982	Darrell Waltrip	1994	Dale Earnhardt
1959	Lee Petty	1971	Richard Petty	1983	Bobby Allison	1995	Jeff Gordon
1960	Rex White	1972	Richard Petty	1984	Terry Labonte		

NASCAR Rookie of the Year

Award presented to rookie driver who accumulates the most Winston Cup points based on his best 15 finishes.

Year		Year		Year		Year	
1958	Shorty Rollins	1968	Pete Hamilton	1978	Ronnie Thomas	1988	Ken Bouchard
1959	Richard Petty	1969	Dick Brooks	1979	Dale Earnhardt	1989	Dick Trickle
1960	David Pearson	1970	Bill Dennis	1980	Jody Ridley	1990	Rob Moroso
1961	Woodie Wilson	1971	Walter Ballard	1981	Ron Bouchard	1991	Bobby Hamilton
1962	Tom Cox	1972	Larry Smith	1982	Geoff Bodine	1992	Jimmy Hensley
1963	Billy Wade	1973	Lennie Pond	1983	Sterling Marlin	1993	Jeff Gordon
1964	Doug Cooper	1974	Earl Ross	1984	Rusty Wallace	1994	Jeff Burton
1965	Sam McQuagg	1975	Bruce Hill	1985	Ken Schrader	1995	Ricky Craven
1966	James Hylton	1976	Skip Manning	1986	Alan Kulwicki		
1967	Donnie Allison	1977	Ricky Rudd	1987	Davey Allison		

IndyCar Circuit

Indianapolis 500

Held every Memorial Day weekend; 200 laps around a 2.5-mile oval at Indianapolis Motor Speedway. First race was held in 1911. Winning drivers are listed with starting positions. Winners who started from pole position are in **bold** type.

Multiple wins: A.J. Foyt, Rick Mears and Al Unser (4); Louis Meyer, Mauri Rose, Johnny Rutherford, Wilbur Shaw and Bobby Unser (3); Emerson Fittipaldi, Gordon Johncock, Tommy Milton, Al Unser Jr., Bill Vukovich and Rodger Ward (2).

Multiple poles: Rick Mears (6); Mario Andretti and A.J. Foyt (4); Rex Mays, Duke Nalon and Tom Sneva (3); Billy Arnold, Bill Cummings, Ralph DePalma, Leon Duray, Walt Faulkner, Parnelli Jones, Jack McGrath, Jimmy Murphy, Johnny Rutherford, Eddie Sachs and Jimmy Snyder (2).

Year	Winner (Pos.)	Car	MPH	Pole Sitter	MPH
1911	Ray Harroun (28)	Marmon Wasp	74.602	Lewis Strang	—
1912	Joe Dawson (7)	National	78.719	Gil Anderson	—
1913	Jules Goux (7)	Peugeot	75.933	Caleb Bragg	—
1914	Rene Thomas (15)	Delage	82.474	Jean Chassagne	—
1915	Ralph DePalma (2)	Mercedes	89.840	Howard Wilcox	98.90
1916-**a**	Dario Resta (4)	Peugeot	84.001	John Aitken	96.69
1917-18	Not held	World War I			
1919	Howdy Wilcox (2)	Peugeot	88.050	Rene Thomas	104.78
1920	Gaston Chevrolet (6)	Monroe	88.618	Ralph DePalma	99.15
1921	Tommy Milton (20)	Frontenac	89.621	Ralph DePalma	100.75
1922	**Jimmy Murphy** (1)	Murphy Special	94.484	Jimmy Murphy	100.50
1923	**Tommy Milton** (1)	H.C.S. Special	90.954	Tommy Milton	108.17
1924	L.L. Corum & Joe Boyer (21)	Duesenberg Special	98.234	Jimmy Murphy	108.037
1925	Peter DePaolo (2)	Duesenberg Special	101.127	Leon Duray	113.196
1926-**b**	Frank Lockhart (20)	Miller Special	95.904	Earl Cooper	111.735
1927	George Souders (22)	Duesenberg	97.545	Frank Lockhart	120.100
1928	Louie Meyer (13)	Miller Special	99.482	Leon Duray	122.391
1929	Ray Keech (6)	Simplex Piston Ring Special	97.585	Cliff Woodbury	120.599
1930	**Billy Arnold** (1)	Miller-Hartz Special	100.448	Billy Arnold	113.268
1931	Louis Schneider (13)	Bowes Seal Fast Special	96.629	Russ Snowberger	112.796
1932	Fred Frame (27)	Miller-Hartz Special	104.144	Lou Moore	117.363
1933	Louie Meyer (6)	Tydol Special	104.162	Bill Cummings	118.530
1934	Bill Cummings (10)	Boyle Products Special	104.863	Kelly Petillo	119.329
1935	Kelly Petillo (22)	Gilmore Speedway Special	106.240	Rex Mays	120.736
1936	Louie Meyer (28)	Ring Free Special	109.069	Rex Mays	119.644
1937	Wilbur Shaw (2)	Shaw-Gilmore Special	113.580	Bill Cummings	123.343
1938	**Floyd Roberts** (1)	Burd Piston Ring Special	117.200	Floyd Roberts	125.681
1939	Wilbur Shaw (3)	Boyle Special	115.035	Jimmy Snyder	130.138
1940	Wilbur Shaw (2)	Boyle Special	114.277	Rex Mays	127.850
1941	Floyd Davis & Mauri Rose (17)	Noc-Out Hose Clamp Special	115.117	Mauri Rose	128.691
1942-45	Not held	World War II			
1946	George Robson (15)	Thorne Engineering Special	114.820	Cliff Bergere	126.471
1947	Mauri Rose (3)	Blue Crown Spark Plug Special	116.338	Ted Horn	126.564
1948	Mauri Rose (3)	Blue Crown Spark Plug Special	119.814	Duke Nalon	131.603
1949	Bill Holland (4)	Blue Crown Spark Plug Special	121.327	Duke Nalon	132.939
1950-**c**	Johnnie Parsons (5)	Wynn's Friction Proofing	124.002	Walt Faulkner	134.343
1951	Lee Wallard (2)	Belanger Special	126.244	Duke Nalon	136.498
1952	Troy Ruttman (7)	Agajanian Special	128.922	Fred Agabashian	138.010
1953	**Bill Vukovich** (1)	Fuel Injection Special	128.740	Bill Vukovich	138.392
1954	Bill Vukovich (19)	Fuel Injection Special	130.840	Jack McGrath	141.033
1955	Bob Sweikert (14)	John Zink Special	128.213	Jerry Hoyt	140.045
1956	**Pat Flaherty** (1)	John Zink Special	128.490	Pat Flaherty	145.596
1957	Sam Hanks (13)	Belond Exhaust Special	135.601	Pat O'Connor	143.948
1958	Jimmy Bryan (7)	Belond AP Parts Special	133.791	Dick Rathmann	145.974
1959	Rodger Ward (6)	Leader Card 500 Roadster	135.857	Johnny Thomson	145.908
1960	Jim Rathmann (2)	Ken-Paul Special	138.767	Eddie Sachs	146.592
1961	A.J. Foyt (7)	Bowes Seal Fast Special	139.130	Eddie Sachs	147.481
1962	Rodger Ward (2)	Leader Card 500 Roadster	140.293	Parnelli Jones	150.370
1963	**Parnelli Jones** (1)	Agajanian-Willard Special	143.137	Parnelli Jones	151.153
1964	A.J. Foyt (5)	Sheraton-Thompson Special	147.350	Jim Clark	158.828
1965	Jim Clark (2)	Lotus Ford	150.686	A.J. Foyt	161.233
1966	Graham Hill (15)	American Red Ball Special	144.317	Mario Andretti	165.899
1967-**d**	A.J. Foyt (4)	Sheraton-Thompson Special	151.207	Mario Andretti	168.982
1968	Bobby Unser (3)	Rislone Special	152.882	Joe Leonard	171.559
1969	Mario Andretti (2)	STP Oil Treatment Special	156.867	A.J. Foyt	170.568

IndyCar Circuit (Cont.)

Indianapolis 500

Year	Winner (Pos.)	Car	MPH	Pole Sitter	MPH
1970	**Al Unser** (1)	Johnny Lightning Special	155.749	Al Unser	170.221
1971	Al Unser (5)	Johnny Lightning Special	157.735	Peter Revson	178.696
1972	Mark Donohue (3)	Sunoco McLaren	162.962	Bobby Unser	195.940
1973-**e**	Gordon Johncock (11)	STP Double Oil Filters	159.036	Johnny Rutherford	198.413
1974	Johnny Rutherford (25)	McLaren	158.589	A.J. Foyt	191.632
1975-**f**	Bobby Unser (3)	Jorgensen Eagle	149.213	A.J. Foyt	193.976
1976-**g**	**Johnny Rutherford** (1)	Hy-Gain McLaren/Goodyear	148.725	Johnny Rutherford	188.957
1977	A.J. Foyt (4)	Gilmore Racing Team	161.331	Tom Sneva	198.884
1978	Al Unser (5)	FNCTC Chaparral Lola	161.363	Tom Sneva	202.156
1979	**Rick Mears** (1)	The Gould Charge	158.899	Rick Mears	193.736
1980	**Johnny Rutherford** (1)	Pennzoil Chaparral	142.862	Johnny Rutherford	192.256
1981-**h**	**Bobby Unser** (1)	Norton Spirit Penske PC-9B	139.084	Bobby Unser	200.546
1982	Gordon Johncock (5)	STP Oil Treatment	162.029	Rick Mears	207.004
1983	Tom Sneva (4)	Texaco Star	162.117	Teo Fabi	207.395
1984	Rick Mears (3)	Pennzoil Z-7	163.612	Tom Sneva	210.029
1985	Danny Sullivan (8)	Miller American Special	152.982	Pancho Carter	212.583
1986	Bobby Rahal (4)	Budweiser/Truesports/March	170.722	Rick Mears	216.828
1987	Al Unser (20)	Cummins Holset Turbo	162.175	Mario Andretti	215.390
1988	**Rick Mears** (1)	Pennzoil Z-7/Penske Chevy V-8	144.809	Rick Mears	219.198
1989	Emerson Fittipaldi (3)	Marlboro/Penske Chevy V-8	167.581	Rick Mears	223.885
1990	Arie Luyendyk (3)	Domino's Pizza Chevrolet	185.981*	Emerson Fittipaldi	225.301
1991	**Rick Mears** (1)	Marlboro Penske Chevy	176.457	Rick Mears	224.113
1992	Al Unser Jr. (12)	Valvoline Galmer '92	134.477	Roberto Guerrero	232.482†
1993	Emerson Fittipaldi (9)	Marlboro Penske Chevy	157.207	Arie Luyendyk	223.967
1994	**Al Unser Jr.** (1)	Marlboro Penske Mercedes	160.872	Al Unser Jr.	228.011
1995	Jacques Villeneuve (5)	Player's Ltd. Reynard Ford	153.616	Scott Brayton	231.604
1996	Buddy Lazier (5)	Reynard Ford	147.956	Tony Stewart	233.100&

*Track record for Winning Time. †Track record for Qualifying Time.
& Scott Brayton won the pole position with an avg. mph of 233.718 but was killed in a practice run. Stewart was given pole position with the next fastest speed.

Notes: a—1916 race scheduled for 300 miles; **b**—rain shortened 1926 race to 400 miles; **c**—rain shortened 1950 race to 345 miles; **d**—1967 race postponed due to rain after 18 laps (May 30), resumed next day (May 31); **e**—rain shortened 1973 race to 332.5 miles; **f**—rain shortened 1975 race to 435 miles; **g**—rain shortened 1976 race to 255 miles; **h**—in 1981, runner-up Mario Andretti was awarded 1st place when winner Bobby Unser was penalized a lap after the race was completed for passing cars illegally under the caution flag. Unser and car-owner Roger Penske appealed the race stewards' decision to the U.S. Auto Club. Four months later, USAC overturned the ruling, saying that the penalty was too harsh and Unser should be fined $40,000 rather than stripped of his championship.

All-Time Leaders

IndyCar's all-time Top 20 drivers in victories, pole positions and earnings, based on records through 1995. Drivers active in 1996 are in **bold** type. Totals include victories, poles and earings before CART was established in 1979.

Victories

	Driver	Wins
1	A.J. Foyt	67
2	Mario Andretti	52
3	Al Unser	39
4	Bobby Unser	35
5	**Al Unser Jr.**	31
6	**Michael Andretti**	30
7	Rick Mears	29
8	Johnny Rutherford	27
9	Roger Ward	26
10	Gordon Johncock	25
11	Ralph DePalma	24
	Bobby Rahal	24
13	Tommy Milton	23
14	Tony Bettenhausen	22
	Emerson Fittipaldi	22
16	Earl Cooper	20
17	Jimmy Bryan	19
	Jimmy Murphy	19
19	Ralph Mulford	17
	Danny Sullivan	17

Pole Positions

	Driver	Poles
1	Mario Andretti	67
2	A.J. Foyt	53
3	Bobby Unser	49
4	Rick Mears	39
5	**Michael Andretti**	30
6	Al Unser	27
7	Johnny Rutherford	23
8	Gordon Johncock	20
9	Rex Mays	19
	Danny Sullivan	19
11	**Bobby Rahal**	18
12	**Emerson Fittipaldi**	17
13	Tony Bettenhausen	14
	Don Branson	14
	Tom Sneva	14
16	Parnelli Jones	12
17	Rodger Ward	11
	Danny Ongais	11
19	Johnny Thompson	10
	Dan Gurney	10
	Nigel Mansell	10

Earnings

	Driver	Earnings
1	**Al Unser Jr.**	$16,738,906
2	**Bobby Rahal**	14,349,710
3	**Emerson Fittipaldi**	13,863,625
4	**Michael Andretti**	12,277,869
5	Mario Andretti	11,552,154
6	Rick Mears	11,050,807
7	**Danny Sullivan**	8,844,129
8	**Arie Luyendyk**	7,372,188
9	Al Unser	6,740,843
10	**Raul Boesel**	5,997,887
11	A.J. Foyt	5,357,589
12	**Scott Brayton**	4,807,214
13	**Roberto Guerrero**	4,468,116
14	**Scott Goodyear**	4,460,711
15	**Paul Tracy**	4,402,770
16	Tom Sneva	4,392,993
17	**Teo Fabi**	4,367,117
18	Johnny Rutherford	4,209,232
19	Jacques Villeneuve	4,097,732
20	**Gordon Johncock**	3,431,414

Indy Racing League Debuted in 1996

The Indy Racing League, a five-race campaign anchored by the Indianapolis 500 and boasting a TV contract with ABC, opened for business in 1996. The brainchild of Indianapolis Motor Speedway president Tony George, the IRL allotted 25 qualifying opositions in the 33-car Indianapolis 500 field to the Top 25 IRL leaders after two races— at Orlando and Phoenix— leaving only eight at large berths for rival IndyCar teams.

PPG Cup Champions

Officially the PPG Indy Car World Series Championship since 1979 and based on official AAA (American Automobile Assn., 1909-55), USAC (U.S. Auto Club, 1956-79), and CART (Championship Auto Racing Teams, 1979-91). CART was renamed IndyCar in 1992.

Multiple titles: A.J. Foyt (7); Mario Andretti (4); Jimmy Bryan, Earl Cooper, Ted Horn, Rick Mears, Louie Meyer, Bobby Rahal, Al Unser (3); Tony Bettenhausen, Ralph DePalma, Peter DePaolo, Joe Leonard, Rex Mays, Tommy Milton, Jimmy Murphy, Wilbur Shaw, Tom Sneva, Al Unser Jr., Bobby Unser and Rodger Ward (2).

AAA

Year		Year		Year		Year	
1909	George Robertson	1920	Tommy Milton	1931	Louis Schneider	1942-45	No racing
1910	Ray Harroun	1921	Tommy Milton	1932	Bob Carey	1946	Ted Horn
1911	Ralph Mulford	1922	Jimmy Murphy	1933	Louie Meyer	1947	Ted Horn
1912	Ralph DePalma	1923	Eddie Hearne	1934	Bill Cummings	1948	Ted Horn
1913	Earl Cooper	1924	Jimmy Murphy	1935	Kelly Petillo	1949	Johnnie Parsons
1914	Ralph DePalma	1925	Peter DePaolo	1936	Mauri Rose	1950	Henry Banks
1915	Earl Cooper	1926	Harry Hartz	1937	Wilbur Shaw	1951	Tony Bettenhausen
1916	Dario Resta	1927	Peter DePaolo	1938	Floyd Roberts	1952	Chuck Stevenson
1917	Earl Cooper	1928	Louie Meyer	1939	Wilbur Shaw	1953	Sam Hanks
1918	Ralph Mulford	1929	Louie Meyer	1940	Rex Mays	1954	Jimmy Bryan
1919	Howard Wilcox	1930	Billy Arnold	1941	Rex Mays	1955	Bob Sweikert

USAC

Year		Year		Year		Year	
1956	Jimmy Bryan	1962	Rodger Ward	1968	Bobby Unser	1974	Bobby Unser
1957	Jimmy Bryan	1963	A.J. Foyt	1969	Mario Andretti	1975	A.J. Foyt
1958	Tony Bettenhausen	1964	A.J. Foyt	1970	Al Unser	1976	Gordon Johncock
1959	Rodger Ward	1965	Mario Andretti	1971	Joe Leonard	1977	Tom Sneva
1960	A.J. Foyt	1966	Mario Andretti	1972	Joe Leonard	1978	A.J. Foyt
1961	A.J. Foyt	1967	A.J. Foyt	1973	Roger McCluskey		

CART/IndyCar

Year		Year		Year		Year	
1979	Rick Mears	1984	Mario Andretti	1989	Emerson Fittipaldi	1994	Al Unser Jr.
1980	Johnny Rutherford	1985	Al Unser	1990	Al Unser Jr.	1995	Jacques Villeneuve
1981	Rick Mears	1986	Bobby Rahal	1991	Michael Andretti	1996	Jimmy Vasser
1982	Rick Mears	1987	Bobby Rahal	1992	Bobby Rahal		
1983	Al Unser	1988	Danny Sullivan	1993	Nigel Mansell		

Indy 500 Rookie of the Year

Voted on by a panel of auto racing media. Award does not necessarily go to highest-finishing first-year driver. Graham Hill won the race on his first try in 1966, but the rookie award went to Jackie Stewart, who led with 10 laps to go only to lose oil pressure and finish 6th.

Father and son winners: Mario and Michael Andretti (1965 and 1984); Bill and Billy Vukovich (1968 and 1988).

Year		Year		Year		Year	
1952	Art Cross	1964	Johnny White	1977	Jerry Sneva	1988	Billy Vukovich III
1953	Jimmy Daywalt	1965	Mario Andretti	1978	Rick Mears & Larry Rice	1989	Bernard Jourdain & Scott Pruett
1954	Larry Crockett	1966	Jackie Stewart	1979	Howdy Holmes	1990	Eddie Cheever
1955	Al Herman	1967	Denis Hulme	1980	Tim Richmond	1991	Jeff Andretti
1956	Bob Veith	1968	Bill Vukovich	1981	Josele Garza	1992	Lyn St. James
1957	Don Edmunds	1969	Mark Donohue	1982	Jim Hickman	1993	Nigel Mansell
1958	George Amick	1970	Donnie Allison	1983	Teo Fabi	1994	Jacques Villeneuve
1959	Bobby Grim	1971	Denny Zimmerman	1984	Michael Andretti & Roberto Guerrero	1995	Christian Fittipaldi
1960	Jim Hurtubise	1972	Mike Hiss	1985	Arie Luyendyk	1996	Tony Stewart
1961	Parnelli Jones & Bobby Marshman	1973	Graham McRae	1986	Randy Lanier		
1962	Jimmy McElreath	1974	Pancho Carter	1987	Fabrizio Barbazza		
1963	Jim Clark	1975	Bill Puterbaugh				
		1976	Vern Schuppan				

CART/IndyCar Rookie of the Year

Award presented to rookie who accumulates the most PPG Cup points among first year drivers. Originally the CART Rookie of the Year; CART was renamed IndyCar in 1992.

Year		Year		Year		Year	
1979	Bill Alsup	1984	Roberto Guerrero	1989	Bernard Jourdain	1994	Jacques Villeneuve
1980	Dennis Firestone	1985	Arie Luyendyk	1990	Eddie Cheever	1995	Gil de Ferran
1981	Bob Lazier	1986	Dominic Dobson	1991	Jeff Andretti	1996	Alex Zanardi
1982	Bobby Rahal	1987	Fabrizio Barbazza	1992	Stefan Johansson		
1983	Teo Fabi	1988	John Jones	1993	Nigel Mansell		

Formula One Circuit

United States Grand Prix

There have been 54 official Formula One races held in the United States since 1950, including the Indianapolis 500 from 1950-60. FISA sanctioned two annual U.S. Grand Prix—USA/East and USA/West—from 1976-80 and 1983. Phoenix was the site of the U.S. Grand Prix from 1989-91.

Indianapolis 500

Officially sanctioned as Grand Prix race from 1950-60 only. See page 887 for details.

U.S. Grand Prix—East

Held from 1959-80 and 1981-88 at the following locations: Sebring, Fla. (1959); Riverside, Calif. (1960); Watkins Glen, N.Y. (1961-80); and Detroit (1982-88). There was no race in 1981. Race discontinued in 1989.

Multiple winners: Jim Clark, Graham Hill and Ayrton Senna (3); James Hunt, Carlos Reutemann and Jackie Stewart (2).

Year		Car
1959	Bruce McLaren, NZE	Cooper Climax
1960	Stirling Moss, GBR	Lotus Climax
1961	Innes Ireland, GBR	Lotus Climax
1962	Jim Clark, GBR	Lotus Climax
1963	Graham Hill, GBR	BRM
1964	Graham Hill, GBR	BRM
1965	Graham Hill, GBR	BRM
1966	Jim Clark, GBR	Lotus BRM
1967	Jim Clark, GBR	Lotus Ford
1968	Jackie Stewart, GBR	Matra Ford
1969	Jochen Rindt, AUT	Lotus Ford
1970	Emerson Fittipaldi, BRA	Lotus Ford
1971	Francois Cevert, FRA	Tyrrell Ford
1972	Jackie Stewart, GBR	Tyrrell Ford
1973	Ronnie Peterson, SWE	Lotus Ford
1974	Carlos Reutemann, ARG	Brabham Ford
1975	Niki Lauda, AUT	Ferrari
1976	James Hunt, GBR	McLaren Ford
1977	James Hunt, GBR	McLaren Ford
1978	Carlos Reutemann, ARG	Ferrari
1979	Gilles Villeneuve, CAN	Ferrari
1980	Alan Jones, AUS	Williams Ford
1981	Not held	
1982	John Watson, GBR	McLaren Ford
1983	Michele Alboreto, ITA	Tyrrell Ford
1984	Nelson Piquet, BRA	Brabham BMW Turbo
1985	Keke Rosberg, FIN	Williams Honda Turbo
1986	Ayrton Senna, BRA	Lotus Renault Turbo
1987	Ayrton Senna, BRA	Lotus Honda Turbo
1988	Ayrton Senna, BRA	McLaren Honda Turbo

U.S. Grand Prix—West

Held from 1976-83 at Long Beach, Calif. Races also held in Las Vegas (1981-82), Dallas (1984) and Phoenix (1989-91). Race discontinued in 1992.

Multiple winners: Alan Jones and Ayrton Senna (2).

Long Beach

Year		Car
1976	Clay Regazzoni, SWI	Ferrari
1977	Mario Andretti, USA	Lotus Ford
1978	Carlos Reutemann, ARG	Ferrari
1979	Gilles Villeneuve, CAN	Ferrari
1980	Nelson Piquet, BRA	Brabham Ford
1981	Alan Jones, AUS	Williams Ford
1982	Niki Lauda, AUT	McLaren Ford
1983	John Watson, GBR	McLaren Ford

Las Vegas

Year		Car
1981	Alan Jones, AUS	Williams Ford
1982	Michele Alboreto, ITA	Tyrrell Ford

Dallas

Year		Car
1984	Keke Rosberg, FIN	Williams Honda Turbo

Phoenix

Year		Car
1989	Alain Prost, FRA	McLaren Honda
1990	Ayrton Senna, BRA	McLaren Honda
1991	Ayrton Senna, BRA	McLaren Honda

All-Time Leaders

The all-time Top 20 Grand Prix winning drivers, based on records through 1995. Listed are starts (Sts), poles won (Pole), wins (1st), second place finishes (2nd), and thirds (3rd). Drivers active in 1996 and career victories are in **bold** type.

		Sts	Pole	1st	2nd	3rd
1	Alain Prost	199	33	**51**	35	20
2	Ayrton Senna	161	65	**41**	23	16
3	**Nigel Mansell**	187	32	**31**	17	11
4	Jackie Stewart	99	17	**27**	11	5
5	Jim Clark	72	33	**25**	1	6
	Niki Lauda	171	24	**25**	20	9
7	Juan-Manuel Fangio	51	28	**24**	10	1
8	Nelson Piquet	204	24	**23**	20	17
9	**M. Schumacher**	69	10	**19**	11	8
10	Stirling Moss	66	16	**16**	5	3
11	Jack Brabham	126	13	**14**	10	7
	Emerson Fittipaldi	144	6	**14**	13	8
	Graham Hill	176	13	**14**	15	7
14	**Damon Hill**	51	11	**13**	12	5
15	Alberto Ascari	32	14	**13**	4	0
16	Mario Andretti	128	18	**12**	2	5
	Alan Jones	116	6	**12**	7	5
	Carlos Reutemann	146	6	**12**	13	20
19	James Hunt	92	14	**10**	6	7
	Ronnie Peterson	123	14	**10**	10	6
	Jody Scheckter	112	3	**10**	14	9

Note: The following five drivers either died or were killed in their final year of competition—Clark in a Formula Two race in West Germany in 1968; Graham Hill in a plane crash in 1975; Ascari in a private practice run in 1955; Peterson following a crash in the 1978 Italian GP; and Senna following a crash in the 1994 San Marino GP.

World Champions

Officially called the World Championship of Drivers and based on Formula One (Grand Prix) records through the 1995 racing season.

Multiple winners: Juan-Manuel Fangio (5); Alain Prost (4); Jack Brabham, Niki Lauda, Nelson Piquet, Ayrton Senna and Jackie Stewart (3); Alberto Ascari, Jim Clark, Emerson Fittipaldi, Graham Hill and Michael Schumacher (2).

Year		Car
1950	Guiseppe Farina, ITA	Alfa Romeo
1951	Juan-Manuel Fangio, ARG	Alfa Romeo
1952	Alberto Ascari, ITA	Ferrari
1953	Alberto Ascari, ITA	Ferrari
1954	Juan-Manuel Fangio, ARG	Maserati/Mercedes
1955	Juan-Manuel Fangio, ARG	Mercedes
1956	Juan-Manuel Fangio, ARG	Ferrari
1957	Juan-Manuel Fangio, ARG	Maserati
1958	Mike Hawthorn, GBR	Ferrari
1959	Jack Brabham, AUS	Cooper Climax
1960	Jack Brabham, AUS	Cooper Climax
1961	Phil Hill, USA	Ferrari
1962	Graham Hill, GBR	BRM
1963	Jim Clark, GBR	Lotus Climax
1964	John Surtees, GBR	Ferrari
1965	Jim Clark, GBR	Lotus Climax
1966	Jack Brabham, AUS	Brabham Repco
1967	Denis Hulme, NZE	Brabham Repco
1968	Graham Hill, GBR	Lotus Ford
1969	Jackie Stewart,GBR	Matra Ford
1970	Jochen Rindt, AUT	Lotus Ford
1971	Jackie Stewart, GBR	Tyrrell Ford
1972	Emerson Fittipaldi, BRA	Lotus Ford
1973	Jackie Stewart, GBR	Tyrrell Ford
1974	Emerson Fittipaldi, BRA	McLaren Ford
1975	Niki Lauda, AUT	Ferrari
1976	James Hunt, GBR	McLaren Ford
1977	Niki Lauda, AUT	Ferrari
1978	Mario Andretti, USA	Lotus Ford
1979	Jody Scheckter, SAF	Ferrari
1980	Alan Jones, AUS	Williams Ford
1981	Nelson Piquet, BRA	Brabham Ford
1982	Keke Rosberg, FIN	Williams Ford
1983	Nelson Piquet, BRA	Brabham BMW Turbo
1984	Niki Lauda, AUT	McL. TAG Porsche Turbo
1985	Alain Prost, FRA	McL. TAG Porsche Turbo
1986	Alain Prost, FRA	McL. TAG Porsche Turbo
1987	Nelson Piquet, BRA	Williams Honda Turbo
1988	Ayrton Senna, BRA	McLaren Honda Turbo
1989	Alain Prost, FRA	McLaren Honda
1990	Ayrton Senna, BRA	McLaren Honda
1991	Ayrton Senna, BRA	McLaren Honda
1992	Nigel Mansell, GBR	Williams Renault
1993	Alain Prost, FRA	Williams-Renault
1994	Michael Schumacher, GER	Benetton Ford
1995	Michael Schumacher, GER	Benetton Renault

ENDURANCE RACES

The 24 Hours of Le Mans

Officially, the Le Mans Grand Prix d'Endurance. First run May 22-23, 1923, and won by Andre Lagache and Rene Leonard in a 3-litre Chenard & Walcker. All subsequent races have been held in June, except in 1956 (July) and 1968 (September). Originally contested over a 10.73-mile track, the circuit was shortened to its present 8.451-mile distance in 1932. The original start of Le Mans, where drivers raced across the track to their unstarted cars, was discontinued in 1970.

Multiple winners: Jacky Ickx (6); Derek Bell (5); Oliver Gendebien and Henri Pescarolo (4); Woolf Barnato, Luigi Chinetti, Yannick Dalmas, Hurley Haywood, Phil Hill, Al Holbert and Klaus Ludwig (3); Sir Henry Birkin, Ivoe Bueb, Ron Flockhart, Jean-Pierre Jaussaud, Gerard Larrousse, Andre Rossignol, Raymond Sommer, Hans Stuck, Gijs van Lennep and Jean-Pierre Wimille (2).

Year	Drivers	Car	MPH
1923	Andre Lagache & Rene Leonard	Chenard & Walcker	57.21
1924	John Duff & Francis Clement	Bentley	53.78
1925	Gerard de Courcelles & Andre Rossignol	La Lorraine	57.84
1926	Robert Bloch & Andre Rossignol	La Lorraine	66.08
1927	J.D. Benjafield & Sammy Davis	Bentley	61.35
1928	Woolf Barnato & Bernard Rubin	Bentley	69.11
1929	Woolf Barnato & Sir Henry Birkin	Bentley Speed 6	73.63
1930	Woolf Barnato & Glen Kidston	Bentley Speed 6	75.88
1931	Earl Howe & Sir Henry Birkin	Alfa Romeo	78.13
1932	Raymond Sommer & Luigi Chinetti	Alfa Romeo	76.48
1933	Raymond Sommer & Tazio Nuvolari	Alfa Romeo	81.40
1934	Luigi Chinetti & Philippe Etancelin	Alfa Romeo	74.74
1935	John Hindmarsh & Louis Fontes	Lagonda	77.85
1936	Not held		
1937	Jean-Pierre Wimille & Robert Benoist	Bugatti 57G	85.13
1938	Eugene Chaboud & Jean Tremoulet	Delahaye	82.36
1939	Jean-Pierre Wimille & Pierre Veyron	Bugatti 57G	86.86
1940-48	Not held	World War II	
1949	Luigi Chinetti & Lord Selsdon	Ferrari	82.28
1950	Louis Rosier & Jean-Louis Rosier	Talbot-Lago	89.71
1951	Peter Walker & Peter Whitehead	Jaguar C	93.50
1952	Hermann Lang & Fritz Reiss	Mercedes-Benz	96.67
1953	Tony Rolt & Duncan Hamilton	Jaguar C	98.65
1954	Froilan Gonzalez & Maurice Trintignant	Ferrari 375	105.13
1955	Mike Hawthorn & Ivor Bueb	Jaguar D	107.05
1956	Ron Flockhart & Ninian Sanderson	Jaguar D	104.47
1957	Ron Flockhart & Ivor Bueb	Jaguar D	113.83
1958	Oliver Gendebien & Phil Hill	Ferrari 250	106.18

Wide World Photos

Mario Andretti (center), who retired from IndyCar racing after the 1994 season, with French teammates **Bob Wollek** (right) and **Eric Helary** (left) after their second place finish in the 1995 running of the 24 Hours of Le Mans. The 55-year-old Andretti has won the Indy 500, Daytona 500 and 24 Hours of Daytona in addition to driving championships in IndyCar and Formula One racing.

Endurance Races (Cont.)

The 24 Hours of Le Mans

Year	Drivers	Car	MPH
1959	Roy Salvadori & Carroll Shelby	Aston Martin	112.55
1960	Oliver Gendebien & Paul Fräre	Ferrari 250	109.17
1961	Oliver Gendebien & Phil Hill	Ferrari 250	115.88
1962	Oliver Gendebien & Phil Hill	Ferrari 250	115.22
1963	Lodovico Scarfiotti & Lorenzo Bandini	Ferrari 250	118.08
1964	Jean Guichel & Nino Vaccarella	Ferrari 275	121.54
1965	Masten Gregory & Jochen Rindt	Ferrari 250	121.07
1966	Bruce McLaren & Chris Amon	Ford Mk. II	125.37
1967	A.J. Foyt & Dan Gurney	Ford Mk. IV	135.46
1968	Pedro Rodriguez & Lucien Bianchi	Ford GT40	115.27
1969	Jacky Ickx & Jackie Oliver	Ford GT40	129.38
1970	Hans Herrmann & Richard Attwood	Porsche 917	119.28
1971	Gijs van Lennep & Helmut Marko	Porsche 917	138.13
1972	Graham Hill & Henri Pescarolo	Matra-Simca	121.45
1973	Henri Pescarolo & Gerard Larrousse	Matra-Simca	125.67
1974	Henri Pescarolo & Gerard Larrousse	Matra-Simca	119.27
1975	Derek Bell & Jacky Ickx	Mirage-Ford	118.98
1976	Jacky Ickx & Gijs van Lennep	Porsche 936	123.49
1977	Jacky Ickx, Jurgen Barth & Hurley Haywood	Porsche 936	120.95
1978	Jean-Pierre Jaussaud & Didier Pironi	Renault-Alpine	130.60
1979	Klaus Ludwig, Bill Wittington & Don Whittington	Porsche 935	108.10
1980	Jean-Pierre Jaussaud & Jean Rondeau	Rondeau-Cosworth	119.23
1981	Jacky Ickx & Derek Bell	Porsche 936	124.94
1982	Jacky Ickx & Derek Bell	Porsche 956	126.85
1983	Vern Schuppan, Hurley Haywood & Al Holbert	Porsche 956	130.70
1984	Klaus Ludwig & Henri Pescarolo	Porsche 956	126.88
1985	Klaus Ludwig, Paolo Barilla & John Winter	Porsche 956	131.75
1986	Derek Bell, Hans Stuck & Al Holbert	Porsche 962	128.75
1987	Derek Bell, Hans Stuck & Al Holbert	Porsche 962	124.06
1988	Jan Lammers, Johnny Dumfries & Andy Wallace	Jaguar XJR	137.75

Year	Drivers	Car	MPH
1989	Jochen Mass, Manuel Reuter & Stanley Dickens	Sauber-Mercedes	136.39
1990	John Nielsen, Price Cobb & Martin Brundle	Jaguar XJR-12	126.71
1991	Volker Weider, Johnny Herbert & Bertrand Gachof	Mazda 787B	127.31
1992	Derek Warwick, Yannick Dalmas & Mark Blundell	Peugeot 905B	123.89
1993	Geoff Brabham, Christophe Bouchut & Eric Helary	Peugeot 905	132.58
1994	Yannick Dalmas, Hurley Haywood & Mauro Baldi	Porsche 962LM	129.82
1995	Yannick Dalmas, J.J. Lehto & Masanori Sekiya	McLaren BMW	105.00
1996	Davy Jones, Manuel Reuter & Alexander Wurz	TWR Porsche	124.65

The 24 Hours of Daytona

Officially, the Rolex 24 at Daytona. First run in 1962 as a three-hour race and won by Dan Gurney in a Lotus 19 Ford. Contested over a 3.56-mile course at Daytona (Fla.) International Speedway. There have been several distance changes since 1962: the event was a three-hour race (1962-63); a 2,000-kilometer race (1964-65); a 24-hour race (1966-71); a six-hour race (1972) and a 24-hour race again since 1973. The race was canceled in 1974 due to a national energy crisis.

Multiple winners: Hurley Haywood (5); Peter Gregg, Pedro Rodriguez and Bob Wollek (4); Derek Bell and Rolf Stommelen (3); A.J. Foyt, Al Holbert, Ken Miles, Brian Redman, Lloyd Ruby and Al Unser Jr. (2).

Year	Drivers	Car	MPH
1962	Dan Gurney	Lotus Ford	104.101
1963	Pedro Rodriguez	Ferrari GTO	102.074
1964	Pedro Rodriguez & Phil Hill	Ferrari GTO	98.230
1965	Ken Miles & Lloyd Ruby	Ford GT	99.944
1966	Ken Miles & Lloyd Ruby	Ford Mk. II	108.020
1967	Lorenzo Bandini & Chris Amon	Ferrari 330	105.688
1968	Vic Elford & Jochen Neerpasch	Porsche 907	106.697
1969	Mark Donohue & Chuck Parsons	Lola Chevrolet	99.268
1970	Pedro Rodriguez & Leo Kinnunen	Porsche 917	114.866
1971	Pedro Rodriguez & Jackie Oliver	Porsche 917K	109.203
1972	Mario Andretti & Jacky Ickx	Ferrari 312P	122.573
1973	Peter Gregg & Hurley Haywood	Porsche Carrera	106.225
1974	Not held		
1975	Peter Gregg & Hurley Haywood	Porsche Carrera	108.531
1976	Peter Gregg, Brian Redman & John Fitzpatrick	BMW CSL	104.040
1977	Hurley Haywood, John Graves & Dave Helmick	Porsche Carrera	108.801
1978	Peter Gregg, Rolf Stommelen & Antoine Hezemans	Porsche Turbo	108.743
1979	Hurley Haywood, Ted Field & Danny Ongais	Porsche Turbo	109.249
1980	Rolf Stommelen, Volkert Merl & Reinhold Joest	Porsche Turbo	114.303
1981	Bobby Rahal, Brian Redman & Bob Garretson	Porsche Turbo	113.153
1982	John Paul Sr., John Paul Jr. & Rolf Stommelen	Porsche Turbo	114.794
1983	A.J. Foyt, Preston Henn, Bob Wollek & Claude Ballot-Lena	Porsche Turbo	98.781
1984	Sarel van der Merwe, Tony Martin & Graham Duxbury	March Porsche	103.119
1985	A.J. Foyt, Bob Wollek, Al Unser Sr. & Thierry Boutsen	Porsche 962	104.162
1986	Al Holbert, Derek Bell & Al Unser Jr.	Porsche 962	105.484
1987	Al Holbert, Derek Bell, Chip Robinson & Al Unser Jr.	Porsche 962	111.599
1988	Raul Boesel, Martin Brundle & John Nielsen	Jaguar XJR-9	107.943
1989	John Andretti, Derek Bell & Bob Wollek	Porsche 962	92.009
1990	Davy Jones, Jan Lammers & Andy Wallace	Jaguar XJR-12	112.857
1991	Hurley Haywood, John Winter, Frank Jelinski, Henri Pescarolo & Bob Wollek	Porsche 962-C	106.633
1992	Masahiro Hasemi, Kazuyoshi Hoshino & Toshio Suzuki	Nissan R-91	112.897
1993	P.J. Jones, Mark Dismore & Rocky Moran	Toyota Eagle	103.537
1994	Paul Gentilozzi, Scott Pruett, Butch Leitzinger & Steve Millen	Nissan 300 ZXT	104.80
1995	Jurgen Lassig, Christophe Bouchut, Giovanni Lavaggi & Marco Werner	Porsche Spyder	102.280
1996	Wayne Taylor, Scott Sharp, & Jim Pace	Oldsmobile Arness MK-111, WSC	103.32

NHRA Drag Racing

NHRA Winston Champions

Based on points earned during the NHRA Winston Drag Racing series. The series began for Top Fuel, Funny Car and Pro Stock in 1975.

Top Fuel

Multiple winners: Joe Amato (5); Don Garlits and Shirley Muldowney (3).

Year		Year		Year		Year	
1975	Don Garlits	1981	Jeb Allen	1987	Dick LaHaie	1993	Eddie Hill
1976	Richard Tharp	1982	Shirley Muldowney	1988	Joe Amato	1994	Scott Kalitta
1977	Shirley Muldowney	1983	Gary Beck	1989	Gary Ormsby	1995	Scott Kalitta
1978	Kelly Brown	1984	Joe Amato	1990	Joe Amato	1996	Kenny Bernstein
1979	Rob Bruins	1985	Don Garlits	1991	Joe Amato		
1980	Shirley Muldowney	1986	Don Garlits	1992	Joe Amato		

Funny Car

Multiple winners: John Force (7); Kenny Bernstein and Don Prudhomme (4); Raymond Beadle (3); Frank Hawley (2).

Year		Year		Year		Year	
1975	Don Prudhomme	1981	Raymond Beadle	1987	Kenny Bernstein	1993	John Force
1976	Don Prudhomme	1982	Frank Hawley	1988	Kenny Bernstein	1994	John Force
1977	Don Prudhomme	1983	Frank Hawley	1989	Bruce Larson	1995	John Force
1978	Don Prudhomme	1984	Mark Oswald	1990	John Force	1995	John Force
1979	Raymond Beadle	1985	Kenny Bernstein	1991	John Force	1996	John Force
1980	Raymond Beadle	1986	Kenny Bernstein	1992	Cruz Pedregon		

Pro Stock

Multiple winners: Bob Glidden (9); Lee Shepherd (4); Warren Johnson (3); Darrell Alderman (2).

Year		Year		Year		Year	
1975	Bob Glidden	1981	Lee Shepherd	1987	Bob Glidden	1993	Warren Johnson
1976	Larry Lombardo	1982	Lee Shepherd	1988	Bob Glidden	1994	Darrell Alderman
1977	Don Nicholson	1983	Lee Shepherd	1989	Bob Glidden	1995	Warren Johnson
1978	Bob Glidden	1984	Lee Shepherd	1990	John Myers	1996	Jim Yates
1979	Bob Glidden	1985	Bob Glidden	1991	Darrell Alderman		
1980	Bob Glidden	1986	Bob Glidden	1992	Warren Johnson		

All-Time Leaders

Career Victories

Top Fuel

1	Don Garlits	35
	Joe Amato	35
3	Gary Beck	19
4	Shirley Muldowney	18
	Darrell Gwynn	18

Funny Car

1	John Force	60
2	Don Prudhomme	35
3	Kenny Bernstein	30
4	Ed McCulloch	18
	Mark Oswald	18

Pro Stock

1	Bob Glidden	85
2	Warren Johnson	59
3	Lee Shepherd	26
4	Darrell Alderman	23
5	Bruce Allen	12

National-Event Victories (pro categories)

Drivers active in 1996 season are in **bold** type.
Totals as of Oct. 13, 1996

1	**Bob Glidden**	85
2	**John Force**	60
3	**Warren Johnson**	59
4	**Don Prudhomme**	49
5	**Kenny Bernstein**	46
6	**Dave Schultz**	41
7	Don Garlits	35
	Joe Amato	35
9	**John Myers**	30
10	Lee Shepherd	26
	Darrell Alderman	26
12	Terry Vance	24
13	Ed McCulloch	22
14	**Mark Oswald**	20
15	Gary Beck	19
16	Shirley Muldowney	18
	Darrell Gwynn	18
18	**Cruz Pedregon**	17
19	**Mike Dunn**	16
20	Dick LaHaie	15
21	Gary Ormsby	14
	Scott Kalitta	14
23	Raymond Beadle	13
	Eddie Hill	13
25	**Bruce Allen**	12
	Al Hofmann	12
	Billy Meyer	12
28	**Frank Iaconio**	11
	Cory McClenathan	11
	Jim Yates	11
	Bill Jenkins	11
32	**Connie Kalitta**	10

Fastest Mile-Per-Hour Speeds

Fastest performances in NHRA major event history as of Oct. 13, 1996.

Top Fuel

MPH	
318.69	Kenny Bernstein, 10/12/96
316.23	Shelly Anderson, 10/12/96
315.67	Scott Kalitta, 7/5/96
315.67	Kenny Bernstein, 7/28/96
314.91	Scott Kalitta, 3/17/96

Funny Car

MPH	
312.60	Cruz Pedregon, 9/27/96
311.20	Cruz Pedregon, 7/7/96
310.66	Cruz Pedregon, 10/12/96
310.45	John Force, 10/13/96
310.34	Cruz Pedregon, 7/7/96

Pro Stock

MPH	
199.15	Warren Johnson, 3/10/95
198.76	Warren Johnson, 3/10/95
198.23	Warren Johnson, 10/15/95
197.97	Warren Johnson, 3/11/95
197.93	Warren Johnson, 8/8/95

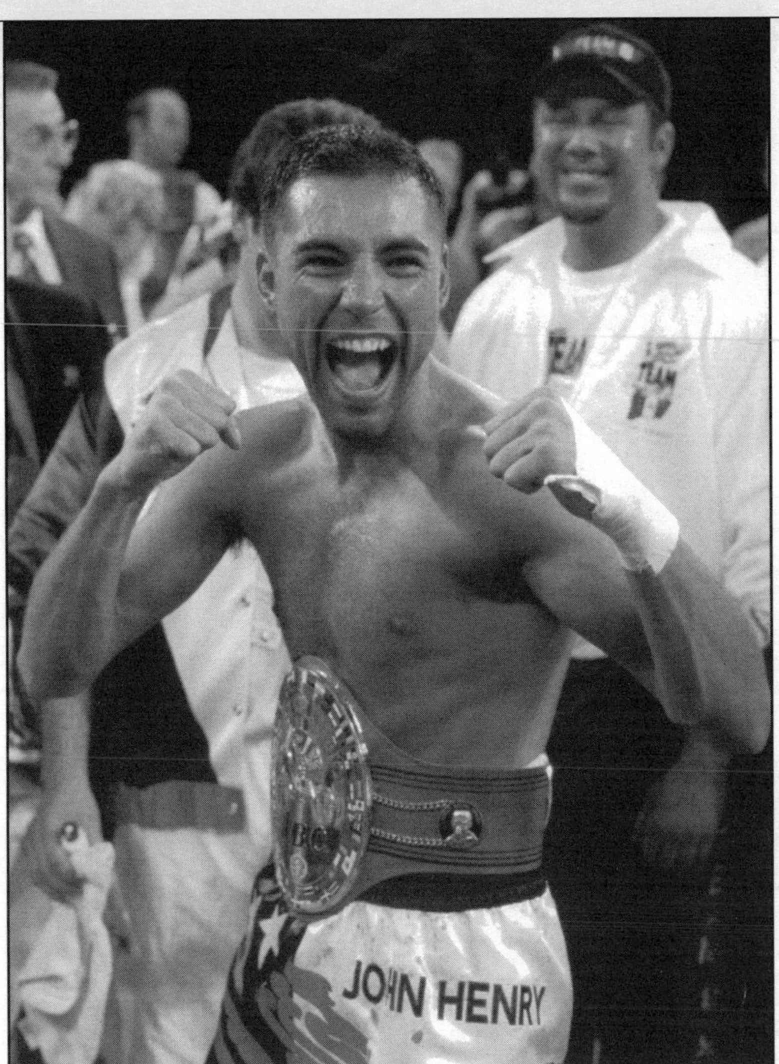

Wide World Photos

A jubilant **Oscar De La Hoya** poses with the belt he won in a June 7, 1996 WBC Super Lightweight title bout with Julio Cesar Chavez.

BOXING

by Bernard Fernanadez

Tyson's Corner

No matter what else happens in boxing, Mike Tyson remains the sport's most compelling figure

Since Mike Tyson was released from prison on March 25, 1995, *The Ring* magazine, the "bible of boxing," has put out two special editions. Both dealt exclusively with Tyson, the most recognizable fighter to walk the earth since Muhammad Ali still was able to float like a butterfly and sting like a bee.

"Tyson sells magazines because people who are marginal– or non-boxing fans have an interest in him and what he does," Nigel Collins, managing editor of *The Ring,* said of the World Boxing Association heavyweight champion's undeniable mystique.

Tyson's comings and goings, both inside and outside the ropes, dominated the boxing landscape over the past year to such an extent that he overshadowed even Oscar De La Hoya, who emerged as the sport's most important non-heavyweight and, indeed, most important fighter of any size not named Michael Gerard Tyson. All Tyson, all the time? Don't be surprised if the Tyson Channel one day is added to your cable system's lineup.

Indeed, any list of the dozen most compelling boxing stories of the year would have to include five or six Tyson-related items, although De La Hoya's watershed stoppage of Julio Cesar Chavez, Riddick Bowe's TKO of Evander Holyfield in their celebrated rubber match, the riot which followed Bowe's disqualification victory over Andrew Golota at Madison Square Garden, Tommy Morrison's revelation that he had tested positive for HIV and David Reid's dramatic, one-punch knockout of a Cuban opponent to win the USA's only gold medal in boxing at the Atlanta Olympics were all major stories.

Tyson made news even when he did nothing. His second comeback bout following his release from an Indiana prison, where he had served three years on a rape conviction, was scheduled for Nov. 4, 1995, against Buster Mathis Jr. at the MGM Grand in Las Vegas. The date is significant in that Bowe's third pairing with Holyfield, the two-time former heavyweight champion, was scheduled for the same night, at more or less the same time, at Caesars Palace, a half-mile down the strip. Talk about a high-stakes game of chicken.

Three days before the mother of all scheduling conflicts, however, Tyson blinked; or perhaps the correct word is winced. Citing a fractured right thumb incurred three weeks earlier in training, he withdrew, leaving the field to Bowe-Holyfield III. Those involved in staging the Caesars Palace show did a bit of gloating, even going so far as to suggest that Tyson's thumb was hurting less than the projected gate for his bout with the hopelessly overmatched Mathis. But Tyson arrived at the press conference to announce the postponement with a note from his doctor. Actually, he brought the doctor himself.

"The injury is basically a break between the main joint of the thumb and the tip of the thumb," Dr. Gary Marrone said. "Our

Bernard Fernanadez has been a sports reporter at the *Philadelphia Daily News* for 21 years and the boxing writer since 1987.

Wide World Photos

Mike Tyson, looking fresh and relaxed, celebrates gracefully after his win by TKO over WBC heavyweight champion Frank Bruno on March 16, 1996.

feeling (Dr. Gerald Higgins also was involved in treating Tyson) at that time was that we weren't sure whether three weeks would be sufficient for Mike to fight. But Mike wanted, under any circumstances, to be able to fight and not have to cancel this ... Unfortunately, he sustained a reinjury to the thumb. At this point, there was no way we could medically release Mike to fight."

But Tyson would have other opportunities to be the dispenser of pain. On Dec. 16, Tyson, his sore thumb presumably feeling much better, finally got around to swapping punches with Mathis. It proved to be the most one-sided bit of trading since Lou Brock for Ernie Broglio. Even though Tyson's performance was ragged in spots, he broke through to knock out Mathis with two sledgehammer right uppercuts in the third round at the CoreStates Spectrum in Philadelphia.

It was Tyson's final appearance in a non-title bout before his March 16 challenge of World Boxing Council champion Frank Bruno, of England, at the MGM Grand. Bruno, sitting at ringside for Tyson-Mathis, was among those giving, uh, a thumbs-down to Tyson's performance.

"Mike Tyson did not look right, man," said Bruno, who had been stopped in five rounds in a Feb. 25, 1989, bout with the then-undisputed champion. "There's something wrong there. He's very, very rusty. He didn't show me much at all. I think he's going through the motions."

Bruno's tough talk served to heighten interest in the rematch, particularly in Europe, but Tyson proved to be even more dominant than he had been seven years earlier. Exactly 2,225 days after he last appeared in a championship bout, Tyson reclaimed the championship he had lent out to others during a meandering, travail-filled journey when he whacked out the terrified Bruno in the third round.

Tyson had been a king without a crown since Feb. 11, 1990, when the combination of James "Buster" Douglas and his own boredom culminated in a 10th-round knockout victory for Douglas in Tokyo, the greatest upset in boxing history. When asked to describe the volley of blows that had brought about his recoronation, Tyson shrugged.

"It just goes snap," Tyson said. "I don't know what it is. Maybe it's maturity, maybe it's just instinct. Sometimes I'll go through two months of training and never use a move. Then in the fight when the move becomes necessary, it comes. I don't think about it. I just fight."

Next up for Tyson was what was supposed to be a unification bout with Bruce Seldon, the WBA champion, but former WBC titlist Lennox Lewis, armed with a ruling from a New Jersey judge, pressed his claim as the WBC's mandatory challenger. Unable to come to a financial agreement with Lewis, Tyson paid him $4 million in step-aside money and fought Seldon on Sept. 7 with just the WBA championship on the line. The WBC later withdrew recognition of Tyson as its champion, citing his inability to come to a satisfactory arrangement with Lewis.

The Lewis flap had Tyson, who had hoped to unify the title as quickly as possible, in a surly mood, which did not bode well for Seldon, whose chin never has been confused with the Rock of Gibraltar.

"I have a temper," Tyson admitted during a remarkably candid prefight session with the media. "It's an extreme temper. I'm pissed off all the time."

Seldon, who, like Bruno, had effected an air of confidence in the weeks leading up to the fight, was blown away like a house of cards in a high wind by the intensity of Tyson's fury. He went down twice in the first round—the first time by a punch that appeared to miss the mark—and was lurching around like a drunken sailor on shore leave when referee Richard Steele stepped in to save him from any more real or imagined damage. "I was hurt," Seldon insisted. "I didn't realize how hard he hit or how fast he was. Mike Tyson is a destroyer. I am a witness to that."

The day after Tyson had brushed off Seldon as he might a bit of lint on the shoulder of a suit jacket, it was announced that Tyson would finally get around to sharing a ring with Holyfield Nov. 9 at the MGM Grand. Twice before the two men had been scheduled to mix it up, but on each occasion the fight fell through, the first time when Tyson lost to Douglas, the second when Tyson injured his ribs in training and subsequently was convicted of rape.

The fact that the 34-year-old Holyfield immediately was installed as a 25-1 underdog by Las Vegas oddsmakers indicated that this much-anticipated matchup had perhaps been on hold too long.

"The only thing that's stopping me from being champ again is time," said Holyfield, obviously believing his chances for success were better than those cited by casino touts.

Tyson and Holyfield have been gravitating toward each other for what seems like forever. Back on Oct. 16, 1987, after he had administered a terrible beating to Tyrell Biggs before stopping him in seven rounds in Atlantic City, Tyson was asked if Holyfield, then the undisputed cruiserweight champion, might someday evolve into a worthy challenger.

"Lock us in a cellar, let us fight, and whoever comes out with the key is the winner," Tyson sneered.

Tyson might be unbeatable in the ring or in the cellar, but he is more vulnerable in the legal arena, where he was only 1-1 over the past year. His win came when prosecutors decided there was insufficient evidence to proceed on charges brought by a Gary, Ind., beautician, LaWanda August, that Tyson had sexually abused her during an encounter on the dance floor at a Chicago nightclub. Tyson said the incident convinced him he was a target.

"I've got to go another route now," he said, noting that any violation of his probation might land him back in prison. "They're going to have to catch me in the library or somewhere like that. No more jitterbugging for me." Jitterbugging?

Kevin Rooney, Tyson's former trainer, also had a beef with Tyson, but he got his day in court and scored big. Although he produced no written contract, Rooney, who claimed he had had a verbal agreement with Tyson's late mentor, Cus D'Amato, that he always would serve as Tyson's trainer, was awarded $4.4 million by an Albany, N.Y., jury. "They just tried to throw me away like I was a piece of garbage," said Rooney, who was dismissed following Tyson's June 27, 1988, first-round blowout of Michael Spinks.

Tyson, who said he had fired Rooney after being angered by the trainer's televised comments about Tyson's marriage to actress Robin Givens, alleged that the judgment for

Rooney was the result of racial bias.

"They think they're doing good justice," Tyson said. "I resent it. I felt like I was discriminated against because of my financial situation."

On the non-Tyson front, De La Hoya's fourth-round TKO of Mexican legend Julio Cesar Chavez, June 7 at Caesars Palace, brought him Chavez's WBC super lightweight title and affirmed his status as boxing's hottest growth property.

For all intents and purposes, De La Hoya, 23, won the fight in the first round when he connected with two stiff jabs followed by a short right. The three-punch combination opened a gaping cut over Chavez's left eye, which bled so profusely that referee Joe Cortez had no choice but to stop the carnage three rounds later.

"Best finisher since Ray Leonard in his prime," an impressed Seth Abraham, president of HBO Sports, said of De La Hoya. "No one else is even close. He's simply a killer." As always, De La Hoya graciously downplayed the triumph which certified him as a superstar.

"I'm still learning," he allowed. "I need many more fights before I become a complete fighter and achieve my goal of becoming a great champion."

De La Hoya also figured in another memorable evening, Dec. 15, when he starched Jesse James Leija in two rounds before a packed house of 17,000-plus in Madison Square Garden. It was the first fight card staged at the Garden, the erstwhile "mecca of boxing," since MSG's management at the time announced in May 1993 that it was disassociating itself from the sport with which it had so long been associated. It says something about De La Hoya's appeal that the Garden's new bosses had him headline its comeback card.

Holyfield and Bowe, who had split two previous battles in what has been described as "the Ali-Frazier of the '90s," put the wraps on their classic rivalry with another fight to remember.

For a moment, it appeared as if Holyfield was on the brink of an upset victory. He dropped the larger, stronger and younger Bowe with a left hook in the sixth round, but he seemed to lack the energy to press his momentary advantage.

"I hurt my [left] shoulder in the third round," Holyfield said later. "I was swinging big shots and trying to get him with the left hook. At times, I thought I had him. But I wasn't able to finish him. He fought smart when he was hurt and he was able to recover."

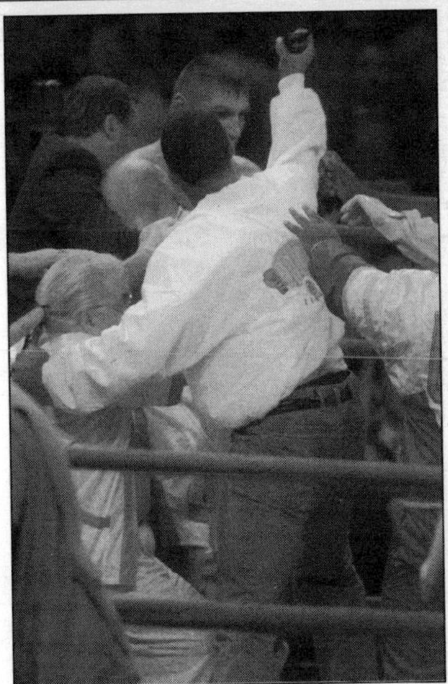

Wide World Photos

As trainer **Lou Duva** tumbles out of the ring (left), **Jason Harris** of Riddick Bowe's entourage prepares to hit **Andrew Golota** with a cellular phone.

Down by a point on all three judges' scorecards through seven rounds, Bowe sent Holyfield to the canvas twice in the eighth round to seize command. After the second knockdown, referee Joe Cortez stepped in to save the valiant Holyfield from additional punishment.

Bowe often has said he is the only man capable of beating Tyson, but being bigger—a career-high 252 pounds—didn't mean better when he squared off against Golota, the little-known Polish national, in their July 11 bout in Madison Square Garden. Golota dominated the out-of-shape Bowe throughout, but, in the seventh round, he slammed one left hook too many below Bowe's belt line. Bowe collapsed in agony and referee Wayne Kelly, who had already taken three points from Golota for low blows, waved the fight to a halt and awarded a disqualification win to the

Wide World Photos

Referee **Mills Lane** escorts **Tommy Morrison** back to his corner after his TKO loss to Lennox Lewis on Oct. 7, 1995. Four months later, Morrison shocked the boxing world when he announced that he had tested positive for the virus that causes AIDS.

former heavyweight champion.

That triggered a number of scuffles in and around the ring. Several members of Bowe's entourage attacked Golota, one of whom, Jason Harris, was observed clubbing Golota on the back of the head with a cellular phone. The melee resulted in 16 arrests and 22 injuries.

"It was a very ugly night for everyone who was involved in the staging of the event," Bowe's controversial manager, Rock Newman, said at a morning-after press conference. "I wholeheartedly apologize for the pain, grief, anguish and embarrassment it has caused all of us."

The New York State Athletic Commission accepted Newman's apology, then fined Bowe $250,000 and suspended Newman for one year.

Morrison sent shock waves through the boxing establishment when, on Feb. 15 in a Tulsa hotel salon, he announced that blood tests had confirmed he was infected with HIV, the virus that leads to AIDS.

"To all my young fans, I'd ask that you no longer see me as a role model, but as an individual that had the opportunity to be a role model and blew it—blew it with irresponsible, irrational, immature decisions ... decisions that one day could cost me my life," the longtime heavyweight contender said in recalling his promiscuous lifestyle. "I thought I was bulletproof. I'm not."

Morrison said he would never fight again, but he held another press conference on Sept. 19 at which he revealed he would enter the ring once more to raise money for children infected with the AIDS virus. Opinion, as might be expected, was divided as to whether an HIV-positive Morrison should be allowed to resume his boxing career.

Reid, the Philadelphia kid competing in the light middleweight division, salvaged U.S. pride at the Olympics when, hopelessly behind in the electronic scoring in the third and final round, he flattened Cuba's Alfredo Duvergel with an overhand right. Reid parlayed the golden bolt from the blue into a ton of greenbacks by signing a five-year, $14.4 million contract with a new promotional company, Amerika Presents.

"This young man is a superstar waiting to happen," Dan Goossen, Amerika Presents' chief operating officer, said of Reid.

Ali, a 1960 Olympic gold medalist, was a surprise and popular choice to be the final torch bearer at the Opening Ceremonies in Atlanta. Old archrival Joe Frazier, though, gave vent to his lingering bitterness at the Games by denigrating's not only Ali's high-profile role at the Games, but "The Greatest" himself.

In other developments, International Boxing Federation super middleweight champion Roy Jones raised eyebrows when he played point guard for the minor-league basketball team the Jacksonville Barracudas a few hours before he successfully defended his title against Eric Lucas ... Buster Douglas ended a five-year retirement with a third-round TKO of Tony LaRosa ... Frans Botha won the vacant IBF heavyweight championship by outpointing Axel Schulz, but was stripped of the title when he tested positive for anabolic steroids. Michael Moorer then claimed the revacated crown by decisioning Schulz ... Wilfred Benitez, Joe Brown, Aaron Pryor, Manuel Ortiz and Emanuel Steward were among the inductees in the International Boxing Hall of Fame in Canastota, N.Y. ❒

BOXING STATISTICS

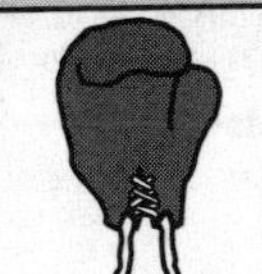

THE SEASON IN REVIEW

1995-1996

CHAMPIONS • TITLE BOUTS

Current Champions

WBA, WBC and IBF Titleholders (through Oct. 16, 1996)

The champions of professional boxing's 17 principal weight divisions, as recognized by the Word Boxing Association (WBA), World Boxing Council (WBC) and International Boxing Federation (IBF).

	Weight Limit	WBA Champion	WBC Champion	IBF Champion
Heavyweight	—	Mike Tyson 45-1-0, 39 KOs	vacant	Michael Moorer 37-1-0, 30 KOs
Cruiserweight	190 lbs	Nate Miller 29-4-0, 25 KOs	Marcelo Dominguez 20-1-1, 11 KOs	Adolpho Washington 26-3-2, 15 KOs
Light Heavyweight	175 lbs	Virgil Hill 42-1-0, 20 KOs	Fabrice Tiozzo 34-1-0, 22 KOs	Henry Maske 30-0-0, 11 KOs
Super Middleweight	168 lbs	Frank Liles 29-1-0, 18 KOs	Robin Reid 22-0-1, 15 KOs	Roy Jones Jr. 33-0-0, 29 KOs
Middleweight	160 lbs	William Joppy 22-0-1, 18 KOs	Keith Holmes 29-1-0, 19 KOs	Bernard Hopkins 30-2-1, 24 KOs
Jr. Middleweight	154 lbs	Laurent Boudouani 32-2-0, 30 KOs	Terry Norris 43-6-0, 27 KOs	Terry Norris 43-6-0, 27 KOs
Welterweight	147 lbs	Ike Quartey 33-0-0, 28 KOs	Pernell Whitaker 39-1-1, 16 KOs	Felix Trinidad 29-0-0, 25 KOs
Jr. Welterweight	140 lbs	Frankie Randall 53-4-1, 41 KOs	Oscar De La Hoya 22-0, 20 KOs	Konstantin Tszyu 18-0-0, 14 KOs
Lightweight	135 lbs	Orzubek Nazarov 23-0-0, 17 KOs	Jean-Baptiste Mendy 49-5-2, 30 KOs	Philip Holiday 28-0-0, 16 KOs
Jr. Lightweight	130 lbs	Choi Yong-Soo 21-2-0, 13 KOs	Azumah Nelson 39-3-2 26 KOs	Arturo Gatti 26-1-0, 22 KOs
Featherweight	126 lbs	Wilfredo Vasquez 47-7-3, 35 KOS	Luisito Espinoza 39-7-0, 20 KO	Tom Johnson 44-2-1, 25 KOs
Jr. Featherweight	122 lbs	Antonio Cermeno 53-7-3, 27 KOs	Daniel Zaragoza 53-7-3, 27 KOs	Vuyani Bungu 29-2-0, 17 KOs
Bantamweight	118 lbs	Nana Yaw Konadu 36-2-1, 29 KOs	Wayne McCullough 20-0-0, 14 KOs	Mbulelo Botile 20-0-0, 13 KOs
Jr. Bantamweight	115 lbs	Yokthai Sith Oar 11-0-0, 7 KOs	Hiroshi Kawashima 20-2-1, 14 KOs	Danny Romero 28-1-0, 25 KOs
Flyweight	112 lbs	Saen Sor Ploenchit 25-0-0, 6 KOs	Yuri Arbachakov 23-0-0, 16 KO	Mark Johnson 30-1-0, 23 KOs
Jr. Flyweight	108 lbs	Keiji Yamaguchi 20-1-0, 7 KOs	Saman Sorjaturong 32-2-1, 26 KOs	Michael Carbajal 43-2-0, 28 KOs
Minimumweight	105 lbs	Rosendo Alvarez 23-0-0, 15 KOs	Ricardo Lopez 42-0-0, 32 KOs	Ratan Voraphin 28-2-1, 22 KOs

Note: the following weight divisions are also known by these names— **Cruiserweight** as Jr. Heavyweight; **Jr. Middleweight** as Super Welterweight; **Jr. Welterweight** as Super Lightweight; **Jr. Lightweight** as Super Featherweight; **Jr. Featherweight** as Super Bantamweight; **Jr. Bantamweight** as Super Flyweight; **Jr. Flyweight** as Light Flyweight; and **Minimum** as Strawweight.

Major Bouts, 1995-96

Division by division, from Oct. 16, 1995 through Oct. 16, 1996.

WBA, WBC and IBF champions are listed in **bold** type. Note the following Result columm abbreviations (in alphabetical order): **Disq.** (won by disqualification); **KO** (knockout); **MDraw** (majority draw); **NC** (no contest); **SDraw** (split draw); **TDraw** (technical draw); **TKO** (technical knockout); **TWs** (won by technical split decision); **TWu** (won by technical unanimous decision); **Wm** (won by majority decision); **Ws** (won by split decision) and **Wu** (won by unanimous decision).

Heavyweights

Date	Winner	Loser	Result	Title	Site
Oct. 19	Danell Nicholson	Jesse Ferguson	TKO 8	Non-title	Las Vegas
Oct. 21	Brian Nielsen	Tony Tubbs	TKO 4	Non-title	Copenhagen, DEN
Oct. 27	Peter McNeeley	Mike Sam	KO 2	Non-title	Boston
Oct. 31	Tim Witherspoon	Everton Davis	TKO 7	Non-title	Phoenix, Ariz
Nov. 4	Riddick Bowe	Evander Holyfield	TKO 8	Non-title	Las Vegas
Nov. 4	David Izonritei	Cleveland Woods	TKO 7	Non-title	Las Vegas
Dec. 5	Bobby Czyz	Ricky Jackson	TKO 6	Non-title	Biloxi, Miss.
Dec. 7	Michael Grant	Mike Dixon	TKO 6	Non-title	Philadelphia
Dec. 9	Frans Botha	Axel Schulz	Wu 12	**IBF**	Stuttgart, GER
Dec. 9	Tyrone Booze	Earl Talley	TKO 3	Non-title	Tuscaloosa, Ala.
Dec. 9	Jose Ribalta	Bruce Johnson	TKO 1	Non-title	Moline, Ill.
Dec. 12	Peter McNeeley	Harold Reitman	TKO 1	Non-title	Punta Gorda, Fla.
Dec. 12	Darroll Wilson	James Stanton	Wu 10	Non-title	Philadelphia
Dec. 13	Jorge Valdez	Marcos Gonzalez	KO 1	Non-title	Atlantic City
Dec. 15	Shannon Briggs	Calvin Jones	TKO 1	Non-title	New York City
Dec. 15	Joe Hipp	Martin Jacques	KO 1	Non-title	Yakima, Wash.
Dec. 16	Henry Akinwande	Tony Tucker	Wu 10	Non-title	Philadelphia
Dec. 16	Mike Tyson	Buster Mathis Jr.	KO 3	Non-title	Philadelphia
Dec. 21	Danell Nicholson	Darren Hayden	Wu 8	Non-title	Bossier City, La.
Jan. 9	Larry Holmes	Curtis Shepherd	KO 4	Non-title	Galveston, Tex.
Jan. 12	Tim Witherspoon	Al Cole	Wu 10	Non-title	New York City
Jan. 13	Obed Sullivan	Jerry Davis	KO 5	Non-title	Atlantic City
Jan. 27	Henry Akinwande	Brian Sargent	TKO 1	Non-title	Phoenix, Ariz.
Feb. 24	Oliver McCall	Oleg Maskaev	TKO 1	Non-title	Richmond, Va.
Mar. 16	Mike Tyson	**Frank Bruno**	TKO 3	**WBC**	Las Vegas
Mar. 23	Crawford Grimsley	Eddie Curry	TKO 1	Non-title	Miami
Mar. 23	Henry Akinwande	Gerald Jones	Disq. 7	Non-title	Miami
Mar. 23	Oliver McCall	James Stanton	TKO 6	Non-title	Miami
Apr. 11	Bonecrusher Smith	Troy Roberts	TKO 3	Non-title	Vancouver
Apr. 16	Larry Holmes	Quinn Navarre	Wu 10	Non-title	Bay St. Louis, Miss.
Apr. 20	Obed Sullivan	Buster Mathis Jr.	NC 4	Non-title	Grand Forks, N.D.
Apr. 26	Trevor Berbick	Kenny Smith	KO 4	Non-title	Westbury, NY
May 10	Tim Witherspoon	Jorge Luis Gonzalez	KO 5	Non-title	New York City
May 10	Lennox Lewis	Ray Mercer	Wm 10	Non-title	New York City
May 10	Evander Holyfield	Bobby Czyz	TKO 5	Non-title	New York City
June 2	Larry Donald	Jorge Valdez	TKO 6	Non-title	Prior Lake, Minn.
June 3	Iran Barkley	Brian Yates	Wu 8	Non-title	Kansas City, Mo.
June 16	Larry Holmes	Anthony Willis	KO 8	Non-title	Bay St. Louis, Miss.
June 22	Michael Moorer	Axel Schulz	Ws 12	**IBF**	Dortmund, GER
June 22	Buster Douglas	Tony LaRosa	TKO 4	Non-title	Atlantic City
June 29	Tony Tucker	Dave Dixon	KO 1	Non-title	Indio, Calif.
June 29	Henry Akinwande	Jeremy Williams	KO 3	(WBO)	Indio, Calif.
July 11	Riddick Bowe	Andew Golota	Disq. 7	Non-title	New York City
July 27	Iran Barkley	Craig Payne	Ws 10	Non-title	Rochester, Wash.
Aug. 8	Larry Donald	Derrick Roddy	TKO 2	Non-title	Lake Charles, La.
Aug. 8	Ahmad Abdin	Marcus Rhode	TKO 4	Non-title	Lake Charles, La.
Sept. 7	Mike Tyson	**Bruce Seldon**	TKO 1	**WBA**	Las Vegas
Oct. 3	Obed Sullivan	Will Hinton	TKO 6	Non-title	Houston, Tex.
Oct. 8	Jimmy Thunder	Quinn Navarre	KO 5	Non-title	Flint, Mich.

Cruiserweights (190 lbs)

(Jr. Heavyweights)

Date	Winner	Loser	Result	Title	Site
Oct. 24	**Marcelo Dominguez**	Sergei Kobozev	SD 12	**WBC**	Levallois-Perret, FRA
Nov. 7	Robert Daniels	Tim St. Clair	TKO 5	Non-title	Chester, W.Va.
Dec. 8	James Toney	Greg Everett	KO 2	Non-title	Ledyard, Conn.
Dec. 8	Kenny Keene	Matthew Charleston	Wu 10	Non-title	Caldwell, Idaho
Dec. 21	Robert Daniels	Tim Knight	TKO 6	Non-title	Ft. Lauderdale, Fla.
Jan. 13	**Nate Miller**	Reynaldo Gimenez	TKO 4	**WBA**	Miami
Feb. 5	Chris Okoh	Darren Westover	TKO 2	Non-title	London, ENG
Mar. 23	**Nate Miller**	Brian LaSpada	TKO 9	**WBA**	Miami

Date	Winner	Loser	Result	Title	Site
Apr. 6	Uriah Grant	Reynaldo Gimenez	TKO 1	Non-title	Miami
Apr. 9	Frank Tate	Everado Armenta	Wu 10	Non-title	Indio, Calif.
Apr. 20	Torsten May	Andrew Maynard	KO 10	Non-title	Dusseldorf, GER
Apr. 20	Alexandre Gurov	Pedro Franco	TKO 3	Non-title	Levallois, FRA
May 25	Akim Tafer	Alexei Iliin	TKO 4	Non-title	St. Petersburg, RUS
June 23	Michael Nunn	Everado Armenta	TKO 8	Non-title	Houston, Tex.
July 2	James Toney	Charles Oliver	Wu 10	Non-title	St. Charles, Mo.
July 5	**Marcelo Dominguez**	Patrice Aouissi	TKO 10	**WBC**	Hyeres, FRA
July 13	Ralf Rocchigiani	Bahsiru Ali	Wu 12	WBO	Essen, GER

Light Heavyweights (175 lbs)

Date	Winner	Loser	Result	Title	Site
Oct. 17	Leslie Stewart	Tyrone Bledsoe	TKO 1	Non-title	Indianapolis, Ind.
Oct. 18	Merqui Sosa	Benito Fernandez	TKO 3	Non-title	Atlantic City, N.J.
Oct. 18	Duran Williams	Fabian Garcia	TKO 2	Non-title	Atlantic City, N.J.
Oct. 25	Frank Tate	Dominick Carter	TKO 8	Non-title	Kenner, Louisiana
Dec. 22	Lenzie Morgan	Jose Gomes	TKO 7	Non-title	Sao Paulo, Brazil
Dec. 28	Ernie Magdaleno	Roman Santos	Wu 10	Non-title	Irvine, Calif.
Feb. 15	Lincoln Carter	David Raban	TKO 7	Non-title	Atlanta, Ga.
Feb. 18	Henry Maske	Duran Williams	Wu 12	**IBF**	Dortmund, GER
Apr. 6	**D. Michalczewski**	Asluddin Umarov	KO 5	**IBF**	Hanover, GER
Apr. 20	**Virgil Hill**	Louis Del Valle	Wu 12	**WBA**	Grand Fork, N.D.
May 4	Fabrice Tiozzo	Leslie Stewart	KO 6	Non-title	Lyons, FRA
May 14	James Toney	Earl Butler	TKO 4	WBU	Ledyard, Conn.
May 25	**Henry Maske**	John Scully	Wu 12	**IBF**	Leipzig, GER
June 8	Dariusz Michalczewski	Christophe Girard	Wu 12	WBO	Cologne, GER
July 11	Merqui Sosa	Karl Willis	TKO 4	Non-title	New York, N.Y.
Aug. 9	James Toney	Duran Williams	TKO 9	Non-title	Bay St. Louis, Miss.
Aug. 10	Dariusz Michalczewski	G. Rocchigiani	Tdraw 7	WBO	Hamburg, GER

Super Middleweights (168 lbs)

Date	Winner	Loser	Result	Title	Site
Oct. 17	Charles Brewer	Mark Buchanan	KO 2	Non-title	Philadelphia
Dec. 8	Michael Nunn	John Scully	Wu 12	Non-title	Ledyard, Conn.
Dec. 9	**Frankie Liles**	Mauricio Amaral	Wu 12	**WBA**	Stuttgart, Germany
Dec. 12	Bryant Brannon	Troy Watson	KO 8	Non-title	Philadelphia
Dec. 16	John David Jackson	Guy Stanford	Wu 10	Non-title	Philadelphia
Dec. 21	Roberto Duran	Wilbur Garst	TKO 4	Non-title	Ft. Lauderdale, Fla.
Jan. 12	Roy Jones Jr.	Merqui Sosa	TKO 2	Non-title	New York City
Jan. 23	Mark Delaney	Darron Griffiths	Wu 12	WBO	Green, ENG
Feb. 20	Roberto Duran	Ray Domenge	Wu 10	Non-title	Miami
Mar. 2	Thulane Malinga	**Nigel Benn**	Ds 12	**WBC**	Newcastle, ENG
May 2	Rodney Toney	Silvio Branco	Ds 12	Non-title	Rome
June 8	**Frankie Liles**	Tim Littles	TKO 3	**WBA**	Las Vegas
June 15	**Roy Jones Jr.**	Eric Lucas	TKO 12	**IBF**	Jacksonville, Fla.
July 6	Vincenzo Nardiello	**Thulane Malinga**	Ws 12	**WBC**	Manchester, ENG
July 6	Steve Collins	Nigel Benn	TKO 4	WBO	Manchester, ENG
Sept. 27	Roberto Duran	Mike Culbert	TKO 6	Non-title	Chester, W.Va.
Oct. 4	**Roy Jones Jr.**	Bryant Brannon	KO 2	**IBF**	New York City
Oct. 12	**Robin Reid**	Vincenzo Nardiello	KO 7	**WBC**	Milan, ITA
Oct. 19	Chris Eubank	Luis Barrera	TKO 5	Non-title	Cairo, EGY

Middleweights (160 lbs)

Date	Winner	Loser	Result	Title	Site
Oct. 27	Dana Rosenblatt	Floyd Williams	Wu 12	Non-title	Boston
Dec. 9	Hector Camacho	Lonnie Horn	TKO 6	Non-title	Moline, Ill.
Dec. 19	Shinji Takehara	**Jorge Castro**	Wu 12	**WBA**	Tokyo
Jan. 27	**Bernard Hopkins**	Steve Frank	KO 1	**IBF**	Phoenix, Ariz.
Feb. 4	Dana Rosenblatt	Pat Lawlor	KO 3	Non-title	Ledyard, Conn.
Feb. 6	Lonnie Bradley	Randy Smith	KO 2	WBO	New York City
Mar. 15	**Bernard Hopkins**	Joe Lipsey	KO 4	**IBF**	Las Vegas
Mar. 16	Keith Holmes	Quincy Taylor	TKO 9	**WBC**	Las Vegas
May 7	Lonnie Bradley	Lonny Beasley	Wu 12	WBO	Steubenville, Ohio
June 12	Buddy McGirt	Alan Watts	Ws 10	Non-title	Atlantic City
June 22	Hector Camacho	Roberto Duran	Wu 12	Non-title	Atlantic City
June 24	William Joppy	**Shinji Takehara**	TKO 9	**WBA**	Yokohama, JPN
July 16	Bernard Hopkins	William James	TKO 11	**IBF**	Atlantic City
Aug. 23	Vinny Pazienza	Dana Rosenblatt	TKO 4	Non-title	Atlantic City, N.J.
Oct. 20	**William Joppy**	Ray McElroy	TKO 6	**WBC**	U. Marlboro, Ind.
Oct. 20	**Keith Holmes**	Richie Woodhall	KO 12	**WBA**	U. Marlboro, Ind.

Junior Middleweights (154 lbs)

(Super Welterweights)

Date	Winner	Loser	Result	Title	Site
Oct. 22	Winky Wright	Young Dick Tiger	KO 9	Non-title	Inglewood, California
Nov. 7	Hector Camacho	Danny Chavez	Wu 10	Non-title	Chester, W.VA.
Dec. 15	Oscar Gonzalez	Greg Haugen	Wu 10	Non-title	Yakima, Wash
Dec. 16	**Julio C. Vasquez**	Carl Daniels	KO 11	**WBA**	Philadelphia
Dec. 16	Terry Norris	Paul Vaden	Wu 12	**IBF/WBC***	Philadelphia
Dec. 21	Anthony Stephens	Tocker Pudwill	TKO 8	Non-title	Bossier City, La.
Dec. 27	Manny Sobral	Rodolfo Gonzalez	TKO 6	Non-title	Rochestern, Wash.
Jan. 27	**Terry Norris**	Jorge Luis Vado	TKO 2	**IBF/WBC**	Phoenix, Ariz.
Feb. 24	**Terry Norris**	Vincent Pettway	TKO 8	**IBF**	Richmond, Va.
May 17	Ronald Wright	Bronco McKart	Ws 12	WBO	Monroe, Mich.
May 18	Laurent Boudouani	Jorge Aquino	KO 5	Non-title	St. Nazaire, FRA
May 19	Mark Breland	Buck Smith	KO 3	Non-title	Auburn Hills, Mich
May 30	Vincent Pettway	Benji Singleton	Wu 10	Non-title	Baltimore, Md.
June 7	Mark Breland	Darryl Lattimore	Wu 10	Non-title	New York City
June 18	Simon Brown	Glenwood Brown	Wu 10	Non-title	Edison, N.J.
Aug. 21	Laurent Boudouani	**Julio C. Vasquez**	KO 5	**WBA**	Cannet, FRA
Oct. 23	Vincent Pettway	Harold Bennet	KO 3	Non-title	Baltimore, Md.

Welterweights (147 lbs)

Date	Winner	Loser	Result	Title	Site
Oct. 21	Giorbis Barthelemy	Alex Quiroga	W 12	Non-title	Miami Beach, Florida
Oct. 21	Roger Mayweather	Clifford Hicks	TKO 3	Non-title	Miami Beach, Florida
Oct. 21	Gary Murray	Luis Maysonet	TKO 5	Non-title	Johannesburg, RSA.
Oct. 28	Vince Phillips	Mauro Guitierrez	TKO 3	Non-title	Las Vegas
Nov. 18	**Pernell Whitaker**	Jake Rodriguez	TKO 6	**WBC**	Atlantic City
Nov. 18	**Felix Trinidad**	Larry Barnes	TKO 4	**IBF**	Atlantic City
Dec. 9	Hector Camacho	Lonnie Horn	TKO 6	Non-title	Moline, Ill.
Jan. 16	Hector Camacho	Sal Lopez	Tdraw 2	Non-title	Ft. Lauderdal, Fla.
Feb. 3	**Ike Quartey**	Jorge R. Aquino	TKO 4	**WBA**	Levallois-Perret, FRA
Feb. 9	Joey Gamache	Tim Payton	KO 4	Non-title	Baraboo, Wisc.
Feb. 10	**Felix Trinidad**	Rodney Moore	KO 4	**IBF**	Las Vegas
Mar. 13	Gabriel Ruelas	Julio C. Herrera	Wu 10	Non-title	Tijuana, MEX
Mar. 23	Carlos Gonzalez	Juam Rodriguez	KO 4	Non-title	Las Vegas
Apr. 12	**Ike Quartey**	Vincent Phillips	TKO 3	**WBA**	St. Maarten
Apr. 12	**Pernell Whitaker**	Wilfredo Rivera	Ws 12	**WBC**	St. Maarten
Apr. 13	Jose Luis Lopez	Eamonn Loughran	TKO 1	WBO	Liverpool, ENG
May 18	**Felix Trinidad**	Fred Pendelton	KO 5	**IBF**	Las Vegas
June 16	Vincent Phillips	Jerry Smith	TKO 3	Non-title	Bay St. Louis, Miss.
Aug. 16	Meldrick Taylor	Kenneth Kidd	TKO 1	Non-title	Altoona, Pa.
Sept. 7	**Felix Trinidad**	Ray Lovato	TKO 6	**IBF**	Las Vegas
Oct. 4	**Ike Quartey**	Oba Carr	W? 12	**WBA**	New York City
Oct. 6	Jose Lopez	Luis Campas	TKO 5	WBO	Los Angeles

Junior Welterweights (140 lbs)

(Super Lightweights)

Date	Winner	Loser	Result	Title	Site
Oct. 22	Sammy Fuentes	Juan Soberanas	TKO 4	WBO	Inglewood, Calif.
Oct. 25	Isaac Cruz	Pedro Saiz	TKO 4	Non-title	Kenner, La.
Oct. 28	Leonardo Mas	Andres Sandoval	TKO 7	Non-title	Miami, Fla.
Oct. 28	Ross Hale	Charlie Kane	KO 2	Non-title	Bristol, ENG
Dec. 11	Sammy Fuentes	Marco Lizarraga	KO 4	Non-title	Inglewood, Calif.
Jan. 13	Juan Martin Coggi	**Frankie Randall**	Tdraw 5	**WBA**	Miami, Fla.
Jan. 20	**Kostya Tszyu**	Hugo Pineda	KO 11	**IBF**	Sydney, AUS
Feb. 9	Oscar De La Hoya	Darryl Tyson	KO 2	Non-title	Las Vegas
Feb. 9	Julio Cesar Chavez	Scott Walker	TKO 2	Non-title	Las Vegas
Apr. 30	Rafael Ruelas	Tomas Barrientes	KO 2	Non-title	San Antonio, Tex.
May 24	**Kostya Tszyu**	Corey Johnson	KO 4	**IBF**	Sydney, AUS
June 7	Oscar De La Hoya	**Julio Cesar Chavez**	TKO 4	**WBC**	Las Vegas
June 20	Giovanni Parisi	Carlos Gonzalez	Ds 12	WBO	Milan, ITA
Aug. 16	Frankie Randall	**Juan M. Coggi**	Wu 12	**WBA**	Buenos Aires, ARG
Oct. 12	Giovanni Parisi	Sergio Rey	KO 4	WBO	Milan, ITA

Lightweights (135 lbs)

Date	Winner	Loser	Result	Title	Site
Oct. 17	Ivan Robinson	Demetrio Cebbalos	Wu 12	Non-title	Philadelphia
Oct. 28	Billy Schwer	Ditau Molefayne	KO 8	Non-title	London
Nov. 4	**Phillip Holiday**	Rocky Martinez	Wu 12	**IBF**	Sun City, S. Afr.
Dec. 15	**Oscar De La Hoya**	Jesse James Leija	TKO 2	WBO	NYC
Feb. 17	**Phillip Holiday**	John Lark	KO 10	**IBF**	Pretoria, S.Afr.
Apr. 15	**Orzubek Nazarov**	Adrianus Taroreh	KO 4	**WBA**	Tokyo
Apr. 20	**Jean Baptiste Mendy**	Lamar Murphy	Wu 12	**WBC**	Levallois, FRA
May 8	Genaro Hernandez	Javier Pichardo	TKO 5	Non-title	Indio, Calif.
May 18	**Phillip Holiday**	Jeff French	TKO 2	**IBF**	Melbourne, AUS
May 18	Leavander Johnson	Jose L. Madrid	TKO 2	Non-title	Las Vegas
Sept. 28	Genaro Hernandez	Antonio Hernandez	Wu 10	Non-title	Ft. Worth, Tex.
Oct. 19	**Phillip Holiday**	Joel Perze	Wu 12	**IBF**	Johannesburg

Junior Lightweights (130 lbs)

(Super Featherweights)

Date	Winner	Loser	Result	Title	Site
Oct. 21	Yongsoo Choi	Victor Paz	KO 10	**WBA**	Salta, Argentina
Oct. 26	**Tracy Patterson**	Bruno Rabanales	KO 6	**IBF**	Hauppage, N.Y.
Nov. 4	Julien Lorcy	Mark Smith	TKO 2	Non-title	Las Vegas
Dec. 1	Azumah Nelson	Gariel Ruelas	TKO 5	**WBC**	Indio, Calif.
Dec. 15	Arturo Gatti	**Tracy Patterson**	Wu 12	**IBF**	New York City
Jan. 27	**Yongsoo Choi**	Yamato Mitani	Wu 12	**WBA**	Tokyo, JPN
Mar. 23	**Arturo Gatti**	Wilson Rodriguez	KO 6	**IBF**	New York City
Apr. 1	Regilio Tuur	Narciso Valenzuela	Wu 12	WBO	Den Bosch, NET
Apr. 14	Tracy Patterson	Harold Warren	Wu 12	Non-title	Ledyard, Conn.
May 11	**Yongsoo Choi**	Orlando Soto	KO 8	**WBA**	Chejudo, KOR
June 1	**Azumah Nelson**	James Leija	TKO 6	**WBC**	Las Vegas
July 11	Arturo Gatti	Feliciano Correa	KO 3	Non-title	New York City
July 25	Tracy Patterson	Joey Figueroa	Wu 10	Non-title	N. Bergen, N.J.
Sept. 9	Saul Duran	Ramon Morlaes	KO 7	WBO	Inglewood, Calif.
Oct. 13	**Yongsoo Choi**	Yamato Mitani	W? 12	**WBA**	Tokyo

Featherweights (126 lbs)

Date	Winner	Loser	Result	Title	Site
Oct. 28	Billy Hardy	Mehdi Labdouani	W 12	Non-title	Fontenay sous Bois, FRA
Oct. 31	Luisito Espinosa	Arnulfo Romero	TKO 3	Non-title	Phoenix, Ariz.
Dec. 9	**Tom Johnson**	Jose Badillo	Ws 12	**IBF**	Stuttgart, GER
Dec. 11	Luisito Espinosa	**Manuel Medina**	Wu 12	**WBC**	Tokyo
Jan. 27	**Eloy Rojas**	Miguel Arrozal	Wu 12	**WBA**	Phoenix, Ariz.
Feb. 2	**Kevin Kelley**	Louie Espinoza	Wu 12	Non-title	Las Vegas
Mar. 1	**Luisito Espinosa**	Alejandro Gonzalez	KO 4	**WBC**	Guadalajara, MEX
Mar. 2	**Tom Johnson**	Ever Beleno	TKO 12	**IBF**	Newcastle, ENG
Mar. 16	Naseem Hamed	Said Lawal	KO 2	WBO	Glasgow, SCOT
Mar. 23	David Santos	Pat Simeon	TKO 1	Non-title	New York, NY
Apr. 27	**Tom Johnson**	Claudio Martinet	KO 7	**IBF**	Antibes, FRA
May 18	**Wilfredo Vasquez**	Eloy Rojas	KO 11	**WBA**	Las Vegas
June 8	Naseem Hamed	Daniel Alicea	TKO 2	WBO	Newcastle, ENG
June 15	Kevin Kelley	Derrick Gainer	KO 8	Non-title	Jacksonville, Fla.
July 6	**Luisito Espinosa**	Cesar Soto	Wu 12	**WBC**	Manila, PHI
July 13	Wayne McCullough	Julio C. Cardona	Wu 10	Non-title	Denver, Colo.
Aug. 31	Naseem Hamed	Manuel Medina	TKO 11	WBO	Dublin, IRE

Junior Featherweights (122 lbs)

(Super Bantamweights)

Date	Winner	Loser	Result	Title	Site
Oct. 21	Daryl Pinckney	Luis Valenzuela	KO 2	Non-title	Miami Beach, Fla.
Oct. 22	Enrique Sanchez	Alejandro Landeros	KO 1	Non-title	Inglewood, Ca.
Nov. 4	Marco A. Barrera	Eddie Croft	TKO 7	WBO	Las Vegas
Nov. 4	Orlando Canizales	Julio Portillo	TKO 2	Non-title	Las Vegas
Jan. 23	**Vuyani Bungu**	John Lewus	Wu 12	**IBF**	Biloxi, Miss.
Feb. 3	Marco A. Barrera	Kennedy McKinney	TKO 12	WBO	Los Angeles
Mar. 23	**Antonio Cermeno**	Yober Ortega	Wu 12	**WBA**	Miami
Mar. 23	Junior Jones	Orlanod Canizales	Ws 12	Non-title	New York City
Apr. 15	**Vuyani Bungu**	Pablo Ozuna	KO 2	**IBF**	Hammanskraal, S. Afr.
May 4	Marco Barrera	Jesse Benavides	KO 2	WBO	Anaheim, Calif.
May 5	Kevin McKinney	John Lewus	Wu 12	Non-title	Biloxi, Miss.
July 14	Marcos A. Barrera	Orlando Fernandez	TKO 7	WBO	Denver, Colo.
July 20	**Daniel Zaragoza**	Tsuyoshi Harada	TKO 7	**WBC**	Osaka, JPN
Aug. 20	**Vuyani Bungu**	Jesus Salud	Wu 12	**IBF**	Hammanskrall, S. Afr.

Bantamweights (118 lbs)

Date	Winner	Loser	Result	Title	Site
Oct. 19	Johnny Tapia	Paul Rios	Wu 10	Non-title	Las Vegas
Oct. 21	Daniel Jimenez	Alfred Kotey	Wu 12	Non-title	London
Jan. 20	Daniel Jimenez	Drew Docherty	Wu 12	WBO	Mansfield, ENG
Jan. 28	Nana Yaw Konadu	Veerapol Sahaprom	TKO 2	**WBA**	Bangkok
Mar. 30	**Wayne McCullough**	Jose Luis Bueno	Ws 12	**WBC**	Dublin, IRE
Apr. 2	**Mbulelo Botile**	Ancee Gedeon	KO 11	**IBF**	Providence, R.I.
Apr. 26	Robbie Regan	Daniel Jimenez	Wu 12	WBO	Cardiff, WAL
Apr. 30	Johnny Tapia	Ramon Gonzalez	KO 2	Non-title	San Antonio, Tex.
May 31	Johnny Bredahl	Alexandre Yagupov	Wu 12	Non-title	Copenhagen, DEN
June 29	**Mbulelo Botile**	Marlon Arios	TKO 9	**IBF**	E. London, S. Afr.
Aug. 10	S. Singmanassak	Jose Luis Bueno	TKO 5	**WBC***	Phitsanulok, THA

*Singmanassak won the WBC interim belt.

Junior Bantamweights (115 lbs)
(Super Flyweights)

Date	Winner	Loser	Result	Title	Site
Oct. 19	Johnny Tapia	Paul Rios	Wu 10	Non-title	Las Vegas
Dec. 1	Johnny Tapia	Willy Salazar	TKO 9	WBO	Indio,.Calif.
Feb. 3	Johnny Tapia	Giovanni Andrade	TKO 2	WBO	Los Angeles
Feb. 24	Alimi Goitia	Hyunchul Lee	TKO 12	**WBA**	Kwangyang, KOR
Apr. 27	Hiroshi Kawashima	Cecilio Espino	Wu 12	**WBC**	Tokyo
Apr. 27	Harold Grey	Carlos Salazar	Wu 12	**IBF**	Cartagena, COL
Apr. 29	Alimi Goitia	Satoshi Lida	TKO 5	**WBA**	Nagoya, JPN
June 7	Johnny Tapia	Ivan Alvaez	TKO 8	WBO	Las Vegas
Aug. 17	Johnny Tapia	Hugo Soto	Wu 12	WBO	Albuquerque, N.M.
Oct. 11	Johnny Tapia	Sammy Stewart	TKO 7	WBO	Las Vegas
Oct. 12	Hiroshi Kawashima	Domingo Sosa	TKO 2	**WBC**	Tokyo

Flyweights (112 lbs)

Date	Winner	Loser	Result	Title	Site
Oct. 17	**Saen Sor Ploenchit**	Hiroki Ioka	TKO 10	**WBA**	Osaka, Japan
Jan. 14	**Saen Sor Ploenchit**	Youngsoon Chang	Wu 12	**WBA**	Bangkok, THA
Feb. 5	Yuri Arbachakov	Raul Juarez	Wu 12	**WBC**	Osaka, JPN
Mar. 23	Alberto Jimenez	Miguel Martinez	TKO 5	WBO	Las Vegas
Mar. 23	**Saen Sor Ploenchit**	Leo Gamez	Ws 12	**WBA**	Bangkok
May 4	Marc Johnson	Francisco Tejedor	KO 1	**IBF**	Anaheim, Calif.
June 1	Alberto Jimenez	Jose Lopez	Wu 12	WBO	Stateline, Nev.
Aug. 5	**Marc Johnson**	Raul Juarez	TKO 8	**IBF**	Inglewood, Calif.
Oct. 10	Will Grigsby	Jesus Lopez	W? 12	Non-title	Rochester, Wash.

Junior Flyweights (108 lbs)
(Light Flyweights)

Date	Winner	Loser	Result	Title	Site
Oct. 21	Jakkrit L.G. Gym	Jesus Chong	Wu 12	Non-title	Bangkok, Thailand
Oct. 28	Manuel Herrera	Carlitos Rodriguez	Wu 12	Non-title	Miami, Florida
Jan. 13	**Carlos Murillo**	Hiyong Choi	Wu 12	**WBA**	Miami, Fla.
Feb. 19	Michael Carbajal	Mauro Diaz	KO 7	Non-title	Tempe, Ariz.
Feb. 24	**S. Sorjatouroung**	Antonio Perez	TKO 4	**WBC**	Chachoensao, THA
Mar. 15	**Carlos Murillo**	Jose Garcia Bernal	KO 10	**WBA**	Panama City, PAN
Mar. 16	Michael Carbajal	Melchor Cob Castro	Wu 12	**IBF**	Las Vegas
Apr. 13	Jacob Matlala	Paul Weir	KO 10	WBO	Liverpool, ENG
Apr. 27	**S. Sorjatouroung**	Joma Gamboa	TKO 7	**WBC**	Maha Saracham, THAI
May 21	Keiji Yamaguchi	Carlos Murillo	Ws 12	**WBA**	Tokyo
July 14	Michael Carbajal	Manuel Sarabia	KO 1	Non-title	Denver, Colo.
Aug. 10	**S. Sorjatouroung**	Shiro Yahiro	TKO 9	**WBC**	Phitsanulok, THAI
Aug. 13	**Keiji Yamaguchi**	Carlos Murillo	Wu 12	**WBA**	Osaka, JPN
Sept. 13	**Michael Carbajal**	Julio Coronell	TKO 8	**IBF**	Des Moines, Iowa
Oct. 12	**Michael Carbajal**	Tomas Rivera	KO 5	**IBF**	Anaheim, Calif.
Oct. 19	**S. Sorjatouroung**	Ali Glavez		**WBC**	Bangkok

Minimumweights (105 lbs)
(Strawweights or Mini-Flyweights)

Date	Winner	Loser	Result	Title	Site
Dec. 2	**Rosendo Alvarez**	Chana Porpaoin	Wu 12	**WBA**	Bangkok
Mar. 16	**Ricardo Lopez**	Ala Villamor	KO 8	**WBC**	Las Vegas
Mar. 30	**Rosendo Alvarez**	Kermin Guardia	KO 3	**WBA**	Managua, NIC
May 18	**Ratan Voraphin**	Jun Arios	Wu 12	**IBF**	Yala, THAI
June 15	**Rosendo Alvarez**	Eric Chavez	Wm 12	**WBA**	Sendai City, JPN
June 29	**Ricardo Lopez**	Kittichai Preecha	KO 3	**WBC**	Indio, Calif.
July 13	**Ratan Voraphin**	Jun Orhaliza	KO 3	**IBF**	Chiangmai, THAI
Sept. 28	**Ratan Voraphin**	O. Andrade	KO 5	**IBF**	Bangkok
Oct. 1	**Rosendo Alvadez**	Takashi Shiohama	KO 8	**WBA**	Kokuka, JPN

1996 U.S. Olympic Box-offs

Apr 18-20 at Augusta, Ga.

The champions of the two brackets (winners and losers) at U.S. Olympic Boxing Trials met at the Olympic Box-offs in April to determine the U.S. Boxing team for the Summer Olympics in Atlanta. If the champion of the winner's bracket beat the champion of the loser's bracket then he automatically makes the team. If the winner of the loser bracket wins in their bout then they fight a second time with the winner of that second bout, earning a place on the team. Champions of the winners bracket at the Trials are in **bold** type.

Wgt		Result
106	Albert Guardado, Topeka, Kan. dec. **Jauquin Gallardo**, San Leandro, Calif.	15-11
	Albert Guardado, Topeka, Kan dec. **Jauquin Gallardo**, San Leandro, Calif.	23-11
112	**Eric Morel**, Madison, Wisc. dec. Ramases Patterson, River Rouge, Mich.	15-15 (43-40) tiebreak
119	**Zahir Raheem**, Philadelphia dec. Steve Carter, Navy/Norfolk, Va.	16-4
125	Floyd Mayweather, Grand Rapids, Mich. dec. **Augustine Sanchez**, Las Vegas	22-8
	Floyd Mayweather, Grand Rapids, Mich. dec. **Augustine Sanchez**, Las Vegas	20-10
132	**Terrance Cauthen**, Philadelphia dec. Jermain Fields, Washington D.C.	11-6
139	**David Diaz**, Chicago dec. Zabdiel Judah, Brooklyn, N.Y.	8-2
147	**Fernando Vargas**, Oxnard, Calif. dec. Brandon Mitchem, Augusta, Ga.	17-14
156	**David Reid**, Philadelphia dec. Darnell Wilson, Lafayette, Ind	20-5
165	**Rhoshii Wells**, Riverdale, Ga. dec. Ronald Simms, USAF/Langley, Va.	18-14
178	**Antonio Tarver**, Orlando, Fla dec. Anthony Stewart, Chicago	17-0
201	**Nate Jones**, Chicago dec. Davarryl Williamson, Washington D.C.	19-10
201+	Joseph Mesi, Tonawanda, N.Y dec. **Lawrence Clay-Bey**, Hartford, Conn.	26-11
	Lawrence Clay-Bey, Hartford, Conn KO'd Joseph Mesi, Tonawanda, N.Y.	(1:36)

Heavyweight Records

The career pro records of heavyweights Mike Tyson, Riddick Bowe, Michael Moorer, and Evander Holyfield,as of Oct. 28, 1996.

Mike Tyson

Born: 6/30/66
Height: 5'11"
Weight: 218
Pro record: 45-1-0, 39 KO
Manager: Don King

No	Date	Opponent, location	Result
1	3/6/85	Hector Mercedes, Albany, N.Y.	KO 1
2	4/10/85	Trent Singleton, Albany, N.Y.	TKO 1
3	5/23/85	Don Halpin, Albany, N.Y.	KO 4
4	6/20/85	Rick Spain, Atlantic City	KO 1
5	7/11/85	John Anderson, Atlantic City	TKO 2
6	7/19/85	Larry Sims, Poughkeepsie, N.Y.	KO 3
7	8/15/85	Lorenzo Canady, Atlantic City	TKO 1
8	9/5/85	Michael Johnson, Atlantic City	KO 1
9	10/9/85	Donnie Long, Atlantic City	KO 1
10	10/25/85	Robert Colay, Atlantic City	KO 1
11	11/1/85	Sterling Benjamin, Latham, N.Y.	TKO 1
12	11/13/85	Eddie Richardson, Houston	KO 1
13	11/22/85	Conroy Nelson, Latham, N.Y.	KO 2
14	12/6/85	Sammy Scaff, New York City	KO 1
15	12/27/85	Mark Young, Latham, N.Y.	KO 1
16	1/10/86	Dave Jaco, Albany, N.Y.	TKO 1
17	1/24/86	Mike Jameson, Atlantic City	TKO 5
18	2/16/86	Jesse Ferguson, Troy, N.Y.	TKO 6
19	3/10/86	Steve Zouski, Uniondale, N.Y.	KO 3
20	5/3/86	James Tillis, Glens Falls, N.Y.	Wu 10
21	5/20/86	Mitchell Green, New York City	Wu 10
22	6/13/86	Reggie Gross, New York City	TKO 1
23	6/28/86	William Hosea, Troy, N.Y.	KO 1
24	7/11/86	Lorenzo Boyd, Swan Lake, N.Y.	KO 2
25	7/26/86	Marvis Frazier, Glens Falls, N.Y.	KO 1
26	8/17/86	Jose Ribalta, Atlantic City	TKO 10
27	9/6/86	Alfonzo Ratliff, Las Vegas	KO 2
28	11/22/86	Trevor Berbick, Las Vegas **(won WBC heavyweight title)**	KO 2
29	3/7/87	Bonecrusher Smith, Las Vegas **(won WBA heavyweight title)**	Wu 12
30	5/30/87	Pinklon Thomas, Las Vegas	TKO 6
31	8/1/87	Tony Tucker, Las Vegas **(won IBF heavyweight title)**	Wu 12
32	10/16/87	Tyrell Biggs, Atlantic City	TKO 7
33	1/22/88	Larry Holmes, Atlantic City	KO 4
34	3/21/88	Tony Tubbs, Tokyo	TKO 2
35	6/27/88	Michael Spinks, Atlantic City	KO 1
36	2/25/89	Frank Bruno, Las Vegas	TKO 5
37	7/21/89	Carl Williams, Atlantic City	TKO 1
38	2/10/90	Buster Douglas, Tokyo **(lost world heavyweight title)**	KO by 10
39	6/16/90	Henry Tillman, Las Vegas	KO 1
40	12/8/90	Alex Stewart, Atlantic City	TKO 1
41	3/18/91	Razor Ruddock, Las Vegas	TKO 7
42	6/28/91	Razor Ruddock, Las Vegas	Wu 12
43	8/19/95	Peter McNeeley, Las Vegas **(first fight since release from prison)**	W disq. 1
44	12/16/95	Buster Mathis Jr., Philadelphia	KO 3
45	3/16/96	Frank Bruno, Las Vegas **(won WBC heavyweight title)**	TKO 3
46	9/7/96	Bruce Seldon, Las Vegas **(won WBA heavyweight title)**	TKO 1

Riddick Bowe

Born: Aug. 10, 1967
Height: 6'5"
Weight: 247 lbs
Olympic medal: 1988 Silver as Super Heavyweight (lost to Lennox Lewis)
Pro record: 39-1-0, 31 KO
Manager: Rock Newman

No	Date	Opponent, location	Result
1	3/6/89	Lionel Butler, Reno	TKO 2
2	4/14/89	Tracy Thomas, Atlantic City	TKO 3
3	5/9/89	Garing Lane, Atlantic City	Wu 4
4	7/2/89	Antonio Whiteside, Fayetteville	TKO 1
5	7/15/89	Lorenzo Canady, Atlantic City	TKO 2
6	9/3/89	Lee Moore, Pensacola, Fla	KO 1

Riddick Bowe (Cont.)

No	Date	Opponent, location	Result
7	9/15/89	Anthony Hayes, Brooklyn	KO 1
8	9/19/89	Earl Lewis, Jacksonville, Fla	KO 1
9	10/19/89	Mike Acey, Atlantic City	TKO 1
10	11/4/89	Garing Lane, Atlantic City	TKO 1
11	11/18/89	Don Askew, Washington, D.C	K0 1
12	11/28/89	Art Card, Buffalo	TKO 3
13	12/14/89	Charles Woodard, St.Joseph, Mo	TKO 2
14	2/20/90	Mike Robinson, Atlantic City	TKO 3
15	4/1/90	Robert Colay, Washington, D.C	TKO 2
16	4/14/90	Eddie Gonzales, Las Vegas	Wu 8
17	5/8/90	Manny Contreras, Atlantic City	KO 1
18	7/8/90	Art Tucker, Atlantic City	TKO 3
19	9/7/90	Pinklon Thomas, Wash, D.C.	TKO 9
20	10/25/90	Bert Cooper, Las Vegas	TKO 2
21	12/14/90	Tony Morrison, Kansas City	KO 1
22	3/2/91	Tyrell Biggs, Atlantic City	TKO 8
23	4/20/91	Tony Tubbs, Atlantic City	Wu 10
24	6/28/91	Rodolfo Marin, Las Vegas	KO 2
25	7/23/91	Phillip Brown, Atlantic City	TKO 3
26	8/9/91	Bruce Seldon, Atlantic City	TKO 7
27	10/29/91	Elijah Tillery, Wash., D.C	W/disq 1
28	12/13/91	Elijah Tillery, Atlantic City	TKO 4
29	4/7/92	Conroy Nelson, Atlantic City	KO 1
30	5/8/92	Everett Martin, Las Vegas	TKO 5
31	7/18/92	Pierre Coetzer, Las Vegas	TKO 7
32	11/13/92	Evander Holyfield, Las Vegas	Wu 12
		(Won undisputed heavyweight title)	
33	2/6/93	Michael Dokes, New York	TKO 1
34	5/22/93	Jesse Ferguson, Wash., D.C	TKO 2
35	11/6/93	Evander Holyfield, Las Vegas	Lm 12
		(Lost IBF/WBA heavyweight titles)	
36	8/13/94	Buster Mathis Jr., Atl. City	NC 4
37	12/3/94	Larry Donald, Syracuse	Wu 12
38	3/11/95	Herbie Hide, Las Vegas	KO 6
		(Won WBO heavyweight title)	
39	6/17/95	Jorge Luis Gonzalez, Las Vegas	KO 2
40	11/4/95	Evander Holyfield, Las Vegas	TKO 8
41	7/11/96	Andrew Golota, New York	Disq 7

Michael Moorer

Born: Nov. 12, 1967
Height: 6′ 2″
Weight: 214 lbs
Pro record: 37-1-0, 30 KO
Manager: John Davimos

No	Date	Opponent, location	Result
1	3/4/88	Adrian Riggs, Las Vegas	TKO 1
2	3/25/88	Bill Lee, Detroit	TKO 1
3	4/29/88	Brett Zywcewinsk, Detroit	KO 1
4	5/10/88	Dennis Fikes, Phoenix	TKO 2
5	6/6/88	Keith McMurray, Las Vegas	TKO 2
6	6/25/88	Lavelle Stanley, Detroit	TKO 2
7	8/6/88	Terrance Walker, Las Vegas	KO 4
8	8/12/88	Jordan Keepers, Milwaukee	TKO 2
9	10/7/88	Jorge Suero, Auburn Hills	KO 2
10	10/17/88	Carl Williams, Tucson	TKO 1
11	11/4/88	Glenn Kennedy, Las Vegas	KO 1
12	12/3/88	Ramzi Hassan, Cleveland	TKO 4
13	12/8/86	Victor Claudio, Auburn Hills	TKO 2
14	1/14/89	Frankie Swindell, Monessen, Pa	TKO 6
15	2/19/89	Fred Delgado, Auburn Hills	TKO 1
16	6/25/89	Leslie Stewart, Atlantic City	TKO 8
17	11/16/89	Jeff Thompson, Atlantic City	TKO 1
18	12/22/89	Mike Sedillo, Auburn Hills	TKO 6
19	2/3/90	Marcellus Allen, Atlantic City	TKO 9
20	4/28/90	Mario Melo, Atlantic City	KO 1
21	8/21/90	Jim MacDonald, Auburn Hills	TKO 3
22	12/15/90	Danny Lindstrom, Pittsburgh	TKO 8
23	4/19/91	Terry Davis, Atlantic City	TKO 2
24	6/25/91	Levi Billups, Auburn Hills	TKO 3
25	7/27/91	Alex Stewart, Norfolk, Va	TKO 4
26	11/23/91	Bobby Crabtree, Atlanta	TKO 1
27	2/1/92	Mike White, Las Vegas	Wu 10
28	3/17/92	Big Foot Martin, Auburn Hills	Wu 10
29	5/15/92	Bert Cooper, Atlantic City	TKO 5
30	11/13/92	Billy Wright, Las Vegas	TKO 2
31	2/27/93	Bonecrusher Smith, Atl.City	Wu 10
32	4/26/93	Frankie Swindell, Detroit	TKO 3
33	6/22/93	James Pritchard, Atlantic City	TKO 3
34	12/4/93	Mike Evans, Reno	Wu 10
35	4/22/94	Evander Holyfield, Las Vegas	Wm 12
		(won IBF/WBA heavyweight titles)	
36	11/5/94	George Foreman, Las Vegas	L, KO 10
		(lost IBF/WBA heavyweight titles)	
37	5/13/95	Melvin Foster, Sacramento	Wu 10
38	6/22/96	Axel Shulz, Dortmund, GER	Ws 12
		(won IBF heavyweight title)	

Evander Holyfield

Born: Oct. 19, 1962
Height: 6′ 2 1/2″
Weight: 217 lbs
Olympic medal: 1984 Bronze as light heavyweight (disqualifed for controversial late knockout punch in semifinal against Kevin Barry of New Zealand)
Pro record: 32-3-0, 23 KO
Manager: Hammer

No	Date	Opponent, location	Result
1	11/15/84	Lionel Byarm, New York	Wu 6
2	1/20/85	Eric Winbush, Atlantic City	Wu 6
3	3/13/85	Freddie Brown, Norfolk	KO 1
4	4/20/85	Mark Rivera, Corpus Christi	KO 2
5	7/20/85	Tyrone Booze, Norfolk	Wu 8
6	8/29/85	Rick Myers, Atlanta	KO 1
7	10/30/85	Jeff Meachem, Atlantic City	KO 5
8	12/21/85	Anthony Davis, Virginia Beach	KO 4
9	3/1/86	Chisanda Mutti, Lancaster, Pa	KO 3
10	4/6/86	Jesse Shelby, Corpus Christi	KO 3
11	5/28/86	Terry Mims, Metairie, LA	KO 5
12	7/20/86	Dwight M. Qwai, Atlanta	Ws 15
		(won WBA cruiserweight title)	
13	12/8/86	Mike Brothers, Paris	KO 3
14	2/14/87	Henry Tillman, Reno	TKO 7
15	5/15/87	Rickey Parkey, Las Vegas	TKO 3
		(won IBF cruiserweight title)	
16	8/15/87	Ossie Ocasio, St.Topez, France	TKO 11
17	12/4/87	Dwight M. Qawi, Atlantic City	TKO 4
18	4/9/88	Carlos DeLeon, Las Vegas	KO 8
		(won WBC cruiserweight title)	
19	7/16/88	James Tillis, Lake Tahoe	KO 5
20	12/9/88	Pinklon Thomas, Atlantic City	TKO 7
21	3/11/89	Michael Dokes, Las Vegas	TKO 10
22	7/15/89	Adilson Rodrigues, Lake Tahoe	KO 2
23	11/4/89	Alex Stewart, Atlantic City	TKO 8
24	6/1/90	Seamus McDonagh, Atlantic City	TKO 4
25	10/25/90	Buster Douglas, Las Vegas	KO 3
		(won undisputed heavyweight title)	
26	4/19/91	George Foreman, Atlantic City	Wu 12
27	11/23/91	Bert Cooper, Atlanta	TKO 7
28	6/19/92	Larry Holmes, Las Vegas	Wu 12
29	11/13/92	Riddick Bowe, Las Vegas	Lu 12
		(lost undisputed heavyweight title)	
30	6/26/93	Alex Stewart, Atlantic City	Wu 12
31	11/6/93	Riddick Bowe, Las Vegas	Wm 12
		(won IBF/WBA heavyweight titles)	
32	4/22/94	Michael Moorer, Las Vegas	Lm 12
		(lost IBF/WBA heavyweight titles)	
33	5/20/95	Ray Mercer, Atlantic City	Wu 10
34	11/4/95	Riddick Bowe, Las Vegas	TKO by 8
35	5/10/96	Bobby Czyz, New York	TKO 5

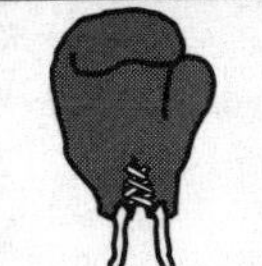

World Heavyweight Championship Fights

Widely accepted world champions in **bold** type. Note following result abbreviations: KO (knockout), TKO (technical knockout), Wu (unanimous decision), Wm (majority decision), Ws (split decision), Ref (referee's decision), ND (no decision), Disq (won on disqualification).

Year	Date	Winner	Age	Wgt	Loser	Wgt	Result	Location
1892	Sept. 7	James J. Corbett	26	178	John L. Sullivan	212	KO 21	New Orleans
1894	Jan. 25	**James J. Corbett**	27	184	Charley Mitchell	158	KO 3	Jacksonville, Fla.
1897	Mar. 17	Bob Fitzsimmons	34	167	**James J. Corbett**	183	KO 14	Carson City, Nev.
1899	June 9	James J. Jeffries	24	206	**Bob Fitzsimmons**	167	KO 11	Coney Island, N.Y.
1899	Nov. 3	**James J. Jeffries**	24	215	Tom Sharkey	183	Ref 25	Coney Island, N.Y.
1900	Apr. 6	**James J. Jeffries**	24	NA	Jack Finnegan	NA	KO 1	Detroit
1900	May 11	**James J. Jeffries**	25	218	James J. Corbett	188	KO 23	Coney Island, N.Y.
1901	Nov. 15	**James J. Jeffries**	26	211	Gus Ruhlin	194	TKO 6	San Francisco
1902	July 25	**James J. Jeffries**	27	219	Bob Fitzsimmons	172	KO 8	San Francisco
1903	Aug. 14	**James J. Jeffries**	28	220	James J. Corbett	190	KO 10	San Francisco
1904	Aug. 25	**James J. Jeffries***	29	219	Jack Munroe	186	TKO 2	San Francisco
1905	July 3	Marvin Hart	28	190	Jack Root	171	KO 12	Reno, Nev.
1906	Feb. 23	Tommy Burns	24	180	**Marvin Hart**	188	Ref 20	Los Angeles
1906	Oct. 2	**Tommy Burns**	25	NA	Jim Flynn	NA	KO 15	Los Angeles
1906	Nov. 28	**Tommy Burns**	25	172	Phila. Jack O'Brien	163½	Draw 20	Los Angeles
1907	May 8	**Tommy Burns**	25	180	Phila. Jack O'Brien	167	Ref 20	Los Angeles
1907	July 4	**Tommy Burns**	26	181	Bill Squires	180	KO 1	Colma, Calif.
1907	Dec. 2	**Tommy Burns**	26	177	Gunner Moir	204	KO 10	London
1908	Feb. 10	**Tommy Burns**	26	NA	Jack Palmer	NA	KO 4	London
1908	Mar. 17	**Tommy Burns**	26	NA	Jem Roche	NA	KO 1	Dublin
1908	Apr. 18	**Tommy Burns**	26	NA	Jewey Smith	NA	KO 5	Paris
1908	June 13	**Tommy Burns**	26	184	Bill Squires	183	KO 8	Paris
1908	Aug. 24	**Tommy Burns**	27	181	Bill Squires	184	KO 13	Sydney
1908	Sept. 2	**Tommy Burns**	27	183	Bill Lang	187	KO 6	Melbourne
1908	Dec. 26	Jack Johnson	30	192	**Tommy Burns**	168	TKO 14	Sydney
1909	Mar. 10	**Jack Johnson**	30	NA	Victor McLaglen	NA	ND 6	Vancouver
1909	May 19	**Jack Johnson**	31	205	Phila. Jack O'Brien	161	ND 6	Philadelphia
1909	June 30	**Jack Johnson**	31	207	Tony Ross	214	ND 6	Pittsburgh
1909	Sept. 9	**Jack Johnson**	31	209	Al Kaufman	191	ND 10	San Francisco
1909	Oct. 16	**Jack Johnson**	31	205½	Stanley Ketchel	170¼	KO 12	Colma, Calif.
1910	July 4	**Jack Johnson**	32	208	James J. Jeffries	227	KO 15	Reno, Nev.
1912	July 4	**Jack Johnson**	34	195½	Jim Flynn	175	TKO 9	Las Vegas, N.M.
1913	Dec. 19	**Jack Johnson**	35	NA	Jim Johnson	NA	Draw 10	Paris
1914	June 27	**Jack Johnson**	36	221	Frank Moran	203	Ref 20	Paris
1915	Apr. 5	Jess Willard	33	230	**Jack Johnson**	205½	KO 26	Havana
1916	Mar. 25	**Jess Willard**	34	225	Frank Moran	203	ND 10	NYC (Mad.Sq. Garden)
1919	July 4	Jack Dempsey	24	187	**Jess Willard**	245	TKO 4	Toledo, Ohio
1920	Sept. 6	**Jack Dempsey**	25	185	Billy Miske	187	KO 3	Benton Harbor, Mich.
1920	Dec. 14	**Jack Dempsey**	25	188¼	Bill Brennan	197	KO 12	NYC (Mad. Sq. Garden)
1921	July 2	**Jack Dempsey**	26	188	Georges Carpentier	172	KO 4	Jersey City, N.J.

*James J. Jeffries retired as champion on May 13, 1905, then came out of retirement to fight Jack Johnson for the title in 1910.

World Heavyweight Championship Fights (Cont.)

Year	Date	Winner	Age	Wgt	Loser	Wgt	Result	Location
1923	July 4	**Jack Dempsey**	28	188	Tommy Gibbons	175½	Ref 15	Shelby, Montana
1923	Sept. 14	**Jack Dempsey**	28	192½	Luis Firpo	216½	KO 2	NYC (Polo Grounds)
1926	Sept. 23	Gene Tunney	29	189½	**Jack Dempsey**	190	Wu 10	Philadelphia
1927	Sept. 22	**Gene Tunney**	30	189½	Jack Dempsey	192½	Wu 10	Chicago
1928	July 26	**Gene Tunney***	31	192	Tom Heeney	203	TKO 11	NYC (Yankee Stadium)
1930	June 12	Max Schmeling	24	188	Jack Sharkey	197	Foul 4	NYC (Yankee Stadium)
1931	July 3	**Max Schmeling**	25	189	Young Stribling	186½	TKO 15	Cleveland
1932	June 21	Jack Sharkey	29	205	**Max Schmeling**	188	Ws 15	Long Island City, N.Y.
1933	June 29	Primo Carnera	26	260½	**Jack Sharkey**	201	KO 6	Long Island City, N.Y.
1933	Oct. 22	**Primo Carnera**	26	259½	Paulino Uzcudun	229¼	Wu 15	Rome
1934	Mar. 1	**Primo Carnera**	27	270	Tommy Loughran	184	Wu 15	Miami
1934	June 14	Max Baer	25	209½	**Primo Carnera**	263¼	TKO 11	Long Island City, N.Y.
1935	June 13	James J. Braddock	29	193¾	**Max Baer**	209½	Wu 15	Long Island City, N.Y.
1937	June 22	Joe Louis	23	197¼	**James J. Braddock**	197	KO 8	Chicago
1937	Aug. 30	**Joe Louis**	23	197	Tommy Farr	204¼	Wu 15	NYC (Yankee Stadium)
1938	Feb. 23	**Joe Louis**	23	200	Nathan Mann	193½	KO 3	NYC (Mad. Sq. Garden)
1938	Apr. 1	**Joe Louis**	23	202½	Harry Thomas	196	KO 5	Chicago
1938	June 22	**Joe Louis**	24	198¾	Max Schmeling	193	KO 1	NYC (Yankee Stadium)
1939	Jan. 25	**Joe Louis**	24	200¼	John Henry Lewis	180¾	KO 1	NYC (Mad. Sq. Garden)
1939	Apr. 17	**Joe Louis**	24	201¼	Jack Roper	204¾	KO 1	Los Angeles
1939	June 28	**Joe Louis**	25	200¾	Tony Galento	233¾	TKO 4	NYC (Yankee Stadium)
1939	Sept. 20	**Joe Louis**	25	200	Bob Pastor	183	KO 11	Detroit
1940	Feb. 9	**Joe Louis**	25	203	Arturo Godoy	202	Ws 15	NYC (Mad. Sq. Garden)
1940	Mar. 29	**Joe Louis**	25	201½	Johnny Paychek	187½	KO 2	NYC (Mad. Sq. Garden)
1940	June 20	**Joe Louis**	26	199	Arturo Godoy	201¼	TKO 8	NYC (Yankee Stadium)
1940	Dec. 16	**Joe Louis**	26	202¼	Al McCoy	180¾	TKO 6	Boston
1941	Jan. 31	**Joe Louis**	26	202½	Red Burman	188	KO 5	NYC (Mad. Sq. Garden)
1941	Feb. 17	**Joe Louis**	26	203½	Gus Dorazio	193½	KO 2	Philadelphia
1941	Mar. 21	**Joe Louis**	26	202	Abe Simon	254½	TKO 13	Detroit
1941	Apr. 8	**Joe Louis**	26	203½	Tony Musto	199½	TKO 9	St. Louis
1941	May 23	**Joe Louis**	27	201½	Buddy Baer	237½	Disq 7	Washington, D.C.
1941	June 18	**Joe Louis**	27	199½	Billy Conn	174	KO 13	NYC (Polo Grounds)
1941	Sept. 29	**Joe Louis**	27	202¼	Lou Nova	202½	TKO 6	NYC (Polo Grounds)
1942	Jan. 9	**Joe Louis**	27	206¾	Buddy Baer	250	KO 1	NYC (Mad. Sq. Garden)
1942	Mar. 27	**Joe Louis**	27	207½	Abe Simon	255½	KO 6	NYC (Mad. Sq. Garden)
1942-45	World War II							
1946	June 9	**Joe Louis**	32	207	Billy Conn	187	KO 8	NYC (Yankee Stadium)
1946	Sept. 18	**Joe Louis**	32	211	Tami Mauriello	198½	KO 1	NYC (Yankee Stadium)
1947	Dec. 5	**Joe Louis**	33	211½	Jersey Joe Walcott	194½	Ws 15	NYC (Mad. Sq. Garden)
1948	June 25	**Joe Louis****	34	213½	Jersey Joe Walcott	194¾	KO 11	NYC (Yankee Stadium)
1949	June 22	**Ezzard Charles**	27	181¾	Jersey Joe Walcott	195½	Wu 15	Chicago
1949	Aug. 10	**Ezzard Charles**	28	180	Gus Lesnevich	182	TKO 8	NYC (Yankee Stadium)
1949	Oct. 14	**Ezzard Charles**	28	182	Pat Valentino	188½	KO 8	San Francisco
1950	Aug. 15	**Ezzard Charles**	29	183¼	Freddie Beshore	184½	TKO 14	Buffalo
1950	Sept. 27	**Ezzard Charles**	29	184½	Joe Louis	218	Wu 15	NYC (Yankee Stadium)
1950	Dec. 5	**Ezzard Charles**	29	185	Nick Barone	178½	KO 11	Cincinnati
1951	Jan. 12	**Ezzard Charles**	29	185	Lee Oma	193	TKO 10	NYC (Mad. Sq. Garden)
1951	Mar. 7	**Ezzard Charles**	29	186	Jersey Joe Walcott	193	Wu 15	Detroit
1951	May 30	**Ezzard Charles**	29	182	Joey Maxim	181½	Wu 15	Chicago
1951	July 18	Jersey Joe Walcott	37	194	**Ezzard Charles**	182	KO 7	Pittsburgh
1952	June 5	**Jersey Joe Walcott**	38	196	Ezzard Charles	191½	Wu 15	Philadelphia
1952	Sept. 23	Rocky Marciano	29	184	**Jersey Joe Walcott**	196	KO 13	Philadelphia
1953	May 15	**Rocky Marciano**	29	184½	Jersey Joe Walcott	197¾	KO 1	Chicago
1953	Sept. 24	**Rocky Marciano**	30	185	Roland LaStarza	184¾	TKO 11	NYC (Polo Grounds)
1954	June 17	**Rocky Marciano**	30	187½	Ezzard Charles	185½	Wu 15	NYC (Yankee Stadium)
1954	Sept. 17	**Rocky Marciano**	31	187	Ezzard Charles	192½	KO 8	NYC (Yankee Stadium)

*Gene Tunney retired as undefeated champion in 1928.

**Joe Louis retired as undefeated champion on Mar. 1, 1949, then came out of retirement to fight Ezzard Charles for the title in 1950.

Year	Date	Winner	Age	Wgt	Loser	Wgt	Result	Location
1955	May 16	**Rocky Marciano**	31	189	Don Cockell	205	TKO 9	San Francisco
1955	Sept. 21	**Rocky Marciano***	32	188¼	Archie Moore	188	KO 9	NYC (Yankee Stadium)
1956	Nov. 30	Floyd Patterson	21	182¼	Archie Moore	187¾	KO 5	Chicago
1957	July 29	**Floyd Patterson**	22	184	Tommy Jackson	192½	TKO 10	NYC (Polo Grounds)
1957	Aug. 22	**Floyd Patterson**	22	187¼	Pete Rademacher	202	KO 6	Seattle
1958	Aug. 18	**Floyd Patterson**	23	184½	Roy Harris	194	TKO 13	Los Angeles
1959	May 1	**Floyd Patterson**	24	182½	Brian London	206	KO 11	Indianapolis
1959	June 26	Ingemar Johansson	26	196	**Floyd Patterson**	182	TKO 3	NYC (Yankee Stadium)
1960	June 20	Floyd Patterson	25	190	**Ingemar Johansson**	194¾	KO 5	NYC (Polo Grounds)
1961	Mar. 13	**Floyd Patterson**	26	194¾	Ingemar Johansson	206½	KO 6	Miami Beach
1961	Dec. 4	**Floyd Patterson**	26	188½	Tom McNeeley	197	KO 4	Toronto
1962	Sept. 25	Sonny Liston	30	214	**Floyd Patterson**	189	KO 1	Chicago
1963	July 22	**Sonny Liston**	31	215	Floyd Patterson	194½	KO 1	Las Vegas
1964	Feb. 25	Cassius Clay**	22	210½	**Sonny Liston**	218	TKO 7	Miami Beach
1965	Mar. 5	Ernie Terrell WBA	25	199	Eddie Machen	192	Wu 15	Chicago
1965	May 25	**Muhammad Ali**	23	206	Sonny Liston	215¼	KO 1	Lewiston, Me.
1965	Nov. 1	Ernie Terrell WBA	26	206	George Chuvalo	209	Wu 15	Toronto
1965	Nov. 22	**Muhammad Ali**	23	210	Floyd Patterson	196¾	TKO 12	Las Vegas
1966	Mar. 29	**Muhammad Ali**	24	214½	George Chuvalo	216	Wu 15	Toronto
1966	May 21	**Muhammad Ali**	24	201½	Henry Cooper	188	TKO 6	London
1966	June 28	Ernie Terrell WBA	27	209½	Doug Jones	187½	Wu 15	Houston
1966	Aug. 6	**Muhammad Ali**	24	209½	Brian London	201½	KO 3	London
1966	Sept. 10	**Muhammad Ali**	24	203½	Karl Mildenberger	194¼	TKO 12	Frankfurt, W. Ger.
1966	Nov. 14	**Muhammad Ali**	24	212¾	Cleveland Williams	210½	TKO 3	Houston
1967	Feb. 6	**Muhammad Ali**	25	212¼	Ernie Terrell WBA	212½	Wu 15	Houston
1967	Mar. 22	**Muhammad Ali**	25	211½	Zora Folley	202½	KO 7	NYC (Mad. Sq. Garden)
1968	Mar. 4	Joe Frazier	24	204½	Buster Mathis	243½	TKO 11	NYC (Mad. Sq. Garden)
1968	Apr. 27	Jimmy Ellis	28	197	Jerry Quarry	195	Wm 15	Oakland
1968	June 24	Joe Frazier NY	24	203½	Manuel Ramos	208	TKO 2	NYC (Mad. Sq. Garden)
1968	Aug. 14	Jimmy Ellis WBA	28	198	Floyd Patterson	188	Ref 15	Stockholm
1968	Dec. 10	Joe Frazier NY	24	203	Oscar Bonavena	207	Wu 15	Philadelphia
1969	Apr. 22	Joe Frazier NY	25	204½	Dave Zyglewicz	190½	KO 1	Houston
1969	June 23	Joe Frazier NY	25	203½	Jerry Quarry	198½	TKO 8	NYC (Mad. Sq. Garden)
1970	Feb. 16	Joe Frazier NY	26	205	Jimmy Ellis WBA	201	TKO 5	NYC (Mad. Sq. Garden)
1970	Nov. 18	Joe Frazier	26	209	Bob Foster	188	KO 2	Detroit
1971	Mar. 8	Joe Frazier	27	205½	**Muhammad Ali**	215	Wu 15	NYC (Mad. Sq. Garden)
1972	Jan. 15	**Joe Frazier**	28	215½	Terry Daniels	195	TKO 4	New Orleans
1972	May 26	**Joe Frazier**	28	217½	Ron Stander	218	TKO 5	Omaha, Neb.
1973	Jan. 22	George Foreman	24	217½	**Joe Frazier**	214	TKO 2	Kingston, Jamaica
1973	Sept. 1	**George Foreman**	24	219½	Jose (King) Roman	196½	KO 1	Tokyo
1974	Mar. 26	**George Foreman**	25	224¾	Ken Norton	212¾	TKO 2	Caracas, Venezuela
1974	Oct. 30	Muhammad Ali	32	216½	**George Foreman**	220	KO 8	Kinshasa, Zaire
1975	Mar. 24	**Muhammad Ali**	33	223½	Chuck Wepner	225	TKO 15	Cleveland
1975	May 16	**Muhammad Ali**	33	224½	Ron Lyle	219	TKO 11	Las Vegas
1975	July 1	**Muhammad Ali**	33	224½	Joe Bugner	230	Wu 15	Kuala Lumpur, Malaysia
1975	Oct. 1	**Muhammad Ali**	33	224½	Joe Frazier	215	TKO 15	Manila, Philippines
1976	Feb. 20	**Muhammad Ali**	34	226	Jean Pierre Coopman	206	KO 5	San Juan, P.R.
1976	Apr. 30	**Muhammad Ali**	34	230	Jimmy Young	209	Wu 15	Landover, Md.
1976	May 24	**Muhammad Ali**	34	220	Richard Dunn	206½	TKO 5	Munich, W. Ger.
1976	Sept. 28	**Muhammad Ali**	34	221	Ken Norton	217½	Wu 15	NYC (Yankee Stadium)
1977	May 16	**Muhammad Ali**	35	221¼	Alfredo Evangelista	209¼	Wu 15	Landover, Md.
1977	Sept. 29	**Muhammad Ali**	35	225	Earnie Shavers	211¼	Wu 15	NYC (Mad. Sq. Garden)
1978	Feb. 15	Leon Spinks	24	197¼	**Muhammad Ali**	224¼	Ws 15	Las Vegas
1978	June 9	Larry Holmes	28	209	Ken Norton WBC‡	220	Ws 15	Las Vegas
1978	Sept. 15	Muhammad Ali†	36	221	**Leon Spinks**	201	Wu 15	New Orleans
1978	Nov. 10	Larry Holmes WBC	29	214	Alfredo Evangelista	208¼	KO 7	Las Vegas

*Rocky Marciano retired as undefeated champion on Apr. 27, 1956.
**After defeating Liston, Cassius Clay announced that he had changed his name to Muhammad Ali. He was later stripped of his title by the WBA and most state boxing commissions after refusing induction into the U.S. Army on Apr. 28, 1967.
†Muhammad Ali retired as champion on June 27, 1979, then came out of retirement to fight Larry Holmes for the title in 1980.
‡WBC recognized Ken Norton as world champion when Leon Spinks refused to meet Norton before Spinks' rematch with Muhammad Ali. Norton had scored a 15-round split decision over Jimmy Young on Nov. 5, 1977 in Las Vegas.

World Heavyweight Championship Fights (Cont.)

Year	Date	Winner	Age	Wgt	Loser	Wgt	Result	Location
1979	Mar. 23	Larry Holmes WBC	29	214	Osvaldo Ocasio	207	TKO 7	Las Vegas
1979	June 22	Larry Holmes WBC	29	215	Mike Weaver	202	TKO 12	NYC (Mad. Sq. Garden)
1979	Sept. 28	Larry Holmes WBC	29	210	Earnie Shavers	211	TKO 11	Las Vegas
1979	Oct. 20	John Tate	24	240	Gerrie Coetzee	222	Wu 15	Pretoria, S. Africa
1980	Feb. 3	Larry Holmes WBC	30	213½	Lorenzo Zanon	215	TKO 6	Las Vegas
1980	Mar. 31	Mike Weaver	27	232	John Tate WBA	232	KO 15	Knoxville, Tenn.
1980	Mar. 31	Larry Holmes WBC	30	211	Leroy Jones	254½	TKO 8	Las Vegas
1980	July 7	Larry Holmes WBC	30	214¼	Scott LeDoux	226	TKO 7	Minneapolis
1980	Oct. 2	Larry Holmes WBC	30	211½	Muhammad Ali	217½	TKO 11	Las Vegas
1980	Oct. 25	Mike Weaver WBA	28	210	Gerrie Coetzee	226½	KO 13	Sun City, Boph'swana
1981	Apr. 11	**Larry Holmes**	31	215	Trevor Berbick	215½	Wu 15	Las Vegas
1981	June 12	**Larry Holmes**	31	212¼	Leon Spinks	200¼	TKO 3	Detroit
1981	Oct. 3	Mike Weaver WBA	29	215	Quick Tillis	209	Wu 15	Rosemont, Ill.
1981	Nov. 6	**Larry Holmes**	32	213¼	Renaldo Snipes	215¾	TKO 11	Pittsburgh
1982	June 11	**Larry Holmes**	32	212½	Gerry Cooney	225½	TKO 13	Las Vegas
1982	Nov. 26	**Larry Holmes**	33	217½	Randall (Tex) Cobb	234¼	Wu 15	Houston
1982	Dec. 10	Michael Dokes	24	216	Mike Weaver WBA	209¾	TKO 1	Las Vegas
1983	Mar. 27	**Larry Holmes**	33	221	Lucien Rodriguez	209	Wu 12	Scranton, Pa.
1983	May 20	Michael Dokes WBA	24	223	Mike Weaver	218½	Draw 15	Las Vegas
1983	May 20	**Larry Holmes**	33	213	Tim Witherspoon	219½	Ws 12	Las Vegas
1983	Sept. 10	**Larry Holmes**	33	223	Scott Frank	211¼	TKO 5	Atlantic City
1983	Sept. 23	Gerrie Coetzee	28	215	Michael Dokes WBA	217	KO 10	Richfield, Ohio
1983	Nov. 25	**Larry Holmes**	34	219	Marvis Frazier	200	TKO 1	Las Vegas
1984	Mar. 9	Tim Witherspoon*	26	220¼	Greg Page	239½	Wm 12	Las Vegas
1984	Aug. 31	Pinklon Thomas	26	216	Tim Witherspoon WBC	217	Wm 12	Las Vegas
1984	Nov. 9	**Larry Holmes** IBF	35	221½	Bonecrusher Smith	227	TKO 12	Las Vegas
1984	Dec. 1	Greg Page	26	236½	Gerrie Coetzee WBA	218	KO 8	Sun City, Boph'swana
1985	Mar. 15	**Larry Holmes**	35	223½	David Bey	233¼	TKO 10	Las Vegas
1985	Apr. 29	Tony Tubbs	26	229	Greg Page WBA	239½	Wu 15	Buffalo
1985	May 20	**Larry Holmes**	35	222¼	Carl Williams	215	Wu 15	Las Vegas
1985	June 15	Pinklon Thomas	27	220¼	Mike Weaver	221¼	KO 8	Las Vegas
1985	Sept. 21	Michael Spinks	29	200	**Larry Holmes** IBF	221½	Wu 15	Las Vegas
1986	Jan. 17	Tim Witherspoon	28	227	Tony Tubbs WBA	229	Wm 15	Atlanta
1986	Mar. 22	Trevor Berbick	33	218½	Pinklon Thomas WBC	222¾	Wu 15	Las Vegas
1986	Apr. 19	**Michael Spinks**	29	205	Larry Holmes	223	Ws 15	Las Vegas
1986	July 19	Tim Witherspoon WBA	28	234¾	Frank Bruno	228	TKO 11	Wembley, England
1986	Sept. 6	**Michael Spinks**	30	201	Steffen Tangstad	214¾	TKO 4	Las Vegas
1986	Nov. 22	Mike Tyson	20	221¼	Trevor Berbick WBC	218½	TKO 2	Las Vegas
1986	Dec. 12	Bonecrusher Smith	33	228½	Tim Witherspoon WBA	233½	TKO 1	NYC (Mad. Sq. Garden)
1987	Mar. 7	Mike Tyson WBC	20	219	Bonecrusher Smith WBA	233	Wu 12	Las Vegas
1987	May 30	Mike Tyson	20	218¾	Pinklon Thomas	217¾	TKO 6	Las Vegas
1987	May 30	Tony Tucker**	28	222¼	Buster Douglas	227¼	TKO 10	Las Vegas
1987	June 15	**Michael Spinks**	30	208¾	Gerry Cooney	238	TKO 5	Atlantic City
1987	Aug. 1	Mike Tyson	21	221	Tony Tucker IBF	221	Wu 12	Las Vegas
1987	Oct. 16	Mike Tyson	21	216	Tyrell Biggs	228¾	TKO 7	Atlantic City
1988	Jan. 22	Mike Tyson	21	215¾	Larry Holmes	225¾	TKO 4	Atlantic City
1988	Mar. 20	Mike Tyson	21	216¼	Tony Tubbs	238¼	KO 2	Tokyo
1988	June 27	Mike Tyson	21	218¼	**Michael Spinks**	212¼	KO 1	Atlantic City
1989	Feb. 25	**Mike Tyson**	22	218	Frank Bruno	228	TKO 5	Las Vegas
1989	July 21	**Mike Tyson**	23	219¼	Carl Williams	218	TKO 1	Atlantic City
1990	Feb. 10	Buster Douglas	29	231½	**Mike Tyson**	220½	KO 10	Tokyo
1990	Oct. 25	Evander Holyfield	28	208	**Buster Douglas**	246	KO 3	Las Vegas
1991	Apr. 19	**Evander Holyfield**	28	208	George Foreman	257	Wu 12	Atlantic City
1991	Nov. 23	**Evander Holyfield**	29	210	Bert Cooper	215	TKO 7	Atlanta
1992	June 19	**Evander Holyfield**	29	210	Larry Holmes	233	Wu 12	Las Vegas
1992	Nov. 13	Riddick Bowe	25	235	**Evander Holyfield**	205	Wu 12	Las Vegas
1993	Feb. 6	**Riddick Bowe**	25	243	Michael Dokes	244	TKO 1	NYC (Mad. Sq. Garden)
1993	May 8	Lennox Lewis WBC†	27	235	Tony Tucker	235	Wu 12	Las Vegas

*WBC recognized winner of Mar. 9, 1984 fight between Tim Witherspoon and Greg Page as world champion after Larry Holmes relinquished title in dispute. IBF then recognized Holmes.

**IBF recognized winner of May 30, 1987 fight between Tony Tucker and James (Buster) Douglas as world champion after Michael Spinks relinquished title in dispute.

†WBC recognized Lennox Lewis as world champion when Riddick Bowe gave up that portion of his title on Dec. 14, 1992, rather than fight Lewis, the WBC's mandatory challenger.

Year	Date	Winner	Age	Wgt	Loser	Wgt	Result	Location
1993	May 22	**Riddick Bowe**	25	244	Jesse Ferguson	224	TKO 2	Washington, D.C.
1993	Oct. 1	Lennox Lewis WBC	28	233	Frank Bruno	238	TKO 7	Cardiff, Wales
1993	Nov. 6	Evander Holyfield	31	217	**Riddick Bowe**	246	Wm 12	Las Vegas
1994	Apr. 22	Michael Moorer	26	214	**Evander Holyfield**	214	Wm 12	Las Vegas
1994	May 6	Lennox Lewis WBC	28	235	Phil Jackson	218	TKO 8	Atlantic City
1994	Sept. 25	Oliver McCall	29	231¼	**Lennox Lewis** WBC	238	TKO 2	London
1994	Nov. 5	George Foreman*	45	250	**Michael Moorer**	222	KO 10	Las Vegas
1995	Apr. 8	Oliver McCall WBC	29	231	Larry Holmes	236	Wu 12	Las Vegas
1995	Apr. 8	Bruce Seldon	28	236	Tony Tucker	240	TKO 7	Las Vegas
1995	Apr. 22	George Foreman*	46	256	Axel Schulz	221	Wm 12	Las Vegas
1995	Aug. 19	Bruce Seldon WBA	28	234	Joe Hipp	223	TKO 10	Las Vegas
1995	Sept. 2	Frank Bruno	33	248	Oliver McCall WBC	235	Wu 12	London
1995	Dec. 9	Frans Botha**	27	227	Axel Schulz	222	Wu 12	Stuttgart, Germany
1996	Mar. 16	Mike Tyson	29	220	Frank Bruno WBC	247	TKO 3	Las Vegas
1996	June 22	Michael Moorer	28	222	Axel Schulz	223	Ws 12	Dortmund, GER
1996	Sept. 7	Mike Tyson WBC*	30	219	Bruce Seldon WBA	229	TKO 1	Las Vegas

*George Foreman won WBA and IBF championships when he beat Michael Moorer on Nov. 5, 1994. He was stripped of WBA title on Mar. 4, 1995, when he refused to fight No. 1 contender Tony Tucker, and he relinquished IBF title on June 29, 1995, rather than give Axel Schulz a rematch. Tucker lost to Bruce Seldon in their April 8 fight for vacant WBA title.

**Botha won the vacant IBF with a controversial 12-round decision over Axel Schulz on Dec. 9, 1995, but after legal sparring was eventually stripped of the IBF belt for using anabolic steriods. Mike Tyson won the WBC belt from Frank Bruno on Mar. 16 and still held it at the time of his Sept. 7 win over Bruce Seldon (although it was not at risk for that fight) but was forced to relinquish title after the bout for not fighting mandatory challenger Lennox Lewis.

Wide World Photos

Cassius Clay (left) stunned the boxing world in 1964 when he beat champion **Sonny Liston** in a seventh round TKO. Clay changed his name to **Muhammad Ali** after winning the title.

All-Time Heavyweight Upsets

Buster Douglas was a 50-1 underdog when he defeated previously-unbeaten heavyweight champion Mike Tyson on Feb. 10, 1990. That 10th-round knockout ranks as the biggest upset in boxing history. By comparison, 45-year-old George Foreman was only a 3-1 underdog before he unexpectedly won the title from Michael Moorer on Nov. 5, 1994.

Here are the best-known upsets in the annals of the heavyweight division. All fights were for the world championship except the Max Schmeling-Joe Louis bout.

Date	Winner	Loser	Result	KO Time	Location
9/7/1892	James J. Corbett	John L. Sullivan	KO 21	1:30	Olympic Club, New Orleans
4/5/1915	Jess Willard	Jack Johnson	KO 26	1:26	Mariano Race Track, Havana
9/23/26	Gene Tunney	Jack Dempsey	Wu 10	—	Sesquicentennial Stadium, Phila.
6/13/35	James J. Braddock	Max Baer	Wu 15	—	Mad.Sq.Garden Bowl, L.I.City
6/19/36	Max Schmeling	Joe Louis	KO 12	2:29	Yankee Stadium, New York
7/18/51	Jersey Joe Walcott	Ezzard Charles	KO 7	0:55	Forbes Field, Pittsburgh
6/26/59	Ingemar Johansson	Floyd Patterson	TKO 3	2:03	Yankee Stadium, New York
2/25/64	Cassius Clay	Sonny Liston	TKO 7	*	Convention Hall, Miami Beach
10/30/74	Muhammad Ali	George Foreman	KO 8	2:58	20th of May Stadium, Zaire
2/15/78	Leon Spinks	Muhammad Ali	Ws 15	—	Hilton Pavilion, Las Vegas
9/21/85	Michael Spinks	Larry Holmes	Wu 15	—	Riviera Hotel, Las Vegas
2/10/90	Buster Douglas	Mike Tyson	KO 10	1:23	Tokyo Dome, Tokyo
11/5/94	George Foreman	Michael Moorer	KO 10	2:03	MGM Grand, Las Vegas

*Liston failed to answer bell for Round 7.

Muhammad Ali's Career Pro Record

Born Cassius Marcellus Clay, Jr. on Jan. 17, 1942, in Louisville; Amateur record of 100-5; won light-heavyweight gold medal at 1960 Olympic Games; Pro record of 56-5-0 with 37 KOs in 61 fights.

1960

Date	Opponent (location)	Result
Oct. 29	Tunney Hunsaker, Louisville	Wu 6
Dec. 27	Herb Siler, Miami Beach	TKO 4

1961

Date	Opponent (location)	Result
Jan. 17	Tony Esperti, Miami Beach	TKO 3
Feb. 7	Jim Robinson, Miami Beach	TKO 1
Feb. 21	Donnie Fleeman, Miami Beach	TKO 7
Apr. 19	Lamar Clark, Louisville	KO 2
June 26	Duke Sabedong, Las Vegas	Wu 10
July 22	Alonzo Johnson, Louisville	Wu 10
Oct. 7	Alex Miteff, Louisville	TKO 6
Nov. 29	Willi Besmanoff, Louisville	TKO 7

1962

Date	Opponent (location)	Result
Feb. 10	Sonny Banks, New York	TKO 4
Feb. 28	Don Warner, Miami Beach	TKO 4
Apr. 23	George Logan, Los Angeles	TKO 4
May 19	Billy Daniels, Los Angeles	TKO 7
July 20	Alejandro Lavorante, Los Angeles	KO 5
Nov. 15	Archie Moore, Los Angeles	KO 4

1963

Date	Opponent (location)	Result
Jan. 24	Charlie Powell, Pittsburgh	KO 3
Mar. 13	Doug Jones, New York	Wu 10
June 18	Henry Cooper, London	TKO 5

1964

Date	Opponent (location)	Result
Feb. 25	Sonny Liston, Miami Beach **(won World Heavyweight title)** After the fight, Clay announces he is a member of the Black Muslim religious sect and has changed his name to Muhammad Ali.	TKO 7

1965

Date	Opponent (location)	Result
May 25	Sonny Liston, Lewiston, Me.	KO 1
Nov. 22	Floyd Patterson, Las Vegas	TKO 12

1966

Date	Opponent (location)	Result
Mar. 29	George Chuvalo, Toronto	Wu 15
May 21	Henry Cooper, London	TKO 6
Aug. 6	Brian London, London	KO 3
Sept.10	Karl Mildenberger, Frankfurt	TKO 12
Nov. 12	Cleveland Williams, Houston	TKO 3

1967

Date	Opponent (location)	Result
Feb. 6	Ernie Terrell, Houston	Wu 15
Mar. 22	Zora Folley, New York	KO 7
Apr. 28	Refuses induction into U.S. Army and is stripped of world title by WBA and most state commissions the next day.	
June 20	Found guilty of draft evasion in Houston; fined $10,000 and sentenced to 5 years; remains free pending appeals, but is barred from the ring.	

1968-69

(Inactive)

1970

Date	Opponent (location)	Result
Feb. 3	Announces retirement.	
Oct. 26	Jerry Quarry, Atlanta	TKO 3
Dec. 7	Oscar Bonavena, New York	TKO 15

1971

Date	Opponent (location)	Result
Mar. 8	Joe Frazier, New York **(for World Heavyweight title)**	Lu 15
June 28	U.S. Supreme Court reverses Ali's 1967 conviction saying he had been drafted improperly.	
July 26	Jimmy Ellis, Houston **(won vacant NABF Heavyweight title)**	TKO 12
Nov. 17	Buster Mathis, Houston	Wu 12
Dec. 26	Jurgen Blin, Zurich	KO 7

1972

Date	Opponent (location)	Result
Apr. 1	Mac Foster, Tokyo	Wu 15
May 1	George Chuvalo, Vancouver	Wu 12
June 27	Jerry Quarry, Las Vegas	TKO 7
July 19	Al (Blue) Lewis, Dublin, Ire.	TKO 11
Sept.20	Floyd Patterson, New York	TKO 7
Nov. 21	Bob Foster, Stateline, Nev.	TKO 8

1973

Date	Opponent (location)	Result
Feb. 14	Joe Bugner, Las Vegas	Wu 12
Mar. 31	Ken Norton, San Diego **(lost NABF Heavyweight title)**	Ls 12
Sept.10	Ken Norton, Inglewood, Calif. **(regained NABF Heavyweight title)**	Ws 12
Oct. 20	Rudi Lubbers, Jakarta, Indonesia	Wu 12

1974

Date	Opponent (location)	Result
Jan. 28	Joe Frazier, New York	Wu 12
Oct. 30	George Foreman, Kinshasa, Zaire **(regained World Heavyweight title)**	KO 8

1975

Date	Opponent (location)	Result
Mar. 24	Chuck Wepner, Cleveland	TKO 15
May 16	Ron Lyle, Las Vegas	TKO 11
June 30	Joe Bugner, Kuala Lumpur, Malaysia	Wu 15
Sept.30	Joe Frazier, Manila	TKO 14

1976

Date	Opponent (location)	Result
Feb. 20	Jean-Pierre Coopman, San Juan	KO 5
Apr. 30	Jimmy Young, Landover, Md	Wu 15
May 24	Richard Dunn, Munich	TKO 5
Sept.28	Ken Norton, New York	Wu 15

1977

Date	Opponent (location)	Result
May 16	Alfredo Evangelista, Landover	Wu 15
Sept.29	Earnie Shavers, New York	Wu 15

1978

Date	Opponent (location)	Result
Feb. 15	Leon Spinks, Las Vegas **(lost World Heavyweight title)**	Ls 15
Sept.15	Leon Spinks, New Orleans **(regained World Heavyweight title)**	Wu 15

1979

Date	
June 27	Announces retirement.

1980

Date	Opponent (location)	Result
Oct. 2	Larry Holmes, Las Vegas	TKO by 11

1981

Date	Opponent (location)	Result
Dec. 11	Trevor Berbick, Nassau (retires after fight)	Lu 10

Foreman and Frazier

The career pro records of George Foreman and Joe Frazier as of Oct. 21, 1996

George Foreman

Born: Jan. 10, 1949 in Marshall, Tex.
Pro record: 74-4-0, 68 KO

No	Date	Opponent, location	Result
1	6/23/69	Don Waldhelm, New York	KO 3
2	7/1/69	Fred Ashew, Houston	KO 1
3	7/14/69	Sylvester Dullaire, Wash., D.C.	KO 1
4	8/18/69	Chuck Wepner, New York	TKO 3
5	9/18/69	John Carroll, Seattle	KO 1
6	9/23/69	Cookie Wallace, Houston	KO 2
7	10/7/69	Vernon Clay, Houston	TKO 2
8	10/31/69	Roberto Davila, New York	Wu 8
9	11/5/69	Leo Peterson, Scranton	KO 4
10	11/18/69	Max Martinez, Houston	KO 2
11	12/6/69	Bob Hazelton, Las Vegas	KO 1
12	12/16/69	Levi Forte, Miami Beach	Wu 10
13	12/18/69	Gary Wilder, Seattle	TKO 1
14	1/6/70	Charley Polite, Houston	KO 4
15	1/26/70	Jack O'Halloran, New York	KO 5
16	2/16/70	Gregorio Peralta, New York	Wu 10
17	3/31/70	Rufus Brassell, Houston	KO 1
18	4/17/70	James J. Woody, New York	TKO 3
19	4/29/70	Aaron Easting, Cleveland	TKO 4
20	5/16/70	George Johnson, Inglewood	TKO 7
21	7/20/70	Roger Russell, Philadelphia	TKO 1
22	8/4/70	George Chuvalo, New York	TKO 3
23	11/3/70	Lou Bailey, Oklahoma City	KO 3
24	11/18/70	Boone Kirkman, New York	TKO 2
25	12/19/70	Mel Turnbow, Seattle	TKO 1
26	2/8/71	Charlie Boston, St. Paul, Minn.	KO 1
27	4/3/71	Stanford Harris, Lake Geneva	KO 2
28	5/10/71	Gregorio Peralta, Oakland	TKO 10
29	9/14/91	Vic Scott, El Paso	KO 1
30	9/21/71	Leroy Caldwell, Beaumont, Tex.	KO 2
31	10/7/71	Ollie Wilson, San Antonio	TKO 2
32	10/29/71	Luis F. Pires, New York	TKO 5
33	2/29/72	Murphy Goodwin, Austin, Tex.	KO 2
34	3/7/72	Clarence Boone, Beaumont, Tex.	TKO 2
35	4/10/72	Ted Gullick, Inglewood	KO 2
36	5/11/72	Miguel A. Paez, Oakland	KO 2
37	10/10/72	Terry Sorrels, Salt Lake City	KO 2
38	1/22/73	Joe Frazier, Kingston, Jamaica	TKO 2
		(won World Heavyweight title)	
39	9/1/73	Jose Roman, Tokyo	KO 1
40	3/26/74	Ken Norton, Caracus, Venezuela	TKO 2
41	10/30/74	Muhammad Ali, Kinshasa, Zaire	KO by 8
		(lost World Heavyweight title)	
42	1/24/76	Ron Lyle, Las Vegas	KO 5
43	6/15/76	Joe Frazier, Uniondale, N.Y.	TKO 5
44	8/14/76	Scott Le Doux, Utica, N.Y.	KO 3
45	10/15/76	Dino Denis, Hollywood, Fla.	TKO 4
46	1/22/77	Pedro Agosto, Pensacola, Fla.	TKO 4
47	3/17/77	Jimmy Young, Hato Rey, P.R.	Lu 12
		(retired after fight)	
48	3/9/87	Steve Zouski, Sacramento	TKO 4
		(first fight of comeback)	
49	7/9/87	Charles Hostetter, Oakland	KO 3
50	9/15/87	Bobby Crabree, Springfield, Mo.	TKO 6
51	11/21/87	Tim Anderson, Orlando	TKO 4
52	12/18/87	Rocky Sekorski, Las Vegas	TKO 3
53	1/23/88	Tom Trimm, Orlando	TKO 1
54	2/5/88	Guido Trane, Las Vegas	TKO 5
55	3/19/88	Dwight Qawi, Las Vegas	TKO 7
56	5/21/88	Frank Williams, Anchorage	KO 3
57	6/26/88	Carlos Hernandez, Atlantic City	TKO 4
58	8/25/88	Ladislao Mijangos, Ft. Myers	TKO 2
59	9/10/88	Bobby Hitz, Auburn Hills, Mich.	KO 1
60	10/27/88	Tony Fulilangi, Marshall, Tex.	TKO 2
61	12/28/88	David Jaco, Bakersfield, Calif.	KO 1
62	1/26/89	Mark Young, Rochester, N.Y.	TKO 7
63	2/16/89	Manuel de Almeida, Orlando	TKO 3
64	4/30/89	J.B. Williamson, Galveston, Tex.	TKO 5
65	6/1/89	Bert Cooper, Phoenix	TKO 3
66	7/20/89	Everett Martin, Tucson	Wu 10
67	1/15/90	Gerry Cooney, Atlantic City	KO 2
68	4/17/90	Mike Jameson, Stateline, Nev.	TKO 4
69	6/16/90	Adilson Rodrigues, Las Vegas	KO 2
70	7/31/90	Ken Lakusta, Edmonton	KO 3
71	9/25/90	Terry Anderson, Millwall, England	KO 1
72	4/19/91	Evander Holyfield, Atlantic City	Lu 12
		(for World Heavyweight title)	
73	12/7/91	Jimmy Ellis, Reno, Nev.	TKO 3
74	4/11/92	Alex Stewart, Las Vegas	Wm 10
75	1/16/93	Pierre Coetzer, Reno, Nev.	TKO 8
76	6/7/93	Tommy Morrison, Las Vegas	Lu 12
77	11/5/94	Michael Moorer, Las Vegas	KO 10
		(won WBA/IBF Heavyweight titles)	
78	4/22/95	Axel Schulz, Las Vegas	Wm 12

Joe Frazier

Born: Jan. 12, 1944 in Beaufort, S.C.
Pro record: 32-4-1, 27 KO

No	Date	Opponent	Result
1	8/16/65	Woody Gross	TKO 1
2	9/20/65	Michael Bruce	KO 3
3	9/28/65	Ray Staples	KO 2
4	11/11/65	Abe Davis	KO 1
5	1/17/66	Mel Turnbow	KO 1
6	3/4/66	Dick Wipperman	TKO 5
7	4/4/66	Charley Polite	TKO 2
8	4/28/66	Don Smith	KO 3
9	5/19/66	Chuck Leslie	KO 3
10	5/26/66	Memphis Jones	KO 1
11	7/25/66	Billy Daniels	TKO 6
12	9/21/66	Oscar Bonavena	Wu 10
13	11/21/66	Eddie Machen	TKO 10
14	2/21/67	Doug Jones	KO 5
15	4/11/67	Jeff Davis	KO 5
16	5/4/67	George Johnson	Wu 10
17	7/19/67	George Chuvalo	TKO 4
18	10/17/67	Tony Doyle	TKO 2
19	12/18/67	Marion Connors	KO 3
20	3/4/68	Buster Mathis	KO 11
21	6/24/68	Manuel Ramos	TKO 2
22	12/10/68	Oscar Bonavena	Wu 15
23	4/22/69	Dave Zyglewicz	KO 1
24	6/23/69	Jerry Quarry	TKO 7
25	2/6/70	Jimmy Ellis	TKO 5
		(won World Heavyweight title)	
26	11/18/70	Bob Foster	KO 2
27	3/8/71	Muhammad Ali	Wu 15
28	1/15/72	Terry Daniels	TKO 4
29	5/25/72	Ron Stander	TKO 5
30	1/22/73	George Foreman	TKO by 2
		(lost World Heavyweight title)	
31	7/2/73	Joe Bugner	Wu 12
32	1/28/74	Muhammad Ali	Lu 12
33	6/17/74	Jerry Quarry	TKO 5
34	4/1/75	Jimmy Ellis	TKO 9
35	9/30/75	Muhammad Ali	TKO by 14
		(for World Heavyweight title)	
36	6/15/76	George Foreman	KO by 5
37	3/12/81	Floyd Cummings	Draw 10

Major Titleholders

Note the following sanctioning body abbreviations: NBA (National Boxing Association), WBA (World Boxing Association), WBC (World Boxing Council), GBR (Great Britain), IBF (International Boxing Federation), plus other national and state commissions. Fighters who retired as champion are indicated by (*) and champions who abandoned or relinquished their titles are indicated by (†).

Heavyweights

Widely accepted champions in CAPITAL letters. Current champions (as of Oct. 14) in **bold** type. Note that Muhammad Ali was stripped of his world title in 1967 after refusing induction into the Army (see page 900). George Foreman was stripped of his WBA and IBF titles in 1995, but remained active as consensus champion (see page 889).

Champion	Held Title
JOHN L. SULLIVAN	1885-92
JAMES J. CORBETT	1892-97
BOB FITZSIMMONS	1897-99
JAMES J. JEFFRIES	1899-1905*
MARVIN HART	1905-06
TOMMY BURNS	1906-08
JACK JOHNSON	1908-15
JESS WILLARD	1915-19
JACK DEMPSEY	1919-26
GENE TUNNEY	1926-28*
MAX SCHMELING	1930-32
JACK SHARKEY	1932-33
PRIMO CARNERA	1933-34
MAX BAER	1934-35
JAMES J. BRADDOCK	1935-37
JOE LOUIS	1937-49*
EZZARD CHARLES	1949-51
JERSEY JOE WALCOTT	1951-52
ROCKY MARCIANO	1952-56*
FLOYD PATTERSON	1956-59
INGEMAR JOHANSSON	1959-60
FLOYD PATTERSON	1960-62
SONNY LISTON	1962-64
CASSIUS CLAY (MUHAMMAD ALI)	1964-70
Ernie Terrell (WBA)	1965-67
Joe Frazier (NY)	1968-70
Jimmy Ellis (WBA)	1968-70
JOE FRAZIER	1970-73
GEORGE FOREMAN	1973-74
MUHAMMAD ALI	1974-78
LEON SPINKS	1978
Ken Norton (WBC)	1978
Larry Holmes (WBC)	1978-80
MUHAMMAD ALI	1978-79*
John Tate (WBA)	1979-80
Mike Weaver (WBA)	1980-82
LARRY HOLMES	1980-85
Michael Dokes (WBA)	1982-83
Gerrie Coetzee (WBA)	1983-84
Tim Witherspoon (WBC)	1984
Pinklon Thomas (WBC)	1984-86
Greg Page (WBA)	1984-85
MICHAEL SPINKS	1985-87
Tim Witherspoon (WBA)	1986
Trevor Berbick (WBC)	1986
Mike Tyson (WBC)	1986-87
James (Bonecrusher) Smith (WBA)	1986-87
Tony Tucker (IBF)	1987
MIKE TYSON (WBC, WBA, IBF)	1987-90
BUSTER DOUGLAS (WBC, WBA, IBF)	1990
EVANDER HOLYFIELD (WBC, WBA, IBF)	1990-92
RIDDICK BOWE (WBA, IBF)	1992-93
Lennox Lewis (WBC)	1992-94
EVANDER HOLYFIELD (WBA, IBF)	1993-94
MICHAEL MOORER (WBA, IBF)	1994
Oliver McCall (WBC)	1994-95
GEORGE FOREMAN (WBA, IBF)	1994-95
Bruce Seldon (WBA)	1995-96
GEORGE FOREMAN	1995-96
Frank Bruno (WBC)	1995-96
Mike Tyson (WBC)	1996
Michael Moorer (IBF)	1996—
Mike Tyson (WBA)	1996—

Note: John L. Sullivan held the Bare Knuckle championship from 1882-85.

Light Heavyweights

Widely accepted champions in CAPITAL letters. Current champions in **bold** type.

Champion	Held Title
JACK ROOT	1903
GEORGE GARDNER	1903
BOB FITZSIMMONS	1903-05
PHILADELPHIA JACK O'BRIEN	1905-12*
JACK DILLON	1914-16
BATTLING LEVINSKY	1916-20
GEORGES CARPENTIER	1920-22
BATTLING SIKI	1922-23
MIKE McTIGUE	1923-25
PAUL BERLENBACH	1925-26
JACK DELANEY	1926-27†
Jimmy Slattery (NBA)	1927
TOMMY LOUGHRAN	1927-29
JIMMY SLATTERY	1930
MAXIE ROSENBLOOM	1930-34
George Nichols (NBA)	1932
Bob Godwin (NBA)	1933
BOB OLIN	1934-35
JOHN HENRY LEWIS	1935-38
MELIO BETTINA (NY)	1939
Len Harvey (GBR)	1939-42
BILLY CONN	1939-40†
ANTON CHRISTOFORIDIS (NBA)	1941
GUS LESNEVICH	1941-48
Freddie Mills (GBR)	1942-46
FREDDIE MILLS	1948-50
JOEY MAXIM	1950-52
ARCHIE MOORE	1952-62

Major Titleholders (Cont.)

Light Heavyweights

Champion	Held Title
Harold Johnson (NBA)	1961
HAROLD JOHNSON	1962-63
WILLIE PASTRANO	1963-65
Eddie Cotton (Mich.)	1963-64
JOSE TORRES	1965-66
DICK TIGER	1966-68
BOB FOSTER	1968-74*
Vicente Rondon (WBA)	1971-72
John Conteh (WBC)	1974-77
Victor Galindez (WBA)	1974-78
Miguel A. Cuello (WBC)	1977-78
Mate Parlov (WBC)	1978
Mike Rossman (WBA)	1978-79
Marvin Johnson (WBC)	1978-79
Matthew (Franklin) Saad Muhammad (WBC)	1979-81
Marvin Johnson (WBA)	1979-80
Eddie (Gregory) Mustapha Muhammad (WBA)	1980-81
Michael Spinks (WBA)	1981-83
Dwight (Braxton) Muhammad Qawi (WBC)	1981-83
MICHAEL SPINKS	1983-85†
J.B.Williamson (WBC)	1985-86
Slobodan Kacar (IBF)	1985-86
Marvin Johnson (WBA)	1986-87
Dennis Andries (WBC)	1986-87
Bobby Czyz (IBF)	1986-87
Leslie Stewart (WBA)	1987
Virgil Hill (WBA)	1987-91
Prince Charles Williams (IBF)	1987-93
Thomas Hearns (WBC)	1987
Donny Lalonde (WBC)	1987-88
Sugar Ray Leonard (WBC)	1988
Dennis Andries (WBC)	1989
Jeff Harding (WBC)	1989-90
Dennis Andries (WBC)	1990-91
Jeff Harding (WBC)	1991-94
Thomas Hearns (WBA)	1991-92
Iran Barkley (WBA)	1992†
Virgil Hill (WBA)	1992—
Henry Maske (IBF)	1993—
Mike McCallum (WBC)	1994-95
Fabrice Tiozzo (WBC)	1995—

Middleweights

Widely accepted champions in CAPITAL letters. Current champions in **bold** type.

Champion	Held Title
JACK (NONPAREIL) DEMPSEY	1884-91
BOB FITZSIMMONS	1891-97
CHARLES (KID) McCOY	1897-98
TOMMY RYAN	1898-1907
STANLEY KETCHEL	1908
BILLY PAPKE	1908
STANLEY KETCHEL	1908-10
FRANK KLAUS	1913
GEORGE CHIP	1913-14
AL McCOY	1914-17†
Jeff Smith (AUS)	1914
Mick King (AUS)	1914
Jeff Smith (AUS)	1914-15
Lee Darcy (AUS)	1915-17
MIKE O'DOWD	1917-20
JOHNNY WILSON	1920-23
Wm. Bryan Downey (Ohio)	1921-22
Dave Rosenberg (NY)	1922
Jock Malone (Ohio)	1922-23
Mike O'Dowd (NY)	1922
Lou Bogash (NY)	1923
HARRY GREB	1923-26
TIGER FLOWERS	1926
MICKEY WALKER	1926-31†
GORILLA JONES	1931-32
MARCEL THIL	1932-37
Ben Jeby (NY)	1932-33
Lou Brouillard (NBA, NY)	1933
Vince Dundee (NBA, NY)	1933-34
Teddy Yarosz (NBA, NY)	1934-35
Babe Risko (NBA, NY)	1935-36
Freddie Steele (NBA, NY)	1936-38
FRED APOSTOLI	1937-39
Al Hostak (NBA)	1938
Solly Krieger (NBA)	1938-39
Al Hostak (NBA)	1939-40
CEFERINO GARCIA	1939-40
KEN OVERLIN	1940-41
Tony Zale (NBA)	1940-41
BILLY SOOSE	1941
TONY ZALE	1941-47
ROCKY GRAZIANO	1947-48
TONY ZALE	1948
MARCEL CERDAN	1948-49
JAKE LA MOTTA	1949-51
SUGAR RAY ROBINSON	1951
RANDY TURPIN	1951
SUGAR RAY ROBINSON	1951-52*
CARL (BOBO) OLSON	1953-55
SUGAR RAY ROBINSON	1955-57
GENE FULLMER	1957
SUGAR RAY ROBINSON	1957
CARMEN BASILIO	1957-58
SUGAR RAY ROBINSON	1958-60
Gene Fullmer (NBA)	1959-62
PAUL PENDER	1960-61
TERRY DOWNES	1961-62
PAUL PENDER	1962-63
Dick Tiger (WBA)	1962-63
DICK TIGER	1963
JOEY GIARDELLO	1963-65
DICK TIGER	1965-66
EMILE GRIFFITH	1966-67
NINO BENVENUTI	1967
EMILE GRIFFITH	1967-68
NINO BENVENUTI	1968-70
CARLOS MONZON	1970-77*
Rodrigo Valdez (WBC)	1974-76
RODRIGO VALDEZ	1977-78
HUGO CORRO	1978-79
VITO ANTUOFERMO	1979-80
ALAN MINTER	1980
MARVELOUS MARVIN HAGLER	1980-87
SUGAR RAY LEONARD	1987
Frank Tate (IBF)	1987-88
Sumbu Kalambay (WBA)	1987-89
Thomas Hearns (WBC)	1987-88
Iran Barkley (WBC)	1988-89
Michael Nunn(IBF)	1988-91
Roberto Duran (WBC)	1989-90*
Mike McCallum (WBA)	1989-91
Julian Jackson (WBC)	1990-93
James Toney (IBF)	1991-93†
Reggie Johnson (WBA)	1992-93

Roy Jones Jr. (IBF)	1993-94†
Gerald McClellan (WBC)	1993-95†
John David Jackson (WBA)	1993-94
Jorge Castro (WBA)	1994-95
Julian Jackson (WBC)	1995
Bernard Hopkins (IBF)	1995—
Quincy Taylor (WBC)	1995-96
Shinji Takehara (WBA)	1995-96
William Joppy (WBA)	1996—
Keith Homes (WBC)	1996—

Welterweights

Widely accepted champions in CAPITAL letters. Current champions in **bold** type.

Champion	Held Title
PADDY DUFFY	1888-90
MYSTERIOUS BILLY SMITH	1892-94
TOMMY RYAN	1894-98
MYSTERIOUS BILLY SMITH	1898-1900
MATTY MATTHEWS	1900
EDDIE CONNOLLY	1900
JAMES (RUBE) FERNS	1900
MATTY MATHEWS	1900-01
JAMES (RUBE) FERNS	1901
JOE WALCOTT	1901-04
THE DIXIE KID	1904-05
HONEY MELLODY	1906-07
MIKE (TWIN) SULLIVAN	1907-08†
Harry Lewis	1908-11
Jimmy Gardner	1908
Jimmy Clabby	1910-11
WALDEMAR HOLBERG	1914
TOM McCORMICK	1914
MATT WELLS	1914-15
MIKE GLOVER	1915
JACK BRITTON	1915
TED (KID) LEWIS	1915-16
JACK BRITTON	1916-17
TED (KID) LEWIS	1917-19
JACK BRITTON	1919-22
MICKEY WALKER	1922-26
PETE LATZO	1926-27
JOE DUNDEE	1927-29
JACKIE FIELDS	1929-30
YOUNG JACK THOMPSON	1930
TOMMY FREEMAN	1930-31
YOUNG JACK THOMPSON	1931
LOU BROUILLARD	1931-32
JACKIE FIELDS	1932-33
YOUNG CORBETT III	1933
JIMMY McLARNIN	1933-34
BARNEY ROSS	1934
JIMMY McLARNIN	1934-35
BARNEY ROSS	1935-38
HENRY ARMSTRONG	1938-40
FRITZIE ZIVIC	1940-41
Izzy Jannazzo (Md.)	1940-41
FREDDIE (RED) COCHRANE	1941-46
MARTY SERVO	1946*
SUGAR RAY ROBINSON	1946-51†
Johnny Bratton	1951
KID GAVILAN	1951-54
JOHNNY SAXTON	1954-55
TONY DeMARCO	1955
CARMEN BASILIO	1955-56
JOHNNY SAXTON	1956
CARMEN BASILIO	1956-57†
VIRGIL AKINS	1958
DON JORDAN	1958-60
BENNY (KID) PARET	1960-61
EMILE GRIFFITH	1961
BENNY (KID) PARET	1961-62
EMILE GRIFFITH	1962-63
LUIS RODRIGUEZ	1963
EMILE GRIFFITH	1963-66†
Charlie Shipes (Calif.)	1966-67
CURTIS COKES	1966-69
JOSE NAPOLES	1969-70
BILLY BACKUS	1970-71
JOSE NAPOLES	1971-75
Hedgemon Lewis (NY)	1972-73
Angel Espada (WBA)	1975-76
JOHN H. STRACEY	1975-76
CARLOS PALOMINO	1976-79
Pipino Cuevas (WBA)	1976-80
WILFREDO BENITEZ	1979
SUGAR RAY LEONARD	1979-80
ROBERTO DURAN	1980
Thomas Hearns (WBA)	1980-81
SUGAR RAY LEONARD	1980-82
Donald Curry (WBA)	1983-85
Milton McCrory (WBC)	1983-85
DONALD CURRY	1985-86
LLOYD HONEYGHAN	1986-87
JORGE VACA (WBC)	1987-88
LLOYD HONEYGHAN (WBC)	1988-89
Mark Breland (WBA)	1987
Marlon Starling (WBA)	1987-88
Tomas Molinares (WBA)	1988-89
Simon Brown (IBF)	1988-91
Mark Breland (WBA)	1989-90
MARLON STARLING (WBC)	1989-90
Aaron Davis (WBA)	1990-91
Maurice Blocker (WBC)	1990-91
Meldrick Taylor (WBA)	1991-92
Simon Brown (WBC)	1991
Maurice Blocker (IBF)	1991-93
Buddy McGirt (WBC)	1991-93
Crisanto Espana (WBA)	1992-94
Pernell Whitaker (WBC)	1993—
Felix Trinidad (IBF)	1993—
Ike Quartey (WBA)	1994—

Lightweights

Widely accepted champions in CAPITAL letters. Current champions in **bold** type.

Champion	Held Title
JACK McAULIFFE	1886-94
GEORGE (KID) LAVIGNE	1896-99
FRANK ERNE	1899-02
JOE GANS	1902-04
JIMMY BRITT	1904-05
BATTLING NELSON	1905-06
JOE GANS	1906-08
BATTLING NELSON	1908-10
AD WOLGAST	1910-12
WILLIE RITCHIE	1912-14
FREDDIE WELSH	1915-17
BENNY LEONARD	1917-25*
JIMMY GOODRICH	1925
ROCKY KANSAS	1925-26
SAMMY MANDELL	1926-30
AL SINGER	1930
TONY CANZONERI	1930-33
BARNEY ROSS	1933-35†
TONY CANZONERI	1935-36
LOU AMBERS	1936-38

Major Titleholders (Cont.)

Lightweights

Champion	Held Title
HENRY ARMSTRONG	1938-39
LOU AMBERS	1939-40
Sammy Angott (NBA)	1940-41
LEW JENKINS	1940-41
SAMMY ANGOTT	1941-42
Beau Jack (NY)	1942-43
Slugger White (Md.)	1943
Bob Montgomery (NY)	1943
Sammy Angott (NBA)	1943-44
Beau Jack (NY)	1943-44
Bob Montgomery (NY)	1944-47
Juan Zurita (NBA)	1944-45
IKE WILLIAMS	1947-51
JAMES CARTER	1951-52
LAURO SALAS	1952
JAMES CARTER	1952-54
PADDY DeMARCO	1954
JAMES CARTER	1954-55
WALLACE (BUD) SMITH	1955-56
JOE BROWN	1956-62
CARLOS ORTIZ	1962-65
Kenny Lane (Mich.)	1963-64
ISMAEL LAGUNA	1965
CARLOS ORTIZ	1965-68
CARLOS TEO CRUZ	1968-69
MANDO RAMOS	1969-70
ISMAEL LAGUNA	1970
KEN BUCHANAN	1970-72
Pedro Carrasco (WBC)	1971-72
Mando Ramos (WBC)	1972
ROBERTO DURAN	1972-79†
Chango Carmona (WBC)	1972
Rodolfo Gonzalez (WBC)	1972-74
Ishimatsu Suzuki (WBC)	1974-76
Esteban De Jesus (WBC)	1976-78
Jim Watt (WBC)	1979-81
Ernesto Espana (WBA)	1979-80
Hilmer Kenty (WBA)	1980-81
Sean O'Grady (WBA,WAA)	1981
Alexis Arguello (WBC)	1981-82
Claude Noel (WBA)	1981
Andrew Ganigan (WAA)	1981-82
Arturo Frias (WBA)	1981-82
Ray Mancini (WBA)	1982-84
ALEXIS ARGUELLO	1982-83
Edwin Rosario (WBC)	1983-84
Choo Choo Brown (IBF)	1984
Livingstone Bramble (WBA)	1984-86
Harry Arroyo (IBF)	1984-85
Jose Luis Ramirez (WBC)	1984-85
Jimmy Paul (IBF)	1985-86
Hector Camacho (WBC)	1985-86
Edwin Rosario (WBA)	1986-87
Greg Haugen (IBF)	1986-87
Julio Cesar Chavez (WBA)	1987-88
Jose Luis Ramirez (WBC)	1987-88
JULIO CESAR CHAVEZ (WBC,WBA)	1988-89
Vinny Pazienza (IBF)	1987-88
Greg Haugen (IBF)	1988-89
Pernell Whitaker (IBF,WBC)	1989-90
Edwin Rosario (WBA)	1989-90
Juan Nazario (WBA)	1990
PERNELL WHITAKER (IBF, WBC, WBA)	1990-92†
Joey Gamache (WBA)	1992
Miguel A. Gonzalez (WBC)	1992-96
Tony Lopez (WBA)	1992-93
Dingaan Thobela (WBA)	1993
Fred Pendleton (IBF)	1993-94
Gussie Nazarov (WBA)	1993—
Rafael Ruelas (IBF)	1994-95
Oscar De La Hoya (IBF)	1995†
Phillip Holiday (IBF)	1995—
Jean-Baptiste Mendez (WBC)	1996—

Featherweights

Widely accepted champions in CAPITAL letters. Current champions in **bold** type.

Champion	Held Title
TORPEDO BILLY MURPHY	1890
YOUNG GRIFFO	1890-92
GEORGE DIXON	1892-97
SOLLY SMITH	1897-98
Ben Jordan (GBR)	1898-99
Eddie Santry (GBR)	1899-1900
DAVE SULLIVAN	1898
GEORGE DIXON	1898-1900
TERRY McGOVERN	1900-01
YOUNG CORBETT II	1901-04
JIMMY BRITT	1904
ABE ATTELL	1904
BROOKLYN TOMMY SULLIVAN	1904-05
ABE ATTELL	1906-12
JOHNNY KILBANE	1912-23
Jem Driscoll (GBR)	1912-13
EUGENE CRIQUI	1923
JOHNNY DUNDEE	1923-24†
LOUIS (KID) KAPLAN	1925-26†
Dick Finnegan (Mass.)	1926-27
BENNY BASS	1927-28
TONY CANZONERI	1928
ANDRE ROUTIS	1928-29
BATTLING BATTALINO	1929-32†
Tommy Paul (NBA)	1932-33
Kid Chocolate (NY)	1932-33
Freddie Miller (NBA)	1933-36
Baby Arizmendi (MEX)	1935-36
Mike Belloise (NY)	1936-37
Petey Sarron (NBA)	1936-37
HENRY ARMSTRONG	1937-38†
Joey Archibald (NY)	1938-39
Leo Rodak (NBA)	1938-39
JOEY ARCHIBALD	1939-40
Petey Scalzo (NBA)	1940-41
Jimmy Perrin (La.)	1940-41
HARRY JEFFRA	1940-41
JOEY ARCHIBALD	1941
Richie Lemos (NBA)	1941
CHALKY WRIGHT	1941-42
Jackie Wilson (NBA)	1941-43
WILLIE PEP	1942-48
Jackie Callura (NBA)	1943
Phil Terranova (NBA)	1943-44
Sal Bartolo (NBA)	1944-46
SANDY SADDLER	1948-49
WILLIE PEP	1949-50
SANDY SADDLER	1950-57*
HOGAN (KID) BASSEY	1957-59
DAVEY MOORE	1959-63
ULTIMINIO (SUGAR) RAMOS	1963-64
VICENTE SALDIVAR	1964-67*
Howard Winstone (GBR)	1968
Raul Rojas (WBA)	1968

Jose Legra (WBC)	1968-69
Shozo Saijyo (WBA)	1968-71
JOHNNY FAMECHON (WBC)	1969-70
VICENTE SALDIVAR (WBC)	1970
KUNIAKI SHIBATA (WBC)	1970-72
Antonio Gomez (WBA)	1971-72
CLEMENTE SANCHEZ (WBC)	1972
Ernesto Marcel (WBA)	1972-74
JOSE LEGRA (WBC)	1972-73
EDER JOFRE (WBC)	1973-74
Ruben Olivares (WBA)	1974
Bobby Chacon (WBC)	1974-75
ALEXIS ARGUELLO (WBA)	1974-76†
Ruben Olivares (WBC)	1975
David (Poison) Kotey (WBC)	1975-76
DANNY (LITTLE RED) LOPEZ (WBC)	1976-80
Rafael Ortega (WBA)	1977
Cecilio Lastra (WBA)	1977-78
Eusebio Pedroza (WBA)	1978-85
SALVADOR SANCHEZ (WBC)	1980-82
Juan LaPorte (WBC)	1982-84
Wilfredo Gomez (WBC)	1984
Min-Keun Oh (IBF)	1984-85
Azumah Nelson (WBC)	1984-88
Barry McGuigan (WBA)	1985-86
Ki-Young Chung (IBF)	1985-86
Steve Cruz (WBA)	1986-87
Antonio Rivera (IBF)	1986-88
Antonio Esparragoza (WBA)	1987-91
Calvin Grove (IBF)	1988
Jorge Paez (IBF)	1988-91†
Jeff Fenech (WBC)	1988-90†
Marcos Villasana (WBC)	1990-91
Yung-Kyun Park (WBA)	1991-93
Troy Dorsey (IBF)	1991
Manuel Medina (IBF)	1991-93
Paul Hodkinson (WBC)	1991-93
Tom Johnson (IBF)	1993—
Goyo Vargas (WBC)	1993
Kevin Kelley (WBC)	1993-95
Eloy Rojas (WBA)	1993-96
Alejandro Gonzalez (WBC)	1995
Manuel Medina (WBC)	1995-96
Wilfredo Vasquez (WBA)	1996—
Luisito Espinoza (WBC)	1995—

Bantamweights

Widely accepted champions in CAPITAL letters. Current champions in **bold** type.

Champion	Held Title
TOMMY (SPIDER) KELLY	1887
HUGHEY BOYLE	1887-88
TOMMY (SPIDER) KELLY	1889
CHAPPIE MORAN	1889-90
Tommy (Spider) Kelly	1890-92
GEORGE DIXON	1890-91
Billy Plummer	1892-95
JIMMY BARRY	1894-99
Pedlar Palmer	1895-99
TERRY McGOVERN	1899-1900
HARRY HARRIS	1901-02
DANNY DOUGHERTY	1900-01
HARRY FORBES	1901-03
FRANKIE NEIL	1903-04
JOE BOWKER	1904-05
JIMMY WALSH	1905-06†
OWEN MORAN	1907-08
MONTE ATTELL	1909-10
FRANKIE CONLEY	1910-11
JOHNNY COULON	1911-14
Digger Stanley (GBR)	1910-12
Charles Ledoux (GBR)	1912-13
Eddie Campi (GBR)	1913-14
KID WILLIAMS	1914-17
Johnny Ertle	1915-18
PETE HERMAN	1917-20
Memphis Pal Moore	1918-19
JOE LYNCH	1920-21
PETE HERMAN	1921
JOHNNY BUFF	1921-22
JOE LYNCH	1922-24
ABE GOLDSTEIN	1924
CANNONBALL EDDIE MARTIN	1924-25
PHIL ROSENBERG	1925-27
Teddy Baldock (GBR)	1927
BUD TAYLOR (NBA)	1927-28†
Willie Smith (GBR)	1927-28
Bushy Graham (NY)	1928-29
PANAMA AL BROWN	1929-35
Sixto Escobar (NBA)	1934-35
BALTAZAR SANGCHILLI	1935-36
Lou Salica (NBA)	1935
Sixto Escobar (NBA)	1935-36
TONY MARINO	1936
SIXTO ESCOBAR	1936-37
HARRY JEFFRA	1937-38
SIXTO ESCOBAR	1938-39*
Georgie Pace (NBA)	1939-40
LOU SALICA	1940-42
MANUEL ORTIZ	1942-47
HAROLD DADE	1947
MANUEL ORTIZ	1947-50
VIC TOWEEL	1950-52
JIMMY CARRUTHERS	1952-54*
ROBERT COHEN	1954-56
Raul Macias (NBA)	1955-57
MARIO D'AGATA	1956-57
ALPHONSE HALIMI	1957-59
JOE BECERRA	1959-60*
Johnny Caldwell (EBU)	1961-62
EDER JOFRE	1961-65
MASAHIKO FIGHTING HARADA	1965-68
LIONEL ROSE	1968-69
RUBEN OLIVARES	1969-70
CHUCHO CASTILLO	1970-71
RUBEN OLIVARES	1971-72
RAFAEL HERRERA	1972
ENRIQUE PINDER	1972-73
ROMEO ANAYA	1973
Rafael Herrera (WBC)	1973-74
ARNOLD TAYLOR	1973-74
SOO-HWAN HONG	1974-75
Rodolfo Martinez (WBC)	1974-76
ALFONSO ZAMORA	1975-77
Carlos Zarate (WBC)	1976-79
JORGE LUJAN	1977-80
Lupe Pintor (WBC)	1979-83
JULIAN SOLIS	1980
JEFF CHANDLER	1980-84
Albert Davila (WBC)	1983-85
RICHARD SANDOVAL	1984-86
Satoshi Shingaki (IBF)	1984-85
Jeff Fenech (IBF)	1985
Daniel Zaragoza (WBC)	1985
Miguel (Happy) Lora (WBC)	1985-88
GABY CANIZALES	1986
BERNARDO PINANGO	1986-87
Wilfredo Vasquez (WBA)	1987-88

Major Titleholders (Cont.)

Bantamweights

Champion	Held Title
Kevin Seabrooks (IBF)	1987-88
Kaokor Galaxy (WBA)	1988
Moon Sung-Kil (WBA)	1988-89
Kaokor Galaxy (WBA)	1989
Raul Perez (WBC)	1988-91
Orlando Canizales (IBF)	1988-94†
Luisito Espinosa (WBA)	1989-91
Greg Richardson	1991
Joichiro Tatsuyoshi (WBC)	1991-92
Israel Contreras (WBA)	1991-92
Eddie Cook (WBA)	1992
Victor Rabanales (WBC)	1992-93
Jorge Julio (WBA)	1992-93
Jung-Il Byun (WBC)	1993
Junior Jones (WBA)	1993-94
Yasuei Yakushiji (WBC)	1993-95
John M. Johnson (WBA)	1994
Daorung Chuvatana (WBA)	1994-95
Harold Mestre (IBF)	1995
Mbulelo Botile (IBF)	1995—
Wayne McCullough (WBC)	1995—
Veeraphol Sahaprom (WBA)	1995-96
Nana Yaw Konadu (WBA)	1996—

Flyweights

Widely accepted champions in CAPITAL letters. Current champions in **bold** type.

Champion	Held Title
Sid Smith (GBR)	1913
Bill Ladbury (GBR)	1913-14
Percy Jones (GBR)	1914
Joe Symonds (GBR)	1914-16
JIMMY WILDE	1916-23
PANCHO VILLA	1923-25
FIDEL LaBARBA	1925-27*
FRENCHY BELANGER (NBA,IBU)	1927-28
IZZY SCHWARTZ (NY)	1927-29
Johnny McCoy (Calif.)	1927-28
Newsboy Brown (Calif.)	1928
FRANKIE GENARO (NBA,IBU)	1928-29
Johnny Hill (GBR)	1928-29
SPIDER PLADNER (NBA,IBU)	1929
FRANKIE GENARO (NBA,IBU)	1929-31
Willie LaMorte (NY)	1929-30
Midget Wolgast (NY)	1930-35
YOUNG PEREZ (NBA,IBU)	1931-32
JACKIE BROWN (NBA,IBU)	1932-35
BENNY LYNCH	1935-38†
Small Montana (NY,Calif.)	1935-37
PETER KANE	1938-43
Little Dado (NBA,Calif.)	1938-40
JACKIE PATERSON	1943-48
RINTY MONAGHAN	1948-50*
TERRY ALLEN	1950
SALVADOR (DADO) MARINO	1950-52
YOSHIO SHIRAI	1953-54
PASCUAL PEREZ	1954-60
PONE KINGPETCH	1960-62
MASAHIKO (FIGHTING) HARADA	1962-63
PONE KINGPETCH	1963
HIROYUKI EBIHARA	1963-64
PONE KINGPETCH	1964-65
SALVATORE BURRINI	1965-66
Horacio Accavallo (WBA)	1966-68
WALTER McGOWAN	1966
CHARTCHAI CHIONOI	1966-69
EFREN TORRES	1969-70
Hiroyuki Ebihara (WBA)	1969
Bernabe Villacampo (WBA)	1969-70
CHARTCHAI CHIONOI	1970
Berkrerk Chartvanchai (WBA)	1970
Masao Ohba (WBA)	1970-73
ERBITO SALAVARRIA	1970-73
Betulio Gonzalez (WBC)	1972
Venice Borkorsor (WBC)	1972-73
VENICE BORKORSOR	1973
Chartchai Chionoi (WBA)	1973-74
Betulio Gonzalez (WBA)	1973-74
Shoji Oguma (WBC)	1974-75
Susumu Hanagata (WBA)	1974-75
Miguel Canto (WBC)	1975-79
Erbito Salavarria (WBA)	1975-76
Alfonso Lopez (WBA)	1976
Guty Espadas (WBA)	1976-78
Betulio Gonzalez (WBA)	1978-79
Chan-Hee Park (WBC)	1979-80
Luis Ibarra (WBA)	1979-80
Tae-Shik Kim (WBA)	1980
Shoji Oguma (WBC)	1980-81
Peter Mathebula (WBA)	1980-81
Santos Laciar (WBA)	1981
Antonio Avelar (WBC)	1981-82
Luis Ibarra (WBA)	1981
Juan Herrera (WBA)	1981-82
Prudencio Cardona (WBC)	1982
Santos Laciar (WBA)	1982-85
Freddie Castillo (WBC)	1982
Eleoncio Mercedes (WBC)	1982-83
Charlie Magri (WBC)	1983
Frank Cedeno (WBC)	1983-84
Soon-Chun Kwon (IBF)	1983-85
Koji Kobayashi (WBC)	1984
Gabriel Bernal (WBC)	1984
Sot Chitalada (WBC)	1984-88
Hilario Zapate (WBA)	1985-87
Chong-Kwan Chung (IBF)	1985-86
Bi-Won Chung (IBF)	1986
Hi-Sup Shin (IBF)	1986-87
Dodie Penalosa (IBF)	1987
Fidel Bassa (WBA)	1987-89
Choi Chang-Ho (IBF)	1987-88
Rolando Bohol (IBF)	1988
Yong-Kang Kim (WBC)	1988-89
Duke McKenzie (IBF)	1988-89
Dave McAuley (IBF)	1989-92
Sot Chitalada (WBC)	1989-91
Jesus Rojas (WBA)	1989-90
Yul-Woo Lee (WBA)	1990
Leopard Tamakuma (WBA)	1990-91
Muangchai Kittikasem (WBC)	1991-92
Yong-Kang Kim (WBA)	1991-92
Rodolfo Blanco (IBF)	1992
Yuri Arbachakov (WBC)	1992—
Aquiles Guzman (WBA)	1992
Phichit Sithbangprachan (IBF)	1992-94†
David Griman (WBA)	1992-94
Saen Sor Ploenchit (WBA)	1994—
Francisco Tejedor (IBF)	1995
Danny Romero (IBF)	1995-96
Marc Johnson (IBF)	1996—

Wide World Photos

The middleweight championship fights between **Carmen Basilio** (left) and **Sugar Ray Robinson** in 1957 and '58 both earned Fight of the Year honors. Above, the two trade blows in the closing moments of their 15-round bout at Yankee Stadium on Sept. 23, 1957. Basilio won the title that night on a split decision. Robinson came back six months later at Chicago Stadium to reclaim the crown on a unanimous decision.

Annual Awards

Ring Magazine Fight of the Year

First presented in 1945 by Nat Fleischer, who started *The Ring* magazine in 1922.

Multiple matchups: Muhammad Ali vs. Joe Frazier, Carmen Basilio vs. Sugar Ray Robinson and Graziano vs. Tony Zale (2).

Multiple fights: Muhammad Ali (6); Carmen Basilio (5); George Foreman and Joe Frazier (4); Rocky Graziano, Rocky Marciano and Tony Zale (3); Nino Benvenuti, Bobby Chacon, Ezzard Charles, Marvin Hagler, Thomas Hearns, Sugar Ray Leonard, Floyd Patterson, Sugar Ray Robinson and Jersey Joe Walcott (2).

Year	Winner	Loser	Result
1945	Rocky Graziano	Red Cochrane	KO 10
1946	Tony Zale	Rocky Graziano	KO 6
1947	Rocky Graziano	Tony Zale	KO 6
1948	Marcel Cerdan	Tony Zale	KO 12
1949	Willie Pep	Sandy Saddler	W 15
1950	Jake LaMotta	Laurent Dauthuille	KO 15
1951	Jersey Joe Walcott	Ezzard Charles	KO 7
1952	Rocky Marciano	Jersey Joe Walcott	KO 13
1953	Rocky Marciano	Roland LaStarza	KO 11
1954	Rocky Marciano	Ezzard Charles	KO 8
1955	Carmen Basilio	Tony DeMarco	KO 12
1956	Carmen Basilio	Johnny Saxton	KO 9
1957	Carmen Basilio	Sugar Ray Robinson	W 15
1958	Sugar Ray Robinson	Carmen Basilio	W 15
1959	Gene Fullmer	Carmen Basilio	KO 14
1960	Floyd Patterson	Ingemar Johansson	KO 5
1961	Joe Brown	Dave Charnley	W 15
1962	Joey Giardello	Henry Hank	W 10
1963	Cassius Clay	Doug Jones	W 10
1964	Cassius Clay	Sonny Liston	KO 7
1965	Floyd Patterson	George Chuvalo	W 12
1966	Jose Torres	Eddie Cotton	W 15
1967	Nino Benvenuti	Emile Griffith	W 15
1968	Dick Tiger	Frank DePaula	W 10
1969	Joe Frazier	Jerry Quarry	KO 7
1970	Carlos Monzon	Nino Benvenuti	KO 12
1971	Joe Frazier	Muhammad Ali	W 15
1972	Bob Foster	Chris Finnegan	KO 14
1973	George Foreman	Joe Frazier	KO 2
1974	Muhammad Ali	George Foreman	KO 8
1975	Muhammad Ali	Joe Frazier	KO 14
1976	George Foreman	Ron Lyle	KO 4
1977	Jimmy Young	George Foreman	W 12
1978	Leon Spinks	Muhammad Ali	W 15
1979	Danny Lopez	Mike Ayala	KO 15
1980	Saad Muhammad	Yaqui Lopez	KO 14
1981	Sugar Ray Leonard	Thomas Hearns	KO 14
1982	Bobby Chacon	Rafael Limon	W 15
1983	Bobby Chacon	C. Boza-Edwards	W 12
1984	Jose Luis Ramirez	Edwin Rosario	KO 4
1985	Marvin Hagler	Thomas Hearns	KO 3
1986	Stevie Cruz	Barry McGuigan	W 15
1987	Sugar Ray Leonard	Marvin Hagler	W 12
1988	Tony Lopez	Rocky Lockridge	W 12
1989	Roberto Duran	Iran Barkley	W 12
1990	Julio Cesar Chavez	Meldrick Taylor	KO 12
1991	Robert Quiroga	Akeem Anifowoshe	W 12
1992	Riddick Bowe	Evander Holyfield	W 12
1993	Michael Carbajal	Humberto Gonzalez	KO 7
1994	Jorge Castro	John David Jackson	TKO 9
1995	Saman Sorjaturong	Chiquita Gonzales	KO 7

Annual Awards (Cont.)

Ring Magazine Fighter of the Year

First presented in 1928 by Nat Fleischer, who started *The Ring* magazine in 1922.

Multiple winners: Muhammad Ali (5); Joe Louis (4); Joe Frazier and Rocky Marciano (3); Ezzard Charles, George Foreman, Marvin Hagler, Thomas Hearns, Ingemar Johansson, Sugar Ray Leonard, Tommy Loughran, Floyd Patterson, Sugar Ray Robinson, Barney Ross, Dick Tiger and Mike Tyson (2).

Year		Year		Year		Year	
1928	Gene Tunney	1945	Willie Pep	1963	Cassius Clay	1980	Thomas Hearns
1929	Tommy Loughran	1946	Tony Zale	1964	Emile Griffith	1981	Sugar Ray Leonard & Salvador Sanchez
1930	Max Schmeling	1947	Gus Lesnevich	1965	Dick Tiger	1982	Larry Holmes
1931	Tommy Loughran	1948	Ike Williams	1966	No award	1983	Marvin Hagler
1932	Jack Sharkey	1949	Ezzard Charles	1967	Joe Frazier	1984	Thomas Hearns
1933	No award	1950	Ezzard Charles	1968	Nino Benvenuti	1985	Donald Curry & Marvin Hagler
1934	Tony Canzoneri & Barney Ross	1951	Sugar Ray Robinson	1969	Jose Napoles	1986	Mike Tyson
1935	Barney Ross	1952	Rocky Marciano	1970	Joe Frazier	1987	Evander Holyfield
1936	Joe Louis	1953	Carl (Bobo) Olson	1971	Joe Frazier	1988	Mike Tyson
1937	Henry Armstrong	1954	Rocky Marciano	1972	Muhammad Ali & Carlos Monzon	1989	Pernell Whitaker
1938	Joe Louis	1955	Rocky Marciano	1973	George Foreman	1990	Julio Cesar Chavez
1939	Joe Louis	1956	Floyd Patterson	1974	Muhammad Ali	1991	James Toney
1940	Billy Conn	1957	Carmen Basilio	1975	Muhammad Ali	1992	Riddick Bowe
1941	Joe Louis	1958	Ingemar Johansson	1976	George Foreman	1993	Michael Carbajal
1942	Sugar Ray Robinson	1959	Ingemar Johansson	1977	Carlos Zarate	1994	Roy Jones Jr.
1943	Fred Apostoli	1960	Floyd Patterson	1978	Muhammad Ali	1995	Oscar De La Hoya
1944	Beau Jack	1961	Joe Brown	1979	Sugar Ray Leonard		
		1962	Dick Tiger				

Note: Cassius Clay changed his name to Muhammad Ali after winning the heavyweight title in 1964.

All-Time Leaders

As compiled by *The Ring Record Book and Encyclopedia.*

Knockouts

		Division	Career	No
1	Archie Moore	Lt. Heavy	1936-63	130
2	Young Stribling	Heavy	1921-33	126
3	Billy Bird	Welter	1920-48	125
4	George Odwel	Welter	1930-45	114
5	Sugar Ray Robinson	Middle	1940-65	110
6	Sandy Saddle	Feather	1944-56	103
7	Sam Langford	Middle	1902-26	102
8	Henry Armstrong	Welter	1931-45	100
9	Jimmy Wilde	Fly	1911-23	98
10	Len Wickwar	Lt. Heavy	1928-47	93

Total Bouts

		Division	Career	No
1	Len Wickwar	Lt. Heavy	1928-47	463
2	Jack Britton	Welter	1905-30	350
3	Johnny Dundee	Feather	1910-32	333
4	Billy Bird	Welter	1920-48	318
5	George Marsden	n/a	1928-46	311
6	Maxie Rosenbloom	Lt. Heavy	1923-39	299
7	Harry Greb	Middle	1913-26	298
8	Young Stribling	Lt. Heavy	1921-33	286
9	Battling Levinsky	Lt. Heavy	1910-29	282
10	Ted (Kid) Lewis	Welter	1909-29	279

Former Champions Who Have Won Back Heavyweight Title

Only eight times since 1892 has the heavyweight championship been lost by a fighter who was able to win it back. Seven men have done it and Muhammad Ali did it twice.

	Lost To	Won Back From
Floyd Patterson	Johansson (1959)	Johansson (1960)
Muhammad Ali	Frazier (1970)	Foreman (1974)
Muhammad Ali	L. Spinks (1978)	L. Spinks (1978)
Tim Witherspoon	Thomas (1984)	Tubbs (1986)
Evander Holyfield	Bowe (1992)	Bowe (1993)
George Foreman	Ali (1974)	Moorer (1994)
Michael Moorer	Foreman (1994)	vacant (1996) vs. Shultz
Mike Tyson	Douglas(1990)	WBC Bruno (1996) WBA Seldon (1996)

Wide World Photos

Triple champion **Henry Armstrong**, the only man to hold the world title in three different weight classes at the same time, puts a hurt on Pedro Montanez in the eighth round of the welterweight title fight in New York. The bout was stopped in the next round and awarded to Armstrong.

Triple Champions

Fighters who have won widely-accepted world titles in more than one division. Henry Armstrong is the only fighter listed to hold three titles simultaneously. Note that (*) indicates title claimant.

Sugar Ray Leonard (5)—WBC Welterweight (1979-80,80-82); WBA Jr. Middleweight (1981); WBC Middleweight (1987); WBC Super Middleweight (1988-90); WBC Light Heavyweight (1988).

Roberto Duran (4)—Lightweight (1972-79); WBC Welterweight (1980); WBA Jr. Middleweight (1983-84); WBC Middleweight (1989-90).

Thomas Hearns (4)—WBA Welterweight (1980-81); WBC Jr. Middleweight (1982-84); WBC Light Heavyweight (1987); WBA Light Heavyweight (1991); WBC Middleweight (1987-88).

Pernell Whitaker (4)—IBF/WBC/WBA Lightweight (1989-92); IBF Jr. Welterweight (1992-93); WBC Welterweight (1993—); WBC Jr. Middleweight (1995).

Alexis Arguello (3)—WBA Featherweight (1974-77); WBC Jr. Lightweight (1978-80); WBC Lightweight (1981-83).

Henry Armstrong (3)—Featherweight (1937-38); Welterweight (1938-40); Lightweight (1938-39).

Iran Barkley (3)—WBC Middleweight (1988-89); IBF Super Middleweight (1992-93); WBA Light Heavyweight (1992).

Wilfredo Benitez (3)—Jr. Welterweight (1976-79); Welterweight (1979); WBC Jr. Middleweight (1981-82).

Tony Canzoneri (3)—Featherweight (1928); Lightweight (1930-33); Jr. Welterweight (1931-32,33).

Julio Cesar Chavez (3)—WBC Jr. Lightweight (1984-87); WBA/WBC Lightweight (1987-89); WBC/IBF Jr. Welterweight (1989-91); WBC Jr. Welterweight (1991-94, 1994—).

Jeff Fenech (3)—IBF Bantamweight (1985); WBC Jr. Featherweight (1986-88); WBC Featherweight (1988-90).

Bob Fitzsimmons (3)—Middleweight (1891-97); Light Heavyweight (1903-05); Heavyweight (1897-99).

Wilfredo Gomez (3)—WBC Super Bantamweight (1977-83); WBC Featherweight (1984); WBA Jr. Lightweight (1985-86).

Emile Griffith (3)—Welterweight (1961,62-63,63-66); Jr. Middleweight (1962-63); Middleweight (1966-67,67-68).

Terry McGovern (3)—Bantamweight (1889-1900); Featherweight (1900-01); Lightweight* (1900-01).

Barney Ross (3)—Lightweight (1933-35); Jr. Welterweight (1933-35); Welterweight (1934, 35-38).

Wide World Photos

The boys from Taiwan give a tip of the cap to the fans at Howard J. Lamade Stadium after winning the **Little League World Series**, 13-3, over Cranston, R.I. on Aug. 24 in Williamsport, Pa.

MISCELLANEOUS SPORTS

by Gerry Brown

Fifty Years Young

Little League World Series turns 50, but players keep it young at heart

Before the game, the 35,000 American fans at Howard J. Lamade Stadium watched the little little leaguers from thousands of miles away line up on the third baseline in South Williamsport, Penn. and do the Macarena. The kids from Kao-Hsuing City, Taiwan almost stole the show before it even began.

But the pride of United States little league, the boys from Cranston, R.I., were planning some moves of their own. The day before the game, they lined up to rub the belly of baseball buddha Kirby Puckett for good luck. The recently-retired Minnesota Twin was in Williamsport to help broadcast the game for ABC and going into the game the U.S. may have entertained thoughts of putting the pint-sized powerhouse in the U.S. East team's home whites. In the end, it might not have made a difference.

After staking their heavily-favored visitors to a 2-0 lead, the US East region champs, a team that sneaked through the crowd and into the championship game, answered with two runs, homers from both ends of their battery. Cranston's leading man, catcher Craig Stinson, and starting pitcher Tom Michael both took Taiwan starting pitcher Chi-Hung Cheng over the fence, producing a tenuous 2-2 tie, and driving him from the game in the first inning after facing just six batters.

The team from the smallest state in the nation was challenging the giants of international little league. Although they would commit five errors in the game, US East would also turn two double plays— especially rare on Little League's 60-foot base paths.

"As I've said all along, I just wanted to see the kids have fun," commented Cranston manager Mike Varrato. "But I knew if we could keep it close, then we might have a chance at the end."

Varrato's team was as much like the biblical David that any baseball team from the United States could be. Cranston arrived at the title game after dodging elimination just when it looked inevitable.

It appeared that the Ocean Staters were sunk after losing to Marshalltown, Iowa, 6-1. But because they won tie-breakers over Marshalltown and Moorpark, Calif. they still could advance if Panama City beat Moorpark that night and scored seven or more runs. Panama City won the game, 10-2, and the undying thanks of Rhode Island little league fans, vaulting Cranston to a United States championship and showdown with terrifying Taiwan.

The team from Kao-Hsuing City was the anti-Cranston, strutting through the international schedule like a playground bully, outscoring their opponents, 49-6.

Ultimately, it didn't take that long for

Gerry Brown is the Associate Editor of the *Information Please Sports Almanac.*

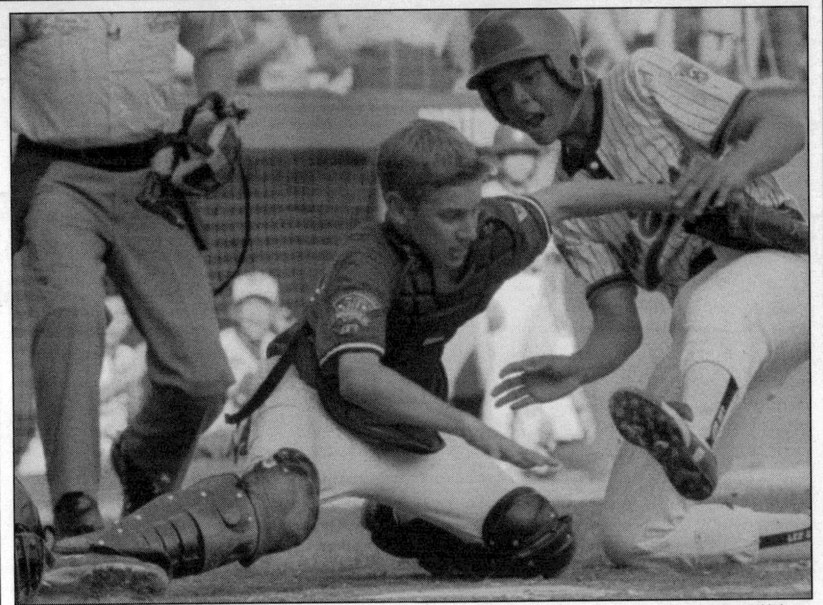

Wide World Photos

Taiwan runner **Chia-Chen Yang** is safe at home as Cranston, R.I. catcher **Craig Stinson** drops the ball in the fourth inning of Taiwan's 13-3 win in the Little League World Series Championship game. Although he had trouble on this play, Stinson's solid work behind the plate along with his hot bat helped get Cranston to the title game.

Taiwan to assert their superiority in the championship game. Taiwan reliever Chiu Chi-Pin settled things down and then, on offense, virtually finished things off, knocking a three-run blast in the decisive fifth. Then 4-foot-9 inch Hsieh Chin-Hsiung set a Little League World Series record, belting his seventh homer of the tournament in his final at-bat. His three-run shot, the one that eclipsed the mark set by his countryman Lin Chih-Hsiang in 1995, put Taiwan on the upside of 13-2 fifth-inning landslide.

The tiny Hsieh (.705, 16 RBI) started slowly in the final (walked, grounded out and struck out in his first three at-bats) but overall he swung the biggest of the big bats from the small island nation. Still, he wasn't taking all the credit. In response to a question about how he was able to hit the record-breaker, Hsieh motioned to his stern and stoic manager, Ho Tung-Yu, and replied through an interpreter, "Because he told me to do it."

"They're all good hitters," said Michael, who set a record of his own, although a dubious one. He became the first pitcher to lose three games in a series.

"If you let up on one, then the next one is going to get you. So, you can't afford to make a mistake against any guy, because they'll all make you pay."

Cranston scored one run in the bottom half of the fifth and, mercifully, the game was ended via the 10-run mercy rule, giving Taiwan its 17th LLWS title.

The American boys were beaten, but not beaten down.

"We're still the U.S. Champions. I mean, I'm not sad and the rest of the team is not sad. We're disappointed we lost. But I mean, jeez, U.S. Champion and second best in the world? You can't be disappointed about that," Michael said after the loss.

"They didn't surprise us. We knew we were the big underdog coming in," explained Varrato, whose team became the first from his state to reach the final and the first from the East bracket to reach the title game since Trumbull, Conn. won it all in 1989.

After the game, the kids who came to play all the way from Taiwan celebrated their impressive victory on Pennsylvania dirt and did the Macarena again. ❐

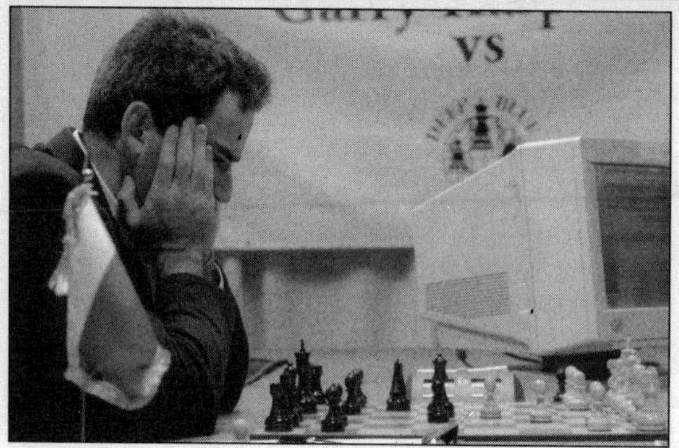

World Chess Champion **Garry Kasparov** plots strategy in his third game with IBM's chess supercomputer Deep Blue, the ACM international computer chess champion, on Feb. 13 at the Convention Center in Philadelphia. The game would end in a draw, but Kasparov would go on to win the final game and the series 4-2.
Wide World Photos

CHESS

World Champions

Anatoly Karpov of Russia successfully defended his FIDE World Championship in a match held June 8-July 12 against 22-year-old American Gata Kamsky. Karpov, 45, won the match, held in Elista, Kalmykia, Russia, by a final score of 10½-7½, earning roughly two-thirds of the $1.1 million prize fund.

PCA champion, and the widely-recognized if unofficial world champion, Garry Kasparov of Russia, defended his honor and earned $400,000 with a victory in a six-game tournament against IBM's supercomputer Deep Blue. After losing Game 1, the 33-year-old Russian bounced back and proved that—for now—the human brain is the ultimate chess computer. "Although I did see some signs of intelligence, it's a weird kind, an inefficient, inflexible kind that makes me think I have a few years left," said Kasparov after his 4-2 win in Philadelphia.

Team IBM partly blamed technical glitches for the loss. In Game 4 the computer crashed, delaying the match temporarily and on several other occasions certain software that would have aided Deep Blue's strategy was either unloaded or loaded improperly. Kasparov and an improved Deep Blue are set for a six-game rematch that begins May 3, 1997. The winner in this man vs. machine meeting will earn $700,000. Kasparov became the youngest man to win the world chess championship when he beat Karpov in 1985 at age 22.

In 1993, Kasparov and then-No. 1 challenger Nigel Short of England broke away from the established International Chess Federation (FIDE) to form the PCA. The FIDE retaliated by stripping Kasparov of their world title and arranging a playoff that was won by Karpov, the former title-holder.

Years	
1866-94	Wilhelm Steinitz, Austria
1894-1921	Emanuel Lasker, Germany
1921-27	Jose Capablanca, Cuba
1927-35	Alexander Alekhine, France
1935-37	Max Euwe, Holland
1937-46	Alexander Alekhine, France
1948-57	Mikhail Botvinnik, USSR
1957-58	Vassily Smyslov, USSR
1958-59	Mikhail Botvinnik, USSR
1960-61	Mikhail Tal, USSR
1961-63	Mikhail Botvinnik, USSR
1963-69	Tigran Petrosian, USSR
1969-72	Boris Spassky, USSR
1972-75	Bobby Fischer, USA*
1975-85	Anatoly Karpov, USSR
1985—	Garry Kasparov, RUS

*Fischer defaulted championship in 1975

U.S. Champions

Cleveland's Alexander Yermolinksy won the 1996 U.S. Chess Championships in the 14-player, round robin tournament that ran July 13-27 in Parsippany, N.J.

Years	
1857-71	Paul Morphy
1871-76	George Mackenzie
1876-80	James Mason
1880-89	George Mackenzie
1889-90	Samuel Lipschutz
1890	Jackson Showalter
1890-91	Max Judd
1891-92	Jackson Showalter
1892-94	Samuel Lipschutz
1894	Jackson Showalter
1894-95	Albert Hodges
1895-97	Jackson Showalter
1897-1906	Harry Pillsbury
1906-09	Vacant
1909-36	Frank Marshall
1936-44	Samuel Reshevsky
1944-46	Arnold Denker
1946-48	Samuel Reshevsky
1948-51	Herman Steiner
1951-54	Larry Evans
1954-57	Arthur Bisguier
1957-61	Bobby Fischer
1961-62	Larry Evans
1962-68	Bobby Fischer
1968-69	Larry Evans
1969-72	Samuel Reshevsky
1972-73	Robert Byrne
1973-74	Lubomir Kavalek & John Grefe
1974-77	Walter Browne
1978-80	Lubomir Kabalek
1980-81	Larry Evans, Larry Christiansen & Walter Browne
1981-83	Walter Browne & Yasser Seirawan
1983	Roman Dzindzichashvili, Larry Christiansen & Walter Browne
1984-85	Lev Alburt
1986	Yasser Seirawan
1987	Joel Benjamin & Nick DeFirmian
1988	Michael Wilder
1989	Roman Dzindzichashvili, Stuart Rachels & Yasser Seirawan
1990	Lev Alburt
1991	Gata Kamsky
1992	Patrick Wolff
1993	Alexander Shabalov & Alex Yermolinsky
1994	Boris Gulko
1995	Alexander Ivanov
1996	Alexander Yermolinsky

DOGS

Iditarod Trail Sled Dog Race

Jeff King, a 39-year-old former Denali National Park ranger, won the 24th annual Iditarod Trail Sled Dog Race on Mar. 12. King, the 1993 winner, reached Nome and the burled arch finish line of the 1,151-mile course in 9 days, 5, hours, 43 minutes and 13 seconds— the second-fastest time ever. The Iditarod began Mar. 2 in Anchorage. In even-numbered years, the trail follows the 1,151-mile long Northern Route, while in odd-numbered years it takes the slightly-different 1,161-mile Southern Route. Rick Swenson, one of the race favorites and the Iditarod's only five-time winner, was disqualified under the race's controversial new "dead dog" rule after one of his dogs, Ariel, died early in the race. King, who finished the race with six of his original 16 dogs, took home $50,000 and a new pickup. Doug Swingley, the 1995 champion and only Non-Alaskan ever to win the race, placed second.

Multiple winners: Rick Swenson (5); Susan Butcher (4); Martin Buser and Rick Mackey (2).

Year		Elapsed Time
1973	Dick Wilmarth	20 days, 00:49:41
1974	Carl Huntington	20 days, 15:02:07
1975	Emmitt Peters	14 days, 14:43:45
1976	Gerald Riley	18 days, 22:58:17
1977	Rick Swenson	16 days, 16:27:13
1978	Dick Mackey	14 days, 18:52:24
1979	Rick Swenson	15 days, 10:37:47
1980	Joe May	14 days, 07:11:51
1981	Rick Swenson	12 days, 08:45:02
1982	Rick Swenson	16 days, 04:40:10
1983	Rick Mackey	12 days, 14:10:44
1984	Dean Osmar	12 days, 15:07:33
1985	Libby Riddles	18 days, 00:20:17
1986	Susan Butcher	11 days, 15:06:00
1987	Susan Butcher	11 days, 02:05:13
1988	Susan Butcher	11 days, 11:41:40
1989	Joe Runyan	11 days, 05:24:34
1990	Susan Butcher	11 days, 01:53:23
1991	Rick Swenson	12 days, 16:34:39
1992	Martin Buser	10 days, 19:17:00
1993	Jeff King	10 days, 15:38:15
1994	Martin Buser	10 days, 13:02:39
1995	Doug Swingley	9 days, 02:42:19*
1996	Jeff King	9 days, 05:43:13

*Course record.

Westminster Kennel Club

Best in Show

Ch, Clussexx Country Sunrise, a 4-year-old clumber spaniel known as Brady, won best in show at the 120th annual Westminster Kennel Club show on Feb. 13 at Madison Square Garden in New York. The 76-pound clumber, owned by Richard and Judith Zaleski of Sorrento, Fla., and handled by Lisa Jane Alston-Myers beat out 2,500 champions from 150 breeds. The judge was D. Roy Holloway. The Westminster show is the most prestigious dog show in the country, and one of America's oldest annual sporting events.

Multiple winners: Ch. Warren Remedy (3); Ch. Chinoe's Adamant James, Ch. Comejo Wycollar Boy, Ch. Flornell Spicy Piece of Halleston; Ch. Matford Vic, Ch. My Own Brucie, Ch. Pendley Calling of Blarney, Ch. Rancho Dobe's Storm (2).

Year		Breed
1907	Warren Remedy	Fox Terrier
1908	Warren Remedy	Fox Terrier
1909	Warren Remedy	Fox Terrier
1910	Sabine Rarebit	Fox Terrier
1911	Tickle Em Jock	Scottish Terrier
1912	Kenmore Sorceress	Airedale
1913	Strathway Prince Albert	Bulldog
1914	Brentwood Hero	Old English Sheepdog
1915	Matford Vic	Old English Sheepdog
1916	Matford Vic	Old English Sheepdog
1917	Comejo Wycollar Boy	Fox Terrier
1918	Haymarket Faultless	Bull Terrier
1919	Briergate Bright Beauty	Airedale
1920	Comejo Wycollar Boy	Fox Terrier
1921	Midkiff Seductive	Cocker Spaniel
1922	Boxwood Barkentine	Airedale
1923	No best-in-show award	
1924	Barberryhill Bootlegger	Sealyham
1925	Governor Moscow	Pointer
1926	Signal Circuit	Fox Terrier
1927	Pinegrade Perfection	Sealyham
1928	Talavera Margaret	Fox Terrier
1929	Land Loyalty of Bellhaven	Collie
1930	Pendley Calling of Blarney	Fox Terrier
1931	Pendley Calling of Blarney	Fox Terrier
1932	Nancolleth Markable	Pointer
1933	Warland Protector of Shelterock	Airedale
1934	Flornell Spicy Bit of Halleston	Fox Terrier
1935	Nunsoe Duc de la Terrace of Blakeen	Standard Poodle
1936	St. Margaret Magnificent of Clairedale	Sealyham
1937	Flornell Spicy Bit of Halleston	Fox Terrier
1938	Daro of Maridor	English Setter
1939	Ferry v.Rauhfelsen of Giralda	Doberman
1940	My Own Brucie	Cocker Spaniel
1941	My Own Brucie	Cocker Spaniel
1942	Wolvey Pattern of Edgerstoune	W. Highland Terrier
1943	Pitter Patter of Piperscroft	Miniature Poodle
1944	Flornell Rarebit of Twin Ponds	Welsh Terrier
1945	Shieling's Signature	Scottish Terrier
1946	Hetherington Model Rhythm	Fox Terrier
1947	Warlord of Mazelaine	Boxer
1948	Rock Ridge Night Rocket	Bedling. Terrier
1949	Mazelaine's Zazarac Brandy	Boxer
1950	Walsing Winning Trick of Edgerstoune	Scot. Terrier
1951	Bang Away of Sirrah Crest	Boxer
1952	Rancho Dobe's Storm	Doberman
1953	Rancho Dobe's Storm	Doberman
1954	Carmor's Rise and Shine	Cocker Spaniel
1955	Kippax Fearnought	Bulldog
1956	Wilber White Swan	Toy Poodle
1957	Shirkhan of Grandeur	Afghan Hound
1958	Puttencove Promise	Standard Poodle
1959	Fontclair Festoon	Miniature Poodle
1960	Chick T'Sun of Caversham	Pekingese
1961	Cappoquin Little Sister	Toy Poodle
1962	Elfinbrook Simon	W. Highland Terrier
1963	Wakefield's Black Knight	English Springer Spaniel
1964	Courtenay Fleetfoot of Pennyworth	Whippet
1965	Carmichaels Fanfare	Scottish Terrier
1966	Zeloy Mooremaides Magic	Fox Terrier
1967	Bardene Bingo	Scottish Terrier
1968	Stingray of Derryabah	Lakeland Terrier

Dogs (Cont.)

Westminster Kennel Club

Best in Show

Year		Breed
1969	Glamoor Good News	Skye Terrier
1970	Arriba's Prima Donna	Boxer
1971	Chinoe's Adamant James	E.S. Spaniel
1972	Chinoe's Adamant James	E.S. Spaniel
1973	Acadia Command Performance	Standard Poodle
1974	Gretchenhof Columbia River	German SH Pointer
1975	Sir Lancelot of Barvan	Old Eng. Sheepdog
1976	Jo Ni's Red Baron of Crofton	Lakeland Terrier
1977	Dersade Bobby's Girl	Sealyham
1978	Cede Higgens	Yorkshire Terrier
1979	Oak Tree's Irishtocrat	Irish Water Spaniel
1980	Sierra Cinnar	Siberian Husky
1981	Dhandy Favorite Woodchuck	Pug
1982	St. Aubrey Dragonora of Elsdon	Pekingese
1983	Kabik's The Challenger	Afghan Hound
1984	Seaward's Blackbeard	Newfoundland
1985	Braeburn's Close Encounter	Scottish Terrier
1986	Marjetta National Acclaim	Pointer
1987	Covy Tucker Hill's Manhattan	German Shepherd
1988	Great Elms Prince Charming II	Pomeranian
1989	Royal Tudor's Wild As The Wind	Doberman
1990	Wendessa Crown Prince	Pekingese
1991	Whisperwind on a Carousel	Stan. Poodle
1992	Lonesome Dove	Fox Terrier
1993	Salilyn's Condor	E.S. Spaniel
1994	Chidley Willum	Norwich Terrier
1995	Gaelforce Post Script	Scottish Terrier
1996	Clussex Country Sunrise	Clumber Spaniel

FISHING

IGFA All-Tackle World Records

All-tackle records are maintained for the heaviest fish of any species caught on any line up to 130-lb (60 kg) class and certified by the International Game Fish Association. Records logged through Oct. 1, 1995. **Address:** 3000 East Las Olas Blvd., Ft. Lauderdale, FL, 33316. **Telephone:** 954-941-3474.

FRESHWATER FISH

Species	Lbs-Oz	Where Caught	Date	Angler
Barramundi	63- 2	Queensland, Australia	Apr. 28, 1991	Scott Barnsley
Bass, Guadalupe	3-11	Lake Travis, TX	Sept. 25, 1983	Allen Christenson Jr.
Bass, largemouth	22- 4	Montgomery Lake, GA	June 2, 1932	George W. Perry
Bass, peacock	27- 0	Rio Negro, Brazil	Dec. 4, 1994	Gerald (Doc) Lawson
Bass, peacock butterfly	9- 8	Kendale Lakes, FL	Mar. 11, 1993	Jerry Gomez
Bass, redeye	8-12	Apalatchicola River, FL	Jan. 28, 1995	Carl W. Davis
Bass, Roanoke	1- 5	Nottoway River, VA	Nov. 11, 1991	Tom Elkins
Bass, rock	3- 0	York River, Ontario	Aug. 1, 1974	Peter Gulgin
Bass, smallmouth	11-15	Dale Hollow Lake, KY	July 9, 1955	David L. Hayes
Bass, spotted	9- 7	Pine Flat Lake, CA	Feb. 25, 1994	Bob E. Shelton
Bass, striped (landlocked)	67- 8	O'Neill Forebay, San Luis, CA	May 7, 1992	Hank Ferguson
Bass, Suwannee	3-14	Suwannee River, FL	Mar. 2, 1985	Ronnie Everett
Bass, white	6-13	Lake Orange, VA	July 31, 1989	Ronald L. Sprouse
Bass, whiterock	24- 8	Lake Chatuge, GA	May 1, 1995	David C. Hobby
Bass, yellow	2- 4	Lake Monroe, IN	Mar. 27, 1977	Donald L. Stalker
Bass, yellow hybrid	2- 5	Kiamichi River, OK	Mar. 26, 1991	George Edwards
Bluegill	4-12	Ketona Lake, AL	Apr. 9, 1950	T.S. Hudson
Bowfin	21- 8	Florence, SC	Jan. 29, 1980	Robert L. Harmon
Buffalo, bigmouth	70- 5	Bussey Brake, Bastrop, LA	Apr. 21, 1980	Delbert Sisk
Buffalo, black	55- 8	Cherokee Lake, TN	May 3, 1984	Edward H. McLain
Buffalo, smallmouth	68- 8	Lake Hamilton, AR	May 16, 1984	Jerry L. Dolezal
Bullhead, black	8- 0	Lake Waccabuc, NY	Aug. 1, 1951	Kani Evans
Bullhead, brown	5-11	Cedar Creek, FL	Mar. 28, 1995	Robert Bengis
Bullhead, yellow	4- 4	Mormon Lake, AZ	May 11, 1984	Emily Williams
Burbot	18- 4	Pickford, MI	Jan. 31, 1980	Tom Courtemanche
Carp	75-11	Lac de St. Cassien, France	May 21, 1987	Leo van der Gugten
Catfish, blue	109- 4	Cooper River, SC	Mar. 14, 1991	George Lijewski
Catfish, channel	58- 0	Santee-Cooper Res., SC	July 7, 1964	W.B. Whaley
Catfish, flathead	91- 4	Lake Lewisville, TX	Mar. 28, 1982	Mike Rogers
Catfish, flatwhiskered	5-13	Cuiaba River, Brazil	June 28, 1992	Sergio Roberto Rothier
Catfish, gilded	85- 8	Amazon River, Brazil	Nov. 15, 1986	Gilberto Fernandes
Catfish, redtail	97- 7	Amazon River, Brazil	July 16, 1988	Gilberto Fernandes
Catfish, sharptoothed	79- 5	Orange River, S. Africa	Dec. 5, 1992	Hennie Moller
Catfish, white	18-14	Inverness, FL	Sept. 21, 1991	Jim Miller
Char, Arctic	32- 9	Tree River, Canada	July 30, 1981	Jeffery Ward
Crappie, black	4- 8	Kerr Lake, VA	Mar. 1, 1981	L. Carl Herring Jr.
Crappie, white	5- 3	Enid Dam, MS	July 31, 1957	Fred L. Bright
Dolly Varden	18- 9	Mashutuk River, AK	July 13, 1993	Richard B. Evans
Dorado	51- 5	Corrientes, Argentina	Sept. 27, 1984	Armando Giudice
Drum, freshwater	54- 8	Nickajack Lake, TN	Apr. 20, 1972	Benny E. Hull

Species	Lbs-Oz	Where Caught	Date	Angler
Gar, alligator	279- 0	Rio Grande, TX	Dec. 2, 1951	Bill Valverde
Gar, Florida	21- 3	Boca Raton, FL	June 3, 1981	Jeff Sabol
Gar, longnose	50- 5	Trinity River, TX	July 30, 1954	Townsend Miller
Gar, shortnose	5-12	Rend Lake, Ill.	July 16, 1995	Donna K. Willmart
Gar, spotted	9-12	Lake Mevia, TX	Apr. 7, 1994	Rick Rivard
Goldfish	6-10	Lake Hodges, CA	Apr. 17, 1996	Florentino M. Abena
Grayling, Arctic	5-15	Katseyedie River, N.W.T.	Aug. 16, 1967	Jeanne P. Branson
Inconnu	53- 0	Pah River, AK	Aug. 20, 1986	Lawrence E. Hudnall
Kokanee	9- 6	Okanagan Lake, Brit.Columbia	June 18, 1988	Norm Kuhn
Muskellunge	67- 8	Hayward, WI	July 24, 1949	Cal Johnson
Muskellunge, tiger	51- 3	Lac Vieux-Desert, WI-MI	July 16, 1919	John A. Knobla
Perch, Nile	191- 8	Lake Victoria, Kenya	Sept. 5, 1991	Andy Davison
Perch, white	4-12	Messalonskee Lake, ME	June 4, 1949	Mrs. Earl Small
Perch, yellow	4- 3	Bordentown, NJ	May, 1865	Dr. C.C. Abbot
Pickerel, chain	9- 6	Homerville, GA	Feb. 17, 1961	Baxley McQuaig Jr.
Pickerel, grass	1- 0	Dewart Lake, Indiana	June 9, 1990	Mike Berg
Pickerel, redfin	1-15	Redhook, NY	Oct. 16, 1988	Bill Stagias
Pike, northern	55- 1	Lake of Grefeern, W.Germany	Oct.16, 1986	Lothar Louis
Redhorse, greater	9- 3	Salmon River, Pulaski, NY	May 11, 1985	Jason Wilson
Redhorse, silver	11- 7	Plum Creek, WI	May 29, 1985	Neal D.G. Long
Salmon, Atlantic	79- 2	Tana River, Norway	1928	Henrik Henriksen
Salmon, chinook	97- 4	Kenai River, AK	May 17, 1985	Les Anderson
Salmon, chum	35- 0	Edye Pass, Brit. Columbia	July 11, 1995	Todd Johansson
Salmon, coho	33- 4	Salmon River, Pulaski, NY	Sept. 27, 1989	Jerry Lifton
Salmon, lake	18- 4	Lake Tanganyika, Zambia	Dec. 1, 1987	Steve Robinson
Salmon, pink	13- 1	St. Mary's River, Ontario	Sept. 23, 1992	Ray Higaki
Salmon, sockeye	15- 3	Kenai River, AK	Aug. 9, 1987	Stan Roach
Sauger	8-12	Lake Sakakawea, ND	Oct. 6, 1971	Mike Fischer
Shad, American	11- 4	Conn.River, S.Hadley, MA	May 19, 1986	Bob Thibodo
Shad, gizzard	4- 6	Lake Michigan, IN	Mar. 2, 1996	Mike Berg
Sturgeon, lake	92- 4	Kettle River, MN	Sept. 11, 1986	James M. DeOtis
Sturgeon, white	468- 0	Benicia, CA	July 9, 1983	Joey Pallotta 3rd
Tigerfish, giant	97- 0	Zaire River, Kinshasa, Zaire	July 9, 1988	Raymond Houtmans
Tilapia	6- 0	Lake Okeechobee, FL	June 24, 1989	Joseph M. Tucker
Trout, Apache	5- 3	White Mountain, AZ	May 29, 1991	John Baldwin
Trout, brook	14- 8	Nipigon River, Ontario	July, 1916	Dr. W.J. Cook
Trout, brown	40- 4	Little Red River, AR	May 9, 1992	Rip Collins
Trout, bull	32- 0	Lake Pond Orielle, ID	Oct. 27, 1949	N.L. Higgins
Trout, cutthroat	41- 0	Pyramid Lake, NV	Dec., 1925	John Skimmerhorn
Trout, golden	11- 0	Cooks Lake, WY	Aug. 5, 1948	Charles S. Reed
Trout, lake	66- 8	Great Bear Lake, N.W.T.	July 19, 1991	Rodney Harback
Trout, rainbow	42- 2	Bell Island, AK	June 22, 1970	David Robert White
Trout, tiger	20-13	Lake Michigan, WI	Aug. 12, 1978	Peter M. Friedland
Walleye	25- 0	Old Hickory Lake, TN	Apr. 1, 1960	Mabry Harper
Warmouth	2- 7	Guess Lake, Holt, FL	Oct. 19, 1985	Tony D. Dempsey
Whitefish, lake	14- 6	Meaford, Ontario	May 21, 1984	Dennis M.Laycock
Whitefish, mountain	5- 6	Rioh River, Saskatchewan	June 15, 1988	John R. Bell
Whitefish, lake	14- 6	Meaford, Ontario	May 21, 1984	Dennis Laycock
Whitefish, round	6- 0	Putahow River, Manitoba	June 14, 1984	Allan J. Ristori
Zander	25- 2	Trosa, Sweden	June 12, 1986	Harry Lee Tennison

SALTWATER FISH

Species	Lbs-Oz	Where Caught	Date	Angler
Albacore	88- 2	Gran Canaria, Canary Islands	Nov. 19, 1977	Siegfried Dickemann
Amberjack, greater	155-10	Challenger Bank, Bermuda	June 24, 1981	Joseph Dawson
Amberjack, pacific	104- 0	Baja Calif., Mexico	July 4, 1984	Richard Cresswell
Barracuda, great	85- 0	Christmas Is., Rep. of Kiribati	Apr. 11, 1992	John W. Helfrich
Barracuda, Mexican	21- 0	Phantom Island, Costa Rica	Mar. 27, 1987	E. Greg Kent
Barracuda, pickhandle	17- 4	Sitra Channel, Bahrain	Nov. 21, 1985	Roger Cranswick
Bass, barred sand	13- 3	Huntington Beach, CA	Aug. 29, 1988	Robert Halal
Bass, black sea	9- 8	Virginia Beach, VA	Jan. 9, 1987	Joe Mizelle Jr.
Bass, European	20-11	Stes Maries de la Mer, France	May 6, 1986	Jean Baptiste Bayle
Bass, giant sea	563- 8	Anacapa Island, CA	Aug. 20, 1968	J.D. McAdam Jr.
Bass, striped	78- 8	Atlantic City, NJ	Sept. 21, 1982	Albert R. McReynolds
Bluefish	31-12	Hatteras, NC	Jan. 30, 1972	James M. Hussey
Bonefish	19- 0	Zululand, South Africa	May 26, 1962	Brian W. Batchelor
Bonito, Atlantic	18- 4	Faial Island, Azores	July 8, 1953	D. Gama Higgs
Bonito, Pacific	14-12	San Benitos Is., Baja Calif., Mexico	Oct. 12, 1980	Jerome H. Rilling
Cabezon	23- 0	Juan de Fuca Strait, WA	Aug. 4, 1990	Wesley Hunter
Cobia	135- 9	Shark Bay, W. Australia	July 9, 1985	Peter W. Goulding
Cod, Atlantic	98-12	Isle of Shoals, NH	June 8, 1969	Alphonse Bielevich

Fishing (Cont.)

IGFA All-Tackle World Records

SALTWATER FISH

Species	Lbs-Oz	Where Caught	Date	Angler
Cod, Pacific	30- 0	Andrew Bay, AK	July 7, 1984	Donald R. Vaughn
Conger	133- 4	South Devon, England	June 5, 1995	Vic Evans
Dolphin	87- 0	Papagallo Gulf, Costa Rica	Sept. 25, 1976	Manuel Salazar
Drum, black	113- 1	Lewes, DE	Sept. 15, 1975	Gerald M. Townsend
Drum, red	94- 2	Avon, NC	Nov. 7, 1984	David G. Deuel
Eel, marbled	36- 1	Durban, S. Africa	June 10, 1984	Ferdie van Nooten
Eel, American	9- 4	Cape May, NJ	Nov. 9, 1995	Jeff Pennick
Flounder, southern	20- 9	Nassau Sound, FL	Dec. 23, 1983	Larenza Mungin
Flounder, summer	22- 7	Montauk, NY	Sept. 15, 1975	Charles Nappi
Grouper, warsaw	436-12	Gulf of Mexico, Destin, FL	Dec. 22, 1985	Steve Haeusler
Haddock	11-11	Perkins Cove, Ogunquit, ME	Sept. 12, 1991	Jim Mailea
Halibut, Atlantic	255- 4	Gloucester, MA	July 28, 1989	Sonny Manley
Halibut, California	53- 4	Santa Rosa Island, CA	July 7, 1988	Russell J. Harmon
Halibut, Pacific	395- 0	Unalaska Bay, Bering Sea	June 21, 1995	Michael J. Golat
Jack, almaco (Pacific)	132- 0	La Paz, Baja Calif., Mexico	July 21, 1964	Howard H. Hahn
Jack, crevalle	57- 5	Barra do Bwanza, Angola	Oct. 10, 1992	Cam Nicolson
Jack, horse-eye	24- 8	Miami, FL	Dec. 20, 1982	Tito Schnau
Jewfish	680- 0	Fernandina Beach, FL	May 20, 1961	Lynn Joyner
Kawakawa	29- 0	Clarion Island, Mexico	Dec. 17, 1986	Ronald Nakamura
Lingcod	69- 0	Langara Is., Brit. Columbia	June 16, 1992	Murray M.Romer
Mackerel, cero	17- 2	Islamorada, FL	Apr. 5, 1986	G. Michael Mills
Mackerel, king	90- 0	Key West, FL	Feb. 16, 1976	Norton I. Thomton
Mackerel, Spanish	13- 0	Ocracoke Inlet, NC	Nov. 4, 1987	Robert Cranton
Marlin, Atlantic blue	1402- 2	Vitoria, Brazil	Feb. 29, 1992	Paulo R.A. Amorim
Marlin, Black	1560- 0	Cabo Blanco, Peru	Aug. 4, 1953	A.C. Glassell Jr.
Marlin, Pacific blue	1376- 0	Kaaiwi Point, Kona, HI	May 31, 1982	Jay W. deBeaubien
Marlin, striped	494- 0	Tutakaka, New Zealand	Jan. 16, 1986	Bill Boniface
Marlin, white	181-14	Vitoria, Brazil	Dec. 8, 1979	Evandro Luiz Coser
Permit	53- 4	Lake Worth, FL	Mar. 25, 1994	Roy Brooker
Pollack	27- 6	Salcombe, Devon, England	Jan. 16, 1986	Robert S. Milkins
Pollock	50- 0	Salstraumen, Norway	Nov. 30, 1996	Thor-Magnus Ukang
Pompano, African	50- 8	Daytona Beach, FL	Apr. 21, 1990	Tom Sargent
Roosterfish	114- 0	La Paz, Baja Calif., Mexico	June 1, 1960	Abe Sackheim
Runner, blue	8- 7	Port Arkansas, TX	Feb. 13, 1995	Allen E. Windecker
Runner, rainbow	37- 9	Clarion Island, Mexico	Nov. 21, 1991	Tom Pfleger
Sailfish, Atlantic	141-10	Luanda, Angola	Feb. 19, 1994	Alfredo de Sousa Neves
Sailfish, Pacific	221- 0	Santa Cruz Is., Ecuador	Feb. 12, 1947	C.W. Stewart
Seabass, white	83-12	San Felipe, Mexico	Mar. 31, 1953	L.C. Baumgardner
Seatrout, spotted	16- 0	Mason's Beach, VA	May 28, 1977	William Katko
Shark, blue	437- 0	Catherine Bay, NSW, Australia	Oct. 2, 1976	Peter Hyde
Shark, great white	2664- 0	Ceduna, S. Australia	Apr. 21, 1959	Alfred Dean
Shark, greenland	1708- 9	Trondheimsfjord, Norway	Oct.18, 1987	Terje Nordtvedt
Shark, hammerhead	991- 0	Sarasota, FL	May 30, 1982	Allen Ogle
Shark, shortfin mako	1115- 0	Black River, Mauritius	Nov. 16, 1988	Patrick Guillanton
Shark, porbeagle	507- 0	Pentland Firth, Scotland	Mar. 9, 1993	Christopher Bennet
Shark, bigeye thresher	802- 0	Tutukaka, New Zealand	Feb. 8, 1981	Dianne North
Shark, tiger	1780- 0	Cherry Grove, SC	June 14, 1964	Walter Maxwell
Snapper, cubera	121- 8	Cameron, LA	July 5, 1982	Mike Hebert
Snapper, red	46- 8	Destin, FL	Oct. 1, 1985	E. Lane Nichols III
Snook	53-10	Parismina Ranch, Costa Rica	Oct. 18, 1978	Gilbert Ponzi
Spearfish, Mediterranean	90-13	Madeira Island, Portugal	June 2, 1980	Joseph Larkin
Swordfish	1182- 0	Iquique, Chile	May 7, 1953	L. Marron
Tarpon	283- 4	Sherbro Is., Sierra Leone	Apr. 16, 1991	Yvon Victor Sebag
Tautog	24- 0	Wachapreague, VA	Aug. 25, 1987	Gregory R. Bell
Tuna, Atlantic bigeye	375- 8	Ocean City, MD	Aug. 26, 1977	Cecil Browne
Tuna, blackfin	42- 8	Duck Key, FL	May 21, 1995	Shawn Snyder
Tuna, bluefin	1496- 0	Aulds Cove, Nova Scotia	Oct. 26, 1979	Ken Fraser
Tuna, longtail	79- 2	Montague Is., NSW, Australia	Apr. 12, 1982	Tim Simpson
Tuna, Pacific bigeye	435- 0	Cabo Blanco, Peru	Apr. 17, 1957	Dr. Russell Lee
Tuna, skipjack	41-14	Pearl Beach, Mauritius	Nov. 12, 1985	Edmund Heinzen
Tuna, southern bluefin	348- 5	Whakatane, New Zealand	Jan. 16, 1981	Rex Wood
Tuna, yellowfin	388-12	San Benedicto Island, Mexico	Apr. 1, 1977	Curt Wiesenhutter
Tunny, little	35- 2	Cape de Garde, Algeria	Dec. 14, 1988	Jean Yves Chatard
Wahoo	155- 8	San Salvador, Bahamas	Apr. 3, 1990	William Bourne
Weakfish	19- 2	Jones Beach, Long Island, NY	Oct. 11, 1984	Dennis R. Rooney
	19- 2	Delaware Bay, DE	May 20, 1989	William E. Thomas

Cochran Lands Second BASS Classic

Using an unorthodox warm-weather strategy, George Cochran won his second BASS Master Classic Championship Aug. 10 on Lay Lake near Birmingham, Ala. Cochran began the third and final day of competition in second place behind leader Mickey Bruce. Fishing as shallow as possible on a large mud flat near Bulley Creek, while most of the competition focused on deep water, the 46-year-old from Hot Springs, Ark. landed five bass weighing a combined 9 pounds, 6 ounces to give him a three-day, 15 bass total of 31 pounds, 14 ounces and put him in first place. His lucky lures were a ⅜-ounce Strike King spinnerbait, tiny Cordell Little O crankbait and a 7-inch Riverside Pro Rib worm. Davey Hite of Prosperity, S.C., placed second, just one pound back from Cochran, with a total of 30 pounds, 14 ounces

Cochran, who also won the Classic in 1987, picked up his $100,000 winner's check from the Bass Anglers Sportsman Society in front of the 19,000 fans in attendance at the final weigh-in ceremony on Saturday at the Birmingham-Jefferson Civic Center.

BASS Masters Classic

The BASS Masters Classic is fishing's version of the Masters golf tournament. Invitees to the three-day event include the 36 top-ranked pros on the BASS tour and five top-ranked amateurs. Anglers may weigh only seven bass per day and each bass must be at least 12 inches long. Competitors are allowed only seven rods and reels and are limited to the tackle they can pack into two tournament-approved tackleboxes. Only artificial lures are permitted. The first Classic, held at Lake Mead, Nevada in 1971, was a $10,000 winner-take-all event.

Multiple winners: Rick Clunn (4); George Cochran, Bobby Murray and Hank Parker (2).

Year		Weight
1971	Bobby Murray, Hot Springs, Ark	43-11
1972	Don Butler, Tulsa, Okla	38-11
1973	Rayo Breckenridge, Paragould, Ark	52- 8
1974	Tommy Martin, Hemphill, Tex	33- 7
1975	Jack Hains, Rayne, La	45- 4
1976	Rick Clunn, Montgomery, Tex	59-15
1977	Rick Clunn, Montgomery, Tex	27- 7
1978	Bobby Murray, Nashville, Tenn	37- 9
1979	Hank Parker, Clover, S.C	31- 0
1980	Bo Dowden, Natchitoches, La	54-10
1981	Stanley Mitchell, Fitzgerald, Ga	35- 2
1982	Paul Elias, Laurel, Miss	32- 8
1983	Larry Nixon, Hemphill, Tex	18- 1
1984	Rick Clunn, Montgomery, Tex	75- 9
1985	Jack Chancellor, Phenix City, Ala	45- 0
1986	Charlie Reed, Broken Bow, Okla	23- 9
1987	George Cochran, N. Little Rock, Ark	15- 5
1988	Guido Hibdon, Gravois Mills, Mo	28- 8
1989	Hank Parker, Denver, N.C	31- 6
1990	Rick Clunn, Montgomery, Tex	34- 5
1991	Ken Cook, Meers, Okla	33- 2
1992	Robert Hamilton Jr., Brandon, Miss	59- 6
1993	David Fritts, Lexington, N.C	48- 6
1994	Bryan Kerchal, Newtown, Conn	36- 7
1995	Mark Davis, Mount Ida, Ark.	47-14
1996	George Cochran, Hot Springs, Ark.	31-14

LITTLE LEAGUE BASEBALL

World Series

See story page 926.

Multiple winners: Taiwan (16); California (5); Connecticut and Pennsylvania (4); Japan and New Jersey (3); Mexico, New York, South Korea and Texas (2).

Year	Winner	Score	Loser
1947	Williamsport, PA	16-7	Lock Haven, PA
1948	Lock Haven, PA	6-5	St. Petersburg, FL
1949	Hammonton, NJ	5-0	Pensacola, FL
1950	Houston, TX	2-1	Bridgeport, CT
1951	Stamford, CT	3-0	Austin, TX
1952	Norwalk, CT	4-3	Monongahela, PA
1953	Birmingham, AL	1-0	Schenectady, NY
1954	Schenectady, NY	7-5	Colton, CA
1955	Morrisville, PA	4-3	Merchantville, NJ
1956	Roswell, NM	3-1	Merchantville, NJ
1957	Monterrey, Mexico	4-0	La Mesa, CA
1958	Monterrey, Mexico	10-1	Kankakee, IL
1959	Hamtramck, MI	12-0	Auburn, CA
1960	Levittown, PA	5-0	Ft. Worth, TX
1961	El Cajon, CA	4-2	El Campo, TX
1962	San Jose, CA	3-0	Kankakee, IL
1963	Granada Hills, CA	2-1	Stratford, CT
1964	Staten Island, NY	4-0	Monterrey, Mex.
1965	Windsor Locks, CT	3-1	Stoney Creek, Can.
1966	Houston, TX	8-2	W. New York, NJ
1967	West Tokyo, Japan	4-1	Chicago, IL
1968	Osaka, Japan	1-0	Richmond, VA
1969	Taipei, Taiwan	5-0	Santa Clara,CA
1970	Wayne, NJ	2-0	Campbell, CA
1971	Tainan, Taiwan	12-3	Gary, IN
1972	Taipei, Taiwan	6-0	Hammond, IN
1973	Tainan City, Taiwan	12-0	Tucson, AZ
1974	Kao Hsiung, Taiwan	12-1	Red Bluff, CA
1975	Lakewood, NJ	4-3*	Tampa, FL
1976	Tokyo, Japan	10-3	Campbell, CA
1977	Li-Teh, Taiwan	7-2	El Cajon, CA
1978	Pin-Tung, Taiwan	11-1	Danville, CA
1979	Hsien, Taiwan	2-1	Campbell, CA
1980	Hua Lian, Taiwan	4-3	Tampa, FL
1981	Tai-Chung, Taiwan	4-2	Tampa, FL
1982	Kirkland, WA	6-0	Hsien, Taiwan
1983	Marietta, GA	3-1	Barahona, D. Rep.
1984	Seoul, S. Korea	6-2	Altamonte, FL
1985	Seoul, S. Korea	7-1	Mexicali, Mex.
1986	Tainan Park, Taiwan	12-0	Tucson, AZ
1987	Hua Lian, Taiwan	21-1	Irvine, CA
1988	Tai Ping, Taiwan	10-0	Pearl City, HI
1989	Trumbull, CT	5-2	Kaohsiung, Taiwan
1990	Taipei, Taiwan	9-0	Shippensburg, PA
1991	Taichung, Taiwan	11-0	Danville, CA
1992	Long Beach, CA	6-0	Zamboanga, Phil.
1993	Long Beach, CA	3-2	Panama
1994	Maracaibo, Venezuela	4-3	Northridge, CA
1995	Tainan, Taiwan	17-3	Spring, TX
1996	Taipei, Taiwan	13-3	Cranston, R.I. (called after 5th inn.)

*Foreign teams were banned from the tournament in 1975, but allowed back in the following year.

Note: In 1992, Zamboanga City of the Philippines beat Long Beach, 15-4, but was stripped of the title a month later when it was discovered that the team had used several players from outside the city limits. Long Beach was then awarded the title by forfeit, 6-0 (one run for each inning of the game).

POWER BOAT RACING

APBA Gold Cup

Dave Villwock took advantage of the absence of hydroplane racing stars Chip Hanauer and Mark Tate and drove Pico/American Dream to a half-mile victory over defending champion Miss Budweiser Sunday evening, June 2 on the Detroit River. Hanauer, normally at the helm of the famed Miss Budweiser, was replaced by driver Mark Evans after sustaining a concussion in preliminary heat. Hanauer barrel-rolled and hit Tate causing considerable damage to both Miss Budweiser and Tate's boat, Smokin' Joe's. Tate, a two-time Gold Cup champ, boat could not be repaired in time for Sunday's final. Villwock, last year's runner-up, averaged a 149.328 mph on the inside lane of the 2.5-mile course earning his first Gold Cup victory in four attempts.

The American Power Boat Association Gold Cup for unlimited hydroplane racing is the oldest active motor sports trophy in North America. The first Gold Cup was competed for on the Hudson River in New York in June and September of 1904. Since then several cities have hosted the race, led by Detroit (28 times, including 1990) and Seattle (14). Note that (*) indicates driver was also owner of the winning boat.

Drivers with multiple wins: Chip Hanauer (10); Bill Muncey (8); Gar Wood (5); Dean Chenoweth (4); Caleb Bragg, Tom D'Eath, Lou Fageol, Ron Musson, George Reis and Jonathon Wainwright (3); Danny Foster, George Henley, Vic Kliesrath, E.J. Schroeder, Bill Schumacher, Zalmon G.Simmons Jr., Joe Taggart, Mark Tate, and George Townsend (2).

Year	Boat	Driver	Avg.MPH
1904	*Standard* (June)	Carl Riotte*	23.160
1904	*Vingt-Et-Un II* (Sept.)	W. Sharpe Kilmer*	24.900
1905	*Chip I*	J. Wainwright*	15.000
1906	*Chip II*	J. Wainwright*	25.000
1907	*Chip II*	J. Wainwright*	23.903
1908	*Dixie II*	E.J. Schroede*	29.938
1909	*Dixie II*	E.J. Schroeder*	29.590
1910	*Dixie III*	F.K. Burnham*	32.473
1911	*MIT II*	J.H. Hayden*	37.000
1912	*P.D.Q. II*	A.G. Miles*	39.462
1913	*Ankle Deep*	Cas Mankowski*	42.779
1914	*Baby Speed Demon II*	Jim Blackton & Bob Edgren	48.458
1915	*Miss Detroit*	Johnny Milot & Jack Beebe	37.656
1916	*Miss Minneapolis*	Bernard Smith	48.860
1917	*Miss Detroit II*	Gar Wood*	54.410
1918	*Miss Detroit II*	Gar Wood	51.619
1919	*Miss Detroit III*	Gar Wood*	42.748
1920	*Miss America I*	Gar Wood*	62.022
1921	*Miss America I*	Gar Wood*	52.825
1922	*Packard Chriscraft*	J.G. Vincent*	40.253
1923	*Packard Chriscraft*	Caleb Bragg	43.867
1924	*Baby Bootlegger*	Caleb Bragg*	45.302
1925	*Baby Bootlegger*	Caleb Bragg*	47.240
1926	*Greenwich Folly*	George Townsend*	47.984
1927	*Greenwich Folly*	George Townsend*	47.662
1928	Not held		
1929	*Imp*	Richard Hoyt*	48.662
1930	*Hotsy Totsy*	Vic Kliesrath*	52.673
1931	*Hotsy Totsy*	Vic Kliesrath*	53.602
1932	*Delphine IV*	Bill Horn	57.775
1933	*El Lagarto*	George Reis*	56.260
1934	*El Lagarto*	George Reis*	55.000
1935	*El Lagarto*	George Reis*	55.056
1936	*Impshi*	Kaye Don	45.735
1937	*Notre Dame*	Clell Perry	63.675
1938	*Alagi*	Theo Rossi*	64.340
1939	*My Sin*	Z.G. Simmons Jr.*	66.133
1940	*Hotsy Totsy III*	Sidney Allen*	48.295
1941	*My Sin*	Z.G. Simmons Jr.*	52.509
1942-45	Not held		
1946	*Tempo VI*	Guy Lombardo*	68.132
1947	*Miss Peps V*	Danny Foster	57.000
1948	*Miss Great Lakes*	Danny Foster	46.845
1949	*My Sweetie*	Bill Cantrell	73.612
1950	*Slo-Mo-Shun IV*	Ted Jones	78.216
1951	*Slo-Mo-Shun V*	Lou Fageol	90.871
1952	*Slo-Mo-Shun IV*	Stan Dollar	79.923
1953	*Slo-Mo-Shun IV*	Joe Taggart & Lou Fageol	99.108
1954	*Slo-Mo-Shun IV*	Joe Taggart & Lou Fageol	92.613
1955	*Gale V*	Lee Schoenith	99.552
1956	*Miss Thirftaway*	Bill Muncey	96.552
1957	*Miss Thriftaway*	Bill Muncey	101.787
1958	*Hawaii Kai III*	Jack Regas	103.000
1959	*Maverick*	Bill Stead	104.481
1960	Not held		
1961	*Miss Century 21*	Bill Muncey	99.678
1962	*Miss Century 21*	Bill Muncey	100.710
1963	*Miss Bardahl*	Ron Musson	105.124
1964	*Miss Bardahl*	Ron Musson	103.433
1965	*Miss Bardahl*	Ron Musson	103.132
1966	*Tahoe Miss*	Mira Slovak	93.019
1967	*Miss Bardahl*	Bill Shumacher	101.484
1968	*Miss Bardahl*	Bill Shumacher	108.173
1969	*Miss Budweiser*	Bill Sterett	98.504
1970	*Miss Budweiser*	Dean Chenoweth	99.562
1971	*Miss Madison*	Jim McCormick	98.043
1972	*Atlas Van Lines*	Bill Muncey	104.277
1973	*Miss Budweiser*	Dean Chenoweth	99.043
1974	*Pay 'n Pak*	George Henley	104.428
1975	*Pay 'n Pak*	George Henley	108.921
1976	*Miss U.S.*	Tom D'Eath	100.412
1977	*Atlas Van Lines*	Bill Muncey*	111.822
1978	*Atlas Van Lines*	Bill Muncey*	111.412
1979	*Atlas Van Lines*	Bill Muncey*	100.765
1980	*Miss Budweiser*	Dean Chenoweth	106.932
1981	*Miss Budweiser*	Dean Chenoweth	116.932
1982	*Atlas Van Lines*	Chip Hanauer	120.050
1983	*Atlas Van Lines*	Chip Hanauer	118.507
1984	*Atlas Van Lines*	Chip Hanauer	130.175
1985	*Miller American*	Chip Hanauer	120.643
1986	*Miller American*	Chip Hanauer	116.523
1987	*Miller American*	Chip Hanauer	127.620
1988	*Miss Circus Circus*	Chip Hanauer & Jim Prevost	123.756
1989	*Miss Budweiser*	Tom D'Eath	131.209
1990	*Miss Budweiser*	Tom D'Eath	143.176
1991	*Winston Eagle*	Mark Tate	137.771
1992	*Miss Budweiser*	Chip Hanauer	136.282
1993	*Miss Budweiser*	Chip Hanauer	141.296
1994	*Smokin' Joe's*	Mark Tate	145.532
1995	*Miss Budweiser*	Chip Hanauer	149.160
1996	*Pico/American Dream*	Dave Villwock	149.328

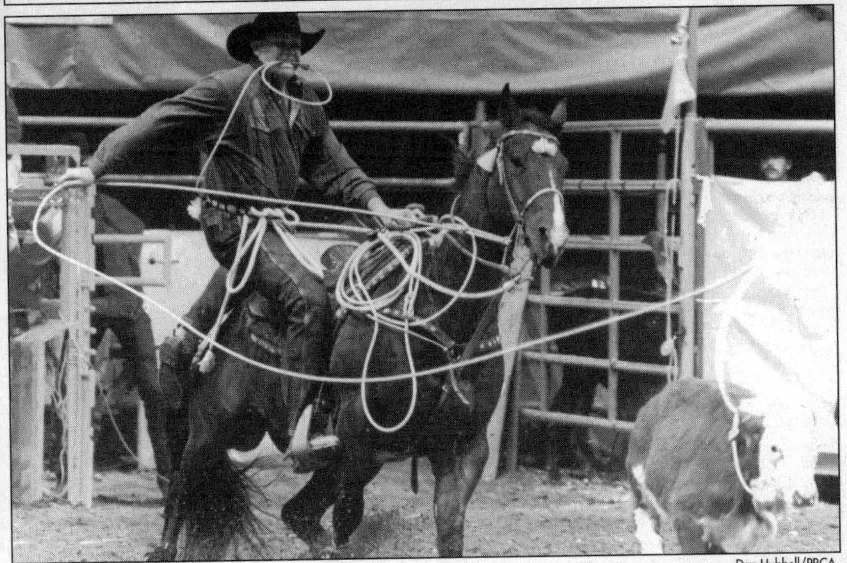

Dan Hubbell/PRCA

Joe Beaver roped his first PRCA all-around cowboy championship in 1995. Beaver, a calf-roping specialist, was unablle, however, to snare the calf-roping world title in 1995, finishing in second.

PRO RODEO

All-Around Champion Cowboy

Joe Beaver of Huntsville, Tex., finally won the title he had understudied for behind six-time champion Ty Murray at the National Finals Rodeo on Dec. 10, 1995 in Las Vegas. Murray was not a factor after suffering a knee injury in June and the 30-year-old Beaver, who finished second to Murray in three of the last four years, claimed the all-around cowboy title with $141,753. Beaver continued his success at the time-event end of the arena but missed out on his sixth calf-roping world title, finishing second behind Fred Whitfield.

The Professional Rodeo Cowboys Association (PRCA) title of All-Around World Champion Cowboy goes to the rodeo athlete who wins the most prize money in a single year in two or more events. Only prize money earned in sanctioned PRCA rodeos is counted. From 1929-44, All-Around champions were named by the Rodeo Association of America (earnings for those years is not available).

Multiple winners: Tom Ferguson, Larry Mahan and Ty Murray (6); Jim Shoulders (5); Lewis Feild and Dean Oliver (3); Everett Bowman, Louis Brooks, Clay Carr, Bill Linderman, Phil Lyne, Gerald Roberts, Casey Tibbs and Harry Tompkins (2).

Year	
1929	Earl Thode
1930	Clay Carr
1931	John Schneider
1932	Donald Nesbit
1933	Clay Carr
1934	Leonard Ward
1935	Everett Bowman
1936	John Bowman
1937	Everett Bowman
1938	Burel Mulkey
1939	Paul Carney
1940	Fritz Truan
1941	Homer Pettigrew
1942	Gerald Roberts
1943	Louis Brooks
1944	Louis Brooks
1945-46	No award

Year		Earnings
1947	Todd Whatley	$18,642
1948	Gerald Roberts	21,766
1949	Jim Shoulders	21,495
1950	Bill Linderman	30,715
1951	Casey Tibbs	29,104
1952	Harry Tompkins	30,934
1953	Bill Linderman	33,674
1954	Buck Rutherford	40,404
1955	Casey Tibbs	42,065
1956	Jim Shoulders	43,381
1957	Jim Shoulders	33,299
1958	Jim Shoulders	32,212
1959	Jim Shoulders	32,905
1960	Harry Tompkins	32,522
1961	Benny Reynolds	31,309
1962	Tom Nesmith	32,611
1963	Dean Oliver	31,329
1964	Dean Oliver	$31,150
1965	Dean Oliver	33,163
1966	Larry Mahan	40,358
1967	Larry Mahan	51,996
1968	Larry Mahan	49,129
1969	Larry Mahan	57,726
1970	Larry Mahan	41,493
1971	Phil Lyne	49,245
1972	Phil Lyne	60,852
1973	Larry Mahan	64,447
1974	Tom Ferguson	66,929
1975	Tom Ferguson	50,300
1976	Tom Ferguson	87,908
1977	Tom Ferguson	65,981
1978	Tom Ferguson	83,734
1979	Tom Ferguson	96,272
1980	Paul Tierney	$105,568
1981	Jimmie Cooper	105,861
1982	Chris Lybbert	123,709
1983	Roy Cooper	153,391
1984	Dee Pickett	122,618
1985	Lewis Feild	130,347
1986	Lewis Feild	166,042
1987	Lewis Feild	144,335
1988	Dave Appleton	121,546
1989	Ty Murray	134,806
1990	Ty Murray	213,772
1991	Ty Murray	244,231
1992	Ty Murray	225,992
1993	Ty Murray	297,896
1994	Ty Murray	246,170
1995	Joe Beaver	141,753

SOAP BOX DERBY

All-American Soap Box Derby

Tim Scrofano won the Master's division at the 59th All-American Soap Box Derby in Akron, Ohio on Aug. 10 in the closest finish in the Derby's history. The 12-year-old edged Akron's Janice Shook in a photo finish to win the Master's title and a $5000 scholarship. Scrofano's winning time clocked in at 28.65 seconds. Jeremy Phillips, 14, took the superstock division in 28.88 while 12-year-old Matt Perez won the stock division with a time of 29.03.

The All-American Soap Box Derby is a coasting race for small gravity-powered cars built by their drivers and assembled within strict guidelines on size, weight and cost. The Derby got its name in the 1930s when most cars were built from wooden soap boxes. Held every summer on the second Saturday of August at Derby Downs in Akron, the Soap Box Derby is open to all boys and girls from 9 to 16 years old who qualify.

There are three competitive divisions: 1. Stock (ages 9-16)— made up of generic, prefab racers that come from Derby - approved kits, can be assembled in four hours and don't exceed 200 pounds when driver, car and wheels are weighed together; 2. Super Stock (ages 10-16)— the same as Stock only with a weight limit of 220 pounds; 3. Masters (ages 11-16)— made up of racers designed by the drivers, but constructed with Derby-approved hardware. The racing ramp at Derby Downs is 953.75 feet with an 11 percent grade.

One champion reigned at the All-American Soap Box Derby each year from 1934-75; Junior and Senior division champions from 1976-87; Kit and Masters champions from 1988-91; and Stock, Kit and Masters champions starting in 1992.

Year		Hometown	Age
1934	Robert Turner	Muncie, IN	11
1935	Maurice Bale Jr.	Anderson, IN	13
1936	Herbert Muench Jr.	St. Louis	14
1937	Robert Ballard	White Plains, NY	12
1938	Robert Berger	Omaha, NE	14
1939	Clifton Hardesty	White Plains, NY	11
1940	Thomas Fisher	Detroit	12
1941	Claude Smith	Akron, OH	14
1942-45	Not held		
1946	Gilbert Klecan	San Diego	14
1947	Kenneth Holmboe	Charleston, WV	14
1948	Donald Strub	Akron, OH	13
1949	Fred Derks	Akron, OH	15
1950	Harold Williamson	Charleston, WV	15
1951	Darwin Cooper	Williamsport, PA	15
1952	Joe Lunn	Columbus, GA	11
1953	Fred Mohler	Muncie, IN	14
1954	Richard Kemp	Los Angeles	14
1955	Richard Rohrer	Rochester, NY	14
1956	Norman Westfall	Rochester, NY	14
1957	Terry Townsend	Anderson, IN	14
1958	James Miley	Muncie, IN	15
1959	Barney Townsend	Anderson, IN	13
1960	Fredric Lake	South Bend, IN	11
1961	Dick Dawson	Wichita, KS	13
1962	David Mann	Gary, IN	14
1963	Harold Conrad	Duluth, MN	12
1964	Gregory Schumacher	Tacoma, WA	14
1965	Robert Logan	Santa Ana, CA	12
1966	David Krussow	Tacoma, WA	12
1967	Kenneth Cline	Lincoln, NE	13
1968	Branch Lew	Muncie, IN	11
1969	Steve Souter	Midland, TX	12
1970	Samuel Gupton	Durham, NC	13
1971	Larry Blair	Oroville, CA	13
1972	Robert Lange Jr.	Boulder, CO	14
1973	Bret Yarborough	Elk Grove, CA	11
1974	Curt Yarborough	Elk Grove, CA	11
1975	Karren Stead	Lower Bucks, PA	11
1976	JR: Phil Raber	Sugarcreek, OH	11
	SR: Joan Ferdinand	Canton, OH	14
1977	JR: Mark Ferdinand	Canton, OH	10
	SR: Steve Washburn	Bristol, CT	15
1978	JR: Darren Hart	Salem, OR	11
	SR: Greg Cardinal	Flint, MI	13
1979	JR: Russell Yurk	Flint, MI	10
	SR: Craig Kitchen	Akron, OH	14
1980	JR: Chris Fulton	Indianapolis	11
	SR: Dan Porul	Sherman Oaks, CA	12
1981	JR: Howie Fraley	Portsmouth, OH	11
	SR: Tonia Schlegel	Hamilton, OH	13
1982	JR: Carol A. Sullivan	Rochester, NH	10
	SR: Matt Wolfgang	Lehigh Val., PA	12
1983	JR: Tony Carlini	Del Mar, CA	10
	SR: Mike Burdgick	Flint, MI	14
1984	JR: Chris Hess	Hamilton, OH	11
	SR: Anita Jackson	St. Louis	15
1985	JR: Michael Gallo	Danbury, CT	12
	SR: Matt Sheffer	York, PA	14
1986	JR: Marc Behan	Dover, NH	9
	SR: Tami Jo Sullivan	Lancaster, OH	13
1987	JR: Matt Margules	Danbury, CT	11
	SR: Brian Drinkwater	Bristol, CT	14
1988	KIT: Jason Lamb	Des Moines, IA	10
	MAS: David Duffield	Kansas City	13
1989	KIT: David Schiller	Dayton, OH	12
	MAS: Faith Chavarria	Ventura, CA	12
1990	MAS: Sami Jones	Salem, OR	13
	KIT: Mark Mihal	Valparaiso, IN	12
1991	MAS: Danny Garland	San Diego, CA	14
	KIT: Paul Greenwald	Saginaw, MI	13
1992	MAS: Bonnie Thornton	Redding, CA	12
	KIT: Carolyn Fox	Sublimity, OR	11
	STK: Loren Hurst	Hudson, OH	10
1993	MAS: Dean Lutton	Delta, OH	14
	KIT: D.M. Del Ferraro	Stow, OH	12
	STK: Owen Yuda	Boiling Springs, PA	10
1994	MAS: D.M. Del Ferraro	Akron, OH	13
	KIT: Joel Endres	Akron, OH	14
	STK: Kristina Damond	Jamestown, NY	13
1995	MAS: J. Fensterbush	Kingman, AZ	11
	SS: Darcie Davisson	Kingman, AZ	11
	STK: Karen Thomas	Jamestown, NY	11
1996	MAS: Tim Scrofano	Conneaut, OH	12
	SS: Jeremy Phillips	Charlestown, WV	14
	STK: Matt Perez	No. Canton, OH	12

Wide World Photos

Welsh full back Justin Thomas, under pressure from the French pack, clears his lines in the early going of their 1996 **Five Nations rugby** match at Cardiff Arms Park on Mar. 16. Wales, holder of a record 33 Five Nations titles, would go on to win the match, 16-15.

Five Nations Rugby

The annual Five Nations rugby union champions first contested by England, Ireland, Scotland and Wales. France made it five nations by joining the competition in 1910. Each team plays each other once and the team with the best record is declared the winner. (*) indicates Grand Slam, meaning team won all four games.

Multiple Winners: Wales (33), England (32), Scotland (20, France and Ireland (18).

Year	
1882	England
1883	England
1884	Not held
1885	Not completed
1886	Scotland & England
1887	Scotland
1888	Not completed
1889	Not completed
1890	England & Scotland
1891	Scotland
1892	England
1893	Wales
1894	Ireland
1895	Scotland
1896	Ireland
1897	Not completed
1898	Not completed
1899	Ireland
1900	Wales
1901	Scotland
1902	Wales
1903	Scotland
1904	Scotland
1905	Wales
1906	Ireland & Wales
1907	Scotland
1908	Wales*
1909	Wales*
1910	England
1911	Wales*
1912	England & Ireland
1913	England*
1914	England*
1915-19	Not held—WW I
1920	England, Scotland & Wales

Year	
1921	England*
1922	Wales
1923	England*
1924	England*
1925	Scotland*
1926	Scotland & Ireland
1927	Scotland & Ireland
1928	England*
1929	Scotland
1930	England
1931	Wales
1932	England, Wales & Ireland
1933	Scotland
1934	England
1935	Ireland
1936	Wales
1937	England
1938	Scotland
1939	England, Wales & Ireland
1940-46	Not held—WW II
1947	Wales & England
1948	Ireland*
1949	Ireland
1950	Wales*
1951	Ireland
1952	Wales*
1953	England
1954	England, France & Wales
1955	France & Wales
1956	Wales
1957	England*
1958	England
1959	France
1960	France & England
1961	France

Year	
1962	France
1963	England
1964	Scotland & Wales
1965	Wales
1966	Wales
1967	France
1968	France*
1969	Wales
1970	France & Wales
1971	Wales*
1972	Not completed
1973	Five way tie
1974	Ireland
1975	Wales
1976	Wales*
1977	France*
1978	Wales*
1979	Wales
1980	England*
1981	France*
1982	Ireland
1983	France & Ireland
1984	Scotland*
1985	Ireland
1986	France & Scotland
1987	France*
1988	Wales & France
1989	France
1990	Scotland*
1991	England*
1992	England*
1993	France
1994	Wales
1995	England*
1996	England

SOFTBALL

Men's and women's national champions since 1933 in Major Fast Pitch, Major Slow Pitch and Super Slow Pitch (men only). Sanctioned by the Amateur Softball Association of America.

MEN

Major Fast Pitch

Multiple winners: Clearwater Bombers (10); Raybestos Cardinals (5); Sealmasters (4); Briggs Beautyware, Pay'n Pak and Zollner Pistons (3); Billard Barbell, Decatur Pride, Hammer Air Field, Kodak Park, National Health Care, Penn Corp and Peterbilt Western (2).

Year
1933 J.L. Gill Boosters, Chicago
1934 Ke-Nash-A, Kenosha, WI
1935 Crimson Coaches, Toledo, OH
1936 Kodak Park, Rochester, NY
1937 Briggs Body Team, Detroit
1938 The Pohlers, Cincinnati
1939 Carr's Boosters, Covington, KY

1940 Kodak Park
1941 Bendix Brakes, South Bend, IN
1942 Deep Rock Oilers, Tulsa, OK
1943 Hammer Air Field, Fresno, CA
1944 Hammer Air Field
1945 Zollner Pistons, Ft. Wayne, IN
1946 Zollner Pistons
1947 Zollner Pistons
1948 Briggs Beautyware, Detroit
1949 Tip Top Tailors, Toronto

1950 Clearwater (FL) Bombers
1951 Dow Chemical, Midland, MI
1952 Briggs Beautyware
1953 Briggs Beautyware
1954 Clearwater Bombers
1955 Raybestos Cardinals, Stratford, CT

Year
1956 Clearwater Bombers
1957 Clearwater Bombers
1958 Raybestos Cardinals
1959 Sealmasters, Aurora, IL

1960 Clearwater Bombers
1961 Sealmasters
1962 Clearwater Bombers
1963 Clearwater Bombers
1964 Burch Tool, Detroit
1965 Sealmasters
1966 Clearwater Bombers
1967 Sealmasters
1968 Clearwater Bombers
1969 Raybestos Cardinals

1970 Raybestos Cardinals
1971 Welty Way, Cedar Rapids, IA
1972 Raybestos Cardinals
1973 Clearwater Bombers
1974 Gianella Bros., Santa Rosa, CA
1975 Rising Sun Hotel, Reading, PA
1976 Raybestos Cardinals
1977 Billard Barbell, Reading, PA
1978 Billard Barbell

Year
1979 McArdle Pontiac/Cadillac, Midland, MI

1980 Peterbilt Western, Seattle
1981 Archer Daniels Midland, Decatur, IL
1982 Peterbilt Western
1983 Franklin Cardinals, Stratford, CT
1984 California Kings, Merced, CA
1985 Pay'n Pak, Seattle
1986 Pay'n Pak
1987 Pay'n Pak
1988 TransAire, Elkhart, IN
1989 Penn Corp, Sioux City, IA

1990 Penn Corp
1991 Gianella Bros., Rohnert Park, CA
1992 National Health Care, Sioux City, IA
1993 National Health Care
1994 Decatur (IL) Pride
1995 Decatur Pride
1996 Green Bay All-Car, Green Bay, WI

Super Slow Pitch

Multiple winners: Howard's/Western Steer, Rich's/Superior and Steele's Sports (3).

Year
1981 Howard's/Western Steer, Denver, NC
1982 Jerry's Catering, Miami
1983 Howard's/Western Steer
1984 Howard's/Western Steer
1985 Steele's Sports, Grafton, OH
1986 Steele's Sports

Year
1987 Steele's Sports
1988 Starpath, Monticello, KY
1989 Ritch's Salvage, Harrisburg, NC
1990 Steele's Silver Bullets
1991 Sun Belt/Worth, Atlanta
1992 Rich's/Superior, Windsor Locks, CT

Year
1993 Rich's/Superior
1994 Bellcorp., Tampa
1995 Lighthouse/Worth, Stone Mt., GA
1996 Rich's/Superior

Major Slow Pitch

Multiple winners: Gatliff Auto Sales, Riverside Paving and Skip Hogan A.C. (3); Campbell Carpets, Hamilton Tailoring and Howard's Furniture (2).

Year
1953 Shields Construction, Newport, KY
1954 Waldneck's Tavern, Cincinnati
1955 Lang Pet Shop, Covington, KY
1956 Gatliff Auto Sales, Newport, KY
1957 Gatliff Auto Sales
1958 East Side Sports, Detroit
1959 Yorkshire Restaurant, Newport, KY

1960 Hamilton Tailoring, Cincinnati
1961 Hamilton Tailoring
1962 Skip Hogan A.C., Pittsburgh
1963 Gatliff Auto Sales
1964 Skip Hogan A.C.
1965 Skip Hogan A.C.
1966 Michael's Lounge, Detroit

Year
1967 Jim's Sport Shop, Pittsburgh
1968 County Sports, Levittown, NY
1969 Copper Hearth, Milwaukee

1970 Little Caesar's, Southgate, MI
1971 Pile Drivers, Va. Beach, VA
1972 Jiffy Club, Louisville, KY
1973 Howard's Furniture, Denver, NC
1974 Howard's Furniture
1975 Pyramid Cafe, Lakewood, OH
1976 Warren Motors, J'ville, FL
1977 Nelson Painting, Okla. City
1978 Campbell Carpets, Concord, CA
1979 Nelco Mfg. Co., Okla. City

1980 Campbell Carpets
1981 Elite Coating, Gordon, CA
1982 Triangle Sports, Minneapolis

Year
1983 No.1 Electric & Heating, Gastonia, NC
1984 Lilly Air Systems, Chicago
1985 Blanton's Fayetteville, NC
1986 Non-Ferrous Metals, Cleveland
1987 Stapath, Monticello, KY
1988 Bell Corp/FAF, Tampa, FL
1989 Ritch's Salvage, Harrisburg, NC

1990 New Construction, Shelbyville,IN
1991 Riverside Paving, Louisville
1992 Vernon's, Jacksonville, FL
1993 Back Porch/Destin (FL) Roofing
1994 Riverside Paving, Louisville
1995 Riverside Paving
1996 Bell II, Orlando, FL

WOMEN

Major Fast Pitch

Multiple winners: Raybestos Brakettes (21); Orange Lionettes (9); Jax Maids (5); Arizona Ramblers and Redding Rebels (3); Hi-Ho Brakettes, J.J. Krieg's and National Screw & Manufacturing (2).

Year	
1933	Great Northerns, Chicago
1934	Hart Motors, Chicago
1935	Bloomer Girls, Cleveland
1936	Nat'l Screw & Mfg., Cleveland
1937	Nat'l Screw & Mfg.
1938	J.J. Krieg's, Alameda, CA
1939	J.J. Krieg's
1940	Arizona Ramblers, Phoenix
1941	Higgins Midgets, Tulsa, OK
1942	Jax Maids, New Orleans
1943	Jax Maids
1944	Lind & Pomeroy, Portland, OR
1945	Jax Maids
1946	Jax Maids
1947	Jax Maids
1948	Arizona Ramblers
1949	Arizona Ramblers
1950	Orange (CA) Lionettes
1951	Orange Lionettes
1952	Orange Lionettes
1953	Betsy Ross Rockets, Fresno, CA
1954	Leach Motor Rockets, Fresno, CA
1955	Orange Lionettes
1956	Orange Lionettes
1957	Hacienda Rockets, Fresno, CA
1958	Raybestos Brakettes, Stratford, CT
1959	Raybestos Brakettes
1960	Raybestos Brakettes
1961	Gold Sox, Whittier, CA
1962	Orange Lionettes
1963	Raybestos Brakettes
1964	Erv Lind Florists, Portland, OR
1965	Orange Lionettes
1966	Raybestos Brakettes
1967	Raybestos Brakettes
1968	Raybestos Brakettes
1969	Orange Lionettes
1970	Orange Lionettes
1971	Raybestos Brakettes
1972	Raybestos Brakettes
1973	Raybestos Brakettes
1974	Raybestos Brakettes
1975	Raybestos Brakettes
1976	Raybestos Brakettes
1977	Raybestos Brakettes
1978	Raybestos Brakettes
1979	Sun City (AZ) Saints
1980	Raybestos Brakettes
1981	Orlando (FL) Rebels
1982	Raybestos Brakettes
1983	Raybestos Brakettes
1984	Los Angeles Diamonds
1985	Hi-Ho Brakettes, Stratford, CT
1986	So. California Invasion, LA
1987	Orange County Majestics, Anaheim, CA
1988	Hi-Ho Brakettes
1989	Whittier (CA) Raiders
1990	Raybestos Brakettes
1991	Raybestos Brakettes
1992	Raybestos Brakettes
1993	Redding (CA) Rebels
1994	Redding Rebels
1995	Redding Rebels
1996	California Commotion, Woodland Hills

Major Slow Pitch

Multiple winners: Spooks (5); Dana Gardens (4); Universal Plastics (3); Cannan's Illusions, Bob Hoffman's Dots and Marks Brothers Dots (2).

Year	
1959	Pearl Laundry, Richmond, VA
1960	Carolina Rockets, High Pt., NC
1961	Dairy Cottage, Covington, KY
1962	Dana Gardens, Cincinnati
1963	Dana Gardens
1964	Dana Gardens
1965	Art's Acres, Omaha, NE
1966	Dana Gardens
1967	Ridge Maintenance, Cleveland
1968	Escue Pontiac, Cincinnati
1969	Converse Dots, Hialeah, FL
1970	Rutenschruder Floral, Cincinnati
1971	Gators, Ft. Lauderdale, FL
1972	Riverside Ford, Cincinnati
1973	Sweeney Chevrolet, Cincinnati
1974	Marks Brothers Dots, Miami
1975	Marks Brothers Dots
1976	Sorrento's Pizza, Cincinnati
1977	Fox Valley Lassies, St. Charles, IL
1978	Bob Hoffman's Dots, Miami
1979	Bob Hoffman's Dots
1980	Howard's Rubi-Otts, Graham, NC
1981	Tifton (GA) Tomboys
1982	Richmond (VA) Stompers
1983	Spooks, Anoka, MN
1984	Spooks
1985	Key Ford Mustangs, Pensacola, FL
1986	Sur-Way Tomboys, Tifton, GA
1987	Key Ford Mustangs
1988	Spooks
1989	Cannan's Illusions, Houston
1990	Spooks
1991	Cannan's Illusions, San Antonio
1992	Universal Plastics, Cookeville, TN
1993	Universal Plastics
1994	Universal Plastics
1995	Armed Forces, Sacramento
1996	Spooks

Other 1996 Champions

Slow Pitch

MEN

Class A—Reece, Springfield, Ky.
Major Industrial—Sikorsky, Stratford, Conn.
Class A Industrial—Luria Bros., Ellwood, Pa.
35-Over—Capital X-Ray, Herndon, Va.
40-Over—ECN Mortgage, Melbourne, Fla.
45-Over—Winchell, Evansville, Ind.
55-Over—Northdurft, St. Claire Shore, Mich.
60-Over—Fairway Ford, Placentia, Calif.
65-Over—Palm Springs 65's, Westminster, Calif.
Major Church—Olive Baptist, Pensacola, Fla.
Class A Church—Cottage Hill, Mobile, Ala.

WOMEN

Class A—Fletch's Softball Club, Newark, Del.
Industrial—Denso Mfg., Maryville, Tenn.
Church—North Gadsden, Gadsden, Ala.
35-Over—Don's Softball Crew, Dothan, Ala.

Fast Pitch

MEN

Class A—Hy-Line Enterprises, Elkhart, Ind.
Class B—D&R Engine, Odessa, Tex.
Class C—Lorain UPC, Lorain, Ohio
40-Over—Knoll Lumber Legends, Mill Creek, Mass.
45-Over—Colt 45's, Clearwater, Fla.
23-Under—Junkers, Garden City, Minn.

WOMEN

Class A—Diamonds, Montclair, Calif.
Class B—Xplosion, Tampa, Fla.
Class C—Pat McKeown Ford, Charlevoix, Mich.

COED

Major—Spaghetti/Station, Spokane, Wash.
Class A—Evansville Blue Crew, Evansville, Ind.

Modified Pitch

Women's Major—Thunderbolts, Keene, N.H.
Men's Major—CBS, New York, N.Y.
Class A—Waves, Cecilton, Md.

TRIATHLON

World Championship

Contested since 1989, the Triathlon World Championship consists of a 1.5 kilometer swim, a 40-kilometer bike ride and a 10-kilometer run. The 1996 championship took place Aug. 24 in Cleveland, Ohio.

Multiple winners: MEN— Simon Lessing (3); Spencer Smith (2). WOMEN— Michelle Jones and Karen Smyers (2).

MEN

Year		Time
1989	Mark Allen, United States	1:58:46
1990	Greg Welch, Australia	1:51:37
1991	Miles Stewart, Australia	1:48:20
1992	Simon Lessing, Great Britain	1:49:04
1993	Spencer Smith, Great Britain	1:51:20
1994	Spencer Smith, Great Britain	1:51:04
1995	Simon Lessing, Great Britain	1:48:29
1996	Simon Lessing, Great Britain	1:39:50

WOMEN

Year		Time
1989	Erin Baker, New Zealand	2:10:01
1990	Karen Smyers, United States	2:03:33
1991	Joanne Ritchie, Canada	2:02:04
1992	Michellie Jones, Australia	2:02:08
1993	Michellie Jones, Australia	2:07:41
1994	Emma Carney, Australia	2:03:19
1995	Karen Smyers, USA	2:04:58
1996	Jackie Gallagher, Australia	1:50:52

Ironman Championship

Contested in Hawaii since 1978, the Ironman Triathlon Championship consists of a 2.4-mile swim, a 112-mile bike ride and 26.2-mile run. The race begins at 7 A.M. and continues all day until the course is closed at midnight. The 1996 Ironman Championship was scheduled for Oct. 26.

MEN

Multiple winners: Mark Allen and Dave Scott (6); Scott Tinley (2).

Year	Date	Winner	Time	Runner-up	Margin	Start	Finish	Location
I	2/18/78	Gordon Haller	11:46	John Dunbar	34:00	15	12	Waikiki Beach
II	1/14/79	Tom Warren	11:15:56	John Dunbar	48:00	15	12	Waikiki Beach
III	1/10/80	Dave Scott	9:24:33	Chuck Neumann	1:08	108	95	Ala Moana Park
IV	2/14/81	John Howard	9:38:29	Tom Warren	26:00	326	299	Kailua-Kona
V	2/6/82	Scott Tinley	9:19:41	Dave Scott	17:16	580	541	Kailua-Kona
VI	10/9/82	Dave Scott	9:08:23	Scott Tinley	20:05	850	775	Kailua-Kona
VII	10/22/83	Dave Scott	9:05:57	Scott Tinley	0:33	964	835	Kailua-Kona
VIII	10/6/84	Dave Scott	8:54:20	Scott Tinley	24:25	1036	903	Kailua-Kona
IX	10/25/85	Scott Tinley	8:50:54	Chris Hinshaw	25:46	1018	965	Kailua-Kona
X	10/18/86	Dave Scott	8:28:37	Mark Allen	9:47	1039	951	Kailua-Kona
XI	10/10/87	Dave Scott	8:34:13	Mark Allen	11:06	1380	1284	Kailua-Kona
XII	10/22/88	Scott Molina	8:31:00	Mike Pigg	2:11	1277	1189	Kailua-Kona
XIII	10/15/89	Mark Allen	8:09:15	Dave Scott	0:58	1285	1231	Kailua-Kona
XIV	10/6/90	Mark Allen	8:28:17	Scott Tinley	9:23	1386	1255	Kailua-Kona
XV	10/19/91	Mark Allen	8:18:32	Greg Welch	6:01	1386	1235	Kailua-Kona
XVI	10/10/92	Mark Allen	8:09:08	Cristian Bustos	7:21	1364	1298	Kailua-Kona
XVII	10/30/93	Mark Allen	8:07:45	Paulli Kiuru	6:37	1438	1353	Kailua-Kona
XVIII	10/15/94	Greg Welch	8:20:27	Dave Scott	4:05	1405	1290	Kailua-Kona
XIX	10/7/95	Mark Allen	8:20:34	Thomas Hellriegel	2:25	1487	1323	Kailua-Kona

WOMEN

Multiple winners: Paula Newby-Fraser (7); Erin Baker and Sylviane Puntous (2).

Year	Winner	Time	Runner-up
1978	No finishers		
1979	Lyn Lemaire	12:55.00	None
1980	Robin Beck	11:21:24	Eve Anderson
1981	Linda Sweeney	12:00:32	Sally Edwards
1982	Kathleen McCartney	11:09:40	Julie Moss
1982	Julie Leach	10:54:08	Joann Dahlkoetter
1983	Sylviane Puntous	10:43:36	Patricia Puntous
1984	Sylviane Puntous	10:25:13	Patricia Puntous
1985	Joanne Ernst	10:25:22	Liz Bulman
1986	Paula Newby-Fraser	9:49:14	Sylviane Puntous
1987	Erin Baker	9:35:25	Sylviane Puntous
1988	Paula Newby-Fraser	9:01:01	Erin Baker
1989	Paula Newby-Fraser	9:00:56	Sylviane Puntous
1990	Erin Baker	9:13:42	P. Newby-Fraser
1991	Paula Newby-Fraser	9:07:52	Erin Baker
1992	Paula Newby-Fraser	8:55:28	Julie Anne White
1993	Paula Newby-Fraser	8:58:23	Erin Baker
1994	Paula Newby-Fraser	9:20:14	Karen Smyers
1995	Karen Smyers	9:16:46	Isabelle Mouthon

Triathlon Added to Olympics

The triathlon will be held for the first time in an Olympic Games at Sydney in 2000. It was developed as a combination of the longest Olympic swimming distance, 1500 meters, the 40 kilometer cycling time trial, and the longest athletic track event of 10,000 meters. The triathlon will start and finish at the Sydney Opera House.

YACHTING

The America's Cup

International yacht racing was launched in 1851 when England's Royal Yacht Squadron staged a 60-mile regatta around the Isle of Wight and offered a silver trophy to the winner. The 101-foot schooner *America*, sent over by the New York Yacht Club, won the race and the prize. Originally called the Hundred-Guinea Cup, the trophy was renamed The America's Cup after the winning boat's owners deeded it to the NYYC with instructions to defend it whenever challenged.

From 1870-1980, the NYYC successfully defended the Cup 25 straight times; first in large schooners and J-class boats that measured up to 140 feet in overall length, then in 12-meter boats. A foreign yacht finally won the Cup in 1983 when *Australia II* beat defender *Liberty* in the seventh and deciding race off Newport, R.I. Four years later, the San Diego Yacht Club's *Stars & Stripes* won the Cup back, sweeping the four races of the final series off Fremantle, Australia.

Then in 1988, New Zealand's Mercury Bay Boating Club, unwilling to wait the usual three- to four-year period between Cup defenses, challenged the SDYC to a match race, citing the Cup's 102-year-old Deed of Gift, which clearly stated that every challenge had to be honored. Mercury Bay announced it would race a 133-foot monohull. San Diego countered with a 60-foot catamaran. The resulting best-of-three series (Sept. 7-8) was a mismatch as the SDYC's catamaran *Stars & Stripes* won two straight by margins of better than 18 and 21 minutes. Mercury Bay syndicate leader Michael Fay protested the outcome and took the SDYC to court in New York State (where the Deed of Gift was first filed) claiming San Diego had violated the spirit of the deed by racing a catamaran instead of a monohull. N.Y. State Supreme Court judge Carmen Ciparick agreed and on March 28, 1989, ordered the SDYC to hand the Cup over to Mercury Bay. The SDYC refused, but did consent to the court's appointment of the New York Yacht Club as custodian of the Cup until an appeal was ruled on.

On Sept. 19, 1989, the Appellate Division of the N.Y. Supreme Court overturned Ciparick's decision and awarded the Cup back to the SDYC. An appeal by Mercury Bay was denied by the N.Y. Court of Appeals on April 26, 1990, ending three years of legal wrangling. To avoid the chaos of 1988-90, a new class of boat—75-foot monohulls with 110-foot masts—has been used by all competing countries since 1992.

Note that (*) indicates skipper was also owner of the boat.

Schooners and J-Class Boats

Year	Winner	Skipper	Series	Loser	Skipper
1851	*America*	Richard Brown	—	—	—
1870	*Magic*	Andrew Comstock	1-0	*Cambria*, GBR	J. Tannock
1871	*Columbia* (2-1)	Nelson Comstock	4-0	*Livonia*, GBR	J.R. Woods
	& *Sappho* (2-0)	Sam Greenwood			
1876	*Madeleine*	Josephus Williams	2-0	*Countess of Dufferin*, CAN	J.E. Ellsworth
1881	*Mischief*	Nathanael Clock	2-0	*Atalanta*, CAN	Alexander Cuthbert*
1885	*Puritan*	Aubrey Crocker	2-0	*Genesta*, GBR	John Carter
1886	*Mayflower*	Martin Stone	2-0	*Galatea*, GBR	Dan Bradford
1887	*Volunteer*	Henry Haff	2-0	*Thistle*, GBR	John Barr
1893	*Vigilant*	William Hansen	3-0	*Valkyrie II*, GBR	Wm. Granfield
1895	*Defender*	HenryHaff	3-0	*Valkyrie III*, GBR	Wm. Granfield
1899	*Columbia*	Charles Barr	3-0	*Shamrock I*, GBR	Archie Hogarth
1901	*Columbia*	Charles Barr	3-0	*Shamrock II*, GBR	E.A. Sycamore
1903	*Reliance*	Charles Barr	3-0	*Shamrock III*, GBR	Bob Wringe
1920	*Resolute*	Charles F. Adams	3-2	*Shamrock IV*, GBR	William Burton
1930	*Enterprise*	Harold Vanderbilt*	4-0	*Shamrock V*, GBR	Ned Heard
1934	*Rainbow*	Harold Vanderbilt*	4-2	*Endeavour*, GBR	T.O.M. Sopwith
1937	*Ranger*	Harold Vanderbilt*	4-0	*Endeavour II*, GBR	T.O.M. Sopwith

12-Meter Boats

Year	Winner	Skipper	Series	Loser	Skipper
1958	*Columbia*	Briggs Cunningham	4-0	*Sceptre*, GBR	Graham Mann
1962	*Weatherly*	Bus Mosbacher	4-1	*Gretel*, AUS	Jock Sturrock
1964	*Constellation*	Bob Bavier & Eric Ridder	4-0	*Sovereign*, AUS	Peter Scott
1967	*Intrepid*	Bus Mosbacher	4-0	*Dame Pattie*, AUS	Jock Sturrock
1970	*Intrepid*	Bill Ficker	4-1	*Gretel II*, AUS	Jim Hardy
1974	*Courageous*	Ted Hood	4-0	*Southern Cross*, AUS	John Cuneo
1977	*Courageous*	Ted Turner	4-0	*Australia*	Noel Robins
1980	*Freedom*	Dennis Conner	4-1	*Australia*	Jim Hardy
1983	*Australia II*	John Bertrand	4-3	*Liberty*, USA	Dennis Conner
1987	*Stars & Stripes*	Dennis Conner	4-0	*Kookaburra III*, AUS	Iain Murray

60-ft Catamaran vs 133-ft Monohull

Year	Winner	Skipper	Series	Loser	Skipper
1988	*Stars & Stripes*	Dennis Conner	2-0	*New Zealand*, NZE	David Barnes

75-ft International America's Cup Class

Year	Winner	Skipper	Series	Loser	Skipper
1992	*America*[3]	Bill Koch* & Buddy Melges	4-1	*Il Moro di Venezia*, ITA	Paul Cayard
1995	*Black Magic*, NZE	Russell Coutts	5-0	*Young America*, USA	Dennis Conner & Paul Cayard

Other Champions

Championships decided in 1996, unless otherwise indicated.

ARCHERY

1997 World Target Championship

at Victoria, Canada (Aug.)

1997 World Indoor Championship

at Istanbul, Turkey (Mar.)

ARENA FOOTBALL

Final AFL Standings

(*) denotes division champion; (+) denotes playoff wild card.

American Conference

Central	W	L	Pct	PF	PA	GB
*Iowa Barnstormers	12	2	.857	712	601	—
†Milwaukee Mustangs	10	4	.714	704	566	2
†St. Louis Stampede	8	6	.571	706	627	4
Memphis Pharaohs	0	14	.000	400	688	12

Western	W	L	Pct	PF	PA	GB
*Arizona Rattlers	11	3	.785	736	646	—
†Anaheim Piranhas	9	5	.643	602	505	2
San Jose SaberCats	6	8	.429	536	540	5
Minnesota Fighting Pike	4	10	.286	471	706	7

National Conference

Eastern	W	L	Pct	PF	PA	GB
*Albany Firebirds	10	4	.714	873	622	—
Charlotte Rage	5	9	.357	591	643	5
Connecticut Coyotes	2	12	.143	540	695	8

Southern	W	L	Pct	PF	PA	GB
*Tampa Bay Storm	12	2	.857	698	504	—
†Orlando Predators	9	5	.643	651	572	3
Florida Bobcats	6	8	.429	598	593	6
Texas Terror	1	13	.071	421	731	11

Quarterfinals

at Tampa Bay 30 .... Anaheim 16
at Albany 79 .... Milwaukee 58
at Iowa 52 .... St. Louis 49
at Arizona 65 .... Orlando 48

Semifinals

at Iowa 62 .... Albany 55
at Tampa Bay 55 .... Arizona 54

ArenaBowl X

Aug. 26 at Veteran's Memorial Auditorium, Des Moines, Iowa; Att: 11,411

Tampa Bay 42 .... Iowa 38

MVP: Steve Thomas, Tampa Bay, 7 catches, 103 yards, 1 INT, 3 TDs

Darts

1997 World Cup

Oct. 2-4, 1997 in Perth, Australia

1996 World Masters Champions

Men .... Erik Clarijs, Belgium
Women .... Sharon Colclough, England

1996 U.S. Champions

Men .... Jim Widmayer, Staten Island, N.Y.
Women .... Lori Verrier, Salem, Ore.

BILLIARDS

PBT World Championships

Pro 8-Ball .... Efren Reyes, Philippines
Pro 9-Ball .... Rodolfo Luat, Philippines
U.S. Open 9-Ball .... Rodney Morris, Honolulu

WPA 9-Ball Championships

1995 Mosconi Cup (Team) .... Europe
Challenge of Champions .... Ralf Souquet, Germany
World Championship ....at Borlänge, Sweden (Oct. 22-28)

CHEERLEADING

High School Champions

UCA

Coed Varsity .... Christian Bros. HS (Memphis, Tenn.)
Large Varsity .... Boyd Co. HS (Ashland, Ky.)
Medium Varsity .... Boaz HS (Boaz, Ala.)
Small Varsity .... Boyd HS (Boyd, Tex.)
Jr. Varsity .... Germantown HS (Germantown, Tenn.)
Jr. High .... Houston HS Freshmen (Germantown, Tenn.)

NCA

Large Coed .... Mater Dei HS (Santa Ana, Calif.)
Small Coed .... Barren County HS (Glasgow, Ky.)
Large Varsity .... Judson HS (Converse, Tex.)
Medium Varsity...Ft. Walton Beach HS (Ft. Walton Beach, Fla.)
Small Varsity.......Floyd Cent. Jr./Sr. HS (Floyds Knobs, Ind.)
Jr. Varsity .... Judson HS (Converse, Tex.)
Jr. High .... Kitty Hawk Jr. High (Universal City, Tex.)
Best Cheerleader .... Shannon Young, Guthrie HS (Guthrie, Okla.)
Best Partner Stunt .... Kelly Stapleton & Tim Pasaquala Aliso Niguel HS (Laguna Niguel, Calif.)
Best Mascot .... Katy O'Halloran, Arlington HS (Arlington, Tex.)

College Champions

UCA

Div.
IA .... Kentucky
I .... Morehead St. (Morehead, Ky.)
II .... Delta St. (Cleveland, Miss.)
JuCo .... Orange Coast CC (Mission Viejo, Calif.)
All Girl .... Sam Houston St. (Huntsville, Tex.)

NCA

Div.
IA .... Louisville
I .... James Madison
II .... Trinity Valley
All Girl .... Oklahoma St.

College Dance Team Champions

UDA

Div.
IA .... Long Beach St.
Open .... Illinois-Chicago

NCA

Div.
I .... Kansas
II .... Stephen F. Austin

CURLING

World Champions

Men ....Canada (skip: Jeff Stoughton)
Women ....Canada (skip: Marilyn Bodogh)

U.S. Champions

Feb. 24-Mar. 2 at Bemidji, MN

Men.............................Superior, Wisc. (skip: Tim Somerville)
Women.................Madison, Wisc. (skip: Lisa Schoeneberg)

FIELD HOCKEY

1997 World Cup

at the Netherlands

HANDBALL

World Four-Wall Championships

1997 in Winnipeg, Manitoba

U.S. Four-Wall Championships

Men ....David Chapman, Springfield, Mo.
Women ....Anna Engele, St. Paul, Minn.
Open doubles ....Octavio Silveyra, Commerce, Calif. & John Bike, Tucson, Ariz.

Team Handball World Cup Final

Jan. 14 at Globen Arena, Stockholm, Sweden

Sweden 23 ....Russia 21

HORSESHOE PITCHING

World Champions

July 22-Aug. 3 at Gillette, Wyo.

Men.......................................Alan Francis, Blythedale, Md.
Women...........................Beverly Nathe, St. Stephen, Minn.

JUDO

1997 World Judo Championships

at Paris, France

1996 Jr. World Championships

(Men under 21 & Women under 19)
Oct. 3-6 at Porto, Portugal

MEN

60 kg ....Kenji Uematsu, Spain
65 kg ....Jozef Krnac, Slovakia
71 kg...Sebastian Pereira, Brazil
78 kg ....Cedric Claverie, France
86 kg..David Alarza, Spain
95 kg ....Tamertan Tmenov, Russia
95+kg ....Ho Sung Jang, S. Korea

WOMEN

48 kg ....Tamara Meyer, Netherlands
52 kg ....Mihoko Nakaya, Japan
56 kg ....Emmy Schapendonk, Netherlands
61 kg ....Kie Kusakabe, Japan
66 kg ....Edith Bosch, Netherlands
72 kg ....Choi Hee Young, S. Korea
72+kg ....Karina Bryant, Great Britain

LACROSSE

Men's 1998 World Cup

July 17-28 at Baltimore, Md.

Women's 1997 World Championship

at Tokyo

Major Indoor Lacrosse League

Final MILL Regular Season Standings

	W	L	Pct	GF	GA
Buffalo Bandits	8	2	.800	172	137
Philadelphia Wings	8	2	.800	165	114
Boston Blazers	6	4	.600	146	113
Rochester Knighthawks	6	4	.600	148	137
Baltimore Thunder	4	6	.400	144	163
New York Saints	3	7	.300	125	144
Charlotte Cobras	0	10	.000	85	186

Semifinals

at Buffalo 18 ....Rochester 10
at Philadelphia 10...Boston 8

Finals

April 12 in Buffalo, N.Y.
Att: 16,230

Buffalo 15...Philadelphia 10

MOTORCYCLE RACING

ROAD RACING

FIM Grand Prix Champions

125 cc..Haruchika Aoki, Japan
250 cc ....Max Biaggi, Italy
500 cc..Mick Doohan, Australia
Super Bike ....Carl Fogerty, England

Note: All four champs repeated in 1996.

MOTOCROSS

Motorcross des Nations

Sept. 22 at Jerez, Spain

Moto One (125/300) ....Steve Lamson, USA/125/Hon
Moto Two (125/250) ....Jeremy McGrath, USA/250/Hon
Moto Three (250/500) ......Jeremy McGrath, USA/250/Hon
Team ....**1.** United States (Jeremy McGrath, Steve Lamson and Jeff Emig), 9 pts.; **2.** France, 21; **3.** Belgium, 30

Grand Prix Champions

125 cc ....Sebastien Tortelli, France
250 cc ....Stefan Everts, Belgium
500 cc..................................Shayne King, New Zealand

1996 American Motorcyclist Association Champions

Road Racing

Superbike ....Doug Chandler, Salinas, Calif., Kawasaki ZX-7
250cc Grand Prix.......................Rich Oliver, Fresno, Calif., Yamaha TZ250
600cc SuperSport.......................Miguel Duhamel, Canada, Honda CBR600
750cc SuperSport ....Aaron Yates, Milledgeville, Ga., Suzuki GSXR750
SuperTwins ....Matt Wait, Lodi, Calif. Harley-Davidson 883 Sportster
SuperTeams ....Erion Racing, Anaheim, Calif. Honda CBR900

Other Champions (Cont.)

Motocross

250cc Motocross ....Jeff Emig, Riverside, Calif.
Kawasaki KX250
125cc Motocross..................Steve Lamson, Riverside, Calif.
Honda CR125

Supercross

AMA Supercross..............Jeremy McGrath, Menifee, Calif.
Honda CR250

Grand National Dirt Track

Grand National ....Scott Parker, Swartz Creek, Mich.
883cc Dirt Track...........Eric Bostrom, Marina del Ray, Calif.
Harley-Davidson 883 Sportster

RAQUETBALL

World Champions

Men ....Todd O'Neil, Dallas, Tex.
Women................................Michelle Gould, Boise, Idaho

U.S. Amateur Champions

Men ....Ruben Gonzalez, Staten Island, N.Y
Women................................Michelle Gould, Boise, Idaho

U.S. Pro Tour Champions

IRT (Men) ....Sudsy Monchik, Staten Island, N.Y.
WIRT (Women).......................Michelle Gould, Boise, Idaho

ROLLER HOCKEY

Roller Hockey International

Final Regular Season standings

(*) denotes division champion; (†) denotes playoff qualifier. Teams receive three points for a win and one point for overtime losses (OTL).

Eastern Conference

Atlantic Div.	W	L	OTL	Pts	GF	GA
*Empire State	16	7	5	37	202	168
†Orlando	17	9	2	36	231	201
Long Island	16	9	3	35	246	211
Philadelphia	16	9	3	35	202	199
New Jersey	7	17	4	18	167	227

Central Div.	W	L	OTL	Pts	GF	GA
*Minnesota	22	6	0	44	246	200
†St. Louis	15	12	1	31	207	209
Montreal	14	11	3	31	177	174
Ottawa	3	22	3	9	174	263

Western Conference

Northwest Div.	W	L	OTL	Pts	GF	GA
*Vancouver	18	7	3	39	217	162
†Oakland	15	11	2	32	187	181
San Jose	15	12	1	31	189	180
Sacramento	10	17	1	21	185	229

Pacific Div.	W	L	OTL	Pts	GF	GA
*Anaheim	22	4	2	46	215	159
†Los Angeles	16	11	1	33	160	155
Oklahoma	13	12	3	29	174	174
San Diego	9	18	1	19	183	233
Denver	8	17	3	19	173	210

Playoffs

First Round (Best of 3)
Orlando def. Empire St., 2 games to 1.
St. Louis def. Minnesota, 2 games to 1.
Vancouver def. Oakland, 2 games to 1.
Anaheim def. Los Angeles, 2 games to 0.

Semifinals (Best of 3)
Orlando def. St. Louis, 2 games to 0.
Anaheim def. Vancouver, 2 games to 1.

Championship (Best of 3)

	W-L	GF	GA
Orlando	2-1	25	19
Anaheim	1-2	19	25

RESULTS: **Aug. 30**— Anaheim, 9-8; **Sept. 1**— Orlando, 9-6; **Sept. 2**— Orlando, 8-4.

Australian Rules Football

AFL Grand Final

at Melbourne Cricket Ground (Sept. 29)
Att: 93,102

North Melbourne 131 ....Sydney 88

RUGBY

Five Nations Championships

1996 Champion: England

	Gm	W	L	T	PF	PA	Pts
England	4	3	1	0	79	54	6
Scotland	4	3	1	0	60	56	6
France	4	2	2	0	89	57	4
Wales	4	1	3	0	62	82	2
Ireland	4	1	3	0	65	106	2

RESULTS: **Jan. 20**—FRANCE 15, England 12; Scotland 16, IRELAND 10; **Feb. 3**—ENGLAND 21, Wales 15; SCOTLAND 19, France 14; **Feb. 17**—Scotland 16, WALES 14; FRANCE 45, Ireland 10; **Mar. 2**—IRELAND 30, Wales 17; England 18, SCOTLAND 9; **Mar. 16**—ENGLAND 28, Ireland 15; WALES 16, France 15.

Note: Home team in ALL CAPS

1995 European Cup

European Clubs Championship

Pool A	W	L	T	PF	PA
Toulouse (France)	2	0	0	72	19
Trevisio (Italy)	1	1	0	95	26
Farul Constanta (Romania)	0	2	0	18	140

RESULTS: **Oct. 31**— Toulouse 54, FARUL CONSTANTA 10; **Nov. 7**— TREVISIO 86, Farul Constanta 8; **Dec. 12**— TOULOUSE 18, Trevision 9.

Pool B	W	L	T	PF	PA
Cardiff (Wales)	1	0	1	60	20
Begles (France)	1	0	1	43	30
Ulster (Ireland)	0	2	0	22	75

RESULTS: **Nov. 21**— BEGLES 14, Cardiff 14; **Nov. 28**— CARDIFF 46, Ulster 6; **Dec. 13**— Begles 29, ULSTER 16.

Pool C	W	L	T	PF	PA
Leinster (Ireland)	2	0	0	47	43
Pontypridd (Wales)	1	1	0	53	35
Milano (Italy)	0	2	0	33	55

RESULTS: **Oct. 31**— Leinster 24, MILANO 21; **Nov. 22**— PONTYPRIDD 31, Milano 12; **Dec. 6**— LEINSTER 23, Pontypridd 22.

Pool D	W	L	T	PF	PA
Swansea (Wales)	1	1	0	35	27
Munster (Ireland)	1	1	0	29	32
Castres (France)	1	1	0	29	34

RESULTS: **Nov. 1**— MUNSTER 17, Swansea 13; **Nov. 8**— CASTRES 19, Munster 12; **Dec. 5**— SWANSEA 22, Castres 10.

Note: Home team in ALL CAPS

Semifinals

Toulousse (France) 30 ....Swansea (Wales) 3
Cardiff (Wales) 23...........................Leinster (Ireland) 14

Final

Jan. 7 at Cardiff, Wales

Toulouse 21 ....OT.......................Cardiff 18

U.S. CHAMPIONS

Club: Men......Old Mission Beach A.C., San Diego
Women...........................Beantown, Boston
College: Men...........................California (Berkeley)
Women ....Princeton
High School: Men..........Highland H.S., Salt Lake City, UT

SHOOTING

U.S. Nationals

PISTOL

Aug. 6-11 at Chino, Calif.

Men

Air Pistol..............................Gregg Derr, Marshfield, Mass.
Center Fire Pistol......................Terry Anderson, Dallas, Tex.
Free Pistol.........................Daryl Szarenski, Saginaw, Mich.
Rapid Fire Pistol......................Dan Iuga, Brentwood, Calif.
Standard Pistol...............George Ross, Santa Clarita, Calif.

Women

Sport Pistol ....Sandra Utasy, Los Angeles, Calif.

RIFLE

Sept. 14-21 at Chino, Calif.

Men

Free Rifle, Prone ....Lance Hopper, Phenix City, Ala.
Free Rifle, 3x40...................Dan Jordan, Franktown, Colo.
Air Rifle....................................Shawn Wells, Miami, Fla.

Women

Standard Rifle, Prone.........Liz Bourland, Wichita Falls, Tex.
Standard Rifle, 3x20..............Jean Foster, Bozeman, Mont.
Air Rifle...Jean Foster

RUNNING TARGET

Aug. 7-13 at Ft. Benning, Ga.

Men

10m Running Target ....Bill Johnson, Woodville, Miss.
50m Running Target.....................Rusty Hill, Sun City, Calif.
10m Running Target, Mixed...Armando Ayala, El Paso, Tex.
50m Running Target, Mixed ....Rusty Hill

Women

10m Running Target ..Betsy Stormont, Oklahoma City, Okla.

SHOTGUN

June 22-29 at Colorado Springs, Colo.

Men

Skeet.......................................Joe Buffa, Flushing, Mich.
Trap...................................Brian Ballard, Culdesac, Idaho
Double Trap ....Mike Herman, Dayton, Wyo.

Women

Skeet.........................Colleen Rumore, Glastonbury, Conn.
Trap ....Joetta Novinski, Renton, Wash.
Double Trap ....Joetta Novinski

SQUASH

1996 World Cup

May 28-June 1 at Kuala Lumpur, Malaysia

Australia 3...England 0

SUMO WRESTLING

5th Sumo World Championship

Dec. 15, 1995 at Ryogoku Kokugikan, Japan

Openweight..............................Emanuel Yarbrough, USA
Heavyweight ....Naohito Saito, Japan
Middleweight ....Ryoji Kumagai, Japan
Lightweight ....Agvaansamdan Suhbat, Mongolia
Team...Japan

1996 Asian Sumo Championship

Oct. 6 at Sakai-city, Osaka, Japan

Openweight...............................B. Bateredene, Mongolia
Heavyweight.......................................Shinchi Taira, Japan
Middleweight.......................................Katsuhito Ito, Japan
Lightweight ....Sadahide Furuichi, Japan
Team...Japan

SURFING

1995 Assn. of Surfing Professionals World Tour Champions

Men ....Kelly Slater, Cocoa Beach, Fla.
Women...................................Lisa Andersen, Ormond, Fla.

1996 U.S. Open

Aug. 11 at Huntington Beach, Calif.
Att: 75,000*

Men	Pts
1 Kelly Slater	21.00
2 Shane Beschen	16.75
Women	**Pts**
1 Layne Beachley	16.00
2 Neridah Falconer	12.75
Longboarding	**Pts**
1 Joel Tudor	22.25
2 Geoff Moysa	21.20
3 Josh Mohr	19.75
4 Colin McPhillips	18.40

*Largest crowd ever for a surfing event in the United States.

SNOOKER

World Championship

May 4 at Sheffield, England

Stephen Hendry, Scotland, def. Peter Ebdon, England, 18-9

TABLE TENNIS

1995 U.S. Nationals

at Las Vegas (Dec. 13-17)

Men's Singles ....David Zhuang, New Brunswick, N.J.
Men's Doubles ....Darko Rop, Houston, Tex.
& Khoa Nguyen, Santa Clara, Calif.
Women's Singles ....Amy Feng, Rockville, Md.
Women's Doubles ....Wei Wang & Lily Yip, Metuchen, N.J.
Mixed Doubles ....David Zhuang & Amy Feng

Other Champions (Cont.)

ULTIMATE

WFDF World Championships

Aug. 10-17 at Jönköping, Sweden

Open....USA (Death or Glory, Boston)
Jrs. (18 and under)....Sweden
Masters (32+)....Sweden
Women....Sweden

1996 Ultimate Players Association

National Championships

Nov. 6-10 at Plano, Texas

VOLLEYBALL

1996 World League

Final Rank

1 Netherlands
2 Italy
3 Russia
4 Cuba

Pro Beach Tours

MEN (AVP)

Manhattan Beach Open....Karch Kiraly/Kent Steffes
Hermosa Beach Tournament....Karch Kiraly/Kent Steffes

WOMEN (WPVA)

U.S. Open....Barbra Fontana Harris/Linda Hanley
Evian Invitational....Lisa Arce/Holly McPeak
National Championships....Lisa Arce/Holly McPeak
Best of the Beach....Lisa Arce/Holly McPeak

Pro Indoor

National Volleyball Association

WOMEN

Semifinals

Orange County def. San Jose....15-7, 15-7, 15-5
San Diego def. Utah....15-11, 15-11, 12-15, 15-6

Championship

Orange County def. San Diego....15-11, 14-16, 15-7, 15-12

WATER SKIING

1997 World Championships

Sept. 13-17 at Medellin, Colombia

U.S. Open Champions

June 22-23 at Greensville, N.C.

Overall: Men....Patrice Martin, France
Women....Brandi Hung, Clermont, Fla.

Cafe de Columbia Water Ski Tour

Men's Slalom....Wade Cox, Orlando, Fla.
Men's Jump....Carl Roberge, Orlando, Fla.
Men's Wakeboarding....Parks Bonifay, Winter Haven, Fla.

World Cup

Men....Jaret Llewellyn, Canada
Women....Toni Neville, Australia

ESPN X GAMES

June 24-30 at Providence, R.I.

Aggressive In-line Skating

Men's Halfpipe....Rene Hulgreen, Munchen, GER
Women's Halfpipe....Fabiola De Silva, Sao Paulo, BRA
Best Trick....Dion Antony, Melbourne, AUS
Street....Arlo Eisenberg, Venice, Calif.

Barefoot Jumping....Ron Scarpa, Winter Haven, Fla.

Bicycle Stunt

Dirt Jumping....Joey Garcia, Gilroy, Calif.
Street....Dave Mirra, Greenville, N.C.
Vert....Matt Hoffman, Oklahoma City, Okla.

Bungy Jumping....Peter Bihun, Ontario, CAN

Extreme Adventure Race....Team KoBeer

Downhill In-line Skating

Men....Dante Muse, W. Des Moines, Iowa
Women....Gypsy Tidwell, Hewitt, Texas

Skateboarding

Best Trick....Gershon Mosely, Boise, Idaho
Street....Rodil de Araujo Jr., Curitahan Carena, BRA
Vert....Andy MacDonald, San Diego, Calif.

Skysurfing....Greiner/Burch, Satellite Beach, Fla.
/Sebastien Beach, Fla.

Sportclimbing

Men's Difficulty....Arnaud Petit, Savoie, FRA
Women's Difficulty....Katie Brown, Paris, Ky.
Men's Speed....Hans Florine, Morega, Calif.
Women's Speed....Cecile Leflem, Vauhallan, FRA

Street Luge

Dual....Shawn Goulart, Stockton, Calif.
Mass....Biker Sherlock, San Diego, Calif.

Wakeboarding....Parks Bonifay, Lake Alfred, Fla.

ARM WRESTLING

World Wristwrestling Championship

Oct. 12 at Petaluma, Calif.

Pro Right

200lbs+....John Brzenk
176-200 lbs....John Brzenk
151-175....Mark Pryor
136-150....Karl Wiggins
under 136....Bryan Senn

Pro Left

200lbs+....Eric Woefel
176-200....John Brzenk
151-175....Marth Anzik
136-150....Blair Pope
under 136....Bryan Senn

Team: Canada

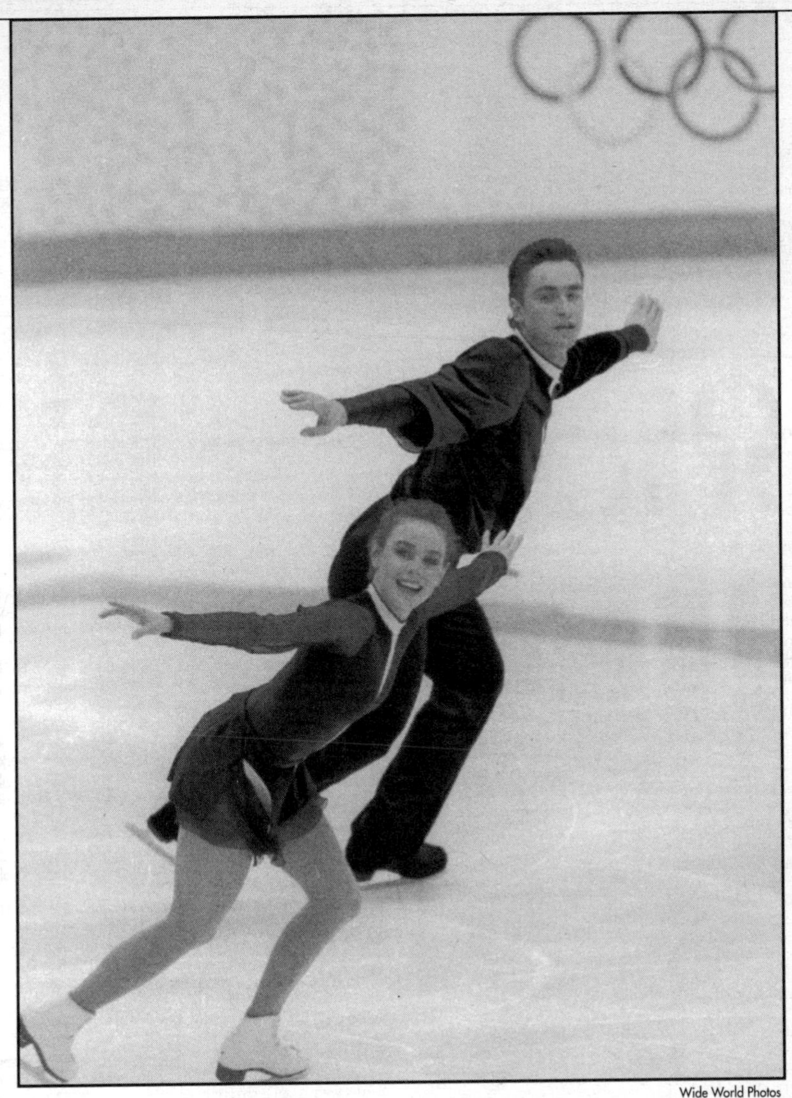

Wide World Photos

Russian figure skater **Sergei Grinkov**, 28, shown with his wife and skating partner Ekaterina Gordeyeva in 1994, died on November 28, 1995 of a heart attack while preparing for a tour.

DEATHS

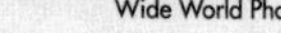

Wide World Photos

Kathy Ahern

Wide World Photos

Johnny Beradino

University of Nebraska

Brook Berringer

Kathy Ahern, 47; joined LPGA tour in 1967 and won three tour championships in the early 1970s, including the 1972 LPGA Championship; member of the LPGA Teaching and Club Professional Division; known for her enjoyment in helping others, she traveled to Vietnam in the 1970s to conduct clinics for U.S. troops; enjoyed caddying for friend Sherri Turner; after a five-year battle with breast cancer; in Phoenix, July 6.

Mel Allen, 83; see story on page 574.

Joe Antenora, 68; commissioner/executive director of the Pro Bowlers Tour from 1972-91; responsible for increasing tournament prize money, instituting the PBA Senior Tour, and securing television coverage for most tour events; inducted into the PBA Hall of Fame in 1993; of a heart attack; in Akron, Ohio; Sept. 2.

Al Barlick, 80; major league baseball umpire from 1940-1972; inducted into the Hall of Fame in 1989, only the sixth umpire at that time to be elected; had his uniform No. 3 retired in Wrigley Field along with two other umpires; known for the loudest ball and strike call in baseball; served as a national league consultant from 1972-1994; of cardiac arrest; in Springfield, Ill., Dec. 27, 1995.

Marlin Barnes, 22; linebacker for Miami Hurricanes football team; selected "Most Improved Player" during spring workouts; graduated North Miami High School and later attended Hargrave Military Academy in Virginia before transferring to Miami; found beaten to death with a shotgun along with girlfriend Timwanika Lumpkins; in Coral Gables, Fla., April 13.

Jeff Beard, 85; Auburn athletic director from 1951-1972; known as the father of the modern Auburn athletics, he developed a virtually nonexistent proagram into one of the nation's perennial powerhouses; Auburn teams won close to 70% of all events during his tenure; after a lengthy illness; in Gold Hill, Ala., Nov. 10, 1995.

Johnny Beradino, 79; major league baseball infielder from 1939-1952; known for his defensive prowess, he hit .249 with 387 RBI in 912 games with the St. Louis Browns, Cleveland Indians and Pittsburgh Pirates; later received three best actor Emmy nominations for his role of Dr. Steve Hardy on "General Hospital"; of cancer; in Los Angeles, May 19.

Brook Berringer, 22; former Nebraska quarterback expected to be chosen in the NFL draft; saw limited playing time as a senior but was instrumental in leading the Huskers to the national championship in 1994, completing over 62% of his passes for 1,295 yards; member of the Fellowship of Christian Athletes; of injuries sustained in a plane crash; in Raymond, Neb., Apr. 18.

Freda Stowe Botkin, 85; headed the Women's International Bowling Congress from 1965-1975; coordinated the international women's bowling championship in 1979, the largest women's sporting event at the time with 50,000 competitors; member of the WIBC Hall of Fame; of colon cancer; in Tuscon; Dec. 20, 1995.

Scott Brayton, 37; Indianapolis 500 polesitter in 1995; raced on the IndyCar circuit from 1981 through 1995 before switching to the new Indy Racing League; earned just under $5 million in 148 career Indy car races including a career best 3rd-place finish in Milwaukee in 1992; earned pole position for the 1996 Indy 500 with an average speed of 233.718 mph; became the 40th driver to be killed at Indianapolis Motor Speedway after a tire deflation caused him to crash into a retaining wall during a practice session; in Indianapolis; May 17.

Ben Brown, 42; track and field gold medal winner in the 1,600-meter relay at the 1976 Montreal Olympics; member of three NCAA champion mile relay teams at UCLA in the early seventies; ran a 45.0 second leg of the 440 relays in 1973, the world's fastest time for that year; worked as an assistant track coach for Cal St. Fullerton; in a car accident; in Fullerton, Calif., Feb. 1.

Valmond (J.B.) Brown, 20; star linebacker for Grambling; led the team with 87 tackles and five sacks in 1995 after registering 89 tackles in 1994; named 2nd team All-Southwestern Athletic Conference and was voted Grambling's most outstanding player; of gun shot wounds to the head and chest allegedly by a former teammate; in Gonzales, La., May 9.

Billy Bruton, 69; major league outfielder whose dramatic 10th inning homer won the first game ever played by the Braves in Milwaukee; led the national league in stolen bases from 1953-55; leading hitter in the 1958 World Series with a .412 average; of a heart attack while driving in Marshallton, Del., Dec. 6, 1995.

Jack Button, 56; served 17 years in the Washington Capitals organization, mostly as director of player personnel; responsible for finding club stars such as Peter Bondra and Jim Carey; formerly GM of the Pittsburgh Penguins in 1974-75, he is credited with keeping the team from being disbanded; of leukemia, in Washington D.C., July 31.

Jim Campbell, 71; executive in the Detroit Tigers organization from 1949-1992; promoted to GM in 1962 and eventually team president in 1978, he oversaw the Tigers' World Series victories in 1968 and 1984; named *The Sporting News* executive of the year in 1968; in Lakeland, Fla., Oct. 31, 1995.

Detroit Tigers

Jim Campbell

Wide World Photos

Charlie Conerly

ESPN

Allan Connal

Michelle Carew, 18; died after a seven-month battle with leukemia; daughter of Hall of Fame baseball player and hitting coach Rod Carew, who organized a well-publicized international drive for a compatible bone marrow donor that drew over 70,000 responses, none of which were the correct match; the search was responsible for increasing the marrow donor registry from 1.1 million to over 2 million; in Orange, Calif., April 17.

Bill Cheesbourg, 68; former driver who raced in the Indianapolis 500 seven times in the late 1950s and early 1960s, finishing the race just once; set a race record in the 1959 Indy 500 by passing 17 cars in the first lap; of cancer; in Tucson, Ariz., Nov. 6, 1995.

Tommy Collins, 67; popular Boston fighter during the 1950s who finished career with a 60-12 record with 43 knockouts; once knocked down ten times in one fight, sparking an outrage that helped to create the three-knock down rule; cried in the ring after demolishing former champ Willie Pep, thinking he had severely injured him; fought four world champions in a 13-month span; after a brief illness; in Boston, June 3.

Charlie Conerly, 74; quarterback who led the New York Giants to a 47-7 rout of the Chicago Bears in the 1956 NFL championship game; NFL's top ranked passer in 1959; established Giant records for completions (1,418) and touchdown passes (173) which were later broken; was reportedly sacked 17 times in one game in a 14-10 loss to Philadelphia; had his number 42 retired by the Giants in 1962; of heart failure; in Memphis; Feb. 13.

Allan (Scotty) Connal, 68; sports telecasting innovator who began his career at NBC as a page in 1947 and ultimately worked his way to become the network's executive producer and senior vice president of sports; left NBC in 1979 to help launch ESPN which has since become a cable giant; his ideas range from placing microphones in golf cups to tinting hockey ice blue; he is known for trying to save football fans from the infamous "Heidi" game in 1968; decided to make Dick Vitale a broadcaster and to put 24 year-old Chris Berman on the air; of a heart attack; in Atlanta; July 30.

Mike Cooke, 49; driver who died from injuries sustained after his car hit a wall en route to his qualifying attempt at the NASCAR Copper World Classic; in Phoenix; Feb. 3.

Jerome Cooper, 81; helped organize the United Soccer Association in 1966, which later merged with another league to become the North American Soccer League; of pneumonia; in Washington; Nov. 30, 1995.

Jerry Cowhig, 74; Notre Dame running back from 1942-46; captained the Fighting Irish squad that broke Army's 25-game winning streak with a 0-0 tie in 1946; played in the NFL from 1947-52 for the LA Rams, Chicago Cardinals, Philadelphia Eagles, and SF 49ers; of natural causes; in Van Nuys, Calif.; Dec. 6, 1995.

Harry Coyle, 74; television director who revolutionized the look of baseball games on T.V. from the late 1940's to the late 1980's; introduced close-ups, hand-held cameras and the center-field camera that is now commonplace; responsible for placing a camera in the left-field scoreboard at Fenway Park that captured the famous coverage of Carlton Fisk's game-winning home run in game 6 of the 1975 World Series; of a heart attack; in Des Moines, Iowa; Feb. 19.

Roger Crozier, 53; former NHL goaltender who was rookie of the year in 1964 with the Detroit Red Wings; won 206 career games and registered 30 shutouts with a 3.04 goals against average during his 14 year NHL stint with Detroit, Buffalo, and Washington; helped popularize the butterfly and flop style of goaltending; served as general manager for the Washington Capitals in 1981-82; of cancer; in Newark, Del.; Jan. 10.

Rodney Culver, 26; NFL running back who carried the ball 47 times for 155 yards and three touchdowns for San Diego in 1995; broke his thumb in the season finale against the New York Giants but stayed in the game and scored the tying touchdown in the Chargers' 27-17 win; drafted by the Indianapolis Colts in 1992 out of Notre Dame; rushed for 1,697 yards as a two-year starter and four-year letterman for the Irish where he was selected team captain as a senior; popular for his unselfishness, leadership, and intangibles he brought to the game; victim along with his wife of ValuJet Flight 592 crash in the Florida Everglades; May 11.

Babe Dahlgren, 84; major league first baseman/utility player known for replacing Lou Gehrig at first base for the New York Yankees, ending his consecutive games streak at 2,130; respected for his stellar play in the field, he batted .261 over a 12 year career with eight different teams; took over for Gehrig on May 2, 1939 in a 22-2 Yankees' romp in Detroit; member of the 1939 World Series champion Yankees team; of natural causes; in Arcadia, Calif.; Sept. 4.

Chris Daniels, 22; University of Dayton basketball 6-foot-10-inch center who, as a fifth-year senior, was averaging 12.9 points per game, six rebounds and was second in the nation in field-goal percentage at 67.9%; scored a season-high 20 points against UMass All-American Marcus Camby; died a natural death due to cardiac arrythmia; in Dayton, Ohio; Feb. 8.

Frank Daniels, 78; harness racing trainer/driver who in 1967 became the first driver in the Maritimes to accumulate 1,000 victories; finished his career with 1,694 wins and $408,135 in career winnings; after a long illness; in Truro, Nova Scotia; Dec. 11, 1995.

Wide World Photos

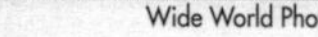
Harry Coyle

Archive Photos

Roger Crozier

Wide World Photos

Al De Rogatis

Willi Daume, 82; former vice-president of the International Olympic Committee from 1972-76 who was instrumental in bringing the Olympic games to Munich in 1972; chairman of German Sports Federation from 1950-1969 and president of National Olympic Committee from 1961-1992; member of German basketball team at the 1936 Olympics in Berlin; of intestinal cancer; in Munich; May 20.

Al DeRogatis, 68; New York Giants lineman from 1949-52 who later became a television and radio broadcaster; originally drafted out of Duke, he was selected to the Pro Bowl team in 1951 and 1952 before a knee injury prematurely ended his career at the age of 25; covered Giants games for WNEW radio for 6 years before switching to television, working the NFL game of the week on NBC with Curt Gowdy; of cancer; in Neptune, NJ; Dec. 26, 1995.

Nikolai Drozdetsky, 38; Soviet hockey star who won an Olympic gold medal and two world championships between the years of 1973-89; forward for the Army Sports Club team and the infamous Central Army team in Moscow; scored 252 goals in just over 300 career games; of complications from diabetes; in St. Petersburg, Russia; Nov. 25, 1995.

Dan Duva, 44; boxing promoter who, along with father, Lou and other family members, was responsible for taking the Main Events promotion company into national prominence; career took off when he acquired promotional rights in 1981 to the Sugar Ray Leonard-Thomas Hearns bout, boxing's highest grossing match in history at the time; went on to promote fights with champions George Foreman, Evander Holyfield, and Pernell Whitaker among others; of cancer; in New York; Jan. 30.

Marty Dye, 28; former South Carolina defensive tackle from 1988-91; registered 77 tackles and four sacks as a senior and was voted the team's defensive most valuable player; of an apparent self-inflicted gunshot wound; in Greenwood, SC; March 30.

Csaba Elthes, 83; international fencing champion from Hungary who later coached the U.S. Olympic teams in five olympic games between 1964-84; coached Peter Westbrook to a bronze medal at the 1984 games; coached at the NY Athletic Club and NY Fencing club in the 1950s after leaving Hungary during the 1956 uprising; of a stroke; in Budapest; Nov. 8, 1995.

Dell Ennis, 70; star outfielder for the 1950 National League champion Philadelphia Phillies who were known as the "Whiz Kids"; broke into the majors in 1946 and became the first Phillie rookie to be selected to the All-Star team; hit 31 home runs in 1950, batting .311 and leading the NL with 126 RBI; finished career after 14 seasons with a .284 average, 2,063 hits and 288 homers; of complications from diabetes; in Huntingdon Valley, Pa.; Feb. 8.

Barney Ewell, 78; gold-medal winning sprinter on the 1948 U.S. Olympic 400-meter relay team in London; also won two silver medals in London in the 100 and 200-meter dashes at the age of 30; won three consecutive collegiate championships at Penn State and set American and world records at 50 yards, 60 yards, and 100 meters; World War II canceled the Olympics in 1940 and 1944, denying him the opportunity to race during his prime; of complications following the partial amputations of both legs; in Lancaster, Pa., April 4.

Joey Fariello, 58; boxing trainer who most recently prepared Buster Mathis, Jr. for his bout with Mike Tyson; got his start in boxing as an assistant to trainer Cus D'Amato; worked with former heavyweight champ Floyd Patterson and featherweight champion Tom (Boom Boom) Johnson; of a stroke; Elmhurst, NY; Dec. 24, 1995.

Minnesota Fats, N/A; legendary pool shark who gained national recognition from the 1960s movie "The Hustler"; made his living in the 1920's and 30's touring the country taking on all challengers; starred in his own television show "Celebrity Billiards" where he played pool against various Hollywood stars and made numerous appearances against other pool legends, most notably Willie Mosconi; usually brash and arrogant, he was known for wearing $100 bills in the handkerchief pockets of his suits; born Rudolf Wanderone Jr., his age continues to be a mystery; of congestive heart failure; in Nashville; Jan. 18.

Charles O. Finley, 77; colorful former major league baseball owner who directed the Oakland A's to three consecutive World Series titles in the 1970s and revolutionized the game with his innovative ideas and promotions; original owner to dress his team in brightly colored uniforms which became hugely popular in the 1970s into the 80s; originated the designated hitter in the American League and World Series night games which have become the norm in today's game; some of his ideas were not quite as successful such as orange baseballs for easy night viewing and sheep grazing behind the right-field fence in Kansas City; purchased the Kansas City A's in 1960 and moved them to Oakland in 1968 due to a lack of attendance; turned the A's into a dynasty when he signed future Hall of Famers Reggie Jackson, Catfish Hunter, and Rollie Fingers although free agency and bitter contract squabbles eventually broke up the team; of heart and vascular disease; in Chicago; Feb. 19.

Chet Forte, 60; original and long-time director of "Monday Night Football"; credited with using creative statistical graphics and innovative camera angles focusing on player and coach's reactions and enthusiastic cheerleaders to develop MNF into the institution it is today; worked 25 years at ABC sports collecting 11 Emmy Awards until a gambling addiction eventually forced the end of his career; All-America basketball player at Columbia despite his 5-foot 7-inch stature; led the nation in 1957 with a 28.9 scoring average, beating Wilt Chamberlain; still holds 11 school records; of a heart attack; in San Diego; May18.

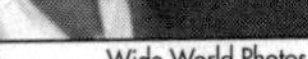
Wide World Photos

Dan Duva

Archive Photos

Dell Ennis

Wide World Photos

Minnesota Fats

Roger Freed, 49; journeyman first baseman from 1970-79; finished career with a .245 average, 22 home runs, and 109 RBI in 344 games with five major league clubs, most recently the St. Louis Cardinals where he had his own fan club; of heart problems; in Chino, Calif.; Jan. 9.

Jack Friel, 97; former coach of the Washington State basketball team who ended his career with 495 wins, the most in school history; led the Cougars to their only NCAA title game in 1941, falling to Wisconsin 39-34; later coached the school's golf team and became the Big Sky conference's first commissioner; of pneumonia; in Pullman, Wash.; Dec. 12, 1995.

Milt Gaston, 100; major league pitcher from 1924-34 known for playing with the most Hall of Fame teammates and managers in history; played with 17 including Babe Ruth, Lou Gehrig, and George Sisler during stints with five clubs; finished with a 97-164 career mark and holds records for most hits allowed (14) while pitching a shutout and being involved with the most double plays (4) in one game by a pitcher; died in his sleep; in Hyannis, Mass., April 26.

Bill Goldsworthy, 51; five-time NHL all-star between 1964-78 and an original member of the Minnesota North Stars; scored 267 goals in 670 games with Minnesota becoming the first expansion player to tally over 250 goals; had his number (8) retired by the club in 1992; also played with Boston, NY Rangers, and Edmonton in the WHA; most recently served as a scout for the San Jose Sharks and a coach for the minor league San Antonio Iguanas; of complications from AIDS; in St. Paul, Minn.; March 29.

Sergei Grinkov, 28; Russian pairs figure skater who won two Olympic gold medals and four world championships with wife and partner Ekaterina Gordeyeva; began his career as a singles skater but was paired with Gordeyeva in 1982; the epitome of majestic Russian pairs skating, the tandem won Olympic gold in Calgary in 1988 and again in Lillehammer in 1994, perfecting their signature quadruple twist and the always impressive double axel; they began dating in 1989, married in 1991 and gave birth to their daughter Daria in 1992; died of a heart attack while practicing for an upcoming tour and the world professional championships; in Lake Placid, NY; Nov. 20, 1995.

Tim Gullikson, 44; renowned tennis coach and former player who teamed with identical twin to become one of the top doubles duos in the world; won four singles and 16 doubles titles (10 with his brother) in the 1970s and 80s; recently coached Pete Sampras to the No. 1 world player ranking and seven grand slam tournament titles; of brain cancer; in Wheaton, Ill.; May 3.

Robert Alexander (Bones) Hamilton, 83; star running back at Stanford from 1933-35; led the Cardinal to a 25-4-2 record during his career and three consecutive Rose Bowls; played on offense, defense, and returned kicks; selected to the Liberty Magazine All-American squad in 1934 and was named Stanford captain as a senior; elected to the College Hall of Fame in 1972; in Palm Springs, Cal.; April 1.

Frank Hammond, 66; first professional and full-time tennis umpire in the 1970s, widely respected as the most reliable in history; known for his booming voice and his habit of leaning forward in his chair and occasionally almost touching his nose to the court to get a better view; disqualified Ilie Nastase in a 1979 U.S. Open match with John McEnroe, sparking a riot in the crowd before he was eventually overruled; of Lou Gehrig's disease; Nov. 23, 1995.

Hord W. Hardin, 84; chairman of the Masters golf tournament from 1980 to 1991; continually fought to uphold the tradition of the Masters and would not allow commercialism to seep into the tournament; an accomplished golfer himself, he competed in the U.S. Open in 1952 and seven U.S. Amateur Championships; served as president of the U.S. Golf Association in 1968-69 and was chairman of the Masters rules committee; after a long illness; in Harbor Springs, Mich.; Aug. 5.

Burt Hawkins, 81; baseball writer and long-time Texas Rangers public relations director; covered the Washington Senators for the Washington Star from 1937-60 and was nominated for a Pulitzer Prize in 1957; hired as PR director for the Senators in 1960 and moved with the team to Texas; retired in 1984 and became the team's official scorer, working the 1995 All-Star game; of a heart attack; in Arlington, Tex.; Nov. 27, 1995.

Jermaine Hopkins, 21; defensive end for Youngstown State football; honor student and member of two Division 1-AA national championship teams; set a school record for sacks with 15 in 1994; of gunshot wounds; in Youngstown Ohio; Jan. 28.

Les Horvath, 74; Ohio State football player who became the first Buckeye to win the Heisman Trophy in 1944; led Ohio State to a 9-0 mark from the quarterback, running back, and defensive back positions; led the Big Ten in rushing in 1944 and finished college career with 1,546 yards and 12 touchdowns on 290 carries; played three years of pro football with the LA Rams and Cleveland Browns before starting his dentistry practice; selected to the National Football Hall of Fame in 1969; of heart failure; in Glendale, Cal.; Nov. 14, 1995.

Frank Howard, 86; all-time winningest football coach in Clemson history; compiled a 165-118-12 record with eight conference titles from 1940-69; served as athletic director from 1969-71 and was inducted into the College Football Hall of Fame in 1989; was a mainstay at all Clemson sporting events; graduated from Alabama where he was a star lineman; of congestive heart failure; in Clemson, SC; Jan. 26.

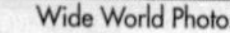

Wide World Photos

Charles O. Finley

Wide World Photos

Chet Forte

Wide World Photos

Bill Goldsworthy

Harry Hyde, 71; colorful NASCAR engineer/crew chief whose life was portrayed by Robert Duval in the movie "Days of Thunder"; won the Winston Cup racing series in 1966 behind the racing of Bobby Isaac; listed 56 Winson Cup victories and 88 poles over his career; of an apparent heart attack; in Charlotte; May 13.

Sandor Iharos, 65; Hungarian distance runner who broke seven world records in 14 months in 1955-56 and set 11 records overall in events ranging from 1,500 meters to 10,000 meters; favorite to win the gold in the 1956 Olympics in Melbourne but was forced to withdraw due to a dislocated ankle; captain in the Hungarian army whose main responsibility was running; cause of death not reported; in Budapest; Jan. 23.

Vic Janowicz, 66; Ohio State multi-dimensional football star who won the 1950 Heisman Trophy; scored five touchdowns and rushed for 314 yards in 1950 as a halfback and threw for 557 yards and 12 touchdowns; he also kicked 23 field goals and 26 extra points, played defensive safety and assumed the punting duties for the Buckeyes as well; after a stint in the Army, he played two years of baseball for the Pittsburgh Pirates before returning to football from 1954-55 with the Washington Redskins; sustained a serious head injury which ended his career and caused partial paralysis; of prostate cancer; in Columbus, Ohio; Feb. 27.

Margaret Jenkins, 92; javelin thrower who competed in two Olympics for the U.S. in 1928 and 1932; broke the U.S. javelin record with a throw of 129 feet, 1 _ inches; finished eighth in the discus in the 1928 Olympics before the javelin became an official event; cause of death not reported; in Jackson, Calif.; Jan. 8.

Charlie Jewtraw, 95; speedskater who won the first event at the first Winter Olympic Games; captured the gold in the 500-meters in the 1924 games in Chamonix, France; won the U.S. sprint championships in 1921 and 1923; later pursued a business career with the Spaulding sports equipment company and worked as a bank security guard; cause of death not reported; in Hobe Sound, Fla.; Jan 26.

Blaine Johnson, 34; drag racing superstar who, with three wins, was leading the 1996 NHRA Winston Top Fuel point standings at the time of his death; set the elapsed-time Top Fuel national record of 4.592 in July 1996 in Topeka, Ks.; died from injuries suffered in a crash while qualifying for the U.S. Nationals in Indianapolis; Aug. 31.

Oscar Judd, 87; major league pitcher from 1941-48 who was the first Canadian to make the American League All-Star team; went 11-6 with a 2.90 ERA in 1941 for the Boston Red Sox; finished his career with a 40-51 mark and threw a no-hitter for Toronto of the International League just before his retirement; selected to the Canadian Baseball Hall of Fame in 1986; cause of death not reported; in Ingersoll, Ont.; Dec. 27, 1995.

Edward J. Keating, 59; sports agent whose clients included Dick Butkus, Arnold Palmer, and Dennis Eckersley; negotiated for Frank Robinson while a member of the International Management Group agency before leaving in the 1970's to start his own agency; of cancer; in Cleveland; April 18.

Robert Kerlan, 74; prominent orthopedic surgeon and former team physician for the St. Louis Rams and Los Angeles Dodgers; treated athletes that included basketball legend Wilt Chamberlain and jockey Bill Shoemaker; graduated from USC and worked 10 years for the Dodgers beginning in 1958, before joining the then Los Angeles Rams; after a long illness; in Santa Monica; Sept. 8.

John Killilea, 67; college scout and director of player personnel for the Houston Rockets since 1988; former assistant coach with the Boston Celtics, where he won two NBA championships and five division titles from 1971-77; also coached with Milwaukee and New Jersey; of a heart attack; in Denver; Jan. 27.

Seymour Knox, 70; chairman and co-founder of the Buffalo Sabres; along with his brother, he brought the expansion Sabres to Buffalo in 1969 and watched the club make it to the Stanley Cup finals vs. Philadelphia in 1975; credited with keeping the team in Buffalo and bringing them into the new state-of-the-art Marine Midland Arena, despite losing millions over the past several years; inducted into the Hockey Hall of Fame in 1993; of cancer; in Buffalo; May 22.

Dr. Hans Kraus, 90; called the father of sports medicine in the United States; developed a widely-used method for treating lower-back pain whereby local anesthetics were injected directly into the problem areas; patients included gold medal skier Billy Kidd, John F. Kennedy, and Yul Brenner; served on the President's Council of Physical Fitness; also considered the father of rock climbing in the United States; cause of death not reported; in Manhattan; March 6.

Richard Kroell, 28; Austrian skier who won the World Cup giant slalom at Alta Badia and Veysonnaz in 1990 and the 1995 Super G in Bormio; in a car accident; in Tirol, Austria; Oct. 5.

Jeff Krosnoff, 31; IndyCar racer who had competed in all possible 11 events for the Arciero-Wells Racing team during his debut season; had previously competed in the Japanese Formula 3000 for five years before joining the IndyCar series; three-time veteran of the prestigious 24 Hours of LeMans; voted 1988 Race Truck Rookie of the Year and Mazda Pro Series "Star of Tomorrow"; graduated from UCLA in 1987 with a degree in psychology; killed along with 44-year-old race course worker Gary Arvin after crashing on the 92nd lap of the 95-lap Toronto Molson-Indy; July 14.

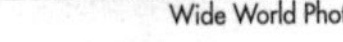

Wide World Photos

Tim Gullikson

Wide World Photos

Hord Hardin

CNN Sports

Bill MacPhail

Paul Labbe, 88; lightweight and welterweight fighter in the 1930s and 40s; lost only 13 of his 489 matches during his 14-year career, including two title bouts to welterweight champion Henry Armstrong; cause of death not reported; in Lewiston, Maine; Nov. 28, 1995.

James Laycock, 81; racing historian who attended every Indianapolis 500 from 1915 until illness eventually forced him to miss the event in 1994; was speedway press room director since 1953 and editor of the Indy 500 record book since 1960; after a long illness; in Avon, Ind.; Nov. 22, 1995.

William Leggett, 64; 30-year *Sports Illustrated* writer who won the Eclipse Award in 1979 for excellence in turf-writing; focused on the horses but also covered baseball, college and pro basketball, and the 1960 U.S. Olympic gold medal hockey team; after a long illness; in New York; Aug. 9.

Richard Long, 46; mountain bike promoter and co-founder of GT Bicycles Inc., the company who produced the $70,000 bicycles used by the United States squad in the Atlanta Olympics; known for his love of fast cars and fast motorcycles; of injuries sustained in a motorcycle crash; in Big Bear, Calif.; July 12.

Billy Lothridge, 54; former All-America quarterback and kicker for Georgia Tech who finished runner-up to Roger Staubach in the 1963 Heisman Trophy race; 1963 Southeastern Conference back of the year; played nine seasons in the NFL as a defensive safety and punter for the Cowboys, Rams, Falcons, and Dolphins; retired in 1972 after winning a Super Bowl ring with Miami; of a heart attack; in Pensacola, Fla.; Feb. 23.

Bill MacPhail, 76; sports television executive responsible for bringing instant replay to television, creating the CNN sports department, and hiring respected sports personalities such as Pat Summerall, Jack Whitaker, and Jim McKay; in his 18 years at CBS as sports director and eventually vice president of sports, he guided the station to purchase rights to the NBA, the Masters golf tournament, and major league baseball, among others; became the first to use instant replay in the 1963 Army-Navy game; left CBS in the mid 1970s and joined CNN where he launched the popular sports division; retired in 1995, serving as a consultant to the cable channel; of complications from heart surgery; in Atlanta; Sept. 4.

Ernie Magdaleno, 33; light heavyweight fighter who was a strong contender for the WBC crown; last fight was a 10-round decision over Roman Santos to improve his career mark to 22-1; lost a title match in March of 1994 to Henry Maske in Germany; an innocent victim caught in a high-speed police chase; in Orange, Calif.; Dec. 31, 1995.

Allan Malamud, 54; popular sports columnist whose column entitled "Notes on a Scorecard" ran for over 20 years in the *Los Angeles Herald Examiner* and then the *Los Angeles Times*; known for his good humor and knowledgeable observations; recently broke the story of Tommy Lasorda's retirement as manager of the Dodgers; appeared in 17 movies including the recently released "Tin Cup"; of natural causes; in Los Angeles; Sept. 16.

Joe Martin, 80; Muhammad Ali's first boxing coach; taught the future champion how to box at the age of 12 and led him six Kentucky Golden Gloves titles, two national AAU championships and the 1960 Olympic gold medal in Rome; combined the once segregated Columbia Gym in Louisville into one gym for both blacks and whites; inducted into the Amateur Boxing Hall of Fame in 1977; cause of death not reported; in Louisville; Sept. 14.

Wayne McDuffie, 51; former University of Georgia assistant coach and Florida State offensive coordinator; had six players earn All-American first team honors during his seven years at Florida State during the 1980's and the Seminoles registered a 32-4 record during his last three years; began at Georgia in 1991 and increased the offensive production by 1,200 yards in his first season en route to a 9-3 mark; served as an assistant coach for the Atlanta Falcons in 1990; of a self-inflicted gun shot wound; in Tallahassee, Fla.; Feb. 16.

Art McKennan, 89; former Pittsburgh Pirates public address announcer who worked every Pirate home game from 1951 to 1976; saw two unassisted triple plays during his tenure and witnessed Bill Mazeroski's infamous World Series winning home run in 1960; fired in 1987 in place of a "more enthusiastic announcer" but tremendous fan support persuaded the team to ultimately hire him back; eventually retired in 1993; cause of death not reported; in Pittsburgh; April 22.

Robert McNulty, 74; one of the eight original owners who brought the expansion North Stars to Minnesota in 1966; designed and built the Met Center in for the club Bloomington and later went on to develop other notable sports arenas, including the Cincinnati Coliseum and the Joe Louis Arena in Detroit; also helped to build such landmarks as Madison Square Garden and London's Wembley Stadium; of congestive heart failure; in Minneapolis; June 30.

Leon McQuay, 45; former running back who played in the Canadian, United States, and National Football leagues; rushed for 2,019 yards in four seasons with CFL's Toronto Argonauts but was best known for his fumble in the final seconds of the 1971 title game with Calgary; played one season for the NY Giants in 1974, accumulating 240 yards and one touchdownon 55 rushes; also played with the New England Patriots before moving to the Tampa Bay Bandits of the U.S.F.L. in 1982; of a heart attack; in Tampa, Fla.; Nov. 29, 1995.

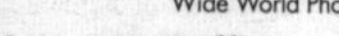

Wide World Photos

Wayne McDuffie

National League

John McSherry

ESPN

Tom Mees

Shannon McPherson, 20; starting point guard for Indiana University-Purdue (Indianapolis) women's basketball team; averaged 3.1 points and 2.1 assists per game for the Metros; killed when the team van crashed after a 71-63 victory over Indiana-Southeast; in Columbus, Ind.; Jan. 30.

John McSherry, 51; major league baseball umpire from 1971-96; worked in two World Series (1977 and 1987), seven league championship series, and three all-star games during his career; got his start umpiring sandlot and high school baseball games; eventually went on to work for the Carolina League, International League and Florida Instructional League before joining the majors as a full-time staff member in 1971; attended St. Johns University; died of severe heart disease after collapsing during the 1996 Cincinnati Reds' season opener at Riverfront Stadium; in Cincinnati; April 1.

Harold (Jug) McSpaden, 87; professional golfer who won five tour tournaments in 1934 and 26 overall in his career; formed a team with Byron Nelson that was known as "The Gold Dust Boys"; of accidental carbon monoxide poisoning; in Kansas City; April 22.

Tom Mees, 46; one of ESPN's original SportsCenter anchors from the show's inception on September 7, 1979 until 1993 when he decided to focus more on his duties as play-by-play hockey announcer for ESPN2; had been host of many popular ESPN shows including Baseball Tonight and This Week in the NHL; also broadcasted numerous major league baseball games and NCAA basketball, football, and hockey games; began his career as sports director at WILM-AM in Wilmington, Del. And then WECA-TV in Tallahassee before becoming a pioneer at ESPN; received a degree in broadcast communications from University of Delaware in 1972; in a drowning accident at a neighbor's swimming pool; in Southington, Conn.; Aug. 14.

Gregory Menton, 20; first and only full scholarship swimmer at UMass; held individual school records in the 100-yard backstroke and the 100-yard butterfly and swam the anchor leg of the record-breaking 200 medley relay; was fourth leading scorer on school's water polo team that went to the Final Four in 1995; held six school swimming records at Newberg High School in Portland, Ore. and was the state's MVP in water polo in 1993; after collapsing during a meet a t Dartmouth College; Jan. 10.

Dell Miller, 83; Hall of Fame harness racer who began his sport in 1929 at the age of 15 and continued racing and training through eight decades and six continents; won 2,442 races and over $11 million in purse money over his career and was widely considered one of the greatest ambassadors of the sport; competed in a record 26 Hambletonians, winning in 1950 with Lusty Song; of heart failure after a long illness; in Washington, Pa.; Aug. 19.

F. Don Miller, 75; former head of the U.S. Olympic Committee from 1973-85; credited for saving the U.S.O.C. after contributions and other funds dried up after the boycott of the 1980 games in Moscow; helped the formation of the U.S. Olympic Foundation which has given $7.5 million per year for athletes' training and $24 million to expand the U.S.O.C Training Center in Colorado Springs; became the first and only president of the foundation; won the 1943 national collegiate boxing title at 155 pounds while at the University of Wisconsin; served 26 years in the Army, winning two purple hearts; of lung cancer; in Colorado Springs; Jan. 17.

Elena Mirochina, 21; Russian diver who won the silver medal in platform diving at the 1992 Olympics in Barcelona; captured sixth place in the 1988 games in Seoul; won the European Championships, the European Cup and the FINA World Cup in 1991; found dead outside of her Moscow apartment; Dec. 18, 1995.

Mike Nunnally, 23; boxer who lost to eventual gold medalist David Reid in the 1996 U.S. Boxing Championships; attended the 1996 Olympics as a coach for a Swaziland boxer; attended Northern Michigan University; in a drowning accident; in Marquette, Mich.; Sept. 2.

Bill Nyrop, 43; NHL defenseman who played on three consecutive Stanley Cup teams from 1975-76 to 1977-78; selected to the NHL All-Star team in 1978; retired from the Canadiens before the 1978-79 season but was lured back by the Minnesota North Stars in 1981; retired again a year later to attend law school and eventually opem a law practice; former owner, president, GM, and coach of the West Palm Beach Blaze of the Southern Hockey League; of cancer; in Minneapolis; Dec. 31, 1995.

Jack O'Hara, 39; former Emmy Award-winning executive producer of ABC Sports; joined ABC Sports in 1983 after a three-year stint as producer for Major League Baseball Productions; became executive producer for ABC in April of 1991; responsibilities included Monday Night Football and Wide World of Sports; graduated from Marquette University in 1979; was killed along with his wife and 13-year-old daughter on the TWA jetliner that exploded off the coast of Long Island; July 17.

Audrey Patterson-Tyler, 69; track sprinter who became America's first black woman to win an Olympic medal when she captured the bronze in the 200-meter dash at the 1948 Olympic games in London; was selected woman athlete of the year by the Amateur Athletic Union in 1949; later founded a youth track club in San Diego and coached over 5,000 youths; graduate of Southern University; died after suffering a stroke and a heart attack; in San Diego; Aug. 23.

Wide World Photos

David Schultz

Wide World Photos

Mike Sharperson

Wide World Photos

Jimmy Snyder

Paul Pryor, 68; National League umpire from 1961-81; worked three all-star games (1963, 71, and 78) and three World Series (1967, 73 and 80); founded a celebrity golf tournament and umpired the "Legends of Baseball" old-timers games in St. Petersburg, Fla.; owned a travel bag company in addition to umping; cause of death not reported; in St. Petersburg; Dec. 15, 1995.

Rodney Rash, 36; horse trainer that accumulated 143 wins and $8,707,331 in 1,061 starts from 1991-1996; began his career at the age of 16 working for Hall of Fame trainer Charlie Whittingham where he eventually became chief assistant before leaving to train on his own; died of complications from a rare blood disease known as Thrombotic Thrombocytopenic Purpura (TTP); in Los Angeles; March 1.

Luis Rodriguez, 59; former Cuban welterweight fighter from 1956-72; won 107 of 120 pro fights with 49 knockouts in becoming the 147-pound champion; defeated the legendary Emile Griffith for the title in 1963 before losing to Griffith later in the same year; Griffith later went on to call Rodriguez "one of the all-time greats"; died after undergoing kidney dialysis for the past two years; in Miami Beach; July 8.

Al Rollins, 69; NHL goaltender who won the Vezina Trophy for the league's top goalie in 1950-51; went 27-5-8 in 1950-51 with a goals against average of 1.77 to lead the Toronto Maple Leafs to the Stanley Cup; three years later with Chicago, he won the Hart Trophy for the league's most valuable player; played 430 games and registered 28 shutouts (including five in 1954) from 1949-1960; cause of death not reported; in Calgary, Alb.; July 27.

Connie Ryan, 75; major league second baseman who later as a scout for the Oakland Athletics discovered future pitching star Vida Blue; hit .248 with 56 homers and 381 RBI in 1,184 games with five teams; was selected to the 1944 NL all-star team in 1944 and was a member of the 1948 pennant-winning Boston Braves in 1948; of a heart attack; in Metarie, La.; Jan. 3.

Ben Schley, 80; renowned fly fisherman credited with popularizing the catch and release approach that has become standard in fly fishing today; began fishing on the Potomac at the age of four and and later became a river guide, directing such luminaries as Dwight D. Eisenhower, Jimmy Carter, and Howard Hughes; was later placed in charge of the nation's fish hatcheries and eventually became a full-time fisherman; cause of death not reported; in Martinsburg, W.Va.; Feb. 17.

Dave Schultz, 36; 1984 Olympic gold medal wrestler often referred to as the "godfather of United States wrestling"; had won almost every wrestling honor possible including the 1983 world championship, the 1986 Goodwill Games championship, and the 1987 Pan American games championship; voted Outstanding Freestyle Wrestler at the 1984, 1987, and 1993 U.S. Nationals; was a California state high school champion in 1977 and attended the University of Oklahoma where he became an NCAA champion in 1982; at the time of his death, he was ranked No. 1 in the U.S. in his weight class and was a top candidate for an Olympic medal in Atlanta; known for his love and loyalty to his sport and willingness to help, he also coached at the University of Wisconsin, Stanford, and Oklahoma; of a gunshot wound; in Newtown Square, Pa.; January 26.

Joe Schultz, 77; manager of the expansion Seattle Pilots in 1969 and the Detroit Tigers in 1973; played nine seasons in the major leagues (six with the St. Louis Browns) and recorded a .259 average in 240 games as a backup catcher; of heart failure; in St. Louis; Jan. 10.

Chung Se-hoon, 22; South Korean judo star who won the men's 65-kilogram title at the 1995 University Games in Japan; was a favorite to win a gold medal at the Olymics in Atlanta; died of a heart attack apparently brought on by a crash diet; in Seoul, S. Korea; Mar. 19.

Bill Serena, 71; Chicago Cubs' infielder from 1949-54; compiled 311 hits with 48 homers and 198 RBI in 408 major league games; of cancer; in Hayward, Calif.; April 17.

Mike Sharperson, 34; veteran major league infielder who was selected to the NL All-Star team in 1992 as a member of the Los Angeles Dodgers; batted .280 over a career that spanned 557 major-league games and hit a career-high .300 in 1992; played parts of six seasons with the Dodgers, winning the world championship in 1988; drafted by the Toronto Blue Jays in the 1981 free agent draft but was traded to L.A. for pitcher Juan Guzman; was playing for the San Diego Padres' Class AAA affiliate in Las Vegas and was scheduled to be called up to the majors at the time of his death; in a car accident; in Las Vegas; May 26.

Matthew Skalsky, 19; basketball guard at University of Maryland-Baltimore County; was averaging 4.9 points per game in his sophomore season for the Retrievers; best game was a 17 point effort (13 in the first half) against Xavier in December of 1994; earned All-Michigan honors as a three-year starter and team captain in high school; of head injuries sustained from a fall; in Darnestown, Md.; Dec. 31, 1995.

Sam Skinner, 56; respected African-American journalist and sports radio host who ended his broadcasts with "if you can't be a good sport, don't bother to play the game"; was one of the first to report the 1972 kidnapping of Israeli athletes at the Munich Olympics and also was instrumental in uncovering Ben Johnson's use of steroids at the 1988 Olympics in Seoul; close friend of many athletes including Muhammad Ali, Carl Lewis, and Joe Montana; after complications from a massive stroke in the summer of 1995; in Burlingame, Calif.; Jan. 11.

C. Arnholt Smith, 97; original owner of the San Diego Padres; brought the team to the National League as an expansion club in 1969; tried to move the team to Washington, D.C. in 1973 but the deal fell through and he subsequently sold the team to McDonald's owner Ray Kroc before the 1974 season; also owner of the now defunct Crocker Bank, he served eight months in prison for grand theft and tax fraud; cause of death not reported, in San Diego; June 8.

Derek Smith, 34; former NBA forward/guard who played nine seasons with the Clippers, Kings, 76ers, and Celtics; most recently, he was serving as assistant coach for the Washington Bullets; best seasons came in 1984-85 when he averaged 22 points a game for the Clippers and 1986-87 when he averaged 16.6 for the Sacramento Kings; starred in college at Louisville where he pumped in 14.8 points a game as a sophomore to help lead the Cardinals to the NCAA National Championship in 1980; died of respiratory arrest while aboard a cruise ship with his family and other teammates; Aug. 10.

George Smith, 83; former head coach of the University of Cincinnati basketball program from 1952-60; recruited and coached such stars as Jack Twyman and the legendary Oscar Robertson and compiled an overall record of 154-56 during his tenure; later became the athletic director and vice president for development before retiring from Cincinnati in 1980; of cancer; in Cincinnati; Jan. 14.

Willie Smith, 24; junior cornerback for Louisiana Tech football team; picked off three passes in a Tech win at Bowling Green and went on to lead the nation in interceptions with eight during the 1995 season; voted Big West Conference Defensive Player of the Year , second-team UPI All-American, and third-team AP All-American; was a star at Garland (Tx.) High School but was shot in the stomach shortly after his senior season; walked on at Louisiana Tech; of an accidental self-inflicted gunshot wound; in Ruston, La.; Dec. 31, 1995.

Pat Smythe, 67; became the first woman show jumper to compete in the Olympic games, winning the bronze at the 1956 games in Stockholm; served as president of the British Show Jumping Association from 1986-89; authored two children's books and two autobiographies; of heart disease; in London; Feb. 27.

Jimmy (The Greek) Snyder, 76; controversial CBS Sports commentator who brought oddsmaking on television into prominence during the late 1970's through the mid 80's; spent 12 years on CBS making predictions on football games and is praised for picking the winner of 18 of 21 Super Bowls through the 70's and 80's; was fired from the network in 1988 after publicly stating his opinion that black athletes were bred to be superior to whites; reportedly got into a fistfight in 1980 with then "NFL Today" host Brent Musburger over a lack of air time; became an oddsmaker and newspaper columnist in Las Vegas during the 1950's and was once pardoned of gambling violations by President Ford; of heart failure after a long illness; in Las Vegas; April 21.

Stan Stamenkovic, 39; former Major Indoor Soccer League standout; won the 1983-84 MISL scoring title and was awarded the league MVP award in leading the Baltimore Blast to the league championship; of a head injury sustained from a fall; in Titova Uzice, Serbia; Jan. 28.

Greg Stokes, 23; linebacker at Division II Angelo State whose 493 career tackles ranks second on the school's all-time list; as captain, he led the team in 1995 with 133 tackles, intercepted two passes, and was selected to the GTE Academic All-American team; was a two-time All-Lone Star Conference choice and was the 1995 Conference Defensive Player of the Year; in a car accident; in San Angelo, Tx.; Nov. 5, 1995.

Leo Strang, 73; former Kent University head football coach and national champion high school coach at Massillon High in Ohio; led Massillon to a 109-26-1 mark and two national titles from 1958-63 before heading up the Kent program from 1964-67 (16-21-1); cause of death not reported; in Akron, Ohio; April 16.

Bill Stroppe, 76; Ford Motor Company car developer for Indy-car races and various other road races; managed the team of Lincolns that took the top three spots at the 1952-53 Pan-Am Road Races in Mexico; died after surgery resulting from a fall; in Long Beach, Calif.; Nov. 8, 1995.

Alvin (Al) Stump, 79; sportswriter specifically chosen by baseball star Ty Cobb to help write his autobiography in 1959 called "My Life in Baseball: The True Record"; after Cobb's death, he wrote another book about the legend that was more truthful and portrayed Cobb as "the meanest man who ever played baseball"; became the subject for the 1994 movie "Cobb"; wrote for publications such as *Esquire, True,* and the *Saturday Evening Post*; of congestive heart failure; in Los Angeles; Dec. 14, 1995.

Earl (Bud) Svendsen, 81; center for the University of Minnesota championship winning football teams of 1934, 35, and 36; former Green Bay Packer center inducted into the Packers' Hall of Fame in 1985; cause of death not reported; in Edina, Minn.; Aug. 6.

Charlie Tate, 77; University of Miami head football coach from 1964 through the frirst two games of the 1970 season; compiled a 34-27-3 record and led the 1966 team to an 8-2-1 mark, the No. 9 ranking in the nation, and a victory over Virginia Tech in the Liberty Bowl; signed Miami's first black football player in 1967; after a long illness; in Blairsville, Ga.; June 10.

Robert (Bennie) Tompkins, 85; South Carolina college basketball star in the 1930s who, at 6-foot-4, was known as one of the "Tall Texans"; their size at the time was enough to dominate the competition as the Gamecocks won a school record 32 consecutive games and the 1933 Southern Conference championship; cause of death not reported; in Columbia, S.C.; Nov. 7, 1995.

Aimee Willard, 22; George Mason soccer and lacrosse star; played on the school's inaugural Division I lacrosse team and in 1996 garnered first team all-conference and second-team All-American honors, leading the club with a team record 50 goals and 18 assists; finished her soccer career with five goals and six assists and was a member of the 1993 team that played in the NCAA championship game; found murdered near her home in Brookhaven, Pa.; June 20.

Kevin Williams, 38; wide receiver for the 1978 national champion USC squad; caught 71 receptions for 1,358 yards and a school record 25 touchdowns during his college career from 1977-80; played one season (1981) with the N.F.L Baltimore Colts, before signing on with the Los Angeles Express of the U.S.F.L. in a freight train crash near Los Angeles; Feb. 1.

Clarence (Cave) Wilson, 70; former player-captain and coach of the Harlem Globetrotters in the late 1940s and 1950s; high school basketball team won 65 consecutive games and two state championships in Kentucky after he pleaded with the principal to form a team; of a stroke; Sept. 18.

Steve Wood, 34; Australian rower who won the bronze medal in the K-4 1,000 meter final at the 1992 Barcelona Olympics; also worked as a part-time coach at the Queensland Academy of Sport; was hoping for a comeback at the 1996 Atlanta Olympics; no official cause of death; in Brisbane, Australia; Nov. 23, 1995.

Al Zarilla, 77; major league outfielder in the 1940s and 50s who played for the St. Louis Browns, Chicago White Sox, and in the same Red Sox outfield with Ted Williams and Dom DiMaggio; finished his ten year career with a .276 average before becoming a major league scout and a coach for the Washington Senators; of cancer; in Honolulu; Sept. 3.

RESEARCH MATERIAL

Many sources were used in the gathering of information for this almanac. Day to day material was almost always found in copies of *USA Today*, *The Boston Globe*, and *The New York Times*.

Several weekly and bi-weekly periodicals were also used in the past year's pursuit of facts and figures, among them—*Baseball America*, *International Boxing Digest*, *The European*, *FIFA News* (Soccer), *The Hockey News*, *The NCAA News*, *On Track*, *Soccer America*, *Sports Illustrated*, *The Sporting News*, *Track & Field News*, and *USA Today Baseball Weekly*.

In addition, the following books provided background material for one or more chapters of the almanac.

Arenas & Ballparks

The Ballparks, by Bill Shannon and George Kalinsky; Hawthorn Books, Inc. (1975); New York.

Diamonds, by Michael Gershman; Houghton Mifflin Co. (1993); Boston.

Green Cathedrals (Revised Edition), by Philip Lowry; Addison-Wesley Publishing Co. (1992); Reading, Mass.

The NFL's Encyclopedic History of Professional Football, Macmillan Publishing Co. (1977); New York.

Take Me Out to the Ballpark, by Lowell Reidenbaugh; The Sporting News Publishing Co. (1983); St. Louis.

24 Seconds to Shoot (An Informal History of the NBA), by Leonard Koppett; Macmillan Publishing Co. (1968); New York.

Plus many major league baseball, NBA, NFL, NHL league and team guides, and college football and basketball guides.

Auto Racing

1996 IndyCar Media Guide, edited by Bob Andrew; Championship Auto Racing Teams; Troy, Mich.

Indy: 75 Years of Racing's Greatest Spectacle, by Rich Taylor; St. Martin's Press (1991); New York.

Marlboro Grand Prix Guide, 1950-95 (1996 Edition), compiled by Jacques Deschenaux and Claude Michele Deschenaux; Charles Stewart & Company Ltd; Brentford, England.

1996 Winston Cup Media Guide, compiled and edited by Chris Powell; NASCAR Winston Cup Series; Winston-Salem, N.C.

Baseball

The All-Star Game (A Pictorial History, 1933 to Present), by Donald Honig; The Sporting News Publishing Co. (1987); St. Louis.

1996 American League Red Book, published by The Sporting News Publishing Co.; St. Louis.

The Baseball Chronology, edited by James Charlton; Macmillian Publishing Co. (1991); New York.

The Baseball Encyclopedia (Ninth Edition), editorial director, Rick Wolff; Macmillan Publishing Co. (1993); New York.

The Complete 1996 Baseball Record Book, edited by Craig Carter; The Sporting News Publishing Co.; St. Louis.

1996 National League Green Book, published by The Sporting News Publishing Co.; St. Louis.

The Scrapbook History of Baseball by Jordan Deutsch, Richard Cohen, Roland Johnson and David Neft; Bobbs-Merrill Company, Inc. (1975); Indianapolis/New York.

1996 Sporting News Official Baseball Guide, edited by Craig Carter and Dave Sloan; The Sporting News Publishing Co.; St. Louis.

1996 Sporting News Official Baseball Register, edited by Sean Stewart and Kyle Veltrop; The Sporting News Publishing Co.; St. Louis.

The Sports Encyclopedia: Baseball (1996 Edition), edited by David Neft and Richard Cohen; St. Martin's Press; New York.

Total Baseball (Fourth Edition), edited by John Thorn and Pete Palmer; HarperPerennial (1995); New York.

College Basketball

All the Moves (A History of College Basketball), by Neil D. Issacs; J.B. Lippincott Company (1975); New York.

1995-96 Blue Ribbon College Basketball Yearbook, edited by Chris Wallace; Christopher Publishing; Buckhannon, W.Va.

College Basketball, U.S.A. (Since 1892), by John D. McCallum; Stein and Day (1978); New York.

Collegiate Basketball: Facts and Figures on the Cage Sport, by Edwin C. Caudle; The Paragon Press (1960); Montgomery, Ala.

The Encyclopedia of the NCAA Basketball Tournament, written and compiled by Jim Savage; Dell Publishing (1990); New York.

The Final Four (Reliving America's Basketball Classic), compiled by Billy Reed; Host Communications, Inc. (1988); Lexington, Ky.

1996 NCAA Final Four Records Book, compiled by Gary Johnson; edited by Stephen R. Hagwell; NCAA Books; Overland Park, Kan.

The Modern Encyclopedia of Basketball (Second Revised Edition), edited by Zander Hollander; Dolphins Books (1979); Doubleday & Company, Inc.; Garden City, N.Y.

1996 NCAA College Basketball Records Book, compiled by Gary Johnson, Richard Campbell, John Painter, Sean Straziscar and James Wright; edited by Laurie Bollig; NCAA Books; Overland Park, Kan.

1996 NIT Tournament Guide, Madison Square Garden; New York.

Plus many 1995-96 NCAA Division I conference guides from the American West to the WAC.

Pro Basketball

The Official NBA Basketball Encyclopedia (Second Edition), edited by Alex Sachare; Villard Books (1994); New York.

1995-96 Sporting News Official NBA Guide, edited by Craig Carter and Alex Sachare; The Sporting News Publishing Co.; St. Louis.

1995-96 Sporting News Official NBA Register, edited by George Puro, Alex Sachare and Kyle Veltrop; The Sporting News Publishing Co.; St. Louis.

Bowling

1995 Bowlers Journal Annual & Almanac; Luby Publishing; Chicago.

1996 LPBT Guide, Ladies Pro Bowlers Tour; Rockford, Ill.

1996 PBA Media Guide; Professional Bowlers Association; Akron, Ohio.

Boxing

The Boxing Record Book (1996), edited by Phill Marder; Fight Fax Inc.; Sicklerville, N.J.

The Ring 1985 Record Book & Boxing Encyclopedia, edited by Herbert G. Goldman; The Ring Publishing Corp.; New York.

The Ring: Boxing, The 20th Century, Steven Farhood, editor-in-chief; BDD Illustrated Books (1993); New York.

College Sports

1994-95 National Collegiate Championships, edited by Ted Breidenthal; NCAA Books; Overland Park, Kan.

1996 NCAA College Basketball Records Book, compiled by Gary Johnson, Richard Campbell, John Painter, Sean Straziscar and James Wright; edited by Laura Bollig; NCAA Books; Overland Park, Kan.

1995 NCAA College Football Records Book, compiled by Richard Campbell, John Painter and Sean Straziscar; edited by J. Gregory Summers; NCAA Books; Overland Park, Kan.

1994-95 NAIA Championships History and Records Book; National Assn. of Intercollegiate Athletics; Tulsa, Okla.

1994-95 National Directory of College Athletics, edited by Kevin Cleary; Collegiate Directories, Inc.; Cleveland.

College Football

Football: A College History, by Tom Perrin; McFarland & Company, Inc. (1987); Jefferson, N.C.

Football: Facts & Figures, by Dr. L.H. Baker; Farrar & Rinehart, Inc. (1945); New York.

Great College Football Coaches of the Twenties and Thirties, by Tim Cohane; Arlington House (1973); New Rochelle, N.Y.

1995 NCAA College Football Records Book, compiled by Richard Campbell, John Painter and Sean Straziscar; edited by J. Gregory Summers; NCAA Books; Overland Park, Kan.

Saturday Afternoon, by Richard Whittingham; Workman Publishing Co., Inc. (1985); New York.

Saturday's America, by Dan Jenkins; Sports Illustrated Books; Little, Brown & Company (1970); Boston.

Tournament of Roses, The First 100 Years, by Joe Hendrickson; Knapp Press (1989); Los Angeles.

Plus numerous college football team and conference guides, especially the 1995 guides compiled by the Atlantic Coast Conference, Southeastern Conference and Southwest Conference.

Pro Football

1995 Canadian Football League Guide, compiled by the CFL Communications Dept.; Toronto.

The Football Encyclopedia (The Complete History of NFL Football from 1892 to the Present), compiled by David Neft and Richard Cohen; St. Martin's Press (1994); New York.

The Official NFL Encyclopedia, by Beau Riffenburgh; New American Library (1986); New York.

Official NFL 1995 Record and Fact Book, compiled by the NFL Communications Dept. and Seymour Siwoff, Elias Sports Bureau; edited by Chris Hardart and Chuck Garrity Jr.; produced by NFL Properties, Inc.; New York.

The Scrapbook History of Pro Football, by Richard Cohen, Jordan Deutsch, Roland Johnson and David Neft; Bobbs-Merrill Company, Inc. (1976); Indianapolis/New York.

1995 Sporting News Football Guide, edited by Craig Carter and Dave Sloan; The Sporting News Publishing Co.; St. Louis.

1995 Sporting News Football Register, edited George Puro and Kyle Veltrop; The Sporting News Publishing Co.; St. Louis.

1995 Sporting News Super Bowl Book, edited by Tom Dienhart, Joe Hoppel and Dave Sloan; The Sporting News Publishing Co.; St. Louis.

Golf

The Encyclopedia of Golf (Revised Edition), compiled by Nevin H. Gibson; A.S. Barnes and Company (1964); New York.

Guinness Golf Records: Facts and Champions, by Donald Steel; Guinness Superlatives Ltd. (1987); Middlesex, England.

The History of the PGA Tour, by Al Barkow; Doubleday (1989); New York.

The Illustrated History of Women's Golf, by Rhonda Glenn, Taylor Publishing Co. (1991); Dallas.

1996 LPGA Player Guide, produced by LPGA Communications Dept.; Ladies Professional Golf Assn. Tour; Daytona Beach, Fla.

1996 PGA Tour Guide, produced by PGA Tour Creative Services; Professional Golfers Assn. Tour; Ponte Vedra, Fla.

Official Guide of the PGA Championships; Triumph Books (1994); Chicago.

The PGA World Golf Hall of Fame Book, by Gerald Astor, Prentice Hall Press (1991); New York.

1996 Senior PGA Tour Guide, produced by PGA Tour Creative Services; Professional Golfers Assn. Tour; Ponte Vedra, Fla.

Pro-Golf 1996, PGA European Tour Media Guide, Virginia Water, Surrey, England.

The Random House International Encyclopedia of Golf, by Malcolm Campbell; Random House (1991); New York.

USGA Record Books (1895-1959, 1960-80 and 1981-90); U.S. Golf Association; Far Hills, N.J.

Hockey

Canada Cup '87: The Official History, No.1 Publications Ltd.; Toronto.

The Complete Encyclopedia of Hockey; edited by Zander Hollander; Visible Ink Press (1993); Detroit.

The Hockey Encyclopedia, by Stan Fischler and Shirley Walton Fischler; research editor, Bob Duff; Macmillan Publishing Co. (1983); New York.

Hockey Hall of Fame (The Official History of the Game and Its Greatest Stars), by Dan Diamond and Joseph Romain; Doubleday (1988); New York.

The National Hockey League, by Edward F. Dolan Jr.; W H Smith Publishers Inc. (1986); New York.

The Official National Hockey League 75th Anniversary Commemorative Book, edited by Dan Diamond; McClelland & Stewart, Inc. (1991); Toronto.

1995-96 Official NHL Guide & Record Book, compiled by the NHL Public Relations Dept.; New York/Montreal/Toronto.

1995-96 Sporting News Complete Hockey Book, edited by Craig Carter, George Puro and Kyle Veltrop; The Sporting News Publishing Co.; St. Louis.

The Stanley Cup, by Joseph Romain and James Duplacey; Gallery Books (1989); New York.

The Trail of the Stanley Cup (Volumns I-III), by Charles L. Coleman; Progressive Publications Inc. (1969); Sherbrooke, Quebec.

Horse Racing

1996 American Racing Manual, compiled by the Daily Racing Form; Hightstown, N.J.

1996 Breeders' Cup Statistics; Breeders' Cup Limited; Lexington, Ky.

1996 Directory and Record Book, Thoroughbred Racing Associations of North America Inc.; Elkton, Md.

1996 NYRA Media Guide, The New York Racing Association Inc.; Jamaica, N.Y.

1996 Preakness Press Guide, compiled and edited by Dale Austin, Craig Sculos and Joe Kelly; Maryland Jockey Club; Baltimore, Md.

1996 Trotting and Pacing Guide, compiled and edited by John Pawlak; United States Trotting Association; Columbus, Ohio.

International Sports

Athletics: A History of Modern Track and Field (1860-1990, Men and Women), by Roberto Quercetani; Vallardi & Associati (1990); Milan, Italy.

1995 International Track & Field Annual, Association of Track & Field Statisticians; edited by Peter Matthews; SportsBooks Ltd.; Surrey, England.

Track & Field News' Little Blue Book; Metric conversion tables; From the editors of Track & Field News (1989); Los Altos, Calif.

Miscellaneous

The America's Cup 1851-1987 (Sailing for Supremacy), by Gary Lester and Richard Sleeman; Lester-Townsend Publishing (1986); Sydney, Australia.

The Encyclopedia of Sports (Fifth Revised Edition), by Frank G. Menke; revisions by Suzanne Treat; A.S. Barnes and Co., Inc. (1975); Cranbury, N.J.

The Great American Sports Book, by George Gipe; Doubleday & Company, Inc. (1978); Garden City, N.Y.

The 1996 Information Please Almanac, edited by Otto Johnson; Houghton Mifflin Co.; Boston.

1996 Official PRCA Media Guide, edited by Steve Fleming; Professional Rodeo Cowboys Association; Colorado Springs.

The Sail Magazine Book of Sailing, by Peter Johnson; Alfred A. Knopf (1989); New York.

"Ten Years of the Ironman," Triathlete Magazine; October, 1988; Santa Monica, Calif.

The 1996 World Almanac and Book of Facts, edited by Robert Famighetti; Funk & Wagnalls; Mahwah, N.J.

Olympics

All That Glitters Is Not Gold (An Irreverent Look at the Olympic Games); by William O. Johnson, Jr.; G.P. Putnam's Sons (1972); New York.

Barcelona/Albertville 1992; edited by Lisa H. Albertson; for U.S. Olympic Committee by Commemorative Publications; Salt Lake City.

Chamonix to Lillehammer (The Glory of the Olympic Winter Games); edited by Lisa H. Albertson; for U.S. Olympic Committee by Commemorative Publication (1994); Salt Lake City.

The Complete Book of the Olympics (1992 Edition); by David Wallechinsky; Little, Brown and Co.; Boston.

The Games Must Go On (Avery Brundage and the Olympic Movement), by Allen Guttmann; Columbia University Press (1984); New York.

The Golden Book of the Olympic Games, edited by Erich Kamper and Bill Mallon; Vallardi & Associati (1992); Milan, Italy.

Hitler's Games (The 1936 Olympics), by Duff Hart-Davis; Harper & Row (1986); New York/London.

An Illustrated History of the Olympics (Third Edition); by Dick Schaap; Alfred A. Knopf (1975); New York.

The Nazi Olympics, by Richard D. Mandell; Souvenir Press (1972); London.

The Official USOC Book of the 1984 Olympic Games, by Dick Schaap; Random House/ABC Sports; New York.

The Olympics: A History of the Games, by William Oscar Johnson; Oxmoor House (1992); Birmingham, Ala.

Pursuit of Excellence (The Olympic Story), by The Associated Press and Grolier; Grolier Enterprises Inc. (1979); Danbury, Conn.

The Story of the Olympic Games (776 B.C. to 1948 A.D.), by John Kieran and Arthur Daley; J.B. Lippincott Company (1948); Philadelphia/New York.

United States Olympic Books (Seven Editions): 1936 and 1948-88; U.S. Olympic Association; New York.

The USA and the Olympic Movement, produced by the USOC Information Dept.; edited by Gayle Plant; U.S. Olympic Committee (1988); Colorado Springs.

Plus official IOC and USOC records from the 1996 Summer Olympics in Atlanta.

Soccer

The American Encyclopedia of Soccer, edited by Zander Hollander; Everest House Publishers (1980); New York.

The European Football Yearbook (1994-95 Edition), edited by Mike Hammond; Sports Projects Ltd; West Midlands, England.

The Guinness Book of Soccer Facts & Feats, by Jack Rollin; Guinness Superlatives Ltd. (1978); Middlesex, England.

History of Soccer's World Cup, by Michael Archer; Chartwell Books, Inc. (1978); Secaucus, N.J.

The Simplest Game, by Paul Gardner; Collier Books (1994); New York.

The Story of the World Cup, by Brian Glanville; Faber and Faber Limited (1993); London/Boston.

1996 MLS Official Media Guide, edited by the MLS Communications staff; Los Angles.

1991-92 MSL Official Guide, Major (Indoor) Soccer League; Overland Park, Kan.

U.S. Soccer 1996 Media Guide, edited by Tom Lang; U.S. Soccer Federation; Chicago.

Tennis

Bud Collins' Modern Encyclopedia of Tennis, edited by Bud Collins and Zander Hollander; Visible Ink Press (1994); Detroit.

The Illustrated Encyclopedia of World Tennis, by John Haylett and Richard Evans; Exeter Books (1989); New York.

Official Encyclopedia of Tennis, edited by the staff of the U.S. Lawn Tennis Assn.; Harper & Row (1972); New York.

1996 ATP Tour Player Guide, compiled by ATP Tour Communications Dept.; Association of Tennis Professionals; Ponte Vedra Beach, Fla.

1996 Corel WTA Tour Media Guide, compiled by WTA Public Relations staff; edited by Renee Bloch Shallouf, Doug Clery and Toni Woods; St. Petersburg, Fla.

Who's Who

The Guiness International Who's Who of Sport, edited by Peter Mathews, Ian Buchanan and Bill Mallon; Guiness Publishing (1993); Middlesex, England

101 Greatest Athletes of the Century, by Will Grimsley and the Associated Press Sports Staff; Bonanza Books (1987); Crown Publishers, Inc.; New York.

The New York Times Book of Sports Legends, edited by Joseph Vecchione; Simon & Shuster (1991); New York.

Superstars, by Frank Litsky; Vineyard Books, Inc. (1975); Secaucus, N.J.

A Who's Who of Sports Champions (Their Stories and Records), by Ralph Hicock, Houghton Mifflin Co. (1995); Boston.

Other Reference Books

Facts & Dates of American Sports, by Gorton Carruth & Eugene Ehrlich; Harper & Row, Publishers, Inc. (1988); New York.

Sports Market Place 1995 (July edition), edited by Richard A. Lipsey; Sportsguide Inc.; Princeton N.J.

The World Book Encyclopedia (1988 Edition); World Book, Inc.; Chicago.

The World Book Yearbook (Annual Supplements, 1954-95); World Book, Inc.; Chicago.

COMING ATTRACTIONS

Olympics

Winter Games

Year	No.	Host City	Dates
1998	XVIII	Nagano, Japan	Feb. 7-22
2002	XIX	Salt Lake City, Utah	Feb. 9-24

Summer Games

Year	No.	Host City	Dates
2000	XXVII	Sydney, Australia	Sept. 16-Oct. 1

All-Star Games

Baseball

Year	Site	Date
1997	Jacobs Field, Cleveland	July 8
1998	Coors Field, Denver	July 7

NBA Basketball

Year	Site	Date
1997	Gund Arena, Cleveland	Feb. 9
1998	Madison Square Garden	Feb. 8

NFL Pro Bowl

Year	Site	Date
1997	Aloha Stadium, Honolulu	Feb. 2
1998	Aloha Stadium, Honolulu	Feb. 1

NHL Hockey

Year	Site	Date
1997	San Jose Arena, San Jose	Jan. 18
1998	GM Place, Vancouver	Jan. 17

Auto Racing

The Daytona 500 stock car race is usually held on the Sunday before the third Monday in February, while the Indianapolis 500 is usually held on the Sunday of Memorial Day weekend in May. Except for 1997, the following dates are tentative.

Year	Daytona 500	Indianapolis 500
1997	Feb. 16	May 25
1998	Feb. 15	May 24
1999	Feb. 14	May 23

NCAA Basketball

Men's Final Four

Year	Site	Date
1997	RCA Dome, Indianapolis	March 29-31
1998	Alamodome, San Antonio	March 28-30
1999	ThunderDome, St. Petersburg	March 27-29
2000	RCA Dome, Indianapolis	April 1-3
2001	Metrodome, Minneapolis	Mar. 31-Apr. 2
2002	Georgia Dome, Atlanta	Mar. 30-Apr. 1

Women's Final Four

Year	Site	Date
1996	Charlotte (N.C.) Coliseum	March 29-31
1997	Riverfront Coliseum, Cincinnati	March 28-29
1998	Kemper Arena, Kansas City	March 28-29
1999	San Jose Arena	TBA
2000	CoreStates Spectrum	TBA

NFL Football

Super Bowl

No.	Site	Date
XXXI	Superdome, New Orleans	Jan. 26, 1997
XXXII	Jack Murphy Stadium, San Diego	Jan. 25, 1998
XXXIII	3Com Park, San Francisco	Jan. 24, 1999
XXXIV	Hollywood Park, Los Angeles	Jan. 23, 2000

Golf

The Masters

Year	Site	Date
1997	Augusta National Ga	April 10-13
1998	Augusta National Ga	April 9-12

U.S. Open

Year	Site	Date
1997	Congressional CC, Bethesda, Md.	June 12-15
1998	Olympic Club, San Francisco	June 18-21
1999	Pinehurst CC, Pinehurst, N.J.	June 17-20
2000	Pebble Beach (Calif.) Golf Links.	June 15-18

U.S. Women's Open

Year	Site	Date
1997	Pumpkin Ridge GC, Cornelius, Ore.	July 10-13
1998	Blackwolf Run GC, Kohler, Wisc.	July 2-5
1999	Old Waverly GC, West Point, Miss.	June 3-6
2000	Merit Club, Libertyville, Ill.	July 20-23

U.S. Senior Open

Year	Site	Date
1997	Olympia Fields GC, Olympia Field, Ill.	June 26-29
1998	Riviera CC, Pacific Palisades, Calif.	July 9-12
1999	Des Moines GC, W. Des Moines, Iowa	July 8-11
2000	Saucon Valley GC, Bethlehem, Pa.	TBA

PGA Championship

Year	Site	Date
1997	Winged Foot GC, Mamaroneck, N.Y.	Aug. 14-17
1998	Sahalee CC, Seattle	Aug. 13-16

British Open

Year	Site	Date
1997	Royal Troon, Scotland	July 17-20
1998	Royal Birkdale, England	July 16-19
1999	Carnoustie, Scotland	July 15-18
2000	Royal Lytham, England	July 20-23

Ryder Cup

Year	Site	Date
1997	Valderrama, Spain	Sept. 20-28
1999	The Country Club, Brookline, Mass.	TBA

Horse Racing

Triple Crown

The Kentucky Derby is always held at Churchill Downs in Louisville on the first Saturday in May, followed two weeks later by the Preakness Stakes at Pimlico Race Course in Baltimore and three weeks after that by the Belmont Stakes at Belmont Park in Elmont, N.Y.

Year	Ky Derby	Preakness	Belmont
1997	May 3	May 17	June 7
1998	May 2	May 16	June 6
1999	May 1	May 15	June 5

Tennis

U.S. Open

Usually held from the last Monday in August through the second Sunday in September, with Labor Day weekend the midway point in the tournament.

Year	Site	Dates
1997	U.S. Tennis Center, NYC	Aug. 25-Sept. 7
1998	U.S. Tennis Center, NYC	Aug. 24-Sept. 6
1999	U.S. Tennis Center, NYC	Aug. 23-Sept. 5